HISTORICAL STATISTICS
OF THE
UNITED STATES

HISTORICAL STATISTICS
OF THE
UNITED STATES

Earliest Times to the Present

MILLENNIAL EDITION

VOLUME FOUR

PART D
ECONOMIC SECTORS

Editors in Chief

Susan B. Carter

Scott Sigmund Gartner

Michael R. Haines

Alan L. Olmstead

Richard Sutch

Gavin Wright

CAMBRIDGE
UNIVERSITY PRESS

CAMBRIDGE UNIVERSITY PRESS
Cambridge, New York, Melbourne, Madrid, Cape Town, Singapore, São Paulo

Cambridge University Press
40 West 20th Street, New York, NY 10011-4211, USA

http://www.cambridge.org
Information on this title: www.cambridge.org/9780521817912

First published 2006

Printed in the United States of America

A catalog record for this publication is available from the British Library.

Library of Congress Cataloging in Publication Data

Historical statistics of the United States : earliest times to the present / Susan B. Carter ... [et al.]. – Millennial ed.
    p. cm.
  Rev. update of: Historical statistics of the United States, colonial times to 1970. Bicentennial ed. Washington : U.S. Dept. of Commerce, Bureau of the Census, 1975.
  Includes bibliographical references and index.
  ISBN 0-521-81791-9 (set)
  1. United States – Statistics. I. Carter, Susan B. II. Historical statistics of the United States, colonial times to 1970. III. Title.

HA202.H57 2006
317.3 – dc22
                                   2005027089

ISBN-13 978-0-521-81791-2 (set of five volumes hardback)
ISBN-10 0-521-81791-9 (set of five volumes hardback)

ISBN-13 978-0-521-58496-8 (volume 1 hardback)
ISBN-10 0-521-58496-5 (volume 1 hardback)

ISBN-13 978-0-521-58540-8 (volume 2 hardback)
ISBN-10 0-521-58540-6 (volume 2 hardback)

ISBN-13 978-0-521-81790-5 (volume 3 hardback)
ISBN-10 0-521-81790-0 (volume 3 hardback)

ISBN-13 978-0-521-85389-7 (volume 4 hardback)
ISBN-10 0-521-85389-3 (volume 4 hardback)

ISBN-13 978-0-521-85390-3 (volume 5 hardback)
ISBN-10 0-521-85390-7 (volume 5 hardback)

ISBN-13 978-0-511-13297-1 (on-line edition)
ISBN-10 0-511-13297-2 (on-line edition)

SUMMARY CONTENTS

DETAILED CONTENTS OF VOLUME FOUR

DETAILED CONTENTS OF VOLUME FOUR

GUIDE TO THE MILLENNIAL EDITION

Monty Hindman and Richard Sutch

Editions and Copyright

Previous editions. This is the fourth edition of *Historical Statistics of the United States*. The U.S. Bureau of the Census published the prior editions in 1949, 1960, and 1975, the last known as the Bicentennial Edition. Cambridge University Press publishes this, the Millennial Edition, with the permission of the Census Bureau. Some of the data and table documentation presented here are used without explicit quotation, but with permission, from the earlier editions. The Census Bureau takes no responsibility for the design of this edition or the accuracy of its content, which rests solely with the contributors, the editors, and Cambridge University Press.

Electronic edition. This edition of *Historical Statistics of the United States* is available in electronic form from Cambridge University Press. A compact disk containing the Bicentennial Edition of *Historical Statistics of the United States* is also available from the Press.

Copyright. Permission to quote or reprint copyright material should be obtained directly from the copyright owner. Much of the data reproduced in this work were originally published by agencies of the U.S. government and are in the public domain. Generally speaking, original data that have been published elsewhere under copyright protection may be freely used for educational, scholarly, or journalistic purposes (but not commercial purposes) with proper citation to the original source under the fair use provision of U.S. copyright law. Cambridge University Press has made every effort to secure, where necessary, permission to reproduce protected material. In almost every case the permission requested was freely granted. In a few instances, however, the copyright owner requested a specific citation. These citations may be found in the listing of Copyright Citations at the end of Volume 5.

Data Revisions and Updates

Reproduction and revision of data from prior editions. Although this volume provides many data series from prior editions of *Historical Statistics of the United States*, users should be aware that some data from these editions have subsequently been revised. Our contributors sought to present the most recently available data, and thus users probably will wish to use the data presented here rather than that in previous editions. In some cases, data from the earlier editions were judged to be unreliable or obsolete and were not reproduced.

Data updates. The data series in *Historical Statistics of the United States* do not have a uniform end date; instead, each table reports the data available at the time the contributor compiled the data. Many series in these volumes are continued on a regular basis with periodic updates and revisions by the agency, group, or individual responsible for the original data. Figures for many of the current series are presented in the *Statistical Abstract of the United States*, published annually by the U.S. Bureau of the Census. The updating of industrial statistics will be complicated by the switch in 1997 from the Standard Industrial Classification (SIC) system to the North American Industrial Classification System (NAICS); see the Introduction to Part D.

Additional data. In many cases, additional data can be found in the source documents, in references mentioned in the table documentation or chapter essays, and through the Internet sites of the groups or agencies noted in the sources for the data presented here.

Errors. In a work as large as this, errors of both commission and omission are likely to have occurred. Users who discover errors are urged to communicate them to Cambridge University Press, 40 West 20th Street, New York, New York 10011-4211, USA.

Data Selection

General principles. The criteria for the selection of data to be included in this edition varied broadly, depending on the particular subject matter. Generally, summary measures or aggregates at gross levels and immediately below were given highest priority for inclusion. Below such levels, selection was governed by the interplay of the following: the amount of space already devoted to a particular subject; the attempt to achieve a relatively balanced presentation among subject fields; whether other data already covered a particular topic; the quantity and quality of the data available; and the extent to which the data might enhance the value of other material in the book. During the early phases of the project these selection criteria were conveyed to our contributors, upon whose judgment we ultimately relied.

Data reliability. Our contributors have attempted to select data that they consider to be generally reliable and to reproduce faithfully the data reported in their sources. They have also provided citations and technical descriptions to assist users in making independent assessments of both the data's reliability and their suitability for a project at hand.

Original versus derived data. Primary emphasis was placed on the presentation of original, unmodified figures rather than derived data because they offer greater flexibility to users. Derived data – for example, averages, percentages, ratios, and index numbers – were provided if they were the accepted standard for presentation (for example, unemployment rates), if the table contributor judged that the derived data would be particularly helpful, or if the use of derived data saved a significant amount of space.

Topical coverage. Because the last thirty years have witnessed the expansion of data collection into areas that were only inadequately covered, if at all, in the 1970s, this edition has a broader topical scope than its predecessors. A tentative list of topics emerged after extensive discussions between the project's editors in chief and Cambridge University Press. The outline was widely circulated to scholars, reference librarians, and government statistical bureaus. After a revision of that outline, the project recruited contributors, who offered additional suggestions. What emerged from this process was an outline for the project that was both designed by the profession and feasible to accomplish.

Temporal coverage. Contributors were asked to take the data series under their charge as far backward and forward in time as possible. They were also encouraged to include important lapsed series – those that begin and terminate in the past – because such series are sometimes available only in out-of-print documents. Most data series in *Historical Statistics of the United States* provide annual or decennial data spanning at least twenty years, with the main exceptions being for special topics (the colonial period and the Confederate States of America), for newly developed series providing the only data available to represent an important subject field, and for short series that served as important extensions of longer series.

Data frequency. Annual data were given preference for inclusion, but certain series are presented only for years in which a national census was conducted and, in some instances, only for scattered dates, as dictated by data availability. When both annual figures and benchmark data exist, both series are sometimes shown. A major exception was made for Chapter Cb, which presents many of its series on a monthly or quarterly basis. Although this volume mainly provides annual data, underlying data are sometimes available more frequently from the original sources.

Geographical coverage. The data in *Historical Statistics of the United States* generally cover the nation as a whole, defined by the recognized borders of the country for the year in question. As new states were admitted to the Union, the coverage of the typical statistical series in this volume expands to include the new additions, without any special notation in the table documentation. The documentation should be consulted to determine if such changes in the boundaries of the United States are likely to have affected the series. When the year of a state's inclusion in a series differs significantly from its year of statehood, this fact was noted in the documentation whenever possible. Refer to Appendix 2 for the dates of statehood.

Subnational data. Because of limitations of space, data are generally not shown for regions, states, or localities. The underlying sources sometimes provide data in finer geographical detail than shown here. Some tables provide data for U.S. census regions or divisions; see Appendix 2 for more information on such regional classifications.

Outlying areas. In almost all cases, outlying areas are not included in the national totals reported here. Refer to Chapter Ef for additional information on such areas.

Organization of the Volume

Arrangement of the data. In this edition of *Historical Statistics of the United States,* data are arranged by broad subjects in five parts, each published in a separate volume and each volume containing several chapters. The tables in most chapters are further organized into various subsections (see the Detailed Table of Contents in each volume).

Essays. Each chapter is introduced by one or more essays that provide a general guide to the data, the sources, and the historical trends that have been emphasized in the scholarly literature. They contain a list of references that may be consulted by those interested in more detail.

Series identifiers. Each data series is assigned a unique alphanumeric identifier. The two letters in the identifier indicate the chapter in which the series resides. Within a chapter, series are numbered sequentially. Sets of contiguous series are identified by means of a series range (for example, series Da42–47). Source citations and table documentation are linked to the data series by means of such identifiers, which may be preferred over page numbers for use in reference citations.

Table identifiers. An entire table is identified by the range of series that it contains. For example, the first two tables in the chapter on vital statistics contain ten and twenty series, respectively; thus, they are identified as Table Ab1–10 and Table Ab11–30. Similarly, a group of contiguous tables is identified by a series range. Using the same example, these two tables could be referred to jointly as Tables Ab1–30.

Table Documentation

Table contributors. Each table provides the names of the contributors who selected, collected, and described the data. The editorial staff also reviewed the data and table documentation for accuracy, completeness, and clarity of presentation.

Sources. In most cases, full citations are given for data sources; however, when numerous issues of a publication were used, the source citations are usually limited to "annual issues" or similar notations. When data are reproduced from the Bicentennial Edition, the source citation lists the original source rather than the Bicentennial Edition, except under special circumstances.

Unpublished data. Nearly all the data reported here have been previously published or accepted for publication. Rare exceptions for previously unpublished data were allowed if a contributor felt that the data were particularly important and if peer review accepted the data for inclusion.

Integrated Public Use Microdata Series. A number of series reported in this edition are extracted from the Integrated Public Use Microdata Series (IPUMS). The IPUMS is composed of representative samples drawn from the returns of the decennial censuses of the population. All censuses from 1850 to 1990 are included, with the exception of 1930, which is under development, and 1890, the manuscripts for which were destroyed by fire. The IPUMS data and documentation are available over the Internet.*

Internet sources. Some data series in *Historical Statistics of the United States* are based on electronic sources; however, owing to the fleeting nature of specific Internet addresses or Web-based

_____

* Steven Ruggles, Matthew Sobek, et al., *Integrated Public Use Microdata Series: Version 2.0* (Historical Census Projects, University of Minnesota, 1997).

file names, we do not use them when identifying sources. Instead, we use more general phrasing to direct users to the Internet source.

Table documentation. Most tables are accompanied by documentation defining relevant terms and concepts, providing methodological and historical background, noting unusual values or comparability issues, explaining methods used to calculate derived data, and providing references to sources containing more detailed data or more extensive discussion. Unlike prior editions, which consolidated table documentation at the beginning of chapters, this edition locates the documentation with the tables, the intent being to increase its visibility, convenience, and thus use. Many tables are fully self-documenting, without cross references to other parts of this work; however, when cross references to other tables or essays are provided, the user is encouraged to follow those references.

Footnotes. There is no sharp demarcation between the type of information conveyed in the ordinary table documentation and that conveyed in the footnotes. Roughly speaking, footnotes are used for two purposes: to draw attention to issues of particular importance (footnotes as warnings) or to comment on matters related to specific columns, rows, or cells in a table.

Footnote order. Within a table, footnotes are numbered sequentially as follows: first the general footnotes that apply to the entire table; then left-to-right across the table header (the footnotes governing specific series); and finally footnotes attached to the table stub and the data area, proceeding in top-to-bottom, then left-to-right fashion (as used here, the directional terms apply to tables with standard page orientation). A footnote's first appearance within a table determines its position within the sequential numbering.

Total and subtotals. In most cases, a table's header structure will clearly indicate the total–subtotal relationships among the series. The typical practice in this volume is to provide the total series first, followed by its components. Often the sum of the components will equal the total, perhaps with small deviations attributable to rounding or other causes; however, sometimes the breakdowns provided in a table are not exhaustive, and the components will add to an amount less than the total. Users should consult the table documentation and exercise caution in this regard.

Race and ethnicity. Many tables provide disaggregations by race or ethnicity. This volume typically uses the terms "white," "black," "Asian" (or "Asian American"), "Indian" (or "Amerindian" or "Native American"), and "Hispanic." Note that a person identified as Hispanic may be of any race. See the essay on definitions and measurement of race and ethnicity in the Introduction to Part A for a discussion of racial classification and identification as it applies to the collection of historical statistics in the United States.

Dates

Date ranges. Throughout the table documentation and the chapter essays, date ranges are inclusive: for example, 1964–1987 includes both 1964 and 1987.

Year of record. The identification of the year of record – in other words, the precise meaning of the years shown in a table stub – was complicated by the failure of some sources to state whether the data were prepared on a calendar year, fiscal year, or some other basis; by changes in the year of record over time; and, in some instances, by imprecision or silence in the source concerning the beginning or ending date for the year of record. Table contributors

attempted to clarify such matters, but ambiguity remains in some tables.

Transition quarters. Sometimes the year of record changes in the middle of a table, and values are provided for the "transition quarter" – the gap between the end of the old year of record and beginning of the new. In such cases, users will see a (TQ) designation in the table stub. Nearly all transition quarters in this volume are associated with the year 1976, when the federal government changed the end of its fiscal year from June 30 to September 30. In rare cases, the (TQ) designation will be for a transition period that is not actually a quarter, but some other fraction of a year.

Units, Measures, and Monetary Values

Units of measure. Series are usually expressed in the units reported in the original source. In some cases, however, units were converted to make two or more data series comparable, or to create a single series when splicing data from multiple sources. The approach taken in these volumes was to restrict the units information to true *measures* and to rely on the table title and layered headers to convey other details about the things being counted or measured. Sometimes series are expressed in units too complex for pithy statement; in these rare cases, a generic unit of measure is given, with further elaboration left to the table documentation.

Billion and trillion. The American and Canadian definitions of billion (10^9) and trillion (10^{12}) are used throughout, not the definitions used in England, Germany, and many other countries.

Index numbers. Some series are expressed in terms of index numbers. In such cases, the base period of the index is provided where the unit of measure would normally be found. For a discussion of index numbers, see the essay on prices and price indexes in Chapter Cc and the essay on national income and product in Chapter Ca.

Weights and measures. Most data series are expressed in American units (the U.S. Customary System) rather than metric units (the International System). For a discussion of these two systems and for conversion information, see Appendix 1.

Monetary values. Unless otherwise noted, monetary values are expressed in current or nominal terms – in other words, the actual historical values (usually U.S. dollars), not adjusted for previous or subsequent changes in prices. This standard was adopted to avoid attaching the word "current" or "nominal" to every reference to a monetary unit. When monetary values have been adjusted in some fashion, this is stated explicitly and the relevant base period is given. For a discussion of monetary values, see Appendix 1 and the essay on prices and price indexes in Chapter Cc.

Data Values

Data precision and significant digits. In making decisions regarding the precision with which data values should be presented, fidelity to sources was our primary consideration. Thus, the underlying data files for *Historical Statistics of the United States* – available in the electronic edition – retain the full precision provided by table contributors, even though this level of detail might be deemed excessive by scientific standards for the reporting of significant digits. In most cases, the detail comes straight from the sources themselves; therefore, exact reproduction provides a valuable check for researchers wanting to trace the provenance of a number or hunt down an anomaly. In other cases, excessive precision comes from spreadsheet calculations made by table contributors (for example, in the computation of derived data). Here, too, we did not impose our judgments concerning the appropriate precision and instead retained the full detail provided by contributors. Users should note that historical sources sometimes change the precision with which they report data over time. Also, some tables contain series reported in the sources at different levels of detail but that, for ease of comparison, are provided here in consistent units. The usual indication of varying precision – whether in a single series or across multiple series within a table – is a run of data values with trailing zeros, either before or after the decimal point. In such cases, users will need to exercise judgment concerning the precision of the data.

Decimal precision for display purposes. While the underlying data files retain all of the detail provided by table contributors, the data displayed in the print edition of *Historical Statistics of the United States* are shown in rounded fashion, typically with no more than three digits following the decimal point. Similarly, tables generated for display purposes by the electronic edition are formatted using the same rounding conventions; however, the underlying files available for downloading provide the values at full precision.

Zero values and (Z). A zero in a data series means exactly that: a reported value of zero. In some cases, an underlying data value may be so small that it rounds to zero when displayed at the level of decimal precision chosen for the series. In such cases, a (Z) marker is used rather than a zero value. Stated more precisely, the (Z) notation indicates a *nonzero value that is not shown or possibly not known*. In the former case – a nonzero value not shown – (Z) means that the value falls below the threshold of our rounding convention: the number rounds to zero, as displayed in this volume (full precision for such values is available through the electronic edition). In the latter case – a nonzero value not known – (Z) means that the original source did not provide a specific value. Owing to these complexities, the meaning of the (Z) marker is specifically documented in every table that uses the device.

Dash as a data value. The "—" marker means that a value is not being reported. There are several possible reasons: the data are not available anywhere; the data were not provided in the source but conceivably could be found with sufficient research; the data were available in the source but the table contributor decided that they should not be reported (for example, unreliable data); or the data might conceivably be reported as a zero, but the table contributor decided for conceptual reasons to represent it as "no value reported" (for example, if a category or program covered by the series did not yet exist). Some sources do not carefully distinguish between zero values and missing data. Table contributors attempted to eliminate such confusion, but in some cases the "—" marker could mean that the value, if shown, would be zero.

Historical Statistics
of the
United States

Millennial Edition
Volume 4

Part D
Economic Sectors

Introduction

INDUSTRIAL CLASSIFICATION

Richard Sutch

Market economies like that of the United States are among the most complex institutions ever devised. Millions of individual transactions are conducted every day; myriad goods and services are produced, transported, and exchanged in hundreds of thousands of different locations. For the most part, market exchange is conducted without an overall plan or central direction. To understand how this complex, decentralized market economy works; to chart its progress; and to make forecasts, we need to be able to track many different exchanges. Statistical tracking schemes that have been devised to record, aggregate, categorize, and simplify the resulting record are called social accounting systems.

The Millennial Edition of *Historical Statistics of the United States* for the most part relies on three accounting systems: national income and product accounting, input accounting, and industrial classification systems. The concepts of national income and product, discussed in Chapter Ca, define a material measure of the productive accomplishments of the economy.

Another concept used to organize aggregate accounting systems is the distinction between outputs and inputs. The outputs included in the national income and product accounts are the goods and services that satisfy the final wants of households, businesses, and government agencies. Inputs are the goods and services that are used to produce the outputs. Yet inputs themselves are a product of economic activity. If wheat is grown to make bread and if bread is produced to satisfy the wants of consumers, then the wheat is an input. Goods used as inputs are called intermediate products. The bread is an output. Such goods are called final products. There are also inputs that are services, not goods. These are the services rendered by the "factors of production," traditionally categorized into three broad groups labeled as land, labor, and capital, where "land" is thought of more broadly as natural resources. The services of labor include the productive power both of human energy and of human skill and knowledge. "Capital" refers to goods produced for the purpose of producing other goods; examples include machines, vehicles, and structures. Capital services raise the productivity of other inputs in the production process. Thus, at a high level of aggregation, the production of final output can be thought of as the result of a production process that employs land, labor, and capital.

Land and other natural resources are treated in Chapters Da and Db. Some factors that influence the productivity of land, such as weather and the environment, are dealt with in Chapter Cf. Labor is covered in Chapter Ba, and two factors that affect the "quality" of labor, education and health, are the subjects of Chapters Bc and Bd. Chapter Ce is concerned with capital. It should be noted that capital itself is an output; only the services of capital are inputs. Because capital raises the productivity of other inputs to the production process, a key issue in any analysis of economic change is how the economy changes its stock of capital. It does that through saving. Output that is not consumed is saved in the form of capital. Chapter Cd treats consumer expenditures, and Chapter Ce focuses on the processes of saving and investment – that is, how the economy partitions the flow of output between final consumption and the creation of new capital (investment).

An industry comprises firms or establishments that produce products or services that are identical, similar, or closely related to each other. Thus, all of the doctors in private practice and all of the health maintenance organizations (HMOs) and all of the hospitals taken collectively might be described as the "health care industry" or "health and medical services industry." By this definition, industries may be defined either narrowly or broadly. "Health care" is an example of a broadly defined industry; "offices and clinics of podiatrists" and "kidney dialysis centers" are examples of narrowly defined industries. Viewed in this way, the industrial structure of an economy consists of a list of broadly defined industrial sectors that are broken into more narrowly defined industries, which in turn may be subdivided still further, in a descending hierarchy.

At the highest level of aggregation, the production units in the economy are conventionally divided into three broad categories:

Primary: agriculture and the extractive industries such as mining and fishing

Secondary: goods-producing industries such as manufacturing and construction

Tertiary: non-goods-producing or service industries

Before World War II, each government agency responsible for collecting statistics on output or employment was free to define the industries under its purview in whatever way suited its own purposes. In many ways, this each-to-its-own approach was, and is, appropriate. Industrial classification, like taxonomies and classification systems in all sciences, must be in the first instance designed to meet the purposes of a specific analysis. During the World War II mobilization, however, economic planners and regulators found the inconsistency of definitions across government agencies a hindrance to their efforts to obtain accurate and comparable data on the nation's productive capacity. Accordingly, in 1945 the U.S. Office of Management and Budget (OMB) standardized the classification of industries and the collection and reporting of data with the Standard Industrial Classification (SIC) system. Although the SIC system underwent revisions several times (the latest in 1987), its basic philosophy and structure remained in force from 1945 to 1997, when it was replaced with a different system.[1] The new system was adopted to facilitate international comparisons.

---

[1] For a description of the SIC system, see U.S. Office of Management and Budget (1987).

The first principle of the SIC system was to define an establishment as an economic unit – usually located at one place – where goods were manufactured, services were performed, or resources were extracted. A single company might consist of many establishments in different physical locations – factories, offices, stores, and warehouses. By SIC definition, establishments include both the production or primary service providers and the "auxiliary workers" who provide services – such as management, data processing, personnel services, and transportation – to other units within the same company. Each establishment was then assigned to one of eleven broad divisions, each designated by a capital letter:

SIC code

A	Agriculture, forestry, and fishing
B	Mining
C	Construction
D	Manufacturing
E	Transportation, communications, and electric, gas, and sanitary utilities
F	Wholesale trade
G	Retail trade
H	Finance, insurance, and real estate (FIRE)
I	Services
J	Public administration
K	Not elsewhere classified (NEC)

These top-level divisions are frequently called economic sectors. The eleven sectors are segmented by OMB into "major industrial groups" and assigned a two-digit numerical code. For example, the division of mining (SIC code B) was divided into five groups:

SIC code

10	Metal mining
11	Anthracite coal mining
12	Bituminous coal mining
13	Oil and gas extraction
14	Extraction of nonmetallic minerals except fuels

These major groups are commonly called two-digit industries. Two-digit industries are broken down into three-digit industries, and three-digit industries are broken down, in turn, into four-digit industries. For example, consider the metal can industry, SIC 3411:

SIC code

D	Manufacturing
34	Fabricated metal products
341	Metal containers
3411	Metal cans
3412	Metal shipping barrels, drums, kegs, and pails

In 1997 the SIC system was replaced by the new North American Industry Classification System (NAICS, pronounced "nakes"). Development of the NAICS system was undertaken jointly by the governments of Canada, Mexico, and the United States to introduce comparability across North American countries in their classification of industries and to aid in the implementation of the North American Free Trade Agreement (NAFTA). Unlike the periodic revisions to the SIC system, the NAICS is a fundamental change. It redefined the concept of an establishment, revised the principles used to assign an establishment to a specific industry, increased the number of economic sectors from eleven to twenty, increased the number of industries defined at the narrowest level, recognizing many new industries in the process, and increased the hierarchical depth from four (expressed with four digits) to five (expressed with six digits).[2]

The major change introduced by NAICS in the definition of an establishment was to disaggregate the SIC establishment into production and "auxiliary" units and to consider the auxiliary units as separate establishments. This moved many workers and their associated output from the primary and tertiary industries into one of the service industries. Next, a single consistent economic principle was adopted to classify each unit. NAICS defines an establishment's industry exclusively on the basis of the production processes it uses. Previously, many establishments were classified on that principle, but others were classified using different principles, such as the class of customer (individuals or firms) or the function of the product or service produced. Doing away with the class-of-customer criteria has greatly affected the boundary between the retail and wholesale trade sectors. Under NAICS, retailers are defined as establishments that sell merchandise in small quantities, generally relying on mass-media advertising, high-traffic locations, self-service, and attractive in-store displays. Examples of retail establishments include grocery stores, department stores, and boutiques. Wholesalers sell goods in large quantities using business-oriented methods such as specialized catalogs, direct customer contacts with sales personnel, and direct delivery to the customer from warehouse or office locations.

The revised, expanded list of top-level economic sectors in NAICS replaces the SIC system's A through K list, as shown in Table Pd-A. For most of the top-level NAICS sectors, a rough indicator of the corresponding two-digit SIC industries is provided. Where no indication is given, the correspondence between the two systems at the two-digit level is too low to provide a helpful comparison. With the sectors where the correspondence is indicated, the changes in the NAICS classifications are greater than the similarity of sector titles would indicate. No NAICS sector corresponds exactly to a collection of SIC sectors, and the lack of correspondence is particularly evident in the service sectors. NAICS sector 55, for example, is almost exclusively made of establishments previously considered auxiliaries of primary establishments in other industries. While the correspondences indicated cannot be used to splice data for an SIC industry to data for a NAICS industry, they are given here as a rough guide to the differences and relationships between the two classification systems. Note that most of the expansion of industrial sectors comes in the service group.

The last economic census taken using the SIC system was in 1992. The data for 1997 has been released with tabulations based on both the 1987 SIC codes and the 1997 NAICS codes. Unfortunately, the federal government has no systematic plans to continue the old SIC system in parallel with the new system or to estimate

---

[2] For an overview of the NAICS system, see U.S. Bureau of the Census (n.d.). The full system is described in National Technical Information Service (1997).

TABLE Pd-A Correspondence between top-level NAICS sectors and two-digit SIC industries

	NAICS	
Code	Sector	SIC code
11	Agriculture, forestry, fishing, and hunting	01–09
21	Mining	10–14
22	Utilities	49
23	Construction	15–17
31–33	Manufacturing	20–39
42	Wholesale trade	50–51
44–45	Retail trade	52–59
48	Transportation	40–47
51	Information	—
52	Finance and insurance	60–64
53	Real estate and rental and leasing	—
54	Professional, scientific, and technical services	—
55	Management of companies and enterprises	—
56	Administrative and support services	—
61	Educational services	82
62	Health care and social assistance	80, 83
71	Arts, entertainment, and recreation	79, 84
72	Accommodation and food services	70
81	Other services, except public administration	—
92	Public administration	91–97

TABLE Pd-B Guide to the coverage of economic sectors in *Historical Statistics of the United States*

Sector	Chapter	NAIC Codes	SIC Codes
Primary			
Crop and animal production	Da	111–112	01–02
Support activities for agriculture	Da	1151–1152	07
Forestry, fishing, and hunting	Db	113–114	08–09
Mining	Db	21	10–14
Secondary			
Electric and gas utilities	Dh	22	491–493
Water, refuse, and sanitary services	Dh	—	494–497
Construction	Dc	23	15–17
Manufacturing	Dd	31–33	20–39
Wholesale trade	De	42	50–51
Retail trade	De	44–45	52–59
Transportation	Df	48	40–47
Service			
Information services	Dg	51	—
Finance and insurance	Cj	52	60–64
Real estate and rental and leasing	Dc	53	—
Professional, scientific, and technical services	Cg	54	—
Management of companies and enterprises	Ch	55	—
Administrative and support services	Ch	56	—
Educational services	Bc	61	82
Health care and social assistance	Bd	62	80, 83
Arts, entertainment, and recreation	Dh	71	79, 84
Accommodation	Dh	721	70
Food service and drinking places	Dh	72	58
Other services, except public administration	Dh	81	—
General government and public administration	Ea	921, 923–926	91, 93, 9411–9651
Justice, public order, and safety activities	Ec	922	92
Space research and technology	Cg	927	9661
National security	Ed	92811	9711
International affairs	Ee	92812	9721

industry aggregates using the NAICS for years before 1997. This will make it difficult or impossible for users to construct a continuous time series for a given economic sector or industry that bridges the SIC–NAICS gap. In some cases, the changes in sectoral differences are small enough that researchers interested in long-term trends will be tempted to splice the new industry data to the old; however, they should do so with caution. For example, construction is the least-changed economic sector, yet three of its twenty-eight detailed industries are new and fourteen are revised. Moreover, significant economic activity has been shifted from auxiliary units once classified as part of the construction industry to one or more service industries.

Of greater interest to users of the *Historical Statistics of the United States* is information on how the economic sectors (however technically defined) are arranged in this work. Because the Millennial Edition was conceived and planned during 1995 and 1996, it is organized more along the lines of the SIC system than the NAICS. Moreover, most of the data are based on the old system because the NAICS was introduced first in 1997 and was not fully implemented across government agencies until 2002. Table Pd-B is a sectoral guide to the material in *Historical Statistics of the United States*.

References

National Technical Information Service. 1997. *The North American Industry Classification System – United States, 1997.*

U.S. Bureau of the Census, Economic Classification Policy Committee. n.d. "New Data for a New Economy."

U.S. Office of Management and Budget. 1987. *Standard Industrial Classification Manual 1987.* U.S. Government Printing Office.

CHAPTER Da

Agriculture

Editor: Alan L. Olmstead

Associate Editors: Julian M. Alston, Bruce L. Gardner, Philip G. Pardey,
Paul W. Rhode, and Daniel A. Sumner

INTRODUCTION

Alan L. Olmstead

Underlying the data in this chapter is one of the epic stories in world history. In the nineteenth and twentieth centuries powerful forces continuously reshaped American agriculture. A hallmark of the nineteenth century was the settlement of the continent with the addition of hundreds of millions of acres of farmland and millions of farms and farmers. In the twentieth century, the amount of farmland changed little, but the growing gap in opportunities between the farm and nonfarm sectors led to a massive exodus from America's farms. In the 1950s alone, more people moved off farms than resided on farms in 2000. Over the course of the past 200 years, mechanical and biological innovations dramatically increased farm productivity and changed the nature of farm work. At the new millennium, the typical farm worker produced more than fifteen times as much output as did a worker in 1900.

New transportation and communications technologies – such as railroads, automobiles, surfaced roads, telephones, radios, and televisions – significantly reduced the distance between farm and urban life. Along with these changes, improvements in the storage and handling of goods and the growth of urban populations broadened the market for farm goods, creating incentives for farmers to specialize. With this came an increase in farm size and income, along with a growing dependence on nonfarm inputs in the production process. Until the 1930s, American agriculture closely approximated the competitive ideal of a large number of producers who were subject to the dictates of the marketplace. This changed in the 1930s as the federal government responded to prolonged agricultural crises by dramatically increasing its role in the farm economy.

The data presented in this chapter documenting these enormous structural, demographic, and economic changes are crucial to our understanding of the past and to our ability to develop appropriate policies for the future. Throughout most of human history, and even in large parts of the world today, the dominant concern has been how to produce enough food and fiber to feed and clothe the population. Unlocking the causal relationships that explain the sources of productivity growth in American agriculture remains one of the important intellectual challenges of our time. This task requires a better understanding of such issues as the linkages between the scientific research community and the farm sector, and of the role of market forces and government policies in the invention and diffusion of new technologies. To grapple with all of these issues, measurement and data are called for.

Agriculture is no stranger to controversy, especially regarding distributional questions and labor market institutions. The information presented in this chapter offers a valuable starting point for the study of such complex issues as the prevalence of tenancy and sharecropping in the American South, the decline in the number of family farms, and the distribution of government support payments. The series on the output and prices of specific crops and livestock provide the basic data for our understanding of the health and performance of the farm economy. The sections dealing with farm structure, productivity, and government policy provide the data or raw materials for analyzing the transformation and integration of the American farm sector over the past two centuries.

The five essays that follow offer an overview of the major trends in American agricultural development. Table Da-A draws on issues relevant to all five to provide a unifying overview of key landmarks

Acknowledgments

Alan L. Olmstead and Paul W. Rhode thank Leslie Maulhardt and Shelagh Mackay for their assistance and valuable comments. In addition, they thank the participants in the Conference on the Agricultural Chapter of the *Historical Statistics of the United States* Millennial Edition Project, held at University of California, Davis, in 1997, for their suggestions. This chapter received financial support from the Farm Foundation and the Cooperative State Research, Education, and Extension Service, U.S. Department of Agriculture. Work on this project was facilitated by a fellowship granted to Alan L. Olmstead by the International Centre for Economic Research (ICER) in Turin, Italy. The chapter editors thank Lisa Cappellari, Susana Iranzo, Claudio Robles, Janine L. F. Wilson, and Leslie Maulhardt for their valuable assistance in assembling and preparing the data. Shelagh Mackay deserves special recognition for her insightful comments and for supervising the day-to-day affairs of the project.

Julian M. Alston and Philip G. Pardey gratefully acknowledge the generous financial assistance they received from the U.S. Farm Foundation, which helped make this research possible.

Bruce Gardner thanks Alan Olmstead for his helpful comments on the essay. He thanks Liesl Koch for assistance in preparing the tables on farm income, prices, and agricultural finance, and Ken Erickson, Howard Elitzak, George Smith, Jerome Stam, and Roger Strickland for their help with particular data issues.

Daniel Sumner appreciates the contributions of research assistants Daniel Hallstrom, Nicolai Kuminoff, and Michele Lee. He also acknowledges the help of many individuals and offices at the U.S. Department of Agriculture, especially at the National Agricultural Statistics Service, Farm Service Agency, Agricultural Marketing Service, Economic Research Service, and Office of Budget and Policy Analysis.

TABLE Da-A   Chronology of U.S. agricultural history: 1609–2000

1609	Settlers at Jamestown learned from Indians how to grow corn.
1769	The orange was introduced into California, but the first grove was not planted until 1804.
1793	Eli Whitney invented the cotton gin, which he patented in 1794.
1820	U.S. population: 9,638,453; 72 percent of workforce in agriculture. Fifty to sixty hours of labor were required to produce one acre (twenty bushels) of wheat with a walking plow, a bundle of brush for a harrow, hand broadcast of seed, harvesting by sickle, and threshing by flail.
1825	Thomas Kensett secured a patent on the use of tin cans in preserving food.
1831	Cyrus McCormick invented his grain reaper, which he patented in 1834.
1836	Hiram Moore and J. Hascall invented the grain combine.
1837	John Deere began manufacturing plows with steel share and smooth wrought iron moldboard.
1840	Justus von Liebig's *Organic Chemistry in Its Applications to Agriculture and Physiology* appeared.
1844	George Easterly patented a grain header.
1846	Robert Reid developed a corn variety (Reid's Yellow Dent) that eventually dominated the Corn Belt.
1850	Thirty to thirty-five man-hours were required to produce one acre (forty bushels) of corn using a walking plow and harrow and planting by hand. Total U.S. population: 23,191,876. Farm population: 11,680,000; 64 percent of the workforce in agriculture.
1856	The first butter factory was established.
1862	President Abraham Lincoln signed legislation that created the U.S. Department of Agriculture. President Lincoln approved the Homestead Act and the Morrill Land-Grant College Act.
1865	Slavery was abolished by the thirteenth amendment to the Constitution.
1867	Oliver Hudson Kelley, an employee of the U.S. Department of Agriculture, organized the Patrons of Husbandry, later known as the National Grange. This was the first general farmers' organization to permit women equality of membership and privilege.
1868	A refrigerator car widely used by railroads in the 1870s was patented by William Davis.
1869	James Oliver patented a plow made of chilled iron. The gypsy moth was brought to the United States and accidentally established in Medford, Massachusetts. David L. Garver of Michigan patented the first practical spring-toothed harrow, which eliminated breaking teeth on roots and stones.
1870	The New York Cotton Exchange opened, followed by one in New Orleans a year later.
1871	The first Granger law regulating railroads and warehouses was passed in Illinois.
1872	Luther Burbank produced the Burbank potato, the first of a long series of new or improved varieties of vegetables, fruits, and flowers.
1873	The "Washington navel" orange was introduced to California from Brazil.
1874	Manufacture of oleomargarine began in the United States. The first important introduction of Turkey wheat by Mennonites into Marion and Harvey Counties, Kansas, was made. The Glidden barbed wire patent was granted. Barbed wire contributed greatly to the agricultural settlement of the Great Plains.
1875	The first state agricultural experiment station in the United States was established in Middletown, Connecticut, through the efforts of Samuel W. Johnson. In the same year, the California Agricultural Experiment Station was founded at the University of California by Eugene W. Hilgard.
1884	An epidemic of a contagious bovine pleuropneumonia of foreign origin led to the adoption by the Congress of the first federal animal quarantine law. The Bureau of Animal Industry was established in accordance with an act of Congress.
1887	The Hatch Experiment Station Act was approved, providing federal grants to states for agricultural experimentation.
1888	Refrigerated rail cars were used to ship meat and to haul fruit from California to New York.
1889	The Bureau of Animal Industry found that cattle fever was carried by ticks. The U.S. Department of Agriculture was raised to cabinet status.
1890	Eight to ten man-hours were required to produce one acre (twenty bushels) of wheat with a gang plow, a seeder, a harrow, a binder, a thresher, wagons, and horses. U.S. population: 62,947,714. Farm population: 26,379,000; 43 percent of the workforce in agriculture.
1892	The first successful gasoline tractor was built by John Froelich. The cotton boll weevil was found near Brownsville, Texas, and began to spread north and east.
1895	Sunkist Growers, Inc., for many years called the California Fruit Growers Exchange, was incorporated as the Southern California Fruit Exchange.
1898	The U.S. Department of Agriculture started to introduce large numbers of soybean varieties. Commercial production of durum wheat began.
1900	Kharkof wheat, a bearded hard red winter variety, was introduced from Russia. Wilt-resistant cotton varieties were developed. U.S. population: 75,994,575. Farm population: 29,414,000; 38 percent of the workforce in agriculture.
1901	The Bureau of Plant Industry (which included Forestry, Chemistry, and Soils) was established under the authority of the appropriation act of March 1901, but not confirmed by an act of Congress until June 3, 1902.
1904	The Holt Company fitted a steam tractor with "caterpillar" tracks.
1906	The Holt Company produced a caterpillar tractor powered by a gasoline engine. The first-known rural electric line was constructed at Hood River, Oregon. The Pure Food and Drug Act was approved.

TABLE Da-A Chronology of U.S. agricultural history: 1609–2000 *Continued*

1907	The U.S. Bureau of Animal Industry at Ames, Iowa, demonstrated a successful hog cholera serum. The American Society of Agricultural Engineers was founded.
1910	U.S. population: 91,972,266. Farm population: 32,077,000; 31 percent of the workforce in agriculture.
1911	The first Farm Bureau was formed in Broome County, New York.
1912	Marquis wheat, which had been developed by A. P. Sanders in Canada in 1892, was introduced into the United States. The Plant Quarantine Act was approved.
1913	The Bull Tractor Company introduced a 4,650-pound machine, the "Bull with the Pull," which was the forerunner of the light tractor.
1914	The Smith–Lever Cooperative Agricultural Extension Act, which formalized cooperative agricultural extension work, was introduced.
1916	The Federal Farm Loan Act, providing for twelve farmland banks, was approved. The law grew out of Country Life Commission recommendations. The U.S. Warehouse Act, authorizing licensing, bonding, and inspection of public warehouses storing agricultural products, was approved.
1917	The European corn borer was discovered near Boston, Massachusetts. Japanese beetles were discovered in New Jersey.
1918	The development of a system for growing modern hybrid seed corn was completed by Donald F. Jones.
1920	U.S. population: 105,710,620. Farm population: 31,614,269; 27 percent of workforce in agriculture. Enclosed gears developed for a tractor. The American Farm Bureau Federation was formally organized and its constitution ratified.
1922	The first electrically heated and electrically regulated incubator used for chickens was patented by Ira M. Petersime. The Capper–Volstead Act declared that a cooperative association was not, by reason of the manner in which it was organized and normally operated, a combination in restraint of trade in violation of the federal antitrust statutes.
1926	Henry Wallace developed commercial hybrid seed corn. The Congress passed the Cooperative Marketing Act, which created a Division of Cooperative Marketing in the U.S. Department of Agriculture.
1928	John D. Rust patented the first successful spindle cotton picker.
1929	W. Gericke invented hydroponics. The Mediterranean fruit fly was discovered in Florida, and an all-out program was instituted to combat it.
1930	U.S. population: 122,775,046. Farm population: 30,445,350; 22 percent of workforce in agriculture. Six to eight man-hours were required to produce one acre (forty bushels) of corn with a two-bottom gang plow, a seven-foot tandem disk, a four-section harrow, a two-row cultivator, a two-row planter, and a two-row picker. Three to four man-hours were required to produce one acre (twenty bushels) of wheat with a tractor, a three-bottom gang plow, a ten-foot tandem disk, a harrow, a twelve-foot combine, and trucks. Fifty-eight percent of all farms had cars; 34 percent had telephones; and 13 percent had electricity, including home generating plants. The estimated average equity of farm operators in the land they farmed was 41 percent. The Plant Patent Act was approved.
1933	The Agricultural Adjustment Act was approved. The Commodity Credit Corporation was established.
1935	The Rural Electrification Administration was established by Executive Order 7037, and it was incorporated into the U.S. Department of Agriculture on June 1, 1939. A one-man combine was developed for harvesting wheat.
1937	The first soil conservation district in the United States was organized.
1938	The Agricultural Adjustment Act of 1938 provided for farm price support and adjustment programs based on an "ever-normal granary" concept. It replaced and invalidated the Agricultural Adjustment Act of 1933.
1940	U.S. population: 131,820,000. Farm population: 30,840,000; 18 percent of workforce in agriculture. Fifty-eight percent of all farms had automobiles; 25 percent had telephones; and 33 percent had electricity.
1946	The Research and Marketing Act was signed.
1949	The usefulness of antibiotics in promoting animal nutrition was demonstrated.
1950	U.S. population: 151,132,000. Farm population: 25,058,000; 11 percent of workforce in agriculture.
1968	Ninety-six percent of all cotton was being harvested mechanically.
1970	The Plant Variety Protection Act was passed. Approximately 70 percent of corn produced in the five principal Corn Belt states was harvested by combines equipped with corn heads.
1985	In the 1980s "no-till" or "low-till" methods of preparing land for planting were used by more farmers on a variety of crops. The objective is to enhance yields while lessening erosion. More herbicides are used than under high-till conditions, and a greater degree of management control is required.
2000	U.S. population: 282,000,000. Farm population: 4,591,000; 2.4 percent of the workforce in agriculture.

Sources

Julian M. Alston and Philip G. Pardey, *Making Science Pay: The Economics of Agricultural R&D Policy* (AEI Press, 1996), pp. 116–21; Maryanna S. Smith and Dennis M. Roth, "Chronological Landmarks in American Agriculture," U.S. Department of Agriculture, Agriculture Information Bulletin number 425, revised (November 1990).

in American agricultural development. This table highlights scientific and technological breakthroughs, the course of labor productivity, and important legislative changes. Together these developments have revolutionized rural life and farm productivity.

FARMS AND FARM STRUCTURE

Alan L. Olmstead and Paul W. Rhode

It is currently popular to conceive of the American economy as undergoing a fundamental transition from an industrial to an information-based economy. Dramatic structural changes associated with globalization, de-industrialization, and rapid technological innovation have generated considerable controversy as old ways of living and doing business have been superseded by the new. History offers evidence on several earlier structural transformations, but few have been as significant as that summarized in the data contained in this chapter. The history of American agriculture is in large part the story of the transformation of the United States from a predominantly rural, agricultural economy to an urban, industrial, and service economy.

Farm Population and the Number of Farms

Figure Da-B displays national statistics on the farm population, the number of farms, and farm employment.[1] As these numbers show, the size of the agricultural sector continued to grow rapidly during the late nineteenth and early twentieth centuries while the country was industrializing. Of course, the farm sector's relative size fell over this period as the nonfarm sector grew even more rapidly. As one indication of these crosscutting trends, the farm population increased from 22 million people in 1880 to 32 million people in 1910 whereas the sector's share of the national population declined from 44 percent to 35 percent during this period.

The size of the farm sector, measured in terms of the value of agricultural output, has continued to grow over the long run. The nominal value of farm products sold rose from about $858 million in 1925 to about $196 billion in 1997 (series Da423). However, the size of the U.S. farm sector, measured in terms of the number of farmers and farms, reached a plateau in the period between 1910 and 1940. The number of farms varied between 6.4 and 6.8 million units throughout this thirty-year period while the farm population hovered in a range of 30.5 to 32.5 million persons. Although U.S. agriculture suffered "hard times" during much of the 1920s and 1930s, there was little tendency for the sector to contract. Indeed, as the figures on off-farm migration indicate, three quarters of a million people, on net, moved "back to the farm" between 1931 and 1933 (series Da3). After World War II, however, U.S. agriculture entered a period of rapid adjustment that witnessed wholesale changes in the labor force and the structure of farming. Between 1945 and 1960, more than 15 million people migrated out of the farm sector. By 1960, there were about 16 million people remaining on the nation's 4 million farms. By the eve of the new millennium, these numbers fell to fewer than 5 million people living on the

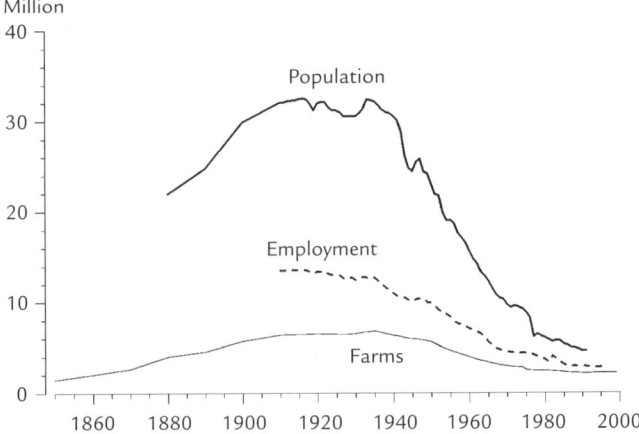

FIGURE Da-B   Farms, farm population, and farm employment: 1850–1999

Sources

Farms: 1850–1900, series Da16; thereafter, series Da4. Population: 1880–1900, series Da14; thereafter, series Da1. Employment: series Da612.

nation's 2 million farms. Although the actual decline in the farm population was largely a post-1940 phenomenon, the decline in the relative size of the farm population dates back to the early nineteenth century. Every decade between 1880 and 2000 has witnessed at least a modest decline in the farm population as a percentage of the total population, with the ratio falling from about 42 percent in 1900, to 15 percent at midcentury, to less than 2 percent in 2000.[2]

The aggregate national data mask significant variations in agricultural development at the regional level (Olmstead and Rhode 1993). By its nature, farming is characterized by substantial differences (e.g., climate, terrain, soil quality, and distance from market) across geographic areas – avocados can be grown in Southern California but not in North Dakota. To highlight these important differences, this chapter departs from the general design of this volume, which focuses on the national picture, by including extensive data at the state and regional levels. The disaggregated series on the farm population and the number of farms included in the census (Tables Da28–158) make clear that over the early twentieth century, when the national aggregates were roughly constant, substantial regional differences existed. For example, the farm population in the (census's) Northeast and North Central states was declining after 1900, whereas that in the South and West continued to expand until 1935. Similarly, the numbers of farms in the Northeast, which peaked in 1880, and the East North Central states, which peaked in 1900, fell steadily during the early twentieth century, whereas those in the West North Central states, the South, and the West continued to grow. It is notable that after World War II, the farm population and the number of farms declined in virtually every state in the nation.

Figure Da-C shows the trends in the acreage of U.S. farmland over the past 150 years. The figure illustrates one of the most significant developments in U.S. agricultural history – the enormous

---

[1] The definitions of the many terms used in this chapter – such as the "farm population," what constitutes a "farm," and "farm employment" – can be found in the text for each table. Such notes also document how many of these definitions have changed over time.

[2] An important caveat is in order when using these data to assess productivity growth. The raw data showing the farm population, the number of farm operators, and farm employment do not take into account the changing productive quality of the agricultural population and thus may significantly overstate the actual decline in labor inputs. On average, farmers today have far more education and skills than did farmers in 1850 or 1900. As a result an hour of agricultural labor in 2000 embodies more inputs than an hour of labor in 1900.

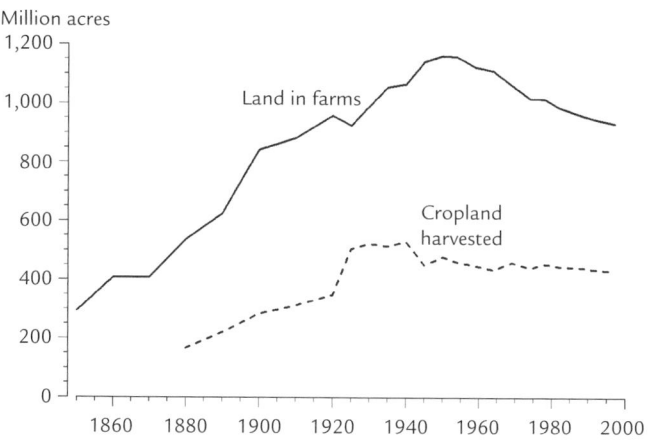

FIGURE Da-C   Land in farms and cropland harvested: 1850–1997

Sources

Series Da17 and Da20.

expansion in total farm acreage. Between 1850 and 1910, land in farms more than tripled. This was not simply the result of the territorial expansion of the country, because throughout the nineteenth and early twentieth centuries a vast amount of land in already settled regions was converted to farmland. This often required a considerable investment in tree clearing or land drainage. The proportion of total U.S. land devoted to farming increased from 16 percent in 1850 to 39 percent in 1910 (and remains at roughly this percentage today).[3]

Two other important signs of intensification – that is, the shift of land to higher value uses – of American agriculture are evident over the late nineteenth and early twentieth centuries. First, the real, that is, inflation-adjusted, value of U.S. farmland per acre more than doubled between 1850 and 1910 (series Da27 shows the nominal value that needs to be adjusted for inflation). Indeed, although farm real estate values have often experienced dramatic fluctuations – such as the sharp run-up in prices during the late 1910s and collapse in the 1920s and a similar episode in the late 1970s and early 1980s – the long-term direction in land prices has been up (series Da13). The second piece of evidence for intensification over the late nineteenth and early twentieth centuries was the rise in the ratio of cropland harvested to total acreage. Between 1880 and 1930 the share of U.S. farmland devoted to crops rose from 31 percent to 53 percent (series Da17 and Da20). Since the 1930s, both acreage in farms and acreage in cropland harvested have contracted modestly, but these reductions have been small compared with the declines in the number of farms, farm population, and farm employment noted previously. For example, between 1940 and 1997, the acreage in farms decreased by 13 percent whereas the number of farms fell by 69 percent. Although acreage in farms has declined, the average quality of the land in farms has improved, as farmers tended to remove their less productive lands from production. More generally, in addition to endeavors in clearing and draining land, there have been enormous investments in leveling and irrigating farmlands, particularly in the western states. Conversely, soil quality in many

areas has declined owing to erosion and the buildup of salt and other toxic chemicals.

Farm Structure

A logical consequence of the decline in the number of farms since 1940, given the relatively constant farmland acreage, has been a major change in farm size and structure. Between 1940 and 1997, the average size of farms in the United States increased from 175 to 487 acres. During this period the proportion of farms with 1,000 or more acres rose from less than 2 percent to more than 9 percent of the total number of units (series Da596). These large-scale operations obviously accounted for a larger fraction of acreage. The share of U.S. farmland in farms with 1,000 or more acres increased from 34 percent in 1940 to 66 percent by 1997 (series Da611). Again, the disaggregated data in Table Da225–290 make it clear that there were substantial differences in average farm sizes across states, but that after 1940, the scale increased in virtually every region (Olmstead and Rhode 2000).

The increase in farm size was dictated by a number of forces. One was the attraction of nonfarm occupations for farmers and especially their children. Productive people would leave agriculture unless agricultural incomes and living standards rose fast enough to remain competitive with those in nonagricultural sectors. Larger farm sizes produced higher farm incomes for those who remained in agriculture (Gardner 1974). Increased mechanization also led to larger farms, given the need to spread the fixed cost of some types of machinery over larger production units. Some observers have expressed concern that the increase in farm size meant the loss of many family farms. It is important to emphasize that much of this concern over the increase in farm size is misplaced in the sense that many of the "lost farms" were never really commercially viable production units that could support a family. Readers are encouraged to consult the census and U.S. Department of Agriculture (USDA) definitions of what constitutes a farm, which are found in the general note for this section (see the text for Table Da1–13). Many of the "lost farms" were only a few acres in size, marketing a few hundred dollars in output per year. Another important cause of the decline in the number of farms stemmed from the decline in sharecropping in the cotton-producing states. The USDA and the census both defined land occupied by a sharecropper as a separate farm even though the landowner usually made many of the farming decisions and the croppers typically had a short tenure on the land. Nevertheless, even accounting for these definitional caveats, the last half of the twentieth century has witnessed a fundamental transformation in farm structure (Gardner 1992).

Another perspective on the change in farm structure comes from the evolution of the census and USDA classifications of farms into different categories based on their gross annual sales. In 1950 the largest sales classification was "$25,000 and above." Adjusting for inflation, this would be equivalent to about $150,000 in 1995 dollars. A farm with receipts of this amount would not be considered a large-scale operation today. Data for 1988, shown in Table Da-D, divide American farms into several sales categories. The largest 1.4 percent of American farms (in terms of cash receipts) accounted for more than 36 percent of cash receipts and 43 percent of all net farm income. At the other end of the spectrum, 47 percent of all farms (those with cash receipts of less than $10,000) accounted for only about 2.5 percent of cash receipts and –0.8 percent of net farm income. These small farmers actually lost money from farming;

---

[3] On this and other issues the inclusion of Alaska after 1960 has a large impact on some trends. Without Alaska, about 50 percent of U.S. land in the 1990s was devoted to farming.

TABLE Da-D   Farm structure in 1988 – percentage distribution of farms, cash receipts, and net income, by farm size

Farm size	Percentage of farms	Percentage of cash receipts	Percentage of net income
$500,000 and over	1.4	36.6	43.3
$250,000 to $499,999	3.5	18.0	19.9
$100,000 to $249,999	9.8	22.0	21.6
$40,000 to $99,999	14.6	13.6	11.2
$10,000 to $39,999	23.9	7.3	4.7
Less than $10,000	46.9	2.4	−0.8
All farms	100	100	100

Source

U.S. Economic Research Service, *Economic Indicators of the Farm Sector: National Financial Summary, 1988*, pp. 39–52.

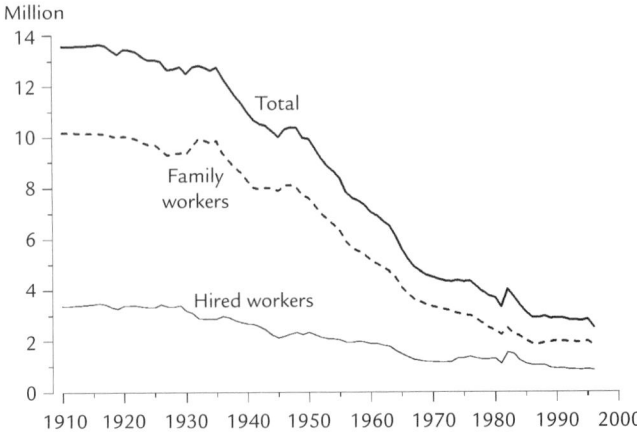

FIGURE Da-E   Farm employment: 1910–1996

Source

Table Da612–614.

their livelihood depended on income earned in off-farm pursuits. At the beginning of the new millennium, the general picture is that about 2 percent of all farms generate about one half of net farm income, while, as a group, one half of all farms typically lose money (USDA 1980; Olmstead and Rhode 2000).

Farms have not only grown in size, they have also become more specialized. Many tasks once done by farmers are now performed by others and traded in the marketplace. As an example, early in the twentieth century farmers typically produced most of their own food and fuel. In 1910 almost 90 percent of American farms reported raising chickens, more than 80 percent tended dairy cows, and more than 75 percent grew their own corn. By the early 1980s, 10 percent raised chickens, 15 percent tended dairy cows, and 32 percent grew corn. Farmers, like most Americans, found it more economical and more convenient to specialize in what they do best and buy much of what they need from someone else. Some may bemoan the loss of self-sufficiency, but the decision not to tend a small corn patch or to raise chickens to supply the family with eggs, meat, and feathers is to a large extent a matter of free choice. More generally, the ratio of purchased to nonpurchased inputs has increased more than sixfold since 1910. A similar increase in the division of labor has occurred on the output side as packagers, fast food chains, truckers, and refrigerated warehouses absorb a growing share of the consumer's food dollar; since 1913 the farmer's share has fallen from about 50 percent to about 20 percent.

It is notable that in one area – agricultural labor – U.S. farmers have not significantly increased their dependence on the market. The data on farm employment show that in 1910, nonpaid or family workers accounted for 75 percent of total employees (Table Da612–614). Despite all of the dramatic structural changes during the twentieth century, this proportion has changed little (see Figure Da-E). In the mid-1990s, nonpaid family workers still comprised roughly 70 percent of farm employment. On this issue, substantial regional variation exists, with the specialty crop producers in some states – such as California, Arizona, and Florida – relying extensively on hired labor, whereas Midwestern farms largely rely on operator and family labor.

Because farming requires detailed knowledge of local conditions, quick managerial response to changing situations, and effective supervision of a dispersed workforce, a decentralized family form of management continues to offer many advantages. In some activities, such as intensive livestock, poultry, and feedlot operations, significant economies of scale offset these advantages, leading to a more concentrated industrial structure (Schertz et al. 1979). But even with the spread of the corporate form of business

organization in agriculture, such concentration is not likely to become a dominant feature of the major cropping industries such as wheat, corn, and soybeans.

As a means of maintaining some control over their inputs and marketing activities, many farmers formed cooperatives in the first decades of the twentieth century (Table Da647–660). The organization of new cooperatives peaked in 1920, with about 2,000 marketing and purchasing associations formed in that year. Encouraged by favorable federal legislation, the movement continued to spread over the 1920s. The total number of co-ops peaked at about 12,000 in 1930; of these, about 10,500 were marketing organizations. Even as the number of organizations started to decline slowly, membership continued to grow, reaching 7.7 million by 1956. Obviously, it is possible for a single farmer to belong to more than one co-op, so this figure undoubtedly overstates the number of individuals involved. At the end of the twentieth century, farmer co-ops continued to play a major role in the farm economy. The roughly 4,000 co-ops in operation, with almost four million members, account for more than one third of the value of farm marketing (Knapp 1973).

Characteristics of Farmers

Characteristics of the typical farmer have changed substantially over time. As series Da541 shows, the number of farms in which the operator was nonwhite fell from almost one million (954,000) in 1920 to fewer than 48,000 today. This represents a decline from about 13 percent of all farm operators to about 2 percent. This trend was especially important in the South, where the number of nonwhite farm operators fell from 665,000 in 1945 to 272,000 in 1959 and then to fewer than 48,000 by 1974 (series Da495). The decline was largely concentrated among tenants. In 1920, nonwhite tenants operated 718,000 farms. This number slipped to 521,000 by 1940 and then fell to 86,000 in 1959 (Atack 1988; Wright 1988). By the early 1990s, nonwhite tenant farmers had virtually disappeared as a category; in 1997, there were only about 7,000 in the entire country.

Another feature of the agricultural transformation in the twentieth century has been a change in where many farmers chose to live and in key demographic characteristics. The series on farm residence show that the share of farm operators who lived off their farms increased from 5 percent in 1940 to almost 22 percent in 1997 (Table Da497–500). The population of farm operators has tended to age and become more fixed in location. In 1910 roughly 29 percent of farm operators were younger than 35, whereas only 8 percent were in this age group by 1997 (Table Da501–512). Similarly in 1910, almost one half (47 percent) of farm operators reported having operated their present farm for less than five years (series Da514). By 1997 this share had fallen to about 11 percent. It is also interesting to note that while the number of male farm operators fell by 19 percent between 1978 and 1997, the number of female farm operators rose by 46 percent over this period (series Da490–491).

Farm Machinery and Farm Chemicals

Nineteenth-century inventors supplied farmers with a marvelous array of labor-saving devices, including steel moldboard plows, multibottom riding plows, seed drills, check-row planters, horse-powered hay forks, and balers, to name but a few (McClelland 1997). The cumulative effect was most impressive because in 1910 the real value of farm implements was almost seven times the value in 1870 (series Da24).[4] Two of the most significant innovations in the history of agriculture were the grain thresher and the mechanical reaper (along with its close cousin, the mechanical mower). These machines, which first arrived on American farms in the 1830s, were nothing short of revolutionary in their day. People would travel for hours just to be able to marvel at early prototypes lumbering through the fields. As one indication of their importance, Cyrus McCormick, the principal inventor of the reaper, received the richly deserved acclaim as the "man who made bread cheap." Even with all the excitement concerning more recent technological breakthroughs, one would be hard pressed to find anything more significant than dramatically lowering the cost of grain in an age when many people still spent as much as one half of their income on basic foodstuffs. The reaper also had profound effects on farm structure, vastly reducing the need for seasonal labor during the small-grain harvest. In a similar fashion, the thresher (which separated the grain from the chaff) dramatically reduced the need to retain a hired man over the winter months (Olmstead and Rhode 1995; McClelland 1997).

These breakthrough inventions often unleashed a wave of subsequent modifications and improvements (Rosenberg 1972). By the end of the nineteenth century, each of the agricultural machines described in the preceding paragraph had undergone numerous modifications that increased its usefulness and reliability. The crowning achievement was the commercial development in the 1880s of the combined harvester, or, as it became known, the combine. The combine merged a reaper and a thresher into one machine. Early combines were huge, cumbersome machines suited only for the large-scale ranches found in the arid West. Some of these harvesters had forty-foot-long cutting bars and were pulled by teams of forty or more draft animals (Olmstead and Rhode 1988).

The evolution of the combine involved making the machines smaller and more versatile, and perfecting its components for use in harvesting corn, beans, peas, and other crops. In the Great Plains combines were not a frequent sight before 1918. The number of combines in the United States grew from 4,000 in 1920 to 61,000 in 1930, and then to 190,000 in 1940 (series Da629). By the late 1930s, combines harvested about one half of all wheat acreage in the United States. In the 1940s there was a reversal in the trend toward smaller machines as specialized custom harvesting services began to thrive. The share of national wheat acreage harvested by combines rose to more than 75 percent by 1945 and to almost 95 percent by 1950. By the 1980s, combines had become the dominant harvesting technology for virtually every grain and field legume (Quick and Buchele 1978).

The gasoline tractor was among the most far-reaching agricultural innovations ever. Like early combines, the first gasoline tractors were behemoths suitable for tasks such as plowing, harrowing, and beltwork. Also, as in the case of combines, the diffusion of tractors required a number of important refinements and the development of a variety of sizes suitable for a number of different tasks. Among the scores of innovations that increased the tractor's appeal was the development of the general-purpose tractor in 1924. This machine could cultivate among growing crops. At about the same time, the power takeoff became available, enabling tractors to transfer power directly to implements under tow. The emergence of pneumatic tires in the 1930s increased the tractor's effective power and enhanced its usefulness in hauling farm goods (Olmstead and Rhode 2001; Gray 1954; Williams 1987).

The number of tractors on American farms grew from about 1,000 machines in 1910 to 246,000 in 1920, and to 920,000 in 1930 (series Da623). With the exception of the first few years of the Great Depression, the number of tractors in use on farms continued to increase, first surpassing the 4 million mark in 1953. Since 1953, the stock of tractors on farms has remained relatively constant at about 4.5 million machines. Data on the number of tractors fail to capture important changes in tractor design and size that have resulted in significant quality improvements over time. As an example, tractor horsepower on farms more than doubled between the mid-1950s and the mid-1980s (when series Da626 ends), while the number of tractors changed little over these three decades. The trend toward larger and more powerful tractors has continued. More generally, in recent decades tractor manufacturers have built more efficient and more versatile machines, offered new driver amenities such as more comfortable seats and enclosed air-conditioned cabs, and added safety features.

There was a regional pattern to diffusion. By and large farmers in the Great Plains and California were the earliest adopters, followed by those in the Midwest and East. The South was the last region to achieve widespread adoption. By 1960, tractors had largely replaced horses on commercial farms across the United States. The stock of farm horses and mules declined from 26.5 million in 1915 to 3.1 million in 1960 (series Da983 and Da985).

The tractor greatly increased the amount of power available to farmers and saved the considerable amount of time that had been devoted to caring for animals. The extra power was particularly valuable during periods of peak activity or when the timeliness of the work was essential, as when plowing had to be finished before bad weather set in. Another effect of the tractor was to add significantly to America's net agricultural output, because about one quarter of U.S. cropland was converted from growing feed for

---

[4] The essay on agricultural productivity in this chapter deals in considerable detail with technological change as a source of agricultural productivity growth. Data on the diffusion of specific mechanical innovations are displayed in Table Da623–634. They pertain to the twentieth century because few consistent time series exist for earlier times. But the lack of quality data does not mean that little happened. On the contrary, American farmers in the nineteenth century were world leaders in the adoption of new agricultural machines and techniques. In fact, much of what came later was a direct consequence of path-breaking advances of an earlier era (Olmstead and Rhode 1988).

work animals to growing products for human consumption (series Da663).

Few innovations have affected the demand for labor as much as the mechanical cotton picker and the milking machine. There had been many attempts to devise a mechanical cotton picker before J. D. Rust succeeded in perfecting a spindle machine in 1928. In 1945, on the eve of diffusion, there were only 107 machines in the United States and almost all of these were employed outside the traditional Cotton South on the irrigated farms of the southwest. The number of cotton picking machines increased to roughly 4,000 in 1950 and then to 38,000 by 1961 (series Da634). By 1970, virtually the entire U.S. cotton crop was mechanically harvested (Street 1957; Musoke and Olmstead 1982). The flip side of the mechanization of the cotton harvest, coupled with the decline in cotton acreage, was to complete the restructuring of Southern rural labor relations that had begun in the 1930s with the spread of tractors. The number of Southern sharecroppers dwindled from 776,000 in 1930 to 121,000 in 1959 (series Da553).

Dairy farming was also a highly labor-intensive activity. As late as 1940, dairying in the United States required more than one and one half times more labor than that devoted to producing cotton. Milking machines employing the intermittent suction principle, introduced in 1905, promised a saving of about one fifth of the annual labor requirement per cow. However, the machines spread slowly at first owing to the structure of dairy farming, the lack of electricity, improper sanitary practices, and "hard times" on the farm. In 1910, about 12,000 farms possessed milking machines; this was less than one of every 400 farms reporting dairy cows. By 1940, the number of farms possessing milking machines had climbed to 190,000. Nonetheless, on the eve of World War II, perhaps 90 percent of all cows were milked by hand. In the postwar period diffusion accelerated, with one half of cows milked mechanically by 1950 and nearly all dairy cows in commercial operations by the mid-1960s. By 1965, some 500,000 farms reported possessing milking machines (series Da634).[5] The spread of milking machines was the most visible part of a larger mechanical revolution on dairy farms (Forste and Frick 1979). Scores of other mechanical inventions, such as refrigeration, electric lights, and improved hay harvesting and handling machinery, transformed the farmer's day-to-day life in the twentieth century. It should be emphasized that, as was the case with tractors, the data showing the number of various types of farm machines do not capture changes in quality. Most machines sold today are better than those of earlier years. A better accounting for quality changes would increase the effective quantity of mechanical inputs in the farm sector. The essay on agricultural productivity in this chapter grapples with just this type of issue.

In addition to the growing use of farm machinery, American agriculture also witnessed what is often called a "biological revolution" after 1930. This was associated with the first significant widespread wave of increasing yields per acre of the major staple crops and was driven by the adoption of improved seeds, such as hybrid corn, and the greater application of farm chemicals (Manglesdorf 1951; Griliches 1957). The use of commercial fertilizer in American agriculture skyrocketed after World War II (Tables Da635–646). Purchases of primary plant nutrients, which

had doubled between 1910 and 1940, increased eightfold over the next thirty years. Accompanying the growth was a shift from low-concentration, phosphate-based, mixed fertilizers to high-concentration, nitrogen-based, straight materials, such as anhydrous ammonia. The increased use of commercial fertilizer after 1945 was the result of several factors. First, the traditional approach of manuring, or using no fertilizer at all, was leading to soil exhaustion in many regions. Second and more important, the real price of fertilizer declined over much of the post-1945 period (the 1970s represented the most notable exception). Active antitrust policies and expansion during World War II of nitrate plants for the munitions industries increased capacity and competition in the postwar fertilizer industry. Third, technological changes such as the development of superphosphates by the Tennessee Valley Authority and the perfection of methods for the direct application of anhydrous ammonia contributed to the advance in fertilizer use. Finally, many of the new crop varieties, such as hybrid corn, were bred to be more responsive to fertilizer applications; thus, there was a high degree of complementarity between higher-yielding plant breeds and the greater use of fertilizer (Markham 1958).

There are strong indications that the biological–genetic revolution is still in its infancy. This is a new frontier, with the U.S. Patent Office extending patent protection to genetically engineered plants in 1985 and to animals in 1988. It is reasonable to assume that the types of productivity advances discussed in the essay on agricultural productivity in this chapter will continue; there will likely be new and better machines, chemicals, and even new sources of power if we look far enough into the future. More generally, one would expect there to be a continuation of the trend to improve the quality of agricultural labor, land, capital, and biological inputs. But the structural transformation is largely complete and the social impacts of any future changes are likely to be relatively small. A major feature of the past transformation was the movement of people off the farms, and today there are few farmers left. Even if half of all current farmers were to leave agriculture it would be a relatively small adjustment compared to what has already occurred. Although the data describe an incredible process of change that has largely run its course, the forces of invention, market restructuring, and changing demands are still reshaping the economy.

References

Atack, Jeremy. 1988. "Tenants and Yeomen in the Nineteenth Century." *Agricultural History* 62 (Summer): 6–32.

Forste, Robert H., and George E. Frick. 1979. "Dairy." In Lyle P. Schertz et al. *Another Revolution in U.S. Farming?* U.S. Department of Agriculture.

Gardner, Bruce L. 1974. "Farm Population Decline and the Income of Rural Families." *American Journal of Agricultural Economics* 56: 600–6.

Gardner, Bruce L. 1992. "Changing Economic Perspectives on the Farm Problem." *Journal of Economic Literature* 30 (March): 62–101.

Gray, R. B. 1954. *Development of the Agricultural Tractor in the United States*. USDA Information Series No. 107.

Griliches, Zvi. 1957. "Hybrid Corn: An Explanation of the Economics of Technological Change." *Econometrica* 25 (4): 501–22.

Knapp, Joseph G. 1973. *The Advance of American Cooperative Enterprise, 1920–1945*. Interstate.

Manglesdorf, Paul G. 1951. "Hybrid Corn." *Scientific American* 185 (2): 39–47.

Markham, Jesse W. 1958. *The Fertilizer Industry: Study of an Imperfect Market*. Vanderbilt University Press.

McClelland, Peter D. 1997. *Sowing Modernity: America's First Agricultural Revolution*. Cornell University Press.

---

[5] Owing to the contraction of the number of dairy operations, this was below the peak of 712,000 farms in 1956.

Musoke, Moses S., and Alan L. Olmstead. 1982. "The Rise of the Cotton Industry in California: A Comparative Perspective." *Journal of Economic History* 42 (June): 385–412.

Olmstead, Alan L., and Paul W. Rhode. 1988. "An Overview of California Agricultural Mechanization, 1870–1930." *Agricultural History* 62: 86–112.

Olmstead, Alan L., and Paul W. Rhode. 1993. "Induced Innovation in American Agriculture: A Reconsideration." *Journal of Political Economy* 101: 100–17.

Olmstead, Alan L., and Paul W. Rhode. 1995. "Beyond the Threshold: An Analysis of the Characteristics and Behavior of Early Reaper Adopters." *Journal of Economic History* 55: 27–57.

Olmstead, Alan L., and Paul W. Rhode. 2000. "The Transformation of Northern Agriculture, 1910–1990." In Stanley Engerman and Robert Gallman, editors. *The Cambridge Economic History of the United States.* Cambridge University Press.

Olmstead, Alan L. and Paul W. Rhode. 2001. "Reshaping the Landscape: The Impact and Diffusion of the Tractor in American Agriculture, 1910–1960." *Journal of Economic History* 61: 663–98.

Quick, Graeme, and Wesley Buchele. 1978. *The Grain Harvesters.* American Society of Agricultural Engineers.

Rosenberg, Nathan. 1972. "Factors Affecting the Diffusion of Technology." *Exploration in Economic History* 10 (Fall): 8.

Schertz, Lyle P., et al. 1979. *Another Revolution in U.S. Farming?* U.S. Department of Agriculture.

Street, James H. 1957. *The New Revolution in the Cotton Economy: Mechanization and Its Consequences.* University of North Carolina Press.

U.S. Department of Agriculture (USDA). 1980. *Farm Structure: A Historical Perspective on Changes in the Number and Size of Farms.* U.S. Senate, Committee on Agriculture, Nutrition, and Forestry, 96th Congress, second session.

Williams, Robert C. 1987. *Fordson, Farmall, and Poppin' Johnny: A History of the Farm Tractor and Its Impact on America.* University of Illinois Press.

Wright, Gavin. 1988. "American Agriculture and the Labor Market: What Happened to Proletarianization?" *Agricultural History* 62 (Summer): 182–209.

CROPS AND LIVESTOCK

Alan L. Olmstead and Paul W. Rhode

The dynamics of American agricultural development have been closely intertwined with the political and social evolution of the country and dependent on changing technological and market forces. This is clearly reflected in the composition of crop and livestock output and the prices that farmers received. The data in this section offer insights into many of the fundamental structural changes that transformed rural America.[1] As examples, one can track the spread of new activities, such as the immense growth in soybean production (series Da677), the takeoff in fruit and vegetable output (Tables Da791–967), and the growing importance of the broiler chicken industry in the twentieth century (series Da1045). The mirror image of these changes has been a fundamental change in the diet of most Americans. The data on commodity prices in this section also help document the extent of the agricultural crises of the 1890s and the 1930s. For example, the data show that between 1890 and 1896, as Populist agitators urged farmers to "grow less corn and raise more hell," nominal corn prices plummeted from 50 cents to 21 cents a bushel (series Da697). In

[1] Atack and Passell (1994, pp. 274–98 and 402–26). These structural changes include factors discussed elsewhere in this chapter such as the change in the location of production, the introduction and spread of new crops, the changes in farming technologies and increases in farm productivity, and the relative (and after 1940, the absolute) decline in the farm population.

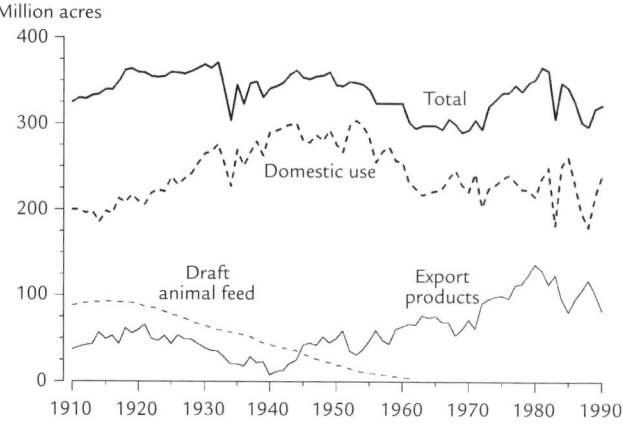

Million acres

FIGURE Da-F   Cropland harvested, by use: 1910–1990

Sources

Series Da661–664.

Documentation

Note that beginning in the early 1960s, as the importance of horses and mules declined, the U.S. Department of Agriculture ceased estimating the amount of cropland required to feed them.

a similar fashion, it is possible to chart the disastrous fall in commodity prices in the Great Depression. For instance, the nominal price of cotton dropped from almost 17 cents per pound in 1929 to less than 6 cents per pound in 1931 (series Da757). The data also reveal the sharp increase in commodity prices – for example, the doubling of wheat prices over the 1972 and 1973 crop years (series Da719) – that led some to call the 1970s the "Era of Limits to Growth."

Crops and Land Utilization

Figure Da-F offers an indication of the change in the market for agricultural output over most of the twentieth century. The figure shows the U.S. Department of Agriculture's (USDA) estimates of the acreage of harvested cropland devoted to three major categories – domestic consumption, feed for draft animals, and the export market – from 1910 to 1990. Over the twentieth century the total area harvested has fluctuated between about 290 and 370 million acres. The fluctuations in this indicator help trace the course of farm prosperity and farm policy. As an example, the sharp drop in acres harvested in the early 1930s was a result of the ravages of the Dust Bowl, the agricultural depression, and the acreage reduction programs discussed in the essay on farm policy in this chapter.[2] The total acreage harvested increased as a result of high demand during World War II and then inched downward with a slackening in demand and more aggressive federal land "conservation" policies.

[2] As a result of prolonged periods of deficient rainfall coupled with farming technologies that made the soil more susceptible to high winds, vast areas of the Great Plains suffered prolonged dust storms beginning in 1933. These storms did terrible damage to Western agriculture, with the dust darkening the sky as far away as New York City. The worst-hit regions included the panhandles of Oklahoma and Texas, eastern Colorado and New Mexico, and western Kansas. This area became known as the Dust Bowl. American agriculture suffered a prolonged period of hard times beginning shortly after World War I and continuing to the early 1940s.

Million acres

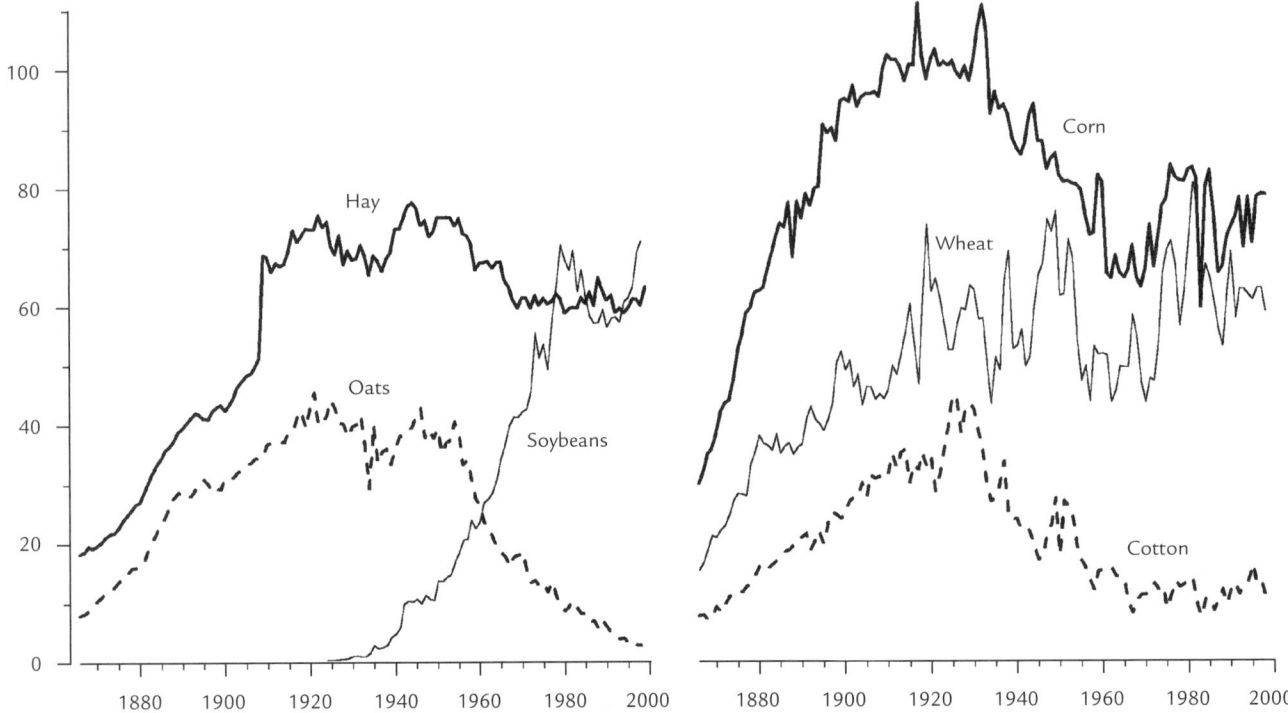

FIGURE Da-G   Acreage of major crops: 1866–1999

Sources

Oats, series Da670; soybeans, series Da676; corn, series Da693; wheat, series Da717; hay, series Da733; and cotton, series Da755.

Documentation

Note that the series for hay represents tame hay (that is, cut from cultivated grasses) through 1908, and all hay thereafter – hence the jump in the series beginning in 1909.

Decomposing the total acreage harvested into its component uses also illustrates some of the most spectacular economic and social changes of the past 100 years. In 1910 about 27 percent of all American cropland harvested was devoted to feeding 24 million horses and mules. (Millions of acres of pastureland also were used to feed horses and mules.) These animals provided the power to make the country's farms and cities tick. The rapid decline after 1930 in the area devoted to grow food for horses and mules offers a graphic indicator of the wholesale adoption of automobiles, trucks, and tractors. The decline in draft animals was the flip side of the growth in the demand for petroleum products. This transformation reflected a significant change in the day-to-day nature of farm life (Olmstead and Rhode 1994).

The data on the acreage devoted to export markets also reflect broader changes in the economic and political landscape. The decline in the 1920s and 1930s signaled the breakdown of the international economy in the interwar years as most European countries raised their tariffs and imposed domestic content provisions requiring bakers and others to use locally grown commodities (Liepmann 1938).

The resurgence in acreage harvested for export crops beginning in 1941 reflects the impact of World War II, which disrupted agriculture in Europe and around the world and led to an increased international demand for U.S. farm products (see Tables Da1323–1336). It also reflects a movement away from the extreme tariff policies of the 1930s. By the 1990s about one third of America's cropland harvested was used to produce food and fiber for export.

The information in Figure Da-G allows us to take a longer-term view of American agricultural evolution by charting the acreage harvested for six leading crops since 1866. The growth in acreage until about 1920 reflects the continued westward expansion and filling in of the agricultural frontier. The settlement of new lands was one of the major features of American agriculture since the time of the first European settlements. As a result the locus of production for all crops inched westward. As an example, in colonial times New York, Pennsylvania, and Virginia were major wheat growing regions. By the time of the Civil War, the Wheat Belt had moved to the Midwest and included such states as Illinois, Michigan, Wisconsin, and Iowa. By the end of the nineteenth century, Kansas, North Dakota, and South Dakota had emerged as leading producers of wheat. With these shifts in the center of production came important shifts in the varieties of wheat grown. The soft wheat varieties that prospered in the East or Midwest were not suited for the harsh winters and relatively arid conditions found in the Great Plains. Thus settlement was dependent on a steady process of scientific inquiry and trial and error as new varieties from around the world were imported. As of 1929 more than 80 percent of the wheat acreage in the United States was planted with varieties (mostly hard winter and spring wheat) that had not existed in the country until the 1870s (Olmstead and Rhode 2002; Dalrymple 1980).

Similarly, the center of cotton cultivation shifted significantly over the nineteenth and twentieth centuries. On the eve of Eli Whitney's invention of the saw gin in 1793, U.S. cotton production was limited chiefly to the coastal regions of South Carolina and Georgia. During the early nineteenth century, the crop spread over the black belt of Alabama and Mississippi and into the rich soils of the Mississippi–Yazoo Delta. Production in many areas of the "Old South" declined. After the Civil War, cotton acreage expanded throughout the South. Further, as the boll weevil began its campaign of destruction in the South after it appeared in 1892, cotton cultivation leapfrogged west to the irrigated valleys of Arizona and California, which were relatively insusceptible to the pest. Circa 1960, Texas, Mississippi, and California, respectively, were the three leading cotton-producing states. As in the case of wheat, the westward expansion of the crop was associated with significant changes in the varieties of cotton grown. As two examples, the expansion of the industry in the Mississippi Delta was largely based on Mexican cotton, introduced in 1806, whereas the growth in the production in California's Central Valley, roughly a century later, was founded on the cultivation of Acala varieties, also imported from Central America (Moore 1988).

For most years, corn has been the predominant crop in the United States in terms of acreage (series Da693). For example, between 1910 and 1925, an average of more than 100 million acres, or roughly three tenths of national cropland harvested, was devoted to raising this one crop. In the 1940s, the land area planted to corn began a prolonged decline. It is important to emphasize that because of productivity changes associated with the diffusion of hybrid seed beginning in the mid-1930s and the increased application of fertilizer, U.S. corn output continued to grow even though acreage fell. By the 1970s the acreage in corn was roughly equal to the acreage in wheat, hay, and soybeans. The meteoric rise in soybean acreage since the 1930s reflects the continued willingness of American farmers to adopt new crops from other parts of the world (series Da676).[3] For the most part, soybeans replaced cotton in the South and corn in the Midwest, providing increased diversification. This was particularly true in the South, where there was a decreased dependence on cotton and a significant increase in cattle and dairy operations.

The search for new products was not limited to introducing new crops such as soybeans, sorghum, and sugar beets. Even "old" crops such as cotton and corn could be put to new uses. For example, over the nineteenth century cotton farmers found a growing market for a previously little-used by-product, cottonseed. Before the Civil War, cottonseed, which is produced in roughly fixed proportions with cotton lint, was typically discarded and represented an environmental hazard. After the war, the seed was increasingly valued as a source of vegetable oil, as a lard substitute (Crisco®), and as an animal feed. By 1909, the dollar value of cottonseed output was more than 15 percent of that of cotton (series Da760). Over the twentieth century, one of America's oldest crops, corn, was consumed in such new forms as oleomargarine, ethanol, and corn sweeteners. In the latter case, scientific breakthroughs allowed for the manufacture of crystallized sugar from corn by 1922. The new product was an instant success and by 1928 150 million pounds of corn sugar were consumed (McMillen 1929, p. 177). Further scientific advances beginning in the 1950s led to the rapid growth of the high-fructose corn syrup industry in the 1970s. These examples illustrate how American farming became more

efficient by finding higher-value uses for crops, animals, and their by-products.

The data on oats and hay acreage also tell an important story (Tables Da667–678 and Da733–745). The rise and fall in oat production roughly tracked the increase and decrease in the horse and mule population (Table Da983–987). The increase in hay acreage was in part a response to the increase in the number of draft animals. But the decrease in the demand for hay stemming from the decline in draft animals was largely offset by the increase in cattle feedlots (Olmstead and Rhode 1997).

Changes in the Livestock Industry

In recent decades the income generated from marketing livestock products has accounted for more than half of the gross value of all farm income (Schertz et al. 1979). Figure Da-H provides an overview of the changes in livestock on farms since 1867. Here one can clearly see the rise in the population of horses and mules on farms up until World War I and its subsequent decline as tractors, trucks, and automobiles became the predominant sources of power on farms. Perhaps somewhat surprising is that the population of dairy cows fell by more than 65 percent between the 1940s and the end of the twentieth century (series Da1020). This decline in the number of cows reflects the enormous improvement in productivity in the dairy industry: despite the radical reduction in the number of animals, the total volume of milk production increased by roughly 30 percent over this same period.

Among the most prominent features of American agricultural development in the twentieth century was the growth in the number of cattle (series Da968). Between 1940 and 1980 the number tripled, rising from about 40 million to about 120 million head. Just as there were important changes in the genetic makeup of the wheat and cotton crops grown in the United States, significant developments also occurred in the genetic composition of the

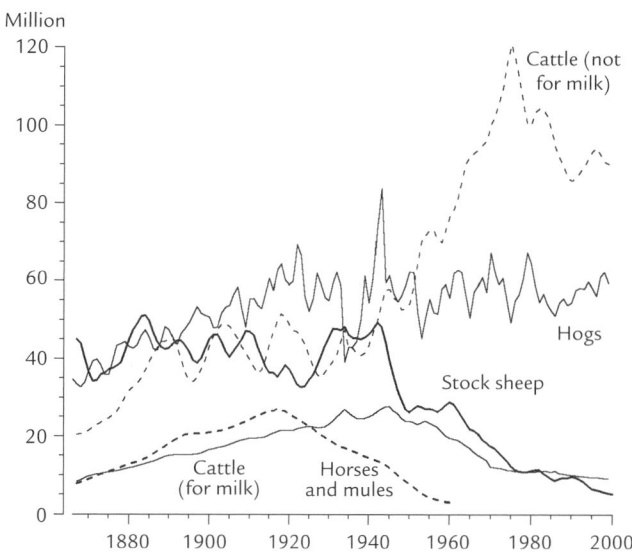

FIGURE Da-H   Livestock on farms: 1866–2000

Source

Cattle (not for milk), series Da968 minus series Da1020; hogs, series Da970; stock sheep, series Da972; cows and heifers kept for milk, series Da1020; and horses and mules, series Da983 and Da985.

---

[3] Sugar beets (series Da783) and grain sorghum (series Da673), not shown in Figure Da-G, represent similar, if less dramatic, examples of the same phenomenon.

cattle population. In the colonial period most cattle (including those used for milking) were tough and sinewy, adapted for surviving in the wild, but not especially well suited for dairy or meat production. The same was true in the nineteenth century. The longhorns that participated in the famed cattle drives from Texas to the railheads in Kansas would be judged to be of very low quality by today's standards. Modern cattle, however, would not have endured the hardships of the wild Texas range and the long cattle drives (Leavitt 1933).

The nineteenth and twentieth centuries saw persistent efforts to improve cattle breeds, often involving the importation of purebred animals from Europe. As examples, statesman Henry Clay of Kentucky reportedly imported the first Hereford cattle into the United States in 1817. The first Guernsey cattle were imported in 1830, and the first Holstein–Friesians in 1857. The next step was for farmers to form registries and breeding associations. In 1846 the first herd book for Shorthorns was compiled and in 1863 an Ayrshire breed association was founded (Smith and Roth 1990). A slow process of transforming the bloodlines of American cattle followed over the next century. The spread of improved cattle breeds, along with better feed and care of dairy cows, led to a major increase in milk production per animal. In 1800 the average cow probably produced less than 1,000 pounds of milk a year. By the mid-1990s annual milk output per cow averaged more than 16,000 pounds (Pirtle 1926; Bateman 1968; Forste and Frick 1979). The improvements in meat quality, although more difficult to quantify, have also been enormous.

The broiler chicken industry also experienced rapid growth and profound technological change during the twentieth century. Between 1934 and 1998 production soared from about thirty-four million to almost eight billion birds a year (series Da1045). Over this same period the average weight of a live broiler increased by about 71 percent, from 2.8 to 4.9 pounds, and the inflation-adjusted price of broilers fell by 86 percent (series Da1047). These changes were made possible by revolutionary advances in the organization and scale of broiler production along with the application of scientific principles to the feeding and care of the birds. Whereas just a few decades ago it was the norm for every farm to raise its own chickens, perhaps marketing a few surplus birds, in the last decades of the twentieth century broiler production became a highly concentrated, capital-intensive industry, with much of the production moving to the Southern states (Rogers 1979). The effect on consumers was enormous. Chicken used to be a luxury item that was more expensive than beef. But the rapid growth in productivity in the poultry industry and the associated increase in output and fall in prices made chickens available to most Americans, more than making good Herbert Hoover's bold 1928 presidential campaign promise of a "chicken in every pot."

Demand and Prices of Farm Products

In addition to supply-side changes that increased productivity in the farm sector, changes in demand have played an important role in determining the mix of farm output. As the real incomes of Americans increased, consumers demanded a different and more varied market basket, in line with the predictions of Engel's Law. Consumption of starches has generally declined while that of more flavorful foods has increased. This has led to relatively more rapid growth in demand for livestock, dairy, and poultry products and for fresh fruits, nuts, and vegetables.[4] In addition to the growth in population and per capita incomes, a number of other changes affected the composition of demand for agricultural goods. Smaller families, the increase in the number and percentage of women working outside the home, and changes in household technologies, such as the change from iceboxes to electric refrigerators, all influenced consumption patterns. Exogenous supply-side changes outside the agricultural sector have also shaped the composition of agricultural output. For example, the development of artificial fibers such as rayon, nylon, and polyester fleece has reduced the demand for natural fibers such as wool, silk, and cotton.

As a final note, this section includes extensive information on commodity prices, typically measured at the farm gate. Movements in these series have attracted much attention over the past 130 years because commodity prices have played a central role affecting the well-being of rural America. These data have many uses, but one must be careful to note that they are in nominal or current value terms and therefore do not adjust for changes in the overall price level. It is important to recall that gross farm income is calculated by multiplying price and quantity. A farmer who increased production might well expect a higher income, but if all farmers increased production, the net effect might be a more than proportional decline in prices and, as a result, a fall in income.[5] In addition, prices often fluctuated significantly as a result of conditions in faraway lands. A comparison of the movement in farm prices with those in other sectors (for example, industrial prices) indicates that farm prices tended to be more volatile, especially before the New Deal. The reason is that the consumption and production of farm goods tended to be relatively unresponsive to price changes in the short run and because agriculture was more susceptible to exogenous shocks such as bad weather that could have significant effects on output. These factors help explain the periodic outbreaks of unrest in the farm sector, even when output was increasing. But it is also important to note that declining prices do not necessarily imply declining well-being of farmers, as the falling prices may be due to declining costs resulting from productivity advances, which are discussed in the essay on agricultural productivity in this chapter. Finally, the price movements after the 1930s reflect more than simply the working of the private market. The essay on farm policy in this chapter offers a more detailed analysis of the operations of federal agricultural policies.

By focusing on how price trends affected suppliers (that is, farmers), perhaps the most important implication of the development of American agriculture is often overlooked. That is the enormous benefits consumers have received. As a result of improved technology and more efficient production and distribution systems, the long-term trend has been to afford consumers a better and more varied bundle of goods at dramatically lower real prices. This is one of the most remarkable achievements of the last two centuries.

References

Atack, Jeremy, and Peter Passell. 1994. *A New Economic View of American History from Colonial Times to 1940.* W. W. Norton.

---

[4] The growing importance of myriad products in the category of fruits, nuts, and vegetables accounts for the greatly expanded coverage in this edition of *Historical Statistics of the United States.*

[5] In more technical terms, this condition would hold if demand were price inelastic.

Bateman, Fred. 1968. "Improvement in American Dairy Farming, 1850–1910: A Quantitative Analysis." *Journal of Economic History* 28 (June): 255–73.

Dalrymple, Dana G. 1980. *Development and Spread of Semi-Dwarf Varieties of Wheat and Rice in the United States: An International Perspective.* Agricultural Economic Report No. 455. U.S. Government Printing Office.

Forste, Robert H., and George E. Frick. 1979. "Dairy." In Lyle P. Schertz et al. *Another Revolution in U.S. Farming?* U.S. Department of Agriculture.

Leavitt, Charles T. 1933. "Attempts to Improve Cattle Breeds in the United States, 1790–1860." *Agricultural History* 7 (April): 51–67.

Liepmann, H. 1938. *Tariff Levels and the Economic Unity of Europe, 1913–1931.* Allen and Unwin.

McMillen, Wheeler. 1929. *Too Many Farmers: The Story of What Is Here and Ahead in Agriculture.* William Morrow.

Moore, John Hebron. 1988. *The Emergence of the Cotton Kingdom in the Old Southwest, Mississippi, 1770–1860.* Louisiana State University Press.

Olmstead, Alan L., and Paul W. Rhode. 1994. "The Agricultural Mechanization Controversy of the Interwar Years." *Agricultural History* 68 (Summer): 35–53.

Olmstead, Alan L., and Paul W. Rhode. 1997. "An Overview of the History of California Agriculture." In *California Agriculture: Issues and Challenges.* University of California, Giannini Foundation.

Olmstead, Alan L., and Paul W. Rhode. 2002. "The Red Queen and the Hard Reds: Productivity Growth in American Wheat, 1800–1940." *Journal of Economic History* 62: 929–66.

Pirtle, T. R. 1926. *History of the Dairy Industry.* Mojonnier Bros.

Rogers, George B. 1979. "Poultry and Eggs." In Lyle P. Schertz et al. *Another Revolution in U.S. Farming?* U.S. Department of Agriculture.

Schertz, Lyle, et al. 1979. *Another Revolution in U.S. Farming?* U.S. Department of Agriculture.

Smith, Maryanna S., and Dennis M. Roth. 1990. "Chronological Landmarks in American Agriculture." USDA *Agriculture Information Bulletin* number 425, revised (November).

AGRICULTURAL PRODUCTIVITY

Julian M. Alston and Philip G. Pardey

One of the most striking and central features of the development of U.S. agriculture has been the increased output per acre, per head of livestock, per farm, and per farm worker, especially during the twentieth century (Bonnen 1986). These are some of the more visible and tangible signs of productivity growth in agriculture arising from investments in the development and adoption of new methods, machines, plant varieties, livestock breeds, and agricultural production know-how.

In the earlier period of expansion of the agricultural land base, production growth came partly from increases in land and labor inputs, as well as from improved technology (Cochrane 1993). During the past 100 years, improved technology has allowed continuing growth in agricultural output from a given or shrinking area of agricultural land, while at the same time using many fewer hours of labor. Labor-saving technology has been critical. Much of the reduction of the agricultural labor force has come about through the consolidation of farms into fewer, more specialized, and larger units. In some instances, especially in intensive livestock and some specialty crops, vertical integration of farming with pre- and post-farm production has been an important element of structural change, facilitated by changes in technologies.

Through these means, U.S. agriculture has been able to supply such an abundance of food and fiber that real, that is, inflation-adjusted, farm-gate prices of food and fiber are much lower than they were 100 years ago, in spite of the growth in demand for most agricultural products that has accompanied the growth in population, per capita income, and trade (Schultz 1956). Productivity growth is the reason why the Malthusian nightmare, in which subsistence defines the entire economy, has not materialized.

Much of the dramatic transformation of U.S. agriculture over the past 100 years, as well as before that time, can be traced to the adoption of new technologies that allowed more to be produced with less (Griliches 1957; Smith and Roth 1990). To understand fully the implications of technological change requires considering and understanding all of the causes and impacts. Such understanding is elusive because the relationships are complex and ever-changing. A first step is to document those aspects that can be measured and more readily understood.

The Measurement of Agricultural Input, Output, and Productivity

The data in this section provide a comprehensive picture of U.S. agricultural productivity during the twentieth century, and some partial but useful measures of productivity extending back into the earlier periods. Economists use the word "productivity" in a technical sense with a meaning similar to that found in common usage, only more specific. The general notion is to measure the *quantity* produced, compared with the *quantity* or the *cost* of the inputs used to produce it.

Some *partial* productivity measures express the quantity of a particular output relative to the quantity of a particular input or resource – output or yield per acre, or output per worker (usually per year). Other measures account for more of the inputs. A *total* productivity measure would express total output relative to the total quantity of all of the inputs used in production, but we rarely have all the data needed to measure the totality of inputs and outputs. More often, what is practical to achieve is a *multifactor* productivity (MFP) measure that expresses aggregate output relative to aggregate input – perhaps omitting certain outputs and inputs that are either difficult to measure or not sufficiently covered by available data. For example, the accumulation of highly localized, within-farm information on soil conditions or improved planting, weeding, and harvesting operations has important productivity consequences. Management skill is another type of unmeasured input that accounts for some productivity growth.

These measures or *indexes* of input, output, and productivity necessarily involve aggregating across different commodities, or different qualities of the same commodity, at a given place and point in time; they usually also involve aggregating to some extent over space and time as well. The measures themselves will depend on the decisions made about how to go about this aggregation, which depend to some degree on the availability of data (Griliches 1960, 1963).

As a related matter, the choice of indexing procedure may be important. The so-called *index number problem* arises when distortions in the aggregate quantity (or price) index result from the use of inappropriate price (or quantity) weights in aggregating the quantities (or prices) of individual goods. For instance, the aggregate price index for agricultural output was computed as a Laspeyres index, in which the series of prices of each of the individual commodities making up the index was multiplied by a weight equal to its individual share of the total value in the base period. This type of index overstates the rise in the cost of living over time because it puts too much weight on the goods that become relatively more expensive over time. Even when this index number problem, associated with the formulation of the index, is avoided or minimized (for example, through the use of Divisia indexes or approximations to Divisia indexes, such as a Fisher–Ideal index), similar problems can arise in aggregating and comparing inputs, outputs, and productivity over space or time. A more complete treatment of these conceptual issues and empirical applications to U.S. agriculture can be found in Acquaye, Alston, and Pardey (2003), AAEA (1980), Ball (1985), Capalbo and Antle (1988), Huffman and Evenson (1993), and Jorgenson and Gollop (1992).

Aggregation bias associated with heterogeneity of inputs and outputs is an issue in developing an accurate sense of the aggregate picture, particularly over long time periods. In aggregating quantities it makes economic sense to use prices as weights, but if the prices and quantities are not perfectly matched (for example, a single national price is used for all states, a single annual price is used for all months or all years, or a single price is used for all grades of a particular output, such as wheat), the picture may be distorted in that changes in quantities of lower- (higher-) value goods will be over- (under-) emphasized (Craig and Pardey 1996; Griliches 1963). For example, over time, the quality of labor and machinery used in agriculture has risen. When we ignore this fact, and just count hours of labor or the number of tractors, our measures overstate the gain in productivity. (Some of the additional output is a result of better inputs; equivalently, a greater quantity of inputs would have been required if input quality had remained constant.)

Aggregate Input, Output, and Productivity Patterns

Long-Term Patterns

In 1990, U.S. agriculture produced, in aggregate terms, more than three times the quantity of output in 1910, implying a compound growth rate of 1.61 percent per year. Over the same time period there were substantial shifts in the mixture of output, reflecting both changes in the composition of demand for food and fiber products as incomes have grown and changes on the supply side, reflecting a host of technological innovations (Table Da1063–1081). In 1910 oil crops accounted for just 0.7 percent of the value of production; by 1997 their share had grown to 9.5 percent. Similarly, greenhouse and nursery products accounted for 5.3 percent of the value of output in 1997, well above their 1.8 percent share in 1924. Other crops have declined in importance. The replacement of the horse with the tractor, especially during the first half of the twentieth century, accounts for a significant shift to reduce production of oats (used to feed horses) and to increase both the production of other crops and the cattle herd.

The 1.61 percent per year increase in output over 1910–1990 was achieved with only a 0.06 percent per year increase in the total quantity of inputs, and, comparing those two figures, agricultural productivity grew by 1.55 percent per year (Table Da1117–1122). The comparatively small change in aggregate input use hides a good deal of variation across different categories of inputs, even for a national index. In 1910, labor accounted for 29 percent of the total cost of inputs, but by 1997, the labor input accounted for only 11.9 percent of total input costs (Table Da1082–1094). As a share of total input costs, energy grew rapidly from 1910 to 1932 and continued to grow gradually thereafter. Fertilizer, lime, and pesticide expenses have generally accounted for between 4.6 and 13.8 percent of total input costs. Beginning in 1950, purchased intermediate inputs grew from 14.5 percent of input costs to 18.7 percent in 1997, with a general decline in inputs purchased from farm origin.

These measured output and especially input trends can be misleading, because important changes in quality have not been taken into account in the measures. Simply counting machines does not capture the fact that machines are much more efficient than they were fifty or even five years ago. Similarly, the composition of the agricultural labor force in agriculture has changed to include more experienced and better educated farmers; hence "hours of work" in agriculture means something quite different today than it did in 1910 (Acquaye, Alston, and Pardey 2003). Nevertheless, labor-saving machinery represented an important element in the overall growth in farm productivity. Important innovations in cropping were introduced when tractors replaced horses and self-propelled combines replaced tractor-drawn combines. In earlier periods, of course, the mechanical reaper and binder replaced the sickle and manual shocking.

Much of the farm mechanization for cereal crops started in the 1800s, with important innovations continuing throughout the 1900s, especially in the first half of the century. In the cotton industry, mechanized picking systems did not appear until after World War II. Innovations to mechanize the harvesting of some other crops were much more recent; for example, mechanical harvesters for canning tomatoes and various tree crops were developed after 1960 (Kislev and Peterson 1981). Other important mechanical innovations include various irrigation technologies; technologies used off the farm to transport and process the harvest, including canning, refrigeration, and other food preservation technologies; and other processing technologies such as Eli Whitney's cotton gin. Electrification was an important development that enabled the adoption of these technologies, in particular in the dairy industry, which was revolutionized by the introduction of milking machines and refrigerated vats.

A significant factor in the aggregate productivity patterns has been the use of biotechnology to improve genetic traits, especially of crops. These changes have led to improved disease resistance; quality improvements such as more uniform grain and fruit, among others; better tolerance for drought, waterlogging, or shorter growing seasons; better adaptation to particular climates or soil conditions; or greater suitability for mechanical harvesting (including more uniform ripening and the ability of the plant or its fruit to withstand mechanical processes) (Olmstead and Rhode 1993). Figure Da-I and Table Da1095–1107 show that per acre yields of crops have grown dramatically, especially during the past fifty years, but with some significant variation among the crops. Genetic improvement is not the only factor, as there have been improvements in chemical fertilizers, irrigation, and weed and pest control, but it is the main factor in many cases, especially for wheat, rice, and corn (Hayami and Ruttan 1970).

Productivity has generally not grown as quickly in the livestock industries as in the cropping industries, partly because genetic improvement has been slower (see Table Da1108–1116). Nevertheless, there have been important innovations in terms of

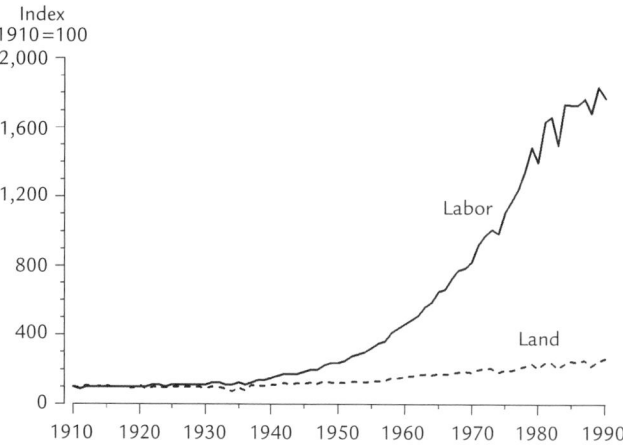

FIGURE Da-J   Indexes of agricultural productivity – labor and land: 1910–1990

Sources

Land productivity: series Da1172. Labor productivity: 1910–1984, series Da1173; thereafter, series Da1174.

Documentation

The values have been reindexed to 1910 = 100.

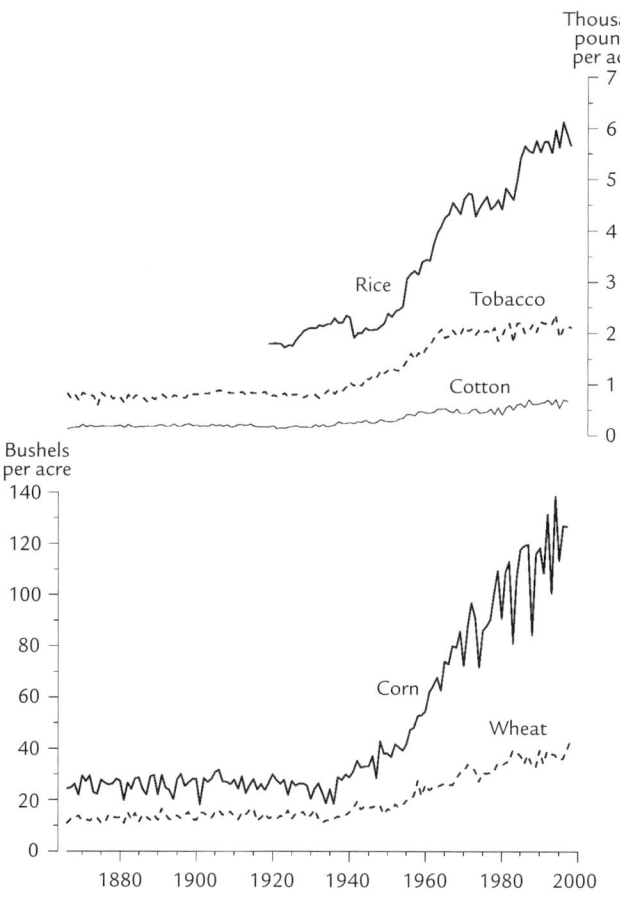

FIGURE Da-I   Average yield per acre for selected crops: 1866–1998

Sources

Series Da1095–1096 and Da1103–1105.

stocking rates, disease control, greater reproductive efficiency, and improved feed conversion efficiency. Such changes have enabled the development, for instance, of intensive large-scale, highly cost-efficient hog and poultry operations. To do so has meant combining elements of improvements in genetics, animal housing, feed, veterinary knowledge and medicines, and, importantly, livestock husbandry. Many of these changes have been somewhat controversial. People concerned with animal welfare have questioned the intensive livestock systems; people concerned about food safety have questioned the use of growth hormones (for example, rBST used to increase milk yield in dairy cattle was very controversial) and transgenic forms of biotechnology in animals or plants (for example, the introduction of a gene from a soil bacterium, *Bacillus thuringiensis*, into corn and cotton to confer pest resistance, or using similar methods to incorporate herbicide tolerance into soybeans).

Another perspective on productivity can be gleaned by considering the aggregate output per acre or per hour of work, as shown in Figure Da-J. Land productivity more than doubled between 1910 and 1990, but this was dwarfed by the nearly twenty-fold increase in labor productivity over the same period (Table Da1172–1174). This comparison reflects a more than trebling of output against a comparatively unchanging land base and a rapidly declining labor force in agriculture. The increases in land and labor productivity occurred mainly after the 1940s, with a slowing in the growth of

both productivity indexes in the 1980s. Increases in the quantities of other inputs, such as fertilizers, herbicides, electricity, fuels, and irrigation, account for some of the growth in output per hour or per acre, but much of the measured growth in productivity reflects changes in technology.

Among the most often cited historical time series of agricultural statistics are the figures on labor requirements for various farming operations. These labor-requirement figures have been updated to the last year before the series were discontinued, and are included here in Table Da1143–1171. Like the measures of labor productivity in Figure Da-J, these labor requirements are partial productivity or factor intensity measures, reflecting the effects of technology and other changes on input–output ratios. For example, in corn production, the figures on the number of hours worked per acre fell from 35.2 in 1910–1914 to 3.1 in 1982–1986, and the number of hours required to produce 100 bushels fell from 135 in 1910–1914 to 3.0 in 1982–1986. The much greater saving in hours per bushel reflects an implied increase in yields from 26.1 bushels per acre in 1910–1914 to 103 in 1982–1986, broadly consistent with the average yields in series Da1096. In turkey production, the figures on the number of hours worked per hundredweight of turkeys fell from 31.4 in 1910–1914 to 0.2 in 1982–1986, a much greater improvement in labor productivity compared with corn, reflecting great changes in input combinations as well as technical improvements.

The labor requirement series were discontinued in 1986 because of concerns over their accuracy and interpretation. It is not known how the figures were derived in the past, but it seems that they were based on expert opinions about best or average practice, and not on any statistical sampling of actual data.[1] The main virtue in these figures is that the series extend back for a long time, into periods for which no alternative data are available on input–output relationships. They might be most useful as indicators of longer-term changes rather than as specific measures of average productivity

---

[1] See USDA (1987), pp. 4–5, which summarizes Short (1986).

at any particular time, and they illustrate the dramatic changes that have taken place, but they must be used with care.

Productivity Patterns, 1949–1991

In aggregate terms, in 1991 U.S. agriculture produced more than double the quantity of output produced in 1949. It did this with marginally less aggregate input, causing an index of MFP to grow faster than the rate of growth in output. In annual rate-of-change terms, we estimate that output increased by 1.71 percent per annum over the 1949–1991 period; inputs used in agriculture declined by 0.19 percent, and so measured MFP grew by 1.90 percent per annum. The comparatively small drop in aggregate input use hides a good deal of variation across different categories of inputs, even for a national index.

The quantity of labor used in U.S. agriculture in 1991 was only 40 percent of the labor used in 1949, an average annual rate of decline of 2.2 percent. Labor quality has changed, too. In 1949, 72 percent of the hours worked by farm operators could be attributed to operators with no more than eight years of schooling. In 1991, operators with this level of educational attainment accounted for only 12 percent of total operator hours. In 1949, less than 5 percent of total operator hours were attributable to individuals with any college-level education, but this share increased to 37 percent in 1991.

The amount of land devoted to agriculture also declined. At the national level, land use is reduced from 0.47 percent to 0.30 percent per annum when one controls for changes in the quality of land used in agriculture. This is, in part, the result of the doubling of irrigated acres in U.S. agriculture over the period from 1949 to 1991. There was a slow overall growth in the capital services used by agriculture, even after accounting for the substantial quality improvements in machinery. Purchased inputs such as energy, seeds, fertilizers, and agricultural chemicals represent the only rapidly growing category of inputs; U.S. farmers have more than doubled the quantity of such inputs used since 1949.

These national trends are broadly consistent with regional developments but there are some significant differences in productivity growth (Table Da1232–1243), and even greater variation in the growth of inputs and, especially, outputs among states. Although land inputs have generally declined, they have increased in quality-adjusted terms in some of the drier Western and Southern states, reflecting a more rapid increase in higher-quality irrigated cropland in those states. Disaggregation of the labor inputs reveals that the temporal pattern of change is not the same in every part of the United States nor is it particularly uniform over time. The reduction in total hours worked was more dramatic in the Southern states than in the rest of the country. But in the West the quantity of labor used in agriculture actually increased over the 1970s and 1980s against a national trend of decreasing labor use.

Research and Development

Policies and Institutions

Over the centuries, much of the innovation in agriculture has been the result of tinkering by farmers and on-farm experimentation – including much breeding and selection of plants and animals and the development of improved methods, practices, tools, and mechan-

ical innovations. Before the modern scientific age, great advances in American agricultural productivity resulted from the efforts of plant prospectors who imported new and improved varieties from foreign lands. Walter Bruling of Mississippi imported a new cotton variety from Mexico in 1806 that would become the mainstay of the early American cotton industry; Agoston Haraszthy helped transform the California wine industry by importing several hundred grape varieties from across Europe, North Africa, and the Middle East in the 1860s. In addition to the efforts of private citizens, the USDA sent its scientists to the far corners of the globe in search of better plant varieties. These efforts were particularly fruitful in introducing varieties of wheat and other crops suitable for the conditions on the Great Plains (Alston 2002; Pardey, Alston, et al. 1996).

Among the inventors who devised some of the more widely known innovations in U.S. agriculture, we can count Eli Whitney, who patented the cotton gin; Cyrus McCormick, whose mechanical reaper "made bread cheap"; John Deere, whose steel-tipped moldboard plows helped tame the prairies; and Hiram Moore, who built the first combined harvester (combining a reaper and a thresher in one machine). The list of biological innovators is less well known, but the legendary Luther Burbank, who developed scores of new and improved varieties, many of which still bear his name, is representative of thousands of farmer-scientists who by careful selection and, in some cases, hybridization, improved the plant varieties available to American farmers. The private sector has continued to emphasize more patentable inventions. In agriculture, in particular, however, it is difficult for individuals to appropriate fully the returns from their research investments, and it is widely held that some government action is warranted to ensure an adequate investment in research and development (R&D) (Alston and Pardey 1996).

In earlier years, agricultural innovation was encouraged primarily by state and local governments and farmer organizations, through the awarding of prizes and demonstrations of best practice at county fairs and such, but with relatively little organized public research. Until 1862, federal government action to encourage investment in agricultural (and other) research was primarily through patent law enabled by article 1, section 8 of the U.S. Constitution, ratified in 1788. Since 1862, which marked both the establishment of the U.S. Department of Agriculture (USDA) and the passage of the Morrill Land Grant College Act, state and federal governments have become progressively more involved through public investments in agricultural R&D.[2]

The first Commissioner of Agriculture – the noncabinet post that originally directed the USDA – was Isaac Newton, who prior to the department's establishment had been the Superintendent of Agriculture at the Patent Office, with responsibility for the collection and distribution of seeds for new plant varieties. One of the first acts of the new commissioner was the appointment of a superintendent of the propagating garden, the USDA's first research facility, on what is now part of the Washington D.C. Mall.

Active intramural USDA research began immediately, with publication of the first research bulletin in 1862, describing the sugar content and suitability for winemaking of several grape varieties.

---

[2] More details and complete references to the history of these institutions may be found in Alston and Pardey (1996), Alston, Pardey, and Smith (1999), Huffman and Evenson (1993), Kerr (1987), National Research Council, Board on Agriculture (1989, 2003), Rasmussen and Baker (1972), and Weaver (1993).

The early years of the USDA were marked by the slow but steady expansion of the department's internal scientific activities, mostly devoted to "service" work rather than the discovery and development of new knowledge, but leading eventually to the establishment of the Agricultural Research Service (ARS). Under the Progressive Era leadership of James "Tama Jim" Wilson, from 1897 to 1913, the USDA budget grew dramatically (by more than 700 percent during Wilson's tenure), and, by 1904, employment of scientists within the USDA surpassed total employment of scientists in the state agricultural experiment stations (SAESs).

Publicly funded research outside the USDA grew out of the state agricultural experiment stations, developed first in Connecticut by Samuel W. Johnson, based on the prototypes developed in Germany in the 1850s. Following work prior to the Civil War to analyze chemical soil enrichers, Johnson was designated state chemist in 1869, with the formal establishment of the Connecticut Agricultural Experiment Station at Wesleyan University in 1875. At about the same time, experimentation directed to the problems of local farmers was beginning at the state land-grant institutions. USDA funding of external (that is, extramural) research followed the passage in 1887 of the Hatch Experiment Station Act. In the following years, agricultural experiment stations, supported by a mixture of federal, state, and some private funds, and generally located at the various land-grant colleges, opened across the country.

In the early years, extension activities provided local information and technology transfer services to farmers. Eventually the importance and popularity of extension activities led to legislative support, through the Smith–Lever Act of 1914, which created the Cooperative Extension Service and instituted a federal role in extension. During the 1930s, state support for the experiment stations fell sharply. In response, the Bankhead–Jones Act of 1935 provided additional federal support for research as well as extension. Several important features of the earlier Smith–Lever Act carried over to the Bankhead–Jones Act, notably the disbursement of federal funds to the states on a formula basis (20 percent of the funds distributed equally among states, 40 percent based on the state's share of the U.S. rural population, and 40 percent according to its share of U.S. farm population), provided the federal dollars were matched by state funds. In the ensuing years there were further legislative changes, as documented in Tables Da-K and Da-L, but the main elements of combined federal and state funding institutions remained unchanged. Importantly, however, the total amount of funding for public agricultural research and extension, and the sources and disposition of those funds, changed dramatically, especially from the 1960s forward.

Spending Patterns

Table Da1244–1252 gives a long-term perspective on agricultural R&D spending. In 1889, shortly after the Hatch Act was passed, federal and state spending appropriations totaled $1,119,136. A little over a century later, in 1997 the public-sector agricultural R&D enterprise had grown to more than $3 billion, an annual rate of growth of 7.99 percent in nominal terms and 4.39 percent in real terms. Intramural USDA research accounted for an increasing share of the national system, until the late 1930s, after which the SAES share grew to 69 percent of total public spending on agricultural R&D by 1997. Of the funds spent in the SAESs in 1997, 31 percent was from federal sources; 47 percent from state government; and

21 percent from industry, income earned from sales and technology licenses, and various other sources.

Along with the growth in research expenditures, the number of research personnel grew substantially as well. In 1998, the SAESs employed about 7,300 full-time equivalent scientists in addition to the 2,270 researchers employed by the USDA.

In 1915, the first year in which federal funds were made available for cooperative extension between the USDA and various state extension agencies, approximately $1.5 million of federal funds were combined with $2.1 million made available from various state and local government sources for a total of $3.6 million (Table Da1260–1265). This total grew by 7 percent per annum to reach $1.6 billion by 1999. The public provision of extension services in the United States is essentially a state or local activity. Consequently funds from within-state sources accounted for 74 percent of the total funds for extension, with federal funds accounting for the remaining 26 percent in 1999, much less than their peak share of 62 percent in 1919.

In 1992, the private sector spent $3.4 billion on in-house agricultural R&D, about 31 percent more than the amount spent by the public sector. Private spending grew by 9.85 percent per annum over the period 1960–1992 (series Da1253), faster than the 8.67 percent per annum for public agricultural R&D spending over the same interval (series Da1244). As a result, for every dollar of publicly conducted research in 1992 the private sector spent $1.31 compared with just 96 cents in the early 1960s.

The long-term trend of rapidly growing total spending on public agricultural R&D (including extension) slowed in the 1990s. An important element of this was a reduction of federal support for SAES research. This has meant a shift in the balance between the private and public elements in both the funding and the conduct of the research, changes in the mix of research being funded, and changes in other aspects of agricultural science policy as well. Some of these changes have come about as part of a shift in funding for all science, some as a result of a shift of public support generally for agriculture, partly driven by changes in agriculture (Pardey and Beintema 2001). In addition, there have been changes in agricultural science encompassing new molecular biotechnologies and concomitant changes in intellectual property and related institutions.

Among the more striking changes has been the broadening of the scope of intellectual property protection to include inventions involving living things. In the United States, the first steps in this direction began with the Plant Patent Act of 1930, which protected asexually reproducing plants, that is, plants such as grape vines, fruit trees, and ornamentals, which are propagated through cuttings and graftings. The patent scope was expanded further in the 1970s and 1980s through the introduction of utility patents for life forms, including asexually and sexually propagated seeds, plants, and tissue culture. Patent protection was complemented by the introduction of the Plant Variety Protection Act in 1970, designed to strengthen intellectual property protection for nonhybrid varieties.

The public investment in agricultural R&D has been credited with much of the strong growth in productivity over the past 100 years, especially the past 50 years. A great many benefit–cost studies have been undertaken to measure the social payoff of the investment. These studies vary in their findings, but generally agree that it has been a highly productive and socially profitable use of U.S. taxpayer funds (Alston, Chan-Kang, et al. 2000).

TABLE Da-K Major legislation affecting federal funding of research in state agricultural experiment stations and other cooperating institutions: 1862–1996

1862	**Legislation**: Act of Congress. **Provisions**: Introduced a Commissioner of Agriculture and the U.S. Department of Agriculture (USDA) to take over agricultural science functions of the Patent Office.
1862	**Legislation**: First Morrill Act. **Provisions**: Each state could establish and maintain at least one college to teach courses related to agriculture and mechanical arts (without excluding other scientific and classical studies, and including military tactics) in order to promote the liberal and practical education of the industrial classes. This provided for the establishment of the land grant system. **Funding**: Each state was to receive 30,000 acres of land for each Senator and Representative in Congress. States where not enough public land was available were given script to public land in other states; the income from the land was to be used for operating expenses (construction, purchase, repair of buildings excluded).
1887	**Legislation**: Hatch Act. **Provisions**: Each state could establish an experiment station to conduct original research or verify experiments on subjects bearing directly to the agricultural industry of the United States. Stations to be established under direction of land-grant colleges, but exceptions were permitted. This provided for the establishment of the state agricultural experiment stations (SAESs). **Funding**: Each qualifying state was to receive $15,000 per year.
1890	**Legislation**: Second Morrill Act. **Provisions**: First proposed in 1872. Gave direct annual appropriations to each state to further support land-grant colleges. Forbade racial discrimination in admission to colleges receiving the funds and gave rise to the so-called "1890 colleges." **Funding**: Congress gave each qualifying state $15,000 in the first year, increasing by $1,000 per year for subsequent years until the annual amount reached $25,000.
1906	**Legislation**: Adams Act. **Provisions**: Each state could receive additional federal funding to pay the necessary expenses of conducting original research and experiments. Emphasis on more science; more accountability; coincides with formation of Experiment Station Committee on Organization and Policy (ESCOP). **Funding**: Each qualifying state could receive a maximum of an additional $15,000 per year. Each state was entitled to an increase of $5,000 for the first year and $2,000 over the previous year's sum for five subsequent years.
1925	**Legislation**: Purnell Act. **Provisions**: Each state could receive additional federal funding for research (a) to establish and maintain a permanent and efficient agricultural industry and (b) to develop and improve the rural home and rural life. Spending on economics, home economics, and sociology was to be given priority. **Funding**: Each qualifying state could receive a maximum of $30,000 per year. Each state was entitled to an increase of $10,000 for the first year and $5,000 over the previous year's sum for four subsequent years.
1935	**Legislation**: Bankhead–Jones Act. **Provisions**: SAESs and the USDA could receive additional funding for research into basic problems of agriculture; research relating to quality improvement, new and improved methods of production and distribution, and new and extended uses and markets for agricultural commodities; and research relating to conservation, development, and recreational use of land and water. This legislation established formula funding and federal-state matching grants for research. **Funding**: A maximum of $5 million per year, with $3 million to the SAESs. A total increment of $1 million per year for each of five years. Funds to be distributed to the states on the basis of their proportions of the rural population of the United States, and each state must match federal contribution with nonfederal funding of the SAES.
1946	**Legislation**: Research and Marketing Act. **Provisions**: SAESs and the U.S. Department of Agriculture could receive additional funding for marketing and utilization research, and for regional research involving two or more states on a problem of regional significance. The stated goal of Congress was to maintain a balanced farming and industrial economy. This legislation introduced open-ended appropriations for research and linked spending in agricultural research and development to national welfare. **Funding**: Title I, Section 9: Total SAES funding up by $2.5 million in 1947 and 1948; $5 million increase for each of 1949, 1950, and 1951; such additional funds as Congress shall deem necessary for additional years. Allocation among states: 20 percent equally among states; 26 percent by formula according to state shares of U.S. rural population; 26 percent by formula according to shares of U.S. farm population; 25 percent for regional research; 3 percent for federal administration. Title I, Section 10: Increased U.S. Department of Agriculture funding for research. Authorized grants for "new uses" research to rise from $3 million in 1947 to $15 million after 1950; funds for cooperative research into farm product utilization to rise from $1.5 million in 1947 to $6 million after 1950; reauthorized $2 million annual Special Research Fund provided for in the Bankhead–Jones Act of 1935. Title II: Authorized an additional $2.5 million in 1947, increasing to $20 million per year after 1950, for marketing research, carried out cooperatively with SAESs and other public and private institutions, on a matching grant basis.
1955	**Legislation**: Amended Hatch Act. **Provisions**: To conduct research contributing to the maintenance of a permanent and effective agricultural industry in the United States, including research basic to the problems of agriculture in its broadest aspects, and research related to the development and improvement of the rural home and rural life and the maximum contribution of agriculture to the welfare of the consumer. Removed restrictions on using funds for building, but Hatch funds still had to be spent within the year awarded. Retained allocation formulas, matching grant requirements, and "open-ended" appropriations. Congress rejected a proposal to reduce marketing research by 20 percent and insisted that earmarking apply to all increases in appropriations. **Funding**: Consolidated federal funding for SAESs into two accounts (formula funds and regional research funds). No set annual amounts were established. Allocation was according to the formula from the Research and Marketing Act: 20 percent of each year's appropriation equally among states; 26 percent by formula according to a state's share of the U.S. rural population; 26 percent by formula according to a state's share of the U.S. farm population; 25 percent for cooperative regional research; 3 percent for federal administration.

TABLE Da–K Major legislation affecting federal funding of research in state agricultural experiment stations and other cooperating institutions: 1862–1996 *Continued*

1962	**Legislation**: McIntire–Stennis Forestry Research Act. **Provisions**: Made funding available for forestry research to SAESs, land grant colleges, and forestry schools – including reforestation, woodlands and related watershed management, outdoor recreation, wildlife habitats, wood utilization, and such other studies as may be necessary to obtain the fullest and most effective use of forest resources. The Cooperative State Research Service (CSRS), formulated as such in 1963 and previously the Cooperative State Experiment Station Service (CSESS) formed in 1961, to administer appropriations under McIntire–Stennis. **Funding**: A formula allocated $10,000 to each state, 40 percent of the remainder according to a state's share of the nation's total commercial forest land, 40 percent according to the value of its timber cut annually, and 20 percent according to its contribution of nonfederal forestry research dollars. In both 1964 and 1965, $1 million was appropriated, 2 percent of CSRS-managed funds (by 1974 this figure had increased to over $6 million annually, 7 percent of CSRS-managed money, and by 1984 it was up to almost $13 million or 6 percent of combined federal funding to the states for agricultural research and development).
1965	**Legislation**: Research Facilities Act. **Provisions**: Earmarked funds to be matched by the states for the construction, acquisition, and remodeling of buildings, laboratories, and other capital facilities. Supported new construction only of facilities for research on hazardous chemicals used in farming. Allowed each station to obligate its annual share over three years for the first time. IR-4 "National Program of Clearances of Chemicals for Minor and Specialty Uses" launched in 1963. Current Research Information System (CRIS) established in the 1960s. **Funding**: The formula resembled that in the amended Hatch Act: one third equally to each state; one third according to the proportion of rural residents; one third according to the proportion of farm population. Total allocations were $3.2 million in 1965, $2 million per year in 1966, 1967, and 1968; none was provided in 1969, and $1 million in 1970, for the last time.
1965	**Legislation**: Public Law 89-106. **Provisions**: Established Specific Research Grants program to finance selected projects, to run for a maximum of five years. Later became the Special Grants program. Earmarked funds to address specific problems of constituent concern or multistate problems. National Agricultural Research Advisory Committee (NARAC) established in 1961. Producer-dominated commodity-oriented research councils declined; they were eliminated in 1970. **Funding**: CSRS would call annually for proposals in areas singled out by Congress for special attention. In 1966, $1.6 million was offered; in 1967–1970, $1.7 million per year. $283,000 per year was allocated to the sixteen "1890 colleges."
1972	**Legislation**: Rural Development Act. **Provisions**: SAESs and the Extension Service could receive funds for rural development and small-farm research and extension. In 1971, Congress granted $75,000 to each of four rural development centers. Recommended that SAESs devote $3 million of Hatch appropriations to Community Improvement research. **Funding**: The 1972 Act authorized $10 million for 1974, $15 million for 1975, and $20 million for 1976. Actual expenditures were much less. $3 million was provided in each of the first three years, split between extension and research, allocated among the SAESs on a basis similar to the Hatch formula except that 10 percent was reserved for interstate projects. Funding continued at $3 million per year for another four years after the initial authorization expired in 1977.
1977	**Legislation**: National Agricultural Research, Extension and Teaching Policy Act (Title XIV of the Food and Agriculture Act of 1977). **Provisions**: Continued and strengthened amended Hatch programs and initiated a new U.S. Department of Agriculture Competitive Grants program for plant science and nutrition research, open to all scientists, to be awarded on a competitive basis to private- and public-sector organizations, including SAESs, all colleges and universities, other research organizations, federal agencies, and individuals. Continued the Special Grants program. Dropped the requirement that 20 percent of amended Hatch funds be earmarked for marketing research. Other new earmarked grants also introduced (for example, energy research, animal health). New mechanisms for more formalized research planning, central (federal) direction, and accountability. **Funding**: Hatch formula funds were strengthened with $120 million called for in 1978 and increases of $25 million per year up to $220 million in 1982. Allocation was basically as by previous arrangements and formulas. The Competitive Grants program authorized additional spending of $25 million in 1978, $30 million in 1979, $35 million in 1980, $40 million in 1981 and $50 million in 1982.
1981	**Legislation**: Amendments to Title XIV (National Agricultural Research, Extension and Teaching Policy Act of 1977). **Provisions**: Primarily extended the 1977 Act for four years. Introduced $10 million annual rangeland research program and $7.5 million annual aquaculture research program. Congress effectively promised not to replace, but to supplement, formula funds with competitive grants. Scope of the competitive grants program was expanded with a biotechnology initiative that included animal science. **Funding**: Same as the 1977 Act. Hatch funds were authorized to rise from $220 million in 1982 to $250 million in 1985. Hatch funds were guaranteed at a minimum of 25 percent of U.S. Department of Agriculture expenditures in cooperative programs.
1985	**Legislation**: National Agricultural Research, Extension and Teaching Policy Act (Title XIV of the Food Security Act of 1981). **Provisions**: Primarily extended the 1981 Act for four years. Added a new subtitle to promote agricultural productivity. Earmarked funds for marketing research were reintroduced ($10 million per year) along with Trade Development Centers at land-grant universities (on a matching basis). U.S. Department of Agriculture permitted to fund competitive grants for facilities at SAESs. **Funding**: Same as 1981 Act. Hatch funds were to grow only 4 percent per year, while Competitive Grants were authorized to increase substantially, especially for biotechnology research. Hatch funding of $270 million in 1986 to increase to $310 million for 1990. Competitive Grants funding to increase from $50 million in 1985 to $70 million in 1986 and subsequent years.

(continued)

TABLE Da-K   Major legislation affecting federal funding of research in state agricultural experiment stations and other cooperating institutions: 1862–1996   Continued

1990	**Legislation**: Food, Agriculture, Conservation and Trade Act of 1990. **Provisions**: Primarily extended the 1985 Act for four years. Inception of the National Initiative for Research on Agriculture, Food and the Environment, commonly called the National Research Initiative (NRI). Congress specified target shares for several types of grants within the NRI; not less than 30 percent for multidisciplinary research; 20 percent for mission-linked research; 10 percent for strengthening grants. The legislation also directed the U.S. Department of Agriculture to emphasize, where appropriate, research that enhanced agricultural sustainability. In FY 1991 NRI was restructured and expanded to include four program areas: plant systems; animal systems; nutrition, food quality, and health; and natural resources and the environment. Grant programs regarding markets, trade, and policy as well as processing for value added were included in the following year.
1994	**Legislation**: Public Law 103-354 Federal Crop Insurance Reform and Department of Agriculture Reorganization Act of 1994. **Provisions**: Merged the Cooperative State Research Service (CSRS) and the Extension Service (ES) into a single agency, the newly created Cooperative State Research, Education and Extension Service (CSREES). National Agricultural Library (NAL) consolidated with the Agricultural Research Service, which, together with CSREES, the Economic Research Service, and the National Academy of Sciences, report to the newly created undersecretary for research, education and economics.
1996	**Legislation**: Public Law 104-127 Federal Agricultural Improvement and Reform (FAIR) Act of 1996. **Provisions**: Merged the three U.S. Department of Agriculture advisory boards, the Agricultural Science and Technology Review Board, the Joint Council on Food and Agricultural Sciences, and the National Agricultural Research and Extension Users Advisory Board to form the National Agricultural Research, Extension, Education, and Economics Advisory Board.

Sources

U.S. Department of Agriculture, *USDA News* 53 (October–November 1994); W. E. Huffman and R. E. Evenson, *Science for Agriculture: A Long-Term Perspective* (Iowa State University Press, 1993), Table 1.6; N. A. Kerr, *The Legacy: A Centennial History of the State Agricultural Experiment Stations, 1887–1987* (Missouri Agricultural Experiment Station, 1987); National Research Council, Board on Agriculture, *Investing in Research: A Proposal to Strengthen the Agricultural, Food, and Environmental System*, 1989; National Research Council, Board on Agriculture, *Investing in Research: An Update of the Competitive Grants Program in the U.S. Department of Agriculture*, 1994; National Research Council, Board on Agriculture and Natural Resources, *Frontiers in Agricultural Research: Food, Health, Environment, and Communities* (National Academy Press, 2003).

TABLE Da-L   Major legislation affecting federal funding of cooperative extension: 1914–1996

1914	**Legislation**: Smith–Lever Act. **Provisions**: Created Cooperative Extension Service to aid in diffusing among the people useful and practical information on subjects relating to agriculture and home economics and to encourage its application. **Funding**: Provided lump sum grants of $10,000 per state ($480,000 total) and additional formula funding. Formula funds were allocated on the basis of a state's share of the U.S. rural population. Formula funding phased in over seven years, maximum of $4.1 million. The formula money was to be matched by state funds.
1928	**Legislation**: Capper–Ketcham Act. **Provisions**: Provided for expansion of Cooperative Extension Service. **Funding**: An additional lump sum grant of $20,000 per state ($980,000 total per year) and an additional $500,000 starting in 1929 to be allocated by formula. Required one third of added funds to be matched in 1923 and full matching after 1928.
1935	**Legislation**: Bankhead–Jones Act. **Provisions**: Provided for expansion of Cooperative Extension Service. **Funding**: An additional lump sum grant of $20,000 per state ($980,000 total per year) and an additional $8 million to be allocated to states by formula in 1936 and $1 million additional for each of the next four years. Formula funds to be allocated by state's share of the U.S. farm population, matching not required.
1945	**Legislation**: Bankhead–Flannagan Act. **Provisions**: Further expansion of Extension. **Funding**: Two percent of the federal appropriation was for federal administration, 4 percent was set aside for the secretary for special need allocation, and 94 percent was distributed by formula according to a state's share in the U.S. farm population.
1953	**Legislation**: Amended Smith–Lever Act. **Provisions**: Consolidated nine existing Acts; provided for appropriations for Federal Extension Staff in the U.S. Department of Agriculture. **Funding**: Provided that subsequent increases be allocated 4 percent to special need, 48 percent based on a state's share of the U.S. rural population, and 48 percent based on a state's share of the U.S. farm population.
1955	**Legislation**: Smith–Lever Amendment. **Provisions**: Special program system established. **Funding**: Provisions added permitting special nonformula funds.
1961	**Legislation**: Amended Smith–Lever Act. **Provisions**: Resource and community development extension added. **Funding**: Provided $700,000 per year for resource and community development work.
1962	**Legislation**: Smith–Lever Amendment. **Funding**: Froze distribution of current federal funds to each state. Subsequent increases to be 4 percent to the Federal Service, and of the remainder, 20 percent in equal proportions to all states, 40 percent according to a state's share of the U.S. rural population, and 40 percent according to its share of the U.S. farm population. Formula remained essentially the same in 1999.
1965	**Legislation**: Smith–Lever Amendment. **Funding**: Section 3(d) used to provide pesticide chemical programs in Appalachia.
1968	**Legislation**: Smith–Lever Amendment. **Funding**: Congress shifted all 3(d) special funds back to formula funding except for $1.6 million for agricultural marketing.

TABLE Da-L Major legislation affecting federal funding of cooperative extension: 1914–1996 *Continued*

1972	**Legislation**: Federal Rural Development Act. **Provisions**: Title V authorized work in rural communities in agriculture and nonagriculture fields. **Funding**: Funds were to be distributed 4 percent for federal administration, 10 percent for multistate work, 20 percent equally distributed among states, and 33 percent according to a state's share of the U.S. rural population and 33 percent according to a state's share of the U.S. farm population.
1977	**Legislation**: Food and Agriculture Act. **Funding**: Changed the Rural Development Title V formula of 1972 to 19 percent for farm research programs and 77 percent for small farm extension programs.
1978	**Legislation**: Passage of the Resource Extension Act. **Provisions**: Authorized funding for extension forestry and other renewable national resources. **Funding**: By appropriation.
1981	**Legislation**: Agriculture and Food Act of 1981. **Funding**: Rural development extension funds became part of Smith–Lever formula appropriation.
1994	**Legislation**: Public Law 103-354 Federal Crop Insurance Reform and Department of Agriculture Reorganization Act of 1994. **Provisions**: Merged the Cooperative State Research Service (CSRS) and the Extension Service (ES) into a single agency, the newly created Cooperative State Research, Education and Extension Service (CSREES). National Agricultural Library (NAL) consolidated with the Agricultural Research Service, which, together with CSREES, the Economic Research Service, and the National Academy of Sciences, report to the newly created undersecretary for research, education, and economics.
1996	**Legislation**: Public Law 104-127 Federal Agricultural Improvement and Reform (FAIR) Act of 1996. **Provisions**: Merged the three U.S. Department of Agriculture advisory boards, the Agricultural Science and Technology Review Board, the Joint Council on Food and Agricultural Sciences, and the National Agricultural Research and Extension Users Advisory Board to form the National Agricultural Research, Extension, Education, and Economics Advisory Board.

Sources

National Research Council, Board on Agriculture and Natural Resources, *Frontiers in Agricultural Research: Food, Health, Environment, and Communities* (National Academy Press, 2003); U.S. Department of Agriculture, *USDA News* 53 (October–November 1994); W. E. Huffman and R. E. Evenson, *Science for Agriculture: A Long-Term Perspective* (Iowa State University Press, 1993), Table 1.7.

References

Acquaye, A. K. A., J. M. Alston, and P. G. Pardey. 2003. "Post-War Productivity Patterns in U.S. Agriculture: Influences of Aggregation Procedures in a State-Level Analysis." *American Journal of Agricultural Economics* 85 (1): 59–80.

Alston, J. M. 2002. "Spillovers." *Australian Journal of Agricultural and Resource Economics* 46 (3): 315–46.

Alston, J. M., C. Chan-Kang, et al. 2000. *A Meta-Analysis of Agricultural R&D Evaluations: Ex Pede Herculem?* Research Report Number 113, International Food Policy Research Institute.

Alston, J. M., and P. G. Pardey. 1996. *Making Science Pay: The Economics of Agricultural R&D Policy.* American Enterprise Institute Press.

Alston, J. M., P. G. Pardey, and V. H. Smith, editors. 1999. *Paying for Agricultural Productivity.* Johns Hopkins University Press.

American Agricultural Economics Association (AAEA) Task Force on Measuring Agricultural Productivity. 1980. *Measurement of U.S. Agricultural Productivity: A Review of Current Statistics and Proposals for Change.* ESCS Technical Bulletin Number 1614. U.S. Department of Agriculture.

Ball, V. E. 1985. "Output, Input and Productivity Measurement in U.S. Agriculture: 1948–79." *American Journal of Agricultural Economics* 67 (3): 475–86.

Bonnen, J. T. 1986. "A Century of Science in Agriculture: Lessons for Science Policy." *American Journal of Agricultural Economics* 68 (5): 1065–80.

Capalbo, S. M., and J. M. Antle, editors. 1988. *Agricultural Productivity: Measurement and Explanation.* Resources for the Future Press.

Cochrane, W. W. 1993. *The Development of American Agriculture: A Historical Analysis.* 2nd edition. University of Minnesota Press.

Craig, B. J., and P. G. Pardey. 1996. "Productivity Measurement in the Presence of Quality Change." *American Journal of Agricultural Economics* 78 (5): 1349–54.

Griliches, Z. 1957. "Hybrid Corn: An Exploration in the Economics of Technological Change." *Econometrica* 25 (4): 501–22.

Griliches, Z. 1960. "Measuring Inputs in Agriculture: A Critical Survey." *Journal of Farm Economics* 42 (5): 1411–27.

Griliches, Z. 1963. "The Sources of Measured Productivity Growth: Agriculture, 1940–1960." *Journal of Political Economy* 71 (4): 331–46.

Hayami, Y., and V. W. Ruttan. 1970. "Factor Prices and Technical Change in Agricultural Development: The United States and Japan, 1880–1960." *Journal of Political Economy* 78 (5): 1115–41.

Huffman, W. E., and R. E. Evenson. 1993. *Science for Agriculture: A Long-Term Perspective.* Iowa State University Press.

Jorgenson, D. W., and F. M. Gollop. 1992. "Productivity Growth in U.S. Agriculture: A Postwar Perspective." *American Journal of Agricultural Economics* 74 (3): 745–50.

Kerr, N. A. 1987. *The Legacy: A Centennial History of the State Agricultural Experiment Stations, 1887–1987.* Missouri Agricultural Experiment Station.

Kislev, Y., and W. Peterson. 1981. "Induced Innovations and Farm Mechanization." *American Journal of Agricultural Economics* 63 (3): 562–5.

National Research Council, Board on Agriculture. 1989. *Investing in Research: A Proposal to Strengthen the Agricultural, Food, and Environmental System.* National Academy Press.

National Research Council, Board on Agriculture and Natural Resources. 2003. *Frontiers in Agricultural Research: Food, Health, Environment, and Communities.* National Academy Press.

Olmstead, A. L., and P. Rhode. 1993. "Induced Innovation in American Agriculture: A Reconsideration." *Journal of Political Economy* 101: 100–18.

Pardey, P. G., J. M. Alston, et al. 1996. *Hidden Harvest: U.S. Benefits from International Research Aid.* IFPRI Food Policy Report. International Food Policy Research Institute.

Pardey, P. G., and N. M. Beintema. 2001. *Slow Magic: Agricultural R&D a Century after Mendel.* IFPRI Food Policy Report. International Food Policy Research Institute.

Rasmussen, W. D., and G. L. Baker. 1972. *The Department of Agriculture.* Praeger.

Schultz, T. W. 1956. "Reflections on Agricultural Production, Output and Supply." *Journal of Farm Economics* 38 (August): 748–62.

Short, Sara. 1986. "Measuring Agricultural Labor Hours and the Rate of Return to Equity in Farm Assets." Paper presented at the annual meeting of the American Agricultural Economics Association, Reno, July.

Smith, M. S., and D. M. Roth. 1990. *Chronological Landmarks in American Agriculture.* USDA-ERS Agricultural Information Bulletin. Revised edition. U.S. Government Printing Office, November.

USDA, Economic Research Service. 1987. *Economic Indicators of the Farm Sector: Production and Efficiency Statistics, 1985.* U.S. Department of Agriculture.

Weaver, R. D., editor. 1993. *U.S. Agricultural Research: Strategic Challenges and Options.* Agricultural Research Institute.

AGRICULTURAL INCOME AND FINANCES

Bruce L. Gardner

The financial situation in agriculture has been a contentious issue in the interpretation of U.S. economic history from the post–Civil War depression of commodity prices to the "farm crisis" of the 1980s. Farmers have tended to see themselves as an economically disadvantaged group, a view that has gained salience among many historians and, of more practical importance, among many politicians. Agricultural economists have developed models of the "farm problem" in which a combination of economic characteristics conspire to bring about chronically unstable and low returns for producers of agricultural products. These include the perfectly competitive nature of farm product markets as contrasted with the market power of agribusinesses with which farmers deal, the price-inelastic supply and demand of farm products, and rapid technological change reducing labor requirements in agricultural production (see Brandow 1977; Gardner 1992; Olmstead and Rhode 2000).

Many of the data series in this chapter were developed, originally by economists in the U.S. Department of Agriculture (USDA), as indicators of the farm income and financial situation. The original impetus for these estimates was legislation that adopted the goal of achieving "income parity" for farmers and nonfarmers, using the period 1910–1914 as a basis for comparison (USDA 1940, 1988). A rapid and sustained drop in farm commodity prices occurred in 1920, following twenty years of prosperity capped with extraordinarily high prices during World War I. Net farm income fell from $9 billion to $3.4 billion between 1919 and 1921 (series Da1295). After a few years of recovery a still greater and more sustained farm income collapse occurred as the nation entered the Great Depression. Data to quantify this situation were developed simultaneously with a search for legislative solutions to farmers' economic problems, which culminated in the commodity programs of the New Deal.

The Farm Income Problem

A notable finding that reinforced political action in the 1930s, and continued to do so for decades afterwards, was documentation that farm incomes were well below those of nonfarm households for most of the twentieth century. But while farm income has been measured in a roughly comparable way for the period 1910 to the present, many issues in comparing farm and nonfarm household incomes have been controversial. Measurements of farmers' incomes from off-farm sources, income in kind from the farm, and cost of living differences between rural and urban areas all pose substantial difficulties (for details see Kirkpatrick 1926; D. Gale Johnson 1953; Thomas Johnson 1985; and Ahearn, Perry, and El-Osta 1993). Data availability and assumptions made about income comparisons have differed at different times, and no fully integrated data series has been published for the whole period. Nonetheless, recent work in the USDA indicates quite strongly that since 1950 farm household incomes have increased from the neighborhood of half of nonfarm incomes to approximate equality with nonfarm incomes after 1990 (see USDA 2000, Table 30). This has changed the underlying conditions for agricultural policy debate considerably.

In addition to farm income measures, the agricultural income and finance tables in this chapter include a variety of statistics that describe agriculture as a sector or industry, as well as details of the economic situation of farm enterprises and rural-farm people. The data include commodity prices, farm input prices, farm credit, farmers' receipts from sales of farm products, marketing margins, exports and imports of agricultural products, and income and balance sheet data for the farm sector.

Net farm income is the most frequently cited indicator of the economic health of U.S. farming. That income excludes off-farm sources of income, which make up the majority of farm households' income. Thus one must sharply distinguish the economic health of farming from the economic well-being of farm people. Estimates of net farm income reported in this volume are not estimated directly by asking farmers about their net returns. While the Current Population Surveys of the Bureau of the Census have asked farm households directly about net income, these estimates have been considered less accurate for sectoral aggregate purposes than indirect estimates, primarily because of understatement of reported net self-employment income (see Grove 1958).

Farm Revenues and Input Costs

Since 1930 the U.S. Census of Agriculture has asked farmers the value of sales of agricultural products from their farms. Data are thus available at five-year intervals since that time (except for the four-year intervals 1974–1978 and 1978–1982). The National Agricultural Statistics Service (NASS) and Economic Research Service, and their predecessor agencies in the USDA, provide annual estimates using census benchmarks and other data from buyers as well as sellers of farm products. Before 1930 all estimates relied on separate production and price information which was then combined to estimate the value of agricultural output. Strauss and Bean provided the first consistently derived long historical aggregate output and gross revenue series, covering 1869 to 1939 (Strauss and Bean 1940). They drew on many sources of information other than the census, and indeed their work crystallized the view that in many respects aggregates directly implied by census data were inaccurate.[1]

Towne and Rasmussen (1960) extended the data series at ten-year intervals back to 1800. Their estimates are provided in Table Da1277–1287. Continuous annual data derived from surveys of output of the agriculture sector, using USDA data in the NIPA accounting framework of the Bureau of Economic Analysis (BEA) of the U.S. Department of Commerce, are available only for the years since 1929. Those data are presented in Table Da1266–1276. The historical data have been revised several times, most recently in 1999, when the methods and definitions used by BEA were finally brought into full conformity with those of USDA.

Prices received by farmers have fluctuated sharply from year to year (see Figure Da-M) and over the longer term have declined in real terms by about half since 1910. This fall is typically attributed primarily to cost-reducing technical progress in agriculture, and has been cited as evidence that consumers rather than farmers have been the main beneficiaries of that progress. Statistics on prices are less well attested than are quantities in census

---

[1] For discussion of problems in the census data, see Johnson (1958) and Grove (1958).

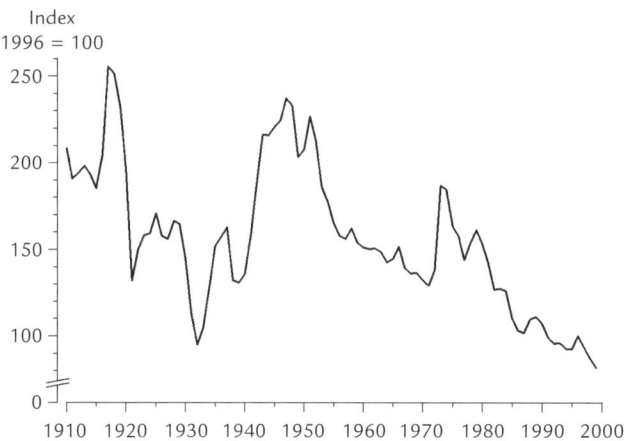

Index
1996 = 100

FIGURE Da-M   Real prices received by farmers: 1910–1999

Sources

Series Da1337 deflated by series Ca13 and converted to an index with 1996 = 100.

data. The USDA began annual surveys of prices received by farmers in 1866 for crops and in 1867 for livestock.[2] At first data collection occurred at only one point during the year, and for a limited number of commodities. In 1908 a significant expansion of the USDA's price data collection efforts was made to obtain monthly estimates. Since that time commodity coverage has been expanded and sampling procedures improved, notably in 1977, to obtain more representative prices. The goal is to obtain prices that, when multiplied by the total quantity of the product sold by U.S. farms, would give the total amount received by farmers for that commodity. The relevant price is an average price received by farmers at the point of first sale to which farmers deliver their product for their sales of all grades, qualities, classes, and locations of a commodity. This price will in general be substantially different from an average spot price on an organized commodity market for any particular specification of a commodity. A more fundamental structural problem is that increasing quantities of farm output are sold under contracts that are only loosely linked to cash commodity prices. For example, in late 1998 cash hog prices fell to levels of $10 to $15 per hundred pounds, a third the level of a year earlier. But many producers had marketing contracts that cushioned them from these low prices through advance pricing or provisions that gave price supplements in low-price periods (to be offset by payback in high-price periods). Indeed, in some markets, notably eggs and broilers, the cash market has become so little used as to call into question the relevance of the prices reported from them.

Information on quantities of inputs used by farmers is less comprehensive, especially in earlier years. Data for farm labor, fertilizers, and other purchased inputs have been published in the Census of Agriculture since 1900. Prices paid by farmers have been estimated by the USDA since 1911. Preparation and publication of these data is currently the responsibility of NASS. Because these estimates were from the beginning associated with efforts to measure the standard of living of farm people, prices paid by farmers for consumption items as well as production expenses were collected

annually until 1976. At that time it was decided that the prices of farm family living items were adequately measured by the Consumer Price Index of the Bureau of Labor Statistics (USDA 1990, p. 7). Since the 1970s the USDA's focus has been on prices of goods and services used in farm production. Prices of farm production items, like those of farm products sold, are an average of all grades, qualities, container sizes, locations, and brands of an item. The location is taken to be at the premises of the seller. Prices are reported by sellers. Surveys are conducted monthly, although not for all items each month, by NASS state offices, using mail, telephone, and personal interviews.[3]

Measurement of farm income uses all of the preceding estimates plus other information on farm credit, farmers' economic activities on farms other than their own, and the costs of owned land, machinery, and other durable inputs that yield services in years beyond the year in which they were purchased. The basic approach to measuring farm income has remained unchanged since the earliest estimates were made. Estimates of farmers' expenditures on inputs used are subtracted from the value of farm output to obtain a net income measure. Expense data needed to estimate net farm income were first collected by land-grant universities and state departments of agriculture in the nineteenth century. Such data were used to construct net income measures for farmers in a series of studies by agricultural economists both in the states and at the USDA. Summaries of their findings were published in the USDA's *Yearbook of Agriculture* and in USDA monographs and articles in economic journals (such as Gray 1923; Kirkpatrick 1926; Black 1928). For purposes of USDA farm income estimation, expenditures on key inputs used in farm production – hired labor, feed, fertilizers, machinery, seeds – were obtained principally from Census of Agriculture data before 1955. But many production expenses have been only irregularly covered by the census. The first comprehensive USDA survey of farm production expenditures was carried out in 1956, and such surveys have been increasingly utilized since that time. The invaluable contribution of the USDA estimates in *The Farm Income Situation* and its successor publications has been to develop consistently constructed farm income estimates for a long historical period.

Agricultural Value Added and Farmers' Wealth

An issue related to but distinct from farm income is agriculture's contribution to the nation's aggregate output (see Figure Da-N). For this purpose the appropriate indicator is value added by farm resources – the land, labor, and capital invested in the sector. The measure used is called "farm national income" (series Da1276). By this measure agriculture has generated increased real product,

---

[2] See USDA (1990) for further details on this and subsequent USDA efforts in farm price estimation.

[3] Indexes of prices received and prices paid were for more than fifty years scaled to a reference period of 1910–1914 = 100, originally because of congressional mandate. This reference period was chosen as an indicator of "parity," the idea being that in 1910–1914 prices received and paid were in an appropriate ratio to indicate market conditions conducive to good economic health for U.S. farming. Consequently, a value of less than 100 in subsequent years could be taken as an indicator of unfavorable economic conditions for farmers. This interpretation is questionable for long-term comparisons because technical change has substantially changed the quantities of inputs used to produce a given level of farm output. In the 1990 Farm Act the 1910–1914 reference point was dropped as a requirement for the USDA's official published estimates.

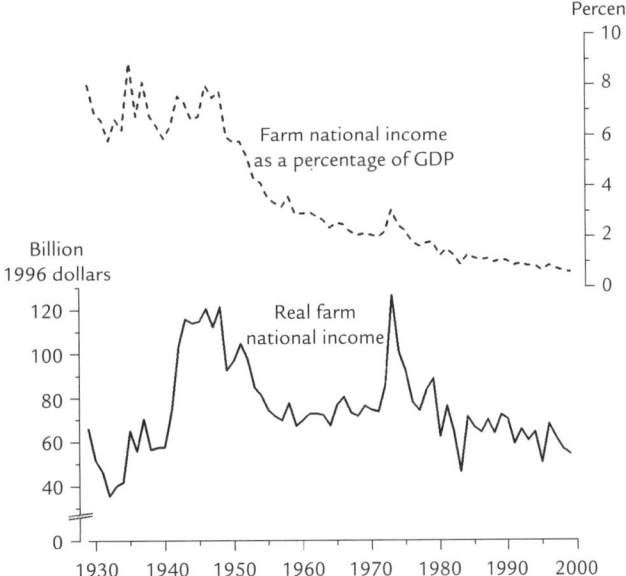

FIGURE Da-N   Farm national income – real and as a percent of gross domestic product: 1929–1999

Sources

Series Da1276 deflated by series Ca13 and also expressed as a percentage of series Ca10.

but a continually declining share of the nation's gross domestic product (GDP), for as long as data have been collected.

A problem that has never been fully resolved is choosing the economic entities whose income should be counted in farm income. Two approaches are reasonable: (1) a product basis, measuring net income generated in the production of farm products, and (2) an establishment basis, measuring net income of entities meeting criteria to be counted as farms (whether owned and operated by a household, a partnership, a corporation, or other institutions, such as prisons and universities).

Net value added (the product-based measure of net income) and net farm income (the establishment-based measure) differ substantially. In 1993 data, for example, only 56 percent of sector net income goes to farm operators, with the rest going to nonfarm suppliers of land, labor, and capital.[4] Thus, the establishment approach to income accounting makes a considerable difference compared to a product-based concept. The 1960 data indicate that at that time the difference between the two approaches was smaller, although still significant. In earlier periods there is still less distinction between farm operators and producers of farm value added.

A longer-term picture of the economic health of farming is given by the balance sheet of farms. Farmers have long been noted for living poor and dying rich, as after a lifetime of paying off mortgage debt and living frugally they often end up with a substantial net wealth position. Information about ownership of farm real estate, machinery, and crop and livestock inventories has been collected in the Census of Agriculture since 1900. The USDA has supplemented these data with information on real estate prices, the value of machinery and equipment on farms, financial assets,

and farmers' debts to estimate a full balance sheet whose "bottom line" is the net worth or "proprietors' equity" in U.S. farms as of January 1 of each year since 1940. Assets and debts exclude those of farm households that are related to business activity other than farming, and exclude personal assets such as corporate bonds and stocks in publicly held companies (but U.S. savings bonds are included). Coverage of the balance sheet data differs in one important respect from that of farm income data; namely, the balance sheet includes farm-related assets and debt of farm landlords who are not farm operators (whereas rents paid to nonfarm landlords are counted as a cost in net farm income accounting) (for further details, see Erickson, Hacklander, et al. 1989).

Marketing Margins and Market Power

Farmers have long complained that, because of the market power of agribusinesses compared to the atomistic competition that prevails in farming, buyers of their products pay too little. Attempts have been made to quantify changes in farmers' economic position with respect to agribusiness by looking at differences in the rates of growth of prices received by farmers and the costs to consumers for food products. The retail cost index, series Da1347, indicates the cost of a market basket of food produced from U.S. farm products compared to the base period 1982–1984. The index is constructed by the Economic Research Service of the USDA using retail price data from the Bureau of Labor Statistics, and differs only slightly from the "food at home" consumer price index (CPI) in series Cc10. The main difference between the two series is that the CPI includes the prices of imported food products and of seafoods and other food products not from farms, while series Da1347 concentrates on foods produced from U.S. domestic farm products. The farm value component in series Da1348 – the cost of the agricultural raw materials going into the market basket – is estimated by the Economic Research Service using raw material requirements for food products in the market basket valued at farm-gate prices. The farm-to-retail price spread is the difference between the retail cost of the food basket and the farm value of raw materials, adjusted for the value of nonfood by-products. Several related indicators of farm-retail price spreads are shown in Tables Da1347–1356. Their value as indicators of farmers' market power compared to that of processors and others in the marketing chain is a subject of debate. Such measures do not directly address the issue of market power, and a decline in the farmers' share does not necessarily have a negative implication for farmers' income (for a discussion see Elitzak 1999 and Wohlgenant 2001). Nonetheless, the data have been widely cited in political debate.

Summary

Overall, the data on agricultural income and finances describe a notable economic success story for the U.S. agricultural sector and for many of the individuals involved in the industry. Indicators of agriculture's success are its continuing international competitiveness as indicated by a strong export position (see Figure Da-O), the rising real incomes of commercial farms, and the declining real cost of domestically produced food in retail outlets (see series Da1347). At the same time, the number of farms has declined, there have been recurrent financial crises in agriculture, and small-scale farm

---

[4] The amount going to hired labor would be even larger – a 19.5 percent share – if $1.9 billion paid to workers in crews supplied by labor contractors were not excluded from farm value added (by both the USDA and the BEA).

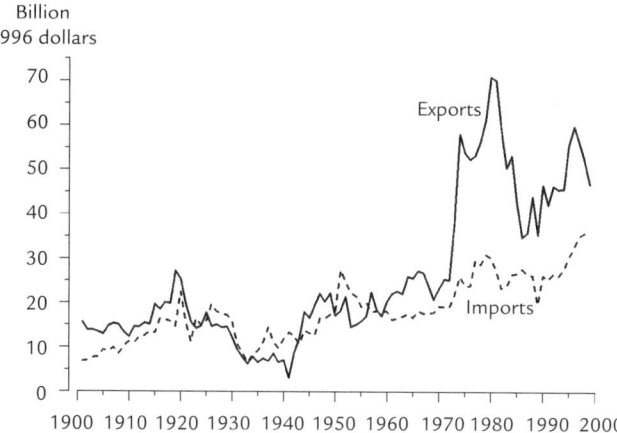

FIGURE Da-O Agricultural exports and imports: 1901–1999

Sources

Series Da1323 and Da1325 deflated by series Ca13.

operations have become increasingly nonviable as commercial enterprises. In a technologically dynamic and competitive industry facing limited demand, it seems inevitable that there will be losers as well as winners.

References

Ahearn, Mary, Janet Perry, and Hisham El-Osta. 1993. "The Economic Well-Being of Farm Operator Households, 1988–90." Agricultural Economic Report No. 666. U.S. Department of Agriculture Economic Research Service.

Black, John D. 1928. "Farm Business Surveys as Sources of Data on Farm Income." *Review of Economic Statistics* 10: 174–81.

Brandow, George E. 1977. "Policy for Commercial Agriculture, 1945–71." In L. Martin, editor. *A Survey of Agricultural Economics Literature*, volume 1. University of Minnesota Press.

Elitzak, Howard. 1999. "Food Cost Review, 1950–97." Agricultural Economic Report No. 780. U.S. Department of Agriculture Economic Research Service.

Erickson, Kenneth, Duane Hacklander, et al. 1989. "The Balance Sheet." *Major Statistical Series of the U.S. Department of Agriculture*, volume 11. Agriculture Handbook No. 671.

Gardner, Bruce. 1992. "Changing Economic Perspectives on the Farm Problem." *Journal of Economic Literature* 30: 62–101.

Gray, L. C. 1923. "Accumulation of Wealth by Farmers." *American Economic Review* 159–78.

Grove, Ernest W. 1958. "Comment." In *Studies in Income and Wealth*, volume 23: *An Appraisal of the 1950 Census Income Data*. Princeton University Press.

Johnson, D. Gale. 1953. "Comparability of Labor Capacities of Farm and Non-farm Labor." *American Economic Review* 43 (3): 296–313.

Johnson, D. Gale. 1958. "An Appraisal of the Data for Farm Families." In *Studies in Income and Wealth*, volume 23, *An Appraisal of the 1950 Census Income Data*. Princeton University Press.

Johnson, Thomas H. 1985. *Agricultural Depression in the 1920s: Economic Fact or Statistical Artifact*. Garland Press.

Kirkpatrick, E. L. 1926. "The Farmer's Standard of Living." Departmental Bulletin No. 1466. U.S. Department of Agriculture.

Olmstead, Alan L., and Paul W. Rhode. 2000. "The Transformation of Northern Agriculture, 1910–1990." In Stanley Engerman and Robert Gallman, editors. *The Cambridge Economic History of the United States*, volume 3. Cambridge University Press.

Strauss, Frederick, and Louis H. Bean. 1940. "Gross Farm Income and Indices of Farm Production and Prices in the United States, 1869–1937." Technical Bulletin No. 703. U.S. Department of Agriculture.

Towne, Marvin E., and Wayne D. Rasmussen. 1960. "Farm Gross Product and Gross Investment in the Nineteenth Century." In *Studies in Income and Wealth*, volume 24, *Trends in the American Economy in the Nineteenth Century*. Princeton University Press.

U.S. Department of Agriculture. 1940. *The Farm Income Situation*. Agricultural Marketing Service, FIS-1.

U.S. Department of Agriculture. 1988. *Major Statistical Series of the U.S. Department of Agriculture*, volume 3, *Farm Income*. Agricultural Handbook number 671.

U.S. Department of Agriculture. 1990. *Major Statistical Series of the U.S. Department of Agriculture*, volume 1, *Agricultural Prices, Expenditures, Farm Employment, and Wages*. Agricultural Handbook number 671.

U.S. Department of Agriculture. 2000. *Agricultural Outlook*.

Wohlgenant, Michael. 2001. "Marketing Margins: Empirical Analysis." In B. Gardner and G. Rausser, editors. *Handbook of Agricultural Economics*. Elsevier.

FARM POLICY

Alan L. Olmstead and Daniel A. Sumner

Government intervention in the farm sector has taken many forms, ranging from investments in public goods to attempts to use price and income supports to raise farm incomes. As the essay on agricultural productivity in this chapter demonstrates, government policies to promote basic and applied research along with farm extension work have raised farm productivity enormously. In addition, a number of government programs, such as transportation systems, rural mail delivery, and rural electrification, have provided rural infrastructure. Land policies, by which the federal government "privatized" much of the continent, represent another class of government policy that has had a major effect on farmers. For example, the Homestead Act of 1862 allowed farmers to acquire 160 acres of federal land free of charge.[1]

This essay concentrates on policies to raise farm incomes or commodity prices through a variety of schemes. These are the policies usually referred to as "farm programs." Collective action to raise agriculture prices in what is now the United States dates back to the early days of colonial Jamestown, when Virginia planters attempted to limit tobacco production. In the nineteenth century, many states experimented with agricultural bounties to encourage the introduction of new crops, and Maine briefly offered subsidies on wheat grown within its borders. But these initiatives were minor aberrations in an era in which farmers grew what they pleased and received prices determined by the law of supply and demand in relatively free markets. (Domestic and foreign tariff policies represented the major market distortions.) In fact, throughout the nineteenth and early twentieth centuries, American agriculture approximated the competitive model, but by the end of the twentieth century many parts of agriculture had become highly regulated and subsidized (Effland 2000). Federal commodity programs, originally justified as emergency measures, have proven difficult to end as farm incomes and land prices have become dependent on government subsidy. Table Da-P shows how the character and extent of government involvement in agriculture has changed over the

---

[1] This act and other land laws are discussed in Chapter Cf.

TABLE Da-P   Major government agricultural programs and policy: 1766–2000

1766	George Washington suggested to Congress the establishment of a National Board of Agriculture.
1789	First tariff act – for revenue only.
1796	Public Land Act of 1796. Authorized federal land sales to the public in minimum 640-acre plots at $2 per acre of credit.
1816	Tariff of 1816. Included protection for wool, sugar, hemp, and flax.
1819	State legislature set up the New York State Board of Agriculture – first organization of this sort.
1820	Agriculture Committee, U.S. House of Representatives, established.
1820	Land Law of 1820. Allowed purchasers to buy as little as eighty acres of public land for a minimum price of $1.25 an acre.
1825	Agriculture Committee, U.S. Senate, established.
1833	Tariff Act of 1833. Began tariff-reducing trend that lasted until the Civil War.
1839	$1,000 appropriated for Patent Office work with agricultural statistics.
1841	Preemption Act. Gave squatters first rights to buy land.
1852	United States Agricultural Society organized.
1862	Homestead Act. Granted 160 acres to settlers who had worked the land five years.
1862	Morrill Act of 1862. Created the land-grant college complex by giving federal lands to the states to endow colleges in the agricultural and mechanical arts.
1862	U.S. Department of Agriculture set up without cabinet status.
1887	Hatch Act of 1887. Provided annual grants to each state for agricultural research, leading to the system of state agricultural experiment stations.
1889	Department of Agriculture raised to cabinet status.
1890	Meat Inspection Acts. Authorized the inspection of salted pork, bacon, and live animals intended for exportation, and the quarantine of imported animals.
1914	Smith–Lever Act of 1914. Created the cooperative federal–state Agricultural Extension Service.
1916	Federal Farm Loan Act of 1916. Created the twelve cooperative federal land banks.
1921	Packers and Stockyards Acts. Authorized the Secretary of Agriculture to regulate meatpackers and livestock trading practiced at public markets having an area of 20,000 square feet or more.
1922	Capper–Volstead Act. Gave cooperatives legal standing.
1922	National Agricultural Conference established to discuss farm policy reform.
1929	Federal Farm Board established.
1933	Agricultural Adjustment Act of 1933 (Public Law 73-10). Introduced price-support programs, including production adjustments, and incorporated the Commodity Credit Corporation (CCC). Price-support loans by the Commodity Credit Corporation were made mandatory for the designated "basic" (storable) commodities (corn, wheat, and cotton). The provisions for production control and processing taxes were later declared unconstitutional.
1934	Taylor Grazing Act. Gave the U.S. Department of the Interior power to regulate grazing on public domain in the West.
1935	Agricultural Adjustment Act of 1935 (Public Law 74-320). Gave the president authority to impose quotas when imports interfered with agricultural adjustment programs.
1936	Soil Conservation and Domestic Allotment Act of 1936 (Public Law 74-461). Provided for soil-conservation and soil-building payments to participating farmers but did not include strong price- and income-support programs.
1938	Agricultural Adjustment Act of 1938 (Public Law 75-430). Made price support mandatory for corn, cotton, and wheat. It also established the Federal Crop Insurance Corporation and is considered part of permanent legislation.
1941	Steagall Amendment of 1941 (Public Law 77-144). Required support for many nonbasic commodities at 85 percent of parity or higher. In 1942, the minimum rate was increased to 90 percent of parity and was required to be continued for two years after the end of World War II.
1946	National School Lunch Act. Authorized assistance to states through grants-in-aid and other means in establishing nonprofit school lunch programs.
1947	General Agreement on Tariffs and Trade (GATT). An agreement originally negotiated in Geneva, Switzerland, in 1947 to increase international trade by reducing tariffs and other trade barriers.
1948	Agricultural Act of 1948 (Public Law 80-897). Made price support mandatory at 90 percent of parity for 1949 basic commodities. Beginning in 1950, parity would be reformulated to take into consideration average prices of the previous ten years, as well as those of the 1910–1914 base period.
1949	Agricultural Act of 1949 (Public Law 89-439). Along with the Agricultural Adjustment Act of 1938, it makes up the major part of permanent agricultural legislation that is still in effect in amended form.
1954	Agricultural Trade Development and Assistance Act of 1954 (Food for Peace) (Public Law 83-480). Established the primary U.S. overseas food assistance program. The program made U.S. agricultural commodities available through long-term credit at low interest rates and provided food donations.
1954	Agricultural Act of 1954 (Public Law 83-690). Established a flexible price support for basic commodities (excluding tobacco) at 82.5–90 percent of parity and authorized a Commodity Credit Corporation reserve for foreign and domestic relief.
1956	Agricultural Act of 1956 (Public Law 84-540). Began the Soil Bank Act, which authorized short- and long-term removal of land from production with annual rental payments to participants. It established the Acreage Reserve Program and a ten-year Conservation Reserve Program.

TABLE Da-P Major government agricultural programs and policy: 1766–2000 *Continued*

1961	Emergency Feed Grain Program of 1961. Launched a voluntary reduction program with payment-in-kind (PIK) provisions.
1962	Food and Agricultural Act of 1962 (Public Law 87-703). Gave the president the power to impose mandatory production controls. This power was subject to approval by two thirds of the producers of a commodity before controls could be put into effect.
1964	Agricultural Act of 1964 (Public Law 88-297). Authorized a two-year voluntary marketing certificate program for wheat and a payment-in-kind (PIK) program for cotton.
1964	Food Stamp Act of 1964 (Public Law 88-525). Provided the basis for the Food Stamp Program. It was later replaced by the food stamp provisions (Title XIII) of the Food and Agricultural Act of 1977.
1965	Food and Agricultural Act of 1965 (Public Law 89-321). The first multiyear farm legislation, providing for four-year commodity programs for wheat, feed grains, and upland cotton. It authorized a Class I milk base plan for the seventy-five federal milk marketing orders, and a long-term diversion of cropland under a Cropland Adjustment Program. It also continued payment and diversion programs for feed grains and cotton and certificate and diversion programs for wheat.
1970	Agricultural Act of 1970 (Public Law 91-524). In effect through 1973, it established the cropland set-aside program and a payment limitation per producer (set at $55,000 per crop). It also amended and extended the authority of the Class I Base Plan in milk marketing order areas.
1973	Agriculture and Consumer Protection Act of 1973 (Public Law 93-86). Established target prices and deficiency payments to replace former price-support payments. It also set payment limitations at $20,000 for all program crops and authorized disaster payments and disaster reserve inventories.
1977	Food and Agriculture Act of 1977 (Public Law 95-113). Increased income and price supports and established a farmer-owned reserve for grain. It also established a new two-tiered pricing program for peanuts.
1977	Food Stamp Act of 1977 (Title XIII). Permanently amended the Food Stamp Act of 1964 by eliminating purchase requirements and simplifying eligibility requirements.
1979	Trade Agreements Act of 1979 (Public Law 96-39). Provided the implementing legislation for the Tokyo Round of multilateral trade agreements in such areas as customs valuation, standards, and government procurement.
1980	Federal Crop Insurance Act of 1980 (Public Law 96-365). Expanded crop insurance into a national program with the authority to cover the majority of crops.
1981	Agriculture and Food Act of 1981 (Public Law 97-98). Set specific target prices for four years, eliminated rice allotments and marketing quotas, and lowered dairy supports.
1982	Omnibus Budget Reconciliation Act of 1982 (Public Law 97-253). Froze dairy price supports and mandated loan rates and acreage reserve programs for the 1983 crops.
1983	Payment-in-Kind (PIK) Program of 1983. Provided voluntary, massive acreage reduction by adding payments in kind to regular acreage reduction payments for grain, upland cotton, and rice; instituted by executive action.
1983	Dairy and Tobacco Adjustment Act of 1983 (Public Law 98-180). Froze tobacco price supports, launched a voluntary dairy diversion program, and established a dairy promotion order.
1984	Agricultural Programs Adjustment Act of 1984 (Public Law 98-258). Froze target price increases provided in the 1981 Act; authorized paid land diversions for feed grains, upland cotton, and rice; and provided a wheat payment-in-kind program for 1984.
1985	Food Security Act of 1985 (Public Law 99-198). Allowed lower price and income supports, lowered dairy supports, established a dairy herd buyout program, and created a Conservation Reserve Program under which the federal government entered into long-term land retirement contracts on qualifying land.
1985	Farm Credit Restructuring and Regulatory Reform Act of 1985 (Public Law 99-205). Implemented interest rate subsidies for farm loans and restructured the Farm Credit Administration.
1988	Disaster Assistance Act of 1988 (Public Law 100-387). Provided assistance to farmers hurt by the drought and other natural disasters in 1988.
1988	United States–Canada Free Trade Agreement Implementation Act of 1988 (Public Law 100-449). Implemented the bilateral agreement between the United States and Canada to phase out tariffs between the two countries over ten years and revise other trade rules, but important import quotas remained.
1990	Omnibus Budget Reconciliation Act of 1990 (Public Law 101-508). Introduced a mandatory 15 percent planting flexibility and assessment on nonprogram crop producers.
1990	Food, Agriculture, Conservation, and Trade Act of 1990 (Public Law 101-624). Froze target prices and allowed more planting flexibility. New titles included rural development, forestry, organic certification, and commodity promotion programs.
1993	North American Free Trade Agreement Implementation Act (Public Law 103-182). Eliminated all nontariff barriers to agricultural trade between the United States and Mexico, and maintained the provisions of the United States–Canada Free Trade Agreement on agricultural trade. Eliminated or scheduled a phase-out of tariffs on a broad range of agricultural products.
1994	Federal Crop Insurance Reform and Department of Agriculture Reorganization Act of 1994 (Public Law 103-354). Supplemented the federal crop insurance program with a new catastrophic coverage level (CAT) and created the Noninsured Assistance Program (NAP), a permanent aid program for crops not covered by crop insurance.
1994	Uruguay Round Agreements (URA) Act (Public Law 103-465). Implemented the trade agreements concluded in the Uruguay Round of multilateral trade negotiations conducted under the auspices of the General Agreement on Tariffs and Trade.

(continued)

TABLE Da-P   Major government agricultural programs and policy: 1766–2000   *Continued*

1996	Federal Agriculture Improvement and Reform (FAIR) Act of 1996 (Public Law 104-127). Removed the link between income support payments and farm prices by providing for predetermined production flexibility contract payments whereby participating producers receive government payments independent of current farm prices and production. It increased planting flexibility by allowing participants to plant 100 percent of their total contract acreage to any crop, except limitations on fruits and vegetables.
2000	Agricultural Risk Protection Act of 2000 (Public Law 106-224). For third year in a row raised contract payments that had been set in the FAIR Act. Also increased crop insurance subsidies and mandated expansion of the program.

Sources
1933–1985. Douglas E. Bowers, Wayne D. Rasmussen, and Gladys L. Baker, "History of Agricultural Price-Support and Adjustment Programs, 1933–84: Background for 1985 Farm Legislation," *Agricultural Information Bulletin* number 485, U.S. Department of Agriculture, Economic Research Service; 1933–1995: U.S. Department of Agriculture, Economic Research Service, "Chrono-logical Landmarks in American Agriculture," *Agriculture Information Bulletin* number 425; 1996: U.S. Department of Agriculture, Economic Research Service, "Provisions of the Federal Improvement and Reform Act of 1996," *Agriculture Information Bulletin* number 729; 2000: Agricultural Risk Protection Act of 2000, Public Law 106-224.

decades and how resistant subsidy programs have been to major reform once they have been introduced.

The Beginnings of Government Intervention

How did we come to this situation? It was only in the 1920s and 1930s that the federal government began to intervene aggressively in the markets for farm inputs and commodities. In 1921 the newly organized "farm bloc" in Congress steered through several bills regulating middlemen and subsidizing loans to farmers. But the main initiative was the "Equity for Agriculture" plan sponsored by Senator Charles McNary and Congressman Gilbert Haugen. Versions of a McNary–Haugen bill were introduced in Congress every year from 1924 to 1928. The concept was to separate the domestic and export markets through tariffs. Domestic "parity prices" would be set, based on the favorable 1905–1914 relationship between farm and nonfarm prices. In 1927 and in 1928 the bills passed both houses of Congress but were vetoed by President Coolidge, who deemed them un-American. In 1928 the Senate failed to override the veto by a scant four votes (Benedict 1953, pp. 194–8, 216–31; Shideler 1957, pp. 76–117; Knapp 1973).

As the farm depression became more severe, the Agricultural Marketing Act of 1929 created the Federal Farm Board, with a $500 million fund to buy and store commodities in order to raise prices. Almost immediately the Farm Board was in trouble, as nominal farm prices fell more than 50 percent between 1929 and 1932. The Board accumulated huge stocks of commodities, bidding up U.S. prices, discouraging exports, and encouraging even more production. With its funds exhausted, the Board unloaded its stocks, shocking commodity markets. In 1933 the Federal Farm Board was abolished (Benedict 1953, pp. 198, 239–66; Shideler 1957, pp. 270, 389; Cochrane 1979; Hamilton 1991).

New Deal Policies

The agricultural situation was grave in March 1933 when Franklin Roosevelt entered the White House; farm income had collapsed, foreclosures were commonplace, and rural banks and farm suppliers were in distress. In all but the most conservative quarters, there was the consensus that drastic action was needed. The first step was a set of emergency credit acts to stem the tide of foreclosures. But the main thrust was to restrict production. The Agricultural Adjustment Act (AAA), signed on May 12, became the foundation for Roosevelt's New Deal agricultural relief programs. The stated goal was to raise the implied purchasing power of most agricultural products to their 1909–1914 parity ratio. Seven "basic" commodities (wheat, cotton, rice, field corn, hogs, tobacco, and dairy products) were originally eligible for production controls. (Eight other commodities were added by 1935.)

The federal government guaranteed prices by granting farmers "nonrecourse loans" secured by commodities stored with the Commodity Credit Corporation (also established in 1933). The farmer could forfeit the commodities and keep the loan money if the price fell below the support level, or reclaim the produce and repay the loan if the price rose above the support level. In addition, farmers could contract with the government to remove land from production in return for a payment as compensation for the foregone output. Because for some commodities production was already underway, the AAA paid farmers to plow up acreage and slaughter piglets and pregnant sows. The destruction of six million baby pigs against a backdrop of massive unemployment and soup kitchens caused a public outcry, ending the slaughter program (Olmstead and Rhode 2000, pp. 729–36).

Between 1932 and 1935 nominal farm income and prices increased substantially, but the AAA's impact is unclear. The severe drought in the Great Plains and changes in international markets also significantly affected farm income. The AAA was a bureaucratic nightmare; huge quantities of information had to be collected, thousands of contracts written, numerous appeals heard, and so forth (Saloutos 1982). The effort to help some farmers sometimes had adverse effects on others. As an example, land withdrawn from the production of basic commodities, such as corn, was often shifted into unregulated uses, such as pasture for cattle, thereby hurting the existing producers. Price support programs and land set aside also cut into U.S. agricultural exports.

In January 1936 the U.S. Supreme Court declared the Agricultural Adjustment Act unconstitutional, but government intervention continued under the Soil Conservation Act (1936) and the second Agricultural Adjustment Act (1938). The second AAA became the basis for many farm support programs over the next several decades. The New Deal also added other crops, created marketing boards for specialty crops, allowed farmers to renegotiate contracts and re-acquire farmsteads lost to banks, and subsidized credit, crop insurance, and exports (Rasmussen and Baker 1979; Gardner 1990). Despite limited programs for a variety of other commodities, farm price supports and related programs affected primarily grains, cotton, tobacco, peanuts, dairy, wool, and sugar. About half of U.S. agriculture, including meat products and most fruits and vegetables, has received relatively little government support.

The stated objective of these farm policies was a desire to boost low commodity prices. The results were mixed, in large part because of the inherent shortcomings of the programs. Low prices were themselves a consequence of the existing supply and demand conditions, and the New Deal policies typically made the situation worse. Higher prices led to more quantity supplied and lower quantity demanded, with the government taking the surplus its policies created. Thus, while providing some relief for farmers, these measures also tended to exacerbate the conditions that perpetuated the "oversupply" problems. It took World War II to bring cash farm income back to its 1929 level (Table Da1288–1295).

The Post–World War II Era

Following World War II there was broad agreement that farm prices might again collapse, and that farm subsidies should continue. Proposals to streamline the programs by replacing price subsidies with direct payments failed to gain approval. The Agricultural Act of 1949, which remains the "permanent" farm legislation to this day, essentially continued the Depression-era programs. Since 1949, basic farm commodity legislation, usually referred to as the "Farm Bill," has taken the form of temporary amendments to the 1949 Act. Programs that began as temporary responses to an emergency have become thoroughly established in the Washington policy landscape and continue to affect the actions of farmers across America. One of the most important effects of the government programs has been to increase farmland values (the program benefits have become capitalized into the price of farmland), thus increasing the wealth of existing landowners, many of whom are not farmers.

The effect of farm programs on the prices received by farmers and on the surpluses accumulated by the government depended on the course of market prices. The thirty-two-year period from 1949 through 1981 saw a few periods of high market prices when programs had relatively little influence. During times when prices were low, stockpiles grew, creating pressure to tighten supply controls. Figure Da-Q provides data for nominal corn prices and the government support prices that show how intervention worked for

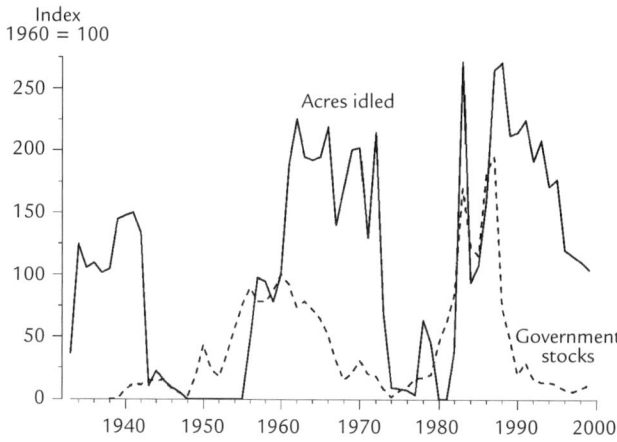

FIGURE Da-R Acreage idled under cropland acreage reduction programs and the value of price-supported commodities owned by the government: 1933–1999

Sources

Crop acres idled, series Da1453. Value of government stocks, series Da1412.

Documentation

For display purposes the values in both series have been expressed as index numbers with 1960 = 100.

this important commodity. In particular, the figure illustrates the jump and subsequent post–World War II fall in nominal corn prices.

Figure Da-R shows the fluctuating pattern of government-held stocks and mandatory land set-asides. Over the post–World War II period stocks rose rapidly, declined briefly during the Korean War, and then reached politically unsustainable levels in the early 1960s (Table Da1403–1415). As a result, there was a significant shift away from commodity loans and stockpiling toward voluntary acreage diversion programs and direct payments when prices were low. Under the new scheme, in addition to a loan program with the government taking physical possession of crops, participating farmers could opt to sell on the open market and receive a "deficiency payment" covering the difference between the market price and a previously announced official "target price." To qualify, farmers had to agree before planting to idle or "set aside" a share (often 10–30 percent) of their base acreage. As Figure Da-R shows, starting in the mid-1950s there was a rapid upswing in the amount of cropland idled, and by 1960 about 60 million acres of cropland were taken out of production under annual commodity programs. An additional several million acres were idled under long-term land bank programs (Table Da1453–1456). With massive land idling programs, stocks were gradually reduced. Then a commodity price boom of the early 1970s eliminated government stocks and allowed the USDA to relax the requirements that farmers leave part of their cropland unplanted. One may see the negative correspondence between these policy measures (stockpiles and land idled on the one hand, and support prices on the other) by juxtaposing Figure Da-R with Figure Da-Q.[2]

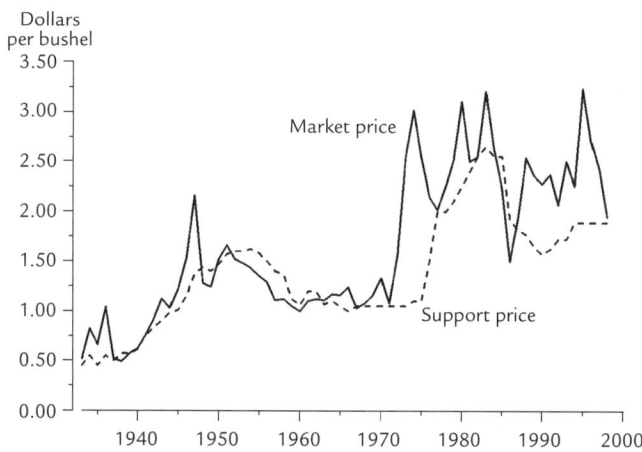

FIGURE Da-Q Corn market price and price support: 1933–1998

Sources

Market price, series Da697; support price, series Da1368.

---

[2] One response to the problem of large stockpiles was the Agricultural Trade Development and Assistance Act of 1954 (Public Law 83-480). The act heavily subsidized the export of surplus commodities to foreign countries as part of the overall foreign aid program. Although this program is generally seen as a humanitarian effort, its longer-term impact was often counterproductive, because it undercut indigenous producers in many receiving nations.

The brief period in the 1970s of low stocks and full production ended when world commodity prices dipped in the early 1980s, and U.S. support prices again exceeded world market prices by a wide margin. Despite significant political changes with the 1980 election, and despite the pro-market positions of the new Reagan administration, the 1981 Farm Act largely continued the 1977 Act. The lack of political resolve to lower high support prices in the early 1980s led to growing stockpiles of wheat, feed grains, and cotton. In response, the Payment-in-Kind (PIK) program added to the already existing acreage reduction programs, allowing farmers to withdraw an additional 10–30 percent of their base acreage in exchange for title to commodities in the Commodity Credit Corporation stockpiles. The result was one of the largest acreage reduction programs in U.S. history, idling 20 percent of U.S. cropland (seventy-seven million acres); PIK was also one of the most expensive programs, with many farmers receiving commodities valued at hundreds of thousands of dollars (series Da1453).

Overall, the four-decade period following World War II was one of numerous adjustments, but relatively little change in the basic structure of U.S. farm commodity programs (Bowers, Rasmussen, and Baker 1984). That changed beginning in 1985.

The Food Security Act of 1985 recognized that lowering price supports was necessary to reduce the accumulation of stocks and increase the competitiveness of American exports. The gradual reduction of support prices and increased planting flexibility signaled a change in policy direction. The Act also allocated more than $1 billion per year to direct export bonuses, mainly for wheat (Tables Da1436–1444). The subsidy of exports was not a new policy but, rather, as Table Da-S shows, export programs have been a recurring feature of U.S. farm policy. A new long-term Conservation Reserve Program paid landlords to remove from production erodible cropland for a ten-year period. In most of the years since 1986, about thirty-six million acres have been idled under this program (series Da1456). Total annual outlays for farm programs peaked at $26 billion in fiscal 1986 and direct payments peaked at $17 billion in fiscal 1987 (series Da1357). In addition, major ad hoc disaster payment programs were enacted in the late 1980s that allocated several billion dollars in direct payments to farmers (series Da1366).

TABLE Da-S Chronology of selected agricultural export programs: 1935–1996

1935	**Price subsidies**: Section 32 for exports (1935–1974). **Credit or guarantees**: Export–Import Bank loans/guarantees (1935–present).
1947	**Market development**: First state check-offs for generic promotion.
1948	**Food aid exports**: Economic Cooperation Act (Marshall Plan). **Other programs**: The Commodity Credit Corporation chartered as a federal corporation.
1949	**Price subsidies**: Cash subsidies to assist wheat under the International Wheat Agreement (1949–1966). **Credit or guarantees**: Special loans to Afghanistan, India, Pakistan, Spain, and the United Kingdom. **Food aid exports**: Section 416 (b) (1950–1954). **Other programs**: Agricultural Act of 1949.
1953	**Food aid exports**: Mutual Security Act.
1954	**Food aid exports**: Public Law 480 (1955–present). **Market development**: Title I of Public Law 80-480 currencies for market development, Cooperator Program (1955–present). **Other programs**: Public Law 80-480 barter (1954–1963).
1956	**Credit or guarantees**: The Commodity Credit Corporation direct credit sales (GSM-5), 1956–1980, 1984–1985.
1958	**Price subsidies**: Payment in kind for wheat, feed grains, cotton exports.
1961	**Market development**: First appropriation for Cooperator Program.
1962	**Price subsidies**: Payment in kind for nonfat dry milk exports.
1963	**Other programs**: Barter under Commodity Credit Corporation Charter Authority (1963–1973).
1971	**Market development**: Export Incentive Program (1971–present).
1979	**Credit or guarantees**: GSM-101 (1979–1981), GSM-201 (1979).
1980	**Credit or guarantees**: GSM-102 (1980–present). **Food aid exports**: Food Security Wheat Reserve Act (1980–present).
1981	**Credit or guarantees**: GSM-301 (1981–1982).
1982	**Food aid exports**: Section 416 (b) reauthorized (1983–present).
1983	**Price subsidies**: Flour sales to Egypt. **Credit or guarantees**: Blended credit (1983–1985).
1984	**Price subsidies**: Commodity Credit Corporation sales to West African countries.
1985	**Price subsidies**: Export Enhancement Program (1985–present), Dairy Export Incentive Program (1986–present). **Credit or guarantees**: GSM-103 (1986–present). **Food aid exports**: Food for Progress (1986–present), and Section 416 (b) expanded. **Market development**: Targeted Export Assistance Program (1986–1990). **Other programs**: Red meat sales (1986–1987), mandated dairy sales (1986–1988), and Agricultural Trade and Development missions (1986–1990).
1988	**Price subsidies**: Sunflowerseed Oil Assistance Program.
1989	**Price subsidies**: Cottonseed Oil Assistance Program.
1990	**Market development**: Market Promotion Program (1991–1996).
1994	**Price subsidies**: Uruguay Round Agreements: limits on export subsidies.
1996	**Market development**: FAIR Act Market Access Program (1996–present).

Source

Karen Z. Ackerman, Mark E. Smith, and Nydia R. Suarez, *Agricultural Export Programs: Background for 1995 Farm Legislation*, U.S. Department of Agriculture, Economic Research Service, Agriculture Economic Report number 716.

Documentation

This table shows the major programs affecting U.S. agricultural exports. The programs are listed under the following categories: price subsidies; credit or guarantees; food aid exports; market development; and other programs.

Budget pressures and moves to further liberalize farm policy led to several reforms in 1990. These included fewer acres eligible for deficiency payments, additional planting flexibility, lower price supports, and frozen nominal target prices used to determine direct payments. Export subsidies and the Conservation Reserve Program were continued with some reforms (Sumner 1995). The 1990 legislation replaced the price support program for grains and oilseeds with a "marketing loan" program under which payments were triggered whenever an average local market price was below the local loan rate. Because loan rates were set at between 75 percent and 85 percent of the moving average of past prices, the expectation was that few payments would be triggered by this new payment scheme. In fact, no payments were made until 1998 (Orden, Paarlberg, and Roe 1999).

As the 1990 farm legislation neared expiration, several forces combined to encourage further reforms (Gardner 1999; Orden, Paarlberg, and Roe 1999). First, farmers and others continued to complain that the programs limited planting flexibility and attempted to control markets. Second, budget pressures continued. Third, farm prices began to rise dramatically while the new law was being developed and farm leaders came to realize they were likely to receive no payments under the traditional target price policy. This last point turned out to be crucial, causing the Federal Agricultural Improvement and Reform (FAIR) Act of 1996 to replace payments linked to market prices with new fixed "contract" payments (Young and Westcott 1996).

Despite widespread accounts to the contrary in sources such as the *New York Times*, the FAIR Act did not schedule a phase-out of farm subsidy programs. Rather, it was an extension of the policy path of the previous decade. Nonetheless, by reinforcing and consolidating previous changes, the FAIR Act changed the form of crop programs by eliminating planting requirements, land set-asides, price supports, and government stockpiles.

The FAIR Act set contract payments in advance for seven years. However, when prices fell and remained depressed, ad hoc legislation raised payments by 50 percent in 1998 and doubled payments for 1999 and 2000 (series Da1366). In all, subsidies jumped from about $4.6 billion in fiscal year 1996 to $19.2 billion in fiscal year 1999 and $32.2 billion in fiscal 2000 (USDA 2001). The FAIR Act turned out to be an excellent contract for farmers. Reforms of the 1980s and 1990s that made farm programs more efficient were not reversed by these bailouts at the end of the century. However, the attempt to limit farm subsidies in times of low farm prices proved politically unsustainable when budget pressures declined. The policy clout of farmers remained powerful entering the new century.

Since World War II there has been a general movement toward freer trade for industrial goods. But for most of this period, agriculture represented a major exception to the general trend, because most industrial nations chose to protect their farmers. This began to change in 1986 when the United States supported a complete global elimination of trade-distorting farm programs at the Uruguay Round of trade negotiations. The Uruguay Round trade agreement was finally signed in 1994 and began to be implemented in 1995. This agreement has received much public attention. It opened some closed markets, eliminated nontariff barriers, began significant reductions in tariffs, and substantially reduced the use of export subsidies. But the implications for domestic farm subsidies were minimal. The agreement contained no binding limits on payment programs, loan rates, or other internal program instruments.

An Evaluation

Farm commodity programs have now been a part of the American political landscape for nearly seventy years. Although numerous administrations have expressed an intent to trim the subsidies, most efforts were abandoned when faced with a downturn in farm prices. Subsidies have become entitlements that have proven very difficult to abolish, even during periods of prosperity. Most estimates suggest that there has been substantial waste in the attempt to manipulate commodity markets to raise farm revenues. For this and other reasons, most economists, including many former advocates of subsidies, have come to question whether there is any remaining rationale for these farm programs (Gardner 1992). In addition, many critics recognize that price support programs have never been very effective tools for helping the rural poor; benefits are based on farm production for selected commodities and the poor simply do not produce much. The result has been a growing intellectual sentiment to eliminate farm subsidies. But so far the political consensus in support of subsidies has held firm; indeed, the nominal 2000 outlays for farm subsidies were higher than ever. Some cows are, indeed, sacred.

References

Benedict, Murray R. 1953. *Farm Policies of the United States, 1790–1950: A Study of Their Origins and Development.* Twentieth Century Fund.

Bowers, Douglas E., Wayne D. Rasmussen, and Gladys L. Baker. 1984. "History of Agricultural Price-Support and Adjustment Programs, 1933–84, Background for 1985 Farm Legislation." *Agricultural Information Bulletin* number 485. U.S. Department of Agriculture, Economic Research Service.

Cochrane, Willard W. 1979. *The Development of American Agriculture: A Historical Analysis.* University of Minnesota Press.

Effland, Anne B. W. 2000. "U.S. Farm Policy: The First 200 Years." In *Agricultural Outlook.* U.S. Department of Agriculture, Economic Research Service.

Gardner, Bruce. 1990. "Why, How, and Consequences of Agricultural Policies: United States." In Fred H. Sanderson, editor. *Agricultural Protectionism in the Industrialized World.* Resources for the Future.

Gardner, Bruce. 1992. "Changing Economic Perspectives on the Farm Problem." *Journal of Economic Literature* 30 (March): 1.

Gardner, Bruce. 1999. "Agricultural Relief Legislation in 1998: The Bell Tolls for Reform." *Regulation* 22 (1): 31–4.

Hamilton, David E. 1991. *From New Day to New Deal: American Farm Policy from Hoover to Roosevelt, 1928–33.* University of North Carolina Press.

Knapp, Joseph G. 1973. *The Advance of American Cooperative Enterprise, 1920–1945.* Interstate.

Olmstead, Alan L., and Paul Rhode. 2000. "The Transformation of Northern Agriculture, 1910–1990." In Stanley Engerman and Robert Gallman, editors. *The Cambridge Economic History of the United States,* volume 3, *The Twentieth Century.* Cambridge University Press.

Orden, David, Robert Paarlberg, and Terry Roe. 1999. *Policy Reform in American Agriculture: Analysis and Prognosis.* University of Chicago Press.

Rasmussen, Wayne, and Gladys L. Baker. 1979. *Price-Support and Adjustment Programs from 1933 through 1978: A Short History.* U.S. Department of Agriculture, Economic Research Service.

Saloutos, Theodore. 1982. *The Farmer and the New Deal.* Iowa State University Press.

Shideler, James H. 1957. *Farm Crisis, 1919–1923.* University of California Press.

Sumner, Daniel A. 1995. "Farm Programs and Related Policy in the United States." In R. M. A. Loyns, Karl Meilke, and Ronald D. Knutson, editors. *Understanding Canada–United States Grain Disputes.* Department of Agricultural Economics and Farm Management, University of Manitoba.

U.S. Department of Agriculture (USDA). 2001. *Agricultural Outlook* AGO-281. U.S. Department of Agriculture, Economic Research Service.

Young, C. Edwin, and P. Westcott. 1996. "The 1996 Farm Act Increases Market Orientation." Agricultural Information Bulletin number 726. U.S. Department of Agriculture, Economic Research Service.

FARMS AND FARM STRUCTURE

Alan L. Olmstead and Paul W. Rhode

TABLE Da1–13   Farms – number, population, land, and value of property: 1910–1999   [Annual]

Contributed by Alan L. Olmstead and Paul W. Rhode

	Farm population				Land in farms		Value of all farm property				Average value of land and buildings		
	Total	As a percentage of total population	Net change through migration	Number of farms	Total	Acreage per farm	Total	Land and buildings	Implements and machinery	Livestock	Per farm	Per acre	Index of value of farm real estate per acre
	Da1	Da2 [1]	Da3	Da4 [1]	Da5 [1,2]	Da6	Da7 [1,3]	Da8 [1]	Da9 [1]	Da10 [1,4]	Da11 [1]	Da12 [1]	Da13
Year	Thousand	Percent	Thousand	Thousand	Thousand acres	Acres	Million dollars	Million dollars	Million dollars	Million dollars	Dollars	Dollars	Index 1967 = 100
1910	32,077	34.9	—	6,406	—	—	41,097	34,801	1,395	4,901	5,433	—	—
1911	32,110	34.3	—	6,425	886,501	138	42,752	36,050	1,452	5,250	5,611	40.67	—
1912	32,210	33.9	—	6,430	894,209	139	43,846	37,306	1,518	5,022	5,802	41.72	27
1913	32,270	33.4	—	6,437	901,918	140	45,691	38,463	1,594	5,634	5,975	42.65	28
1914	32,320	32.8	—	6,447	909,627	141	47,395	39,586	1,678	6,131	6,140	43.52	28
1915	32,440	32.4	—	6,458	917,335	142	47,635	39,597	1,762	6,276	6,131	43.17	28
1916	32,530	32.0	—	6,463	925,044	143	50,511	42,271	1,899	6,341	6,540	45.70	30
1917	32,430	31.5	—	6,478	932,752	144	54,587	45,531	2,016	7,040	7,029	48.81	33
1918	31,950	30.6	—	6,488	940,461	145	60,977	49,987	2,469	8,521	7,705	53.15	36
1919	31,200	29.7	—	6,506	948,169	146	66,765	54,539	3,241	8,985	8,383	57.52	39
1920	31,974	30.1	−366	6,518	958,677	147	78,688	66,316	3,891	8,481	10,174	69.17	48
1921	32,123	29.7	−564	6,511	949,566	146	71,989	61,477	4,133	6,379	9,442	64.74	44
1922	32,109	29.3	−1,137	6,500	943,253	145	62,491	54,017	3,404	5,070	8,310	57.27	39
1923	31,490	28.2	−807	6,492	936,941	144	60,931	52,710	2,856	5,365	8,119	56.26	37
1924	31,177	27.5	−487	6,480	930,628	144	58,526	50,468	2,987	5,071	7,788	54.23	36
1925	31,190	27.0	−702	6,471	924,319	143	57,422	49,468	2,933	5,021	7,645	53.52	35
1926	30,979	26.5	−907	6,462	936,806	145	57,461	49,052	3,023	5,386	7,591	52.36	34
1927	30,530	25.7	−457	6,458	949,297	147	56,298	47,634	3,144	5,520	7,376	50.18	33
1928	30,548	25.4	−422	6,470	961,787	149	56,647	47,495	3,127	6,025	7,341	49.38	22
1929	30,580	25.2	−477	6,512	974,277	150	57,717	47,880	3,245	6,592	7,353	49.14	32
1930	30,529	24.9	−61	6,546	990,112	151	57,822	47,880	3,428	6,514	7,314	48.36	31
1931	30,845	24.9	156	6,609	1,000,317	151	52,108	43,993	3,256	4,859	6,657	43.98	28
1932	31,388	25.2	607	6,687	1,013,865	152	43,742	37,236	2,950	3,556	5,568	36.73	24
1933	32,393	25.8	−463	6,741	1,027,415	152	36,171	30,724	2,464	2,983	4,558	29.90	19
1934	32,305	25.6	−527	6,776	1,040,963	154	37,272	31,933	2,170	3,169	4,713	30.68	20
1935	32,161	25.3	−799	6,814	1,054,515	155	38,548	32,859	2,211	3,478	4,822	31.16	21
1936	31,737	24.8	−834	6,739	1,055,780	157	41,456	33,910	2,362	5,184	5,032	32.12	22
1937	31,266	24.3	−661	6,636	1,057,047	159	42,438	34,757	2,616	5,065	5,238	32.88	23
1938	30,980	23.9	−545	6,527	1,058,315	162	42,794	34,747	3,013	5,034	5,324	32.83	23
1939	30,840	23.6	−703	6,441	1,059,582	165	42,204	33,931	3,181	5,092	5,268	32.02	23
1940	30,547	23.2	−788	6,350	1,065,114	168	41,893	33,642	3,118	5,133	5,298	31.59	21
1941	30,118	22.6	−1,587	6,293	1,077,002	171	43,376	34,475	3,575	5,326	5,478	32.01	21
1942	28,914	21.5	−3,145	6,202	1,093,155	176	49,128	37,669	4,386	7,073	6,074	34.46	23
1943	26,186	19.2	−1,740	6,089	1,109,308	182	56,658	41,725	5,290	9,643	6,853	37.61	25
1944	24,815	18.0	−748	6,003	1,125,461	187	63,902	48,455	5,763	9,684	8,072	43.05	28
1945	24,420	17.5	671	5,967	1,141,615	191	69,905	54,606	6,288	9,011	9,151	47.83	31
1946	25,403	18.0	−44	5,926	1,145,003	193	77,424	61,411	6,296	9,717	10,363	53.63	35
1947	25,829	18.0	−1,889	5,871	1,148,394	196	87,867	69,339	6,612	11,916	11,810	60.38	39
1948	24,383	16.7	−586	5,803	1,151,784	198	96,060	74,405	8,398	13,257	12,822	64.60	43
1949	24,194	16.3	−1,537	5,722	1,155,174	202	102,454	77,119	10,909	14,426	13,478	66.76	44
1950	23,048	15.3	−1,531	5,648	1,202,019	213	104,800	75,400	12,300	17,100	13,350	62.73	43
1951	21,890	14.2	−483	5,428	1,203,500	222	117,600	83,800	14,300	19,500	15,438	69.63	49
1952	21,748	13.9	−2,201	5,198	1,204,930	232	114,900	85,100	15,000	14,800	16,372	70.63	55
1953	19,874	12.5	−1,151	4,984	1,205,740	242	111,600	84,300	15,600	11,700	16,914	69.92	55
1954	19,019	11.8	−210	4,798	1,206,355	251	114,700	87,800	15,700	11,200	18,299	72.78	53
1955	19,078	11.6	−627	4,654	1,201,900	258	119,900	93,000	16,300	10,600	19,983	77.38	57
1956	18,712	11.2	−1,295	4,514	1,197,070	265	128,200	100,300	16,900	11,000	22,220	83.79	57
1957	17,656	10.4	−748	4,372	1,191,340	272	127,300	106,400	17,000	13,900	24,337	89.31	61
1958	17,128	9.9	−740	4,233	1,184,944	280	150,400	114,600	18,100	17,700	27,073	96.71	65
1959	16,592	9.4	−1,142	4,104	1,182,563	288	155,700	121,200	19,300	15,200	29,532	102.49	71

Notes appear at end of table

(continued)

TABLE Da1–13   Farms – number, population, land, and value of property: 1910–1999   [Annual]   *Continued*

	Farm population				Land in farms		Value of all farm property				Average value of land and buildings		
	Total	As a percentage of total population	Net change through migration	Number of farms	Total	Acreage per farm	Total	Land and buildings	Implements and machinery	Livestock	Per farm	Per acre	Index of value of farm real estate per acre
	Da1	Da2 [1]	Da3	Da4 [1]	Da5 [1,2]	Da6	Da7 [1,3]	Da8 [1]	Da9 [1]	Da10 [1,4]	Da11 [1]	Da12 [1]	Da13
	Thousand	Percent	Thousand	Thousand	Thousand acres	Acres	Million dollars	Million dollars	Million dollars	Million dollars	Dollars	Dollars	Index 1967 = 100
Year													
1960	15,635	8.7	−1,000	3,963	1,175,646	297	157,956	123,280	19,068	15,608	31,108	104.86	72
1961	14,803	8.1	−646	3,825	1,167,699	305	164,795	129,097	19,270	16,428	33,751	110.56	74
1962	14,313	7.7	−1,086	3,692	1,159,383	314	171,823	134,614	19,902	17,307	36,461	116.11	78
1963	13,367	7.1	−533	3,572	1,151,572	322	178,591	142,353	20,373	15,865	39,852	123.62	77
1964	12,954	6.8	−703	3,457	1,146,106	332	186,202	150,486	21,247	14,469	43,531	131.30	82
1965	12,363	6.4	−858	3,356	1,139,597	340	201,539	161,525	22,429	17,585	48,130	141.74	87
1966	11,595	5.9	−793	3,257	1,131,844	348	214,274	171,233	24,067	18,974	52,574	151.29	94
1967	10,875	5.5	−481	3,162	1,123,456	355	226,099	180,943	26,310	18,846	57,224	161.06	100
1968	10,454	5.3	−198	3,071	1,115,231	363	237,382	189,389	27,744	20,249	61,670	169.82	107
1969	10,307	5.1	−642	3,000	1,107,811	369	246,782	195,309	28,634	22,839	65,103	176.30	113
1970	9,712	4.8	−330 [6]	2,949	1,102,371	374	256,487	202,417	30,364	23,706	68,639	183.62	117
1971	9,425	4.5	—	2,902	1,096,863	378	277,261	217,563	32,434	27,264	74,970	198.35	—
1972	9,610	4.6	156	2,860	1,092,065	382	311,325	243,002	34,644	33,679	84,966	222.52	—
1973	9,472	4.5	−164	2,823	1,087,923	385	380,342	298,301	39,671	42,370	105,668	274.19	—
1974	9,264	4.3	−233	2,795	1,084,433	388	408,577	335,556	48,454	24,567	120,056	309.43	—
1975	8,864	4.1	−425	2,521	1,059,420	420	470,334	383,560	57,417	29,357	152,146	362.05	—
1976	8,253	3.8	−635	2,497	1,054,075	422	551,862	459,539	63,275	29,048	184,036	435.96	—
1977	6,194 [5]	2.8 [5]	−474	2,455	1,047,785	427	610,559	509,308	69,320	31,931	207,457	486.08	—
1978	6,501 [5]	2.9 [5]	—	2,436	1,044,790	429	720,353	601,773	68,474	50,106	247,033	575.98	—
1979	6,241 [5]	2.8 [5]	—	2,437	1,042,015	428	842,834	706,064	75,384	61,386	289,727	677.59	—
1980	6,051 [5]	2.7 [5]	—	2,440	1,038,885	426	923,799	782,819	80,347	60,633	320,827	753.52	—
1981	5,850 [5]	2.5 [5]	—	2,440	1,034,190	424	924,624	785,561	85,519	53,544	321,951	759.59	—
1982	5,628 [5]	2.4 [5]	—	2,407	1,027,795	427	889,005	750,023	85,989	52,993	311,601	729.74	—
1983	5,787 [5]	2.5 [5]	—	2,379	1,023,425	430	888,784	753,394	85,849	49,541	316,685	736.15	—
1984	5,754	2.4	—	2,334	1,017,803	436	796,363	661,796	85,041	49,526	283,546	650.22	—
1985	5,355	2.2	—	2,293	1,012,073	441	715,350	586,190	82,901	46,259	255,643	579.20	—
1986	5,226	2.2	—	2,250	1,005,333	447	671,944	542,330	81,863	47,751	241,036	539.45	—
1987	4,986	2.1	—	2,213	998,923	451	700,150	563,487	78,686	57,977	254,626	564.09	—
1988	4,951	2.1	—	2,201	994,423	452	725,849	582,662	80,976	62,211	264,726	585.93	—
1989	4,801	2.0	—	2,175	990,723	456	751,113	600,809	84,091	66,213	276,234	606.43	—
1990	4,591	1.9	—	2,146	986,850	460	776,303	619,149	86,298	70,856	288,513	627.40	—
1991	4,632	1.9	—	2,117	981,736	464	778,779	624,769	85,890	68,120	295,120	636.39	—
1992	—	—	—	2,108	978,503	464	797,134	640,791	85,381	70,962	303,981	654.87	—
1993	—	—	—	2,202	968,845	440	836,768	677,578	86,411	72,779	307,710	699.37	—
1994	—	—	—	2,198	965,935	439	860,199	704,138	88,149	67,912	320,354	728.97	—
1995	—	—	—	2,196	962,515	438	887,709	740,491	89,440	57,778	337,200	769.33	—
1996	—	—	—	2,191	958,675	438	919,696	769,536	89,845	60,315	351,226	802.71	—
1997	—	—	—	2,191	956,010	436	965,371	808,229	90,067	67,075	368,886	845.42	—
1998	—	—	—	2,191	953,500	435	995,367	841,777	90,199	63,391	384,198	882.83	—
1999	—	—	—	2,194	947,340	432	1,029,671	870,021	89,042	70,608	396,546	918.38	—

[1] Overlapping data from *Historical Statistics of the United States* (1975) and new U.S. Department of Agriculture source do not coincide.

[2] Intercensal estimates derived from straight-line interpolation.

[3] Data through 1970 may not be completely comparable with that for later years; see text.

[4] Livestock coverage changes over time; see text.

[5] Based on a different definition of a farm, that is, any establishment that sells or normally would sell at least $1,000 of agricultural products in a calendar year.

[6] Unable to verify source; see source text.

Sources

Series Da1–2. 1910–1970: U.S. Rural Development Service, *Farm Population Estimates, 1910–70*, Statistical Bulletin number 523, Table 1; 1971–1991: *Economic Report of the President, February 1996*, Table B-96.

Series Da3. 1920–1970: U.S. Rural Development Service, *Farm Population Estimates, 1910–70*, Statistical Bulletin number 523, Table 6 (Statistical Bulletin number 523 ends in 1969. U.S. Bureau of the Census, *Historical Statistics of the United States* (1975), provides a value for 1970 without noting the source.

That value is reproduced here although its source could not be verified.); 1972–1977: Vera J. Banks, *Farm Population Estimates*, annual issues, published variously by the U.S. Department of Agriculture, Economic Research Service, the U.S. Rural Development Service, the *Agricultural Economic Report*, and the *Rural Development Report*.

Series Da4. 1910–1958: U.S. Crop Reporting Board, *Number of Farms 1910–1959, Land in Farms 1950–1959 by States*, Statistical Bulletin number 316; 1959–1968: U.S. Crop Reporting Board, *Farms: Revised Estimates, 1959–1970*, Statistical Bulletin number 507; 1969–1974: U.S. Crop Reporting Board, *Farms and Land in Farms, Final Estimates by States, 1969–1975*, Statistical Bulletin number 594; 1975–1978: U.S. Crop Reporting Board, *Number of Farms, Land in Farms, Revised Estimates for 1975–1980*, Farm Numbers, December 1980; 1979–1987: U.S. Agricultural Statistics Board, *Farms and Land in Farms, Final Estimates 1979–87*, Statistical Bulletin number 792; 1988–1992: U.S. Agricultural Statistics Board, *Farms and Land in Farms, Final Estimates 1988–92*, Statistical Bulletin number 895; 1993–1997: U.S. National Agricultural Statistics Service, *Farms and Land in Farms, Final Estimates 1993–97*, Statistical Bulletin number 955; 1998–1999: U.S. National Agricultural

TABLE Da1–13 Farms – number, population, land, and value of property: 1910–1999 [Annual] *Continued*

Statistics Service, *Farms and Land in Farms*, February 2000, p. 3, downloaded January 10, 2000, from U.S. Department of Agriculture, Economics and Statistics System Internet site.

Series Da5. Same as series Da4 except 1911–1949, U.S. Department of Agriculture, unpublished data obtained by straight-line interpolations.

Series Da6. Based on series Da4–5.

Series Da7–10. 1910–1949: U.S. Department of Agriculture, *Agricultural Statistics 1952*, Table 651; 1950–1959: *Economic Report of the President, 2000*, Table B-96 (source: U.S. Department of Agriculture, Economic Research Service); 1960–1999: U.S. Department of Agriculture, Economic Research Service, *Farm Business Balance Sheet*, 1960–1999, Table 1, downloaded January 10, 2001, from the U.S. Department of Agriculture, Economic Research Service Internet site.

Series Da11–12. Based on series Da4–5 and Da8.

Series Da13. *Farm Real Estate Market Developments*, August 1971, p. 48.

See also *Major Statistical Series of the U.S. Department of Agriculture*, Agriculture Handbook number 365, volume 6, for a more complete description of methods used and limitations.

Documentation
General Note for Tables Da1–660

Basic statistics on agriculture are, for the most part, prepared by the U.S. Bureau of the Census, which conducts the Census of Agriculture, and by the Statistical Reporting Service and the Economic Research Service of the U.S. Department of Agriculture, which prepare current estimates.

Annual agricultural statistics have been issued by the Department of Agriculture since May 1, 1863. Statistics compiled by the Statistical Reporting Service on crops, livestock and livestock products, agricultural prices, farm employment, and related subjects are based mainly on data obtained by mail and by personal interview of farmers and ranchers. Mailed questionnaires are returned from nearly three quarters of a million respondents, mostly farmers. More than 50,000 farmers are interviewed to obtain agricultural data. They are located in almost all the counties in the United States and usually report on one or more items during a year.

Beginning 1840, a Census of Agriculture has been taken every ten years and, beginning 1925, a mid-decade Census of Agriculture has also been taken. Census information was obtained by a personal canvass of individual farms until 1969, when for the first time the Census Bureau shifted to a questionnaire mailed to persons or organizations associated with agricultural operations in the nation to be completed by them and returned by mail.

The first census was limited in scope. It included such items as an inventory of the principal classes of domestic animals, the production of wool, the value of poultry, the value of dairy products, and the production of principal crops. The number of farms and the acreage and value of farmland were first included in 1850 and information on farm tenure was first obtained in 1880. A detailed classification of farmland according to use was first obtained in 1925; in earlier censuses, farmland was classified only as improved land, woodland, and other unimproved land. For brief discussions of the comparability of various agricultural data, census to census, see Bureau of the Census, *U.S. Census of Agriculture: 1969*, volume II, chapter 1.

For each decade from 1840 through 1900, the Census of Agriculture was taken as of June 1. The five decennial censuses since then have been taken as of April 15, 1910; January 1, 1920; and April 1, 1930, 1940, and 1950. The 1925, 1935, and 1945 quinquennial censuses of agriculture were taken as of January 1; the 1954, 1959, and 1964 censuses were taken during October and November. For the 1969 census the report forms were mailed to farm operators in the last week of December 1969. The reports covered production and sales for the 1969 calendar year, with livestock inventories as of December 31, 1969. For 1969, data for farms with less than $2,500 in sales are based on a 50 percent sample of these farms. In general, data for 1974 are comparable with data from earlier censuses only for farms with $2,500 or more total value of sales, because data for these farms were not affected by the change in the definition of a farm (see below). Data for all farms for 1974 are based on the new definition so they are not directly comparable to earlier censuses.

Evaluation studies of the 1969 and 1974 Censuses, which were conducted primarily by mail, indicated that lists used to create the census mailing list were not adequate to ensure complete coverage in the census. The 1978 Census was conducted primarily by mail, supplemented by a personal canvass of a statistical area segment sample for maximum completeness of coverage. Owing to budget reductions, the direct enumeration area sample was eliminated for 1982. The U.S., region, and state data for 1978 shown in the 1978 Census included data for farms represented on the mail list plus estimates from the area sample for farms not on the mail list. Therefore, they are not directly comparable to other censuses. To provide comparable data for 1982 and 1978, estimates from the 1978 area sample have been subtracted from the 1978 data. Thus, the 1978 data in the 1982 Census include only farms represented on the mail list. Data on acreages and inventories for 1982, 1987, and 1992 are generally comparable. For comparability, the 1978 data shown in the 1987 Census include only farms on the mail list.

The definition of a farm has varied as follows from census to census. For the 1959, 1964, and 1969 Censuses, census farms comprised places on which agricultural operations were conducted at any time under the control or supervision of one person, a partnership, or a manager. Places of less than ten acres were counted as farms if the estimated sales of agricultural products for the year amounted or normally would amount to at least $250. Places of ten or more acres were counted as farms if the estimated sales of agricultural products for the year amounted or normally would amount to at least $50. In 1974, there was a change in the definition of a farm. For the 1974 and later censuses, a farm is considered to be any establishment that during the census year had or normally would have had sales of agricultural products of $1,000 or more.

For the 1954 Census of Agriculture, places of three or more acres were counted as farms if the annual value of agricultural products for sale or home use (exclusive of home-garden products) amounted to $150 or more. Places of less than three acres were counted as farms only if the annual value of sales of agricultural products amounted to $150 or more. Places for which the value of agricultural products for 1954 was less than these minimums because of crop failure or other unusual conditions and places operated for the first time in 1954 were counted as farms if normally they could be expected to produce these minimum quantities of agricultural products.

If a place had croppers or other tenants, the land assigned each one was considered a separate farm, even though the landlord handled the entire holding as one operating unit with respect to supervision, equipment, rotation practice, purchase of supplies, or sale of products. Land retained by the landlord and worked by him with the help of his family and/or hired labor was likewise considered a farm.

For the 1950 Census of Agriculture, the definition of a farm was the same as for 1954. For the 1945 and earlier censuses, the definition of a farm was somewhat more inclusive. For 1925–1945, farms included (1) places of three or more acres on which there were agricultural operations and (2) places of less than three acres if the agricultural products for home use or for sale were valued at $250 or more. The only reports excluded from the 1925–1940 tabulations were those taken in error and those with very limited agricultural production, such as only a small home garden, a few fruit trees, a very small flock of chickens, and so forth. In 1945, reports for places of three acres or more with limited agricultural operations were retained only if (1) there were three or more acres of cropland and pasture or (2) the value of products in 1944 amounted to $150 or more.

The definition of a farm in the 1910 and 1920 Censuses was similar to that used from 1925 to 1940 but was even more inclusive. In those years, farms of less than three acres with products valued at less than $250 were to be included provided they required the continuous services of at least one person. In 1900, there were no acreage or production limits. Market, truck, and fruit gardens, orchards, nurseries, cranberry marshes, greenhouses, and city dairies were to be included provided the entire time of at least one person was devoted to their care. For 1870, 1880, and 1890, no tract of less than three acres was to be reported as a farm unless $500 worth of produce was sold from it during the year. For 1860, no definition was given to enumerators. For 1850, no acreage qualification was given, but there was a lower limit of $100 for the value of products.

(continued)

TABLE Da1–13 Farms – number, population, land, and value of property: 1910–1999 [Annual] *Continued*

Series Da1–12. Beginning 1959, data include Alaska and Hawai'i.

Series Da1–3

For 1880–1970, the estimates relate to the rural civilian population living on farms, regardless of occupation. For convenience, the term "farm population" is used without qualification, although the relatively few members of the armed forces living on farms are excluded. Beginning in 1960, the farm population has been defined as all persons living in rural territory on places of ten or more acres, if as much as $50 worth of agricultural products were sold from the place in the reporting year. It also includes those living on places of under ten acres, if as much as $250 worth of agricultural products were sold from the place in the reporting year. Prior to 1960, no specific criteria of acreage operated or value of products sold from a place were used to classify a farm population. The change in definition in 1960 was largely stimulated by the fact that an increasing number of families whose livelihood was not gained directly from agriculture were living in the open country. In 1974, the definition of a farm changed again. As of 1974, a farm is considered any establishment that during the year had or normally would have had sales of agricultural products of $1,000 or more.

In the farm population, where the flow of migrants is responsive to many influences such as employment opportunities, mechanization, and technological advancements, migration, rather than the balance of births and deaths, becomes the dominant factor in population change. Net change through migration, series Da3, includes not only those persons who make a physical move from farm to nonfarm areas, but also the loss that occurred when agricultural operations ceased on a place, and the occupants of the related dwelling units were reclassified from farm to nonfarm. Although exact figures are not available, actual migration is considered to be the larger of these two components.

The farm population estimates are based on data obtained from three principal sources: (1) the Current Population Survey (CPS) of the Bureau of the Census, which provides the annual estimate of the U.S. farm population; (2) the censuses of population, from which benchmark data for states, geographic divisions, and regions are derived; and (3) annual surveys of the farm population, conducted for the Economic Research Service by the Statistical Reporting Service, on which annual estimates of geographic distributions are based for intercensal years, and from which estimates of components of farm population change are derived annually. The Economic Research Service and its predecessor agencies conducted an annual survey of the farm population and its components of change from 1923 to 1969. Utilizing the U.S. Department of Agriculture's crop reporting system, reports were collected through a mailed questionnaire. Respondents reported on the number of persons who were living on their own and neighboring farms at the beginning and end of a specified twelve-month period. They also reported on births, deaths, and changes through migration that occurred during this period.

Farm populations estimated are based on U.S. Department of Agriculture questionnaire survey data, tied to benchmark figures from complete censuses, and adjusted total estimates of farm population obtained from the CPS. The reliability of these estimates is dependent on the reliability of the U.S. estimate and the mail survey data. Annual estimates of the U.S. total farm population are obtained from the CPS. As these estimates are based on a sample, they may differ somewhat from figures that would have been obtained if a complete census had been taken using the same schedules, instructions, and enumerators. As in any survey work, the results are subject to error of response and of reporting as well as to sampling variability. The reliability of data from the mail survey alone cannot be assessed in terms of sample error. Reliability depends in part on state-to-state variations in the size and representativeness of the mailing list, as well as on variations in rate, representativeness, and accuracy of returns. In general, it should be noted that small figures, small changes, and trends over a short period of time may have less reliability than larger numbers and changes and trends over a period of several years.

The total farm population series was discontinued in 1992.

Overlapping data on farm population as a percent of total population, series Da2, from the *Economic Report of the President, February 1996* from 1948 to 1970 were the same as data from *Historical Statistics of the United States* (1975) for the following years only: 1951–1953, 1960–1963, 1965–1967, and 1969.

Series Da4

Estimates are based on trend and indications of change in acreage and livestock surveys, in annual assessors' censuses in a number of states, in Agricultural Stabilization and Conservation records, and in other miscellaneous verifying data.

The U.S. Department of Agriculture defines a farm as any establishment that sells or normally would sell at least $1,000 of agricultural products in a calendar year. The Census of Agriculture adopted this farm definition in 1974, and the U.S. Department of Agriculture began using it in the 1975 series. Overlapping data on number of farms from the *Economic Indicators of the Farm Sector: National Financial Summary, 1993* from 1950 to 1970 were the same as data from *Historical Statistics of the United States* (1975) for the following years only: 1951–1953, 1955–1958, 1963, and 1965–1968.

Series Da5

The acreage in each farm was allocated by the farm operator among the various land-use categories. Any acreage that had two or more uses during the year was classified according to the first use on the report form. For example, if a crop was harvested from an acreage and the same acreage was then pastured, the acreage was included as land from which crops were harvested but not as pasture.

The U.S. Department of Agriculture defines a farm as any establishment that sells or normally would sell at least $1,000 of agricultural products in a calendar year. The Census of Agriculture adopted this farm definition in 1974, and the U.S. Department of Agriculture began using it in the 1975 series. Overlapping data on number of farms from the *Economic Indicators of the Farm Sector: National Financial Summary, 1993* from 1950 to 1970 were the same as data from *Historical Statistics of the United States* (1975) for the following years only: 1951–1953, 1955–1958, 1963, and 1965–1968.

Information on farmland values in scattered local areas is found in P. W. Bidwell and H. I. Falconer, *History of Agriculture in the Northern United States, 1620–1860* (Carnegie Institution, 1925), pp. 70–71, 242, and 328. Similar information for Southern states is found in L. C. Gray, *History of Agriculture in the Southern United States to 1860* (Carnegie Institution, 1933), volume I, pp. 403–6, and volume II, pp. 640–45.

Excludes the District of Columbia.

Series Da6

This series equals series Da5 divided by series Da4.

For 1983–1993, a farm is any establishment from which $1,000 or more of agricultural products were sold or would normally be sold during the year. Data from 1971 to 1982 are unavailable; therefore the series from 1850 to 1970 may not be directly comparable with the series from 1983 to 1993.

Series Da7

For 1910–1970, current market values of farm real estate, machinery and equipment, and livestock only are combined in this series. Estimates of the value of farm real estate are based on census reports and the annual index of farm real estate values. Inventory values for machinery and equipment and for livestock are based in part on census reports and supplemental estimates made by the Statistical Reporting Service and Economic Research Service. Data for 1971–1999 are the sum of three series contained in the *Farm Business Balance Sheet*: real estate, livestock and poultry, and machinery and motor vehicles. Therefore, data before and after 1970 may not be completely comparable. A complete accounting of physical farm assets would include crops, purchased inputs, and financial assets. The historical treatment of these latter categories is inconsistent.

Series Da8 and Da11–12

Figures for 1910–1970 intercensal years are estimates derived by applying the change in the index of average value of land and buildings per acre to census benchmarks, recognizing changes in acres of land in farms. All farm operators were asked to estimate the market value of their farms in each census from 1910 through 1969. In the 1950, 1954, 1959, and 1964 Censuses, data were obtained from all large farms and from a 20 percent sample of other farms. In the 1969 Census, all operators who received a form were asked to estimate the present market value of land and buildings.

For series Da8, figures for census years are as of date of enumeration, and for intercensal years as of March 1. The series excludes the District of Columbia.

TABLE Da1–13   Farms – number, population, land, and value of property: 1910–1999   [Annual]   *Continued*

Average value of land and buildings per farm is obtained by dividing series Da8 by series Da4, using rounded data. Average value of land and buildings per acre is obtained by dividing series Da8 by series Da5, using unrounded data.

Series Da9

Figures for 1971–1999 are the value of machinery and motor vehicles, which are estimated for four main components: tractors, trucks, automobiles, and other farm machinery. The value of equipment leased from dealers and manufacturers is not part of this account. The 1971–1999 series may not be entirely comparable to the 1910–1970 values, which measure the value of implements and machinery.

A perpetual inventory method is used to estimate December 31 stocks for each machinery component. This method considers current ending stocks to be equal to the previous period's ending stocks, plus capital expenditures, less accidental damage, value of losses, and depreciation.

At the state level, only the value of machinery and motor vehicles is published. The state values are derived from the U.S. total value by using distributors based on machinery and motor vehicle values per farm from the latest Census of Agriculture multiplied by the number of farms published by the National Agricultural Statistical Service. These distributors are adjusted for the intercensal years when a new Census of Agriculture is released.

Figures for 1910–1970 represent inventory value at the beginning of the year. They are closely tied to the values presented in the censuses of agriculture, the figures for intercensal years being estimated from information on manufacture and sales with due allowance for wear and tear and then adjusted for changes in price levels.

Series Da10

Livestock comprises all cattle, hogs, all sheep (prior to 1920, stock sheep only), horses, mules, chickens, and turkeys (beginning with 1929); beginning with 1950 excludes commercial broilers; beginning with 1959 excludes horses, mules, and broilers.

Estimates in this series generally are as of January 1 for 1910 through 1949, and generally as of December 31 from 1950 to 1999.

Series Da13

This index, which is available also by states, is designed to measure changes in the market value of farm real estate, including land, buildings, and such other permanent improvements as are customarily included when farms are sold. The index is constructed from estimates of average value of farm real estate per acre obtained from the regular crop reporters of the Department of Agriculture. It is not based on the value of farm real estate obtained in the census. Between 15,000 and 20,000 reporters supply estimates of the market value of farms per acre in their localities as of March 1 and November 1. Although they undoubtedly base their estimates in part on actual sales, no sales data are used directly in computing the index. Averages for crop-reporting districts are weighted by acres of land in farms as taken from the 1945, 1950, 1954, 1959, 1964, and 1969 Censuses to obtain weighted state averages, which are, in turn, weighted by acres of land in farms to obtain regional and national averages. The weighted dollar values per acre are then expressed as index numbers.

Data for Alaska and Hawai'i are excluded.

TABLE Da14–27   Farms – number, population, land, and value of property: 1850–1997   [Census years]

Contributed by Alan L. Olmstead and Paul W. Rhode

	Farm population			Land in farms					Value of all farm property				Average value of land and buildings	
	Total	As a percentage of total population	Number of farms	Total	As a percentage of total land area	Acreage per farm	Cropland	Pastureland	Total	Land and buildings	Implements and machinery	Livestock	Per farm	Per acre
	Da14	Da15	Da16	Da17 [1]	Da18 [1,2]	Da19 [1]	Da20 [1,2]	Da21 [1,2]	Da22	Da23 [1]	Da24	Da25	Da26	Da27
Year	Thousand	Percent	Thousand	Thousand acres	Percent	Acres	Thousand acres	Thousand acres	Million dollars	Million dollars	Million dollars	Million dollars	Dollars	Dollars
1850	—	—	1,449	293,561	15.6	203	—	—	3,967	3,272	152	544	2,258	11.14
1860	—	—	2,044	407,213	21.4	199	—	—	7,980	6,645	246	1,089	3,251	16.32
1870 [3]	—	—	2,660	407,735	21.4	153	—	—	9,412	7,444	271	1,230	2,799	18.26
1880	21,973	43.8	4,009	536,082	28.2	134	166,187 [5]	—	12,404	10,197	407	1,577	2,544	19.02
1890	24,771	39.3	4,565	623,219	32.7	137	219,706 [5]	—	16,439	13,279	494	2,309	2,909	21.31
1900	29,875	39.3	5,740	841,202	37.0	147	283,218 [5]	—	20,365	16,675	750	3,059	2,905	19.82
1910	32,077	34.9	6,366	881,431	38.8	139	311,293 [5]	—	40,959	34,885	1,265	4,887	5,480	39.58
1920	31,614	29.9	6,454	958,677	42.2	149	348,549 [5]	—	78,386	66,446	3,595	7,977	10,295	69.31
1925	31,049	25.0	6,372	924,319	48.6	145	505,027	217,687	57,439	49,468	2,692	4,829	7,764	53.52
1930	30,445	24.8	6,295	990,112	43.6	157	522,396	269,673	57,689	47,994	3,302	6,048	7,624	48.47
1935	31,801	25.0	6,812	1,054,515	55.4	155	513,914	311,226	38,959	32,859	—	3,413	4,823	31.16
1940	27,805	21.1	6,102	1,065,114	46.8	175	530,191	393,544	—	33,758	3,060	4,533	5,532	31.69
1945	24,493	17.8	5,859	1,141,615	59.9	195	450,694	481,017	—	46,389	5,147	8,472	7,917	40.63
1950	23,332 [4]	15.5	5,388	1,161,420	51.1	216	478,315	416,802	—	75,462	—	11,667	14,005	64.97
1954	21,890	13.5	4,782	1,158,192	60.8	242	459,649	459,879	—	97,583	—	11,245	20,405	84.25
1959	13,445	7.5	3,711	1,123,508	49.5	303	448,087	466,225	—	129,005 [6]	—	15,187	34,826 [6]	115.08 [6]
1964	—	—	3,158	1,110,187	49.0	352	434,232	490,307	—	159,932	—	14,080	50,646	143.81
1969	—	—	2,730	1,062,893	47.0	390	458,990	—	—	206,717	25,343	22,822	75,714	194.49
1974	—	—	2,314	1,017,030	44.9	440	440,039	—	—	342,099	48,403	22,186	147,838	336.37
1978	—	—	2,258	1,014,777	44.8	449	453,874	433,317	—	631,434	77,601	49,277	279,672	622.24
1982	—	—	2,241	986,797	43.6	440	445,362	418,264	—	774,158	93,663	51,090	345,869	784.52
1987	—	—	2,088	964,471	42.6	462	443,318	410,329	—	604,168	85,801	59,005	289,387	626.42
1992	—	—	1,925	945,532	41.8	491	435,366	410,835	—	687,432	93,316	—	357,076	727.03
1997	—	—	1,912	931,795	41.2	487	431,145	396,885	—	859,839	110,256	—	449,748	922.78

Notes appear on next page

(continued)

TABLE Da14–27   Farms – number, population, land, and value of property: 1850–1997   [Census years]   *Continued*

[1] Excludes the District of Columbia.

[2] Intercensal estimates derived from straight-line interpolation.

[3] Value in gold – approximately one fifth less than reported currency values published in the 1870 report.

[4] Farm population was determined largely by the residents themselves; see text.

[5] Cropland harvested only.

[6] Excludes Hawai'i.

Sources

Series Da14–15. 1880–1950, U.S. Bureau of the Census, *Farm Population: 1880 to 1950*, Technical Paper number 3, Tables 1–2; 1954–1959, U.S. Bureau of the Census, *U.S. Census of Agriculture, 1959*, volume 2, Table 2.

Series Da16–17 and Da19. 1850–1959, U.S. Bureau of the Census, *U.S. Census of Agriculture, 1964, General Report*, volume 2, Table 5, p. 15; 1964–1997, U.S. Bureau of the Census, *U.S. Census of Agriculture: 1997*, volume 1, part 51, Table 1, pp. 10–11.

Series Da19. Derived from series Da16–17.

Series Da18. 1850–1959, U.S. Bureau of the Census, *Census of Agriculture, 1964, General Report*, volume 2, Table 5, p. 15; 1964–1997, U.S. Bureau of the Census, *Census of Agriculture*, 1982–1997.

Series Da20–21. U.S. Bureau of the Census, *Census of Agriculture, 1935*, volume 3, pp. 18–19; *1945*, volume 2, pp. 8; *1964*, volume 2, pp. 12–13; *1982*, volume 1, part 51, p. 1; *1997*, volume 1, part 51, p. 19.

Series Da22. U.S. Bureau of the Census, *Historical Statistics of the United States* (1975).

Series Da23 and Da26–27. 1850–1969, U.S. Bureau of the Census, *U.S. Census of Agriculture, 1969*, volume 2, chapter 2, p. 20; 1974, *U.S. Census of Agriculture, 1974*, volume 1, part 51, p. xiii; 1978–1982, *U.S. Census of Agriculture, 1987*, volume 1, part 51, p. 18; 1987–1997, *U.S. Census of Agriculture, 1997*, volume 1, part 51, p. 22.

Series Da24. 1850–1945, U.S. Bureau of the Census, *U.S. Census of Agriculture, 1945*, volume 2, p. 311; 1950–1997, *U.S. Census of Agriculture, 1969*, volume 2, p. 12, *U.S. Census of Agriculture, 1997*, volume I, part 51, p. 10.

Series Da25. U.S. Bureau of the Census, *U.S. Census of Agriculture*: 1850–1910, *1945*, volume 2, chapter 7, p. 341; 1920–1954, *1954*, volume 2, p. 443; *1959*, volume 2, p. 497; 1964, *1969*, volume 2, chapter 7, p. 2; 1969–1974, *1974*, volume 2, p. 5; 1978–1987, *1987*, volume 1, part 51, p. 25.

Documentation

See the text for Table Da1–13 for a general note.

Series Da14–15. The main value of this table is that it provides farm population estimates prior to 1910. In various sources the Bureau of the Census estimates for a given year varied from one census to the next. Thus, if one were to go to the specific census year one would be likely to find a different number than that reported here. Data for Hawai'i and Alaska are not included.

Series Da14–15. In the 1950 Census, farm population was determined largely by the residents themselves. If the respondent, in reply to a direct inquiry, considered his house located on a farm, the house was, in most cases, considered a farm dwelling and the occupants were considered part of the farm population. See U.S. Census Bureau, *U.S. Census of Agriculture, 1950*, volume 2, pp. 15–17, for further details.

Series Da16–23. Data for Hawai'i and Alaska are not included for 1850–1890, 1925, 1935, 1945, and 1954.

Series Da19. Equals series Da17 divided by series Da16.

Series Da22. Data could not be found and verified in the source given by *Historical Statistics of the United States* (1975). The values are simply reproduced here.

Series Da23. Data as of date of enumeration.

Series Da24–25. Data for Hawai'i and Alaska are not included.

Series Da25. Estimates as of January 1.

TABLE Da28–92   Farm population, by region and state: 1890–1969

Contributed by Alan L. Olmstead and Paul W. Rhode

		Northeast										
		Total	New England								Middle Atlantic	
	United States		Total	Maine	New Hampshire	Vermont	Massachusetts	Rhode Island	Connecticut		Total	New York
	Da28	Da29	Da30	Da31	Da32	Da33	Da34	Da35	Da36		Da37	Da38
Year	Thousand	Thousand	Thousand	Thousand	Thousand	Thousand	Thousand	Thousand	Thousand		Thousand	Thousand
1890	24,771	3,194	878	283	130	148	167	26	123		2,317	1,076
1900	29,875	3,364	892	267	131	152	183	28	131		2,472	1,113
1910	32,077	2,901	764	247	102	142	140	20	112		2,137	922
1920	31,974	2,537	633	200	77	127	120	15	94		1,904	806
1925	31,190	2,435	617	190	72	122	125	16	92		1,818	768
1930	30,529	2,287	575	171	63	113	124	17	87		1,712	722
1935	32,161	2,633	718	187	77	123	165	22	144		1,915	789
1940	30,547	2,411	623	176	71	107	147	17	105		1,788	730
1945	24,420	1,906	446	125	51	75	111	12	71		1,460	601
1950	23,048	1,791	403	122	47	81	80	10	63		1,388	578
1954	19,019	1,397	301	86	32	66	61	8	47		1,095	467
1959	16,592	1,175	246	66	23	60	52	6	39		929	408
1964	12,954	929	183	46	17	45	39	5	30		747	321
1969	10,307	741	138	33	12	34	30	4	25		603	254

TABLE Da28–92   Farm population, by region and state: 1890–1969 *Continued*

	Northeast		North Central									
	Middle Atlantic			East North Central							West North Central	
	New Jersey	Pennsylvania	Total	Total	Ohio	Indiana	Illinois	Michigan	Wisconsin		Total	Minnesota
	Da39	Da40	Da41	Da42	Da43	Da44	Da45	Da46	Da47		Da48	Da49
Year	Thousand	Thousand	Thousand	Thousand	Thousand	Thousand	Thousand	Thousand	Thousand		Thousand	Thousand
1890	155	1,085	9,995	5,144	1,241	998	1,289	843	773		4,851	641
1900	176	1,183	11,094	5,653	1,354	1,071	1,341	982	904		5,441	856
1910	165	1,050	10,714	5,275	1,245	997	1,219	912	902		5,440	833
1920	145	953	10,158	4,953	1,149	914	1,107	856	927		5,205	903
1925	138	912	9,805	4,637	1,060	848	1,033	807	889		5,168	908
1930	131	859	9,583	4,501	1,016	815	1,002	785	883		5,082	898
1935	145	981	9,951	4,808	1,136	860	1,026	847	939		5,143	934
1940	143	915	9,349	4,638	1,089	816	979	871	883		4,711	915
1945	112	746	7,767	3,866	893	696	808	704	765		3,901	753
1950	105	705	7,433	3,703	853	667	763	695	725		3,729	740
1954	85	543	6,732	3,276	717	606	694	590	668		3,457	698
1959	75	446	6,191	2,974	607	569	652	510	636		3,217	671
1964	61	365	5,246	2,519	515	493	565	410	537		2,727	572
1969	50	300	4,496	2,147	434	432	492	324	464		2,349	502

	North Central						South				
	West North Central						South Atlantic				
	Iowa	Missouri	North Dakota	South Dakota	Nebraska	Kansas	Total	Total	Delaware	Maryland	District of Columbia
	Da50	Da51	Da52	Da53	Da54	Da55	Da56	Da57	Da58	Da59	Da60
Year	Thousand	Thousand	Thousand	Thousand	Thousand	Thousand	Thousand	Thousand	Thousand	Thousand	Thousand
1890	1,047	1,318	139	240	615	851	10,723	4,209	47	221	2
1900	1,139	1,475	239	274	619	838	14,226	5,271	50	254	1
1910	1,053	1,352	369	371	631	830	16,657	6,212	58	297	1
1920	991	1,219	398	364	588	742	17,063	6,496	52	283	—
1925	990	1,172	397	380	588	733	16,762	6,215	49	261	—
1930	981	1,118	398	391	587	709	16,364	5,914	47	238	—
1935	974	1,192	389	360	585	709	17,162	6,283	50	245	—
1940	931	1,125	328	307	498	607	16,400	6,060	46	246	—
1945	815	882	277	261	417	495	12,740	4,891	39	201	—
1950	783	863	254	254	391	444	11,896	4,633	34	183	—
1954	767	747	235	238	370	401	9,139	3,573	29	150	—
1959	755	630	220	228	349	364	7,613	2,984	26	135	—
1964	645	515	187	201	301	306	5,513	2,106	21	108	—
1969	565	417	161	178	263	263	4,058	1,483	16	84	—

	South										
	South Atlantic						East South Central				
	Virginia	West Virginia	North Carolina	South Carolina	Georgia	Florida	Total	Kentucky	Tennessee	Alabama	Mississippi
	Da61	Da62	Da63	Da64	Da65	Da66	Da67	Da68	Da69	Da70	Da71
Year	Thousand	Thousand	Thousand	Thousand	Thousand	Thousand	Thousand	Thousand	Thousand	Thousand	Thousand
1890	748	429	998	628	950	185	3,833	1,024	1,007	909	892
1900	952	535	1,258	835	1,183	203	4,860	1,267	1,246	1,166	1,181
1910	1,065	544	1,409	970	1,594	273	5,291	1,286	1,278	1,383	1,344
1920	1,078	484	1,520	1,088	1,706	285	5,257	1,324	1,290	1,355	1,288
1925	1,020	466	1,566	1,001	1,566	286	5,163	1,249	1,249	1,343	1,322
1930	953	450	1,604	919	1,423	280	5,109	1,180	1,219	1,344	1,366
1935	1,066	569	1,645	960	1,424	324	5,409	1,326	1,326	1,405	1,352
1940	986	533	1,659	917	1,368	305	5,283	1,261	1,276	1,343	1,403
1945	831	445	1,360	709	1,052	254	4,271	1,038	1,046	1,068	1,119
1950	732	411	1,377	701	962	233	4,048	974	1,016	960	1,097
1954	579	264	1,126	543	697	186	3,146	768	818	708	852
1959	502	165	1,006	455	530	165	2,641	652	715	553	721
1964	356	117	710	282	371	140	1,933	550	538	367	477
1969	259	84	507	165	251	117	1,433	474	412	240	308

(continued)

TABLE Da28–92   Farm population, by region and state: 1890–1969   *Continued*

	South					West					
	West South Central						Mountain				
	Total	Arkansas	Louisiana	Oklahoma	Texas	Total	Total	Montana	Idaho	Wyoming	Colorado
	Da72	Da73	Da74	Da75	Da76	Da77	Da78	Da79	Da80	Da81	Da82
Year	Thousand	Thousand	Thousand	Thousand	Thousand	Thousand	Thousand	Thousand	Thousand	Thousand	Thousand
1890	2,681	804	431	44	1,401	859	312	32	39	18	97
1900	4,095	956	608	587	1,943	1,192	502	67	81	30	115
1910	5,154	1,107	732	1,022	2,293	1,805	918	111	148	52	203
1920	5,310	1,165	798	1,033	2,314	2,216	1,179	228	203	68	268
1925	5,384	1,153	823	1,045	2,363	2,188	1,119	209	189	69	267
1930	5,341	1,122	833	1,027	2,359	2,295	1,143	205	189	74	284
1935	5,470	1,198	872	1,031	2,369	2,415	1,199	197	201	76	278
1940	5,057	1,113	854	930	2,160	2,387	1,118	176	203	73	253
1945	3,578	798	608	651	1,520	2,008	905	134	161	53	191
1950	3,215	802	567	567	1,292	1,929	859	136	165	57	198
1954	2,420	595	414	404	1,007	1,751	780	128	159	54	175
1959	1,988	483	326	318	860	1,613	719	123	158	52	154
1964	1,474	327	240	258	650	1,265	577	106	128	41	122
1969	1,141	245	173	219	503	1,011	471	94	107	35	99

	West									
	Mountain				Pacific					
	New Mexico	Arizona	Utah	Nevada	Total	Washington	Oregon	California	Alaska	Hawai'i
	Da83	Da84	Da85	Da86	Da87	Da88	Da89	Da90	Da91	Da92
Year	Thousand	Thousand	Thousand	Thousand	Thousand	Thousand	Thousand	Thousand	Thousand	Thousand
1890	43	11	66	7	546	123	141	283	—	—
1900	61	33	106	9	690	171	180	339	—	—
1910	184	85	122	13	887	260	210	417	—	—
1920	163	92	141	16	1,037	289	219	529	—	—
1925	154	92	124	15	1,069	291	217	561	—	—
1930	159	99	116	17	1,152	306	224	622	—	—
1935	192	101	139	15	1,216	342	253	621	—	—
1940	178	114	105	16	1,270	340	259	670	—	—
1945	149	101	102	14	1,102	304	233	565	—	—
1950	132	77	81	13	1,070	274	228	568	—	—
1954	103	74	74	13	971	242	200	529	—	—
1959	76	73	69	13	894	216	176	502	—	—
1964	60	55	53	11	689	170	145	362	2	9
1969	48	37	41	10	541	140	124	268	2	7

Sources

1880–1910: U.S. Bureau of the Census, *Farm Population: 1880 to 1950*, Technical Paper number 3; 1920–1970: U.S. Department of Agriculture, Rural Development Service, *Farm Population Estimates, 1910–70*, Statistical Bulletin number 523.

Documentation

See the text for Table Da1–13 for a general note.

TABLE Da93–158   Farms, by region and state: 1850–1997

Contributed by Alan L. Olmstead and Paul W. Rhode

			Northeast								
			New England							Middle Atlantic	
	United States	Total	Total	Maine	New Hampshire	Vermont	Massachusetts	Rhode Island	Connecticut	Total	New York
	Da93	Da94	Da95	Da96	Da97	Da98	Da99	Da100	Da101	Da102	Da103
Year	Thousand	Thousand	Thousand	Thousand	Thousand	Thousand	Thousand	Thousand	Thousand	Thousand	Thousand
1850	1,449	490	168	47	29	30	34	5	22	322	171
1860	2,044	565	184	56	31	32	36	5	25	381	197
1870	2,660	602	181	60	30	34	27	5	26	421	216
1880	4,009	696	207	64	32	36	38	6	31	489	241
1890	4,565	659	190	62	29	33	34	6	26	469	226
1900	5,740	678	192	59	29	33	38	5	27	486	227
1910	6,366	657	187	60	27	33	37	5	27	468	216
1920	6,454	582	157	48	21	29	32	4	23	425	193
1925	6,372	578	159	50	21	28	33	4	23	419	189
1930	6,295	483	125	39	15	25	26	3	17	358	160
1935	6,812	556	158	42	18	27	35	4	32	398	177
1940	6,102	483	135	39	17	24	32	3	21	348	153
1945	5,859	498	150	42	19	26	37	4	22	347	149
1950	5,388	400	103	30	13	19	22	3	16	297	125
1954	4,782	339	82	23	10	16	17	2	13	257	106
1959	3,711	255	57	17	7	12	11	1	8	198	82
1964	3,158	202	42	13	5	9	8	1	6	160	67
1969	2,730	152	29	8	3	7	6	1	4	123	52
1974	2,314	128	22	6	2	6	4	1	3	104	44
1978	2,258	132	24	7	3	6	5	1	4	107	43
1982	2,240	132	26	7	3	6	5	1	4	106	42
1987	2,088	123	26	6	3	6	6	1	4	98	38
1992	1,925	109	22	6	2	5	5	1	3	86	32
1997	1,912	112	26	6	3	6	6	1	4	86	32

(continued)

	Northeast		North Central									
	Middle Atlantic			East North Central							West North Central	
	New Jersey	Pennsylvania	Total	Total	Ohio	Indiana	Illinois	Michigan	Wisconsin	Total	Minnesota
	Da104	Da105	Da106	Da107	Da108	Da109	Da110	Da111	Da112	Da113	Da114
Year	Thousand	Thousand	Thousand	Thousand	Thousand	Thousand	Thousand	Thousand	Thousand	Thousand	Thousand
1850	24	128	438	368	144	94	76	34	20	69	(Z)
1860	28	156	772	587	180	132	143	62	69	185	18
1870	31	174	1,125	762	196	161	203	99	103	363	47
1880	34	214	1,698	985	247	194	256	154	134	713	92
1890	31	212	1,924	1,009	251	198	241	172	146	915	117
1900	35	224	2,197	1,136	277	222	264	203	170	1,061	155
1910	33	219	2,233	1,123	272	215	252	207	177	1,110	156
1920	30	202	2,182	1,085	257	205	237	196	189	1,097	178
1925	30	200	2,163	1,052	245	196	226	192	193	1,111	188
1930	25	172	2,079	967	219	182	214	169	182	1,113	185
1935	29	191	2,264	1,084	255	201	231	197	200	1,180	203
1940	26	169	2,097	1,006	234	185	213	188	187	1,091	197
1945	26	172	1,986	954	221	176	204	175	178	1,032	189
1950	25	147	1,868	885	199	167	195	156	169	983	179
1954	23	129	1,704	799	177	154	176	139	154	905	165
1959	15	100	1,461	666	140	128	155	112	131	795	146
1964	11	83	1,277	574	120	108	133	94	119	704	131
1969	8	63	1,152	513	111	101	124	78	99	639	111
1974	7	53	1,017	445	92	88	111	64	89	573	99
1978	8	56	976	424	89	82	105	60	87	552	99
1982	8	56	933	403	87	77	98	59	82	529	94
1987	9	52	862	365	79	71	89	51	75	497	85
1992	9	45	777	326	71	63	78	47	68	451	75
1997	9	45	750	312	69	58	73	46	66	438	73

(continued)

TABLE Da93–158   Farms, by region and state: 1850–1997   *Continued*

	North Central							South			
	West North Central								South Atlantic		
	Iowa	Missouri	North Dakota	Dakota Territory: 1870	South Dakota	Nebraska	Kansas	Total	Total	Delaware	Maryland
	Da115	Da116	Da117	Da118	Da119	Da120	Da121	Da122	Da123	Da124	Da125
Year	Thousand	Thousand	Thousand	Thousand	Thousand	Thousand	Thousand	Thousand	Thousand	Thousand	Thousand
1850	15	54	—	—	—	—	—	515	248	6	22
1860	61	93	—	—	—	3	10	672	302	7	25
1870	116	148	—	2	—	12	38	885	374	8	27
1880	185	216	4	—	14	63	139	1,531	644	9	41
1890	202	238	28	—	50	114	167	1,836	750	9	41
1900	229	285	45	—	53	122	173	2,620	962	10	46
1910	217	277	74	—	78	130	178	3,098	1,112	11	49
1920	213	263	78	—	75	124	165	3,207	1,159	10	48
1925	213	260	76	—	80	128	166	3,131	1,108	10	49
1930	215	256	78	—	83	129	166	3,224	1,058	10	43
1935	222	278	85	—	83	134	175	3,422	1,147	10	44
1940	213	256	74	—	72	121	156	3,007	1,019	9	42
1945	209	243	70	—	69	112	141	2,881	1,043	9	41
1950	203	230	65	—	66	107	131	2,652	959	7	36
1954	193	202	62	—	63	101	120	2,317	859	6	33
1959	175	169	55	—	56	90	104	1,646	592	5	25
1964	154	147	49	—	50	80	92	1,373	468	4	21
1969	140	137	46	—	46	72	86	1,161	371	4	17
1974	126	116	43	—	43	68	79	930	296	3	15
1978	121	115	40	—	39	64	74	898	282	3	16
1982	115	112	36	—	37	60	73	897	274	3	16
1987	105	106	35	—	36	61	69	824	240	3	15
1992	97	98	31	—	34	53	63	775	223	3	13
1997	91	99	31	—	31	51	62	785	217	2	12

	South										
	South Atlantic						East South Central				
	Virginia	Virginia and West Virginia	West Virginia	North Carolina	South Carolina	Georgia	Florida	Total	Kentucky	Tennessee	Alabama	Mississippi
	Da126	Da127	Da128	Da129	Da130	Da131	Da132	Da133	Da134	Da135	Da136	Da137
Year	Thousand	Thousand	Thousand	Thousand	Thousand	Thousand	Thousand	Thousand	Thousand	Thousand	Thousand	Thousand
1850	—	77	—	57	30	52	4	223	75	73	42	34
1860	—	93	—	75	33	62	7	271	91	82	55	43
1870	74	—	40	94	52	70	10	372	118	118	67	68
1880	119	—	63	158	94	139	23	570	166	166	136	102
1890	128	—	73	178	115	171	34	656	179	174	158	144
1900	168	—	93	225	155	225	41	903	235	225	223	221
1910	184	—	97	254	176	291	50	1,042	259	246	263	274
1920	186	—	87	270	193	311	54	1,052	271	253	256	272
1925	194	—	90	283	173	249	59	1,006	259	253	238	257
1930	171	—	83	280	158	256	59	1,062	246	246	257	313
1935	198	—	105	301	166	251	73	1,137	278	274	273	312
1940	175	—	99	278	138	216	62	1,023	253	248	232	291
1945	173	—	98	287	148	226	61	960	239	234	223	264
1950	151	—	81	289	139	198	57	913	218	232	212	251
1954	136	—	69	268	124	166	58	790	193	203	177	216
1959	98	—	44	191	78	106	45	563	151	158	116	138
1964	80	—	35	148	56	83	41	468	133	133	93	109
1969	65	—	23	119	40	67	36	392	125	121	72	73
1974	53	—	17	91	29	55	32	306	102	94	57	54
1978	50	—	17	82	27	51	36	284	102	87	51	44
1982	52	—	19	73	25	50	36	283	102	91	48	42
1987	45	—	17	59	21	44	37	250	92	80	43	34
1992	42	—	17	52	20	41	35	235	90	75	38	32
1997	41	—	18	49	20	40	35	231	82	77	41	31

TABLE Da93–158   Farms, by region and state: 1850–1997   *Continued*

	South					West					
	West South Central						Mountain				
	Total	Arkansas	Louisiana	Oklahoma	Texas	Total	Total	Montana	Idaho	Wyoming	Colorado
	Da138	Da139	Da140	Da141	Da142	Da143	Da144	Da145	Da146	Da147	Da148
Year	Thousand	Thousand	Thousand	Thousand	Thousand	Thousand	Thousand	Thousand	Thousand	Thousand	Thousand
1850	43	18	13	—	12	7	5	—	—	—	—
1860	99	39	17	—	43	35	9	—	—	—	—
1870	139	49	28	—	61	48	14	1	(Z)	(Z)	2
1880	317	94	48	—	174	84	25	2	2	(Z)	5
1890	431	125	69	9 [1]	228	146	49	6	7	3	16
1900	755	179	116	108 [1]	352	245	101	13	17	6	25
1910	943	215	121	190	418	378	183	26	31	11	46
1920	996	233	135	192	436	484	244	58	42	16	60
1925	1,017	222	132	197	466	499	233	47	41	16	58
1930	1,103	242	161	204	495	510	241	47	42	16	60
1935	1,138	253	170	213	501	571	271	51	45	17	64
1940	964	217	150	180	418	515	233	42	44	15	51
1945	878	199	129	165	385	494	213	38	41	13	48
1950	780	182	124	142	332	468	195	35	40	13	46
1954	668	145	111	119	293	423	180	33	39	11	41
1959	491	95	74	95	227	349	149	29	34	10	33
1964	436	80	62	89	205	306	134	27	30	9	30
1969	399	60	42	83	214	265	120	25	25	9	28
1974	328	51	33	70	174	239	112	23	24	8	26
1978	331	52	31	72	175	254	117	24	24	8	27
1982	340	51	32	72	185	280	122	24	25	9	27
1987	335	48	27	70	189	278	124	25	24	9	27
1992	317	44	26	67	181	264	118	23	22	9	27
1997	337	45	24	74	194	263	120	24	22	9	28

	West									
	Mountain				Pacific					
	New Mexico	Arizona	Utah	Nevada	Total	Washington	Oregon	California	Alaska	Hawai'i
	Da149	Da150	Da151	Da152	Da153	Da154	Da155	Da156	Da157	Da158
Year	Thousand	Thousand	Thousand	Thousand	Thousand	Thousand	Thousand	Thousand	Thousand	Thousand
1850	4	—	1	—	2	—	1	1	—	—
1860	5	—	4	(Z)	26	1	6	19	—	—
1870	4	(Z)	5	1	34	3	8	24	—	—
1880	5	1	9	1	59	7	16	36	—	—
1890	4	1	11	1	96	18	26	53	—	—
1900	12	6	19	2	144	33	36	73	(Z)	2
1910	36	9	22	3	194	56	46	88	(Z)	4
1920	30	10	26	3	240	66	50	118	(Z)	5
1925	32	11	26	4	266	73	56	136	—	—
1930	31	14	27	3	268	71	55	136	1	6
1935	41	19	31	4	300	84	65	150	—	—
1940	34	18	25	4	282	82	62	133	1	5
1945	30	13	26	3	282	80	63	139	—	—
1950	24	10	24	3	273	70	60	137	1	6
1954	21	9	23	3	243	65	54	123	—	—
1959	16	7	18	2	200	52	43	99	(Z)	6
1964	14	6	16	2	171	46	40	81	(Z)	5
1969	12	6	13	2	145	34	29	78	(Z)	4
1974	11	6	12	2	127	29	27	68	(Z)	3
1978	12	6	13	2	137	31	29	73	(Z)	4
1982	13	7	14	3	158	36	34	82	1	5
1987	14	8	14	3	154	34	32	83	1	5
1992	14	7	14	3	146	30	32	78	1	5
1997	14	6	14	3	143	29	34	74	1	5

Notes appear on next page

(continued)

TABLE Da93–158   Farms, by region and state: 1850–1997   *Continued*

(Z) Fewer than 500 farms.

[1] Oklahoma Territory only (1890); Oklahoma Territory and Indian Territory (1900).

Sources

U.S. Bureau of the Census, *U.S. Census of Agriculture: 1925*, Summary Statistics, by States; *1945*, volume 2; *1950*, volume 2; *1954*, volume 2; *1959*, volume 2; *1964*, volume 2; *1969*, volume 2; *1974*, volume 1, part 51, pp. II-1–2; *1978*,

volume 1, part 51, pp. 118–19; *1982*, volume 1, part 51, pp. 134–40; *1987*, volume 1, part 51, pp. 179–85; *1992*, volume 1, part 51, pp. 214–20; and *1997*, volume 1, part 51, pp. 241–9.

Documentation

See the text for Table Da1–13 for a general note. Also see the text for series Da4.

TABLE Da159–224   Land in farms, by region and state: 1850–1997

Contributed by Alan L. Olmstead and Paul W. Rhode

						Northeast					
					New England					Middle Atlantic	
Year	United States	Total	Total	Maine	New Hampshire	Vermont	Massachusetts	Rhode Island	Connecticut	Total	New York
	Da159	Da160	Da161	Da162	Da163	Da164	Da165	Da166	Da167	Da168	Da169
	Thousand acres	Thousand acres	Thousand acres	Thousand acres	Thousand acres	Thousand acres	Thousand acres	Thousand acres	Thousand acres	Thousand acres	Thousand acres
1850	293,561	55,163	18,367	4,555	3,392	4,126	3,356	554	2,384	36,795	19,119
1860	407,213	61,082	20,111	5,728	3,745	4,274	3,339	521	2,504	40,971	20,975
1870	407,735	62,744	19,570	5,838	3,606	4,529	2,730	502	2,364	43,175	22,191
1880	536,082	67,986	21,484	6,553	3,721	4,883	3,359	515	2,454	46,502	23,781
1890	623,219	62,744	19,756	6,180	3,459	4,396	2,998	469	2,253	42,988	21,962
1900	841,202	65,409	20,549	6,300	3,610	4,724	3,147	456	2,312	44,860	22,648
1910	881,431	62,906	19,715	6,297	3,249	4,664	2,876	443	2,186	43,191	22,030
1920	958,677	57,564	16,991	5,426	2,604	4,236	2,494	332	1,899	40,573	20,633
1925	924,319	53,349	15,858	5,161	2,262	3,926	2,368	309	1,832	37,491	19,270
1930	990,112	49,330	14,283	4,640	1,960	3,896	2,005	279	1,502	35,047	17,980
1935	1,054,515	51,919	15,463	4,722	2,116	4,043	2,196	308	2,080	36,455	18,686
1940	1,065,114	47,010	13,371	4,223	1,809	3,667	1,938	222	1,512	33,639	17,170
1945	1,141,615	48,903	14,497	4,613	2,017	3,931	2,078	265	1,593	34,406	17,568
1950	1,161,420	44,402	12,547	4,182	1,714	3,527	1,660	191	1,272	31,855	16,017
1954	1,158,192	41,019	11,121	3,614	1,457	3,318	1,439	155	1,138	29,898	15,071
1959	1,123,508	36,047	9,316	3,082	1,124	2,945	1,142	138	884	26,730	13,490
1964	1,110,187	31,979	7,744	2,590	903	2,524	902	104	721	24,235	12,275
1969	1,062,893	25,683	5,599	1,760	613	1,916	701	69	541	20,085	10,148
1974	1,017,030	23,359	4,801	1,524	506	1,668	602	61	440	18,558	9,411
1978	1,014,777	23,749	4,757	1,500	485	1,633	617	66	456	18,992	9,461
1982	986,797	23,036	4,632	1,469	470	1,574	613	62	444	18,404	9,190
1987	964,471	21,426	4,249	1,343	426	1,408	615	59	398	17,177	8,416
1992	945,532	19,353	3,857	1,258	386	1,279	526	50	359	15,495	7,458
1997	931,795	19,073	3,820	1,212	415	1,262	518	55	359	15,253	7,254

TABLE Da159–224 Land in farms, by region and state: 1850–1997 *Continued*

	Northeast		North Central								
	Middle Atlantic			East North Central						West North Central	
	New Jersey	Pennsylvania	Total	Total	Ohio	Indiana	Illinois	Michigan	Wisconsin	Total	Minnesota
	Da170	Da171	Da172	Da173	Da174	Da175	Da176	Da177	Da178	Da179	Da180
Year	Thousand acres	Thousand acres	Thousand acres	Thousand acres	Thousand acres	Thousand acres	Thousand acres	Thousand acres	Thousand acres	Thousand acres	Thousand acres
1850	2,753	14,923	62,686	50,189	17,997	12,793	12,037	4,384	2,977	12,498	29
1860	2,984	17,012	107,900	72,697	20,472	16,388	20,912	7,031	7,894	35,203	2,712
1870	2,990	17,994	139,215	87,449	21,712	18,120	25,883	10,019	11,715	51,766	6,484
1880	2,930	19,791	206,982	105,785	24,529	20,421	31,674	13,807	15,353	101,198	13,403
1890	2,662	18,364	256,587	105,787	23,352	20,363	30,498	14,786	16,788	150,800	18,664
1900	2,841	19,371	317,349	116,341	24,502	21,620	32,795	17,562	19,863	201,009	26,248
1910	2,574	18,587	350,577	117,929	24,106	21,300	32,523	18,941	21,060	232,648	27,676
1920	2,283	17,658	374,708	117,735	23,516	21,063	31,975	19,033	22,148	256,973	30,222
1925	1,925	16,296	360,834	112,752	22,219	19,915	30,732	18,035	21,851	248,081	30,059
1930	1,758	15,309	376,379	110,891	21,514	19,689	30,695	17,119	21,874	265,488	30,913
1935	1,914	15,855	390,034	116,957	22,858	20,519	31,661	18,460	23,459	273,077	32,818
1940	1,874	14,594	388,078	113,655	21,908	19,801	31,033	18,038	22,876	274,423	32,607
1945	1,818	15,020	398,812	115,564	21,928	20,027	31,602	18,392	23,615	283,248	33,140
1950	1,725	14,113	396,427	112,098	20,969	19,659	30,978	17,270	23,221	284,329	32,883
1954	1,665	13,162	393,458	108,597	19,992	19,233	30,399	16,467	22,507	284,861	32,285
1959	1,379	11,862	385,394	103,386	18,507	18,613	30,327	14,783	21,156	282,007	30,796
1964	1,156	10,804	383,090	99,486	17,619	17,933	29,958	13,599	20,378	283,603	30,805
1969	1,036	8,901	373,309	94,607	17,111	17,573	29,913	11,901	18,109	278,701	28,785
1974	961	8,186	362,939	90,005	15,668	16,785	29,095	10,832	17,625	272,934	27,605
1978	987	8,544	362,518	90,963	15,789	16,824	29,472	11,038	17,839	271,555	28,460
1982	916	8,298	354,218	88,601	15,404	16,294	28,726	10,942	17,234	265,618	27,708
1987	894	7,866	350,468	86,618	14,997	16,171	28,527	10,317	16,607	263,849	26,574
1992	848	7,190	343,561	82,669	14,248	15,619	27,250	10,088	15,464	260,892	25,667
1997	833	7,168	342,503	81,190	14,103	15,111	27,205	9,873	14,900	261,313	25,995

	North Central							South			
	West North Central							South Atlantic			
	Iowa	Missouri	North Dakota	Dakota Territory	South Dakota	Nebraska	Kansas	Total	Total	Delaware	Maryland
	Da181	Da182	Da183	Da184	Da185	Da186	Da187	Da188 [1]	Da189 [1]	Da190	Da191
Year	Thousand acres	Thousand acres	Thousand acres	Thousand acres	Thousand acres	Thousand acres	Thousand acres	Thousand acres	Thousand acres	Thousand acres	Thousand acres
1850	2,736	9,733	—	—	—	—	—	171,047	93,402	956	4,634
1860	10,070	19,985	—	26	—	631	1,778	225,514	106,521	1,004	4,836
1870	15,542	21,707	—	302	—	2,074	5,657	189,556	90,213	1,052	4,513
1880	24,753	27,879	1,028	—	2,773	9,945	21,417	234,920	101,420	1,090	5,120
1890	30,492	30,780	7,660	—	11,396	21,593	30,214	256,606	100,158	1,056	4,952
1900	34,574	33,998	15,543	—	19,071	29,912	41,663	362,036	104,298	1,066	5,170
1910	33,931	34,591	28,427	—	26,017	38,622	43,385	354,453	103,782	1,039	5,057
1920	33,475	34,775	36,215	—	34,636	42,225	45,425	350,122	97,775	945	4,758
1925	33,281	32,642	34,327	—	32,018	42,025	43,729	324,189	88,571	900	4,433
1930	34,019	33,743	38,658	—	36,470	44,709	46,976	343,086	86,363	901	4,374
1935	34,359	35,055	39,118	—	37,102	46,616	48,010	376,206	95,987	921	4,384
1940	34,149	34,740	37,936	—	39,474	47,344	48,174	370,168	92,555	896	4,198
1945	34,454	35,278	41,001	—	43,032	47,753	48,589	377,795	96,601	923	4,200
1950	34,265	35,123	41,194	—	44,786	47,467	48,611	393,215	102,170	851	4,056
1954	34,045	34,195	41,877	—	44,949	47,487	50,024	386,289	98,259	814	3,897
1959	33,831	33,155	41,466	—	44,851	47,756	50,153	357,448	83,339	763	3,457
1964	33,758	32,692	42,717	—	45,567	47,793	50,271	346,228	76,959	717	3,181
1969	33,570	32,420	43,118	—	45,584	45,834	49,390	332,808	68,031	674	2,803
1974	33,045	29,801	42,387	—	45,978	46,172	47,946	305,670	60,939	631	2,634
1978	33,258	30,099	41,702	—	44,422	46,114	47,500	305,123	59,750	670	2,614
1982	32,612	29,267	40,206	—	43,811	44,961	47,052	293,794	57,226	655	2,558
1987	31,638	29,209	40,337	—	44,158	45,305	46,629	281,243	51,199	608	2,397
1992	31,347	28,547	39,438	—	44,828	44,393	46,672	277,046	48,577	589	2,223
1997	31,167	28,826	39,359	—	44,355	45,525	46,089	279,166	49,206	580	2,155

Notes appear at end of table

(continued)

TABLE Da159–224   Land in farms, by region and state: 1850–1997   *Continued*

South

							South Atlantic					East South Central			
	Virginia	Virginia and West Virginia	West Virginia	North Carolina	South Carolina	Georgia	Florida	Total	Kentucky	Tennessee	Alabama	Mississippi			
	Da192	Da193	Da194	Da195	Da196	Da197	Da198	Da199	Da200	Da201	Da202	Da203			
Year	Thousand acres	Thousand acres	Thousand acres	Thousand acres	Thousand acres	Thousand acres	Thousand acres	Thousand acres	Thousand acres	Thousand acres	Thousand acres	Thousand acres			
1850	—	26,152	—	20,997	16,218	22,821	1,595	58,562	16,950	18,984	12,138	10,490			
1860	—	31,117	—	23,763	16,196	26,650	2,920	74,777	19,163	20,669	19,105	15,840			
1870	18,146	—	8,528	19,835	12,105	23,648	2,374	66,324	18,660	19,581	14,961	13,121			
1880	19,836	—	10,194	22,364	13,458	26,043	3,297	76,873	21,495	20,667	18,855	15,855			
1890	19,105	—	10,321	22,652	13,185	25,200	3,674	78,999	21,412	20,162	19,853	17,573			
1900	19,908	—	10,655	22,749	13,985	26,392	4,364	81,248	21,979	20,342	20,685	18,241			
1910	19,496	—	10,026	22,439	13,512	26,953	5,254	81,521	22,189	20,042	20,732	18,558			
1920	18,561	—	9,570	20,022	12,427	25,441	6,047	78,897	21,613	19,511	19,577	18,197			
1925	17,210	—	8,980	18,594	10,639	21,945	5,865	70,607	19,913	17,901	16,739	16,053			
1930	16,729	—	8,802	18,055	10,393	22,079	5,027	72,817	19,927	18,003	17,555	17,332			
1935	17,645	—	9,424	19,936	12,330	25,297	6,048	79,101	20,699	19,086	19,661	19,655			
1940	16,445	—	8,909	18,845	11,239	23,684	8,338	77,086	20,294	18,493	19,143	19,156			
1945	16,358	—	8,720	18,618	11,022	23,676	13,084	76,198	19,725	17,789	19,068	19,617			
1950	15,572	—	8,215	19,318	11,879	26,751	16,528	79,576	19,442	18,534	20,889	20,711			
1954	14,686	—	7,352	18,260	11,069	24,019	18,162	77,202	18,034	17,654	20,810	20,702			
1959	13,126	—	6,063	15,888	9,149	19,658	15,237	68,285	17,031	16,081	16,543	18,630			
1964	12,002	—	5,279	14,382	8,101	17,887	15,411	64,509	16,265	15,266	15,226	17,752			
1969	10,650	—	4,341	12,734	6,992	15,806	14,032	60,719	15,968	15,057	13,654	16,040			
1974	9,678	—	3,497	11,244	6,177	13,878	13,199	53,688	14,432	13,103	11,853	14,300			
1978	9,459	—	3,529	10,999	6,046	13,417	13,016	51,646	14,606	12,681	11,148	13,211			
1982	9,437	—	3,559	10,321	5,590	12,292	12,814	49,276	14,179	12,475	10,201	12,422			
1987	8,676	—	3,373	9,448	4,759	10,745	11,194	45,636	14,013	11,731	9,146	10,746			
1992	8,297	—	3,267	8,936	4,473	10,026	10,766	43,474	13,666	11,169	8,451	10,188			
1997	8,228	—	3,456	9,122	4,593	10,671	10,454	43,284	13,334	11,122	8,704	10,125			

South						West					
West South Central							Mountain				
Total	Arkansas	Louisiana	Oklahoma	Texas		Total	Total	Montana	Idaho	Wyoming	Colorado
Da204	Da205	Da206	Da207	Da208		Da209	Da210	Da211	Da212	Da213	Da214
Thousand acres	Thousand acres	Thousand acres	Thousand acres	Thousand acres		Thousand acres	Thousand acres	Thousand acres	Thousand acres	Thousand acres	Thousand acres
19,084	2,598	4,989	—	11,496		4,664	337	—	—	—	—
44,216	9,574	9,299	—	25,344		12,718	1,561	—	—	—	—
33,020	7,597	7,026	—	18,397		16,219	1,754	140	77	4	320
56,627	12,062	8,274	—	36,292		26,194	3,976	406	328	124	1,165
77,449	14,891	9,544	1,606 [2]	51,407		47,282	14,766	1,964	1,302	1,830	4,599
176,491	16,637	11,059	22,988 [2]	125,807		96,407	46,397	11,844	3,205	8,125	9,475
169,150	17,416	10,439	28,859	112,435		113,495	59,533	13,546	5,284	8,543	13,532
173,449	17,457	10,020	31,952	114,021		176,283	117,337	35,071	8,376	11,809	24,462
165,013	15,632	8,838	30,869	109,674		185,947	131,689	32,736	8,116	18,663	24,167
183,906	16,053	9,355	33,791	124,707		221,316	157,450	44,659	9,347	23,525	28,876
201,118	17,742	10,444	35,335	137,597		236,356	173,881	47,512	9,952	28,162	29,978
200,527	18,045	9,996	34,803	137,683		259,857	191,901	46,452	10,298	28,026	31,527
204,995	17,456	10,040	36,162	141,338		316,105	244,577	58,787	12,503	33,117	36,218
211,469	18,871	11,202	36,007	145,389		327,377	250,213	59,247	13,224	34,421	37,953
210,828	17,944	11,441	35,630	145,813		337,426	260,942	61,469	14,364	34,989	38,385
205,824	16,457	10,347	35,801	143,218		344,620	264,429	64,081	15,232	36,200	38,787
204,760	16,565	10,411	36,077	141,706		348,936	268,003	65,834	15,302	37,053	38,259
204,058	15,695	9,789	36,008	142,567		331,092	256,525	62,918	14,417	35,476	36,697
191,043	14,642	9,133	33,083	134,185		325,062	253,021	62,158	14,274	34,272	35,902
193,727	15,075	9,295	33,737	135,620		323,387	252,609	61,691	14,699	33,627	35,253
187,291	14,683	8,929	32,369	131,310		315,929	246,101	60,539	13,922	33,500	33,538
184,408	14,356	8,007	31,542	130,503		311,334	244,063	60,204	13,932	33,595	34,048
184,995	14,128	7,838	32,143	130,887		305,572	240,746	59,643	13,469	32,876	33,983
186,676	14,365	7,877	33,219	131,308		290,891	228,245	58,608	11,830	34,089	32,634

Notes appear at end of table

TABLE Da159–224   Land in farms, by region and state: 1850–1997   *Continued*

	West									
	Mountain				Pacific					
	New Mexico	Arizona	Utah	Nevada	Total	Washington	Oregon	California	Alaska	Hawai'i
	Da215	Da216	Da217	Da218	Da219	Da220	Da221	Da222	Da223	Da224
Year	Thousand acres	Thousand acres	Thousand acres	Thousand acres	Thousand acres	Thousand acres	Thousand acres	Thousand acres	Thousand acres	Thousand acres
1850	291	—	47	—	4,327	—	433	3,894	—	—
1860	1,415	—	90	56	11,157	366	2,061	8,730	—	—
1870	834	22	148	209	14,465	649	2,389	11,427	—	—
1880	631	136	656	531	22,218	1,409	4,215	16,594	—	—
1890	788	1,297	1,324	1,661	32,516	4,179	6,910	21,427	—	—
1900	5,131	1,935	4,117	2,566	50,009	8,499	10,071	28,829	(Z)	2,610
1910	11,270	1,247	3,398	2,715	53,962	11,712	11,685	27,931	43	2,591
1920	24,410	5,802	5,050	2,357	58,946	13,245	13,542	29,366	91	2,702
1925	27,850	11,065	5,001	4,091	54,258	12,610	14,131	27,517	—	—
1930	30,822	10,527	5,613	4,081	63,866	13,534	16,549	30,443	526	2,815
1935	34,397	14,019	6,239	3,622	62,476	14,680	17,358	30,438	—	—
1940	38,860	25,651	7,302	3,785	67,956	15,182	17,988	30,524	1,776	2,486
1945	49,608	37,856	10,309	6,178	71,529	16,720	19,754	35,054	—	—
1950	47,522	39,916	10,865	7,064	77,164	17,369	20,328	36,613	422	2,432
1954	49,451	41,790	12,262	8,231	76,484	17,641	21,047	37,795	—	—
1959	46,293	40,203	12,689	10,943	80,191	18,717	21,236	36,888	888	2,461
1964	47,647	40,559	12,867	10,483	80,887	19,053	20,509	37,011	1,959	2,354
1969	46,792	38,203	11,313	10,708	74,568	17,559	18,018	35,328	1,604	2,058
1974	47,046	37,944	10,610	10,814	72,041	16,662	18,241	33,386	1,633	2,119
1978	47,935	38,506	10,471	10,427	70,778	16,722	18,054	32,727	1,286	1,988
1982	47,096	37,753	9,773	9,980	69,828	16,650	17,740	32,157	1,324	1,958
1987	46,018	36,288	9,989	9,989	67,271	16,116	17,809	30,598	1,027	1,722
1992	46,849	35,038	9,624	9,264	64,826	15,726	17,609	28,979	923	1,589
1997	45,787	26,867	12,025	6,409	62,646	15,180	17,449	27,699	881	1,439

(Z) Fewer than 500 acres.

[1] Washington, D.C., is not reported separately but is included in the totals for the South and South Atlantic.

[2] Oklahoma Territory only (1890); Oklahoma Territory and Indian Territory (1900).

Sources

U.S. Bureau of the Census, *U.S. Census of Agriculture: 1925*, Summary Statistics, by States; *1945*, volume 2; *1950*, volume 2; *1954*, volume 2; *1959*, volume 2; *1964*, volume 2; *1969*, volume 2; *1974*, volume 1, part 51, pp. II-1–2; *1978*, volume 1, part 51, pp. 118–19; *1982*, volume 1, part 51, pp. 134–40; *1987*, volume 1, part 51, pp. 179–85; *1992*, volume 1, part 51, pp. 214–20; and *1997*, volume 1, part 51, pp. 241–49.

Documentation

See the text for Table Da1–13 for a general note. Also see the text for series Da5–6.

TABLE Da225-290   Average acreage per farm, by region and state: 1850-1997[1]

Contributed by Alan L. Olmstead and Paul W. Rhode

					Northeast						
					New England					Middle Atlantic	
	United States	Total	Total	Maine	New Hampshire	Vermont	Massachusetts	Rhode Island	Connecticut	Total	New York
	Da225	Da226	Da227	Da228	Da229	Da230	Da231	Da232	Da233	Da234	Da235
Year	Acres	Acres	Acres	Acres	Acres	Acres	Acres	Acres	Acres	Acres	Acres
1850	203	113	110	97	116	139	99	103	106	114	112
1860	199	108	109	103	123	136	94	96	100	108	107
1870	153	104	108	98	122	134	103	94	93	103	103
1880	134	98	104	102	116	138	88	83	80	95	99
1890	137	95	104	100	119	135	87	85	86	92	97
1900	147	97	107	106	123	143	83	83	86	92	100
1910	139	96	104	105	120	143	78	84	82	92	102
1920	149	99	109	113	127	146	78	81	84	95	107
1925	145	92	99	103	107	141	71	79	79	90	102
1930	157	102	114	119	132	157	78	84	87	98	113
1935	155	93	98	113	120	149	63	71	65	92	106
1940	175	97	99	108	109	156	61	74	72	97	112
1945	195	98	96	109	107	148	56	74	72	99	118
1950	216	112	122	138	128	185	75	74	82	107	128
1954	242	121	136	155	140	208	83	77	89	116	143
1959	303	142	164	178	172	243	102	99	107	124	164
1964	352	158	185	201	194	273	113	94	119	141	185
1969	389	169	195	221	211	279	123	98	121	163	196
1974	440	183	206	237	210	282	134	102	129	178	215
1978	449	181	196	221	193	279	125	98	130	177	220
1982	440	175	178	210	170	249	113	86	118	174	218
1987	462	174	169	214	169	240	99	84	111	175	223
1992	491	177	168	218	158	235	100	76	105	180	231
1997	487	172	156	209	141	217	93	75	97	177	228

	Northeast		North Central								
	Middle Atlantic			East North Central						West North Central	
	New Jersey	Pennsylvania	Total	Total	Ohio	Indiana	Illinois	Michigan	Wisconsin	Total	Minnesota
	Da236	Da237	Da238	Da239	Da240	Da241	Da242	Da243	Da244	Da245	Da246
Year	Acres	Acres	Acres	Acres	Acres	Acres	Acres	Acres	Acres	Acres	Acres
1850	115	117	143	136	125	136	158	129	148	180	184
1860	108	109	140	124	114	124	146	113	114	190	149
1870	98	103	124	115	111	112	128	101	114	143	139
1880	85	93	122	107	99	105	124	90	114	142	145
1890	86	87	133	105	93	103	127	86	115	165	160
1900	82	86	145	102	89	97	124	86	117	190	170
1910	77	85	157	105	89	99	129	92	119	210	177
1920	77	87	172	109	92	103	135	97	117	234	169
1925	65	81	167	107	91	102	136	94	113	223	160
1930	69	89	181	115	98	108	143	101	120	239	167
1935	65	83	172	108	90	102	137	94	117	231	161
1940	73	86	185	113	94	107	145	96	123	252	165
1945	69	87	201	121	99	114	155	105	133	275	175
1950	70	96	212	127	105	118	159	111	138	289	184
1954	73	102	231	136	113	125	173	119	147	315	195
1959	89	119	264	155	132	145	196	132	161	355	211
1964	109	130	300	173	146	166	226	145	172	403	235
1969	122	142	324	184	154	173	242	153	183	436	260
1974	130	154	357	202	170	191	262	169	197	477	280
1978	124	152	372	215	177	204	282	183	206	492	288
1982	111	149	388	231	177	211	292	187	210	502	294
1987	99	153	407	237	189	229	321	202	221	531	312
1992	93	160	442	254	201	249	351	217	228	578	342
1997	91	158	457	261	206	261	372	215	227	597	354

Notes appear at end of table

TABLE Da225–290 Average acreage per farm, by region and state: 1850–1997 *Continued*

	North Central							South			
	West North Central								South Atlantic		
	Iowa	Missouri	North Dakota	Dakota Territory	South Dakota	Nebraska	Kansas	Total	Total	Delaware	Maryland
	Da247	Da248	Da249	Da250	Da251	Da252	Da253	Da254	Da255	Da256	Da257
Year	Acres	Acres	Acres	Acres	Acres	Acres	Acres	Acres	Acres	Acres	Acres
1850	185	179	—	—	—	—	—	332	376	158	212
1860	165	215	—	215	—	226	171	335	353	151	190
1870	134	146	—	176	—	169	148	214	241	138	167
1880	134	129	271	—	203	157	155	153	157	125	126
1890	151	129	277	—	227	190	181	140	134	113	121
1900	151	119	343	—	362	246	241	138	108	110	112
1910	156	125	382	—	335	298	244	114	93	96	103
1920	157	132	466	—	464	339	275	109	84	93	99
1925	156	125	452	—	403	329	264	104	80	88	91
1930	158	132	496	—	439	345	283	106	82	93	101
1935	155	126	462	—	445	349	275	110	84	89	99
1940	160	136	513	—	545	391	308	123	91	100	100
1945	165	145	590	—	626	427	344	131	93	99	102
1950	169	153	630	—	674	443	370	148	107	114	112
1954	177	170	676	—	719	471	416	167	114	129	120
1959	194	197	755	—	805	528	481	217	141	146	138
1964	219	222	875	—	917	596	544	252	164	163	153
1969	239	237	930	—	997	634	574	287	184	182	163
1974	262	258	992	—	1,074	683	605	329	206	185	174
1978	274	262	1,033	—	1,147	723	640	340	212	197	168
1982	283	260	1,104	—	1,179	746	642	328	209	196	158
1987	301	275	1,143	—	1,214	749	680	341	214	205	162
1992	325	291	1,267	—	1,316	839	738	357	218	224	171
1997	343	292	1,290	—	1,418	885	748	354	225	236	178

	South											
	South Atlantic							East South Central				
	Virginia	Virginia and West Virginia	West Virginia	North Carolina	South Carolina	Georgia	Florida	Total	Kentucky	Tennessee	Alabama	Mississippi
	Da258	Da259	Da260	Da261	Da262	Da263	Da264	Da265	Da266	Da267	Da268	Da269
Year	Acres	Acres	Acres	Acres	Acres	Acres	Acres	Acres	Acres	Acres	Acres	Acres
1850	—	340	—	369	541	441	371	262	227	261	289	309
1860	—	336	—	316	488	430	444	276	211	251	347	370
1870	246	—	214	212	233	338	232	178	158	166	222	193
1880	167	—	163	142	143	188	141	135	129	125	139	156
1890	150	—	142	127	115	147	107	121	119	116	126	122
1900	119	—	115	101	90	118	107	90	94	91	93	83
1910	106	—	104	88	77	93	105	78	86	82	79	68
1920	100	—	110	74	65	82	112	75	80	77	76	67
1925	89	—	99	66	62	88	99	70	77	71	70	62
1930	98	—	107	65	66	86	85	69	81	73	68	55
1935	89	—	90	66	75	101	83	70	74	70	72	63
1940	94	—	90	68	82	110	134	75	80	75	83	66
1945	95	—	89	65	75	105	214	79	83	76	85	74
1950	103	—	101	67	85	130	290	87	89	80	99	82
1954	108	—	107	68	89	145	316	98	93	87	118	96
1959	135	—	138	83	117	185	338	121	113	102	143	135
1964	149	—	153	97	144	215	380	138	122	114	165	163
1969	165	—	188	107	177	234	394	155	128	124	188	221
1974	184	—	207	123	211	253	407	175	141	140	209	267
1978	189	—	202	135	226	261	360	182	143	146	220	300
1982	182	—	190	142	224	248	353	174	140	138	211	293
1987	194	—	196	159	232	247	306	182	152	147	211	315
1992	197	—	192	172	221	246	306	185	151	149	223	318
1997	200	—	194	185	228	265	300	187	162	145	210	323

(continued)

TABLE Da225–290   Average acreage per farm, by region and state: 1850–1997   *Continued*

	South						West				
	West South Central						Mountain				
	Total	Arkansas	Louisiana	Oklahoma	Texas	Total	Total	Montana	Idaho	Wyoming	Colorado
	Da270	Da271	Da272	Da273	Da274	Da275	Da276	Da277	Da278	Da279	Da280
Year	Acres	Acres	Acres	Acres	Acres	Acres	Acres	Acres	Acres	Acres	Acres
1850	440	146	372	—	943	695	72	—	—	—	—
1860	446	245	537	—	591	367	177	—	—	—	—
1870	238	154	247	—	301	336	127	164	186	25	184
1880	179	128	171	—	208	313	159	267	174	272	259
1890	180	119	138	182 [2]	225	324	299	351	197	586	281
1900	234	93	95	213 [2]	357	393	458	886	183	1,333	384
1910	179	81	87	152	269	300	325	517	172	778	293
1920	174	75	74	166	262	364	481	608	199	750	408
1925	162	70	67	157	236	373	564	698	200	1,203	417
1930	167	66	58	166	252	434	653	940	224	1,469	482
1935	177	70	61	166	275	414	641	940	221	1,610	471
1940	208	83	67	194	329	504	822	1,111	236	1,866	613
1945	234	88	78	219	367	639	1,151	1,557	301	2,533	761
1950	271	103	90	253	439	700	1,284	1,689	328	2,729	833
1954	316	124	103	300	498	798	1,450	1,859	371	3,069	942
1959	419	173	139	378	631	987	1,774	2,213	452	3,715	1,162
1964	469	207	167	407	691	1,142	1,998	2,437	516	4,100	1,284
1969	511	260	232	434	668	1,240	2,139	2,522	566	4,014	1,313
1974	582	287	275	475	771	1,360	2,262	2,665	603	4,274	1,408
1978	586	291	296	467	773	1,274	2,168	2,618	606	4,182	1,310
1982	551	291	282	446	710	1,129	2,021	2,568	563	3,781	1,237
1987	551	298	293	449	691	1,118	1,965	2,451	577	3,650	1,248
1992	583	322	306	480	725	1,158	2,037	2,613	609	3,772	1,252
1997	553	318	331	448	676	1,100	1,881	2,414	530	3,692	1,154

	West									
	Mountain				Pacific					
	New Mexico	Arizona	Utah	Nevada	Total	Washington	Oregon	California	Alaska	Hawai'i
	Da281	Da282	Da283	Da284	Da285	Da286	Da287	Da288	Da289	Da290
Year	Acres	Acres	Acres	Acres	Acres	Acres	Acres	Acres	Acres	Acres
1850	78	—	51	—	2,125	—	372	4,466	—	—
1860	278	—	25	617	432	275	355	466	—	—
1870	186	127	30	201	420	208	315	482	—	—
1880	125	177	69	378	379	216	260	462	—	—
1890	177	910	126	1,301	337	231	271	405	—	—
1900	417	333	212	1,175	348	256	281	397	13	1,148
1910	316	135	157	1,010	278	208	257	317	192	600
1920	818	582	197	745	246	200	270	250	249	511
1925	879	1,024	192	1,054	—	172	253	202	—	—
1930	982	743	207	1,186	238	191	300	224	1,052	428
1935	832	745	203	980	—	174	268	202	—	—
1940	1,139	1,389	287	1,059	241	186	291	230	2,850	498
1945	1,671	2,881	392	1,802	—	209	313	252	—	—
1950	2,014	3,834	449	2,271	283	249	340	267	803	423
1954	2,347	4,483	537	2,881	—	271	387	307	—	—
1959	2,908	5,558	712	4,649	401	363	499	372	2,421	394
1964	3,354	6,262	817	4,862	472	418	516	458	5,129	484
1969	4,020	6,486	867	5,070	514	516	620	454	4,832	528
1974	4,170	6,539	871	5,209	567	567	682	493	5,612	702
1978	3,894	6,114	820	4,346	515	540	633	447	3,359	461
1982	3,493	5,148	699	3,671	441	456	520	390	2,323	426
1987	3,230	4,732	710	3,300	436	480	556	368	1,789	353
1992	3,281	5,173	712	3,205	445	520	552	373	1,803	298
1997	3,249	4,379	848	2,266	438	523	513	374	1,608	263

TABLE Da225–290   Average acreage per farm, by region and state: 1850–1997   *Continued*

[1] Starting in 1978 average acreage per farm was not reported by region in the Census of Agriculture. Numbers reported here were calculated from state data.

[2] Oklahoma Territory only (1890); Oklahoma Territory and Indian Territory (1900).

Sources

U.S. Bureau of the Census, *U.S. Census of Agriculture: 1925*, Summary Statistics, by States; *1945*, volume 2; *1950*, volume 2; *1954*, volume 2; *1959*, volume 2; *1964*, volume 2; *1969*, volume 2; *1974*, volume 1, part 51, pp. II-1-2; *1978*, volume 1, part 51, pp. 118–19; *1982*, volume 1, part 51, pp. 134–40; *1987*,

volume 1, part 51, pp. 179-85; *1992*, volume 1, part 51, pp. 214–20; and *1997*, volume 1, part 51, pp. 241-9.

Documentation

See the text for Table Da1–13 for a general note. Also see the text for series Da5-6.

For years before 1978 data are as reported by the U.S. Census. For reasons that cannot be determined, if one wants to calculate averages for regions from the underlying data, results would often be different.

TABLE Da291–356   Value of farmland and buildings, by region and state: 1850–1997[1]

Contributed by Alan L. Olmstead and Paul W. Rhode

			Northeast									
			New England								Middle Atlantic	
	United States	Total	Total	Maine	New Hampshire	Vermont	Massachusetts	Rhode Island	Connecticut	Total	New York
	Da291	Da292	Da293	Da294	Da295	Da296	Da297	Da298	Da299	Da300	Da301
Year	Million dollars	Million dollars	Million dollars	Million dollars	Million dollars	Million dollars	Million dollars	Million dollars	Million dollars	Million dollars	Million dollars
1850	3,272	1,455	372	55	55	63	109	17	73	1,083	555
1860	6,645	2,122	476	79	70	94	123	20	91	1,646	803
1870	7,444	2,527	468	82	64	111	93	17	99	2,059	1,018
1880	10,197	2,803	581	102	76	109	146	26	121	2,223	1,056
1890	13,279	2,539	490	99	66	80	128	22	95	2,050	968
1900	16,675	2,477	528	97	70	83	158	23	97	1,949	888
1910	34,885	3,161	719	160	86	113	194	28	138	2,443	1,185
1920	66,446	3,920	917	204	90	159	248	26	190	3,002	1,425
1925	49,468	3,705	906	197	87	137	255	28	202	2,800	1,367
1930	47,994	3,758	941	194	77	146	261	35	227	2,818	1,316
1935	32,859	3,043	901	144	67	116	256	35	284	2,141	1,045
1940	33,758	2,780	741	124	62	111	212	26	205	2,039	947
1945	46,389	3,328	939	160	80	135	265	36	263	2,389	1,088
1950	75,462	4,708	1,222	227	125	196	315	44	315	3,485	1,467
1954	97,583	5,409	1,253	219	125	202	322	53	331	4,156	1,675
1959	129,005	6,293	1,414	256	118	240	354	52	393	4,879	1,971
1964	159,932	6,901	1,459	257	118	275	349	51	409	5,442	2,181
1969	206,717	9,025	1,803	283	146	429	396	50	499	7,222	2,772
1974	342,099	15,460	2,915	519	286	770	578	92	671	12,545	4,800
1978	631,434	24,079	4,339	800	426	1,065	907	159	983	19,740	6,315
1982	774,158	28,272	5,385	1,054	555	1,305	1,111	173	1,187	22,887	7,512
1987	604,168	32,045	7,866	1,321	900	1,521	2,154	295	1,674	24,179	8,263
1992	687,432	38,305	8,834	1,396	836	1,730	2,421	313	2,138	29,472	9,130
1997	859,839	40,651	9,241	1,456	945	1,876	2,535	325	2,104	31,410	9,117

Notes appear at end of table

(continued)

TABLE Da291–356   Value of farmland and buildings, by region and state: 1850–1997   *Continued*

	Northeast		North Central								
	Middle Atlantic			East North Central						West North Central	
	New Jersey	Pennsylvania	Total	Total	Ohio	Indiana	Illinois	Michigan	Wisconsin	Total	Minnesota
	Da302	Da303	Da304	Da305	Da306	Da307	Da308	Da309	Da310	Da311	Da312
Year	Million dollars	Million dollars	Million dollars	Million dollars	Million dollars	Million dollars	Million dollars	Million dollars	Million dollars	Million dollars	Million dollars
1850	120	408	752	672	359	136	96	52	29	80	(Z)
1860	180	662	2,130	1,736	678	357	409	161	131	394	28
1870	206	835	3,452	2,647	844	508	736	319	240	804	78
1880	191	976	5,129	3,629	1,127	635	1,010	499	358	1,500	194
1890	159	922	7,070	4,101	1,050	755	1,263	556	478	2,968	340
1900	163	898	9,564	4,913	1,037	842	1,766	583	686	4,651	670
1910	217	1,041	20,489	8,874	1,654	1,594	3,523	901	1,202	11,615	1,262
1920	250	1,327	39,407	14,938	2,661	2,654	5,998	1,437	2,188	24,469	3,301
1925	263	1,170	27,555	11,024	1,946	1,696	4,199	1,284	1,899	16,531	2,394
1930	299	1,203	24,495	9,337	1,693	1,416	3,336	1,161	1,732	15,159	2,125
1935	234	862	15,982	6,597	1,278	1,040	2,206	826	1,247	9,385	1,383
1940	228	864	16,130	7,334	1,444	1,251	2,537	913	1,189	8,796	1,443
1945	293	1,009	22,074	9,959	1,868	1,794	3,663	1,199	1,434	12,115	1,834
1950	505	1,513	33,748	14,704	2,859	2,691	5,395	1,701	2,057	19,044	2,777
1954	672	1,809	42,616	18,942	3,707	3,733	7,036	2,195	2,271	23,673	3,478
1959	717	2,190	55,469	24,737	4,573	4,933	9,580	2,855	2,796	30,732	4,749
1964	782	2,479	64,182	27,909	5,221	5,582	10,744	3,182	3,180	36,272	5,125
1969	1,131	3,319	86,383	36,683	6,819	7,136	14,643	3,883	4,201	49,701	6,502
1974	1,737	6,008	150,978	61,406	11,056	12,078	24,628	5,989	7,656	89,572	11,855
1978	2,549	10,877	304,720	130,814	23,495	26,660	54,933	10,585	15,146	173,906	25,762
1982	2,840	12,539	339,761	134,967	23,290	26,129	53,071	13,389	19,120	204,794	32,335
1987	3,579	12,337	228,073	96,291	18,023	18,716	35,779	10,034	13,740	131,782	18,616
1992	5,590	14,752	263,320	110,003	20,626	21,732	41,844	11,517	14,285	153,317	23,319
1997	5,403	16,890	349,313	150,771	28,450	30,853	56,475	16,490	18,503	198,542	29,927

	North Central							South			
	West North Central							South Atlantic			
	Iowa	Missouri	North Dakota	Dakota Territory	South Dakota	Nebraska	Kansas	Total	Total	Delaware	Maryland
	Da313	Da314	Da315	Da316	Da317	Da318	Da319	Da320	Da321	Da322	Da323
Year	Million dollars	Million dollars	Million dollars	Million dollars	Million dollars	Million dollars	Million dollars	Million dollars	Million dollars	Million dollars	Million dollars
1850	17	63	—	—	—	—	—	1,056	577	19	87
1860	120	231	—	—	—	4	12	2,323	1,009	31	146
1870	314	314	—	2	—	24	72	1,289	610	37	136
1880	567	376	9	—	14	106	235	1,873	892	37	166
1890	858	626	75	—	107	402	560	2,575	1,135	40	175
1900	1,498	844	199	—	220	578	644	3,279	1,206	34	175
1910	3,257	1,716	823	—	1,005	1,813	1,738	7,353	2,486	53	242
1920	7,602	3,063	1,489	—	2,473	3,712	2,830	15,157	5,202	65	387
1925	4,954	2,003	1,020	—	1,437	2,523	2,198	11,539	4,099	60	341
1930	4,225	1,796	951	—	1,285	2,495	2,281	12,344	3,852	67	356
1935	2,462	1,099	707	—	692	1,563	1,479	8,737	2,792	51	243
1940	2,691	1,107	490	—	505	1,138	1,421	9,716	3,160	55	274
1945	3,611	1,527	708	—	764	1,699	1,971	13,149	4,239	73	355
1950	5,507	2,236	1,189	—	1,402	2,785	3,199	22,955	7,160	97	507
1954	6,770	2,785	1,493	—	1,767	3,400	3,980	29,549	9,555	128	691
1959	8,587	3,727	2,141	—	2,277	4,234	5,017	39,011	12,832	180	982
1964	9,181	4,928	2,854	—	2,814	5,232	6,138	52,068	16,157	235	1,349
1969	13,150	7,269	4,045	—	3,815	7,076	7,843	69,664	20,513	336	1,793
1974	23,754	11,811	8,268	—	6,656	13,017	14,211	110,362	34,987	612	2,791
1978	51,831	21,972	14,565	—	11,466	24,417	23,895	186,098	57,395	964	4,645
1982	54,361	25,103	17,740	—	15,563	32,094	28,167	236,638	69,751	1,218	5,378
1987	29,830	18,634	12,934	—	11,871	20,828	19,068	207,777	64,886	1,096	5,419
1992	38,063	22,070	13,163	—	12,264	22,713	21,725	222,294	76,544	1,351	6,570
1997	51,438	30,589	15,635	—	15,236	29,200	26,517	276,716	91,941	1,500	6,824

TABLE Da291–356 Value of farmland and buildings, by region and state: 1850–1997 *Continued*

						South						

			South Atlantic					East South Central				
Year	Virginia	Virginia and West Virginia	West Virginia	North Carolina	South Carolina	Georgia	Florida	Total	Kentucky	Tennessee	Alabama	Mississippi
	Da324	Da325	Da326	Da327	Da328	Da329	Da330	Da331	Da332	Da333	Da334	Da335
	Million dollars	Million dollars	Million dollars	Million dollars	Million dollars	Million dollars	Million dollars	Million dollars	Million dollars	Million dollars	Million dollars	Million dollars
1850	—	216	—	68	82	96	6	372	155	98	64	55
1860	—	372	—	143	140	157	16	929	291	271	176	191
1870	170	—	81	63	36	76	8	544	249	175	54	65
1880	216	—	133	136	69	112	20	678	299	207	79	93
1890	254	—	152	184	99	152	73	828	346	243	111	127
1900	272	—	168	195	127	183	41	934	382	265	135	152
1910	532	—	264	457	333	479	118	1,738	635	481	288	334
1920	1,024	—	411	1,076	813	1,138	281	3,664	1,305	1,025	544	790
1925	887	—	356	926	458	588	479	2,481	847	759	415	459
1930	856	—	342	844	379	577	423	2,685	871	743	502	568
1935	594	—	238	623	286	430	321	1,915	620	556	368	371
1940	675	—	270	737	338	480	324	2,325	776	664	409	475
1945	869	—	341	1,003	441	654	498	3,094	1,016	871	560	648
1950	1,277	—	487	1,906	820	1,115	946	5,169	1,572	1,432	1,017	1,148
1954	1,551	—	497	2,346	965	1,442	1,935	6,086	1,722	1,635	1,206	1,523
1959	1,819	—	450	2,949	1,226	1,908	3,317	7,855	2,305	2,095	1,480	1,974
1964	2,215	—	478	3,622	1,403	2,431	4,423	10,251	2,958	2,737	1,902	2,655
1969	3,047	—	589	4,244	1,826	3,701	4,976	14,540	4,041	4,028	2,725	3,746
1974	5,396	—	1,050	6,634	2,887	6,576	9,041	22,006	6,158	6,117	4,310	5,421
1978	8,572	—	2,082	11,558	4,581	10,291	14,700	39,460	12,705	10,884	7,021	8,849
1982	10,633	—	2,425	13,673	5,198	11,171	20,088	46,466	14,680	12,601	8,295	10,935
1987	10,409	—	2,255	11,845	4,127	9,852	19,884	38,811	12,545	11,648	7,284	7,333
1992	13,534	—	2,810	13,950	5,093	11,437	21,801	45,055	14,775	13,977	8,350	7,952
1997	15,813	—	3,790	18,566	6,558	15,842	23,048	61,904	18,943	20,066	12,340	10,555

		South						West				

		West South Central						Mountain			
Year	Total	Arkansas	Louisiana	Oklahoma	Texas	Total	Total	Montana	Idaho	Wyoming	Colorado
	Da336	Da337	Da338	Da339	Da340	Da341	Da342	Da343	Da344	Da345	Da346
	Million dollars	Million dollars	Million dollars	Million dollars	Million dollars	Million dollars	Million dollars	Million dollars	Million dollars	Million dollars	Million dollars
1850	108	15	76	—	17	9	2	—	—	—	—
1860	385	92	205	—	88	70	4	—	—	—	—
1870	135	32	55	—	48	177	9	1	(Z)	(Z)	3
1880	304	74	59	—	170	391	58	3	3	1	25
1890	613	119	85	9 [2]	400	1,095	199	26	17	14	85
1900	1,139	135	141	171 [2]	692	1,355	339	62	42	27	106
1910	3,129	309	238	739	1,843	3,881	1,319	252	245	98	409
1920	6,291	753	474	1,364	3,700	7,963	3,163	777	582	235	866
1925	4,959	541	325	1,049	3,045	6,668	2,173	455	373	173	592
1930	5,806	548	418	1,243	3,597	7,397	2,458	528	417	207	629
1935	4,030	376	296	784	2,574	5,097	1,772	376	307	167	419
1940	4,232	457	354	831	2,590	5,133	1,780	350	339	159	388
1945	5,816	663	472	1,106	3,575	7,839	2,756	518	493	232	565
1950	10,626	1,136	921	1,851	6,718	14,052	5,513	999	923	455	1,212
1954	13,908	1,378	1,278	2,256	8,997	20,009	7,775	1,476	1,296	535	1,529
1959	18,324	1,797	1,766	3,002	1,759	28,233	10,878	2,223	1,701	774	2,053
1964	25,660	2,935	2,413	4,366	15,945	36,781	13,650	2,791	2,022	1,043	2,687
1969	34,611	4,081	3,145	6,214	21,170	41,645	17,444	3,748	2,545	1,445	3,471
1974	53,369	6,135	4,679	9,992	32,563	65,299	32,028	6,952	4,833	2,751	6,734
1978	89,243	11,446	9,111	17,038	51,649	116,536	56,761	12,084	8,449	4,812	11,220
1982	120,421	14,470	12,076	22,601	71,443	169,488	76,181	15,980	11,368	6,494	15,249
1987	104,079	10,884	7,348	15,102	70,746	136,274	62,906	12,418	8,126	4,909	12,519
1992	100,695	12,407	7,474	15,754	65,060	163,514	69,720	13,578	9,077	5,242	14,568
1997	122,871	16,255	9,077	20,188	77,351	193,155	84,935	16,970	11,983	7,460	19,993

Notes appear at end of table   (continued)

TABLE Da291–356   Value of farmland and buildings, by region and state: 1850–1997   *Continued*

	West									
	Mountain				Pacific					
	New Mexico	Arizona	Utah	Nevada	Total	Washington	Oregon	California	Alaska	Hawai'i
	Da347	Da348	Da349	Da350	Da351	Da352	Da353	Da354	Da355	Da356
Year	Million dollars	Million dollars	Million dollars	Million dollars	Million dollars	Million dollars	Million dollars	Million dollars	Million dollars	Million dollars
1850	2	—	(Z)	—	7	—	3	4	—	—
1860	3	—	1	(Z)	66	2	15	49	—	—
1870	2	(Z)	2	1	168	4	22	141	—	—
1880	6	1	14	5	333	14	57	262	—	—
1890	8	7	28	12	896	83	116	697	—	—
1900	21	14	51	16	1,016	116	132	708	—	60
1910	112	47	118	40	2,562	572	456	1,451	1	83
1920	222	172	244	66	4,800	920	675	3,074	1	129
1925	175	144	192	68	4,495	727	616	3,152	—	—
1930	208	184	221	64	4,939	774	631	3,419	3	112
1935	170	133	158	43	3,325	551	449	2,325	—	—
1940	188	154	154	48	3,353	593	477	2,166	4	113
1945	327	288	262	72	5,083	900	698	3,485	—	—
1950	713	604	471	136	8,538	1,470	1,216	5,650	7	195
1954	1,055	1,075	586	223	12,233	2,022	1,643	8,569	—	—
1959	1,086	1,951	755	334	17,355	2,455	1,857	13,026	18	—
1964	1,663	2,141	910	393	23,131	2,931	2,349	17,352	18	481
1969	1,960	2,664	1,040	571	24,201	3,930	2,707	16,932	20	611
1974	3,649	4,197	1,998	915	33,271	5,828	4,552	21,793	69	1,029
1978	6,634	7,550	4,087	1,922	59,775	11,114	8,588	38,152	140	1,784
1982	8,343	10,974	5,449	2,517	93,307	15,275	12,668	61,565	264	3,577
1987	8,291	10,111	4,259	2,272	73,367	11,948	9,597	48,567	317	2,938
1992	9,220	10,984	4,704	2,347	93,794	14,178	11,824	63,689	249	3,854
1997	8,801	10,360	6,894	2,474	108,220	18,409	16,316	69,768	267	3,460

(Z) Less than $500,000.

[1] Data are based on a sample of farms.

[2] Oklahoma Territory only (1890); Oklahoma Territory and Indian Territory (1900).

Sources

U.S. Bureau of the Census, *U.S. Census of Agriculture: 1925*, Summary Statistics, by States; *1945*, volume 2; *1950*, volume 2; *1954*, volume 2; *1959*, volume 2; *1964*, volume 2; *1969*, volume 2, p. 14; *1974*, volume 1, part 51, pp. IV-1, II-1-2; *1978*, volume 1, part 51, pp. 118-19; *1982*, volume 1, part 51, pp. 134-40; *1987*, volume 1, part 51, pp. 18, 179-85; *1992*, volume 1, part 51, pp. 214-20; and *1997*, volume 1, part 51, pp. 241-9.

Documentation

See the text for Table Da1–13 for a general note. Also see the text for series Da8.

Data were calculated from state and regional data on number of farms and average value of land and buildings: 1850-1964, data from U.S. Bureau of the Census, *Historical Statistics of the United States* (1975); 1969-1982, calculations provided by the table contributors; and 1987-1997, data from *U.S. Census of Agriculture, 1992* and *1997*.

TABLE Da357–422   Value of land and buildings per farm, by region and state: 1850–1997[1]

Contributed by Alan L. Olmstead and Paul W. Rhode

			Northeast								
			New England							Middle Atlantic	
	United States	Total	Total	Maine	New Hampshire	Vermont	Massachusetts	Rhode Island	Connecticut	Total	New York
	Da357	Da358	Da359	Da360	Da361	Da362	Da363	Da364	Da365	Da366	Da367
Year	Dollars	Dollars	Dollars	Dollars	Dollars	Dollars	Dollars	Dollars	Dollars	Dollars	Dollars
1850	2,258	2,971	2,221	1,173	1,890	2,129	3,202	3,170	3,240	3,361	3,250
1860	3,251	3,756	2,589	1,413	2,285	2,988	3,462	3,616	3,607	4,319	4,078
1870	2,799	4,201	2,591	1,377	2,175	3,296	3,515	3,215	3,897	4,892	4,709
1880	2,544	4,027	2,802	1,592	2,356	3,078	3,807	4,164	3,957	4,546	4,381
1890	2,909	3,856	2,577	1,589	2,270	2,469	3,710	3,977	3,605	4,374	4,280
1900	2,905	3,656	2,753	1,627	2,391	2,509	4,190	4,206	3,615	4,013	3,917
1910	5,480	4,811	3,806	2,660	3,176	3,442	5,260	5,278	5,158	5,216	5,495
1920	10,295	6,738	5,860	4,232	4,385	5,473	7,737	6,463	8,399	7,061	7,376
1925	7,764	6,407	5,678	3,943	4,113	4,940	7,611	7,139	8,689	6,684	7,243
1930	7,624	7,789	—	4,981	5,190	5,861	10,205	10,388	13,226	—	8,234
1935	4,823	5,473	—	3,425	3,783	4,286	7,285	8,144	8,828	—	5,905
1940	5,532	5,751	5,478	3,183	3,758	4,712	6,647	8,737	9,675	5,858	6,180
1945	7,917	6,685	6,244	3,785	4,280	5,080	7,167	9,883	11,826	6,875	7,275
1950	14,005	11,771	11,839	7,462	9,323	10,314	14,163	17,062	20,189	11,747	11,742
1954	20,405	15,950	15,303	9,392	11,989	12,662	18,552	26,475	25,971	16,156	15,844
1959	34,768	24,702	24,860	14,756	18,046	19,837	31,692	37,571	47,372	24,657	23,936
1964	50,646	34,130	34,762	19,979	25,402	29,733	43,492	46,030	67,429	33,964	32,797
1969	75,714	59,426	62,937	35,496	50,418	62,347	69,362	72,033	111,071	58,609	53,399
1974	147,838	121,227	125,278	80,656	118,421	130,338	128,535	153,390	196,135	120,322	109,884
1978	279,671	183,066	178,763	118,027	169,736	181,939	183,339	236,436	279,270	184,040	146,597
1982	345,456	214,218	207,446	150,487	201,171	206,616	205,677	237,141	316,317	215,876	177,988
1987	289,386	259,510	312,647	210,777	358,279	258,713	346,530	420,279	467,677	245,914	218,932
1992	357,052	350,632	384,216	241,816	342,607	318,131	460,410	481,783	624,135	341,680	282,546
1997	449,740	366,612	376,140	251,074	323,523	323,107	455,014	442,402	571,074	363,900	286,620

	Northeast		North Central								
	Middle Atlantic			East North Central						West North Central	
	New Jersey	Pennsylvania	Total	Total	Ohio	Indiana	Illinois	Michigan	Wisconsin	Total	Minnesota
	Da368	Da369	Da370	Da371	Da372	Da373	Da374	Da375	Da376	Da377	Da378
Year	Dollars	Dollars	Dollars	Dollars	Dollars	Dollars	Dollars	Dollars	Dollars	Dollars	Dollars
1850	5,030	3,197	1,718	1,824	2,495	1,453	1,261	1,522	1,414	1,153	1,032
1860	6,520	4,234	2,758	2,958	3,770	2,706	2,854	2,577	1,893	2,126	1,513
1870	6,721	4,796	3,068	3,475	4,305	3,149	3,631	3,225	2,335	2,215	1,683
1880	5,564	4,569	3,021	3,683	4,561	3,274	3,948	3,241	2,663	2,105	2,097
1890	5,166	4,359	3,675	4,065	4,176	3,809	5,247	3,227	3,262	3,245	2,910
1900	4,692	4,006	4,354	4,325	3,746	3,793	6,684	2,866	4,041	4,385	4,329
1910	6,484	4,747	9,174	7,899	6,080	7,899	13,986	4,354	6,784	10,464	8,085
1920	8,428	6,560	18,063	13,771	10,368	12,937	25,289	7,313	11,558	22,307	18,496
1925	8,848	5,838	12,740	10,483	7,951	8,661	18,615	6,676	9,830	14,875	12,717
1930	11,776	6,977	11,781	—	7,720	7,796	15,553	6,853	9,526	—	11,471
1935	7,977	4,505	7,061	—	5,007	5,180	9,536	4,205	6,238	—	6,803
1940	8,818	5,113	7,693	7,289	6,176	6,781	11,887	4,865	6,365	8,065	7,312
1945	11,171	5,872	11,116	10,441	8,470	10,197	17,933	6,843	8,069	11,739	9,705
1950	20,343	10,299	18,065	16,607	14,341	16,151	27,628	10,935	12,203	19,379	15,507
1954	29,635	14,039	25,010	23,717	20,937	24,303	40,083	15,800	14,789	26,151	21,051
1959	46,397	21,892	37,974	37,132	32,583	38,489	61,946	25,535	21,309	38,680	32,605
1964	73,487	29,836	50,244	48,656	43,373	51,645	80,894	34,027	26,765	51,539	39,075
1969	133,202	52,829	74,993	71,465	61,251	70,316	118,507	49,821	42,448	77,829	58,714
1974	234,469	112,992	148,401	138,086	119,964	137,385	221,774	93,435	85,560	156,410	120,311
1978	319,183	193,558	312,455	309,081	263,585	323,213	524,718	175,171	175,095	315,042	261,096
1982	343,137	225,794	372,204	351,974	267,899	338,549	538,886	228,238	232,606	386,858	342,593
1987	396,198	239,333	264,591	263,903	227,341	265,446	402,970	196,065	182,950	265,096	218,808
1992	615,430	328,795	339,022	337,827	291,766	346,199	539,181	247,370	210,179	339,885	310,612
1997	594,206	371,740	466,347	484,503	414,773	532,663	773,141	358,166	282,135	453,443	407,863

Notes appear at end of table

(continued)

TABLE Da357–422   Value of land and buildings per farm, by region and state: 1850–1997   *Continued*

	North Central							South			
	West North Central								South Atlantic		
	Iowa	Missouri	North Dakota	Dakota Territory	South Dakota	Nebraska	Kansas	Total	Total	Delaware	Maryland
	Da379	Da380	Da381	Da382	Da383	Da384	Da385	Da386 [2]	Da387 [2]	Da388	Da389
Year	Dollars	Dollars	Dollars	Dollars	Dollars	Dollars	Dollars	Dollars	Dollars	Dollars	Dollars
1850	1,125	1,161	—	—	—	—	—	2,051	2,323	3,114	3,988
1860	1,960	2,485	—	784	—	1,391	1,179	3,455	3,340	4,720	5,726
1870	2,701	2,119	—	970	—	1,967	1,892	1,456	1,632	4,907	5,048
1880	3,061	1,742	2,263	—	1,013	1,671	1,697	1,224	1,384	4,205	4,085
1890	4,247	2,629	2,728	—	2,143	3,542	3,359	1,402	1,515	4,220	4,291
1900	6,550	2,963	4,385	—	4,183	4,753	3,718	1,251	1,254	3,555	3,807
1910	15,008	6,190	11,063	—	12,945	13,983	9,770	2,374	2,236	4,905	4,941
1920	35,616	11,646	19,160	—	33,132	29,836	17,122	4,727	4,488	6,386	8,070
1925	23,207	7,691	13,428	—	18,071	19,760	13,250	3,685	3,699	5,818	6,966
1930	19,655	7,018	12,199	—	15,455	19,274	13,738	3,829	—	6,896	8,244
1935	11,092	3,948	8,358	—	8,305	11,696	8,469	2,553	—	4,959	5,465
1940	12,614	4,324	6,628	—	6,976	9,399	9,092	3,231	3,099	6,104	6,506
1945	17,284	6,285	10,189	—	11,124	15,205	13,962	4,564	4,062	7,820	8,596
1950	27,105	9,720	18,178	—	21,095	25,517	24,344	8,654	7,466	13,043	14,048
1954	35,090	13,815	24,110	—	28,263	33,713	33,117	12,755	11,123	20,287	21,258
1959	49,150	22,094	38,978	—	40,852	46,796	48,084	23,702	21,671	34,551	39,095
1964	59,553	33,451	58,450	—	56,615	65,268	66,397	37,931	34,496	53,443	64,999
1969	93,694	53,034	87,222	—	83,427	97,931	91,131	59,983	55,356	90,632	104,370
1974	188,370	102,074	193,574	—	155,415	192,574	179,454	118,656	118,158	180,023	184,079
1978	427,161	191,130	360,902	—	295,953	382,902	322,165	207,448	203,331	283,593	298,920
1982	471,011	223,247	486,939	—	418,940	532,741	384,197	263,930	254,727	364,843	332,301
1987	283,597	175,612	366,475	—	326,333	344,253	278,047	252,202	270,713	369,751	366,788
1992	394,267	225,015	422,936	—	360,111	429,188	343,312	286,683	343,293	514,156	503,828
1997	566,587	309,430	512,734	—	487,039	567,468	430,533	350,994	419,619	609,974	563,605

	South											
	South Atlantic							East South Central				
	Virginia	Virginia and West Virginia	West Virginia	North Carolina	South Carolina	Georgia	Florida	Total	Kentucky	Tennessee	Alabama	Mississippi
	Da390	Da391	Da392	Da393	Da394	Da395	Da396	Da397	Da398	Da399	Da400	Da401
Year	Dollars	Dollars	Dollars	Dollars	Dollars	Dollars	Dollars	Dollars	Dollars	Dollars	Dollars	Dollars
1850	—	2,810	—	1,192	2,751	1,850	1,469	1,665	2,073	1,345	1,533	1,612
1860	—	4,014	—	1,906	4,210	2,533	2,502	3,428	3,210	3,294	3,189	4,453
1870	2,308	—	2,043	669	691	1,081	777	1,461	2,103	1,481	804	961
1880	1,823	—	2,124	862	732	807	866	1,190	1,798	1,248	581	912
1890	1,994	—	2,087	1,031	862	889	2,125	1,262	1,932	1,392	704	883
1900	1,618	—	1,812	867	816	816	1,000	1,034	1,628	1,180	603	688
1910	2,891	—	2,735	1,800	1,887	1,647	2,362	1,668	2,452	1,953	1,096	1,218
1920	5,501	—	4,706	3,990	4,222	3,663	5,212	3,484	4,823	4,055	2,123	2,903
1925	4,578	—	3,941	3,267	2,649	2,359	8,088	2,466	3,278	3,006	1,746	1,785
1930	5,016	—	4,138	3,018	2,401	2,259	7,179	—	3,535	3,025	1,952	1,818
1935	3,005	—	2,269	2,069	1,725	1,715	4,407	—	2,229	2,030	1,347	1,190
1940	3,860	—	2,718	2,647	2,461	2,223	5,211	2,272	3,070	2,683	1,764	1,632
1945	5,021	—	3,494	3,490	2,982	2,896	8,149	3,224	4,259	3,715	2,506	2,457
1950	8,458	—	5,983	6,605	5,886	5,623	16,617	5,662	7,196	6,182	4,809	4,566
1954	11,369	—	7,248	8,758	7,769	8,710	33,627	7,709	8,900	8,049	6,816	7,053
1959	18,635	—	10,230	15,475	15,685	17,944	73,554	13,962	15,269	13,288	12,780	14,292
1964	27,572	—	13,882	24,442	24,948	29,155	109,053	21,897	22,235	20,509	20,552	24,322
1969	47,191	—	25,450	35,551	46,171	54,883	139,818	37,135	32,309	33,176	37,596	51,611
1974	102,388	—	62,094	72,672	98,609	119,766	278,479	71,914	60,344	65,308	76,049	101,102
1978	171,658	—	119,153	141,464	171,558	200,201	407,118	138,914	124,233	125,238	138,257	200,646
1982	205,034	—	129,390	187,840	208,524	225,092	552,586	164,150	144,427	139,141	171,210	257,819
1987	232,374	—	130,802	199,781	201,169	226,217	543,830	155,519	135,696	146,126	168,161	215,209
1992	320,488	—	165,088	269,000	251,583	280,562	619,295	191,511	163,660	186,171	220,265	248,479
1997	384,979	—	212,832	375,895	324,834	392,577	662,538	267,066	230,274	261,209	298,244	337,081

Notes appear at end of table

TABLE Da357–422   Value of land and buildings per farm, by region and state: 1850–1997   *Continued*

	South					West					
	West South Central						Mountain				
	Total	Arkansas	Louisiana	Oklahoma	Texas	Total	Total	Montana	Idaho	Wyoming	Colorado
	Da402	Da403	Da404	Da405	Da406	Da407	Da408	Da409	Da410	Da411	Da412
Year	Dollars	Dollars	Dollars	Dollars	Dollars	Dollars	Dollars	Dollars	Dollars	Dollars	Dollars
1850	2,481	860	5,649	—	1,357	1,295	420	—	—	—	—
1860	3,876	2,350	11,818	—	2,054	2,033	493	—	—	—	—
1870	969	648	1,916	—	787	3,662	651	685	952	83	1,558
1880	958	786	1,222	—	979	4,669	2,319	2,129	1,503	1,829	5,572
1890	1,421	950	1,232	972 [3]	1,753	7,506	4,019	4,553	2,640	4,627	5,189
1900	1,509	757	1,217	1,582 [3]	1,964	5,329	3,342	4,639	2,422	4,424	4,305
1910	3,317	1,440	1,971	3,884	4,412	10,271	7,192	9,599	7,955	8,912	8,848
1920	6,316	3,238	3,499	7,104	8,486	16,455	12,958	13,468	13,811	14,907	14,449
1925	4,875	2,436	2,451	5,318	6,540	13,364	9,310	9,709	9,197	11,132	10,211
1930	—	2,261	2,590	6,096	7,260	14,518	—	11,109	10,012	12,919	10,497
1935	—	1,486	1,736	3,677	5,137	8,928	—	7,433	6,814	9,537	6,580
1940	4,388	2,108	2,359	4,625	6,196	9,962	7,623	8,373	7,768	10,585	7,550
1945	6,626	3,334	3,653	6,713	9,286	15,853	12,969	13,720	11,888	17,746	11,855
1950	13,616	6,225	7,416	13,016	20,263	30,029	28,294	28,475	22,920	36,060	26,588
1954	20,817	9,496	11,497	18,964	30,711	47,334	43,191	44,653	33,466	46,935	37,513
1959	37,306	18,915	23,719	31,710	51,787	80,870	72,967	76,761	50,528	79,447	61,494
1964	58,826	36,734	38,636	49,212	77,756	120,383	101,780	103,271	68,178	115,355	90,183
1969	86,681	67,532	74,414	74,838	99,133	157,091	145,486	150,222	99,916	163,529	124,180
1974	162,717	120,382	140,754	143,320	187,073	273,199	286,303	298,070	204,091	343,063	264,065
1978	269,818	221,156	290,454	235,858	294,473	458,966	487,082	512,791	348,408	598,623	416,988
1982	354,497	286,402	381,817	311,642	386,138	606,239	625,575	677,995	459,965	732,875	562,479
1987	311,049	225,604	268,630	215,024	374,742	489,411	506,450	505,526	336,615	533,284	458,906
1992	317,480	282,389	291,332	235,359	360,153	619,728	589,974	594,881	410,206	601,437	536,510
1997	364,084	360,114	380,871	271,996	398,126	730,209	700,021	699,069	536,521	808,346	707,165

	West									
	Mountain				Pacific					
	New Mexico	Arizona	Utah	Nevada	Total	Washington	Oregon	California	Alaska	Hawai'i
	Da413	Da414	Da415	Da416	Da417	Da418	Da419	Da420	Da421	Da422
Year	Dollars	Dollars	Dollars	Dollars	Dollars	Dollars	Dollars	Dollars	Dollars	Dollars
1850	441	—	337	—	3,302	—	2,448	4,443	—	—
1860	532	—	367	3,322	2,559	1,668	2,618	2,603	—	—
1870	404	750	375	1,434	4,866	1,272	2,946	5,953	—	—
1880	1,091	1,471	1,483	3,852	5,672	2,120	3,509	7,293	—	—
1890	1,826	5,065	2,701	9,663	9,291	4,622	4,537	13,180	—	—
1900	1,697	2,355	2,619	7,150	6,751	3,482	3,693	9,759	—	26,410
1910	3,135	5,125	5,423	14,730	13,050	10,179	10,012	16,447	3,908	19,197
1920	7,432	17,276	9,499	20,947	19,941	13,885	13,449	26,122	3,329	24,438
1925	5,520	13,332	7,395	17,512	16,926	9,921	11,019	23,111	—	—
1930	6,619	12,999	8,135	18,626	—	10,911	11,438	25,203	5,714	18,771
1935	4,113	7,047	5,157	11,518	—	6,527	6,922	15,466	—	—
1940	5,498	8,321	6,074	13,321	11,720	7,264	7,712	16,331	6,165	22,580
1945	11,004	21,905	9,947	20,985	18,028	11,268	11,054	25,084	—	—
1950	30,228	57,996	19,492	43,700	31,266	21,057	20,327	41,192	12,465	33,961
1954	50,078	115,330	25,652	78,162	50,406	31,018	30,178	69,620	—	—
1959	68,233	269,724	42,391	141,974	89,632	47,590	43,608	131,212	48,379	—
1964	117,042	330,549	57,747	182,436	134,929	64,304	59,079	214,650	47,150	98,936
1969	168,336	452,241	79,705	270,507	166,674	115,487	93,134	217,429	61,541	156,800
1974	323,418	723,169	163,989	440,806	261,669	198,154	170,145	322,034	237,938	340,569
1978	538,888	1,198,843	320,234	801,173	435,116	358,679	301,308	521,240	364,527	413,948
1982	618,708	1,496,334	389,678	925,540	591,317	423,352	371,644	746,577	463,849	778,471
1987	582,012	1,317,765	302,838	749,936	475,689	355,976	299,755	583,668	553,000	603,435
1992	645,677	1,621,530	347,982	811,941	643,867	468,482	370,938	820,063	486,550	722,189
1997	625,307	1,689,258	486,235	876,417	755,790	634,619	479,385	941,170	486,827	632,281

Notes appear on next page

(continued)

TABLE Da357–422 Value of land and buildings per farm, by region and state: 1850–1997 *Continued*

[1] Data are based on a sample of farms.

[2] Washington, D.C., is not reported separately but is included in the totals for the South and South Atlantic.

[3] Oklahoma Territory only (1890), Oklahoma Territory and Indian Territory (1900).

Sources

U.S. Bureau of the Census, *U.S. Census of Agriculture: 1925*, Summary Statistics, by States; *1945*, volume 2; *1950*, volume 2; *1954*, volume 2; *1959*, volume 2; *1964*, volume 2; *1969*, volume 2; *1974*, volume 1, part 51, pp. II-1–2; *1978*, volume 1, part 51, pp. 118–19; *1982*, volume 1, part 51, pp. 134–40; *1987*,

volume 1, part 51, pp. 179–85; *1992*, volume 1, part 51, pp. 214–20; and *1997*, volume 1, part 51, pp. 241–9.

Documentation

See the text for Table Da1–13 for a general note. Also see the text for series Da11.

Beginning in 1978 regional data was calculated: value of land and buildings for all states in region divided by total number of farms for all states in region.

TABLE Da423–486 Value of farm products sold, by region and state: 1925–1997

Contributed by Alan L. Olmstead and Paul W. Rhode

		Northeast											
		New England								Middle Atlantic			
	United States	Total	Total	Maine	New Hampshire	Vermont	Massachusetts	Rhode Island	Connecticut	Total	New York	New Jersey	Pennsylvania
	Da423	Da424	Da425	Da426	Da427	Da428	Da429	Da430	Da431	Da432	Da433	Da434	Da435
Year	Million dollars	Million dollars	Million dollars	Million dollars	Million dollars	Million dollars	Million dollars	Million dollars	Million dollars	Million dollars	Million dollars	Million dollars	Million dollars
1925 [1]	858	71	21	4	(Z)	4	4	1	8	50	38	2	10
1930	9,610	978	278	81	24	48	68	9	48	699	343	83	273
1940	6,682	723	208	42	19	33	63	8	44	515	242	74	198
1945	16,231	1,490	425	96	39	70	115	15	89	1,065	504	166	396
1950	22,217	1,922	532	126	46	87	135	16	121	1,391	630	214	546
1954	24,645	2,049	535	140	45	86	125	15	123	1,514	668	242	604
1959	30,493	2,292	593	171	48	109	126	18	120	1,699	755	231	713
1964	35,292	2,575	716	256	49	115	139	19	139	1,859	853	216	791
1969 [2]	45,564	2,822	683	198	49	136	139	16	146	2,138	979	214	945
1974	81,526	4,291	1,028	360	72	208	180	22	187	3,263	1,462	297	1,503
1978	107,073	5,594	1,216	394	88	271	212	26	226	4,378	1,861	350	2,167
1982	131,900	7,180	1,468	399	103	369	281	30	285	5,711	2,427	436	2,848
1987	136,049	7,639	1,624	405	107	376	340	38	358	6,015	2,442	496	3,078
1992	162,608	8,412	1,687	430	114	415	351	40	337	6,725	2,622	533	3,570
1997	196,865	9,516	1,987	439	149	476	454	48	422	7,529	2,835	697	3,998

		North Central										
		East North Central						West North Central				
	Total	Total	Ohio	Indiana	Illinois	Michigan	Wisconsin	Total	Minnesota	Iowa	Missouri	North Dakota
	Da436	Da437	Da438	Da439	Da440	Da441	Da442	Da443	Da444	Da445	Da446	Da447
Year	Million dollars	Million dollars	Million dollars	Million dollars	Million dollars	Million dollars	Million dollars	Million dollars	Million dollars	Million dollars	Million dollars	Million dollars
1925 [1]	437	145	28	17	53	20	27	292	73	81	33	17
1930	4,140	1,608	315	265	455	227	346	2,531	361	621	329	194
1940	2,923	1,302	254	217	415	178	239	1,620	301	512	215	100
1945	7,047	2,953	533	492	954	366	608	4,094	637	1,152	506	365
1950	9,733	4,044	712	732	1,362	474	765	5,689	961	1,635	720	401
1954	10,647	4,594	844	906	1,506	545	793	6,053	984	1,840	734	376
1959	13,002	5,203	863	946	1,811	623	961	7,799	1,212	2,284	1,012	469
1964	14,838	6,105	1,013	1,105	2,123	766	1,097	8,733	1,376	2,597	1,053	570
1969 [2]	20,080	7,544	1,246	1,400	2,612	829	1,455	12,536	1,748	3,656	1,460	749
1974	36,357	13,385	2,263	2,613	4,665	1,491	2,353	22,972	3,470	6,320	2,304	1,803
1978	47,318	17,484	2,860	3,358	5,906	1,914	3,445	29,834	4,523	8,173	3,311	1,784
1982	59,335	22,371	3,387	4,227	7,314	2,588	4,855	36,964	5,940	9,829	3,607	2,294
1987	57,633	21,333	3,434	4,068	6,377	2,545	4,910	36,299	5,676	8,927	3,645	2,188
1992	67,567	24,172	3,914	4,633	7,337	3,029	5,260	43,395	6,477	10,100	4,303	2,746
1997	78,701	27,618	4,684	5,230	8,556	3,568	5,580	51,083	8,290	11,948	5,368	2,869

Notes appear at end of table

TABLE Da423–486   Value of farm products sold, by region and state: 1925–1997   Continued

	North Central			South									
	West North Central				South Atlantic								
	South Dakota	Nebraska	Kansas	Total	Total	Delaware	Maryland	Virginia	West Virginia	North Carolina	South Carolina	Georgia	Florida
	Da448	Da449	Da450	Da451	Da452	Da453	Da454	Da455	Da456	Da457	Da458	Da459	Da460
Year	Million dollars	Million dollars	Million dollars	Million dollars	Million dollars	Million dollars	Million dollars	Million dollars	Million dollars	Million dollars	Million dollars	Million dollars	Million dollars
1925 [1]	19	33	37	199	73	(Z)	7	21	1	13	9	9	13
1930	212	398	418	2,903	922	18	77	155	53	221	117	197	83
1940	96	192	204	1,921	700	16	55	108	30	199	87	122	80
1945	286	543	604	4,632	1,735	62	137	248	63	489	192	302	240
1950	430	778	765	6,359	2,125	76	172	310	82	557	214	375	339
1954	436	881	802	7,025	2,631	82	195	364	90	733	252	448	466
1959	514	1,198	1,111	8,884	3,248	86	231	424	99	797	303	607	700
1964	629	1,334	1,175	10,586	4,142	108	276	470	92	1,068	349	826	954
1969 [2]	958	2,148	1,818	13,328	4,873	129	340	570	105	1,195	362	1,040	1,132
1974	1,660	3,733	3,682	23,364	8,520	251	620	960	133	2,121	676	1,860	1,899
1978	1,898	5,149	4,996	32,423	11,762	321	785	1,261	194	2,980	855	2,341	3,026
1982	2,478	6,626	6,191	37,391	14,008	371	1,029	1,607	242	3,501	969	2,768	3,522
1987	2,719	6,667	6,477	40,267	14,878	444	989	1,589	271	3,541	879	2,815	4,351
1992	3,244	8,210	8,316	49,474	18,837	560	1,169	2,056	364	4,834	1,066	3,521	5,266
1997	3,570	9,832	9,207	61,908	25,024	691	1,312	2,344	447	7,677	1,588	4,993	6,005

	South										West		
	East South Central					West South Central						Mountain	
	Total	Kentucky	Tennessee	Alabama	Mississippi	Total	Arkansas	Louisiana	Oklahoma	Texas	Total	Total	Montana
	Da461	Da462	Da463	Da464	Da465	Da466	Da467	Da468	Da469	Da470	Da471	Da472	Da473
Year	Million dollars	Million dollars	Million dollars	Million dollars	Million dollars	Million dollars	Million dollars	Million dollars	Million dollars	Million dollars	Million dollars	Million dollars	Million dollars
1925 [1]	50	28	7	7	8	76	7	9	21	39	151	35	3
1930	727	170	162	165	230	1,255	187	137	264	666	1,589	672	129
1940	428	128	107	77	115	793	118	90	146	439	1,115	449	84
1945	1,082	338	247	213	284	1,815	269	178	369	1,000	3,062	1,068	223
1950	1,371	417	341	274	340	2,863	393	246	471	1,753	4,203	1,631	279
1954	1,542	425	353	304	460	2,853	492	310	409	1,642	4,924	1,810	339
1959	1,972	518	475	414	566	3,664	639	335	581	2,109	6,315	2,356	377
1964	2,382	592	529	537	724	4,063	830	407	601	2,225	7,293	2,537	390
1969 [2]	2,725	770	623	647	685	5,730	973	496	969	3,291	9,334	3,839	576
1974	4,537	1,252	933	1,122	1,229	10,308	1,881	1,194	1,595	5,638	17,514	6,820	1,033
1978	6,403	1,813	1,396	1,531	1,664	14,258	2,487	1,212	2,330	8,229	21,745	8,706	1,177
1982	7,683	2,377	1,684	1,704	1,918	15,699	2,826	1,406	2,530	8,936	27,995	10,461	1,547
1987	7,464	2,076	1,618	1,908	1,863	17,924	3,320	1,340	2,715	10,549	30,509	11,194	1,547
1992	9,303	2,664	1,934	2,369	2,337	21,334	4,160	1,608	3,563	12,004	37,155	13,422	1,730
1997	11,460	3,064	2,178	3,099	3,127	25,424	5,480	2,031	4,146	13,767	46,695	15,405	1,871

Notes appear at end of table

(continued)

TABLE Da423–486   Value of farm products sold, by region and state: 1925–1997 *Continued*

West

	Mountain							Pacific					
	Idaho	Wyoming	Colorado	New Mexico	Arizona	Utah	Nevada	Total	Washington	Oregon	California	Alaska	Hawai'i
	Da474	Da475	Da476	Da477	Da478	Da479	Da480	Da481	Da482	Da483	Da484	Da485	Da486
Year	Million dollars	Million dollars	Million dollars	Million dollars	Million dollars	Million dollars	Million dollars	Million dollars	Million dollars	Million dollars	Million dollars	Million dollars	Million dollars
1925 [1]	3	1	21	3	2	2	(Z)	116	21	8	87	—	—
1930	127	59	177	56	47	59	19	916	184	125	608	—	—
1940	84	46	102	43	43	39	40	11	666	117	99	452	—	—
1945	215	83	251	82	95	97	23	1,994	354	239	1,400	—	—
1950	281	122	426	155	204	130	34	2,571	365	298	1,742	2	165
1954	332	115	380	155	328	127	34	3,113	506	346	2,261	—	—
1959	438	162	580	197	388	156	57	3,959	569	412	2,822	3	152
1964	478	151	612	227	469	159	51	4,756	637	428	3,499	4	188
1969 [2]	650	249	1,101	359	611	213	81	5,495	771	531	3,904	4	286
1974	1,381	361	1,970	522	1,081	339	133	10,694	1,658	1,025	7,395	7	610
1978	1,633	530	2,590	792	1,311	465	199	13,039	2,075	1,262	9,274	8	419
1982	2,232	606	2,941	851	1,527	555	203	17,533	2,831	1,641	12,491	11	559
1987	2,269	677	3,143	1,060	1,629	618	250	19,316	2,920	1,846	13,922	18	610
1992	2,964	824	4,116	1,259	1,515	725	288	23,734	3,821	2,293	17,052	15	552
1997	3,346	899	4,534	1,618	1,903	877	357	31,290	4,768	2,969	23,032	25	497

(Z) Less than $500,000.

[1] Products sold through cooperative marketing organizations only.

[2] Procedures used differ from previous years; see text.

Sources

U.S. Bureau of the Census, *U.S. Census of Agriculture: 1925*, Summary Statistics, by States; *1945*, volume 2; *1950*, volume 2; *1954*, volume 2; *1959*, volume 2; *1964*, volume 2; *1969*, volume 2; *1974*, volume 1, part 51, pp. IV-2–IV-380; *1978*, volume 1, part 51, pp. 211, 221–506; *1982*, volume 1, part 51, pp. 148–54; *1987*, volume 1, part 51, pp. 151–7; *1992*; volume 1, part 51, pp. 176–82; and *1997*, volume 1, part 51, pp. 193–201.

Documentation

See the text for Table Da1–13 for a general note.

Data for the value of farm products sold in 1969 were obtained by direct questioning. This procedure was a departure from the one used in previous censuses, in which data on value of sales were obtained by enumeration for some products and by estimation for others.

For 1969, value of farm products sold excludes income that the farm operator and members of the operator's family received from providing hunting, fishing, picnicking, camping, boarding and lodging, or other recreational services on the farm; for 1964 and prior censuses, recreation income was included. The value of farm products sold does not include government payments received by farm operators for participation in wheat, feed grains, and other government programs.

TABLE Da487–496   Farm operators, by sex, race, and region: 1880–1997[1]

Contributed by Alan L. Olmstead and Paul W. Rhode

		Race		Sex			Residence				
								South			
	Total	White	Nonwhite	Male	Female	North	Total	White	Nonwhite	West
	Da487	Da488	Da489	Da490	Da491	Da492	Da493	Da494	Da495	Da496
Year	Number	Number	Number	Number	Number	Number	Number	Number	Number	Number
1880	4,008,907	—	—	—	—	2,394,107	1,531,077	—	—	83,723
1890	4,564,641	—	—	—	—	2,582,391	1,836,372	—	—	145,878
1900	5,739,657	4,970,129	769,528	—	—	2,874,073	2,620,391	1,879,721	740,670	245,193
1910	6,361,502	5,440,619	920,883	—	—	2,890,618	3,097,547	2,207,406	890,141	373,337
1920	6,453,991	5,499,707	954,284	—	—	2,763,406	3,206,664	2,283,750	922,914	483,921
1925	6,371,640	—	—	—	—	2,741,243	3,131,418	2,299,963	831,455	498,979
1930	6,295,103	5,373,703	921,400	—	—	2,561,785	3,223,816	2,342,129	881,687	509,502
1935	6,812,350	5,956,795	855,555	—	—	2,819,468	3,421,923	2,606,176	815,747	570,959
1940	6,102,417	5,378,913	723,504	—	—	2,579,959	3,007,170	2,326,904	680,266	515,288
1945	5,859,169	5,169,954	689,215	—	—	2,483,578	2,881,135	2,215,722	665,413	494,456

Note appears on next page

TABLE Da487–496 Farm operators, by sex, race, and region: 1880–1997 *Continued*

		Race		Sex			Residence			
								South		
	Total	White	Nonwhite	Male	Female	North	Total	White	Nonwhite	West
	Da487	Da488	Da489	Da490	Da491	Da492	Da493	Da494	Da495	Da496
Year	Number	Number	Number	Number	Number	Number	Number	Number	Number	Number
1950	5,388,437	4,802,520	585,917	—	—	2,268,066	2,652,423	2,093,333	559,090	467,948
1954	4,782,416	4,298,766	483,650	—	—	2,043,092	2,316,607	1,851,391	465,216	422,717
1959	3,710,503	3,419,672	290,831	—	—	1,715,441	1,645,949	1,374,350	271,599	349,113
1964	3,157,857	2,957,905	199,952	—	—	1,479,581	1,372,732	1,188,154	184,578	305,544
1969	2,730,250	2,639,744	90,506	—	—	1,303,750	1,161,399	1,076,150	85,249	265,101
1974	2,314,013	2,254,642	59,371	—	—	1,144,898	930,099	882,895	47,204	239,016
1978	2,257,775	2,199,787	57,988	2,144,976	112,799	—	—	—	—	—
1982	2,240,976	2,186,609	54,367	2,119,377	121,599	—	—	—	—	—
1987	2,087,759	2,043,119	44,640	1,956,118	131,641	—	—	—	—	—
1992	1,925,300	1,881,813	43,487	1,780,144	145,156	—	—	—	—	—
1997	1,911,859	1,864,201	47,658	1,746,757	165,102	—	—	—	—	—

[1] Excludes Alaska and Hawai'i: 1910, 1925, 1935, 1945, and 1954.

Sources

U.S. Bureau of the Census, *U.S. Census of Agriculture: 1969*, volume 2, chapter 3, p. 14; *1974*, volume 2, part 3, p. I-84; *1978*, volume 1, part 51, p. 2, *1987*, volume 1, part 51, p. 20; and *1997*, volume 1, part 51, p. 24.

Documentation

See the text for Table Da1–13 for a general note.

The term "farm operator" is used to designate a person who operates a farm, either doing the work him- or herself or directly supervising the work. The farm operator may be the owner; a member of the owner's household; a salaried manager; or a tenant, renter, or sharecropper. If the operator rents land to others or has land worked on shares by others, he or she is considered operator only of the land retained for his or her own operation. In the case of a partnership, only one partner is counted as an operator. For census purposes the number of farm operators, series Da487, is the same as the number of farms. A farm operator may spend a few hours a week on a "farm" producing only a few hundred dollars worth of farm products while partly or fully employed elsewhere, or be working full time as operator of a "farm" producing hundreds of thousands of dollars worth of farm products a year.

Generally, data from the 1974 Census and later censuses are comparable. The 1974 and later censuses, however, are not comparable to earlier censuses because of the change in the definition of a farm. Before 1974, the definition of a farm was any place with less than ten acres from which $250 or more of agricultural products were sold or normally would have been sold during the census year, or any place of ten acres or more from which $50 or more of agricultural products were sold or normally would have been sold during the census year. The current definition of a farm, first used in the 1974 Census, is any establishment that during the census year had or normally would have had sales of agricultural products of $1,000 or more.

For the most part, data from the 1969 Census and earlier censuses are comparable. However, a difference in timing and the change from personal interview to mail enumeration affect the comparability of some of the data from 1969 and later censuses with those from earlier censuses. Starting in 1969, the census was conducted by mailout/mailback. Generally the quality of data on reports completed by operators exceeds that of reports filled out by enumerators. The 1969 Census forms were mailed just prior to January 1, 1970. Extensive mail, telephone, and enumerator follow-up procedures extended the data-collection phase through September 1970. Prior censuses were taken by enumerators, each assigned to a specific geographic area. Field work for the 1964 Census was completed largely in November and December 1964, whereas most of the field work for 1959 was accomplished during October and November. In censuses prior to 1959, the time of enumeration varied from late fall to April 1 to January 1 and even to June 1.

All censuses since 1969 were conducted primarily by mail. To improve the coverage of the 1978 Census, the mailout/mailback enumeration was supplemented by the direct enumeration of all households in approximately 6,400 sample segments in rural area in all states, except Alaska and Hawai'i. The data for 1978 shown in the 1978 Census of Agriculture publications included data for farms represented on the mail list plus estimates from the area sample for farms not on the mail list. To provide comparable data for 1978 and later censuses, estimates from the 1978 area sample have been subtracted from the 1978 data. Thus, the 1978 data in the 1982 and 1987 Censuses include only farms represented on the mail list. All 1978 figures are taken from the 1987 or 1982 Censuses of Agriculture to ensure comparability.

Classification by race of the farm operator was first made in the Census of 1900. Since 1900, the race classification has consisted of two major groups, "white" and "all other," and for a limited number of items, a more detailed breakdown by race. The detailed breakdown, since 1954, has provided for a separate count of black and other races. For decennial censuses prior to 1954, separate totals are available for black, American Indian, Chinese, Japanese, Filipino, and other races.

Classification of farm operators by gender began in 1978.

See Appendix 2 regarding the composition of census regions and divisions. The North, in series Da492, represents the sum of the Northeast and North Central regions.

TABLE Da497–500 Farm operators, by residence on or off farm: 1940–1997[1]

Contributed by Alan L. Olmstead and Paul W. Rhode

	Total	On farm	Off farm	Not reporting
	Da497	Da498	Da499	Da500
Year	Number	Number	Number	Number
1940	6,102,417	5,506,322	313,598	276,879
1945	5,859,169	5,459,841	336,893	62,435
1950	5,388,437	4,987,134	269,546	131,757
1954	4,782,416	4,392,205	289,876	100,335
1959	3,710,503	3,236,247	266,988	207,268
1964	3,157,857	2,773,815	290,971	93,071
1969	2,730,250	1,982,738	457,679	289,833
1974 [2]	2,314,013	1,502,488	371,833	439,692
1978 [3]	2,257,775	1,585,704	421,790	250,281
1982	2,240,976	1,581,101	429,322	230,553
1987	2,087,759	1,487,937	442,613	157,209
1992	1,925,300	1,378,701	408,560	138,039
1997	1,911,859	1,361,766	412,554	137,539

[1] Excludes Alaska and Hawai'i: 1940, 1945, and 1954.

[2] Data apply only to individual or family operations (sole proprietorships) and partnerships.

[3] Data taken from the 1987 Census; see text for Table Da487–496.

Sources

U.S. Bureau of the Census, *U.S. Census of Agriculture: 1969*, volume 2, chapter 3, p. 174; *1974*, volume 2, part 3, p. III-20; *1982*, volume 1, part 2, p. 3, *1987*, volume 1, part 51, p. 20; *1992*, volume 1, part 51, p. 22; and *1997*, volume 1, part 51, p. 24.

Documentation

See the text for Table Da487–496. See also the text for Table Da1–13 for a general note.

Farm operators were classified by residence on the basis of their reporting whether or not they lived on the farm operated. Data as to residence of the farm operators have been collected for the last seven censuses of agriculture, beginning with 1940. Except for 1964, when the instructions were to include operators who lived on the farm "any time" during the year, the inquiries have been similar and no time limitations were used. The instructions used for 1964 did not have a significant effect on the comparability of the 1964 data with other censuses.

TABLE Da501–512 Farm operators, by age: 1890–1997[1]

Contributed by Alan L. Olmstead and Paul W. Rhode

	Total	Under 25	25–34	35–44	45–54	55–64	55 or older	65–69	65 or older	70 or older	Average age	Age not reported
	Da501	Da502	Da503	Da504	Da505	Da506	Da507	Da508	Da509	Da510	Da511	Da512
Year	Number	Number	Number	Number	Number	Number	Number	Number	Number	Number	Years	Number
1890 [2]	4,564,641	218,531	1,082,620	1,182,056	1,034,792	—	1,249,180	—	—	—	—	—
1900 [2]	5,739,657	275,098	1,194,482	1,409,829	1,296,147	864,769	—	—	595,422	—	—	13,000
1910	6,361,502	419,330	1,413,876	1,571,469	1,432,707	947,524	—	—	554,570	—	—	22,000
1920	6,453,991	383,680	1,333,020	1,587,519	1,482,494	993,771	—	—	583,679	—	—	84,000
1925	6,371,640	—	—	—	—	—	—	—	—	—	—	—
1930	6,295,103	371,679	1,049,052	1,452,425	1,459,959	1,064,034	—	—	676,374	—	—	215,000
1935	6,812,350	—	—	—	—	—	—	—	—	—	—	—
1940	6,102,417	233,492	949,931	1,252,038	1,429,148	1,147,903	—	—	828,933	—	—	261,000
1945	5,859,169	147,296	854,058	1,323,786	1,432,434	1,173,014	—	—	867,047	—	48.7	61,000
1950	5,388,437	163,966	792,352	1,188,211	1,158,553	1,001,627	—	—	745,337	—	—	335,000
1954	4,782,416	90,856	619,984	1,100,458	1,153,679	951,310	—	—	779,282	—	49.6	87,000
1959	3,710,503	61,527	403,410	806,106	980,018	802,658	—	—	617,270	—	50.5	37,000
1964	3,157,857	53,182	309,203	653,509	851,338	742,334	—	—	548,291	—	51.3	—
1969	2,730,250	52,905	273,662	522,698	723,977	704,014	—	—	452,994	—	51.2	—
1974 [3]	2,314,013	52,418	239,674	400,059	577,064	588,584	—	—	421,471	—	51.7	—
1978	2,257,775	66,575	285,420	433,900	549,159	552,175	—	—	370,546	—	50.3	—
1982	2,240,976	62,336	293,810	443,420	505,412	536,402	—	—	399,596	—	50.5	—
1987	2,087,759	35,851	242,688	411,153	454,910	495,816	—	191,435	—	255,906	52.0	—
1992	1,925,300	27,906	178,826	381,746	429,333	429,839	—	188,165	—	289,485	53.3	—
1997	1,911,859	20,850	128,455	371,442	466,729	427,354	—	179,858	—	317,171	54.3	—

TABLE Da501–512   Farm operators, by age: 1890–1997   *Continued*

[1] Excludes Alaska and Hawai'i: 1900–1920, 1930, 1945, and 1954.

[2] Figures are for occupants of farm homes. In 1900, the number of occupants of farm homes was 88,364 less than the number of farm operators, while in 1890, occupants exceeded operators by 202,358.

[3] Data apply only to individuals or family operations (sole proprietorships) and partnerships.

Sources

U.S. Bureau of the Census, *U.S. Census of Agriculture: 1925*, Summary Statistics, by States; *1945*, volume 2; *1950*, volume 2; *1954*, volume 2; *1959*, volume 2; *1964*, volume 2; *1969*, volume 2, chapter 3, p. 179; *1982*, volume 1, part 51, p. 4; *1987*, volume 1, part 51, p. 20; *1992*, volume 1, part 51, p. 22; *1997*, volume 1, part 51, p. 24.

Documentation

See the text for Table Da487–496. See also the text for Table Da1–13 for a general note.

Data on age of farm operators have been obtained in each of the decennial censuses beginning with 1910 and also in the Censuses of Agriculture for 1945, 1954, 1959, 1964, and 1969. No data on age of operators were obtained in the Censuses of 1925 and 1935. For both 1964 and 1969, the operator's age was imputed if it was not reported. Tabulated data for 1964 and 1969 therefore show an age for each farm operator. The number of operators for which age was not reported is shown for prior censuses. Average age of operators was tabulated in 1945 and 1954 through 1997.

TABLE Da513–517   Farm operators, by years on present farm: 1910–1997[1]

Contributed by Alan L. Olmstead and Paul W. Rhode

	Total	Years on present farm			
		Less than 5	5–9	10 or more	Not reported
	Da513	Da514 [2]	Da515	Da516	Da517
Year	Number	Number	Number	Number	Number
1910	6,361,502	2,999,760	992,468	1,802,540	566,734
1920	6,453,991	2,956,690	1,086,458	2,184,391	220,804
1925	6,371,640	2,984,560	1,215,291	2,018,628	153,161
1930	6,295,103	2,710,092	939,418	2,393,650	251,943
1935	6,812,350	2,909,174	1,080,447	2,687,621	135,108
1940	6,102,417	2,148,786	944,513	2,517,295	491,823
1945	5,859,169	2,432,860	957,489	2,336,194	132,346
1950	5,388,437	1,857,874	1,012,262	2,194,113	321,276
1954	4,782,416	1,010,935	1,171,866	2,487,488	112,732
1959	3,710,503	638,599	629,773	2,339,976	99,625
1964	3,157,857	611,862	469,147	1,905,801	171,047
1969	2,730,250	429,456	330,645	1,385,261	584,888
1974	2,314,013	—	—	—	—
1978	2,257,775	—	—	—	—
1982	2,240,976	319,890	360,458	1,097,660	462,968
1987	2,087,759	249,027	303,875	1,163,336	371,521
1992	1,925,300	227,790	258,767	1,112,827	325,916
1997	1,911,859	219,365	263,642	1,113,839	315,013

[1] Excludes Alaska and Hawai'i: 1910–1925, 1935, 1945, and 1954.

[2] Beginning 1982, values are the sum of the categories "two years or less" and "three or four years."

Sources

U.S. Bureau of the Census, *U.S. Census of Agriculture: 1925*, Summary Statistics, by States; *1945*, volume 2; *1950*, volume 2; *1954*, volume 2; *1959*, volume 2; *1964*, volume 2, chapter 5, p. 518; *1969*, volume 2, chapter 3, p. 178; *1978*, volume 1, part 51, p. 3; *1982*, volume 1, part 51, p. 4; *1992*, volume 1, part 51, p. 22; *1997*, volume 1, part 51, p. 24.

Documentation

See the text for Table Da487–496. See also the text for Table Da1–13 for a general note.

The data for years on present farm reflect the continuity of operators on particular farms. They do not refer to years of farm experience. Information for years on farm has been obtained for each Census of Agriculture beginning with 1910. In the Censuses of 1925, 1930, and 1950 through 1964, the inquiry called for the month as well as the year of occupancy. For 1935, 1940, and 1945, only the year of occupancy was asked. The report forms for 1910 and 1920 asked for the number of years and months the operator had operated the farm occupied at the time of the census. For each census, the data for years on farm have been summarized by groups of "years on present farm." The number of years or months comprising these groups of "years on present farm" have not always been the same, largely owing to changes in the date of census enumeration. The group "less than five years" has been subdivided for some censuses. The difference between censuses in elapsed time from the beginning of the calendar year to the date the census reports were completed affects the data for the "less than five years" group more than that for the other groups.

TABLE Da518–529   Farm operators, by number of days worked off farm: 1930–1997[1]

Contributed by Alan L. Olmstead and Paul W. Rhode

Year	Total	Worked off the farm								Did not work off the farm or did not report	Did not work off the farm	Did not report
		Any days	1–49 days	50–99 days	Less than 100 days	100–149 days	150–199 days	100–199 days	200 or more days			
	Da518	Da519	Da520	Da521	Da522	Da523	Da524	Da525	Da526	Da527	Da528	Da529
	Number	Number	Number	Number	Number	Number	Number	Number	Number	Number	Number	Number
1930	6,295,103	1,902,898	844,170	335,459	1,179,629	—	—	326,565	396,704	4,385,750	—	—
1935	6,812,350	2,077,474	956,100	360,602	1,316,702	—	—	348,151	412,621	4,734,876	—	—
1940	6,102,417	1,749,296	543,855	260,047	803,902	—	—	379,309	566,085	4,352,498	—	—
1945	5,859,169	1,570,357	312,832	178,471	491,303	—	—	244,475	834,579	4,288,812	—	—
1950	5,388,437	2,092,922	574,173 [3]	261,499 [3]	835,672	—	—	313,353 [4]	943,897 [4]	3,292,603	—	—
1954	4,782,416	2,153,737	570,675	249,337	820,012	—	—	306,377	1,027,348	2,629,284	—	—
1959	3,710,503	1,663,841	380,254	175,981	556,235	—	—	229,787	877,819	2,044,132	—	—
1964	3,157,857	1,462,183	—	—	448,983	—	—	189,027	824,173	1,695,674	—	—
1969	2,730,250	1,482,292	273,387	118,403	391,790	—	—	219,687	870,815 [5]	1,248,000	—	—
1974 [2]	2,314,013	1,011,476	134,205	62,716	196,921	61,615	94,969	156,584	657,971	—	829,843	437,951
1978	2,257,775	1,203,286	181,471	71,000	252,471	72,852	107,918	180,770	770,045	—	942,803	111,686
1982	2,240,976	1,187,374	156,421	67,312	223,733	74,300	114,497	188,797	774,844	—	861,798	191,804
1987	2,087,759	1,115,560	135,116	64,915	200,031	70,622	107,701	178,323	737,206	—	844,476	127,723
1992	1,925,300	992,773	110,437	54,743	165,180	60,100	101,923	162,023	665,570	—	801,881	130,646
1997	1,911,859	1,042,158	107,680	57,277	164,957	61,268	106,654	167,922	709,279	—	755,254	114,447

[1] Excludes Alaska and Hawai'i: 1930, 1935, 1945, and 1954.

[2] Data apply only to individual or family operations (sole proprietorships) and partnerships.

[3] 92 farms in Alaska reporting 1–99 days included with 1–49 days.

[4] 239 farms in Alaska reporting 100 days or more included.

[5] Unable to verify source for data; value taken directly from *Historical Statistics of the United States* (1975).

Sources

U.S. Bureau of the Census, *U.S. Census of Agriculture: 1925*, Summary Statistics, by States; *1945*, volume 2; *1950*, volume 2; *1954*, volume 2; *1959*, volume 2; *1964*, volume 2, chapter 5, p. 518; *1969*, volume 2, chapter 3, p. 178; *1978*, volume 1, part 51, p. 3; *1982*, volume 1, part 51, p. 3; *1992*, volume 1, part 51, p. 22; and *1997*, volume 1, part 1, p. 24.

Documentation

See the text for Table Da487–496. See also the text for Table Da1–13 for a general note.

Information on work off the farm by farm operators has been obtained for each agriculture census beginning with 1930. Farm operators reporting off-farm work vary from those who supplement their farm incomes with odd or spare-time jobs to those operators who have regular nonfarm jobs and use the farm to supplement their regular income or as a residence. The operators with odd or spare-time jobs usually consider their nonfarm employment to be of secondary importance; they may work part time on someone else's farm or work at seasonal nonfarm jobs. Many persons who may be employed in cities or have other regular nonfarm jobs live in rural areas and conduct sufficient agricultural operations for their places to meet the definition of a farm. Some use the farm income to supplement their regular nonfarm income. Some farm operators working off their farms may be using their nonfarm income as a source of capital for expanding their farming operations.

TABLE Da530–545   Farms, by race and tenure of operator: 1880–1997[1]

Contributed by Alan L. Olmstead and Paul W. Rhode

	All farms						Farms with white operators					Farms with non-white operators				
	Total	Owner			Manager	Tenant	Total	Owner		Manager	Tenant	Total	Owner		Manager	Tenant
		Full	Full, part, or manager	Part				Full	Part				Full	Part		
	Da530	Da531	Da532	Da533	Da534	Da535	Da536	Da537	Da538	Da539	Da540	Da541	Da542	Da543	Da544	Da545
Year	Number	Number	Number	Number	Number	Number	Number	Number	Number	Number	Number	Number	Number	Number	Number	Number
1880	4,008,907	—	2,984,306	—	—	1,024,601	—	—	—	—	—	—	—	—	—	—
1890	4,564,641	—	3,269,728	—	—	1,294,913	—	—	—	—	—	—	—	—	—	—
1900	5,739,657	3,202,643	—	451,515	59,213	2,026,286	4,970,129	3,026,214	420,916	57,353	1,465,646	769,528	176,429	30,599	1,860	560,640
1910	6,361,502	3,355,731	—	593,954	58,353	2,357,784	5,441,372	3,159,560	548,457	56,679	1,676,676	924,450	196,171	45,497	1,674	681,108
1920	6,453,991	3,368,146 [3]	—	558,708	68,583	2,458,554	5,499,707 [4]	3,174,675	517,820	66,317	1,740,534	954,284 [4]	193,126	40,888	2,258	718,009
1930	6,295,103	2,913,052 [3]	—	657,109	56,131	2,668,811	5,373,703 [4]	2,753,187 [5]	612,887	52,890	1,954,247	921,400 [4]	159,894 [5]	43,863	3,202	714,433
1940	6,102,417	3,085,491	—	615,502	36,501	2,364,923	5,378,913	2,917,255	581,678	35,750	1,844,230	723,504	168,236	33,824	751	520,693
1945	5,859,169	3,301,361	—	660,502	38,885	1,858,421	5,169,954	3,126,212	629,734	38,263	1,375,745	689,215	175,149	30,768	622	482,676
1950	5,388,437	3,091,666	—	825,670	23,646	1,447,455	4,802,520	2,936,960	769,751	23,140	1,072,669	585,917	154,706	55,919	506	374,786
1954 [2]	4,782,416	2,744,708	—	868,180	20,894	1,149,239	4,301,420	2,604,730	814,112	20,236	862,342	481,601	139,978	54,068	658	286,897
1959 [2]	3,710,503	2,116,594	—	834,470	21,060	735,849	3,423,361 [4]	2,016,808	792,422	20,457	592,417	284,612 [4]	97,388	40,733	489	141,017
1964 [2]	3,157,857	1,818,254	—	781,884	17,798	539,921	2,957,905	1,739,721	747,051	17,402	453,731	199,952	78,533	34,833	396	86,190
1969	2,730,250	1,705,720	—	671,607	—	352,923	2,639,744	1,650,290	655,379	—	334,075	90,506	55,430	16,228	—	18,848
1974	2,314,013	1,423,953	—	628,224	—	261,836	2,254,642	1,385,172	615,908	—	253,562	59,371	38,781	12,316	—	8,274
1978	2,257,775	1,297,902	—	681,112	—	278,761	2,199,787	1,263,752	666,086	—	269,949	57,988	34,150	15,026	—	8,812
1982	2,240,976	1,325,773	—	656,249	—	258,954	2,186,609	1,291,808	643,156	—	251,645	54,367	33,965	13,093	—	7,309
1987	2,087,759	1,238,547	—	609,012	—	240,200	2,043,119	1,210,140	599,016	—	233,963	44,640	28,407	9,996	—	6,237
1992	1,925,300	1,111,738	—	596,657	—	216,905	1,881,813	1,085,073	586,064	—	210,676	43,487	26,665	10,593	—	6,229
1997	1,911,859	1,146,891	—	573,839	—	191,129	1,864,201	1,117,494	562,367	—	184,340	47,658	29,397	11,472	—	6,789

[1] Excludes Alaska in 1910, and Alaska and Hawai'i in 1945, 1954, and 1959.

[2] Data for 1954, for 1959, and for tenants for 1964 are based on sample reports.

[3] Figures for 1920 and 1930 include 345 and 330 owners, respectively, for whom no differentiation was made between full and part owners.

[4] Totals by race include the following operators for whom tenure distribution was not available: 361 white and 3 nonwhite (1920, Alaska); 492 white and 8 nonwhite (1930, Alaska); 1,257 white and 4,985 nonwhite (1959, Hawai'i).

[5] Includes 369 part owners for Hawai'i; tenure distribution by race for Hawai'i for that year made no differentiation between full and part owners.

Sources

U.S. Bureau of the Census, *U.S. Census of Agriculture: 1954*, volume 2, pp. 956, 958; *1969*, volume 2, chapter 3, pp. 11, 14; *1978*, volume 1, part 51, p. 2; *1987*, volume 1, part 51, p. 20; *1997*, volume 1, part 1, p. 24.

Partial data, not reported here, are available for 1925 and 1935. See *1969 Census*, volume 2, chapter 3, p. 14.

Documentation

See the text for Table Da1–13 for a general note. See also the text for Table Da487–496.

Data on farm-operator status were not collected until the Census of 1880. Studies of land tenure before 1860 are based, necessarily, on fragments of information. See P. W. Bidwell and H. I. Falconer, *History of Agriculture in the Northern United States, 1620–1860* (Carnegie Institution, 1925), and L. C. Gray, *History of Agriculture in the Southern United States to 1860* (Carnegie Institution, 1933).

The 1900 Census of Agriculture covered the ownership of rented farms, with particular reference to absentee ownership and the concentration of ownership. On a sample basis, the U.S. Department of Agriculture made a study of ownership of rented farms in 1920; the results were published as Bulletins 1432 and 1433. The Bureau of the Census and the Department of Agriculture cooperated on sample surveys in 1945, 1950, and 1954 that were designed to show the portion of all farmland owned by each major class of owner. The results of these studies were published in U.S. Department of Agriculture, *Agricultural Economics Research* 5 (4) (1953), and in Agricultural Research Service and Bureau of the Census, *Graphic Summary of Tenure* (1954). A complete study of farmland ownership in the United States was made in 1945 and published as U.S. Department of Agriculture Miscellaneous Publication no. 699.

For the Censuses of 1880 and 1890 only the number of farms was classified by tenure. Classifications by the race of the farm operator and cross-classifications by race and tenure were first made in the Census of 1900.

According to the census definition, a farm operator is a person who operates a farm, either performing the labor him- or herself or directly supervising it. The census definition of a farm is based on operating units, rather than ownership tracts. A farm may consist of a number of separate tracts held under different tenures, some owned and some rented. Similarly, when a landowner has several tenants, renters, or croppers, the land operated by each is considered a separate farm. Therefore, the number of farm operators, for all practical purposes, is identical with the number of farms, series Da4, and these items are used interchangeably.

(continued)

TABLE Da530–545   Farms, by race and tenure of operator: 1880–1997   *Continued*

In the race classification of farm operators, Mexicans and others of Hispanic origin are reported as white. The black and other race group includes blacks, American Indians, Chinese, Japanese, and other races not classified as white.

Each farm was classified according to the tenure under which the operator controlled the land. Land was considered owned if the operator or the operator's spouse held it under title, homestead law, purchase contract, or as one of the heirs or as trustee of an undivided estate. If both an owned and a rented tract were farmed by the same operator, the tracts were to be considered as one farm even though they were not contiguous and each was locally called a farm. Farm operators were classified in the following four categories: (1) Full owners who own all the land they operate. (2) Part owners who own a part and rent from others the rest of the land they operate. (3) Managers who operate farms for others and receive wages or salaries for their services. Persons acting merely as caretakers or hired laborers were not classified as managers, and farms operated for institutions or corporations were considered to be managed even where no person was specifically indicated as being employed as the farm manager. In the 1969 Census, managers were no longer classified separately because of the difficulty in identifying managed farms in the mail enumeration procedures used; farms that may have had a manager were classified by tenure based on the tenure of the individual, partnership, or firm that hired the manager and controlled the land. (4) Tenants who operate hired or rented land only.

Croppers are share tenants to whom landlords furnish all of the work animals or tractor power in lieu of work animals (see Tables Da546–577). Croppers were first classified separately in the 1920 census. In the 1920, 1925, and 1930 Censuses, croppers were defined as share tenants whose landlords furnished the work animals. The 1935 Census schedule carried no inquiry on the method of paying rent and, therefore, croppers for that year included all tenants whose landlords furnished the work animals. The fur-

nishing of tractor power was not taken into account in classifying croppers until the 1940 Census.

The greatest difficulties in making a classification by tenure resulted from the sharecropper system. In brief, the question was whether the sharecropper should be considered merely a type of laborer or a farm operator. In reality, croppers had some of the characteristics of both laborers and tenants. Because of the decreasing importance of the cropper system in the South, croppers have not been classified separately since 1959.

In 1916, the Bureau of the Census published *Plantation Farming in the United States* from a 1910 Census study of plantations in 325 selected counties in eleven Southern states. In the selected plantation area, 39,073 plantations were reported as having five or more tenants. Another study of plantations was made in connection with the 1940 Census, but the results were not published. In 1947, the Bureau of the Census published *Multiple Unit Operations* from a study made in connection with the 1945 Census of Agriculture. The Bureau has also published volumes on multiple unit operations from the 1950 and 1954 Censuses of Agriculture. In 1924, the Bureau of Agricultural Economics issued Department Bulletin 1269, the results of a study by C. O. Brannen, *Relation of Land Tenure to Plantation Organization*.

All censuses since 1969 were conducted primarily by mail. To improve the coverage of the 1978 census, the mailout/mailback enumeration was supplemented by the direct enumeration of all households in approximately 6,400 sample segments in rural areas in all states, except Alaska and Hawai'i. The data for 1978 shown in the 1978 Census of Agriculture publications included data for farms represented on the mail list plus estimates from the area sample for farms not on the mail list. To provide comparable data for 1978 and later censuses, estimates from the 1978 area sample have been subtracted from the 1978 data. Thus, the 1978 data in the 1982 and 1987 Censuses include only farms represented on the mail list. All 1978 figures are taken from the 1987 or 1982 Censuses of Agriculture to ensure comparability.

TABLE Da546–565   Farms in the South, by race and tenure of operator: 1880–1974[1]

Contributed by Alan L. Olmstead and Paul W. Rhode

		Farms in the South									
		All farms								Farms with white operators		
			Owner				Tenant				Owner	
	Total farms in the United States	Total	Full	Full, part, or manager	Part	Manager	Total	Cropper	Total	Full	Part
	Da546	Da547	Da548	Da549	Da550	Da551	Da552	Da553	Da554	Da555	Da556
Year	Number	Number	Number	Number	Number	Number	Number	Number	Number	Number	Number
1880	4,008,907	1,531,077	—	977,229	—	—	553,848	—	—	—	—
1890	4,564,641	1,836,372	—	1,130,029	—	—	706,343	—	—	—	—
1900	5,739,657	2,620,391	1,237,114	—	133,368	18,765	1,231,144	—	1,879,721	1,078,635	105,171
1910	6,361,502	3,097,547	1,329,390	—	215,121	16,284	1,536,752	—	2,207,406	1,154,100	171,944
1920	6,453,991	3,206,664	1,405,762	—	191,463	18,318	1,591,121	561,091	2,283,750	1,227,204	152,432
1930	6,295,103	3,223,816	1,190,683	—	224,992	17,358	1,790,783	776,278	2,342,129	1,050,187	183,469
1940	6,102,417	3,007,170	1,327,690	—	216,607	13,580	1,449,293	541,291	2,326,904	1,185,788	185,246
1945	5,859,169	2,881,135	1,509,056	—	193,607	13,193	1,165,279	446,556	2,215,722	1,348,076	165,355
1950	5,388,437	2,652,423	1,411,123	—	325,999	9,979	905,322	346,765	2,093,333	1,269,641	274,135
1954 [2]	4,782,416	2,317,296	1,275,226	—	351,016	9,571	681,483	267,662	1,853,820	1,145,372	300,280
1959 [2]	3,710,503	1,645,028	946,613	—	322,952	9,196	366,267	121,037	1,379,407	856,864	285,418
1964 [2]	3,157,857	1,372,732	808,500	—	303,612	7,120	253,500	—	1,188,154	737,701	272,349
1969	2,730,250	1,161,399	779,731	—	245,280	—	136,388	—	1,076,150	727,138	229,906
1974	2,314,013	930,099	623,219	—	214,061	—	92,819	—	882,895	591,646	204,347

Notes appear on next page

TABLE Da546–565   Farms in the South, by race and tenure of operator: 1880–1974 *Continued*

	Farms in the South								
	Farms with white operators			Farms with nonwhite operators					
		Tenant			Owner			Tenant	
	Manager	Total	Cropper	Total	Full	Part	Manager	Total	Cropper
	Da557	Da558	Da559	Da560	Da561	Da562	Da563	Da564	Da565
Year	Number	Number	Number	Number	Number	Number	Number	Number	Number
1880	—	—	—	—	—	—	—	—	—
1890	—	—	—	—	—	—	—	—	—
1900	17,172	678,743	—	740,670	158,479	28,197	1,593	552,401	—
1910	15,084	866,278	—	890,141	175,290	43,177	1,200	670,474	—
1920	16,548	887,566	227,378	922,914	178,558	39,031	1,770	703,555	333,713
1930	16,529	1,091,944	383,381	881,687	140,496	41,523	829	698,839	392,897
1940	13,215	942,655	242,173	680,266	141,902	31,361	365	506,638	299,118
1945	12,751	689,540	176,290	665,413	160,980	28,252	442	475,739	270,296
1950	9,740	539,817	148,708	559,090	141,482	51,864	239	365,505	198,057
1954 [2]	9,190	398,978	107,416	463,476	129,854	50,736	381	282,505	160,246
1959 [2]	8,906	228,219	47,650	265,621	89,749	37,534	290	138,048	73,387
1964 [2]	6,975	171,129	—	184,578	70,799	31,263	145	82,371	—
1969	—	119,106	—	85,249	52,593	15,374	—	17,282	—
1974	—	86,902	—	47,204	31,573	9,714	—	5,917	—

[1] Excludes Alaska (1910) and Alaska and Hawai'i (1945, 1954, and 1959).

[2] Data for 1954, for 1959, and for tenants for 1964 are based on sample reports.

Sources

U.S. Bureau of the Census, *U.S. Census of Agriculture: 1954*, volume 2, pp. 956, 958; *1969*, volume 2, chapter 3, pp. 11, 14; and *1974*, volume 1, part 51, p. IV-19.

Documentation

See the text for Tables Da487–496 and Da530–545. For a general note, see the text for Table Da1–13.

TABLE Da566–577   Land in farms and value per farm of farmland and buildings, by tenure of operator: 1900–1997[1,2]

Contributed by Alan L. Olmstead and Paul W. Rhode

	Land in farms						Value per farm of farmland and buildings					
		Tenure of operator						Tenure of operator				
		Owner			Tenant			Owner			Tenant	
	Total	Full	Part	Manager	Total	Cropper	Total	Full	Part	Manager	Total	Cropper
	Da566	Da567	Da568	Da569	Da570	Da571	Da572 [3]	Da573 [3]	Da574 [3]	Da575	Da576	Da577 [3]
Year	Acres	Acres	Acres	Acres	Acres	Acres	Dollars	Dollars	Dollars	Dollars	Dollars	Dollars
1900	838,592,000	431,261,000	124,779,000	87,518,000	195,034,000	—	2,896	2,851	4,347	13,114	2,345	—
1910	878,798,000	464,923,000	133,631,000	53,731,000	226,513,000	—	5,471	5,160	8,515	25,075	4,662	—
1920	955,974,000	461,327,000 [4]	175,525,000	54,141,000	264,982,000	22,531,000	10,284	9,122 [6]	16,387	38,936	9,689	2,633
1930	990,112,000	372,575,000 [4]	246,605,000	63,626,000	307,306,000	31,605,000	7,623	7,253 [6]	12,400	41,307	6,143	1,802
1940	1,065,114,000	382,184,000	300,782,000	68,939,000	313,209,000	23,313,000	5,532	4,959	9,936	42,208	4,566	1,433
1945	1,141,615,000	412,358,000	371,251,000	106,372,000	251,634,000	18,922,000	7,917	6,393	15,184	60,552	6,941	1,981
1950	1,161,420,000	419,109,000	422,812,000	107,296,000	212,204,000	14,166,000	13,932	10,719	25,137	153,043	12,926	3,333
1954	1,160,044,000	397,214,000	472,465,000	100,003,000	190,362,000	9,413,000	19,761	14,511	35,764	165,800	19,464	3,972
1959	1,123,378,000	346,483,000	503,682,000	109,990,000	163,223,000	5,097,000	33,175 [5]	22,478 [5]	56,660 [5]	244,714 [5]	36,159 [5]	7,040 [5]
1964	1,110,187,000	318,876,209	533,043,590	113,361,000	144,906,402	—	50,646	—	—	—	—	—
1969	1,062,892,501	375,091,955	550,100,786	—	137,699,760	—	75,725	47,578	137,606	—	94,007	—
1974	1,017,030,357	359,375,934	535,300,914	—	122,353,509	—	147,838	86,730 [7]	262,016 [7]	—	175,753 [7]	—
1978	1,014,777,234	331,920,878	561,138,719	—	121,717,637	—	259,133	195,107	370,458	—	299,113	—
1982	986,796,579	342,448,434	530,703,476	—	113,644,669	—	341,230	213,198	588,562	—	362,705	—
1987	964,470,625	317,787,149	519,814,523	—	126,868,953	—	289,387	191,962	476,532	—	323,068	—
1992	945,531,506	296,242,076	526,612,012	—	122,677,418	—	357,056	232,849	571,548	—	406,480	—
1997	931,795,255	316,044,548	507,673,344	—	108,077,363	—	449,748	294,011	744,861	—	508,111	—

[1] Beginning with 1969, data for series Da566–568 and Da570 use the most recent source available, which sometimes revised previous figures. However, data for series Da572–574 and Da576 are reported only for the year of the census, so these averages are based on the unadjusted data.

[2] Excludes Alaska and Hawai'i (1900–1910, 1945, and 1954), Hawai'i (1920), and Alaska (1950, 1959, and 1964).

[3] Data are based on a sample of farms; see text.

[4] Data for 1920 and 1930 include 77,288 and 63,626 acres, respectively, for Alaska, for which no differentiation was made between full and part owners.

[5] Excludes Hawai'i.

[6] Figures for 1920 and 1930 include 345 and 330 Alaska owners, respectively, for whom no differentiation was made between full and part owners.

(continued)

TABLE Da566–577   Land in farms and value per farm of farmland and buildings, by tenure of operator: 1900–1997
Continued

[7] Data for farms with sales of $2,500 or more only. The figures included here were estimated by applying the same ratio of $2,500 farms and all farms found for 1978.

Sources
U.S. Bureau of the Census, *U.S. Census of Agriculture: 1954*, volume 2, pp. 956, 958; *1969*, volume 2, chapter 3, pp. 11, 12, 14; *1974*, volume 1, part 51, pp. I-2, I-5, I-28; *1978*, volume 1, part 51, pp. 1, 22; *1982*, volume 1, part 51, pp. 3, 26; *1987*, volume 1, part 51, pp. 20, 48; *1992*, volume 1, part 51, p. 52; and *1997*, volume 1, part 1, pp. 24, 56.

Documentation
See the text for Tables Da487–496 and Da530–545. For a general note, see the text for Table Da1–13.

For censuses since 1978, data on the average value of land and buildings, series Da572–574 and Da577, were collected from only a sample of farms. These data are subject to sampling error. For 1992, the sample form was mailed to approximately 29 percent of all farms, including all large and specialized farms (based on expected sales, acres, or standard industrial classification), all farms in Alaska, Hawai'i, and Rhode Island, and a sample of all other farms. For 1987 and 1982, the sample form was mailed to all large and specialized farms, all farms in Alaska and Hawai'i, and approximately 17 percent of all other farms. The 1978 sample consisted of all certainty (large) farms and approximately 20 percent of all other farms.

TABLE Da578–579   Farms operated by full owners – percent mortgaged, and mortgage debt as a percentage of value of land and buildings: 1890–1961

Contributed by Alan L. Olmstead and Paul W. Rhode

Year	Percentage of farms mortgaged Da578 Percent	Mortgage debt as a percentage of value of land and buildings Da579 Percent
1890	28	36 [3]
1910	30 [1]	27 [4]
1920	35 [2]	29 [4]
1925	34	42
1930	42	40
1935	40	50
1940	41	43
1945	30	33
1950	29	28
1956	33	27
1961	35	28

[1] Forty-nine states; no data for Alaska.

[2] Includes 345 owners for Alaska, for whom no differentiation was made between full and part owners.

[3] Figures for 1890 include estimates, since at that census the farm homes for which no mortgage report was secured were distributed between the two groups, "mortgaged" and "free from mortgage."

[4] Figures include only farms consisting wholly of land owned by the operator and reporting amount of mortgage debt.

Sources
U.S. Census Division, *Abstract of the Eleventh Census: 1890*, p. 231; U.S. Bureau of the Census, *Fourteenth Census of the United States Taken in the Year 1920*, volume 5, p. 489; U.S. Bureau of the Census, *United States Census of Agriculture 1925*, part 3, p. 16; U.S. Department of Agriculture, Economic Research Service, *United States Census of Agriculture 1959*, volume 5, part 4, *Special Reports, Farm Mortgage Debt and Farm Taxes*, p. 4.

Documentation
Information on the number of mortgaged farms has been collected by both the Bureau of the Census and the Agricultural Research Service, or, more recently, the Economic Research Service. Generally speaking, such data have been published with the data on amount of debt in census years, except in 1900 when no information on amount of debt was obtained. For a historical summary and an analysis of the data on number of mortgaged owner-operated farms for 1890–1935, see Donald C. Horton, "Number and Percentage of Farms under Mortgage," *Agricultural Finance Review* 1 (2) (1938): 39–53. The sources cited above also include state data on the number of mortgaged farms in each tenure class for 1940, 1945, 1950, 1956, and 1961.

Farm-mortgage debt includes the unpaid principal of mortgages, deeds of trust, sales contracts, vendors' liens, and all other debt for which farm real estate is pledged as security. Any farm that has a real estate mortgage is classified as a mortgaged farm even though only a portion of it is mortgaged.

Estimates for 1930–1961 are based on information obtained in the census of agriculture for owner-operated farms, mail surveys of samples of farm owners (including both operators and landlords), and reports from farm-mortgage lenders.

For each of the years shown, mortgage information was obtained from full-owner farm operators in the Census of Agriculture. Similar information was obtained by the Bureau of the Census for part owners for 1940, 1945, 1950, 1956, and 1961. This information was supplemented by data obtained in mail surveys for land operated by part owners, tenants, and managers. The 1930 mail survey was conducted by the Bureau of Agricultural Economics. Later surveys were cooperative undertakings of the Bureau of the Census and the Bureau of Agricultural Economics or the Agricultural Research Service.

Data for 1966 were collected in a supplementary survey for the 1964 Census of Agriculture of approximately 16,000 farms. The survey was taken in 1966 and the farms included in the survey were selected from the 1964 Census of Agriculture and from the records of the coverage evaluation survey for the 1964 Census. Comparable data for the tenure breakdown for 1966 are not available because of procedures used in the processing of the data.

For information by states and geographic divisions and descriptions of procedures, see the sources cited and U.S. Census of Agriculture: 1950, volume 5, part 8, and 1959, volume 5, part 4.

See also the text for Table Da530–545 for a definition of tenure.

Series Da579. Figures are mortgage debt as a percentage of the value of land and buildings of mortgaged farms operated by full owners.

TABLE Da580–596   Farms, by size: 1880–1997[1]

Contributed by Alan L. Olmstead and Paul W. Rhode

	Total	Less than 10	Less than 3	3–9	10–29	10–49	30–49	50–99	100–179	50–179	100–259	100–499	180–259	180–499	260–499	500–999	1,000 and over
	Da580	Da581	Da582	Da583	Da584	Da585	Da586	Da587	Da588	Da589	Da590	Da591	Da592	Da593	Da594	Da595	Da596
Year	Thousand	Thousand	Thousand	Thousand	Thousand	Thousand	Thousand	Thousand	Thousand	Thousand	Thousand	Thousand	Thousand	Thousand	Thousand	Thousand	Thousand
1880	4,009	139	4	135	—	1,036	—	1,033	—	—	—	1,696	—	—	—	76	29
1890	4,565	150	—	—	—	1,168	—	1,122	—	—	—	2,009	—	—	—	84	32
1900	5,740	268	42	227	—	1,665	—	1,366	—	—	—	2,291	—	—	—	103	47
1910	6,362	335	18	317	—	1,918	—	1,438	—	—	2,051	—	—	—	444	125	50
1920	6,454	292 ²	21 ²	270 ²	—	2,014	—	1,475	—	—	—	2,457	—	—	—	150	67
1925	6,372	379	15	363	—	2,039	—	1,421	—	—	1,887	—	—	—	440	144	63
1930	6,295	362	44	318	—	2,002	—	1,375	—	—	—	2,315	—	—	—	160	81
1935	6,812	571	36	535	1,241	—	1,882	1,444	1,438	—	—	—	507	—	473	167	89
1940	6,102	509	37	472	—	1,782	—	1,291	—	—	—	2,255	—	—	—	164	101
1945	5,859	595	99	496	946	—	709	1,157	1,200	—	—	—	493	—	473	174	113
1950	5,388	489	78	410	855	—	625	1,048	—	—	—	2,068	—	—	—	182	121
1954	4,782	484	100	384	713	—	499	864	953	—	—	—	464	—	482	192	130
1959	3,711	244	79	165	—	813	—	658	773	—	—	—	415	—	472	200	136
1964	3,158	183	60	123	—	637	—	542	633	—	—	—	355	—	451	210	145
1969	2,730	162	79	83	—	473	—	460	542	—	—	—	307	—	419	216	151
1974	2,314	128	—	—	—	380	—	—	—	828	—	—	—	616	—	207	155
1978	2,258	151	—	—	—	392	—	—	—	759	—	—	—	582	—	213	161
1982	2,241	188	—	—	—	449	—	—	—	712	—	—	—	527	—	204	162
1987	2,088	183	—	—	—	412	—	—	—	645	—	—	—	478	—	200	169
1992	1,925	166	—	—	—	388	—	—	—	584	—	—	—	428	—	186	173
1997	1,912	153	—	—	—	411	—	—	—	593	—	—	—	403	—	176	176

Size of farm (acres)

[1] Excludes Alaska and Hawai'i: 1910, 1925, 1935, 1945, and 1954.
[2] Excludes Alaska.

Sources

U.S. Bureau of the Census, *U.S. Census of Agriculture: 1954*, volume 2, pp. 352–54; *1959*, volume 2, pp. 390, 392; *1969*, volume 2, chapter 2, pp. 65–9; *1978*, volume 1, part 51, p. 2; *1982*, volume 1, part 51, p. 3; *1987*, volume 1, part 51, p. 16; *1992*, volume 1, part 51, p. 18; and *1997*, volume 1, part 51, p. 20.

Documentation

See the text for Table Da1–13 for a general note regarding changes in the definition of farm.

TABLE Da597-611   Land in farms, by farm size: 1900-1997[1]

Contributed by Alan L. Olmstead and Paul W. Rhode

	Total	Less than 10	Less than 3	3-9	10-29	10-49	30-49	50-99	100-179	100-259	100-499	180-259	260-499	500-999	1,000 and over
	Da597	Da598	Da599	Da600	Da601	Da602	Da603	Da604	Da605	Da606	Da607	Da608	Da609	Da610	Da611
Year	Thousand acres	Thousand acres	Thousand acres	Thousand acres	Thousand acres	Thousand acres	Thousand acres	Thousand acres	Thousand acres	Thousand acres	Thousand acres	Thousand acres	Thousand acres	Thousand acres	Thousand acres
1900	841,202	1,482	80	1,402	—	47,253	—	98,600	—	295,978	—	—	129,686	67,878	200,324
1910	878,798	—	—	—	—	—	—	103,121	—	—	470,770	—	—	83,653	167,082
1920	955,884	1,600	33	1,567	—	55,553	—	105,631	—	307,244	—	—	164,244	100,976	220,636
1925	924,319	2,097	23	2,074	—	54,465	—	101,906	—	292,180	—	—	151,731	97,468	224,472
1930	990,112	1,922	63	1,859	—	54,085	—	98,700	—	290,525	—	—	159,273	108,940	276,667
1935	1,054,515	3,057	51	3,006	22,272	—	33,691	104,016	194,804	—	—	108,462	164,268	114,244	309,701
1940	1,065,114	2,679	52	2,627	—	47,538	—	93,336	177,558	—	—	104,289	161,995	111,946	365,772
1945	1,141,615	2,805	141	2,664	16,864	—	27,074	83,206	162,375	—	—	105,802	164,647	118,836	460,006
1950	1,162,643 [2]	2,443	—	—	—	39,372	—	75,647	149,991	—	—	105,403	168,944	125,988	494,856
1954	1,158,192	2,260	—	—	12,704	—	19,165	62,725	130,120	—	—	99,863	168,368	131,505	531,482
1959	1,123,508	1,053	—	—	—	21,850	—	47,950	105,732	—	—	89,503	165,438	137,351	554,631
1964	1,110,185	778	—	—	—	17,327	—	39,590	86,588	—	—	76,854	159,597	144,598	584,847
1969	1,062,893	568	—	—	—	13,253	—	33,621	74,005	—	—	66,378	149,309	147,801	577,958
1974	1,017,030	451	—	—	—	10,839	—	28,057	60,452	—	—	54,768	129,780	142,309	590,375
1978	1,014,777	555	—	—	—	10,949	—	25,865	54,975	—	—	50,577	124,642	146,698	600,516
1982	986,797	728	—	—	—	12,095	—	24,837	49,935	—	—	45,718	113,074	140,505	599,904
1987	964,471	674	—	—	—	11,061	—	22,461	45,333	—	—	41,504	102,917	138,541	601,981
1992	945,532	661	—	—	—	10,340	—	20,426	40,715	—	—	37,170	91,711	129,265	615,243
1997	931,795	649	—	—	—	10,964	—	21,231	40,238	—	—	35,482	85,444	122,093	615,694

[1] Excludes Alaska and Hawai'i: 1910, 1920, 1925, 1935, 1945, and 1954.

[2] Based on sample data; therefore differs from series Da5 and Da159.

Sources

U.S. Bureau of the Census, *U.S. Census of Agriculture: 1954*, volume 2, pp. 352-4; *1959*, volume 2, pp. 390, 392; *1969*, volume 2, chapter 2, pp. 65-9; *1974*, volume 1, part 51, p. I-1; *1978*, volume 1, part 51, p. 2; *1982*, volume 1, part 51, p. 3; *1987*, volume 1, part 51, p. 16; *1992*, volume 1, part 51, p. 18; and *1997*, volume 1, part 51, p. 20.

Documentation

See the text for Table Da1-13 for a general note regarding changes in the definition of farm.

TABLE Da612–614   Farm employment: 1910–1999[1, 2, 3]

Contributed by Alan L. Olmstead and Paul W. Rhode

Year	Total Da612 [4] Thousand	Unpaid farm workers Da613 [5] Thousand	Hired workers Da614 Thousand	Year	Total Da612 [4] Thousand	Unpaid farm workers Da613 [5] Thousand	Hired workers Da614 Thousand
1910	13,555	10,174	3,381	1955	8,381	6,345	2,036
1911	13,539	10,169	3,370	1956	7,852	5,900	1,953
1912	13,559	10,162	3,397	1957	7,600	5,660	1,940
1913	13,572	10,158	3,414	1958	7,503	5,521	1,982
1914	13,580	10,147	3,433	1959	7,342	5,390	1,952
1915	13,592	10,140	3,452	1960	7,057	5,172	1,885
1916	13,632	10,144	3,488	1961	6,919	5,029	1,890
1917	13,568	10,121	3,447	1962	6,700	4,873	1,827
1918	13,391	10,053	3,338	1963	6,518	4,738	1,780
1919	13,243	9,968	3,275	1964	6,110	4,506	1,604
1920	13,432	10,041	3,391	1965	5,610	4,128	1,482
1921	13,398	10,001	3,397	1966	5,214	3,854	1,360
1922	13,337	9,936	3,401	1967	4,903	3,650	1,253
1923	13,162	9,798	3,364	1968	4,749	3,535	1,213
1924	13,031	9,705	3,326	1969	4,596	3,419	1,176
1925	13,036	9,715	3,321	1970	4,523	3,348	1,175
1926	12,976	9,526	3,450	1971	4,436	3,275	1,161
1927	12,642	9,278	3,364	1972	4,373	3,228	1,146
1928	12,691	9,340	3,351	1973	4,337	3,169	1,168
1929	12,763	9,360	3,403	1974	4,389	3,075	1,314
1930	12,497	9,307	3,190	1975	4,342	3,026	1,317
1931	12,745	9,642	3,103	1976	4,374	2,997	1,377
1932	12,816	9,922	2,894	1977	4,170	2,863	1,307
1933	12,739	9,874	2,865	1978	3,957	2,689	1,268
1934	12,627	9,765	2,862	1979	3,774	2,501	1,273
1935	12,733	9,855	2,878	1980	3,705	2,402	1,303
1936	12,331	9,350	2,981	1981	3,330	2,236	1,094
1937	11,978	9,054	2,924	1982	4,043	2,494	1,549
1938	11,622	8,815	2,807	1983	3,749	2,271	1,478
1939	11,338	8,611	2,727	1984	3,405	2,175	1,230
1940	10,979	8,300	2,679	1985	3,116	2,017	1,098
1941	10,669	8,017	2,652	1986	2,912	1,873	1,039
1942	10,504	7,949	2,555	1987	2,897	1,846	1,044
1943	10,446	8,010	2,436	1988	2,954	1,917	1,037
1944	10,219	7,988	2,231	1989	2,863	1,936	928
1945	10,000	7,881	2,119	1990	2,891	1,999	892
1946	10,295	8,106	2,189	1991	2,877	1,967	910
1947	10,382	8,115	2,267	1992	2,810	1,944	866
1948	10,363	8,026	2,337	1993	2,800	1,943	857
1949	9,964	7,712	2,252	1994	2,769	1,929	840
1950	9,926	7,597	2,329	1995	2,836	1,967	869
1951	9,546	7,310	2,236	1996	2,523	1,834	832
1952	9,149	7,005	2,144	1997	—	—	879
1953	8,864	6,775	2,089	1998	—	—	880
1954	8,651	6,570	2,081	1999	—	—	929

[1] For 1910–1974, these annual averages are simple averages of last-of-month employment estimates; for 1975–1981, figures are simple averages of quarterly employment estimates.

[2] Beginning July 1984, surveys were conducted in the forty-eight contiguous states and Hawai'i. Hawai'i is included in U.S. average beginning 1978.

[3] Average of January and April surveys (1981); July survey (1982–1983); July and October surveys (1984); April, July, and October surveys (1985–1988); January, April, July, and October surveys (1989–1994); and January and April surveys (1996, series Da612–613 only).

[4] Through 1979, equals the sum of family and hired workers, series Da613–614. Beginning 1980, it was defined as the total of self-employed workers, unpaid workers, and hired workers. Agricultural service workers were not included.

[5] Includes farm operators and members of their families doing farm work without wages. In 1982, the "family workers" series was split up into "self-employed workers" and "unpaid workers"; see text.

Sources

1910–1972, U.S. National Agricultural Statistics Service, *Farm Employment and Wage Rates, 1910–1990*, Statistical Bulletin number 822, p. 7; 1973–1994, U.S. National Agricultural Statistics Service, *Agricultural Statistics, 1988*, p. 386; *1995–96*, p. IX-15; 1995–1999, U.S. Agricultural Statistics Board, *Farm Labor*, quarterly issues, February 1995–May 2000.

Documentation

See the text for Table Da1–13 for a general note.

For detailed descriptions of farm employment concepts, see *Major Statistical Series of the U.S. Department of Agriculture*, Agriculture Handbook number 365, volume 7, pp. 7–12. See source publications for regional, state, and monthly data.

These data are based on (1) data from the census of population used as benchmarks for 1910, 1920, and 1930, and data from the Census of

(continued)

TABLE Da612–614   Farm employment: 1910–1999   *Continued*

Agriculture used for 1940, 1950, 1954, and 1959; (2) nationwide annual sample surveys made by the Statistical Reporting Service since 1965; (3) estimates of farm employment from nationwide enumerative sample surveys made at intervals during 1945–1948, together with historical data on the seasonal distributions of man-hour labor requirements in farm production, used to develop measures of seasonal variation; (4) returns from the crop reporters of the monthly mailed questionnaire on employment on farms, available since 1925; and (5) annual estimates of the number of farms by states and regions used to expand "adjusted" average employment per farm to obtain regional and national estimates of total farm employment and of the family and hired worker components of the total.

From 1910 to 1981, the U.S. Department of Agriculture estimated the number of family workers, series Da613, employed on farms. Family workers included farm operators doing one or more hour of farm work and members of their families working fifteen hours or more during the survey week without cash wages. Starting in July 1982, the family workers series was split up into two series: self-employed workers and unpaid workers. Self-employed workers are defined as a farm operator or partner(s) who did at least one hour of unpaid agricultural work on the farm during the survey week. Unpaid workers are anyone, other than a self-employed worker, who did at least fifteen hours of unpaid agricultural work on a farm during the survey week. Thus, series Da613 was entitled "family workers" from 1910 to 1981; from 1982 to the present it is the sum of "self-employed" and "unpaid" workers.

All persons working one hour or more during the survey week for pay at farm work or chores are classified as hired farm workers, series Da614. Members of the operator's family receiving wages for work on their farms are counted as hired workers. Sharecroppers are considered family workers when working on their own crops but are classified as hired workers when doing farm work for pay off their tracts. A person employed as both a family worker and a hired worker during the survey week on the same farm is counted as a hired worker.

The survey week is the last complete calendar week in the month, but when that week includes the last day of the month the survey week is the next-to-last full calendar week.

The average number of hired and family workers per farm is computed for the reporting farms for the conterminous United States. The averages are then adjusted by factors based on comparisons with the last census level, labor requirements data, and the estimated seasonal pattern of employment based on the latest census and special studies in selected states. The adjusted averages are then multiplied by the estimated number of farms in each state to estimate the number of family and hired workers employed. Data from the census, state assessors' reports, Agricultural Stabilization and Conservation records, and indications of change from the larger acreage and livestock surveys are used in estimating the number of farms. Annual averages of employment are simple averages of last-of-month employment estimates.

Farm employment data were first collected through crop reporters in October 1923. In 1938, the National Research Project of the Works Progress Administration developed monthly farm employment estimates for 1925–1936 from the crop reporter data. See E. C. Shaw and J. A. Hopkins, *Trends in Employment in Agriculture, 1909–1936* (Works Progress Administration, November 1938). Monthly estimates have been made by the Agricultural Marketing Service and the former Bureau of Agricultural Economics from crop reporter data for 1936–1970, using the methods developed in the Works Progress Administration project, plus certain recent refinements. Following the 1950 Census of Agriculture, the entire historical series was reexamined and revised. Data for 1950–1970 reflect revisions following the 1959 and 1964 Censuses of Agriculture and enumerative area surveys made by the Statistical Reporting Service.

TABLE Da615–622 Deaths on farms per 100,000 farm workers, by type of injury: 1951–1996[1]

Contributed by Alan L. Olmstead and Paul W. Rhode

	Total farm employment		Deaths on farms per 100,000 workers						
		All causes	Machinery-related	Drowning	Firearms	Falls	Struck by an object	Other causes
	Da615	Da616	Da617 [2]	Da618	Da619 [3]	Da620 [4]	Da621 [2]	Da622
Year	Thousand	Per 100,000	Per 100,000	Per 100,000	Per 100,000	Per 100,000	Per 100,000	Per 100,000
1951	9,546.0	27.0	9.0	3.0	3.0	3.0	2.0	7
1952	9,149.0	—	—	—	—	—	—	—
1953	8,864.0	29.0	10.0	4.0	4.0	3.0	2.0	7
1954	8,651.0	—	—	—	—	—	—	—
1955	8,381.0	30.0	10.0	5.0	3.0	3.0	2.0	7
1956	7,852.0	—	—	—	—	—	—	—
1957	7,600.0	32.0	12.0	5.0	4.0	3.0	2.0	7
1958	7,503.0	—	—	—	—	—	—	—
1959	7,342.0	33.0	12.0	5.0	4.0	3.0	2.0	7
1960	7,057.0	—	—	—	—	—	—	—
1961	6,919.0	35.0	13.0	5.0	4.0	3.0	2.0	8
1962	6,700.0	34.0	13.0	5.0	3.0	3.0	2.0	7
1963	6,518.0	35.0	14.0	6.0	4.0	3.0	2.0	8
1964	6,110.0	37.0	14.0	6.0	4.0	2.0	3.0	8
1965	5,610.0	41.0	17.0	7.0	4.0	3.0	2.0	9
1966	5,214.0	42.0	17.0	6.0	4.0	3.0	3.0	9
1967	4,903.0	45.0	19.0	7.0	4.0	3.0	3.0	9
1968	4,749.0	—	—	—	—	—	—	—
1969	4,596.0	43.0	10.0	7.0	4.0	3.0	8.0	11
1970	4,523.0	40.0	10.0	6.0	3.0	3.0	7.0	11
1971	4,436.3	39.0	10.0	6.0	3.0	3.0	6.0	11
1972	4,373.4	39.0	10.0	6.0	3.0	3.0	6.0	11
1973	4,336.7	41.0	10.0	6.0	3.0	3.0	7.0	12
1974	4,388.9	37.0	9.0	5.0	2.0	3.0	7.0	11
1975	4,342.1	39.0	11.0	5.0	3.0	2.0	7.0	11
1976	4,373.9	33.0	9.0	4.0	2.0	2.0	6.0	10
1977	4,169.9	33.0	8.0	4.0	2.0	2.0	7.0	11
1978	3,956.6	34.0	8.0	4.0	2.0	2.0	7.0	10
1979	3,774.2	34.0	17.0	4.0	2.0	1.0	3.0	7
1980	3,705.3	35.0	15.0	5.0	2.0	2.0	3.0	8
1981	3,330.0	36.0	17.0	4.0	3.0	2.0	3.0	8
1982	4,043.4	30.0	13.0	4.0	2.0	2.0	3.0	7
1983	3,749.0	29.0	14.0	3.0	2.0	1.0	2.0	6
1984	3,404.5	29.0	14.0	3.0	2.0	1.0	3.0	6
1985	3,115.7	32.3	15.3	3.2	2.8	1.8	3.3	6
1986	2,912.0	33.4	15.7	3.7	1.9	1.8	2.7	8
1987	2,896.7	32.6	15.8	3.2	1.5	1.9	3.0	7
1988	2,954.3	28.1	13.7	2.6	1.6	2.0	2.6	6
1989	2,863.3	26.9	12.4	3.5	1.8	1.5	2.0	6
1990	2,891.3	26.9	13.9	2.1	1.5	1.7	2.3	5
1991	2,877.3	25.8	13.2	2.1	1.6	1.9	2.3	5
1992	2,810.0	25.8	12.9	2.1	1.4	1.2	2.2	6
1993	2,799.8	28.3	13.8	1.8	1.5	2.1	2.3	7
1994	2,768.5	25.5	12.4	1.8	1.2	2.0	2.7	5
1995	2,835.6	23.9	11.1	1.8	1.1	2.0	2.0	6
1996	2,523.0	—	—	—	—	—	—	—

[1] Data on agricultural employment, the denominator for the death rate series, are highly controversial owing to problems in measuring migrant and part-time workers.

[2] Classification changed in 1969 and 1979; consequently, data for 1951–1968, 1969–1978, and 1979–1995 are not comparable.

[3] Data beginning 1969 are not comparable to previous years owing to classification changes.

[4] Data beginning 1979 are not comparable to previous years owing to classification changes.

Sources

Series Da615. 1951–1972, U.S. National Agricultural Statistics Service, *Farm Employment and Wage Rates, 1910–1990*, Statistical Bulletin number 822, p. 7; 1973–1994, U.S. National Agricultural Statistics Service, *Agricultural Statistics, 1988*, p. 386; *1995–96*, p. IX-15; 1995–1999, U.S. Agricultural Statistics Board, *Farm Labor*, quarterly issues, February 1995–May 2000.

Series Da616–622. 1951–1953, National Safety Council, *Accident Facts*, 1971 edition, p. 88; 1955–1962, *Accident Facts*, 1979 edition, p. 88; 1963–1966, *Accident Facts*, 1985 edition, p. 88; 1967–1981, *Accident Facts*, 1989 edition, p. 99; 1982–1992, *Accident Facts*, 1995 edition, p. 137; 1993–1995, *Accident Facts*, 1998 edition, p. 137.

Documentation

Data are farm deaths from unintentional injuries that occurred on farms to all persons, primarily farm residents, but include others such as nonresident workers, hunters, and visitors. Excluded are farm home accidental deaths, transport deaths, and deaths of farm residents that occurred off farm property. Tabulations are understated, as not all death certificates indicate the place of accident.

Series Da616–622 are the number of deaths on farms divided by farm employment, series Da615. See the text for Table Da612–614 for a discussion of the farm employment series.

TABLE Da623–634   Farm machinery and equipment: 1910–1998[1]

Contributed by Alan L. Olmstead and Paul W. Rhode

	Tractors			Total horsepower	Motor trucks	Automobiles	Grain combines	Cornpickers	Pickup balers	Field forage harvesters	Cottonpickers	Farms with milking machines
	Total	Wheel	Crawler									
Year	Da623 [2]	Da624	Da625	Da626	Da627	Da628	Da629 [3]	Da630 [4]	Da631 [5]	Da632 [6]	Da633	Da634
	Thousand	Thousand	Thousand	Million	Thousand	Thousand	Thousand	Thousand	Thousand	Thousand	Number	Thousand
1910	1	—	—	—	—	50	1	—	—	—	—	12
1911	4	—	—	—	2	100	—	—	—	—	—	—
1912	8	—	—	—	5	175	—	—	—	—	—	—
1913	14	—	—	—	10	258	—	—	—	—	—	—
1914	17	—	—	—	15	343	—	—	—	—	—	—
1915	25	—	—	—	25	472	—	—	—	—	—	—
1916	37	—	—	—	40	687	—	—	—	—	—	—
1917	51	—	—	—	60	966	—	—	—	—	—	—
1918	85	—	—	—	89	1,502	—	—	—	—	—	—
1919	158	—	—	—	111	1,760	—	—	—	—	—	—
1920	246 [8]	—	—	—	139 [8]	2,146 [8]	4	10	—	—	—	55
1921	343	—	—	—	207	2,382	—	—	—	—	—	—
1922	372	—	—	—	263	2,425	—	—	—	—	—	—
1923	428	—	—	—	316	2,618	—	—	—	—	—	—
1924	496	—	—	—	363	3,004	—	—	—	—	—	—
1925	549	—	—	—	459	3,283	—	—	—	—	—	—
1926	621	—	—	—	559	3,605	—	—	—	—	—	—
1927	693	—	—	—	662	3,820	—	—	—	—	—	—
1928	782	—	—	—	753	3,820	—	—	—	—	—	—
1929	827	—	—	—	840	3,970	—	—	—	—	—	—
1930	920 [8]	—	—	—	900 [8]	4,135 [8]	61	50	—	—	—	100
1931	997	—	—	—	920	4,077	—	—	—	—	—	—
1932	1,022	—	—	—	910	3,798	—	—	—	—	—	—
1933	1,019	—	—	—	865	3,399	—	—	—	—	—	—
1934	1,016	—	—	—	875	3,399	—	—	—	—	—	—
1935	1,048	—	—	—	890	3,642	—	—	—	—	—	—
1936	1,125	—	—	—	923	3,735	—	—	—	—	—	—
1937	1,230	—	—	—	990	3,962	—	—	—	—	—	—
1938	1,370	—	—	—	1,042	4,109	—	—	—	—	—	—
1939	1,445	—	—	—	1,020	4,030	—	—	—	—	—	—
1940	1,567 [8]	—	—	42	1,047 [8]	4,144 [8]	190	110	—	—	—	175
1941	1,665	—	—	45	1,095	—	225	120	—	—	—	210
1942	1,860	—	—	50	1,160	—	275	130	25	—	—	255
1943	2,055	—	—	55	1,280	—	320	138	31	—	—	275
1944	2,160	—	—	58	1,385	—	345	146	34	—	—	300
1945	2,354 [8]	2,255	99	61	1,490 [8]	4,148 [8]	375 [8]	168	42	20	107	365 [8]
1946	2,480	2,374	106	64	1,550	—	420	203	54	25	756	440
1947	2,613	2,500	113	69	1,700	—	465	236	65	30	1,522	525
1948	2,821	2,700	121	77	1,900	—	535	299	90	45	2,423	575
1949	3,123	2,990	133	85	2,065	—	620	372	135	60		610

Year	Tractors				Motor trucks	Automobiles	Grain combines	Cornpickers	Pickup balers	Field forage harvesters	Cottonpickers	Farms with milking machines
	Total	Wheel	Crawler	Total horsepower								
	Da623 [2]	Da624	Da625	Da626	Da627	Da628	Da629 [3]	Da630 [4]	Da631 [5]	Da632 [6]	Da633	Da634
	Thousand	Thousand	Thousand	Million	Thousand	Thousand	Thousand	Thousand	Thousand	Thousand	Number	Thousand
1950	3,394 [8]	3,250	144	93	2,207 [8]	4,100 [8]	714 [8]	456 [8]	196 [8]	81	3,940	636 [8]
1951	3,678	3,531	147	101	2,325	—	810	522	240	102	7,369	655
1952	3,907	3,756	151	108	2,430	—	887	588	298	124	11,959	675
1953	4,100	3,946	154	115	2,535	—	930	630	345	148	—	690
1954	4,243	4,086	157	121	2,610	—	965	660	395	175	—	705
1955	4,345 [8]	4,185	160	126	2,675	4,140	980 [8]	688 [8]	448 [8]	202 [8]	18,644	712 [8]
1956	4,480	4,310	170	134	2,707	—	1,005	715	505	220	—	—
1957	4,570	4,392	178	139	2,745	—	1,015	740	560	240	—	—
1958	4,620	4,434	186	144	2,775	—	1,030	755	600	258	—	—
1959	4,673	4,481	192	150	2,800	—	1,045	775	645	270	—	—
1960	4,685 [8]	4,489	199	153	2,825 [8]	3,629 [8]	1,042 [8]	792 [8]	680 [8]	291 [8]	—	666 [8]
1961	4,695	4,547	196	158	2,850	—	980	740	685	291	37,870 [8,9]	—
1962	4,710	4,570	193	162	2,885	—	960	730	703	300	—	—
1963	4,730	4,588	190	167	2,925	—	940	720	718	307	—	—
1964	4,755	4,598	188	172	2,970	—	920	705	734	312	—	—
1965	4,783 [8]	4,601	186	176	3,023 [8]	3,587 [8]	910 [8]	690 [8]	751 [8]	316 [8]	—	500 [8]
1966	4,800	4,594	189	182	3,060	—	895	675	765	320	—	—
1967	4,815	4,593	193	189	3,100	—	880	655	775	322	—	—
1968	4,822	4,570	196	195	3,130	—	870	640	785	325	—	—
1969	4,810	4,513	199	199	3,160	—	860	630	790	328	—	—
1970	4,790	4,416	203	203	3,185	—	850	620	795	331	—	—
1971	4,614	4,421	193	206	2,994	—	739	630	700	300	43,542 [8,9]	—
1972	4,566	4,383	183	209	3,003	—	683	625	690	298	—	—
1973	4,512	4,339	173	212	3,013	—	620	621	684	292	—	—
1974	4,480	4,316	164	219	3,023	—	579	618	672	295	—	—
1975	4,469 [8]	4,312	158	222	3,038 [8]	—	524 [8]	615 [8]	667 [8]	255 [8]	—	—
1976	4,562	4,409	153	228	3,113	—	524	610	695	263	—	—
1977	4,668	4,526	142	232	3,195	—	569	605	718	270	—	—
1978	4,779	4,628	151	259	3,276	—	610	695	741	295	—	—
1979 [7]	4,776 [8]	4,626	150	301	3,358 [8]	—	655 [8]	706 [8]	744 [8]	295 [8]	41,435 [8]	—
1980	4,780	4,632	148	304	3,377	—	656	701	756	293	—	—
1981	4,740	4,594	146	306	3,397	—	650	696	778	291	—	—
1982	4,696	4,551	145	306	3,416	—	647	690	803	288	—	—
1983 [7]	4,669 [8]	4,524	145	309	3,435 [8]	—	644 [8]	684 [8]	800 [8]	285 [8]	49,563 [8]	—
1984	4,671	4,525	144	311	3,436	—	643	684	800	285	—	—
1985	4,676	4,545	143	311	3,436	—	651	684	814	285	—	—
1986	4,670	4,586	142	311	3,436	—	661	683	818	281	—	—
1987	—	4,611	—	—	3,437	—	666	—	820	—	—	—
1988 [7,8]	—	4,609	—	—	3,437	—	667	—	823	—	42,914	—
1993 [7,8]	—	4,305	—	—	3,295	—	569	—	790	—	36,795	—
1998 [7,8]	—	3,936	—	—	3,498	—	461	—	717	—	38,294	—

Notes appear on next page

(continued)

TABLE Da623–634   Farm machinery and equipment: 1910–1998   *Continued*

[1] Non-census-year data are U.S. Department of Agriculture estimates; see text. Interpolations between census years are discontinued in 1989.

[2] Excludes steam or garden types.

[3] Beginning in 1975, only self-propelled combines.

[4] Beginning in 1971, includes corn pickers and shellers.

[5] Beginning in 1971, includes pickup balers producing bales up to 200 pounds.

[6] Beginning in 1976, does not include flail-type forage harvesters.

[7] Data are based on a sample of farms; see text.

[8] Census data.

[9] Weighted sum of machines in which two-row models are counted as two one-row models.

Sources

Series Da623–632 and Da634. 1910–1970, U.S. Department of Agriculture, Economic Research Service (USDA ERS), *Changes in Farm Production and Efficiency*, Statistical Bulletin number 233, July 1964 and June 1971 issues; 1971–1988, USDA ERS, *Selected Farm Machinery Statistics*, September 1991, Table 18, downloaded August 25, 2000, from the USDA Economics and Statistics System; 1993–1997, U.S. Bureau of the Census, *1997 Census of Agriculture*, volume 1, part 51, p. 22.

Series Da633. 1946–1952, James Street, *The New Revolution in the Cotton Economy* (University of North Carolina Press, 1957), p. 133; 1955, James Street, "Mechanizing the Cotton Harvest," *Agricultural History* 31 (1957): 17; 1961, U.S. Department of Labor, Bureau of Employment Security, *Cotton Harvest Mechanization: Effect on Seasonal Hired Labor*, B.E.S. number 209 (June 1962), p. 5; 1971, U.S. Bureau of the Census, *1969 Census of Agriculture*, volume 5, *Special Reports*, part 3, *Cotton*, p. 37; 1979–1998, U.S. Bureau of the Census, *Census of Agriculture, 1982*, volume 1, part 51, p. 9; *1987*, volume 1, part 51, p. 18; *1992*, volume 1, part 51, p. 20; and *1997*, volume 1, part 51, p. 22.

Documentation

Census counts of tractors and motor trucks were first made in the 1920 Census of Agriculture; of grain combines in the 1945 Census; of cornpickers and pickup balers in the 1950 Census; and of field forage harvesters in the 1954 Census. Estimates for intercensal years and before census data were available are as of January 1.

Before 1950, figures of machines shipped by manufacturers for farm use, with an allowance for disappearance, were used mainly as the basis for these estimates. Figures for motor trucks were based on annual registrations for a limited number of agricultural states, and a few special sample surveys that were nationwide. Since 1950, the annual series is based on census count, production, imports and shipments of machines, survey data (mainly a questionnaire to Statistical Reporting Service crop reporters in February), trends in census data, and estimated annual discard rates.

For censuses since 1978, data on farm machinery were collected from only a sample of farms. These data are subject to sampling error. For 1992, the sample form was mailed to approximately 29 percent of all farms, including all large and specialized farms (based on expected sales, acres, or standard industrial classification), all farms in Alaska, Hawai'i, and Rhode Island, and a sample of all other farms. For 1987 and 1982, the sample form was mailed to all large and specialized farms, all farms in Alaska and Hawai'i, and approximately 17 percent of all other farms. The 1978 sample consisted of all certainty (large) farms and approximately 20 percent of all other farms.

The estimates for cotton harvesters, series Da633, for 1946 to 1952 rely on the National Cotton Council data for the cumulative number of machines sold. These figures probably significantly overstate the number of machines in use, because no account is taken of obsolete or discarded machines.

The user should be aware of unusual dating in these series. The data for years through 1988 come from the USDA publications noted in series Da623–632 and Da634. These publications used the Agricultural Census for census years without providing alternative USDA estimates. The USDA consistently presented census data in the year following the census year. For example, data from the 1978 Census were listed in 1979 in the USDA presentation. The USDA tabulations ceased in 1988. This table supplements the USDA data with three additional years of census data. For consistency, it continues the USDA practice of offsetting the data by one year.

TABLE Da635–642   Fertilizer – quantity used, by primary plant nutrient: 1947–1993[1]

Contributed by Alan L. Olmstead and Paul W. Rhode

	Quantity used				Index of quantity used			
	Total	Nitrogen	Phosphate	Potash	Total	Nitrogen	Phosphate	Potash
	Da635	Da636	Da637	Da638	Da639	Da640	Da641	Da642
Year	Thousand short tons	Thousand short tons	Thousand short tons	Thousand short tons	Index 1977 = 100	Index 1977 = 100	Index 1977 = 100	Index 1977 = 100
1947	3,490	836	1,775	879	16	8	32	15
1948	3,640	841	1,843	956	17	8	33	16
1949	3,860	912	1,884	1,064	18	9	34	18
1950	4,058	1,005	1,950	1,103	18	9	35	19
1951	4,728	1,238	2,110	1,380	21	12	38	24
1952	5,205	1,425	2,199	1,581	24	13	39	27
1953	5,646	1,637	2,271	1,738	26	15	40	30
1954	5,896	1,847	2,235	1,814	27	17	40	31
1955	6,109	1,960	2,284	1,865	28	18	41	32
1956	6,055	1,933	2,247	1,875	27	18	40	32
1957	6,377	2,135	2,305	1,937	29	20	41	33
1958	6,512	2,284	2,293	1,935	30	21	41	33
1959	7,414	2,672	2,551	2,191	34	25	45	38
1960	7,463	2,738	2,572	2,153	34	26	46	37
1961	7,844	3,031	2,645	2,168	36	28	47	37
1962	8,448	3,370	2,807	2,271	38	32	50	39
1963	9,505	3,929	3,073	2,503	43	37	55	43
1964	10,460	4,353	3,377	2,730	47	41	60	47
1965	10,987	4,639	3,513	2,835	50	44	62	49
1966	12,445	5,326	3,898	3,221	56	50	69	55
1967	13,974	6,027	4,305	3,642	63	57	76	62
1968	15,035	6,788	4,454	3,793	68	64	79	65
1969	15,515	6,958	4,665	3,892	70	65	83	67
1970	16,068	7,459	4,574	4,035	73	70	81	69
1971	17,168	8,134	4,803	4,231	78	76	85	73
1972	17,212	8,022	4,865	4,325	78	75	86	74
1973	18,029	8,295	5,085	4,649	82	78	90	80
1974	19,338	9,157	5,099	5,083	88	86	91	87
1975	17,572	8,608	4,511	4,453	80	81	80	76
1976	20,849	10,412	5,228	5,210	94	98	93	89
1977	22,111	10,647	5,630	5,834	100	100	100	100
1978	20,587	9,965	5,096	5,526	93	94	91	95
1979	22,565	10,715	5,606	6,244	102	101	100	107
1980	23,083	11,407	5,432	6,245	104	107	97	107
1981	23,678	11,924	5,434	6,320	107	112	97	108
1982	21,429	10,984	4,814	5,631	97	103	86	97
1983	18,096	9,127	4,138	4,831	82	86	74	83
1984	21,790	11,092	4,901	5,797	99	104	87	99
1985	21,703	11,493	4,658	5,552	98	108	83	95
1986	19,655	10,424	4,178	5,053	89	98	74	87
1987	19,054	10,209	4,008	4,837	86	96	71	83
1988	19,613	10,512	4,129	4,973	89	99	73	85
1989	19,548	10,593	4,117	4,838	88	100	73	83
1990	20,624	11,076	4,345	5,203	93	104	77	89
1991	20,489	11,287	4,201	5,001	—	—	—	—
1992	20,706	11,446	4,218	5,042	—	—	—	—
1993	20,926	11,358	4,458	5,110	—	—	—	—

[1] Calendar year for 1947–1949. Fertilizer year ending June 30 for 1950–1987.

Sources

1947–1989, U.S. Department of Agriculture, Economic Research Service, *Economic Indicators of the Farm Sector: Production and Efficiency Statistics, 1990,* April 1992, downloaded August 24, 2000, from the U.S. Department of Agriculture, Economics and Statistics System; 1990–1993, U.S. Department of Agriculture, Economic Research Service, *Fertilizer Use and Price Statistics, 1960–93,* Statistical Bulletin number 893, 1994.

Documentation

Data include the fifty states and Puerto Rico.

Series Da635 and Da639. Include material for nonfarm use.

Series Da637 and Da641. To convert P_2O_5 to P, multiply P_2O_5 by 0.43642.

Series Da638 and Da642. To convert K_2O to K, multiply K_2O by 0.83016.

TABLE Da643–646   Fertilizer – farmers' expenditures, commercial fertilizer consumption, and liming materials used: 1850–1999[1]

Contributed by Alan L. Olmstead and Paul W. Rhode

Year	Farmers' expenditure for fertilizer and lime Da643 [2,3] Million dollars	Commercial fertilizer consumed Da644 Thousand short tons	Liming materials Quantity Da645 Thousand short tons	Liming materials Index Da646 Index 1977 = 100	Year	Farmers' expenditure for fertilizer and lime Da643 [2,3] Million dollars	Commercial fertilizer consumed Da644 Thousand short tons	Liming materials Quantity Da645 Thousand short tons	Liming materials Index Da646 Index 1977 = 100
1850	—	53	—	—	1945	657	15,128	23,055	—
1860	—	164	—	—	1946	683	15,128	29,462	—
1870	—	321	—	—	1947	755	16,839	30,283	97
1880	—	753	—	—	1948	826	17,818	25,686	82
1890	—	1,390	—	—	1949	895	18,542	27,902	89
1891	—	1,584	—	—	1950	975	18,343	29,842	95
1892	—	1,504	—	—	1951	1,064	20,991	27,583	88
1893	—	1,715	—	—	1952	1,184	22,432	27,252	87
1894	—	1,773	—	—	1953	1,178	23,413	20,669	66
1895	—	1,578	—	—	1954	1,209	22,773	18,975	61
1896	—	1,888	—	—	1955	1,185	22,726	20,659	66
1897	—	2,131	—	—	1956	1,166	22,194	22,021	70
1898	—	2,333	—	—	1957	1,166	22,709	22,476	72
1899	—	2,603	—	—	1958	1,206	22,516	23,215	74
1900	—	2,730	—	—	1959	1,332	25,313	22,726	72
1901	—	3,044	—	—	1960	1,344	24,877	22,614	72
1902	—	3,084	—	—	1961	1,437	25,567	22,612	72
1903	—	3,382	—	—	1962	1,544	26,615	23,616	75
1904	—	3,704	—	—	1963	1,712	28,844	26,119	83
1905	—	3,913	—	—	1964	1,888	30,681	27,002	86
1906	—	4,249	—	—	1965	1,994	31,836	28,075	90
1907	—	4,307	—	—	1966	2,219	34,532	30,461	97
1908	—	4,449	—	—	1967	2,429	37,081	29,202	93
1909	120	4,821	—	—	1968	2,434	38,743	30,536	97
1910	152	5,547	946	—	1969	2,312	38,949	28,380	90
1911	168	6,108	1,116	—	1970	2,435	39,589	25,901	83
1912	161	5,852	1,286	—	1971	2,654	41,118	23,703	76
1913	175	6,416	1,456	—	1972	2,721	41,206	25,122	80
1914	195	7,194	1,626	—	1973	3,503	43,288	23,657	75
1915	165	5,418	1,796	—	1974	6,053	47,094	27,807	89
1916	193	5,214	1,966	—	1975	6,660	42,484	31,128	99
1917	232	6,087	2,136	—	1976	6,468	49,189	38,147	122
1918	311	6,580	2,306	—	1977	6,529	51,624	31,381	100
1919	358	6,751	2,476	—	1978	6,620	47,497	30,697	98
1920	390	7,176	2,653	—	1979	7,369	51,480	30,979	99
1921	249	4,854	2,794	—	1980	9,491	52,787	34,402	110
1922	234	5,680	2,935	—	1981	9,409	53,988	29,647	95
1923	263	6,435	3,076	—	1982	8,018	48,669	23,237	74
1924	264	6,833	3,217	—	1983	7,055	41,813	25,383	81
1925	299	7,329	3,359	—	1984	8,361	50,056	26,592	85
1926	298	7,326	3,330	—	1985	7,513	49,109	—	—
1927	267	6,844	3,798	—	1986	6,820	44,071	—	—
1928	318	7,989	3,806	—	1987	6,453	42,964	—	—
1929	300	7,982	3,907	—	1988	7,679	44,527	—	—
1930	297	8,171	3,588	—	1989	8,176	44,787	—	—
1931	202	6,306	2,611	—	1990	8,208	47,705	—	—
1932	118	4,336	1,811	—	1991	8,667	46,816	—	—
1933	120	4,872	1,548	—	1992	8,333	—	—	—
1934	176	5,547	2,748	—	1993	8,398	—	—	—
1935	188	6,275	3,505	—	1994	9,150	—	—	—
1936	261	6,956	6,566	—	1995	10,000	—	—	—
1937	279	8,139	7,199	—	1996	10,900	—	—	—
1938	258	7,471	7,859	—	1997	10,900	—	—	—
1939	273	7,728	9,066	—	1998	10,600	—	—	—
1940	306	9,360	14,406	—	1999	9,900	—	—	—
1941	334	9,296	15,916	—					
1942	417	10,125	19,838	—					
1943	505	11,516	19,935	—					
1944	576	13,045	24,568	—					

TABLE Da643–646   Fertilizer – farmers' expenditures, commercial fertilizer consumption, and liming materials used: 1850–1999   *Continued*

[1] Calendar year for 1910–1949. Fiscal year ending June 30 for 1950–1987.

[2] Method of deriving estimates changes over time. See text.

[3] The 1959–1970 values presented here differ from those in *Historical Statistics of the United States* (1975). The data were taken from the most recent available source.

Sources

For a detailed discussion of concepts, coverage, and methods, see *Major Statistical Series of the U.S. Department of Agriculture*, Agriculture Handbook number 365, volume 3.

Series Da643. 1909–1929, U.S. Department of Agriculture, Agricultural Marketing Service, *The Farm Income Situation*, July 1958 (No. 174); 1930–1958, U.S. Department of Agriculture, Economic Research Service (USDA ERS), *Farm Income Situation*, July 1971, number 218; 1959–1990, USDA ERS, *Economic Indicators of the Farm Sector, National Financial Summary, 1993*, p. 38; 1991–1993, USDA ERS, *Farm Business Economics Report, 1994*, p. 9; 1994–1999, USDA ERS, *Farm Production Expenditures, 1999 Summary*, p. 21, downloaded August 30, 2000, from the U.S. Department of Agriculture, Economics and Statistics System.

Series Da644. 1850–1944, U.S. Department of Agriculture, Agricultural Research Service, *Statistics on Fertilizers and Liming Materials in the United States*, Statistical Bulletin number 191, April 1957; 1945–1969, U.S. Department of Agriculture, Statistical Reporting Service, *Consumption of Commercial Fertilizer and Primary Plant Nutrients in the United States*, Statistical Bulletin number 472, June 1971; 1970–1991, Tennessee Valley Authority, National Fertilizer and Environmental Research Center, *Commercial Fertilizers, 1991*, p. 4.

Series Da645. 1910–1946, USDA ERS, *Economic Indicators of the Farm Sector: Production and Efficiency Statistics, 1979*, Table 27; 1947–1984, National Stone Association, in *Economic Indicators of the Farm Sector: Production and Efficiency Statistics, 1990*, April 1992, Table 27, downloaded August 24, 2000, from the U.S. Department of Agriculture, Economics and Statistics System.

Series Da646. National Stone Association, in *Economic Indicators of the Farm Sector: Production and Efficiency Statistics, 1990*, April 1992, Table 27, downloaded August 24, 2000, from the U.S. Department of Agriculture, Economics and Statistics System.

Documentation

Series Da643. Beginning with 1991, estimates are based on the Farm Costs and Returns Survey (FCRS). FCRS data for 1991 and later years use revised nonresponse and undercoverage procedures that make them more representative of the entire farm sector. Estimates for 1988–1990 were derived using interpolation factors between prior 1987 estimates and the new 1991 results. FCRS data used in 1987 estimates were adjusted to represent the USDA number of farms in sales classes under $100,000. FCRS data used in estimates prior to 1987 are usually as published in annual *Farm Production Expenditures* summaries.

Series Da643. Expenses for operator dwellings are included only if the operator dwelling is located on the farm. For 1984 and later years, operator dwelling expenses are based on data derived from the Farm Costs and Returns Survey.

Series Da645–646. Excludes Alaska and Hawai'i.

TABLE Da647–660   Farmers' cooperatives – number, memberships, and business, by type of cooperative: 1913–1998[1]

Contributed by Alan L. Olmstead and Paul W. Rhode

	Cooperatives				Membership				Marketing and farm supply cooperatives, volume and service receipts		Marketing cooperatives, volume		Farm supply cooperatives, volume	
	Total	Marketing	Related service	Farm supply	Total	Marketing	Related service	Farm supply	Gross business	Net business	Gross business	Net business	Gross business	Net business
	Da647	Da648[2]	Da649[2]	Da650	Da651	Da652	Da653[3]	Da654	Da655[4]	Da656[4,5]	Da657[4]	Da658[4,5]	Da659[4]	Da660[4,5]
Year	Number	Number	Number	Number	Thousand	Thousand	Thousand	Thousand	Million dollars	Million dollars	Million dollars	Million dollars	Million dollars	Million dollars
1913	3,099	2,988	—	111	—	—	—	—	310	—	304	—	6	—
1915	5,424	5,149	—	275	651	592	—	59	636	—	624	—	12	—
1921	7,374	6,476	—	898	—	—	—	—	1,256	—	1,198	—	58	—
1926	10,803	9,586	—	1,217	2,700	2,453	—	247	2,400	—	2,265	—	135	—
1929	12,000	10,546	—	1,454	3,100	2,630	—	470	2,500	—	2,310	—	190	—
1930	11,950	10,362	—	1,588	3,000	2,608	—	392	2,400	—	2,185	—	215	—
1931	11,900	10,255	—	1,645	3,200	2,667	—	533	1,925	—	1,744	—	181	—
1932	11,000	9,352	—	1,648	3,000	2,457	—	543	1,340	—	1,200	—	140	—
1933	10,900	9,052	—	1,848	3,156	2,464	—	692	1,365	—	1,213	—	152	—
1934	10,700	8,794	—	1,906	3,280	2,490	—	790	1,530	—	1,343	—	187	—
1935	10,500	8,388	—	2,112	3,660	2,710	—	950	1,840	—	1,586	—	254	—
1936	10,743	8,142	—	2,601	3,270	2,414	—	856	2,196	—	1,883	—	313	—
1937	10,900	8,300	—	2,600	3,400	2,500	—	900	2,400	—	2,050	—	350	—
1938	10,700	8,100	—	2,600	3,300	2,410	—	890	2,100	—	1,765	—	335	—
1939	10,700	8,051	—	2,649	3,200	2,300	—	900	2,087	—	1,729	—	358	—
1940	10,600	7,943	—	2,657	3,400	2,420	—	980	2,280	—	1,911	—	369	—
1941	10,550	7,824	—	2,726	3,600	2,430	—	1,170	2,840	—	2,360	—	480	—
1942	10,450	7,708	—	2,742	3,850	2,580	—	1,270	3,780	—	3,180	—	600	—
1943	10,300	7,522	—	2,778	4,250	2,730	—	1,520	5,160	—	4,430	—	730	—
1944	10,150	7,400	—	2,750	4,505	2,895	—	1,610	5,645	—	4,835	—	810	—
1945	10,150	7,378	—	2,772	5,010	3,150	—	1,860	6,070	—	5,147	—	923	—
1946	10,125	7,268	—	2,857	5,436	3,378	—	2,058	7,116	—	6,005	—	1,111	—
1947	10,135	7,159	—	2,976	5,890	3,630	—	2,260	8,635	—	7,195	—	1,440	—
1948	10,075	6,993	—	3,082	6,384	3,973	—	2,411	9,320	—	7,700	—	1,620	—
1949	10,035	6,922	—	3,113	6,584	4,075	—	2,509	8,726	—	7,083	—	1,643	—
1950	10,064	6,519	262	3,283	7,091	4,118	94	2,879	—	8,147	—	6,362	—	1,685
1951	10,179	6,594	261	3,324	7,364	4,229	102	3,033	—	9,410	—	7,377	—	1,919
1952	10,128	6,501	249	3,378	7,475	4,247	89	3,139	—	9,521	—	7,366	—	2,013
1953	10,072	6,457	241	3,374	7,608	4,273	82	3,252	—	9,475	—	7,339	—	1,978
1954	9,903	6,330	227	3,346	7,604	4,213	68	3,323	—	9,642	—	7,425	—	2,022
1955	9,894	6,284	235	3,375	7,732	4,223	65	3,444	—	9,756	—	7,495	—	2,046
1956	9,891	6,284	234	3,373	7,673	4,122	62	3,489	—	10,380	—	7,999	—	2,146
1957	9,735	6,119	233	3,383	7,486	3,880	63	3,543	—	10,753	—	8,318	—	2,188
1958	9,658	6,042	229	3,387	7,559	3,861	54	3,644	—	11,747	—	9,103	—	2,371
1959	9,345	5,828	220	3,297	7,273	3,622	51	3,600	—	12,036	—	9,330	—	2,408
1960	9,163	5,727	214	3,222	7,203	3,473	50	3,680	—	12,409	—	9,631	—	2,472
1961	9,039	5,626	207	3,206	7,099	3,420	44	3,635	—	13,024	—	10,161	—	2,561
1962	8,907	5,502	194	3,211	7,219	3,582	41	3,596	—	13,842	—	10,834	—	2,705
1963	8,847	5,421	200	3,226	7,080	3,613	42	3,425	—	14,354	—	11,209	—	2,832
1964	8,583	5,305	193	3,085	7,082	3,791	40	3,251	—	14,742	—	11,516	—	2,910
1965	8,329	5,194	186	2,949	6,826	3,636	36	3,154	—	15,608	—	12,198	—	3,085
1966	8,125	5,076	178	2,871	6,502	3,299	34	3,169	—	16,557	—	12,900	—	3,339
1967	7,940	4,929	176	2,835	6,445	3,225	34	3,186	—	17,050	—	13,189	—	3,545
1968	7,747	4,773	181	2,793	6,364	3,141	33	3,189	—	17,387	—	13,421	—	3,615
1969	7,790	4,834	181	2,775	6,355	3,103	30	3,222	—	19,080	—	14,816	—	3,873

Year	Cooperatives				Membership				Marketing and farm supply cooperatives, volume and service receipts		Marketing cooperatives, volume		Farm supply cooperatives, volume	
	Total	Marketing	Related service	Farm supply	Total	Marketing	Related service	Farm supply	Gross business	Net business	Gross business	Net business	Gross business	Net business
	Da647	Da648 [2]	Da649 [2]	Da650	Da651	Da652	Da653 [3]	Da654	Da655 [4]	Da656 [4,5]	Da657 [4]	Da658 [4,5]	Da659 [4]	Da660 [4,5]
	Number	Number	Number	Number	Thousand	Thousand	Thousand	Thousand	Million dollars	Million dollars	Million dollars	Million dollars	Million dollars	Million dollars
1970	7,995	5,097	167	2,731	6,158	3,105	25	3,028	—	20,556	—	15,802	—	4,340
1971	7,797	4,864	152	2,781	6,147	3,134	22	2,991	—	21,665	—	16,463	—	4,740
1972	7,854	4,897	156	2,801	6,128	3,118	22	2,988	—	25,991	—	19,573	—	5,915
1973	7,755	4,822	155	2,778	6,105	3,111	22	2,972	—	35,366	—	26,944	—	7,764
1974	7,645	4,770	146	2,729	6,123	3,127	25	2,971	—	41,342	—	31,937	—	8,660
1975	7,535	4,658	146	2,731	5,906	2,812	38	3,056	—	40,050	—	29,783	—	9,412
1976 [6]	6,736	4,008	135	2,593	5,758	2,655	37	3,066	—	43,584	—	32,134	—	10,557
1977 [6]	6,736	4,008	135	2,593	5,758	2,655	37	3,066	—	43,584	—	32,134	—	10,557
1978	6,600	3,930	120	2,550	5,695	2,595	37	3,063	—	47,305	—	35,306	—	11,052
1979 [7]	6,445	3,825	113	2,507	5,627	2,531	36	3,060	—	56,268	—	41,693	—	13,521
1980	6,293	3,808	116	2,369	5,379	2,542	32	2,804	—	66,254	—	48,911	—	16,134
1981	6,211	3,743	112	2,356	5,335	2,452	27	2,856	—	71,534	—	53,285	—	17,059
1982	6,125	3,714	112	2,299	5,135	2,444	25	2,666	—	69,150	—	51,394	—	16,362
1983	5,989	3,647	134	2,208	4,955	2,308	95	2,553	—	66,755	—	49,344	—	15,943
1984	5,782	3,514	132	2,136	4,842	2,317	128	2,397	—	73,047	—	54,556	—	16,969
1985	5,625	3,441	148	2,036	4,781	2,214	169	2,398	—	65,601	—	47,321	—	16,641
1986	5,369	3,260	138	1,971	4,600	2,140	150	2,310	—	58,395	—	41,540	—	15,095
1987	5,109	3,054	114	1,941	4,440	2,026	132	2,282	—	60,318	—	44,156	—	14,271
1988 [8]	4,937	2,988	113	1,836	4,195	1,912	141	2,142	—	66,430	—	49,067	—	15,424
1989 [8]	4,799	2,550	446	1,803	4,134	1,856	243	2,035	—	72,129	—	53,247	—	16,907
1990	4,663	2,519	427	1,717	4,119	1,882	232	2,006	—	77,266	—	57,831	—	17,088
1991	4,494	2,384	421	1,689	4,059	1,842	191	2,025	—	76,636	—	56,203	—	17,916
1992	4,315	2,218	479	1,618	4,072	1,839	212	2,020	—	79,284	—	58,196	—	18,513
1993	4,244	2,214	483	1,547	4,023	1,830	216	1,977	—	82,872	—	60,930	—	19,218
1994	4,174	2,173	505	1,496	3,986	1,805	245	1,936	—	89,309	—	65,545	—	20,779
1995	4,006	2,074	474	1,458	3,767	1,712	210	1,846	—	93,818	—	69,321	—	21,213
1996	3,884	2,012	469	1,403	3,664	1,682	187	1,795	—	106,182	—	79,429	—	23,653
1997	3,791	1,941	464	1,386	3,424	1,498	183	1,743	—	106,670	—	77,843	—	25,181
1998 [9]	3,651	1,863	441	1,347	3,353	1,398	181	1,774	—	104,667	—	76,642	—	24,551

[1] Through 1977, reports of cooperatives apply to fiscal years; dates shown are the ending date of the fiscal year. Reports of cooperatives are included for the calendar year beginning 1978.

[2] Increase in 1989 figures for series Da649 is attributable to a reclassification of cotton ginning cooperatives from series Da648 beginning that year.

[3] Number of memberships increased significantly in 1983 owing to inclusion of additional related service cooperatives.

[4] Beginning 1950, method of reporting revised. See text.

[5] Estimated net business figures beginning 1951 cannot be compared with figures for previous years. See text.

[6] Data for 1976 and 1977 are identical. See text.

[7] Estimated.

[8] Revised.

[9] Preliminary data.

Sources

1913–1926, U.S. Farmer Cooperative Service, *Statistics of Farmer Cooperatives, 1954–1955; 1930–1997*, U.S. Department of Agriculture, Economic Research Service, *Agricultural Statistics, 1957, 1967, 1972, 1982, 1987, 1990, 1997*, and *2000* editions.

Documentation

The U.S. Department of Agriculture (USDA) reported the data reproduced in this table on a fiscal year basis until 1976. They then switched to calendar year reporting. The presentation in this table follows that format. Owing to the change in reporting year, the data for 1976 and for 1977 were presented as a single "year," 1976/77. The USDA data for "1976/77" appear to have been annualized. Otherwise, some values would be much higher than average in this "year." To provide a consistent series we have reproduced the 1976/77 data in both 1976 and 1977.

These data were first compiled in 1913–1915 from questionnaires collected by mail from all cooperatives known to exist in the period 1912–1915. In 1919, data on the extent of cooperative marketing and farm supply purchasing were collected as a part of the Census of Agriculture. Other nationwide surveys were conducted in 1922 and for the fiscal years 1925–1926 and 1927–1928. Beginning with 1929–1930, annual nationwide surveys have been taken of farmer marketing, farm supply, and related services cooperatives. Data were collected by mail in each of these surveys except for 1936–1937, for which information was collected in the field by the Farm Credit Administration in cooperation with the banks for cooperatives and thirty-three state agricultural colleges.

A farmer cooperative is defined as one which meets the following requirements: (1) farmers or associations of agricultural producers hold the controlling interest; (2) each member is limited to one

(continued)

TABLE Da647–660   Farmers' cooperatives – number, memberships, and business, by type of cooperative: 1913–1998   *Continued*

vote regardless of the amount of stock or membership capital he owns therein, unless dividends on stock or membership capital are limited to 8 percent a year or less, in which case the number of votes per member can vary; and (3) the value of products handled for nonmembers is not greater in value than the amount handled for members. All active farmer cooperatives that meet the above criteria, and that provide information indicating they market farm products, handle farm supplies, or perform related services, are included in the annual survey.

As cooperatives tended increasingly to diversify their operations, the annual survey figures became less satisfactory. Therefore, beginning with the survey covering fiscal year 1951, revised questionnaires were used to develop information on a functional and commodity basis. The questionnaires were revised further in 1960 to limit the scope of questions on service organizations.

Series Da647–650. Includes independent local cooperatives, centralized cooperatives, federations of cooperatives, and cooperatives with mixed organizational structures. Cooperatives are classified according to their major activity. If, for example, more than 50 percent of a cooperative's business is derived from marketing activities, it is included as a marketing cooperative.

Series Da649 and Da653. In 1950, a separate category was set up for cooperatives whose major activity is providing services related to marketing and farm-supply activities. The series include cooperatives whose major activity is providing services related to marketing and farm supply activities.

Series Da651–654. Includes members (those entitled to vote for directors) but does not include nonvoting patrons. Some duplication exists because some farmers belong to more than one cooperative.

Series Da655. Equals the sum of series Da657 and Da659, and gross service receipts.

Series Da655–660. Estimated gross business includes all business reported between cooperatives, such as the wholesale business of farm supply cooper-

atives with other cooperatives or terminal market sales for local cooperatives. Estimated net business represents the value at the first level at which cooperatives transact business for farmers. Figures are adjusted for duplication resulting from intercooperative business.

Series Da655–660. Prior to 1950, total dollar volume of the marketing cooperatives was classified as marketing business even though a portion of this volume was derived from handling supplies or performing services for patrons. Similarly, the total volume of farm-supply cooperatives was classified as farm-supply business even though a portion of their business originated from the sale of various farm commodities or from performing trucking and other services for patrons. In 1950, the method of reporting was revised so that cooperatives reported sales of each major commodity marketed, the value of each major type of supply purchased, and receipts from major types of services performed for patrons. Beginning with 1950, the total marketing volume, therefore, consists only of the value of products actually marketed and farm-supply volume consists only of the value of individual supplies purchased.

Series Da655, Da657, and Da659. Includes service receipts for cooperatives rendering essential services either in marketing or farm-supply purchasing.

Series Da656. Equals the sum of series Da658 and Da660, and net service receipts.

Series Da656, Da658, and Da660. The estimated net business figures for 1951 and subsequent years cannot be compared with the estimated business for previous years because previous figures included some supply sales at the wholesale level for other cooperatives and some terminal market sales for local cooperatives. Estimated net business represents the value at the first level at which cooperatives transact business for farmers. Figures are adjusted for duplication resulting from intercooperative business.

Alan L. Olmstead and Paul W. Rhode

TABLE Da661–666 Cropland – acreage harvested and indexes of cropland use and production per acre: 1910–1990 *Continued*

Year	Acreage of harvested crops, by use				Index of cropland used for crops	Index of crop production per acre
	Total	Export products	Feed for horses and mules	Products for domestic use		
	Da661	Da662	Da663	Da664	Da665	Da666
	Million acres	Million acres	Million acres	Million acres	Index 1967 = 100	Index 1967 = 100
1910	325	37	88	200	96	55
1911	330	40	90	200	98	54
1912	329	42	91	196	98	62
1913	333	43	92	198	99	53
1914	334	57	92	185	100	58
1915	340	49	93	198	101	60
1916	340	53	92	195	101	54
1917	349	44	92	213	104	56
1918	362	62	92	208	108	54
1919	364	56	91	217	109	54
1920	360	60	90	210	107	60
1921	359	66	87	206	107	51
1922	355	50	86	219	106	56
1923	354	47	84	223	106	56
1924	355	53	81	221	106	55
1925	360	44	78	238	108	56
1926	359	54	76	229	108	57
1927	358	49	73	236	109	56
1928	361	49	70	242	110	58
1929	365	44	67	254	110	56
1930	369	39	65	265	111	52
1931	365	36	62	267	112	58
1932	371	35	60	276	112	55
1933	340	28	59	253	110	49
1934	304	20	57	227	109	41
1935	345	20	56	269	110	54
1936	323	18	54	251	109	45
1937	347	29	52	266	110	62
1938	349	22	48	279	108	59
1939	331	23	45	263	106	60
1940	341	8	43	290	107	62
1941	344	12	40	292	107	64
1942	348	13	39	296	108	70
1943	357	21	37	299	110	64
1944	362	25	36	301	110	68
1945	354	42	32	280	108	68
1946	352	45	29	278	108	70
1947	355	42	26	287	109	67
1948	356	52	24	280	110	75
1949	360	45	22	293	113	70
1950	345	50	19	276	110	69
1951	344	59	18	267	111	69
1952	349	36	15	298	111	73
1953	348	31	13	304	111	73
1954	346	37	11	298	111	71
1955	340	47	10	283	110	74
1956	324	60	9	255	107	77
1957	324	48	8	268	104	77
1958	324	44	7	273	103	86
1959	324	61	6	257	104	86

(continued)

TABLE Da661–666   Cropland – acreage harvested and indexes of cropland use and production per acre: 1910–1990   *Continued*

Year	Acreage of harvested crops, by use				Index of cropland used for crops	Index of crop production per acre
	Total	Export products	Feed for horses and mules	Products for domestic use		
	Da661	Da662	Da663	Da664	Da665	Da666
	Million acres	Million acres	Million acres	Million acres	Index 1967 = 100	Index 1967 = 100
1960	324	64	5	255	104	88
1961	302	67	4	232	99	92
1962	295	66	—	225	97	95
1963	298	77	—	217	98	97
1964	298	74	—	220	98	95
1965	298	76	—	222	98	100
1966	294	69	—	225	96	99
1967	306	69	—	237	100	100
1968	300	54	—	246	99	104
1969	290	61	—	229	97	107
1970	293	72	—	221	98	102
1971	305	62	—	243	100	112
1972	294	91	—	203	98	115
1973	321	96	—	225	103	115
1974	328	99	—	229	107	102
1975	336	100	—	236	108	112
1976	337	97	—	240	109	109
1977	345	112	—	233	111	116
1978	338	114	—	224	108	122
1979	348	125	—	223	111	131
1980	352	137	—	215	112	116
1981	366	129	—	237	113	134
1982	362	113	—	249	112	135
1983	306	124	—	182	98	116
1984	348	96	—	252	110	130
1985	342	81	—	261	109	140
1986	325	96	—	229	104	135
1987	302	106	—	196	98	143
1988	297	118	—	180	97	123
1989	318	103	—	216	100	138
1990 [1]	322	83	—	239	100	148

[1] Preliminary.

Sources

Series Da661. 1910–1960, U.S. Department of Agriculture, Economic Research Service (USDA ERS), *Changes in Farm Production and Efficiency*, Statistical Bulletin number 233, July 1964 and June 1971; 1961–1990, U.S. Department of Agriculture, *Economic Indicators of the Farm Sector: Production and Efficiency Statistics*, 1990, p. 18.

Series Da662. 1910–1970, USDA ERS, *Changes in Farm Production and Efficiency*, Statistical Bulletin number 233, July 1964 and June 1971; 1971–1990, *Economic Indicators of the Farm Sector: Production and Efficiency Statistics*, 1990, p. 18.

Series Da663. USDA ERS, *Changes in Farm Production and Efficiency*, Statistical Bulletin No. 233, July 1964 and June 1971.

Series Da664. 1910–1961, USDA ERS, *Changes in Farm Production and Efficiency*, Statistical Bulletin No. 233, July 1964 and June 1971; 1962–1990, *Economic Indicators of the Farm Sector: Production and Efficiency Statistics*, 1990, p. 18.

Series Da665–666. 1910–1949, unpublished data; 1950–1970, USDA ERS, *Changes in Farm Production and Efficiency*, Statistical Bulletin number 233, June 1971; 1971–1990, *Economic Indicators of the Farm Sector: Production and Efficiency Statistics*, 1990, p. 19.

Related data up to 1994 can be found at the U.S. Department of Agriculture, Economics and Statistics System Internet site.

Documentation

Acreages for harvested crops do not include pasture.

For a more detailed explanation of these series, see *Major Statistical Series of the U.S. Department of Agriculture*, Agriculture Handbook number 365, volume 2.

Series Da661. Total crop acres harvested consists of acreages of the fifty-nine crops harvested, as reported by the Crop Reporting Board (excluding duplication) plus acreages in tree fruits, small fruits, tree nuts, and farm gardens. Acreages of several minor crops, which are not included, have accounted for about 0.5 million acres in recent years.

Series Da662

Acreages used for production of crop exports are determined by dividing the quantity yield per acre. Two steps are necessary in computing the acreages of crops used to produce each of the livestock products exported. The first consists of estimating the quantities of each feed crop used to produce 100 pounds of pork, 100 pounds of milk, 100 dozen eggs, and so on. The second consists of determining the quantity of each feed crop used to produce the products exported, and then determining the acreages needed to produce each feed crop, at average yields per acre. Periodic five-year average yields rather than yields for each year are used.

Yield data for the export estimates are from reports of the Crop Reporting Board. Data for volume of exports prior to 1940 are from *Agricultural Statistics*. For 1940–1970, export data are from reports and records of the Economic Research Service.

Data are for the year beginning July 1 through 1974; October 1 thereafter.

TABLE Da661–666   Cropland – acreage harvested and indexes of cropland use and production per acre: 1910–1990 *Continued*

Series Da663

Covers feed used on farms and in cities and mines. The estimates of feed consumed by horses and mules are based on the following average rations of corn, oats, and all hay. For 1910–1919, the calculations allow 800 pounds of oats, 1,600 pounds of shelled corn, and 1.8 short tons of hay per head for farm horses and mules three years old and over and animal-unit equivalents for younger animals. For 1920–1940, it was assumed that as farm horses were worked less, they consumed less grain and more hay. Consequently, the rate of feeding corn was decreased ten pounds per head per year and the rate of feeding hay was increased twenty pounds. Beginning with 1941, it was assumed that horses and mules would work less each year, and that on average they would be fed less corn, oats, and hay and would consume more pasture.

For nonfarm horses and mules it was assumed that, for 1910–1931, the quantities of grain and hay consumed per head per year were a third more than those consumed by farm work animals. Since 1932, the computations have rounded out to one million acres used in producing feed for nonfarm horses and mules.

Prior to 1960, basic data on horses and mules were from publications of the Economic Research Service. Estimates of horses and mules on farms were discontinued in 1960. The rations for horses and mules are based on data from many sources, especially from Bureau of Agricultural Economics, *Work Performed and Feed Utilized by Horses and Mules*, Farm Management 44, 1944, and on the judgment of workers familiar with the subject.

Series Da664. Includes products used by U.S. military forces in this country and abroad and by domestic civilian population.

Series Da665

Consists of three components: acres of harvested cropland (land from which one or more crops were harvested), crop failure, and summer fallow. The index excludes idle cropland and land in soil-improvement crops during the entire year and not harvested. These figures are based on estimates of principal crops harvested and crop losses prepared by the former Bureau of Agricultural Economics (BAE) and the Statistical Reporting Service (SRS) and on data from the 1925–1954 Censuses of Agriculture. Data from the 1950–1964 Censuses of Agriculture were adjusted to cover some of the undernumeration indicated by postenumeration surveys.

Acreages of crop failure were derived from the 1925–1945 Censuses of Agriculture, and interpolations for intervening years were based on BAE estimates of crop losses or differences between planted and harvested acreages of principal crops. Acreages of crop failure for recent years are based chiefly on crop losses as reported by the SRS. Reported acreages of crop losses are adjusted for the replanting of part of the acreage on which winter wheat is abandoned. Hay land that produced nothing but pasture in some dry seasons is not included in crop failure in recent years.

Estimates of acreage of cultivated summer fallow were made only for the geographic divisions west of the Mississippi River.

Series Da666. Indexes of total crop production were divided by indexes of cropland used for crops to derive indexes of crop production per acre. Indexes of crop production were developed as one step in the calculation of farm output; see series Da1210–1217.

TABLE Da667–678   Rice, oats, sorghum, and soybeans – acreage, production, and price: 1866–1998   [Annual]

Contributed by Alan L. Olmstead and Paul W. Rhode

	Rice			Oats			Sorghum			Soybeans		
	Acreage harvested	Production	Price	Acreage harvested	Production	Price	Acreage harvested	Production	Price	Acreage harvested	Production	Price
	Da667	Da668	Da669 [1]	Da670 [2]	Da671 [2]	Da672 [2,3]	Da673 [4]	Da674 [4]	Da675 [4]	Da676	Da677	Da678 [1]
Year	Thousand acres	Thousand hundredweight	Dollars per hundredweight	Thousand acres	Thousand bushels	Dollars per bushel	Thousand acres	Thousand bushels	Dollars per bushel	Thousand acres	Thousand bushels	Dollars per bushel
1866	—	—	—	7,935	232,360	0.47	—	—	—	—	—	—
1867	—	—	—	8,176	222,605	0.59	—	—	—	—	—	—
1868	—	—	—	8,897	229,676	0.54	—	—	—	—	—	—
1869	—	—	—	9,555	284,004	0.46	—	—	—	—	—	—
1870	—	—	—	10,348	267,947	0.43	—	—	—	—	—	—
1871	—	—	—	11,061	306,218	0.39	—	—	—	—	—	—
1872	—	—	—	11,789	326,759	0.32	—	—	—	—	—	—
1873	—	—	—	12,010	306,906	0.37	—	—	—	—	—	—
1874	—	—	—	12,775	272,501	0.52	—	—	—	—	—	—
1875	—	—	—	13,616	364,967	0.37	—	—	—	—	—	—
1876	—	—	—	14,589	327,212	0.35	—	—	—	—	—	—
1877	—	—	—	14,816	435,330	0.29	—	—	—	—	—	—
1878	—	—	—	15,830	443,365	0.24	—	—	—	—	—	—
1879	—	—	—	15,955	415,440	0.33	—	—	—	—	—	—
1880	—	—	—	16,414	417,942	0.35	—	—	—	—	—	—
1881	—	—	—	16,916	446,125	0.46	—	—	—	—	—	—
1882	—	—	—	19,075	540,462	0.37	—	—	—	—	—	—
1883	—	—	—	20,621	605,576	0.32	—	—	—	—	—	—
1884	—	—	—	21,974	640,520	0.27	—	—	—	—	—	—
1885	—	—	—	23,351	674,151	0.28	—	—	—	—	—	—
1886	—	—	—	24,426	682,312	0.29	—	—	—	—	—	—
1887	—	—	—	26,272	696,175	0.30	—	—	—	—	—	—
1888	—	—	—	27,807	773,139	0.27	—	—	—	—	—	—
1889	—	—	—	28,697	831,047	0.22	—	—	—	—	—	—
1890	—	—	—	28,275	609,122	0.42	—	—	—	—	—	—
1891	—	—	—	27,756	836,789	0.31	—	—	—	—	—	—
1892	—	—	—	28,168	721,824	0.32	—	—	—	—	—	—
1893	—	—	—	29,266	707,129	0.29	—	—	—	—	—	—
1894	—	—	—	29,556	750,009	0.32	—	—	—	—	—	—
1895	292	3,341	—	30,905	924,858	0.19	—	—	—	—	—	—
1896	270	2,340	—	30,248	774,929	0.18	—	—	—	—	—	—
1897	290	3,084	—	28,829	829,525	0.21	—	—	—	—	—	—
1898	314	3,737	—	29,327	842,205	0.25	—	—	—	—	—	—
1899	338	4,029	—	29,254	937,173	0.25	—	—	—	—	—	—
1900	361	4,407	—	31,049	945,483	0.25	—	—	—	—	—	—
1901	423	5,702	—	30,891	799,812	0.40	—	—	—	—	—	—
1902	545	6,541	—	31,358	1,076,899	0.30	—	—	—	—	—	—
1903	547	8,590	—	32,187	885,469	0.34	—	—	—	—	—	—
1904	574	8,647	1.46	32,749	1,011,556	0.31	—	—	—	—	—	—
1905	457	7,217	2.10	33,426	1,104,395	0.29	—	—	—	—	—	—
1906	505	7,999	2.01	33,688	1,022,715	0.32	—	—	—	—	—	—
1907	563	9,338	1.91	34,439	801,144	0.44	—	—	—	—	—	—
1908	596	10,079	1.80	34,310	829,308	0.49	—	—	—	—	—	—
1909	662	10,614	1.76	35,062	1,013,909	0.42	—	—	—	—	—	—

	Rice			Oats			Sorghum			Soybeans		
	Acreage harvested	Production	Price	Acreage harvested	Production	Price	Acreage harvested	Production	Price	Acreage harvested	Production	Price
	Da667	Da668	Da669 [1]	Da670 [2]	Da671 [2]	Da672 [2,3]	Da673 [4]	Da674 [4]	Da675 [4]	Da676	Da677	Da678 [1]
Year	Thousand acres	Thousand hundredweight	Dollars per hundredweight	Thousand acres	Thousand bushels	Dollars per bushel	Thousand acres	Thousand bushels	Dollars per bushel	Thousand acres	Thousand bushels	Dollars per bushel
1910	666	11,129	1.47	36,844	1,106,162	0.34	—	—	—	—	—	—
1911	636	10,198	1.75	37,149	885,527	0.44	—	—	—	—	—	—
1912	643	10,665	1.98	37,244	1,353,273	0.33	—	—	—	—	—	—
1913	722	10,894	1.98	37,245	1,039,131	0.37	—	—	—	—	—	—
1914	646	10,565	1.98	37,213	1,066,328	0.43	—	—	—	—	—	—
1915	740	11,748	1.86	38,802	1,435,270	0.37	—	—	—	—	—	—
1916	843	17,795	2.19	39,098	1,138,969	0.47	—	—	—	—	—	—
1917	953	15,621	4.26	41,604	1,442,519	0.68	—	—	—	—	—	—
1918	1,101	17,999	3.99	42,464	1,428,611	0.66	—	—	—	—	—	—
1919	1,083	19,310	5.46	39,601	1,106,603	0.75	—	—	—	—	—	—
1920	1,299	23,242	2.48	42,732	1,444,291	0.52	—	—	—	—	—	—
1921	990	17,673	2.18	45,539	1,045,270	0.30	—	—	—	—	—	—
1922	1,053	18,748	2.19	40,324	1,147,905	0.36	—	—	—	—	—	—
1923	874	14,957	2.49	40,245	1,227,184	0.39	—	—	—	—	—	—
1924	838	14,689	2.99	41,857	1,416,120	0.47	—	—	—	448	4,947	2.50
1925	853	14,866	3.30	44,240	1,405,268	0.37	—	—	—	415	4,875	2.34
1926	1,016	18,911	2.51	42,854	1,152,911	0.39	—	—	—	466	5,239	2.00
1927	1,027	20,024	2.02	40,350	1,093,221	0.46	—	—	—	568	6,938	1.80
1928	972	19,725	2.03	40,128	1,312,914	0.39	—	—	—	579	7,880	1.86
1929	860	17,790	2.22	38,153	1,112,949	0.40	3,523	49,967	0.76	708	9,438	1.86
1930	966	20,218	1.74	39,847	1,274,592	0.31	3,477	37,561	0.57	1,074	13,929	1.34
1931	965	20,076	1.08	40,193	1,124,232	0.20	4,443	71,914	0.30	1,141	17,260	0.48
1932	874	18,729	0.93	41,700	1,254,584	0.15	4,400	66,097	0.31	1,001	15,158	0.53
1933	798	16,943	1.73	36,528	736,309	0.33	4,354	54,386	0.51	1,044	13,509	0.92
1934	812	17,571	1.76	29,455	544,247	0.46	2,396	19,209	0.87	1,556	23,157	0.96
1935	817	17,753	1.60	40,109	1,210,229	0.26	4,597	57,610	0.55	2,915	48,901	0.71
1936	981	22,419	1.85	33,654	792,583	0.43	2,793	30,270	0.92	2,359	33,721	1.25
1937	1,099	24,040	1.46	35,542	1,176,744	0.30	4,915	69,948	0.51	2,586	46,164	0.84
1938	1,076	23,628	1.42	36,042	1,089,383	0.23	4,699	67,210	0.41	3,035	61,906	0.66
1939	1,045	24,328	1.62	33,460	957,704	0.31	4,760	53,280	0.58	4,315	90,141	0.80
1940	1,069	24,495	1.80	35,431	1,246,450	0.30	6,374	85,824	0.49	4,807	78,045	0.89
1941	1,214	23,095	3.01	38,161	1,182,509	0.41	6,015	113,543	0.58	5,889	107,197	1.55
1942	1,457	29,082	3.61	38,197	1,342,681	0.48	5,991	109,653	0.79	9,894	187,524	1.60
1943	1,472	29,264	3.96	38,914	1,139,831	0.71	6,889	109,536	1.14	10,397	190,133	1.81
1944	1,480	30,974	3.93	39,741	1,149,240	0.69	9,386	184,978	0.91	10,245	192,121	2.05
1945	1,499	30,668	3.98	41,739	1,523,851	0.65	6,324	96,063	1.20	10,740	193,167	2.08
1946	1,582	32,497	5.00	42,812	1,477,573	0.81	6,669	106,025	1.40	9,932	203,395	2.57
1947	1,708	35,217	5.97	37,855	1,176,142	1.04	5,480	93,217	1.83	11,411	186,451	3.33
1948	1,804	38,275	4.88	39,280	1,450,186	0.72	7,317	131,384	1.28	10,682	227,217	2.27
1949	1,858	40,769	4.10	37,794	1,220,118	0.66	6,602	148,494	1.13	10,482	234,194	2.16
1950	1,637	38,820	5.09	39,306	1,369,199	0.79	10,346	233,536	1.05	13,807	299,249	2.47
1951	1,996	46,089	4.82	35,233	1,277,647	0.82	8,544	162,863	1.32	13,615	283,777	2.73
1952	1,997	48,193	5.87	37,012	1,217,433	0.79	5,326	90,741	1.58	14,435	298,839	2.72
1953	2,159	52,834	5.19	37,536	1,153,205	0.74	6,295	115,719	1.32	14,829	269,169	2.72
1954	2,550	64,193	4.57	40,551	1,409,601	0.71	11,718	235,575	1.26	17,047	341,075	2.46

Notes appear at end of table

(continued)

TABLE Da667–678 Rice, oats, sorghum, and soybeans – acreage, production, and price: 1866–1998 [Annual] *Continued*

	Rice			Oats			Sorghum			Soybeans		
	Acreage harvested	Production	Price	Acreage harvested	Production	Price	Acreage harvested	Production	Price	Acreage harvested	Production	Price
	Da667	Da668	Da669 [1]	Da670 [2]	Da671 [2]	Da672 [2,3]	Da673 [4]	Da674 [4]	Da675 [4]	Da676	Da677	Da678 [1]
Year	Thousand acres	Thousand hundredweight	Dollars per hundredweight	Thousand acres	Thousand bushels	Dollars per bushel	Thousand acres	Thousand bushels	Dollars per bushel	Thousand acres	Thousand bushels	Dollars per bushel
1955	1,826	55,902	4.81	39,027	1,495,978	0.60	12,891	242,638	0.98	18,620	373,682	2.22
1956	1,569	49,459	4.86	33,333	1,151,398	0.69	9,209	204,881	1.15	20,620	449,251	2.18
1957	1,340	42,935	5.11	34,065	1,289,880	0.60	19,682	567,506	0.97	20,857	483,425	2.07
1958	1,415	44,760	4.68	31,247	1,401,410	0.58	16,524	581,012	1.00	23,993	580,250	2.00
1959	1,586	53,647	4.59	27,758	1,050,051	0.65	15,406	555,441	0.86	22,631	532,899	1.96
1960	1,595	54,591	4.55	26,588	1,153,332	0.60	15,601	619,954	0.84	23,655	555,085	2.13
1961	1,589	54,198	5.14	23,886	1,010,314	0.64	10,985	480,208	1.01	27,003	678,554	2.28
1962	1,773	66,045	5.04	22,377	1,012,197	0.62	11,571	510,284	1.02	27,608	669,186	2.34
1963	1,771	70,269	5.01	21,308	965,510	0.62	13,326	585,394	0.98	28,615	699,165	2.51
1964	1,786	73,166	4.90	19,759	852,257	0.63	11,742	489,796	1.05	30,793	700,921	2.62
1965	1,793	76,281	4.93	18,522	929,554	0.62	13,029	672,698	0.98	34,449	845,608	2.54
1966	1,967	85,020	4.77	17,877	803,324	0.67	12,813	714,992	1.02	36,546	928,481	2.75
1967	1,970	89,379	4.97	16,110	793,800	0.66	14,988	755,344	0.99	39,805	976,439	2.49
1968	2,353	104,142	5.00	17,708	950,689	0.60	13,890	731,277	0.95	41,391	1,106,958	2.43
1969	2,128	91,904	4.95	17,971	965,863	0.58	13,437	729,919	1.07	41,337	1,133,120	2.35
1970	1,815	83,805	5.17	18,594	915,236	0.62	13,568	683,179	1.14	42,249	1,127,100	2.85
1971	1,818	85,768	5.34	15,705	878,079	0.60	16,142	867,997	1.04	42,705	1,176,101	3.03
1972	1,818	85,439	6.73	13,410	690,616	0.72	13,212	801,350	1.37	45,683	1,270,608	4.37
1973	2,170	92,765	13.80	13,770	659,136	1.18	15,700	923,224	2.14	55,667	1,547,543	5.68
1974	2,531	112,386	11.20	12,608	600,655	1.53	13,809	622,711	2.77	51,341	1,216,287	6.64
1975	2,818	128,437	8.35	13,038	638,960	1.45	15,403	754,354	2.36	53,617	1,548,344	4.92
1976	2,480	115,648	7.02	11,834	540,441	1.56	14,466	710,797	2.03	49,401	1,288,608	6.81
1977	2,249	99,223	9.49	13,485	752,774	1.09	13,797	780,944	1.82	57,830	1,767,267	5.88
1978	2,970	133,170	8.16	11,126	581,657	1.20	13,410	731,270	2.01	63,663	1,868,754	6.66
1979	2,869	131,947	10.50	9,682	526,748	1.36	12,901	807,422	2.34	70,343	2,260,665	6.28
1980	3,312	146,150	12.80	8,657	458,792	1.79	12,513	579,343	2.94	67,813	1,797,543	7.57
1981	3,792	182,742	9.05	9,407	509,529	1.89	13,677	875,835	2.39	66,163	1,989,110	6.04
1982	3,262	153,637	8.11	10,258	592,630	1.49	14,137	835,083	2.47	69,442	2,190,297	5.69
1983	2,169	99,720	8.76	9,062	476,471	1.62	10,001	487,521	2.74	62,525	1,635,772	7.81
1984	2,802	138,810	8.06	8,163	473,661	1.67	15,355	866,241	2.32	66,113	1,860,863	5.78
1985	2,492	134,913	6.53	8,147	518,490	1.23	16,782	1,120,271	1.93	61,599	2,099,056	5.05
1986	2,360	133,356	3.75	6,840	384,996	1.21	13,862	938,869	1.37	58,312	1,942,558	4.78
1987	2,333	129,603	7.27	6,888	373,713	1.56	10,531	730,809	1.70	57,172	1,937,722	5.88
1988	2,900	159,897	6.83	5,533	217,600	2.61	9,042	576,686	2.27	57,373	1,548,841	7.42
1989	2,687	154,487	7.35	6,882	373,587	1.49	11,103	615,420	2.10	59,538	1,923,666	5.69
1990	2,823	156,088	6.70	5,945	357,524	1.14	9,089	573,303	2.12	56,512	1,925,947	5.74
1991	2,781	159,367	7.58	4,806	243,451	1.21	9,870	584,860	2.35	58,011	1,986,539	5.58
1992	3,132	179,658	5.89	4,496	294,229	1.32	12,050	875,022	1.89	58,233	2,190,354	5.56
1993	2,833	156,110	7.98	3,803	206,731	1.36 [5]	8,916	534,172	2.40	57,307	1,869,718	6.40
1994	3,316	197,779	6.78	4,008	228,844	1.22 [5]	8,882	645,741	2.40	60,809	2,514,869	5.48
1995	3,093	173,871	9.15	2,952	161,094	1.67 [5]	8,253	458,648	3.15	61,544	2,174,254	6.72
1996	2,804	171,599	9.96	2,655	153,245	1.96	11,811	795,274	2.35	63,349	2,380,274	7.35
1997	3,103	182,992	9.70	2,813	167,246	1.60	9,158	633,545	2.21	69,110	2,688,750	6.47
1998	3,317	188,051	8.50	2,765	167,122	1.10	7,723	519,933	1.75	70,811	2,756,794	5.35

¹ Through 1985 includes adjustments for outstanding loans and government purchases.

² Coverage changes over time; see text.

³ December 1 price through 1907; season average price, 1908–1985; marketing year average price beginning 1986. Prices are weighted by production through 1908, and by sales thereafter.

⁴ The source used here deviated from its normal procedure (and the procedure normally used here) and spliced census data in with U.S. Department of Agriculture data.

⁵ Unrevised.

Source

U.S. Department of Agriculture, National Agricultural Statistics Service, Crops Branch, Field Crops Section, *Track Records: United States Crop Production*, May 1999, downloaded October 20, 2000, from the U.S. Department of Agriculture, Economics and Statistics System.

Documentation

For many crops, estimates of acreage, production, and prices begin in 1866, the year in which the U.S. Department of Agriculture (USDA) began making regular reports. *Agricultural Statistics*, particularly the issues of 1941 and 1952, presents most of the available statistics, chiefly on a national basis, covering every phase, from acreage and production of individual commodities to utilization and consumption. *Crop Production* (Crop Reporting Board) presents monthly forecasts for the current season, beginning in March and carrying through the growing season. The December issue provides a summary for the current season, revisions for the previous season, and comparisons with previous years. These data appear also in the USDA's publication *Crops and Markets*.

Crop estimates are based chiefly on reports from volunteer farmer-reporters who represent every part of every state. Check information is gathered from processors, from transportation and storage facilities, from buyers of farm products, from annual state farm enumerations, from various farm programs, and from other governmental agencies such as the Bureau of the Census, the Internal Revenue Service, and the Bureau of Customs.

Season average prices are averages of the mid-month prices weighted by the quantity sold each month in the crop-marketing season, which is the twelve-month period following the harvesting of the crop. This season may vary for different crops, and for any crop it may vary by state. The season average price of any crop is the average of all the state prices, weighted by the production of each state. Thus,

it may be applied to production in any given year to obtain a measure of the value of that production. State season average prices may be weighted by quantities sold in each state to obtain an average for the United States, which may be applied to total quantities sold in the nation to measure value of sales in the crop season. In neither case, however, should the computed value be confused with calendar-year income from the crop. Monthly estimates of quantity sold are based on reports of receipts by the chief purchasers of the commodity – in the case of grains, the interior mills, and elevators.

Mid-month prices received by farmers are estimated by the Crop Reporting Board and are based upon reports from thousands of firms dealing directly with farmers (such as elevators, truckers, processors, produce dealers, etc.) and from farmers themselves.

Season average prices for each state and the United States are summed up in the December issue of *Crop Values* (USDA) and in *Field and Seed Crops Farm Production, Farm Disposition, and Value* (Crop Reporting Board) issued each May. Data for season average prices begins for most commodities in 1908, but is supplemented for preceding years by the December 1 price series based on farmers' estimates on December 1 of average prices for the season's sales.

Series Da670–672. For 1866–1948, oats for grain figures include the acreage cut ripe and fed unthreshed; for 1949–1970, they include only the acreage and production harvested by combine or threshed. Estimates of harvested acreage exclude oats cut green for hay for all years, and oats cut ripe and fed unthreshed, 1949–1970.

Series Da673–675. Sorghum grain includes both grain sorghums for grain, and sweet sorghums for grain or seed. Price is based on the reported price of grain sorghums. It is obtained by weighting state prices by quantity sold and includes allowance for unredeemed loans and purchases by the government valued at the average loan and purchase rate, by state.

Series Da675. Prices weighted by sales.

Series Da676–678. Soybean price figures are season average prices prepared by weighting the mid-month prices received by farmers. Figures for acreage grown for all purposes, alone and interplanted, and acreage and production of soybeans for hay are also estimated by the Crop Reporting Board. Data on farm stocks and stocks in off-farm positions, 1942–1970, are also available in publications of the same agency.

TABLE Da679–692   Rice, oats, sorghum, and soybeans – acreage, production, and price: 1839–1997[1]   [Census years]

Contributed by Alan L. Olmstead and Paul W. Rhode

	Rice			Oats for grain			Sorghum — For all purposes			Sorghum — For grain or seed		Soybeans for beans		
	Da679	Da680	Da681[2]	Da682	Da683	Da684[2]	Da685	Da686	Da687[2]	Da688	Da689	Da690	Da691	Da692[2]
	Acreage harvested	Production	Price	Acreage harvested	Production	Price	Acreage harvested	Production	Price	Acreage harvested	Production	Acreage harvested	Production	Price
Year	Thousand acres	Thousand hundredweight	Dollars per hundredweight	Thousand acres	Million bushels	Dollars per bushel	Thousand acres	Million bushels	Dollars per bushel	Thousand acres	Million bushels	Thousand acres	Million bushels	Dollars per bushel
1839	—	—	—	—	123	—	—	—	—	—	—	—	—	—
1849	—	—	—	—	147	—	—	—	—	—	—	—	—	—
1859	—	—	—	—	173	—	—	—	—	—	—	—	—	—
1869	—	—	—	—	282	—	—	—	—	—	—	—	—	—
1879	—	—	—	16,145	408	—	—	—	—	—	—	—	—	—
1889	—	—	—	28,321	809	—	—	—	—	—	—	—	—	—
1899	351	4,386	1.80	29,540	943	0.23	—	—	—	—	—	—	—	—
1909	620	10,246	1.67	35,159	1,007	0.41	—	—	—	—	—	2	(Z)	1.25
1919	917	16,195	6.10	37,991	1,055	0.81	3,630	74	—	—	—	113	1.1	4.10
1924	744	13,286	3.20	37,650	1,305	0.47	3,519	61	—	—	—	—	—	—
1929	743	15,137	2.18	33,466	993	0.41	3,522	49	—	—	—	—	8.7	1.67
1934	706	14,831	1.72	24,589	458	0.47	2,396	19	0.95	—	—	—	23.0	1.01
1939	852	19,732	1.63	29,934	870	0.31	4,760	53	0.57	—	—	4,274	87.6	0.81
1944	1,394	29,270	3.90	35,425	1,041	0.69	9,386	185	0.91	—	—	—	187.7	2.07
1949	1,819	40,251	3.94	35,344	1,137	0.65	6,602	148	1.13	—	—	10,148	212.4	2.12
1954	2,498	65,284	4.53	37,921	1,314	0.71	11,718	236	1.26	—	—	16,444	324.1	2.52
1959	1,617	54,403	4.58	26,573	1,001	0.64	15,406	555	0.86	—	—	22,080	515.6	1.97
1964	1,815	74,824	4.93	18,936	808	0.63	11,742	490	1.05	11,168	463	29,844	669.7	2.66
1969	2,131	91,544	4.91	16,354	880	0.58	13,437	730	1.07	12,954	682	38,550	1,041.5	2.35
1974	2,547	114,286	—	11,143	526	—	14,596	—	—	12,929	554	48,119	1,145.8	—
1978	3,002	133,715	—	10,122	513	—	13,994	—	—	12,900	659	61,340	1,722.2	—
1982	3,233	154,953	—	9,131	506	—	13,514	—	—	12,679	726	64,833	1,990.0	—
1987	2,425	131,716	—	5,981	313	—	—	—	—	9,761	633	55,291	1,838.1	—
1992	3,118	175,942	—	4,188	250	—	—	—	—	10,887	733	56,351	2,053.2	—
1997	3,122	182,231	—	2,681	151	—	—	—	—	8,470	559	66,148	2,504.3	—

(Z) Less than 50,000 bushels.

[1] Data beginning in 1969 are not comparable with previous censuses; data are only for farms with farm products sales of $2,500 or more beginning that year.

[2] Through 1899, December 1 price received by farmers; season average price thereafter.

Sources

U.S Bureau of the Census, *U.S. Census of Agriculture, 1964,* volume 2, Table 5, p. 313; *1969,* volume 2, chapter 6; *1974,* volume 1, part 51, p. I-22, and volume 2, part 6, pp. 28, 70; *1978,* volume 1, part 51, p. 17; *1982,* volume 1, part 51, p. 20; *1987,* volume 1, part 51, p. 36; *1992,* volume 1, part 51, p. 37; and *1997,* volume 1, part 51, p. 39.

Documentation

For years before 1866, information from trade sources is available for rice. See the text for Table Da667-678.

TABLE Da693–706   Corn, barley, and flaxseed – acreage, production, price, and corn stocks: 1866–1999   [Annual]

Contributed by Alan L. Olmstead and Paul W. Rhode

	Corn								Barley			Flaxseed		
	For all purposes		Harvested for grain			Harvested for silage		Farm stocks						
	Acreage harvested	Production	Acreage	Production	Price	Acreage	Production		Acreage harvested	Production	Price	Acreage harvested	Production	Price
	Da693	Da694 [1]	Da695	Da696 [1]	Da697 [2]	Da698	Da699 [1]	Da700 [3]	Da701	Da702	Da703 [2,4]	Da704 [5]	Da705 [5]	Da706 [5,6]
Year	Thousand acres	Million bushels	Thousand acres	Thousand bushels	Dollars per bushel	Thousand acres	Thousand tons	Million bushels	Thousand acres	Thousand bushels	Dollars per bushel	Thousand acres	Thousand bushels	Dollars per bushel
1866	30,017	731	—	—	0.66	—	—	—	754	18,095	0.95	—	1,800	—
1867	32,116	794	—	—	0.78	—	—	—	1,058	23,850	1.22	—	1,900	—
1868	35,116	920	—	—	0.62	—	—	—	1,064	23,200	1.49	—	2,000	—
1869	35,833	782	—	—	0.73	—	—	—	1,238	29,099	0.87	—	2,100	—
1870	38,388	1,125	—	—	0.52	—	—	—	1,331	29,047	0.85	—	2,400	—
1871	42,002	1,142	—	—	0.46	—	—	—	1,348	27,690	0.77	—	2,800	—
1872	43,584	1,279	—	—	0.38	—	—	—	1,421	32,005	0.74	—	3,400	—
1873	44,084	1,008	—	—	0.48	—	—	—	1,473	30,536	0.96	—	4,800	—
1874	47,640	1,059	—	—	0.64	—	—	—	1,628	36,125	0.96	—	5,400	—
1875	52,446	1,450	—	—	0.42	—	—	—	1,702	32,812	0.86	—	5,400	—
1876	55,277	1,478	—	—	0.36	—	—	—	1,973	40,711	0.69	—	5,800	—
1877	58,799	1,516	—	—	0.36	—	—	—	1,962	39,173	0.63	—	7,000	—
1878	59,659	1,565	—	—	0.31	—	—	—	1,848	37,448	0.58	—	7,000	—
1879	62,229	1,752	—	—	0.36	—	—	—	1,926	42,369	0.60	—	7,171	—
1880	62,545	1,707	—	—	0.39	—	—	—	1,990	45,261	0.66	—	7,500	—
1881	63,026	1,245	—	—	0.63	—	—	—	2,201	48,984	0.82	—	7,800	—
1882	66,157	1,755	—	—	0.48	—	—	—	2,434	60,072	0.63	—	8,600	—
1883	68,834	1,948	—	—	0.35	—	—	—	2,474	57,126	0.59	—	8,600	—
1884	71,854	2,058	—	—	0.32	—	—	—	2,694	67,919	0.48	—	9,500	—
1885	73,911	1,783	—	—	0.36	—	—	—	2,862	63,963	0.56	—	9,300	—
1886	73,296	1,605	—	—	0.43	—	—	—	3,027	73,503	0.53	—	10,000	—
1887	77,474	2,251	—	—	0.33	—	—	—	3,258	72,395	0.52	—	9,800	—
1888	68,168	1,652	—	—	0.42	—	—	—	3,283	75,980	0.59	1,344	10,000	—
1889	77,656	2,294	—	—	0.28	—	—	—	3,352	80,790	0.42		10,614	—
1890	74,785	1,650	—	—	0.50	—	—	—	3,250	69,880	0.62	2,283	19,176	—
1891	78,855	2,336	—	—	0.40	—	—	—	3,590	94,160	0.52	2,040	16,732	—
1892	76,914	1,897	—	—	0.39	—	—	—	3,857	95,170	0.47	1,423	11,807	—
1893	79,832	1,900	—	—	0.36	—	—	—	3,689	87,109	0.40	1,287	10,421	—
1894	80,069	1,615	—	—	0.45	—	—	—	3,639	74,211	0.44	1,457	10,490	—
1895	90,479	2,535	—	—	0.25	—	—	—	4,185	104,475	0.33	2,039	21,414	—
1896	89,074	2,671	—	—	0.21	—	—	—	4,131	97,479	0.30	1,848	17,738	—
1897	89,965	2,288	—	—	0.26	—	—	—	4,120	102,575	0.34	1,365	13,238	—
1898	87,784	2,351	—	—	0.29	—	—	—	4,113	98,174	0.39	1,889	18,516	—
1899	94,591	2,646	—	—	0.30	—	—	—	4,472	118,161	0.39	2,102	19,969	0.98
1900	94,852	2,662	—	—	0.35	—	—	—	4,703	96,588	0.41	2,762	16,017	—
1901	94,422	1,716	—	—	0.60	—	—	—	4,963	123,800	0.45	3,173	27,605	—
1902	97,177	2,774	—	—	0.40	—	—	—	5,474	146,207	0.45	3,878	36,080	1.05
1903	93,555	2,515	—	—	0.42	—	—	—	6,231	149,335	0.45	3,180	25,360	0.81
1904	95,228	2,687	—	—	0.44	—	—	—	6,579	166,103	0.41	2,092	22,625	0.99

Notes appear at end of table

(continued)

TABLE Da693-706   Corn, barley, and flaxseed – acreage, production, price, and corn stocks: 1866-1999   [Annual]   Continued

	Corn								Barley			Flaxseed		
	For all purposes		Harvested for grain			Harvested for silage								
	Acreage harvested	Production	Acreage	Production	Price	Acreage	Production	Farm stocks	Acreage harvested	Production	Price	Acreage harvested	Production	Price
Year	Da693	Da694 [1]	Da695	Da696 [1]	Da697 [2]	Da698	Da699 [1]	Da700 [3]	Da701	Da702	Da703 [2,4]	Da704 [5]	Da705 [5]	Da706 [5,6]
	Thousand acres	Million bushels	Thousand acres	Thousand bushels	Dollars per bushel	Thousand acres	Thousand tons	Million bushels	Thousand acres	Thousand bushels	Dollars per bushel	Thousand acres	Thousand bushels	Dollars per bushel
1905	95,746	2,954	—	—	0.41	—	—	—	6,658	171,639	0.39	2,439	28,692	0.84
1906	95,624	3,033	—	—	0.39	—	—	—	6,744	179,148	0.42	2,568	27,635	1.02
1907	96,094	2,614	—	—	0.51	—	—	—	6,854	150,584	0.67	2,699	23,793	0.96
1908	95,285	2,567	—	—	0.65	—	—	—	7,409	170,780	0.57	2,351	20,627	1.16
1909	100,200	2,611	—	—	0.62	—	—	—	7,697	173,069	0.57	2,081	19,511	1.42
1910	102,267	2,853	—	—	0.52	—	—	—	7,546	142,419	0.60	2,222	11,384	2.27
1911	101,393	2,475	—	—	0.68	—	—	—	7,613	145,074	0.81	2,631	18,537	1.97
1912	101,451	2,948	—	—	0.55	—	—	—	7,542	196,927	0.51	2,941	28,139	1.29
1913	100,206	2,273	—	—	0.70	—	—	—	7,673	158,820	0.53	1,954	15,099	1.23
1914	97,796	2,524	—	—	0.71	—	—	—	7,653	177,712	0.53	1,561	12,940	1.31
1915	100,623	2,829	—	—	0.68	—	—	—	7,279	206,976	0.51	1,116	11,270	1.68
1916	100,561	2,425	—	—	1.14	—	—	—	7,623	159,157	0.79	1,298	11,829	2.31
1917	110,893	2,908	—	—	1.46	—	—	—	8,453	182,209	1.22	1,881	8,402	3.11
1918	102,195	2,441	—	—	1.52	—	—	—	9,198	225,067	0.96	1,783	12,779	3.57
1919	98,145	2,679	87,487	2,341,870	1.51	3,554	26,866	—	6,579	131,086	1.28	1,293	6,770	4.41
1920	101,359	3,071	90,149	2,695,085	0.64	3,682	27,996	—	7,439	171,042	0.91	1,647	10,900	2.33
1921	103,155	2,928	91,939	2,556,924	0.52	3,486	26,979	—	7,074	132,702	0.50	1,143	8,107	1.66
1922	100,345	2,707	84,858	2,229,496	0.73	3,663	27,568	—	6,601	152,908	0.51	1,113	10,520	2.08
1923	101,123	2,875	87,493	2,429,551	0.81	3,983	29,874	—	7,151	158,994	0.55	2,015	16,563	2.12
1924	100,420	2,223	84,119	1,860,112	1.06	4,307	28,737	—	7,038	165,318	0.74	3,535	31,220	2.18
1925	101,331	2,798	86,825	2,382,288	0.70	3,681	29,343	262.1	8,186	192,466	0.62	3,022	22,334	2.26
1926	99,452	2,547	83,275	2,140,207	0.74	4,350	29,493	192.5	7,917	166,030	0.57	2,736	18,531	2.03
1927	98,357	2,616	83,915	2,218,189	0.85	4,268	29,926	87.2	9,465	239,071	0.70	2,763	25,174	1.92
1928	100,336	2,666	85,832	2,260,990	0.84	3,985	30,000	142.4	12,735	328,351	0.59	2,611	19,118	1.94
1929	97,805	2,516	83,194	2,135,038	0.80	4,021	29,335	—	13,564	280,637	0.56	3,049	15,924	2.81
1930	101,465	2,080	85,525	1,757,297	0.60	4,875	30,026	134.4	12,629	301,619	0.42	3,780	21,673	1.61
1931	106,866	2,576	91,131	2,229,903	0.32	4,710	32,875	162.6	11,181	200,280	0.35	2,431	11,755	1.17
1932	110,577	2,930	97,213	2,578,685	0.32	4,293	32,073	251.7	13,206	299,394	0.23	1,988	11,511	0.88
1933	105,918	2,398	92,130	2,104,725	0.52	4,864	32,705	326.8	9,641	152,839	0.43	1,341	6,904	1.63
1934	92,193	1,449	61,245	1,146,734	0.82	7,132	35,093	274.0	6,577	117,390	0.64	1,002	5,719	1.70
1935	95,974	2,299	82,551	2,001,367	0.66	5,309	37,563	61.4	12,436	288,667	0.38	2,126	14,914	1.42
1936	93,154	1,506	67,833	1,258,673	1.04	8,539	33,690	171.6	8,329	147,740	0.75	1,125	5,331	1.90
1937	93,930	2,643	81,222	2,349,425	0.52	5,543	37,522	60.0	9,969	221,889	0.55	927	7,070	1.87
1938	92,160	2,549	82,788	2,300,095	0.49	4,456	35,187	351.5	10,610	256,620	0.38	905	8,032	1.59
1939	88,279	2,581	78,307	2,341,602	0.57	4,514	33,200	553.8	12,739	278,193	0.40	2,171	19,606	1.46
1940	86,429	2,457	76,443	2,206,882	0.62	4,735	34,615	541.4	13,525	311,278	0.39	3,182	30,924	1.42
1941	85,357	2,652	77,404	2,414,445	0.75	4,023	33,751	473.5	14,276	362,568	0.55	3,266	32,133	1.79
1942	87,367	3,069	79,213	2,801,819	0.92	3,841	33,445	422.0	16,958	429,450	0.63	4,408	40,976	2.36
1943	92,060	2,966	81,906	2,668,490	1.12	4,162	33,518	355.2	14,900	322,913	1.00	5,691	50,009	2.83
1944	94,014	3,088	85,002	2,801,612	1.03	4,476	34,888	202.7	12,301	276,275	1.01	2,610	21,665	2.91

	Corn							Farm stocks	Barley			Flaxseed		
	For all purposes		Harvested for grain			Harvested for silage								
	Acreage harvested	Production	Acreage	Production	Price	Acreage	Production		Acreage harvested	Production	Price	Acreage harvested	Production	Price
	Da693	Da694[1]	Da695	Da696[1]	Da697[2]	Da698	Da699[1]	Da700[3]	Da701	Da702	Da703[2,4]	Da704[5]	Da705[5]	Da706[5,6]
Year	Thousand acres	Million bushels	Thousand acres	Thousand bushels	Dollars per bushel	Thousand acres	Thousand tons	Million bushels	Thousand acres	Thousand bushels	Dollars per bushel	Thousand acres	Thousand bushels	Dollars per bushel
1945	87,625	2,869	77,928	2,577,449	1.23	4,495	35,214	293.4	10,454	266,994	1.01	3,785	34,557	2.89
1946	87,585	3,217	78,410	2,916,089	1.53	4,577	36,031	151.9	10,380	265,059	1.38	2,432	22,588	4.03
1947	82,888	2,355	73,802	2,108,320	2.16	4,637	34,290	251.8	10,955	281,868	1.73	4,129	40,618	6.15
1948	84,778	3,605	76,840	3,307,038	1.28	4,317	37,592	112.1	11,905	315,537	1.16	4,973	54,803	5.71
1949	85,595	3,238	77,106	2,946,206	1.24	4,513	40,386	696.1	9,872	237,071	1.06	5,048	42,976	3.63
1950	81,818	3,075	72,398	2,764,071	1.52	4,937	41,002	470.1	11,155	303,772	1.19	4,090	40,236	3.34
1951	80,729	2,926	71,191	2,628,937	1.66	4,809	38,949	313.1	9,424	257,213	1.26	3,904	34,696	3.72
1952	80,940	3,292	71,353	2,980,793	1.52	5,361	43,174	172.0	8,236	228,168	1.37	3,304	30,184	3.73
1953	80,459	3,210	70,738	2,881,801	1.48	6,102	47,855	330.0	8,680	246,723	1.17	4,570	37,656	3.64
1954	80,186	3,058	68,668	2,707,913	1.43	7,114	52,559	359.4	13,370	379,254	1.09	5,663	41,274	3.05
1955	79,367	3,220	68,462	2,872,959	1.35	6,961	52,974	313.8	14,523	403,065	0.92	4,914	40,415	2.90
1956	75,247	3,445	64,877	3,075,336	1.29	6,535	54,571	299.3	12,852	376,661	0.99	5,473	47,037	2.99
1957	71,864	3,400	63,065	3,045,355	1.11	6,122	54,072	418.9	14,872	442,761	0.89	4,793	25,113	2.94
1958	72,224	3,725	63,549	3,356,205	1.12	6,284	55,612	343.0	14,791	477,368	0.90	3,679	37,409	2.69
1959	81,902	4,197	72,091	3,824,598	1.05	7,017	59,708	325.0	14,869	420,203	0.86	2,932	21,237	3.00
1960	80,678	4,314	71,422	3,906,949	1.00	7,176	65,429	452.0	13,856	429,005	0.84	3,342	30,402	2.65
1961	65,405	—	57,634	3,597,803	1.10	6,261	66,064	588.1	12,806	392,441	0.98	2,514	22,178	3.26
1962	64,474	—	55,726	3,606,311	1.12	7,201	76,753	578.3	12,214	427,726	0.92	2,808	32,230	2.83
1963	68,317	—	59,227	4,019,238	1.11	7,692	82,926	533.8	11,236	392,833	0.90	3,172	31,041	2.76
1964	65,388	—	55,369	3,484,253	1.17	8,620	83,551	681.1	10,277	386,059	0.95	2,825	24,401	2.82
1965	64,616	—	55,392	4,102,867	1.16	8,054	84,447	581.5	9,166	393,055	1.02	2,775	35,402	2.80
1966	65,867	—	57,002	4,167,608	1.24	7,934	89,683	531.2	10,250	392,108	1.06	2,576	23,390	2.89
1967	70,034	—	60,694	4,860,372	1.03	8,363	94,783	572.2	9,230	373,745	1.01	1,975	20,036	2.95
1968	64,605	—	55,980	4,449,542	1.08	7,879	93,652	788.2	9,732	426,151	0.92	2,092	26,983	2.81
1969	63,063	—	54,574	4,687,057	1.16	7,892	99,161	732.3	9,557	427,055	0.89	2,605	34,929	2.65
1970	66,086	—	57,358	4,152,243	1.33	8,078	94,084	575.6	9,712	416,091	0.97	2,836	29,416	2.40
1971	73,631	—	64,123	5,646,260	1.08	8,814	109,302	426.7	10,104	462,423	0.99	1,545	18,198	2.38
1972	66,384	—	57,513	5,579,832	1.57	8,307	109,343	751.9	9,645	421,719	1.21	1,149	13,883	3.10
1973	71,733	—	62,143	5,670,712	2.55	8,252	114,267	403.9	9,013	417,434	2.14	735	10,278	7.56
1974	76,875	—	65,405	4,701,402	3.02	9,023	115,705	288.7	10,295	298,669	2.81	1,700	16,408	9.67
1975	78,033	—	67,625	5,840,757	2.54	9,848	116,087	193.2	8,617	379,162	2.42	1,511	15,553	6.57
1976	83,642	—	71,506	6,289,169	2.15	11,281	118,547	233.2	8,439	383,007	2.25	955	7,580	7.08
1977	81,537	—	71,614	6,505,041	2.02	9,314	117,743	447.8	9,728	427,784	1.78	1,239	14,280	4.54
1978	80,987	—	71,930	7,267,927	2.25	8,624	118,132	666.7	9,248	454,759	1.92	687	8,614	5.74
1979	80,777	—	72,400	7,928,139	2.52	7,989	114,799	794.5	7,527	383,201	2.29	878	12,014	5.97
1980	82,844	—	72,961	6,639,396	3.11	9,299	111,990	920.5	7,260	361,135	2.84	663	7,728	7.20
1981	83,192	—	74,524	8,118,650	2.50	8,307	117,891	489.9	9,038	473,512	2.44	577	7,289	6.73
1982	81,278	—	72,719	8,235,101	2.55	8,252	117,782	1,243.3	9,013	515,935	2.18	735	10,278	5.19
1983	59,587	—	51,479	4,174,251	3.21	7,808	96,238	1,510.4	9,721	508,269	2.47	580	6,903	6.80
1984	79,761	—	71,897	7,672,130	2.63	7,535	104,491	347.9	11,218	598,034	2.29	538	7,022	6.09
1985	82,670	—	75,209	8,875,453	2.23	7,155	102,664	678.9	11,591	590,213	1.98	584	8,293	5.05
1986	75,325	—	68,907	8,225,764	1.50	6,418	90,227	—	11,974	608,532	1.61	683	11,538	3.47
1987	65,499	—	59,505	7,131,300	1.94	5,994	86,442	2,284.5	9,957	521,499	1.81	463	7,444	3.39
1988	66,551	—	58,250	4,928,681	2.54	8,301	78,911	2,002.8	7,636	289,994	2.80	226	1,615	7.56
1989	71,389	—	64,783	7,531,953	2.36	6,606	86,111	967.5	8,313	404,203	2.42	163	1,215	7.20

Notes appear at end of table

(continued)

TABLE Da693–706   Corn, barley, and flaxseed – acreage, production, price, and corn stocks: 1866–1999   [Annual]   Continued

	Corn								Barley			Flaxseed		
	For all purposes		Harvested for grain			Harvested for silage		Farm stocks						
	Acreage harvested	Production	Acreage	Production	Price	Acreage	Production		Acreage harvested	Production	Price	Acreage harvested	Production	Price
	Da693	Da694 [1]	Da695 [1]	Da696 [1]	Da697 [2]	Da698	Da699 [1]	Da700 [3]	Da701	Da702	Da703 [2,4]	Da704 [5]	Da705 [5]	Da706 [5,6]
Year	Thousand acres	Million bushels	Thousand acres	Thousand bushels	Dollars per bushel	Thousand acres	Thousand tons	Million bushels	Thousand acres	Thousand bushels	Dollars per bushel	Thousand acres	Thousand bushels	Dollars per bushel
1990	73,075	—	66,952	7,934,028	2.28	6,123	86,820	754.8	7,529	422,196	2.14	253	3,812	5.27
1991	74,962	—	68,822	7,474,765	2.37	6,140	81,216	691.2	8,413	464,326	2.10	342	6,200	3.52
1992	78,146	—	72,077	9,476,698	2.07	6,069	87,663	605.5	7,285	455,090	2.04	165	3,288	4.12
1993	69,756	—	62,933	6,337,730	2.50	6,823	81,131	1,070.7	6,753	398,041	1.99	191	3,482	4.25
1994	78,231	—	72,514	10,050,520	2.26	5,717	90,170	395.4	6,667	374,862	2.03	171	2,922	4.63
1995	70,531	—	65,210	7,400,051	3.24	5,321	78,181	740.9	6,279	359,376	2.89	147	2,212	5.19
1996	78,251	—	72,644	9,232,557	2.71	5,607	86,581	196.6	6,707	392,433	2.74	92	1,602	6.37
1997	78,725	—	72,671	9,206,832	2.43	6,054	97,192	475.0	6,198	359,878	2.38	146	2,420	5.81
1998	78,523	—	72,604	9,761,085	1.95	5,919	94,525	640.0	5,867	352,445	1.95	329	6,708	5.10
1999	—	—	—	—	—	—	—	797.0	—	—	—	—	—	—

[1] Beginning with 1961, figures represent corn harvested for grain only.

[2] Through 1907, December 1 price received by farmers; season average price 1908–1985; marketing year price beginning with 1986.

[3] 1926–1985, old crop only, October 1 stock; beginning with 1987, September 1 stock, year beginning previous December.

[4] Prices weighted by production, 1866–1908; weighted by sales thereafter.

[5] Through 1990 includes only Minnesota, North Dakota, and South Dakota; thereafter includes all states except Alaska and Hawai'i.

[6] December 1 price through 1907; season average price 1908–1985; marketing year average price beginning 1986. U.S. prices weighted by sales from 1909 to date; weighted by production from 1866–1908.

Sources

Series Da693. 1866–1918, U.S. Department of Agriculture, Statistical Reporting Service, *Agricultural Statistics, 1967 and 1972 editions*; 1919–1998, U.S. National Agricultural Statistics Service, Crops Branch, Field Crops Section, *Track Records: United States Crop Production*, March 1999, downloaded October 3, 2000, from the U.S. Department of Agriculture, Economics and Statistics System.

Series Da694. *Agricultural Statistics, 1967 and 1972 editions*.

Series Da695–696 and Da698–699. U.S. National Agricultural Statistics Service, Crops Branch, Field Crops Section, *Track Records: United States Crop Production*, March 1999, downloaded October 3, 2000, from the U.S. Department of Agriculture, Economics and Statistics System.

Series Da697. 1866–1948, *Agricultural Statistics, 1967 and 1972 editions*; 1949–1998, U.S. National Agricultural Statistics Service, Crops Branch, Field Crops Section, *Track Records: United States Crop Production*, March 1999, downloaded October 3, 2000, from the U.S. Department of Agriculture, Economics and Statistics System.

Series Da700. *Agricultural Statistics, 1952, 1957, 1962, 1967, 1973, 1983, 1988, 1995–96, and 2000 editions*.

Series Da701–705. U.S. National Agricultural Statistics Service, Crops Branch, Field Crops Section, *Track Records: United States Crop Production*, March 1999, downloaded October 3, 2000, from the U.S. Department of Agriculture, Economics and Statistics System.

Series Da706. 1899, *Agricultural Statistics, 1941 edition*; 1902–1998, U.S. National Agricultural Statistics Service, Crops Branch, Field Crops Section, *Track Records: United States Crop Production*, March 1999, downloaded October 3, 2000, from the U.S. Department of Agriculture, Economics and Statistics System.

Documentation

See the text for Table Da667–678.

Series Da693–699. Corn figures include not only the production of corn on the acreage harvested for grain, but also an allowance for that harvested for silage and for forage, including some harvested by grazing farm animals (commonly called hogging off). U.S. Department of Agriculture data on corn exclude Hawai'i; corn is not grown in Alaska.

Series Da700. The Crop Reporting Board has estimated farm stocks, by state, quarterly since 1926 from reports of a large number of farmers. Farm stocks represent the farm carryover for crops of previous years, which become a part of the feed supply for the new season. In addition to farm stocks of corn, stocks in all off-farm positions have been estimated since 1943. Comparison with the farm-stocks data indicates that the bulk of carryover stocks of corn on October 1 of any year is still on farms.

Series Da701–703. Barley cut for hay is excluded. Figures on farm stocks are available from 1933 to 1970, and stocks in off-farm positions have been estimated since 1943.

Series Da704–706. Flax grown for fiber is not included in the production estimates. Estimates of fiber flax are available in publications of the Crop Reporting Board. Farm-stocks data and stocks in off-farm positions, 1942–1970, are also available from the same source.

TABLE Da707–716   Corn, barley, and flaxseed – acreage, production, and price: 1839–1997   [Census years]
Contributed by Alan L. Olmstead and Paul W. Rhode

	Corn				Barley for grain			Flaxseed		
	For all purposes, acreage harvested	For grain or seed			Acreage harvested	Production	Price	Acreage harvested	Production	Price
		Acreage harvested	Production	Price						
	Da707	Da708	Da709	Da710 [1]	Da711	Da712	Da713 [1]	Da714	Da715	Da716 [1]
Year	Thousand acres	Thousand acres	Million bushels	Dollars per bushel	Thousand acres	Million bushels	Dollars per bushel	Thousand acres	Million bushels	Dollars per bushel
1839	—	—	378	—	—	4	—	—	—	—
1849	—	—	592	—	—	5	—	—	0.6	—
1859	—	—	839	—	—	16	—	—	0.6	—
1869	—	—	761	—	—	30	—	—	1.7	—
1879	—	62,369	1,755	—	1,998	44	—	—	7.2	—
1889	—	72,088	2,122	—	3,221	78	—	1,319	10.3	—
1899	—	94,917	2,666	0.31	4,470	120	0.35	2,111	20.0	0.78
1909	—	98,386	2,552	0.56	7,699	173	0.53	2,083	19.5	1.48
1919	91,781	87,778	2,346	1.50	6,473	122	1.31	1,261	6.7	4.41
1924	98,402	82,329	1,824	1.02	6,767	159	0.77	3,435	28.2	2.34
1929	97,742	83,163	2,131	0.77	12,891	264	0.53	2,966	15.0	2.86
1934	87,476	62,247	1,169	0.82	6,193	110	0.67	998	5.6	1.70
1939	86,991	77,433	2,311	0.56	12,025	261	0.41	2,081	18.8	1.46
1944	92,259	84,349	2,788	1.08	11,694	261	1.00	2,477	20.8	2.91
1949	83,337	75,133	2,778	1.24	9,180	221	1.05	4,813	40.2	3.60
1954	78,123	66,793	2,613	1.44	12,556	355	1.08	5,179	35.5	3.04
1959	79,616	70,065	3,697	1.05	14,199	398	0.86	2,848	19.6	3.04
1964	63,515	53,751	3,361	1.16	9,805	362	0.93	2,651	21.7	2.81
1969	60,402	52,540	4,442	—	8,925	394	0.88	2,490	32.0	2.63
1974	72,330	61,654	4,397	—	9,568	355	—	1,452	12.3	—
1978	78,350	70,043	6,805	—	8,944	428	—	426	5.3	—
1982	77,883	69,858	7,509	—	8,650	468	—	633	8.2	—
1987	—	58,702	6,725	—	9,178	458	—	430	6.3	—
1992	—	69,340	8,697	—	6,818	397	—	157	2.8	—
1997	—	69,797	8,579	—	5,945	336	—	140	2.3	—

[1] Through 1899, December 1 price received by farmers; season average price thereafter.

Sources
U.S. Bureau of the Census, *U.S. Census of Agriculture, 1964*, volume 2, Table 5, p. 313; *1969*, volume 2, chapter 6; *1974*, volume 1, part 51, pp. IV-5 and I-5; *1974*, volume 2, part 6, pp. 62 and 65; *1978*, volume 1, part 51, p. 17; *1982*, volume 1, part 51, p. 20; *1987*, volume 1, part 51, p. 36; *1992*, volume 1, part 51, p. 37; and *1997*, volume 1, part 51, p. 39.

Documentation
See the text for Table Da667–678.

TABLE Da717–729 Wheat, spring wheat, and winter wheat – acreage, production, price, and stocks: 1866–1999 [Annual]

Contributed by Alan L. Olmstead and Paul W. Rhode

	All wheat					Spring wheat						Winter wheat	
				Stocks		All		Durum wheat		Other			
Year	Acreage harvested	Production	Price	On farms	Off farms	Acreage harvested	Production	Acreage harvested	Production	Acreage harvested	Production	Acreage harvested	Production
	Da717	Da718	Da719 [1]	Da720 [2]	Da721 [2]	Da722	Da723	Da724 [3]	Da725 [3]	Da726 [4]	Da727 [4]	Da728	Da729
	Thousand acres	Million bushels	Dollars per bushel	Million bushels	Million bushels	Thousand acres	Million bushels	Thousand acres	Million bushels	Thousand acres	Million bushels	Thousand acres	Million bushels
1866	15,408	170	2.06	—	—	—	—	—	—	—	—	—	—
1867	16,738	211	2.01	—	—	—	—	—	—	—	—	—	—
1868	19,140	246	1.46	—	—	—	—	—	—	—	—	—	—
1869	21,194	290	0.92	—	—	—	—	—	—	—	—	—	—
1870	20,945	254	1.04	—	—	—	—	—	—	—	—	—	—
1871	22,230	272	1.25	—	—	—	—	—	—	—	—	—	—
1872	22,962	271	1.24	—	—	—	—	—	—	—	—	—	—
1873	24,866	322	1.17	—	—	—	—	—	—	—	—	—	—
1874	27,310	356	0.95	—	—	—	—	—	—	—	—	—	—
1875	28,382	314	1.01	—	—	—	—	—	—	—	—	—	—
1876	28,283	309	1.04	—	—	—	—	—	—	—	—	—	—
1877	27,963	396	1.09	—	—	—	—	—	—	—	—	—	—
1878	33,379	449	0.77	—	—	—	—	—	—	—	—	—	—
1879	35,347	459	1.11	—	—	—	—	—	—	—	—	—	—
1880	38,096	502	0.95	—	—	—	—	—	—	—	—	—	—
1881	36,795	406	1.20	—	—	—	—	—	—	—	—	—	—
1882	36,496	552	0.89	—	—	—	—	—	—	—	—	—	—
1883	35,587	439	0.91	—	—	—	—	—	—	—	—	—	—
1884	38,485	571	0.65	—	—	—	—	—	—	—	—	—	—
1885	35,095	400	0.77	—	—	—	—	—	—	—	—	—	—
1886	36,312	514	0.69	—	—	—	—	—	—	—	—	—	—
1887	36,873	491	0.68	—	—	—	—	—	—	—	—	—	—
1888	34,969	424	0.93	—	—	—	—	—	—	—	—	—	—
1889	36,098	504	0.70	—	—	—	—	—	—	—	—	—	—
1890	36,686	449	0.84	—	—	—	—	—	—	—	—	—	—
1891	41,090	678	0.83	—	—	—	—	—	—	—	—	—	—
1892	42,979	612	0.62	—	—	—	—	—	—	—	—	—	—
1893	40,790	506	0.53	—	—	—	—	—	—	—	—	—	—
1894	40,167	542	0.49	—	—	—	—	—	—	—	—	—	—
1895	38,998	542	0.51	—	—	—	—	—	—	—	—	—	—
1896	40,828	523	0.72	—	—	—	—	—	—	—	—	—	—
1897	43,413	606	0.81	—	—	—	—	—	—	—	—	—	—
1898	50,506	768	0.58	—	—	—	—	—	—	—	—	—	—
1899	52,342	655	0.59	—	—	—	—	—	—	—	—	—	—
1900	49,203	599	0.62	—	—	—	—	—	—	—	—	—	—
1901	50,847	763	0.63	—	—	—	—	—	—	—	—	—	—
1902	46,244	687	0.63	—	—	—	—	—	—	—	—	—	—
1903	48,456	663	0.69	—	—	—	—	—	—	—	—	—	—
1904	43,155	556	0.93	—	—	—	—	—	—	—	—	—	—
1905	46,306	706	0.75	—	—	—	—	—	—	—	—	—	—
1906	46,230	741	0.66	—	—	—	—	—	—	—	—	—	—
1907	44,139	629	0.87	—	—	—	—	—	—	—	—	—	—
1908	45,102	643	0.97	—	—	—	—	—	—	—	—	—	—
1909	44,262	684	0.99	—	—	17,244	266	—	—	—	—	27,018	418
1910	45,793	625	0.91	—	—	17,641	196	—	—	—	—	28,152	430
1911	49,894	618	0.87	—	—	20,114	189	—	—	—	—	29,780	429
1912	48,413	730	0.80	—	—	20,007	327	—	—	—	—	28,406	403
1913	52,012	751	0.79	—	—	20,050	250	—	—	—	—	31,962	501
1914	55,613	897	0.98	—	—	19,410	227	—	—	—	—	36,203	671
1915	60,303	1,009	0.96	—	—	20,706	368	—	—	—	—	39,597	641
1916	53,510	635	1.43	—	—	19,432	178	—	—	—	—	34,078	456
1917	46,787	620	2.04	—	—	19,962	230	—	—	—	—	26,825	390
1918	61,068	904	2.05	—	—	23,897	348	—	—	—	—	37,171	557
1919	73,700	952	2.16	—	—	23,296	204	3,684	27	19,612	176	50,404	748

Notes appear at end of table

TABLE Da717–729   Wheat, spring wheat, and winter wheat – acreage, production, price, and stocks: 1866–1999 [Annual]   *Continued*

	All wheat					Spring wheat						Winter wheat	
				Stocks		All		Durum wheat		Other			
	Acreage harvested	Production	Price	On farms	Off farms	Acreage harvested	Production	Acreage harvested	Production	Acreage harvested	Production	Acreage harvested	Production
	Da717	Da718	Da719 [1]	Da720 [2]	Da721 [2]	Da722	Da723	Da724 [3]	Da725 [3]	Da726 [4]	Da727 [4]	Da728	Da729
Year	Thousand acres	Million bushels	Dollars per bushel	Million bushels	Million bushels	Thousand acres	Million bushels	Thousand acres	Million bushels	Thousand acres	Million bushels	Thousand acres	Million bushels
1920	62,358	843	1.82	—	—	21,949	230	4,032	39	17,917	191	40,409	613
1921	64,566	819	1.03	—	—	21,406	216	5,629	50	15,777	166	43,160	603
1922	61,397	847	0.96	—	—	19,748	275	5,380	78	14,368	197	41,649	571
1923	56,920	759	0.92	—	—	18,208	204	3,936	38	14,272	167	38,712	555
1924	52,463	842	1.24	—	—	17,045	268	3,596	58	13,449	210	35,418	574
1925	52,443	669	1.43	—	—	20,479	268	4,094	57	16,385	211	31,964	401
1926	56,616	832	1.21	24	73	19,019	201	4,563	42	14,456	158	37,597	632
1927	59,628	875	1.18	27	83	21,433	327	5,430	78	16,003	249	38,195	548
1928	59,226	914	0.99	20	93	22,373	335	6,775	95	15,598	240	36,853	579
1929	63,392	824	1.03	44	183	22,151	237	5,539	54	16,612	183	41,241	587
1930	62,637	887	0.66	63	229	21,526	253	4,669	57	16,857	196	41,111	634
1931	57,704	942	0.38	37	275	14,216	116	2,943	21	11,273	95	43,488	825
1932	57,851	756	0.38	94	282	21,750	265	3,943	40	17,807	224	36,101	492
1933	49,424	552	0.74	83	295	19,076	174	2,262	16	16,814	158	30,348	378
1934	43,347	526	0.84	61	212	8,664	87	845	6	7,819	81	34,683	439
1935	51,305	628	0.83	44	102	17,703	159	2,228	23	15,475	135	33,602	469
1936	49,125	630	1.02	43	97	11,181	106	1,543	8	9,638	98	37,944	524
1937	64,169	874	0.96	22	61	17,094	185	2,785	28	14,309	157	47,075	689
1938	69,197	920	0.56	59	94	19,630	235	3,484	40	16,146	195	49,567	685
1939	52,669	741	0.69	88	162	14,988	176	2,965	32	12,023	143	37,681	566
1940	53,273	815	0.67	80	200	17,178	222	3,029	32	14,149	190	36,095	593
1941	55,935	942	0.94	87	298	16,157	268	2,524	41	13,633	228	39,778	674
1942	49,773	969	1.09	163	468	13,753	267	2,109	41	11,644	226	36,020	702
1943	51,355	844	1.35	190	429	16,792	306	2,078	34	14,714	273	34,563	537
1944	59,749	1,060	1.41	104	213	18,624	308	2,057	30	16,567	279	41,125	752
1945	65,167	1,108	1.49	88	192	18,143	291	2,004	33	16,139	258	47,024	817
1946	67,105	1,152	1.91	42	59	18,734	283	2,453	36	16,281	247	48,371	870
1947	74,519	1,359	2.29	41	43	19,584	300	2,948	44	16,636	256	54,935	1,059
1948	72,418	1,295	1.98	95	102	19,455	305	3,220	45	16,235	260	52,963	990
1949	75,910	1,098	1.88	67	241	21,496	240	3,570	39	17,926	201	54,414	858
1950	61,607	1,019	2.00	66	359	18,357	279	2,829	37	15,528	241	43,250	741
1951	61,873	988	2.11	76	324	21,780	337	2,518	35	19,262	303	40,093	651
1952	71,130	1,306	2.09	63	193	20,235	241	2,174	22	18,061	219	50,895	1,065
1953	67,840	1,173	2.04	79	526	20,907	288	1,865	13	19,042	275	46,933	885
1954	54,356	984	2.12	103	830	15,138	183	1,309	5	13,829	178	39,218	801
1955	47,290	937	1.98	41	996	13,583	231	1,348	20	12,237	210	33,700	705
1956	49,768	1,005	1.97	67	966	14,236	265	2,310	39	11,920	225	35,554	741
1957	43,754	956	1.93	60	849	12,084	244	2,281	40	9,810	200	31,715	711
1958	53,047	1,457	1.75	51	830	12,024	284	906	22	11,118	262	41,023	1,174
1959	51,716	1,118	1.76	115	1,180	12,219	203	1,141	20	11,013	180	39,562	918
1960	51,879	1,355	1.74	96	1,218	11,900	247	1,650	34	10,202	209	40,027	1,111
1961	51,571	1,232	1.83	137	1,274	10,852	160	1,624	21	9,193	136	40,754	1,075
1962	43,688	1,092	2.04	102	1,220	9,965	273	2,367	70	7,587	199	33,734	823
1963	45,506	1,147	1.85	96	1,100	10,637	234	1,999	51	8,700	181	34,807	914
1964	49,762	1,283	1.37	76	826	11,455 [5]	266 [5]	2,467	68	9,220	194	38,075	1,021
1965	49,560	1,316	1.35	133	685	—	—	2,296	70	9,678	229	37,586	1,017
1966	49,613	1,305	1.63	131	404	—	—	2,423	63	8,574	185	38,616	1,057
1967	58,353	1,508	1.39	145	280	—	—	2,754	66	10,560	247	45,039	1,194
1968	54,765	1,557	1.24	230	309	—	—	3,621	100	9,215	239	41,929	1,218
1969	47,146	1,443	1.25	326	491	—	—	3,420	108	7,423	203	36,303	1,131
1970	43,564	1,352	1.33	307	578	—	—	2,105	53	8,757	207	32,702	1,092
1971	47,685	1,619	1.34	240	491	—	—	2,864	92	12,451	382	32,370	1,145
1972	47,303	1,546	1.76	355	508	—	—	2,550	73	9,894	287	34,859	1,186
1973	54,148	1,711	3.95	134	305	—	—	2,884	78	12,517	354	38,747	1,278
1974	65,368	1,782	4.09	89	158	—	—	4,099	81	14,491	325	46,778	1,376

Notes appear at end of table

(continued)

TABLE Da717–729   Wheat, spring wheat, and winter wheat – acreage, production, price, and stocks: 1866–1999
[Annual] *Continued*

	All wheat					Spring wheat						Winter wheat	
				Stocks		All		Durum wheat		Other			
Year	Acreage harvested	Production	Price	On farms	Off farms	Acreage harvested	Production	Acreage harvested	Production	Acreage harvested	Production	Acreage harvested	Production
	Da717	Da718	Da719 [1]	Da720 [2]	Da721 [2]	Da722	Da723	Da724 [3]	Da725 [3]	Da726 [4]	Da727 [4]	Da728	Da729
	Thousand acres	Million bushels	Dollars per bushel	Million bushels	Million bushels	Thousand acres	Million bushels	Thousand acres	Million bushels	Thousand acres	Million bushels	Thousand acres	Million bushels
1975	69,499	2,127	3.55	133	194	—	—	4,680	123	13,443	361	51,376	1,643
1976	70,927	2,149	2.73	236	430	—	—	4,584	135	16,765	450	49,578	1,564
1977	66,686	2,046	2.33	527	686	—	—	3,025	80	14,889	425	48,772	1,540
1978	56,495	1,776	2.97	494	684	—	—	4,024	133	13,980	420	38,491	1,222
1979	62,454	2,134	3.78	484	440	—	—	3,932	107	15,095	426	43,427	1,601
1980	71,125	2,381	3.91	377	525	—	—	4,840	108	14,650	371	51,635	1,902
1981	80,642	2,785	3.66	414	575	—	—	5,655	183	16,511	505	58,476	2,097
1982	77,937	2,765	3.45	576	583	—	—	4,177	146	16,127	546	57,633	2,074
1983	61,390	2,420	3.51	669	846	—	—	2,492	73	11,314	359	47,584	1,988
1984	66,928	2,595	3.39	592	807	—	—	3,219	103	12,196	431	51,513	2,060
1985	64,704	2,424	3.08	582	843	—	—	3,094	113	13,687	485	47,923	1,827
1986	60,688	2,091	2.42	681	1,224	—	—	2,877	98	14,641	472	43,170	1,520
1987	55,945	2,108	2.57	560	1,261	—	—	3,279	93	13,334	450	39,332	1,565
1988	53,189	1,812	3.72	525	736	—	—	2,847	45	10,542	205	39,800	1,562
1989	62,189	2,037	3.72	289	413	—	—	3,673	92	17,007	490	41,509	1,455
1990	69,103	2,730	2.61	213	324	—	—	3,507	122	15,875	583	49,721	2,024
1991	57,803	1,980	3.00	341	527	—	—	3,197	104	15,100	505	39,506	1,372
1992	62,761	2,467	3.24	145	330	—	—	2,519	100	18,119	758	42,123	1,609
1993	62,712	2,396	3.26	184	347	—	—	2,100	70	16,801	566	43,811	1,760
1994	61,770	2,321	3.45	175	393	—	—	2,715	97	17,700	562	41,355	1,662
1995	60,955	2,183	4.55	163	343	—	—	3,356	102	16,612	535	40,987	1,545
1996	62,819	2,277	4.30	75	301	—	—	3,556	116	19,689	692	39,574	1,470
1997	62,840	2,481	3.38	155	289	—	—	3,177	88	18,323	548	41,340	1,846
1998	59,002	2,550	2.70	224	498	—	—	—	141	—	529	—	1,881
1999	—	—	—	278	668	—	—	—	—	—	—	—	—

[1] Through 1984, season average price; thereafter, marketing year average. Prices weighted by production, 1866–1908; weighted by sales thereafter.

[2] 1926–1975: July 1 stock for year beginning the previous October; old crop only. 1976–1986: June 1 stock for year beginning previous October; old crop only. Beginning 1987: June 1 stock for year beginning previous September.

[3] Through 1953, covers only Minnesota, North Dakota, and South Dakota; includes Montana beginning with 1954 and California beginning with 1956.

[4] Includes small quantities of durum wheat grown in states other than Minnesota, North Dakota, and South Dakota.

[5] Data in original source appear to be in error but cannot be corrected.

Sources
Series Da717–719. U.S. National Agricultural Statistics Service, Crops Branch, Field Crops Section, *Track Records: United States Crop Production*, March 1999, downloaded October 3, 2000, from the U.S. Department of Agriculture, Economics and Statistics System.

Series Da720. *Agricultural Statistics*, 1952, 1957, 1962, 1967, 1972, 1973, 1985, 1992, and 2000 editions.

Series Da721. 1926–1933, *Agricultural Statistics*, 1941 and 1946; 1934, Agricultural Marketing Service, Statistical Bulletin number 203, January 1957 (processed); 1935–1995, *Agricultural Statistics*, 1957, 1962, 1967, 1972, 1973, 1985, 1992, and 2000 editions.

Series Da722–723. U.S. National Agricultural Statistics Service, *Agricultural Statistics 1940, 1952, 1955, 1960,* and *1965* editions.

Series Da724–729. 1909–1964, *Agricultural Statistics, 1952, 1955, 1960,* and *1968* editions; 1965–1998, *Track Records: United States Crop Production*, March 1999, downloaded October 3, 2000, from the U.S. Department of Agriculture, Economics and Statistics System.

Documentation
See the text for Table Da667–678.

U.S. Department of Agriculture data exclude Alaska; wheat is not grown in Hawai'i.

Series Da717–719. Figures are the combined estimates for winter, durum, and other spring wheat harvested for grain. Wheat acreage harvested for hay is not included.

Series Da720. Farm stocks of all wheat, by state, have been estimated quarterly since 1926 from reports of a large number of farmers. Farm stocks represent the farm carryover from previous crops at the beginning of a new crop year. The carryover added to the new crop is the supply for the new season.

Series Da721. Includes stocks at mills, elevators, warehouses, terminals, and processors.

Series Da724–725. Includes "red durum."

TABLE Da730–732   Wheat for grain – acreage, production, and price: 1839–1997[1]   [Census years]

Contributed by Alan L. Olmstead and Paul W. Rhode

	Acreage harvested	Production	Price
	Da730	Da731	Da732 [2]
Year	Thousand acres	Million bushels	Dollars per bushel
1839	—	85	—
1849	—	100	—
1859	—	173	—
1869	—	288	—
1879	35,430	459	—
1889	33,580	468	—
1899	52,589	659	0.56
1909	44,263	683	0.96
1919	73,099	945	2.19
1924	50,862	801	1.30
1929	62,000	801	1.05
1934	41,943	513	0.86
1939	50,527	709	0.69
1944	58,286	1,033	1.41
1949	71,163	1,007	1.86
1954	51,362	909	2.13
1959	49,567	1,056	1.77
1964	47,958	1,218	1.37
1969	44,075	1,296	1.34
1974	62,594	1,683	—
1978	54,155	1,608	—
1982	70,910	2,373	—
1987	53,224	1,887	—
1992	59,089	2,207	—
1997	58,836	2,204	—

[1] Data beginning 1969 not comparable with previous censuses; data are only for farms with farm products sales of $2,500 or more beginning that year.

[2] Through 1899, December 1 price received by farmers; season average price thereafter.

Sources

U.S Bureau of the Census, *U.S. Census of Agriculture, 1954*, volume 2, p. 633; *1964*, volume 2, Table 5, p. 313; *1969*, volume 2, chapter 6; *1974*, volume 1, part 51, p. I-22; *1982*, volume 1, part 51, p. 20; *1987*, volume 1, part 51, p. 36; *1992*, volume 1, part 51, p. 37; and *1997*, volume 1, part 51, p. 39.

Documentation

See the text for Table Da667–678.

TABLE Da733–745　Hay, rye, and buckwheat – acreage, production, and price: 1866–1999　[Annual]

Contributed by Alan L. Olmstead and Paul W. Rhode

	Hay							Rye			Buckwheat		
	All			Alfalfa		Other							
	Acreage harvested	Production	Price	Acreage harvested	Production	Acreage harvested	Production	Acreage harvested	Production	Price	Acreage harvested	Production	Price
	Da733 [1]	Da734 [1]	Da735 [1,2]	Da736	Da737	Da738	Da739	Da740	Da741	Da742 [2]	Da743	Da744	Da745 [2]
Year	Thousand acres	Thousand tons	Dollars per short ton	Thousand acres	Thousand tons	Thousand acres	Thousand tons	Thousand acres	Thousand bushels	Dollars per bushel	Thousand acres	Thousand bushels	Dollars per bushel
1866	18,250	21,000	14.48	—	—	—	—	1,509	17,619	1.06	772	11,861	0.94
1867	18,641	23,000	14.30	—	—	—	—	1,649	19,595	1.31	811	11,184	1.06
1868	19,568	23,000	13.90	—	—	—	—	1,620	17,218	1.20	781	10,520	1.04
1869	19,310	25,000	12.76	—	—	—	—	1,631	17,906	0.87	761	10,437	0.87
1870	19,719	21,000	14.45	—	—	—	—	1,559	15,637	0.81	739	9,249	0.80
1871	20,270	22,000	16.57	—	—	—	—	1,588	16,975	0.77	725	9,271	0.82
1872	21,081	24,000	15.35	—	—	—	—	1,563	16,776	0.74	769	10,337	0.84
1873	21,597	24,000	14.40	—	—	—	—	1,553	16,141	0.76	751	10,370	0.82
1874	21,861	25,000	13.85	—	—	—	—	1,568	17,305	0.86	747	10,031	0.80
1875	22,662	26,000	12.75	—	—	—	—	1,647	16,927	0.76	793	10,991	0.70
1876	23,986	29,000	9.80	—	—	—	—	1,770	19,266	0.68	815	9,613	0.72
1877	24,749	30,000	8.72	—	—	—	—	1,844	21,860	0.61	839	11,854	0.69
1878	25,627	33,000	7.32	—	—	—	—	1,905	21,755	0.55	838	12,000	0.53
1879	26,641	31,000	9.63	—	—	—	—	1,825	19,789	0.67	842	11,742	0.60
1880	27,011	33,000	11.82	—	—	—	—	1,752	19,306	0.75	818	11,009	0.59
1881	28,619	35,000	12.25	—	—	—	—	1,749	19,181	0.92	800	8,678	0.87
1882	30,373	39,000	9.99	—	—	—	—	2,080	26,747	0.63	800	10,678	0.73
1883	32,077	44,000	8.77	—	—	—	—	2,123	25,407	0.58	804	7,143	0.82
1884	33,448	43,000	8.99	—	—	—	—	2,100	26,627	0.53	782	10,139	0.58
1885	34,507	43,000	10.07	—	—	—	—	1,897	21,714	0.58	826	11,567	0.56
1886	35,771	45,000	8.72	—	—	—	—	1,918	23,854	0.53	802	10,771	0.54
1887	36,480	42,000	10.09	—	—	—	—	1,985	22,530	0.54	799	9,666	0.57
1888	37,411	47,000	9.24	—	—	—	—	2,181	28,440	0.59	812	9,729	0.63
1889	38,867	50,000	7.74	—	—	—	—	2,248	29,524	0.42	809	11,654	0.51
1890	39,613	51,000	8.11	—	—	—	—	2,116	26,378	0.62	821	11,979	0.57
1891	40,350	51,000	8.65	—	—	—	—	2,180	29,569	0.77	829	12,863	0.57
1892	41,328	53,000	8.78	—	—	—	—	2,239	28,718	0.54	840	12,119	0.52
1893	42,083	53,000	9.48	—	—	—	—	2,162	26,700	0.50	806	10,330	0.58
1894	41,864	48,000	8.98	—	—	—	—	2,166	26,758	0.49	805	11,024	0.55
1895	41,153	40,000	9.63	—	—	—	—	2,400	29,614	0.41	801	12,426	0.45
1896	40,971	51,000	7.60	—	—	—	—	2,599	31,852	0.37	856	13,791	0.39
1897	42,396	56,000	7.21	—	—	—	—	2,323	31,129	0.43	827	14,318	0.42
1898	43,083	60,000	6.52	—	—	—	—	2,204	29,044	0.44	794	12,187	0.45
1899	43,395	54,000	8.20	—	—	—	—	2,059	26,001	0.50	803	11,197	0.56
1900	42,488	50,000	9.78	—	—	—	—	2,127	27,413	0.50	791	11,709	0.56
1901	43,555	53,000	9.88	—	—	—	—	2,409	30,773	0.55	807	15,145	0.56
1902	44,716	59,000	9.05	—	—	—	—	2,444	33,862	0.50	810	13,547	0.60
1903	46,650	64,000	9.18	—	—	—	—	2,260	28,932	0.54	824	14,263	0.61
1904	47,480	66,000	8.82	—	—	—	—	2,205	28,461	0.69	831	15,489	0.63
1905	48,333	67,000	8.49	—	—	—	—	2,297	31,173	0.60	825	15,997	0.58
1906	48,650	60,000	10.40	—	—	—	—	2,154	29,609	0.59	821	14,806	0.59
1907	49,833	66,000	11.60	—	—	—	—	2,073	28,247	0.73	833	14,225	0.70
1908	51,487	72,000	9.08	—	—	—	—	2,130	28,650	0.73	842	14,675	0.78
1909	68,703	87,000	10.20	—	—	—	—	2,212	30,083	0.73	871	14,762	0.72
1910	68,332	75,000	11.66	—	—	—	—	2,262	29,098	0.73	840	14,536	0.68
1911	65,885	65,000	14.11	—	—	—	—	2,452	31,396	0.81	805	13,888	0.76
1912	67,395	86,000	10.80	—	—	—	—	2,724	37,911	0.65	804	15,095	0.68
1913	66,873	77,000	11.37	—	—	—	—	3,089	40,390	0.61	774	10,208	0.76
1914	67,337	83,000	10.64	—	—	—	—	3,144	42,120	0.82	752	12,919	0.81
1915	69,518	91,000	10.26	—	—	—	—	3,417	46,752	0.84	754	12,523	0.82
1916	72,918	99,000	11.13	—	—	—	—	3,528	43,089	1.12	786	10,302	1.27
1917	71,017	85,000	16.53	—	—	—	—	5,064	60,381	1.73	926	13,605	1.67
1918	71,909	82,000	19.62	—	—	—	—	6,709	83,586	1.50	1,018	14,404	1.64
1919	73,156	92,000	20.92	8,647	19,380	—	—	7,187	78,849	1.46	733	12,707	1.59
1920	73,033	92,000	16.50	9,015	20,458	—	—	4,843	62,113	1.47	729	12,193	1.25
1921	73,070	85,000	11.61	9,165	20,071	—	—	4,865	61,205	0.84	640	11,822	0.88
1922	75,432	95,000	11.63	9,275	20,110	—	—	6,770	101,142	0.64	729	11,776	0.89
1923	73,545	89,000	13.08	9,764	21,630	—	—	4,946	56,091	0.59	689	11,596	0.96
1924	74,459	91,000	12.68	10,352	20,828	64,107	70,626	3,943	58,470	0.95	737	12,508	1.08

Notes appear at end of table

TABLE Da733–745 Hay, rye, and buckwheat – acreage, production, and price: 1866–1999 [Annual] *Continued*

	Hay							Rye			Buckwheat		
	All			Alfalfa		Other							
	Acreage harvested	Production	Price	Acreage harvested	Production	Acreage harvested	Production	Acreage harvested	Production	Price	Acreage harvested	Production	Price
	Da733 [1]	Da734 [1]	Da735 [1,2]	Da736	Da737	Da738	Da739	Da740	Da741	Da742 [2]	Da743	Da744	Da745 [2]
Year	Thousand acres	Thousand tons	Dollars per short ton	Thousand acres	Thousand tons	Thousand acres	Thousand tons	Thousand acres	Thousand bushels	Dollars per bushel	Thousand acres	Thousand bushels	Dollars per bushel
1925	70,105	79,000	12.80	10,388	21,821	59,717	57,011	3,807	42,418	0.79	742	12,559	0.87
1926	68,795	76,000	13.27	10,721	21,529	58,074	54,496	3,427	34,968	0.83	679	10,976	0.88
1927	72,131	98,000	10.29	11,277	25,454	60,854	72,697	3,466	51,196	0.84	764	12,820	0.87
1928	67,185	84,000	11.28	11,123	23,882	56,062	59,960	3,320	38,055	0.84	679	10,117	0.90
1929	69,531	87,000	10.90	11,529	23,787	58,002	63,570	3,138	35,411	0.86	629	8,710	0.96
1930	67,947	75,000	11.10	11,609	22,713	56,338	51,814	3,646	45,383	0.44	574	6,967	0.79
1931	68,160	75,000	8.73	11,740	21,396	56,420	53,807	3,159	32,777	0.34	507	8,910	0.42
1932	70,412	84,000	6.20	12,607	25,924	57,805	57,797	3,350	39,099	0.28	454	6,727	0.43
1933	68,439	75,000	8.09	12,713	24,113	55,726	50,959	2,405	20,573	0.63	460	7,816	0.56
1934	65,387	60,000	13.20	11,691	19,036	53,696	41,449	1,921	16,285	0.72	475	8,994	0.59
1935	68,550	90,000	7.52	13,548	28,564	55,002	61,800	4,066	56,938	0.40	505	8,488	0.55
1936	67,732	70,000	1.20	14,062	24,737	53,670	45,277	2,694	24,239	0.81	379	6,440	0.85
1937	66,001	83,000	8.74	13,533	26,685	52,468	56,317	3,825	48,862	0.69	421	6,808	0.67
1938	68,175	91,000	6.78	13,366	28,503	54,809	62,917	4,087	55,984	0.34	448	6,763	0.54
1939	69,243	87,000	10.20	13,257	26,953	55,986	59,598	3,822	38,562	0.44	370	5,736	0.62
1940	73,058	96,000	9.82	14,023	30,286	59,035	65,764	3,204	39,725	0.42	388	6,476	0.54
1941	73,136	96,000	12.20	15,195	32,917	57,941	62,837	3,573	43,878	0.54	337	6,038	0.67
1942	74,827	108,000	13.70	16,199	37,162	58,628	70,555	3,792	52,929	0.60	375	6,636	0.85
1943	77,004	103,000	18.60	15,518	33,442	61,486	69,686	2,652	28,680	0.98	505	8,830	1.26
1944	77,639	103,000	21.40	15,254	33,323	62,385	69,566	2,132	22,525	1.09	508	8,956	0.96
1945	76,697	107,000	20.30	15,095	33,858	61,602	73,580	1,850	23,708	1.36	401	6,467	1.16
1946	73,741	100,000	22.70	14,187	31,092	59,554	68,426	1,597	18,487	1.92	383	6,812	1.46
1947	74,666	101,000	22.90	14,555	32,489	60,111	68,087	1,991	25,497	2.28	505	7,177	1.90
1948	71,817	96,000	24.30	14,669	32,710	57,148	63,462	2,058	25,886	1.43	330	6,085	1.08
1949	72,821	97,000	21.10	18,423	39,101	54,398	57,889	1,554	18,102	1.20	269	4,956	0.92
1950	75,150	104,000	21.10	19,901	42,673	55,249	61,147	1,753	21,403	1.31	253	4,424	1.08
1951	75,063	110,000	25.70	21,094	46,844	53,969	62,658	1,722	21,517	1.52	199	3,296	1.39
1952	75,147	106,000	26.90	21,569	47,348	53,578	59,038	1,393	16,146	1.72	163	3,232	1.40
1953	74,997	108,000	21.90	23,337	50,673	51,660	57,572	1,430	18,894	1.29	178	3,199	0.90
1954	73,721	108,000	21.90	26,576	56,364	47,145	51,470	1,795	25,963	1.21	150	2,692	1.24
1955	74,956	113,000	22.50	28,320	59,101	46,636	53,706	2,049	29,089	1.06	107	1,822	1.16
1956	72,292	108,000	22.20	29,103	60,940	43,189	47,038	1,624	21,288	1.16	100	1,832	1.19
1957	71,912	120,000	19.30	29,826	68,761	42,086	51,282	1,718	28,516	1.08	98	1,664	1.10
1958	70,547	120,000	18.80	28,941	66,522	41,606	53,578	1,797	33,182	1.02	86	1,533	1.02
1959	66,266	111,000	22.30	27,383	63,312	38,883	47,664	1,457	23,076	1.00	60	1,012	1.05
1960	67,313	118,000	21.70	27,580	67,083	39,733	51,075	1,688	33,108	0.88	48	847	1.16
1961	67,376	117,000	20.70	28,265	66,946	39,111	50,011	1,543	27,336	1.01	46	864	1.15
1962	67,563	122,000	21.80	28,257	71,731	39,306	50,028	1,981	40,698	0.95	41	828	1.31
1963	66,428	118,000	24.60	28,490	70,037	37,938	47,500	1,588	29,178	1.08	45	952	1.42
1964	67,375	119,000	23.90	29,384	71,304	37,991	47,474	1,696	32,476	1.04	50	1,020	1.08
1965	67,496	125,610	23.20	29,705	74,854	37,791	50,756	1,473	33,307	0.98	—	—	—
1966	64,356	120,930	25.00	28,950	73,073	35,406	47,857	1,276	27,791	1.06	—	—	2.49
1967	63,303	125,134	24.50	27,997	74,260	35,306	50,874	1,063	23,949	1.07	—	—	2.75
1968	60,922	124,244	23.60	26,964	73,632	33,958	50,612	996	22,971	1.02	—	—	2.43
1969	59,716	126,026	24.70	26,634	75,883	33,082	50,143	1,291	30,204	1.01	—	—	2.31
1970	61,467	126,969	26.10	27,276	75,573	34,191	51,396	1,427	36,840	0.99	—	—	—
1971	61,355	129,132	28.10	27,599	77,285	33,756	51,847	1,751	49,223	0.90	—	—	—
1972	59,680	128,565	31.30	27,187	78,226	32,493	50,339	1,050	28,256	0.96	—	—	—
1973	61,828	134,217	41.60	27,826	78,805	34,002	55,412	955	24,677	1.91	—	—	—
1974	60,195	126,384	50.90	26,877	74,368	33,318	52,016	784	17,506	2.51	—	—	—
1975	61,353	132,397	52.10	27,288	78,183	34,065	54,214	728	15,924	2.36	—	—	—
1976	60,377	120,125	60.20	26,674	69,960	33,703	50,165	719	14,891	2.47	—	—	—
1977	60,988	132,211	53.70	27,150	80,814	33,383	51,397	677	16,543	2.06	—	—	—
1978	62,113	143,817	49.80	27,864	87,294	34,249	56,523	926	24,065	1.99	—	—	—
1979	61,279	147,307	59.40	27,550	88,110	33,729	59,197	850	21,887	2.07	—	—	—
1980	58,870	130,740	71.00	26,174	79,963	32,696	50,777	650	15,958	2.63	—	—	—
1981	59,599	142,520	67.30	26,243	83,696	33,356	58,824	685	18,187	3.00	—	—	—
1982	59,812	149,241	69.30	26,188	88,385	33,624	60,856	677	19,533	2.39	—	—	—
1983	59,694	140,738	75.80	25,729	82,255	33,965	58,483	892	27,008	2.17	—	—	—
1984	61,414	150,582	72.70	26,818	90,144	34,596	60,438	979	32,407	2.00	—	—	—

Notes appear at end of table

(continued)

TABLE Da733–745   Hay, rye, and buckwheat – acreage, production, and price: 1866–1999   [Annual]   *Continued*

	Hay							Rye			Buckwheat		
	All			Alfalfa		Other							
	Acreage harvested	Production	Price	Acreage harvested	Production	Acreage harvested	Production	Acreage harvested	Production	Price	Acreage harvested	Production	Price
	Da733 [1]	Da734 [1]	Da735 [1,2]	Da736	Da737	Da738	Da739	Da740	Da741	Da742 [2]	Da743	Da744	Da745 [2]
Year	Thousand acres	Thousand tons	Dollars per short ton	Thousand acres	Thousand tons	Thousand acres	Thousand tons	Thousand acres	Thousand bushels	Dollars per bushel	Thousand acres	Thousand bushels	Dollars per bushel
1985	60,461	148,719	67.60	25,647	85,121	34,814	63,598	708	20,373	2.03	—	—	—
1986	62,334	155,385	59.80	26,911	91,865	35,423	63,520	661	19,067	1.48	—	—	—
1987	60,133	147,457	65.00	25,435	84,225	34,698	63,232	671	19,526	1.62	—	—	—
1988	64,771	125,736	85.20	26,751	69,306	38,020	56,430	595	14,689	2.52	—	—	—
1989	62,722	144,706	85.40	25,796	77,059	36,926	67,647	484	13,647	2.06	—	—	—
1990	61,030	146,212	80.60	25,346	83,413	35,684	62,799	375	10,176	2.09	—	—	—
1991	61,834	152,073	71.20	25,414	83,319	36,420	68,754	395	9,734	2.20	—	—	—
1992	58,903	146,903	74.30	24,070	79,140	34,833	67,763	391	11,440	2.38	—	—	—
1993	59,689	146,699	84.70	24,673	80,115	35,016	66,584	381	10,340	2.55	—	—	—
1994	58,815	150,136	86.70	24,138	81,130	34,677	69,006	407	11,341	2.70	—	—	—
1995	59,764	154,239	82.20	24,404	84,138	35,360	70,101	385	10,064	2.90	—	—	—
1996	61,169	149,779	95.80	24,206	79,139	36,963	70,640	345	8,936	3.70	—	—	—
1997	61,084	152,536	100.00	23,551	78,535	37,533	74,001	316	8,132	3.75	—	—	—
1998	60,076	151,780	84.60	—	—	—	—	—	11,795	2.49	—	—	—
1999	63,160 [3]	159,077 [3]	77.00	—	—	—	—	—	—	2.28	—	—	—

[1] Tame hay (that is, cut from cultivated grasses) through 1908; all hay thereafter.

[2] Method of determining price changes over time; see text.

[3] Preliminary.

Sources

Series Da733–734. 1866–1964, U.S. Department of Agriculture, Statistical Reporting Service, *Agricultural Statistics, 1967* and *1972* editions; 1965–1999, U.S. National Agricultural Statistics Service, Crops Branch, Field Crops Section, *Track Records: United States Crop Production*, March 1999, downloaded October 3, 2000, from the U.S. Department of Agriculture, Economics and Statistics System, and *Agricultural Statistics, 2000*.

Series Da735. *Agricultural Statistics, 1967, 1972, 1978, 1982, 1987, 1992, 1995–96,* and *2000* editions.

Series Da736–737. 1919–1964, *Agricultural Statistics, 1937, 1952, 1960,* and *1968* editions; 1965–1997, *Track Records: United States Crop Production*, March 1997, downloaded October 3, 2000, from the U.S. Department of Agriculture, Economics and Statistics System.

Series Da738–739. 1924–1964, *Agricultural Statistics, 1952, 1960,* and *1968* editions; 1965–1997, *Track Records: United States Crop Production*, March 1997, downloaded October 3, 2000, from the U.S. Department of Agriculture, Economics and Statistics System.

Series Da740–741. 1866–1964, *Agricultural Statistics, 1941, 1952, 1957, 1962, 1967,* and *1972* editions; 1965–1998, *Track Records: United States Crop Production*, March 1999, downloaded October 3, 2000, from the U.S. Department of Agriculture, Economics and Statistics System.

Series Da742. *Agricultural Statistics, 1941, 1952, 1957, 1962, 1967, 1972, 1983, 1988, 1993, 1995–96,* and *2000* editions.

Series Da743–745. 1866–1923, U.S. Agricultural Marketing Service, *Rice, Popcorn and Buckwheat Acreage, Yield, Production, Price and Value, 1866–1953,* Statistical Bulletin number 238, October 1958. Series Da743–744 for 1924–1961, and series Da745 for 1924–1964, *Agricultural Statistics, 1962, 1967,* and *1971* editions. Series Da743–744, 1962–1964, U.S. Department of Agriculture, Statistical Reporting Service, *Crop Production, 1971 Annual Summary,* January 14, 1972. Series Da745, 1966–1969, U.S. Department of Agriculture, Statistical Reporting Service, *Crop Values, 1966* and subsequent annual issues.

Documentation

Figures for stocks of hay are published in U.S. National Agricultural Statistics Service, *Agricultural Statistics.* Data on farm stocks of rye are available from 1933, and on stocks in off-farm positions from 1943.

See the text for Table Da667–678.

Series Da735. December 1 average price through 1908; season average price thereafter. Loose hay price, 1909–1938; baled hay price thereafter.

Series Da742. Through 1907, December 1 price received by farmers. For 1908–1983, figures are season average price per bushel received by farmers; includes allowance for loans outstanding and purchases by the government valued at the average loan and purchase rate, by state, where applicable. Beginning 1984, figures are marketing year average price per bushel received by farmers.

Series Da745. Through 1907, December 1 price received by farmers; season average price thereafter.

TABLE Da746–754   Hay, rye, and buckwheat – acreage, production, and price: 1839–1997   [Census years]

Contributed by Alan L. Olmstead and Paul W. Rhode

	Hay			Rye for grain			Buckwheat		
	Acreage harvested	Production	Price	Acreage harvested	Production	Price	Acreage harvested	Production	Price
	Da746 [1]	Da747 [1]	Da748 [1,2]	Da749 [3]	Da750 [3]	Da751 [2,3]	Da752 [3]	Da753 [3]	Da754 [2,3]
Year	Thousand acres	Million tons	Dollars per short ton	Thousand acres	Thousand bushels	Dollars per bushel	Thousand acres	Thousand bushels	Dollars per bushel
1839	—	10	—	—	18,646	—	—	7,292	—
1849	—	14	—	—	14,189	—	—	8,957	—
1859	—	19	—	—	21,101	—	—	17,572	—
1869	—	27	—	—	16,919	—	—	9,822	—
1879	30,631	35	—	1,842	19,832	—	848	11,817	—
1889	52,949	67	—	2,172	28,421	—	837	12,110	—
1899	61,691	79	6.11	2,054	25,569	0.48	807	11,234	0.51
1909	68,227	87	8.90	2,196	29,520	0.69	878	14,849	0.63
1919	70,936	89	21.50	7,679	75,992	1.53	743	12,690	1.55
1924	74,692	88	12.18	3,744	55,674	1.04	717	12,004	1.07
1929	67,823	82	11.45	3,033	34,303	0.86	622	8,359	0.96
1934	63,156	54	13.82	1,914	16,234	0.73	—	—	—
1939	61,229	74	8.74	3,556	35,844	0.44	361	5,589	0.62
1944	73,402	95	18.06	2,023	21,349	1.09	—	—	—
1949	67,470	89	21.62	1,418	16,563	1.22	236	4,318	0.94
1954	69,940	104	22.22	1,450	21,844	1.22	128	2,277	0.97
1959	63,549	107	20.46	1,392	21,809	1.02	56	923	1.08
1964	66,160	117	23.71	1,640	30,916	1.04	48	986	1.07
1969	53,204	112	24.70	1,115	25,703	1.00	38	680	1.00
1974	56,236	115	—	637	14,167	—	60	1,143	—
1978	60,241	131	—	433	11,347	—	56	1,071	—
1982	56,744	128	—	449	12,828	—	83	1,330	—
1987	57,968	129	—	546	15,106	—	81	1,556	—
1992	56,596	127	—	336	9,287	—	65	900	—
1997	60,800	139	—	268	6,502	—	25	733	—

[1] Tame hay (that is, cut from cultivated grasses) through 1908; all hay thereafter.

[2] Method of determining price changes over time; see text.

[3] Data for 1969 and 1974 are not comparable with other census years; data are only for farms with farm products sales of $2,500 or more.

Sources

U.S. Bureau of the Census, *U.S. Census of Agriculture, 1964*, volume 2, Table 5, p. 313; *1969*, volume 2, chapter 6; *1974*, volume 1, part 51, p. I-5; *1974*, volume 2, part 6, pp. 62, 67; *1982*, volume 1, part 51, pp. 20, 311; *1987*, volume 1, part 51, pp. 35, 327; *1992*, volume 1, part 51, pp. 37, 370; and *1997*, volume 1, part 51, pp. 39, 436.

Documentation

See the text for Table Da667–678.

Series Da748. Through 1899, December 1 average price; season average price thereafter. Loose hay price 1909–1938; baled hay price thereafter.

Series Da751 and Da754. Through 1899, December 1 price received by farmers; season average price thereafter.

TABLE Da755–765   Cotton, cottonseed, shorn wool, and tobacco – acreage, production, price, and cotton stocks: 1790–1999   [Annual]

Contributed by Alan L. Olmstead and Paul W. Rhode

	Cotton				Cottonseed		Shorn wool		Tobacco		
	Acreage harvested	Production	Price	Stocks	Production	Price	Production	Price	Acreage harvested	Production	Price
	Da755	Da756 [1]	Da757 [2]	Da758 [3]	Da759	Da760 [2]	Da761 [4,5]	Da762 [2,4]	Da763	Da764	Da765 [2]
Year	Thousand acres	Thousand bales	Cents per pound	Thousand bales	Thousand short tons	Dollars per short ton	Million pounds	Cents per pound	Thousand acres	Million pounds	Cents per pound
1790	—	3	—	—	—	—	—	—	—	—	—
1791	—	4	—	—	—	—	—	—	—	—	—
1792	—	6	—	—	—	—	—	—	—	—	—
1793	—	10	—	—	—	—	—	—	—	—	—
1794	—	17	—	—	—	—	—	—	—	—	—
1795	—	17	—	—	—	—	—	—	—	—	—
1796	—	21	—	—	—	—	—	—	—	—	—
1797	—	23	—	—	—	—	—	—	—	—	—
1798	—	31	—	—	—	—	—	—	—	—	—
1799	—	42	—	—	—	—	—	—	—	—	—
1800	—	73	—	—	—	—	—	—	—	—	—
1801	—	100	—	—	—	—	—	—	—	—	—
1802	—	115	—	—	—	—	—	—	—	—	—
1803	—	126	—	—	—	—	—	—	—	—	—
1804	—	136	—	—	—	—	—	—	—	—	—
1805	—	146	—	—	—	—	—	—	—	—	—
1806	—	167	—	—	—	—	—	—	—	—	—
1807	—	167	—	—	—	—	—	—	—	—	—
1808	—	157	—	—	—	—	—	—	—	—	—
1809	—	172	—	—	—	—	—	—	—	—	—
1810	—	178	—	—	—	—	—	—	—	—	—
1811	—	167	—	—	—	—	—	—	—	—	—
1812	—	157	—	—	—	—	—	—	—	—	—
1813	—	157	—	—	—	—	—	—	—	—	—
1814	—	146	—	—	—	—	—	—	—	—	—
1815	—	209	—	—	—	—	—	—	—	—	—
1816	—	259	—	—	—	—	—	—	—	—	—
1817	—	272	—	—	—	—	—	—	—	—	—
1818	—	262	—	—	—	—	—	—	—	—	—
1819	—	349	—	—	—	—	—	—	—	—	—
1820	—	335	—	—	—	—	—	—	—	—	—
1821	—	377	—	—	—	—	—	—	—	—	—
1822	—	439	—	—	—	—	—	—	—	—	—
1823	—	387	—	—	—	—	—	—	—	—	—
1824	—	450	—	—	—	—	—	—	—	—	—
1825	—	533	—	—	—	—	—	—	—	—	—
1826	—	732	—	—	—	—	—	—	—	—	—
1827	—	565	—	—	—	—	—	—	—	—	—
1828	—	680	—	—	—	—	—	—	—	—	—
1829	—	764	—	—	—	—	—	—	—	—	—
1830	—	732	—	—	—	—	—	—	—	—	—
1831	—	805	—	—	—	—	—	—	—	—	—
1832	—	816	—	—	—	—	—	—	—	—	—
1833	—	931	—	—	—	—	—	—	—	—	—
1834	—	962	—	—	—	—	—	—	—	—	—
1835	—	1,062	—	—	—	—	—	—	—	—	—
1836	—	1,129	—	—	—	—	—	—	—	—	—
1837	—	1,428	—	—	—	—	—	—	—	—	—
1838	—	1,093	—	—	—	—	—	—	—	—	—
1839	—	1,654	—	—	—	—	—	—	—	—	—
1840	—	1,348	—	—	—	—	—	—	—	—	—
1841	—	1,398	—	—	—	—	—	—	—	—	—
1842	—	2,035	—	—	—	—	—	—	—	—	—
1843	—	1,750	—	—	—	—	—	—	—	—	—
1844	—	2,079	—	—	—	—	—	—	—	—	—
1845	—	1,806	—	—	—	—	—	—	—	—	—
1846	—	1,604	—	—	—	—	—	—	—	—	—
1847	—	2,128	—	—	—	—	—	—	—	—	—
1848	—	2,615	—	—	—	—	—	—	—	—	—
1849	—	2,066	—	—	—	—	—	—	—	—	—

Notes appear at end of table

TABLE Da755–765   Cotton, cottonseed, shorn wool, and tobacco – acreage, production, price, and cotton stocks: 1790–1999   [Annual]   *Continued*

	Cotton				Cottonseed		Shorn wool		Tobacco		
	Acreage harvested	Production	Price	Stocks	Production	Price	Production	Price	Acreage harvested	Production	Price
	Da755	Da756 [1]	Da757 [2]	Da758 [3]	Da759	Da760 [2]	Da761 [4,5]	Da762 [2,4]	Da763	Da764	Da765 [2]
Year	Thousand acres	Thousand bales	Cents per pound	Thousand bales	Thousand short tons	Dollars per short ton	Million pounds	Cents per pound	Thousand acres	Million pounds	Cents per pound
1850	—	2,136	—	—	—	—	—	—	—	—	—
1851	—	2,799	—	—	—	—	—	—	—	—	—
1852	—	3,130	—	—	—	—	—	—	—	—	—
1853	—	2,766	—	—	—	—	—	—	—	—	—
1854	—	2,708	—	—	—	—	—	—	—	—	—
1855	—	3,221	—	—	—	—	—	—	—	—	—
1856	—	2,874	—	—	—	—	—	—	—	—	—
1857	—	3,012	—	—	—	—	—	—	—	—	—
1858	—	3,758	—	—	—	—	—	—	—	—	—
1859	—	4,508	—	—	—	—	—	—	—	—	—
1860	—	3,841	—	—	—	—	—	—	—	—	—
1861	—	4,491	—	—	—	—	—	—	—	—	—
1862	—	1,597	—	—	—	—	—	—	—	—	—
1863	—	449	—	—	—	—	—	—	—	—	—
1864	—	299	—	—	—	—	—	—	—	—	—
1865	—	2,094	—	—	—	—	—	—	—	—	—
1866	7,666	2,097	—	—	864	—	—	—	394	316	11.6
1867	7,864	2,520	—	—	1,042	—	—	—	370	260	11.6
1868	6,973	2,366	—	—	974	—	—	—	369	286	12.2
1869	7,751	3,011	—	—	1,118	—	162	22.2	395	264	10.9
1870	9,238	4,352	—	—	1,786	—	162	22.2	424	345	9.7
1871	8,285	2,974	—	—	1,223	—	160	27.4	420	327	10.2
1872	9,580	3,933	—	—	1,621	—	150	31.7	492	385	10.7
1873	10,998	4,168	—	—	1,718	—	158	26.5	513	382	8.6
1874	10,753	3,836	—	—	1,567	—	170	25.7	378	217	13.7
1875	11,348	4,631	—	—	1,909	—	181	25.7	746	609	7.7
1876	11,747	4,474	9.7	—	1,826	—	192	19.7	625	466	7.3
1877	12,606	4,773	8.5	—	1,994	—	200	21.4	789	621	5.4
1878	13,539	5,074	8.2	—	2,106	—	208	18.8	651	455	5.8
1879	14,474	5,756	10.3	—	2,425	—	211	18.0	633	472	6.1
1880	15,921	6,606	9.8	—	2,822	—	233	23.1	650	469	8.1
1881	16,483	5,456	10.7	—	2,280	—	240	22.2	698	426	9.6
1882	15,638	6,949	9.1	—	3,033	—	272	20.5	744	579	8.5
1883	16,295	5,713	9.1	—	2,450	—	290	17.1	750	509	8.8
1884	16,849	5,682	9.2	—	2,427	—	300	14.5	754	580	8.1
1885	17,922	6,576	8.4	—	2,828	—	308	14.5	815	611	7.5
1886	18,370	6,505	8.1	—	2,802	—	302	16.3	848	609	7.2
1887	18,793	7,047	8.6	—	3,056	—	285	18.0	722	469	10.5
1888	19,520	6,938	8.5	—	3,074	—	269	17.1	891	661	7.9
1889	20,191	7,473	8.6	—	3,318	—	265	18.0	758	525	6.6
1890	20,937	8,653	8.6	—	3,802	—	276	17.1	851	648	8.0
1891	21,503	9,035	7.2	—	3,967	—	285	16.3	955	747	8.2
1892	18,869	6,700	8.3	—	2,956	—	294	16.3	1,039	757	8.9
1893	20,256	7,493	7.0	—	3,297	—	349	14.5	1,096	767	7.9
1894	21,886	9,091	4.6	—	4,448	—	325	11.1	993	767	6.6
1895	19,839	7,162	7.6	—	3,174	—	294	10.3	1,006	745	6.8
1896	23,230	8,533	6.7	—	3,778	—	272	10.3	1,038	760	5.5
1897	25,131	10,899	6.7	—	4,878	—	259	11.1	978	703	7.4
1898	24,715	11,278	5.7	—	5,120	—	267	13.7	1,116	909	6.1
1899	24,163	9,346	7.0	—	4,152	—	272	14.5	1,102	870	7.1
1900	24,886	10,124	9.2	—	4,500	—	260	13.7	1,086	852	6.7
1901	27,050	9,508	7.0	—	4,226	—	266	13.7	1,098	886	7.2
1902	27,561	10,630	7.6	—	4,729	—	274	13.7	1,189	960	6.9
1903	27,762	9,851	10.5	—	4,379	—	245	15.4	1,212	976	6.7
1904	30,077	13,438	9.0	—	5,967	—	250	16.3	1,026	857	7.8
1905	27,753	10,576	10.8	—	4,700	—	253	22.2	1,103	939	8.2
1906	31,404	13,274	9.6	1,299	5,898	—	257	23.1	1,123	973	9.6
1907	30,729	11,106	10.4	1,465	4,931	—	256	20.5	1,042	886	10.0
1908	31,091	13,241	9.0	1,161	5,883	—	270	16.3	1,009	836	10.2
1909	30,555	10,005	13.5	1,469	4,442	24.35	310	22.2	1,292	1,054	10.1

Notes appear at end of table

(continued)

TABLE Da755-765   Cotton, cottonseed, shorn wool, and tobacco – acreage, production, price, and cotton stocks: 1790-1999 [Annual] Continued

	Cotton				Cottonseed		Shorn wool		Tobacco		
	Acreage harvested	Production	Price	Stocks	Production	Price	Production	Price	Acreage harvested	Production	Price
	Da755	Da756 [1]	Da757 [2]	Da758 [3]	Da759	Da760 [2]	Da761 [4,5]	Da762 [2,4]	Da763	Da764	Da765 [2]
Year	Thousand acres	Thousand bales	Cents per pound	Thousand bales	Thousand short tons	Dollars per short ton	Million pounds	Cents per pound	Thousand acres	Million pounds	Cents per pound
1910	31,508	11,609	14.0	940	5,156	26.11	306	21.7	1,398	1,142	9.3
1911	34,916	15,694	9.7	1,275	6,970	17.18	302	15.8	1,133	941	9.3
1912	32,557	13,703	11.5	1,652	6,037	18.36	278	17.3	1,335	1,117	10.7
1913	35,206	14,153	12.5	1,511	6,286	21.96	266	16.7	1,284	992	12.8
1914	35,615	16,112	7.4	1,366	7,155	15.51	251	16.6	1,258	1,037	9.7
1915	29,951	11,172	11.2	3,936	4,963	30.15	241	22.1	1,419	1,157	9.0
1916	33,071	11,448	17.4	3,140	5,085	45.63	244	26.1	1,483	1,207	14.8
1917	32,245	11,284	27.1	2,720	5,012	64.28	237	41.6	1,616	1,326	24.0
1918	35,038	12,018	28.9	3,509	5,341	65.23	254	57.7	1,720	1,445	27.9
1919	32,906	11,141	35.3	4,445	5,069	65.59	270	49.5	1,959	1,444	31.2
1920	34,408	13,429	15.9	3,824	5,966	25.65	251	45.5	1,935	1,509	17.3
1921	28,678	7,945	17.0	6,896	3,528	29.07	242	17.3	1,340	1,005	19.5
1922	31,361	9,755	22.9	3,322	4,330	30.33	228	27.1	1,616	1,254	22.8
1923	35,550	10,140	28.7	2,325	4,503	41.21	230	39.4	1,855	1,518	19.0
1924	39,501	13,630	22.9	1,556	6,050	33.25	238	36.6	1,702	1,245	19.0
1925	44,386	16,105	19.6	1,610	7,150	31.69	253	39.5	1,751	1,376	16.8
1926	44,608	17,978	12.5	3,543	7,989	22.08	269	34.0	1,628	1,289	17.9
1927	38,342	12,956	20.2	3,762	5,758	34.86	289	30.3	1,556	1,211	20.7
1928	42,434	14,477	18.0	2,536	6,319	34.21	315	36.2	1,864	1,373	20.0
1929	43,232	14,825	16.8	2,312	6,406	30.93	328	30.2	1,980	1,533	18.3
1930	42,444	13,932	9.5	4,530	6,028	22.07	352	19.5	2,124	1,648	12.8
1931	38,704	17,097	5.7	6,370	7,310	8.98	376	13.6	1,988	1,565	8.2
1932	35,891	13,003	6.5	9,678	5,815	10.35	351	8.6	1,405	1,018	10.5
1933	29,383	13,047	10.2	8,165	5,511	12.91	374	20.6	1,739	1,372	13.0
1934	26,866	9,636	12.4	7,744	4,256	33.03	369	21.9	1,273	1,085	21.3
1935	27,509	10,638	11.1	7,208	4,634	30.54	362	19.3	1,439	1,302	18.4
1936	29,755	12,399	12.4	5,409	5,472	33.30	353	26.9	1,441	1,163	23.6
1937	33,623	18,946	8.4	4,499	7,844	19.50	356	32.0	1,753	1,569	20.4
1938	24,248	11,943	8.6	11,533	4,950	21.79	360	19.1	1,601	1,386	19.6
1939	23,805	11,817	9.1	13,033	4,869	21.14	362	22.3	2,000	1,881	15.4
1940	23,861	12,566	9.9	10,564	5,286	21.72	372	28.4	1,410	1,460	16.1
1941	22,236	10,744	17.0	12,166	4,553	47.65	388	35.5	1,307	1,262	26.4
1942	22,602	12,817	19.1	10,640	5,202	45.60	388	40.1	1,377	1,408	36.9
1943	21,610	11,427	19.9	10,657	4,688	52.10	379	41.6	1,458	1,406	40.5
1944	19,617	12,230	20.7	10,744	4,902	52.70	338	42.3	1,750	1,951	42.0
1945	17,029	9,015	22.5	11,164	3,664	51.10	308	41.9	1,821	1,991	42.6
1946	17,584	8,640	32.6	7,326	3,514	72.00	281	42.3	1,960	1,315	45.1
1947	21,330	11,860	31.9	2,530	4,682	85.90	251	42.0	1,852	2,107	43.6
1948	22,911	14,877	30.4	3,080	5,945	67.20	232	49.2	1,554	1,980	48.2
1949	27,439	16,128	28.6	5,287	6,559	43.40	213	49.4	1,623	1,969	45.9
1950	17,843	10,014	40.1	6,846	4,105	86.60	217	62.1	1,599	2,030	51.7
1951	26,949	15,149	37.9	2,278	6,286	69.30	228	97.1	1,780	2,332	51.1
1952	25,921	15,139	34.6	2,789	6,190	69.60	233	54.1	1,772	2,256	49.9
1953	24,341	16,465	32.3	5,605	6,748	52.70	232	54.9	1,633	2,059	52.3
1954	19,251	13,697	33.6	9,728	5,709	60.30	236	53.2	1,668	2,244	51.1
1955	16,928	14,721	32.3	11,205	6,043	44.60	241	42.7	1,495	2,193	53.2
1956	15,615	13,310	31.8	14,529	5,407	53.40	242	44.3	1,364	2,176	53.7
1957	13,558	10,964	29.7	11,323	4,609	51.10	239	53.4	1,122	1,668	56.1
1958	11,849	11,512	33.2	8,737	4,798	43.80	244	36.4	1,078	1,736	59.9
1959	15,117	14,558	31.7	8,885	5,991	38.80	260	43.2	1,153	1,796	58.3
1960	15,309	14,272	30.2	7,559	5,886	42.60	265	42.0	1,142	1,944	60.9
1961	15,634	14,318	32.9	7,228	5,978	51.10	259	42.9	1,174	2,061	63.8
1962	15,569	14,867	31.9	7,831	6,139	47.90	247	47.7	1,224	2,315	58.9
1963	14,212	15,334	32.2	11,216	6,192	50.70	232	48.4	1,176	2,344	57.7
1964	14,055	15,145	31.1	12,378	6,237	47.10	212	53.2	1,078	2,228	59.2
1965	13,613	14,938	29.4	14,291	6,086	46.70	201	47.1	977	1,855	65.1
1966	9,553	9,557	21.8	16,862	3,960	65.90	195	52.1	972	1,885	66.4
1967	7,997	7,443	26.7	12,533	3,210	55.20	189	39.8	960	1,968	66.8
1968	10,159	10,926	23.1	6,448	4,638	50.50	178	40.5	879	1,710	69.5
1969	11,051	9,990	22.0	6,521	4,068	41.10	166	41.9	918	1,803	71.8

Notes appear at end of table

TABLE Da755-765   Cotton, cottonseed, shorn wool, and tobacco – acreage, production, price, and cotton stocks: 1790–1999   [Annual]   *Continued*

	Cotton				Cottonseed		Shorn wool		Tobacco		
	Acreage harvested	Production	Price	Stocks	Production	Price	Production	Price	Acreage harvested	Production	Price
	Da755	Da756 [1]	Da757 [2]	Da758 [3]	Da759	Da760 [2]	Da761 [4,5]	Da762 [2,4]	Da763	Da764	Da765 [2]
Year	Thousand acres	Thousand bales	Cents per pound	Thousand bales	Thousand short tons	Dollars per short ton	Million pounds	Cents per pound	Thousand acres	Million pounds	Cents per pound
1970	11,155	10,192	22.0	5,760	4,066	56.50	162	35.5	898	1,906	72.9
1971	11,471	10,477	28.2	4,252	4,240	56.80	160	19.6	838	1,705	78.6
1972	12,984	13,704	27.3	3,234	5,393	49.50	159	35.0	842	1,749	83.0
1973	11,970	12,974	44.6	3,929	5,016	100.00	144	82.7	887	1,742	90.1
1974	12,547	11,540	42.9	3,743	4,510	135.50	131	59.2	963	1,990	108.6
1975	8,796	8,302	51.3	5,481	3,218	97.00	120	44.8	1,086	2,182	102.6
1976	10,914	10,581	64.1	3,594	4,122	103.00	111	66.0	1,045	2,137	112.5
1977	13,275	14,389	52.3	2,920	5,521	70.30	107	72.0	958	1,914	118.6
1978	12,400	10,856	58.4	5,326	4,269	114.00	103	74.5	964	2,025	132.4
1979	12,831	14,629	62.5	3,782	5,778	121.00	105	86.3	828	1,527	141.1
1980	13,215	11,122	74.7	3,027	4,471	129.00	105	88.1	921	1,786	152.3
1981	13,841	15,646	54.3	2,595	6,397	86.00	110	94.5	977	2,064	170.6
1982	9,734	11,963	59.6	6,399	4,744	77.00	106	68.6	913	1,994	176.4
1983	7,348	7,771	66.6	7,561	3,076	166.00	103	61.3	789	1,429	174.6
1984	10,379	12,982	58.9	2,906	5,149	100.00	96	79.5	792	1,728	180.6
1985	10,229	13,432	56.3	4,088	5,279	66.00	88	63.3	688	1,512	164.5
1986	8,468	9,731	52.4	9,041	3,801	80.00	84	66.8	581	1,162	152.4
1987	10,030	14,760	64.3	4,797	5,769	83.00	85	91.7	586	1,189	157.3
1988	11,948	15,412	56.6	5,684	6,062	118.00	90	138.0	634	1,370	164.6
1989	9,538	12,196	66.2	6,984	4,677	105.00	89	124.0	678	1,367	170.8
1990	11,732	15,505	68.2	3,109	5,969	121.00	88	80.0	733	1,625	173.8
1991	12,960	17,614	58.1	2,389	6,926	71.00	88	55.0	764	1,663	177.1
1992	11,123	16,219	54.9	3,569	6,230	98.00	83	74.0	784	1,722	177.7
1993	12,783	16,134	58.4	4,482	6,343	113.00	78	51.0	746	1,613	175.4
1994	13,322	19,662	72.0	3,509	7,604	101.00	69	78.0	671	1,583	175.8
1995	16,007	17,900	76.5	2,608	6,849	106.00	64	104.0	664	1,270	182.0
1996	12,888	18,942	70.5	2,695	7,144	126.00	57	70.0	733	1,519	188.2
1997	13,406	18,793	66.2	3,895	6,935	121.00	54	84.0	836	1,787	180.2
1998	10,723	13,796	65.3	4,079	5,365	123.00 [6]	49	60.0 [6]	718	1,480	182.8
1999	—	—	—	3,866 [6]	6,210	—	—	—	644 [6]	1,275 [6]	183.1

[1] Coverage and conversion factors change over time; see text.

[2] Method of determining price changes over time; see text.

[3] See text for discussion of changes in series over time and for information on treatment of domestic and foreign stocks.

[4] See text for information on geographic coverage and comparability of the series over time.

[5] Includes shearing at commercial feeding yards.

[6] Preliminary.

Sources

Series Da755 and Da757. U.S. National Agricultural Statistics Service, Crops Branch, Field Crops Section, *Track Records: United States Crop Production*, March 1999, downloaded October 3, 2000, from the U.S. Department of Agriculture, Economics and Statistics System.

Series Da756. 1790–1865: U.S. Department of Agriculture, Bureau of Statistics, Circular number 32, August 1912; 1866–1998, *Track Records: United States Crop Production*, March 1999, downloaded October 3, 2000, from the U.S. Department of Agriculture, Economics and Statistics System.

Series Da758. U.S. National Agricultural Statistics Service, *Agricultural Statistics, 1941, 1952, 1956, 1957, 1967, 1971, 1983, 1990,* and *2000* editions.

Series Da759. 1866–1966, *Agricultural Statistics, 1967* and *1971* editions; 1967–1999, U.S. Department of Agriculture, Commercial Agriculture Division, Research Service, *1997 Oil Crops Situation and Outlook Yearbook*, January 1998, updated November 1999, Table 25, downloaded October 3, 2000, from the U.S. Department of Agriculture, Economics and Statistics System.

Series Da760. 1909–1918, U.S. Agricultural Marketing Service, Statistical Bulletin number 164, June 1955 (processed); 1919–1970, *Agricultural Statistics, 1957, 1962,* and *1972* editions; 1971–1976, U.S. National Agricul-

tural Statistics Service, Agricultural Commodities Section, *Prices Received by Commodity, Historic Data Series, and Indexes*, June 24, 1994, downloaded October 3, 2000, from the U.S. Department of Agriculture, Economics and Statistics System; 1977–1998, *1997 Oil Crops Situation and Outlook Yearbook*, January 1998, updated November 1999, Table 26, downloaded October 3, 2000, from the U.S. Department of Agriculture, Economics and Statistics System.

Series Da761. 1869–1908, U.S. Department of Agriculture, *Agriculture Yearbook*, 1923; 1909–1939, U.S. Department of Agriculture, *Livestock and Meat Statistics*, Statistical Bulletin number 230, July 1958; 1940–1978, *Agricultural Statistics, 1967, 1972, 1983,* and *1988* editions; 1979–1998, U.S. Department of Agriculture, Economic Research Service, Commercial Agriculture Division, *1997 Cotton and Wool Situation and Outlook Yearbook*, November 1997, updated December 1999, downloaded October 3, 2000, from the U.S. Department of Agriculture, Economics and Statistics System.

Series Da762. 1869–1908, U.S. Department of Agriculture, *Gross Farm Income and Indices of Farm Production and Prices in the United States, 1869–1937*, Technical Bulletin number 703, December 1940; 1909–1939, *Livestock and Meat Statistics*, Statistical Bulletin number 230, July 1958; 1940–1970, *Agricultural Statistics, 1967* and *1972* editions; 1971–1991, *Prices Received by Commodity, Historic Data Series, and Indexes*, June 24, 1994, downloaded October 3, 2000, from the U.S. Department of Agriculture, Economics and Statistics System; 1992–1998, *Agricultural Statistics, 2000*.

Series Da763. 1866–1964, *Agricultural Statistics, 1967* and *1972* editions; 1965–1997, *Track Records: United States Crop Production*, March 1997, downloaded October 3, 2000, from the U.S. Department of Agriculture, Economics and Statistics System; 1998–1999, *Agricultural Statistics, 2000*.

(continued)

TABLE Da755–765   Cotton, cottonseed, shorn wool, and tobacco – acreage, production, price, and cotton stocks: 1790–1999   [Annual]   *Continued*

Series Da764. 1866-1964, *Agricultural Statistics: 1967* and *1972* editions; 1965-1997, *Track Records: United States Crop Production*, March 1997, downloaded October 3, 2000, from the U.S. Department of Agriculture, Economics and Statistics System; 1998-1999, *Agricultural Statistics, 2000*.

Series Da765. *Agricultural Statistics: 1967, 1972, 1983, 1988, 1993*, and *2000* editions.

Documentation
See the text for Table Da667-678.

Series Da755–760. The crop-marketing season for both cotton and cottonseed begins August 1 for all states except Texas, where it begins about mid-July.

Series Da756
Cotton production estimates are defined by statute as cotton actually ginned. For 1913-1924, annual ginnings as published by the Bureau of the Census included some cotton produced in lower California and Mexico and ginned in California; however, it is not included in U.S. production for those years. For those years, also, cotton ginned in the United States exceeds production by the quantity of the cross-border movement of seed cotton into this country. For all other years, beginning in 1899, production of cotton is the quantity of census ginnings by states adjusted for cross-state movement of seed cotton and rounded to thousands of bales. U.S. production is obtained by adding rounded state estimates and therefore differs slightly from the Census Bureau report on ginnings.

Production figures are in running bales through 1898; 500-pound gross weight bales, 1899-1953; and 480-pound net weight bales thereafter.

Before 1899, cotton production figures were compiled from various current sources including exports and imports, rail and water shipments, mill receipts, and so forth, together with the decennial enumerations of the Bureau of the Census. These production estimates are the same as those in Department of Agriculture, Bureau of Statistics, Circular 32, cited in the Sources section, except for minor adjustments caused by rounding state estimates.

Series Da757 and Da760. The season average prices for 1908-1970 for both cotton and cottonseed are the weighted averages of midmonth prices. Through 1908, cottonseed prices are not available. Through 1907, cotton prices were based on farmers' estimates on December 1 of average prices for the season.

Series Da757. Figures are gross weight prices, including bagging and ties, except that beginning 1922 American Egyptian cotton is included at net weight. Through 1907 prices are as of December 1. Season average price is derived.

Series Da758
Figures for stocks are in running bales, except that any small quantity of foreign cotton included is in equivalent 500-pound gross-weight bales. Through 1913, stocks are as of September 1; August 1 thereafter. Data for 1906-1922 are from the New York Cotton Exchange Service; the Bureau of the Census compiled those for 1923-1970.

These data are the carryovers from the previous season. In earlier figures from *Agricultural Statistics*, this was the reporting procedure used (that is, "carryover, at the beginning of the season"). However, by 1951, *Agricultural Statistics* had changed the reporting standard. The data are now reported in the previous year, as "carryovers at the end of the season."

Series Da759. Cottonseed production for 1866-1927 was computed from net lint production using a uniform ratio of 65 pounds of cottonseed for each 35 pounds of net lint. Beginning in 1928, ratios were estimated from data collected from cotton ginners.

Series Da760. Season average price, 1909-1974; thereafter, prices are for year beginning August 1.

Series Da761–762. Beginning with 1961, includes Alaska; no estimates made for Hawai'i. The original source of shorn wool data for 1869-1908 was the National Association of Wool Manufacturers. Estimates have been made by the Department of Agriculture since 1909. Wool production is estimated by ascertaining the number of sheep and lambs shorn and the average weight per fleece, and using data from the censuses of agriculture as periodic benchmarks. Extensive revisions of production estimates back through 1909 were made in 1936. The figures for 1869-1908 are not comparable to these revised estimates. To illustrate the lack of comparability, the unrevised production estimate of 287 million pounds for 1909, published in the *Agriculture Yearbook* for 1923, may be compared with the revised estimate of 310 million pounds.

Series Da762. The average price is related to calendar year through 1942, April-March marketing season for 1943-1962, April-December for 1963, and calendar year thereafter. Beginning 1953, the price includes allowance for unredeemed wool.

Series Da763–765. Production figures are on farm-sales-weight basis. Consumer and Marketing Service publications also present estimates of stocks of tobacco, 1929-1970, and of acreage and production of tobacco, by types, 1919-1970.

Series Da765. Through 1918, December 1 price; 1919-1972, season average price; beginning 1973, marketing year average price received by farmers.

**TABLE Da766-767   Cotton – acreage and production:
1839–1997   [Census years]**

Contributed by Alan L. Olmstead and Paul W. Rhode

Year	Acreage harvested Da766 Thousand acres	Production Da767 [1] Thousand bales
1839	—	1,976
1849	—	2,469
1859	—	5,387
1869	—	3,012
1879	14,480	5,755
1889	20,175	7,473
1899	24,275	9,535
1909	32,044	10,649
1919	33,740	11,376
1924	39,204	13,683
1929	43,228	14,574
1934	26,754	9,472
1939	22,811	11,481
1944	18,962	11,838
1949	26,599	15,419
1954	18,858	12,921
1959	14,649	13,914
1964	13,917	14,734
1969	11,496	10,360
1974	12,224	10,887
1978	12,694	10,686
1982	9,781	11,376
1987	9,826	13,280
1992	10,962	15,370
1997	13,235	17,879

[1] Definition of series changes over time, affecting comparability; see text.

Sources

U.S. Bureau of the Census, *U.S. Census of Agriculture, 1964*, volume 2, chapter 4, Table 5, p. 313; *1969*, volume 2, chapter 6; *1992*, volume 1, part 51, p. 9; and *1997*, volume 1, part 51, p. 11.

Documentation

See the text for Table Da667–678.

Series Da767. Note that census-year production figures in this table are not comparable with the annual production estimates shown in series Da756. Annual production estimates prior to 1962 are shown in 500-pound gross-weight bales; beginning with 1962, 480-pound net-weight bales. Figures for census years are shown in running bales. The net weight per running bale was 383 pounds in 1839, 496.1 pounds in 1944, 482.0 pounds in 1954, 501.1 pounds in 1964, and 503.6 pounds in 1969.

TABLE Da768–773   Irish potatoes and sweet potatoes – acreage, production, and price: 1866–1998   [Annual]

Contributed by Alan L. Olmstead and Paul W. Rhode

	Irish potatoes			Sweet potatoes		
	Acreage harvested	Production	Price	Acreage harvested	Production	Price
	Da768	Da769	Da770 [1]	Da771	Da772	Da773 [1,2]
Year	Thousand acres	Thousand hundredweight	Dollars per hundredweight	Thousand acres	Thousand hundredweight	Dollars per hundredweight
1866	1,225	66,969	1.11	—	—	—
1867	1,289	59,798	1.51	—	—	—
1868	1,400	72,175	1.31	325	15,706	1.93
1869	1,479	86,759	0.85	351	12,492	2.12
1870	1,443	64,725	1.18	352	17,001	1.61
1871	1,496	80,833	0.96	375	15,451	1.52
1872	1,559	80,144	1.00	379	14,931	1.52
1873	1,543	77,698	1.16	392	18,298	1.42
1874	1,654	78,668	1.12	406	16,582	1.44
1875	1,789	107,887	0.64	425	17,885	1.34
1876	1,783	73,567	1.10	460	21,018	—
1877	1,878	104,221	0.74	454	19,358	—
1878	1,879	86,018	0.98	479	21,287	—
1879	1,961	101,663	0.72	451	18,618	1.00
1880	1,968	99,095	0.80	469	22,070	0.92
1881	2,036	76,544	1.52	441	13,656	—
1882	2,216	118,390	0.91	469	22,958	1.09
1883	2,373	136,253	0.69	470	17,103	1.02
1884	2,307	124,789	0.64	476	17,807	1.04
1885	2,335	118,286	0.73	474	22,061	0.93
1886	2,393	117,045	0.76	481	21,484	0.97
1887	2,466	95,769	1.15	494	21,190	1.02
1888	2,604	143,785	0.65	515	24,661	0.86
1889	2,603	130,760	0.60	521	24,628	0.95
1890	2,557	102,065	1.26	531	24,730	0.96
1891	2,633	158,170	0.60	537	25,175	0.90
1892	2,519	114,120	1.09	544	25,500	—
1893	2,614	122,534	0.98	545	25,088	—
1894	2,869	118,614	0.89	548	27,322	—
1895	3,090	181,269	0.44	545	24,687	0.87
1896	2,968	157,641	0.48	557	23,101	0.78
1897	2,809	118,904	0.92	531	22,873	0.88
1898	2,877	144,209	0.70	547	27,909	—
1899	2,939	163,541	0.67	531	23,235	0.96
1900	2,997	155,813	0.72	542	25,126	0.92
1901	2,950	124,447	1.28	558	26,486	1.04
1902	3,077	177,941	0.79	558	26,936	1.05
1903	3,079	165,770	1.02	565	29,079	1.06
1904	3,208	209,695	0.76	570	30,533	1.10
1905	3,263	180,421	1.02	574	32,208	1.06
1906	3,254	204,876	0.85	585	31,762	1.13
1907	3,333	199,875	1.01	596	31,533	1.28
1908	3,417	183,148	1.16	621	34,264	1.21
1909	3,675	234,100	0.95	639	32,447	1.38
1910	3,644	205,231	0.97	634	33,170	1.40
1911	3,532	181,628	1.55	603	30,407	1.72
1912	3,505	243,729	0.92	586	31,154	1.69
1913	3,477	199,468	1.11	596	30,799	1.50
1914	3,417	220,949	0.91	572	29,780	1.59
1915	3,433	202,056	1.14	627	34,783	1.38
1916	3,274	162,233	2.51	658	33,850	1.79
1917	3,801	239,192	2.11	725	40,022	2.37
1918	3,597	207,668	1.96	738	37,720	2.89
1919	3,300	178,405	3.18	791	43,050	3.13

Notes appear at end of table

TABLE Da768–773   Irish potatoes and sweet potatoes – acreage, production, and price: 1866–1998   [Annual]   Continued

	Irish potatoes			Sweet potatoes		
	Acreage harvested	Production	Price	Acreage harvested	Production	Price
	Da768	Da769	Da770 [1]	Da771	Da772	Da773 [1,2]
Year	Thousand acres	Thousand hundredweight	Dollars per hundredweight	Thousand acres	Thousand hundredweight	Dollars per hundredweight
1920	3,301	221,342	2.11	767	42,349	2.68
1921	3,598	195,187	1.84	817	40,539	2.19
1922	3,901	249,224	1.11	817	43,101	1.82
1923	3,378	219,814	1.56	674	35,129	2.38
1924	3,106	230,500	1.14	564	24,686	2.79
1925	2,810	177,880	2.83	636	27,576	3.08
1926	2,811	192,964	2.16	645	34,815	2.07
1927	3,182	221,786	1.66	724	38,993	1.96
1928	3,499	256,349	0.88	636	32,548	2.12
1929	3,030	200,035	2.17	647	35,758	2.15
1930	3,139	206,290	1.47	670	30,017	2.01
1931	3,490	230,590	0.75	854	37,023	1.21
1932	3,568	224,815	0.63	1,059	47,627	0.86
1933	3,423	205,922	1.34	907	41,040	1.29
1934	3,599	243,889	0.71	959	42,722	1.41
1935	3,469	227,337	0.98	944	44,687	1.25
1936	2,960	194,373	1.87	769	32,871	1.70
1937	3,055	225,869	0.84	768	37,479	1.41
1938	2,870	213,509	0.90	793	37,732	1.31
1939	2,813	205,423	1.16	728	33,959	1.35
1940	2,832	226,152	0.85	648	28,434	1.59
1941	2,693	213,418	1.31	731	34,384	1.71
1942	2,671	221,339	1.91	687	36,008	2.22
1943	3,239	275,332	2.10	857	39,128	3.86
1944	2,780	230,356	2.41	726	37,538	3.41
1945	2,664	251,639	2.30	646	33,692	3.63
1946	2,527	292,389	2.01	637	33,454	3.88
1947	2,001	233,391	2.67	547	27,303	3.86
1948	1,981	269,937	2.54	455	23,702	3.93
1949	1,755	240,950	2.10	472	24,804	3.88
1950	1,698	259,112	1.50	489	27,269	2.99
1951	1,349	195,776	2.68	312	15,998	5.55
1952	1,397	211,095	3.21	322	16,040	5.99
1953	1,536	231,679	1.31	343	18,998	4.44
1954	1,413	219,547	2.15	332	17,198	4.20
1955	1,405	227,696	1.77	342	21,608	3.27
1956	1,371	245,792	2.02	276	17,381	4.01
1957	1,359	242,522	1.91	274	18,057	4.18
1958	1,428	266,897	1.31	256	17,571	3.76
1959	1,331	245,272	2.27	257	18,865	3.26
1960	1,386	257,104	2.00	191	14,858	4.09
1961	1,480	293,166	1.36	183	14,415	4.30
1962	1,347	264,810	1.67	203	17,120	3.54
1963	1,323	271,158	1.78	171	14,356	4.03
1964	1,272	241,076	3.50	151	12,969	5.09
1965	1,383	291,109	2.53	168	15,469	4.22
1966	1,463	307,242	2.04	154	13,699	4.56
1967	1,460	305,766	1.87	140	13,486	4.48
1968	1,383	295,401	2.24	135	13,378	4.89
1969	1,416	312,578	2.24	136	14,070	4.18
1970	1,421	325,716	2.21	127	13,164	4.38
1971	1,391	319,329	1.90	113	11,494	5.22
1972	1,256	296,359	3.02	113	12,170	5.73
1973	1,307	300,013	4.90	112	12,156	7.32
1974	1,392	342,395	4.01	118	13,339	7.34

Notes appear at end of table

(continued)

TABLE Da768–773   Irish potatoes and sweet potatoes – acreage, production, and price: 1866–1998   [Annual]   *Continued*

	Irish potatoes			Sweet potatoes		
	Acreage harvested	Production	Price	Acreage harvested	Production	Price
	Da768	Da769	Da770 [1]	Da771	Da772	Da773 [1,2]
Year	Thousand acres	Thousand hundredweight	Dollars per hundredweight	Thousand acres	Thousand hundredweight	Dollars per hundredweight
1975	1,260	321,978	4.48	114	12,891	8.59
1976	1,371	357,666	3.59	115	13,273	7.50
1977	1,360	355,334	3.55	107	11,885	10.50
1978	1,375	366,314	3.38	112	13,115	10.60
1979	1,258	342,447	3.44	114	13,370	8.92
1980	1,148	303,905	6.55	102	10,953	13.60
1981	1,232	340,623	5.42	110	12,799	13.60
1982	1,267	355,131	4.45	115	14,833	8.03
1983	1,242	333,726	5.82	102	12,083	13.60
1984	1,298	362,039	5.69	103	12,902	14.00
1985	1,359	406,609	3.92	103	14,573	8.81
1986	1,220	361,743	5.03	91	12,368	11.00
1987	1,293	389,320	4.38	89	11,611	11.60
1988	1,259	356,438	6.00	86	10,945	12.90
1989	1,282	370,444	7.35	86	11,358	16.40
1990	1,371	402,110	6.08	90	12,594	9.70
1991	1,374	417,622	4.96	78	11,203	13.30
1992	1,315	425,367	5.52	82	12,005	12.20
1993	1,321	430,349	6.17 [3]	80	11,027	15.10
1994	1,385	469,425	5.58 [3]	83	13,380	14.00
1995	1,376	445,099	6.77 [3]	83	12,821	15.90
1996	1,426	499,254	4.92 [3]	84	13,216	14.40
1997	1,354	467,091	5.62 [3]	82	13,327	15.80
1998	1,394	477,754	5.24	84	11,887	15.80

[1] December 1 price through 1908; season average price thereafter.

[2] Prices weighted by sales, 1909–1984; otherwise, prices weighted by production.

[3] Unrevised.

Sources

Series Da768–770. U.S. National Agricultural Statistics Service, Crops Branch, Field Crops Section, *Track Records: United States Crop Production*, March 1999, downloaded October 3, 2000, from the U.S. Department of Agriculture, Economics and Statistics System.

Series Da771–773. U.S. National Agricultural Statistics Service, Crops Branch, Field Crops Section, *Track Records: United States Crop Production*, March 1999, downloaded October 3, 2000, from the U.S. Department of Agriculture, Economics and Statistics System.

Documentation

See the text for Table Da667–678.

Estimates of potatoes and sweet potatoes relate to the total crop harvested and include quantities used on farms where grown, and losses from shrinkage, cullage, and dumping after harvest.

The potato crop is divided into six seasonal groups: winter, early spring, late spring, early summer, late summer, and fall. The seasonal estimates are based on the usual time of harvest. The schedule of estimates and the classification of states are shown in Agriculture Handbook number 127, June 1967.

TABLE Da774-779   Irish potatoes and sweet potatoes – acreage, production, and price: 1849-1997   [Census years]

	Irish potatoes			Sweet potatoes		
	Acreage harvested	Production	Price	Acreage harvested	Production	Price
	Da774	Da775	Da776 [2]	Da777 [3]	Da778	Da779 [2]
Year	Thousand acres	Thousand hundredweight	Dollars per hundredweight	Thousand acres	Thousand bushels	Dollars per bushel
1849	—	39,479	—	—	21,047	—
1859	—	66,660	—	—	23,152	—
1869	—	86,002	—	—	11,940	—
1879	—[4]	101,675	—	—[4]	18,358	—
1889	2,601	130,528	—	525	24,173	—
1899	2,939	163,997	0.60	537	23,390	0.85
1909	3,669	233,527	0.71	642	32,590	1.09
1919	3,253	174,293	3.67	803	42,951	2.91
1924	2,911	211,477	1.06	467	20,594	2.62
1929	3,945	193,480	2.14	650	35,856	1.89
1934	3,582	242,052	0.80	967	42,891	1.47
1939	2,645	190,999	1.14	697	35,195	1.35
1944	2,537	213,928	2.43	673	37,973	3.40
1949	1,515	219,917	2.13	393	23,654	3.85
1954	1,211	204,113	2.16	261	15,068	4.53
1959	1,200	224,140	2.14	218	16,162	3.33
1964	1,174	221,874	3.43	112	10,123	5.11
1969	1,261	273,644	2.00	99	19,643	2.49
1974	1,345	316,164	—	86	17,269	—
1978	1,386	351,217	—	88	18,856	—
1982	1,268	334,621	—	95	20,440	—
1987	1,310	367,199	—	73	15,953	—
1992	1,351	410,509	—	81	19,579	—
1997	1,355	459,886	—	77	20,763	—

[1] Data beginning 1969 not comparable with previous censuses; data are only for farms with farm products sales of $2,500 or more beginning that year.

[2] December 1 price, 1899-1908; season average price thereafter.

[3] In censuses prior to 1950, the acreage of sweet potatoes was to be reported in all cases, even when the quantity harvested was small. Therefore, acres harvested for censuses prior to 1950 are not fully comparable with those of the last four censuses.

[4] Acreage reporting incomplete: 13 states reported 911,325 acres of Irish potatoes; 23 states reported 444,817 acres of sweet potatoes.

Sources

U.S. Bureau of the Census, *U.S. Census of Agriculture, 1964*, volume 2, Table 5, p. 313; *1969*, volume 2, chapter 6; *1974*, volume 1, part 51, p. I-5; *1982*, volume 1, part 51, pp. 19, 20; *1987*, volume 1, part 51, p. 35; *1992*, volume 1, part 51, p. 37; and *1997*, volume 1, part 51, pp. 39, 445.

Documentation

See the text for Table Da667-678.

TABLE Da780-788   Sugarcane, sugar beets, and peanuts – acreage, production, and price: 1909-1999   [Annual]

Contributed by Alan L. Olmstead and Paul W. Rhode

	Sugarcane			Sugar beets			Peanuts harvested for nuts		
	Acreage harvested for sugar	Production of raw sugar	Price	Acreage harvested	Production	Price	Acreage harvested	Production	Price
	Da780 [1]	Da781 [1]	Da782 [1,2]	Da783	Da784	Da785 [2]	Da786	Da787	Da788
Year	Thousand acres	Thousand tons	Dollars per short ton	Thousand acres	Thousand tons	Dollars per short ton	Thousand acres	Million pounds	Cents per pound
1909	292.0	338	3.83	420	4,240	5.06	537	355	4.1
1910	311.0	362	3.69	398	4,138	5.45	464	384	4.0
1911	317.1	368	4.29	474	5,062	5.50	472	366	4.2
1912	205.0	166	3.73	555	5,648	5.82	480	362	4.4
1913	255.0	307	3.13	580	5,886	5.69	465	383	4.5
1914	216.5	252	3.75	483	5,585	5.45	526	421	4.2
1915	184.0	141	4.55	611	6,511	5.67	617	481	4.1
1916	227.3	317	5.29	665	6,228	6.12	878	666	4.8
1917	246.0	251	7.10	665	5,980	7.39	1,314	989	7.0
1918	234.1	290	7.28	594	5,949	10.00	1,326	946	6.5
1919	180.0	125	14.00	692	6,421	11.74	957	688	9.3

Notes appear at end of table

(continued)

TABLE Da780–788   Sugarcane, sugar beets, and peanuts – acreage, production, and price: 1909–1999
[Annual]   *Continued*

	Sugarcane			Sugar beets			Peanuts harvested for nuts		
	Acreage harvested for sugar	Production of raw sugar	Price	Acreage harvested	Production	Price	Acreage harvested	Production	Price
	Da780 [1]	Da781 [1]	Da782 [1,2]	Da783	Da784	Da785 [2]	Da786	Da787	Da788
Year	Thousand acres	Thousand tons	Dollars per short ton	Thousand acres	Thousand tons	Dollars per short ton	Thousand acres	Million pounds	Cents per pound
1920	189.3	180	5.76	872	8,538	11.63	995	696	4.8
1921	228.9	334	3.63	815	7,782	6.35	980	678	3.8
1922	242.5	302	5.83	530	5,183	7.91	821	523	5.3
1923	217.5	168	7.09	657	7,006	8.99	797	568	6.5
1924	163.0	90	5.58	816	7,508	7.95	1,084	713	5.8
1925	190.0	142	4.05	648	7,381	6.39	996	722	4.3
1926	128.0	48	4.92	677	7,223	7.61	860	662	5.0
1927	73.0	72	4.61	721	7,753	7.67	1,086	844	5.2
1928	130.7	136	3.86	644	7,101	7.11	1,213	844	4.9
1929	191.7	218	3.73	688	7,315	7.08	1,262	898	3.7
1930	187.2	215	3.31	776	9,199	7.14	1,073	697	3.5
1931	182.1	184	3.21	713	7,903	5.94	1,440	1,056	1.6
1932	220.6	265	2.98	764	9,070	5.26	1,501	941	1.6
1933	211.4	250	3.14	983	11,030	5.13	1,217	820	2.9
1934	235.8	262	2.33	770	7,519	5.16	1,514	1,014	3.3
1935	253.1	382	3.15	763	7,908	5.76	1,497	1,153	3.1
1936	243.6	438	3.67	776	9,028	6.05	1,660	1,260	3.7
1937	285.2	459	2.90	753	8,759	5.26	1,538	1,233	3.3
1938	296.2	584	2.71	925	11,497	4.65	1,692	1,289	3.3
1939	254.1	506	2.84	918	10,781	4.76	1,908	1,213	3.4
1940	240.1	332	2.88	912	12,194	5.11	2,052	1,767	3.3
1941	254.8	416	3.95	755	10,342	6.43	1,900	1,475	4.7
1942	290.2	458	4.40	954	11,685	6.84	3,355	2,193	6.1
1943	284.2	497	4.57 [4]	550	6,547	8.81	3,528	2,175	7.1
1944	273.1	437	4.95 [4]	555	6,718	10.60	3,068	2,081	8.0
1945	265.4	475	5.67 [4]	713	8,616	10.20	3,160	2,042	8.3
1946	286.8	425	6.62	802	10,582	11.10	3,141	2,038	9.1
1947	293.6	377	7.17	879	12,503	11.80	3,377	2,182	10.1
1948	309.2	477	5.76	694	9,424	10.60	3,296	2,336	10.5
1949	424.4	1,477	6.25	687	10,196	10.80	2,308	1,865	10.4
1950	419.8	1,525	7.80	925	13,535	11.20	2,262	2,035	10.9
1951	406.4	1,415	6.37	691	10,482	11.70	1,982	1,659	10.4
1952	425.9	1,625	6.96	665	10,169	12.00	1,443	1,356	10.9
1953	432.8	1,729	7.25	745	12,084	11.60	1,515	1,574	11.1
1954	393.1	1,687	6.95	876	14,082	10.80	1,387	1,008	12.2
1955	373.0	1,714	6.51	740	12,231	11.16	1,669	1,548	11.7
1956	341.1	1,661	8.04	785	12,995	11.94	1,384	1,607	11.2
1957	365.3	1,619	6.90	878	15,505	11.22	1,481	1,436	10.4
1958	337.5	1,344	7.48	891	15,150	11.74	1,516	1,814	10.6
1959	406.8	1,591	7.13	906	17,015	11.24	1,435	1,523	9.6
1960	407.5	1,566	7.41	957	16,421	11.58	1,395	1,718	10.0
1961	441.4	1,950	7.71	1,077	17,704	11.16	1,185	1,657	10.9
1962	477.2	1,972	8.40	1,103	18,251	12.78	1,401	1,719	11.0
1963	542.8	2,284	10.20	1,235	23,328	12.22	1,396	1,942	11.2
1964	655.9	2,326	6.93	1,395	23,389	11.80	1,397	2,099	11.2
1965	583.3	2,322	7.90	1,249	20,918	11.90	1,438	2,390	11.4
1966	590.2	2,448	8.49	1,161	20,342	12.80	1,421	2,416	11.3
1967	596.2	2,648	9.38	1,122	19,197	13.50	1,404	2,477	11.4
1968	577.3	2,447	9.34	1,410	25,363	13.80	1,438	2,547	11.9
1969	502.8	2,254	9.94	1,541	27,736	12.70	1,456	2,535	12.3
1970	551.1	2,416	10.50	1,413	26,378	14.80	1,469	2,983	12.8
1971	606.7	2,436	11.10	1,342	27,096	15.40	1,455	3,005	13.6
1972	664.3	2,740	11.60	1,329	28,410	16.00	1,486	3,275	14.5
1973	703.0	2,549	20.90	1,218	24,499	29.60	1,496	3,474	16.2
1974	689.9	2,512	48.60	1,213	22,123	46.80	1,472	3,668	17.9
1975	734.7	2,934	21.50	1,517	29,704	27.60	1,500	3,847	19.6
1976	704.0	2,724	15.20	1,479	29,386	21.00	1,518	3,739	20.0
1977	719.3	2,684	17.70	1,216	25,007	24.20	1,512	3,715	21.0
1978	699.8	2,611	19.50	1,269	25,725	25.20	1,509	3,952	21.1
1979	689.7	2,700	26.00	1,120	21,996	33.90	1,520	3,969	20.6

Notes appear at end of table

TABLE Da780–788   Sugarcane, sugar beets, and peanuts – acreage, production, and price: 1909–1999 [Annual] *Continued*

Year	Sugarcane			Sugar beets			Peanuts harvested for nuts		
	Acreage harvested for sugar	Production of raw sugar	Price	Acreage harvested	Production	Price	Acreage harvested	Production	Price
	Da780 [1]	Da781 [1]	Da782 [1,2]	Da783	Da784	Da785 [2]	Da786	Da787	Da788
	Thousand acres	Thousand tons	Dollars per short ton	Thousand acres	Thousand tons	Dollars per short ton	Thousand acres	Million pounds	Cents per pound
1980	683.6	2,728	38.50	1,190	23,502	47.20	1,400	2,303	25.1
1981	715.6	2,833	24.90	1,228	27,538	29.20	1,489	3,982	26.9
1982	700.4	3,063	26.50	1,027	20,894	35.40	1,277	3,440	25.1
1983	733.4	2,930	27.80	1,056	20,992	37.00	1,374	3,296	24.7
1984	700.7	3,007	28.20	1,096	22,134	33.90	1,528	4,406	27.9
1985	722.8	3,033	26.70	1,103	22,529	33.80	1,467	4,123	24.3
1986	750.7	3,281	27.30	1,191	25,162	35.90	1,535	3,697	29.2
1987	778.3	3,333	29.10	1,252	28,072	38.20	1,547	3,616	28.0
1988	793.6	3,398	29.40	1,301	24,310	41.20	1,628	3,981	27.9
1989	803.3	3,176	29.20	1,295	25,085	42.10	1,645	3,990	28.0
1990	726.4	3,152	30.80	1,378	27,593	43.00	1,816	3,604	34.7
1991	849.6	3,430	29.00	1,387	28,203	38.50	2,016	4,927	28.3
1992	870.4	3,373	28.10	1,412	29,143	41.40	1,669	4,284	30.0
1993	893.3	3,482	28.50	1,409	26,249	39.00	1,690	3,392	30.4
1994	881.7	—	29.20	1,443	31,853	38.80	1,619	4,248	28.9
1995	874.7	—	29.50	1,420	28,065	38.10	1,517	3,461	29.3
1996	829.5	—	28.30	1,323	26,680	45.40	1,380	3,661	28.1
1997	860.3	—	28.10	1,428	29,886	38.80	1,414	3,537	28.3
1998	888.3	—	27.30	1,451	32,499	36.40	1,467	3,611	28.4
1999 [3]	939.4	—	—	1,527	33,319	—	1,428	—	25.6

[1] Beginning with 1959, data include Hawai'i.

[2] Prices do not include government payments under the Sugar Act.

[3] Preliminary.

[4] Includes average support payments of $0.34, $0.83, and $1.50 for the years 1943–1945, respectively.

Sources

Series Da780–781. 1909–1970, U.S. Department of Agriculture, Statistical Reporting Service, *Agricultural Statistics*, various issues; 1971–1989, U.S. Department of Agriculture, Economic Research Service, *U.S. Sugar Statistical Compendium*, October 1991, Tables 9 and 12, downloaded October 11, 2000, from the U.S. Department of Agriculture, Economics and Statistics System; 1990–1999, *Agricultural Statistics, 2000*.

Series Da782. 1909–1974, *Agricultural Statistics, 1983* and various issues; 1975–1991, U.S. Department of Agriculture, Economic Research Service, Agricultural Commodities Section, *Prices Received by Commodity, Historic Data Series, and Indexes,* June 1994, downloaded October 11, 2000, from the U.S. Department of Agriculture, Economics and Statistics System; 1992–1998, *Agricultural Statistics, 2000*.

Series Da783–784. 1909–1973, *Agricultural Statistics, 1952, 1957, 1962, 1972, 1973,* and *1983* editions; 1974–1990, *U.S. Sugar Statistical Compendium*, October 1991, Tables 27 and 29, downloaded October 11, 2000, from the U.S. Department of Agriculture, Economics and Statistics System; 1991–1999, *Agricultural Statistics, 2000*.

Series Da785. 1909–1974, *Agricultural Statistics, 1952, 1957, 1962, 1972, 1973,* and *1983* editions; 1975–1991, *Prices Received by Commodity, Historic Data Series, and Indexes,* June 1994, downloaded October 11, 2000, from the

U.S. Department of Agriculture, Economics and Statistics System; 1992–1998, *Agricultural Statistics, 2000*.

Series Da786. 1909–1969, *Agricultural Statistics, 1952, 1957, 1962, 1972,* and *1973* editions; 1970–1996, U.S. Department of Agriculture, Economic Research Service, Commercial Crops Division, Research Service, *Oil Crops Situation Yearbook,* November 1999, OCS-1999, Table 4, downloaded October 11, 2000, from the U.S. Department of Agriculture, Economics and Statistics System; 1997–1999, *Agricultural Statistics, 2000*.

Series Da787. 1909–1969, *Agricultural Statistics, 1952, 1957, 1962, 1972,* and *1973* editions; 1970–1998, U.S. Department of Agriculture, Economic Research Service, Commercial Crops Division, Research Service, *Oil Crops Situation Yearbook,* November 1999, OCS-1999, Table 4, downloaded October 11, 2000, from the U.S. Department of Agriculture, Economics and Statistics System.

Series Da788. 1909–1976: *Agricultural Statistics, 1952, 1957, 1962, 1972, 1973,* and *1983* editions; 1977–1996, *Oil Crops Situation Yearbook,* November 1999, OCS-1999, Table 5, downloaded October 11, 2000, from the U.S. Department of Agriculture, Economics and Statistics System; 1997–1999, *Agricultural Statistics, 2000*.

Documentation

See the text for Table Da667–678.

Series Da781. Raw value is the equivalent in terms of 96-degree sugar, as defined in the Sugar Act of 1948.

Series Da787. Net weight basis.

Series Da788. Obtained by weighting state prices by quantity sold.

TABLE Da789–790   Sugarcane – acreage and price: 1929–1997[1]   [Census years]

Contributed by Alan L. Olmstead and Paul W. Rhode

| | Acreage harvested | Price |
| | Da789 | Da790 |
Year	Thousand acres	Dollars per short ton
1929	341.3	—
1939	383.9	3.64
1944	269.1	5.05
1949	427.8	—
1954	278.6	6.70
1959	408.4	7.32
1964	643.4	8.15
1969	519.2 [2]	—
1974	668.3 [2]	—
1978	766.1	—
1982	713.1	—
1987	779.2	—
1992	883.9	—
1997	875.2	—

[1] Beginning 1959, includes Hawai'i.

[2] Data for 1969 and 1974 are not comparable with other census years; data are only for farms with farm products sales of $2,500 or more.

Sources

U.S. Bureau of the Census, *U.S. Census of Agriculture, 1964*, volume 2, Table 5, p. 313; *1969*, volume 2, chapter 6, Table 62; *1974*, volume 1, part 51, chapter 3, Table 9; *1982*, volume 1, part 51, p. 20; *1992*, volume 1, part 51, p. 37; and *1997*, volume 1, part 51, p. 39.

Documentation

See the text for Table Da667–678.

TABLE Da791–795   Fruit and tree nuts – bearing acreage: 1929–1998[1]

Contributed by Alan L. Olmstead and Paul W. Rhode

		Fruits			
	Total	Citrus	Major deciduous	Miscellaneous noncitrus	Tree nuts
	Da791	Da792	Da793	Da794	Da795
Year	Thousand acres	Thousand acres	Thousand acres	Thousand acres	Thousand acres
1929	—	—	4,247.2	82.1	171.1
1930	4,935.0	471.7	4,201.2	82.7	179.4
1931	4,922.6	494.3	4,158.2	84.3	185.8
1932	4,930.1	536.3	4,117.8	85.8	190.2
1933	4,922.1	576.1	4,065.3	85.4	195.3
1934	4,027.5	608.5	3,134.9	85.6	198.5
1935	3,966.6	647.0	3,031.7	84.9	203.0
1936	3,902.8	678.3	2,931.9	85.8	206.8
1937	3,865.6	703.2	2,862.2	87.5	212.7
1938	3,826.2	725.7	2,795.5	87.9	217.1
1939	3,806.9	743.0	2,756.2	88.0	219.7
1940	3,806.3	753.3	2,742.3	87.4	223.3
1941	3,816.3	766.6	2,736.2	87.1	226.4
1942	3,833.8	782.2	2,735.6	86.3	229.7
1943	3,850.6	796.6	2,734.6	86.2	233.2
1944	3,873.4	807.3	2,730.1	86.8	249.2
1945	3,820.2	815.0	2,661.4	87.3	256.5
1946	3,740.5	829.5	2,562.6	86.4	262.0
1947	3,644.6	837.3	2,454.3	85.9	267.1
1948	3,543.6	845.5	2,348.9	83.8	265.4
1949	3,457.6	852.7	2,259.7	81.9	263.3

Note appears on next page

TABLE Da791–795   Fruit and tree nuts – bearing acreage: 1929–1998   Continued

		Fruits			
	Total	Citrus	Major deciduous	Miscellaneous noncitrus	Tree nuts
	Da791	Da792	Da793	Da794	Da795
Year	Thousand acres	Thousand acres	Thousand acres	Thousand acres	Thousand acres
1950	3,342.5	811.4	2,190.8	81.3	259.0
1951	3,251.2	815.0	2,097.6	80.3	258.3
1952	3,122.4	780.4	2,001.8	81.2	259.0
1953	3,054.4	792.3	1,921.2	82.7	258.2
1954	2,982.8	797.0	1,847.8	85.1	252.9
1955	2,946.6	822.7	1,789.0	86.6	248.3
1956	2,893.0	825.6	1,736.0	86.5	244.9
1957	2,851.1	821.1	1,696.2	86.8	247.0
1958	2,806.8	775.0	1,694.0	88.0	249.8
1959	2,806.7	776.9	1,694.0	85.6	250.2
1960	2,818.2	798.0	1,682.2	88.2	249.8
1961	2,811.1	806.6	1,668.0	88.7	247.8
1962	2,854.6	838.4	1,676.6	89.0	250.6
1963	2,785.9	775.4	1,668.7	89.3	252.5
1964	2,798.1	781.4	1,666.6	90.2	259.9
1965	2,837.0	830.3	1,645.7	86.4	274.6
1966	2,870.1	881.1	1,624.4	84.3	280.3
1967	2,928.6	951.7	1,606.1	83.5	287.3
1968	2,983.8	1,001.5	1,602.1	81.9	298.3
1969	3,060.1	1,065.2	1,598.3	81.3	315.3
1970	3,103.4	1,122.6	1,560.0	81.4	339.4
1971	3,164.7	1,180.8	1,540.4	82.7	360.8
1972	3,139.5	1,154.0	1,521.6	84.9	379.0
1973	3,183.5	1,174.5	1,527.9	87.5	393.6
1974	3,246.9	1,177.8	1,562.3	90.8	416.0
1975	3,412.4	1,181.3	1,700.5	94.8	435.8
1976	3,373.2	1,178.4	1,645.5	100.7	448.6
1977	3,571.4	1,180.2	1,674.2	234.1	482.9
1978	3,602.7	1,161.2	1,657.3	264.8	519.4
1979	3,605.9	1,149.5	1,627.7	272.8	555.9
1980	3,641.5	1,161.8	1,629.7	284.3	565.7
1981	3,613.5	1,148.0	1,612.1	292.0	561.4
1982	3,584.7	1,124.3	1,640.3	241.0	579.1
1983	3,615.3	1,091.6	1,674.4	250.3	599.0
1984	3,588.5	1,007.9	1,703.8	253.0	623.8
1985	3,537.8	899.3	1,725.0	256.4	657.1
1986	3,476.3	818.9	1,727.7	260.2	669.5
1987	3,503.9	826.2	1,739.1	263.2	675.4
1988	3,514.2	832.9	1,730.4	264.6	686.3
1989	3,506.9	847.5	1,714.1	258.7	686.6
1990	3,504.7	851.8	1,709.5	252.0	691.4
1991	3,486.4	849.9	1,701.8	247.3	687.4
1992	3,586.7	886.1	1,721.3	299.3	680.0
1993	3,675.6	946.7	1,738.3	290.1	700.5
1994	3,767.9	977.8	1,756.7	307.8	725.6
1995	3,824.7	1,054.0	1,762.9	289.2	718.6
1996	3,920.7	1,104.5	1,796.2	287.9	732.1
1997	4,004.4	1,152.5	1,811.0	292.3	748.6
1998	4,015.9	1,125.3	1,833.4	295.6	761.6

[1] Crop coverage changes over time; see text.

Sources

1929–1976, U.S. Department of Agriculture, Statistical Reporting Service, *Agricultural Statistics, 1967, 1974,* and *1978* editions; 1977–1998, U.S. Department of Agriculture, Economic Research Service, *Fruit Situation and Outlook Yearbook,* December 2000, Table A-2, downloaded October 15, 2000, from the U.S. Department of Agriculture, Economics and Statistics System.

Documentation

Fruit production is estimated as total production, the quantity of fruit harvested plus quantities that would have been acceptable for fresh market or processing but were not harvested or utilized because of economic and other factors. Losses from natural causes, such as windstorms, freezes, and so forth, are not included in production. Before 1964, several fruit production series included quantities not marketed that were excluded in computing value; they are noted. Production relates to the crop produced on all farms, except for apples and strawberries. In accordance with congressional enactment, the USDA estimates of apple production since 1938 have related only to commercial production. The estimates for strawberries cover production on areas where the fruit is grown primarily for sale.

(continued)

TABLE Da791–795   Fruit and tree nuts – bearing acreage: 1929–1998   *Continued*

The annual estimates are checked and adjusted at the end of each marketing season on the basis of shipment and processing records from transportation agencies, processors, cooperative marketing associations, and other industry organizations. The estimates are reviewed (and revised if necessary) at five-year intervals, when the Census of Agriculture data become available. The Department's available statistics exclude some states for which census data indicate production is of only minor importance.

Series Da791. Equals the crude sum of series Da792–795. Owing to the discrepancy reported in the text for series Da792, these figures differ from those in the *Agricultural Statistics* publications prior to 1970.

Series Da792. Includes grapefruit, lemons, limes, oranges, tangelos (beginning with 1954), tangerines, temples, and K-early (beginning with the 1992–1993 season). Acreage is for the year harvest was completed. Prior to 1970, the acreage reported in the original source was for the year of bloom. Starting 1970 the acreage reported is for the year the harvest is completed (see *Agricultural Statistics 1970*, footnote 1 in Table 299, p. 207). This table adopts

the later standard and reports the acreage for the year of harvest. Thus in the *Agricultural Statistics* publications prior to 1970, this data is off by a year with respect to the figures presented here.

Series Da793. Includes commercial apples, apricots, cherries, grapes, peaches, pears, plums, prunes, and beginning with 1977, nectarines (before that date nectarines were reported together with fruits in series Da794).

Series Da794. Includes avocados, bananas (beginning with 1977), berries (until 1979 and after 1992), cranberries (beginning with 1977), dates, figs, guavas (beginning with 1977), kiwifruit (beginning with 1977), olives, papayas (beginning with 1977), persimmons (until 1977), pineapples (beginning with 1977), pomegranates (until 1989), and strawberries (beginning with 1977). For many years the data in this series were listed as "Minor Fruits" in *Agricultural Statistics*.

Series Da795. Includes almonds, hazelnuts (beginning with 1977), macadamia nuts (beginning with 1977), walnuts, pistachios (beginning with 1977), and filberts (until 1977).

TABLE Da796–805   Apples, avocados, grapes, and peaches – production and price: 1889–1999

Contributed by Alan L. Olmstead and Paul W. Rhode

	Apples				Avocados		Grapes		Peaches	
	Total		Commercial							
	Production	Price	Production	Price	Production	Price	Production	Price	Production	Price
	Da796 [1]	Da797	Da798	Da799 [2]	Da800 [1,3]	Da801 [2,3]	Da802 [1]	Da803 [2]	Da804 [1]	Da805 [2]
Year	Thousand short tons	Dollars per short ton	Million pounds	Cents per pound	Short tons	Dollars per short ton	Thousand short tons	Dollars per short ton	Million pounds	Cents per pound
1889	3,431	—	—	—	—	—	—	—	—	—
1890	1,923	—	—	—	—	—	—	—	—	—
1891	4,774	—	—	—	—	—	—	—	—	—
1892	2,893	—	—	—	—	—	—	—	—	—
1893	2,755	—	—	—	—	—	—	—	—	—
1894	3,232	—	—	—	—	—	—	—	—	—
1895	5,270	—	—	—	—	—	—	—	—	—
1896	5,582	—	—	—	—	—	—	—	—	—
1897	3,929	—	—	—	—	—	—	—	—	—
1898	2,833	—	—	—	—	—	—	—	—	—
1899	4,208	—	—	—	—	—	—	—	741	—
1900	4,942	—	—	—	—	—	—	—	2,373	—
1901	3,252	—	—	—	—	—	—	—	2,229	—
1902	5,096	—	—	—	—	—	—	—	1,816	—
1903	4,696	—	—	—	—	—	—	—	1,385	—
1904	5,607	—	—	—	—	—	—	—	1,971	—
1905	3,269	—	—	—	—	—	—	—	1,758	—
1906	5,201	—	—	—	—	—	—	—	2,117	—
1907	2,869	—	—	—	—	—	—	—	1,081	—
1908	3,575	—	—	—	—	—	—	—	2,311	—
1909	3,489	32.50	—	—	—	—	1,133	—	1,696	1.7
1910	3,358	33.33	—	—	—	—	968	—	2,097	2.1
1911	5,051	28.33	—	—	—	—	1,175	—	1,570	2.5
1912	5,401	25.83	—	—	—	—	1,197	—	2,369	2.0
1913	3,242	37.08	—	—	—	—	988	—	2,004	2.2
1914	5,600	23.75	—	—	—	—	1,215	—	2,513	2.1
1915	4,841	28.33	—	—	—	—	1,268	—	2,897	1.7
1916	4,349	34.17	—	—	—	—	1,267	—	1,802	2.3
1917	3,729	46.25	—	—	—	—	1,426	—	2,282	2.8
1918	3,876	53.33	—	—	—	—	1,317	—	1,820	3.5
1919	3,375	74.17	—	—	—	—	1,574	—	2,523	3.9
1920	4,961	51.67	—	—	—	—	1,520	—	2,173	4.5
1921	2,295	68.33	—	—	—	—	1,268	—	1,607	3.2
1922	4,546	41.25	—	—	—	—	2,084	—	2,799	2.9
1923	4,342	45.83	—	—	—	—	2,226	—	2,192	3.1
1924	3,851	51.25	—	—	100	—	1,774	38	2,520	2.7

Notes appear at end of table

TABLE Da796–805   Apples, avocados, grapes, and peaches – production and price: 1889–1999   *Continued*

	Apples				Avocados		Grapes		Peaches	
	Total		Commercial							
	Production	Price	Production	Price	Production	Price	Production	Price	Production	Price
	Da796 [1]	Da797	Da798	Da799 [2]	Da800 [1,3]	Da801 [2,3]	Da802 [1]	Da803 [2]	Da804 [1]	Da805 [2]
Year	Thousand short tons	Dollars per short ton	Million pounds	Cents per pound	Short tons	Dollars per short ton	Thousand short tons	Dollars per short ton	Million pounds	Cents per pound
1925	3,658	52.50	—	—	200	—	2,200	33	2,213	3.3
1926	5,512	36.67	—	—	600	—	2,384	26	3,229	2.2
1927	2,777	61.67	—	—	300	—	2,592	27	2,105	2.6
1928	4,268	45.42	—	—	1,200	—	2,653	20	3,199	2.1
1929	3,242	57.92	—	—	800	394	2,086	27	2,177	3.1
1930	3,759	42.92	—	—	2,800	245	2,458	20	2,707	2.1
1931	4,930	26.67	—	—	3,400	161	1,647	23	3,737	1.3
1932	3,523	25.42	—	—	3,100	134	2,233	13	2,117	1.3
1933	3,567	32.92	—	—	4,700	135	1,939	18	2,215	1.7
1934	3,077	37.08	5,088	1.3	11,300	85	1,958	20	2,333	1.8
1935	4,186	30.42	6,740	1.1	6,200	160	2,477	15	2,661	1.9
1936	2,804	43.33	4,706	1.6	6,800	129	1,897	21	2,340	2.1
1937	4,835	27.92	7,352	0.9	7,300	136	2,726	20	2,882	2.2
1938	3,011 [5]	34.58 [5]	5,074	1.2	17,000	83	2,671	15	2,588	1.6
1939	—	—	6,684	1.0	10,000	127	2,449	16	3,083	1.7
1940	—	—	5,348	1.3	15,500	106	2,466	17	2,776	1.6
1941	—	—	5,866	1.5	19,800	101	2,725	24	3,617	1.9
1942	—	—	6,082	2.2	17,700	203	2,396	36	3,203	3.1
1943	—	—	4,190	4.0	25,900	209	2,965	62	2,053	5.6
1944	—	—	5,820	3.6	17,400	393	2,712	79	3,753	4.8
1945	—	—	3,200	5.2	27,200	279	2,767	59	3,803	4.6
1946	—	—	5,708	4.1	20,100	384	3,137	93	3,977	4.3
1947	—	—	5,418	3.1	20,900	378	3,020	39	3,668	3.4
1948	—	—	4,288	3.8	17,500	361	3,061	39	2,909	4.1
1949	—	—	6,446	2.3	20,500	373	2,614	36	3,296	3.1
1950	—	—	5,940	2.8	27,900	302	2,678	68	2,398	4.3
1951	—	—	5,366	3.2	34,500	239	3,378	40	3,034	4.2
1952	—	—	4,516	4.5	31,900	286	3,157	40	2,997	4.2
1953	—	—	4,598	4.8	31,900	282	2,690	48	3,092	4.0
1954	—	—	5,370	4.2	57,000	190	2,563	52	2,960	4.1
1955	—	—	5,100	3.4	34,300	292	3,242	43	2,479	4.6
1956	—	—	4,864	4.4	26,600	319	2,911	52	3,338	4.4
1957	—	—	5,724	3.1	61,100	174	2,594	63	2,980	4.5
1958	—	—	6,120	3.1	55,600	166	3,023	68	3,424	4.0
1959	—	—	5,738	3.8	76,000	109	3,216	54	3,598	4.0
1960	—	—	4,918	4.8	37,300	275	3,069	54	3,583	3.8
1961	—	—	5,696	4.1	56,100	209	3,255	55	3,770	4.0
1962	—	—	5,689	4.3	51,700	239	3,239	63	3,611	3.9
1963	—	—	5,753	4.1	60,700	232	3,793	53	3,540	4.4
1964	—	—	6,319	3.9	36,700	402	3,478	63	3,453	4.6
1965	—	—	6,140	4.3	60,800	271	4,351	45	3,474	4.4
1966	—	—	5,761	4.5	80,300	204	3,733	56	3,389	5.1
1967	—	—	5,436	5.6	52,100	383	3,069	69	2,688	6.3
1968	—	—	5,469	6.1	73,700	289	3,549	67	3,637	5.3
1969	—	—	6,820	4.1	47,000	561	3,898	73	3,688	5.2
1970	—	—	6,398	4.5	85,800	357	3,119	95	3,001	6.0
1971	—	—	6,373	4.9	45,400	691	3,994	96	2,883	6.1
1972	—	—	5,879	6.4	89,300	499	2,579	165	2,372	6.9
1973	—	—	6,265	8.8	73,700	672	4,198	162	2,591	8.3
1974	—	—	6,580	8.4	127,400	450	4,199	139	2,917	9.5
1975	—	—	7,530	6.5	87,400	826	4,366	142	2,836	10.4
1976	—	—	6,472	9.1	141,100	566	4,398	155	3,018	9.6
1977	—	—	6,740	10.6	117,700	735	4,298	194	2,955	9.8
1978	—	—	7,597	10.4	146,100	645	4,567	233	2,653	12.0
1979	—	—	8,126	10.9	102,300	1,256	4,989	236	2,939	11.6

Notes appear at end of table

(continued)

TABLE Da796–805   Apples, avocados, grapes, and peaches – production and price: 1889–1999   *Continued*

	Apples				Avocados		Grapes		Peaches	
	Total		Commercial							
	Production	Price	Production	Price	Production	Price	Production	Price	Production	Price
	Da796 [1]	Da797	Da798	Da799 [2]	Da800 [1,3]	Da801 [2,3]	Da802 [1]	Da803 [2]	Da804 [1]	Da805 [2]
Year	Thousand short tons	Dollars per short ton	Million pounds	Cents per pound	Short tons	Dollars per short ton	Thousand short tons	Dollars per short ton	Million pounds	Cents per pound
1980	—	—	8,818	8.7	268,800	377	5,595	240	3,069	12.4
1981	—	—	7,740	11.1	182,800	662	4,458	297	2,771	13.3
1982	—	—	8,122	10.0	236,700	463	6,555	232	2,286	14.0
1983	—	—	8,379	10.5	274,000	379	5,521	199	1,855	14.4
1984	—	—	8,324	11.1	229,500	557	5,208	190	2,660	12.6
1985	—	—	7,915	11.7	188,500	953	5,616	172	2,148	14.4
1986	—	—	7,859	13.4	302,700	344	5,228	226	2,307	14.0
1987	—	—	10,742	8.6	209,000	1,030	5,267	259	2,382	13.8
1988	—	—	9,128	12.7	192,000	1,140	6,034	266	2,622	15.6
1989	—	—	9,963	10.4	138,500	1,809	5,931	314	2,363	16.4
1990	—	—	9,657	15.1	155,600	1,319	5,660	295	2,242	17.4
1991	—	—	9,707	17.9	184,300	1,063	5,556	312	2,696	15.7
1992	—	—	10,569	13.6	291,200	405	6,052	306	2,672	15.2
1993	—	—	10,685	12.9	143,400	1,780	6,023	333	2,644	15.9
1994	—	—	11,501	12.9	175,000	1,384	5,874	321	2,509	13.3
1995	—	—	10,578	17.0	190,000	1,296	5,921	346	2,290	18.4
1996	—	—	10,382	15.9	190,500	1,431	5,554	429	2,105	19.1
1997	—	—	10,324	15.4	178,000	1,559	7,291	429	2,625	17.7
1998	—	—	11,648 [4]	12.3 [4]	156,000 [4]	2,126 [4]	5,820	454	2,401	19.2
1999 [4]	—	—	10,741	16.0	—	—	6,169	478	2,521	19.2

[1] See text for information on excess cullage or on quantities not harvested for economic reasons.

[2] Method of determining price changes over time; see text.

[3] Covers California and Florida production only.

[4] Preliminary.

[5] Data in the original source appear to be in error but cannot be corrected.

Sources

Series Da796. 1889–1918, U.S. Bureau of Agricultural Economics, *Fruits (Noncitrus): Production, Farm Disposition, Value, and Utilization of Sales, 1889–1944*, Statistical Bulletin number CS-27, May 1948, pp. 3, 15; 1919–1938, U.S. Department of Agriculture, Statistical Reporting Service, *Agricultural Statistics, 1944* and *1967* editions.

Series Da797. *Agricultural Statistics, 1952.*

Series Da798–799. *Agricultural Statistics, 1967, 1974, 1982, 1987, 1992, 1994,* and *2000* editions.

Series Da800. *Agricultural Statistics, 1944, 1967, 1974, 1982, 1992,* and *2000* editions.

Series Da801. *Agricultural Statistics, 1967, 1974, 1982, 1992,* and *2000* editions.

Series Da802. 1909–1944, *Fruits (Noncitrus): Production, Farm Disposition, Value, and Utilization of Sales, 1889–1944*, Statistical Bulletin number CS-27, May 1948, pp. 67, 95; 1945–1969, *Agricultural Statistics, 1944, 1967, 1970,* and *1975* editions; 1970–1992, U.S. Department of Agriculture, Economic Research Service, *U.S.–Mexico Fruit and Vegetable Trade,* March 1995, Table 41, downloaded October 15, 2000, from the U.S. Department of Agriculture, Economics and Statistics System; 1993 to date, *Agricultural Statistics, 1999* and *2000* editions.

Series Da803. 1924–1944, *Fruits (Noncitrus): Production, Farm Disposition, Value, and Utilization of Sales, 1889–1944*, Statistical Bulletin number CS-27, May 1948, p. 67; 1945–1999, *Agricultural Statistics, 1967, 1975, 1982, 1987, 1992, 1994,* and *2000* editions.

Series Da804–805. Prior to 1945, *Fruits (Noncitrus): Production, Farm Disposition, Value, and Utilization of Sales, 1889–1944*, Statistical Bulletin number CS-27, May 1948, p. 30; 1945–1999, *Agricultural Statistics, 1967, 1974, 1982, 1987, 1992, 1994, 1995–96,* and *2000* editions.

Documentation

See the text for Table Da791–795.

Series Da796. Estimates of quantities not harvested on account of economic conditions, which are included in estimates of total production (in thousand short tons): 7 in 1924; 177 in 1926; 50 in 1931; 101 in 1932; 110 in 1933; 8 in 1934; 132 in 1935; 6 in 1936; 276 in 1937; and 46 in 1938. Estimates of quantities harvested but not utilized because of abnormal cullage, which are included in estimates of total production (in thousand short tons): 24 in 1934; 99 in 1935; 16 in 1936; 98 in 1937; and 55 in 1938. The official U.S. Department of Agriculture conversion factor estimates that one bushel of either apples or peaches is equivalent to 48 pounds (or 0.024 short tons). Data for 1889–1918 were converted from bushels to short tons by multiplying the number of bushels by 0.024.

Series Da797. Data are season average prices. Data were converted from dollars per bushel to dollars per short ton by dividing dollars per short ton by 0.024.

Series Da798. Includes production for all uses, as well as quantities not harvested for economic reasons and excess cullage of harvested fruit. Estimates of the commercial crop refer to production in orchards of 100 or more bearing-age trees.

Series Da799. Data are season average prices. Fresh fruit prices are equivalent returns at packinghouse door for Washington, Oregon, California, and New York starting in 1977; for other states, returns at point of first sale. Beginning with 1963, processing prices are equivalent returns at processing plant door. Beginning with 1944, the price was obtained by weighting state prices by quantity sold; prior to 1944, prices were weighted by production. Data from 1934 to 1958 were converted from dollars per bushel to cents per pound by dividing dollars per bushel by 0.48.

Series Da800. Covers production having value. Data are based on the year of bloom. The season runs from November 1 to November 30 (of the following year) for California and June 20 to February 28 for Florida. Production is the amount sold or utilized. The data include excess cullage of harvested fruit as follows (in short tons): 500 in 1954; 875 in 1955; 1,125 in 1956; 545 in 1957; 400 in 1958; 950 in 1959; and 660 in 1964.

TABLE Da796–805 Apples, avocados, grapes, and peaches – production and price: 1889–1999 *Continued*

Series Da801. Beginning with 1944, the price was obtained by weighting state prices by quantity sold; prior to 1944, prices were weighted by production. Avocado prices are equivalent returns per short ton for bulk fruit at the first delivery point. Beginning with 1963, quantities processed are priced at the equivalent processing plant door level.

Series Da802. Most of the *Agricultural Statistics* volumes distinguish between "Total Production" and "Utilized Production." The series here reproduces "Total Production." For 1954–1969, *Agricultural Statistics* only reported "Utilized Production," so the contributors of this table made some adjustments so that the series was consistent with the other years. The series includes the following quantities not harvested on account of economic conditions or excess cullage of harvested fruit (in thousand short tons): 54 in 1915; 100 in 1922; 138 in 1925; 15 in 1926; 142 in 1927; 153 in 1928; 433 in 1930, which include 316 of California raisin varieties purchased but left on the vines in accordance with marketing agreements; 10 in 1931; 154 in 1932; 3 in 1933; 9 in 1937; 2 in 1940; 3 in 1950; 2 in 1951; 6 in 1957; 61 in 1963; 25 in 1965; and 7 in 1967. The series also includes losses of California raisins laid but not harvested due to severe weather damage: 65,000 short tons (293,000 short tons fresh equivalent) in 1976; 56,300 short tons (248,000 short tons fresh equivalent) in 1978; and losses in total U.S. grape (short tons fresh equivalent): 1977, 1,550; 1978, 248,000; 1979, 300; 1980, 300; 1981, 600; 1982, 690,200; 1983, 145,500; 1984, 25,100; 1985, 100; 1986, 600; 1987, 13,500; 1988, 1,600; 1989, 800; 1990, 120; 1991, 630; 1992, 19,500; 1993, 8,600; 1994, 4,400; and 1995, 9,550.

Series Da803. Beginning with 1963, quantities processed are priced at the equivalent processing plant door level. Beginning with 1944, the price was obtained by weighting state prices by quantity sold; prior to 1944, prices were weighted by production. Through 1970, fresh fruit prices are equivalent packinghouse-door returns for Washington, equivalent returns for bulk fruit at the first delivery point for California, and the average prices as sold for other states. Beginning with 1971, prices are equivalent packinghouse-door returns for California and Washington and the average price as sold for other states.

Series Da804. This series contains all production, including quantities not harvested on account of economic reasons or excess cullage of harvested fruit. The following are estimates of quantities not harvested on account of economic conditions, which are included in estimates of total production (in million pounds): 67 in 1926; 130 in 1927; 190 in 1928; 501 in 1930; 407 in 1931; 370 in 1932; 171 in 1933; 120 in 1934; 5 in 1937; 61 in 1938; 36 in 1939; 32 in 1940; 74 in 1941; 12 in 1942; 14 in 1943; and 116 in 1944. The above figures include the following quantities of California Clingstones purchased but not harvested (in million pounds): 297 in 1930; 189 in 1931; and 67 in 1933. The following are estimates of quantities harvested but not utilized because of abnormal cullage that are included in total production (in million pounds): 4 in 1935; 13 in 1939; 6 in 1940; 35 in 1941; 37 in 1942; and 2 in 1944. For the period 1959–1970, *Agricultural Statistics* distinguishes between "Production" – quantity sold or utilized – and "Not Utilized." For consistency with the rest of the data, the series here presents the sum of both categories, "Production" and "Not Utilized." The differences are the quantities not harvested on account of economic reasons or excess cullage of harvested fruit, as follows (in million pounds): 45 in 1959; 27 in 1960; 66.5 in 1961; 63.5 in 1962; 29 in 1963; 24 in 1964; 143.5 in 1964; 25 in 1965; 5 in 1967; 69 in 1968; 46 in 1969; and 13.5 in 1970. Data from 1899 to 1918 were converted from thousands of bushels to millions of pounds by multiplying thousands of bushels by 0.048.

Series Da805. Data are season average prices. Beginning with 1944, the price was obtained by weighting state prices by quantity sold; prior to 1944, prices were weighted by production. Beginning with 1963, quantities processed are priced at the equivalent processing plant-door level. Fresh fruit prices are equivalent packinghouse-door returns for California and Washington except equivalent returns for bulk fruit at the first delivery point for California Clingstone, and the average price as sold for other states. Data for 1909–1958 were converted from dollars per bushel to cents per pound by dividing dollars per bushel by 0.48.

TABLE Da806–820 Grapefruit, oranges, lemons, and limes – acreage, production, and price: 1910–1999

Contributed by Alan L. Olmstead and Paul W. Rhode

	Grapefruit			Oranges						Lemons			Limes		
								California					Acreage harvested (Florida)		
	Acreage harvested	Production	Price	Acreage harvested	Production	Price	Juice production	Production	Price	Acreage harvested	Production	Price		Production	Price
	Da806	Da807 [1,2]	Da808 [1,2,3]	Da809	Da810 [2,4]	Da811 [2,3,4]	Da812	Da813 [2,4]	Da814 [2,4]	Da815	Da816 [2]	Da817 [3]	Da818	Da819	Da820 [3]
Year	Thousand acres	Thousand boxes	Dollars per box	Thousand acres	Thousand boxes	Dollars per box	Thousand tons	Thousand boxes	Dollars per box	Thousand acres	Thousand boxes	Dollars per box	Thousand acres	Thousand boxes	Dollars per box
1910	—	1,119	1.53	—	—	—	—	12,239	1.31	—	1,751	3.14	—	—	—
1911	—	1,236	1.33	—	—	—	—	17,078	1.27	—	2,447	2.61	—	—	—
1912	—	1,214	2.84	—	—	—	—	15,273	1.26	—	2,282	2.62	—	—	—
1913	—	2,085	1.32	—	—	—	—	6,870	1.88	—	973	4.98	—	—	—
1914	—	2,307	1.72	—	—	—	—	19,688	1.05	—	1,295	3.12	—	—	—
1915	—	2,539	0.62	—	—	—	—	17,407	1.29	—	2,750	1.12	—	—	—
1916	—	2,559	1.24	—	—	—	—	17,147	1.59	—	2,901	2.77	—	—	—
1917	—	2,688	1.49	—	—	—	—	21,315	1.37	—	3,210	2.59	—	—	—
1918	—	2,227	1.84	—	—	—	—	8,267	3.81	—	2,683	4.41	—	—	—
1919	—	3,880	2.06	—	—	—	—	18,315	2.93	—	4,446	2.56	—	—	—
1920	—	6,295	1.60	—	—	—	—	16,632	3.29	—	4,532	1.41	—	28	2.95
1921	—	6,234	1.63	—	—	—	—	23,771	1.94	—	5,641	2.48	—	26	2.60
1922	—	7,103	1.54	—	—	—	—	14,021	3.17	—	4,377	2.59	—	33	2.25
1923	—	8,289	1.17	—	—	—	—	21,283	1.93	—	3,783	3.44	—	35	2.40
1924	—	9,023	0.58	—	—	—	—	24,153	1.75	—	6,432	1.27	—	40	2.50
1925	—	9,693	0.96	—	—	—	—	18,506	3.28	—	5,301	3.04	—	36	2.50
1926	—	8,550	1.95	—	—	—	—	24,200	2.72	—	7,317	1.85	—	30	3.00
1927	—	9,753	1.30	—	—	—	—	28,252	2.86	—	6,861	2.07	—	12	5.50
1928	—	8,920	2.10	—	—	—	—	22,737	4.01	—	5,419	3.44	—	(Z)	—
1929	—	13,236	1.06	—	—	—	—	39,159	1.89	—	7,620	2.80	—	6	3.50
1930	—	11,215	1.89	—	30,979	3.64	—	21,195	4.35	—	6,109	3.65	—	8	4.50
1931	—	18,690	0.73	—	52,660	1.38	—	35,179	1.44	—	7,950	2.20	—	8	4.00
1932	—	15,181	0.80	—	47,902	1.24	—	34,658	1.14	—	7,696	1.82	—	9	3.50
1933	—	15,004	0.58	—	49,715	0.89	—	34,265	0.93	—	6,704	2.15	—	10	3.00
1934	—	14,647	0.83	—	44,197	1.41	—	28,439	1.64	—	7,295	2.45	—	12	2.50
1935	—	21,166	0.55	—	60,593	1.16	—	45,047	1.22	—	10,747	1.44	—	15	3.00
1936	—	18,313	0.88	—	49,359	1.53	—	32,809	1.64	—	7,787	3.17	—	12	3.75
1937	—	30,570	0.58	—	50,515	1.83	—	29,827	2.02	—	7,579	3.06	—	45	3.25
1938	—	31,103	0.57	—	70,781	0.83	—	45,914	0.84	—	9,304	1.84	—	70	3.25
1939	—	39,820	0.32	—	72,182	0.78	—	41,420	0.83	—	11,106	1.48	—	95	2.60
1940	—	34,846	0.44	—	72,106	0.95	—	44,425	1.11	—	11,983	1.59	—	95	2.80
1941	—	42,879	0.43	—	81,488	1.21	—	50,778	1.36	—	16,734	1.20	—	80	2.85
1942	—	40,257	0.75	—	82,301	1.56	—	52,155	1.73	—	11,720	1.60	—	150	2.22
1943	—	50,479	1.15	—	84,495	2.46	—	44,329	2.97	—	14,880	2.47	—	175	2.27
1944	—	56,088	1.53	—	102,221	2.58	—	51,961	3.17	—	11,050	3.31	—	190	4.49
1945	—	52,177	1.69	—	107,589	2.70	—	60,500	2.83	—	12,550	2.75	—	250	4.46
1946	—	63,448	1.37	—	99,419	2.94	—	44,010	3.27	—	14,450	1.94	—	200	3.57
1947	—	55,484	0.86	—	112,001	1.54	—	53,530	1.77	—	13,800	2.67	—	170	3.92
1948	—	54,670	0.50	—	109,547	1.31	—	45,830	1.80	—	12,870	2.58	—	170	3.31
1949	—	45,482	0.83	—	98,839	1.75	—	37,010	1.94	—	10,010	4.25	—	200	3.05

Year	Grapefruit Acreage harvested Da806	Grapefruit Production Da807 [1,2]	Grapefruit Price Da808 [1,2,3]	Oranges Acreage harvested Da809	Oranges Production Da810 [2,4]	Oranges Price Da811 [2,3,4]	Oranges Juice production Da812	California Production Da813 [2,4]	California Price Da814 [2,4]	Lemons Acreage harvested Da815	Lemons Production Da816 [2]	Lemons Price Da817 [3]	Limes Acreage harvested (Florida) Da818	Limes Production Da819	Limes Price Da820 [3]
	Thousand acres	Thousand boxes	Dollars per box	Thousand acres	Thousand boxes	Dollars per box	Thousand tons	Thousand boxes	Dollars per box	Thousand acres	Thousand boxes	Dollars per box	Thousand acres	Thousand boxes	Dollars per box
1950	—	36,499	1.81	—	102,581	2.24	—	41,860	2.02	—	11,360	3.59	—	260	3.73
1951	—	46,567	1.09	—	116,311	1.97	—	45,210	2.06	—	13,450	2.82	—	280	2.60
1952	—	37,500	0.86	—	117,427	1.50	—	38,410	2.13	—	12,800	3.46	—	260	3.80
1953	—	38,358	1.08	—	119,737	1.71	—	46,030	1.79	—	12,590	3.90	—	320	4.19
1954	—	47,070	0.85	—	123,167	1.93	—	32,400	2.78	—	16,130	2.73	—	370	5.81
1955	—	42,184	0.99	—	127,532	1.93	—	39,420	2.39	—	14,000	2.79	—	380	2.97
1956	—	45,377	0.95	—	128,928	2.41	—	38,370	2.83	—	13,100	3.14	—	400	3.02
1957	—	44,787	1.21	—	128,725	2.08	—	35,900	2.88	—	16,200	2.27	—	400	4.17
1958	—	39,777	1.42	—	107,383	3.07	—	23,200	4.71	—	16,900	2.19	—	350	3.10
1959	—	43,797	1.43	—	125,940	3.24	—	40,200	3.08	—	17,240	1.93	—	200	4.87
1960	—	41,591	1.38	—	122,510	2.75	—	30,800	3.78	—	18,230	1.92	—	320	3.96
1961	—	43,370	1.27	—	112,325	3.60	—	25,000	4.32	—	14,340	2.49	—	310	3.75
1962	—	42,490	1.06	—	133,025	2.68	—	20,500	4.50	—	16,740	2.17	—	340	3.80
1963	—	34,738	1.64	—	102,385	3.46	—	28,600	4.19	—	12,990	4.00	—	400	3.89
1964	—	34,207	2.63	—	88,505	4.67	—	31,700	4.15	—	19,040	2.67	—	450	4.39
1965	—	41,027	1.90	—	116,410	3.15	—	31,200	3.58	—	14,210	3.31	—	560	3.64
1966	—	46,695	1.95	—	135,470	2.48	—	—	—	—	15,770	3.29	—	415	4.90
1967	—	55,676	1.38	—	182,850	1.84	—	—	—	—	17,910	3.28	—	420	6.44
1968	—	44,058	2.54	—	124,490	3.08	—	—	—	—	16,850	3.85	—	720	4.49
1969	—	54,170	1.68	—	183,760	2.43	—	—	—	—	15,810	4.41	—	700	4.51
1970	—	53,910	2.24	—	185,770	2.09	8,023	—	—	—	15,120	4.85	—	725	5.71
1971	—	60,560	2.40	—	189,430	2.45	8,205	—	—	—	16,450	4.98	—	880	4.70
1972	—	64,250	2.89	—	191,450	2.87	8,237	—	—	—	16,680	4.81	—	1,100	5.49
1973	—	65,640	2.70	—	224,660	2.69	9,737	—	—	—	22,200	4.38	—	1,100	6.10
1974	—	65,500	2.41	—	216,210	2.78	9,386	—	—	—	17,800	6.17	—	1,050	7.20
1975	—	61,610	2.51	—	237,810	2.75	10,241	—	—	—	29,400	3.85	—	1,100	7.62
1976	—	70,080	2.21	—	242,780	2.80	10,493	—	—	—	17,620	5.79	—	1,080	9.27
1977	—	74,600	2.35	—	242,950	3.34	10,546	—	—	—	26,000	3.56	—	1,000	11.61
1978	—	74,660	2.54	—	220,120	5.45	9,546	—	—	—	26,100	4.24	—	460	19.11
1979	192.8	67,380	3.43	801.2	210,600	6.15	9,160	—	—	68.9	19,600	6.87	4.1	720	16.16
1980	199.9	73,200	4.13	806.0	273,630	4.85	11,832	—	—	70.1	20,750	8.11	4.7	1,100	12.55
1981	197.0	67,860	4.74	794.6	244,580	5.30	10,487	—	—	71.9	31,300	4.83	5.3	1,200	11.10
1982	199.1	70,550	3.24	777.7	176,690	6.53	7,600	—	—	75.8	24,800	4.26	6.4	1,300	12.44
1983	199.3	61,200	3.06	750.8	225,180	5.96	9,519	—	—	71.5	25,000	4.37	7.3	1,700	13.09
1984	191.6	53,840	4.09	688.2	169,440	7.68	7,243	—	—	69.8	20,750	5.66	7.0	1,440	12.16
1985	162.8	56,150	5.47	617.7	158,350	9.16	6,719	—	—	66.6	25,450	6.61	6.7	1,640	12.13
1986	145.2	57,870	5.87	561.5	175,440	6.18	7,476	—	—	65.3	18,200	11.93	6.8	1,725	12.70
1987	147.9	63,775	6.53	569.5	181,175	7.29	7,697	—	—	63.9	28,600	6.37	6.7	1,450	13.50
1988	148.7	68,700	7.01	574.5	200,250	8.92	8,551	—	—	64.5	20,650	9.78	7.0	1,300	17.93
1989	150.2	69,500	6.00	588.7	209,050	8.90	8,949	—	—	63.9	20,000	11.75	6.6	1,250	17.18
1990	147.3	49,300	7.49	597.8	184,415	7.96	7,745	—	—	63.3	18,600	15.04	6.7	1,650	13.87
1991	133.2	55,500	7.16	612.7	178,950	8.70	7,848	—	—	62.1	18,900	15.32	6.2	1,450	19.21
1992	136.6	55,265	7.84	640.1	209,610	7.43	8,906	—	—	62.1	20,200	12.73	6.3	1,600	14.27
1993	145.6	68,375	4.40	688.2	255,760	5.77	—	—	—	62.1	24,800	9.67	6.3	1,000	6.55
1994	154.7	65,100	5.26	711.9	240,450	6.37	—	—	—	61.1	25,900	9.94	1.9	200	18.46

Notes appear at end of table

(continued)

TABLE Da806–820 Grapefruit, oranges, lemons, and limes – acreage, production, and price: 1910–1999 *Continued*

	Grapefruit			Oranges				California		Lemons			Limes		
	Acreage harvested	Production	Price	Acreage harvested	Production	Price	Juice production	Production	Price	Acreage harvested	Production	Price	Acreage harvested (Florida)	Production	Price
Year	Da806	Da807 [1,2]	Da808 [1,2,3]	Da809	Da810 [2,4]	Da811 [2,3,4]	Da812	Da813 [2,4]	Da814 [2,4]	Da815	Da816 [2]	Da817 [3]	Da818	Da819	Da820 [3]
	Thousand acres	Thousand boxes	Dollars per box	Thousand acres	Thousand boxes	Dollars per box	Thousand tons	Thousand boxes	Dollars per box	Thousand acres	Thousand boxes	Dollars per box	Thousand acres	Thousand boxes	Dollars per box
1995	166.1	71,050	4.29	771.2	263,605	6.08	—	—	—	61.0	23,600	11.16	1.9	230	14.47
1996	174.3	66,200	4.33	808.8	263,890	6.85	—	—	—	61.3	26,100	10.01	2.0	300	13.05
1997	182.0	70,100	4.00	843.6	293,020	6.16	—	—	—	61.9	25,300	12.00	2.1	320	11.93
1998	171.7	63,150	4.13	828.8	315,525	6.13	—	—	—	62.7	23,600	10.21	2.7	440	11.90
1999 [5]	156.5	61,400	5.36	830.1	226,280	7.85	—	—	—	61.6	19,650	13.25	2.7	500	16.43

(Z) Fewer than 1,000 boxes.
[1] See text for information on changing or restricted geographic coverage.
[2] Conversion factors differ over time or among locations; see text.
[3] Method of determining price changes over time; see text.
[4] Crop coverage changes over time; see text.
[5] Preliminary.

Sources

Series Da806, Da809, Da815, and Da818. U.S. Department of Agriculture, Economic Research Service (USDA ERS), *Fruit Situation and Outlook Yearbook*, December 1996, updated December 2000, downloaded January 8, 2001, from the U.S. Department of Agriculture, Economics and Statistics System.

Series Da807–808. 1910–1929: U.S. Department of Agriculture, Statistical Reporting Service, Crop Reporting Board, *Citrus Fruits by States, 1909–10 to 1964–65, Revised Estimates*, Statistical Bulletin number 380, January 1967, p. 77; 1930–1999, USDA ERS, *Agricultural Statistics, 1967, 1972, 1982, 1987, 1992, 1995–96*, and *2000* editions.

Series Da810–811. *Agricultural Statistics, 1967, 1972, 1982, 1987, 1992, 1995–96*, and *2000* editions.

Series Da812. USDA ERS, *U.S.–Mexico Fruit and Vegetable Trade, 1970–1992*, March 1995, Table 38, downloaded January 12, 2001, from the U.S. Department of Agriculture, Economics and Statistics System.

Series Da813–814. *Citrus Fruits by States, 1909–10 to 1964–65, Revised Estimates*, Statistical Bulletin number 380, January 1967, pp. 38–9.

Series Da816–817. 1910–1929: U.S. Department of Agriculture, Statistical Reporting Service, Crop Reporting Board, *Citrus Fruits by States, 1909–10 to 1964–65, Revised Estimates*, Statistical Bulletin number 380, January 1967, p. 108; 1930–1999, USDA ERS, *Agricultural Statistics, 1967, 1972, 1982, 1987, 1992, 1995–96*, and *2000* editions.

Series Da819–820. 1910–1929: U.S. Department of Agriculture, Statistical Reporting Service, Crop Reporting Board, *Citrus Fruits by States, 1909–10 to 1964–65, Revised Estimates*, Statistical Bulletin number 380, January 1967, p. 117; 1930–1999, USDA ERS, *Agricultural Statistics, 1967, 1972, 1982, 1987, 1992, 1995–96*, and *2000* editions.

Documentation

See the text for Table Da791–795.

Typically the U.S. Department of Agriculture (USDA) reports the production for a span of two years (for example, 1975–1976) because the crop year begins with the bloom in one year and ends with the completion of the harvest the following year. When attributing production to just one year, recent convention is to attribute it to the year of the harvest. This is the procedure used here. For oranges, harvest in California usually starts in late October of the first year shown and continues into September of the following year. In other states, harvest of oranges begins about October 1 and ends in early summer. Grapefruit harvest for the California desert and for all other states begins in the fall and ends by early summer. Harvest of other California grapefruit begins in March of the year after bloom and continues through October. California lemons are harvested from August 1 to July 31; Arizona lemons are harvested from August 15 to February 1. Florida limes are picked mostly from April through March.

Series Da807–808. Through 1919, the estimates relate to California and Florida only; production in other states for those years was negligible and estimates are not available. Data are based on the following net weights per box of grapefruit: Florida, 80 pounds (prior to 1949) and 85 pounds (beginning with 1949); Texas, 80 pounds; California Desert Valleys and Arizona, 65 pounds (prior to 1954) and 64 pounds (beginning with 1954); and other California areas, 68 pounds (prior to 1954) and 67 pounds (beginning with 1954). Price figures are marketing year average prices.

Series Da807, Da810, Da816, and Da819. Figures cover production having value (the quantity sold or utilized).

Series Da808, Da811, Da817, and Da820. Through 1977, figures are season average returns per box; beginning with 1978, figures are marketing year average returns per box. Data are equivalent returns per box at the intake packinghouse door for all methods of sale. When sale represents fruit sold at points other than intake packinghouse door, prices of fruit as sold are converted by additions or subtractions of necessary charges to or from prices of fruit as actually sold. Beginning with 1944, prices were obtained by weighting state prices by quantity sold; prior to 1944, prices were weighted by production.

Series Da810–811. Includes small quantities of tangerines in Texas; prior to 1964, includes tangerines in Louisiana and Arizona; prior to 1961, includes tangerines in California. Excludes Florida temples beginning 1953; in earlier years temples are included with oranges. One box of oranges is equivalent to 90 pounds in Florida; 85 in Texas; and 75 in California and Arizona (prior to 1954, the conversion rate was 77 pounds to one box).

Series Da812. Includes production for all uses. Production is based on a crop year. Year stated is when crop was harvested.

Series Da813–814. Includes small quantities of tangerines prior to 1962. One box is equivalent to approximately 75 pounds. Prior to 1954, the conversion rate was 77 pounds to one box. Price figures are equivalent packinghouse-door returns.

Series Da816. One box of lemons is equivalent to 76 pounds in California and Arizona. Prior to 1954, the net weight used by the USDA was 79 pounds.

Series Da818. Season beginning April.

Series Da819. One box of Florida limes is equivalent to 88 pounds.

TABLE Da821–836   Nectarines, strawberries, watermelon, and cantaloupe – acreage, production, and price: 1918–1999

Contributed by Alan L. Olmstead and Paul W. Rhode

	Nectarines		Strawberries							
			Fresh and processed			Fresh		Processed		
	Production	Price	Acreage harvested	Production	Price	Production	Price	Production	Price
	Da821	Da822 [1]	Da823	Da824 [2]	Da825 [1]	Da826 [3]	Da827 [1]	Da828	Da829 [1]
Year	Thousand short tons	Dollars per short ton	Acres	Thousand hundredweight	Dollars per hundredweight	Thousand hundredweight	Dollars per hundredweight	Thousand hundredweight	Dollars per hundredweight
1918	—	—	94,120	2,251	12.4	—	—	—	—
1919	—	—	88,320	2,398	13.3	—	—	—	—
1920	—	—	94,580	2,325	13.5	—	—	—	—
1921	—	—	110,880	2,823	12.9	—	—	—	—
1922	—	—	133,570	3,860	9.4	—	—	—	—
1923	—	—	149,170	3,869	10.1	—	—	—	—
1924	—	—	176,440	4,405	9.4	—	—	—	—
1925	—	—	146,130	3,207	11.6	—	—	—	—
1926	—	—	153,960	3,673	11.6	—	—	—	—
1927	—	—	191,940	4,518	10.0	—	—	—	—
1928	—	—	207,630	4,638	8.9	—	—	—	—
1929	—	—	206,890	4,639	8.7	—	—	—	—
1930	—	—	178,470	3,291	11.1	—	—	—	—
1931	—	—	156,190	4,150	8.8	—	—	—	—
1932	—	—	190,990	4,712	5.4	—	—	—	—
1933	—	—	197,490	4,387	4.8	—	—	—	—
1934	—	—	197,260	3,766	5.7	—	—	—	—
1935	—	—	159,000	3,892	6.5	—	—	—	—
1936	10	—	155,320	3,242	7.8	—	—	—	—
1937	11	—	143,550	3,891	8.2	—	—	—	—
1938	10	—	155,310	3,590	7.6	—	—	—	—
1939	13	—	174,800	4,439	6.8	3,956	7.0	482	5.3
1940	8	—	166,350	4,509	6.9	3,856	7.3	614	4.6
1941	10	—	170,570	4,468	6.9	3,661	7.3	730	5.3
1942	12	58	156,080	4,706	8.8	3,883	8.9	560	8.4
1943	12	147	109,340	2,366	17.6	2,142	18.0	217	13.7
1944	17	89	76,900	1,647	22.1	1,376	22.7	268	18.6
1945	13	95	75,400	1,866	23.9	1,520	24.8	343	20.1
1946	16	106	90,250	2,551	27.0	1,955	27.1	595	26.9
1947	15	100	112,350	3,238	20.8	2,456	21.6	764	18.3
1948	13	93	116,650	3,777	22.2	2,349	23.5	1,413	20.1
1949	17	87	116,150	3,119	20.0	2,188	22.1	921	15.1
1950	12	147	126,030	3,936	20.9	2,230	21.1	1,707	20.7
1951	12	148	139,120	4,054	18.5	2,583	19.4	1,442	16.8
1952	15	147	123,350	4,169	18.6	2,287	20.8	1,882	15.9
1953	13	150	99,600	4,276	19.3	2,147	22.1	2,130	16.5
1954	19	128	96,200	4,115	19.4	1,844	23.7	2,228	15.8
1955	24	148	100,490	4,467	20.0	1,874	24.7	2,593	16.7
1956	19	181	114,710	5,480	17.9	2,411	22.0	3,070	14.5
1957	36	148	122,170	5,506	14.3	2,763	19.1	2,679	9.3
1958	34	149	109,230	5,314	16.0	2,647	20.0	2,660	12.0
1959	39	115	96,560	4,798	17.9	2,391	22.3	2,407	13.6
1960	44	106	92,200	4,659	19.2	2,370	23.7	2,289	14.7
1961	54	103	88,390	5,073	17.5	2,859	21.9	2,214	11.9
1962	51	108	87,910	5,204	18.0	2,905	22.4	2,299	12.5
1963	57	95	80,070	5,099	18.7	2,951	23.6	2,148	12.1
1964	75	95	74,850	5,490	20.0	3,098	24.5	2,392	14.2
1965	67	86	67,940	4,328	22.1	2,629	25.6	1,699	16.8
1966	68	142	66,180	4,644	22.2	2,659	26.2	1,985	16.8
1967	55	157	63,700	4,740	20.5	2,818	24.5	1,922	14.5
1968	64	147	58,700	5,256	21.3	3,373	24.3	1,883	16.0
1969	66	140	53,500	4,862	22.6	3,154	25.9	1,708	16.4
1970	67	152	50,400	4,960	21.5	3,164	24.8	1,796	15.6
1971	70	155	47,780	5,207	22.5	3,404	25.4	1,803	14.5
1972	87	177	43,410	4,602	24.0	3,211	27.1	1,391	16.8
1973	87	255	40,610	4,796	27.6	3,164	31.0	1,632	21.0
1974	117	228	39,260	5,388	28.8	3,706	32.5	1,682	20.7

Notes appear at end of table

(continued)

TABLE Da821–836   Nectarines, strawberries, watermelon, and cantaloupe – acreage, production, and price: 1918–1999 *Continued*

	Nectarines		Strawberries							
			Fresh and processed			Fresh		Processed		
	Production	Price	Acreage harvested	Production	Price	Production	Price	Production	Price	
	Da821	Da822 [1]	Da823	Da824 [2]	Da825 [1]	Da826 [3]	Da827 [1]	Da828	Da829 [1]	
Year	Thousand short tons	Dollars per short ton	Acres	Thousand hundredweight	Dollars per hundredweight	Thousand hundredweight	Dollars per hundredweight	Thousand hundredweight	Dollars per hundredweight	
1975	111	275	39,590	5,506	30.6	3,774	35.5	1,732	19.9	
1976	128	245	34,450	5,807	32.9	3,695	37.7	2,112	24.5	
1977	155	205	35,650	6,619	33.2	4,298	39.1	2,321	22.4	
1978	148	307	37,600	6,592	31.7	4,779	36.7	1,813	18.8	
1979	172	197	36,500	6,383	38.7	4,360	43.4	2,023	28.5	
1980	191	231	36,050	7,017	41.2	4,821	47.9	2,196	26.3	
1981	182	229	37,000	7,416	42.0	5,375	47.1	2,041	28.3	
1982	178	249	40,250	8,830	48.1	5,896	55.2	2,934	33.8	
1983	185	299	43,400	8,968	45.5	5,887	52.9	3,081	31.5	
1984	183	316	43,300	9,937	41.7	7,510	49.0	2,427	19.3	
1985	210	327	44,350	10,218	44.3	7,571	52.6	2,647	20.4	
1986	172	440	44,750	10,232	49.5	7,387	57.6	2,845	28.4	
1987	191	343	46,120	11,173	49.4	7,804	58.5	3,369	28.5	
1988	200	394	47,150	11,791	46.2	8,555	54.1	3,236	25.2	
1989	220	398	46,100	11,420	47.1	8,616	53.9	2,804	26.1	
1990	232	474	46,080	12,537	47.0	8,636	55.3	3,901	28.7	
1991	215	402	46,080	13,656	46.2	9,682	54.0	3,974	27.4	
1992	236	312	49,530	13,348	52.3	9,997	61.5	3,351	24.7	
1993	205	500	51,230	14,465	46.3	10,108	54.0	4,357	28.4	
1994	242	282	48,830	16,486	50.7	11,477	60.2	5,009	29.1	
1995	176	534	48,080	16,020	50.7	11,456	60.4	4,564	26.2	
1996	247	474	47,670	16,259	47.3	12,126	56.5	4,133	20.4	
1997	264	375	44,260	16,278	55.5	12,018	65.6	4,260	27.1	
1998	224	471	45,230	16,397	61.1	11,338	74.1	5,059	31.9	
1999	276 [6]	411 [6]	45,560 [6]	18,126 [6]	61.7 [6]	12,642 [6]	73.5 [6]	5,484 [6]	34.4 [6]	

	Strawberries	Watermelon			Cantaloupe		
	Frozen production	Acreage harvested	Production	Price	Acreage harvested	Production	Price
	Da830	Da831 [3]	Da832 [2,3,4]	Da833 [1,3,4]	Da834 [3,5]	Da835 [2,3,4,5]	Da836 [3,4,5]
Year	Thousand tons	Acres	Thousand hundredweight	Dollars per hundredweight	Acres	Thousand hundredweight	Dollars per hundredweight
1918	—	80,930	7,383	0.62	51,640	4,708	3.20
1919	—	121,660	10,600	0.68	65,020	5,915	2.53
1920	—	148,930	14,736	0.74	72,500	6,285	2.66
1921	—	155,190	15,718	0.71	78,830	6,778	2.29
1922	—	210,840	18,123	0.62	99,520	7,637	3.03
1923	—	157,780	10,967	1.01	80,430	6,697	3.26
1924	—	185,560	14,577	0.63	93,930	7,997	2.40
1925	—	171,290	14,033	0.96	93,710	8,409	2.47
1926	—	204,560	17,849	0.54	102,310	8,570	2.19
1927	—	185,580	14,364	0.70	105,230	8,959	2.47
1928	—	212,900	15,911	0.63	89,540	8,016	2.16
1929	—	226,570	18,386	0.69	95,060	8,279	2.47
1930	—	255,060	21,377	0.47	111,170	7,639	2.27
1931	—	253,610	19,478	0.40	121,670	8,647	1.61
1932	—	247,910	16,748	0.32	118,020	8,197	1.37
1933	—	218,250	14,096	0.37	97,200	6,295	1.34
1934	—	281,930	15,014	0.42	92,190	6,237	1.71
1935	—	268,220	16,592	0.38	101,400	6,674	1.49
1936	—	250,710	15,636	0.51	101,340	6,687	1.70
1937	—	254,890	17,732	0.42	104,020	7,158	1.89
1938	—	263,630	17,711	0.44	109,490	7,367	1.73
1939	—	319,100	18,858	0.48	133,800	9,439	1.37

Notes appear at end of table

TABLE Da821–836   Nectarines, strawberries, watermelon, and cantaloupe – acreage, production, and price:
1918–1999   *Continued*

Year	Strawberries Frozen production Da830 Thousand tons	Watermelon Acreage harvested Da831 [3] Acres	Watermelon Production Da832 [2,3,4] Thousand hundredweight	Watermelon Price Da833 [1,3,4] Dollars per hundredweight	Cantaloupe Acreage harvested Da834 [3,5] Acres	Cantaloupe Production Da835 [2,3,4,5] Thousand hundredweight	Cantaloupe Price Da836 [3,4,5] Dollars per hundredweight
1940	—	316,450	21,799	0.43	124,900	9,151	1.51
1941	—	305,600	18,269	0.54	124,950	9,489	1.67
1942	—	248,050	17,216	0.91	107,250	7,840	2.81
1943	—	203,100	16,732	1.69	82,850	7,558	4.98
1944	—	295,930	22,695	1.43	106,700	9,245	3.62
1945	—	348,100	24,358	1.54	119,800	9,453	3.68
1946	—	417,950	25,645	1.47	144,300	11,808	3.66
1947	—	383,850	26,203	1.18	141,300	10,917	3.88
1948	—	344,700	23,932	1.47	134,100	11,114	3.69
1949	—	383,800	25,692	1.15	128,300	10,913	3.27
1950	—	372,400	24,995	1.22	130,000	11,474	3.68
1951	—	349,200	25,769	1.38	119,800	11,303	3.83
1952	—	357,600	25,967	1.73	118,850	11,082	4.44
1953	—	424,850	29,289	1.55	125,870	12,197	4.31
1954	—	443,950	31,567	1.15	139,370	13,197	4.00
1955	—	433,400	34,156	1.29	138,070	12,937	4.18
1956	—	397,300	30,495	1.44	127,500	12,333	4.19
1957	—	393,100	27,487	1.69	119,850	11,110	5.13
1958	—	398,550	34,195	1.07	131,350	12,424	3.98
1959	—	327,990	26,995	1.74	123,850	12,870	4.38
1960	—	332,290	31,112	1.29	125,900	12,562	4.33
1961	—	307,580	29,083	1.58	120,450	12,765	5.01
1962	—	298,280	28,961	1.47	128,850	13,343	4.23
1963	—	286,310	31,102	1.44	122,150	13,409	4.96
1964	—	280,400	27,575	1.70	121,450	12,162	5.02
1965	—	286,320	29,603	1.60	109,600	11,439	5.51
1966	—	275,640	28,436	1.87	103,800	10,745	6.28
1967	—	273,260	27,790	2.10	107,200	12,539	6.26
1968	—	283,880	27,616	1.88	115,350	13,543	5.78
1969	—	272,400	25,950	2.05	124,300	13,697	5.61
1970	248	266,200	27,373	2.21	109,710	13,282	6.16
1971	260	252,400	27,094	2.51	100,400	12,382	6.54
1972	230	267,600	25,280	2.50	97,750	13,045	7.26
1973	240	240,400	26,170	2.95	93,000	11,302	8.07
1974	269	212,700	23,466	3.81	69,800	9,720	9.99
1975	275	210,700	24,395	4.00	75,660	9,858	10.50
1976	290	234,100	26,459	3.27	75,730	10,140	11.00
1977	331	225,200	26,885	3.44	80,000	10,899	10.60
1978	330	212,400	25,270	3.99	99,820	13,318	9.64
1979	319	205,300	24,076	4.55	91,420	12,421	11.30
1980	351	184,500	22,716	6.59	86,350 [6]	12,242	13.60
1981	371	203,600	26,128	6.09	—	13,346	14.10
1982	442	207,115	27,339	5.63	—	16,824	10.15
1983	447	191,971	25,340	6.47	—	14,537	11.70
1984	495	241,707	31,905	5.34	—	16,516	12.25
1985	509	218,979	30,438	4.94	—	18,743	9.45
1986	510	199,291	29,296	6.24	—	20,562	10.50
1987	559	205,187	28,931	7.13	—	20,273	9.80
1988	590	207,000	31,155	6.50	—	16,916	15.45
1989	571	208,479	30,949	5.23	—	21,714	12.55
1990	627	203,976	31,871	6.66	—	18,567	14.65
1991	684	190,765	30,974	8.87	—	16,640	12.25
1992	656	215,240	37,783	5.91	—	18,111	13.90
1993	—	205,430	36,920	6.90	—	18,980	15.60
1994	—	207,890	39,240	6.80	—	17,960	16.60
1995	—	203,880	39,420	8.90	—	18,960	18.20
1996	—	207,500	42,720	6.30	—	21,580	18.20
1997	—	—	39,920 [7]	7.64	—	20,840 [7]	18.00
1998	—	—	36,980 [7]	7.71	—	21,492 [7]	17.80
1999	—	—	41,320	6.49	—	22,980	17.10

Notes appear on next page

(continued)

TABLE Da821–836   Nectarines, strawberries, watermelon, and cantaloupe – acreage, production, and price: 1918–1999 *Continued*

[1] Method of determining price changes over time; see text.

[2] See text for information on excess cullage or on quantities not harvested or marketed for economic reasons.

[3] Data for 1918–1938 are not strictly comparable to later years; see text.

[4] Economic Research Service estimates, 1982–1991; see text.

[5] Crop coverage changes over time; see text.

[6] Preliminary.

[7] Data in original source have been revised.

Sources

Series Da821–822. U.S. National Agricultural Statistics Service, *Agricultural Statistics, 1956, 1967, 1970, 1975, 1982, 1987, 1992,* and *2000* editions.

Series Da823–825. *Agricultural Statistics, 1952, 1967, 1975, 1982, 1987, 1992,* and *2000* editions.

Series Da826–829. *Agricultural Statistics, 1967, 1975, 1982, 1987, 1992,* and *2000* editions.

Series Da830. U.S. Department of Agriculture, Economic Research Service (USDA ERS), *U.S.–Mexico Fruit and Vegetable Trade, 1970–1992,* March 1995, Table 46, downloaded October 15, 2000, from the U.S. Department of Agriculture, Economics and Statistics System.

Series Da831. 1918–1949, *Agricultural Statistics, 1952* and *1967* editions; 1950–1996, USDA ERS, *The U.S. Watermelon Industry,* October 1994, updated March 1998, Table A25, downloaded October 15, 2000, from the U.S. Department of Agriculture, Economics and Statistics System.

Series Da832 and Da835. 1918–1969, *Agricultural Statistics, 1952, 1967,* and *1977* editions; 1970–1981, *U.S.–Mexico Fruit and Vegetable Trade, 1970–1992,* March 1995, Tables 34 and 33, downloaded October 15, 2000, from the U.S. Department of Agriculture, Economics and Statistics System; 1982–1999, USDA ERS, *Vegetable Yearbook,* July 1997, updated August 2000, Tables 60 and 61, downloaded October 15, 2000, from the U.S. Department of Agriculture, Economics and Statistics System.

Series Da833 and Da836. 1918–1975, *Agricultural Statistics, 1952, 1967,* and *1977* editions; 1976–1999, *Vegetable Yearbook,* July 1997, updated August 2000, Tables 60 and 61, downloaded October 15, 2000, from the U.S. Department of Agriculture, Economics and Statistics System.

Series Da834. *Agricultural Statistics, 1952, 1967, 1974, 1978,* and *1981* editions.

Documentation

See the text for Table Da791–795.

Series Da821. Covers production having value. Includes production for all uses.

Series Da822. Fresh fruit prices are equivalent returns at first delivery point. Processing fruit prices are at first delivery point prior to 1963; beginning with 1963, they are equivalent returns at processing plant door.

Series Da824. Includes the following quantities not marketed, which were excluded in computing value (in thousand pounds): 11,000 in 1932; 10,100 in 1933; 2,900 in 1934; 4,800 in 1938; 1,000 in 1939; 3,960 in 1940; 7,668 in 1941; 26,316 in 1942; 720 in 1943; 324 in 1944; 360 in 1945; 1,800 in 1947; 1,440 in 1948; 1,106 in 1949; 2,880 in 1951; 4,248 in 1954; 6,483 in 1957; 700 in 1958; 500 in 1959; 7,700 in 1964; 30,112 in 1965; and 400 in 1966. Excludes the following quantities not harvested and not marketed because of economic conditions (in thousand hundredweight): 77 in 1964; 302 in 1965; 4 in 1966; 44 in 1967; 70 in 1969; 100 in 1970; 1 in 1977; 1 in 1978; 28 in 1979; 48 in 1980; 22 in 1981; 11 in 1982; 21 in 1983; 19 in 1984; 35 in 1985; 11 in 1986; 239 in 1987; 4 in 1988; 9 in 1989; 13 in 1990; 7 in 1991; 8 in 1992; 6 in 1993; and 50 in 1995. The official U.S. Department of Agriculture conversion factor estimates that one crate

of strawberries is equivalent to 36 pounds. Data from 1918 to 1938 were converted from crates to hundredweights by multiplying crates by 0.36.

Series Da825. Data from 1918 to 1938 were converted from dollars per crate to dollars per hundredweight by dividing dollars per crate by 0.36.

Series Da825, Da827, and Da829. Beginning with 1954, figures are fresh market price on an f.o.b. (free on board) basis. Beginning with 1964, figures are processing price at processing plant door; prior to 1964, average price received by growers at receiving point.

Series Da826–827. Figures are mostly for fresh market, but include some quantities used for processing in states for which processing estimates are not prepared.

Series Da826 and Da831–836. Data for 1918–1938 are not strictly comparable to later years. In the earlier period, estimates were frequently made only for well-recognized commercial areas from which substantial quantities were shipped – usually by rail – to distant terminal markets. In many states, local-market or market garden areas near large population centers were excluded from the 1918–1938 estimates.

Series Da830. Includes production for all uses.

Series Da832. Includes some quantities not marketed and excluded in computing value (in thousand short tons): 71 in 1930; 22 in 1931; 116 in 1932; 17 in 1933; 2 in 1934; 31 in 1935; 5 in 1936; 31 in 1937; 50 in 1938; 8 in 1939; 53 in 1940; 81 in 1947; 5 in 1949; 92 in 1950; 6 in 1951; 51 in 1954; 100 in 1955; 48 in 1956; 200 in 1958; 4 in 1959; 72 in 1960; 136 in 1962; and 96 in 1963. Excludes the following quantities not marketed (in thousand short tons): 3 in 1964; 2 in 1965; 30 in 1966; and 5 in 1968. The official U.S. Department of Agriculture conversion factor estimates that one watermelon is equivalent to 25 pounds (or 0.0125 short tons). Data from 1918 to 1938 were converted from melons to short tons by multiplying melons by 0.0125.

Series Da832–833 and Da835–836. Production data were estimated by the Economic Research Service (ERS) for 1982–1991 based on available state data adjusted to the national level. Includes all uses.

Series Da833. Beginning 1954, price figures are on an f.o.b. basis. The season-average price data for 1982–1991 was estimated by the ERS using state data. Beginning with 1991, the source is the National Agricultural Statistics Service (NASS). Data from 1918 to 1938 were converted from dollars per melon to dollars per hundredweight by dividing dollars per melon by 250.

Series Da834–836. Includes casaba, persian, honeyball, and honeydew melons (1918–1928); includes casaba and persian melons, but not honeyball or honeydew melons (1929–1969); excludes casaba, crenshaw, persian, honeyball, and honeydew melons (1966–1980).

Series Da835. Includes the following quantities not marketed, which were excluded in computing value (in thousand hundredweights): 266 in 1931; 1,155 in 1932; 291 in 1933; 210 in 1935; 249 in 1936; 897 in 1938; 100 in 1940; 191 in 1941; 17 in 1942; 12 in 1944; 23 in 1945; 55 in 1946; 33 in 1947; 144 in 1948; 63 in 1949; 63 in 1950; and 193 in 1962. Excludes the following quantities not harvested or not marketed because of economic conditions (in thousand hundredweights): 240 in 1965, 10 in 1971, 203 in 1973, and 46 in 1974. The official U.S. Department of Agriculture conversion factor (see *Agricultural Statistics, 1952*) estimates that one crate of cantaloupe is equivalent to 70 pounds (or 0.035 short tons). Note that the conversion factor changed later to one crate approximately equal to 83 pounds. Data from 1918 to 1938 were converted from crates to short tons by multiplying crates by 0.035.

Series Da836. Data from 1918 to 1938 were converted from dollars per crate to dollars per hundredweight by dividing dollars per crate by 0.70. The source for the season-average price data is the NASS, except 1982–1991, which was estimated by the ERS using state data.

TABLE Da837–843   Plums, prunes, and pears – production and price: 1909–1999

Contributed by Alan L. Olmstead and Paul W. Rhode

		Plums and prunes				Pears	
		California					
		Plums		Prunes, dry basis			
	U.S. production	Production	Price	Production	Price	Production	Price
	Da837 [1]	Da838 [1]	Da839 [2]	Da840 [1,3]	Da841	Da842 [1,3]	Da843 [2]
Year	Thousand short tons	Thousand short tons	Dollars per short ton	Thousand short tons	Dollars per short ton	Thousand short tons	Dollars per short ton
1909	—	21	55	75	65	226	—
1910	—	21	55	40	105	271	—
1911	—	22	76	95	115	300	—
1912	—	27	66	102	90	323	—
1913	—	24	72	48	105	266	—
1914	—	28	54	56	115	320	—
1915	—	32	40	92	95	306	—
1916	—	29	69	78	120	303	—
1917	—	41	63	109	140	339	—
1918	—	37	85	45	170	330	—
1919	494	44	86	140	240	366	82
1920	378	38	138	98	170	430	67
1921	382	44	76	100	145	284	72
1922	511	49	56	126	150	504	43
1923	504	71	52	114	100	426	56
1924	503	42	95	139	110	461	64
1925	504	54	69	146	120	496	60
1926	641	74	49	151	100	602	41
1927	750	58	79	225	75	449	63
1928	717	67	67	221	100	602	50
1929	566	40	113	103	160	534	70
1930	944	82	49	274	63	668	34
1931	757	65	42	214	50	622	31
1932	661	68	31	172	55	603	20
1933	649	57	37	182	80	591	28
1934	665	62	45	171	60	691	33
1935	906	48	54	258	58	638	30
1936	636	64	41	159	80	672	32
1937	786	66	58	249	54	719	31
1938	919	63	37	288	42	780	23
1939	750	71	46	185	67	720	30
1940	617	69	53	184	55	728	30
1941	660	71	63	188	75	717	42
1942	618	72	93	172	146	744	63
1943	703	76	169	196	184	596	96
1944	604	92	117	159	218	771	89
1945	784	71	138	226	210	800	80
1946	794	100	137	214	256	823	89
1947	674	74	157	200	148	838	70
1948	615	67	150	176	152	615	94
1949	635	90	105	151	168	795	38
1950	502	77	180	149	245	688	76
1951	639	97	144	176	171	701	90
1952	485	53	246	135	233	719	58
1953	547	84	161	146	222	677	67
1954	595	71	179	175	217	721	75
1955	518	86	174	131	277	717	72
1956	689	100	145	191	196	778	78
1957	573	81	204	165	201	763	66
1958	361	61	202	96	390	699	78
1959	536	93	155	139	361	722	72
1960	463	82	192	139	391	624	88
1961	511	87	188	139	333	659	92
1962	546	84	170	148	283	711	73
1963	490	106	162	133	305	472	111
1964	647	113	107	180	230	728	92

Notes appear at end of table

(continued)

TABLE Da837–843   Plums, prunes, and pears – production and price: 1909–1999   Continued

Year	Plums and prunes					Pears	
	U.S. production	California					
		Plums		Prunes, dry basis			
		Production	Price	Production	Price	Production	Price
	Da837 [1]	Da838 [1]	Da839 [2]	Da840 [1,3]	Da841	Da842 [1,3]	Da843 [2]
	Thousand short tons	Thousand short tons	Dollars per short ton	Thousand short tons	Dollars per short ton	Thousand short tons	Dollars per short ton
1965	606	113	97	167	240	500	132
1966	492	95	182	132	325	748	88
1967	584	98	180	164	276	464	164
1968	534	106	178	153	301	624	135
1969	496	67	237	130	288	727	101
1970	787	123	160	200	216	549	133
1971	582	101	229	131	287	749	95
1972	359	96	248	77	535	612	139
1973	783	97	321	205	462	730	138
1974	659	143	275	142	440	742	169
1975	656	124	279	149	402	748	143
1976	666	115	380	148	412	839	124
1977	727	157	313	159	499	782	146
1978	634	154	370	132	696	723	219
1979	661	175	277	136	812	855	204
1980	821	160	449	168	683	897	196
1981	765	198	309	160	654	897	187
1982	573	118	620	126	679	802	183
1983	674	159	435	145	667	774	170
1984	721	225	212	148	693	708	229
1985	648	167	514	141	680	745	269
1986	491	152	657	99	819	767	267
1987	977	245	308	229	732	938	198
1988	738	216	475	151	782	861	274
1989	1,018	216	445	226	779	917	277
1990	729	223	603	147	873	964	279
1991	831	218	449	187	940	904	303
1992	822	250	252	184	1,030	926	295
1993	588	185	508	121	1,120	948	245
1994	879	247	321	193	1,090	1,046	223
1995	744	124	950	181	1,040	948	272
1996	952	228	420	223	839	821	376
1997	899	246	312	205	883	1,043	276
1998	543 [4]	188	529	103	764	955 [4]	292
1999 [4]	773	196	419	173	—	982	304

[1] See text for information on excess cullage or on quantities not harvested for economic reasons.

[2] Method of determining price changes over time; see text.

[3] Conversion factors differ over time or among locations; see text.

[4] Data are preliminary.

Sources

Series Da837. 1919–1944, *Fruits (Noncitrus): Production, Farm Disposition, Value, and Utilization of Sales, 1889–1944*, Statistical Bulletin number CS-27, May 1948, p. 95; 1945–1949, *Fruits (Noncitrus): Production, Farm Disposition, Value, and Utilization of Sales, 1944–1949*, Statistical Bulletin number 114, October 1952, p. 36; 1950–1959, *Fruits (Noncitrus), by States, 1954–1959*, Statistical Bulletin number 292, August 1961, p. 94; 1960–1969, *Agricultural Statistics, 1967* and *1979* editions; 1970–1992, U.S. Department of Agriculture, Economic Research Service, *U.S.–Mexico Fruit and Vegetable Trade, 1970–1992*, March 1995, Table 44, downloaded January 12, 2001, from the U.S. Department of Agriculture, Economics and Statistics System; 1993–1999, *Agricultural Statistics, 2000* edition.

Series Da838–839. 1909–1944, U.S. Bureau of Agricultural Economics, *Fruits (Noncitrus): Production, Farm Disposition, Value, and Utilization of Sales, 1889–1944*, Statistical Bulletin number CS-27, May 1948, p. 96; 1945–1948, *Fruits (Noncitrus): Production, Farm Disposition, Value, and Utilization of Sales, 1944–1949*, Statistical Bulletin number 114, October 1952, p. 37;

1949–1953, *Fruits (Noncitrus): Production, Farm Disposition, Value, and Utilization of Sales, 1949–1955*, Statistical Bulletin number 192, p. 62; 1954–1958, *Fruits (Noncitrus): Production, Farm Disposition, Value, and Utilization of Sales, 1954–1959*, Statistical Bulletin number 292, p. 85; 1959–1999, U.S. Department of Agriculture, Economic Research Service, *Agricultural Statistics, 1974, 1982, 1992, 1995–96,* and *2000* editions.

Series Da840–841. 1909–1944, *Fruits (Noncitrus): Production, Farm Disposition, Value, and Utilization of Sales, 1889–1944*, Statistical Bulletin number CS-27, May 1948, p. 98; 1945–1948, *Fruits (Noncitrus): Production, Farm Disposition, Value, and Utilization of Sales, 1944–1949*, Statistical Bulletin number 114, p. 37; 1949–1953, *Fruits (Noncitrus): Production, Farm Disposition, Value, and Utilization of Sales, 1949–1955*, Statistical Bulletin number 192, p. 64; 1954–1958, *Fruits (Noncitrus): Production, Farm Disposition, Value, and Utilization of Sales, 1954–1959*, Statistical Bulletin number 292, p. 87; 1959–1999, *Agricultural Statistics, 1974, 1987, 1990,* and *2000* editions.

Series Da842. 1909–1944, *Fruits (Noncitrus): Production, Farm Disposition, Value, and Utilization of Sales, 1889–1944*, Statistical Bulletin number CS-27, May 1948, p. 46; 1945–1969, *Agricultural Statistics, 1967, 1974,* and *1978* editions; 1970–1992, *U.S.–Mexico Fruit and Vegetable Trade, 1970–1992*, March 1995, Table 43, downloaded January 12, 2001, from the U.S. Department of Agriculture, Economics and Statistics System; 1993–1999, *Agricultural Statistics, 2000.*

TABLE Da837–843   Plums, prunes, and pears – production and price: 1909–1999   *Continued*

Series Da843. 1919–1944, *Fruits (Noncitrus): Production, Farm Disposition, Value, and Utilization of Sales, 1889–1944,* Statistical Bulletin number CS-27, May 1948, p. 46; 1945–1999, *Agricultural Statistics, 1967, 1974, 1978, 1986, 1987, 1992, 1995–96,* and *2000* editions.

Documentation

See the text for Table Da791–795.

Series Da837. Includes production for all uses. Covers production from Michigan, Idaho, Washington, Oregon, and California. The following are estimates of plum and prune quantities not harvested from Idaho, Washington, Oregon, and California, on account of economic conditions, which are included in estimates of total production (in short tons): 2,000 in 1924; 1,000 in 1926; 3,000 in 1929; 56,500 in 1930; 7,000 in 1931; 37,000 in 1932; 10,500 in 1933; 8,200 in 1934; 9,600 in 1935; 3,400 in 1937; 183,300 in 1938; 25,700 in 1939; 33,600 in 1940; 30,500 in 1941; 22,900 in 1942; 5,330 in 1943; and 5,300 in 1944. The following are estimates of prune quantities harvested but not utilized because of abnormal cullage, which are included in estimates of production (from Idaho, Washington, and Oregon, in short tons): 400 in 1930; 5,000 in 1931; 1,100 in 1932; 4,800 in 1933; 2,300 in 1934; 600 in 1935; 500 in 1936; 1,600 in 1937; 2,300 in 1938; 3,200 in 1939; 400 in 1940; 4,300 in 1941; 600 in 1942; and 100 in 1943.

Series Da838–839. Includes some quantities of fresh prunes. Estimates of quantities not harvested on account of economic conditions that are included in estimates of total production (in short tons): 7,000 in 1931; 10,000 in 1932; 7,000 in 1933; 7,000 in 1939; 5,000 in 1940; 5,000 in 1941; 6,000 in 1942; and 2,000 in 1944. Prices are season average price for 1959–1976, and marketing year average price thereafter. Fresh fruit prices are equivalent returns at point of first sale. Prior to 1963, processing fruit prices were at first delivery point; beginning with 1963, they are equivalent returns at the processing plant door.

Series Da840–841. Covers all production utilized. Prior to 1944, production also includes the following estimates of quantities not harvested on account of economic conditions, in short tons (dry basis): 13,000 in 1930;

4,000 in 1932; 64,000 in 1938 (including 4,000 short tons lost in the drying process); 9,000 in 1940; 10,000 in 1941; and 1,000 in 1942. Through 1971, the drying ratio is approximately 2.5 pounds of fresh fruit to one pound of dried fruit; for 1972–1995 the drying ratio is approximately 3 pounds of fresh fruit to 1 pound of dried fruit. Prices in series Da841 represent equivalent returns at the processing plant door.

Series Da842. Includes production for all uses. The following are estimated quantities not harvested on account of economic conditions that are included in estimate of total production (New York, Pennsylvania, Ohio, Florida, Washington, Oregon, and California, in thousand short tons): 2 in 1927; 2 in 1928; 32 in 1930; 15 in 1931; 85 in 1932; 56 in 1933; 18 in 1934; 5 in 1935; 8 in 1936; 24 in 1937; 59 in 1938; 22 in 1939; 19 in 1940; 1 in 1941; 10 in 1942; 5 in 1943; and 11 in 1944. The following are estimated quantities harvested but not utilized because of abnormal cullage, which are included in estimates of total production (Washington and Oregon, in thousand short tons): 2 in 1935; 2 in 1937; 15 in 1938; 10 in 1939; 12 in 1940; and 4 in 1941. There are two official U.S. Department of Agriculture conversion factors for pears; one bushel of California pears is equivalent to 48 pounds (or 0.024 short tons), and one bushel of "other" pears is equivalent to 50 pounds (or 0.025 short tons). Data in bushels and in short tons from 1919–1961 provided an implied conversion rate of 1 bushel to 49.2 pounds (or 0.0246 short tons). Data from 1909–1918 were converted from bushels to short tons by multiplying bushels by 0.0246.

Series Da843. Figures are season average prices for 1959–1985, and marketing year average prices thereafter. Beginning with 1944, the price was obtained by weighting state prices by quantity sold; prior to 1944, prices were weighted by production. Figures are November 15 prices for 1919–1924, except for Washington, Oregon, and California. Fresh fruit prices are equivalent packinghouse-door returns for California, Oregon, and Washington, and the average price as sold for other states. Quantities processed are priced at the equivalent processing plant-door level. Data from 1919 to 1958 were converted from price per bushel to price per short ton by dividing price per bushel by 0.0246.

TABLE Da844–860 Sunflower seeds, oils, and lard – acreage, production, and price: 1962–1999

Contributed by Alan L. Olmstead and Paul W. Rhode

Year	Sunflower seeds Acreage harvested Da844 [1] (Thousand acres)	Sunflower seeds Production Da845 [1] (Thousand pounds)	Sunflower seeds Price Da846 [1] (Dollars per hundredweight)	Oil Production Da847 (Thousand hundredweight)	Oil Price Da848 (Dollars per hundredweight)	Corn oil Production Da849 (Million pounds)	Corn oil Price Da850 (Cents per pound)	Soybean oil Production Da851 (Million pounds)	Soybean oil Price Da852 (Cents per pound)	Linseed oil Production Da853 (Million pounds)	Linseed oil Price Da854 (Cents per pound)	Cottonseed oil Production Da855 (Million pounds)	Cottonseed oil Price Da856 [2] (Cents per pound)	Canola Seed production Da857 (Million pounds)	Canola Oil production Da858 (Million pounds)	Lard Production Da859 [3] (Million pounds)	Lard Price Da860 (Cents per pound)
1962	13	12,250	5.50	—	—	—	—	—	—	—	—	—	—	—	—	—	—
1963	30	29,100	4.35	—	—	—	—	—	—	—	—	—	—	—	—	—	—
1964	40	25,760	4.12	—	—	—	—	—	—	—	—	—	—	—	—	—	—
1965	46	38,050	4.87	—	—	—	—	5,800	11.83	—	—	—	—	—	—	—	—
1966	73	65,240	5.63	—	—	—	—	6,076	10.13	—	—	—	—	—	—	—	—
1967	216	223,960	4.82	—	—	—	—	6,032	8.42	—	—	—	—	—	—	—	—
1968	151	155,670	4.30	—	—	—	—	6,531	8.42	301	12.18	—	—	—	—	—	—
1969	185	171,430	4.59	—	—	—	—	7,904	11.18	290	11.85	—	—	—	—	—	—
1970	207	186,670	4.91	—	—	—	—	8,265	12.84	363	9.86	1,235	15.21	—	—	—	—
1971	392	411,680	5.09	—	—	—	—	7,892	11.27	428	8.80	1,308	12.27	—	—	—	—
1972	692	633,560	4.86	—	—	—	—	7,501	16.46	393	9.69	1,564	16.52	—	—	—	—
1973	666	719,070	8.52	—	—	—	—	8,995	31.53	344	27.67	1,552	33.32	—	—	—	—
1974	548	524,705	15.90	—	—	—	—	7,375	30.69	263	45.60	1,335	31.71	—	—	—	—
1975	709	786,010	10.80	—	—	—	—	9,630	18.30	231	32.20	920	23.46	—	—	1,060	17.8
1976	810	857,100	11.00	—	—	—	—	8,578	23.87	217	28.18	1,198	24.81	—	—	1,038	21.3
1977	2,205	2,760,470	10.20	—	—	—	—	10,288	24.51	232	25.06	1,453	25.43	—	—	1,006	23.2
1978	2,798	3,817,920	10.70	—	—	737	32.76	11,323	27.15	259	24.21	1,282	31.63	—	—	1,129	25.6
1979	5,410	7,296,110	9.05	4,938	26.08	791	27.38	12,105	24.32	256	30.10	1,423	25.34	—	—	1,207	20.7
1980	3,683	3,741,640	11.10	6,570	26.94	864	25.22	11,270	22.73	251	30.02	1,195	25.86	—	—	1,159	20.3
1981	3,811	4,487,410	10.80	3,020	24.95	873	23.42	10,979	18.95	237	30.50	1,551	20.10	—	—	1,011	—
1982	4,724	5,332,820	8.88	6,680	22.45	981	23.82	12,040	20.62	182	25.20	1,134	21.80	—	—	973	28.2
1983	3,063	3,198,500	13.10	4,497	33.61	1,054	28.62	10,872	30.55	265	30.10	777	32.80	—	—	939	19.6
1984	3,692	3,744,530	11.10	4,828	29.98	1,194	29.14	11,468	29.51	194	32.00	1,174	29.20	—	—	927	13.7
1985	2,844	3,153,020	7.93	5,842	19.10	1,253	18.46	11,617	18.00	205	30.80	1,070	16.91	—	—	876	14.8
1986	1,955	2,675,750	6.90	5,864	16.01	1,400	21.43	12,783	15.40	201	26.30	781	17.67	—	—	863	16.3
1987	1,775	2,608,150	8.34	8,311	23.59	1,435	23.27	12,974	22.67	217	24.70	1,204	21.67	—	—	932	14.1
1988	1,921	1,792,090	12.10	5,181	22.68	1,415	21.01	11,737	21.10	170	39.40	1,243	19.71	—	—	935	13.3
1989	1,786	1,759,760	10.60	4,740	24.40	1,470	24.82	13,004	22.30	165	40.20	1,039	23.30	95	130	919	13.5
1990	1,851	2,274,405	10.80	5,357	23.59	1,656	27.50	13,408	21.00	176	38.00	1,154	22.30	97	18	952	13.3
1991	2,673	3,613,030	8.69	9,105	21.59	1,821	25.82	14,345	19.10	182	32.00	1,279	20.10	191	32	1,025	15.4
1992	2,043	2,564,985	9.74	7,297	25.31	1,878	20.90	13,778	21.40	172	31.50	1,137	30.07	144	49	1,005	17.5
1993	2,486	2,572,063	12.90	5,798	30.98	1,906	27.17	13,951	27.10	174	31.80	1,119	30.30	252	406	1,034	20.3
1994	3,430	4,835,825	10.70	11,640	28.21	2,227	27.17	15,613	27.60	171	33.70	1,312	29.23	447	299	1,040	21.9
1995	3,368	4,009,332	11.50	8,598	25.40	2,139	26.47	15,240	24.75	180	36.50	1,229	26.53	548	356	998	23.4
1996	2,479	3,559,343	11.70	8,400	22.54	2,231	25.24	15,752	22.50	200	36.00	1,216	25.58	481	342	993	17.9
1997	2,792	3,676,952	11.60	9,590 [4]	27.58	2,335	24.05	18,143	25.84	210	36.30	1,223	28.84	781 [4]	451	1,091	—
1998	3,476	5,246,701	10.20	11,243 [4]	20.23 [4]	2,374	28.94	18,105 [4]	19.90 [4]	212	37.75	820 [4]	28.00 [4]	1,589 [4]	556 [4]	—	—
1999	—	—	—	—	—	2,420	—	—	—	—	—	—	—	—	—	—	—

[1] 1975–1976, includes only North Dakota and Minnesota; 1977–1987, also includes South Dakota and Texas; 1988–1990, also includes Kansas; beginning 1991, includes all states except Alaska and Hawai'i.

[2] Prime Bleachable Summer Yellow basis, Greenwood, Mississippi, beginning 1992.

[3] Economic Research Service estimates after 1989; U.S. Census Bureau ended publication of lard production in July 1989.

[4] Preliminary.

Sources

Series Da844–846. 1962–1974, U.S. National Agricultural Statistics Service, *Agricultural Statistics 1980*; 1975–1998, U.S. National Agricultural Statistics Service, Crops Branch, Field Crops Section, *Track Records: United States Crop Production*, March 1999, downloaded October 3, 2000, from the U.S. Department of Agriculture, Economics and Statistics System.

Series Da847–848. U.S. Department of Agriculture, Economic Research Service, *Oil Crops Yearbook*, January 1998, updated November 1999, Table 36, downloaded October 3, 2000, from the U.S. Department of Agriculture, Economics and Statistics System.

Series Da849–850. U.S. Department of Agriculture, Economic Research Service, *Oil Crops Yearbook*, January 1998, updated November 1999, Table 10, downloaded October 3, 2000, from the U.S. Department of Agriculture, Economics and Statistics System.

Series Da851–852. U.S. Department of Agriculture, Economic Research Service, *Oil Crops Yearbook*, January 1998, updated November 1999, Table 18, downloaded October 3, 2000, from the U.S. Department of Agriculture, Economics and Statistics System.

Series Da853–854. U.S. Department of Agriculture, Economic Research Service, *Oil Crops Yearbook*, January 1998, updated November 1999, Table 15, downloaded October 3, 2000, from the U.S. Department of Agriculture, Economics and Statistics System.

Series Da855–856. U.S. Department of Agriculture, Economic Research Service, *Oil Crops Yearbook*, January 1998, updated November 1999, Table 28, downloaded October 3, 2000, from the U.S. Department of Agriculture, Economics and Statistics System.

Series Da857. U.S. Department of Agriculture, Economic Research Service, *Oil Crops Yearbook*, January 1998, updated November 1999, Table 37, downloaded October 3, 2000, from the U.S. Department of Agriculture, Economics and Statistics System.

Series Da858. U.S. Department of Agriculture, Economic Research Service, *Oil Crops Yearbook*, January 1998, updated November 1999, Table 38, downloaded October 3, 2000, from the U.S. Department of Agriculture, Economics and Statistics System.

Series Da859–860. U.S. Department of Agriculture, Economic Research Service, *Oil Crops Yearbook*, January 1998, updated November 1999, Table 51, downloaded October 3, 2000, from the U.S. Department of Agriculture, Economics and Statistics System.

Documentation

Series Da847. Figures converted from thousands of metric tons to thousand hundredweight by multiplying thousands of metric tons by 22.046.

Series Da847–852. Year beginning October 1.

Series Da848. Average price of crude sunflowerseed oil, Minneapolis. Figures converted from price per metric ton to price per hundredweight by dividing price per metric ton by 22.046.

Series Da850. Average price of corn oil, Chicago.

Series Da852. Price of crude soybean oil, Decatur, Illinois.

Series Da854. Price of linseed oil, Minneapolis.

Series Da855. Year beginning October 1.

Series Da856. Average price of cottonseed oil, Valley Points. Data are for year beginning October 1.

Series Da857–858. Year beginning June 1.

Series Da860. Loose, average wholesale, tanks, Chicago.

TABLE Da861–876 Almonds, hazelnuts, macadamia nuts, pecans, and walnuts – acreage, production, and price: 1909–1999

Contributed by Alan L. Olmstead and Paul W. Rhode

	Almonds, California					Hazelnuts, Oregon and Washington			Macadamia nuts, Hawai'i			Pecans		Walnuts, California		
	In-shell			Shelled												
	Bearing acreage	Production	Price	Production	Price	Bearing acreage	Production	Price	Bearing acreage	Production	Price	Production	Price	Bearing acreage	Production	Price
	Da861	Da862	Da863 [1]	Da864 [2]	Da865 [2]	Da866	Da867 [3]	Da868 [1]	Da869	Da870 [3]	Da871	Da872 [4]	Da873 [1,4]	Da874	Da875	Da876
Year	Thousand acres	Short tons	Dollars per short ton	Million pounds	Cents per pound	Acres	Short tons	Dollars per short ton	Acres	Thousand pounds	Cents per pound	Thousand pounds	Cents per pound	Acres	Short tons	Dollars per short ton
1909	—	1,700	—	—	—	—	—	—	—	—	—	—	—	—	9,800	—
1910	—	3,300	—	—	—	—	—	—	—	—	—	—	—	—	10,000	—
1911	—	1,700	—	—	—	—	—	—	—	—	—	—	—	—	12,800	—
1912	—	3,000	—	—	—	—	—	—	—	—	—	—	—	—	13,000	—
1913	—	1,300	—	—	—	—	—	—	—	—	—	—	—	—	21,400	—
1914	—	2,300	—	—	—	—	—	—	—	—	—	—	—	—	9,600	—
1915	—	3,500	—	—	—	—	—	—	—	—	—	—	—	—	15,200	—
1916	—	3,400	—	—	—	—	—	—	—	—	—	—	—	—	15,300	—
1917	—	4,000	—	—	—	—	—	—	—	—	—	—	—	—	17,000	—
1918	—	5,100	—	—	—	—	—	—	—	—	—	—	—	—	22,000	—
1919	—	7,900	440	—	—	—	—	—	—	—	—	69,110	19.5	—	30,000	550
1920	—	6,000	360	—	—	—	—	—	—	—	—	10,375	25.7	—	22,700	400
1921	—	6,200	320	—	—	—	—	—	—	—	—	48,155	17.6	—	23,000	400
1922	—	9,000	290	—	—	—	—	—	—	—	—	11,355	26.5	—	29,000	360
1923	—	11,000	260	—	—	—	—	—	—	—	—	58,030	19.3	—	26,500	400
1924	—	8,000	300	—	—	—	—	—	—	—	—	37,998	23.4	—	24,200	460
1925	—	7,500	400	—	—	—	—	—	—	—	—	52,463	22.1	—	36,000	440
1926	—	16,000	300	—	—	—	—	—	—	—	—	95,861	15.6	—	15,300	480
1927	—	12,000	320	—	—	—	60	320	—	—	—	36,504	20.6	—	51,000	330
1928	—	14,000	340	—	—	—	200	380	—	—	—	68,550	16.6	—	25,900	420
1929	—	4,700	480	—	—	—	200	300	—	—	—	53,340	14.7	—	42,000	320
1930	—	13,500	200	—	—	—	300	340	—	—	—	57,135	14.9	—	29,400	410
1931	—	14,800	176	—	—	—	420	250	—	—	—	88,463	7.8	—	31,600	219
1932	—	14,000	165	—	—	—	490	202	—	—	—	68,234	6.0	—	45,900	175
1933	—	12,900	186	—	—	—	1,070	297	—	—	—	78,812	8.0	—	32,700	222
1934	—	12,000	180	—	—	—	1,210	202	—	—	—	56,172	12.6	—	44,000	187
1935	—	12,700	280	—	—	—	1,240	263	—	—	—	124,485	6.8	—	53,300	201
1936	—	10,700	402	—	—	—	2,100	270	—	—	—	59,787	12.4	—	44,200	216
1937	—	24,600	275	—	—	—	2,570	217	—	—	—	107,190	7.7	—	59,800	180
1938	—	18,400	258	—	—	—	2,440	225	—	—	—	74,323	9.4	—	49,000	222
1939	—	28,700	209	—	—	—	3,890	226	—	—	—	97,060	9.7	—	57,400	168
1940	—	15,000	324	—	—	—	3,210	250	—	—	—	122,884	8.9	—	46,400	233
1941	—	9,500	704	—	—	—	5,750	306	—	—	—	121,781	10.3	—	63,000	253
1942	—	31,500	442	—	—	—	4,270	352	—	—	—	77,374	17.1	—	57,600 [6]	308
1943	—	20,500	732	—	—	—	7,030	499	—	—	—	133,042	23.0	—	58,500	483
1944	—	31,700	744	—	—	—	6,520	540	—	—	—	142,104	21.5	—	65,000	446
1945	—	32,000	720	—	—	—	5,320	551	—	630	15.2	138,854	23.8	—	64,000	514
1946	—	47,200	486	—	—	—	8,450	384	—	680	16.9	76,225	33.7	—	63,000	570
1947	—	35,700	558	—	—	—	8,800	252	—	—	16.9	119,602	22.3	—	59,000	388
1948	—	36,500	422	—	—	—	6,380	259	—	700	17.0	176,043	12.2	—	62,000	442
1949	—	43,300	330	—	—	—	10,800	219	—	680	16.9	125,690	18.8	—	80,200	363

Almonds, California — Hazelnuts, Oregon and Washington — Macadamia nuts, Hawai'i — Pecans — Walnuts, California

Year	Da861 Bearing acreage (Thousand acres)	Da862 In-shell Production (Short tons)	Da863 In-shell Price [1] (Dollars per short ton)	Da864 Shelled Production [2] (Million pounds)	Da865 Shelled Price [2] (Cents per pound)	Da866 Bearing acreage (Acres)	Da867 Production [3] (Short tons)	Da868 Price [1] (Dollars per short ton)	Da869 Bearing acreage (Acres)	Da870 Production [3] (Thousand pounds)	Da871 Price (Cents per pound)	Da872 Production [4] (Thousand pounds)	Da873 Price [1,4] (Cents per pound)	Da874 Bearing acreage [1] (Acres)	Da875 Production (Short tons)	Da876 Price (Dollars per short ton)
1950	—	37,700	546	—	—	—	6,570	350	—	755	17.0	124,630	28.8	—	58,000	392
1951	—	42,700	472	—	—	—	6,740	351	—	850	16.9	156,735	19.7	—	68,300	440
1952	—	36,400	464	—	—	—	11,790	298	—	965	17.1	151,436	22.1	—	75,600	400
1953	—	38,600	476	—	—	—	4,900	344	—	970	17.0	214,170	16.3	—	54,800	415
1954	—	43,200	498	—	—	—	8,620	320	—	930	17.1	94,600	28.6	—	67,000	360
1955	—	38,300	861	—	—	—	7,710	420	—	903	17.9	147,300	32.8	—	72,000	555
1956	—	58,600	804	—	—	—	3,040	510	—	1,027	18.4	174,400	18.5	—	69,000	442
1957	—	37,500	505	—	—	—	12,510	300	—	1,329	18.7	141,600	23.7	—	61,300	427
1958	—	19,800	772	—	—	—	7,540	380	—	1,832	18.5	173,350	28.1	—	82,200	377
1959	—	82,800	466	—	—	—	10,100	376	—	2,112	18.2	145,500	32.5	—	58,500	483
1960	—	53,000	526	—	—	—	8,950	420	—	2,579	18.4	187,500	31.0	—	70,300	535
1961	—	66,400	561	—	—	—	11,760	380	—	3,761	18.5	253,550	18.1	—	61,200	473
1962	—	48,000	654	—	—	—	7,780	440	—	5,194	18.4	75,300	35.2	—	77,000	469
1963	—	59,700	591	—	—	—	6,960	470	2,390	6,011	17.7	376,400	18.4	—	79,300	460
1964	—	75,400	630	—	—	—	8,090	440	2,520	7,655	15.6	178,600	22.6	—	86,100	458
1965	—	72,900	617	80	56.5	—	7,740	450	2,780	8,538	19.4	251,100	17.9	—	79,000	432
1966	—	85,100	610	95	54.4	—	12,220	391	2,950	8,726	21.0	161,600	28.9	—	92,000	460
1967	—	76,600	582	83	53.8	—	7,540	492	3,340	7,972	24.6	231,900	33.6	—	74,000	560
1968	—	74,500	597	80	55.3	—	7,600	518	3,680	10,444	22.8	192,500	37.5	—	92,000	650
1969	—	122,000	606	132	56.0	—	7,400	550	4,030	10,057	24.6	226,100	29.8	—	103,000	420
1970	170	124,000	646	149	53.8	16,300	9,260	570	4,115	13,216	21.7	155,100	39.0	—	108,000	407
1971	188	134,000	650	162	53.8	16,600	11,370	414	4,900	14,448	24.7	246,200	33.0	—	135,000	420
1972	199	125,000	785	151	65.0	17,000	10,150	508	5,000	13,110	23.3	183,100	42.4	—	116,000	564
1973	214	134,000	1,490	155	128.8	17,000	12,250	573	5,080	12,124	25.5	275,700	36.7	—	174,000	605
1974	231	189,000	900	230	74.0	16,900	6,700	560	5,760	16,370	32.0	137,100	47.2	146,500	155,000	419
1975	249	160,000	740	186	63.7	17,800	12,120	610	6,080	18,210	31.6	246,800	39.8	150,400	198,000	456
1976	258	233,000	810	284	64.8	17,900	7,170	640	6,300	18,990	36.9	103,100	81.5	157,600	183,000	627
1977	277	249,000 [5]	1,030	313	84.5	17,600	11,750	687	6,300	19,680	40.8	236,600	57.7	158,200	192,000	725
1978	308	—	—	181	145.0	17,600	14,050	806	9,200	20,980	53.8	249,900	60.5	163,200	160,000	1,302
1979	324	—	—	376	153.0	17,600	13,000	951	9,600	26,660	62.9	210,600	55.4	165,800	208,000	847
1980	327	—	—	322	147.0	22,000	15,400	1,152	10,000	33,390	72.4	183,500	78.1	169,800	197,000	936
1981	326	—	—	408	78.0	22,000	14,700	786	10,000	33,360	79.3	339,100	54.5	176,300	225,000	1,014
1982	339	—	—	347	94.0	22,000	18,800	680	10,200	36,720	73.9	218,600	67.5	176,000	234,000	1,020
1983	360	—	—	242	104.0	21,300	8,200	558	10,600	36,420	65.7	270,000	58.7	181,400	199,000	631
1984	381	—	—	590	77.4	22,000	13,400	621	12,000	37,700	69.2	232,400	62.3	179,200	213,000	730
1985	409	—	—	465	80.0	23,300	24,600	680	13,500	42,000	72.5	244,400	68.0	179,000	219,000	798
1986	416	—	—	250	192.0	24,900	15,100	726	14,400	44,000	80.0	272,700	72.1	180,000	180,000	1,080
1987	417	—	—	660	100.0	25,800	21,800	959	15,600	42,700	84.0	262,200	53.1	176,000	247,000	984
1988	419	—	—	590	105.0	26,500	16,500	853	16,600	45,500	90.0	308,200	54.1	177,000	209,000	922
1989	411	—	—	490	102.0	27,460	13,000	820	18,200	50,500	89.0	250,500	71.5	179,000	229,000	1,070
1990	411	—	—	660	93.0	27,300	21,700	784	18,400	50,000	82.0	205,000	121.0	181,000	227,000	1,040
1991	405	—	—	490	119.0	27,470	25,500	726	18,200	49,500	70.0	299,000	104.0	181,000	259,000	1,060
1992	401	—	—	548	130.0	27,030	27,700	552	17,500	48,000	68.0	166,000	145.0	178,000	203,000	1,410
1993	413	—	—	490	194.0	27,030	41,000	633	18,500	48,500	68.0	365,000	58.6	185,000	260,000	1,390
1994	433	—	—	735	134.0	27,550	21,200	835	18,500	52,500	69.0	199,000	104.0	189,000	232,000	1,030

Notes appear at end of table

(continued)

TABLE Da861-876   Almonds, hazelnuts, macadamia nuts, pecans, and walnuts – acreage, production, and price: 1909–1999   *Continued*

	Almonds, California					Hazelnuts, Oregon and Washington			Macadamia nuts, Hawai'i			Pecans		Walnuts, California		
	In-shell			Shelled												
Year	Bearing acreage Da861	Production Da862	Price Da863 [1]	Production Da864 [2]	Price Da865	Bearing acreage Da866	Production Da867 [3]	Price Da868 [1]	Bearing acreage Da869	Production Da870 [3]	Price Da871	Production Da872 [4]	Price Da873 [1,4]	Bearing acreage Da874	Production Da875	Price Da876
	Thousand acres	Short tons	Dollars per short ton	Million pounds	Cents per pound	Acres	Short tons	Dollars per short ton	Acres	Thousand pounds	Cents per pound	Thousand pounds	Cents per pound	Acres	Short tons	Dollars per short ton
1995	418	—	—	370	248.0	27,980	39,000	913	19,300	51,000	74.0	267,500	101.0	193,000	234,000	1,400
1996	428	—	—	510	208.0	28,600	19,000	860	19,200	56,500	78.0	209,500	64.1	192,000	208,000	1,580
1997	442	—	—	759	156.0	29,000	47,000	899	19,200	58,000	75.0	335,000	77.4	193,000	269,000	1,430
1998	460	—	—	520	141.0	29,530	15,500	964	19,200	57,500	65.0	146,400	121.0	193,000	227,000	1,050
1999	480	—	—	830	85.0	29,200	38,000	882	18,900	53,000	67.0	341,700	83.3		283,000 [7]	—

1 Method of determining price changes over time; see text.

2 Price is based on edible portion of the crop only. Inedible quantities of no value are included in production figures beginning 1982. See text.

3 See text for information on excess cullage or quantities not harvested for economic reasons.

4 Production and price for North Carolina, South Carolina, Georgia, Florida, Alabama, Mississippi, Arkansas, Louisiana, Oklahoma, Texas, and, through 1943, Illinois and Missouri. California added to program in 1988. Arizona, Kansas, Missouri, and Tennessee added to program in 1989. Missouri and Tennessee discontinued in 1996.

5 Data in original source appear to be in error but cannot be corrected.

6 Includes 2,500 short tons unharvested on account of economic conditions and/or excess cullage of harvested nuts.

7 Preliminary.

Sources

Series Da861. 1970–1974, U.S. Department of Agriculture, Economic Research Service (USDA ERS), *Fruit and Tree Nuts, Situation and Outlook Report Yearbook*, August 1990, p. 63; 1975–1989, *Fruit and Tree Nuts, Situation and Outlook Report Yearbook*, September 1995, p. 58; 1990–1999, USDA ERS, *Agricultural Statistics, 2000*.

Series Da862–863. 1909–1918, U.S. Department of Agriculture, Statistical Reporting Service, *Tree Nuts by States, 1909–65, Revised Estimates*, Statistical Bulletin number 473, p. 3; 1919–1977, USDA ERS, *Agricultural Statistics, 1952, 1967 and 1978* editions.

Series Da864–865. USDA ERS, *Agricultural Statistics, 1982, 1992, and 2000* editions.

Series Da866. 1970–1977, *Fruit and Tree Nuts, Situation and Outlook Report Yearbook*, August 1990, p. 65; 1978–1999, USDA ERS, *Fruit Situation and Outlook Yearbook*, December 2000, Table E-9, downloaded January 19, 2001, from the U.S. Department of Agriculture, Economics and Statistics System.

Series Da867–868. 1927–1930, *Tree Nuts by States, 1909–65, Revised Estimates*, Statistical Bulletin number 473, p. 6; 1931–1999, *Agricultural Statistics, 1967, 1982, 1992, and 2000* editions.

Series Da869. *Agricultural Statistics, 1978, 1982, 1992, and 2000* editions.

Series Da870–871. 1946–1962, *Tree Nuts by States, 1909–65, Revised Estimates*, Statistical Bulletin number 473, p. 10; 1963–1999, *Agricultural Statistics, 1978, 1982, 1992, and 2000* editions.

Series Da872–873. *Agricultural Statistics, 1952, 1967, 1982, 1992, and 2000* editions.

Series Da874. 1970–1974, *Fruit and Tree Nuts, Situation and Outlook Report Yearbook*, August 1990, p. 69; 1975–1989, *Fruit and Tree Nuts, Situation and Outlook Report Yearbook*, September 1995, p. 55, Table E-1; 1990–1998, *Fruit and Tree Nuts, Situation and Outlook Report Yearbook*, October 1999, p. 68, Table E-17.

Series Da875. 1909–1918, U.S. Department of Agriculture, Statistical Reporting Service, *Tree Nuts by States, 1909–65, Revised Estimates*, Statistical Bulletin number 473, p. 51; 1919–1999, USDA ERS, *Agricultural Statistics, 1952, 1967, 1982, 1992, and 2000* editions.

Series Da876. USDA ERS, *Agricultural Statistics, 1952, 1967, 1982, 1992, and 2000* editions.

Documentation

Figures include nuts for all uses. Estimates for tree nuts are for in-shell nuts. Production estimates are the quantity sold or utilized. Commercial production of almonds, hazelnuts, and walnuts is limited to the Pacific Coast states. Commercial production of macadamia nuts is limited to Hawai'i. Almond production is limited almost entirely to California. Most of the country's hazelnuts are produced in Oregon; the rest are produced in Washington. English walnuts are produced in both California and Oregon, with most of the production in California. Pecan growing is limited to the Southeastern, South Central, and Southwestern states.

Series Da863. Equivalent returns for bulk nuts at first delivery point, beginning with 1949. Prior years are all methods of sales.

Series Da864. Included in production are inedible quantities of no value as follows (million pounds): 16.0 in 1982; 19.0 in 1983; 13.5 in 1984; 14.3 in 1985; 9.8 in 1986; 12.0 in 1987; 18.5 in 1988; 18.5 in 1989; 17.0 in 1990; 15.9 in 1991; 16.2 in 1992; 10.3 in 1993; 14.7 in 1994; 14.8 in 1995; 20.4 in 1996; 15.0 in 1997; 21.0 in 1998; and 33.2 in 1999.

Series Da867. Production is the quantity sold or utilized. Includes the following quantities unharvested on account of economic conditions (short tons): Oregon – 100 in 1942; 100 in 1943; 100 in 1944; 200 in 1948; 100 in 1949; 650 in 1950; 250 in 1951; 220 in 1952; 100 in 1953; 150 in 1954; and 200 in 1957; Washington – 120 in 1948; 110 in 1949; 130 in 1950; and 40 in 1951. Excludes unharvested production for Oregon as follows: 500 short tons in 1974.

Series Da868. Equivalent returns per ton at first delivery point beginning with 1949. Prior years are all methods of sales. Total U.S. prices obtained by weighting state prices by quantity sold from 1944 to date; prior to 1944, weighted by production.

Series Da870. Additional quantities of nuts not harvested for economic reasons and excess cullage of harvested nuts are as follows (thousands of pounds): 10 in 1956; 14 in 1957; 4 in 1958; 2 in 1959; 30 in 1960; 10 in 1961; 4 in 1963; 217 in 1964; 111 in 1965; and 150 in 1966.

Series Da871. Price per pound is derived from value of sales and the quantity sold.

Series Da873. November 1 price for 1922; December 1 price for 1923–1936. Through 1943, weighted by production; thereafter, obtained by weighting state prices by quantity sold.

Series Da875. Production is the quantity sold or utilized.

Series Da876. Equivalent returns for bulk nuts at first delivery point.

TABLE Da877–884   Greenhouse and nursery crops – grower cash receipts: 1960–1996

Contributed by Alan L. Olmstead and Paul W. Rhode

	Total greenhouse and nursery crops	Floriculture crops						Environmental horticulture crops
		Total	Cut flowers	Plants			Cut cultivated greens	
				Flowering	Foliage	Bedding and garden		
	Da877	Da878 [1]	Da879	Da880	Da881	Da882	Da883	Da884
Year	Thousand dollars	Thousand dollars	Thousand dollars	Thousand dollars	Thousand dollars	Thousand dollars	Thousand dollars	Thousand dollars
1960	661,308	—	—	—	—	—	—	—
1961	678,984	—	—	—	—	—	—	—
1962	709,479	—	—	—	—	—	—	—
1963	726,295	—	—	—	—	—	—	—
1964	771,552	—	—	—	—	—	—	—
1965	823,058	—	—	—	—	—	—	—
1966	826,659	182,565	142,702	—	23,988	—	—	644,094
1967	860,924	191,774	147,519	—	26,079	—	—	669,150
1968	894,833	213,183	167,209	—	26,412	—	—	681,650
1969	928,233	249,939	198,843	—	29,158	—	—	678,294
1970	958,375	250,157	198,559	—	27,073	—	—	708,218
1971	1,014,314	268,099	203,710	—	37,586	—	—	746,215
1972	1,120,956	300,326	221,230	—	48,428	—	—	820,630
1973	1,322,917	329,682	227,604	—	67,982	—	—	993,235
1974	1,466,515	386,595	234,420	—	113,503	—	—	1,079,920
1975	1,689,422	420,399	193,264	—	184,898	—	—	1,269,023
1976	2,039,231	690,931	209,136	144,274	243,427	94,094	—	1,348,300
1977	2,251,465	760,169	213,490	156,403	275,300	114,976	—	1,491,296
1978	2,637,342	814,786	230,655	172,473	281,919	129,739	—	1,822,556
1979	2,983,313	858,228	242,701	182,603	283,928	148,996	—	2,125,085
1980	3,418,788	953,286	250,093	209,931	312,968	180,294	—	2,465,502
1981	3,656,621	1,022,187	252,759	232,346	329,160	207,922	—	2,634,434
1982	4,015,485	—	—	—	—	—	—	—
1983	4,529,351	—	—	—	—	—	—	—
1984	5,175,509	1,272,598	271,317	226,517	429,641	345,123	—	3,902,911
1985	5,407,382	1,685,360	371,509	291,334	468,495	487,289	66,733	3,722,022
1986	5,983,052	1,906,937	359,826	388,727	521,374	560,126	76,884	4,076,115
1987	6,736,606	2,293,449	439,473	511,169	515,332	739,004	88,471	4,443,157
1988	7,248,384	2,293,248	457,854	507,731	481,631	755,261	90,761	4,955,136
1989	7,776,728	2,504,996	482,531	538,227	488,851	896,536	110,517	5,271,732
1990	8,676,784	2,652,007	467,720	550,176	474,930	829,103	106,584	6,024,777
1991	9,034,986	2,795,438	471,556	569,163	447,567	942,449	110,039	6,239,548
1992	9,285,078	3,022,388	458,455	645,989	427,009	1,118,171	111,524	6,262,690
1993	9,588,379	3,073,126	423,911	683,346	417,049	1,170,011	115,979	6,515,253
1994	10,007,196	3,246,912	442,297	662,490	489,306	1,280,087	119,247	6,760,284
1995	10,423,121	3,328,632	423,630	681,107	498,969	1,356,967	113,124	7,094,489
1996	10,912,455	3,421,083	446,500	686,191	507,897	1,412,955	121,015	7,491,372

[1] Data for 1986–1991 include twenty-eight crops in twenty-eight states; data for 1992–1996 include thirty-six states; other years are not comparable. Data include only commercial growers with $10,000 or more in gross sales.

Sources

Series Da877. 1960–1965, U.S. Department of Agriculture, Economic Research Service (USDA ERS), *Floriculture and Environmental Horticulture Products: A Production and Marketing Review*, July 1990, Table 1, downloaded January 19, 2001, from the U.S. Department of Agriculture, Economics and Statistics System; 1966–1996, USDA ERS, *Floriculture and Environmental Horticulture*, February 1998, Table 4, downloaded January 19, 2001, from the U.S. Department of Agriculture, Economics and Statistics System.

Series Da878–884. USDA ERS, *Floriculture and Environmental Horticulture*, February 1998, Table 4, downloaded January 19, 2001, from the U.S. Department of Agriculture, Economics and Statistics System.

Documentation

Greenhouse and nursery production is concentrated in the West and the South, owing mostly to climatic factors, but also owing to demand factors stemming from proximity to population centers. However, greenhouse and nursery production is also important in the Northeast and the Midwest, and has also been increasing in states with minor production. Ten states account for more than two thirds of U.S. output. The most important states ranked by their respective share (percent) of U.S. receipts are: California (20), Florida (11), North Carolina and Texas (8 each), Ohio and Oregon (5 each), and Michigan, Pennsylvania, Oklahoma, and New York (2–4 each).

Series Da877. Includes all floriculture and environmental horticulture crops except cut Christmas trees, seeds, and food crops grown under cover. This series is the total of series Da878 and Da884.

Series Da878. Includes cut flowers, potted flowering and foliage plants, bedding plants, and cut cultivated greens. This total, Floriculture crops, does not equal the sum of these parts.

Series Da884. Includes greenhouse and nursery environmental crops such as annuals and perennials, bulbs, sod, nursery stock, and other greenhouse and nursery products not shown separately, except cut Christmas trees.

TABLE Da885–888   Commercial vegetables – acreage and production for fresh market and processing: 1939–1999

Contributed by Alan L. Olmstead and Paul W. Rhode

Year	Acreage		Production	
	For fresh market	For processing	For fresh market	For processing
	Da885 [1]	Da886	Da887 [1,2]	Da888
	Acres	Acres	Tons	Tons
1939	1,926,580	1,154,710	7,314,050	3,435,200
1940	1,861,370	1,400,170	7,404,500	4,017,900
1941	1,829,290	1,656,060	7,112,750	5,048,400
1942	1,798,070	1,978,470	7,594,350	5,750,400
1943	1,733,320	1,928,620	7,471,650	4,983,700
1944	2,055,080	1,939,720	8,809,800	5,302,500
1945	2,066,080	1,918,960	9,197,400	5,267,500
1946	2,219,060	2,057,870	9,798,050	6,311,500
1947	2,001,460	1,867,500	8,699,650	5,549,800
1948	1,973,250	1,699,050	9,141,500	5,467,100
1949	2,140,040	1,712,730	9,449,600	5,422,300
1950	2,148,920	1,573,580	10,028,550	5,175,000
1951	1,954,150	1,846,000	9,550,950	7,206,700
1952	1,969,950	1,802,070	9,672,600	6,695,900
1953	2,045,460	1,800,330	10,354,450	6,600,000
1954	2,076,280	1,707,660	10,354,550	5,901,000
1955	2,026,760	1,694,280	10,472,850	6,178,400
1956	1,987,110	1,811,710	10,731,300	8,376,320
1957	1,945,300	1,740,540	10,142,850	6,808,540
1958	1,952,160	1,629,910	10,533,550	7,496,310
1959	1,861,800	1,572,040	10,321,600	6,935,740
1960	1,815,670	1,567,700	11,024,800	7,373,080
1961	1,739,985	1,718,160	10,682,600	8,170,310
1962	1,700,490	1,714,780	10,679,200	9,356,700
1963	1,703,035	1,604,820	10,998,150	8,021,760
1964	1,668,580	1,604,960	10,525,150	8,136,230
1965	1,644,150	1,642,790	10,915,000	8,348,670
1966	1,613,300	1,804,040	10,617,200	8,941,280
1967	1,631,380	1,936,130	11,142,850	9,979,460
1968	1,624,820	2,012,230	11,290,050	12,105,870
1969	1,699,810	1,629,630	11,175,950	9,297,350
1970	1,673,670	1,531,160	11,357,800	9,297,200
1971	1,609,960	1,558,460	11,361,050	9,922,550
1972	1,648,110	1,584,490	11,578,050	10,241,600
1973	1,636,610	1,727,010	11,907,200	10,661,650
1974	1,557,570	1,775,810	12,016,750	11,794,050
1975	1,542,110	1,874,480	11,993,700	13,533,250
1976	1,577,350	1,624,640	12,509,950	11,048,850
1977	1,578,830	1,638,120	12,741,050	12,612,450
1978	1,643,650	1,611,960	13,140,000	11,323,490
1979	1,645,520	1,652,480	13,480,750	12,576,010
1980	1,617,770	1,427,130	13,339,650	10,806,620
1981	1,617,950	1,353,540	13,858,450	10,416,530
1982	939,350	1,250,440	10,360,150	11,179,590
1983 [3]	935,350	1,197,350	9,905,400	10,270,050
1984	1,071,930	1,369,760	10,803,700	12,013,020
1985	1,070,740	1,391,780	10,859,650	11,791,860
1986	1,069,730	1,239,200	10,809,700	11,621,740
1987	1,122,320	1,312,260	11,683,900	12,235,130
1988	1,130,750	1,341,540	12,012,450	11,383,320
1989	1,149,490	1,474,970	12,720,900	14,450,860
1990	1,126,990	1,544,500	12,701,950	15,444,970
1991	1,073,330	1,570,430	12,136,650	16,151,030
1992	1,876,870	1,446,320	19,662,500	14,236,320
1993	1,855,000	1,405,190	19,526,400	14,914,797
1994	1,943,400	1,588,450	21,114,150	18,316,538
1995	1,851,860	1,580,400	19,856,250	17,543,177
1996	1,886,780	1,485,020	20,600,500	17,547,062
1997	1,847,330	1,422,940	21,483,150	16,227,819
1998	1,855,070	1,443,510	21,002,600	15,476,230
1999 [4]	1,899,310	1,508,700	22,559,650	19,039,620

TABLE Da885–888   Commercial vegetables – acreage and production for fresh market and processing: 1939–1999 *Continued*

[1] Crop coverage changes over time. See text.

[2] Treatment of quantities not marketed changes over time; see text.

[3] Owing to program modification, 1983 data are not comparable with other years for fresh market vegetables.

[4] Data are preliminary.

Sources

U.S. National Agricultural Statistics Service, *Agricultural Statistics, 1967, 1974, 1982, 1987, 1992, 1995–96*, and *2000* editions.

Documentation

Annual estimates of national commercial production of all vegetables are presented in this table. The estimates for fresh market vegetables include the following: production for sale of principal fresh market crops in major producing states for which regular seasonal estimates are prepared; allowances for production of principal crops in minor producing states; greenhouse vegetable production in all states; and production of minor vegetables in all states.

The seasonal nature of the production of vegetables and melons for fresh market and their perishability created a need for information on supplies available during specific periods of the year to facilitate orderly marketing. Vegetable and melon estimates are classified according to the season or period within the season when the bulk of each crop is usually harvested. The forecasts and estimate of acreage and production therefore provide a measure of supplies available in specific seasonal periods. The seasonal groupings used are as follows: Winter – January, February, March; Spring – April, May, June; Summer – July, August, September; Fall – October, November, December.

The seasonal patterns of harvest do not correspond precisely in all states to the quarterly estimating period or periods designated. In some cases, only one seasonal group is shown for a state, but marketing may be active in earlier or later months. Because of the small volume from this earlier or later period, the crop estimate has been placed in the seasonal group in which the largest portion is harvested.

For processing vegetables, the estimates relate to production used by commercial canners, freezers, and other processors, except dehydrators. These estimates include raw products grown by processors themselves and those grown under contract or purchased on the open market. This production is not duplicated in the fresh market estimates for the same commodities. The production of those vegetables used for processing for which regular processing estimates are not made is included in the fresh market estimates. However, with the vegetable program modifications implemented in 1973, the processed segment of production for asparagus, broccoli, carrots, and cauliflower, combined with fresh market production during the year, is published at the end of the season, separately. Annual production estimates for the portion processed are published beginning with 1971.

Commercial vegetables for fresh market include principal vegetable and melon crops in the major producing states. These estimates relate to crops that are grown primarily for sale, and they do not include vegetables and melons produced in farm and nonfarm gardens. The bulk of the production of the principal vegetable and melon crops is for consumption in the fresh state. However, during certain years, quantities used by processors of several vegetables are included, and separate estimates of commercial processing are not made for these crops. They include celery and onions (beginning with 1939), garlic (1922–1964), and bell peppers (1939–1964). The commercial estimates of the principal crops include local market production from areas near consuming centers as well as production from well-recognized commercial areas that specialize in producing supplies for shipment to distant markets. Estimates of commercial vegetables for fresh market prepared for years prior to 1939 are not strictly comparable with the series for 1939 and later years, as the earlier series pertain largely to important commercial shipping areas and for the most part do not include local market production from areas near consuming centers.

Aggregate data for the years 1985–1991 lack comparability with data from other years because of program changes altering the crops included.

Series Da885. Area for fresh market is area for harvest, including any partially harvested or not harvested because of low prices or other economic factors.

Series Da885–888. Beginning with 1971, asparagus for processing included in fresh market segment.

Series Da885 and Da887. Area and production for fresh market includes the following crops, for which regular seasonal estimates are prepared in major producing states: artichokes, asparagus, lima beans, snap beans, beets, broccoli, Brussels sprouts, cabbage, cantaloupes, carrots, cauliflower, celery, sweet corn, cucumbers, eggplant, escarole/endive, garlic, honeyball melons (prior to 1954), honeydew melons, kale, lettuce, onions, green peas, green peppers, shallots, spinach, tomatoes, and watermelons. Lima beans, beets, kale, green peas, and shallots discontinued in 1968.

Series Da885 and Da887. Beginning with crop year 1982, acreage and production estimates were discontinued for the following fresh market crops: artichokes, asparagus, snap beans, Brussels sprouts, cabbage, cantaloupes, cucumbers, eggplant, escarole/endive, garlic, bell peppers, spinach, and watermelons; processing vegetables: asparagus, lima beans, beets, cabbage for sauerkraut, cucumbers (pickles), and spinach. Estimates for these crops are not in *Agricultural Statistics*. Estimates for asparagus and cucumbers for pickles were reinstated with the 1984 crop. Beginning with the 1992 crop year, acreage and production estimates were reinstated for the following fresh market crops: artichokes, lima beans, snap beans, Brussels sprouts, cabbage, cantaloupes, cucumbers, eggplant, escarole/endive, garlic, leaf lettuce, romaine lettuce, bell peppers, spinach, and watermelons; and for the processing market, lima beans, beets, cabbage for sauerkraut, and spinach.

Series Da886. Area for processing is area harvested.

Series Da887. Production for fresh market prior to 1964 includes some quantities not marketed because of low prices or other economic factors, which are excluded in computing value. Production since 1964 is the quantity sold and excludes some quantities not marketed because of low prices or other economic factors.

Series Da886 and Da888. Area and production for processing includes the following crops in all states: asparagus (discontinued in 1971), lima beans, snap beans, beets, cabbage (sauerkraut), carrots, sweet corn, cucumbers (pickles), green peas, pimientos (prior to 1954), spinach, and tomatoes. Production of other vegetables processed included in fresh market series of estimates.

TABLE Da889–908   Asparagus, snap beans, and broccoli – acreage, production, and price: 1918–1999[1]

Contributed by Alan L. Olmstead and Paul W. Rhode

	Asparagus						Snap beans		
	Fresh			For processing			Fresh		
Total, acreage harvested	Acreage harvested	Production	Price	Acreage harvested	Production	Price	Acreage harvested	Production	Price
Da889	Da890 [2]	Da891 [2,3]	Da892 [2,4]	Da893	Da894 [5]	Da895 [6]	Da896	Da897 [7]	Da898 [4]
Year	Acres	Acres	Thousand hundredweight	Dollars per hundredweight	Acres	Short tons	Dollars per short ton	Acres	Thousand hundredweight	Dollars per hundredweight
1918	—	13,120	340	9.37	11,340	22,570	65	21,310	998	4.63
1919	—	12,140	271	10.30	14,460	25,740	85	26,080	1,026	5.87
1920	—	14,410	303	10.77	15,860	25,530	110	26,320	1,096	5.80
1921	—	14,590	278	10.80	17,930	22,230	70	28,970	1,215	5.97
1922	—	14,240	269	12.03	20,380	30,980	85	39,450	1,274	6.57
1923	—	17,670	347	11.83	23,010	37,970	100	47,370	1,569	7.33
1924	—	26,860	499	11.17	24,100	44,830	100	61,860	1,783	6.37
1925	—	34,610	659	10.07	29,720	43,390	78	67,570	1,908	5.53
1926	—	42,880	838	8.70	40,760	55,840	66	69,240	1,821	5.93
1927	—	45,190	862	8.37	43,430	52,550	70	87,120	2,062	5.27
1928	—	53,990	1,060	9.70	41,570	58,610	79	90,230	2,148	5.87
1929	—	50,320	966	9.37	42,540	66,790	82	110,630	3,074	5.23
1930	—	55,750	1,200	8.90	41,990	66,760	81	127,330	3,363	4.57
1931	—	65,710	1,313	7.27	37,400	43,760	75	127,490	3,557	4.00
1932	—	79,430	1,511	5.20	32,100	35,310	51	135,410	3,590	3.17
1933	—	69,640	1,390	4.60	48,790	54,160	46	154,020	4,095	2.83
1934	—	73,540	1,584	4.57	42,410	50,040	67	177,020	4,475	3.00
1935	—	64,550	1,347	5.20	48,500	56,740	76	175,280	4,214	3.40
1936	—	68,060	1,590	5.50	42,220	59,110	79	177,750	3,995	3.87
1937	—	67,170	1,573	5.93	43,750	51,190	91	157,900	3,674	4.47
1938	—	68,330	1,520	5.90	47,510	44,660	71	182,270	4,927	2.73
1939	124,440	60,010	1,438	5.62	59,920	64,070	80	184,100	5,387	3.23
1940	132,910	67,080	1,682	6.33	61,870	72,040	92	180,900	5,462	3.57
1941	130,790	70,670	1,644	7.03	59,630	63,970	108	184,900	4,889	4.90
1942	131,950	58,880	1,494	7.65	72,670	81,970	123	176,950	5,345	5.57
1943	130,750	61,110	1,470	10.83	69,740	80,050	156	205,350	5,963	7.43
1944	127,330	53,900	1,376	11.30	74,350	91,940	159	215,400	5,365	7.57
1945	122,480	43,680	1,234	13.26	77,700	100,470	172	198,800	5,691	8.47
1946	118,810	41,940	1,292	12.51	75,270	109,860	189	199,350	6,069	7.83
1947	117,230	47,190	1,322	12.35	68,900	90,810	143	197,850	5,660	7.20
1948	119,390	46,240	1,142	11.56	75,350	86,290	167	192,200	5,738	8.13
1949	127,290	40,820	1,152	12.15	86,300	106,260	180	188,400	5,788	7.34
1950	131,620	43,530	1,197	12.90	88,670	106,190	211	185,900	5,623	7.53
1951	131,120	39,210 [9]	1,018	14.13	—	105,410	243	184,250	5,932	8.13
1952	131,830	—	1,111	13.47	—	97,030	210	161,400	4,935	9.23
1953	134,940	—	1,165	12.89	—	93,620	203	151,050	5,081	9.08
1954	143,700	—	1,025	13.43	—	102,140	226	152,800	5,262	8.18
1955	151,340	—	1,007	14.86	—	129,280	246	151,700	5,527	7.93
1956	152,730	—	1,151	14.19	—	117,140	226	133,380	4,644	9.17
1957	155,700	—	1,333	12.94	—	114,470	187	126,370	4,731	9.21
1958	158,090	—	1,307	12.84	—	111,400	194	123,700	4,410	8.05
1959	161,150	—	1,243	13.66	—	119,220	199	119,300	4,258	9.26
1960	156,960	—	1,230	13.63	—	126,600	219	121,030	4,494	8.74
1961	147,650	—	1,098	15.15	—	129,700	241	117,870	4,484	8.84
1962	145,970	—	1,043	15.80	—	133,900	249	111,110	4,118	9.52
1963	145,170	—	1,037	16.33	—	135,950	263	106,730	4,106	9.67
1964	144,730	—	1,000	14.80	—	126,150	238	102,440	3,854	10.10
1965	131,230	—	1,040	16.30	—	112,000 [12]	287	96,430	3,756	10.70
1966	128,110	—	847 [10]	20.10	—	123,600 [12]	331	97,410	3,618	12.00
1967	125,920	—	850	21.00	—	109,900	332	97,790	3,785	11.50
1968	121,360	—	892	21.80	—	115,500	352	94,440	3,520	12.60
1969	115,350	—	778 [10]	23.60	—	101,850	362	88,320	3,290	13.00
1970	112,260	—	944	22.30	—	90,550	373	85,350	3,120	13.10
1971	114,170	—	833	29.20	—	97,900	406	83,610	3,096	14.40
1972	119,070	—	922	26.70	—	98,450	439	86,700	3,137	14.80
1973	115,380	—	860	31.10	—	84,250	471	85,870	3,033	17.90
1974	112,490	—	824	33.40	—	89,000	526	82,990	2,920	18.60

Notes appear at end of table

TABLE Da889-908   Asparagus, snap beans, and broccoli – acreage, production, and price: 1918–1999   *Continued*

	Asparagus							Snap beans		
	Fresh				For processing			Fresh		
	Total acreage harvested	Acreage harvested	Production	Price	Acreage harvested	Production	Price	Acreage harvested	Production	Price
	Da889	Da890 [2]	Da891 [2,3]	Da892 [2,4]	Da893	Da894 [5]	Da895 [6]	Da896	Da897 [7]	Da898 [4]
Year	Acres	Acres	Thousand hundredweight	Dollars per hundredweight	Acres	Short tons	Dollars per short ton	Acres	Thousand hundredweight	Dollars per hundredweight
1975	102,570	—	874	34.00	—	63,350	501	84,630	3,200	19.60
1976	92,580	—	962	38.10	—	69,150	536	86,210	3,183	19.90
1977	87,520	—	767	47.00	—	73,350	638	79,550	2,963	21.10
1978	83,830	—	717	52.20	—	58,000	771	86,280	2,921	26.00
1979	80,660	—	648	64.40	—	63,500	900	85,510	2,928	27.10
1980	82,950	—	789	58.10	—	44,410	824	95,700 [9]	3,044	27.10 [9]
1981	81,990	—	821	70.50	—	44,640	950	—	2,926	—
1982	—	—	894 [11]	—	—	—	—	—	—	—
1983	—	—	980 [11]	—	—	—	—	—	—	—
1984	89,930	—	1,043	73.70	—	42,690	928	—	—	—
1985	91,450	—	1,152	79.30	—	49,210	938	—	—	—
1986	96,180	—	1,387	70.60	—	42,080	927	—	—	—
1987	99,840	—	1,388	65.60	—	47,880	932	—	—	—
1988	100,910	—	1,481	70.50	—	47,030	1,010	—	—	—
1989	98,510	—	1,492	68.20	—	50,140	955	—	—	—
1990	94,600	—	1,424	68.60	—	50,600	987	—	—	—
1991	89,300	—	1,370	78.90	—	43,820	955	—	—	—
1992	86,120	—	1,376	92.00	—	48,720	948	—	346,100	—
1993	81,150	—	1,252	95.70	—	47,540	1,010	—	—	—
1994	76,750	—	1,311	100.00	—	44,300	1,050	—	—	—
1995	72,340	—	1,100	113.00	—	46,180	1,150	—	—	36.50
1996	73,560	—	1,114	92.90	—	43,780	1,210	—	—	41.80
1997	74,030	—	1,248	108.00	—	38,920	1,220	—	—	40.60
1998	74,430	—	1,264	124.00	—	35,720	1,200	—	—	48.90
1999	75,890 [8]	—	1,455	131.00 [8]	—	36,820 [8]	1,180 [8]	—	—	46.20 [8]

	Snap beans			Broccoli						
	For freezing			Total			Fresh		For processing	
	Acreage harvested	Production	Price	Acreage harvested	Production	Price	Production	Price	Production	Price
	Da899	Da900	Da901 [6]	Da902	Da903	Da904	Da905 [3]	Da906	Da907	Da908
Year	Acres	Short tons	Dollars per short ton	Acres	Thousand hundredweight	Dollars per hundredweight	Thousand pounds	Dollars per hundredweight	Short tons	Dollars per short ton
1918	12,650	33,600	56.90	—	—	—	—	—	—	—
1919	15,590	39,500	55.32	—	—	—	—	—	—	—
1920	11,680	23,700	62.87	—	—	—	—	—	—	—
1921	8,850	20,300	60.79	—	—	—	—	—	—	—
1922	12,460	29,300	58.74	—	—	—	—	—	—	—
1923	16,410	34,300	64.31	—	—	—	—	—	—	—
1924	25,030	44,300	66.03	—	—	—	—	—	—	—
1925	35,940	73,800	63.55	—	—	—	—	—	—	—
1926	31,970	48,100	60.31	—	—	—	—	—	—	—
1927	34,960	54,100	62.46	—	—	—	—	—	—	—
1928	45,640	70,200	61.47	—	—	—	—	—	—	—
1929	65,040	92,300	62.73	—	—	—	—	—	—	—
1930	78,690	90,400	62.15	—	—	—	—	—	—	—
1931	52,710	68,700	52.98	—	—	—	—	—	—	—
1932	31,460	43,900	37.97	—	—	—	—	—	—	—
1933	40,770	60,200	38.59	—	—	—	—	—	—	—
1934	45,100	66,100	41.41	—	—	—	—	—	—	—
1935	49,590	81,500	43.06	—	—	—	—	—	—	—
1936	50,180	76,500	44.46	—	—	—	—	—	—	—
1937	63,720	107,000	47.94	—	—	—	—	—	—	—
1938	73,570	128,400	44.84	—	—	—	—	—	—	—
1939	54,170	96,370	42.04	9,000	517	3.43	—	—	—	—

Notes appear at end of table

(continued)

TABLE Da889–908   Asparagus, snap beans, and broccoli – acreage, production, and price: 1918–1999 *Continued*

	Snap beans			Broccoli						
	For freezing			Total			Fresh		For processing	
	Acreage harvested	Production	Price	Acreage harvested	Production	Price	Production	Price	Production	Price
	Da899	Da900	Da901 [6]	Da902	Da903	Da904	Da905 [3]	Da906	Da907	Da908
Year	Acres	Short tons	Dollars per short ton	Acres	Thousand hundredweight	Dollars per hundredweight	Thousand pounds	Dollars per hundredweight	Short tons	Dollars per short ton
1940	62,600	114,250	43.60	8,400	435	3.71	—	—	—	—
1941	88,500	146,560	54.83	9,400	486	4.79	—	—	—	—
1942	137,260	237,460	75.66	9,200	443	6.60	—	—	—	—
1943	162,340	265,150	96.12	11,600	551	9.95	—	—	—	—
1944	160,570	222,820	99.31	13,200	712	8.38	—	—	—	—
1945	129,210	213,050	104.94	13,650	705	10.26	—	—	—	—
1946	124,970	214,870	113.38	18,700	930	8.69	—	—	—	—
1947	104,380	173,080	103.73	15,900	756	9.17	—	—	—	—
1948	106,360	193,020	122.22	17,600	839	9.38	—	—	—	—
1949	126,450	264,200	111.70	39,550	1,833	9.04	—	—	—	—
1950	121,220	263,820	106.40	39,950	1,865	8.36	—	—	—	—
1951	120,520	273,510	113.50	35,950	1,631	9.38	—	—	—	—
1952	114,920	240,470	121.20	42,830	2,272	8.57	—	—	—	—
1953	149,040	319,390	124.70	42,720	2,159	7.82	—	—	—	—
1954	153,900	346,430	119.50	35,700	1,763	7.82	—	—	—	—
1955	134,490	305,690	111.10	39,660	2,105	7.91	—	—	—	—
1956	137,810	338,630	119.00	44,200	2,356	7.79	—	—	—	—
1957	153,380	361,310	117.00	39,570	1,857	7.36	—	—	—	—
1958	153,360	365,000	110.50	40,580	2,168	7.73	—	—	—	—
1959	162,270	365,860	106.55	41,550	2,065	7.87	—	—	—	—
1960	173,680	406,970	108.31	41,980	2,372	7.92	—	—	—	—
1961	189,260	478,550	104.95	40,950	2,362	8.02	—	—	—	—
1962	182,610	450,790	101.81	37,350	2,064	8.22	—	—	—	—
1963	194,040	474,430	99.68	41,450	2,448	7.85	—	—	—	—
1964	216,930	469,880	102.00	38,100	2,323	7.97	—	—	—	—
1965	230,660	540,530	96.60	37,470	2,211	8.31	—	—	—	—
1966	245,070	521,330	101.00	39,280	2,677	8.68	—	—	—	—
1967	273,590	635,920	102.00	43,360	2,782	8.88	—	—	—	—
1968	267,070	626,630	99.80	42,950	3,080	8.93	—	—	—	—
1969	238,290	568,450	99.50	37,360	2,487	10.10	81,100	13.0	83,800	174
1970	227,770	570,150	95.60	41,140	3,138 [14]	9.71	97,700	13.4	108,050	161
1971	240,200	596,650	92.60	42,770	3,171	11.20	128,600	14.8	94,250	176
1972	255,440	613,400	100.00	47,300	3,644	10.80	137,500	14.1	113,450	176
1973	292,180	741,650	103.00	53,940	3,502 [14]	12.10	149,700	15.7	100,250	189
1974	291,080	748,350	157.00	49,400	3,933	14.20	159,000	17.1	117,150	245
1975	273,580	665,200	153.00	49,650	3,940	15.10	203,500	17.4	95,250	253
1976	237,170	590,700	139.00	52,800	4,289	15.90	234,800	19.0	102,750	250
1977	257,640	675,450	145.00	70,890	5,694	16.30	270,300	19.7	156,100	270
1978	280,350	716,600	146.00	68,300	5,399	18.10	271,500	21.7	137,600	293
1979	285,420	769,130	153.00	70,900	6,301	19.20	329,700	22.2	152,300	319
1980	255,690	704,230	156.00	77,850	6,753	21.40	381,900	23.5	147,900	374
1981	218,300	672,170	166.00	78,520	7,522	23.30	453,100	26.3	150,240	376
1982	204,410	643,860	166.00	92,000	8,819	24.00	541,400	26.7	170,220	390
1983	196,730	587,410	160.00	91,500 [13]	8,326 [13]	25.30 [13]	558,200 [13]	28.2 [13]	137,220 [13]	385 [13]
1984	216,640	666,110	171.00	106,500	10,282	23.10	674,000	25.1	177,090	389
1985	222,160	702,490	169.00	109,500	10,627	22.50	715,400	24.2	173,660	382
1986	190,560	609,400	160.00	119,100	11,529	20.80	844,200	21.9	154,350	357
1987	224,010	685,830	160.00	121,700	11,510	20.80	855,900	21.9	145,540	353
1988	217,650	588,280	168.00	114,400	12,793	22.80	1,002,300	24.0	138,480	374
1989	249,000	869,700	174.00	116,800	13,513	20.40	1,074,400	21.0	138,450	365
1990	243,130	787,470	183.00	110,800	12,345	21.70	989,300	22.3	122,600	390
1991	231,550	767,820	176.00	101,000	11,190	21.60	936,800	22.0	91,100	391
1992	192,390	645,900	173.00	111,400	12,447	22.90	1,060,200	23.5	92,290	386
1993	196,530	661,600	178.00	119,200	12,059	25.80	1,068,500	26.6	68,710	386
1994	221,900	816,830	166.00	134,100	15,714	26.70	1,415,200	27.5	78,100	383
1995	216,040	705,540	173.00	129,400	15,815	28.00	1,384,300	29.3	98,600	386
1996	207,050	784,920	178.00	133,500	15,693	26.50	1,442,800	27.1	63,250	387
1997	195,080	729,250	176.00	130,800	16,880	28.50	1,574,400	29.1	56,800	423
1998	198,700	730,990	172.00	134,300	17,351	29.50	1,622,800	30.2	56,150	388
1999	212,150 [8]	778,430 [8]	173.00 [8]	137,300 [8]	19,910 [8]	22.80 [8]	1,876,600	23.0 [8]	57,200	400 [8]

TABLE Da889–908   Asparagus, snap beans, and broccoli – acreage, production, and price: 1918–1999   *Continued*

[1] See text for information on changing or restricted geographic coverage.

[2] Includes quantities used for processing in states other than California for 1918–1938.

[3] Production data were adjusted by Economic Research Service for 1970–1981 to account for states not included in the National Agricultural Statistics Service estimates.

[4] Beginning 1954, price on an f.o.b. (free on board) basis.

[5] Includes production that can easily be diverted to either fresh or processing uses.

[6] Beginning with 1964, price at the processing plant door.

[7] For select years, includes quantities not marketed and excluded in computing value. In other years excludes quantities not marketed. See text.

[8] Preliminary.

[9] Data in original source appear to be in error but cannot be corrected.

[10] Excludes the following quantities not marketed because of economic conditions: 91,000 hundredweight in 1966 and 80,000 hundredweight in 1969.

[11] Economic Research Service estimates.

[12] Excludes the following quantities not harvested or not marketed because of economic conditions (short tons): 6,000 in 1965 and 4,550 in 1966.

[13] Owing to program modifications, 1983 data are not comparable with those for other years.

[14] Excludes the following quantities not harvested or not marketed because of economic conditions (thousands of hundredweight): 46 in 1970 and 22 in 1973.

Sources

Series Da889, Da892, and Da894. *Agricultural Statistics, 1952, 1967, 1974, 1981, 1992, 1995–96,* and *2000* editions.

Series Da890. U.S. Department of Agriculture, Statistical Reporting Service, *Agricultural Statistics, 1952.*

Series Da891. 1918–1969, *Agricultural Statistics, 1952, 1967, 1974,* and *1981* editions; 1970–1975, U.S. Department of Agriculture, Economic Research Service, *U.S.–Mexico Fruit and Vegetable Trade,* March 1995, Table 4, downloaded January 21, 2001, from the U.S. Department of Agriculture, Economics and Statistics System; 1976–1999, U.S. Department of Agriculture, Economic Research Service, *Vegetable Yearbook,* August 2000, Table 49, downloaded January 21, 2001, from the U.S. Department of Agriculture, Economics and Statistics System.

Series Da893. U.S. Bureau of Agricultural Economics, "Vegetables for Commercial Processing," *Statistical Bulletin* number 132, June 1953, pp. 23, 24.

Series Da895. 1918–1950, U.S. Bureau of Agricultural Economics, "Vegetables for Commercial Processing," *Statistical Bulletin* number 132, June 1953, pp. 23, 25; 1951–1999: *Agricultural Statistics, 1967, 1974, 1981, 1992, 1995–96,* and *2000* editions.

Series Da896. *Agricultural Statistics, 1952, 1967, 1974,* and *1981* editions.

Series Da897. 1918–1969, *Agricultural Statistics, 1952, 1967, 1974,* and *1981* editions; 1970–1992, *U.S.–Mexico Fruit and Vegetable Trade,* March 1995, Table 7, downloaded January 21, 2001, from the U.S. Department of Agriculture, Economics and Statistics System.

Series Da898. *Agricultural Statistics, 1952, 1967, 1974, 1981, 1998,* and *2000* editions.

Series Da899–901. *Agricultural Statistics, 1952, 1967, 1974, 1981, 1992, 1995–96,* and *2000* editions.

Series Da902–904. *Agricultural Statistics, 1967, 1974, 1981, 1992, 1995–96,* and *2000* editions.

Series Da905. 1969, *Agricultural Statistics, 1981;* 1970–1975, *U.S.–Mexico Fruit and Vegetable Trade,* March 1995, Table 10, downloaded January 21, 2001, from the U.S. Department of Agriculture, Economics and Statistics System; 1976–1999, *Vegetable Yearbook,* August 2000, Table 47, downloaded

January 21, 2001, from the U.S. Department of Agriculture, Economics and Statistics System.

Series Da906 and Da908. *Agricultural Statistics, 1981, 1992, 1995–96,* and *2000* editions.

Series Da907. 1969, *Agricultural Statistics, 1981;* 1970–1975, *U.S.–Mexico Fruit and Vegetable Trade,* March 1995, Table 11, downloaded January 21, 2001, from the U.S. Department of Agriculture, Economics and Statistics System; 1976–1999, *Vegetable Yearbook,* August 2000, Table 63, downloaded January 21, 2001, from the U.S. Department of Agriculture, Economics and Statistics System.

Documentation

See the text for Table Da885–888.

Series Da890. Data are for large commercial areas.

Series Da891–892. The official U.S. Department of Agriculture conversion factor estimates that one crate of asparagus is equivalent to 30 pounds. Data from 1918 to 1938 were converted from crates to hundredweight by multiplying the number of crates by 0.3.

Series Da891–892 and Da896–898. Data for 1918–1938 are not strictly comparable with those from 1939 to date. In the earlier period, estimates were frequently made only for well-recognized commercial areas from which substantial quantities were shipped – usually by rail – to distant terminal markets. In many states, local-market or market garden areas near large population centers were excluded from these 1918–1938 estimates. This feature makes this early series less complete than that from 1939 to 1999.

Series Da893–895. California only from 1918 to 1938. Additional states included, beginning with 1939, so that the total is now twenty states.

Series Da894–895. Production and price data are on an "as sold" or "pay-weight" basis. The pay weight is field-cut asparagus trimmed to a specified maximum length, usually seven inches. Overlength and culls not paid for are not included in the estimates.

Series Da895 and Da901. The season falls in the calendar year.

Series Da897. Includes the following quantities not marketed and excluded in computing value (in thousand hundredweight): 115 in 1930; 58 in 1931; 223 in 1932; 206 in 1933; 222 in 1934; 48 in 1935; 112 in 1938; 13 in 1939; 41 in 1940; 23 in 1943; 30 in 1944; 269 in 1945; 278 in 1946; 528 in 1947; 360 in 1948; 141 in 1949; 102 in 1950; 529 in 1951; 44 in 1953; 18 in 1954; 208 in 1955; 73 in 1956; 43 in 1957; 150 in 1958; 44 in 1959; 35 in 1960; 85 in 1961; 35 in 1962; and 45 in 1963. Excludes the following quantities not marketed (in thousand hundredweight): 143 in 1964; 152 in 1965; and 38 in 1968.

Series Da897–898. The official U.S. Department of Agriculture conversion factor estimates that one bushel of snap beans is equivalent to 30 pounds. Data from 1918 to 1939 were converted from bushels to hundredweight by multiplying bushels by 0.3, and were converted from dollars per bushel to dollars per hundredweight by dividing dollars per bushel by 0.3.

Series Da902–908. Sprouting broccoli only. Does not include broccoli rabe or heading (cauliflower) broccoli. Sprouting broccoli is a branching cauliflower that produces a head of functional florets at the end of each main branch, which is cut for food while the florets are tight green or purplish buds. Heading or cauliflower broccoli is a cauliflower that is larger, hardier, and a better keeper than the common cauliflower. Prior to 1949, data pertain to Arizona, Pennsylvania, and California only.

Series Da906. Price at the processing plant door.

Series Da908. Price on an f.o.b. basis.

TABLE Da909–928   Cabbage, carrots, and cauliflower – acreage, production, and price: 1918–1999

Contributed by Alan L. Olmstead and Paul W. Rhode

	Cabbage					
	Fresh			For sauerkraut		
Year	Acreage harvested Da909 [1,2]	Production Da910 [1,2,3,4]	Price Da911 [1,2,5]	Acreage harvested Da912	Production Da913	Price Da914 [6]
	Acres	Thousand hundredweight	Dollars per hundredweight	Acres	Short tons	Dollars per short ton
1918	100,050	15,032	1.22	14,770	115,800	10.79
1919	86,470	11,668	1.33	7,700	47,500	11.26
1920	113,410	20,340	0.91	8,260	66,600	9.46
1921	95,780	12,770	1.27	7,220	64,800	13.50
1922	117,450	18,422	0.67	15,610	161,000	6.60
1923	88,960	13,738	1.21	17,620	166,600	9.50
1924	108,320	19,074	0.90	11,210	121,500	7.09
1925	113,730	17,940	0.99	8,770	90,200	7.44
1926	115,560	18,768	0.92	11,290	117,100	6.65
1927	118,120	20,272	0.79	12,720	157,300	6.68
1928	117,530	17,018	1.17	17,210	153,300	9.54
1929	136,790	19,668	1.01	20,530	173,000	10.22
1930	132,690	17,206	1.07	28,100	213,800	7.74
1931	148,360	19,650	0.57	19,210	136,500	6.03
1932	144,700	19,894	0.63	16,160	151,900	4.11
1933	136,110	15,778	1.05	16,440	95,400	11.21
1934	204,310	26,652	0.52	25,710	215,700	6.35
1935	152,580	20,340	0.70	16,500	134,800	5.17
1936	165,090	19,726	0.98	18,980	115,100	13.17
1937	160,060	19,826	0.75	24,840	148,900	9.68
1938	158,720	24,542	0.46	17,740	195,400	5.29
1939	159,180	19,704	0.84	19,710	146,600	7.59
1940	170,390	23,066	0.62	21,020	186,700	5.45
1941	153,330	20,108	1.08	23,480	211,000	9.70
1942	180,110	25,930	0.94	15,000	161,300	7.96
1943	182,260	22,122	2.40	13,790	106,900	21.92
1944	230,000	29,142	1.68	16,640	117,500	14.83
1945	199,150	30,960	1.41	22,660	232,800	13.30
1946	178,690	27,244	1.53	24,380	268,800	13.14
1947	163,530	22,552	2.15	9,820	72,300	17.22
1948	175,760	25,318	1.51	19,380	203,400	14.51
1949	152,380	22,631	1.60	17,500	176,600	12.40
1950	158,550	27,003	1.33	18,080	246,400	9.60
1951	129,770	21,491	2.58	14,990	184,200	12.60
1952	125,350	20,566	2.92	15,580	176,600	19.90
1953	140,240	23,413	1.57	17,030	221,100	13.40
1954	132,200	21,811	1.68	15,830	208,600	12.00
1955	120,910	18,679	2.48	13,250	160,700	18.20
1956	121,950	21,994	1.86	16,370	258,900	11.80
1957	109,830	18,325	2.38	11,460	170,000	15.00
1958	113,890	19,728	2.27	11,950	203,000	11.60
1959	112,010	18,091	2.65	10,870	149,280	15.22
1960	114,055	20,105	2.30	14,200	220,460	15.51
1961	116,275	18,980	2.11	13,090	215,700	12.74
1962	109,940	18,845	3.10	12,130	211,270	13.25
1963	106,105	19,080	2.65	11,530	197,260	13.04
1964	106,010	18,345	2.81	10,280	162,850	15.40
1965	102,360	18,130	2.83	12,750	238,910	13.60
1966	99,820	17,799	3.74	10,760	179,560	20.00
1967	99,900	19,037	2.86	14,280	273,400	17.00
1968	94,210	18,948	3.25	12,560	231,850	18.00
1969	95,100	18,058	3.42	12,780	222,500	19.00
1970	96,830	18,661	4.06	12,980	266,100	17.70
1971	98,180	19,215	3.87	11,460	234,950	17.50
1972	94,630	18,611	4.00	10,800	198,100	21.40
1973	97,530	19,907	5.87	13,040	219,150	24.80
1974	93,480	19,712	4.60	13,910	281,450	31.00

Notes appear at end of table

TABLE Da909–928   Cabbage, carrots, and cauliflower – acreage, production, and price: 1918–1999   *Continued*

	Cabbage					
	Fresh			For sauerkraut		
	Acreage harvested	Production	Price	Acreage harvested	Production	Price
	Da909 [1,2]	Da910 [1,2,3,4]	Da911 [1,2,5]	Da912	Da913	Da914 [6]
Year	Acres	Thousand hundredweight	Dollars per hundredweight	Acres	Short tons	Dollars per short ton
1975	92,040	20,197	5.37	11,810	239,750	31.40
1976	87,860	19,122	5.87	11,470	232,050	31.20
1977	81,510	19,174	8.91	10,530	234,750	30.50
1978	86,380	20,134	8.37	10,570	217,790	31.50
1979	82,820	19,369	8.09	9,800	237,820	31.60
1980	84,780	18,849	8.10	9,140	209,020	34.10
1981	82,440	19,811	7.16	10,160	246,090	36.80
1982	—	20,877	9.20	—	—	—
1983	—	19,750	8.90	—	—	—
1984	—	20,023	11.90	—	—	—
1985	—	21,322	8.80	—	—	—
1986	—	21,434	8.20	—	—	—
1987	—	22,759	7.90	—	—	—
1988	—	22,512	7.70	—	—	—
1989	—	21,465	7.60	—	—	—
1990	—	21,634	7.70	—	—	—
1991	—	21,871	8.30	—	—	—
1992	72,290	23,267	9.10	5,520	172,720	38.00
1993	71,790	24,813	11.40	5,320	134,520	46.60
1994	—	24,783	9.32	—	—	—
1995	—	22,104	11.50	—	—	—
1996	—	22,900	10.20	—	—	—
1997	—	25,267 [7]	11.10 [7]	—	—	—
1998	—	23,946 [7]	12.90 [7]	—	—	—
1999	—	22,069	10.60	—	—	—

	Carrots						
	Total			Fresh		For processing	
	Acreage harvested	Production	Price	Production	Price	Production	Price
	Da915 [1]	Da916 [1,3]	Da917 [1]	Da918 [4]	Da919	Da920	Da921
Year	Acres	Thousand hundredweight	Dollars per hundredweight	Thousand hundredweight	Dollars per hundredweight	Short tons	Dollars per short ton
1918	—	—	—	—	—	—	—
1919	—	—	—	—	—	—	—
1920	—	—	—	—	—	—	—
1921	—	—	—	—	—	—	—
1922	—	—	—	—	—	—	—
1923	7,860	1,293	1.80	—	—	—	—
1924	10,730	1,887	1.66	—	—	—	—
1925	14,200	1,900	1.26	—	—	—	—
1926	15,920	2,390	1.26	—	—	—	—
1927	20,290	3,165	1.22	—	—	—	—
1928	22,590	3,197	1.60	—	—	—	—
1929	32,770	5,637	1.36	—	—	—	—
1930	34,820	5,911	1.36	—	—	—	—
1931	34,040	5,645	1.20	—	—	—	—
1932	35,650	5,452	1.30	—	—	—	—
1933	37,420	5,333	1.18	—	—	—	—
1934	40,960	6,353	1.24	—	—	—	—
1935	39,800	6,391	1.36	—	—	—	—
1936	45,090	6,906	1.26	—	—	—	—
1937	46,810	7,411	1.38	—	—	—	—
1938	50,980	8,107	1.18	—	—	—	—
1939	58,020	8,969	1.32	—	—	—	—

Notes appear at end of table

(continued)

TABLE Da909–928   Cabbage, carrots, and cauliflower – acreage, production, and price: 1918–1999   *Continued*

				Carrots			
	Total			Fresh		For processing	
	Acreage harvested	Production	Price	Production	Price	Production	Price
	Da915 [1]	Da916 [1,3]	Da917 [1]	Da918 [4]	Da919	Da920	Da921
Year	Acres	Thousand hundredweight	Dollars per hundredweight	Thousand hundredweight	Dollars per hundredweight	Short tons	Dollars per short ton
1940	62,940	9,696	1.38	—	—	—	—
1941	64,510	10,318	1.54	—	—	—	—
1942	70,400	11,387	2.30	—	—	—	—
1943	96,070	16,523	2.48	—	—	—	—
1944	91,440	15,296	2.40	—	—	—	—
1945	97,300	17,765	2.46	—	—	—	—
1946	90,650	15,895	2.56	—	—	—	—
1947	80,650	13,332	3.30	—	—	—	—
1948	87,370	15,312	3.42	—	—	—	—
1949	93,200	14,536	2.80	—	—	—	—
1950	91,870	15,788	2.48	—	—	—	—
1951	73,450	14,346	3.61	—	—	—	—
1952	77,760	14,886	3.06	—	—	—	—
1953	81,000	13,315	3.22	—	—	—	—
1954	79,750	15,113	3.92	—	—	—	—
1955	79,880	14,838	3.93	—	—	—	—
1956	79,040	16,253	3.49	—	—	—	—
1957	79,490	15,095	4.05	—	—	—	—
1958	82,240	16,363	3.50	—	—	—	—
1959	80,750	15,480	3.55	—	—	—	—
1960	83,625	18,335	3.12	—	—	—	—
1961	73,970	15,797	3.86	—	—	—	—
1962	83,340	16,808	3.33	—	—	—	—
1963	91,170	18,015	2.91	—	—	—	—
1964	82,510	16,216	3.46	—	—	—	—
1965	79,680	17,469	3.50	—	—	—	—
1966	79,680	17,215	4.02	—	—	—	—
1967	81,290	17,501	4.16	—	—	—	—
1968	72,200	19,142	4.31	—	—	—	—
1969	79,000	18,380	4.37	11,168	6.2	360,600	29.8
1970	77,570	18,156	3.63	10,952	5.1	360,200	28.2
1971	72,330	18,866	5.02	11,671	7.2	359,750	30.5
1972	75,800	19,605	5.14	12,571	7.2	351,700	28.7
1973	83,800	22,284	4.76	12,857	7.2	471,350	28.6
1974	78,550	22,924	5.28	13,289	7.7	481,750	40.1
1975	70,080	19,016	6.88	12,423	9.4	329,650	43.6
1976	73,460	19,278	5.88	13,997	8.1	346,250	39.2
1977	69,630	19,271	7.20	12,163	11.2	426,800	43.7
1978	76,770	19,824	6.74	12,131	10.0	422,520	45.7
1979	86,040	22,124	7.16	13,308	10.6	462,200	46.5
1980	81,800	20,888	8.33	13,932	11.3	359,170	53.0
1981	84,350	21,831	9.11	14,632	12.3	365,960	55.2
1982	86,850	24,081	8.68	15,685	11.9	419,830	55.0
1983	87,300	23,106	9.37	15,234 [9]	12.7	393,570	59.8
1984	93,740	23,606	10.60	15,616	14.4	399,520	63.9
1985	89,800	22,772	9.05	15,345	11.9	371,370	64.4
1986	86,600	23,540	10.00	16,060	13.3	373,970	62.4
1987	99,600	28,720	8.66	20,896	10.8	391,220	58.9
1988	97,550	24,845	10.50	17,857	13.3	349,390	66.1
1989	101,900	29,560	10.30	20,386	13.6	458,710	60.3
1990	94,900	29,938	9.37	21,106	11.9	441,610	64.9
1991	98,000	28,573	11.20	19,973	14.6	430,020	64.2
1992	106,900	32,792	10.80	21,698	14.5	554,700	68.9
1993	103,400	31,683	9.34	28,880	11.9	498,150	75.6
1994	110,070	36,132	9.48	33,509	12.1	549,960	71.5
1995	109,020	38,065 [8]	11.80 [8]	29,518	16.8	585,550	79.3
1996	116,980	—	—	33,236	13.3	566,580	67.2
1997	133,740	—	—	38,589	12.9	569,450	67.4
1998	135,880	—	—	37,233	12.0	549,280	68.3
1999	—	—	—	37,837	—	—	—

Notes appear at end of table

TABLE Da909–928   Cabbage, carrots, and cauliflower – acreage, production, and price: 1918–1999   *Continued*

				Cauliflower			
		Total			Fresh	For processing	
	Acreage harvested	Production	Price	Production	Price	Production	Price
	Da922 [1]	Da923 [1,3]	Da924 [1,5]	Da925 [4]	Da926	Da927	Da928
Year	Acres	Thousand hundredweight	Dollars per hundredweight	Thousand hundredweight	Dollars per hundredweight	Short tons	Dollars per short ton
1918	6,330	721	2.95	—	—	—	—
1919	7,010	727	3.16	—	—	—	—
1920	8,630	910	3.46	—	—	—	—
1921	8,350	897	3.14	—	—	—	—
1922	9,790	1,017	4.16	—	—	—	—
1923	11,920	1,218	3.97	—	—	—	—
1924	13,100	1,095	3.32	—	—	—	—
1925	14,930	1,321	3.46	—	—	—	—
1926	22,330	2,199	2.30	—	—	—	—
1927	18,440	1,686	2.97	—	—	—	—
1928	21,830	1,996	2.62	—	—	—	—
1929	26,350	2,596	2.19	—	—	—	—
1930	30,120	2,519	2.30	—	—	—	—
1931	29,960	2,796	2.03	—	—	—	—
1932	32,060	2,821	1.65	—	—	—	—
1933	30,340	2,652	1.51	—	—	—	—
1934	29,150	2,511	1.57	—	—	—	—
1935	27,890	2,543	1.76	—	—	—	—
1936	29,790	2,822	1.92	—	—	—	—
1937	29,470	3,210	1.92	—	—	—	—
1938	27,830	3,058	1.54	—	—	—	—
1939	30,650	3,893	1.68	—	—	—	—
1940	32,060	4,190	1.43	—	—	—	—
1941	29,930	3,284	2.22	—	—	—	—
1942	27,880	3,517	2.81	—	—	—	—
1943	27,070	3,438	4.73	—	—	—	—
1944	32,100	3,981	3.87	—	—	—	—
1945	34,820	4,565	4.22	—	—	—	—
1946	40,460	5,124	3.59	—	—	—	—
1947	34,590	4,510	3.89	—	—	—	—
1948	35,550	5,008	3.51	—	—	—	—
1949	34,150	5,051	3.07	—	—	—	—
1950	32,850	4,591	3.13	—	—	—	—
1951	28,650	4,511	3.62	—	—	—	—
1952	29,550	4,737	3.64	—	—	—	—
1953	29,850	4,498	3.12	—	—	—	—
1954	27,650	2,072	6.47	—	—	—	—
1955	29,380	2,536	6.75	—	—	—	—
1956	32,430	2,894	6.03	—	—	—	—
1957	32,570	2,678	6.08	—	—	—	—
1958	30,220	2,579	6.73	—	—	—	—
1959	28,320	2,259	6.31	—	—	—	—
1960	30,520	2,930	5.90	—	—	—	—
1961	28,400	2,576	6.36	—	—	—	—
1962	26,830	2,570	7.45	—	—	—	—
1963	27,780	2,596	7.48	—	—	—	—
1964	26,460	2,507	7.69	—	—	—	—
1965	24,800	2,473	8.22	—	—	—	—
1966	25,950	2,526	8.62	—	—	—	—
1967	26,250	2,445	8.77	—	—	—	—
1968	27,350	2,737	8.77	—	—	—	—
1969	27,300	2,615	9.47	1,650	11.8	48,250	109
1970	24,060	2,298	9.48	1,354	12.4	47,200	106
1971	24,960	2,456	10.20	1,274	14.5	59,100	113
1972	28,080	2,989	10.60	1,611	14.6	68,900	116
1973	31,780	2,940	11.50	1,442	16.4	74,900	137
1974	32,220	3,033	13.10	1,553	17.8	74,000	161

Notes appear at end of table

(continued)

TABLE Da909–928   Cabbage, carrots, and cauliflower – acreage, production, and price: 1918–1999   *Continued*

	Cauliflower						
	Total			Fresh		For processing	
	Acreage harvested	Production	Price	Production	Price	Production	Price
	Da922 [1]	Da923 [1,3]	Da924 [1,5]	Da925 [4]	Da926	Da927	Da928
Year	Acres	Thousand hundredweight	Dollars per hundredweight	Thousand hundredweight	Dollars per hundredweight	Short tons	Dollars per short ton
1975	31,880	2,987	15.20	1,744	20.0	62,150	169
1976	33,500	3,071	16.80	2,243	21.3	54,100	173
1977	37,210	3,674	17.50	2,383	23.2	78,050	196
1978	41,450	3,808	18.20	1,933	26.4	99,550	213
1979	42,750	4,117	19.70	2,711	25.2	74,530	201
1980	43,320	4,255	22.50	2,846	28.2	72,720	230
1981	46,020	5,209	24.10	3,517	30.0	86,590	242
1982	51,400	5,370	24.50	3,420	31.2	97,530	252
1983	54,600 [9]	5,414 [9]	25.80 [9]	3,704 [9]	32.0 [9]	85,510 [9]	252 [9]
1984	60,800	6,688	26.20	4,817	31.1	93,560	266
1985	61,200	6,664	25.40	4,905	29.8	87,940	264
1986	67,800	7,527	25.50	5,906	28.8	81,060	269
1987	66,100	7,375	25.40	5,928	28.3	72,330	274
1988	62,300	7,824	25.70	6,465	28.2	68,690	280
1989	67,200	7,805	26.10	6,622	28.1	59,630	297
1990	65,000	7,764	24.20	6,540	25.1	61,730	388
1991	55,100	6,903	26.80	6,157	27.1	37,850	483
1992	55,300	6,904	28.10	6,072	29.0	31,240	433
1993	60,600	7,884	30.00	7,011	31.0	43,660	440
1994	58,800	8,190	28.30	7,345	28.8	42,290	470
1995	53,350	7,315	33.30	6,484	34.7	41,550	451
1996	48,200	7,354	32.30	6,801	33.0	27,640	477
1997	43,500	6,889	31.60	6,323 [7]	32.3	28,300	480
1998	44,200	6,897	32.80	5,468 [7]	34.5	71,450	533
1999	46,400 [8]	7,742 [8]	28.10 [8]	7,368	28.3 [8]	18,690 [8]	483 [8]

[1] Data for 1918–1938 not strictly comparable with later years; see text.

[2] Includes production for dehydration, 1918–1938 and 1943–1945.

[3] See text for information on quantities not harvested or not marketed for economic reasons.

[4] Data adjusted or estimated by the Economic Research Service; see text.

[5] Beginning with 1954, f.o.b. (free on board) basis.

[6] Beginning with 1964, processing value per short ton at the processing plant door.

[7] Data from original source have been revised.

[8] Preliminary.

[9] Because of program modifications, 1983 data are not comparable with those of other years.

Sources

Series Da909. 1918–1959, U. S. Department of Agriculture, Statistical Reporting Service, *Agricultural Statistics, 1952* and *1967* editions; 1960–1993, U.S. National Agricultural Statistics Service (NASS), *U.S. Cabbage Statistics, 1960–93*, October 1994, Table 1, downloaded January 27, 2001, from the U.S. Department of Agriculture, Economics and Statistics System.

Series Da910–911. 1918–1959, *Agricultural Statistics, 1952 and 1967* editions; 1960–1975, NASS, *U.S. Cabbage Statistics, 1960–93*, October 1994, Table 1, downloaded January 27, 2001, from the U.S. Department of Agriculture, Economics and Statistics System; 1976–1999, U.S. Department of Agriculture, Economic Research Service, *Vegetable Yearbook*, July 1997, NASS, *U.S. Cabbage Statistics, 1960–93*, August 2000, Table 52, downloaded January 27, 2001, from the U.S. Department of Agriculture, Economics and Statistics System.

Series Da912–914. 1918–1959, *Agricultural Statistics, 1952* and *1967* editions; 1960–1993, NASS, *U.S. Cabbage Statistics, 1960–93*, October 1994, Table 2, downloaded January 27, 2001, from the U.S. Department of Agriculture, Economics and Statistics System.

Series Da915–917. *Agricultural Statistics, 1952, 1967, 1982, 1992, 1995–96, 1998,* and *2000* editions.

Series Da918. 1969, *Agricultural Statistics, 1982*; 1970–1975, U.S. Department of Agriculture, Economic Research Service, *U.S.–Mexico Fruit and Vegetable Trade*, March 1995, Table 13, downloaded January 27, 2001, from the U.S. Department of Agriculture, Economics and Statistics System; 1976–1999, *Vegetable Yearbook*, August 2000, Table 46, downloaded January 27, 2001, from the U.S. Department of Agriculture, Economics and Statistics System.

Series Da919–921, Da926, and Da928. *Agricultural Statistics, 1982, 1992, 1995–96, 1998,* and *2000* editions.

Series Da922–924. *Agricultural Statistics, 1952, 1967, 1982, 1992, 1995–96,* and *2000* editions.

Series Da925. 1969, *Agricultural Statistics, 1982*; 1970–1975, *U.S.–Mexico Fruit and Vegetable Trade*, March 1995, Table 14, downloaded January 27, 2001, from the U.S. Department of Agriculture, Economics and Statistics System; 1976–1999, *Vegetable Yearbook*, August 2000, Table 48, downloaded January 27, 2001, from the U.S. Department of Agriculture, Economics and Statistics System.

Series Da927. 1969, *Agricultural Statistics, 1982*; 1970–1992, *U.S.–Mexico Fruit and Vegetable Trade*, March 1995, Table 15, downloaded January 27, 2001, from the U.S. Department of Agriculture, Economics and Statistics System; 1993–1999, *Agricultural Statistics, 2000*.

Documentation

See the text for Table Da885–888.

Series Da909–911, Da915–917, and Da922–924. Data for 1918–1938 are not strictly comparable with those for later years. In the earlier period, estimates were frequently made only for well-recognized commercial areas from which substantial quantities were shipped – usually by rail – to distant terminal markets. In many states, local-market or market garden areas near large population centers were excluded from these 1918–1938 estimates. This feature makes this early series less complete than that from 1939 to date.

TABLE Da929–949   Cabbage, carrots, and cauliflower – acreage, production, and price: 1918–1999   *Continued*

Series Da910. For 1982–1991, U.S. production and price were estimated by the Economic Research Service based on available state reports. The series covers largely head cabbage. End of year stocks and shrinkage are not included. Prior to 1964, the series includes the following quantities not harvested or not marketed, which were excluded in computing value (thousands of hundredweight): (1) due to economic factors: 632 in 1931; 656 in 1932; 130 in 1933; 2236 in 1934; 98 in 1935; 1040 in 1936; 436 in 1937; 1104 in 1938; 540 in 1939; 340 in 1940; 80 in 1941; 2218 in 1942; 122 in 1943; 2,230 in 1944; 2,102 in 1945; 2,382 in 1946; 408 in 1947; 1,682 in 1948; 1,195 in 1949; 5,076 in 1950; 1,591 in 1951; 294 in 1952; 2,479 in 1953; 1,573 in 1954; 516 in 1955; 1,003 in 1956; 112 in 1957; 629 in 1958; 432 in 1959; 504.4 in 1960; 523.3 in 1961; 156.4 in 1962; and 145.6 in 1963; (2) loss due to shrinkage and waste in the New York storage crop: 142 in 1959; 338 in 1960; 133 in 1961; 165 in 1962; 228 in 1963; and 164 in 1964.

Series Da916. Covers production mostly for fresh market use, but includes some quantities used for processing and for dehydration. Includes the following quantities not marketed and excluded in computing value (thousands of hundredweight): 118 in 1929; 528 in 1931; 133 in 1932; 4 in 1935; 3 in 1936; 41 in 1938; 107 in 1943; 39 in 1944; 43 in 1945; 373 in 1946; 233 in 1947; 414 in 1948; 418 in 1949; 743 in 1950; 124 in 1951; 294 in 1953; 321 in 1954; 135 in 1955; 110 in 1956; 289 in 1958; 871.8 in 1960; 0.5 in 1961; 0.6 in 1962; and 110.4 in 1963. Excludes the following quantities not harvested or not marketed because of economic conditions (thousands of hundredweight): 170 in 1975; 243 in 1976; 5 in 1977; and 37 in 1978. The official U. S. Department of Agriculture conversion factor estimates that one bushel of carrots is equivalent to fifty pounds. Data from 1923 to 1938 were converted from bushels to hundredweight by multiplying bushels by 0.5.

Series Da917. Data from 1923 to 1938 were converted from dollars per bushels to dollars per hundredweight by dividing dollars per bushels by 0.5.

Series Da918. Production data were adjusted by the Economic Research Service for 1973–1981 to account for states not included in the USDA NASS estimates.

Series Da922–928. Estimates include heading broccoli or cauliflower broccoli. Heading or cauliflower broccoli is a cauliflower that is larger, hardier, and a better keeper than the common cauliflower.

Series Da923. Includes production for fresh market and processing. Includes the following quantities not marketed and excluded in computing value (thousands of hundredweight): 124 in 1932; 47 in 1935; 11 in 1944; 47 in 1946; 27 in 1948; 100 in 1949; 138 in 1950; 8 in 1953; and 20 in 1957. Excludes the following quantities not harvested or not marketed because of economic conditions (thousands of hundredweight): 42 in 1970 and 27 in 1973. The official U.S. Department of Agriculture conversion factor estimates that one crate of cauliflower is equivalent to thirty-seven pounds. Data from 1918–1938 were converted from crates to hundredweight by multiplying bushels by 0.37.

Series Da924. Data from 1918 to 1938 were converted from dollars per crate to dollars per hundredweight by dividing dollars per crate by 0.37.

Series Da925. Data were adjusted by the Economic Research Service for 1980–1981 to account for states not included in the NASS estimates.

Series Da926. Price on an f.o.b. basis.

Series Da928. Price at the processing plant door.

TABLE Da929–949   Celery, sweet corn, cucumbers, eggplant, and garlic – acreage, production, and price: 1918–1999

Contributed by Alan L. Olmstead and Paul W. Rhode

	Celery, fresh			Sweet corn					
				Fresh			For processing		
	Acreage harvested	Production	Price	Acreage harvested	Production	Price	Acreage harvested	Production	Price
	Da929	Da930 [1]	Da931 [2,3]	Da932 [4]	Da933 [1,4]	Da934 [4]	Da935 [2]	Da936 [2]	Da937 [3]
Year	Acres	Thousand hundredweight	Dollars per hundredweight	Acres	Thousand hundredweight	Dollars per hundredweight	Acres	Short tons	Dollars per short ton
1918	14,080	1,895	3.92	—	—	—	274,930	536,000	18.0
1919	14,240	1,888	5.36	—	—	—	250,230	587,500	17.7
1920	15,670	2,138	4.42	—	—	—	261,750	595,300	19.3
1921	16,000	2,245	4.08	—	—	—	136,280	360,600	13.5
1922	18,800	2,394	4.31	—	—	—	197,600	474,700	11.0
1923	21,570	2,713	3.64	—	—	—	252,590	603,300	12.5
1924	23,560	3,086	4.06	—	—	—	302,790	527,800	14.2
1925	25,070	3,412	4.03	—	—	—	393,910	1,014,100	15.0
1926	25,690	3,264	4.36	—	—	—	317,310	816,000	13.2
1927	27,210	3,426	3.39	—	—	—	223,350	415,900	12.0
1928	29,060	4,258	3.58	—	—	—	310,020	599,500	12.6
1929	35,220	5,375	3.33	—	—	—	359,800	706,900	13.1
1930	35,050	5,426	3.36	—	—	—	376,760	661,400	13.2
1931	35,180	4,812	3.86	—	—	—	358,030	785,100	11.1
1932	34,220	4,988	2.36	—	—	—	165,130	387,200	7.5
1933	34,890	4,937	2.53	—	—	—	199,670	394,300	8.0
1934	36,130	5,017	2.75	—	—	—	287,630	498,000	8.5
1935	35,840	4,416	3.83	—	—	—	401,610	859,900	9.3
1936	38,120	5,034	3.53	—	—	—	372,420	607,500	10.2
1937	40,180	5,467	3.56	—	—	—	438,810	978,100	11.6
1938	40,190	5,889	2.81	—	—	—	345,160	882,800	10.0
1939	40,660	10,198	1.92	62,700	2,659	1.04	251,160	667,100	8.4

Notes appear at end of table

(continued)

TABLE Da929–949   Celery, sweet corn, cucumbers, eggplant, and garlic – acreage, production, and price: 1918–1999
Continued

	Celery, fresh			Sweet corn					
				Fresh			For processing		
	Acreage harvested	Production	Price	Acreage harvested	Production	Price	Acreage harvested	Production	Price
	Da929	Da930 [1]	Da931 [2,3]	Da932 [4]	Da933 [1,4]	Da934 [4]	Da935 [2]	Da936 [2]	Da937 [3]
Year	Acres	Thousand hundredweight	Dollars per hundredweight	Acres	Thousand hundredweight	Dollars per hundredweight	Acres	Short tons	Dollars per short ton
1940	40,350	10,195	2.17	60,800	2,796	1.49	320,400	738,100	8.8
1941	41,750	11,126	2.58	67,500	3,286	1.53	445,270	1,137,500	9.7
1942	41,510	10,357	3.43	66,500	3,358	1.73	485,610	1,282,500	13.5
1943	38,840	9,605	5.58	71,500	3,091	2.56	510,110	1,170,600	18.4
1944	39,290	10,447	4.65	79,900	3,423	2.64	489,920	1,043,500	19.4
1945	42,780	11,381	5.55	76,000	3,539	3.36	487,270	1,139,400	19.3
1946	49,220	13,262	3.50	72,500	3,270	3.24	505,210	1,251,300	19.8
1947	41,180	11,332	5.18	70,000	3,174	2.51	494,990	1,097,200	20.7
1948	41,180	12,542	3.55	78,300	3,846	3.64	466,500	1,262,100	23.2
1949	38,310	12,678	4.03	211,300	10,541	2.99	460,880	1,408,300	20.3
1950	35,770	13,376	3.69	217,300	11,090	3.28	336,030	958,100	18.0
1951	36,860	14,091	3.82	203,700	10,800	3.49	436,400	1,197,900	23.2
1952	36,750	14,118	4.06	209,750	11,205	3.72	489,000	1,526,100	23.9
1953	35,690	14,335	3.61	200,500	11,365	3.97	503,340	1,514,100	23.4
1954	35,770	15,126	3.31	209,700	12,214	3.63	453,210	1,488,800	20.7
1955	33,000	15,304	3.94	197,900	12,315	3.20	389,520	1,174,000	19.5
1956	35,600	16,232	3.29	187,600	11,719	3.86	449,030	1,710,000	20.3
1957	34,740	15,137	3.86	193,900	11,524	4.32	441,910	1,524,500	19.9
1958	35,130	14,260	4.43	207,750	12,756	3.43	388,000	1,329,900	18.8
1959	37,670	15,534	3.28	215,260	13,023	3.72	418,650	1,582,170	19.1
1960	36,210	15,169	3.32	200,160	12,696	4.04	411,890	1,390,960	19.2
1961	31,390	14,957	3.26	200,110	13,204	4.01	450,520	1,726,270	19.4
1962	30,450	14,084	4.70	207,170	13,189	3.92	442,800	1,799,250	20.1
1963	30,890	14,297	3.60	207,240	13,347	4.00	392,320	1,679,140	20.0
1964	30,540	13,882	4.58	197,850	12,198	4.52	353,040	1,480,700	20.4
1965	30,790	13,977	4.43	199,480	13,198	4.38	376,690	1,613,600	22.4
1966	32,710	14,680	4.88	194,860	12,204	5.06	445,650	1,962,400	22.7
1967	32,660	14,684	4.75	190,100	13,219	4.83	470,550	2,101,900	25.0
1968	32,910	15,465	4.65	182,880	12,670	5.21	519,160	2,479,300	25.6
1969	33,180	15,790	5.61	189,100	12,996	4.93	448,700	2,109,350	25.1
1970	33,080	15,531	5.39	190,000	13,102	5.27	413,650	1,888,200	23.9
1971	33,540	15,909	5.46	184,800	12,654	5.83	424,600	2,054,200	24.2
1972	33,220	16,021	6.42	182,400	13,284	6.28	429,830	2,119,500	25.8
1973	33,480	16,784	6.04	179,800	14,008	6.77	456,100	2,190,450	29.8
1974	32,690	16,476	5.70	177,400	13,909	7.80	462,150	2,069,450	54.3
1975	31,750	15,826	7.46	179,400	14,398	8.41	508,700	2,393,100	53.6
1976	33,660	16,904	7.89	184,100	14,921	8.16	460,980	2,233,100	48.2
1977	33,760	16,561	8.51	176,800	14,343	8.07	453,980	2,376,200	49.6
1978	36,830	17,201	11.90	181,100	14,061	8.84	429,610	2,434,700	49.9
1979	35,720	17,603	9.15	179,800	14,033	9.89	417,640	2,463,940	51.3
1980	37,250	18,655	9.11	180,450	14,281	10.70	375,400	2,158,010	53.7
1981	36,720	18,628	10.80	183,700	14,288	11.60	401,000	2,378,170	63.1
1982	36,440	19,139	10.20	186,100	14,435	12.20	446,900	2,740,450	61.4
1983	34,780	18,287	13.70	190,900	14,874	12.50	399,800	2,227,060	59.8
1984	35,050	18,757	12.20	193,300	15,607	13.10	427,200	2,552,170	63.7
1985	33,860	18,349	10.30	191,100	15,754	12.70	435,300	2,640,000	63.4
1986	33,340	17,614	12.00	185,200	15,050	13.90	413,380	2,559,440	58.9
1987	33,940	17,847	11.10	194,300	15,664	12.90	430,920	2,866,630	59.3
1988	33,980	19,423	11.90	181,700	14,401	14.80	446,200	2,420,400	60.8
1989	35,330	20,276	13.20	182,200	16,135	16.90	464,450	2,949,340	66.9
1990	37,660	19,816	10.80	193,400	16,955	15.00	490,080	3,120,610	69.6
1991	33,010	19,090	10.80	183,200	14,995	17.00	545,860	3,396,080	71.0
1992	35,580	18,909	12.30	221,200	17,196	14.60	486,370	3,251,570	64.5
1993	28,220	18,215	14.80	209,800	18,848	17.80	472,060	2,721,190	72.4
1994	28,500	18,798	11.80	225,900	22,121	17.20	516,100	3,731,040	68.6
1995	27,550	18,120	16.30	225,200	21,792	18.30	483,910	3,324,150	75.6
1996	27,840	19,015	10.50	227,800	23,127	16.90	474,200	3,296,330	78.5
1997	26,910	18,119	14.70	236,400	23,641	17.70	465,800	3,342,330	74.9
1998	27,200	18,000	12.30	237,400	26,311	17.20	467,300	3,255,560	73.3
1999	27,500 [7]	18,727 [7]	11.70 [7]	242,300 [7]	27,248 [7]	16.80 [7]	466,800 [7]	3,297,910 [7]	71.1 [7]

Notes appear at end of table

TABLE Da929–949   Celery, sweet corn, cucumbers, eggplant, and garlic – acreage, production, and price: 1918–1999
Continued

	Cucumbers					
	Fresh			For pickles		
	Acreage harvested	Production	Price	Acreage harvested	Production	Price
	Da938 [2]	Da939 [1,2,5]	Da940 [2,3,5]	Da941 [2]	Da942 [1,2]	Da943 [2,3]
Year	Acres	Thousand hundredweight	Dollars per hundredweight	Acres	Short tons	Dollars per short ton
1918	12,200	963	5.10	64,430	86,256	35.83
1919	15,430	1,228	4.44	50,200	70,752	37.08
1920	17,570	1,158	3.69	50,570	46,128	40.83
1921	20,480	1,327	3.25	63,220	108,144	43.33
1922	26,500	1,846	2.75	52,830	62,904	38.75
1923	29,620	1,743	4.33	64,480	79,536	47.50
1924	39,080	2,321	2.85	85,410	61,176	47.50
1925	39,240	2,527	2.75	100,880	164,832	42.92
1926	35,890	2,235	3.13	70,740	89,352	40.00
1927	38,440	2,393	2.65	55,930	62,640	39.17
1928	45,840	2,482	2.44	73,970	107,784	34.58
1929	45,990	2,401	3.25	78,180	91,152	33.75
1930	62,940	3,302	2.19	114,520	175,080	32.92
1931	53,210	2,431	1.63	82,470	133,128	29.17
1932	48,100	2,016	1.52	30,910	41,448	20.83
1933	45,360	1,845	1.58	54,660	83,016	18.75
1934	47,030	2,079	1.83	77,470	100,536	19.58
1935	48,070	2,409	1.67	86,970	114,912	21.25
1936	48,350	2,046	1.98	86,020	145,104	23.33
1937	45,040	2,024	2.23	108,070	186,264	25.00
1938	44,850	2,331	1.67	82,290	146,232	24.58
1939	45,600	2,481	2.02	55,710	90,600	27.08
1940	43,500	2,310	2.31	91,340	147,600	24.17
1941	43,400	2,390	2.62	109,780	196,800	28.33
1942	41,800	2,291	3.31	107,610	199,200	33.33
1943	33,930	1,896	5.81	84,700	149,800	39.58
1944	38,200	1,910	4.56	98,870	183,600	45.83
1945	44,150	2,601	5.23	101,230	191,900	49.17
1946	55,950	3,276	5.10	134,260	251,800	58.33
1947	55,050	2,961	4.56	126,950	245,400	56.25
1948	49,650	3,168	5.02	124,760	236,300	67.50
1949	51,750	3,356	4.40	136,110	284,300	59.58
1950	49,850	3,361	4.75	108,790	175,800	67.92
1951	47,250	3,650	4.89	142,840	275,100	64.58
1952	45,400	3,633	5.47	150,690	331,400	65.00
1953	46,200	3,695	5.73	146,260	326,600	64.58
1954	52,850	4,210	4.73	138,310	301,000	59.17
1955	51,550	4,237	4.48	125,400	311,600	54.17
1956	49,250	3,961	5.41	115,960	323,000	55.00
1957	56,970	4,576	5.08	129,280	369,900	54.16
1958	52,800	4,432	4.50	119,150	356,300	53.33
1959	52,480	4,057	5.76	98,960	329,820	50.85
1960	53,690	4,401	5.10	90,230	336,060	54.33
1961	49,690	4,590	5.14	103,100	408,930	55.77
1962	49,220	4,197	6.00	98,960	401,520	53.39
1963	52,590	4,860	5.20	107,720	466,680	55.36
1964	52,280	4,954	5.72	108,900	425,790	65.80
1965	50,500	4,932	5.92	108,210	429,220	76.00
1966	48,190	4,728	6.74	131,020	537,800	81.60
1967	50,380	4,990	6.37	156,200	599,350	91.20
1968	53,590	4,449	7.12	148,320	564,460	92.10
1969	48,580	4,422	7.21	135,020	517,000	91.90
1970	47,670	4,478	6.42	133,580	588,800	94.10
1971	46,550	4,326	7.57	127,600	563,100	93.20
1972	48,960	4,702	8.14	128,830	571,150	94.00
1973	43,890	4,206	9.34	125,930	598,800	99.30
1974	45,690	4,676	10.40	132,010	597,000	131.00

Notes appear at end of table

(continued)

TABLE Da929–949   Celery, sweet corn, cucumbers, eggplant, and garlic – acreage, production, and price: 1918–1999
Continued

	Cucumbers					
	Fresh			For pickles		
	Acreage harvested	Production	Price	Acreage harvested	Production	Price
	Da938 [2]	Da939 [1,2,5]	Da940 [2,3,5]	Da941 [2]	Da942 [1,2]	Da943 [2,3]
Year	Acres	Thousand hundredweight	Dollars per hundredweight	Acres	Short tons	Dollars per short ton
1975	47,450	4,969	10.50	140,170	674,250	129.00
1976	48,960	5,109	9.67	128,380	633,800	126.00
1977	51,710	5,647	10.00	123,790	623,850	126.00
1978	53,460	5,931	12.10	134,740	685,450	130.00
1979	50,720	5,921	14.70	131,680	668,970	145.00
1980	54,160 [8]	6,143	13.70	116,410	609,170	166.00
1981	—	6,037	15.20	97,530	575,380	175.00
1982	—	7,222	12.70	—	—	—
1983	—	7,286	14.05	—	—	—
1984	—	7,661	13.45	103,580	618,240	168.00
1985	—	7,232	12.75	115,200	694,430	178.00
1986	—	7,457	12.75	110,510	639,550	177.00
1987	—	8,133	15.60	109,630	635,450	180.00
1988	—	8,349	15.75	118,870	651,580	200.00
1989	—	8,052	17.00	124,170	642,690	204.00
1990	—	8,576	15.80	115,490	653,480	209.00
1991	—	8,541	19.75	104,240	623,030	210.00
1992	—	9,156	19.10	102,510	558,070	211.00
1993	—	9,335	18.10	109,150	586,980	215.00
1994	—	9,415	16.00	116,640	633,518	219.00
1995	59,780	10,002	16.50	117,090	611,180	222.00
1996	56,000	9,836	19.00	105,200	536,689	248.00
1997	57,450	11,571 [9]	17.70 [9]	103,370	620,100	234.00
1998	57,280	11,263 [9]	20.00 [9]	102,870	593,720	237.00
1999	59,900 [7]	11,921	18.20	102,800 [7]	612,650 [7]	240.00 [7]

	Eggplant, fresh			Garlic, fresh		
	Acreage harvested	Production	Price	Acreage harvested	Production	Price
	Da944 [2]	Da945 [1,2]	Da946 [3]	Da947 [2]	Da948 [6]	Da949 [2]
Year	Acres	Thousand hundredweight	Dollars per hundredweight	Acres	Thousand hundredweight	Dollars per hundredweight
1918	—	—	—	—	—	—
1919	—	—	—	—	—	—
1920	—	—	—	—	—	—
1921	2,420	292	4.42	—	—	—
1922	2,170	281	4.61	1,200	84	4.00
1923	2,700	304	6.27	1,600	93	5.48
1924	2,470	236	3.24	1,740	52	6.52
1925	3,120	291	2.30	2,200	158	4.01
1926	2,290	196	3.30	3,700	202	2.00
1927	2,750	239	2.79	1,850	122	3.50
1928	2,960	205	3.21	2,250	135	4.25
1929	4,090	325	3.21	2,220	124	4.10
1930	4,400	289	2.30	4,230	142	3.54
1931	3,750	289	2.42	3,330	113	3.81
1932	4,100	298	1.79	4,500	139	2.61
1933	4,050	275	1.79	4,110	123	3.22
1934	3,850	256	1.58	3,600	124	3.65
1935	3,030	220	2.52	3,160	123	3.97
1936	3,700	317	1.52	3,900	149	4.11
1937	3,650	266	2.48	4,250	187	2.68
1938	4,350	354	1.70	4,460	182	3.01
1939	4,650	343	2.03	4,300	179	3.15

Notes appear at end of table

TABLE Da929–949   Celery, sweet corn, cucumbers, eggplant, and garlic – acreage, production, and price: 1918–1999
Continued

	Eggplant, fresh			Garlic, fresh		
	Acreage harvested	Production	Price	Acreage harvested	Production	Price
	Da944 [2]	Da945 [1,2]	Da946 [3]	Da947 [2]	Da948 [6]	Da949 [2]
Year	Acres	Thousand hundredweight	Dollars per hundredweight	Acres	Thousand hundredweight	Dollars per hundredweight
1940	3,800	270	2.58	3,890	142	7.43
1941	5,150	413	2.76	3,860	153	9.67
1942	4,050	304	3.67	4,320	210	4.18
1943	5,450	403	5.85	2,730	123	10.76
1944	5,850	469	4.18	2,780	142	16.63
1945	6,000	516	5.82	2,810	169	18.38
1946	7,100	621	4.61	3,500	196	13.41
1947	5,350	357	5.76	3,460	178	9.81
1948	6,260	518	4.36	2,350	122	20.30
1949	5,900	486	4.03	2,600	132	9.96
1950	5,250	468	4.64	3,040	178	8.48
1951	4,500	432	5.53	2,460	141	8.49
1952	5,300	545	4.86	2,050	124	16.03
1953	4,400	435	4.86	1,450	109	15.99
1954	4,700	466	4.84	1,950	146	11.45
1955	4,550	507	4.27	2,500	212	10.13
1956	4,000	442	5.20	2,400	216	10.43
1957	4,800	499	4.86	2,300	196	9.24
1958	4,600	422	5.56	2,900	218	10.41
1959	4,900	497	6.29	3,200	272	9.47
1960	4,850	479	5.51	5,400	459	8.45
1961	4,550	570	5.24	3,600	288	8.76
1962	3,500	547	5.56	2,700	284	10.79
1963	4,100	513	5.41	4,100	410	9.06
1964	3,850	517	6.25	4,400	506	9.38
1965	3,650	558	5.88	4,600	552	8.40
1966	3,350	510	7.40	3,500	350	8.27
1967	3,550	551	6.58	4,400	506	10.10
1968	2,900	424	10.70	6,400	800	8.99
1969	3,350	478	8.62	7,300	876	8.44
1970	3,000	467	8.03	5,600	728	8.39
1971	2,770	437	9.18	3,700	481	9.32
1972	3,100	522	8.68	5,100	663	9.84
1973	2,800	527	9.80	6,900	897	11.70
1974	3,250	605	11.60	9,000	1,170	12.20
1975	3,350	701	10.40	10,800	1,404	13.10
1976	3,450	702	10.40	8,800	924	13.00
1977	3,150	641	11.00	10,400	1,144	14.30
1978	3,550	669	12.70	13,000	1,560	15.80
1979	3,700	671	14.70	14,200	1,846	15.20
1980	3,900 [8]	719	14.50 [8]	15,200 [8]	1,976	17.10 [8]
1981	—	707	—	—	1,650	—
1982	—	—	—	—	—	—
1983	—	—	—	—	—	—
1984	—	—	—	—	—	—
1985	—	—	—	—	—	—
1986	—	—	—	—	—	—
1987	—	—	—	—	—	—
1988	—	—	—	—	—	—
1989	—	—	—	—	—	—
1990	—	—	—	—	—	—
1991	—	—	—	—	—	—
1992	—	828	—	23,000	3,795	—
1993	—	—	—	26,000	4,160	—
1994	—	—	—	27,000	4,590	—
1995	3,300	633	25.60	28,000	4,620	—
1996	3,100	713	26.90	35,000	6,125	—
1997	3,300	793	23.90	33,000	5,610	—
1998	3,200	768	28.50	38,000	5,510	—
1999	2,800 [7]	712 [7]	30.20 [7]	40,000	6,600	—

Notes appear on next page

(continued)

TABLE Da929–949   Celery, sweet corn, cucumbers, eggplant, and garlic – acreage, production, and price: 1918–1999
Continued

[1] See text for information on quantities not harvested or not marketed for economic reasons.

[2] Data for 1918–1938 not strictly comparable with later years; see text.

[3] Method of determining price changes over time; see text.

[4] 1944–1947, includes only New Jersey, New York, and Pennsylvania; 1948, also includes Florida and Massachusetts; thereafter, includes twenty-six commercially important states.

[5] For 1982–1991, U.S. production was estimated by the Economic Research Service based on available state reports.

[6] Louisiana, Texas, and California, 1922–1952; California only, 1953 to date. Includes production for fresh market and processing.

[7] Preliminary.

[8] Data in the original source appear to be in error but cannot be corrected.

[9] Data from original source have been revised.

Sources

Series Da929 and Da931. U.S. Department of Agriculture, Economic Research Service (USDA ERS), *Agricultural Statistics, 1952, 1967, 1974, 1982, 1992,* and *2000* editions.

Series Da930. 1918–1969, *Agricultural Statistics, 1952, 1967, 1974,* and *1982* editions; 1970–1992, USDA ERS, *U.S.–Mexico Fruit and Vegetable Trade,* March 1995, Table 16, downloaded January 27, 2001, from the U.S. Department of Agriculture, Economics and Statistics System; 1993–1999, *Agricultural Statistics, 2000.*

Series Da932 and Da934–937. *Agricultural Statistics, 1952, 1967, 1974, 1982, 1992, 1995–96,* and *2000* editions.

Series Da933. 1939–1969, *Agricultural Statistics, 1967, 1974,* and *1982* editions; 1970–1992, *U.S.–Mexico Fruit and Vegetable Trade,* March 1995, Table 17, downloaded January 27, 2001, from the U.S. Department of Agriculture, Economics and Statistics System; 1993–1999, *Agricultural Statistics, 2000.*

Series Da938. *Agricultural Statistics, 1952, 1967, 1974, 1981,* and *2000* editions.

Series Da939. 1918–1969, *Agricultural Statistics, 1952, 1967, 1974,* and *1981* editions; 1970–1981, *U.S.–Mexico Fruit and Vegetable Trade,* March 1995, Table 20, downloaded January 27, 2001, from the U.S. Department of Agriculture, Economics and Statistics System; 1982–1999, USDA ERS, *Vegetable Yearbook,* August 2000, Table 51, downloaded January 27, 2001, from the U.S. Department of Agriculture, Economics and Statistics System.

Series Da940. 1918–1975, *Agricultural Statistics, 1952, 1967, 1974,* and *1981* editions; 1976–1999, *Vegetable Yearbook,* August 2000, Table 51, downloaded January 27, 2001, from the U.S. Department of Agriculture, Economics and Statistics System.

Series Da941–943. *Agricultural Statistics, 1952, 1967, 1974, 1981, 1992,* and *2000* editions.

Series Da944 and Da946. *Agricultural Statistics, 1952, 1967, 1974, 1981, 1998, 1999,* and *2000* editions.

Series Da945. 1921–1969, *Agricultural Statistics, 1952, 1967,* and *1976* editions; 1970–1992, *U.S.–Mexico Fruit and Vegetable Trade,* March 1995, Table 21, downloaded January 27, 2001, from the U.S. Department of Agriculture, Economics and Statistics System; 1995–1999, *Agricultural Statistics, 1998, 1999,* and *2000* editions.

Series Da947 and Da949. *Agricultural Statistics, 1952, 1967, 1974, 1981, 1994, 1995–96, 1998,* and *2000* editions.

Series Da948. 1922–1969, *Agricultural Statistics, 1952, 1967, 1974,* and *1981* editions; 1970–1992, *U.S.–Mexico Fruit and Vegetable Trade,* March 1995, Table 22, downloaded January 27, 2001, from the U.S. Department of Agriculture, Economics and Statistics System; 1993–1999, *Agricultural Statistics, 1994, 1995–96, 1998,* and *2000* editions.

Documentation

See the text for Table Da885–888.

Series Da930. The official U.S. Department of Agriculture conversion factor estimates that one crate of celery is equivalent to sixty pounds. Data from 1918 to 1938 were converted from crates to hundredweight by multiplying crates by 0.6. This series covers production mostly for fresh market use, but includes quantities used for processing. Prior to 1964, includes the follow-

ing quantities not marketed, which were excluded in computing value (in thousands of hundredweight): 167 in 1932; 208 in 1933; 254 in 1938; 31 in 1943; 240 in 1944; 61 in 1945; 488 in 1946; 557 in 1947; 231 in 1949; 257 in 1950; 124 in 1951; 68 in 1952; 183 in 1953; 405 in 1954; 66 in 1955; 859 in 1956; 825 in 1959; 136 in 1961; and 253 in 1963. Excludes the following quantities not harvested or not marketed because of economic conditions (thousands of hundredweight): 183 in 1964; 134 in 1965; 297 in 1966; 823 in 1967; 351 in 1968; 128 in 1969; 22 in 1970; 70 in 1971; 56 in 1973; and 109 in 1974.

Series Da931, Da935–936, Da938–945, Da947, and Da949. Data for 1918–1938 are not strictly comparable with those for later years. In the earlier period, estimates were frequently made only for well-recognized commercial areas from which substantial quantities were shipped – usually by rail – to distant terminal markets. In many states, local-market or market garden areas near large population centers were excluded from these 1918–1938 estimates. This feature makes this early series less complete than that from 1939 to 1999.

Series Da931. The official U.S. Department of Agriculture conversion factor estimates that one crate of celery is equivalent to sixty pounds. Data from 1918 to 1938 were converted from dollars per crate to dollars per hundredweight by dividing dollars per crate by 0.6.

Series Da931, Da940, and Da946. Beginning with 1954, price on an f.o.b. (free on board) basis.

Series Da933. Prior to 1964, includes the following quantities not marketed, which were excluded in computing value (thousands of hundredweight): 138 in 1947; 194 in 1949; 428 in 1950; 99 in 1951; 88 in 1952; 233 in 1955; 13 in 1956; 180 in 1958; 105 in 1959; 242 in 1961; 50 in 1962; and 226 in 1963. Excludes the following quantities not harvested or not marketed because of economic conditions (thousands of hundredweight): 157 in 1964; 46 in 1965; 89 in 1966; 30 in 1967; 49 in 1969; 120 in 1970; 349 in 1971; 77 in 1972; and 56 in 1978.

Series Da934. Price on an f.o.b. basis.

Series Da937 and Da943. Beginning with 1964, at processing plant door; prior to 1964, average price received by growers at receiving point.

Series Da939 and Da942. Excludes some quantities not marketed (thousands of hundredweight): 101 in 1964; 3 for fresh market and 13,630 tons for processing in 1965; 40 in 1977. Prior to 1964 includes the following quantities not marketed, which were excluded in computing value (thousands of hundredweight): 744 in 1930; 60 in 1931; 48 in 1932; 109 in 1935; 23 in 1939; 20 in 1941; 3 in 1945; 61 in 1946; 96 in 1947; 30 in 1948; 115 in 1949; 165 in 1950; 260 in 1951; 31 in 1953; 247 in 1954; 146 in 1955; 30 in 1956; 98 in 1957; 308 in 1958; 156 in 1959; 141 in 1960; 80 in 1961; 81 in 1962; and 106 in 1963.

Series Da939. The official U.S. Department of Agriculture conversion factor estimates that one bushel of cucumbers is equivalent to forty-eight pounds (or 0.024 short tons). Data from 1918–1938 were converted from bushels to hundredweight by multiplying bushels by 0.48.

Series Da940. Data from 1918 to 1938 were converted from dollars per bushels to dollars per hundredweight by dividing dollars per bushels by 0.48. Comparable grower prices are not available for 1982–1990.

Series Da942. Data from 1918 to 1938 were converted from thousands of bushels to short tons by multiplying thousands of bushels by 24.

Series Da943. Data from 1918 to 1938 were converted from dollars per bushels to dollars per short ton by dividing dollars per bushels by 0.024.

Series Da945. Includes some quantities not marketed and excluded in computing value (thousands of hundredweight): 30 in 1944; 20 in 1945; 59 in 1946; 79 in 1948; 28 in 1949; 24 in 1950; 3 in 1954; 29 in 1955; 5 in 1956; 11 in 1957; 13 in 1958; and 14 in 1961. Excludes the following quantities not harvested or not marketed because of economic conditions (thousands of hundredweight): 20 in 1964; 20 in 1965; and 21 in 1966. The official U.S. Department of Agriculture conversion factor estimates that one bushel of eggplant is equivalent to thirty-three pounds. Data from 1922 to 1938 were converted from bushels to hundredweight by multiplying bushels by 0.33.

Series Da946. Data from 1922 to 1938 were converted from dollars per bushel to dollars per hundredweight by dividing dollars per bushel by 0.33.

TABLE Da950–967   Lettuce, honeydew, onions, peppers, and tomatoes – acreage, production, and price: 1918–1999[1]

Contributed by Alan L. Olmstead and Paul W. Rhode

	Lettuce, fresh head			Honeydew, fresh			Onions		
	Acreage harvested	Production	Price	Acreage harvested	Production	Price	Acreage harvested	Production	Price
	Da950	Da951 [2, 3]	Da952 [4]	Da953	Da954 [3]	Da955 [4]	Da956	Da957 [3]	Da958 [4]
Year	Acres	Thousand hundredweight	Dollars per hundredweight	Acres	Thousand hundredweight	Dollars per hundredweight	Acres	Thousand hundredweight	Dollars per hundredweight
1918	15,840	2,651	2.33	—	—	—	66,260	10,851	1.82
1919	19,570	3,031	2.73	—	—	—	54,030	8,167	3.04
1920	32,520	5,392	2.19	—	—	—	69,390	11,869	1.44
1921	31,180	5,050	2.70	—	—	—	59,740	7,910	2.80
1922	46,870	6,504	2.69	—	—	—	66,510	10,502	1.78
1923	56,430	7,258	2.29	—	—	—	65,870	9,796	2.26
1924	64,470	8,695	2.24	—	—	—	68,740	10,810	1.92
1925	80,640	10,097	2.09	—	—	—	67,330	11,002	2.20
1926	103,990	11,389	2.40	—	—	—	81,460	12,246	1.68
1927	121,680	13,041	1.91	—	—	—	84,550	13,380	1.68
1928	123,930	12,926	2.43	13,340	1,416	1.83	97,990	12,045	2.30
1929	139,860	13,992	2.63	12,680	1,514	1.60	104,190	15,234	1.48
1930	171,580	13,874	2.46	15,110	1,447	2.51	96,450	15,393	0.96
1931	173,300	13,541	2.11	15,200	1,562	1.49	101,890	11,414	1.86
1932	162,650	12,499	1.84	16,400	1,735	1.23	124,950	15,649	0.82
1933	141,350	12,166	1.86	10,650	993	1.66	107,560	12,621	1.28
1934	155,630	13,374	2.00	8,150	922	2.11	116,780	13,602	1.34
1935	151,720	13,477	2.09	12,110	1,137	1.63	146,370	14,765	1.42
1936	164,530	14,773	2.09	12,780	1,201	1.71	175,280	17,344	0.86
1937	151,750	14,518	2.26	13,320	1,327	1.71	136,710	15,120	1.32
1938	147,540	13,437	2.17	12,310	1,075	1.83	140,770	15,423	1.10
1939	169,670	17,057	1.91	13,700	1,221	1.45	135,820	18,311	0.90
1940	148,810	15,601	2.11	14,400	1,085	2.11	112,890	16,443	1.40
1941	157,440	16,628	2.53	11,000	1,258	2.05	100,760	15,614	2.20
1942	156,590	17,292	3.64	8,750	981	3.45	138,100	19,454	1.98
1943	137,720	18,866	4.44	8,780	1,133	5.93	113,300	15,671	3.36
1944	165,950	21,599	3.50	13,050	1,607	4.16	181,760	23,970	2.40
1945	173,880	22,534	3.94	17,000	2,186	4.39	143,570	18,834	3.38
1946	200,410	26,119	3.41	20,150	2,036	4.02	160,690	25,223	1.78
1947	190,350	26,673	4.21	14,930	1,504	4.59	120,980	18,357	4.16
1948	202,590	26,526	4.04	11,750	1,446	4.21	132,580	21,247	2.64
1949	202,320	26,674	4.84	9,850	1,198	4.13	122,760	19,604	2.94
1950	227,680	28,940	3.48	8,900	1,242	4.06	136,290	22,091	1.75
1951	204,350	27,944	4.44	10,000	1,412	4.58	101,410	20,045	3.34
1952	214,180	30,437	4.13	9,500	1,440	5.21	116,350	20,020	4.62
1953	208,600	30,844	4.00	10,700	1,618	4.80	131,850	25,253	1.37
1954	206,420	31,255	4.03	13,000	1,756	4.78	116,060	22,174	2.26
1955	210,900	32,937	4.20	13,600	1,559	4.74	114,130	21,388	2.49
1956	229,080	35,693	3.76	12,700	1,647	4.44	123,750	24,426	2.88
1957	234,050	34,506	4.05	9,250	1,227	5.32	110,410	24,364	2.99
1958	225,100	34,349	3.80	11,170	1,270	4.66	107,000	23,784	3.51
1959	221,610	35,182	3.94	8,860	1,251	5.58	113,530	25,609	2.52
1960	222,590	38,631	4.14	9,900	1,379	4.95	102,580	26,457	2.44
1961	218,040	38,054	3.45	9,500	1,322	5.64	91,340	23,600	4.05
1962	198,020	37,554	4.36	9,500	1,237	4.63	96,330	25,789	2.85
1963	214,940	39,328	4.22	8,150	1,299	5.81	95,650	25,781	3.51
1964	212,590	39,137	4.40	9,800	1,312	5.49	99,660	25,267	2.86
1965	214,940	40,884	4.61	10,300	1,496	5.62	97,170	28,078	3.21
1966	216,960	41,534	5.31	9,100	1,216	6.63	93,780	24,723	4.89
1967	221,150	42,966	4.99	11,300	1,577	5.82	102,680	28,579	3.95
1968	220,980	44,273	4.51	10,300	1,379	6.71	105,920	28,769	3.60
1969	228,570	44,874	5.41	13,800	1,971	5.86	100,000	28,234	4.13
1970	234,740	46,540	4.75	13,200	1,931	5.66	101,000	30,493	3.67
1971	216,750	47,367	6.31	12,300	2,039	6.23	98,800	29,803	3.88
1972	220,470	48,720	5.73	13,200	2,307	6.24	94,470	28,355	6.48
1973	224,950	50,535	7.40	14,000	2,453	7.47	104,990	29,689	7.57
1974	228,320	51,431	6.93	12,400	2,185	8.23	109,730	33,151	4.87

Notes appear at end of table   (continued)

TABLE Da950–967   Lettuce, honeydew, onions, peppers, and tomatoes – acreage, production, and price: 1918–1999 Continued

	Lettuce, fresh head			Honeydew, fresh			Onions		
	Acreage harvested	Production	Price	Acreage harvested	Production	Price	Acreage harvested	Production	Price
	Da950	Da951 [2, 3]	Da952 [4]	Da953	Da954 [3]	Da955 [4]	Da956	Da957 [3]	Da958 [4]
Year	Acres	Thousand hundredweight	Dollars per hundredweight	Acres	Thousand hundredweight	Dollars per hundredweight	Acres	Thousand hundredweight	Dollars per hundredweight
1975	228,750	53,658	6.71	12,570	2,395	9.31	103,080	31,418	9.35
1976	225,020	56,400	8.26	13,950	2,346	10.60	109,520	35,288	6.93
1977	231,380	60,432	6.94	15,480	2,591	9.87	108,550	34,583	6.76
1978	239,090	60,528	9.90	18,520	3,413	9.62	121,920	36,174	7.81
1979	245,850	61,439	9.20	20,500	3,477	10.90	123,910	38,602	6.98
1980	236,460	63,363	8.91	17,700	3,180	13.50	113,160	33,526	11.40
1981	223,840	62,682	10.90	19,600	3,419	15.40	112,030	35,155	14.70
1982	216,050	62,949	12.10	24,900	3,780	14.10	125,920	41,861	8.24
1983	205,730 [6]	57,755 [6]	12.30 [6]	23,800	3,918	13.20	123,640	39,166	12.50
1984	218,280	63,976	10.90	23,300	4,031	13.90	128,450	43,068	10.60
1985	221,990	61,334	10.80	25,700	4,758	12.20	122,760	45,059	9.08
1986	211,460	58,290	12.00	28,800	5,438	12.70	115,540	43,615	11.10
1987	224,920	67,877	14.80	28,600	4,811	14.40	123,720	45,113	12.50
1988	239,760	70,505	14.80	31,200	5,241	14.40	128,950	46,733	9.75
1989	243,260	75,231	12.60	29,900	5,131	12.10	132,660	47,902	11.40
1990	231,300	73,201	11.50	26,400	4,503	18.00	138,340	52,781	10.50
1991	222,140	70,778	11.40	25,900	3,737	18.40	133,970	50,702	12.50
1992	215,120	70,810	12.50	26,200	4,740	13.50	141,730	54,213	13.00
1993	207,810	67,811	16.00	23,300	3,792	18.20	158,080	60,124	16.50
1994	220,950	70,058	13.30	27,100	4,724	16.40	164,650	65,313	10.80
1995	197,160	62,349	23.50	26,000	4,332	20.60	166,800	65,374	11.10
1996	217,600	62,072	14.70	27,300	4,737	17.00	166,210	64,106	10.50
1997	203,000	68,794	17.50	26,600	4,828 [8]	18.90	165,910	68,769	12.60
1998	198,400	63,401	16.10	25,500	4,887 [8]	21.10	166,340	66,024	13.85
1999	199,100 [7]	72,799	13.30 [7]	28,500 [7]	6,132	20.70 [7]	169,200 [7]	71,379 [7]	10.20 [7]

	Peppers, fresh bell			Tomatoes					
				Fresh			For processing		
	Acreage harvested	Production	Price	Acreage harvested	Production	Price	Acreage harvested	Production	Price
	Da959	Da960 [2, 3]	Da961 [4]	Da962	Da963 [3]	Da964 [4]	Da965	Da966 [3]	Da967 [5]
Year	Acres	Thousand hundredweight	Dollars per hundredweight	Acres	Thousand hundredweight	Dollars per hundredweight	Acres	Short tons	Dollars per short ton
1918	—	—	—	75,080	5,587	2.79	354,090	1,565,900	21.73
1919	—	—	—	82,860	5,684	2.85	276,960	1,111,100	18.50
1920	—	—	—	81,540	6,170	3.08	235,780	1,099,800	19.80
1921	7,480	673	6.48	73,510	5,384	3.34	94,340	456,900	11.65
1922	8,010	670	6.72	101,860	7,625	3.74	235,150	1,199,200	12.62
1923	8,650	786	6.28	98,930	7,281	4.40	268,700	1,165,300	13.56
1924	9,870	793	4.60	128,320	8,119	3.79	291,270	1,190,200	15.71
1925	12,850	803	5.00	127,790	8,975	3.92	355,130	1,809,200	14.79
1926	12,230	768	4.64	116,000	7,238	3.83	263,300	998,600	14.71
1927	13,800	844	4.04	135,420	8,857	3.11	267,970	1,195,900	14.31
1928	14,000	865	4.32	149,310	9,129	3.09	270,850	997,200	14.19
1929	16,400	944	4.44	157,640	10,759	3.26	323,720	1,543,700	15.25
1930	19,590	1,084	3.76	170,730	10,334	2.98	407,950	1,757,500	15.05
1931	17,900	1,127	3.08	168,140	10,041	2.08	296,120	976,400	11.80
1932	17,020	955	2.88	173,380	10,772	1.85	280,510	1,199,300	10.08
1933	18,650	1,169	2.08	171,330	10,205	2.08	280,150	1,081,300	11.39
1934	18,350	912	2.68	193,680	11,637	2.26	368,660	1,425,700	12.03
1935	17,870	920	3.04	189,960	11,932	2.13	471,730	1,700,200	11.73
1936	20,320	1,184	2.48	193,060	11,177	2.47	419,070	1,987,500	12.59
1937	20,600	1,201	2.92	203,360	11,664	2.47	451,000	1,926,300	13.11
1938	22,560	1,362	2.52	219,910	13,607	2.02	392,350	1,742,600	12.41
1939	22,800	1,428	3.40	232,500	15,232	2.57	365,220	2,022,500	12.14

Notes appear at end of table

TABLE Da950–967   Lettuce, honeydew, onions, peppers, and tomatoes – acreage, production, and price: 1918–1999
Continued

	Peppers, fresh bell			Tomatoes					
				Fresh			For processing		
	Acreage harvested	Production	Price	Acreage harvested	Production	Price	Acreage harvested	Production	Price
	Da959	Da960 [2, 3]	Da961 [4]	Da962	Da963 [3]	Da964 [4]	Da965	Da966 [3]	Da967 [5]
Year	Acres	Thousand hundredweight	Dollars per hundredweight	Acres	Thousand hundredweight	Dollars per hundredweight	Acres	Short tons	Dollars per short ton
1940	22,200	1,291	3.40	217,850	14,156	2.28	412,150	2,282,900	11.80
1941	23,300	1,263	3.96	209,860	13,677	3.00	445,310	2,689,300	15.13
1942	21,900	1,261	5.20	231,100	15,398	3.98	582,920	3,067,900	19.77
1943	24,600	1,241	8.92	228,600	15,373	5.43	523,650	2,530,000	26.35
1944	26,550	1,431	6.96	260,850	15,678	5.81	525,200	2,919,300	27.18
1945	29,200	1,693	8.12	283,100	18,191	6.26	515,390	2,545,200	27.64
1946	35,400	1,990	7.20	290,250	18,544	5.45	556,820	3,366,970	30.65
1947	33,650	1,599	9.76	238,250	16,170	6.02	499,770	3,229,400	28.67
1948	36,600	2,050	7.52	234,080	16,547	6.10	391,200	2,882,950	27.92
1949	41,190	2,368	7.41	241,290	17,700	5.58	324,500	2,469,100	23.89
1950	41,490	2,419	6.76	234,240	17,667	6.41	336,150	2,628,060	25.30
1951	38,430	2,330	8.56	228,170	18,372	6.58	419,330	4,257,950	31.40
1952	37,000	2,364	9.94	225,840	18,380	7.57	373,200	3,546,250	29.10
1953	41,010	2,514	8.95	223,480	18,208	7.06	304,500	3,268,400	27.30
1954	47,950	2,902	7.45	236,450	19,776	6.94	262,950	2,690,690	24.30
1955	45,140	3,240	7.19	232,230	20,951	7.03	330,500	3,278,320	24.90
1956	40,540	3,044	8.20	221,600	19,868	8.10	354,480	4,638,010	25.70
1957	44,930	3,240	8.93	218,280	20,147	7.73	304,320	3,314,130	25.20
1958	40,640	2,881	9.22	212,650	18,463	6.61	343,650	4,281,190	25.40
1959	46,590	3,318	9.08	193,170	19,486	7.70	296,930	3,539,030	24.46
1960	45,880	3,633	7.97	161,520	19,006	8.00	279,950	4,053,770	26.12
1961	47,230	3,989	7.76	163,530	21,121	7.61	304,550	4,257,900	29.65
1962	43,280	3,715	8.67	158,430	20,877	7.53	327,900	5,393,900	28.42
1963	44,110	3,985	7.83	155,920	20,012	7.68	250,460	4,099,690	26.74
1964	43,050	3,874	9.73	155,270	20,527	8.85	273,350	4,583,310	30.70
1965	45,530	3,891	9.82	152,180	20,420	9.45	257,520	4,411,340	37.20
1966	48,470	4,024	10.20	150,650	20,326	9.39	299,830	4,662,270	35.70
1967	46,990	4,328	10.60	148,450	20,555	9.51	327,060	5,189,550	42.80
1968	51,620	4,916	10.50	143,110	19,446	11.60	370,550	6,967,600	40.20
1969	51,600	4,361	12.10	147,580	19,249	11.60	266,590	4,901,650	34.70
1970	47,660	3,872	11.70	147,100	18,234	11.20	245,090	5,058,950	34.00
1971	48,900	4,072	12.30	136,360	17,827	13.90	258,130	5,515,550	35.50
1972	47,750	4,651	12.70	145,170	19,925	14.80	265,020	5,803,700	35.20
1973	47,930	4,738	13.90	138,990	19,556	16.00	295,100	5,934,550	42.00
1974	48,840	5,251	14.50	124,160	20,081	17.30	337,700	7,019,850	64.50
1975	50,480	5,106	16.60	124,680	21,114	18.70	384,250	8,503,750	63.20
1976	53,950	5,269	16.80	127,590	21,772	19.10	308,960	6,471,750	58.00
1977	56,300	5,370	16.40	124,420	19,895	20.60	346,660	7,779,150	64.10
1978	55,200	5,201	19.40	130,220	22,408	19.70	295,560	6,367,700	64.20
1979	61,300	5,819	19.90	125,200	23,292	22.50	312,030	7,329,510	67.60
1980	55,500 [9]	5,494	22.70	126,250	25,393	20.70	263,030	6,210,590	61.00
1981	—	5,875	23.80	126,960	25,981	21.40	253,920	5,716,130	67.50
1982	—	5,927	20.91	119,690	26,769	22.50	295,300	7,298,990	71.60
1983	—	6,987	23.94	123,100	27,262	24.20	292,020	7,029,840	68.40
1984	—	7,150	21.66	122,580	28,163	25.60	291,870	7,681,160	67.40
1985	—	7,652	19.52	123,380	29,740	24.20	265,500	7,177,130	66.30
1986	—	8,593	19.46	125,710	31,361	25.10	252,330	7,398,470	63.90
1987	—	9,176	27.95	129,600	32,414	25.90	257,400	7,607,690	59.10
1988	—	9,905	22.31	139,700	35,889	27.10	274,920	7,409,920	60.70
1989	—	10,144	25.50	141,240	35,904	33.20	320,850	9,484,470	69.30
1990	—	10,505	24.59	134,590	33,800	27.40	354,700	10,355,260	67.80
1991	—	12,361	27.78	131,710	33,988	31.70	355,980	10,872,990	66.40
1992	66,600	14,428	26.80	131,910	39,033	35.80	273,910	8,777,430	58.00
1993	64,950	14,498	30.30	134,250	36,663	31.60	307,470	9,676,667	60.10
1994	64,500	15,422	29.70	135,220	37,387	27.40	340,060	11,539,710	62.10
1995	67,600	14,431	31.40	131,020	34,098	25.20	344,380	11,285,007	63.20
1996	68,500	16,639	28.00	120,640	33,634	28.20	339,140	11,407,301	62.30
1997	56,200	14,959	32.10	115,190	32,777	31.70	283,390	9,973,259	60.70
1998	56,680	14,556	34.80	121,710	32,628	35.20	299,960	9,402,010	65.30
1999	58,220 [7]	15,321	30.40	131,680 [7]	35,492 [7]	25.90 [7]	350,410 [7]	12,836,020 [7]	71.10 [7]

Notes appear on next page

(continued)

TABLE Da950–967   Lettuce, honeydew, onions, peppers, and tomatoes – acreage, production, and price: 1918–1999   *Continued*

[1] Data for 1918–1938 not strictly comparable with later years; see text.

[2] Data adjusted or estimated by the Economic Research Service; see text.

[3] See text for information on quantities not harvested or not marketed for economic reasons.

[4] Beginning 1954, price on an f.o.b. (free on board) basis.

[5] Through 1963, average price received by growers at receiving point; thereafter, price at the processing plant door.

[6] Owing to program modifications, 1983 data are not comparable with other data.

[7] Preliminary.

[8] Data from original source have been revised.

[9] Data in the original source appear to be in error but cannot be corrected.

Sources

Series Da950, Da953, and Da956–958. U.S. Department of Agriculture, Economic Research Service, *Agricultural Statistics, 1952, 1967, 1974, 1982, 1992,* and *2000* editions.

Series Da951–952. 1918–1975, *Agricultural Statistics, 1952, 1967, 1974,* and *1982* editions; 1976–1999, U.S. Department of Agriculture, Economic Research Service, *Vegetable Yearbook,* August 2000, Table 43, downloaded January 27, 2001, from the U.S. Department of Agriculture, Economics and Statistics System.

Series Da954–955. 1928–1975, *Agricultural Statistics, 1952, 1967, 1974,* and *1982* editions; 1976–1999, *Vegetable Yearbook,* August 2000, Table 59, downloaded January 27, 2001, from the U.S. Department of Agriculture, Economics and Statistics System.

Series Da959. *Agricultural Statistics, 1952, 1967, 1974, 1981, 1993, 1995–96, 1998,* and *2000* editions.

Series Da960–961. 1921–1975, *Agricultural Statistics, 1952, 1967, 1974,* and *1981* editions; 1976–1999, *Vegetable Yearbook,* August 2000, Table 42, downloaded January 27, 2001, from the U.S. Department of Agriculture, Economics and Statistics System.

Series Da962 and Da965. *Agricultural Statistics, 1952, 1967, 1974, 1982, 1992,* and *2000* editions.

Series Da963–964 and Da966–967. 1918–1975, *Agricultural Statistics, 1952, 1967, 1974,* and *1982* editions; 1976–1999, *Vegetable Yearbook,* August 2000, Tables 41 and 69, downloaded February 7, 2001, from the U.S. Department of Agriculture, Economics and Statistics System.

Documentation

See the text for Table Da885–888.

Data for 1918–1938 are not strictly comparable with those from 1939 to 1999. In the earlier period, estimates were frequently made only for well-recognized commercial areas from which substantial quantities were shipped – usually by rail – to distant terminal markets. In many states, local-market or market garden areas near large population centers were excluded from these 1918–1938 estimates. This feature makes this early series less complete than that from 1939 to 1999.

Series Da951. Production data were adjusted by the Economic Research Service for 1970–1981 to account for states not included in the National Agricultural Statistics Service estimates.

Series Da951. The official U.S. Department of Agriculture conversion rate estimates that one crate of lettuce is equivalent to seventy pounds. Data for 1918–1938 were converted from crates to hundredweight by multiplying crates by 0.7. The series includes the following quantities not marketed and excluded in computing value (thousands of hundredweight): 330 in 1932; 63 in 1933; 210 in 1934; 351 in 1936; 77 in 1937; 197 in 1938; 1,352 in 1939; 27 in 1940; 11 in 1942; 33 in 1943; 110 in 1944; 23 in 1945; 185 in 1946; 98 in 1947; 562 in 1948; 641 in 1949; 1,340 in 1950; 119 in 1951; 144 in 1952; 195 in 1953; 205 in 1954; 398 in 1956; 130 in 1957; 397 in 1958; 1,047 in 1959; 3,744 in 1960; 1,857 in 1961; 446 in 1962; and 119.6 in 1963. Excludes the following quantities not marketed (thousands of hundredweight): 7.2 in 1964; 46 in 1965; 673 in 1966; 124 in 1967; 735 in 1968; 576 in 1969; 915 in 1970; 338 in 1971; and 82 in 1972.

Series Da952. Data from 1918 to 1938 were converted from dollars per crate to dollars per hundredweight by dividing dollars per crate by 0.7.

Series Da954. Includes the following quantities not marketed and excluded in computing value (thousands of hundredweight): 84 in 1931; 564 in 1932; and 153 in 1933. The official U.S. Department of Agriculture conversion factor estimates that one crate of honeydew melons is equivalent to thirty-five pounds. Data from 1928 to 1938 were converted from crates to hundredweight by multiplying crates by 0.35.

Series Da955. Data from 1928 to 1938 were converted from dollars per crate to dollars per hundredweight by dividing dollars per crate by 0.35.

Series Da956–961. Mostly for fresh market use, but includes some quantities used for processing.

Series Da957. Includes onions for all uses. Includes storage crop onions harvested but not sold because of shrinkage and waste. Includes the following quantities not harvested and excluded in computing value (thousands of hundredweight) because of low prices, labor shortage, lack of transportation, and other economic factors: 88 in 1928; 83 in 1929; 43 in 1930; 364 in 1931; 750 in 1932; 99 in 1934; 267 in 1935; 925 in 1936; 246 in 1937; 492 in 1938; 476 in 1939; 45 in 1940; 493 in 1942; 557 in 1944; 124 in 1945; 1,276 in 1946; 198 in 1948; 646 in 1950; 200 in 1951; 1,202 in 1953; 98 in 1954; 1,006 in 1956; 384 in 1957; 563 in 1958; 573 in 1959; 380 in 1960; and 35 in 1961. Excludes the following quantities not harvested or not marketed because of economic conditions (thousands of hundredweight): 644 in 1964; 257 in 1967; 39 in 1970; and 30 in 1976. The official U.S. Department of Agriculture conversion rate estimates that one sack of onions is equivalent to fifty pounds. Data before 1939 were converted from sacks to hundredweight by multiplying sacks by 0.5.

Series Da958. Data before 1939 were converted from dollars per sack to dollars per hundredweight by dividing sacks by 0.5.

Series Da960. Includes the following quantities not marketed, which are excluded in computing value (thousands of hundredweight): 15 in 1931; 29 in 1936; 17 in 1944; 2 in 1945; 99 in 1946; 63 in 1948; 68 in 1950; 59 in 1951; 59 in 1954; 130 in 1955; 44 in 1958; 59 in 1960; and 55 in 1961. Excludes the following quantities not marketed (thousands of hundredweight): 17 in 1964; 96 in 1965; and 62 in 1966. The official U.S. Department of Agriculture conversion factor estimates that one bushel of peppers is equivalent to twenty-five pounds. Data from 1921 to 1938 were converted from bushels to hundredweight by multiplying bushels by 0.25. From 1982 to 1991, U.S. production was estimated by the Economic Research Service based on available state reports.

Series Da961. Data from 1921 to 1938 were converted from dollars per bushel to dollars per hundredweight by dividing dollars per bushel by 0.25.

Series Da963. Includes the following quantities not marketed, which are excluded in computing value (thousands of hundredweight): 68 in 1931; 27 in 1932; 38 in 1933; 517 in 1934; 40 in 1935; 81 in 1938; 22 in 1940; 27 in 1941; 8 in 1942; 21 in 1943; 181 in 1945; 169 in 1946; 42 in 1948; 105 in 1949; 59 in 1951; 102 in 1954; 110 in 1955; 100 in 1956; 541 in 1958; 1 in 1962; and 1 in 1963. Excludes the following quantities not harvested or not marketed because of economic conditions (thousands of hundredweight): 1 in 1964; 56 in 1965; 406 in 1966; 1 in 1967; 100 in 1970; 19 in 1973; and 44 in 1977. In 1968, includes some quantities not delivered because of economic conditions. The official U.S. Department of Agriculture conversion rate estimates that one bushel of tomatoes is equivalent to fifty-three pounds. Data from 1918 to 1938 were converted from bushels to hundredweight by dividing bushels by 0.53.

Series Da964. Data from 1918 to 1938 were converted from dollars per bushel to dollars per hundredweight by dividing dollars per bushel by 0.53.

Series Da966. Excludes the following quantities not marketed (thousands of short tons): 90.6 in 1965 and 200 in 1976. In 1968, includes some quantities not delivered because of economic conditions.

TABLE Da968–982 Cattle, hogs, and sheep – number, value per head, production, and price: 1866–2000 [Annual]

Contributed by Alan L. Olmstead and Paul W. Rhode

	Number and value per head							Live weight production and price						
	Cattle		Hogs		Stock (breeding) sheep / Sheep		Sheep and lambs, value per head	Cattle			Hogs		Sheep		Lambs, price
	Number	Value per head	Number	Value per head	Number	Value per head		Cattle, production	Beef cattle, price	Veal calves, price	Production	Price	Production	Price	
Year	Da968	Da969	Da970	Da971 [1]	Da972 [2]	Da973	Da974 [2]	Da975 [3]	Da976	Da977	Da978 [3]	Da979	Da980 [3]	Da981	Da982
	Thousand	Dollars	Thousand	Dollars	Thousand	Dollars	Dollars	Million pounds	Dollars per hundredweight	Dollars per hundredweight	Million pounds	Dollars per hundredweight	Million pounds	Dollars per hundredweight	Dollars per hundredweight
1866	28,636	—	34,489	3.95	—	—	—	—	—	—	—	—	—	—	—
1867	29,238	21.55	33,304	5.43	44,997	3.37	—	—	—	—	—	—	—	—	—
1868	30,060	20.86	32,570	4.55	43,808	2.52	—	—	—	—	—	—	—	—	—
1869		25.12	33,781	6.26	39,892	2.17	—	—	—	—	—	—	—	—	—
1870	31,082	22.54	36,688	6.99	36,449	2.28	—	—	—	—	—	—	—	—	—
1871	32,107	22.81	39,296	6.19	34,063	2.32	—	—	—	—	—	—	—	—	—
1872	33,078	19.61	39,794	4.36	34,312	2.80	—	—	—	—	—	—	—	—	—
1873	33,830	20.06	38,377	4.09	35,782	2.96	—	—	—	—	—	—	—	—	—
1874	34,821	19.15	35,834	4.36	36,234	2.61	—	—	—	—	—	—	—	—	—
1875	35,361	18.68	35,715	5.34	37,237	2.79	—	—	—	—	—	—	—	—	—
1876	36,140	19.04	39,333	6.80	37,477	2.60	—	—	—	—	—	—	—	—	—
1877	37,333	17.10	43,375	6.09	38,147	2.27	—	—	—	—	—	—	—	—	—
1878	39,396	17.14	43,767	4.98	38,942	2.25	—	—	—	—	—	—	—	—	—
1879	41,420	15.39	44,327	3.18	41,678	2.07	—	—	—	—	—	—	—	—	—
1880	43,347	17.80	43,076	4.80	44,867	2.18	—	—	—	—	—	—	—	—	—
1881	44,501	18.67	42,566	6.00	47,371	2.35	—	—	—	—	—	—	—	—	—
1882	45,738	20.93	43,440	6.74	48,883	2.35	—	—	—	—	—	—	—	—	—
1883	47,387	23.87	45,961	5.64	50,935	2.53	—	—	—	—	—	—	—	—	—
1884	49,804	25.26	47,330	5.06	51,101	2.40	—	—	—	—	—	—	—	—	—
1885	52,463	24.40	45,457	4.30	49,620	2.19	—	—	—	—	—	—	—	—	—
1886	54,868	22.20	42,563	4.60	46,654	1.95	—	—	—	—	—	—	—	—	—
1887	56,602	21.18	42,134	5.12	44,217	2.05	—	—	—	—	—	—	—	—	—
1888	58,599	19.39	44,508	5.80	43,011	2.06	—	—	—	—	—	—	—	—	—
1889	59,178	18.77	48,130	4.80	42,365	2.14	—	—	—	—	—	—	—	—	—
1890	60,014	16.95	47,435	4.24	42,693	2.29	—	—	—	—	—	—	—	—	—
1891	59,968	16.49	45,165	4.65	43,882	2.51	—	—	—	—	—	—	—	—	—
1892	58,126	16.81	43,652	6.37	44,628	2.60	—	—	—	—	—	—	—	—	—
1893	55,119	17.00	46,522	6.06	44,567	2.64	—	—	—	—	—	—	—	—	—
1894	51,713	16.84	47,628	5.09	43,414	1.97	—	—	—	—	—	—	—	—	—
1895	49,510	16.56	49,154	4.50	41,827	1.57	—	—	—	—	—	—	—	—	—
1896	49,205	17.86	51,232	4.36	39,609	1.71	—	—	—	—	—	—	—	—	—
1897	50,447	18.62	53,282	4.70	38,891	1.84	—	—	—	—	—	—	—	—	—
1898	52,868	22.79	51,558	4.67	40,097	2.51	—	—	—	—	—	—	—	—	—
1899	55,927	24.53	51,055	5.36	42,688	2.80	—	—	—	—	—	—	—	—	—
1900	59,739	26.50	50,681	6.08	45,065	2.97	—	—	—	—	—	—	—	—	—
1901	62,576	22.68	47,858	6.95	46,126	2.96	—	—	—	—	—	—	—	—	—
1902	64,418	21.48	48,100	7.69	46,196	2.62	—	—	—	—	—	—	—	—	—
1903	66,004	21.55	51,623	6.08	44,436	2.62	—	—	—	—	—	—	—	—	—
1904	66,442	19.69	53,176	5.89	41,908	2.55	—	—	—	—	—	—	—	—	—

Notes appear at end of table

(continued)

TABLE Da968–982   Cattle, hogs, and sheep – number, value per head, production, and price: 1866–2000   [Annual]   *Continued*

	Number and value per head							Live weight production and price							
	Cattle		Hogs		Stock (breeding) sheep		Sheep and lambs, value per head	Cattle		Veal calves, price	Hogs		Sheep		Lambs, price
	Number	Value per head	Number	Value per head	Number	Value per head		Cattle, production	Beef cattle, price		Production	Price	Production	Price	
	Da968	Da969	Da970 [1]	Da971	Da972 [2]	Da973	Da974 [2]	Da975 [3]	Da976	Da977	Da978 [3]	Da979	Da980 [3]	Da981	Da982
Year	Thousand	Dollars	Thousand	Dollars	Thousand	Dollars	Dollars	Million pounds	Dollars per hundredweight	Dollars per hundredweight	Million pounds	Dollars per hundredweight	Million pounds	Dollars per hundredweight	Dollars per hundredweight
1905	66,111	18.39	53,633	6.07	40,410	2.77	—	—	—	—	—	—	—	—	—
1906	65,009	19.65	56,543	7.54	41,965	3.51	—	—	—	—	—	—	—	—	—
1907	63,754	20.91	58,388	5.99	43,460	3.81	—	—	—	—	—	—	—	—	—
1908	61,989	20.92	52,508	6.45	45,095	3.87	—	—	—	—	—	—	—	—	—
1909	60,774	21.99	48,072	9.05	47,098	3.42	—	13,081	—	—	11,027	6.62	1,272	—	—
1910	58,993	24.54	55,366	9.33	46,939	4.06	—	12,672	4.86	6.40	12,025	8.14	1,150	4.99	6.16
1911	57,225	27.22	55,394	7.99	46,055	3.83	—	12,586	4.57	5.97	12,517	6.21	1,128	4.01	5.17
1912	55,675	27.68	53,747	9.89	42,972	3.42	—	13,807	5.43	6.49	11,945	6.73	1,275	4.25	5.62
1913	56,592	33.07	52,853	10.51	40,544	3.87	—	14,866	6.20	7.51	12,220	7.54	1,187	4.52	5.99
1914	59,461	38.97	56,600	9.95	38,059	3.91	—	15,562	6.52	7.85	12,594	7.52	1,271	4.83	6.36
1915	63,849	40.67	60,596	8.48	36,263	4.39	—	15,136	6.26	7.70	13,935	6.47	1,254	5.30	6.98
1916	67,438	40.10	57,578	11.82	36,260	5.10	—	15,933	6.76	8.37	13,582	8.37	1,118	6.28	8.34
1917	70,979	43.34	62,931	19.69	35,246	7.06	—	16,764	8.54	10.40	12,928	13.90	1,126	9.58	12.70
1918	73,040	50.01	64,326	22.18	36,704	11.76	—	15,658	9.88	11.70	14,792	16.10	1,238	10.80	14.00
1919	72,094	54.65	60,159	20.00	38,360	11.49	—	13,387	9.97	12.70	13,986	16.40	1,143	9.26	12.80
1920	70,400	52.64	58,942	13.63	37,328	10.59	10.44	12,403	8.71	11.80	13,533	12.90	926	8.17	11.60
1921	68,714	39.07	59,849	10.58	35,426	6.34	6.26	12,817	5.63	7.85	14,132	7.63	1,146	4.55	7.13
1922	68,795	30.39	69,304	12.29	33,365	4.79	4.79	13,185	5.73	7.64	16,518	8.40	1,080	5.96	9.90
1923	67,546	31.66	66,576	10.30	32,597	7.50	7.48	13,174	5.84	7.90	17,008	6.94	1,253	6.55	10.50
1924	65,996	32.11	55,770	13.15	32,859	7.94	7.87	13,402	5.84	7.83	15,388	7.34	1,459	6.57	10.80
1925	63,373	31.72	52,105	15.66	34,469	9.63	9.66	12,953	6.53	8.59	14,168	10.91	1,508	7.56	12.40
1926	60,576	36.80	55,496	17.19	35,719	10.53	10.46	12,605	6.75	9.34	14,909	11.79	1,609	7.20	11.70
1927	58,178	39.98	61,873	13.17	38,067	9.79	9.65	12,072	7.62	10.14	16,340	9.64	1,664	7.01	11.50
1928	57,322	50.63	59,042	12.93	40,689	10.36	10.20	12,327	9.52	11.75	16,189	8.54	1,773	7.65	12.20
1929	58,877	58.47	55,705	13.45	43,481	10.71	10.57	12,754	9.47	12.16	15,582	9.42	1,823	7.19	11.90
1930	61,003	56.36	54,835	11.35	45,577	9.00	8.93	13,263	7.71	9.68	15,176	8.84	1,965	4.74	7.76
1931	63,030	38.99	59,301	6.13	47,720	5.40	5.35	13,386	5.53	6.95	16,541	5.73	2,052	3.11	5.64
1932	65,801	26.39	62,127	4.21	47,682	3.44	3.40	14,232	4.25	4.95	16,368	3.34	1,829	2.24	4.47
1933 [4]	70,280	19.74	58,621	4.09	47,303	2.91	2.91	15,405	3.75	4.64	16,566	3.53	1,860	2.38	5.04
1934 [4]	74,369	17.78	39,066	6.31	48,244	3.77	3.78	14,538	4.13	4.92	12,385	4.14	1,911 [6]	2.85	5.90
1935 [4]	68,846	20.20	42,975	12.71	46,139	4.33	4.31	13,651	6.04	7.16	10,673	8.65	1,835	3.75	7.28
1936	67,847	34.06	43,083	11.89	45,435	6.35	6.38	14,438	5.82	7.20	12,976	9.37	1,852	3.77	8.05
1937	66,098	34.06	44,525	11.26	45,251	6.02	6.00	13,746	7.00	8.10	12,506	9.50	1,932	4.52	8.88
1938	65,249	36.58	50,012	11.18	44,972	6.13	6.11	14,047	6.54	7.90	14,372	7.74	2,038	3.58	7.05
1939	66,029	38.44	61,165	7.78	45,463	5.74	5.74	15,177	7.14	8.40	17,079	6.23	2,029	3.90	7.78
1940	68,309	40.60	54,353	8.34	46,266	6.35	6.31	15,702	7.56	8.83	17,043	5.39	2,101	3.95	8.10
1941	71,755	43.20	60,607	15.60	47,441	6.77	6.73	17,029	8.82	10.30	17,489	9.09	2,251	5.06	9.58
1942	76,025	55.00	73,881	22.50	49,346	8.66	8.60	18,568	10.70	12.30	21,105	13.04	2,313	5.80	11.70
1943	81,204	69.30	83,741	17.50	48,196	9.68	9.66	19,159	11.90	13.30	25,375	13.69	2,108	6.57	13.00
1944	85,334	68.40	59,373	20.60	44,270	8.68	8.71	19,708	10.80	12.40	20,584	13.06	1,938	6.01	12.50

	Number and value per head							Live weight production and price						
	Cattle		Hogs		Sheep			Cattle			Hogs		Sheep		
					Stock (breeding) sheep										
	Number	Value per head	Number	Value per head	Number	Value per head	Sheep and lambs, value per head	Cattle, production	Beef cattle, price	Veal calves, price	Production	Price	Production	Price	Lambs, price
	Da968	Da969	Da970 [1]	Da971 [1]	Da972 [2]	Da973	Da974 [2]	Da975 [3]	Da976	Da977	Da978 [3]	Da979	Da980 [3]	Da981	Da982
Year	Thousand	Dollars	Thousand	Dollars	Thousand	Dollars	Dollars	Million pounds	Dollars per hundredweight	Dollars per hundredweight	Million pounds	Dollars per hundredweight	Million pounds	Dollars per hundredweight	Dollars per hundredweight
1945	85,573	66.90	61,306	24.00	39,609	8.45	8.57	19,517	12.10	13.00	18,843	14.00	1,912	6.38	13.10
1946	82,235	76.20	56,810	36.00	35,525	9.57	9.69	18,999	14.50	15.20	18,744	17.50	1,762	7.48	15.60
1947	80,554	97.50	54,590	42.90	31,805	12.20	12.60	19,130	18.40	20.40	18,159	24.10	1,567	8.39	20.50
1948	77,171	117.00	56,257	38.30	29,486	15.00	15.40	18,402	22.20	24.40	18,222	23.10	1,383	9.69	22.80
1949	76,830	135.00	58,937	27.10	26,940	17.00	17.20	19,274	19.80	22.60	19,457	18.10	1,278	9.27	22.40
1950	77,963	124.00	62,269	33.30	26,182	17.80	17.80	21,185	23.30	26.30	20,214	18.00	1,336	11.60	25.10
1951	82,083	160.00	62,117	29.90	27,251	26.50	26.40	22,990	28.70	31.90	21,436	20.00	1,372	16.00	31.00
1952	88,072	179.00	51,755	26.10	27,944	28.00	27.90	24,933	24.30	25.80	19,727	17.80	1,471	10.00	24.30
1953	94,241	128.00	45,114	36.60	27,593	15.70	15.90	27,405	16.30	16.70	16,800	21.40	1,538	6.67	19.30
1954	95,679	92.00	50,474	30.60	27,079	13.80	13.90	27,580	16.00	16.50	18,218	21.60	1,607	6.14	19.10
1955	96,592	88.20	55,354	17.70	27,137	14.90	14.90	28,099	15.60	16.80	20,154	15.00	1,618	5.78	18.40
1956	95,900	88.10	51,897	24.70	26,890	14.30	14.20	27,531	14.90	16.10	19,089	14.40	1,569	5.60	18.50
1957	92,860	91.60	51,517	30.20	26,348	14.90	15.00	26,555	17.20	18.70	18,413	17.80	1,534	6.05	19.90
1958	91,176	120.00	58,045	32.00	27,167	19.40	19.20	26,764	21.90	25.30	19,180	19.60	1,657	7.20	21.00
1959	93,322	153.00	59,026	18.50	28,108	20.30	20.10	28,280	22.60	26.70	21,273	14.10	1,713	6.00	18.70
1960	96,236	137.00	55,560	27.20	28,849	16.50	16.50	28,796	20.40	22.90	19,203	15.30	1,628	5.60	17.90
1961	97,700	134.00	61,837	27.50	28,320	14.60	14.60	29,902	20.20	23.70	20,167	16.60	1,646	5.20	15.80
1962	100,369	140.00	62,726	27.50	26,719	12.90	12.90	30,775	21.30	25.10	20,275	16.30	1,491	5.63	17.85
1963	104,488	142.00	62,060	23.40	25,122	14.40	14.60	32,777	19.90	24.00	20,960	14.90	1,403	5.76	18.10
1964	107,903	127.00	56,106	24.50	23,455	14.00	14.10	34,836	18.00	20.40	20,217	14.80	1,331	6.00	19.90
1965	109,000	113.00	50,519	45.20	21,843	15.80	16.00	34,003	19.90	22.00	18,252	19.60	1,217	6.34	22.80
1966	108,862	133.00	57,125	33.20	21,456	19.70	19.80	34,950	22.20	26.00	19,149	23.50	1,249	6.84	23.40
1967	108,783	149.00	58,818	28.30	20,677	19.70	19.80	36,122	22.30	26.30	20,636	19.10	1,154	6.35	22.10
1968	109,371	148.00	60,829	30.50	19,108	19.10	19.20	36,515	23.40	27.60	21,034	18.50	1,166	6.58	24.40
1969	110,015	158.00	57,046	39.00	18,355	22.00	22.00	37,153	26.20	31.60	20,600	22.20	1,065	8.10	27.20
1970	112,369	179.00	67,285	23.50	17,433	24.80	25.10	39,343	27.10	34.50	21,823	22.70	1,099	7.52	26.40
1971	114,578	184.00	62,412	28.50	16,946	—	23.60	39,434	29.00	36.40	22,832	17.50	1,071	6.56	25.90
1972	117,862	208.00	59,017	42.00	15,845	—	22.90	41,225	33.50	44.70	20,919	25.10	1,004	7.26	29.10
1973	121,539	252.00	60,614	60.40	14,768	—	26.70	44,231	42.80	56.60	20,154	38.40	896	12.90	35.10
1974	127,788	293.00	54,693	44.90	13,685	—	32.80	42,761	35.60	35.20	19,976	34.20	807	11.20	37.00
1975	132,028	159.00	49,267	80.40	12,436	—	30.50	40,901	32.20	27.20	16,835	46.10	785	11.30	42.10
1976	127,980	190.00	54,934	47.00	11,427	—	37.30	41,398	33.70	34.10	18,160	43.30	733	13.10	46.90
1977	122,810	206.00	56,539	63.20	10,991	—	42.50	40,745	34.40	36.90	19,021	39.40	706	13.50	51.30
1978	116,375	232.00	60,356	83.20	10,798	—	51.60	39,971	48.50	59.10	19,466	46.60	687	21.80	62.80
1979	110,864	403.00	67,318	56.00	10,786	—	72.10	38,803	66.10	88.70	22,617	41.80	705	26.30	66.70
1980	111,242	502.00	64,462	74.70	11,077	—	78.20	40,284	62.40	76.80	23,402	38.00	746	21.30	63.60
1981	114,351	473.00	58,698	70.10	11,298	—	69.90	41,178	58.60	64.00	21,813	43.90	772	21.20	54.90
1982	115,444	415.00	54,534	89.90	11,433	—	57.10	40,715	56.70	59.80	19,658	52.30	785	19.50	53.10
1983	115,001	406.00	56,694	58.80	10,479	—	51.80	40,356	55.50	61.70	21,206	46.80	769	15.70	53.90
1984	113,360	396.00	54,073	75.00	9,841	—	52.10	40,055	57.30	59.90	20,200	47.10	700	16.40	60.10

Notes appear at end of table

(continued)

TABLE Da968–982   Cattle, hogs, and sheep – number, value per head, production, and price: 1866–2000 [Annual] *Continued*

	Number and value per head							Live weight production and price							
	Cattle		Hogs		Sheep			Cattle			Hogs		Sheep		Lambs
					Stock (breeding) sheep										
	Number	Value per head [1]	Number	Value per head [1]	Number	Value per head	Sheep and lambs, value per head	Cattle, production	Beef cattle, price	Veal calves, price	Production	Price	Production	Price	Lambs, price
	Da968	Da969	Da970 [1]	Da971 [1]	Da972 [2]	Da973 [2]	Da974 [2]	Da975 [3]	Da976	Da977	Da978 [3]	Da979	Da980 [3]	Da981	Da982
Year	Thousand	Dollars	Thousand	Dollars	Thousand	Dollars	Dollars	Million pounds	Dollars per hundredweight	Dollars per hundredweight	Million pounds	Dollars per hundredweight	Million pounds	Dollars per hundredweight	Dollars per hundredweight
1985	109,582	402.00	52,314	69.60	9,130	—	61.10	40,121	53.70	62.10	20,167	44.00	704	23.90	67.70
1986	105,378	391.00	51,001	91.90	8,658	—	67.40	40,589	52.60	61.10	19,461	49.30	726	25.60	69.00
1987	102,118	407.00	54,384	76.00	9,059	—	75.70	40,502	61.10	78.50	20,446	51.20	733	29.50	77.60
1988	99,622	523.00	55,466	66.30	9,364	—	90.00	39,714	66.60	89.20	21,697	42.30	731	25.60	69.10
1989	96,740	581.00	53,788	79.10	9,207	—	82.40	38,850	69.50	90.80	21,907	42.50	811	24.40	66.10
1990	95,816	616.00	54,416	85.40	9,596	—	79.30	39,202	74.60	95.60	21,287	53.70	781	23.20	55.50
1991	96,393	655.00	57,649	68.80	9,444	—	65.60	39,764	72.70	98.00	22,727	49.10	796	19.70	52.20
1992	97,556	630.00	58,202	71.20	8,965	—	61.20	40,253	71.30	89.00	23,947	41.60	746	25.80	59.50
1993	99,176	649.00	57,940	75.00	8,305	—	70.60	41,140	72.60	91.20	23,777	45.20	739	28.60	64.40
1994	100,974	659.00	59,738	53.00	7,236	—	69.90	41,573	66.70	87.20	24,448	39.90	635	30.90	65.60
1995	102,785	615.00	58,201	71.00	6,518	—	74.70	42,534	61.80	73.10	24,427	40.50	602	28.00	78.20
1996	103,548	503.00	56,124	94.00	6,226	—	86.50	40,884	58.70	58.40	23,080	51.90	572	29.90	88.20
1997	101,656	525.00	61,158	82.00	5,919	—	96.00	41,111	63.10	78.90	23,979	52.90	603	37.90	90.30
1998	99,744	603.00	62,206	44.00	5,611	—	102.00	41,565 [5]	59.60 [5]	78.80 [5]	25,766 [5]	34.40 [5]	556 [5]	30.60 [5]	72.30 [5]
1999	99,115	594.00	59,407 [5]	72.00 [5]	5,299	—	88.00	—	—	—	—	—	—	—	—
2000 [5]	98,048	683.00	—	—	5,163	—	95.00	—	—	—	—	—	—	—	—

[1] U.S. Department of Agriculture data prior to 1967 adjusted for purpose of consistency. See text.

[2] Beginning with 1994, includes new crop lambs.

[3] Includes adjustments for livestock shipped in and inventory changes. See text.

[4] Government purchases included in figures for all cattle, 1935 and 1934; for hogs, 1933.

[5] Data are preliminary.

[6] Includes government purchases.

Sources

Series Da968. 1867–1969, U.S. Department of Agriculture, Statistical Reporting Service, *Agricultural Statistics, 1967* and *1978*; 1970–2000, U.S. Department of Agriculture, Economic Research Service, *Red Meat Yearbook*, September 2000, Table 103, downloaded November 6, 2000, from U.S. Department of Agriculture, Economics and Statistics System.

Series Da969, Da971, and Da973–974. 1867–1879, *Reports of the Commissioner of Agriculture, 1866–1878*; 1880–2000, *Agricultural Statistics, 1967, 1970, 1972, 1973, 1978, 1982, 1987, 1992, 1995–96*, and *2000* editions.

Series Da970 and Da972. 1866–1992, U.S. National Agricultural Statistics Service, *Cattle, Hogs, Chickens, and Sheep – Inventory by State*, July 1995, downloaded November 6, 2000, from U.S. Department of Agriculture, Economics and Statistics System; 1993–2000, *Agricultural Statistics 2000*.

Series Da975, Da978, and Da980. 1909–1923, U.S. Bureau of Agricultural Economics, *Meat Animals, Farm Production, and Income, 1924–1944*, September 1947; 1924–1998, *Agricultural Statistics, 1952, 1967, 1982, 1987, 1992, 1995–96*, and *2000* editions.

Series Da976–977, Da979, and Da981–982. 1909–1923, U.S. Agricultural Marketing Service, "Prices Received by Farmers, 1908–1955," *Statistical Bulletin* number 180, June 1956; 1924–1994,

Agricultural Statistics, 1952, 1957, 1962, 1967, 1972, 1978, 1982, 1987, 1992, 1995–96, and *2000* editions.

Documentation

Data include Alaska and Hawai'i beginning 1961.

Series Da968. January inventory.

Series Da968–969 and Da975. Cattle include milk cows, dairy heifers, beef cows, beef heifers, other heifers, steers over 500 pounds, bulls, and calves.

Series Da968–974

These estimates have been made by the U.S. Department of Agriculture (USDA) since 1867. The early estimates were based on reports of the percentage change in numbers from the previous year by field agents and crop reporters. At ten-year intervals, the Census of Agriculture furnished the basic figures to which these percentage changes were applied. Beginning with 1920, a national agriculture census has been taken every five years. Since 1920, the USDA's annual estimates are based primarily on survey returns from livestock producers who reported on the number of livestock, by classes, on their own farms about December 1 each year. Records of livestock assessed for taxation in the various states have furnished indications of the annual percentage change in numbers, and records of marketings and slaughter have been used both by states and for the United States as check information.

Comparison with Table Da988–994 will show that there are few census years when the USDA estimates and the census data are in close agreement. One of the main reasons for these differences is that there are only a few times when the census was taken as of January 1. In the mid-1930s, the USDA undertook a general revision of all estimates prior to 1920 to correct for irregularities in the early series and to utilize more fully the records of numbers assessed for taxation and other information not considered in preparing the original estimates.

TABLE Da968-982   Cattle, hogs, and sheep – number, value per head, production, and price: 1866–2000   [Annual]
Continued

Prior to 1920, crop reporters provided a single estimate of the value per head for a given species. Since 1920, the estimates are weighted averages based on values per head reported separately for the different age and sex classes of a given species, using as weights the estimated number in the respective class.

Series Da969, Da971, and Da973. The data for 1866–1879 were compiled from the *Reports of the Commissioner of Agriculture*. The data differ from those reported in the previous editions of *Historical Statistics of the United States* and many USDA publications because they are expressed in greenback rather than gold values for this period. The USDA originally presented these data in greenback values but later converted them to gold values. Almost all crops series in this and other sources are expressed in terms of greenback values. For consistency it is important that livestock values are reported in the same standard as crop values.

Series Da970. December 1 inventory.

Series Da970–971. Prior to 1967 the USDA reported hog inventory numbers and value per head as of January 1 of a given year. Beginning with 1967 the USDA reported these data as of December 1 of a given year. This table presents the hog inventory series as of December 1 back to 1866 by moving the USDA values back one year, that is, the 1937 hog inventory and value per head numbers presented here would line up with the 1938 data reported in *Historical Statistics of the United States* (1975). This is consistent with recent USDA publications. In the early 1980s the USDA revised the hog inventory values for 1961–1966. The revised numbers are between 8 and 10 percent greater than those originally published. The U.S. Department of Agriculture did not revise the value per head numbers.

Series Da973. Series was discontinued in 1971.

Series Da975, Da978, and Da980. Production in live weight relates to the total poundage produced on farms and ranches during a calendar year. The estimate of production is derived by determining for each state a balance sheet that shows, as debit items, the inventory at the beginning of the year, the births, and inshipments; and, as credit items, the marketings, farm slaughter, death losses, and numbers on hand at the end of the year. Estimates of average live weight are based on reports from slaughterers, collected by the Department of Agriculture and in the Census of Manufactures, and on records obtained from stockyards. Reports have also been obtained from farmers on the average weight of livestock slaughtered on farms. The total live weight for beginning and end of year is obtained by multiplying estimates of the different age and sex classes for a species by an estimate of their respective average live weight. Live weight of marketings, farm slaughter, and inshipments is determined by multiplying the estimate for these items by the respective average live weight. To obtain production, the total weight of inshipments is subtracted from the combined weight of marketings and farm slaughter. Then the difference in the inventory weight between the beginning and end of year is added or subtracted as the case might be.

Series Da976–977, Da979, and Da981–982. Price information is obtained from voluntary price reporters who furnish average local market prices each month. The estimates of monthly prices are weighted by monthly estimates of marketings to obtain the annual average. The monthly marketings are based on reports from stockyards and packers on monthly receipts of livestock by state of origin.

TABLE Da983–987   Horses and mules – number on farms and value per head: 1867–1960[1]   [Annual]

Contributed by Alan L. Olmstead and Paul W. Rhode

	Horses		Mules				Horses		Mules		
	Number	Value per head	Number	Value per head	Work stock		Number	Value per head	Number	Value per head	Work stock
	Da983	Da984	Da985	Da986	Da987		Da983	Da984	Da985	Da986	Da987
Year	Thousand	Dollars	Thousand	Dollars	Thousand	Year	Thousand	Dollars	Thousand	Dollars	Thousand
1867	6,820	79.46	1,000	92.52	—	1915	21,431	103.23	5,062	112.19	—
1868	7,051	75.16	1,057	77.61	—	1916	21,334	101.45	5,200	113.78	—
1869	7,304	84.16	1,130	106.74	—	1917	21,306	102.64	5,853	118.45	—
1870	7,633	81.36	1,245	109.51	—	1918	21,238	103.97	5,485	128.97	—
1871	8,054	78.51	1,305	101.52	—	1919	20,922	97.94	5,568	135.58	—
1872	8,441	73.37	1,360	94.82	—	1920	20,091	96.45	5,651	148.29	22,386
1873	8,767	74.36	1,419	95.24	—	1921	19,369	84.48	5,768	117.37	22,348
1874	9,055	71.45	1,485	89.22	—	1922	18,764	71.01	5,824	88.99	22,271
1875	9,333	68.01	1,548	80.00	—	1923	18,125	70.49	5,893	86.87	22,050
1876	9,606	64.96	1,608	75.33	—	1924	17,378	65.39	5,907	85.89	21,578
1877	9,910	60.08	1,674	68.91	—	1925	16,651	64.28	5,918	82.91	21,038
1878	10,230	58.16	1,746	63.70	—	1926	16,083	65.31	5,903	81.51	20,491
1879	10,574	52.41	1,816	56.06	—	1927	15,388	63.73	5,804	74.51	19,765
1880	10,903	53.74	1,878	61.74	—	1928	14,792	66.71	5,656	79.84	19,120
1881	11,187	57.91	1,912	68.84	—	1929	14,234	69.68	5,510	82.45	18,514
1882	11,444	58.75	1,928	71.69	—	1930	13,742	69.98	5,382	83.93	17,981
1883	11,794	69.92	1,975	77.79	—	1931	13,195	60.64	5,273	69.23	17,375
1884	12,215	73.80	2,047	83.53	—	1932	12,664	53.48	5,148	60.70	16,822
1885	12,700	72.94	2,102	81.88	—	1933	12,291	54.12	5,046	60.42	16,404
1886	13,276	70.62	2,162	78.96	—	1934	12,052	66.88	4,945	82.42	15,984
1887	13,821	71.59	2,213	78.39	—	1935	11,861	77.05	4,822	99.34	15,473
1888	14,490	72.03	2,260	79.06	—	1936	11,598	96.73	4,628	120.63	14,839
1889	15,064	72.39	2,295	78.95	—	1937	11,342	99.14	4,460	130.25	14,330
1890	15,732	69.27	2,322	77.61	—	1938	10,995	90.89	4,250	123.39	13,690
1891	16,329	67.19	2,377	76.93	—	1939	10,629	84.32	4,163	118.58	13,273
1892	16,846	64.56	2,459	74.31	—	1940	10,444	77.30	4,034	116.00	13,000
1893	17,289	60.72	2,550	69.18	—	1941	10,193	68.20	3,911	107.00	12,651
1894	17,709	46.63	2,632	60.65	—	1942	9,873	64.70	3,782	107.00	12,346
1895	17,849	35.57	2,708	47.23	—	1943	9,605	79.80	3,626	127.00	12,117
1896	17,876	32.34	2,782	44.08	—	1944	9,192	78.60	3,421	143.00	11,668
1897	17,803	30.92	2,836	40.49	—	1945	8,715	64.90	3,235	134.00	11,116
1898	17,698	33.35	2,918	42.31	—	1946	8,081	57.50	3,027	133.00	10,434
1899	17,728	36.61	3,012	43.52	—	1947	7,340	59.30	2,789	141.00	9,578
1900	17,856	43.56	3,139	51.46	—	1948	6,704	55.70	2,575	133.00	8,800
1901	17,955	53.03	3,190	53.47	—	1949	6,096	52.50	2,402	116.00	8,074
1902	17,968	58.52	3,264	67.23	—	1950	5,548	46.00	2,233	99.10	7,415
1903	18,121	62.27	3,353	71.73	—	1951	7,036	54.60	—	—	6,732
1904	18,331	67.59	3,465	78.02	—	1952	6,150	53.90	—	—	5,887
1905	18,491	69.73	3,586	87.06	—	1953	5,403	53.00	—	—	5,166
1906	18,806	79.77	3,680	97.75	—	1954	4,791	52.90	—	—	4,572
1907	19,090	92.85	3,814	111.46	—	1955	4,309	56.20	—	—	4,101
1908	19,444	92.76	3,949	107.81	—	1956	3,958	62.60	—	—	3,757
1909	19,731	95.13	4,085	108.20	—	1957	3,632	71.80	—	—	3,436
1910	19,972	107.70	4,239	119.98	—	1958	3,415	84.40	—	—	3,220
1911	20,418	111.11	4,429	125.73	—	1959	3,189	102.00	—	—	2,988
1912	20,726	105.58	4,551	120.33	—	1960	3,089	113.00	—	—	2,883
1913	21,008	110.58	4,683	124.10	—						
1914	21,308	109.27	4,870	123.47	—						

[1] Beginning with 1951, mules included with horses.

Sources

Reports of the Commissioner of Agriculture, 1867–1879; U.S. Department of Agriculture, *Agricultural Statistics, 1957* and *1962*.

Documentation

See the text for series Da968–974. These series were discontinued in 1961.

Series Da983–986. Includes colts.

Series Da984 and Da986. The data for 1867–1879 were compiled from the *Reports of the Commissioner of Agriculture*. The data differ from those reported in previous editions of *Historical Statistics of the United States* and many U.S. Department of Agriculture (USDA) publications because they are expressed in greenback rather than gold values for this period. The USDA originally presented these data in greenback values but later converted them to gold values. Almost all crops series in this and other sources are expressed in terms of greenback values. For consistency it is important to have livestock values reported in the same standard as crop values.

Series Da987. Animals two years old and over.

TABLE Da988–994   Cattle, hogs, sheep, horses, and mules – number on farms: 1850–1997[1,2]   [Census years]

Contributed by Alan L. Olmstead and Paul W. Rhode

	Number on farms						Cows and heifers kept for milk
	All cattle	Hogs	Stock sheep	Horses	Mules	Work stock	
	Da988	Da989	Da990	Da991 [3]	Da992 [3]	Da993	Da994
Year	Thousand	Thousand	Thousand	Thousand	Thousand	Thousand	Thousand
1850	18,379	30,354	21,723	4,337	559	—	6,385
1860	25,620	33,513	22,471	6,249	1,151	—	8,586
1870	23,821	25,135	28,478	7,145	1,125	—	8,935
1880	39,676	49,773	42,192	10,357	1,813	—	12,443
1890	57,649	57,427	40,876	15,266	2,252	—	16,512
1900	67,822	62,876	61,606	18,280	3,271	—	17,140
1910	61,950	58,206	52,525	19,849	4,218	—	20,633
1920	66,777	59,371	35,077	19,783	5,441	21,873	19,680
1925	60,760	50,854	35,590	16,401	5,681	20,619	20,900
1930	64,036	56,319	57,014	13,523	5,383	17,612 [9]	20,124
1935	68,284	37,213	48,358	11,858	4,818	15,467 [9]	24,582
1940	60,818 [4]	34,070 [5]	40,173 [6]	10,098 [7,8]	3,849 [4,7]	13,029 [9]	21,937
1945	82,654	46,735	41,224	8,499	3,130	—	22,803
1950	76,920	55,789	31,406	5,409	2,204	—	21,233
1954	95,027	57,093	31,619	4,141	—	—	20,183
1959	92,534	67,949	33,945	2,955	—	—	16,552
1964	105,558	54,080	25,472	—	—	—	14,623
1969	106,346	55,455	21,611	2,238	—	—	11,174
1974	113,175	45,504	15,380	1,596	—	—	10,222
1978	103,865	57,697	12,243	1,957	—	—	10,655
1982	104,476	55,366	12,438	2,261	—	—	10,850
1987	95,847	52,271	11,059	2,457	—	—	10,085
1992	96,136	57,563	10,770	2,050	—	—	9,492
1997	98,989	61,206	7,822	2,427	—	—	9,095

[1] Reporting year ends December 31/January 1, except as follows: 1850–1900 (June 1); 1910 (April 15); 1930, 1940, and 1950 (April 1); 1954–1959 (October/November); 1964 (November/December).

[2] Data for Alaska and Hawai'i are not included in the following years: 1850–1890, 1925, 1935, 1945, and 1954.

[3] Beginning with 1954, mules included with horses.

[4] Animals more than three months old only.

[5] Hogs more than four months old only.

[6] Sheep and lambs more than six months old only.

[7] Includes ponies.

[8] Figures are for horses and ponies more than three months old only.

[9] More than twenty-seven months old.

Sources

U.S. Bureau of the Census, *U.S. Census of Agriculture*, various years, including: *1959*, volume 3, chapter 6, volume 2, pp. 494, 530–531; *1964*, volume 2, chapter 2; *1969*, volume 2, chapter 5, pp. 6–9; *1974*, volume 1, part 51, p. I-4; *1982*, volume 1, part 51, p. 11; *1987*, volume 1, part 51, pp. 27–34; *1992*, volume 1, part 51, pp. 28–34; and *1997*, volume 1, part 51, pp. 30–7.

Documentation

See the text for series Da968–974.

For the years prior to 1970 the numbers reported here sometimes differ slightly from those found in *Historical Statistics of the United States* (1975). The editors of that edition "adjusted" the census numbers to provide a January 1 estimate. These adjustments were inconsistent and not reproducible. Users should be aware that data reported for June of a given year will normally be higher than if the number were adjusted to January 1, owing to the addition of spring-born animals.

Series Da991–992. Includes colts.

Series Da993. The table contributors were unable to verify the numbers for work-stock given in series K574 of *Historical Statistics of the United States* (1975). These data are estimates of horse and mule populations excluding colts and ponies.

Series Da993–994. Animals two years old and over.

Series Da994. As of January 1.

TABLE Da995–1019   Beef, veal, pork, and lamb – slaughtering, production, and price: 1899–1999

Contributed by Alan L. Olmstead and Paul W. Rhode

	Beef								Veal			
	Cattle slaughtered		Production		Price	Steers	Calves slaughtered		Production		Price	
	Total	Commercial	Total	Commercial		Price, choice 2–4	Total	Commercial	Total	Commercial	Calves	Vealer, choice
	Da995	Da996 [1]	Da997	Da998	Da999	Da1000 [2,3]	Da1001	Da1002 [1]	Da1003	Da1004	Da1005	Da1006
Year	Thousand	Thousand	Million pounds	Million pounds	Dollars per hundredweight	Dollars per hundredweight	Thousand	Thousand	Million pounds	Million pounds	Dollars per hundredweight	Dollars per hundredweight
1899	—	—	5,522	—	5.30	—	—	—	387	—	—	—
1900	10,792	—	5,628	—	5.15	—	4,105	—	397	—	—	—
1901	11,526	—	5,814	—	5.25	—	4,318	—	422	—	5.61	—
1902	11,751	—	5,649	—	6.20	—	4,854	—	476	—	6.35	—
1903	12,266	—	6,240	—	4.80	—	5,044	—	492	—	6.20	—
1904	12,257	—	6,176	—	4.95	—	5,076	—	491	—	5.60	—
1905	13,096	—	6,504	—	5.05	—	5,731	—	556	—	5.75	—
1906	13,456	—	6,537	—	5.30	—	6,187	—	598	—	6.25	—
1907	13,886	—	6,544	—	5.80	—	6,395	—	626	—	6.40	—
1908	13,569	—	6,662	—	6.10	—	6,546	—	637	—	6.50	—
1909	14,135	—	6,915	—	6.35	—	6,864	—	660	—	7.10	—
1910	14,140	—	6,647	—	6.80	—	6,917	—	667	—	8.25	—
1911	13,817	—	6,549	—	6.40	—	6,855	—	666	—	7.91	—
1912	13,386	—	6,234	—	7.75	—	6,828	—	662	—	8.94	—
1913	12,989	—	6,182	—	8.25	—	6,305	—	608	—	10.20	—
1914	12,676	—	6,017	—	8.65	—	5,927	—	569	—	10.10	—
1915	12,901	—	6,075	—	8.40	—	6,054	—	590	—	10.08	—
1916	13,793	—	6,460	—	9.50	—	6,628	—	655	—	10.98	—
1917	15,741	—	7,239	—	11.60	—	7,372	—	744	—	13.78	—
1918	17,093	—	7,726	—	14.65	—	7,485	—	760	—	15.75	—
1919	15,027	—	6,756	—	15.50	—	8,201	—	819	—	16.83	—
1920	13,470	12,520	6,306	—	13.30	—	8,481	7,556	842	—	14.58	—
1921	12,428	11,478	6,022	—	8.20	—	8,394	7,469	820	—	9.36	—
1922	13,706	12,756	6,588	—	8.65	—	8,832	7,932	852	—	9.15	—
1923	14,283	13,383	6,721	—	9.40	—	9,327	8,427	916	—	9.66	—
1924	14,750	13,917	6,877	—	9.24	—	9,804	8,971	972	—	9.86	—
1925	14,704	13,975	6,878	—	10.16	—	9,936	9,131	989	—	10.87	—
1926	14,781	14,132	7,089	—	9.47	—	9,354	8,575	955	—	11.61	—
1927	13,413	12,820	6,395	—	11.36	—	8,478	7,743	867	—	12.90	—
1928	12,028	11,544	5,771	—	13.91	—	7,651	6,997	773	—	14.56	—
1929	12,038	11,578	5,871	—	13.43	—	7,406	6,779	761	—	14.76	—
1930	12,056	11,569	5,917	—	10.95	—	7,761	7,084	792	—	11.51	—
1931	12,096	11,576	6,009	—	8.06	—	8,057	7,302	823	—	8.33	—
1932	11,980	11,263	5,789	—	6.70	—	7,970	7,178	822	—	6.21	—
1933 [5]	13,107	12,317	6,440	—	5.42	—	8,564	7,722	891	—	5.88	—
1934 [6]	15,071	18,681	8,343 [7]	—	6.76	—	10,106	10,774	1,246	—	6.10	—
1935 [6]	14,566	14,173	6,608	—	10.26	—	9,580	8,766	1,023	—	8.88	—
1936 [6]	15,897	15,288	7,358	—	8.82	—	10,008	9,120	1,075	—	9.30	—
1937	15,254	14,684	6,798	—	11.47	—	10,304	9,519	1,108	—	10.07	—
1938	14,822	14,253	6,908	—	9.39	—	9,306	8,581	994	—	9.00	—
1939	14,621	14,050	7,011	—	9.75	—	9,191	8,436	991	—	9.82	—

	Beef								Veal			
	Cattle slaughtered		Production		Steers		Calves slaughtered		Production		Price	
	Total	Commercial	Total	Commercial	Price	Price, choice 2–4	Total	Commercial	Total	Commercial	Calves	Vealer, choice
	Da995	Da996 [1]	Da997	Da998	Da999	Da1000 [2,3]	Da1001	Da1002 [1]	Da1003	Da1004	Da1005	Da1006
Year	Thousand	Thousand	Million pounds	Million pounds	Dollars per hundredweight	Dollars per hundredweight	Thousand	Thousand	Million pounds	Million pounds	Dollars per hundredweight	Dollars per hundredweight
1940	14,958	14,387	7,175	—	10.43	—	9,089	8,361	981	—	10.61	—
1941	16,419	15,848	8,082	—	11.33	—	9,252	8,568	1,036	—	12.18	—
1942	18,033	17,387	8,843	—	13.79	—	9,718	9,077	1,151	—	14.48	—
1943	17,845	17,137	8,571	—	15.30	—	9,940	9,320	1,167	—	15.18	—
1944	19,844	18,990	9,112	—	15.44	—	14,242	13,518	1,738	—	14.86	—
1945	21,694	20,775	10,276	—	16.18	—	13,657	12,904	1,664	—	15.12	—
1946	19,824	18,881	9,373	—	19.16	—	12,176	11,410	1,443	—	16.87	—
1947	22,404	21,533	10,432	—	25.83	—	13,726	13,013	1,605	—	24.98	—
1948	19,177	18,386	9,075	—	30.88	—	12,378	11,767	1,423	—	29.02	—
1949	18,765	18,013	9,439	—	25.80	—	11,398	10,828	1,334	—	27.64	—
1950	18,614	17,901	9,534	—	29.35	—	10,501	9,973	1,230	—	31.08	—
1951	17,084	16,376	8,837	—	35.72	—	8,902	8,418	1,059	—	37.19	—
1952	18,625	17,856	9,650	—	32.38	—	9,388	8,894	1,169	—	34.42	—
1953	24,465	23,605	12,407	—	23.62	—	12,200	11,668	1,546	—	25.04	—
1954	25,889	25,017	12,963	12,601	24.23	—	13,270	12,746	1,647	1,551	23.07	—
1955	26,587	25,722	13,569	13,213	22.59	—	12,864	12,377	1,578	1,487	24.80	—
1956	27,755	26,862	14,462	14,090	22.00	—	12,999	12,512	1,632	1,541	23.62	—
1957	27,068	26,232	14,202	13,852	23.48	—	12,353	11,904	1,526	1,442	25.93	—
1958	24,368	23,555	13,330	12,983	27.09	27.07	9,738	9,315	1,186	1,103	32.20	—
1959	23,723	22,930	13,580	13,233	27.53	27.67	8,072	7,683	1,008	929	31.91	—
1960	26,029	25,224	14,728	14,374	25.93	25.90	8,615	8,225	1,109	1,025	28.07	—
1961	26,471	25,635	15,300	14,930	24.46	24.43	8,080	7,701	1,044	960	—	—
1962	26,911	26,083	15,298	14,931	27.20	26.92	7,857	7,494	1,015	936	—	—
1963	28,070	27,232	16,428	16,049	23.79	23.58	7,204	6,833	929	847	—	—
1964	31,678	30,818	18,429	18,037	22.86	22.41	7,632	7,254	1,013	928	—	—
1965	33,171	32,347	18,693	18,325	25.81	24.99	7,788	7,420	1,018	936	—	—
1966	34,171	33,727	19,694	19,493	26.17	25.71	6,861	6,647	910	862	—	—
1967	34,295	33,869	20,184	19,991	25.97	25.29	6,107	5,919	792	749	—	—
1968	35,414	35,026	20,846	20,662	27.65	26.87	5,613	5,443	734	696	—	—
1969	35,576	35,237	21,126	20,960	30.48	29.45	5,009	4,863	673	640	—	—
1970	35,354	35,025	21,652	21,472	30.20	29.36	4,203	4,072	588	558	—	—
1971	35,895	35,585	21,868	21,697	—	32.39	3,821	3,689	546	517	—	—
1972	36,083	35,779	22,387	22,218	—	35.78	3,184	3,053	459	429	—	—
1973	34,026	33,687	21,277	21,089	—	44.54	2,376	2,249	357	325	—	—
1974	37,327	36,812	23,138	22,844	—	41.89	3,172	2,987	486	442	—	—
1975	41,464	40,911	23,974	23,671	—	44.61	5,406	5,209	873	827	—	49.94
1976	43,196	42,654	25,969	25,667	—	39.11	5,528	5,350	853	812	—	58.18
1977	42,381	41,856	25,279	24,986	—	40.38	5,692	5,517	834	793	—	58.28
1978	39,970	39,552	24,242	24,010	—	52.34	4,302	4,170	632	599	—	74.07
1979	34,008	33,678	21,446	21,262	—	67.67	2,924	2,824	434	411	—	102.82

Notes appear at end of table

(continued)

TABLE Da995–1019 Beef, veal, pork, and lamb – slaughtering, production, and price: 1899–1999 Continued

	Cattle slaughtered		Beef Production		Steers		Calves slaughtered		Veal Production		Veal Price	
	Total	Commercial [1]	Total	Commercial	Price	Price, choice 2–4	Total	Commercial [1]	Total	Commercial	Calves	Vealer, choice
	Da995	Da996	Da997	Da998	Da999	Da1000 [2,3]	Da1001	Da1002 [1]	Da1003	Da1004	Da1005	Da1006
Year	Thousand	Thousand	Million pounds	Million pounds	Dollars per hundredweight	Dollars per hundredweight	Thousand	Thousand	Million pounds	Million pounds	Dollars per hundredweight	Dollars per hundredweight
1980	34,116	33,807	21,644	21,469	—	66.96	2,679	2,588	400	379	—	94.04
1981	35,265	34,953	22,389	22,214	—	63.84	2,884	2,798	436	414	—	88.76
1982	36,155	35,843	22,536	22,366	—	64.22	3,103	3,021	448	423	—	83.36
1983	36,974	36,649	23,241	23,058	—	62.52	3,162	3,077	454	428	—	85.45
1984	37,892	37,582	23,596	23,416	—	65.34	3,377	3,297	495	479	—	79.56
1985	36,593	36,293	23,728	23,557	—	58.37	3,455	3,385	514	499	—	78.88
1986	37,568	37,288	24,371	24,213	—	57.74	3,478	3,408	524	509	—	78.29
1987	35,890	35,647	23,566	23,405	—	64.60	2,902	2,815	429	417	—	87.00
1988	35,324	35,079	23,590	23,425	—	69.58	2,565	2,506	395	387	—	95.82
1989	34,106	33,917	23,088	22,975	—	72.52	2,223	2,172	355	344	—	97.57
1990	33,439	33,243	22,743	22,634	—	77.40	1,838	1,789	327	316	—	97.61
1991	32,885	32,689	22,917	22,800	—	73.83	1,483	1,436	306	296	—	94.66
1992	33,069	32,874	23,204	23,086	—	74.65	1,420	1,371	322	299	—	87.01
1993	33,504	33,324	23,049	22,942	—	75.60	1,242	1,195	286	267	—	89.11
1994	34,376	34,196	24,386	24,278	—	67.55	1,315	1,268	293	283	—	88.01
1995	35,817	35,639	25,224	25,117	—	—	1,477	1,430	318	308	—	—
1996	36,760	36,584	25,527	25,421	—	—	1,815	1,768	379	367	—	—
1997	36,492	36,318	25,490	25,384	—	—	1,619	1,575	333	324	—	—
1998	35,637	35,465	25,760	25,653	—	—	1,501	1,458	261	252	—	—
1999	36,320	36,150	26,492	26,385	—	—	1,322	1,282	233	226	—	—

	Hogs slaughtered		Pork Production		Pork Price		Sheep and lambs Slaughtered			Lamb and mutton production		Slaughter lamb price	
	Total	Commercial [1]	Total	Commercial	Slaughter hogs	Barrow and gilt	Total	Commercial [1]	Lambs and yearlings, commercial	Total	Commercial	Chicago, IL	Choice, San Angelo, TX
	Da1007	Da1008	Da1009	Da1010	Da1011 [4]	Da1012	Da1013	Da1014 [1]	Da1015	Da1016	Da1017	Da1018	Da1019
Year	Thousand	Thousand	Million pounds	Million pounds	Dollars per hundredweight	Dollars per hundredweight	Thousand	Thousand	Thousand	Million pounds	Million pounds	Dollars per hundredweight	Dollars per hundredweight
1899	—	—	6,310	—	4.05	—	—	—	—	487	—	—	—
1900	51,885	—	6,329	—	5.05	—	12,000	—	—	493	—	—	—
1901	53,898	—	6,357	—	5.85	—	13,200	—	—	548	—	4.80	—
1902	48,306	—	5,936	—	6.85	—	13,700	—	—	564	—	5.50	—
1903	48,548	—	6,067	—	6.00	—	13,800	—	—	563	—	5.45	—
1904	52,072	—	6,387	—	5.15	—	13,100	—	—	538	—	5.60	—
1905	54,433	—	6,629	—	5.25	—	13,100	—	—	530	—	6.80	—
1906	54,698	—	6,793	—	6.25	—	13,800	—	—	543	—	6.85	—
1907	56,527	—	7,059	—	6.10	—	13,799	—	—	553	—	7.05	—
1908	63,463	—	7,535	—	5.70	—	14,200	—	—	559	—	6.35	—
1909	54,986	—	6,557	—	7.35	—	15,464	—	—	608	—	7.40	—

	Pork						Lamb						
	Hogs slaughtered		Production		Price		Sheep and lambs Slaughtered		Lambs and yearlings, commercial	Lamb and mutton production		Slaughter lamb price	
	Total	Commercial	Total	Commercial	Slaughter hogs [4]	Barrow and gilt	Total	Commercial		Total	Commercial	Chicago, IL	Choice, San Angelo, TX
Year	Da1007	Da1008 [1]	Da1009	Da1010	Da1011	Da1012	Da1013	Da1014 [1]	Da1015	Da1016	Da1017	Da1018	Da1019
	Thousand	Thousand	Million pounds	Million pounds	Dollars per hundredweight	Dollars per hundredweight	Thousand	Thousand	Thousand	Million pounds	Million pounds	Dollars per hundredweight	Dollars per hundredweight
1910	48,215	—	6,087	—	8.90	—	15,332	—	—	597	—	7.55	—
1911	57,000	—	6,961	—	6.70	—	18,177	—	—	693	—	5.95	—
1912	55,500	—	6,822	—	7.55	—	19,131	—	—	735	—	7.20	—
1913	57,000	—	6,979	—	8.35	—	18,375	—	—	706	—	7.70	—
1914	55,000	—	6,824	—	8.30	—	18,035	—	—	693	—	8.00	—
1915	62,000	—	7,616	—	7.10	—	15,576	—	—	605	—	9.00	—
1916	67,000	—	8,207	—	9.60	—	15,160	—	—	585	—	10.75	—
1917	56,500	—	7,055	—	15.10	—	12,128	—	—	463	—	15.60	—
1918	65,100	—	8,349	—	17.45	—	13,220	—	—	506	—	16.60	—
1919	65,795	—	8,477	—	17.85	—	15,784	—	—	590	—	16.00	—
1920	61,502	44,806	7,648	—	13.91	—	13,984	13,494	—	538	—	14.60	—
1921	61,818	45,937	7,697	—	8.51	—	16,742	16,252	—	639	—	9.86	—
1922	66,201	50,998	8,145	—	9.22	—	14,373	13,863	—	553	—	13.68	—
1923	77,508	62,808	9,483	—	7.55	—	15,146	14,631	—	588	—	13.89	—
1924	76,809	62,314	9,149	—	8.11	—	15,578	15,035	—	597	—	14.57	—
1925	65,508	51,284	8,128	—	11.81	—	15,430	14,922	—	603	—	15.66	—
1926	62,585	48,674	7,966	—	12.34	—	16,444	15,932	—	639	—	14.26	—
1927	66,195	52,340	8,430	—	9.95	—	16,113	15,625	—	629	—	14.12	—
1928	72,889	59,294	9,041	—	9.22	—	17,076	16,594	—	663	—	14.99	—
1929	71,012	57,759	8,833	—	10.16	—	17,483	17,020	—	682	—	14.62	—
1930	67,272	53,732	8,482	—	9.47	—	21,125	20,651	—	825	—	9.69	—
1931	69,233	54,895	8,739	—	6.16	—	23,133	22,542	—	885	—	7.26	—
1932	71,425	55,845	8,923	—	3.83	—	23,043	22,319	—	884	—	5.92	—
1933 [5]	73,270	64,437	9,234	—	3.94	—	21,833	21,067	—	852	—	6.65	—
1934 [6]	68,760	53,650	8,397	—	4.65	—	20,444	20,994	—	851	—	8.01	—
1935 [6]	46,011	32,663	5,919	—	9.27	—	22,000	21,320	—	877	—	9.02	—
1936 [6]	58,730	44,435	7,474	—	9.89	—	21,555	20,918	—	854	—	9.91	—
1937	53,715	40,382	6,951	—	10.02	—	21,455	20,857	—	852	—	10.78	—
1938	58,927	45,602	7,680	—	8.09	—	22,423	21,813	—	897	—	8.50	—
1939	66,561	52,581	8,660	—	6.57	—	21,614	21,017	—	872	—	9.33	—
1940	77,610	63,455	10,044	—	5.71	—	21,571	21,000	—	876	—	9.66	—
1941	71,397	58,608	9,528	—	9.45	—	22,309	21,727	—	923	—	11.28	—
1942	78,547	66,014	10,876	—	13.70	—	25,585	25,007	—	1,042	—	13.82	—
1943	95,226	81,210	13,640	—	14.31	—	27,073	26,497	—	1,104	—	14.91	—
1944	98,068	84,517	13,304	—	13.57	—	25,355	24,793	—	1,024	—	14.52	—
1945	71,891	58,260	10,697	—	14.66	—	24,639	24,068	—	1,054	—	14.90	—
1946	76,115	62,300	11,136	—	18.40	—	22,788	22,234	—	968	—	18.40	—
1947	74,001	61,929	10,502	—	24.45	—	18,706	18,207	—	799	—	22.63	—
1948	70,869	59,669	10,055	—	23.14	—	17,371	16,897	—	747	—	25.04	—
1949	74,997	64,761	10,286	—	18.12	—	13,780	13,376	—	603	—	25.54	—

Notes appear at end of table

(continued)

TABLE Da995–1019   Beef, veal, pork, and lamb – slaughtering, production, and price: 1899–1999   Continued

	Pork						Lamb						
	Hogs slaughtered		Production		Price		Sheep and lambs			Lamb and mutton production		Slaughter lamb price	
	Total	Commercial	Total	Commercial	Slaughter hogs	Barrow and gilt	Slaughtered		Lambs and yearlings, commercial	Total	Commercial	Chicago, IL	Choice, San Angelo, TX
							Total	Commercial					
Year	Da1007	Da1008 [1]	Da1009	Da1010	Da1011 [4]	Da1012	Da1013	Da1014 [1]	Da1015	Da1016	Da1017	Da1018	Da1019
	Thousand	Thousand	Million pounds	Million pounds	Dollars per hundredweight	Dollars per hundredweight	Thousand	Thousand	Thousand	Million pounds	Million pounds	Dollars per hundredweight	Dollars per hundredweight
1950	79,263	69,543	10,714	—	18.20	18.11	13,244	12,852	—	597	—	27.54	—
1951	85,540	76,061	11,481	—	20.12	20.21	11,416	11,075	—	521	—	34.31	—
1952	86,572	77,690	11,527	—	17.94	17.71	14,304	13,962	—	648	—	26.76	—
1953	74,368	66,913	10,006	—	21.65	21.57	16,321	15,967	—	729	—	22.46	—
1954	71,495	64,827	9,870	8,932	21.32	21.77	16,255	15,920	—	734	721	21.59	—
1955	81,051	74,216	10,990	10,027	14.80	14.72	16,553	16,215	—	758	744	20.95	—
1956	85,064	78,513	11,200	10,284	14.35	14.56	16,328	15,993	—	741	728	21.12	—
1957	78,636	72,585	10,424	9,579	17.89	18.16	15,292	14,957	—	707	694	22.37	—
1958	76,822	70,965	10,454	9,618	19.80	20.03	14,495	14,164	—	688	674	22.58	—
1959	87,606	81,582	11,993	11,131	14.12	14.53	15,528	15,180	—	738	724	20.93	—
1960	84,150	79,036	11,598	10,863	15.50	15.88	16,240	15,899	—	768	754	19.26	—
1961	81,970	77,335	11,399	10,730	16.71	17.07	17,537	17,190	—	832	818	17.07	—
1962	83,424	79,334	11,819	11,229	16.44	16.75	17,168	16,837	—	808	795	19.45	—
1963	87,117	83,324	12,419	11,863	15.03	15.36	16,147	15,822	—	770	757	18.69	—
1964	86,284	83,018	12,503	12,019	14.89	15.24	14,895	14,595	—	715	703	21.93	—
1965	76,462	73,784	11,165	10,736	20.78	20.99	13,300	13,006	—	651	639	24.29	—
1966	75,386	74,011	11,328	11,130	22.61	23.25	13,005	12,737	—	650	639	25.00	—
1967	83,425	82,124	12,572	12,377	18.88	19.17	13,036	12,791	—	646	636	23.48	—
1968	86,422	85,160	13,055	12,867	18.65	19.01	12,121	11,884	—	602	592	26.02	—
1969	84,972	83,838	12,946	12,774	23.09	23.55	10,924	10,691	—	550	540	28.35	—
1970	87,052	85,817	13,429	14,500	—	21.75	10,801	10,552	9,803	551	540	—	27.45
1971	95,648	94,438	14,783	15,815	—	18.24	10,965	10,729	9,871	555	545	—	27.16
1972	85,865	84,707	13,631	14,241	—	26.36	10,525	10,301	9,599	543	533	—	30.70
1973	77,890	76,795	12,751	13,043	—	39.83	9,799	9,597	8,776	514	502	—	38.14
1974	83,083	81,762	13,805	14,100	—	34.65	9,064	8,847	8,260	465	453	—	40.51
1975	69,880	68,687	11,503	11,585	—	47.93	8,047	7,835	7,255	410	400	—	44.45
1976	74,959	73,784	12,415	12,488	—	42.60	6,916	6,714	6,280	371	361	—	49.87
1977	78,447	77,303	13,247	13,052	—	40.65	6,554	6,356	5,843	351	340	—	54.17
1978	78,401	77,315	13,393	13,209	—	48.29	5,543	5,369	4,994	309	301	—	65.48
1979	90,169	89,099	15,450	15,271	—	41.56	5,189	5,017	4,672	293	282	—	68.63
1980	97,174	96,074	16,615	16,433	—	39.08	5,745	5,579	5,167	318	310	—	67.00
1981	92,470	91,575	15,875	15,717	—	43.87	6,197	6,008	5,589	338	328	—	59.18
1982	82,845	82,190	14,229	14,121	—	54.87	6,644	6,449	5,984	365	356	—	56.95
1983	88,101	87,584	15,202	15,117	—	47.32	6,790	6,619	6,126	376	367	—	57.94
1984	85,641	85,168	14,812	14,720	—	48.53	6,900	6,759	6,224	380	371	—	62.82
1985	84,938	84,492	14,805	14,728	—	44.47	6,300	6,165	5,750	357	352	—	68.80
1986	79,956	79,598	14,063	13,998	—	50.30	5,762	5,635	5,313	337	331	—	69.71
1987	81,422	81,081	14,374	14,311	—	50.88	5,312	5,200	4,919	316	309	—	78.09
1988	88,136	87,795	15,684	15,623	—	42.98	5,392	5,293	4,989	335	329	—	68.84
1989	89,007	88,691	15,811	15,759	—	43.75	5,559	5,465	5,122	348	341	—	67.30

Pork

Year	Hogs slaughtered Total Da1007 Thousand	Hogs slaughtered Commercial Da1008 [1] Thousand	Production Total Da1009 Million pounds	Production Commercial Da1010 Million pounds	Price Slaughter hogs Da1011 [4] Dollars per hundredweight	Price Barrow and gilt Da1012 Dollars per hundredweight
1990	85,431	85,136	15,353	15,300	—	57.38
1991	88,445	88,169	16,000	15,948	—	48.52
1992	95,157	94,889	17,282	17,184	—	42.44
1993	93,296	93,068	17,087	17,030	—	42.44
1994	95,905	95,697	17,697	17,658	—	39.76
1995	96,535	96,326	17,848	17,811	—	41.87
1996	92,569	92,394	17,116	17,085	—	53.29
1997	92,125	91,960	17,275	17,244	—	51.79
1998	101,194	101,029	19,011	18,980	—	—
1999	101,694	101,544	19,306	19,278	—	—

Lamb

Year	Sheep and lambs Slaughtered Total Da1013 Thousand	Sheep and lambs Slaughtered Commercial Da1014 [1] Thousand	Lambs and yearlings, commercial Da1015 Thousand	Lamb and mutton production Total Da1016 Million pounds	Lamb and mutton production Commercial Da1017 Million pounds	Slaughter lamb price Chicago, IL Da1018 Dollars per hundredweight	Slaughter lamb price Choice, San Angelo, TX Da1019 Dollars per hundredweight
1990	5,750	5,654	5,321	362	358	—	55.42
1991	5,813	5,721	5,377	362	358	—	53.21
1992	5,585	5,496	5,178	354	343	—	61.00
1993	5,259	5,182	4,878	337	329	—	65.85
1994	5,014	4,938	4,634	310	304	—	—
1995	4,629	4,560	4,272	288	281	—	75.86
1996	4,249	4,184	3,904	269	264	—	85.27
1997	3,969	3,907	3,683	260	257	—	87.95
1998	3,861	3,804	3,586	252	248	—	74.20
1999	3,766	3,701	3,503	247	244	—	75.96

[1] Beginning with 1966, custom slaughter in plants for farmers is included in commercial slaughter.

[2] Omaha, Nebraska. Through 1985, 900–1,100 pounds; thereafter, 1,000–1,100 pounds. Simple average of Choice 900 (or 1,000 after 1985) to 1,100-pound price quotations.

[3] Prior to 1992, seven-market average; 1992–1993, six-market average.

[4] Excludes processing tax of $0.50 per 100 pounds from November 5 to 30, 1933; $1.00 from December 1, 1933, to January 31, 1934; $1.50 from February 1 to 28, 1934; and $2.25 from March 1, 1934, to January 6, 1936.

[5] Excludes purchases on government account for the Emergency Hog Production Control Program from August 22 to October 7, 1933.

[6] Excludes cattle and calves purchased for slaughter for Federal Surplus Relief Corporation from June 1934 to February 1935 and for August 1936; excludes also cattle thus purchased for September 1936.

[7] Includes slaughter under the Emergency Government Relief Purchase Program in 1934–1935.

Sources

Series Da995, Da1001, Da1007, and Da1013–1014. 1900–1939, U.S. Department of Agriculture, Production and Marketing Administration, Livestock Market News, Statistics and Related Data, 1946, September 1947; 1940–1964, U.S. Department of Agriculture, Economic Research Service (USDA ERS), Livestock and Meat Statistics, annual issues, and U.S. Department of Agriculture, Statistical Reporting Service, Agricultural Statistics, annual issues; 1965–1994, Agricultural Statistics, 1982, 1987, 1992, 1995–96, and 2000 editions.

Series Da996, Da1002, Da1008, and Da1015. 1920–1969, Agricultural Statistics, 1957, 1962, 1967, and 1982 editions; 1970–1999, USDA ERS, Red Meat Yearbook, September 2000, downloaded October 9, 2000, from the U.S. Department of Agriculture, Economics and Statistics System.

Series Da997, Da1003, Da1009, and Da1016. 1899–1939, Livestock Market News, Statistics and Related Data, 1946, September 1947; 1940–1970, Livestock and Meat Statistics, annual issues, and Agricultural Statistics, annual issues; 1971–1999, Agricultural Statistics, 1982, 1990, 1995–96, and 2000 editions.

Series Da998, Da1004, Da1010, and Da1017. 1954–1969, Livestock and Meat Statistics, Statistical Bulletin number 230, 1961, p. 80, and 1972, p. 196; 1970–1999, USDA ERS, Red Meat Yearbook, September 2000, downloaded October 9, 2000, from the U.S. Department of Agriculture, Economics and Statistics System.

Series Da999, Da1005, Da1011, and Da1018. 1899–1939, Livestock Market News, Statistics and Related Data, 1946, September 1947; 1940–1970, Livestock and Meat Statistics, annual issues, and Agricultural Statistics, annual issues.

Series Da1000. Livestock and Meat Statistics, 1983, Statistical Bulletin number 715, p. 127; and USDA ERS, Red Meat Yearbook, September 2000, downloaded November 20, 2000, from the U.S. Department of Agriculture, Economics and Statistics System.

Series Da1006. USDA ERS, Red Meat Yearbook, September 2000, downloaded November 20, 2000, from the U.S. Department of Agriculture, Economics and Statistics System.

Series Da1012. Agricultural Statistics, 1967, 1972, 1978, 1982, 1987, 1992, 1995–96, and 1998 editions.

Series Da1019. USDA ERS, Red Meat Yearbook, September 2000, downloaded October 9, 2000, from the U.S. Department of Agriculture, Economics and Statistics System.

Documentation

Figures for slaughter include federally inspected slaughter and estimates of all other slaughter (other commercial slaughter and farm slaughter). Before 1944, this information was obtained largely on an annual basis from various sources, but, beginning in 1944, information was collected by months, first under the slaughter control program of the War Food Administration and later under the slaughter and meat control programs of the Office of Price Administration. Current data on federally inspected slaughter, which includes animals condemned as unfit for human food, are compiled by the Consumer and Marketing Service in connection with its regulatory functions on meat inspection. The number of animals slaughtered in other commercial channels is estimated by the National Agricultural Statistics Service from monthly reports made by slaughterers who are not under federal inspection. Estimates of farm slaughter are based on annual voluntary reports from livestock producers with periodic data from the Census of Agriculture as benchmarks. Production of the different kinds of meat is computed from estimated average live weights and dressing yields and, except for pork, is shown on a carcass weight basis. Pork production represents carcass weight excluding the raw fat rendered into lard.

(continued)

TABLE Da995–1019   Beef, veal, pork, and lamb – slaughtering, production, and price: 1899–1999   *Continued*

The data on production under federal inspection are based on records of production and yields reported monthly by slaughterers operating under federal inspection. Monthly estimates of production under federal inspection are not available prior to 1921. Reports of the biennial census of manufactures on slaughter were used as a basis for annual production estimates for years for which they are available. In other years, the estimates were based on information obtained from market records and other sources. Currently, information on weights and yields for other commercial slaughter is based on monthly reports from commercial slaughterers who are not under federal inspection.

Prices of the different species of livestock at Chicago for the early years are from records published in the Drovers Journal Yearbook. Beginning in 1922, the price of beef steers at Chicago is based on records of all steers sold out of first hands for slaughter. The number of head, live weight, and total value of steers, by grades, are compiled by weeks. The annual prices represent the weighted average of all grades of steers sold during the year for slaughter. Since 1919, the average price for veal calves is based on the

average of daily quotations. The average price of hogs at Chicago has been obtained from different sources; since 1920, it is the weighted average of packer and shipper purchases at the Chicago market. Since 1921, the price of lambs at Chicago represents an average computed from the bulk of sales price data.

Series Da995, Da1001, Da1007, and Da1013. Slaughter totals include inspected, noninspected, retail, and farm slaughter.

Series Da1006. Price in Albany, New York. A vealer is a calf suitable for veal, especially one less than three months old and largely or wholly milk-fed.

Series Da1011. Average cost for all packer and shipper purchases, Chicago, Illinois.

Series Da1012. Average cost in Omaha, Nebraska. A barrow is a male hog castrated before it reaches sexual maturity. A gilt is a young sow usually prior to production of her first litter but sometimes until bred to produce a second litter.

TABLE Da1020–1038   Dairy products – production, price, and livestock kept for milk: 1830–1999

Contributed by Alan L. Olmstead and Paul W. Rhode

	Cows and heifers kept for milk			Production of dairy products					
				Evaporated and condensed milk		Butter			
	Number	Value per head	Milk produced on farms	Total production	Case goods, unskimmed	Total farm and factory	Creamery	Cheese	Hard ice cream
	Da1020	Da1021	Da1022	Da1023 [1]	Da1024	Da1025	Da1026 [2]	Da1027 [3]	Da1028
Year	Thousand	Dollars	Million pounds	Million pounds	Thousand pounds	Million pounds	Thousand pounds	Million pounds	Million gallons
1830	—	—	—	—	—	—	—	—	—
1831	—	—	—	—	—	—	—	—	—
1832	—	—	—	—	—	—	—	—	—
1833	—	—	—	—	—	—	—	—	—
1834	—	—	—	—	—	—	—	—	—
1835	—	—	—	—	—	—	—	—	—
1836	—	—	—	—	—	—	—	—	—
1837	—	—	—	—	—	—	—	—	—
1838	—	—	—	—	—	—	—	—	—
1839	—	—	—	—	—	—	—	—	—
1840	—	—	—	—	—	—	—	—	—
1841	—	—	—	—	—	—	—	—	—
1842	—	—	—	—	—	—	—	—	—
1843	—	—	—	—	—	—	—	—	—
1844	—	—	—	—	—	—	—	—	—
1845	—	—	—	—	—	—	—	—	—
1846	—	—	—	—	—	—	—	—	—
1847	—	—	—	—	—	—	—	—	—
1848	—	—	—	—	—	—	—	—	—
1849	—	—	—	—	—	313	—	106	—
1850	—	—	—	—	—	—	—	—	—
1851	—	—	—	—	—	—	—	—	—
1852	—	—	—	—	—	—	—	—	—
1853	—	—	—	—	—	—	—	—	—
1854	—	—	—	—	—	—	—	—	—
1855	—	—	—	—	—	—	—	—	—
1856	—	—	—	—	—	—	—	—	—
1857	—	—	—	—	—	—	—	—	—
1858	—	—	—	—	—	—	—	—	—
1859	—	—	—	—	—	460	—	104	(Z)

Notes appear at end of table

TABLE Da1020–1038   Dairy products – production, price, and livestock kept for milk: 1830–1999   *Continued*

	Cows and heifers kept for milk			Production of dairy products					
				Evaporated and condensed milk		Butter			
Year	Number	Value per head	Milk produced on farms	Total production	Case goods, unskimmed	Total farm and factory	Creamery	Cheese	Hard ice cream
	Da1020	Da1021	Da1022	Da1023 [1]	Da1024	Da1025	Da1026 [2]	Da1027 [3]	Da1028
	Thousand	Dollars	Million pounds	Million pounds	Thousand pounds	Million pounds	Thousand pounds	Million pounds	Million gallons
1860	—	—	—	—	—	—	—	—	—
1861	—	—	—	—	—	—	—	—	—
1862	—	—	—	—	—	—	—	—	—
1863	—	—	—	—	—	—	—	—	—
1864	—	—	—	—	—	—	—	—	—
1865	—	—	—	—	—	—	—	—	—
1866	—	—	—	—	—	—	—	—	—
1867	8,263	29.40	—	—	—	—	—	—	—
1868	8,705	26.96	—	—	—	—	—	—	—
1869	9,205	28.86	—	4	—	514	—	163	(Z)
1870	9,672	31.89	—	—	—	412	—	181	—
1871	9,941	33.62	—	—	—	470	—	164	—
1872	10,191	29.18	—	—	—	434	—	187	—
1873	10,348	26.32	—	—	—	566	—	212	—
1874	10,562	25.20	—	—	—	585	—	206	—
1875	10,714	25.29	—	—	—	556	—	233	—
1876	10,821	25.20	—	—	—	677	—	214	—
1877	11,004	25.14	—	—	—	696	—	235	—
1878	11,222	25.70	—	—	—	726	—	303	—
1879	11,486	21.55	—	13	—	807	—	243	(Z)
1880	11,754	23.31	—	—	—	816	—	270	—
1881	11,977	23.82	—	—	—	803	—	304	—
1882	12,234	26.12	—	—	—	743	—	261	—
1883	12,571	30.47	—	—	—	844	—	281	—
1884	12,883	31.58	—	—	—	869	—	275	—
1885	13,213	29.88	—	—	—	933	—	260	—
1886	13,478	27.52	—	—	—	989	—	244	—
1887	13,888	26.23	—	—	—	978	—	268	—
1888	14,350	24.82	—	—	—	978	—	286	—
1889	14,706	24.03	44,807	45	—	1,292	—	301	1
1890	15,000	22.30	—	—	—	1,171	—	318	—
1891	15,133	21.73	—	—	—	1,091	—	293	—
1892	15,177	21.53	—	—	—	1,058	—	318	—
1893	15,164	21.90	—	—	—	1,047	—	254	—
1894	15,237	21.86	—	—	—	1,063	—	257	—
1895	15,230	22.11	—	—	—	1,297	—	234	—
1896	15,266	22.53	—	—	—	1,604	—	240	—
1897	15,382	23.08	—	—	—	1,533	—	311	—
1898	15,641	27.34	—	—	—	1,473	—	281	—
1899	16,094	29.46	62,486	187	—	1,493	—	299	5
1900	16,544	31.30	—	207	—	1,540	—	324	—
1901	16,708	29.88	—	228	—	1,575	—	362	—
1902	16,992	29.08	—	252	—	1,401	—	318	—
1903	17,217	30.06	—	279	—	1,485	—	323	—
1904	17,485	29.00	—	308	—	1,540	—	331	12
1905	17,823	27.19	—	339	—	1,667	—	327	—
1906	18,230	29.34	—	373	—	1,545	—	292	—
1907	18,629	30.63	—	410	—	1,537	—	286	—
1908	18,992	30.48	—	450	—	1,763	—	313	—
1909	19,201	32.09	64,211	495	—	1,622	—	313	30
1910	19,450	35.40	—	556	—	1,706	—	355	—
1911	19,422	40.07	—	624	—	1,762	—	345	—
1912	19,517	39.42	—	701	—	1,592	—	323	—
1913	19,580	45.04	—	787	—	1,608	—	359	—
1914	19,821	53.91	—	883	—	1,685	—	367	72

Notes appear at end of table

(continued)

TABLE Da1020-1038   Dairy products – production, price, and livestock kept for milk: 1830–1999   *Continued*

	Cows and heifers kept for milk			Production of dairy products					
				Evaporated and condensed milk		Butter			
	Number	Value per head	Milk produced on farms	Total production	Case goods, unskimmed	Total farm and factory	Creamery	Cheese	Hard ice cream
	Da1020	Da1021	Da1022	Da1023 [1]	Da1024	Da1025	Da1026 [2]	Da1027 [3]	Da1028
Year	Thousand	Dollars	Million pounds	Million pounds	Thousand pounds	Million pounds	Thousand pounds	Million pounds	Million gallons
1915	20,270	55.30	—	1,028	—	1,751	—	440	—
1916	20,752	53.81	—	1,196	—	1,793	—	422	94
1917	21,212	59.51	—	1,391	—	1,644	—	472	106
1918	21,536	70.63	—	1,619	—	1,503	—	415	143
1919	21,545	78.37	67,124	1,883	—	1,647	—	486	153
1920	21,455	81.51	—	1,416	—	1,574	—	423	171
1921	21,456	61.19	—	1,324	—	1,748	—	434	175
1922	21,851	48.68	—	1,281	—	1,870	—	432	191
1923	22,138	48.65	—	1,585	—	1,993	—	471	214
1924	22,331	49.91	89,240	1,507	—	2,066	—	474	213
1925	22,575	48.34	90,699	1,548	—	2,082	1,361,526	503	240
1926	22,410	54.65	93,325	1,456	—	2,132	1,451,766	468	238
1927	22,251	59.15	95,172	1,576	1,435,170	2,188	1,496,495	462	251
1928	22,231	73.38	95,843	1,604	1,476,099	2,120	1,487,049	479	254
1929	22,440	83.89	98,988	1,849	1,645,566	2,184	1,597,027	499	277
1930	23,032	82.70	100,158	1,761	1,570,775	2,149	1,595,231	510	255
1931	23,820	57.03	103,029	1,682	1,526,462	2,239	1,667,452	499	226
1932	24,896	39.51	103,810	1,780	1,640,900	2,307	1,694,132	491	168
1933	25,936	29.18	104,762	1,899	1,770,580	2,375	1,762,688	548	162
1934	26,931	27.00	101,621	1,908	1,772,222	2,286	1,694,708	587	192
1935	26,082	30.17	101,205	2,032	1,891,875	2,211	1,632,380	628	219
1936	25,196	49.32	102,410	2,270	2,091,120	2,168	1,629,407	650	259
1937	24,649	50.45	101,908	2,131	1,949,991	2,135	1,623,971	653	291
1938	24,466	54.52	105,807	2,322	2,145,737	2,252	1,786,172	726	286
1939	24,600	55.73	106,792	2,367	2,205,333	2,210	1,781,737	710	306
1940	24,940	57.30	109,412	2,731	2,526,623	2,240	1,836,826	785	318
1941	25,453	60.90	115,088	3,555	3,361,319	2,268	1,872,183	956	390
1942	26,313	77.90	118,533	3,782	3,580,957	2,130	1,764,054	1,112	464
1943	27,138	99.50	117,017	3,344	3,174,521	2,015	1,673,788	993	412
1944	27,704	102.00	117,023	3,750	3,567,234	1,818	1,488,502	1,017	445
1945	27,770	99.40	119,828	4,126	3,919,689	1,699	1,363,717	1,117	477
1946	26,521	112.00	117,697	3,333	3,164,549	1,502	1,171,339	1,106	714
1947	25,842	145.00	116,814	3,630	3,372,760	1,640	1,329,094	1,183	631
1948	24,615	164.00	112,671	3,755	3,509,188	1,504	1,210,324	1,098	576
1949	23,862	193.00	116,103	3,106	2,856,682	1,688	1,412,111	1,199	558
1950	23,853	177.00	116,602	3,205	2,944,448	1,648	1,386,408	1,191	554
1951	23,568	219.00	114,681	3,228	2,955,319	1,443	1,202,981	1,161	569
1952	23,060	252.00	114,671	3,165	2,894,474	1,402	1,188,170	1,170	593
1953	23,549	203.00	120,221	2,875	2,594,803	1,607	1,412,109	1,344	605
1954	23,896	147.00	122,094	2,845	2,559,344	1,628	1,448,872	1,383	597
1955	23,462	134.00	122,945	2,922	2,613,512	1,545	1,382,914	1,367	629
1956	22,912	139.00	124,860	2,953	2,609,866	1,553	1,413,344	1,388	641
1957	22,325	147.00	124,628	2,872	2,507,497	1,533	1,414,060	1,407	651
1958	21,265	177.00	123,220	2,752	2,355,386	1,486	1,389,575	1,399	658
1959	20,132	221.00	121,989	2,743	2,328,607	1,411	1,334,385	1,383	699
1960	19,527	210.00	123,109	2,666	2,245,097	1,436	1,372,901	1,478	700
1961	19,271	208.00	125,707	2,632	2,187,304	1,536	1,484,126	1,635	699
1962	18,963	212.00	126,251	2,409	2,002,896	1,579	1,537,143	1,592	704
1963	18,379	206.00	125,202	2,369	2,066,234	1,454	1,419,688	1,632	718
1964	17,647	194.00	126,967	2,395	1,982,683	1,469	1,441,502	1,724	739
1965	16,981	188.00	124,180	2,178	1,788,922	1,346	1,324,582	1,755	757
1966	15,973	208.00	119,912	2,196	1,837,861	1,128	1,112,009	1,854	751
1967	15,129	247.00	118,732	1,886	1,557,542	1,238	1,224,949	1,919	745
1968	14,456	251.00	117,225	1,800	1,447,386	1,175	1,164,829	1,938	773
1969	13,821	270.00	116,108	1,776	1,483,754	1,129	1,118,228	1,990	766

Notes appear at end of table

TABLE Da1020–1038   Dairy products – production, price, and livestock kept for milk: 1830–1999   *Continued*

	Cows and heifers kept for milk			Production of dairy products					
					Evaporated and condensed milk		Butter			
	Number	Value per head	Milk produced on farms	Total production	Case goods, unskimmed	Total farm and factory	Creamery	Cheese	Hard ice cream
	Da1020	Da1021	Da1022	Da1023 [1]	Da1024	Da1025	Da1026 [2]	Da1027 [3]	Da1028
Year	Thousand	Dollars	Million pounds	Million pounds	Thousand pounds	Million pounds	Thousand pounds	Million pounds	Million gallons
1970	12,091	300.00	117,006	1,517	1,268,325	1,143	1,137,020	2,201	762
1971	11,909	—	118,565	—	1,268,086	1,144 [9]	1,143,695	2,374	766
1972	11,776	—	120,025	—	1,183,298	1,102	1,101,910	2,605	768
1973	11,622	—	115,491	—	1,102,183	919	918,618	2,685	774
1974	11,297	—	115,586	—	1,035,209	962 [10]	961,724	2,937	782
1975	11,220	—	115,398	—	926,923	—	983,791	2,811	837
1976	11,071	—	120,180	—	932,123	—	978,631	3,320	818
1977	10,998	—	122,655	—	818,927	—	1,085,595	3,359	810
1978	10,896	—	121,461	—	787,866	—	994,290	3,520	815
1979	10,790	—	123,350	—	796,076	—	984,604	3,717	811
1980	10,758	—	128,406	—	724,665	—	1,145,254	3,984	830
1981	10,849	—	132,770	—	757,919	—	1,228,190	4,277	832
1982	10,986	—	135,506	—	734,921	—	1,256,964 [11]	4,542 [11]	852 [11]
1983	11,047	—	139,588	—	694,185	—	1,299,247	4,819	882
1984	11,059	—	135,351	—	647,663	—	1,103,316	4,674	894
1985	10,777	—	143,012	—	635,292	—	1,247,792	5,081	901
1986	11,116	—	143,125	—	584,426	—	1,202,392	5,209	887
1987	10,466	—	142,709	—	579,722	—	1,104,135	5,344	887
1988	10,311	—	145,035	—	590,113	—	1,207,540	5,572	844
1989	10,138	—	143,893	—	525,128	—	1,295,409	5,615	789
1990	10,015	—	147,720	—	602,647	—	1,302,177	6,061	775
1991	9,966	—	147,696	—	543,094	—	1,335,782	6,055	817
1992	9,728	—	150,847	—	582,115	—	1,365,164	6,488	822
1993	9,658	—	150,636	—	534,507	—	1,315,198	6,528	826
1994	9,507	—	153,602	—	537,881	—	1,295,942	6,735	836
1995	9,482	—	155,292	—	476,656	—	1,264,474	6,917	822
1996	9,420	—	154,006	—	463,613	—	1,174,475	7,218	825
1997	9,318	—	156,091	—	549,129	—	1,151,250	7,030	854
1998	9,199	—	157,441	—	468,070 [8]	—	1,081,879	7,502	866
1999	9,133	—	—	—	—	—	—	—	—

			Prices							
									Cheddar cheese (Wisconsin)	
	Milk equivalent of manufactured products, milkfat basis	Utilization (milk equivalent), total manufactured products	Whole milk				Butter			
			Sold to plants and dealers	Sold directly to consumers	Milkfat in cream	Marketings of milk and cream	All butter, farm price	Bulk, wholesale (Grade A, 92-score), New York	Primary markets	Assembly points
	Da1029 [4]	Da1030	Da1031	Da1032	Da1033	Da1034 [5]	Da1035	Da1036 [6]	Da1037 [7]	Da1038
Year	Million pounds	Million pounds	Dollars per hundredweight	Cents per quart	Cents per pound	Dollars per pound	Cents per pound	Cents per pound	Cents per pound	Dollars per pound
1830	—	—	—	—	—	—	—	13.9	—	—
1831	—	—	—	—	—	—	—	14.9	—	—
1832	—	—	—	—	—	—	—	15.2	—	—
1833	—	—	—	—	—	—	—	15.8	—	—
1834	—	—	—	—	—	—	—	14.4	—	—
1835	—	—	—	—	—	—	—	19.2	—	—
1836	—	—	—	—	—	—	—	23.9	—	—
1837	—	—	—	—	—	—	—	21.6	—	—
1838	—	—	—	—	—	—	—	23.4	—	—
1839	—	—	—	—	—	—	—	22.9	—	—
1840	—	—	—	—	—	—	—	17.4	—	—
1841	—	—	—	—	—	—	—	18.6	—	—
1842	—	—	—	—	—	—	—	16.5	—	—
1843	—	—	—	—	—	—	—	13.3	—	—
1844	—	—	—	—	—	—	—	15.2	—	—

Notes appear at end of table

(continued)

TABLE Da1020–1038   Dairy products – production, price, and livestock kept for milk: 1830–1999   *Continued*

				Prices					Cheddar cheese (Wisconsin)	
	Milk equivalent of manufactured products, milkfat basis	Utilization (milk equivalent), total manufactured products	Whole milk				Butter			
			Sold to plants and dealers	Sold directly to consumers	Milkfat in cream	Marketings of milk and cream	All butter, farm price	Bulk, wholesale (Grade A, 92-score), New York	Primary markets	Assembly points
	Da1029 [4]	Da1030	Da1031	Da1032	Da1033	Da1034 [5]	Da1035	Da1036 [6]	Da1037 [7]	Da1038
Year	Million pounds	Million pounds	Dollars per hundredweight	Cents per quart	Cents per pound	Dollars per pound	Cents per pound	Cents per pound	Cents per pound	Dollars per pound
1845	—	—	—	—	—	—	—	17.7	—	—
1846	—	—	—	—	—	—	—	16.7	—	—
1847	—	—	—	—	—	—	—	20.7	—	—
1848	—	—	—	—	—	—	—	20.1	—	—
1849	7,636	—	—	—	—	—	—	18.9	—	—
1850	—	—	—	—	—	—	—	19.6	—	—
1851	—	—	—	—	—	—	—	18.4	—	—
1852	—	—	—	—	—	—	—	23.6	—	—
1853	—	—	—	—	—	—	—	23.0	—	—
1854	—	—	—	—	—	—	—	23.0	—	—
1855	—	—	—	—	—	—	—	26.4	—	—
1856	—	—	—	—	—	—	—	25.8	—	—
1857	—	—	—	—	—	—	—	25.7	—	—
1858	—	—	—	—	—	—	—	23.8	—	—
1859	10,690	—	—	—	—	—	—	23.9	—	—
1860	—	—	—	—	—	—	—	21.9	—	—
1861	—	—	—	—	—	—	—	19.4	—	—
1862	—	—	—	—	—	—	—	20.9	—	—
1863	—	—	—	—	—	—	—	28.2	—	—
1864	—	—	—	—	—	—	—	43.7	—	—
1865	—	—	—	—	—	—	—	39.8	—	—
1866	—	—	—	—	—	—	—	42.7	—	—
1867	—	—	—	—	—	—	—	34.8	—	—
1868	—	—	—	—	—	—	—	44.7	—	—
1869	12,484	—	—	—	—	—	—	43.3	—	—
1870	10,472	—	—	—	—	—	—	38.1	—	—
1871	11,527	—	—	—	—	—	—	33.6	—	—
1872	10,997	—	—	—	—	—	—	32.0	—	—
1873	14,029	—	—	—	—	—	—	35.4	—	—
1874	14,347	—	—	—	—	—	—	36.2	—	—
1875	14,029	—	—	—	—	—	—	32.8	—	—
1876	16,390	—	—	—	—	—	—	31.3	—	—
1877	16,995	—	—	—	—	—	—	28.5	—	—
1878	18,307	—	—	—	—	—	—	27.3	—	—
1879	19,402	—	—	—	—	—	—	24.2	8.0	—
1880	19,861	—	—	—	—	—	—	30.5	12.5	—
1881	19,934	—	—	—	—	—	—	31.8	12.4	—
1882	18,248	—	—	—	—	—	—	35.6	11.9	—
1883	20,584	—	—	—	—	—	—	31.2	11.0	—
1884	21,061	—	—	—	—	—	—	30.3	11.1	—
1885	22,258	—	—	—	—	—	—	26.6	8.7	—
1886	23,283	—	—	—	—	—	—	26.8	9.6	—
1887	23,301	—	—	—	—	—	—	26.7	10.8	—
1888	23,494	—	—	—	—	—	—	27.5	8.1	—
1889	30,260	—	—	—	—	—	—	24.4	8.7	—
1890	27,906	—	—	—	—	—	—	23.7	9.0	—
1891	25,990	—	—	—	—	—	—	26.2	8.9	—
1892	25,561	—	—	—	—	—	—	26.3	9.3	—
1893	24,718	—	—	—	—	—	—	27.1	9.6	—
1894	25,113	—	—	—	—	—	—	23.0	10.2	—
1895	29,828	—	—	—	—	—	—	21.2	7.4	—
1896	36,385	—	—	—	—	—	—	18.5	7.7	—
1897	35,640	—	—	—	—	—	—	19.0	8.5	—
1898	34,145	—	—	—	—	—	—	19.6	7.6	—
1899	34,806	—	—	—	—	—	—	21.3	10.6	—

Notes appear at end of table

TABLE Da1020-1038 Dairy products – production, price, and livestock kept for milk: 1830–1999 *Continued*

			Prices								
			Whole milk					Butter		Cheddar cheese (Wisconsin)	
Year	Milk equivalent of manufactured products, milkfat basis	Utilization (milk equivalent), total manufactured products	Sold to plants and dealers	Sold directly to consumers	Milkfat in cream	Marketings of milk and cream	All butter, farm price	Bulk, wholesale (Grade A, 92-score), New York	Primary markets	Assembly points
	Da1029 [4]	Da1030	Da1031	Da1032	Da1033	Da1034 [5]	Da1035	Da1036 [6]	Da1037 [7]	Da1038
	Million pounds	Million pounds	Dollars per hundredweight	Cents per quart	Cents per pound	Dollars per pound	Cents per pound	Cents per pound	Cents per pound	Dollars per pound
1900	36,106	—	—	—	—	—	—	22.2	10.0	—
1901	37,280	—	—	—	—	—	—	21.4	9.8	—
1902	33,248	—	—	—	—	—	—	24.7	11.2	—
1903	35,159	—	—	—	—	—	—	23.4	11.1	—
1904	36,468	—	—	—	—	—	—	21.7	9.3	—
1905	39,210	—	—	—	—	—	—	24.6	11.7	—
1906	36,403	—	—	—	—	—	—	24.6	11.8	—
1907	36,290	—	—	—	—	—	—	28.1	13.4	—
1908	41,439	—	—	—	—	—	—	27.6	12.2	—
1909	38,715	—	—	6.4	25.5	—	24.0	29.9	14.6	—
1910	41,132	—	1.58	6.6	26.4	—	25.5	31.1	14.7	—
1911	42,464	—	1.52	6.7	23.2	—	22.9	27.9	12.7	—
1912	38,963	—	1.59	6.9	26.7	—	25.7	31.6	15.6	—
1913	40,010	—	1.61	7.1	27.4	—	26.7	32.2	14.3	—
1914	42,101	—	1.60	7.2	25.5	—	25.1	29.8	14.6	—
1915	44,677	—	1.58	7.1	25.9	—	25.7	29.8	14.2	—
1916	45,927	—	1.73	7.4	29.4	—	28.0	34.0	17.5	—
1917	44,010	—	2.38	8.9	38.0	—	35.9	42.7	22.5	—
1918	40,077	—	2.96	10.6	45.4	—	42.7	51.5	25.9	—
1919	45,388	—	3.29	11.9	53.3	—	50.3	60.7	29.0	—
1920	42,446	—	3.22	12.8	55.5	—	54.3	61.4	24.9	—
1921	45,759	—	2.30	11.2	37.0	—	37.0	43.3	18.3	—
1922	48,629	—	2.11	10.4	35.9	—	35.3	40.6	19.3	—
1923	52,204	—	2.49	10.9	42.2	—	40.4	46.9	22.1	—
1924	52,417	—	2.22	11.1	40.4	—	39.5	42.6	18.2	—
1925	53,434	—	2.38	11.2	42.4	—	40.5	45.3	21.5	—
1926	53,902	—	2.38	11.3	41.6	—	40.9	44.4	20.1	—
1927	55,409	—	2.51	11.3	44.5	—	41.5	47.3	22.7	—
1928	54,261	—	2.52	11.5	46.1	—	42.6	47.4	22.1	—
1929	56,625	—	2.53	11.5	45.2	0.61	42.2	45.0	20.2	—
1930	55,581	—	2.21	11.3	34.5	0.53	36.3	36.5	16.4	—
1931	56,686	—	1.69	10.1	24.8	0.41	27.2	28.3	12.5	—
1932	57,433	—	1.28	8.9	17.9	0.32	20.8	21.0	10.0	—
1933	59,557	—	1.30	8.6	18.8	0.32	20.1	21.6	10.2	—
1934	58,479	—	1.55	9.4	22.7	0.38	22.7	25.7	11.8	—
1935	57,881	46,950	1.72	9.8	28.1	0.43	26.7	29.8	14.3	—
1936	58,250	48,087	1.88	10.1	32.2	0.46	28.8	33.1	15.3	—
1937	57,548	48,000	1.99	10.5	33.3	0.49	29.6	34.4	15.9	—
1938	60,989	51,816	1.73	10.3	26.3	0.42	26.6	28.0	12.6	—
1939	60,455	51,802	1.69	10.3	23.9	0.40	25.0	26.0	12.8	—
1940	62,845	54,716	—	10.3	28.0	0.44	26.6	29.5	14.3	—
1941	67,832	59,865	2.19	10.8	34.2	0.51	30.4	34.3	19.4	—
1942	67,996	60,631	2.58	11.8	39.6	0.60	35.2	40.1	21.6	—
1943	63,724	56,864	3.12	12.7	49.9	0.73	43.7	44.8	23.2	—
1944	61,566	54,945	3.21	13.2	50.3	0.76	43.8	42.2	23.2	—
1945	61,859	55,145	3.19	13.4	50.3	0.76	45.3	42.8	23.2	—
1946	58,325	51,768	3.99	15.2	64.3	0.96	58.3	62.8	34.8	—
1947	61,716	55,562	4.27	17.5	71.8	1.04	63.3	71.3	36.0	—
1948	57,669	51,861	4.88	18.8	79.9	1.17	66.7	75.8	40.7	—
1949	60,764	55,324	3.95	18.6	61.6	0.96	58.0	61.5	30.4	—
1950	60,330	55,170	3.89	18.5	62.0	0.95	56.8	62.2	31.9	—
1951	56,349	51,603	4.58	19.9	71.2	1.12	60.8	69.9	38.9	—
1952	55,783	51,544	4.85	20.8	75.0	1.20	—	73.0	40.3	—
1953	61,492	57,597	4.32	20.9	66.5	1.08	—	66.6	37.2	—
1954	62,266	58,681	3.97	20.6	58.7	1.00	—	60.5	33.9	—

Notes appear at end of table

(continued)

TABLE Da1020–1038 Dairy products – production, price, and livestock kept for milk: 1830–1999 *Continued*

			Prices								
			Whole milk					Butter		Cheddar cheese (Wisconsin)	
Year	Milk equivalent of manufactured products, milkfat basis	Utilization (milk equivalent), total manufactured products	Sold to plants and dealers	Sold directly to consumers	Milkfat in cream	Marketings of milk and cream	All butter, farm price	Bulk, wholesale (Grade A, 92-score), New York	Primary markets	Assembly points
	Da1029 [4]	Da1030	Da1031	Da1032	Da1033	Da1034 [5]	Da1035	Da1036 [6]	Da1037 [7]	Da1038
	Million pounds	Million pounds	Dollars per hundredweight	Cents per quart	Cents per pound	Dollars per pound	Cents per pound	Cents per pound	Cents per pound	Dollars per pound
1955	61,272	58,027	4.01	20.8	57.8	1.01	—	58.2	33.1	—
1956	62,220	59,406	4.14	21.0	59.4	1.05	—	59.9	34.3	—
1957	61,640	59,212	4.21	21.3	60.6	1.08	—	60.7	34.8	—
1958	60,847	58,746	4.13	21.3	59.3	1.08	—	59.7	33.7	—
1959	60,010	58,217	4.16	21.5	60.1	1.09	—	60.6	33.2	—
1960	61,088	59,751	4.21	21.7	60.5	1.11	—	59.9	36.4	—
1961	64,695	63,580	4.22	21.7	61.5	1.12	—	61.2	37.2	—
1962	65,056	64,141	4.09	21.9	59.4	1.10	—	59.4	—	—
1963	63,410	62,667	4.10	22.2	59.5	1.11	—	59.0	36.6	—
1964	65,133	64,538	4.15	22.3	60.2	1.13	—	59.9	37.6	—
1965	62,240	61,768	4.23	22.3	61.1	1.15	—	61.0	38.3	—
1966	58,234	57,900	4.81	23.2	67.2	1.31	—	67.2	45.9	—
1967	60,062	59,770	5.01	24.0	68.2	1.37	—	67.7	45.1	0.45
1968	59,664	59,230	5.24	24.8	68.7	1.44	—	67.9	47.3	0.45
1969	58,499	58,315	5.49	25.8	68.9	1.51	—	68.5	51.5	—
1970	60,330	60,013	5.71	27.0	70.0	1.58	—	70.6	54.6	—
1971	—	61,614	5.87	27.9	69.1	1.62	—	69.4	— [13]	—
1972	—	62,319	6.07	27.8	67.8	1.67	—	69.7	— [13]	—
1973	—	58,678	7.14	31.0	67.3	1.97	—	70.6	74.9	0.73
1974	—	61,327	8.33	34.9	63.2	2.29	—	67.4	83.2	0.80
1975	—	60,524	8.75	35.4	70.3	2.41	—	81.8	90.7	0.87
1976	—	64,673	9.66	36.4	83.4	2.66	—	94.4	—	0.96
1977	—	67,068	9.72	36.7	92.0	2.68	—	101.5	—	0.97
1978	—	65,944	10.60	38.8	102.0	2.91	—	114.1	—	1.07
1979	—	67,504	12.02	42.3	—	3.31	—	127.2	—	1.24
1980	—	73,327	13.05	45.3	—	3.60	—	144.8	—	1.33
1981	—	77,916	13.77	48.3	—	3.81	—	153.5 [12]	—	1.39
1982	—	80,583	13.61	48.1	—	3.75	—	—	—	1.38
1983	—	83,992	13.58	48.4	—	3.74	—	—	—	1.38
1984	—	77,292	13.46	49.2	—	3.69	—	—	—	1.38
1985	—	83,537	12.76	48.7	—	3.50	—	—	—	1.28
1986	—	83,226	12.51	48.3	—	3.43	—	—	—	1.27
1987	—	81,945	12.54	48.6	—	3.46	—	—	—	1.23
1988	—	84,775	12.26	50.0	—	3.36	—	—	—	1.24
1989	—	84,738	13.56	53.9	—	3.70	—	—	—	1.39
1990	—	88,940	13.74	56.1	—	3.79	—	—	—	1.37
1991	—	88,817	12.27	55.6	—	3.38	—	—	—	1.24
1992	—	92,207	13.15	58.2	—	3.60	—	—	—	1.32
1993	—	90,559	12.84	58.4	—	3.53	—	—	—	1.32
1994	—	92,493	13.01	63.6	—	3.59	—	—	—	1.31
1995	—	92,795	12.78	64.7	—	3.53	—	—	—	1.33
1996	—	91,585	14.75	78.4	—	4.05	—	—	—	1.49
1997	—	92,970	13.36	73.3	—	3.70	—	—	—	1.32
1998	—	93,435	15.41 [8]	81.4 [8]	—	4.25 [8]	—	—	—	1.58
1999	—	—	—	—	—	—	—	—	—	—

(Z) Less than 500,000 gallons.

[1] Through 1918, includes total production of all condensed and evaporated milk as interpolated from census enumerations. For 1919–1970 includes all evaporated and condensed whole milk as compiled by the former Bureau of Agricultural Economics and Agricultural Marketing Service.

[2] Beginning with 1931, includes whey butter.

[3] Includes all types of cheese except cottage, pot, and bakers' cheese; full-skim American cheese excluded since 1908. Farm output not estimated since 1926.

[4] For 1849–1923, computed from data on estimated production of manufactured dairy products, using average milk equivalent factors; 1924–1970, as published by Agricultural Marketing Service.

[5] Through 1949, includes farm-churned butter sold.

[6] Change over time in method for deriving figures; see text.

[7] Through 1949, includes cheeses in addition to cheddar. For 1878–1899, September figure shown because annual averages not available.

[8] Preliminary.

[9] Creamery butter only.

[10] Data in source appear to be in error but cannot be corrected.

[11] April–December estimates based on published quarterly data.

[12] January–March only. Reporting of New York bulk butter prices were discontinued April 20.

[13] Insufficient prices to compute annual average.

Sources

Series Da1020. 1867–1960, U.S. Department of Agriculture, Statistical Reporting Service, *Agricultural Statistics, 1967* and *1972* editions; 1961–1990,

TABLE Da1020-1038   Dairy products – production, price, and livestock kept for milk: 1830-1999   *Continued*

U.S. National Agricultural Statistics Service, *Cattle, Hogs, Chickens, and Sheep – Inventory by State,* July 1995, downloaded November 20, 2000, from the U.S. Department of Agriculture, Economics and Statistics System; 1991-1999, *Agricultural Statistics, 2000.*

Series Da1021. U.S. Department of Agriculture, Statistical Reporting Service, *Agricultural Statistics, 1967* and *1972* editions.

Series Da1022. 1889-1919, U.S. Bureau of the Census, various Census of Agriculture reports; 1924-1944, U.S. Agricultural Marketing Service, "Milk-Farm Production, Disposition, and Income," *Statistical Bulletin* number 175, April 1956; 1945-1969, *Agricultural Statistics, 1967* and *1972* editions; 1970-1998, U.S. Department of Agriculture, Economic Research Service, *Dairy Yearbook,* October 1999, Table 1, downloaded November 20, 2000, from the U.S. Department of Agriculture, Economics and Statistics System.

Series Da1023 and Da1029. 1849-1916, E. E. Vial, "Production and Consumption of Manufactured Dairy Products," U.S. Department of Agriculture, *Technical Bulletin* number 722, April 1940; 1917-1939, U.S. Agricultural Marketing Service, *Revisions in the Production of Creamery Butter, Cheese, and Ice Cream by States, 1916–1939,* and *Production and Utilization of Milk, United States, 1924–1952*; 1940-1949, *Production of Manufactured Dairy Products*; 1950-1970, *Agricultural Statistics, 1964,* and subsequent annual issues.

Series Da1024. *Agricultural Statistics, 1936, 1944, 1950, 1957, 1962, 1967, 1972, 1978, 1982, 1985, 1990, 1995–96,* and *2000.*

Series Da1025. 1849-1916, E. E. Vial, "Production and Consumption of Manufactured Dairy Products," U.S. Department of Agriculture, *Technical Bulletin* number 722, April 1940; 1917-1939, U.S. Agricultural Marketing Service, *Revisions in the Production of Creamery Butter, Cheese, and Ice Cream by States, 1916–1939,* and *Production and Utilization of Milk, United States, 1924–1952*; 1940-1949, *Production of Manufactured Dairy Products*; 1950-1974, *Agricultural Statistics, 1964,* and subsequent annual issues.

Series Da1026. 1927-1969, *Agricultural Statistics, 1936, 1938, 1944, 1947, 1954, 1959, 1964, 1971,* and *1973* editions; 1970-1998, *Dairy Yearbook,* October 1999, Table 11, downloaded November 20, 2000, from the U.S. Department of Agriculture, Economics and Statistics System.

Series Da1027. 1849-1916, E. E. Vial, "Production and Consumption of Manufactured Dairy Products," U.S. Department of Agriculture, *Technical Bulletin* number 722, April 1940; 1917-1939, U.S. Agricultural Marketing Service, *Revisions in the Production of Creamery Butter, Cheese, and Ice Cream by States, 1916–1939,* and *Production and Utilization of Milk, United States, 1924–1952*; 1940-1949, *Production of Manufactured Dairy Products*; 1950-1969, *Agricultural Statistics, 1964,* and subsequent annual issues; 1970-1998, U.S. Department of Agriculture, Economic Research Service, *Dairy Yearbook,* March 1996, Table 16, downloaded October 5, 2000, from the U.S. Department of Agriculture, Economics and Statistics System.

Series Da1028. 1849-1916, E. E. Vial, "Production and Consumption of Manufactured Dairy Products," U.S. Department of Agriculture, *Technical Bulletin* number 722, April 1940; 1917-1939, U.S. Agricultural Marketing Service, *Revisions in the Production of Creamery Butter, Cheese, and Ice Cream by States, 1916–1939,* and *Production and Utilization of Milk, United States, 1924–1952*; 1940-1949, *Revisions of Ice Cream and Ice Milk Data, by States, 1940–1949*; 1950-1969, *Agricultural Statistics, 1964,* and subsequent annual issues; 1970-1998, U.S. Department of Agriculture, Economic Research Service, *Dairy Yearbook,* March 1996, Table 39, downloaded September 19, 2000, from the U.S. Department of Agriculture, Economics and Statistics System.

Series Da1030. *Agricultural Statistics, 1957, 1962, 1972, 1982, 1985, 1992, 1995–96,* and *2000* editions.

Series Da1031-1032. 1909-1944, "Prices Received by Farmers," *Statistical Bulletin* number 180, June 1956; 1945-1998, *Agricultural Statistics, 1967, 1972, 1982, 1987, 1995–96,* and *2000* editions.

Series Da1033. 1909-1944, "Prices Received by Farmers," *Statistical Bulletin* number 180, June 1956; 1945-1978, *Agricultural Statistics, 1967, 1972, 1982,* and *1985* editions.

Series Da1034. *Agricultural Statistics, 1957, 1962, 1972, 1982, 1987, 1995–96,* and *2000* editions.

Series Da1035. 1909-1944, U.S. Agricultural Marketing Service, "Prices Received by Farmers," *Statistical Bulletin* number 180, June 1956; 1945-1951, *Agricultural Statistics, 1967* and *1972* editions.

Series Da1036. U.S. Department of Agriculture, Consumer and Marketing Service, unpublished data, and *Agricultural Statistics, 1972, 1975, 1978,* and *1982* editions.

Series Da1037. U.S. Department of Agriculture, Consumer and Marketing Service, unpublished data, and *Agricultural Statistics, 1974* and *1976* editions.

Series Da1038. *Agricultural Statistics, 1977, 1978,* and *1982* editions.

Documentation

Early development of the dairy industry in the United States is indicated by export statistics of 1790, which showed the New England states, New York, and Pennsylvania producing considerable amounts of butter and cheese in excess of their consumption requirements. The growth and spread of the industry between that time and 1849, when statistics on dairying were first available through the national census of agriculture, are described in the *U.S. Department of Agriculture's Agriculture Yearbook,* 1922, pp. 297-306. At the middle of the nineteenth century, milk cows were rather generally distributed over the eastern half of the United States as far west as southern Wisconsin, eastern Iowa, western Missouri and Arkansas, and the eastern third of Texas. By 1860, there were appreciable numbers of milk cows in the Pacific Coast states. In later years, they gradually spread over the intervening territory.

Dairy products sold by farmers in the early period were limited mainly to whole milk, farm-made butter, and farm-made cheese. Prior to 1850, these products were produced mainly on farms. The 1850 Census showed the bulk of cheese production for 1849 coming from farms in the area extending from northeastern Ohio eastward through New York and New England. Factory cheese production was in an experimental stage shortly before 1850, and made considerable progress during the next two decades. Although some butter was made in early cheese plants, the first commercial creamery was not established until 1861. Since that time, factories have largely supplanted farms in the production of both cheese and butter.

The first condensery was established in 1856, but little interest was given the product until the Civil War. Unsweetened condensed milk was first produced in 1885; the canned unsweetened product (evaporated milk) now makes up about nine tenths of all evaporated and condensed whole milk. Ice cream was produced and sold by some retail stores in the first half of the nineteenth century, and wholesale plant distribution to dealers began about the middle of the century.

Series Da1020-1021. Animals two years old and over, as of January 1. The estimates are based on interpretation of data from the Census of Agriculture, tax assessors, and other state agencies, together with the analysis of changes taking place in herds kept by a large sample of livestock reporters. With respect to the data on milk cow numbers obtained in the Censuses of Agriculture, the wording of the census questions has not necessarily been comparable with the definitions represented by the annual estimates and has varied somewhat from one census enumeration to another.

Series Da1022. Excludes milk suckled by calves. Beginning with 1924, the figures represent calendar-year estimates. The estimates are based on interpretations of census data, analysis of annual and monthly survey data on milk cows and milk production, and checks against information on milk utilization obtained from dairy plants and other sources. For 1919 and earlier years, the data are based on Censuses of Agriculture and converted from gallons to pounds by use of a conversion factor of 8.6 pounds per gallon. For 1889, the census totals are the reported figures. For 1899, they include estimates for incomplete reports, and for 1909 and 1919, they include estimates of production on farms that reported milk cows but failed to report milk produced. The 1889 and 1899 data were enumerated as of the following June, the 1909 data as of April 15, 1910, and the 1919 data as of January 1, 1920.

Series Da1023-1028. For 1940-1970, data are from the annual survey of output of dairy plants. For 1916-1939, data are based on the annual survey of dairy plants supplemented by estimates for incompleteness in some states based on data from the Census of Manufactures or from state sources. For the years prior to 1916 or 1917, the level of the figures was based mainly on

(continued)

TABLE Da1020–1038   Dairy products – production, price, and livestock kept for milk: 1830–1999   *Continued*

the Census Bureau's survey of the output of dairy plants with interpolations for intervening years for some products (see Vial 1940, cited in the sources).

Series Da1023. Evaporated and condensed milk production includes evaporated whole milk, bulk unsweetened condensed whole milk, and case and bulk sweetened condensed whole milk. Production figures for 1879, 1899, 1904, 1909, and 1914 are census totals for all condensed and evaporated milk. For 1889, the census data were revised upward to allow for incompleteness. Data for 1869 are estimated; those for the noncensus years before 1919 represent an estimated trend of production based on intervening census data.

Series Da1025. Butter production data represent farm and factory production combined. Factory butter figures for 1917–1970 are for production of creamery butter and include some estimates for incompleteness. Figures for factory production for 1849, 1859, 1869, 1879, 1899, 1904, 1909, and 1914 are from the Census of Manufactures. The 1889 census data were revised upward to allow for incompleteness. Annual figures on factory butter production for the intercensal years were interpolated on the basis of receipts of butter at major central markets for 1879–1919 and on factory production for 1917–1970.

Series Da1027. Cheese production figures include both farm and factory cheese production prior to 1927. Since 1926, farm cheese was negligible and is excluded. For 1909–1917, cheese figures exclude full-skim American. For 1918–1970, data are from plant reports of all types of cheese manufactured except cottage, pot, and bakers' cheese and full-skim American. For 1849, 1859, 1869, 1879, 1889, and 1909 the figures for total cheese production are from the decennial censuses. The census data for 1889 were revised upward to allow for incompleteness. Estimates for the intercensal years 1869–1899 were interpolated on the basis of market receipts. Data on factory production of cheese for 1904 and 1914 are from the Census of Manufactures; data for the intercensal years 1869–1919 were interpolated on the basis of market receipts. Production of farm cheese for the intercensal years 1899–1926 was roughly projected on the basis of average change between census years and added to the factory product to obtain total cheese figures.

Series Da1028. Ice cream production figures for 1916–1970 are based on the annual survey of dairy manufacturing plants supplemented by estimates for incompleteness in some states based on data from the Census of Manufactures or state sources. For 1914, data were estimated from the Census of Manufactures. For 1909 and earlier years, the data represent merely an estimated trend of production.

Series Da1029–1030. Both of these series attempt to provide a summary measure of the volume of milk used in manufactured products. Series Da1030 is drawn from U.S. Department of Agriculture sources and is reproducible. Series Da1029 has been copied from *Historical Statistics of the United States* (1975). In constructing this series the authors made a number of adjustments for "conversion factors" and "duplications" that were not defined. Thus the precise definition of this series is unclear and it is not possible to contrast this series with the more modern series Da1030.

Series Da1029. Series uses milkfat basis of measurement. Data include farm butter. For 1849–1923, the figures are based on national production of manufactured dairy products converted to milk equivalent on the basis of somewhat less refined conversion factors than those used for later years. As such they include no allowance for shifts in production between states or areas of high- or low-testing milk, and they assume standard butterfat content of the products for all years. For 1930–1970, data were based on information of products made in each state and state conversion factors for each product. Duplication of milk usage involving the production of butter from whey fat recovered from cheese making and the use of butter and condensed milk in the production of ice cream was eliminated.

Series Da1030. Includes net milk equivalent of butter and frozen dairy products to avoid double counting of milk from which fat was reused in making a second dairy product.

Series Da1031–1033 and Da1035. Prices received by farmers for milkfat in cream, wholesale milk, and retail milk are estimates based on averages of survey data reported by dealers and farmers for their local market areas. Prices of milkfat in cream, series Da1033, represent the butterfat in farm-skimmed cream sold by farmers; survey information was not collected prior to 1920, and estimates were extrapolated on the basis of trends in butter prices.

Series Da1031. Wholesale milk prices are for milk sold by farmers to plants and dealers including such establishments as cheese factories, condenseries, creameries, or market milk plants. Prior to 1923, these prices were asked on a per-gallon basis and since that time on a per hundred-pounds basis. Additional historic information on wholesale milk-price series was collected by direct plant contacts during the mid-1930s when the state estimates were revised.

Series Da1032. Retail milk prices represent the milk retailed by farmers directly to consumers. Before 1923, survey information was collected on a price per gallon rather than per quart basis. Some of the increase in price between 1909 and 1945 probably represents additional services rendered in the process of distributing the milk.

Series Da1033. Figures are prices received by farmers, per pound of fat.

Series Da1034. Figures are average return per pound milkfat – cash receipts divided by milkfat represented in combined marketings of milk and cream. The figures are computed from the value of milk and cream sold, divided by the quantity of milk or milkfat used in the preparation of these products for the market.

Series Da1036–1037. The wholesale prices of cheese represent averages of weekly quotations prior to 1950 on American twins and thereafter on cheddar cheese only, on the Wisconsin cheese exchange at Plymouth. The wholesale price of butter is for the New York City market. Since 1830, the data for butter differ somewhat in definition and source.

Series Da1036. Figures are annual averages of monthly figures from sources and for grades as follows: 1830–1879, average of high and low for two days each week, high grade, New York shipping and commercial list; 1880–1895, average of monthly range, creamery extras, annual reports of New York Chamber of Commerce; 1896–1920, average of daily quotations for extra fresh, specials, extras and firsts, or fresh extras, *New York Produce Review* and *American Creamery*, published by Urner-Barry Company; 1921–1970, ninety-two score creamery, daily market reports of U.S. Department of Agriculture.

Series Da1037. Figures are from the Wisconsin cheese exchange, based on weekly prices established on Friday each week. Wisconsin prices are carload and truckload prices paid f.o.b. (free on board) at Wisconsin assembly points.

Series Da1038. Price per pound, f.o.b., for forty-pound blocks.

**TABLE Da1039–1058   Chickens, turkeys, and eggs – number, production, price, sales, and value per head: 1909–1999
[Annual]**

Contributed by Alan L. Olmstead and Paul W. Rhode

										Eggs	
	Number on farms	Value per head	Production		Sales, liveweight	Price per pound, liveweight	Production		Price per pound, liveweight	Produced	Price per dozen
			Number	Liveweight			Number	Liveweight			
	Da1039	Da1040	Da1041 [1]	Da1042 [1]	Da1043 [1]	Da1044 [1,2]	Da1045	Da1046	Da1047 [2,3]	Da1048 [1]	Da1049 [1,2]
Year	Million	Dollars	Million	Million pounds	Thousand pounds	Cents per pound	Thousand	Thousand pounds	Cents per pound	Million	Cents
1909	340	0.44	498	—	—	—	—	—	—	25,300	20.0
1910	356	0.47	543	—	—	—	—	—	—	27,000	20.9
1911	382	0.46	517	—	—	—	—	—	—	29,400	17.5
1912	367	0.42	513	—	—	—	—	—	—	28,300	20.2
1913	365	0.47	514	—	—	—	—	—	—	28,100	19.4
1914	367	0.49	531	—	—	—	—	—	—	27,900	20.5
1915	379	0.46	514	—	—	—	—	—	—	29,900	19.4
1916	369	0.49	501	—	—	—	—	—	—	28,800	22.1
1917	359	0.59	509	—	—	—	—	—	—	27,700	31.8
1918	363	0.77	543	—	—	—	—	—	—	28,000	36.0
1919	391	0.96	527	—	—	—	—	—	—	30,500	41.3
1920	381	0.97	514	—	—	—	—	—	—	29,700	43.5
1921	370	0.89	556	—	—	—	—	—	—	30,800	28.3
1922	395	0.81	585	—	—	—	—	—	—	33,000	25.0
1923	415	0.75	610	—	—	—	—	—	—	35,000	26.5
1924	435	0.76	605	2,197	1,428,000	19.4	—	—	—	34,592	26.7
1925	435	0.79	626	2,275	1,489,000	20.5	—	—	—	34,969	30.4
1926	438	0.89	665	2,409	1,535,000	22.1	—	—	—	37,248	28.9
1927	461	0.91	694	2,507	1,649,000	20.2	—	—	—	38,627	25.1
1928	475	0.86	640	2,316	1,635,000	21.4	—	—	—	38,659	28.1
1929	449	0.91	692	2,506	1,641,000	22.8	—	—	—	37,921	29.8
1930	468	0.93	714	2,553	1,815,000	18.4	—	—	—	39,067	23.7
1931	450	0.70	647	2,368	1,634,000	15.8	—	—	—	38,532	17.6
1932	437	0.62	673	2,489	1,616,000	11.7	—	—	—	36,298	14.2
1933	445	0.45	685	2,524	1,696,000	9.5	—	—	—	35,514	13.8
1934	434	0.42	578	2,105	1,545,000	11.1	34,030	96,594	19.3	34,429	17.0
1935	390	0.54	598	2,210	1,414,000	14.9	42,890	122,637	20.0	33,609	23.4
1936	403	0.75	651	2,410	1,536,000	15.0	53,155	152,217	20.6	34,534	21.8
1937	424	0.66	533	2,032	1,417,000	16.0	67,915	195,633	21.4	37,564	21.3
1938	390	0.76	583	2,185	1,282,000	14.8	82,420	239,126	19.0	37,356	20.3
1939	419	0.70	621	2,338	1,481,000	13.2	105,630	306,132	17.0	38,843	17.4
1940	438	0.60	556	2,158	1,508,000	13.0	142,762	413,474	17.3	39,707	18.0
1941	423	0.65	664	2,586	1,673,000	15.6	191,502	558,905	18.4	41,894	23.5
1942	477	0.83	752	3,005	2,046,000	18.7	228,187	674,087	22.9	48,610	30.0
1943	542	1.04	914	3,679	2,836,000	24.3	285,293	832,837	28.6	54,547	37.1
1944	582	1.18	725	3,009	2,645,000	23.7	274,149	817,605	28.8	58,537	32.5
1945	516	1.21	799	3,315	2,616,000	25.9	365,572	1,107,174	29.5	56,221	37.7
1946	523	1.27	646	2,715	2,318,000	27.6	292,527	883,855	32.7	55,962	37.6
1947	467	1.44	636	2,668	2,144,000	26.5	310,168	936,442	32.3	55,384	45.3
1948	500	1.44	536	2,289	1,804,000	30.1	370,515	1,126,643	36.0	54,899	47.2
1949	431	1.66	623	2,643	1,954,000	25.4	513,296	1,570,197	28.2	56,154	45.2
1950	457	1.36	535	2,310	1,859,000	22.2	631,458	1,944,524	27.4	58,954	36.3
1951	431	1.46	540	2,312	1,791,000	25.0	788,601	2,414,767	28.5	58,063	47.7
1952	427	1.53	473	2,025	1,637,000	22.1	860,891	2,623,934	28.8	58,068	41.6
1953	398	1.41	464	2,046	1,582,000	22.1	946,533	2,904,174	27.1	57,891	47.7
1954	397	1.43	455	1,948	1,508,000	16.8	1,047,798	3,236,248	23.1	58,933	36.6
1955	391	1.05	375	1,623	1,215,000	18.6	1,091,684	3,349,555	25.2	59,526	39.5
1956	384	1.26	386	1,639	1,157,000	16.0	1,343,660	4,269,502	19.6	61,113	39.3
1957	391	1.17	310	1,339	1,006,000	13.7	1,447,528	4,682,738	18.9	61,026	35.9
1958	374	1.26	344	1,490	1,037,000	14.0	1,659,519	5,430,674	18.5	61,607	38.5
1959	387	1.26	311	1,346	1,087,000	11.0	1,736,922	5,762,951	16.1	63,335	31.4
1960	369	1.06	260	1,142	866,173	12.2	1,794,933	6,017,217	16.9	61,462	36.1
1961	366	1.25	275	1,224	902,079	10.1	1,990,906	6,831,932	13.9	62,423	35.6
1962	377	1.15	257	1,157	920,132	10.2	2,023,373	6,907,076	15.2	63,569	33.8
1963	376	1.16	254	1,147	907,567	10.0	2,102,023	7,276,008	14.6	63,500	34.5
1964	382	1.16	255	1,170	936,634	9.2	2,161,172	7,521,269	14.2	65,215	33.8

Notes appear at end of table

(continued)

TABLE Da1039–1058   Chickens, turkeys, and eggs – number, production, price, sales, and value per head: 1909–1999 [Annual]   Continued

		Chickens								Eggs	
		Nonbroilers					Broilers				
			Production					Production			
Number on farms	Value per head	Number	Liveweight	Sales, liveweight	Price per pound, liveweight	Number	Liveweight	Price per pound, liveweight	Produced	Price per dozen
Da1039	Da1040	Da1041 [1]	Da1042 [1]	Da1043 [1]	Da1044 [1,2]	Da1045	Da1046	Da1047 [2,3]	Da1048 [1]	Da1049 [1,2]
Year	Million	Dollars	Million	Million pounds	Thousand pounds	Cents per pound	Thousand	Thousand pounds	Cents per pound	Million	Cents
1965	394	1.17	240	1,117	969,288	8.9	2,333,633	8,111,426	15.0	65,560	33.7
1966	393	1.21	279	1,262	1,031,688	9.7	2,570,516	8,988,508	15.3	66,205	39.1
1967	429	1.20	263	1,258	1,156,613	7.9	2,591,850	9,183,426	13.3	69,327	31.3
1968	425	1.14	244	1,109	1,090,428	8.2	2,619,855	9,326,341	14.2	68,156	34.0
1969	422	1.28	252	1,144	1,062,969	9.7	2,788,732	10,047,769	15.2	67,546	40.0
1970	433	1.21	264	1,196	1,120,603	9.1	2,986,769	10,818,916	13.6	68,212	39.1
1971	422	1.23	258	1,212	1,192,639	7.8	2,945,348	10,817,657	13.8	69,649	31.4
1972	404	1.28	233	1,118	1,128,813	8.9	3,074,921	11,480,101	14.1	69,219	30.9
1973	409	1.62	251	1,172	1,121,546	15.1	3,008,667	11,219,885	24.0	66,039	52.5
1974	394	1.70	242	1,186	1,202,562	9.7	2,992,820	11,320,396	21.5	65,620	53.2
1975	380	1.74	233	1,067	1,047,000	9.9	2,950,099	11,096,015	26.3	64,626	52.4
1976	378	1.70	229	1,109	1,046,091	13.0	3,273,556	12,481,136	23.6	64,511	58.3
1977	387	1.69	245	1,172	1,082,313	12.3	3,393,897	12,961,942	23.6	64,602	55.6
1978	397	1.75	242	1,136	1,050,474	12.4	3,613,647	13,999,702	26.3	67,157	52.2
1979	401	1.81	251 [7]	1,216 [7]	1,147,638	13.9 [7]	3,951,297	15,521,728	26.0	69,209 [7]	58.3
1980	392	1.88	241	1,178	1,167,017	11.0	3,963,211	15,538,573	27.7	69,686	56.3
1981	385	1.89	242	1,215	1,187,255	11.1	4,147,521	16,519,568	28.4	69,825	63.1
1982	379	1.85	246	1,172	1,158,703	10.3	4,148,970	16,759,860	26.9	69,718	59.5
1983	365	1.96	232	1,137	1,158,551	12.7	4,183,660	17,037,998	28.6	68,169	61.1
1984	374	2.02	242	1,138	1,066,652	15.9	4,283,020	17,861,023	33.7	68,222	72.3
1985	369	1.90	—	—	1,025,146	14.8	4,469,578	18,809,938	30.1	68,445	57.2
1986	369	1.87	—	—	1,025,716	12.5	4,648,520	19,661,110	34.5	69,106	61.5
1987	378	1.87	—	—	1,018,400	11.0	5,003,560	21,523,356	28.7	70,356	54.7
1988	357	2.04	—	—	1,050,658	9.4	5,237,901	22,464,479	33.1	69,878	52.8
1989	357	2.16	—	—	943,732	15.1	5,516,521	23,978,816	36.6	67,503	68.9
1990	353	2.29	—	—	985,007	9.6	5,864,150	25,630,960	32.6	68,134	70.8
1991	364	2.30	—	—	953,281	7.6	6,137,150	27,202,862	30.8	69,465	67.6
1992	371	2.26	—	—	978,255	9.1	6,402,490	28,828,872	31.8	70,749	57.6
1993	380	2.37	—	—	964,356	10.0	6,694,310	30,617,600	34.0	71,936	63.4
1994	386	2.34	—	—	922,840	7.4	7,017,540	32,528,500	35.0	73,903	61.5
1995	388	2.41	—	—	924,036	6.5	7,325,670	34,222,000	34.4	74,764	62.5
1996	393	2.65	—	—	900,652	6.6	7,596,760	36,479,100	38.1	76,377	75.0
1997	410	2.72	—	—	925,499	7.7	7,764,200	37,540,750	37.7	77,532	70.3
1998	425	2.69	—	—	934,568	8.0	7,934,280 [6]	38,553,600 [6]	39.3 [6]	79,690	65.5
1999	436 [6]	2.65 [6]	—	—	—	—	—	—	—	82,707 [6]	—

		Turkeys							
		Total (breeder hens and other)					Breeder hens		
				Production			Number on farms		
Number on farms	Value per head	Number raised	Number	Liveweight	Price per pound, liveweight	January 1	December 1	Value per head
Da1050	Da1051	Da1052	Da1053	Da1054	Da1055 [4]	Da1056	Da1057 [5]	Da1058 [5]
Year	Thousand	Dollars	Thousand	Thousand	Thousand pounds	Cents	Thousand	Thousand	Dollars
1909	—	—	—	—	—	—	—	—	—
1910	—	—	—	—	—	—	—	—	—
1911	—	—	—	—	—	—	—	—	—
1912	—	—	—	—	—	—	—	—	—
1913	—	—	—	—	—	—	—	—	—
1914	—	—	—	—	—	—	—	—	—
1915	—	—	—	—	—	—	—	—	—
1916	—	—	—	—	—	—	—	—	—
1917	—	—	—	—	—	—	—	—	—
1918	—	—	—	—	—	—	—	—	—
1919	—	—	—	—	—	—	—	—	—

Notes appear at end of table

TABLE Da1039–1058   Chickens, turkeys, and eggs – number, production, price, sales, and value per head: 1909–1999 [Annual] *Continued*

	Turkeys								
	Total (breeder hens and other)						Breeder hens		
				Production			Number on farms		
	Number on farms	Value per head	Number raised	Number	Liveweight	Price per pound, liveweight	January 1	December 1	Value per head
	Da1050	Da1051	Da1052	Da1053	Da1054	Da1055 [4]	Da1056	Da1057 [5]	Da1058 [5]
Year	Thousand	Dollars	Thousand	Thousand	Thousand pounds	Cents	Thousand	Thousand	Dollars
1920	—	—	—	—	—	—	—	—	—
1921	—	—	—	—	—	—	—	—	—
1922	—	—	—	—	—	—	—	—	—
1923	—	—	—	—	—	—	—	—	—
1924	—	—	—	—	—	—	—	—	—
1925	—	—	—	—	—	—	—	—	—
1926	—	—	—	—	—	—	—	—	—
1927	—	—	—	—	—	—	—	—	—
1928	—	—	—	—	—	—	—	—	—
1929	5,541	3.55	18,476	18,136	239,128	24.5	—	—	—
1930	5,969	3.00	17,419	17,052	228,147	20.2	—	—	—
1931	5,318	2.60	18,249	17,923	243,983	19.3	—	—	—
1932	5,946	2.43	22,333	21,964	302,930	12.8	—	—	—
1933	6,852	1.41	23,241	22,813	319,259	11.6	—	—	—
1934	6,309	1.48	21,702	21,310	299,598	15.1	—	—	—
1935	5,499	2.18	20,821	20,487	297,961	20.1	—	—	—
1936	5,731	2.82	27,981	27,642	405,418	15.6	—	—	—
1937	6,358	2.06	25,755	25,391	375,828	18.1	3,481	—	—
1938	6,096	2.49	26,887	26,547	395,017	17.5	3,222	—	—
1939	6,489	2.56	33,587	33,201	494,019	15.7	3,914	—	—
1940	8,569	2.14	33,791	33,316	501,916	15.2	4,607	—	—
1941	7,150	2.27	32,607	32,204	512,075	19.9	3,848	—	—
1942	7,447	3.08	32,504	32,064	521,534	27.5	3,962	—	—
1943	6,584	4.47	31,803	31,360	509,214	32.7	3,897	—	—
1944	7,294	5.35	35,132	34,700	584,010	33.9	4,198	—	—
1945	7,082	5.79	42,900	42,470	740,462	33.7	4,505	—	—
1946	7,862	5.75	40,142	39,746	714,450	36.3	4,841	—	—
1947	5,879	6.54	33,975	33,693	610,737	36.5	3,779	—	—
1948	3,959	6.97	31,541	31,346	573,918	46.8	2,537	—	—
1949	4,622	8.80	41,266	41,019	769,351	35.2	3,148	—	—
1950	5,124	6.34	44,393	44,134	817,482	32.9	3,270	—	—
1951	5,037	6.48	53,298	53,055	949,865	37.5	3,201	—	—
1952	5,725	6.99	62,327	62,117	1,049,218	33.6	3,694	—	—
1953	5,086	6.15	59,822	59,626	1,007,995	33.7	3,162	—	—
1954	4,956	6.32	67,693	67,507	1,160,544	28.8	3,095	—	—
1955	4,917	5.33	65,659	65,471	1,090,735	30.2	3,012	—	—
1956	4,937	5.50	76,777	76,569	1,274,297	27.2	3,181	—	—
1957	5,828	5.05	81,447	81,232	1,356,043	23.4	3,605	—	—
1958	5,612	4.67	79,552	79,333	1,356,220	23.9	3,336	—	—
1959	6,105	4.65	84,493	84,294	1,433,055	23.9	3,662	—	—
1960	5,633	4.89	84,458	84,271	1,488,649	25.4	3,327	—	—
1961	7,008	4.91	107,749	107,496	1,871,494	18.9	4,316	—	—
1962	6,423	3.79	92,088	91,837	1,626,049	21.6	3,823	—	—
1963	6,374	4.40	94,063	93,849	1,686,355	22.3	3,777	—	—
1964	5,996	4.28	101,105	100,892	1,826,035	21.0	3,636	—	—
1965	6,100	4.40	105,914	105,914	1,915,331	22.2	3,555	—	—
1966	6,905	5.26	116,538	116,538	2,123,484	23.1	3,920	—	—
1967	7,811	5.13	126,577	126,577	2,343,339	19.5	4,142	—	—
1968	7,279	4.65	106,709	106,709	2,014,589	20.5	3,372	—	—
1969	6,537	4.96	106,736	106,736	2,029,315	22.4	3,225	3,331	5.97
1970	6,715	5.51	116,139	—	2,197,916	22.6	3,346	3,173	5.82
1971	7,701	5.31	119,657	—	2,255,614	22.1	3,450	2,999	6.18
1972	—	—	128,664	—	2,423,618	22.2	—	3,135	6.46
1973	—	—	132,231	—	2,451,848	38.2	—	3,148	9.47
1974	—	—	131,909	—	2,437,121	28.0	—	2,970	9.81

Notes appear at end of table

(continued)

TABLE Da1039–1058   Chickens, turkeys, and eggs – number, production, price, sales, and value per head: 1909–1999 [Annual]   *Continued*

			Turkeys						
		Total (breeder hens and other)					Breeder hens		
			Production				Number on farms		
Number on farms	Value per head	Number raised	Number	Liveweight	Price per pound, liveweight	January 1	December 1	Value per head
Da1050	Da1051	Da1052	Da1053	Da1054	Da1055 [4]	Da1056	Da1057 [5]	Da1058 [5]
Year	Thousand	Dollars	Thousand	Thousand	Thousand pounds	Cents	Thousand	Thousand	Dollars
1975	—	—	124,165	—	2,276,504	34.8	—	3,014	10.81
1976	—	—	140,021	—	2,606,265	31.7	—	3,069	11.13
1977	—	—	136,390	—	2,562,825	35.5	—	3,038	11.39
1978	—	—	138,939	—	2,654,788	43.6	—	3,370	12.53
1979	—	—	156,457	—	2,957,612	41.1	—	3,705	13.57
1980	—	—	165,243	—	3,076,858	41.3	—	3,749	14.11
1981	—	—	170,875	—	3,264,463	38.2	—	3,514	15.35
1982	—	—	165,464	—	3,175,060	39.5	—	3,429	14.60
1983	—	—	170,723	—	3,335,519	38.0	—	3,155	17.59
1984	—	—	171,296	—	3,384,393	48.9	—	3,159	16.54
1985	—	—	185,427	—	3,703,994	49.1	—	—	—
1986	—	—	207,232	—	4,147,168	47.0	—	—	—
1987	—	—	240,438	—	4,894,858	34.8	—	—	—
1988	—	—	242,421	—	5,059,056	38.6	—	—	—
1989	—	—	261,394	—	5,467,629	40.9	—	—	—
1990	—	—	282,445	—	6,043,155	39.6	—	—	—
1991	—	—	284,910	—	6,114,620	38.5	—	—	—
1992	—	—	289,880	—	6,355,293	37.7	—	—	—
1993	—	—	287,650	—	6,432,577	39.0	—	—	—
1994	—	—	286,585	—	6,540,295	40.4	—	—	—
1995	—	—	292,356	—	6,761,327	41.0	—	—	—
1996	—	—	302,713	—	7,222,834	43.3	—	—	—
1997	—	—	301,251	—	7,225,059	39.9	—	—	—
1998	—	—	283,503 [6]	—	7,002,768 [6]	38.0 [6]	—	—	—
1999	—	—	—	—	—	—	—	—	—

[1] Beginning with 1970, data reported on December–November marketing year.

[2] Average annual price received by farmers.

[3] Liveweight equivalent price.

[4] Liveweight equivalent price to producers.

[5] Major producing states.

[6] Preliminary.

[7] Included are layers destroyed because of possible polychlorinated biphenyl (PCB) contamination.

Sources

Series Da1039–1040. U.S. National Agricultural Statistics Service (NASS), *Agricultural Statistics, 1957, 1962, 1967, 1971, 1972, 1973, 1985, 1990, 1995–96,* and *2000* editions.

Series Da1041–1042. 1909–1939, NASS, "Farm Production, Disposition, and Income from Chickens and Eggs, 1909–44," *Statistical Bulletin* number 133, July 1953; 1940–1984: NASS, *Agricultural Statistics, 1957, 1967, 1973, 1981,* and *1986* editions.

Series Da1043–1044. 1924–1929, U.S. Bureau of Agricultural Economics, "Farm Production, Disposition, and Income from Chickens and Eggs, 1909–44," *Statistical Bulletin* number 133, July 1953; 1930–1989, U.S. Department of Agriculture, Economic Research Service, *Poultry Yearbook,* March 1997, Table 115, downloaded January 22, 2001, from the U.S. Department of Agriculture, Economics and Statistics System; 1990–1998, *Agricultural Statistics, 2000.*

Series Da1045–1047. 1934–1989, *Poultry Yearbook,* March 1997, Table 65, downloaded January 22, 2001, from the U.S. Department of Agriculture, Economics and Statistics System; 1990–1998, *Agricultural Statistics, 2000.*

Series Da1048–1049. 1909–1919, U.S. Bureau of Agricultural Economics, "Farm Production, Disposition, and Income from Chickens and Eggs," *Statistical Bulletin* number 133, July 1953; 1920–1924, *Agricultural Statistics 1952*; 1925–1989, *Poultry Yearbook,* March 1997, Table 2, downloaded January 22, 2001, from the U.S. Department of Agriculture, Economics and Statistics System; 1990–1999, *Agricultural Statistics, 2000.*

Series Da1050–1051 and Da1056–1058. NASS, *Agricultural Statistics, 1972, 1973, 1985,* and *1990* editions.

Series Da1052 and Da1054–1055. 1929–1959, *Agricultural Statistics, 1957* and *1972* editions; 1960–1989, *Poultry Yearbook,* March 1997, Table 131, downloaded January 22, 2001, from the U.S. Department of Agriculture, Economics and Statistics System; 1990–1998, *Agricultural Statistics, 2000.*

Series Da1053. *Agricultural Statistics, 1957, 1972,* and *1973* editions.

Documentation

The estimates are believed to indicate, within reasonable limits of accuracy, the actual number of farm chickens and turkeys; the production of chickens, turkeys, and eggs; and, with greater accuracy, the direction and extent of the changes from year to year.

Complete surveys of the hatchery industry are made every year in all states. Monthly estimates of the production of baby chicks, based on returns from about 70 percent of total hatchery capacity, are also made. These figures of hatchery output give a dependable check on the actual level of chicken production.

Series Da1039

Estimates of inventory numbers of chickens on farms are primarily based on census enumerations. Enumerations for 1910–1955 were adjusted for changes between January 1 and the average date of enumeration in each state, and cover only farm flocks as defined by the Census Bureau. Estimates of change in numbers from year to year through 1967 were based on annual surveys made in December of each year, covering about 150,000 livestock farms, and on changes in flocks belonging to about 30,000 crop reporters, plus assessor and state farm census data where available. Since 1967, estimates of change in numbers from year to year are based on annual surveys in December of each year covering about 40,000 flock owners (contractors and independents), which account for nearly half of all birds in the country.

TABLE Da1039–1058 Chickens, turkeys, and eggs – number, production, price, sales, and value per head: 1909–1999 [Annual] *Continued*

Although census enumerations of chickens on farms were made in 1880, 1890, and 1900, the Department of Agriculture did not make annual estimates until 1909 because data showing annual changes were not available.

Series Da1040. Figures as of January 1.

Series Da1041. Figures are the quantity available for utilization during the year, that is, sales plus home consumption plus or minus the change in inventory.

Series Da1041 and Da1053. Chickens and turkeys produced on farms are computed from the number raised during the year, minus the death loss of chickens and of turkeys that were on hand at the beginning of the year. Young chickens and young turkeys of the current year's hatchings that die are also excluded.

Series Da1045–1047. Marketing year December 1 previous year through November 30.

Series Da1045. Broilers are young chickens of the heavy breeds and other meat-type birds, to be marketed at two to five pounds liveweight, and from which no pullets are kept for egg production. These figures are not included in farm production of chickens.

Series Da1048. Egg production is estimated from returns from about 30,000 crop respondents and 5,000 commercial egg producers (contractors and independents) reporting on the first of each month for their own flocks, the number of layers on hand, and the eggs produced yesterday. Beginning with the estimated total number of layers on hand at the beginning of the year, the change in numbers from month to month is estimated from the changes shown by these survey operations. The monthly average number of layers and

total egg production is revised at the end of the year if the change in number of layers shown by the annual survey in December differs from the change estimated from monthly returns. Adjustment is also made for change in the number of chicken farms on an annual basis.

Series Da1050. Estimates are based primarily on the census enumerations of turkeys on farms January 1, 1935, and April 1, 1940, adjusted for changes in numbers between January 1 and the date of enumeration. Turkeys on farms were not reported in the 1945 Census. The number on January 1, 1945, was estimated from the relationship between turkeys raised in 1944 and the number on hand January 1, 1945, as reported by crop and livestock reporters, using as a base the revised estimates of turkeys raised in 1944 based on the census enumeration. Annual changes in the estimates for intervening years are based mainly on the numbers on hand as reported on January 1 by crop and livestock reporters. Estimates of turkeys raised from 1954 to 1970 are based on poultry placement data secured from hatcheries. In recent years coverage has been virtually complete. Although census enumerations of turkeys on farms were made in 1890, 1900, 1910, and 1920, the U.S. Department of Agriculture did not make annual estimates for years prior to 1929 because data showing annual changes were not available.

Series Da1051. Figures as of January 1.

Series Da1052. Figures based on turkeys placed September 1–August 31. Figures are total poults hatched less death loss of poults and young turkeys during the year.

Series Da1053. Figures are turkeys raised less death loss during the year of breeder hens on hand January 1.

Series Da1058. Figures as of December 1.

TABLE Da1059–1062   Chickens and turkeys – number and value per head: 1910–1997   [Census years]

Contributed by Alan L. Olmstead and Paul W. Rhode

	Chickens		Turkeys	
	Number	Value per head	Number	Value per head
	Da1059	Da1060	Da1061	Da1062
Year	Million	Dollars	Million	Dollars
1910	280	0.50	3,689	—
1920	360	1.04	3,627	—
1925	409	0.93	—	—
1930	379	0.85	—	—
1935	372	0.52	5,382	2.17
1940	338	0.56	4,362	1.71
1945	433	1.23	—	—
1950	343	1.09	2,849	4.51
1954	376	1.04	2,278 [1]	3.76 [1]
1959	351	1.06	—	—
1964	343	1.17	—	—
1969	371	1.31	—	—
1974	336	—	—	—
1978	354	—	—	—
1982	362	—	—	—
1987	374	—	—	—
1992	351	—	—	—
1997	367	—	—	—

[1] Data for October–November.

Sources

Series Da1059–1060. U.S. Bureau of the Census, *U.S. Census of Agriculture 1940, Special Poultry Report*, p. 4; *U.S. Census of Agriculture, 1945*, volume 2, p. 407; *1964*, volume 2, chapter 2, Table 5; *1969*, volume 2, chapter 5, Table 20; *1974*, volume 1, part 51, p. I-4; *1982*, volume 1, part 51, p. 11; *1987*, volume 1, part 51, p. 25; *1992*, volume 1, part 51, p. 26; *1997*, volume 1, part 51, p. 28.

Series Da1061–1062. *U.S. Census of Agriculture, 1954*, volume 2, p. 556.

Documentation

In census data, age limitations for chickens and turkeys are as follows: no age limit (1920–1925); at least four months old (1940–1964); at least three months old (all other years).

PRODUCTIVITY AND INVESTMENTS

Julian M. Alston and Philip G. Pardey

TABLE Da1063–1081   Agricultural output – gross and net value, by crop and livestock: 1910–1998[1]

Contributed by Albert K. A. Acquaye, Julian M. Alston, and Philip G. Pardey

	Gross value			Net value						
					Crops					
	Total	Crops	Livestock products	Total	Total	Food grains	Feed crops	Cotton	Oil crops	Tobacco
	Da1063	Da1064	Da1065	Da1066	Da1067	Da1068	Da1069	Da1070	Da1071	Da1072
Year	Thousand dollars	Thousand dollars	Thousand dollars	Thousand dollars	Thousand dollars	Thousand dollars	Thousand dollars	Thousand dollars	Thousand dollars	Thousand dollars
1910	7,262,000	3,598,632	3,663,368	5,780,000	2,929,000	532,000	601,000	880,000	38,000	102,000
1911	6,489,000	3,135,552	3,353,448	5,584,000	2,905,000	482,000	559,000	855,000	43,000	96,000
1912	7,791,000	4,082,420	3,708,580	6,008,000	3,095,000	532,000	621,000	852,000	49,000	108,000
1913	7,194,000	3,067,446	4,126,554	6,238,000	3,077,000	537,000	567,000	968,000	37,000	135,000
1914	7,681,000	3,503,411	4,177,589	6,036,000	2,899,000	716,000	555,000	602,000	31,000	99,000
1915	7,911,000	3,871,324	4,039,676	6,392,000	3,263,000	822,000	618,000	830,000	32,000	93,000
1916	8,792,000	3,962,322	4,829,678	7,746,000	4,035,000	912,000	715,000	1,148,000	48,000	139,000
1917	13,725,000	7,250,951	6,474,049	10,736,000	5,642,000	1,187,000	1,043,000	1,604,000	75,000	242,000
1918	15,655,000	7,730,173	7,924,827	13,467,000	6,974,000	1,703,000	1,428,000	1,784,000	94,000	343,000
1919	16,585,000	8,096,235	8,488,765	14,538,000	7,603,000	1,743,000	1,166,000	2,282,000	92,000	500,000
1920	15,797,000	8,351,547	7,445,453	12,600,000	6,644,000	1,535,000	1,220,000	1,476,000	68,000	295,000
1921	9,239,000	4,085,968	5,153,032	8,058,000	4,106,000	907,000	634,000	852,000	36,000	253,000
1922	10,190,000	4,954,846	5,235,154	8,575,000	4,300,000	749,000	613,000	1,148,000	42,000	249,000
1923	11,272,000	5,705,209	5,566,791	9,545,000	4,865,000	679,000	692,000	1,569,000	61,000	276,000
1924	11,448,000	5,706,395	5,741,605	10,225,000	5,413,000	889,000	906,000	1,664,000	100,000	260,000
1925	13,213,000	6,594,606	6,618,394	11,021,000	5,545,000	910,000	776,000	1,762,000	87,000	260,000
1926	12,440,000	5,524,557	6,915,443	10,558,000	4,875,000	901,000	668,000	1,222,000	65,000	240,000
1927	12,283,000	5,607,337	6,675,663	10,733,000	5,125,000	969,000	668,000	1,500,000	87,000	245,000
1928	12,855,000	5,694,192	7,160,808	10,991,000	4,956,000	840,000	757,000	1,453,000	84,000	247,000
1929	12,903,000	5,471,798	7,431,202	11,312,000	5,130,000	788,000	694,000	1,511,000	85,000	279,000
1930	10,338,000	4,035,610	6,302,390	9,055,000	3,868,000	500,000	557,000	826,000	73,000	244,000
1931	8,107,000	3,366,338	4,740,662	6,382,000	2,540,000	298,000	312,000	497,000	38,000	157,000
1932	5,852,000	2,386,118	3,465,882	4,749,000	1,996,000	220,000	245,000	461,000	30,000	115,000
1933	6,169,000	2,750,581	3,418,419	5,333,000	2,486,000	335,000	327,000	578,000	33,000	157,000
1934	6,552,000	2,620,817	3,931,183	6,357,000	3,021,000	348,000	355,000	863,000	53,000	236,000
1935	9,138,000	4,143,075	4,994,925	7,120,000	2,977,000	418,000	302,000	712,000	69,000	243,000
1936	8,980,000	3,343,445	5,636,555	8,392,000	3,649,000	500,000	473,000	904,000	77,000	243,000
1937	11,114,000	5,241,773	5,872,227	8,864,000	3,924,000	659,000	446,000	886,000	85,000	320,000
1938	9,090,000	3,587,866	5,502,134	7,723,000	3,200,000	468,000	444,000	655,000	92,000	294,000
1939	9,177,000	3,833,996	5,343,004	7,873,000	3,336,000	465,000	507,000	627,000	111,000	271,000
1940	9,873,000	4,005,407	5,867,593	8,382,000	3,469,000	479,000	600,000	638,000	126,000	242,000
1941	12,960,000	5,056,444	7,903,556	11,111,000	4,619,000	689,000	626,000	1,006,000	238,000	323,000
1942	18,422,000	7,678,045	10,743,955	15,565,000	6,526,000	977,000	839,000	1,272,000	525,000	476,000
1943	21,820,000	9,100,293	12,719,707	19,620,000	8,127,000	1,068,000	1,135,000	1,301,000	703,000	538,000
1944	22,307,000	9,664,237	12,642,763	20,536,000	9,185,000	1,375,000	1,271,000	1,548,000	590,000	690,000
1945	23,580,000	10,523,369	13,056,631	21,663,000	9,655,000	1,563,000	1,509,000	1,208,000	615,000	898,000
1946	27,493,000	12,180,467	15,312,533	24,802,000	11,016,000	1,841,000	1,679,000	1,473,000	715,000	969,000
1947	30,625,000	12,288,452	18,336,548	29,620,000	13,093,000	2,753,000	2,265,000	2,245,000	917,000	1,032,000
1948	34,692,000	15,577,920	19,114,080	30,227,000	13,098,000	2,629,000	2,026,000	2,553,000	1,053,000	945,000
1949	29,168,942	11,958,465	17,210,477	27,805,258	12,396,118	2,255,020	2,161,019	2,637,027	854,008	903,010
1950	31,336,354	13,191,987	18,144,367	28,461,015	12,356,063	1,940,979	2,142,987	2,434,012	935,000	1,061,071
1951	36,346,213	14,030,178	22,316,035	32,857,700	13,238,882	2,003,981	2,090,981	2,857,975	985,991	1,189,991
1952	35,669,853	15,325,715	20,344,138	32,527,960	14,289,984	2,557,996	2,270,997	2,975,997	1,080,999	1,090,999
1953	32,385,134	14,149,475	18,235,659	31,001,355	14,078,164	2,456,027	2,397,027	3,179,039	959,011	1,094,014
1954	32,112,360	14,424,209	17,688,151	29,832,162	13,556,074	2,327,012	2,549,013	2,702,015	942,005	1,161,007
1955	31,383,344	14,254,993	17,128,351	29,490,453	13,523,205	1,990,032	2,555,040	2,580,039	1,131,018	1,225,014
1956	31,530,553	14,435,649	17,094,905	30,401,612	14,038,282	2,148,044	2,648,054	2,500,050	1,155,023	1,162,022
1957	31,815,494	13,655,236	18,160,258	29,714,250	12,338,104	1,868,016	2,395,020	1,756,015	1,181,010	971,008
1958	35,785,887	15,008,026	20,777,861	33,455,907	14,228,960	2,441,993	2,903,992	2,137,994	1,409,996	1,019,997
1959	34,950,144	14,766,091	20,184,053	33,647,298	14,743,131	2,232,020	2,770,025	2,686,024	1,274,011	1,060,009

Note appears at end of table

(continued)

TABLE Da1063–1081   Agricultural output – gross and net value, by crop and livestock: 1910–1998   *Continued*

	Gross value			Net value						
					Crops					
Year	Total	Crops	Livestock products	Total	Total	Food grains	Feed crops	Cotton	Oil crops	Tobacco
	Da1063	Da1064	Da1065	Da1066	Da1067	Da1068	Da1069	Da1070	Da1071	Da1072
	Thousand dollars	Thousand dollars	Thousand dollars	Thousand dollars	Thousand dollars	Thousand dollars	Thousand dollars	Thousand dollars	Thousand dollars	Thousand dollars
1960	35,543,966	15,671,747	19,872,219	34,012,148	15,023,157	2,449,734	2,986,268	2,361,326	1,362,194	1,153,637
1961	36,608,669	15,820,618	20,788,051	35,163,481	15,650,202	2,467,780	2,775,865	2,468,863	1,622,695	1,324,661
1962	38,080,872	16,659,426	21,421,446	36,468,521	16,310,282	2,507,226	2,964,177	2,551,522	1,789,046	1,320,886
1963	39,027,164	17,933,907	21,093,257	37,477,136	17,430,414	2,562,030	3,414,323	2,837,842	1,951,258	1,269,262
1964	37,343,698	16,873,477	20,470,221	37,325,734	17,378,304	1,992,918	3,446,592	2,521,225	2,145,264	1,413,839
1965	41,217,713	19,023,665	22,194,048	39,364,894	17,478,711	2,041,543	3,692,712	2,330,343	2,173,491	1,186,240
1966	44,175,780	18,313,430	25,862,350	43,435,086	18,408,572	2,373,279	4,334,205	1,588,097	2,703,036	1,210,581
1967	44,210,161	19,217,687	24,992,474	42,817,365	18,434,350	2,361,377	4,392,911	1,095,043	2,794,891	1,391,388
1968	45,026,468	18,922,397	26,104,071	44,183,457	18,696,185	2,087,560	4,311,446	1,315,896	2,845,178	1,173,312
1969	49,009,052	19,683,018	29,326,034	48,179,167	19,605,897	2,214,442	4,576,319	1,363,934	3,048,864	1,296,371
1970	51,290,674	20,523,152	30,767,522	50,508,794	20,976,583	2,542,148	5,109,008	1,254,304	3,590,651	1,387,861
1971	54,888,909	23,427,562	31,461,347	52,748,097	22,269,174	2,484,650	5,525,479	1,487,471	3,787,290	1,327,798
1972	62,855,363	25,951,434	36,903,929	61,105,694	25,522,512	3,498,002	5,854,320	1,841,892	4,392,745	1,442,144
1973	91,407,139	43,051,994	48,355,145	86,886,069	41,114,026	7,193,603	10,605,357	2,798,252	7,579,771	1,569,715
1974	91,969,596	49,152,408	42,817,188	92,390,659	51,064,734	8,580,735	13,934,676	2,892,788	9,963,167	2,097,147
1975	93,429,381	50,441,137	42,988,244	88,901,843	45,813,080	8,195,336	12,183,354	2,310,744	7,480,458	2,155,022
1976	94,989,546	48,361,480	46,628,066	95,355,208	49,031,967	7,111,900	13,127,058	3,476,558	9,442,757	2,309,587
1977	98,475,304	51,154,258	47,321,046	96,234,850	48,600,035	6,055,076	11,906,226	3,470,205	9,721,764	2,330,578
1978	115,466,462	56,611,100	58,855,362	112,360,224	53,198,007	5,839,238	11,426,989	3,537,561	13,022,922	2,603,928
1979	137,850,560	66,654,722	71,195,838	131,529,228	62,293,103	9,046,893	14,040,490	4,330,142	14,299,674	2,270,706
1980	134,676,027	64,357,745	70,318,282	139,736,457	71,745,935	10,402,389	18,307,595	4,447,096	15,492,540	2,671,956
1981	149,318,490	78,910,683	70,407,807	141,615,829	72,465,286	11,619,493	17,770,261	4,055,091	13,852,529	3,250,271
1982	142,310,261	71,811,066	70,499,195	142,563,080	72,304,687	11,411,973	17,408,588	4,456,545	13,816,529	3,341,519
1983	126,909,998	56,873,064	70,036,934	136,770,378	67,164,500	9,712,997	15,558,855	3,704,896	13,545,553	2,751,797
1984	149,767,820	77,740,918	72,026,902	142,783,951	69,888,890	9,730,562	16,137,705	3,674,246	13,640,509	2,812,570
1985	142,794,655	74,104,786	68,689,869	144,137,764	74,315,945	8,990,497	22,591,363	3,686,502	12,474,816	2,721,865
1986	134,079,109	63,330,892	70,748,217	135,384,884	63,831,405	5,723,375	16,992,713	3,371,188	10,614,011	1,917,914
1987	140,220,617	64,478,001	75,742,616	141,796,554	65,800,113	5,790,126	14,634,697	4,189,135	11,282,517	1,815,568
1988	147,880,073	69,249,156	78,630,917	151,243,067	71,603,326	7,469,449	14,280,830	4,525,060	13,500,523	2,068,552
1989	165,269,256	81,496,934	83,772,322	160,809,780	76,892,196	8,246,637	17,049,052	5,025,638	11,866,212	2,410,192
1990	173,472,849	83,274,660	90,198,189	169,526,257	80,306,309	7,479,840	18,669,328	5,488,395	12,258,130	2,733,496
1991	168,298,690	81,007,524	87,291,166	167,863,702	82,077,344	7,325,424	19,327,296	5,236,401	12,697,874	2,881,115
1992	176,094,991	89,005,811	87,089,180	171,321,830	85,684,851	8,467,473	20,098,376	5,192,067	13,285,937	2,958,005
1993	174,289,768	82,329,556	91,960,212	177,892,557	87,447,053	8,179,932	20,198,978	5,249,680	13,218,312	2,947,785
1994	190,100,568	100,405,367	89,695,201	181,263,955	93,085,441	9,545,012	20,310,443	6,737,709	14,651,639	2,656,352
1995	183,544,380	95,837,722	87,706,658	188,055,457	100,954,117	10,416,611	24,519,598	6,851,079	15,492,562	2,548,399
1996	207,577,140	115,434,735	92,142,405	199,137,778	106,181,913	10,719,281	27,184,853	6,983,119	16,343,659	2,794,668
1997	208,684,644	112,141,794	96,542,850	207,611,196	111,075,945	10,137,190	27,101,492	6,345,614	19,673,407	2,874,251
1998	196,227,774	101,951,629	94,276,145	196,761,410	102,222,386	8,733,840	22,926,687	6,013,197	17,198,474	2,989,298

	Net value								
	Crops				Livestock products				
Year	Fruits and nuts	Vegetables	Other	Greenhouse and nursery products	Total	Meat animals	Dairy products	Poultry and eggs	Miscellaneous livestock
	Da1073	Da1074	Da1075	Da1076	Da1077	Da1078	Da1079	Da1080	Da1081
	Thousand dollars	Thousand dollars	Thousand dollars	Thousand dollars	Thousand dollars	Thousand dollars	Thousand dollars	Thousand dollars	Thousand dollars
1910	243,000	271,000	262,000	—	2,851,000	1,626,000	597,000	484,000	144,000
1911	283,000	306,000	281,000	—	2,679,000	1,500,000	577,000	452,000	150,000
1912	295,000	363,000	275,000	—	2,913,000	1,641,000	630,000	482,000	160,000
1913	264,000	294,000	275,000	—	3,161,000	1,855,000	669,000	479,000	158,000
1914	300,000	318,000	278,000	—	3,137,000	1,814,000	667,000	500,000	156,000
1915	297,000	286,000	285,000	—	3,129,000	1,768,000	686,000	499,000	176,000
1916	330,000	412,000	331,000	—	3,711,000	2,208,000	764,000	554,000	185,000
1917	403,000	660,000	428,000	—	5,094,000	3,109,000	1,030,000	739,000	216,000
1918	505,000	603,000	514,000	—	6,493,000	4,091,000	1,250,000	872,000	280,000
1919	632,000	593,000	595,000	—	6,935,000	4,045,000	1,522,000	1,106,000	262,000

TABLE Da1063–1081   Agricultural output – gross and net value, by crop and livestock: 1910–1998   *Continued*

	Net value								
	Crops				Livestock products				
	Fruits and nuts	Vegetables	Other	Greenhouse and nursery products	Total	Meat animals	Dairy products	Poultry and eggs	Miscellaneous livestock
	Da1073	Da1074	Da1075	Da1076	Da1077	Da1078	Da1079	Da1080	Da1081
Year	Thousand dollars	Thousand dollars	Thousand dollars	Thousand dollars	Thousand dollars	Thousand dollars	Thousand dollars	Thousand dollars	Thousand dollars
1920	702,000	712,000	636,000	—	5,956,000	3,079,000	1,529,000	1,148,000	200,000
1921	514,000	477,000	433,000	—	3,952,000	1,841,000	1,200,000	820,000	91,000
1922	584,000	488,000	427,000	—	4,275,000	2,204,000	1,171,000	796,000	104,000
1923	559,000	553,000	476,000	—	4,680,000	2,229,000	1,425,000	889,000	137,000
1924	561,000	572,000	461,000	183,783	4,812,000	2,364,000	1,405,000	909,000	134,000
1925	619,000	677,000	454,000	194,081	5,476,000	2,777,000	1,515,000	1,039,000	145,000
1926	618,000	708,000	453,000	194,018	5,683,000	2,883,000	1,566,000	1,095,000	139,000
1927	602,000	617,000	437,000	191,958	5,608,000	2,771,000	1,685,000	1,019,000	133,000
1928	633,000	514,000	428,000	194,024	6,035,000	2,995,000	1,755,000	1,123,000	162,000
1929	631,000	711,000	431,000	191,596	6,182,000	3,016,000	1,839,000	1,184,000	143,000
1930	577,000	687,000	404,000	170,139	5,187,000	2,481,000	1,608,000	998,000	100,000
1931	455,000	471,000	312,000	139,002	3,842,000	1,742,000	1,277,000	748,000	75,000
1932	321,000	347,000	257,000	104,839	2,753,000	1,158,000	986,000	560,000	49,000
1933	343,000	423,000	290,000	97,122	2,847,000	1,228,000	1,004,000	515,000	100,000
1934	398,000	468,000	300,000	111,374	3,336,000	1,465,000	1,146,000	617,000	108,000
1935	432,000	468,000	333,000	126,204	4,143,000	1,897,000	1,310,000	805,000	131,000
1936	473,000	597,000	382,000	143,826	4,743,000	2,271,000	1,478,000	818,000	176,000
1937	540,000	586,000	402,000	156,097	4,940,000	2,350,000	1,525,000	866,000	199,000
1938	403,000	471,000	373,000	146,976	4,523,000	2,190,000	1,388,000	799,000	146,000
1939	439,000	527,000	389,000	152,177	4,537,000	2,271,000	1,346,000	771,000	149,000
1940	446,000	559,000	379,000	162,710	4,913,000	2,391,000	1,521,000	828,000	173,000
1941	604,000	692,000	441,000	183,335	6,492,000	3,233,000	1,900,000	1,143,000	216,000
1942	844,000	1,028,000	565,000	216,889	9,039,000	4,767,000	2,330,000	1,726,000	216,000
1943	1,273,000	1,472,000	637,000	233,758	11,493,000	5,834,000	2,785,000	2,574,000	300,000
1944	1,528,000	1,484,000	699,000	268,317	11,351,000	5,705,000	2,915,000	2,468,000	263,000
1945	1,498,000	1,611,000	753,000	—	12,008,000	5,900,000	3,021,000	2,817,000	270,000
1946	1,759,000	1,591,000	989,000	—	13,786,000	7,041,000	3,709,000	2,754,000	282,000
1947	1,199,000	1,632,000	1,050,000	—	16,527,000	9,295,000	4,013,000	2,957,000	262,000
1948	1,128,000	1,712,000	1,052,000	—	17,129,000	9,354,000	4,389,000	3,135,000	251,000
1949	929,009	1,616,015	1,041,010	—	15,409,140	8,325,075	3,748,034	3,110,029	226,002
1950	1,188,005	1,436,005	1,218,004	—	16,104,952	9,280,943	3,719,002	2,839,008	265,999
1951	1,156,990	1,727,984	1,224,989	577,700	19,618,818	11,359,894	4,253,961	3,604,967	399,996
1952	1,096,999	2,022,998	1,192,999	596,018	18,237,976	10,060,986	4,566,994	3,329,996	280,000
1953	1,197,014	1,662,019	1,134,013	604,472	16,923,191	8,678,097	4,366,050	3,602,041	277,003
1954	1,220,007	1,548,009	1,107,006	538,583	16,276,088	8,868,047	4,114,022	3,013,017	281,002
1955	1,276,020	1,683,026	1,083,016	551,509	15,967,248	8,255,130	4,217,065	3,224,049	271,004
1956	1,358,027	1,873,038	1,194,024	—	16,363,330	8,321,169	4,485,090	3,254,065	303,006
1957	1,292,011	1,710,014	1,165,010	—	17,376,146	9,336,078	4,628,039	3,076,026	336,003
1958	1,393,996	1,735,995	1,184,997	634,182	19,226,947	11,046,970	4,556,987	3,352,991	269,999
1959	1,514,013	1,861,017	1,346,012	658,867	18,904,167	10,952,097	4,604,041	2,991,026	357,003
1960	1,529,219	1,980,237	1,200,542	661,308	18,988,991	10,574,228	4,759,957	3,292,406	362,400
1961	1,609,810	1,910,025	1,470,503	678,984	19,513,279	11,009,249	4,932,290	3,212,189	359,551
1962	1,577,590	2,028,794	1,571,041	709,479	20,158,239	11,662,568	4,859,636	3,262,454	373,581
1963	1,678,424	2,003,843	1,713,432	726,295	20,046,722	11,458,825	4,860,891	3,344,018	382,988
1964	1,800,756	2,313,604	1,744,106	771,552	19,947,430	11,136,640	5,026,833	3,381,069	402,888
1965	1,649,951	2,617,477	1,786,954	823,058	21,886,183	12,877,904	5,037,727	3,583,594	386,958
1966	1,746,585	2,611,943	1,840,846	826,659	25,026,514	14,932,375	5,533,398	4,146,032	414,709
1967	1,816,996	2,679,604	1,902,140	860,924	24,383,015	14,660,726	5,742,231	3,622,082	357,976
1968	2,043,026	2,892,888	2,026,879	894,833	25,487,272	15,373,702	5,957,282	3,797,660	358,628
1969	2,171,435	2,841,946	2,092,586	928,233	28,573,270	17,657,295	6,195,672	4,377,083	343,220
1970	2,070,621	2,813,521	2,208,469	958,375	29,532,211	18,444,848	6,526,563	4,248,146	312,654
1971	2,305,137	3,010,833	2,340,516	1,014,314	30,478,923	19,420,312	6,812,035	3,952,460	294,116
1972	2,558,094	3,285,439	2,649,876	1,120,956	35,583,182	23,906,975	7,135,682	4,181,995	358,530
1973	3,444,532	4,350,796	3,572,000	1,322,917	45,772,043	30,254,799	8,090,160	6,909,738	517,346
1974	3,440,554	5,335,513	4,820,154	1,466,515	41,325,925	25,159,282	9,453,647	6,219,591	493,405
1975	3,562,768	5,346,116	4,579,282	1,689,422	43,088,763	25,822,403	9,922,533	6,810,241	533,586
1976	3,714,069	5,230,823	4,619,215	2,039,231	46,323,241	27,174,374	11,428,455	7,155,287	565,125
1977	4,603,435	5,609,314	4,903,437	2,251,465	47,634,815	27,893,080	11,751,730	7,212,464	777,541
1978	5,763,881	6,127,461	4,876,027	2,637,342	59,162,217	37,454,759	12,724,074	8,109,932	873,452
1979	6,462,233	6,480,010	5,362,955	2,983,313	69,236,125	44,553,625	14,641,918	8,923,106	1,117,476

(continued)

TABLE Da1063–1081   Agricultural output – gross and net value, by crop and livestock: 1910–1998   *Continued*

				Net value					
	Crops				Livestock products				
	Fruits and nuts	Vegetables	Other	Greenhouse and nursery products	Total	Meat animals	Dairy products	Poultry and eggs	Miscellaneous livestock
	Da1073	Da1074	Da1075	Da1076	Da1077	Da1078	Da1079	Da1080	Da1081
Year	Thousand dollars	Thousand dollars	Thousand dollars	Thousand dollars	Thousand dollars	Thousand dollars	Thousand dollars	Thousand dollars	Thousand dollars
1980	6,557,399	7,306,561	6,560,399	3,418,788	67,990,522	41,232,593	16,364,999	9,159,704	1,233,226
1981	6,602,930	8,771,913	6,542,798	3,656,621	69,150,543	39,748,208	18,095,226	9,949,077	1,358,032
1982	6,803,791	8,075,970	6,989,772	4,015,485	70,258,393	40,917,288	18,233,554	9,520,028	1,587,523
1983	6,055,869	8,472,456	7,362,077	4,529,351	69,605,878	39,073,636	18,747,732	9,980,581	1,803,929
1984	6,733,621	9,151,841	8,007,836	5,175,509	72,895,061	40,750,146	17,931,425	12,245,116	1,968,374
1985	6,946,379	8,571,814	8,332,709	5,407,382	69,821,819	38,549,985	18,054,865	11,208,531	2,008,438
1986	7,251,672	8,859,353	9,101,179	5,983,052	71,553,479	39,080,780	17,723,533	12,701,143	2,048,023
1987	8,055,991	9,890,880	10,141,199	6,736,606	75,996,441	44,477,969	17,726,646	11,515,483	2,276,343
1988	9,032,090	9,792,069	10,934,773	7,248,384	79,639,741	46,701,062	17,631,666	12,868,435	2,438,578
1989	9,151,178	11,561,722	11,581,565	7,776,728	83,917,584	46,686,153	19,357,305	15,377,284	2,496,842
1990	9,415,969	11,463,655	12,797,496	8,676,784	89,219,048	51,241,678	20,152,604	15,289,018	2,536,648
1991	9,922,858	11,624,743	13,061,633	9,034,986	85,786,358	50,132,104	18,006,612	15,153,546	2,494,096
1992	10,178,673	11,806,335	13,697,985	9,286,612	85,636,979	47,748,299	19,736,250	15,523,553	2,628,877
1993	10,263,142	13,667,004	13,722,220	9,592,179	90,445,504	50,968,787	19,261,516	17,349,132	2,866,069
1994	10,315,280	14,185,266	14,683,740	10,021,195	88,178,514	46,661,451	19,983,347	18,460,610	3,073,106
1995	11,096,953	15,040,257	14,988,658	10,440,668	87,101,340	44,865,160	19,879,611	19,050,734	3,305,835
1996	11,928,309	14,439,005	15,789,019	10,887,058	92,955,865	44,154,386	22,785,017	22,431,653	3,584,809
1997	13,073,571	14,961,302	16,909,118	10,942,816	96,535,251	49,681,635	20,940,261	22,233,945	3,679,410
1998	11,727,041	15,337,346	17,296,503	—	94,539,024	43,604,486	24,312,307	22,806,366	3,815,865

[1] U.S. Department of Agriculture estimates and publishes individual cash receipt values only for major commodities and major producing states. The U.S. receipts for individual commodities, computed as the sum of the reported states, may understate the value of sales for some commodities, with the balance included in the appropriate category labeled "other" or "miscellaneous." The degree of underestimation in some of the minor commodities can be substantial.

Sources

U.S. Department of Agriculture, Economic Research Service Internet site, Farm Business Economics Briefing Room, Table 1. Value added to the U.S. economy by the agricultural sector via the production of goods and services, 1910–1989, downloaded February 1998, last updated August 1997; 1990–1998 downloaded May 2000, last updated February 2000. Table 5, Cash Receipts, by Commodity Groups and Selected Commodities, United States and States 1924–97, downloaded January 1998, last updated September 1997, and *1997 Census of Agriculture*, National Agricultural Statistics Service, and Economic Research Service, U.S. Department of Agriculture.

Documentation

Outputs (and inputs) are heterogeneous, and so an aggregation procedure must be used to form an aggregate measure of output (and input) quantities. For many analytical purposes, one would like to distinguish between changes in the aggregate quantity of output that simply reflect a change in the mix of outputs attributable to changes in relative prices, and changes in the quantity of output attributable to other factors, such as technological change. To form such an output quantity aggregate requires disaggregated price and quantity data, but what is more readily accessible are pre-aggregated measures of the value of output.

There are different ways of forming an estimate of the value of output. Two such measures are reported in this table: gross value and net value.

Series Da1063–1065, gross value. Reports the gross value of agricultural output, calculated as a simple sum of the calendar year sales of particular commodities (valued at the price received by farmers), plus a U.S. Department of Agriculture estimate of the value of home consumption and adjustments for changes in on-farm inventories. These series represent a production measure of the value of output.

Series Da1066–1081, net value. Represents the value of farm sales net of the value of home consumption and adjustments for changes in on-farm inventories. These series are more appropriately thought of as an income measure of the value of output, but are the more readily available series reporting various commodity sub-aggregate measures of output.

Series Da1066. Total output includes all crops (series Da1067), all livestock products (series Da1077), and greenhouse and nursery products (series Da1076).

Series Da1068, food grains. Includes crops such as rice, rye, buckwheat, and wheat.

Series Da1069, feed crops. Includes crops such as barley, corn, hay, oats, sorghum (grain) and silage.

Series Da1070, cotton. Includes all lint cotton and cottonseed.

Series Da1071, oil crops. Includes crops such as flaxseed, peanuts, soybeans, sunflower, and sesame.

Series Da1073, fruits and nuts. Includes grapefruit, lemons, limes, oranges, tangelos, tangerines, apples, apricots, avocados, cherries, dates, figs, grapes, nectarines, olives, peaches, pears, persimmons, pineapples, plums and prunes, pomegranates, coffee, bananas, papayas, kiwifruit, mangos, guavas, cranberries, strawberries, blueberries, raspberries, blackberry group, other berries, almonds, filberts, pecans, walnuts, macadamia nuts, pistachios, and miscellaneous fruits and nuts.

Series Da1074, vegetables. Includes dry beans, dry peas, lentils, potatoes, sweet potatoes, taro, ginger root, artichokes, asparagus, green lima beans, snap beans, beets, broccoli, Brussels sprouts, cabbage, carrots, cauliflower, celery, sweet corn, cucumbers, all eggplants, escarole, garlic, kale/collards, lettuce, onions, green peas, chili peppers, green peppers, spinach, tomatoes, radishes, squash, miscellaneous vegetables, cantaloupes, honeydews, casaba melons, crenshaw melons, and watermelons.

Series Da1075, other crops. Includes maple products, sugar beets, cane for sugar, alfalfa, bentgrass, bluegrass-Kentucky, crimson clover, fescue, orchard grass, red clover, ryegrass, sorghum (Sudan crosses), other seeds, hops, mint, popcorn, other field crops, Christmas trees, and mushrooms.

Series Da1076, greenhouse and nursery products. Are also included in the output total, and a separate series for this group was taken from the Internet site noted in the source.

Series Da1078, meat animals. Includes cattle, calves, hogs, sheep, and lambs.

Series Da1079, dairy products. Includes retailed milk and wholesale milk.

Series Da1080, poultry and eggs. Includes broilers, farm chickens, chicken eggs, turkeys, ducks, and other poultry.

Series Da1081, miscellaneous livestock products. Includes honey, horses and mules, mohair, wool, aquaculture, and other livestock.

TABLE Da1082–1094 Expenditures on farm inputs: 1910–1998

Contributed by Albert K. A. Acquaye, Julian M. Alston, and Philip G. Pardey

	Purchases from farm origin				Manufactured inputs					Other intermediate expenses	Hired and contract labor	Capital consumption
	Total	Total	Feed	Livestock and poultry	Seed	Total	Fertilizers and lime	Pesticides	Petroleum fuel and oil	Electricity			
	Da1082	Da1083	Da1084	Da1085	Da1086	Da1087	Da1088	Da1089	Da1090	Da1091	Da1092 [1]	Da1093 [1]	Da1094
Year	Thousand dollars	Thousand dollars	Thousand dollars	Thousand dollars	Thousand dollars	Thousand dollars	Thousand dollars	Thousand dollars	Thousand dollars	Thousand dollars	Thousand dollars	Thousand dollars	Thousand dollars
1910	2,605,703	681,000	426,000	199,000	56,000	171,000	152,000	7,000	11,000	1,000	582,988	754,715	416,000
1911	2,599,258	603,000	350,000	188,000	65,000	190,000	168,000	7,000	14,000	1,000	605,384	757,873	443,000
1912	2,791,284	710,000	419,000	217,000	74,000	187,000	161,000	7,000	18,000	1,000	635,975	789,309	469,000
1913	2,858,561	718,000	406,000	250,000	62,000	205,000	175,000	7,000	22,000	1,000	650,129	804,432	481,000
1914	2,871,327	691,000	414,000	215,000	62,000	227,000	195,000	7,000	23,000	2,000	666,876	804,451	482,000
1915	2,915,217	680,000	411,000	207,000	62,000	205,000	165,000	7,000	31,000	2,000	690,862	815,355	524,000
1916	3,383,359	853,000	517,000	260,000	76,000	250,000	193,000	8,000	47,000	2,000	779,230	904,129	597,000
1917	4,230,971	1,150,000	614,000	414,000	122,000	315,000	232,000	11,000	69,000	3,000	924,910	1,127,061	714,000
1918	5,513,992	1,760,000	1,106,000	522,000	132,000	428,000	311,000	14,000	100,000	3,000	1,086,903	1,337,089	902,000
1919	6,055,946	1,802,000	1,097,000	567,000	138,000	507,000	358,000	20,000	126,000	3,000	1,192,607	1,514,339	1,040,000
1920	6,667,462	1,854,000	1,254,000	422,000	178,000	592,000	390,000	16,000	182,000	4,000	1,219,569	1,789,893	1,212,000
1921	4,586,827	1,035,000	710,000	202,000	123,000	415,000	249,000	14,000	147,000	5,000	927,122	1,170,705	1,039,000
1922	4,507,599	1,104,000	676,000	319,000	109,000	399,000	234,000	14,000	145,000	6,000	943,920	1,126,678	934,000
1923	4,918,694	1,234,000	819,000	304,000	111,000	443,000	263,000	16,000	157,000	7,000	1,047,962	1,250,731	943,000
1924	5,273,788	1,549,000	1,116,000	313,000	120,000	462,000	264,000	19,000	171,000	8,000	1,062,486	1,248,302	952,000
1925	5,266,402	1,506,000	988,000	382,000	136,000	540,000	299,000	22,000	210,000	9,000	1,081,233	1,267,168	872,000
1926	5,346,969	1,429,000	891,000	396,000	142,000	581,000	298,000	25,000	249,000	9,000	1,120,963	1,330,006	886,000
1927	5,346,729	1,497,000	892,000	465,000	140,000	552,000	267,000	29,000	246,000	10,000	1,105,268	1,302,461	890,000
1928	5,654,330	1,699,000	977,000	588,000	134,000	636,000	318,000	33,000	270,000	15,000	1,129,449	1,289,881	900,000
1929	5,566,222	1,545,000	919,000	504,000	122,000	658,000	300,000	37,000	304,000	17,000	1,146,826	1,300,396	916,000
1930	5,059,089	1,277,000	791,000	362,000	124,000	654,000	297,000	33,000	306,000	18,000	995,622	1,177,467	955,000
1931	3,943,056	818,000	448,000	253,000	117,000	494,000	202,000	28,000	245,000	19,000	862,006	914,050	855,000
1932	3,123,019	620,000	348,000	193,000	79,000	387,000	118,000	27,000	227,000	15,000	712,368	669,651	734,000
1933	3,069,393	686,000	422,000	199,000	65,000	388,000	120,000	27,000	226,000	15,000	734,860	616,479	644,000
1934	3,408,569	829,000	542,000	183,000	104,000	474,000	176,000	30,000	251,000	17,000	776,070	679,499	650,000
1935	3,775,116	948,000	528,000	312,000	108,000	508,000	188,000	31,000	273,000	16,000	879,832	775,284	664,000
1936	4,289,578	1,185,000	755,000	283,000	147,000	596,000	261,000	33,000	284,000	18,000	912,830	867,748	728,000
1937	4,836,759	1,331,000	805,000	332,000	194,000	660,000	279,000	36,000	325,000	20,000	1,062,020	987,739	796,000
1938	4,646,493	1,131,000	557,000	368,000	206,000	646,000	258,000	38,000	329,000	21,000	1,056,928	979,565	833,000
1939	4,911,920	1,366,000	732,000	465,000	169,000	662,000	273,000	41,000	323,000	25,000	1,114,872	988,048	781,000
1940	5,447,481	1,712,000	998,000	517,000	197,000	728,000	306,000	44,000	350,000	28,000	1,181,030	1,029,451	797,000
1941	6,135,035	1,927,000	1,089,000	635,000	203,000	812,000	334,000	47,000	402,000	29,000	1,277,350	1,248,685	870,000
1942	8,163,979	2,803,000	1,625,000	877,000	301,000	948,000	417,000	52,000	444,000	35,000	1,446,938	1,631,041	1,335,000
1943	9,608,822	3,449,000	2,135,000	908,000	406,000	1,071,000	505,000	58,000	474,000	34,000	1,692,740	2,027,082	1,369,000
1944	10,344,629	3,679,000	2,427,000	812,000	440,000	1,184,000	576,000	63,000	509,000	36,000	1,854,628	2,202,001	1,425,000
1945	11,007,696	4,184,000	2,738,000	1,011,000	435,000	1,309,000	657,000	68,000	544,000	40,000	1,906,051	2,298,645	1,310,000
1946	12,081,099	4,620,000	3,022,000	1,170,000	428,000	1,454,000	683,000	77,000	643,000	51,000	2,286,174	2,531,925	1,189,000
1947	14,405,003	5,639,000	3,746,000	1,379,000	514,000	1,732,000	755,000	98,000	823,000	56,000	2,698,441	2,782,562	1,553,000
1948	16,122,399	6,166,000	3,996,000	1,589,000	581,000	2,026,000	826,000	118,000	1,009,000	73,000	2,939,079	2,989,320	2,002,000
1949	15,393,990	5,095,229	3,023,841	1,528,501	542,887	2,254,070	895,161	139,300	1,133,708	85,901	2,873,476	2,806,215	2,365,000
1950	16,635,061	5,804,328	3,282,965	2,003,706	517,657	2,417,731	975,009	179,400	1,192,491	70,831	2,936,662	2,811,340	2,665,000
1951	19,233,047	7,131,332	4,143,644	2,436,864	550,824	2,603,682	1,063,832	194,800	1,249,951	95,099	3,429,956	2,921,077	3,147,000
1952	19,493,302	6,842,346	4,330,788	1,917,403	594,155	2,762,518	1,183,379	190,000	1,287,889	101,250	3,705,435	2,857,003	3,326,000
1953	18,342,931	5,640,065	3,769,931	1,319,671	550,463	2,791,603	1,178,402	154,600	1,338,270	120,331	3,721,256	2,736,007	3,454,000
1954	18,698,634	5,993,531	3,906,048	1,563,033	524,450	2,865,190	1,208,874	166,700	1,366,244	123,372	3,662,478	2,596,435	3,581,000
1955	19,055,007	5,985,224	3,880,500	1,538,969	565,755	2,910,265	1,184,709	199,800	1,402,775	122,981	3,844,592	2,614,926	3,700,000
1956	19,429,691	6,023,515	3,894,500	1,610,464	518,551	2,996,612	1,165,620	269,100	1,433,715	128,177	4,045,736	2,640,828	3,723,000
1957	20,373,133	6,478,296	4,034,600	1,934,027	509,669	2,955,822	1,165,534	194,100	1,464,029	132,159	4,291,531	2,734,484	3,913,000
1958	22,158,460	7,750,923	4,541,000	2,701,645	508,278	3,020,167	1,206,605	226,200	1,447,111	140,251	4,534,556	2,841,814	4,011,000
1959	23,369,546	7,928,158	4,743,822	2,693,083	491,253	3,226,915	1,331,923	286,400	1,446,926	161,666	5,057,952	2,905,521	4,251,000
1960	23,293,477	7,577,208	4,551,642	2,505,982	519,584	3,293,984	1,343,877	289,600	1,483,761	176,746	5,023,021	3,062,264	4,337,000
1961	24,125,133	8,036,748	4,763,117	2,729,065	544,566	3,475,466	1,436,930	330,200	1,508,324	200,012	5,032,406	3,192,513	4,388,000
1962	25,485,025	8,856,621	5,186,722	3,104,463	565,436	3,639,491	1,544,066	368,100	1,511,941	215,384	5,159,788	3,299,125	4,530,000
1963	26,401,429	9,235,118	5,690,326	2,926,007	618,785	3,853,947	1,712,126	378,900	1,534,560	228,361	5,216,179	3,400,185	4,696,000
1964	26,360,133	8,591,951	5,511,813	2,419,416	660,722	4,082,312	1,887,926	402,200	1,549,234	242,952	5,300,204	3,482,666	4,903,000
1965	27,695,920	9,305,163	5,673,623	2,911,938	719,602	4,283,597	1,993,655	474,100	1,567,194	248,648	5,393,028	3,603,132	5,111,000
1966	30,049,565	10,704,052	6,400,630	3,543,580	759,842	4,648,708	2,219,279	561,600	1,616,020	251,809	5,629,958	3,682,847	5,384,000
1967	31,487,977	10,891,042	6,646,461	3,430,687	813,894	5,126,793	2,429,528	791,100	1,656,695	249,470	5,966,526	3,722,616	5,781,000
1968	32,344,306	10,864,107	6,356,643	3,676,245	831,219	5,185,682	2,434,452	827,100	1,661,529	262,601	6,174,939	3,919,578	6,200,000
1969	34,442,138	12,197,047	7,100,396	4,225,183	871,468	5,213,223	2,311,472	906,400	1,717,492	277,859	6,306,209	4,151,658	6,574,000

Note appears at end of table

(continued)

TABLE Da1082–1094   Expenditures on farm inputs: 1910–1998   *Continued*

	Purchases from farm origin					Manufactured inputs					Other intermediate expenses	Hired and contract labor	Capital consumption
	Total	Total	Feed	Livestock and poultry	Seed	Total	Fertilizers and lime	Pesticides	Petroleum fuel and oil	Electricity			
	Da1082	Da1083	Da1084	Da1085	Da1086	Da1087	Da1088	Da1089	Da1090	Da1091	Da1092 [1]	Da1093 [1]	Da1094
Year	Thousand dollars	Thousand dollars	Thousand dollars	Thousand dollars	Thousand dollars	Thousand dollars	Thousand dollars	Thousand dollars	Thousand dollars	Thousand dollars	Thousand dollars	Thousand dollars	Thousand dollars
1970	36,322,032	13,279,891	8,028,500	4,323,819	927,572	5,409,992	2,434,907	960,211	1,710,766	304,108	6,416,747	4,311,506	6,903,896
1971	38,710,673	14,244,483	8,049,001	5,123,372	1,072,110	5,855,135	2,654,273	1,142,651	1,721,526	336,685	6,854,219	4,340,836	7,416,000
1972	41,884,107	16,179,742	8,396,924	6,668,282	1,114,536	6,146,001	2,720,627	1,366,633	1,688,035	370,706	7,121,477	4,527,887	7,909,000
1973	52,128,468	22,906,243	13,224,140	8,065,142	1,616,961	7,202,314	3,502,811	1,414,120	1,876,596	408,787	7,919,569	5,154,342	8,946,000
1974	57,977,211	21,584,450	14,512,649	5,130,801	1,941,000	10,756,853	6,053,076	1,513,139	2,689,925	500,713	9,020,448	6,075,460	10,540,000
1975	61,322,628	19,999,026	12,906,703	4,954,323	2,138,000	12,354,208	6,659,913	1,782,512	3,318,117	593,666	10,029,052	6,586,342	12,354,000
1976	68,294,514	22,619,572	14,369,707	5,883,865	2,366,000	13,400,100	6,468,108	2,107,839	3,966,413	857,740	10,986,576	7,510,266	13,778,000
1977	73,146,522	23,522,259	13,966,634	7,071,625	2,484,000	13,891,445	6,528,931	1,937,972	4,355,985	1,068,557	12,286,392	7,953,426	15,493,000
1978	85,302,585	28,823,712	16,035,546	10,150,166	2,638,000	15,274,490	6,619,474	2,656,273	4,609,472	1,389,271	15,962,880	8,278,503	16,963,000
1979	100,014,357	35,230,162	19,314,395	13,011,704	2,904,063	17,886,093	7,368,904	3,435,990	5,634,568	1,446,631	18,571,120	8,981,982	19,345,000
1980	106,711,628	34,861,062	20,971,331	10,669,704	3,220,027	22,434,223	9,490,263	3,538,624	7,879,364	1,525,972	18,648,563	9,293,780	21,474,000
1981	108,960,995	33,281,909	20,854,817	8,999,111	3,427,981	23,926,769	9,408,571	4,200,816	8,569,898	1,747,484	19,247,386	8,931,931	23,573,000
1982	108,783,692	31,447,301	18,591,984	9,683,565	3,171,752	22,076,493	8,018,434	4,282,213	7,734,462	2,041,384	21,692,136	9,379,127	24,188,635
1983	108,302,298	32,081,271	20,573,263	8,817,895	2,690,113	20,118,193	7,054,974	3,870,115	7,211,000	1,982,104	23,407,577	8,937,530	23,757,727
1984	108,195,027	32,255,954	19,383,352	9,486,536	3,386,066	22,403,712	8,360,374	4,687,759	7,296,045	2,059,534	23,113,373	9,427,175	20,994,813
1985	101,465,612	29,261,312	16,948,977	9,184,113	3,128,222	20,159,256	7,512,393	4,333,680	6,435,525	1,877,658	22,597,159	10,007,545	19,440,340
1986	97,765,775	30,418,013	17,472,339	9,757,935	3,187,739	18,249,265	6,820,243	4,323,730	5,310,029	1,795,263	21,688,522	9,484,000	17,925,975
1987	102,587,096	32,554,111	17,463,152	11,832,068	3,258,891	18,076,962	6,452,500	4,512,189	4,956,645	2,155,628	24,762,018	9,975,471	17,218,534
1988	111,763,025	37,341,501	20,246,184	13,035,827	4,059,490	18,985,833	7,677,808	4,147,721	4,800,045	2,360,259	26,922,757	10,906,721	17,606,213
1989	117,495,807	38,075,828	20,743,579	12,935,089	4,397,160	20,604,514	8,173,912	5,011,460	4,771,505	2,647,637	28,669,165	12,028,833	18,117,467
1990	123,593,793	39,547,160	20,387,812	14,641,549	4,517,799	21,965,344	8,206,264	5,363,181	5,789,706	2,606,193	29,830,913	14,118,804	18,131,572
1991	125,084,462	38,575,156	19,332,763	14,129,138	5,113,255	23,227,539	8,666,114	6,320,505	5,607,471	2,633,449	31,188,968	13,902,779	18,190,020
1992	124,024,884	38,620,505	20,132,962	13,574,171	4,913,372	22,710,022	8,330,714	6,470,627	5,298,420	2,610,261	30,368,823	14,008,501	18,317,033
1993	132,301,845	41,336,072	21,431,234	14,741,954	5,162,884	23,147,056	8,397,509	6,723,326	5,349,450	2,676,771	34,456,586	15,008,840	18,353,291
1994	136,988,631	41,304,337	22,631,209	13,300,041	5,373,087	24,398,774	9,179,680	7,225,032	5,311,323	2,682,739	37,351,421	15,310,370	18,623,729
1995	142,932,113	41,800,924	23,829,253	12,509,962	5,461,709	26,155,393	10,032,833	7,726,463	5,426,321	2,969,776	39,748,535	16,293,790	18,933,471
1996	147,725,415	42,744,917	25,234,162	11,298,761	6,211,994	28,601,758	10,933,968	8,526,302	5,977,628	3,163,860	39,719,785	17,428,509	19,230,446
1997	156,256,921	46,860,165	26,331,646	13,817,720	6,710,799	29,234,672	10,933,386	9,027,261	6,230,104	3,043,921	42,259,515	18,609,381	19,293,188
1998	155,090,760	44,933,819	25,031,399	12,691,302	7,211,118	28,274,134	10,652,644	9,127,938	5,585,168	2,908,384	43,156,554	19,278,084	19,448,169

[1] Contract labor was deducted from the reported other intermediate expenses, series Da1092, and added to the reported hired labor series to estimate hired and contract labor, series Da1093.

Source

U.S. Department of Agriculture, Economic Research Service Internet site, Farm Business Economics Briefing Room, Farm Income, Net Value-Added, Table 1, Value Added to the U.S. Economy by the Agricultural Sector via the Production of Goods and Services, 1910–1949, downloaded February 1998, last updated August 1997; 1950–1998, downloaded May 2000, last updated February 2000.

Documentation

Starting in 1991, all production expenses are based on the Farm Costs and Returns Survey (FCRS), except livestock and poultry purchased, series Da1085, dairy assessment fees (part of other intermediate expenses, series Da1092), and capital consumption, series Da1094. FCRS data for 1991 and later years use various procedures designed to deal with sampling problems (for example, nonresponse and undercoverage) to make the data more representative of the entire farm sector. Estimates for 1988–1990 were derived by U.S. Department of Agriculture (USDA) using interpolation factors between the 1987 and 1991 estimates. FCRS data used to develop the 1987 estimates were adjusted to represent the USDA number of farms in sales classes under $100,000. FCRS data used in estimates prior to 1987 are published in the annual Farm Production Expenditures summaries.

Series Da1086. Seed includes bulbs, plants, and trees for replanting.

Series Da1090. The final estimates for petroleum fuel and oil subtract federal and state refunds of excise taxes from total expenditures.

Series Da1090–1091. Includes only the proportion of the cost of respective inputs used in the farm business.

Series Da1092

Other intermediate expenses include insurance, registration, and licensing fees for automobiles and trucks, repair and maintenance of capital items, machine hire and custom work, marketing, storage, and transportation, and other miscellaneous expenses. The procedure by which other intermediate expenses were calculated has varied over the years.

Before 1978, estimates on cotton ginning expenses (part of other intermediate expenses) are based on cotton production and ginning costs per bale. From 1978 to 1986, ginning expenses as reported in the FCRS crop marketing cells are used. Starting in 1987, the value of cottonseed, which is usually given to mills as payment for ginning, is added to FCRS machine hire and custom work (part of other intermediate expenses).

Estimates for marketing, storage, and transportation expenses (part of other intermediate expenses) for 1978 and later years are based on the FCRS and include all marketing, storage, and transportation expenses for all commodities. Estimates before 1978 are based on various data sources and include only expenses for fruit and vegetable containers, cotton ginning, livestock marketing, and milk hauling. Estimates are not compatible between the two periods.

Estimates for miscellaneous expenses (part of other intermediate expenses series) for 1978 and later years are based on the FCRS and include such items as livestock health and breeding services and supplies, grazing fees, custom feeding fees paid by operators, irrigation water fees, farm supplies, tools, noncapital equipment, other general production expenses, motor vehicle registration and licensing fees, telephone and water, and other farm business management expenses. Other miscellaneous livestock purchases, livestock rental fees, custom feeding fees paid by non-operators, and dairy assessment fees are included beginning in 1982. Net insurance cost (including relevant motor vehicles costs), which equal gross insurance less indemnities,

TABLE Da1082–1094   Expenditures on farm inputs: 1910–1998   *Continued*

is included from 1978 through 1986. For 1987 and later years, gross insurance costs (including motor vehicle insurance) are included while indemnities are reported as part of farm-related income.

Estimates of other intermediate expenses before 1978 are based on various data sources and include spending on items such as binding materials, dairy supplies, net insurance excluding motor vehicles, greenhouse and nursery, grazing fees, harness and saddlery, blacksmithing, hardware, hand tools, electricity, telephones, veterinary fees and supplies, and other miscellaneous expenses. Estimates are not compatible between the two periods. Estimates of operator dwelling insurance for 1984 and later years are not compatible with earlier estimates.

Series Da1093. Hired and contract labor includes contract labor, cash wages, employers' contribution to Social Security, and perquisites. Procedures and data sources for hired labor for 1982 and later years are not strictly compatible with those before 1982.

Series Da1094. Estimates on capital consumption are based on current replacement costs rather than acquisition costs. A new calculation procedure for operator dwelling capital consumption was implemented starting in 1984 and estimates for 1984 and later years are not compatible with earlier estimates.

TABLE Da1095–1107   Average yield of selected crops: 1800–1998

Contributed by Albert K. A. Acquaye, Julian M. Alston, and Philip G. Pardey

	Wheat	Corn	Soybeans	Sorghum Grain	Sorghum For silage	Barley	Oats	Peanuts	Cotton	Tobacco	Rice	Rye	Buckwheat
	Da1095	Da1096	Da1097	Da1098	Da1099	Da1100	Da1101	Da1102 [1]	Da1103	Da1104	Da1105	Da1106	Da1107
Year	Bushels per acre	Bushels per acre	Bushels per acre	Bushels per acre	Tons per acre	Bushels per acre	Bushels per acre	Pounds per acre	Pounds per acre	Pounds per acre	Pounds per acre	Bushels per acre	Bushels per acre
1800	15.0	25.0	—	—	—	—	—	—	147	—	—	—	—
1840	15.0	25.0	—	—	—	—	—	—	147	—	—	—	—
1866	11.0	24.3	—	—	—	24.0	29.3	—	122	803	—	—	—
1867	12.6	24.7	—	—	—	22.5	27.2	—	143	703	—	—	—
1868	12.9	26.2	—	—	—	21.8	25.8	—	151	775	—	—	—
1869	13.7	21.8	—	—	—	23.5	29.7	—	155	668	—	—	—
1870	12.1	29.3	—	—	—	21.8	25.9	—	208	814	—	—	—
1871	12.2	27.2	—	—	—	20.5	27.7	—	159	777	—	—	—
1872	11.8	29.4	—	—	—	22.5	27.7	—	182	782	—	—	—
1873	12.9	22.9	—	—	—	20.7	25.6	—	168	745	—	—	—
1874	13.0	22.2	—	—	—	22.2	21.3	—	157	575	—	—	—
1875	11.1	27.7	—	—	—	19.3	26.8	—	181	817	—	—	—
1876	10.9	26.7	—	—	—	20.6	22.4	—	168	746	—	—	—
1877	14.1	25.8	—	—	—	20.0	29.4	—	170	787	—	—	—
1878	13.5	26.2	—	—	—	20.3	28.0	—	168	700	—	—	—
1879	13.0	28.2	—	—	—	22.0	26.0	—	181	746	—	—	—
1880	13.2	27.3	—	—	—	22.7	25.5	—	191	722	—	—	—
1881	11.0	19.8	—	—	—	22.3	26.4	—	149	610	—	—	—
1882	15.1	26.5	—	—	—	24.7	28.3	—	209	778	—	—	—
1883	12.3	24.2	—	—	—	23.1	29.4	—	162	679	—	—	—
1884	14.8	28.3	—	—	—	25.2	29.1	—	155	769	—	—	—
1885	11.4	28.6	—	—	—	22.3	28.9	—	170	749	—	—	—
1886	14.1	24.1	—	—	—	24.3	27.9	—	164	718	—	—	—
1887	13.3	21.9	—	—	—	22.2	26.5	—	175	649	—	—	—
1888	12.1	29.1	—	—	—	23.1	27.8	—	170	742	—	—	—
1889	14.0	29.5	—	—	—	24.1	29.0	—	177	692	—	—	—
1890	12.2	22.1	—	—	—	21.5	21.5	—	196	761	—	—	—
1891	16.5	29.6	—	—	—	26.2	30.1	—	199	783	—	—	—
1892	14.2	24.7	—	—	—	24.7	25.6	—	169	728	—	—	—
1893	12.4	23.8	—	—	—	23.6	24.2	—	175	700	—	—	—
1894	13.5	20.2	—	—	—	20.4	25.4	—	219	772	—	—	—
1895	13.9	28.0	—	—	—	25.0	29.9	—	172	741	—	—	—
1896	12.8	30.0	—	—	—	23.6	25.6	—	175	732	—	—	—
1897	14.0	25.4	—	—	—	24.9	28.8	—	209	719	—	—	—
1898	15.2	26.8	—	—	—	23.9	28.7	—	223	815	—	—	—
1899	12.5	28.0	—	—	—	26.4	32.0	—	185	790	—	—	—
1900	12.2	28.1	—	—	—	20.5	30.5	—	195	785	—	—	—
1901	15.0	18.2	—	—	—	24.9	25.9	—	168	807	—	—	—
1902	14.9	28.5	—	—	—	26.7	34.3	—	185	807	—	—	—
1903	13.7	26.9	—	—	—	24.0	27.5	—	170	806	—	—	—
1904	12.9	28.2	—	—	—	25.2	30.9	—	214	835	—	—	—

Note appears at end of table

(continued)

TABLE Da1095–1107   Average yield of selected crops: 1800–1998   *Continued*

	Wheat	Corn	Soybeans	Sorghum Grain	Sorghum For silage	Barley	Oats	Peanuts	Cotton	Tobacco	Rice	Rye	Buckwheat
	Da1095	Da1096	Da1097	Da1098	Da1099	Da1100	Da1101	Da1102 [1]	Da1103	Da1104	Da1105	Da1106	Da1107
Year	Bushels per acre	Bushels per acre	Bushels per acre	Bushels per acre	Tons per acre	Bushels per acre	Bushels per acre	Pounds per acre	Pounds per acre	Pounds per acre	Pounds per acre	Bushels per acre	Bushels per acre
1905	15.2	30.9	—	—	—	25.8	33.0	—	182	851	—	—	—
1906	16.0	31.7	—	—	—	26.6	30.4	—	202	866	—	—	—
1907	14.2	27.2	—	—	—	22.0	23.3	—	173	850	—	—	—
1908	14.3	26.9	—	—	—	23.1	24.2	—	204	828	—	—	—
1909	15.5	26.1	—	—	—	22.5	28.9	660	157	816	—	—	—
1910	13.7	27.9	—	—	—	18.9	30.0	827	176	817	—	—	—
1911	12.4	24.4	—	—	—	19.1	23.8	775	215	830	—	—	—
1912	15.1	29.1	—	—	—	26.1	36.3	753	201	837	—	—	—
1913	14.4	22.7	—	—	—	20.7	27.9	824	192	772	—	—	—
1914	16.1	25.8	—	—	—	23.2	28.7	801	216	824	—	—	—
1915	16.7	28.1	—	—	—	28.4	37.0	779	179	816	—	—	—
1916	11.9	24.1	—	—	—	20.9	29.1	758	166	814	—	—	—
1917	13.2	26.2	—	—	—	21.6	34.7	752	167	820	—	—	—
1918	14.8	23.9	—	—	—	24.5	33.6	713	164	840	—	—	—
1919	12.9	26.8	—	—	—	19.9	27.9	719	166	737	1,783	11.0	17.3
1920	13.5	29.9	—	—	—	23.0	33.8	699	187	780	1,789	12.8	16.7
1921	12.7	27.8	—	—	—	18.8	23.0	692	133	750	1,785	12.6	18.5
1922	13.8	26.3	—	—	—	23.2	28.5	637	149	776	1,780	14.9	16.2
1923	13.3	27.8	—	—	—	22.2	30.5	713	136	818	1,711	11.3	16.8
1924	16.0	22.1	11.0	—	—	23.5	33.8	658	165	731	1,753	14.8	17.0
1925	12.8	27.4	11.7	—	—	23.5	31.8	725	174	786	1,743	11.1	16.9
1926	14.7	25.7	11.2	—	—	21.0	26.9	770	193	792	1,861	10.2	16.2
1927	14.7	26.4	12.2	—	—	25.3	27.1	777	162	779	1,950	14.8	16.8
1928	15.4	26.3	13.6	—	—	25.8	32.7	695	163	737	2,029	11.5	14.9
1929	13.0	25.7	13.3	14.1	6.1	20.7	29.2	712	164	774	2,069	11.3	13.8
1930	14.2	20.5	13.0	10.8	5.4	23.9	32.0	650	157	776	2,093	12.4	12.1
1931	16.3	24.5	15.1	16.2	5.8	17.9	28.0	733	212	787	2,080	10.4	17.6
1932	13.1	26.5	15.1	15.0	5.8	22.7	30.1	627	174	725	2,143	11.7	14.8
1933	11.2	22.8	12.9	12.5	4.7	15.9	20.2	674	213	789	2,123	8.6	17.0
1934	12.1	18.7	14.9	8.0	2.7	17.8	18.5	670	172	852	2,164	8.5	18.9
1935	12.2	24.2	16.8	12.5	4.7	23.2	30.2	770	185	905	2,173	14.0	16.8
1936	12.8	18.6	14.3	10.8	3.8	17.7	23.6	759	199	807	2,285	9.0	17.0
1937	13.6	28.9	17.9	14.2	5.1	22.3	33.1	802	270	895	2,187	12.8	16.2
1938	13.3	27.8	20.4	14.3	6.1	24.2	30.2	762	236	866	2,196	13.7	15.1
1939	14.1	29.9	20.9	11.2	4.8	21.8	28.6	636	238	940	2,328	10.1	15.5
1940	15.3	28.9	16.2	13.5	5.8	23.0	35.2	861	253	1,036	2,291	12.4	16.7
1941	16.8	31.2	18.2	18.9	6.4	25.4	31.0	776	232	966	1,902	12.3	17.9
1942	19.5	35.4	19.0	18.3	6.5	25.3	35.2	654	272	1,023	1,996	14.0	17.7
1943	16.4	32.6	18.3	15.9	5.2	21.7	29.3	617	254	964	1,988	10.8	17.5
1944	17.7	33.0	18.8	19.7	6.4	22.5	28.9	678	299	1,115	2,093	10.6	17.6
1945	17.0	33.1	18.0	15.2	5.3	25.5	36.5	646	254	1,094	2,046	12.8	16.1
1946	17.2	37.2	20.5	15.9	5.8	25.5	34.5	649	236	1,181	2,054	11.6	17.8
1947	18.2	28.6	16.3	17.0	5.1	25.7	31.1	646	267	1,138	2,062	12.8	14.2
1948	17.9	43.0	21.3	18.0	7.2	26.5	36.9	709	311	1,274	2,122	12.6	18.4
1949	14.5	38.2	22.3	22.5	7.1	24.0	32.3	808	282	1,213	2,194	11.6	18.4
1950	16.5	38.2	21.7	22.6	7.3	27.2	34.8	900	269	1,269	2,371	12.2	17.5
1951	16.0	36.9	20.8	19.1	6.9	27.3	36.3	837	269	1,310	2,309	12.5	16.6
1952	18.4	41.8	20.7	17.0	5.3	27.7	32.9	940	280	1,273	2,413	11.6	19.8
1953	17.3	40.7	18.2	18.4	6.0	28.4	30.7	1,039	324	1,261	2,447	13.2	18.0
1954	18.1	39.4	20.0	20.1	5.6	28.4	34.8	727	341	1,346	2,517	14.4	17.9
1955	19.8	42.0	20.1	18.8	5.5	27.8	38.3	928	417	1,466	3,061	14.2	17.0
1956	20.2	47.4	21.8	22.2	6.2	29.3	34.5	1,161	409	1,596	3,151	13.0	18.3
1957	21.8	48.3	23.2	28.8	8.3	29.8	37.9	969	388	1,486	3,204	16.3	17.0
1958	27.5	52.8	24.2	35.2	9.3	32.3	44.8	1,197	466	1,611	3,137	18.2	17.8
1959	21.6	53.1	23.5	36.1	8.6	28.3	37.8	1,061	461	1,558	3,382	15.8	16.9
1960	26.1	54.7	23.5	39.7	9.1	31.0	43.4	1,232	446	1,703	3,423	19.6	17.6
1961	23.9	62.4	25.1	43.7	10.0	30.6	42.3	1,185	438	1,755	3,411	17.7	18.8
1962	25.0	64.7	24.2	44.1	10.5	35.0	45.2	1,228	457	1,891	3,726	20.5	19.7
1963	25.2	67.9	24.4	43.9	10.1	35.0	45.3	1,391	517	1,994	3,968	18.4	20.7
1964	25.8	62.9	22.8	41.7	9.4	37.6	43.1	1,502	517	2,067	4,098	19.1	20.0

Note appears at end of table

TABLE Da1095–1107   Average yield of selected crops: 1800–1998   *Continued*

	Wheat	Corn	Soybeans	Sorghum Grain	Sorghum For silage	Barley	Oats	Peanuts	Cotton	Tobacco	Rice	Rye	Buckwheat
	Da1095	Da1096	Da1097	Da1098	Da1099	Da1100	Da1101	Da1102 [1]	Da1103	Da1104	Da1105	Da1106	Da1107
Year	Bushels per acre	Bushels per acre	Bushels per acre	Bushels per acre	Tons per acre	Bushels per acre	Bushels per acre	Pounds per acre	Pounds per acre	Pounds per acre	Pounds per acre	Bushels per acre	Bushels per acre
1965	26.5	74.1	24.5	51.6	10.3	42.9	50.2	1,661	527	1,898	4,255	22.6	—
1966	26.3	73.1	25.4	55.8	10.9	38.3	44.9	1,700	480	1,939	4,322	21.8	—
1967	25.8	80.1	24.5	50.4	9.9	40.5	49.3	1,765	447	2,050	4,537	22.5	—
1968	28.4	79.5	26.7	52.6	10.7	43.8	53.7	1,770	516	1,945	4,425	23.1	—
1969	30.6	85.9	27.4	54.3	11.7	44.7	53.7	1,742	434	1,964	4,318	23.4	—
1970	31.0	72.4	26.7	50.4	9.7	42.8	49.2	2,031	438	2,122	4,618	25.8	—
1971	33.9	88.1	27.5	53.8	10.9	45.8	55.9	2,066	438	2,035	4,718	28.1	—
1972	32.7	97.0	27.8	60.7	11.8	43.7	51.5	2,203	507	2,076	4,700	26.9	—
1973	31.6	91.3	27.8	58.8	11.4	40.5	47.9	2,323	520	1,965	4,274	25.8	—
1974	27.3	71.9	23.7	45.1	9.8	37.7	47.6	2,491	442	2,067	4,440	22.3	—
1975	30.6	86.4	28.9	49.0	9.8	44.0	49.0	2,564	453	2,008	4,558	21.9	—
1976	30.3	88.0	26.1	49.1	9.2	45.4	45.7	2,464	465	2,041	4,663	20.7	—
1977	30.7	90.8	30.6	56.6	10.9	44.0	55.8	2,456	520	1,982	4,412	24.4	—
1978	31.4	101.0	29.4	54.5	10.9	49.2	52.3	2,619	420	2,101	4,484	26.0	—
1979	34.2	109.5	32.1	62.6	11.8	50.9	54.4	2,611	547	1,844	4,599	25.7	—
1980	33.5	91.0	26.5	46.3	9.5	49.7	53.0	1,645	404	1,939	4,413	24.6	—
1981	34.5	108.9	30.1	64.0	12.0	52.4	54.2	2,675	542	2,113	4,819	26.6	—
1982	35.5	113.2	31.5	59.1	12.3	57.2	57.8	2,693	590	2,185	4,710	28.9	—
1983	39.4	81.1	26.2	48.7	10.3	52.3	52.6	2,399	508	1,811	4,598	30.3	—
1984	38.8	106.7	28.1	56.4	10.6	53.3	58.0	2,883	600	2,183	4,954	33.1	—
1985	37.5	118.0	34.1	66.8	12.3	50.9	63.6	2,810	630	2,197	5,414	28.8	—
1986	34.4	119.4	33.3	67.7	11.8	50.8	56.3	2,408	552	2,001	5,651	28.8	—
1987	37.7	119.8	33.9	69.4	12.4	52.4	54.3	2,337	706	2,028	5,555	29.1	—
1988	34.1	84.6	27.0	63.8	10.1	38.0	39.3	2,445	619	2,160	5,514	24.7	—
1989	32.7	116.3	32.3	55.4	10.4	48.6	54.3	2,426	614	2,016	5,749	28.2	—
1990	39.5	118.5	34.1	63.1	10.2	56.1	60.1	1,985	634	2,218	5,529	27.1	—
1991	34.3	108.6	34.2	59.3	10.0	55.2	50.6	2,444	652	2,179	5,731	24.6	—
1992	39.3	131.5	37.6	72.6	12.1	62.5	65.4	2,567	700	2,195	5,736	29.3	—
1993	38.2	100.7	32.6	59.9	11.2	58.9	54.4	2,008	606	2,161	5,510	27.1	—
1994	37.6	138.6	41.4	72.7	11.9	56.2	57.1	2,624	708	2,359	5,964	27.9	—
1995	35.8	113.5	35.3	55.6	10.3	57.2	54.7	2,282	537	1,914	5,621	26.1	—
1996	36.3	127.1	37.6	67.3	11.8	58.5	57.7	2,653	705	2,072	6,120	25.9	—
1997	39.5	126.7	38.9	69.1	13.1	58.1	59.5	2,503	673	2,137	5,897	25.7	—
1998	43.2	—	38.9	—	—	—	—	—	—	2,104	5,669	28.2	—

[1] Applies only to peanuts picked and threshed.

Sources

Series Da1095–1102. 1800–1840, U.S. Department of Agriculture, "Progress of Farm Mechanization," *Miscellaneous Publication* number 630, 1947 (data for 1800 and 1840 are estimates by the authors of that publication); 1866–1996, *Agricultural Statistics, 1938, 1945, 1960, 1974, 1988, 1995–96,* and *1999.* Series Da1095–1101, 1866–1997, and series Da1102, 1909–1997, are available in electronic form on the Cornell University Library Internet site, Crops by State (downloaded June 2000).

Series Da1103–1106. 1800–1840, U.S. Department of Agriculture, "Progress of Farm Mechanization," *Miscellaneous Publication* number 630, 1947 (data for 1800 and 1840 are estimates by the authors of that publication); 1866–1995, *Agricultural Statistics, 1957, 1960, 1973, 1987, 1995–96,* and *1999.*

Series Da1107. U.S. Department of Agriculture, *Agricultural Statistics, 1957,* and *1966.*

Documentation

Series Da1096. Corn harvested area for 1866–1918 includes corn grain, silage, forage, and grazed and hogged down area planted to corn. The production and yield data for corn for the period 1866–1918 include a conversion to a grain equivalent for corn produced on so-called non-grain acreage.

Series Da1107. Data series was discontinued in 1965.

TABLE Da1108–1116   Partial productivity indicators for selected livestock products: 1909–1998

Contributed by Albert K. A. Acquaye, Julian M. Alston, and Philip G. Pardey

	Average live weight of animals slaughtered			Average live weight		Production per cow		Eggs produced	
	Cattle	Calves	Hogs	Turkeys	Broilers	Milk	Butterfat	Per layer (at year end)	Per layer (average number of layers)
	Da1108 [1]	Da1109 [1,2]	Da1110 [1]	Da1111	Da1112	Da1113	Da1114	Da1115	Da1116
Year	Pounds	Pounds	Pounds	Pounds	Pounds	Pounds	Pounds	Number	Number
1909	—	—	—	—	—	—	—	83	—
1910	—	—	—	—	—	—	—	85	—
1911	—	—	—	—	—	—	—	86	—
1912	—	—	—	—	—	—	—	86	—
1913	—	—	—	—	—	—	—	86	—
1914	—	—	—	—	—	—	—	85	—
1915	—	—	—	—	—	—	—	88	—
1916	—	—	—	—	—	—	—	87	—
1917	—	—	—	—	—	—	—	86	—
1918	—	—	—	—	—	—	—	86	—
1919	—	—	—	—	—	—	—	87	—
1920	—	—	—	—	—	—	—	87	—
1921	—	—	—	—	—	—	—	93	—
1922	—	—	—	—	—	—	—	93	—
1923	—	—	—	—	—	—	—	94	—
1924	—	—	—	—	—	4,167	163	89	—
1925	—	—	—	—	—	4,218	165	90	—
1926	—	—	—	—	—	4,379	172	95	—
1927	—	—	—	—	—	4,491	176	93	—
1928	—	—	—	—	—	4,516	177	91	—
1929	955	176	—	13.2	—	4,579	180	94	—
1930	956	175	—	13.4	—	4,508	177	93	121
1931	958	175	—	13.6	—	4,459	175	96	127
1932	943	175	—	13.8	—	4,307	169	94	121
1933	954	179	—	14.0	—	4,180	164	91	118
1934	928	185	—	14.1	2.8	4,033	159	89	118
1935	910	189	232	14.5	2.9	4,184	165	96	122
1936	921	194	221	14.7	2.9	4,316	170	95	121
1937	899	190	234	14.8	2.9	4,366	173	99	130
1938	921	189	234	14.9	2.9	4,558	180	106	135
1939	943	191	234	14.9	2.9	4,589	182	103	134
1940	940	191	237	15.1	2.9	4,625	184	101	134
1941	961	196	242	15.9	2.9	4,741	188	110	139
1942	954	208	255	16.3	3.0	4,740	188	114	142
1943	955	207	246	16.2	2.9	4,606	183	112	142
1944	924	218	254	16.8	3.0	4,578	182	112	148
1945	948	214	261	17.4	3.0	4,797	191	118	151
1946	943	199	258	17.9	3.0	4,891	195	117	155
1947	928	209	251	18.1	3.0	4,997	199	127	158
1948	945	209	251	18.2	3.0	5,038	201	129	162
1949	976	209	244	18.7	3.1	5,243	208	137	165
1950	989	206	246	18.6	3.1	5,314	210	136	174
1951	992	209	243	17.9	3.1	5,333	210	—	177
1952	990	221	240	16.9	3.0	5,374	210	—	181
1953	970	227	242	16.9	3.1	5,542	215	—	185
1954	958	223	243	17.2	3.1	5,657	219	—	188
1955	975	218	235	16.7	3.1	5,842	225	—	192
1956	989	225	236	16.6	3.2	6,090	233	—	197
1957	992	214	235	16.7	3.2	6,303	240	—	199
1958	1,018	210	239	17.1	3.3	6,585	249	—	202
1959	1,045	208	238	17.0	3.3	6,815	256	—	207
1960	1,032	210	241	17.6	3.4	7,029	264	—	209
1961	1,043	209	241	17.4	3.4	7,290	273	—	210
1962	1,027	205	241	17.7	3.4	7,496	280	—	212
1963	1,046	200	242	18.0	3.5	7,700	286	—	213
1964	1,041	204	241	18.1	3.5	8,099	300	—	217
1965	1,016	203	244	18.1	3.5	8,304	307	—	218
1966	1,031	201	242	18.3	3.5	8,507	314	—	218
1967	1,039	191	241	18.6	3.5	8,797	325	—	221
1968	1,030	195	239	18.9	3.6	8,992	330	—	220
1969	1,030	197	242	19.1	3.6	9,166	337	—	220

Notes appear at end of table

TABLE Da1108–1116   Partial productivity indicators for selected livestock products: 1909–1998   *Continued*

	Average liveweight of animals slaughtered			Average liveweight		Production per cow		Eggs produced	
	Cattle	Calves	Hogs	Turkeys	Broilers	Milk	Butterfat	Per layer (at year end)	Per layer (average number of layers)
	Da1108 [1]	Da1109 [1,2]	Da1110 [1]	Da1111	Da1112	Da1113	Da1114	Da1115	Da1116
Year	Pounds	Pounds	Pounds	Pounds	Pounds	Pounds	Pounds	Number	Number
1970	1,049	199	240	18.9	3.6	9,385	343	—	218
1971	1,040	206	240	18.9	3.7	9,609	353	—	223
1972	1,048	210	240	18.8	3.7	10,015	367	—	227
1973	1,054	207	242	18.5	3.7	10,259	377	—	227
1974	1,052	211	245	18.5	3.8	10,119	370	—	230
1975	1,009	227	240	18.3	3.8	10,293	377	—	232
1976	1,030	223	238	18.6	3.8	10,360	381	—	235
1977	1,033	207	237	18.8	3.8	10,894	399	—	235
1978	1,043	206	240	19.1	3.9	11,206	410	—	239
1979	1,068	210	242	18.9	3.9	11,243	412	—	240
1980	1,080	214	242	18.6	3.9	11,492	420	—	242
1981	1,083	218	243	19.1	4.0	11,891	435	—	243
1982	1,071	208	243	19.2	4.0	12,183	444	—	243
1983	1,077	213	243	19.5	4.1	12,306	450	—	247
1984	1,072	225	244	19.8	4.2	12,585	460	—	245
1985	1,103	234	245	20.0	4.2	13,024	478	—	247
1986	1,105	239	246	20.0	4.2	13,285	487	—	248
1987	1,109	239	248	20.4	4.3	13,819	505	—	248
1988	1,124	251	249	20.9	4.3	14,185	521	—	251
1989	1,138	259	249	20.9	4.3	14,323	528	—	250
1990	1,140	280	250	21.4	4.4	14,782	539	—	251
1991	1,167	345	252	21.5	4.4	15,031	550	—	252
1992	1,172	376	253	21.9	4.5	15,570	573	—	254
1993	1,164	388	254	22.4	4.6	15,722	575	—	253
1994	1,193	383	255	22.8	4.6	16,179	592	—	254
1995	1,187	371	257	23.1	4.7	16,405	601	—	254
1996	1,173	340	254	23.9	4.8	16,433	608	—	256
1997	1,177	335	257	—	—	—	—	—	255
1998	1,207	282	257	—	—	—	—	—	—

[1] Slaughtered under federal inspection.

[2] Average number during the year. Heifers not freshened are excluded. Includes allowances for seasonal variation and trend during the year.

Sources

Series Da1108–1109. U.S. Department of Agriculture (USDA), *Agricultural Statistics, 1940, 1942, 1951, 1972, 1986, 1995–96,* and *1999.*

Series Da1110. USDA, *Agricultural Statistics, 1957, 1972, 1986, 1995–96,* and *1999.*

Series Da1111. 1929–1940, USDA, *Agricultural Statistics, 1942,* Table 669, liveweight estimated by dividing production (in pounds) by number of turkeys sold, plus the number consumed in households of farm producers, plus or minus changes in inventory; 1941–1970, USDA, *Agricultural Statistics, 1951,* Table 582, and *Agricultural Statistics, 1972,* Table 609; 1971–1996, USDA, *Agricultural Statistics, 1986,* Table 521, USDA, *Agricultural Statistics, 1995–96,* Table 512, and USDA, *Agricultural Statistics, 1999,* Table 8-54, liveweight estimated by dividing total (liveweight) pounds produced by total poults hatched less death loss of poults and young turkeys during the year.

Series Da1112. USDA, *Agricultural Statistics, 1972, 1986, 1995–96,* and *1999.*

Series Da1113–1114. USDA, *Agricultural Statistics, 1942, 1972, 1986, 1995–96,* and *1999.*

Series Da1115–1116. USDA, *Agricultural Statistics, 1942, 1951, 1972, 1986, 1995–96,* and *1999.*

Documentation

Series Da1108–1109. Beginning 1942, includes slaughter in plants to which federal inspection was extended by the Fulmer Act and in plants operating under limited inspection. 1950–1970, excludes slaughter in Alaska, Hawai'i, and the U.S. Virgin Islands.

Series Da1110. Beginning 1942, includes slaughter in plants to which federal inspection was extended by the Fulmer Act. Obtained from monthly surveys of slaughtering plants, all of which were under federal inspection prior to July 1943. 1950–1970, excludes slaughter in Alaska, Hawai'i, and the U.S. Virgin Islands.

Series Da1111. 1929–1940, liveweight estimated by dividing production (in pounds) by number of turkeys sold, plus the number consumed in households of farm producers, plus or minus changes in inventory; 1971–1996, liveweight estimated by dividing total (liveweight) pounds produced by total poults hatched less death loss of poults and young turkeys during the year.

Series Da1112. Broilers are young chickens of the heavy breeds and other meat-type birds, to be marketed at two to five pounds liveweight, and from which no pullets are kept for egg production. These figures are not included in farm production of chickens. Beginning with 1961, data include Hawai'i. Obtained by dividing (live) weight of broilers produced by number of broilers. 1970 to date, commercial broilers were changed to a December 1 through November 30 marketing year.

Series Da1113–1114. Beginning with 1960, Alaska and Hawai'i included. Excludes milk suckled by calves and milk produced by cows not on farms. To convert pounds of milk to gallons, divide by 8.6.

Series Da1115. Calculated as the number of eggs produced during the year, divided by number of all hens and pullets on hand January 1. The series was discontinued in 1950.

Series Da1116. Calculated as the number of eggs produced during the year divided by the average number of hens and pullets of laying age on hand during the year. Beginning with 1961 all series include Alaska and Hawai'i.

TABLE Da1117–1122   Indexes of farm output, input, and productivity: 1870–1990

Contributed by Albert K. A. Acquaye, Julian M. Alston, and Philip G. Pardey

Year	1870–1984 indexes			1947–1990 indexes		
	Output	Input	Productivity	Output	Input	Productivity
	Da1117	Da1118	Da1119 [1]	Da1120	Da1121	Da1122 [1]
	Index 1977 = 100	Index 1977 = 100	Index 1977 = 100	Index 1977 = 100	Index 1977 = 100	Index 1977 = 100
1870	14	39	35	—	—	—
1880	22	51	42	—	—	—
1890	25	61	42	—	—	—
1900	33	70	47	—	—	—
1910	36	84	43	—	—	—
1911	35	86	41	—	—	—
1912	40	88	45	—	—	—
1913	36	88	40	—	—	—
1914	39	91	43	—	—	—
1915	40	90	45	—	—	—
1916	37	90	41	—	—	—
1917	39	91	43	—	—	—
1918	39	93	42	—	—	—
1919	39	93	42	—	—	—
1920	42	96	44	—	—	—
1921	37	93	40	—	—	—
1922	41	94	43	—	—	—
1923	41	95	44	—	—	—
1924	41	96	43	—	—	—
1925	42	97	44	—	—	—
1926	44	99	44	—	—	—
1927	44	97	45	—	—	—
1928	45	99	46	—	—	—
1929	44	100	45	—	—	—
1930	43	99	44	—	—	—
1931	47	99	48	—	—	—
1932	46	95	48	—	—	—
1933	42	94	45	—	—	—
1934	36	88	41	—	—	—
1935	43	89	49	—	—	—
1936	39	91	43	—	—	—
1937	48	96	50	—	—	—
1938	48	94	51	—	—	—
1939	48	96	51	—	—	—
1940	50	97	52	—	—	—
1941	52	97	54	—	—	—
1942	58	100	58	—	—	—
1943	57	102	57	—	—	—
1944	59	103	58	—	—	—
1945	58	100	58	—	—	—
1946	60	99	60	—	—	—
1947	58	99	58	58	104	55
1948	63	100	63	63	104	60
1949	62	102	61	62	108	57
1950	61	101	61	61	106	58
1951	63	104	61	63	106	60
1952	66	104	63	66	105	62
1953	66	103	64	66	103	64
1954	66	102	65	66	102	65
1955	69	102	67	69	104	66
1956	69	101	68	69	103	67
1957	67	98	69	67	100	67
1958	73	98	74	73	98	74
1959	74	99	74	74	101	73
1960	76	98	77	76	99	76
1961	76	97	78	76	98	78
1962	77	97	79	77	98	78
1963	80	97	82	80	98	82
1964	79	97	81	79	98	81

Note appears at end of table

TABLE Da1117–1122   Indexes of farm output, input, and productivity: 1870–1990
Continued

	1870–1984 indexes			1947–1990 indexes		
	Output	Input	Productivity	Output	Input	Productivity
	Da1117	Da1118	Da1119 [1]	Da1120	Da1121	Da1122 [1]
Year	Index 1977 = 100	Index 1977 = 100	Index 1977 = 100	Index 1977 = 100	Index 1977 = 100	Index 1977 = 100
1965	82	96	86	82	97	84
1966	79	96	83	79	96	83
1967	83	98	86	83	98	85
1968	85	97	87	85	97	87
1969	85	97	88	85	96	88
1970	84	97	87	84	96	87
1971	92	98	94	92	97	95
1972	91	97	94	91	97	94
1973	93	98	95	93	98	95
1974	88	98	90	88	98	90
1975	95	96	99	95	97	99
1976	97	99	98	97	98	98
1977	100	100	100	100	100	100
1978	104	102	102	104	102	101
1979	111	105	105	111	105	105
1980	103	103	101	104	103	101
1981	118	102	116	118	102	116
1982	116	99	117	116	98	119
1983	95	95	100	96	96	100
1984	111	96	116	112	95	118
1985	—	—	—	118	91	129
1986	—	—	—	111	89	124
1987	—	—	—	110	89	124
1988	—	—	—	102	87	116
1989	—	—	—	114	87	130
1990	—	—	—	119	88	135

[1] Calculated from unrounded values.

Sources

Series Da1117–1119. 1870–1938, U.S. Department of Agriculture, Economic Research Service (USDA ERS), *Economic Indicators of the Farm Sector: Production and Efficiency Statistics, 1981*; 1939–1984, USDA ERS, *Economic Indicators of the Farm Sector: Production and Efficiency Statistics, 1984*.

Series Da1120–1122. USDA ERS, *Economic Indicators of the Farm Sector: Production and Efficiency Statistics, 1990*, and also in electronic form on the Cornell University Library/Economic Research Service Internet site, Production and Efficiency Statistics, Table 48, Indexes of Farm Output, Input, and Productivity, United States, 1947–90, downloaded March 1998.

Documentation

These series are formed as Laspeyres indexes that use base-period prices to weight both current and base-period quantities. Index number procedures used to construct these series are described in USDA ERS, *Economic Indicators of the Farm Sector: Production and Efficiency Statistics, 1979*. Specifically, the indexes are calculated by the weighted aggregate method, which requires two distinct steps. First, to arrive at quantity-price aggregates, quantities of each commodity produced each year are multiplied by weighted average prices received by farmers during the weight period. Second, the indexes are formed by expressing the quantity-price aggregates as percentages of the average quantity-price aggregates in the reference (or base) period. These series were discontinued in 1990.

Three general features of the weighting system and method of calculation should be noted if the indexes are to be clearly understood:

(1) The farm output, crop production, and livestock production indexes are calculated annually beginning in 1939 for each of the ten farm production regions, as well as for the United States from 1910 to date. In addition, farm output indexes are calculated for the United States at decade intervals from 1870 to 1900. Weighted average prices received by farmers in a given region are used as weights in constructing the indexes for the region. The quantity-price aggregates for the ten farm production regions are summed

each year beginning with 1939 to obtain the quantity-price aggregates on which the index for the United States is based.

(2) The indexes were originally based with 1933 equal to 100 and later rebased with 1977 equal to 100. For weight periods, multiyear average prices received by farmers were used to reduce the effects of extreme weather conditions in any single year. Three weight periods are used for the regional indexes, and four weight periods for the U.S. indexes. Average 1967–1969 prices received by farmers in each farm production region are used as weights for 1965 and subsequent years; average 1957–1959 prices are used for 1955–1965; average 1957–1959 prices are used for 1939–1955. In the U.S. indexes, for years preceding 1939, average 1935–1939 prices are used.

Because more than one price weight period is used in computing the indexes, the indexes for the various subperiods are spliced together using overlapping calculations for specific years. Splicing years are 1955 and 1965 for the ten farm production regions and the United States. The U.S. series is also spliced at 1939.

(3) The chief sources of data for production and prices are official reports of the Economics and Statistics Service Crop Reporting Board. The main item of production omitted in the farm output series is production from farm forests. This, plus other minor items omitted, are insignificant parts of the total farm output.

USDA ERS, *Economic Indicators of the Farm Sector: Production and Efficiency Statistics, 1981* reports that all index number series have been converted to the reference base period (1977 = 100). In addition, data have been aligned with Census of Agriculture benchmarks, and a more recent weight period (1976–1978) and splice year (1975) have been used. The reference period for federal government general purpose statistical index numbers is updated about every ten years in an effort to ensure that the index is timely and based on a reasonable estimate of the current structure of the economy.

Two input, output, and productivity series are presented because the treatment of labor input in the 1939–1984 series obtained from USDA ERS, *Economic Indicators of the Farm Sector: Production and Efficiency Statistics, 1981* and *1984* differs slightly from that included in the 1947–1990 series obtained

(continued)

TABLE Da1117–1122 Indexes of farm output, input, and productivity: 1870–1990 *Continued*

from USDA ERS, *Economic Indicators of the Farm Sector: Production and Efficiency Statistics, 1990*. Hence, these two series are not entirely compatible.

The 1939–1984 series included published estimates of the hours of labor used in each of twelve enterprise groups (namely, feed grains, hay and forage, food grains, vegetables, fruits and nuts, sugar crops, cotton, tobacco, oil crops, meat animals, milk cows, and poultry) and ten regions. These labor use or input data were largely estimated by multiplying a set of "labor requirements" coefficients (developed by the Economic Research Service in consultation with state agriculture experts) by the corresponding Agricultural Statistics Board estimates of planted acreage (for preharvest labor), harvested acreage (for harvest labor), or weight units of production or animal numbers (for livestock). This labor input estimate was then scaled up by 13–15 percent (depending on the region in question) to incorporate a so-called overhead labor component in the reported total hours of labor series. This labor-requirements procedure for estimating labor use was last done comprehensively in 1964, and before that in agricultural census years. After 1964, modifications in the base labor requirement coefficients occurred sporadically, formed by subjective judgments based on changes in yields and developments in mechanization. Documentation to justify these modifications was not provided, nor was there any uniformity in the way these estimates were implemented (USDA ERS, *Economic Indicators of the Farm Sector: Production and Efficiency Statistics, 1985*).

In the 1947–1990 series, U.S. and regional labor hours (including, operator, unpaid family, and hired labor) for 1984 to date were derived using information from the Economic Research Service's Farm Cost and Returns Survey, which was first conducted in 1984. The Bureau of Labor Statistics national estimates for 1947–1983 were disaggregated by region, based on the prevailing percentage distributions then used by the Economic Research Service (effectively based on the regional shares of the corresponding national total for each type of labor). Regional labor input totals were calculated by aggregating across the three types of labor (USDA ERS, *Economic Indicators of the Farm Sector: Production and Efficiency Statistics, 1985*). For more details about the construction of these indexes, see *Major Statistical Series of the U.S. Department of Agriculture*, Agriculture Handbook number 671, volume 2.

The output series Da1117 and Da1120 are ostensibly the same but differ in the years 1983–1984 owing to revisions in the underlying data that were incorporated into series Da1120 but not the earlier series Da1117. Output includes all livestock and livestock products, made up of clipped wool, mohair, and, for 1950 to date, honey and beeswax, as well as meat animals, including cattle, calves, sheep, lamps, and hogs; dairy products, including butter, butterfat, wholesale milk, retail milk, and milk consumed on farms; poultry and eggs, which include chickens, eggs, commercial broilers, and turkeys; and all crops.

All crops include hayseeds, pasture seeds, cover crop seeds, and some miscellaneous crop production not included in separate groups of crops; feed grains, which include corn for grain; oats, barley, and sorghum grain; hay and forage, including all hay, sorghum forage, corn silage, and, for 1950 to date, sorghum silage; and food grains, made up of all wheat, rye, and rice. Buckwheat was excluded after 1964.

Other items included in crops are vegetables, including potatoes, sweet potatoes, dry edible beans, dry field peas, truck crops for processing, and truck crops for fresh market; fruits and nuts, made up of fruit, berries, and tree nuts; sugar crops, which include sugar beets, sugarcane for sugar and seed, sugarcane syrup, and maple syrup; and oil crops made up of soybeans, peanuts for nuts, cottonseed, flaxseed, and, for 1950 to 1964, tung nuts, and peanuts hogged. Citrus production is reported by year of harvest, 1960 to date; earlier years are reported by year of bloom. Farm gardens are excluded after 1964.

Inputs included are farm labor, including hired, operator, and unpaid family labor; farm real estate, including all land in farms, service buildings, grazing fees, and repairs on service buildings; mechanical power and machinery, including interest and depreciation on mechanical power and machinery, repairs, licenses, and fuel; agricultural chemicals, including fertilizer, lime, and pesticides; feed, seed, and livestock purchases, which includes nonfarm value of feed, seed, and livestock purchases; taxes and interest, including real estate and personal property taxes and interest on livestock and crop inventory; and miscellaneous inputs, including such things as insurance, telephone, and veterinary fees, containers, and building materials.

TABLE Da1123–1142   Indexes of farm output per unit of input, by region: 1939–1990

Contributed by Albert K. A. Acquaye, Julian M. Alston, and Philip G. Pardey

	Index of output per unit of input, 1939–1983									
	Northeast	Lake States	Corn Belt	Northern Plains	Appalachians	Southeast	Delta States	Southern Plains	Mountain	Pacific
	Da1123	Da1124	Da1125	Da1126	Da1127	Da1128	Da1129	Da1130	Da1131	Da1132
Year	Index 1977 = 100	Index 1977 = 100	Index 1977 = 100	Index 1977 = 100	Index 1977 = 100	Index 1977 = 100	Index 1977 = 100	Index 1977 = 100	Index 1977 = 100	Index 1977 = 100
1939	51	46	56	39	61	54	47	46	56	52
1940	52	48	55	45	60	56	44	50	59	54
1941	52	47	58	53	60	53	47	49	65	55
1942	56	50	62	62	65	59	51	53	67	56
1943	55	49	61	57	61	61	49	50	68	57
1944	57	48	59	59	65	62	51	56	67	58
1945	57	52	61	62	65	63	49	50	67	57
1946	62	53	66	62	70	62	47	52	68	61
1947	61	52	56	63	66	61	49	59	70	59
1948	62	56	70	66	69	64	57	55	72	59
1949	62	56	65	55	65	59	49	66	67	60
1950	65	55	65	63	65	61	49	55	69	62
1951	66	57	63	59	68	67	50	53	70	63
1952	66	59	67	63	66	63	52	56	74	65
1953	69	59	65	58	66	70	57	58	79	67
1954	71	60	67	60	69	64	57	60	73	70
1955	72	61	70	57	72	76	66	62	76	69
1956	76	64	72	57	77	76	62	60	76	70
1957	74	64	72	66	69	71	58	64	81	71
1958	81	68	77	79	75	75	60	73	86	71
1959	80	69	78	69	76	77	68	72	82	73
1960	84	71	81	81	79	80	67	77	83	72
1961	87	74	82	74	81	84	71	79	83	72
1962	84	73	82	80	83	85	72	75	86	74
1963	87	77	86	80	86	89	78	76	88	76
1964	89	75	83	82	86	86	80	78	86	78
1965	93	77	88	84	86	92	83	85	95	81
1966	88	78	85	84	83	84	78	77	93	82
1967	96	79	89	86	88	94	78	76	96	78
1968	94	82	87	89	87	88	87	83	99	85
1969	98	81	87	93	92	92	83	77	100	85
1970	100	83	82	87	91	92	85	79	101	86
1971	103	89	97	102	95	102	88	73	103	88
1972	95	88	95	101	98	99	90	82	102	91
1973	97	90	93	102	99	100	88	91	101	93
1974	100	83	83	88	101	105	84	78	103	99
1975	104	89	99	93	105	112	92	92	109	105
1976	104	82	97	89	108	113	94	92	110	105
1977	100	100	100	100	100	100	100	100	100	100
1978	106	99	104	103	105	109	97	88	109	98
1979	102	98	109	110	100	113	104	100	103	104
1980	104	100	102	96	97	104	84	86	113	113
1981	117	106	113	120	118	124	108	114	129	119
1982	112	105	113	121	118	130	117	102	123	115
1983	108	92	84	103	93	117	93	90	119	113
1984	—	—	—	—	—	—	—	—	—	—
1985	—	—	—	—	—	—	—	—	—	—
1986	—	—	—	—	—	—	—	—	—	—
1987	—	—	—	—	—	—	—	—	—	—
1988	—	—	—	—	—	—	—	—	—	—
1989	—	—	—	—	—	—	—	—	—	—
1990	—	—	—	—	—	—	—	—	—	—

(continued)

TABLE Da1123–1142   Indexes of farm output per unit of input, by region: 1939–1990   *Continued*

	Northeast	Lake States	Corn Belt	Northern Plains	Appalachians	Southeast	Delta States	Southern Plains	Mountain	Pacific
	Da1133	Da1134	Da1135	Da1136	Da1137	Da1138	Da1139	Da1140	Da1141	Da1142
	Index	Index	Index	Index	Index	Index	Index	Index	Index	Index
Year	1977 = 100	1977 = 100	1977 = 100	1977 = 100	1977 = 100	1977 = 100	1977 = 100	1977 = 100	1977 = 100	1977 = 100
1939	—	—	—	—	—	—	—	—	—	—
1940	—	—	—	—	—	—	—	—	—	—
1941	—	—	—	—	—	—	—	—	—	—
1942	—	—	—	—	—	—	—	—	—	—
1943	—	—	—	—	—	—	—	—	—	—
1944	—	—	—	—	—	—	—	—	—	—
1945	—	—	—	—	—	—	—	—	—	—
1946	—	—	—	—	—	—	—	—	—	—
1947	58	49	53	60	62	57	44	55	67	58
1948	60	54	67	64	65	60	52	52	69	59
1949	60	52	62	53	60	55	45	62	64	59
1950	63	53	62	61	61	57	45	52	66	61
1951	65	56	61	59	66	65	48	52	69	64
1952	66	58	66	63	64	62	51	55	73	67
1953	70	59	65	59	66	70	56	58	79	70
1954	71	61	66	61	68	64	56	60	73	72
1955	70	60	68	57	70	75	63	60	74	70
1956	74	62	70	56	74	74	60	58	74	71
1957	73	63	70	65	67	70	56	63	79	72
1958	81	67	75	80	74	74	58	73	86	73
1959	79	68	77	69	74	76	66	71	81	74
1960	83	69	79	81	77	79	65	76	83	73
1961	86	73	81	75	80	83	69	79	83	74
1962	83	72	81	81	82	84	71	74	85	76
1963	86	77	86	81	85	88	77	76	88	78
1964	88	74	82	82	86	85	79	78	86	80
1965	91	75	86	84	84	90	81	84	94	81
1966	87	77	84	84	82	83	77	77	93	83
1967	95	78	88	86	88	94	78	76	96	80
1968	93	81	87	89	87	88	87	84	99	86
1969	98	81	86	94	92	93	83	77	100	87
1970	100	83	83	88	92	93	86	80	101	88
1971	104	90	97	103	97	104	89	74	104	90
1972	95	88	94	102	98	100	90	82	102	92
1973	97	90	93	102	99	101	88	91	101	93
1974	100	83	83	87	100	105	84	78	102	98
1975	103	89	99	93	104	111	91	91	109	105
1976	104	82	97	89	108	113	94	93	110	106
1977	100	100	100	100	100	100	100	100	100	100
1978	105	99	104	103	104	108	97	87	108	98
1979	102	98	108	111	101	113	104	100	102	104
1980	105	100	101	97	98	103	84	87	113	112
1981	117	106	113	120	117	125	108	113	126	118
1982	121	110	116	124	121	136	120	106	126	116
1983	115	98	87	107	93	118	95	92	119	109
1984	109	102	111	127	127	156	122	95	121	134
1985	114	109	138	144	127	162	125	105	118	134
1986	110	110	131	145	115	137	117	98	131	126
1987	112	107	124	139	115	141	124	101	129	143
1988	108	90	103	118	121	153	140	104	126	146
1989	118	116	136	129	134	153	131	102	136	142
1990	120	119	136	151	134	149	139	113	140	146

The header above the column-group row reads: **Index of output per unit of input, 1947–1990**

Sources

Series Da1123–1132. U.S. Department of Agriculture, Economic Research Service, *Economic Indicators of the Farm Sector: Production and Efficiency Statistics, 1984.*

Series Da1133–1142. U.S. Department of Agriculture, Economic Research Service, *Economic Indicators of the Farm Sector: Production and Efficiency Statistics, 1990.* Data can also be found in electronic form at the Cornell University Library/Economic Research Service Internet site, Production and Efficiency Statistics, Table 47, Farm Productivity: Indexes of Output per Unit of Input, by Region, 1947–90, downloaded in March 1998.

Documentation

These series are Laspeyres indexes that use base-period prices to weight a ratio of current and base-period quantities. See the text for Table Da1117–1122 for further details about this index number procedure and the labor data for these series. For a list of states included in the ten U.S. Department of Agriculture subregions, see the text for Table Da1232–1243.

The series in this table began in 1939 and were discontinued in 1990.

TABLE Da1143–1171 Labor hours per unit of production and related factors, by commodity: 1800–1986

Contributed by Albert K. A. Acquaye, Julian M. Alston, and Philip G. Pardey

	Corn for grain		Sorghum grain		Wheat		Hay		Potatoes		Sugar beets		Cotton	
	Per acre	Per 100 bushels	Per acre	Per 100 bushels	Per acre	Per 100 bushels	Per acre	Per ton	Per acre	Per ton	Per acre	Per ton	Per acre	Per bale
	Da1143	Da1144	Da1145	Da1146	Da1147	Da1148	Da1149	Da1150	Da1151	Da1152	Da1153	Da1154	Da1155	Da1156
Year(s)	Hours	Hours	Hours	Hours	Hours	Hours	Hours	Hours	Hours	Hours	Hours	Hours	Hours	Hours
1800	86.0	344	—	—	56.0	373	—	—	—	—	—	—	185	601
1840	69.0	276	—	—	35.0	233	—	—	—	—	—	—	135	438
1880	46.0	180	—	—	20.0	152	—	—	—	—	—	—	119	303
1900	38.0	147	—	—	15.0	108	—	—	—	—	—	—	112	284
1910–1914	35.2	135	—	—	15.2	106	11.9	10.3	76	25	128	12.1	116	276
1915–1919	34.2	132	—	—	13.6	98	13.0	10.4	74	26	125	13.0	105	299
1920–1924	32.7	122	—	—	12.4	90	12.5	10.2	75	23	—	—	96	296
1925–1929	30.3	115	17.5	104	10.5	74	12.0	9.8	73	21	109	10.0	96	268
1930–1934	28.2	123	—	—	9.4	70	10.3	9.5	68	21	—	—	97	252
1935–1939	28.1	108	13.1	102	8.8	67	11.3	9.1	70	20	98	8.4	99	209
1940–1944	25.5	79	—	—	7.5	44	11.0	8.1	69	17	—	—	99	182
1945–1949	19.2	53	8.8	49	5.7	34	8.4	6.2	69	12	85	6.3	83	146
1950–1954	13.3	34	—	—	4.6	27	6.3	4.4	63	8	—	—	66	107
1955–1959	9.9	20	5.9	20	3.8	17	6.0	3.7	53	6	51	2.9	66	74
1960–1964	7.0	11	—	—	3.0	12	5.0	2.8	48	5	—	—	47	47
1965–1969	5.8	7	4.2	8	2.9	11	3.8	1.9	45	4	33	1.9	30	30
1975–1979	3.6	4	3.8	7	2.8	9	3.4	1.6	38	3	26	1.3	8	8
1977–1981	3.4	3	3.7	6	2.7	8	3.3	1.4	36	3	24	1.2	6	6
1981–1985	3.1	3	3.5	6	2.6	7	3.0	1.3	33	2	21	1.0	6	5
1982–1986	3.1	3	3.5	6	2.5	7	3.0	1.2	33	2	20	1.0	5	5

(continued)

TABLE Da1143–1171 Labor hours per unit of production and related factors, by commodity: 1800–1986 Continued

Year(s)	Tobacco Per acre Da1157[1] Hours	Tobacco Per 100 pounds Da1158[1] Hours	Soybeans Per acre Da1159 Hours	Soybeans Per 100 bushels Da1160 Hours	Milk Per milk cow Da1161 Hours	Milk Per hundredweight Da1162 Hours	Beef, hundredweight Da1163[2,3] Hours	Hogs, hundredweight Da1164[3] Hours	Eggs Per 100 layers Da1165 Hours	Eggs Per 100 eggs Da1166 Hours	Chickens Farm raised Per 100 Da1167 Hours	Chickens Farm raised Per hundredweight Da1168[3] Hours	Chickens Broilers Per 100 Da1169 Hours	Chickens Broilers Per hundredweight Da1170[3] Hours	Turkeys, hundredweight Da1171[3] Hours
1800	—	—	—	—	—	—	—	—	—	—	—	—	—	—	—
1840	—	—	—	—	—	—	—	—	—	—	—	—	—	—	—
1880	—	—	—	—	—	—	—	—	—	—	—	—	—	—	—
1900	—	—	—	—	—	—	—	—	—	—	—	—	—	—	—
1910–1914	356	44	—	—	146	3.8	4.6	3.6	—	—	33	9.5	—	—	31.4
1915–1919	353	44	19.9	143	141	3.7	4.5	3.6	—	—	33	9.4	—	—	31.1
1920–1924	353	46	—	—	142	3.6	4.5	3.5	—	—	32	9.3	—	—	30.0
1925–1929	370	48	15.9	126	145	3.3	4.3	3.3	218	1.9	32	9.4	—	—	28.5
1930–1934	370	47	—	—	147	3.4	4.3	3.2	225	1.9	31	9.3	—	—	26.7
1935–1939	415	47	11.8	64	148	3.4	4.2	3.2	221	1.7	30	9.0	25.0	8.5	23.7
1940–1944	442	43	—	—	142	3.1	4.0	3.0	223	1.6	29	8.2	23.0	7.7	19.6
1945–1949	460	39	8.0	41	129	2.6	4.0	3.0	240	1.5	29	7.7	16.0	5.1	13.1
1950–1954	464	36	—	—	121	2.2	3.6	2.7	232	1.3	27	7.3	8.0	2.4	6.8
1955–1959	475	31	5.2	23	109	1.7	3.2	2.4	175	0.9	23	6.7	4.0	1.3	4.4
1960–1964	493	26	—	—	93	1.2	2.6	1.9	126	0.6	17	4.7	3.0	0.8	2.4
1965–1969	427	22	4.8	19	78	0.9	2.1	1.4	97	0.4	14	3.7	2.0	0.5	1.3
1975–1979	254	13	3.7	12	45	0.4	1.3	0.5	60	0.3	12	2.9	0.6	0.2	0.5
1977–1981	242	12	3.5	12	38	0.3	1.2	0.4	49	0.2	11	2.7	0.5	0.1	0.4
1981–1985	223	11	3.2	11	27	0.2	0.9	0.3	46	0.2	10	2.5	0.4	0.1	0.3
1982–1986	218	10	3.2	10	24	0.2	0.9	0.3	44	0.2	10	2.5	0.4	0.1	0.2

[1] Per acre harvested.

[2] Production includes beef produced as a by-product of milk cow enterprise.

[3] Liveweight production.

Sources

Series Da1143–1160. 1800–1900, U.S. Department of Agriculture, "Progress of Farm Mechanization," *Miscellaneous Publication* number 630, 1947; 1910–1959, U.S. Department of Agriculture, Economic Research Service, "Labor Used to Produce Field Crops," *Statistical Bulletin* number 346, 1964, and unpublished data.

Series Da1161–1171. U.S. Department of Agriculture, 1910–1949, "Gains in Productivity of Farm Labor," *Technical Bulletin* number 1020, 1950; 1950–1959, "Labor Used to Produce Livestock," Estimates by States, Statistical Bulletin number 336, 1963.

Series Da1143–1171. U.S. Department of Agriculture, Economic Research Service, *Agricultural Statistics, 1972, 1982, 1988,* and unpublished data, 1960–1986.

Documentation

For discussion on labor requirements measures, see the text for Table Da1117–1122. The series in this table were discontinued – the last year of data is 1986.

Estimates for series Da1143–1160 pertaining to acreage represent labor hours per acre harvested, including preharvest work on acreage abandoned, grazed, and turned under.

TABLE Da1172–1174   Indexes of agricultural land and labor productivity: 1910–1990

Contributed by Albert K. A. Acquaye, Julian M. Alston, and Philip G. Pardey

Year	Land Da1172 Index 1977 = 100	Labor, 1910–1984 Da1173 Index 1977 = 100	Labor, 1947–1990 Da1174 Index 1977 = 100	Year	Land Da1172 Index 1977 = 100	Labor, 1910–1984 Da1173 Index 1977 = 100	Labor, 1947–1990 Da1174 Index 1977 = 100
1910	48	8	—	1955	63	26	30
1911	45	7	—	1956	64	28	31
1912	52	8	—	1957	65	29	33
1913	46	8	—	1958	73	33	39
1914	50	8	—	1959	72	35	39
1915	51	8	—	1960	77	37	42
1916	46	8	—	1961	78	39	44
1917	48	8	—	1962	81	41	46
1918	46	8	—	1963	83	45	51
1919	45	8	—	1964	81	47	52
1920	52	8	—	1965	85	52	56
1921	43	8	—	1966	83	53	59
1922	47	9	—	1967	86	58	64
1923	47	9	—	1968	89	62	68
1924	46	8	—	1969	91	63	72
1925	48	9	—	1970	88	66	74
1926	49	9	—	1971	96	74	85
1927	47	9	—	1972	99	78	83
1928	49	9	—	1973	99	81	86
1929	48	9	—	1974	88	79	81
1930	44	9	—	1975	96	89	90
1931	49	10	—	1976	94	94	97
1932	47	10	—	1977	100	100	100
1933	43	9	—	1978	105	108	104
1934	35	9	—	1979	113	119	113
1935	46	10	—	1980	100	112	109
1936	38	9	—	1981	115	131	123
1937	53	10	—	1982	116	133	125
1938	51	11	—	1983	100	120	99
1939	51	11	—	1984	112	139	121
1940	53	12	—	1985	120	—	139
1941	54	13	—	1986	116	—	139
1942	59	14	—	1987	123	—	142
1943	55	14	—	1988	106	—	135
1944	58	14	—	1989	119	—	147
1945	57	15	—	1990	127	—	142
1946	60	16	—				
1947	57	16	18				
1948	64	18	21				
1949	60	19	20				
1950	59	19	22				
1951	59	20	24				
1952	62	22	26				
1953	62	23	28				
1954	61	24	29				

Sources

Series Da1172. 1910–1938, U.S. Department of Agriculture, Economic Research Service (USDA ERS), *Economic Indicators of the Farm Sector: Production and Efficiency Statistics, 1981*, Table 13; 1939–1946, USDA ERS, *Economic Indicators of the Farm Sector: Production and Efficiency Statistics, 1984*, Table 13; 1947–1990, USDA ERS, *Economic Indicators of the Farm Sector: Production and Efficiency Statistics, 1990*, and the Cornell University Library Internet site, Production and Efficiency Statistics, Table 13, Cropland Used for Crops and Index of Crop Production per Acre, United States, 1947–90, downloaded March 1998.

Series Da1173. 1910–1938, USDA ERS, *Economic Indicators of the Farm Sector: Production and Efficiency Statistics, 1981*, Table 45; 1939–1984, USDA ERS, *Eco-*

nomic Indicators of the Farm Sector: Production and Efficiency Statistics, 1984, Table 45.

Series Da1174. USDA ERS, *Economic Indicators of the Farm Sector: Production and Efficiency Statistics, 1990*, and the Cornell University Library Internet site (downloaded March 1998).

Documentation

These series are Laspeyres indexes that use base-period prices to weight both current and base-period quantities. For further details about this index number procedure and the labor data for these series, see the text for Table Da1117–1122.

Series Da1172 and Da1174 were discontinued in 1990; series Da1173 was discontinued in 1984.

TABLE Da1175–1204 Indexes of agricultural land and labor productivity, by region: 1939–1990

Contributed by Albert K. A. Acquaye, Julian M. Alston, and Philip G. Pardey

	Land										Labor (1984 estimates)				
	Northeast	Lake States	Corn Belt	Northern Plains	Appalachian	Southeast	Delta States	Southern Plains	Mountain	Pacific	Northeast	Lake States	Corn Belt	Northern Plains	Appalachian
	Da1175	Da1176	Da1177	Da1178	Da1179	Da1180	Da1181	Da1182	Da1183	Da1184	Da1185	Da1186	Da1187	Da1188	Da1189
Year	Index 1977 = 100	Index 1977 = 100	Index 1977 = 100	Index 1977 = 100	Index 1977 = 100	Index 1977 = 100	Index 1977 = 100	Index 1977 = 100	Index 1977 = 100	Index 1977 = 100	Index 1977 = 100	Index 1977 = 100	Index 1977 = 100	Index 1977 = 100	Index 1977 = 100
1939	64	47	48	30	69	50	76	43	56	48	13	11	10	10	16
1940	65	49	45	37	68	53	71	49	61	49	14	11	10	12	16
1941	63	45	47	46	66	47	75	47	68	51	14	11	11	14	16
1942	68	51	52	57	70	54	87	51	72	50	15	12	12	16	18
1943	63	45	47	49	65	57	80	45	70	51	16	12	12	15	17
1944	63	46	46	53	76	60	87	55	67	52	16	12	12	16	18
1945	63	49	47	54	77	62	83	44	67	51	17	13	12	18	19
1946	75	50	53	51	87	61	74	45	68	57	19	14	14	18	20
1947	73	47	40	51	81	61	78	57	70	55	20	15	12	20	20
1948	78	53	57	55	86	66	104	50	71	55	21	16	16	22	22
1949	78	52	53	41	79	59	83	68	63	55	23	17	16	20	21
1950	81	51	51	49	82	62	82	49	64	58	24	18	17	23	22
1951	80	53	49	44	87	72	86	48	63	61	25	19	17	23	23
1952	77	56	55	50	84	64	90	50	67	63	26	21	19	26	23
1953	80	56	52	44	82	71	100	53	73	63	28	21	19	24	25
1954	80	56	53	44	85	63	90	54	64	64	29	22	20	25	26
1955	78	57	56	41	89	81	112	55	68	64	30	23	22	25	29
1956	84	62	59	41	97	79	103	51	67	67	32	25	24	27	32
1957	78	62	58	54	83	72	87	61	76	67	33	26	25	31	31
1958	90	65	64	69	95	81	89	76	82	67	37	29	28	39	35
1959	87	66	65	54	95	80	112	72	80	72	38	30	30	37	36
1960	93	67	67	69	100	91	109	78	81	70	41	32	32	45	38
1961	97	71	73	59	107	99	115	82	79	70	43	35	34	43	40
1962	90	71	75	70	116	107	115	75	82	75	44	35	36	48	43
1963	91	73	80	64	121	110	128	75	84	75	47	39	40	49	45
1964	92	69	75	63	121	106	129	78	81	79	50	39	41	52	48
1965	98	70	84	69	112	118	124	91	85	78	54	41	47	57	51
1966	90	78	84	71	109	105	108	81	83	81	53	45	49	61	52
1967	106	77	87	72	108	116	100	80	88	76	61	48	53	62	59
1968	102	83	89	79	101	101	110	93	91	84	61	52	56	67	62
1969	109	86	93	84	114	113	101	80	92	87	66	54	58	74	67
1970	108	85	82	75	111	91	106	87	92	84	71	58	58	70	72
1971	107	89	100	94	106	99	108	78	95	87	75	64	71	82	79
1972	92	91	102	94	112	121	113	97	93	88	75	67	74	87	86
1973	102	90	95	97	110	120	109	107	96	94	80	72	76	88	89
1974	106	78	77	77	108	122	109	77	98	97	85	70	70	77	90
1975	103	83	97	87	111	125	99	84	97	97	90	78	87	87	93
1976	102	70	94	81	113	121	93	89	103	98	99	77	93	85	95
1977	100	100	100	100	100	100	100	100	100	100	100	100	100	100	100
1978	109	102	108	110	109	114	100	88	109	95	113	106	111	108	111
1979	109	105	116	119	102	120	112	109	107	107	117	114	124	122	116

Land

Year	Northeast Da1175 Index 1977 = 100	Lake States Da1176 Index 1977 = 100	Corn Belt Da1177 Index 1977 = 100	Northern Plains Da1178 Index 1977 = 100	Appalachian Da1179 Index 1977 = 100	Southeast Da1180 Index 1977 = 100	Delta States Da1181 Index 1977 = 100	Southern Plains Da1182 Index 1977 = 100	Mountain Da1183 Index 1977 = 100	Pacific Da1184 Index 1977 = 100
1980	104	100	102	92	95	102	81	79	111	113
1981	112	106	114	116	118	130	110	106	117	112
1982	114	114	117	120	120	133	118	91	116	115
1983	104	101	88	102	88	122	98	97	110	114
1984	116	110	105	118	116	129	118	100	107	121
1985	120	114	124	129	111	135	114	105	104	124
1986	113	114	124	131	96	122	106	93	112	122
1987	115	122	123	127	97	143	120	114	125	147
1988	101	80	85	100	106	154	133	119	114	149
1989	115	116	115	107	111	149	126	101	124	148
1990	126	125	120	133	115	142	132	114	131	154

Labor

1984 estimates

Year	Northeast Da1185 Index 1977 = 100	Lake States Da1186 Index 1977 = 100	Corn Belt Da1187 Index 1977 = 100	Northern Plains Da1188 Index 1977 = 100	Appalachian Da1189 Index 1977 = 100
1980	120	120	117	105	110
1981	142	135	132	132	132
1982	137	137	133	138	134
1983	137	131	101	127	111
1984	—	—	—	—	—
1985	—	—	—	—	—
1986	—	—	—	—	—
1987	—	—	—	—	—
1988	—	—	—	—	—
1989	—	—	—	—	—
1990	—	—	—	—	—

Labor

1984 estimates

Year	Southeast Da1190 Index 1977 = 100	Delta States Da1191 Index 1977 = 100	Southern Plains Da1192 Index 1977 = 100	Mountain Da1193 Index 1977 = 100	Pacific Da1194 Index 1977 = 100
1939	11	8	10	14	19
1940	12	8	11	15	19
1941	12	8	11	16	20
1942	13	9	12	16	21
1943	14	9	12	18	22
1944	14	9	13	18	23
1945	15	10	13	19	24
1946	15	10	14	20	25
1947	16	10	16	21	26
1948	17	12	15	23	28
1949	17	11	20	23	29
1950	19	12	17	24	31
1951	21	13	17	26	32
1952	21	14	19	29	35
1953	25	15	20	32	38
1954	25	17	22	29	41
1955	30	20	23	32	41
1956	32	21	24	33	43
1957	33	21	27	36	44
1958	37	23	32	40	45
1959	38	27	33	41	48

1990 estimates

Year	Northeast Da1195 Index 1977 = 100	Lake States Da1196 Index 1977 = 100	Corn Belt Da1197 Index 1977 = 100	Northern Plains Da1198 Index 1977 = 100	Appalachian Da1199 Index 1977 = 100	Southeast Da1200 Index 1977 = 100	Delta States Da1201 Index 1977 = 100	Southern Plains Da1202 Index 1977 = 100	Mountain Da1203 Index 1977 = 100	Pacific Da1204 Index 1977 = 100
1939	—	—	—	—	—	—	—	—	—	—
1940	—	—	—	—	—	—	—	—	—	—
1941	—	—	—	—	—	—	—	—	—	—
1942	—	—	—	—	—	—	—	—	—	—
1943	—	—	—	—	—	—	—	—	—	—
1944	—	—	—	—	—	—	—	—	—	—
1945	—	—	—	—	—	—	—	—	—	—
1946	—	—	—	—	—	—	—	—	—	—
1947	22	17	14	23	22	18	11	17	24	31
1948	25	19	19	26	24	20	13	17	26	33
1949	25	19	18	23	22	19	12	21	25	34
1950	27	20	19	27	23	22	13	19	27	36
1951	30	23	21	27	26	25	14	20	30	40
1952	32	25	23	32	27	26	16	23	34	43
1953	35	26	24	31	29	31	18	25	39	49
1954	36	27	25	31	30	30	20	27	35	51
1955	35	27	26	29	32	34	22	26	36	49
1956	37	29	27	31	34	36	22	26	37	50
1957	38	30	28	36	34	38	22	30	40	52
1958	44	34	32	47	39	43	25	36	46	55
1959	44	35	34	43	39	44	29	36	46	57

(continued)

TABLE Da1175–1204 Indexes of agricultural land and labor productivity, by region: 1939–1990 *Continued*

Labor

	1984 estimates					1990 estimates									
	Southeast	Delta States	Southern Plains	Mountain	Pacific	Northeast	Lake States	Corn Belt	Northern Plains	Appalachian	Southeast	Delta States	Southern Plains	Mountain	Pacific
	Da1190	Da1191	Da1192	Da1193	Da1194	Da1195	Da1196	Da1197	Da1198	Da1199	Da1200	Da1201	Da1202	Da1203	Da1204
	Index	Index	Index	Index	Index	Index	Index	Index	Index	Index	Index	Index	Index	Index	Index
Year	1977 = 100	1977 = 100	1977 = 100	1977 = 100	1977 = 100	1977 = 100	1977 = 100	1977 = 100	1977 = 100	1977 = 100	1977 = 100	1977 = 100	1977 = 100	1977 = 100	1977 = 100
1960	40	28	37	43	50	47	37	36	51	41	46	29	41	48	57
1961	44	30	39	45	51	50	40	39	50	44	51	33	44	51	60
1962	46	35	41	47	54	49	40	40	55	46	52	37	45	52	63
1963	49	38	44	50	57	54	45	46	57	49	56	41	49	57	67
1964	52	43	47	51	60	57	45	47	60	52	59	46	52	57	70
1965	59	46	55	60	64	58	45	50	61	55	64	50	59	64	70
1966	57	52	56	62	65	59	50	54	67	58	63	53	62	68	73
1967	66	50	55	66	67	68	54	59	70	66	74	57	62	74	75
1968	65	59	63	69	71	68	57	62	74	68	73	66	69	77	79
1969	69	58	59	70	72	75	60	65	83	75	78	65	65	79	82
1970	73	64	62	75	76	80	65	66	78	81	83	72	69	84	86
1971	84	69	60	80	79	86	73	80	93	90	96	79	67	91	91
1972	87	73	69	84	84	80	71	79	92	91	92	78	74	89	90
1973	89	77	81	85	83	84	75	80	93	93	94	81	84	90	88
1974	96	77	71	90	90	88	72	72	78	92	99	79	72	92	92
1975	102	86	83	97	96	92	79	88	87	94	103	87	84	98	98
1976	108	91	90	104	103	102	79	96	88	104	111	94	93	107	106
1977	100	100	100	100	100	100	100	100	100	100	100	100	100	100	100
1978	116	109	96	114	104	109	102	105	104	106	110	104	92	109	99
1979	129	122	111	111	110	112	109	117	117	111	122	116	105	105	106
1980	110	99	99	122	119	116	115	112	102	106	106	95	95	117	115
1981	134	126	126	136	128	133	128	124	124	124	130	118	119	128	121
1982	144	135	115	133	122	134	133	123	129	127	139	127	112	126	116
1983	133	113	111	132	121	118	112	84	105	93	112	94	95	110	101
1984	—	—	—	—	—	83	80	95	125	159	258	154	92	113	197
1985	—	—	—	—	—	87	87	127	160	166	274	176	111	109	185
1986	—	—	—	—	—	88	96	114	166	166	221	178	118	140	166
1987	—	—	—	—	—	99	90	112	167	161	222	183	135	123	210
1988	—	—	—	—	—	93	80	103	145	165	243	204	108	141	211
1989	—	—	—	—	—	97	97	131	151	179	229	193	130	142	187
1990	—	—	—	—	—	91	91	117	171	165	230	197	120	136	187

Sources

Series Da1175–1184. 1939–1946, U.S. Department of Agriculture, Economic Research Service (USDA ERS), *Economic Indicators of the Farm Sector: Production and Efficiency Statistics, 1984*; 1947–1990, USDA ERS, *Economic Indicators of the Farm Sector: Production and Efficiency Statistics, 1990*, and also in electronic form at the Cornell University Library/Economic Research Service Internet site (downloaded February 1998).

Series Da1185–1194. USDA ERS, *Economic Indicators of the Farm Sector: Production and Efficiency Statistics, 1984*.

Series Da1195–1204. USDA ERS, *Economic Indicators of the Farm Sector: Production and Efficiency Statistics, 1990*, and also in electronic form at the Cornell University Library/Economic Research Service Internet site (downloaded February 1998).

Documentation

These series are Laspeyres indexes that use base-period prices to weight a ratio of current and base-period quantities. For further details about this index number procedure and the labor data for these

series, see the text for Table Da1117–1122. For a list of states included in the ten U.S. Department of Agriculture subregions, see the text for Table Da1232–1243.

The series in this table began in 1939 and were discontinued in 1990.

Series Da1185–1204. The two sets of series for labor productivity were both published by USDA-ERS in different editions of the *Economic Indicators of the Farm Sector: Production and Efficiency Statistics*, in 1984 and 1990, respectively. The first set, labeled "1984 estimates" (Da1185–1194), covers the interval 1939–1983. The second set, labeled "1990 estimates" (Da1195–1204), covers the interval 1947–1990. The two sets overlap for the years 1947–1983 and the indexes differ slightly between the two sets in those years for which both are available. In making use of these indexes, it is good practice to use only one set (i.e., either the 1984 estimates or the 1990 estimates). If either index covers all the years of interest, the 1990 estimates may be preferable.

TABLE Da1205–1231   Indexes of agricultural output, input, and total factor productivity: 1948–1996

Contributed by Albert K. A. Acquaye, Julian M. Alston, and Philip G. Pardey

		Livestock and livestock products					Crops						
	All farm outputs	All livestock and livestock products	Meat animals	Dairy products	Poultry and eggs	All crops	Food grains	Feed crops	Oil crops	Sugar crops	Cotton and cottonseed	Vegetables and melons	Fruits and tree nuts
	Da1205	Da1206	Da1207	Da1208	Da1209	Da1210	Da1211	Da1212	Da1213	Da1214	Da1215	Da1216	Da1217
Year	Index 1948 = 100	Index 1948 = 100	Index 1948 = 100	Index 1948 = 100	Index 1948 = 100	Index 1948 = 100	Index 1948 = 100	Index 1948 = 100	Index 1948 = 100	Index 1948 = 100	Index 1948 = 100	Index 1948 = 100	Index 1948 = 100
1948	100	100	100	100	100	100	100	100	100	100	100	100	100
1949	100	106	105	103	114	95	86	91	91	105	110	103	89
1950	99	110	113	97	123	91	80	93	107	132	68	103	86
1951	104	116	121	98	131	95	79	90	98	105	104	94	95
1952	107	118	123	98	134	98	101	93	97	109	103	91	93
1953	107	120	122	103	137	98	93	92	94	123	114	101	95
1954	108	124	128	104	145	95	82	95	106	137	95	99	98
1955	111	127	134	105	143	99	77	100	121	123	104	103	102
1956	112	130	130	106	159	99	81	98	142	125	92	102	104
1957	111	128	126	106	162	98	76	107	141	145	76	104	106
1958	117	129	128	105	172	107	112	114	172	142	80	103	97
1959	120	135	138	104	178	109	90	115	152	159	101	107	106
1960	122	134	135	105	175	113	107	120	164	195	101	100	112
1961	125	140	140	108	189	113	98	111	190	218	100	111	115
1962	126	141	143	108	188	115	91	114	193	224	104	108	117
1963	130	145	150	107	192	119	96	119	202	279	107	109	113
1964	130	149	155	109	199	115	106	109	203	284	106	99	115
1965	132	144	147	107	205	123	109	124	243	260	103	101	121
1966	133	147	152	103	217	121	110	123	261	260	66	112	124
1967	138	152	159	102	227	127	124	135	273	254	54	113	123
1968	140	152	161	101	221	130	131	131	308	298	72	120	121
1969	142	152	162	100	226	134	121	135	314	300	85	115	143
1970	142	158	171	101	236	129	113	126	319	292	72	114	136
1971	151	160	174	102	239	144	133	153	354	299	72	115	142
1972	152	162	175	104	246	143	127	149	356	314	94	117	127
1973	158	164	182	99	239	153	140	154	428	294	88	115	153
1974	149	161	177	100	239	140	149	129	343	269	80	120	157
1975	158	152	161	100	234	160	176	153	431	318	63	120	168
1976	161	160	168	104	253	159	175	154	363	328	79	125	162
1977	170	163	169	106	259	173	165	165	493	295	95	129	172
1978	173	163	168	105	272	178	153	178	524	297	73	137	169
1979	184	166	172	106	277	195	179	189	638	269	99	140	180
1980	177	174	178	111	297	177	199	160	491	283	74	140	196
1981	194	177	178	114	308	204	235	192	559	315	106	143	193
1982	194	175	171	117	309	205	228	197	608	277	78	151	192
1983	170	179	174	120	311	160	194	129	458	283	54	145	191
1984	192	176	170	116	319	200	214	191	527	277	88	154	189

(continued)

TABLE Da1205–1231 Indexes of agricultural output, input, and total factor productivity: 1948–1996 *Continued*

Index of output

		Livestock and livestock products				Crops								
	All farm outputs	All livestock and livestock products	Meat animals	Dairy products	Poultry and eggs	All crops	Food grains	Feed crops	Oil crops	Sugar crops	Cotton and cottonseed	Vegetables and melons	Fruits and tree nuts	
	Da1205	Da1206	Da1207	Da1208	Da1209	Da1210	Da1211	Da1212	Da1213	Da1214	Da1215	Da1216	Da1217	
	Index	Index	Index	Index	Index	Index	Index	Index	Index	Index	Index	Index	Index	
Year	1948 = 100	1948 = 100	1948 = 100	1948 = 100	1948 = 100	1948 = 100	1948 = 100	1948 = 100	1948 = 100	1948 = 100	1948 = 100	1948 = 100	1948 = 100	
1985	200	181	170	123	333	210	200	211	581	281	89	165	187	
1986	194	182	170	123	347	198	176	201	536	298	65	165	181	
1987	197	186	172	123	378	201	177	178	533	328	100	180	207	
1988	185	190	175	125	387	176	160	131	437	312	104	164	222	
1989	200	191	175	124	403	202	175	179	530	313	81	172	212	
1990	210	193	174	127	427	217	226	185	529	318	104	188	210	
1991	211	198	180	127	446	215	172	181	568	330	118	196	209	
1992	224	203	181	130	467	235	211	212	605	345	109	201	217	
1993	211	204	181	129	487	210	202	161	515	326	109	196	233	
1994	240	218	186	148	511	249	204	216	695	366	132	228	240	
1995	227	223	188	150	531	225	189	176	598	338	120	217	221	
1996	237	222	181	149	557	242	196	207	649	323	127	225	222	

Index of input

		Intermediate inputs					Labor			Capital				Index of total factor productivity
	All farm inputs	All intermediate inputs	Fertilizer	Pesticides	Fuels and electricity	Feed, seed, and livestock	All labor	Hired	Self-employed	All capital	Durable equipment	Real estate	Inventories	
	Da1218	Da1219	Da1220	Da1221	Da1222	Da1223	Da1224	Da1225	Da1226	Da1227	Da1228	Da1229	Da1230	Da1231
	Index	Index	Index	Index	Index	Index	Index	Index	Index	Index	Index	Index	Index	Index
Year	1948 = 100	1948 = 100	1948 = 100	1948 = 100	1948 = 100	1948 = 100	1948 = 100	1948 = 100	1948 = 100	1948 = 100	1948 = 100	1948 = 100	1948 = 100	1948 = 100
1948	100	100	100	100	100	100	100	100	100	100	100	100	100	100
1949	106	112	103	120	111	104	98	93	99	111	118	102	108	94
1950	106	113	124	152	114	103	94	97	93	121	136	103	107	94
1951	107	118	123	127	117	108	90	94	89	129	152	105	110	97
1952	107	119	130	133	123	107	88	91	86	137	165	106	115	100
1953	106	119	126	161	126	109	83	89	81	141	172	107	118	102
1954	102	112	130	180	125	100	81	84	80	145	180	108	116	105
1955	107	122	131	241	128	113	82	82	82	147	183	109	119	104
1956	107	126	139	328	128	117	77	75	78	148	184	109	121	105
1957	106	130	140	238	126	123	72	72	72	147	181	110	118	105
1958	106	135	138	283	123	130	69	73	68	146	178	110	122	110
1959	109	143	158	375	125	131	69	71	68	147	178	110	126	110
1960	108	143	162	393	127	130	67	71	66	147	180	110	128	113
1961	106	140	168	529	129	125	65	71	63	144	177	107	130	118
1962	106	142	144	579	131	129	64	70	63	143	174	105	134	119
1963	107	146	160	531	133	133	63	70	60	144	174	106	138	122
1964	105	145	179	558	136	130	59	63	58	144	176	105	140	124

		Index of input												
	All farm inputs	Intermediate inputs					Labor			Capital				Index of total factor productivity
		All intermediate inputs	Fertilizer	Pesticides	Fuels and electricity	Feed, seed, and livestock	All labor	Hired	Self-employed	All capital	Durable equipment	Real estate	Inventories	
	Da1218	Da1219	Da1220	Da1221	Da1222	Da1223	Da1224	Da1225	Da1226	Da1227	Da1228	Da1229	Da1230	Da1231
Year	Index 1948 = 100	Index 1948 = 100	Index 1948 = 100	Index 1948 = 100	Index 1948 = 100	Index 1948 = 100	Index 1948 = 100	Index 1948 = 100	Index 1948 = 100	Index 1948 = 100	Index 1948 = 100	Index 1948 = 100	Index 1948 = 100	Index 1948 = 100
1965	104	145	189	603	137	128	58	60	57	144	179	105	135	128
1966	105	154	216	652	140	138	54	54	54	146	184	104	142	127
1967	104	156	216	871	139	138	51	50	51	150	191	107	143	132
1968	102	151	164	797	140	140	49	48	50	151	200	105	146	137
1969	103	156	178	850	142	148	48	49	48	151	203	104	149	138
1970	103	158	183	936	142	153	48	49	47	151	205	104	150	137
1971	103	156	184	1,027	139	148	47	49	46	153	207	106	147	147
1972	103	160	185	1,273	138	152	46	48	46	152	207	104	156	147
1973	105	163	214	1,179	140	152	47	49	46	157	211	108	159	150
1974	105	165	236	1,126	133	151	43	52	40	162	223	110	165	142
1975	103	159	211	1,023	156	144	43	53	40	163	232	108	160	154
1976	106	169	228	1,218	176	151	43	54	39	165	237	109	169	151
1977	105	166	230	1,104	184	144	41	52	38	167	244	109	163	162
1978	110	189	234	1,429	193	166	39	51	36	167	250	108	170	157
1979	113	198	246	1,709	176	177	38	51	34	170	258	109	173	163
1980	114	202	294	1,702	171	187	37	50	33	174	266	111	182	155
1981	111	192	261	1,753	164	177	37	50	34	173	266	111	171	174
1982	109	184	198	1,693	155	183	36	45	33	171	261	109	184	179
1983	105	185	195	1,500	150	187	35	49	31	161	249	102	180	161
1984	105	180	224	1,795	155	167	35	45	31	164	236	107	160	183
1985	102	175	221	1,724	139	170	32	40	30	161	224	107	172	196
1986	98	171	255	1,707	130	171	30	40	28	155	208	104	166	198
1987	97	173	215	1,892	144	167	30	40	27	147	192	100	162	204
1988	96	172	198	1,615	144	165	31	47	28	144	182	99	156	193
1989	96	171	192	1,902	143	157	31	38	29	144	174	101	147	210
1990	97	178	197	1,853	142	171	30	38	28	142	169	100	154	217
1991	98	179	199	2,056	143	171	32	38	29	141	166	99	159	216
1992	96	178	203	2,053	142	172	30	36	28	140	161	99	159	234
1993	96	186	226	2,001	142	174	29	35	26	137	155	98	165	219
1994	97	190	221	2,105	146	176	29	35	26	136	151	98	157	247
1995	97	193	173	1,926	154	187	28	38	24	135	147	97	171	235
1996	96	183	181	2,176	148	164	30	38	27	135	143	98	165	247

Source

Data available in electronic form from the Cornell University Library Internet site, Agricultural Productivity in the U.S. (Table 11, Indexes of Farm Output, Input Use and Productivity, 1948–1996, downloaded June 2000). These indexes form the basis for the discussion in "Agricultural Productivity Continues Healthy Growth," *Agricultural Outlook*, AGO-251, U.S. Department of Agriculture, Economic Research Service, May 1998, pp. 30–3.

Documentation

The aggregate output and input indexes reported here, series Da1205–1230, represent Fisher indexes formed as a geometric average of corresponding Laspeyres and Pasche indexes. For these indexes, national output and input prices were used to weight corresponding national quantities. Particulars

regarding the treatment and sources of much of the data that underlie this version of the U.S. Department of Agriculture productivity series can be found in U.S. Department of Agriculture, Economic Research Service, "Major Statistical Series of the U.S. Department of Agriculture: Agricultural Production and Efficiency," *Agriculture Handbook 671*, volume 2, 1989.

The output index is based on disaggregated data for physical quantities and market prices of crops and livestock compiled by the Economic Research Service, Resource Economics Division. The quantity data exclude production used on the farm as an input but include the quantities of commodities sold off the farm (including unredeemed Commodity Credit Corporation loans) plus net additions to inventory and quantities consumed as part of final demand in farm households during the calendar year.

(continued)

TABLE Da1205–1231 Indexes of agricultural output, input, and total factor productivity: 1948–1996 *Continued*

Prices corresponding to each disaggregated output reflect the value of that output to the producer; that is, subsidies are added and indirect taxes are subtracted from market values. Prices received by farmers, as reported in *Agricultural Prices*, include an allowance for net Commodity Credit Corporation loans and purchases by the government valued at the average loan rate. However, direct payments under federal commodity programs are not reflected in the data. To prices for wool, mohair, and program crops are added government payments per unit of production; dairy assessments are subtracted from receipts for milk.

Series Da1205. Includes all livestock and livestock products, series Da1206, and all crops, series Da1210.

Series Da1206. Includes series Da1206–1209 in addition to wool, mohair, horses, mules, honey, beeswax, bees, goats, rabbits, aquaculture, and fur animals. These items are not included in the separate groups of livestock and livestock products shown.

Series Da1210. Includes series Da1211–1217 in addition to tobacco, floriculture and ornamentals, Christmas trees, forest products, mushrooms, legume and grass seeds, hops, mint, broomcorn, popcorn, hemp fiber and seed, and flax fiber, none of which are shown separately.

Series Da1218. Includes all intermediate, labor, and capital inputs, series Da1219–1230, in addition to purchased services such as contract labor services, custom machine services, machine and building maintenance and repairs, irrigation fees paid to public sellers of water, and miscellaneous farm production items.

Series Da1220–1221. Hedonic price series for fertilizers and pesticides were developed to capture quality differences in these input aggregates.

Series Da1223. Livestock includes broiler- and egg-type chicks and turkey poults and imports of livestock for purposes other than immediate slaughter.

Series Da1224–1226. Adjustments for changes in labor quality were made when calculating labor input series.

Series Da1227. The capital aggregate includes machinery (passenger autos, motor trucks, wheel-type farm tractors, and other equipment), land in farms (excluding set-aside land), and the on-farm stocks of livestock and grain.

Series Da1231. Total factor productivity is formed as a ratio of the output quantity index, series Da1205, in a particular year to the corresponding input quantity index, series Da1218.

TABLE Da1232–1243 Indexes of agricultural multifactor productivity, by region: 1949–1991

Contributed by Albert K. A. Acquaye, Julian M. Alston, and Philip G. Pardey

Year	United States Da1232 Index 1949 = 100	New England Da1233 Index 1949 = 100	Middle Atlantic Da1234 Index 1949 = 100	Corn Belt Da1235 Index 1949 = 100	Lake States Da1236 Index 1949 = 100	Northern Plains Da1237 Index 1949 = 100	Appalachian Da1238 Index 1949 = 100	Southeast Da1239 Index 1949 = 100	Delta States Da1240 Index 1949 = 100	Southern Plains Da1241 Index 1949 = 100	Mountain Da1242 Index 1949 = 100	Pacific Da1243 Index 1949 = 100
1949	100	100	100	100	100	100	100	100	100	100	100	100
1950	98	111	104	97	97	111	99	99	93	76	102	101
1951	101	113	108	96	100	107	111	118	102	78	105	106
1952	106	119	109	103	105	117	108	112	108	82	110	112
1953	107	135	115	102	106	106	108	125	118	86	116	114
1954	110	141	123	105	112	109	113	114	114	89	110	118
1955	112	136	119	106	113	106	114	134	132	87	113	117
1956	113	139	124	109	115	102	123	134	126	87	111	118
1957	112	136	118	106	116	115	109	126	115	91	117	119
1958	121	136	126	113	123	140	116	133	118	107	126	121
1959	122	138	123	116	122	124	120	140	140	107	122	123
1960	121	138	125	113	117	135	122	140	136	108	119	119
1961	123	146	129	115	122	123	126	152	147	108	118	119
1962	123	153	128	114	116	130	131	146	148	98	119	125
1963	127	158	129	120	122	130	135	156	163	98	122	127
1964	126	164	131	114	120	130	136	160	168	98	120	129
1965	128	165	137	116	118	132	130	164	169	106	123	129
1966	129	169	131	115	123	138	128	170	172	101	127	135
1967	136	171	142	123	127	144	138	185	182	103	132	136
1968	139	177	140	124	132	150	136	172	198	110	139	143
1969	142	183	148	124	131	157	146	183	193	109	143	149
1970	143	191	149	121	137	152	147	187	203	118	148	150
1971	155	201	154	140	146	174	152	210	214	112	155	156
1972	156	194	146	140	146	171	156	211	216	122	154	159
1973	163	197	153	141	154	180	162	221	225	136	156	172
1974	159	210	163	127	143	163	169	243	228	132	164	180
1975	170	204	164	143	149	168	179	261	252	145	171	186
1976	167	197	165	140	139	163	185	258	253	143	172	184
1977	176	194	166	148	167	183	181	242	276	159	164	181
1978	171	191	170	151	162	175	184	242	262	134	165	166
1979	182	199	176	166	168	183	184	257	290	148	163	183

TABLE Da1232–1243   Indexes of agricultural multifactor productivity, by region: 1949–1991   *Continued*

Year	United States	New England	Middle Atlantic	Corn Belt	Lake States	Northern Plains	Appalachian	Southeast	Delta States	Southern Plains	Mountain	Pacific
	Da1232	Da1233	Da1234	Da1235	Da1236	Da1237	Da1238	Da1239	Da1240	Da1241	Da1242	Da1243
	Index 1949 = 100	Index 1949 = 100	Index 1949 = 100	Index 1949 = 100	Index 1949 = 100	Index 1949 = 100	Index 1949 = 100	Index 1949 = 100	Index 1949 = 100	Index 1949 = 100	Index 1949 = 100	Index 1949 = 100
1980	182	194	181	160	176	173	187	257	256	143	178	201
1981	206	205	201	179	190	207	226	299	320	170	194	211
1982	209	222	209	179	195	209	231	310	337	170	191	211
1983	182	216	200	138	172	182	185	293	281	153	188	207
1984	206	224	214	169	193	211	225	317	328	161	190	222
1985	216	228	229	194	208	232	222	305	327	164	189	217
1986	209	224	226	186	203	224	207	292	306	157	193	212
1987	212	223	218	181	207	226	205	290	324	163	195	232
1988	197	225	215	148	161	201	214	308	340	167	190	230
1989	213	213	216	185	207	219	228	296	318	161	199	227
1990	220	207	221	189	208	247	239	306	329	177	209	221
1991	222	214	223	181	206	245	258	334	348	181	218	216

Sources

Data underlying these estimates are from A. K. A. Acquaye, J. M. Alston, and P. G. Pardey, "Post-War Productivity Patterns in U.S. Agriculture: Influences of Aggregation Procedures in a State-Level Analysis," *American Journal of Agricultural Economics* 85 (1) (2003): 59–80, and updated from B. Craig and P. G. Pardey, "Productivity Measurement in the Presence of Quality Change," *American Journal of Agricultural Economics* 78 (5) (1996): 1349–54. These regional and related state data can be downloaded from P. Pardey's home page at the Internet site of the Department of Applied Economics, University of Minnesota.

Documentation

The quantity indexes reported here represent Fisher Ideal approximations of a Divisia index, in which changes in the quantity variables used to construct a particular aggregate are weighted by the appropriate (and changing) relative output and input prices. State-specific price weights were used to construct the regional output and input quantity indexes that formed the multifactor productivity indexes reported here.

The output index includes fifty-five types of output, further differentiated in the state in which they were produced. The commodity categories are field crops including barley, corn, cotton, flax, oats, peanuts, rice, rye, sugar beets, sugarcane, sorghum, soybeans, tobacco, tomatoes for processing, and wheat; fruits and nuts including almonds, apples, apricots, avocados, cherries, cranberries, grapefruit, grapes, lemon, oranges, pears, peaches, pecans, strawberries, and walnuts; vegetables including beans, broccoli, carrots, cauliflower, celery, cucumbers, fresh tomatoes, lettuce, onions, peas, potatoes, and sweet corn (fresh, and for processing); greenhouse and nursery products; and livestock including broilers, cattle, eggs, hogs, honey, milk, sheep, turkeys, and wool. In addition, revenues from machines rented out for hire and returns from crop reserve program (CRP) acreages were included as part of output.

The input quantity aggregate includes fifty-eight types of inputs further differentiated in the state in which each was used. There are thirty-two distinct types of labor in agriculture, which factor in days worked off farm by farm operators who were grouped into various age-education classes. Hours worked by hired workers and family members were also included.

The land input is the service flow from three basic types: pasture or rangeland, non-irrigated crop land, and irrigated crop land. Capital inputs are included as service flows and consist of seven classes of physical capital (trucks, automobiles, tractors, combines, pickup balers, mower conditioners, and buildings) and five classes of biological capital (dairy cows, beef cows, ewes, chickens, and sows). Adjustments for changes in the quality of tractors and combines were made. Fertilizers are broken down into three distinct elements (nitrogen, phosphorus, and potash). Also included are implicit quantities of purchased seed, purchased feed, a preaggregated pesticides, herbicides, and fungicides category, fuels and oils, electricity, repairs and machine hire, plus a miscellaneous input category that preaggregates a list of disparate inputs such as fencing, irrigation fees, hand tools, veterinary services, and insurance costs, among others.

Regional groupings of states correspond to the U.S. Department of Agriculture farm production subregions except for the Northeast, which is split in two subregions. The regions are defined as follows: New England ("Northeast 1" in source) – Connecticut, Maine, Massachusetts, New Hampshire, Rhode Island, and Vermont; Middle Atlantic ("Northeast 2" in source) – Delaware, Maryland, New Jersey, New York, and Pennsylvania; Corn Belt – Illinois, Indiana, Iowa, Missouri, and Ohio; Lake States – Michigan, Minnesota, and Wisconsin; Northern Plains – Kansas, Nebraska, North Dakota, and South Dakota; Appalachian – Kentucky, North Carolina, Tennessee, Virginia, and West Virginia; Southeast – Alabama, Florida, Georgia, and South Carolina; Delta States – Arkansas, Louisiana, and Mississippi; Southern Plains – Oklahoma and Texas; Mountain – Arizona, Colorado, Idaho, Montana, New Mexico, Nevada, Utah, and Wyoming; and Pacific – California, Oregon, and Washington (excludes Alaska and Hawai'i).

TABLE Da1244–1252   Agricultural research and development appropriations – federal and state: 1889–1999

Contributed by Albert K. A. Acquaye, Julian M. Alston, and Philip G. Pardey

						Federal obligations for agricultural research		
	Appropriations to agricultural research and development							
		State agricultural experiment stations						
	Total federal and state	All sources	Federal sources	State sources	Miscellaneous, fees, and sales	U.S. Department of Agriculture	Total	Basic	Applied
	Da1244	Da1245	Da1246	Da1247	Da1248	Da1249	Da1250	Da1251	Da1252
Year	Thousand dollars	Thousand dollars	Thousand dollars	Thousand dollars	Thousand dollars	Thousand dollars	Thousand dollars	Thousand dollars	Thousand dollars
1889	1,119	716	585	75	56	403	—	—	—
1890	1,359	1,015	653	269	94	344	—	—	—
1891	—	943	678	191	74	—	—	—	—
1892	—	1,000	690	155	155	—	—	—	—
1893	—	967	705	178	84	—	—	—	—
1894	1,442	990	720	168	102	452	—	—	—
1895	1,512	1,041	720	209	113	471	—	—	—
1896	1,709	1,096	720	244	132	613	—	—	—
1897	1,677	1,092	720	262	110	585	—	—	—
1898	1,809	1,160	720	320	120	649	—	—	—
1899	1,839	1,110	720	231	159	728	—	—	—
1900	1,955	1,153	720	239	194	802	—	—	—
1901	2,184	1,275	720	366	189	909	—	—	—
1902	2,441	1,395	720	475	200	1,047	—	—	—
1903	2,965	1,455	720	486	249	1,510	—	—	—
1904	3,129	1,529	720	576	232	1,600	—	—	—
1905	3,510	1,456	720	522	214	2,054	—	—	—
1906	4,060	1,975	960	736	279	2,086	—	—	—
1907	3,678	2,257	1,056	795	406	1,421	—	—	—
1908	4,935	2,832	1,152	1,118	562	2,103	—	—	—
1909	5,956	3,031	1,248	1,225	558	2,925	—	—	—
1910	6,993	3,470	1,344	1,489	636	3,523	—	—	—
1911	6,226	3,513	1,440	1,441	632	2,712	—	—	—
1912	6,936	4,336	1,440	2,231	665	2,600	—	—	—
1913	7,275	4,368	1,440	1,979	949	2,906	—	—	—
1914	7,949	4,659	1,426	2,539	694	3,290	—	—	—
1915	9,116	4,858	1,440	2,340	1,077	4,259	—	—	—
1916	8,552	5,213	1,440	2,622	1,151	3,339	—	—	—
1917	10,446	5,107	1,440	2,267	1,399	5,340	—	—	—
1918	10,988	5,683	1,440	2,744	1,499	5,305	—	—	—
1919	12,489	6,370	1,440	2,716	2,214	6,119	—	—	—
1920	14,415	6,899	1,440	3,694	1,765	7,515	—	—	—
1921	13,778	6,918	1,440	3,787	1,691	6,860	—	—	—
1922	15,446	7,839	1,440	5,187	1,211	7,608	—	—	—
1923	16,516	8,518	1,440	5,539	1,539	7,998	—	—	—
1924	18,536	9,989	1,440	6,646	1,904	8,546	—	—	—
1925	19,195	9,378	1,440	5,904	2,034	9,818	—	—	—
1926	21,150	11,373	2,400	6,607	2,367	9,777	—	—	—
1927	22,088	11,895	2,880	6,459	2,556	10,193	—	—	—
1928	25,734	14,210	3,360	8,055	2,795	11,524	—	—	—
1929	30,482	15,059	3,840	8,191	3,028	15,423	—	—	—
1930	33,107	16,168	4,320	8,773	3,075	16,939	—	—	—
1931	34,239	16,264	4,320	9,167	2,777	17,976	—	—	—
1932	35,569	16,127	4,320	9,487	2,319	19,442	—	—	—
1933	31,573	14,105	4,320	7,727	2,058	17,468	—	—	—
1934	29,293	13,310	4,320	6,695	2,296	15,983	—	—	—
1935	27,675	13,703	4,320	6,608	2,774	13,972	—	—	—
1936	30,010	14,876	4,905	7,448	2,523	15,135	—	—	—
1937	31,040	15,972	5,490	7,671	2,810	15,068	—	—	—
1938	36,670	18,026	6,075	9,327	2,624	18,644	—	—	—
1939	43,804	18,688	6,367	9,597	2,723	25,116	—	—	—
1940	43,608	19,294	6,660	9,739	2,895	24,315	—	—	—
1941	40,081	20,228	6,660	10,306	3,263	19,852	—	—	—
1942	40,143	19,784	6,719	9,711	3,354	20,359	—	—	—
1943	40,718	21,582	6,719	10,479	4,384	19,136	—	—	—
1944	45,635	23,194	6,719	11,744	4,731	22,441	—	—	—

TABLE Da1244–1252   Agricultural research and development appropriations – federal and state: 1889–1999
Continued

	Appropriations to agricultural research and development					Federal obligations for agricultural research		
		State agricultural experiment stations						
	Total federal and state	All sources	Federal sources	State sources	Miscellaneous, fees, and sales	U.S. Department of Agriculture	Total	Basic	Applied
	Da1244	Da1245	Da1246	Da1247	Da1248	Da1249	Da1250	Da1251	Da1252
Year	Thousand dollars	Thousand dollars	Thousand dollars	Thousand dollars	Thousand dollars	Thousand dollars	Thousand dollars	Thousand dollars	Thousand dollars
1945	51,787	24,209	6,719	12,422	5,068	27,577	—	—	—
1946	58,826	28,545	6,914	16,042	5,589	30,281	—	—	—
1947	66,562	35,428	6,914	21,360	7,154	31,134	—	—	—
1948	76,135	44,349	9,261	26,670	8,418	31,786	—	—	—
1949	87,976	50,050	10,936	29,600	9,515	37,925	—	—	—
1950	96,426	58,478	12,745	36,142	9,591	37,948	—	—	—
1951	106,999	62,718	13,072	38,063	11,583	44,281	55,076	—	—
1952	125,509	69,551	12,707	44,147	12,697	55,959	55,291	6,796	—
1953	119,208	72,355	12,068	47,094	13,193	46,853	56,045	6,951	—
1954	128,944	80,289	13,012	54,435	12,842	48,655	59,459	7,791	—
1955	137,890	87,879	18,333	55,962	13,584	50,010	72,176	11,477	—
1956	156,403	100,165	23,315	62,245	14,606	56,238	83,038	15,159	67,879
1957	196,534	108,983	27,711	64,982	16,291	87,550	99,794	19,203	75,831
1958	205,038	124,594	28,487	78,060	18,048	80,444	110,242	23,865	81,488
1959	226,712	130,489	29,591	80,613	20,285	96,223	120,697	29,266	86,805
1960	259,414	141,056	29,565	90,260	21,230	118,359	125,759	33,606	87,159
1961	284,928	145,613	30,494	95,671	19,448	139,314	143,443	40,556	97,047
1962	292,680	157,264	33,269	104,162	19,834	135,416	157,167	49,666	100,755
1963	313,307	166,751	35,196	110,823	20,732	146,556	168,038	56,020	104,312
1964	336,470	186,169	38,493	125,164	22,513	150,300	189,034	67,989	113,805
1965	383,074	200,036	44,913	130,422	24,701	183,038	224,552	90,254	127,570
1966	411,763	226,108	49,922	147,074	29,113	185,654	234,896	93,902	133,907
1967	436,731	237,525	54,020	153,860	29,645	199,205	252,642	100,199	137,130
1968	461,911	263,718	56,059	176,972	30,686	198,193	253,540	99,657	139,817
1969	482,438	277,547	56,819	186,638	34,089	204,891	260,066	106,636	144,674
1970	539,566	301,112	58,887	207,794	34,430	238,454	281,157	115,709	156,216
1971	597,165	325,345	65,378	224,152	35,815	271,820	304,902	118,414	173,738
1972	656,279	354,813	85,166	230,093	39,554	301,466	349,573	137,311	199,858
1973	694,612	393,466	100,343	248,749	44,373	301,146	366,522	142,726	211,380
1974	741,081	439,652	108,334	277,653	53,665	301,429	378,706	145,611	219,453
1975	822,815	484,638	122,395	308,025	54,218	338,177	420,082	154,184	247,760
1976	933,308	525,236	151,314	299,386	74,536	408,072	462,449	171,371	270,853
1977	1,023,738	604,560	181,416	330,750	92,394	419,178	546,963	204,450	319,570
1978	1,128,090	661,152	202,286	363,233	95,633	466,938	621,282	242,704	351,780
1979	1,219,436	746,836	235,903	401,486	109,447	472,600	663,025	256,420	375,500
1980	1,361,007	832,007	255,173	443,570	133,264	529,000	687,586	275,650	381,785
1981	1,486,680	919,080	282,534	487,246	149,300	567,600	773,958	314,128	426,856
1982	1,624,277	1,034,577	334,304	532,454	167,819	589,700	797,274	330,755	435,708
1983	1,686,072	1,071,872	329,908	562,591	179,373	614,200	847,605	362,019	455,539
1984	1,782,694	1,139,494	342,251	606,866	190,377	643,200	866,171	392,649	442,238
1985	1,901,956	1,230,656	358,938	662,341	209,377	671,300	942,979	445,388	465,552
1986	2,000,533	1,332,533	385,429	724,576	222,528	668,000	928,528	432,857	463,549
1987	2,119,034	1,416,034	402,215	761,562	252,257	703,000	947,858	445,464	473,443
1988	2,253,870	1,508,270	439,410	806,093	262,767	745,600	1,016,627	480,588	504,618
1989	2,425,343	1,644,343	463,950	877,091	303,302	781,000	1,038,279	484,928	517,294
1990	2,604,773	1,766,073	500,857	927,149	338,067	838,700	1,108,380	519,190	542,096
1991	2,793,394	1,852,594	532,148	961,727	358,719	940,800	1,236,646	557,578	617,887
1992	2,909,867	1,914,867	582,056	956,293	376,518	995,000	1,327,112	595,153	665,843
1993	2,946,333	1,980,333	632,391	960,407	387,535	966,000	1,327,795	615,941	635,784
1994	3,080,741	2,085,741	683,123	987,453	415,165	995,000	1,399,883	606,328	716,172
1995	3,160,713	2,147,713	708,013	1,024,254	415,446	1,013,000	1,380,218	595,034	703,796
1996	3,137,163	2,169,163	698,461	1,025,192	445,510	968,000	1,300,326	549,980	670,024
1997	3,253,549	2,234,549	703,462	1,059,071	472,016	1,019,000	1,388,619	590,097	700,009
1998	—	—	—	—	—	1,086,000	1,441,937	598,033	741,318
1999	—	—	—	—	—	1,068,000	1,425,628	608,797	711,838

(continued)

TABLE Da1244–1252   Agricultural research and development appropriations – federal and state: 1889–1999
Continued

Sources

Series Da1244. Derived from series Da1245 and Da1249.

Series Da1245–1248. 1889, U.S. Department of Agriculture, Office of Experiment Stations (USDA OES), *Organization of the Agricultural Experiment Stations in the United States*, February 1889, Experiment Station Bulletin number 1, and U.S. Department of Agriculture, *Report of the Director of the Office of Experiment Stations, 1889*; 1890, U.S. Department of Agriculture, *Report of the Director of the Office of Experiment Stations, 1890*; 1891–1896, USDA OES, *Statistics of Land-Grant Colleges and Agricultural Experiment Stations*, annual issues; 1897–1900, USDA OES, *A Report of the Work and Expenditures of the Agricultural Experiment Stations*, annual issues; 1901–1912, U.S. Department of Agriculture, *Annual Report of the Office of Experiment Stations*, annual issues; 1913–1915, U.S. Department of Agriculture, *Report on Agricultural Experiment Stations and Cooperative Agricultural Extension Work in the United States*, annual issues; 1916–1924, USDA OES, *Work and Expenditure of the Agricultural Experiment Stations*, annual issues; 1925–1959, U.S. Department of Agriculture, Agricultural Research Service, *Report of the State Agricultural Experiment Stations*, annual issues; 1960–1975, U.S. Department of Agriculture, Cooperative State Research Service, *Funds for Research at State Agricultural Experiment Stations and Other Cooperating Institutions*, annual issues; 1976–1997, U.S. Department of Agriculture, Cooperative State Research Service, *Inventory of Agricultural Research: Current Research Information System*, annual issues.

Series Da1249. 1889–1977, compiled from appropriations data reported for each agency within the U.S. Department of Agriculture from the U.S. Treasury Department, *Combined Statement of Receipts and Expenditures*, annually, 1889–1977. Significant efforts were made to exclude regulatory and other nonresearch functions from the series; 1978–1999, unpublished U.S. Department of Agriculture annual budgetary tables - Table 9, fiscal year 1986 for years 1978–1981; Table 9, fiscal year 1991 for years 1982–1990, and Table 8, fiscal year 1999 for years 1991–1999.

Series Da1250–1252. National Science Foundation Internet site, Federal Funds Survey, Detailed Historical Tables, Fiscal Years 1951–99, Table A, Federal Obligations for Research and Development, by Character of Work, Research and Development Plant, and Major Agency: Fiscal Years 1951–1999, downloaded on July 2000.

Documentation

Series Da1244. Equals the sum of series Da1245 and Da1249.

Series Da1245–1248. Data represent appropriations to and funds obligated by the agricultural experiment stations and cooperating institutions located in the forty-eight contiguous states (excludes data for Alaska and Hawai'i).

Series Da1249. This series approximates intramural research by the U.S. Department of Agriculture and consists of total appropriations to the Agricultural Research Service, the Economic Research Service, the Forest Service, and the Agricultural Cooperative Research Service less appropriations to contracts, grants, and cooperative agreements with State Agricultural Experiment Stations made by the U.S. Department of Agriculture agencies.

Series Da1250–1252. These series report federal funds obligated to research in the agricultural, forestry, fisheries, and related sciences undertaken by the U.S. Department of Agriculture, including intramural U.S. Department of Agriculture research and research undertaken elsewhere with funds disbursed from or managed by agencies within the U.S. Department of Agriculture

Series Da1250. Includes series Da1251–1252, as well as funds obligated to research development activities not classified as either basic or applied research.

TABLE Da1253–1259   Private-sector spending on agricultural research and development: 1960–1992

Contributed by Albert K. A. Acquaye, Julian M. Alston, and Philip G. Pardey

		Input oriented					Food and kindred products
	Total	Total	Plant breeding	Agricultural chemicals	Farm machinery	Animal health	
	Da1253	Da1254	Da1255	Da1256	Da1257	Da1258	Da1259
Years	Million dollars	Million dollars	Million dollars	Million dollars	Million dollars	Million dollars	Million dollars
1960	206	114	6	27	75	6	92
1961	212	120	6	38	65	11	92
1962	230	132	6	42	70	14	98
1963	245	143	7	45	76	15	102
1964	273	155	8	48	79	20	118
1965	323	192	9	64	96	23	131
1966	346	216	11	77	100	28	130
1967	355	221	12	72	102	35	134
1968	392	227	17	78	96	36	165
1969	421	239	22	85	99	34	182
1970	464	258	26	98	89	45	206
1971	487	276	29	109	90	48	211
1972	507	280	32	104	93	52	227
1973	576	333	39	113	120	62	243
1974	669	386	45	136	131	74	283
1975	709	436	50	169	138	79	273
1976	818	510	55	200	168	87	308
1977	954	606	58	243	221	84	348
1978	1,079	694	69	290	249	86	385
1979	1,204	784	81	312	295	96	420
1980	1,453	965	97	395	363	111	488
1981	1,468	976	105	469	278	125	492
1982	1,652	1,055	118	527	281	129	596
1983	1,794	1,158	138	584	290	147	636
1984	2,046	1,243	154	624	311	154	803
1985	2,167	1,326	179	683	304	159	842
1986	2,321	1,381	204	691	307	179	940
1987	2,278	1,388	222	682	292	191	891
1988	2,583	1,699	245	938	295	221	884
1989	2,772	1,825	283	979	320	243	947
1990	3,012	2,046	314	1,127	360	245	965
1991	3,173	2,227	342	1,227	382	276	946
1992	3,416	2,379	400	1,279	394	306	1,038

Source

U.S. Department of Agriculture, Economic Research Service, *AREI Updates: Agricultural Research, 1995*, number 5 revised, Table 2.

Documentation

Numbers may not sum owing to rounding.

Series Da1253. The estimate of total investment in agricultural research by the private sector is conservative, and may have been as much as $200–300 million more in 1992, owing to lack of data on research investment in animal breeding, biotechnology, and other areas.

TABLE Da1260-1265   Funds for cooperative extension, by source: 1915-1999

Contributed by Albert K. A. Acquaye, Julian M. Alston, and Philip G. Pardey

	Total	State sources				Federal appropriation
		Total	State government appropriation	County appropriation	Nontax	
	Da1260	Da1261	Da1262	Da1263	Da1264	Da1265
Year	Thousand dollars	Thousand dollars	Thousand dollars	Thousand dollars	Thousand dollars	Thousand dollars
1915	3,597	2,111	1,044	780	287	1,486
1916	4,864	2,721	1,471	973	277	2,143
1917	6,150	3,431	1,928	1,258	245	2,719
1918	11,303	4,827	2,469	1,864	494	6,476
1919	14,662	5,623	2,961	2,291	371	9,039
1920	14,658	8,767	5,229	2,866	627	5,891
1921	16,792	10,358	6,044	3,294	1,021	6,434
1922	17,182	10,455	6,528	2,973	954	6,727
1923	18,485	11,384	7,054	3,420	910	7,101
1924	18,879	11,955	7,040	4,259	659	6,924
1925	19,250	12,388	7,203	3,858	1,326	6,862
1926	19,417	12,526	7,327	4,055	1,144	6,891
1927	19,748	12,832	7,423	4,363	1,046	6,916
1928	20,398	13,469	7,767	4,673	1,029	6,929
1929	22,513	13,940	6,406	6,282	1,252	8,573
1930	23,804	15,006	6,865	7,036	1,105	8,798
1931	25,581	15,876	7,243	7,523	1,110	9,705
1932	25,331	15,683	7,189	7,365	1,129	9,716
1933	23,405	13,752	6,390	6,394	967	9,653
1934	19,896	10,520	4,889	4,844	787	9,376
1935	20,042	11,042	5,045	5,152	844	9,000
1936	28,780	11,844	5,465	5,569	811	16,936
1937	29,764	12,508	5,795	5,888	825	17,256
1938	31,027	13,486	6,467	6,241	778	17,541
1939	32,116	14,148	6,582	6,676	890	17,968
1940	32,764	14,179	6,427	6,665	1,087	18,585
1941	33,194	14,603	6,707	6,807	1,089	18,591
1942	34,111	15,155	7,141	6,960	1,054	18,956
1943	34,865	15,908	7,312	7,442	1,154	18,957
1944	36,740	17,743	8,466	8,168	1,110	18,997
1945	37,836	18,839	9,158	8,480	1,201	18,997
1946	44,548	21,141	10,738	9,059	1,345	23,407
1947	52,993	25,670	12,855	11,076	1,739	27,323
1948	58,163	31,006	17,174	12,268	1,564	27,457
1949	65,733	35,202	18,867	14,214	2,121	30,531
1950	73,394	41,234	23,464	15,528	2,242	32,160
1951	75,983	43,809	24,942	16,534	2,333	32,174
1952	79,999	47,908	27,693	17,859	2,356	32,091
1953	84,593	52,443	30,544	19,644	2,255	32,150
1954	89,531	57,368	33,875	21,166	2,327	32,163
1955	100,671	60,942	35,998	22,403	2,541	39,675
1956	109,912	64,437	37,840	24,282	2,315	45,475
1957	119,195	69,330	40,516	26,502	2,312	49,865
1958	128,060	77,345	46,993	28,358	1,994	50,715
1959	134,836	81,121	49,517	30,102	1,502	53,715
1960	140,071	86,356	53,583	31,231	1,542	53,715
1961	150,098	93,383	57,895	32,782	2,706	56,715
1962	159,227	99,637	62,226	34,530	2,881	59,590
1963	168,621	105,191	65,704	36,402	3,085	63,430
1964	177,920	110,812	69,907	37,804	3,101	67,108
1965	188,884	117,200	74,341	39,776	3,083	71,684
1966	201,223	126,039	80,345	41,941	3,753	75,184
1967	213,669	135,413	87,461	44,096	3,856	78,256
1968	225,477	147,595	96,752	46,600	4,243	77,882
1969	241,952	161,190	106,326	50,288	4,576	80,762
1970	290,688	177,969	116,115	53,485	5,369	112,719
1971	331,897	193,706	129,562	58,613	5,531	138,191
1972	354,359	205,839	136,090	63,582	6,167	148,520
1973	385,091	221,987	148,218	66,387	7,382	163,104
1974	407,452	241,847	161,897	71,744	8,206	165,605

TABLE Da1260–1265   Funds for cooperative extension, by source: 1915–1999
Continued

Year	Total	State sources				Federal appropriation
		Total	State government appropriation	County appropriation	Nontax	
	Da1260	Da1261	Da1262	Da1263	Da1264	Da1265
	Thousand dollars	Thousand dollars	Thousand dollars	Thousand dollars	Thousand dollars	Thousand dollars
1975	448,334	269,513	181,848	79,126	8,539	178,821
1976	498,452	307,498	206,854	91,805	8,839	190,954
1977	525,362	326,130	220,906	93,612	11,612	199,232
1978	586,744	371,444	245,638	111,019	14,787	215,300
1979	624,923	403,847	270,047	119,193	14,607	221,076
1980	682,698	451,878	304,883	130,630	16,356	230,820
1981	746,515	497,580	335,723	142,390	19,467	248,935
1982	853,908	550,988	368,846	157,671	24,471	302,920
1983	897,303	581,106	389,423	164,706	26,977	316,197
1984	937,823	615,604	415,521	171,335	28,748	322,219
1985	996,629	655,690	452,866	182,253	30,571	330,939
1986	1,039,029	722,569	489,424	200,912	32,233	316,460
1987	1,052,026	729,717	500,601	194,693	34,423	322,309
1988	1,145,159	801,940	552,933	210,688	38,319	343,219
1989	1,207,757	860,519	587,801	299,070	43,648	347,238
1990	1,264,046	909,507	620,471	235,742	53,294	354,557
1991	1,365,437	983,170	662,866	261,074	59,230	382,267
1992	1,385,893	984,696	651,689	267,290	65,717	401,197
1993	1,393,110	982,789	642,517	269,190	71,083	410,321
1994	1,429,156	1,009,756	659,921	274,272	75,563	419,400
1995	1,476,456	1,055,124	683,075	286,063	85,985	421,332
1996	1,480,740	1,070,748	695,667	287,457	87,624	409,992
1997	1,529,687	1,120,909	719,760	307,571	93,578	408,778
1998	1,533,291	1,127,060	732,001	303,838	91,221	406,231
1999	1,631,466	1,210,791	787,189	318,530	105,072	420,676

Sources

1915-1990, unpublished data from F. Woods (Cooperative State Research, Education, and Extension Service) as reported in W. E. Huffman and R. E. Evenson, *Science for Agriculture: A Long-Term Perspective* (Iowa State University Press, 1993), Table A4.3; 1991–1992, unpublished data from F. Woods (Cooperative State Research, Education, and Extension Service) as reported in J. M. Alston and P. G. Pardey, *Making Science Pay: The Economics of Agricultural R&D Policy* (AEI Press, 1996), Table 2-A6; 1993–1999, unpublished data from D. Prindle (Cooperative State Research, Education, and Extension Service).

Documentation

Includes data for the specified places beginning on the date indicated: Hawai'i, 1929; Puerto Rico, 1930; Alaska, 1931; Guam and Virgin Islands, 1974;

American Samoa and Micronesia, 1981; and Northern Mariana, 1987.

Cooperative extension entails cooperation between federal, state, and county agencies in the provision of agricultural extension services.

INCOME AND FINANCES

Bruce L. Gardner

TABLE Da1266–1276   Farm output, gross product, net product, and national income: 1929–1999

Contributed by Bruce L. Gardner

	Farm output				Less: intermediate goods and services purchased	Equals: gross farm product	Less: consumption of fixed capital	Equals: net farm product	Less: indirect business tax and nontax liability	Plus: government subsidies to operators	Equals: farm national income
	Total	Cash receipts from farm marketings and CCC loan forfeitures	Other farm output	Change in farm inventories							
	Da1266	Da1267	Da1268	Da1269	Da1270	Da1271	Da1272	Da1273	Da1274	Da1275	Da1276
Year	Million dollars	Million dollars	Million dollars	Million dollars	Million dollars	Million dollars	Million dollars	Million dollars	Million dollars	Million dollars	Million dollars
1929	13,816	11,312	2,626	−122	4,160	9,656	788	8,868	538	0	8,330
1930	11,203	9,055	2,417	−269	3,564	7,639	785	6,854	535	0	6,319
1931	8,881	6,381	2,040	460	2,603	6,278	720	5,558	485	0	5,073
1932	6,515	4,748	1,657	110	2,042	4,473	634	3,839	418	0	3,421
1933	6,782	5,237	1,644	−99	2,186	4,596	589	4,007	362	113	3,758
1934	7,192	6,202	1,765	−775	2,524	4,668	597	4,071	349	397	4,119
1935	9,821	7,090	2,003	728	2,850	6,971	577	6,394	354	498	6,538
1936	9,672	8,466	2,087	−881	3,274	6,398	603	5,795	364	242	5,673
1937	11,847	8,756	2,167	924	3,611	8,236	669	7,567	378	283	7,472
1938	9,835	7,409	1,980	446	3,290	6,545	718	5,827	375	377	5,829
1939	9,917	8,088	1,950	−121	3,624	6,293	706	5,587	382	661	5,866
1940	10,617	8,172	1,954	491	4,170	6,447	725	5,722	382	626	5,966
1941	13,727	11,144	2,196	387	4,803	8,924	811	8,113	397	472	8,188
1942	19,243	15,396	2,579	1,268	6,211	13,032	921	12,111	403	563	12,271
1943	22,699	19,793	3,132	−226	7,393	15,306	939	14,367	418	563	14,512
1944	23,262	20,446	3,136	−320	7,933	15,329	992	14,337	438	687	14,586
1945	24,632	22,076	3,408	−852	8,652	15,980	1,041	14,939	499	659	15,099
1946	28,796	25,025	3,965	−194	9,950	18,846	1,196	17,650	542	683	17,791
1947	32,021	29,600	4,212	−1,791	11,848	20,173	1,463	18,710	645	277	18,342
1948	36,119	29,218	4,238	2,663	12,859	23,260	1,816	21,444	714	227	20,957
1949	30,443	27,408	3,638	−603	11,767	18,676	2,107	16,569	773	161	15,957
1950	32,684	29,222	3,547	−85	12,824	19,860	2,357	17,503	810	249	16,942
1951	38,017	33,066	3,953	998	15,103	22,914	2,706	20,208	864	250	19,594
1952	37,477	32,070	4,026	1,381	15,335	22,142	2,899	19,243	906	240	18,577
1953	33,981	29,401	3,856	724	13,924	20,057	3,001	17,056	925	186	16,317
1954	33,877	30,076	3,601	200	14,346	19,531	3,058	16,473	942	224	15,755
1955	33,352	30,374	3,542	−564	14,717	18,635	3,131	15,504	975	200	14,729
1956	33,328	30,832	3,460	−964	14,897	18,431	3,289	15,142	1,013	486	14,615
1957	33,600	30,068	3,440	91	15,299	18,301	3,394	14,907	1,069	891	14,729
1958	37,600	32,042	3,588	1,970	17,139	20,461	3,544	16,917	1,100	988	16,805
1959	37,075	35,090	3,547	−1,562	18,174	18,901	3,626	15,275	1,191	615	14,699
1960	37,814	33,786	3,476	553	17,999	19,815	3,691	16,124	1,268	632	15,488
1961	38,934	34,501	3,554	880	18,873	20,061	3,725	16,336	1,324	1,324	16,336
1962	40,369	36,278	3,508	583	20,186	20,183	3,798	16,385	1,354	1,540	16,571
1963	41,570	37,511	3,566	492	21,193	20,377	3,899	16,478	1,383	1,488	16,583
1964	40,102	37,668	3,614	−1,178	20,839	19,263	4,024	15,239	1,426	1,898	15,711
1965	44,068	39,567	3,679	822	22,182	21,886	4,227	17,659	1,459	2,143	18,343
1966	47,229	43,888	3,839	−500	24,362	22,867	4,511	18,356	1,553	2,871	19,674
1967	47,441	42,592	3,967	885	25,209	22,232	4,819	17,413	1,640	2,703	18,476
1968	48,357	42,906	4,078	1,372	25,665	22,692	5,141	17,551	1,757	3,030	18,824
1969	52,543	48,190	4,336	18	27,387	25,156	5,504	19,652	1,861	3,319	21,110
1970	55,051	51,302	4,586	−838	28,851	26,200	5,848	20,352	1,973	3,266	21,645
1971	58,912	52,423	4,829	1,660	30,848	28,064	6,290	21,774	2,045	2,782	22,511
1972	67,087	61,581	5,217	289	34,461	32,626	6,738	25,888	2,121	3,524	27,291
1973	95,076	87,909	5,639	1,526	45,322	49,754	7,444	42,310	2,175	2,335	42,470
1974	95,929	92,775	5,936	−2,781	48,575	47,354	8,618	38,736	2,351	478	36,863
1975	98,356	88,898	6,096	3,359	49,573	48,783	10,232	38,551	2,462	732	36,821
1976	100,201	94,697	6,340	−839	53,775	46,426	11,348	35,078	2,709	670	33,039
1977	103,806	92,677	6,597	4,533	56,601	47,205	12,607	34,598	2,829	1,657	33,426
1978	122,207	113,313	7,522	1,371	67,462	54,745	14,066	40,679	2,792	2,483	40,370
1979	145,305	133,417	8,318	3,568	80,855	64,450	16,145	48,305	3,013	1,015	46,307

TABLE Da1266–1276   Farm output, gross product, net product, and national income: 1929–1999 *Continued*

	Farm output				Less: intermediate goods and services purchased	Equals: gross farm product	Less: consumption of fixed capital	Equals: net farm product	Less: indirect business tax and nontax liability	Plus: government subsidies to operators	Equals: farm national income
	Total	Cash receipts from farm marketings and CCC loan forfeitures	Other farm output	Change in farm inventories							
	Da1266	Da1267	Da1268	Da1269	Da1270	Da1271	Da1272	Da1273	Da1274	Da1275	Da1276
Year	Million dollars	Million dollars	Million dollars	Million dollars	Million dollars	Million dollars	Million dollars	Million dollars	Million dollars	Million dollars	Million dollars
1980	142,872	140,266	8,717	−6,114	86,766	56,106	18,622	37,484	2,983	1,006	35,507
1981	157,846	139,607	9,478	8,760	87,950	69,896	20,424	49,472	3,246	1,488	47,714
1982	152,017	135,278	10,985	5,755	86,874	65,143	21,595	43,548	2,966	2,153	42,735
1983	135,078	140,186	10,248	−15,355	85,926	49,152	21,458	27,694	3,220	7,515	31,989
1984	159,957	144,605	9,623	5,728	91,425	68,532	21,378	47,154	3,149	7,043	51,048
1985	152,653	136,348	10,550	5,754	85,553	67,100	20,978	46,122	3,302	6,294	49,114
1986	144,035	135,294	10,193	−1,450	81,077	62,958	20,799	42,159	3,310	9,546	48,395
1987	151,968	147,777	10,609	−6,418	86,893	65,075	20,570	44,506	3,622	13,512	54,395
1988	158,502	159,608	10,772	−11,877	94,701	63,801	20,728	43,073	3,709	11,744	51,108
1989	177,232	166,715	10,531	−14	101,002	76,230	21,395	54,836	3,916	9,309	60,229
1990	185,266	172,132	10,754	2,380	105,691	79,575	22,065	57,510	4,276	7,548	60,782
1991	180,401	170,477	11,031	−1,107	107,201	73,200	22,585	50,615	4,352	6,768	53,031
1992	187,903	172,276	10,650	4,977	107,434	80,469	23,379	57,090	4,554	7,685	60,222
1993	187,441	182,042	11,288	−5,889	113,875	73,567	23,473	50,093	4,426	11,278	56,945
1994	203,332	181,043	11,487	10,802	119,765	83,567	23,722	59,845	4,666	6,605	61,784
1995	197,858	194,165	12,871	−9,178	124,671	73,187	24,619	48,567	4,962	6,106	49,711
1996	222,597	201,227	13,520	7,850	130,405	92,192	25,388	66,804	4,950	6,199	68,052
1997	226,317	208,607	14,788	2,922	138,054	88,262	26,313	61,949	5,186	6,330	63,094
1998	214,645	198,214	15,812	619	133,884	80,761	27,397	53,364	5,191	10,292	58,465
1999	208,384	190,714	17,917	−246	134,173	74,211	29,225	44,986	5,629	17,591	56,947

Source

U.S. Department of Commerce, Bureau of Economic Analysis, unpublished data.

Documentation

Series Da1268. Consists of farm housing, farm products consumed on farms, and other farm income.

Series Da1269. Represents change in quantities of commodities held by farms, including quantities under Commodity Credit Corporation loan, but not including changes in prices of commodities held.

Series Da1271. Equals series Da1266 minus series Da1270.

Series Da1273. Equals series Da1271 minus series Da1272.

Series Da1276. Equals series Da1273, minus series Da1274, plus series Da1275.

TABLE Da1277–1287   Farm gross output and product: 1800–1900

Contributed by Bruce L. Gardner

	Total gross output	Sales and home consumption of farm products			Livestock inventory changes	Gross rental value of farm dwellings	Intermediate products consumed	Farm gross product including improvements and home manufactures	Farm gross product	Improvements to farms	Value of home manufactures
		Total	Livestock	Crops							
	Da1277	Da1278	Da1279	Da1280	Da1281	Da1282	Da1283	Da1284	Da1285	Da1286	Da1287
Year	Million dollars	Million dollars	Million dollars	Million dollars	Million dollars	Million dollars	Million dollars	Million dollars	Million dollars	Million dollars	Million dollars
1800	236	220	127	93	6	10	6	255	230	7	18
1810	336	311	186	125	9	16	12	363	324	9	30
1820	338	308	178	130	10	20	15	364	323	12	29
1830	466	427	251	176	15	24	21	491	445	17	29
1840	757	699	431	268	14	44	37	769	720	22	27
1850	904	837	414	423	10	57	53	914	851	34	29
1860	1,579	1,469	700	769	21	89	95	1,556	1,484	47	25
1870	2,774	2,553	1,393	1,160	52	169	232	2,631	2,542	67	22
1880	3,263	3,021	1,498	1,523	39	203	296	3,045	2,967	68	10
1890	3,397	3,106	1,515	1,591	44	247	362	3,107	3,035	67	5
1900	4,298	3,912	2,047	1,865	79	307	499	3,857	3,799	55	3

Source

M. W. Towne and W. E. Rasmussen, "Farm Gross Product and Gross Investment during the Nineteenth Century," in *Studies in Income and Wealth*, volume 24 (National Bureau of Economic Research, 1960).

Documentation

Series Da1277. Total gross output is the sum of sales and consumption of farm products (series Da1278), livestock inventory changes (series Da1281), and gross rent from farm dwellings (Series Da1282).

Series Da1283. Intermediate products are goods and services purchased for production purposes from the nonfarm sector.

Series Da1285. Farm gross product is total farm gross output (series Da1277) less intermediate products consumed (series Da1283). It represents the share of gross national product originating in agricultural activities on farms.

TABLE Da1288–1295   Farm income and expenses: 1910–1999

Contributed by Bruce L. Gardner

Year	Cash marketing receipts Da1288 Million dollars	Direct government payments Da1289 Million dollars	Value of farm goods consumed Da1290 Million dollars	Gross rental value of farm housing Da1291 Million dollars	Other farm-related income Da1292 Million dollars	Value of change in commodity inventories Da1293 Million dollars	Production expenses Da1294 Million dollars	Net farm income Da1295 Million dollars
1910	5,780	—	1,270	445	—	212	2,771	4,176
1911	5,584	—	1,165	464	—	−260	2,795	3,370
1912	6,008	—	1,204	498	—	579	2,999	4,456
1913	6,238	—	1,222	518	—	−266	3,121	3,739
1914	6,036	—	1,228	529	—	417	3,168	4,182
1915	6,392	—	1,192	563	—	327	3,246	4,307
1916	7,746	—	1,384	614	—	−338	3,807	4,571
1917	10,736	—	2,003	671	—	986	4,854	8,305
1918	13,467	—	2,341	739	—	−153	6,033	8,888
1919	14,538	—	2,556	824	—	−509	6,648	9,079
1920	12,600	—	2,509	835	—	688	6,965	7,794
1921	8,058	—	1,746	769	—	−565	5,070	3,369
1922	8,575	—	1,717	767	—	−102	5,147	4,342
1923	9,545	—	1,772	850	—	−45	5,504	5,068
1924	10,220	—	1,706	854	—	−483	5,882	4,855
1925	10,996	—	1,827	868	—	365	5,854	6,734
1926	10,564	—	1,875	869	—	7	5,853	5,938
1927	10,756	—	1,725	878	—	−175	5,927	5,700
1928	11,072	—	1,724	883	—	140	6,211	5,983
1929	11,303	—	1,713	913	—	−122	6,079	6,152
1930	9,055	—	1,552	863	—	−269	5,408	4,257
1931	6,382	—	1,265	775	—	460	4,184	3,344
1932	4,750	—	993	664	—	110	3,351	2,033
1933	5,333	131	1,030	614	—	−194	3,426	2,556
1934	6,357	446	1,125	640	—	−930	3,663	2,923
1935	7,086	573	1,320	683	—	698	4,001	5,277
1936	8,372	278	1,394	693	—	−806	4,452	4,310
1937	8,860	336	1,434	733	—	816	4,886	6,003
1938	7,686	446	1,235	745	—	132	4,605	4,361
1939	7,879	763	1,209	741	—	95	4,991	4,417
1940	8,343	723	1,210	744	—	281	5,566	4,481
1941	11,157	544	1,429	767	—	420	6,388	6,489
1942	15,316	650	1,758	821	—	1,099	8,124	9,854
1943	19,340	645	2,253	879	—	−53	9,603	11,735
1944	19,790	776	2,181	955	—	−410	10,267	11,704
1945	21,663	742	2,356	1,052	—	−439	11,074	12,313
1946	24,802	772	2,662	1,303	—	29	12,497	15,067
1947	29,620	314	2,765	1,447	—	−1,760	14,605	15,353
1948	30,227	257	2,733	1,505	—	1,732	15,904	17,664
1949	27,805	185	2,230	1,408	—	−866	14,861	12,780
1950	28,461	283	2,063	1,464	20	812	16,038	13,648
1951	32,858	286	2,304	1,608	42	1,184	18,396	15,933
1952	32,528	275	2,220	1,736	70	922	18,625	14,961
1953	31,001	213	2,007	1,765	84	−623	17,187	12,980
1954	29,832	257	1,789	1,711	101	491	17,414	12,373
1955	29,490	229	1,678	1,741	123	215	17,666	11,305
1956	30,402	554	1,585	1,734	141	−456	18,185	11,254
1957	29,714	1,016	1,484	1,787	169	618	18,972	11,085
1958	33,456	1,089	1,505	1,860	222	825	20,944	13,168
1959	33,647	682	1,289	2,031	227	14	22,040	10,713
1960	34,012	702	1,135	2,098	243	397	22,394	11,212
1961	35,163	1,493	1,109	2,202	242	336	23,489	11,957
1962	36,469	1,747	993	2,258	257	620	25,046	12,064
1963	37,477	1,696	921	2,360	285	629	26,187	11,770
1964	37,326	2,181	835	2,443	336	−817	26,200	10,492
1965	39,365	2,463	811	2,481	387	1,042	27,864	12,899
1966	43,435	3,277	824	2,599	416	−83	30,398	13,960
1967	42,817	3,079	736	2,747	484	657	31,665	12,339
1968	44,183	3,462	719	2,838	520	124	32,609	12,322
1969	48,179	3,794	731	3,046	559	99	34,763	14,293

(continued)

TABLE Da1288–1295   Farm income and expenses: 1910–1999   *Continued*

Year	Cash marketing receipts Da1288 Million dollars	Direct government payments Da1289 Million dollars	Value of farm goods consumed Da1290 Million dollars	Gross rental value of farm housing Da1291 Million dollars	Other farm-related income Da1292 Million dollars	Value of change in commodity inventories Da1293 Million dollars	Production expenses Da1294 Million dollars	Net farm income Da1295 Million dollars
1970	50,509	3,717	776	3,268	542	6	36,752	14,366
1971	52,748	3,145	744	3,475	610	1,397	38,828	15,012
1972	61,106	3,961	889	3,712	615	861	42,883	19,455
1973	86,886	2,607	1,115	4,147	749	3,406	54,682	34,356
1974	92,391	530	1,190	4,942	805	−1,611	59,343	27,267
1975	88,902	807	1,128	5,355	998	3,399	61,563	25,547
1976	95,355	734	1,182	6,115	1,079	−1,548	67,677	20,175
1977	96,235	1,819	1,160	7,250	1,222	1,080	71,884	19,881
1978	112,360	3,030	1,214	8,057	1,893	1,892	84,615	25,198
1979	131,529	1,375	1,346	9,256	2,238	4,975	102,524	27,415
1980	139,736	1,286	1,234	11,045	2,273	−6,294	110,093	16,141
1981	141,616	1,932	1,214	12,597	2,475	6,488	114,466	26,879
1982	142,563	3,492	1,129	13,121	5,225	−1,382	114,430	23,842
1983	136,770	9,295	1,049	12,593	5,057	−10,909	114,147	14,247
1984	142,784	8,430	1,017	4,881	4,901	5,966	120,085	25,960
1985	144,138	7,704	926	4,689	6,035	−2,269	112,154	28,648
1986	135,385	11,813	895	4,567	5,689	−2,201	106,387	30,926
1987	141,797	16,747	743	5,041	6,412	−2,319	112,896	37,427
1988	151,243	14,480	732	7,695	7,858	−4,095	121,045	38,006
1989	160,810	10,887	672	7,182	8,596	3,788	127,494	45,274
1990	169,526	9,298	688	7,181	8,110	3,258	134,240	44,620
1991	167,864	8,214	642	7,156	8,281	−207	134,116	38,530
1992	171,266	9,169	620	7,211	8,022	4,156	133,535	47,669
1993	177,915	13,402	598	8,071	8,958	−4,198	141,188	44,333
1994	181,138	7,879	550	9,025	9,037	8,283	147,354	48,793
1995	187,962	7,253	503	9,410	10,540	−5,018	153,213	36,893
1996	199,142	7,340	480	9,852	10,927	7,956	159,761	54,914
1997	207,596	7,495	528	10,092	12,035	696	168,618	48,601
1998	196,575	12,209	494	10,815	13,862	−738	167,248	44,623
1999	188,610	20,594	508	10,869	15,839	−899	170,426	43,398

Source

U.S. Department of Agriculture, Economic Research Service Internet site.

Documentation

Series Da1288. Includes net Commodity Credit Corporation loans and excludes forest product sales from farms beginning 1978.

Series Da1289. Includes cash payments and payment-in-kind entitlements.

Series Da1292. Includes machine hire and custom work performed, and, starting in 1978, forest product sales.

Series Da1293. Includes changes in quantities of commodities held, but unlike series Da1269 excludes quantities held under Commodity Credit Corporation loans.

Series Da1295. Net farm income is not equal to receipts minus cash expenses because cash expenses omit capital depreciation.

TABLE Da1296–1311   Cash receipts from farm marketings, by crop and livestock: 1910–1999

Contributed by Bruce L. Gardner

	Crops								Livestock							
	Cotton (lint and seed)	Tobacco	Food grains	Oil crops	Feed crops	Vegetables	Fruits and tree nuts	Other crops and residual	Hogs	Cattle and calves	Sheep and lambs	Wool	Dairy products	Eggs	Chickens	Other livestock
	Da1296	Da1297	Da1298	Da1299	Da1300	Da1301 [1]	Da1302 [1]	Da1303	Da1304	Da1305	Da1306	Da1307	Da1308	Da1309	Da1310	Da1311
Year	Million dollars	Million dollars	Million dollars	Million dollars	Million dollars	Million dollars	Million dollars	Million dollars	Million dollars	Million dollars	Million dollars	Million dollars	Million dollars	Million dollars	Million dollars	Million dollars
1910	880	102	532	38	601	271	243	262	670	851	105	66	597	330	127	105
1911	855	96	482	43	559	306	283	281	617	784	99	48	577	304	123	127
1912	852	108	532	49	621	363	295	275	647	885	109	48	630	338	120	136
1913	968	135	537	37	567	294	264	275	741	999	115	44	669	321	132	140
1914	602	99	716	31	555	318	300	278	713	985	116	42	667	336	138	140
1915	830	93	822	32	618	286	297	285	691	966	111	53	686	341	134	147
1916	1,148	139	912	48	715	412	330	331	949	1,132	127	64	764	375	152	148
1917	1,604	242	1,187	75	1,043	660	403	428	1,299	1,651	159	98	1,030	523	184	150
1918	1,784	343	1,703	94	1,428	603	505	514	1,866	2,029	196	147	1,250	599	232	174
1919	2,282	500	1,743	92	1,166	593	632	595	1,911	1,921	213	134	1,522	762	296	176
1920	1,476	295	1,535	68	1,220	712	702	636	1,385	1,528	166	114	1,529	781	317	136
1921	852	253	907	36	634	477	514	433	857	876	108	42	1,200	528	251	90
1922	1,148	249	749	42	613	488	584	427	1,024	1,037	143	62	1,171	506	250	82
1923	1,569	276	679	61	692	553	559	476	1,027	1,042	160	91	1,425	583	262	90
1924	1,663	260	889	103	906	589	546	457	1,064	1,119	181	87	1,406	585	278	86
1925	1,762	260	915	88	773	684	589	455	1,319	1,252	207	100	1,515	682	305	90
1926	1,222	240	908	65	664	731	607	452	1,407	1,271	205	92	1,566	695	340	98
1927	1,500	246	974	87	660	664	590	436	1,237	1,336	197	88	1,685	626	333	96
1928	1,453	247	838	84	748	629	622	424	1,218	1,556	221	114	1,756	709	350	104
1929	1,512	279	790	85	706	710	621	423	1,297	1,495	224	99	1,838	740	374	110
1930	824	244	504	72	553	685	561	425	1,136	1,184	161	69	1,607	606	333	92
1931	497	157	296	39	298	490	460	299	774	838	130	51	1,277	434	258	80
1932	461	115	219	31	235	358	331	249	445	621	93	30	986	324	189	65
1933	578	157	335	32	302	446	350	287	524	599	104	77	1,004	309	161	69
1934	863	236	348	51	332	498	398	295	521	815	131	81	1,146	373	189	80
1935	712	243	416	66	286	402	444	411	682	1,062	152	70	1,310	502	232	98
1936	905	243	498	73	451	651	462	374	991	1,114	165	95	1,478	481	271	122
1937	883	321	657	82	435	647	546	386	925	1,239	186	114	1,525	517	267	129
1938	647	294	443	92	418	533	405	358	870	1,162	157	69	1,388	485	241	123
1939	627	271	473	112	477	590	443	373	810	1,290	172	81	1,346	437	249	127
1940	647	241	477	127	572	591	442	372	836	1,381	180	106	1,516	465	256	132
1941	1,045	323	755	232	594	630	613	526	1,302	1,718	227	139	1,897	658	338	161
1942	1,237	474	941	433	799	1,087	826	533	2,191	2,293	307	157	2,336	1,005	485	213
1943	1,318	540	944	675	1,126	1,592	1,203	582	2,942	2,581	342	160	2,809	1,426	835	263
1944	1,490	717	1,187	477	1,116	1,469	1,476	671	2,796	2,607	303	147	2,969	1,336	740	289
1945	1,208	898	1,563	615	1,509	1,611	1,498	753	2,263	3,318	319	126	3,021	1,518	1,004	439
1946	1,473	969	1,841	715	1,679	1,591	1,759	989	2,917	3,761	363	119	3,709	1,508	928	481
1947	2,245	1,032	2,753	917	2,265	1,632	1,199	1,050	3,926	4,967	402	105	4,013	1,813	870	431
1948	2,553	945	2,629	1,053	2,026	1,712	1,128	1,052	3,660	5,285	409	110	4,389	1,884	948	444
1949	2,637	903	2,255	854	2,161	1,616	929	1,041	3,125	4,849	351	101	3,748	1,857	939	439

Note appears at end of table

(continued)

TABLE Da1296–1311   Cash receipts from farm marketings, by crop and livestock: 1910–1999   Continued

	Crops								Livestock							
	Cotton (lint and seed)	Tobacco	Food grains	Oil crops	Feed crops	Vegetables	Fruits and tree nuts [1]	Other crops and residual	Hogs	Cattle and calves	Sheep and lambs	Wool	Dairy products	Eggs	Chickens	Other livestock
	Da1296	Da1297	Da1298	Da1299	Da1300	Da1301 [1]	Da1302 [1]	Da1303	Da1304	Da1305	Da1306	Da1307	Da1308	Da1309	Da1310	Da1311
Year	Million dollars	Million dollars	Million dollars	Million dollars	Million dollars	Million dollars	Million dollars	Million dollars	Million dollars	Million dollars	Million dollars	Million dollars	Million dollars	Million dollars	Million dollars	Million dollars
1950	2,434	1,061	1,941	935	2,143	1,436	1,188	1,218	3,214	5,680	387	131	3,719	1,579	946	449
1951	2,858	1,190	2,004	986	2,091	1,728	1,157	1,225	3,900	6,998	462	275	4,254	2,225	956	549
1952	2,976	1,091	2,558	1,081	2,271	2,023	1,097	1,193	3,480	6,194	386	125	4,567	1,811	1,132	543
1953	3,179	1,094	2,456	959	2,397	1,662	1,197	1,134	3,546	4,823	309	130	4,366	2,122	1,118	509
1954	2,702	1,161	2,327	942	2,549	1,548	1,220	1,107	3,455	5,088	325	131	4,114	1,627	1,000	536
1955	2,580	1,225	1,990	1,131	2,555	1,683	1,276	1,083	2,715	5,220	319	103	4,217	1,774	1,067	551
1956	2,500	1,162	2,148	1,155	2,648	1,873	1,358	1,194	2,632	5,358	331	110	4,485	1,817	1,033	597
1957	1,756	971	1,868	1,181	2,395	1,710	1,292	1,165	2,854	6,185	297	104	4,628	1,686	1,041	581
1958	2,138	1,020	2,442	1,410	2,904	1,736	1,394	1,185	3,377	7,319	352	83	4,557	1,808	1,171	561
1959	2,686	1,060	2,232	1,274	2,770	1,861	1,514	1,346	2,784	7,834	334	137	4,604	1,549	1,046	616
1960	2,361	1,154	2,450	1,362	2,986	1,980	1,529	1,201	2,869	7,380	325	108	4,760	1,738	1,122	687
1961	2,469	1,325	2,468	1,623	2,776	1,910	1,610	1,471	3,152	7,560	297	109	4,932	1,750	1,039	675
1962	2,552	1,321	2,507	1,789	2,964	2,029	1,578	1,571	3,162	8,182	319	114	4,860	1,703	1,142	676
1963	2,838	1,269	2,562	1,951	3,414	2,004	1,678	1,713	3,033	8,113	312	112	4,861	1,747	1,154	714
1964	2,521	1,414	1,993	2,145	3,447	2,314	1,801	1,744	3,034	7,785	318	113	5,027	1,770	1,156	745
1965	2,330	1,186	2,042	2,173	3,693	2,617	1,650	1,787	3,608	8,942	329	95	5,038	1,785	1,304	787
1966	1,588	1,211	2,373	2,703	4,334	2,612	1,747	1,841	4,169	10,430	334	101	5,533	2,106	1,471	883
1967	1,095	1,391	2,361	2,795	4,393	2,680	1,817	1,902	3,809	10,550	302	75	5,742	1,765	1,314	826
1968	1,316	1,173	2,088	2,845	4,311	2,893	2,043	2,027	3,795	11,264	315	72	5,957	1,893	1,415	776
1969	1,364	1,296	2,214	3,049	4,576	2,842	2,171	2,093	4,742	12,572	343	70	6,196	2,212	1,635	804
1970	1,254	1,388	2,542	3,591	5,109	2,814	2,071	2,208	4,478	13,633	334	57	6,527	2,109	1,564	831
1971	1,487	1,328	2,485	3,787	5,525	3,011	2,305	2,341	4,112	14,986	323	31	6,812	1,782	1,585	848
1972	1,842	1,442	3,498	4,393	5,854	3,285	2,558	2,650	5,317	18,237	354	56	7,136	1,800	1,751	933
1973	2,798	1,570	7,194	7,580	10,605	4,351	3,445	3,572	7,529	22,336	390	120	8,090	2,947	2,908	1,451
1974	2,893	2,097	8,581	9,963	13,935	5,336	3,441	4,820	6,947	17,844	369	79	9,454	2,854	2,558	1,223
1975	2,311	2,155	8,195	7,480	12,183	5,346	3,563	4,579	7,916	17,520	386	54	9,923	2,814	3,063	1,413
1976	3,477	2,310	7,112	9,443	13,127	5,231	3,714	4,619	7,488	19,294	393	73	11,428	3,135	3,050	1,462
1977	3,470	2,331	6,055	9,722	11,906	5,609	4,603	4,903	7,281	20,225	386	77	11,752	2,919	3,235	1,760
1978	3,538	2,604	5,839	13,023	11,427	6,127	5,764	4,876	8,754	28,248	453	76	12,724	2,939	3,845	2,124
1979	4,330	2,271	9,047	14,300	14,040	6,480	6,462	5,363	9,058	35,025	470	91	14,642	3,329	4,190	2,431
1980	4,447	2,672	10,402	15,493	18,308	7,307	6,557	6,560	8,943	31,819	471	93	16,365	3,247	4,431	2,622
1981	4,055	3,250	11,619	13,853	17,770	8,772	6,603	6,543	9,794	29,538	416	104	18,095	3,648	4,778	2,777
1982	4,457	3,342	11,412	13,817	17,409	8,076	6,804	6,990	10,659	29,813	445	72	18,234	3,439	4,580	3,016
1983	3,705	2,752	9,713	13,546	15,559	8,472	6,056	7,362	9,790	28,861	423	63	18,748	3,451	5,020	3,251
1984	3,674	2,813	9,731	13,641	16,138	9,152	6,734	8,008	9,701	30,589	460	74	17,931	4,110	6,190	3,839
1985	3,687	2,722	8,990	12,475	22,591	8,572	6,946	8,333	9,033	29,002	514	56	18,055	3,262	5,820	4,079
1986	3,371	3,250	5,723	10,614	16,993	8,859	7,252	9,101	9,734	28,865	481	57	17,724	3,543	6,912	4,238
1987	4,189	1,816	5,790	11,283	14,635	9,891	8,056	10,141	10,337	33,583	558	77	17,727	3,208	6,289	4,218
1988	4,525	2,069	7,469	13,501	14,281	9,792	9,032	10,935	9,221	36,958	522	125	17,632	3,067	7,530	4,585
1989	5,026	2,410	8,247	11,866	17,049	11,562	9,151	11,582	9,770	36,429	487	110	19,357	3,862	8,916	4,986

	Crops								Livestock							
	Cotton (lint and seed)	Tobacco	Food grains	Oil crops	Feed crops	Vegetables	Fruits and tree nuts	Other crops and residual	Hogs	Cattle and calves	Sheep and lambs	Wool	Dairy products	Eggs	Chickens	Other livestock
	Da1296	Da1297	Da1298	Da1299	Da1300	Da1301 [1]	Da1302 [1]	Da1303	Da1304	Da1305	Da1306	Da1307	Da1308	Da1309	Da1310	Da1311
Year	Million dollars	Million dollars	Million dollars	Million dollars	Million dollars	Million dollars	Million dollars	Million dollars	Million dollars	Million dollars	Million dollars	Million dollars	Million dollars	Million dollars	Million dollars	Million dollars
1990	5,488	2,733	7,480	12,258	18,669	11,464	9,416	12,797	11,525	39,302	414	69	20,153	4,010	8,456	5,291
1991	5,236	2,881	7,325	12,698	19,327	11,625	9,923	13,062	11,036	38,697	399	47	18,007	3,901	8,450	5,249
1992	5,192	2,958	8,467	13,287	20,098	11,765	10,145	13,701	10,017	37,272	459	60	19,736	3,384	9,259	5,464
1993	5,250	2,949	8,180	13,219	20,199	13,677	10,263	13,734	10,948	39,487	533	39	19,262	3,779	10,512	5,884
1994	6,738	2,656	9,545	14,652	20,310	14,043	10,312	14,690	9,898	36,252	511	52	19,983	3,790	11,445	6,259
1995	6,851	2,548	10,356	15,495	24,516	14,979	11,097	15,006	10,255	34,044	566	64	19,880	3,893	11,822	6,589
1996	6,983	2,795	10,795	16,357	27,189	14,444	11,928	15,814	12,565	30,977	612	40	22,785	4,776	13,964	7,119
1997	6,345	2,874	10,411	19,802	27,048	14,653	13,134	16,866	13,054	36,000	628	45	20,940	4,540	14,231	7,026
1998	6,101	2,803	8,892	17,483	22,666	15,145	12,238	17,136	9,444	33,415	477	21	24,114	4,439	15,220	6,981
1999	4,696	2,273	7,292	13,555	19,752	15,164	12,975	17,441	8,623	36,522	456	18	23,204	4,323	15,197	7,122

[1] Melons included in series Da1302, 1910–1948; in series Da1301 thereafter.

Sources

1910–1923: U.S. Department of Agriculture, Economic Research Service, *Farm Income Situation*, various issues. 1924–1999: U.S. Department of Agriculture, Economic Research Service Internet site, accessed May 1, 2001.

Documentation

Series Da1303. Other crops include sugar crops, greenhouse and nursery products, Christmas trees, legume and grass seeds, hops, mint, broomcorn, popcorn, hemp fiber and seed, flax fiber, mushrooms,

and maple products. The residual is the remaining difference between the U.S. Department of Agriculture's estimate of total crop receipts and individual crop items.

Series Da1311. Includes turkeys, horses, mules, mohair, honey, beeswax, bees, goats, rabbits, fur animals, ducks, geese, guineas, pigeons, quail, pheasants, other animals, and aquaculture.

TABLE Da1312–1322   Balance sheet of the farming sector: 1940–1998[1]

Contributed by Bruce L. Gardner

	Assets							Claims			
									Debt		
	Total	Real estate	Livestock and poultry	Machinery and motor vehicles	Crops stored on and off farms	Purchased inputs	Financial	Total	Real estate	Non–real estate	Proprietors' equities
	Da1312	Da1313	Da1314 [2]	Da1315	Da1316	Da1317	Da1318	Da1319	Da1320	Da1321	Da1322
Year	Billion dollars	Billion dollars	Billion dollars	Billion dollars	Billion dollars	Billion dollars	Billion dollars	Billion dollars	Billion dollars	Billion dollars	Billion dollars
1940	52.9	33.6	5.1	3.1	2.7	—	—	10.0	6.6	3.4	42.9
1941	55.0	34.4	5.3	3.3	3.0	—	—	10.4	6.5	3.9	44.6
1942	62.9	37.5	7.1	4.0	3.8	—	—	10.5	6.4	4.1	52.4
1943	73.7	41.6	9.6	4.9	5.1	—	—	10.0	6.0	4.0	63.7
1944	84.6	48.2	9.7	5.4	6.1	—	—	8.9	5.4	3.5	75.7
1945	94.2	53.9	9.0	6.5	6.7	—	—	8.3	4.9	3.4	85.9
1946	103.5	61.0	9.7	5.4	6.3	—	—	8.0	4.8	3.2	95.5
1947	116.4	68.5	11.9	5.3	7.1	—	—	8.5	4.9	3.6	107.9
1948	127.9	73.7	13.3	7.4	9.0	—	—	9.3	5.1	4.2	118.6
1949	134.9	76.6	14.4	10.1	8.6	—	—	11.4	5.3	6.1	123.5
1950	132.5	75.3	12.9	12.2	7.6	—	—	12.4	5.6	6.8	120.1
1951	151.5	86.6	17.1	14.1	7.9	—	—	13.1	6.1	7.0	138.4
1952	167.0	95.1	19.5	16.7	8.8	—	—	14.7	6.7	8.0	152.8
1953	164.3	96.5	14.8	17.4	9.0	—	—	16.1	7.2	8.9	148.2
1954	161.2	95.0	11.7	18.4	9.2	—	—	16.9	7.7	9.2	144.3
1955	165.1	98.2	11.2	18.6	9.6	—	—	17.6	8.2	9.4	147.5
1956	169.6	102.9	10.6	19.3	8.4	—	—	18.8	9.0	9.8	150.8
1957	177.9	110.4	11.0	20.2	8.3	—	—	19.3	9.8	9.5	158.6
1958	185.8	115.9	13.9	20.2	7.6	—	—	20.4	10.4	10.0	165.4
1959	202.1	124.4	17.7	21.8	9.3	—	—	23.6	11.1	12.5	178.5
1960 [1]	203.5	130.2	15.5	22.7	7.7	—	—	24.8	12.1	12.7	178.7
1960 [1]	174.4	123.3	15.6	19.1	6.4	0.0	10.0	22.4	11.3	11.1	151.9
1961	181.6	129.1	16.4	19.3	6.5	0.0	10.4	24.1	12.3	11.8	157.5
1962	188.9	134.6	17.3	19.9	6.5	0.0	10.5	26.7	13.5	13.2	162.2
1963	196.7	142.4	15.9	20.4	7.4	0.0	10.7	29.6	15.0	14.6	167.1
1964	204.2	150.5	14.5	21.2	7.0	0.0	11.0	32.2	16.9	15.3	172.1
1965	220.8	161.5	17.6	22.4	7.9	0.0	11.4	35.8	18.9	16.9	185.0
1966	234.0	171.2	19.0	24.1	8.1	0.0	11.6	39.2	20.7	18.5	194.8
1967	246.1	180.9	18.8	26.3	8.0	0.0	12.0	42.2	22.6	19.6	203.9
1968	257.2	189.4	20.2	27.7	7.4	0.0	12.4	43.9	24.7	19.2	213.2
1969	267.8	195.3	22.8	28.6	8.3	0.0	12.8	46.4	26.4	20.0	221.4
1970	278.9	202.4	23.7	30.4	8.7	0.0	13.7	48.8	27.5	21.2	230.1
1971	301.7	217.6	27.3	32.4	10.0	0.0	14.5	53.2	29.3	24.0	248.5
1972	339.9	243.0	33.7	34.6	12.9	0.0	15.7	58.7	32.0	26.7	281.2
1973	418.5	298.3	42.4	39.7	21.4	0.0	16.8	67.6	36.1	31.6	350.9
1974	449.2	335.6	24.6	48.5	22.5	0.0	18.1	75.9	40.8	35.1	373.3
1975	510.8	383.6	29.4	57.4	20.5	0.0	19.9	85.0	45.3	39.7	425.8
1976	590.7	456.5	29.0	63.3	20.6	0.0	21.3	96.1	50.5	45.6	494.7
1977	651.5	509.3	31.9	69.3	20.4	0.0	20.5	110.9	58.4	52.4	540.7
1978	767.4	601.8	50.1	68.5	23.8	0.0	23.2	127.4	66.7	60.7	640.0
1979	898.1	706.1	61.4	75.4	29.9	0.0	25.4	151.6	79.7	71.8	746.6
1980	983.3	782.8	60.6	80.3	32.8	0.0	26.7	166.8	89.7	77.1	816.5
1981	982.3	785.6	53.5	85.5	29.5	0.0	28.2	182.4	98.8	83.6	799.9
1982	944.6	750.0	53.0	86.0	25.9	0.0	29.7	188.8	101.8	87.0	755.8
1983	943.4	753.4	49.5	85.8	23.7	0.0	30.9	191.1	103.2	87.9	752.3
1984	857.1	661.8	49.5	85.0	26.1	2.0	32.6	193.8	106.7	87.1	663.3
1985	772.7	586.2	46.3	82.9	22.9	1.2	33.3	177.6	100.1	77.5	595.1
1986	724.8	542.3	47.8	81.9	16.3	2.1	34.5	157.0	90.4	66.6	567.8
1987	756.3	563.5	58.0	78.7	17.8	3.2	35.1	144.4	82.4	62.0	611.9
1988	788.4	582.7	62.2	81.0	23.7	3.5	35.4	139.6	77.8	61.7	648.8
1989	814.4	600.8	66.2	84.1	23.9	2.6	36.8	137.9	76.0	61.9	676.6
1990	840.6	619.1	70.9	86.3	23.2	2.8	38.3	138.0	74.7	63.2	702.6
1991	844.2	624.8	68.1	85.9	22.2	2.6	40.5	139.2	74.9	64.3	705.0
1992	868.3	640.8	71.0	85.4	24.2	3.9	43.1	139.1	75.4	63.6	729.3
1993	910.2	677.6	72.8	86.5	23.3	3.8	46.3	142.0	76.0	65.9	768.3
1994	935.5	704.1	67.9	87.5	23.3	5.0	47.6	146.8	77.7	69.1	788.7

Notes appear at end of table

TABLE Da1312–1322   Balance sheet of the farming sector: 1940–1998   *Continued*

	Assets							Claims			
									Debt		
	Total	Real estate	Livestock and poultry	Machinery and motor vehicles	Crops stored on and off farms	Purchased inputs	Financial	Total	Real estate	Non–real estate	Proprietors' equities
	Da1312	Da1313	Da1314 [2]	Da1315	Da1316	Da1317	Da1318	Da1319	Da1320	Da1321	Da1322
Year	Billion dollars	Billion dollars	Billion dollars	Billion dollars	Billion dollars	Billion dollars	Billion dollars	Billion dollars	Billion dollars	Billion dollars	Billion dollars
1995	966.7	740.5	57.8	88.5	27.4	3.4	49.1	150.8	79.3	71.5	815.9
1996	1,003.9	769.5	60.3	88.9	31.7	4.4	49.0	156.1	81.7	74.4	847.8
1997	1,051.6	808.4	67.1	89.0	32.2	5.1	49.7	165.4	85.4	80.1	886.2
1998	1,064.3	822.8	62.0	88.6	30.1	5.3	55.4	172.9	89.6	83.2	891.4

[1] Post-1960 data have been revised by the U.S. Department of Agriculture, and 1940–1960 data are no longer fully consistent with the revised data. Both revised and unrevised data are shown for 1960, to show the consequences of revision.

[2] Beginning with 1961, excludes horses and mules.

Sources

U.S. Department of Agriculture, *The Balance Sheet of the Farming Sector* (formerly *The Balance Sheet of Agriculture*), annual issues, and U.S. Department of Agriculture, Economic Research Service Internet site, accessed May 2001.

Documentation

Series Da1316. Includes crops held on farms and crops held off farms by farmers as security for Commodity Credit Corporation loans.

TABLE Da1323-1326   Exports and imports of farm products: 1901-1999

Contributed by Bruce L. Gardner

	Exports, domestic products		Imports, for consumption			Exports, domestic products		Imports, for consumption	
	Total	As a percentage of all exports	Total	As a percentage of all imports		Total	As a percentage of all exports	Total	As a percentage of all imports
	Da1323	Da1324	Da1325	Da1326		Da1323	Da1324	Da1325	Da1326
Fiscal year	Million dollars	Percent	Million dollars	Percent	Fiscal year	Million dollars	Percent	Million dollars	Percent
1901	949	65	418	51	1955	3,144	21	3,781	36
1902	855	63	436	48	1956	3,496	21	4,086	34
1903	877	63	484	47	1957	4,728	23	3,800	30
1904	858	60	499	50	1958	4,003	21	3,929	31
					1959	3,719	21	4,004	29
1905	825	55	601	54					
1906	975	57	597	49	1960	4,519	24	4,010	26
1907	1,053	57	683	48	1961	4,946	24	3,645	26
1908	1,016	55	573	48	1962	5,142	24	3,762	24
1909	901	55	696	53	1963	5,078	23	3,907	24
					1964	6,068	25	4,096	23
1910	869	51	787	51					
1911	1,029	51	767	50	1965	6,097	23	3,986	20
1912	1,048	48	882	53	1966	6,676	23	4,454	19
1913	1,121	46	909	50	1967	6,771	22	4,453	17
1914	1,112	48	993	52	1968	6,311	20	4,656	16
					1969	5,741	16	4,931	14
1915	1,474	54	992	59					
1916	1,516	35	1,342	61	1970	6,721	16	5,592	15
1917	1,966	32	1,592	60	1971	7,758	18	5,828	14
1918	2,279	39	1,822	62	1972	8,047	18	6,048	12
1919	3,579	51	1,930	62	1973	12,902	22	7,324	12
					1974	21,293	25	9,549	12
1920	3,850	48	3,410	65					
1921	2,606	41	2,059	56	1975	21,578	21	9,579	9
1922	1,915	52	1,370	53	1976	22,147	20	10,107	10
1923	1,798	46	2,077	55	1977	23,974	20	13,357	9
1924	1,867	44	1,875	53	1978	27,289	21	13,886	8
					1979	31,979	19	16,186	8
1925	2,280	48	2,057	54					
1926	1,892	41	2,529	57	1980	40,481	19	17,276	7
1927	1,908	39	2,281	54	1981	43,780	19	17,218	7
1928	1,815	38	2,194	53	1982	39,097	18	15,485	6
1929	1,847	35	2,177	51	1983	34,769	18	16,373	7
					1984	38,027	18	18,916	6
1930	1,496	32	1,900	49					
1931	1,038	34	1,162	48	1985	31,201	15	19,740	6
1932	752	39	834	48	1986	26,312	13	20,884	6
1933	590	42	614	52	1987	27,876	12	20,650	5
1934	787	39	839	50	1988	35,316	12	21,014	5
					1989	29,471	12	16,426	4
1935	669	32	934	52					
1936	766	32	1,141	52	1990	40,365	11	22,705	5
1937	732	26	1,537	53	1991	37,780	10	22,728	5
1938	891	27	1,155	50	1992	42,625	10	24,488	5
1939	683	24	999	48	1993	42,879	10	24,634	4
					1994	43,960	9	26,603	4
1940	738	20	1,239	51					
1941	350	9	1,474	53	1995	54,725	10	29,865	4
1942	1,032	16	1,503	49	1996	59,891	10	32,577	4
1943	1,497	15	1,342	45	1997	57,365	9	35,798	4
1944	2,305	16	1,774	47	1998	53,730	8	37,007	4
					1999	49,102	8	37,447	4
1945	2,191	17	1,729	44					
1946	2,857	34	1,878	45					
1947	3,610	28	2,704	50					
1948	3,505	25	2,862	45					
1949	3,830	30	3,001	43					
1950	2,986	30	3,177	45					
1951	3,411	27	5,147	48					
1952	4,053	26	4,699	45					
1953	2,819	19	4,303	40					
1954	2,936	19	4,176	40					

Sources

U.S. Department of Agriculture, *Agricultural Statistics, 1937*, Table 463; *1952*, Table 817; *1957*, Table 808; *1972*, Table 817; corresponding tables in later annual volumes.

TABLE Da1327–1336   Exports and imports of farm products, by commodity: 1940–1998

Contributed by Bruce L. Gardner

	Exports						Imports			
	Feed grains	Food grains	Oilseeds and products	Cotton	Tobacco	Animals and products	Crops, fruits and vegetables	Animals and products	Coffee	Cocoa beans and products
	Da1327	Da1328	Da1329	Da1330	Da1331	Da1332	Da1333	Da1334	Da1335	Da1336
Year	Billion dollars	Billion dollars	Billion dollars	Billion dollars	Billion dollars	Billion dollars	Billion dollars	Billion dollars	Billion dollars	Billion dollars
1940	(Z)	(Z)	(Z)	0.2	(Z)	0.1	(Z)	0.2	0.1	(Z)
1941	(Z)	0.1	(Z)	0.1	0.1	0.3	0.1	0.3	0.2	(Z)
1942	(Z)	(Z)	(Z)	0.1	0.1	0.8	(Z)	0.5	0.2	(Z)
1943	(Z)	0.1	0.1	0.2	0.2	1.2	0.1	0.4	0.3	(Z)
1944	(Z)	0.1	0.1	0.1	0.1	1.3	0.1	0.3	0.3	(Z)
1945	(Z)	0.4	(Z)	0.3	0.2	0.9	0.1	0.4	0.3	(Z)
1946	0.1	0.7	(Z)	0.5	0.4	0.9	0.2	0.4	0.5	0.1
1947	0.4	1.4	0.1	0.4	0.3	0.7	0.1	0.4	0.6	0.2
1948	0.1	1.5	0.2	0.5	0.2	0.5	0.2	0.6	0.7	0.2
1949	0.3	1.1	0.3	0.9	0.3	0.4	0.2	0.4	0.8	0.1
1950	0.2	0.6	0.2	1.0	0.3	0.3	0.2	0.7	1.1	0.2
1951	0.3	1.1	0.3	1.1	0.3	0.5	0.2	1.1	1.4	0.2
1952	0.3	1.1	0.2	0.9	0.2	0.3	0.2	0.7	1.4	0.2
1953	0.3	0.7	0.2	0.5	0.3	0.4	0.2	0.6	1.5	0.2
1954	0.2	0.5	0.3	0.8	0.3	0.5	0.2	0.5	1.5	0.3
1955	0.3	0.6	0.4	0.5	0.4	0.6	0.2	0.5	1.4	0.2
1956	0.4	1.0	0.5	0.7	0.3	0.7	0.2	0.4	1.4	0.2
1957	0.3	1.0	0.5	1.0	0.4	0.7	0.2	0.5	1.4	0.2
1958	0.5	0.8	0.4	0.7	0.4	0.5	0.2	0.7	1.2	0.2
1959	0.6	0.9	0.6	0.4	0.3	0.6	0.2	0.8	1.1	0.2
1960	0.5	1.2	0.6	1.0	0.4	0.6	0.2	0.6	1.0	0.2
1961	0.5	1.4	0.6	0.9	0.4	0.6	0.2	0.7	1.0	0.2
1962	0.8	1.3	0.7	0.5	0.4	0.6	0.2	0.9	1.0	0.2
1963	0.8	1.5	0.8	0.6	0.4	0.7	0.3	0.9	1.0	0.2
1964	0.9	1.7	1.0	0.7	0.4	0.8	0.3	0.8	1.2	0.2
1965	1.1	1.4	1.2	0.5	0.4	0.8	0.3	0.9	1.1	0.1
1966	1.3	1.8	1.2	0.4	0.5	0.7	0.4	1.2	1.1	0.1
1967	1.1	1.5	1.3	0.5	0.5	0.7	0.4	1.1	1.0	0.2
1968	0.9	1.4	1.3	0.5	0.5	0.7	0.5	1.3	1.2	0.2
1969	0.9	1.2	1.3	0.3	0.6	0.8	0.5	1.4	0.9	0.2
1970	1.1	1.4	1.9	0.4	0.5	0.9	0.5	1.6	1.2	0.3
1971	1.0	1.3	2.2	0.6	0.5	1.0	0.6	1.5	1.2	0.2
1972	1.5	1.8	2.4	0.5	0.7	1.1	0.7	1.8	1.3	0.2
1973	3.5	4.7	4.3	0.9	0.7	1.6	0.8	2.6	1.7	0.3
1974	4.6	5.4	5.7	1.3	0.8	1.8	0.8	2.2	1.6	0.5
1975	5.2	6.2	4.5	1.0	0.9	1.7	0.8	1.8	1.7	0.5
1976	6.0	4.7	5.1	1.0	0.9	2.4	0.9	2.3	2.9	0.6
1977	4.9	3.6	6.6	1.5	1.1	2.7	1.2	2.3	4.2	1.0
1978	5.9	5.5	8.2	1.7	1.4	3.0	1.5	3.1	4.0	1.4
1979	7.7	6.3	8.9	2.2	1.2	3.8	1.7	3.9	4.2	1.2
1980	9.8	7.9	9.4	2.9	1.3	3.8	1.7	3.8	4.2	0.9
1981	9.4	9.6	9.6	2.3	1.5	4.2	2.0	3.5	2.9	0.9
1982	6.4	7.9	9.1	2.0	1.5	3.9	2.3	3.7	2.9	0.7
1983	7.3	7.4	8.7	1.8	1.5	3.8	2.3	3.8	2.8	0.8
1984	8.1	7.5	8.4	2.4	1.5	4.2	3.1	4.1	3.3	1.1
1985	6.0	4.5	5.8	1.6	1.5	4.1	3.5	4.2	3.3	1.4
1986	3.1	3.8	6.5	0.8	1.2	4.5	3.6	4.5	4.6	1.1
1987	3.8	3.8	6.4	1.6	1.1	5.2	3.6	4.9	2.9	1.2
1988	5.9	5.9	7.7	2.0	1.3	6.4	3.8	5.2	2.5	1.0
1989	7.7	7.1	6.3	2.2	1.3	6.4	4.2	5.0	2.4	1.0
1990	7.0	4.8	5.7	2.8	1.4	6.7	4.9	5.6	1.9	1.1
1991	5.7	4.2	6.4	2.5	1.4	7.1	4.8	5.5	1.9	1.1
1992	5.7	5.4	7.2	2.0	1.7	8.0	4.9	5.7	1.7	1.1
1993	5.0	5.6	7.3	1.5	1.3	8.1	5.0	5.9	1.5	1.0
1994	4.7	5.3	7.2	2.7	1.3	9.3	5.4	5.8	2.5	1.0
1995	8.2	6.7	8.9	3.7	1.4	11.0	5.9	6.0	3.3	1.1
1996	9.4	7.4	10.8	2.7	1.4	11.3	6.9	6.1	2.8	1.4
1997	6.0	5.2	12.1	2.7	1.6	11.5	7.2	6.5	3.9	1.5
1998	5.0	5.0	9.5	2.5	1.5	10.7	7.9	7.0	3.4	1.7

(Z) Less than $50 million.

Source

Economic Report of the President, 2000, Table B-100, p. 421.

Documentation

Series Da1328. Includes rice, wheat, and wheat flour.

Series Da1333. Includes nuts, fruits, and vegetable preparations.

TABLE Da1337–1346   Prices received and paid by farmers – indexes and parity ratio: 1909–1999

Contributed by Bruce L. Gardner

	Prices received by farmers			Prices paid by farmers						Parity ratio
							Payable per acre			
Year	All farm products	Crops	Livestock and products	All prices paid	Living expenses	Production	Interest	Taxes	Wage rates	
	Da1337	Da1338	Da1339	Da1340	Da1341	Da1342	Da1343	Da1344	Da1345	Da1346
	Index 1910–1914 = 100	Index 1910–1914 = 100	Index 1910–1914 = 100	Index 1910–1914 = 100	Index 1910–1914 = 100	Index 1910–1914 = 100	Index 1910–1914 = 100	Index 1910–1914 = 100	Index 1910–1914 = 100	Index 1910–1914 = 100
1909	—	101	100	—	—	—	—	—	—	—
1910	104	106	102	97	99	97	83	90	96	107
1911	95	101	88	98	99	98	91	91	98	97
1912	99	101	98	101	100	102	101	99	101	98
1913	102	98	105	101	100	101	109	103	104	101
1914	101	96	107	103	102	102	116	117	101	98
1915	99	96	102	105	104	104	122	118	101	94
1916	119	120	117	116	115	115	132	128	112	103
1917	178	191	165	148	143	156	145	136	141	120
1918	206	220	194	173	170	180	159	151	177	119
1919	217	230	206	197	202	195	180	160	206	110
1920	211	235	190	214	228	195	216	200	241	99
1921	124	121	127	155	164	128	248	244	156	80
1922	131	136	126	151	153	127	260	259	154	87
1923	142	156	129	159	156	138	261	261	172	89
1924	143	159	128	160	156	140	250	266	182	89
1925	156	164	149	163	161	145	236	265	181	96
1926	145	139	151	161	158	141	228	270	183	90
1927	141	134	146	159	155	141	223	271	185	89
1928	149	142	155	162	156	148	219	277	184	92
1929	148	135	159	161	154	147	213	279	184	92
1930	125	115	134	153	144	135	206	281	187	82
1931	87	75	98	131	124	113	197	277	179	66
1932	65	57	72	113	106	99	185	254	139	58
1933	70	71	70	109	108	99	164	220	104	64
1934	90	98	81	120	122	114	147	188	88	75
1935	109	103	114	124	124	122	135	178	99	88
1936	114	109	119	124	124	122	125	180	107	92
1937	123	118	126	131	128	132	117	181	115	94
1938	97	81	112	124	122	122	110	187	129	78
1939	95	82	107	123	120	121	106	185	130	77
1940	100	91	109	124	121	123	102	189	127	81
1941	124	108	138	133	130	131	98	187	129	93
1942	159	145	171	152	149	148	94	189	151	105
1943	193	187	198	171	166	165	84	185	196	113
1944	197	199	196	182	175	173	79	185	263	108
1945	207	202	211	190	182	176	75	192	318	109
1946	236	228	243	208	202	191	74	213	359	113
1947	276	263	288	240	237	224	76	237	387	115
1948	287	255	315	260	251	250	78	276	419	110
1949	250	224	273	251	243	238	82	298	442	100
1950	258	233	280	256	246	246	89	320	430	101
1951	302	265	336	282	268	273	98	335	425	107
1952	288	267	306	287	271	274	108	350	470	100
1953	255	240	268	277	269	256	116	367	503	92
1954	246	242	249	278	270	255	125	384	513	88
1955	233	231	234	276	270	251	136	403	510	84
1956	230	235	226	278	274	250	151	432	516	83
1957	235	225	244	287	282	257	166	462	536	82
1958	250	223	273	294	287	264	182	494	558	85
1959	240	222	257	298	288	266	200	532	558	81
1960	239	223	253	299	290	265	221	586	574	80
1961	240	227	251	302	291	266	242	620	588	79
1962	244	233	255	307	295	270	268	651	636	79
1963	243	240	245	312	298	273	300	675	641	78
1964	237	239	236	313	300	270	340	700	660	76

TABLE Da1337–1346 Prices received and paid by farmers – indexes and parity ratio: 1909–1999 *Continued*

	Prices received by farmers			Prices paid by farmers						
	All farm products	Crops	Livestock and products	All prices paid	Living expenses	Production	Payable per acre		Wage rates	Parity ratio
							Interest	Taxes		
	Da1337	Da1338	Da1339	Da1340	Da1341	Da1342	Da1343	Da1344	Da1345	Da1346
Year	Index 1910–1914 = 100	Index 1910–1914 = 100	Index 1910–1914 = 100	Index 1910–1914 = 100	Index 1910–1914 = 100	Index 1910–1914 = 100	Index 1910–1914 = 100	Index 1910–1914 = 100	Index 1910–1914 = 100	Index 1910–1914 = 100
1965	245	230	260	322	305	277	387	740	677	76
1966	264	238	290	335	314	289	435	795	693	79
1967	250	225	275	341	320	290	486	849	728	73
1968	255	225	286	349	334	290	437	932	785	73
1969	268	217	322	366	348	302	607	1,020	847	73
1970	274	225	325	382	363	313	665	1,095	919	72
1971	281	242	323	400	379	328	724	1,158	1,011	70
1972	313	257	372	425	394	351	799	1,206	1,083	74
1973	447	394	502	491	426	424	920	1,236	1,139	91
1974	481	504	454	558	484	481	1,103	1,305	1,205	86
1975	466	436	477	613	530	532	1,207	1,400	1,314	76
1976	475	428	491	654	561	570	1,333	1,518	1,506	73
1977	462	409	489	695	573	594	1,688	1,614	1,915	66
1978	529	438	599	759	616	648	1,871	1,612	2,053	70
1979	600	484	693	862	683	740	2,229	1,730	2,262	70
1980	624	527	683	978	775	822	2,733	1,859	2,421	64
1981	634	549	685	1,081	858	888	3,161	1,988	2,626	59
1982	598	484	694	1,133	915	915	3,314	1,998	2,760	53
1983	625	534	678	1,133	944	897	3,138	2,085	2,836	55
1984	641	547	701	1,163	985	908	3,100	2,142	2,872	55
1985	579	481	656	1,131	1,016	878	2,649	2,143	2,934	51
1986	554	430	675	1,109	1,041	833	2,449	2,157	3,049	50
1987	563	426	697	1,139	1,072	844	2,399	2,326	3,174	49
1988	627	516	713	1,191	1,117	874	2,518	2,375	3,267	53
1989	659	537	764	1,299	1,169	922	2,645	2,442	3,538	51
1990	660	507	804	1,332	1,229	958	2,685	2,543	3,583	50
1991	632	496	757	1,347	1,287	973	2,516	2,707	3,757	47
1992	626	498	743	1,353	1,327	979	2,321	2,789	3,930	47
1993	643	505	768	1,384	1,369	1,006	2,191	2,886	4,055	47
1994	634	520	727	1,419	1,404	1,030	2,367	2,828	4,140	45
1995	646	553	707	1,456	1,447	1,051	2,548	2,915	4,278	44
1996	712	624	761	1,540	1,490	1,118	2,652	3,001	4,389	47
1997	679	570	755	1,585	1,525	1,151	2,621	3,093	4,591	43
1998	642	523	740	1,528	1,548	1,093	2,617	3,185	4,838	42
1999	612	484	728	1,525	1,582	1,083	2,663	3,214	5,037	40

Source

U.S. Department of Agriculture, National Agricultural Statistics Service, *Agricultural Prices: Annual Summary*, various issues.

Documentation

Series Da1346. Equals the ratio of prices received to prices paid: series Da1337 divided by series Da1340.

TABLE Da1347–1350   Indexes of the retail cost of food and the farm-value component of retail cost: 1913–1999

Contributed by Bruce L. Gardner

Year	Index of retail cost of food Da1347 Index 1982–1984 = 100	Index of farm value component of retail cost Da1348 Index 1982–1984 = 100	Farm-to-retail price spread index Da1349 Index 1982–1984 = 100	Share of retail price accounted for by farm value Da1350 Percent	Year	Index of retail cost of food Da1347 Index 1982–1984 = 100	Index of farm value component of retail cost Da1348 Index 1982–1984 = 100	Farm-to-retail price spread index Da1349 Index 1982–1984 = 100	Share of retail price accounted for by farm value Da1350 Percent
1913	12	16	10	46	1960	34	38	32	39
1914	13	16	11	45	1961	34	37	33	39
1915	12	15	11	44	1962	34	38	33	39
1916	15	19	13	44	1963	34	36	33	38
1917	20	27	17	47	1964	34	36	34	36
1918	21	30	16	51	1965	35	40	33	38
1919	24	32	19	48	1966	37	43	34	39
1920	26	31	23	43	1967	37	40	35	39
1921	20	22	19	40	1968	38	42	36	38
1922	19	21	18	39	1969	40	46	37	39
1923	19	21	18	39	1970	42	46	40	37
1924	19	21	18	40	1971	43	46	41	37
1925	20	24	18	42	1972	45	50	42	38
1926	21	24	19	41	1973	52	68	45	44
1927	20	23	19	41	1974	60	73	53	42
1928	20	24	18	42	1975	64	76	58	40
1929	20	23	18	42	1976	65	72	61	38
1930	20	21	19	38	1977	66	72	63	37
1931	15	15	16	35	1978	74	83	68	38
1932	13	12	14	31	1979	82	92	77	38
1933	13	12	13	32	1980	88	97	84	37
1934	14	14	14	34	1981	95	100	92	36
1935	16	17	15	38	1982	98	99	98	35
1936	16	18	15	40	1983	99	97	100	34
1937	17	19	15	41	1984	103	104	103	35
1938	15	17	14	38	1985	104	96	108	32
1939	15	16	14	38	1986	106	95	112	31
1940	15	17	14	40	1987	112	97	120	30
1941	16	20	14	44	1988	116	100	125	30
1942	19	25	15	47	1989	125	107	134	30
1943	21	30	16	51	1990	134	113	145	30
1944	21	30	16	51	1991	137	106	154	27
1945	21	32	16	53	1992	138	103	157	26
1946	24	36	19	53	1993	142	105	162	26
1947	29	43	22	52	1994	145	101	169	24
1948	32	46	24	51	1995	149	103	175	24
1949	30	40	25	47	1996	156	111	180	25
1950	30	40	25	47	1997	160	106	189	23
1951	33	46	26	49	1998	163	103	195	22
1952	34	44	28	47	1999	167	98	205	21
1953	32	41	28	45					
1954	32	39	28	43					
1955	31	36	29	41					
1956	32	36	29	40					
1957	33	37	30	40					
1958	35	40	32	41					
1959	34	37	32	39					

Sources

1913–1951, U.S. Department of Agriculture, Economic Research Service, "Farm–Retail Spreads for Food Products," *Miscellaneous Publication* number 741. 1952–1999, U.S. Department of Agriculture, Economic Research Service, "Food Cost Review," *Agricultural Economic Report* number 780, Table 4, updated using U.S. Department of Agriculture, Economic Research Service, unpublished data for 1998 and 1999.

Documentation

Data are based on retail prices for a market basket of domestically produced farm foods. Data exclude food purchased at eating places outside the home, imported food products, and seafood and other foods not of farm origin.

Series Da1349. The price spread is the difference between the retail cost of U.S. Department of Agriculture's "market basket" of food products minus the farm value of agricultural products that go into the market basket.

Series Da1350. The farm share is the percentage of the value of the retail market basket accounted for by the farm value of agricultural products that go into the market basket.

TABLE Da1351–1356   Consumer expenditures on food – by location and by farm value and marketing bill components: 1913–1997[1]

Contributed by Bruce L. Gardner

Year	Total Da1351 [2] Billion dollars	Location At home Da1352 Billion dollars	Location Away from home Da1353 Billion dollars	Farm value Da1354 Billion dollars	Marketing bill Da1355 Billion dollars	Farm value share Da1356 Percent
1913	7.4	—	—	3.5	3.9	47.3
1914	7.9	—	—	3.6	4.3	45.6
1915	8.0	—	—	3.6	4.4	45.0
1916	9.5	—	—	4.4	5.1	46.3
1917	12.4	—	—	6.1	6.3	49.2
1918	13.2	—	—	6.9	6.3	52.3
1919	15.2	—	—	7.6	7.6	50.0
1920	16.5	—	—	7.4	9.1	44.8
1921	12.6	—	—	5.1	7.5	40.5
1922	12.9	—	—	5.2	7.7	40.3
1923	14.0	—	—	5.6	8.4	40.0
1924	14.5	—	—	5.9	8.6	40.7
1925	15.7	—	—	6.8	8.9	43.3
1926	16.4	—	—	7.0	9.4	42.7
1927	16.2	—	—	6.7	9.5	41.4
1928	16.3	—	—	6.9	9.4	42.3
1929	17.1	—	—	7.2	9.9	42.1
1929 [3]	18.0	—	—	7.5	10.5	41.7
1930	16.2	—	—	6.3	9.9	38.9
1931	13.1	—	—	4.7	8.4	35.9
1932	10.6	—	—	3.4	7.2	32.1
1933	10.9	—	—	3.6	7.3	33.0
1934	12.5	—	—	4.3	8.2	34.4
1935	12.9	—	—	5.0	7.9	38.8
1935 [3]	13.8	—	—	5.2	8.6	37.7
1936	14.3	—	—	5.8	8.5	40.6
1937	14.2	—	—	6.0	8.2	42.3
1938	13.4	—	—	5.2	8.2	38.8
1939	13.4	—	—	5.2	8.2	38.8
1939 [3]	15.3	—	—	5.4	9.9	35.3
1940	14.1	—	—	5.6	8.5	39.7
1941	16.3	—	—	7.1	9.2	43.6
1942	19.8	—	—	9.3	10.5	47.0
1943	22.3	—	—	11.4	11.1	51.1
1944	22.5	—	—	11.6	11.4	51.6
1945	24.4	—	—	12.6	12.5	51.6
1946	30.8	—	—	15.7	15.6	51.0
1947 [1]	36.5	—	—	18.7	17.8	51.2
1947 [1]	41.9	—	—	19.3	22.6	46.1
1948	44.8	—	—	19.9	24.9	44.4
1949	43.4	—	—	17.4	26.0	40.1
1950	44.0	—	—	18.0	26.0	40.9
1951	49.2	—	—	20.5	28.7	41.7
1952	50.9	—	—	20.4	30.5	40.1
1953	51.0	—	—	19.5	31.5	38.2
1954	51.1	—	—	18.8	32.3	36.8
1955	53.1	—	—	18.7	34.4	35.2
1956	55.5	—	—	19.2	36.3	34.6
1957	58.3	—	—	20.4	37.9	35.0
1958	61.0	—	—	21.4	39.6	35.1
1959	63.6	—	—	21.2	42.4	33.3
1960	66.9	—	—	22.3	44.6	33.3
1961	68.7	—	—	23.0	45.7	33.5
1962	71.3	—	—	23.7	47.6	33.2
1963	74.0	56.0	18.0	24.1	49.9	32.6
1964	77.5	58.5	19.0	24.9	52.6	32.1
1965	81.1	60.2	20.9	27.1	54.0	33.4
1966	86.9	64.0	22.9	29.8	57.1	34.3
1967	91.6	66.8	24.8	29.2	62.4	31.9
1968	96.8	69.5	27.3	30.9	65.9	31.9
1969	102.6	73.1	29.5	34.3	68.3	33.4

Notes appear at end of table   (continued)

TABLE Da1351-1356   Consumer expenditures on food – by location and by farm value and marketing bill components: 1913-1997 *Continued*

	Total	Location		Farm value and marketing components		
		At home	Away from home	Farm value	Marketing bill	Farm value share
	Da1351 [2]	Da1352	Da1353	Da1354	Da1355	Da1356
Year	Billion dollars	Billion dollars	Billion dollars	Billion dollars	Billion dollars	Percent
1970	110.6	78.2	32.4	35.5	75.1	32.1
1971	114.6	80.6	34.0	36.1	78.5	31.5
1972	122.2	85.4	36.8	39.8	82.4	32.6
1973	138.8	98.5	40.3	51.7	87.1	37.2
1974	154.6	109.5	45.1	56.4	98.2	36.5
1975	167.0	116.2	50.8	55.6	111.4	33.3
1976	183.3	127.2	56.1	58.3	125.0	31.8
1977	190.9	130.8	60.1	58.2	132.7	30.5
1978	216.9	149.2	67.7	69.5	147.4	32.0
1979	245.2	169.4	75.8	79.2	166.0	32.3
1980	264.4	180.1	84.3	81.7	182.7	30.9
1981	287.7	194.0	93.7	81.7	206.0	28.4
1982	298.9	196.7	102.2	81.4	217.5	27.2
1983	315.0	204.6	110.4	85.3	229.7	27.1
1984	332.0	213.1	118.9	89.8	242.2	27.0
1985	345.4	220.8	124.6	86.4	259.0	25.0
1986	359.6	226.0	133.6	88.8	270.8	24.7
1987	375.5	230.2	145.3	90.4	285.1	24.1
1988	398.8	242.1	156.7	96.8	301.9	24.3
1989	419.4	255.5	163.9	103.8	315.6	24.7
1990	449.8	276.2	173.6	106.2	343.6	23.6
1991	465.1	286.1	179.0	101.6	363.5	21.8
1992	474.5	289.6	184.9	105.1	369.4	22.1
1993	489.2	294.9	194.3	109.6	379.6	22.4
1994	512.2	308.7	203.5	109.6	402.6	21.4
1995	529.5	316.9	212.6	113.8	415.7	21.5
1996	546.7	328.0	218.7	122.2	424.5	22.4
1997	561.1	334.7	226.4	120.0	441.1	21.4

[1] Beginning with 1947, new series based on 1958 benchmark estimate. Two values are given for 1947, the first comparable with earlier years, the second with later years.

[2] For 1913-1947, consumer expenditures for farm foods eaten away from home are based on retail food store prices.

[3] Revised figures, comparable to 1947-1970 data based on 1958 benchmark estimate.

Sources

1913-1947: U.S. Department of Agriculture, Agricultural Marketing Service, "Farm-Retail Spreads for Food Products," Miscellaneous Publication number 741, 1957; Economic Research Service, revised figures for 1929, 1935, and 1939, "The Farm Food Marketing Bill and Its Components," *Agricultural Economic Report* 105 (1967). 1947-1952: U.S. Department of Agriculture, Economic Research Service, *Marketing and Transportation Situation* (August 1971). 1953-1997: U.S. Department of Agriculture, Economic Research Service, *Agricultural Economic Report* 780 (June 1999).

Documentation

Series Da1351. Consumer expenditures on food exclude alcoholic beverages, food consumed on the farm where produced, and imported foods.

Series Da1352. Includes food purchased primarily at retail food stores.

Series Da1353. Includes food purchased at restaurants, fast-food outlets, and other public eating places, and food served in institutions, such as hospitals, schools, and rest homes.

Series Da1354. Farm value is the value of agricultural products, priced at the farm level, that are used to produce domestically consumed food products.

Series Da1355. The marketing bill is an estimate of the total cost of transporting, processing, and distributing U.S. farm products consumed domestically. It is estimated as a residual between the retail value of food and the farm value of food raw materials. The main difference between the marketing bill and the price spread of series Da1349 is that the price spread is calculated for fixed quantities in a basket of food products, while the marketing bill incorporates changes over time in the quantities of final goods and in quantities of farm products used.

Daniel A. Sumner

TABLE Da1357–1367 Direct commodity program and other payments, by commodity or purpose: 1933–1999

Contributed by Daniel A. Sumner

Year	Total Da1357 Dollars	Feed grain Da1358 Dollars	Wheat Da1359 Dollars	Rice Da1360 Dollars	Cotton Da1361 Dollars	Wool Da1362 Dollars	Sugar Da1363 Dollars	Dairy Da1364 Dollars	Conservation and environment Da1365 Dollars	Emergency and disaster Da1366 Dollars	Other (and adjustments) Da1367 Dollars
1933	131,000,000	—	—	—	—	—	—	—	—	—	131,000,000
1934	446,000,000	—	—	—	51,000,000	—	—	—	—	—	395,000,000
1935	573,000,000	—	—	—	15,000,000	—	—	—	—	—	558,000,000
1936	278,000,000	—	—	—	41,000,000	—	—	—	24,000,000	—	213,000,000
1937	336,000,000	—	—	—	—	—	—	—	324,000,000	—	11,000,000
1938	446,000,000	—	—	—	114,000,000	—	22,000,000	—	309,000,000	—	0
1939	763,000,000	—	—	—	8,000,000	—	28,000,000	—	527,000,000	—	201,000,000
1940	723,000,000	—	—	—	—	—	27,000,000	—	496,000,000	—	200,000,000
1941	544,000,000	—	—	—	—	—	27,000,000	—	382,000,000	—	134,000,000
1942	650,000,000	—	—	—	—	—	25,000,000	—	450,000,000	—	175,000,000
1943	645,000,000	—	—	—	—	—	36,000,000	—	332,000,000	—	276,000,000
1944	776,000,000	—	—	—	—	—	27,000,000	—	378,000,000	—	371,000,000
1945	742,000,000	—	—	—	—	—	24,000,000	—	259,000,000	—	459,000,000
1946	772,000,000	—	—	—	—	—	31,000,000	—	285,000,000	—	456,000,000
1947	314,000,000	—	—	—	—	—	37,000,000	—	277,000,000	—	0
1948	257,000,000	—	—	—	—	—	39,000,000	—	218,000,000	—	0
1949	185,000,000	—	—	—	—	—	30,000,000	—	156,000,000	—	0
1950	283,000,000	—	—	—	—	—	37,000,000	—	246,000,000	—	0
1951	286,000,000	—	—	—	—	—	40,000,000	—	246,000,000	—	0
1952	275,000,000	—	—	—	—	—	33,000,000	—	242,000,000	—	0
1953	213,000,000	—	—	—	—	—	32,000,000	—	181,000,000	—	0
1954	257,000,000	—	—	—	—	—	40,000,000	—	217,000,000	—	0
1955	229,000,000	—	—	—	—	—	41,000,000	—	188,000,000	—	0
1956	554,000,000	—	—	—	—	54,000,000	37,000,000	—	463,000,000	—	0
1957	1,016,000,000	—	—	—	—	53,000,000	32,000,000	—	930,000,000	—	0
1958	1,089,000,000	—	—	—	—	14,000,000	44,000,000	—	1,030,000,000	—	0
1959	682,000,000	—	—	—	—	82,000,000	44,000,000	—	556,000,000	—	0
1960	702,000,000	—	—	—	—	51,000,000	59,000,000	—	593,000,000	—	0
1961	1,493,000,000	772,000,000	42,000,000	—	—	56,000,000	53,000,000	—	570,000,000	—	0
1962	1,747,000,000	841,000,000	253,000,000	—	—	54,000,000	64,000,000	—	534,000,000	—	0
1963	1,696,000,000	843,000,000	215,000,000	—	—	37,000,000	67,000,000	—	535,000,000	—	0
1964	2,181,000,000	1,163,000,000	438,000,000	—	39,000,000	25,000,000	79,000,000	—	435,000,000	—	0
1965	2,463,000,000	1,391,000,000	525,000,000	—	70,000,000	18,000,000	75,000,000	—	384,000,000	—	0
1966	3,276,823,050	1,293,390,403	679,018,508	—	772,520,404	33,697,090	71,355,132	149,705	426,691,808	—	0
1967	3,078,829,336	865,449,960	730,530,696	—	932,055,340	29,118,966	69,982,737	274,818	451,416,819	—	0
1968	3,462,053,537	1,366,034,715	747,407,190	—	786,518,386	65,555,042	75,281,965	193,641	421,062,598	—	0
1969	3,793,718,234	1,643,299,042	857,505,109	—	828,137,201	61,350,896	78,125,515	111,385	325,189,086	—	0

(continued)

TABLE Da1357–1367 Direct commodity program and other payments, by commodity or purpose: 1933–1999 Continued

Year	Total Da1357 Dollars	Feed grain Da1358 Dollars	Wheat Da1359 Dollars	Rice Da1360 Dollars	Cotton Da1361 Dollars	Wool Da1362 Dollars	Sugar Da1363 Dollars	Dairy Da1364 Dollars	Conservation and environment Da1365 Dollars	Emergency and disaster Da1366 Dollars	Other (and adjustments) Da1367 Dollars
1970	3,717,371,216	1,503,863,652	871,465,570	—	919,001,738	49,424,760	88,248,313	179,800	279,681,093	5,506,290	0
1971	3,144,655,329	1,053,800,489	877,874,918	—	822,194,216	68,771,375	80,120,367	105,871	236,328,214	3,497,382	1,962,497
1972	3,961,109,307	1,845,383,693	855,844,734	—	812,641,442	109,797,308	81,831,329	34,127	249,320,110	125,200	6,131,364
1973	2,607,191,437	1,142,048,321	474,294,210	—	718,416,112	64,958,855	81,683,111	126,898	119,526,815	−717	6,137,832
1974	530,566,294	100,494,390	70,088,435	—	41,980,642	34,553	77,947,418	278,385	235,046,620	−820	4,696,671
1975	807,080,903	278,766,088	76,975,665	—	138,238,152	12,920,086	61,100,821	139,534	234,160,515	0	4,780,042
1976	733,624,077	195,545,415	135,369,726	87,154	108,288,966	39,263,832	634,429	120,735	238,754,729	0	15,559,091
1977	1,818,878,932	187,287,580	887,307,282	130,252,733	88,990,817	5,361,588	65,439,238 [4]	41,123	343,513,152	73,294,145	37,391,274
1978	2,716,997,024	1,172,015,220	962,644,265	2,623,102	126,723,203	27,174,478	0 [5]	76,738	257,276,022	163,998,029	4,465,967
1979	1,415,266,992	493,951,837	113,541,182	58,751,210	184,948,836	33,265,987	—	53,619	219,124,188	58,649,206	252,980,927
1980	1,285,672,350	382,060,806	211,343,941	1,948,162	171,762,111	28,166,175	—	50,841	240,448,006	86,845,989	163,046,319
1981	1,932,184,219	242,949,597	624,545,929	1,751,427	221,964,221	35,040,221	—	39,528	229,619,577	266,676,811	309,596,908
1982	3,491,965,052	713,314,870	652,267,501	155,910,747	800,210,572	46,041,667	—	13,714	204,261,113	12,186,394	907,758,474
1983 [1]	9,295,099,404	3,904,539,215	2,837,694,693	545,183,178	1,104,983,990	83,550,073	—	6,121,375	209,779,034	26,006	603,221,840
1984 [2]	8,388,485,585	3,589,269,994	2,301,206,379	284,309,078	924,905,704	117,578,000	—	536,071,565	214,393,817	41,682	420,709,366
1985 [3]	7,703,954,092	2,860,552,256	2,040,424,299	577,234,157	1,106,243,569	97,395,741	—	428,568,438	213,267,888	22,642	380,445,102
1986	11,813,350,848	5,158,038,195	3,499,720,896	422,769,007	1,042,392,476	111,922,460	—	624,393,746	291,848,780	29,712,618	632,552,670
1987	16,746,732,102	8,489,993,234	2,931,265,769	474,852,545	1,204,298,456	143,724,447	—	507,756,548	1,552,393,708	621,930,806	820,516,589
1988	14,479,808,333	7,219,460,128	1,841,882,665	464,547,617	923,863,299	116,777,275	—	217,766,540	1,629,358,649	1,510,766,975	555,385,185
1989	10,886,701,858	3,140,795,555	602,997,161	670,981,143	1,183,815,499	81,402,972	—	182,476,678	1,793,473,246	3,153,503,577	77,256,027
1990	9,348,080,038	2,701,172,726	2,311,300,022	464,878,518	440,757,135	96,195,387	—	178,198,930	1,921,766,825	1,002,631,722	231,178,773
1991	8,214,399,204	2,648,653,002	2,165,671,995	550,028,731	406,902,839	153,519,465	—	80,426,537	1,884,857,243	129,730,482	194,608,910
1992	9,168,920,387	2,499,272,562	1,402,687,527	512,299,504	751,177,428	188,082,261	—	23,524,418	1,927,647,982	1,325,793,315	538,435,390
1993	13,397,444,589	4,844,009,108	1,904,791,161	707,572,854	1,225,618,233	173,249,004	—	222,386	1,999,848,078	1,583,038,521	959,095,244
1994	7,879,128,525	1,446,938,521	1,155,839,714	337,076,803	826,377,286	201,946,522	—	80,409,641	2,009,992,671	1,668,173,915	152,373,452
1995	7,253,372,120	3,023,945,418	587,194,222	784,459,145	29,688,293	98,254,586	—	73,021,089	1,916,844,849	658,009,625	81,954,893
1996	7,280,677,708	2,819,525,137	1,095,287,630	680,708,242	589,776,536	55,689,040	—	82,292,939	1,810,925,187	96,463,128	50,009,869
1997	7,460,412,311	2,723,292,111	1,598,269,036	518,349,386	705,958,468	13,955	—	16,741,870	1,737,525,255	104,647,688	55,614,543
1998	12,544,950,000	4,828,066,668	2,363,628,462	762,373,689	1,046,801,181	90,000	—	447,000	1,548,256,000	10,374,000	1,984,913,000
1999	20,065,075,879	6,010,898,400	2,942,695,600	949,148,200	1,303,257,800	10,000,000	—	96,462,000	1,595,134,215	317,442,028	6,840,037,636

[1] Payment-in-kind (PIK) payments for 1983 were $1,973,515,949 to wheat, $267,555,058 to rice, $2,224,523,735 to corn, $333,982,695 to sorghum, and $442,695,000 to upland cotton.

[2] PIK payments from the 1983 program made in calendar year 1984 were $245,331,588 to wheat, $92,526,160 to rice, $2,998,242,805 to corn, $224,288,586 to sorghum, and $650,248,000 to upland cotton. For the 1984 and 1985 crops, only wheat was authorized for PIK. The 1984 PIK payment to wheat was $260,723,874.

[3] PIK disbursements to wheat were $90,603,356.09.

[4] Payments shown were made to producers by processors.

[5] No new payments were made for the Sugar Act program. There were prior year adjustments that are reflected in the "Other" category. The Sugar Act program was discontinued in 1979.

Sources

Series Da1357–1367. 1933–1965: U.S. Department of Agriculture, Economic Research Service, *Farm Income Statistics,* 1974; 1966–1992: U.S. Department of Agriculture, Agricultural Stabilization and Conservation Service, *Payments to Producers by State and Programs,* various issues; 1993–1998: U.S. Department of Agriculture, Economic Research Service, *Agricultural Statistics,* various issues.

Series Da1357–1361. 1999: U.S. Department of Agriculture, Farm Service Agency, *Production Flexibility Contracts, Marketing Loss Assistance Payments, and Marketing Assistance Loans,* February 1999.

Series Da1362–1367. 1999: U.S. Department of Agriculture, Farm Service Agency, Producer Payments Reporting System, unpublished data.

Other source: U.S. Department of Agriculture, Economic Research Service, "Provisions of the Federal Agriculture Improvement and Reform Act of 1996," *Agriculture Information Bulletin* number 729.

Documentation

Data from 1933 to 1965 are from *Farm Income Statistics.* Details may not add to totals due to rounding. After 1965, data were taken from the Agricultural Stabilization and Conservation Service, *Payments to Producers by State and Programs,* and adjusted to include Great Plains Conservation Payments and to exclude payments made to territories.

For all these series and for others in this section, the specific programs under which payments were made change often and irregularly. We have categorized the payments in this table into ten series and total. Other categorization would provide alternative pictures.

TABLE Da1357–1367   Direct commodity program and other payments, by commodity or purpose: 1933–1999
Continued

Direct government payments to farmers are those made in connection with farm programs. These payments do not involve commodity transactions in the form of nonrecourse loans but are made directly to farmers who participate in specified farm programs.

For the years 1983–1985, the payments-in-kind made under the wheat, rice, corn and sorghum (which are included in feed grains), and upland cotton programs are included in the payments for each individual commodity.

For the years since 1996, the allocation of total production flexibility payments to each commodity under the Federal Agriculture Improvement and Reform (FAIR) Act is as follows: wheat: 26.26 percent; cotton: 11.63 percent; rice: 8.47 percent; and feed grains: 53.64 percent (corn: 46.22 percent; barley: 2.16 percent; sorghum: 5.11 percent; oats: .15 percent).

Series Da1357. Equals the sum of series Da1358–1367.

Series Da1358. Payments under the feed grains program include payments to farmers participating in the corn, oats, sorghum grain, and barley programs.

Series Da1361. Cotton payments include both upland and extra long staple.

Series Da1362. Wool program payments include mohair.

Series Da1363. Sugar Act payments began in 1938 and ended in 1979.

Series Da1364. Series shows payments for the dairy program, which is comprised of Milk/Dairy Indemnity payments, Milk Diversion payments, Dairy Termination payments, and Milk Marketing Fee payments for the years that apply.

Series Da1365. Series shows program payments for conservation and environment, which consist of Agricultural Conservation under the Rural Environmental Assistance Program (REAP) and the Rural Environmental Conservation Program (RECP), Forestry Incentive, Great Plains Conservation, Soil Bank, Appalachian Conservation, Conservation Reserve, Drought and Flood Conservation, Emergency Conservation, Cropland Conversion, Water Bank, Cropland Adjustment, Colorado River Salinity, Arkansas Beaver Lake, Wetland Reserve, Naval Stores, Environment Quality Incentives, Rural Clean Water Program, Clean Lakes, and Regional Development for the years that apply.

Series Da1366. Payments to the emergency and disaster programs include Emergency Feed, Emergency Livestock Feed, Emergency Preparedness, and Disaster payments for the years that apply.

Series Da1367. Other payments include a variety of programs such as Beekeepers Indemnity, Potato Diversion, Rental and Benefits 1933–1937, Price Adjustment and Parity 1939–1944, Wartime Production Subsidy 1943–1946, Extended Storage, PIK Storage, Wild Hemp Elimination, Hay and Cattle Transportation payments, Animal Waste Management, Producer Storage, Karnal Bunt Fungus, Noninsured Assistance, Public Access, Loan Deficiency payments, Options Pilot Program, Interest, 90-Day Rule, Market Gains payments, and prior year adjustments and credit for the years that apply.

TABLE Da1368–1385   Selected commodity program provisions – corn, wheat, rice, and upland cotton: 1933–1999[1,2]
Contributed by Daniel A. Sumner

	Corn					Wheat				
				Acres idled					Acres idled	
Year	Loan rate	Target price	Total	As a percentage of total acres	Farmer-owned reserves	Loan rate	Target price	Total	As a percentage of total acres	Farmer-owned reserves
	Da1368[3]	Da1369	Da1370	Da1371	Da1372	Da1373	Da1374	Da1375	Da1376	Da1377
	Dollars per bushel	Dollars per bushel	Acres	Percent	Bushels	Dollars per bushel	Dollars per bushel	Acres	Percent	Bushels
1933	0.45	—	—	—	—	—	—	—	—	—
1934	0.55	—	—	—	—	—	—	—	—	—
1935	0.45	—	—	—	—	—	—	—	—	—
1936	0.55	—	—	—	—	—	—	—	—	—
1937	0.50	—	—	—	—	—	—	—	—	—
1938	0.57	—	—	—	—	0.59	—	—	—	—
1939	0.57	—	—	—	—	0.63	—	—	—	—
1940	0.61	—	—	—	—	0.64	—	—	—	—
1941	0.75	—	—	—	—	0.98	—	—	—	—
1942	0.83	—	—	—	—	1.14	—	—	—	—
1943	0.90	—	—	—	—	1.23	—	—	—	—
1944	0.98	—	—	—	—	1.35	—	—	—	—
1945	1.01	—	—	—	—	1.38	—	—	—	—
1946	1.15	—	—	—	—	1.49	—	—	—	—
1947	1.37	—	—	—	—	1.84	—	—	—	—
1948	1.44	—	—	—	—	2.00	—	—	—	—
1949	1.40	—	—	—	—	1.95	—	—	—	—
1950	1.47	—	—	—	—	1.99	—	—	—	—
1951	1.57	—	—	—	—	2.18	—	—	—	—
1952	1.60	—	—	—	—	2.20	—	—	—	—
1953	1.60	—	—	—	—	2.21	—	—	—	—
1954	1.62	—	—	—	—	2.24	—	—	—	—

Notes appear at end of table

(continued)

TABLE Da1368–1385   Selected commodity program provisions – corn, wheat, rice, and upland cotton: 1933–1999
Continued

	Corn					Wheat				
			Acres idled					Acres idled		
	Loan rate	Target price	Total	As a percentage of total acres	Farmer-owned reserves	Loan rate	Target price	Total	As a percentage of total acres	Farmer-owned reserves
	Da1368 [3]	Da1369	Da1370	Da1371	Da1372	Da1373	Da1374	Da1375	Da1376	Da1377
	Dollars per bushel	Dollars per bushel				Dollars per bushel	Dollars per bushel			
Year			Acres	Percent	Bushels			Acres	Percent	Bushels
1955	1.58	—	—	—	—	2.08	—	—	—	—
1956	1.50	—	—	—	—	2.00	—	—	—	—
1957	1.40	—	—	—	—	2.00	—	—	—	—
1958	1.36	—	—	—	—	1.82	—	—	—	—
1959	1.12	—	—	—	—	1.81	—	—	—	—
1960	1.06	—	—	—	—	1.78	—	—	—	—
1961	1.20	—	19,114,600	22.5	—	1.79	—	—	—	—
1962	1.20	—	20,263,010	23.8	—	2.00	—	10,699,164	17.8	—
1963	1.07	—	17,160,951	20.0	—	1.82	—	7,160,739	11.8	—
1964	1.10	—	22,221,645	25.2	—	1.30	—	5,122,778	8.4	—
1965	1.05	—	23,976,440	26.9	280,000,000 [7]	1.25	—	7,184,662	11.1	—
1966	1.00	—	27,871,971	29.6	176,000,000 [7]	1.25	—	8,257,415	13.2	—
1967	1.05	—	16,158,966	18.5	296,000,000 [7]	1.25	—	—	—	—
1968	1.05	—	25,427,074	28.1	350,000,000 [7]	1.25	—	—	—	—
1969	1.05	—	27,171,694	29.7	293,000,000 [7]	1.25	—	11,097,411	17.2	—
1970	1.05	—	26,101,902	28.1	203,000,000 [7]	1.25	—	15,723,479	24.4	—
1971	1.05	—	14,092,829	16.0	515,000,000 [7]	1.25	—	13,499,827	20.1	—
1972	1.05	—	24,411,658	26.7	48,000,000 [7]	1.25	—	20,105,882	26.8	—
1973	1.05	—	5,993,794	7.7	—	1.25	—	7,372,030	11.1	—
1974	1.10	1.38	—	—	—	1.37	2.05	—	—	—
1975	1.10	1.38	—	—	—	1.37	2.05	—	—	—
1976	1.50	1.57	—	—	—	2.25	2.29	—	—	—
1977	2.00	2.00	—	—	212,000,000	2.25	2.90	—	—	342,000,000
1978	2.00	2.10	6,133,100	7.0	585,000,000	2.35	3.40	9,464,806	12.5	393,000,000
1979	2.10	2.20	2,877,422	3.4	670,000,000	2.50	3.40	8,297,669	10.4	260,000,000
1980	2.25 [4]	2.35 [5]	—	—	0	3.00 [4]	3.63 [5]	—	—	360,000,000
1981	2.40	2.40	—	—	1,276,000,000	3.20	3.81	—	—	562,000,000
1982	2.55	2.70	2,090,222	2.5	1,890,000,000	3.55	4.05	5,831,908	6.3	1,061,000,000
1983	2.65	2.86	20,985,281	25.8	447,000,000	3.65	4.30	31,607,913	29.5	611,000,000
1984	2.55	3.03	3,877,119	4.6	389,000,000	3.30	4.38	18,606,409	19.0	654,000,000
1985	2.55	3.03	5,446,092	6.1	711,000,000	3.30	4.38	18,825,009	19.9	433,000,000
1986	1.92	3.03	12,746,161	14.3	1,498,000,000	2.40	4.38	21,014,243	22.6	463,000,000
1987	1.82	3.03	23,169,301	25.9	1,127,000,000	2.28	4.38	23,931,737	26.7	467,000,000
1988	1.77	2.93	20,476,655	23.2	724,000,000	2.21	4.23	22,462,977	25.5	287,000,000
1989	1.65	2.84	10,755,563	13.0	387,000,000	2.06	4.10	9,580,557	11.1	100,000,000
1990	1.57	2.75	10,671,116	12.6	3,000,000	1.95	4.00	8,520,564	9.9	0
1991	1.62	2.75	7,451,026 [6]	8.9	0	2.04	4.00	15,924,272	18.5	0
1992	1.72	2.75	5,274,762 [6]	6.2	13,000,000	2.21	4.00	7,321,461	9.2	0
1993	1.72	2.75	10,908,764 [6]	13.0	119,000,000	2.45	4.00	5,696,746	7.3	0
1994	1.89	2.75	2,042,291 [6]	2.5	150,000,000	2.58	4.00	4,565,693	6.1	0
1995	1.89	2.75	6,183,034 [6]	8.0	0	2.58	4.00	3,786,558	5.2	0
1996	1.89	—	0	0.0	0	2.58	—	0	0.0	0
1997	1.89	—	0	0.0	0	2.58	—	0	0.0	0
1998	1.89	—	0	0.0	0	2.58	—	0	0.0	0
1999	1.89	—	0	0.0	0	2.58	—	0	0.0	0

Notes appear at end of table

TABLE Da1368–1385   Selected commodity program provisions – corn, wheat, rice, and upland cotton: 1933–1999
Continued

	Rice				Upland cotton			
	Loan rate	Target price	Acres idled		Loan rate	Target price	Acres idled	
			Total	As a percentage of total acres			Total	As a percentage of total acres
	Da1378	Da1379	Da1380	Da1381	Da1382	Da1383	Da1384	Da1385
Year	Dollars per hundredweight	Dollars per hundredweight	Acres	Percent	Cents per pound	Cents per pound	Acres	Percent
1933	—	—	—	—	10.00	—	—	—
1934	—	—	—	—	12.00	—	—	—
1935	—	—	—	—	10.00	—	—	—
1936	—	—	—	—	—	—	—	—
1937	—	—	—	—	9.00	—	—	—
1938	—	—	—	—	8.30	—	—	—
1939	—	—	—	—	8.70	—	—	—
1940	—	—	—	—	8.90	—	—	—
1941	2.04	—	—	—	14.02	—	—	—
1942	2.33	—	—	—	17.02	—	—	—
1943	— [8]	—	—	—	18.41	—	—	—
1944	— [8]	—	—	—	20.03 [9]	—	—	—
1945	2.82	—	—	—	19.84 [9]	—	—	—
1946	— [8]	—	—	—	22.83	—	—	—
1947	3.76	—	—	—	26.49	—	—	—
1948	4.08	—	—	—	28.79	—	—	—
1949	3.96	—	—	—	27.23	—	—	—
1950	4.56	—	—	—	27.90	—	—	—
1951	5.00	—	—	—	30.46	—	—	—
1952	5.04	—	—	—	30.91	—	—	—
1953	4.84	—	—	—	30.80	—	—	—
1954	4.92	—	—	—	31.58	—	—	—
1955	4.66	—	—	—	31.70	—	—	—
1956	4.57	—	—	—	29.34	—	—	—
1957	4.72	—	—	—	28.81	—	—	—
1958	4.42	—	—	—	31.23	—	—	—
1959	4.38	—	—	—	30.40 [10]	—	—	—
1960	4.48	—	—	—	28.97	—	—	—
1961	4.71	—	—	—	31.88	—	—	—
1962	4.71	—	—	—	31.88	—	—	—
1963	4.71	—	—	—	31.72	—	—	—
1964	4.71	—	—	—	29.30	—	—	—
1965	4.50	—	—	—	28.31	—	—	—
1966	4.50	—	—	—	20.21	—	4,561,799	30.8
1967	4.55	—	—	—	19.47	—	4,847,075	34.1
1968	4.60	—	—	—	19.69	—	3,318,167	23.4
1969	4.72	—	—	—	19.71	—	11,097,000	48.5
1970	4.86	—	—	—	20.15	—	15,723,000	57.0
1971	5.07	—	—	—	19.50	—	13,500,000	52.4
1972	5.27	—	—	—	19.50	—	20,106,000	59.1
1973	6.07	—	—	—	19.50	—	7,372,000	37.3
1974	7.54	—	—	—	27.06	38.00	—	—
1975	8.52	—	—	—	36.12	38.00	—	—
1976	6.19	8.25	—	—	38.92	43.20	—	—
1977	6.19	8.25	—	—	44.63	47.80	—	—
1978	6.40	8.53	—	—	48.00	52.00	16,800,000	55.8
1979	6.79	9.05	—	—	50.23	57.70	682,886	4.7
1980	7.12	9.49	—	—	48.00	58.40	—	—
1981	8.01	10.68	—	—	52.46	70.87	—	—
1982	8.14	10.85	422,395	11.4	57.08	71.00	1,580,488	12.3
1983	8.14	11.40	1,825,600	45.5	55.00	76.00	6,805,200	46.4
1984	8.00	11.90	812,362	22.3	55.00	81.00	2,472,146	18.3
1985	8.00	11.90	1,259,034	33.4	57.30	81.00	3,611,816	25.4
1986	7.20	11.90	1,479,128	38.3	55.00	81.00	4,041,448	28.9
1987	6.84	11.66	1,565,854	39.9	52.25	79.40	3,860,531	27.3
1988	6.63	11.15	1,087,872	27.1	51.80	75.90	2,161,372	14.9
1989	6.50	10.80	1,183,574	30.2	50.00	73.40	3,513,025	25.6

Notes appear at end of table   (continued)

TABLE Da1368–1385   Selected commodity program provisions – corn, wheat, rice, and upland cotton: 1933–1999
Continued

	Rice				Upland cotton			
			Acres idled				Acres idled	
	Loan rate	Target price	Total	As a percentage of total acres	Loan rate	Target price	Total	As a percentage of total acres
	Da1378	Da1379	Da1380	Da1381	Da1382	Da1383	Da1384	Da1385
Year	Dollars per hundredweight	Dollars per hundredweight	Acres	Percent	Cents per pound	Cents per pound	Acres	Percent
1990	6.50	10.71	1,022,465	26.1	50.27	72.90	1,956,181	13.9
1991	6.50	10.71	850,126	22.8	50.77	72.90	1,229,597	8.2
1992	6.50	10.71	446,023	12.3	52.35	72.90	1,705,892	11.6
1993	6.50	10.71	679,805	18.9	52.35	72.90	1,378,707	9.4
1994	6.50	10.71	258,520	7.2	50.00	72.90	1,711,796	11.2
1995	6.50	10.71	453,474	12.5	51.92	72.90	158,183	1.0
1996	6.50	—	0	0.0	51.92	—	0	—
1997	6.50	—	0	0.0	51.92	—	0	—
1998	6.50	—	0	0.0	51.92	—	0	—
1999	6.50	—	0	0.0	51.92	—	0	—

[1] Data are actual loan rates for 1933–1996. Upper limits on loan rates established by the Federal Agriculture Improvement and Reform (FAIR) Act are reported as the loan rate in this table from 1997 forward for wheat, corn, and cotton. Actual loan rates are to be no lower than the level calculated as 85 percent of a moving average of previous prices, subject to fixed upper limits and fixed lower limits also established by the FAIR Act.

[2] In addition to the upper limits on loan rates shown in the table, minimum loan rates were also set under the 1996 FAIR Act; fifty cents per pound for upland cotton.

[3] Loan rate for corn is the announced loan rate and not the basic loan rate.

[4] Loan rate for regular loans. An alternative loan rate applied to crops placed in the farmer-owned reserve in 1980–1982 and 1986. See text.

[5] Target price if crop planted within normal crop acreage. An alternative price applied if the amount planted exceeded normal crop acreage. See text.

[6] For 1991–1995, 50–92 and 0–92 program acreage includes program acreage planted to minor oilseeds.

[7] For 1965–1972, the grains were stored under the Reseal Program.

[8] In the years 1943, 1944, and 1946, the rice loan rate was not announced.

[9] Prices subject to Stabilization Extension Act of June 30, 1944. See text for series. The price shown is the beginning purchase price. The purchase price increased five points monthly for seven months in 1944 and for ten months in 1945.

[10] Cotton grown by farmers electing Choice A acreage allotments. Corresponding support level for Choice B for 1959 was 24.70 cents (65 percent of parity); for 1960, it was 23.18 cents (60 percent of parity).

Sources

1933–1960: U.S. Department of Agriculture, Agricultural Stabilization and Conservation Service, "Farm Commodity and Related Programs," *Agriculture Handbook* number 345, revised, March 1976. 1961–1989: Robert C. Green, "Program Provisions for Program Crops: A Database for 1961–90," U.S. Department of Agriculture, Economic Research Service, Agriculture and Trade Analysis Division, *Staff Report* number AGES 9010. 1990–1995: U.S. Department of Agriculture, Economic Research Service, *Agricultural Outlook*, various issues, and U.S. Department of Agriculture, Farm Service Agency, unpublished data. 1996–1999: U.S. Department of Agriculture, Economic Research Service, "Provisions of the Federal Agriculture Improvement and Reform Act of 1996," *Agriculture Information Bulletin* number 729.

Documentation

Series Da1368, Da1373, Da1378, and Da1382. The loan rates are the prices per unit at which the government will provide loans to farmers on crops that may either be sold later or forfeited to the government under "nonrecourse" provisions.

Series Da1369, Da1374, Da1379, and Da1383. The target prices are the prices established by law for wheat, corn, grain sorghum, barley, oats, rice, and extra long staple and upland cotton. Prior to 1996, farmers participat-

ing in these programs received deficiency payments based on the difference between the target price and the higher of the national market price during a specified time period, or the price support (nonrecourse) loan rate. The 1996 Federal Agriculture Improvement and Reform (FAIR) Act eliminated target prices.

Series Da1368–1369 and Da1373–1374. There were alternate loan rates for corn and wheat in 1980–1982 and 1986 (series Da1368 and Da1373) if the crop was placed in the farmer-owned reserve (FOR). There was also an alternative target price for these two crops in 1980 (series Da1369 and Da1374), if the amount planted exceeded the normal crop acreage (NCA). The alternative rates for the years in question are recorded in the following table.

	Corn loan rate FOR Series Da1368	Wheat loan rate FOR Series Da1373	Corn target price exceeded NCA Series Da1369	Wheat target price exceeded NCA Series Da1374
1980	2.40	3.30	2.05	3.08
1981	2.55	3.50	—	—
1982	2.90	4.00	—	—
1986	1.89	2.30	—	—

Series Da1370, Da1375, Da1380, and Da1384. Consists of acres idled under the Acreage Reduction Program (ARP), Paid Land Diversion (PLD), Payment-in-Kind (PIK), Set-aside, 50/92, and 0/85–92 for the crops to which these programs may apply. For a data series on the Conservation Reserve Program – which applies after 1985 – and previous conservation programs, see Table Da1453–1456.

Series Da1371, Da1376, Da1381, and Da1385. Calculated as total acres idled divided by the sum of planted acres and diverted acres.

Series Da1372 and Da1377. The Farmer-Owned Reserve (FOR) program provided storage payments for wheat and feed grains when market prices were low and stocks abundant. FOR stocks are ending stocks.

Series Da1382. For 1944 and 1945, section 3 of the Stabilization Act of 1942, as amended by the Stabilization Extension Act of June 30, 1944, required that all lawful action be taken to assure producers of certain commodities, including cotton, the higher of (1) the parity or comparable price, or (2) the highest price received by producers for the commodity between January 1 and September 15, 1942. Inasmuch as 100 percent of the parity was higher than the loan level, it was to the advantage of cotton producers to redeem cotton previously placed under loan and to resell to the Commodity Credit Corporation at the higher price. This course was followed by most producers.

TABLE Da1386–1398 Selected commodity program provisions – soybeans, peanuts, tobacco, sugarcane, sugar beets, honey, wool, and milk: 1938–1999

Contributed by Daniel A. Sumner

Year	Soybeans, loan rate	Peanuts — Loan rate for quota	Peanuts — National marketing poundage quota	Flue-cured tobacco — Loan rate	Flue-cured tobacco — National marketing poundage quota	Burley tobacco — Loan rate	Burley tobacco — National marketing poundage quota	Raw sugarcane, target price/loan rate	Refined sugar beet, loan rate	Honey, loan rate	Wool — Support level	Wool — Payment rate	Milk, support level
	Da1386 [1,2]	Da1387	Da1388	Da1389	Da1390	Da1391	Da1392	Da1393 [3]	Da1394	Da1395	Da1396	Da1397	Da1398 [4]
	Dollars per bushel	Cents per pound	Thousand pounds	Cents per pound	Thousand pounds	Cents per pound	Thousand pounds	Cents per pound	Cents per bushel	Cents per pound	Cents per pound	Percent	Dollars per hundredweight
1938	—	—	—	—	—	—	—	—	—	—	18.0	—	—
1939	—	—	—	15.4	—	—	—	—	—	—	18.0	—	—
1940	—	—	—	15.0	—	16.4	—	—	—	—	—	—	—
1941	1.05	4.350	—	19.6	—	20.0	—	—	—	—	—	—	—
1942	1.60	6.600	—	23.7	—	24.6	—	—	—	—	—	—	—
1943	1.80	7.100	—	27.6	—	27.0	—	—	—	—	41.7	—	—
1944	2.04	7.300	—	28.9	—	28.2	—	—	—	—	42.4	—	—
1945	2.04	7.500	—	29.7	—	29.0	—	—	—	—	41.9	—	—
1946	2.04	8.600	—	32.1	—	33.6	—	—	—	—	42.3	—	—
1947	2.04	10.000	—	40.0	—	40.3	—	—	—	—	42.3	—	—
1948	2.18	10.800	—	43.9	—	42.4	—	—	—	—	42.3	—	—
1949	2.11	10.530	—	42.5	—	40.3	—	—	—	—	42.3	—	—
1950	2.06	10.800	1,286,000	45.0	—	45.7	—	—	—	9.0 [10]	45.2	—	—
1951	2.45	11.280	1,300,000	50.7	—	49.8	—	—	—	10.1	50.7	—	—
1952	2.56	11.970	1,300,000	50.6	—	49.5	—	—	—	11.4	54.2	—	—
1953	2.56	11.880	1,326,000	47.9	—	46.6	—	—	—	10.5	53.1	—	—
1954	2.22	12.240	1,348,000	47.9	—	46.4	—	—	—	10.2	53.2	—	—
1955	2.04	12.240	1,592,000	48.3	—	46.2	—	—	—	9.9	62.0	—	—
1956	2.15	11.350	1,500,000	48.9	—	48.1	—	—	—	9.7	62.0	—	—
1957	2.09	11.070	1,451,000	50.8	—	51.7	—	—	—	9.7	62.0	—	—
1958	2.09	10.660	1,652,000	54.6	—	55.4	—	—	—	9.6	62.0	—	—
1959	1.85	9.675	1,772,000	55.5	—	57.2	—	—	—	8.3	62.0	—	—
1960	1.85	10.062	1,868,000	55.5	—	57.2	—	—	—	8.6	62.0	—	—
1961	2.30	11.050	1,940,000	55.5	—	57.2	—	6.40	—	11.2	62.0	44.5	3.06
1962	2.25	11.070	2,012,000	56.1	—	57.8	—	6.51	—	11.2	62.0	30.0	3.40
1963	2.25	11.200	2,012,000	56.6	—	58.3	—	6.61	—	11.2	62.0	27.8	3.11
1964	2.25	11.200	2,133,000	57.2	—	58.9	—	6.63	—	11.2	62.0	16.5	3.14
1965	2.25	11.200	2,375,000	57.7	1,126,000	59.5	—	6.80	—	11.2	65.0	31.6	3.15
1966	2.50	11.350	2,737,000	58.8	1,135,000	60.6	—	7.08	—	11.4	66.0	24.8	3.24
1967	2.50	11.350	2,858,000	59.9	1,126,000	61.8	—	7.25	—	12.5	67.0	65.8	3.50
1968	2.50	12.012	2,978,000	61.6	1,128,000	63.5	—	7.52	—	12.5	67.0	65.4	4.00
1969	2.25	12.375	3,099,000	63.8	1,072,000	65.8	—	7.91	—	13.0	69.0	65.1	4.28
1970	2.25	12.750	3,075,000	66.6	1,072,000	68.6	—	8.27	—	13.0	72.0	102.8	4.28
1971	2.25	13.425	3,107,000	69.4	1,072,000	71.5	555,000	8.69	—	14.0	72.0	271.1	4.66
1972	2.25	14.250	3,268,000	72.7	1,071,000	74.9	532,000	9.10	—	14.0	72.0	105.7	4.93
1973	2.25	16.425	3,542,000	76.6	1,179,000	78.9	560,000	10.38	—	16.1	72.0	—	4.93
1974	2.25	18.300	3,703,000	83.3	1,297,000	85.9	606,000	12.19	—	20.6	72.0	21.8	5.29

Notes appear at end of table

(continued)

TABLE Da1386–1398   Selected commodity program provisions – soybeans, peanuts, tobacco, sugarcane, sugar beets, honey, wool, and milk: 1938–1999
Continued

Year	Soybeans, loan rate [1,2] Da1386 Dollars per bushel	Peanuts Loan rate for quota Da1387 Cents per pound	Peanuts National marketing poundage quota Da1388 Thousand pounds	Flue-cured tobacco Loan rate Da1389 Cents per pound	Flue-cured tobacco National marketing poundage quota Da1390 Thousand pounds	Burley tobacco Loan rate Da1391 Cents per pound	Burley tobacco National marketing poundage quota Da1392 Thousand pounds	Raw sugarcane, target price/loan rate [3] Da1393 Cents per pound	Refined sugar beet, loan rate Da1394 Cents per bushel	Honey, loan rate Da1395 Cents per pound	Wool Support level Da1396 Cents per pound	Wool Payment rate Da1397 Percent	Milk, support level [4] Da1398 Dollars per hundredweight
1975	—	19.725	3,800,000	93.2	1,491,000	96.1	670,000	—	—	25.5	72.0	61.1	6.57
1976	2.50	20.700	4,009,000	106.0	1,268,000	109.3	635,000	—	—	29.4	72.0	9.6	7.24
1977	3.50	21.525	4,138,000	113.8	1,116,500	117.3	636,200	13.50	14.24 [9]	32.7	99.0	37.5	8.13
1978	4.50	21.000	3,330,000	121.0	1,117,200	124.7	614,200	14.73	16.99	36.8	108.0	45.0	9.43
1979	4.50	21.000	3,192,000	129.3	1,094,900	133.3	614,200	13.00	15.15	43.9	115.0	33.3	10.76
1980	5.02	22.750	3,032,000	141.5	1,094,400	145.9	614,400	— [5]	— [5]	50.3	123.0	39.6	12.36
1981	5.02	22.750	2,880,000	158.7	1,012,900	163.6	660,100	16.75 [6]	19.70 [6]	57.4	135.0	42.9	13.49
1982	5.02	27.500	2,400,000	169.9	1,013,000	175.1	680,300	17.00	20.15	60.4	137.0	100.3	13.10
1983	5.02	27.500	2,335,000	169.9	910,500	175.1	646,300	17.50	20.86	62.2	153.0	149.6	13.10
1984	5.02	27.500	2,269,000	169.9	804,300	175.1	581,800	17.75	20.76	65.8	165.0	107.5	12.10
1985	5.02	27.950	2,200,000	169.9	775,000	148.8	524,400	18.00	21.06	65.3	165.0	160.7	11.60
1986	4.77	30.370	2,711,000	143.8	728,500	148.8	493,200	18.00 [7]	21.09 [7]	64.0	178.0	166.5	11.60
1987	4.77	30.370	2,711,000	143.5	707,000	148.8	463,900	18.00	21.16	61.0	181.0	97.4	11.10
1988	4.77	30.800	2,804,400	144.2	754,300	150.0	473,200	18.00 [8]	21.37 [8]	59.1	178.0	29.0	11.10
1989	4.53	30.800	2,880,000	146.8	890,500	153.2	586,900	18.00 [8]	21.54 [8]	56.4	177.0	42.7	10.60
1990	4.50	31.570	3,120,000	148.8	877,700	155.8	601,300	18.00 [8]	21.93 [8]	53.8	182.0	127.5	10.10
1991	5.02	32.140	3,100,000	152.8	877,600	158.4	724,100	18.00	22.85	53.8	188.0	241.8	10.10
1992	5.02	33.370	3,080,000	156.0	891,800	164.9	668,500	18.00	23.33	53.8	197.0	166.2	10.10
1993	5.02	33.370	2,992,000	157.7	891,200	168.3	603,000	18.00	23.62	53.8	204.0	300.0	10.10
1994	4.92	33.920	2,700,000	158.3	802,600	171.4	542,700	18.00	23.43	50.0	209.0	167.9	10.10
1995	4.92	33.920	2,700,000	159.7	934,600	172.5	549,000	18.00	22.90	50.0	212.0	0.0	10.10
1996	4.97	30.500	2,200,000	160.1	823,600	173.7	633,800	18.00	22.90	—	—	0.0	10.35
1997	5.26	30.500	2,266,000	162.1	973,800	176.0	704,500	18.00	22.90	—	—	0.0	10.20
1998	5.26	30.500	2,334,000	162.8	807,600	177.8	637,000	18.00	22.90	—	—	0.0	10.05
1999	5.26	30.500	2,360,000	163.2	666,200	178.9	452,900	18.00	22.90	—	—	0.0	9.90

1 Data are actual loan rates for 1933–1996. Upper limits on loan rates established by the Federal Agriculture Improvement and Reform (FAIR) Act are reported as the loan rate in this table from 1997 forward for soybeans. Actual loan rates are to be no lower than the level calculated as 85 percent of a moving average of immediate prices, subject to fixed upper limits and fixed lower limits also established by the FAIR Act.

2 In addition to the upper limits on loan rates shown in the table, minimum loan rates were also set under the 1996 FAIR Act; $4.92 per bushel for soybeans.

3 The series records the target price for raw cane sugar until 1977, at which point it records the loan rate.

4 Milk support level is as of April 1 with the following exceptions: for the years 1981, 1983, 1986, 1987, and 1989–1999, the support level is as of October 1.

5 No program was established, but the price continued to be supported.

6 Represents data for price support purchase programs for sugar produced from December 22, 1981, through March 31, 1982. The sugar was statutorily defined as part of the 1982 crop.

7 Loan proceeds were reduced 4.3 percent as the result of the Balanced Budget and Emergency Deficit Control Act.

8 For the years 1988–1990, loan proceeds were reduced 1.4 percent as the result of the Balanced Budget and Emergency Deficit Control Act.

9 The value reported is the initial setting; the value for the final setting was 15.57 cents per bushel.

10 On March 22, 1951, support for most flavors of honey was announced at 10 cents per pound with about a dozen flavors of limited commercial acceptability supported at 9 cents. On April 5, 1951, it was announced that the support price for honey of wide table use acceptability would be increased from 10.0 to 10.1 cents per pound.

Sources

1950–1960, series Da1388: Robert C. Green, U.S. Department of Agriculture, Economic Research Service, Agriculture and Trade Analysis Division, unpublished data.

1933–1960, all other series: U.S. Department of Agriculture, Agricultural Stabilization and Conservation Service, "Farm Commodity and Related Programs," Agriculture Handbook number 345, revised, March 1976 (1933–1960).

1961–1989: Robert C. Green, "Program Provisions for Rye, Dry Edible Beans, Oil Crops, Tobacco, Sugar, Honey, Wool, Mohair, Gum Naval Stores, and Dairy Products: A Database for 1961–90," U.S. Department of Agriculture, Economic Research Service, Agricultural and Trade Analysis Division, Staff Report number AGES 9128.

TABLE Da1386–1398 Selected commodity program provisions – soybeans, peanuts, tobacco, sugarcane, sugar beets, honey, wool, and milk: 1938–1999 *Continued*

1990–1997: U.S. Department of Agriculture, Economic Research Service, *Agricultural Statistics*, various issues.

1998–1999: U.S. Department of Agriculture, Farm Service Agency, Tobacco and Peanuts Division, unpublished data.

Other sources: U.S. Department of Agriculture, Economic Research Service, *Provisions of the Federal Improvement and Reform Act of 1996*, Agriculture Information Bulletin number 729.

Documentation

Series Da1386–1387, Da1389, Da1391, and Da1393–1395. The loan rates are the prices per unit at which the government will provide loans to farmers to enable them to hold their crops for later sale.

Series Da1388. Provides the basic national marketing poundage quota for peanuts.

Series Da1390 and Da1392. Provides the basic national marketing quota and allotment for flue-cured tobacco and burley tobacco.

Series Da1396 and Da1398. The support price is a legislated minimum price for a particular commodity, maintained through a variety of mechanisms, such as nonrecourse loans and purchase programs. The milk support level is at the national average milkfat.

Series Da1397. Gives the wool payment rate as a percentage of the market price. The payment rate is the amount paid per unit of production to each participating farmer for eligible payment production under the 1996 FAIR Act.

TABLE Da1399–1402 Federal government outlays for agriculture, natural resources, and the environment: 1962–1999

Contributed by Daniel A. Sumner

		Agriculture		
	Natural resources and environment	Total	Farm income stabilization	Agricultural research and services
	Da1399	Da1400	Da1401	Da1402
Year	Million dollars	Million dollars	Million dollars	Million dollars
1962	2,044	3,562	3,222	340
1963	2,251	4,384	4,047	337
1964	2,364	4,609	4,241	369
1965	2,531	3,955	3,551	404
1966	2,719	2,447	2,004	444
1967	2,869	2,990	2,515	475
1968	2,988	4,545	4,032	512
1969	2,900	5,826	5,304	521
1970	3,065	5,166	4,589	577
1971	3,915	4,290	3,651	639
1972	4,241	5,259	4,553	706
1973	4,775	4,854	4,099	755
1974	5,697	2,230	1,458	772
1975	7,346	3,036	2,160	876
1976	8,184	3,170	2,249	921
(TQ)	2,524	983	743	240
1977	10,032	6,787	5,735	1,052
1978	10,983	11,357	10,228	1,129
1979	12,135	11,236	9,895	1,340
1980	13,858	8,839	7,441	1,398
1981	13,568	11,323	9,783	1,540
1982	12,998	15,944	14,344	1,599
1983	12,672	22,901	21,323	1,578
1984	12,593	13,613	11,877	1,736
1985	13,357	25,565	23,751	1,813
1986	13,639	31,449	29,608	1,841
1987	13,363	26,606	24,742	1,864
1988	14,606	17,210	15,246	1,964
1989	16,182	16,919	14,817	2,102
1990	17,080	11,958	9,761	2,197
1991	18,559	15,183	12,924	2,259
1992	20,025	15,205	12,666	2,539
1993	20,239	20,363	17,720	2,643
1994	21,064	15,046	12,350	2,695
1995	22,078	9,778	7,020	2,758
1996	21,614	9,159	6,477	2,682
1997	21,227	9,032	6,272	2,780
1998	22,300	12,206	9,297	2,909
1999	23,968	23,011	20,020	2,991

(TQ) Transition quarter.

Sources

1962–1997, *Historical Tables, Budget of the United States Government, Fiscal Year 1999*; 1998–1999, Budget of the U.S. Government, Office of Management and Budget, Outlays by Function and Subfunction: 1962–2005, online data.

Documentation

This table shows federal government outlays (on-budget) according to their functional classification. Each function, in turn, is divided into basic group-ings of programs titled subfunctions. In arraying data on a functional basis, outlays are classified according to the primary purpose of the activity. To the extent feasible, this classification is made without regard to agency or organizational distinctions.

The function numbers associated with each series are as follows: series Da1399, function number 300; series Da1400, function number 350 (the sum of 351 and 352); series Da1401, subfunction number 351; and series Da1402, subfunction number 352.

TABLE Da1403–1415   Commodity Credit Corporation – loans, acquisitions, and commodities owned of wheat, corn, and cotton: 1934–1999[1],[2]

Contributed by Daniel A. Sumner

	New loans made	Value of loans Outstanding				Cost of acquisitions				Value of commodities owned			
		Total	Wheat	Corn	Cotton	Total	Wheat	Corn	Cotton	Total	Wheat	Corn	Cotton
Year	Da1403 [3],[4]	Da1404	Da1405	Da1406	Da1407	Da1408	Da1409	Da1410	Da1411	Da1412	Da1413 [5]	Da1414	Da1415
	Dollars	Dollars	Dollars	Dollars	Dollars	Dollars	Dollars	Dollars	Dollars	Dollars	Dollars	Dollars	Dollars
1934	260,000,000	205,000,000	—	117,000,000	88,000,000	—	—	—	—	—	—	—	—
1935	311,000,000	152,000,000	—	1,000,000	139,000,000	—	—	—	—	—	—	—	—
1936	29,000,000	243,000,000	—	5,000,000	226,000,000	—	—	—	—	—	—	—	—
1937	1,000,000	123,000,000	—	(Z)	114,000,000	—	—	—	—	—	—	—	—
1938	280,000,000	241,000,000	—	7,000,000	220,000,000	—	—	—	—	9,000,000	—	9,000,000	—
1939	457,000,000	360,000,000	10,000,000	26,000,000	292,000,000	—	—	—	—	11,000,000	4,000,000	7,000,000	—
1940	308,000,000	168,000,000	7,000,000	106,000,000	36,000,000	—	—	—	—	473,000,000	1,000,000	58,000,000	369,000,000
1941	453,000,000	359,000,000	27,000,000	185,000,000	108,000,000	—	—	—	—	726,000,000	133,000,000	142,000,000	351,000,000
1942	609,000,000	336,000,000	100,000,000	154,000,000	65,000,000	—	—	—	—	678,000,000	325,000,000	46,000,000	239,000,000
1943	841,000,000	479,000,000	161,000,000	67,000,000	230,000,000	—	—	—	—	896,000,000	315,000,000	22,000,000	199,000,000
1944	531,000,000	436,000,000	24,000,000	5,000,000	399,000,000	—	—	—	—	861,000,000	160,000,000	5,000,000	191,000,000
1945	534,000,000	309,000,000	31,000,000	17,000,000	252,000,000	—	—	—	—	922,000,000	154,000,000	20,000,000	448,000,000
1946	185,000,000	48,000,000	4,000,000	(Z)	32,000,000	—	—	—	—	490,000,000	53,000,000	14,000,000	141,000,000
1947	278,000,000	121,000,000	1,000,000	17,000,000	2,000,000	424,000,000	—	—	82,000,000	294,000,000	(Z)	—	1,000,000
1948	289,000,000	144,000,000	8,000,000	1,000,000	5,000,000	373,000,000	(Z)	—	(Z)	150,000,000	(Z)	(Z)	(Z)
1949	2,169,000,000	1,270,000,000	40,000,000	456,000,000	609,000,000	1,617,000,000	622,000,000	14,000,000	3,000,000	1,082,000,000	529,000,000	10,000,000	(Z)
1950	2,023,000,000	923,000,000	65,000,000	554,000,000	122,000,000	2,716,000,000	601,000,000	601,000,000	633,000,000	2,624,000,000	760,000,000	506,000,000	580,000,000
1951	771,000,000	354,000,000	22,000,000	180,000,000	1,000,000	908,000,000	203,000,000	266,000,000	19,000,000	1,433,000,000	483,000,000	643,000,000	16,000,000
1952	949,000,000	390,000,000	47,000,000	55,000,000	48,000,000	502,000,000	256,000,000	72,000,000	1,000,000	1,073,000,000	364,000,000	500,000,000	(Z)
1953	2,129,000,000	1,163,000,000	97,000,000	468,000,000	290,000,000	1,598,000,000	855,000,000	8,000,000	78,000,000	2,158,000,000	1,090,000,000	324,000,000	31,000,000
1954	3,355,000,000	2,368,000,000	198,000,000	641,000,000	1,157,000,000	2,396,000,000	965,000,000	516,000,000	(Z)	3,430,000,000	1,813,000,000	581,000,000	17,000,000
1955	2,377,000,000	2,137,000,000	32,000,000	470,000,000	1,129,000,000	2,985,000,000	1,075,000,000	586,000,000	271,000,000	4,572,000,000	2,297,000,000	934,000,000	266,000,000
1956	3,024,000,000	2,319,000,000	90,000,000	654,000,000	979,000,000	3,150,000,000	552,000,000	461,000,000	1,166,000,000	5,384,000,000	2,205,000,000	1,136,000,000	1,184,000,000
1957	2,445,000,000	1,994,000,000	28,000,000	710,000,000	603,000,000	3,086,000,000	346,000,000	611,000,000	1,025,000,000	4,738,000,000	1,883,000,000	1,297,000,000	845,000,000
1958	2,135,000,000	1,600,000,000	68,000,000	511,000,000	366,000,000	2,999,000,000	378,000,000	695,000,000	604,000,000	4,703,000,000	1,862,000,000	1,609,000,000	179,000,000
1959	3,543,000,000	2,480,000,000	158,000,000	513,000,000	1,060,000,000	2,802,000,000	892,000,000	359,000,000	335,000,000	5,259,000,000	2,416,000,000	1,576,000,000	150,000,000
1960	1,507,000,000	1,347,000,000	163,000,000	646,000,000	9,000,000	4,020,000,000	371,000,000	361,000,000	2,507,000,000	6,021,000,000	2,452,000,000	1,700,000,000	880,000,000
1961	1,814,000,000	1,523,000,000	223,000,000	782,000,000	12,000,000	3,066,000,000	498,000,000	449,000,000	1,226,000,000	5,563,000,000	2,484,000,000	1,696,000,000	340,000,000
1962	2,662,000,000	2,255,000,000	149,000,000	1,040,000,000	591,000,000	1,969,000,000	257,000,000	431,000,000	(Z)	4,474,000,000	2,143,000,000	737,000,000	249,000,000
1963	3,070,000,000	2,602,000,000	161,000,000	1,044,000,000	751,000,000	2,771,000,000	454,000,000	709,000,000	566,000,000	4,726,000,000	2,168,000,000	604,000,000	719,000,000
1964	2,776,000,000	2,815,000,000	115,000,000	759,000,000	1,012,000,000	2,305,000,000	212,000,000	541,000,000	760,000,000	4,338,000,000	1,683,000,000	906,000,000	739,000,000
1965	2,144,000,000	2,534,000,000	136,000,000	616,000,000	775,000,000	2,005,000,000	169,000,000	140,000,000	952,000,000	3,892,000,000	1,297,000,000	595,000,000	1,123,000,000
1966	1,971,000,000	2,231,000,000	111,000,000	451,000,000	731,000,000	1,540,000,000	55,000,000	191,000,000	767,000,000	3,113,000,000	680,000,000	344,000,000	1,497,000,000
1967	1,411,000,000	1,536,000,000	96,000,000	296,000,000	153,000,000	1,351,000,000	24,000,000	111,000,000	742,000,000	1,858,000,000	195,000,000	168,000,000	1,051,000,000
1968	2,052,000,000	2,345,000,000	298,000,000	606,000,000	61,000,000	599,000,000	9,000,000	3,000,000	132,000,000	913,000,000	149,000,000	162,000,000	101,000,000
1969	2,964,000,000	3,493,000,000	583,000,000	656,000,000	324,000,000	939,000,000	96,000,000	179,000,000	7,000,000	1,244,000,000	225,000,000	306,000,000	27,000,000
1970	2,388,000,000	2,952,000,000	576,000,000	632,000,000	170,000,000	1,518,000,000	217,000,000	49,000,000	304,000,000	1,858,000,000	405,000,000	293,000,000	225,000,000
1971	1,777,828,653	1,989,458,326	245,902,126	435,657,739	31,236,929	1,128,750,947	211,206,846	19,848,022	128,379,413	1,206,471,683	488,372,312	102,737,172	48,391,771
1972	2,801,113,594	2,474,178,009	436,033,207	856,208,788	23,411,515	946,604,852	81,132,698	89,601,546	1,607,476	1,090,095,157	487,877,721	172,381,239	5,482,911
1973	1,580,177,122	1,418,051,271	77,314,655	451,391,404	25,942,521	576,438,178	55,736,799	42,610,547	26,333	478,657,337	194,450,239	98,957,131	523,336
1974	1,256,282,329	720,182,509	9,829,830	115,367,424	34,039,118	402,308,582	2,057	5,519,242	7,980	114,206,015	26,418,474	11,006,970	0

Notes appear at end of table

(continued)

TABLE Da1403–1415   Commodity Credit Corporation – loans, acquisitions, and commodities owned of wheat, corn, and cotton: 1934–1999   Continued

	Value of loans					Cost of acquisitions				Value of commodities owned			
	Outstanding												
Year	New loans made Da1403 [3,4]	Total Da1404	Wheat Da1405	Corn Da1406	Cotton Da1407	Total Da1408	Wheat Da1409	Corn Da1410	Cotton Da1411	Total Da1412	Wheat Da1413 [5]	Corn Da1414	Cotton Da1415
	Dollars	Dollars	Dollars	Dollars	Dollars	Dollars	Dollars	Dollars	Dollars	Dollars	Dollars	Dollars	Dollars
1975	852,074,379	532,240,378	3,750,617	38,939,253	142,820,481	735,330,535	3,799,524	1,925,313	13,476	416,111,014	1,659,642	447,302	10,689
1976	339,512,137	859,847,547	77,789,401	25,550,500	3,935,325	146,843,123	8,412,800	409,933	0	607,153,958	48,588	280,854	0
1977	3,621,171,829	3,244,515,883	1,814,239,971	239,387,763	13,118,568	997,410,014	72,299,696	2,503,432	268	984,856,403	22,802,599	49,536	0
1978	6,385,155,099	5,029,641,683	1,318,305,520	1,280,363,077	153,416,878	911,299,368	135,255,177	31,264,028	94,523	1,029,021,929	118,575,070	26,654,235	84,347
1979	4,575,568,631	5,209,956,621	816,108,932	1,300,669,795	80,254,459	1,007,378,565	40,041,471	194,699,552	435,625	1,162,202,085	118,230,713	208,648,059	187,202
1980	4,228,183,215	5,118,966,279	837,249,315	1,617,077,763	36,241,615	2,759,203,401	601,266,291	415,677,850	579,078	2,736,992,838	705,388,998	596,429,212	676,794
1981	5,849,100,832	5,192,725,933	1,871,208,671	629,255,268	76,132,662	2,506,657,381	27,987,093	20,506,531	137,558	3,726,847,568	678,712,878	555,161,502	761,025
1982	11,453,929,000	11,633,284,000	3,321,269,000	4,209,643,000	713,927,000	2,968,000,000	26,881,000	179,340,000	1,061,000	5,103,162,000	678,869,000	708,858,000	1,817,000
1983	13,710,254,000	15,083,861,000	4,162,017,000	5,273,883,000	959,668,000	8,633,527,000	1,599,885,000	3,131,970,000	175,001,000	10,227,424,000	1,533,024,000	3,392,474,000	173,922,000
1984	5,131,112,000	8,571,481,000	3,413,508,000	1,235,993,000	66,670,000	8,741,305,000	1,983,043,000	2,590,900,000	1,056,079,000	7,358,172,000	1,509,971,000	1,044,584,000	73,531,000
1985	10,186,532,000	12,630,878,000	4,591,226,000	2,765,619,000	376,156,000	4,294,435,000	919,158,000	191,912,000	53,029,000	6,920,924,000	1,951,115,000	757,339,000	46,027,000
1986	17,391,019,000	18,668,431,000	3,753,434,000	7,878,357,000	1,075,747,000	9,911,737,000	2,196,036,000	2,286,713,000	558,813,000	11,049,610,000	3,491,148,000	1,756,790,000	226,056,000
1987	16,566,286,000	15,173,610,000	2,835,950,000	7,423,572,000	449,374,000	17,616,466,000	1,802,186,000	10,217,650,000	1,273,399,000	11,734,889,000 [6]	3,272,227,000	4,172,148,000	23,546,000
1988	13,302,054,000	8,007,387,000	1,608,113,000	3,803,007,000	568,837,000	12,166,648,000	1,050,965,000	8,483,676,000	138,341,000	4,476,773,000	1,208,129,000	2,196,542,000	1,622,000
1989	—	—	—	—	—	3,193,074,000	294,264,000	1,418,447,000	72,848,000	2,967,437,000	697,447,000	1,253,444,000	33,733,000
1990	5,816,909,000	2,581,194,000	796,124,000	1,031,223,000	41,662,000	2,129,711,000	306,766,000	851,883,000	32,766,000	1,178,492,000	505,054,000	625,441,000	7,193,000
1991	6,630,783,000	1,571,967,000	499,499,000	149,404,000	18,977,000	2,726,156,000	435,759,000	995,759,000	1,385,000	1,782,155,000	639,036,000	962,264,000	198,000
1992	6,594,285,000	1,480,267,000	360,859,000	132,236,000	48,351,000	1,606,781,000	385,845,000	67,932,000	66,494,000	952,464,000	582,934,000	322,303,000	954,000
1993	9,050,194,000	2,649,059,000	451,326,000	904,653,000	105,539,000	1,773,393,000	593,771,000	166,869,000	180,201,000	809,051,000	561,708,000	144,827,000	27,354,000
1994	6,430,072,000	2,664,215,000	439,180,000	290,679,000	35,255,000	1,690,533,000	328,623,000	77,252,000	147,034,000	808,254,000	538,206,000	110,281,000	60,949,000
1995	—	2,368,502,000	216,609,000	452,433,000	1,804,000	636,009,000	182,623,000	43,827,000	—	701,523,000	528,122,000	105,214,000	52,000
1996	5,137,411,000	1,254,467,000	241,754,000	26,386,000	47,894,000	628,223,287	148,040,477	35,973,884	84,000	485,288,000	407,510,000	75,208,000	61,000
1997	5,333,116,260	1,350,910,347	355,200,723	144,797,269	15,571,703	727,124,000	122,195,000	51,838,000	6,582,846	376,776,074	346,333,677	6,362,686	100,209
1998	7,189,198,000	2,218,679,000	618,638,000	210,632,000	40,422,000	995,982,000	756,936,000	68,077,000	1,698,000	531,249,000	369,967,000	20,085,000	0
1999	8,357,612,807	2,439,774,242	277,998,175	342,148,256	118,844,654					714,184,000	425,695,000	39,554,000	2,190,000

(Z) Less than $500,000.

1 All values and costs are as of June 30 for 1934-1975. 1976 values and costs include a transition quarter and end on September 30. Thereafter, all values and costs are as of September 30.

2 Cotton consists of upland and extra long staple.

3 Beginning in 1985, new loans are not authorized to be made under the Storage Facility and Equipment program, but adjustments and additional costs on existing loans are still present.

4 In 1993, the Storage Facility and Equipment loans program was closed out.

5 Beginning in 1992, wheat inventory excludes wheat set aside for Food Security Wheat Reserve.

6 Some financial transactions were omitted from the accounts. See text for the series.

Sources

1934-1970: U.S. Department of Agriculture, Agricultural Stabilization and Conservation Service, *Commodity Credit Corporation Report of Financial Condition and Operations*, annual issues; 1971-1997: U.S. Department of Agriculture, National Agricultural Statistics Service, *Agricultural Statistics*, various issues; 1998-1999: U.S. Department of Agriculture, Farm Service Agency, Financial Management Division, unpublished data.

Documentation

The Commodity Credit Corporation (CCC) is a wholly owned government corporation. Originally incorporated October 17, 1933, with a capitalization of three million dollars, the CCC was initially managed and operated in close affiliation with the Reconstruction Finance Corporation, which funded its ongoing operations. On July 1, 1939, it was transferred to the Department of Agriculture by the President's Reorganization Plan I, and on July 1, 1948, it was reincorporated as a federal corporation within the Department of Agriculture by the Commodity Credit Corporation Charter Act. The management of the CCC is vested in a board of directors, subject to the general supervision and direction of the Secretary of Agriculture. The board consists of six members, in addition to the Secretary as chairman, who are appointed by the president of the United States by and with the advice and consent of the Senate.

The CCC's price support programs, and domestic acquisition and disposal activities for price support commodities, are carried out entirely through the Agricultural Stabilization and Conservation Service, which is now the Farm Service Agency. These support operations are handled primarily through loan, purchase, and payment programs.

TABLE Da1403–1415 Commodity Credit Corporation – loans, acquisitions, and commodities owned of wheat, corn, and cotton: 1934–1999 *Continued*

The CCC is directed to utilize, to the maximum extent practicable, the customary channels, facilities, and arrangements of trade and commerce in carrying on purchasing and selling activities, and in conducting warehousing, transporting, processing, and handling operations. The CCC may contract for the use of plants and facilities for the handling, storing, processing, servicing, and transporting of agricultural commodities subject to its control; it has authority to acquire personal property and to rent or lease office space necessary for the conduct of its business.

Commodities from the price support inventory have been moved into consumption outlets in various ways. Some commodities were sold for domestic uses in the United States, and some were sold for export, including those under the CCC Export Sales Program and programs authorized under Title I of Public Law 480. Some commodities were bartered for goods and services to fill U.S. government needs abroad, and for foreign-produced strategic and critical materials for stockpiling. In addition, commodities were donated through federal, state, and private agencies for use in child nutrition programs and in the assistance of needy persons in the United States; commodities were transferred for donation through U.S. welfare organizations and intergovernmental organizations to needy persons and child feeding programs abroad; and dairy products were transferred for use by the Veterans Administration and by the Department of Defense. Some grains were donated to aid livestock producers in declared acute economic distress and major disaster areas; some grains were sold at reduced prices to livestock producers in areas where feed was short due to drought, flood, hurricane, or other catastrophe.

Series Da1403. Shows the value of new loans made on price-support commodities and includes new loans made on storage facility and equipment. The storage capacity of new loans varies annually.

Series Da1404–1407. Shows the value of price-support loans and storage facility and equipment loans outstanding by commodity and total. Beginning in 1988, the total of loans outstanding is reduced by allowances for losses and doubtful accounts, which is the net change in allowance for doubtful accounts between the beginning and the end of the fiscal year.

Series Da1408–1411. Shows the cost of acquisitions for price-support commodities only by commodity and total. Cost of acquisitions is the sum of purchases and collateral acquired for the price-support program.

Series Da1412–1415. Shows the value of price-support program commodities owned by the CCC by commodity and total. Beginning in 1988, total ending inventory operations is reduced by allowances for inventory losses and adjustments for lag activity, which is current year activity not processed during the regular operating cycle or inventory disposed of during the current fiscal year activity. Inventories of commodities, as shown, include commodities committed to sale or otherwise obligated. Prior to 1953, inventory dollar transactions include costs incurred subsequent to acquisition of title, such as storage, handling, transportation, and cost of storing certain grains while under extended loan for cost of acquisitions and value of commodities owned.

Series Da1412. In 1987, the accounts of the Commodity Credit Corporation were closed promptly at the end of the fiscal year, causing some financial transactions to be omitted from the accounts. After closing the books, but before release of these financial statements, CCC became aware of the approximate dollar value of transactions representing amounts not recorded or given full effect in the accounts. This resulted in an adjustment to commodity inventories for unallocated loan forfeitures of $891,275,000 for fiscal year 1987 and $1,789,573,000 for October 1, 1986. The commodity inventories balance, net of allowance for losses on Schedule A-2, for fiscal year 1987 is $9,679,489,000 and for fiscal year 1986 is $8,730,858,000.

TABLE Da1416   U.S. Department of Agriculture – gross budget authority: 1839–1999

Contributed by Daniel A. Sumner

	USDA gross budget authority Da1416 [1]		USDA gross budget authority Da1416 [1]		USDA gross budget authority Da1416 [1]		USDA gross budget authority Da1416 [1]
Year	Dollars	Year	Dollars	Year	Dollars	Year	Dollars
1839	1,000	1885	878,430	1930	213,433,271	1975	15,775,616,687
1840	0	1886	825,300	1931	371,637,435	1976	15,604,124,833
1841	0	1887	873,642	1932	288,619,220	(TQ)	3,256,375,000
1842	1,000	1888	1,866,719	1933	425,364,786	1977	16,377,354,000
1843	0	1889	1,976,293	1934	626,641,157	1978	17,180,059,908
1844	2,000	1890	2,021,195	1935	1,080,686,179	1979	25,668,399,000
1845	2,000	1891	2,137,075	1936	710,466,889	1980	26,029,756,009
1846	3,000	1892	3,538,865	1937	789,413,616	1981	30,146,791,000
1847	0	1893	3,323,061	1938	931,730,732	1982	58,254,081,000
1848	3,000	1894	3,708,856	1939	1,529,222,831	1983	72,782,233,000
1849	4,500	1895	3,612,149	1940	1,655,528,298	1984	47,822,020,000
1850	4,500	1896	3,989,150	1941	1,548,165,658	1985	62,951,441,000
1851	4,500	1897	3,636,264	1942	1,610,106,202	1986	60,424,763,000
1852	5,500	1898	3,573,552	1943	1,130,755,417	1987	53,799,223,000
1853	5,000	1899	4,089,416	1944	1,184,718,511	1988	56,697,996,000
1854	15,000	1900	4,131,597	1945	1,169,037,137	1989	57,360,872,000
1855	25,000	1901	4,427,105	1946	1,257,983,678	1990	56,828,313,000
1856	55,000	1902	5,091,440	1947	1,291,850,424	1991	61,380,149,000
1857	75,000	1903	6,216,818	1948	1,240,763,606	1992	67,142,877,000
1858	63,500	1904	6,745,801	1949	1,198,386,320	1993	68,694,015,000
1859	60,000	1905	6,767,251	1950	1,506,516,626	1994	66,615,313,000
1860	40,000	1906	9,189,152	1951	1,310,777,244	1995	59,929,000,000
1861	60,000	1907	12,695,293	1952	1,364,988,114	1996	59,873,000,000
1862	64,000	1908	13,881,219	1953	1,317,955,341	1997	62,073,000,000
1863	80,000	1909	16,588,790	1954	1,504,101,594	1998	58,299,000,000
1864	119,770	1910	17,684,134	1955	1,344,968,168	1999	67,551,000,000
1865	150,604	1911	19,450,339	1956	1,601,834,663		
1866	168,088	1912	21,103,646	1957	3,583,284,445		
1867	199,100	1913	25,415,013	1958	6,871,043,612		
1868	279,020	1914	25,065,218	1959	5,899,878,841		
1869	210,198	1915	29,917,951	1960	5,650,543,909		
1870	156,440	1916	29,074,869	1961	5,534,821,766		
1871	188,180	1917	37,365,506	1962	7,420,078,889		
1872	197,070	1918	73,372,284	1963	7,513,185,749		
1873	202,440	1919	117,290,605	1964	7,878,690,521		
1874	277,690	1920	149,393,310	1965	8,504,131,902		
1875	357,380	1921	151,674,763	1966	8,089,868,464		
1876	264,120	1922	134,508,050	1967	8,964,131,795		
1877	313,687	1923	87,479,246	1968	7,730,700,728		
1878	347,640	1924	89,906,499	1969	8,813,536,368		
1879	215,900	1925	79,841,104	1970	10,777,128,688		
1880	212,000	1926	168,469,395	1971	10,358,523,399		
1881	264,300	1927	155,029,990	1972	13,486,996,088		
1882	392,365	1928	150,972,824	1973	12,678,400,148		
1883	686,942	1929	166,790,201	1974	13,329,035,337		
1884	648,982						

(TQ) Transition quarter.

[1] Amounts for 1839–1862 were appropriated to the Patent Office and the Department of the Interior; thereafter, appropriations were made to the U.S. Department of Agriculture. See text.

Sources

1839–1997: Historical Agricultural Appropriation Data compiled and adjusted by U.S. Department of Agriculture, Office of Budget and Program Analysis from the official budget authority figures in *Historical Tables, Budget of the United States Government, Fiscal Year 1999*; 1998–1999: U.S. Department of Agriculture, Office of the Budget and Program Analysis, Budget Summary.

Documentation

Budget authority is the authority to enter into obligations that will result in immediate or future outlays of government funds. It may differ from actual budget outlays because it is recorded as a dollar amount in the year when it first becomes available. Under certain circumstances, not-obligated balances of budget authority may be carried over into the next year. These balances are not recorded as budget authority again. They do, however, constitute a budgetary resource that is available for obligation. Budget authority is heterogeneous, varying significantly from one program to another. As a result, it is not additive – either across programs or agencies for a year or, in many cases, for an agency or program across a series of years. Budget authority can take the form of appropriations, authority to borrow, or contract authority. The form of budget authority is usually determined in the authorizing statute for a program. Most programs are funded by appropriations.

The U.S. Department of Agriculture (USDA) gross budget authority shows authority for all USDA programs, excluding spending authority from offsetting collections. USDA historical totals have been adjusted to include the budget authority for programs now carried out by the USDA that were not officially listed as part of the USDA, but were operated for USDA. Hence,

TABLE Da1416   U.S. Department of Agriculture – gross budget authority: 1839–1999   *Continued*

series Da1416 reflects a consistent measure of the budget for programs that have been historically associated with the USDA.

Amounts shown for fiscal years 1839 to 1862, inclusive, were appropriated to the Patent Office and the Department of the Interior for collection of agricultural statistics, procurement, propagation and distribution of seeds,

and other agricultural purposes. The Act of May 15, 1862 (12 Stat. 387), established the agricultural activities of the federal government independently under a Commissioner of Agriculture, and thereafter appropriations were made to the Department of Agriculture.

TABLE Da1417–1418   U.S. Department of Agriculture – outlays: 1921–1999

Contributed by Daniel A. Sumner

Year	Total Da1417 Million dollars	As a percentage of government outlays Da1418 Percent	Year	Total Da1417 Million dollars	As a percentage of government outlays Da1418 Percent	Year	Total Da1417 Million dollars	As a percentage of government outlays Da1418 Percent
1921	120	2.4	1955	4,636	6.8	1985	55,523	5.9
1922	143	4.3	1956	5,177	7.3	1986	58,679	5.9
1923	126	4.0	1957	5,006	6.5	1987	49,600	4.9
1924	141	4.8	1958	4,875	5.9	1988	44,003	4.1
1925	165	5.6	1959	7,091	7.7	1989	48,316	4.2
1926	155	5.3	1960	5,419	5.9	1990	46,012	3.7
1927	156	5.5	1961	5,929	6.1	1991	54,119	4.1
1928	160	5.4	1962	6,437	6.0	1992	56,437	4.1
1929	171	5.5	1963	7,414	6.7	1993	63,144	4.5
1930	178	5.4	1964	7,569	6.4	1994	60,753	4.2
1931	297	8.3	1965	6,940	5.9	1995	56,665	3.7
1932	319	6.8	1966	5,633	4.2	1996	54,344	3.5
1933	251	5.5	1967	5,952	3.8	1997	52,547	3.3
1934	791	12.1	1968	7,430	4.2	1998	53,947	3.3
1935	1,158	18.1	1969	8,446	4.6	1999	62,834	3.7
1936	924	11.2	1970	8,412	4.3			
1937	1,059	14.0	1971	8,673	4.1			
1938	614	9.0	1972	11,053	4.8			
1939	1,321	14.5	1973	10,200	4.2			
1940	1,614	17.0	1974	10,338	3.8			
1941	1,349	9.9	1975	15,556	4.7			
1942	2,125	6.0	1976	17,743	4.8			
1943	2,887	3.7	(TQ)	5,020	5.2			
1944	3,237	3.5	1977	23,341	5.7			
1945	2,333	2.5	1978	30,235	6.6			
1946	3,668	6.6	1979	31,758	6.3			
1947	1,623	4.7	1980	34,785	5.9			
1948	1,225	4.1	1981	41,624	6.1			
1949	2,750	7.1	1982	45,700	6.1			
1950	2,956	6.9	1983	52,404	6.5			
1951	834	1.8	1984	42,015	4.9			
1952	1,242	1.8						
1953	3,217	4.2						
1954	2,915	4.1						

(TQ) Transition quarter.

Source

U.S. Department of Agriculture, Office of Budget and Program Analysis, Agricultural Appropriations Background Material compiled by Office of Budget and Program Analysis, unpublished data.

Documentation

This table shows the value of outlays by the U.S. Department of Agriculture and the share of total government outlays they comprise.

TABLE Da1419–1424   U.S. Department of Agriculture – farm, food, and other outlays: 1960–1999

Contributed by Daniel A. Sumner

	Outlays			As a percentage of total		
	Farm	Food	Other	Farm	Food	Other
	Da1419	Da1420	Da1421	Da1422	Da1423	Da1424
Year	Million dollars	Million dollars	Million dollars	Percent	Percent	Percent
1960	2,071.1	323.7	3,024.2	38.2	6.0	55.8
1961	1,573.1	357.7	3,998.2	26.5	6.0	67.5
1962	2,268.3	383.9	3,784.8	35.2	6.0	58.8
1963	3,126.6	376.5	3,910.9	42.2	5.1	52.7
1964	3,099.9	548.2	3,920.9	41.0	7.2	51.8
1965	2,563.2	572.5	3,804.3	36.9	8.2	54.9
1966	1,526.1	480.9	3,626.0	27.1	8.5	64.4
1967	1,951.4	563.9	3,436.7	32.8	9.5	57.7
1968	3,339.3	680.0	3,410.7	44.9	9.2	45.9
1969	4,400.0	1,001.6	3,044.4	52.1	11.9	36.0
1970	3,745.8	1,409.2	3,257.0	44.5	16.8	38.7
1971	2,888.8	2,580.9	3,203.3	33.3	29.8	36.9
1972	4,267.0	3,218.2	3,567.8	38.6	29.1	32.3
1973	3,822.6	3,641.0	2,736.4	37.5	35.7	26.8
1974	1,197.4	4,433.1	4,707.5	11.6	42.9	45.5
1975	2,132.4	6,643.2	6,780.4	13.7	42.7	43.6
1976	2,099.8	7,959.0	7,684.2	11.8	44.9	43.3
(TQ)	656.8	1,824.0	2,539.2	13.1	36.3	50.6
1977	5,554.0	8,527.3	9,259.7	23.8	36.5	39.7
1978	10,394.6	8,926.2	10,914.2	34.4	29.5	36.1
1979	9,502.8	10,787.0	11,495.2	29.9	33.9	36.2
1980	7,250.3	14,016.4	13,518.3	20.8	40.3	38.9
1981	9,599.2	16,204.5	15,820.3	23.1	38.9	38.0
1982	14,296.9	15,580.8	15,822.3	31.3	34.1	34.6
1983	21,284.5	17,879.3	13,240.2	40.6	34.1	25.3
1984	11,778.6	18,045.2	12,191.2	28.0	42.9	29.1
1985	23,629.1	18,520.3	13,373.6	42.6	33.4	24.0
1986	29,591.0	18,562.3	10,525.7	50.4	31.6	18.0
1987	25,425.5	18,872.5	5,302.0	51.3	38.0	10.7
1988	15,489.2	20,012.1	8,501.7	35.2	45.5	19.3
1989	14,613.8	21,228.5	12,473.7	30.2	43.9	25.9
1990	9,599.0	23,999.1	12,405.0	20.9	52.2	27.0
1991	12,876.0	28,516.5	12,722.0	23.8	52.7	23.5
1992	11,872.0	32,652.1	11,898.0	21.0	57.9	21.1
1993	16,960.0	35,224.9	10,949.0	26.9	55.8	17.3
1994	11,900.0	36,762.6	12,091.0	19.6	60.5	19.9
1995	6,526.0	37,464.0	12,676.0	11.5	66.1	22.4
1996	5,814.0	37,833.0	10,697.0	10.7	69.6	19.7
1997	7,564.0	35,961.0	9,022.0	14.4	68.4	17.2
1998	10,887.0	33,485.0	9,575.0	20.2	62.1	17.7
1999	20,357.0	33,047.0	9,430.0	32.4	52.6	15.0

(TQ) Transition quarter.

Source

U.S. Department of Agriculture, Office of Budget and Program Analysis, Agricultural Appropriations Background Material compiled by Office of Budget and Program Analysis, unpublished data.

Documentation

This table compares the amount of U.S. Department of Agriculture (USDA) outlays made for farm sector programs with the amount of outlays made for food-assistance programs. From 1960 to about 1973 farm sector outlays as a percentage of total outlays were higher than food-based outlays. After 1973, there was a reversal of that trend and on average, food-based outlays as a percentage of total outlays were higher.

Series Da1419. Shows total USDA outlays to the farm sector and consists of outlays by the Commodity Credit Corporation (CCC), Agricultural Credit Insurance Fund (ACIF), and Federal Crop Insurance Corporation (FCIC).

Series Da1420. Shows total USDA outlays for food-assistance programs, which includes the Food and Nutrition Service (FNS) and Section 32 domestic food program payments.

Series Da1421. Shows USDA outlays to all other programs. These include research, administration, food inspection, and market regulation.

TABLE Da1425   U.S. Department of Agriculture – employees: 1861–1999

Contributed by Daniel A. Sumner

Year	USDA employees Da1425 [1] Number	Year	USDA employees Da1425 [1] Number	Year	USDA employees Da1425 [1] Number	Year	USDA employees Da1425 [1] Number
1861	9	1910	12,480	1940	100,167	1970	116,012
1863	29	1911	12,704	1941	90,169	1971	117,699
1867	99	1912	13,858	1942	91,141	1972	114,975
1871	84	1913	14,478	1943	104,510	1973	111,285
1873	92	1914	16,061	1944	77,720	1974	116,203
1875	90	1915	16,223	1945	81,993	1975	118,981
1877	77	1916	17,167	1946	96,603	1976	125,842
1879	93	1917	18,751	1947	87,483	1977	125,900
1881	103	1918	25,239	1948	82,134	1978	126,715
1883	239	1919	24,299	1949	86,247	1979	126,346
1885	214	1920	19,373	1950	84,097	1980	127,437
1887	328	1921	18,748	1951	81,062	1981	127,291
1889	488	1922	19,704	1952	78,249	1982	120,200
1891	1,577	1923	20,261	1953	78,097	1983	122,786
1893	1,870	1924	20,665	1954	76,276	1984	117,384
1895	2,043	1925	20,587	1955	85,503	1985	117,562
1896	2,205	1926	20,742	1956	89,398	1986	112,001
1897	2,444	1927	21,661	1957	95,998	1987	116,993
1899	2,965	1928	22,189	1958	101,139	1988	120,869
		1929	24,020	1959	97,220	1989	122,062
1900	3,128	1930	25,741	1960	98,694	1990	122,594
1901	3,388	1931	28,163	1961	102,557	1991	125,640
1902	3,789	1932	27,350	1962	110,511	1992	128,324
1903	4,200	1933	26,544	1963	112,488	1993	124,199
1904	4,504	1934	38,623	1964	108,476	1994	119,558
1905	5,446	1935	44,080	1965	113,017	1995	113,321
1906	6,242	1936	53,522	1966	118,585	1996	109,586
1907	9,107	1937	106,217	1967	121,871	1997	106,539
1908	10,420	1938	100,125	1968	122,715	1998	107,143
1909	11,140	1939	105,591	1969	122,860	1999	107,893

[1] Beginning in 1987, data switched from ceiling end-of-year to total end-of-year.

Sources

1861–1998: Historical data on U.S. Department of Agriculture employees compiled by Office of Budget and Program Analysis from the official employee figures in *Historical Tables, Budget of the United States Government, Fiscal Year 1999* (U.S. Government Printing Office, 1998); 1999: U.S. Department of Agriculture, Office of Budget and Program Analysis, unpublished data.

Documentation

This series shows the total number of U.S. Department of Agriculture employees at the end of the year. Although the U.S. Department of Agriculture began in 1862, the data show employees prior to that because they were associated with and are considered attributable to the programs that were transferred to and have long been associated with the U.S. Department of Agriculture.

TABLE Da1426–1432   U.S. Department of Agriculture – employees, by function: 1948–1999

Contributed by Daniel A. Sumner

Year	Farm and foreign agricultural service Da1426 [1] Number	Natural resources and environment Da1427 Number	Food safety and nutrition Da1428 [2] Number	Research, statistics, and extension Da1429 Number	Agricultural marketing and cooperative service Da1430 Number	Credit and rural development Da1431 Number	Administration and all other Da1432 Number
1948	5,613	26,011	279	13,939	5,091	7,604	2,278
1949	6,237	26,572	310	15,120	5,627	7,777	1,420
1950	7,255	28,209	279	16,078	6,045	8,279	1,402
1951	7,067	27,329	238	14,960	5,849	8,868	1,826
1952	5,436	26,854	221	13,708	6,115	8,639	1,839
1953	5,510	27,581	177	12,906	6,164	8,588	1,553
1954	6,485	29,123	167	12,931	6,159	7,620	1,205
1955	6,883	28,286	165	14,414	6,342	7,207	1,197
1956	7,527	30,781	155	15,550	6,857	7,612	1,225
1957	8,238	32,648	158	16,449	7,642	8,105	1,223
1958	7,666	34,937	196	15,908	9,016	7,627	2,135
1959	7,781	37,298	218	15,756	9,574	7,493	2,104

Notes appear at end of table

(continued)

TABLE Da1426–1432   U.S. Department of Agriculture – employees, by function: 1948–1999
Continued

Year	Farm and foreign agricultural service Da1426 [1] Number	Natural resources and environment Da1427 Number	Food safety and nutrition Da1428 [2] Number	Research, statistics, and extension Da1429 Number	Agricultural marketing and cooperative service Da1430 Number	Credit and rural development Da1431 Number	Administration and all other Da1432 Number
1960	7,983	39,137	385	15,192	10,059	6,914	2,081
1961	7,805	42,138	421	15,822	10,260	6,761	2,144
1962	7,467	45,012	467	16,765	10,492	6,968	2,185
1963	7,493	48,466	495	17,541	10,804	7,365	2,417
1964	31,411	48,337	506	17,869	10,912	7,478	2,505
1965	30,470	46,416	11,497	12,173	6,826	7,714	3,459
1966	28,825	47,564	12,297	12,681	6,574	8,531	4,950
1967	27,414	48,867	13,121	13,247	6,552	8,912	5,617
1968	24,419	50,173	14,407	13,459	6,647	9,286	5,928
1969	23,799	47,004	15,307	13,106	6,104	9,174	5,733
1970	23,465	47,209	17,913	13,001	3,683	9,385	4,369
1971	22,378	48,876	18,598	13,159	3,629	10,190	3,044
1972	21,055	50,588	18,676	13,201	3,549	10,413	3,135
1973	20,060	50,550	19,621	12,566	3,331	10,265	3,222
1974	15,305	49,499	19,664	12,348	3,026	9,908	3,167
1975	14,986	51,696	19,635	12,383	2,773	10,262	3,258
1976	13,731	56,014	20,353	13,003	2,800	10,401	3,310
1977	14,338	57,582	20,998	13,525	2,908	11,310	3,538
1978	17,923	60,907	22,449	12,818	2,835	12,158	3,525
1979	18,013	62,924	24,297	12,511	2,821	12,755	3,505
1980	16,976	67,197	20,591	11,562	4,750	13,358	3,670
1981	16,219	60,188	19,698	11,387	4,572	14,163	3,592
1982	15,102	57,208	18,740	11,074	4,408	13,165	3,548
1983	17,659	56,006	17,997	10,885	4,287	13,295	3,492
1984	17,414	54,460	17,714	10,620	4,288	14,272	3,443
1985	17,121	52,797	17,814	10,602	4,202	13,938	3,458
1986	18,828	49,812	17,401	10,473	4,158	13,799	3,396
1987	22,033	49,139	17,481	10,525	4,059	13,792	3,387
1988	21,712	52,577	17,862	10,550	4,189	13,596	3,462
1989	21,863	54,867	17,996	10,619	4,195	13,966	3,592
1990	20,354	55,860	18,256	10,623	4,167	13,827	3,677
1991	19,313	55,331	18,349	10,610	4,335	13,683	3,748
1992	19,758	56,951	18,817	10,962	4,554	13,736	3,950
1993	17,739	54,538	19,094	10,542	4,355	13,538	4,032
1994	21,114	53,891	19,465	10,201	4,021	10,914	4,150
1995	19,875	50,493	19,062	9,736	3,842	10,108	3,757
1996	18,364	49,044	18,559	9,632	3,644	10,089	3,686
1997	16,516	48,218	18,491	9,582	3,524	9,458	3,622
1998	15,736	46,714	18,435	9,513	3,517	9,135	3,675
1999	16,530	46,086	18,257	9,583	3,389	9,097	3,530

[1] Beginning in 1964, nonfederal county Agricultural Stabilization and Conservation Service/Farm Service Agency employees are included.

[2] Beginning with 1965, meat and other food safety inspectors that are paid by private firms are included.

Source
U.S. Department of Agriculture, Office of Budget and Program Analysis, unpublished data.

Documentation
Series Da1426. Consists of the Agricultural Stabilization and Conservation Service/Farm Service Agency (including nonfederal county employees), Consolidated Farm Service Agency, Foreign Agricultural Service, Office of International Cooperation and Development, and Risk Management Agency.

Series Da1427. Consists of Forest Service, Soil Conservation Service, and Natural Resources Conservation Service.

Series Da1428. Consists of the Food and Nutrition Service, Human Nutrition Information Service, Food and Consumer Service, Federal Grain Inspection Service, Animal and Plant Health Inspection Service, Food Safety and Inspection Service, and Packers and Stockyards Administration.

Series Da1429. Consists of Agricultural Research Service, Cooperative State Research Service, Extension Service, National Agricultural Library, Economic Research Service, National Agricultural Statistics Service, and World Agricultural Outlook Board.

Series Da1430. Consists of Agricultural Cooperative Service and Agricultural Marketing Service.

Series Da1431. Consists of Farmers Home Administration, Rural Development Administration, Rural Electrification Administration, Rural Housing and Community Development Service, Office of Rural Development Policy, and Federal Crop Insurance Corporation.

Series Da1432. Consists of Office of the Secretary, Departmental Administration, Office of Budget and Program Analysis, Office of Public Affairs, Alternative Agricultural Research Commercialization Center, Office of the Inspector General, Office of the General Counsel, Office of Economic Opportunity Program, Office of the Chief Economist, Commodity Exchange Authority 1948–1966, Defense Production Activities 1951–1953, and Miscellaneous for Prior Year Programs 1948–1950.

TABLE Da1433–1435   Raw sugar prices – New York and world: 1929–1999

Contributed by Daniel A. Sumner

Year	New York Da1433 Cents per pound	World Da1434 Cents per pound	Percentage difference Da1435 Percent	Year	New York Da1433 Cents per pound	World Da1434 Cents per pound	Percentage difference Da1435 Percent	Year	New York Da1433 Cents per pound	World Da1434 Cents per pound	Percentage difference Da1435 Percent
1929	3.76	1.77	112	1955	5.95	3.24	84	1980	30.11	29.02	4
1930	3.36	1.27	165	1956	6.09	3.48	75	1981	19.73	16.93	17
1931	3.33	1.13	195	1957	6.24	5.16	21	1982	19.92	8.42	137
1932	2.93	0.78	276	1958	6.27	3.50	79	1983	22.04	8.49	160
1933	3.22	0.86	274	1959	6.24	2.97	110	1984	21.74	5.18	320
1934	3.02	0.91	232	1960	6.30	3.14	101	1985	20.34	4.04	403
1935	3.23	0.88	267	1961	6.30	2.91	116	1986	20.95	6.05	246
1936	3.59	0.88	308	1962	6.45	2.98	116	1987	21.83	6.71	225
1937	3.44	1.13	204	1963	8.18	8.50	−4	1988	22.12	10.17	118
1938	2.94	1.00	194	1964	6.90	5.87	18	1989	22.81	12.79	78
1939	2.99	1.43	109	1965	6.75	2.12	218	1990	23.26	12.55	85
1940	2.79	1.11	151	1966	6.99	1.86	276	1991	21.57	9.04	139
1941	3.38	1.46	132	1967	7.28	1.99	266	1992	21.31	9.09	134
1942	3.74 [1]	2.69	39	1968	7.52	1.98	280	1993	21.62	10.03	116
1943	3.74 [1]	2.69	39	1969	7.75	3.37	130	1994	22.04	12.13	82
1944	3.74 [1]	2.69	39	1970	8.07	3.75	115	1995	22.96	13.44	71
1945	3.75 [1]	3.14	19	1971	8.52	4.52	88	1996	22.40	12.24	83
1946	4.59 [1]	4.24	8	1972	9.09	7.43	22	1997	21.96	12.06	82
1947	6.21 [1]	5.03	23	1973	10.29	9.61	7	1998	22.06	9.68	128
1948	5.54	4.23	31	1974	29.50	29.99	−2	1999	21.16	6.54	224
1949	5.81	4.16	40	1975	22.47	20.49	10				
1950	5.93	4.98	19	1976	13.31	11.58	15				
1951	6.06	5.67	7	1977	11.00	8.11	36				
1952	6.26	4.17	50	1978	13.93	7.82	78				
1953	6.29	3.41	84	1979	15.56	9.66	61				
1954	6.09	3.26	87								

[1] From 1942 to 1947, the raw sugar price reflects the average duty-paid delivered price charged U.S. refiners by the Commodity Credit Corporation.

Sources

1929–1968: U.S. Department of Agriculture, Agricultural Stabilization and Conservation Services, Sugar Division, *Sugar Statistics and Related Data: Compiled in the Administration of the U.S. Sugar Acts*, volume 1, Statistical Bulletin number 293, revised December 1969; 1969–1999: U.S. Department of Agriculture, Economic Research Service, *Sugar and Sweetener Situation and Outlook*, various issues.

Documentation

Series show the U.S. price and the world price of sugar and then the difference as a percentage of the world price as indications of the amount of protection U.S. sugar producers receive.

Series Da1433. 1929–1947 Lamborn Sugar Market Report. 1948–1960 New York Coffee and Sugar Exchange, number 6 Contract plus 0.5-cent duty. Quotations beginning in 1961 are for Exchange Contract number 7 raw sugar in bulk, duty paid New York, which from November 21, 1966, to October 1977 was replaced by Contract number 10. Duty 1961–present, 0.625 cents. November 1977 through December 1978: London daily price, c.i.f. (cost, insurance, and freight) U.K., bulk basis, converted to duty-paid, New York. 1979 to May 1985: Contract number 12, c.i.f. duty/fee paid, New York. June 1985–December 1985: prices are for nearby number 12 futures. Starting January 1986, 1997 prices are for Contract number 14, duty/fee paid New York.

Series Da1434. Cost and freight London basic converted to c. & f. (cost and freight) New York basis, by Chadbourne Committee, 1929–1930; Lamborn Sugar Market Report, 1931–1941, less freight from Cuba to New York. 1929–1947 prices are those paid to Cuba by the Commodity Credit Corporation plus the Commodity Credit Corporation's expense markup. Prices paid to Cuba for various crops were: 1942-1944, 2.65 cents per pound; 1945, 4.18 cents; 1947, 4.96 cents. 1948–1960 New York Coffee and Sugar Exchange, number 4 Contract. 1961–1969 f.o.b. (free on board) and stowed at Greater Caribbean ports, including Brazil. 1970, Contract number 8 – f.o.b. stowed Caribbean port, including Brazil, bagged. 1971 through October 1977, Contract number 11 – f.o.b. stowed Caribbean port, including Brazil, bulk. November 1977 through December 1978, International Sugar Agreement price, f.o.b. stowed Caribbean port, in bulk. 1979–1999, Contract number 11 – f.o.b. stowed Caribbean port, including Brazil, bulk spot price.

Series Da1435. Equals the difference between series Da1433-1434, divided by series Da1434, expressed as a percentage.

TABLE Da1436–1439   Federal expenditures on export programs: 1936–1999

Contributed by Daniel A. Sumner

	CCC commodity export payments	International Wheat Agreement and EEP	Public Law 480 expenditures	Section 32 expenditures		CCC commodity export payments	International Wheat Agreement and EEP	Public Law 480 expenditures	Section 32 expenditures
	Da1436	Da1437 [1]	Da1438 [2]	Da1439		Da1436	Da1437 [1]	Da1438 [2]	Da1439
Year	Million dollars	Million dollars	Million dollars	Million dollars	Year	Million dollars	Million dollars	Million dollars	Million dollars
1936	—	—	—	0.9	1970	100.7	—	937.2	5.3
1937	—	—	—	0.9	1971	176.1	—	918.2	3.9
1938	—	—	—	0.9	1972	116.9	—	993.2	2.9
1939	—	—	—	9.8	1973	349.3	—	753.9	1.1
					1974	57.0	—	638.9	0.0
1940	—	—	—	47.2					
1941	—	—	—	10.2	1975	3.1	—	933.9	0.0
1942	—	—	—	10.3	1976	—	—	691.1	0.0
1943	—	—	—	6.7	(TQ)	—	—	420.9	0.0
1944	—	—	—	1.3	1977	—	—	850.2	0.0
					1978	—	—	808.2	0.0
1945	—	—	—	4.2	1979	—	—	975.9	0.0
1946	—	—	—	20.3					
1947	—	—	—	33.7	1980	—	—	1,073.4	0.0
1948	—	—	—	19.9	1981	—	—	1,253.8	0.0
1949	—	75.5	—	27.0	1982	—	—	929.4	0.0
					1983	—	—	992.0	0.0
1950	—	178.2	—	24.6	1984	—	—	1,085.4	0.0
1951	—	166.9	—	24.3					
1952	—	125.8	—	17.1	1985	—	22.8	1,715.1	0.0
1953	—	55.9	—	11.8	1986	—	300.0	1,095.3	0.0
1954	—	98.4	—	11.9	1987	—	900.0	969.9	0.0
					1988	—	1,000.0	773.6	10.0
1955	—	89.7	—	4.6	1989	—	349.0	1,157.2	8.2
1956	—	86.4	—	4.1					
1957	81.6	78.6	—	8.5	1990	—	325.0	887.1	3.8
1958	96.0	46.7	—	0.0	1991	—	971.0	753.1	0.0
1959	122.4	65.3	—	0.0	1992	—	1,068.0	970.7	0.0
					1993	—	1,161.0	852.2	0.0
1960	301.9	74.4	—	10.9	1994	—	1,292.0	1,144.3	0.0
1961	288.9	89.9	1,827.2	0.0					
1962	244.1	73.8	1,961.5	1.5	1995	—	25.4	704.6	0.0
1963	178.0	124.9	2,039.5	3.0	1996	—	110.3	513.8	0.0
1964	212.0	34.1	2,049.2	2.0	1997	—	99.6	376.6	0.0
					1998	—	131.0	441.3	0.0
1965	98.7	10.2	1,851.8	0.4	1999	—	128.0	865.3	0.0
1966	208.3	—	1,784.5	0.1					
1967	167.6	—	1,451.7	0.0					
1968	73.5	—	1,204.3	0.4					
1969	33.0	—	974.5	4.8					

(TQ) Transition quarter.

[1] Figures for 1949–1965 are for the International Wheat Agreement. See text.

[2] Public Law 480 began in 1955, however, the budget outlays presented here are only from 1961 forward.

Sources

Series Da1436 and Da1438–1439. 1936–1952, 1962–1996: U.S. Department of Agriculture, Commodity Credit Corporation, *History of Budgetary Expenditures of the Commodity Credit Corporation, Books 1, 2, and 3*, internal sources; 1953–1961: U.S. Department of Agriculture, Commodity Credit Corporation, *Revised Comparative Financial Data, Fiscal Years 1953–1961*; 1997–1999: U.S. Department of Agriculture, Office of Budget and Program Analysis Internet site, budget summaries.

Series Da1437. 1949–1965: U.S. Department of Agriculture, *Agricultural Statistics, 1967*; 1966–1995: U.S. Department of Agriculture, Commodity Credit Corporation, 'History of Budgetary Expenditures of the Commodity Credit Corporation, Books 1, 2, and 3,' internal sources; 1996–1998: U.S. Department of Agriculture, Foreign Agricultural Service, Country Allocation and Status Reports for the Export Enhancement Program (EEP) and Dairy Export Incentive Program (DEIP), Press Releases 0416-96, 0591-97, 0432-98, U.S. Department of Agriculture Internet site; 1999: U.S. Department of Agriculture, Office of Budget and Program Analysis Internet site, budget summaries.

Documentation

Series Da1437. Shows expenditures under the EEP, including the International Wheat Agreement. Expenditures on the Wheat Agreement from 1949 to 1965 are the sum of commercial export payments and exports from Commodity Credit Corporation stocks. The EEP was initiated in May 1985 under the Commodity Credit Corporation Charter Act and was included in the Food Security Act of 1985 later that year. Under the EEP, exporters are awarded payments that enable them to sell certain commodities to specified countries at subsidized prices. Payments for the EEP were initially made in kind. After 1991, payments were made in cash.

Series Da1438. Shows Public Law 480 (P.L. 480) expenditures, the common name for the Agricultural Trade Development and Assistance Act of 1954, also called the Food for Peace Program. Title I of P.L. 480 makes U.S. agricultural commodities available by financing export sales on concessional terms. Donations for emergency food relief and nonemergency humanitarian assistance are provided under Title II. Title III authorizes a Food for Development program that provides government-to-government grant food assistance to least developed countries. P.L. 480 expenditures are the sum of sales for foreign currency, long-term credit sales, and foreign donations.

Series Da1439. Shows Section 32 expenditures. Section 32 of Public Law 370 became law in 1935. It provided funds for below-cost commodity sales in both domestic and export markets.

TABLE Da1440-1444   Value of commodities exported under U.S. Department of Agriculture programs: 1955-1996

Contributed by Daniel A. Sumner

Year	Total	GSM programs	Export enhancement programs	Concessional programs	Commodity Credit Corporation programs
	Da1440	Da1441	Da1442	Da1443	Da1444
	Million dollars	Million dollars	Million dollars	Million dollars	Million dollars
1955	384.4	—	—	259.8	124.6
1956	986.3	1.4	—	686.5	298.4
1957	1,529.7	4.6	—	1,124.6	400.5
1958	992.9	11.9	—	881.2	99.8
1959	1,056.0	38.7	—	885.0	132.3
1960	1,116.7	0.8	—	966.7	149.2
1961	1,334.8	18.4	—	1,172.4	144.0
1962	1,528.3	32.8	—	1,297.1	198.4
1963	1,532.9	76.6	—	1,408.8	47.4
1964	1,536.4	118.4	—	1,374.5	43.5
1965	1,665.0	94.5	—	1,538.6	31.9
1966	1,555.9	210.0	—	1,313.8	32.1
1967	1,610.1	339.3	—	1,248.3	22.5
1968	1,420.1	140.6	—	1,273.1	6.3
1969	1,154.6	116.0	—	1,037.2	1.4
1970	1,267.1	211.3	—	1,055.8	0.0
1971	1,413.8	390.8	—	1,023.0	0.0
1972	1,428.6	371.6	—	1,057.0	0.0
1973	1,974.9	1,028.5	—	946.4	0.0
1974	1,163.8	297.9	—	865.9	0.0
1975	1,347.7	248.6	—	1,099.1	0.0
1976	1,861.0	956.9	—	904.1	0.0
1977	1,858.9	755.3	—	1,103.6	0.0
1978	2,672.2	1,582.5	—	1,072.8	16.9
1979	2,795.6	1,527.4	—	1,187.2	81.0
1980	2,800.0	717.9	—	1,341.6	740.5
1981	3,379.2	1,744.2	—	1,333.0	302.0
1982	2,525.1	1,386.5	—	1,107.6	31.0
1983	5,359.1	3,420.2	—	1,194.7	744.1
1984	5,167.7	3,172.7	—	1,505.9	489.1
1985	4,849.1	2,709.6	86.5	1,905.8	147.2
1986	4,202.1	2,416.5	715.7	1,345.0	111.7
1987	5,125.5	2,784.4	1,684.4	1,077.2	157.0
1988	7,819.9	3,879.9	3,313.5	1,469.2	108.6
1989	8,368.6	5,057.0	2,826.7	1,311.4	137.0
1990	7,347.9	4,299.6	2,384.2	1,434.5	7.1
1991	6,964.3	4,111.3	2,009.3	1,323.9	39.9
1992	8,802.7	5,564.7	3,296.8	1,516.0	133.3
1993	8,979.8	3,831.5	3,733.5	2,363.7	15.9
1994	6,493.4	2,948.5	3,118.9	1,167.3	19.2
1995	5,581.3	2,547.1	2,408.0	892.4	18.3
1996	4,234.9	3,240.2	135.2	869.5	0.0

Sources

1955-1996: U.S. Department of Agriculture, Foreign Agricultural Service, *Commodity Exports by USDA Programs: Concessional and Other Authorized Government Programs for Fiscal Years 1955–1997*. 1997-1999, update provided by Fred Blott, U.S. Department of Agriculture, Office of Budget and Program Analysis.

Other sources: U.S. Department of Agriculture, Economic Research Service, *Provisions of the Federal Agriculture Improvement and Reform Act of 1996, Agriculture Information Bulletin* number 729.

Documentation

Each data series is the total value of agricultural exports shipped under each program.

Series Da1441. GSM programs (administered by the General Sales Manager of the USDA's Foreign Agricultural Service) are credit guarantees for agricultural exports. Covers selected GSM programs (the sum of GSM-5, GSM-102, and GSM-103). The Export Credit Guarantee program (GSM-102) is the largest U.S. agricultural export promotion program, functioning since 1980. It guarantees repayment of private, short-term credit for up to three years. The Intermediate Export Credit Guarantee Program (GSM-103) is a program established by the Food Security Act of 1985 that complements GSM-102, but guarantees repayment of private credit for three to ten years. GSM-5 is a short-term direct credit program in effect for 1956–1981.

Series Da1442. The value of exports in this series include shipments made under the Export Enhancement Program (EEP), the Sunflower Oil Assistance Program (SOAP), the Cottonseed Oil Assistance Program (COAP), and the Dairy Export Incentive Program (DEIP). Under the EEP, exporters are awarded cash payments that enable them to sell certain commodities to specified countries at subsidized prices. The SOAP and the COAP are the two programs under which bonuses were awarded to exporters of U.S. vegetable oil to assist in exports to targeted markets. Funds for the programs were authorized to be made available under Section 32 of the Agricultural Adjustment Act of 1935.

Series Da1443. The value for concessional programs is equal to the sum of value of exports shipped under P.L. 480, 416(b), and Food for Progress

(continued)

TABLE Da1440–1444   Value of commodities exported under U.S. Department of Agriculture programs: 1955–1996
Continued

(FFP). Food for Progress is a food aid program originally authorized by the Food Security Act of 1985 to provide commodities to developing countries.

Series Da1444. Commodity Credit Corporation (CCC) programs include the value of exports shipped under GSM-101, GSM-201, GSM-301, Blended Credit, Supplier Credit, and the Barter programs or shipped directly out of Commodity Credit Corporation stocks.

TABLE Da1445–1448   Federal milk marketing orders: 1936–1999
Contributed by Daniel A. Sumner

Year	Number (Da1445)	Percentage of milk covered by federal marketing orders (Da1446)	Margin of Class I price over the basic formula price — Chicago (and successor) orders (Da1447 [1])	Margin of Class I price over the basic formula price — New York (and successor) orders (Da1448 [1])	Year	Number (Da1445)	Percentage of milk covered by federal marketing orders (Da1446)	Margin of Class I price over the basic formula price — Chicago (and successor) orders (Da1447 [1])	Margin of Class I price over the basic formula price — New York (and successor) orders (Da1448 [1])
	Number	Percent	Dollars per hundredweight	Dollars per hundredweight		Number	Percent	Dollars per hundredweight	Dollars per hundredweight
1936	6	—	—	—	1970	62	79	1.21	2.39
1937	8	—	—	—	1971	62	80	1.25	2.39
1938	11	—	—	—	1972	62	78	1.18	2.32
1939	15	—	—	—	1973	61	78	0.89	2.04
1940	20	—	0.59	1.26	1974	61	78	1.46	2.60
1941	21	—	0.52	0.88	1975	56	78	0.91	2.04
1942	22	—	0.67	1.07	1976	50	79	1.38	2.52
1943	22	—	0.70	0.91	1977	47	80	1.16	2.28
1944	25	—	0.70	1.06	1978	47	80	0.98	1.98
1945	28	—	0.70	1.10	1979	47	80	1.14	2.13
1946	30	—	0.70	0.88	1980	47	80	1.05	2.04
1947	29	—	0.67	1.42	1981	48	80	1.26	2.25
1948	30	—	0.81	1.69	1982	49	81	1.26	2.25
1949	33	—	0.91	2.40	1983	46	82	1.31	2.29
1950	39	41	0.73	2.05	1984	45	81	1.22	2.21
1951	44	44	0.77	2.02	1985	44	80	1.50	2.48
1952	49	46	1.03	1.72	1986	44	80	1.24	2.33
1953	49	49	0.92	1.99	1987	43	80	1.51	2.66
1954	53	49	0.73	2.13	1988	42	79	1.23	2.34
1955	63	51	0.77	2.17	1989	41	75	0.99	2.13
1956	68	51	0.95	2.18	1990	42	77	2.18	3.31
1957	68	53	0.74	2.50	1991	40	76	1.07	2.11
1958	74	56	0.70	2.57	1992	40	77	1.52	2.53
1959	77	60	0.67	2.63	1993	38	73	1.22	2.24
1960	80	64	0.69	2.42	1994	38	75	1.57	2.58
1961	81	67	0.66	2.06	1995	33	75	1.20	2.22
1962	83	70	0.66	2.37	1996	32	72	1.65	2.64
1963	82	70	0.66	2.12	1997	31	70	1.12	2.15
1964	77	70	0.66	2.10	1998	31	66	0.73	1.80
1965	73	70	0.76	2.02	1999	31	70	2.59	3.67
1966	71	70	0.71	2.15					
1967	74	71	—	2.01					
1968	67	74	1.31	2.27					
1969	67	77	1.22	2.38					

[1] Changes occurred over time affecting the series; see text.

Sources

Series Da1445–1446. 1936–1946, 1980–1998: U.S. Department of Agriculture, Marketing and Regulatory Programs, Agricultural Marketing Service, Dairy Programs, *Federal Milk Order Market Statistics*; 1947–1979: U.S. Department of Agriculture, Agricultural Marketing Service, "The Federal Milk Marketing Order Program," *Marketing Bulletin* number 27; 1999: U.S. Department of Agriculture, Agricultural Marketing Service, Dairy Programs, Market Information Branch.

Series Da1447–1448. 1936–1998: U.S. Department of Agriculture, Marketing and Regulatory Programs, Agricultural Marketing Service, Dairy Programs, "Federal Milk Order Market Statistics," *Marketing Bulletin* number 27; 1999: U.S. Department of Agriculture, Agricultural Marketing Service, Dairy Programs, Market Information Branch.

Documentation

A federal milk marketing order is a regulation issued by the Secretary of Agriculture and established under the authority of the Agricultural Marketing Agreement Act of 1937, as amended. It places certain requirements on the handling of milk in the area it covers and includes provisions for a classified pricing plan. A classified pricing plan establishes different classes and prices for milk in different uses. Milk used in fluid products is placed in Class 1, which is the highest priced class. Each order requires milk handlers in a marketing area to pay not less than certain minimum class prices established according to how the milk is utilized. Such price levels reflect local and general economic conditions affecting the supply and demand for milk. It also requires that payments for milk be pooled and paid to individual farmers or cooperative associations of farmers on the basis of a uniform or "blend" price. A milk order, including the pricing provisions, becomes effective only after approval by dairy farmers.

TABLE Da1445–1448   Federal milk marketing orders: 1936–1999   *Continued*

Series Da1445. Shows the number of marketing agreements and orders in effect at the end of the year based on the date on which pricing provisions become effective. An individual marketing order is for a region in which federal rules place certain requirements on the handling of milk and payments to producers.

Series Da1446. Shows the percentage of fluid-grade milk that is covered by marketing orders – receipts of milk covered as a percentage of milk sold to plants and dealers. The decrease in these percentages beginning in 1988 results from handlers electing, because of disadvantageous price relationships and qualification circumstances, not to pool milk that normally would have been pooled under federal milk orders. The estimated volume of milk in federal order areas not pooled in 1997 was 7.7 billion pounds. The decline also reflects growth in the share of milk produced in California under the state milk marketing order.

Series Da1447–1448. Shows how much the annual average Class 1 price exceeded the national price for manufacturing-use milk in two representative federal milk marketing orders. Prior to August 1969, the fluid (Class I) differential in the Chicago (and successor) orders was subject to supply/demand and other adjustments or varied during the year. Since then, the fluid differentials have been as follows: August 1969 through April 1986, $1.26; thereafter, $1.40. The Chicago order was terminated April 30, 1966, and the Chicago Regional order was formed July 1, 1968. The New York price is for a 201–210-mile zone. In the New York (and successor) orders, an economic index was used in lieu of a fluid differential. Prior to August 1969, the fluid differentials have been as follows: August 1969 through October 1977, $2.40; November 1977 through April 1986, $2.25; May 1986 through March 1991, $2.55; thereafter, $2.42.

TABLE Da1449–1452   Grazing fees and use of grazing district lands: 1936–1999

Contributed by Daniel A. Sumner

	Grazing fees						Grazing fees			
	Public	Private	Ratio of private to public	Permitted use of grazing district lands			Public	Private	Ratio of private to public	Permitted use of grazing district lands
	Da1449	Da1450	Da1451	Da1452 [1]			Da1449	Da1450	Da1451	Da1452 [1]
Year	Dollars per animal unit month	Dollars per animal unit month	Ratio	Animal unit months		Year	Dollars per animal unit month	Dollars per animal unit month	Ratio	Animal unit months
1936	0.05	—	—	—		1970	0.44	—	—	10,980,535
1937	0.05	—	—	—		1971	0.64	—	—	10,286,574
1938	0.05	—	—	—		1972	0.66	—	—	10,409,608
1939	0.05	—	—	—		1973	0.78	—	—	10,382,996
1940	0.05	—	—	—		1974	1.00	—	—	10,393,079
1941	0.05	—	—	—		1975	1.00	—	—	10,239,189
1942	0.05	—	—	—		1976	1.51	—	—	10,227,730
1943	0.05	—	—	—		1977	1.51	—	—	9,094,194
1944	0.05	—	—	—		1978	1.51	—	—	9,385,393
1945	0.05	—	—	—		1979	1.89	8.80	4.66	9,172,945
1946	0.05	—	—	—		1980	2.36	8.67	3.67	8,875,380
1947	0.08	—	—	—		1981	2.31	9.71	4.20	9,025,011
1948	0.08	—	—	—		1982	1.86	9.75	5.24	9,152,028
1949	0.08	—	—	—		1983	1.40	9.59	6.85	8,898,897
1950	0.08	—	—	—		1984	1.37	9.56	6.98	9,612,517
1951	0.12	—	—	—		1985	1.35	9.06	6.71	9,768,829
1952	0.12	—	—	—		1986	1.35	8.33	6.17	8,994,391
1953	0.12	—	—	—		1987	1.35	8.09	5.99	9,720,254
1954	0.12	—	—	—		1988	1.54	8.98	5.83	8,720,257
1955	0.15	—	—	—		1989	1.86	10.06	5.41	9,576,034
1956	0.15	—	—	—		1990	1.81	10.86 [2]	6.00	9,382,959
1957	0.15	—	—	—		1991	1.97	9.78	4.96	8,320,845
1958	0.19	—	—	—		1992	1.92	10.46	5.45	8,750,136
1959	0.22	—	—	—		1993	1.86	10.60	5.70	8,401,369
1960	0.22	—	—	—		1994	1.98	11.30	5.71	8,587,695
1961	0.19	—	—	12,096,998		1995	1.61	11.20	6.96	8,606,381
1962	0.19	—	—	12,000,057		1996	1.55	11.40	7.35	8,423,344
1963	0.30	—	—	12,051,772		1997	1.35	11.70	8.67	8,166,877
1964	0.30	—	—	11,861,242		1998	1.35	12.30	9.11	8,920,973
1965	0.30	—	—	11,773,097		1999	1.35	12.30	9.11	8,788,056
1966	0.33	—	—	11,801,304						
1967	0.33	—	—	11,634,505						
1968	0.33	—	—	11,665,024						
1969	0.44	—	—	11,237,706						

Notes appear at end of table

(continued)

TABLE Da1449–1452 Grazing fees and use of grazing district lands: 1936–1999 *Continued*

[1] Based on calendar year through 1977; a grazing-fee year for 1978–1982; and a fiscal year thereafter.

[2] Data in the original source have been corrected or revised.

Sources

Series Da1449. 1936–1946, 1969–1998: U.S. Department of the Interior, Bureau of Land Management, Rangeland, Soils, Water and Wild Horse and Burros Group, unpublished data; 1947–1968: U.S. Department of Commerce, Public Land Law Review Commission, *User Fees and Charges for Public Lands and Resources*, PB 195-846, December 1970.

Series Da1450. U.S. Department of Agriculture, National Agricultural Statistics Service, Agricultural Statistics Board, *Agricultural Price Summary*, various issues.

Series Da1452. U.S. Department of the Interior, Bureau of Land Management, *Public Land Statistics*, various issues.

Documentation

An animal unit is a standardized unit of measurement for range livestock, equivalent to one cow, one horse, five sheep, five goats, or four reindeer – all more than six months of age. An animal unit month is a standardized unit of measurement of the amount of forage necessary for the complete sustenance of one animal unit for a period of one month. It is also a unit of measurement of grazing privileges that represents the privilege of grazing one animal unit for a period of one month.

Series Da1450. Data represent the sixteen-state average cattle grazing rates on privately owned nonirrigated land. The sixteen states are Arizona, California, Colorado, Idaho, Kansas, Montana, Nebraska, Nevada, New Mexico, North Dakota, Oklahoma, Oregon, South Dakota, Utah, Washington, and Wyoming. The fee includes animal unit plus cow/calf rates: cow/calf rate is converted to animal unit months (aum) rates using aum = 0.833*(cow-calf rate).

Series Da1451. A ratio of series Da1450 to series Da1449.

Series Da1452. Data represent the total use of grazing district (Section 3) lands for cattle, yearlings, horses, burros, mules, sheep, and goats for Arizona, California, Colorado, Idaho, Montana, Nevada, New Mexico, Oregon, Utah, and Wyoming. It does not include authorized non-use, trailing, or exchange of use. A grazing district is an administrative subdivision of the rangelands under jurisdiction of the Bureau of Land Management, established pursuant to Section 1 of the Taylor Grazing Act, to facilitate management of their resources. A grazing permit is an authorization that permits grazing of the specified number and class of livestock on a designated area of grazing district lands during specified seasons each year.

TABLE Da1453–1456   Acreage idled under cropland acreage reduction programs: 1933–1999

Contributed by Daniel A. Sumner

Year	Total	As a share of total cropland	Under Conservation Adjustment Act, Agricultural Conservation Program, and annual commodity programs	Under Soil Bank, Conservation Reserve Program, and Cropland Adjustment Program
	Da1453	Da1454	Da1455	Da1456
	Million acres	Ratio	Million acres	Million acres
1933	10.5	0.030	10.5	0.0
1934	35.8	0.105	35.8	0.0
1935	30.3	0.081	30.3	0.0
1936	31.4	0.089	31.4	0.0
1937	29.1	0.077	29.1	0.0
1938	30.0	0.079	30.0	0.0
1939	41.5	0.111	41.5	0.0
1940	42.4	0.111	42.4	0.0
1941	43.0	0.111	43.0	0.0
1942	38.3	0.099	38.3	0.0
1943	3.1	0.009	3.1	0.0
1944	6.4	0.017	6.4	0.0
1945	4.1	0.011	4.1	0.0
1946	2.7	0.008	2.7	0.0
1947	1.6	0.004	1.6	0.0
1948	0.0	0.000	0.0	0.0
1949	0.0	0.000	0.0	0.0
1950	0.0	0.000	0.0	0.0
1951	0.0	0.000	0.0	0.0
1952	0.0	0.000	0.0	0.0
1953	0.0	0.000	0.0	0.0
1954	0.0	0.000	0.0	0.0
1955	0.0	0.000	0.0	0.0
1956	13.6	0.040	0.0	13.6
1957	27.9	0.079	0.0	27.9
1958	27.1	0.077	0.0	27.1
1959	22.5	0.065	0.0	22.5
1960	28.7	0.081	0.0	28.7
1961	53.7	0.151	25.2	28.5
1962	64.7	0.180	38.9	25.8
1963	55.9	0.158	31.7	24.3
1964	55.1	0.156	37.6	17.4
1965	55.9	0.158	41.9	14.0
1966	62.9	0.176	47.6	15.3
1967	40.2	0.116	25.2	15.0
1968	49.0	0.140	35.7	13.2
1969	57.5	0.165	50.2	7.3
1970	57.9	0.165	53.1	4.8
1971	37.2	0.109	33.8	3.4
1972	61.5	0.173	58.7	2.8
1973	19.6	0.058	16.8	2.8
1974	2.7	0.008	0.0	2.7
1975	2.4	0.007	0.0	2.4
1976	2.1	0.006	0.0	2.1
1977	1.0	0.003	0.0	1.0
1978	18.2	0.051	18.2	0.0
1979	13.0	0.036	13.0	0.0
1980	0.0	0.000	0.0	0.0
1981	0.0	0.000	0.0	0.0
1982	11.1	0.030	11.1	0.0
1983	77.9	0.203	77.9	0.0
1984	27.0	0.072	27.0	0.0
1985	30.7	0.082	30.7	0.0
1986	46.1	0.124	46.1	2.0
1987	76.2	0.201	60.5	15.7
1988	77.7	0.207	53.3	24.5
1989	60.8	0.161	30.9	29.9
1990	61.6	0.161	27.7	33.9
1991	64.5	—	30.1	34.4
1992	54.9	—	19.5	35.4
1993	59.8	—	23.4	36.4
1994	49.2	—	12.8	36.4
1995	50.8	—	14.4	36.4
1996	34.4	—	0.0	34.4
1997	33.0	—	0.0	33.0
1998	31.7	—	0.0	31.7
1999	29.9	—	0.0	29.9

Sources

1933–1995: W. M. Crosswhite and C. L. Sandretto, "Trends in Resource Protection Policies in Agriculture," pp. 42–6 in *Agricultural Resources: Cropland, Water, and Conservation Situation and Outlook Report*, AR-23, U.S. Department of Agriculture, Economic Research Service, 1991. Series updated based on data from the Farm Services Agency, U.S. Department of Agriculture, and U.S. Department of Agriculture, Economic Research Service, "Provisions of the Federal Agriculture Improvement and Reform Act of 1996," *Agriculture Information Bulletin* number 729. 1996–1999: U.S. Department of Agriculture, Farm Service Agency, Conservation Reserve Program, *Active Contract Reports*, 2000.

Documentation

Series Da1453. Equals the sum of series Da1455–1456.

Series Da1454. Equals the ratio of crop acres idled to the sum of total crop acres idled and cropland planted to principal crops – in other words, series Da1453 divided by the sum of series Da661 and Da1453. This provides an indication of the relative importance of the idling and diversion programs.

Series Da1455. Equals the sum of acres idled under the Conservation Adjustment Act (CAA), Agricultural Conservation Program (ACP), and Annual Commodity Programs. The Conservation Adjustment Act began in 1933 and the Agricultural Conservation Program began in 1936, and both were annual programs. The Acreage Reduction Program (ARP) was an annual voluntary land retirement system in which participating farmers idled a prescribed portion of their crop acreage base of wheat, feed grains, cotton, or rice. Farmers were required to participate in the ARP to be eligible for benefits such as Commodity Credit Corporation loans and deficiency payments. The 1996 Federal Agriculture Improvement and Reform (FAIR) Act repealed or did not reauthorize the ARP.

Series Da1456. Equals the sum of acres idled under the Soil Bank, Conservation Reserve Program, and Cropland Adjustment Program. The Soil Bank was established in 1956 and consisted of the Acreage Reserve Program that ended in 1958 and the Conservation Reserve Program (CRP) for which enrollment ended in 1961. Farmers enrolled land for three- to ten-year contracts. The 1985 Food Security Act enacted the CRP again, but it was different

(continued)

TABLE Da1453–1456   Acreage idled under cropland acreage reduction programs: 1933–1999   *Continued*

from the CRP of the Soil Bank in that it was targeted at highly erosive land. It was created to reduce erosion and protect water quality on up to forty-five million acres of farmland. Under the program, landowners who sign contracts agree to convert environmentally sensitive land to approved permanent conserving uses for ten to fifteen years. In exchange, the landowner receives an annual rental payment and cash or payments-in-kind to share up to 50 percent of the cost of establishing permanent vegetative cover. The 1996 FAIR Act capped maximum CRP acreage at 36.4 million acres. The

Cropland Adjustment Program was enacted in 1965 and was an acreage diversion program in which the Secretary of Agriculture made five- to ten-year contracts with farmers who agreed to convert cropland into uses for conservation. For 1966–1970, there was an overlap between the Soil Bank and Cropland Adjustment Program. The acres idled under the Cropland Adjustment Program were 2 million in 1966, 4 million in 1967, 4 million in 1968, 3.9 million in 1969, and 3.8 million in 1970. The Soil Bank ended in 1970.

TABLE Da1457–1465   Crop insurance programs – number, coverage, premiums, indemnities, and loss ratio: 1948–1999

Contributed by Daniel A. Sumner

	County programs	Insured units	Total acreage insured	Value of maximum insured production	Total premiums	Indemnities			Loss ratio
						Number	Acreage indemnified	Value paid	
	Da1457	Da1458	Da1459	Da1460	Da1461	Da1462	Da1463	Da1464	Da1465
Year	Number	Number	Thousand acres	Thousand dollars	Thousand dollars	Number	Thousand acres	Thousand dollars	Ratio
1948	375	194,151	8,923	153,997	12,684	16,802	909	6,780	0.53
1949	394	198,655	11,067	163,495	11,732	34,561	2,541	15,531	1.32
1950	624	361,460	15,275	240,448	14,104	61,847	1,364	12,799	0.91
1951	810	383,022	16,186	317,463	19,111	58,820	2,820	21,338	1.12
1952	874	384,597	16,445	350,216	21,201	42,943	2,776	20,609	0.97
1953	922	477,093	20,617	437,514	27,098	79,288	4,007	31,056	1.15
1954	884	429,615	16,491	354,573	22,655	64,606	3,581	28,031	1.24
1955	888	407,603	14,347	309,924	22,330	52,156	3,032	25,505	1.14
1956	948	425,406	14,398	306,743	22,139	62,079	2,998	27,890	1.26
1957	989	366,957	11,459	242,106	17,407	44,337	1,402	12,004	0.69
1958	1,213	344,262	11,165	242,712	17,617	16,811	497	4,505	0.26
1959	1,488	373,233	11,709	270,828	18,462	45,000	1,823	14,138	0.77
1960	1,550	356,754	11,006	265,929	17,796	29,292	890	10,316	0.58
1961	1,597	341,509	10,215	271,709	18,150	36,791	1,638	16,092	0.89
1962	1,967	390,214	10,382	356,552	21,853	45,683	1,234	24,022	1.10
1963	2,379	466,224	13,089	496,999	30,374	46,245	1,728	23,524	0.77
1964	2,689	496,758	14,663	542,117	33,846	62,170	2,157	30,347	0.90
1965	2,781	493,279	15,290	590,392	35,993	74,241	2,733	40,739	1.13
1966	3,023	503,142	15,156	605,525	36,816	49,634	1,517	25,185	0.68
1967	3,245	505,322	17,932	775,749	43,454	81,956	3,281	55,100	1.27
1968	3,398	524,583	18,693	872,948	48,857	63,611	2,653	51,251	1.05
1969	3,558	504,852	17,303	916,959	48,720	55,430	2,099	52,791	1.08
1970	3,537	470,643	15,986	850,815	44,296	49,931	1,838	41,812	0.94
1971	3,549	464,647	18,502	944,634	47,797	34,136	1,415	28,545	0.60
1972	3,548	413,140	15,898	853,821	41,992	28,009	1,194	25,254	0.60
1973	3,587	396,721	17,399	1,007,411	47,530	25,995	1,680	28,302	0.60
1974	3,574	388,536	18,605	1,148,811	53,964	60,343	3,636	63,336	1.17
1975	3,678	421,610	20,898	1,570,494	73,360	46,640	2,304	63,329	0.86
1976	3,684	447,787	23,551	1,982,116	90,824	85,514	4,944	142,240	1.57
1977	3,686	467,120	25,405	2,090,841	101,789	67,084	4,555	148,943	1.46
1978	4,010	421,217	21,520	1,992,418	93,592	26,544	1,437	47,265	0.51
1979	4,084	404,192	21,416	2,138,809	102,714	32,782	2,203	65,257	0.64
1980	4,651	506,962	26,503	3,029,272	157,085	130,257	8,222	358,873	2.28
1981	5,994	868,397	44,928	5,981,820	376,863	138,490	8,826	406,646	1.08
1982	14,548	801,052	42,703	6,127,513	396,406	134,987	8,605	527,661	1.33
1983	15,415	641,865	27,761	4,358,709	284,941	188,016	8,311	579,830	2.03
1984	17,879	832,886	42,255	6,546,324	428,729	199,331	12,544	618,710	1.44
1985	18,903	868,180	48,321	7,122,343	438,470	159,717	12,414	652,995	1.49
1986	19,064	855,134	48,631	6,216,977	379,370	456,986	11,953	615,062	1.62
1987	19,263	903,495	49,126	6,077,377	364,640	134,407	8,368	369,701	1.01
1988	19,675	929,459	50,464	6,307,997	394,131	379,434	30,025	953,770	2.42
1989	20,507	1,854,297	101,826	13,617,359	819,488	461,072	39,156	1,215,571	1.48

TABLE Da1457–1465   Crop insurance programs – number, coverage, premiums, indemnities, and loss ratio: 1948–1999 _Continued_

Year	County programs	Insured units	Total acreage insured	Value of maximum insured production	Total premiums	Indemnities Number	Indemnities Acreage indemnified	Indemnities Value paid	Loss ratio
	Da1457	Da1458	Da1459	Da1460	Da1461	Da1462	Da1463	Da1464	Da1465
	Number	Number	Thousand acres	Thousand dollars	Thousand dollars	Number	Thousand acres	Thousand dollars	Ratio
1990	21,347	1,886,428	101,342	12,818,972	835,780	299,255	24,424	1,029,706	1.23
1991	21,373	1,581,464	82,319	11,211,672	736,610	339,313	26,800	957,817	1.30
1992	21,391	1,549,958	83,107	11,333,810	758,748	245,160	21,944	918,036	1.21
1993	21,568	1,564,552	83,707	11,353,208	755,642	458,223	35,997	1,695,281	2.24
1994	16,620	1,815,714	99,565	13,607,259	949,523	190,050	17,376	598,064	0.63
1995	17,413	3,684,860	220,608	23,821,125	1,550,266	568,421	47,994	1,598,668	1.03
1996	18,271	3,205,226	204,864	26,891,247	1,840,144	504,440	46,834	1,492,291	0.81
1997	27,429	2,802,581	182,395	25,717,774	1,779,575	307,649	24,846	990,351	0.56
1998	29,043	2,696,050	181,956	27,892,934	1,875,520	391,896	34,444	1,733,786	0.92
1999	35,789	2,892,690	196,176	29,109,659	2,289,909	536,525	47,245	2,362,678	1.03

Sources

U.S. Department of Agriculture, _Agricultural Statistics_, annual issues.

Other sources: U.S. Department of Agriculture, Economic Research Service, "Provisions of the Federal Agriculture Improvement and Reform Act of 1996," _Agriculture Information Bulletin_ number 729.

Documentation

The federal crop insurance program is a subsidized insurance program paying farmers an indemnity payment when crop yield – or, in some cases, revenue – falls below a specified level. The amendments to the Federal Crop Insurance Act made by the Federal Crop Insurance Reform Act of 1994 broadened coverage and were in effect beginning with 1995 crops.

This table aggregates all commodities under crop insurance programs to show the amount of coverage, the premium, and the indemnities.

Series Da1457. Data represent the number of county crop combinations that were eligible for enrollment in the federal crop insurance program.

Series Da1458. Acreage can be subdivided and some units can stand alone as an insurable unit. The criteria for breaking down acreage into insurable units differ by crop. The data represent the number of farms on which the insured crop was planted, including duplication where both the landlord and tenant are insured. Insured farms on which no insured crop was planted are not included.

Series Da1459. Figures are acres covered by crop insurance policies, whereas series Da1463 gives acres that were paid out.

Series Da1461. Values represent the total value of premiums paid by farmers plus the federal subsidy.

Series Da1464. An indemnity payment is the payment that eligible producers receive if they realize a qualifying crop loss under the federal crop insurance program.

Series Da1465. The loss ratio is the ratio of the value of indemnities to the value of the premium. Here the ratio is losses to total premium including the premium paid on a subsidy by the government.

TABLE Da1466–1470   Farm real estate debt – Farm Credit System, Farm Service Agency, and Commodity Credit Corporation: 1918–1999[1]

Contributed by Daniel A. Sumner

	Held by			As a percentage of total farm real estate debt				Held by			As a percentage of total farm real estate debt	
	Farm Credit System	Farm Service Agency and prior agencies	Commodity Credit Corporation storage and drying facilities	Farm Credit System	Farm Service Agency		Farm Credit System	Farm Service Agency and prior agencies	Commodity Credit Corporation storage and drying facilities	Farm Credit System	Farm Service Agency
	Da1466 [2]	Da1467 [3]	Da1468	Da1469	Da1470		Da1466 [2]	Da1467 [3]	Da1468	Da1469	Da1470
Year	Million dollars	Million dollars	Million dollars	Percent	Percent	Year	Million dollars	Million dollars	Million dollars	Percent	Percent
1918	41	—	—	0.6	—	1960	2,335	676	44	19.3	5.6
1919	165	—	—	2.3	—	1961	2,539	723	48	19.7	5.6
1920	354	—	—	4.2	—	1962	2,803	948	69	20.1	6.8
1921	428	—	—	4.2	—	1963	3,024	1,058	74	19.8	6.9
1922	518	—	—	4.8	—	1964	3,282	1,171	60	19.5	6.9
1923	858	—	—	8.0	—	1965	3,687	1,285	44	19.5	6.8
1924	1,190	—	—	11.2	—	1966	4,240	1,497	34	20.0	7.1
1925	1,370	—	—	13.8	—	1967	4,915	1,663	32	21.3	7.2
1926	1,544	—	—	15.9	—	1968	5,563	1,847	61	22.1	7.3
1927	1,701	—	—	17.6	—	1969	6,081	2,058	147	22.1	7.5
1928	1,815	—	—	18.6	—	1970	6,671	2,280	170	22.7	7.8
1929	1,839	—	—	18.8	—	1971	7,145	2,440	146	23.4	8.0
1930	1,840	—	—	19.1	—	1972	7,880	2,618	190	24.3	8.1
1931	1,803 [4]	—	—	19.2	—	1973	9,050	2,835	266	25.6	8.0
1932	1,733	—	—	19.1	—	1974	10,901	3,013	278	27.4	7.6
1933	1,622	—	—	19.2	—	1975	13,470	3,215	217	30.0	7.2
1934	1,741	—	—	22.7	—	1976	16,029	3,369	170	32.2	6.8
1935	2,842	—	—	37.5	—	1977	18,565	3,657	144	33.5	6.6
1936	3,108	—	—	41.9	—	1978	21,541	3,982	492	33.7	6.2
1937	3,152	—	—	44.1	—	1979	24,816	4,120	1,148	34.1	5.7
1938	3,084	—	—	44.3	—	1980	29,820	6,875	1,391	34.4	7.9
1939	2,978	10	—	43.9	0.1	1981	36,196	8,163	1,456	37.1	8.4
1940	2,815	32	—	42.7	0.5	1982	43,825	8,977	1,342	40.9	8.3
1941	2,716 [5]	66	—	41.8	1.0	1983	47,822	9,170	1,127	43.0	8.2
1942	2,572	116	—	40.3	1.8	1984	48,929	9,550	888	43.0	8.4
1943	2,299	159	—	38.6	2.7	1985	49,078	10,073	623	43.7	9.0
1944	1,893	174	—	35.1	3.2	1986	44,584	10,427	307	42.2	9.9
1945	1,562	196	—	31.6	4.0	1987	37,758	10,349	123	39.4	10.8
1946	1,322	184	—	27.8	3.9	1988	32,638	10,083	46	37.2	11.5
1947	1,125	192	—	23.0	3.9	1989	30,327	9,607	21	36.6	11.6
1948	997	198	—	19.7	3.9	1990	28,507	8,720	12	35.4	10.8
1949	947	197	—	17.9	3.7	1991	27,390	8,093	7	34.7	10.3
1950	965	202	7	17.3	3.6	1992	26,760	7,462	4	33.7	9.4
1951	991	257	18	16.2	4.2	1993	26,886	6,780	2	33.4	8.4
1952	1,027	291	26	15.4	4.4	1994	26,460	6,216	0	32.6	7.7
1953	1,095	330	28	15.1	4.5	1995	26,300	5,853	0	31.7	7.1
1954	1,187	352	29	15.3	4.5	1996	26,530	5,403	0	31.4	6.4
1955	1,280	378	41	15.4	4.6	1997	27,462	5,025	0	31.5	5.8
1956	1,480	413	37	16.4	4.6	1998	28,923	4,914	0	31.7	5.4
1957	1,722	463	29	17.5	4.7	1999	29,521	3,837	0	32.7	4.3
1958	1,897	541	25	18.2	5.2						
1959	2,065	608	31	18.6	5.5						

[1] Data on the amount of debt held has been adjusted from December 31 to January 1.

[2] Known as Federal Land Banks debt prior to 1988. Includes loans of the Federal Farm Mortgage Corporation, 1935–1955, and joint-stock land banks, 1917–1950. See text.

[3] Covers the Farmers Home Administration prior to 1994. See text.

[4] Joint Stock Land Bank Loans were $638 million or 6.6 percent of the total farm mortgage debt.

[5] Federal Farm Mortgage Corporation loans were $713 million or 10.8 percent of the total farm mortgage debt.

Sources

1917–1938: U.S. Department of Agriculture, Economic Research Service (USDA ERS), *Agricultural Finance Statistics*, AFS-3, July 1976; 1939–1993: USDA ERS, *Economic Indicators of the Farm Sector; National Financial Summary*, various issues; 1994–1999: USDA ERS, *Agricultural Income and Finance: Situation and Outlook Report*, various issues.

Other sources: USDA ERS, "Agricultural Finance Statistics, 1960–83," *Statistical Bulletin* number 706, April 1984.

Documentation

Farm-mortgage credit has been referred to as farm-real-estate credit, long-term credit, or capital credit.

Series Da1466. Prior to 1988, the Farm Credit System was known as federal land banks and includes loans of the Federal Farm Mortgage Corporation and joint-stock land banks. The federal land banks were organized pursuant to the Federal Farm Loan Act of 1916 and became important lenders in the farm-mortgage field, particularly after 1933. Land Bank Commissioner loans, first made under the authority of the Emergency Farm-Mortgage Act of 1933, were taken over by the Federal Farm Mortgage Corporation on its creation in 1934 and were continued until July 1, 1947, when authority to make new loans, except those incidental to liquidation, expired. In 1955,

TABLE Da1466–1470   Farm real estate debt – Farm Credit System, Farm Service Agency, and Commodity Credit Corporation: 1918–1999   *Continued*

the remaining outstanding loans of the Corporation were sold to the federal land banks. The joint-stock land banks also authorized under the Federal Loan Act of 1916 were under federal supervision and regulation but differed from the federal land banks in that they were privately owned.

Series Da1467. Prior to 1994, the debt held by the Farm Service Agency was held by the Farmers Home Administration. Debt held by the Farmers Home Administration, formerly the Farm Security Administration, includes farm-

purchase, farm-enlargement, farm-development, project-liquidation, and direct soil and water loans to individuals, loans for these purposes from State Corporation trust funds, and rural-housing loans to farmers. The origins of the Farmers Home Administration go back to Executive Order 7072, signed April 30, 1935, creating the Resettlement Administration as an independent agency. Farm loans originated with the Bankhead–Jones Farm Tenant Act of July 22, 1937.

TABLE Da1471–1474   Non–real estate loans outstanding – Farmers Home Administration and Farm Credit System: 1922–1999

Contributed by Daniel A. Sumner

	Held by		As a percentage of total loans outstanding				Held by		As a percentage of total loans outstanding	
	Farmers Home Administration	Farm Credit System	Farmers Home Administration	Farm Credit System		Farmers Home Administration	Farm Credit System	Farmers Home Administration	Farm Credit System
	Da1471 [1]	Da1472	Da1473	Da1474		Da1471 [1]	Da1472	Da1473	Da1474
Year	Million dollars	Million dollars	Percent	Percent	Year	Million dollars	Million dollars	Percent	Percent
1922	3	—	—	—	1965	643	2,401	3.9	14.7
1923	3	—	—	—	1966	717	2,717	4.0	15.0
1924	2	9	—	—	1967	737	3,171	3.7	16.0
1925	2	18	—	—	1968	798	3,693	3.8	17.7
1926	2	25	—	—	1969	821	4,005	4.0	19.6
1927	2	38	—	—	1970	785	4,711	3.7	22.3
1928	2	42	—	—	1971	795	5,516	3.6	24.8
1929	2	43	—	—	1972	771	6,315	3.1	25.1
1930	7	47	—	—	1973	780	6,859	2.8	24.5
1931	8	62	—	—	1974	877	8,145	2.7	24.6
1932	49	71	—	—	1975	1,044	9,905	2.8	27.0
1933	114	79	—	—	1976	1,772	11,120	4.3	26.7
1934	235	60	—	—	1977	1,877	12,617	3.9	26.4
1935	203	115	—	—	1978	3,141	13,893	5.7	25.3
1936	278	139	—	—	1979	5,780	15,477	9.1	24.2
1937	321	144	—	—	1980	9,305	18,778	12.3	24.8
1938	305	175	—	—	1981	11,397	20,539	14.0	25.3
1939	351	178	—	—	1982	14,438	22,116	16.4	25.1
1940	418	185	—	—	1983	14,746	21,379	16.1	23.3
1941	459	203	—	—	1984	14,608	20,164	15.8	21.7
1942	485	222	—	—	1985	15,613	18,809	17.0	20.4
1943	525	220	—	—	1986	16,720	14,562	20.3	17.7
1944	519	230	—	—	1987	16,392	10,735	23.2	15.2
1945	452	217	—	—	1988	16,049	9,768	24.3	14.8
1946	413	220	14.4	7.7	1989	14,659	9,131	22.3	13.9
1947	400	261	11.6	7.6	1990	12,322	9,942	18.8	15.2
1948	370	326	9.0	8.0	1991	10,652	10,258	15.9	15.4
1949	342	421	6.9	8.5	1992	9,332	10,648	13.8	15.7
1950	346	437	6.7	8.5	1993	8,118	10,777	12.1	16.1
1951	329	512	5.4	8.4	1994	7,090	10,979	10.2	15.8
1952	304	638	4.1	8.6	1995	6,841	11,646	9.4	16.0
1953	337	681	4.4	8.9	1996	5,786	12,992	7.7	17.3
1954	375	604	5.5	8.9	1997	5,243	14,599	6.7	18.7
1955	417	634	5.8	8.8	1998	3,993	16,812	4.8	20.2
1956	405	705	5.1	8.9	1999	4,048	17,088	4.9	20.7
1957	430	759	5.4	9.5					
1958	435	952	4.9	10.8					
1959	405	1,197	4.0	11.9					
1960	397	1,450	3.4	12.6					
1961	419	1,567	3.5	13.1					
1962	496	1,738	3.9	13.7					
1963	556	1,947	3.9	13.7					
1964	593	2,230	3.8	14.3					

Note appears on next page

(continued)

TABLE Da1471–1474 Non-real estate loans outstanding – Farmers Home Administration and Farm Credit System: 1922–1999 *Continued*

[1] Includes operating loans, emergency loans, emergency crop and feed loans, and, beginning 1966, economic opportunity loans; prior to 1933, covers only emergency crop and feed loans. For 1922–1931, data are from July 1 of the previous year.

Sources

U.S. Department of Agriculture, *Agricultural Statistics*, various issues, and data provided by Jerome M. Stam, U.S. Department of Agriculture, Economic Research Service.

Documentation

Data for loans outstanding held by the Farmers Home Administration and the Farm Credit System for 1922–1970 are from *Historical Statistics of the United States* (1975). Data for total non-real estate loans outstanding for 1946–1998 is from Jerome M. Stam.

Non-real estate credit, variously called short-term credit, personal and collateral credit, or production credit, is obtained by farmers from many sources, including banks, federal and federally sponsored credit agencies, merchants, dealers, commission men, finance companies, landlords, and individuals. Commercial banks have provided the bulk of this type of credit extended by credit institutions although, since the early 1930s, federal and federally sponsored agencies and finance companies have become important in this lending field.

The federal government first entered the non-real estate agricultural credit field in 1918 when it made available $5 million for direct loans to farmers in the Northwest and Southwest where there had been two successive crop failures. During the 1920s, seed and feed loans were made available

from time to time in certain "distressed" areas by special acts of Congress. In the early 1930s, the basis for lending was broadened and the Emergency Crop and Feed Loan Office came to be the more-or-less-permanent source of credit for farmers in distress. The Farmers Home Administration Act of 1946 transferred the activities of the Emergency Crop and Feed Loan Office from the Farm Credit Administration to the newly created Farmers Home Administration (successor to the Farm Security Administration) and provided for the liquidation of these loans.

The Agricultural Credit Act of 1923 created the federal intermediate credit banks, the first permanent federally sponsored credit agencies making non-real estate loans available to farmers. These banks make no loans directly to farmers, but they do make loans to and discount loans for private financing institutions (agricultural credit corporations and livestock loan companies). The same 1923 Act also authorized the federal intermediate credit banks to provide loans to and discounts for agricultural cooperatives, that is, direct loans to marketing cooperatives on the security of commodities. In 1933, special legislation authorized the creation of the "banks for cooperatives," which, by 1936, had largely taken over the function of the intermediate credit banks in making loans to cooperatives. A part of the loan funds of the "banks for cooperatives," however, is supplied by the federal intermediate credit banks.

Except as indicated, data are for loans outstanding as of January 1.

Series Da1472. The Farm Credit System includes the production credit association, banks for cooperatives, and federal intermediate credit banks.

TABLE Da1475–1476   Agricultural regulation laws – number: 1884–1970

Contributed by Daniel A. Sumner

	Total	Excluding New Deal laws		Total	Excluding New Deal laws		Total	Excluding New Deal laws
	Da1475	Da1476		Da1475	Da1476		Da1475	Da1476
Year	Number	Number	Year	Number	Number	Year	Number	Number
1884	1	1	1915	1	1	1945	8	1
1885	0	0	1916	2	2	1946	11	4
1886	1	1	1917	3	3	1947	17	7
1887	0	0	1918	2	2	1948	14	7
1888	0	0	1919	1	1	1949	15	4
1889	0	0	1920	1	1	1950	11	6
1890	1	1	1921	4	4	1951	9	5
1891	0	0	1922	3	3	1952	5	3
1892	0	0	1923	3	3	1953	9	4
1893	0	0	1924	2	2	1954	15	6
1894	1	1	1925	0	0	1955	29	5
1895	0	0	1926	4	4	1956	31	12
1896	0	0	1927	4	4	1957	16	3
1897	0	0	1928	4	4	1958	34	10
1898	0	0	1929	6	6	1959	11	2
1899	0	0	1930	5	5	1960	17	6
1900	0	0	1931	6	6	1961	16	3
1901	0	0	1932	4	4	1962	25	6
1902	1	1	1933	9	7	1963	10	2
1903	1	1	1934	17	4	1964	11	3
1904	0	0	1935	16	5	1965	10	3
1905	0	0	1936	26	7	1966	9	6
1906	3	3	1937	14	8	1967	11	3
1907	1	1	1938	22	9	1968	13	9
1908	0	0	1939	26	8	1969	5	2
1909	0	0	1940	23	8	1970	16	6
1910	0	0	1941	13	3			
1911	0	0	1942	18	3			
1912	1	1	1943	10	1			
1913	0	0	1944	14	3			
1914	1	1						

Source

Gary Libecap, "The Great Depression and the Regulating State: Federal Government Regulation of Agriculture, 1884–1970," in Michael D. Bordo, Claudia Goldin, and Eugene N. White, editors, *The Defining Moment: The Great Depression and the American Economy in the Twentieth Century* (University of Chicago Press, 1998), pp. 181–224.

Documentation

Series Da1475. Gives the total number of new laws relating to agricultural regulation between 1884 and 1970.

Series Da1476. Gives the total number of new laws relating to agricultural regulation between 1884 and 1970 excluding legislation creating, revising, or building on New Deal Programs in the years 1933–1970.

CHAPTER Db
Natural Resource Industries

Editor: Gavin Wright

MINING, ENERGY, FISHERIES, AND FORESTRY

Gavin Wright

From the beginnings of European settlement, a substantial portion of American economic activity has been closely tied to natural resources. Products of the forest – naval stores, gums, resins, turpentine, and timber – were vital to the British mercantile economy. New Englanders engaged in ocean-going cod and mackerel fishing during the colonial era extensively enough for Adam Smith to write in 1776: "The New England fishery in particular was before the late disturbances one of the most important perhaps in the world." (volume 2, p. 90). The minerals economy rose to prominence in the nineteenth century, forming the backbone of America's world leadership in manufacturing.

Resource-based industries became less economically central in the twentieth century, as measured by shares of employment or gross domestic product. But the problem of energy was critical, and energy issues in turn were linked to long historical trends in the production and trade of essential minerals, in technology, and in the pressure of environmental concerns. The tables in this chapter provide basic historical information about these trends and their implications.

Minerals and the American Economy

Mining and mineral products were an important part of America's rise to world economic preeminence by the end of the nineteenth century, both directly as a source of production value and indirectly as a stimulus to manufacturing, to technology, and to regional development. At its peak in 1919, employment in mineral operations exceeded one million persons (series Db5–6). This amounted, however, to less than 3 percent of the total number of production workers in the economy at that time, about the same as the share of mining in national income. Although the minerals sector was not nearly as large as agriculture or manufacturing, its economic contribution was in many ways central. Contrary to the intuition that the importance of natural resources should decline over time, the share of mining in the labor force rose until 1909, and its contribution to the national product increased until the 1920s. The

relative price of material inputs declined, and American manufacturing exports became more resource intensive between 1880 and 1920, the very period in which the country rose to a position of world economic leadership. Econometric studies have found a significant materials-using bias in technological change in manufacturing during this era, including many of the most prominent and successful U.S. industries (Cain and Paterson 1986). It is arguable, indeed, that resource-intensity and materials-using biases are persistent characteristics of the American economy down to the present day.

The quantitative record of rising U.S. mineral production is displayed in the various series on the physical volume of output, grouped into fuel minerals (Table Db25–33), metals (Tables Db73–103), and nonmetal minerals (Table Db112–121). The modern sources for these data begin in 1880, shortly after the establishment of the U.S. Geological Survey, which issued an annual report entitled *Mineral Resources of the United States*. (Beginning in 1924, the Bureau of Mines assumed responsibility for the report, and the title changed to *Minerals Yearbook* in 1932.) Longer-term series such as coal, lead, iron ore, gold, silver, and copper have been estimated not only from the decennial census but also from state and industry sources, which generally reflect the smelter or refining (or minting) phase rather than direct measurement of production at the mines. As such, they probably underestimate total production for the early years.

Despite the deficiencies of the data, the growing interest in mineral statistics seems to have reflected the rising importance of minerals in the economy. Virtually without exception, the longer-term series such as coal, lead, and iron ore (proxied by shipments of pig iron) show rapid increases from near-zero levels early in the nineteenth century. Other series, such as gold, silver, and copper, begin only in the 1830s or 1840s because mining of these items was negligible or nonexistent before that time. Thus, the country was not always minerals-rich. Writing in 1790, Benjamin Franklin declared: "Gold and silver are not the produce of North America, which has no mines" (quoted in Rickard 1932, p. 2). (In the eighteenth century, the term "mine" meant an outcropping or deposit of a mineral, not an operation for actually extracting the mineral from the ground.) A century later, however, the United States had achieved world leadership or near-leadership in the production of coal, petroleum, copper, iron ore, antimony, magnesite, mercury, nickel, gold, silver, and zinc. On one or another of these minerals, production in another country may have rivaled that of the United

Acknowledgments
Gavin Wright thanks Giulio Pontecorvo and Mark Holliday for helpful advice on fisheries and Peter Berck for suggestions on forestry. He also thanks Courtney M. Grey, Christopher Kingston, Slavi Slavov, and Ritesh Shah for research assistance. The tables on forests were jointly edited by Wright and

by Peter Berck of the University of California, Berkeley. They thank Georgina Moreno for assistance with this work. The project was facilitated by a grant from the Office of Technology Licensing at Stanford University.

States. But no other country in the world possessed the depth and range of mineral supplies found in the United States during the first decades in the twentieth century.[1] Mineral abundance was particularly important for the rise of American manufacturing in an era during which technologies were resource dependent and transportation costs were high by modern standards (see Wright 1990).

It has long been conventional in economics to view mineral deposits as an exogenous "resource endowment" to the economy; indeed, they are the classic illustration of *nonrenewable* resources, available only in fixed supply and destined for inevitable rising scarcity and exhaustion. The U.S. historical record is precisely the opposite of this scenario. For almost all major minerals, new deposits were continually discovered, and production continued to rise, well into the twentieth century – for the country as a whole, if not for every mining area considered separately. To some extent, this growth was a function of the size of the country and its relatively unexplored condition prior to the westward migration of the nineteenth century. But mineral discoveries were not mere byproducts of territorial expansion. Some of the most dramatic production growth occurred not in the Far West but in the older parts of the country: copper in Michigan, coal in Pennsylvania and Illinois, and oil in Pennsylvania and later Indiana, for examples. Many other countries in the world were large and (as we now know) well endowed with minerals. But no other country exploited its geological potential to the same extent. Using modern geological estimates, Paul David and Gavin Wright show that the U.S. share of world mineral production in 1913 was far in excess of its share of world reserves (David and Wright 1997, p. 205). Mineral development was thus an integral part of the broader process of national development.

David and Wright identify three major elements in the rise of the American minerals economy: (1) an accommodating legal environment; (2) investment in the infrastructure of public knowledge; and (3) education in mining and metallurgy (David and Wright 1997).

U.S. mineral law was novel in that the government claimed no ultimate legal title to the nation's minerals, not even on the public domain. All other major mining systems retained the influence of the ancient tradition whereby minerals were the personal property of the lord or ruler, who granted user rights as concessions if he so chose. This liberality was not entirely intentional. The Land Ordinance of 1785 did claim for the federal government "one third part of all gold, silver, lead and copper mines" on the public domain, and between 1807 and 1846 a federal leasing system for lead mines was in operation (see Wright 1966). The system collapsed in the 1830s and 1840s because of noncompliance and fraud, and leasing was discontinued in 1846. Thus, the great California gold rush that began in 1848 took place in a legal vacuum, only partially filled by the rules of local mining districts and the intervention of state courts. The federal Mining Laws of 1866, 1870, and 1872 ultimately codified what by then was an established tradition of minimal federal engagement: open access for exploration; exclusive rights to mine a specific site upon proof of discovery; and the requirement that the claim be worked at some frequency or be subject to forfeit. Although the fuel minerals coal and oil have received

separate treatment in the twentieth century, for most minerals, the Mining Law of 1872 remains the basic mineral law of the country (Mayer and Riley 1985).

This discussion may convey the impression that the rise of U.S. mineral production was primarily an exercise in rapid exhaustion of a nonrenewable resource in a common-property setting. Although elements of such a scenario were sometimes on display during periodic mineral "rushes," resource extraction in America was also associated with ongoing processes of learning, investment, technological progress, and cost reduction, generating a many-fold expansion rather than depletion of the nation's resource base. The point is illustrated by the work of the U.S. Geological Survey (USGS). Established in 1879, the USGS was the most ambitious and productive governmental science project of the nineteenth century. The agency was successor to many state-sponsored surveys and to a number of more narrowly focused federal efforts. It proved to be highly responsive to the concerns of Western mining interests, and the practical value of its detailed mineral maps gave the USGS, in turn, a powerful constituency in support of its scientific research. The early twentieth-century successes of the USGS in petroleum were instrumental in transforming the attitudes of the oil industry from hunches and folklore toward trained geologists and applied geological science (Williamson, Andreano, et al. 1963).

The third force was education. By the late nineteenth century, the United States emerged as the world's leading educator in mining engineering and metallurgy. The early leader was the Columbia School of Mines, opened in 1864; some twenty schools granted degrees in mining by 1890. After a surge in enrollment during the decades bracketing the turn of the century, the University of California at Berkeley became the largest mining college in the world. A manpower survey for military purposes in 1917 identified 7,500 mining engineers in the country, with a remarkably broad range of professional experience, domestic and foreign. The most famous American mining engineer, Herbert Hoover, maintained that the increasing assignment of trained engineers to positions of combined financial and managerial, as well as technical responsibility, was largely an American development (Hoover 1909).

Trends in Mineral Scarcity and Self-Sufficiency

The preceding discussion implies that informative as the long-term mineral production series may be, they can only be given an economic-historical interpretation in conjunction with supplementary information on technology, costs, reserves, international trade, and other aspects of the subject. Some data of this sort are presented in these tables, but specialists will want to consult a wider range of statistical and technical sources. As in most economic problems, the first step in interpreting evidence on quantities is to examine the trends in mineral prices, relative to the general price level. This information may be extracted from the tables by dividing the *value* of production (Tables Db34–39, Db104–111, and Db122–131) by the corresponding series on quantity. Unfortunately, USGS reports on the value of output beginning in 1880. Some longer-term price data are presented for coal and petroleum in Tables Db56–72; many other historical mineral price series are collected in Schmitz (1979); for more recent years price and cost data are readily available in the *Minerals Yearbooks* and other sources.

---

[1] Comparative international statistics are conveniently collected in Schmitz (1979).

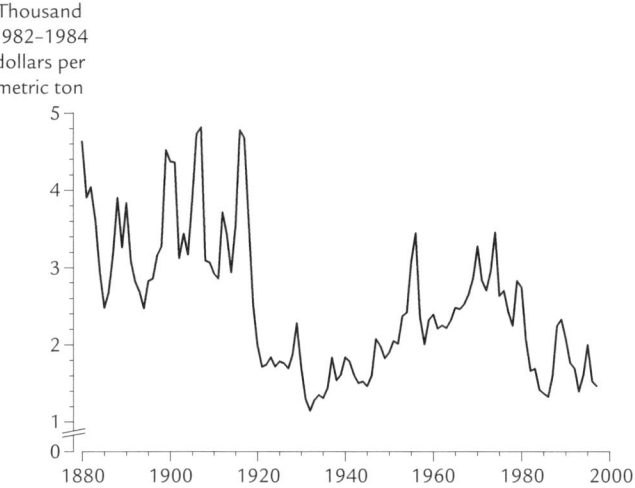

Thousand
1982–1984
dollars per
metric ton

FIGURE Db-A   Real price of copper: 1880–1997

Sources
Series Db106, divided by series Db75, and then deflated by series Cc1.

The procedure for constructing real prices from the value of output is illustrated in Figure Db-A for the case of copper. Series Db105 has been divided by series Db75, and the resulting nominal price series (dollars per metric ton) was then deflated by the David-Solar all-commodity consumer price index, series Cc1. The graph indicates that although the course of real copper prices has by no means been smooth, the long-term trend has been downward.

Similar long-term declines in relative prices have been observed for virtually all nonrenewable minerals, as shown in a 1963 study by Howard Barnett and Chandler Morse. The downward trend appeared to be at an end during the 1970s, when restrictions on oil production generated fears of impending material scarcities, but it was subsequently renewed in the 1980s and 1990s. This record is contrary to the predictions of economic theory, which hold that prices of nonrenewable resources must inevitably begin to rise.[2]

What forces have staved off mineral exhaustion across two centuries? Until World War II, the dominant factor was technological progress in the minerals industries. This category includes not just the discovery of new deposits but also advances in the techniques of search, in the methods for extracting ores from the ground, and in the processes used to separate the metal from the ore (smelting and refining). In the example of copper, U.S. firms pioneered the use of electrolytic refining and the oil flotation process for concentrating the ore. These metallurgical methods were complementary to the application of the Jackling method of large-scale, nonselective copper mining in the first decade of the twentieth century, using highly mechanized techniques to remove all material from the mineralized area. Together, this technological revolution allowed U.S. firms to drive the margin for commercially profitable cooper ore below 2 percent, at a time when yields in copper-rich Chile averaged between 10 and 13 percent. Knowing only the yields, we might interpret this comparison as a sign of worsening scarcity. But the fact that the real price of copper was declining during this period confirms that the fall in yields was an indication of

technological progress; it was, in effect, an expansion of the national resource base.

Since World War II, the continuing fall in U.S. minerals prices no longer derived primarily from an expansion in domestic production but reflected an increased reliance on imports from abroad. The shift of the United States to a position of net minerals importer may be traced in the tables for fuel minerals (Tables Db56–72), for selected metals (Table Db132–149), and for selected nonfuel and nonmetal minerals (Table Db150–154). Bauxite became a net import even before the war. Lead, zinc, and copper followed in the late 1940s. Imports of crude oil and iron ore became significant in the 1950s. By the 1980s, the country was a net importer of most minerals, the only major exceptions being bituminous coal and phosphate rock.

During the first postwar decade, many national leaders viewed these trends with alarm. Their concerns led to the appointment of the President's Material Policy Commission (the Paley Commission), whose 1952 report was entitled *Resources for Freedom*. The commission called for liberalization of international trade in raw materials as well as intensification of domestic resource development. As events took their course, the ready availability of imports largely allayed fears of impending scarcity. The obvious exception is petroleum, for which the Organization of Petroleum Exporting Countries (OPEC) embargo and the resulting economic turbulence of the 1970s vividly displayed the potential drawbacks to reliance on imports. Taking a long view, however, the rise of a global market in minerals – petroleum included – has been an important contributor to world economic growth during the modern era. Although depletion of domestic supplies has been a factor in some cases, the more important force has been the fall in transportation costs and the development of new ore deposits around the world. Thus, the United States is now a net importer even of minerals for which domestic production continues at or near historic peaks, such as zinc, molybdenum, and copper.

In addition to increased supplies, impending mineral scarcities have also been forestalled by adjustments on the demand side, including substitutions of relatively abundant resources for those that are relatively scarce and conservation in the uses of certain metals. Issues concerning energy are discussed in the next section of the essay. An interesting illustration of conservation may be found in the present section in the trend toward secondary production of a number of metals, using both new and old scrap. The growing importance of recycling may be seen for aluminum, magnesium, lead, zinc, nickel, and copper (see Tables Db73–103). Generally, scrap is categorized as old or new, where "new" indicates preconsumer sources and "old" suggests postconsumer sources. When metal is converted into shapes, new scrap is generated in the form of turnings, stampings, cuttings, and off-specification parts. After a product completes its useful life, it becomes old scrap. An example is used aluminum beverage cans, which now account for approximately one half of the old aluminum scrap consumed in the United States. More than three fourths of the refined lead produced in the United States in 1997 was recovered from recycled scrap, of which a major source was spent lead-acid storage batteries. Not only does recycling of metals contribute to the sustainability of their use, but the practice also has environmental benefits in the form of reduced volumes of waste and reduced emissions. Detailed industry reports on the status of recycling are issued each year by the U.S. Geological Survey in the *Minerals Yearbook*.

---

[2] The classic article is Hotelling (1931). An excellent review of concepts and evidence is Krautkraemer (1998).

Energy in American Economic History

Whereas the tables discussed in the previous section reported mineral production either in physical units or aggregated in terms of dollar values, Tables Db155–181 report many of the same commodities reduced to the common denominator of energy, the British thermal unit (BTU) – the quantity of heat required to raise the temperature of one pound of water one degree Fahrenheit, at or near its point of maximum density. Why do we need this alternative mode of social accounting? Textbooks commonly explain that "energy is essential to life" and imply by extension that high levels of energy consumption are essential to economic life at modern standards of living. But a distinct and voluminous body of historical statistics would hardly be justified by the mere need for the economy to conform to the laws of physics. The more compelling explanation for the study of energy is historical. At recurring points through American history, fears of impending energy scarcities have become widespread, generally because of disruptions to or doubts about future supplies of a major energy source. In light of these episodes, it is informative to analyze the sources of energy more comprehensively and to consider the ways in which these sources have changed through history in response to changes in incentives and in technology.

There are, however, a number of drawbacks to this form of aggregation. First, historical accounts of the production and consumption of "energy" are by no means comprehensive from a scientific standpoint: animal power, wind power for sailing vessels, and even "direct" industrial water power are typically not included. Second, conversion into BTUs does not reflect the different thermal efficiencies of the various fuels. This problem is most serious with respect to wood, long the nation's dominant fuel source, but one that involved an especially low thermal efficiency. Thus the series on fuelwood consumption, superseded by the series on biomass production and consumption, probably overstates energy *consumed* – as opposed to the energy *produced* – from this source (see series Db171, Db174, and Db179). Third, the conversion of hydroelectric power represents a special problem. Because the energy exerted by the flowing water is not measured directly, the energy provided by hydroelectric power is typically constructed by estimating the "fuel equivalent" of the kilowatt hours generated (see, for example, series Db163). But this procedure means that the series on hydroelectric power is influenced by the changing efficiency of converting fuel into electricity elsewhere in the economy. The time profile of hydroelectric power looks quite different in tables in which the electricity generated is measured directly in kilowatt hours, as in series Db224.

The general point is that tables like these involve a considerable amount of construction, some of which is arbitrary. Students of energy history will want to use them in conjunction with the full range of information on the volume and value of production in the minerals section. More technical researchers will want to turn to the underlying sources (such as the *Minerals Yearbook* and the *Annual Energy Review*) to analyze the definition and historical evolution of the conversion factors themselves.

Despite these shortcomings, Tables Db155–171 do provide a quantitative rendition of the two major historical revolutions in American energy: the transition from wood to coal in the nineteenth century and the shift from coal to petroleum in the twentieth century. The first of these was fundamental to the Industrial Revolution of eighteenth-century England, releasing the economy from the constraints of the "organic economy" (Wrigley 1988). So long as energy had to be obtained from vegetable sources such as timber, its supply was either limited to an annual harvest or subject to rising costs because it had to come from greater and greater distances. The replacement of wood by coal, however, opened up for human use a vast inventory of already-stored energy. Because major coal deposits are geographically concentrated, moreover, specialized transportation systems could carry these materials to appropriately located establishments for use. Cheap, concentrated energy thus served to relax geographic limits on the scale of production and to increase the return on fixed investments in all sectors.

Ironically, in the United States this transition was delayed by an abundance of forestland, which readily generated timber as a byproduct in the ongoing process of clearing forests for farmland. As late as 1870, wood fuel constituted as much as 75 percent of U.S. energy consumption (Table Db164–171). Cheap timber helped give the United States world leadership in shipbuilding during the era of wooden ships, and Americans developed woodworking expertise and a wood-based lifestyle unique in the world at that time. But reliance on wood fuels consigned industries to what were then outmoded technologies, such as charcoal-using iron foundries. According to Alfred Chandler, it was not until the opening of the anthracite fields of eastern Pennsylvania that large-scale, steam-powered factories were feasible in America (Chandler 1972). Only with the rise of bituminous coal in the 1850s did American blast furnaces begin to adopt coke-using technologies. Making up for lost time, U.S. coal production surpassed that of Britain and Germany by the end of the nineteenth century. This development coincided with the rise of the United States to the position of the world's largest industrial nation, a transition forecast in W. S. Jevons's classic, *The Coal Question* (1866).

Figure Db-B shows that through 1890 the rise of coal was largely a substitute for wood energy; thereafter, the country's energy consumption rose to a new plateau of nearly 200 million BTU per

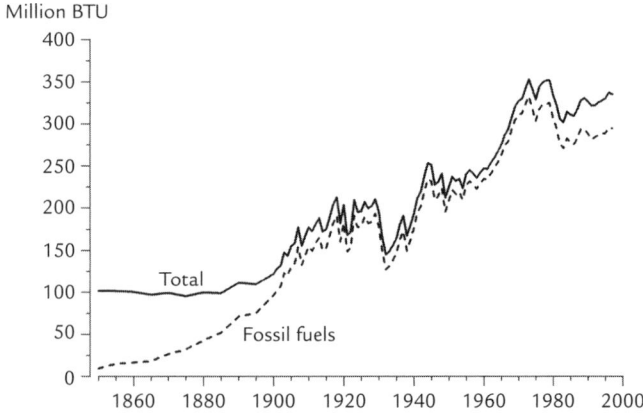

FIGURE Db-B   Energy consumption per capita: 1850–1998

Sources

Fossil fuels: series Db164. Total: sum of series Db164 and Db168–171. Population: series Aa7.

Documentation

The gap between fossil fuels and the total in the nineteenth century is explained by the use of wood for fuel. Wood's share of non-fossil-fuel energy consumption declined steadily during the twentieth century, from nearly 100 percent in 1890 to 50 percent by 1941, 25 percent by 1961, and less than 10 percent beginning 1971.

capita by 1920, easily the highest in the world at that time. This was the era during which coal was dominant – as fuel for household heating (primarily anthracite) and transportation (primarily railroads) and as an industrial energy source (dominated by the giant steel industry). Forecasters projected an enormous expansion in the demand for coal by the mid-twentieth century, but relative to gross domestic product, coal's share peaked during the 1910–1920 decade. The transition to petroleum energy was already underway.

The Era of Petroleum

World petroleum production was dominated by the United States for nearly a century, from the time of Edwin Drake's first oil strike near Titusville, Pennsylvania, in 1859 until the 1950s. Through most of the nineteenth century, petroleum's chief use was as an illuminant, a role claimed by electricity after 1900. In the twentieth century, oil became the nation's primary source of energy: as fuel oil for industry, heating oil for homes, and gasoline and diesel fuel for transportation. One of the advantages of oil over coal was its cost, but the primary advantage was transportability, both in relocating from the point of origin to the point of use and in moving the vehicles themselves. Industrialization in California, which had been held back by an absence of coal, flourished under the new oil regime. And California became a symbol of the oil-using, high-mobility American lifestyle of the twentieth century. Primarily through automobiles and electrification of the household, per capita energy consumption nearly doubled again between the 1920s and the 1970s, peaking at more than 350 million BTU per person.

The American love affair with oil was first prompted by a series of major new fields developed between 1900 and 1930, allaying (at least temporarily) the recurring fear that domestic supplies would run out. New discoveries led to an ever-widening range of uses (see Table Db45–55). Nonetheless, by the 1950s, the long-delayed exploitation of the vast oil fields in the Middle East was finally underway, and the United States became a major net importer of petroleum energy (Tables Db182–197). Although oil allowed great flexibility to firms and households, the nation as a whole became quite committed to it through massive investments in an infrastructure of pipelines and roads and through its commercial and household capital stock. The availability of cheap imports sustained the growth of consumption. But this commitment proved to be a heavy burden during the oil shocks of 1973 and 1979, brought on by the steep rise in prices resulting from cutbacks in production coordinated by OPEC. The effects of this traumatic decade may be traced in virtually all of the minerals and energy tables presented here.

It is interesting to reflect on the historical roots of the oil crisis of the 1970s for the nation and for the world in light of changing perceptions about oil supplies and energy requirements. Table Db198–205 displays estimates of crude oil reserves for the major regions of the world, between 1948 and 2000. (A longer-term U.S. series may be found in series Db59.) Such data must be taken with considerable skepticism. Because new reserves are added to the totals every year, geologists understand that these figures do not represent the ultimate oil energy potential of the earth; they are more like a working inventory, subject to discretionary financial and technical decisions over time. International reserve estimates are particularly subject to guesswork and variability. Nonetheless, when viewed over an extended period, reserve

estimates convey some important lessons. Although U.S. oil formerly dominated both world and national production, U.S. reserves at the turn of the twenty-first century are an extremely minor part of the world picture. U.S. reserve levels peaked in 1971 (when the Alaskan Prudhoe Bay discovery was recorded) and have gently declined ever since. One may note, however, that estimates of aggregate world reserves have continued to increase rather than decrease. This perhaps surprising phenomenon reflects the ongoing processes of exploration and development, which draw upon increasingly sophisticated branches of geological and geophysical science. Indeed, if one were to accumulate the entire volume of oil ever extracted from U.S. wells and put it back in the ground, the totals would still constitute a relatively small part of the modern world oil reserve picture. Thus, data on oil production and reserves should not be evaluated hastily. Far more detailed studies may be pursued using the voluminous information issued each year in the *Annual Energy Review*, the *Petroleum Supply Annual*, the *Crude Oil, Natural Gas and Gas Liquids Report*, and other publications of the Energy Information Administration.

With hindsight, in other words, the crisis of the 1970s reflected short-term vulnerability rather than an impending long-term energy scarcity. With some lags in adjustment, the tables show that patterns of energy production and consumption have demonstrated a remarkable range of flexibility and responsiveness to incentives. In addition to the discoveries and developments of oil reserves around the world, American homes and industries have moved away from exclusive dependence on oil, currently favoring natural gas or electricity (mainly generated by coal). The overall efficiency of energy use has dramatically improved, with per capita consumption leveling off or declining from the peaks of the 1970s. Table Db206–217 shows that even the gas-guzzling American automobile has increased its fuel efficiency since 1960, albeit prompted by federal legislation as well as heightened consumer sensitivity to gas mileage.

Responsiveness to incentives is a double-edged sword, however. The tables also show that many of the energy initiatives of the 1970s have stagnated as oil prices have declined. The record of renewable energy sources can only be considered disappointing to their advocates (Tables Db172–181 and Db242–260). Improvements in average gasoline mileage have largely come to an end, with the growing popularity of minivans and sport-utility vehicles (series Db211). The U.S. transport sector continues to consume far more oil than do its counterparts in other advanced industrial nations, American drivers responding not just to low world oil prices but to uniquely low gasoline taxes in the country. Nonetheless, the record indicates that a considerable array of alternative energy sources and margins for energy improvement does exist and could be called upon should another crisis occur.

Electrification and Energy Efficiency

Across the twentieth century, a steadily rising share of America's energy consumption has been provided through the medium of electricity. Electricity is not a primary energy source because it is itself produced from fuels through costly conversion processes. Table Db218–227 traces the sources net generation by electrical utilities since 1920. One may see that although generation from all sources has increased (including nuclear and hydroelectric energy), the dominant fuel source for electricity throughout the century has

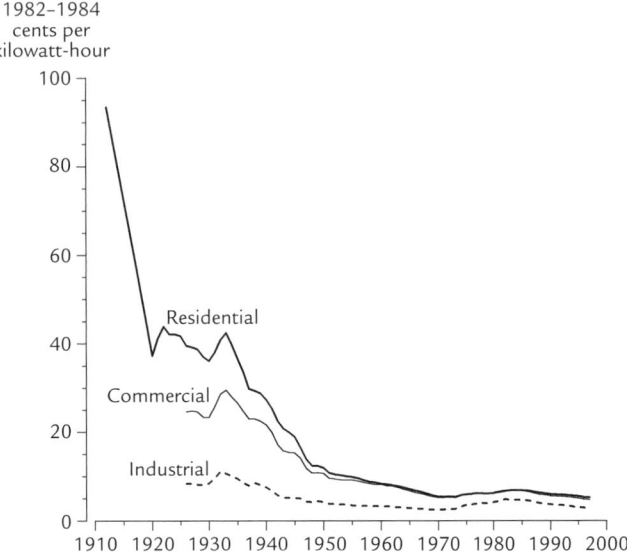

1982–1984
cents per
kilowatt-hour

**FIGURE Db-C   Real electricity prices, by type of use:
1912–1997**

Sources
Series Db235–237, deflated by series Cc1.

been coal. This persistence is a clear demonstration of the broader proposition that what is most important for the energy economy is the form, flexibility, and convenience through which energy is supplied, as contrasted with the cost or price of a unit of energy per se. Electrification is an indirect form of energy supply and, therefore, contributes to increased costs. Yet electrification has also been a major contributor to the long trend toward greater efficiency in energy utilization for the economy as a whole.[3]

Table Db228–233 presents data on sales and use of electricity since 1902, showing a steady expansion in residential, commercial, and industrial markets. The surge of electrification that began in the 1920s was triggered by the rapid decline in electricity prices during the 1910–1920 decade and sustained by the real price fall that continued into the 1960s. These trends may be seen in Figure Db-C, which uses price data from Table Db234–241, deflated by the David-Solar index of consumer prices. The price fall was driven by the scale economies made possible by central power stations in which giant generators were driven by high-speed steam turbines and by integration and extension of power transmission networks over an expanded territory. In comparison with these dramatic developments of the first half of the century, the price increases after the 1970s were moderate and soon reversed.

Series Db238 shows that the diffusion of electric service to American households was essentially complete by the early 1950s. The process was somewhat delayed in rural areas but was encouraged by the loans and assistance provided by the Rural Electrification Administration established in 1936; electrification in farm households had nearly closed the gap by 1950 (series Db239). After service was established, electricity use per household steadily increased, its growth slowing only moderately in response to the price increases of the 1970s and 1980s (series Db241).

How then has electricity contributed to improved energy efficiency? The greatest impact has been on the manufacturing sector, where electrification actually predated that of households, in part because high-volume industrial rates came down much earlier (series Db237). During the 1920s, purchased electricity replaced steam power as the primary power source in manufacturing. The transition had begun earlier, but only with the favorable investment conditions of that decade were manufacturing firms in position to implement the thorough restructuring of plant design and machine layout that would allow them to take advantage of electricity's potential to increase the productivity of both capital and labor. This episode has been identified by Paul David as a classic example of an innovation whose major impact is delayed by the need for accommodating changes in the structure of markets and of the workplace. For electrification, the crucial step was the shift from "group drive" (in which electric power simply replaced steam in a plant that retained the huge shafts and belts of the earlier era) to "unit drive" (in which each machine was equipped with its own electric motor).[4] By improving the reliability and flexibility of power, electrification thus made possible a fuller utilization of the nation's manufacturing capital stock, as well as its labor force. According to Murray F. Foss, this trend continued into the 1970s and played a significant role in generating the high rates of total-factor-productivity growth enjoyed during that era (Foss 1997).

For present purposes, the important point is that electrification was an essential background prerequisite for an entire set of technological and efficiency improvements in the economy; however, this progress had little to do with reducing the unit price of energy to its users. Thermal efficiency has indeed continued to improve, but the more important impact came through the "efficiency of energy utilization," adaptations made possible by electricity's ease of transport, convenience, and flexibility. The result has been an overall reduction in the energy intensity of the economy, or an increase in the productivity of energy.

Forest Areas of the United States

Americans have long been concerned about the disappearance of their forests. Unfortunately, careful surveys of woodland areas date only from the emergence of this concern at or shortly after the turn of the twentieth century. Earlier, of an estimated original forestland of some 900 million acres, only 470 million acres remained in 1920, and the majority of these had been disrupted to such an extent that they were no longer self-restoring. The most rapid destruction occurred between 1800 and 1920, the very period when Americans were so ingeniously adding to the country's mineral resource base. The last phase of this process may be traced in series Cf107 and Cf115, where the sum of these two forest land categories declines from 558 million acres in 1880 to 328 million in 1920. Although forests have always been renewable in principle, during most of this era they were viewed by settlers and lumber companies as a one-time gift of nature, and the abundance of American forest products supported expertise in woodworking technology and a wood-based lifestyle unique in the world at that time.[5]

The tide began to turn early in the twentieth century. Table Cf135–144 shows a remarkable increase in both public

---

[3] This apparent paradox is persuasively elaborated in Schurr, Burwell, et al. (1990).

[4] For fuller accounts, see David (1991) and Devine (1983).

[5] A good historical account may be found in Williams (1989).

and privately owned forest land, the largest jumps occurring between 1940 and 1970. Although precise comparisons are difficult, it seems accurate to say that at the end of the twentieth century, U.S. forest acreage was higher than it was a century before. Table Db379–386 shows that two thirds of the forest acreage is commercial timberland, a share that has been stable since the 1960s. Of this, nearly three fourths is privately owned.

Nonetheless, changes in public policy have played an important role in reversing the trend. In 1891, the first legislation was passed permitting the president to set aside public forest reservations (see Table Db387–389). Subsequent laws led to the creation of the Forest Service in 1905, with Gifford Pinchot as its first director. Under Pinchot's aggressive leadership, national forest acreage rose to 172 million acres by 1909, very close to its modern levels. The gross area within the national forest system boundaries, however, continued to expand until the late 1930s (Table Db390–397).

The national forest system was never intended, and has not functioned, to protect wooded lands from commercial uses. Although the conservation movement provided political pressure, the Act of 1891 intended no more than a temporary withdrawal of land from sale to the public, to protect area water supplies. Throughout his tenure, Pinchot argued that the national forests could be run at a profit, serving as a kind of model of enlightened, farsighted business practices. Thus, from the beginning in 1905, a considerable volume of timber has been cut and sold commercially from the national forest system (series Db390–392 and Db399). Grazing use receipts have also been important; in fact, until the 1920s, they were larger than timber sales (series Db400). Taking advantage of the regenerative capacities of previously logged-over and abandoned land, managing the annual timber harvest became a major activity of the Forest Service by the 1950s, with commercial sales peaking in the late 1980s. The goal of a profit for the system as a whole, however, has been elusive. Reliable long-term cost data are not readily available, but the evidence suggests that these operations have generally made losses, serving as an implicit subsidy to the lumber industry.[6]

Under budgetary and political pressure, the Forest Service has gradually grown into a wider set of noncommercial mandates, including improved tree breeding, habitat restoration, wilderness preservation and recreation, and forest conservation. The Multiple Use–Sustained Yield Act of 1960 was something of a landmark in this evolution, identifying timber as only one among many Forest Service goals. The Wilderness Act of 1964 went much further, mandating a system of wilderness lands reserved from all forms of development. These broadened responsibilities were to be shared with the National Park Service and the Fish and Wildlife Service. In the 1990s, as a result, clear-cut harvests on the national forests were substantially reduced, and the number of visitor-days to national forest system lands steadily increased (series Db402). The Forest Service now claims to be the single largest supplier of public outdoor recreation in the nation. A sense of its emerging institutional identity may be gained from the *Report of the Forest Service*, published annually.

Eventually, attitudes and practices in the private forest sector also gravitated toward longer-term sustainability. The diffusion of sustainable private-sector practices depended on improvement in the general knowledge base and level of training in forest management, as well as on attainment of sufficiently long organizational

time horizons to make these investments worthwhile. A major factor in this transition was the conquest of forest fires, which were frequent and devastating in the nineteenth century, adding to the motivation for realizing revenue quickly. When the early forest surveys of the 1920s reported surprisingly rapid regeneration, they also found that in roughly half the area surveyed, timber drain exceeded timber growth. The prime culprit was fire, the direct or indirect cause of three fourths of pine timber mortality. The problem had a strong regional component: the South accounted for some 85 percent of all forest fires in the country during the 1920s and 1930s, though the region contained less than one third of the nation's forest area. Roughly 40 percent of these fires were of suspected incendiary origin, reflecting the time-honored tradition of annual woods-burning, practiced in order to improve livestock grazing and eliminate pests. Between the 1920s and the 1950s, an ambitious federal–state–voluntary cooperative program undertook to transform the regional culture through education and prosecution and to expand the forest area under federal protection.

The success of the program may be seen in series Db404, which shows that the total burned-over forest area peaked in 1930 at more than 50 million acres and declined to less than one tenth of this level by the 1950s. The decline in the number of fires was somewhat less, reflecting success at fire containment as well as prevention (series Db403). As a result, the Federal Reserve Board amended its regulations in 1953 to allow financial institutions to make loans on timberland. This step was a significant milestone in the restoration and expansion of the South's forest industries.[7]

In recent years, enlightened forestry opinion has developed an appreciation of some of the benefits of controlled forest fires, for certain ecosystems and for the moderation of uncontrolled fires. A policy of complete fire exclusion can create a multistoried forest structure with a continuous vertical fuel arrangement, allowing what would be a surface fire to spread into the trees and become a crown fire. An unusually severe fire can seriously diminish the long-term sustainability of the land. Further, fire exclusion sometimes favors nonnative species in fire-dependent areas. For these reasons, many authorities actively favor the reintroduction of forest fire on a controlled basis.[8] From a century-long standpoint, these modern discussions are possible only because of the prior demise of the uncontrolled fire regime.

Forest Products Industries

Production and consumption of forest products are unusual in American history in that they have gone through a long cycle of decline and rebirth. The longest statistical series is for lumber production, which shows a peak at 46 billion board feet in 1906–1907 (series Db423). If we convert this into a series on consumption per capita, by adding imports (series Db426), subtracting exports (series Db429), and dividing by the national population, we can see that the country underwent a spectacular nineteenth-century expansion of its use of wood, followed by an equally precipitous decline in the first half of the twentieth century (see Figure Db-D).

---

[6] For an informed discussion, see Wolf (1997).

[7] Greater detail on the regional incidence and causes of forest fires may be found in the sources for Table Db403–408.

[8] See the multiagency Federal Wildland Fire Policy memorandum of 1995, available at the Forest Service Internet site.

FIGURE Db-D   Lumber consumption per capita: 1799–1997

Sources

Lumber consumption: series Db423, plus series Db426, minus series Db429.
Population: series Aa7.

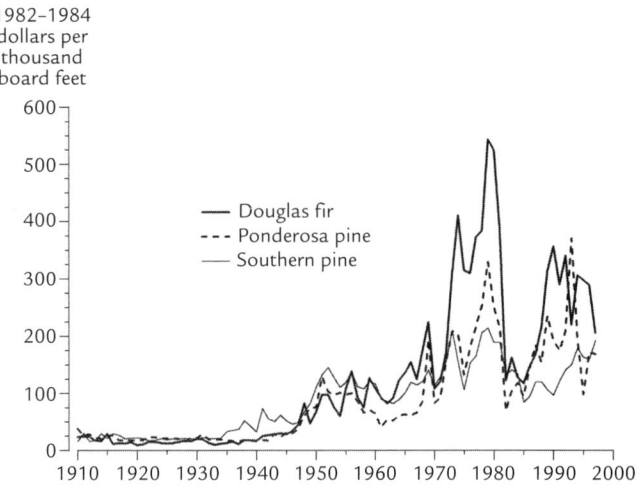

FIGURE Db-E   Real stumpage prices: 1910–1997

Sources

Series Db454–455 and Db457, deflated by series Cc1.

Remarkably, the decline ended during World War II, and per capita lumber consumption has been largely stable since then. Since the 1970s, imports of lumber have increased, overwhelmingly from Canada. But for most timber products, the growth of consumption has closely tracked the growth of domestic production, the most impressive growth sector being pulp products (Table Db409–422).

Largely occurring in the South, this expansion is a reflection of a revolution in technology and practice that has converted that region's forest economy into an advanced form of tree farming. Important enabling factors included the invention of the kraft or sulfate pulping process in Germany and successes at the U.S. Forest Products Laboratories in showing that suitable paper could be made from young, resinous pine trees, using the kraft process. Having then conquered the forest fire problem, firms relocating in the South could draw upon tree breeding and improvement programs first developed in Sweden and other European countries. Federal–state–industry collaboration subsequently led to the creation of a network of state nurseries in the South, and in recent years, university–industry programs like the North Carolina State Cooperative have led to remarkable advances in genetically based artificial regeneration. Some indication of this regional progress is visible in the data on lumber from principal tree species, which show that production from southern pine has nearly tripled from its low in the early 1960s, while nearly all other softwoods show decline (Table Db432–445). Pulpwood has also expanded, the South now accounting for about three fourths of the U.S. total and over half of paper and board production (Table Db446–453).[9]

The behavior of resource prices over the past two centuries has confounded the predictions of economic theory, which holds that nonrenewables should become more costly over time as they become more scarce, while the price of renewables should stabilize at the cost of production. As we have seen in the section on minerals, the price trend for most nonrenewables has been downward. Prices of lumber and forest products, on the other hand, despite the fact that they are renewable, show a long-term upward trend over the past two centuries. Peter Berck and William R. Bentley

(1997) show that Hotelling's theory of rising *non*renewable prices provides a good fit for the historical record for redwoods, a variety of which the old-growth supply is essentially fixed for practical purposes.[10]

What could possibly be the last phase of this era of rising scarcity may be seen in the first part of Figure Db-E, which graphs stumpage prices since 1910 for three major tree species, deflated by the David-Solar consumer price index. The continued increase during the first half of the century is evident. However, even though price levels since the 1950s have been highly volatile, the figure suggests that the long-term rising trend may have come to end. This is particularly so for the southern pine, which was the high-price variety before the 1960s but has now become relatively less expensive because its production has been placed on a sustainable and renewable basis.

This historical overview puts into somewhat different perspective the debate over preservation of the old-growth forests in the Pacific Northwest. These areas are often portrayed as the last vestiges of a once-vast American woodland, a characterization that is far from accurate. Because the cycle of regeneration is much longer in this region than in the South, logging still retains much of the character of the old once-over pattern and is less amenable to change through incentives. The issues largely turn, however, not on the need to conserve timber resources for future generations, nor on the vital importance of timber to the national economy, but on the social value of preserving the unique ecosystems that the old-growth forests represent, particularly as habitats for diverse plant and animal life. The annual harvest of Douglas fir declined precipitously between the 1980s and the 1990s because of the demands of the Endangered Species Act (series Db434).[11] These ecological values are subject to great uncertainty and wide differences of opinion. But compromise is difficult because of the probable irreversibility of many of the ecological consequences, unlike the highly regenerative quality that other American forests have displayed.

---

[9] For a compelling account, see Boyd (2001).

[10] Price data for the nineteenth century may be found in U.S. Forest Service (1948).

[11] This history is recounted by Yaffee (1994).

Fisheries

The term "fishery" has at least two distinct meanings: (1) the business of catching, packing, or selling fish or other products of lakes, rivers, or the sea; and (2) a place where fish and the like are caught – a fishing ground. It may also refer to a legal right to catch fish in certain waters or at certain times, or a place where fish are bred. All these meanings come into play in American history, but the first two have been paramount in the statistics collected since the founding of the U.S. Fish Commission in 1871. Following in this tradition, the main focus of these tables is the record of the quantity and value of fish and related products generated by the U.S. domestic industry, with some attention to the question of sustainability, in light of the fact that fish are a renewable natural resource subject to depletion. Because most fish populations swim in international waters, however, it is inherently difficult to draw inferences about resource stocks from trends in the annual catch by fishermen of a single nation.

The American fishing industry long predates the statistical tables presented here. Aided by a federal bounty enacted in the 1790s, East Coast fishing experienced a considerable expansion in the first half of the nineteenth century.[12]

This period of growth was followed by contraction after the Civil War. The latter stages of this decline may be seen in the series on total domestic yield of fishery products (series Db273), and especially in the fall in the landed catch of Atlantic cod between 1887 and 1905, and in the landed catch of Atlantic mackerel between 1880 and 1910 (Table Db283–300). It is not clear that this development reflected a deterioration of fishery resources. Other important historical factors would include the abolition of the federal fishing bounty in 1866; the rise of Canadian competition in the Grand Banks of Newfoundland and other international waters; the increase in U.S. tariffs, which raised the cost of imported curing salt; changes in consumer preferences; and the rise of new regional fishing industries in the South, the Great Lakes, and the Pacific.[13] Note that the U.S. whaling industry went through a similar rise-and-fall cycle, which does not seem to be attributable to pressures on stocks of the major hunted whale species (Table Db371–376).[14]

After 1900, the aggregate figures show alternating periods of growth and stagnation in the domestic yield of fishery products, with a pronounced upward trend across the century as a whole (Tables Db273–282 and Db311–314). The growth of the fish catch allocated toward industrial purposes (primarily animal feed) began to decline after the early 1980s, but the fish yield for human consumption resumed its positive long-term trend at roughly the same time. Both fish product imports and exports have grown, reflecting the general expansion of world trade rather than generalized pressures on domestic supplies (Table Db273–282). Constructed series on unit values (obtained by dividing value figures by the corresponding quantity figures) show no indication of an increase in the average price of fish, relative to the general price level. Perhaps as a result, per capita consumption levels have drifted upward across the century (Table Db342–352).

When we turn to the record for particular fish species, the picture is more mixed (Table Db283–300). Although the total landed catch of fish increased between the 1960s and the 1990s, many individual species show evidence of recurrent overfishing. The yield of Atlantic mackerel all but disappeared from the 1950s to the 1980s, before recovering moderately in the 1990s. The yield of Pacific mackerel peaked at 176 million pounds in 1947, falling to 18 million pounds in 1973; after a resurgence in the 1980s, the catch fell once again to a low of 23 million pounds in 1995. The collapse of tuna and haddock has been even more precipitous. The virtual disappearance of the Pacific sardine fishery in the 1950s is recounted in detail by Arthur F. McEvoy (McEvoy 1986). According to McEvoy, that episode represented an extreme example of failure by federal and state authorities to "manage" fish stocks successfully, a failure attributable to the use of inadequate single-stock biological models to estimate maximum sustainable yield (MSY) and an inability to forecast changes in climatic conditions bearing on fish stock dynamics. In most cases where the fish catch declines, however, it is difficult to assign precise responsibility to overfishing, as opposed to other factors, such as pressures on habitats arising either from human actions or from natural causes.

The record for shellfish is broadly similar (Table Db301–310). Most of the species for which long-term data are available – clams, lobster, Atlantic and Pacific squid – show rising trends in landed catch over more than a century. Shrimp is a partial exception, showing rising yields until the 1970s, followed by decline in the 1990s to levels that were typical during the 1950s. The series on oysters begins only in 1929, but it clearly deviates from the others. From yields greater than 90 million pounds in the 1930s, the landed catch of oysters has declined to less than 40 million pounds per year in the 1990s. Consistent with this downward trend, the relative price of oysters has been rising in recent years. Nonetheless, the total landed catch of shellfish grew markedly between 1960 and 1991, though it subsequently declined.

In recent years, the National Marine Fisheries Service (NMFS) has expanded and improved its statistical reporting services. One new initiative is reflected in Table Db334–341, the effort to monitor recreational fishing in coastal waters. The figures suggest that the number of recreational fishing trips per year was relatively stable from the 1970s to the 1990s, but the number and weight of fish caught actually declined during this period.

Another new development is the emergence of commercial aquaculture, which has been monitored by the Department of Agriculture since 1983 (Tables Db353–370). The total value of U.S. aquaculture production tripled between 1983 and 1997, possibly an important factor in restraining increases in market prices generally. The most rapid increase has been catfish, which in 1997 accounted for two thirds of aquaculture production by weight, though only 40 percent by value. Salmon aquaculture also shows a large increase between 1983 and 1995, though the share of aquaculture in total domestic salmon supply is still relatively small (compare series Db294 and Db357). Shellfish aquaculture has grown very slowly, and its share in total shellfish supply also remains relatively small (compare series Db359–361 and Table Db301–310).

Perhaps the most important new responsibility of the NMFS is to report each year on the status of fisheries by geographic area and to identify those fisheries that are overfished or are approaching a condition of being overfished. This charge was established by the Sustainable Fisheries Act of 1996, which reauthorized and amended the Magnuson–Stevens Fishery Conservation

---

[12] Accounts of this growth may be found in Innis (1954) and O'Leary (1996). The latter work presents numerous statistical tables with state data and references to available national series.

[13] The best recent discussion of these trends is in O'Leary (1996).

[14] See the discussion in Davis, Gallman, and Gleiter (1997).

and Management Act of 1976. This Act reflected the prevalent view among informed observers that the high catch levels of the 1990s are not sustainable but instead represent an intensified exploitation of fishery resources. Such conclusions have been documented by various international studies, such as the Food and Agricultural Organization's *Chronicles of Marine Fisheries Landings (1950–1994)*, which showed that a growing number of world marine fisheries were in either a "mature" or "senescent" stage of declining yield (Food and Agricultural Organization 1996). In its "Reports on the Status of Fisheries of the United States," the NMFS estimates of "overfished" species increased from 86 in 1997 to 98 in 1999. The number of species classified "not overfished" decreased from 183 in 1997 to 127 in 1999. However, the status of the largest number of fish species (674 in 1999) was unknown.[15]

References

Barnett, Howard, and Chandler Morse. 1963. *Scarcity and Growth*. Johns Hopkins University Press.

Berck, Peter, and William R. Bentley. 1997. "Hotelling's Theory, Enhancement, and the Taking of the Redwood National Park." *American Journal of Agricultural Economics* 79 (May): 287–98.

Boyd, William. 2001. "The Forest Is the Future." In Philip Scranton, editor. *The Second Wave: Southern Industrialization, 1940–1970s*. University of Georgia Press.

Cain, Louis P., and Donald G. Paterson. 1986. "Biased Technical Change, Scale and Factor Substitution in American Industry, 1850–1919." *Journal of Economic History* 46 (September): 153–64.

Chandler, Alfred. 1972. "Anthracite Coal and the Beginnings of the Industrial Revolution in the United States." *Business History Review* 46 (Summer): 141–81.

David, Paul A. 1991. "Computer and Dynamo." In *Technology and Productivity: The Challenge for Economic Policy*. Organization for Economic Cooperation and Development.

David, Paul, and Gavin Wright. 1997. "Increasing Returns and the Genesis of American Resource Abundance." *Industrial and Corporate Change* 6: 205–12.

Davis, Lance E., Robert E. Gallman, and Karin Gleiter. 1997. *In Pursuit of Leviathan*. University of Chicago Press.

Devine, Jr., Warren. 1983. "From Shafts to Wires." *Journal of Economic History* 43: 347–72.

Food and Agricultural Organization. 1996. *Chronicles of Marine Fisheries Landings (1950–1994)*. FAO Technical Paper number 359.

Foss, Murray F. 1997. *Shiftwork, Capital Hours and Productivity Change*. Kluwer Academic Press.

Hoover, Herbert. 1909. *Principles of Mining*. Hill Publishing Company.

Hotelling, Harold. 1931. "The Economics of Exhaustible Resources." *Journal of Political Economy* 39: 137–75.

Innis, Harold A. 1954 [1940]. *The Cod Fisheries*. University of Toronto Press.

Jevons, W. S. 1866. *The Coal Question*. Macmillan.

Krautkraemer, Jeffrey A. 1998. "Nonrenewable Resource Scarcity." *Journal of Economic Literature* 36: 2065–107.

Mayer, C. J., and G. A. Riley. 1985. *Public Domain, Private Dominion*. Sierra Club.

McEvoy, Arthur F. 1986. *The Fisherman's Problem*. Cambridge University Press.

O'Leary, Wayne M. 1996. *Maine Sea Fisheries*. Northeastern University Press.

Rickard, Thomas A. 1932. *A History of American Mining*. McGraw-Hill.

Schmitz, C. J. 1979. *World Non-Ferrous Metal Production and Prices, 1799–1976*. Cass.

Schurr, Sam, Calvin C. Burwell, et al. 1990. *Electricity in the American Economy*. Greenwood Press.

Smith, Adam. 1976 [1776]. *An Inquiry into the Nature and Causes of the Wealth of Nations*. University of Chicago Press.

U.S. Forest Service. 1948. *Lumber Production in the United States, 1799–1946*. Miscellaneous Publication number 669.

Williams, Michael. 1989. *Americans and Their Forests*. Cambridge University Press.

Williamson, H. F., R. Andreano, et al. 1963. *The American Petroleum Industry: The Age of Energy 1899–1959*. Northwestern University Press.

Wolf, Robert. 1997. "National Forest Timber Sales and the Legacy of Gifford Pinchot." In Char Miller, editor. *American Forests*. University Press of Kansas.

Wright, Gavin. 1990. "The Origins of American Industrial Success, 1879–1940." *American Economic Review* 80 (September): 651–68.

Wright, J. E. 1966. *The Galena Lead District: Federal Policy and Practice 1824–1847*. University of Wisconsin Press.

Wrigley, E. A. 1988. *Continuity, Chance and Change*. Cambridge University Press.

Yaffee, Steven Lewis. 1994. *The Wisdom of the Spotted Owl*. Island Press.

---

[15] The 1999 report and other relevant material may be found at the NMFS Internet site.

Gavin Wright

TABLE Db1–11 Mineral operations – establishments, receipts, value added, employment, and expenses: 1880–1997[1,2]

Contributed by Gavin Wright

	Establishments	Value of shipments and receipts		Value added in mining	Persons engaged		Man-hours (production, development, and exploration workers)	Wages and salaries		Cost of supplies and purchased machinery installed	Capital expenditures
		Gross	Net		Production and development	All other activities		Production, development, and exploration workers	Other workers		
	Db1	Db2	Db3	Db4	Db5	Db6	Db7	Db8	Db9	Db10 [3]	Db11
Year	Number	Million dollars	Million dollars	Million dollars	Thousand	Thousand	Million man-hours	Million dollars	Million dollars	Million dollars	Million dollars
1880	—	—	256	221	301.2 [6]	— [6]	—	95 [6]	— [6]	35	—
1889	—	—	416	336	529.6 [6]	— [6]	—	217 [6]	— [6]	80	—
1902	52,123	—	773	628	582.0 [7]	39.9	—	376	41	144	—
1909	25,698	1,233	1,205	928	961.1	45.4	—	576	54	305	—
1919	22,347	3,174	3,138	2,399	989.8	75.7	—	1,310	152	774	—
1939 [4]	24,703	—	3,433	2,680	774.1	81.9	1,288	971	204	753	—
1954	37,641	15,160	14,226	11,559	648.3	138.8	1,252	2,580	815	6,099	2,726
1958	36,392	18,463	16,373	13,385	565.4	168.5	1,080	2,623	1,126	7,521	2,804
1963	38,651	22,030	18,804	15,910	481.5	134.1	973	2,680	1,063	8,974	3,264
1967	28,579	26,208	22,784 [5]	19,330	432.6	134.7	892	2,888	1,299	10,576	4,058
1972	25,269	—	36,319	26,471	442.9	152.2	909	4,250	1,975	14,884	5,036
1977	31,359	—	96,375	68,013	592.8	206.0	1,183	9,082	4,085	46,079	17,718
1982	42,241	—	250,000	188,055	762.2	351.4	1,578	18,030	10,608	109,697	47,753
1987	33,617	—	157,964	110,959	451.1	247.0	942	12,443	9,296	62,423	15,418
1992	30,828	—	162,339	113,780	414.0	223.0	873	13,874	10,429	64,602	16,043
1997	25,251	—	173,985	133,636	389.0	120.0 [8]	808	15,316	5,482 [8]	71,404	16,043

[1] Prior to 1954, figures are for "Mineral industries, including operations in manufactures"; thereafter, they represent "Mineral industries" only.

[2] Beginning 1967, excludes data for single unit establishments without paid employees.

[3] Through 1939, excludes purchased machinery installed.

[4] Excludes Alaska.

[5] Includes gross shipments for ferroalloy ores and metallic ores, not elsewhere classified. In 1963, difference between gross and net shipments for these industries was about $7.6 million.

[6] "Other" employees included with production and exploration workers.

[7] Figures for average employment converted to a 300-day basis for establishments operating for a shorter period.

[8] See text and the Introduction to Part D regarding NAICS and comparability with earlier data.

Source

U.S. Bureau of the Census, *Census of Mineral Industries; 1997 Economic Census: Mining.*

Documentation

In general, figures include data for mining operations at manufacturing establishments (until 1977). For all years prior to 1935, they exclude common clay, shale, and peat (except as noted) and contract service operations; for years prior to 1929, they exclude sand and gravel operations and crushed stone quarries at manufacturing plants.

In 1902, operators of mineral properties reported an average of 8,527 employees performing contract service operations for metal mines; 6,906 for coal mines; 12,143 for oil and gas field operations; and 592 for nonmetallic minerals (except fuels). These are not included in the employment series shown.

Beginning in 1967, data for single-unit establishments without paid employees were excluded from the census. For 1963, for mining as a whole, there were 6,543 such establishments, accounting for approximately 3 percent of value added. The number of such establishments in 1963 for metal mining was 460; for coal mining, 1,347; for oil and gas extraction, 3,714; and for nonmetallic minerals (except fuels), 1,022.

The adoption of the North American Industry Classification System (NAICS, see the Introduction to Part D) had only a minor effect on the comparability of data between the 1992 and 1997 census. However, data for central administrative offices associated with mining are no longer included in the mining data, which may affect comparability for series Db6 and Db9.

Series Db1. Figures for the number of establishments are much less comparable from year to year than the other series in this table.

Series Db2–3. Includes the estimated value of mineral produced and used in making manufactured products.

TABLE Db12-24   Employees of mining firms, by industry division: 1939–1999

Contributed by Susan B. Carter

Year	Total	Metal			Coal		Oil and gas			Nonmetallic minerals			
		Total	Iron	Copper	Total	Bituminous coal and lignite	Oil and gas extraction	Crude oil and natural gas	Oil and gas field service	Total	Crushed and broken stone	Sand and gravel	Mineral chemical and fertilizer
	Db12	Db13	Db14	Db15	Db16	Db17	Db18	Db19	Db20	Db21	Db22	Db23	Db24
	Thousand	Thousand	Thousand	Thousand	Thousand	Thousand	Thousand	Thousand	Thousand	Thousand	Thousand	Thousand	Thousand
1939	854	103	—	—	—	368	198	—	—	76	—	—	—
1940	925	115	—	—	—	412	203	—	—	81	—	—	—
1941	957	128	—	—	—	408	211	—	—	94	—	—	—
1942	992	132	—	—	—	449	196	—	—	100	—	—	—
1943	925	126	—	—	—	414	189	—	—	90	—	—	—
1944	892	106	—	—	—	397	207	—	—	80	—	—	—
1945	836	89	—	—	—	363	215	—	—	75	—	—	—
1946	862	88	—	—	—	353	231	—	—	90	—	—	—
1947	955	103	34	28	—	403	249	164	—	98	—	—	—
1948	994	104	37	27	—	413	274	174	—	100	—	—	—
1949	930	98	34	26	—	372	266	173	—	95	—	—	—
1950	901	97	36	26	—	348	266	167	—	95	—	—	—
1951	929	101	38	26	—	352	284	169	—	102	—	—	—
1952	898	100	34	27	—	310	303	177	—	104	—	—	—
1953	866	106	40	29	—	274	311	181	—	106	—	—	—
1954	791	99	35	28	—	216	318	185	—	105	—	—	—
1955	792	102	34	29	—	207	332	189	—	108	—	—	—
1956	822	109	35	33	—	216	340	192	—	115	—	—	—
1957	828	111	39	32	—	218	344	195	—	114	—	—	—
1958	751	93	32	28	215	183	328	192	135	115	40	39	—
1959	732	84	28	23	198	169	330	185	144	120	42	42	—
1960	712	94	33	28	186	160	309	178	131	123	44	42	—
1961	672	87	27	29	161	139	303	171	132	120	42	41	—
1962	650	82	25	29	152	133	298	168	130	118	42	41	—
1963	635	80	24	28	149	130	289	164	125	117	41	40	—
1964	634	80	25	27	147	129	291	160	131	116	41	39	—
1965	632	84	26	30	141	125	287	157	131	120	41	40	—
1966	627	87	26	32	137	123	282	153	129	121	41	40	—
1967	613	79	26	25	139	125	276	150	126	120	40	39	—
1968	606	82	25	28	132	120	276	148	128	116	40	38	—
1969	619	89	26	34	135	123	280	146	134	115	40	37	—
1970	623	93	26	37	145	132	270	145	125	115	41	37	—
1971	609	87	25	34	146	133	264	145	119	115	42	36	—
1972	628	83	22	37	161	149	268	140	125	116	43	37	19
1973	642	87	24	40	162	150	274	136	135	119	44	38	19
1974	697	95	24	44	180	167	300	141	156	122	44	38	21
1975	752	94	24	39	213	198	329	151	174	117	41	35	23
1976	779	94	25	37	225	210	346	157	184	115	40	34	23
1977	813	90	19	34	225	210	381	166	211	116	39	35	23
1978	851	94	24	30	210	196	429	178	247	119	39	36	24
1979	958	101	25	33	259	242	474	193	276	124	41	38	25

		Metal			Coal		Oil and gas			Nonmetallic minerals			
	Total	Total	Iron	Copper	Total	Bituminous coal and lignite	Oil and gas extraction	Crude oil and natural gas	Oil and gas field service	Total	Crushed and broken stone	Sand and gravel	Mineral chemical and fertilizer
	Db12	Db13	Db14	Db15	Db16	Db17	Db18	Db19	Db20	Db21	Db22	Db23	Db24
Year	Thousand	Thousand	Thousand	Thousand	Thousand	Thousand	Thousand	Thousand	Thousand	Thousand	Thousand	Thousand	Thousand
1980	1,027	98	22	30	246	230	560	220	334	123	40	36	27
1981	1,139	104	21	36	225	209	692	254	430	119	37	34	27
1982	1,128	73	13	24	237	221	708	266	435	110	35	32	24
1983	952	56	10	19	194	180	598	258	333	104	34	32	21
1984	966	55	11	16	196	182	606	254	346	109	36	33	21
1985	927	46	10	13	187	175	583	247	329	110	38	34	20
1986	777	41	7	12	176	164	450	219	226	110	39	35	18
1987	717	44	7	13	162	151	402	199	197	110	40	34	17
1988	713	50	8	14	151	140	400	196	199	112	41	35	17
1989	692	56	8	14	144	134	381	193	184	111	41	35	17
1990	709	58	8	15	147	137	395	192	198	110	41	34	17
1991	689	56	9	16	136	127	393	192	196	105	38	33	16
1992	635	53	9	15	127	118	353	182	165	102	38	32	15
1993	610	50	9	15	109	101	350	171	174	102	38	32	14
1994	601	49	9	14	112	104	337	162	169	104	39	33	14
1995	581	51	9	16	104	97	320	151	164	105	40	34	13
1996	580	54	9	16	98	91	322	147	171	106	40	35	13
1997	596	54	9	16	96	90	339	144	190	108	42	36	12
1998	590	49	8	15	92	86	339	141	194	110	43	36	12
1999	535	45	8	14	85	80	293	133	156	112	45	37	11

Source

U.S. Bureau of Labor Statistics Internet site, National Current Employment Statistics.

Documentation

See the text for Table Ba840–848.

Series Db12. Equals series Ba841.

Series Db21. Excludes fuels.

TABLE Db25–33   Fuel mineral production: 1800–2000

Contributed by Gavin Wright

	Coal				Crude petroleum	Natural gasoline and cycle products	Liquefied petroleum gases	Natural gas, marketed	Uranium concentrate
	Bituminous	Subbituminous	Lignite	Pennsylvania anthracite					
	Db25 [1]	Db26 [1]	Db27 [1]	Db28	Db29	Db30 [2]	Db31 [2]	Db32	Db33 [3]
Year	Thousand short tons	Thousand short tons	Thousand short tons	Thousand short tons	Thousand 42-gallon barrels	Million 42-gallon barrels	Million 42-gallon barrels	Billion cubic feet	Short tons
1800	108	—	—	—	—	—	—	—	—
1801	114	—	—	—	—	—	—	—	—
1802	122	—	—	—	—	—	—	—	—
1803	127	—	—	—	—	—	—	—	—
1804	141	—	—	—	—	—	—	—	—
1805	146	—	—	—	—	—	—	—	—
1806	152	—	—	—	—	—	—	—	—
1807	159	—	—	—	—	—	—	—	—
1808	165	—	—	1	—	—	—	—	—
1809	170	—	—	1	—	—	—	—	—
1810	176	—	—	2	—	—	—	—	—
1811	188	—	—	2	—	—	—	—	—
1812	203	—	—	2	—	—	—	—	—
1813	218	—	—	2	—	—	—	—	—
1814	235	—	—	2	—	—	—	—	—
1815	253	—	—	2	—	—	—	—	—
1816	278	—	—	2	—	—	—	—	—
1817	303	—	—	2	—	—	—	—	—
1818	330	—	—	3	—	—	—	—	—
1819	320	—	—	3	—	—	—	—	—
1820	330	—	—	4	—	—	—	—	—
1821	349	—	—	4	—	—	—	—	—
1822	360	—	—	6	—	—	—	—	—
1823	370	—	—	10	—	—	—	—	—
1824	414	—	—	15	—	—	—	—	—
1825	437	—	—	43	—	—	—	—	—
1826	493	—	—	61	—	—	—	—	—
1827	532	—	—	80	—	—	—	—	—
1828	569	—	—	103	—	—	—	—	—
1829	607	—	—	149	—	—	—	—	—
1830	646	—	—	235	—	—	—	—	—
1831	695	—	—	258	—	—	—	—	—
1832	771	—	—	502	—	—	—	—	—
1833	823	—	—	663	—	—	—	—	—
1834	912	—	—	512	—	—	—	—	—
1835	1,059	—	—	760	—	—	—	—	—
1836	1,067	—	—	925	—	—	—	—	—
1837	1,070	—	—	1,164	—	—	—	—	—
1838	1,141	—	—	978	—	—	—	—	—
1839	1,251	—	—	1,072	—	—	—	—	—
1840	1,345	—	—	1,129	—	—	—	—	—
1841	1,355	—	—	1,262	—	—	—	—	—
1842	1,473	—	—	1,441	—	—	—	—	—
1843	1,615	—	—	1,656	—	—	—	—	—
1844	1,794	—	—	2,128	—	—	—	—	—
1845	2,097	—	—	2,626	—	—	—	—	—
1846	2,328	—	—	3,032	—	—	—	—	—
1847	2,631	—	—	3,726	—	—	—	—	—
1848	3,080	—	—	4,001	—	—	—	—	—
1849	3,518	—	—	4,172	—	—	—	—	—
1850	4,029	—	—	4,327	—	—	—	—	—
1851	4,590	—	—	5,814	—	—	—	—	—
1852	4,909	—	—	6,412	—	—	—	—	—
1853	6,100	—	—	6,653	—	—	—	—	—
1854	7,359	—	—	7,668	—	—	—	—	—
1855	7,543	—	—	8,607	—	—	—	—	—
1856	7,992	—	—	8,960	—	—	—	—	—
1857	8,775	—	—	8,618	—	—	—	—	—
1858	8,846	—	—	8,808	—	—	—	—	—
1859	9,127	—	—	10,092	2	—	—	—	—

Notes appear at end of table

TABLE Db25–33   Fuel mineral production: 1800–2000   *Continued*

	Coal								
	Bituminous	Subbituminous	Lignite	Pennsylvania anthracite	Crude petroleum	Natural gasoline and cycle products	Liquefied petroleum gases	Natural gas, marketed	Uranium concentrate
	Db25 [1]	Db26 [1]	Db27 [1]	Db28	Db29	Db30 [2]	Db31 [2]	Db32	Db33 [3]
Year	Thousand short tons	Thousand short tons	Thousand short tons	Thousand short tons	Thousand 42-gallon barrels	Million 42-gallon barrels	Million 42-gallon barrels	Billion cubic feet	Short tons
1860	9,057	—	—	10,984	500	—	—	—	—
1861	8,756	—	—	10,245	2,114	—	—	—	—
1862	9,384	—	—	10,186	3,057	—	—	—	—
1863	10,480	—	—	12,267	2,611	—	—	—	—
1864	11,415	—	—	13,027	2,116	—	—	—	—
1865	12,349	—	—	12,077	2,498	—	—	—	—
1866	13,015	—	—	15,784	3,598	—	—	—	—
1867	13,837	—	—	16,067	3,347	—	—	—	—
1868	16,244	—	—	17,708	3,646	—	—	—	—
1869	19,903	—	—	18,341	4,215	—	—	—	—
1870	20,471	—	—	19,958	5,261	—	—	—	—
1871	22,857	—	—	19,465	5,205	—	—	—	—
1872	27,311	—	—	24,734	6,293	—	—	—	—
1873	31,601	—	—	25,627	9,894	—	—	—	—
1874	30,733	—	—	24,267	10,927	—	—	—	—
1875	32,657	—	—	23,121	12,163	—	—	—	—
1876	31,822	—	—	22,793	9,133	—	—	—	—
1877	34,385	—	—	25,660	13,350	—	—	—	—
1878	36,418	—	—	21,690	15,397	—	—	—	—
1879	40,425	—	—	30,208	19,914	—	—	—	—
1880	50,757	—	—	28,650	26,286	—	—	—	—
1881	51,945	—	—	31,920	27,661	—	—	—	—
1882	58,917	—	—	35,121	30,350	—	—	—	—
1883	64,860	—	—	38,457	23,450	—	—	—	—
1884	71,737	—	—	37,157	24,218	—	—	—	—
1885	71,773	—	—	38,336	21,859	—	—	—	—
1886	74,645	—	—	39,035	28,065	—	—	—	—
1887	88,562	—	—	42,088	28,283	—	—	—	—
1888	102,040	—	—	46,620	27,612	—	—	—	—
1889	95,685	—	—	45,547	35,164	—	—	—	—
1890	111,302	—	—	46,469	45,824	—	—	—	—
1891	117,901	—	—	50,665	54,293	—	—	—	—
1892	126,857	—	—	52,473	50,515	—	—	—	—
1893	128,385	—	—	53,968	48,431	—	—	—	—
1894	118,820	—	—	51,921	49,344	—	—	—	—
1895	135,118	—	—	57,999	52,892	—	—	—	—
1896	137,640	—	—	54,346	60,960	—	—	—	—
1897	147,618	—	—	52,612	60,476	—	—	—	—
1898	166,594	—	—	53,383	55,364	—	—	—	—
1899	193,323	—	—	60,418	57,071	—	—	—	—
1900	212,316	—	—	57,368	63,621	—	—	128	—
1901	225,828	—	—	67,472	69,389	—	—	180	—
1902	260,217	—	—	41,374	88,767	—	—	206	—
1903	282,749	—	—	74,607	100,461	—	—	239	—
1904	278,660	—	—	73,157	117,081	—	—	257	—
1905	315,063	—	—	77,660	134,717	—	—	320	—
1906	342,875	—	—	71,282	126,494	—	—	389	—
1907	394,759	—	—	85,604	166,095	—	—	407	—
1908	332,574	—	—	83,269	178,527	—	—	402	—
1909	379,744	—	—	81,070	183,171	—	—	481	—
1910	417,111	—	—	84,485	209,557	—	—	509	—
1911	405,907	—	—	90,464	220,449	(Z)	—	513	25
1912	450,105	—	—	84,362	222,935	(Z)	—	562	26
1913	478,435	—	—	91,525	248,446	1	—	582	41
1914	422,704	—	—	90,822	265,763	1	—	592	87
1915	442,624	—	—	88,995	281,104	2	—	629	20
1916	502,520	—	—	87,578	300,767	2	—	753	134
1917	551,791	—	—	99,612	335,316	5	—	795	103
1918	579,386	—	—	98,826	355,928	7	—	721	106
1919	465,860	—	—	88,092	378,367	8	—	746	113

Notes appear at end of table

(continued)

TABLE Db25–33   Fuel mineral production: 1800–2000   *Continued*

	Coal					Natural gasoline and	Liquefied	Natural gas,	Uranium
	Bituminous	Subbituminous	Lignite	Pennsylvania anthracite	Crude petroleum	cycle products	petroleum gases	marketed	concentrate
	Db25 [1]	Db26 [1]	Db27 [1]	Db28	Db29	Db30 [2]	Db31 [2]	Db32	Db33 [3]
Year	Thousand short tons	Thousand short tons	Thousand short tons	Thousand short tons	Thousand 42-gallon barrels	Million 42-gallon barrels	Million 42-gallon barrels	Billion cubic feet	Short tons
1920	568,667	—	—	89,598	442,929	9	—	812	169
1921	415,922	—	—	90,473	472,183	11	—	674	109
1922	422,268	—	—	54,683	557,531	12	—	776	27
1923	564,565	—	—	93,339	732,407	19	—	1,025	22
1924	483,687	—	—	87,927	713,940	22	—	1,162	—
1925	520,053	—	—	61,817	763,743	27	—	1,210	17
1926	573,367	—	—	84,437	770,874	32	—	1,336	(Z)
1927	517,763	—	—	80,096	901,129	39	—	1,471	(Z)
1928	500,745	—	—	75,348	901,474	43	—	1,596	1
1929	534,989	—	—	73,828	1,007,323	53	—	1,952	1
1930	467,526	—	—	69,385	898,011	53	—	1,979	1
1931	382,089	—	—	59,646	851,081	44	—	1,722	1
1932	309,710	—	—	49,855	785,159	36	—	1,594	2
1933	333,631	—	—	49,541	905,656	34	—	1,597	1
1934	359,368	—	—	57,168	908,065	37	—	1,816	4
1935	372,373	—	—	52,159	996,596	39	—	1,969	13
1936	439,088	—	—	54,580	1,099,687	43	—	2,225	11
1937	445,531	—	—	51,856	1,279,160	49	—	2,473	12
1938	348,545	—	—	46,099	1,214,355	51	—	2,358	31
1939	394,855	—	—	51,487	1,264,962	52	—	2,538	35
1940	460,772	—	—	51,485	1,353,214	56	—	2,734	10
1941	514,149	—	—	56,368	1,402,228	64	17	2,894	11
1942	582,693	—	—	60,328	1,386,645	65	18	3,146	—
1943	590,177	—	—	60,644	1,505,613	66	22	3,516	—
1944	619,576	—	—	63,701	1,677,904	72	28	3,815	—
1945	577,617	—	—	54,934	1,713,655	78	34	4,042	—
1946	533,922	—	—	60,507	1,733,939	82	34	4,153	—
1947	630,624	—	—	57,190	1,856,987	87	45	4,582	—
1948	599,518	—	—	57,140	2,020,185	94	53	5,148	—
1949	437,868	—	—	42,702	1,841,940	99	58	5,420	180
1950	516,311	—	—	44,077	1,973,574	110	72	6,282	460
1951	533,665	—	—	42,670	2,247,711	118	86	7,457	770
1952	466,841	—	—	40,583	2,289,836	121	102	8,013	870
1953	457,290	—	—	30,949	2,357,082	127	112	3,397	1,160
1954	391,706	—	—	29,083	2,314,988	128	124	8,743	1,700
1955	464,633	—	—	26,205	2,484,428	139	142	9,405	2,780
1956	500,874	—	—	28,900	2,617,283	138	154	10,082	5,960
1957	492,704	—	—	25,338	2,616,901	137	158	10,680	8,480
1958	410,446	—	—	21,171	2,448,937	133	162	11,030	12,440
1959	412,028	—	—	20,649	2,574,590	133	187	12,046	16,240
1960	415,512	—	—	18,817	2,574,933	139	201	12,771	17,640
1961	402,977	—	—	17,446	2,621,758	145	216	13,182	17,350
1962	422,149	—	—	16,894	2,676,189	149	224	13,801	17,010
1963	458,928	—	—	18,267	2,752,723	156	245	14,667	14,220
1964	486,998	—	—	17,184	2,786,822	167	256	15,462	11,850
1965	512,088	—	—	14,866	2,848,514	174	268	16,040	10,440
1966	533,881	—	—	12,941	3,027,763	179	289	17,207	10,590
1967	552,626	—	—	12,256	3,216,715	188	327	18,171	11,255
1968	545,245	—	—	11,461	3,329,042	199	351	19,322	12,370
1969	547,200	8,300	5,000	10,473	3,371,751	202	378	20,698	11,610
1970	578,500	16,400	8,000	9,729	3,517,450	206	400	21,921	12,905
1971	521,300	22,200	8,700	8,727	3,453,995	200	418	22,493	12,275
1972	556,800	27,500	11,000	7,106	3,455,406	193	445	22,532	12,900
1973	543,500	33,900	14,300	6,830	3,360,920	187	447	22,648	13,235
1974	545,700	42,200	15,500	6,617	3,202,510	168	448	21,601	11,530
1975	577,500	51,100	19,800	6,203	3,056,875	152	444	20,109	11,600
1976	588,400	64,800	25,500	6,228	2,976,312	150	437	19,952	12,745
1977	581,000	82,100	28,200	5,861	3,009,425	147	443	20,025	14,940
1978	534,000	96,800	34,400	5,037	3,178,055	141	431	19,974	18,485
1979	612,300	121,500	42,500	4,835	3,121,480	134	444	20,471	18,735

Notes appear at end of table

TABLE Db25-33   Fuel mineral production: 1800-2000   *Continued*

Year	Coal Bituminous Db25 [1] Thousand short tons	Coal Subbituminous Db26 [1] Thousand short tons	Coal Lignite Db27 [1] Thousand short tons	Pennsylvania anthracite Db28 Thousand short tons	Crude petroleum Db29 Thousand 42-gallon barrels	Natural gasoline and cycle products Db30 [2] Million 42-gallon barrels	Liquefied petroleum gases Db31 [2] Million 42-gallon barrels	Natural gas, marketed Db32 Billion cubic feet	Uranium concentrate Db33 [3] Short tons
1980	628,800	147,700	47,200	6,056	3,146,502	135	441	20,180	21,850
1981	608,000	159,700	50,700	5,423	3,128,780	129	458	19,956	19,235
1982	620,200	160,900	52,400	4,588	3,156,885	107	459	18,582	13,435
1983	568,600	151,000	58,300	4,089	3,171,120	91	480	16,884	10,580
1984	649,500	179,200	63,100	4,162	3,249,714	108	488	18,304	7,440
1985	613,900	192,700	72,400	4,708	3,274,415	108	479	17,270	5,655
1986	620,100	189,600	76,400	4,292	3,168,200	100	466	16,859	6,755
1987	636,600	200,200	78,400	3,560	3,047,385	108	475	17,433	6,495
1988	638,100	223,500	85,100	3,555	2,979,240	112	483	17,918	6,565
1989	659,800	231,200	86,400	3,348	2,778,745	113	452	18,095	6,920
1990	693,200	244,300	88,100	3,506	2,684,575	113	456	18,594	4,445
1991	650,700	255,300	86,500	3,445	2,707,205	—	606	18,532	3,975
1992	651,900	252,100	90,100	3,500	2,624,586	—	621	18,712	2,822
1993	576,700	274,900	89,500	4,300	2,499,155	—	633	18,982	1,532
1994	640,300	300,500	88,100	4,646	2,431,630	—	630	19,710	1,676
1995	613,765	327,998	86,500	4,711	2,394,268	—	643	19,506	3,022
1996	644,900	322,200	91,600	4,751	2,366,017	—	547	19,812	3,161
1997	653,828	345,071	86,341	4,678	2,354,831	—	547	19,866	2,822
1998	640,370	386,147	85,767	5,252	2,281,919	—	529	19,961	2,353
1999	601,732	406,714	87,218	4,768	2,146,732	—	564	19,804	2,306
2000	574,276	409,203	85,561	4,572	2,130,707	—	587	20,002	1,979

(Z) Series Db30, less than 500,000 barrels. Series Db33, less than 0.5 tons.

[1] Through 1968, subbituminous and lignite coal are included with bituminous.

[2] Beginning 1991, series Db30-31 are aggregated. Thus, series Db31 after 1990 is total U.S. natural gas liquids production.

[3] Content of ore shipments, 1911-1941; recoverable content of ore shipments, 1948-1970.

Sources

Series Db25. 1800-1885: H. N. Eavenson, *The First Century and a Quarter of the American Coal Industry* (Waverly Press, 1942), pp. 426-34. 1886-1931: U.S. Bureau of Mines, *Mineral Resources of the United States* (annual). 1932-1976: U.S. Bureau of Mines, *Minerals Yearbook* (annual). 1977-1997: U.S. Energy Information Agency, *Coal Industry Annual* (U.S. Department of Energy, annual).

Series Db26-27. U.S. Energy Information Agency, *Coal Industry Annual*.

Series Db28. 1800-1885: Eavenson (1942), pp. 426-34. 1886-1931: U.S. Bureau of Mines, *Mineral Resources of the United States*. 1932-1976: U.S. Bureau of Mines, *Minerals Yearbooks*. 1977-2000: U.S. Energy Information Agency, *Coal Industry Annual*.

Series Db29. 1859-1931: U.S. Bureau of Mines, *Mineral Resources of the United States* (annual). 1932-1976: U.S. Bureau of Mines, *Minerals Yearbooks*. 1977-2000: U.S. Energy Information Agency, *Petroleum Supply Annual* (U.S. Department of Energy, annual).

Series Db30-31. 1911-1976: U.S. Bureau of Mines, *Minerals Yearbooks*, except series Db31 for 1943, U.S. Bureau of Mines, *Monthly Petroleum Statement*, number 402. 1977-1990: U.S. Energy Information Agency, *Annual Energy Review 1991* (U.S. Department of Energy) (converted from figures in barrels per day). 1991-2000: U.S. Energy Information Agency, *Petroleum Supply Annual* (U.S. Department of Energy, annual).

Series Db32. 1911-1976: U.S. Bureau of Mines, *Minerals Yearbooks Annual*, except series Db31 for 1943, U.S. Bureau of Mines, *Monthly Petroleum Statement Annual*, no. 402. 1977-2000: U.S. Energy Information Agency, *Historical Natural Gas Annual* (annual).

Series Db33. 1911-1931: U.S. Bureau of Mines, *Mineral Resources of the United States*; 1932-1941: U.S. Bureau of Mines, *Minerals Yearbooks*; 1949-2000: U.S.

Energy Information Agency, *Annual Energy Review 1991* (U.S. Department of Energy) and *Uranium Industry Annuals* (U.S. Department of Energy, annual).

Documentation

Series Db25. Bituminous coal or "soft coal" production data are based on detailed annual reports furnished by producers to the Bureau of Mines. Prior to 1969, subbituminous and lignite production was included with bituminous. Prior to 1886, production figures shown are those as derived by Eavenson and considered superior to the early Geological Survey figures, which appear in *Mineral Resources of the United States*. Eavenson's estimates were made on an individual state basis and were derived from state, county, newspaper, census, and any other documented records available.

Series Db28. Coverage of anthracite or "hard coal" is limited to Pennsylvania. Some anthracite production occurred between 1800 and 1807, but it amounted to less than 500 tons annually. Until 1951, production estimates made no attempt to include "bootleg" operations - mining of anthracite near the surface of the earth without consent of the owner of the mineral rights. Beginning in 1951, output of these independent operators (no longer called "bootleggers" because they operated under legal agreements with landowners) is included, so these figures are not strictly comparable with those for earlier years.

Series Db29. Data are included for Alaska beginning 1959 and Hawai'i, 1960.

Series Db30-31. Natural gasoline and cycle products include all natural gas liquids except liquefied petroleum gases and ethane. Examples include natural gasoline mixtures, finished gasoline, naphtha, plant condensate, kerosene, and distillate fuel produced from natural gas. Ethane is included in series Db31. The distinction between the two columns is not always firm. Beginning 1954, for example, isopentane, previously in liquefied petroleum gases, was included in natural gasoline and cycle products. After 1991, only total natural gas liquids production is reported.

Series Db32. Figures are estimated as gross production minus repressuring, vented and wasted gas. Figures for 1900-1919 are not strictly comparable with those for later years because neither net storage change nor transmission loss was included.

TABLE Db34–39   Fuel mineral production – value: 1880–2000

Contributed by Gavin Wright

	Fossil fuels					Uranium
	Total	Bituminous coal and lignite	Pennsylvania anthracite	Petroleum	Marketed natural gas	
	Db34	Db35	Db36	Db37	Db38	Db39
Year	Million dollars	Million dollars	Million dollars	Million dollars	Million dollars	Million dollars
1880	120	53	42	25	—	—
1881	149	60	64	25	—	—
1882	171	76	71	24	(Z)	—
1883	185	82	77	26	(Z)	—
1884	165	77	66	21	1	—
1885	183	82	77	19	5	—
1886	184	78	76	20	10	—
1887	218	98	85	19	16	—
1888	232	102	89	18	23	—
1889	209	95	66	27	21	—
1890	230	110	66	35	19	—
1891	238	117	74	31	16	—
1892	248	125	82	26	15	—
1893	252	123	86	29	14	—
1894	236	108	78	36	14	—
1895	269	116	82	58	13	—
1896	269	115	82	59	13	—
1897	254	120	79	41	14	—
1898	267	133	75	44	15	—
1899	341	168	88	65	20	—
1900	407	221	86	76	24	—
1901	442	236	113	66	27	—
1902	469	291	76	71	31	—
1903	635	352	152	95	36	—
1904	583	305	139	101	38	—
1905	603	335	142	84	42	—
1906	652	381	132	92	47	—
1907	789	451	164	120	54	—
1908	716	374	158	129	55	—
1909	745	405	149	128	63	—
1910	828	469	160	128	71	—
1911	835	451	175	134	75	—
1912	945	518	178	164	85	—
1913	1,085	565	195	237	88	—
1914	989	493	188	214	94	—
1915	967	502	185	179	101	—
1916	1,318	665	202	331	120	—
1917	2,198	1,249	284	523	142	—
1918	2,686	1,492	336	704	154	—
1919	2,447	1,161	365	760	161	—
1920	4,121	2,130	434	1,361	196	—
1921	2,642	1,200	452	815	175	—
1922	2,666	1,275	274	895	222	—
1923	3,240	1,515	507	978	240	—
1924	2,817	1,063	477	1,023	254	—
1925	2,785	1,060	328	1,285	112	—
1926	3,230	1,183	474	1,448	125	—
1927	2,751	1,030	421	1,173	127	—
1928	2,523	934	394	1,055	140	—
1929	2,777	953	386	1,280	158	—
1930	2,367	795	355	1,070	147	—
1931	1,544	589	296	551	108	—
1932	1,408	407	222	680	99	—
1933	1,358	446	207	608	97	—
1934	1,883	628	244	905	106	—
1935	1,939	658	210	961	110	—
1936	2,317	771	227	1,200	119	—
1937	2,698	864	198	1,513	123	—
1938	2,347	679	181	1,373	114	—
1939	2,330	728	187	1,294	120	—

Note appears at end of table

TABLE Db34–39   Fuel mineral production – value: 1880–2000   *Continued*

		Fossil fuels			
	Total	Bituminous coal and lignite	Pennsylvania anthracite	Petroleum	Marketed natural gas	Uranium
	Db34	Db35	Db36	Db37	Db38	Db39
Year	Million dollars	Million dollars	Million dollars	Million dollars	Million dollars	Million dollars
1940	2,589	879	205	1,385	120	—
1941	3,106	1,125	240	1,602	139	—
1942	3,443	1,374	272	1,643	154	—
1943	3,878	1,585	307	1,809	177	—
1944	4,389	1,811	355	2,033	190	—
1945	4,377	1,768	324	2,094	191	—
1946	4,904	1,836	413	2,443	212	—
1947	6,886	2,620	413	3,578	275	—
1948	9,035	2,990	467	5,245	333	—
1949	7,511	2,134	358	4,675	344	—
1950	8,261	2,497	392	4,963	409	—
1951	9,261	2,622	406	5,690	543	—
1952	9,072	2,283	380	5,785	624	—
1953	9,649	2,248	299	6,327	775	—
1954	9,326	1,770	248	6,425	883	—
1955	10,146	2,092	206	6,870	978	—
1956	11,030	2,412	237	7,297	1,084	—
1957	12,013	2,504	228	8,079	1,202	—
1958	10,881	1,996	188	7,380	1,317	—
1959	11,168	1,966	172	7,473	1,557	—
1960	11,307	1,950	147	7,420	1,790	—
1961	11,547	1,845	140	7,566	1,996	—
1962	11,945	1,892	134	7,774	2,145	—
1963	12,461	2,013	154	7,966	2,328	—
1964	12,720	2,166	149	8,017	2,388	—
1965	13,051	2,276	122	8,158	2,495	—
1966	13,951	2,421	101	8,726	2,703	—
1967	14,926	2,555	96	9,376	2,899	—
1968	15,607	2,546	97	9,795	3,169	—
1969	16,774	2,797	94	10,427	3,456	—
1970	18,797	3,772	105	11,174	3,746	—
1971	19,798	3,905	103	11,693	4,097	—
1972	20,557	4,562	85	11,707	4,203	—
1973	23,092	5,050	90	13,058	4,894	—
1974	38,071	9,502	145	21,581	6,573	—
1975	44,731	12,472	198	23,116	8,945	—
1976	49,200	13,189	209	24,230	11,572	—
1977	55,516	13,700	200	25,790	15,826	—
1978	61,450	14,490	180	28,600	18,085	—
1979	120,480	18,360	200	39,450	24,114	—
1980	160,660	20,200	260	67,930	32,044	—
1981	160,701	21,510	240	99,400	39,551	1,333
1982	158,534	22,620	230	90,030	45,654	1,031
1983	147,144	20,110	210	83,050	43,774	808
1984	155,640	22,750	200	84,100	48,590	485
1985	144,503	22,060	220	78,880	43,343	355
1986	93,537	21,000	190	39,630	32,717	405
1987	97,148	21,050	160	46,930	29,008	356
1988	88,757	20,830	160	37,480	30,287	393
1989	96,107	21,270	140	44,070	30,627	271
1990	107,805	22,270	140	53,770	31,755	140
1991	96,518	21,290	130	44,770	30,328	109
1992	95,531	20,870	120	41,970	32,571	76
1993	93,181	18,620	140	35,610	38,811	40
1994	88,676	19,900	170	32,070	36,536	35
1995	84,694	19,270	190	35,000	30,234	67
1996	106,220	19,510	170	43,680	42,860	87
1997	106,227	19,630	170	40,340	46,087	73
1998	83,670	19,523	227	24,800	39,120	58
1999	95,070	18,138	162	33,400	43,370	54
2000	148,760	17,832	188	56,930	73,810	45

(continued)

TABLE Db34–39   Fuel mineral production – value: 1880–2000   *Continued*

(Z) Less than $500,000.

Sources

Series Db34. Derived from series Db35–38.

Series Db35–37. 1880–1931: U.S. Bureau of Mines, *Mineral Resources of the United States* (annual). 1932–1976: U.S. Bureau of Mines, *Minerals Yearbooks* (annual). 1977–2000: U.S. Energy Information Agency, *Annual Energy Review* (U.S. Department of Energy, annual).

Series Db38. 1880–1931: U.S. Bureau of Mines, *Mineral Resources of the United States*. 1932–1976: U.S. Bureau of Mines, *Minerals Yearbooks*. 1977–1997: U.S. Energy Information Agency, *Natural Gas Annual 1997*.

Series Db39. U.S. Energy Information Agency, *Annual Energy Review*.

Documentation

Series Db34–38. These mineral value figures present two overlapping series: the "old basis" series runs through 1924, whereas the "new basis" is the series as compiled since 1925. A significant factor making for lack of long-run comparability is the failure of the basic source to use a consistent stage of production at which to measure value. The totals and subtotals for any year are to some extent a mixture of values at different stages in the production process. However, double counting has generally been avoided by including a product at not more than one stage in the production process.

Series Db34. Equals the sum of series Db35–38.

Series Db35. Coal and lignite figures are total value of production, f.o.b. (free on board) mine. (This means the buyer is responsible for transportation and insurance costs incurred beginning at the mine.)

Series Db36. Anthracite data beginning 1951 are not strictly comparable with earlier years because they include output of independent operators, formerly called "bootleggers."

Series Db37. Represents value of crude oil at the well.

Series Db38. Represents the total value of "marketed production" (that is, gross withdrawals less repressuring, vented and wasted gas). The most important discontinuity between the old and new basis occurs here, as value was measured at the point of consumption until 1924, and at the well beginning 1925. (The value at the point of consumption was $265 million in 1925.) For 1885–1890, the value shown is for coal and fuel wood displaced by natural gas rather than the value of gas consumed as actually reported.

Series Db39. Values are constructed by multiplying domestic production by the average price for domestic purchases.

TABLE Db40–44   Petroleum refineries – input: 1916–2000

Contributed by Gavin Wright

	Petroleum						Petroleum			
	Total	Crude			Natural gas liquids		Total	Crude			Natural gas liquids
		Total	Domestic	Foreign				Total	Domestic	Foreign	
	Db40	Db41	Db42	Db43	Db44		Db40	Db41	Db42	Db43	Db44
Year	Thousand barrels	Thousand barrels	Thousand barrels	Thousand barrels	Thousand barrels	Year	Thousand barrels	Thousand barrels	Thousand barrels	Thousand barrels	Thousand barrels
1916	—	246,992	—	—	—	1960	3,119,327	—	2,581,568	370,966	166,793
1917	—	315,132	—	—	—	1961	3,156,605	—	2,604,127	383,031	169,447
1918	328,476	—	324,618	1,407	2,451	1962	3,252,478	—	2,659,826	409,805	182,847
1919	364,477	—	327,533	33,987	2,957	1963	3,360,875	—	2,758,168	412,484	190,223
1920	437,068	—	372,779	61,136	3,153	1964	3,436,622	—	2,785,895	437,434	213,293
1921	445,880	—	368,037	75,326	2,517	1965	3,526,531	—	2,847,821	453,021	225,689
1922	504,368	—	425,823	74,883	3,662	1966	3,682,803	—	3,000,789	446,404	235,610
1923	586,725	—	538,252	42,986	5,487	1967	3,827,401	—	3,174,004	408,590	244,807
1924	656,390	—	597,954	45,765	12,671	1968	4,037,073	—	3,308,044	466,316	262,713
1925	759,556	—	698,582	41,338	19,636	1969	4,148,406	—	3,363,602	516,003	268,801
1926	806,960	—	734,301	44,963	27,696	1970	4,252,075	—	3,485,332	482,171	284,572
1927	860,997	—	778,729	50,106	32,162	1971	4,378,780	—	3,481,543	606,226	291,011
1928	948,518	—	835,711	77,584	35,223	1972	4,593,426	—	3,473,880	806,983	312,563
1929	1,034,165	—	912,191	75,517	46,457	1973	4,845,452	—	3,359,946	1,177,308	308,198
1930	970,617	—	866,615	60,832	43,170	1974	4,714,199	—	3,168,596	1,260,130	285,473
1931	929,724	—	847,671	46,937	35,116	1975	4,814,524	—	3,047,014	1,494,412	273,098
1932	846,329	—	777,696	42,301	26,332	1976	5,189,640	—	2,989,129	1,921,111	279,400
1933	886,600	—	825,786	35,468	25,346	1977	5,594,016	—	2,932,150	2,397,733	264,133
1934	923,798	—	860,776	34,860	28,162	1978	5,632,159	—	3,099,938	2,279,815	252,406
1935	996,815	—	933,659	32,131	31,025	1979	5,548,745	—	3,018,049	2,328,339	202,357
1936	1,102,387	—	1,034,637	33,933	33,817	1980	5,119,287	—	3,023,366	1,910,803	185,118
1937	1,222,821	—	1,157,444	25,996	39,381	1981	4,761,258	4,551,725	3,128,780	1,604,540	209,533
1938	1,204,976	—	1,138,828	26,187	39,961	1982	4,504,532	4,297,355	3,156,885	1,273,120	207,177
1939	1,277,446	—	1,204,350	33,490	39,606	1983	4,452,282	4,265,068	3,171,120	1,215,085	187,214
1940	1,333,709	—	1,252,364	41,798	39,547	1984	4,607,777	4,408,183	3,240,835	1,250,490	199,594
1941	1,457,017	—	1,358,246	50,946	47,825	1985	4,586,557	4,380,741	3,274,415	1,168,365	205,816
1942	1,390,698	—	1,319,507	14,596	56,595	1986	4,837,171	4,641,296	3,168,200	1,524,970	195,875
1943	1,490,936	—	1,417,559	12,179	61,198	1987	4,885,096	4,691,783	3,047,385	1,669,510	193,313
1944	1,732,891	—	1,622,514	43,170	67,207	1988	5,054,592	4,848,175	2,971,100	1,864,055	206,417
1945	1,789,858	—	1,645,862	73,672	70,324	1989	5,095,247	4,891,381	2,778,745	2,132,695	203,866
1946	1,793,058	—	1,645,845	84,352	62,861	1990	5,093,610	4,894,379	2,684,575	2,151,310	199,231
1947	1,922,938	—	1,754,987	97,259	70,692	1991	5,058,896	4,855,016	2,707,205	2,110,430	203,880
1948	2,124,567	—	1,924,335	124,014	76,218	1992	5,128,222	4,908,603	2,617,415	2,220,295	219,619
1949	2,029,678	—	1,789,756	154,465	85,457	1993	5,218,007	4,968,641	2,499,155	2,477,255	249,366
1950	2,189,506	—	1,918,854	176,013	94,639	1994	5,303,584	5,061,111	2,431,630	2,577,995	242,473
1951	2,469,654	—	2,188,677	181,727	99,250	1995	5,379,584	5,100,317	2,394,268	2,604,301	279,267
1952	2,545,157	—	2,235,198	206,061	103,898	1996	5,474,537	5,195,265	2,366,017	2,797,628	279,272
1953	2,666,158	—	2,321,820	233,045	111,293	1997	5,628,500	5,351,466	2,354,831	2,962,991	277,034
1954	2,657,113	—	2,300,766	238,798	117,549	1998	5,892,561	5,434,383	2,256,799	3,177,584	274,802
1955	2,856,600	—	2,446,833	283,385	126,382	1999	5,877,651	5,403,450	2,219,828	3,183,622	269,869
1956	3,040,168	—	2,563,655	341,451	135,062	2000	5,964,012	5,514,395	2,197,585	3,316,810	272,970
1957	3,040,526	—	2,529,672	360,764	150,090						
1958	2,926,673	—	2,444,229	345,175	137,269						
1959	3,070,984	—	2,565,504	352,157	153,323						

Sources

1916–1930: U.S. Bureau of Mines, *Petroleum Refinery Statistics, 1930*, Bulletin 367, p. 15; 1931–1976: U.S. Bureau of Mines, *Minerals Yearbook* (annual); 1977–1980: U.S. Energy Information Administration, *Energy Data Reports: Petroleum Statement* (U.S. Department of Energy, 1977, 1979, 1980); 1981–2000: U.S. Energy Information Administration, *Petroleum Supply Annuals* (U.S. Department of Energy, annual).

Documentation

Refineries take in materials as inputs, which appear in this table, and refine them into outputs, which appear in Table Db45–55. One could calculate the difference in total inputs and outputs to find the processing gain or loss each year.

Series Db40. Total petroleum refineries input includes domestic and foreign crude petroleum, natural gas liquids, and other hydrocarbons/oxygenates; it excludes unfinished oils rerun (net).

Series Db41. Consists of domestic and foreign crude petroleum inputs. It does not always equal the sum of series Db42–43 because of unaccounted-for inputs.

TABLE Db45-55   Petroleum refineries – output: 1916–2000

Contributed by Gavin Wright

Year	Total Db45 Thousand barrels	Gasoline Db46 [1] Thousand barrels	Kerosene Db47 [2] Thousand barrels	Fuel oil Distillate Db48 [3] Thousand barrels	Fuel oil Residual Db49 [3] Thousand barrels	Lubricating oil Db50 Thousand barrels	Wax Db51 Thousand barrels	Coke Db52 Thousand barrels	Asphalt Db53 [4] Thousand barrels	Still gas Db54 Thousand barrels	Road oil Db55 [4] Thousand barrels
1916	—	49,021	34,655	—	111,045	14,870	—	—	—	—	—
1917	—	67,870	41,114	—	155,079	17,947	—	—	—	—	—
1918	—	85,007	43,461	—	174,319	20,035	—	—	—	—	—
1919	—	94,235	55,753	—	181,602	20,161	—	—	—	—	—
1920	—	116,251	55,240	—	210,987	24,938	—	—	—	—	—
1921	—	122,704	46,318	—	230,091	20,896	—	—	—	—	—
1922	—	147,672	54,913	—	254,910	23,304	—	—	—	—	—
1923	572,814	179,903	55,927	—	287,481	26,128	1,684	3,717	12,888	—	—
1924	649,720	213,326	60,026	—	320,476	27,498	1,861	4,085	14,196	—	—
1925	745,863	259,601	59,689	—	364,991	31,055	2,135	5,281	15,067	—	—
1926	791,100	299,734	61,768	—	365,195	32,293	2,310	5,316	16,454	—	—
1927	845,480	330,435	56,113	—	393,066	31,721	2,089	5,858	18,793	—	—
1928	935,448	376,945	59,353	—	427,237	34,658	2,257	7,344	18,252	—	—
1929	1,013,070	435,078	55,940	—	448,949	34,359	2,261	7,390	19,169	—	—
1930	931,372	432,241	49,208	81,551	290,947	34,201	1,956	9,895	18,194	—	5,425
1931	914,023	431,510	42,446	83,882	253,085	26,704	1,705	10,363	16,371	38,630	5,177
1932	827,538	392,623	43,836	69,467	225,283	22,433	1,639	9,123	13,612	40,905	6,879
1933	865,297	401,591	48,977	78,920	237,519	23,775	1,677	7,900	12,757	45,212	5,534
1934	908,883	416,932	53,855	94,972	240,381	26,373	1,674	6,500	15,623	44,391	6,310
1935	986,702	457,842	55,813	100,235	259,826	27,853	1,608	7,290	17,133	51,184	6,030
1936	1,102,144	504,811	56,082	125,906	287,968	30,927	1,689	6,891	21,278	57,046	7,398
1937	1,224,624	559,141	65,308	146,706	312,064	35,321	1,863	6,533	23,001	64,218	8,087
1938	1,206,880	556,012	64,580	151,774	294,890	30,826	1,555	8,011	23,878	65,890	7,543
1939	1,283,993	596,501	68,521	161,746	305,944	35,036	1,659	8,332	27,248	68,779	7,868
1940	1,333,342	597,375	73,882	183,304	316,221	36,765	1,833	7,633	29,406	75,950	7,771
1941	1,460,252	671,110	72,586	189,177	342,367	39,539	2,393	8,244	36,067	83,354	9,149
1942	1,387,591	586,971	67,474	196,714	358,901	38,626	2,502	6,692	34,631	78,924	8,039
1943	1,477,707	592,425	72,270	211,516	417,306	38,679	2,697	6,942	37,162	86,755	2,295
1944	1,715,385	722,718	78,344	239,152	461,455	41,106	2,883	9,017	38,479	102,239	1,556
1945	1,793,523	774,460	81,024	249,224	469,492	41,867	2,921	10,115	39,196	103,458	2,686
1946	1,793,086	748,411	104,385	287,896	431,364	45,645	3,003	10,621	44,911	88,136	6,175
1947	1,918,959	814,841	110,412	312,173	447,795	51,765	3,624	12,077	49,286	85,564	7,074
1948	2,118,252	895,986	121,914	379,340	479,988	51,416	3,515	14,494	51,919	81,159	7,916
1949	2,039,517	939,051	102,152	340,825	424,909	45,389	3,208	16,959	49,007	82,621	7,691
1950	2,196,866	998,093	118,512	398,912	425,217	51,735	4,462	17,224	58,240	83,743	6,928
1951	2,484,022	1,108,880	135,742	475,801	469,377	61,489	4,814	18,977	66,302	96,294	6,100
1952	2,551,845	1,141,467	128,767	517,920	453,897	55,600	4,331	18,123	70,312	95,275	6,998
1953	2,673,764	1,233,954	123,200	528,111	449,979	52,545	4,978	21,607	72,409	102,243	6,594
1954	2,673,555	1,232,989	122,305	542,278	416,757	53,243	5,290	24,284	74,912	102,552	7,213
1955	2,880,187	1,331,528	117,137	602,547	420,331	55,836	5,293	28,337	83,121	116,506	8,482
1956	3,059,880	1,396,787	123,480	665,687	426,699	59,211	5,367	31,095	90,636	121,993	8,027
1957	3,055,685	1,415,335	108,929	668,573	415,656	55,723	5,461	33,466	85,683	125,720	7,209
1958	2,982,358	1,411,956	110,008	631,405	363,358	51,298	5,252	37,808	89,380	125,951	5,925
1959	3,128,361	1,473,430	110,662	678,938	347,900	56,111	5,630	41,117	97,643	126,958	6,493

Year	Total Db45 Thousand barrels	Gasoline Db46 [1] Thousand barrels	Kerosene Db47 [2] Thousand barrels	Fuel oil — Distillate Db48 [3] Thousand barrels	Fuel oil — Residual Db49 [3] Thousand barrels	Lubricating oil Db50 Thousand barrels	Wax Db51 Thousand barrels	Coke Db52 Thousand barrels	Asphalt Db53 [4] Thousand barrels	Still gas Db54 Thousand barrels	Road oil Db55 [4] Thousand barrels
1960	3,194,703	1,510,134	135,772	667,050	332,147	59,389	5,896	60,010	98,671	129,480	5,970
1961	3,241,294	1,512,324	141,410	696,015	315,577	59,254	5,781	75,333	101,819	127,537	5,820
1962	3,344,112	1,570,553	156,373	719,590	295,679	61,467	5,353	78,724	109,576	130,829	7,079
1963	3,466,519	1,603,896	164,805	764,597	275,910	63,086	5,126	80,688	111,948	129,598	6,792
1964	3,543,279	1,675,278	93,474	742,046	266,825	63,668	5,352	84,325	114,879	131,257	6,371
1965	3,638,883	1,722,475	93,149	765,071	268,567	62,925	5,456	86,040	123,604	135,295	6,565
1966	3,806,970	1,813,334	100,849	784,717	263,961	65,407	5,772	88,054	129,579	135,459	7,247
1967	3,968,230	1,865,434	99,061	804,429	275,956	64,870	5,719	90,933	127,767	140,034	6,978
1968	4,179,916	1,961,470	100,545	839,373	275,814	65,684	5,887	95,190	135,460	149,796	6,826
1969	4,305,477	2,050,804	101,738	846,863	265,906	65,080	6,362	102,868	135,691	160,363	9,086
1970	4,421,218	2,130,107	94,635	895,656	257,510	66,183	6,294	107,871	146,658	163,905	9,393
1971	4,561,831	2,225,775	86,256	910,727	274,684	65,473	6,939	109,114	157,039	156,967	8,755
1972	4,787,105	2,347,864	79,027	962,405	292,519	65,349	6,148	119,765	155,294	170,993	7,943
1973	5,056,708	2,431,704	79,422	1,029,343	354,597	68,742	6,768	132,290	167,884	176,758	7,326
1974	4,926,805	2,369,745	56,646	973,764	390,491	70,694	6,929	123,746	164,237	175,724	7,162
1975	4,994,970	2,419,878	55,495	968,436	450,957	56,221	5,665	129,241	143,957	175,351	4,944
1976	5,371,914	2,548,661	55,591	1,070,032	503,953	61,803	7,008	130,145	139,706	180,666	3,240
1977	5,793,922	2,611,949	62,498	1,196,143	640,140	64,484	6,655	134,739	154,058	191,257	3,299
1978	5,827,760	2,666,596	56,274	1,155,969	608,634	69,466	6,935	134,581	172,899	200,028	3,212
1979	5,753,598	2,543,289	66,750	1,150,594	615,579	70,983	6,892	137,274	168,785	205,069	1,571
1980	5,351,668	2,422,925	50,023	973,981	578,426	65,124	6,322	135,472	141,155	206,422	2,520
1981	5,106,374	2,372,736	43,521	953,732	482,088	60,561	6,943	142,430	123,452	206,399	531
1982	4,887,757	2,339,215	41,937	951,242	390,377	51,642	5,135	149,538	119,406	202,147	610
1983	4,795,353	2,341,297	39,977	896,504	310,863	53,808	5,535	153,305	135,659	200,707	—
1984	5,006,527	2,390,720	41,808	980,727	326,189	58,253	5,388	160,655	141,339	204,713	—
1985	5,018,612	2,370,029	34,475	980,351	321,997	53,081	5,506	166,019	146,332	213,181	—
1986	5,300,676	2,495,967	32,647	1,020,716	324,349	58,165	5,613	184,513	149,739	233,966	—
1987	5,338,657	2,527,028	28,691	996,119	323,201	60,870	5,879	186,902	158,434	234,529	—
1988	5,498,146	2,576,838	28,770	1,045,786	338,734	62,291	6,166	199,056	162,066	245,351	—
1989	5,538,702	2,572,144	26,938	1,057,975	348,148	61,387	6,223	197,665	154,887	248,658	—
1990	5,574,458	2,568,402	16,281	1,067,485	346,576	61,161	6,193	201,660	163,970	245,535	—
1991	5,568,548	2,572,802	13,952	1,081,018	341,080	57,001	6,681	207,463	156,840	237,759	—
1992	5,635,507	2,612,709	14,768	1,088,324	326,511	57,635	6,738	217,988	153,191	241,160	—
1993	5,762,251	2,693,589	17,438	1,143,075	304,780	58,285	7,328	226,016	164,714	238,365	—
1994	5,763,584	2,648,257	21,138	1,169,688	301,436	62,089	7,637	227,059	164,789	239,901	—
1995	5,837,945	2,748,452	19,182	1,151,735	287,601	63,690	7,713	229,955	170,394	236,242	—
1996	5,974,675	2,794,104	22,758	1,213,563	265,544	63,346	9,380	242,985	167,823	239,515	—
1997	6,116,870	2,852,490	23,887	1,238,041	258,290	65,889	8,372	251,619	177,019	241,184	—
1998	6,216,008	2,880,521	27,848	1,249,881	277,957	67,263	8,355	260,061	181,910	239,539	—
1999	6,201,141	2,895,989	24,353	1,240,783	254,839	66,784	7,075	260,115	184,280	239,520	—
2000	6,310,904	2,910,056	23,860	1,310,158	254,843	65,587	6,478	266,107	192,223	241,365	—

1 Includes special naphtha; beginning 1952, includes unfinished gasoline production.

2 Beginning 1964, kerosene-type jet fuel is included with other finished products.

3 Through 1929, data for distillate fuel oil are included with residual fuel oil.

4 Beginning 1983, data for road oil are included with asphalt.

Sources

1916–1930: U.S. Bureau of Mines, *Petroleum Refinery Statistics, 1930*, Bulletin 367, p. 15. 1931–1976: U.S. Bureau of Mines, *Minerals Yearbook* (annual). 1977–1980: U.S. Energy Information Administration, *Energy Data Reports: Petroleum Statement* (1977, 1979, 1980). 1981–2000: U.S. Energy Information Administration, *Petroleum Supply Annuals* (U.S. Department of Energy, annual).

(continued)

TABLE Db45–55   Petroleum refineries – output: 1916–2000   *Continued*

Documentation

Refineries take in materials as inputs, which appear in Table Db40–44, and refine them into outputs, which appear in this table. One could calculate the difference in total inputs and outputs to find the processing gain or loss each year.

Series Db45 represents the sum of all finished products, including some not shown separately. The only series containing data on unfinished products is series Db46, which includes unfinished gasoline beginning in 1952.

Also beginning in 1952, jet fuel components are excluded from series Db46–48, though they are included in the total. Prior to 1981, some still gas used as petrochemical feedstocks was excluded from series Db54, though it was included in the total.

The conversion factors used for series Db50–54 are as follows: wax, 280 pounds = 1 barrel; coke, 1 short ton = 5 barrels; asphalt, 1 short ton = 5.5 barrels; still gas, 3,600 cubic feet = 1 barrel.

TABLE Db56–59   Crude petroleum – average value, foreign trade, and proved reserves: 1859–2001

Contributed by Gavin Wright

Year	Average value at well — Db56 — Dollars per barrel	Imports — Db57 — Thousand 42-gallon barrels	Exports — Db58 — Thousand 42-gallon barrels	Estimated proved reserves — Db59 [1] — Thousand 42-gallon barrels	Year	Average value at well — Db56 — Dollars per barrel	Imports — Db57 — Thousand 42-gallon barrels	Exports — Db58 — Thousand 42-gallon barrels	Estimated proved reserves — Db59 [1] — Thousand 42-gallon barrels
1859	16.00	—	—	—	1905	0.62	—	3,004	3,800,000
1860	9.59	—	—	—	1906	0.73	—	3,525	3,800,000
1861	0.49	—	—	—	1907	0.72	—	3,007	3,900,000
1862	1.05	—	—	—	1908	0.72	—	3,552	4,000,000
1863	3.15	—	—	—	1909	0.70	—	4,056	4,200,000
1864	8.06	—	—	—	1910	0.61	—	4,288	4,500,000
1865	6.59	—	—	—	1911	0.61	—	4,806	5,000,000
1866	3.74	—	—	—	1912	0.74	—	4,493	5,400,000
1867	2.41	—	—	—	1913	0.95	17,809	4,633	5,500,000
1868	3.62	—	—	—	1914	0.81	17,247	2,970	5,400,000
1869	5.64	—	—	—	1915	0.64	18,140	3,768	5,500,000
1870	3.86	—	248	—	1916	1.10	30,570	4,096	5,900,000
1871	4.34	—	269	—	1917	1.56	30,127	4,098	5,900,000
1872	3.64	—	390	—	1918	1.98	37,736	4,901	6,200,000
1873	1.83	—	468	—	1919	2.01	52,822	6,019	6,700,000
1874	1.17	—	344	—	1920	3.07	106,175	9,295	7,200,000
1875	1.35	—	394	—	1921	1.73	125,364	9,627	7,800,000
1876	2.52	—	603	—	1922	1.61	127,308	10,805	7,600,000
1877	2.38	—	685	—	1923	1.34	82,015	17,534	7,600,000
1878	1.17	—	573	—	1924	1.43	77,775	18,239	7,500,000
1879	0.86	—	681	—	1925	1.68	61,824	13,337	8,500,000
1880	0.94	—	875	—	1926	1.88	60,382	15,407	8,800,000
1881	0.92	—	963	—	1927	1.30	53,383	15,844	10,500,000
1882	0.78	—	1,072	—	1928	1.17	79,767	18,966	11,000,000
1883	1.10	—	1,405	—	1929	1.27	78,933	26,401	13,200,000
1884	0.85	—	1,897	—	1930	1.19	62,129	23,705	13,600,000
1885	0.88	—	1,939	—	1931	0.65	47,250	25,535	13,000,000
1886	0.71	—	1,818	—	1932	0.87	44,682	27,393	12,300,000
1887	0.67	—	1,920	—	1933	0.67	31,893	36,584	12,000,000
1888	0.65	—	1,846	—	1934	1.00	35,558	41,127	12,177,000
1889	0.77	—	2,028	—	1935	0.97	32,239	51,430	12,400,000
1890	0.77	—	2,299	—	1936	1.09	32,327	50,313	13,063,400
1891	0.56	—	2,303	—	1937	1.18	27,484	67,234	15,507,268
1892	0.51	—	2,486	—	1938	1.13	26,412	77,254	17,348,146
1893	0.60	—	2,660	—	1939	1.02	33,095	72,076	18,483,012
1894	0.72	—	2,903	—	1940	1.02	42,738	51,495	19,024,515
1895	1.09	—	2,650	—	1941	1.14	50,606	33,238	19,559,296
1896	0.96	—	2,641	—	1942	1.19	12,297	33,834	20,082,793
1897	0.68	—	2,893	—	1943	1.20	13,833	41,342	20,064,152
1898	0.80	—	2,736	—	1944	1.21	44,805	34,238	20,453,231
1899	1.13	—	2,802	2,500,000	1945	1.22	74,337	32,998	20,826,813
1900	1.19	—	3,290	2,900,000	1946	1.41	86,066	42,436	20,873,560
1901	0.96	—	3,024	3,000,000	1947	1.93	97,532	45,355	21,487,685
1902	0.80	—	3,458	3,200,000	1948	2.60	129,093	39,736	23,280,444
1903	0.94	—	3,012	3,400,000	1949	2.54	153,686	33,069	24,649,489
1904	0.86	—	2,647	3,600,000					

Note appears at end of table

TABLE Series Db56–59   Crude petroleum – average value, foreign trade, and proved reserves: 1859–2001   *Continued*

Year	Average value at well Db56 Dollars per barrel	Imports Db57 Thousand 42-gallon barrels	Exports Db58 Thousand 42-gallon barrels	Estimated proved reserves Db59 [1] Thousand 42-gallon barrels	Year	Average value at well Db56 Dollars per barrel	Imports Db57 Thousand 42-gallon barrels	Exports Db58 Thousand 42-gallon barrels	Estimated proved reserves Db59 [1] Thousand 42-gallon barrels
1950	2.51	177,714	34,823	25,268,398	1980	21.59	1,926,162	104,935	29,805,000
1951	2.53	179,073	28,604	27,468,031	1981	31.77	1,604,703	83,166	29,426,000
1952	2.53	209,591	26,696	27,960,554	1982	28.52	1,273,214	86,279	27,858,000
1953	2.68	236,455	19,931	28,944,828	1983	26.19	1,215,225	59,948	27,735,000
1954	2.77	239,479	13,564	29,560,746	1984	25.88	1,253,949	66,234	28,446,000
1955	2.77	235,421	11,571	30,012,170	1985	24.09	1,168,297	74,513	28,416,000
1956	2.79	341,833	28,624	30,434,649	1986	12.51	1,524,978	56,205	26,889,000
1957	3.09	373,255	50,243	30,300,405	1987	15.40	1,705,922	54,964	27,256,000
1958	3.01	348,007	4,346	30,535,917	1988	12.58	1,869,005	56,714	26,825,000
1959	2.90	352,344	2,526	31,719,347	1989	15.86	2,132,761	51,683	26,501,000
1960	2.88	371,575	3,087	31,613,211	1990	20.03	2,151,387	39,654	26,254,000
1961	2.89	381,548	3,227	31,758,505	1991	16.54	2,110,532	42,384	24,682,000
1962	2.90	411,039	1,790	31,389,223	1992	15.99	2,229,935	32,474	23,745,000
1963	2.89	412,660	1,698	30,969,990	1993	14.25	2,477,230	35,833	22,957,000
1964	2.88	438,643	1,363	30,990,510	1994	13.19	2,578,072	36,019	22,457,000
1965	2.86	452,040	1,097	31,352,391	1995	14.62	2,638,810	34,509	22,351,000
1966	2.88	447,120	1,477	31,452,127	1996	18.46	2,747,839	40,211	22,017,000
1967	2.92	411,649	26,541	31,376,670	1997	17.23	3,002,299	39,308	22,546,000
1968	2.94	472,323	1,802	30,707,117	1998	10.88	3,177,584	40,102	21,034,000
1969	3.09	514,114	1,436	29,631,862	1999	15.56	3,183,622	43,031	21,765,000
1970	3.18	483,293	4,991	39,001,335	2000	26.72	3,316,810	18,351	22,045,000
1971	3.39	613,417	503	38,062,957	2001	21.84	3,400,982	7,386	22,446,000
1972	3.39	811,135	187	36,339,408					
1973	3.89	1,183,996	697	35,299,839					
1974	6.87	1,269,155	1,074	34,249,956					
1975	7.67	1,498,181	2,146	32,682,127					
1976	8.19	1,935,012	2,941	30,942,166					
1977	8.57	2,414,327	18,255	31,780,000					
1978	9.00	2,319,826	57,728	31,355,000					
1979	12.64	2,379,541	85,707	29,810,000					

[1] There is a discontinuity associated with the change in source in 1976–1977. The later figures include lease condensate. Also, Prudhoe Bay, Alaska, was added to Reserves in 1970 (9.6 billion barrels).

Sources

Series Db56. 1859–1931: U.S. Bureau of Mines, *Mineral Resources of the United States* (annual). 1932–1976: U.S. Bureau of Mines, *Minerals Yearbooks* (annual). 1977–2001: U.S. Energy Information Administration, *Monthly Energy Review*.

Series Db57. 1913–1931: U.S. Bureau of Mines, *Mineral Resources of the United States*. 1932–1976: U.S. Bureau of Mines, *Minerals Yearbooks*. 1977–2001: U.S. Energy Information Administration, *Petroleum Supply Annual* (U.S. Department of Energy, annual).

Series Db58. 1870–1931: U.S. Bureau of Mines, *Mineral Resources of the United States*. 1932–1976: U.S. Bureau of Mines, *Minerals Yearbooks*. 1977–2001: U.S. Energy Information Administration, *Petroleum Supply Annual* (U.S. Department of Energy, annual).

Series Db59. 1899–1948: American Petroleum Institute, *Petroleum Facts and Figures* (American Petroleum Institute, 1950), p. 182. 1949–1955: American Petroleum Institute, *Petroleum Facts and Figures* (American Petroleum Institute, 1956), p.164. 1956–1976: U.S. Bureau of Mines, *Minerals Yearbooks*. 1977–2001: U.S. Energy Information Administration, *U.S. Crude Oil, Natural Gas and Natural Gas Liquids Reserves Annual Report* (U.S. Department of Energy, annual).

Documentation

Series Db57. Crude petroleum imports are shown only from 1913 because crude and topped oil were reported separately only since July 1912. Since 1920, the figures include shipments from Puerto Rico and other areas administered by the United States.

Series Db58. For 1916 and earlier years, the crude petroleum exports figures include all crude mineral oils. For 1928 and earlier years, reexports of foreign crude petroleum are included; prior to 1919 such reexports were negligible. From 1920, the figures include shipments to Puerto Rico and other areas administered by the United States.

Series Db59

The Energy Information Administration defines proved reserves as "those volumes of oil and gas that geological and engineering data demonstrate with reasonable certainty to be recoverable in future years from known reservoirs under existing economic and operating conditions. Proved reserves are either proved producing or proved nonproducing (that is, resident in reservoirs that did not produce during the report year). The latter may represent a substantial fraction of total proved reserves" (*U.S. Crude Oil, Natural Gas, and Natural Gas Liquids Reserves Annual Report*, 1995, p. 121). They do not include other categories of estimated reserves, variously known as measured, indicated, inferred, probable, and possible reserves. Because these other reserves are generally less wellknown and therefore less precisely quantifiable, their eventual recovery is less assured.

The reported estimates for 1899–1934 are estimates of the American Petroleum Institute and are not based on geological surveys. Except for 1936, the figures for 1935–1955 are estimates of the Committee on Petroleum Reserves of the American Petroleum Institute. (The estimate for 1936 was taken by the American Petroleum Institute from *The Lamp*, a publication of Standard Oil Company of New Jersey.) Prior to 1946, the estimates included some condensate. Estimates for all years are as of December 31. Figures differ from those given in series Db199 because values there are as of January 1.

TABLE Db60–66   Bituminous coal – production, employment, foreign trade, and average value: 1800–2000

Contributed by Gavin Wright

	Production		Employment	Average value	Imports for consumption	Exports	Mines
	Total	Underground					
	Db60	Db61	Db62	Db63	Db64	Db65 [1]	Db66
Year	Thousand short tons	Thousand short tons	Number	Dollars per ton	Thousand short tons	Thousand short tons	Number
1800	108	—	—	—	—	—	—
1801	114	—	—	—	—	—	—
1802	122	—	—	—	—	—	—
1803	127	—	—	—	—	—	—
1804	141	—	—	—	—	—	—
1805	146	—	—	—	—	—	—
1806	152	—	—	—	—	—	—
1807	159	—	—	—	—	—	—
1808	165	—	—	—	—	—	—
1809	170	—	—	—	—	—	—
1810	176	—	—	—	—	—	—
1811	188	—	—	—	—	—	—
1812	203	—	—	—	—	—	—
1813	218	—	—	—	—	—	—
1814	235	—	—	—	—	—	—
1815	253	—	—	—	—	—	—
1816	278	—	—	—	—	—	—
1817	303	—	—	—	—	—	—
1818	330	—	—	—	—	—	—
1819	320	—	—	—	—	—	—
1820	330	—	—	—	—	—	—
1821	349	—	—	—	—	—	—
1822	360	—	—	—	—	—	—
1823	370	—	—	—	—	—	—
1824	414	—	—	—	—	—	—
1825	437	—	—	—	—	—	—
1826	493	—	—	—	—	—	—
1827	532	—	—	—	—	—	—
1828	569	—	—	—	—	—	—
1829	607	—	—	—	—	—	—
1830	646	—	—	—	—	—	—
1831	695	—	—	—	—	—	—
1832	771	—	—	—	—	—	—
1833	823	—	—	—	—	—	—
1834	912	—	—	—	—	—	—
1835	1,059	—	—	—	—	—	—
1836	1,067	—	—	—	—	—	—
1837	1,070	—	—	—	—	—	—
1838	1,141	—	—	—	—	—	—
1839	1,251	—	—	—	—	—	—
1840	1,345	—	—	—	—	—	—
1841	1,355	—	—	—	—	—	—
1842	1,473	—	—	—	—	—	—
1843	1,615	—	—	—	—	—	—
1844	1,794	—	—	—	—	—	—
1845	2,097	—	—	—	—	—	—
1846	2,328	—	—	—	—	—	—
1847	2,631	—	—	—	—	—	—
1848	3,080	—	—	—	—	—	—
1849	3,518	—	—	—	—	—	—
1850	4,029	—	—	—	—	—	—
1851	4,590	—	—	—	—	—	—
1852	4,909	—	—	—	—	—	—
1853	6,100	—	—	—	—	—	—
1854	7,359	—	—	—	—	—	—
1855	7,543	—	—	—	—	—	—
1856	7,992	—	—	—	—	—	—
1857	8,775	—	—	—	—	—	—
1858	8,846	—	—	—	—	—	—
1859	9,127	—	—	—	—	—	—

Note appears at end of table

TABLE Db60–66   Bituminous coal – production, employment, foreign trade, and average value: 1800–2000   *Continued*

Year	Production Total	Production Underground	Employment	Average value	Imports for consumption	Exports	Mines
	Db60	Db61	Db62	Db63	Db64	Db65 [1]	Db66
	Thousand short tons	Thousand short tons	Number	Dollars per ton	Thousand short tons	Thousand short tons	Number
1860	9,057	—	—	—	—	—	—
1861	8,756	—	—	—	—	—	—
1862	9,384	—	—	—	—	—	—
1863	10,480	—	—	—	—	—	—
1864	11,415	—	—	—	—	—	—
1865	12,349	—	—	—	—	—	—
1866	13,015	—	—	—	—	—	—
1867	13,837	—	—	—	571	103	—
1868	16,244	—	—	—	441	97	—
1869	19,903	—	—	—	490	—	—
1870	20,471	—	—	—	466	120	—
1871	22,857	—	—	—	482	149	—
1872	27,311	—	—	—	543	158	—
1873	31,601	—	—	—	515	272	—
1874	30,733	—	—	—	551	405	—
1875	32,657	—	—	—	489	228	—
1876	31,822	—	—	—	449	258	—
1877	34,385	—	—	—	555	360	—
1878	36,418	—	—	—	642	382	—
1879	40,425	—	—	—	545	309	—
1880	50,757	—	—	1.25	528	249	—
1881	51,945	—	—	1.12	731	214	—
1882	58,917	—	—	1.12	891	352	—
1883	64,860	—	—	1.07	723	519	—
1884	71,737	—	—	0.94	839	724	—
1885	71,773	—	—	1.13	861	765	—
1886	74,645	—	—	1.05	909	610	—
1887	88,562	—	—	1.11	918	791	—
1888	102,040	—	—	1.00	1,216	964	—
1889	95,685	—	—	0.99	1,122	1,047	—
1890	111,302	—	192,204	0.99	1,047	1,272	—
1891	117,901	—	205,803	0.99	1,182	1,652	—
1892	126,857	—	212,893	0.99	1,492	1,905	—
1893	128,385	—	230,365	0.96	1,234	1,986	—
1894	118,820	—	244,603	0.91	1,286	2,440	—
1895	135,118	—	239,962	0.86	1,411	2,660	2,555
1896	137,640	—	244,171	0.83	1,393	2,516	2,599
1897	147,618	—	247,817	0.81	1,443	2,670	2,454
1898	166,594	—	255,717	0.80	1,426	3,004	2,862
1899	193,323	—	271,027	0.87	1,410	3,898	3,245
1900	212,316	—	304,375	1.04	1,912	6,061	—
1901	225,828	—	340,235	1.05	2,215	6,455	—
1902	260,217	—	370,056	1.12	2,174	6,049	—
1903	282,749	—	415,777	1.24	4,044	5,836	—
1904	278,660	—	437,832	1.10	2,180	7,207	4,650
1905	315,063	—	460,629	1.06	1,705	7,513	5,060
1906	342,875	—	478,425	1.11	2,039	8,014	4,430
1907	394,759	—	513,258	1.14	1,893	9,870	4,550
1908	332,574	—	516,264	1.12	2,219	11,071	4,730
1909	379,744	—	543,152	1.07	1,375	10,101	5,775
1910	417,111	—	555,533	1.12	1,820	11,663	5,818
1911	405,907	—	549,775	1.11	1,973	13,260	5,887
1912	450,105	—	548,632	1.15	1,456	16,475	5,747
1913	478,435	—	571,882	1.18	1,768	18,013	5,776
1914	422,704	421,423	583,506	1.17	1,521	17,590	5,592
1915	442,624	439,792	557,456	1.13	1,704	18,777	5,502
1916	502,520	498,587	561,102	1.32	1,714	21,255	5,726
1917	551,791	546,001	603,143	2.26	1,448	23,840	6,939
1918	579,386	571,093	615,305	2.58	1,457	22,351	8,319
1919	465,860	460,225	621,998	2.49	1,012	20,114	8,994

Note appears at end of table   (continued)

TABLE Db60–66 Bituminous coal – production, employment, foreign trade, and average value: 1800–2000 *Continued*

Year	Production Total	Production Underground	Employment	Average value	Imports for consumption	Exports	Mines
	Db60	Db61	Db62	Db63	Db64	Db65 [1]	Db66
	Thousand short tons	Thousand short tons	Number	Dollars per ton	Thousand short tons	Thousand short tons	Number
1920	568,667	559,807	639,547	3.75	1,245	38,517	8,921
1921	415,922	410,865	663,754	2.89	1,258	23,131	8,038
1922	422,268	412,059	687,958	3.02	5,060	12,413	9,299
1923	564,565	552,625	704,793	2.68	1,882	21,454	7,331
1924	483,687	470,080	619,604	2.20	417	17,100	7,586
1925	520,053	503,182	588,493	2.04	602	17,462	7,144
1926	573,367	556,444	593,647	2.06	486	35,272	7,177
1927	517,763	499,385	593,918	1.99	550	18,012	7,011
1928	500,745	480,956	522,150	1.86	547	16,164	6,450
1929	534,989	514,721	502,993	1.78	495	17,429	6,057
1930	467,526	447,684	493,202	1.70	241	15,877	5,891
1931	382,089	363,157	450,213	1.54	206	12,126	5,642
1932	309,710	290,069	406,380	1.31	187	8,814	5,427
1933	333,631	315,360	418,703	1.34	197	9,037	5,555
1934	359,368	338,578	458,011	1.75	180	10,869	6,258
1935	372,373	348,726	462,403	1.77	202	9,742	6,315
1936	439,088	410,962	477,204	1.76	272	10,655	6,875
1937	445,531	413,780	491,864	1.94	258	13,145	6,548
1938	348,545	318,138	441,333	1.95	241	10,490	5,777
1939	394,855	357,133	421,788	1.84	355	11,590	5,820
1940	460,772	417,604	439,075	1.91	372	16,466	6,324
1941	514,149	459,078	456,981	2.19	390	20,740	6,822
1942	582,693	515,490	461,991	2.36	498	22,943	6,972
1943	590,177	510,492	416,007	2.69	758	25,836	6,620
1944	619,576	518,678	393,347	2.92	634	26,032	6,928
1945	577,617	467,630	383,100	3.06	467	27,956	7,033
1946	533,922	420,958	396,434	3.44	435	41,197	7,333
1947	630,624	491,229	419,182	4.16	290	68,667	8,700
1948	599,518	460,012	441,631	4.99	291	45,930	9,079
1949	437,868	331,823	433,698	4.88	315	27,842	8,559
1950	516,311	392,844	415,582	4.84	347	25,468	9,429
1951	533,665	415,842	372,897	4.92	292	56,722	8,009
1952	466,841	356,425	335,217	4.90	262	47,643	7,275
1953	457,290	349,551	293,106	4.92	227	33,760	6,671
1954	391,706	289,112	227,397	4.52	199	31,041	6,130
1955	464,633	343,465	225,093	4.50	337	51,277	7,856
1956	500,874	265,774	228,163	4.82	356	68,553	8,520
1957	492,704	360,649	228,635	5.08	367	76,446	8,539
1958	410,446	286,884	197,402	4.86	307	50,293	8,264
1959	412,028	283,434	179,636	4.77	375	37,253	7,719
1960	415,512	284,888	169,400	4.69	260	36,541	7,865
1961	402,977	272,766	150,474	4.58	164	34,970	7,648
1962	422,149	281,266	143,822	4.48	232	38,413	7,740
1963	458,928	302,256	141,646	4.39	267	47,078	7,940
1964	486,998	321,808	128,698	4.45	293	47,969	7,630
1965	512,088	332,661	133,732	4.44	184	50,181	7,228
1966	533,881	338,524	131,752	4.54	178	49,302	6,749
1967	552,626	349,133	131,523	4.62	227	49,528	5,873
1968	545,245	344,142	127,894	4.67	224	50,637	5,327
1969	560,505	347,132	124,532	4.99	109	56,234	5,118
1970	602,930	338,788	140,140	6.26	36	70,944	5,601
1971	552,192	275,888	145,664	7.07	111	56,633	5,149
1972	595,386	304,103	149,265	7.66	47	55,997	4,879
1973	591,738	299,353	148,121	8.53	127	52,903	4,744
1974	603,406	277,309	166,701	15.75	2,080	59,926	5,247
1975	648,438	292,826	189,880	19.23	940	65,669	6,168
1976	678,685	294,880	202,280	19.43	1,203	59,406	6,161
1977	691,344	265,950	221,428	19.82	1,647	54,312	6,077
1978	665,127	242,177	242,295	21.78	2,953	40,714	6,230
1979	776,299	320,321	224,203	23.65	2,059	66,042	5,837

Note appears at end of table

TABLE Db60–66   Bituminous coal – production, employment, foreign trade, and average value: 1800–2000   *Continued*

Year	Production — Total	Production — Underground	Employment	Average value	Imports for consumption	Exports	Mines
	Db60	Db61	Db62	Db63	Db64	Db65 [1]	Db66
	Thousand short tons	Thousand short tons	Number	Dollars per ton	Thousand short tons	Thousand short tons	Number
1980	823,644	336,925	224,938	24.52	1,194	91,742	5,596
1981	818,352	315,875	226,250	26.29	1,043	112,541	5,569
1982	833,523	338,572	214,400	27.14	742	106,277	5,363
1983	778,003	299,892	173,543	25.85	1,271	77,772	4,265
1984	891,759	351,474	175,746	25.51	1,286	81,483	—
1985	878,930	350,073	167,009	25.10	1,952	92,680	4,547
1986	886,023	359,800	152,668	23.70	2,212	85,518	3,870
1987	915,202	372,238	141,065	23.00	1,747	79,607	—
1988	946,710	381,546	133,913	22.00	2,134	95,023	3,462
1989	977,381	393,322	130,103	21.76	2,851	100,815	3,429
1990	1,025,570	424,119	129,619	21.71	2,699	105,804	3,243
1991	992,539	406,901	119,441	21.45	3,390	108,969	2,590
1992	994,062	406,815	108,979	20.98	3,803	102,516	2,580
1993	941,118	350,637	100,099	19.79	7,309	74,519	2,327
1994	1,028,883	398,760	96,317	19.34	7,584	71,359	2,211
1995	1,028,292	395,821	89,183	18.74	7,201	88,547	1,970
1996	1,059,105	409,458	82,291	18.42	7,126	90,473	1,776
1997	1,085,254	420,238	80,229	18.11	7,487	83,545	1,697
1998	1,112,857	417,320	84,137	17.55	8,724	78,048	1,603
1999	1,095,678	391,413	77,397	16.55	9,089	58,476	1,480
2000	1,069,040	373,350	70,452	16.68	12,513	58,489	1,341

[1] Beginning 1978, figures are for total coal exports (includes small amount of anthracite).

Sources

Series Db60. 1800–1885: H. N. Eavenson, *The First Century and a Quarter of the American Coal Industry* (Waverly Press, 1942), pp. 426–34. 1886–1931: U.S. Bureau of Mines, *Mineral Resources of the United States* (annual). 1932–1970: U.S. Bureau of Mines, *Minerals Yearbooks* (annual). 1971–1993: U.S. Energy Information Administration, *Coal Data: A Reference* (biennial). 1994–2000: U.S. Energy Information Administration, *Coal Industry Annual* (U.S. Department of Energy, annual).

Series Db61–62. 1890–1931: U.S. Bureau of Mines, *Mineral Resources of the United States*. 1932–1970: U.S. Bureau of Mines, *Minerals Yearbooks*. 1971–1993: U.S. Energy Information Administration, *Coal Data*. 1994–2000: *Coal Industry Annual*.

Series Db63. 1880–1931: U.S. Bureau of Mines, *Mineral Resources of the United States*. 1932–1970: U.S. Bureau of Mines, *Minerals Yearbooks*. 1971–1993: U.S. Energy Information Administration, *Coal Data*. 1994–2000: U.S. Energy Information Agency, *Annual Energy Review* (U.S. Department of Energy, annual).

Series Db64–66. 1867–1931: U.S. Bureau of Mines, *Mineral Resources of the United States*. 1932–1976: U.S. Bureau of Mines, *Minerals Yearbooks*. 1977–2000: U.S. Energy Information Administration, *Coal Industry Annual*.

Documentation

Bituminous coal is also known as "soft coal," with an ignition temperature of 750–800 degrees Fahrenheit. Coverage of bituminous includes all subbituminous coal and lignite and a small amount of anthracite and semianthracite produced outside of Pennsylvania.

Series Db60. Prior to 1886, production figures are those as derived by Eavenson and are considered superior to the early Geological Survey figures, which appear in *Mineral Resources of the United States*.

Series Db62. Beginning with 1946, the figures on employment represent the average number of men working daily, excluding periods when the mine is closed and not in operation. Before 1946, each mine was asked to report the average number of men on the rolls per pay period and the number of days the mine worked. Men employed were multiplied by number of days to determine total man-shifts. Beginning 1978, employment figures exclude miners employed at mines that produced less than 10,000 tons.

Series Db63. Values are f.o.b. (free on board) mine (the buyer is responsible for costs of transportation and insurance from the mine). For 1880–1936, figures exclude selling expenses. Beginning in 1937, selling expenses are included. This change occurred in the wake of the Bituminous Coal Act of 1937, which, among other things, shifted responsibility for the collection of statistics on bituminous coal from the Bureau of Mines to the Coal Commission, who decided to explicitly include selling costs in the calculation of the average value per ton.

Series Db66. The number of mines excludes those producing less than 1,000 tons per year. The original source, *Coal Industry Annual*, excludes those producing less than 10,000 tons per year.

TABLE Db67–72 Anthracite coal – production, employment, foreign trade, and average value: 1808–2000

Contributed by Gavin Wright

Year	Production Total	Production Underground	Average value	Exports	Imports for consumption	Employment
	Db67	**Db68**	**Db69** [1]	**Db70**	**Db71**	**Db72** [2]
	Thousand short tons	Thousand short tons	Dollars per ton	Thousand short tons	Thousand short tons	Number
1808	1	—	—	—	—	—
1809	1	—	—	—	—	—
1810	2	—	—	—	—	—
1811	2	—	—	—	—	—
1812	2	—	—	—	—	—
1813	2	—	—	—	—	—
1814	2	—	—	—	—	—
1815	2	—	—	—	—	—
1816	2	—	—	—	—	—
1817	2	—	—	—	—	—
1818	3	—	—	—	—	—
1819	3	—	—	—	—	—
1820	4	—	—	—	—	—
1821	4	—	—	—	—	—
1822	6	—	—	—	—	—
1823	10	—	—	—	—	—
1824	15	—	—	—	—	—
1825	43	—	—	—	—	—
1826	61	—	—	—	—	—
1827	80	—	—	—	—	—
1828	103	—	—	—	—	—
1829	149	—	—	—	—	—
1830	235	—	—	—	—	—
1831	258	—	—	—	—	—
1832	502	—	—	—	—	—
1833	663	—	—	—	—	—
1834	512	—	—	—	—	—
1835	760	—	—	—	—	—
1836	925	—	—	—	—	—
1837	1,164	—	—	—	—	—
1838	978	—	—	—	—	—
1839	1,072	—	—	—	—	—
1840	1,129	—	—	—	—	—
1841	1,262	—	—	—	—	—
1842	1,441	—	—	—	—	—
1843	1,656	—	—	—	—	—
1844	2,128	—	—	—	—	—
1845	2,626	—	—	—	—	—
1846	3,032	—	—	—	—	—
1847	3,726	—	—	—	—	—
1848	4,001	—	—	—	—	—
1849	4,172	—	—	—	—	—
1850	4,327	—	—	—	—	—
1851	5,814	—	—	—	—	—
1852	6,412	—	—	—	—	—
1853	6,653	—	—	—	—	—
1854	7,668	—	—	—	—	—
1855	8,607	—	—	—	—	—
1856	8,960	—	—	—	—	—
1857	8,618	—	—	—	—	—
1858	8,808	—	—	—	—	—
1859	10,092	—	—	—	—	—
1860	10,984	—	—	—	—	—
1861	10,245	—	—	—	—	—
1862	10,186	—	—	—	—	—
1863	12,267	—	—	—	—	—
1864	13,027	—	—	—	—	—

Notes appear at end of table

TABLE Db67–72   **Anthracite coal – production, employment, foreign trade, and average value: 1808–2000**   *Continued*

Year	Production Total	Production Underground	Average value	Exports	Imports for consumption	Employment
	Db67	Db68	Db69 [1]	Db70	Db71	Db72 [2]
	Thousand short tons	Thousand short tons	Dollars per ton	Thousand short tons	Thousand short tons	Number
1865	12,077	—	—	—	—	—
1866	15,784	—	—	—	—	—
1867	16,067	—	—	216	—	—
1868	17,708	—	—	215	—	—
1869	18,341	—	—	318	—	—
1870	19,958	—	—	136	—	35,600
1871	19,465	—	—	151	1	37,488
1872	24,734	—	—	291	—	44,745
1873	25,627	—	—	383	2	48,199
1874	24,267	—	—	450	1	53,402
1875	23,121	—	—	354	—	69,966
1876	22,793	—	—	378	2	70,474
1877	25,660	—	—	469	1	66,842
1878	21,690	—	—	358	—	63,964
1879	30,208	—	—	433	1	68,847
1880	28,650	—	1.47	440	—	73,373
1881	31,920	—	2.01	518	1	76,031
1882	35,121	—	2.01	620	—	82,200
1883	38,457	—	2.01	625	1	91,421
1884	37,157	—	1.79	727	2	101,073
1885	38,336	—	2.00	659	6	100,324
1886	39,035	—	1.95	747	2	103,044
1887	42,088	—	2.01	925	16	106,517
1888	46,620	—	1.91	1,086	27	122,218
1889	45,547	—	1.44	961	23	123,676
1890	46,469	—	1.43	890	17	126,000
1891	50,665	—	1.46	965	42	126,350
1892	52,473	—	1.57	954	73	129,050
1893	53,968	—	1.59	1,493	60	132,944
1894	51,921	—	1.51	1,614	101	131,603
1895	57,999	—	1.41	1,647	158	142,917
1896	54,346	—	1.50	1,512	114	148,991
1897	52,612	—	1.51	1,455	27	149,884
1898	53,383	—	1.41	1,513	4	145,504
1899	60,418	—	1.46	1,913	(Z)	139,608
1900	57,368	—	1.49	1,853	(Z)	144,206
1901	67,472	—	1.67	2,233	(Z)	145,309
1902	41,374	—	1.84	1,017	191	148,141
1903	74,607	—	2.04	2,250	197	150,483
1904	73,157	—	1.90	2,496	81	155,861
1905	77,660	—	1.83	2,498	38	165,406
1906	71,282	—	1.85	2,483	36	162,355
1907	85,604	—	1.91	3,022	11	167,234
1908	83,269	—	1.90	3,083	18	174,174
1909	81,070	—	1.84	3,184	4	171,195
1910	84,485	—	1.90	3,384	9	169,497
1911	90,464	—	1.94	3,980	3	172,585
1912	84,362	—	2.11	4,131	2	174,030
1913	91,525	—	2.13	4,653	1	175,745
1914	90,822	—	2.07	4,290	18	179,679
1915	88,995	83,973	2.07	3,965	1	176,552
1916	87,578	80,931	2.31	4,666	6	159,859
1917	99,612	90,164	2.85	6,007	13	154,174
1918	98,826	87,802	3.40	4,968	37	147,121
1919	88,092	81,055	4.14	4,977	83	154,571
1920	89,598	80,454	4.85	5,404	32	145,074
1921	90,473	85,900	5.00	4,677	9	159,499
1922	54,683	49,533	5.01	2,649	234	156,849
1923	93,339	83,009	5.43	5,090	300	157,743
1924	87,927	82,869	5.43	4,018	118	160,009

Notes appear at end of table

(continued)

TABLE Db67–72   Anthracite coal – production, employment, foreign trade, and average value: 1808–2000 *Continued*

Year	Production		Average value	Exports	Imports for consumption	Employment
	Total	Underground				
	Db67	Db68	Db69 [1]	Db70	Db71	Db72 [2]
	Thousand short tons	Thousand short tons	Dollars per ton	Thousand short tons	Thousand short tons	Number
1925	61,817	57,152	5.30	3,179	383	160,312
1926	84,437	78,059	5.62	4,030	814	165,386
1927	80,096	73,658	5.26	3,326	119	165,259
1928	75,348	69,725	5.22	3,336	385	160,681
1929	73,828	69,964	5.22	3,406	487	151,501
1930	69,385	64,925	5.11	2,552	675	150,804
1931	59,646	53,460	4.97	1,778	638	139,431
1932	49,855	43,834	4.46	1,303	607	121,243
1933	49,541	41,032	4.17	1,035	456	104,633
1934	57,168	48,575	4.27	1,298	478	109,050
1935	52,159	43,783	4.03	1,609	571	103,269
1936	54,580	44,727	4.16	1,678	615	102,081
1937	51,856	42,566	3.81	1,914	396	99,085
1938	46,099	38,142	3.92	1,909	363	96,417
1939	51,487	42,572	3.64	2,590	298	93,138
1940	51,485	41,517	3.99	2,668	135	91,313
1941	56,368	43,877	4.26	3,380	75	88,054
1942	60,328	45,237	4.50	4,439	140	82,121
1943	60,644	42,736	5.06	4,139	166	79,153
1944	63,701	41,775	5.57	4,186	12	77,591
1945	54,934	34,886	5.90	3,591	(Z)	72,842
1946	60,507	38,084	6.83	6,497	10	78,145
1947	57,190	36,963	7.22	8,510	10	78,600
1948	57,140	37,175	8.17	6,676	1	76,215
1949	42,702	27,031	8.38	4,943	—	75,377
1950	44,077	28,156	8.90	3,892	18	72,624
1951	42,670	26,342	9.51	5,956	27	68,995
1952	40,583	24,748	9.36	4,592	29	65,923
1953	30,949	17,893	9.67	2,724	31	57,862
1954	29,083	16,852	8.52	2,851	6	43,996
1955	26,205	14,499	7.86	3,152	(Z)	33,523 [4]
1956	28,900	15,055	8.19	5,244	(Z)	31,516
1957	25,338	12,616	8.99	4,332	1	30,825
1958	21,171	10,699	8.88	2,280	4	26,540
1959	20,649	9,415	8.35	1,788	3	23,294
1960	18,817	7,696	7.82	1,440	1	19,051
1961	17,446	6,785	8.04	1,435	1	15,792
1962	16,894	6,673	7.94	1,802	8	14,010
1963	18,267	6,715	8.40	3,357	5 [3]	13,498
1964	17,184	5,889	8.65	1,575	—	13,144
1965	14,866	5,297	8.21	851	—	11,132
1966	12,941	4,088	7.78	766	—	9,292
1967	12,256	3,258	7.85	595	—	7,750
1968	11,461	2,450	8.48	518	—	6,932
1969	10,473	2,106	9.62	627	—	5,927
1970	9,729	1,742	10.83	789	—	5,938
1971	8,727	1,287	12.08	671	—	5,800
1972	7,106	944	12.40	743	—	4,783
1973	6,830	726	13.65	717	—	4,083
1974	6,617	657	22.19	735	—	3,847
1975	6,203	641	32.26	640	—	3,907
1976	6,228	584	33.92	615	—	3,686
1977	5,861	642	34.86	—	—	3,655
1978	5,037	595	35.25	—	—	3,472
1979	4,835	570	41.06	—	—	3,094
1980	6,056	583	42.51	—	—	3,631
1981	5,423	621	44.28	—	—	3,052
1982	4,588	579	49.85	—	—	2,717
1983	4,089	487	52.29	—	—	2,099
1984	4,162	576	48.22	—	—	2,102

Notes appear at end of table

TABLE Db67–72   Anthracite coal – production, employment, foreign trade, and average value: 1808–2000   *Continued*

	Production		Average value	Exports	Imports for consumption	Employment
	Total	Underground				
	Db67	Db68	Db69 [1]	Db70	Db71	Db72 [2]
Year	Thousand short tons	Thousand short tons	Dollars per ton	Thousand short tons	Thousand short tons	Number
1985	4,708	727	45.80	—	—	2,272
1986	4,292	638	44.12	—	—	1,977
1987	3,560	636	43.65	—	—	1,602
1988	3,555	610	44.16	—	—	1,453
1989	3,348	513	42.93	—	—	1,394
1990	3,506	427	39.40	—	—	1,687
1991	3,445	324	36.34	—	—	1,161
1992	3,483	424	34.24	—	—	1,217
1993	4,306	416	32.94	—	—	1,124
1994	4,621	343	36.07	—	—	1,183
1995	4,682	428	39.78	—	—	1,069
1996	4,751	391	36.78	—	—	1,171
1997	4,678	419	34.01	—	—	1,287
1998	5,252	408	42.91	—	—	1,185
1999	4,768	377	35.13	—	—	1,326
2000	4,572	309	40.90	—	—	1,070

(Z) Less than 500 short tons.

[1] For 1971–1978, prices are f.o.b. (free on board, that is, before charges for transportation, insurance, and any taxes) preparation plants. See text.

[2] Beginning 1979, excludes miners employed at mines that produced less than 10,000 tons.

[3] For period January–August. Beginning September 1963, data are not available separately because of a change in import commodity classification.

[4] Estimated.

Sources

Series Db67. 1800–1885: H. N. Eavenson, *The First Century and a Quarter of the American Coal Industry* (Waverly Press, 1942), pp. 426–34. 1886–1931: U.S. Bureau of Mines, *Mineral Resources of the United States* (annual). 1932–1970: U.S. Bureau of Mines, *Minerals Yearbooks* (annual). 1971–1993: U.S. Energy Information Administration, *Coal Data: A Reference* (biennial). 1994–2000: U.S. Energy Information Administration, *Coal Industry Annual* (U.S. Department of Energy, annual).

Series Db68. 1890–1931: U.S. Bureau of Mines, *Mineral Resources of the United States*. 1932–1970: U.S. Bureau of Mines, *Minerals Yearbooks*. 1971–1993: U.S. Energy Information Administration, *Coal Data*. 1994–2000: *Coal Industry Annual*.

Series Db69. 1890–1931: U.S. Bureau of Mines, *Mineral Resources of the United States*. 1932–1970: U.S. Bureau of Mines, *Minerals Yearbooks*. 1971–1993: U.S. Energy Information Administration, *Coal Data*. 1994–2000: U.S. Energy Information Agency, *Annual Energy Review* (U.S. Department of Energy, annual).

Series Db70–71. 1890–1931: U.S. Bureau of Mines, *Mineral Resources of the United States*. 1932–1976: U.S. Bureau of Mines, *Minerals Yearbooks*.

Series Db72. 1867–1931: U.S. Bureau of Mines, *Mineral Resources of the United States*. 1932–1970: U.S. Bureau of Mines, *Minerals Yearbooks*. 1971–1993: U.S. Energy Information Administration, *Coal Data*. 1994–2000: *Coal Industry Annual*.

Documentation

Series Db67. Anthracite or "hard coal" is limited to Pennsylvania. Some anthracite production occurred during 1800–1807, but it amounted to less than 500 tons annually. Until 1951, production estimates made no attempt to include "bootleg" operations, or mining of anthracite near the surface of the earth without consent of the owner of the mineral rights. Beginning in 1951, output of these independent operators (no longer called "bootleggers" since they operated under legal agreements with landowners) is included, so these figures are not strictly comparable with those for earlier years. Small amounts of anthracite and semianthracite produced outside of Pennsylvania are included in data on bituminous coal production in series Db60.

Series Db69. Except as noted for 1971–1978, prices are f.o.b. mines. In 1970, the price at f.o.b. preparation plants was 11.03. Free on board (f.o.b.) means the buyer is responsible for transportation and insurance costs from the point specified.

Series Db72. Beginning in 1946, the figures represent the average number of men working daily, excluding periods when the mine was closed and not in operation. Before 1946, each mine was asked to report the average number of men on the rolls per pay period and the number of days the mine worked. Men employed were multiplied by number of days to determine total man-shifts.

TABLE Db73–78 Metal production – iron ore, pig iron, and copper: 1810–2000

Contributed by Gavin Wright

			Copper			
	Iron ore production	Pig iron shipments	Production from mines (recoverable content)	Primary copper refined from domestic and foreign ores	Secondary production	
					Total	From old scrap
	Db73	Db74 [1]	Db75	Db76	Db77	Db78
Year	Thousand metric tons	Thousand metric tons	Metric tons	Metric tons	Metric tons	Metric tons
1810	—	55	—	—	—	—
1820	—	20	—	—	—	—
1828	—	132	—	—	—	—
1829	—	144	—	—	—	—
1830	—	168	—	—	—	—
1831	—	194	—	—	—	—
1832	—	203	—	—	—	—
1840	—	292	—	—	—	—
1842	—	218	—	—	—	—
1845	—	—	102	—	—	—
1846	—	777	152	—	—	—
1847	—	813	305	—	—	—
1848	—	813	508	—	—	—
1849	—	660	711	—	—	—
1850	—	572	660	—	—	—
1851	—	—	914	—	—	—
1852	—	508	1,118	—	—	—
1853	—	—	2,032	—	—	—
1854	—	668	2,286	—	—	—
1855	—	711	3,048	—	—	—
1856	—	801	4,064	—	—	—
1857	—	723	4,877	—	—	—
1858	—	639	5,588	—	—	—
1859	—	763	6,401	—	—	—
1860	2,919	834	7,316	—	—	—
1861	—	664	7,620	—	—	—
1862	—	715	9,598	—	—	—
1863	—	860	8,636	—	—	—
1864	—	1,030	8,128	—	—	—
1865	—	845	8,636	—	—	—
1866	—	1,224	9,043	—	—	—
1867	—	1,326	10,160	—	—	—
1868	—	1,454	11,786	—	—	—
1869	—	1,739	12,701	—	—	—
1870	3,893	1,692	12,802	—	—	—
1871	—	1,734	13,209	—	—	—
1872	—	2,590	12,701	—	—	—
1873	—	2,602	15,749	—	—	—
1874	—	2,440	17,781	—	—	—
1875	4,082	2,056	18,289	—	—	—
1876	—	1,899	19,305	—	—	—
1877	—	2,100	21,337	—	—	—
1878	—	2,338	21,845	—	—	—
1879	—	2,786	23,369	—	—	—
1880	7,234	3,897	27,433	—	—	—
1881	7,234	4,212	32,514	—	—	—
1882	9,144	4,697	41,116	—	—	—
1883	8,535	4,670	52,402	—	—	—
1884	8,332	4,164	65,746	—	—	—
1885	7,722	4,110	75,240	—	—	—
1886	10,160	5,744	71,560	—	—	—
1887	11,481	6,520	82,317	—	—	—
1888	12,257	6,594	102,676	—	—	—
1889	14,751	7,726	102,864	—	—	—
1890	16,293	9,351	117,827	—	—	—
1891	14,825	8,412	128,876	—	—	—
1892	16,559	9,304	156,489	—	—	—
1893	11,774	7,238	149,393	—	—	—
1894	12,071	6,764	160,657	—	—	—

Notes appear at end of table

TABLE Db73–78   Metal production – iron ore, pig iron, and copper: 1810–2000
Continued

Year	Iron ore production Db73 Thousand metric tons	Pig iron shipments Db74 [1] Thousand metric tons	Copper			
			Production from mines (recoverable content) Db75 Metric tons	Primary copper refined from domestic and foreign ores Db76 Metric tons	Secondary production Total Db77 Metric tons	From old scrap Db78 Metric tons
1895	16,214	9,598	172,644	—	—	—
1896	16,262	8,761	208,681	—	—	—
1897	17,799	9,808	224,110	—	—	—
1898	19,746	11,963	238,822	—	—	—
1899	24,995	13,840	257,943	—	—	—
1900	27,738	14,010	274,931	—	—	—
1901	29,059	16,134	273,095	—	—	—
1902	35,866	18,107	299,148	—	—	—
1903	35,358	18,298	316,628	—	—	—
1904	27,941	16,762	368,561	—	—	—
1905	43,080	23,361	403,146	—	—	—
1906	48,516	25,713	415,932	489,450	—	—
1907	52,551	26,195	384,262	468,342	—	—
1908	36,560	16,192	434,015	516,171	—	—
1909	52,117	26,210	510,982	630,957	—	—
1910	57,930	27,102	493,617	645,027	85,729	58,513
1911	44,581	23,630	505,649	650,395	97,069	68,946
1912	56,035	30,665	566,580	711,280	124,738	97,069
1913	62,975	30,877	560,445	732,583	123,831	83,007
1914	42,105	22,620	520,920	695,712	116,013	79,725
1915	56,417	30,873	674,978	741,263	177,978	109,939
1916	76,374	39,754	909,850	1,024,841	317,515	158,757
1917	76,497	39,233	859,755	1,098,508 [2]	347,815	176,810
1918	70,776	38,663	866,372	1,086,036	319,937	160,272
1919	61,943	30,715	549,906	802,935	260,534	138,436
1920	68,689	36,283	555,447	692,257	283,459	153,278
1921	29,964	16,295	211,460	431,266	197,131	119,739
1922	47,885	25,067	437,528	569,493	304,723	183,977
1923	70,464	38,978	670,292	898,039	372,762	245,756
1924	55,138	31,562	728,545	1,025,154	352,260	241,493
1925	62,901	37,405	761,182	999,978	381,208	264,000
1926	68,708	38,794	782,572	1,053,462	435,267	305,994
1927	62,732	35,426	748,409	1,054,949	444,702	307,899
1928	63,195	38,919	820,910	1,128,360	486,614	331,576
1929	74,200	42,216	904,967	1,242,894	568,397	421,251
1930	59,346	30,431	639,633	978,426	423,837	310,439
1931	31,632	18,099	479,787	681,043	314,793	237,047
1932	10,005	8,656	216,011	308,837	225,145	164,182
1933	17,835	14,584	172,948	336,374	306,719	236,140
1934	24,983	15,877	215,367	404,024	342,372	282,044
1935	31,030	21,519	350,619	534,155	407,235	328,129
1936	49,572	31,293	557,480	746,150	439,622	347,180
1937	73,251	35,789	763,848	967,798	482,713	370,948
1938	28,903	18,495	505,994	718,895	326,405	242,491
1939	52,562	32,606	660,721	915,817	453,320	260,271
1940	74,879	42,601	796,586	1,191,638	482,664	302,900
1941	93,893	50,098	869,218	1,265,803	658,976	374,394
1942	107,219	53,616	979,815	1,283,269	841,645	387,479
1943	102,873	55,145	989,574	1,251,247	985,245	387,841
1944	95,628	55,335	882,282	1,107,843	862,680	414,320
1945	89,794	48,321	701,158	1,005,704	913,096	450,957
1946	71,980	40,892	552,237	797,109	728,965	368,728
1947	94,586	52,950	768,896	1,052,307	872,477	456,655
1948	102,624	54,477	757,330	1,004,658	882,499	458,549
1949	86,300	48,007	682,883	841,801	646,953	347,949

Notes appear at end of table

(continued)

TABLE Db73-78   Metal production – iron ore, pig iron, and copper: 1810-2000
Continued

			Copper			
	Iron ore production	Pig iron shipments	Production from mines (recoverable content)	Primary copper refined from domestic and foreign ores	Secondary production	
					Total	From old scrap
	Db73	Db74 [1]	Db75	Db76	Db77	Db78
Year	Thousand metric tons	Thousand metric tons	Metric tons	Metric tons	Metric tons	Metric tons
1950	99,618	58,628	824,942	1,124,759	886,536	440,176
1951	118,375	63,729	842,167	1,094,961	845,752	415,603
1952	99,489	55,551	839,472	1,068,388	819,367	376,151
1953	119,888	67,280	840,460	1,173,096	869,504	389,534
1954	79,383	52,420	757,928	1,099,435	761,951	369,284
1955	104,656	70,127	905,888	1,217,859	897,210	466,824
1956	99,448	68,139	1,001,674	1,308,735	844,284	425,006
1957	107,851	69,751	985,982	1,319,207	763,747	403,236
1958	68,796	51,635	888,433	1,226,986	723,378	373,186
1959	61,243	55,560	748,288	996,313	844,199	427,290
1960	90,209	59,522	979,913	1,377,948	790,510	389,513
1961	72,474	59,246	1,057,011	1,406,263	770,145	372,953
1962	72,982	59,627	1,114,405	1,462,137	836,268	377,093
1963	74,780	65,509	1,100,566	1,448,186	883,985	382,690
1964	86,197	77,740	1,131,060	1,502,657	991,572	429,571
1965	88,842	80,187	1,226,273	1,552,913	1,136,930	465,781
1966	91,594	82,448	1,296,505	1,552,179	1,210,411	485,217
1967	85,530	78,761	865,513	1,027,824	1,052,250	437,861
1968	87,243	80,817	1,092,814	1,303,975	1,105,260	472,437
1969	89,745	86,611	1,401,219	1,581,056	1,247,827	521,532
1970	91,200	82,801	1,560,047	1,601,267	1,131,806	457,286
1971	82,058	73,783	1,380,902	1,444,041	1,088,731	403,840
1972	76,644	80,788	1,510,318	1,699,369	1,180,223	415,667
1973	89,076	92,195	1,558,489	1,695,064	1,190,503	441,086
1974	85,709	87,036	1,448,776	1,501,081	1,219,547	438,562
1975	80,132	71,885	1,282,184	1,309,411	881,752	334,908
1976	81,277	78,647	1,456,561	1,396,437	1,038,975	380,225
1977	56,645	74,745	1,364,374	1,357,316	1,085,425	409,928
1978	82,892	80,325	1,357,586	1,449,057	1,247,235	501,650
1979	87,091	79,634	1,446,586	1,516,655	1,552,525	604,301
1980	70,730	62,999	1,181,116	1,215,188	1,437,427	613,458
1981	74,348	67,329	1,538,160	1,544,017	1,407,397	591,805
1982	36,002	39,416	1,146,975	1,226,778	1,187,466	517,726
1983	38,165	44,526	1,038,098	1,182,090	1,083,579	449,478
1984	52,092	47,322	1,102,613	1,174,078	1,119,914	460,695
1985	49,533	45,368	1,104,823	1,057,241	1,139,084	503,407
1986	39,486	40,254	1,144,213	1,073,981	1,126,528	479,213
1987	47,648	43,824	1,243,596	1,126,908	1,214,059	497,937
1988	57,515	50,571	1,416,928	1,406,020	1,306,891	518,179
1989	59,032	50,687	1,497,818	1,476,833	1,308,455	547,561
1990	56,408	49,668	1,587,742	1,576,633	1,309,245	536,732
1991	56,761	44,123	1,630,000	1,580,000	1,200,000	518,401
1992	55,593	47,377	1,760,000	1,710,000	1,280,000	554,608
1993	55,676	48,155	1,800,000	1,790,000	1,290,000	543,000
1994	58,454	49,400	1,850,000	1,840,000	1,330,000	500,000
1995	62,501	50,900	1,850,000	1,930,000	1,320,000	442,000
1996	62,083	49,400	1,920,000	2,010,000	1,320,000	428,000
1997	62,971	49,600	1,940,000	2,070,000	1,460,000	498,000
1998	62,931	48,200	1,860,000	2,140,000	1,420,000	466,000
1999	57,749	46,300	1,600,000	1,890,000	1,330,000	381,000
2000	63,089	47,900	1,440,000	1,590,000	1,310,000	363,000

[1] For 1810-1909, figures represent production; for 1910-1986, shipments; thereafter, production.

[2] Includes some refined copper imports.

Sources

Series Db73. 1860-1898 and 1907-1997: U.S. Bureau of Mines, *Mineral Resources of the United States* (annual); U.S. Bureau of Mines, *Minerals Yearbooks* (annual). 1899-1906: Harold Barger and Sam H. Schurr, *The Mining Industries, 1899-1939: A Study of Output, Employment and Productivity* (National Bureau of Economic Research, 1944), pp. 354-5.

Series Db74-78. 1810-1931: U.S. Bureau of Mines, *Mineral Resources of the United States* (annual). 1932-2000: U.S. Bureau of Mines, *Minerals Yearbooks* (annual).

TABLE Db73–78   Metal production – iron ore, pig iron, and copper: 1810–2000   *Continued*

Documentation

Series Db73. Coverage is restricted beginning in 1907 to ores containing less than 5 percent manganese. The Barger-Schurr series assures comparability back to 1899. For 1860 to 1898, the figures very probably include ores with a higher manganese content.

Series Db74. Pig iron shipments for 1854–1909 were collected by the American Iron and Steel Association. Those for 1810, 1840, and 1850 are census figures; those for other years are largely estimates by early statisticians.

Series Db75. Copper mine production for 1845–1905 is smelter production of copper from domestic ores. Beginning 1906, the figures refer to the estimated recoverable copper content of domestically mined ores. The statistical differences between the two data series are slight.

Series Db77. Represents secondary production from both new and old scrap.

TABLE Db79–86   Metal production – lead and zinc: 1801–2000

Contributed by Gavin Wright

	Lead				Zinc			
	Mine (recoverable content)	Primary, refined from domestic and foreign ores	Secondary		Mine (recoverable content)	Primary smelter slab from domestic and foreign ores	Secondary	
			Total	From old scrap			Total	From old scrap
	Db79	Db80 [1]	Db81	Db82	Db83	Db84	Db85	Db86
Year	Metric tons	Metric tons	Metric tons	Metric tons	Metric tons	Metric tons	Metric tons	Metric tons
1801	—	907	—	—	—	—	—	—
1802	—	907	—	—	—	—	—	—
1803	—	907	—	—	—	—	—	—
1804	—	907	—	—	—	—	—	—
1805	—	907	—	—	—	—	—	—
1806	—	907	—	—	—	—	—	—
1807	—	907	—	—	—	—	—	—
1808	—	907	—	—	—	—	—	—
1809	—	907	—	—	—	—	—	—
1810	—	907	—	—	—	—	—	—
1811	—	1,361	—	—	—	—	—	—
1812	—	1,361	—	—	—	—	—	—
1813	—	1,361	—	—	—	—	—	—
1814	—	1,361	—	—	—	—	—	—
1815	—	1,361	—	—	—	—	—	—
1816	—	1,361	—	—	—	—	—	—
1817	—	1,361	—	—	—	—	—	—
1818	—	1,361	—	—	—	—	—	—
1819	—	1,361	—	—	—	—	—	—
1820	—	1,361	—	—	—	—	—	—
1821	—	1,724	—	—	—	—	—	—
1822	—	1,724	—	—	—	—	—	—
1823	—	1,876	—	—	—	—	—	—
1824	—	1,803	—	—	—	—	—	—
1825	—	2,025	—	—	—	—	—	—
1826	—	2,158	—	—	—	—	—	—
1827	—	4,073	—	—	—	—	—	—
1828	—	6,760	—	—	—	—	—	—
1829	—	7,775	—	—	—	—	—	—
1830	7,260	7,257	—	—	—	—	—	—
1831	6,800	6,804	—	—	—	—	—	—
1832	9,070	9,072	—	—	—	—	—	—
1833	9,980	9,979	—	—	—	—	—	—
1834	10,880	10,886	—	—	—	—	—	—
1835	11,800	11,793	—	—	—	—	—	—
1836	13,600	13,608	—	—	—	—	—	—
1837	12,250	12,247	—	—	—	—	—	—
1838	13,600	13,608	—	—	—	—	—	—
1839	15,880	15,876	—	—	—	—	—	—
1840	15,420	15,422	—	—	—	—	—	—
1841	18,600	18,597	—	—	—	—	—	—
1842	21,770	21,772	—	—	—	—	—	—
1843	22,680	22,680	—	—	—	—	—	—
1844	23,590	23,587	—	—	—	—	—	—

Notes appear at end of table   *(continued)*

TABLE Db79–86   Metal production – lead and zinc: 1801–2000   *Continued*

	Lead				Zinc			
	Mine (recoverable content)	Primary, refined from domestic and foreign ores	Secondary		Mine (recoverable content)	Primary smelter slab from domestic and foreign ores	Secondary	
			Total	From old scrap			Total	From old scrap
	Db79	Db80 [1]	Db81	Db82	Db83	Db84	Db85	Db86
Year	Metric tons	Metric tons	Metric tons	Metric tons	Metric tons	Metric tons	Metric tons	Metric tons
1845	27,220	27,216	—	—	—	—	—	—
1846	22,680	25,401	—	—	—	—	—	—
1847	25,400	25,401	—	—	—	—	—	—
1848	22,680	22,680	—	—	—	—	—	—
1849	21,320	21,319	—	—	—	—	—	—
1850	19,960	19,958	—	—	—	—	—	—
1851	16,780	16,783	—	—	—	—	—	—
1852	14,240	14,243	—	—	—	—	—	—
1853	15,240	15,241	—	—	—	—	—	—
1854	14,970	14,969	—	—	—	—	—	—
1855	14,330	14,334	—	—	—	—	—	—
1856	14,520	14,515	—	—	—	—	—	—
1857	14,330	14,334	—	—	—	—	—	—
1858	13,880	13,880	—	—	—	18	—	—
1859	14,880	14,878	—	—	—	45	—	—
1860	14,150	14,152	—	—	—	726	—	—
1861	12,790	12,791	—	—	—	1,361	—	—
1862	12,880	12,882	—	—	—	1,361	—	—
1863	13,420	13,426	—	—	—	1,542	—	—
1864	13,880	13,880	—	—	—	1,633	—	—
1865	13,330	13,336	—	—	—	1,905	—	—
1866	14,600	14,606	—	—	—	1,814	—	—
1867	13,790	13,789	—	—	—	2,903	—	—
1868	14,880	14,878	—	—	—	3,357	—	—
1869	15,880	15,876	—	—	—	3,901	—	—
1870	16,175	16,175	—	—	—	4,899	—	—
1871	18,145	18,116	—	—	—	6,260	—	—
1872	23,480	23,333	—	—	—	7,076	—	—
1873	38,590	38,047	—	—	—	8,709	—	—
1874	47,245	46,475	—	—	—	11,884	—	—
1875	54,105	53,152	—	—	—	15,150	—	—
1876	58,125	57,098	—	—	—	15,422	—	—
1877	74,300	72,920	—	—	—	14,152	—	—
1878	82,610	80,857	—	—	—	17,781	—	—
1879	84,170	82,409	—	—	—	19,323	—	—
1880	88,745	86,840	—	—	—	22,770	—	—
1881	106,218	103,868	—	—	—	27,450	—	—
1882	120,556	117,734	—	—	—	30,631	—	—
1883	130,596	127,275	—	—	—	33,450	—	—
1884	126,912	123,647	—	—	—	34,967	—	—
1885	117,401	114,479	—	—	—	36,912	—	—
1886	123,041	119,920	—	—	—	38,683	—	—
1887	132,177	142,092	—	—	—	45,668	—	—
1888	137,819	141,534	—	—	—	50,714	—	—
1889	141,881	161,803	—	—	—	53,397	—	—
1890	130,299	143,194	—	—	—	57,772	—	—
1891	161,982	179,952	—	—	—	73,367	—	—
1892	157,220	188,897	—	—	—	79,161	—	—
1893	158,762	203,500	—	—	—	71,515	—	—
1894	147,586	193,820	—	—	—	68,336	—	—
1895	154,220	213,934	—	—	—	81,362	—	—
1896	170,550	233,588	—	—	—	73,935	—	—
1897	192,320	255,979	—	—	—	90,700	—	—
1898	201,400	274,104	—	—	—	104,688	—	—
1899	190,960	270,384	—	—	—	117,073	—	—
1900	245,687	333,638	—	—	—	112,387	—	—
1901	245,575	336,595	—	—	—	127,752	—	—
1902	244,940	333,746	—	—	—	142,362	—	—
1903	255,825	334,696	—	—	—	144,441	—	—
1904	278,500	356,934	—	—	—	169,373	—	—

Notes appear at end of table

TABLE Db79–86   Metal production – lead and zinc: 1801–2000   *Continued*

	Lead				Zinc			
	Mine (recoverable content)	Primary, refined from domestic and foreign ores	Secondary		Mine (recoverable content)	Primary smelter slab from domestic and foreign ores	Secondary	
			Total	From old scrap			Total	From old scrap
	Db79	Db80 [1]	Db81	Db82	Db83	Db84	Db85	Db86
Year	Metric tons	Metric tons	Metric tons	Metric tons	Metric tons	Metric tons	Metric tons	Metric tons
1905	273,970	352,266	—	—	—	184,929	—	—
1906	317,654	367,180	—	—	—	203,908	—	—
1907	340,206	375,020	23,131	—	229,533	226,669	23,162	—
1908	305,191	359,757	16,813	—	212,339	190,893	21,070	—
1909	361,092	405,429	37,818	—	274,308	232,022	43,755	—
1910	358,622	426,624	50,278	—	294,331	244,200	62,594	—
1911	400,214	441,780	49,246	—	300,746	259,932	67,809	—
1912	414,915	436,260	60,934	—	349,830	307,360	85,376	—
1913	453,763	419,537	66,074	—	375,415	314,499	81,218	—
1914	474,360	491,805	55,395	—	377,184	320,281	76,748	—
1915	509,512	499,002	71,577	—	533,479	444,084	98,702	—
1916	565,154	518,124	87,362	—	637,905	606,310	117,208	—
1917	590,531	554,080	84,822	—	647,328	607,426	119,748	—
1918	527,668	580,775	88,088	—	577,052	469,855	124,284	—
1919	402,513	437,463	110,767	—	497,905	422,515	118,206	—
1920	450,702	480,497	113,081	—	532,993	420,368	127,913	—
1921	376,020	406,953	94,148	—	232,820	181,891	84,368	—
1922	433,301	483,223	144,750	—	428,220	321,395	146,057	—
1923	496,427	560,932	176,438	—	554,009	463,058	148,778	—
1924	540,744	626,405	185,519	—	578,763	469,322	142,428	—
1925	620,913	695,783	205,822	—	644,870	519,768	141,521	—
1926	620,439	724,787	251,562	—	702,672	561,023	152,407	—
1927	603,722	722,600	250,383	—	651,850	537,521	152,679	—
1928	568,944	708,576	279,957	—	630,648	546,652	164,835	—
1929	587,851	702,735	282,135	—	657,236	567,396	159,846	—
1930	506,493	583,350	232,058	—	540,161	451,819	115,575	—
1931	367,067	401,669	212,916	—	372,234	264,894	92,533	—
1932	265,776	255,773	179,895	—	258,757	187,921	64,047	—
1933	247,368 [2]	239,203	203,663	—	348,613	278,671	108,862	—
1934	260,670 [2]	282,349	189,057	—	398,006	329,843	86,183	—
1935	300,372	294,436	245,303	—	469,834	381,593	117,027	—
1936	338,307	362,108	238,499	—	522,152	446,455	146,057	—
1937	421,743	423,943	249,567	—	568,226	505,215	150,593	—
1938	335,410	348,059	204,025	—	468,745	404,914	107,955	—
1939	375,556	439,109	219,085	191,235	529,621	460,157	172,038	40,914
1940	414,939	483,692	236,182	205,553	603,340	612,599	201,407	58,245
1941	418,599	517,973	360,530	344,984	679,595	745,724	257,610	73,622
1942	450,181	514,228	293,022	279,946	696,741	809,093	299,848	66,213
1943	411,239	426,025	310,343	281,865	675,124	854,848	334,287	76,408
1944	378,170	421,626	300,656	263,023	651,941	788,617	313,404	102,658
1945	354,556	402,414	329,344	281,090	557,337	693,598	326,989	82,795
1946	304,338	306,807	356,330	312,610	521,480	660,668	272,774	70,056
1947	348,560	400,078	464,452	403,314	578,429	728,011	281,947	68,020
1948	354,234	368,947	453,657	392,569	571,506	714,647	294,507	67,304
1949	371,862	433,034	373,926	330,342	538,145	739,158	215,740	46,857
1950	390,840	461,135	437,513	387,840	565,517	765,180	295,769	67,220
1951	352,137	378,925	470,022	400,666	617,965	799,804	285,198	61,846
1952	353,949	428,964	427,551	373,607	604,186	820,529	281,611	67,735
1953	310,841	424,464	441,561	388,956	496,620	831,076	267,327	58,273
1954	295,215	441,538	436,288	385,542	429,526	727,948	246,549	65,913
1955	306,651	434,684	455,453	407,495	466,902	874,076	276,487	75,794
1956	320,078	491,974	459,721	404,165	492,003	892,316	255,241	66,901
1957	306,824	484,013	443,821	391,798	482,382	894,299	239,591	69,662
1958	242,560	426,518	364,495	311,408	373,765	708,734 [3]	208,954	63,436
1959	231,864	309,287	409,492	356,308	385,829	724,537 [3]	250,613	66,994
1960	223,774	346,940	426,289	370,492	395,013	725,309 [3]	241,148	62,023
1961	237,611	407,839	410,766	354,290	421,288	768,199 [3]	215,880	53,893
1962	214,963	341,159	402,973	356,781	458,574	797,774 [3]	237,698	56,021
1963	229,853	358,095	447,669	387,539	480,131	809,739	243,357	56,757
1964	259,464	407,715	491,315	426,069	521,503	865,531	270,698	61,747

Notes appear at end of table

(continued)

TABLE Db79–86   Metal production – lead and zinc: 1801–2000   *Continued*

	Lead				Zinc			
	Mine (recoverable content)	Primary, refined from domestic and foreign ores	Secondary		Mine (recoverable content)	Primary smelter slab from domestic and foreign ores	Secondary	
			Total	From old scrap			Total	From old scrap
	Db79	Db80 [1]	Db81	Db82	Db83	Db84	Db85	Db86
Year	Metric tons	Metric tons	Metric tons	Metric tons	Metric tons	Metric tons	Metric tons	Metric tons
1965	273,196	379,429	522,374	449,722	554,429	902,107	320,566	74,397
1966	296,983	399,828	519,666	440,283	519,416	929,924	326,778	78,276
1967	287,515	344,634	502,374	432,605	498,419	851,692	290,162	72,855
1968	325,821	423,937	499,749	427,526	480,305	926,137	321,799	72,391
1969	461,769	579,378	547,854	468,050	501,786	944,014	341,456	74,051
1970	518,698	604,847	541,943	459,204	484,560	796,337	308,014	65,456
1971	524,852	589,684	541,405	444,322	455,899	695,297	325,818	72,614
1972	561,470	617,248	559,368	451,517	433,924	574,411	351,771	72,010
1973	547,054	611,911	593,558	488,601	434,408	529,323	347,688	80,792
1974	602,253	610,557	633,848	545,168	453,477	503,658	307,066	68,410
1975	563,783	577,080	597,341	511,872	425,792	397,394	256,916	69,616
1976	552,971	592,280	659,132	564,481	439,543	452,554	338,281	86,538
1977	537,499	548,700	757,592	637,234	407,889	408,364	329,978	82,460
1978	529,661	565,173	769,236	649,500	302,669	406,698	338,821	76,788
1979	525,569	575,611	801,368	672,743	267,341	472,481	370,030	81,235
1980	550,366	547,590	675,578	581,387	317,103	340,456	304,363	65,532
1981	445,535	495,323	641,105	578,031	312,418	346,563	340,850	85,511
1982	512,516	512,160	571,276	521,272	303,160	228,176	284,969	62,314
1983	449,295	519,167	503,501	451,978	275,294	235,694	348,627	76,253
1984	322,677	389,398	633,374	585,749	252,768	253,132	398,569	80,764
1985	413,955	494,003	615,695	569,732	226,545	261,209	347,023	69,248
1986	339,793	370,288	624,769	575,271	202,983	253,369	341,971	71,055
1987	311,381	373,610	710,067	657,532	216,327	261,345	351,908	81,510
1988	384,983	392,087	736,401	691,127	244,314	241,294	336,953	97,327
1989	410,915	396,455	891,341	841,729	275,883	260,305	347,026	117,138
1990	483,704	403,657	922,197	874,093	515,355	262,200	341,400	108,945
1991	465,931	345,714	884,624	829,654	518,000	253,600	353,000	119,000
1992	397,076	304,791	916,341	860,917	523,000	271,800	366,000	132,000
1993	355,185	335,014	893,000	838,000	488,000	240,000	355,000	109,000
1994	363,000	351,400	931,000	877,000	570,000	216,600	361,000	116,000
1995	386,000	374,000	1,020,000	963,000	614,000	232,000	353,000	112,000
1996	426,000	326,000	1,070,000	1,060,000	586,000	225,000	377,000	113,000
1997	448,000	343,000	1,110,000	1,040,000	592,000	227,000	368,000	89,000
1998	481,000	337,000	1,120,000	1,060,000	709,000	234,000	434,000	89,900
1999	503,000	350,000	1,110,000	1,060,000	771,000	241,000	399,000	78,100
2000	457,000	341,000	1,130,000	1,080,000	786,000	228,000	436,000	66,900

[1] Through 1820, estimated based on 5-year averages.

[2] Excludes output of Virginia (Bureau of Mines was not at liberty to publish).

[3] Includes production of zinc in concentration used directly in alloying operations.

Sources

Series Db79. 1830–1990: U.S. Geological Survey, *Statistical Compendium* (U.S. Geological Survey, annual). 1991–1996: U.S. Bureau of Mines, *Minerals Yearbooks* (annual). 1997–2000: U.S. Geological Survey, *Minerals Yearbooks* (U.S. Department of Mines, annual).

Series Db80. 1801–1927: L. A. Smith, "Summarized Data of Lead Production," U.S. Bureau of Mines, Economic Paper number 5 (1929), pp. 12–14. 1928–1931: U.S. Bureau of Mines, *Mineral Resources of the United States* (annual). 1932–1996: U.S. Bureau of Mines, *Minerals Yearbooks*. 1997–2000: U.S. Geological Survey, *Minerals Yearbooks*.

Series Db81–82. 1907–1931: U.S. Bureau of Mines, *Mineral Resources of the United States* (annual). 1932–1996: U.S. Bureau of Mines, *Minerals Yearbooks*. 1997–2000: U.S. Geological Survey, *Minerals Yearbooks*.

Series Db83 and Db85–86. 1907–1931: U.S. Bureau of Mines, *Mineral Resources of the United States*. 1932–1996: U.S. Bureau of Mines, *Minerals Yearbooks*. 1997–2000: U.S. Geological Survey, *Minerals Yearbooks*.

Series Db84. 1858–1881: E. W. Pehrson, "Summarized Data of Zinc Production," U.S. Bureau of Mines, Economic Paper number 2 (1929), p. 19. 1882–1931: U.S. Bureau of Mines, *Mineral Resources of the United States*. 1932–

1996: U.S. Bureau of Mines, *Minerals Yearbooks*. 1997–2000: U.S. Geological Survey, *Minerals Yearbooks*.

Documentation

Series Db79–80. Figures in series Db79 for 1830–1906 represent lead recovered from domestic ores; for 1907–1995, they represent recoverable mine production. Series Db80 differs from series Db79 by the amount of ore imported into this country for domestic refining (covered in series Db80) and by the amount of lead ore and concentrates consumed outside the refineries for such products as antimonial lead and lead pigments and salts (covered in series Db79). Other smaller differences between the two reflect time lags and differences in stock changes at the two stages of production.

Series Db81. Data represent secondary production from both new and old scrap.

Series Db83–84. Series Db83 represents the estimated recoverable zinc content of domestic mine output; series Db84, the total primary smelter output (including electrolytic plants) from both domestic and foreign ores and base bullion. The two differ by the amounts of ore and unsmelted zinc imported into this country for domestic smelting (covered in series Db84) and by consumption of zinc ore and concentrates outside the smelter directly in the production of zinc dust and zinc pigments and salts (covered in series Db85). Other smaller differences between the two series reflect time lags and differences in stock changes at the two stages of production.

TABLE Db87–95   Metal production – bauxite, aluminum, magnesium, gold, and silver: 1834–2000

Contributed by Gavin Wright

Year	Bauxite	Aluminum Primary	Aluminum Secondary Total	Aluminum Secondary From old scrap	Magnesium Primary	Magnesium Secondary Total	Magnesium Secondary From old scrap	Gold	Silver
	Db87	Db88	Db89	Db90	Db91	Db92	Db93	Db94	Db95
	Thousand metric tons	Thousand metric tons	Thousand metric tons	Thousand short tons	Thousand metric tons	Thousand metric tons	Thousand metric tons	Kilograms	Metric tons
1834	—	—	—	—	—	—	—	—	(Z)
1835	—	—	—	—	—	—	—	1,213	1
1836	—	—	—	—	—	—	—	809	1
1837	—	—	—	—	—	—	—	498	1
1838	—	—	—	—	—	—	—	746	1
1839	—	—	—	—	—	—	—	715	1
1840	—	—	—	—	—	—	—	746	1
1841	—	—	—	—	—	—	—	933	1
1842	—	—	—	—	—	—	—	1,337	1
1843	—	—	—	—	—	—	—	1,804	1
1844	—	—	—	—	—	—	—	1,711	1
1845	—	—	—	—	—	—	—	1,524	1
1846	—	—	—	—	—	—	—	1,711	1
1847	—	—	—	—	—	—	—	1,337	1
1848	—	—	—	—	—	—	—	10,182	1
1849	—	—	—	—	—	—	—	20,856	1
1850	—	—	—	—	—	—	—	83,503	1
1851	—	—	—	—	—	—	—	102,800	1
1852	—	—	—	—	—	—	—	104,758	1
1853	—	—	—	—	—	—	—	102,989	1
1854	—	—	—	—	—	—	—	91,531	1
1855	—	—	—	—	—	—	—	79,025	1
1856	—	—	—	—	—	—	—	88,477	1
1857	—	—	—	—	—	—	—	85,583	1
1858	—	—	—	—	—	—	—	82,433	1
1859	—	—	—	—	—	—	—	83,236	2
1860	—	—	—	—	—	—	—	75,874	4
1861	—	—	—	—	—	—	—	69,984	51
1862	—	—	—	—	—	—	—	69,207	124
1863	—	—	—	—	—	—	—	73,437	243
1864	—	—	—	—	—	—	—	76,734	326
1865	—	—	—	—	—	—	—	83,359	319
1866	—	—	—	—	—	—	—	86,967	307
1867	—	—	—	—	—	—	—	81,400	351
1868	—	—	—	—	—	—	—	74,495	328
1869	—	—	—	—	—	—	—	72,535	324
1870	—	—	—	—	—	—	—	73,748	393
1871	—	—	—	—	—	—	—	64,697	554
1872	—	—	—	—	—	—	—	59,285	663
1873	—	—	—	—	—	—	—	57,792	892
1874	—	—	—	—	—	—	—	62,302	939
1875	—	—	—	—	—	—	—	63,515	981
1876	—	—	—	—	—	—	—	69,984	1,110
1877	—	—	—	—	—	—	—	73,437	1,089
1878	—	—	—	—	—	—	—	73,437	1,158
1879	—	—	—	—	—	—	—	56,734	1,058
1880	—	—	—	—	—	—	—	54,774	1,060
1881	—	—	—	—	—	—	—	51,322	1,181
1882	—	—	—	—	—	—	—	47,838	1,244
1883	—	—	—	—	—	—	—	44,697	1,202
1884	—	—	—	—	—	—	—	44,386	1,308
1885	—	—	—	—	—	—	—	45,443	1,373
1886	—	(Z)	—	—	—	—	—	52,379	1,229
1887	—	(Z)	—	—	—	—	—	53,281	1,291
1888	—	(Z)	—	—	—	—	—	58,383	1,423
1889	1	(Z)	—	—	—	—	—	55,988	1,555

Notes appear at end of table

(continued)

TABLE Db87–95   Metal production – bauxite, aluminum, magnesium, gold, and silver: 1834–2000   *Continued*

Year	Bauxite	Aluminum Primary	Aluminum Secondary Total	Aluminum Secondary From old scrap	Magnesium Primary	Magnesium Secondary Total	Magnesium Secondary From old scrap	Gold	Silver
	Db87	Db88	Db89	Db90	Db91	Db92	Db93	Db94	Db95
	Thousand metric tons	Thousand metric tons	Thousand metric tons	Thousand short tons	Thousand metric tons	Thousand metric tons	Thousand metric tons	Kilograms	Metric tons
1890	2	(Z)	—	—	—	—	—	52,815	1,701
1891	4	(Z)	—	—	—	—	—	49,953	1,813
1892	11	(Z)	—	—	—	—	—	49,642	1,974
1893	9	(Z)	—	—	—	—	—	54,184	1,861
1894	11	(Z)	—	—	—	—	—	59,940	1,550
1895	17	(Z)	—	—	—	—	—	70,109	1,734
1896	18	1	—	—	—	—	—	79,907	1,841
1897	21	1	—	—	—	—	—	86,376	1,680
1898	25	1	—	—	—	—	—	97,045	1,714
1899	34	2	—	—	—	—	—	119,191	1,718
1900	23	3	—	—	—	—	—	119,113	1,811
1901	20	3	—	—	—	—	—	118,367	1,717
1902	27	3	—	—	—	—	—	120,357	1,726
1903	46	3	—	—	—	—	—	110,716	1,689
1904	52	4	—	—	—	—	—	121,632	1,742
1905	58	5	—	—	—	—	—	132,642	1,750
1906	72	6	—	—	—	—	—	146,263	1,784
1907	96	7	—	—	—	—	—	131,460	1,633
1908	51	5	—	—	—	—	—	137,929	1,582
1909	134	14	—	—	—	—	—	149,218	1,782
1910	153	16	—	—	—	—	—	142,594	1,791
1911	160	17	—	—	—	—	—	145,735	1,900
1912	164	19	—	—	—	—	—	138,893	2,054
1913	214	22	5	—	—	—	—	134,072	2,214
1914	223	26	5	—	—	—	—	137,400	2,165
1915	305	41	7	—	(Z)	—	—	147,849	2,250
1916	432	53	17	—	(Z)	—	—	137,369	2,452
1917	578	59	15	—	(Z)	—	—	121,290	2,198
1918	616	56	14	—	(Z)	—	—	99,924	2,117
1919	383	58	17	—	(Z)	—	—	85,618	1,614
1920	529	63	15	—	(Z)	—	—	74,111	1,758
1921	142	24	8	—	(Z)	—	—	72,930	1,436
1922	315	34	15	—	(Z)	—	—	71,312	1,904
1923	531	58	19	—	(Z)	—	—	74,796	2,188
1924	354	68	24	—	(Z)	—	—	76,008	1,993
1925	322	64	40	—	(Z)	—	—	71,748	2,075
1926	398	67	40	—	(Z)	—	—	69,446	1,943
1927	326	74	42	—	(Z)	—	—	65,528	1,854
1928	381	95	44	—	(Z)	—	—	66,803	1,800
1929	372	103	44	—	(Z)	—	—	64,035	1,893
1930	336	104	35	—	(Z)	—	—	66,523	1,484
1931	199	81	27	—	(Z)	—	—	69,198	929
1932	98	47	22	—	(Z)	—	—	70,566	708
1933	156	39	31	—	1	—	—	71,281	719
1934	172	34	42	—	2	—	—	86,427	1,020
1935	249	54	46	—	2	—	—	100,671	1,509
1936	386	102	47	—	2	—	—	117,651	1,902
1937	432	132	57	—	2	—	—	128,039	2,221
1938	316	130	35	—	2	—	—	132,704	1,919
1939	381	149	49	38	3	—	—	145,330	2,002
1940	446	187	73	46	5	—	—	151,457	2,191
1941	952	280	97	43	15	2	(Z)	147,756	2,085
1942	2,644	473	178	42	44	5	(Z)	107,513	1,682
1943	6,333	835	285	33	167	10	(Z)	42,420	1,289
1944	2,869	704	296	23	142	13	(Z)	31,038	1,072
1945	997	449	270	27	30	8	1	29,701	903
1946	1,122	372	252	91	5	5	1	48,983	713
1947	1,221	519	313	164	11	9	5	65,590	1,114
1948	1,480	565	260	96	9	7	4	62,635	1,185
1949	1,167	547	164	45	11	5	3	61,951	1,078

Notes appear at end of table

TABLE Db87–95   Metal production – bauxite, aluminum, magnesium, gold, and silver: 1834–2000   *Continued*

	Bauxite	Aluminum Primary	Aluminum Secondary Total	Aluminum Secondary From old scrap	Magnesium Primary	Magnesium Secondary Total	Magnesium Secondary From old scrap	Gold	Silver
	Db87	Db88	Db89	Db90	Db91	Db92	Db93	Db94	Db95
Year	Thousand metric tons	Thousand metric tons	Thousand metric tons	Thousand short tons	Thousand metric tons	Thousand metric tons	Thousand metric tons	Kilograms	Metric tons
1950	1,356	652	221	76	15	8	5	74,453	1,320
1951	1,879	759	266	77	37	11	5	61,609	1,237
1952	1,694	850	277	71	96	10	6	58,872	1,227
1953	1,605	1,136	335	79	84	11	5	60,894	1,168
1954	2,027	1,325	265	60	64	7	3	57,131	1,149
1955	1,817	1,421	305	76	55	9	5	55,980	1,157
1956	1,772	1,523	308	72	62	10	5	56,820	1,204
1957	1,439	1,495	328	72	73	10	5	55,793	1,187
1958	1,332	1,421	263	64	27	8	5	54,083	1,061
1959	1,727	1,773	327	78	28	9	5	49,853	970
1960	2,030	1,827	298	63	36	9	4	51,844	957
1961	1,248	1,727	308	102	37	7	5	48,143	1,082
1962	1,391	1,921	419	129	63	9	3	47,987	1,144
1963	1,549	2,098	459	116	69	8	2	45,219	1,096
1964	1,627	2,316	501	124	72	11	4	45,282	1,130
1965	1,681	2,498	581	160	73	13	4	53,026	1,238
1966	1,825	2,692	629	137	73	14	5	56,073	1,514
1967	1,681	2,966	633	129	88	12	4	49,262	1,006
1968	1,692	2,953	741	155	89	15	3	45,966	1,018
1969	1,873	3,441	817	148	91	12	3	53,896	1,303
1970	2,115	3,607	907	179	102	11	3	54,207	1,400
1971	2,020	3,561	953	196	112	13	3	46,495	1,293
1972	1,841	3,739	1,022	227	110	14	3	47,272	1,158
1973	1,909	4,109	1,126	240	111	16	4	36,574	1,166
1974	1,980	4,448	1,163	276	— [1]	13	5	35,050	1,050
1975	1,800	3,519	1,121	305	109	25	9	32,717	1,087
1976	1,989	3,856	1,334	371	109	28	10	32,593	1,068
1977	2,013	4,118	1,456	482	114	30	11	34,210	1,187
1978	1,669	4,358	1,518	522	136	33	13	31,069	1,225
1979	1,821	4,557	1,612	557	147	34	13	29,980	1,179
1980	1,559	4,654	1,577	617	154	37	16	30,164	1,005
1981	1,510	4,489	1,789	758	140	42	22	42,897	1,265
1982	732	3,274	1,666	782	93	39	21	45,588	1,252
1983	679	3,353	1,773	820	105	42	22	62,286	1,351
1984	856	4,099	1,760	825	144	44	24	64,839	1,387
1985	674	3,500	1,762	850	136	41	24	75,495	1,227
1986	510	3,037	1,773	784	126	42	23	116,297	1,074
1987	576	3,343	1,986	852	124	45	23	153,870	1,241
1988	588	3,944	2,122	1,045	142	50	28	200,914	1,661
1989	— [1]	4,030	2,054	1,011	152	51	28	265,731	2,008
1990	— [1]	4,048	2,393	1,359	139	55	31	294,189	2,121
1991	— [1]	4,121	2,290	1,320	131	51	27	294,062	1,855
1992	— [1]	4,042	2,760	1,610	137	57	31	330,212	1,804
1993	— [1]	3,695	2,940	1,630	132	59	31	331,013	1,645
1994	— [1]	3,299	3,090	1,500	128	62	30	327,000	1,490
1995	— [1]	3,375	3,190	1,510	142	65	30	317,000	1,560
1996	— [1]	3,577	3,310	1,580	133	71	30	326,000	1,570
1997	— [1]	3,603	3,550	1,530	125	78	31	362,000	2,180
1998	— [1]	3,713	3,440	1,500	106	77	32	366,000	2,060
1999	— [1]	3,779	3,690	1,570	— [1]	87	34	341,000	1,950
2000	— [1]	3,668	3,450	1,370	— [1]	82	30	330,000	1,860

(Z) Series Db88, Db91, and Db93, fewer than 500 tons. Series Db95, fewer than 0.5 tons.

[1] Withheld to avoid disclosing individual company data.

Sources

Series Db87–93. 1886–1931: U.S. Bureau of Mines, *Mineral Resources of the United States* (annual). 1932–1996: U.S. Bureau of Mines, *Minerals Yearbooks* (annual). 1997–2000: U.S. Geological Survey, *Minerals Yearbooks* (U.S. Department of the Interior, annual).

Series Db94. 1835–1844: R. H. Ridgway, "Summarized Data of Gold Production," U.S. Bureau of Mines, Economic Paper number 6 (1929), p. 14. 1845–1847, and 1901–1903: U.S. Bureau of the Mint, *Annual Report of the Director of the Mint, 1910*, p. 99. 1848–1900: Thomas Senior Berry, *Early California: Gold, Prices, Trade* (Bostwick Press, 1984), pp. 74, 76, 78. 1904–1938: U.S. Bureau of Mines, unpublished data. 1939–1996: U.S. Bureau of Mines, *Minerals Yearbooks*. 1997–2000: U.S. Geological Survey, *Minerals Yearbooks*.

(continued)

TABLE Db87-95   Metal production – bauxite, aluminum, magnesium, gold, and silver: 1834–2000   *Continued*

Series Db95. 1835–1844: C. W. Merrill, "Summarized Data for Silver Production," U.S. Bureau of Mines, Economic Paper number 8, 1930, p. 18. 1845–1860 and 1901–1904: U.S. Bureau of the Mint, *Annual Report of the Director of the Mint, 1910*, p. 99. 1861–1900: Berry (1984), p. 78. 1904–1938: U.S. Bureau of Mines, unpublished data. 1939–1996: U.S. Bureau of Mines, *Minerals Yearbooks*. 1997–2000: U.S. Geological Survey, *Minerals Yearbooks*.

Documentation

Series Db87. For 1889 to 1934, data refer to bauxite "as shipped"; beginning 1935, they are in terms of "dried bauxite equivalent." Because of widely differing moisture content of the different forms (crude, dried, and calcined), dried bauxite equivalent yields a more comparable measure of quantity.

Series Db89. Represents recoverable content from both old and new aluminum scrap processed. Beginning 1954, these figures represent recoverable aluminum content and are not strictly comparable with those for previous years, which are for recoverable aluminum–alloy content.

Series Db91. Represents magnesium production beginning 1939; for 1915 to 1938, data are for new ingot sold or used.

Series Db92–93. Secondary magnesium production is expressed in terms of ingot equivalent and represents the recoverable magnesium and magnesium-alloy content of scrap processed.

Series Db94. The 1910 Mint Director's report also presented estimates of aggregate production for the years 1792 to 1834 (677,000 fine ounces, or 21,055 kilograms), and 1835–1844 (363,000 fine ounces, or 11,289 kilograms). The latter figure is not entirely consistent with the sum of the annual series for these years. Figures prior to 1904 originate from information on coinage at U.S. mints. Pre-1848 estimates are highly suspect, owing to the absence of official per annum deposit information by state of origin for the branch mints during this period. (See David A. Martin, "U.S. Gold Production Prior to the California Gold Rush," *Explorations in Economic History* 13

(1976): 437–49. Martin writes: "The information required to generate direct annual output figures does not exist and cannot be deduced from the extant records.") Berry's estimates are a thorough revision of available evidence from California during the Gold Rush period, 1848 to 1860. For 1861 to 1900, Berry's figures represent a reconciliation of various earlier estimates; his series is presented in millions of kilograms at the constant official price of $20.67 per fine ounce. Data include both lode and placer production. Beginning 1904, the figures represent production measured at the mining stage.

Series Db95. The 1910 Mint Director's report also reported aggregate silver production for the years 1835 to 1844 at 193,000 fine ounces, or about 6 metric tons. Production for 1840 to 1849 was crudely estimated at 19,000 fine ounces per year and for 1850 to 1858, at 39,000 per year. Both are represented here by the rounded estimate of one metric ton. Berry's figures reconcile various earlier estimates; his series is presented in millions of dollars, converted here to metric tons using average prices in the New York market. Berry writes:

> The silver data . . . may reflect an upward bias between 1861 and 1870, at least, and the gold data . . . may show a corresponding downward bias. This is due to the fact that Wells Fargo always reported Nevada shipments as "silver bullion"; and various observers assumed this to be all silver. George F. Becker, a noted geologist, remarked that the Nevada output up to 1880 was 43 percent gold and 57 percent silver over a period of 21 years; and this was confirmed by a survey of 12 mines showing gold percentages varying between 32 and 50 percent and averaging 45 percent.

The citation is to Becker, *Geology of the Comstock Lode and the Washoe District* (U.S. Government Printing Office, 1882), pp. 6–9.

TABLE Db96-103   Metal production – manganese, chromite, tungsten, molybdenum, vanadium, and nickel: 1880–2000

Contributed by Gavin Wright

							Nickel	
	Manganese ore	Chromite	Tungsten concentrates	Molybdenum ores and concentrates	Vanadium ores and concentrates	Primary	Secondary (nonferrous)	Secondary (ferrous)
	Db96 [1]	Db97	Db98	Db99	Db100	Db101	Db102	Db103
Year	Short tons	Short tons	Metric tons	Metric tons	Metric tons	Metric tons	Metric tons	Metric tons
1880	6,452	2,563	—	—	—	—	—	—
1881	5,482	2,240	—	—	—	—	—	—
1882	5,076	2,800	—	—	—	—	—	—
1883	6,894	3,360	—	—	—	—	—	—
1884	11,402	2,240	—	—	—	—	—	—
1885	26,049	3,024	—	—	—	—	—	—
1886	33,816	2,240	—	—	—	—	—	—
1887	38,667	3,360	—	—	—	—	—	—
1888	32,702	1,680	—	—	—	—	—	—
1889	27,101	2,240	—	—	—	—	—	—
1890	21,602	4,031	—	—	—	—	—	—
1891	25,146	1,537	—	—	—	—	—	—
1892	15,246	1,680	—	—	—	—	—	—
1893	8,644	1,624	—	—	—	—	—	—
1894	7,065	4,122	—	—	—	—	—	—
1895	10,693	1,949	—	—	—	—	—	—
1896	11,299	880	—	—	—	—	—	—
1897	12,441	—	—	—	—	—	—	—
1898	17,872	—	—	—	—	—	—	—
1899	11,127	—	—	—	—	—	—	—

Notes appear at end of table

TABLE Db96–103   Metal production – manganese, chromite, tungsten, molybdenum, vanadium, and nickel: 1880–2000   _Continued_

Year	Manganese ore	Chromite	Tungsten concentrates	Molybdenum ores and concentrates	Vanadium ores and concentrates	Nickel Primary	Nickel Secondary (nonferrous)	Nickel Secondary (ferrous)
	Db96 [1]	Db97	Db98	Db99	Db100	Db101	Db102	Db103
	Short tons	Short tons	Metric tons	Metric tons	Metric tons	Metric tons	Metric tons	Metric tons
1900	13,184	157	20	—	—	—	—	—
1901	13,434	412	77	—	—	—	—	—
1902	8,375	353	80	—	—	—	—	—
1903	3,164	168	126	—	—	—	—	—
1904	3,523	138	319	—	—	—	—	—
1905	4,612	25	347	—	—	—	—	—
1906	7,751	120	401	—	—	—	—	—
1907	6,276	325	708	—	—	—	—	—
1908	6,881	402	289	—	—	—	—	—
1909	1,729	670	699	—	—	—	—	—
1910	2,529	230	786	—	—	—	—	—
1911	2,752	134	492	—	275	—	—	—
1912	1,863	225	574	—	300	—	—	—
1913	4,534	286	664	—	432	—	—	—
1914	2,951	662	427	1	452	—	—	—
1915	10,705	3,675	1,041	83	627	—	—	—
1916	35,250	52,679	2,558	93	460	—	798	—
1917	144,873	48,972	2,653	159	484	—	841	—
1918	342,573	92,322	2,185	391	276	—	1,363	—
1919	61,552	5,688	365	135	284	—	2,394	—
1920	105,750	2,802	93	15	527	—	2,153	—
1921	15,155	316	3	—	202	—	925	—
1922	15,013	398	—	—	26	—	1,479	—
1923	35,280	254	103	10	64	—	1,517	—
1924	63,297	323	135	135	—	—	2,192	—
1925	110,124	121	513	523	216	—	2,250	—
1926	51,810	158	597	650	331	—	2,984	—
1927	50,110	225	503	1,035	—	—	3,307	—
1928	52,483	739	522	1,510	—	—	4,403	—
1929	67,625	301	358	1,771	—	—	4,256	—
1930	75,080	90	303	1,706	—	—	2,838	—
1931	43,951	300	606	1,432	—	—	2,025	—
1932	19,910	174	171	1,076	271	—	1,419	—
1933	21,444	944	386	2,613	2	—	1,614	—
1934	29,697	413	885	4,253	7	—	1,810	—
1935	29,599	577	1,034	4,941	26	—	1,908	—
1936	35,974	301	1,128	8,147	70	—	1,923	—
1937	45,071	2,600	1,511	13,663	543	—	2,348	—
1938	28,360	909	1,315	11,670	807	—	2,250	—
1939	32,824	4,048	1,851	14,704	992	—	2,857	—
1940	44,038	2,982	2,296	11,489	1,082	—	4,063	—
1941	87,795	14,259	2,835	17,407	1,257	—	5,201	—
1942	190,748	112,876	4,029	30,135	2,220	—	4,053	—
1943	205,173	160,120	5,156	24,474	2,793	—	6,768	—
1944	247,616	45,629	4,439	17,882	1,764	—	4,228	—
1945	182,337	13,973	2,389	14,753	1,482	—	6,343	—
1946	143,635	4,107	2,242	7,395	636	—	8,070	—
1947	131,627	948	1,335	10,065	1,059	—	9,336	—
1948	131,100	3,619	1,741	13,457	895	—	8,659	—
1949	126,135	433	1,194	10,560	1,581	—	5,558	—
1950	134,451	404	2,081	20,205	2,298	828	7,979	—
1951	105,007	7,056	2,709	17,217	3,040	686	7,804	—
1952	115,379	21,304	3,286	19,376	3,589	574	6,785	—
1953	157,536	58,817	4,140	24,414	4,643	11	7,577	—
1954	206,128	163,365	5,910	29,039	4,930	1,820	7,806	—
1955	287,255	153,253	7,085	29,352	4,983	4,002	10,469	—
1956	344,735	207,662	6,363	25,912	5,636	6,706	13,481	—
1957	366,334	66,157	2,383	25,920	7,294	11,703	10,920	—
1958	327,309	143,795	1,636	19,200	7,266	12,238	6,723	—
1959	229,199	105,000	1,576	23,407	7,392	12,133	8,562	—

Notes appear at end of table

(continued)

TABLE Db96-103   Metal production – manganese, chromite, tungsten, molybdenum, vanadium, and nickel: 1880-2000 *Continued*

Year	Manganese ore Db96 [1] Short tons	Chromite Db97 Short tons	Tungsten concentrates Db98 Metric tons	Molybdenum ores and concentrates Db99 Metric tons	Vanadium ores and concentrates Db100 Metric tons	Nickel Primary Db101 Metric tons	Nickel Secondary (nonferrous) Db102 Metric tons	Nickel Secondary (ferrous) Db103 Metric tons
1960	80,021	107,000	3,162	31,725	8,047	12,772	8,556	—
1961	46,088	82,000	3,560	30,279	6,359	11,914	9,696	—
1962	24,758	—	3,639	22,909	7,647	11,893	10,077	—
1963	10,622	—	2,442	29,865	6,047	12,151	17,233	—
1964	26,058	—	3,991	29,528	5,184	13,989	20,969	—
1965	29,258	—	3,432	35,067	5,641	12,256	17,606	—
1966	14,406	—	3,250	41,581	5,685	12,008	24,292	—
1967	12,585	—	3,557	37,011	5,088	13,259	18,802	—
1968	11,378	—	4,101	42,296	7,105	13,826	12,756	—
1969	5,630	—	3,588	46,725	5,737	14,343	17,032	—
1970	4,737	—	4,224	50,068	5,793	14,114	21,010	—
1971	142	—	3,096	44,399	5,547	14,201	26,904	—
1972	578	—	3,195	46,356	4,699	1,271	32,592	—
1973	239	—	3,202	61,279	4,117	12,605	29,601	—
1974	—	—	3,554	53,598	5,240	12,785	18,987	—
1975	—	—	2,490	47,704	5,213	13,012	16,220	—
1976	—	—	2,662	51,949	8,076	12,582	12,041	—
1977	—	—	2,731	56,687	7,565	11,700	11,294	—
1978	—	—	3,130	59,282	4,446	10,249	11,162	—
1979	—	—	3,014	65,093	5,841	10,606	11,976	—
1980	—	—	2,738	67,727	5,832	10,183	16,777	27,939
1981	—	—	3,545	53,940	5,852	9,349	15,982	31,261
1982	—	—	1,575	34,534	4,093	3,135	11,734	27,246
1983	—	—	1,016	22,138	— [2]	—	17,941	27,285
1984	—	—	1,173	46,450	— [2]	3,992	17,606	32,441
1985	—	—	983	50,773	— [2]	4,990	15,381	33,285
1986	—	—	817	43,094	— [2]	1,066	7,626	32,042
1987	—	—	34	31,692	— [2]	—	7,613	24,718
1988	—	—	— [2]	45,240	— [2]	—	3,357	37,682
1989	—	—	— [2]	61,733	— [2]	—	7,491	32,293
1990	—	—	— [2]	61,580	— [2]	330	6,317	27,398
1991	—	—	— [2]	53,607	— [2]	5,520	8,700	44,800
1992	—	—	— [2]	45,098	— [2]	6,670	8,140	47,700
1993	—	—	— [2]	39,209	— [2]	2,460	7,460	46,600
1994	—	—	— [2]	46,000	— [2]	—	9,690	48,900
1995	—	—	— [2]	60,900	— [2]	1,560	10,200	54,400
1996	—	—	— [2]	54,900	— [2]	1,330	10,500	48,800
1997	—	—	— [2]	60,100	— [2]	— [2]	10,200	58,200
1998	—	—	— [2]	53,300	— [2]	— [2]	10,400	52,700
1999	—	—	— [2]	42,400	— [2]	— [2]	12,400	58,600
2000	—	—	— [2]	40,900	— [2]	— [2]	12,200	71,700

[1] Through 1914, 40 percent or more manganese.

[2] Withheld to avoid disclosing individual company data.

Sources

1880-1931: U.S. Bureau of Mines, *Mineral Resources of the United States* (annual). 1932-1996: U.S. Bureau of Mines, *Minerals Yearbooks* (annual). 1997-2000: U.S. Geological Survey, *Minerals Yearbook* (U.S. Department of the Interior, annual).

Documentation

A number of series end before the most recent dates, either because domestic production ceased, or because figures were withheld to avoid disclosing individual company data. Domestic mine production of chromite ceased in 1961 when the federal government's last Defense Production Act contract was concluded. Manganese ore was largely replaced after 1973 by manganiferous ore (5 to 35 percent manganese), but these figures are withheld to avoid disclosing individual company data.

Values are shown in the following terms: series Db96, short tons, 40 percent content; series Db97, gross weight; and series Db98-103, metal content.

Series Db97. Cumulative production prior to 1880 equaled 224,000 short tons.

Series Db98. Tungsten figures for 1900 to 1909 were converted from concentrate to content on the basis that one short ton of 60 percent tungstic trioxide (WO_3), which is the ordinary commercial basis in the United States, contained 951.72 pounds of tungsten.

Series Db101. Primary production of nickel refers to metal derived directly from ore.

Series Db102-103. Secondary production of nickel refers to metal recovered from scrap metal, sweepings, skimmings, and drosses. Secondary metal does not, however, imply the metal is of inferior quality.

TABLE Db104–111   Metal production – value: 1880–2000

Contributed by Gavin Wright

Year	Total metals Db104 Million dollars	Iron ore Db105 Million dollars	Copper Db106 Million dollars	Lead Db107 Million dollars	Zinc Db108 Million dollars	Gold Db109 Million dollars	Silver Db110 Million dollars	Molybdenum Db111 Million dollars
1880	125	23	13	10	3	36	35	—
1881	130	24	13	11	3	35	38	—
1882	144	31	17	13	4	32	41	—
1883	136	26	19	12	3	30	40	—
1884	130	21	19	10	3	31	42	—
1885	129	19	18	10	3	32	43	—
1886	138	28	18	12	4	35	39	—
1887	153	34	25	13	5	33	41	—
1888	164	29	38	13	5	33	43	—
1889	164	33	31	12	6	33	47	—
1890	187	35	41	13	7	33	57	—
1891	184	32	36	15	8	33	58	—
1892	186	33	40	14	8	33	56	—
1893	158	19	36	12	6	36	47	—
1894	136	14	34	10	5	40	31	—
1895	161	18	41	10	6	47	36	—
1896	185	23	50	11	6	53	40	—
1897	193	19	59	14	8	57	32	—
1898	213	22	65	15	11	64	32	—
1899	272	35	97	18	15	71	33	—
1900	319	67	101	23	11	79	36	—
1901	299	49	101	22	12	79	33	—
1902	295	65	80	22	15	80	29	—
1903	309	66	96	24	17	74	29	—
1904	309	43	104	26	19	80	33	—
1905	392	75	139	29	24	88	34	—
1906	477	101	177	38	24	94	38	—
1907	501	132	174	37	26	90	37	—
1908	376	82	124	26	18	95	28	—
1909	439	110	142	30	25	100	28	—
1910	470	141	137	33	27	96	31	—
1911	432	87	137	35	31	97	33	—
1912	537	107	205	35	45	93	39	—
1913	538	131	190	36	38	89	40	—
1914	446	72	153	40	35	95	40	(Z)
1915	677	101	243	48	114	101	37	(Z)
1916	1,107	182	474	76	151	93	49	(Z)
1917	1,228	238	515	94	119	84	59	(Z)
1918	1,179	244	471	77	90	69	66	1
1919	744	197	239	45	66	60	64	(Z)
1920	866	285	222	76	73	51	61	(Z)
1921	344	90	65	36	20	50	53	—
1922	524	158	128	52	40	49	56	—
1923	778	241	211	76	69	52	60	(Z)
1924	682	151	214	91	67	52	44	(Z)
1925	715	161	238	114	84	50	46	1
1926	721	174	244	109	92	48	39	1
1927	622	151	221	84	74	45	34	2
1928	655	156	263	73	72	46	34	2
1929	802	197	353	85	81	46	33	2
1930	507	146	181	57	47	47	20	2
1931	287	74	95	29	22	50	9	2
1932	128	13	34	15	12	51	7	1
1933	205	64	29	19	26	65	8	4
1934	277	66	39	22	31	108	21	7
1935	365	83	63	25	36	126	33	7
1936	516	132	112	36	49	153	49	12
1937	756	208	202	52	72	168	56	21
1938	460	74	110	31	42	178	41	18
1939	631	159	148	40	51	196	44	22

Note appears at end of table

(continued)

TABLE Db104–111   Metal production – value: 1880–2000   *Continued*

	Total metals	Iron ore	Copper	Lead	Zinc	Gold	Silver	Molybdenum
	Db104	Db105	Db106	Db107	Db108	Db109	Db110	Db111
Year	Million dollars	Million dollars	Million dollars	Million dollars	Million dollars	Million dollars	Million dollars	Million dollars
1940	752	189	205	43	74	210	49	17
1941	890	250	228	54	98	209	51	26
1942	999	279	257	59	110	131	40	47
1943	987	269	258	52	102	49	29	38
1944	900	257	237	50	99	36	25	28
1945	774	244	185	46	80	33	21	24
1946	729	215	173	49	82	51	19	12
1947	1,084	318	356	111	153	64	32	15
1948	1,219	391	362	140	168	62	34	20
1949	1,101	378	297	130	149	62	31	19
1950	1,351	483	378	116	179	74	38	38
1951	1,671	630	449	134	249	61	36	36
1952	1,617	590	448	126	223	58	36	41
1953	1,811	790	532	90	125	69	34	52
1954	1,518	526	493	89	102	64	33	64
1955	2,055	749	745	101	127	66	34	67
1956	2,358	750	939	111	149	64	35	64
1957	2,137	866	654	97	123	63	35	68
1958	1,594	569	515	63	84	61	31	50
1959	1,570	514	506	59	98	56	28	65
1960	2,022	724	693	58	112	58	28	87
1961	1,927	651	699	54	107	54	32	88
1962	1,937	618	757	44	116	54	40	69
1963	2,002	678	747	55	123	51	45	91
1964	2,366	802	813	75	156	51	47	97
1965	2,544	801	957	94	178	60	51	121
1966	2,703	854	1,034	99	166	63	56	144
1967	2,333	818	729	89	152	55	50	134
1968	2,968	836	1,008	95	143	58	70	151
1969	3,333	929	1,468	152	162	72	75	174
1970	3,928	942	1,984	179	164	63	80	190
1971	3,403	891	1,583	160	162	62	64	165
1972	3,642	950	1,705	186	169	85	63	171
1973	4,362	1,164	2,044	196	198	115	96	218
1974	5,501	1,388	2,469	299	359	180	159	235
1975	5,191	1,621	1,815	267	366	170	154	259
1976	6,086	1,871	2,235	282	359	131	149	333
1977	5,810	1,423	2,009	364	309	163	176	450
1978	—	2,401	1,990	394	207	193	213	608
1979	8,536	2,814	2,967	610	220	297	420	871
1980	8,921	2,544	2,667	515	262	594	667	1,344
1981	8,842	2,915	2,886	359	307	634	428	946
1982	5,517	1,492	1,841	289	257	551	320	504
1983	5,857	1,945	1,751	215	251	849	497	167
1984	6,004	2,248	1,625	182	271	752	363	327
1985	5,629	2,077	1,631	174	202	771	242	348
1986	5,824	1,473	1,666	165	170	1,377	189	240
1987	7,438	1,503	2,262	247	200	2,216	277	179
1988	10,209	1,717	3,764	315	324	2,831	349	267
1989	11,863	1,940	4,324	356	499	3,269	355	421
1990	12,442	1,570	4,311	491	847	3,641	329	346
1991	11,022	1,900	3,931	344	602	3,435	241	250
1992	11,547	1,730	4,179	307	674	3,662	229	190
1993	10,800	1,570	3,636	249	497	3,841	227	165
1994	12,100	1,600	4,430	298	619	4,050	253	284
1995	14,000	1,730	5,640	359	756	3,950	271	651
1996	13,000	1,770	4,610	459	674	4,090	259	456
1997	13,100	1,890	4,580	460	860	3,850	262	203
1998	11,200	1,970	3,220	480	804	3,480	368	200
1999	9,810	1,550	2,680	485	909	3,070	329	251
2000	10,200	1,560	2,810	439	1,020	3,180	300	232

TABLE Db104–111   Metal production – value: 1880–2000   *Continued*

(Z) Less than $500,000.

Sources

U.S. Bureau of Mines, *Mineral Resources of the United States* (annual). 1880-1996: U.S. Bureau of Mines, *Minerals Yearbooks* (annual). U.S. Geological Survey, *Minerals Yearbooks* (U.S. Department of the Interior, annual).

Documentation

Series Db104. Includes the value of some metals not shown separately.

Series Db105. The value of iron ore represents the total value of ore shipments. Figures for 1881, 1890, and 1891 were estimated by multiplying the arithmetic mean of the average value of the preceding year and the following year by the quantity of output for the year to be estimated. Beginning 1906, the data exclude ore containing 5 percent or more of manganese, and for 1916–1941, ore for paint.

Series Db106–108. The value of copper, lead, and zinc for 1880–1946 is the value of smelter output from domestic ores. Beginning in 1947, figures

represent the average price of refined metal multiplied by mine production of recoverable copper.

Series Db109. The value of gold for 1880–1946 is refinery or mint output multiplied by the official price. The official price of gold was $20.67 until 1933; from 1934 until March 15, 1968, it was $35. For 1947 until March 15, 1968, the figures represent the recoverable content of ore (mine output) multiplied by the official price per fine ounce, and by Engelhard selling quotations thereafter.

Series Db110. The value of silver for 1880–1946 is refinery or mint output multiplied by the price. Beginning 1947, the figures represent the recoverable ore content multiplied by the New York market price of refined metal.

Series Db111. The value of molybdenum is the value of shipments of molybdenum concentrates.

TABLE Db112–121   Nonmetal mineral production: 1818–2000

Contributed by Gavin Wright

Year(s)	Cement shipments	Crude gypsum mined	Lime sold by producers	Sand and gravel, sold or used	Stone sold or used by producers	Sulfur production from Frasch mines	Pyrites production	Salt sold or used by producers	Potash sold by producers	Phosphate rock sold or used by producers
	Db112 [1]	Db113	Db114	Db115	Db116	Db117	Db118	Db119	Db120	Db121
	Thousand metric tons	Thousand metric tons	Thousand metric tons	Thousand metric tons	Thousand metric tons	Thousand metric tons	Thousand metric tons	Thousand metric tons	Thousand metric tons	Thousand metric tons
1818–1829	51	—	—	—	—	—	—	—	—	—
1830–1839	171	—	—	—	—	—	—	—	—	—
1840–1849	725	—	—	—	—	—	—	—	—	—
1850–1859	1,876	—	—	—	—	—	—	—	—	—
1860–1869	2,800	—	—	—	—	—	—	—	—	—
1870–1879	3,766	—	—	—	—	—	—	—	—	—
1880	354	82	2,540	—	—	1	2	757	—	214
1881	426	77	2,722	—	—	1	10	787	—	271
1882	554	91	2,812	—	—	1	12	815	—	337
1883	715	82	2,903	—	—	1	25	787	—	384
1884	682	82	3,357	—	—	(Z)	36	827	—	439
1885	708	82	3,629	—	—	1	50	894	—	684
1886	767	86	3,856	—	—	2	56	979	—	438
1887	1,184	86	4,241	—	—	3	53	1,017	—	489
1888	1,109	100	4,453	—	—	—	55	1,023	—	459
1889	1,165	243	—	—	—	(Z)	96	1,017	—	555
1890	1,326	166	—	—	—	—	102	1,128	—	518
1891	1,402	189	—	—	—	1	109	1,268	—	598
1892	1,494	232	—	—	—	2	112	1,486	—	693
1893	1,364	230	—	—	—	1	77	1,511	—	956
1894	1,426	217	—	—	—	(Z)	108	1,647	—	1,013
1895	1,489	241	—	—	—	2	102	1,736	—	1,056
1896	1,625	203	—	—	—	5	117	1,759	—	946
1897	1,882	262	—	—	—	2	145	2,028	—	1,056
1898	2,106	265	—	—	—	1	196	2,237	—	1,330
1899	2,704	441	—	—	—	4	178	2,503	—	1,540
1900	2,939	539	—	—	—	3	208	2,651	—	1,515
1901	3,423	575	—	—	—	7	239	2,612	—	1,508
1902	4,392	740	—	1,676	—	7 [2]	203 [2]	3,029	—	1,514
1903	5,099	945	—	1,915	—	7 [2]	230 [2]	2,409	—	1,608
1904	5,402	854	2,457	9,689	—	86	210	2,798	—	1,904
1905	6,839	946	2,707	21,051	—	224	257	3,298	—	1,979
1906	8,698	1,398	2,901	29,875	—	300	265	3,578	—	2,115
1907	8,909	1,589	2,806	37,967	—	192	251	3,773	—	2,302
1908	9,025	1,562	2,510	33,762	—	370	227	3,660	—	2,424
1909	11,373	2,044	3,162	54,037	—	278	251	3,824	—	2,376

Notes appear at end of table   (continued)

TABLE Db112–121   Nonmetal mineral production: 1818–2000   *Continued*

Year(s)	Cement shipments Db112 [1] Thousand metric tons	Crude gypsum mined Db113 Thousand metric tons	Lime sold by producers Db114 Thousand metric tons	Sand and gravel, sold or used Db115 Thousand metric tons	Stone sold or used by producers Db116 Thousand metric tons	Sulfur production from Frasch mines Db117 Thousand metric tons	Pyrites production Db118 Thousand metric tons	Salt sold or used by producers Db119 Thousand metric tons	Potash sold by producers Db120 Thousand metric tons	Phosphate rock sold or used by producers Db121 Thousand metric tons
1910	13,266	2,158	3,181	62,967	—	251	246	3,849	—	2,698
1911	13,567	2,108	3,078	60,642	—	208	306	3,961	—	3,102
1912	14,655	2,269	3,201	62,010	—	801	357	4,232	—	3,021
1913	15,271	2,359	3,261	72,172	—	499	346	4,369	—	3,161
1914	14,881	2,246	3,067	71,923	—	425	342	4,421	—	2,778
1915	14,955	2,221	3,287	69,493	—	529	400	4,855	1	1,865
1916	16,269	2,502	3,695	80,823	83,307	660	446	5,772	9	2,014
1917	15,578	2,446	3,435	69,326	75,818	1,152	491	6,330	30	2,625
1918	12,168	1,866	2,908	56,086	62,199	1,376	471	6,567	35	2,531
1919	14,691	2,195	3,021	64,025	59,456	1,210	428	6,244	42	2,309
1920	16,557	2,839	3,239	74,426	71,238	1,275	316	6,205	37	4,169
1921	16,380	2,623	2,297	72,434	57,641	1,909	160	4,519	4	2,097
1922	20,226	3,429	3,302	86,062	72,767	1,860	176	6,162	10	2,457
1923	23,396	4,312	3,698	126,944	93,729	2,069	194	6,469	17	3,055
1924	25,151	4,575	3,694	141,729	93,607	1,241	171	6,172	20	2,914
1925	27,125	5,151	4,156	156,036	105,098	1,432	197	6,711	24	3,538
1926	28,007	5,112	4,137	166,106	112,940	1,920	231	6,688	23	3,261
1927	29,680	4,851	4,005	179,126	123,690	2,146	308	6,866	45	3,222
1928	30,366	4,628	4,044	189,709	121,444	2,014	318	7,325	54	3,557
1929	29,339	4,550	3,874	201,913	128,012	2,400	338	7,751	53	3,821
1930	27,432	3,149	3,074	178,762	115,208	2,600	354	7,306	52	3,989
1931	21,895	2,321	2,457	139,233	88,843	2,163	336	6,675	58	2,575
1932	13,877	1,285	1,778	108,896	64,087	904	193	5,813	51	1,735
1933	11,045	1,211	2,058	97,753	63,704	1,429	289	6,899	126	2,530
1934	13,060	1,393	2,175	105,788	83,519	1,444	440	6,905	103	2,880
1935	13,004	1,727	2,710	112,421	75,440	1,659	522	7,191	204	3,091
1936	19,547	2,461	3,401	161,778	119,218	2,048	556	8,009	202	3,406
1937	19,729	2,774	3,741	172,056	120,785	2,786	593	8,384	242	4,020
1938	18,452	2,435	3,036	164,490	113,252	2,431	565	7,281	259	3,799
1939	21,328	2,927	3,859	205,030	133,761	2,125	527	8,417	332	3,817
1940	22,661	3,356	4,433	216,188	139,464	2,776	637	9,398	357	4,067
1941	29,056	4,344	5,515	261,917	166,112	3,189	655	11,540	482	4,765
1942	32,032	4,262	5,537	276,097	177,702	3,517	732	12,422	618	4,718
1943	22,083	3,518	5,985	212,338	155,439	2,580	815	13,802	664	5,208
1944	16,303	3,412	5,873	176,703	141,139	3,270	802	14,258	742	5,463
1945	18,391	3,458	5,371	177,376	139,166	3,813	735	13,965	789	5,900
1946	29,352	5,106	5,437	230,543	162,251	3,922	826	13,727	842	6,971
1947	32,475	5,632	6,150	260,959	188,290	4,512	956	14,564	955	9,172
1948	35,419	6,582	6,590	289,632	204,601	4,947	944	14,880	1,037	8,808
1949	35,699	5,995	5,732	289,485	203,233	4,821	902	14,127	1,017	9,131
1950	39,563	7,432	6,784	336,070	228,706	5,275	946	15,086	1,158	10,418
1951	41,721	7,862	7,490	363,447	259,038	5,363	1,034	18,331	1,277	11,223
1952	43,459	7,634	7,324	395,188	273,593	5,378	1,010	17,731	1,450	11,506
1953	45,082	7,523	8,776	399,521	278,361	5,238	938	18,859	1,571	12,719
1954	47,478	8,161	7,828	504,880	373,813	5,604	924	18,751	1,740	13,253
1955	52,912	9,692	9,507	537,190	427,510	5,831	1,023	20,597	1,820	13,397
1956	55,540	9,359	9,595	568,344	460,404	6,527	1,087	21,968	1,908	14,337
1957	51,973	8,341	9,320	573,570	483,911	5,579	1,084	21,640	1,939	14,831
1958	54,919	8,709	8,356	620,963	486,179	4,718	990	19,878	2,119	14,994
1959	60,046	9,888	11,340	662,428	529,941	4,627	1,074	22,825	2,246	16,323
1960	55,784	8,913	11,734	643,910	559,535	5,022	1,032	23,114	2,360	17,478
1961	57,198	8,618	12,019	682,004	555,138	5,472	1,003	23,321	2,256	18,128
1962	59,201	9,044	12,476	704,608	595,976	5,065	931	26,133	2,469	19,366
1963	62,293	9,424	13,173	745,566	624,472	4,960	838	27,797	2,458	20,178
1964	65,366	9,692	14,596	787,622	658,235	5,312	861	28,688	2,762	22,435
1965	66,802	9,102	15,235	823,765	707,820	6,214	889	31,467	2,659	26,344
1966	67,787	8,751	16,381	847,743	737,877	7,114	886	33,079	2,842	33,060
1967	66,561	8,521	16,316	822,854	712,674	7,127	875	35,331	2,836	34,323
1968	70,742	9,088	16,907	832,309	743,523	7,580	886	37,443	2,643	33,855
1969	72,864	8,964	18,333	850,182	782,796	7,261	834	40,138	2,784	33,321

Notes appear at end of table

TABLE Db112–121 Nonmetal mineral production: 1818–2000 *Continued*

Year(s)	Cement shipments Db112 [1] Thousand metric tons	Crude gypsum mined Db113 Thousand metric tons	Lime sold by producers Db114 Thousand metric tons	Sand and gravel, sold or used Db115 Thousand metric tons	Stone sold or used by producers Db116 Thousand metric tons	Sulfur production from Frasch mines Db117 Thousand metric tons	Pyrites production Db118 Thousand metric tons	Salt sold or used by producers Db119 Thousand metric tons	Potash sold by producers Db120 Thousand metric tons	Phosphate rock sold or used by producers Db121 Thousand metric tons
1970	69,295	8,560	17,951	856,325	788,515	7,196	859	41,636	2,421	35,167
1971	74,749	9,451	17,812	834,237	794,802	7,138	821	39,986	2,351	36,551
1972	77,365	11,184	18,445	829,457	834,990	7,407	753	40,843	2,375	39,694
1973	82,306	12,299	19,171	892,329	961,724	7,727	568	39,834	2,599	40,854
1974	75,218	10,885	19,636	820,677	946,657	8,028	431	42,217	2,309	43,931
1975	64,123	8,846	17,381	716,161	817,733	7,327	635	37,222	1,900	42,120
1976	68,244	10,868	18,377	802,996	818,005	6,365	762	40,089	2,268	40,522
1977	74,039	12,147	18,132	842,952	866,720	5,915	442	39,383	2,233	47,437
1978	79,831	13,509	18,583	903,733	953,447	5,648	778	38,890	2,307	48,774
1979	79,063	13,272	19,035	888,139	998,670	6,357	1,049	41,543	2,388	53,063
1980	70,510	11,227	17,270	719,122	893,405	6,390	847	36,607	2,217	54,581
1981	66,201	10,430	17,137	653,152	792,813	6,348	797	35,296	1,908	45,526
1982	59,015	9,560	12,802	563,722	717,688	4,210	676	34,377	1,784	38,571
1983	65,195	11,688	13,519	618,443	782,616	3,202	— [3]	31,364	1,513	46,839
1984	73,629	12,990	14,475	728,720	868,300	4,193	— [3]	35,584	1,639	53,277
1985	76,198	13,076	14,255	752,534	908,908	5,011	— [3]	36,348	1,266	46,634
1986	80,488	13,973	13,152	825,915	929,189	4,043	— [3]	33,260	1,147	41,776
1987	82,034	14,163	14,295	838,425	1,089,777	3,202	— [3]	33,106	1,485	43,673
1988	82,020	14,869	15,492	863,527	1,133,032	3,174	— [3]	35,326	1,427	48,441
1989	79,480	15,988	15,584	840,511	1,101,923	3,888	— [3]	35,250	1,536	49,280
1990	79,547	14,883	15,858	851,852	1,109,718	3,730	— [3]	36,916	1,716	49,754
1991	68,833	14,021	15,694	731,100	997,957	2,870	— [3]	35,902	1,709	44,707
1992	70,500	14,759	16,226	859,195	1,054,840	2,320	— [3]	34,784	1,766	45,113
1993	74,079	15,812	16,700	894,920	1,117,000	1,900	— [3]	38,200	1,484	40,051
1994	80,490	17,200	17,400	918,300	1,230,000	2,960	— [3]	39,700	1,470	43,900
1995	76,900	16,600	18,500	938,200	1,260,000	3,070	— [3]	40,800	1,480	43,500
1996	79,270	17,500	19,200	941,800	1,330,000	— [3]	— [3]	42,900	1,390	45,400
1997	82,530	18,600	19,600	980,500	1,420,000	— [3]	— [3]	40,600	2,900	45,900
1998	83,890	19,000	20,100	1,198,200	1,510,000	— [3]	— [3]	40,800	3,000	44,200
1999	85,980	22,400	19,600	1,138,900	1,640,000	— [3]	— [3]	44,400	2,500	40,600
2000	87,830	19,500	19,600	1,148,400	1,560,000	— [3]	— [3]	43,300	2,600	38,600

(Z) Less than 500 long tons.

[1] Beginning 1993, includes Puerto Rico.

[2] Tonnage calculated from combined total of domestic sulfur and sulfur content of pyrites produced.

[3] Withheld to avoid disclosing individual company data.

Sources

1818–1931: U.S. Bureau of Mines, *Mineral Resources of the United States* (annual). 1932–1996: U.S. Bureau of Mines, *Minerals Yearbooks* (annual). 1997–2000: U.S Geological Survey, *Minerals Yearbooks* (U.S. Department of the Interior, annual).

Documentation

Only the more important of the nonmetals (excluding fuels), for which adequate data exist, are included here.

Series Db112. Represents cement production for 1818–1911. Beginning in 1912, it is shipments of hydraulic cement. Figures for 1818–1890 are estimated; beginning in 1891, they are based on practically complete returns from all producers. Coverage includes natural cement since 1818, portland cement beginning 1870, slag cement (formerly referred to as puzzolan cement) beginning 1896, and hydraulic lime cement beginning 1934. It also includes prepared masonry cement made at natural and slag cement plants and, beginning in 1955, prepared masonry cement made at portland cement plants.

Series Db113. Represents crude gypsum mined and ready for calcining or for uncalcined use. The figures exclude by-product gypsum.

Series Db114. Includes quicklime, hydrated lime, and dead-burned dolomite. For 1921–1952, only small quantities of "captive" lime tonnage were included, but beginning in 1953, coverage is essentially complete. Figures for 1880–1889 are considered too high, but there is no adequate means of explaining the discrepancy.

Series Db115. Sand and gravel are produced primarily for construction, but industrial production is included as well.

Series Db116. Includes both dimension and crushed or broken stone, but for 1916–1953, it excludes abrasive stone, bituminous limestone and sandstone, and ground soapstone.

Series Db117. Includes only sulfur produced by the Frasch hotwater method, which is used to mine native sulfur associated with the cap-rock of salt domes and in sedimentary deposits. The native sulfur is melted underground and brought to the surface by compressed air. Figures in the series represent the major portion of sulfur production for most years. Other sources of sulfur production not encompassed here include recovered sulfur (as a by-product of petroleum refining, natural gas processing, and coking plants) and by-product sulfuric acid (from copper, lead, molybdenum, and zinc roasters and smelters).

Series Db118. Pyrites production figures for 1922–1927 have been corrected for flotation concentrates. Canvassing of pyrites was discontinued in 1994.

Series Db119. Salt sold or used by producers includes evaporated salt, rock salt, and the salt content of brine production.

Series Db120. Expressed in terms of K_2O equivalent.

TABLE Db122–131   Nonmetal mineral production – value: 1880–2000

Contributed by Gavin Wright

Year	Total nonmetal minerals Db122 Million dollars	Cement Db123 Million dollars	Raw clay Db124 Million dollars	Clay products Db125 Million dollars	Lime Db126 Million dollars	Sand and gravel Db127 [1] Million dollars	Crushed stone (including slate) Db128 [1] Million dollars	Phosphate rock Db129 Million dollars	Salt Db130 Million dollars	Sulfur Db131 Million dollars
1880	56	2	—	—	19	—	22	1	5	(Z)
1881	61	3	—	—	20	—	24	2	4	(Z)
1882	64	4	—	—	22	—	23	2	4	(Z)
1883	61	4	—	—	19	—	22	2	4	(Z)
1884	58	4	—	—	18	—	21	2	4	(Z)
1885	62	3	—	—	20	—	21	4	5	(Z)
1886	67	4	—	—	21	—	22	2	5	(Z)
1887	77	6	—	—	23	—	28	2	4	(Z)
1888	80	5	—	—	25	—	29	2	4	(Z)
1889	83	5	—	—	8	—	46	3	4	(Z)
1890	81	5	—	—	— [3]	—	50 [3]	3	5	(Z)
1891	83	5	—	—	— [3]	—	50 [3]	4	5	(Z)
1892	90	5	—	—	— [3]	—	52 [3]	3	6	(Z)
1893	70	4	—	—	— [3]	—	36 [3]	4	4	(Z)
1894	127	5	—	65	8	—	30	3	5	(Z)
1895	126	5	—	65	7	—	29	4	4	(Z)
1896	120	6	—	63	6	—	27	3	4	(Z)
1897	128	8	—	62	6	—	30	3	5	(Z)
1898	151	10	—	74	7	—	32	3	6	(Z)
1899	185	13	—	96	7	—	39	5	7	(Z)
1900	188	13	—	96	7	—	41	5	7	(Z)
1901	219	16	—	110	8	—	52	5	7	1
1902	254	25	—	122	9	1	60	5	6	1
1903	272	32	—	131	9	1	64	5	5	1
1904	274	26	—	131	10	6	64	7	6	1
1905	319	36	—	150	11	11	69	7	6	3
1906	362	55	—	161	12	13	72	9	7	3
1907	376	56	—	159	13	14	77	11	8	5
1908	325	44	—	133	11	13	72	11	8	4
1909	386	54	—	166	14	18	77	11	8	5
1910	410	69	—	170	14	21	83	11	8	5
1911	407	67	—	162	14	21	83	12	8	5
1912	430	70	—	173	14	23	84	12	9	5
1913	467	90	—	181	15	24	90	12	10	6
1914	431	81	—	165	13	24	83	10	10	6
1915	429	75	—	163	14	23	80	5	12	5
1916	554	105	—	207	19	30	84	6	14	12
1917	666	123	—	233	24	35	88	8	20	24
1918	648	114	—	221	27	38	88	8	27	28
1919	752	147	—	275	29	46	103	12	27	10
1920	1,025	196	—	374	38	66	142	25	30	30
1921	780	182	—	271	25	56	114	12	25	17
1922	921	208	—	321	33	65	131	10	27	22
1923	1,157	260	—	425	40	91	172	12	28	26
1924	1,174	266	—	416	40	97	174	10	26	25
1925	1,187	281	—	423	43	108	187	12	26	29
1926	1,219	281	—	430	42	111	201	11	25	37
1927	1,201	282	—	404	39	116	210	11	25	38
1928	1,163	279	—	374	36	119	208	12	27	38
1929	1,166	255	—	373	33	133	214	13	27	44
1930	973	231	—	275	26	115	187	14	25	36
1931	671	143	—	178	19	86	141	9	22	25
1932	412	83	—	89	12	58	92	6	20	20
1933	432	86	—	95	14	53	84	8	22	30
1934	520	118	—	116	17	61	102	10	23	29
1935	564	115	—	156	22	62	91	11	22	29
1936	685	173	16	95	27	90	147	11	23	35
1937	711	171	18	109	30	97	152	13	24	44
1938	622	157	13	89	24	86	145	13	23	27
1939	754	184	17	123	30	106	165	12	25	36

Notes appear at end of table

TABLE Db122-131   Nonmetal mineral production – value: 1880-2000   *Continued*

Year	Total nonmetal minerals	Cement	Raw clay	Clay products	Lime	Sand and gravel	Crushed stone (including slate)	Phosphate rock	Salt	Sulfur
	Db122	Db123	Db124	Db125	Db126	Db127 [1]	Db128 [1]	Db129	Db130	Db131
	Million dollars	Million dollars	Million dollars	Million dollars	Million dollars	Million dollars	Million dollars	Million dollars	Million dollars	Million dollars
1940	784	193	20	114	34	111	166	12	26	41
1941	989	251	27	135	43	147	203	16	34	54
1942	1,056	287	27	103	44	188	211	17	38	50
1943	916	202	40	75	49	153	189	19	42	47
1944	836	152	37	65	49	125	181	21	44	56
1945	888	175	43	86	46	129	185	24	44	61
1946	1,243	297	61	179	51	171	243	31	45	66
1947	1,338	357	74	219	63	213	298	47	52	85
1948	1,552	446	85	268	75	252	340	51	54	90
1949	1,559	475	79	—	69	246	352	51	54	86
1950	1,822	538	95	—	83	293	402	63	60	106
1951	2,079	612	129	—	97	330	448	65	70	112
1952	2,163	638	131	—	95	345	473	72	71	117
1953	2,350	698	125	—	112	374	489	77	78	150
1954	2,733	763	123	446	102	503	622 [4]	87	105	155
1955	3,076	884	140	525	127	536	715 [4]	75	123	177
1956	3,391	989	163	—	136	602	775 [4]	98	136	166
1957	3,387	961	156	—	135	600	825	88	149	124
1958	3,466	1,039	143	525	121	653	827	94	141	111
1959	3,861	1,145	160	589	164	729	912	99	156	123
1960	3,868	1,089	162	560	173	720	953	117	161	117
1961	3,946	1,106	157	558	177	751	947	131	160	120
1962	4,117	1,129	163	591	187	795	1,026	134	175	109
1963	4,316	1,157	181	593	199	847	1,068	140	185	99
1964	4,623	1,209	193	650	223	893	1,135	161	201	121
1965	4,933	1,221	205	651	233	957	1,204	193	216	165
1966	5,176	1,227	222	640	240	985	1,261	261	230	201
1967	5,206	1,211	224	616	240	981	1,240	266	251	252
1968	5,449	1,295	247	672	250	1,020	1,318	251	272	271
1969	5,624	1,354 [2]	264	681	281	1,070	1,425	209	288	174
1970	5,712	1,336 [2]	268	642	286	1,116	1,470	203	305	154
1971	6,058	1,528	274	725	308	1,149	1,501	204	304	118
1972	6,482	1,724	303	799	339	1,201	1,582	208	297	132
1973	7,413	1,975	354	839	366	1,359	1,904	239	306	139
1974	8,639	2,151	423	767	474	1,417	2,086	501	361	241
1975	9,570	2,159	425	810	524	1,340	2,022	1,122	368	305
1976	10,616	2,510	529	927	609	1,774	2,117	949	431	300
1977	11,701	2,932	579	1,142	666	2,028	2,353	822	452	295
1978	—	3,544	717	1,283	750	2,302	2,773	929	499	280
1979	15,438	3,992	846	1,359	862	2,427	3,265	1,046	538	449
1980	16,213	3,886	899	1,256	843	2,289	3,266	1,257	656	721
1981	16,446	3,723	989	1,207	884	2,290	3,125	1,438	638	716
1982	14,150	3,264	825	1,116	696	1,998	2,918 [5]	950	671	435
1983	15,263	3,534	931	1,352	758	2,270	3,327	1,021	597	414
1984	17,164	4,152	1,032	1,676	811	2,581	3,755 [5]	1,182	675	546
1985	17,678	4,286	1,011	1,897	809	2,812	4,053	1,236	740	574
1986	17,647	4,408	1,095	2,149	758	3,107	4,255 [5]	897	665	509
1987	18,904	4,394	1,202	1,930	786	3,367	5,248	793	684	387
1988	19,805	4,370	1,391	1,977	818	3,514	5,558 [5]	888	699	431
1989	20,357	4,243	1,515	1,966	852	3,659	5,325	1,084	777	379
1990	20,992	4,280	1,620	1,951	902	3,704	5,591 [5]	1,075	827	335
1991	20,080	3,832	1,456	1,785	890	3,196	5,348	1,109	802	272
1992	20,574	3,779	1,470	1,854	950	3,776	5,786 [5]	1,058	803	151
1993	21,200	4,175	1,470	1,972	965	3,985	5,930	759	904	101
1994	23,000	4,981	1,590	2,084	1,020	4,228	6,620 [5]	869	990	162
1995	24,600	5,227	1,730	2,102	1,100	4,412	6,740	947	1,000	207
1996	25,800	5,631	1,710	2,411	1,160	4,497	7,180 [5]	1,060	1,060	— [6]
1997	27,400	6,049	1,670	—	1,200	4,778	8,070	1,080	993	— [6]
1998	28,200	6,421	1,663	—	1,250	5,423	8,130	1,130	986	— [6]
1999	29,300	6,732	1,555	—	1,180	5,788	8,240	1,240	1,110	— [6]
2000	29,200	6,891	1,529	—	1,180	5,946	8,390	932	1,040	— [6]

Notes appear on next page   (continued)

TABLE Db122–131   Nonmetal mineral production – value: 1880–2000   *Continued*

(Z) Less than $500,000.

[1] Beginning 1954, sand and sandstone (ground) included with series Db127 (sand and gravel) and series Db128 (stone), respectively.

[2] Excludes natural and slag cement.

[3] Data for lime not available separately; included with value of stone.

[4] Includes value of stone used for cement or lime, excluded from total nonmetals, series Db122, to avoid duplication.

[5] Data in original source appears to be in error, but cannot be corrected.

[6] Withheld to avoid disclosing individual company data.

Sources

1818–1931: U.S. Bureau of Mines, *Mineral Resources of the United States* (annual). 1932–1996: U.S. Bureau of Mines, *Minerals Yearbooks* (annual), except series Db125, 1954–1996, which is from U.S. Bureau of the Census, *Annual Survey of Manufactures* (annual) and *1967 Census of Manufactures* (1971). 1997–2000: U.S. Geological Survey, *Minerals Yearbooks* (U.S. Department of the Interior, annual), except series Db125, 1997–2000, which is from *Annual Survey of Manufactures* and *1967 Census of Manufactures*.

Documentation

Figures for the value of nonmetals are heavily weighted by the value of products normally classified as manufactures. For example, cement and lime are included in the data instead of their raw material components. Integrated operations make it difficult to obtain a value for the raw materials, which usually are not purchased on the open market.

Series Db122. Includes additional mineral products not shown separately.

Series Db123. The value of cement is f.o.b. (free on board) mill excluding the cost of the container. (This means the buyer is responsible for costs of transportation and insurance from the mill.) Included are portland, natural, masonry-neutral, slag (formerly referred to as puzzolan), and hydraulic lime cements. After 1912, figures represent the total value of shipments; for 1880–1911, figures are for value of production. For 1880–1890, the figures are estimates. Early decade valuation estimates not shown include: 1818–1829, $0.2 million; 1830–1839, $1 million; 1840–1849, $4 million; 1850–1859, $9 million; 1860–1869, $14 million; and 1870–1879, $19 million.

Series Db124–125. Raw clay and clay products in are both shown because total nonmetals, series Db122, includes one or the other, or parts of both, at different times. Prior to 1944, raw clay, series Db124, was mainly restricted to "merchant clay" marketed as raw clay, excluding the very great amounts of clay converted into brick and other products before sale. Figures for clay products in series Db125 are incomplete prior to 1894, though they are included in the totals. Until 1936, the series represents the total value of clay products; beginning in 1936, the figures represent the value of heavy clay products other than potteries and refractories.

Series Db126. The value of lime is f.o.b. plant, excluding the cost of the container. Data from 1953 are not strictly comparable with those for earlier years. Prior to 1953, the series has only partial coverage of captive plants; beginning in 1953, coverage is essentially complete.

Series Db127. The value of sand and gravel is the value at the pit (or source). Coverage includes commercial and noncommercial (government and contractor) operations. Values of industrial sand, ground and unground, are also included.

Series Db128. The value of stone and slate is f.o.b. quarries or nearest point of shipment. Stone coverage includes granite, basalt and related rocks (traprock), marble, limestone, sandstone and other stone. From 1954, data include ground sandstone, quartz and quartzite used for abrasives and other purposes (formerly included elsewhere in value of nonmetals), stone for cement and lime (value excluded from nonmetals total), and shell (not formerly covered). Both dimension stone and nondimension (crushed) stone are included. Slate includes roofing slate, millstock, flagstones, granules, flour and other. Data for 1880–1888 are incomplete, representing building stone only.

Series Db129. The value of phosphate rock is f.o.b. mine. Beginning 1950, the figures refer to marketable production; for earlier years, they refer to phosphate rock sold or used.

Series Db130. The value of salt is f.o.b. mine or refinery of common salt sold or used by producers, excluding the cost of cooperage or container. Included are dry salt, both evaporated (manufactured) and rock, and also salt in brine.

Series Db131. The value of sulfur represents the total value of shipments. Frasch process mine output is included since 1945 and recovered elemental sulfur since 1950.

TABLE Db132–149 Metals – selected imports and exports: 1851–2000

Contributed by Gavin Wright

Year	Bauxite – imports	Aluminum, crude and semicrude – imports	Manganese ore (gross weight) – imports	Chromite (gross weight) – imports	Tungsten concentrates – imports	Vanadium ores and concentrates – imports [1]	Nickel (nickel content) – imports	Molybdenum ores and concentrates – exports	Refined copper Imports	Refined copper Exports	Iron ore Imports	Iron ore Exports	Pig iron Imports	Pig iron Exports	Refined lead Imports	Refined lead Exports	Refined zinc Imports	Refined zinc Exports
	Db132	Db133	Db134	Db135	Db136	Db137	Db138	Db139	Db140	Db141	Db142	Db143	Db144	Db145	Db146	Db147	Db148	Db149
	Thousand metric tons	Thousand metric tons	Metric tons	Metric tons	Metric tons	Metric tons	Metric tons	Metric tons	Metric tons	Metric tons	Thousand metric tons	Thousand metric tons	Thousand metric tons	Thousand metric tons	Metric tons	Metric tons	Metric tons	Metric tons
1851	—	—	—	—	—	—	—	—	—	—	—	—	—	—	—	104	—	—
1852	—	—	—	—	—	—	—	—	—	—	—	—	—	—	—	339	—	—
1853	—	—	—	—	—	—	—	—	—	—	—	—	—	—	—	45	—	—
1854	—	—	—	—	—	—	—	—	—	—	—	—	—	—	—	183	—	—
1855	—	—	—	—	—	—	—	—	—	—	—	—	—	—	—	75	—	—
1856	—	—	—	—	—	—	—	—	—	—	—	—	—	—	—	141	—	—
1857	—	—	—	—	—	—	—	—	—	—	—	—	—	—	—	395	—	—
1858	—	—	—	—	—	—	—	—	—	—	—	—	—	—	—	408	—	—
1859	—	—	—	—	—	—	—	—	—	—	—	—	—	—	—	142	—	—
1860	—	—	—	—	—	—	—	—	—	—	—	—	—	—	—	410	—	—
1861	—	—	—	—	—	—	—	—	—	—	—	—	—	—	—	50	—	—
1862	—	—	—	—	—	—	—	—	—	—	—	—	—	—	—	36	—	—
1863	—	—	—	—	—	—	—	—	—	—	—	—	—	—	—	108	—	—
1864	—	—	—	—	—	—	—	—	—	—	—	—	—	—	—	102	—	44
1865	—	—	—	—	—	—	—	—	—	—	—	—	—	—	—	386	—	83
1866	—	—	—	—	—	—	—	—	—	—	—	—	—	—	—	12	—	64
1867	—	—	1,033	—	—	—	—	—	—	—	—	—	—	—	29,630	45	2,609	142
1868	—	—	496	—	—	—	—	—	—	—	—	—	—	—	28,692	199	4,231	464
1869	—	—	—	—	—	—	—	—	—	—	—	—	—	—	39,855	—	5,993	—
1870	—	—	1,424	—	—	—	—	—	—	—	—	—	—	—	38,962	—	4,183	50
1871	—	—	1,073	—	—	—	—	—	—	—	24	—	—	—	41,502	—	5,062	34
1872	—	—	1,226	—	—	—	—	—	—	—	24	—	—	—	33,151	—	5,353	28
1873	—	—	1,048	—	—	—	—	—	—	—	47	—	—	—	32,851	—	3,103	34
1874	—	—	795	—	—	—	—	—	—	—	59	—	—	—	20,958	—	1,630	20
1875	—	—	206	—	—	—	—	—	—	—	58	—	—	—	14,864	—	923	17
1876	—	—	418	—	—	—	—	—	—	—	17	—	—	—	6,500	—	430	61
1877	—	—	905	—	—	—	—	—	—	—	31	—	—	—	6,615	—	574	644
1878	—	—	636	—	—	—	—	—	—	—	28	—	—	—	3,047	—	576	1,155
1879	—	—	1,916	—	—	—	—	—	—	—	289	—	—	—	552	—	644	967
1880	—	—	2,214	—	—	—	—	—	—	—	501	—	—	—	3,050	—	3,670	621
1881	—	—	1,731	—	—	—	—	—	—	—	765	—	—	—	1,960	—	1,297	677
1882	—	—	908	—	—	—	—	—	—	—	599	—	—	—	2,758	—	8,350	676
1883	—	—	1,347	2,720	—	—	—	—	—	—	499	—	—	—	1,832	—	7,742	386
1884	—	—	612	—	—	—	—	—	—	—	496	—	—	—	1,393	—	2,663	57
1885	—	—	1,711	12	—	—	—	—	—	—	397	—	—	—	2,659	—	1,595	46
1886	—	—	1,847	3,410	—	—	—	—	—	—	1,056	—	—	—	7,975	—	1,950	416
1887	—	—	1,657	1,426	—	—	—	—	—	—	1,213	—	—	—	3,500	—	3,805	62
1888	—	—	1,201	4,511	—	—	—	—	—	—	596	—	—	—	1,171	—	1,735	28
1889	—	—	4,354	5,562	—	—	—	—	—	—	868	—	—	—	1,258	—	931	399

Notes appear at end of table

(continued)

TABLE Db132–149   Metals – selected imports and exports: 1851–2000   Continued

Year	Bauxite imports — Db132 (Thousand metric tons)	Aluminum, crude and semicrude imports — Db133 (Thousand metric tons)	Manganese ore (gross weight) imports — Db134 (Metric tons)	Chromite (gross weight) imports — Db135 (Metric tons)	Tungsten concentrates imports — Db136 (Metric tons)	Vanadium ores and concentrates imports — Db137 [1] (Metric tons)	Nickel (nickel content) imports — Db138 (Metric tons)	Molybdenum ores and concentrates exports — Db139 (Metric tons)	Refined copper Imports — Db140 (Metric tons)	Refined copper Exports — Db141 (Metric tons)	Iron ore Imports — Db142 (Thousand metric tons)	Iron ore Exports — Db143 (Thousand metric tons)	Pig iron Imports — Db144 (Thousand metric tons)	Pig iron Exports — Db145 (Thousand metric tons)	Refined lead Imports — Db146 (Metric tons)	Refined lead Exports — Db147 (Metric tons)	Refined zinc Imports — Db148 (Metric tons)	Refined zinc Exports — Db149 (Metric tons)
1890	—	—	34,702	4,423	—	—	—	—	—	—	1,267	—	—	—	8,771	—	906	1,495
1891	—	—	29,288	4,530	—	—	—	—	—	—	928	—	—	—	1,539	—	367	1,948
1892	—	—	59,512	5,009	—	—	—	—	—	—	820	—	—	—	703	—	135	5,667
1893	—	—	69,206	6,456	—	—	—	—	—	—	535	—	—	—	1,796	—	193	3,377
1894	—	—	45,372	3,525	—	—	—	—	—	—	170	—	—	—	17,766	—	176	1,637
1895	—	—	87,493	5,314	—	—	—	—	—	—	532	—	—	—	49,692	769	337	1,388
1896	—	—	31,995	8,808	—	—	—	—	—	—	694	—	—	—	4,786	7,421 [6]	472	9,190
1897	—	—	121,886	11,755	—	—	—	—	—	—	498	—	—	—	7,280	3,504 [6]	1,318	12,923
1898	1	—	116,728	16,565	—	—	—	—	—	—	190	—	—	—	142	54	1,187	9,525
1899	7	—	191,372	16,046	—	—	—	—	—	—	685	42	—	—	1,576	43	1,263	6,128
1900	9	—	260,364	17,823	—	—	—	—	—	—	912	52	—	—	1,666	904	802	20,330
1901	18	—	168,382	20,434	—	—	—	—	—	—	983	66	—	—	1,635	2,171	252	3,075
1902	16	—	239,356	40,205	—	—	—	—	—	—	1,184	89	—	—	5,645	2,967	406	2,937
1903	15	—	148,400	23,300	—	—	—	—	—	—	996	82	—	—	4,070	51	183	1,380
1904	15	—	110,260	24,616	—	—	—	—	—	—	496	217	—	—	7,863	32	309	9,205
1905	12	—	261,158	55,307	—	—	—	—	—	—	860	211	—	—	4,708	57	388	5,004
1906	18	—	224,810	44,138	—	—	—	—	—	—	1,077	269	—	—	11,286	67	926	4,237
1907	25	—	212,376	42,663	—	—	—	—	—	—	1,249	283	—	—	7,107	50	1,550	511
1908	22	—	181,062	28,323	—	—	—	—	—	—	789	314	—	—	2,425	—	704	2,395
1909	19	3	216,179	40,260	—	—	—	—	—	—	1,722	463	—	—	3,219	—	8,545	2,328
1910	16	5	246,237	39,198	—	—	13,531	—	—	—	2,633	761	—	—	3,074	—	897	3,620
1911	44	2	179,690	38,143	—	—	—	—	—	—	1,841	780	—	—	3,226	—	293	6,234
1912	26	10	305,485	54,794	748	—	21,009	—	—	—	2,139	1,215	—	—	2,355	—	9,724	6,018
1913	21	12	350,628	66,226	407	—	21,521	—	—	—	2,637	1,059	—	—	2,097	—	4,686	7,061
1914	25	8	287,840	75,884	271	—	15,920	—	—	—	1,373	561	—	—	261	53,272	177	58,787
1915	3	5	325,925	77,682	1,611	—	25,673	—	3,816	325,052	1,363	719	—	—	453	115,144	57	119,184
1916	(Z)	3	585,570	117,805	3,604	—	32,953	—	3,063	467,554	1,347	1,203	—	—	2,898	100,135	19	175,861
1917	8	(Z)	640,082	73,220	4,423	—	34,258	—	17,276	312,992	988	1,150	—	—	797	82,862	16	183,222
1918	4	1	499,181	101,749	10,659	804	33,215	—	15,938	198,746	800	1,276	—	—	517	91,850	10	78,415
1919	6	6	338,693	62,389	8,535	2,945	16,629	—	—	—	484	1,013	—	—	4,615	46,707	29	110,678
1920	44	18	609,389	152,686	1,768	10,105	21,996	—	49,325	250,032	1,293	1,163	—	—	31,253	18,228	—	92,694
1921	28	15	398,906	83,149	1,464	5,038	1,994	—	31,411	270,395	321	447	—	—	28,082	24,153	5,986	2,730
1922	24	20	432,001	91,527	1,498	299	6,778	—	46,785	296,044	1,153	612	389	32	3,885	34,635	36	27,475
1923	121	19	425,724	131,774	—	2,042	18,505	—	72,898 [2]	330,841	2,812	1,135	374	33	19,471	46,026	1	44,643
1924	205	15	513,104	120,242	—	6,900	16,821	—	66,184	457,958	2,080	605	212	42	12,411	74,471	10	65,846
1925	360	19	624,869	152,142	387	2,315	19,596	—	45,257	439,107	2,226	641	448	34	7,014	93,911	—	69,264
1926	287	33	749,843	218,922	1,149	8,180	17,509	—	77,367	388,331	2,596	883	453	25	11,052	65,259	—	38,936
1927	363	28	632,049	225,928	984	6,787	16,239	—	46,847	418,424	2,663	913	134	52	4,506	113,640	35	41,454
1928	356	17	434,572	220,068	1,295	540	27,488	—	38,433	430,674	2,492	1,303	143	86	9,293	105,477	—	22,942
1929	387	23	674,928	322,727	2,710	9,540	37,648	—	60,788	373,059	3,189	1,325	150	47	9,153	66,452	205	13,073
1930	417	12	594,965	331,858	1,676	5,658	22,952	—	39,104	269,486	2,820	764	140	14	518	43,823	255	4,203
1931	311	6	510,582	215,938	76	—	13,698	—	79,129	183,885	1,490	443	86	7	9 [3]	19,654	249	583
1932	209	4	112,409	90,573	42	—	8,528	—	76,110	100,677	591	84	132	3	40	21,333	281	5,870
1933	152	7	159,352	118,380	141	—	19,867	—	4,928	113,019	875	157	161	3	41	20,716	1,715	1,039
1934	170	8	346,817	195,383	384	202	19,051	—	24,872	238,014	1,451	619	116	5	259 [4]	5,361	1,565	4,631

Year	Bauxite imports Db132 (Thousand metric tons)	Aluminum, crude and semicrude imports Db133 (Thousand metric tons)	Manganese ore (gross weight) imports Db134 (Metric tons)	Chromite (gross weight) imports Db135 (Metric tons)	Tungsten concentrates imports Db136 (Metric tons)	Vanadium ores and concentrates imports Db137 [1] (Metric tons)	Nickel (nickel content) imports Db138 (Metric tons)	Molybdenum ores and concentrates exports Db139 (Metric tons)	Refined copper Imports Db140 (Metric tons)	Refined copper Exports Db141 (Metric tons)	Iron ore Imports Db142 (Thousand metric tons)	Iron ore Exports Db143 (Thousand metric tons)	Pig iron Imports Db144 (Thousand metric tons)	Pig iron Exports Db145 (Thousand metric tons)	Refined lead Imports Db146 (Metric tons)	Refined lead Exports Db147 (Metric tons)	Refined zinc Imports Db148 (Metric tons)	Refined zinc Exports Db149 (Metric tons)
1935	203	10	389,654	263,221	368	46	31,026	—	16,394	236,535	1,516	672	133	5	1,241	6,334	4,032	1,467
1936	328	12	826,414	329,461	1,627	168	43,182	—	4,338	199,935	2,268	655	169	5	1,795	16,613	10,578	34
1937	515	21	926,556	562,805	2,523	616	43,998	—	6,792	267,678	2,481	1,284	113	795	2,136	18,226	33,755	226
1938	463	8	491,346	357,735	73	676	23,768	—	1,635	336,153	2,156	602	31	440	1,815	41,609 [4]	6,559 [4]	—
1939	528	13	637,192	322,606	674	1,043	52,798	—	14,754	338,178	2,452	1,074	39	180	4,329	67,487	28,086	4,096
1940	640	16	1,302,652	668,243	2,545	1,259	75,986	2,986	61,994	323,349	2,519	1,408	10	562	33,459	21,550	9,204	71,750
1941	1,135	12	1,555,442	1,011,776	5,226	1,046	96,327	3,465	314,788	93,986	2,382	1,939	4	525	295,741	13,026	36,549	81,020
1942	898	102	1,436,096	890,499	6,498	1,184	103,569	5,260	364,177	119,210	743	2,555	—	101	351,709	1,760	32,978	121,507
1943	1,567	123	1,371,328	842,390	8,821	1,004	111,123	4,569	365,380	159,537	405	2,464	1	131	221,383	1,817	50,943	88,395
1944	565	93	1,193,562	769,647	8,344	628	107,314	2,715	446,693	62,027	471	2,193	5	147	202,646	14,082	57,721	19,573
1945	749	308	1,189,633	839,951	2,165	758	97,462	1,298	482,048	44,056	1,217	2,096	19	83	206,213	1,277	87,779	7,060
1946	865	52	1,373,972	687,094	3,116	387	83,915	256	140,043	47,744	2,798	1,530	13	87	94,423	542	94,406	42,841
1947	1,872	28	1,177,519	1,003,483	2,730	481	73,226	1,356	135,604	133,939	4,975	2,856	30	10	143,975	1,382	65,374	96,769
1948	2,599	146	1,336,694	1,398,993	3,424	514	87,888	1,874	226,002	129,363	6,190	3,130	199	6	221,981	362	83,910	59,454
1949	2,774	113	1,291,743	1,092,116	2,846	270	82,620	2,413	250,212	125,035	7,510	2,464	91	73	247,151	879	113,910	53,260
1950	2,579	232	1,746,465	1,182,709	7,325	713	82,869	2,828	287,907	131,144	8,414	2,592	730	6	394,090	2,481	140,915	11,718
1951	2,865	147	1,726,245	1,295,369	2,892	481	84,541	1,692	216,792	120,932	10,303	4,398	968	6	162,405	1,162	79,871	33,121
1952	3,518	137	1,999,023	1,550,351	7,900	510	98,747	2,800	314,757	157,973	9,918	5,205	345	13	463,316	1,598	102,560	52,357
1953	4,298	326	2,825,902	2,019,966	12,728	351	107,716	3,192	248,669	99,409	11,252	4,320	535	17	343,931	728	206,524	16,301
1954	5,068	221	2,035,361	1,334,503	10,971	194	119,552	6,144	195,152	195,908	16,045	3,196	264	9	248,828	541	145,275	22,674
1955	4,960	217	2,053,728	1,391,621	9,389	91	128,820	6,613	183,534	181,273	23,849	4,589	258	32	239,476	366	176,955	16,392
1956	5,761	240	2,016,182	1,973,178	9,462	—	129,403	8,157	174,009	202,396	30,899	5,596	297	244	237,868	4,198	222,012	7,995
1957	7,212	234	2,303,500	2,070,850	6,358	—	127,006	11,551	147,244	313,909	34,191	5,082	204	800	291,849	3,936	243,873	9,784
1958	8,042	266	1,631,683	1,146,171	2,967	3	81,647	5,428	116,541	349,146	27,986	3,630	191	93	319,110	1,233	168,458	1,881
1959	8,280	274	1,703,752	1,409,354	2,466	3	101,605	8,551	194,190	144,186	36,189	3,015	635	9	238,256	2,500	149,197	10,550
1960	8,879	178	2,065,633	1,257,923	1,599	—	93,440	13,718	129,463	393,502	35,133	5,358	300	102	193,545	1,784	109,701	68,170
1961	9,354	231	1,947,900	1,205,768	963	—	115,212	16,176	60,650	388,927	26,219	5,038	342	377	224,462	1,935	113,567	45,409
1962	10,745	342	1,786,745	1,311,404	1,828	12	111,584	7,055	89,648	305,290	33,945	5,993	454	140	233,932	1,912	123,373	32,751
1963	9,408	423	2,167,737	1,262,000	1,388		107,955	12,041	108,154	282,569	33,797	6,921	585	64	199,942	987	120,050	30,711
1964	10,518	411	2,743,542	1,295,252	1,428		117,027	11,313	126,982	286,879	43,089	7,075	668	160	191,543	9,231	121,670	24,054
1965	11,601	562	3,497,740	1,377,413	1,641		147,871	13,469	124,686	294,803	45,827	7,199	800	25	202,720	7,086	139,667	5,388
1966	11,928	616	2,405,783	1,691,000	1,950	70	127,913	11,242	149,076	247,726	47,001	7,904	1,077	11	259,263	4,931	254,290	1,276
1967	12,330	489	1,869,926	1,125,000	771	41	129,727	13,608	299,889	144,563	45,327	6,001	549	6	329,849	5,929	201,397	15,249
1968	12,006	719	1,661,246	983,000	791	30	134,218	13,157	363,126	218,400	44,646	5,978	713	8	306,284	7,512	276,407	29,947
1969	13,132	506	1,777,775	1,003,000	682		117,328	25,209	118,996	181,681	41,386	5,243	367	40	252,989	4,507	294,616	8,435
1970	13,039	425	1,574,016	1,275,000	582		141,749	25,282	119,878	200,679	45,611	5,580	226	281	221,918	7,028	235,988	261
1971	12,837	626	1,736,592	1,178,000	190		128,986	20,994	148,767	170,237	40,768	3,110	278	31	174,697	5,375	294,159	12,107
1972	12,803	720	1,469,868	958,000	2,603		157,732	20,576	174,523	165,782	36,335	2,129	578	14	222,803	7,599	468,691	3,923
1973	13,618	557	1,369,662	845,000	4,914	2,578	162,744	33,547	184,118	171,817	43,991	2,791	405	14	161,584	60,397	535,920	13,214
1974	15,216	571	1,111,332	1,000,000	5,033	2,429	200,175	35,680	284,465	114,782	48,800	2,360	310	92	107,381	56,229	493,333	17,293
1975	11,714	499	1,427,950	1,136,000	2,890	2,830	145,610	28,400	128,914	156,422	47,493	2,578	434	54	89,860	19,283	340,124	6,257
1976	12,749	679	1,194,592	1,157,000	2,405	2,931	170,684	28,338	345,948	101,502	45,102	2,960	376	53	128,802	5,332	630,642	3,187
1977	12,989	758	844,541	1,173,000	3,138	2,749	176,692	29,786	360,870	46,745	38,514	2,177	338	46	230,069	8,931	503,621	215
1978	13,847	980	496,974	919,000	4,145	2,184	212,601	31,366	402,673	91,923	34,155	4,281	594	46	225,406	8,225	622,470	723
1979	13,780	762	453,395	929,000	5,149	2,387	160,758	32,768	203,855	73,677	34,318	5,231	432	95	182,550	10,646	524,130	279

Notes appear at end of table

(continued)

TABLE Db132–149   Metals – selected imports and exports: 1851–2000   Continued

Year	Bauxite imports — Db132 Thousand metric tons	Aluminum, crude and semicrude — imports — Db133 Thousand metric tons	Manganese ore (gross weight) — imports — Db134 Metric tons	Chromite (gross weight) — imports — Db135 Metric tons	Tungsten concentrates — imports — Db136 Metric tons	Vanadium ores and concentrates — Db137 [1] Metric tons	Nickel (nickel content) — imports — Db138 Metric tons	Molybdenum ores and concentrates — exports — Db139 Metric tons	Refined copper Imports — Db140 Metric tons	Refined copper Exports — Db141 Metric tons	Iron ore Imports — Db142 Thousand metric tons	Iron ore Exports — Db143 Thousand metric tons	Pig iron Imports — Db144 Thousand metric tons	Pig iron Exports — Db145 Thousand metric tons	Refined lead Imports — Db146 Metric tons	Refined lead Exports — Db147 Metric tons	Refined zinc Imports — Db148 Metric tons	Refined zinc Exports — Db149 Metric tons
1980	14,087	647	632,776	891,000	5,158	1,746	171,629	30,943	426,948	14,489	25,460	5,780	363	66	81,300	164,458	410,163	302
1981	12,802	848	579,819	815,000	5,331	2,380	189,609	23,292	330,625	24,397	28,783	5,635	425	15	100,108	23,320	612,007	323
1982	10,122	878	215,691	460,000	3,528	1,087	117,741	22,581	258,439	30,558	14,734	3,229	292	49	94,855	55,629	456,233	341
1983	7,601	1,091	334,000	173,000	2,861	57	138,194	21,350	459,567	81,397	13,459	3,842	220	5	134,357	24,351	617,679	427
1984	9,435	1,477	307,000	276,000	5,807	619	160,313	28,742	444,699	91,414	17,463	5,073	637	52	161,489	16,563	639,228	760
1985	7,158	1,420	351,000	376,000	4,746	296	143,054	28,966	377,723	37,937	16,024	5,114	307	29	131,353	37,322	610,900	1,011
1986	6,456	1,967	420,000	443,000	2,522	1,968	117,112	22,295	501,984	12,452	17,012	4,554	268	37	140,221	19,778	665,126	1,938
1987	9,156	1,850	309,000	490,000	4,414	2,054	134,511	18,377	469,159	9,197	16,849	5,093	322	45	185,673	13,586	705,985	1,082
1988	9,944	1,620	464,000	615,000	8,045	3,616	140,039	23,499	333,072	58,325	20,183	5,285	635	65	148,604	29,077	749,130	482
1989	10,893	1,470	580,000	525,000	7,896	4,210	127,880	51,231	300,110	130,189	19,596	5,365	443	11	115,681 [5]	43,837 [5]	711,554	5,532
1990	12,142	1,514	307,000	306,000	6,429	3,830	133,545	41,380	261,672	211,164	18,054	3,199	347	14	90,638	76,749	631,742	1,238
1991	11,900	1,490	234,000	212,000	7,837	882	132,446	33,424	288,586	263,217	13,335	4,045	434	15	116,473	113,872	549,137	1,253
1992	10,900	1,730	247,000	219,000	2,477	838	118,760	33,439	289,077	176,913	12,504	5,055	497	33	190,723	71,733	644,482	565
1993	11,600	2,540	232,000	255,000	1,720	1,450	126,352	28,280	343,375	126,741	14,097	5,060	828	27	195,572	60,300	723,563	1,410
1994	10,700	3,380	331,000	201,000	2,960	1,900	127,000	33,600	470,000	157,000	17,500	4,980	2,500	56	231,000	74,200	793,000	6,310
1995	10,100	1,980	394,000	253,000	4,660	2,530	157,200	44,600	429,000	217,000	17,600	5,270	2,360	56	264,000	65,300	856,000	3,080
1996	10,200	2,810	478,000	250,000	4,190	2,270	157,000	45,000	543,000	169,000	18,400	6,260	2,660	60	268,000	121,000	927,000	1,970
1997	10,700	3,080	510,000	303,000	4,850	2,950	154,600	57,200	647,000	92,900	18,600	6,350	6,350	86	265,000	94,000	876,000	3,630
1998	11,393	3,550	160,000	358,000	4,750	4,280	156,500	41,700	217,000	135,000	16,900	6,000	5,150	87	267,000	91,100	879,000	2,330
1999	10,189	4,000	224,000	252,000	2,870	2,950	148,480	27,900	313,000	150,000	14,300	6,120	4,990	83	311,000	101,000	966,000	1,880
2000	8,860	3,910	222,000	268,000	2,370	3,380	166,700	23,600	397,000	188,000	15,700	6,150	4,970	72	356,000	80,700	915,000	2,770

(Z) Series Db132, less than 500 long tons. Series Db133, less than 500 short tons.

1 Beginning 1973, vanadium concentrate.

2 Imports of refined copper from Chile, as reported by the Chile Exploration Company, were included by Mineral Resources of the United States in place of those of the Bureau of Foreign and Domestic Commerce, which were considered too low.

3 Comprises reclaimed scrap; no recorded imports of pigs and bars.

4 Includes sheets and pipes; figures not available separately.

5 Because of the implementation of the Harmonised Tariff system in January 1989, import and export categories for 1989 and after are not necessarily comparable with those in previous years.

6 Part of this is foreign lead mistakenly designated by customs collectors as domestic lead.

Sources

Series Db132. 1898–1931: U.S. Bureau of Mines, Mineral Resources of the United States (annual). 1932–1969: Minerals Yearbooks (annual). 1970–1990: Statistical Compendium (U.S. Geological Survey). 1991–1996: U.S. Bureau of Mines, Minerals Yearbooks (annual). 1997–2000: U.S. Geological Survey, Minerals Yearbooks (U.S. Department of the Interior, annual).

Series Db133–141. 1868–1931: U.S. Bureau of Mines, Mineral Resources of the United States. 1932–1996: U.S. Bureau of Mines, Minerals Yearbooks. 1997–2000: U.S. Geological Survey, Minerals Yearbooks.

Series Db142–149. 1851–1931: Mineral Resources of the United States. 1932–1996: U.S. Bureau of Mines, Minerals Yearbooks. 1997–2000: U.S. Geological Survey, Minerals Yearbooks.

Documentation

Series Db132. For 1934–1950, the figures are in terms of "dried bauxite equivalent," an adjustment in the Department of Commerce series made by the Bureau of Mines. Figures are not adjusted for moisture content for other years, except from Jamaica, beginning 1952. The figures do not include calcined bauxite. Bauxite exports are not reported because they are insignificant.

Series Db133. Aluminum imports include metals and alloys, crude; scrap; and plates, sheets, bars, etc.

Series Db134. Manganese ore imports are reported by gross weight. Prior to 1915, the figures are restricted to ores containing at least 40 percent manganese; beginning in 1915, the cut-off point is reduced to 35 percent. For 1868–1888, figures are Canadian imports only; totals are not available.

Series Db135. Reported by gross weight of chromite ore.

Series Db136–139. Weights expressed in terms of metallic content.

Series Db136. Tungsten concentrate imports are reported by gross weight for 1912–1922 and by tungsten content thereafter.

Series Db137. Vanadium ores and concentrates imports are reported by gross weight for 1918–1933 and by vanadium content thereafter. (For 1934, the vanadium content equaled 207 short tons compared to the gross weight of 1754 short tons.) Imports of vanadium ores ceased after 1968. Beginning in 1973, the figures are imports of slags and residues (vanadium content).

TABLE Db132–149   Metals – selected imports and exports: 1851–2000   *Continued*

Series Db138. Nickel import figures represent nickel content.

Series Db139. Molybdenum ores and concentrates exports represent molybdenum content, and include roasted concentrates, metals and alloys, crude, and scrap. Export figures are not available before 1940, though molybdenum exports were of substantial importance.

Series Db140–141. Imports and exports of refined copper only. Imports of copper ore, concentrates, and various unrefined copper metallic materials have historically been larger than imports of refined copper. Neither imports nor exports of unmanufactured copper, however, have been tabulated separately until the 1980s.

Series Db144–145. Prior to 1922, pig iron imports and exports were not shown separately from ferroalloys.

Series Db146–147. Although the figures for imports and exports of refined lead purport to refer to refined lead in pigs and bars, the specific items included changed frequently over the long period and can be identified only by referring to the original sources. For example, for 1867–1934, imports of old lead were also included. For 1914 and 1915, exports of lead refined domestically from foreign ores were not included.

Series Db148–149. Figures for imports and exports of refined zinc represent zinc in blocks, pigs, and slabs. The specific items included, however, changed frequently over the long period and can be identified only by referring to the original sources.

TABLE Db150–154   Nonfuel nonmetals – selected imports and exports: 1867–2000

Contributed by Gavin Wright

	Sulfur						Sulfur				
	Crude imports	Crude exports	Pyrites imports	Potash imports	Phosphate rock exports		Crude imports	Crude exports	Pyrites imports	Potash imports	Phosphate rock exports
	Db150	Db151 [1]	Db152	Db153	Db154		Db150	Db151 [1]	Db152	Db153	Db154
Year	Thousand metric tons	Thousand metric tons	Thousand metric tons	Thousand metric tons	Thousand metric tons	Year	Thousand metric tons	Thousand metric tons	Thousand metric tons	Thousand metric tons	Thousand metric tons
1867	25	—	—	—	—	1905	84	12	512	117	—
1868	18	—	—	—	—	1906	73	14	598	142	—
1869	24	—	—	—	—	1907	20	37	628	131	1,034
1870	27	—	—	—	—	1908	20	28	668	123	1,207
1871	37	—	—	—	—	1909	29	38	689	157	1,038
1872	25	—	—	—	—	1910	29	31	804	254	1,100
1873	47	—	—	—	—	1911	24	28	1,006	249	1,267
1874	42	—	—	—	—	1912	27	59	971	230	1,227
1875	41	—	—	—	—	1913	15	90	851	247	1,389
1876	47	—	—	—	—	1914	24	100	1,027	188	980
1877	44	—	—	—	—	1915	25	38	965	44	257
1878	49	—	—	—	—	1916	21	131	1,245	7	248
1879	71	—	—	—	—	1917	1	155	967	7	169
1880	89	—	—	—	—	1918	(Z)	133	497	7	145
1881	107	—	—	—	—	1919	(Z)	229	389	36	385
1882	100	—	—	—	—	1920	(Z)	485	333	204	1,087
1883	97	—	—	—	—	1921	(Z)	291	216	72	745
1884	107	—	17	—	—	1922	(Z)	494	279	182	730
1885	99	—	6	—	—	1923	(Z)	481	264	191	841
1886	120	—	2	—	—	1924	1	490	247	181	832
1887	99	—	17	—	—	1925	(Z)	639	276	234	884
1888	100	—	—	—	—	1926	(Z)	586	366	241	761
1889	138	—	—	—	—	1927	3	802	251	221	933
1890	166	—	—	—	—	1928	5	696	457	299	914
1891	119	—	101	—	—	1929	1	869	514	295	1,161
1892	103	—	152	—	—	1930	(Z)	603	355	310	1,246
1893	108	—	195	—	—	1931	—	415	352	195	966
1894	127	—	164	—	—	1932	—	359	253	103	623
1895	123	—	190	—	—	1933	5	531	373	156	842
1896	140	—	200	—	—	1934	6	515	366	156	1,009
1897	139	—	260	—	—	1935	2	408	397	220	1,121
1898	153	—	253	—	—	1936	1	556	429	192	1,228
1899	142	—	270	—	—	1937	(Z)	686	524	318	1,070
1900	170	—	322	—	—	1938	(Z)	588	334	176	1,159
1901	177	—	404	—	—	1939	(Z)	638	482	91	964
1902	174	—	440	—	—						
1903	192	—	420	—	—						
1904	130	3	423	—	—						

Notes appear at end of table

(continued)

TABLE Db150–154   Nonfuel nonmetals – selected imports and exports: 1867–2000   *Continued*

	Sulfur							Sulfur				
	Crude imports	Crude exports	Pyrites imports	Potash imports	Phosphate rock exports			Crude imports	Crude exports	Pyrites imports	Potash imports	Phosphate rock exports
	Db150	Db151 [1]	Db152	Db153	Db154			Db150	Db151 [1]	Db152	Db153	Db154
Year	Thousand metric tons	Thousand metric tons	Thousand metric tons	Thousand metric tons	Thousand metric tons		Year	Thousand metric tons	Thousand metric tons	Thousand metric tons	Thousand metric tons	Thousand metric tons
1940	—	758	407	108	763		1975	1,927	1,309	—	3,445	11,131
1941	—	741	369	15	1,036		1976	1,755	1,202	—	4,168	9,433
1942	—	577	300	4	537		1977	2,009	1,076	—	4,605	13,230
1943	—	668	256	15	364		1978	2,177	827	—	4,707	12,870
1944	—	664	181	5	446		1979	2,494	1,963	—	5,165	14,358
1945	—	934	187	5	499		1980	2,523	1,673	—	4,972	14,276
1946	—	1,208	183	4	710		1981	2,522	1,392	—	4,796	10,395
1947	—	1,320	127	24	1,671		1982	1,905	961	—	3,858	9,842
1948	—	1,283	107	24	1,033		1983	1,695	992	—	4,440	12,010
1949	(Z)	1,454	121	17	1,338		1984	2,557	1,334	—	4,829	11,528
1950	—	1,464	209	182	1,788		1985	2,104	1,365	—	4,593	9,136
1951	2	1,309	221	285	1,704		1986	1,347	1,895	—	4,212	7,848
1952	5	1,325	296	171	1,424		1987	1,599	1,242	—	4,073	8,454
1953	1	1,262	190	122	2,095		1988	1,996	1,223	—	4,217	8,092
1954	(Z)	1,671	47 [2]	108	2,315		1989	2,260	1,024	—	3,410 [3]	7,842
1955	36	1,627	80 [2]	161	2,218		1990	2,571	972	—	4,164	6,238
1956	215	1,677	73 [2]	164	2,728		1991	3,020	1,196	—	4,158	5,082
1957	507	1,603	71 [2]	165	3,058		1992	2,725	966	—	4,248	3,723
1958	600	1,603	343	181	2,737		1993	2,039	656	—	4,363	3,198
1959	652	1,638	281	212	3,097		1994	1,650	899	—	4,800	2,800
1960	753	1,805	306	205	4,058		1995	2,510	906	—	4,820	2,760
1961	849	1,611	282	238	3,981		1996	1,960	855	—	4,940	1,570
1962	1,057	1,562	302	309	3,997		1997	2,060	703	—	5,490	335
1963	1,373	1,629	194	539	4,620		1998	2,270	889	—	7,870	378
1964	1,485	1,951	120	669	5,782		1999	2,580	685	—	7,360	272
1965	1,510	2,666	160	1,005	6,643		2000	2,330	762	—	7,580	299
1966	1,538	2,363	160	1,353	8,390							
1967	1,498	2,076	165	1,549	9,137							
1968	1,597	1,574	140	1,965	10,976							
1969	1,702	1,574	120	2,116	10,284							
1970	1,562	1,452	130	2,363	10,649							
1971	1,320	1,557	130	2,509	11,419							
1972	1,156	1,877	50	2,686	12,950							
1973	1,242	1,799	—	3,254	12,585							
1974	2,185	2,621	—	3,924	12,605							

(Z) Less than 500 long tons.

[1] Beginning 1981, includes exports from the Virgin Islands to foreign countries.

[2] Data for 1954–1957 not strictly comparable with years before or after. Estimated comparable totals for those years should include an additional 232,920, 277,860, 292,520, and 282,000 long tons, respectively.

[3] Imports probably underreported.

Sources

1851–1931: U.S. Bureau of Mines, *Mineral Resources of the United States*. 1932–1996: U.S. Bureau of Mines, *Minerals Yearbooks* (annual). 1997–2000: U.S. Geological Survey, *Minerals Yearbooks* (U.S. Department of the Interior, annual).

Documentation

Series Db150. Crude imports of sulfur represent imports of crude sulfur and sulfur ore. Also includes elemental Frasch and recovered imports. For 1867–1883, pyrites imports are presumably included. Although no imports of sulfur ore are reported for most of the 1940s, processors stated that during 1941–1945 at least 2,000 tons of sulfur ore were imported from Mexico.

Figures for 1867–1887 are on a fiscal year basis ending June 30; beginning in 1888, they are on a calendar year basis.

Series Db151. Exports of crude sulfur have been separately classified since 1905. The first shipment occurred in 1904 when 3,000 tons were shipped from Louisiana to France.

Series Db152. Imports of pyrites were included with sulfur ore prior to 1884; for 1888–1890, they were included under imports of iron ores. Imports of pyrites ended in 1972 because the product was no longer competitive with elemental sulfur.

Series Db153. Potash imports represent crude and refined potash materials, expressed in terms of approximate K_2O equivalent.

Series Db154. Exports of phosphate rock generally include high-grade hard rock, land pebble, and other (colloidal matrix, soft phosphate rock, and Tennessee, Idaho, and Montana rock). Sintered matrix is included only for selected years. For 1942–1946, Florida soft rock, colloidal, and sintered matrix are excluded.

ENERGY

Gavin Wright

TABLE Db155–163   Energy production, by source: 1800–2001[1]

Contributed by Gavin Wright

Year	Fossil fuel Db155 [2] Trillion BTU	Coal Db156 [2] Trillion BTU	Crude petroleum Db157 Trillion BTU	Natural gas Total Db158 [3] Trillion BTU	Dry Db159 Trillion BTU	Liquids Db160 Trillion BTU	Nuclear electric power Db161 Trillion BTU	Geothermal energy Db162 Trillion BTU	Hydroelectric power Db163 [4] Trillion BTU
1800	3	3	—	—	—	—	—	—	—
1805	4	4	—	—	—	—	—	—	—
1810	5	5	—	—	—	—	—	—	—
1815	7	7	—	—	—	—	—	—	—
1820	9	9	—	—	—	—	—	—	—
1825	12	12	—	—	—	—	—	—	—
1830	23	23	—	—	—	—	—	—	—
1835	47	47	—	—	—	—	—	—	—
1840	64	64	—	—	—	—	—	—	—
1845	122	122	—	—	—	—	—	—	—
1850	216	216	—	—	—	—	—	—	—
1855	417	417	—	—	—	—	—	—	—
1860	519	516	3	—	—	—	—	—	—
1865	645	631	14	—	—	—	—	—	—
1870	1,074	1,043	31	—	—	—	—	—	—
1875	1,494	1,443	51	—	—	—	—	—	—
1880	2,210	2,058	152	—	—	—	—	—	—
1885	3,063	2,854	127	82	—	—	—	—	—
1890	4,619	4,096	266	257	—	—	—	—	—
1895	5,467	5,013	307	147	—	—	—	—	—
1900	7,643	7,020	369	254	—	—	—	—	250
1901	8,316	7,631	402	283	—	—	—	—	264
1902	8,685	7,869	515	301	—	—	—	—	289
1903	10,205	9,303	583	319	—	—	—	—	321
1904	10,171	9,159	679	333	—	—	—	—	354
1905	11,386	10,228	781	377	—	—	—	—	386
1906	11,946	10,794	734	418	—	—	—	—	414
1907	13,917	12,517	963	437	—	—	—	—	441
1908	12,295	10,828	1,035	432	—	—	—	—	476
1909	13,587	12,008	1,062	517	—	—	—	—	513
1910	14,836	13,074	1,215	547	—	—	—	—	539
1911	14,763	12,933	1,279	551	—	—	—	—	565
1912	15,833	13,936	1,293	604	—	—	—	—	585
1913	16,927	14,860	1,441	626	—	—	—	—	609
1914	15,559	13,382	1,541	636	—	—	—	—	636
1915	16,163	13,857	1,630	676	—	—	—	—	659
1916	17,944	15,390	1,744	810	—	—	—	—	681
1917	19,787	16,987	1,945	855	—	—	—	—	700
1918	20,529	17,690	2,064	775	—	—	—	—	701
1919	17,441	14,444	2,195	802	—	—	—	—	718
1920	20,627	17,175	2,569	883	—	—	—	—	738
1921	16,666	13,195	2,739	732	—	—	—	—	620
1922	16,529	12,452	3,234	843	—	—	—	—	643
1923	22,524	17,163	4,248	1,113	—	—	—	—	685
1924	20,309	14,905	4,141	1,263	—	—	—	—	648
1925	20,939	15,195	4,430	1,314	—	—	—	—	668
1926	23,088	17,165	4,471	1,452	—	—	—	—	728
1927	22,424	15,599	5,227	1,598	—	—	—	—	776
1928	21,997	15,034	5,229	1,734	—	—	—	—	854
1929	28,852	15,892	5,842	2,118	—	—	—	—	816
1930	21,367	14,011	5,208	2,148	—	—	—	—	752
1931	18,331	11,526	4,936	1,869	—	—	—	—	668
1932	15,663	9,380	4,554	1,729	—	—	—	—	713
1933	16,985	9,999	5,253	1,733	—	—	—	—	711
1934	18,104	10,867	5,267	1,970	—	—	—	—	698

Notes appear at end of table

(continued)

TABLE Db155–163   Energy production, by source: 1800–2001   *Continued*

Year	Fossil fuel Db155 [2] Trillion BTU	Coal Db156 [2] Trillion BTU	Crude petroleum Db157 Trillion BTU	Natural gas Total Db158 [3] Trillion BTU	Natural gas Dry Db159 Trillion BTU	Natural gas Liquids Db160 Trillion BTU	Nuclear electric power Db161 Trillion BTU	Geothermal energy Db162 Trillion BTU	Hydroelectric power Db163 [4] Trillion BTU
1935	18,997	11,081	5,780	2,136	—	—	—	—	806
1936	21,679	12,890	6,378	2,411	—	—	—	—	812
1937	23,093	12,990	7,419	2,684	—	—	—	—	871
1938	19,911	10,303	7,043	2,565	—	—	—	—	866
1939	21,753	11,653	7,337	2,763	—	—	—	—	838
1940	24,208	13,380	7,849	2,979	—	—	—	—	880
1941	26,198	14,903	8,133	3,162	—	—	—	—	934
1942	28,278	16,799	8,043	3,436	—	—	—	—	1,136
1943	29,575	17,003	8,733	3,839	—	—	—	—	1,304
1944	31,759	17,851	9,732	4,176	—	—	—	—	1,344
1945	30,891	16,529	9,939	4,423	—	—	—	—	1,442
1946	30,133	15,526	10,057	4,550	—	—	—	—	1,406
1947	33,758	17,975	10,771	5,012	—	—	—	—	1,296
1948	34,490	17,158	11,717	5,615	—	—	—	—	1,369
1949	28,748	11,974	10,683	6,091	5,377	714	—	—	1,425
1950	32,563	14,060	11,447	7,056	6,233	823	—	—	1,415
1951	35,792	14,419	13,037	8,336	7,416	920	—	—	1,424
1952	34,977	12,735	13,281	8,962	7,964	998	—	—	1,466
1953	35,349	12,278	13,671	9,401	8,339	1,062	—	—	1,413
1954	33,764	10,542	13,427	9,795	8,682	1,113	—	—	1,360
1955	37,364	12,370	14,410	10,585	9,345	1,240	—	—	1,360
1956	39,771	13,306	15,180	11,285	10,002	1,283	—	—	1,435
1957	40,133	13,061	15,178	11,894	10,605	1,289	(Z)	—	1,422
1958	37,216	10,783	14,204	12,229	10,942	1,287	2	—	1,592
1959	39,045	10,778	14,933	13,335	11,952	1,383	2	—	1,551
1960	39,869	10,817	14,935	14,117	12,656	1,461	6	1	1,608
1961	40,307	10,447	15,206	14,654	13,105	1,549	20	2	1,656
1962	41,732	10,901	15,522	15,310	13,717	1,593	26	2	1,816
1963	44,037	11,849	15,966	16,222	14,513	1,709	38	4	1,768
1964	45,789	12,524	16,164	17,101	15,298	1,803	40	5	1,886
1965	47,235	13,055	16,521	17,658	15,775	1,883	43	4	2,059
1966	50,036	13,468	17,561	19,007	17,011	1,996	64	4	2,062
1967	52,597	13,826	18,651	20,120	17,943	2,177	88	7	2,347
1968	54,306	13,608	19,308	21,389	19,068	2,321	142	9	2,349
1969	56,286	13,864	19,556	22,866	20,446	2,420	154	13	2,648
1970	59,186	14,607	20,401	24,178	21,666	2,512	239	11	2,630
1971	58,041	13,185	20,033	24,824	22,280	2,544	413	12	2,820
1972	58,938	14,091	20,041	24,806	22,208	2,598	584	31	2,860
1973	58,242	13,993	19,493	24,756	22,187	2,569	910	43	2,860
1974	56,331	14,074	18,575	23,681	21,210	2,471	1,272	53	3,180
1975	54,734	14,990	17,729	22,014	19,640	2,374	1,900	70	3,150
1976	54,723	15,654	17,262	21,807	19,480	2,327	2,111	78	2,980
1977	55,101	15,755	17,454	21,892	19,565	2,327	2,702	77	2,330
1978	55,074	14,910	18,434	21,730	19,485	2,245	3,024	64	2,940
1979	58,005	17,539	18,104	22,362	20,076	2,286	2,776	84	2,930
1980	59,007	18,597	18,249	22,162	19,908	2,254	2,739	110	2,900
1981	58,529	18,376	18,146	22,006	19,699	2,307	3,008	123	2,760
1982	57,458	18,639	18,309	20,510	18,319	2,191	3,131	105	3,260
1983	54,416	17,246	18,392	18,777	16,593	2,184	3,203	129	3,500
1984	58,849	19,719	18,848	20,282	18,008	2,274	3,553	165	3,310
1985	57,539	19,325	18,992	19,221	16,980	2,241	4,149	198	2,940
1986	56,576	19,510	18,376	18,690	16,541	2,149	4,471	219	3,030
1987	57,167	20,142	17,675	19,351	17,136	2,215	4,906	229	2,635
1988	57,874	20,737	17,279	19,859	17,599	2,260	5,661	217	2,334
1989	57,468	21,345	16,117	20,005	17,847	2,158	5,677	321	2,839
1990	58,564	22,456	15,571	20,537	18,362	2,175	6,161	344	3,033
1991	57,829	21,594	15,701	20,535	18,229	2,306	6,579	349	3,008
1992	57,590	21,629	15,223	20,738	18,375	2,363	6,607	361	2,619
1993	55,736	20,249	14,494	20,992	18,584	2,408	6,519	375	2,893
1994	57,952	22,111	14,103	21,739	19,348	2,391	6,837	370	2,685

Notes appear at end of table

TABLE Db155–163   Energy production, by source: 1800–2001   *Continued*

Year	Fossil fuel Db155 [2] Trillion BTU	Coal Db156 [2] Trillion BTU	Crude petroleum Db157 Trillion BTU	Natural gas — Total Db158 [3] Trillion BTU	Natural gas — Dry Db159 Trillion BTU	Natural gas — Liquids Db160 Trillion BTU	Nuclear electric power Db161 Trillion BTU	Geothermal energy Db162 Trillion BTU	Hydroelectric power Db163 [4] Trillion BTU
1995	57,458	22,029	13,887	21,542	19,101	2,441	7,177	321	3,209
1996	58,236	22,684	13,723	21,830	19,300	2,530	7,168	339	3,593
1997	58,758	23,211	13,658	21,889	19,394	2,495	6,678	322	3,718
1998	59,204	23,935	13,235	22,033	19,613	2,420	7,157	327	3,345
1999	57,505	23,186	12,451	21,869	19,341	2,528	7,736	335	3,305
2000	57,054	22,623	12,358	22,072	19,461	2,611	8,009	319	2,883
2001	58,262	23,574	12,282	22,406	19,859	2,547	8,167	312	2,245

(Z) Less than 500 billion BTU.

[1] Discontinuity in some series between 1989 and 1990 because of changes in coverage of renewable energy sources.

[2] Discontinuity between 1948 and 1949 because of a change in source.

[3] Data prior to 1920 are not strictly comparable with those for later years because net storage change and transmission losses were not included.

[4] Beginning 1990, pumped storage is removed from hydroelectric power production.

Sources

Series Db155. Based on series Db156–157 and Db159.

Series Db156. 1800–1849: production series from H. N. Eavenson, *The First Century and a Quarter of American Coal Industry* (Waverly Press, 1942), converted to BTU at the same rate as data for more recent years. 1850–1885: Resources for the Future, *Energy in the American Economy* (Johns Hopkins University Press, 1960). 1890–1948: converted to BTU from physical quantities shown in successive volumes of U.S. Bureau of Mines, *Mineral Resources of the United States* (annual) and *Minerals Yearbooks* (annual). 1949–2001: U.S. Energy Information Administration, *Annual Energy Review* (U.S. Department of Energy, annual).

Series Db157. 1860–1895, converted to BTU from physical quantities shown in successive volumes of U.S. Bureau of Mines, *Mineral Resources of*

the United States. 1900–1948: *Minerals Yearbooks.* 1949–2001: U.S. Energy Information Administration, *Annual Energy Review.*

Series Db158. 1885–1948: Resources for the Future, *Energy in the American Economy.* 1949–2001: based on series Db159–160.

Series Db159–162. *Annual Energy Review.*

Series Db163. 1900–1949: U.S. Bureau of Mines, *Minerals Yearbooks.* 1949–2001: *Annual Energy Review.*

Documentation

A British thermal unit (BTU) is the quantity of heat required to raise the temperature of one pound of water one degree Fahrenheit, at or near its point of maximum density.

Series Db155. Equals the sum of series Db156–157 and Db159.

Series Db156. Bituminous coal (including lignite) plus Pennsylvania anthracite coal.

Series Db157. Includes lease condensate.

Series Db158. For 1949–1998, equals the sum of series Db159–160. Data represent marketed production of wet and dry gas. Prior to 1900, the figures are based on the estimated quantity of coal and fuel wood displaced, rather than measures of gas produced.

TABLE Db164–171   Energy consumption, by energy source: 1850–2001[1]

Contributed by Gavin Wright

Year	Fossil fuels — Total Db164 [2] Trillion BTU	Fossil fuels — Coal Db165 [3] Trillion BTU	Fossil fuels — Petroleum Db166 [4] Trillion BTU	Natural gas Db167 Trillion BTU	Hydroelectric power Db168 [5] Trillion BTU	Nuclear electric power Db169 Trillion BTU	Geothermal energy Db170 Trillion BTU	Fuel wood Db171 Trillion BTU
1850	219	219	—	—	—	—	—	2,138
1855	421	421	—	—	—	—	—	2,389
1860	521	518	3	—	—	—	—	2,641
1865	642	632	10	—	—	—	—	2,767
1870	1,059	1,048	11	—	—	—	—	2,893
1875	1,451	1,440	11	—	—	—	—	2,872
1880	2,150	2,054	96	—	—	—	—	2,851
1885	2,962	2,840	40	82	—	—	—	2,683
1890	4,475	4,062	156	257	22	—	—	2,515
1895	5,265	4,950	168	147	90	—	—	2,306
1900	7,322	6,841	229	252	250	—	—	1,703
1901	7,996	7,465	250	281	264	—	—	1,686
1902	8,426	7,763	364	299	289	—	—	1,669
1903	9,924	9,158	449	317	321	—	—	1,654
1904	9,816	8,952	534	330	354	—	—	1,637
1905	10,983	10,001	610	372	386	—	—	1,611
1906	11,507	10,541	555	411	414	—	—	1,591
1907	13,390	12,177	781	432	441	—	—	1,580
1908	11,762	10,515	820	427	476	—	—	1,573
1909	13,018	11,663	844	511	513	—	—	1,567

Notes appear at end of table

(continued)

TABLE Db164–171   Energy consumption, by energy source: 1850–2001   *Continued*

	Fossil fuels			Hydroelectric power	Nuclear electric power	Geothermal energy	Fuel wood
	Total	Coal	Petroleum	Natural gas				
Year	Db164 [2]	Db165 [3]	Db166 [4]	Db167	Db168 [5]	Db169	Db170	Db171
	Trillion BTU	Trillion BTU	Trillion BTU	Trillion BTU	Trillion BTU	Trillion BTU	Trillion BTU	Trillion BTU
1910	14,261	12,714	1,007	540	539	—	—	1,587
1911	14,027	12,442	1,041	544	597	—	—	1,593
1912	15,093	13,440	1,059	594	615	—	—	1,543
1913	16,074	14,241	1,213	620	645	—	—	1,529
1914	14,858	12,901	1,325	632	676	—	—	1,539
1915	15,385	13,294	1,418	673	691	—	—	1,498
1916	17,052	14,737	1,508	807	729	—	—	1,520
1917	18,842	16,213	1,779	850	755	—	—	1,490
1918	19,686	16,973	1,942	771	750	—	—	1,506
1919	16,792	13,801	2,198	793	766	—	—	1,476
1920	19,400	15,504	3,069	827	775	—	—	1,471
1921	16,096	12,348	3,066	682	656	—	—	1,456
1922	16,859	12,628	3,446	785	675	—	—	1,387
1923	21,347	15,806	4,509	1,032	727	—	—	1,348
1924	20,232	14,731	4,331	1,170	685	—	—	1,334
1925	20,683	14,706	4,765	1,212	701	—	—	1,304
1926	22,275	15,915	5,025	1,335	765	—	—	1,251
1927	21,663	14,992	5,206	1,465	815	—	—	1,261
1928	22,202	14,940	5,674	1,588	890	—	—	1,261
1929	23,509	15,427	6,140	1,942	847	—	—	1,270
1930	21,999	13,639	6,391	1,969	785	—	—	1,325
1931	18,446	11,227	5,504	1,715	692	—	—	1,378
1932	15,906	9,324	4,988	1,594	726	—	—	1,461
1933	16,470	9,583	5,287	1,600	729	—	—	1,506
1934	17,534	10,418	5,297	1,819	721	—	—	1,476
1935	18,576	10,634	5,968	1,974	831	—	—	1,437
1936	20,879	12,048	6,610	2,221	841	—	—	1,422
1937	22,246	12,566	7,212	2,468	905	—	—	1,392
1938	19,437	9,959	7,130	2,348	899	—	—	1,412
1939	21,203	11,116	7,548	2,539	872	—	—	1,417
1940	23,166	12,535	7,905	2,726	917	—	—	1,368
1941	25,839	14,281	8,707	2,851	975	—	—	1,348
1942	27,040	15,584	8,354	3,102	1,177	—	—	1,159
1943	29,405	17,007	8,917	3,481	1,347	—	—	1,110
1944	31,096	16,956	10,365	3,775	1,387	—	—	1,130
1945	30,635	15,972	10,690	3,973	1,486	—	—	1,096
1946	29,331	14,479	10,763	4,089	1,446	—	—	1,075
1947	30,747	14,600	11,629	4,518	1,326	—	—	1,091
1948	32,634	14,897	12,704	5,033	1,393	—	—	1,100
1949	29,002	11,981	11,883	5,145	1,449	0	0	1,095
1950	31,632	12,347	13,315	5,968	1,440	0	0	1,017
1951	34,008	12,553	14,428	7,049	1,454	0	0	1,002
1952	33,800	11,306	14,956	7,550	1,496	0	0	978
1953	34,826	11,373	15,556	7,907	1,439	0	0	931
1954	33,877	9,715	15,839	8,330	1,388	0	0	885
1955	37,410	11,167	17,255	8,998	1,407	0	0	838
1956	38,888	11,350	17,937	9,614	1,487	0	0	792
1957	38,926	10,821	17,932	10,191	1,557	(Z)	0	746
1958	38,717	9,533	18,527	10,663	1,629	2	0	702
1959	40,550	9,518	19,323	11,717	1,587	2	0	656
1960	42,137	9,838	19,919	12,385	1,657	6	1	612
1961	42,758	9,623	20,216	12,926	1,680	20	2	569
1962	44,681	9,906	21,049	13,731	1,822	26	2	524
1963	46,509	10,413	21,701	14,403	1,772	38	4	507
1964	48,543	10,965	22,301	15,288	1,907	40	5	489
1965	50,576	11,580	23,246	15,769	2,058	43	4	468
1966	53,514	12,143	24,401	16,995	2,073	64	4	447
1967	55,127	11,914	25,284	17,945	2,344	88	7	424
1968	58,502	12,330	26,979	19,210	2,342	142	9	396
1969	61,362	12,382	28,338	20,678	2,659	154	13	364

Notes appear at end of table

TABLE Db164–171   Energy consumption, by energy source: 1850–2001   *Continued*

Year	Fossil fuels Total Db164 [2] Trillion BTU	Fossil fuels Coal Db165 [3] Trillion BTU	Fossil fuels Petroleum Db166 [4] Trillion BTU	Fossil fuels Natural gas Db167 Trillion BTU	Hydroelectric power Db168 [5] Trillion BTU	Nuclear electric power Db169 Trillion BTU	Geothermal energy Db170 Trillion BTU	Fuel wood Db171 Trillion BTU
1970	63,522	12,264	29,521	21,795	2,654	239	11	329
1971	64,596	11,599	30,561	22,469	2,861	413	12	303
1972	67,696	12,077	32,947	22,698	2,944	584	31	286
1973	70,316	12,971	34,840	22,512	3,010	910	43	302
1974	67,906	12,663	33,455	21,732	3,309	1,272	53	317
1975	65,355	12,663	32,731	19,948	3,219	1,900	70	341
1976	69,104	13,584	35,175	20,345	3,066	2,111	78	363
1977	70,989	13,922	37,122	19,931	2,515	2,702	77	385
1978	71,856	13,765	37,965	20,000	3,141	3,024	64	—
1979	72,892	15,039	37,123	20,666	3,141	2,776	84	—
1980	69,984	15,423	34,202	20,394	3,118	2,739	110	—
1981	67,750	15,907	31,931	19,928	3,105	3,008	123	—
1982	64,037	15,322	30,232	18,505	3,572	3,131	105	—
1983	63,290	15,894	30,054	17,357	3,899	3,203	129	—
1984	66,617	17,071	31,051	18,507	3,800	3,553	165	—
1985	66,221	17,478	30,922	17,834	3,398	4,149	198	—
1986	66,148	17,261	32,196	16,708	3,446	4,471	219	—
1987	68,626	18,008	32,865	17,744	3,117	4,906	229	—
1988	71,660	18,846	34,222	18,552	2,662	5,661	217	—
1989	72,551	18,925	34,211	19,384	2,982	5,677	332	—
1990	71,955	19,101	33,553	19,296	3,124	6,161	355	—
1991	71,231	18,770	32,845	19,606	3,208	6,579	365	—
1992	72,842	19,158	33,527	20,131	2,863	6,607	379	—
1993	74,461	19,776	33,841	20,827	3,147	6,519	393	—
1994	76,006	19,960	34,735	21,288	2,971	6,837	395	—
1995	76,877	20,024	34,663	22,163	3,474	7,177	339	—
1996	79,364	20,940	35,864	22,560	3,913	7,168	352	—
1997	80,387	21,444	36,381	22,530	3,922	6,678	322	—
1998	80,538	21,667	36,934	21,937	3,569	7,157	328	—
1999	81,840	21,677	37,960	22,203	3,512	7,736	335	—
2000	83,947	22,432	38,404	23,111	3,152	8,009	319	—
2001	81,603	21,800	38,333	21,470	2,404	8,167	312	—

(Z) Less than 500 billion BTU.

[1] Discontinuity between 1948 and 1949 because of a change in source. Discontinuity in some series between 1989 and 1990 because of changes in coverage of renewable energy consumption.

[2] Equals the sum of series Db165–167. Beginning in 1949, also includes coke net imports.

[3] Beginning 1992, independent power producers' use of coal is included.

[4] Petroleum products supplied, including natural gas plant liquids and crude oil burned as fuel. Includes net trade in oil products before 1920.

[5] Includes all net imports of electricity through 1989; thereafter, includes only the portion of net imports of electricity that is derived from hydroelectric power.

Sources

Series Db164. Based on series Db165–167, plus U.S. Energy Information Administration, *Annual Energy Review* (U.S. Department of Energy, annual).

Series Db165–170. 1850–1919: Resources for the Future, *Energy in the American Economy* (Johns Hopkins University Press, 1960). 1920–1948: U.S. Bureau of Mines, *Minerals Yearbooks* (annual). 1949–2001: U.S. Energy Information Administration, *Annual Energy Review* (U.S. Department of Energy, annual).

Series Db171. 1800–1945: Resources for the Future, *Energy in the American Economy*. 1946–1977: based on U.S. Forest Service data as used in U.S. Bureau of the Census and U.S. Bureau of Mines, *Raw Materials in the United States Economy 1900–1977*, Technical Paper number 47 (1980).

Documentation

A British thermal unit (BTU) is the quantity of heat required to raise the temperature of one pound of water one degree Fahrenheit, at or near its point of maximum density.

TABLE Db172–181   Renewable energy production and consumption, by energy source: 1949–2001[1]

Contributed by Gavin Wright

	Production					Consumption				
	Conventional hydroelectric power	Geothermal energy	Wood and waste	Solar energy	Wind energy	Conventional hydroelectric power	Geothermal energy	Wood and waste	Solar energy	Wind energy
	Db172	Db173	Db174 [2]	Db175	Db176	Db177	Db178	Db179 [2]	Db180	Db181
Year	Trillion BTU	Trillion BTU	Trillion BTU	Trillion BTU	Trillion BTU	Trillion BTU	Trillion BTU	Trillion BTU	Trillion BTU	Trillion BTU
1949	1,425	0	1,549	0	0	1,449	0	1,549	0	0
1950	1,415	0	1,562	0	0	1,440	0	1,562	0	0
1951	1,424	0	1,535	0	0	1,454	0	1,535	0	0
1952	1,466	0	1,474	0	0	1,496	0	1,474	0	0
1953	1,413	0	1,419	0	0	1,439	0	1,419	0	0
1954	1,360	0	1,394	0	0	1,388	0	1,394	0	0
1955	1,360	0	1,424	0	0	1,407	0	1,424	0	0
1956	1,435	0	1,416	0	0	1,487	0	1,416	0	0
1957	1,516	0	1,334	0	0	1,557	0	1,334	0	0
1958	1,592	0	1,323	0	0	1,629	0	1,323	0	0
1959	1,548	0	1,353	0	0	1,587	0	1,353	0	0
1960	1,608	1	1,320	0	0	1,657	1	1,320	0	0
1961	1,656	2	1,295	0	0	1,680	2	1,295	0	0
1962	1,816	2	1,300	0	0	1,822	2	1,300	0	0
1963	1,771	4	1,323	0	0	1,772	4	1,323	0	0
1964	1,886	5	1,337	0	0	1,907	5	1,337	0	0
1965	2,059	4	1,335	0	0	2,058	4	1,335	0	0
1966	2,062	4	1,369	0	0	2,073	4	1,369	0	0
1967	2,347	7	1,340	0	0	2,344	7	1,340	0	0
1968	2,349	9	1,419	0	0	2,342	9	1,419	0	0
1969	2,648	13	1,440	0	0	2,659	13	1,440	0	0
1970	2,634	11	1,429	0	0	2,654	11	1,429	0	0
1971	2,824	12	1,430	0	0	2,861	12	1,430	0	0
1972	2,864	31	1,501	0	0	2,944	31	1,501	0	0
1973	2,861	43	1,527	0	0	3,010	43	1,527	0	0
1974	3,177	53	1,538	0	0	3,309	53	1,538	0	0
1975	3,155	70	1,497	0	0	3,219	70	1,497	0	0
1976	2,976	78	1,711	0	0	3,066	78	1,711	0	0
1977	2,333	77	1,837	0	0	2,515	77	1,837	0	0
1978	2,937	64	2,036	0	0	3,141	64	2,036	0	0
1979	2,931	84	2,150	0	0	3,141	84	2,150	0	0
1980	2,900	110	2,483	0	0	3,118	110	2,483	0	0
1981	2,758	123	2,590	0	0	3,105	123	2,590	0	0
1982	3,266	105	2,615	0	0	3,572	105	2,615	0	0
1983	3,527	129	2,831	0	(Z)	3,899	129	2,831	0	(Z)
1984	3,386	165	2,880	0	(Z)	3,800	165	2,880	(Z)	(Z)
1985	2,970	198	2,862	0	(Z)	3,398	198	2,862	(Z)	(Z)
1986	3,071	219	2,840	0	(Z)	3,446	219	2,840	(Z)	(Z)
1987	2,635	229	2,822	0	(Z)	3,117	229	2,822	(Z)	(Z)
1988	2,334	217	2,940	0	(Z)	2,662	217	2,940	(Z)	(Z)
1989	2,828	306	3,062	55	19	2,987	317	3,062	55	19
1990	3,030	325	2,661	60	24	3,128	337	2,661	60	24
1991	3,001	336	2,702	63	27	3,139	351	2,702	63	27
1992	2,618	349	2,847	64	30	2,818	368	2,847	64	30
1993	2,893	364	2,804	66	31	3,119	382	2,804	66	31
1994	2,683	338	2,939	69	36	2,993	368	2,939	69	36
1995	3,205	294	3,068	70	33	3,480	312	3,068	70	33
1996	3,590	316	3,127	71	33	3,889	329	3,127	71	33
1997	3,640	325	3,006	70	34	3,881	325	3,006	70	34
1998	3,297	328	2,835	70	31	3,518	329	2,835	70	31
1999	3,268	331	2,872	69	46	3,472	332	2,872	69	46
2000	2,811	317	2,948	66	57	3,077	317	2,948	66	57
2001	2,219	313	2,869	64	59	2,376	315	2,869	64	59

(Z) Less than 500 billion BTU.

[1] Discontinuity in some series between 1989 and 1990 because of changes in coverage of renewable energy.

[2] Values are estimated. For all years, includes wood consumption in all sectors. Beginning in 1970, includes electric utility waste. Beginning in 1981, includes industrial sector waste, and transportation sector use of ethanol blended into motor gasoline. Beginning in 1989, includes expanded coverage of nonutility wood and waste.

Documentation

A British thermal unit (BTU) is the quantity of heat required to raise the temperature of one pound of water one degree Fahrenheit, at or near its point of maximum density.

The difference between production and consumption represents international trade.

Source

Energy Information Administration, *Annual Energy Review* (U.S. Department of Energy, annual).

TABLE Db182–189   Energy imports and exports, by type of fuel: 1949–2001

Contributed by Gavin Wright

	Imports				Exports			
	Total energy	Coal	Natural gas (dry)	Petroleum	Total energy	Coal	Natural gas (dry)	Petroleum
	Db182	Db183	Db184	Db185	Db186	Db187	Db188	Db189
Year	Trillion BTU	Trillion BTU	Trillion BTU	Trillion BTU	Trillion BTU	Trillion BTU	Trillion BTU	Trillion BTU
1949	1,470	10	—	1,430	1,590	880	20	680
1950	1,930	10	—	1,890	1,470	790	30	640
1951	1,920	10	—	1,870	2,620	1,680	30	890
1952	2,170	10	10	2,110	2,370	1,400	30	910
1953	2,340	10	10	2,280	1,870	980	30	840
1954	2,370	10	10	2,320	1,700	910	30	750
1955	2,830	10	10	2,750	2,290	1,460	30	770
1956	3,250	10	10	3,170	2,950	1,980	40	910
1957	3,570	10	40	3,460	3,450	2,170	40	1,200
1958	3,920	10	140	3,720	2,060	1,420	40	580
1959	4,110	10	140	3,910	1,540	1,050	20	450
1960	4,230	10	160	4,000	1,480	1,020	10	430
1961	4,460	(Z)	230	4,190	1,380	980	10	370
1962	5,010	10	420	4,560	1,480	1,080	20	360
1963	5,100	10	420	4,650	1,850	1,360	20	440
1964	5,490	10	460	4,960	1,840	1,340	20	430
1965	5,920	(Z)	470	5,400	1,850	1,380	30	390
1966	6,180	(Z)	500	5,630	1,850	1,350	30	410
1967	6,190	10	580	5,560	2,150	1,350	80	650
1968	6,930	10	670	6,210	2,030	1,380	100	490
1969	7,710	(Z)	750	6,900	2,150	1,530	50	490
1970	8,390	(Z)	850	7,470	2,660	1,940	70	550
1971	9,580	(Z)	960	8,540	2,180	1,550	80	470
1972	11,460	(Z)	1,050	10,300	2,140	1,530	80	470
1973	14,730	(Z)	1,060	13,470	2,050	1,430	80	490
1974	14,410	50	990	13,130	2,220	1,620	80	460
1975	14,110	20	980	12,950	2,360	1,760	70	440
1976	16,840	30	990	15,670	2,190	1,600	70	470
1977	20,090	40	1,040	18,760	2,070	1,440	60	510
1978	19,250	70	990	17,820	1,930	1,080	50	770
1979	19,620	50	1,300	17,930	2,870	1,750	60	1,000
1980	15,970	30	1,010	14,660	3,720	2,420	50	1,160
1981	13,970	30	920	12,640	4,330	2,940	60	1,260
1982	12,090	20	950	10,780	4,630	2,790	50	1,730
1983	12,030	30	940	10,650	3,720	2,040	60	1,570
1984	12,760	30	850	11,430	3,800	2,150	60	1,540
1985	12,100	50	950	10,610	4,230	2,440	60	1,660
1986	14,430	60	750	13,200	4,050	2,250	60	1,670
1987	15,760	40	990	14,160	3,850	2,090	50	1,630
1988	17,560	50	1,300	15,750	4,410	2,500	70	1,740
1989	18,950	70	1,390	17,160	4,770	2,640	110	1,840
1990	18,990	70	1,550	17,120	4,910	2,770	90	1,820
1991	18,350	80	1,710	16,250	5,190	2,850	120	2,130
1992	19,660	100	2,160	16,970	5,020	2,680	220	2,010
1993	21,540	180	2,400	18,510	4,350	1,960	140	2,120
1994	22,710	190	2,680	19,250	4,120	1,880	160	1,990
1995	22,570	180	2,900	18,860	4,580	2,320	160	1,990
1996	24,010	180	3,000	20,270	4,640	2,370	160	2,060
1997	25,510	190	3,060	21,750	4,560	2,190	160	2,100
1998	26,850	220	3,220	22,910	4,370	2,090	160	1,970
1999	27,540	230	3,660	23,130	3,800	1,530	160	1,950
2000	29,310	310	3,870	24,530	4,090	1,530	250	2,150
2001	29,950	490	4,120	24,880	3,920	1,270	400	2,060

(Z) Less than 5 trillion BTU.

Series Db182 and Db186. Totals include other fuel types not shown separately.

Source

U.S. Energy Information Administration, *Annual Energy Review* (U.S. Department of Energy, annual).

Documentation

A British thermal unit (BTU) is the quantity of heat required to raise the temperature of one pound of water one degree Fahrenheit, at or near its point of maximum density.

TABLE Db190–197   Selected mineral fuels – imports and exports: 1867–2001

Contributed by Gavin Wright

	Coal		Crude oil		Petroleum products		Natural gas	
	Imports	Exports	Imports	Exports	Imports	Exports	Imports	Exports
	Db190	Db191	Db192	Db193	Db194	Db195	Db196	Db197
Year	Thousand short tons	Thousand short tons	Thousand barrels	Thousand barrels	Thousand barrels	Thousand barrels	Million cubic feet	Million cubic feet
1867	571	319	—	—	—	—	—	—
1868	441	312	—	—	—	—	—	—
1869	490	318	—	—	—	—	—	—
1870	466	256	—	248	—	—	—	—
1871	483	300	—	269	—	—	—	—
1872	543	449	—	390	—	—	—	—
1873	517	655	—	468	—	—	—	—
1874	552	855	—	344	—	—	—	—
1875	489	582	—	394	—	—	—	—
1876	451	636	—	603	—	—	—	—
1877	556	829	—	685	—	—	—	—
1878	642	740	—	573	—	—	—	—
1879	546	742	—	681	—	—	—	—
1880	528	689	—	875	—	—	—	—
1881	732	732	—	963	—	—	—	—
1882	891	972	—	1,072	—	—	—	—
1883	724	1,144	—	1,405	—	—	—	—
1884	841	1,451	—	1,897	—	—	—	—
1885	867	1,424	—	1,939	—	—	—	—
1886	911	1,357	—	1,818	—	—	—	—
1887	934	1,716	—	1,920	—	—	—	—
1888	1,243	2,050	—	1,846	—	—	—	—
1889	1,145	2,008	—	2,028	—	—	—	—
1890	1,064	2,162	—	2,299	—	—	—	—
1891	1,224	2,617	—	2,303	—	—	—	—
1892	1,565	2,859	—	2,486	—	—	—	—
1893	1,294	3,479	—	2,660	—	—	—	—
1894	1,387	4,054	—	2,903	—	—	—	—
1895	1,569	4,307	—	2,650	—	—	—	—
1896	1,507	4,028	—	2,641	—	—	—	—
1897	1,470	4,125	—	2,893	—	—	—	—
1898	1,430	4,517	—	2,736	—	—	—	—
1899	1,410	5,811	—	2,802	—	—	—	—
1900	1,912	7,914	—	3,290	—	—	—	—
1901	2,215	8,688	—	3,024	—	—	—	—
1902	2,365	7,066	—	3,458	—	—	—	—
1903	4,241	8,086	—	3,012	—	—	—	—
1904	2,261	9,703	—	2,647	—	—	—	—
1905	1,743	10,011	—	3,004	—	—	—	—
1906	2,075	10,497	—	3,525	—	—	—	—
1907	1,904	12,892	—	3,007	—	—	—	—
1908	2,237	14,154	—	3,552	—	—	—	—
1909	1,379	13,285	—	4,056	—	—	—	—
1910	1,829	15,047	—	4,288	—	—	—	—
1911	1,976	17,240	—	4,806	—	—	—	—
1912	1,458	20,606	—	4,493	—	—	—	—
1913	1,769	22,666	17,809	4,633	—	—	—	—
1914	1,539	21,880	17,247	2,970	—	—	—	—
1915	1,705	22,742	18,140	3,768	—	—	—	—
1916	1,720	25,921	30,570	4,096	—	—	—	—
1917	1,461	29,847	30,127	4,098	—	—	—	—
1918	1,494	27,319	37,736	4,901	—	—	—	—
1919	1,095	25,091	52,822	6,019	—	—	—	—
1920	1,277	43,921	106,175	9,295	2,647	70,281	—	—
1921	1,267	27,808	125,364	9,627	3,428	62,025	—	—
1922	5,294	15,062	127,308	10,805	8,665	63,539	—	—
1923	2,182	26,544	82,015	17,534	17,638	84,447	—	—
1924	535	21,118	77,775	18,239	16,806	98,905	—	—

TABLE Db190–197   Selected mineral fuels – imports and exports: 1867–2001   *Continued*

	Coal		Crude oil		Petroleum products		Natural gas	
	Imports	Exports	Imports	Exports	Imports	Exports	Imports	Exports
	Db190	Db191	Db192	Db193	Db194	Db195	Db196	Db197
Year	Thousand short tons	Thousand short tons	Thousand barrels	Thousand barrels	Thousand barrels	Thousand barrels	Million cubic feet	Million cubic feet
1925	985	20,641	61,824	13,337	16,376	100,497	—	—
1926	1,300	39,302	60,382	15,407	20,938	116,543	—	—
1927	669	21,338	53,383	15,844	13,353	125,805	—	—
1928	932	19,500	79,767	18,966	11,782	135,991	—	—
1929	982	20,835	78,933	26,401	29,777	136,719	—	—
1930	916	18,429	62,129	23,705	43,489	132,794	21	1,798
1931	844	13,904	47,250	25,535	38,837	98,859	44	2,231
1932	794	10,117	44,682	27,393	29,812	74,263	38	1,693
1933	653	10,072	31,893	36,584	13,501	67,572	83	2,158
1934	658	12,167	35,558	41,127	14,936	71,737	68	5,801
1935	773	11,351	32,239	51,430	20,396	74,343	106	6,800
1936	887	12,333	32,327	50,313	24,777	79,133	152	7,436
1937	654	15,059	27,484	67,234	29,673	102,077	289	4,868
1938	604	12,399	26,412	77,254	27,896	116,474	372	1,837
1939	653	14,180	33,095	72,076	25,965	116,883	131	3,122
1940	507	19,134	42,738	51,495	41,089	78,970	0	5,563
1941	465	24,120	50,606	33,238	46,536	75,592	0	7,466
1942	638	27,382	12,297	33,834	23,669	83,073	0	8,702
1943	924	29,975	13,833	41,342	49,579	108,615	0	11,210
1944	646	30,218	44,805	34,238	47,506	173,378	0	14,576
1945	467	31,547	74,337	32,998	39,282	149,985	0	18,207
1946	445	47,694	86,066	42,436	51,610	110,687	0	17,675
1947	300	77,177	97,532	45,355	61,857	118,122	0	18,149
1948	292	52,606	129,093	39,736	59,051	94,938	0	18,704
1949	315	32,785	153,686	33,069	81,873	86,307	0	20,054
1950	365	29,360	177,714	34,823	132,547	76,483	0	25,727
1951	319	62,678	179,073	28,604	129,121	125,448	0	24,163
1952	291	52,235	209,591	26,696	138,916	131,492	7,807	27,456
1953	258	36,484	236,455	19,931	141,044	126,660	9,225	28,322
1954	205	33,892	239,479	13,564	144,476	116,134	6,847	28,726
1955	337	54,429	235,421	11,571	170,143	122,617	10,888	31,029
1956	356	73,797	341,833	28,624	183,758	128,762	10,380	35,963
1957	368	80,778	373,255	50,243	201,334	156,944	37,941	41,655
1958	311	52,573	348,007	4,346	272,582	96,292	135,797	38,719
1959	378	39,041	352,344	2,526	297,239	74,541	133,990	18,413
1960	261	37,981	371,575	3,087	292,536	70,819	155,646	11,332
1961	165	36,405	381,548	3,227	318,118	60,336	218,860	10,747
1962	240	40,215	411,039	1,790	348,754	59,600	401,534	15,814
1963	272	50,435	412,660	1,698	362,053	74,216	406,204	16,957
1964	293	49,544	438,643	1,363	388,093	72,516	443,326	19,603
1965	184	51,032	452,040	1,097	448,732	67,191	456,394	26,132
1966	178	50,068	447,120	1,477	492,042	70,923	479,780	24,639
1967	227	50,123	411,649	26,541	514,342	85,519	564,226	81,614
1968	224	51,155	472,323	1,802	567,046	82,742	651,885	93,745
1969	109	56,861	514,114	1,436	641,437	83,449	726,951	51,304
1970	36	71,697	483,293	4,991	764,769	89,467	820,780	69,813
1971	111	57,304	613,417	500	819,463	81,345	934,548	80,212
1972	47	56,740	811,135	187	924,179	81,202	1,019,496	78,013
1973	127	53,587	1,183,996	697	1,099,497	83,716	1,032,901	77,169
1974	2,080	60,661	1,269,155	1,074	961,792	79,417	959,284	76,789
1975	940	66,309	1,498,181	2,146	712,154	74,282	953,008	72,675
1976	1,203	60,021	1,935,012	2,941	741,399	78,658	963,768	64,711
1977	1,647	54,312	2,406,787	18,255	800,319	70,333	1,011,002	55,626
1978	2,953	40,714	2,261,028	57,728	732,819	74,329	965,545	52,532
1979	2,059	66,042	2,356,107	85,707	706,946	86,149	1,253,383	55,673
1980	1,194	91,742	1,910,095	104,934	622,541	94,322	984,767	48,731
1981	1,043	112,541	1,511,405	81,551	583,716	135,473	903,949	59,372
1982	742	106,277	1,213,021	80,716	593,144	216,798	933,336	51,728
1983	1,271	77,772	1,129,940	53,212	628,519	216,642	918,407	54,639
1984	1,286	81,483	1,181,911	55,282	735,986	208,795	843,060	54,753

(continued)

TABLE Db190–197 Selected mineral fuels – imports and exports: 1867–2001 *Continued*

	Coal		Crude oil		Petroleum products		Natural gas	
	Imports	Exports	Imports	Exports	Imports	Exports	Imports	Exports
	Db190	Db191	Db192	Db193	Db194	Db195	Db196	Db197
Year	Thousand short tons	Thousand short tons	Thousand barrels	Thousand barrels	Thousand barrels	Thousand barrels	Million cubic feet	Million cubic feet
1985	1,952	92,680	1,125,173	62,542	681,211	222,527	949,715	55,268
1986	2,212	85,518	1,507,415	45,994	746,604	240,379	750,449	61,271
1987	1,747	79,607	1,679,405	54,964	731,456	223,768	992,532	54,020
1988	2,134	95,023	1,850,247	56,712	840,135	241,754	1,293,812	73,638
1989	2,851	100,815	2,112,413	51,683	809,338	261,777	1,381,520	106,871
1990	2,699	105,804	2,141,615	39,653	775,008	273,018	1,532,259	85,565
1991	3,390	108,969	2,110,430	42,340	673,060	323,025	1,773,313	129,244
1992	3,803	102,516	2,220,295	32,485	658,825	314,265	2,137,504	216,282
1993	7,309	74,519	2,477,255	35,770	669,045	329,960	2,350,115	140,183
1994	7,584	71,359	2,577,995	40,150	705,545	307,695	2,623,839	161,739
1995	7,201	88,547	2,638,810	34,509	585,825	312,075	2,841,048	154,119
1996	7,126	90,473	2,747,839	40,211	721,386	318,786	2,937,413	153,393
1997	7,487	83,545	3,002,299	39,308	706,275	327,040	2,994,173	157,006
1998	8,724	78,048	3,177,584	40,102	730,730	304,775	3,152,058	159,007
1999	9,089	58,476	3,183,622	43,031	536,867	284,379	3,585,505	163,415
2000	12,513	58,489	3,316,810	18,352	648,141	343,154	3,781,603	243,716
2001	19,787	48,666	3,397,508	7,386	636,026	332,949	4,011,027	363,600

Sources

Series Db190–191. 1867–1972: U.S. Bureau of Mines, *Mineral Resources of the United States* (annual), and *Minerals Yearbooks* (annual). 1973–2001: U.S. Energy Information Administration, *Monthly Energy Review* (U.S. Department of Energy), Table 6.1.

Series Db192–193. 1870–1974: U.S. Bureau of Mines, *Mineral Resources of the United States* (annual), and *Minerals Yearbooks* (annual). 1975–2001: U.S. Energy Information Administration, *Annual Petroleum Statement* (U.S. Department of Energy, annual), *Petroleum Supply Annual* (U.S. Department of Energy, annual), and *Petroleum Supply Monthly* (U.S. Department of Energy, annual).

Series Db194–195. 1920–1937: U.S. Bureau of Mines, *Monthly Petroleum Statement* number 402. 1938–1974: U.S. Bureau of Mines, *Minerals Year-books* (annual). 1975–2001: US Energy Information Administration, *Annual Petroleum Statement, Petroleum Supply Annual,* and *Petroleum Supply Monthly.*

Series Db196–197. 1930–1975: U.S. Bureau of Mines, *Minerals Yearbook*; 1976–2001: U.S. Energy Information Administration, *Natural Gas Annual* (U.S. Department of Energy, annual) and *Natural Gas Monthly* (U.S. Department of Energy, annual).

Documentation

Series Db190–191. Includes bituminous and anthracite. Figures for 1867–1885 and 1890–1914 are for fiscal years ending June 30.

TABLE Db198–205 Crude oil reserves, by country and region: 1948–2002

Contributed by Gavin Wright

	Total world	United States	Canada	Latin America	Middle East	Africa	Asia and Pacific	Western Europe
	Db198	Db199 [1]	Db200	Db201	Db202	Db203	Db204	Db205
Year	Million barrels	Million barrels	Million barrels	Million barrels	Million barrels	Million barrels	Million barrels	Million barrels
1948	68,198	21,488	125	10,085	28,550	100	1,300	50
1949	73,599	23,280	500	10,880	32,621	122	1,372	179
1950	76,453	24,650	1,200	11,401	32,413	203	1,557	289
1951	89,926	25,268	1,203	11,525	41,567	188	1,765	445
1952	103,445	27,468	1,377	12,711	51,320	175	1,966	502
1953	118,454	27,961	1,680	11,884	64,825	163	2,062	473
1954	134,970	28,945	1,845	13,182	78,160	158	2,583	642
1955	157,500	29,561	2,208	14,356	97,459	112	2,708	1,049
1956	189,571	30,012	2,510	15,515	126,271	169	3,000	1,261
1957	227,958	30,435	2,849	17,474	144,470	285	6,140	1,305
1958	260,640	30,300	2,875	21,004	169,566	814	8,578	1,304
1959	272,403	30,536	3,166	21,843	173,951	4,119	9,647	1,437
1960	290,035	31,719	3,497	24,436	181,436	7,274	10,176	1,496
1961	297,744	31,613	3,679	25,062	183,160	8,100	10,907	1,722
1962	305,407	31,759	4,174	24,706	188,204	9,710	10,868	1,736
1963	309,514	31,389	4,481	24,226	193,975	12,346	11,331	1,791
1964	326,947	30,970	4,882	24,305	207,368	16,376	11,621	1,926

Note appears at end of table

TABLE Db198–205   Crude oil reserves, by country and region: 1948–2002   *Continued*

Year	Total world Db198 Million barrels	United States Db199 [1] Million barrels	Canada Db200 Million barrels	Latin America Db201 Million barrels	Middle East Db202 Million barrels	Africa Db203 Million barrels	Asia and Pacific Db204 Million barrels	Western Europe Db205 Million barrels
1965	338,668	30,991	6,178	25,525	212,180	19,396	11,614	2,036
1966	348,222	31,352	6,711	25,171	215,360	23,049	11,009	2,085
1967	381,885	31,452	7,792	27,100	235,615	32,356	11,809	1,925
1968	407,553	31,377	8,169	26,907	249,209	42,285	11,816	2,017
1969	454,735	30,707	8,382	28,783	270,760	44,569	13,720	1,937
1970	530,534	29,632	8,620	29,180	333,506	54,680	13,138	1,779
1971	611,195	39,001	8,559	26,185	344,575	74,758	14,409	3,709
1972	632,554	38,063	8,333	31,559	367,386	58,886	15,605	14,222
1973	664,220	36,399	8,020	32,602	355,852	106,402	14,922	12,082
1974	626,707	35,300	7,674	31,640	350,163	67,304	15,635	15,991
1975	712,419	34,250	7,171	40,578	403,858	68,300	21,048	25,814
1976	657,921	32,682	6,653	35,368	368,411	65,085	21,234	25,488
1977	642,639	33,502	6,247	29,609	367,681	60,570	19,391	24,539
1978	647,999	31,780	5,971	40,270	366,166	59,200	19,749	26,863
1979	645,323	31,355	6,860	41,247	369,996	57,892	20,007	23,966
1980	644,933	29,810	6,800	56,473	361,947	57,072	19,355	23,476
1981	651,930	29,805	6,400	69,490	362,071	55,148	19,631	23,085
1982	670,350	29,426	7,300	84,982	362,840	56,172	19,151	24,635
1983	668,262	27,858	7,020	78,482	369,286	57,822	19,756	22,924
1984	669,738	27,735	6,730	81,676	370,101	56,907	18,969	23,020
1985	699,813	28,446	7,075	83,316	398,381	55,541	18,530	24,426
1986	700,567	28,416	6,500	84,242	398,036	56,734	18,856	26,413
1987	699,779	26,889	6,850	88,755	401,879	55,194	19,024	21,938
1988	889,345	27,256	6,825	114,332	564,680	55,250	19,354	22,448
1989	907,768	26,825	6,786	121,951	571,519	56,964	21,367	18,557
1990	1,002,213	26,501	6,134	125,027	660,247	58,837	22,545	18,822
1991	999,114	26,254	5,783	121,091	662,598	59,892	50,242	14,476
1992	991,011	24,682	5,588	119,766	661,571	60,488	44,073	14,503
1993	997,042	23,745	5,292	123,811	661,791	61,872	44,572	15,829
1994	999,124	22,957	5,096	125,784	662,866	61,963	44,647	16,643
1995	999,761	22,457	5,038	129,573	660,295	62,177	44,453	16,572
1996	1,007,475	22,351	4,898	128,801	659,555	73,154	43,953	15,573
1997	1,018,849	22,017	4,894	127,943	676,352	67,555	42,299	18,361
1998	1,019,546	22,546	4,893	126,170	676,952	70,063	43,014	18,128
1999	1,034,668	21,034	4,931	137,317	673,647	75,442	42,275	18,719
2000	1,016,041	21,765	4,931	117,200	675,636	74,889	43,985	18,611
2001	1,028,458	22,045	4,706	122,529	683,515	74,889	43,957	17,185
2002	1,031,101	22,446	4,858	122,511	685,592	76,677	43,779	17,135

[1] Beginning 1971, figures include 1968 discovery in Prudhoe Bay, Alaska.

Sources

Series Db198 and Db201–205. 1948–1976: Estimates generated by the American Petroleum Institute's Committee on Reserves and Productive Capacity, published in American Petroleum Institute, *Basic Petroleum Data Book, 1981.* 1977–2002: *Oil and Gas Journal,* "Worldwide Report" and "Worldwide Production Report" issues.

Series Db199. 1948–1976: American Petroleum Institute's Committee on Reserves and Productive Capacity. 1977–2002: U.S. Energy Information Administration, *Crude Oil, Natural Gas and Gas Liquids Report* (U.S. Department of Energy, annual – listed as December 31 of preceding year).

Series Db200. 1948–1976: American Petroleum Institute's Committee on Reserves and Productive Capacity. 1977–1991: Estimates generated by the Canadian Petroleum Association, published in American Petroleum Institute,

Basic Petroleum Data Book (1993). 1992–2002: *Oil and Gas Journal,* "Worldwide Report" and "Worldwide Production Report" issues.

Documentation

Data are estimates of proved crude oil reserves. Proved reserves are defined by the Energy Information Administration (EIA) as "those volumes of oil that geological and engineering data demonstrate with reasonable certainty to be recoverable in future years from known reservoirs under existing economic and operating conditions." Methods of estimation vary widely internationally and are best regarded as rough approximations.

Values shown are as of January 1. Figures for the United States differ from those given in series Db59 because values there are as of December 31.

In recent years, the *Oil and Gas Journal* has followed the practice of listing the EIA estimate for U.S. reserves as its U.S. figure for the following year, contributing to some confusion over precise dates.

TABLE Db206–217   Motor vehicle fuel efficiency, and alternative-fuel vehicles in use: 1960–2001

Contributed by Gavin Wright

	All motor vehicles			Passenger vehicles			Alternative-fuel vehicles in use					
		Fuel consumption			Fuel consumption			Liquefied petroleum gases	Compressed natural gas	Methanol	Ethanol	Electricity
	Miles per vehicle	Per vehicle	Miles per gallon	Miles per vehicle	Per vehicle	Miles per gallon	Total					
	Db206	Db207	Db208	Db209 [1]	Db210 [1]	Db211 [1]	Db212	Db213	Db214	Db215	Db216	Db217
Year	Miles	Gallons	Miles per gallon	Miles	Gallons	Miles per gallon	Number	Number	Number	Number	Number	Number
1960	9,732	784	12.4	9,518	668	14.3	—	—	—	—	—	—
1961	9,708	781	12.4	9,521	663	14.4	—	—	—	—	—	—
1962	9,687	779	12.4	9,494	662	14.3	—	—	—	—	—	—
1963	9,737	780	12.5	9,587	655	14.6	—	—	—	—	—	—
1964	9,805	787	12.5	9,665	661	14.6	—	—	—	—	—	—
1965	9,826	787	12.5	9,603	661	14.5	—	—	—	—	—	—
1966	9,675	780	12.4	9,733	688	14.1	—	—	—	—	—	—
1967	9,751	786	12.4	9,849	699	14.1	—	—	—	—	—	—
1968	9,864	805	12.2	9,922	714	13.9	—	—	—	—	—	—
1969	9,885	821	12.0	9,921	727	13.6	—	—	—	—	—	—
1970	9,976	830	12.0	9,989	737	13.5	—	—	—	—	—	—
1971	10,133	839	12.1	10,097	743	13.6	—	—	—	—	—	—
1972	10,279	857	12.0	10,171	754	13.5	—	—	—	—	—	—
1973	10,099	850	11.9	9,884	737	13.4	—	—	—	—	—	—
1974	9,493	788	12.0	9,221	677	13.6	—	—	—	—	—	—
1975	9,627	790	12.2	9,309	665	14.0	—	—	—	—	—	—
1976	9,774	806	12.1	9,418	681	13.8	—	—	—	—	—	—
1977	9,978	814	12.3	9,517	676	14.1	—	—	—	—	—	—
1978	10,077	816	12.4	9,500	665	14.3	—	—	—	—	—	—
1979	9,722	776	12.5	9,062	620	14.6	—	—	—	—	—	—
1980	9,458	712	13.3	8,813	551	16.0	—	—	—	—	—	—
1981	9,477	697	13.6	8,873	538	16.5	—	—	—	—	—	—
1982	9,644	686	14.1	9,050	535	16.9	—	—	—	—	—	—
1983	9,760	686	14.2	9,118	534	17.1	—	—	—	—	—	—
1984	10,017	691	14.5	9,248	530	17.4	—	—	—	—	—	—
1985	10,020	685	14.6	9,419	538	17.5	—	—	—	—	—	—
1986	10,143	692	14.7	9,464	543	17.4	—	—	—	—	—	—
1987	10,453	694	15.1	9,720	539	18.0	—	—	—	—	—	—
1988	10,721	688	15.6	9,972	531	18.8	—	—	—	—	—	—
1989	10,932	688	15.9	10,157	533	19.0	—	—	—	—	—	—
1990	11,107	677	16.4	10,277	506	20.3	—	—	—	—	—	—
1991	11,294	669	16.9	10,322	487	21.2	—	—	—	—	—	—
1992	11,558	683	16.9	10,571	502	21.0	251,352	221,000	23,191	5,254	210	1,607
1993	11,595	693	16.7	10,545	512	20.6	314,848	269,000	32,714	10,677	468	1,690
1994	11,683	698	16.7	10,759	517	20.8	324,472	264,000	41,227	15,899	638	2,224
1995	11,793	700	16.8	11,203	530	21.1	333,049	259,000	50,218	18,705	1,663	2,860
1996	11,813	700	16.9	11,330	534	21.2	352,421	263,000	60,144	20,437	897	3,280
1997	12,107	711	17.0	11,581	539	21.5	367,526	263,000	68,571	21,212	477	4,453
1998	12,211	721	16.9	11,754	544	21.6	383,847	266,000	78,782	19,848	802	5,243
1999	12,206	732	16.7	11,848	553	21.4	406,841	267,000	89,556	19,162	22,478	6,964
2000	12,164	720	16.9	11,976	547	21.9	432,344	268,000	100,530	18,560	34,693	8,661
2001	11,800	692	17.1	11,766	532	22.1	456,306	269,000	109,730	17,102	48,035	10,400

[1] For 1960–1965, passenger cars category also includes motorcycles.

Sources
Series Db206–211. 1960–2001: U.S. Energy Information Administration, *Annual Energy Review* (U.S. Department of Energy, annual), from data compiled by the Federal Highway Administration.

Series Db212–217. 1992–2001: U.S. Energy Information Administration, *Annual Energy Review*.

Documentation
Data on alternative-fuel vehicles were collected beginning 1992, pursuant to the Energy Policy Act of that year.

Series Db206–208. Includes passenger cars, motorcycles, buses, other two-axle vehicles (including vans, minivans, pickup trucks, and sport-utility vehicles), single-unit trucks with six or more tires, and combination trucks.

Series Db212–217. Vehicles in use represent lower bound estimates, rounded to the nearest thousand.

Series Db212. Includes other fuel types not shown separately.

Series Db215. Includes both 85 percent methanol and neat methanol-fueled vehicles.

Series Db216. Includes both 85 percent and 95 percent ethanol-fueled vehicles.

TABLE Db218–227   Electric utilities – power generation and fossil fuel consumption, by energy source: 1920–2000

Contributed by Gavin Wright

	Net generation							Consumption		
	Total	Fossil fuels				Nuclear	Hydroelectric	Coal	Natural gas	Petroleum
		Total	Coal	Natural gas	Petroleum					
	Db218	Db219	Db220	Db221	Db222	Db223	Db224	Db225	Db226	Db227
Year	Million kilowatt-hours	Million kilowatt-hours	Million kilowatt-hours	Million kilowatt-hours	Million kilowatt-hours	Million kilowatt-hours	Million kilowatt-hours	Thousand short tons	Million cubic feet	Thousand barrels
1920	39,405	23,495	—	—	—	—	15,760	31,640	22,136	12,690
1921	37,180	22,343	—	—	—	—	14,703	26,604	21,701	11,505
1922	43,633	26,561	—	—	—	—	16,876	29,193	24,996	12,443
1923	51,229	32,088	—	—	—	—	18,940	33,636	29,340	13,925
1924	54,662	34,963	—	—	—	—	19,490	32,790	47,301	16,060
1925	61,451	39,443	—	—	—	—	21,798	35,615	45,472	9,794
1926	69,353	43,472	—	—	—	—	25,603	36,842	52,647	8,999
1927	75,418	46,660	—	—	—	—	28,474	38,199	62,485	6,552
1928	82,794	49,622	—	—	—	—	32,874	38,042	77,155	6,818
1929	92,180	59,154	—	—	—	—	32,648	41,827	112,353	9,783
1930	91,112	59,583	—	—	—	—	31,190	40,278	119,553	8,805
1931	87,350	58,014	—	—	—	—	29,028	36,115	138,458	7,922
1932	79,393	46,422	—	—	—	—	32,878	28,056	107,103	7,583
1933	81,740	48,170	—	—	—	—	33,457	28,543	101,985	9,606
1934	87,258	54,418	—	—	—	—	32,684	34,414	127,071	10,258
1935	95,287	56,688	—	—	—	—	38,372	32,715	124,118	11,257
1936	109,316	69,823	—	—	—	—	39,058	40,085	154,084	14,079
1937	118,913	74,502	—	—	—	—	44,013	42,929	169,127	13,829
1938	113,812	69,255	—	—	—	—	44,279	38,394	165,504	12,942
1939	127,642	83,628	—	—	—	—	43,564	44,539	188,878	17,139
1940	141,837	93,963	—	—	—	—	47,321	51,474	180,096	16,325
1941	164,788	113,272	—	—	—	—	50,863	62,668	201,763	20,077
1942	185,979	121,585	—	—	—	—	63,870	66,257	235,208	15,236
1943	217,759	143,785	—	—	—	—	73,632	77,301	301,937	17,986
1944	228,189	153,868	—	—	—	—	73,945	80,084	358,784	20,862
1945	222,486	142,331	—	—	—	—	79,970	74,725	326,212	20,228
1946	223,178	144,555	—	—	—	—	78,406	72,197	306,942	36,316
1947	255,739	176,983	—	—	—	—	78,426	89,531	373,054	45,309
1948	282,698	199,796	—	—	—	—	82,470	99,586	478,097	42,645
1949	291,100	200,965	135,000	37,000	29,000	—	89,748	83,963	550,121	66,301
1950	329,141	232,813	155,000	45,000	34,000	—	95,938	91,871	628,919	75,420
1951	370,673	270,531	185,204	56,616	28,712	—	99,750	105,768	763,898	63,945
1952	399,224	293,640	195,437	68,453	29,750	—	105,103	107,071	910,117	67,218
1953	442,665	337,042	218,846	79,791	38,404	—	105,233	115,897	1,034,272	82,238
1954	471,686	364,354	239,146	93,688	31,520	—	107,069	118,385	1,165,498	66,745
1955	547,038	433,786	301,363	95,285	37,138	—	112,975	143,759	1,153,280	75,274
1956	600,668	478,487	338,503	104,037	35,947	—	122,029	158,279	1,239,311	72,711
1957	631,507	501,108	346,386	114,212	40,500	10	130,232	160,769	1,336,141	79,693
1958	645,098	504,497	344,366	119,759	40,372	165	140,262	155,724	1,372,853	77,668
1959	710,006	571,883	378,424	146,619	46,840	188	137,782	168,423	1,628,509	88,263
1960	753,350	607,142	403,067	157,970	46,105	518	145,516	176,634	1,724,762	85,340
1961	792,039	638,277	421,871	169,286	47,120	1,692	151,850	182,121	1,825,117	85,736
1962	852,314	681,533	450,249	184,301	46,983	2,270	168,283	193,238	1,965,974	85,768
1963	916,793	751,919	493,927	201,602	52,001	3,212	165,755	211,332	2,144,473	93,314
1964	983,990	803,222	526,230	220,038	56,954	3,343	177,073	225,425	2,322,896	101,141
1965	1,055,252	857,286	570,926	221,559	64,801	3,657	193,851	244,788	2,321,101	115,203
1966	1,144,350	943,352	613,475	251,151	78,926	5,520	194,758	266,477	2,609,949	140,949
1967	1,214,365	984,560	630,483	264,806	89,271	7,655	221,518	274,185	2,746,352	161,278
1968	1,329,443	1,093,614	684,905	304,433	104,276	12,528	222,491	297,779	3,147,909	188,642
1969	1,442,182	1,177,127	706,001	333,279	137,847	13,928	250,193	310,641	3,487,642	251,027
1970	1,531,609	1,261,474	706,102	372,884	182,488	21,797	247,456	320,818	3,931,996	335,504
1971	1,613,936	1,307,310	714,676	374,026	218,608	37,899	266,320	327,878	3,975,972	396,438
1972	1,747,323	1,421,136	772,871	375,735	272,530	54,031	272,734	352,391	3,976,762	493,663
1973	1,856,216	1,492,644	845,986	336,001	310,657	83,334	271,634	388,190	3,640,756	559,842
1974	1,866,436	1,449,070	829,839	319,935	299,296	113,727	300,928	392,344	3,429,072	536,140
1975	1,917,619	1,342,476	852,837	199,766	288,873	172,506	300,065	406,032	3,157,591	506,081
1976	2,037,674	1,558,266	943,877	294,610	319,779	191,107	283,734	448,431	3,080,627	556,583
1977	2,124,166	1,648,775	985,465	305,444	357,866	250,882	220,446	477,215	3,190,571	623,826
1978	2,206,313	1,646,163	976,618	305,392	364,153	276,403	280,432	481,624	3,188,370	635,829
1979	2,247,359	1,708,029	1,075,595	329,486	302,948	255,155	279,790	527,317	3,490,517	523,256

(continued)

TABLE Db218–227   Electric utilities – power generation and fossil fuel consumption, by energy source: 1920–2000
Continued

	Net generation							Consumption		
	Total	Fossil fuels				Nuclear	Hydroelectric	Coal	Natural gas	Petroleum
		Total	Coal	Natural gas	Petroleum					
	Db218	Db219	Db220	Db221	Db222	Db223	Db224	Db225	Db226	Db227
Year	Million kilowatt-hours	Million kilowatt-hours	Million kilowatt-hours	Million kilowatt-hours	Million kilowatt-hours	Million kilowatt-hours	Million kilowatt-hours	Thousand short tons	Million cubic feet	Thousand barrels
1980	2,286,414	1,753,749	1,161,969	346,233	245,547	251,121	276,039	569,453	3,681,595	420,214
1981	2,294,812	1,755,401	1,203,554	345,777	206,070	272,674	260,684	596,936	3,640,154	351,111
1982	2,241,211	1,644,062	1,192,379	305,260	146,423	282,773	309,213	593,666	3,225,518	249,771
1983	2,310,285	1,678,021	1,259,424	274,098	144,499	293,677	332,130	625,211	2,910,767	245,497
1984	2,416,304	1,758,883	1,341,681	297,394	119,808	327,634	321,150	664,399	3,111,342	204,479
1985	2,469,841	1,794,276	1,402,128	291,946	100,202	383,691	281,149	693,841	3,044,083	173,414
1986	2,487,310	1,770,924	1,385,831	248,508	136,585	414,038	290,844	685,056	2,602,370	230,482
1987	2,572,127	1,854,895	1,463,781	272,621	118,493	455,270	249,695	717,894	2,844,051	199,378
1988	2,704,250	1,942,354	1,540,653	252,801	148,900	526,973	222,940	758,372	2,635,613	248,096
1989	2,784,304	1,978,577	1,553,661	266,598	158,318	529,355	265,063	766,888	2,787,012	267,451
1990	2,808,151	1,940,712	1,559,606	264,089	117,017	576,862	279,926	773,549	2,787,332	196,054
1991	2,825,023	1,926,802	1,551,167	264,172	111,463	612,565	275,519	772,268	2,789,014	184,886
1992	2,797,219	1,928,683	1,575,895	263,872	88,916	618,776	239,559	779,860	2,765,608	147,335
1993	2,882,525	1,997,605	1,639,151	258,915	99,539	610,291	265,063	813,508	2,682,440	162,454
1994	2,910,712	2,017,647	1,635,493	291,115	91,039	640,440	243,693	817,270	2,987,146	151,004
1995	2,994,529	2,021,064	1,652,914	307,306	60,844	673,402	296,153	829,007	3,196,507	102,150
1996	3,077,400	2,066,797	1,737,500	262,335	66,962	674,729	324,541	874,616	2,727,173	112,565
1997	3,122,500	2,148,023	1,787,800	283,108	77,115	628,420	333,455	898,332	2,955,694	124,739
1998	3,212,171	2,226,860	1,807,480	309,222	110,158	673,702	304,403	910,867	3,258,054	178,614
1999	3,173,674	2,150,989	1,767,679	296,381	86,929	725,036	293,932	894,120	3,113,419	143,830
2000	3,105,383	2,059,514	1,696,619	290,715	72,180	705,433	248,195	859,335	3,043,094	120,129

Sources

Series Db218 and Db223–224. 1920–1992: Edison Electric Institute (EEI), *Historical Statistics of the Electric Utility Industry* (EEI, 1995). 1993–1995: EEI, *Statistical Yearbook of the Electric Utility Industry* (EEI, annual). The EEI figures are compiled from federal sources: Federal Power Commission (1920–1970) and U.S. Energy Information Administration (1971–2000). Less complete series are reported in U.S. Energy Information Administration, *Annual Energy Review* (U.S. Department of Energy, annual).

Series Db219–222. 1920–1948: U.S. Federal Power Commission, *Fuel Consumption of Electric Power Plants* (monthly and annual reports). 1949–2000: U.S. Energy Information Administration, *Annual Energy Review* (U.S. Department of Energy, annual).

Series Db225–227. 1920–1970: U.S. Federal Power Commission, *Fuel Consumption of Electric Power Plants.* 1971–1992: EEI, *Historical Statistics of the Electric Utility Industry through 1992* (EEI, 1995). 1993–2000: EEI, *Statistical Yearbook of the Electric Utility Industry* 1995. The EEI figures are compiled from the U.S. Energy Information Administration. Less complete series are reported in *Annual Energy Review.*

Documentation

Series Db218. Includes other fuel types not shown separately: geothermal, wood, waste, wind, and solar.

TABLE Db228–233   Electrical energy – sales and use: 1902–2000[1]

Contributed by Gavin Wright

	Electric energy use				Electric utility sales to ultimate customers	
	Total	Residential	Commercial	Industrial	Total	Industrial
	Db228	Db229	Db230	Db231	Db232	Db233
Year	Million kilowatt-hours	Million kilowatt-hours	Million kilowatt-hours	Million kilowatt-hours	Million kilowatt-hours	Million kilowatt-hours
1902	5,969	—	—	—	—	—
1907	14,121	—	—	—	—	—
1912	25,283	910	4,076	11,250	—	—
1917	44,645	1,731	5,213	23,750	—	—
1920	57,499	3,190	6,150	31,500	—	—
1921	54,134	3,532	6,125	28,000	—	—
1922	62,170	3,916	7,180	32,200	—	—
1923	72,730	4,580	8,027	38,250	—	—
1924	77,182	5,080	8,634	40,300	—	—
1925	85,939	6,020	9,345	45,500	—	—
1926	95,715	6,827	9,485	52,750	56,089	31,993
1927	103,009	7,676	11,489	57,383	61,251	34,540
1928	109,642	8,619	12,880	59,750	66,988	37,715
1929	118,170	9,773	14,461	63,279	75,295	42,971
1930	116,229	11,018	15,417	61,023	74,906	40,148
1931	110,582	11,738	15,057	56,512	74,901	36,937
1932	100,003	11,875	13,304	48,614	63,711	30,965
1933	103,622	11,747	12,833	52,358	65,916	33,857
1934	111,638	12,658	13,710	56,695	71,082	36,944
1935	120,272	13,978	14,799	63,265	77,596	40,865
1936	137,562	15,659	17,083	70,500	90,044	48,655
1937	148,303	17,691	19,745	73,300	99,359	51,359
1938	143,763	19,371	20,714	65,850	93,731	43,140
1939	163,202	21,084	22,603	78,603	105,767	51,108
1940	182,021	23,317	24,364	92,390	118,643	59,557
1941	210,637	25,124	26,980	113,931	140,060	76,061
1942	235,564	26,937	30,123	133,899	159,407	88,378
1943	270,037	28,621	31,188	155,671	185,889	106,657
1944	282,040	31,266	33,210	156,365	198,160	115,187
1945	273,817	34,184	34,107	146,261	193,558	107,490
1946	272,000	38,571	37,447	137,308	190,795	98,885
1947	309,315	44,171	43,930	157,197	217,581	113,523
1948	338,353	50,978	49,520	172,658	240,740	124,088
1949	346,654	58,139	53,646	169,274	248,542	120,766
1950	390,460	67,030	57,846	194,835	280,539	139,065
1951	435,545	77,024	65,757	214,522	318,168	157,827
1952	465,324	86,780	70,616	224,487	342,524	167,358
1953	516,177	97,063	78,821	254,260	384,244	190,010
1954	546,985	108,465	83,549	263,527	410,904	200,155
1955	633,078	120,524	87,005	334,088	480,921	253,711
1956	689,352	133,851	93,987	364,779	530,128	281,501
1957	719,957	147,059	101,317	372,476	557,829	287,849
1958	728,070	159,047	107,100	358,099	569,161	280,220
1959	798,858	173,414	199,683	394,770	626,743	308,789
1960	848,723	189,911	126,145	415,699	683,199	339,951
1961	883,749	209,021	134,864	424,235	720,728	347,427
1962	947,018	226,414	144,095	449,270	776,088	373,916
1963	1,011,515	241,692	166,516	477,325	830,811	388,399
1964	1,085,696	262,010	183,539	508,991	890,356	409,356
1965	1,157,442	280,970	202,112	534,297	953,414	433,365
1966	1,250,536	306,572	225,878	571,613	1,038,982	465,077
1967	1,317,001	331,525	242,492	588,560	1,107,023	486,043
1968	1,435,398	367,692	265,151	628,657	1,202,321	518,834
1969	1,553,829	407,922	286,686	672,345	1,307,178	557,220
1970	1,641,731	447,795	312,750	685,693	1,391,359	572,522
1971	1,719,358	479,080	333,752	—	1,466,441	592,700
1972	1,861,889	511,423	361,859	—	1,577,714	639,467
1973	1,973,023	554,171	396,903	—	1,703,203	687,235
1974	1,980,702	554,960	392,716	—	1,700,769	689,435

Note appears at end of table

(continued)

TABLE Db228-233   Electrical energy – sales and use: 1902-2000   *Continued*

	Electric energy use				Electric utility sales to ultimate customers	
	Total	Residential	Commercial	Industrial	Total	Industrial
	Db228	Db229	Db230	Db231	Db232	Db233
Year	Million kilowatt-hours	Million kilowatt-hours	Million kilowatt-hours	Million kilowatt-hours	Million kilowatt-hours	Million kilowatt-hours
1975	2,009,166	586,149	418,069	—	1,733,024	661,558
1976	2,133,369	613,072	440,625	—	1,849,625	725,169
1977	2,229,156	652,345	469,227	—	1,950,791	757,168
1978	2,304,608	679,156	480,748	—	2,017,818	782,141
1979	2,339,068	694,266	493,494	—	2,079,221	815,586
1980	2,375,284	734,411	524,122	—	2,126,094	793,812
1981	2,392,842	730,479	521,698	—	2,150,674	819,641
1982	2,333,031	732,678	516,959	—	2,099,741	770,398
1983	2,403,293	750,293	545,601	—	2,159,787	782,984
1984	2,527,485	782,608	578,083	—	2,280,585	835,486
1985	2,609,255	792,875	605,865	—	2,305,882	820,301
1986	2,635,215	820,015	628,965	—	2,354,744	818,982
1987	2,765,074	846,457	658,445	—	2,435,483	843,709
1988	2,910,272	886,070	697,832	—	2,554,161	881,790
1989	2,996,151	898,802	715,915	—	2,621,003	912,772
1990	3,042,912	915,799	738,869	—	2,683,976	931,877
1991	3,122,507	948,807	753,296	—	2,736,586	934,906
1992	3,135,294	929,290	755,658	—	2,734,929	949,259
1993	3,238,349	994,144	804,094	—	2,849,755	956,611
1994	3,326,919	1,008,492	833,508	—	2,930,063	990,254
1995	3,441,795	1,042,399	863,501	—	3,007,469	1,006,178
1996	3,510,893	1,082,358	887,086	—	3,093,984	1,028,427
1997	3,567,686	1,078,605	929,031	—	3,138,604	1,027,667
1998	3,754,782	1,127,735	966,528	—	3,239,818	1,040,038
1999	3,733,538	1,140,761	970,601	—	3,235,899	1,017,783
2000	3,830,469	1,183,137	1,000,865	—	3,309,550	1,017,723

[1] In 1937, a new "Uniform System of Accounts" was prescribed by the electric utility companies. Data beginning 1937 are not directly comparable with the data for earlier years.

Sources

Series Db228. 1902-1992: Edison Electric Institute (EEI), *Historical Statistics of the Electric Utility Industry through 1992* (EEI, 1995). 1993-2000: EEI, *Statistical Yearbook of the Electric Utility Institute* (EEI, annual).

Series Db229-230. 1912-1925: based on *Electrical World* (McGraw-Hill, annual). 1926-1992: EEI, *Historical Statistics of the Electrical Utility Industry through 1992*. 1993-2000: EEI, *Statistical Yearbook of the Electric Utility Industry*.

Series Db231. 1912-1938: U.S. Bureau of the Census reports of the Census of Manufactures and *Census of Mineral Industries* (1919, 1929, 1939). 1939-1946: reports of the Census of Manufactures; U.S. Federal Power Commission report, *Industrial Electric Power 1939–1946*; and *Census of Mineral Industries* (1939). 1947-1962, unpublished data. 1963-1970: U.S. Federal Power Commission, *Sales of Electric Energy by Class of Service* (annual).

Series Db232-233. 1926-1992: EEI, *Historical Statistics of the Electric Utility Industry through 1992*. 1993-2000: EEI, *Statistical Yearbook of the Electric Utility Industry*.

Documentation

Series Db228. Represents "electricity made available in the United States" and is comprised of total generation by the electric utility industry plus "other sources" (generation of industrial, mine and railway electric power plants, whether or not these entered into market transactions) plus net imports. This series differs slightly from that published in *Historical Statistics of the United States* (1975), but it is derived from the same federal sources (Census reports through 1937, Federal Power Commission and Energy Information Administration thereafter).

Series Db230-231. Commercial and industrial are not wholly comparable on a year-to-year basis because of changes in classification. Prior to 1960, rural service was included in the commercial sector. Industrial "use" differs from "sales to industrial customers" because it includes self-generated electricity used in non–electric utility industries.

TABLE Db234–241   Electrical energy – retail prices, residential use, and service coverage: 1902–2000

Contributed by Gavin Wright

	Average price				Percentage of dwelling units with electrical service			Annual use per residential customer
	All services	Residential	Commercial	Industrial	All	Farm	Urban and rural nonfarm	
	Db234	Db235	Db236	Db237	Db238	Db239	Db240	Db241
Year	Cents per kilowatt-hour	Cents per kilowatt-hour	Cents per kilowatt-hour	Cents per kilowatt-hour	Percent	Percent	Percent	Kilowatt-hours
1902	—	16.20	—	—	—	—	—	—
1907	2.70	10.50	—	—	8.0	—	—	—
1912	—	9.10	—	—	15.9	—	—	264
1917	2.10	7.52	—	—	24.3	—	—	268
1920	—	7.45	—	—	34.7	1.6	47.4	339
1921	—	7.39	—	—	37.8	2.0	—	347
1922	2.83	7.38	—	—	40.0	2.5	—	359
1923	—	7.20	—	—	44.2	3.0	—	368
1924	—	7.20	—	—	48.6	3.5	—	378
1925	—	7.30	—	—	53.2	3.9	69.4	396
1926	2.71	7.00	4.35	1.49	57.9	4.8	—	430
1927	2.71	6.82	4.32	1.46	63.1	5.9	—	446
1928	2.66	6.63	4.20	1.40	65.0	7.3	—	463
1929	2.57	6.33	4.00	1.38	67.9	9.2	—	502
1930	2.66	6.03	3.89	1.41	68.2	10.4	84.8	547
1931	2.75	5.78	3.92	1.47	67.4	10.7	—	583
1932	2.85	5.60	3.93	1.53	67.0	11.2	—	601
1933	2.66	5.52	3.84	1.38	66.7	11.8	—	600
1934	2.58	5.33	3.75	1.35	67.1	12.1	—	629
1935	2.46	5.01	3.65	1.30	68.0	12.6	83.9	677
1936	2.27	4.67	3.44	1.19	70.3	14.5	—	735
1937	2.17	4.30	3.31	1.14	73.1	18.3	—	805
1938	2.30	4.14	3.24	1.20	74.9	23.9	—	853
1939	2.16	4.00	3.12	1.12	77.3	27.4	—	897
1940	2.06	3.84	3.03	1.06	78.7	32.6	90.8	952
1941	1.90	3.73	2.93	1.00	80.0	35.0	—	986
1942	1.79	3.67	2.80	0.94	81.2	37.8	—	1,022
1943	1.66	3.60	2.73	0.90	81.3	40.0	—	1,070
1944	1.65	3.51	2.71	0.91	84.0	42.2	—	1,151
1945	1.73	3.41	2.76	0.93	85.0	48.0	93.0	1,229
1946	1.81	3.22	2.75	0.98	85.5	53.3	—	1,329
1947	1.77	3.09	2.63	0.97	86.2	60.2	—	1,438
1948	1.79	3.01	2.61	1.01	89.6	66.8	—	1,563
1949	1.86	2.95	2.59	1.05	93.0	72.9	—	1,684
1950	1.81	2.88	2.58	1.01	94.0	77.7	96.6	1,845
1951	1.78	2.81	2.49	1.00	95.2	82.2	—	2,021
1952	1.79	2.77	2.50	1.01	96.1	86.9	—	2,186
1953	1.77	2.74	2.47	0.99	97.2	91.4	—	2,369
1954	1.77	2.70	2.47	0.99	97.9	93.0	—	2,573
1955	1.67	2.65	2.46	0.93	98.4	94.4	98.8	2,773
1956	1.64	2.61	2.44	0.91	98.8	95.9	99.2	2,989
1957	1.67	2.56	2.42	0.94	—	—	—	3,198
1958	1.71	2.54	2.42	0.96	—	—	—	3,389
1959	1.69	2.51	2.37	0.96	—	—	—	3,618
1960	1.69	2.47	2.43	0.96	—	—	—	3,854
1961	1.69	2.45	2.35	0.97	—	—	—	4,019
1962	1.68	2.41	2.37	0.96	—	—	—	4,259
1963	1.65	2.37	2.28	0.93	—	—	—	4,442
1964	1.62	2.31	2.19	0.91	—	—	—	4,703
1965	1.59	2.25	2.13	0.90	—	—	—	4,933
1966	1.56	2.20	2.06	0.89	—	—	—	5,265
1967	1.56	2.17	2.04	0.90	—	—	—	5,577
1968	1.55	2.12	2.00	0.90	—	—	—	6,057
1969	1.54	2.09	1.99	0.91	—	—	—	6,571
1970	1.59	2.10	2.01	0.95	—	—	—	7,066
1971	1.69	2.19	2.12	1.03	—	—	—	7,380
1972	1.77	2.29	2.22	1.09	—	—	—	7,691
1973	1.86	2.38	2.30	1.17	—	—	—	8,079
1974	2.30	2.83	2.85	1.55	—	—	—	7,907

(continued)

TABLE Db234–241   Electrical energy – retail prices, residential use, and service coverage: 1902–2000   *Continued*

	Average price				Percentage of dwelling units with electrical service			Annual use per residential customer
	All services	Residential	Commercial	Industrial	All	Farm	Urban and rural nonfarm	
	Db234	Db235	Db236	Db237	Db238	Db239	Db240	Db241
Year	Cents per kilowatt-hour	Cents per kilowatt-hour	Cents per kilowatt-hour	Cents per kilowatt-hour	Percent	Percent	Percent	Kilowatt-hours
1975	2.70	3.21	3.23	1.92	—	—	—	8,176
1976	2.89	3.45	3.46	2.07	—	—	—	8,360
1977	3.21	3.78	3.84	2.33	—	—	—	8,693
1978	3.46	4.03	4.10	2.59	—	—	—	8,849
1979	3.82	4.43	4.40	2.85	—	—	—	8,843
1980	4.49	5.12	5.22	3.44	—	—	—	9,025
1981	5.16	5.86	6.00	4.03	—	—	—	8,825
1982	5.79	6.44	6.61	4.66	—	—	—	8,743
1983	6.00	6.83	6.80	4.68	—	—	—	8,814
1984	6.27	7.17	7.14	4.88	—	—	—	8,978
1985	6.47	7.39	7.27	5.04	—	—	—	8,906
1986	6.47	7.43	7.22	4.99	—	—	—	9,090
1987	6.39	7.45	7.10	4.82	—	—	—	9,236
1988	6.36	7.49	7.04	4.71	—	—	—	9,498
1989	6.47	7.65	7.20	4.79	—	—	—	9,470
1990	6.57	7.83	7.33	4.81	—	—	—	9,508
1991	6.76	8.05	7.55	4.91	—	—	—	9,719
1992	6.85	8.22	7.67	4.93	—	—	—	9,392
1993	6.94	8.29	7.73	4.87	—	—	—	9,864
1994	6.91	8.38	7.73	4.73	—	—	—	9,868
1995	6.89	8.40	7.70	4.66	—	—	—	10,042
1996	6.86	8.36	7.64	4.61	—	—	—	10,275
1997	6.85	8.43	7.58	4.54	—	—	—	10,072
1998	6.74	8.26	7.41	4.48	—	—	—	10,275
1999	6.66	8.16	7.26	4.43	—	—	—	10,388
2000	6.78	8.21	7.36	4.57	—	—	—	10,707

Sources

Series Db234–237. 1902–1925: U.S. Bureau of the Census, *Census of Electrical Industries* (1917, 1922, 1927). 1926–1959: Edison Electrical Institute (EEI), *Edison Electric Institute Statistical Bulletin* (EEI, 1952, 1970). 1960–2000: EEI, *Statistical Yearbook of the Electric Utility Industry* (EEI, annual).

Series Db238–240. Census years: U.S. Bureau of the Census, census of housing (decennial) and census of agriculture (quinquennial). Intercensal years: National Electric Light Association, *Statistical Supplement to the Electric Light and Power Industry in the United States*; *Electrical World*, and *Edison Electric Institute Statistical Bulletin*.

Series Db241. 1912: U.S. Bureau of the Census, *Census of Electrical Industries* (1912). 1917–1925: National Electric Light Association, *Statistical Supplement to the Electric Light and Power Industry in the United States*. 1926–1970: Edison Electric Institute, *Statistical Bulletin* (1952 and 1970 issues). 1971–2000: EEI, *Statistical Yearbook of the Electric Utility Industry*.

Documentation

Series Db234–237. These averages indicate the average revenue from electric services and do not reflect variation with use and rate levels. Beginning in 1950, the figures were revised to allocate rural service to other appropriate classes, and so are not fully comparable with earlier years.

Series Db238–240. These percentages are generally based on the relationship between the number of residential electric customers and population in census years. For intercensal years, variation in percentages of farms electrified, as estimated in different sources, may be caused by the inclusion or exclusion of farms without permanent dwelling units, farms with their own electric power plants, farms without service where the distribution lines are within a quarter-mile of the dwelling unit, or the interpolation procedures used for estimating the number of farms between census years.

TABLE Db242–245   Nuclear power plants – number, capacity, and generation: 1957–2001

Contributed by Gavin Wright

	Nuclear power plants					Nuclear power plants		
	Operable nuclear generating units	Net summer capability	Net generation	Capacity factor		Operable nuclear generating units	Net summer capability	Net generation	Capacity factor
	Db242	Db243	Db244	Db245		Db242	Db243	Db244	Db245
Year	Number	Million kilowatt-hours	Million kilowatt-hours	Percent	Year	Number	Million kilowatt-hours	Million kilowatt-hours	Percent
1957	1	0.1	(Z)	—	1980	70	51.8	251,100	56.3
1958	1	0.1	200	—	1981	75	56.0	250,900	58.2
1959	2	0.1	200	—	1982	78	60.0	276,400	56.6
1960	3	0.4	500	—	1983	81	63.0	255,200	54.4
1961	3	0.4	1,700	—	1984	86	69.7	327,600	56.3
1962	5	0.7	2,300	—	1985	95	79.4	383,700	58.0
1963	6	0.8	3,200	—	1986	100	85.2	414,000	56.9
1964	6	0.8	3,300	—	1987	107	93.6	455,300	57.4
1965	6	0.8	3,700	—	1988	108	94.7	527,000	63.5
1966	8	1.7	5,500	—	1989	110	98.2	529,400	62.2
1967	10	1.7	7,700	—	1990	110	99.6	576,900	66.0
1968	11	2.7	12,500	—	1991	111	99.6	612,600	70.2
1969	14	4.4	13,900	—	1992	109	99.0	618,800	70.9
1970	18	7.0	21,800	—	1993	110	99.0	610,300	70.5
1971	21	9.0	38,100	—	1994	109	99.1	640,400	73.8
1972	29	14.5	54,100	—	1995	109	99.5	673,400	77.4
1973	39	22.7	83,500	53.5	1996	109	100.8	674,700	76.2
1974	48	31.9	114,000	47.8	1997	107	99.7	628,600	71.1
1975	54	37.3	172,500	55.9	1998	104	97.1	673,700	78.2
1976	61	43.8	191,100	54.7	1999	104	97.4	728,300	85.3
1977	65	46.3	250,900	63.3	2000	104	97.9	753,900	88.1
1978	70	50.8	276,400	64.5	2001	104	98.1	768,800	89.4
1979	68	49.7	255,200	58.4					

(Z) Less than 50 million kilowatt-hours.

Source

U.S. Energy Information Administration, *Annual Energy Review* (U.S. Department of Energy, annual).

Documentation

Series Db242. As of the end of year.

Series Db243. Net summer capability is the peak steady hourly output that generating equipment is expected to supply to system load, exclusive of auxi-liary and other power plant, as demonstrated by test at the time of summer peak demand.

Series Db245. The annual capacity factor is the weighted average of monthly capacity factors. Monthly factors are derived by dividing actual monthly generation by the maximum possible generation for the month (hours in month multiplied by the net maximum dependable capacity).

TABLE Db246–250   Uranium production and foreign trade, and discharged commercial reactor fuel: 1949–2001

Contributed by Gavin Wright

	Uranium concentrate			Discharged commercial reactor fuel			Uranium concentrate			Discharged commercial reactor fuel	
	Production	Exports	Imports	Annual discharge	Year-end inventory		Production	Exports	Imports	Annual discharge	Year-end inventory
	Db246	Db247	Db248	Db249	Db250		Db246	Db247	Db248	Db249	Db250
Year	Million pounds	Million pounds	Million pounds	Metric tons	Metric tons	Year	Million pounds	Million pounds	Million pounds	Metric tons	Metric tons
1949	0.36	0.00	4.30	—	—	1975	23.20	1.00	1.40	499	1,538
1950	0.92	0.00	5.50	—	—	1976	25.49	1.20	3.60	—	—
1951	1.54	0.00	6.10	—	—	1977	29.88	4.00	5.60	—	—
1952	1.74	0.00	5.70	—	—	1978	36.97	6.80	5.20	—	—
1953	2.32	0.00	3.80	—	—	1979	37.47	6.20	3.00	—	—
1954	3.40	0.00	6.50	—	—	1980	43.70	5.80	3.60	1,193	6,434
1955	5.56	0.00	7.60	—	—	1981	38.47	4.40	6.60	1,077	7,511
1956	11.92	0.00	12.50	—	—	1982	26.87	6.20	17.10	1,014	8,525
1957	16.96	0.00	17.10	—	—	1983	21.16	3.30	8.20	1,224	9,749
1958	24.88	0.00	32.30	—	—	1984	14.88	2.20	12.50	1,257	11,006
1959	32.48	0.00	36.30	—	—	1985	11.31	5.30	11.70	1,330	12,481
1960	35.28	0.00	36.00	—	—	1986	13.51	1.60	13.50	1,431	13,881
1961	34.70	0.00	29.00	—	—	1987	12.99	1.00	15.10	1,625	15,506
1962	34.02	0.00	24.20	—	—	1988	13.13	3.30	15.80	1,672	17,178
1963	28.44	0.00	22.40	—	—	1989	13.84	2.10	13.10	1,914	19,092
1964	23.70	0.00	12.10	—	—	1990	8.89	2.00	23.70	2,084	21,029
1965	20.88	0.00	8.00	—	—	1991	7.95	3.50	16.30	1,794	22,914
1966	21.18	0.80	4.60	—	—	1992	5.65	2.80	23.30	2,192	24,937
1967	22.51	1.40	0.00	—	—	1993	3.06	3.00	21.00	2,102	27,039
1968	24.74	1.60	0.00	—	—	1994	3.35	17.70	36.60	1,809	28,848
1969	23.22	1.00	0.00	—	—	1995	6.04	9.80	41.30	2,292	31,140
1970	25.81	4.20	0.00	82	118	1996	6.32	11.50	45.40	2,174	31,140
1971	24.55	0.40	0.00	—	—	1997	5.64	17.00	43.00	—	—
1972	25.80	0.20	0.00	—	—	1998	4.71	15.10	43.70	—	—
1973	26.47	1.20	0.00	—	—	1999	4.61	8.50	47.60	—	—
1974	23.06	3.00	0.00	—	—	2000	3.96	13.60	44.90	—	—
						2001	2.64	11.70	46.70	—	—

Sources

Series Db246–248. U.S. Energy Information Administration, *Annual Energy Review* (U.S. Department of Energy, annual) and *Uranium Industry Annual* (U.S. Department of Energy, annual).

Series Db249–250. Nuclear Assurance Corporation, Atlanta, Georgia, as reported in U.S. Census Bureau, *Statistical Abstract of the United States*.

TABLE Db251-260   Solar collectors – manufacturers and shipments, by type, use, and market sector: 1974-2000[1]

Contributed by Gavin Wright

		Shipments								
		Type			End use			Market sector		
	Manufacturers	Total	Low-temperature	Medium-temperature, special, and other	Pool heating	Hot water	Space heating	Residential	Commercial	Industrial
	Db251	Db252	Db253	Db254	Db255	Db256	Db257	Db258	Db259	Db260
Year	Number	Thousand square feet	Thousand square feet	Thousand square feet	Thousand square feet	Thousand square feet	Thousand square feet	Thousand square feet	Thousand square feet	Thousand square feet
1974	45	1,274	1,137	137	—	—	—	—	—	—
1975	131	3,743	3,026	717	—	—	—	—	—	—
1976	222	5,801	3,876	1,925	—	—	—	—	—	—
1977	349	10,312	4,743	5,569	6,334	1,713	1,699	7,978	1,680	105
1978	273	10,860	5,872	4,988	5,970	2,513	1,736	8,095	1,848	263
1979	341	14,251	8,395	5,857	8,551	2,958	1,722	11,387	2,015	314
1980	329	19,398	12,233	7,165	12,029	4,790	1,688	16,077	2,417	488
1981	338	20,133	8,677	11,456	9,781	7,204	2,017	15,773	2,561	1,518
1982	309	18,621	7,476	11,145	7,035	7,444	2,367	13,729	3,789	560
1983	234	16,828	4,853	11,975	4,839	9,323	2,082	11,780	3,039	1,665
1984	254	17,191	4,479	11,939	4,427	8,930	2,370	13,980	2,091	289
1986	109	9,360	3,751	1,111	3,494	1,181	127	4,131	703	13
1987	62	7,269	3,157	957	3,111	964	23	3,775	305	11
1988	53	8,174	3,326	732	3,304	726	7	3,796	255	7
1989	46	11,482	4,283	1,989	4,688	1,374	205	5,804	424	42
1990	53	11,378	3,621	2,519	5,016	1,091	2	5,835	294	22
1991	57	6,574	5,585	989	5,535	989	24	6,322	225	13
1992	50	7,086	6,187	897	6,210	801	35	6,832	204	27
1993	46	6,928	6,025	931	6,040	880	15	6,694	215	31
1994	47	7,627	6,823	803	6,813	790	19	7,026	583	16
1995	40	7,666	6,813	840	6,763	755	132	6,966	604	82
1996	33	7,616	6,821	785	6,787	765	57	6,873	682	54
1997	34	8,138	7,524	606	7,528	595	9	7,360	768	7
1998	31	7,756	7,292	443	7,201	463	67	7,165	517	62
1999	33	8,583	8,152	427	8,141	373	42	7,774	785	18
2000	27	8,354	7,948	400	7,863	367	99	7,473	810	57

[1] Declines for 1984-1989 are primarily the result of the expiration of the federal energy
    tax credit and industry consolidation.

Source

U.S. Energy Information Administration, *Solar Collector Manufacturing Activity*,
Annual Energy Review (U.S. Department of Energy, annual).

Documentation

A solar collector is a device for intercepting sunlight, converting the light to
heat, and carrying the heat to where it will be either used or stored.

Series Db252. Includes other end uses and market sectors not shown separately.

TABLE Db261–272 Gas utility customers, sales, and revenues, by type of service: 1932–2000[1]

Contributed by Gavin Wright

	Customers				Sales				Revenues			
	Total	Residential	Commercial	Industrial	Total	Residential	Commercial	Industrial	Total	Residential	Commercial	Industrial
	Db261	Db262	Db263	Db264	Db265	Db266	Db267	Db268	Db269	Db270	Db271	Db272
Year	Thousand	Thousand	Thousand	Thousand	Million therms	Million therms	Million therms	Million therms	Million dollars	Million dollars	Million dollars	Million dollars
1932	15,532	14,452	999	73	10,441	4,672	1,193	4,534	723	537	93	91
1933	15,195	14,141	978	68	10,531	4,237	1,150	5,114	680	495	88	95
1934	15,512	14,440	990	74	12,063	4,202	1,102	6,699	703	494	87	119
1935	15,819	14,725	1,014	72	12,924	4,445	1,211	7,221	727	503	91	130
1936	16,170	15,026	1,058	77	14,693	4,784	1,369	8,280	770	516	97	151
1937	16,605	15,466	1,056	74	15,773	4,987	1,382	9,041	802	528	100	167
1938	16,876	15,697	1,094	75	14,682	4,956	1,380	7,941	777	523	101	145
1939	17,128	15,926	1,121	73	15,927	5,289	1,469	8,768	814	538	105	165
1940	17,600	16,381	1,138	73	17,235	5,823	1,598	9,544	872	573	112	182
1941	18,126	16,904	1,137	78	19,009	5,862	1,650	11,206	914	575	114	220
1942	18,734	17,511	1,137	78	20,849	6,679	1,990	11,723	994	623	127	238
1943	19,064	17,838	1,141	77	23,415	7,001	2,083	13,582	1,064	648	128	277
1944	19,585	18,320	1,177	82	25,120	7,313	2,208	14,635	1,108	667	133	293
1945	19,977	18,607	1,278	80	25,868	7,749	2,497	14,523	1,153	705	149	281
1946	20,636	19,157	1,377	87	26,379	8,482	2,630	14,602	1,213	754	161	284
1947	21,416	19,835	1,474	91	29,882	10,087	3,107	15,792	1,396	862	191	326
1948	22,245	20,562	1,571	94	33,885	11,153	3,535	17,981	1,579	958	221	377
1949	23,035	21,264	1,657	97	35,790	11,827	3,724	18,979	1,689	1,031	238	396
1950	24,001	22,146	1,739	100	42,090	13,839	4,104	22,887	1,948	1,177	266	480
1951	24,953	23,042	1,787	101	48,222	16,205	4,559	25,522	2,228	1,335	294	557
1952	25,850	23,852	1,869	104	52,392	17,348	4,929	27,990	2,466	1,457	321	639
1953	26,705	24,647	1,926	107	56,073	18,033	4,980	30,373	2,716	1,574	339	739
1954	27,528	25,398	1,990	112	61,026	20,031	5,405	33,096	3,049	1,783	378	821
1955	28,479	26,283	2,048	121	66,586	22,387	6,029	35,351	3,450	2,007	424	938
1956	29,536	27,241	2,141	125	72,541	24,643	6,558	38,687	3,850	2,237	471	1,066
1957	30,476	28,101	2,211	132	77,034	25,985	6,989	40,476	4,134	2,379	506	1,150
1958	31,242	28,786	2,287	134	80,285	28,125	7,649	40,764	4,568	2,658	571	1,229
1959	32,066	29,530	2,364	136	87,917	29,739	8,275	45,631	5,065	2,870	633	1,431
1960	33,054	30,418	2,458	141	92,877	31,881	9,198	47,094	5,617	3,177	723	1,563
1961	33,831	31,118	2,529	147	95,890	33,210	9,881	47,856	5,993	3,377	789	1,658
1962	34,683	31,893	2,598	156	102,348	35,369	10,929	51,001	6,445	3,603	874	1,796
1963	35,551	32,711	2,640	162	107,663	36,680	11,366	54,381	6,727	3,728	910	1,906
1964	36,463	33,551	2,712	159	115,912	38,697	12,735	59,120	7,133	3,895	998	2,049
1965	37,338	34,341	2,790	166	119,803	39,990	13,448	61,465	7,407	4,030	1,054	2,148
1966	38,228	35,142	2,868	174	128,591	41,754	14,628	66,533	7,870	4,195	1,135	2,335
1967	39,077	35,915	2,934	181	134,883	43,653	15,776	70,143	8,261	4,383	1,224	2,461
1968	39,930	36,691	3,004	188	144,724	45,527	17,049	75,951	8,781	4,567	1,315	2,675
1969	40,854	37,538	3,074	193	153,916	48,204	18,781	81,358	9,480	4,883	1,459	2,919
1970	41,482	38,097	3,131	199	160,435	49,237	20,066	84,392	10,283	5,207	1,620	3,181
1971	42,242	38,789	3,199	205	166,857	50,401	21,555	86,455	11,357	5,635	1,829	3,569
1972	42,955	39,428	3,264	209	170,821	51,418	22,757	87,757	12,465	6,094	2,064	3,943
1973	43,711	40,116	3,331	209	164,799	49,936	22,808	83,708	12,987	6,247	2,172	4,197
1974	44,267	40,627	3,392	194	160,003	48,648	22,934	81,532	15,242	6,899	2,539	5,391
1975	44,555	40,950	3,367	184	148,629	49,910	23,868	68,371	19,101	8,445	3,303	6,745
1976	44,941	41,338	3,372	180	148,135	50,142	24,226	71,920	23,701	9,941	4,075	9,435
1977	45,274	41,682	3,371	173	143,409	49,463	24,094	67,964	28,303	11,541	4,980	11,455
1978	45,789	42,183	3,370 [2]	189	147,484	51,067	24,995	69,315	32,150	12,939	5,696	13,139
1979	46,478	42,821	3,423	189	154,403	50,831	24,858	76,414	38,947	14,833	6,624	17,045
1980	47,223	43,489	3,498	187	154,132	48,261	24,534	79,659	48,303	17,432	8,183	22,240
1981	47,948	44,149	3,565	187	153,748	46,097	23,754	82,393	56,110	19,180	9,286	27,124
1982	48,415	44,552	3,631	186	141,827	47,698	24,713	67,943	63,200	23,700	11,666	27,200
1983	48,799	44,894	3,676	182	128,575	44,496	22,982	59,694	65,837	26,173	12,659	26,315
1984	49,325	45,367	3,730	180	131,617	46,283	23,960	59,910	67,496	27,485	13,205	26,094
1985	49,971	45,929	3,816	179	126,152	45,130	23,380	56,347	63,293	26,864	12,722	23,086
1986	50,704	46,583	3,892 [3]	178	111,251	43,808	22,389	43,382	51,201	24,759	11,274	14,495
1987	51,576	47,363	3,980	180	105,434	43,850	21,559	38,479	45,492	23,622	10,271	11,068
1988	52,422	48,133	4,069	168	107,053	46,950	23,060	35,441	46,162	24,828	10,681	10,113
1989	53,356	48,981	4,161	168	105,511	47,980	23,218	32,434	47,493	26,172	11,074	9,666

Notes appear at end of table

TABLE Db261–272   Gas utility customers, sales, and revenues, by type of service: 1932–2000 *Continued*

	Customers				Sales				Revenues			
	Total	Residential	Commercial	Industrial	Total	Residential	Commercial	Industrial	Total	Residential	Commercial	Industrial
	Db261	Db262	Db263	Db264	Db265	Db266	Db267	Db268	Db269	Db270	Db271	Db272
Year	Thousand	Thousand	Thousand	Thousand	Million therms	Million therms	Million therms	Million therms	Million dollars	Million dollars	Million dollars	Million dollars
1990	54,261	49,802	4,246	166	98,418	44,684	21,920	30,104	45,153	25,000	10,604	8,996
1991	55,174	50,634	4,322	168	96,014	45,463	21,981	26,313	44,647	25,729	10,669	7,576
1992	56,132	51,525	4,397	165	99,065	46,944	22,087	27,722	46,178	26,702	10,865	7,913
1993	57,028	52,358	4,428	181	101,509	50,538	23,966	25,330	50,137	29,787	12,076	7,642
1994	57,936	53,219	4,475	180	92,484	48,448	22,529	19,921	49,852	30,552	12,276	6,428
1995	58,728	53,955	4,530	181	92,207	48,027	22,814	19,189	46,436	28,742	11,573	5,571
1996	59,820	54,968	4,616	183	95,319	51,984	23,951	17,906	51,115	32,021	12,726	5,821
1997	59,790	54,992	4,539	170	88,801	50,129	22,343	15,105	51,531	33,175	12,632	5,236
1998	62,421	57,465	4,755	164	86,297	48,277	21,570	15,277	47,930	31,333	11,523	4,684
1999	64,071	58,939	4,920	174	88,889	48,647	20,867	18,682	48,423	31,476	11,133	5,547
2000	64,115	59,061	4,813	161	90,523	49,405	21,164	19,042	59,667	37,446	13,648	8,069

[1] Through 1975, some electric generation is included in the "other" class of service; thereafter, all electric generation is included in the industrial category.

[2] Some customers reclassified from commercial to industrial.

[3] Some customers reclassified from commercial to other.

Sources

1932–1959: American Gas Association (AGA), *Historical Statistics of the Gas Industry* (AGA, 1965). 1960–1970: AGA, *Gas Facts* (AGA, 1971). 1971–2000: AGA, *Gas Facts* (AGA, annual).

Documentation

A therm is equivalent to 100,000 British thermal units.

Series Db261, Db265, and Db269. Totals include other customers, sales, or revenues not shown separately.

Series Db265–268. Excludes sales for resale.

FISHERIES

Gavin Wright

TABLE Db273–282   Yield, imports, and exports of fishery products: 1880–2000
Contributed by Gavin Wright

	Domestic yield				Imports			Exports		
	Volume					Value			Value	
	Total	For human food	For industrial use	Value	Volume, edible	Edible	Nonedible	Volume, edible	Edible	Nonedible
	Db273	Db274	Db275	Db276	Db277	Db278 [1]	Db279 [1]	Db280	Db281 [1]	Db282 [1,2]
Year	Million pounds	Million pounds	Million pounds	Million dollars	Million pounds	Million dollars	Million dollars	Million pounds	Million dollars	Million dollars
1880	1,706	—	—	39.1	—	—	—	—	—	—
1889	1,685	—	—	39.0	—	—	—	—	—	—
1890	1,758	—	—	41.3	—	—	—	—	—	—
1891	1,709	—	—	42.3	—	—	—	—	—	—
1892	1,652	—	—	40.7	—	—	—	—	—	—
1905	2,002	—	—	57.3	—	—	—	—	—	—
1906	2,046	—	—	59.3	—	—	—	—	—	—
1907	1,930	—	—	60.9	—	—	—	—	—	—
1908	2,053	—	—	62.7	—	—	—	—	—	—
1917	2,676	—	—	71.1	—	—	—	—	—	—
1921	2,255	1,451	804	—	—	—	—	—	—	—
1922	2,619	1,677	942	—	—	—	—	—	—	—
1923	2,726	1,807	919	—	—	—	—	—	—	—
1924	2,461	1,874	587	—	285	29.3	17.1	165	20.3	0.5
1925	2,891	2,029	862	105.1	263	29.1	20.0	161	20.7	0.5
1926	2,871	2,198	673	106.7	309	32.5	17.6	164	19.9	0.4
1927	2,806	2,172	634	111.5	312	34.9	20.8	158	18.3	0.4
1928	3,061	2,370	691	114.3	361	37.4	21.5	171	20.8	0.4
1929	3,491	2,601	890	125.8	357	38.8	27.8	213	23.5	0.3
1930	3,224	2,478	746	109.0	338	35.0	15.8	167	17.0	0.3
1931	2,630	2,129	501	77.0	277	28.9	14.1	114	11.4	0.2
1932	2,612	1,864	748	56.0	260	21.7	7.9	87	7.7	0.2
1933	2,997	2,087	911	61.1	284	21.8	8.7	80	7.4	1.0
1934	4,104	2,434	1,670	76.8	287	23.2	7.6	116	12.0	1.8
1935	4,135	2,583	1,552	82.8	325	27.5	8.7	120	12.9	1.5
1936	4,826	2,854	1,972	94.8	371	30.4	11.5	111	12.3	1.0
1937	4,353	2,703	1,650	101.4	365	33.9	16.7	119	13.7	0.8
1938	4,254	2,639	1,615	94.2	303	28.3	11.0	118	13.8	0.6
1939	4,445	2,713	1,732	97.6	346	32.4	13.6	125	13.6	0.6
1940	4,060	2,675	1,385	96.1	303	29.1	12.8	145	17.1	0.7
1941	4,900	3,062	1,838	129.0	306	28.0	12.9	216	21.5	0.5
1942	3,875	2,683	1,192	170.3	277	29.0	10.6	167	27.9	4.0
1943	4,162	2,737	1,425	204.0	324	43.7	23.5	239	43.2	5.3
1944	4,533	2,865	1,668	213.0	339	53.4	25.0	112	31.9	4.0
1945	4,598	3,167	1,431	269.9	405	76.4	24.8	136	30.9	7.7
1946	4,467	3,049	1,418	313.0	474	90.0	39.7	200	38.4	1.6
1947	4,349	3,020	1,329	312.0	408	83.3	26.7	207	49.3	3.6
1948	4,513	3,146	1,367	371.1	473	111.7	45.0	95	21.0	3.4
1949	4,804	3,305	1,499	342.7	471	113.8	37.9	147	29.2	5.8
1950	4,901	3,307	1,594	347.4	640	158.4	39.9	122	18.9	8.6
1951	4,433	3,048	1,385	364.8	647	158.4	54.1	166	27.1	8.7
1952	4,432	2,778	1,654	363.6	705	183.1	57.3	62	15.5	6.4
1953	4,487	2,519	1,968	356.1	726	195.9	49.6	69	17.1	10.8
1954	4,762	2,705	2,057	359.3	804	203.7	48.7	63	16.2	15.3
1955	4,809	2,579	2,230	338.9	780	209.0	49.9	110	24.9	15.1
1956	5,268	2,690	2,578	372.2	802	234.7	48.0	102	22.9	16.6
1957	4,789	2,475	2,314	353.7	900	252.8	46.5	85	20.5	15.4
1958	4,747	2,651	2,096	373.3	1,020	283.8	47.0	65	19.4	11.6
1959	5,122	2,369	2,753	346.1	1,141	314.7	55.5	81	26.7	17.5
1960	4,942	2,498	2,444	353.6	1,095	310.6	52.7	61	25.6	18.5
1961	5,187	2,490	2,697	362.2	1,087	339.3	61.3	40	19.6	15.1
1962	5,354	2,540	2,814	396.4	1,256	405.8	84.0	57	22.5	13.3
1963	4,847	2,556	2,291	377.2	1,197	399.9	100.8	65	30.4	26.2
1964	4,541	2,497	2,044	389.5	1,318	433.7	130.6	95	42.9	21.3

Notes appear at end of table

TABLE Db273-282   Yield, imports, and exports of fishery products: 1880-2000   *Continued*

	Domestic yield				Imports			Exports		
	Volume					Value			Value	
	Total	For human food	For industrial use	Value	Volume, edible	Edible	Nonedible	Volume, edible	Edible	Nonedible
	Db273	Db274	Db275	Db276	Db277	Db278 [1]	Db279 [1]	Db280	Db281 [1]	Db282 [1,2]
Year	Million pounds	Million pounds	Million pounds	Million dollars	Million pounds	Million dollars	Million dollars	Million pounds	Million dollars	Million dollars
1965	4,777	2,587	2,190	445.7	1,399	479.4	121.5	96	49.3	20.2
1966	4,366	2,573	1,794	472.3	1,594	568.1	151.6	110	62.9	21.9
1967	4,055	2,368	1,687	439.6	1,470	538.3	169.6	108	67.5	14.7
1968	4,160	2,347	1,814	497.3	1,741	643.2	179.5	91	56.8	10.9
1969	4,337	2,321	2,016	526.5	1,707	704.8	139.5	141	86.5	18.1
1970	4,917	2,537	2,380	613.1	1,873	812.5	224.9	140	93.9	23.6
1971	5,018	2,441	2,577	651.0	1,785	887.1	187.1	172	113.6	25.6
1972	4,806	2,435	2,371	748.0	2,341	1,233.3	261.1	172	134.2	23.7
1973	4,858	2,398	2,460	937.0	2,416	1,398.5	184.6	239	241.9	57.3
1974	4,967	2,496	2,471	932.0	2,267	1,495.4	215.5	178	195.0	67.2
1975	4,877	2,465	2,412	977.0	1,913	1,367.2	269.9	218	267.4	37.4
1976	5,388	2,775	2,613	1,349.0	2,228	1,913.9	414.3	241	329.8	54.9
1977	5,271	2,952	2,319	1,554.0	2,176	2,078.2	555.4	331	473.4	47.1
1978	6,028	3,177	2,851	1,854.0	2,411	2,256.3	829.6	448	831.7	73.9
1979	6,267	3,318	2,949	2,234.0	2,359	2,671.9	1,136.9	554	1,022.3	62.2
1980	6,482	3,654	2,828	2,237.0	2,145	2,686.7	961.7	574	904.4	101.8
1981	5,977	3,547	2,430	2,388.0	2,272	3,034.2	1,171.8	669	1,072.8	84.2
1982	6,367	3,285	3,082	2,390.0	2,225	3,202.4	1,321.2	657	998.9	60.0
1983	6,439	3,238	3,201	2,355.0	2,387	3,626.7	1,502.7	624	961.2	116.2
1984	6,438	3,320	3,118	2,350.0	2,454	3,742.3	2,141.1	598	893.9	107.4
1985	6,258	3,294	2,964	2,326.0	2,754	4,064.3	2,614.3	673	1,064.3	74.9
1986	6,031	3,393	2,638	2,763.0	2,979	4,813.5	2,812.8	754	1,325.6	68.2
1987	6,896	3,946	2,950	3,115.0	3,201	5,711.2	3,106.5	806	1,625.4	96.7
1988	7,192	4,588	2,604	3,520.0	2,968	5,441.6	3,430.4	1,086	2,213.3	125.1
1989	8,463	6,204	2,259	3,238.0	3,243	5,497.8	4,106.5	1,406	2,355.6	2,582.5
1990	9,404	7,041	2,363	3,522.0	2,885	5,233.2	3,814.5	1,947	2,881.3	3,084.7
1991	9,484	7,031	2,453	3,308.0	3,015	5,671.9	3,763.2	2,059	3,155.8	3,386.0
1992	9,637	7,618	2,019	3,678.0	2,894	5,705.9	4,165.4	2,088	3,465.7	3,654.0
1993	10,467	8,214	2,253	3,471.0	2,917	5,848.7	4,773.6	1,986	3,076.8	3,847.9
1994	10,461	7,936	2,525	3,809.0	3,035	6,645.1	5,341.7	1,979	3,126.1	4,254.7
1995	9,788	7,667	2,121	3,770.0	3,066	6,791.7	5,659.9	2,047	3,262.2	5,005.9
1996	9,565	7,475	2,090	3,487.0	3,170	6,729.6	6,330.7	2,112	3,032.3	5,621.2
1997	9,842	7,244	2,598	3,448.0	3,339	7,754.2	6,774.1	2,019	2,713.1	6,640.6
1998	9,194	7,173	2,021	3,128.0	3,647	8,173.2	7,459.5	1,689	2,268.0	6,437.4
1999	9,339	6,832	2,507	3,467.1	3,888	9,013.9	8,025.7	1,961	2,848.6	7,158.3
2000	9,069	6,912	2,157	3,549.5	3,978	10,054.1	8,959.4	2,172	2,964.9	7,934.1

[1] Data include Puerto Rico; beginning 1955, imports also include landings of tuna by foreign vessels in American Samoa, and imports of tuna into U.S. outlying areas.

[2] Increase in 1989 partially attributable to reclassification of commodities that are considered to be based on fishery products including fish, shellfish, aquatic plants and animals, and any products thereof, including processed and manufactured products.

Sources

1880: U.S. Commission of Fish and Fisheries, *The Fisheries and Fishery Industries of the United States* (1887); 1889-1917: H. F. Taylor, *Economics of the Fisheries of North Carolina*, part 3, "Survey of Marine Fisheries of North Carolina" (University of North Carolina Press, 1951); 1921-1938: U.S. Bureau of Fisheries, *Fishery Industries of the United States* (annual); 1939-2000: U.S. National Marine Fisheries Service (NMFS) and predecessor agencies, *Fishery Statistics of the United States* (NMFS, annual), and *Fisheries of the United States* (NMFS, annual).

Documentation

Since 1880, complete or partial surveys have been made of the various regions of the United States, except for the Mississippi River, with sufficient frequency to produce satisfactory annual estimates of the yield and value of the U.S. fisheries. Because of the relative stability and low magnitude of the Mississippi River production, the inclusion of interpolated estimates for that region does not significantly affect the national totals.

Prior to 1921, except for 1909-1914, Taylor (1951) provides a well-validated and statistically satisfactory series of annual figures by summation of critically adjusted and interpolated data based upon various individual state and regional data published by the U.S. Bureau of Fisheries or its predecessor, the Commission of Fish and Fisheries. No statistically satisfactory national totals can be provided for 1909 to 1914 (Taylor 1951). A satisfactory Alaska total is provided by J. N. Cobb, *Products of the Commercial Fisheries of the United States*, Transactions of the American Fisheries Society (AFS), volume 48 (AFS, 1919), which, added to Taylor's 1917 U.S. total, provides a combined total for that year.

Prior to 1908, records of salt fish were not converted to equivalent fresh round weights except for 1880. It was estimated (Taylor 1951) that such salt fish in 1887 represented at least 20 percent of the national total catch of food-fish species. By 1920, this proportion had declined to about 1 percent. Estimated corrections back to 1908 (derived from Taylor 1951, Figure 7, p. 379) have been added to the estimates of national totals (Taylor 1951, p. 480).

For recent years, details on commercial landings at major U.S. ports and territorial possessions may be found in the source.

Series Db275. The domestic yield for industrial purposes represents the weight of fishery products determined to have been processed into meal, oil, solubles, and shell products or used as bait or animal food.

TABLE Db283–300 Landed catches of principal fish species: 1880–2000

Contributed by Gavin Wright

Year	Total Db283	Atlantic cod Db284	Pacific cod Db285	Flounder Db286	Pacific (whiting) hake Db287	Halibut Db288	Atlantic sea herring Db289	Pacific sea herring Db290	Menhaden Db291	Pollock Db292	Sablefish Db293	Pacific salmon Db294	Swordfish Db295	Tuna Db296	Atlantic mackerel Db297	Pacific mackerel Db298	Haddock Db299	Pacific sardine Db300
	Million pounds	Million pounds	Million pounds	Million pounds	Million pounds	Million pounds	Million pounds	Million pounds	Million pounds	Million pounds	Million pounds	Million pounds	Million pounds	Million pounds	Million pounds	Million pounds	Million pounds	Million pounds
1880	—	—	—	—	—	—	—	—	520	—	—	—	—	—	131	—	49	—
1881	—	—	—	—	—	—	—	—	304	—	—	—	—	—	147	—	—	—
1882	—	—	—	—	—	—	—	—	232	—	—	—	—	—	142	—	—	—
1883	—	—	—	—	—	—	—	—	411	—	—	—	—	—	85	—	—	—
1884	—	—	—	—	—	—	—	—	575	—	—	—	—	—	179	—	—	—
1885	—	—	—	—	—	—	—	—	321	—	—	—	—	—	124	—	—	—
1886	—	—	—	—	—	—	—	—	190	—	—	—	—	—	30	—	—	—
1887	—	207	—	—	—	2	43	—	223	—	—	—	—	—	33	—	47	—
1888	—	196	—	—	—	—	53	—	294	—	—	—	—	—	20	—	53	—
1889	—	164	—	—	—	1	—	—	372	—	—	—	—	—	10	—	52	—
1890	—	—	—	—	—	1	—	—	358	—	—	—	—	—	11	—	—	—
1891	—	—	—	—	—	1	—	—	238	—	—	—	—	—	20	—	58	1
1892	—	—	—	—	—	2	—	24	150	—	—	47	—	—	22	—	—	—
1893	—	—	—	—	—	—	—	—	245	—	—	—	—	—	25	—	53	—
1894	—	—	—	—	—	—	—	—	357	—	—	—	—	—	23	—	67	—
1895	—	—	—	—	—	2	—	10	309	—	—	78	—	—	12	—	62	1
1896	—	—	—	—	—	—	—	—	269	—	—	—	—	—	35	—	49	—
1897	—	—	—	—	—	—	—	—	391	—	—	—	—	—	11	—	50	—
1898	—	125	—	—	—	—	—	—	363	—	—	129	—	—	10	—	54	—
1899	—	—	—	—	—	—	—	10	—	—	—	—	—	—	13	—	53	2
1900	—	—	—	—	—	—	—	—	610	—	—	—	—	—	46	—	52	—
1901	—	—	—	—	—	—	—	—	—	—	—	—	—	—	35	—	48	—
1902	—	124	—	—	—	—	—	—	—	—	—	—	—	—	23	—	55	—
1903	—	—	—	—	—	—	—	—	—	—	—	—	—	—	26	—	60	—
1904	—	—	—	—	—	—	—	18	—	—	—	107	—	—	20	—	70	1
1905	—	94	—	—	—	—	—	—	—	—	—	—	—	—	22	—	89	—
1906	—	—	—	—	—	—	—	—	—	—	—	—	—	—	12	—	85	—
1907	—	—	—	—	—	49	122	—	—	—	—	—	—	—	24	—	63	—
1908	—	95	—	—	—	—	—	16	—	—	—	86	—	—	21	—	70	5
1909	—	—	—	—	—	—	—	—	—	—	—	—	—	—	17	—	64	—
1910	—	—	—	—	—	—	—	—	—	—	—	—	—	—	6	—	72	—
1911	—	—	—	—	—	—	—	—	—	—	—	—	—	1	12	—	79	—
1912	—	—	—	—	—	—	—	—	711	—	—	—	—	3	10	—	88	—
1913	—	—	—	—	—	59	—	—	—	—	—	—	—	7	14	—	76	—
1914	—	—	—	—	—	—	—	—	—	—	—	—	—	18	21	—	81	—
1915	—	—	—	—	—	67	—	17	—	—	—	127	—	21	23	—	85	4
1916	—	—	—	—	—	51	—	—	—	—	—	—	—	43	30	1	78	—
1917	—	—	—	—	—	52	—	—	306	—	—	—	—	32	37	3	68	—
1918	—	—	—	—	—	42	—	—	259	—	—	—	—	17	20	4	85	158
1919	—	89	—	—	—	44	—	—	439	—	—	—	—	36	16	3	114	154

Year	Total Db283 Million pounds	Atlantic cod Db284 Million pounds	Pacific cod Db285 Million pounds	Flounder Db286 Million pounds	Pacific (whiting) hake Db287 Million pounds	Halibut Db288 Million pounds	Atlantic sea herring Db289 Million pounds	Pacific sea herring Db290 Million pounds	Menhaden Db291 Million pounds	Pollock Db292 Million pounds	Sablefish Db293 Million pounds	Pacific salmon Db294 Million pounds	Swordfish Db295 Million pounds	Tuna Db296 Million pounds	Atlantic mackerel Db297 Million pounds	Pacific mackerel Db298 Million pounds	Haddock Db299 Million pounds	Pacific sardine Db300 Million pounds
1920	—	—	—	—	—	51	—	—	—	—	—	344	—	39	19	3	109	119
1921	—	—	—	—	—	56	—	—	691	—	—	218	—	20	10	3	91	59
1922	—	—	—	—	—	45	—	83	812	—	—	415	—	35	13	3	99	93
1923	—	—	—	—	—	56	—	87	744	—	—	491	—	38	34	4	105	159
1924	—	93	—	—	—	58	—	101	344	—	—	505	—	27	27	3	114	243
1925	—	—	—	—	—	58	—	184	532	—	—	484	—	53	49	4	129	315
1926	—	—	—	—	—	59	—	182	383	—	—	593	—	43	68	4	135	287
1927	—	—	—	—	—	62	—	130	393	—	—	415	—	69	60	5	192	342
1928	—	90	—	—	—	58	—	166	362	—	—	548	—	63	45	36	248	420
1929	—	87	—	—	—	64	107	188	442	—	—	553	—	72	64	59	294	652
1930	—	102	—	—	—	56	84	190	410	—	—	491	—	100	52	17	271	494
1931	—	93	—	—	—	48	64	121	236	—	—	548	—	57	47	15	195	300
1932	—	86	—	—	—	50	39	150	375	—	—	482	—	61	61	13	167	312
1933	—	100	—	—	—	52	49	174	358	—	—	506	—	69	42	70	166	510
1934	—	—	—	—	—	50	—	204	517	—	—	653	—	94	52	115	155	1,136
1935	—	120	—	—	—	49	55	228	434	—	—	498	—	118	65	156	202	1,168
1936	—	—	—	—	—	52	—	211	516	—	—	708	—	125	52	105	185	1,503
1937	—	135	—	—	—	51	53	263	529	—	—	609	—	156	26	67	177	1,140
1938	—	118	—	—	—	50	22	232	518	—	—	592	—	138	43	84	176	1,110
1939	—	105	—	—	—	51	76	231	575	—	—	482	—	172	33	85	179	1,241
1940	—	82	—	—	—	55	46	113	635	—	—	457	—	206	41	122	156	914
1941	—	—	—	—	—	54	—	157	775	—	—	613	—	125	46	80	186	1,328
1942	—	65	—	—	—	52	101	46	483	—	—	470	—	117	51	58	146	975
1943	—	66	—	—	—	54	—	92	616	—	—	467	—	126	59	88	126	997
1944	—	94	—	—	—	53	85	140	686	—	—	429	—	167	74	96	141	1,147
1945	—	141	—	—	—	52	96	154	759	—	—	449	—	183	59	63	155	850
1946	—	89	—	—	—	56	—	218	916	—	—	413	—	216	52	69	155	531
1947	—	64	—	—	—	43	130	198	948	—	—	454	—	256	59	176	166	272
1948	—	68	—	—	—	50	194	180	1,008	—	—	379	—	320	51	112	156	373
1949	—	59	—	—	—	49	171	37	1,073	—	—	443	—	334	42	101	135	634
1950	—	57	7	—	—	52	197	170	1,000	26	—	323	1	391	22	166	159	715
1951	—	50	10	—	—	47	67	94	1,104	23	—	377	(Z)	319	16	123	154	329
1952	—	44	11	—	—	51	155	56	1,384	27	—	356	1	323	18	167	161	14
1953	—	33	9	—	—	47	111	41	1,696	24	—	323	(Z)	303	9	63	140	9
1954	—	37	17	—	—	58	130	37	1,738	20	—	335	(Z)	323	4	43	155	137
1955	—	36	13	—	—	50	106	67	1,868	23	—	282	1	282	4	59	135	146
1956	—	35	10	—	—	56	148	110	2,097	23	—	297	1	343	4	126	152	70
1957	—	34	12	—	—	48	162	121	1,690	22	—	266	1	305	2	144	134	46
1958	—	42	13	—	—	48	179	100	1,549	33	—	307	2	328	5	50	120	207
1959	—	47	13	—	—	54	121	115	2,203	25	—	202	2	286	4	75	113	74
1960	4,250	42	5	127	1	51	155	84	2,018	22	11	235	1	298	3	112	119	58
1961	4,550	49	3	133	0	54	58	54	2,315	21	7	310	1	326	3	142	134	43
1962	4,709	50	3	155	0	54	159	42	2,348	16	9	315	1	312	2	139	134	15
1963	4,122	53	6	177	1	46	155	39	1,816	15	6	294	3	322	3	136	124	7
1964	3,829	45	6	176	1	35	64	52	1,570	13	8	352	3	306	4	117	133	13

Note appears at end of table

(continued)

TABLE Db283–300   Landed catches of principal fish species: 1880–2000   Continued

Year	Total Db283	Atlantic cod Db284	Pacific cod Db285	Flounder Db286	Pacific (whiting) hake Db287	Halibut Db288	Atlantic sea herring Db289	Pacific sea herring Db290	Menhaden Db291	Pollock Db292	Sablefish Db293	Pacific salmon Db294	Swordfish Db295	Tuna Db296	Atlantic mackerel Db297	Pacific mackerel Db298	Haddock Db299	Pacific sardine Db300
	Million pounds	Million pounds	Million pounds	Million pounds	Million pounds	Million pounds	Million pounds	Million pounds	Million pounds	Million pounds	Million pounds	Million pounds	Million pounds	Million pounds	Million pounds	Million pounds	Million pounds	Million pounds
1965	3,947	43	10	180	3	41	76	35	1,726	12	7	327	3	319	3	74	134	2
1966	3,487	40	10	175	12	41	72	24	1,308	9	7	388	2	269	4	46	133	2
1967	3,190	44	9	159	29	40	70	18	1,164	7	7	217	1	328	7	40	99	(Z)
1968	3,362	49	6	158	9	26	92	15	1,375	7	4	328	1	294	6	57	71	(Z)
1969	3,519	57	4	162	9	33	69	22	1,546	10	6	268	1	325	8	54	46	(Z)
1970	4,007	53	3	169	9	35	67	12	1,837	9	6	410	2	393	8	48	27	(Z)
1971	4,054	54	6	157	11	29	76	11	2,190	11	6	332	(Z)	346	5	59	22	(Z)
1972	3,815	47	11	169	4	27	89	13	1,939	13	12	232	(Z)	387	4	53	12	(Z)
1973	3,825	50	8	163	3	24	59	41	1,890	15	12	222	2	347	4	18	8	(Z)
1974	3,971	59	10	156	2	18	72	48	1,979	20	16	201	4	392	3	22	8	(Z)
1975	3,934	56	12	156	3	22	80	40	1,803	21	19	202	5	393	4	30	16	(Z)
1976	4,350	56	13	165	3	21	111	40	2,039	24	17	310	4	491	6	39	13	(Z)
1977	4,062	77	11	170	4	18	112	44	1,796	29	26	377	4	334	3	110	28	(Z)
1978	4,857	87	11	181	7	18	111	43	2,595	43	29	404	10	409	4	93	39	(Z)
1979	5,132	99	12	209	31	21	143	66	2,604	40	48	536	9	364	4	94	42	(Z)
1980	5,328	118	26	217	12	19	184	107	2,497	43	22	614	14	399	6	129	55	(Z)
1981	4,826	102	56	201	11	27	139	108	2,105	44	28	648	11	341	6	116	22	(Z)
1982	5,389	117	85	228	16	33	73	129	2,766	37	47	607	14	261	7	120	45	(Z)
1983	5,539	112	125	254	17	45	51	129	2,963	34	40	639	14	279	6	113	33	(Z)
1984	5,456	97	117	220	15	48	74	105	2,891	64	50	691	16	212	7	117	26	(Z)
1985	5,214	83	92	196	16	61	57	142	2,739	129	63	727	16	83	7	96	14	(Z)
1986	4,871	61	93	169	26	78	79	131	2,391	214	85	659	12	88	9	119	11	(Z)
1987	5,708	59	142	200	39	76	85	123	2,712	524	103	562	13	100	10	120	7	(Z)
1988	5,906	76	249	229	16	82	90	131	2,086	1,177	108	606	16	111	15	123	6	(Z)
1989	7,145	79	332	202	17	75	90	119	1,989	2,216	98	786	17	89	18	117	4	(Z)
1990	8,091	96	479	255	21	70	113	108	1,962	2,874	90	733	15	62	23	92	5	(Z)
1991	7,993	93	554	405	56	66	107	123	1,977	3,369	84	783	17	36	37	67	4	(Z)
1992	8,174	62	551	646	124	69	123	159	1,644	3,094	75	716	19	57	26	44	5	(Z)
1993	8,999	51	483	599	310	63	110	107	1,983	3,271	77	888	19	55	10	28	2	(Z)
1994	9,132	39	460	427	557	58	101	113	2,324	3,133	71	901	14	72	20	28	1	29
1995	8,520	30	591	423	390	45	147	117	1,847	2,860	66	1,021	12	64	19	23	1	94
1996	8,273	31	605	460	431	49	197	120	1,755	2,630	60	877	13	85	35	26	1	72
1997	8,397	29	661	566	500	70	211	137	2,027	2,522	53	568	14	83	34	44	3	94
1998	7,888	25	556	391	502	73	180	92	1,706	2,729	44	644	15	85	28	48	6	94
1999	7,812	21	524	331	478	80	175	91	1,989	2,336	48	815	16	58	27	27	7	132
2000	7,690	25	531	413	453	75	160	75	1,760	2,616	50	629	18	51	12	56	9	150

(Z) Less than 500,000 pounds.

Sources

U.S. National Marine Fisheries Service (NMFS) and predecessor agencies, *Fishery Statistics of the United States* (NMFS, annual), and *Fisheries of the United States* (NMFS, annual).

Fishery Statistics of the United States and more recently *Fisheries of the United States* publish historical statistics sections on particular species from time to time. Pre-1960 data for series Db284–285 come from *Fisheries of the United States* (1995). Pre-1960 data for series Db288 come from *Fishery Statistics of the United States* (1960). Pre-1966 data for series Db289–290, Db296, and Db299 come from *Fishery Statistics of the United States* (1965). Pre-1968 data for series Db291 come from *Fishery Statistics of the United States* (1965). Pre-1968 data for series Db287–298 come from *Fishery Statistics of the United States* (1968). Pre-1960 data for series Db297–298 come from *Fishery Statistics of the United States* (1961, 1962).

Documentation

Landings are reported in round (live) weight for all items. The data do not include landings for Mississippi River drainage area states; landings by U.S.-flag vessels at Puerto Rico and other ports outside the fifty states; or catches by U.S.-flag vessels transferred to internal water processing vessels in the U.S. waters. Aquaculture products are also not included.

These data are frequently subject to revision after initial publication. The figures here attempt to present the latest information available and therefore may not match previously published data.

Series Db300. This series was dropped from *Fisheries of the United States* in 1974, after falling below the threshold figure of 500,000 pounds in 1967; sardines returned to the list in 1994.

TABLE Db301–310   Landed catches of principal shellfish species: 1880–2000

Contributed by Gavin Wright

Year	Total	Clams	Crabs	American lobsters	Oysters	Calico scallops	Sea scallops	Shrimp	Atlantic squid	Pacific squid
	Db301	Db302	Db303	Db304	Db305	Db306	Db307	Db308	Db309	Db310
	Million pounds	Million pounds	Million pounds	Million pounds	Million pounds	Million pounds	Million pounds	Million pounds	Million pounds	Million pounds
1880	—	—	—	—	—	—	—	0.821	—	—
1887	—	—	—	28.883	—	—	—	0.010	0.511	—
1888	—	—	—	28.109	—	—	—	4.917	0.486	—
1889	—	—	—	30.772	—	—	—	9.049	0.607	—
1890	—	—	—	—	—	—	—	8.205	0.039	—
1891	—	—	—	—	—	—	—	0.009	0.041	—
1892	—	—	—	—	—	—	—	5.316	—	—
1895	—	—	—	—	—	—	—	5.461	—	—
1897	—	—	—	—	—	—	—	7.423	0.151	—
1898	—	—	—	—	—	—	—	0.003	1.205	—
1899	—	—	—	—	—	—	—	6.535	—	1.869
1900	—	—	—	15.768	—	—	—	—	—	—
1901	—	—	—	—	—	—	—	0.008	0.199	—
1902	—	—	—	—	—	—	—	16.185	5.497	—
1904	—	—	—	—	—	—	—	3.443	0.174	0.754
1905	—	—	—	—	—	—	—	0.002	0.945	—
1908	—	15.961 [1]	—	15.278	—	—	—	18.776	2.452	0.110
1913	—	—	—	12.267	—	—	—	—	—	—
1915	—	—	—	—	—	—	—	0.684	—	6.226
1916	—	—	—	—	—	—	—	0.164	—	—
1917	—	—	—	—	—	—	—	0.114	—	—
1918	—	—	—	—	—	—	—	63.657	0.001	0.362
1919	—	—	—	—	—	—	—	1.191	6.517	3.689
1920	—	—	—	—	—	—	—	1.518	0.042	0.508
1921	—	—	—	—	—	—	—	3.174	0.764	0.433
1922	—	—	—	—	—	—	—	3.154	—	0.209
1923	—	—	—	—	—	—	—	74.848	0.006	1.180
1924	—	—	—	—	—	—	—	4.897	3.077	6.831
1925	—	—	—	—	—	—	—	4.744	0.454	1.891
1926	—	—	—	—	—	—	—	4.589	1.576	3.136
1927	—	—	—	—	—	—	—	103.679	0.002	6.014
1928	—	—	—	—	—	—	—	120.949	7.927	1.352
1929	—	19.691	—	11.747	90.064	—	—	115.323	6.733	4.660
1930	—	25.780	—	13.916	86.874	—	—	94.447	7.505	10.980
1931	—	24.452	—	12.461	74.210	—	—	101.411	5.415	1.744
1932	—	22.643	—	11.157	68.467	—	—	92.985	5.643	4.230
1933	—	—	—	9.812	47.372	—	—	4.254	2.012	0.825
1934	—	—	—	—	59.989	—	—	123.530	0.114	1.536
1935	—	—	—	11.496	60.307	—	—	6.121	6.256	0.835
1936	—	—	—	—	57.698	—	—	123.152	0.122	0.962
1937	—	32.637	—	11.576	95.627	—	—	145.436	5.833	0.503
1938	—	32.563	—	11.984	86.932	—	—	144.983	4.563	1.615
1939	—	32.498	—	11.985	93.005	—	—	152.149	6.160	1.198
1940	—	33.003	—	11.761	89.383	—	—	155.013	4.677	1.863
1941	—	—	—	—	48.030	—	—	3.755	0.283	1.640
1942	—	—	—	12.300	54.464	—	—	2.845	2.002	0.961
1943	—	—	—	—	23.467	—	—	1.315	2.132	9.166
1944	—	—	—	17.929	53.706	—	—	1.658	2.021	10.939
1945	—	32.369	—	22.728	75.628	—	—	191.378	3.048	15.228
1946	—	—	—	—	48.957	—	—	2.901	1.186	38.025
1947	—	—	—	23.927	63.084	—	—	3.252	2.482	14.551
1948	—	—	—	20.987	61.609	—	—	4.121	4.555	19.258
1949	—	—	—	24.656	74.777	—	—	130.625	6.933	6.860
1950	—	39.571	—	23.198	76.415	—	19.980	191.695	2.441	5.996
1951	—	41.831	—	25.946	72.990	—	18.746	225.188	5.598	12.383
1952	—	38.996	—	25.032	82.242	—	18.630	228.210	2.067	3.672
1953	—	36.544	—	28.115	79.719	—	23.618	261.504	5.627	8.917
1954	—	31.536	—	27.481	81.922	—	17.631	269.517	3.629	8.156

Notes appear at end of table

(continued)

TABLE Db301–310   Landed catches of principal shellfish species: 1880–2000   *Continued*

Year	Total Db301 Million pounds	Clams Db302 Million pounds	Crabs Db303 Million pounds	American lobsters Db304 Million pounds	Oysters Db305 Million pounds	Calico scallops Db306 Million pounds	Sea scallops Db307 Million pounds	Shrimp Db308 Million pounds	Atlantic squid Db309 Million pounds	Pacific squid Db310 Million pounds
1955	—	33.032	—	28.954	77.515	—	22.158	245.779	4.144	14.272
1956	—	38.099	—	26.520	75.133	—	20.069	224.557	3.059	19.484
1957	—	39.782	—	30.155	71.658	—	20.994	205.535	6.039	12.449
1958	—	36.364	—	27.227	66.396	—	18.977	213.843	4.353	7.475
1959	—	44.916	—	29.085	64.710	—	24.644	240.182	3.674	19.694
1960	682.154	49.483	221.681	31.168	60.010	0.112	26.599	249.452	3.649	2.562
1961	624.508	50.625	231.606	27.998	62.305	0.026	27.461	174.530	3.397	10.286
1962	635.585	54.169	234.340	29.497	56.037	0.017	24.634	191.105	4.819	9.382
1963	717.650	63.403	252.334	30.724	58.444	— [2]	19.939	240.473	4.746	11.562
1964	701.105	64.464	270.442	30.958	60.534	— [2]	16.914	211.804	2.266	16.435
1965	821.279	70.849	335.407	30.246	54.686	0.872	20.070	243.618	2.611	18.620
1966	872.507	72.751	372.425	29.541	51.224	1.857	15.975	239.037	2.702	19.026
1967	858.230	71.500	322.184	26.745	59.958	1.410	10.242	307.782	3.883	17.010
1968	791.524	67.246	254.523	32.558	61.886	0.089	12.070	299.287	3.799	24.934
1969	812.760	80.745	257.325	33.787	52.199	0.199	7.410	318.534	3.311	20.779
1970	900.096	99.204	277.218	34.152	53.602	1.833	5.852	367.464	2.365	24.591
1971	915.408	84.489	276.374	33.688	57.938	1.574	5.406	390.902	2.775	31.521
1972	895.351	90.689	281.077	32.244	56.058	1.352	5.850	387.461	2.933	20.159
1973	907.329	107.540	291.882	28.991	51.931	0.558	5.291	379.722	3.953	12.129
1974	968.151	121.693	329.282	28.543	50.176	1.131	6.017	373.573	5.494	28.906
1975	907.735	113.387	300.950	30.200	53.227	1.992	9.753	346.731	4.425	20.339
1976	1,000.389	82.532	344.810	31.483	54.395	2.268	19.588	406.394	8.506	23.662
1977	1,136.019	97.339	398.539	31.773	50.088	1.114	25.831	476.452	5.884	28.245
1978	1,170.304	87.711	449.142	15.214	54.100	0.948	31.168	422.875	3.797	37.829
1979	1,134.760	92.050	489.184	37.200	50.362	0.863	29.650	335.950	13.280	44.055
1980	1,153.940	95.369	523.111	37.215	50.826	— [2]	28.162	339.704	9.903	39.917
1981	1,151.114	120.631	445.995	37.494	52.612	14.641	25.955	354.471	6.590	51.842
1982	977.930	108.305	349.602	39.445	56.189	11.010	19.936	283.627	16.489	36.035
1983	899.261	115.405	316.992	44.206	54.048	9.606	19.234	249.665	33.623	4.407
1984	981.589	132.921	312.953	43.967	54.774	39.330	17.191	301.354	31.757	2.219
1985	1,043.279	150.551	337.632	46.152	50.881	12.513	14.958	333.641	26.214	24.407
1986	1,159.931	145.393	355.660	46.053	48.769	1.616	19.262	400.185	35.701	46.946
1987	1,187.511	134.357	386.368	45.558	39.807	8.155	31.403	363.142	38.741	44.066
1988	1,286.992	131.740	455.629	48.643	31.892	11.868	30.301	330.873	46.790	82.084
1989	1,317.926	138.166	458.378	52.926	29.250	6.580	33.332	351.414	68.493	90.250
1990	1,312.503	139.198	499.416	61.017	29.193	1.135	39.169	346.494	60.039	62.718
1991	1,490.920	134.243	649.993	63.337	31.859	0.286	39.302	320.087	71.415	83.163
1992	1,463.120	142.449	624.322	55.841	36.156	— [2]	33.528	337.765	81.944	30.436
1993	1,467.753	147.752	604.437	56.613	33.575	— [2]	18.116	292.887	90.809	71.550
1994	1,329.112	131.427	446.942	66.416	38.086	7.162	18.228	282.626	93.389	122.395
1995	1,267.468	134.224	363.639	66.406	40.380	0.957	18.316	306.869	74.248	155.280
1996	1,292.179	123.239	391.797	71.641	38.007	— [2]	18.162	316.879	65.248	174.785
1997	1,244.970	114.184	429.963	83.921	37.116	1.613	13.789	290.255	66.177	157.606
1998	1,218.615	107.959	552.716	79.642	33.538	— [2]	13.061	277.757	93.245	6.208
1999	1,318.176	112.230	458.307	87.469	26.983	4.109	23.038	304.173	58.310	199.888
2000	1,255.261	118.482	299.006	83.190	41.146	— [2]	32.747	332.486	57.520	259.508

[1] Excludes Pacific Coast region.

[2] Data are confidential, but are included in total landed catch of shellfish.

Sources

U.S. National Maritime Fisheries Service (NMFS) and predecessor agencies, *Fishery Statistics of the United States* (NMFS, annual), and *Fisheries of the United States* (NMFS, annual).

Fishery Statistics of the United States and, more recently, *Fisheries of the United States*, publish historical statistics sections on particular species from time to time. Pre-1967 data for series Db302 come from *Fishery Statistics of the United States* (1966). Pre-1930 data for series Db304 come from *Fishery Statistics of the United States* (1965), while data for 1930–1989 come from *Fisheries of the United States* (1989). Pre-1989 data for series Db305 come from *Fisheries of the United States* (1988). Pre-1987 data for series Db307 come from *Fisheries of the United States* (1991). Pre-1988 data for series Db308 come from *Fisheries*

of the United States (1987). Pre-1994 data for series Db309–310 come from *Fisheries of the United States* (1993).

Documentation

Landings are reported in round (live) weight for all items except univalve and bivalve mollusks such as clams, oysters, and scallops, which are reported in weight of meats (excluding the shell). Data do not include aquaculture products, except oysters and clams.

The data do not include landings for Mississippi River drainage area states; nor landings by U.S.-flag vessels at Puerto Rico and other ports outside the fifty states, nor catches by U.S.-flag vessels transferred to internal water processing vessels in the U.S. waters.

Regional figures (often for earlier historical periods) may be found in the sources. The figures here attempt to present the latest available information and therefore may not match previously published data.

TABLE Db311–314   Disposition of landed catches, by major product group: 1921–2000

Contributed by Gavin Wright

Year	Fresh and frozen Db311 Million pounds	Canned Db312 Million pounds	Cured for human food Db313 Million pounds	Industrial Db314 Million pounds	Year	Fresh and frozen Db311 Million pounds	Canned Db312 Million pounds	Cured for human food Db313 Million pounds	Industrial Db314 Million pounds
1921	788	483	180	804	1965	1,469	1,042	76	2,190
1922	801	696	180	942	1966	1,490	1,006	77	1,793
1923	845	782	180	919	1967	1,290	1,001	77	1,687
1924	900	799	175	587	1968	1,263	1,017	67	1,813
1925	990	864	175	862	1969	1,320	933	68	2,016
1926	1,085	938	175	673	1970	1,316	1,150	71	2,380
1927	1,119	878	175	634	1971	1,536	1,063	75	2,344
1928	1,125	1,095	150	691	1972	1,632	915	71	2,188
1929	1,165	1,286	150	890	1973	1,693	918	71	2,176
1930	1,256	1,077	145	746	1974	1,670	924	74	2,299
1931	1,037	962	130	501	1975	1,701	935	69	2,172
1932	937	787	140	748	1976	1,893	1,094	53	2,348
1933	961	991	135	911	1977	2,098	1,078	55	2,040
1934	1,011	1,293	130	1,670	1978	2,237	1,099	52	2,640
1935	1,233	1,220	130	1,552	1979	2,394	1,046	94	2,733
1936	1,260	1,459	135	1,972	1980	2,621	1,161	96	2,604
1937	1,217	1,356	130	1,650	1981	2,547	1,118	90	2,222
1938	1,275	1,234	130	1,615	1982	2,550	891	85	2,841
1939	1,302	1,281	130	1,732	1983	2,304	1,087	80	2,968
1940	1,264	1,280	130	1,385	1984	2,558	906	82	2,892
1941	1,292	1,645	125	1,838	1985	2,242	1,232	70	2,714
1942	1,338	1,230	115	1,192	1986	2,487	1,134	60	2,350
1943	1,458	1,165	114	1,425	1987	3,157	1,009	89	2,641
1944	1,530	1,225	110	1,668	1988	3,813	1,017	86	2,276
1945	1,827	1,230	110	1,431	1989	5,585	798	128	1,952
1946	1,672	1,277	100	1,418	1990	6,501	751	126	2,026
1947	1,536	1,384	100	1,329	1991	6,541	674	119	2,150
1948	1,558	1,488	100	1,367	1992	7,288	543	110	1,696
1949	1,542	1,663	100	1,499	1993	7,744	649	115	1,959
1950	1,487	1,720	100	1,594	1994	7,475	622	95	2,269
1951	1,638	1,326	84	1,385	1995	7,099	769	90	1,830
1952	1,445	1,248	85	1,654	1996	7,054	678	93	1,740
1953	1,441	993	85	1,968	1997	6,873	648	108	2,213
1954	1,461	1,159	85	2,057	1998	6,870	516	129	1,679
1955	1,454	1,039	86	2,230	1999	6,416	712	133	2,078
1956	1,401	1,202	87	2,578	2000	6,657	530	119	1,763
1957	1,270	1,117	88	2,314					
1958	1,356	1,210	85	2,096					
1959	1,309	977	83	2,753					
1960	1,373	1,043	82	2,444					
1961	1,439	970	81	2,697					
1962	1,486	974	80	2,814					
1963	1,405	1,073	78	2,291					
1964	1,393	1,033	71	2,044					

Sources

U.S. National Marine Fisheries Service (NMFS), *Fishery Statistics of the United States* (NMFS, annual); *Imports and Exports of Fishery Products*, Annual Summary (NMFS, 1970), p. 8; and *Fisheries of the United States* (NMFS, annual).

Documentation

Series Db311. Fresh and frozen catch is derived as a residual from the total catch figures, series Db273, and the canned, cured, and industrial catch figures, series Db312–314.

Series Db312. Canned catch represents a computed amount of fish or other aquatic organisms that were heat processed in cans.

Series Db313. Cured products represent an estimated amount of fish and other living aquatic animals that were dried or dehydrated, salted, smoked, or pickled.

Series Db314. Industrial products represents the weight of fish and other aquatic products determined to have been manufactured into fish meal, oil, fish solubles, homogenized condensed fish, shell products, or used as bait or for animal food, and other miscellaneous items.

TABLE Db315–321   Domestic production of processed fishery products: 1921–2000[1]

Contributed by Gavin Wright

	Canned fishery products		Groundfish fillets and steaks, quantity	Dried fish meal and scrap		Fish and other marine oils	
	Quantity	Value		Quantity	Value	Quantity	Value
	Db315	Db316	Db317 [2]	Db318 [3]	Db319	Db320	Db321
Year	Million cases	Million dollars	Million pounds	Million pounds	Million dollars	Million gallons	Million dollars
1921	—	46.635	—	212.000	3.600	7.000	2.100
1922	—	60.465	—	232.000	4.400	11.000	4.200
1923	—	72.445	—	228.000	4.400	11.000	5.100
1924	—	72.165	—	164.000	2.900	9.000	4.300
1925	—	80.577	—	238.000	4.600	13.000	6.500
1926	—	86.193	—	186.000	3.600	11.000	5.000
1927	12.282	81.384	—	184.000	4.400	11.000	4.900
1928	15.630	95.872	—	208.000	5.400	12.000	5.200
1929	17.310	101.065	—	286.000	6.800	15.000	6.800
1930	14.767	82.858	—	280.000	6.100	15.000	4.200
1931	12.581	62.949	—	168.000	3.000	9.000	1.600
1932	10.495	43.749	—	204.000	2.400	12.000	1.400
1933	13.117	59.800	—	260.000	3.900	18.000	2.600
1934	17.379	80.021	—	394.000	6.100	30.000	6.400
1935	17.435	74.999	—	426.000	5.700	32.000	13.100
1936	20.098	94.564	—	486.000	7.700	40.000	15.300
1937	19.531	105.175	—	440.000	7.500	36.000	16.400
1938	17.004	83.446	—	410.000	7.400	35.000	13.500
1939	19.487	96.628	99.000	452.000	9.100	36.000	14.700
1940	18.909	94.182	91.000	388.000	7.900	25.000	12.000
1941	23.555	138.684	123.000	474.000	13.200	29.000	29.600
1942	18.077	144.997	105.000	342.000	11.600	21.000	22.600
1943	16.716	141.189	87.000	382.000	13.700	23.000	29.800
1944	18.521	152.914	109.000	426.000	15.200	28.000	31.000
1945	18.555	152.801	126.000	402.000	14.400	25.000	27.200
1946	20.486	227.629	127.000	404.000	20.500	20.000	34.700
1947	21.868	310.679	116.000	374.000	22.400	17.000	31.800
1948	23.734	336.181	138.000	400.000	23.100	17.000	31.000
1949	25.650	295.504	140.000	474.000	35.700	18.000	17.400
1950	29.837	331.335	137.000	480.000	29.300	22.000	17.500
1951	24.563	301.210	149.000	420.000	25.400	18.000	16.600
1952	26.260	305.829	133.000	443.000	27.200	16.000	9.400
1953	26.007	306.874	112.000	478.000	29.600	20.000	11.500
1954	28.166	331.018	122.000	514.000	32.800	22.000	12.800
1955	26.315	303.165	105.000	529.000	34.700	25.000	14.900
1956	30.962	349.516	107.000	592.000	37.900	27.000	17.300
1957	31.063	335.829	97.000	528.000	32.600	20.000	12.600
1958	34.483	388.582	99.000	496.000	31.800	22.000	12.300
1959	31.781	348.251	91.000	613.000	35.900	25.000	13.100
1960	34.917	387.595	94.000	580.000	25.300	28.000	13.400
1961	33.395	422.836	93.000	623.000	31.900	34.000	14.400
1962	36.843	456.866	94.000	625.000	35.600	33.000	11.000
1963	34.571	421.607	83.000	512.000	30.200	24.000	10.800
1964	35.752	436.660	75.000	471.000	28.000	23.000	13.300
1965	38.349	495.231	77.000	508.000	35.700	25.000	14.900
1966	40.784	563.708	75.000	448.000	32.300	21.000	12.500
1967	41.241	525.563	71.000	422.000	26.000	16.000	6.100
1968	43.006	583.908	55.000	470.000	30.300	22.000	7.300
1969	40.744	575.533	47.000	505.000	39.800	22.000	9.300
1970	46.188	741.760	43.000	538.000	46.400	27.000	18.200
1971	45.991	770.597	43.808	585.624	44.501	34.252	20.831
1972	57.413	994.922	39.266	571.012	48.289	24.315	13.117
1973	59.180	1,167.160	46.974	575.034	119.905	28.985	25.563
1974	57.506	1,305.847	45.337	601.428	84.380	30.707	49.216
1975	48.990	1,067.067	36.822	580.862	65.545	31.697	32.603
1976	54.997	1,418.514	40.564	619.388	96.815	26.398	31.156
1977	51.700	1,543.152	59.942	564.582	97.239	17.185	28.239
1978	58.891	1,884.124	65.573	725.820	121.207	38.231	60.701
1979	51.936	1,743.331	74.568	748.586	131.528	34.574	54.087

Notes appear at end of table

(continued)

TABLE Db315–321   Domestic production of processed fishery products: 1921–2000 *Continued*

Year	Canned fishery products		Groundfish fillets and steaks, quantity	Dried fish meal and scrap		Fish and other marine oils	
	Quantity	Value		Quantity	Value	Quantity	Value
	Db315	Db316	Db317 [2]	Db318 [3]	Db319	Db320	Db321
	Million cases	Million dollars	Million pounds	Million pounds	Million dollars	Million gallons	Million dollars
1980	53.731	1,927.656	67.221	723.844	133.669	40.324	57.936
1981	54.008	1,953.710	78.788	637.018	118.746	23.781	33.032
1982	46.292	1,457.483	72.885	746.854	122.642	44.840	53.570
1983	49.964	1,534.478	82.556	763.536	130.093	51.527	66.814
1984	51.392	1,577.463	102.142	751.528	113.467	48.104	60.961
1985	43.852	1,360.314	93.292	721.682	83.846	36.784	41.921
1986	50.122	1,484.590	133.552	702.194	83.476	43.446	43.731
1987	47.478	1,561.900	199.743	786.978	121.711	38.516	35.507
1988	45.290	1,485.614	206.786	643.796	130.677	28.998	43.595
1989	54.715	1,991.879	211.498	618.382	115.049	29.094	23.526
1990	45.205	1,561.793	258.809	577.498	120.735	36.381	28.994
1991	50.162	1,644.279	264.323	612.716	128.131	34.496	30.523
1992	55.802	1,577.434	252.358	644.512	122.056	23.835	27.268
1993	59.785	1,687.974	233.755	750.744	131.161	37.865	40.789
1994	61.434	1,795.498	220.357	807.833	134.560	37.662	37.156
1995	67.198	1,887.050	216.699	667.240	122.210	31.218	42.260
1996	74.985	1,799.880	220.102	638.500	142.163	32.051	43.945
1997	58.281	1,593.190	220.403	724.668	173.936	36.565	55.287
1998	58.701	1,765.730	269.004	613.434	112.881	28.735	55.700
1999	67.483	1,861.428	362.303	686.250	146.970	36.926	41.884
2000	63.070	1,622.512	369.311	638.240	114.901	24.819	20.914

[1] Includes production of U.S. outlying areas.

[2] Includes Alaska for all years and Hawai'i beginning 1959.

[3] Includes Hawai'i beginning 1952; Puerto Rico, 1953; and American Samoa, 1954.

Sources

Series Db315–316. 1921–1935: U.S. Bureau of Fisheries, *Fishery Industries of the United States* (annual issues). 1939–1968: *Canned Fishery Products, Annual Summary 1970* (annual). 1936–1938 and 1969–2000: U.S. National Marine Fisheries Service (NMFS) and predecessor agencies, *Fishery Statistics of the United States* (NMFS, annual), and *Fisheries of the United States* (NMFS, annual).

Series Db317. 1939–1956: U.S. Fish and Wildlife Service, *Packaged Fish – 1956*, Current Fishery Statistics, number 1518. 1957–2000: *Fishery Statistics of the United States* and *Fisheries of the United States*.

Series Db318–321. 1921–1938: *Fishery Industries of the United States*. 1939–2000: *Fishery Statistics of the United States* and *Fisheries of the United States*.

Documentation

In addition to the nine products for which figures were separately presented as series L 340–357 in *Historical Statistics of the United States* (1975) and which have represented over the period of record (up to 1970) from 85 percent to 97 percent of production of all canned fishery products, these totals include very substantial packs of clams and clam products, large and valuable packs of crabs, and small but valuable packs of fish roes and of shrimp and oyster specialty products, and many other less important items. These data are the latest revised figures and all are equated to units of the latest defined standard case for each product. A history of conversion factors that have been used and their present definitions appears in *Fishery Statistics of the United States*, Statistical Digest number 64 (1970).

Series Db317. The term "groundfish" refers to fish caught on or near the ocean floor. Here, it includes the following species, Atlantic and Pacific: cod, hake, ocean perch, and pollock; cusk; and haddock.

Series Db318–319. Includes acidulated scrap, which has been of negligible importance since 1941. To convert pounds into tons of fish meal divide by 2000.

Series Db318 and Db320. In contrast to series Db273, which includes only the products of U.S. land-based whaling, these data include the meal and oil yields from the United States Antarctica and West Australia factory-ship whaling in 1935–1939.

Series Db319 and Db321. Excludes the value of imported items that may be further processed.

Series Db320. To convert gallons into pounds of oil multiply by 7.75.

TABLE Db322–333   Supply of selected fishery products: 1939–2000

Contributed by Gavin Wright

	Canned				Crab		Lobsters					
	Sardines	Salmon	Tuna	Crabmeat	King	Snow (tanner)	American	Spiny	Clams	Oysters	Scallops	Shrimp
	Db322	Db323	Db324	Db325	Db326	Db327	Db328	Db329	Db330	Db331	Db332	Db333
Year	Million pounds	Million pounds	Million pounds	Million pounds	Million pounds	Million pounds	Million pounds	Million pounds	Million pounds	Million pounds	Million pounds	Million pounds
1939	—	—	80.370	14.147	—	—	—	—	—	—	—	—
1940	—	—	89.522	—	—	—	—	—	—	—	—	—
1947	—	—	114.654	—	—	—	—	—	—	—	—	—
1948	—	—	140.459	5.570	—	—	—	—	—	—	—	—
1949	—	—	143.229	—	—	—	—	—	—	—	—	—
1950	—	—	210.253	6.725	—	—	—	—	—	—	—	—
1951	—	—	168.336	4.845	—	—	—	—	—	—	—	—
1952	78.537	222.406	198.472	3.725	—	—	—	—	—	—	—	—
1953	115.380	197.657	220.070	6.203	—	—	—	—	—	—	—	—
1954	156.886	203.954	244.597	5.861	—	—	—	—	—	—	—	—
1955	77.554	162.070	231.975	6.866	—	—	—	—	—	—	25.670	—
1956	75.546	191.839	267.660	8.054	—	—	—	—	—	—	23.716	—
1957	93.515	171.630	276.842	9.169	—	—	—	—	—	—	26.690	—
1958	169.867	199.133	323.335	8.658	—	—	—	—	—	—	25.151	—
1959	58.419	135.658	338.326	10.246	—	—	—	—	—	—	30.943	—
1960	80.615	143.238	353.143	8.622	—	—	—	—	—	—	35.615	—
1961	71.322	177.424	369.275	9.237	—	—	—	—	—	—	37.847	—
1962	101.595	180.300	392.225	9.126	—	—	—	—	—	—	39.373	—
1963	78.367	149.175	384.206	12.652	—	—	—	—	—	—	34.853	—
1964	67.067	159.754	404.481	11.075	—	—	—	—	—	—	34.976	—
1965	71.714	149.622	409.366	13.291	—	—	—	127.002	—	—	39.296	—
1966	85.265	189.266	455.828	10.849	—	—	—	125.779	73.454	—	36.324	—
1967	80.326	79.051	454.166	—	—	—	—	120.732	72.208	—	26.211	—
1968	96.323	164.719	463.130	—	—	—	—	145.596	67.995	—	29.979	—
1969	67.673	109.125	471.553	8.011	—	—	—	154.411	83.656	—	25.947	363.286
1970	64.227	169.096	509.902	7.662	—	14.473	—	130.560	104.160	74.564	27.667	409.198
1971	71.370	151.770	498.583	6.896	—	12.880	—	143.388	87.936	75.457	27.615	390.432
1972	103.414	83.094	676.309	5.039	—	30.135	—	152.445	95.817	86.951	31.221	433.001
1973	88.719	62.666	674.475	4.156	—	61.719	—	135.254	111.807	78.282	27.805	386.348
1974	92.441	88.022	713.091	6.022	—	63.906	—	144.294	126.606	73.810	27.174	442.944
1975	54.773	58.793	581.074	4.277	—	46.856	—	150.397	115.822	73.769	33.440	388.375
1976	76.938	108.024	658.084	5.495	—	80.771	—	173.738	89.237	78.077	48.964	464.990
1977	72.312	114.988	582.640	7.817	—	55.956	—	157.333	105.762	79.862	58.299	502.187
1978	72.898	116.366	756.574	7.184	—	66.436	—	149.137	93.842	84.826	61.662	430.689
1979	77.895	98.279	673.936	7.165	—	44.104	—	157.375	99.323	77.493	59.258	423.771
1980	68.761	126.106	665.609	8.545	—	53.545	—	127.073	102.277	72.558	50.605	424.878
1981	83.945	151.231	697.820	6.612	—	42.778	—	133.807	130.151	78.381	71.815	434.289
1982	66.803	70.991	626.082	6.885	—	24.682	—	127.347	119.427	83.718	54.975	458.012
1983	46.424	126.533	712.871	7.866	23.134	29.953	92.655	136.908	126.411	84.823	66.702	540.833
1984	57.652	150.269	776.594	7.191	12.845	22.409	100.235	153.372	144.034	90.860	86.755	583.881
1985	76.139	112.622	758.941	7.996	10.549	44.699	107.818	153.888	162.559	96.807	70.592	632.531
1986	68.307	86.944	873.452	9.319	18.694	48.453	113.346	151.872	161.030	98.807	69.054	705.964
1987	76.981	75.750	865.668	8.104	14.026	28.874	115.765	151.461	150.841	91.892	79.364	772.731
1988	63.253	58.954	842.685	7.829	10.419	30.350	121.281	139.237	145.154	78.306	73.664	766.776
1989	60.530	159.490	1,027.984	7.854	18.345	57.542	85.146	89.545	149.557	65.822	78.987	743.292
1990	61.155	148.215	856.155	8.824	19.356	37.098	95.335	88.598	152.067	55.735	74.331	733.643
1991	51.833	130.593	933.220	10.937	19.907	60.051	107.233	85.040	143.586	61.667	62.185	743.704
1992	41.258	72.532	922.253	8.887	14.773	87.707	94.844	80.719	155.049	61.888	68.977	819.736
1993	41.190	114.162	834.628	9.219	7.755	66.339	91.729	75.654	155.522	60.688	66.464	807.923
1994	48.492	117.019	850.166	9.358	11.982	40.014	100.719	75.587	144.317	60.792	76.155	847.207
1995	44.074	146.573	874.561	12.230	21.186	41.981	93.742	88.988	144.016	62.672	61.931	831.994
1996	46.391	103.899	858.987	12.529	29.883	45.694	97.101	80.870	134.131	58.067	70.692	841.624
1997	49.426	81.713	829.236	15.346	45.177	110.253	111.692	75.518	123.713	57.994	65.759	923.106
1998	49.856	82.671	911.943	21.529	62.202	253.631	110.369	99.934	119.307	61.236	58.305	1,001.580
1999	56.936	122.688	1,020.408	26.405	52.359	216.285	121.545	90.586	124.647	54.948	64.275	1,083.600
2000	—	95.280	980.044	28.681	39.480	121.701	124.419	97.368	132.623	71.434	77.307	1,171.768

TABLE Db322–333   Supply of selected fishery products: 1939–2000   *Continued*

Source
U.S. National Marine Fisheries Service (NMFS), *Fisheries of the United States* (NMFS, annual).

Documentation
Supply is defined as U.S. commercial landings plus imports minus exports.

A record of the conversion factors that have been used for series Db326–331 and Db333 appears in the "Supply of Fishery Products" section of *Fisheries of the United States*, Current Fishery Statistics number 9600 (1996).

Weight measurements are as follows: series Db322–325, canned weight; series Db326–329, round weight; series Db330–332, meat weight; series Db333, heads-off weight.

Series Db324. Data include pack from landings by U.S.-flag vessels in Puerto Rico and American Samoa as well as tuna canned in American Samoa from foreign-caught fish.

Series Db328. Only imports from Canada and St. Pierre and Miquelon are considered American lobster.

Series Db332. May include small amounts of canned or cured scallops.

TABLE Db334–341   Marine recreational fisheries – participants, fishing trips, catch, and harvest: 1955–1998[1]

Contributed by Gavin Wright

	Participants		Fishing trips		Fish caught		Fish harvested	
	Atlantic and Gulf coasts	Pacific coast	Atlantic and Gulf coasts	Pacific coast	Atlantic and Gulf coasts	Pacific coast	Atlantic and Gulf coasts	Pacific coast
	Db334	Db335	Db336	Db337	Db338	Db339	Db340	Db341
Year	Million	Million	Million	Million	Million	Million	Million pounds	Million pounds
1955	3.420	1.137	—	—	—	—	—	—
1960	4.820	1.472	—	—	—	—	—	—
1965	6.262	2.043	—	—	—	—	—	—
1970	7.282	2.178	—	—	—	—	—	—
1979	9.153	—	63.000	8.000 [2]	439.000	49.293 [2]	—	—
1980	—	—	74.000	14.732	436.000	83.927	—	—
1981	5.976	—	40.392	10.923	269.674	50.640	278.215	—
1982	6.044	—	50.041	10.921	305.381	53.027	315.360	—
1983	8.202	—	60.109	10.825	369.379	44.522	339.150	—
1984	7.449	—	55.809	10.137	319.325	46.839	261.966	—
1985	7.077	—	52.552	9.923	300.302	43.179	264.227	—
1986	7.438	—	60.266	11.029	407.319	55.312	367.623	—
1987	6.697	—	53.545	9.974	286.078	46.000	289.976	—
1988	7.153	—	59.201	12.415	290.654	51.215	251.314	—
1989	6.327	—	49.380	9.446	249.113	41.292	223.324	—
1990	6.511	—	45.777	—	250.402	—	173.004	—
1991	7.510	—	58.338	—	384.980	—	228.241	—
1992	6.779	—	52.736	—	291.884	—	182.401	—
1993	7.063	1.661	55.742	6.893	316.784	30.922	185.244	20.935
1994	7.622	1.671	59.950	7.187	341.854	27.619	183.436	17.924
1995	7.031	1.678	57.958	7.220	311.526	27.609	202.157	24.313
1996	6.619	1.783	56.400	7.849	279.728	34.047	185.354	22.963
1997	12.482	2.091	60.953	7.186	337.359	28.820	208.129	26.000
1998	11.336	1.982	53.241	7.017	283.798	28.459	162.714	31.917

[1] Series for Atlantic and Gulf Coasts exclude Texas data. Series for Pacific Coast excludes Washington data for 1993–1995.

[2] July through December only.

Source
U.S. National Marine Fisheries Service (NMFS), *Fisheries of the United States* (NMFS, annual).

Documentation
The NMFS began a new comprehensive Marine Recreational Fishery Statistical Survey in 1979. The data consist of an intercept survey of anglers in the field and an independent telephone survey of coastal county households. Estimates of catch, fishing effort, and participation are generated by subregion, state, species, mode, and area of fishing. "Fish caught" includes both those harvested and those released. The Pacific region was not surveyed during 1990–1992. Procedures were updated in 1995, resulting in revisions of earlier estimates.

TABLE Db342–352   Per capita consumption of fishery products: 1909–1998

Contributed by Gavin Wright

	All commercial fish and shellfish				Canned salmon	Canned sardines	Canned tuna	Canned shellfish	Fillets and steaks	Sticks and portions	Shrimp, all preparation
	Total	Fresh and frozen	Canned	Cured							
	Db342	Db343	Db344	Db345	Db346	Db347	Db348	Db349	Db350	Db351	Db352
Year	Pounds	Pounds	Pounds	Pounds	Pounds	Pounds	Pounds	Pounds	Pounds	Pounds	Pounds
1909	11.0	4.3	2.7	4.0	—	—	—	—	—	—	—
1910	11.2	4.5	2.8	3.9	—	—	—	—	—	—	—
1911	11.3	4.8	2.8	3.7	—	—	—	—	—	—	—
1912	11.3	5.0	2.9	3.4	—	—	—	—	—	—	—
1913	11.5	5.3	2.9	3.3	—	—	—	—	—	—	—
1914	11.7	5.6	3.0	3.1	—	—	—	—	—	—	—
1915	11.2	5.8	2.4	3.0	—	—	—	—	—	—	—
1916	11.0	6.0	2.2	2.8	—	—	—	—	—	—	—
1917	10.9	6.2	2.0	2.7	—	—	—	—	—	—	—
1918	10.9	6.4	2.0	2.5	—	—	—	—	—	—	—
1919	11.6	6.4	2.8	2.4	—	—	—	—	—	—	—
1920	11.8	6.3	3.2	2.3	—	—	—	—	—	—	—
1921	10.5	6.2	2.2	2.1	1.1	0.7	0.1	0.2	—	—	—
1922	11.3	6.1	3.2	2.0	2.1	0.7	0.1	0.2	—	—	—
1923	10.7	6.0	2.9	1.8	1.9	0.6	0.2	0.2	—	—	—
1924	11.0	6.1	3.2	1.7	2.1	0.8	0.1	0.2	—	—	—
1925	11.1	6.3	3.2	1.6	2.0	0.8	0.2	0.2	—	—	—
1926	11.4	6.6	3.4	1.4	2.1	0.8	0.2	0.2	—	—	—
1927	12.2	7.0	3.9	1.3	2.6	0.8	0.2	0.2	—	—	—
1928	12.1	7.1	3.9	1.1	2.4	1.1	0.2	0.2	—	—	—
1929	11.9	6.9	3.9	1.1	2.1	1.0	0.3	0.3	—	—	—
1930	10.2	5.8	3.4	1.0	2.1	0.6	0.3	0.2	—	—	—
1931	8.8	4.9	3.2	0.7	2.1	0.5	0.2	0.2	—	—	—
1932	8.4	4.3	3.4	0.7	2.3	0.5	0.3	0.2	—	—	—
1933	8.7	4.2	3.9	0.6	2.3	0.7	0.3	0.2	—	—	—
1934	9.2	4.3	4.2	0.7	2.3	0.8	0.4	0.2	—	—	—
1935	10.5	5.1	4.7	0.7	2.2	1.0	0.5	0.2	—	—	—
1936	11.7	5.2	5.8	0.7	3.0	1.3	0.4	0.4	—	—	0.4
1937	11.8	5.6	5.3	0.9	2.6	1.3	0.5	0.4	—	—	0.5
1938	10.8	5.2	4.8	0.8	2.4	1.0	0.5	0.4	—	—	0.5
1939	10.7	5.3	4.7	0.7	2.1	1.1	0.6	0.5	—	—	0.5
1940	11.0	5.7	4.6	0.7	2.0	1.0	0.6	0.5	—	—	0.5
1941	11.2	6.3	4.2	0.7	2.3	0.9	0.5	0.2	—	—	—
1942	8.7	5.2	2.9	0.6	1.2	0.8	0.4	0.2	—	—	—
1943	7.9	5.5	1.8	0.6	0.7	0.4	0.4	0.2	—	—	—
1944	8.7	5.5	2.6	0.6	0.8	0.9	0.5	0.1	—	—	—
1945	9.9	6.6	2.6	0.7	0.9	0.8	0.6	0.1	—	—	—
1946	10.8	5.9	4.2	0.7	1.4	1.1	0.7	0.4	—	—	0.8
1947	10.3	5.8	3.8	0.7	1.3	0.9	0.8	0.2	—	—	0.7
1948	11.1	6.0	4.4	0.7	1.6	1.1	0.9	0.3	—	—	0.7
1949	10.9	5.8	4.5	0.6	1.6	1.2	0.9	0.3	—	—	0.7
1950	11.8	6.3	4.9	0.6	1.4	1.4	1.1	0.4	1.9	—	0.8
1951	11.2	6.3	4.3	0.6	1.4	0.8	1.2	0.4	2.2	—	0.9
1952	11.2	6.2	4.3	0.7	1.4	0.5	1.3	0.3	2.1	—	0.9
1953	11.4	6.4	4.3	0.7	1.3	0.7	1.4	0.4	2.0	—	0.9
1954	11.2	6.2	4.3	0.7	1.1	0.8	1.4	0.4	2.2	—	0.9
1955	10.5	5.9	3.9	0.7	1.0	0.6	1.4	0.4	1.8	—	1.0
1956	10.4	5.7	4.0	0.7	1.1	0.4	1.6	0.4	1.8	—	0.9
1957	10.2	5.5	4.0	0.7	1.0	0.4	1.6	0.4	1.9	—	0.8
1958	10.6	5.7	4.3	0.6	1.1	0.6	1.8	0.4	1.8	0.5	0.9
1959	10.9	5.9	4.4	0.6	0.9	0.6	1.9	0.5	1.7	0.6	1.0
1960	10.3	5.7	4.0	0.6	0.7	0.4	2.0	0.4	1.6	0.6	1.1
1961	10.7	5.9	4.3	0.5	0.8	0.5	2.1	0.4	1.7	0.7	1.0
1962	10.6	5.8	4.3	0.5	0.9	0.3	2.1	0.4	1.8	0.8	1.0
1963	10.7	5.8	4.4	0.5	0.9	0.4	2.0	0.5	1.6	0.9	1.2
1964	10.5	5.9	4.1	0.5	0.7	0.3	2.0	0.5	1.6	1.0	1.2
1965	10.8	6.0	4.3	0.5	0.9	0.3	2.3	0.5	1.7	1.1	1.2
1966	10.9	6.1	4.3	0.5	0.8	0.4	2.3	0.4	1.7	1.1	1.2
1967	10.6	5.8	4.3	0.5	0.7	0.4	2.4	0.5	1.6	1.2	1.3
1968	11.0	6.2	4.3	0.5	0.7	0.4	2.4	0.5	1.9	1.3	1.4
1969	11.2	6.6	4.2	0.4	0.7	0.4	2.4	0.5	2.0	1.6	1.3

TABLE Db342-352   Per capita consumption of fishery products: 1909-1998 *Continued*

	All commercial fish and shellfish				Canned salmon	Canned sardines	Canned tuna	Canned shellfish	Fillets and steaks	Sticks and portions	Shrimp, all preparation
	Total	Fresh and frozen	Canned	Cured							
	Db342	Db343	Db344	Db345	Db346	Db347	Db348	Db349	Db350	Db351	Db352
Year	Pounds	Pounds	Pounds	Pounds	Pounds	Pounds	Pounds	Pounds	Pounds	Pounds	Pounds
1970	11.8	6.9	4.5	0.4	0.7	0.4	2.5	0.5	2.2	1.7	1.5
1971	11.5	6.7	4.3	0.5	0.7	0.4	2.4	0.5	2.0	1.6	1.4
1972	12.5	7.1	4.9	0.5	0.7	0.4	2.9	0.5	2.3	1.8	1.4
1973	12.8	7.4	5.0	0.4	0.4	0.5	3.1	0.5	2.5	2.0	1.4
1974	12.1	6.9	4.7	0.5	0.3	0.4	3.1	0.5	2.1	1.8	1.5
1975	12.2	7.5	4.3	0.4	0.3	0.2	2.9	0.5	2.4	1.8	1.4
1976	12.9	8.2	4.2	0.5	0.3	0.3	2.8	0.4	2.5	2.0	1.5
1977	12.7	7.7	4.6	0.4	0.5	0.3	2.8	0.6	2.5	2.0	1.6
1978	13.4	8.1	5.0	0.3	0.6	0.3	3.3	0.5	2.7	2.2	1.5
1979	13.0	7.8	4.8	0.4	0.5	0.3	3.2	0.5	2.7	2.2	1.3
1980	12.5	7.9	4.3	0.3	0.5	0.3	3.0	0.4	2.4	2.0	1.4
1981	12.7	7.8	4.6	0.3	0.5	0.4	3.0	0.4	2.4	1.8	1.5
1982	12.5	7.9	4.3	0.3	0.5	0.3	2.8	0.4	2.5	1.7	1.5
1983	13.4	8.4	4.7	0.3	0.5	0.2	3.2	0.4	2.7	1.8	1.7
1984	14.2	9.0	4.9	0.3	0.6	0.2	3.2	0.4	3.0	1.8	1.9
1985	15.1	9.8	5.0	0.3	0.5	0.3	3.3	0.5	3.2	1.8	2.0
1986	15.5	9.8	5.4	0.3	0.5	0.3	3.6	0.5	3.4	1.8	2.2
1987	16.2	10.7	5.2	0.3	0.4	0.3	3.5	0.5	3.6	1.7	2.4
1988	15.2	10.0	4.9	0.3	0.3	0.3	3.6	0.4	3.2	1.5	2.4
1989	15.6	10.2	5.1	0.3	0.3	0.3	3.9	0.4	3.1	1.5	2.3
1990	15.0	9.6	5.1	0.3	0.4	0.3	3.7	0.3	3.1	1.5	2.2
1991	14.9	9.7	4.9	0.3	0.5	0.2	3.6	0.4	3.0	1.2	2.4
1992	14.8	9.9	4.6	0.3	0.5	0.2	3.5	0.3	2.9	0.9	2.5
1993	15.0	10.2	4.5	0.3	0.4	0.2	3.5	0.3	2.9	1.0	2.5
1994	15.2	10.4	4.5	0.3	0.4	0.2	3.3	0.3	3.1	0.9	2.6
1995	15.0	10.0	4.7	0.3	0.5	0.2	3.4	0.3	2.9	1.2	2.5
1996	14.8	10.0	4.5	0.3	0.5	0.2	3.2	0.3	3.0	1.0	2.5
1997	14.6	9.9	4.4	0.3	0.4	0.2	3.1	0.3	3.0	1.0	2.7
1998	14.9	10.2	4.4	0.3	0.3	0.2	3.4	0.3	3.2	0.9	2.8

Source

U.S. National Marine Fisheries Service (NMFS), *Fisheries of the United States* (NMFS, annual).

Documentation

All figures are expressed as pounds of edible meat.

The NMFS calculation of per capita consumption is based on a "disappearance" model. The total U.S. supply of imports and landings is converted to edible weight and decreases in supply such that exports and inventories are subtracted out. These consumption estimates are divided by the total civilian resident population as of July 1 of each year.

These consumption figures refer only to consumption of fish and shellfish entering commercial channels, and they do not include data on consumption of recreationally caught fish and shellfish, which since 1970 is estimated to be between 3 and 4 pounds (edible meat) per person annually. The figures are calculated on the basis of raw edible meat (that is, excluding bones, viscera, shells, and so on). Domestic landings used in calculating these data are preliminary after 1977.

The 1909 estimates are based on the 1908 Census and foreign trade data.

Series Db343. Fresh and frozen fish consumption from 1910 to 1928 is estimated. Beginning in 1973, data include consumption of artificially cultivated catfish.

Series Db344. Canned fish consumption for 1911 to 1920 is estimated. Beginning in 1921, it is based on production reports, packer stocks, and foreign trade statistics for individual years.

Series Db345. Cured fish consumption for 1910 to 1928 is estimated.

Series Db350-351. Figures represent product weight.

Series Db350. Filets and steaks data include groundfish and other species. Data do not include blocks, but fillets could be made into blocks from which sticks and portions could be produced.

Series Db352. Figures are the edible (meat) weight of shrimp.

TABLE Db353-361   Aquaculture production – estimated weight, by species: 1983-2000

Contributed by Gavin Wright

	Total	Finfish					Shellfish		
		Total	Baitfish	Catfish	Salmon	Trout	Total	Crawfish	Oysters
	Db353	Db354	Db355	Db356	Db357	Db358	Db359	Db360	Db361
Year	Million pounds	Million pounds	Million pounds	Million pounds	Million pounds	Million pounds	Million pounds	Million pounds	Million pounds
1983	308.394	209.532	22.046	137.250	1.836	48.400	91.862	69.498	19.416
1984	335.728	230.468	23.598	154.255	2.675	49.940	95.043	66.280	25.365
1985	375.777	270.944	24.807	191.616	3.921	50.600	90.566	65.011	21.906
1986	408.521	293.451	25.807	213.756	2.878	51.000	99.402	69.834	24.475
1987	484.172	367.172	26.000	280.496	4.024	56.247	100.155	70.000	23.926
1988	500.242	385.198	26.400	295.109	6.777	56.032	95.638	65.848	24.398
1989	548.030	430.957	24.005	341.900	8.504	55.528	92.743	66.000	22.255
1990	572.531	449.520	21.610	360.435	9.069	56.816	99.463	71.000	22.192
1991	604.106	490.477	21.182	390.870	16.753	59.422	88.738	60.585	20.632
1992	691.182	571.236	20.618	457.367	23.937	56.264	95.991	63.032	23.986
1993	678.801	577.958	20.574	459.013	25.279	54.642	94.230	56.784	24.399
1994	665.635	558.372	21.709	439.269	24.714	52.075	86.801	49.080	28.016
1995	690.950	579.284	21.759	446.886	31.315	55.428	88.307	58.146	23.221
1996	693.693	601.064	20.849	472.123	30.657	53.620	72.816	46.584	18.546
1997	766.673	666.593	19.929	524.929	39.745	56.710	78.741	49.232	15.737
1998	789.708	695.440	16.389	564.355	32.107	55.103	70.773	37.945	18.157
1999	841.982	739.898	16.389	596.628	39.114	60.283	77.390	42.889	18.662
2000	822.519	747.330	13.954	593.603	49.372	59.164	48.982	17.025	16.822

Source

U.S. National Marine Fisheries Service (NMFS), *Fisheries of the United States* (NMFS, annual).

Documentation

Weights usually represent final sales of products to processors and dealers. Oysters are reported as meat weights (excludes shell), while other identified species are reported as whole (live) weights.

Series Db357. Only pen-reared aquaculture production is indicated for salmon.

Series Db361. Some oyster aquaculture production is reported in series Db305, U.S. commercial oyster landings.

TABLE Db362-370   Aquaculture production – estimated value, by species: 1983-2000

Contributed by Gavin Wright

	Total	Finfish					Shellfish		
		Total	Baitfish	Catfish	Salmon	Trout	Total	Crawfish	Oysters
	Db362	Db363	Db364	Db365	Db366	Db367	Db368	Db369	Db370
Year	Million dollars	Million dollars	Million dollars	Million dollars	Million dollars	Million dollars	Million dollars	Million dollars	Million dollars
1983	260.824	180.408	44.000	83.860	2.548	50.000	73.416	32.664	32.034
1984	307.086	211.793	47.045	106.899	3.414	54.435	83.695	27.936	47.906
1985	347.500	250.821	51.280	138.922	5.465	55.154	75.138	29.350	38.882
1986	372.460	254.495	51.522	142.789	4.399	55.590	95.567	35.009	49.666
1987	437.092	310.678	71.500	173.347	7.462	57.556	93.692	29.400	49.549
1988	520.282	376.857	71.000	225.463	20.467	57.927	103.323	24.364	58.900
1989	539.501	393.587	62.489	245.142	23.742	60.041	99.950	20.460	58.082
1990	655.112	421.659	53.978	273.210	26.341	64.640	134.545	34.000	77.949
1991	636.228	410.971	55.948	246.639	44.156	59.142	122.938	33.285	63.463
1992	724.187	482.350	61.183	273.506	75.193	53.942	147.630	34.860	82.432
1993	782.394	541.027	63.033	325.432	68.358	54.309	144.135	28.518	76.139
1994	751.109	562.733	68.714	344.475	61.915	52.569	129.831	26.994	69.928
1995	815.284	604.951	72.522	351.222	75.991	52.659	134.730	34.714	70.628
1996	885.635	597.414	70.254	364.951	60.995	56.958	136.052	34.820	64.368
1997	909.655	622.630	73.580	372.497	65.053	60.212	109.031	29.300	39.031
1998	938.643	650.305	57.392	419.054	62.694	59.710	121.650	23.649	47.951
1999	987.080	686.612	57.392	438.936	76.778	64.954	140.458	28.267	55.635
2000	972.833	687.120	45.790	445.919	99.208	63.690	117.724	27.626	42.419

Source

U.S. National Marine Fisheries Service (NMFS), *Fisheries of the United States* (NMFS, annual).

Documentation

Values usually represent final sales of products to processors and dealers.

Series Db366. Only pen-reared aquaculture production is indicated for salmon.

Series Db370. Some oyster aquaculture production is reported in series Db305, U.S. commercial oyster landings.

TABLE Db371–376   Output of whaling products: 1816–1905

Contributed by Gavin Wright

	U.S. fleet			New Bedford fleet		
	Sperm oil	Whale oil	Whalebone	Sperm oil	Whale oil	Whalebone
	Db371	Db372	Db373	Db374	Db375	Db376
Year	Barrels	Barrels	Pounds	Barrels	Barrels	Pounds
1816	7,539	9,350	796	1,150	0	0
1817	32,650	18,471	19,440	6,007	8,300	0
1818	18,625	19,303	65,446	2,850	9,950	14,000
1819	21,323	38,232	83,843	1,297	15,580	0
1820	34,708	44,757	78,879	12,330	21,130	17,045
1821	43,099	38,524	62,893	14,201	7,724	10,409
1822	42,900	51,427	50,799	4,080	15,105	3,231
1823	93,281	53,887	103,404	28,038	21,787	16,568
1824	98,129	58,198	133,427	24,980	28,872	9,314
1825	61,089	52,902	152,534	16,547	22,873	141,665
1826	29,200	35,182	79,368	5,839	18,172	131,889
1827	93,920	35,525	106,225	40,613	19,192	147,636
1828	78,577	50,533	137,323	24,494	29,058	230,651
1829	74,608	71,635	563,654	32,767	22,957	196,081
1830	110,541	89,883	514,991	37,258	34,261	294,628
1831	115,452	114,596	279,279	42,210	36,959	43,200
1832	73,002	181,076	442,881	27,536	46,629	67,200
1833	104,437	163,592	266,432	35,448	45,590	65,000
1834	123,542	131,582	343,324	55,123	23,950	37,000
1835	164,493	125,406	965,192	66,422	32,453	109,000
1836	133,334	136,568	1,028,773	46,134	37,717	32,000
1837	169,179	202,857	1,753,104	58,625	69,001	269,702
1838	132,356	226,552	2,200,000	62,655	68,001	57,500
1839	142,336	229,783	2,000,000	52,450	61,506	156,094
1840	157,791	207,908	2,000,000	51,258	61,883	31,586
1841	159,034	207,348	2,000,000	54,066	58,063	8,400
1842	165,637	161,041	1,600,000	72,895	53,375	143,314
1843	166,985	206,727	2,000,000	62,098	42,434	393,683
1844	139,594	262,047	2,532,445	58,002	109,263	887,243
1845	157,917	272,730	3,167,142	52,130	87,548	782,318
1846	95,217	207,493	2,276,939	40,138	89,146	580,862
1847	120,753	313,150	3,341,680	57,682	101,338	749,845
1848	107,976	280,656	2,003,000	52,254	116,876	975,686
1849	100,944	248,492	2,281,100	49,205	79,292	583,610
1850	92,892	200,608	2,869,200	43,645	90,370	911,508
1851	99,591	328,483	3,906,500	47,613	153,025	1,940,827
1852	78,872	84,211	1,259,900	41,248	30,177	397,575
1853	103,077	260,114	5,652,300	45,481	89,900	1,228,238
1854	76,696	319,837	3,445,200	40,471	155,760	2,116,773
1855	72,649	184,015	2,707,500	33,502	119,131	1,617,010
1856	80,941	197,890	2,592,700	50,572	91,666	1,161,090
1857	78,440	230,941	2,058,900	53,865	123,639	1,406,865
1858	81,941	182,223	1,540,600	42,013	73,195	789,666
1859	91,408	190,411	1,923,850	54,913	80,288	863,461
1860	73,708	140,005	1,337,650	39,101	101,499	1,159,464
1861	68,932	133,717	1,038,450	44,845	76,450	827,285
1862	55,641	100,487	763,500	37,361	71,464	729,551
1863	65,055	62,974	488,750	42,567	55,767	573,131
1864	64,372	71,863	760,450	56,877	35,594	427,743
1865	32,242	76,238	619,350	24,363	33,939	368,442
1866	36,663	74,302	920,375	17,249	24,196	304,896
1867	43,433	89,289	1,001,397	21,297	47,991	610,450
1868	47,174	65,575	900,850	29,872	44,374	531,461
1869	47,936	85,011	603,606	29,244	56,093	803,240
1870	55,183	72,691	708,365	40,215	38,577	381,760
1871	41,534	75,152	600,655	38,769	81,907	887,821
1872	45,201	31,075	193,793	25,450	15,671	83,226
1873	42,053	40,014	206,396	28,299	16,175	93,015
1874	32,203	37,782	345,560	27,415	21,355	141,254

(continued)

TABLE Db371–376   Output of whaling products: 1816–1905
Continued

	U.S. fleet			New Bedford fleet		
	Sperm oil	Whale oil	Whalebone	Sperm oil	Whale oil	Whalebone
	Db371	Db372	Db373	Db374	Db375	Db376
Year	Barrels	Barrels	Pounds	Barrels	Barrels	Pounds
1875	42,617	34,594	372,303	30,044	25,412	218,341
1876	39,811	33,010	150,628	28,509	18,417	157,334
1877	41,119	27,191	160,220	22,347	13,960	65,129
1878	43,508	33,778	207,259	42,717	27,223	176,887
1879	41,308	23,334	286,280	28,297	18,989	183,586
1880	37,614	34,776	464,028	35,068	42,726	488,034
1881	30,598	31,677	368,322	36,265	37,094	332,801
1882	29,884	23,371	271,999	23,615	27,328	291,610
1883	24,595	24,170	254,037	14,089	11,941	102,696
1884	22,099	24,670	426,968	19,585	20,610	133,765
1885	24,203	41,586	463,990	18,735	17,343	199,900
1886	23,312	27,249	352,490	25,330	15,360	152,400
1887	18,873	34,171	585,011	15,159	20,113	254,468
1888	16,265	17,185	334,572	8,534	10,815	135,900
1889	18,727	14,247	253,113	12,720	6,529	83,550
1890	14,480	17,565	309,700	20,339	9,049	115,805
1891	13,015	14,837	297,768	9,915	6,365	86,100
1892	12,944	13,382	369,885	7,275	6,150	112,510
1893	15,253	8,110	411,315	5,245	3,405	69,250
1894	16,333	8,720	278,800	10,285	2,310	37,000
1895	16,585	4,009	114,960	10,135	1,585	34,700
1896	15,124	4,800	207,850	11,285	2,290	54,850
1897	10,050	3,600	178,010	19,195	1,690	24,780
1898	12,520	5,295	246,120	5,755	840	11,820
1899	11,903	3,827	320,100	7,515	1,995	45,400
1900	18,525	5,510	207,650	11,395	4,055	18,500
1901	14,910	2,930	99,050	17,325	1,420	11,600
1902	21,970	4,725	109,980	18,860	4,020	17,000
1903	18,109	1,260	74,850	10,815	265	0
1904	17,050	3,750	123,300	14,820	1,420	15,000
1905	12,985	1,755	79,900	6,140	1,340	62,400

Source

Lance E. Davis, Robert E. Gallman, and Karin Gleiter, *In Pursuit of Leviathan* (University of Chicago Press, 1997), pp. 379–80.

Documentation

The figures for the U.S. fleet are originally from Walter S. Tower, *A History of the American Whale Fishery*, Series in Political Economy and Public Law, number 20 (University of Pennsylvania, 1907), adjusted so that oil amounts are expressed in all years in barrels.

The New Bedford figures are developed by Davis, Gallman, and Gleiter (1997) from a manuscript prepared by Joseph Dias, found in the Baker Library at Harvard University. The two sets of output figures are not fully comparable with respect to timing: Tower's data report output in the year when the output, not the vessel, arrived in port. Davis, Gallman, and Gleiter date the output with the return of the vessel.

TABLE Db377–378   Sealskin harvesting and whale processing – Pribilof Islands and Pacific Coast stations: 1910–1985

Contributed by Gavin Wright

Year	Sealskins taken from the Pribilof Islands Db377 Number	Whales processed at Pacific Coast land-based stations Db378 Number	Year	Sealskins taken from the Pribilof Islands Db377 Number	Whales processed at Pacific Coast land-based stations Db378 Number	Year	Sealskins taken from the Pribilof Islands Db377 Number	Whales processed at Pacific Coast land-based stations Db378 Number
1910	12,964	—	1935	57,296	583	1960	40,616	271
1911	12,138	—	1936	52,446	483	1961	95,974	343
1912	3,191	1,003	1937	55,180	413	1962	77,915	248
1913	2,406	397	1938	58,364	174	1963	85,254	259
1914	2,735	697	1939	60,473	232	1964	64,206	274
1915	3,947	864	1940	65,263	29	1965	51,020	241
1916	6,468	657	1941	95,013	24	1966	52,866	221
1917	8,170	673	1942	150	26	1967	65,672	246
1918	34,890	637	1943	117,164	29	1968	58,532	202
1919	27,821	1,004	1944	47,652	5	1969	38,805	183
1920	26,648	1,270	1945	76,964	0	1970	42,228	73
1921	23,681	129	1946	64,523	0	1971	31,740	53
1922	31,156	1,170	1947	61,447	38	1972	37,221	39
1923	15,920	908	1948	70,142	67	1973	28,582	37
1924	17,219	687	1949	70,891	49	1974	33,027	21
1925	19,860	638	1950	60,090	0	1975	28,849	15
1926	22,131	719	1951	60,689	40	1976	23,188	48
1927	24,942	1,102	1952	63,922	0	1977	28,444	30
1928	31,099	706	1953	66,673	0	1978	24,483	14
1929	40,068	722	1954	63,888	0	1979	—	16
1930	42,500	655	1955	65,638	0	1980	—	18
1931	49,524	—	1956	122,826	145	1981	—	17
1932	49,336	319	1957	93,618	237	1982	—	10
1933	54,550	382	1958	78,919	261	1983	—	11
1934	53,470	669	1959	57,810	309	1984	—	12
						1985	—	12

Sources

Series Db377. 1910–1938: U.S. Bureau of Fisheries, *Alaska Fishery and Fur-Seal Industries*, Administrative Reports; 1939–1957: U.S. Fish and Wildlife Service, *Alaska Fishery and Fur-Seal Industries, Statistical Digest*; 1958–1978: U.S. National Marine Fisheries Service (NMFS) and predecessor organizations, *Fishery Statistics of the United States* (NMFS, annual), and *Fisheries of the United States* (NMFS, annual).

Series Db378. 1912–1936: *Historical Statistics of the United States* (1976), which gives source as *Pacific Fisherman*, "Annual Statistical Numbers"; 1937–1964: U.S. National Oceanic and Atmospheric Administration and predecessor organizations, *Fishery Statistics of the United States*; 1965–1985: Committee for Whaling Statistics (CWS), *International Whaling Statistics* (CWS, annual).

Documentation

Series Db377. Figures are for sealskins taken from the Pribilof Islands. Under the terms of the 1911 and succeeding treaties or agreements with Canada, Japan, and Russia, the take of seal on the Pribilof Islands in the Bering Sea was administered by the U.S. government. The sealskin figures represent the total take before partitioning of the yield among the several countries involved. The figures for 1910 and 1911 are pretreaty and represent skins taken directly by the U.S. government, as the U.S. lease to the private company that had engaged in the operation since 1867 had expired early in 1910. The arrangement was terminated by international agreement and statute in the early 1980s.

Series Db378. Figures are for whales processed at Alaska and Pacific Coast states land-based stations. Present century participation by the United States in the whaling industry has been relatively inconsequential compared to that of other countries and to the American high-seas whaling of the nineteenth century. It has been largely restricted to land-based operations, chiefly in Alaska, Washington, and California. Washington whaling terminated in 1925; Alaska, in 1939. In 1969, the International Whaling Commission recommended that all member countries establish quotas for the commercial catch of some types of whales. At its thirty-fourth Annual Meeting in July 1982, the Commission agreed that the "catch limits for the killing for commercial purposes from all stocks for the 1986 coastal and the 1985/86 pelagic seasons and thereafter shall be zero." Although not all countries are party to this agreement, the statistical compilation by the Commission was terminated at that time.

FORESTRY

Peter Berck and Gavin Wright

TABLE Db379–386   Forest land – acreage, sawtimber, and grow stock: 1952–1997

Contributed by Gavin Wright

Year	Total forest land	Commercial timberland ownership				Net volume of sawtimber		Net volume of grow stock
		All	Federally owned/ managed	State, county, municipal	Private	Softwood	Hardwood	
	Db379	Db380	Db381	Db382	Db383	Db384	Db385	Db386
	Million acres	Million acres	Million acres	Million acres	Million acres	Billion board feet	Billion board feet	Billion cubic feet
1952	664	509	125	27	356	2,089	431	610
1962	759	515	125	27	363	2,062	496	659
1970	753	500	107	29	363	1,905	515	649
1977	736	482	105	30	347	1,985	594	711
1987	731	485	97	34	354	2,040	813	766
1992	737	490	97	35	358	2,047	945	786
1997	747	503	96	50	358	4,134	3,239	836

Sources

1952, 1962: U.S. Forest Service, *Forest Statistics of the United States* (U.S. Department of Agriculture, 1987). 1970: U.S. Forest Service, *The Outlook for Timber in the United States* (U.S. Department of Agriculture, 1973). 1977: U.S. Forest Service, *An Analysis of the Timber Situation in the United States, 1952–2030* (U.S. Department of Agriculture, 1984). 1987–1997: U.S. Forest Service, *Forest Resources of the United States* (U.S. Department of Agriculture, 1992, 1997).

Documentation

To be classified as forest land, an area must be at least 10 percent stocked by trees of any size, or formerly have had such tree cover and not currently be developed for nonforest use. Timberland is forest land that is producing or is capable of producing crops of industrial wood and is not withdrawn from timber utilization by statute or administrative regulation. Currently inaccessible and inoperable areas are included. Sawtimber is timber suitable for sawing into lumber. Growing stock is the net volume of live trees of commercial species meeting specified standards of quality or vigor.

Regional detail is available in the source.

TABLE Db387–389 National forest system – forests and acreage: 1891–2001

Contributed by Gavin Wright

	National forests	National forest system			National forests	National forest system			National forests	National forest system	
		Acreage	Gross area within unit boundaries			Acreage	Gross area within unit boundaries			Acreage	Gross area within unit boundaries
	Db387	Db388	Db389		Db387	Db388	Db389		Db387	Db388	Db389
Year	Number	Acres	Acres	Year	Number	Acres	Acres	Year	Number	Acres	Acres
1891	1	1,239,000	—	1930	149	160,090,817	183,976,000	1970	154	182,571,102	226,064,000
1892	6	3,254,000	—	1931	151	160,787,687	185,252,000	1971	154	182,578,296	225,000,000
1893	15	13,417,000	—	1932	148	161,360,691	186,215,000	1972	155	182,773,942	225,000,000
1894	17	17,928,000	—	1933	148	162,009,145	186,837,000	1973	155	183,014,294	226,171,000
1895	17	17,928,000	—	1934	145	162,591,124	188,037,000	1974	155	182,045,476	226,000,000
1896	17	17,928,000	—	1935	142	163,310,002	188,292,000	1975	155	183,280,072	226,000,000
1897	29	39,103,000	—	1936	147	165,978,691	197,435,000	1976	154	183,280,072	226,000,000
1898	31	40,866,000	—	1937	157	171,403,306	226,621,000	1977	154	183,447,427	226,000,000
1899	37	46,168,000	—	1938	158	172,451,394	227,280,000	1978	154	183,186,893	226,000,000
1900	38	46,515,000	—	1939	158	173,225,983	228,784,000	1979	154	183,186,893	226,344,000
1901	41	46,234,000	—	1940	160	174,769,543	228,174,000	1980	155	183,060,464	226,000,000
1902	54	51,896,000	—	1941	160	175,763,793	228,309,000	1981	155	186,441,602	229,694,000
1903	53	63,211,000	—	1942	160	176,593,251	228,725,000	1982	155	186,559,221	230,000,000
1904	59	62,611,000	—	1943	160	176,925,027	228,633,000	1983	155	186,531,949	229,971,000
1905	83	75,352,000	85,693,000	1944	158	177,422,436	228,643,000	1984	156	186,383,802	230,000,000
1906	106	94,159,000	106,994,000	1945	155	177,641,903	228,703,000	1985	156	186,315,499	229,979,000
1907	159	132,732,000	150,832,000	1946	152	177,768,552	228,760,000	1986	156	186,463,004	230,000,000
1908	165	147,820,000	167,977,000	1947	153	178,595,882	228,810,000	1987	156	186,454,781	230,220,000
1909	150	172,230,000	194,505,000	1948	152	178,595,882	228,936,000	1988	156	186,245,659	230,000,000
1910	149	168,029,000	192,931,000	1949	152	179,339,893	229,175,000	1989	156	186,905,252	230,839,000
1911	153	168,165,000	190,608,000	1950	151	179,685,328	229,341,000	1990	156	187,083,200	231,443,000
1912	163	165,027,000	187,406,000	1951	151	179,947,794	229,258,000	1991	156	186,996,286	231,443,000
1913	163	165,516,518	186,617,000	1952	153	180,168,800	229,165,000	1992	156	187,114,116	231,502,000
1914	163	163,848,524	185,321,000	1953	153	180,386,928	229,112,000	1993	155	187,226,244	231,553,000
1915	162	162,773,280	184,506,000	1954	152	180,358,491	235,694,000	1994	155	187,269,551	231,761,000
1916	153	155,399,809	176,089,000	1955	149	180,302,398	235,728,000	1995	155	187,239,503	231,605,000
1917	152	155,166,619	176,340,000	1956	149	180,354,267	232,118,000	1996	155	187,281,319	231,744,000
1918	151	155,374,602	175,951,000	1957	149	180,335,417	231,293,000	1997	155	187,419,277	231,808,000
1919	151	153,933,460	174,261,000	1958	148	180,378,544	231,080,000	1998	155	187,485,759	232,075,000
1920	152	156,032,053	180,300,000	1959	148	180,468,001	227,359,000	1999	155	187,669,299	232,170,000
1921	149	156,666,045	181,820,000	1960	151	180,843,513	226,623,000	2000	155	187,737,334	232,444,000
1922	148	156,837,282	181,800,000	1961	154	181,050,808	226,110,000	2001	155	187,811,680	232,434,000
1923	146	157,236,807	182,100,000	1962	154	181,635,371	225,613,000				
1924	146	157,502,793	182,817,000	1963	154	181,974,887	225,584,000				
1925	159	158,395,056	184,126,000	1964	154	182,078,340	225,743,000				
1926	160	158,759,210	184,124,000	1965	154	182,138,750	226,434,000				
1927	159	158,800,424	183,938,000	1966	154	182,272,997	226,519,000				
1928	151	159,480,856	184,404,000	1967	154	182,507,377	227,721,000				
1929	150	159,750,520	184,565,000	1968	154	182,615,576	226,502,000				
				1969	154	182,340,141	226,045,000				

Source

U.S. Forest Service, *Land Areas of the National Forest System* (U.S. Department of Agriculture, annual).

Documentation

Series Db388. For 1891–1905, the figures in are gross acreage, which means the total land area within the authorized boundaries of the units formally designated or proclaimed as national forests. After 1905, this series includes only national forest lands formally established and permanently held for national forest purposes, which is the narrowest definition.

Series Db389. Comprises all publicly and privately owned land within authorized boundaries of national forests, purchase units, national grasslands, land utilization projects, research and experimental areas, and other areas. The source provides a detailed breakdown for recent years.

TABLE Db390–397   National forest system – volume and value of timber cut: 1905–2000

Contributed by Gavin Wright

		Commercial sales			Land exchange		Free use	
		Timber		Miscellaneous forest products value				
	Total value	Volume	Value	value	Volume	Value	Volume	Value
	Db390	Db391	Db392	Db393	Db394	Db395	Db396	Db397
Year	Million dollars	Million board feet	Million dollars	Million dollars	Million board feet	Million dollars	Million board feet	Million dollars
1905	0.086	68	0.086	—	—	—	—	—
1906	0.203	139	0.203	—	—	—	—	—
1907	0.338	195	0.338	—	—	—	—	—
1908	0.964	393	0.794	—	—	—	132	0.169
1909	0.847	352	0.678	—	—	—	105	0.169
1910	1.082	380	0.906	—	—	—	105	0.176
1911	1.040	375	0.843	—	—	—	123	0.197
1912	1.139	431	0.943	—	—	—	123	0.197
1913	1.267	496	1.075	—	—	—	122	0.192
1914	1.454	626	1.271	—	—	—	121	0.183
1915	1.386	566	1.179	—	—	—	123	0.207
1916	1.439	595	1.255	—	—	—	119	0.185
1917	1.683	736	1.533	—	—	—	113	0.150
1918	1.655	730	1.527	—	—	—	97	0.128
1919	1.635	705	1.515	0.008	—	—	91	0.113
1920	1.887	805	1.764	0.010	—	—	88	0.113
1921	2.081	800	1.896	0.008	—	—	180	0.177
1922	1.859	723	1.752	0.008	—	—	90	0.099
1923	2.680	995	2.570	0.011	—	—	97	0.098
1924	3.203	1,144	3.095	0.014	—	—	89	0.094
1925	2.895	1,022	2.808	0.005	—	—	78	0.082
1926	3.477	1,193	3.371	0.010	—	—	88	0.097
1927	3.944	1,161	3.306	0.007	199	0.540	81	0.091
1928	3.610	1,168	3.209	0.012	104	0.299	82	0.090
1929	4.456	1,353	3.892	0.031	144	0.437	87	0.098
1930	4.930	1,488	4.340	0.023	165	0.449	116	0.117
1931	3.527	1,048	2.888	0.017	174	0.460	168	0.162
1932	1.767	545	1.326	0.021	67	0.193	270	0.227
1933	1.333	389	0.838	0.019	84	0.239	266	0.237
1934	1.845	599	1.397	0.026	76	0.213	248	0.210
1935	2.260	668	1.719	0.041	84	0.219	317	0.281
1936	2.892	815	2.119	0.030	206	0.471	293	0.272
1937	3.505	1,097	2.740	0.039	194	0.449	318	0.277
1938	3.539	1,075	2.662	0.052	213	0.547	301	0.279
1939	3.687	1,017	2.685	0.052	273	0.691	268	0.260
1940	5.168	1,371	3.825	0.057	369	0.982	326	0.304
1941	6.084	1,552	4.529	0.062	515	1.233	284	0.260
1942	6.429	1,560	4.523	0.079	645	1.586	219	0.241
1943	8.907	1,864	6.835	0.060	495	1.837	169	0.175
1944	14.517	2,840	12.416	0.150	493	1.739	181	0.213
1945	13.291	2,732	11.682	0.104	413	1.334	154	0.171
1946	11.811	2,470	10.494	0.150	260	0.997	138	0.170
1947	16.780	3,472	14.955	0.183	363	1.445	128	0.197
1948	21.389	3,451	19.842	0.145	307	1.212	116	0.189
1949	29.163	3,380	26.928	0.224	360	1.821	114	0.190
1950	31.140	3,195	29.084	0.211	307	1.630	121	0.215
1951	48.227	4,422	46.533	0.178	266	1.284	106	0.233
1952	59.759	4,232	58.275	0.193	186	1.066	98	0.225
1953	71.039	4,982	69.727	0.226	179	0.889	101	0.196
1954	65.887	5,180	64.149	0.255	185	1.259	109	0.224
1955	71.231	6,225	70.105	0.266	103	0.656	106	0.204
1956	98.107	6,813	96.865	0.268	94	0.755	104	0.219
1957	116.098	6,910	115.093	0.312	68	0.474	108	0.219
1958	94.762	6,335	93.777	0.346	85	0.411	121	0.228
1959	114.579	8,262	113.509	0.366	79	0.387	184	0.316
1960	157.094	9,302	156.132	0.454	65	0.292	123	0.216
1961	125.170	8,308	123.957	0.477	73	0.495	150	0.241
1962	129.654	8,946	128.514	0.522	86	0.392	149	0.226
1963	135.173	9,957	134.148	0.514	69	0.258	164	0.253
1964	151.880	10,911	150.711	0.529	43	0.363	186	0.276

TABLE Db390–397   National forest system – volume and value of timber cut: 1905–2000
Continued

		Commercial sales			Land exchange		Free use	
		Timber		Miscellaneous forest products value				
	Total value	Volume	Value		Volume	Value	Volume	Value
	Db390	Db391	Db392	Db393	Db394	Db395	Db396	Db397
Year	Million dollars	Million board feet	Million dollars	Million dollars	Million board feet	Million dollars	Million board feet	Million dollars
1965	161.880	11,229	160.809	0.494	15	0.296	191	0.280
1966	196.427	12,138	195.590	0.572	—	—	181	0.265
1967	189.563	10,851	188.711	0.575	—	—	170	0.277
1968	240.226	12,129	239.311	0.622	—	—	175	0.293
1969	327.944	11,783	326.997	0.665	—	—	168	0.282
1970	308.638	11,527	307.610	0.695	—	—	179	0.333
1971	258.400	10,341	257.000	0.600	—	—	190	0.800
1972	382.900	11,700	382.000	0.500	—	—	179	0.400
1973	480.100	12,357	479.200	0.500	—	—	190	0.400
1974	509.900	10,958	509.000	0.500	—	—	449	0.800
1975	368.400	9,174	366.000	1.400	—	—	618	1.100
1976	495.400	9,575	492.000	1.200	—	—	1,080	2.100
1977	735.900	10,482	733.000	1.000	—	—	1,028	2.400
1978	858.500	10,080	855.000	1.200	—	—	1,221	2.600
1979	973.000	10,377	968.000	1.100	—	—	1,637	3.800
1980	737.000	9,178	730.000	1.100	—	—	2,070	5.700
1981	728.900	8,036	720.900	1.600	—	—	2,107	6.400
1982	348.700	6,747	339.200	2.000	—	—	2,343	7.500
1983	655.900	9,244	649.700	1.700	—	—	1,071	4.500
1984	763.889	10,549	759.577	1.669	—	—	570	2.600
1985	724.505	10,941	720.636	1.703	—	—	399	2.200
1986	789.878	11,786	786.906	1.592	—	—	308	1.400
1987	1,018.977	12,712	1,015.995	1.905	—	—	209	1.100
1988	1,242.988	12,649	1,239.788	2.031	—	—	223	1.200
1989	1,313.186	11,951	1,309.732	2.239	—	—	214	1.200
1990	1,191.209	10,500	1,187.618	2.580	—	—	151	1.000
1991	1,012.342	8,475	1,008.586	2.747	—	—	121	1.000
1992	937.991	7,290	934.504	2.655	—	—	80	0.800
1993	918.225	5,917	914.646	2.791	—	—	80	0.800
1994	796.926	4,815	783.038	3.138	—	—	80	0.800
1995	619.732	3,866	616.117	2.935	—	—	—	—
1996	547.428	3,725	544.349	3.262	—	—	—	—
1997	500.896	3,285	497.957	3.262	—	—	—	—
1998	448.752	3,298	445.774	3.262	—	—	—	—
1999	342.599	2,939	302.934	3.262	—	—	—	—
2000	305.921	2,542	302.934	3.262	—	—	—	—

Source

U.S. Forest Service, *Agricultural Statistics* (U.S. Department of Agriculture, annual).

Documentation

Series Db390 equals the sum of series Db392–393, Db395, and Db397, including materials not measurable in board feet, such as Christmas trees, tanbark, turpentine, seedlings, and Spanish moss.

Commercial sales, series Db391–393, include all sales from the national forests for which a charge is made. Some timber from the national forest is exchanged for land (series Db394–395), but these have been included with commercial sales since 1966. Some timber is disposed of under free- and administrative-use permits to settlers, miners, residents, and other similar users (series Db396–397).

TABLE Db398–402   National forest system – receipts, payments to states, and visitor-days: 1905–1998

Contributed by Gavin Wright

	Receipts			Payments to states and outlying areas	Thousand
	Total	From timber use	From grazing use		
	Db398	Db399	Db400	Db401 [1]	Db402
Year	Million dollars	Million dollars	Million dollars	Million dollars	Thousand
1905	0.073	0.073	—	—	—
1906	0.758	0.237	0.513	0.076	—
1907	1.530	0.654	0.857	0.153	—
1908	1.788	0.811	0.947	0.447	—
1909	1.766	0.702	1.023	0.442	—
1910	2.041	1.011	0.970	0.511	—
1911	1.969	0.952	0.928	0.515	—
1912	2.109	1.028	0.961	0.554	—
1913	2.392	1.271	0.999	0.633	—
1914	2.438	1.311	1.002	0.640	—
1915	2.481	1.183	1.130	0.649	—
1916	2.824	1.422	1.210	0.737	—
1917	3.457	1.640	1.550	0.911	—
1918	3.575	1.630	1.726	0.946	—
1919	4.358	1.535	2.609	1.149	—
1920	4.793	2.045	2.486	1.253	—
1921	4.152	1.770	2.132	1.083	—
1922	3.422	1.813	1.316	0.882	—
1923	5.336	2.722	2.341	1.371	—
1924	5.252	3.036	1.916	1.347	—
1925	5.000	2.940	1.725	1.271	—
1926	5.156	3.367	1.422	1.300	—
1927	5.167	3.253	1.531	1.311	—
1928	5.442	3.325	1.714	1.387	—
1929	6.300	4.109	1.740	1.606	—
1930	6.752	4.390	1.943	1.719	—
1931	4.993	2.608	1.961	1.272	—
1932	2.294	1.049	0.830	0.589	—
1933	2.626	0.783	1.498	0.679	—
1934	3.315	1.522	1.359	0.844	—
1935	3.289	1.729	1.151	0.838	—
1936	4.063	2.203	1.441	1.028	—
1937	4.936	2.924	1.580	1.243	—
1938	4.671	2.518	1.696	1.167	—
1939	4.908	2.857	1.574	1.216	—
1940	5.863	3.943	1.463	1.456	—
1941	6.638	4.737	1.429	1.556	—
1942	7.177	5.100	1.595	1.693	—
1943	10.095	7.634	1.973	2.503	—
1944	15.879	12.872	2.459	4.177	—
1945	16.302	11.813	2.159	4.039	—
1946	14.168	10.802	2.060	3.463	—
1947	18.721	15.745	2.294	4.596	—
1948	25.013	21.243	2.898	6.069	—
1949	32.149	27.889	3.276	7.858	—
1950	34.551	30.269	3.385	8.479	—
1951	57.622	52.512	4.166	14.126	—
1952	71.452	65.407	5.023	17.536	—
1953	76.042	70.040	4.890	18.865	—
1954	68.993	63.146	3.930	16.543	—
1955	81.139	73.353	3.760	19.573	—
1956	116.997	110.583	3.729	28.665	—
1957	113.324	107.088	3.367	27.128	—
1958	93.461	86.473	3.711	22.370	—
1959	123.454	115.541	4.487	29.904	—
1960	148.213	140.126	4.507	35.672	—
1961	106.100	98.443	3.899	25.279	—
1962	114.174	106.160	3.806	27.440	—
1963	126.224	117.390	4.028	30.225	—
1964	137.514	127.962	3.790	33.083	—

Note appears at end of table

**TABLE Db398–402   National forest system – receipts, payments to states, and
visitor-days: 1905–1998   *Continued***

Year	Receipts			Payments to states and outlying areas	Thousand
	Total	From timber use	From grazing use		
	Db398	Db399	Db400	Db401 [1]	Db402
	Million dollars	Million dollars	Million dollars	Million dollars	Thousand
1965	149.239	138.772	3.521	35.757	—
1966	175.616	164.940	3.861	41.942	—
1967	184.517	172.791	4.184	43.912	—
1968	218.323	205.627	4.083	52.326	—
1969	321.254	306.815	4.438	78.013	—
1970	299.703	283.907	4.371	71.897	—
1971	236.200	217.000	5.400	56.650	—
1972	350.000	330.000	5.500	84.676	—
1973	469.700	446.700	6.200	113.669	—
1974	485.700	459.900	7.800	117.506	—
1975	373.100	341.300	7.700	89.770	—
1976	454.700	418.600	10.900	—	—
1977	691.600	652.100	11.400	109.523	—
1978	765.400	723.300	11.400	224.098	—
1979	881.000	827.600	12.500	238.863	—
1980	703.000	625.000	16.000	276.982	—
1981	680.700	581.400	14.900	233.623	—
1982	350.200	251.000	12.400	230.486	—
1983	495.300	398.500	10.200	132.601	—
1984	637.349	544.265	9.617	192.711	227,554
1985	635.947	514.560	9.040	224.937	225,407
1986	831.774	745.132	8.617	212.241	226,533
1987	898.393	807.941	8.104	239.887	238,458
1988	980.162	888.374	8.738	285.314	242,316
1989	1,050.816	909.517	10.950	317.290	252,495
1990	971.387	849.468	10.419	360.923	263,051
1991	771.644	667.073	11.457	344.788	278,849
1992	614.288	520.003	10.780	321.527	287,690
1993	503.578	425.105	10.518	308.059	295,473
1994	514.867	431.615	11.056	309.160	330,348
1995	386.745	303.046	8.756	273.483	345,083
1996	273.535	195.000	7.352	255.720	341,200
1997	284.754	197.194	6.972	234.322	—
1998	293.799	207.938	6.992	229.032	—

[1] Prior to 1976, data cover the period from July 1 to June 30; thereafter, the period is October 1 to September 30.

Source

U.S. Forest Service, *Agricultural Statistics* (U.S. Department of Agriculture, annual).

Documentation

Series Db398–400. Receipts from the national forests are derived from timber and other forest products sales, settlement and trespass; grazing and grazing trespass; plus land uses such as power lines, resort and summer homesites, ski lifts, and mineral leases. Series Db399 includes receipts from California and Oregon Railroad Grant Lands.

Series Db401. Payments to states and outlying areas consist primarily of the "25-percent fund" under legislative acts of May 23, 1908 (as amended), July 24, 1956, and October 22, 1976. These are payments from gross receipts from each national forest to the state or outlying area in which the forest is situated for the benefit of public roads and schools. This series also includes payments from timber receipts from the Tongass National Forest to Alaska for public schools and public roads, under an act approved July 24, 1956. Total payments include Arizona and New Mexico School Fund on account of school section lands administered by the Forest Service, and payments from an area of the Superior National Forest, on account of which the State of Minnesota is paid (for the counties) 0.75 percent of the appraised valuation in lieu of 25 percent of the receipts. These components are no longer reported separately in *Agricultural Statistics*. Note that the national totals as reported in Agricultural Statistics for 1994–1996 are not correct. The totals reported here are the corrected sums of the state figures.

Series Db402. A visitor-day is twelve visitor-hours of recreational use of national forest land and water. This may entail one person for twelve hours, twelve persons for one hour, or any equivalent combination.

TABLE Db403-408   Forest fires – number and acreage burned: 1926-2000[1]

Contributed by Gavin Wright

	Total		Protected areas			
			Federal		State and private	
	Fires	Area burned	Fires	Area burned	Fires	Area burned
	Db403	Db404	Db405	Db406	Db407	Db408
Year	Number	Acres	Number	Acres	Number	Acres
1926	91,793	24,316,000	—	—	33,867	4,755,000
1927	158,438	38,531,000	—	—	35,300	2,784,000
1928	175,934	43,542,000	—	—	39,260	4,111,000
1929	134,895	46,230,000	—	—	44,076	4,876,000
1930	190,980	52,266,000	—	—	70,832	5,809,000
1931	187,214	51,607,000	5,715	551,000	56,459	5,856,000
1932	166,399	42,063,000	4,933	419,000	55,567	3,234,000
1933	140,722	43,890,000	4,517	380,000	48,770	3,343,000
1934	162,663	41,821,000	8,064	658,000	61,254	3,515,000
1935	140,297	30,335,000	7,962	228,000	54,592	2,311,000
1936	226,285	43,207,000	11,144	425,000	73,709	3,792,000
1937	185,209	21,981,000	9,468	90,000	54,292	1,254,000
1938	232,229	33,815,000	9,873	316,000	76,326	2,623,000
1939	212,671	30,449,000	12,356	523,000	85,677	3,266,000
1940	195,427	25,848,000	14,076	482,000	73,527	2,934,000
1941	199,702	26,405,000	10,002	437,000	80,994	3,138,000
1942	208,218	31,854,000	9,940	576,000	75,849	3,863,000
1943	210,326	32,333,000	9,892	702,000	78,815	3,860,000
1944	131,229	16,549,000	8,985	375,000	56,148	2,301,000
1945	124,728	17,681,000	8,539	445,000	48,176	2,456,000
1946	172,278	20,691,000	9,670	321,000	66,103	2,253,000
1947	200,799	23,226,000	8,928	318,000	71,442	2,814,000
1948	174,189	16,557,000	6,681	312,000	61,095	1,962,000
1949	193,774	15,397,000	9,592	317,000	78,649	2,320,000
1950	208,402	15,519,000	8,418	391,000	96,578	3,408,000
1951	164,090	10,781,000	8,638	471,000	97,230	3,055,000
1952	188,277	14,187,000	9,634	281,000	118,363	6,347,000
1953	154,160	9,976,000	10,149	318,000	94,446	2,534,000
1954	176,891	8,833,000	8,592	176,000	118,681	2,787,000
1955	145,180	8,069,000	6,830	364,000	80,774	2,448,000
1956	143,485	6,606,000	11,341	372,000	82,997	1,613,000
1957	83,392	3,410,000	6,219	188,000	59,483	1,099,000
1958	97,910	3,280,000	12,942	288,000	67,366	1,173,000
1959	104,662	4,156,000	8,935	897,000	77,802	1,681,000
1960	103,387	4,478,000	12,090	622,000	77,537	1,909,000
1961	98,517	3,036,000	14,122	303,000	72,247	1,125,000
1962	115,345	4,079,000	10,421	270,000	94,487	1,646,000
1963	164,183	7,121,000	11,493	209,000	134,427	3,108,000
1964	116,358	4,197,000	8,877	194,000	90,480	1,670,000
1965	113,684	2,652,000	9,073	146,000	91,495	1,206,000
1966	122,500	4,574,000	11,571	1,265,000	98,157	1,908,000
1967	125,025	4,659,000	11,495	342,000	102,267	1,926,000
1968	125,371	4,232,000	10,027	1,205,000	107,689	1,633,000
1969	113,351	6,689,000	10,112	4,112,000	97,393	1,582,000
1970	121,736	3,279,000	14,968	719,000	101,455	1,541,000
1971	108,398	4,278,472	13,167	1,719,000	91,673	1,826,586
1972	124,554	2,641,166	15,937	1,232,172	83,010	1,050,309
1973	117,957	1,915,273	12,806	675,902	78,877	1,086,222
1974	145,868	2,879,095	15,040	1,200,030	105,835	1,511,447
1975	134,872	1,791,327	12,272	407,884	91,026	1,119,427
1976	241,699	5,109,926	15,800	518,789	157,035	2,118,709
1977	173,998	3,152,644	16,273	802,136	142,577	2,096,349
1978	218,842	3,910,913	14,090	201,959	130,798	1,552,622
1979	163,200	2,987,000	13,900	1,237,000	104,400	1,317,000
1980	234,892	5,260,825	14,264	750,642	141,035	2,348,190
1981	189,159	4,180,468	15,351	945,766	173,808	3,234,702
1982	101,650	1,432,086	10,686	332,212	90,964	1,099,874
1983	161,500	5,081,000	—	1,017,000	—	944,000
1984	118,636	2,266,134	14,163	941,684	104,473	1,324,422

Note appears at end of table

TABLE Db403–408   Forest fires – number and acreage burned: 1926–2000   *Continued*

Year	Total		Protected areas			
	Fires	Area burned	Federal		State and private	
			Fires	Area burned	Fires	Area burned
	Db403	Db404	Db405	Db406	Db407	Db408
	Number	Acres	Number	Acres	Number	Acres
1985	133,840	4,434,748	14,789	2,330,548	119,051	2,104,188
1986	139,980	3,308,133	16,201	1,595,545	123,779	1,712,550
1987	143,877	4,152,575	19,533	1,768,156	124,344	2,384,405
1988	154,573	7,398,889	20,024	4,785,352	134,549	2,613,536
1989	121,714	3,264,191	17,932	1,031,353	103,782	2,232,773
1990	122,763	5,454,773	18,248	2,979,391	104,515	—
1991	118,941	2,236,818	17,331	432,806	99,610	1,804,012
1992	103,830	2,457,665	19,998	1,246,806	83,832	1,210,859
1993	97,030	2,309,418	15,101	1,149,571	81,929	1,159,847
1994	114,066	4,727,272	24,072	2,643,341	89,994	2,083,931
1995	130,019	2,316,595	16,501	992,218	113,518	1,324,377
1996	115,166	6,701,842	20,792	3,441,098	94,374	3,260,744
1997	89,517	3,662,357	13,937	1,775,800	75,580	1,886,557
1998	81,043	2,329,709	—	—	—	—
1999	93,702	5,661,976	—	—	—	—
2000	122,827	8,422,237	18,818	4,720,479	104,009	3,701,758

[1] Through 1930, federal lands included under state and privately protected areas.

Sources

1926–1967: U.S. Forest Service, *Forest Fire Statistics* (U.S. Department of Agriculture, annual); 1968–1982 and 1984–1990: U.S. Forest Service, *Wildfire Statistics* (U.S. Department of Agriculture, annual); 1983: *Statistical Abstract of the United States* (1987); 1991–2000: U.S. Forest Service, *Wildland Fire Statistics* (U.S. Department of Agriculture, annual).

Documentation

Data are based on reports submitted by the office of the State Foresters, by the Regional Officers of the Forest Service, the Department of Interior, and the Tennessee Valley Authority. The statistics are for forest land and nonforest watershed lands in federal ownership, and for state and privately owned lands that are included in the Cooperative Forest Fire Control Program authorized by section 2 of the Clarke–McNary Act of 1924.

Protected areas, series Db405–408, include all forest lands that receive some organized fire protection. The difference between the totals (series Db403–404) and the figures for protected areas represents fires on unprotected state and private lands.

The sources contain detailed data on state and regional incidence and on causes of wildland fires.

TABLE Db409–422   Production, exports, and imports of timber products, by use: 1900–2000

Contributed by Gavin Wright

	Industrial timber products			Industrial roundwood used for										
				Lumber			Plywood and veneer			Pulp products			Logs	
	Domestic production	Imports	Exports	Domestic production	Imports	Exports	Domestic production	Imports	Exports	Domestic production	Imports	Exports	Imports	Exports
Year	Db409	Db410 [1]	Db411 [2]	Db412	Db413 [1]	Db414 [2]	Db415	Db416 [1]	Db417 [2]	Db418	Db419 [1]	Db420	Db421	Db422
	Million cubic feet	Million cubic feet	Million cubic feet	Million cubic feet	Million cubic feet	Million cubic feet	Million cubic feet	Million cubic feet	Million cubic feet	Million cubic feet	Million cubic feet	Million cubic feet	Million cubic feet	Million cubic feet
1900	7,285	—	140	5,680	—	175	5	—	—	135	35	—	—	—
1901	7,580	—	110	5,930	—	150	5	—	—	150	40	—	—	—
1902	7,880	—	60	6,180	—	110	10	—	—	160	50	—	—	—
1903	8,215	—	140	6,445	—	195	15	—	—	175	55	—	—	—
1904	8,490	—	150	6,675	—	205	20	—	—	190	60	—	—	—
1905	8,625	—	90	6,755	—	155	35	—	—	195	65	—	—	—
1906	9,225	—	95	7,145	—	170	60	—	—	225	75	—	—	—
1907	9,555	—	115	7,145	—	215	65	—	—	235	100	—	—	—
1908	8,725	—	80	6,520	—	160	70	—	—	205	80	—	—	—
1909	9,275	—	50	6,910	—	155	80	—	—	230	105	—	—	—
1910	9,295	—	80	6,910	—	215	90	—	—	220	135	—	—	—
1911	9,020	—	150	6,980	—	290	80	—	—	240	140	—	—	—
1912	9,330	—	145	6,990	—	295	80	—	—	250	150	—	—	—
1913	9,170	—	165	6,835	—	320	80	—	—	260	155	—	—	—
1914	8,565	—	15	6,290	—	185	85	—	—	265	170	—	—	—
1915	8,020	—	135	5,750	—	35	85	—	—	300	170	—	—	—
1916	8,530	165	—	6,185	—	10	90	—	—	325	175	—	—	—
1917	7,940	170	—	5,570	5	—	90	—	—	345	165	—	—	—
1918	7,310	180	—	4,955	20	—	95	—	—	335	160	—	—	—
1919	7,725	125	—	5,370	—	55	105	—	—	330	180	—	—	—
1920	7,770	205	—	5,440	—	55	80	—	—	360	260	—	—	—
1921	6,560	165	—	4,505	—	80	75	—	—	260	245	—	—	—
1922	7,605	290	—	5,480	—	60	90	—	—	340	350	—	—	—
1923	8,535	345	—	6,375	—	75	115	—	—	340	420	—	—	—
1924	8,250	285	—	6,140	—	155	115	—	—	340	440	—	—	—
1925	8,350	360	—	6,375	—	120	135	—	—	345	480	—	—	—
1926	8,215	375	—	6,180	—	145	145	—	—	400	520	—	—	—
1927	7,780	340	—	5,790	—	205	175	(Z)	—	380	545	—	—	—
1928	7,670	290	—	5,710	—	275	175	—	5	400	570	—	—	—
1929	8,045	330	—	6,020	—	255	200	—	5	445	590	—	—	—
1930	6,305	400	—	4,560	—	175	155	—	5	395	580	—	—	—
1931	4,600	335	—	3,105	—	150	125	—	5	400	490	—	—	—
1932	3,400	305	—	2,100	—	120	120	—	(Z)	350	425	—	—	—
1933	4,040	345	—	2,665	—	145	125	—	5	415	495	—	—	—
1934	4,340	355	—	2,925	—	165	130	—	5	430	525	—	—	—
1935	5,090	420	—	3,565	—	135	145	—	5	485	560	—	—	—
1936	5,990	560	—	4,295	—	95	165	—	5	555	660	—	—	—
1937	6,360	610	—	4,505	—	115	195	—	5	640	730	—	—	—
1938	5,570	470	—	3,860	—	70	195	(Z)	—	595	540	—	—	—
1939	6,370	535	—	4,470	—	60	210	(Z)	—	725	595	—	—	—

Year	Industrial timber products Domestic production Db409 Million cubic feet	Imports Db410 [1] Million cubic feet	Exports Db411 [2] Million cubic feet	Lumber Domestic production Db412 Million cubic feet	Imports Db413 [1] Million cubic feet	Exports Db414 [2] Million cubic feet	Plywood and veneer Domestic production Db415 Million cubic feet	Imports Db416 [1] Million cubic feet	Exports Db417 [2] Million cubic feet	Pulp products Domestic production Db418 Million cubic feet	Imports Db419 [1] Million cubic feet	Exports Db420 Million cubic feet	Logs Imports Db421 Million cubic feet	Exports Db422 Million cubic feet
1940	6,990	420	—	4,845	—	35	235	5	—	930	440	—	35	10
1941	8,055	650	—	5,680	105	—	265	5	—	1,075	500	—	55	5
1942	8,085	705	—	5,645	170	—	305	—	5	1,130	515	—	30	5
1943	7,560	565	—	5,325	85	—	280	—	15	1,030	480	—	20	5
1944	7,455	555	—	5,115	100	—	270	—	10	1,160	445	—	25	5
1945	6,605	685	—	4,365	100	—	250	—	10	1,140	575	—	25	5
1946	7,705	810	—	5,295	90	—	255	—	5	1,260	700	—	25	(Z)
1947	8,090	815	—	5,500	5	—	275	—	5	1,370	805	—	30	10
1948	8,375	1,090	—	5,750	190	—	290	(Z)	—	1,470	865	—	45	10
1949	7,355	935	—	5,000	140	—	320	(Z)	—	1,275	875	—	30	10
1950	8,525	1,525	140	5,905	535	80	345	5	(Z)	1,500	935	50	45	10
1951	8,740	1,465	260	5,780	390	155	390	10	(Z)	1,825	1,025	90	35	15
1952	8,775	1,375	215	5,820	385	115	435	10	(Z)	1,810	945	85	30	10
1953	8,790	1,425	190	5,710	430	100	475	15	(Z)	1,910	935	70	40	20
1954	8,755	1,465	270	5,635	480	110	480	30	(Z)	1,960	920	135	35	25
1955	9,225	1,610	340	5,785	560	130	575	40	(Z)	2,200	975	175	35	25
1956	9,620	1,640	315	5,920	530	120	590	45	(Z)	2,475	1,040	160	30	30
1957	8,615	1,495	340	5,100	460	130	560	45	(Z)	2,350	960	185	25	25
1958	8,530	1,495	310	5,160	530	115	615	50	(Z)	2,165	895	165	15	30
1959	9,390	1,700	355	5,745	635	120	720	75	5	2,355	970	195	20	35
1960	8,920	1,680	455	5,080	610	135	705	60	(Z)	2,575	985	275	20	45
1961	8,745	1,745	500	4,945	665	120	765	60	(Z)	2,475	1,000	295	20	75
1962	9,035	1,910	505	5,120	760	120	800	75	(Z)	2,565	1,055	340	20	85
1963	9,560	1,990	640	5,355	830	135	870	80	5	2,670	1,060	395	15	150
1964	10,170	2,035	735	5,635	815	150	960	90	5	2,865	1,120	380	10	170
1965	10,540	2,105	740	5,670	815	145	1,030	100	5	3,095	1,175	420	10	190
1966	10,645	2,230	835	5,645	810	160	1,030	115	5	3,190	1,290	460	15	220
1967	10,410	2,165	1,020	5,360	800	175	1,030	110	10	3,190	1,240	525	15	310
1968	11,025	2,400	1,235	5,630	960	180	1,120	165	10	3,385	1,260	570	15	405
1969	11,000	2,515	1,295	5,535	980	180	1,050	180	20	3,585	1,340	720	15	375
1970	11,115	2,430	1,540	5,355	955	195	1,065	170	15	3,835	1,280	620	25	430
1971	11,035	2,670	1,295	5,385	1,130	165	1,175	210	15	3,560	1,310	625	15	390
1972	11,440	3,060	1,545	5,535	1,415	215	1,300	270	25	3,520	1,365	640	5	535
1973	11,925	3,150	1,755	5,670	1,460	300	1,320	225	40	3,755	1,460	805	5	575
1974	11,540	2,755	1,805	5,095	1,115	270	1,150	155	50	4,220	1,470	715	15	455
1975	10,575	2,215	1,685	4,890	930	255	1,165	170	70	3,485	1,105	710	15	455
1976	11,920	2,840	1,870	5,585	1,290	290	1,355	215	65	3,805	1,320	725	15	555
1977	12,185	3,310	1,795	5,950	1,675	260	1,425	210	35	3,645	1,395	720	30	525
1978	12,565	3,755	1,845	6,155	1,910	275	1,460	230	40	3,745	1,595	805	20	585
1979	12,950	3,655	2,135	6,115	1,800	340	1,370	195	45	4,110	1,635	1,070	25	670

Notes appear at end of table

(continued)

TABLE Db409–422   Production, exports, and imports of timber products, by use: 1900–2000   *Continued*

	Industrial timber products			Industrial roundwood used for										
				Lumber			Plywood and veneer			Pulp products			Logs	
Year	Domestic production	Imports [1]	Exports [2]	Domestic production	Imports [1]	Exports [2]	Domestic production	Imports [1]	Exports [2]	Domestic production	Imports [1]	Exports	Imports	Exports
	Db409	Db410	Db411	Db412	Db413	Db414	Db415	Db416	Db417	Db418	Db419	Db420	Db421	Db422
	Million cubic feet	Million cubic feet	Million cubic feet	Million cubic feet	Million cubic feet	Million cubic feet	Million cubic feet	Million cubic feet	Million cubic feet	Million cubic feet	Million cubic feet	Million cubic feet	Million cubic feet	Million cubic feet
1980	12,120	3,250	2,350	5,300	1,540	395	1,175	120	45	4,390	1,565	995	25	560
1981	11,150	3,165	2,090	4,780	1,490	380	1,180	140	70	4,125	1,515	900	20	425
1982	10,910	3,015	1,995	4,635	1,460	320	1,135	115	50	3,980	1,415	965	20	550
1983	12,065	3,710	2,110	5,370	1,915	360	1,365	160	65	4,165	1,605	930	30	565
1984	12,725	4,165	2,060	5,770	2,130	340	1,400	145	45	4,355	1,860	920	30	600
1985	12,515	3,430	1,533	5,665	2,251	295	1,420	195	25	4,165	968	454	20	655
1986	13,845	3,404	1,687	6,545	2,173	363	1,505	199	45	4,545	1,020	544	15	620
1987	14,670	3,561	1,941	6,990	2,240	485	1,650	241	57	4,670	1,067	584	15	705
1988	14,985	3,421	2,441	6,920	2,088	686	1,630	201	72	4,885	1,121	697	15	825
1989	14,664	3,314	2,791	7,206	2,023	618	1,406	115	98	4,875	1,170	780	6	753
1990	14,124	3,000	2,714	6,892	1,786	570	1,368	96	110	4,645	1,114	784	4	674
1991	14,894	2,808	2,393	6,444	1,726	565	1,216	83	95	5,397	969	746	2	601
1992	15,280	3,090	2,344	6,793	1,970	540	1,265	100	107	5,516	992	801	7	525
1993	15,011	3,465	2,143	6,636	2,246	504	1,257	101	101	5,423	1,065	724	15	460
1994	15,306	3,632	2,139	7,323	2,420	482	1,310	95	88	5,576	1,102	758	18	429
1995	15,430	3,917	2,265	7,034	2,556	461	1,297	108	91	5,972	1,226	888	13	451
1996	15,258	3,899	2,239	7,028	2,615	449	1,284	122	87	5,753	1,114	865	18	422
1997	14,790	3,864	2,136	7,103	2,620	452	1,211	114	103	5,183	1,063	775	20	329
1998	14,899	3,979	1,812	7,298	2,690	350	1,201	131	55	5,187	1,082	679	30	316
1999	15,032	4,231	1,825	7,629	2,810	404	1,208	160	46	4,962	1,167	627	47	326
2000	14,789	4,310	1,811	7,713	2,832	421	1,172	155	42	4,857	1,215	664	61	331

(Z) Less than 2.5 million cubic feet.

[1] Through 1949, net imports; thereafter, total imports.

[2] Through 1947, net exports; thereafter, total exports.

Sources

1900–1949: U.S. Forest Service, *The Demand and Price Situation for Forest Products* (U.S. Department of Agriculture), 1963); 1950–1994: U.S. Forest Service, *U.S. Timber Production, Trade, Consumption, and Price Statistics 1950–1985*, updated for 1960–1988 and 1965–1994 (U.S. Department of Agriculture); 1995–2000: *Agricultural Statistics* (U.S. Department of Agriculture, annual).

Documentation

Data are expressed in roundwood equivalents, meaning the volume of logs or other round product required to produce the lumber, plywood, woodpulp, and the like.

Estimates for lumber have been converted to cubic-feet roundwood on the basis of 156 cubic feet per 1,000 board-feet softwoods and 153 cubic feet per 1,000 board-feet hardwoods lumber tally. Veneer logs commonly reported in board feet, log scale, have been converted to cubic-feet roundwood on the basis of 170 cubic feet per 1,000 board feet. Pulp products include pulpwood and pulpwood equivalent of woodpulp, paper and board; these have been converted on the basis of 77 cubic feet per cord.

Series Db409. Includes other industrial products not listed separately, such as cooperage logs, poles and piling, fence posts, hewn ties, round mine timbers, box bolts, excelsior bolts, chemical wood, shingle bolts, and miscellaneous items.

TABLE Db423–431   Lumber production, imports, and exports, by softwoods and hardwoods: 1799–2000

Contributed by Gavin Wright

	Domestic production			Imports			Exports		
	Total	Softwoods	Hardwoods	Total	Softwoods	Hardwoods	Total	Softwoods	Hardwoods
	Db423	Db424	Db425	Db426	Db427	Db428	Db429	Db430	Db431
Year	Billion board feet	Billion board feet	Billion board feet	Billion board feet	Billion board feet	Billion board feet	Billion board feet	Billion board feet	Billion board feet
1799	0.4	0.3	—	—	—	—	—	—	—
1809	0.4	0.3	0.1	—	—	—	—	—	—
1819	0.6	0.5	0.1	—	—	—	—	—	—
1829	0.8	0.7	0.1	—	—	—	—	—	—
1839	1.6	1.3	0.3	—	—	—	—	—	—
1849	5.4	4.1	1.3	—	—	—	—	—	—
1859	8.0	5.8	2.2	—	—	—	—	—	—
1869	12.8	9.3	3.5	—	—	—	—	—	—
1879	18.1	13.3	4.8	—	—	—	—	—	—
1889	27.0	20.0	7.0	—	—	—	—	—	—
1899	35.1	26.2	8.9	0.7	—	—	1.5	—	—
1900	—	—	—	0.5	—	—	1.7	—	—
1901	—	—	—	0.6	—	—	1.5	—	—
1902	—	—	—	0.7	—	—	1.4	—	—
1903	—	—	—	0.6	—	—	1.9	—	—
1904	43.0	32.5	10.5	0.6	—	—	2.0	—	—
1905	43.5	33.0	10.5	0.8	—	—	1.8	—	—
1906	46.0	34.9	11.0	1.0	—	—	2.1	—	—
1907	46.0	34.9	11.1	0.9	—	—	2.3	—	—
1908	42.0	31.9	10.1	0.8	—	—	1.8	—	—
1909	44.5	33.9	10.6	1.0	—	—	2.0	—	—
1910	44.5	34.0	10.5	1.0	—	—	2.3	—	—
1911	43.0	33.0	10.0	0.8	—	—	2.7	2.5	0.2
1912	45.0	34.7	10.3	1.0	—	—	2.9	2.5	0.4
1913	44.0	34.1	10.0	1.0	—	—	3.0	2.6	0.4
1914	40.5	31.5	9.0	0.9	—	—	2.1	1.9	0.2
1915	37.0	29.5	7.5	1.1	—	—	1.3	1.1	0.2
1916	39.8	31.3	8.5	1.2	—	—	1.3	1.2	0.1
1917	35.8	29.2	6.6	1.2	—	—	1.1	1.0	0.1
1918	31.9	25.7	6.2	1.2	1.2	—	1.1	0.9	0.2
1919	34.5	27.4	7.1	1.1	1.1	—	1.5	1.1	0.4
1920	35.0	27.6	7.4	1.4	1.3	(Z)	1.7	1.5	0.2
1921	29.0	23.4	5.6	0.8	0.8	(Z)	1.3	1.2	0.1
1922	35.2	28.9	6.3	1.6	1.5	(Z)	2.0	1.7	0.3
1923	41.0	33.2	7.8	2.0	1.9	0.1	2.5	2.2	0.3
1924	39.5	31.5	8.0	1.7	1.7	0.1	2.7	2.4	0.3
1925	41.0	33.3	7.7	1.8	1.7	0.1	2.6	2.2	0.4
1926	39.8	32.1	7.7	1.9	1.8	0.1	2.8	2.5	0.4
1927	37.3	30.0	7.3	1.7	1.6	0.1	3.1	2.6	0.4
1928	36.8	29.9	6.9	1.5	1.4	0.1	3.2	2.8	0.5
1929	38.7	30.8	7.9	1.5	1.4	0.1	3.2	2.7	0.5
1930	29.4	23.2	6.1	1.2	1.2	(Z)	2.4	1.9	0.4
1931	20.0	15.9	4.1	0.7	0.7	(Z)	1.7	1.4	0.3
1932	13.5	10.8	2.7	0.4	0.4	(Z)	1.2	0.9	0.2
1933	17.2	13.8	3.4	0.4	0.3	(Z)	1.3	1.0	0.3
1934	18.8	14.6	4.2	0.3	0.3	(Z)	1.3	1.1	0.3
1935	22.9	18.2	4.7	0.4	0.4	0.1	1.3	1.0	0.3
1936	27.6	22.0	5.6	0.7	0.6	0.1	1.3	0.9	0.3
1937	29.0	23.1	5.9	0.7	0.6	0.1	1.4	1.1	0.4
1938	24.8	20.0	4.9	0.5	0.5	0.1	1.0	0.7	0.3
1939	28.8	23.3	5.5	0.7	0.6	0.1	1.1	0.8	0.3
1940	31.2	25.6	5.5	0.7	0.6	0.1	1.0	0.8	0.2
1941	36.5	29.9	6.7	1.4	1.2	0.2	0.7	0.5	0.1
1942	36.3	29.5	6.8	1.5	1.4	0.1	0.5	0.4	0.1
1943	34.3	26.9	7.4	0.9	0.7	0.1	0.3	0.2	0.1
1944	32.9	25.2	7.8	1.0	0.8	0.1	0.4	0.3	0.1
1945	28.1	21.1	7.0	1.1	0.9	0.2	0.4	0.3	0.1
1946	34.1	25.9	8.3	1.2	1.0	0.2	0.6	0.6	0.1
1947	35.4	27.9	7.5	1.3	1.1	0.2	1.4	1.2	0.2
1948	37.0	29.6	7.4	1.9	1.7	0.2	0.6	0.6	0.1
1949	32.2	26.5	5.7	1.6	1.4	0.1	0.7	0.5	0.1

Note appears at end of table

(continued)

TABLE Db423–431   Lumber production, imports, and exports, by softwoods and hardwoods: 1799–2000   *Continued*

Year	Domestic production			Imports			Exports		
	Total	Softwoods	Hardwoods	Total	Softwoods	Hardwoods	Total	Softwoods	Hardwoods
	Db423	Db424	Db425	Db426	Db427	Db428	Db429	Db430	Db431
	Billion board feet	Billion board feet	Billion board feet	Billion board feet	Billion board feet	Billion board feet	Billion board feet	Billion board feet	Billion board feet
1950	38.0	30.6	7.4	3.4	3.1	0.3	0.5	0.4	0.1
1951	37.2	29.5	7.7	2.5	2.3	0.3	1.0	0.9	0.1
1952	37.5	30.2	7.2	2.5	2.3	0.2	0.7	0.6	0.2
1953	36.7	29.6	7.2	2.8	2.5	0.2	0.6	0.5	0.1
1954	36.4	29.3	7.1	3.1	2.9	0.2	0.7	0.6	0.1
1955	37.4	29.8	7.6	3.6	3.3	0.3	0.8	0.7	0.2
1956	38.2	30.2	8.0	3.4	3.2	0.3	0.8	0.6	0.2
1957	32.9	27.1	5.8	3.0	2.7	0.2	0.8	0.6	0.2
1958	33.4	27.4	6.0	3.4	3.2	0.2	0.7	0.6	0.2
1959	37.2	30.5	6.7	4.1	3.8	0.3	0.8	0.6	0.2
1960	32.9	26.7	6.3	3.9	3.6	0.3	0.9	0.7	0.2
1961	32.0	26.1	6.0	4.3	4.0	0.2	0.8	0.6	0.2
1962	33.2	26.8	6.4	4.9	4.6	0.3	0.8	0.6	0.1
1963	34.7	27.6	7.2	5.3	5.0	0.3	0.9	0.7	0.1
1964	36.6	29.3	7.3	5.2	4.9	0.3	1.0	0.8	0.1
1965	36.8	29.3	7.5	5.2	4.9	0.3	0.9	0.8	0.1
1966	36.6	28.8	7.7	5.2	4.8	0.4	1.0	0.9	0.2
1967	34.7	27.3	7.4	5.1	4.8	0.3	1.1	1.0	0.2
1968	36.5	29.3	7.2	6.2	5.8	0.3	1.2	1.0	0.1
1969	35.8	28.3	7.5	6.3	5.9	0.4	1.1	1.0	0.1
1970	34.7	27.5	7.1	6.1	5.8	0.3	1.3	1.2	0.1
1971	36.9	30.0	6.9	7.6	7.2	0.4	1.1	0.9	0.2
1972	37.8	31.0	6.8	9.4	9.0	0.4	1.4	1.2	0.2
1973	38.6	31.6	7.0	9.5	9.0	0.5	2.0	1.8	0.2
1974	34.6	27.7	6.9	7.2	6.8	0.4	1.8	1.6	0.2
1975	32.6	26.7	5.9	6.0	5.7	0.3	1.6	1.4	0.2
1976	37.0	30.6	6.4	8.3	8.0	0.3	1.8	1.6	0.2
1977	39.4	32.7	6.7	10.7	10.4	0.3	1.6	1.4	0.2
1978	40.5	33.5	7.0	12.3	11.9	0.4	1.8	1.4	0.4
1979	40.6	33.3	7.3	11.6	11.2	0.4	2.2	1.8	0.4
1980	35.3	28.2	7.1	9.9	9.6	0.3	2.5	2.0	0.5
1981	31.7	25.4	6.3	9.5	9.2	0.3	2.4	1.9	0.5
1982	30.0	24.9	5.1	9.3	9.1	0.2	2.0	1.6	0.4
1983	34.5	28.9	5.6	12.3	12.0	0.3	2.3	1.8	0.5
1984	37.1	30.8	6.3	13.6	13.3	0.3	2.1	1.6	0.5
1985	40.2	31.3	8.9	15.0	14.6	0.4	1.9	1.5	0.4
1986	46.2	35.3	10.9	14.6	14.3	0.3	2.4	1.9	0.5
1987	50.2	38.2	12.0	15.2	14.7	0.5	3.2	2.4	0.8
1988	49.6	38.1	11.4	14.2	13.8	0.4	4.5	3.3	1.2
1989	48.5	37.5	11.0	13.9	13.6	0.3	4.2	3.3	1.0
1990	46.5	35.8	10.7	12.3	12.1	0.2	3.8	3.0	0.9
1991	43.4	33.2	10.2	11.9	11.7	0.28	3.8	2.9	0.9
1992	45.7	34.5	11.2	13.7	13.4	0.3	3.6	2.7	1.0
1993	45.1	33.3	11.8	15.5	15.2	0.3	3.4	2.4	1.0
1994	43.7	32.7	11.0	16.8	16.4	0.4	3.3	2.2	1.0
1995	44.4	32.0	12.4	17.8	17.4	0.4	3.2	2.0	1.1
1996	46.8	33.9	12.8	18.6	18.2	0.4	3.2	1.9	1.1
1997	47.4	34.5	12.9	18.5	18.0	0.5	3.2	1.8	1.3
1998	48.3	34.8	13.5	19.3	18.7	0.6	2.6	1.3	1.1
1999	51.0	36.7	14.3	19.9	19.2	0.7	2.9	1.4	1.2
2000	51.6	35.9	15.7	20.3	19.4	0.8	2.8	1.4	1.3

(Z) Less than 50 million board feet.

Sources

Series Db423–425. 1799–1945: U.S. Forest Service, *Lumber Production in the United States, 1799–1946* (U.S. Department of Agriculture, 1948); 1946–1949: U.S. Bureau of the Census, *Facts for Industry* (annual); 1950–1988: U.S. Forest Service, *U.S. Timber Production, Trade, Consumption, and Price Statistics, 1950–1980*, updated for 1960–1988 (U.S. Department of Agriculture); 1989–2000: *Agricultural Statistics*, from data published by the American Forest and Paper Association (U.S. Department of Agriculture, annual).

Series Db426–431. 1899–1946: U.S. Bureau of the Census, *Foreign Commerce and Navigation of the United States* (annual); 1947–1949: U.S. Bureau of the Census, *United States Imports of Merchandise for Consumption* (annual); *United States Exports of Domestic and Foreign Merchandise* (annual); 1950–1994: U.S. Forest Service, *U.S. Timber Production, Trade, Consumption and Price Statistics, 1950–1980*, updated for 1960–1988, and 1965–1994 (U.S. Department of Agriculture); 1995–2000: American Forest and Paper Association (AFPA), *Wood Statistical Roundup*, from U.S. Commerce Department data (AFPA, annual).

TABLE Db423–431   Lumber production, imports, and exports, by softwoods and hardwoods: 1799–2000 *Continued*

Documentation

Data on lumber were first collected by the Census Office in the Census of 1810 (for the year 1809), and decennially for census years 1819 and 1839–1899. Estimates for 1799 and 1829 are mainly extensions of trends developed for other years.

Softwood refers to coniferous trees, usually evergreen, having needles or scalelike leaves. Hardwood refers to dicotyledonous trees, usually broad-leaved and deciduous.

Series Db423–425. Since 1904, production has been estimated for most years. Prior to 1869, census reports gave only the value of lumber produced;

national lumber production by softwoods and hardwoods for these years has been estimated on the basis of values reported by the census and available records of lumber prices. Since 1899, lumber production has been reported in quantity terms by states and species, although in recent years such reporting, based on sampling of the industry, has been restricted to major species and principal producing states.

Series Db426–431. Figures for international trade are the summation of import entries and warehouse withdrawals prepared by importers or their brokers, and of export declarations prepared by their authorized agents or brokers.

TABLE Db432–445   Lumber production, by species: 1869–1996

Contributed by Gavin Wright

		Softwoods							Hardwoods					
	Total	Total	Douglas fir	Southern pine	Western pine	Hemlock	Redwood	Eastern white pine	Total	Oak	Yellow poplar	Sweetgum	Maple	Cottonwood and aspen
	Db432	Db433	Db434	Db435	Db436 [1]	Db437	Db438	Db439	Db440	Db441	Db442	Db443 [2]	Db444	Db445
Year	Million board feet	Million board feet	Million board feet	Million board feet	Million board feet	Million board feet	Million board feet	Million board feet	Million board feet	Million board feet	Million board feet	Million board feet	Million board feet	Million board feet
1869	12,756	9,252	196	1,378	321	770	—	5,770	3,504	2,014	320	4	410	—
1879	18,125	13,334	289	2,379	366	1,200	—	7,863	4,791	2,943	496	24	447	—
1889	27,039	20,024	1,206	4,220	741	2,533	—	9,409	7,015	3,804	783	69	636	—
1899	35,078	26,179	1,739	9,670	1,011	3,421	360	7,747	8,898	4,553	1,118	299	662	417
1904	34,127	27,345	2,928	11,522	1,402	3,269	519	5,316	6,782	2,903	854	524	588	322
1905	30,503	24,915	4,319	8,772	1,227	2,804	412	4,868	5,588	1,834	583	317	609	236
1906	37,551	30,235	4,970	11,661	1,636	3,537	660	4,469	7,315	2,820	683	454	883	264
1907	40,256	31,001	4,749	13,215	1,747	3,373	569	4,088	9,255	3,719	863	689	939	293
1908	33,224	25,546	3,675	11,236	1,522	2,531	405	3,198	7,678	2,772	654	589	875	232
1909	44,510	33,897	4,856	16,277	1,826	3,051	522	3,695	10,613	4,414	858	707	1,107	266
1910	40,018	31,161	5,204	14,143	1,940	2,836	543	3,104	8,857	3,522	735	610	1,007	220
1911	37,003	28,902	5,054	12,897	1,808	2,555	490	2,904	8,101	3,098	659	583	952	199
1912	39,158	30,526	5,175	14,737	1,737	2,427	497	2,775	8,632	3,319	623	694	1,021	227
1913	38,387	30,303	5,556	14,839	1,768	2,320	510	2,229	8,084	3,212	620	773	901	209
1914	37,346	29,407	4,764	14,473	1,808	2,166	535	2,307	7,939	3,279	519	675	910	195
1915	31,242	25,441	4,122	12,177	1,810	2,026	419	1,872	5,801	2,070	377	478	771	138
1916	34,791	28,576	5,413	13,411	2,262	1,987	491	1,952	6,215	2,165	395	652	809	135
1917	33,193	27,130	5,351	12,483	2,267	1,968	487	1,794	6,063	1,968	326	731	802	179
1918	29,362	24,100	5,819	9,942	2,113	1,696	443	1,687	5,262	1,659	242	652	697	148
1919	34,552	27,407	5,902	13,063	2,203	1,755	410	1,425	7,145	2,708	329	851	857	144
1920	29,878	24,254	6,957	8,964	2,785	1,685	476	1,039	5,624	1,854	270	685	768	138
1921	26,961	22,186	4,642	10,960	1,853	1,201	468	998	4,775	1,592	235	683	610	122
1922	31,569	26,644	6,832	11,501	2,700	1,535	566	972	4,925	1,605	274	808	640	114
1923	37,166	30,904	8,223	12,949	3,511	1,873	592	1,109	6,262	2,028	353	1,016	842	158
1924	35,931	29,406	7,462	12,487	3,347	1,879	604	1,056	6,525	2,077	351	1,071	857	167
1925	38,339	31,710	8,154	13,236	3,949	2,140	511	1,031	6,628	2,129	376	1,101	922	142
1926	36,936	30,469	8,807	11,752	3,964	2,159	488	911	6,467	2,191	322	1,133	829	122
1927	34,532	28,443	8,443	10,891	3,614	2,071	570	824	6,090	2,013	335	1,101	774	104
1928	34,142	28,345	8,449	10,610	3,837	2,222	487	838	5,797	1,830	328	968	743	144
1929	36,886	29,813	8,689	11,630	4,207	2,099	486	709	7,073	2,574	436	1,104	824	165
1930	26,051	21,323	6,453	7,450	3,375	1,517	403	564	4,729	1,662	258	694	601	158
1931	16,523	13,852	4,648	4,430	2,364	960	211	305	2,671	954	172	343	328	77
1932	10,151	8,746	2,904	3,069	1,590	337	136	198	1,406	516	86	202	160	49
1933	13,961	11,899	3,969	4,446	2,082	416	164	236	2,062	698	111	386	221	108
1934	15,494	12,735	4,066	4,473	2,304	478	282	388	2,758	1,083	163	393	311	109
1935	19,539	16,248	4,772	5,960	3,209	578	329	383	3,291	1,195	182	482	404	98
1936	24,355	20,242	6,321	7,113	3,861	813	403	442	4,113	1,535	260	606	490	137
1937	25,997	21,589	6,555	7,691	4,264	862	436	449	4,408	1,582	299	578	525	146
1938	21,646	18,293	5,216	7,196	3,474	578	317	408	3,353	1,204	221	454	389	140
1939	25,148	21,408	6,494	7,749	4,214	665	345	514	3,741	1,432	276	383	445	130

Notes appear at end of table   (continued)

TABLE Db432–445   Lumber production, by species: 1869–1996   *Continued*

		Softwoods							Hardwoods					
	Total	Total	Douglas fir	Southern pine	Western pine	Hemlock	Redwood	Eastern white pine	Total	Oak	Yellow poplar	Sweetgum	Maple	Cottonwood and aspen
	Db432	Db433	Db434	Db435	Db436 [1]	Db437	Db438	Db439	Db440	Db441	Db442	Db443 [2]	Db444	Db445
Year	Million board feet	Million board feet	Million board feet	Million board feet	Million board feet	Million board feet	Million board feet	Million board feet	Million board feet	Million board feet	Million board feet	Million board feet	Million board feet	Million board feet
1940	28,934	24,903	7,121	10,163	4,571	716	389	577	4,031	1,467	376	479	463	154
1941	33,613	28,032	8,532	10,339	5,196	1,005	456	916	5,581	2,208	433	589	619	231
1942	36,332	29,510	8,550	11,761	4,830	1,089	462	1,083	6,822	2,763	543	840	642	283
1943	34,289	26,917	7,951	9,962	4,568	1,213	461	1,045	7,371	3,038	589	1,044	581	244
1944	32,938	25,160	7,864	8,132	4,465	1,201	462	1,244	7,778	3,292	641	1,017	634	297
1945	28,122	21,140	6,237	7,210	3,596	1,039	444	1,023	6,982	2,859	578	971	522	209
1946	34,112	25,857	7,640	9,376	4,314	1,216	243	1,165	8,256	3,378	827	1,080	598	312
1947	35,404	27,937	9,043	9,473	4,534	1,244	530	1,119	7,467	3,193	636	803	630	381
1948	37,000	29,600	9,794	—	4,926	—	—	793	7,400	—	—	—	—	—
1949	32,178	26,472	9,074	8,259	4,491	1,177	744	820	5,704	2,518	556	515	508	217
1950	38,007	30,633	9,984	9,939	4,632	1,508	875	950	7,374	3,347	833	758	546	225
1951	37,204	29,493	10,372	8,495	— [5]	1,502	860	— [5]	7,711	3,590	753	792	584	241
1952	37,462	30,234	10,569	8,572	4,142	1,525	900	976	7,228	3,353	671	567	566	404
1953	36,742	29,562	10,367	7,581	4,506	1,441	969	1,064	7,180	3,339	709	530	551	406
1954	36,356	29,282	10,328	7,332	4,544	1,337	958	1,036	7,074	3,451	592	522	575	280
1955	37,380	29,815	10,414	7,360	4,362	1,568	991	796	7,565	3,716	690	529	568	327
1956	38,199	30,231	10,195	7,740	4,279	1,322	1,125	848	7,968	3,928	752	516	593	230
1957	32,901	27,100	9,094	6,568	3,262	1,242	953	— [5]	5,801	2,796	539	346	487	173
1958	33,385	27,379	9,329	6,420	3,868	1,386	917	— [5]	6,006	2,882	615	412	572	176
1959	37,166	30,509	10,265	6,716	4,075	1,658	1,221	— [5]	6,657	3,369	655	432	450	149
1960	32,926	26,672	8,832	5,660	3,909	2,032	1,000	— [5]	6,254	2,789	592	331	602	206
1961	32,019	26,066	8,378	5,622	3,824	2,031	1,011	— [5]	5,953	2,817	541	316	526	167
1962	33,174	26,812	8,504	5,733	3,995	2,279	1,024	— [5]	6,362	3,068	619	328	523	178
1963	34,706	27,552	8,353	6,055	4,305	2,486	1,138	— [5]	7,154	3,170	644	418	556	192
1964	36,559	29,284	8,868	6,414	4,598	2,490	1,199	— [5]	7,275	3,417	645	380	642	205
1965	36,762	29,295	8,783	6,628	4,666	2,576	1,087	— [5]	7,467	3,356	681	387	786	198
1966	36,584	28,847	8,528	6,609	4,713	2,490	1,038	— [5]	7,737	3,675	692	434	658	211
1967	34,741	27,311	7,822	6,511	4,469	2,257	939	— [5]	7,430	3,424	666	385	715	202
1968	36,473	29,285	8,532	6,901	4,763	2,186	1,049	— [5]	7,188	3,319	662	364	704	190
1969	35,824	28,342	8,059	7,181	4,523	1,902	1,083	— [5]	7,482	3,410	644	390	746	220
1970	34,668	27,530	7,727	7,063	4,327	1,980	1,078	— [5]	7,138	3,250	606	376	742	229
1971	36,988	30,039	8,211	7,734	4,716	2,367	1,141	— [5]	6,949	3,177	600	340	735	218
1972	37,745	30,975	8,533	8,053	4,861	2,688	1,242	— [5]	6,770	3,133	628	344	628	273
1973	38,595	31,586	8,686	7,895	4,876	2,711	1,277	— [5]	7,009	3,227	701	342	623	326
1974	34,608	27,704	7,901	6,921	4,155	2,105	1,170	— [5]	6,904	3,160	710	294	574	312
1975	32,619	26,747	7,329	6,967	4,215	2,020	1,054	— [5]	5,872	2,724	555	245	531	253
1976	36,295	29,878	8,207	7,598	4,766	2,454	1,128	— [5]	6,417	2,996	596	283	604	309
1977	37,882	31,203	8,543	8,293	4,898	2,439	1,148	— [5]	6,679	3,103	605	377	563	355
1978	38,270	31,273	8,601	8,267	4,847	2,728	917	— [5]	6,997	3,220	645	412	561	372
1979	37,678	30,411	8,425	7,928	4,577	2,715	896	— [5]	7,267	3,461	673	401	217 [6]	374
1980	35,354	28,239	6,853	6,740	3,787	2,058	770	— [5]	7,115	3,356	661	371	225 [6]	303
1981	31,672	25,420	5,868	6,824	3,349	1,575	730	— [5]	6,252	1,922	409	231	426	155
1982	30,010	24,949	5,524	8,754	2,662	1,333	760	— [5]	5,061	1,855	399	193	367	105
1983	34,553	28,926	6,434	10,181	3,311	1,690	852	— [5]	5,627	2,163	475	181	524	197
1984	37,065	30,801	7,740	10,648	4,975	— [5]	999	— [5]	6,264	2,786	569	300	538	233
1985	36,445	30,479	7,751	10,230	5,144	— [5]	1,155	— [5]	5,966	2,793	544	293	532	216
1986	41,999	34,815	9,600	11,443	5,471	— [5]	984	— [5]	7,184	3,410	724	375	587	247
1987	44,886	37,410	10,422	12,043	6,009	— [5]	1,157	— [5]	7,476	3,684	805	330	636	235
1988	44,576	36,845	9,986	12,474	5,697	— [5]	1,157	— [5]	7,731	3,790	828	356	619	234
1989	43,576	36,040	10,045	12,031	4,312	— [5]	1,048	— [5]	7,536	3,546	802	306	589	217
1990 [3]	43,466	36,224	8,831	12,989	4,047	— [5]	1,077	— [5]	7,242	2,615	666	219	543	167
1991	39,830	33,064	7,804	12,318	3,690	— [5]	876	453	6,741	2,439	630	170	516	155
1992	40,754	33,704	7,638	13,224	3,369	— [5]	828	503	7,050	2,538	708	179	513	152
1993 [4]	45,356	34,725	7,059	14,698	3,133	— [5]	714	460	10,631	2,717	805	249	569	238
1994	46,466	35,556	6,959	15,221	3,053	— [5]	808	464	10,910	2,798	858	243	272	262
1995	43,971	33,043	6,386	14,706	2,575	— [5]	762	464	10,928	2,878	871	217	614	232
1996	44,699	34,025	6,792	15,027	2,375	— [5]	714	466	10,674	2,843	866	187	599	214

TABLE Db432–445   Lumber production, by species: 1869–1996   *Continued*

[1] Includes Idaho white pine, ponderosa pine, and sugar pine; prior to 1957 and from 1984 to 1987, also includes lodgepole pine.

[2] Beginning 1984, includes black and tupelo gum.

[3] Change in Forest Service sample of establishments and estimating procedures in this year.

[4] A large number of revisions of previously published figures occurred in this year, as a result of a reconciliation among *Current Industrial Reports* (series MA24T), the 1992 Census of Manufactures, and state sawmill directories.

[5] Separate data not available; included in totals, series Db432–433.

[6] Excludes hard maple.

Sources

1869–1945: U.S. Forest Service, *Lumber Production in the United States, 1799–1946* (U.S. Department of Agriculture, 1948); 1946–1956: U.S. Bureau of the Census, *Facts for Industry* (annual); 1957–1996: U.S. Bureau of Census, *Current Industrial Reports*, Series MA24T, "Lumber Production and Mill Stocks" (annual).

TABLE Db446–453   Production, exports, and imports of pulpwood, woodpulp, paper and board, and newsprint: 1809–1999

Contributed by Gavin Wright

	Pulpwood			Woodpulp			Paper and board, domestic production	Newsprint, domestic production
	Domestic production	Imports	Exports	Domestic production	Imports	Exports		
	Db446	Db447 [1]	Db448	Db449	Db450 [1]	Db451	Db452	Db453
Year	Thousand cords	Thousand cords	Thousand cords	Thousand tons	Thousand tons	Thousand tons	Thousand tons	Thousand metric tons
1809	—	—	—	—	—	—	3	—
1819	—	—	—	—	—	—	12	—
1839	—	—	—	—	—	—	38	—
1849	—	—	—	—	—	—	78	—
1859	—	—	—	—	—	—	127	—
1869	2	—	—	1	—	—	386	—
1879	41	—	—	23	—	—	452	—
1889	583	—	—	306	—	—	935	—
1899	1,617	369	—	1,180	37	—	2,168	—
1904	2,477	574	—	1,922	169	—	3,107	—
1905	2,547	645	—	—	—	—	—	—
1906	2,922	739	—	—	—	—	—	—
1907	3,037	925	—	2,548	284	—	—	—
1908	2,652	695	—	2,119	239	—	—	—
1909	3,095	910	—	2,496	361	—	4,121	—
1910	3,160	930	—	2,534	498	—	—	—
1911	3,440	890	—	2,686	553	—	—	—
1912	—	—	—	—	526	—	—	—
1913	—	—	—	—	522	—	—	—
1914	3,470	1,000	—	2,893	663	—	5,153	—
1915	—	—	—	—	548	—	—	—
1916	4,130	1,100	—	3,435	644	—	—	—
1917	4,450	1,030	—	3,510	639	—	5,804	—
1918	3,880	1,370	—	3,314	556	—	5,938	—
1919	4,430	1,045	—	3,518	596	—	5,966	—
1920	4,875	1,240	—	3,822	874	—	7,185	—
1921	3,475	1,080	—	2,876	669	—	5,333	—
1922	4,535	1,010	—	3,522	1,234	—	6,875	—
1923	4,540	1,335	—	3,789	1,360	—	7,871	—
1924	4,515	1,250	—	3,723	1,491	—	7,930	—
1925	4,625	1,470	—	3,962	1,626	—	9,002	—
1926	5,405	1,365	—	4,395	1,697	—	9,794	—
1927	5,215	1,540	—	4,313	1,644	—	10,002	—
1928	5,640	1,520	—	4,511	1,721	—	10,403	—
1929	6,345	1,300	—	4,863	1,827	—	11,140	—
1930	5,745	1,450	—	4,630	1,782	—	10,169	—
1931	5,780	940	—	4,409	1,543	—	9,382	—
1932	5,015	620	—	3,760	1,434	—	7,998	—
1933	5,870	710	—	4,276	1,862	—	9,190	—
1934	5,840	960	—	4,436	1,663	—	9,187	—

Note appears at end of table

(continued)

TABLE Db446-453   Production, exports, and imports of pulpwood, woodpulp, paper and board, and newsprint: 1809-1999   *Continued*

	Pulpwood			Woodpulp			Paper and board, domestic production	Newsprint, domestic production
	Domestic production	Imports	Exports	Domestic production	Imports	Exports		
	Db446	Db447 [1]	Db448	Db449	Db450 [1]	Db451	Db452	Db453
Year	Thousand cords	Thousand cords	Thousand cords	Thousand tons	Thousand tons	Thousand tons	Thousand tons	Thousand metric tons
1935	6,620	1,010	—	4,926	1,761	—	10,479	827
1936	7,525	1,190	—	5,695	2,084	—	11,976	836
1937	8,895	1,500	—	6,573	2,072	—	12,837	858
1938	7,955	1,240	—	5,934	1,570	—	11,381	744
1939	9,735	1,080	—	6,993	1,887	—	13,510	852
1940	12,370	1,375	—	8,960	744	—	14,484	919
1941	14,175	1,560	—	10,375	829	—	17,762	921
1942	14,905	1,660	—	10,783	858	—	17,084	865
1943	13,580	1,355	—	9,680	1,005	—	17,036	730
1944	15,350	1,350	—	10,108	853	—	17,183	653
1945	15,255	1,520	—	10,167	1,619	—	17,371	657
1946	16,965	1,675	—	10,607	1,766	—	19,278	699
1947	18,545	1,750	—	11,946	2,192	—	21,102	749
1948	20,025	1,980	—	12,872	2,082	—	21,897	787
1949	17,620	1,410	—	12,207	1,641	—	20,315	816
1950	20,715	1,410	25	14,849	2,385	96	24,375	921
1951	25,130	2,510	15	16,524	2,361	202	26,047	1,021
1952	25,045	2,125	15	16,473	1,937	212	24,418	1,041
1953	26,320	1,550	10	17,537	2,158	162	26,605	983
1954	26,970	1,605	40	18,302	2,051	442	28,876	1,099
1955	30,950	1,765	60	20,740	2,214	631	30,178	1,408
1956	35,195	1,870	110	22,131	2,332	525	31,441	1,558
1957	34,420	1,765	100	21,800	2,101	622	30,666	1,657
1958	33,240	1,370	100	21,796	2,105	515	30,823	1,595
1959	36,715	1,175	120	24,383	2,431	653	34,015	1,782
1960	40,010	1,320	160	25,316	2,389	1,142	34,444	1,849
1961	40,270	1,350	190	26,523	2,467	1,178	35,749	1,900
1962	42,770	1,405	115	27,908	2,789	1,186	37,541	1,954
1963	44,710	1,635	90	30,121	2,775	1,422	39,230	2,012
1964	48,600	1,470	75	32,415	2,942	1,580	41,703	2,051
1965	52,320	1,305	155	33,993	3,130	1,402	44,080	1,978
1966	56,070	1,385	280	36,603	3,357	1,572	47,113	2,185
1967	57,470	1,590	640	36,677	3,170	1,721	49,926	2,377
1968	61,670	1,425	1,190	40,892	3,532	1,902	51,245	2,663
1969	66,910	980	1,660	42,813	4,040	2,103	54,187	2,932
1970	70,460	1,120	1,965	43,546	3,518	3,095	53,516	3,003
1971	68,340	1,225	1,530	43,903	3,515	1,275	55,086	2,990
1972	71,250	1,020	1,975	46,767	3,728	2,252	59,457	3,175
1973	77,170	1,200	2,670	48,327	4,002	2,344	61,304	3,084
1974	81,850	965	3,135	48,349	4,123	2,802	59,930	3,230
1975	69,030	765	2,645	43,084	3,078	2,782	52,521	3,348
1976	77,410	1,115	3,270	47,721	3,727	2,518	59,898	3,389
1977	79,770	1,350	3,370	49,132	3,871	2,640	62,722	3,511
1978	80,080	1,675	3,055	50,020	4,023	2,599	64,333	3,418
1979	86,200	1,405	3,790	51,177	4,318	2,935	66,329	3,716
1980	88,590	1,590	3,700	52,958	4,051	3,806	65,834	4,238
1981	85,250	1,490	2,955	52,790	4,087	3,678	66,440	4,752
1982	81,730	1,405	2,355	50,986	3,656	3,395	62,699	4,574
1983	87,520	1,715	2,040	54,055	4,093	3,644	68,801	4,688
1984	91,540	1,825	1,920	57,747	4,490	3,594	72,099	5,025
1985	87,330	650	1,870	57,693	4,466	3,796	70,654	4,924
1986	93,380	630	1,945	60,562	4,594	4,459	74,090	5,108
1987	95,820	430	2,015	62,392	4,848	4,869	77,591	5,300
1988	95,030	735	2,765	63,798	4,938	5,528	79,617	5,427
1989	93,831	988	2,204	62,598	5,004	5,766	78,573	5,523
1990	93,936	917	2,293	63,649	4,893	5,905	80,445	5,997
1991	93,246	1,025	2,346	64,237	4,997	6,338	81,234	6,206
1992	95,239	857	2,453	65,943	5,029	7,222	84,701	6,425
1993	92,759	745	2,509	63,505	5,413	6,499	86,693	6,412
1994	95,327	544	2,612	65,095	5,650	6,728	91,109	6,335

Note appears at end of table

TABLE Db446–453   Production, exports, and imports of pulpwood, woodpulp, paper and board, and newsprint: 1809–1999   Continued

Year	Pulpwood — Domestic production Db446	Pulpwood — Imports Db447 [1]	Pulpwood — Exports Db448	Woodpulp — Domestic production Db449	Woodpulp — Imports Db450 [1]	Woodpulp — Exports Db451	Paper and board, domestic production Db452	Newsprint, domestic production Db453
	Thousand cords	Thousand cords	Thousand cords	Thousand tons	Thousand tons	Thousand tons	Thousand tons	Thousand metric tons
1995	99,258	303	2,290	65,789	5,969	8,621	91,369	6,352
1996	92,560	334	2,527	64,191	5,691	7,170	92,054	6,304
1997	87,400	357	3,083	64,254	6,397	6,990	95,127	—
1998	85,335	231	3,011	65,163	5,984	6,025	94,526	—
1999	82,912	144	3,084	62,914	6,650	5,438	96,611	—

[1] Through 1949, data are net imports; export data not available separately.

Sources

Series Db446, Db449, and Db452. 1809–1949: U.S. Bureau of the Census, *Census of Manufactures*, various reports; *Facts for Industry* (annual); unpublished U.S. Forest Service data used for 1905, 1916–1918, and 1920; 1950–1994: *U.S. Timber Production, Trade, Consumption, and Price Statistics 1955–1980*, updated for 1960–1988, and 1965–1999 (U.S. Department of Agriculture).

Series Db447–448 and Db450–451. 1899–1946: U.S. Bureau of the Census, *Foreign Commerce and Navigation of the United States* (annual); 1947–1949: U.S. Bureau of the Census, *U.S. Imports of Merchandise for Consumption*, and *U.S. Exports of Domestic and Foreign Merchandise*; 1950–1994: *U.S. Timber Production, Trade, Consumption, and Price Statistics 1950–1980*, updated for 1960–1988, and 1965–1994 (U.S. Department of Agriculture); 1995–1997: U.S. Forest Service, as reported in *Statistical Abstract of the United States 1998*.

Series Db453. 1935–1993: U.S. Bureau of Economic Analysis, *Survey of Current Business* (monthly); 1994–1996: American Forest and Paper Association (AFPA), *Statistics of Paper, Paperboard, and Wood Pulp* (AFPA, annual).

Documentation

Pulpwood refers to woods used in the making of pulp for paper. Woodpulp refers to the pulp extracted from wood via mechanical or chemical processes and then used to make paper and other products.

Series Db447–448 and Db450–451. For nearly all years, statistics are based on a mail canvass of woodpulp and paper producers.

Series Db453. Data are from trade associations and cover virtually the entire industry in the United States, including Alaska beginning in 1961.

TABLE Db454–457   Stumpage prices, by selected species: 1910–1999

Contributed by Gavin Wright

Year	Douglas fir Db454	Southern pine Db455	Sugar pine Db456	Ponderosa pine Db457	Year	Douglas fir Db454	Southern pine Db455	Sugar pine Db456	Ponderosa pine Db457
	Dollars per thousand board feet	Dollars per thousand board feet	Dollars per thousand board feet	Dollars per thousand board feet		Dollars per thousand board feet	Dollars per thousand board feet	Dollars per thousand board feet	Dollars per thousand board feet
1910	2.2	1.5	4.3	3.6	1930	3.3	3.2	6.3	3.6
1911	2.3	2.8	2.5	2.5	1931	2.9	3.4	4.6	4.2
1912	2.3	1.5	3.5	2.7	1932	1.7	2.8	3.7	2.6
1913	1.7	1.7	3.3	2.2	1933	1.2	2.7	—	—
1914	1.6	2.9	3.0	2.0	1934	1.5	2.9	3.5	2.5
1915	2.9	2.1	3.4	2.5	1935	1.7	4.5	3.1	2.4
1916	1.2	3.2	3.5	2.9	1936	2.1	—	2.8	2.2
1917	1.6	3.4	2.8	2.2	1937	1.6	5.3	2.8	2.2
1918	1.8	3.0	3.4	2.7	1938	2.5	7.3	3.5	2.5
1919	2.4	3.7	3.4	3.0	1939	—	5.8	3.1	2.4
1920	1.8	4.4	5.0	3.7	1940	2.3	4.5	3.0	2.2
1921	1.9	3.7	4.2	3.2	1941	3.6	10.8	3.4	2.6
1922	2.5	2.8	3.8	4.0	1942	—	8.9	4.8	2.7
1923	2.5	3.0	4.4	3.9	1943	—	8.7	4.2	5.0
1924	2.2	3.5	4.2	3.5	1944	5.2	10.9	5.2	4.0
1925	2.1	3.2	4.4	3.6	1945	5.0	9.3	7.3	5.6
1926	2.2	3.6	4.5	3.7	1946	6.6	8.9	7.2	5.8
1927	2.5	3.5	4.0	3.4	1947	9.9	10.9	12.5	8.3
1928	2.9	3.6	3.2	2.5	1948	19.9	16.4	16.2	14.6
1929	2.7	3.5	4.6	3.6	1949	11.1	19.7	18.9	17.6

(continued)

TABLE Db454–457   Stumpage prices, by selected species: 1910–1999   *Continued*

Year	Douglas fir Db454 Dollars per thousand board feet	Southern pine Db455 Dollars per thousand board feet	Sugar pine Db456 Dollars per thousand board feet	Ponderosa pine Db457 Dollars per thousand board feet	Year	Douglas fir Db454 Dollars per thousand board feet	Southern pine Db455 Dollars per thousand board feet	Sugar pine Db456 Dollars per thousand board feet	Ponderosa pine Db457 Dollars per thousand board feet
1950	16.4	26.7	25.0	18.3	1975	169.5	57.0	99.2	71.2
1951	25.4	34.6	40.4	33.6	1976	176.2	87.0	187.2	101.8
1952	25.8	38.5	36.4	27.4	1977	225.9	100.3	169.6	131.4
1953	20.2	34.2	30.2	25.9	1978	250.3	134.5	159.6	164.7
1954	16.2	29.7	31.2	27.2	1979	394.4	155.2	365.0	239.0
1955	28.9	32.0	30.0	26.1	1980	432.2	155.4	666.6	206.1
1956	37.7	37.4	34.9	27.2	1981	350.2	172.0	225.2	195.2
1957	26.2	31.5	30.0	24.2	1982	118.2	127.2	71.9	66.9
1958	21.8	31.1	23.5	19.1	1983	161.6	140.6	137.7	104.0
1959	36.8	35.2	26.7	20.6	1984	132.9	139.4	84.3	122.7
1960	32.0	34.5	29.0	19.1	1985	126.2	90.7	109.7	101.4
1961	27.6	26.8	18.4	12.1	1986	160.7	103.6	169.6	156.6
1962	24.8	26.0	20.0	16.1	1987	190.2	135.7	287.6	209.3
1963	27.9	25.1	19.2	15.8	1988	256.0	141.9	260.4	182.1
1964	38.1	27.8	23.3	19.0	1989	389.8	131.4	289.0	292.0
1965	42.6	31.7	23.3	19.8	1990	466.4	126.7	285.0	252.2
1966	50.0	38.6	24.9	19.8	1991	395.0	166.1	241.0	237.6
1967	41.7	38.3	23.5	22.2	1992	477.2	198.4	492.0	292.3
1968	61.2	42.2	35.0	30.2	1993	317.8	217.2	598.0	535.2
1969	82.2	51.7	75.2	71.0	1994	453.0	265.9	625.0	291.4
1970	41.9	44.1	38.5	32.1	1995	453.5	248.5	397.0	149.9
1971	49.0	52.2	48.0	37.6	1996	453.0	251.1	318.0	270.0
1972	71.7	65.6	66.2	65.8	1997	331.4	307.3	—	270.2
1973	138.1	93.4	89.2	92.3	1998	254.2	287.8	—	204.9
1974	202.4	76.2	104.0	100.6	1999	314.7	268.5	—	181.0

Sources

1910–1949: U.S. Forest Service, *The Demand and Price Situation for Forest Products* (U.S. Department of Agriculture, 1963); 1950–1994: U.S. Forest Service, *U.S. Timber Production, Trade, Consumption, and Price Statistics, 1950–1985*, updated to 1960–1988, and 1965–1999 (U.S. Department of Agriculture).

Documentation

National Forest prices are for timber sold on a Scribner Decimal C log rule basis, except in the Northeastern states where international 1/4-inch log rule is used. Prices include specified road costs and kilovolt payments and exclude timber sold by land exchanges and from land utilization project lands. Prior to 1984, prices are statistical high bid prices. Beginning in 1984, data are high bid prices that include specified road costs.

Series Db454. Douglas fir prices are for western Washington and western Oregon.

Series Db455. Southern pine figures include privately owned second growth southern pine timber prior to 1935.

Series Db456–457. Sugar and ponderosa pine prices represent national-forest sales for these species in the Pacific Southwest region (prior to 1979 called the California region).

CHAPTER Dc

Construction, Housing, and Mortgages

Editor: Kenneth A. Snowden

CONSTRUCTION, HOUSING, AND MORTGAGES

Kenneth A. Snowden

Construction is the fabrication of new buildings and structures or the substantial modification of those that were previously built. These activities are ordinary, everyday features of our landscape – houses are built, neighborhood schools are renovated, shopping complexes take shape, industrial plants are erected, and roads are improved. Buildings and structures are familiar because they represent the basic physical infrastructure used to house and to move all persons, goods, and services. The statistics presented in this chapter document the role that construction has played in the American economy for more than a century. The first two groups of tables include series that measure aggregate construction and its major components (Tables Dc1–255 and Dc256–509). In the last two sections of the chapter, the focus is sharpened to residential housing and series that document how we have built, occupied, owned, and financed this most enduring symbol of the American Dream (Tables Dc510–902 and Dc903–1288).

The goal is to present historical series related to construction, housing, and mortgages, and to connect these series to similar data from the modern period. Along these lines, a special focus of this chapter is to connect the official "value-in-place" construction output series that are currently compiled by the U.S. Bureau of the Census to their pre-1964 counterparts that are no longer updated or supported by the Bureau. The last section of this essay provides an overview of this issue.

Construction as Investment

Every society faces a fundamental trade-off: by consuming less of its output today, it can produce and consume more in future periods. The choice arises because some goods that could be produced today, such as machines, houses, or roads, will yield productive services many years into the future. These are referred to as "real" investment goods. When society allocates scarce resources to produce these types of goods, it must reduce the amount of resources

it uses to produce goods that will be consumed today. Investment goods that were produced in the past and that remain productive today are collectively referred to as the nation's capital stock. The buildings and structures represented in this chapter comprise the largest single component of the capital stock in the United States.

To appreciate the magnitudes involved, consider that total U.S. output in 1999 was just less than $9.3 trillion (output measured here by gross domestic product, GDP). More than 9 percent of this output – some $0.85 trillion – was invested in buildings and structures. At the end of the year, moreover, the value of the stock of usable buildings and structures was $20.5 trillion, or more than double the value of the total output produced during the year. Importantly, 1999 was not an exceptional year. Between 1929 and 1999 an average of one out of every ten dollars of output in the United States was spent on construction investment. Over the same period, the value of buildings and structures has been, on average, 2.5 times larger than the value of annual output.

Simon Kuznets's (1961) groundbreaking investigation of the history of the American capital stock revealed that investment in buildings and structures represented an even larger share of aggregate activity before 1929. Kuznets's annual estimates of construction output for the 1889–1955 period are presented in Tables Dc78–105; they are shown in Figure Dc-A as shares of total current-dollar output (gross national product, GNP) for overlapping decades that run from 1869–1878 to 1944–1953. These data show that a peak in the relative importance of construction occurred between 1884 and 1908, when nearly one out of every six dollars of output was invested in buildings and structures.

The surge in construction that Kuznets identified suggests that investment in building and structures played a key role in late nineteenth-century economic growth. Not surprisingly, the connection between the two has been an active area of research ever since. A primary focus has been on investments that were made during the period in transportation, communications, and city building. Fogel (1964) initiated a major debate when he measured the broad social benefits that were attributable to investments in railroads, while others compared these social benefits to the costs of the subsidies that were used to encourage their expansion (Fishlow 2000 provides a survey). The reduction in transport costs attributable to the railroad has also been linked to the nation's emerging leadership in manufacturing and to improvements in business organization

Acknowledgments

Ken Snowden thanks Lyda Bigelow and Lee Wright for assistance in the preparation of Tables Dc1–509. The Center for Real Estate and Urban Economics, University of California at Berkeley, and a Joseph M. Bryan School of Business and Economics research award provided financial support for this work. Snowden acknowledges Dr. Ellen Merry of the Division of Research and Statistics at the Board of Governors of the Federal Reserve System for guidance

and documentation on Table Dc950–982; David Middaugh of the Department of Housing and Urban Development (HUD) for supplying the Survey of Mortgage Lending Activity data files and background information used in Tables Dc996–1104; and Dr. William F. Shaw (HUD and Federal Housing Authority) and Kathleen Mangold (Department of Veterans Affairs) for unpublished data and valuable guidance used to prepare Table Dc1105–1121.

Percent

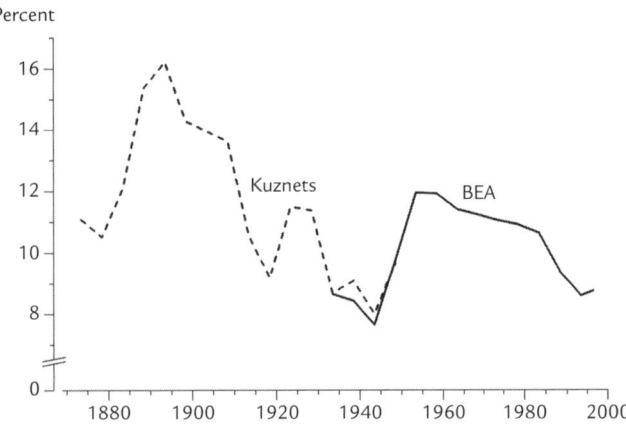

FIGURE Dc-A Gross construction as a share of gross national product: 1869–1999

Sources

Simon Kuznets, *Capital in the American Economy: Its Formation and Financing* (Princeton University Press, 1961), Tables R-11 and R-14, pp. 520 and 524. Data downloaded from the Internet site of the U.S. Bureau of Economic Analysis (BEA), June 28, 2002: Table 1.3, "Gross Domestic Product by Major Type of Product," and Table 1.9 "Relation of Gross Domestic Product, Gross National Product, Net National Product, National Income, and Personal Income."

Documentation

Shares are computed from figures expressed in current dollars. The values displayed are for overlapping decades: 1869–1878, 1874–1883, and so forth, ending with a six-year period for 1994–1999. The midpoint of each period is used to plot the values on the graph.

during the period (Chandler 1959; Atack 1985; Wright 1990). Field (1987, 1992) extends the argument to show that nineteenth-century investments in transportation and communication (for example, the telegraph) improved both financial market efficiency and inventory management practices. Rapid urbanization during the late nineteenth century, meanwhile, required substantial investments in housing, transportation, and facilities for education and public health (Gaspari and Woolf 1985; Snowden 1987; Troesken 1999; see Cain 1997 for a survey). In this chapter, series that measure construction investment for broad sectors and aggregates back to the late nineteenth century are presented in Tables Dc78–131 and Dc510–530.[1]

Kuznets's data have been extended in Figure Dc-A with decadal shares of construction between 1929 and 1999 that have been calculated from official national income statistics. The modern data make the sustained surge in building activity between 1880 and 1910 look even more singular, episodic, and remarkable, as construction claimed 14 percent or more of total output for nearly the entire period. In contrast, investment in building and structures represented an average of 10 percent of output between 1910 and 1990, and wandered above and below this average for extended periods of time.

During the 1930s and 1940s, for example, the construction sector saw its share of total output fall far below its long-term average. This resulted from two sharp collapses in construction expenditure – by a little more than 60 percent between 1929 and 1933, and a little less than 60 percent between 1941 and 1944.

The earlier decline has been blamed on the residential construction boom of the 1920s, which, it is alleged, left the economy with an excess supply of housing at the end of the 1920s, and with prospects for only a slow recovery for the remainder of the 1930s (Hickman 1973; Mercer and Morgan 1973). The decline in residential construction, in fact, was staggering. Constant-dollar residential construction fell by 80 percent between 1929 and 1933, and the sector had not fully recovered even by 1939 (see Tables Dc256–271 and Dc510–530). However, the housing sector was not unique. Nonresidential building and public utility construction also decreased by 80 percent between 1929 and 1933, and both recovered more slowly than residential housing (see Tables Dc282–302 and Dc321–338). The collapse in private construction activity during the 1930s was systemic and profound, and is likely to stimulate continued discussion and explanation. The collapse in private construction between 1941 and 1944, on the other hand, was nearly as severe, but was clearly attributable to the exigencies of war.

The decline in the share of total construction in aggregate output between 1929 and 1948 would have been even more severe had public investments in building and structures not increased and partially offset the severe decline in private construction. The impacts of the Great Depression on public and private construction were so different, in fact, that the composition of the nation's stock of buildings and structures changed rapidly and permanently. Figure Dc-B shows the shares of building and structures that were privately and publicly owned (separate shares shown for private residential and private nonresidential). Eighty-five percent of the total was in private hands in 1925, with equal shares dedicated to residential and nonresidential uses. Over the next twenty years the share of publicly owned buildings and structures increased by 10 percentage points while the share of private nonresidential building and structures decreased by the same amount. Although the expansion of military infrastructure during World War II played a role in the transition, most of the change had already occurred during the 1930s. Moreover, after the public share of buildings and structures fell for a few years immediately following the war, it gradually increased throughout the 1950s and 1960s because of increased public investments in highways and educational facilities (see Tables Dc351–509). As a result, by 1975 the publicly

Percent

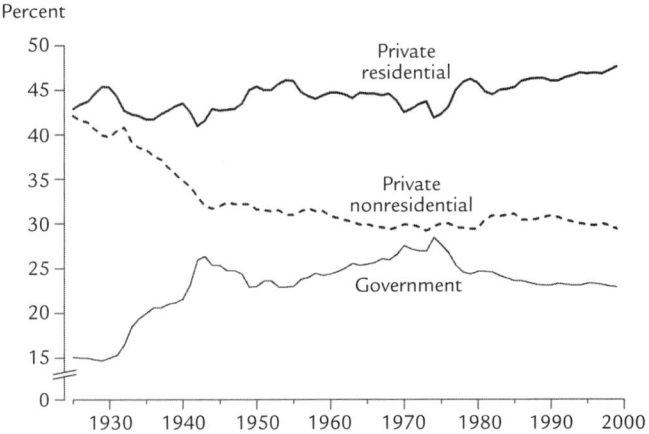

FIGURE Dc-B Composition of the net stock of structures: 1925–1999

Sources

Series Dc55–56 and Dc62.

---

[1] Those interested in data for more specific types of investments during the period should consult Ulmer (1960) and Lipsey and Preston (1966).

owned stock of buildings and structures had become nearly equal in size to the privately owned stock that was held for nonresidential uses.

The surge in public infrastructure investment during the 1950s, combined with a robust homebuilding industry, produced a postwar "golden age" for the American construction industry. Between 1950 and 1965 investment in new buildings and structures grew apace with real GDP and claimed a share of output that was higher than it had been since the 1920s (refer to Figure Dc-A). During the late 1960s, however, the share of construction in output began to fall, and then declined for twenty-five years. The decrease in the relative importance of construction after 1970 can be measured either in current dollars (as in Figure Dc-A) or in constant dollars (see Table Dc44–53). By either measure, construction activity represented a smaller share of output during the 1990s than it did at any other time in the twentieth century except the 1930s and 1940s.

As the importance of total construction decreased through the 1970s and 1980s, so did the share of buildings and structures that were publicly owned (see Figure Dc-B). The major part of this decline was related to reduced levels of investment in transportation, education, and public health facilities. As we have seen, similar types of infrastructure investments appear to have supported rapid economic growth during the late nineteenth century. Aschauer (1989) reversed the logic for the modern era by connecting the decline in public infrastructure investment that began in the 1970s to a simultaneous slowdown in aggregate productivity growth. His conjecture stimulated a heated discussion about the impact of infrastructure investments on growth that occupied the academic and policymaking communities; Gramlich (1994) reviews this debate and finds that it was inconclusive. However, for a few years construction was once again on center stage.

Construction, Long Swings, and the Business Cycle

John Maynard Keynes argued during the 1930s that changes in the amount of investment spending played a critical role in propagating economy-wide fluctuations in production, income, and employment. Given their own Depression-era perspective, it was natural for investigators in the United States to focus more narrowly on the role that construction investment played in the business cycle. Through their efforts, several indexes of total building activity that reached well back into the nineteenth century were compiled; most are presented and described in Table Dc78–91. One of them is shown in Figure Dc-C for the period between 1830 and 1933. Also shown in the figure is a similar "building index" running from 1920 to 1999 that has been fashioned out of three distinct segments of the Census Bureau's constant-dollar, value-in-place measure of total construction activity. These two series summarize much of what we know about annual fluctuations in aggregate construction activity over the past 170 years.

On the basis of similar evidence, Alvin Hansen (1964) argued that a fifteen- to eighteen-year "building cycle" had been a key determinant of the depth and severity of business cycle contractions in the United States before 1940. He noted, in particular, that all three "super-depressions" during the period (those beginning in 1873, 1893, and 1929) had occurred just after a peak in the building cycle, while four relatively mild contractions (those in 1882, 1907, 1920,

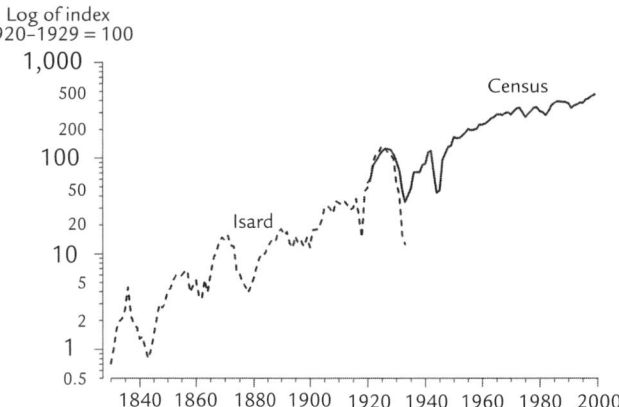

FIGURE Dc-C Indexes of construction activity: 1830–1999

Sources

Isard: 1830–1933, series Dc108. U.S. Census Bureau's value-in-place series: series Dc22 for 1920–1946, series Dc33 for 1947–1963, and series Dc44 for 1964–1999, with the series linked at 1947 and 1964 to form an index with the same base as the Isard series (1920–1929 = 100).

Documentation

See Tables Dc22–53 and Dc106–131 for details. The indexes are graphed on a logarithmic scale.

and 1937) had occurred when building activity was on a long-term upswing. From a broader perspective, Moses Abramovitz (1964, 1968) argued that the historical building cycle had been integral to the "long swing" movement of aggregate growth rates in the United States between 1840 and 1914. Abramovitz described these fluctuations as sequences of short spurts (two to four years) of vigorous growth, followed by seven to eleven years of steady but declining growth during which population-sensitive and transportation-related construction spending reached "towering heights." Each long swing ended with a severe depression in construction that lasted four to seven years and, as Hansen observed, a severe general business cycle contraction.

Hansen and Abramovitz were not alone; the behavior of construction was central to most early thinking about the American business cycle (see also, for example, Clark 1935; Silberling 1943; and, for a critical view, Colean and Newcomb 1952). Nowadays, building cycles and long swings play virtually no role in business cycle theory. The reason for the change can be clearly seen in Figure Dc-C: the building cycle or long swing disappeared after World War II. Abramovitz (1968) attributed its "passing" to changes in the demographic forces that determined residential housing demand (free immigration was shut off in the 1920s), and to changes in the structure of private business investment (the railroads were no longer dominant). Hickman (1973) examined the historical pattern of building starts (presented here in Tables Dc510–553), and found support for Abramovitz's conjecture that immigration restrictions were responsible in part for the disappearance of the long swing in residential housing.

Even though building cycles or long swings have diminished, we continue to examine the impact that changes in broad construction aggregates have on more general macroeconomic conditions. Most notably, Gordon and Veitch (1986) found that changes in building and structures investment between 1919 and 1983 were autonomous shocks that originated within the construction sector, not responses to general business conditions. Green (1997) found that residential construction leads the general business cycle, whereas nonfarm business construction tends to lag it. It makes sense to focus on the macroeconomic impacts of the homebuilding sector, in any case, because it is the largest component of the construction industry. Investigators in the modern era tend to explain changes in the volume of residential construction activity as a response to changes in the supply, cost, and availability of mortgage credit and, therefore, to monetary policy (Swan 1970; Jaffee and Rosen 1979; Ryding 1990). However, whatever causes them to change, a variety of statistical measures of residential construction activity besides actual expenditures (see Tables Dc256–281) is regularly used to assess general macroeconomic conditions – housing starts (Tables Dc510–565), new house completions and sales (Tables Dc566–652), and housing vacancies (Table Dc810–825).

In recent years, construction statistics have also figured prominently in literature that assesses changes in the severity of the American business cycle over time. Christina Romer (1986, 1989) started this line of inquiry by challenging the evidence that had been used for decades to show that the U.S. economy had become more stable after World War II than it had been before World War I. Balke and Gordon (1989) countered that Romer's argument relied too heavily on a commodity output series and ignored high-quality series that measured output for the construction, transportation, and communication sectors (see Table Dc106–131). Balke and Gordon used these data to derive a new historical GNP series that supported the conventional view that aggregate output was more volatile before 1929 than after World War II (see Series Ca213-215). Particularly important, it turned out, was the reduction in the volatility of construction after World War II that was described earlier in this essay. Stock and Watson reached a similar conclusion for the modern era. They report evidence that a discrete reduction in general macroeconomic variability that occurred around 1985 was attributable in part to a marked reduction in the variability of construction around the same time (Stock and Watson 2002).

Housing Trends and Patterns

The first enumeration of dwelling units in the United States was conducted within the Population Census of 1890; in that year 12.7 million units were occupied by slightly fewer than 63 million persons. By 1990 the population had nearly quadrupled, but the number of occupied housing units had increased sevenfold to nearly 92 million. In the first decadal Census of Housing (1940), the Census Bureau began to collect information about the characteristics of housing units in addition to just counting them. We learned in that year, for example, that 64 percent of the nation's housing units were detached, single-family homes – that share increased to nearly 70 percent by 1960, before falling back to 60 percent by 1999 owing to the increasing importance of multifamily units and mobile homes. Largely because of the efforts of the Census Bureau, our knowledge about the places we call home has increased steadily, especially over the past century.[2]

Tables Dc653–669 and Dc683–696 provide national and regional totals of the number and types of occupied and vacant housing units over the past century. More detailed information about characteristics of the housing stock is available in the decadal

TABLE Dc-D   Housing characteristics: 1940–1990

		Percentage of households			
Year	Lacking complete plumbing facilities	In crowded units (more than one person per room)	In single-person household	Heating with fuel oil, coal, or wood	Without a telephone
1940	45.3	20.2	7.7	87.5	—
1950	35.5	15.7	9.3	67.2	—
1960	16.8	11.5	13.3	48.8	21.5
1970	6.9	8.2	17.6	30.2	13.0
1980	2.7	4.5	22.7	22.0	7.1
1990	1.1	4.9	24.6	16.7	5.2

Source

U.S. Census Bureau, "Housing: Then and Now – 50 Years of Decennial Censuses," U.S. Census Bureau's Web site, accessed May 2003.

Censuses of Housing Data and in the biennial American Housing Survey that has been conducted by the U.S. Department of Housing and Urban Development since 1973. A sample of the information available about the housing stock is shown in Table Dc-D. During the half-century covered in this table, the nation's housing units became less crowded, were heated with safer and cleaner fuels, and almost universally came to offer modern plumbing and communication facilities.

The quality of a housing unit is determined by many more of its characteristics than those shown in Table Dc-D – it also depends, of course, on the attributes of the property, the neighborhood, and the general locale where the unit is situated. In the housing market, the value of all of these characteristics is captured in a single number – the market price of the housing unit (Kain and Quigley 1970; Kutty 1999). This feature of housing prices must be kept in mind when using or interpreting the single-family home price indexes that are included in this chapter (Tables Dc826–878). These series measure national or regional trends in average home prices for both new and existing homes, but they are not all designed to capture the same information. Indexes such as series Dc829 and Dc863 measure changes in the average prices of homes that were actually built or sold within a given year; these indexes capture changes in both the characteristics of the average home and the implicit market price of these characteristics. Other indexes, such as series Dc597 and Dc869, capture only changes in the prices of characteristics by tracking the price of homes whose characteristics do not change.[3]

However they are measured, general movements in single-family home prices have a profound impact on households throughout the economy. Changes in home prices could affect some households as they decide whether to rent or buy a home; for many others, a change in home prices affects the amount of wealth they hold in the form of residential property. In this chapter, residential wealth series are presented for 1889–1953 (Table Dc879–888) and for 1925–1999 (Table Dc889–902). The stakes are large when residential wealth changes – during the 1990s residential wealth represented nearly 60 percent of the nonfinancial wealth of households and more than 30 percent of their total wealth (Aizcorbe, Kennickell, and Moore 2003). Because it is so large in amount and so widely distributed, residential housing wealth has recently been examined

---

[2] To read more about the historical development of housing statistics in the United States, refer to Colean (1944), Housing and Home Finance Agency (1948), Grebler, Blank, and Winnick (1956), and Beyer (1965). For the modern era, refer to Simmons (2001).

[3] More detailed information concerning the appropriate interpretation and uses of the home price indexes presented in this chapter can be found in the table documentation, and in Wallace (1996) and Englund, Quigley, and Redfearn (1999).

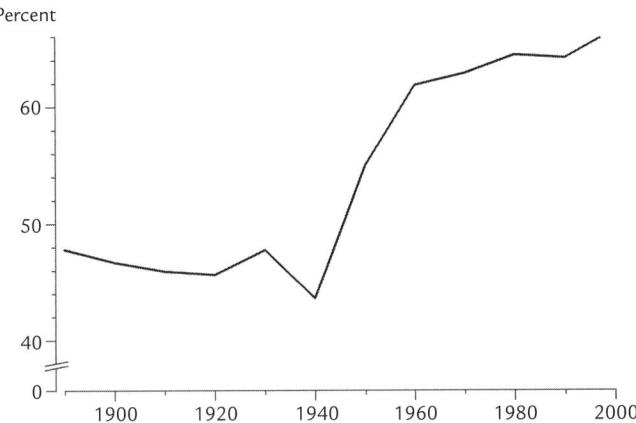

FIGURE Dc-E   Homeownership – owner-occupied units as a percentage of all occupied housing units: 1900–1990

Sources
Series Dc729 expressed as a percentage of series Dc713.

as a determinant of household decisions concerning consumption, saving, and retirement planning (Haines and Goodman 1993; Skinner 1996; Hoynes and McFadden 1997; Moore and Mitchell 2000). Changes in residential wealth have even been investigated as a determinant of household demand for corporate equity and, therefore, stock market prices (Case, Shiller, and Quigley 2001).

One must own a home to hold residential wealth, of course, and no other benchmark of economic and social well-being represents the aspirations of households in the United States better than homeownership. The proportion of households that owned their home is shown for each decade in the twentieth century in Figure Dc-E. The data reveal a surge in homeownership that begins in the middle decades of the century. Prior to 1940, between 45 and 50 percent of all households owned the dwelling in which they lived, but by 1960 the share of owner-occupants jumped to more than 60 percent, and from there gradually increased to just under two thirds by 1990.

Changes in the aggregate rate of homeownership such as these need to be interpreted carefully. The overall rate can change either because the proportion of homeowners has changed for specific groups within the population or because the relative importance of the specific groups has changed. The apparent stability of the aggregate homeownership rate between 1900 and 1930 shown in Figure Dc-E provides an interesting case in point. During this period the proportion of nonfarm households that owned their homes increased throughout the United States. At the same time, however, there was a decrease in the share of households living on farms. Because rates of homeownership were generally higher among farm households, the two developments had offsetting influences on the aggregate homeownership rate (Snowden 2003). Rates of homeownership are presented in Tables Dc697–809 for different regions, for farm and nonfarm families, for urban and rural areas, and for groups of different ages, races, ethnic background, and marital status.[4]

There is a well-established literature that investigates the causes of changes in homeownership rates over time and of differences in

homeownership rates across groups. Most of these studies examine household-level data so that tenure status can be explained by income, age, marital status, labor market experience, and race, among many other influences. Haines and Goodman (1992) tackle the issue for the late nineteenth century, for example, with survey data that were collected from urban industrial workers in 1889. Collins and Margo (2001) examine racial differences in homeownership rates across the entire twentieth century using household-level data that were drawn from the Integrated Public Use Microdata Samples of the decadal censuses; they also used these data to calculate the homeownership rates by racial group that appear in Table Dc761–780. Examinations of homeownership patterns for the modern era are too numerous to list here, but most attention has been spent trying to explain the persistent differences in rates of homeownership across racial groups and between native and immigrant households (Wachter and Megbolugbe 1992; Painter, Gabriel, and Myers 2001; Borjas 2002).

Government policy is generally acknowledged to have pushed homeownership rates higher in the United States during the twentieth century through favorable tax treatment of home mortgage interest paid by homeowners and the "rental" housing services that they receive (Martinez 2000). In recent years academicians and policymakers have confronted an interesting but difficult question: Do the social benefits that can be attributed to the increased rate of homeownership in the twentieth century justify the social costs of the related housing subsidies?[5]

The Residential Mortgage Market

Thirty-seven percent of nonfarm homes were owner-occupied in 1890, and fewer than three out of ten of them were mortgaged. By 1990, the homeownership rate had increased to 65 percent, and two thirds of these homes were mortgage-financed. Homeownership and the residential mortgage market have grown together in the United States over the past century – we have learned to live the American dream by borrowing it. The series in Tables Dc903–1288 document three distinct phases in the institutional development of the American residential mortgage market over the past century.

During the first phase, from the late 1800s to 1930, financial intermediaries displaced individual investors as the predominant source of residential mortgage finance. Mutual savings banks and building and loan associations were the first important institutional home mortgage lenders in the United States. Together, they held one third of the outstanding residential mortgage debt in 1900, but this still represented only two thirds of the amount held by individual investors. By 1930, the combined share of mutual savings banks and building and loans equaled that of noninstitutional investors (about 40 percent each), and all financial institutions taken together held 60 percent of the nation's residential mortgage debt. Mortgage lending shares before 1930 for a variety of institutions can be found in Table Dc903–928. Other annual series of mortgage holdings are available for this period but were not included in this chapter because they focus on particular institutions or groups of intermediaries.[6]

---

[4] Refer to Chevan (1989) or Bostic and Surrette (2001) to see how group-specific rates like these reveal important patterns and trends in homeownership over the past century.

[5] For a brief review, see Coulson (2002).

[6] See Lintner (1948), Payne and Davis (1956), and Olmstead (1976) for mutual savings banks; Zartman (1906) for life insurance companies; and Bodfish (1931) for building and loans.

We have access to detailed benchmark data from the historical mortgage market because the federal government conducted a series of national surveys of homeownership and indebtedness (in 1890 and 1920), of building and loan associations (in 1893), and of all outstanding mortgages (in 1890). These data provide snapshots of what Lance Davis (1965) identified as a segmented national mortgage market. Davis documented substantial variations in mortgage loan rates across regions of the country, and attributed the differences to legal and information-related barriers that restricted the geographic movement of funds. As a result, mortgage rates were low in the savings-rich East, and high in the South and West, where mortgage loan demand was strongest. Davis focused on segmentation in the farm loan market, but it turns out that the barriers between local and regional markets were even greater in the residential mortgage market (Snowden 1987, 1988, 1997).

The second phase in the development of the residential mortgage market, 1930–1970, can itself be broken into two segments. During the first fifteen years, the market was rapidly, and nearly completely, federalized; over the next quarter-century the new federal structure financed the greatest surge in homeownership in the nation's modern history. Federal involvement began early in the Depression when building and loan associations (B&Ls) advocated for the establishment of a Federal Home Loan Bank (FHLB) system to discount their mortgage loans and to act as a "lender of last resort" just as the Federal Reserve System did for commercial banks. B&Ls needed a separate facility, they argued, because they held long-term (ten- to twelve-year), fully amortized mortgage loans. Other lenders issued short-term mortgage loans that matured, and were rolled over, every three to five years. Nearly all members of the new FHLB system were B&Ls when it began operations in 1932. Soon thereafter, most of these institutions converted into savings and loan associations (S&Ls) that were federally regulated and issued federally insured deposit contracts, which became the predominant institutional home mortgage lenders in the post–World War II era (Snowden 2003).

The FHLB system figures prominently in this chapter because it produced a wealth of statistical data about the residential mortgage market. Its estimates of home mortgage loans held by institutional lenders between 1925 and 1950, for example, are embedded in Table Dc903–928. The FHLB also produced annual estimates of new residential mortgage loans made by each major group of institutional mortgage lenders – the earliest systematic record of mortgage loan originations that is available (see Table Dc983–989). Both data series were discontinued in 1950 when the Federal Reserve began to assemble more comprehensive estimates of outstanding residential mortgage debt (see Tables Dc929–982). However, the FHLB system continued to compile annual series on nonfarm mortgage loan recordings until 1964 (Table Dc990–995), and a nonfarm mortgage foreclosure index until 1975 (Table Dc1255–1270). Finally, beginning in 1963 the FHLB system established its Monthly Interest Rate Survey (MIRS), which remains the most comprehensive source of information on new, conventional mortgage interest rates and loan terms (Table Dc1210–1254).

The FHLB system was not established to collect data, of course. Its main focus was to regulate member institutions and to support them by making loans, which were called advances. FHLB advances provided S&Ls with liquidity in times of crisis, but were more regularly used as a roundabout secondary market – S&Ls could borrow against mortgages they had previously made and use these funds to make new mortgage loans. These advances were

then repaid when new funds flowed into the S&L from the savings deposit market. A more straightforward secondary market was established in 1938 in the form of the Federal National Mortgage Association (FNMA). FNMA bought and sold residential mortgage loans (only federally insured or guaranteed loans; see the next two paragraphs) from qualified institutional lenders – most FNMA business involved banks, life insurance companies, and mortgage companies that were not members of the FHLB system. A third federally financed secondary mortgage market facility was established in 1933 to serve an important, but temporary, function. Between 1933 and 1937 the Home Owners Loan Corporation (HOLC) bailed out financial institutions of all kinds by "buying" billions of dollars of mortgages from them. It did so, and saved many institutions from failure, by agreeing to refinance their weakest mortgage loans. The "secondary market" activities of each of these agencies – FHLB, FNMA, and HOLC – are presented in Table Dc1138–1153.

The federalization of the residential mortgage market during the 1930s also involved a change in the basic residential mortgage loan contract. The Federal Housing Authority (FHA) was established in 1933 with the authority to insure individual mortgage loans on single- and multifamily residential mortgage structures. FHA insurance required that the residential property securing the loan meet minimum safety, construction, and zoning standards. In this way the program sought to improve the quality of the nation's residential housing stock. Importantly, FHA-insured loans were structured quite differently from most conventional residential mortgage loans. They could be written for much higher loan-to-value ratios (so down payment requirements were reduced), for terms of twenty years or more (so monthly payments were reduced), and with full amortization (so that borrowers gradually paid off the principal of the loan). Prior to FHA, only B&Ls and S&Ls had regularly used fully amortized mortgage loan contracts. Soon after FHA began lending, however, the familiar modern mortgage contract became popular even in the noninsured, or conventional, mortgage market (see Table Dc1192–1209).

FHA-insured loans also proved popular in the secondary mortgage market. This was particularly important for loans on multifamily structures, loans on single-family structures that were built in large developments, and loans on properties located in areas of the country with insufficient local supplies of mortgage credit. In all of these cases, the provision of mortgage credit normally involved two or more institutions that specialized either in financing housing projects during construction or in permanently financing the home for the owner. Veterans Administration–guaranteed loans were also used extensively in these complex mortgage transactions after being introduced soon after World War II. Finally, by the mid-1960s a private mortgage insurance industry emerged to provide similar services in the conventional mortgage market. The activities of both the government and private mortgage loan insurance programs are shown in Tables Dc1105–1137.

The federalization of the residential mortgage market provided liquidity and lowered lending risk for financial institutions, liberalized mortgage lending terms for borrowers, and stimulated the development of a secondary mortgage market for home mortgage loans. Over the next two decades the rate of homeownership increased from 43 percent in 1940 to 62 percent in 1960 (refer to Figure Dc-E). The magnitude and rapidity of the change were impressive: the number of occupied housing units increased by 18.1 million between 1940 and 1960, and 17.6 million of these, or

97 percent, were owner-occupied (see Table Dc697–760). Many factors – such as pent-up demand for housing, postwar increases in income, and the development of large, suburban developments – played a role in doubling the number of owner-occupied housing units in the United States between 1940 and 1960. However, for any of these influences to operate, mortgage loans had to be made. The new federalized residential mortgage market was up to the task.

Those interested in the post–World War II residential mortgage market will find a wealth of information, analysis, and comment available beyond the statistical series presented in this chapter. Most noteworthy is a series of ten monographs produced under the auspices of the National Bureau of Economic Research that chronicles the development of the postwar urban mortgage market (see especially Colean 1950; Morton 1956; Klaman 1961). More detailed annual and monthly statistics of residential mortgage lending activity during the period are available in the *Savings and Home Financing Source Book* (published by the FHLB system) and the annual *Fact Books* of the U.S. Savings and Loan League.

The third phase of development in the residential market – between 1970 and 1999 – was ushered in under some troubling signs. After performing so impressively in the 1950s, some cracks had appeared in the residential mortgage system during the 1960s. Early in that decade, Jones and Grebler (1961) argued that the formal secondary market – by then largely controlled by FNMA – was failing to provide sufficient liquidity and marketability to lenders, and had not yet fully mobilized residential mortgage funds across regional and sectoral lines. After a surprisingly severe downturn in residential construction in 1966, moreover, the FHLB system commissioned a wide-ranging examination of the S&L industry that pointed out several important shortcomings with the federal structure (Friend 1969). Matters took a turn for the worse in the 1970s when institutions holding fixed-rate mortgage loans, especially savings and loans, saw profits disappear as inflation lowered the real return on their existing mortgage loan portfolios. A movement to save the S&L industry by deregulating it led to a disastrous wave of failures in the 1980s that exhausted the industry's deposit insurance fund and resulted in the dismantling of the FHLB regulatory system (Kane 1989; Barth 1991; White 1991).

The S&L debacle of the 1970s and 1980s was a visible manifestation of a more fundamental change within the nation's residential mortgage market. The federalized structure of the post–World War II era was dominated by financial institutions that originated mortgage loans and held them until they were paid off. Mortgages are now regularly bundled into packages after they have been originated, and then used as security for mortgage-backed bonds that are issued and traded in the formal capital market. As the underlying mortgage loans are paid off, so are the security holders.[7]

Mortgage securitization is arguably the most important financial innovation of the late twentieth century – it hardly existed at all in 1970, but financed 60 percent of all outstanding residential mortgage loans by 1999 (see Table Dc950–982). The securitization movement has redefined the role of all institutions that operated in the residential mortgage market before 1970, and has encouraged new types of institutions to enter the market since then. That process is documented in this chapter in two sets of tables. Changes in the mix of institutions that originate mortgage loans can be examined with the data in Tables Dc996–1104. These annual series were

taken from the Survey of Mortgage Lending, which was sponsored by the U.S. Department of Housing and Urban Development before being discontinued in 1997. The activities of institutions that create, market, and sell mortgage-backed securities are documented in Tables Dc1154–1191. Chief among these are three government-sponsored enterprises that dominate the market – FannieMae and GinnieMae, entities that were created out of the old FNMA, and FreddieMac, a privately owned entity that was created under the auspices of the FHLB system. See the documentation for these tables for a more detailed description of the functions performed by these most important institutions.

Appendix: A Guide to the Value-in-Place Series

The Value of Construction Put in Place series that are produced by the Manufacturing and Construction Division of the U.S. Bureau of the Census are the most comprehensive and reliable statistical record of construction activity in the United States. These series are produced using data on building permits and housing starts, a national database of construction contract awards, and direct reports by federal agencies on their construction activities. The value-in-place program is a clearinghouse, in effect, for all of the construction-related data that are generated by public and private agencies within the United States. For this reason, the value-in-place series are featured prominently in Tables Dc1–240 and Dc256–509.

These two sets of tables have been designed as a general reference to the historical value-in-place series. The Census Bureau determined during the mid-1970s that it would no longer revise or update value-in-place estimates for years before 1964 when it introduced new methods and procedures. Some twenty-five years later, substantial discontinuities now appear between the value-in-place estimates that the Census Bureau currently produces going back to 1964, and earlier value-in-place estimates for the years 1915–1964. In addition to these breaks in the statistical series, however, a break in documentation also occurred: no source explained how the post-1964 value-in-place series differ from their pre-1964 counterparts. The table documentation in this chapter is intended to serve as a reference guide that links these two extremely rich, but now disconnected, segments of construction statistics. The remainder of this discussion provides general information about the value-in-place series to provide context for the more detailed and technical material included in the table documentation.

What Are They?

The value-in-place series were designed and first assembled for the 1915–1937 period by the Construction and Real Property Section of the U.S. Commerce Department's Division of Economic Research (Chawner 1938). The data and methodology used to compile the series have evolved continually since then, but the six principal categories of construction activity have remained the same:

Private construction
1. Residential
2. Nonresidential building
3. Nonresidential farm
4. Public utility

---

[7] For a concise, readable introduction to modern mortgage securitization, see Kendall and Fishman (1996).

Public construction
 5. Federal
 6. State and local

Except for the nonresidential farm category, each of these series is an aggregate of separate subcomponents that estimate specific types of construction activity – seventeen for the private sector and eighteen for the public sector. Each subcomponent, in turn, is estimated from different types of primary data using one of several different methods of estimation. The unifying feature of all of these estimates is that they are designed to measure either construction or the value of construction put in place:

> *Construction* – defined as new buildings and structures (including mechanical, electrical, heating, and plumbing systems and some types of fixed equipment), additions and alterations to existing buildings and structures, and the preparation of the construction site. Construction excludes maintenance and repairs, land acquisition, the costs of purchasing and installing most types of production machinery and equipment, and the drilling of oil and gas wells.

> *Value of construction put in place* – a measure of the value of construction installed or erected during a given month, quarter, or year. For a given project this includes the cost of materials installed and labor used, the profits of contractors, fees paid to architects and engineers, and the overhead costs, interest, and taxes paid during the construction project. Total value-in-place for a given period is the sum of the value of work done on all projects currently underway in the United States regardless of when the project was started or will be completed, or whether payment for the work has been made to contractors.

How Are They Compiled?

Direct measures of total construction activity, as defined above, would be prohibitively expensive to collect for the hundreds of thousands of construction projects that are ongoing in the United States at any one time. The value-in-place series, in fact, are a set of estimates of the value of work performed that the Census Bureau assembles for nearly forty separate categories of construction activity. The data and methodologies that are used to compile these estimates vary across these many categories, but can be thought of as falling into three broad groups. More specific details about estimates for particular components can be found in the table documentation and in the sources cited at the end of this essay.

Residential housing construction is the largest of the six major value-in-place categories (46 percent of the 1999 total), and forms a methodological category of its own. Included here is work on new single- and multifamily housing units, and improvements to existing residential structures. Each of these is estimated from survey data that are collected by the Census Bureau. The Survey of Construction (SOC), for example, collects information directly from residential home builders on housing starts, completions, and sales for a sample of residential projects that are chosen from the Census Bureau's Building Permits Survey. These data are used to estimate the total value of single-unit residential projects that are started each month. This total value is then allocated as work performed for each of the next twelve months. Monthly estimates of work performed on multifamily residential projects, on the other hand, are estimated directly from construction progress reports that

are collected each month for a sample of the two-or-more-unit residential projects that are identified from the SOC data. Finally, the value-in-place estimate for residential improvements on owner-occupied units is derived from data collected in the Consumer Expenditure Survey, while information on improvements on rental units is collected in a separate follow-up survey.

The second broad methodological category encompasses the value-in-place estimates for eight types of nonresidential buildings (26 percent of the 1999 value-in-place), nine separate categories of state and local government construction activity (21 percent of the 1999 value-in-place), and a very small "all other private construction" category. All eighteen of these series are derived from data gathered in monthly construction progress reports that are submitted by project owners (or the responsible government agency) for a sample of projects. The samples in these cases are drawn from a comprehensive list of nonresidential projects authorized by permit or begun each month that is compiled from data supplied by the F. W. Dodge Corporation (see Tables Dc132–156) and a Census Bureau canvass of projects located in non-permit-issuing places and Hawai'i.

The third methodological approach is the most direct: value-in-place estimates are assembled from reports of actual expenditures made on construction projects during a given year or month. This method is used to derive the value-in-place series for all privately owned public utilities except telephones, and for all federal government construction activities. The expenditure data for the utilities groups are reported by trade associations, while federal expenditures on construction are reported to the Census Bureau by the relevant agencies. Also directly reported to the Census Bureau are estimates of nonresidential farm construction expenditures that are compiled independently by the U.S. Department of Agriculture. Taken together, the components that are directly reported to the Census Bureau represented the remaining 7 percent of total volume of construction in 1999.

Why Are They Reported Here in Two Discontinuous Segments?

Historical value-in-place estimates for the United States are available back to 1915. In this chapter, however, all current-dollar value-in-place series are reported separately in two segments: from 1915 to 1964 and from 1964 to 1999 (see below for an explanation of an additional break in 1947 in the constant-dollar series). For these statistics to be used appropriately for historical analysis, users of these series must take account of these breaks in the series.

Prior to 1959, the value-in-place series were compiled jointly by the Department of Commerce and the Department of Labor, but on July 1 of that year the Bureau of the Census assumed full responsibility for the series. Over the ensuing four decades new methodologies and revised data series have regularly been introduced to improve the accuracy and reliability of the estimates. Until 1974, these revisions and new methods were regularly carried back to 1946, or in some cases to 1958, in order to maintain historical continuity. Since then, revisions to all value-in-place series have been carried back only to 1964, so significant breaks now appear in many of the value-in-place series.

When assembling the value-in-place tables that are presented in this chapter, the last published value-in-place estimate was used for each year between 1915 and 1999. The value-in-place estimates shown for the 1915–1964 period, therefore, are identical to those that appeared in the 1980 supplement cited below (C30-80S). For the 1964–1999 period, on the other hand, the data were taken from the May 2000 value-in-place publication (C30-00-5) and the Census Bureau's Internet site (see the sources for Table Dc12–21). The two segments for each series are shown separately in the chapter, although one year of overlap (1964) is presented for each series so that the breaks in the series can be identified. No attempt has been made here to eliminate the 1964 breaks in any of the affected subcomponents.

Four types of revisions are responsible for nearly all of the 1964 breaks in the value-in-place series. The simplest occurred when an external agency revised its own data on construction expenditures that it had been reporting directly to the Census Bureau. Most of these revisions were undertaken by federal agencies or public utilities trade groups at the request of the Census Bureau; after 1980 these organizations were no longer encouraged to carry the revisions back further than 1964. A second, and more infrequent, type of revision occurred when the Census Bureau reassigned a particular type of project to a new value-in-place subcomponent. The most important revision of this kind occurred in 1968, when projects began to be assigned to value-in-place subcomponents on an establishment basis rather than a building-type basis. The detailed information that would have been required to perform a similar revision on pre-1964 estimates was not available.

The most important type of revision that has created breaks in the value-in-place series occurred as the Census Bureau gradually replaced the "indirect" methods of estimation on which the program relied before 1959. During these early years, estimates for residential housing, nonresidential buildings, and state and local government construction were formed by applying fixed patterns of monthly construction progress to a set of projects that had been identified in surveys of building permits and reports of construction contract that had been awarded. Value-in-place estimates for all of these categories are now based on field survey data and actual monthly progress reports. The implementation of these improvements (for single-family and nonresidential buildings in 1964; for multifamily residences in 1974; and for state and local construction projects in 1975) is responsible for breaks in 1964 for each of these important subcomponents of the value-in-place estimates.

The fourth type of revision involved changes in the procedures that are used to convert current-dollar value-in-place estimates to constant-dollar series. The most important revision of this kind occurred in 1974, when the Census Bureau adopted new cost indexes for many value-in-place subcomponents. Particularly important at this time was a revision of the Census Bureau's own cost index for new single-family homes. Variants of the new indexes were used at the time to revise the constant-dollar value-in-place series back to 1947, but these estimates have not been updated since. As a result, the constant-dollar value-in-place series presented in this chapter are reported in three separate segments: for 1915–1947 (in 1957–1959 dollars), for 1947–1964 (in 1967 dollars), and for 1964–1999 (in 1996 dollars).

The value-in-place estimates that appeared in *Historical Statistics of the United States* (1975) were reported as continuous series for the 1915–1970 period (except for breaks in several current-dollar series in 1946). When these data were assembled, revisions were still being carried back to years before 1964 to preserve historical continuity. The existence of this longer continuous span of data suggests a solution that could be used when breaks in the series presented here are particularly inconvenient: an investigator could use the older, continuous version of the value-in-place series that was assembled before revisions created breaks in the series. This approach could be used to employ continuous value-in-place estimates that begin in 1915 and end in 1957, 1966, 1974, or 1980. These opportunities are identified in the table documentation.

Where Can One Find More Information?

To prepare the documentation that appears in the value-in-place tables, many different sources were relied on. For the 1915–1964 segment, the technical notes from the 1975 edition of *Historical Statistics* (Chapter N) were used extensively and amended, where required, by information drawn from the U.S. Bureau of the Census, *Construction Reports Supplement* titled "Value of New Construction Put in Place 1964 to 1980" (series C30-80S), July 1981. For the series that span the 1964–1999 period, documentation was drawn from the U.S. Bureau of the Census, *Construction Report* titled "Value of New Construction Put in Place: May 2000" (series C30/00-5), July 2000.

These sources provide "snapshots" of the data and methodologies that were used at different points in time to assemble the Value Put in Place series. They do not tell the full story, however, about the historical development of the series. To trace this process in detail, refer to the following sources: Chawner (1938); Lipsey and Preston (1966); U.S. Department of Commerce and U.S. Department of Labor (1956); U.S. Department of Commerce (1964); U.S. Bureau of the Census (1975); U.S. Bureau of the Census (1967); U.S. Bureau of the Census (1981); and U.S. Bureau of the Census, *Construction Reports* (series C30), various years since 1980.

References

Abramovitz, Moses. 1964. "Evidences of Long Swings in Aggregate Construction since the Civil War." NBER Occasional Paper number 90. National Bureau of Economic Research.

Abramovitz, Moses. 1968. "The Passing of the Kuznets Cycle." *Economica* (new series) 35: 349–67.

Aizcorbe, Ana M., Arthur B. Kennickell, and Kevin B. Moore. 2003. "Recent Changes in U.S. Family Finances: Evidence from the 1998 and 2001 Survey of Consumer Finances." *Federal Reserve Bulletin* 89: 1–32.

Aschauer, David A. 1989. "Is Public Expenditure Productive?" *Journal of Monetary Economics* 23 (2): 177–200.

Atack, Jeremy. 1985. "Industrial Structure and the Emergence of the Modern Industrial Corporation." *Explorations in Economic History* 22: 29–53.

Balke, Nathan, and Robert J. Gordon. 1989. "The Estimation of Prewar Gross National Product: Methodology and New Evidence." *Journal of Political Economy* 97: 38–92.

Barth, James R. 1991. *The Great Savings and Loan Debacle*. American Enterprise Institute Press.

Beyer, Glenn. 1965. *Housing and Society*. Macmillan.

Bodfish, Morton. 1931. *History of the Building and Loan in the United States*. United States Building and Loan League.

Borjas, George J. 2002. "Homeownership in the Immigrant Population." *Journal of Urban Economics* 52: 448–76.

Bostic, Raphael W., and Brian J. Surette. 2001. "Have the Doors Opened Wider? Trends in Homeownership Rates by Race and Income." *Journal of Real Estate Finance and Economics* 23: 411–34.

Cain, Louis P. 1997. "Historical Perspective on Infrastructure and US Economic Development." *Regional Science and Urban Economics* 27 (2): 117–38.

Case, Karl E., Robert J. Shiller, and John M. Quigley. 2001. "Comparing Wealth Effects: The Stock Market versus the Housing Market." National Bureau of Economic Research Working Paper number w8606.

Chandler, Alfred. 1959. "The Beginnings of 'Big Business' in American Industry." *Business History Review* 33: 1–31.

Chawner, Lowell J. 1938. "Construction Activity in the United States 1915–37." U.S. Department of Commerce Domestic Commerce Series number 99.

Chevan, Albert. 1989. "The Growth of Home Ownership: 1940–1980." *Demography* 26: 249–66.

Clark, John Maurice. 1935. *Strategic Factors in Business Cycles.* National Bureau of Economic Research.

Colean, Miles. 1944. *American Housing: Problems and Prospects.* Twentieth Century Fund.

Colean, Miles. 1950. *The Impact of Government on Real Estate Finance in the United States.* National Bureau of Economic Research.

Colean, Miles, and Robinson Newcomb. 1952. *Stabilizing Construction: The Record and Potential.* McGraw-Hill.

Collins, William J., and Robert A. Margo. 2001. "Race and Home Ownership: A Century-Long View." *Explorations in Economic History* 38: 68–92.

Coulson, N. Edward. 2002. "Housing Policy and the Social Benefits of Homeownership." *Federal Reserve Bank of Philadelphia Business Review* 2nd Quarter: 7–16.

Davis, Lance. 1965. "The Investment Market, 1870–1914: The Evolution of a National Market." *Journal of Economic History* 25 (3): 355–99.

Englund, Peter, John M. Quigley, and Christian L. Redfearn. 1999. "The Choice of Methodology for Computing Housing Price Indexes." *Journal of Real Estate Finance and Economics* 19 (2): 91–112.

Federal Home Loan Bank Board. *Savings and Home Financing Source Book.* Various years.

Field, Alexander J. 1987. "Modern Business Enterprise as a Capital-Saving Innovation." *Journal of Economic History* 47 (2): 473–85.

Field, Alexander James. 1992. "The Magnetic Telegraph, Price and Quantity Data, and the New Management of Capital." *Journal of Economic History* 52 (2): 401–13.

Fishlow, Albert. 2000. "Internal Transportation in the Nineteenth and Twentieth Centuries." In Stanley L. Engerman and Robert E. Gallman, editors. *The Cambridge Economic History of the United States*, volume 2, *The Long Nineteenth Century.* Cambridge University Press.

Friend, Irwin, editor. 1969. *Study of the Saving and Loan Industry.* 4 volumes. U.S. Government Printing Office.

Gaspari, K. Celeste, and Arthur G. Woolf. 1985. "Income, Public Works, and Mortality in Early Twentieth-Century American Cities." *Journal of Economic History* 45 (2): 355–61.

Gordon, Robert J., and John M. Veitch. 1986. "Fixed Investment in the American Business Cycle." In Robert J. Gordon, editor. *The American Business Cycle: Continuity and Change.* University of Chicago Press.

Gramlich, E. M. (1994). "Infrastructure Investment: A Review Essay." *Journal of Economic Literature* 32: 1176–96.

Grebler, Leo, David Blank, and Louis Winnick. 1956. *Capital Formation in Residential Real Estate.* Princeton University Press.

Green, Richard K. 1997. "Follow the Leader: How Changes in Residential and Non-Residential Investment Predict Changes in GDP." *Real Estate Economics* 25 (2): 253–70.

Haines, Michael R., and Allen C. Goodman. 1992. "Housing Demand in the United States in the Late Nineteenth Century: Evidence from the Commissioner of Labor Survey, 1889/1890." *Journal of Urban Economics* 31: 99–122.

Haines, Michael, and Allen C. Goodman. 1993. "A Home of One's Own: Aging and Homeownership in the United States in the Late Nineteenth and Early Twentieth Centuries." In David I. Kertzer and Peter Laslett, editors. *Aging in the Past: Demography, Society, and Old Age.* University of California Press.

Hansen, Alvin H. 1964. *Business Cycles and National Income.* Norton.

Hickman, Bert G. 1973. "What Became of the Building Cycle?" In P. David and M. Reder, editors. *Nations and Households in Economic Growth: Essays in Honor of Moses Abramovitz.* Academic Press.

Housing and Home Finance Agency. 1948. *Housing Statistics Yearbook.* U.S. Government Printing Office.

Hoynes, Hilary Williamson, and Daniel McFadden. 1997. "The Impact of Demographics on Housing and Non-Housing Wealth in the United States." In Michael D. Hurd and Naohiro Yashiro, editors. *The Economic Effects of Aging in the United States and Japan.* University of Chicago Press.

Jaffee, Dwight M., and Kenneth T. Rosen. 1979. "Mortgage Credit Availability and Residential Construction." *Brookings Papers on Economic Activity* 1979 (2): 333–76.

Jones, Oliver, and Leo Grebler. 1961. *The Secondary Mortgage Market.* Real Estate Research Program, University of California, Los Angeles.

Kain, John F., and John M. Quigley. 1970. "Measuring the Value of Housing Quality." *Journal of American Statistical Association* 65: 532–48.

Kane, Edward J. 1989. *The S&L Insurance Mess: How Did It Happen?* Urban Institute Press.

Kendall, Leon T., and Michael J. Fishman, editors. 1996. *A Primer on Securitization.* MIT Press.

Klaman, Saul B. 1961. *The Postwar Residential Mortgage Market.* Princeton University Press.

Kutty, Nandinee K. 1999. "Determinants of Structural Adequacy of Dwellings." *Journal of Housing Research* 10: 27–43.

Kuznets, Simon. 1961. *Capital in the American Economy: Its Formation and Financing.* Princeton University Press.

Lintner, John. 1948. *Mutual Savings Banks in the Savings and Mortgage Markets.* Harvard University Press.

Lipsey, Robert E., and Doris Preston. 1966. *Source Book of Statistics Related to Construction.* Columbia University Press.

Martinez, Sylvia C. 2000. "The Housing Act of 1949: Its Place in the Realization of the American Dream of Homeownership." *Housing Policy Debate* 11: 467–87.

Mercer, Lloyd J., and W. Douglas Morgan. 1973. "Housing Surplus in the 1920s? Another Evaluation." *Explorations in Economic History* 10: 295–303.

Moore, James F., and Olivia S. Mitchell. 2000. "Projected Retirement Wealth and Savings Adequacy in the Health and Retirement Study." In O. S. Mitchell, B. Hammond, and A. Rappaport, editors. *Forecasting Retirement Needs and Retirement Wealth.* University of Pennsylvania Press.

Morton, J. E. 1956. *Urban Mortgage Lending: Comparative Markets and Experience.* Princeton University Press.

Olmstead, Alan L. 1976. *New York City Mutual Savings Banks, 1819–1861.* University of North Carolina Press.

Painter, Gary, Stuart Gabriel, and Dowell Myers. 2001. "Race, Immigrant Status, and Housing Tenure Choice." *Journal of Urban Economics* 49: 150–67.

Payne, Peter, and Lance Davis. 1956. *The Savings Bank of Baltimore, 1818–1866.* Johns Hopkins University Press.

Romer, Christina D. 1986. "Is the Stabilization of the Postwar Economy a Figment of the Data?" *American Economic Review* 76: 314–34.

Romer, Christina D. 1989. "The Prewar Business Cycle Reconsidered: New Estimates of Gross National Product." *Journal of Political Economy* 97: 1–37.

Ryding, John. 1990. "Housing Finance and the Transmission of Monetary Policy." *Federal Reserve Bank of New York Quarterly Review* 15 (2): 1–9.

Silberling, Norman J. 1943. *The Dynamics of Business.* McGraw-Hill.

Skinner, Jonathan. 1996. "Is Housing Wealth a Sideshow?" In D. Wise, editor. *Advances in the Economics of Aging.* University of Chicago Press.

Snowden, Kenneth. 1987. "Mortgage Rates and American Capital Market Development in the Late Nineteenth Century." *Journal of Economic History* 47: 671–91.

Snowden, Kenneth. 1988. "Mortgage Lending and American Urbanization, 1880–1890." *Journal of Economic History* 48: 273–85.

Snowden, Kenneth. 1997. "Building and Loan Associations in the U.S.: The Origins of Localization in Residential Mortgage Market." *Research in Economics* 51: 227–50.

Snowden, Kenneth. 2003. "The Transition from Building and Loan to Savings and Loan, 1890–1940." In S. L. Engerman, P. T. Hoffman, J. Rosenthal, and K. L. Sokoloff, editors. *Finance, Intermediaries, and Economic Development.* Cambridge University Press.

Stock, James, and Mark Watson. 2002. "Has the Business Cycle Changed and Why?" National Bureau of Economic Research Working Paper number 9127.

Swan, Craig. 1970. "Homebuilding: A Review of the Evidence." *Brookings Papers on Economic Activity* 1970 (1): 48–70.

Troesken, Werner. 1999. "Typhoid Rates and the Public Acquisition of Private Waterworks, 1880–1920." *Journal of Economic History* 59 (4): 927–48.

Ulmer, Melville J. 1960. *Capital in Transportation, Communications and Public Utilities: Its Formation and Financing.* Princeton University Press.

U.S. Bureau of the Census. 1923. *Mortgages on Homes.*

U.S. Bureau of the Census. 1967. *Construction Reports: Value of New Construction Put in Place* (series C30-66S, October 1967).

U.S. Bureau of the Census. 1975. *Construction Reports: Value of New Construction Put in Place 1947 to 1974* (series C30-74S, December 1975).

U.S. Bureau of the Census. 1981. *Construction Reports. Value of New Construction Put in Place 1964 to 1980* (series C30-80S, July 1981).

U.S. Bureau of the Census. 1999. *Construction Statistics Data Users' Conference*, October 28, 1997. MCD/99 CSDUC.

U.S. Bureau of the Census. Various years. *Construction Reports* (series C30-XX/5).

U.S. Department of Commerce. 1964. *Construction Reports: Value of New Construction Put in Place: 1946–63 Revised* (Supplement C30-61, October 1964).

U.S. Department of Commerce and U.S. Department of Labor. 1956. *Construction Volume and Costs, 1915–56: A Statistical Supplement to Construction Review*.

U.S. Savings and Loan League. *Fact Books*. Published annually.

Wachter, Susan M., and Isaac F. Megbolugbe. 1992. "Racial and Ethnic Disparities in Homeownership." *Housing Policy Debate* 3: 333–70.

Wallace, Nancy E. 1996. "Hedonic-Based Price Indexes for Housing: Theory, Estimation, and Index Construction." *San Francisco Federal Reserve Bank Economic Review* 3: 34–48.

White, Lawrence. 1991. *The S&L Debacle*. Oxford University Press.

Wright, Gavin. 1990. "The Origins of American Industrial Success, 1879–1940." *American Economic Review* 80 (4): 651–68.

Zartman, Lester. 1906. *The Investments of Life Insurance Companies*. Henry Holt.

TOTAL CONSTRUCTION: OUTPUT AND COSTS

Kenneth A. Snowden

TABLE Dc1–11   Value of new construction – major components: 1915–1964[1]   [Current dollars]

Contributed by Kenneth A. Snowden

		Private						Public			
	Total	Total	Residential buildings	Nonresidential buildings	Farm nonresidential	Privately owned public utilities	Other	Total	Buildings	Military facilities	Other
	Dc1	Dc2	Dc3	Dc4	Dc5	Dc6	Dc7	Dc8	Dc9	Dc10	Dc11
Year	Million dollars	Million dollars	Million dollars	Million dollars	Million dollars	Million dollars	Million dollars	Million dollars	Million dollars	Million dollars	Million dollars
1915	3,262	2,543	1,220	478	229	549	67	719	217	17	485
1916	3,849	3,141	1,375	716	324	658	68	708	207	21	480
1917	4,569	3,290	1,190	800	449	788	63	1,279	192	608	479
1918	5,118	2,880	915	731	478	697	59	2,238	227	1,555	456
1919	6,296	4,320	1,850	1,082	653	673	62	1,976	260	1,089	627
1920	6,749	5,397	2,015	1,964	566	771	81	1,352	283	161	908
1921	6,004	4,440	2,105	1,434	223	604	74	1,564	387	49	1,128
1922	7,647	5,963	3,360	1,457	269	787	90	1,684	481	25	1,178
1923	9,332	7,710	4,400	1,697	317	1,191	105	1,622	481	16	1,125
1924	10,407	8,506	5,060	1,675	298	1,356	117	1,901	494	9	1,398
1925	11,439	9,301	5,515	2,060	311	1,302	113	2,138	573	8	1,557
1926	12,082	9,938	5,600	2,513	297	1,415	113	2,144	603	11	1,530
1927	12,034	9,625	5,160	2,534	355	1,450	126	2,409	596	12	1,801
1928	11,641	9,156	4,770	2,573	331	1,372	110	2,485	638	15	1,832
1929	10,793	8,307	3,625	2,694	307	1,578	103	2,486	659	19	1,808
1930	8,741	5,883	2,075	2,003	193	1,527	85	2,858	660	29	2,169
1931	6,427	3,768	1,565	1,099	97	946	61	2,659	612	40	2,007
1932	3,538	1,676	630	502	37	467	40	1,862	415	34	1,413
1933	2,879	1,231	470	406	49	261	45	1,648	230	36	1,382
1934	3,720	1,509	625	456	66	326	36	2,211	364	47	1,800
1935	4,232	1,999	1,010	472	126	363	28	2,233	337	37	1,859
1936	6,497	2,981	1,565	713	161	518	24	3,516	762	29	2,725
1937	6,999	3,903	1,875	1,085	207	705	31	3,096	643	37	2,416
1938	6,980	3,560	1,990	764	171	605	30	3,420	707	62	2,651
1939	8,198	4,389	2,680	786	212	683	28	3,809	1,035	125	2,649
1940	8,682	5,054	2,985	1,025	240	771	33	3,628	815	385	2,428
1941	11,957	6,206	3,510	1,482	310	872	32	5,751	2,076	1,620	2,055
1942	14,075	3,415	1,715	635	260	786	19	10,660	4,230	5,016	1,414
1943	8,301	1,979	885	233	284	570	7	6,322	2,749	2,550	1,023
1944	5,259	2,186	815	351	283	725	12	3,073	1,572	837	664
1945	5,809	3,411	1,276	1,020	267	827	21	2,398	1,017	690	691
1946	14,308	12,077	6,247	3,362	1,161	1,255	52	2,231	728	188	1,315
1947	20,041	16,722	9,850	3,243	1,434	2,126	69	3,319	791	204	2,324
1948	26,078	21,374	13,128	3,765	1,640	2,776	65	4,704	1,447	158	3,099
1949	26,722	20,453	12,428	3,383	1,570	2,994	78	6,269	2,408	137	3,724
1950	33,575	26,709	18,126	3,904	1,522	3,045	112	6,866	2,732	177	3,957
1951	35,435	26,180	15,881	5,279	1,599	3,357	64	9,255	4,091	887	4,277
1952	36,828	26,049	15,803	5,014	1,614	3,533	85	10,779	4,812	1,387	4,580
1953	39,136	27,894	16,594	5,680	1,527	3,973	120	11,242	4,906	1,290	5,046
1954	41,380	29,668	18,187	6,250	1,425	3,685	121	11,712	4,945	1,003	5,764
1955	46,519	34,804	21,877	7,611	1,385	3,770	161	11,715	4,462	1,287	5,966
1956	47,601	34,869	20,178	8,818	1,392	4,361	120	12,732	4,368	1,360	7,004
1957	49,139	35,080	19,006	9,556	1,411	4,908	199	14,059	5,013	1,287	7,759
1958	50,047	34,590	19,789	8,675	1,249	4,688	189	15,457	5,499	1,402	8,556
1959	55,392	39,322	24,251	8,859	1,484	4,521	207	16,070	5,476	1,465	9,129
1960	54,738	38,875	22,975	10,149	849	4,621	281	15,863	5,511	1,366	8,986
1961	56,445	39,297	23,107	10,734	871	4,335	250	17,148	6,011	1,371	9,766
1962	60,205	42,336	25,150	11,617	962	4,330	277	17,869	6,092	1,266	10,511
1963	64,812	45,455	27,874	11,646	958	4,667	310	19,357	6,534	1,179	11,644
1964	68,048	47,665	28,010	12,955	1,331	5,031	338	20,383	7,177	910	12,296

TABLE Dc1–11   Value of new construction – major components: 1915–1964   *Continued*

[1] See text for a discussion of issues relating to the comparability of the series over time.

Source

U.S. Bureau of the Census, *Value of New Construction Put in Place 1964 to 1980, Construction Reports*: C30-80S, July 1981, Table D-1, pp. 182–6.

Documentation

This table presents current-dollar estimates of construction activity in the United States broken down into its major components. Construction activity is measured here (and in Tables Dc12–53 and Dc256–509) as the value of new construction put in place. These estimates, which are produced by the U.S. Bureau of the Census, are the most comprehensive and reliable statistical record of total construction activity and its components. "New construction" includes new buildings and structures (including site development, building service systems (such as heating and plumbing), and specific types of major and fabricated equipment), as well as major additions and alterations to existing building and structures. It excludes maintenance and repair, land acquisition, mobile structures, the installation of special-purpose equipment, and the drilling of oil and gas wells. "Value put in place" includes the costs of labor and materials, the contractor's profit, the owner's overhead costs, interest and taxes, and architectural and engineering fees. The total value-in-place for the nation in a given year is the sum of the value-in-place for any project underway in that year regardless of when it was started or when payments for the work were actually made. The essay in this chapter provides a general overview of the purpose, structure, and historical development of the value-in-place estimates.

Before July 1, 1959, the U.S. Departments of Commerce and Labor shared responsibility for compiling value-in-place estimates for new construction; after this date full responsibility devolved to the Commerce Department. The Census Bureau soon began to make improvements to the value-in-place estimates and on several occasions made revisions to pre-1960 estimates to maintain the historical continuity of the series. Since the source was published in 1981, however, major revisions of historical value-in-place estimates have been carried back no further than 1964. As a result, substantial discontinuities now exist between value-in-place estimates for the pre-1964 period and those for 1964–1999 that are currently reported and maintained by the Census Bureau.

Annual value-in-place estimates for the entire 1915–1999 period are presented in this chapter; however, the focus of the presentation is to clarify the differences between the pre- and post-1964 segments of these data. To this end, the value-in-place series for the two periods are presented in separate tables throughout this chapter with a one-year overlap (1964) so that the existence and magnitude of discontinuities can be assessed easily. The descriptions of tables for the earlier period, like this one, discuss the data and methods that were used to compile the 1915–1964 estimates and any substantial breaks in series that appear within this time frame. Details about breaks in the series that appear in 1964 owing to revisions made after 1980, on the other hand, appear in descriptions of the value-in-place series for the 1964–1999 period.

The 1964 breaks in the value-in-place series are of serious consequence for historical analysis. Many of the series measuring specific categories of construction, and nearly all of the aggregated components, are affected. The source presents current-dollar estimates for the 1964–1980 period that were then considered to be directly comparable to the 1915–1964 series shown in this chapter. These could be used to form a longer continuous value-in-place series for applications in which the breaks of comparability in 1964 are particularly troublesome. This approach would involve, of course, using 1964–1980 estimates that have since been substantially revised and improved.

The current-dollar 1915–1964 value-in-place estimates in Table Dc1–11 can be thought of as having been produced in the following three stages.

1915–1945. These estimates were compiled jointly by the Departments of Commerce and Labor. Until 1938, annual data were compiled directly, whereas after 1939 annual figures were derived as the sum of monthly value-in-place estimates. The original source for this period is Lowell J. Chawner, *Construction Activity in the United States, 1915–1937*, Domestic Commerce Series

number 99, Bureau of Foreign and Domestic Commerce (U.S. Department of Commerce, 1938). Revisions to these series, and annual estimates for 1939–1945, appeared in annual editions of the *Statistical Abstract of the United States*. Estimates for the entire 1915–1945 period have not changed since they appeared in U.S. Bureau of the Census, *Construction Statistics, 1915–56: A Supplement to Construction Review,* which was published in 1957. See this source for detailed descriptions of sources and methods.

1946–1957. After taking full responsibility for the value-in-place series in 1959, the Census Bureau incorporated new data and procedures that created discontinuities in a number of individual series within the residential, farm nonresidential, and public utility components. To restore historical comparability and continuity back to at least 1946, major revisions were made to these subcomponents in 1964. These revisions, of course, created new breaks between 1945 and 1946. Refer to U.S. Bureau of the Census, *Value of New Construction Put in Place: 1946–63 Revised*, Construction Reports: C30-64S (October 1964, for details of these revisions and an assessment of the breaks in comparability in 1946.

1958–1964. Between 1964 and 1975 revisions were made to the 1958–1964 estimates for several value-in-place series to maintain historical continuity as new procedures and data were introduced. The series affected were farm nonresidential (1958–1963), residential buildings (1960–1964), nonresidential buildings (1962–1964), and state and local public construction (1962–1964). These revisions appeared in 1966 and 1970 supplements to the C30 series, and all revised estimates were reported in U.S. Bureau of the Census, *Value of New Construction Put in Place: 1947–74*, Construction Reports: C30-74S (December 1975).

The 1915–1964 current-dollar value-in-place estimates shown in this chapter have not changed since they were presented in the 1975 edition of *Historical Statistics of the United States* (a minor exception is a revised 1964 estimate for the farm nonresidential series). The presentation of the series, however, differs from that of the 1975 edition in three important respects. First, the 1915–1964 and 1964–1999 value-in-place estimates are shown here as separate series in separate tables, whereas the 1915–1970 estimates were presented as single, continuous series in the 1975 edition. As explained above, the latter approach is no longer appropriate because of substantial revisions made after 1980 to estimates for 1964 and following years. Second, the value-in-place series names and categories appear here as they were shown in the 1980 source. These differ in several respects from the 1964 conventions that were employed in the 1975 edition. Finally, the Census Bureau was still revising and publishing pre-1964 value-in-place estimates when the 1975 edition of *Historical Statistics of the United States* was assembled. Moreover, the comparability of these data with estimates for later years was regularly discussed in official sources when new procedures were implemented. There is now no longer an authoritative or readily available source of information concerning the appropriate use of the 1915–1964 value-in-place estimates of aggregate construction activity. In fact, no systematic treatment of the relationship between the pre- and post-1964 value-in-place series has appeared since the 1975 edition of *Historical Statistics* was published. This chapter offers an expanded and more detailed discussion of the pre-1964 value-in-place series in an attempt to meet this need.

Value-in-place series are referred to here as either "subcomponents" or "aggregates." The former term is reserved for specific categories of construction for which value-in-place estimates are compiled from underlying data. The term "value-in-place aggregates," on the other hand, refers to broader categories of construction, which represent the sum of a related set of subcomponents or aggregates. In this table, for example, aggregate series Dc1 is the sum of total private and total public construction, series Dc2 and Dc8. The latter two are also aggregates that combine value-in-place estimates on the basis of ownership of the project while it is being built – and not the source of financing.

The new private housing unit subcomponent of the residential building series shown here should be interpreted as including estimates for Alaska and Hawai'i beginning in 1946. All other components include Alaska and Hawai'i beginning in 1959.

(continued)

TABLE Dc1–11   Value of new construction – major components: 1915–1964   *Continued*

The source presents the data with no documentation of definitions or methods for the 1915–1963 period. For these details and monthly and seasonally adjusted monthly values, see the following. For 1915–1945 (current dollars; monthly data 1939–1945) and for 1939–1945 (1947–1949 dollars), see U.S. Business and Defense Services Administration, Department of Commerce, and U.S. Bureau of Labor Statistics, Department of Labor, *Construction Volume and Costs, 1915–56: A Statistical Supplement to Construction Review*, volume 3 (1957). For 1915–1947 (1957–1959 dollars), see U.S. Business and Defense Services Administration, Department of Commerce, *Construction Statistics, 1915–64: A Supplement to Construction Review* (January 1966). For 1946–1958 (current dollars) and for 1946–1957 (in 1957–1959 dollars), see U.S. Bureau of the Census, *Value of New Construction Put in Place: 1946–63 Revised*, Construction Reports: C30-61S (October 1964). For 1958–1964 (current dollars), and for 1947–1964 (1967 dollars), see U.S. Bureau of the Census, *Value of New Construction Put in Place: 1947–74*, Construction Reports: C30-74S (December 1975). Alternatively, for the 1915–1958 period, see U.S. Business and Defense Services Administration, Department of Commerce, *Construction Statistics, 1915–64: A Supplement to Construction Review* (January 1966).

Series Dc2–7. Total privately owned construction, series Dc2, is composed of five types of construction activity: series Dc3, residential buildings, which is an aggregate that combines construction of new housing units, additions, and alterations to existing units, and non-housekeeping residential structures (see Table Dc256–271); series Dc4, nonresidential buildings, which includes industrial, office and commercial, religious, educational, hospital and institutional, and miscellaneous nonresidential buildings (see Table Dc282–302); series Dc5, farm nonresidential construction; series Dc6, privately owned public utility construction, which combines buildings and structures in the telephone and telegraph, gas, electric light and power, railroad, and petroleum pipeline sectors (see Table Dc321–338); and series Dc7, all other private construction. The data and procedures used to compile the value-in-place estimates for privately owned construction are discussed in this chapter when the individual subcomponent series are presented – in the tables indicated for the first three aggregates listed above and directly below for the farm nonresidential and all other private subcomponents.

Series Dc4 and Dc9. It was not possible to segregate industrial nonresidential building construction into public and private before 1933. It is included in private nonresidential building because the amount of public construction of this type before 1933 is believed to have been negligible.

Series Dc5. Farm nonresidential construction includes buildings and structures, such as barns, storage houses, smoke houses, wells, and fences, that were constructed on places classified as farms. These annual estimates were prepared by the U.S. Department of Agriculture based on surveys of construc-

tion expenditures of farm operators for 1934–1937, 1939, 1946, 1949, and 1955. Estimates for other years were based on data reported in U.S. Bureau of the Census, *Current Industrial Reports*, and on regression analyses of selected series of farm income and construction expenditures in the benchmark years. Curiously, farm residential housing is included in the "nonresidential farm" component before 1960. This is because nonfarm and farm residential buildings were combined into a single category in 1970; however, the pre-1960 estimates prepared by the Department of Agriculture could not be appropriately decomposed into a residential and a nonresidential component (see Construction Reports: C30-70S, October 1971). The combined 1915–1959 series continued to be referred to as "farm nonresidential," however, to be compatible with post-1960 categories. Substantial revisions were made in 1964 to the farm nonresidential series for the 1946–1963 period (see Construction Reports: C30-64S, October 1964). The revised estimate for 1946 was $305 million (or 36 percent) higher than its previous level, and so a substantial break in the series occurs at this date. Additional revisions for the 1958–1963 period followed in 1975; however, these introduced no other discontinuities in the series (see Construction Reports: C30-74S, December 1975).

Series Dc7. All other private construction includes unclassified items such as private dams and reservoirs not owned by public utility companies, sewer and water installations, roads, bridges, parks, playgrounds, and airfields. The series was estimated indirectly using compilations of contracts awarded for projects of these types as reported by the F. W. Dodge Corporation. The procedures used to derive value-in-place estimates from these data were also used to estimate the nonresidential buildings subcomponents. See the text for Table Dc282–302 for details.

Series Dc8–11. The total public construction aggregate, series Dc8, has been broken into three components for this table. Series Dc9, public buildings, includes construction on both federally and state and locally owned housing, industrial, educational, hospital and "other public" buildings. On the other hand, series Dc10, military facilities, is an exclusively federal subcomponent shown separately here because of its importance during World War II. Series Dc11, all other public, is an aggregate compiled specifically for this table as the sum of federal and nonfederal construction on highways and streets, conservation and development projects, sewer systems, water supply facilities, and miscellaneous buildings and structures. Current-dollar estimates of all public value-in-place subcomponents are presented and discussed in detail in Table Dc351–363, while value-in-place estimates for the 1915–1964 period are presented separately for federal versus state and local governments in Tables Dc390–441.

Series Dc8. Includes work relief expenditures on construction for 1933–1943.

TABLE Dc12–21   Value of new construction – major components: 1964–1999[1]   [Current dollars]

Contributed by Kenneth A. Snowden

		Private						Public		
	Total	Total	Residential buildings	Nonresidential buildings	Farm nonresidential	Privately owned public utilities	Other	Total	Federal	State and local
	Dc12	Dc13	Dc14	Dc15	Dc16	Dc17	Dc18	Dc19	Dc20	Dc21
Year	Million dollars	Million dollars	Million dollars	Million dollars	Million dollars	Million dollars	Million dollars	Million dollars	Million dollars	Million dollars
1964	75,097	54,893	30,526	17,385	1,331	5,314	338	20,203	3,718	16,485
1965	81,886	59,966	30,235	21,896	1,387	6,032	416	21,920	3,872	18,048
1966	85,753	61,907	28,611	24,238	1,484	7,090	484	23,846	3,803	20,043
1967	87,221	61,844	28,737	23,117	1,702	7,834	454	25,377	3,316	22,061
1968	96,824	69,386	34,172	23,811	1,598	9,232	573	27,437	3,199	24,238
1969	104,944	77,151	37,214	27,741	1,689	9,766	741	27,793	3,150	24,643
1970	105,890	77,982	35,863	28,171	1,875	11,127	946	27,908	3,110	24,798
1971	122,414	92,715	48,514	29,307	1,916	11,985	992	29,699	3,810	25,889
1972	139,126	109,096	60,693	32,375	1,785	13,301	941	30,030	4,244	25,786
1973	153,781	121,433	65,085	37,639	2,525	15,272	912	32,348	4,700	27,648
1974	155,170	117,038	55,967	39,889	3,249	16,933	1,000	38,132	5,091	33,042

Notes appear at end of table

TABLE Dc12–21   Value of new construction – major components: 1964–1999   [Current dollars]   *Continued*

		Private						Public		
	Total	Total	Residential buildings	Nonresidential buildings	Farm nonresidential	Privately owned public utilities	Other	Total	Federal	State and local
	Dc12	Dc13	Dc14	Dc15	Dc16	Dc17	Dc18	Dc19	Dc20	Dc21
Year	Million dollars	Million dollars	Million dollars	Million dollars	Million dollars	Million dollars	Million dollars	Million dollars	Million dollars	Million dollars
1975	152,635	109,342	51,581	35,409	3,731	17,553	1,068	43,293	6,088	37,205
1976	172,132	128,153	68,273	34,628	3,971	20,204	1,078	43,980	6,783	37,196
1977	200,501	157,418	92,004	38,245	4,431	21,437	1,301	43,083	7,088	35,994
1978	239,867	189,721	109,838	48,824	5,209	24,567	1,283	50,146	8,146	42,000
1979	272,873	216,228	116,444	64,765	5,588	27,978	1,452	56,646	8,564	48,081
1980	273,936	210,290	100,381	72,480	5,274	30,905	1,250	63,646	9,642	54,004
1981	289,070	224,378	99,241	85,569	4,612	33,688	1,268	64,691	10,413	54,278
1982	279,332	216,268	84,676	92,690	3,692	33,942	1,269	63,064	10,008	53,056
1983	311,887	248,437	125,833	87,069	3,255	30,817	1,464	63,450	10,557	52,893
1984	370,190	299,952	155,015	107,680	3,161	32,191	1,905	70,238	11,240	58,998
1985	403,416	325,601	160,520	127,466	2,197	32,692	2,726	77,815	12,004	65,811
1986	433,454	348,872	190,677	120,917	2,072	32,931	2,275	84,582	12,412	72,170
1987	446,643	355,994	199,652	123,247	2,605	27,862	2,628	90,648	14,052	76,596
1988	462,012	367,277	204,496	130,854	2,394	27,412	2,121	94,735	12,264	82,471
1989	477,502	379,328	204,255	139,953	2,531	30,129	2,460	98,174	12,155	86,018
1990	476,778	369,300	191,103	143,506	2,801	28,933	2,957	107,478	12,099	95,379
1991	432,592	322,483	166,251	116,570	2,753	33,966	2,943	110,109	12,845	97,264
1992	463,661	347,814	199,393	105,646	2,398	36,807	3,570	115,847	14,376	101,471
1993	493,260	377,300	225,067	110,635	3,392	34,925	3,281	115,960	14,424	101,535
1994	539,232	419,038	258,561	120,289	3,226	34,071	2,890	120,193	14,440	105,753
1995	555,591	425,658	247,351	136,541	3,658	35,859	2,893	129,933	15,751	114,181
1996	613,535	474,273	281,115	153,912	3,815	33,156	2,431	139,263	15,325	123,938
1997	656,630	501,749	289,014	172,990	4,284	33,638	2,292	154,882	14,087	140,795
1998 [2]	711,759	552,236	314,607	190,711	4,451	40,028	2,606	159,523	14,317	145,207
1999 [2]	764,233	591,561	348,826	195,776	3,084	39,607	2,901	172,673	14,056	158,617

[1] See text for a discussion of issues relating to the comparability of the series over time.

[2] Estimates are subject to normal revisions for three years because several series are benchmarked to data that appear in other annual or biennial reports; see text.

Sources

1964–1995: Downloaded February 9, 2001, from the U.S. Census Bureau's Internet site. 1995–1999: U.S. Census Bureau, *Current Construction Reports*, C30/00-5, *Value of Construction Put in Place: May 2000* (issued July 2000), Tables 1 and 2.

Documentation

Previous editions of *Current Construction Reports*, C30, contain data for earlier years that have subsequently been revised as shown in the table. Refer to the May issues of the monthly C30 reports each year after 1980 for complete details about revisions that have been made to the annual value-in-place series; the discussion here summarizes major revisions made to the series before 2000. Refer to essay in this chapter, the source, and the text for Table Dc1–11 for more details about the structure, purpose, and historical development of the value of new construction put in place estimates of aggregate construction activity.

This table presents current-dollar estimates of the total value of new construction put in place in the United States, broken down into major components (for constant-dollar estimates see Table Dc44–53). Most of these components are aggregates of several related, but individually compiled, value-in-place estimates that measure more specific categories of construction. The estimates for all but two of these underlying subcomponents are presented and described in Tables Dc256–509. The two exceptions are series Dc17–18, farm nonresidential and other private, which are not included in any other value-in-place aggregates.

Since taking responsibility for the value-in-place program in 1959, the Census Bureau has incorporated better data and new procedures on an almost continuous basis to provide improved value-in-place estimates. Any future revisions to the 1964–1999 series presented here, or their subcomponents that are presented in Tables Dc256–509, will be presented and documented in the C30 series of the *Current Construction Reports* (revisions to annual historical data are reported in the May issue).

Of particular concern to users of historical statistics are the numerous and substantial breaks in the value-in-place series that occur in 1964. These breaks have appeared because the Census Bureau determined in 1980 that further revisions of the series would be carried back to 1964, but to no earlier years. Nearly all of the major value-in-place components shown in this table have been affected by these revisions and so have significant breaks with their 1915–1964 value-in-place counterparts shown in Table Dc1–11. Moreover, these breaks also occur for many of the value-in-place subcomponent series that underlie the major components shown in this table; for breaks in these series, refer to Tables Dc256–509. All of the value-in-place tables presented in this chapter are designed to help identify major breaks in the series while the accompanying discussions explain the nature of the revisions and the magnitudes of the discontinuities they have caused. The user can check if any individual value-in-place series shown in this chapter is affected by these breaks by comparing the 1964 values from its 1964–1999 and 1915–1964 segments.

The distinction between private and public construction in the value-in-place series is made on the basis of the ownership of the project while it is being built – regardless of the source of financing.

Series Dc14. The residential building aggregate is composed of three subcomponents: new single- and multiunit housing units, and residential improvements (see Table Dc272–281).

Series Dc15. No fewer than eight separate subcomponents are incorporated into the aggregate for private nonresidential buildings: industrial, office, hotels and motels, other commercial, religious, educational, hospital and institutional, and miscellaneous nonresidential buildings (see Table Dc303–320).

Series Dc16. Farm nonresidential construction includes buildings, structures, and fences that are constructed on establishments having annual agricultural sales of $1,000 or more. Also included are land improvements, and the construction of dikes, ponds, flood control systems, and roads and lanes. Value-in-place estimates for new farm nonresidential construction are extrapolated from the annual U.S. Department of Agriculture (USDA) report *Income and Balance Sheet Statistics*. Monthly or quarterly estimates are not available.

(continued)

TABLE Dc12-21   Value of new construction – major components: 1964-1999   [Current dollars]   *Continued*

Series Dc17. The public utilities aggregate is composed of telecommunications, gas, electric light and power, railroad, and petroleum pipelines (see Table Dc339-350).

Series Dc18. Includes all privately owned nonbuilding projects (other than those built for public utility companies) that are not classified elsewhere. These include streets and bridges, parking areas not associated with a building project, dams and reservoirs, sewer and water facilities, golf courses, parks and playgrounds, and airfields, among others. Prior to May 1995, monthly estimates for this series were indirectly measured by applying fixed monthly construction progress patterns to construction contract award data compiled by F. W. Dodge. Beginning with data for May 1995, estimates for this series are based on a monthly sample survey of projects drawn from the same F. W. Dodge contract data.

Series Dc19-21. Note that the distinction between federal and state-local is made on the basis of ownership, not financing. Federal and state-local construction are each estimated with nine separate subcomponents, seven of which are common to both: public housing (and redevelopment in the case of state and local), highways and streets, conservation and development, miscellaneous public construction, educational buildings, hospital buildings, and other public buildings. The two exclusively federal subcomponents are industrial buildings and military facilities. Sewer systems and water facilities, on the other hand, are estimated as separate components only for state and local governments. The current-dollar estimates for these subcomponents are presented in Tables Dc442-475.

TABLE Dc22-43   Value of new construction – major components: 1915-1964[1]   [Constant dollars]

Contributed by Kenneth A. Snowden

		Private						Public			
	Total	Total	Residential buildings	Nonresidential buildings	Farm nonresidential	Privately owned public utilities	Other	Total	Buildings	Military facilities	Other
	Dc22 [2]	Dc23 [2]	Dc24 [2]	Dc25 [2]	Dc26 [2]	Dc27 [2]	Dc28 [2]	Dc29 [2]	Dc30 [2]	Dc31 [2]	Dc32 [2]
Year	Million 1957–1959 dollars	Million 1957–1959 dollars	Million 1957–1959 dollars	Million 1957–1959 dollars	Million 1957–1959 dollars	Million 1957–1959 dollars	Million 1957–1959 dollars	Million 1957–1959 dollars	Million 1957–1959 dollars	Million 1957–1959 dollars	Million 1957–1959 dollars
1915	—	—	6,122	—	1,001	2,357	417	—	—	73	1,884
1916	—	—	6,489	—	1,249	2,508	336	—	—	81	1,562
1917	—	—	4,802	—	1,447	2,364	232	—	—	2,027	1,254
1918	—	—	3,097	—	1,274	1,780	198	—	—	4,515	1,041
1919	—	—	5,389	—	1,465	1,688	190	—	—	2,755	1,275
1920	14,753	12,333	4,553	4,657	1,157	1,770	196	2,420	685	321	1,414
1921	16,167	12,745	5,925	4,441	629	1,525	225	3,422	1,223	122	2,077
1922	22,524	18,420	10,279	4,813	741	2,284	303	4,104	1,641	66	2,397
1923	25,011	21,415	12,008	5,040	837	3,222	308	3,596	1,464	38	2,094
1924	28,022	23,796	14,010	5,004	780	3,659	343	4,226	1,522	22	2,682
1925	31,323	26,366	15,428	6,246	800	3,552	340	4,957	1,801	20	3,136
1926	33,113	28,038	15,504	7,569	765	3,860	340	5,075	1,896	27	3,152
1927	33,238	27,528	14,496	7,712	917	4,025	378	5,710	1,874	30	3,806
1928	32,113	26,127	13,344	7,812	867	3,774	330	5,986	2,007	39	3,940
1929	29,213	23,157	9,715	8,144	798	4,194	306	6,056	2,072	50	3,934
1930	24,511	17,200	5,710	6,437	522	4,273	258	7,311	2,250	81	4,980
1931	19,559	11,998	4,672	4,001	303	2,826	196	7,561	2,346	124	5,091
1932	12,350	6,111	2,222	2,078	133	1,531	147	6,239	1,827	123	4,289
1933	9,232	4,570	1,657	1,725	177	847	164	4,662	1,028	122	3,512
1934	10,815	5,089	2,028	1,738	212	993	118	5,726	1,454	145	4,127
1935	12,780	6,764	3,358	1,809	403	1,102	92	6,016	1,371	115	4,530
1936	18,938	9,771	5,029	2,609	505	1,552	76	9,167	2,939	88	6,140
1937	19,051	11,504	5,392	3,443	616	1,963	90	7,547	2,111	104	5,332
1938	18,775	10,361	5,556	2,477	522	1,719	87	8,414	2,326	177	5,911
1939	22,379	12,600	7,350	2,567	650	1,946	87	9,779	3,394	354	6,031
1940	23,217	14,105	7,924	3,200	731	2,149	101	9,112	2,442	1,055	5,615
1941	30,144	16,049	8,614	4,228	848	2,274	85	14,095	5,544	4,144	4,407
1942	31,777	8,234	4,014	1,628	631	1,911	50	23,543	10,009	10,796	2,738
1943	17,866	4,474	1,965	563	609	1,314	23	13,392	6,227	5,144	2,021
1944	11,525	4,803	1,673	861	547	1,687	35	6,722	3,685	1,758	1,279
1945	12,251	7,181	2,429	2,353	488	1,868	43	5,070	2,344	1,434	1,292
1946	25,668	21,787	10,785	6,498	1,933	2,465	106	3,881	1,351	329	2,201
1947	29,573	24,682	14,044	4,994	1,939	3,584	121	4,891	1,223	293	3,375

Notes appear at end of table

TABLE Dc22–43   Value of new construction – major components: 1915–1964   [Constant dollars]   *Continued*

		Private						Public			
	Total	Total	Residential buildings	Nonresidential buildings	Farm nonresidential	Privately owned public utilities	Other	Total	Buildings	Military facilities	Other
	Dc33 [3]	Dc34 [3]	Dc35 [3]	Dc36 [3]	Dc37 [3]	Dc38 [3]	Dc39 [3]	Dc40 [3]	Dc41 [3]	Dc42 [3]	Dc43 [3]
Year	Million 1967 dollars	Million 1967 dollars	Million 1967 dollars	Million 1967 dollars	Million 1967 dollars	Million 1967 dollars	Million 1967 dollars	Million 1967 dollars	Million 1967 dollars	Million 1967 dollars	Million 1967 dollars
1947	31,142	25,896	14,400	5,240	2,232	3,918	106	5,246	1,247	313	3,686
1948	36,890	30,177	17,669	5,474	2,308	4,637	89	6,713	2,087	219	4,407
1949	37,826	28,776	16,505	5,048	2,231	4,885	107	9,050	3,535	194	5,321
1950	46,737	36,412	23,480	5,870	2,155	4,741	166	10,325	4,036	260	6,029
1951	45,256	33,114	19,204	6,992	2,041	4,794	83	12,142	5,348	1,126	5,668
1952	45,777	32,115	18,569	6,469	2,006	4,966	105	13,662	6,135	1,710	5,817
1953	48,351	34,052	19,386	7,291	1,839	5,336	150	14,299	6,234	1,615	6,450
1954	51,594	36,200	21,123	8,245	1,789	4,886	157	15,394	6,470	1,299	7,625
1955	56,932	41,498	24,832	9,885	1,712	4,855	214	15,434	5,751	1,667	8,016
1956	55,046	39,766	22,297	10,536	1,616	5,172	145	15,280	5,192	1,617	8,471
1957	55,356	39,231	20,886	10,973	1,593	5,552	227	16,125	5,730	1,473	8,922
1958	56,852	38,868	21,748	10,202	1,472	5,227	219	17,984	6,403	1,624	9,957
1959	63,059	44,115	26,652	10,531	1,765	4,925	242	18,944	6,418	1,714	10,812
1960	62,568	43,582	25,111	12,107	1,012	5,016	336	18,986	6,500	1,622	10,864
1961	64,589	44,173	25,253	12,817	1,040	4,766	297	20,416	7,087	1,618	11,711
1962	68,075	47,278	27,341	13,716	1,135	4,767	319	20,797	7,103	1,463	12,231
1963	72,746	50,628	30,555	13,480	1,109	5,133	351	22,118	7,529	1,339	13,250
1964	75,660	52,668	30,557	14,711	1,513	5,508	379	22,992	8,132	1,020	13,840

[1] See text for a discussion of issues relating to the comparability of the series over time.

[2] Series ends after 1947.

[3] Series begins in 1947.

Source
See the source for Table Dc1–11.

Documentation
This table presents constant-dollar value-in-place estimates for the current-dollar figures in Table Dc1–11. Refer to the discussion there for a description of each series and general information about the 1915–1964 current-dollar value-in-place estimates.

Constant-dollar value-in-place estimates represent an indirect way of measuring the actual physical volume of construction for a given period. These estimates are derived by deflating the current-dollar estimates for each value-in-place subcomponent by an index chosen to represent the prices actually paid for the construction projects included in that category. Many of the indexes used to deflate value-in-place subcomponents for the 1915–1964 period are presented in Table Dc207–226, while the constant-dollar estimates of the subcomponents are presented in Tables Dc256–509. The two exceptions are the farm nonresidential and other private subcomponents, which are presented in this table and discussed below.

There is a discrete break in 1947 in all of the constant-dollar estimates shown in this chapter for the 1915–1964 period. The tables showing these data reflect the break by presenting the 1915–1947 and 1947–1964 estimates for each value-in-place aggregate or subcomponent as separate series that differ in two important respects. First, the set of deflating indexes used in constructing the constant-dollar estimates before 1947 is in almost all cases different from those used for the later period. Second, the estimates for the two subperiods are measured in different constant-dollar units: the base year for the early period is 1957–1959, and for the later period it is 1967. As a result, estimates drawn from the two subperiods, even for the same series, cannot be directly compared. Moreover, neither series can be directly compared to the 1964–1999 constant-dollar estimates shown in separate tables throughout this chapter because they all are expressed in 1992 constant dollars.

This break in the constant-dollar series resulted from the adoption of a new set of construction deflators in 1975, which was used to revise all constant-dollar value-in-place estimates back to 1947. The rationale for this important change in procedure was reported in U.S. Department of Commerce, "Revised Deflators for New Construction," *Survey of Current Business* 54 (8), part 1 (August 1974): 18–26, and is discussed in more detail in the

text for Table Dc44–53. Revisions were carried back no further than 1947 because some of the new deflators were not available for earlier periods (see Construction Reports: C30-74S, December 1975). Prior to this major revision, constant-dollar estimates for the 1915–1946 period had last been reported using the old set of deflators that were scaled to 1957–1959 dollars (see Construction Report: C30-61S, October 1964, pp. 4–5). The revised 1947–1964 estimates were reported in Construction Reports: C30-74S (December 1975).

The breaks in the constant-dollar series at 1947 and 1964 will be troublesome in many applications, but two alternatives can be considered when longer continuous series are required for analysis.

The first is to use earlier sets of constant-dollar estimates that were compiled prior to the revisions that created the breaks: for 1915–1956 (in 1947–1949 constant dollars), see U.S. Bureau of the Census, *Construction Volume and Costs, 1915–1956*, Tables 9 and 10; for 1915–1970 (in 1957–1959 dollars), see the U.S. Bureau of the Census, *Historical Statistics of the United States* (1975), series N30-60 (these include the 1915–1947 estimates shown here); and for 1947–1974 (in 1967 dollars), see U.S. Bureau of the Census, Construction Reports: C30-74S (December 1975), Table 2. Each of these alternative sets of estimates has drawbacks, however, which should be kept in mind. The first two series were compiled using the old set of deflators, and users should be aware of the criticisms of them in the 1974 *Survey of Current Business* article cited above (see the text for Table Dc44–53 for a brief summary). In addition, the 1915–1970 series in the 1975 edition of *Historical Statistics* is based on the same current-dollar series shown in Table Dc1–11, which, as discussed in the text for that table, has breaks of its own in 1946. Finally, all three of these alternative sets of series are based in part on current-dollar estimates that were later revised and improved: for the 1946–1956 period in the first case, for 1964–1970 in the case of *Historical Statistics of the United States* (1975), and for 1964–1974 for the data that appear in C30-74S.

A second alternative is to rescale the separate segments of the constant-dollar series shown here to remove the "jumps" that appear in 1947 and 1964; one year of overlap has been shown at each break for this purpose. To rescale the segments, multiply the 1915–1946 constant-dollar estimates for any series by the ratio of (a) its 1947 value measured in 1967 dollars to (b) its 1947 value measured in 1957–1959 dollars. This approach has the advantage of linking together the levels of constant-dollar estimates that have been compiled using the most recently published current-dollar estimates and the "best" set of deflators available for each year. It does not, however, resolve the underlying differences between the 1915–1947 and

(continued)

TABLE Dc22–43 **Value of new construction – major components: 1915–1964** **[Constant dollars]** *Continued*

1947–1964 segments that stem from differences in the indexes used to deflate the series. As a result, caution should be exercised when performing analysis across the 1947 break or when comparing the time series behavior between these two segments.

It should also be noted that the rescaling procedure described in the preceding paragraph essentially adjusts for differences in the levels of the implicit annual deflators between the two periods (the deflator is simply the ratio of current-dollar to constant-dollar value-in-place). This is not equivalent to rescaling the annual deflating indexes to a common base year and then recalculating the constant-dollar series. From 1939 on, the constant-dollar value-in-place estimates were compiled each month and then summed to annual totals. The implicit deflator in this case is a weighted average of the monthly values of the appropriate deflating index, with the weight each month equal to its share in current-dollar value-in-place for the year. The important implication of this rather technical point is that the base year used to measure annual constant-dollar value-in-place estimates after 1939 can be changed only by recalculating all monthly value-in-place series as well. Any other method of rescaling the annual data will introduce some approximation error.

Series Dc26 and Dc37. As noted in the text for Table Dc1–11, the current dollar farm nonresidential series contains both residential and nonresiden-

tial farm construction through 1959. These two components were deflated separately throughout the period. The indexes used for 1915–1947 were specifically designed and compiled by the Agricultural Marketing Service of the U.S. Department of Agriculture to measure the construction costs for farm service buildings and farm operators' dwellings. The new set of deflators for the 1947–1964 period that was adopted in 1975 did not include indexes specifically designed for agricultural construction. Instead, under the new system, nonfarm residential construction was deflated by the same index used for nonfarm residential construction, while farm nonresidential construction was deflated by the index used for privately owned nonresidential buildings. These indexes are described in the text for Tables Dc256–271 and Dc282–302.

Series Dc28 and Dc39. For the 1915–1947 period, series Dc28 was deflated by an average of two privately produced indexes of general construction costs, one compiled by the Associated General Contractors and the other by the *Engineering News-Record*. For the revised 1947–1964 period, series Dc39, an average of the composite cost indexes compiled by the U.S. Bureau of Public Roads and the U.S. Bureau of Reclamation was used.

TABLE Dc44–53   Value of new construction – major components: 1964–1999[1]   [Constant dollars]

Contributed by Kenneth A. Snowden

		Private						Public		
	Total	Total	Residential buildings	Nonresidential buildings	Farm nonresidential	Privately owned public utilities	Other	Total	Federal	State and local
	Dc44	Dc45	Dc46	Dc47	Dc48	Dc49	Dc50	Dc51	Dc52	Dc53
Year	Million 1996 dollars	Million 1996 dollars	Million 1996 dollars	Million 1996 dollars	Million 1996 dollars	Million 1996 dollars	Million 1996 dollars	Million 1996 dollars	Million 1996 dollars	Million 1996 dollars
1964	405,864	300,372	169,635	96,497	7,386	25,169	1,685	105,492	19,402	86,090
1965	428,899	317,740	162,872	117,762	7,471	27,618	2,016	111,159	19,655	91,504
1966	430,631	314,197	147,243	125,310	7,676	31,689	2,278	116,434	18,563	97,872
1967	424,218	303,880	143,091	116,120	8,552	34,065	2,052	120,338	15,553	104,784
1968	446,145	323,080	161,347	112,547	7,563	39,157	2,466	123,065	14,240	108,825
1969	452,092	335,399	165,261	121,159	7,384	38,602	2,993	116,693	13,193	103,500
1970	429,041	321,940	155,113	115,372	7,681	40,305	3,469	107,101	11,956	95,144
1971	465,633	360,011	197,987	110,450	7,226	40,950	3,397	105,623	13,574	92,049
1972	498,463	397,677	231,139	114,173	6,298	43,012	3,055	100,786	14,251	86,535
1973	506,572	405,815	226,131	122,703	8,240	45,992	2,748	100,757	14,699	86,058
1974	449,424	346,260	177,074	113,590	9,256	43,731	2,610	103,164	13,836	89,328
1975	404,132	298,555	149,410	96,407	10,155	40,155	2,427	105,577	14,993	90,584
1976	435,292	332,773	185,804	90,480	10,375	43,786	2,329	102,518	15,941	86,577
1977	470,439	375,319	225,518	92,949	10,774	43,375	2,703	95,120	15,716	79,404
1978	505,446	404,508	237,131	107,029	11,444	46,420	2,484	100,938	16,526	84,412
1979	513,753	413,220	224,697	127,420	11,012	47,630	2,462	100,533	15,542	84,991
1980	464,144	364,101	175,822	129,275	9,395	47,755	1,855	100,043	15,660	84,383
1981	455,260	361,069	162,706	140,569	7,577	48,486	1,732	94,191	15,604	78,588
1982	423,729	333,894	134,605	145,054	5,781	46,743	1,710	89,835	14,472	75,363
1983	465,073	375,193	195,028	131,289	4,907	41,974	1,995	89,880	15,109	74,770
1984	534,557	437,325	231,396	155,261	4,560	43,535	2,573	97,232	15,694	81,538
1985	567,689	463,854	234,955	178,925	3,087	43,342	3,544	103,835	16,292	87,543
1986	588,804	479,623	266,481	163,740	2,805	43,722	2,875	109,182	16,322	92,860
1987	585,103	470,575	267,063	160,363	3,391	36,476	3,281	114,528	18,010	96,518
1988	583,396	467,599	263,385	164,191	3,004	34,448	2,570	115,797	15,199	100,598
1989	579,583	463,541	252,745	169,173	3,059	35,688	2,876	116,042	14,516	101,526
1990	560,802	436,999	228,943	167,896	3,276	33,505	3,379	123,803	14,064	109,739
1991	503,711	378,245	197,526	135,389	3,197	38,830	3,303	125,467	14,731	110,736
1992	533,322	401,567	232,134	120,921	2,744	41,745	4,024	131,755	16,331	115,424
1993	546,757	418,037	249,757	122,222	3,746	38,671	3,641	128,720	15,932	112,788
1994	574,302	445,460	274,956	127,593	3,424	36,372	3,114	128,842	15,406	113,435
1995	567,900	434,450	251,937	139,711	3,084	36,740	2,979	133,450	16,151	117,298
1996	613,454	474,307	281,229	153,866	3,657	33,124	2,431	139,147	15,328	123,819
1997	635,765	486,273	280,748	166,754	3,675	32,884	2,212	149,493	13,592	135,901
1998	670,859	520,613	297,886	177,639	3,989	38,616	2,482	150,246	13,503	136,743
1999	692,477	535,625	315,757	175,048	3,977	38,166	2,678	156,852	12,824	144,028

[1] See text for a discussion of issues relating to the comparability of the series over time.

Source

See the source for Table Dc12–21.

Documentation

This table presents constant-dollar estimates for the current-dollar figures in Table Dc12–21. Refer to the discussion there for a description of the series and general information about the current-dollar value-in-place estimates.

Measurement of construction expenditures in constant dollars is an indirect way of approximating changes in the actual physical volume of construction. The estimates are derived by deflating the current-dollar estimate of each value-in-place subcomponent by an index chosen to represent the prices paid each year for the type of construction projects covered by the current-dollar series. Price indexes that are ideal for this purpose are difficult to compile because each value-in-place subcomponent contains a heterogeneous collection of complex buildings and structures. In fact, some of the deflating indexes used by the Census Bureau, especially in the case of private nonresidential buildings, do not measure actual prices of construction output. Instead, they measure changes over time in the prices of the inputs used in the construction project (primarily labor and materials). A constant-dollar series derived with this type of "input price" index tends to understate the growth over time in the production of "physical units" of construction because the downward impact of productivity improvements on construction

output prices is not captured. For detailed discussions of the indexes used to deflate current-dollar value-in-place estimates, see U.S. Department of Commerce, "Revised Deflators for New Construction," *Survey of Current Business* 54 (8), part 1 (August 1974):18–26, and U.S. Bureau of the Census, *Construction Statistics Data Users' Conference* (March 1999), pp. 11–3. For a description of the indexes currently used as deflators and the indexes themselves, see Table Dc227–240.

The indexes used to construct constant-dollar value-in-place estimates are converted to a common base year – 1996 as this chapter was being prepared. Constant-dollar values are first calculated for the monthly estimates of each value-in-place subcomponent, which are then combined to form monthly constant-dollar estimates for the major components shown here. The annual constant-dollar estimates reported in this chapter are formed by adding up these monthly estimates for each subcomponent and aggregates of those components. Annual averages of all indexes used as deflators in the value-in-place program are reported by the Census Bureau and shown in Table Dc227–240, but these are not directly used to deflate annual current-dollar value-in-place estimates.

The constant-dollar estimates for the subcomponents of each of these aggregates are presented in Tables Dc256–509, along with descriptions of the deflating indexes.

TABLE Dc54–65   Net stock of structures, by type: 1925–1999

Contributed by Kenneth A. Snowden

		Private							Government			
			Nonresidential							Federal		
Year	Total	Residential	Total	Buildings, excluding farm	Privately owned public utilities	Farm-related	Mining	Other nonfarm	Total	Defense	Nondefense	State and local
	Dc54	Dc55	Dc56	Dc57	Dc58	Dc59	Dc60	Dc61	Dc62	Dc63	Dc64	Dc65
	Million dollars	Million dollars	Million dollars	Million dollars	Million dollars	Million dollars	Million dollars	Million dollars	Million dollars	Million dollars	Million dollars	Million dollars
1925	198,198	100,037	98,161	35,182	46,563	8,463	3,621	4,332	35,170	4,472	2,301	28,397
1926	204,525	104,386	100,139	37,092	47,075	7,609	3,865	4,497	36,078	4,401	2,334	29,343
1927	210,023	107,849	102,174	38,272	47,934	7,567	4,039	4,362	36,951	4,216	2,371	30,365
1928	217,865	114,023	103,842	39,407	48,518	7,469	4,196	4,252	37,768	4,039	2,427	31,302
1929	221,500	117,911	103,589	39,499	48,188	7,361	4,337	4,203	38,125	3,804	2,481	31,840
1930	210,737	112,244	98,493	37,211	45,573	6,972	4,720	4,018	37,084	3,448	2,470	31,166
1931	185,504	96,959	88,546	32,868	41,505	6,129	4,509	3,535	33,564	3,023	2,358	28,182
1932	167,764	85,848	81,916	30,037	39,126	5,176	4,383	3,194	33,186	2,856	2,412	27,918
1933	172,830	89,671	83,160	31,426	39,746	4,532	4,067	3,389	39,286	3,101	3,056	33,102
1934	179,225	93,585	85,640	32,979	40,506	4,768	3,818	3,569	43,059	3,295	3,664	36,100
1935	182,738	95,238	87,500	33,661	40,983	5,246	3,967	3,643	45,702	3,462	4,498	37,742
1936	196,060	103,104	92,956	36,463	43,186	5,241	4,298	3,768	51,015	3,791	5,583	41,641
1937	208,143	110,721	97,422	38,911	44,466	5,276	4,936	3,833	53,863	3,975	6,495	43,392
1938	210,127	113,605	96,522	38,607	43,933	5,298	4,904	3,779	55,729	4,031	7,022	44,676
1939	215,100	117,912	97,188	38,569	44,868	5,103	4,917	3,732	57,837	4,153	7,360	46,323
1940	229,867	127,679	102,188	41,162	47,379	4,700	5,088	3,858	63,437	4,904	8,035	50,498
1941	252,945	140,237	112,707	46,547	51,637	4,783	5,685	4,056	76,578	9,282	8,569	58,727
1942	272,880	151,127	121,753	49,468	55,634	5,653	6,771	4,226	95,781	20,845	9,007	65,929
1943	289,207	163,417	125,790	50,169	56,688	6,801	7,877	4,254	103,615	26,606	9,879	67,129
1944	305,847	175,915	129,931	50,918	58,261	7,800	8,618	4,335	104,280	28,409	10,264	65,607
1945	331,334	189,402	141,933	55,811	64,099	8,427	8,911	4,684	112,590	32,477	11,924	68,189
1946	392,523	223,560	168,963	70,067	74,499	9,718	9,398	5,281	129,594	38,435	14,783	76,376
1947	462,893	264,427	198,466	83,442	86,471	11,928	10,666	5,959	152,872	44,465	16,899	91,507
1948	503,412	289,176	214,236	88,688	93,451	14,231	11,659	6,207	162,089	43,849	18,827	99,413
1949	524,488	305,674	218,814	87,748	97,953	15,216	12,017	5,879	155,398	41,547	19,065	94,786
1950	572,568	337,483	235,085	94,307	105,744	15,382	13,615	6,037	171,156	44,976	19,468	106,712
1951	625,367	367,749	257,617	105,445	113,420	16,735	15,510	6,508	192,731	51,940	20,653	120,137
1952	658,455	387,538	270,917	110,125	119,048	18,456	6,720	6,568	203,409	53,544	22,619	127,246
1953	681,891	403,669	278,221	111,514	123,526	19,094	17,670	6,417	202,214	54,074	22,383	125,758
1954	709,957	424,499	285,458	113,734	127,467	19,205	18,849	6,203	211,464	57,317	23,087	131,060
1955	760,735	454,490	306,245	123,614	135,517	19,358	21,300	6,456	227,034	56,819	24,926	145,289
1956	814,395	478,661	335,733	138,060	146,088	20,649	23,985	6,951	254,890	63,384	26,416	165,090
1957	846,757	493,204	353,553	145,687	153,173	22,182	25,273	7,238	266,802	65,865	27,988	172,948
1958	872,249	508,777	363,472	148,114	157,425	24,429	26,305	7,198	283,727	70,036	28,893	184,798
1959	907,124	530,858	376,266	152,840	163,855	24,843	27,842	6,886	289,822	69,088	29,792	190,943
1960	932,831	551,809	381,022	157,591	164,117	25,104	27,230	6,980	300,337	69,372	31,066	199,899
1961	964,477	572,067	392,410	166,936	164,264	25,981	28,038	7,191	315,838	71,220	32,790	211,828
1962	998,505	593,440	405,065	177,189	164,707	27,030	28,661	7,478	334,859	72,735	35,379	226,745
1963	1,025,515	608,409	417,106	187,231	165,761	28,040	28,283	7,790	353,736	74,033	38,002	241,700
1964	1,097,301	657,393	439,907	203,554	169,055	29,707	29,576	8,015	372,685	75,009	40,094	257,582

	Private								Government			
			Nonresidential							Federal		
Year	Total	Residential	Total	Buildings, excluding farm	Privately owned public utilities	Farm-related	Mining	Other nonfarm	Total	Defense	Nondefense	State and local
	Dc54	Dc55	Dc56	Dc57	Dc58	Dc59	Dc60	Dc61	Dc62	Dc63	Dc64	Dc65
	Million dollars	Million dollars	Million dollars	Million dollars	Million dollars	Million dollars	Million dollars	Million dollars	Million dollars	Million dollars	Million dollars	Million dollars
1965	1,167,473	698,950	468,523	222,203	175,290	31,224	31,303	8,502	400,400	76,430	43,697	280,274
1966	1,259,909	755,746	504,163	245,519	182,337	33,262	33,869	9,176	436,296	79,233	47,568	309,494
1967	1,343,066	805,824	537,242	266,186	190,576	35,253	35,407	9,820	473,865	85,136	50,752	337,977
1968	1,477,566	891,514	586,052	297,399	201,965	38,424	37,614	10,651	519,319	88,973	55,072	375,274
1969	1,599,318	954,338	644,981	332,765	218,624	41,648	39,980	11,964	579,678	95,288	60,334	424,057
1970	1,718,240	1,008,902	709,338	370,429	238,133	45,290	41,759	13,727	653,459	103,800	65,516	484,143
1971	1,924,469	1,133,357	791,112	421,279	259,222	50,472	44,761	15,378	717,734	110,904	71,951	534,879
1972	2,136,901	1,270,694	866,207	469,111	277,526	54,738	47,962	16,870	789,672	125,648	77,752	586,272
1973	2,433,507	1,458,373	975,133	530,013	312,542	60,487	52,907	19,183	901,820	144,407	85,278	672,135
1974	2,828,975	1,656,037	1,172,938	627,241	376,984	70,919	73,296	24,497	1,125,862	171,637	101,991	852,234
1975	3,061,400	1,791,838	1,269,562	661,934	421,034	75,273	84,977	26,345	1,175,578	172,404	113,751	889,423
1976	3,373,872	1,988,725	1,385,146	710,666	467,572	81,302	97,758	27,848	1,236,218	188,396	121,159	926,662
1977	3,850,728	2,322,070	1,528,658	786,906	499,647	90,715	121,379	30,012	1,309,050	189,731	130,580	988,739
1978	4,406,160	2,681,402	1,724,758	885,865	551,838	102,687	151,671	32,697	1,435,163	205,695	143,037	1,086,432
1979	5,097,680	3,115,959	1,981,721	1,030,525	622,348	118,585	171,924	38,340	1,646,605	235,477	160,839	1,250,289
1980	5,767,875	3,512,102	2,255,773	1,182,507	686,638	133,397	207,558	45,673	1,894,191	259,336	182,669	1,452,185
1981	6,346,136	3,775,982	2,570,153	1,318,385	744,419	144,619	310,516	52,213	2,076,587	261,827	203,386	1,611,373
1982	6,679,817	3,942,844	2,736,973	1,434,834	786,762	151,240	307,869	56,268	2,184,075	266,893	215,649	1,701,533
1983	6,910,671	4,102,122	2,808,549	1,526,085	806,874	155,340	262,912	57,338	2,210,521	273,470	219,512	1,717,539
1984	7,314,273	4,334,068	2,980,206	1,652,267	831,814	161,126	274,586	60,413	2,292,095	287,088	226,176	1,778,831
1985	7,700,402	4,564,634	3,135,768	1,782,703	842,444	163,888	279,710	67,023	2,384,954	294,874	233,376	1,856,704
1986	8,191,759	4,928,093	3,263,666	1,925,810	850,405	168,356	245,690	73,405	2,526,518	309,678	241,183	1,975,657
1987	8,684,281	5,240,876	3,443,405	2,066,680	891,092	172,956	232,607	80,070	2,657,492	316,450	251,325	2,089,717
1988	9,230,428	5,560,496	3,669,932	2,215,477	939,666	177,106	253,116	84,566	2,782,907	337,723	260,769	2,184,416
1989	9,748,642	5,863,816	3,884,827	2,372,571	984,912	181,232	254,708	91,403	2,922,906	352,683	273,381	2,296,843
1990	10,167,935	6,087,209	4,080,726	2,514,333	1,005,177	184,074	277,903	99,239	3,052,800	358,350	284,389	2,410,061
1991	10,347,220	6,209,567	4,137,653	2,576,360	1,021,031	182,944	251,943	105,376	3,141,998	369,154	293,399	2,479,445
1992	10,821,457	6,542,842	4,278,615	2,676,059	1,050,917	184,597	254,687	112,356	3,275,577	386,682	301,219	2,587,675
1993	11,433,804	6,935,300	4,498,504	2,816,644	1,109,184	189,928	262,917	119,831	3,440,829	409,065	313,902	2,717,862
1994	12,152,607	7,413,546	4,739,061	2,992,267	1,148,421	197,135	272,537	128,700	3,650,459	426,004	329,414	2,895,040
1995	12,664,633	7,723,255	4,941,378	3,125,084	1,190,239	199,988	287,339	138,730	3,847,446	438,816	348,883	3,059,747
1996	13,306,251	8,131,219	5,175,032	3,285,623	1,229,002	204,381	311,244	144,783	4,032,853	450,089	368,867	3,213,897
1997	14,067,850	8,580,822	5,487,028	3,498,851	1,264,691	210,670	360,760	152,056	4,249,361	462,134	386,397	3,400,830
1998	14,873,309	9,124,270	5,749,039	3,742,207	1,285,425	218,117	346,044	157,245	4,446,187	472,084	397,576	3,576,528
1999	15,801,630	9,765,940	6,035,690	3,990,849	1,310,846	224,494	345,230	164,272	4,695,672	486,924	413,231	3,795,517

Source

These data were reported in "Fixed Assets and Consumer Durable Goods for 1925–99," *Survey of Current Business* 80 (9)(2000): 19–30. The figures presented here were released by the U.S. Bureau of Economic Analysis (BEA) on November 17, 2000, and were downloaded from the BEA's Internet site on February 6, 2001.

Documentation

The BEA forms annual year-end estimates of the nation's gross stock of structures, depreciation on home structures, and (shown here) the stock of structures net of depreciation for use in the national

income and product accounts (NIPA). Depreciation of reproducible fixed capital shows up in the NIPA as consumption of fixed capital (CFC) – the decline in the value of structures and equipment used in the production of output that results from wear and tear, obsolescence, accidental damage, and aging. Capital consumption, therefore, is a cost incurred in the production of gross domestic product, just like the compensation of employees and other components of gross domestic income. CFC is deducted from gross domestic product and income to derive net domestic product and net domestic income – rough measures of the level of income or consumption that can be maintained while leaving the economy's capital stock intact. The BEA also uses current-cost estimates of depreciation on structures

(continued)

TABLE Dc54-65   Net stock of structures, by type: 1925–1999   *Continued*

and other fixed assets to derive a capital consumption adjustment for fixed private capital that is used to estimate corporate profits and other business income in the NIPA.

To estimate depreciation on structures for a given year, the BEA must derive estimates of the stock of structures for that year. The series in this table measure the current market value of the stock of each type of structure after adjustment has been made for depreciation. In principle, these estimates represent the market value for which these structures could have been bought or sold at each year-end and the present value, in equilibrium, of all expected future services embodied in existing structures. The 1994 estimates in the table, for instance, value the net stock of structures in place that year at the prices that prevailed in the market at year-end 1994; similarly, the 1925 estimates value the net stock of structures in place at that time at year-end 1925 prices. The BEA refers to this measure as current-cost valuation. The source also reports the net stock of structures in terms of historical cost and real cost (for the latter, see Table Dc66-77), and the net stock of structures by industry and ownership as well as by the type-of-structure aggregates shown here.

The estimates of the net stock of structures shown here are not derived from actual inventories of structures. Instead, the BEA produces estimates of the net stock of structures in real terms by applying the perpetual inventory method to annual investment data and assumed patterns of depreciation. The current-cost series shown here are then formed by converting the real-cost estimates of the net stock to market prices for each year as measured by average annual price indexes for each type of structure. See the text for Table Dc66-77 for an explanation of how the real-cost estimates of the net stock of structures are derived, and the source for details about the price indexes that are used to form the current-cost estimates.

These estimates incorporate the results of the annual revision of the NIPA that were reported in Eugene P. Seskin and David F. Sullivan, "Annual Revision of the National Income and Product Accounts: Annual Estimates 1997–99 and Quarterly Estimates, 1997:I–2000:I," *Survey of Current Business* 80 (August 2000): 6-33.

For detailed discussion of the methods used to derive the net stocks of structures, see U.S. Bureau of Economic Analysis, *Fixed Reproducible Tangible Wealth in the United States, 1925–94* (U.S. Government Printing Office, August 1999), pp. M-1 to M-36; and Shelby W. Herman, "Fixed Assets and Consumer Durable Goods: Estimates for 1925–98 and New NIPA Table – Changes in Net Stock of Produced

Assets," *Survey of Current Business* 80 (April 2000): 17-30. Additional data on investment, depreciation, net stock, and age of structures will be reported in the BEA's *Fixed Assets and Consumer Durable Goods in the United States, 1925–97* (2003). The volume includes additional estimates by industry, type of structure, and legal form of organization.

Series Dc55. Includes new single- and multifamily units, mobile homes, improvements to existing residential units and an "other residential" category that consists primarily of dormitories and fraternity and sorority houses.

Series Dc56. Equals the sum of series Dc57–61. Private nonresidential buildings include new industrial, commercial, and office buildings (except those owned by privately owned public utilities). Also included are buildings used for religious, educational, and other institutional purposes, as well as hospitals, hotels, and recreational buildings. The nonresidential building category, finally, includes privately owned mobile structures, passenger terminals, greenhouses, and animal hospitals.

Series Dc57. Consists of office buildings, except those occupied by electric and gas utility companies.

Series Dc58 and Dc60. Series Dc58 encompasses privately owned railroad, telecommunication, electric light and power, and gas and petroleum pipeline facilities. It also includes office buildings owned by electric and natural gas producers. In contrast, petroleum and natural gas drilling facilities, as well as all other mining facilities, are included under mining structures, series Dc60.

Series Dc61. Consists primarily of privately owned streets, dams, reservoirs, sewer and water facilities, parks, and airfields.

Series Dc62-65. Consists of the fixed capital of general government and government enterprises.

Series Dc63-64. Federal defense structures include residential and industrial buildings used for military purposes and U.S. Department of Defense military facilities. Nondefense structures include all other federally owned nonresidential buildings, garages, passenger terminals, highways and streets, conservation and development facilities, transit systems, and airfields.

Series Dc65. State and local governments own a wide range of buildings as well as highways and streets, sewer and water systems, and structures used for conservation and development.

TABLE Dc66-77　Net stock of structures, by type: 1925–1999　[Chain-type quantity indexes]

Contributed by Kenneth A. Snowden

	Private								Government			
		Nonresidential								Federal		
Year	Total	Residential	Total	Buildings, excluding farm	Privately owned public utilities	Farm-related	Mining	Other nonfarm	Total	Defense	Nondefense	State and local
	Dc66	Dc67	Dc68	Dc69	Dc70	Dc71	Dc72	Dc73	Dc74	Dc75	Dc76	Dc77
	Index 1996 = 100	Index 1996 = 100	Index 1996 = 100	Index 1996 = 100	Index 1996 = 100	Index 1996 = 100	Index 1996 = 100	Index 1996 = 100	Index 1996 = 100	Index 1996 = 100	Index 1996 = 100	Index 1996 = 100
1925	20.92	17.50	26.60	15.59	51.11	62.03	14.99	34.22	10.65	17.77	7.87	9.95
1926	21.69	18.26	27.39	16.43	52.02	61.71	15.91	34.32	11.10	17.49	8.00	10.48
1927	22.42	18.96	28.17	17.27	52.90	61.68	16.52	34.54	11.63	17.22	8.13	11.11
1928	23.08	19.58	28.89	18.07	53.65	61.50	17.18	34.66	12.21	16.97	8.33	11.78
1929	23.64	19.98	29.71	18.92	54.70	61.22	18.02	34.73	13.00	16.76	8.66	12.66
1930	23.94	20.12	30.30	19.53	55.61	60.41	18.40	34.68	13.78	16.63	9.17	13.53
1931	24.02	20.19	30.39	19.69	55.86	59.29	18.16	34.46	14.59	16.58	9.91	14.39
1932	23.89	20.10	30.20	19.61	55.52	57.99	18.11	34.11	15.25	16.53	11.13	15.02
1933	23.69	19.99	29.84	19.39	54.89	56.81	17.91	33.84	15.70	16.49	13.14	15.33
1934	23.53	19.92	29.55	19.18	54.35	55.72	18.05	33.43	16.33	16.55	15.12	15.73
1935	23.45	19.94	29.30	18.99	53.87	55.00	18.43	32.94	16.90	16.55	18.07	16.07
1936	23.46	20.03	29.20	18.93	53.60	54.45	19.06	32.40	17.90	17.08	20.64	16.89
1937	23.57	20.14	29.28	19.01	53.53	54.07	20.12	31.92	18.71	17.78	22.85	17.52
1938	23.60	20.26	29.19	18.92	53.30	53.57	20.81	31.45	19.62	18.35	24.78	18.30
1939	23.75	20.53	29.13	18.84	53.20	53.19	21.40	30.98	20.64	18.80	26.58	19.25
1940	23.95	20.87	29.07	18.70	53.22	52.64	22.18	30.55	21.58	21.09	28.17	19.95
1941	24.24	21.24	29.21	18.87	53.25	52.27	23.00	30.12	23.18	35.25	29.60	20.35
1942	24.21	21.31	29.03	18.63	53.21	51.81	23.17	29.59	26.13	70.14	30.54	20.41
1943	24.07	21.26	28.73	18.27	53.01	51.54	23.21	28.97	27.44	87.41	31.24	20.26
1944	23.96	21.20	28.53	17.92	53.05	51.25	23.66	28.39	27.81	93.80	31.57	20.06
1945	23.90	21.13	28.49	17.82	53.11	50.90	24.25	27.88	27.98	97.26	31.81	19.90
1946	24.44	21.70	28.98	18.38	53.18	53.14	24.92	27.54	27.84	96.01	31.26	19.92
1947	25.10	22.50	29.37	18.58	53.81	55.15	25.79	27.27	27.89	94.38	31.36	20.14
1948	25.92	23.48	29.91	18.92	54.63	56.90	27.11	26.94	28.17	93.23	32.06	20.51
1949	26.66	24.35	30.41	19.18	55.47	58.52	28.40	26.67	28.77	92.07	33.47	21.16
1950	27.70	25.63	31.03	19.60	56.24	60.13	30.13	26.60	29.52	91.17	35.07	21.96
1951	28.58	26.62	31.71	20.15	57.01	61.53	31.91	26.26	30.48	92.99	36.33	22.78
1952	29.42	27.58	32.35	20.60	57.77	63.07	33.99	26.01	31.62	96.92	37.55	23.60
1953	30.32	28.56	33.10	21.15	58.68	64.25	36.31	25.90	32.82	100.91	38.42	24.53
1954	31.30	29.64	33.90	21.85	59.37	65.31	38.95	25.82	34.14	103.80	39.32	25.71
1955	32.44	30.93	34.80	22.73	59.98	66.20	41.84	25.90	35.46	105.51	40.17	27.03
1956	33.55	32.06	35.86	23.82	60.81	67.15	44.35	25.80	36.78	106.96	41.11	28.35
1957	34.56	33.07	36.88	24.88	61.66	67.90	46.46	25.95	38.18	108.44	42.15	29.75
1958	35.49	34.08	37.70	25.74	62.33	68.60	48.15	26.03	39.79	110.30	43.60	31.33
1959	36.67	35.45	38.57	26.71	62.89	70.08	49.85	26.22	41.40	111.99	45.17	32.92
1960	37.80	36.66	39.57	27.91	63.44	71.76	51.17	26.70	42.98	113.23	46.95	34.49
1961	38.92	37.86	40.57	29.19	63.84	73.29	52.49	27.04	44.72	114.71	48.88	36.21
1962	40.16	39.21	41.63	30.53	64.21	75.09	53.93	27.45	46.46	115.48	51.13	37.97
1963	41.51	40.77	42.68	31.87	64.64	76.89	55.00	27.95	48.32	115.64	53.63	39.91
1964	43.01	42.41	43.94	33.45	65.23	78.60	56.32	28.51	50.26	115.21	56.36	41.98

(continued)

	Private								Government			
			Nonresidential						Federal			
Year	Total	Residential	Total	Buildings, excluding farm	Privately owned public utilities	Farm-related	Mining	Other nonfarm	Total	Defense	Nondefense	State and local
	Dc66	Dc67	Dc68	Dc69	Dc70	Dc71	Dc72	Dc73	Dc74	Dc75	Dc76	Dc77
	Index 1996 = 100	Index 1996 = 100	Index 1996 = 100	Index 1996 = 100	Index 1996 = 100	Index 1996 = 100	Index 1996 = 100	Index 1996 = 100	Index 1996 = 100	Index 1996 = 100	Index 1996 = 100	Index 1996 = 100
1965	44.57	43.96	45.54	35.50	66.01	80.31	57.53	29.31	52.34	114.55	59.30	44.22
1966	46.04	45.28	47.24	37.66	66.96	82.08	58.46	30.27	54.54	113.97	62.15	46.60
1967	47.42	46.50	48.85	39.54	68.21	84.22	59.18	31.04	56.75	113.26	63.98	49.14
1968	48.94	47.97	50.47	41.34	69.70	85.88	59.88	32.10	59.00	112.54	65.36	51.79
1969	50.53	49.47	52.20	43.32	71.15	87.44	60.73	33.50	61.03	112.00	66.30	54.20
1970	52.00	50.81	53.88	45.16	72.69	89.12	61.28	35.24	62.78	111.17	67.16	56.32
1971	53.77	52.69	55.47	46.92	74.21	90.54	61.51	36.89	64.45	110.74	68.08	58.29
1972	55.78	54.96	57.08	48.65	75.92	91.39	62.00	38.24	65.97	110.18	69.24	60.07
1973	57.85	57.20	58.90	50.60	77.79	93.10	62.69	39.46	67.46	109.64	70.66	61.80
1974	59.45	58.75	60.57	52.39	79.22	95.50	64.04	40.55	68.87	108.94	71.95	63.47
1975	60.69	59.95	61.87	53.59	80.50	98.06	66.02	41.57	70.23	108.19	73.16	65.08
1976	62.21	61.64	63.16	54.69	81.89	100.71	68.24	42.61	71.52	107.33	74.39	66.64
1977	64.09	63.86	64.52	55.83	83.23	103.51	71.03	43.92	72.65	106.52	75.64	67.99
1978	66.20	66.25	66.19	57.35	84.64	106.63	74.51	45.52	73.99	105.77	77.07	69.58
1979	68.34	68.46	68.23	59.42	86.04	109.69	78.20	47.54	75.35	104.84	78.29	71.25
1980	70.12	69.96	70.46	61.54	87.41	111.55	84.95	49.22	76.71	104.12	79.55	72.88
1981	71.88	71.22	73.00	63.97	88.68	112.64	93.07	50.85	77.85	103.34	81.24	74.18
1982	73.31	72.03	75.35	66.51	89.62	112.72	99.53	52.52	78.77	102.81	82.41	75.24
1983	74.98	73.64	77.12	68.68	90.11	112.41	103.28	54.59	79.65	102.63	83.30	76.25
1984	77.12	75.63	79.48	71.54	90.95	112.00	108.12	57.65	80.74	102.41	84.28	77.50
1985	79.40	77.61	82.23	74.97	92.29	110.84	111.28	62.41	82.04	102.58	85.18	78.98
1986	81.67	79.97	84.36	77.95	93.50	109.59	109.84	65.91	83.49	102.88	86.30	80.61
1987	83.91	82.31	86.42	80.78	94.61	108.62	108.35	69.89	85.01	103.35	87.68	82.27
1988	86.04	84.58	88.36	83.66	95.15	107.48	107.08	72.64	86.53	103.68	88.23	84.04
1989	88.08	86.69	90.28	86.56	95.67	106.25	105.35	75.90	88.01	103.58	88.82	85.81
1990	90.00	88.52	92.34	89.49	96.41	105.31	104.49	79.87	89.70	103.35	89.66	87.84
1991	91.37	89.86	93.76	91.41	97.07	104.34	103.86	83.58	91.43	102.65	90.86	89.95
1992	92.78	91.50	94.79	92.83	97.66	102.97	102.20	88.33	93.16	102.10	92.07	92.04
1993	94.45	93.50	95.94	94.30	98.33	102.20	101.77	92.35	94.79	101.43	93.48	94.01
1994	96.16	95.65	96.97	95.81	98.49	101.44	101.13	95.42	96.35	100.88	94.77	95.90
1995	97.92	97.67	98.31	97.71	99.13	100.53	100.06	98.21	98.10	100.41	96.63	97.94
1996	100.00	100.00	100.00	100.00	100.00	100.00	100.00	100.00	100.00	100.00	100.00	100.00
1997	102.21	102.31	102.04	102.71	100.88	99.42	101.65	101.40	101.93	99.34	100.92	102.41
1998	104.73	104.94	104.39	105.70	102.40	99.01	102.56	103.19	103.86	98.60	102.09	104.80
1999	107.30	107.78	106.54	108.55	103.64	98.14	102.55	105.30	105.93	97.81	103.11	107.39

Source

See the source for Table Dc54–65.

Documentation

The series shown in this table are identical in composition to those described in the text for Table Dc54–65.

The indexes shown in this table are year-end estimates of the nation's net stock of structures measured in "real" or "physical volume" terms. The U.S. Bureau of Economic Analysis (BEA) refers to these chained indexes as real-cost estimates because identical structures are assigned equal value in base-year (1996) prices regardless of the level of prices that prevailed in the years in which they were actually acquired. A separate index is shown here for every major type of structure. The source reports indexes for subaggregates of these categories. Each index is derived by applying the perpetual inventory method described below to deflated investment flows so that the effects of price changes are removed.

The BEA adopted the use of chained quantity indexes during its 1996 comprehensive revision of the national income and product accounts (NIPA). The indexes were chosen to replace the more familiar "constant-dollar" series, which were produced by deflating current-dollar series with fixed-weight price indexes. A problem with constant-dollar series is that the growth rate between any two dates will generally change when the base year changes. The problem becomes more severe during periods of rapid price changes or when growth rates are measured for periods far away in time from the base year.

TABLE Dc66–77   Net stock of structures, by type: 1925–1999   [Chain-type quantity indexes]   *Continued*

The chain indexes shown here avoid this problem by multiplying (or "chaining" together) separate year-to-year changes for all of the years in the series. This provides a more accurate estimate of the growth rate between any two years because the weights used for every year reflect the actual composition of structures in the market during that year. Furthermore, although the levels of chained indexes change when their base period is updated, the growth rates of the various series do not.

Unlike constant-dollar series, however, chained indexes are not additive and so cannot be directly used to calculate the relative importance individual components play in a total series (for example, the share of telecommunications in all nonresidential structures). It is possible, however, to combine the indexes shown here with the current-cost estimates shown in Table Dc54–65 to derive chained 1996-dollar estimates that are reliable over fairly short intervals of time. See J. Steven Landefeld and Robert P. Parker, "BEA's Chain Indexes, Time Series, and Measures of Long-Term Economic Growth," *Survey of Current Business* 77 (5)(1997): 58–68, for an explanation of this procedure and a general discussion of the relative merits and different uses of constant-dollar and chained weight indexes.

The perpetual inventory method the BEA employs to derive the chained indexes shown in this table is derived in three steps. The first step involves forming estimates of the gross stock of structures for each year by cumulating real investments in each type of structure for past years. The BEA uses its own current-dollar NIPA investment estimates deflated by base year 1996 price indexes as the real investment series (see below for more on the underlying investment series). The second step consists of forming estimates of real-cost depreciation for each year and each type of structure by assuming that a unit of each type of real investment "wears out" according to a declining geometric pattern that is based on empirical studies (see U.S. Bureau of Economic Analysis, *Fixed Reproducible Tangible Wealth in the United States, 1925–94* (August 1999), pp. M-27 to M-31). Real depreciation is then cumulated

over all vintages of a given type of structure and subtracted from the gross stock to obtain estimates of the real net stock of structures for each year and type of structure. The third, and final, step is to calculate the year-to-year percentage changes in each net stock series and to "chain" these together to construct the indexes shown in the table.

The annual chain-type quantity indexes of the net stock of structures, therefore, are actually weighted summations of real investments flows. The principal advantage of the perpetual inventory method over the alternative of counting the actual physical inventory of structures each year is that comprehensive, detailed, and relatively reliable estimates of flows of new investment are available (the NIPA measures of real purchases of new structures by consumers, business, and government).

The NIPA estimates are closely related to the annual estimates of the value of construction put in place produced by the Census Bureau that are shown in Tables Dc1–53, but the two series differ in several important respects including coverage, estimation procedures, classification, and the timing when revisions are incorporated. These differences include investment in some types of structures that are captured in the NIPA estimates but are excluded from value-in-place series – expenditures on new manufactured homes, drilling and exploration of petroleum and natural gas wells, construction on mines, and brokers' commissions on the sale of new and existing structures. On the other hand, the value-in place estimates make allowance for imputed interest on funds used during construction of public utility plants whereas the NIPA estimates do not. The NIPA estimates also adjust for the net value of used structures purchased from the public sector by the private sector, and include expenditures on federal government structures located outside the United States. For more detailed information concerning the differences between the NIPA measures of investment in structures and the value-in-place series, see the *Survey of Current Business* (January/February 1996): 5 and Tables 5.6 and 5.14, and Current Construction Report C30/99-5, in U.S. Census Bureau, *Value of Construction Put in Place* (May 1999).

TABLE Dc78–91   Expenditures for new construction – gross and net, by type: 1889–1955[1]   [Current dollars]

Contributed by Kenneth A. Snowden

		Gross								Net				
		Private					Public			Private		Public	
		Nonfarm residential			Other						Nonfarm			
Year	Total	Total excluding oil and gas well drilling	Total	New	Additions and alterations	Total	Oil and gas well drilling	Nonmilitary	Military	Total	residential	Other	Nonmilitary	Military
	Dc78	Dc79	Dc80	Dc81	Dc82	Dc83	Dc84	Dc85	Dc86	Dc87	Dc88	Dc89	Dc90	Dc91
	Million dollars	Million dollars	Million dollars	Million dollars	Million dollars	Million dollars	Million dollars	Million dollars	Million dollars	Million dollars	Million dollars	Million dollars	Million dollars	Million dollars
1889	1,645	1,601	891	806	85	635	44	119	—	787	712	12	63	—
1890	2,393	2,339	875	790	85	1,394	54	124	—	1,555	682	807	66	—
1891	2,141	2,112	694	612	82	1,320	29	127	—	1,293	493	732	68	—
1892	2,718	2,701	843	763	80	1,743	17	132	—	1,859	636	1,152	71	—
1893	2,190	2,173	662	583	79	1,390	17	138	—	1,303	444	785	74	—
1894	2,093	2,060	672	594	78	1,282	33	139	—	1,202	452	675	75	—
1895	2,192	2,127	756	679	77	1,295	65	141	—	1,276	528	674	74	—
1896	1,875	1,800	683	606	77	1,046	75	146	—	918	444	399	75	—
1897	2,088	2,030	719	643	76	1,219	58	150	—	1,125	474	573	78	—
1898	1,982	1,934	646	574	72	1,174	48	162	—	962	381	497	84	—
1899	2,069	1,969	679	608	71	1,205	100	185	—	911	386	429	96	—
1900	2,471	2,346	503	433	70	1,761	125	207	—	1,244	186	948	110	—
1901	2,705	2,598	683	610	73	1,809	107	213	—	1,463	365	984	114	—
1902	3,107	2,986	648	572	76	2,228	121	231	—	1,797	311	1,363	123	—
1903	3,063	2,918	691	607	84	2,085	145	287	—	1,675	335	1,170	170	—
1904	3,023	2,870	788	690	98	1,903	153	332	—	1,598	428	960	210	—

Note appears at end of table

(continued)

TABLE Dc78-91   Expenditures for new construction – gross and net, by type: 1889-1955   [Current dollars]
Continued

			Gross								Net				
			Private					Public			Private			Public	
			Nonfarm residential			Other									
	Total	Total excluding oil and gas well drilling	Total	New	Additions and alterations	Total	Oil and gas well drilling	Nonmilitary	Military	Total	Nonfarm residential	Other	Nonmilitary	Military
	Dc78	Dc79	Dc80	Dc81	Dc82	Dc83	Dc84	Dc85	Dc86	Dc87	Dc88	Dc89	Dc90	Dc91
Year	Million dollars	Million dollars	Million dollars	Million dollars	Million dollars	Million dollars	Million dollars	Million dollars	Million dollars	Million dollars	Million dollars	Million dollars	Million dollars	Million dollars
1905	3,327	3,197	1,264	1,154	110	1,721	130	342	—	1,766	872	688	206	—
1906	3,951	3,792	1,281	1,170	111	2,307	159	363	—	2,216	831	1,177	208	—
1907	4,342	4,169	1,148	1,037	111	2,750	173	444	—	2,487	661	1,552	274	—
1908	3,891	3,747	1,148	1,034	114	2,245	144	498	—	2,037	662	1,052	324	—
1909	4,467	4,308	1,390	1,272	118	2,589	159	488	—	2,515	869	1,346	300	—
1910	4,425	4,293	1,140	1,028	112	2,764	132	521	—	2,373	581	1,474	317	—
1911	4,144	4,022	1,109	1,000	109	2,459	122	576	—	2,008	545	1,104	359	—
1912	4,546	4,392	1,221	1,113	108	2,765	154	560	—	2,310	630	1,353	327	—
1913	4,988	4,754	1,214	1,108	106	3,183	234	591	—	2,637	631	1,666	340	—
1914	3,659	3,454	1,187	1,081	106	1,808	205	645	19	1,276	587	283	388	18
1915	3,509	3,382	1,300	1,192	108	1,490	127	702	17	1,011	671	−100	425	16
1916	4,162	3,905	1,371	1,255	116	2,083	257	687	21	1,300	685	243	353	18
1917	4,641	4,323	879	769	110	2,483	318	671	608	1,038	68	134	247	589
1918	5,126	4,729	481	391	90	2,407	397	683	1,555	693	−480	−466	161	1,477
1919	6,396	5,919	1,398	1,258	140	3,022	477	887	1,089	1,200	285	−277	264	928
1920	6,727	6,076	1,212	1,072	140	4,163	651	1,191	161	365	−231	302	376	−82
1921	6,359	6,004	1,980	1,795	185	2,815	355	1,515	49	1,094	813	−394	825	−150
1922	8,016	7,647	3,155	2,955	200	3,177	369	1,659	25	3,058	2,053	184	985	−164
1923	9,732	9,332	4,170	3,960	210	3,940	400	1,606	16	4,131	2,878	642	808	−196
1924	10,792	10,407	4,805	4,575	230	4,086	385	1,892	9	5,030	3,462	701	1,068	−201
1925	11,891	11,439	5,160	4,910	250	4,593	452	2,130	8	6,039	3,748	1,199	1,283	−191
1926	12,584	12,082	5,190	4,920	270	5,250	502	2,133	11	6,485	3,685	1,748	1,247	−195
1927	12,439	12,034	4,830	4,540	290	5,200	405	2,397	12	6,161	3,269	1,626	1,458	−192
1928	11,988	11,641	4,510	4,195	315	4,993	347	2,470	15	5,490	2,876	1,299	1,495	−180
1929	11,193	10,793	3,380	3,040	340	5,327	400	2,467	19	4,323	1,623	1,437	1,438	−175
1930	9,041	8,741	1,875	1,570	305	4,308	300	2,829	29	2,276	207	430	1,793	−155
1931	6,627	6,427	1,495	1,320	175	2,473	200	2,619	40	220	−45	−1,216	1,608	−127
1932	3,738	3,538	590	485	105	1,286	200	1,828	34	−2,110	−706	−2,225	932	−112
1933	3,079	2,879	435	290	145	996	200	1,612	36	−2,843	−847	−2,363	488	−121
1934	3,920	3,720	580	380	200	1,129	200	2,164	47	−2,590	−795	−2,515	847	−127
1935	4,532	4,232	960	710	250	1,339	300	2,196	37	−1,859	−363	−2,219	860	−136
1936	6,797	6,497	1,505	1,210	295	1,776	300	3,487	29	156	124	−1,825	2,007	−149
1937	7,499	6,999	1,795	1,475	320	2,608	500	3,059	37	240	255	−1,350	1,473	−138
1938	7,380	6,980	1,915	1,620	295	2,045	400	3,358	62	−54	324	−2,046	1,724	−56
1939	8,566	8,198	2,590	2,270	320	2,167	368	3,684	125	1,224	959	−1,804	2,002	66
1940	9,080	8,682	2,895	2,560	335	2,557	398	3,243	385	1,482	1,166	−1,513	1,490	339
1941	12,380	11,957	3,415	3,040	375	3,214	423	4,131	1,620	4,251	1,522	−929	2,134	1,524
1942	14,381	14,075	1,665	1,440	225	2,056	306	5,644	5,016	5,405	−350	−2,148	3,172	4,731
1943	8,648	8,301	870	710	160	1,456	347	3,772	2,550	−1,218	−1,222	−3,128	1,082	2,049
1944	5,785	5,259	790	570	220	1,922	526	2,236	837	−4,564	−1,460	−3,015	−359	271
1945	6,231	5,633	1,060	720	340	2,773	598	1,708	690	−4,570	−1,310	−2,446	−895	81
1946	12,653	12,000	3,870	3,300	570	6,421	653	2,174	188	427	1,248	510	−774	−556
1947	17,462	16,689	6,185	5,450	735	7,844	773	3,229	204	2,384	2,959	384	−241	−719
1948	22,729	21,670	8,425	7,500	925	9,479	1,059	4,667	158	5,650	4,754	1,090	675	−869
1949	23,858	22,804	8,082	7,257	825	9,371	1,054	6,268	137	6,459	4,415	675	2,248	−879
1950	29,733	28,472	12,425	11,525	900	10,308	1,261	6,823	177	11,419	8,417	1,198	2,662	−858
1951	32,750	31,259	10,783	9,849	934	12,549	1,491	8,531	887	12,376	6,310	2,481	3,847	−262
1952	34,624	32,941	10,915	9,870	1,045	12,808	1,683	9,513	1,388	13,323	6,187	2,526	4,460	150
1953	37,172	35,308	11,663	—	—	14,115	1,864	10,087	1,307	14,725	6,718	3,259	4,765	−17
1954	39,792	37,749	13,200	—	—	14,663	2,043	10,899	1,030	16,675	8,133	3,535	5,353	−346
1955	45,153	42,832	16,256	—	—	16,478	2,321	11,122	1,297	20,526	10,827	4,795	5,074	−170

[1]   See text for a discussion of issues relating to the comparability of the series over time and for differences between these figures and the official Census Bureau value-in-place estimates.

Sources
All series, except those noted. Robert E. Lipsey and Doris Preston, *Source Book of Statistics Related to Construction* (Columbia University Press, 1966), Section C, pp. 29–40.

Series on the subcomponents (new, and additions and alterations) of nonfarm residential construction. Leo Grebler, David Blank, and Louis Winnick, *Capital Formation in Residential Real Estate* (Princeton University Press, 1956), Tables B-3 and B-4, pp. 336-7. See also David M. Blank, *The Volume of Residential Construction 1889-1950*, National Bureau of Economic Research, Technical Paper number 9, 1954.

TABLE Dc78–91   Expenditures for new construction – gross and net, by type: 1889–1955   [Current dollars]
Continued

Series on gross public military construction. Simon Kuznets, *Capital in the American Economy: Its Formation and Financing* (Princeton University Press, 1961), Table R-6, p. 494.

Most series shown here are available at the Internet site of the National Bureau of Economic Research.

Documentation

Tables Dc78–105 present Simon Kuznets's estimates of gross and net construction expenditures in both current and constant 1929 dollars.

Kuznets reported decadal and five-year moving averages of annual estimates of construction activity in his monumental examination, *Capital in the American Economy* (1961). Kuznets was interested in examining long-term trends in the rate and composition of real investment activity between 1869 and 1955 and so focused on five- and ten-year moving averages of his construction series. Lipsey and Preston (1966) used Kuznets's notes and original tables to recover his estimates of annual construction expenditures and published these series for the first time, along with extensive explanatory notes. Kuznets's own documentation of these estimates appears on pages 490-3 and 576-95 of *Capital in the American Economy*.

For the 1915–1955 period, Kuznets's general approach was to adopt the Commerce Department's official value of construction put-in-place estimates. There are several differences worth noting, however, between the post-1915 estimates shown in these tables and the official value-in-place figures shown in Tables Dc1–11 and Dc22–43.

(1) Kuznets included the cost of drilling oil and gas wells in his estimates of construction, whereas these activities were excluded from the official value-in-place series. Total construction is reported in these tables both including and excluding expenditures for drilling oil and gas wells to facilitate comparison between Kuznets's estimates and the official value-in-place series. For the derivation of the current-dollar estimates shown here, see Lipsey and Preston (1966), p. 280.

(2) Kuznets included expenditures for "nonhousekeeping" residential units (such as hotels and dormitories) in his private construction excluding residential aggregates, series Dc83 and Dc89 in the current-dollar table and series Dc97 and Dc103 in the constant-dollar table. The Commerce Department, in contrast, included them as a component of the nonfarm residential aggregate.

(3) Kuznets used Grebler, Blank, and Winnick's (1956) estimates of nonfarm residential construction (excluding nonhousekeeping) for 1915–1920 rather than the official value-in-place estimates (see discussion below).

Except for these three elements, Kuznets's estimates for the 1915–1955 period were identical to official Commerce Department value-in-place estimates as they stood when *Capital in the American Economy* was being written. In the early 1960s, however, major revisions were made to the official series for the 1946–1955 period that created additional differences between official estimates and Kuznets's series. The most important was a substantial upward revision made in 1960 to the residential construction series going back to 1946. Kuznets's estimates for 1946–1955 differ significantly, therefore, from the official revised Commerce Department estimates.

Users of these data should consider that the original, unrevised 1945–1955 estimates used by Kuznets and shown in this table maintain backward continuity with the Commerce Department's official estimates for earlier years. The revisions made to the official series in the early 1960s, in contrast, were designed to bring data from 1945–1959 in line with the new procedures implemented in and after 1960. As a result, the original Kuznets series are shown here in their entirety even though they embody official value-in-place estimates for the 1945–1955 period that have since been revised.

Kuznets's important contribution was to extend the official Commerce Department's construction estimates backward from 1915 to 1889. He did so in several steps, described in the following list. Note that these series were first estimated in constant 1929 dollars, as shown in Table Dc92–105, and then expressed in current dollars, as shown in Table Dc78–91. See Lipsey and Preston (1966) for a discussion of the price indexes that were used to convert Kuznets's constant-dollar series to current-dollar estimates.

(1) Kuznets first estimated total construction expenditure excluding oil and gas drilling for each year from a measure of construction materials consumed each year. (a) For the 1921–1955 period, he used the official constant-dollar value-in-place total construction series after it had been rebased to constant 1929 dollars. (b) For the 1915–1920 period, the level and changes in series Dc93 differ from the official estimates because Kuznets chose to use Grebler, Blank, and Winnick's (1956) data for the nonfarm residential category rather than official value-in-place estimates. (c) For the 1889–1914 period, Kuznets constructed his own estimates of series Dc93 by extrapolating from total domestic consumption of construction materials for each year as reported by William H. Shaw, *Value of Commodity Output since 1869* (National Bureau of Economic Research, 1947), Table I1, p. 64. Kuznets first rescaled Shaw's series to 1929 prices and multiplied it by 1.4576 to account for transportation and distribution costs. The resulting series was then adjusted by the net changes in construction inventories each year to capture only the total flow of construction materials consumed in each year in 1929 prices. These totals were then multiplied by 1.54056, the ratio of total new construction cost to the cost of construction materials consumed in 1919-1933. The method of estimation and data sources are described in Kuznets (1961), Table R-30, notes to column 10, and Kuznets, *National Product since 1869* (National Bureau of Economic Research, 1946), Table II-5, notes to column 7.

(2) Kuznets also had to assemble estimates of the other component of his constant-dollar total gross construction series – the constant-dollar cost of oil and gas wells drilled, series Dc98. For 1929–1955 this series was based on current-dollar drilling expenditures series and price indexes, all rebased to 1929, that had been reported in various Commerce Department publications. For 1919–1928, data were extrapolated from the 1929 figure by the series described in Kuznets, *National Income and Its Composition, 1919–1938* (National Bureau of Economic Research, 1941), p. 645. This series is based on individual state data for number of wells drilled and 1935 costs. For years before 1919, the constant-dollar estimates for oil and gas wells were extrapolated from the 1919 figure by the number of wells drilled each year. For further details concerning the derivation of series Dc98, see Kuznets (1961), pp. 492-3, 526-7, and Lipsey and Preston (1966), p. 280.

(3) Kuznets summed series Dc93 and Dc98 to form constant-dollar total gross construction, and then decomposed this total into three major subcomponents – private nonfarm residential, private excluding nonfarm residential, and public. Additional information on these subcomponents is provided in the following sections.

Nonfarm Residential Construction

As noted above, these series cover only housekeeping units.

Grebler, Blank, and Winnick's (1956) nonfarm residential construction series that Kuznets used was the sum of two other series that are also reported here. The new housekeeping units subcomponent was originally estimated and reported for the 1889–1920 period by Blank (1954, Table 18) in order to extend the official value-in-place residential construction series back before 1915. Blank used pre-1920 city-level building permit data for new construction that were collected and compiled during the 1930s by the Bureau of Labor Statistics and the Works Progress Administration. Blank argued that his source material was more comprehensive and his techniques more refined than those that had been used to construct official estimates for the 1915–1920 period, but accepted the official series beginning in 1921. Grebler, Blank, and Winnick (1956) constructed their own estimates of additions and alterations to housekeeping units for the 1889–1920 period, and extended it to 1952 by the official value-in-place series for this component. Kuznets accepted all of Grebler, Blank, and Winnick's series for the 1889–1952 period and used official Commerce estimates then available for 1953–1955. Kuznets also accepted Grebler, Blank, and Winnick's current-dollar annual estimates of depreciation and demolition for residential real estate, and their net expenditures on nonfarm residential construction. See the Grebler, Blank, and Winnick source for details about the residential series.

(continued)

TABLE Dc78–91   Expenditures for new construction – gross and net, by type: 1889–1955   [Current dollars]   *Continued*

Public Construction

For 1915–1955, Kuznets simply rebased official constant-dollar military and nonmilitary value-in-place estimates to 1929 dollars.

For the pre-1915 period, Kuznets assembled his own current-dollar estimates for gross public construction using, whenever possible, sources and methodology that were similar to those that underlie the official value-in-place estimates starting in 1915. Kuznets calculated constant-dollar figures for public construction by deflating the various components of his current-dollar public construction series with separate price indexes (see Kuznets 1961, Table R-30, for details.) Note that through 1913, the public construction figures include some small amount of military construction. Kuznets formed this series by adding together separate estimates of federal, state, and local government construction. The federal series was derived from annual expenditures on construction by federal agencies, while the state and local government expenditures came from the Census Bureau's reports on government finances for the years 1902–1913, which were then extrapolated back using population and wealth estimates for the 1889–1901 period. A detailed description is given in Kuznets (1961), notes to Table R-30, pp. 580–4. Separate estimates for state and local government construction before 1915 appear in Lipsey and Preston (1966), p. 39.

Also note that Kuznets reports gross military construction expenditures rounded to $10 million. The estimates here (rounded to $1 million) were calculated as a residual and checked against official Census Bureau value-in-place series.

Private Construction Excluding Nonfarm Residential

Kuznets estimated this major subcomponent as a residual – namely, the difference between (a) total gross construction and (b) the sum of the other two major subcomponents, private nonfarm residential and public.

Net Construction Expenditures

Total net expenditure on construction, series Dc101, was derived as the sum of constant-dollar net expenditures on its four subcomponents. Kuznets intended to capture not only physical depreciation, but also depletion, obsolescence, accidental loss or damage, and demolition in his annual estimates of capital consumption. Each capital consumption series was calculated in constant dollars and on a replacement cost basis. Net constant-dollar expenditure on nonfarm residential, series Dc102, was calculated by subtracting annual constant-dollar estimates of capital consumption from gross constant-dollar expenditure on residential housing, series Dc94. Kuznets used Grebler, Blank, and Winnick's (1956) annual capital consumption estimates for nonfarm residential structures for 1889–1952, and extended their method to 1955 (see Grebler, Blank, and Winnick 1956, Appendix E, for details). For capital consumption on private nonresidential structures, and publicly owned military and nonmilitary structures alike, Kuznets relied on a variety of authors and procedures. For an overview, see Lipsey and Preston (1966), pp. 253–5; for details, see Kuznets (1961), notes to Tables R-6, R-8, R-31, and R-32.

To form the current-dollar net construction series, each of these capital consumption series was reflated into current dollars by the use of appropriate price indexes and subtracted from gross construction. Lipsey and Preston (1966, pp. 253–5) provide details about the price indexes used in the procedures. Total net construction was then formed as the sum of the components.

TABLE Dc92–105 Expenditures for new construction – gross and net, by type: 1889–1955¹ [Constant dollars]

Contributed by Kenneth A. Snowden

			Gross							Net				
			Private					Public			Private		Public	
			Nonfarm residential			Other									
Year	Total	Total excluding oil and gas well drilling	Total	New	Additions and alterations	Total	Oil and gas well drilling	Nonmilitary	Military	Total	Nonfarm residential	Other	Nonmilitary	Military
	Dc92	Dc93	Dc94	Dc95	Dc96	Dc97	Dc98	Dc99	Dc100	Dc101	Dc102	Dc103	Dc104	Dc105
	Million 1929 dollars	Million 1929 dollars	Million 1929 dollars	Million 1929 dollars	Million 1929 dollars	Million 1929 dollars	Million 1929 dollars	Million 1929 dollars	Million 1929 dollars	Million 1929 dollars	Million 1929 dollars	Million 1929 dollars	Million 1929 dollars	Million 1929 dollars
1889	3,735	3,641	2,284	2,067	217	1,181	94	270	—	1,985	1,826	12	147	—
1890	5,451	5,336	2,232	2,015	217	2,937	115	282	—	3,595	1,736	1,706	153	—
1891	5,033	4,969	1,831	1,615	216	2,904	64	298	—	3,073	1,301	1,609	163	—
1892	6,570	6,532	2,290	2,073	217	3,962	38	318	—	4,521	1,727	2,618	176	—
1893	5,338	5,299	1,804	1,589	215	3,199	39	335	—	3,203	1,210	1,807	186	—
1894	5,300	5,221	1,898	1,678	220	3,051	79	351	—	3,083	1,277	1,611	195	—
1895	5,598	5,443	2,167	1,946	221	3,073	155	358	—	3,295	1,515	1,586	194	—
1896	4,744	4,568	1,945	1,726	219	2,435	176	364	—	2,354	1,264	898	192	—
1897	5,493	5,352	2,090	1,869	221	3,014	141	389	—	3,010	1,379	1,422	209	—
1898	5,118	5,003	1,800	1,599	201	2,908	115	410	—	2,547	1,063	1,263	221	—
1899	4,866	4,647	1,763	1,579	184	2,678	219	425	—	2,204	1,003	974	227	—
1900	5,562	5,302	1,239	1,067	172	3,866	260	457	—	2,811	459	2,103	249	—
1901	6,241	6,012	1,703	1,521	182	4,058	229	480	—	3,404	909	2,233	262	—
1902	6,964	6,713	1,561	1,378	183	4,897	251	506	—	4,046	748	3,020	278	—
1903	6,632	6,340	1,607	1,412	195	4,420	292	605	—	3,627	778	2,485	364	—
1904	6,625	6,314	1,855	1,624	231	4,047	311	723	—	3,529	1,007	2,054	468	—
1905	6,968	6,716	2,840	2,593	247	3,414	252	714	—	3,766	1,960	1,363	443	—
1906	7,615	7,330	2,620	2,393	227	4,288	285	707	—	4,294	1,700	2,173	421	—
1907	8,049	7,750	2,246	2,029	217	4,980	299	823	—	4,611	1,293	2,798	520	—
1908	7,496	7,238	2,319	2,089	230	4,210	258	967	—	3,941	1,337	1,960	645	—
1909	8,471	8,190	2,705	2,475	230	4,832	281	934	—	4,799	1,691	2,517	591	—
1910	8,234	8,006	2,143	1,932	211	5,118	228	973	—	4,436	1,093	2,734	609	—
1911	7,678	7,468	2,113	1,905	208	4,496	210	1,069	—	3,761	1,039	2,040	682	—
1912	8,280	8,019	2,270	2,069	201	4,982	261	1,028	—	4,242	1,172	2,453	617	—
1913	8,879	8,490	2,339	2,135	204	5,481	389	1,059	—	4,717	1,216	2,876	625	—
1914	6,701	6,350	2,274	2,071	203	3,210	351	1,186	31	2,409	1,124	529	726	30
1915	6,363	6,148	2,430	2,228	202	2,646	215	1,259	28	1,941	1,255	−109	769	26
1916	6,783	6,409	2,406	2,202	204	3,275	374	1,071	31	2,226	1,203	443	553	27
1917	6,090	5,735	1,320	1,155	165	3,148	355	853	769	1,392	102	232	312	745
1918	5,676	5,286	608	494	114	2,617	390	737	1,714	818	−605	−384	179	1,628
1919	6,300	5,857	1,518	1,366	152	2,919	443	817	1,046	1,219	309	−223	242	891
1920	5,414	4,887	1,021	903	118	3,414	527	857	122	241	−195	235	263	−62
1921	6,341	6,004	2,076	1,882	194	2,870	337	1,349	46	1,102	853	−335	727	−142
1922	8,768	8,376	3,597	3,369	228	3,524	392	1,622	25	3,385	2,340	250	960	−165
1923	9,653	9,258	4,242	4,028	214	3,985	395	1,412	14	4,120	2,928	657	712	−177
1924	10,752	10,386	4,958	4,721	237	4,092	366	1,694	8	5,047	3,572	704	955	−184

Note appears at end of table

(continued)

TABLE Dc92–105   Expenditures for new construction–gross and net, by type: 1889–1955   [Constant dollars]   Continued

	Gross									Net				
			Private					Public			Private		Public	
			Nonfarm residential			Other						Nonfarm			
Year	Total	Total excluding oil and gas well drilling	Total	New	Additions and alterations	Total	Oil and gas well drilling	Nonmilitary	Military	Total	residential	Other	Nonmilitary	Military
	Dc92	Dc93	Dc94	Dc95	Dc96	Dc97	Dc98	Dc99	Dc100	Dc101	Dc102	Dc103	Dc104	Dc105
	Million 1929 dollars	Million 1929 dollars	Million 1929 dollars	Million 1929 dollars	Million 1929 dollars	Million 1929 dollars	Million 1929 dollars	Million 1929 dollars	Million 1929 dollars	Million 1929 dollars	Million 1929 dollars	Million 1929 dollars	Million 1929 dollars	Million 1929 dollars
1925	12,066	11,625	5,364	5,104	260	4,712	441	1,982	8	6,147	3,896	1,241	1,194	−184
1926	12,773	12,278	5,356	5,077	279	5,382	495	2,025	10	6,597	3,803	1,792	1,184	−182
1927	12,699	12,292	5,052	4,749	303	5,343	407	2,293	11	6,301	3,419	1,669	1,395	−182
1928	12,268	11,915	4,703	4,374	328	5,113	353	2,437	15	5,626	2,999	1,332	1,474	−179
1929	11,193	10,793	3,380	3,040	340	5,327	400	2,467	19	4,324	1,623	1,438	1,438	−175
1930	9,352	9,039	1,923	1,610	313	4,380	313	3,018	31	2,382	212	419	1,915	−165
1931	7,457	7,238	1,663	1,468	195	2,668	219	3,079	47	365	−50	−1,325	1,890	−151
1932	4,845	4,607	775	637	138	1,444	238	2,579	47	−2,291	−928	−2,523	1,313	−153
1933	3,673	3,436	571	381	190	1,160	237	1,896	46	−3,471	−1,111	−2,777	573	−156
1934	4,214	3,996	699	458	241	1,203	218	2,257	55	−2,943	−960	−2,720	886	−149
1935	5,026	4,702	1,193	882	311	1,468	324	2,321	44	−2,175	−451	−2,461	898	−161
1936	7,295	6,979	1,787	1,437	350	1,933	316	3,542	33	8	147	−2,017	2,050	−172
1937	7,540	7,055	1,916	1,574	342	2,594	485	2,990	40	157	272	−1,387	1,419	−147
1938	7,385	6,994	1,988	1,682	306	1,979	391	3,351	67	−45	336	−2,022	1,702	−61
1939	8,683	8,323	2,643	2,316	327	2,175	360	3,729	136	1,200	979	−1,845	1,994	72
1940	9,065	8,682	2,846	2,517	329	2,520	383	3,293	406	1,462	1,146	−1,518	1,476	358
1941	11,642	11,259	3,116	2,774	342	3,187	383	3,749	1,590	3,830	1,389	−912	1,857	1,496
1942	12,115	11,858	1,438	1,244	194	2,091	257	4,447	4,139	3,984	−302	−2,095	2,477	3,904
1943	6,926	6,641	718	586	132	1,339	285	2,900	1,969	−1,415	−1,008	−2,854	865	1,582
1944	4,653	4,224	598	431	167	1,636	429	1,750	669	−3,799	−1,105	−2,591	−319	216
1945	4,836	4,363	752	511	241	2,209	473	1,328	547	−3,636	−930	−2,016	−754	64
1946	8,492	—	2,479	2,114	365	4,357	—	1,530	126	114	799	252	−564	−373
1947	9,667	—	3,270	2,881	388	4,321	—	1,965	111	1,073	1,565	46	−145	−393
1948	11,309	—	4,002	3,563	439	4,754	—	2,475	78	2,512	2,258	351	334	−430
1949	12,031	—	3,956	3,552	404	4,672	—	3,334	69	3,023	2,161	159	1,145	−442
1950	14,406	—	5,763	5,346	417	4,964	—	3,591	88	5,205	3,904	381	1,346	−426
1951	14,680	—	4,648	4,245	403	5,584	—	4,043	405	5,232	2,720	895	1,736	−119
1952	15,032	—	4,582	4,144	439	5,535	—	4,301	614	5,466	2,597	872	1,930	67
1953	15,694	—	4,813	—	—	5,825	—	4,489	567	5,898	2,772	1,082	2,052	−8
1954	16,852	—	5,489	—	—	5,990	—	4,926	447	6,809	3,382	1,163	2,414	−150
1955	18,585	—	6,557	—	—	6,534	—	4,946	548	8,241	4,367	1,593	2,353	−72

[1] See text for a discussion of issues relating to the comparability of the series over time and for differences between these figures and the official U.S. Census Bureau value-in-place estimates.

Source
See the source for Table Dc78–91.

Documentation
See the text for Table Dc78–91.

TABLE Dc106–131 Measures of construction activity – building permits and units built: 1830–1939

Contributed by Kenneth A. Snowden

	Riggleman		Isard – index of	Indexes of total construction			New building permits — Long				Newman – indexes of total value of permits		Blank – urban dwelling units	
	Permit value per capita		total value of permits				Indexes of residential construction		Indexes of nonresidential construction					
	Current dollars	Constant dollars		Number of permits	Value of permits	Value of permits (Colean-Newcomb)	Number of permits	Value of permits	Number of permits	Value of permits	Current prices	Constant prices	Index of number of units	Index of total value of permits
	Dc106	Dc107	Dc108	Dc109	Dc110	Dc111	Dc112	Dc113	Dc114	Dc115	Dc116	Dc117	Dc118	Dc119
Year	Dollars	1913 dollars	1920–1929 = 100	1920–1930 = 100	1920–1930 = 100	1920–1929 = 100	1920–1929 = 100	1920–1929 = 100	1920–1930 = 100	1920–1929 = 100	1920–1930 = 100	1913 = 100	1929 = 100	1929 = 100
1830	10.05	14.57	0.71	—	—	—	—	—	—	—	—	—	—	—
1831	14.04	19.23	1.02	—	—	—	—	—	—	—	—	—	—	—
1832	21.69	28.92	1.63	—	—	—	—	—	—	—	—	—	—	—
1833	25.22	34.55	1.97	—	—	—	—	—	—	—	—	—	—	—
1834	25.78	37.91	2.10	—	—	—	—	—	—	—	—	—	—	—
1835	30.73	39.90	2.61	—	—	—	—	—	—	—	—	—	—	—
1836	50.22	52.31	4.45	—	—	—	—	—	—	—	—	—	—	—
1837	24.60	25.36	2.27	—	—	—	—	—	—	—	—	—	—	—
1838	18.84	21.41	1.82	—	—	—	—	—	—	—	—	—	—	—
1839	16.72	19.22	1.70	—	—	—	—	—	—	—	—	—	—	—
1840	12.00	16.67	1.28	—	—	—	—	—	—	—	—	—	—	—
1841	12.04	17.20	1.35	—	—	—	—	—	—	—	—	—	—	—
1842	8.64	14.40	1.01	—	—	—	—	—	—	—	—	—	—	—
1843	6.46	12.67	0.80	—	—	—	—	—	—	—	—	—	—	—
1844	7.65	14.43	0.99	—	—	—	—	—	—	—	—	—	—	—
1845	10.33	17.51	1.41	—	—	—	—	—	—	—	—	—	—	—
1846	14.53	24.22	2.08	—	—	—	—	—	—	—	—	—	—	—
1847	19.68	30.28	2.96	—	—	—	—	—	—	—	—	—	—	—
1848	17.18	30.14	2.71	—	—	—	—	—	—	—	—	—	—	—
1849	19.15	34.20	3.01	—	—	—	—	—	—	—	—	—	—	—
1850	24.63	42.10	4.04	—	—	—	—	—	—	—	—	—	—	—
1851	25.36	44.10	4.35	—	—	—	—	—	—	—	—	—	—	—
1852	29.27	49.19	5.28	—	—	—	—	—	—	—	—	—	—	—
1853	31.39	51.04	5.96	—	—	—	—	—	—	—	—	—	—	—
1854	30.35	47.80	6.07	—	—	—	—	—	—	—	—	—	—	—
1855	24.05	44.13	5.94	—	—	—	—	—	—	—	—	—	—	—
1856	25.04	45.12	6.46	21	—	—	23	—	16	—	—	—	—	—
1857	24.91	41.52	6.70	18	—	—	19	—	16	—	—	—	—	—
1858	14.46	26.53	3.95	18	—	—	19	—	12	—	—	—	—	—
1859	16.17	28.37	4.61	22	—	—	25	—	16	—	—	—	—	—
1860	17.83	30.37	5.29	27	—	—	30	—	12	—	—	—	—	—
1861	12.06	20.13	3.68	18	—	—	22	—	4	—	—	—	—	—
1862	10.68	17.45	3.34	26	—	—	32	—	12	—	—	—	—	—
1863	16.80	21.00	5.34	28	—	—	31	—	23	—	—	—	—	—
1864	11.37	12.55	3.91	16	—	—	16	—	16	—	—	—	—	—

(continued)

TABLE Dc106–131   Measures of construction activity – building permits and units built: 1830–1939   _Continued_

	Riggleman		Isard – index of total value of permits	Indexes of total construction			Long — New building permits					Newman – indexes of total value of permits		Blank – urban dwelling units	
	Permit value per capita						Indexes of residential construction		Indexes of nonresidential construction						
	Current dollars	Constant dollars		Number of permits	Value of permits	Value of permits (Colean-Newcomb)	Number of permits	Value of permits	Number of permits	Value of permits	Current prices	Constant prices	Index of number of units	Index of total value of permits
	Dc106	Dc107	Dc108	Dc109	Dc110	Dc111	Dc112	Dc113	Dc114	Dc115	Dc116	Dc117	Dc118	Dc119
Year	Dollars	1913 dollars	1920–1929 = 100	1920–1930 = 100	1920–1930 = 100	1920–1929 = 100	1920–1929 = 100	1920–1929 = 100	1920–1930 = 100	1920–1929 = 100	1920–1930 = 100	1913 = 100	1929 = 100	1929 = 100
1865	17.77	18.04	6.10	22	—	—	22	—	23	—	—	—	—	—
1866	25.33	24.50	8.92	29	—	—	31	—	28	—	—	—	—	—
1867	29.55	28.44	10.55	38	—	—	44	—	26	—	—	—	—	—
1868	34.33	32.91	13.25	47	10	8	56	14	26	5	—	—	—	—
1869	37.53	35.61	14.88	54	11	10	66	15	26	8	—	—	—	—
1870	33.93	35.60	13.79	52	10	8	64	14	26	5	—	—	27.8	16.0
1871	37.69	37.92	15.41	62	12	10	78	18	26	6	—	—	39.3	20.2
1872	29.31	29.55	12.30	52	8	7	58	12	37	4	—	—	27.3	13.0
1873	27.80	28.66	11.97	47	7	7	58	8	26	6	—	—	25.8	8.9
1874	22.12	24.52	6.42	30	5	4	41	7	13	2	—	—	24.5	8.0
1875	20.27	24.72	6.22	29	6	5	41	8	12	3	5.4	20	24.9	8.5
1876	16.19	20.49	5.12	25	5	4	34	7	12	3	4.6	18	21.0	7.1
1877	13.94	18.94	4.55	26	4	3	37	6	9	1	4.5	19	17.5	6.6
1878	11.58	16.61	3.90	19	4	4	26	7	10	2	4.0	17	16.3	7.3
1879	13.03	19.36	4.53	19	6	5	23	10	12	2	4.1	19	21.4	10.8
1880	15.71	21.46	5.64	14	8	6	19	13	8	2	5.4	22	32.1	12.4
1881	19.33	24.91	7.33	18	11	10	27	16	9	7	6.7	27	36.4	16.9
1882	22.91	28.11	8.99	20	12	10	30	19	9	5	8.9	33	38.2	18.6
1883	24.94	30.45	10.13	24	12	10	37	17	10	6	10.4	39	52.9	19.6
1884	23.51	32.07	9.97	27	11	9	42	17	11	5	10.5	44	63.5	20.2
1885	26.33	36.01	11.60	33	12	9	53	20	12	4	11.2	47	71.8	25.6
1886	29.03	37.17	13.24	37	16	13	60	26	12	6	12.9	51	82.1	29.1
1887	29.84	38.35	14.40	34	17	13	64	24	15	8	11.8	47	91.1	32.8
1888	27.58	36.68	13.83	30	15	13	61	18	14	11	11.2	46	74.7	25.2
1889	32.93	43.73	17.06	36	19	15	74	24	16	12	15.4	63	88.3	33.3
1890	35.35	48.23	18.11	34	21	18	70	24	15	16	17.5	75	84.5	31.7
1891	29.85	42.10	15.75	30	16	14	56	18	13	14	17.6	76	67.9	24.7
1892	30.73	43.34	17.02	35	18	16	65	21	16	15	19.3	84	77.8	29.3
1893	22.58	31.76	12.87	26	16	15	50	16	12	16	12.6	55	55.1	20.5
1894	19.70	28.47	11.56	24	14	13	46	16	13	12	12.2	55	54.4	20.9
1895	25.22	36.13	15.26	27	20	18	56	23	13	17	16.5	73	73.6	27.7
1896	20.36	29.81	12.64	25	17	17	49	17	13	18	13.3	60	58.7	23.3
1897	21.36	32.12	13.57	26	19	17	55	21	11	17	14.5	67	75.4	28.0
1898	18.11	26.83	11.93	20	14	12	36	17	10	9	12.7	58	65.3	25.0
1899	23.34	31.37	14.89	24	22	19	38	25	11	17	16.7	70	84.9	33.6
1900	17.36	21.71	11.69	17	13	12	28	13	9	12	11.6	46	49.3	20.8
1901	25.58	30.59	15.75	23	21	20	36	20	13	22	17.0	66	75.1	30.3
1902	25.22	30.10	17.99	22	19	21	33	13	14	27	18.4	69	49.5	21.7
1903	24.88	29.62	18.29	24	19	20	36	16	16	24	19.8	71	59.9	24.1
1904	29.15	33.35	22.09	29	24	22	48	26	17	22	22.9	80	83.6	32.6

	Riggleman		Isard – index of	Indexes of total construction			Long – New building permits				Newman – indexes of total value of permits		Blank – urban dwelling units	
	Permit value per capita		total value of permits				Indexes of residential construction		Indexes of nonresidential construction					
	Current dollars	Constant dollars		Number of permits	Value of permits	Value of permits (Colean-Newcomb)	Number of permits	Value of permits	Number of permits	Value of permits	Current prices	Constant prices	Index of number of units	Index of total value of permits
	Dc106	Dc107	Dc108	Dc109	Dc110	Dc111	Dc112	Dc113	Dc114	Dc115	Dc116	Dc117	Dc118	Dc119
Year	Dollars	1913 dollars	1920–1929 = 100	1920–1930 = 100	1920–1930 = 100	1920–1929 = 100	1920–1929 = 100	1920–1929 = 100	1920–1930 = 100	1920–1929 = 100	1920–1930 = 100	1913 = 100	1929 = 100	1929 = 100
1905	37.94	41.88	29.66	39	36	31	66	43	20	27	31.9	106	134.0	53.2
1906	39.61	41.65	31.92	42	34	30	72	38	21	28	34.6	109	121.3	52.7
1907	35.66	35.45	29.63	39	28	27	65	29	21	27	31.4	98	102.9	45.6
1908	30.84	31.73	26.43	37	24	22	60	24	19	23	27.3	89	92.0	43.5
1909	40.43	44.48	35.68	46	36	33	79	41	20	30	38.8	125	118.5	60.4
1910	37.42	38.86	33.97	46	34	33	72	34	28	34	34.5	109	106.7	53.3
1911	35.28	37.77	32.79	46	33	34	71	30	29	37	33.2	104	106.4	50.9
1912	37.19	41.00	35.37	46	36	37	66	32	29	41	35.6	108	105.9	52.7
1913	33.02	33.02	32.12	43	30	30	60	28	28	33	33.1	100	96.2	47.2
1914	28.97	29.47	28.81	42	27	26	61	27	29	27	29.9	92	93.2	44.4
1915	29.81	29.54	30.26	48	30	28	69	32	34	28	31.2	94	101.0	50.4
1916	36.18	31.30	37.56	52	38	38	69	36	41	40	37.2	100	101.3	54.2
1917	22.70	15.89	24.10	36	23	26	34	16	36	32	26.2	59	48.3	26.9
1918	13.59	7.95	14.74	23	11	14	14	6	32	18	14.5	27	24.6	13.5
1919	40.46	19.01	44.84	67	46	48	65	38	70	56	47.9	70	68.6	55.3
1920	43.19	17.19	48.93	58	46	54	37	27	75	71	50.9	58	47.2	43.6
1921	52.63	26.08	60.81	81	60	58	75	61	83	59	61.1	90	94.2	83.3
1922	78.47	44.97	92.49	112	94	85	123	105	103	80	94.3	151	155.5	140.3
1923	94.10	43.97	113.20	133	113	101	143	128	121	93	116.4	167	193.7	178.5
1924	93.98	43.63	115.50	139	122	111	149	133	129	106	119.9	173	193.9	187.1
1925	108.27	52.38	135.95	144	144	136	164	151	128	136	137.7	204	208.1	207.0
1926	100.54	48.33	128.49	128	138	129	133	147	122	127	130.9	194	192.3	190.1
1927	90.44	43.86	113.36	102	117	112	101	117	106	116	118.5	176	172.8	173.3
1928	82.55	39.92	109.16	89	119	115	87	120	93	118	114.3	170	155.5	153.9
1929	72.54	35.04	97.55	67	92	99	54	72	80	118	100.3	149	100.0	100.0
1930	39.86	19.65	54.49	48	54	61	32	38	60	76	56.5	86	—	—
1931	29.95	16.51	41.55	43	42	45	31	33	52	54	40.5	71	—	—
1932	11.20	7.13	15.77	20	15	18	10	6	29	26	14.0	28	—	—
1933	8.84	5.20	12.63	15	8	8	7	7	22	8	10.8	22	—	—
1934	—	—	—	15	9	11	7	5	23	14	—	—	—	—
1935	—	—	—	23	18	18	18	15	28	21	—	—	—	—
1936	—	—	—	—	—	—	32	31	35	24	—	—	—	—
1937	—	—	—	—	—	—	—	—	—	—	—	—	—	—
1938	—	—	—	—	—	—	—	—	—	—	—	—	—	—
1939	—	—	—	—	—	—	—	—	—	—	—	—	—	—

(continued)

TABLE Dc106–131   Measures of construction activity – building permits and units built: 1830–1939   *Continued*

	Value of new construction		Indexes of new construction						Construction output and value			
			Value of new construction				Physical volume of construction				Value of nonfarm building activity	
			Current prices		Constant prices							
							Abramovitz					
Year	Current prices	Constant prices	Segment 1	Segment 2	Segment 1	Segment 2	Segment 1	Segment 2	Housing units built	Total	Residential	Nonresidential
	Dc120	Dc121	Dc122	Dc123	Dc124	Dc125	Dc126	Dc127	Dc128	Dc129	Dc130	Dc131
	1920–1929 = 100	1913 = 100	1870–1897 = 100	1889–1918 = 100	1870–1897 = 100	1889–1918 = 100	1856–1897 = 100	1889–1918 = 100	Thousand	Million dollars	Million dollars	Million dollars
1830	—	—	—	—	—	—	—	—	—	—	—	—
1831	1.1	—	—	—	—	—	—	—	—	—	—	—
1832	1.5	—	—	—	—	—	—	—	—	—	—	—
1833	1.9	—	—	—	—	—	—	—	—	—	—	—
1834	2.2	—	—	—	—	—	—	—	—	—	—	—
1835	3.1	—	—	—	—	—	—	—	—	—	—	—
1836	3.1	—	—	—	—	—	—	—	—	—	—	—
1837	2.3	—	—	—	—	—	—	—	—	—	—	—
1838	1.9	—	—	—	—	—	—	—	—	—	—	—
1839	1.6	—	—	—	—	—	—	—	—	—	—	—
1840	1.4	—	—	—	—	—	—	—	36	—	—	—
1841	1.2	—	—	—	—	—	—	—	41	—	—	—
1842	1.1	—	—	—	—	—	—	—	34	—	—	—
1843	0.9	—	—	—	—	—	—	—	34	—	—	—
1844	1.1	—	—	—	—	—	—	—	38	—	—	—
1845	1.5	—	—	—	—	—	—	—	46	—	—	—
1846	2.2	—	—	—	—	—	—	—	58	—	—	—
1847	2.6	—	—	—	—	—	—	—	72	—	—	—
1848	2.9	—	—	—	—	—	—	—	70	—	—	—
1849	3.3	—	—	—	—	—	—	—	82	—	—	—
1850	3.8	—	—	—	—	—	—	—	94	184.7	82.4	102.3
1851	4.6	—	—	—	—	—	—	—	109	212.8	96.2	116.6
1852	5.2	—	—	—	—	—	—	—	121	257.7	107.4	150.3
1853	5.8	28.6	—	—	—	—	—	—	133	290.0	118.8	171.2
1854	6.0	28.6	—	—	—	—	—	—	138	270.9	124.0	146.9
1855	6.2	34.5	—	—	—	—	59.4	—	138	233.1	124.6	108.5
1856	6.4	34.9	—	—	—	—	54.9	—	135	216.5	122.7	93.8
1857	5.7	28.8	—	—	—	—	46.1	—	142	241.6	129.8	111.8
1858	5.1	28.4	—	—	—	—	59.6	—	103	168.3	94.8	73.5
1859	4.6	24.5	—	—	—	—	—	—	98	167.1	87.2	79.9
1860	4.5	23.2	—	—	—	—	61.4	—	93	163.0	75.4	87.6
1861	4.1	20.7	—	—	—	—	38.5	—	76	140.0	64.0	76.0
1862	4.1	20.3	—	—	—	—	60.8	—	79	128.8	75.3	53.5
1863	4.2	15.9	—	—	—	—	77.4	—	74	122.7	78.9	43.8
1864	5.1	17.0	—	—	—	—	53.7	—	60	130.7	67.5	63.2
1865	6.3	19.4	—	—	—	—	69.7	—	81	161.6	82.7	78.9
1866	8.5	24.9	—	—	—	—	90.7	—	114	220.7	110.1	110.6
1867	10.9	31.8	—	—	—	—	105.0	—	140	272.6	134.1	138.5
1868	12.9	37.5	—	—	—	—	122.3	—	166	315.0	169.5	145.5
1869	14.0	40.2	—	—	—	—	137.8	—	169	309.8	173.3	136.5

	Value of new construction		Indexes of new construction — Abramovitz						Construction output and value			
	Current prices	Constant prices	Value of new construction — Current prices		Constant prices		Physical volume of construction		Housing units built	Value of nonfarm building activity		
										Total	Residential	Nonresidential
	Dc120	Dc121	Dc122	Dc123	Dc124	Dc125	Dc126	Dc127	Dc128	Dc129	Dc130	Dc131
	1920–1929 = 100	1913 = 100	1870–1897 = 100	1889–1918 = 100	1870–1897 = 100	1889–1918 = 100	1856–1897 = 100	1889–1918 = 100	Thousand	Million dollars	Million dollars	Million dollars
Year												
1870	14.7	46.8	133.2	—	119.6	—	138.1	—	158	359.6	164.4	195.2
1871	13.8	42.1	148.4	—	131.8	—	162.3	—	188	407.2	191.7	215.5
1872	13.2	40.3	123.2	—	102.1	—	159.2	—	168	336.0	170.9	165.1
1873	10.2	31.9	108.4	—	88.1	—	134.0	—	174	334.8	186.0	148.8
1874	8.2	27.6	58.9	—	51.7	—	87.5	—	124	259.0	143.7	115.3
1875	5.9	21.8	53.0	—	48.7	—	85.4	—	127	292.5	155.6	136.9
1876	5.3	20.3	45.5	—	43.7	—	78.7	—	102	242.1	123.8	118.3
1877	4.5	18.5	43.1	—	44.5	—	75.0	—	103	213.0	125.7	87.3
1878	4.3	18.7	38.4	—	41.9	—	66.2	—	81	196.0	98.4	97.6
1879	5.0	22.5	43.8	—	48.4	—	72.3	—	90	266.6	108.8	157.8
1880	7.0	29.0	68.0	—	68.1	—	76.0	—	127	330.4	148.3	182.1
1881	10.0	39.0	96.3	—	95.4	—	98.4	—	191	410.5	215.0	195.5
1882	11.0	40.9	103.0	—	97.8	—	94.3	—	208	473.3	226.9	246.4
1883	11.0	40.7	98.3	—	93.9	—	91.8	—	237	494.1	259.9	234.2
1884	10.0	41.3	88.1	—	86.3	—	93.0	—	246	463.7	283.3	180.4
1885	11.0	45.6	93.8	—	93.6	—	106.2	—	267	493.6	319.0	174.6
1886	13.0	50.4	110.9	—	110.1	—	132.4	—	278	572.1	326.9	245.2
1887	14.0	54.5	126.0	—	127.1	—	158.6	—	326	615.9	377.3	238.6
1888	15.0	60.4	119.6	—	119.1	—	131.7	—	320	605.8	387.1	218.7
1889	16.0	64.4	138.7	67.1	139.4	77.2	151.6	87.9	368	729.1	480.9	248.2
1890	17.0	70.3	146.2	71.3	147.2	83.1	154.8	88.4	278	810.9	384.7	426.2
1891	17.0	72.7	131.0	61.1	136.1	73.9	119.9	75.0	252	765.5	354.9	410.6
1892	16.0	68.4	157.8	79.8	168.8	99.9	141.6	93.8	323	825.6	460.5	365.1
1893	16.0	68.2	132.8	73.9	143.4	93.3	106.6	67.2	226	702.1	327.5	374.6
1894	16.0	70.1	97.9	58.7	109.4	76.1	100.4	67.0	225	629.5	330.8	298.7
1895	17.0	73.8	109.7	62.2	123.1	80.7	119.8	76.6	262	782.4	386.7	395.7
1896	18.0	79.9	89.9	58.9	99.9	75.7	105.3	66.4	218	659.9	317.7	342.2
1897	16.0	72.9	96.1	60.7	111.0	80.3	121.3	73.7	247	691.8	364.8	327.0
1898	17.0	76.3	—	52.4	—	67.5	—	70.0	222	622.0	335.2	286.8
1899	15.0	61.1	—	68.5	—	81.4	—	77.7	239	829.9	365.0	464.9
1900	18.0	68.3	—	57.1	—	65.6	—	61.9	230	784.8	345.4	439.4
1901	19.0	68.9	—	75.9	—	88.1	—	85.6	330	1,179.0	494.9	684.1
1902	21.0	75.9	—	81.4	—	92.1	—	86.2	320	1,216.1	497.6	718.5
1903	22.0	79.4	—	82.6	—	90.8	—	92.0	347	1,226.0	559.8	666.2
1904	25.0	86.7	—	87.7	—	96.6	—	89.6	403	1,458.1	704.9	753.2
1905	30.0	100.3	—	122.3	—	127.9	—	134.6	535	1,957.6	1,028.2	929.4
1906	31.0	98.8	—	135.0	—	131.0	—	139.2	524	2,021.8	1,045.7	976.1
1907	28.0	84.3	—	133.5	—	125.3	—	127.3	471	1,795.7	959.7	836.0
1908	29.0	90.4	—	125.7	—	121.6	—	104.9	462	1,568.8	952.4	634.4
1909	31.0	103.3	—	147.0	—	137.6	—	128.3	576	2,095.5	1,259.3	836.2

(continued)

TABLE Dc106–131   Measures of construction activity – building permits and units built: 1830–1939   _Continued_

	Value of new construction		Indexes of new construction				Abramovitz		Construction output and value			
			Value of new construction				Physical volume of construction		Housing units built	Value of nonfarm building activity		
	Current prices	Constant prices	Current prices		Constant prices					Total	Residential	Nonresidential
			Segment 1	Segment 2	Segment 1	Segment 2	Segment 1	Segment 2				
	Dc120	Dc121	Dc122	Dc123	Dc124	Dc125	Dc126	Dc127	Dc128	Dc129	Dc130	Dc131
	1920–1929 = 100	1913 = 100	1870–1897 = 100	1889–1918 = 100	1870–1897 = 100	1889–1918 = 100	1856–1897 = 100	1889–1918 = 100	Thousand	Million dollars	Million dollars	Million dollars
Year												
1910	35.0	110.1	—	149.4	—	137.4	—	130.2	477	2,042.9	1,119.8	923.1
1911	37.0	120.0	—	149.2	—	136.9	—	122.9	472	2,037.9	1,146.1	981.8
1912	36.0	120.3	—	159.9	—	144.0	—	132.7	510	2,207.6	1,247.0	978.0
1913	33.0	100.0	—	149.1	—	132.4	—	132.5	477	1,895.6	1,200.7	694.9
1914	30.0	92.5	—	128.7	—	115.9	—	119.9	467	1,672.6	1,151.3	521.3
1915	33.0	99.1	—	122.1	—	107.8	—	129.5	474	1,968.9	1,233.9	735.0
1916	39.0	102.3	—	145.6	—	116.3	—	144.5	467	2,078.9	1,201.9	877.0
1917	47.0	99.7	—	140.3	—	92.2	—	110.4	291	1,500.0	722.0	778.0
1918	52.0	92.2	—	93.3	—	51.1	—	83.5	169	978.1	368.1	610.0
1919	64.0	91.1	—	—	—	—	—	—	415	1,684.1	945.1	739.0
1920	69.0	83.2	—	—	—	—	—	—	250	1,536.1	553.1	983.0
1921	61.0	91.6	—	—	—	—	—	—	491	2,148.4	1,094.4	1,045.0
1922	78.0	135.4	—	—	—	—	—	—	767	3,151.7	1,918.7	1,233.0
1923	95.0	134.5	—	—	—	—	—	—	950	3,586.1	2,336.1	1,250.0
1924	106.0	149.1	—	—	—	—	—	—	963	3,972.1	2,707.1	1,265.0
1925	117.0	171.5	—	—	—	—	—	—	1,048	4,617.1	3,035.1	1,582.0
1926	123.0	179.2	—	—	—	—	—	—	1,010	5,062.3	3,211.3	1,851.0
1927	123.0	180.8	—	—	—	—	—	—	837	4,435.2	2,609.2	1,826.0
1928	119.0	174.4	—	—	—	—	—	—	741	4,124.7	2,288.7	1,836.0
1929	110.0	161.0	—	—	—	—	—	—	573	3,690.4	1,819.4	1,871.0
1930	89.0	132.9	—	—	—	—	—	—	485	2,828.2	1,258.2	1,570.0
1931	65.0	108.6	—	—	—	—	—	—	373	2,233.2	1,146.2	1,087.0
1932	36.0	69.5	—	—	—	—	—	—	197	1,170.9	497.9	673.0
1933	29.0	51.7	—	—	—	—	—	—	137	779.4	298.4	481.0
1934	38.0	—	—	—	—	—	—	—	185	917.5	357.5	560.0
1935	43.0	—	—	—	—	—	—	—	325	1,264.5	705.5	559.0
1936	66.0	—	—	—	—	—	—	—	469	2,109.7	1,178.7	931.0
1937	71.0	—	—	—	—	—	—	—	494	2,193.3	1,245.3	948.0
1938	71.0	—	—	—	—	—	—	—	597	2,175.2	1,338.2	837.0
1939	84.0	—	—	—	—	—	—	—	757	3,049.4	2,035.4	1,014.0

Sources

Series Dc106–108. Miles L. Colean and Robinson Newcomb, _Stabilizing Construction: The Record and Potential_ (McGraw-Hill, 1952), Appendix N, Tables 2 and 4. Colean and Newcomb reported data that originally appeared in John R. Riggleman, "Variations in Building Activity in United States Cities" (Ph.D. dissertation, Johns Hopkins University, 1934), and Walter Isard, "The Economic Dynamics of Transport Technology" (Ph.D. dissertation, Yale University, 1947).

Series Dc109–110 and Dc112–115. Clarence D. Long Jr., _Building Cycles and the Theory of Investment_ (Princeton University Press, 1940), pp. 213–23.

Series Dc111 and Dc120. Miles L. Colean and Robinson Newcomb, _Stabilizing Construction: The Record and Potential_ (McGraw-Hill, 1952), Appendix N, Tables 2 and 3.

Series Dc116–117. William H. Newman, "The Building Industry and Business Cycles," _Journal of Business_ 8 (3, part 2) (1935): 63–71.

Series Dc118–119. David M. Blank, _The Volume of Residential Construction, 1889–1950_, National Bureau of Economic Research, Technical Paper number 9, 1954, Table 11.

Series Dc121–127. Moses Abramovitz, _Evidences of Long Swings in Aggregate Construction since the Civil War_, National Bureau of Economic Research Occasional Paper number 90, 1964, Table A-1.

Series Dc128. Manuel Gottlieb, _Estimates of Residential Building in the United States, 1840–1939_, NBER, Technical Paper number 17, 1964, Table 15.

TABLE Dc106–131   Measures of construction activity – building permits and units built: 1830–1939   *Continued*

Series Dc129–131. Manuel Gottlieb, "New Measures of Value of Nonfarm Building for the United States, Annually 1850-1939," *Review of Economics and Statistics* (November 1965): 412-9.

Documentation

This table presents a broad range of indicators of construction activity that have been assembled to investigate periods earlier than those covered by official value-in-place estimates (see Table Dc1-11).

One way of understanding the scope of these historical series is by differentiating them according to the activities they are designed to measure. The earliest available records of construction activity are building permits that are held in local jurisdictions – and all of the series shown in this table are based at least in part on local building permit data. The majority of the series presented here (series Dc106-119) were constructed from permit data that were unadjusted – these measure the total number of permits, or the total value shown on them, as indexes either on a per capita basis or in current or constant dollars. This first group of series does not purport to provide comprehensive or accurate measures of actual construction activity; they are designed, instead, to reflect general changes over time and trends in building activity. This limitation arises for two reasons. First, building permits measure the number and estimated costs of projects before they are begun and so are noisy indicators of building activity actually completed. Moreover, during the eighteenth and early nineteenth centuries, building permit data consistently understated the amount of work performed because permits were generally required for private, and not public, construction; for building, and not non-building, construction; and for urban, and neither rural nor farm, building activity. Riggleman, Long, Newman, Blank, and Colean and Newcomb all understood that their indexes were affected by these limitations, and so should users of their series.

A second group of the series shown in the table (series Dc120-127) was compiled to derive more accurate measures of total actual construction activity than the series based solely on unadjusted permit data. To this end both Abramovitz and Colean and Newcomb either supplemented building permit data with other information or manipulated the basic permit data. These eight series are also expressed as index numbers, and so do not explicitly measure total construction amounts or costs. However, both authors used their series to extend official value-in-place construction estimates back before 1915 after the latter had also been converted to an index. In fact, only the third and last group of series in this table – those produced by Gottlieb (series Dc128-131) – represents estimates of actual units of production or dollars of costs. As a result, only the Gottlieb series represent an alternative to Kuznets's estimates of aggregate construction expenditures for the same period, shown in Tables Dc78-105.

A second way of understanding the differences and similarities among the series shown in this table is to appreciate when and why each was assembled. For this purpose, the series fall into three distinct groups:

(1) Series Dc106-117 were assembled soon after aggregate construction had collapsed during the Great Depression. At the time it was believed that the building boom of the 1920s and bust of the 1930s was the most recent in a series of "building cycles" that had played a large part in overall economic instability in the United States since the mid-1800s. To investigate this conjecture, Riggleman (1933), Newman (1935), and Long (1940) assembled municipal records of building permits back into the nineteenth century.

(2) Interest in the building cycle was renewed during the 1950s and 1960s after Kuznets's identified fifteen- to twenty-year "long swings" in economic growth. This led Colean and Newcomb (1952) and Abramovitz (1964) to reexamine the building permit data that had been originally assembled in the 1930s in an attempt to uncover variations in the long-term trends in construction activity. This second group – series Dc120-127 – therefore, represents later manipulations of data assembled by Riggleman, Long, and others. Users of this second group of series should consult the discussion below, along with sources, for details of the data transformations that were employed, because these affect the time series behavior of the underlying annual building permit data.

(3) Finally, series Dc118-119 and Dc128-131 were derived from data that the authors of the series assembled and used in an attempt to better measure actual construction activity. Blank's indexes of the number and value of urban dwellings authorized by permit were assembled from municipal building permit data records and special censuses of building permits that were conducted during the 1930s. These indexes represent Blank's first step in deriving estimates of total nonfarm housing starts and values for the period before 1920, which were ultimately carried back only to 1889. The indexes of unadjusted permit data shown here, therefore, should not be confused with Blank's other series that were based on them – nonfarm housing starts (see Table Dc510-530), and expenditures on nonfarm residential construction (see Tables Dc78-105). Gottlieb (1964) originally offered his urban housing production series as an improvement and extension of the Bureau of Labor Statistics official housing start series and then used it to develop independent estimates of the total value of new nonfarm construction and its two major components (Gottlieb 1965). Nathan Balke and Robert J. Gordon recently deemed Gottlieb's aggregate, series Dc129, a better measure of pre-World War I construction than Kuznets's pre-1915 expenditure data shown in series Dc78, and they used it in their analysis of the changing variability of the U.S. business cycle. See Nathan Balke and Robert J. Gordon, "The Estimation of Prewar Gross National Product: Methodology and New Evidence," *Journal of Political Economy* 97 (1) (1989): 65-7.

Those interested in these historical construction series will find three sources particularly useful. Robert Lipsey and Doris Preston (*Source Book of Statistics Relating to Construction* (National Bureau of Economic Research, 1966)) provide an extended discussion of Long's and Riggleman's building permit series. Abramovitz (1964, pp. 195-225) provides an authoritative discussion and critique of all the series shown above. Finally, additional historical building permit series for regions and individual cities can be found at the Internet site of the National Bureau of Economic Research (NBER).

Series Dc106–107. Riggleman's principal contribution was to assemble historical building permit data for a sample of cities: Manhattan, Boston, and Washington, D.C., for 1830-1848, ten cities by 1868, and seventy cities beginning in 1900 (counting the five boroughs of New York City separately). The permits were for residential and nonresidential building, and included additions and alterations as well as new construction. The series were dominated by Manhattan before 1870, and in the early years based largely on estimates. For a list of cities covered, see Colean and Newcomb (1952), Appendix N, Table 4, p. 240. Riggleman originally presented his permit series in per capita terms by using city population estimates that were interpolated from decadal census figures. The annual per capita figures were then expressed as deviations from a long-term trend. The current- and constant-dollar per capita series shown in this table are not detrended and were first published in Colean and Newcomb (1952), Appendix N, Tables 2 and 4. The constant 1913 dollar series was derived by applying a building cost index that Riggleman based on the industrial building cost index of the American Appraisal Company for 1852-1903, and the *Engineering News-Record*'s construction cost index thereafter. For the pre-1852 period, Colean and Newcomb extended Riggleman's cost index with their own unweighted average of building trade wage rates and softwood lumber prices.

Series Dc108. In order to construct a building permit index that was comparable to Long's, Isard eliminated Riggleman's population adjustment and weighted each year of data on the basis of the relative volume of activity from 1920 to 1929 in the areas covered. This index first appeared in Isard's unpublished dissertation; the source used here is Colean and Newcomb (1952), Appendix N, Table 2.

Series Dc109–115. Long compiled the underlying data from published reports of municipal building departments before 1920 and from reports by the Bureau of Labor Statistics after that date. The annual value for each of Long's indexes was calculated relative to a base equal to its average value between 1920 and 1930. His indexes for the value of building permits cover only one city (Manhattan) beginning in 1868 and expand in coverage to twenty-seven cities by 1911. Over the same period, the coverage of the indexes for number of buildings increases from one to twenty-nine cities. For a list of cities and years covered, see Long (1940), Appendix B. Long's series are indexes of urban construction only, and they primarily cover large Eastern cities before 1898. Long also reports an annual index of the value of additions and

(continued)

TABLE Dc106–131 Measures of construction activity – building permits and units built: 1830–1939 *Continued*

alterations in the same twenty-seven cities, 1868–1935; the value of permits for detached dwellings, multifamily dwellings, public buildings, nonresidential buildings, and additions and alterations for fourteen cities, 1868–1935; and a monthly index of all construction (including public buildings and additions and alterations) for one to thirty-five cities, 1868–1939.

Series Dc111. Colean and Newcomb (1952, pp. 219–25) criticize the composition of Long's total value of new building, series Dc110, as being too heavily weighted toward residential construction (Long assumed a weight of approximately one half). Their adjustment to Long's series reduces the weight of new residential buildings to one third, and used 1920–1929 as the base period. See Colean and Newcomb (1952), Appendix N, Table 2.

Series Dc116–117. Newman (1935) took a different approach in assembling his series of building permit values. For the 1900–1933 period, his current-dollar index is an amalgam of three commercially produced indexes: Bradstreet's building permit values in 120 identical cities for 1911–1933, Babson's monthly values of building permits in 20 cities for 1903–1910, and Ayres's index of permits in 50 cities for 1900–1902. For the 1875–1899 period, Newman used permit data drawn directly from the records of thirteen cities. His constant-dollar index, series Dc117, was obtained by deflating the current-dollar series by the American Appraisal Company's building construction cost index for 1913–1933; an arithmetic average of the American Appraisal Company's cost indexes for frame, brick, and reinforced concrete buildings for 1900–1913; and an average of the cost indexes for frame and brick buildings for earlier years. Newman cites his unpublished dissertation (available at the University of Chicago Library) for additional explanation and details.

Series Dc118–119. Blank (1954, pp. 42–3) offered his indexes of the number and valuation of urban dwelling units authorized by permit as a direct summary of the permit data for the cities he examined – that is, before the adjustments he made to derive estimates of housing starts (see Table Dc510–530) and residential construction expenditures (as shown in Tables Dc78–105). Blank's analysis was based on transcriptions of building permit data in 314 cities that was undertaken during the 1930s as a WPA project. The cities include only Manhattan for 1870–1874, and Boston; Philadelphia; Jersey City; and Quincy, Illinois, for the rest of that decade. The coverage increases to 20 cities by 1889, 67 by 1900, and 314 in 1929. For a list of cities and years covered, see Blank (1954, Table 23, pp. 75–7). The figures here are chain indexes that were computed by first deriving relatives of the aggregate number of dwelling units authorized and their aggregate permit valuation in identical groups of cities between pairs of successive years. These series were unadjusted for lapses of building permits (with certain exceptions for New York City), for understatement of valuations in building permits, or to reflect actual construction expenditures.

Series Dc120. Colean and Newcomb's (1952) series was assembled to investigate the "long cycle" in new construction over the longest time period available. It links three-year moving averages of the Isard figures in series Dc108 for 1831–1878 to their adjusted version of Long's data, series Dc111, for 1879–1914. The source (Appendix N, Table 3) extends the index to 1951 by using the official value-in-place estimates of new construction expenditures, series Dc1, but the index is shown here only through 1939. Colean and Newcomb argued that their modifications to the Isard and Long indexes dampened excess year-to-year fluctuations in earlier building permit series, so they were more closely comparable to the official construction expenditures series that begin in 1915. The authors also questioned the reliability of the pre-1914 raw permit data, and cautioned that their own index was only "suggestive."

Series Dc121. Abramowitz (1964, Table A-1, pp. 146–50, 192) converted Colean and Newcomb's current-dollar figures shown in series Dc120 into a constant-dollar index for the 1853–1933 period by using Riggleman's building cost index as modified by Colean and Newcomb.

Series Dc122–127. Abramovitz assembled annual indexes of the value of aggregate construction from 1870 to 1918 in both current and constant

dollars, and indexes of the physical volume of aggregate construction from 1856 to 1918. Each of the three series was reported in two segments, and all six segments represent weighted averages of what Abramovitz believed were the most reliable estimates of residential building, nonresidential building, and public utility construction activity for each period. Abramovitz compiled these indexes as alternatives to Kuznets's estimates of pre-1915 construction expenditures (see Tables Dc78–105). After cataloguing several potential biases in Kuznets's approach, Abramovitz (1964, pp. 217–22) argued that his indexes had the advantage of having been derived from series that directly measured construction, permits, or contracts. Although he offered these indexes as measures of aggregate construction, Abramovitz notes that most of the series he used provided incomplete coverage of public sector construction. In deriving all of his indexes, Abramovitz first expressed the underlying component series as an index relative to its overall average for the relevant time segment before weighting and combining them. For an extended discussion on all of Abramovitz's series, see part III of his Appendix (1964, pp. 195–227).

Series Dc122 and Dc124. Segment 1 uses the Isard index, series Dc108, to represent both residential and nonresidential buildings (corrected for price changes before being used in the constant-dollar series). This component was given a weight of 0.75 in the indexes and then added to an annual series of gross capital expenditures in the regulated industries (given a weight of 0.25). The latter series was drawn from Melville Ulmer, *Capital in the Transportation, Communications and Public Utilities: Its Formation and Financing* (Princeton University Press, 1960).

Series Dc123 and Dc125. Segment 2 combines Blank's estimates of expenditures on new nonfarm housekeeping units, series Dc81 (weight of 0.41), Long's index of the value of nonresidential building permits, series Dc115 (weight of 0.23), and Ulmer's gross capital expenditure for the regulated industries (weight of 0.36).

Series Dc126–127. Both segments 1 and 2 of Abramovitz's physical volume series combined Long's index of the number of nonresidential building permits, series Dc114, and a series of rail consumption to represent the public utilities sector, albeit with slightly differing weights. The physical volume of residential construction for the earlier segment (1856–1897) was measured by Long's index of the number of residential building permits, series Dc112, and Blank's series of dwelling units started after 1889 (see Table Dc510–530).

Series Dc128. Gottlieb was the last major contributor to the measurement of historical construction statistics, and he introduced both a new approach and new data. Rather than relying on building permits, Gottlieb assembled his housing production series from housing stock and vintage data that were collected in the 1940 Census of Housing and from an almost complete inventory of housing in Ohio before 1890. His method was first to estimate decadal totals of new housing, and then distribute these by using weighted averages of the annual indexes of Isard (series Dc108), Long (series Dc110), Blank (see Table Dc510–530), and his own Ohio data. Gottlieb (1964) provides a detailed description of the methodology, along with comparisons of his estimates with the others shown in this table.

Series Dc129–131. Gottlieb's aggregate building series for the pre-1915 period was assembled using a method similar to that used for series Dc128. In this case, Gottlieb connected the decadal increments in wealth and the nonfarm labor force in Ohio to estimates of building for that state, and then used these to extrapolate nationwide estimates of building from aggregate decadal labor force and wealth data. After 1915 the total value of building (series Dc129) is simply the sum of the residential and nonresidential components. Gottlieb's residential building series was based up to 1912 on his Ohio housing production series for new homes, and Grebler, Blank, and Winnick's figures for later years (see Table Dc78–91). Gottlieb's nonresidential building series before 1915 is simply a residual of series Dc129–130, and the official value-in-place estimates thereafter.

TABLE Dc132–144 Construction contracts awarded – value, by type of construction: 1901–1998[1,2]

Contributed by Kenneth A. Snowden

		Nonresidential buildings										Residential buildings	Nonbuilding construction
	Total	Total	Commercial	Manufacturing	Educational and science	Public and institutional	Hospital	Public	Religious	Social and recreational	Miscellaneous		
	Dc132	Dc133	Dc134 [3]	Dc135	Dc136	Dc137	Dc138	Dc139	Dc140	Dc141	Dc142	Dc143	Dc144
Year	Million dollars	Million dollars	Million dollars	Million dollars	Million dollars	Million dollars	Million dollars	Million dollars	Million dollars	Million dollars	Million dollars	Million dollars	Million dollars
1901	120	—	—	—	—	—	—	—	—	—	—	—	—
1902	119	—	—	—	—	—	—	—	—	—	—	—	—
1903	104	—	—	—	—	—	—	—	—	—	—	—	—
1904	97	—	—	—	—	—	—	—	—	—	—	—	—
1905	107	—	—	—	—	—	—	—	—	—	—	—	—
1906	125	—	—	—	—	—	—	—	—	—	—	—	—
1907	129	—	—	—	—	—	—	—	—	—	—	—	—
1908	112	—	—	—	—	—	—	—	—	—	—	—	—
1909	166	—	—	—	—	—	—	—	—	—	—	—	—
1910	859	—	—	—	—	—	—	—	—	—	—	—	—
1911	828	—	—	—	—	—	—	—	—	—	—	—	—
1912	923	—	—	—	—	—	—	—	—	—	—	—	—
1913	917	—	—	—	—	—	—	—	—	—	—	—	—
1914	775	—	—	—	—	—	—	—	—	—	—	—	—
1915	978	—	—	—	—	—	—	—	—	—	—	418	—
1916	1,413	—	—	—	—	—	—	—	—	—	—	483	—
1917	1,691	—	—	—	—	—	—	—	—	—	—	355	—
1918	1,767	—	—	—	—	—	—	—	—	—	—	305	—
1919	2,580	1,213	406	498	—	266	—	—	—	—	—	849	517
1920	2,564	1,394	444	555	—	345	—	—	—	—	—	570	600
1921	2,355	998	332	153	—	461	—	—	—	—	—	879	479
1922	3,344	1,395	496	278	—	599	—	—	—	—	—	1,340	609
1923	3,992	1,456	518	313	—	601	—	—	—	—	—	1,736	801
1924	4,479	1,583	591	233	—	721	—	—	—	—	—	2,052	844
1925	6,006	2,202	872	327	419	—	111	55	153	253	12	2,748	1,057
1926	6,381	2,418	921	471	373	—	133	67	149	252	52	2,671	1,292
1927	6,303	2,439	933	376	369	—	163	80	157	261	102	2,573	1,291
1928	6,628	2,438	885	509	390	—	165	76	128	219	67	2,788	1,402
1929	5,751	2,425	929	546	370	—	152	121	106	147	55	1,916	1,410
1930	4,523	1,822	616	257	366	—	163	140	93	117	71	1,101	1,599
1931	3,093	1,141	311	116	223	—	121	181	53	99	36	811	1,141
1932	1,351	488	123	44	81	—	48	118	27	34	13	280	583
1933	1,256	417	99	128	39	—	37	51	18	27	19	249	589
1934	1,543	551	151	116	112	—	37	56	18	46	15	249	743
1935	1,845	681	165	109	168	—	47	98	24	55	16	479	685
1936	2,675	960	249	198	219	—	74	102	28	75	14	802	914
1937	2,913	1,156	297	314	223	—	82	105	37	84	15	905	852
1938	3,197	1,072	216	121	334	—	116	114	36	108	28	986	1,139
1939	3,551	966	247	175	201	—	83	110	38	82	29	1,334	1,251
1940	4,004	1,295	318	442	147	—	94	80	46	63	104	1,597	1,112
1941	6,007	2,316	471	1,182	141	—	89	89	53	78	214	1,954	1,738
1942	8,255	3,897	302	2,228	148	—	185	102	24	101	808	1,818	2,541
1943	3,274	1,424	121	766	62	—	111	25	7	58	274	868	982
1944	1,994	899	81	473	69	—	59	12	12	33	161	348	746
1945	3,299	1,850	346	1,027	100	—	113	16	35	60	153	563	885
1946	7,490	2,716	773	1,317	221	—	131	25	68	93	88	3,142	1,631
1947	9,175	2,716	785	941	392	—	192	73	118	122	92	4,569	1,890
1948	11,121	3,666	975	840	725	—	405	84	245	232	161	5,299	2,155
1949	11,826	3,644	885	559	824	—	555	119	276	222	204	5,706	2,476
1950	16,592	5,182	1,209	1,142	1,180	—	655	124	336	261	274	8,832	2,578
1951	17,151	6,823	915	2,883	1,335	—	581	158	299	136	515	7,605	2,723
1952	18,070	6,695	979	2,558	1,472	—	444	233	318	153	538	7,963	3,412
1953	18,804	6,956	1,489	2,051	1,720	—	434	203	385	222	452	7,840	4,008
1954	20,596	7,110	1,816	1,274	2,063	—	519	249	486	252	452	9,344	4,142
1955	24,632	8,497	2,359	1,878	2,134	—	475	301	551	270	530	11,072	5,063
1956	31,612	11,208	3,140	2,381	2,883	—	678	428	681	422	595	12,862	7,542
1957	32,173	11,293	3,267	2,168	2,936	—	870	470	699	429	455	13,039	7,841
1958	35,090	10,948	3,197	1,400	2,907	—	879	655	746	500	664	14,696	9,446
1959	36,269	11,387	3,496	1,880	2,666	—	865	605	799	601	474	17,150	7,732

Notes appear at end of table   (continued)

TABLE Dc132–144   Construction contracts awarded – value, by type of construction: 1901–1998   *Continued*

| | | | | Nonresidential buildings | | | | | | | | |
Year	Total	Total	Commercial	Manufacturing	Educational and science	Public and institutional	Hospital	Public	Religious	Social and recreational	Miscellaneous	Residential buildings	Nonbuilding construction
	Dc132	Dc133	Dc134 [3]	Dc135	Dc136	Dc137	Dc138	Dc139	Dc140	Dc141	Dc142	Dc143	Dc144
	Million dollars	Million dollars	Million dollars	Million dollars	Million dollars	Million dollars	Million dollars	Million dollars	Million dollars	Million dollars	Million dollars	Million dollars	Million dollars
1960	36,318	12,240	3,725	2,114	3,005	—	832	679	789	631	464	15,105	8,973
1961	37,135	12,115	3,797	1,814	3,015	—	985	671	805	623	403	16,123	8,897
1962	41,303	13,010	4,216	2,086	3,060	—	1,079	677	811	704	377	18,039	10,255
1963	45,546	14,377	4,445	2,274	3,314	—	1,485	964	755	648	493	20,502	10,667
1964	47,330	15,522	4,572	2,970	3,554	—	1,625	789	814	599	598	20,565	11,244
1965	49,272	17,219	5,457	3,064	4,164	—	1,515	842	783	800	596	21,248	10,805
1966	50,150	19,393	5,835	3,623	4,939	—	1,721	939	825	855	656	17,827	12,930
1967	54,514	20,139	6,080	3,701	5,216	—	1,873	959	793	834	683	21,155	13,220
1968	61,732	22,513	7,645	3,768	5,347	—	2,114	1,112	778	954	795	24,838	14,382
1969	68,294	25,949	9,786	3,915	5,543	—	2,817	1,154	674	1,116	944	25,633	16,710
1970	68,294	24,455	9,056	3,664	5,253	—	2,811	1,007	575	1,137	952	24,837	19,001
1971	80,188	25,590	9,610	2,619	5,649	—	3,188	1,493	603	1,296	1,132	34,714	19,883
1972	90,979	27,021	11,369	3,005	4,760	—	3,516	1,490	640	1,237	1,003	44,975	18,983
1973	99,304	31,534	12,846	4,841	5,061	—	3,324	2,014	705	1,508	1,235	45,696	22,074
1974	93,685	33,131	11,751	5,595	6,334	—	3,818	2,070	778	1,562	1,222	33,567	26,988
1975	92,659	31,647	9,233	6,834	5,876	—	3,680	2,143	813	1,617	1,452	31,261	29,751
1976	110,000	31,300	11,100	4,500	5,300	—	4,500	2,000	900	1,500	1,600	42,900	35,800
1977	141,000	37,000	14,900	5,400	5,500	—	4,500	2,000	1,000	1,800	1,800	60,800	43,200
1978	160,600	47,400	22,300	9,300	6,100	—	3,900	1,600	1,200	2,100	900	73,200	40,000
1979	170,900	53,500	26,900	7,800	6,900	—	4,800	1,600	1,300	2,700	1,500	71,900	45,500
1980	151,800	56,900	27,700	9,200	7,400	—	5,400	1,600	1,200	2,700	1,700	60,400	34,500
1981	157,300	65,500	35,200	9,300	6,600	—	6,400	1,400	1,200	3,400	2,000	56,300	35,400
1982	157,100	64,600	32,300	9,600	6,800	—	8,000	1,900	1,200	2,800	2,000	55,000	37,500
1983	194,100	67,900	38,300	5,400	7,100	—	8,500	2,100	1,500	2,900	2,100	88,400	37,800
1984	214,300	82,100	48,200	7,900	8,500	—	7,400	2,700	1,700	3,300	2,400	95,300	36,900
1985	235,600	92,100	54,600	8,100	10,000	—	7,800	3,100	2,000	4,000	2,500	102,100	41,400
1986	249,300	91,600	52,400	7,300	11,700	—	7,900	3,200	2,100	4,200	2,800	115,600	42,100
1987	259,000	98,800	53,700	8,600	13,200	—	9,000	4,700	2,100	4,300	3,200	114,100	46,100
1988	262,200	97,900	51,600	9,500	14,100	—	8,200	4,400	2,200	4,700	3,200	116,200	48,100
1989	271,300	106,100	53,600	12,700	15,900	—	8,800	5,200	2,000	5,000	2,900	116,200	49,000
1990	246,000	95,400	44,800	8,400	16,600	—	9,200	5,700	2,200	5,300	3,100	100,900	49,700
1991	230,800	86,200	32,700	8,300	19,000	—	9,600	6,200	2,400	5,100	3,000	94,400	50,200
1992	252,200	87,000	32,800	8,900	17,600	—	10,900	5,800	2,500	5,500	3,100	110,600	54,600
1993	271,500	88,800	34,200	9,000	19,300	—	10,500	3,900	2,400	6,800	2,600	123,900	58,900
1994	296,700	101,500	40,800	11,200	21,000	—	10,500	6,100	2,500	6,500	3,000	133,600	61,600
1995	306,500	114,200	46,600	13,800	22,900	—	10,800	6,300	2,800	7,100	3,800	127,800	64,400
1996	331,800	120,300	51,800	13,100	22,900	—	11,100	6,300	2,900	8,100	4,000	146,400	65,100
1997	358,400	136,500	58,600	14,100	27,800	—	11,500	6,900	3,700	9,800	4,000	152,600	69,400
1998	375,300	134,000	63,900	10,100	26,900	—	10,800	6,000	3,800	9,300	3,100	173,000	68,200

[1] For 1919–1924, series Dc137 combines series Dc138–142. For the same period, the totals include theaters, which are not shown separately.

[2] Changing geographical coverage over time; see text.

[3] Beginning in 1976, includes nonindustrial warehouses.

Sources

1901–1924: Robert E. Lipsey and Doris Preston, *Source Book of Statistics Relating to Construction* (National Bureau of Economic Research, 1966), pp. 15–21. 1925–1999: F. W. Dodge Division, McGraw-Hill Information Systems Company, New York (proprietary data provided by special permission).

Documentation

These series – except the part of residential buildings comprising privately owned one- and two-family houses – are based on daily reports by the F. W. Dodge field staff. This field staff contacts owners, architects, engineers, contractors, financial institutions, real estate brokers, and others able to supply reliable information on construction projects. The series include new construction, additions, and major alterations within sixty days of work start. They exclude maintenance and repair work, farm building, ship building, and a part of force-account work done by firms and public agencies. These data have been relied on to formulate estimates for several of the U.S. Census Bureau's value-in-place categories throughout the history of the program.

Geographic coverage has been increased in several steps since the series began. The earliest data beginning in 1901 cover total construction in the New England states. Data covering twenty-seven northeastern states and the District of Columbia are available for the years from 1910; the addition of nine Southern states between 1920 and 1923 brought the total to thirty six. Note, however, that the figures for 1919–1920 cover only twenty-five states (the totals, in million dollars, for twenty-seven states are 2,699 in 1919 and 2,635 in 1920). Texas was added in 1924. The thirty-seven states covered then excluded Montana, Idaho, Wyoming, Colorado, New Mexico, Arizona, Utah, Nevada, Washington, Oregon, and California. For the remaining eleven Western states, information gathered from permit places, publications, and a sample of areas was used. From 1956 to 1969, the forty-eight conterminous states were covered; beginning in 1970, all fifty states were covered.

Valuation represents, as nearly as possible, actual construction costs, including subcontracts for items such as plumbing, heating, electrical work, roofing, and normal connecting utilities, and excluding land and architects' fees. Cost of industrial equipment not an integral part of the structure is excluded, except for special-purpose equipment in petroleum refineries; outdoor chemical plants; electrical generating, power, and heating plants; and water and sewage treatment plants.

Note that beginning in 1976 the source reports the data in billion dollars, with one digit of precision after the decimal point.

TABLE Dc145–156 Construction contracts awarded – building floor space, by type of construction: 1919–1998[1,2]

Contributed by Kenneth A. Snowden

		Nonresidential buildings										Residential buildings
	Total	Total	Commercial	Manufacturing	Educational and science	Public and institutional	Hospital	Public	Religious	Social and recreational	Miscellaneous	Residential buildings
	Dc145	Dc146	Dc147 [3]	Dc148	Dc149	Dc150	Dc151	Dc152	Dc153	Dc154	Dc155	Dc156
Year	Million square feet	Million square feet	Million square feet	Million square feet	Million square feet	Million square feet	Million square feet	Million square feet	Million square feet	Million square feet	Million square feet	Million square feet
1919	557	315	110	152	—	47	—	—	—	—	—	242
1920	402	264	84	125	—	49	—	—	—	—	—	138
1921	385	180	65	35	—	74	—	—	—	—	—	205
1922	570	259	95	62	—	98	—	—	—	—	—	312
1923	674	281	110	68	—	99	—	—	—	—	—	393
1924	695	274	112	48	—	109	—	—	—	—	—	422
1925	936	362	160	67	61	—	14	8	19	32	1	559
1926	884	356	152	76	54	—	15	8	16	30	4	521
1927	851	351	142	68	54	—	19	10	17	34	7	495
1928	967	394	159	93	61	—	20	11	15	28	6	568
1929	791	398	161	106	59	—	20	13	13	22	6	388
1930	510	272	97	48	57	—	19	17	11	16	7	230
1931	366	171	50	20	37	—	17	24	6	14	3	190
1932	156	80	24	9	14	—	7	16	4	6	1	74
1933	147	73	23	19	6	—	6	10	3	6	2	73
1934	152	86	28	18	17	—	4	9	3	7	1	64
1935	252	114	35	21	26	—	6	14	4	8	1	135
1936	410	183	57	40	42	—	10	14	4	13	1	223
1937	446	204	62	61	36	—	11	12	6	14	1	236
1938	429	186	42	25	57	—	17	16	5	18	6	241
1939	513	179	49	44	34	—	12	15	6	12	6	333
1940	690	268	67	95	25	—	14	12	7	12	37	421
1941	941	440	106	188	24	—	15	14	9	15	69	503
1942	1,296	848	74	446	31	—	34	20	3	23	216	449
1943	448	245	22	106	12	—	20	5	1	13	66	201
1944	229	156	12	84	10	—	8	2	1	5	33	74
1945	397	285	63	158	13	—	11	2	5	8	26	111
1946	946	432	119	235	26	—	15	2	8	11	15	516
1947	1,060	349	100	143	41	—	20	6	12	14	12	707
1948	1,060	385	101	110	72	—	35	6	21	22	18	673
1949	1,038	344	86	61	79	—	42	8	25	21	22	694
1950	1,475	483	122	115	111	—	45	10	29	24	28	989
1951	1,279	470	77	148	110	—	38	11	25	11	50	805
1952	1,288	441	82	115	107	—	26	15	22	12	62	845
1953	1,306	490	123	112	124	—	23	13	28	17	50	814
1954	1,486	532	138	100	154	—	28	16	34	19	44	953
1955	1,695	604	173	125	155	—	23	18	37	20	53	1,089
1956	2,017	823	244	192	200	—	33	27	48	30	48	1,194
1957	2,003	809	245	176	207	—	40	27	50	31	33	1,195
1958	2,101	768	243	113	201	—	38	37	51	37	47	1,333
1959	2,337	824	281	158	181	—	38	34	54	43	35	1,512
1960	2,154	854	283	178	196	—	36	33	53	44	31	1,300
1961	2,203	838	293	150	194	—	44	33	53	41	29	1,364
1962	2,414	894	326	174	191	—	49	34	53	40	27	1,520
1963	2,711	958	347	187	197	—	65	43	48	38	32	1,753
1964	2,738	1,024	360	239	202	—	67	34	50	36	36	1,714
1965	2,843	1,132	415	265	225	—	60	36	45	47	38	1,711
1966	2,643	1,227	442	312	245	—	60	37	45	47	40	1,416
1967	2,820	1,165	424	270	242	—	66	37	41	42	43	1,654
1968	3,129	1,254	496	284	234	—	69	39	39	46	47	1,876
1969	3,249	1,374	573	317	221	—	87	36	33	53	54	1,874
1970	2,938	1,157	530	212	195	—	75	29	27	47	42	1,781
1971	3,437	1,157	552	175	189	—	76	40	26	52	46	2,279
1972	4,052	1,255	643	211	156	—	84	39	27	51	44	2,797
1973	4,013	1,439	717	293	156	—	76	49	28	63	57	2,574
1974	2,938	1,282	594	246	176	—	75	47	27	58	59	1,657

Notes appear at end of table

(continued)

TABLE Dc145–156   Construction contracts awarded – building floor space, by type of construction: 1919–1998
Continued

	Total	Nonresidential buildings										Residential buildings
		Total	Commercial	Manufacturing	Educational and science	Public and institutional	Hospital	Public	Religious	Social and recreational	Miscellaneous	
	Dc145	Dc146	Dc147 [3]	Dc148	Dc149	Dc150	Dc151	Dc152	Dc153	Dc154	Dc155	Dc156
Year	Million square feet	Million square feet	Million square feet	Million square feet	Million square feet	Million square feet	Million square feet	Million square feet	Million square feet	Million square feet	Million square feet	Million square feet
1975	2,390	949	409	146	152	—	63	46	28	51	54	1,441
1976	2,810	978	463	151	128	—	71	38	31	45	51	1,832
1977	3,542	1,135	600	176	119	—	66	38	32	49	55	2,407
1978	4,114	1,338	798	220	112	—	54	23	35	54	43	2,776
1979	3,919	1,444	871	246	110	—	58	20	34	54	53	2,475
1980	3,102	1,263	738	220	103	—	55	18	28	49	52	1,839
1981	2,805	1,243	787	188	83	—	60	14	25	46	41	1,562
1982	2,455	1,015	631	119	82	—	71	19	25	38	30	1,440
1983	3,387	1,111	716	112	84	—	84	20	29	36	31	2,276
1984	3,661	1,350	901	157	100	—	70	23	29	37	34	2,311
1985	3,854	1,530	1,039	165	111	—	73	28	32	44	38	2,324
1986	3,935	1,454	960	148	129	—	73	30	32	44	39	2,481
1987	3,756	1,469	933	160	139	—	78	42	32	46	38	2,288
1988	3,594	1,413	883	162	142	—	71	38	32	49	37	2,181
1989	3,516	1,400	867	158	151	—	72	41	27	48	35	2,115
1990	3,020	1,203	694	128	152	—	69	47	29	51	32	1,817
1991	2,635	981	476	100	177	—	72	50	29	45	33	1,653
1992	2,800	936	462	95	156	—	77	41	30	42	32	1,864
1993	3,062	971	481	110	165	—	75	30	30	51	29	2,091
1994	3,411	1,144	600	143	172	—	72	45	30	51	31	2,267
1995	3,453	1,281	700	163	186	—	70	40	33	56	33	2,172
1996	3,773	1,295	721	155	177	—	77	41	32	60	32	2,478
1997	4,076	1,510	838	188	199	—	86	47	41	76	34	2,566
1998	4,483	1,581	974	149	194	—	81	38	42	74	29	2,902

[1] For 1919–1924, series Dc150 combines series Dc151–155. For the same period, the totals include theaters, which are not shown separately.

[2] Changing geographical coverage over time; see text.

[3] Beginning in 1976, includes nonindustrial warehouses. Also, for early years, includes a small amount of floor space reported for public works and utilities.

Source

See the source for Table Dc132–144.

Documentation

See the text for Table Dc132–144.

Floor space figures represent footage under roof, exclusive of basement. Where building permit data are the basis of the statistics, floor area is estimated from construction costs, with local building cost differentials applied to nationally established cost-per-square-foot rates.

TABLE Dc157–166   Indexes of wholesale prices for construction materials: 1926–1946

Contributed by Kenneth A. Snowden

Year	Prepared paint	Lumber	Millwork	Nonferrous metals	Plumbing fixtures and brass fittings	Concrete ingredients and related products — Overall	Portland cement	Concrete products	Asphalt felt and coatings — Overall	Prepared asphalt, tar roofing, and siding products
	Dc157	Dc158	Dc159	Dc160	Dc161	Dc162	Dc163	Dc164	Dc165	Dc166
	Index 1982 = 100	Index 1982 = 100	Index 1982 = 100	Index 1982 = 100	Index 1982 = 100	Index 1982 = 100	Index 1982 = 100	Index 1982 = 100	Index 1982 = 100	Index 1982 = 100
1926	18.6	8.1	10.7	16.5	26.2	14.9	15.1	23.7	21.2	23.6
1927	18.6	7.6	10.7	15.3	23.4	14.5	14.4	23.7	20.0	22.3
1928	18.3	7.3	10.7	15.5	23.8	16.4	14.0	23.7	17.9	20.0
1929	18.1	7.6	10.8	17.5	22.5	16.5	13.5	23.3	15.8	17.6
1930	18.1	6.9	10.2	13.6	21.3	16.6	13.6	23.6	16.1	18.0
1931	16.6	5.6	8.5	10.2	20.1	15.1	11.3	22.3	16.7	18.7
1932	15.3	4.8	8.4	8.2	16.4	14.4	11.2	20.5	15.3	17.1
1933	14.8	5.7	8.8	9.8	16.1	15.6	13.3	20.9	15.7	17.5
1934	15.9	6.8	9.2	11.2	16.8	16.6	14.1	20.9	16.9	18.9
1935	15.9	6.6	9.1	11.3	14.7	16.6	14.0	19.0	17.7	19.8
1936	15.9	7.0	9.7	11.8	16.8	16.7	13.9	20.2	17.4	19.5
1937	15.9	8.1	11.7	14.8	17.1	16.6	13.4	20.3	19.1	21.3
1938	17.3	7.1	10.5	12.0	16.9	16.7	13.6	18.7	15.4	17.2
1939	17.3	7.5	10.3	12.9	16.9	16.7	13.8	18.6	15.9	17.8
1940	17.5	8.3	11.2	13.4	17.9	16.6	13.7	16.6	17.4	19.4
1941	17.8	9.9	12.8	13.9	18.3	16.8	13.9	19.2	17.9	20.1
1942	18.5	10.7	14.0	14.1	20.3	17.3	14.2	19.9	17.5	19.6
1943	18.5	11.4	14.1	14.2	19.7	17.3	14.2	19.9	17.5	19.5
1944	18.5	12.4	14.6	14.1	19.0	17.5	14.5	19.9	17.6	19.7
1945	18.5	12.5	14.7	14.1	18.8	18.0	15.0	19.9	18.0	20.1
1946	19.3	14.4	16.6	16.3	20.1	18.7	15.7	21.1	18.8	21.0

Source

Downloaded June 14, 2000, from the U.S. Bureau of Labor Statistics (BLS) Internet site.

Documentation

The series in this table represent the construction-related commodity group price indexes that extend back to 1926 and are currently maintained by the BLS. See series Cc92 for the overall building materials price index for the period covered in this table. Indexes for some of these series for the period

1913–1946 (with the 1926 base year) can be found in Housing and Home Finance Agency, *Housing Statistics Handbook* (1948), p. 27.

The continuation of series Dc159, Dc161–162, Dc164, and Dc166 for the 1947–1999 period can be found in Table Dc167–195. With the exception of series Dc163, the remaining series in the table are broader in scope than the classes of goods currently included in the special construction materials grouping.

See the text for Table Dc167–195 for additional information.

TABLE Dc167–195   Indexes of wholesale prices for construction materials: 1947–1999

Contributed by Kenneth A. Snowden

Year	Overall group index	Interior solvent-based paint	Plastic products	Lumber — Softwood lumber — Douglas fir, dressed	Southern pine, dressed	Millwork	Plywood — Softwood	Hardwood	Softwood veneer	Building paper and building board mill products
	Dc167	Dc168	Dc169	Dc170	Dc171	Dc172	Dc173	Dc174	Dc175	Dc176
	1982 = 100	1982 = 100	1982 = 100	1982 = 100	1982 = 100	1982 = 100	1982 = 100	1982 = 100	1982 = 100	1982 = 100
1947	23.5	22.3	—	26.8	27.8	21.3	40.6	54.7	—	29.4
1948	26.0	23.0	—	30.6	30.5	25.7	52.3	57.1	—	32.5
1949	25.5	23.7	—	26.7	27.5	26.3	45.4	50.2	—	32.9
1950	27.4	23.8	—	33.0	30.9	28.0	52.5	54.7	—	34.0
1951	29.9	26.5	—	36.1	33.1	31.7	55.8	59.8	—	35.9
1952	29.6	26.8	—	35.7	33.4	31.0	50.9	54.6	—	36.5
1953	30.0	26.9	—	32.9	33.1	32.1	51.0	58.4	—	38.4
1954	30.1	27.2	—	33.5	31.7	31.8	49.4	54.1	—	40.4
1955	31.4	27.7	—	36.6	32.9	31.4	50.8	55.4	—	41.4
1956	32.7	29.6	—	36.4	34.1	31.5	46.5	56.5	—	43.3
1957	32.7	31.4	—	32.8	32.8	31.3	42.0	56.0	—	44.8
1958	32.6	32.0	—	32.2	32.3	31.2	42.4	56.3	—	45.3
1959	33.7	32.1	—	36.7	33.4	33.1	45.1	57.3	—	46.3
1960	33.2	32.2	—	33.5	32.8	33.3	40.1	58.1	—	46.1
1961	32.5	32.6	—	32.2	31.4	32.5	39.0	57.3	—	45.8
1962	32.4	32.7	—	33.1	31.4	32.5	37.7	55.3	—	44.2
1963	32.5	32.8	—	34.4	31.3	33.2	38.6	55.0	—	43.6
1964	32.9	33.0	—	35.0	31.3	34.6	37.4	55.7	—	42.7
1965	33.3	33.4	—	34.7	31.9	34.4	37.5	55.5	—	42.1
1966	34.3	33.8	—	36.4	35.0	35.1	37.6	56.0	—	42.1
1967	34.7	35.2	—	37.6	35.0	35.8	35.4	55.2	—	41.8
1968	36.7	36.9	—	45.2	39.8	37.9	45.8	55.5	—	42.1
1969	38.8	38.6	—	49.5	44.1	42.2	49.3	57.5	—	44.1
1970	39.1	40.1	65.5	40.8	40.1	41.5	40.3	56.6	—	42.2
1971	41.5	41.3	63.7	52.7	46.9	43.2	45.0	55.6	—	42.9
1972	44.0	42.4	62.9	60.5	53.0	46.0	54.9	57.6	61.1	44.4
1973	48.1	43.9	63.4	78.7	65.7	51.6	68.8	62.3	75.8	47.1
1974	55.9	52.5	80.1	80.3	64.5	56.2	66.2	71.9	80.6	51.6
1975	60.4	60.2	83.5	79.6	61.3	57.4	71.1	66.0	75.2	53.1
1976	65.1	65.8	85.7	94.2	76.0	63.3	87.8	67.7	96.6	57.9
1977	71.1	69.2	89.7	109.5	91.8	69.3	104.9	70.5	106.8	65.6
1978	79.3	73.7	91.8	127.6	106.5	84.3	115.7	77.4	126.8	78.2
1979	87.3	79.7	99.4	144.2	113.4	91.0	114.2	93.4	135.7	76.2
1980	92.5	91.3	103.9	132.6	104.0	93.2	109.5	97.5	126.0	86.1
1981	98.2	97.4	104.3	117.1	102.0	97.8	108.7	99.3	118.9	96.7
1982	100.0	100.0	100.0	100.0	100.0	100.0	100.0	100.0	100.0	100.0
1983	103.4	100.0	110.1	135.8	111.9	108.2	110.0	99.3	103.1	104.4
1984	106.4	103.9	115.5	123.2	111.9	110.2	107.6	99.6	103.3	108.2
1985	107.6	107.3	108.6	126.5	105.2	111.7	107.4	89.9	100.1	107.4
1986	107.3	109.9	106.4	124.5	104.9	113.7	109.4	91.0	105.9	108.8
1987	109.5	111.6	108.4	125.1	114.1	117.7	109.8	92.9	108.4	111.2
1988	115.7	120.3	121.1	135.7	112.4	121.9	109.1	94.2	117.3	113.3
1989	119.5	128.8	120.1	151.6	108.0	127.3	124.2	99.8	142.1	115.6
1990	119.6	133.0	117.2	138.4	111.2	130.4	119.6	102.7	142.3	112.2
1991	120.4	140.2	115.1	139.6	111.0	135.5	120.8	102.8	138.5	111.8
1992	122.5	141.7	112.7	169.5	130.6	143.3	147.2	106.9	168.3	119.6
1993	128.6	142.9	116.6	237.6	168.8	156.6	169.7	115.4	216.0	132.7
1994	133.8	148.1	122.9	236.2	182.6	162.4	176.8	122.3	207.8	144.1
1995	138.8	164.5	133.8	198.8	166.9	163.8	188.1	122.2	203.5	144.9
1996	139.6	175.6	130.9	227.1	177.9	166.6	173.7	124.9	189.3	137.2
1997	142.1	180.5	128.2	221.3	201.2	170.9	175.5	127.1	201.7	129.6
1998	141.4	185.7	126.2	186.1	177.3	171.1	174.9	126.9	180.1	132.9
1999	142.8	188.0	128.0	212.1	185.7	174.7	207.0	128.6	197.4	141.6

TABLE Dc167–195   Indexes of wholesale prices for construction materials: 1947–1999   *Continued*

					Metal and metal products					
					Fabricated structural metal products			Lighting fixtures		
Year	Steel pipes and tubes	Builders hardware	Plumbing fixtures and brass fittings	Heating equipment	Metal doors, sash, and trim	Siding, aluminum	Architectural and ornamental metalwork	Commercial fluorescent fixtures	Outdoor lighting equipment	Fabricated ferrous wire products
	Dc177	Dc178	Dc179	Dc180	Dc181	Dc182	Dc183	Dc184	Dc185	Dc186
	June 1982 = 100	1982 = 100	1982=100	1982 = 100	1982 = 100	December 1982 = 100	December 1983 = 100	1982 = 100	June 1985 = 100	June 1982 = 100
1947	—	—	24.0	35.8	24.7	—	—	—	—	—
1948	—	—	26.1	38.0	25.8	—	—	—	—	—
1949	—	—	26.1	38.9	26.4	—	—	—	—	—
1950	—	—	27.4	39.4	28.2	—	—	—	—	—
1951	—	—	31.1	43.0	31.0	—	—	—	—	—
1952	—	—	29.8	42.7	30.2	—	—	—	—	—
1953	—	—	29.4	43.1	31.5	—	—	—	—	—
1954	—	—	30.0	42.9	33.2	—	—	—	—	—
1955	—	—	31.8	43.2	35.8	—	—	—	—	—
1956	—	—	34.0	44.6	37.3	—	—	—	—	—
1957	—	—	33.0	45.7	36.1	—	—	—	—	—
1958	—	—	31.4	45.3	36.4	—	—	—	—	—
1959	—	—	33.0	45.5	34.7	—	—	—	—	—
1960	—	—	33.5	44.6	34.0	—	—	—	—	—
1961	—	—	33.5	42.9	33.9	—	—	47.9	—	—
1962	—	33.9	32.5	42.4	33.7	—	—	45.5	—	—
1963	—	33.9	32.5	42.2	32.9	—	—	44.3	—	—
1964	—	33.9	32.8	41.8	33.0	—	—	44.2	—	—
1965	—	34.2	33.5	41.7	32.8	—	—	43.6	—	—
1966	—	35.9	35.2	42.1	33.6	—	—	44.7	—	—
1967	—	37.0	35.9	42.2	34.4	—	—	45.4	—	—
1968	—	37.6	37.1	43.3	35.8	—	—	47.1	—	—
1969	—	39.0	38.5	44.4	37.3	—	—	49.1	—	—
1970	—	41.7	39.9	46.6	38.9	—	—	51.1	—	—
1971	—	43.6	41.8	48.6	40.5	—	—	51.5	—	—
1972	—	44.5	43.0	49.8	41.5	—	—	51.6	—	—
1973	—	46.0	45.1	50.8	42.9	—	—	52.0	—	—
1974	—	52.2	53.5	56.9	50.7	—	—	58.4	—	—
1975	—	58.7	58.2	63.5	55.9	—	—	61.0	—	—
1976	—	60.7	62.5	66.6	59.0	—	—	61.1	—	—
1977	—	64.9	67.0	69.8	64.9	—	—	62.1	—	—
1978	—	69.4	71.4	73.5	71.5	—	—	64.7	—	—
1979	—	75.8	77.9	78.9	79.0	—	—	74.3	—	—
1980	—	84.9	88.5	87.0	87.8	—	—	81.8	—	—
1981	—	94.4	96.0	94.5	96.0	—	—	93.4	—	—
1982	—	100.0	100.0	100.0	100.0	—	—	100.0	—	—
1983	92.2	104.8	103.8	102.7	102.8	101.3	—	99.5	—	96.2
1984	94.2	109.3	108.6	106.6	106.6	112.4	101.1	103.3	—	97.5
1985	93.3	113.5	111.9	109.5	107.3	110.1	104.5	104.6	—	99.3
1986	89.4	115.8	115.5	113.0	108.9	104.8	104.5	105.9	101.0	100.3
1987	90.9	117.4	119.7	115.5	112.0	104.4	106.2	104.9	100.8	101.0
1988	99.3	122.5	128.7	119.2	122.4	116.8	113.7	105.7	103.5	107.0
1989	102.6	127.8	137.7	125.1	130.0	—	117.5	110.5	110.9	111.9
1990	102.6	133.0	144.3	131.6	131.4	—	118.7	113.0	113.0	114.6
1991	100.8	138.1	149.7	134.1	134.6	—	119.2	116.5	114.7	115.9
1992	94.1	141.4	153.1	137.3	135.0	116.7	117.7	117.6	115.3	117.5
1993	92.8	144.9	155.9	140.4	136.6	117.2	119.5	117.4	115.5	119.3
1994	96.9	148.0	159.6	142.5	142.0	119.4	123.4	116.2	115.4	122.6
1995	104.4	153.2	166.0	147.5	156.5	132.4	128.0	121.0	120.8	125.7
1996	103.2	156.5	171.1	151.2	159.3	125.5	131.3	123.4	122.9	126.8
1997	106.9	158.4	174.5	152.4	161.0	132.1	133.5	122.8	123.2	128.0
1998	109.4	160.8	175.1	153.3	161.3	134.5	135.4	119.0	122.8	130.1
1999	102.5	161.9	176.7	154.0	162.2	135.4	136.2	118.7	122.3	130.6

TABLE Dc167–195   Indexes of wholesale prices for construction materials: 1947–1999   *Continued*

	Stamped metal switch and receptacle box	Elevators, escalators, and other lifts	Nonmetallic mineral products						
			Concrete ingredients and related products	Concrete products	Clay products	Prepared asphalt, tar roofing, and siding products	Gypsum products	Insulation materials	Paving mixtures and blocks
	Dc187	Dc188	Dc189	Dc190	Dc191	Dc192	Dc193	Dc194	Dc195
Year	1982 = 100	1982 = 100	1982 = 100	1982 = 100	1982 = 100	1982 = 100	1982 = 100	1982 = 100	1982 = 100
1947	—	23.6	20.5	23.9	23.9	24.0	27.5	29.2	—
1948	—	25.1	22.4	25.1	25.7	26.3	30.0	30.7	—
1949	—	26.2	23.2	25.7	26.5	26.2	29.7	29.9	—
1950	—	26.2	23.5	26.3	27.6	25.8	30.4	30.2	—
1951	—	28.3	24.9	28.0	29.9	26.7	34.1	31.1	—
1952	—	28.5	24.9	28.0	29.8	26.2	34.2	31.5	—
1953	—	28.9	25.8	28.7	30.4	27.3	35.2	32.3	—
1954	—	29.4	26.6	29.2	30.9	26.5	35.5	32.8	—
1955	—	30.2	27.5	29.5	32.1	27.0	35.5	31.9	—
1956	—	32.0	28.7	30.6	33.8	28.5	36.9	30.4	—
1957	—	34.5	29.9	31.4	34.3	31.2	36.9	30.7	—
1958	—	34.8	30.6	31.9	34.5	28.8	38.4	31.1	17.4
1959	—	34.8	30.9	32.3	35.4	29.7	38.7	30.8	17.4
1960	—	35.0	31.3	32.6	35.9	27.3	38.7	31.1	17.4
1961	—	35.2	31.3	32.6	36.1	29.4	39.4	29.3	17.4
1962	—	34.8	31.5	32.7	36.4	28.3	39.9	29.2	17.4
1963	—	35.2	31.4	32.4	36.6	26.9	40.0	28.0	17.4
1964	—	35.7	31.3	32.1	36.7	26.5	41.1	28.1	17.4
1965	—	35.9	31.5	32.3	37.0	27.7	39.5	27.3	17.4
1966	—	35.9	31.6	32.8	37.7	29.0	38.9	27.7	17.3
1967	26.7	36.5	32.3	33.6	38.3	28.3	39.1	28.0	17.1
1968	27.6	37.3	33.3	34.5	39.3	29.4	40.5	29.8	17.4
1969	29.1	38.6	34.4	35.8	40.7	29.3	40.5	32.4	17.6
1970	30.1	42.3	36.3	37.7	42.1	28.8	38.9	34.6	18.1
1971	—	44.2	39.3	40.5	43.9	35.8	42.7	36.9	20.9
1972	—	44.6	40.9	42.2	45.0	37.8	44.8	38.4	21.2
1973	—	45.1	42.3	44.2	47.3	39.2	47.2	38.5	21.6
1974	—	51.5	48.0	50.9	51.8	53.8	53.7	43.9	38.2
1975	—	62.0	55.6	57.3	58.0	61.7	56.2	55.0	44.0
1976	—	66.3	60.2	60.5	62.7	65.5	60.3	59.6	45.4
1977	61.0	69.7	64.2	64.4	69.0	69.8	71.7	66.2	47.7
1978	69.2	74.5	70.2	71.9	75.6	81.7	89.5	70.3	53.4
1979	76.1	78.7	78.7	82.0	83.6	89.2	98.5	71.9	63.6
1980	83.9	87.3	88.4	92.0	88.8	105.5	100.1	80.7	83.7
1981	92.7	92.7	95.6	97.8	95.8	101.6	100.1	—	100.5
1982	100.0	100.0	100.0	100.0	100.0	100.0	100.0	100.0	100.0
1983	102.3	97.3	101.1	101.4	106.5	94.1	111.7	103.7	100.9
1984	110.4	97.1	105.1	103.9	110.0	97.7	135.4	104.0	106.1
1985	116.3	97.7	108.5	107.5	113.5	100.5	132.3	105.2	111.6
1986	132.9	99.2	109.4	109.2	118.0	96.8	137.0	105.7	104.9
1987	138.5	100.4	110.4	109.4	121.4	91.9	125.2	105.0	100.8
1988	145.5	103.6	112.0	110.0	124.9	94.4	112.9	105.8	102.7
1989	151.0	107.1	113.2	111.2	127.0	95.6	110.0	106.7	101.0
1990	158.0	110.1	115.3	113.5	129.9	95.8	105.2	108.4	101.2
1991	160.8	108.7	118.4	116.6	130.2	96.2	99.3	110.8	103.2
1992	166.5	109.4	119.4	117.2	132.0	94.3	99.9	102.3	100.2
1993	172.9	110.7	123.4	120.2	135.1	94.9	108.3	105.8	102.0
1994	179.1	112.4	128.7	124.6	138.3	92.9	136.1	111.9	103.2
1995	183.5	113.0	134.7	129.4	141.3	97.8	154.5	118.8	105.8
1996	186.3	113.7	138.8	133.2	142.3	97.4	154.0	118.9	107.6
1997	189.0	114.8	142.5	136.0	143.5	96.5	170.8	117.7	113.2
1998	191.5	116.0	147.6	140.0	144.9	95.7	177.6	119.7	112.5
1999	192.8	117.5	152.1	143.7	148.3	95.2	208.0	131.7	112.9

Source

Downloaded June 14, 2000, from the U.S. Bureau of Labor Statistics Internet site.

Documentation

For details about the construction of the wholesale price indexes, see U.S. Bureau of Labor Statistics, *Handbook of Methods*, Chapter 14, "Producer Prices,"

Bulletin number 2490 (1997). See series Cc100 for the stage-of-processing index for construction materials and components for the same period.

The indexes in this table conform to the Bureau of Labor Statistics's commodity classification structure in which products are organized by similarity of end use or material composition, regardless of whether they are primary or secondary products in their industry of origin. Series Dc167 is a special

TABLE Dc167–195   Indexes of wholesale prices for construction materials: 1947–1999   *Continued*

commodity grouping index because it combines weighted indexes of products that are used in construction but belong to seven of the thirteen major industrial commodity groupings in the classification system (chemicals, rubber and plastic, lumber and wood, pulp and paper, metals and metal products, machinery and equipment, and nonmetallic mineral products). To be included in this index, materials need to be incorporated as integral parts of a building, or normally installed during construction and not readily removable. As a result, consumer durables such as kitchen ranges or refrigerators are excluded.

Series Dc167 should not be confused with the commodity-based stage-of-processing index for intermediate materials and components for construction (series Cc100) or the industry-based index for material inputs to construction industries (series Dc196). The index in series Cc100 is a major component of the overall intermediate goods stage-of-processing index and is designed to capture and measure how changes in input prices are passed through to the price of final goods, whereas the index in series Dc196 weights material inputs according to their actual use in the construction industry.

In contrast to series Dc157, series Dc167 combines price indexes of construction-related commodities using weights that correspond to total shipment values even when some shipments go to sectors other than construction. In contrast to series Cc100, moreover, the index in this table combines prices of commodity groups at different stages of processing. This leads

to some double-counting of price changes (for example, concrete ingredients, series Dc189, and concrete products, series Dc190, are both included). Series Dc167, therefore, should not be used to measure inflation or to deflate current-dollar series into constant dollars.

The other series shown in the table represent a limited subset of all the construction-related commodities or commodity groups that are combined in series Dc167. Among these are eight relatively broad three-digit commodity subgroups (millwork, building paper and board, plumbing fixtures, heating equipment, concrete ingredients, concrete products, clay construction products, and gypsum) and nine four-digit product classes (plastic construction, three plywood series, metal doors and sashes, fabricated ferrous wire products, asphalt roofing and siding, and insulation and paving materials). The remaining series are either six-digit subproduct or eight-digit product classes, which are the narrowest groupings in the BLS commodity classification system. A complete listing of the classification system is available at the BLS Internet site.

Series Dc174. Covers hardwood plywood and related products.

Series Dc175. Covers softwood plywood veneer, excluding reinforced or backed.

Series Dc184. Covers commercial fluorescent fixtures (recessed nonair).

Series Dc191. Covers clay construction products, excluding refractories.

TABLE Dc196–206   Indexes of material input prices, by type of construction: 1987–1999

Contributed by Kenneth A. Snowden

		New construction industries								Maintenance and repair construction		
			Residential									
	All construction industries	Overall	Single-unit	Multiunit	Nonresidential building	Highway and street	Water and sewer supply	Other heavy	Overall	Residential	Nonresidential
	Dc196	Dc197	Dc198	Dc199	Dc200	Dc201	Dc202	Dc203	Dc204	Dc205	Dc206
Year	1986 = 100	1986 = 100	June 1986 = 100	June 1986 = 100	June 1986 = 100	June 1986 = 100	June 1986 = 100	June 1986 = 100	June 1986 = 100	June 1986 = 100	June 1986 = 100
1987	101.5	101.6	101.8	101.4	101.4	100.8	101.1	101.9	101.3	101.0	101.4
1988	106.1	106.1	105.6	105.5	106.2	103.4	105.7	108.6	106.0	105.6	106.2
1989	111.0	111.0	110.3	109.8	110.8	107.0	110.2	115.4	110.9	110.3	111.1
1990	113.4	113.3	112.3	111.8	113.1	110.7	113.4	117.9	113.6	113.1	113.9
1991	114.8	114.6	114.2	113.4	114.2	110.6	115.8	118.1	115.1	114.8	115.3
1992	116.7	116.9	118.4	116.3	115.0	110.0	116.8	118.5	116.2	116.2	116.3
1993	121.4	122.2	126.5	122.1	117.8	111.7	118.8	120.6	119.4	119.5	119.3
1994	125.0	125.9	130.4	126.2	121.4	114.3	122.0	124.3	122.3	122.5	122.2
1995	129.1	129.8	133.3	130.2	126.1	118.4	126.8	129.8	127.1	127.5	126.9
1996	131.2	131.8	135.0	131.7	128.2	122.1	130.0	132.3	129.3	129.6	129.2
1997	133.8	134.6	138.3	134.6	130.5	124.6	132.8	134.6	131.5	131.7	131.4
1998	133.5	134.3	137.5	134.7	131.2	123.5	134.1	133.3	131.3	131.8	131.0
1999	136.1	137.0	141.2	137.7	133.0	126.6	136.2	134.8	133.3	134.1	132.9

Source

Downloaded June 14, 2000, from the U.S. Bureau of Labor Statistics Internet site.

Documentation

For general details about the construction of the wholesale price indexes, see U.S. Bureau of Labor Statistics, *Handbook of Methods*, Chapter 14, "Producer Prices," Bulletin number 2490 (1997). For a description of these specific indexes, see U.S. Bureau of Labor Statistics, *Producer Price Indexes* (July 1986), p. 190.

The series in this table comprise a set of price indexes for material inputs into the construction industry that the BLS began to publish on a monthly basis in July 1986. These indexes include only inputs to construction that are produced by the mining and manufacturing sectors of the economy, and they exclude capital equipment. The indexes are not comprehensive measures of input costs, therefore, because they do not capture costs of labor or capital.

The indexes in the table are weighted combinations of producer price indexes for the net output of industries that supply materials to the construction industry. The weights are derived from input/output tables published by the U.S. Department of Commerce, and so correspond to each construction sector's actual use of material input. This is in substantial contrast to the special commodity grouping price index for construction materials in series Dc167, which weights the price indexes for construction-related commodity groups according to total shipment values even when some shipments go to sectors other than construction.

The indexes in this table are also more broadly defined than either the special commodity group index, series Dc167, or the stage-of-processing construction materials and components index, series Cc100. The latter two indexes include only durable products that are physically encompassed in a finished structure. The indexes here also include nondurable inputs (such as fuels) that are consumed during the course of construction.

TABLE Dc207–226   Indexes of construction costs: 1913–1970[1]

Contributed by Kenneth A. Snowden

	Department of Commerce composite	American Appraisal Co.	Associated General Contractors	E.H. Boeckh and Associates			Engineering News-Record		Department of Agriculture, Economic Research Service	
				Residences	Apartments, hotels, and office buildings	Commercial and factory buildings	Building	Construction	Farm housing	Other farm
	Dc207	Dc208	Dc209	Dc210	Dc211	Dc212	Dc213	Dc214	Dc215	Dc216
Year	1967 = 100	1967 = 100	1967 = 100	1967 = 100	1967 = 100	1967 = 100	1967 = 100	1967 = 100	1967 = 100	1967 = 100
1913	—	—	—	—	—	—	—	—	—	—
1914	—	—	—	—	—	—	—	—	—	—
1915	16	11	15	15.6	14.6	14.8	14.2	8.7	18	22
1916	18	13	17	16.6	16.4	17.2	19.5	12.1	20	25
1917	23	16	23	19.5	19.7	21.0	24.9	16.9	24	30
1918	27	20	27	23.2	22.3	23.1	23.7	17.7	29	36
1919	30	26	30	26.9	25.4	25.4	23.6	18.5	36	41
1920	37	31	37	34.7	32.4	31.6	30.8	23.5	39	46
1921	30	24	34	27.9	26.1	25.9	24.7	18.8	28	33
1922	27	23	28	25.7	24.5	24.0	23.1	16.3	29	33
1923	30	25	30	28.7	27.1	26.8	27.7	20.0	31	35
1924	30	24	31	28.3	26.5	26.7	27.6	20.1	31	36
1925	30	24	30	28.0	26.8	26.5	27.2	19.3	31	37
1926	30	24	30	28.3	27.0	26.7	27.6	19.5	31	36
1927	30	24	30	27.9	26.6	26.4	27.7	19.2	31	36
1928	30	24	30	28.0	26.8	26.4	28.0	19.3	31	35
1929	30	24	31	29.3	27.4	27.2	28.4	19.4	31	36
1930	29	23	30	28.5	26.9	26.8	27.6	19.0	30	34
1931	27	20	30	26.3	24.9	24.8	25.3	17.0	25	30
1932	23	17	26	22.2	21.2	21.4	21.0	14.7	22	26
1933	25	17	24	22.2	21.7	21.9	22.0	15.9	22	26
1934	28	17	27	24.2	23.9	23.9	24.8	18.5	25	30
1935	27	18	27	23.6	23.6	23.5	24.7	18.3	25	30
1936	28	19	27	24.4	24.3	24.2	25.7	19.2	25	30
1937	30	22	29	27.3	27.1	27.0	29.2	21.9	27	31
1938	30	22	29	28.1	28.2	28.0	29.3	22.0	25	31
1939	28	23	29	28.6	28.5	28.3	29.4	22.0	25	30
1940	29	23	29	29.6	29.0	28.7	30.2	22.6	26	31
1941	31	24	30	31.9	30.4	30.2	31.5	24.1	29	33
1942	35	26	32	33.8	32.0	31.6	33.1	25.9	33	39
1943	38	28	33	35.2	33.3	32.9	34.1	27.1	38	43
1944	37	29	34	38.3	35.5	35.2	35.0	27.9	42	47
1945	39	30	35	41.1	37.8	37.3	35.6	28.8	45	50
1946	45	35	39	45.1	41.3	40.7	39.1	32.3	49	54
1947	54	47	45	54.6	48.6	47.8	46.6	38.6	62	67
1948	60	54	51	61.4	54.8	54.0	51.3	43.0	67	73
1949	60	54	52	59.8	55.5	54.6	52.4	44.5	64	72
1950	62	55	55	63.0	58.0	56.8	55.9	47.7	69	69
1951	68	59	58	68.0	62.5	61.4	59.7	50.7	76	76
1952	69	61	59	69.7	64.6	63.5	61.9	53.2	77	78
1953	71	64	62	71.0	66.6	65.7	64.1	56.0	78	79
1954	71	65	64	70.4	67.2	66.5	66.4	58.7	77	78
1955	73	67	67	72.5	69.2	68.7	69.9	61.6	79	80
1956	77	70	70	75.7	72.5	72.3	73.1	64.7	82	83
1957	80	73	73	77.2	74.8	74.9	75.7	67.6	84	86
1958	81	75	76	77.9	76.1	76.4	78.2	71.0	84	87
1959	82	77	78	80.5	78.7	79.1	81.6	74.5	86	90
1960	83	80	81	81.8	80.3	80.4	83.3	76.9	88	91
1961	84	81	83	82.1	81.3	81.1	84.6	79.2	88	91
1962	86	83	84	83.4	83.2	82.8	86.3	81.5	89	91
1963	88	86	86	85.2	85.2	84.6	88.5	84.2	90	92
1964	90	88	90	87.6	87.7	87.1	91.1	87.4	90	91
1965	93	91	93	90.4	90.7	90.0	93.3	90.8	92	93
1966	96	95	96	94.3	94.3	93.9	96.9	95.2	96	96
1967	100	100	100	100.0	100.0	100.0	100.0	100.0	100	100
1968	106	107	105	107.3	107.0	106.8	107.4	107.9	108	106
1969	114	116	114	116.2	116.1	114.5	117.7	118.7	—	115
1970	122	124	126	122.4	124.4	123.1	124.4	128.9	—	118

Note appears at end of table

TABLE Dc207–226   Indexes of construction costs: 1913–1970   *Continued*

	George A. Fuller Co.—commercial buildings	Handy–Whitman public utility			ICC—railroad	Bell System Telephone plant, telephone, telegraph		Federal Highway Administration	Turner Construction Company	Average of contractor indexes
		Buildings	Gas plant	Electric light and power plant		Buildings	Outside plant			
	Dc217	Dc218	Dc219	Dc220	Dc221	Dc222	Dc223	Dc224	Dc225	Dc226
Year	1967 = 100	1967 = 100	1967 = 100	1967 = 100	1967 = 100	1967 = 100	1967 = 100	1967 = 100	1967 = 100	1913 = 100
1913	—	—	—	—	—	—	—	—	—	100
1914	—	—	—	—	—	—	—	—	—	102
1915	19	17	13	15	25	—	—	33.5	14	113
1916	21	19	15	18	27	—	—	35.5	18	128
1917	23	28	21	22	33	—	—	40.7	21	151
1918	23	29	25	26	39	—	—	49.2	24	176
1919	25	29	27	27	44	—	—	54.5	28	184
1920	31	34	29	30	53	—	—	70.8	36	232
1921	28	26	27	27	43	—	—	58.7	26	187
1922	26	23	22	27	39	—	—	53.5	25	174
1923	28	26	24	26	42	—	—	59.6	28	196
1924	29	29	26	27	42	—	—	57.1	28	198
1925	29	27	25	27	41	—	—	54.3	28	199
1926	29	27	24	26	41	—	—	52.2	28	200
1927	29	26	24	26	40	—	—	51.5	28	195
1928	29	26	23	26	40	—	—	48.1	28	193
1929	29	26	23	28	40	—	—	46.6	27	192
1930	29	25	23	26	38	26.4	35.7	43.3	24	182
1931	26	23	23	26	35	23.3	35.7	38.8	21	163
1932	23	21	21	25	32	20.9	34.8	30.9	20	147
1933	23	21	21	25	31	20.2	34.8	38.8	20	148
1934	26	24	23	27	32	21.7	35.7	42.4	23	163
1935	25	24	23	28	32	22.5	34.8	40.7	23	163
1936	25	24	24	28	33	23.3	34.8	41.9	24	169
1937	27	27	27	31	35	25.6	37.4	40.1	28	189
1938	29	26	27	31	34	26.4	37.4	36.8	27	187
1939	29	26	27	31	34	26.4	37.4	36.6	26	184
1940	29	26	27	32	35	27.1	37.4	36.1	28	191
1941	30	29	28	33	37	27.9	38.3	41.1	31	210
1942	34	31	30	34	43	30.2	40.9	55.0	35	229
1943	35	31	30	34	46	30.2	42.6	63.1	37	236
1944	36	32	31	34	46	31.0	44.3	57.1	35	237
1945	36	33	31	35	49	35.7	46.1	55.1	38	246
1946	43	38	36	40	53	46.1	53.0	60.1	46	292
1947	52	45	43	46	60	53.0	65.0	68.3	55	346
1948	56	51	48	51	67	58.2	67.8	76.4	61	375
1949	57	54	50	54	67	60.2	68.6	73.7	59	371
1950	56	56	52	58	68	61.2	67.7	66.6	61	379
1951	60	61	57	65	73	64.9	74.3	81.7	68	413
1952	61	61	58	67	76	66.7	76.4	84.1	71	—
1953	64	65	60	69	79	68.8	77.7	81.0	72	—
1954	66	67	64	72	79	70.7	78.5	76.4	71	—
1955	68	70	67	74	81	72.8	81.5	74.2	71	—
1956	71	76	73	81	87	76.6	86.0	84.0	78	—
1957	74	82	77	86	91	78.9	85.9	87.7	83	—
1958	78	84	81	88	93	81.0	84.4	85.5	83	—
1959	81	87	84	89	95	82.6	86.4	82.0	84	—
1960	82	87	85	89	96	83.5	88.9	80.0	85	—
1961	85	87	86	88	95	83.6	87.1	80.7	86	—
1962	89	88	88	89	95	84.4	87.2	84.3	87	—
1963	91	90	90	89	95	86.5	89.3	86.4	89	—
1964	94	92	92	90	95	88.9	89.8	86.9	91	—
1965	96	93	94	94	96	91.9	91.1	90.3	94	—
1966	98	97	97	96	98	95.7	96.5	96.1	97	—
1967	100	100	100	100	100	100.0	100.0	100.0	100	—
1968	105	105	104	104	—	105.5	104.5	103.4	106	—
1969	116	113	110	110	—	114.7	111.2	111.8	117	—
1970	127	121	117	119	—	125.0	124.0	125.6	129	—

(continued)

TABLE Dc207-226   Indexes of construction costs: 1913-1970   *Continued*

[1] Excludes Alaska and Hawai'i for all years.

Sources

U.S. Bureau of the Census, *Historical Statistics of the United States* (1975), series N118-137, which were based on the following sources:

1915-1968: U.S. Bureau of the Census, unpublished data. The indexes for series Dc221, 1915-1968; series Dc222-223, 1946-1968; series Dc224, 1962-1968; and series Dc225, 1967-1968, were provided on a 1967 base by the source agencies; all other indexes, except series Dc226, represent conversions of those given on a 1957-1959 base in U.S. Business and Defense Services Administration, *Construction Statistics, 1915-1964*, pp. 58-9, and in U.S. Bureau of the Census, *Construction Reports*, series C 30, various issues.

1969-1970: U.S. Bureau of the Census, *Construction Reports*, series C 30-74-7, p. 8.

Series Dc226, all years: Miles L. Colean and Robinson Newcomb, *Stabilizing Construction: The Record and Potential* (McGraw-Hill, 1952), Appendix Q.

Documentation

The construction cost indexes shown in this table were assembled by the U.S. Commerce Department specifically for the Bicentennial Edition of *Historical Statistics*. The source provides no additional published references and so the discussion below is drawn from the source. The indexes shown were used to convert current-dollar measures of the value of new construction put in place for the 1947-1964 period (see Table Dc1-11) into constant-dollar series (see Table Dc22-43). Refer to the text for Tables Dc256-509 for details concerning the use of these indexes as deflators for specific components of construction. Some of these indexes continue to be used to deflate value-in-place series and for these the series shown here can be linked to the indexes shown in Table Dc227-240 to form an index for the entire 1915-1999 period. These include the census composite, *Engineering News-Record*, Handy-Whitman, Federal Highway Administration, and Turner indexes – series Dc207, Dc213-214, Dc218-220, and Dc224-225. To acquire post-1970 data for the other series, contact the source agency noted below.

Construction cost indexes are useful in the conversion of construction expenditure data from current prices to constant prices and in the study of cost trends. However, no single cost index is satisfactory for all types of construction because the movements of cost differ for different types of construction. Series Dc207, however, is a composite index weighted by the relative importance of the major classes of construction.

Construction cost indexes generally are not fully adequate for making cost comparisons over an extended period of time. Changes in the productivity and the proportions used of the various productive factors cannot be allowed for easily in the assignment of weights to labor, materials, and other cost items. An aggregative index proportional to the total construction cost of a standardized project, or a component part thereof, is not easily computed for most types of construction and suffers from the disadvantage of the probable eventual obsoleteness of any adequately specified standard project. For further discussion, see Chapter 4 of the Colean and Newcomb source; Lowell J. Chawner, "Construction Cost Indexes as Influenced by Technological Changes and Other Factors," *Journal of the American Statistical Association*, 30 (1935): 561-76; and Leo Grebler, David M. Blank, and Louis Winnick, *Capital Formation in Residential Real Estate* (Princeton University Press, 1956), Appendix C.

Series Dc207, Department of Commerce composite cost index. This index is a combination of various indexes weighted by the relative importance of the major classes of construction. It is an implicit index computed by dividing the total estimate of new construction activity in current prices by the total expressed in 1967 prices. Because the total in 1967 prices is obtained by adding the estimates for the separately deflated classes of construction, the composite cost index is the equivalent of a variably weighted index, reflecting changes not only in the component indexes, but also in the relative importance of the major classes of construction, which are used as weights. For 1945-1970, the index is an average of the twelve monthly indexes.

Series Dc208, American Appraisal Company index. This index is compiled on the basis of a detailed bill of quantities of material and labor required for four representative types of buildings – frame, brick, concrete, and steel – with allowances for contractor's overhead and profit, in various cities throughout the United States. Workmen's compensation and liability insurance, unemployment insurance, and old-age pension factors are included. The index covers the structural portion of the buildings, but does not include the fixtures such as plumbing, heating, lighting, sprinkler systems, and elevators. The material and labor costs are recomputed monthly in accordance with average prices and wages supplemented by personal investigation of appraisers and information from clients and others regarding actual costs. These computations automatically result in weighted averages for the individual buildings. Arithmetic averages are computed for the individual buildings and cities to obtain the city and national averages. The latter covers twenty-four cities prior to 1925 and thirty cities since that time. The index reflects changes in average price levels but does not reflect costs resulting from overtime wages and bonuses during boom periods or sacrifice prices and omissions of overhead costs and profits during depression periods.

Series Dc209, Associated General Contractors index. This index is a combination of indexes of wages and materials weighted in the proportion of 40 percent for wages and 60 percent for materials. Wages used in computing this index are for hod carriers and common laborers, and the material prices are those for sand, gravel, crushed stone, portland cement, common brick, lumber (each with a weight of 1), hollow tile (weighted $1/2$), and structural and reinforcing steel (each with a weight of $1/4$). Wages and prices are reported by the twelve district offices of the Association as of the fifteenth of each month.

Series Dc210-212, E. H. Boeckh and Associates indexes. These indexes are based on separate computations for ten types of buildings in twenty cities (comparable indexes are available from the compilers for a total of more than forty cities). The basic list of items covered includes current local prices for common brick, common lumber, portland cement, structural steel, common labor, brick masons, carpenters, structural ironworkers, plasterers, and miscellaneous (which includes many specialized items such as heating and plumbing equipment, paint, glass, and hardware). Wage rates are adjusted to reflect efficiency of local labor. State and local sales taxes and Social Security payroll taxes are included. The weights assigned to the different items vary among the ten types of buildings. An unweighted arithmetic average of the individual indexes for the twenty cities for each of the ten types of buildings has been computed and these have been further consolidated into the three series shown here. The residential index is an unweighted average of the indexes for frame residences and for brick residences; the apartment, hotel, and office building index is an unweighted average of the indexes for brick and wood, brick and concrete, and brick and steel apartment, hotel, and office buildings; the commercial and factory buildings index is an unweighted average of the indexes for wood, steel, brick and wood, brick and steel, and brick and concrete commercial and factory buildings.

Series Dc213-214, *Engineering News-Record* (ENR) indexes. The index of construction costs comprises the following: (1) steel, which before 1938 is the base price of structural steel shapes at Pittsburgh and, beginning in 1938, is a weighted average of steel prices at Pittsburgh, Gary, and Birmingham; (2) cement, which before 1948 is the consumers' net price, f.o.b. (free on board) Chicago, and, beginning in 1948, is the ENR twenty-city average of bulk cement prices; (3) lumber, which before 1936 is 12 × 12 long leaf yellow pine, wholesale, at New York, and beginning in 1936 is a composite twenty-city price average of a 2 × 4 Douglas fir and southern or local pine in carload lots; and (4) common labor rate paid in the steel industry for 1913-1920 and since 1920 the average common labor rate in construction (ENR twenty-city average of wage rates in force). The four components are weighted according to their relative importance in the national economy in 1910, 1913, 1916, and 1919. The index of building costs is identical to the index of construction costs for all components except wage rates, where the trend of skilled labor wage rates is substituted for common labor wage rates. For a detailed description of these two indexes, see U.S. Office of Business Economics, *Business Statistics* (1971), p. 53.

TABLE Dc207–226   Indexes of construction costs: 1913–1970   *Continued*

Series Dc215–216, U.S. Department of Agriculture, Economic Research Service, indexes. These are weighted indexes of farm wage rates and prices paid for materials. In compiling the index of farm housing construction costs, prices paid by farmers for building materials are given a weight of 73 percent, and farm wage rates are given a weight of 27 percent. For other farm building construction, the corresponding weights are 78 and 22 percent. The wages paid by farmers for labor for building construction and repairs are higher than the wages paid for ordinary agricultural labor, but they probably fluctuate more comparably to farm labor wage rates than to urban union wage rates.

Series Dc217, George A. Fuller Company index. This is a composite index of thirty-six major cost elements in three commercial type buildings, including structural elements, elevators, wiring, heating, plumbing, ventilating, and employee benefit costs. The index is adjusted for changes in productivity from job-cost reports showing the number of man-hours of skilled and unskilled labor required. The indexes are simple averages of the quarterly indexes from the job-cost reports made by the compiler.

Series Dc218–220, Handy–Whitman public utility construction cost indexes. These indexes (compiled by Whitman, Requardt, and Associates, Baltimore) measure changes in construction costs of utility buildings, gas plants, and electric plants. Cost trends of reinforced concrete utility building construction and brick utility building construction are reported semiannually by geographic regions. A single index is computed by averaging the figures for the first, middle, and end of each year for each region and then combining the regions for a U.S. average. Cost trends of gas plant construction and of steam-operated electric plant construction are also reported semiannually by geographic regions. A single index for each is computed in the same manner as for utility buildings.

Series Dc221, U.S. Interstate Commerce Commission railroad construction cost index. The index is the weighted average (for the entire United States) of thirty-one separate indexes for individual operations important in railroad construction. Separate indexes covering items such as grading, tunnel excavation, bridges, ballast haul, and track laying and surfacing were developed largely from analysis of major construction contracts covering a period of more than thirty years. The indexes for material accounts – such as ties, rails, other track material, ballast, and fences – were based on studies of carriers' returns, joint studies made with the various railroad committees, well-known engineering and trade publications, contracts covering major construction projects over a period of thirty years, and other information furnished by individual carriers.

Series Dc222–223, Bell Telephone System plant indexes. The American Telephone and Telegraph Company compiled separate annual cost indexes for construction of telephone company "buildings" and "outside plant," for example, poles, cable, aerial wire, and underground conduits. These indexes represent changes in the total installed cost of telephone buildings or plant.

The outside plant index reflects the effect of price changes in the cost of telephone apparatus and the cost of associated installation and engineering.

Series Dc224, Federal Highway Administration index. This index is based on a record of quarterly variations in contract unit bid prices maintained by the Federal Highway Administration and its predecessor, Public Roads Administration, since 1922. Cost indexes are based on average annual construction of state and federal aid highway systems during 1925–1929. Average costs for these years are taken as 100 percent. For this period, the total quantity and contract cost of each of the principal cost-controlling contract items were summarized and divided by the total mileage of construction. This operation provided average quantities of each type of work involved per average gross or composite mile of construction. As unit prices and construction volumes vary not only from state to state but also from year to year, the percentage of each item contributed during this five-year period by each state was adopted as the contributing state base. The index thus indicates the relative costs at which the average quantities placed per mile in 1925–1929, with the same state distribution, could be replaced at current contract bid prices. Figures for 1915–1922 were extrapolated by the Department of Commerce by means of a weighted average of the Interstate Commerce Commission indexes for grading; tunnel and subway excavation; bridges, culverts, and trestles; and ballast. This index is a composite derived from average unit bid prices for fixed amounts of the following items put in place: common excavation, surfacing, and structures. The base quantities involved in measuring this index are as follows: 3,641,885,000 cubic yards of roadway excavation; 154,953,000 square yards of portland cement concrete surfacing with average thickness of 9.1 inches; 111,516,000 tons of bituminous concrete surfacing; 2,206,879,000 pounds of reinforcing steel for structures; 2,581,462,000 pounds of structural steel; and 14,583,000 cubic yards of structural concrete.

Series Dc225, Turner Construction Company index. This index is based on the building cost experience of the Turner Construction Company in Eastern cities applied to the following factors: labor rates, material prices, productivity of labor, efficiency of plant and management, and competitive conditions. The series also reflects the payment of sales taxes and employee benefit costs.

Series Dc226, average of contractor indexes of construction cost. This is an average of four contractor indexes shown separately in the underlying source. In contrast to the common indexes of construction costs, which usually represent a combination of wages and materials prices according to a fixed relationship and may not take adequate account of changes in efficiency, the contractor indexes are based on estimates of the actual cost for erecting comparable structures. The comparison of these indexes with the common indexes may suggest changes in cost that result from changes in efficiency. For a fuller discussion, see the source, pp. 69–74, and Grebler, Blank, and Winnick (1956), Appendix C.

TABLE Dc227–240 Indexes of construction costs: 1964–1999

Contributed by Kenneth A. Snowden

	U.S. Census Bureau							Handy–Whitman					Engineering News-Record	
	Total construction		Single-family houses											
Year	Fixed-weighted price index	Implicit price deflator	Fixed-weighted price index	Price deflator	Turner Construction Company	Federal Highway Administration composite	Bureau of Reclamation composite	Utilities buildings	Electric light and power plants	Gas plants	Water facilities	Turner – telephone plant	Buildings	Construction
	Dc227	Dc228	Dc229	Dc230	Dc231	Dc232	Dc233	Dc234	Dc235	Dc236	Dc237	Dc238	Dc239	Dc240
	1992 = 100	1992 = 100	1996 = 100	1996 = 100	1996 = 100	1996 = 100	1996 = 100	1996 = 100	1996 = 100	1996 = 100	1996 = 100	1996 = 100	1996 = 100	1996 = 100
1964	18.5	18.5	18.0	18.0	18	19.7	20	20	19	21	19	29	19.1	16.6
1965	19.1	19.1	18.6	18.6	19	20.5	21	20	19	21	20	30	19.6	17.3
1966	19.9	19.9	19.5	19.5	19	21.5	21	21	20	22	20	32	20.3	18.1
1967	20.5	20.6	20.1	20.2	20	22.5	22	21	21	22	21	33	21.0	19.0
1968	21.7	21.7	21.3	21.2	21	25.3	23	22	22	23	22	34	22.5	20.5
1969	23.2	23.2	22.6	22.6	23	28.5	24	24	23	24	23	36	24.7	22.6
1970	24.5	24.7	23.2	23.2	26	30.2	26	26	24	25	25	39	26.1	24.6
1971	26.2	26.3	24.5	24.5	29	31.5	28	28	26	28	28	40	29.6	28.1
1972	28.0	27.9	26.2	26.3	30	31.6	31	31	28	30	31	41	32.7	31.2
1973	30.4	30.4	28.8	28.8	32	34.8	32	34	30	31	33	44	35.5	33.7
1974	34.3	34.5	31.7	31.7	38	47.5	36	41	36	35	39	51	37.6	35.9
1975	37.2	37.8	34.5	34.5	39	47.6	42	45	42	40	43	53	40.8	39.3
1976	39.1	39.5	36.7	36.7	40	46.1	45	46	44	43	45	56	44.5	42.7
1977	42.5	42.6	41.1	40.6	41	49.0	48	49	47	47	48	59	48.2	45.8
1978	47.1	47.5	46.2	46.1	44	58.0	51	53	50	51	52	63	52.2	49.4
1979	53.0	53.1	52.1	51.7	49	70.1	56	59	55	55	57	70	56.8	53.4
1980	59.3	59.0	58.0	57.0	54	79.7	62	66	60	60	64	79	60.6	57.6
1981	63.9	63.5	62.1	61.0	60	77.2	68	69	66	66	68	80	65.5	62.9
1982	65.7	65.9	63.3	62.8	64	72.5	72	69	69	71	70	82	69.7	68.0
1983	67.2	67.1	65.1	64.5	68	71.8	73	71	71	73	72	79	74.4	72.3
1984	69.8	69.3	68.1	67.0	71	75.9	74	74	73	76	75	76	75.5	73.7
1985	71.8	71.1	69.8	68.3	74	83.6	75	76	74	75	76	77	75.8	74.6
1986	74.8	73.6	73.4	71.4	76	82.9	76	78	74	73	78	76	77.5	76.4
1987	77.7	76.3	76.8	74.7	79	82.0	77	79	75	75	79	77	79.3	78.4
1988	80.4	79.2	79.5	77.7	82	87.4	79	82	80	80	81	78	81.1	80.4
1989	83.2	82.4	82.2	80.8	84	88.3	82	84	84	84	84	85	82.2	82.1
1990	85.5	85.0	84.6	83.4	87	88.9	85	85	86	86	85	87	84.4	84.2
1991	86.2	85.9	84.8	84.1	89	88.1	88	83	88	87	85	87	85.9	86.0
1992	86.7	86.9	85.8	85.8	89	86.1	89	84	89	89	87	87	88.5	88.7
1993	90.1	90.2	90.0	90.0	91	88.8	91	89	92	91	91	89	93.5	92.7
1994	93.9	93.9	94.1	94.0	94	94.3	94	94	95	97	95	90	97.1	96.2
1995	97.7	97.8	98.1	98.1	97	99.8	98	97	98	99	98	96	97.1	97.3
1996	100.0	100.0	100.0	100.0	100	100.0	100	100	100	100	100	100	100.0	100.0
1997	103.2	103.3	102.9	102.9	104	107.5	103	103	102	102	102	102	105.0	103.6
1998	106.0	106.1	105.6	105.6	109	105.2	105	104	104	104	104	102	105.8	105.3
1999	110.3	110.4	110.4	110.4	113	112.7	107	107	105	107	107	101	107.9	107.8

measure changes over time in the price of an identical new single-family house that is assumed to be under construction each month and year. This index is calculated using the "hedonic" or regression methodology whereby physical characteristics of new houses are regressed against house values each month to obtain current market "prices" of those characteristics (the regression data is drawn from the Census Bureau's Survey of Construction discussed in the text for Tables Dc531–584). These derived prices are then used to compute the construction value of a new house each month that is built with the same characteristics as the average house in the base year. This type of fixed-basket index (called the Laspeyres) reflects only changes in prices. The annual index is computed independent of the monthly indexes, and may not equal the average of the monthly indexes. The price deflator in series Dc230 is calculated based on the same data and regression analysis, but is formed using the Fisher ideal chain-type annual-weighted index methodology. This type of index is preferred for use as a price deflator because it captures changes in the characteristics of residential housing that occur over time rather than imposing the fixed basket of characteristics assumption, which can bias the Laspeyres approach. For more details and discussion about the differences between the Census Bureau's single-family residential construction indexes, see the source.

Series Dc231. The Turner Construction Company (New York) compiles a national building construction index each quarter. The index is derived from the firm's current cost experience with labor rates and productivity, material prices, and the competitive condition of the marketplace. The annual index is an average of the quarterly indexes and is available at the Internet site of the Turner Construction Company.

Series Dc232. The Federal Highway Administration compiles its composite index on a quarterly basis. The index is derived from average unit bid prices for fixed amounts of common excavation, surfacing (portland cement concrete and bituminous concrete), and structures (reinforcing steel, structural steel, and structural concrete). To eliminate erratic quarter-to-quarter movement in the Federal Highway Administration composite index, the quarterly index is adjusted with the application of twelve-quarter phasing patterns based on highway construction activity. The annual index is a weighted average of the indicator items for the composite index.

Series Dc233. The U.S. Department of the Interior's Bureau of Reclamation (Denver, Colorado) compiles its composite index quarterly. This index reflects the Bureau of Reclamation's cost of constructing dams and reclamation projects in seventeen Western states. The index is a weighted average of costs of labor, materials, and equipment furnished by contractors and the government and, when possible, is based on actual bid prices from contracts. These data are supplemented by components of the Federal Highway Administration index, Bureau of Labor Statistics wholesale indexes, quotations of wage rates published in *Engineering News-Record*, and judgment of Bureau of Reclamation analysts. The index reflects the cost of labor, materials, and equipment for eleven categories of reclamation work, including dams, canals, hydroelectric power plants, concrete pipelines, and substations. The relative weights for each cost component and each category of work are held constant to those derived from contracts awarded during the period 1930–1946. The Census Bureau computes an annual index by averaging the quarterly indexes. This index is available from the Internet site of the Bureau of Reclamation.

Series Dc234–237. These annual indexes are computed by the U.S. Census Bureau from semiannual cost indexes compiled by Whitman, Requardt, and Associates (Baltimore) for four types of construction – utility buildings, steam-powered electric light and power plants, gas plants, and water. The source company compiles these indexes separately for six different geographical regions and the Census Bureau then computes simple averages of these to form national cost indexes for each type of construction. Each of the original regional source indexes is based on prices for materials, labor costs, and prices of mechanical and electrical equipment that have been drawn from standard publications or actual transactions.

(continued)

Source

U.S. Census Bureau, *Current Construction Reports*, C30/00-5, Value of Construction Put in Place: May 2000 (issued July 2000), Tables D-4, D-5, and D-6. The source provides all indexes shown for 1995–1999 and the fixed-weight index and price deflator of the Census Bureau for the entire 1964–1999 period. For the remaining indexes, data were downloaded April 6, 2001, from the Census Bureau's Internet site.

Documentation

The value-in-place estimates in current dollars (shown in Table Dc12-21) were converted to constant-dollar series (shown in Table Dc44–53) using the set of cost indexes presented in this table. The current-dollar value-in-place series are deflated into constant dollars on a monthly basis and then summed across months to form the annual constant-dollar series shown in Tables Dc44–53 and Dc256–509. The annual indexes shown here, on the other hand, are generally unweighted averages of the monthly or quarterly values for each index. As a result, the annual constant-dollar value-in-place series is not generally equal to the annual current-dollar series deflated by these annual indexes. The index or combinations of indexes that are used to deflate individual categories of construction are shown in Table D-3 of the source, and are discussed in this chapter with the constant-dollar series.

Beginning in May 2000, the base year for the value-in-place program was changed to 1996 from 1992, and the price indexes shown here and the constant-dollar value-in-place series shown elsewhere reflect this revision. The Census Bureau constructs its own price index and deflator for total construction (series Dc227–228) and for single-family residential construction (series Dc229–230). The other value-in-place indexes are deflated by indexes or combinations of indexes that the Census Bureau secures from private companies or federal agencies and then converts to a 1996 base year. The sources of the original indexes are noted in the following paragraphs, and the indexes expressed in the original base year used by the company or agency source (generally not 1996) can be found on the Census Bureau's Internet site.

A discussion of the choice of deflators used by the Census Bureau appears in U.S. Department of Commerce, *Survey of Current Business* (August 1974), part 1. At that time it was deemed appropriate to reduce the number of independent indexes used to deflate the value-in-place series, and since then the choice of the indexes and the procedures used for developing the deflators are jointly determined by the Bureau of Economic Analysis and the Census Bureau. Several of the indexes that were used to deflate value-in-place series for pre-1964 periods continue to be employed in the program; in these cases the index shown in this table can be linked to its pre-1964 counterpart shown in Table Dc207–226 to form a single, continuous index for the 1915–1999 period. These include the census composite, Turner, FHA, Handy–Whitman, and *Engineering News-Record* indexes – series Dc227, Dc231–232, Dc234–236, and Dc239–240.

Series Dc227–228. The census composite fixed-weighted price index is a weighted average of the individual price indexes that are used to deflate the subcomponents of the value-in-place series. In calculating the index each month, the weights are held constant (to reflect the composition of current-dollar value-in-place in 1992 by category of construction). Consequently, this index reflects only changes in prices. In contrast, the census implicit price deflator, series Dc228, is a derived ratio of total current-dollar to total constant-dollar value put in place (multiplied by 100); it is also, therefore, a weighted average of the individual price indexes. For this series, however, the weights change each month with changes in the composition of the total value put in place. Consequently, the implicit price deflator reflects not only changes in prices, but also changes in the composition of value put in place, and its use as a measure of price change is discouraged.

Series Dc229–230. A similar distinction should be made between the Census Bureau's single-family houses under construction fixed-weighted price index and price deflator. The former is designed to

TABLE Dc227–240   Indexes of construction costs: 1964–1999   *Continued*

Series Dc238. AUS Consultants Inc. (Harrisburg, Pennsylvania) has compiled the source data used to compute the C. A. Turner telephone plant index since 1977 and has published the index through its publications division, C. A. Turner, since 1990. Before then, the index was published as the Handy-Whitman index of public utility construction cost for the telephone industry through an affiliation with Whitman, Requardt, and Associates. The telephone plant index covers each major FCC plant account and is compiled semiannually from data provided by operating companies and suppliers. The index is published for the six geographic regions.

Series Dc239–240. The *Engineering News-Record* (McGraw-Hill) compiles monthly national cost indexes for buildings and for construction. Both indexes have four components – structural steel (a twenty-city average of wholesale prices), cement (a twenty-city average of f.o.b. [free on board] bulk prices), lumber (a twenty-city average wholesale prices for pine and fir), and labor (twenty-city averages of common labor rate for the construction index, or of the skilled labor rate for the building index). A complete description of the quantities, unit prices, and labor rates used in developing both indexes was published in *Business Statistics* (1963), a supplement to the *Survey of Current Business*, published by the Office of Business Economics (now the Bureau of Economic Analysis), U.S. Department of Commerce. Annual indexes are averages of the monthly indexes. More information and the annual indexes themselves can be found at the Internet site of the *Engineering News-Record*.

TABLE Dc241–255   Employees of construction firms, by industry division: 1958–1999

Contributed by Susan B. Carter

		Building construction				Heavy construction, except building			Special trade contractors						
	Total	Total	Residential	Operative	Nonresidential	Total	Highway and street	Except highway and street	Total	Plumbing, heating, and air conditioning	Painting and paper hanging	Electrical	Masonry, stonework, and plastering	Carpeting and floorwork	Roofing, siding, and sheet metal work
	Dc241	Dc242	Dc243	Dc244	Dc245	Dc246	Dc247	Dc248	Dc249	Dc250	Dc251	Dc252	Dc253	Dc254	Dc255
Year	Thousand	Thousand	Thousand	Thousand	Thousand	Thousand	Thousand	Thousand	Thousand	Thousand	Thousand	Thousand	Thousand	Thousand	Thousand
1958	2,817	861	—	46	—	—	—	—	—	312	138	189	—	—	99
1959	3,004	928	—	54	—	—	—	—	—	328	153	195	—	—	108
1960	2,926	877	—	49	—	—	—	—	—	323	146	200	—	—	108
1961	2,859	848	—	52	—	—	—	—	—	322	137	196	—	—	102
1962	2,948	858	—	56	—	—	—	—	—	333	141	206	—	—	103
1963	3,010	889	—	57	—	—	—	—	—	343	141	212	—	—	106
1964	3,097	920	—	56	—	—	—	—	—	354	140	219	—	—	108
1965	3,232	961	—	55	—	—	—	—	—	366	143	234	—	—	110
1966	3,317	992	—	50	—	—	—	—	—	373	142	249	—	—	112
1967	3,248	947	—	48	—	—	—	—	—	375	135	258	—	—	113
1968	3,350	976	—	53	—	—	—	—	—	392	133	267	—	—	112
1969	3,575	1,071	—	61	—	—	—	—	—	415	134	287	—	—	118
1970	3,588	1,066	—	63	—	—	—	—	—	430	130	298	—	—	115
1971	3,704	1,102	—	78	—	—	—	—	—	455	124	299	—	—	117
1972	3,889	1,165	578	94	493	774	—	505	1,951	479	125	335	323	125	126
1973	4,097	1,221	594	102	525	790	—	530	2,087	503	134	362	339	134	135
1974	4,020	1,192	576	92	524	799	—	544	2,029	494	132	357	310	113	135
1975	3,525	1,012	480	68	464	734	—	507	1,779	434	116	317	264	103	124
1976	3,576	1,022	514	67	442	747	—	537	1,806	435	119	317	267	109	127
1977	3,851	1,108	578	75	455	760	—	549	1,983	473	125	340	308	123	134
1978	4,229	1,229	637	82	509	828	—	603	2,173	520	138	369	338	133	155
1979	4,463	1,272	625	83	564	898	—	661	2,293	542	148	399	360	131	164

Year	Total	Building construction				Heavy construction, except building			Total	Special trade contractors					
		Total	Residential	Operative	Nonresidential	Total	Highway and street	Except highway and street		Plumbing, heating, and air conditioning	Painting and paper hanging	Electrical	Masonry, stonework, and plastering	Carpeting and floorwork	Roofing, siding, and sheet metal work
	Dc241	Dc242	Dc243	Dc244	Dc245	Dc246	Dc247	Dc248	Dc249	Dc250	Dc251	Dc252	Dc253	Dc254	Dc255
	Thousand	Thousand	Thousand	Thousand	Thousand	Thousand	Thousand	Thousand	Thousand	Thousand	Thousand	Thousand	Thousand	Thousand	Thousand
1980	4,346	1,173	554	67	552	895	—	667	2,278	533	142	412	353	122	166
1981	4,188	1,094	508	60	526	865	—	659	2,229	523	132	415	327	117	156
1982	3,904	990	447	48	496	795	—	612	2,119	499	124	407	307	104	155
1983	3,946	1,019	493	55	472	753	—	557	2,174	505	131	404	327	120	165
1984	4,380	1,161	579	58	524	758	—	549	2,462	565	151	449	382	143	184
1985	4,668	1,251	623	58	570	765	—	543	2,652	605	160	487	413	155	192
1986	4,810	1,289	665	57	567	750	—	520	2,771	619	162	516	437	170	198
1987	4,958	1,318	692	54	572	739	—	505	2,901	633	171	526	470	186	207
1988	5,098	1,350	711	47	593	743	227	516	3,005	650	171	545	492	195	206
1989	5,171	1,332	681	42	609	767	234	534	3,072	658	176	550	493	209	210
1990	5,120	1,298	643	38	617	770	239	532	3,051	655	176	549	481	198	210
1991	4,650	1,140	554	31	556	727	218	508	2,783	612	159	513	409	176	191
1992	4,492	1,077	528	27	521	711	215	497	2,704	606	153	500	387	176	189
1993	4,668	1,120	561	27	532	713	222	490	2,836	633	161	522	395	186	202
1994	4,986	1,188	605	28	556	740	226	514	3,058	681	172	564	422	210	206
1995	5,160	1,207	609	27	572	752	228	524	3,201	716	182	604	418	223	214
1996	5,418	1,257	642	26	589	777	236	541	3,384	759	190	636	441	237	230
1997	5,691	1,310	673	27	610	799	243	556	3,582	795	199	682	467	255	241
1998	6,020	1,377	706	28	643	840	257	583	3,804	833	207	735	501	276	249
1999	6,404	1,450	767	30	653	869	278	592	4,084	884	226	799	540	300	256

Source

U.S. Bureau of Labor Statistics Internet site, National Current Employment Statistics.

Documentation

See the text for Table Ba840–848.

The series correspond to Standard Industrial Classification (SIC) codes as follows: series Dc241, codes 15–19; series Dc242, code 15; series Dc243, code 152; series Dc244, code 153; series Dc245, code 154; series Dc246, code 16; series Dc247, code 161; series Dc248, code 162; series Dc249, code 17; series Dc250, code 171; series Dc251, code 172; series Dc252, code 173; series Dc253, code 174; series Dc254, code 175; series Dc255, code 176. See the Introduction to Part D for a discussion of SIC codes.

Series Dc241. Equals series Ba842.

CONSTRUCTION, BY SECTOR

Kenneth A. Snowden

TABLE Dc256–271 Value of new construction – private residential buildings, by type: 1915–1964[1]

Contributed by Kenneth A. Snowden

	New housing units										New housing units					
	Total	By number of units in structure		Additions and alterations	Nonhousekeeping residential buildings	Total	New housing units	Additions and alterations	Nonhousekeeping residential buildings	Total	Total	By number of units in structure		Additions and alterations	Nonhousekeeping residential buildings
			One	Two or more									One	Two or more		
	Total	Total	One	Two or more	Additions and alterations	Nonhousekeeping residential buildings	Total	New housing units	Additions and alterations	Nonhousekeeping residential buildings	Total	Total	One	Two or more	Additions and alterations	Nonhousekeeping residential buildings
	Dc256	Dc257	Dc258	Dc259	Dc260	Dc261	Dc262	Dc263	Dc264	Dc265	Dc266	Dc267	Dc268	Dc269	Dc270	Dc271
Year	Million dollars	Million dollars	Million dollars	Million dollars	Million dollars	Million dollars	Million 1957–1959 dollars	Million 1957–1959 dollars	Million 1957–1959 dollars	Million 1957–1959 dollars	Million 1967 dollars	Million 1967 dollars	Million 1967 dollars	Million 1967 dollars	Million 1967 dollars	Million 1967 dollars
1915	1,220	1,040	—	—	140	40	6,122	5,219	702	201	—	—	—	—	—	—
1916	1,375	1,170	—	—	145	60	6,489	5,521	685	283	—	—	—	—	—	—
1917	1,190	1,000	—	—	125	65	4,802	4,036	505	261	—	—	—	—	—	—
1918	915	760	—	—	110	45	3,097	2,571	373	153	—	—	—	—	—	—
1919	1,850	1,645	—	—	130	75	5,389	4,792	379	218	—	—	—	—	—	—
1920	2,015	1,710	—	—	175	130	4,553	3,865	395	293	—	—	—	—	—	—
1921	2,105	1,795	—	—	185	125	5,925	5,053	520	352	—	—	—	—	—	—
1922	3,360	2,955	—	—	200	205	10,279	9,040	612	627	—	—	—	—	—	—
1923	4,400	3,960	—	—	210	230	12,008	10,807	574	627	—	—	—	—	—	—
1924	5,060	4,575	—	—	230	255	14,010	12,666	638	706	—	—	—	—	—	—
1925	5,515	4,910	—	—	250	355	15,428	13,736	699	993	—	—	—	—	—	—
1926	5,600	4,920	—	—	270	410	15,504	13,621	748	1,135	—	—	—	—	—	—
1927	5,160	4,540	—	—	290	330	14,496	12,754	815	927	—	—	—	—	—	—
1928	4,770	4,195	—	—	315	260	13,344	11,734	882	728	—	—	—	—	—	—
1929	3,625	3,040	—	—	340	245	9,715	8,147	911	657	—	—	—	—	—	—
1930	2,075	1,570	—	—	305	200	5,710	4,320	839	551	—	—	—	—	—	—
1931	1,565	1,320	—	—	175	70	4,672	3,940	523	209	—	—	—	—	—	—
1932	630	485	—	—	105	40	2,222	1,711	370	141	—	—	—	—	—	—
1933	470	290	—	—	145	35	1,657	1,022	512	123	—	—	—	—	—	—
1934	625	380	—	—	200	45	2,028	1,233	649	146	—	—	—	—	—	—
1935	1,010	710	—	—	250	50	3,358	2,361	831	166	—	—	—	—	—	—
1936	1,565	1,210	—	—	295	60	5,029	3,889	947	193	—	—	—	—	—	—
1937	1,875	1,475	—	—	320	80	5,392	4,241	921	230	—	—	—	—	—	—
1938	1,990	1,620	—	—	295	75	5,556	4,523	824	209	—	—	—	—	—	—
1939	2,680	2,270	—	—	320	90	7,350	6,223	879	248	—	—	—	—	—	—
1940	2,985	2,560	—	—	335	90	7,924	6,794	890	240	—	—	—	—	—	—
1941	3,510	3,040	—	—	375	95	8,614	7,460	921	233	—	—	—	—	—	—
1942	1,715	1,440	—	—	225	50	4,014	3,358	531	125	—	—	—	—	—	—
1943	885	710	—	—	160	15	1,965	1,579	354	32	—	—	—	—	—	—
1944	815	570	—	—	220	25	1,673	1,170	452	51	—	—	—	—	—	—

	New housing units					Nonhousekeeping residential buildings		New housing units						New housing units				Nonhousekeeping residential buildings
			By number of units in structure		Additions and alterations		Total	New housing units	Additions and alterations		Total	Total	By number of units in structure		Additions and alterations	
	Total	Total	One	Two or more									One	Two or more		
	Dc256	Dc257	Dc258	Dc259	Dc260	Dc261	Dc262	Dc263	Dc264	Dc265	Dc266	Dc267	Dc268	Dc269	Dc270	Dc271
Year	Million dollars	Million dollars	Million dollars	Million dollars	Million dollars	Million dollars	Million 1957–1959 dollars	Million 1957–1959 dollars	Million 1957–1959 dollars	Million 1957–1959 dollars	Million 1967 dollars	Million 1967 dollars	Million 1967 dollars	Million 1967 dollars	Million 1967 dollars	Million 1967 dollars
1945	1,276	720	—	—	516	40	2,429	1,372	982	75	—	—	—	—	—	—
1946	6,247	4,795	—	—	1,307	145	10,785	8,266	2,269	250	—	—	—	—	—	—
1947	9,850	7,765	—	—	1,960	125	14,044	11,066	2,797	181	14,400	11,352	—	—	2,865	183
1948	13,128	10,506	—	—	2,467	155	—	—	—	—	17,669	14,140	—	—	3,320	209
1949	12,428	10,043	—	—	2,200	185	—	—	—	—	16,505	13,337	—	—	2,922	246
1950	18,126	15,551	—	—	2,400	175	—	—	—	—	23,480	20,144	—	—	3,109	227
1951	15,881	13,207	—	—	2,484	190	—	—	—	—	19,204	15,970	—	—	3,004	230
1952	15,803	12,851	—	—	2,767	185	—	—	—	—	18,569	15,101	—	—	3,251	217
1953	16,594	13,411	—	—	2,916	267	—	—	—	—	19,386	15,667	—	—	3,407	312
1954	18,187	14,931	—	—	2,960	296	—	—	—	—	21,123	17,341	—	—	3,438	344
1955	21,877	18,242	—	—	3,296	339	—	—	—	—	24,832	20,706	—	—	3,741	385
1956	20,178	16,143	—	—	3,588	447	—	—	—	—	22,297	17,838	—	—	3,965	494
1957	19,006	14,736	—	—	3,769	501	—	—	—	—	20,886	16,193	—	—	4,142	551
1958	19,789	15,445	—	—	3,711	633	—	—	—	—	21,748	16,973	—	—	4,079	696
1959	24,251	19,233	—	—	4,253	765	—	—	—	—	26,652	21,135	—	—	4,674	843
1960	22,975	17,279	14,648	2,631	4,831	865	—	—	—	—	25,111	18,884	16,010	2,874	5,281	946
1961	23,107	17,074	13,758	3,316	4,973	1,060	—	—	—	—	25,253	18,663	15,038	3,625	5,434	1,156
1962	25,150	19,443	14,601	4,842	4,484	1,223	—	—	—	—	27,341	21,136	15,872	5,264	4,874	1,331
1963	27,874	21,735	15,297	6,438	4,798	1,341	—	—	—	—	30,555	23,827	16,768	7,059	5,260	1,468
1964	28,010	21,786	15,337	6,449	4,767	1,457	—	—	—	—	30,557	23,767	16,731	7,036	5,198	1,592

[1] See text for a discussion of issues relating to the comparability of the series over time.

Source

U.S. Bureau of the Census, *Value of New Construction Put in Place 1964 to 1980*, Construction Reports: C30-81S (July 1981), Tables D-1 and D-2, pp. 182–91.

Documentation

For additional details on the value-in-place estimates for this period, see the text for Tables Dc1–11 and Dc22–43. For specific treatments of the residential building estimates, see the following. For 1946–1958: U.S. Bureau of the Census, *Value of New Construction Put in Place: 1946–63 Revised*, Construction Reports: C30-61S (October 1964), pp. 2–4; for 1960–1964: U.S. Bureau of the Census, *Value of New Construction Put in Place*, Construction Reports: C30-70S (October 1971), pp. 1, 69.

This table presents current- and constant-dollar value-in-place estimates for aggregate residential building construction. Residential building has been the largest category of new construction throughout the twentieth century, but is also the most difficult to estimate. After taking full responsibility for the value-in-place estimates in 1959, the Census Bureau spent the next decade implementing major changes in the procedures used to estimate the new housing unit subcomponent. Throughout this period revisions were made to pre-1964 estimates in an attempt to maintain the historical continuity of the series. The cumulative effect, however, was to leave substantial breaks in the current-dollar estimates of the new residential housing unit series in 1946 and 1960, which were compounded in the constant-dollar series when a new residential deflator was used to revise estimates for this series back to 1947. The addition and alteration subcomponent was also revised during the 1960s, but in this case no substantial discontinuity was created between the pre-1964 data shown here and the series in later years. Additional details concerning revisions are provided in the following sections.

Series Dc257–259

The new housing unit value-in-place series covers all new houses and apartments at all levels of value and quality, such as prefabricated units, shell houses, basement (or capped) houses, and houses built of used materials. The subcomponent excludes, however, group and transient accommodations, residential units in buildings that are primarily nonresidential, new housing units provided by conversion of residential or nonresidential space, mobile homes, house trailers, and houseboats. From the inception of the value-in-place program, current-dollar value-in-place estimates for this subcomponent have been derived by: (1) securing an estimate of the value of housing units started each period, and (2) allocating the value of work started over subsequent periods by applying fixed patterns of construction progress.

(continued)

TABLE Dc256–271 Value of new construction – private residential buildings, by type: 1915–1964 *Continued*

Most revisions and changes in procedures have been directed toward obtaining better estimates of the value of houses started each period, and many resulted from improvements in the procedures used to compile the underlying official estimates of building permits and housing starts that are shown in Tables Dc510–553. The procedures used to estimate new housing unit series for the period shown in this table follow.

1915–1940. This earliest period predates the official housing start program, so for most of these years the Bureau of Labor Statistics simply collected and reported building permit data – for the nation's largest 257 cities beginning in 1921 and then increasing to 2,400 cities with populations greater than 1,000 by 1938. From these data, several different estimates of the number and value of housing starts were developed for the 1920–1939 period (for a critical review of these efforts, see David L. Wickens, *Residential Real Estate* (National Bureau of Economic Research, 1941), pp. 56–61, 295–7). Among these were the original value-in-place estimates of the new housing units series; see Lowell J. Chawner, *Construction Activity in the United States, 1915–1937*, Domestic Commerce Series number 99, Bureau of Foreign and Domestic Commerce (U.S. Department of Commerce, 1938), pp. 38–45, for details. In brief, estimates for the 1921–1940 period were derived by roughly adjusting the value of permits issued each year to account for nonpermit and non-permit-reporting areas of the country, to compensate for the typical understatement of construction costs in permits, and to allow for lapses of permits that were not started. For this period only slight adjustment was made for year-to-year differences in the amount of carryover of expenditures for units started near the end of the year. The estimates for 1915–1920 were derived by using link relatives, which measured the annual changes in the value of residential building contracts reported by the F. W. Dodge Corporation, to project back from the 1921–1922 average.

1941–1959. Regular monthly estimates of housing starts began to be produced by the Bureau of Labor Statistics in 1940. When these data became available, value-in-place estimates of the new housing units series began to be based on monthly reports of the value of new housing units authorized by local building permits and on monthly field surveys in a sample of areas not issuing building permits. The total construction cost of housing units started in both permit- and non-permit-issuing places was estimated first, and then adjusted to include architectural and engineering fees, and site development costs that were not measured elsewhere. This final estimate of the total value of work started each month was then allocated to subsequent months by the application of a fixed monthly expenditure pattern, and these monthly estimates were summed together to form the annual series shown here.

1959–1964. A 1959 change in the procedures used in the housing starts program yielded much larger estimates of new starts in nonpermit areas of the country (see Construction Reports: C30-61S, October 1964). This break in the housing start series, of course, was also reflected in the value-in-place estimates for new housing units. To restore historical comparability, revised estimates of housing starts and the new housing unit series were introduced in 1964 for the 1946–1958 period. The revised current-dollar estimate for 1946 (shown in the table as $4.795 billion) turned out to be 45 percent higher than its previous, unrevised level ($3.3 billion), and represented a substantial break in this series. Moreover, this single series raised the previous estimates of current-dollar total private construction for 1946 by 14 percent, and total construction by nearly 12 percent. The Census Bureau noted that "even without these breaks in the series beginning with 1946, a substantial discontinuity in the economic significance of the data was occasioned at this time by the war period" (C30-61S, p. 4). It also cautioned that in comparisons of pre- and postwar value-in-place estimates "some adjustment will be necessary on the part of the user to make allowances for the break in the series at 1946" (C30-61S, p. 4).

Post-1964. Additional modifications to the new housing unit estimates for the years 1960–1964 followed in 1966 when separate estimates for single-

and multiunit structures were derived going back to 1960, and in 1970 when estimates including new farm housing units (also going back to 1960) were published for the first time (see Construction Reports: C30-70S, October 1971). The first change introduced no new break in continuity for the total new housing units series, but the latter requires some adjustment if the 1960–1964 estimates shown above are to be compared to earlier ones.

Series Dc260

Private residential additions and alterations includes all remodeling of, or additions to, housing units subsequent to their original completion, the construction of additional housing units in existing residential structures, the finishing of basements or attics, the modernization of kitchens, bathrooms, and so forth. Work representing normal maintenance and repair is not included. Private residential construction is the only type of construction activity for which value-in-place estimates of additions and alterations are reported separately, and the data cover housekeeping structures only. For a discussion of the problems of estimating residential additions and alterations, particularly prior to 1960, see Marvin Wilkerson, "Revised Estimates of Residential Additions and Alterations, 1945–56," *Construction Review* (June 1957). This subcomponent was also substantially revised in 1964, but in a way that did not affect its historical continuity. Beginning in 1960, a quarterly survey of residential additions and alterations was initiated by the Census Bureau (reported in its Construction Reports: C50 series), and the 1960–1964 estimates for this category were derived based on imputations from this survey as it was being tested and reformulated (see Construction Reports: C30-61S, October 1964, p. 2; and Construction Reports: C30-66S, October 1967, pp. 47, 68).

Series Dc261

The non-housekeeping residential buildings subcomponent includes fixed structures providing residential facilities other than housekeeping units such as hotels, motels, dormitories, and nursing homes. Throughout this period, the current-dollar estimates were derived from compilations of construction contract awards using the same procedures that were used for all subcomponents of private nonresidential buildings construction. Refer to text for Table Dc282–302, where these methods are described in detail. Note also that the non-housekeeping residential subcomponent has been moved to the nonresidential buildings category in the 1964–1999 official value-in-place series.

Series Dc262–271

The 1915–1947 constant-dollar series for all the value-in-place estimates shown in this table were calculated by deflating the current-dollar estimates with the E. H. Boeckh index of building materials and labor costs for brick and frame residences (shown for this period in Table Dc207–226). In fact, the Boeckh residential series continued to be used to deflate residential value-in-place estimates until the Census Bureau's price index of new single-family houses became available in the mid-1960s. Several alternatives to the Boeckh index were considered during the Census Bureau's comprehensive review of construction deflators in 1974 (described in the text for Table Dc227–240); in the end an unweighted average of two price indexes derived for Federal Housing Administration–insured houses was chosen for the 1947–1962 period, while the Census Bureau's price index for new single-family houses sold was adopted for 1963 and later years. (See "Revised Deflators for New Construction, 1947–73," *Survey of Current Business* (August 1974), pp. 22–5.) At the time the Census Bureau's price index used regression analysis to estimate the price of major structural characteristics from a large sample of actual current sales prices. These estimates were used to calculate the price of a basic reference home with a set of fixed characteristics. The 1915–1947 and 1947–1964 constant-dollar estimates shown in the table cannot be directly compared because they were derived using different deflators that were measured in different base years.

TABLE Dc272–281   Value of new construction – private residential buildings, by type: 1964–1999[1]

Contributed by Kenneth A. Snowden

	New housing units						New housing units			
		By number of units in structure						By number of units in structure		
	Total	Total	One	Two or more	Improvements	Total	Total	One	Two or more	Improvements
	Dc272	Dc273	Dc274	Dc275	Dc276	Dc277	Dc278	Dc279	Dc280	Dc281
Year	Million dollars	Million dollars	Million dollars	Million dollars	Million dollars	Million 1996 dollars	Million 1996 dollars	Million 1996 dollars	Million 1996 dollars	Million 1996 dollars
1964	30,526	24,098	17,649	6,449	6,428	169,635	133,916	98,078	35,837	35,719
1965	30,235	23,846	17,839	6,007	6,389	162,872	128,428	96,078	32,349	34,445
1966	28,611	21,811	16,568	5,243	6,800	147,243	112,287	85,300	26,987	34,956
1967	28,737	21,541	16,817	4,724	7,196	143,091	107,222	83,721	23,501	35,870
1968	34,172	26,723	19,520	7,203	7,449	161,347	126,127	92,169	33,958	35,220
1969	37,214	29,224	19,696	9,528	7,990	165,261	129,773	87,473	42,300	35,488
1970	35,863	27,059	17,541	9,518	8,804	155,113	117,100	75,894	41,206	38,013
1971	48,514	38,670	25,806	12,864	9,844	197,987	157,758	105,239	52,519	40,229
1972	60,693	50,095	32,848	17,247	10,598	231,139	190,743	125,056	65,687	40,396
1973	65,085	54,619	35,181	19,438	10,466	226,131	189,826	122,229	67,597	36,305
1974	55,967	43,420	29,701	13,720	12,547	177,074	137,440	93,836	43,604	39,634
1975	51,581	36,317	29,639	6,679	15,264	149,410	105,194	85,775	19,419	44,216
1976	68,273	50,771	43,860	6,910	17,502	185,804	138,094	119,283	18,811	47,711
1977	92,004	72,231	62,214	10,017	19,773	225,518	176,934	152,335	24,599	48,584
1978	109,838	85,601	72,769	12,832	24,237	237,131	184,758	157,053	27,705	52,373
1979	116,444	89,272	72,257	17,015	27,172	224,697	172,251	139,456	32,795	52,446
1980	100,381	69,629	52,921	16,708	30,752	175,822	121,964	92,640	29,324	53,858
1981	99,241	69,424	51,965	17,460	29,817	162,706	113,853	85,217	28,636	48,853
1982	84,676	57,001	41,462	15,538	27,675	134,605	90,599	65,889	24,710	44,006
1983	125,833	94,961	72,514	22,447	30,872	195,028	147,174	112,384	34,790	47,854
1984	155,015	114,616	86,395	28,221	40,399	231,396	171,119	128,985	42,134	60,277
1985	160,520	115,888	87,350	28,539	44,632	234,955	169,631	127,856	41,776	65,324
1986	190,677	135,169	104,131	31,038	55,508	266,481	188,917	145,497	43,420	77,564
1987	199,652	142,668	117,216	25,452	56,984	267,063	190,842	156,777	34,065	76,222
1988	204,496	142,391	120,093	22,298	62,105	263,385	183,394	154,670	28,724	79,991
1989	204,255	143,232	120,929	22,304	61,023	252,745	177,265	149,651	27,613	75,480
1990	191,103	132,137	112,886	19,250	58,966	228,943	158,319	135,253	23,066	70,625
1991	166,251	114,575	99,427	15,148	51,676	197,526	136,121	118,110	18,011	61,405
1992	199,393	135,070	121,976	13,094	64,323	232,134	157,254	141,990	15,264	74,879
1993	225,067	150,911	140,123	10,788	74,156	249,757	167,467	155,488	11,979	82,290
1994	258,561	176,389	162,309	14,081	82,172	274,956	187,561	172,609	14,952	87,395
1995	247,351	171,404	153,515	17,889	75,947	251,937	174,585	156,363	18,222	77,352
1996	281,115	191,113	170,790	20,324	90,002	281,229	191,212	170,865	20,347	90,018
1997	289,014	198,063	175,179	22,883	90,951	280,748	192,386	170,154	22,232	88,362
1998 [2]	314,607	223,983	199,409	24,574	90,624	297,886	212,068	188,785	23,283	85,818
1999 [2]	348,826	249,536	222,280	27,256	99,290	315,757	225,896	201,210	24,686	89,860

[1] See text for a discussion of issues relating to the comparability of the series over time.

[2] Estimates are subject to normal revisions for three years because several series are benchmarked to data that appear in other annual or biennial reports; see text.

Source

See the source for Table Dc12–21.

Documentation

Refer to the essay in this chapter and the text for Tables Dc12–21 and Dc44–53 for general information about the 1964–1999 value-in-place series.

This table presents current- and constant-dollar estimates of private residential construction activity in the United States. Total residential building construction in the value-in-place program is defined as the sum of new housing units and improvements to existing residential units. The new housing units subcomponent includes the costs of building new houses, apartments, condominiums, and townhouses, but excludes mobile homes, houseboats, and residential units in buildings that are primarily nonresidential.

Several major revisions were made in 1986 to the residential building value-in-place category and its subcomponents. The composition of the category was redefined to exclude the "non-housekeeping residential buildings" subcomponent (composed largely of hotels, motels, and dormitories), which was moved to the nonresidential buildings category (see Table Dc303–320).

Moreover, new procedures and revised estimates were incorporated into the single-family and improvements series that substantially raised the levels of both subcomponents. All of these revisions were carried back no further than 1964, and the current-dollar estimate of total residential buildings, series Dc272, for that year is now 9 percent higher than the prerevision level. This represents a substantial break with the 1915–1964 series shown in Table Dc1–11.

Series Dc274. The estimate for new one-unit houses is calculated from data drawn from the Census Bureau's single-family housing starts survey (see Table Dc531–553). This survey yields the number of units started each month and the average cost per unit, which is estimated separately for homes to be sold or rented versus homes built for or by the owner. The average unit cost for each type of house is adjusted to exclude a variety of "nonconstruction" expenditures and multiplied by the number of units started each month to estimate the total construction cost for each type of single-unit house. These are added together to form an estimate of the total construction cost for single units started each month. These estimates, in turn, are distributed across the next twelve months by applying fixed patterns of monthly construction progress (see Table B-4 in the source). For any given month, therefore, the value-in-place estimate of work performed on new housing units is the sum

(continued)

TABLE Dc272–281 Value of new construction – private residential buildings, by type: 1964–1999 *Continued*

of work done on houses started that month and work done on all houses that were started during the preceding eleven months. These monthly estimates are summed together to yield the annual estimates shown in the table. The procedural changes made in 1986 were designed to improve the estimated value of units started and to expand coverage by including land development undertaken by builders. The combination of the two raised the 1964 value-in-place estimate for the new one-unit subcomponent 15 percent above its previous level, and represents a substantial break from the pre-1964 one-unit housing series Dc258. See Construction Reports: C30-85-5 (May 1985), Appendix B, for details of the 1986 revisions.

Series Dc275. For 1964–1973, the general procedure described above was also used to derive the value-in-place estimates for new housing units in two-or-more-unit structures. Beginning with the 1974 data, however, this series has been estimated by different procedures. Each month a subsample of new residential building projects with two or more units is selected from the housing starts survey, and the owners of these projects are requested to submit monthly construction progress reports until the project is completed. A total of approximately 2,100 ongoing two-or-more-unit projects are currently reported on each month. Estimates of value put in place for the nation are then compiled as a weighted sum of the reported value of the work performed on the sample projects during that month. The weight for each project incorporates the probability of its being selected for the sample and an adjustment to inflate the owner's reported value for unreported architectural and engineering fees and other miscellaneous costs. The monthly estimates are summed together to form the annual estimates shown in the table.

Series Dc276. Improvements to residential buildings include remodeling, additions, and major replacements to properties subsequent to completion of the original building. It includes projects such as adding a housing unit to an existing residential structure, finishing a basement or attic, modernizing a kitchen or bathroom, adding a swimming pool or garage, and replacing major heating or cooling equipment. Maintenance and repair work is not included. The data used to estimate the value of improvements put in place through 1984 were collected as part of the Bureau's Quarterly Household Survey of Residential Alterations and Repairs. Beginning in 1985, data from the Consumer Expenditure Surveys (conducted by the Bureau of the Census for the Bureau of Labor Statistics) have been used to estimate expenditures for improvements made on owner-occupied properties. A separate survey of a sample of owners of rented and vacant residential buildings is conducted each quarter to collect data that are used to estimate the value of improvements made on these types of properties. Before 1986 this subcomponent was referred to as "residential alterations and additions." The name of the series was changed when the residential improvements series was substantially revised in 1986 to include major replacements (such as a roof or heating system) that extended the life of the property. The revision was carried back to 1964 and increased the estimate in that year by 35 percent, which represents a substantial break with the 1915–1964 alterations and additions series.

Series Dc281. The Census Bureau's "single-family houses under construction price deflator" is used to convert current-dollar estimates to constant-dollar series for all subcomponents of residential buildings. See Table Dc227–240.

TABLE Dc282–302   Value of new construction – private nonresidential buildings, by type: 1915–1964[1]

Contributed by Kenneth A. Snowden

	Current dollars							1957–1959 dollars			
	Total	Industrial	Office and commercial	Religious	Educational	Hospital and institutional	Miscellaneous	Total	Industrial	Office and commercial	Religious
	Dc282	Dc283	Dc284	Dc285	Dc286	Dc287	Dc288	Dc289	Dc290	Dc291	Dc292
Year	Million dollars	Million dollars	Million dollars	Million dollars	Million dollars	Million dollars	Million dollars	Million 1957–1959 dollars	Million 1957–1959 dollars	Million 1957–1959 dollars	Million 1957–1959 dollars
1915	478	197	—	—	—	—	—	—	1,107	—	—
1916	716	262	—	—	—	—	—	—	1,263	—	—
1917	800	364	—	—	—	—	—	—	1,431	—	—
1918	731	449	—	—	—	—	—	—	1,563	—	—
1919	1,082	621	—	—	—	—	—	—	1,831	—	—
1920	1,964	1,099	625	55	22	30	133	4,657	2,536	1,540	134
1921	1,434	574	570	71	32	44	143	4,441	1,812	1,713	224
1922	1,457	467	613	103	61	53	160	4,813	1,543	1,984	352
1923	1,697	549	716	117	83	57	175	5,040	1,618	2,106	356
1924	1,675	460	740	130	91	63	191	5,004	1,370	2,172	400
1925	2,060	513	940	165	108	79	255	6,246	1,523	2,814	519
1926	2,513	727	1,107	177	108	83	311	7,569	2,156	3,277	556
1927	2,534	696	1,145	179	106	106	302	7,712	2,118	3,415	564
1928	2,573	802	1,121	168	107	100	275	7,812	2,440	3,327	529
1929	2,694	949	1,135	147	120	104	239	8,144	2,970	3,256	462
1930	2,003	532	893	135	118	109	216	6,437	1,865	2,600	464
1931	1,099	221	454	87	100	71	166	4,001	880	1,495	334
1932	502	74	223	45	53	34	73	2,078	314	861	198
1933	406	176	130	22	15	10	53	1,725	728	543	100
1934	456	191	173	21	14	9	48	1,738	691	657	89
1935	472	158	211	28	17	10	48	1,809	564	810	118
1936	713	266	290	34	40	17	66	2,609	910	1,069	137
1937	1,085	492	387	44	42	31	89	3,443	1,481	1,251	153
1938	764	232	285	51	40	35	121	2,477	714	914	174
1939	786	254	292	48	39	31	122	2,567	806	944	164
1940	1,025	442	348	59	50	33	93	3,200	1,310	1,106	198
1941	1,482	801	409	62	58	46	106	4,228	2,160	1,214	195
1942	635	346	155	31	24	29	50	1,628	829	418	87
1943	233	156	33	6	6	11	21	563	351	92	17
1944	351	208	56	11	11	26	39	861	491	143	29
1945	1,020	642	203	26	31	37	81	2,353	1,426	489	65
1946	3,362	1,689	1,153	76	123	85	236	6,498	3,050	2,348	160
1947	3,243	1,702	957	126	174	110	174	4,994	2,595	1,474	198
1948	3,765	1,397	1,397	251	253	126	341	—	—	—	—
1949	3,383	972	1,182	360	269	202	398	—	—	—	—
1950	3,904	1,062	1,415	409	294	344	380	—	—	—	—
1951	5,279	2,117	1,498	452	345	419	448	—	—	—	—
1952	5,014	2,320	1,137	399	351	394	413	—	—	—	—
1953	5,680	2,229	1,791	472	426	317	445	—	—	—	—
1954	6,250	2,030	2,212	593	529	337	549	—	—	—	—
1955	7,611	2,399	3,218	734	492	351	417	—	—	—	—
1956	8,818	3,084	3,631	768	536	328	471	—	—	—	—
1957	9,556	3,557	3,564	868	525	525	517	—	—	—	—
1958	8,675	2,382	3,589	863	574	600	667	—	—	—	—
1959	8,859	2,106	3,930	947	525	570	781	—	—	—	—
1960	10,149	2,851	4,180	1,013	566	605	934	—	—	—	—
1961	10,734	2,780	4,674	1,003	609	771	897	—	—	—	—
1962	11,617	2,842	5,144	1,033	680	985	933	—	—	—	—
1963	11,646	2,906	4,995	1,001	678	1,030	1,036	—	—	—	—
1964	12,955	3,565	5,396	992	697	1,291	1,014	—	—	—	—

Note appears at end of table

(continued)

TABLE Dc282–302   Value of new construction – private nonresidential buildings, by type: 1915–1964   *Continued*

	1957–1959 dollars			1967 dollars						
	Educational	Hospital and institutional	Miscellaneous	Total	Industrial	Office and commercial	Religious	Educational	Hospital and institutional	Miscellaneous
	Dc293	Dc294	Dc295	Dc296	Dc297	Dc298	Dc299	Dc300	Dc301	Dc302
Year	Million 1957–1959 dollars	Million 1957–1959 dollars	Million 1957–1959 dollars	Million 1967 dollars	Million 1967 dollars	Million 1967 dollars	Million 1967 dollars	Million 1967 dollars	Million 1967 dollars	Million 1967 dollars
1915	—	—	—	—	—	—	—	—	—	—
1916	—	—	—	—	—	—	—	—	—	—
1917	—	—	—	—	—	—	—	—	—	—
1918	—	—	—	—	—	—	—	—	—	—
1919	—	—	—	—	—	—	—	—	—	—
1920	54	73	320	—	—	—	—	—	—	—
1921	102	139	451	—	—	—	—	—	—	—
1922	209	182	543	—	—	—	—	—	—	—
1923	253	174	533	—	—	—	—	—	—	—
1924	280	193	589	—	—	—	—	—	—	—
1925	340	248	802	—	—	—	—	—	—	—
1926	340	262	978	—	—	—	—	—	—	—
1927	334	334	947	—	—	—	—	—	—	—
1928	336	314	866	—	—	—	—	—	—	—
1929	378	327	751	—	—	—	—	—	—	—
1930	407	376	725	—	—	—	—	—	—	—
1931	384	273	635	—	—	—	—	—	—	—
1932	234	150	321	—	—	—	—	—	—	—
1933	68	45	241	—	—	—	—	—	—	—
1934	60	38	203	—	—	—	—	—	—	—
1935	73	42	202	—	—	—	—	—	—	—
1936	161	68	264	—	—	—	—	—	—	—
1937	144	108	306	—	—	—	—	—	—	—
1938	138	121	416	—	—	—	—	—	—	—
1939	134	105	414	—	—	—	—	—	—	—
1940	167	109	310	—	—	—	—	—	—	—
1941	182	144	333	—	—	—	—	—	—	—
1942	68	83	143	—	—	—	—	—	—	—
1943	17	29	57	—	—	—	—	—	—	—
1944	29	68	101	—	—	—	—	—	—	—
1945	77	93	203	—	—	—	—	—	—	—
1946	258	179	503	—	—	—	—	—	—	—
1947	276	175	276	5,240	2,750	1,546	204	281	178	281
1948	—	—	—	5,474	2,031	2,031	365	368	183	496
1949	—	—	—	5,048	1,451	1,764	537	401	301	594
1950	—	—	—	5,870	1,597	2,128	615	442	517	571
1951	—	—	—	6,992	2,804	1,984	599	457	555	593
1952	—	—	—	6,469	2,994	1,467	514	453	508	533
1953	—	—	—	7,291	2,861	2,299	606	547	407	571
1954	—	—	—	8,245	2,678	2,918	782	698	445	724
1955	—	—	—	9,885	3,116	4,179	953	639	456	542
1956	—	—	—	10,536	3,685	4,338	918	640	392	563
1957	—	—	—	10,973	4,084	4,092	997	603	603	594
1958	—	—	—	10,202	2,799	4,222	1,016	676	704	785
1959	—	—	—	10,531	2,501	4,672	1,127	625	676	930
1960	—	—	—	12,107	3,401	4,986	1,209	675	723	1,113
1961	—	—	—	12,817	3,322	5,580	1,196	727	921	1,071
1962	—	—	—	13,716	3,355	6,072	1,220	804	1,162	1,103
1963	—	—	—	13,480	3,361	5,782	1,159	786	1,192	1,200
1964	—	—	—	14,711	4,049	6,126	1,125	792	1,465	1,154

[1] See the text for a discussion of issues relating to the comparability of the series over time.

Source

U.S. Bureau of the Census, *Value of New Construction Put in Place 1964 to 1980*, Construction Reports: C30-80S (July 1981), Tables D-1 and D-2, pp. 182–91.

Documentation

For additional details on the value-in-place estimates for this period, see the text for Tables Dc1–11 and Dc22–43. For specific details about the non-residential buildings series, see the following: Lowell J. Chawner, *Construction Activity in the United States, 1915–1937*, Domestic Commerce Series number 99, U.S. Bureau of Foreign and Domestic Commerce, Department of Commerce (1938), pp. 45–60; U.S. Business and Defense Services Administration, Department of Commerce, and U.S. Bureau of Labor Statistics, Department of Labor, *Construction Volume and Costs, 1915–56: A Statistical Supplement to Construction Review*, volume 3 (1957), pp. 71, 82; and Construction Reports: C30-66S (October 1967), pp. 47–55, 69–72.

This table presents the current- and constant-dollar estimates of private nonresidential buildings construction and its constituent subcomponent categories. Throughout the 1915–1964 period, the current-dollar estimates were based on reports of construction contracts awarded that were compiled by

TABLE Dc282–302   Value of new construction – private nonresidential buildings, by type: 1915–1964   *Continued*

the F. W. Dodge Corporation of McGraw-Hill, using a basic two-step procedure. Although there were some important modifications within this general structure during the period, no substantial discontinuities appear in the current-dollar estimates shown in the preceding.

The first step in deriving value-in-place estimates for nonresidential buildings involved constructing national estimates of work started from Dodge reports of contracts awarded in thirty-seven Eastern states and the District of Columbia. To do so, adjustments were made for architectural and engineering fees, for geographical areas not covered by the Dodge reports, and for Dodge's undercoverage of smaller projects. Contracts also had to be classified into the six subcomponent categories shown in this table (see below). The procedures used in this first step of estimating value-in-place estimates for nonresidential buildings remained virtually unchanged between 1925 and 1964. Before 1925, however, the Dodge report covered fewer states and with insufficient specificity before 1920 to allow separate estimation of the subcomponents shown here. Moreover, publicly owned and privately owned commercial and industrial buildings could not be segregated before 1932, and so they all were included in the private nonresidential subcomponents. For a detailed account of the procedures used to construct nonresidential buildings value-in-place estimates for the pre-1925 period, see Chawner (1938).

The second step in deriving these series involved forming estimates of the value of work put in place each period by distributing the estimates of the value of work started over time. Up to 1938, when only annual estimates were constructed, one half of the work started in each year was assumed to have been actually completed and put in place during that year for most subcomponents of nonresidential buildings. The exception was industrial building for which two thirds of the work was assumed to have been completed during the first year. The remaining one half of the work (one third for industrial buildings) was assumed to have been put in place the following year.

A modification to this second step occurred in 1938 when monthly value-in-place estimates began to be compiled. This was done by distributing the value of work started each month into the value of work put in place in subsequent months according to fixed monthly progress patterns that differed by subcomponent and the season the work started. These monthly value-in-place estimates were then summed to form the annual estimates shown above.

A final change in the procedure used in the second step of estimating these series was implemented in 1963 to permit a more direct estimate of value-in-place for nonresidential building construction. The thirty-seven-state Dodge report continued to be the basis of the estimates, but a sample of these projects was selected each month to submit monthly construction progress reports until the project was completed. The survey results were used to estimate more precisely the actual start dates for contracts awarded each month, to distribute more accurately the work performed over subsequent months, and to adjust for changes in the costs of the projects after the contracts were awarded. These new procedures were introduced gradually to maintain continuity with the pre-1963 estimates.

Throughout the 1920–1964 period, a building project was classified into one of the nonresidential subcomponents according to its own function, even if it was intended to serve as an auxiliary unit of a parent organization. For example, a cafeteria building at a hospital or an industrial plant was classified as a commercial structure instead of either a hospital or an industrial building. Refer to *Construction Volume and Costs, 1915–56*, as cited above, and Construction Reports: C30-61S (October 1964), pp. 72–3, for discussions of the classification issue.

Series Dc283

Before 1964, as noted, the industrial category was designed to include only those buildings and structures that housed the production, assembly, and warehousing activities of a manufacturing establishment. Auxiliary facilities at an industrial location (such as buildings for administration, or sewer, water, and parking facilities) were supposed to be excluded but in practice often could not be segregated. These types of auxiliary facilities that were owned by public utilities were excluded entirely from the nonresidential buildings categories and placed in the relevant public utility subcomponent (see Table Dc321–338).

Industrial building construction could not be segregated into public and private before 1933. It is all included in private nonresidential building because the amount of public construction of this type before 1933 is believed to have been negligible.

Series Dc284 and Dc288

The Census Bureau reported two separate subcomponents of the office and commercial series until 1964 – "office buildings and warehouses" and "stores, restaurants, garages, etc." Separate estimates for these series are reported in U.S. Business and Defense Services Administration, Department of Commerce, *Construction Statistics, 1915–64: A Supplement to Construction Review* (January 1966), p. 4. The 1980 source from which the data in this table were drawn combined the two, presumably to more closely replicate post-1964 categories (see Table Dc303–320).

Another subcomponent that was reported separately until 1964, "social and recreational buildings," was subsumed in the source, and reported here, as part of miscellaneous nonresidential buildings. In addition to the social and recreational projects, therefore, the miscellaneous subcomponent includes privately owned fire stations, bus and air passenger terminals, some commercial warehouses (until 1955), and other projects not elsewhere classified.

Series Dc289–302

Constant-dollar estimates for the entire 1915–1964 period were originally compiled using different deflators for the industrial building (the Turner Construction Company Index), commercial building (the Fuller Company Index), and all other nonresidential buildings subcomponents (the American Appraisal Index). Annual values of all of these indexes are included in Table Dc207–226. As a result of the comprehensive revision of construction cost indexes in 1975 (see the text for Tables Dc22–53 and Dc227–240), a single new deflating index was chosen for all subcomponents of nonresidential buildings. The new deflator was constructed as an unweighted average of the Turner Construction Company Index of general building costs, the Bureau of Public Roads cost index for structures, and the new residential buildings deflator adopted by the Census Bureau at that time (see the text for Table Dc256–271 and Table Dc227–240 for the annual cost indexes). This new deflator was used to revise constant-dollar estimates back to 1947, in 1967 dollars. In the table these estimates are shown separately from the unrevised 1915–1947 estimates because the two cannot be directly compared.

TABLE Dc303–320   Value of new construction – private nonresidential buildings, by type: 1964–1999[1]

Contributed by Kenneth A. Snowden

Year	Total	Industrial	Office	Hotels and motels	Other commercial	Religious	Educational	Hospital and institutional	Miscellaneous
	Dc303	Dc304	Dc305	Dc306	Dc307	Dc308	Dc309	Dc310	Dc311
	Million dollars	Million dollars	Million dollars	Million dollars	Million dollars	Million dollars	Million dollars	Million dollars	Million dollars
1964	17,385	5,028	—	1,548	6,330	1,044	822	1,485	1,128
1965	21,896	7,182	—	1,579	7,865	1,263	861	1,603	1,543
1966	24,238	9,261	—	1,511	7,933	1,205	1,080	1,637	1,612
1967	23,117	8,400	—	1,345	7,956	1,118	1,147	1,532	1,618
1968	23,811	8,492	—	1,315	9,104	1,135	1,255	1,816	694
1969	27,741	9,600	—	1,469	11,066	1,044	1,185	2,502	876
1970	28,171	9,316	—	1,458	11,560	988	1,011	2,938	899
1971	29,307	7,754	—	1,502	13,819	867	1,103	3,341	921
1972	32,375	6,730	6,841	2,158	9,813	907	1,163	3,725	1,038
1973	37,639	9,021	7,799	2,537	11,378	877	1,075	3,714	1,238
1974	39,889	11,454	7,998	1,844	11,846	993	806	3,784	1,164
1975	35,409	11,659	6,521	1,220	9,472	941	714	3,805	1,077
1976	34,628	10,473	6,263	1,028	9,692	1,040	785	4,037	1,311
1977	38,245	11,309	6,968	1,084	11,603	1,144	812	3,934	1,392
1978	48,824	16,155	8,712	1,349	14,655	1,367	940	4,010	1,635
1979	64,765	22,034	12,576	2,480	18,954	1,701	986	4,242	1,791
1980	72,480	20,522	17,815	3,401	20,510	1,811	1,430	4,893	2,100
1981	85,569	25,413	23,515	4,340	20,820	1,853	1,541	5,970	2,117
1982	92,690	26,082	31,262	4,828	17,805	1,730	1,721	7,204	2,057
1983	87,069	19,454	28,333	6,139	18,902	2,009	1,869	8,089	2,274
1984	107,680	20,901	35,577	8,036	28,036	2,418	1,958	7,808	2,946
1985	127,466	24,139	43,599	8,749	35,709	2,751	2,251	6,969	3,297
1986	120,917	20,984	39,361	8,903	35,763	3,076	2,774	6,749	3,307
1987	123,247	21,210	36,886	8,939	37,341	3,178	4,126	7,614	3,952
1988	130,854	23,203	39,307	8,265	38,852	3,271	3,511	9,147	5,298
1989	139,953	28,786	40,116	9,275	39,833	3,449	3,991	9,559	4,945
1990	143,506	33,636	35,055	10,679	40,047	3,566	4,616	10,868	5,040
1991	116,570	31,424	25,951	6,939	29,355	3,521	4,193	10,567	4,619
1992	105,646	29,029	20,271	3,691	29,197	3,485	4,474	11,487	4,012
1993	110,635	26,482	20,920	4,565	32,453	3,887	4,649	12,492	5,188
1994	120,289	28,952	22,178	4,648	37,551	3,869	4,822	12,268	6,002
1995	136,541	34,024	25,613	7,112	42,654	4,326	5,493	11,248	6,071
1996	153,912	36,220	27,886	10,912	48,188	4,534	6,742	11,780	7,650
1997	172,990	36,739	34,305	12,898	51,809	5,777	8,693	13,546	9,223
1998 [2]	190,711	40,484	42,226	14,816	53,598	6,594	9,698	13,793	9,501
1999 [2]	195,776	34,894	46,570	15,939	57,143	7,497	9,784	13,624	10,327

Year	Total	Industrial	Office	Hotels and motels	Other commercial	Religious	Educational	Hospital and institutional	Miscellaneous
	Dc312	Dc313	Dc314	Dc315	Dc316	Dc317	Dc318	Dc319	Dc320
	Million 1996 dollars	Million 1996 dollars	Million 1996 dollars	Million 1996 dollars	Million 1996 dollars	Million 1996 dollars	Million 1996 dollars	Million 1996 dollars	Million 1996 dollars
1964	96,497	27,901	—	8,599	35,118	5,793	4,565	8,242	6,279
1965	117,762	38,612	—	8,500	42,293	6,796	4,632	8,632	8,297
1966	125,310	47,861	—	7,821	41,011	6,225	5,581	8,469	8,342
1967	116,120	42,203	—	6,758	39,955	5,615	5,762	7,696	8,130
1968	112,547	40,115	—	6,215	43,023	5,371	5,945	8,588	3,291
1969	121,159	41,942	—	6,422	48,306	4,564	5,184	10,919	3,822
1970	115,372	38,143	—	5,976	47,338	4,046	4,144	12,038	3,686
1971	110,450	29,299	—	5,653	52,005	3,271	4,154	12,594	3,473
1972	114,173	23,742	24,126	7,605	34,601	3,200	4,104	13,140	3,655
1973	122,703	29,356	25,441	8,284	37,083	2,860	3,512	12,125	4,042
1974	113,590	32,573	22,796	5,274	33,720	2,826	2,301	10,788	3,313
1975	96,407	31,738	17,762	3,324	25,788	2,560	1,945	10,360	2,932
1976	90,480	27,385	16,363	2,685	25,316	2,714	2,050	10,543	3,424
1977	92,949	27,487	16,952	2,642	28,153	2,780	1,974	9,583	3,378
1978	107,029	35,354	19,104	2,964	32,134	2,996	2,061	8,826	3,590
1979	127,420	43,439	24,715	4,867	37,219	3,348	1,938	8,375	3,518

TABLE Dc303–320   Value of new construction – private nonresidential buildings, by type: 1964–1999 *Continued*

Year	Total Dc312 Million 1996 dollars	Industrial Dc313 Million 1996 dollars	Office Dc314 Million 1996 dollars	Hotels and motels Dc315 Million 1996 dollars	Other commercial Dc316 Million 1996 dollars	Religious Dc317 Million 1996 dollars	Educational Dc318 Million 1996 dollars	Hospital and institutional Dc319 Million 1996 dollars	Miscellaneous Dc320 Million 1996 dollars
1980	129,275	36,635	31,742	6,065	36,594	3,228	2,544	8,719	3,748
1981	140,569	41,727	38,616	7,130	34,219	3,046	2,535	9,810	3,484
1982	145,054	40,835	48,911	7,553	27,872	2,705	2,692	11,268	3,218
1983	131,289	29,357	42,726	9,251	28,481	3,027	2,819	12,201	3,427
1984	155,261	30,137	51,290	11,597	40,403	3,486	2,825	11,274	4,249
1985	178,925	33,885	61,207	12,282	50,116	3,860	3,160	9,787	4,628
1986	163,740	28,415	53,328	12,053	48,417	4,160	3,754	9,137	4,475
1987	160,363	27,589	48,006	11,640	48,579	4,134	5,370	9,906	5,140
1988	164,191	29,107	49,325	10,375	48,745	4,105	4,406	11,480	6,647
1989	169,173	34,778	48,518	11,212	48,134	4,169	4,823	11,559	5,980
1990	167,896	39,350	41,027	12,497	46,847	4,169	5,398	12,710	5,897
1991	135,389	36,496	30,143	8,064	34,092	4,088	4,869	12,273	5,363
1992	120,921	33,233	23,209	4,225	33,401	3,988	5,124	13,149	4,593
1993	122,222	29,264	23,129	5,044	35,834	4,292	5,134	13,799	5,726
1994	127,593	30,696	23,537	4,934	39,801	4,104	5,120	13,029	6,373
1995	139,711	34,814	26,218	7,274	43,636	4,426	5,621	11,512	6,209
1996	153,866	36,215	27,875	10,909	48,170	4,531	6,737	11,778	7,650
1997	166,754	35,411	33,058	12,438	49,948	5,565	8,375	13,066	8,892
1998 [2]	177,639	37,715	39,333	13,794	49,915	6,139	9,039	12,853	8,850
1999 [2]	175,048	31,214	41,643	14,262	51,067	6,701	8,743	12,183	9,235

[1] See text for a discussion of issues relating to the comparability of the series over time.

[2] Estimates are subject to normal revisions for three years because several series are benchmarked to data that appear in other annual or biennial reports; see text.

Source
See the source for Table Dc12–21.

Documentation
Refer to the essay in this chapter and the text for Tables Dc12–21 and Dc44–53 for general information about the 1964–1999 value-in-place series.

This table presents value-in-place estimates for nonresidential buildings construction in both current and constant dollars. Each aggregate is formed as the sum of the eight nonresidential buildings subcomponents. The primary data source for compiling these estimates is the value of contracts on nonresidential buildings that is collected and compiled by the F. W. Dodge subsidiary of McGraw-Hill (see the Dodge series in Table Dc132–144).

Substantial revisions were made in 1986 and 1996 to the coverage of the nonresidential aggregate and the procedures used to construct all of its subcomponents. These revisions were made back only to 1964 so that substantial breaks now appear in the levels of all the nonresidential building series shown here and their 1915–1964 counterparts shown in Table Dc282–302.

The 1986 revision transferred what had been the non-housekeeping residential subcomponent of the residential buildings category to the nonresidential buildings aggregate shown here. Most of this activity was included in a new hotels and motels subcomponent, while the remainder was transferred to the educational subcomponent. This first revision increased the 1964 estimate of total nonresidential buildings by 11 percent, but left the series unchanged for earlier years. The 1996 revision, in turn, increased the 1964 total nonresidential buildings estimate by another 23 percent relative to its level shown in Table Dc282–302. This latter revision incorporated new weights to derive nonresidential value-in-place estimates from monthly survey reports (see below) and began to benchmark estimates of the industrial building series to the Census Bureau's Annual Capital Expenditures Survey (ACES).

The Bureau of the Census conducts a monthly Construction Progress Reporting Survey for estimating the value of private nonresidential building construction in the United States. This survey identifies nonresidential projects started each month from contracts awarded throughout the United States (except Hawai'i), from building permit notifications in Hawai'i, and for projects in a sample of areas not covered by a contract survey or a building permit system. A sample of these projects is chosen to represent all subcomponents of the nonresidential buildings category and the owner of each sample project is requested to complete and submit a monthly construction progress report until the project is completed. A total of 5,500 projects are in the survey at any one time. Estimates of value put in place are derived each month by adjusting the reported work performed on the sample projects to include costs not covered by the survey, by weighting the reported work performed for each sample project by its probability of being selected for the survey, and to account for an undercoverage of projects in the Dodge reports. The adjusted and weighted reports from sample participants are summed by categories to form the value-in-place estimates for all subcomponents in that month. These monthly estimates are then summed to form the annual estimates shown in this table.

The survey of nonresidential buildings construction has been used to estimate value in place since 1962 (see Construction Reports: C30-65S (January 1966), pp. 69–72). At that time the Dodge reports covered only thirty-seven states, and national estimates were derived by inflating the data to represent the other thirteen states. Between 1966 and 1970 the Census Bureau began to conduct its own survey of the states not covered by Dodge while other modifications were incorporated gradually so as to maintain the historical continuity of the series after 1964 (see Construction Reports: C30-70S (October 1971), p. 152).

Series Dc304. The industrial subcomponent includes all buildings and structures at manufacturing sites. Office buildings and warehouses owned by industrial companies, but not constructed at an industrial site, are classified as office and other commercial buildings, respectively.

Series Dc305. Includes office and professional buildings used primarily for office space. This category excludes office buildings at industrial sites or those built by public utilities for their own use because classification is on an establishment basis (so the former is classified as industrial and the latter is included in the relevant public utility subcomponents). The office subcomponent does include, however, office buildings owned by an industrial company but not located at an industrial site.

Series Dc306. Includes resort lodging, tourist courts and cabins, and similar facilities.

Series Dc307. Includes buildings and structures that are intended for use by wholesale, retail, or service trade establishments (such as shopping centers, department stores, low-rise banks, parking garages, auto service stations, and restaurants). Also included are warehouses and storage buildings, cold storage plants, grain elevators and silos, except such facilities at industrial sites.

(continued)

TABLE Dc303–320   Value of new construction – private nonresidential buildings, by type: 1964–1999   *Continued*

Series Dc308. Includes houses of worship and other religious buildings, but not educational or charitable institutions, hospitals, or publishing houses that are owned by religious organizations.

Series Dc309. Includes schools, universities, and associated buildings (such as libraries, cafeteria, dormitories, and student unions). Noncommercial museums and art galleries are also included, but beauty and dance schools are classified in the other commercial subcomponent.

Series Dc310. Includes health care and institutional facilities, as well as nursing homes and similar establishments providing prolonged care. Surgical or outpatient clinics affiliated with a hospital are also part of this category. Buildings that are used primarily for doctors' offices are placed in the office buildings series.

Series Dc311. Includes buildings that are not classified in any of the above categories, such as studios, theaters, casinos, and buildings that provide amusement and recreational services. Also included are bus and airline terminal buildings.

Series Dc312–320. The constant-dollar series for all of the nonresidential buildings subcomponents are derived by an index that is an unweighted average of the Turner Company's national construction cost index and the single-family houses under construction deflator that is produced by the Census Bureau (see these indexes in Table Dc227–240).

TABLE Dc321–338   Value of new construction – privately owned public utilities, by type: 1915–1964[1]

Contributed by Kenneth A. Snowden

	Current dollars							1957–1959 dollars		
	Total	Telephone and telegraph	Gas	Electric light and power	Railroad	Petroleum pipeline		Total	Telephone and telegraph	Gas
	Dc321	Dc322	Dc323	Dc324	Dc325	Dc326		Dc327	Dc328	Dc329
Year	Million dollars	Million dollars	Million dollars	Million dollars	Million dollars	Million dollars		Million 1957–1959 dollars	Million 1957–1959 dollars	Million 1957–1959 dollars
1915	549	43	41	92	353	20		2,357	150	253
1916	658	61	70	117	390	20		2,508	176	355
1917	788	85	45	123	515	20		2,364	208	167
1918	697	73	26	102	472	24		1,780	166	84
1919	673	76	56	156	329	56		1,688	166	167
1920	771	124	78	262	266	41		1,770	232	215
1921	604	102	66	163	243	30		1,525	192	200
1922	787	117	139	229	261	41		2,284	260	508
1923	1,191	158	133	412	435	53		3,222	303	443
1924	1,356	196	206	463	421	70		3,659	394	639
1925	1,302	210	171	421	445	55		3,552	464	550
1926	1,415	227	248	362	542	36		3,860	521	810
1927	1,450	212	257	362	539	80		4,025	468	860
1928	1,372	246	212	338	523	53		3,774	537	735
1929	1,578	354	185	350	592	97		4,194	771	631
1930	1,527	333	181	377	606	30		4,273	799	620
1931	946	166	117	225	361	77		2,826	433	420
1932	467	87	66	109	168	37		1,531	260	258
1933	261	45	35	59	115	7		847	136	137
1934	326	47	43	66	158	12		993	136	150
1935	363	52	48	87	156	20		1,102	146	166
1936	518	67	77	139	194	41		1,552	184	256
1937	705	102	80	218	238	67		1,963	271	243
1938	605	92	65	267	160	21		1,719	257	197
1939	683	93	61	303	191	35		1,946	260	188
1940	771	122	91	311	217	30		2,149	328	275
1941	872	179	111	305	217	60		2,274	451	316
1942	786	155	87	255	209	80		1,911	362	234
1943	570	61	63	144	225	77		1,314	134	169
1944	725	83	146	163	262	71		1,687	187	388
1945	827	117	141	245	282	42		1,868	243	366
1946	1,255	305	197	425	265	63		2,465	506	439
1947	2,126	510	394	761	340	121		3,584	694	740
1948	2,776	713	499	1,016	398	150		—	—	—
1949	2,994	533	637	1,313	354	157		—	—	—
1950	3,045	440	859	1,240	309	197		—	—	—
1951	3,357	487	1,010	1,315	372	173		—	—	—
1952	3,533	570	710	1,537	449	267		—	—	—
1953	3,973	615	818	1,805	405	330		—	—	—
1954	3,685	655	723	1,717	366	224		—	—	—

Note appears at end of table

TABLE Dc321-338   Value of new construction – privately owned public utilities, by type: 1915-1964

	Current dollars						1957–1959 dollars		
	Total	Telephone and telegraph	Gas	Electric light and power	Railroad	Petroleum pipeline	Total	Telephone and telegraph	Gas
	Dc321	Dc322	Dc323	Dc324	Dc325	Dc326	Dc327	Dc328	Dc329
Year	Million dollars	Million dollars	Million dollars	Million dollars	Million dollars	Million dollars	Million 1957–1959 dollars	Million 1957–1959 dollars	Million 1957–1959 dollars
1955	3,770	805	922	1,572	341	130	—	—	—
1956	4,361	1,066	1,031	1,720	421	123	—	—	—
1957	4,908	1,068	1,116	2,168	397	159	—	—	—
1958	4,688	904	1,065	2,291	272	156	—	—	—
1959	4,521	951	1,214	2,007	218	131	—	—	—
1960	4,621	1,088	1,105	2,026	270	132	—	—	—
1961	4,335	980	1,147	1,886	213	109	—	—	—
1962	4,330	996	1,031	1,899	201	203	—	—	—
1963	4,667	1,128	948	2,066	253	272	—	—	—
1964	5,031	1,314	1,073	2,211	267	166	—	—	—

	1957–1959 dollars			1967 dollars					
	Electric light and power	Railroad	Petroleum pipeline	Total	Telephone and telegraph	Gas	Electric light and power	Railroad	Petroleum pipeline
	Dc330	Dc331	Dc332	Dc333	Dc334	Dc335	Dc336	Dc337	Dc338
Year	Million 1957–1959 dollars	Million 1957–1959 dollars	Million 1957–1959 dollars	Million 1967 dollars	Million 1967 dollars	Million 1967 dollars	Million 1967 dollars	Million 1967 dollars	Million 1967 dollars
1915	537	1,316	101	—	—	—	—	—	—
1916	554	1,337	86	—	—	—	—	—	—
1917	468	1,452	69	—	—	—	—	—	—
1918	339	1,118	73	—	—	—	—	—	—
1919	503	699	153	—	—	—	—	—	—
1920	752	468	103	—	—	—	—	—	—
1921	520	523	90	—	—	—	—	—	—
1922	757	630	129	—	—	—	—	—	—
1923	1,358	961	157	—	—	—	—	—	—
1924	1,497	930	199	—	—	—	—	—	—
1925	1,365	1,013	160	—	—	—	—	—	—
1926	1,191	1,232	106	—	—	—	—	—	—
1927	1,220	1,239	238	—	—	—	—	—	—
1928	1,119	1,223	160	—	—	—	—	—	—
1929	1,105	1,398	289	—	—	—	—	—	—
1930	1,255	1,506	93	—	—	—	—	—	—
1931	769	951	253	—	—	—	—	—	—
1932	398	485	130	—	—	—	—	—	—
1933	208	342	24	—	—	—	—	—	—
1934	213	455	39	—	—	—	—	—	—
1935	277	449	64	—	—	—	—	—	—
1936	434	549	129	—	—	—	—	—	—
1937	620	633	196	—	—	—	—	—	—
1938	766	437	62	—	—	—	—	—	—
1939	861	534	103	—	—	—	—	—	—
1940	873	585	88	—	—	—	—	—	—
1941	812	540	155	—	—	—	—	—	—
1942	657	454	204	—	—	—	—	—	—
1943	368	452	191	—	—	—	—	—	—
1944	416	525	171	—	—	—	—	—	—
1945	618	542	99	—	—	—	—	—	—
1946	925	466	129	—	—	—	—	—	—
1947	1,413	523	214	3,918	820	716	1,595	567	220
1948	—	—	—	4,637	1,090	768	1,954	594	231
1949	—	—	—	4,885	797	937	2,392	528	231
1950	—	—	—	4,741	658	1,210	2,142	454	277
1951	—	—	—	4,794	667	1,347	2,039	510	231
1952	—	—	—	4,966	763	922	2,343	591	347
1953	—	—	—	5,336	809	1,010	2,597	513	407
1954	—	—	—	4,886	852	893	2,401	463	277

(continued)

TABLE Dc321–338   Value of new construction – privately owned public utilities, by type: 1915–1964   *Continued*

	1957–1959 dollars				1967 dollars					
	Electric light and power	Railroad	Petroleum pipeline	Total	Telephone and telegraph	Gas	Electric light and power	Railroad	Petroleum pipeline
	Dc330	Dc331	Dc332	Dc333	Dc334	Dc335	Dc336	Dc337	Dc338
Year	Million 1957–1959 dollars	Million 1957–1959 dollars	Million 1957–1959 dollars	Million 1967 dollars	Million 1967 dollars	Million 1967 dollars	Million 1967 dollars	Million 1967 dollars	Million 1967 dollars
1955	—	—	—	4,855	1,015	1,124	2,136	421	159
1956	—	—	—	5,172	1,271	1,146	2,134	484	137
1957	—	—	—	5,552	1,268	1,151	2,533	436	164
1958	—	—	—	5,227	1,080	1,074	2,626	291	156
1959	—	—	—	4,925	1,110	1,206	2,248	230	131
1960	—	—	—	5,016	1,239	1,093	2,269	283	132
1961	—	—	—	4,766	1,134	1,139	2,158	226	109
1962	—	—	—	4,767	1,151	1,039	2,161	213	203
1963	—	—	—	5,133	1,270	981	2,336	265	281
1964	—	—	—	5,508	1,466	1,155	2,430	279	178

[1] See text for a discussion of issues relating to the comparability of the series over time.

Source

U.S. Bureau of the Census, *Value of New Construction Put in Place 1964 to 1980*, Construction Reports: C30-80S (July 1981), Table D-2, pp. 187–91.

Documentation

For additional details on the value-in-place estimates for this period, see the text for Tables Dc1–11 and Dc22–43.

This table presents current- and constant-dollar value-in-place estimates of construction activity on privately owned public utilities. The definitions and methodology used to compile the annual value-in-place series for subcomponents of privately owned public utilities changed very little over this period. The current-dollar series for each subcomponent was generally based on annual capital expenditures as reported to federal regulatory agencies or cooperating private organizations (exceptions are noted below). Value-in-place estimates were derived from these data by excluding expenditures on land, equipment, and other nonconstruction items. Monthly estimates (which are available beginning in 1939) were derived using a variety of techniques to break down annual construction expenditures over the year.

The 1946–1963 estimates for three of the subcomponents shown above were modified in the 1964 comprehensive revision of the value-in-place series. These revisions led to breaks in series Dc325, railroads (the previous 1946 estimate was decreased by 10.7 percent); series Dc324, electric light and power (a decrease of 4 percent); and series Dc323, gas (a decrease of 27 percent). These discontinuities, although substantial for the series shown here, created only modest breaks in estimates of total private and total construction. For details, see Construction Report: C30-53S (December 1963), and Construction Report: C30-61S (October 1964).

Series Dc322. Estimates were derived from annual capital expenditures reported by the American Telephone and Telegraph (AT&T) Company (for 1915–1964), the Western Union Telegraph Company (for 1927–1964), and the Postal Telegraph and Cable Company (for 1919–1943). The AT&T data included both expenditures for Bell System companies and estimates for independent telephone companies, while the telegraph estimates for 1915–1918 had to be extrapolated on the basis of annual increments in the value of plant and equipment.

Series Dc323. Estimates were based on reports of the Federal Power Commission and data compiled by the American Gas Association. For 1929–1964, annual data published by the American Gas Association were adjusted to eliminate equipment expenditures. For 1915-1928, estimates were obtained by extrapolation on the basis of year-to-year changes in the fixed capital accounts of fifty large gas companies.

Series Dc324. Based on reports of annual capital expenditures submitted to the Federal Power Commission by privately owned electric companies and on data reported to the Rural Electrification Administration (REA) by REA cooperative companies. For 1937–1964, annual additions to electric plants reported to the Federal Power Commission were adjusted to include smaller companies that were not required to report to the agency and to allow for

work in progress and property purchases. For 1921–1936, data from the Edison Electric Institute were used. For 1915–1920, the data are based on an estimated year-by-year distribution of the five-year increments in plant and equipment derived from data reported in the Census of Electrical Industries for 1912, 1917, and 1922.

Series Dc325. Estimates were based on annual summaries of construction expenditures prepared by the Interstate Commerce Commission from reports by all class I railroads. These data were adjusted to include estimates for class II railroads and for railroad investment in roads and certain equipment. Prior to 1955, local transit estimates of capital and maintenance expenditures were also included as reported in the annual *Transit Fact Book* of the American Transit Association. Outlays by municipally owned transit companies were deducted from these expenditures and included in a public construction subcomponent. The estimates for 1955–1958 are projections based on an assumed gradual decline in expenditure from the 1954 level to zero in 1959. For both railroads and local transit, the estimates for 1915–1921 are extrapolations based on miles of track added or rebuilt.

Series Dc326. Estimates were derived from data on expenditures on pipelines for 1919–1964 as reported to the Interstate Commerce Commission. Adjustments to these data were made for the purchase of existing lines and for expenditures by companies not required to file information with the Commission. The 1915–1918 current-dollar pipeline data represent rough estimates by the U.S. Bureau of Foreign and Domestic Commerce.

Series Dc328–331 and Dc334–337. A description of most of the cost indexes that were used to derive the constant-dollar series in this table, as well as annual values of the indexes, can be found in Table Dc207–226.

Series Dc328 and Dc334. The constant-dollar telephone and telegraph series in both 1957–1959 and 1967 dollars were derived using a weighted average of the Bell Telephone System's construction cost indexes for buildings and outside plants.

Series Dc329, Dc332, Dc335, and Dc338. For the 1915–1947 period, different deflating indexes were used to construct the constant-dollar estimates for these two components: for series Dc329, gas, an average of the Handy–Whitman gas and utility building indexes was used; and for series Dc332, petroleum pipelines, the same two indexes were averaged with the Handy–Whitman electric, and the Interstate Commerce Commission's railroad, cost indexes. For the 1947–1964 period, however, the same deflator was used for both series Dc335 and Dc338 – a pipeline construction cost index compiled by the Interstate Commerce Commission.

Series Dc330 and Dc336. The constant-dollar electric light and power series were derived using a weighted average of an electric plant and a utility building cost index that was produced by the Handy–Whitman Company.

Series Dc331 and Dc337. The constant-dollar railroad series were derived by deflating the current-dollar estimates with the Interstate Commerce Commission's railroad construction cost index.

TABLE Dc339–350   Value of new construction – privately owned public utilities, by type: 1964–1999[1]

Contributed by Kenneth A. Snowden

	Current dollars						1996 dollars					
	Total	Telecommunications	Gas	Electric light and power	Railroad	Petroleum pipeline	Total	Telecommunications	Gas	Electric light and power	Railroad	Petroleum pipeline
	Dc339	Dc340	Dc341	Dc342	Dc343	Dc344	Dc345	Dc346	Dc347	Dc348	Dc349	Dc350
Year	Million dollars	Million dollars	Million dollars	Million dollars	Million dollars	Million dollars	Million 1996 dollars	Million 1996 dollars	Million 1996 dollars	Million 1996 dollars	Million 1996 dollars	Million 1996 dollars
1964	5,314	1,314	493	2,211	1,130	166	25,169	4,581	2,458	11,842	5,483	805
1965	6,032	1,463	572	2,589	1,286	122	27,618	4,840	2,774	13,386	6,047	572
1966	7,090	1,609	698	3,060	1,581	142	31,689	5,096	3,271	15,356	7,309	657
1967	7,834	1,638	604	3,777	1,503	312	34,065	4,978	2,727	18,193	6,766	1,401
1968	9,232	1,704	762	4,421	1,988	357	39,157	4,987	3,276	20,595	8,735	1,565
1969	9,766	2,203	835	4,692	1,803	233	38,602	6,177	3,377	20,512	7,560	975
1970	11,127	2,968	561	5,628	1,686	284	40,305	7,594	2,064	22,897	6,640	1,110
1971	11,985	3,005	538	6,391	1,627	424	40,950	7,608	1,833	24,078	5,900	1,532
1972	13,301	3,301	661	7,160	1,897	283	43,012	8,111	2,141	25,378	6,426	955
1973	15,272	3,965	779	8,228	1,992	309	45,992	8,948	2,341	27,296	6,415	992
1974	16,933	4,279	1,061	8,813	1,995	785	43,731	8,419	2,748	24,641	5,737	2,187
1975	17,553	3,810	949	9,192	1,658	1,944	40,155	7,233	2,153	21,874	4,101	4,794
1976	20,204	3,940	1,071	10,679	1,627	2,887	43,786	7,077	2,309	24,045	3,737	6,618
1977	21,437	4,529	1,361	12,456	1,894	1,197	43,375	7,650	2,828	26,256	4,054	2,588
1978	24,567	5,640	2,197	13,825	2,371	534	46,420	8,992	4,225	27,524	4,642	1,036
1979	27,978	6,918	2,195	15,324	2,950	591	47,630	9,816	3,718	27,686	5,342	1,068
1980	30,905	7,768	2,319	16,468	3,542	809	47,755	9,832	3,414	27,235	5,925	1,348
1981	33,688	8,205	2,260	18,295	4,186	742	48,486	10,241	3,089	27,747	6,294	1,114
1982	33,942	8,509	2,595	18,606	3,854	377	46,743	10,395	3,498	26,908	5,415	528
1983	30,817	7,641	2,951	17,185	2,583	457	41,974	9,706	4,022	24,100	3,524	622
1984	32,191	8,085	3,513	17,431	2,892	271	43,535	10,697	4,747	23,918	3,816	357
1985	32,692	8,397	4,046	16,460	3,517	272	43,342	10,807	5,258	22,271	4,648	359
1986	32,931	9,106	2,891	17,375	3,273	286	43,722	11,950	3,647	23,257	4,478	390
1987	27,862	9,194	2,451	12,660	3,188	369	36,476	11,936	3,060	16,756	4,235	490
1988	27,412	9,556	2,382	11,441	3,656	377	34,448	12,347	2,884	14,186	4,561	470
1989	30,129	9,614	2,650	13,137	4,386	342	35,688	11,291	3,097	15,666	5,227	408
1990	28,933	9,803	2,600	11,299	4,820	411	33,505	11,346	2,969	13,083	5,627	480
1991	33,966	8,962	2,406	16,293	5,555	750	38,830	10,275	2,698	18,662	6,340	856
1992	36,807	8,993	2,928	17,136	6,901	849	41,745	10,330	3,299	19,422	7,742	953
1993	34,925	9,619	3,108	15,567	5,645	986	38,671	10,857	3,445	17,069	6,216	1,084
1994	34,071	10,121	3,340	14,918	4,694	998	36,372	11,225	3,592	15,688	4,837	1,031
1995	35,859	11,093	3,509	14,049	6,279	929	36,740	11,556	3,609	14,310	6,329	936
1996	33,156	11,810	4,398	11,211	4,722	1,015	33,124	11,791	4,391	11,209	4,720	1,013
1997	33,638	12,416	4,922	11,325	4,006	969	32,884	12,159	4,745	11,122	3,911	947
1998 [2]	40,028	13,328	5,736	12,381	7,318	1,265	38,616	13,036	5,463	11,885	7,020	1,213
1999 [2]	39,607	15,223	4,918	14,057	3,920	1,489	38,166	15,142	4,540	13,393	3,690	1,401

[1] See text for a discussion of issues relating to the comparability of the series over time.

[2] Estimates are subject to normal revisions for three years because several series are benchmarked to data that appear in other annual or biennial reports; see text.

Source

See the source for Table Dc12–21.

Documentation

Refer to the essay in this chapter and the text for Tables Dc12–21 and Dc44–53 for general information about the 1964–1999 value-in-place series.

This table presents value-in-place estimates of privately owned public utility construction. Also shown are the five subcomponents that comprise the public utility aggregate. Between 1986 and

(continued)

TABLE Dc339–350 Value of new construction – privately owned public utilities, by type: 1964–1999 *Continued*

1990, important revisions were made to the gas and railroad subcomponents that were carried back only to 1964. As a result, a significant break appears between several of the series shown here and the 1964 values of the same indexes over the 1915–1964 period (see Table Dc321–338).

For each subcomponent of the privately owned public utility category (including those cooperatively owned), construction expenditures are classified in terms of the industry, and not the function, of the building or structure. The estimates include not only the type of construction peculiar to the operation of the utility, but also other types of nonresidential building and nonbuilding construction built by these companies for their own use, such as office buildings. The definitions of the various subcomponents are straightforward with the exception of telecommunications, as noted below.

Estimates of construction put in place are based on annual capital expenditure reports compiled by federal regulatory agencies and private organizations, except as noted below for the telephone industry.

Series Dc340. For most of the period covered here, this series was known as "telephone and telegraph" and it included construction performed within only these two industries. The series was redefined in 1989 to include television cable construction, renamed, and revised back to 1975. Value-in-place estimates for the telephone industry are based on reports of actual monthly construction progress.

Series Dc343. In 1985 the Interstate Commerce Commission revised its historical estimates of annual construction expenditures made by railroads to include expenditures for track replacement. These new data were used to revise the value-in-place estimates for railroads back to 1964, and increased the current-dollar value in that year by nearly 85 percent, creating a substantial break with the 1915–1964 estimates shown in Table Dc321–338.

Series Dc341. New historical data were received from the American Gas Association in 1986, just as a new procedure was implemented to benchmark the value-in-place estimates for this series to the U.S. Bureau of Economic Analysis's Plant and Equipment Expenditures Survey. The combination of these revisions led to a substantial upward revision of the gas series back to 1964. These were followed with changes in procedures in 1990 that led to a substantial downward revision in the same series. All told, the 1964 current-dollar estimate for the gas subcomponent has been increased approximately 5 percent above its unrevised value that is shown in the 1915–1964 series in Table Dc321–338.

Series Dc345–350. A variety of deflators are used to derive the constant-dollar estimates for the public utilities subcomponents (see Table Dc207–226 for descriptions and annual values of these indexes). An average of composite construction costs indexes compiled by the Federal Highway Administration and the U.S. Bureau of Reclamation is used for the railroad series. Telecommunications, on the other hand, is deflated by the Turner Company's index of construction costs for telephone plants. The gas, electric power and light, and petroleum pipeline series are each derived using indexes of construction costs for similar classes of utility projects that are compiled by the Handy-Whitman organization.

TABLE Dc351–363   Value of new construction – public, by type: 1915–1964[1]   [Current dollars]

Contributed by Kenneth A. Snowden

		Buildings						Highway		Conservation			
								and	Military	and		Water	
	Total	Total	Housing and redevelopment	Industrial	Educational	Hospital	Other	streets	facilities	development	Sewer	facilities	Miscellaneous
	Dc351	Dc352	Dc353	Dc354	Dc355	Dc356	Dc357	Dc358	Dc359	Dc360	Dc361	Dc362	Dc363
Year	Million dollars	Million dollars	Million dollars	Million dollars	Million dollars	Million dollars	Million dollars	Million dollars	Million dollars	Million dollars	Million dollars	Million dollars	Million dollars
1915	719	217	0	—	—	—	—	302	17	36	52	54	41
1916	708	207	0	—	—	—	—	314	21	28	46	49	43
1917	1,279	192	0	—	—	—	—	320	608	27	45	46	41
1918	2,238	227	28	—	—	—	—	296	1,555	29	38	56	37
1919	1,976	260	14	—	—	—	—	429	1,089	39	53	71	35
1920	1,352	283	0	—	190	33	60	656	161	55	67	86	44
1921	1,564	387	0	—	274	40	73	853	49	52	78	100	45
1922	1,684	481	0	—	342	60	79	876	25	48	88	113	53
1923	1,622	481	0	—	346	55	80	805	16	65	90	113	52
1924	1,901	494	0	—	353	60	81	987	9	79	108	155	69
1925	2,138	573	0	—	400	61	112	1,082	8	73	133	145	124
1926	2,144	603	0	—	399	68	136	1,067	11	61	145	140	117
1927	2,409	596	0	—	367	80	149	1,222	12	63	174	138	204
1928	2,485	638	0	—	378	108	152	1,289	15	72	183	117	171
1929	2,486	659	0	—	389	101	169	1,266	19	115	127	126	174
1930	2,858	660	0	—	364	118	178	1,516	29	137	142	201	173
1931	2,659	612	0	—	285	110	217	1,355	40	156	114	156	226
1932	1,862	415	0	—	130	83	202	958	34	150	69	87	149
1933	1,648	230	0	2	52	49	127	847	36	359	45	50	81
1934	2,211	364	1	11	148	51	153	1,000	47	518	102	71	109
1935	2,233	337	9	2	153	38	135	845	37	700	101	74	139
1936	3,516	762	61	4	366	74	257	1,362	29	658	230	112	363
1937	3,096	643	93	2	253	73	222	1,226	37	605	209	102	274
1938	3,420	707	35	12	311	97	252	1,421	62	551	235	120	324
1939	3,809	1,035	65	23	468	127	352	1,381	125	570	243	128	327
1940	3,628	815	200	164	156	54	241	1,302	385	528	184	154	260
1941	5,751	2,076	430	1,280	158	42	166	1,066	1,620	500	118	134	237
1942	10,660	4,230	545	3,437	128	35	85	734	5,016	357	76	93	154 [2]
1943	6,322	2,749	739	1,870	63	44	33	446	2,550	285	37	70	185 [2]
1944	3,073	1,572	211	1,230	41	58	32	362	837	163	26	53	60 [2]
1945	2,398	1,017	80	755	59	85	38	398	690	130	37	60	66
1946	2,231	728	374	113	101	85	55	764	188	260	97	97	97
1947	3,319	791	200	96	287	77	131	1,344	204	424	188	163	205
1948	4,704	1,447	156	196	618	213	264	1,661	158	670	300	235	233
1949	6,269	2,408	359	177	934	458	480	2,015	137	852	354	265	238
1950	6,866	2,732	345	224	1,133	499	531	2,134	177	942	383	276	222
1951	9,255	4,091	595	974	1,513	527	482	2,355	887	912	425	350	235
1952	10,779	4,812	654	1,684	1,619	495	360	2,677	1,387	900	435	355	213
1953	11,242	4,906	556	1,771	1,714	369	496	3,021	1,290	892	520	363	250
1954	11,712	4,945	336	1,506	2,134	333	636	3,714	1,003	773	568	414	295
1955	11,715	4,462	266	721	2,442	300	733	3,852	1,287	701	615	470	328
1956	12,732	4,368	292	453	2,556	300	767	4,415	1,360	826	701	574	488
1957	14,059	5,013	506	473	2,825	354	855	4,934	1,287	971	781	563	510
1958	15,457	5,499	846	408	2,875	390	980	5,545	1,402	1,019	836	551	605
1959	16,070	5,476	962	368	2,656	428	1,062	5,761	1,465	1,121	906	561	780
1960	15,863	5,511	716	407	2,818	401	1,169	5,437	1,366	1,175	882	605	887
1961	17,148	6,011	842	472	3,052	369	1,276	5,854	1,371	1,384	914	667	947
1962	17,869	6,092	938	422	2,984	397	1,351	6,365	1,266	1,523	1,072	682	869
1963	19,357	6,534	531	440	3,477	426	1,660	7,084	1,179	1,694	947	882	1,037
1964	20,383	7,177	567	403	3,790	469	1,948	7,133	910	1,750	1,325	956	1,132

[1] See text for a discussion of issues relating to the comparability of the series over time.

[2] Includes petroleum pipelines as follows: $25 million in 1942, $125 million in 1943, and $4 million in 1944.

Source

U.S. Bureau of the Census, *Value of New Construction Put in Place 1964 to 1980*, Construction Reports: C30-80S (July 1981), Table D-1, pp. 182–6.

Documentation

For additional details on the value-in-place estimates for this period, see the text for Tables Dc1–11 and Dc22–43. For details on estimates of public construction see Lowell J. Chawner, *Construction Activity in the United States 1915–37*, U.S. Department of Commerce, Domestic Commerce Series number 99 (1938), pp. 70–89; U.S. Department of Commerce and U.S. Department of Labor, *Construction Volume and Costs, 1915–56: A Supplement to Construction Review*, pp. 83–6; U.S. Department of Commerce, *Value of New Construction Put in Place: 1946–63 Revised*, Construction Report C30-61S (October 1964),

(continued)

TABLE Dc351–363   Value of new construction – public, by type: 1915–1964   [Current dollars]   *Continued*

pp. 74–5, 79–80; and U.S. Department of Commerce, *Value of New Construction Put in Place, 1962–66,* Construction Report: C30-66S (October 1967), pp. 55, 75–80.

This table presents the current-dollar value-in-place estimates for total public construction, disaggregated by type of activity. Table Dc364–389 presents the constant-dollar estimates for the same series. The distinction between private and public construction in the value-in-place series was made on the basis of ownership at the time the work was performed rather than by source of financing. These estimates do not include, therefore, work on projects that were built by private nonprofit organizations but were financed with federal, state, or local government aid. As a result, the public construction estimates shown above do not account for all public expenditures for new construction.

Three subcomponents shown in the table measure construction activity that is exclusively federally owned within the value-in-place classification system: industrial buildings, military facilities, and conservation and development – series Dc354 and Dc359–360. On the other hand, sewer and water facilities – series Dc361–362 – are exclusively state and local in ownership. The remaining components include both federally and nonfederally owned construction projects, but construction activity for the two levels of government was compiled using different data and methods even within the same subcomponent. To sharpen the distinction between the levels of government, the current-dollar estimates shown above are disaggregated into federal versus state and local ownership in Tables Dc390–441.

Throughout the period shown in the table, value-in-place estimates for federally owned projects were based on reports made by the responsible agency. Before 1939, annual reports were adequate because this was the frequency of the value-in-place series; by the early 1940s, all federal agencies supervising major construction programs submitted monthly reports of construction progress and expenditures.

The data underlying the state and local government value-in-place estimates, on the other hand, were drawn from a variety of sources: (1) annual reports of state and local construction expenditures compiled by the Census Bureau or other federal agencies; (2) reports by federal agencies supervising federally aided, but state- and locally owned construction projects; (3) data on publicly owned construction contracts that were compiled by F. W. Dodge, other private agencies, and government organizations; and, (4) a Census Bureau survey of the construction activities of state and local governments. The mix among these four data sources changed considerably over the 1915–1964 period.

The original 1915–1936 estimates for state and local highways and streets, sewer and water facilities, and public service enterprises were based on data drawn from the Census Bureau's *Financial Statistics of States* and *Financial Statistics of Cities,* and the annual reports of the Bureau of Public Roads (see Chawner 1938, pp. 70–81). Other state and local subcomponents during this period (primarily nonresidential buildings and miscellaneous construction) were estimated from F. W. Dodge contracts awarded data. Chawner's original estimates were extended through 1939, and remained the official value-in-place estimates for public construction until 1950, with relatively minor revision. In 1951, however, major upward revisions were incorporated in both the federal and the nonfederal value-in-place estimates for the 1933–1943 period to account for work relief programs (see *Construction and Construction Materials,* Statistical Supplement, May 1950, as cited in the *Statistical Abstract of the United States, 1951,* p. 707).

Between 1941 and 1962 there was much less reliance on published federal reports to derive value-in-place estimates for projects owned by state and local governments. Instead, the series were compiled indirectly by (1) collecting information each month about the value of construction contracts that had been awarded by state and local governments; (2) adjusting the data to form national estimates of the value of construction work started; and (3) distributing the work started over subsequent months by the application of fixed monthly construction progress patterns (see *Construction Volume and Costs, 1915–56: A Supplement to Construction Review,* pp. 83–6). Published reports of state and local construction expenditures, on the other hand, were used to compile value-in-place estimates only for public housing and highways, and a few specific types of federally aided construction (hospitals and airports).

In 1966 the methods used to estimate state and local construction changed once again, this time for estimates beginning in 1963. A quarterly survey of state and local government was initiated and used to secure direct value-in-place estimates for all subcomponents (see Construction Report: C30-66S). At the same time a new classification system for both federal and nonfederal construction was employed. Before 1963, each project was classified into a subcomponent based on its own function rather than that of the agency that was responsible for the project. Beginning in 1963, agencies were placed in subcomponents based on their primary function, and all of the construction work of each agency went into its category regardless of the individual project type. The implementation of the new survey and classification system did not create a break in the overall levels of total public construction in 1963, but breaks appeared in some subcomponents between 1962 and 1963 as work was shifted among them by the reclassification.

In general, the public value-in-place series shown in this table do not suffer from the substantial breaks that appear in several of the private construction components for the 1915–1964 period. Nonetheless, these data were compiled using different methodologies and approaches over time. The impact of these on specific subcomponents are noted in the series descriptions that follow.

Series Dc353. Estimates for public housing and redevelopment construction were based on reports of the Public Housing Administration, the New York City Housing Authority, and other state and local agencies. They include direct federal construction during World War I, the Depression of the 1930s, and the defense and World War II periods (1940s); federally aided low-rent public housing programs executed by state and local agencies with federal loans and grants; similar programs executed by state and local agencies without federal aid; and military family housing (but not barracks). Estimates for federally owned residential construction were based primarily on monthly reports from federal bureaus and agencies. For state and local residential construction prior to 1963, on the other hand, the estimates are based on data compiled from various sources, such as the F. W. Dodge Corporation, the Public Housing Administration, regional offices of the Housing and Home Finance Agency, and state and local agencies responsible for construction of public housing. For 1963–1964, the estimates are based on expenditures collected in the Census Bureau's quarterly survey of state and local construction activity.

Series Dc354–357. For 1940 and earlier years, estimates of the four remaining nonresidential buildings subcomponents (federal and nonfederal) were based on compilations of contract awards reported by the F. W. Dodge Corporation. Before 1932, however, all industrial and commercial buildings contracts were classified as privately owned because public construction on these types of buildings was negligible. Beginning in 1941, estimates for federally owned and federally aided nonresidential buildings construction were based on reports of federal agencies. For years beginning in 1963, results of the Census Bureau's quarterly survey of state and local construction activity was used. The industrial buildings series is exclusively federally owned and was dominated after 1940 by military ordinance and Atomic Energy Commission facilities. The bulk of educational and hospital buildings, on the other hand, were owned by state and local governments.

Series Dc358. The highway subcomponent includes roads, streets, bridges, vehicular tunnels, viaducts, and forest and park roads owned by state and local governments or federal agencies other than the U.S. Department of Defense. It also includes culverts, right-of-way drainage, erosion control, lighting, guard rails, and earthwork protective structures if built in connection with a federal road. Estimates for 1915–1919 were derived from the 1920 *Yearbook of Agriculture,* and for 1920 by straight-line interpolation. For 1921–1962, estimates for state-administered highways are based on annual reports of the U.S. Bureau of Public Roads adjusted to include expenditures by county, municipal, and other local bodies. The adjustments are based on ratios developed from the analysis of total highway construction and state highway construction. For years beginning in 1963, the quarterly survey of state and local construction activity was used.

TABLE Dc351–363　　Value of new construction – public, by type: 1915–1964　　[Current dollars]

Series Dc359. Most of the projects owned by the Department of Defense were included in the military facilities series for this period. Included are the construction of troop housing, administration and training buildings, warehouses, mess halls, recreation centers, educational facilities, airfields, and airport buildings. The construction of Coast Guard facilities was also covered. Estimates for 1940–1964 were based on monthly reports by the Department of Defense. Navy Department construction expenditures for 1915–1936 were derived from special tabulations of the U.S. Bureau of Supplies and Accounts. Expenditures of the Navy for 1937–1939 and the War Department for 1915–1939 were compiled from expenditures shown in various issues of U.S. Bureau of the Budget, *Budget of the United States Government*.

Series Dc360. Conservation and development construction projects during this period were almost exclusively federally owned. Expenditures for reclamation, improvement of rivers and harbors, and flood control work were derived from annual reports of the U.S. Army Corps of Engineers and the U.S. Bureau of Reclamation, and beginning in 1943, annual reports from the Tennessee Valley Authority were also used. For Bureau of Indian Affairs, Forest Service, National Park Service, Soil Conservation Service, Bonneville Power Administration, Office of Saline Water, Southwestern Power Administration, International Boundary and Water Commission, and St. Lawrence Seaway Development Corporation, expenditures were derived from special tabulations prepared by those agencies and from the Office of Management and Budget, *Budget of the United States Government*, various issues. The estimates, with minor exceptions for earlier years, include only expenditures by

the federal government. State and local government expenditures for conservation and development are included under miscellaneous, series Dc363.

Series Dc361–362. Sewer and water facilities projects were exclusively state and locally owned. For 1915–1942 the estimates were based on data published annually in U.S. Bureau of the Census, *Financial Statistics of Cities*. For 1943–1962, estimates are based on contracts awarded, as reported by the F. W. Dodge Corporation, with adjustments for undercoverage. Beginning in 1963, data were secured from the quarterly survey of state and local construction activity.

Series Dc363. The miscellaneous public series is an aggregate of two series that were reported separately before 1964. "Miscellaneous public service enterprises" included state- and locally owned electric utilities, airports, and transit projects. Prior to 1963, outlays on these enterprises were obtained directly from the municipalities or estimated from information reported in U.S. Bureau of the Census, *Financial Statistics of Cities*. Before 1964 the second subcomponent was "all other public." Included here were construction expenditures by federal, state, and local agencies that were not covered by other series. Expenditures on federally owned miscellaneous projects were compiled from monthly or quarterly reports of the responsible agencies or, in a few cases, derived from fiscal-year data as reported in the *Budget of the United States Government*. Prior to 1963, estimates for nonfederal "all other" construction were derived from contract-award data compiled by a variety of private and public agencies. Beginning in 1963, the data were drawn from the quarterly survey of state and local government construction activity.

TABLE Dc364–389 Value of new construction – public, by type: 1915–1964[1] [Constant dollars]

Contributed by Kenneth A. Snowden

	Total	Total	Buildings					Highway and streets	Military facilities	Conservation and development	Sewer	Water facilities	Miscellaneous
			Housing and redevelopment	Industrial	Educational	Hospital	Other						
Year	Dc364 [2]	Dc365 [2]	Dc366 [2]	Dc367 [2]	Dc368 [2]	Dc369 [2]	Dc370 [2]	Dc371 [2]	Dc372 [2]	Dc373 [2]	Dc374 [2]	Dc375 [2]	Dc376 [2]
	Million 1957–1959 dollars	Million 1957–1959 dollars	Million 1957–1959 dollars	Million 1957–1959 dollars	Million 1957–1959 dollars	Million 1957–1959 dollars	Million 1957–1959 dollars	Million 1957–1959 dollars	Million 1957–1959 dollars	Million 1957–1959 dollars	Million 1957–1959 dollars	Million 1957–1959 dollars	Million 1957–1959 dollars
1915	—	—	0	—	—	—	—	763	73	224	324	335	238
1916	—	—	0	—	—	—	—	749	81	138	232	238	205
1917	—	—	0	—	—	—	—	663	2,027	100	166	169	156
1918	—	—	95	—	—	—	—	507	4,515	97	127	187	123
1919	—	—	40	—	—	—	—	665	2,755	119	163	217	111
1920	2,420	685	0	—	459	80	146	783	321	134	163	209	125
1921	3,422	1,223	0	—	866	126	231	1,228	122	159	219	325	146
1922	4,104	1,641	0	—	1,167	205	269	1,384	66	161	296	380	176
1923	3,596	1,464	0	—	1,053	167	244	1,141	38	190	262	332	169
1924	4,226	1,522	0	—	1,087	185	250	1,459	22	232	314	456	221
1925	4,957	1,801	0	—	1,258	192	351	1,681	20	219	396	440	400
1926	5,075	1,896	0	—	1,255	214	427	1,725	27	184	436	422	385
1927	5,710	1,874	0	—	1,154	251	469	2,004	30	188	520	415	679
1928	5,986	2,007	0	—	1,189	340	478	2,260	39	216	546	356	562
1929	6,056	2,072	0	—	1,223	318	531	2,296	50	341	377	374	546
1930	7,311	2,250	0	—	1,241	402	607	2,958	81	415	428	610	569
1931	7,561	2,346	0	—	1,093	421	832	2,951	124	502	362	507	769
1932	6,239	1,827	0	—	572	366	889	2,623	123	551	253	320	542
1933	4,662	1,028	0	9	228	218	573	1,819	122	1,101	164	166	262
1934	5,726	1,454	3	40	584	208	619	1,899	145	1,422	332	179	295
1935	6,016	1,371	29	7	628	155	552	1,681	115	1,932	332	208	377
1936	9,167	2,939	196	14	1,441	289	999	2,497	88	1,794	734	209	906
1937	7,547	2,111	268	6	853	246	738	2,396	104	1,513	610	188	625
1938	8,414	2,326	98	37	1,037	323	831	2,893	177	1,397	679	200	742
1939	9,779	3,394	174	76	1,555	434	1,155	2,877	354	1,441	708	238	767
1940	9,112	2,442	529	481	484	182	766	2,797	1,055	1,336	530	325	627
1941	14,095	5,544	1,056	3,406	464	134	484	2,019	4,144	1,230	245	364	549
1942	23,543	10,009	1,260	8,048	366	102	233	1,081	10,796	913	163	237	344
1943	13,392	6,227	1,647	4,195	171	121	93	599	5,144	702	95	169	456
1944	6,722	3,685	436	2,904	109	155	81	535	1,758	390	61	129	164
1945	5,070	2,344	154	1,730	147	215	98	611	1,434	299	87	138	157
1946	3,881	1,351	634	209	213	182	113	1,067	329	529	198	199	208
1947	4,891	1,223	300	145	449	121	208	1,652	293	737	329	284	373

		Buildings										
	Total	Total	Housing and redevelopment	Industrial	Educational	Hospital	Other	Highway and streets	Military facilities	Conservation and development	Sewer	Water facilities	Miscellaneous
	Dc377 [3]	Dc378 [3]	Dc379 [3]	Dc380 [3]	Dc381 [3]	Dc382 [3]	Dc383 [3]	Dc384 [3]	Dc385 [3]	Dc386 [3]	Dc387 [3]	Dc388 [3]	Dc389 [3]
Year	Million 1967 dollars	Million 1967 dollars	Million 1967 dollars	Million 1967 dollars	Million 1967 dollars	Million 1967 dollars	Million 1967 dollars	Million 1967 dollars	Million 1967 dollars	Million 1967 dollars	Million 1967 dollars	Million 1967 dollars	Million 1967 dollars
1947	5,246	1,247	292	155	464	124	212	1,962	313	684	405	321	314
1948	6,713	2,087	210	285	898	310	384	2,163	219	957	570	400	317
1949	9,050	3,535	477	264	1,394	684	716	2,719	194	1,183	658	435	326
1950	10,325	4,036	447	337	1,704	750	798	3,204	260	1,385	677	433	330
1951	12,142	5,348	719	1,290	2,003	698	638	2,879	1,126	1,267	700	516	306
1952	13,662	6,135	769	2,173	2,089	639	465	3,183	1,710	1,169	693	508	264
1953	14,299	6,234	650	2,273	2,200	474	637	3,730	1,615	1,129	786	493	312
1954	15,394	6,470	390	1,987	2,815	439	839	4,861	1,299	991	835	556	382
1955	15,434	5,751	302	936	3,171	390	952	5,184	1,667	922	861	613	436
1956	15,280	5,192	323	541	3,054	358	916	5,256	1,617	1,007	927	693	588
1957	16,125	5,730	556	543	3,243	406	982	5,626	1,473	1,103	976	636	581
1958	17,984	6,403	929	481	3,380	461	1,152	6,476	1,624	1,170	1,009	605	697
1959	18,944	6,418	1,055	438	3,155	509	1,261	6,953	1,714	1,283	1,059	603	914
1960	18,986	6,500	781	484	3,358	481	1,396	6,782	1,622	1,353	1,021	645	1,063
1961	20,416	7,087	917	563	3,644	440	1,523	7,264	1,618	1,574	1,042	707	1,124
1962	20,797	7,103	1,016	497	3,523	471	1,596	7,593	1,463	1,704	1,205	725	1,004
1963	22,118	7,529	581	511	4,022	492	1,923	8,218	1,339	1,873	1,042	942	1,175
1964	22,992	8,132	624	459	4,304	532	2,213	8,207	1,020	1,902	1,437	1,032	1,262

[1] See text for a discussion of issues relating to the comparability of the series over time.

[2] Series ends after 1947.

[3] Series begins in 1947.

Source

U.S. Bureau of the Census, *Value of New Construction Put in Place 1964 to 1980*, Construction Reports: C30-80S (July 1981), Table D-2, pp. 187–91.

Documentation

For additional details on the value-in-place estimates for this period, see the text for Tables Dc1–11 and Dc22–43.

This table presents the constant-dollar value-in-place estimates for public construction and its subcomponents. The current-dollar estimates that underlie these series include estimates of construction work owned by both the federal and state and local governments (see the text for Table Dc351–363 for the methods used to compile these estimates). Measurement of construction expenditures in constant dollars is an indirect way of approximating changes in the physical volume of construction. The estimates shown above were compiled by deflating the current-dollar estimates for each public value-in-place subcomponent by an appropriate construction cost index. Two separate constant-dollar series are shown for each category of construction because of a comprehensive revision of construction deflators that was implemented in 1974 going back to 1947. As explained in the text for Table Dc22–43, the two separate series for each subcomponent are not directly comparable because they differ in base years, and in almost all cases were derived using different deflating indexes. The cost indexes that were used to deflate the current-dollar series are identified below; many of them are described and presented in Table Dc207–226.

For 1938 and earlier years all series were compiled annually, but beginning in 1939 monthly constant-dollar estimates were constructed for each subcomponent and aggregate series, and then summed to form the annual series shown here.

Series Dc366–370 and Dc379–383. For both the 1915–1947 and 1947–1964 subperiods, the five public building subcomponents were deflated with the same indexes that were used for private residential and nonresidential buildings (see Tables Dc256–271 and Dc282–302 for details). During the earlier period, the deflators that were used included the Boeckh residential cost index (for housing and redevelopment, series Dc366), the Turner Company's construction cost index (for industrial buildings, series Dc367), and the American Appraisal Company's index (for educational, hospital, and other public buildings, series Dc368–370). After 1947, a price index for new Federal Housing Administration–insured houses (1947–1962) and the U.S. Census Bureau's index of new home prices (1963–1964) were used to deflate current-dollar housing and redevelopment construction (series Dc379), while an average of the Turner Company index, the revised residential index, and the U.S. Bureau of Public Roads' cost index for structures were applied to all four of the public nonresidential buildings subcomponents (Tables Dc460–475 and Dc494–509; series Dc380–381).

Series Dc371–372 and Dc384–385. The series for highways and streets were deflated by a composite cost index compiled by the Bureau of Public Roads for both the 1915–1947 and 1947–1964 subperiods. The same composite was combined with American Appraisal's, Turner's, and Fuller's cost indexes to deflate current-dollar military facilities before 1948 (series Dc372), and averaged with the revised residential and nonresidential buildings indexes described above to form constant-dollar military construction estimates for the 1947–1964 period (series Dc385).

Series Dc373–375 and Dc386–388. The 1915–1947 constant-dollar series for conservation and development, sewer, and water facilities were all derived using an unweighted average of construction cost indexes produced by the Associated General Contractors and the *Engineering News-Record*. For the estimates in 1967 dollars, a more specific deflator was used in each case: the U.S. Bureau of Reclamation's composite index for conservation and development, the Environmental Protection Agency's (EPA's) sewers and sewage treatment plant indexes for sewers, and an average of the EPA's sewer composite and the U.S. Interstate Commerce Commission's pipeline cost index for water facilities.

Series Dc375 and Dc388. Constant-dollar miscellaneous public construction for the earlier period was derived using a deflator that combined a cost index for private electric utilities construction with the cost index that was used for private miscellaneous construction. The revised miscellaneous public construction deflator – used to compile series Dc388 – was a simple average of the composite cost indexes produced by the Bureau of Public Roads and the Bureau of Reclamation.

TABLE Dc390–418   Value of new construction – public, by type, ownership, and financing: 1915–1946[1]   [Current dollars]
Contributed by Kenneth A. Snowden

	Total				Buildings								Highways and streets	
					Residential				Nonresidential					
Year	Total	Federal direct	Federal aid	State and local	Total	Federal direct	Federal aid	State and local	Total	Federal direct	Federal aid	State and local	Total	Federal direct
	Dc390	Dc391	Dc392	Dc393	Dc394	Dc395	Dc396	Dc397	Dc398	Dc399	Dc400	Dc401	Dc402	Dc403
	Million dollars	Million dollars	Million dollars	Million dollars	Million dollars	Million dollars	Million dollars	Million dollars	Million dollars	Million dollars	Million dollars	Million dollars	Million dollars	Million dollars
1915	719	71	0	648	0	0	0	0	217	17	0	200	302	0
1916	708	66	0	642	0	0	0	0	207	16	0	191	314	0
1917	1,279	654	5	620	0	0	0	0	192	18	0	174	320	0
1918	2,238	1,634	10	594	28	28	0	0	199	20	0	179	296	1
1919	1,976	1,162	65	749	14	14	0	0	246	16	0	230	429	3
1920	1,352	232	95	1,025	0	0	0	0	283	11	0	272	656	4
1921	1,564	122	78	1,364	0	0	0	0	387	17	0	370	853	3
1922	1,684	100	78	1,506	0	0	0	0	481	21	0	460	876	4
1923	1,622	108	77	1,437	0	0	0	0	481	18	0	463	805	7
1924	1,901	111	100	1,690	0	0	0	0	494	13	0	481	987	9
1925	2,138	100	89	1,949	0	0	0	0	573	8	0	565	1,082	10
1926	2,144	92	82	1,970	0	0	0	0	603	8	0	595	1,067	10
1927	2,409	98	81	2,230	0	0	0	0	596	10	0	586	1,222	10
1928	2,485	122	85	2,278	0	0	0	0	638	14	0	624	1,289	11
1929	2,486	155	80	2,251	0	0	0	0	659	26	0	633	1,266	11
1930	2,858	209	104	2,545	0	0	0	0	660	43	0	617	1,516	17
1931	2,659	271	235	2,153	0	0	0	0	612	65	0	547	1,355	22
1932	1,862	333	111	1,418	0	0	0	0	415	133	0	282	958	21
1933	1,648	516	286	846	0	0	0	0	230	94	9	127	847	44
1934	2,211	626	721	864	1	1	0	0	363	64	61	238	1,000	61
1935	2,233	814	567	852	9	9	0	0	328	59	72	197	845	64
1936	3,516	797	1,566	1,153	61	61	0	0	701	76	314	311	1,362	53
1937	3,096	776	1,117	1,203	93	93	0	0	550	82	233	235	1,226	42
1938	3,420	717	1,320	1,383	35	32	0	3	672	85	213	374	1,421	37
1939	3,809	759	1,377	1,673	65	4	0	61	970	80	367	523	1,381	35
1940	3,628	1,182	946	1,500	200	4	0	196	615	233	172	210	1,302	30
1941	5,751	3,751	697	1,303	430	215	0	215	1,646	1,357	97	192	1,066	26
1942	10,660	9,313	475	872	545	363	0	182	3,685	3,500	69	116	734	17
1943	6,322	5,609	268	445	739	694	0	45	2,010	1,909	32	69	446	7
1944	3,073	2,505	126	442	211	203	0	8	1,361	1,271	28	62	362	7
1945	2,398	1,737	99	562	80	80	0	0	937	808	29	100	398	11
1946	2,231	—	—	—	374	248	61	65	354	156	0	198	764	—

Year	Highways and streets — Federal aid	Highways and streets — State and local	Conservation and development — Total	Conservation and development — Federal direct	Conservation and development — Federal aid	Conservation and development — State and local	Sewer and water systems — Total	Sewer and water systems — Federal direct	Sewer and water systems — Federal aid	Sewer and water systems — State and local	Military facilities (federal direct)	Miscellaneous — Total	Miscellaneous — Federal direct	Miscellaneous — Federal aid	Miscellaneous — State and local
	Dc404	Dc405	Dc406	Dc407	Dc408	Dc409	Dc410	Dc411	Dc412	Dc413	Dc414	Dc415	Dc416	Dc417	Dc418
	Million dollars	Million dollars	Million dollars	Million dollars	Million dollars	Million dollars	Million dollars	Million dollars	Million dollars	Million dollars	Million dollars	Million dollars	Million dollars	Million dollars	Million dollars
1915	0	302	106	0	0	106	36	0	0	36	17	41	1	0	40
1916	0	314	95	0	0	95	28	0	0	28	21	43	1	0	42
1917	5	315	91	0	0	91	27	0	0	27	608	41	1	0	40
1918	10	285	94	0	0	94	29	0	0	29	1,555	37	1	0	36
1919	65	361	124	0	0	124	39	0	0	39	1,089	35	1	0	34
1920	95	557	153	0	0	153	55	0	0	55	161	44	1	0	43
1921	78	772	178	0	0	178	52	0	0	52	49	45	1	0	44
1922	78	794	201	0	0	201	48	0	0	48	25	53	2	0	51
1923	77	721	203	0	0	203	65	0	0	65	16	52	2	0	50
1924	100	878	263	0	0	263	79	0	0	79	9	69	1	0	68
1925	89	983	278	0	0	278	73	0	0	73	8	124	1	0	123
1926	82	975	285	0	0	285	61	0	0	61	11	117	2	0	115
1927	81	1,131	312	0	0	312	63	0	0	63	12	204	3	0	201
1928	85	1,193	300	0	0	300	72	0	0	72	15	171	10	0	161
1929	80	1,175	253	0	0	253	115	29	0	86	19	174	13	0	161
1930	104	1,395	343	0	0	343	137	26	0	111	29	173	9	0	164
1931	235	1,098	270	0	0	270	156	21	0	135	40	226	9	0	217
1932	111	826	156	0	0	156	150	11	0	139	34	149	6	0	143
1933	232	571	95	0	14	81	359	5	16	338	36	81	4	15	62
1934	476	463	173	0	69	104	518	11	62	445	47	114	13	53	48
1935	326	455	175	0	63	112	700	18	45	637	37	139	8	61	70
1936	766	543	342	2	209	131	658	39	50	569	29	363	7	227	129
1937	538	646	311	2	158	151	605	56	39	510	37	274	10	149	115
1938	716	668	355	2	174	179	551	37	30	484	62	324	15	187	122
1939	603	743	371	0	195	176	570	40	35	495	125	327	20	177	130
1940	513	759	338	0	129	209	528	12	21	495	385	260	35	111	114
1941	391	649	252	0	84	168	500	5	7	488	1,620	237 ²	45	118	74
1942	278	439	169	17	57	95	357	3	4	350	5,016	154 ²	50	67	37
1943	192	247	107	29	37	41	285	0	0	285	2,550	185 ²	135	7	43
1944	84	271	79	10	14	55	163	0	0	163	837	60 ²	14	0	46
1945	59	328	97	7	11	79	130	0	0	130	690	66	11	0	55
1946	—	—	194	2	3	189	260	20	0	240	188	97	10	0	87

1 See text for a discussion of issues relating to the comparability of the series over time.

2 Includes petroleum pipelines as follows: $25 million in 1942, $125 million in 1943, and $4 million in 1944.

Source

U.S. Department of Commerce and U.S. Department of Labor, *Construction Volume and Costs, 1915–56: A Supplement to Construction Review*, Table 4, pp. 10–13.

Documentation

For additional details on the value-in-place estimates for public construction for this period, see the text for Tables Dc1–11 and Dc22–43.

The current-dollar value-in-place estimates for public construction presented in Table Dc351–363 are disaggregated here into federal direct construction (federally owned and financed), federally aided (federally financed but owned by state and local government), and state and local (nonfederally owned and financed). The sum of the first two (that is, federal direct and federally aided construction) represents total federal construction spending, while the sum of the last two (that is, federally aided and state and local construction) represent the official value-in-place estimates for state and local construction.

Public construction estimates disaggregated by ownership are available for the post-1947 period (see Table Dc419–441), but not by the sources of finance. The more detailed breakdown shown here was adopted from the source in order to facilitate the examination of intergovernmental relationships during the 1930s, and, especially, the impact of New Deal federal aid programs on state and local construction activity.

See Lowell J. Chawner, *Construction Activity in the United States, 1915–37*, U.S. Department of Commerce, Domestic Commerce Series number 99 (1938), pp. 70–89, for the original derivation of the public value-in-place estimates. Chawner's original estimates went through several relatively minor revisions during the 1940s. In 1951, a major revision of Chawner's estimates that incorporated previously excluded work relief expenditures for 1933–1943 appeared in the *Statistical Abstract of the United States, 1951*, Table 847 (see also *Construction and Construction Materials*, Statistical Supplement (May 1950), for details). The 1946 estimate for highways and streets shown here was revised again in 1964, but at that time estimates were not decomposed by ownership or source of funds in published reports.

Series Dc398. The source reports only aggregates for nonresidential buildings. This series equals the sum of the industrial, educational, hospital, and other public buildings subcomponents reported separately in series Dc354–357.

Series Dc410. The source reports only aggregates for sewer and water systems. This series combines the sewer and the water facilities figures shown separately in series Dc361–362.

TABLE Dc419–441   Value of new construction – public, by type and ownership: 1947–1964[1]   [Current dollars]

Contributed by Kenneth A. Snowden

	Total			Buildings								
				Total		Housing and redevelopment		Industrial (federal)	Educational		Hospital	
	Total	Federal	State and local	Federal	State and local	Federal	State and local		Federal	State and local	Federal	State and local
	Dc419	Dc420	Dc421	Dc422	Dc423	Dc424	Dc425	Dc426	Dc427	Dc428	Dc429	Dc430
Year	Million dollars	Million dollars	Million dollars	Million dollars	Million dollars	Million dollars	Million dollars	Million dollars	Million dollars	Million dollars	Million dollars	Million dollars
1947	3,319	840	2,479	200	591	9	191	96	58	229	30	47
1948	4,704	1,177	3,527	346	1,101	33	123	196	3	615	98	115
1949	6,269	1,488	4,781	496	1,912	33	326	177	0	934	169	289
1950	6,866	1,624	5,242	514	2,218	15	330	224	0	1,133	146	353
1951	9,255	2,981	6,274	1,193	2,898	10	585	974	2	1,511	132	395
1952	10,779	4,185	6,594	1,887	2,925	16	638	1,684	18	1,601	113	382
1953	11,242	4,139	7,103	1,949	2,957	21	535	1,771	9	1,705	66	303
1954	11,712	3,428	8,284	1,646	3,299	5	331	1,506	9	2,125	35	298
1955	11,715	2,769	8,946	804	3,658	2	264	721	6	2,436	22	278
1956	12,732	2,726	10,006	600	3,768	17	275	453	8	2,548	37	263
1957	14,059	2,974	11,085	755	4,258	155	351	473	8	2,817	45	309
1958	15,457	3,387	12,070	964	4,535	357	489	408	11	2,864	35	355
1959	16,070	3,724	12,346	1,148	4,328	488	474	368	11	2,645	58	370
1960	15,863	3,622	12,241	1,024	4,487	288	428	407	20	2,798	56	345
1961	17,148	3,879	13,269	1,097	4,914	290	552	472	28	3,024	55	314
1962	17,869	3,913	13,956	1,091	5,001	201	737	422	29	2,955	55	342
1963	19,357	4,001	15,356	1,226	5,308	137	394	440	26	3,451	89	337
1964	20,383	3,898	16,485	1,375	5,802	105	462	403	24	3,766	102	367

	Buildings Other		Highways and streets			Conservation and development		Sewer and water systems (state and local)		Miscellaneous	
	Federal	State and local	Federal	State and local	Military facilities (federal)	Federal	State and local	Sewer	Water supply	Federal	State and local
	Dc431	Dc432	Dc433	Dc434	Dc435	Dc436	Dc437	Dc438	Dc439	Dc440	Dc441
Year	Million dollars	Million dollars	Million dollars	Million dollars	Million dollars	Million dollars	Million dollars	Million dollars	Million dollars	Million dollars	Million dollars
1947	7	124	34	1,310	204	394	30	188	163	8	197
1948	16	248	39	1,622	158	629	41	300	235	5	228
1949	117	363	57	1,958	137	793	59	354	265	5	233
1950	129	402	45	2,089	177	881	61	383	276	7	215
1951	75	407	41	2,314	887	853	59	425	350	7	228
1952	56	304	50	2,627	1,387	854	46	435	355	7	206
1953	82	414	63	2,958	1,290	830	62	520	363	7	243
1954	91	545	65	3,649	1,003	704	69	568	414	10	285
1955	53	680	70	3,782	1,287	598	103	615	470	10	318
1956	85	682	77	4,338	1,360	675	151	701	574	14	474
1957	74	781	100	4,834	1,287	818	153	781	563	14	496
1958	153	827	113	5,432	1,402	885	134	836	551	23	582
1959	223	839	94	5,667	1,465	972	149	906	561	45	735
1960	253	916	136	5,301	1,366	1,005	170	882	605	91	796
1961	252	1,024	134	5,720	1,371	1,200	184	914	667	77	870
1962	384	967	160	6,205	1,266	1,297	226	1,072	682	99	770
1963	534	1,126	183	6,901	1,179	1,337	357	947	882	76	961
1964	741	1,207	173	6,960	910	1,390	360	1,325	956	50	1,082

[1] See the text for a discussion of issues relating to the comparability of the series over time.

Source

U.S. Bureau of the Census, *Value of New Construction Put in Place 1964 to 1980*, Construction Reports: C30-80S (July 1981), Table D-3, p. 192.

Documentation

For additional details on the value-in-place estimates for this period, see the text for Tables Dc1–11 and Dc22–43. See the text for Table Dc351–363 for details concerning the compilation of these series, and Table Dc476–493 for a similar breakdown of public construction for the 1964–1999 period.

TABLE Dc419–441   Value of new construction – public, by type and ownership: 1947–1964   [Current dollars]
Continued

This table presents the current-dollar value-in-place estimates of public construction for the 1947–1964 period disaggregated into its federal versus state and local components. The distinction between the two was made on the basis of ownership at the time work was performed rather than by source of funds.

During this period, federal grants represented a substantial source of finance for several categories of state- and locally owned construction projects. To this extent, the federal value-in-place construction estimates do not account for all federal expenditures for new construction, and the state and local estimates overstate state and local contributions toward the financing of their construction activities.

TABLE Dc442–459   Value of new construction – public, by type and ownership: 1964–1999[1]   [Current dollars]
Contributed by Kenneth A. Snowden

	Total			Buildings			Highways and streets		
	Total	Federal	State and local	Total	Federal	State and local	Total	Federal	State and local
	Dc442	Dc443	Dc444	Dc445	Dc446	Dc447	Dc448	Dc449	Dc450
Year	Million dollars	Million dollars	Million dollars	Million dollars	Million dollars	Million dollars	Million dollars	Million dollars	Million dollars
1964	20,203	3,718	16,485	6,997	1,195	5,802	7,133	173	6,960
1965	21,920	3,872	18,048	7,751	1,318	6,433	7,550	169	7,381
1966	23,846	3,803	20,043	8,759	1,120	7,639	8,405	248	8,157
1967	25,377	3,316	22,061	9,823	832	8,991	8,591	244	8,347
1968	27,437	3,199	24,238	10,271	768	9,503	9,321	233	9,088
1969	27,793	3,150	24,643	11,065	842	10,224	9,251	213	9,039
1970	27,908	3,110	24,798	10,473	720	9,753	9,982	254	9,728
1971	29,699	3,810	25,889	11,223	903	10,320	10,657	288	10,369
1972	30,030	4,244	25,786	11,351	983	10,368	10,429	299	10,130
1973	32,348	4,700	27,648	12,842	1,177	11,665	10,505	269	10,236
1974	38,132	5,091	33,042	14,788	1,302	13,487	12,065	257	11,808
1975	43,293	6,088	37,205	15,912	1,664	14,249	13,147	307	12,840
1976	43,980	6,783	37,196	15,690	1,894	13,796	12,371	339	12,032
1977	43,083	7,088	35,994	14,578	2,066	12,512	12,460	396	12,064
1978	50,146	8,146	42,000	16,129	2,225	13,903	14,169	421	13,748
1979	56,646	8,564	48,081	17,661	2,343	15,318	17,088	528	16,560
1980	63,646	9,642	54,004	20,427	2,818	17,610	18,209	456	17,753
1981	64,691	10,413	54,278	20,776	3,151	17,625	18,405	751	17,654
1982	63,064	10,008	53,056	21,203	2,986	18,217	17,274	518	16,756
1983	63,450	10,557	52,893	21,832	3,390	18,442	17,904	468	17,436
1984	70,238	11,240	58,998	23,949	3,796	20,153	21,556	516	21,040
1985	77,815	12,004	65,811	27,466	4,215	23,251	23,741	469	23,272
1986	84,582	12,412	72,170	30,528	4,157	26,370	25,318	402	24,916
1987	90,648	14,052	76,596	32,216	4,801	27,415	27,073	405	26,668
1988	94,735	12,264	82,471	35,193	4,141	31,052	29,126	431	28,695
1989	98,174	12,155	86,018	38,235	3,986	34,249	28,747	234	28,513
1990	107,478	12,099	95,379	43,615	4,689	38,926	32,105	227	31,877
1991	110,109	12,845	97,264	47,406	5,886	41,520	32,042	236	31,806
1992	115,847	14,376	101,471	49,986	5,964	44,022	33,106	220	32,886
1993	115,960	14,424	101,535	48,559	5,695	42,865	34,299	338	33,961
1994	120,193	14,440	105,753	49,446	5,142	44,303	37,419	428	36,991
1995	129,933	15,751	114,181	57,754	6,043	51,711	37,616	308	37,308
1996	139,263	15,325	123,938	63,471	6,230	57,240	39,464	368	39,096
1997	154,882	14,087	140,795	71,867	6,107	65,760	44,105	255	43,850
1998 [2]	159,523	14,317	145,207	73,277	6,031	67,246	48,515	251	48,264
1999 [2]	172,673	14,056	158,617	77,690	5,470	72,220	53,532	318	53,214

Notes appear at end of table

(continued)

TABLE Dc442-459   Value of new construction – public, by type and ownership: 1964-1999   [Current dollars]
Continued

Year	Military facilities (federal)	Conservation and development			Sewer and water systems (state and local)		Miscellaneous		
		Total	Federal	State and local	Sewer	Water supply	Total	Federal	State and local
	Dc451	Dc452	Dc453	Dc454	Dc455	Dc456	Dc457	Dc458	Dc459
	Million dollars	Million dollars	Million dollars	Million dollars	Million dollars	Million dollars	Million dollars	Million dollars	Million dollars
1964	910	1,750	1,390	360	1,325	956	1,132	50	1,082
1965	830	2,019	1,506	513	1,195	1,266	1,309	49	1,260
1966	727	2,194	1,665	529	1,300	1,066	1,395	43	1,352
1967	695	2,124	1,497	627	1,058	1,270	1,816	48	1,768
1968	808	1,973	1,363	610	1,551	1,514	1,999	27	1,972
1969	877	1,780	1,189	591	1,342	1,336	2,141	29	2,111
1970	717	1,907	1,367	540	1,543	1,093	2,192	51	2,142
1971	901	2,097	1,646	451	1,829	997	1,995	71	1,924
1972	1,088	2,170	1,761	409	1,700	1,077	2,216	114	2,103
1973	1,167	2,311	1,955	356	1,954	1,067	2,503	133	2,370
1974	1,186	2,741	2,246	495	2,682	1,381	3,290	100	3,189
1975	1,389	3,261	2,638	622	4,175	1,535	3,874	90	3,784
1976	1,630	3,868	2,839	1,029	4,704	1,443	4,274	81	4,193
1977	1,429	3,966	3,088	877	4,269	1,441	4,939	109	4,831
1978	1,502	4,494	3,860	635	5,275	2,074	6,503	138	6,365
1979	1,647	4,678	3,915	764	6,027	2,056	7,488	131	7,357
1980	1,880	5,178	4,270	908	6,775	3,082	8,094	217	7,877
1981	1,964	5,462	4,404	1,058	5,949	3,011	9,124	143	8,981
1982	2,205	5,286	4,119	1,167	5,771	3,024	8,301	181	8,120
1983	2,544	5,054	4,000	1,054	5,601	2,219	8,298	156	8,141
1984	2,839	4,909	3,927	982	6,567	2,757	7,660	162	7,498
1985	3,235	5,126	3,844	1,282	7,291	2,704	8,252	241	8,011
1986	3,868	4,926	3,675	1,251	8,097	3,368	8,478	310	8,168
1987	4,324	5,531	3,961	1,570	9,517	3,885	8,102	561	7,541
1988	3,579	4,768	3,606	1,163	9,521	4,319	8,229	507	7,722
1989	3,520	5,098	3,698	1,400	9,814	4,179	8,581	718	7,864
1990	2,665	4,686	3,657	1,029	10,276	4,909	9,223	861	8,362
1991	1,837	5,011	3,603	1,408	10,039	4,981	8,793	1,283	7,510
1992	2,502	5,952	4,533	1,419	9,663	5,162	9,477	1,157	8,320
1993	2,453	5,937	4,217	1,719	8,863	5,085	10,765	1,722	9,043
1994	2,318	6,363	4,376	1,988	8,700	4,647	11,301	2,176	9,125
1995	3,011	6,308	4,167	2,140	8,420	4,709	12,116	2,223	9,893
1996	2,591	6,008	3,845	2,163	9,798	5,618	12,313	2,291	10,022
1997	2,556	5,739	3,368	2,371	10,392	6,419	13,803	1,800	12,002
1998 [2]	2,529	5,447	3,536	1,911	10,168	6,830	12,755	1,969	10,787
1999 [2]	2,111	6,003	4,009	1,993	11,181	7,602	14,555	2,148	12,407

[1] See text for a discussion of issues relating to the comparability of the series over time.

[2] Estimates are subject to normal revisions for three years because several series are benchmarked to data that appear in other annual or biennial reports; see text.

Source

See the source for Table Dc12-21.

Documentation

Refer to the essay in this chapter and the text for Tables Dc12-21 and Dc44-53 for general information about the 1964-1999 value-in-place series.

This table presents current-dollar value-in-place estimates of public construction. Classification by governmental level is determined by ownership at the time work is performed on a new construction project and not according to the actual source of finance. For example, all of the work performed on a state highway project appears under state and local highways and streets even if a substantial share of the project is financed with a federal grant.

The federal and state and local value-in-place subcomponents are compiled using different data and different procedures. Value-in-place estimates for federally owned construction are, with few exceptions, based on monthly progress reports supplied to the U.S. Census Bureau by each federal agency involved in construction activities. These monthly estimates are summed to form the annual series. This general approach has been in use in the value-in-place program since 1940. For a small number of agencies, however, budget

totals from federal documents have been secured and prorated over the fiscal year to derive monthly estimates.

Between 1963 and 1975, the value-in-place estimates of all state and local subcomponents were based on a monthly (quarterly before 1968) Census Bureau survey of construction expenditures for a sample of state agencies and local jurisdictions. Since 1975, however, state and local government value-in-place estimates have been based on a monthly Construction Progress Report Survey that is similar in all procedural respects to the one used for private nonresidential buildings (see Table Dc303-320). In particular, a sample of state and locally owned building projects are selected from F. W. Dodge contracts-awarded data (see Table Dc132-144), and construction progress reports are requested each month from the agency in charge of the sample project until it is completed. At any one time, close to 9,000 projects are surveyed by the program. Weighted sums of monthly activity reports are organized by construction type using the same procedure as for private nonresidential buildings, and then increased by 5 percent to account for construction projects not covered by the F. W. Dodge data. To form the annual estimates shown in the table, these monthly value-in-place estimates are summed together and benchmarked to annual construction expenditures collected in the Census Bureau's Annual Survey of Public Finances (see Current Construction Reports: C30-9005, August 1990, p. 1).

TABLE Dc442–459   Value of new construction – public, by type and ownership: 1964–1999   [Current dollars]
Continued

The implementation of the survey-based estimation procedure in 1975 also involved a change in the definitions of some state and local government subcomponents and a reclassification of work performed among these categories (see Construction Reports: C30-80S, July 1981, pp. 156-7). These modifications created a break in all the state and local value-in-place series within the 1964–1999 time span, but no break in the 1915–1964 state and local value-in-place estimates. In fact, the 1947–1962 state and local government value-in-place estimates shown in Table Dc419–441 were also derived from the F. W. Dodge data, but by applying fixed monthly progress patterns to distribute construction costs over the months subsequent to the project's start.

The value-in-place estimates for federal and state and local construction are each classified into nine separate subcomponents. Federal construction is generally classified into subcomponents according to the principal function of the agency responsible for the work, while state and local construction is classified by the major function of the project itself. There are also differences in the nature of the work undertaken by different levels of government within the same nominal category. For these reasons the subcomponents presented here are defined separately for federal versus state and local construction.

Series Dc445–447. This table presents the combined public buildings aggregates for both levels of government. The underlying subcomponents of public buildings are presented in Table Dc460–475. Only one of these subcomponents, federal industrial buildings, has been substantially revised since 1980 in such a way as to create a break with the pre-1964 value-in-place series – there is a break, therefore, between the federal (and total) building series

shown here and the same series for the 1915–1964 period shown in Table Dc419–441.

Series Dc449–450. Includes streets, bridges, tunnels, and forest and park roads owned by federal agencies other than the U.S. Department of Defense. Also included are structures associated with roads such as those that provide drainage, lighting, and protection for motorists.

Series Dc451. Military facilities are, of course, an exclusively federal value-in-place category, which includes, with a few exceptions, all of the construction owned by the Department of Defense and the Coast Guard. Those activities specifically excluded from military facilities are family housing for the armed services, civil works by the U.S. Army Corps of Engineers, industrial facilities, military hospitals, and Soldiers Homes. The first three of these were placed in federal public buildings and are described in the text for Table Dc460–475.

Series Dc453–454. Work done by the Corps of Engineers, and other agencies that are primarily engaged in the maintenance and supervision of natural resources (such as the Tennessee Valley Authority and the Bureau of Reclamation), comprise the federal conservation and development series. The nonfederal conservation and development figures are dominated by construction intended for water resources protection and control.

Series Dc458. Includes construction at Soldiers Homes and Veterans Administration cemeteries, along with work done on a variety of facilities such as airports and fish and wildlife preserves.

Series Dc459. Covers "open" projects such as amusement and recreational facilities, power generating facilities, subway and streetcar construction, airport runways, and open parking facilities.

TABLE Dc460–475   Value of new construction – public buildings, by type and ownership: 1964–1999¹   [Current dollars]

Contributed by Kenneth A. Snowden

	Total			Housing and redevelopment			Industrial (federal)	Educational			Hospital			Other		
	Total	Federal	State and local	Total	Federal	State and local		Total	Federal	State and local	Total	Federal	State and local	Total	Federal	State and local
	Dc460	Dc461	Dc462	Dc463	Dc464	Dc465	Dc466	Dc467	Dc468	Dc469	Dc470	Dc471	Dc472	Dc473	Dc474	Dc475
Year	Million dollars	Million dollars	Million dollars	Million dollars	Million dollars	Million dollars	Million dollars	Million dollars	Million dollars	Million dollars	Million dollars	Million dollars	Million dollars	Million dollars	Million dollars	Million dollars
1964	6,997	1,195	5,802	567	105	462	223	3,790	24	3,766	469	102	367	1,948	741	1,207
1965	7,751	1,318	6,433	603	148	455	226	4,284	14	4,270	520	121	399	2,118	809	1,309
1966	8,759	1,120	7,639	655	81	574	208	5,333	13	5,320	511	130	381	2,052	688	1,364
1967	9,823	832	8,991	709	31	678	249	5,988	22	5,966	637	97	540	2,240	433	1,807
1968	10,271	768	9,503	746	60	686	351	6,061	14	6,047	698	69	629	2,415	274	2,141
1969	11,065	842	10,224	1,046	139	907	358	5,867	11	5,856	802	95	708	2,991	238	2,754
1970	10,473	720	9,753	1,106	93	1,013	316	5,619	16	5,604	838	130	708	2,594	166	2,428
1971	11,223	903	10,320	1,136	124	1,013	402	5,561	17	5,544	982	150	832	3,142	210	2,932
1972	11,351	983	10,368	874	142	732	389	5,718	25	5,694	1,007	158	849	3,363	269	3,094
1973	12,842	1,177	11,665	941	130	811	454	6,647	58	6,589	1,001	156	845	3,799	379	3,420
1974	14,788	1,302	13,487	1,006	190	816	564	7,310	47	7,263	1,238	170	1,068	4,670	331	4,339
1975	15,912	1,664	14,249	1,356	281	1,074	687	7,776	16	7,760	1,749	262	1,486	4,345	417	3,928
1976	15,690	1,894	13,796	1,263	269	994	672	7,245	6	7,238	2,085	361	1,724	4,427	587	3,840
1977	14,578	2,066	12,512	1,478	255	1,222	838	6,215	10	6,205	1,921	410	1,511	4,127	553	3,574
1978	16,129	2,225	13,903	1,384	178	1,205	932	6,654	22	6,632	1,908	466	1,442	5,251	626	4,625
1979	17,661	2,343	15,318	1,656	103	1,553	1,112	7,806	40	7,766	1,803	450	1,353	5,284	639	4,645
1980	20,427	2,818	17,610	1,983	148	1,835	1,441	8,902	39	8,862	1,921	519	1,402	6,181	671	5,510
1981	20,776	3,151	17,625	2,347	100	2,247	1,655	7,936	30	7,906	2,342	640	1,702	6,496	726	5,770
1982	21,203	2,986	18,217	2,277	186	2,091	1,632	7,606	22	7,584	2,379	626	1,753	7,309	520	6,789
1983	21,832	3,390	18,442	2,617	198	2,419	1,809	6,904	18	6,886	2,518	633	1,885	7,984	732	7,252
1984	23,949	3,796	20,153	2,651	257	2,394	1,828	7,833	11	7,823	2,496	724	1,772	9,140	976	8,165
1985	27,466	4,215	23,251	2,893	298	2,595	1,968	9,084	10	9,074	2,471	802	1,669	11,050	1,137	9,913
1986	30,528	4,157	26,370	3,029	354	2,675	1,657	10,456	14	10,441	2,323	887	1,437	13,063	1,245	11,818
1987	32,216	4,801	27,415	3,268	460	2,808	1,457	10,627	4	10,623	2,573	1,039	1,534	14,292	1,842	12,450
1988	35,193	4,141	31,052	3,292	419	2,873	1,413	12,823	3	12,820	2,756	884	1,872	14,909	1,422	13,487
1989	38,235	3,986	34,249	3,441	500	2,941	1,300	14,696	8	14,688	2,652	829	1,823	16,146	1,349	14,797
1990	43,615	4,689	38,926	3,808	438	3,370	1,434	16,055	11	16,044	2,860	826	2,034	19,458	1,981	17,478
1991	47,406	5,886	41,520	3,587	213	3,374	1,824	19,203	20	19,183	2,829	703	2,125	19,965	3,127	16,838
1992	49,986	5,964	44,022	4,138	161	3,977	1,876	20,647	30	20,617	3,383	757	2,626	19,943	3,141	16,801
1993	48,559	5,695	42,865	4,011	236	3,775	1,718	19,129	21	19,108	3,710	906	2,804	19,991	2,814	17,177
1994	49,446	5,142	44,303	3,835	446	3,389	1,465	20,361	26	20,335	3,951	851	3,099	19,834	2,354	17,480
1995	57,754	6,043	51,711	4,698	576	4,122	1,508	25,784	27	25,757	4,236	1,041	3,195	21,529	2,891	18,638
1996	63,470	6,230	57,240	5,048	681	4,367	1,389	28,590	12	28,578	4,616	1,159	3,457	23,827	2,989	20,838
1997	71,867	6,107	65,760	5,231	677	4,554	999	34,385	19	34,366	5,152	1,251	3,901	26,100	3,161	22,939
1998 ²	73,277	6,031	67,246	5,124	543	4,581	1,010	36,234	15	36,219	3,906	1,009	2,897	27,004	3,454	23,550
1999 ²	77,690	5,470	72,220	5,618	424	5,194	925	39,724	15	39,709	3,968	850	3,118	27,454	3,255	24,199

¹ See text for a discussion of issues relating to the comparability of the series over time.

² Estimates are subject to normal revisions for three years because several series are benchmarked to data that appear in other annual or biennial reports; see text.

Source

See the source for Table Dc12–21.

Documentation

Refer to the essay in this chapter and the text for Tables Dc12–21 and Dc44–53 for general information about the 1964–1999 value-in-place series.

This table presents the individual subcomponents of the public buildings series presented in Table Dc442–459. Refer to the discussion there for the methods used to construct all current-dollar state and local government subcomponents.

Of the nine value-in-place subcomponents shown here, only series Dc466, federal industrial buildings, has been substantially revised back to 1964, and so a break now appears between this series and its counterpart for the 1947–1964 period shown in Table Dc419–441. Also affected, of course, are any aggregates in Tables Dc442–475 that include series Dc466.

Series Dc464. Federal housing includes new family housing units and the rehabilitation of existing units constructed for the armed services. Military barracks, bachelor officers' quarters, and family housing for Coast Guard personnel are classified under federal military facilities, series Dc451, while housing for forest rangers and national park employees is classified under federal conservation and development, series Dc453.

Series Dc465. Includes houses, apartment buildings, and all other residential structures.

Series Dc466. The industrial building category is exclusively federal and covers primarily construction carried out at U.S. Department of Energy research and development facilities, and buildings and their related facilities at sites such as arsenals, ordnance works, and shipyards that house manufacturing, assembly, and processing activities. In 1982 this series was revised back to 1964 to exclude expenditures on capital equipment not related to construction. The revision reduced the 1964 value by 45 percent, which represents a substantial break in continuity with the unrevised industrial public buildings series for the 1915–1964 period shown in Table Dc351–363.

Series Dc468. Includes academic and associated buildings, laboratories and science buildings, libraries, art galleries, and museums, except for those built by the U.S. Department of Defense. Federally owned schools on Indian reservations are included in this category.

Series Dc469 and Dc472. Includes state or locally owned buildings at primary, secondary, and postsecondary institutions as well as facilities such as public libraries, museums and galleries, and observatories and gardens. Excluded from this category, however, are institutional buildings for the handicapped or teaching hospitals. These are grouped with health care and institutional facilities such as hospitals, clinics, infirmaries, and nursing homes in state and local hospitals, series Dc472.

Series Dc471. Health care and institutional facilities such as veterans' hospitals and clinics comprise the federal hospital buildings series

Series Dc474. Covers general office buildings, customs houses, courthouses, jails, and prisons, except for those owned by the Department of Defense.

Series Dc475. Covers a wide range of commercial, industrial, and miscellaneous buildings not classified elsewhere, such as general administrative buildings; police, fire, and rescue buildings; courthouses, jails and prisons; and, bus, streetcar, subway, and railroad garages.

TABLE Dc476–493   Value of new construction – public, by type and ownership: 1964–1999[1]   [Constant dollars]

Contributed by Kenneth A. Snowden

	Total			Buildings			Highways and streets			Military facilities (federal)	Conservation and development			Sewer and water systems (state and local)		Miscellaneous		
	Total	Federal	State and local	Total	Federal	State and local	Total	Federal	State and local		Total	Federal	State and local	Sewer	Water supply	Total	Federal	State and local
	Dc476	Dc477	Dc478	Dc479	Dc480	Dc481	Dc482	Dc483	Dc484	Dc485	Dc486	Dc487	Dc488	Dc489	Dc490	Dc491	Dc492	Dc493
Year	Million 1996 dollars	Million 1996 dollars	Million 1996 dollars	Million 1996 dollars	Million 1996 dollars	Million 1996 dollars	Million 1996 dollars	Million 1996 dollars	Million 1996 dollars	Million 1996 dollars	Million 1996 dollars	Million 1996 dollars	Million 1996 dollars	Million 1996 dollars	Million 1996 dollars	Million 1996 dollars	Million 1996 dollars	Million 1996 dollars
1964	105,492	19,402	86,090	38,868	6,638	32,230	36,026	874	35,152	4,810	8,601	6,831	1,770	6,515	5,029	5,642	249	5,393
1965	111,159	19,655	91,504	41,711	7,096	34,615	36,934	827	36,107	4,258	9,705	7,238	2,467	5,748	6,453	6,353	238	6,115
1966	116,434	18,563	97,872	45,270	5,799	39,471	39,331	1,160	38,171	3,571	10,316	7,831	2,485	6,117	5,285	6,544	202	6,342
1967	120,338	15,553	104,784	49,312	4,182	45,130	39,070	1,109	37,961	3,311	9,555	6,734	2,821	4,762	6,112	8,215	217	7,998
1968	123,065	14,240	108,825	48,605	3,637	44,968	40,184	1,004	39,180	3,636	8,463	5,846	2,617	6,649	6,935	8,592	116	8,476
1969	116,693	13,193	103,500	48,481	3,689	44,792	37,419	860	36,559	3,692	7,235	4,832	2,403	5,462	5,700	8,704	120	8,584
1970	107,101	11,956	95,144	43,150	2,970	40,180	35,819	913	34,906	2,744	7,179	5,142	2,037	5,806	4,331	8,072	187	7,885
1971	105,623	13,574	92,049	42,684	3,438	39,246	35,639	962	34,677	3,190	7,317	5,741	1,576	6,384	3,580	6,828	243	6,585
1972	100,786	14,251	86,535	40,281	3,510	36,771	33,469	959	32,510	3,651	7,100	5,763	1,337	5,569	3,534	7,182	368	6,814
1973	100,757	14,699	86,058	42,138	3,867	38,271	31,149	799	30,350	3,633	7,092	6,000	1,092	5,991	3,190	7,564	400	7,164
1974	103,164	13,836	89,328	42,451	3,767	38,684	31,013	664	30,349	3,221	7,229	5,920	1,309	7,103	3,550	8,597	264	8,333
1975	105,577	14,993	90,584	43,544	4,579	38,965	29,010	681	28,329	3,391	7,574	6,136	1,438	9,724	3,559	8,774	205	8,569
1976	102,518	15,941	86,577	41,169	4,984	36,185	26,203	718	25,485	3,814	8,515	6,251	2,264	10,356	3,233	9,229	175	9,054
1977	95,120	15,716	79,404	35,533	5,041	30,492	25,982	825	25,157	3,214	8,230	6,409	1,821	8,859	3,025	10,276	226	10,050
1978	100,938	16,526	84,412	35,370	4,888	30,482	27,071	809	26,262	3,088	8,703	7,473	1,230	10,193	3,965	12,548	268	12,280
1979	100,533	15,542	84,991	34,723	4,628	30,095	27,846	861	26,985	2,960	8,202	6,870	1,332	10,544	3,570	12,687	222	12,465

Notes appear at end of table   (continued)

TABLE Dc476–493   Value of new construction – public, by type and ownership: 1964–1999   [Constant dollars]   Continued

Year	Total			Buildings			Highways and streets			Military facilities (federal)	Conservation and development			Sewer and water systems (state and local)		Miscellaneous		
	Total	Federal	State and local	Total	Federal	State and local	Total	Federal	State and local		Total	Federal	State and local	Sewer	Water supply	Total	Federal	State and local
	Dc476	Dc477	Dc478	Dc479	Dc480	Dc481	Dc482	Dc483	Dc484	Dc485	Dc486	Dc487	Dc488	Dc489	Dc490	Dc491	Dc492	Dc493
	Million 1996 dollars	Million 1996 dollars	Million 1996 dollars	Million 1996 dollars	Million 1996 dollars	Million 1996 dollars	Million 1996 dollars	Million 1996 dollars	Million 1996 dollars	Million 1996 dollars	Million 1996 dollars	Million 1996 dollars	Million 1996 dollars	Million 1996 dollars	Million 1996 dollars	Million 1996 dollars	Million 1996 dollars	Million 1996 dollars
1980	100,043	15,660	84,383	36,349	5,022	31,327	25,110	630	24,480	2,937	8,182	6,749	1,433	10,693	4,820	11,953	322	11,631
1981	94,191	15,604	78,588	34,134	5,184	28,950	23,719	967	22,752	2,840	7,953	6,415	1,538	8,653	4,420	12,472	196	12,276
1982	89,835	14,472	75,363	33,232	4,676	28,556	22,549	675	21,874	3,136	7,366	5,741	1,625	8,036	4,327	11,188	244	10,944
1983	89,880	15,109	74,770	33,040	5,121	27,919	24,124	631	23,493	3,616	6,984	5,528	1,456	7,734	3,070	11,312	213	11,099
1984	97,232	15,694	81,538	34,673	5,489	29,184	28,960	693	28,267	3,950	6,678	5,343	1,335	8,928	3,687	10,356	219	10,137
1985	103,835	16,292	87,543	38,730	5,936	32,794	29,925	592	29,333	4,306	6,859	5,144	1,715	9,750	3,541	10,723	313	10,410
1986	109,182	16,322	92,860	41,451	5,649	35,802	30,563	485	30,078	4,938	6,510	4,858	1,652	10,695	4,321	10,701	391	10,310
1987	114,528	18,010	96,518	42,052	6,270	35,782	32,451	485	31,966	5,396	7,206	5,159	2,047	12,397	4,910	10,116	700	9,416
1988	115,797	15,199	100,598	44,268	5,212	39,056	33,959	503	33,456	4,330	6,002	4,539	1,463	11,986	5,288	9,963	615	9,348
1989	116,042	14,516	101,526	46,306	4,832	41,474	32,655	266	32,389	4,124	6,139	4,455	1,684	11,818	4,965	10,036	839	9,197
1990	123,803	14,064	109,739	51,117	5,498	45,619	35,880	254	35,626	3,050	5,482	4,278	1,204	12,010	5,730	10,534	984	9,550
1991	125,467	14,731	110,736	55,144	6,841	48,303	35,376	261	35,115	2,081	5,714	4,109	1,605	11,448	5,840	9,864	1,439	8,425
1992	131,755	16,331	115,424	57,315	6,834	50,481	37,405	249	37,156	2,844	6,694	5,099	1,595	10,874	5,939	10,683	1,305	9,378
1993	128,720	15,932	112,788	53,685	6,292	47,393	38,573	380	38,193	2,735	6,497	4,617	1,880	9,705	5,594	11,932	1,909	10,023
1994	128,842	15,406	113,435	52,436	5,454	46,982	40,886	468	40,418	2,497	6,751	4,643	2,108	9,231	4,868	12,172	2,344	9,828
1995	133,450	16,151	117,298	59,074	6,183	52,891	38,952	319	38,633	3,102	6,444	4,257	2,187	8,600	4,809	12,467	2,290	10,177
1996	139,147	15,328	123,819	63,446	6,234	57,212	39,413	368	39,045	2,593	6,000	3,841	2,159	9,778	5,609	12,310	2,293	10,017
1997	149,493	13,592	135,901	69,319	5,892	63,427	42,535	246	42,289	2,466	5,541	3,252	2,289	10,034	6,275	13,322	1,735	11,587
1998 [2]	150,246	13,503	136,743	68,333	5,628	62,706	45,877	237	45,640	2,377	5,219	3,387	1,832	9,743	6,552	12,144	1,873	10,271
1999 [2]	156,852	12,824	144,028	69,497	4,896	64,601	48,827	290	48,537	1,909	5,603	3,743	1,860	10,438	7,142	13,436	1,986	11,450

[1] See text for a discussion of issues relating to the comparability of the series over time.

[2] Estimates are subject to normal revisions for three years because several series are benchmarked to data that appear in other annual or biennial reports; see text.

Source

See the source for Table Dc12–21.

Documentation

Refer to the essay in this chapter and the text for Tables Dc12–21 and Dc44–53 for general information about the 1964–1999 value-in-place series.

This table presents the constant-dollar estimates for the series presented in Table Dc442–459. See the text for that table for a description of each subcomponent

Refer to the text for Table Dc44–53 for general details concerning the derivation of constant-dollar value-in-place estimates, and the text for Table Dc227–240 for the deflators that were used to deflate the public buildings subcomponents. Three indexes used to deflate current-dollar public building construction have been designed specifically for the task: the Handy–Whitman cost index for structures and improvements at water facilities (used for series Dc490); the Federal Highway Administration's

(FHA's) composite index of bids on excavation, surfacing, and highway-related structural components (used for series Dc484–485); and the U.S. Bureau of Reclamation's composite index of bid prices on eleven different categories of water resource–related construction activities (used for series Dc487–488).

The last index is also used to deflate current-dollar state and local sewer systems, series Dc489, and is averaged with the FHA's composite to produce the constant-dollar estimates for the subcomponents of miscellaneous public construction, series Dc492–493. The index used for military facilities, series Dc485, is a weighted average of the FHA composite, the U.S. Census Bureau's single-family houses under construction price deflator, and the Turner Construction Company's index of national building construction costs.

Series Dc479–481. Constant-dollar estimates of the underlying subcomponents of public building construction are reported in Table Dc494–509. None of the 1996 constant-dollar series shown in this table are directly comparable to the constant-dollar estimates for the same value-in-place series for earlier years as shown in Table Dc364–389 – different deflators and base years have been used for the two periods.

TABLE Dc494-509 Value of new construction – public buildings, by type and ownership: 1964–1999¹ [Constant dollars]

Contributed by Kenneth A. Snowden

	Total			Housing and redevelopment			Industrial (federal)	Educational			Hospital			Other		
	Total	Federal	State and local	Total	Federal	State and local		Total	Federal	State and local	Total	Federal	State and local	Total	Federal	State and local
	Dc494	Dc495	Dc496	Dc497	Dc498	Dc499	Dc500	Dc501	Dc502	Dc503	Dc504	Dc505	Dc506	Dc507	Dc508	Dc509
Year	Million 1996 dollars	Million 1996 dollars	Million 1996 dollars	Million 1996 dollars	Million 1996 dollars	Million 1996 dollars	Million 1996 dollars	Million 1996 dollars	Million 1996 dollars	Million 1996 dollars	Million 1996 dollars	Million 1996 dollars	Million 1996 dollars	Million 1996 dollars	Million 1996 dollars	Million 1996 dollars
1964	38,868	6,638	32,230	3,150	582	2,568	1,241	21,050	133	20,917	2,606	567	2,039	10,822	4,115	6,707
1965	41,711	7,096	34,615	3,243	796	2,447	1,219	23,055	75	22,980	2,799	651	2,148	11,392	4,353	7,039
1966	45,270	5,799	39,471	3,368	420	2,948	1,075	27,559	67	27,492	2,643	673	1,970	10,626	3,565	7,061
1967	49,312	4,182	45,130	3,538	154	3,384	1,251	30,082	110	29,972	3,195	488	2,707	11,246	2,179	9,067
1968	48,605	3,637	44,968	3,515	283	3,232	1,662	28,702	67	28,635	3,305	327	2,978	11,422	1,298	10,124
1969	48,481	3,689	44,792	4,647	618	4,029	1,568	25,669	50	25,619	3,506	414	3,092	13,093	1,040	12,053
1970	43,150	2,970	40,180	4,781	403	4,378	1,292	23,016	64	22,952	3,438	532	2,906	10,622	678	9,944
1971	42,684	3,438	39,246	4,654	504	4,150	1,516	20,968	65	20,903	3,700	565	3,135	11,847	789	11,058
1972	40,281	3,510	36,771	3,334	543	2,791	1,372	20,155	87	20,068	3,559	559	3,000	11,861	949	10,912
1973	42,138	3,867	38,271	3,266	451	2,815	1,479	21,715	190	21,525	3,266	508	2,758	12,412	1,239	11,173
1974	42,451	3,767	38,684	3,179	600	2,579	1,606	20,852	135	20,717	3,529	485	3,044	13,285	942	12,343
1975	43,544	4,579	38,965	3,930	816	3,114	1,872	21,162	43	21,119	4,759	713	4,046	11,821	1,135	10,686
1976	41,169	4,984	36,185	3,445	735	2,710	1,756	18,941	16	18,925	5,450	943	4,507	11,577	1,533	10,044
1977	35,533	5,041	30,492	3,642	631	3,011	2,041	15,123	24	15,099	4,687	998	3,689	10,040	1,347	8,693
1978	35,370	4,888	30,482	2,980	388	2,592	2,050	14,601	49	14,552	4,202	1,026	3,176	11,537	1,375	10,162
1979	34,723	4,628	30,095	3,193	200	2,993	2,196	15,365	79	15,286	3,557	888	2,669	10,411	1,265	9,146
1980	36,349	5,022	31,327	3,477	259	3,218	2,571	15,857	70	15,787	3,422	924	2,498	11,022	1,197	9,825
1981	34,134	5,184	28,950	3,847	164	3,683	2,724	13,045	49	12,996	3,848	1,052	2,796	10,669	1,195	9,474
1982	33,232	4,676	28,556	3,620	294	3,326	2,554	11,903	35	11,868	3,724	979	2,745	11,432	814	10,618
1983	33,040	5,121	27,919	4,057	307	3,750	2,729	10,416	27	10,389	3,796	955	2,841	12,041	1,103	10,938
1984	34,673	5,489	29,184	3,957	384	3,573	2,638	11,296	15	11,281	3,601	1,044	2,557	13,180	1,407	11,773
1985	38,730	5,936	32,794	4,234	437	3,797	2,765	12,752	13	12,739	3,469	1,125	2,344	15,509	1,596	13,913
1986	41,451	5,649	35,802	4,236	495	3,741	2,245	14,139	20	14,119	3,149	1,201	1,948	17,683	1,689	15,994
1987	42,052	6,270	35,782	4,373	615	3,758	1,898	13,830	5	13,825	3,347	1,352	1,995	18,604	2,400	16,204
1988	44,268	5,212	39,056	4,240	540	3,700	1,774	16,086	4	16,082	3,459	1,109	2,350	18,710	1,786	16,924
1989	46,306	4,832	41,474	4,259	619	3,640	1,571	17,758	10	17,748	3,205	1,002	2,203	19,513	1,630	17,883
1990	51,117	5,498	45,619	4,560	525	4,035	1,677	18,772	12	18,760	3,347	967	2,380	22,760	2,316	20,444
1991	55,144	6,841	48,303	4,264	253	4,011	2,117	22,294	23	22,271	3,285	817	2,468	23,183	3,630	19,553
1992	57,315	6,834	50,481	4,818	187	4,631	2,146	23,638	34	23,604	3,873	866	3,007	22,840	3,600	19,240
1993	53,685	6,292	47,393	4,465	262	4,203	1,898	21,145	23	21,122	4,098	1,002	3,096	22,078	3,106	18,972
1994	52,436	5,454	46,982	4,072	473	3,599	1,555	21,573	28	21,545	4,196	904	3,292	21,040	2,494	18,546
1995	59,074	6,183	52,891	4,786	586	4,200	1,544	26,374	27	26,347	4,335	1,066	3,269	22,035	2,960	19,075
1996	63,446	6,234	57,212	5,047	682	4,365	1,390	28,577	12	28,565	4,618	1,161	3,457	23,815	2,989	20,826
1997	69,319	5,892	63,427	5,084	658	4,426	965	33,137	19	33,118	4,970	1,206	3,764	25,165	3,045	22,120
1998 ²	68,334	5,628	62,706	4,853	515	4,338	941	33,743	14	33,729	3,642	941	2,701	25,155	3,217	21,938
1999 ²	69,497	4,896	64,601	5,088	384	4,704	828	35,497	14	35,483	3,547	762	2,785	24,537	2,909	21,628

(continued)

¹ See text for a discussion of issues relating to the comparability of the series over time.

² Estimates are subject to normal revisions for three years because several series are benchmarked to data that appear in other annual or biennial reports; see text.

Source

See the source for Table Dc12–21.

TABLE Dc494–509   Value of new construction – public buildings, by type and ownership: 1964–1999 [Constant dollars]   *Continued*

Documentation

Refer to the essay in this chapter and the text for Tables Dc12–21 and Dc44–53 for general information about the 1964–1999 value-in-place series.

This table presents the constant 1996 dollar estimates for subcomponents of the public buildings aggregates shown in Table Dc476–493. See the text for Table Dc460–475 for a description of each subcomponent and Table Dc227–240 for the cost indexes that were used as deflators.

The U.S. Census Bureau's single-family houses under construction price deflator is used to derive the constant-dollar value-in-place estimates for the public housing subcomponents. An unweighted average of this deflator and the Turner Construction Company's index of national construction costs is used to derive the constant-dollar value-in-place estimates for all of the nonresidential public buildings subcomponents shown in this table.

HOUSING

Kenneth A. Snowden

TABLE Dc510–530   Housing units started and authorized by permit, by metropolitan location, region, and number of units in structure: 1889–1958[1,2]   [BLS; privately owned, nonfarm]

Contributed by Kenneth A. Snowden

		Number of units in structure			Urban–rural location		Metropolitan location		Region	
	Total	One	Two	Three or more	Urban	Rural	Metropolitan	Nonmetropolitan	Northeast	North Central
	Dc510[3]	Dc511	Dc512	Dc513	Dc514	Dc515	Dc516	Dc517	Dc518	Dc519
Year	Thousand	Thousand	Thousand	Thousand	Thousand	Thousand	Thousand	Thousand	Thousand	Thousand
1889	342.0	—	—	—	193.0	149.0	—	—	—	—
1890	328.0	—	—	—	185.0	143.0	—	—	—	—
1891	298.0	—	—	—	169.0	129.0	—	—	—	—
1892	381.0	—	—	—	215.0	166.0	—	—	—	—
1893	267.0	—	—	—	151.0	116.0	—	—	—	—
1894	265.0	—	—	—	150.0	115.0	—	—	—	—
1895	309.0	—	—	—	175.0	134.0	—	—	—	—
1896	257.0	—	—	—	145.0	112.0	—	—	—	—
1897	292.0	—	—	—	165.0	127.0	—	—	—	—
1898	262.0	—	—	—	148.0	114.0	—	—	—	—
1899	282.0	—	—	—	159.0	123.0	—	—	—	—
1900	189.0	123.0	31.0	35.0	124.0	65.0	—	—	—	—
1901	275.0	177.0	32.0	66.0	180.0	95.0	—	—	—	—
1902	240.0	171.0	32.0	37.0	157.0	83.0	—	—	—	—
1903	253.0	175.0	30.0	48.0	166.0	87.0	—	—	—	—
1904	315.0	207.0	45.0	63.0	206.0	109.0	—	—	—	—
1905	507.0	336.0	64.0	107.0	332.0	175.0	—	—	—	—
1906	487.0	316.0	69.0	102.0	319.0	168.0	—	—	—	—
1907	432.0	291.0	59.0	82.0	283.0	149.0	—	—	—	—
1908	416.0	286.0	65.0	65.0	272.0	144.0	—	—	—	—
1909	492.0	328.0	73.0	91.0	322.0	170.0	—	—	—	—
1910	387.0	251.0	57.0	79.0	283.0	104.0	—	—	—	—
1911	395.0	249.0	62.0	84.0	288.0	107.0	—	—	—	—
1912	426.0	258.0	71.0	97.0	311.0	115.0	—	—	—	—
1913	421.0	264.0	72.0	85.0	307.0	114.0	—	—	—	—
1914	421.0	263.0	72.0	86.0	308.0	113.0	—	—	—	—
1915	433.0	262.0	73.0	98.0	316.0	117.0	—	—	—	—
1916	437.0	267.0	69.0	101.0	319.0	118.0	—	—	—	—
1917	240.0	166.0	31.0	43.0	175.0	65.0	—	—	—	—
1918	118.0	91.0	13.0	14.0	86.0	32.0	—	—	—	—
1919	315.0	239.0	36.0	40.0	230.0	85.0	—	—	—	—
1920	247.0	202.0	24.0	21.0	196.0	51.0	—	—	55.0	70.0
1921	449.0	316.0	70.0	63.0	359.0	90.0	—	—	121.0	109.0
1922	716.0	437.0	146.0	133.0	574.0	142.0	—	—	224.0	186.0
1923	871.0	513.0	175.0	183.0	698.0	173.0	—	—	278.0	244.0
1924	893.0	534.0	173.0	186.0	716.0	177.0	—	—	302.0	244.0
1925	937.0	573.0	157.0	208.0	752.0	185.0	—	—	314.0	252.0
1926	849.0	491.0	117.0	241.0	681.0	168.0	—	—	300.0	231.0
1927	810.0	454.0	99.0	257.0	643.0	167.0	—	—	301.0	213.0
1928	753.0	436.0	78.0	239.0	594.0	159.0	—	—	263.0	196.0
1929	509.0	316.0	51.0	142.0	400.0	109.0	—	—	156.0	140.0
1930	330.0	227.0	29.0	74.0	236.0	94.0	—	—	—	—
1931	254.0	187.0	22.0	45.0	174.0	80.0	—	—	—	—
1932	134.0	118.0	7.0	9.0	64.0	70.0	—	—	—	—
1933	93.0	76.0	5.0	12.0	45.0	48.0	—	—	—	—
1934	126.0	109.0	5.0	12.0	49.0	77.0	—	—	—	—
1935	215.7	182.2	7.7	25.8	112.6	103.1	—	—	—	—
1936	304.2	238.5	13.3	52.4	197.6	106.6	—	—	—	—
1937	332.4	265.8	15.3	51.3	214.4	118.0	—	—	—	—
1938	399.3	316.4	18.0	64.9	255.3	144.0	—	—	—	—
1939	458.4	373.0	19.7	65.7	303.5	154.9	—	—	—	—

Notes appear at end of table

(continued)

TABLE Dc510–530   Housing units started and authorized by permit, by metropolitan location, region, and number of units in structure: 1889–1958   [BLS; privately owned, nonfarm]   *Continued*

						Units started				
		Number of units in structure			Urban–rural location		Metropolitan location		Region	
	Total	One	Two	Three or more	Urban	Rural	Metropolitan	Nonmetropolitan	Northeast	North Central
	Dc510 [3]	Dc511	Dc512	Dc513	Dc514	Dc515	Dc516	Dc517	Dc518	Dc519
Year	Thousand	Thousand	Thousand	Thousand	Thousand	Thousand	Thousand	Thousand	Thousand	Thousand
1940	529.6	447.6	25.6	56.4	333.2	196.4	—	—	—	—
1941	619.5	533.2	28.4	57.9	369.5	250.0	—	—	—	—
1942	301.2	252.3	17.5	31.4	184.9	116.3	—	—	—	—
1943	183.7	136.3	17.8	29.6	119.7	64.0	—	—	—	—
1944	138.7	114.6	10.6	13.5	93.2	45.5	—	—	—	—
1945	208.1	184.6	8.8	14.7	132.7	75.4	—	—	—	—
1946	662.5	590.0	24.3	48.2	395.7	266.8	—	—	—	—
1947	845.6	740.2	33.9	71.5	476.4	369.2	—	—	—	—
1948	913.5	763.2	46.3	104.0	510.0	403.5	—	—	185.2	202.4
1949	988.8	792.4	34.7	161.7	556.6	432.2	—	—	217.2	224.2
1950	1,352.2	1,150.7	42.3	159.2	785.6	566.6	987.0	365.2	297.7	332.7
1951	1,020.1	892.2	40.4	87.5	531.3	488.8	723.1	297.0	224.2	258.1
1952	1,068.5	939.1	45.9	83.5	554.6	513.9	750.6	317.9	229.8	253.7
1953	1,068.3	932.8	41.5	94.0	533.2	535.1	776.9	291.4	241.5	265.4
1954	1,201.7	1,077.3	34.2	90.2	—	—	879.4	322.3	233.8	321.6
1955	1,309.5	1,190.0	32.8	86.7	—	—	960.1	349.4	263.5	351.9
1956	1,093.9	980.7	30.9	82.3	—	—	766.5	327.4	219.5	297.3
1957	992.8	840.2	33.1	119.5	—	—	677.4	315.4	183.7	252.3
1958	1,141.5	932.5	38.9	170.1	—	—	789.0	352.5	192.2	275.8

	Units started			Construction cost			Authorization of units by building permit						
	Region							Units authorized			Valuation of authorized units		
									Number of units in structure			Number of units in structure	
	South	West	Total	Per unit	Permit-issuing places	Total	One	Two or more	Total	One	Two or more		
	Dc520	Dc521	Dc522	Dc523	Dc524	Dc525	Dc526	Dc527	Dc528	Dc529	Dc530		
Year	Thousand	Thousand	Million dollars	Dollars	Number	Thousand	Thousand	Thousand	Million dollars	Million dollars	Million dollars		
1889	—	—	806.0	2,350	—	193	—	—	430	—	—		
1890	—	—	790.0	2,400	—	185	—	—	409	—	—		
1891	—	—	612.0	2,050	—	169	—	—	309	—	—		
1892	—	—	763.0	2,000	—	215	—	—	407	—	—		
1893	—	—	583.0	2,175	—	151	—	—	292	—	—		
1894	—	—	594.0	2,250	—	150	—	—	311	—	—		
1895	—	—	679.0	2,200	—	175	—	—	358	—	—		
1896	—	—	606.0	2,350	—	145	—	—	311	—	—		
1897	—	—	643.0	2,200	—	165	—	—	337	—	—		
1898	—	—	574.0	2,200	—	148	—	—	295	—	—		
1899	—	—	608.0	2,150	—	159	—	—	319	—	—		
1900	—	—	433.0	2,300	—	124	—	—	241	—	—		
1901	—	—	610.0	2,225	—	180	—	—	368	—	—		
1902	—	—	572.0	2,375	—	157	—	—	329	—	—		
1903	—	—	607.0	2,400	—	166	—	—	356	—	—		
1904	—	—	690.0	2,200	—	206	—	—	407	—	—		
1905	—	—	1,154.0	2,275	—	332	—	—	701	—	—		
1906	—	—	1,170.0	2,400	—	319	—	—	679	—	—		
1907	—	—	1,037.0	2,400	—	283	—	—	596	—	—		
1908	—	—	1,034.0	2,475	—	272	—	—	603	—	—		
1909	—	—	1,272.0	2,575	—	322	—	—	756	—	—		
1910	—	—	1,028.0	2,650	—	283	—	—	630	—	—		
1911	—	—	1,000.0	2,525	—	288	—	—	631	—	—		
1912	—	—	1,113.0	2,625	—	311	—	—	710	—	—		
1913	—	—	1,108.0	2,625	—	307	—	—	698	—	—		
1914	—	—	1,081.0	2,575	—	308	—	—	681	—	—		

Notes appear at end of table

TABLE Dc510–530 Housing units started and authorized by permit, by metropolitan location, region, and number of units in structure: 1889–1958 [BLS; privately owned, nonfarm] *Continued*

	Units started		Construction cost			Authorization of units by building permit						
	Region					Units authorized			Valuation of authorized units		
							Number of units in structure			Number of units in structure	
	South	West	Total	Per unit	Permit-issuing places	Total	One	Two or more	Total	One	Two or more
	Dc520	Dc521	Dc522	Dc523	Dc524	Dc525	Dc526	Dc527	Dc528	Dc529	Dc530
Year	Thousand	Thousand	Million dollars	Dollars	Number	Thousand	Thousand	Thousand	Million dollars	Million dollars	Million dollars
1915	—	—	1,192.0	2,750	—	316	—	—	746	—	—
1916	—	—	1,255.0	2,875	—	319	—	—	781	—	—
1917	—	—	769.0	3,200	—	175	—	—	438	—	—
1918	—	—	391.0	3,325	—	86	—	—	262	—	—
1919	—	—	1,258.0	4,000	—	230	—	—	865	—	—
1920	78.0	44.0	1,068.0	4,325	3,165	196	—	—	—	—	—
1921	132.0	87.0	1,771.0	3,950	3,165	359	—	—	—	—	—
1922	178.0	128.0	2,957.0	4,125	3,165	574	—	—	—	—	—
1923	194.0	155.0	3,775.0	4,325	3,165	698	—	—	—	—	—
1924	207.0	140.0	4,065.0	4,550	3,165	716	—	—	—	—	—
1925	228.0	143.0	4,475.0	4,775	3,165	752	—	—	—	—	—
1926	196.0	122.0	4,112.0	4,850	3,165	681	—	—	—	—	—
1927	185.0	111.0	3,910.0	4,825	3,165	643	—	—	—	—	—
1928	188.0	106.0	3,613.0	4,800	3,165	594	—	—	—	—	—
1929	132.0	81.0	2,453.0	4,825	3,165	400	—	—	—	—	—
1930	—	—	1,494.0	4,525	3,464	236	—	—	—	—	—
1931	—	—	1,105.0	4,350	3,464	174	—	—	—	—	—
1932	—	—	407.0	3,050	3,464	64	—	—	—	—	—
1933	—	—	285.0	3,075	3,464	45	—	—	—	—	—
1934	—	—	368.0	2,925	3,464	49	—	—	—	—	—
1935	—	—	732.0	3,400	3,464	113	—	—	—	—	—
1936	—	—	1,194.0	3,925	3,464	198	—	—	—	—	—
1937	—	—	1,366.0	4,100	3,464	214	—	—	—	—	—
1938	—	—	1,562.0	3,900	3,464	255	—	—	—	—	—
1939	—	—	1,764.0	3,850	3,464	304	—	—	—	—	—
1940	—	—	2,072.0	3,925	3,464	333	262	71	—	—	—
1941	—	—	2,531.0	4,075	3,464	369	295	75	—	—	—
1942	—	—	1,134.0	3,775	3,464	185	139	46	599	479	120
1943	—	—	660.0	3,600	3,464	120	79	41	374	260	115
1944	—	—	483.0	3,475	3,464	93	71	22	287	220	67
1945	—	—	959.3	4,625	3,464	149	125	24	618	536	81
1946	—	—	3,713.8	5,600	3,464	430	358	72	2,115	1,830	285
1947	—	—	5,617.4	6,650	3,464	502	394	108	2,885	2,362	524
1948	314.6	211.4	7,029.0	7,700	3,464	516	393	123	3,423	2,745	677
1949	353.5	194.1	7,374.3	7,450	3,464	575	414	161	3,725	2,845	879
1950	437.2	284.7	11,418.4	8,450	3,464	798	624	174	5,819	4,851	969
1951	325.4	212.4	9,186.1	9,000	3,464	535	135	99	4,280	3,818	562
1952	343.8	241.2	9,706.3	9,075	3,464	563	457	105	4,643	4,050	593
1953	314.0	247.4	10,181.2	9,525	3,464	537	426	112	4,646	3,993	652
1954	356.8	289.6	12,309.2	10,250	6,600	1,057	928	129	9,696	8,917	780
1955	385.3	308.8	14,345.8	10,950	6,600	1,133	1,014	118	11,386	10,643	743
1956	327.4	249.7	12,814.8	11,725	6,600	925	811	114	9,962	9,211	751
1957	320.8	236.0	12,126.8	12,225	6,600	820	669	151	8,939	7,923	1,016
1958	390.4	283.1	13,678.5	11,975	6,600	960	748	211	10,305	8,886	1,418

[1] Through 1954, the series on the authorization of units by building permit cover only urban places; thereafter, both rural and urban places covered.

[2] Beginning in 1935 units started (series Dc510–521) were reported with one significant decimal place; a similar level of precision was introduced into series Dc522 in 1945.

[3] For 1949–1956, includes 82,595 privately owned low-cost units built under the Wherry amendment to the National Housing Act for voluntary rental occupancy by military and defense-connected personnel.

Sources

Series Dc510–515. 1889–1944: U.S. Bureau of the Census, *Housing Construction Statistics: 1889 to 1964* (1966) Tables A-2. 1945–1958: U.S. Bureau of Labor Statistics, "Nonfarm Housing Starts, 1889 to 1958," Bulletin number 1260 (1959), Table 2.

Series Dc514–515. 1889–1944: U.S. Bureau of the Census, *Housing Construction Statistics: 1889 to 1964,* Tables A-2. 1945–1953: U.S. Bureau of Labor Statistics, "Nonfarm Housing Starts, 1889 to 1958," Bulletin number 1260 (1959), Table 7.

Series Dc516–517. 1950–1958: U.S. Bureau of Labor Statistics, "Nonfarm Housing Starts, 1889 to 1958," Bulletin number 1260 (1959), Table 7.

Series Dc518–521. 1920–1929: U.S. Bureau of the Census, *Housing Construction Statistics: 1889 to 1964,* Table A-2. 1948–1958: Computed for this table from data reported in *Housing Construction Statistics: 1889 to 1964,* Table A-3, and "Nonfarm Housing Starts, 1889 to 1958," Bulletin number 1260 (1959), Table 9. See explanation below.

(continued)

TABLE Dc510–530 Housing units started and authorized by permit, by metropolitan location, region, and number of units in structure: 1889–1958 [BLS; privately owned, nonfarm] *Continued*

Series Dc522–523. 1889–1944: U.S. Bureau of the Census, *Housing Construction Statistics: 1889 to 1964*, Table A-5. 1945–1958: U.S. Bureau of Labor Statistics, "Nonfarm Housing Starts, 1889 to 1958," Bulletin number 1260 (1959), Tables 18 and 19.

Series Dc524–530. U.S. Bureau of the Census, *Housing Construction Statistics: 1889 to 1964*, Table B-1.

Documentation

The most important official measures of privately owned nonfarm residential building activity are the building permit and housing start series shown in this table. During the period covered by this table, the U.S. Geological Survey (before 1920) and the U.S. Bureau of Labor Statistics (1920–1958) were responsible for collecting the basic building permit data, and the Bureau of Labor Statistics (BLS) was charged with deriving estimates of housing starts from them. In 1959 responsibility for collecting building permit data and estimating housing starts was shifted to the U.S. Bureau of the Census, which introduced significant improvements in procedures and estimation methods. Among these modifications was a substantial revision of the BLS housing start estimates for the 1945–1958 period, which are shown in Table Dc531–553. The unrevised, original BLS housing start series for the 1945–1958 period are shown in this table because these were assembled using procedures and methods similar to those used for the pre-1945 period. As a result, the data shown here represent a continuous sixty-nine-year record of residential building activity. Table Dc531–553, in contrast, presents data on building permits and starts between 1945 and 1958 that are comparable with the post-1958 estimates produced by the Census Bureau.

The BLS estimates shown here do not include farm housing starts because before 1959 these were estimated separately by the U.S. Department of Agriculture. The series shown in this table, moreover, include only privately owned housing units. For public housing starts, see Table Dc554–565. Finally, see Table Dc256–271 for an explanation of how the housing start series shown here were used in the compilation of the value-in-place estimates of residential construction.

In 1920 the BLS began to collect data from local officials who issued building permits. The U.S. Geological Survey (USGS) had collected building permit data before then to document the types and amounts of building materials that were being used in the nation; these earliest permit data were not used to construct estimates of housing starts as they were being collected. When the USGS suspended its permit collection program, the BLS started its own to provide a statistical record of the number and value of new family dwellings that were produced in the economy. By the mid-1930s this program had expanded to produce national estimates of both building permit and housing start data. This table presents the most important statistical series measuring privately owned nonfarm residential building activity that were compiled by the BLS, or were adopted by the BLS as its official estimates. The BLS national housing start series for the 1889–1958 period, therefore, are actually an amalgam of work done by Blank and Wickens (see below) for the period before 1930, and BLS estimates and revisions to Wickens's estimates for the period after 1930.

To understand the connection between building permit and housing start data, note that a permit stating the builder's intentions will normally be applied for before the actual construction project is undertaken. A housing start, on the other hand, was defined by the BLS (and by the Census Bureau in later years) to commence with the excavation for a basement or a foundation. As a result of the difference in timing, adjustments must be made to convert building permit data into estimates of housing starts. These include accounting for time lags between the issue of a building permit and the beginning of construction, and for cases when a project is abandoned altogether and the permit is allowed to lapse. The valuation shown on a building permit, moreover, normally understates the true cost of construction after the house has been started. The BLS was aware of all of these considerations early on, and conducted periodic surveys during the 1930s to assess the importance of lags, lapses, and undervaluations. Few systematic adjustments were made to the building permit data that were reported, however, until the BLS instituted regular studies of building permit use immediately after World War II.

A second early impediment the BLS faced in compiling national measures of building activity derived from the poor coverage provided by its building permit program – many localities that required building permits did not report to the BLS, and many more, especially those in rural areas, did not even require a permit to build. In 1921 the BLS received semiannual building permit reports from only 257 of the 289 cities with populations greater than 25,000, and even by 1932 the number stood at only 360 out of a possible 376 cities of the same size. The "nonreporting" areas were so numerous and important, in fact, that the BLS did not even attempt to construct national estimates of either building permits or housing starts. Beginning in 1929 it simply published monthly building permit information for selected large cities. The dramatic expansion in the BLS program occurred when the permit-reporting universe was extended to include cities with populations greater than 10,000 in 1933, to cities greater than 2,500 in 1936, and to 2,400 different localities with populations of 1,000 or more in 1938. By this time the BLS used permit data to estimate housing starts for at least its permit-reporting universe. The expansion of the program continued after World War II as the reporting universe was increased to encompass all permit-issuing places that could be identified – 2,513 cities and 2,660 rural nonfarm places as of 1947, and nearly 7,000 places by 1954. By the end of the period shown in this table, the BLS permit reporting program covered places holding 80 percent of the nation's nonfarm population and 85 percent of privately owned nonfarm residential construction activity.

The breakthrough in the derivation of national estimates of residential building activity from incomplete building permit data is credited to David L. Wickens and Ray R. Foster ("Non-Farm Residential Construction, 1920–1936," National Bureau of Economic Research, Bulletin number 65, 1937) for work done under the auspices of the National Bureau of Economic Research (see also David L. Wickens, *Residential Real Estate* (National Bureau of Economic Research, 1941)). Wickens relied heavily on the building permit activity of the 257 cities for which data had been continuously reported since 1921 to construct separate estimates for 1920–1936 of building permits and housing starts for nonreporting urban localities and the entire nonfarm rural sector. Wickens's estimates were derived by identifying the relationship between population growth rates and permit activity in reporting urban areas and then using these to project building activity on the basis of population trends in nonreporting areas. These estimates were then combined with adjusted permit data from urban reporting areas to construct national estimates of authorized dwelling units and starts. The BLS adopted Wickens's estimates for 1920–1936 as its official housing start series, and then employed similar techniques to construct estimates for the 1937–1944 period. In 1942 BLS used the results of the 1940 Census of Housing to revise Wickens's estimates for 1930–1936 and its own estimates for 1937–1939.

The building permit and housing start series were extended even further back in time when the BLS adopted David M. Blank's annual estimates for 1889–1919 as its official housing starts series for that period (Blank, "The Volume of Residential Construction 1889 to 1950," National Bureau of Economic Research, Technical Paper number 9, 1954). Blank constructed his estimates from pre-1920 building permit data that had been collected during the mid-1930s under the auspices of a Works Progress Administration project. Like Wickens, Blank relied on relationships between population and building permits to derive his estimates, but his approach was considerably more sophisticated (see Blank 1954, Chapters 4 and 5, for a complete description of his methodology).

The BLS implemented several methodological improvements after World War II in the methods it used to estimate housing starts in non-permit-issuing places, and especially in rural, nonfarm localities. In 1945 a field canvass of homebuilding in rural, nonreporting areas was begun so that housing start estimates for these areas were no longer derived by assuming relationships between population growth and building permits. Then in 1954 a completely new design was implemented that yielded estimates for starts in urban as well as rural nonreporting areas. The new approach designated nearly sixty "primary sampling units," which together made a representative national sample of urban and rural localities, as well as both permit-reporting and nonreporting areas. These samples were used to identify the relationship

TABLE Dc510–530   Housing units started and authorized by permit, by metropolitan location, region, and number of units in structure: 1889–1958   [BLS; privately owned, nonfarm]   *Continued*

between homebuilding activity in permit-reporting and nonreporting areas, which was then applied to scale the reported building permit and housing starts data up to national estimates. As was noted earlier, by this time non-permit-reporting areas represented less than 20 percent of the national total.

Immediately after World War II, the BLS also initiated a systematic survey of permit use so it could adjust the building permit data in reporting areas for lags and lapses. As a result, by the 1950s the BLS had established all of the basic methodological elements that the Census Bureau implemented when it took over responsibility for the building permit and housing starts programs in 1959. Information drawn from the 1940 and 1950 Censuses of Housing and special intercensal surveys of housing indicated, however, that BLS estimates substantially understated total housing starts in the economy even after the major revision to its methodology in 1954. This led the Census Bureau to improve several important dimensions of the BLS methodology after taking responsibility for the program in 1959, and to a break between the BLS and Census Bureau housing start series in that year.

The Census Bureau determined that the undercount in the BLS housing start series up to 1958 was so severe and persistent that it eventually (in 1964) substantially revised the total housing start series shown here for the 1945–1958 period. Because of data requirements, however, the revision could not be extended to the detailed housing start components (such as type of structure, urban versus rural location, inside and outside metropolitan areas, and region) that are presented here. As a result, the estimates shown in this table can be used as continuous series over the time period shown here, but should not be directly compared with the post-1959 series shown in Table Dc531–553. Instead, the revised 1945–1958 estimates shown in Table Dc531–553 should be used to examine trends or changes in the number of housing starts across the 1959 break. Moreover, it should be noted that the unrevised 1945–1958 BLS data shown in this table were not reported in *Historical Statistics of the United States* (1975) – only the Census Bureau's revisions for the 1945–1958 period were presented there.

In this table both housing starts and building permits are measured only for permanent, nonfarm housekeeping units that were built in new, privately owned residential structures (including those started with Federal Housing Administration–guaranteed or Veterans Administration–insured mortgage loans). Excluded are housing units that were created through conversions of existing structures as well as those that were intended for temporary, non-housekeeping or transient uses (including motels, hotels, dormitories, trailers, and houseboats). Also excluded are mobile homes, although pre-fabricated homes are included so long as they were permanent.

The sources are compilations of previously reported data and provide extended discussions of the derivations of the series and additional bibliographic information. Among the most important of these references are Blank (1954) (for housing starts and building permit data, 1889–1919); Wickens and Foster (1937), and Wickens (1941), Chapter 5 (for the derivation of housing starts, 1920–1936); and U.S. Department of Labor, *Construction, 1948 in Review*, Bulletin number 983 (1950) (for revisions of the 1930–1936 data reported by Wickens). Monthly and seasonally adjusted monthly data on housing starts are available in the BLS Bulletin number 1260 (1959) for the 1939–1958 period. Estimates of regional housing starts for the 1930–1950 period that are consistent with the national figures shown here are presented in Leo Grebler, David M. Blank, and Louis Winnick, *Capital Formation in Residential Real Estate* (Princeton University Press, 1956), Table H-1, pp. 396-7.

Series Dc511–513. A single-family dwelling unit, series Dc511, was generally a detached structure, although a unit that was attached to another structure was counted if it had a separate entrance from the outside, an individual heating plant, and walls that separated the unit from all others from ground to roof. Units in multifamily structures, series Dc512-513, shared a common entrance, stairway, heating plant, or basement, but could be arranged side-by-side, one above the others, or in any other manner. For most of the period, the BLS reported multifamily housing structures separately for two-and three-unit structures. The breakdown along the more modern distinction (buildings with two to four units versus those with five or more units) is available in the source only for 1954–1958. A structure with three of more

dwelling units, series Dc513, provided common structural elements with at least two other dwelling units, while a two-unit structure, series Dc512, contained either two dwelling units or a single dwelling unit and commercial space (such as a store).

Series Dc514–517. For most of the period shown in the table, the BLS classified housing starts as urban or rural in general in accordance with definitions established in decadal Censuses of Population. In rural areas, moreover, nonfarm residence also followed Census of Population criteria. Before 1930 urban areas were incorporated places with populations of 2,500 or more; all other places were rural. Definitions from the 1940 Census were used for the 1930–1953 period, which resulted in the addition of a small number of densely populated but unincorporated places to the urban category. When the Census Bureau adopted more complex urban and rural definitions in 1950, however, the BLS switched its categorization scheme to conform to the new census definitions of metropolitan and nonmetropolitan. The 168 standard metropolitan areas defined in 1950 each represented contiguous groups of counties that contained at least one city with 50,000 inhabitants or more, and a few densely populated areas in New England that did not contain such a city. For more details about the 1950 Census place of residence categories, see the text for Table Dc653–669.

Series Dc518–521. The regional categorizations shown in the table conform to post-1940 census definitions (see Table Ap-G in Appendix 2 regarding the composition of census regions and divisions). Regional housing start figures for all nonfarm units were reported for the 1948–1958 period in the BLS Bulletin number 1260 (1959), Table 9. These were converted into regional starts for privately owned units by subtracting regional publicly owned housing start estimates as reported in Table A-3 of *Housing Construction Statistics: 1889 to 1964*.

Series Dc522. The total construction cost of new dwelling units was computed by adjusting permit valuations for typical understatements. The estimates cover the cost of labor, materials, and subcontracted work, and that part of the builder's overhead and profit chargeable to the building of nonfarm dwelling units started in a specified period. These estimates were used during the period to derive the value of new construction on new housing units (series Dc257), but the two differ because the value-in-place estimates are constructed to include engineering and architectural fees, which are excluded here, and the costs of site development. In addition, value-in-place estimates are constructed by allocating the total cost of construction over the duration of projects according to assumed patterns of building progress, whereas the construction costs given here are for the year in which the project was started.

Series Dc523. These figures were rounded in published reports for all years and, in later years, represent the rounded average of monthly estimates. They are therefore only approximately equal to the average total cost that could be computed by dividing series Dc522 by series Dc510.

Series Dc524–530. Series Dc524 reports the number of reporting localities used to construct series Dc525–530 for each year. This is generally much larger than the number of cities reporting because often several permit-issuing offices were located in just one city. Through 1919, the number of urban places to which the series relate is not reported in Blank (1954). At its maximum it is fewer than 3,165 places, and it is reduced to a smaller number at either the midpoint or end of each decade. Also note that before 1954, the BLS produced its building permit series only for urban areas, and the user should note that that series Dc514 equals series Dc525 through 1944 (save for rounding); and for 1945–1953 the small differences between the two represent adjustments made for lapsed permits and lags between the date of permit issue and the start of construction. When the BLS abandoned the urban–rural distinction for housing starts in 1954, it also began to construct a series for units authorized by permit for all reporting offices – both urban and rural. The BLS also began to report the number of units and total valuation separately for multifamily structures containing two to four or five or more units; before then, multifamily units were divided into those with two units and those with three or more units. For purposes of this table, the data for units in all multifamily structures were combined.

TABLE Dc531–553   Housing units started and authorized by permit, by metropolitan location, region, and number of units in structure: 1945–1999[1,2]   [Census; privately owned]

Contributed by Kenneth A. Snowden

		Units started									
		Number of units in structure				Metropolitan location		Region			
	Total	One	Two	Three to four	Five or more	Metropolitan	Nonmetropolitan	Northeast	North Central	South	West
	Dc531 [3]	Dc532	Dc533	Dc534	Dc535	Dc536	Dc537	Dc538	Dc539	Dc540	Dc541
Year	Thousand	Thousand	Thousand	Thousand	Thousand	Thousand	Thousand	Thousand	Thousand	Thousand	Thousand
1945	325.0	—	—	—	—	—	—	—	—	—	—
1946	1,015.0	—	—	—	—	—	—	—	—	—	—
1947	1,265.0	—	—	—	—	—	—	—	—	—	—
1948	1,344.0	—	—	—	—	—	—	—	—	—	—
1949	1,430.0	—	—	—	—	—	—	—	—	—	—
1950	1,908.0	—	—	—	—	—	—	—	—	—	—
1951	1,420.0	—	—	—	—	—	—	—	—	—	—
1952	1,446.0	—	—	—	—	—	—	—	—	—	—
1953	1,402.0	—	—	—	—	—	—	—	—	—	—
1954	1,532.0	—	—	—	—	—	—	—	—	—	—
1955	1,627.0	—	—	—	—	—	—	—	—	—	—
1956	1,325.0	—	—	—	—	—	—	—	—	—	—
1957	1,175.0	—	—	—	—	—	—	—	—	—	—
1958	1,314.0	—	—	—	—	—	—	—	—	—	—
1959	1,517.0	1,234.0	55.9	—	227.0	1,054.9	462.1	268.7	367.4	511.4	369.5
1960	1,252.2	994.7	44.0	—	213.5	864.5	387.7	221.4	292.0	429.4	309.4
1961	1,313.0	974.3	43.9	—	294.8	913.6	399.4	246.3	277.7	472.7	316.3
1962	1,462.9	991.4	49.2	—	422.3	1,034.1	428.8	263.8	289.6	531.2	378.3
1963	1,603.2	1,012.4	52.9	—	537.8	1,125.4	477.8	261.0	329.2	586.2	426.8
1964	1,528.8	970.5	53.9	54.5	450.0	1,079.8	449.0	254.5	339.7	577.8	356.9
1965	1,472.8	963.7	50.8	35.8	422.5	1,011.9	460.9	270.2	361.5	574.7	266.3
1966	1,164.9	778.6	34.6	26.5	325.1	787.7	377.1	206.5	288.3	472.5	197.6
1967	1,291.6	843.9	41.4	30.2	376.1	902.9	388.7	214.9	337.1	519.5	220.1
1968	1,507.6	899.4	46.0	34.9	527.3	1,096.4	411.2	226.8	368.6	618.5	293.7
1969	1,466.8	810.6	43.0	42.0	571.2	1,078.7	388.0	206.1	348.7	588.4	323.5
1970	1,433.6	812.9	42.4	42.4	535.9	1,017.9	415.7	217.9	293.5	611.6	310.5
1971	2,052.2	1,151.0	55.1	65.2	780.9	1,501.8	550.4	263.8	434.1	868.7	485.6
1972	2,356.6	1,309.2	67.1	74.2	906.2	1,720.4	636.2	329.5	442.8	1,057.0	527.4
1973	2,045.3	1,132.0	54.2	64.1	795.0	1,495.4	549.9	277.3	439.7	899.4	428.8
1974	1,337.7	888.1	33.2	34.9	381.6	922.5	415.3	183.2	317.3	552.8	284.5
1975	1,160.4	892.2	34.5	29.5	204.3	760.3	400.1	149.2	294.0	442.1	275.1
1976	1,537.5	1,162.4	44.0	41.9	289.2	1,043.5	494.1	169.2	400.1	568.5	399.6
1977	1,987.1	1,450.9	60.7	61.0	414.4	1,377.3	609.8	201.6	464.6	783.1	537.9
1978	2,020.3	1,433.3	62.2	62.8	462.0	1,432.1	588.2	200.3	451.2	823.7	545.2
1979	1,745.1	1,194.1	56.1	65.9	429.0	1,240.6	504.6	177.9	349.2	747.5	470.5
1980	1,292.2	852.2	48.8	60.7	330.5	913.6	378.7	125.4	218.1	642.7	306.0
1981	1,084.2	705.4	38.2	52.9	287.7	759.8	324.3	117.3	165.2	561.6	240.0
1982	1,062.2	662.6	31.9	48.1	319.6	784.8	277.4	116.7	149.1	591.0	205.4
1983	1,703.0	1,067.6	41.8	71.7	522.0	1,351.1	351.9	167.6	217.9	935.2	382.3
1984	1,749.5	1,084.2	38.6	82.8	544.0	1,414.6	334.9	204.1	243.4	866.0	436.0
1985	1,741.8	1,072.4	37.0	56.4	576.1	1,493.9	247.9	251.7	239.7	782.3	468.2
1986	1,805.4	1,179.4	36.1	47.9	542.0	1,546.3	259.1	293.5	295.8	733.1	483.0
1987	1,620.5	1,146.4	27.8	37.5	408.7	1,372.2	248.2	269.0	297.9	633.9	419.8
1988	1,488.1	1,081.3	23.4	35.4	348.0	1,243.0	245.1	235.3	274.0	574.9	403.9
1989	1,376.1	1,003.3	19.9	35.3	317.6	1,128.1	248.0	178.5	265.8	536.2	395.7
1990	1,192.7	894.8	16.1	21.4	260.4	946.9	245.7	131.3	253.2	479.3	328.9
1991	1,013.9	840.4	15.5	20.1	137.9	789.2	224.7	112.9	233.0	414.1	254.0
1992	1,199.7	1,029.9	12.4	18.3	139.0	931.5	268.2	126.7	287.8	496.9	288.3
1993	1,287.6	1,125.7	11.1	18.3	132.6	1,031.9	255.8	126.5	297.7	561.8	301.7
1994	1,457.0	1,198.4	14.8	20.2	223.5	1,183.1	273.9	138.2	328.9	639.1	350.8
1995	1,354.1	1,076.2	14.3	19.4	244.1	1,106.4	247.6	117.7	290.1	615.0	331.3
1996	1,476.8	1,160.9	16.4	28.8	270.8	1,211.4	265.5	132.1	321.5	661.9	361.4
1997	1,474.0	1,133.7	18.1	26.4	295.8	1,221.3	252.7	136.8	303.6	670.3	363.3
1998	1,616.9	1,271.4	15.7	26.9	302.9	1,349.9	267.0	148.5	330.5	743.0	394.9
1999	1,666.5	1,334.9	13.4	18.5	299.7	1,404.5	261.9	153.7	356.4	760.3	396.1

Notes appear at end of table

TABLE Dc531–553   Housing units started and authorized by permit, by metropolitan location, region, and number of units in structure: 1945–1999   [Census; privately owned]   *Continued*

							Authorization of units by building permit					
							Units authorized					
			Number of units in structure				**Metropolitan location**		**Region**			
	Permit-issuing places	Total	One	Two	Three to four	Five or more	Metropolitan	Nonmetropolitan	Northeast	North Central	South	West
	Dc542	Dc543	Dc544	Dc545	Dc546	Dc547	Dc548	Dc549	Dc550	Dc551	Dc552	Dc553
Year	Thousand	Thousand	Thousand	Thousand	Thousand	Thousand	Thousand	Thousand	Thousand	Thousand	Thousand	Thousand
1945	—	—	—	—	—	—	—	—	—	—	—	—
1946	—	—	—	—	—	—	—	—	—	—	—	—
1947	—	—	—	—	—	—	—	—	—	—	—	—
1948	—	—	—	—	—	—	—	—	—	—	—	—
1949	—	—	—	—	—	—	—	—	—	—	—	—
1950	—	—	—	—	—	—	—	—	—	—	—	—
1951	—	—	—	—	—	—	—	—	—	—	—	—
1952	—	—	—	—	—	—	—	—	—	—	—	—
1953	—	—	—	—	—	—	—	—	—	—	—	—
1954	—	—	—	—	—	—	—	—	—	—	—	—
1955	—	—	—	—	—	—	—	—	—	—	—	—
1956	—	—	—	—	—	—	—	—	—	—	—	—
1957	—	—	—	—	—	—	—	—	—	—	—	—
1958	—	—	—	—	—	—	—	—	—	—	—	—
1959	10	1,208.3	938.3	77.1	—	192.9	—	—	222.4	285.8	355.8	344.3
1960	10	998.0	746.1	64.6	—	187.4	—	—	199.0	228.3	283.0	287.7
1961	10	1,064.2	722.8	67.6	—	273.8	—	—	229.4	226.1	299.4	309.4
1962	10	1,186.6	716.2	87.1	—	383.3	—	—	242.5	238.3	342.8	363.0
1963	12	1,334.7	750.2	51.0	67.9	465.6	1,080.8	253.8	239.4	268.8	403.2	423.3
1964	12	1,285.8	720.1	49.1	51.7	464.9	1,034.4	251.4	243.4	286.9	401.4	354.2
1965	12	1,239.8	709.9	47.3	37.5	445.1	992.3	247.5	252.7	310.5	407.5	269.1
1966	12	971.9	563.2	36.3	24.7	347.7	775.2	196.8	209.8	250.9	331.1	180.2
1967	13	1,141.0	650.6	42.5	30.5	417.5	918.0	223.0	222.6	309.8	390.8	217.8
1968	13	1,353.4	694.7	45.1	39.2	574.4	1,104.6	248.8	234.8	350.1	477.3	291.1
1969	13	1,323.7	625.9	44.7	40.5	612.7	1,074.1	249.6	215.8	317.0	470.5	320.4
1970	13	1,351.5	646.8	43.0	45.1	616.7	1,067.6	284.0	218.3	287.4	502.9	342.9
1971	13	1,924.6	906.1	61.8	71.1	885.7	1,597.6	327.0	303.6	421.1	725.4	474.6
1972	14	2,218.9	1,033.1	68.1	80.5	1,037.2	1,798.0	420.9	333.3	440.8	905.4	539.3
1973	14	1,819.5	882.1	53.8	63.2	820.5	1,483.5	336.0	271.9	361.4	763.2	423.1
1974	14	1,074.4	643.8	32.6	31.7	366.2	835.0	239.4	165.4	241.3	390.1	277.6
1975	14	939.2	675.5	34.1	29.8	199.8	704.1	235.1	129.5	241.5	292.7	275.5
1976	14	1,296.2	893.6	47.5	45.6	309.5	1,001.9	294.2	152.4	326.1	401.7	416.0
1977	14	1,690.0	1,126.1	62.1	59.2	442.7	1,326.3	363.7	181.9	402.4	561.1	544.6
1978	16	1,800.5	1,182.6	64.5	66.1	487.3	1,398.6	401.9	194.4	388.0	667.6	550.5
1979	16	1,551.8	981.5	59.5	65.9	444.8	1,210.6	341.2	166.9	289.1	628.0	467.7
1980	16	1,190.6	710.4	53.8	60.7	365.7	911.0	279.6	117.9	192.0	561.9	318.9
1981	16	985.5	564.3	44.6	57.2	319.4	765.2	220.4	109.8	133.3	491.1	251.3
1982	16	1,000.5	546.4	38.4	49.9	365.8	812.6	187.9	106.7	126.3	543.5	224.1
1983	16	1,605.2	901.5	57.5	76.1	570.1	1,359.7	245.5	164.1	187.8	862.9	390.4
1984	17	1,681.8	922.4	61.9	80.7	616.8	1,456.2	225.7	200.8	211.7	812.1	457.3
1985	17	1,733.3	956.6	54.0	66.1	656.6	1,507.6	225.6	259.7	237.0	752.6	483.9
1986	17	1,769.4	1,077.6	50.4	58.0	583.5	1,551.3	218.1	283.3	290.0	686.5	509.7
1987	17	1,534.8	1,024.4	40.8	48.5	421.1	1,319.5	215.2	271.8	282.3	574.7	406.0
1988	17	1,455.6	993.8	35.0	40.7	386.1	1,239.7	215.9	230.2	266.3	543.5	415.6
1989	17	1,338.4	931.7	31.7	35.3	339.8	1,127.6	210.8	179.0	252.1	505.3	402.1
1990	17	1,110.8	793.9	26.7	27.6	262.6	910.9	199.9	125.8	233.8	426.2	324.9
1991	17	948.8	753.5	22.0	21.1	152.1	766.8	182.0	109.8	215.4	375.7	247.9
1992	17	1,094.9	910.7	23.3	22.5	138.4	888.5	206.5	124.8	259.0	442.5	268.6
1993	17	1,199.1	986.5	26.7	25.6	160.2	1,009.0	190.1	133.5	276.6	500.7	288.2
1994	19	1,371.6	1,068.5	31.4	30.8	241.0	1,144.1	227.5	138.5	305.2	585.5	342.4
1995	19	1,332.5	997.3	32.2	31.5	271.5	1,116.8	215.8	124.2	296.6	583.2	328.5
1996	19	1,425.6	1,069.5	33.6	32.2	290.3	1,200.0	225.6	136.9	317.8	623.4	347.4
1997	19	1,441.1	1,062.4	34.9	33.6	310.3	1,220.2	220.9	141.9	299.8	635.9	363.5
1998	19	1,612.3	1,187.6	33.2	36.0	355.5	1,377.9	234.4	159.4	327.2	724.5	401.2
1999	19	1,663.5	1,246.7	32.5	33.3	351.1	1,427.4	236.1	164.9	345.4	748.9	404.3

[1] Beginning in 1992, estimates of housing starts include units in structures being totally rebuilt on existing foundations.

[2] Through 1963 (for starts) and 1962 (for authorizations), figures for three- and four-unit structures are included with the figures for structures of five units or more.

[3] Through 1958, figures are the 1964 Bureau of Census revisions of the original Bureau of Labor Statistics total starts series shown in series Dc510; see text.

Sources

1945–1958: U.S. Bureau of the Census, *Housing Starts*, C20-60 (June 1964). 1959–1998: downloaded from the Internet site of the Census Bureau. 1999: U.S. Bureau of the Census, *Housing Starts*, C20-00/5 (May 2000).

(continued)

TABLE Dc531–553   Housing units started and authorized by permit, by metropolitan location, region, and number of units in structure: 1945–1999   [Census; privately owned]   *Continued*

Documentation

This table presents estimates of housing starts and housing units authorized by building permits that are compiled and reported by the U.S. Bureau of the Census. These are among the most closely watched of all aggregate economic time series because of the importance of residential housing construction to the national economy, and the sensitivity of the sector to changes in interest rates, income, and employment. Series for both housing units authorized by permit (before construction has begun) and units actually started are shown. These differ primarily because of time lags in starting a project after it has been authorized and because some projects are never started after a permit is received. A housing start, according to the Census Bureau, occurs only when excavation begins for the structure's footings or foundation. All units in a multifamily building are considered to be started when excavation for the building has begun.

Responsibility for compiling estimates of housing starts and housing units authorized by permit was shifted from the U.S. Bureau of Labor Statistics (BLS) to the Census Bureau in 1959. The Census Bureau adopted the basic approach and methodology that the BLS had employed (see the text for Table Dc510–530), but it immediately revised and improved the BLS methods along several lines: (1) privately owned farm as well as nonfarm housing units were included in the series; (2) the number of permit-issuing places surveyed was increased from 6,600 to 10,000; (3) continuous, regular monthly surveys were instituted to estimate lags and lapses between permit issue and actual housing starts; and (4) improvements were made in the surveys used to estimate housing starts in areas that did not issue building permits. Between 1959 and 1999, the number of permit-issuing places surveyed has gradually increased, as shown in series Dc542. Otherwise, there have been only relatively modest changes in methods and definitions, and there are no significant "breaks" in these series.

The combined impact of the 1959 changes created a break with the housing start series produced by the BLS for earlier years, and so in 1964 the Census Bureau derived revised estimates of total nonfarm housing starts for the 1945–1958 period that were consistent with the new post-1958 Census Bureau estimates. Complete details of the revision appear in the C20-60 report cited above. In brief, the revisions were formed by using the 1950 and 1960 Censuses of Housing, the 1956 National Housing Inventory, and the 1959 Survey of Components of Change in Housing to estimate the total number of additions to the housing stock between 1945 and 1950, 1950 and 1956, and 1957 and 1958. These were adjusted for definitional differences between sources and then allocated by individual years to reflect the same year-to-year movements as the unrevised BLS estimates. The Census Bureau determined that high-quality data were not available to revise the BLS estimates before 1945, or to revise detailed components of the total housing starts series (by units in structure, metropolitan status, and region). In the description of the revisions, however, the Census Bureau noted that most, and perhaps nearly all, of the upward revisions were applicable to single-family housing starts with little change in starts for structures with three or more units. Revised monthly estimates for the 1945–1958 period can be found in U.S. Bureau of the Census, *Housing Starts, 1959 to 1971* (December 1972), pp. 68–9.

The estimates of building permits and housing starts beginning in 1959 are the product of two closely related surveys of residential building activity that are conducted by the Census Bureau. The Building Permits Survey currently collects information from 19,000 jurisdictions on the number of building permits issued that authorize the construction of housing units, and the number and value of the units authorized in each permit. These data are collected monthly for a sample of about 8,500 jurisdictions to produce estimates that are widely used as a leading economic indicator. The annual data shown in this table are formed by surveying all remaining jurisdictions once each year and then adding the total permit activity in these areas to annual totals of the monthly activities in the sample jurisdictions. In the mid-1960s it was estimated that more than 85 percent of all housing construction took place in the permit-issuing jurisdictions surveyed by the Census Bureau, while fully 97 percent of home construction takes place within the 19,000 places that have been surveyed since the mid-1990s. Building Permit Survey data are not confidential, and the Census Bureau will produce detailed tables for specific jurisdictions on request and for a fee.

The results of the Building Permits Survey are relied on heavily in the Survey of Construction (SOC), which is conducted by the Bureau of the Census to gather information on housing starts, completions, and sales. The SOC comprises two different surveys – the Survey of Use of Permit (SUP), which collects information from the builders on a selection of building permits drawn from the Building Permits Survey, and the Nonpermit Survey, which collects information from a sample of active residential builders who are identified by field representatives in non-permit-issuing jurisdictions. Both surveys are conducted within the Primary Sampling Units, which are currently employed in the Current Population Survey. For purposes of compiling housing start estimates, information is collected on a monthly basis from each builder in the two samples until the project has been started or is designated as abandoned. (Projects actually remain in the SOC survey until completed and sold; see the text for Table Dc566–584. Annual data on completions and sales are shown in Tables Dc566–607.)

The housing start estimates are compiled for permit-issuing places by calculating start ratios from the SUP sample data – the ratio of the number of units started to the number of units covered by permits. Separate ratios are calculated for each month in which permits were issued (the current month and each preceding month in the sample) and for each type of structure. To derive estimates of housing starts, these ratios are then applied to the number of units authorized by permit for the monthly sample of 8,500 permit-issuing places and all 19,000 permit-issuing places on an annual basis. Adjustments are then made to account for single-family units started without authorization in permit-issuing areas (assumed to be an additional 3.3 percent) and for all units started prior to authorization or for which monthly SOC reports are late. These estimates are reported for total housing starts, series Dc531, as well as by type of structure, for areas inside and outside Metropolitan Statistical Areas, and by region, as currently defined by the Bureau of the Census (see Table Ap-G in Appendix 2 regarding the composition of census regions and divisions). The components of each of these three decompositions sum to equal series Dc531. Seasonally adjusted and unadjusted housing starts are reported each month, and the annual starts equal the sum of the unadjusted monthly series.

A housing unit is a single room or group of rooms intended for occupancy as separate living quarters by a family, a person living alone, or a group of unrelated persons living together. Separate living quarters are those that have direct access from the outside of a building or through a common hall that is used by occupants of another unit. Only new housekeeping units are measured, so group quarters (such as dormitories and rooming houses), transient accommodations (such as transient hotels and motels), and units in relocated or converted structures are excluded. Housing units may be "stick-built," prefabricated, panelized, sectional, or modular, but mobile homes are excluded (see Table Dc637–652 for data on "manufactured homes"). Publicly owned housing units are excluded from the housing starts and building permit series, but units built by private developers with subsidies or those that are for sale upon completion to a local public housing authority under the Department of Housing and Urban Development's turnkey program are included.

See the text for Table Dc272–281 for information on the use of these data in the compilation of the Census Bureau's value-in-place estimates for residential construction.

For additional documentation, see "Housing Starts," C20-11 (May 1960); and "Housing Starts, 1959 to 1971" C20 supplement (December 1972). For an excellent overview of all Census Bureau construction statistics programs, see Bureau of the Census, *Construction Statistics Data Users' Conference*, October 28, 1997, MCD/99 CSDUC (March 1999).

Series Dc532–535 and Dc544–547. The one-unit structure category includes units built in fully detached and semidetached side-by-side structures, so long as each unit is separated from adjacent units by a ground-to-roof wall and the units do not share heating or air-conditioning systems, or water, sewage, and electrical lines. All other side-by-side units and units built one upon the other are classified according to the number of units in the structure. Apartment buildings are defined as structures containing five or more units.

TABLE Dc554-565   Housing units started, by metropolitan location, region, and number of units in structure: 1935-1977   [Publicly owned]

Contributed by Kenneth A. Snowden

	Total	Number of units in structure			Urban–rural location		Metropolitan location		Region			
		One	Two	Three or more	Urban	Rural	Metropolitan	Nonmetropolitan	Northeast	North Central	South	West
	Dc554	Dc555	Dc556	Dc557	Dc558	Dc559	Dc560	Dc561	Dc562	Dc563	Dc564	Dc565
Year	Thousand	Thousand	Thousand	Thousand	Thousand	Thousand	Thousand	Thousand	Thousand	Thousand	Thousand	Thousand
1935	5.3	0.8	0.3	4.2	4.4	0.9	—	—	—	—	—	—
1936	14.8	5.5	0.7	8.6	13.4	1.4	—	—	—	—	—	—
1937	3.6	1.2	0.7	1.7	3.6	0.0	—	—	—	—	—	—
1938	6.7	0.6	0.0	6.1	6.7	0.0	—	—	—	—	—	—
1939	56.6	26.0	9.3	21.3	55.5	1.1	—	—	—	—	—	—
1940	73.0	38.1	11.7	23.2	63.4	9.6	—	—	—	—	—	—
1941	86.6	70.3	5.9	10.4	64.8	21.8	—	—	—	—	—	—
1942	54.8	40.5	2.6	11.7	42.5	12.3	—	—	—	—	—	—
1943	7.3	7.3	(Z)	(Z)	4.7	2.6	—	—	—	—	—	—
1944	3.1	3.1	(Z)	(Z)	3.0	0.1	—	—	—	—	—	—
1945	1.2	(Z)	0.0	1.2	1.2	0.0	—	—	—	—	—	—
1946	8.0	(Z)	0.0	8.0	8.0	0.0	—	—	—	—	—	—
1947	3.4	(Z)	0.0	3.4	3.4	0.0	—	—	—	—	—	—
1948	18.1	3.4	0.6	14.1	14.9	3.2	—	—	12.8	2.4	1.1	1.7
1949	36.3	1.9	1.8	32.6	32.2	4.1	—	—	30.6	1.6	2.3	1.6
1950	43.6	3.4	2.5	37.9	42.2	1.6	34.5	9.2	25.3	4.2	11.7	2.5
1951	71.2	7.8	0.0	63.4	64.0	7.2	53.7	17.5	25.5	4.6	36.2	4.9
1952	58.5	3.4	0.0	55.1	55.0	3.5	44.3	14.2	21.6	8.4	23.2	5.3
1953	35.5	5.0	0.0	30.5	31.8	3.7	26.6	8.9	13.2	5.1	13.6	3.6
1954	18.6	0.6	0.0	18.1	—	—	17.5	1.2	9.3	4.2	2.9	2.2
1955	19.6	4.5	0.0	15.0	—	—	15.8	3.7	9.6	4.1	3.7	2.0
1956	24.2	9.1	0.0	15.1	—	—	13.3	10.9	9.3	5.8	6.8	2.3
1957	49.1	32.4	0.2	16.5	—	—	22.3	26.8	11.8	6.1	25.5	5.7
1958	67.9	42.5	0.1	25.3	—	—	38.0	29.9	18.7	13.8	22.9	12.5
1959	36.7	16.6	2.9	17.2	—	—	22.1	14.6	11.3	7.3	9.9	8.2
1960	43.9	14.0	6.5	23.4	—	—	24.6	19.3	15.1	11.7	11.9	5.2
1961	52.0	14.5	6.2	31.3	—	—	34.1	17.9	18.6	11.6	14.6	7.2
1962	29.7	4.7	6.9	18.1	—	—	19.7	10.0	10.0	5.4	9.9	4.3
1963	31.8	0.9	7.7	23.2	—	—	22.4	9.3	10.5	6.6	9.6	5.0
1964	33.3	1.5	8.5	23.3	—	—	19.1	14.1	8.2	7.1	12.4	5.5
1965	36.9	1.2	7.5	28.3	—	—	23.2	13.7	11.1	7.1	13.9	4.9
1966	30.9	0.9	6.1	24.0	—	—	20.6	10.3	9.2	8.9	10.4	2.5
1967	30.3	1.1	6.4	22.9	—	—	17.4	12.9	8.6	6.8	11.9	2.9
1968	37.8	1.0	7.5	29.3	—	—	19.8	18.0	9.6	8.4	15.2	4.6
1969	32.8	0.6	5.3	26.9	—	—	17.7	15.1	6.9	7.8	14.4	3.6
1970	35.4	2.2	5.6	27.5	—	—	16.5	18.9	6.2	7.9	17.3	4.0
1971	32.3	1.9	8.5	22.0	—	—	16.7	15.7	7.2	5.8	15.1	4.3
1972	21.9	1.5	5.3	15.2	—	—	12.2	9.6	4.7	2.5	10.6	4.1
1973	12.2	1.1	3.5	7.6	—	—	6.3	5.9	1.1	2.4	6.3	2.4
1974	14.8	1.1	5.6	8.0	—	—	9.7	5.1	0.2	2.5	8.0	3.9
1975	10.9	3.3	1.6	6.1	—	—	6.4	4.5	0.6	1.4	6.2	2.7
1976	10.1	4.0	0.9	5.2	—	—	4.8	5.3	0.3	0.6	6.3	2.8
1977	2.7	1.2	0.2	1.2	—	—	0.6	2.1	0.1	0.4	1.4	0.8

(Z) Fewer than 50.

Sources

1935–1963: U.S. Bureau of the Census, *Housing Construction Statistics: 1889–1964* (1966), Table A-3. For series Dc558–559, 1950–1953 figures are from U.S. Bureau of Labor Statistics, "Nonfarm Housing Starts, 1889 to 1958," Bulletin number 1260 (1959), Table 7.

1964–1977: U.S. Bureau of the Census, *Housing Starts*, C20-78-7 (July 1978), Table 4.

Documentation

A breakdown into federally versus state- and locally owned units is reported by program for the years 1949-1964 in *Housing Construction Statistics: 1889–1964*, Table A-5. Similar detailed data appear for the 1964–1970 period in U.S. Census Bureau, *Historical Statistics of the United States* (1975), series N172-179. For documentation and monthly data beginning in 1959, see U.S. Bureau of the Census, *Housing Starts: 1959–1971*, C-20 supplement (December 1972), and subsequent C-20 reports.

These series represent actual counts of publicly owned housing starts as reported by the U.S. Public Housing Administration, the U.S. Defense Department, the New York City Housing Authority, and other state and local housing authorities before 1965 and the U.S. Department of Housing and Urban Development (HUD) thereafter. Publicly owned housing starts were not counted separately until 1935, but before this the volume of permanent, publicly owned housing units was considered to be insignificant. Housing provided under the federal emergency programs, including those during and for World War II, consisted largely of units in temporary or converted structures and, therefore, were not included in the permanent units shown here.

To be counted as publicly owned, a housing unit had to be located within a nonfarm residential structure that was owned by a public agency during and after the construction period. Not counted are units in structures built by private developers that after completion were intended to be, or actually were, sold to a public agency (for example, under HUD's turnkey program). Moreover, housing started under various federal, state, and local government insurance programs was not considered publicly owned housing.

(continued)

TABLE Dc554–565   Housing units started, by metropolitan location, region, and number of units in structure: 1935–1977   [Publicly owned]   *Continued*

Publicly owned housing starts were reported in the Census Bureau's regular monthly C-20 report until July 1978, when these series were discontinued without comment. The discontinuation may well have been connected to the change in the method of compiling the public building components of the value-in-place program that was adopted in 1975. For a description of those changes, see the text for Table Dc442–459. No similar compilation for years after 1977 has been located.

See Table Ab-G in Appendix 2 regarding the composition of census regions and divisions.

TABLE Dc566–584   Housing units started, by construction status, purpose, and number of units in structure: 1964–1999[1]   [Privately owned]

Contributed by Kenneth A. Snowden

	Units started								
		Number of units in structure							
		One					Two or more		
			Built for owner occupancy						
	Total	Total	Built for sale	Contractor-built	Owner-built	Built for rent	Total	Built for sale	Built for rent
	Dc566	Dc567	Dc568	Dc569	Dc570	Dc571	Dc572	Dc573	Dc574
Year	Thousand	Thousand	Thousand	Thousand	Thousand	Thousand	Thousand	Thousand	Thousand
1964	1,529	970	571	185	190	24	558	—	—
1965	1,473	964	596	181	171	16	509	—	—
1966	1,165	779	445	176	144	13	386	—	—
1967	1,292	844	509	170	150	15	448	—	—
1968	1,508	899	544	181	160	14	608	—	—
1969	1,467	811	489	172	137	12	656	—	—
1970	1,434	813	502	168	134	9	621	—	—
1971	2,052	1,151	749	226	162	14	901	—	—
1972	2,037	1,309	859	256	180	14	1,047	—	—
1973	2,045	1,132	693	245	183	11	913	—	—
1974	1,338	888	501	205	174	8	450	131	319
1975	1,160	892	531	190	164	7	268	45	223
1976	1,538	1,162	705	240	209	8	375	63	312
1977	1,987	1,451	904	298	240	9	536	90	446
1978	2,020	1,433	901	287	231	14	587	131	456
1979	1,745	1,194	742	213	222	17	551	173	378
1980	1,292	852	526	149	164	12	440	163	277
1981	1,084	705	426	122	148	10	379	158	221
1982	1,062	663	409	108	133	12	400	140	259
1983	1,703	1,068	713	151	179	24	635	210	425
1984	1,750	1,084	728	157	165	33	665	206	459
1985	1,742	1,072	713	177	157	26	669	154	515
1986	1,805	1,179	782	204	166	27	626	143	483
1987	1,620	1,146	732	208	178	28	474	130	344
1988	1,488	1,081	709	196	154	22	407	99	307
1989	1,376	1,003	648	192	144	19	373	87	286
1990	1,193	895	529	196	147	22	298	56	241
1991	1,014	840	490	198	138	14	174	41	132
1992	1,200	1,030	618	224	168	19	170	41	128
1993	1,288	1,126	716	225	162	22	162	44	118
1994	1,457	1,198	763	245	169	22	259	52	206
1995	1,354	1,076	712	199	133	33	278	51	227
1996	1,477	1,161	774	218	144	25	316	59	257
1997	1,474	1,134	784	189	131	29	341	59	282
1998	1,617	1,271	882	209	144	36	346	59	287
1999	1,665	1,333	938	213	143	40	331	64	267

Notes appear at end of table

TABLE Dc566–584 Housing units started, by construction status, purpose, and number of units in structure: 1964–1999 [Privately owned] *Continued*

	Units under construction					Units completed				
	Total	Number of units in structure				Total	Number of units in structure			
		One	Two	Three or four	Five or more		One	Two	Three or four	Five or more
	Dc575	Dc576	Dc577 [2]	Dc578 [2]	Dc579	Dc580	Dc581	Dc582	Dc583	Dc584
Year	Thousand	Thousand	Thousand	Thousand	Thousand	Thousand	Thousand	Thousand	Thousand	Thousand
1964	—	—	—	—	—	—	—	—	—	—
1965	—	—	—	—	—	—	—	—	—	—
1966	—	—	—	—	—	—	—	—	—	—
1967	—	—	—	—	—	—	—	—	—	—
1968	—	—	—	—	—	1,319.8	858.6	44.2	33.4	383.6
1969	884.8	349.6	49.2	—	486.0	1,399.0	807.5	44.0	35.4	512.1
1970	922.0	381.1	50.1	—	490.8	1,418.4	801.8	42.9	42.2	531.5
1971	1,254.0	504.9	64.5	—	684.6	1,706.1	1,014.0	50.9	55.2	586.1
1972	1,542.1	612.5	36.4	46.4	846.8	2,003.9	1,160.2	54.0	64.9	724.7
1973	1,454.4	521.7	31.0	48.0	853.6	2,100.5	1,197.2	59.9	63.6	779.8
1974	1,000.8	441.1	19.4	29.1	511.3	1,728.5	940.3	43.5	51.8	692.9
1975	794.3	447.5	20.1	27.4	299.4	1,317.2	874.8	31.5	29.1	381.8
1976	922.0	562.6	22.7	31.8	304.9	1,377.2	1,034.2	40.8	36.5	265.8
1977	1,208.0	729.8	34.0	44.9	399.3	1,657.1	1,258.4	48.9	46.1	303.7
1978	1,310.2	764.5	36.1	47.3	462.2	1,867.5	1,369.0	59.0	57.2	382.2
1979	1,140.1	638.7	31.3	46.7	423.4	1,870.8	1,301.0	60.5	64.4	444.9
1980	896.1	514.5	28.3	40.3	313.1	1,501.6	956.7	51.4	67.2	426.3
1981	682.4	381.7	16.5	29.0	255.3	1,265.7	818.5	49.2	62.4	335.7
1982	720.0	399.7	16.5	24.9	278.9	1,005.5	631.5	29.8	51.1	293.1
1983	1,002.8	523.9	19.0	39.1	420.8	1,390.3	923.7	37.0	55.2	374.4
1984	1,050.5	556.0	20.9	42.5	431.0	1,652.2	1,025.1	35.0	77.3	514.8
1985	1,062.5	538.6	20.6	34.9	468.4	1,703.3	1,072.5	36.4	60.7	533.6
1986	1,073.5	583.1	19.3	28.4	442.7	1,756.4	1,120.2	35.0	51.0	550.1
1987	987.3	590.6	17.3	22.5	356.9	1,668.8	1,122.8	29.0	42.4	474.6
1988	919.4	569.6	16.1	24.1	309.5	1,529.8	1,084.6	23.5	33.2	388.6
1989	850.3	535.1	11.9	25.1	278.1	1,422.8	1,026.3	24.1	34.6	337.9
1990	711.4	449.1	10.9	15.1	236.3	1,308.0	966.0	16.5	28.2	297.3
1991	606.3	433.5	9.1	14.5	149.2	1,090.8	837.6	16.9	19.7	216.6
1992	612.4	472.7	5.6	11.3	122.8	1,157.5	963.6	15.1	20.8	158.0
1993	680.1	543.0	6.5	12.4	118.2	1,192.7	1,039.4	9.5	16.7	127.1
1994	762.2	557.8	9.1	12.9	182.5	1,346.9	1,160.3	12.1	19.5	154.9
1995	775.9	547.2	8.4	12.7	207.7	1,312.6	1,065.5	14.8	19.8	212.4
1996	792.3	550.0	9.0	19.1	214.3	1,412.9	1,128.5	13.6	19.5	251.3
1997	846.7	554.6	11.2	20.7	260.2	1,400.5	1,116.4	13.6	23.4	247.1
1998	970.8	659.1	8.3	20.5	282.9	1,474.2	1,159.7	16.2	24.4	273.9
1999	992.6	679.0	8.2	13.8	291.6	1,636.1	1,037.2	12.0	25.2	291.8

[1] Housing units for which the purpose of construction was not reported have been distributed in the same proportion as those for which the information was reported.

[2] Through 1971, units in three- and four-unit structures that are reported with units in two-unit structures.

Sources

Series Dc566–574. U.S. Bureau of the Census, *Housing Starts*, C-20 report.

Series Dc575–584. U.S. Bureau of the Census, *Housing Completions*, C-22 report. Data were downloaded on August 8, 2000, from the Internet site of the Census Bureau.

Documentation

As explained in the text for Table Dc531–553, the Census Bureau conducts the Survey of Construction (SOC) on a sample of recently authorized building permits each month. The primary function of the SOC is to derive ratios of permits to starts for a nationally representative sample of residential building projects, which can be used to derive official housing start estimates. Once a project has been selected for inclusion in the SOC, however, the Census Bureau's surveys collect information not only about a project's start date, but also about the building's structural characteristics; whether the unit was built to be sold, to be occupied by its current owner, or to be rented; the status of the project until it is completed; and, if the project is a single-family home, its market status until it is sold. The data in this table represent national estimates of the number of housing units that have been started, the number of those started that were still under construction, and the number of those started that had been completed. Because all of these estimated series are based on the SOC sample, users of these data should refer to the source publications for details of the procedures used to derive these estimates and an assessment of the sampling and nonsampling errors that affect them. The sources also contain information about the standard errors and confidence intervals that are associated with these estimates.

A unit built in a one-unit structure is counted as started when excavation has begun for the footings and foundations; all units in a multifamily residential structure are counted as started as soon as excavation for its footings and foundations is underway. A one-unit structure is counted as completed when all finished flooring has been installed or, if earlier, at the time of occupancy. In buildings with two or more units, all units are counted as completed when 50 percent or more of the units are occupied or are available for occupancy. A housing unit is under construction between its start and completion dates. For more complete definitions of structures by number of units, see the text for Table Dc531–553.

Greater detail and regional data by purpose of construction are reported annually in the February issue of the C-20 report.

TABLE Dc585–607   Single-family houses for sale and sold – number, prices, and time on market, by construction status and region: 1963–1999[1]

Contributed by Kenneth A. Snowden

	Houses for sale at end of year					Houses sold during year					Sales price	
		Construction status					Construction status					
	Total	Completed	Under construction	Not yet started	Median months on sales market	Total	Completed	Under construction	Not started	Median months on sales market	Median	Average
	Dc585	Dc586	Dc587	Dc588	Dc589	Dc590	Dc591	Dc592	Dc593	Dc594	Dc595	Dc596
Year	Thousand	Thousand	Thousand	Thousand	Number	Thousand	Thousand	Thousand	Thousand	Number	Dollars	Dollars
1963	265	—	—	—	4.4	560	258	186	116	3.4	18,000	19,300
1964	250	—	—	—	5.3	565	255	190	120	3.7	18,900	20,500
1965	228	—	—	—	4.5	575	247	194	134	3.7	20,000	21,500
1966	196	—	—	—	6.1	461	198	160	103	3.8	21,400	23,300
1967	190	—	—	—	3.8	487	200	174	113	3.1	22,700	24,600
1968	218	—	—	—	4.0	490	196	194	100	3.3	24,700	26,600
1969	228	—	—	—	5.0	448	198	176	74	4.0	25,600	27,900
1970	227	—	—	—	4.2	485	195	198	92	3.3	23,400	26,600
1971	294	—	—	—	3.4	656	232	302	123	2.7	25,200	28,300
1972	416	—	—	—	4.4	718	252	348	119	3.1	27,600	30,500
1973	422	80	239	104	5.4	634	288	255	90	4.5	32,500	35,500
1974	350	101	190	59	6.6	519	265	194	60	5.2	35,900	38,900
1975	316	87	178	50	5.0	549	253	212	84	4.4	39,300	42,600
1976	358	87	215	56	4.3	646	254	276	116	3.6	44,200	48,000
1977	408	87	256	65	4.0	819	271	366	183	3.5	48,800	54,200
1978	419	99	258	62	4.6	817	273	367	177	4.0	55,700	62,500
1979	402	117	227	59	5.6	709	264	306	139	4.7	62,900	71,800
1980	342	107	182	53	5.5	545	238	199	109	5.5	64,600	76,400
1981	278	105	126	48	8.3	436	192	160	84	5.1	68,900	83,000
1982	255	81	125	49	6.8	412	150	154	107	3.9	69,300	83,900
1983	304	85	170	49	4.5	623	191	261	171	2.9	75,300	89,800
1984	358	111	197	49	5.2	639	200	273	166	3.4	79,900	97,600
1985	350	116	177	58	5.5	688	229	276	183	3.9	84,300	100,800
1986	361	103	194	64	5.2	750	220	312	218	3.6	92,000	111,900
1987	370	100	212	57	5.4	671	201	289	182	3.9	104,500	127,200
1988	371	111	204	57	5.9	676	213	286	177	4.0	112,500	138,300
1989	366	109	188	69	6.5	650	215	263	172	4.3	120,000	148,800
1990	321	119	145	57	7.8	534	193	199	142	4.5	122,900	149,800
1991	284	104	130	51	6.8	509	184	172	154	4.4	120,000	147,200
1992	267	86	135	46	5.2	610	196	211	202	3.5	121,500	144,100
1993	295	83	166	47	4.4	666	198	225	243	3.6	126,500	147,700
1994	340	108	189	42	4.9	670	220	230	220	3.8	130,000	154,500
1995	374	123	199	52	5.3	667	238	223	205	4.3	133,900	158,700
1996	326	101	185	40	4.8	757	275	254	228	4.2	140,000	166,400
1997	287	92	161	34	4.9	804	236	295	273	3.7	146,000	176,200
1998	300	72	185	43	4.0	886	228	334	324	3.5	152,500	181,900
1999	326	84	201	42	4.2	907	215	367	325	3.3	160,000	195,800

Note appears at end of table

TABLE Dc585–607   Single-family houses for sale and sold – number, prices, and time on market, by construction status and region: 1963–1999   *Continued*

	Sales price			Houses sold during year — By region							
	Estimated according to house characteristics			Number sold				Median sales price			
	1977 characteristics	1992 characteristics	Price index	Northeast	North Central	South	West	Northeast	North Central	South	West
	Dc597	Dc598	Dc599	Dc600	Dc601	Dc602	Dc603	Dc604	Dc605	Dc606	Dc607
Year	Dollars	Dollars	Thousand chained 1992 dollars	Thousand	Thousand	Thousand	Thousand	Dollars	Dollars	Dollars	Dollars
1963	23,400	—	—	87	134	199	141	20,300	17,900	16,100	18,800
1964	23,600	—	—	90	146	200	129	20,300	19,400	16,700	20,400
1965	24,000	—	—	94	142	210	129	21,500	23,600	17,500	21,600
1966	25,100	—	—	84	113	166	99	23,500	23,200	18,200	23,200
1967	25,800	—	—	77	112	179	119	25,400	25,100	19,400	24,100
1968	27,100	—	—	73	119	177	121	27,700	27,400	21,500	25,100
1969	29,200	—	—	62	97	175	114	31,600	27,600	22,800	25,300
1970	30,000	—	—	61	100	203	121	30,300	24,400	20,300	24,000
1971	31,600	—	—	82	127	270	176	30,600	27,200	22,500	25,500
1972	33,600	—	—	96	130	305	187	31,400	29,300	25,800	27,500
1973	36,600	—	—	95	120	257	161	37,100	23,900	30,900	32,400
1974	40,000	—	—	69	103	207	139	40,100	36,100	34,500	35,800
1975	44,300	—	—	71	106	222	150	44,000	39,600	37,300	40,600
1976	48,100	—	—	72	128	247	199	47,300	44,800	40,500	47,200
1977	54,200	67,400	—	86	162	317	255	51,600	51,500	44,100	53,500
1978	62,100	77,400	—	78	145	331	262	58,100	59,200	50,300	61,300
1979	70,900	89,100	59.5	67	112	304	225	65,500	63,900	57,300	69,600
1980	78,700	98,100	65.4	50	81	267	145	69,500	63,400	59,600	72,300
1981	85,900	105,900	70.3	46	60	219	112	76,000	65,900	64,400	77,800
1982	87,600	108,400	73.2	47	48	219	99	78,200	68,900	66,100	75,000
1983	89,700	110,700	75.3	76	71	323	152	82,200	79,500	70,900	80,100
1984	93,300	115,100	78.1	94	76	309	160	88,600	85,400	72,000	87,300
1985	97,100	116,600	80.1	112	82	323	171	103,300	80,300	75,000	92,600
1986	—	121,200	83.8	136	96	322	196	125,000	88,300	80,200	95,700
1987	—	127,700	88.7	117	97	271	186	140,000	95,000	88,000	111,000
1988	—	132,400	92.1	101	97	276	202	149,000	101,600	92,000	126,500
1989	—	137,800	95.8	86	102	260	202	159,600	108,800	96,400	139,000
1990	—	140,400	97.4	71	89	225	149	159,000	107,900	99,000	147,500
1991	—	142,200	98.6	57	93	215	144	155,900	110,000	100,000	141,100
1992	—	144,100	100.0	65	116	259	170	169,000	115,600	105,500	130,400
1993	—	150,300	104.5	60	123	295	188	162,600	125,000	115,000	135,000
1994	—	157,500	109.6	61	123	295	191	169,000	132,900	116,900	140,400
1995	—	161,900	112.5	55	125	300	187	180,000	134,000	124,500	141,000
1996	—	165,100	114.9	74	137	337	209	186,000	138,000	126,200	153,900
1997	—	170,600	118.2	78	140	363	223	190,000	149,900	129,600	160,000
1998	—	175,000	121.0	81	164	398	243	200,000	157,500	135,800	163,500
1999	—	184,000	127.1	75	173	408	249	210,000	164,000	145,200	174,000

[1] Houses for which sales prices were not reported are distributed in the same proportion as those for which sales prices were reported.

Sources

Series Dc585–588, Dc590–593, and Dc600–603. U.S. Bureau of the Census, Current Construction Reports, *New One-Family Houses Sold* (published monthly) and *Characteristics of New Housing* (published annually), C25, as follows: 1963–1970, C25-71-6 (June 1971); 1974–1984, C25-85-3 (March 1985); 1985–1988, C25/96-1 (December 1995/January 1996); and 1989–1999, C25/00-3 (March 2000).

Series Dc589, Dc594–596, Dc599, and Dc604–607. Downloaded on August 8, 2000, from the Internet site of the Bureau of the Census.

Series Dc597. U.S. Bureau of the Census, Current Construction Reports, *New One-Family Houses Sold*, C25-85-3 (1985).

Series Dc598. U.S. Bureau of the Census, Current Construction Reports, *Characteristics of New Housing*, C25/99-A (1999).

Documentation

Once selected for the U.S. Census Bureau's Survey of Construction (SOC), a privately owned, one-family house that is built for sale remains in the SOC sample until it is sold (see the text for Table Dc531–553 for a description of the SOC). Information is collected each month to determine if each sample home remains for sale, and, if not, the price at which the home finally sold. This table presents estimates of the number of new single-family housing units for sale at the end of each year, the number sold during the year, and the average and median prices at which these homes sold. All of these estimates are subject to sampling error, and the sources should be consulted for a description of the methodology, the standard errors, and the confidence intervals associated with them. The estimates shown here are primarily drawn from monthly C25 reports, *Characteristics of New Housing*. The annual publication in this series provides additional and extensive detail about the physical characteristics of one-family houses that have been completed and sold during the year.

(continued)

TABLE Dc585–607   Single-family houses for sale and sold – number, prices, and time on market, by construction status and region: 1963–1999   *Continued*

In the SOC a one-family house must be either detached or, if attached, separated from other houses by a ground to roof wall (such as in a townhouse). Such houses are considered to be for sale: (1) if they have been authorized by permit (or have been started in areas where permits are not required); (2) if a sales contract has not been signed or a deposit has not been taken; and (3) if a sales price has been set that includes both the house and the land on which it has been built. The house is considered sold when a contract has been signed or a down payment accepted, regardless of the stage of construction. The units in both the for sale and sold categories are also classified into one of three stages of construction – completed, under construction, or not yet started.

Series Dc589 and Dc594. Median months on the sales market is defined as the period between the month in which the home was started and the current month if it has not yet been sold, or, if it has been sold, between the month of start and sale.

Series Dc595–596 and Dc604–607. The median sale price of a new home represents the midpoint of all sales prices (50 percent above, 50 percent below), whereas the average sale price is simply the arithmetic average of all sales prices. The distribution of home sales prices is generally not symmetric – it is positively skewed with a longer "tail" of high-priced homes than low-priced homes. In this case, the median sales price will be lower than the average (or mean) sales price, and it is generally thought to be a better overall measure of housing prices. In keeping with this practice, the median

sales prices for the United States and its regions are shown in this table, but the average sales price for the United States is also shown for purposes of comparison. Changes in both median and average sales prices over time reflect changes in the market prices of specific characteristics of new houses (such as the price per square foot of living space) as well as changes in the actual characteristics of houses that are sold (such as a trend toward larger or smaller homes).

Series Dc597–599. To isolate changes in the prices of single-family characteristics, each year the Bureau of the Census estimates the sales price of a home with a fixed set of characteristics. For series Dc597 this "fixed characteristics" home is chosen to be identical in several important characteristics to the "average" home bought in 1977; for series Dc598 the base home for comparison is the average home sold in 1992. In 1997 the Bureau of the Census introduced a chain-type annual-weighted price index, series Dc599, to provide yet another measure of price changes over time, and computed it back to 1977. The change in this price index between any two years reflects the combined effects of changes in the price of housing characteristics and changes in the actual characteristics of the homes sold in that year. An extensive discussion of the derivation and interpretation of these different types of new home price indexes can be found in the March 1997 issue of the source (C25/97-3).

Series Dc600–607. See Table Ap-G in Appendix 2 regarding the composition of census regions and divisions.

TABLE Dc608–636 Multifamily housing units – number completed, asking rent, and absorption rate, by metropolitan location, region, and type of unit: 1970–1999[1]

Contributed by Kenneth A. Snowden

	Total	Apartment units completed										Cooperatives and condominiums	Other units	Median asking rent—unfurnished apartments
		Total	Unfurnished apartments							Furnished apartments	Federally subsidized units			
			Metropolitan location			Region								
			Central city	Suburban	Nonmetropolitan	Northeast	North Central	South	West					
	Dc608	Dc609	Dc610	Dc611	Dc612	Dc613	Dc614	Dc615	Dc616	Dc617	Dc618	Dc619	Dc620	Dc621
Year	Number	Number	Number	Number	Number	Number	Number	Number	Number	Number	Number	Number	Number	Dollars
1970	526,000	328,400	136,800	179,100	12,500	37,600	84,100	142,300	64,400	48,200	55,900	72,500	21,000	188
1971	583,400	334,400	111,500	198,600	24,300	35,800	78,300	125,400	94,900	32,200	104,800	49,100	63,000	187
1972	718,200	497,900	161,300	291,800	44,800	65,200	123,300	183,500	126,000	37,700	93,800	57,300	31,400	191
1973	774,800	531,700	180,200	289,000	62,400	64,600	141,100	211,600	114,400	36,200	82,000	98,100	26,800	191
1974	685,400	405,500	171,400	195,300	39,000	37,500	91,700	197,900	78,400	20,700	75,400	159,000	25,000	197
1975	371,400	223,100	85,600	118,900	18,700	31,100	55,600	91,800	44,500	11,100	38,900	84,600	13,800	211
1976	258,200	157,000	64,900	67,500	24,700	16,000	54,500	48,300	38,200	12,800	32,000	46,300	10,000	219
1977	289,400	195,600	78,400	79,000	38,200	11,200	59,800	60,800	63,800	16,200	26,000	43,000	8,700	232
1978	362,700	228,700	91,700	111,500	25,500	13,400	66,800	89,500	59,000	11,200	54,100	54,500	14,300	251
1979	439,300	241,200	102,400	100,400	38,500	20,500	54,000	111,200	55,400	12,100	87,500	91,800	6,700	272
1980	418,900	196,100	80,300	93,900	21,900	14,200	43,800	91,500	46,600	9,700	79,900	122,800	10,500	308
1981	332,500	135,400	52,400	50,300	32,700	4,900	36,900	68,400	25,100	6,000	66,100	112,600	12,500	347
1982	288,200	117,000	51,400	45,000	20,600	4,600	21,900	66,800	23,700	5,400	48,000	107,900	10,000	385
1983	370,700	191,500	76,800	76,200	38,400	3,500	41,100	115,100	31,800	4,700	47,700	111,800	15,100	386
1984	506,000	313,200	141,600	133,400	38,200	3,800	41,200	194,400	73,900	9,800	28,500	143,600	10,700	393
1985	533,300	364,500	157,100	188,400	18,900	8,200	53,900	166,400	135,900	7,400	12,000	135,800	13,700	432
1986	550,200	407,600	187,900	197,800	21,900	16,900	64,500	171,700	154,500	11,600	23,300	101,700	6,000	457
1987	474,200	345,600	146,800	179,300	19,500	11,300	66,000	124,500	143,900	7,900	17,000	92,300	11,300	517
1988	388,600	284,500	121,400	156,100	7,000	8,700	60,400	91,700	123,800	4,300	15,200	76,200	8,400	550 [2]
1989	337,900	246,400	102,100	132,100	12,000	13,100	45,200	85,900	102,000	4,900	19,800	59,700	7,200	550 [2]
1990	294,400	214,300	86,700	114,700	12,900	12,700	44,300	77,200	80,000	2,900	13,800	52,600	10,800	600
1991	216,500	165,300	68,000	84,600	12,700	6,800	37,900	63,600	57,000	2,800	9,600	35,300	3,500	614
1992	155,200	110,200	41,500	53,700	15,000	10,900	34,000	37,400	28,000	700	7,000	31,100	6,000	586
1993	124,800	77,200	33,900	33,500	9,800	3,700	25,300	27,700	20,500	2,700	7,700	32,000	5,200	573
1994	154,900	104,000	46,900	46,600	10,500	3,700	32,200	44,500	23,600	1,100	11,800	34,400	3,600	576
1995	212,400	155,000	67,100	73,500	14,500	7,100	31,700	78,500	37,700	1,600	13,700	36,400	5,700	655
1996	251,300	191,300	89,900	90,300	11,200	6,100	37,200	96,900	51,100	2,400	14,200	36,900	6,400	672
1997	247,100	189,200	75,400	100,400	13,400	7,700	34,100	96,100	51,300	3,000	14,100	35,800	5,000	724
1998	273,900	209,900	85,500	111,400	13,000	10,600	35,500	115,100	48,700	3,000	20,000	34,500	6,600	735
1999	291,800	225,900	93,200	121,200	11,400	16,700	27,500	124,200	57,500	7,700	13,600	34,200	10,400	791

Notes appear at end of table

(continued)

TABLE Dc608–636 Multifamily housing units – number completed, asking rent, and absorption rate, by metropolitan location, region, and type of unit: 1970–1999 Continued

Absorption rate

	Cooperatives and condominiums				Unfurnished apartments										
						Three-month									
							Metropolitan location			Region						
Year	Three-month	Six-month	Nine-month	Twelve-month	Overall	Central city	Suburban	Nonmetropolitan	Northeast	North Central	South	West	Six-month	Nine-month	Twelve-month
	Dc622	Dc623	Dc624	Dc625	Dc626	Dc627	Dc628	Dc629	Dc630	Dc631	Dc632	Dc633	Dc634	Dc635	Dc636
	Percent	Percent	Percent	Percent	Percent	Percent	Percent	Percent	Percent	Percent	Percent	Percent	Percent	Percent	Percent
1970	—	—	—	—	73	74	72	84	79	74	73	71	87	93	96
1971	—	—	—	—	68	68	68	60	75	69	65	67	85	92	95
1972	—	—	—	—	68	70	66	72	74	66	70	64	84	92	96
1973	—	—	—	—	70	68	70	74	74	67	72	66	85	93	96
1974	57	—	—	—	68	66	68	73	68	72	65	69	83	90	94
1975	44	—	—	—	70	69	69	80	63	74	68	73	85	92	95
1976	53	—	—	—	80	82	82	71	85	76	81	84	93	97	99
1977	71	—	—	—	80	85	80	72	74	81	81	80	94	97	99
1978	77	—	—	—	82	84	80	83	88	84	81	81	93	97	99
1979	74	—	—	—	82	82	80	88	87	82	82	81	93	97	99
1980	72	—	—	—	75	75	73	80	77	77	74	75	90	95	98
1981	62	—	—	—	80	80	78	85	85	86	78	75	92	96	97
1982	54	—	—	—	72	69	69	87	74	79	70	72	87	93	96
1983	66	—	—	—	69	69	62	82	73	86	63	69	85	92	96
1984	69	82	87	91	67	69	66	65	64	79	63	70	84	92	96
1985	65	77	85	89	65	62	65	83	68	73	59	68	84	92	95
1986	74	82	87	91	66	64	67	68	70	70	62	67	84	92	96
1987	74	83	88	92	63	62	64	59	73	65	59	64	82	90	94
1988	64	76	83	86	66	64	67	87	52	73	58	69	84	91	95
1989	66	77	82	86	70	68	70	79	74	75	67	69	86	93	96
1990	60	74	80	85	67	71	65	53	66	75	64	65	85	93	96
1991	60	74	80	86	70	70	70	70	83	78	65	68	87	93	97
1992	68	81	87	90	74	78	73	73	75	80	72	70	91	96	98
1993	76	85	90	93	75	77	74	71	37	81	76	73	88	94	96
1994	77	87	91	93	80	82	80	76	96	78	78	85	93	97	98
1995	74	83	89	92	73	76	75	51	74	75	72	73	89	94	97
1996	80	90	94	97	72	73	70	88	61	77	69	75	88	95	98
1997	80	92	95	97	73	74	73	72	55	81	72	72	91	95	97
1998	79	88	92	94	72	73	70	86	77	74	69	77	89	95	98
1999	75	86	91	93	72	73	72	69	85	73	69	74	89	95	98

1 Use caution when comparing data beginning with 1990 to earlier data, because of a change in methodology; see text.

2 The median asking rent for these years is greater than $550 – the highest rent interval reported.

Sources

1970–1994: U.S. Bureau of the Census, *Market Absorption of Apartments: Annual 1995 Absorptions,* Current Housing Reports, H130/95-A (June 1996), Tables 8, 10–15, 17–18.

1995–1999: U.S. Bureau of the Census, *Market Absorption of Apartments: Annual Absorptions,* Current Housing Reports H130/YY-A (annual issues) Tables 1, 2, 5.

Historical data for the 1975–1999 period are reported in U.S. Bureau of the Census, *Market Absorption of Apartments: Annual 2000 Absorptions,* Current Housing Reports H130/00-A (April 2001). Also see U.S. Census Bureau, *Characteristics of Apartments Completed: 1999,* Current Housing Reports H131/99-A (August 2000), Tables 1–3, 5.

Documentation

This table presents annual estimates of the different types of multifamily housing units that have been completed each year since 1970 and estimates of the rates at which newly completed unfurnished apartments, condominiums, and cooperative units have been rented or sold (absorbed) in a variety of markets. The relative importance of multifamily home building fluctuated widely over the period shown in the table – from one third of all housing starts in the early 1970s to generally less than 20 percent of housing starts in the 1980s (see Tables Dc531–553 and Dc566–584). For annual vacancy rates for all (new and existing) rental housing, see Table Dc810–825.

The estimates of new multifamily units by type of unit are a breakdown of the annual estimates of the number of units completed in five-or-more-unit structures that are produced from the Census

All data are available at the Internet site of the Bureau of the Census.

Bureau's Survey of Construction (SOC, see series Dc584). These estimates cover only those localities within the SOC sample for which building permit information was available, but since the late 1980s this has included nearly all areas in which five-or-more-unit structures have been built. These multifamily units are placed in one of several categories: privately financed furnished and unfurnished apartments, cooperatives and condominiums, federally subsidized units, and other types of multifamily units. The categories are defined below. Note that the data on privately financed units include privately owned housing subsidized by state and local governments.

The Census Bureau conducts an auxiliary survey within the SOC (sponsored by the U.S. Department of Housing and Urban Development) to measure how quickly new multifamily housing units are rented or sold. The sample for the Survey of Market Absorption (SOMA) is composed of units that are identified within SOC as unfurnished apartments, condominiums, and cooperatives. The SOMA collects information each quarter on how many of the sample multifamily units have been rented or sold (absorbed) at three-, six-, nine-, and twelve-month intervals after completion. These data are then used to construct estimates of the percentage of all units absorbed (or the absorption rate) for each of these intervals. Quarterly absorption rates are reported in the series Current Housing Reports H130/YY-MM, and are averaged to form the annual rates as reported in the source. Absorption rates are also reported in SOMA by region, metropolitan status, number of bedrooms, asking rents and sales prices, and several kinds of amenities and structural characteristics associated with multifamily housing units – all of them at three-, six-, nine- and twelve-month intervals.

Absorption rates are not available for types of multifamily units that lie outside the scope of SOMA – such as federally subsidized, furnished, or "other" multifamily units. The SOMA is limited to measuring absorptions in privately financed, nonsubsidized, unfurnished apartments, series Dc609, and condominiums and cooperatives, series Dc622, in newly constructed buildings with five or more units. Together, these categories represented at least three quarters of all multifamily completions before the mid-1980s, and about 90 percent since then.

The reported absorption rates for each category are based on the first time an apartment is rented after completion or the first time a condominium or cooperative apartment is sold after completion.

An apartment is counted as a rental unit even if it was initially intended to be sold as condominium or cooperative but has, instead, been offered for rent by the builder or building owner.

SOMA estimates at first were constructed separately for the nation and for each region. The Census Bureau modified its estimation procedure in 1990 so that national estimates of completions and absorptions were constructed as the sum of the four regional results. The change in procedure results in estimates of completed units each quarter that are consistent with published figures from the SOC and to some extent reduces the sampling variability of the estimates. The three-month absorption rate is shown in the table for each region and metropolitan status; rates for longer intervals in these areas are reported in the source. Annual absorption rates are obtained by computing a weighted average of the four quarterly estimates (for example, in 1997, separate three-month absorption rates for unfurnished apartment units completed in the first, second, third, and fourth quarters). Absorption rates for units not included in the SOMA sample or otherwise not accounted for are assumed to be identical to the rates for units for which data were obtained. The non-interviewed and not-accounted-for cases constitute less than 2 percent of the sample of housing units in this survey.

The estimated absorption rates are subject to sampling error and the source should be consulted for a description of the methodology, the standard errors, and the confidence intervals associated with them. Users should also keep in mind that the absorption rates reported for units completed in a given year (for example, 1997) can represent a weighted average of market conditions for that year and the next (for example, 1998), because sample units in the SOMA are tracked for up to an entire year after completion.

See Table Ap-G in Appendix 2 regarding the composition of census regions and divisions.

Series Dc618. Newly constructed units categorized as federally subsidized are those built under the Section 8 (Low Income Housing Assistance) and Section 202 (Citizens Housing Direct Loans) programs of the Department of Housing and Urban Development, or those units located in buildings containing apartments in the Federal Housing Administration rent supplement program.

Series Dc619. Includes time-sharing units, continuing care retirement units, and turnkey units (privately built for and sold to local public housing authorities after completion).

TABLE Dc637–652   Manufactured homes – shipments, placements, inventories, and sales prices, by region: 1947–1999[1]

Contributed by Kenneth A. Snowden

Year	Shipments	Homes placed for residential use					Homes on dealer lots					Average sales price – homes placed for residential use				
		Total	Region				Total	Region				Overall	Region			
			Northeast	Midwest	South	West		Northeast	Midwest	South	West		Northeast	Midwest	South	West
	Dc637	Dc638	Dc639	Dc640	Dc641	Dc642	Dc643	Dc644	Dc645	Dc646	Dc647	Dc648	Dc649	Dc650	Dc651	Dc652
	Thousand	Thousand	Thousand	Thousand	Thousand	Thousand	Thousand	Thousand	Thousand	Thousand	Thousand	Dollars	Dollars	Dollars	Dollars	Dollars
1947	60.0	—	—	—	—	—	—	—	—	—	—	—	—	—	—	—
1948	85.5	—	—	—	—	—	—	—	—	—	—	—	—	—	—	—
1949	46.2	—	—	—	—	—	—	—	—	—	—	—	—	—	—	—
1950	63.1	—	—	—	—	—	—	—	—	—	—	—	—	—	—	—
1951	67.3	—	—	—	—	—	—	—	—	—	—	—	—	—	—	—
1952	83.0	—	—	—	—	—	—	—	—	—	—	—	—	—	—	—
1953	76.9	—	—	—	—	—	—	—	—	—	—	—	—	—	—	—
1954	76.0	—	—	—	—	—	—	—	—	—	—	—	—	—	—	—
1955	111.9	—	—	—	—	—	—	—	—	—	—	—	—	—	—	—
1956	124.3	—	—	—	—	—	—	—	—	—	—	—	—	—	—	—
1957	119.3	—	—	—	—	—	—	—	—	—	—	—	—	—	—	—
1958	102.0	—	—	—	—	—	—	—	—	—	—	—	—	—	—	—
1959	120.5	—	—	—	—	—	—	—	—	—	—	—	—	—	—	—
1960	103.7	—	—	—	—	—	—	—	—	—	—	—	—	—	—	—
1961	90.2	—	—	—	—	—	—	—	—	—	—	—	—	—	—	—
1962	118.0	—	—	—	—	—	—	—	—	—	—	—	—	—	—	—
1963	150.8	—	—	—	—	—	—	—	—	—	—	—	—	—	—	—
1964	191.3	—	—	—	—	—	—	—	—	—	—	—	—	—	—	—
1965	216.5	—	—	—	—	—	—	—	—	—	—	—	—	—	—	—
1966	217.3	—	—	—	—	—	—	—	—	—	—	—	—	—	—	—
1967	240.4	—	—	—	—	—	—	—	—	—	—	—	—	—	—	—
1968	318.0	—	—	—	—	—	—	—	—	—	—	—	—	—	—	—
1969	412.7	—	—	—	—	—	—	—	—	—	—	—	—	—	—	—
1970	401.2	—	—	—	—	—	—	—	—	—	—	—	—	—	—	—
1971	491.7	—	—	—	—	—	—	—	—	—	—	—	—	—	—	—
1972	575.9	—	—	—	—	—	—	—	—	—	—	—	—	—	—	—
1973	579.9	—	—	—	—	—	—	—	—	—	—	—	—	—	—	—
1974	338.3	332.0	23.3	67.5	170.8	70.4	91.6	7.1	19.1	45.9	19.5	9,300	9,400	9,300	8,300	11,600
1975	212.7	229.3	14.7	48.5	110.8	55.2	64.3	5.3	15.3	30.0	13.7	10,600	10,500	10,700	9,000	13,600
1976	246.1	249.6	16.8	51.5	114.8	66.5	67.2	5.3	14.7	28.4	18.8	12,300	11,600	11,600	10,600	16,000
1977	265.6	257.5	16.7	50.7	112.5	77.7	69.7	5.2	14.5	29.7	20.3	14,200	12,900	13,500	12,100	18,100
1978	275.7	279.9	17.4	49.5	135.3	77.7	74.3	4.4	14.6	33.9	21.3	15,900	14,300	15,100	13,700	20,600
1979	277.4	279.9	16.9	47.3	145.2	70.5	75.8	3.6	13.7	39.2	19.4	17,600	15,800	16,100	15,600	23,100
1980	221.6	233.7	12.3	32.3	140.3	48.7	56.0	2.8	8.6	33.1	11.5	19,800	18,500	18,600	18,200	25,400
1981	240.9	229.2	12.0	30.1	143.5	43.6	57.9	2.4	8.8	36.0	10.6	19,900	19,000	18,900	18,400	25,600
1982	239.5	234.1	12.4	25.6	161.1	35.0	58.3	2.9	7.7	38.4	9.2	19,700	19,800	20,000	18,500	24,700
1983	295.8	278.1	16.3	34.3	186.0	41.4	73.2	4.2	10.1	48.5	10.4	21,000	21,400	20,400	19,700	27,000
1984	295.4	287.9	19.8	35.2	193.4	39.4	81.7	4.3	11.0	55.9	10.5	21,500	22,200	21,100	20,200	27,400
1985	283.5	283.4	20.2	38.6	187.6	36.9	77.6	4.3	9.6	55.1	8.6	21,800	22,700	21,500	20,400	28,700
1986	244.3	256.1	21.2	37.2	162.3	35.4	67.1	5.3	10.0	45.3	6.4	22,400	24,400	21,800	20,700	29,900
1987	232.8	239.2	23.6	40.0	145.5	30.1	60.6	5.5	9.3	39.2	6.6	23,700	25,600	23,700	21,900	31,000
1988	218.3	224.3	22.7	39.1	130.7	31.8	58.0	5.7	10.9	34.9	6.5	25,100	27,000	24,600	22,700	33,900
1989	198.1	202.8	20.2	39.1	112.8	30.6	55.5	5.5	10.6	33.1	6.3	27,200	30,200	26,700	24,100	37,800

Year	Shipments Total Dc637 Thousand	Homes placed for residential use — Total Dc638 Thousand	Region Northeast Dc639 Thousand	Region Midwest Dc640 Thousand	Region South Dc641 Thousand	Region West Dc642 Thousand	Homes on dealer lots — Total Dc643 Thousand	Region Northeast Dc644 Thousand	Region Midwest Dc645 Thousand	Region South Dc646 Thousand	Region West Dc647 Thousand	Average sales price — Overall Dc648 Dollars	Region Northeast Dc649 Dollars	Region Midwest Dc650 Dollars	Region South Dc651 Dollars	Region West Dc652 Dollars
1990	188.3	195.4	18.8	37.7	108.4	30.6	49.0	4.1	9.9	29.2	5.8	27,800	30,000	27,000	24,500	39,300
1991	170.9	174.3	14.3	35.4	97.6	27.0	49.3	4.4	10.0	29.1	5.9	27,700	30,400	27,600	24,500	38,600
1992	210.5	212.0	15.0	42.2	124.4	30.4	50.9	3.9	9.1	31.7	6.2	28,400	30,900	28,800	25,400	39,000
1993	254.3	242.5	15.4	44.5	146.7	35.9	61.4	4.2	10.6	39.2	7.3	30,500	32,000	31,400	27,700	40,500
1994	303.9	290.9	16.3	53.3	177.7	43.6	69.9	3.6	12.2	45.5	8.6	32,800	32,900	34,000	30,200	41,900
1995	339.9	319.4	15.0	57.5	203.2	43.7	81.7	4.1	14.4	53.2	11.3	35,300	35,800	35,700	33,300	44,100
1996	363.3	337.7	16.2	58.8	218.2	44.4	89.0	3.6	13.5	60.5	11.4	37,200	37,300	38,000	35,500	45,000
1997	353.7	336.3	14.3	55.3	219.4	47.3	91.5	3.4	13.3	65.1	9.7	39,800	41,300	40,300	38,000	47,300
1998	373.1	373.7	14.7	58.3	250.3	50.4	83.0	2.6	11.4	62.0	7.0	41,600	42,200	42,400	40,100	48,400
1999	348.1	338.2	13.7	52.4	229.1	43.1	87.9	3.4	12.1	64.3	8.1	43,400	44,300	44,400	41,900	49,700

1 Through 1979, average sales prices were computed using the intended sales prices of homes leased or not yet sold; thereafter, average sales prices were computed for homes sold at or before placement.

Sources

1956–1963: U.S. Bureau of the Census, *Historical Statistics of the United States* (1975), series N170, which was taken from U.S. Department of Housing and Urban Development, *HUD Statistical Yearbook*, annual issues. 1964–1979: U.S. Census Bureau, Current Construction Reports, *Housing Starts*: C20-82-6 (June 1982). 1980–1993: Data downloaded from the Internet site of the Census Bureau on August 8, 2000. 1994–1999: Revised figures downloaded from the Internet site of the Census Bureau on August 14, 2001.

Documentation

A manufactured home is defined as a movable dwelling, eight feet or more wide and forty feet or more long, designed to be towed on its own chassis, with transportation gear integral to the unit when it leaves the factory, and without need of a permanent foundation. These manufactured homes include multi-wides and expandable manufactured homes, but not travel trailers, motor homes, or modular housing units.

Mass production of ten-foot-wide homes began in 1955 and of twelve-foot-wide homes in 1962. Statistics on shipments of new mobile homes have been compiled for the period shown in the table – the U.S. Census Bureau throughout the period shown in the table – the Mobile Home Manufacturers Association before 1970, the Manufactured Housing Institute for 1970–1977, and the National Conference of States on Building Codes and Standards since then.

The shipments figures are based on reports submitted by manufacturers on the number of manufactured homes actually shipped during the survey month. These data have not been adjusted by the Census Bureau for lags that may have occurred as units were placed in use or for the number of manufactured housing units that were used as seasonal homes, second homes, or for nonresidential purposes. Units such as these do not add to the supply of housing units occupied as usual places of residence, but the number of shipped mobile homes that fall into these categories was not known.

Beginning in 1974, the Census Bureau began to conduct the Manufactured Homes Survey (MHS) under the sponsorship of the Department of Housing and Urban Development. Between 1974 and 1979 the survey collected information each month on new manufactured homes from a sample of manufactured home dealers who were drawn from within 137 geographic areas or primary sampling units. The dealers were requested to provide data on the number of manufactured homes received from manufacturers, the number placed on a site for residential use, and the number held in inventory. Procedures were modified in 1979, when the Census Bureau began to follow a sample of new manufactured homes each month that was drawn from those shipped by manufacturers. Dealers who received the sample units were contacted by telephone and asked about the status of the unit. This was (and is) done each month until that unit is reported as placed.

Each month the MHS produces regional estimates of manufactured homes placed for residential use, the average price at which the units sold, and dealers' inventories of new manufactured homes. More detailed quarterly and annual estimates including selected characteristics of new manufactured homes can be found in the sources.

The standard census geographic regions are used here. See Table Ap-G in Appendix 2 regarding the composition of census regions and divisions.

The user of these data should note that the series in this table are estimates, and so are prone to both sampling and nonsampling errors. See the sources for information on standard errors and confidence intervals.

Until April 1999, information on annual and quarterly shipments, placements, and sales of manufactured homes appeared in U.S. Census Bureau, Current Construction Reports, *Housing Starts*: C20. Beginning in August 1999, data on manufactured homes are available only through the Internet site of the Census Bureau. Monthly and seasonally adjusted monthly data can also be found at this site.

Series Dc648–652. The sales prices of new manufactured homes shown in the table include self-reported dealer setup costs. In some cases, there may also be additional costs associated with preparing the unit for occupancy that are not included in the sales prices. Beginning in 1980, average sales prices are computed from data for manufactured homes sold at or before the time they are placed on a site. Prices (values) of manufactured homes leased or sold after placement are not collected. The average sales price computation for manufactured homes placed prior to 1980 included not only the price of those actually sold, but also the intended sales price of those that remained for sale and the value of leased manufactured homes.

TABLE Dc653–669   Housing units, by occupancy and ownership: 1890–1997[1]

Contributed by Kenneth A. Snowden

| | Housing units | Vacant | Vacant — For sale or rent | Vacant — For sale or rent | Vacant — For sale or rent | Vacant | Vacant | Occupied | Occupied — Units reporting tenure | Occupied — Units reporting tenure | Occupied — Units reporting tenure | Percentage of housing units | Percentage of housing units | Percentage of housing units | Vacancy rate | Vacancy rate | |
| | Total | Total | Total | For sale only | For rent | Other | Seasonal | Total | Total | Owner-occupied | Renter-occupied | Vacant | Seasonal | Occupied | Homeowner | Rental | Homeownership rate |
Year	Dc653 Number	Dc654 Number	Dc655 Number	Dc656 Number	Dc657 Number	Dc658 Number	Dc659 Number	Dc660 Number	Dc661 Number	Dc662 Number	Dc663 Number	Dc664 Percent	Dc665 Percent	Dc666 Percent	Dc667 Percent	Dc668 Percent	Dc669 Percent
1890	—	—	—	—	—	—	—	12,690,152	12,690,152	6,066,417	6,623,735	—	—	—	—	—	47.8
1900	—	—	—	—	—	—	—	15,963,965	15,428,987	7,205,212	8,223,775	—	—	—	—	—	46.7
1910	—	—	—	—	—	—	—	20,255,555	19,781,606	9,083,711	10,697,895	—	—	—	—	—	45.9
1920	—	—	—	—	—	—	—	24,351,676	23,810,558	10,866,960	12,943,598	—	—	—	—	—	45.6
1930	—	—	—	—	—	—	—	29,904,663	29,321,891	14,002,074	15,319,817	—	—	—	—	—	47.8
1940	37,325,470	1,731,344	1,475,374	—	—	—	—	34,854,532	34,854,532	15,195,763	19,658,769	4.6	2.0	93.4	—	—	43.6
1950	45,983,398	2,106,651	731,721	215,077	516,644	1,374,930	1,050,466	42,826,281	42,826,281	23,559,966	19,266,315	4.6	2.3	93.1	0.9	2.6	55.0
1960	58,326,357	3,560,017	1,974,826	521,780	1,453,046	1,585,191	1,742,465	53,023,875	53,023,875	32,796,720	20,227,155	6.1	3.0	90.9	1.6	6.7	61.9
1970	68,679,030	4,206,819	2,132,761	477,371	1,655,390	2,074,058	1,022,465	63,449,747	63,449,747	39,885,180	23,564,567	6.1	1.5	92.4	1.2	6.6	62.9
1980	88,411,263	6,303,150	3,127,270	948,469	2,178,801	3,175,880	1,718,440	80,389,673	80,389,673	51,794,545	28,595,128	7.1	1.9	90.9	1.8	7.1	64.4
1990	102,263,678	7,199,401	4,306,871	1,260,233	3,046,638	2,892,530	3,116,867	91,947,410	91,947,410	59,024,811	32,922,599	7.0	3.0	89.9	2.1	8.5	64.2
1997	112,357,000	9,704,000	4,680,000	1,043,000	3,637,000	5,024,000	3,166,000	99,487,000	99,487,000	65,487,000	34,000,000	8.6	2.8	88.5	1.6	9.7	66.2

[1] Terminology, methodology, and basic unit of enumeration changed over time; see text.

Sources

1890: U.S. Census Office, *The Report on Farm and Home Proprietorship and Indebtedness* (1895).

1900–1930: Reports on "Dwellings and Families," in the U.S. Census of Population (1900: volume 7, part 2; 1910: volume 1, Chapter 15; 1920: volume 2; 1930: volume 6).

1940–1990: "United States Summary" in the U.S. Census of Housing: (1940: volume 2, part 1; 1950: volume 1, part 1; 1960: volume 1, part 1; 1970: volume 1, part 1; 1980: volume 1, part 1; 1990: CH-1-1).

1997: U.S. Census Bureau, Current Housing Reports, series H150/97, *American Housing Survey in the United States*.

Documentation

For 1890–1940 data, see also U.S. Housing and Finance Agency, *Housing Statistics Yearbook* (U.S. Government Printing Office, 1948), part 2, Chapter 2. Data by states as well as measures of housing quality drawn from the 1940–1990 Census of Housing are available at the Internet site of the U.S. Census Bureau.

See Tables Dc781–825 for recent annual data on vacancy and homeownership.

Information about the number, occupancy, and ownership of the nation's residential housing stock has been collected since 1890 as part of each decennial U.S. Census of Population. Since 1940 this component of the population census has been tabulated and reported separately as the Decennial Census of Housing. This table, along with Tables Dc670–682 and Dc697–760, uses data drawn from these sources to provide a broad picture of the composition and ownership of the nation's residential housing since 1890. Also included in these tables are comparable data drawn from the American Housing Survey for 1997.

The definitions and concepts used in the census enumerations of housing have evolved since 1890 (where possible, the vocabulary of the 1990 Census of Housing is used here). They have consistently been designed, however, to count the number of living quarters of all families, single individuals, or groups of related or unrelated persons. The 1990 Census notes that the concept of a "dwelling unit" was first established in the 1940 Census (the basic unit of measure in the 1940 and 1950 Censuses was the dwelling unit), and that it has remained essentially comparable since then despite slight modifications and the change in name. A "housing unit" is currently defined as a house, an apartment, a mobile home or trailer, a group of rooms, or a single room that is occupied as separate living quarters or, if vacant, intended for occupancy as separate living quarters. The definition excludes recreational vehicles, boats, vans, tents, and the like unless they are occupied as a usual place of residence. The more substantial modifications of the definition of dwelling or housing unit over the 1940 to 1990 period are noted; for other modifications, see the source.

Before 1940 the census enumerated "families" and not housing unit (the number of "private" families is reported for 1900 and 1930 and the number of "total" families for 1890, 1910, and 1920). However, the two concepts are closely related: a census family was defined in 1930 as a single person living alone, a small group of unrelated persons sharing living accommodations, or, more normally, a group of related persons who live together as one household. Despite differences in terminology, therefore, the basic notion of a family, dwelling unit, or housing unit has provided essentially comparable measures of the residential housing stock since 1890.

There has also been continuity in the definition of "quasi families" (before 1940) and "group quarters" (from 1940 onward). These represent groups of persons who live together in institutions, prisons, "large" rooming houses, dormitories, or military quarters. Group quarters have consistently been excluded from the count of housing units since 1940. Before then such families were included in "total families" and excluded from the "private families" aggregate. In 1890, 1910, and 1920 the census reported statistics only on total families; in 1900 for both total and private families; and in 1930 for private families only. In this table the private family aggregate is reported for both 1900 and 1930, and the total family data (including quasi families) for 1890, 1910, and 1920. The resulting overstatement in housing units for these early years is relatively modest. In 1900 there were some 223,000 quasi families, and the population living in group quarters in 1940 and 1950 represented only between 2 and 4 percent of the total population living in housing units (and, because these groups were of large average size, would have represented an even smaller percentage of housing units had they been included). The enumeration of quasi families for these early years, therefore, does not materially compromise the continuity of the total housing unit series.

Before 1940, information was collected and reported only on occupied living quarters, but beginning with the first Census of Housing in 1940, enumerators collected and reported information on both vacant and seasonal housing units. Since that time these two categories, along with occupied housing units, sum to total housing units.

The American Housing Survey was first conducted by the Bureau of the Census in 1973 in order to collect intercensal information on the nation's residential housing stock. The survey was originally named the Annual Housing Survey and was conducted each year between 1973 and 1981. Since 1981 the survey has been held every other year and its name was changed to the American Housing Survey (AHS) in 1984. Over the years the national sample has covered an average of about 55,000 homes in each survey, and published tabulations are reported in thousands of units. The AHS returns to the same housing units year after year to gather data, and so is ideal for analyzing the flow of households through the housing stock. The concepts and definitions used in the AHS are compatible with those used in the 1990 Census of Housing. Unlike the census data, however, the AHS estimates are based on a sample, and so they will differ from the figures that would have been obtained if a complete census had been taken using the same questionnaires, instructions, and enumerators. See the series H150 source for a discussion of the sampling and nonsampling errors associated with these data and the standard errors of the estimates.

Series Dc654–658. Total vacant units comprise three subcomponents – vacant units "for sale only," vacant units "for rent or sale," and "all other" vacant units. The first two of these categories are used to calculate the homeowner and rental vacancy rates (see below); the third includes housing units that remain vacant after having been sold or rented, units held for occasional, nonseasonal use (for example, a second, weekend home), or vacant units held off the market for other reasons (such as to house a caretaker or janitor or during probate). Beginning in 1990 dilapidated vacant units have also been included in the "all other" vacant category, series Dc658; in 1940 and before, these had been excluded from the housing enumeration altogether. Beginning in 1980, vacant units were defined to include mobile homes that were vacant but intended for year-round occupancy at the current site (excluded, therefore, were mobile homes on dealers' lots).

Series Dc659. Seasonal units are intended for specific recreational uses (such as beach houses or hunting lodges) or work uses (for example, herding and logging) that are seasonal in nature. Since 1960, seasonal units have also explicitly included housing units used to house migratory workers. See the source for other modifications to the definitions of vacant and seasonal housing between 1940 and 1990.

Series Dc660–663. An occupied housing unit is one that serves as the "usual place of residence" for the person or group living in it at the time of enumeration.

Series Dc662–663. A primary goal of all housing enumerations has been to examine homeownership. To be owner-occupied has always meant that at least one member of a family, or one person who uses the living quarters as a usual place of residence, has at least a partial ownership interest in the housing unit. A housing unit was considered owner-occupied whether the unit was owned free and clear or mortgaged. All units not occupied by an owner were considered renter-occupied, whether or not a cash rental payment was made. Some families did not report tenure information in years prior to 1940. The Census Office distributed those not reporting tenure between the owner-occupied and renter-occupied categories in the published 1890 report. For all other years, families or housing units reporting tenure are shown in series Dc661, so that this series is the sum of series Dc662-663.

Series Dc667–668. Since 1940, the vacancy rates for both owner-occupied and renter-occupied housing units have been reported. The vacancy rate for homeowner units equals series Dc656 expressed as a percentage of the sum of series Dc656 and Dc662. The vacancy rate for rental units equals series Dc657 expressed as a percentage of the sum of series Dc657 and Dc663. Note that the 1997 AHS reported a rental vacancy rate of 7.8 percent based on vacant units "for rent only." Reported here is the rental vacancy rate consistent with those reported in the Census of Housing, which accounts for units for rent only and those "for sale or rent."

Series Dc669. The traditional measure of the extent of homeownership is shown in this series. It equals series Dc662 expressed as a percentage of series Dc660.

TABLE Dc670–682   Housing units, by type of structure: 1940–1997[1]

Contributed by Kenneth A. Snowden

	Housing units									Percentage of housing units in			
										One- to four-unit structures		Five-or-more-unit structures	Mobile homes
	Total	One unit, detached	One unit, attached	One to two units, semi-detached	Two to four units	One to four units, attached to business	Five or more units	Mobile homes	Other	One-unit detached	Other		
	Dc670	Dc671	Dc672	Dc673	Dc674	Dc675	Dc676	Dc677 [2]	Dc678	Dc679	Dc680	Dc681	Dc682
Year	Number	Number	Number	Number	Number	Number	Number	Number	Number	Percent	Percent	Percent	Percent
1940	37,325,470	23,730,637	1,178,318	1,656,858	5,723,658	940,726	3,928,298	—	166,975	63.6	25.5	10.5	—
1950	45,983,398	29,115,698	1,209,730	1,588,902	8,676,183	—	5,077,667	315,218	—	63.3	25.0	11.0	0.7
1960	58,314,784	40,103,346	3,655,210	—	7,551,865	—	6,237,798	766,565	—	68.8	19.2	10.7	1.3
1970 [3]	67,699,084	44,800,684	1,989,867	—	9,006,950	—	9,828,696	2,072,887	—	66.2	16.2	14.5	3.1
1980 [3]	86,758,717	53,595,586	3,587,019	—	9,681,832	—	15,478,306	4,415,974	—	61.8	15.3	17.8	5.1
1990	102,263,678	60,383,409	5,378,243	—	9,876,407	—	18,104,610	7,399,855	1,121,154	59.0	14.9	17.7	7.2
1997	112,357,000	68,109,000	6,778,000	—	10,363,000	—	18,806,000	8,301,000	—	60.6	15.3	16.7	7.4

[1] Terminology and methodology changed over time; see text.

[2] Through 1970, only occupied (and not vacant) mobile homes were enumerated.

[3] Units in structure were not reported for seasonal units or units used to house migratory workers; see text.

Source

See the source for Table Dc653–669.

Documentation

See the text for Table Dc653–669 for additional information on the Census of Housing and the American Housing Survey, including information on changes in terminology and methodology over time. The American Housing Survey (AHS) is the source for the 1997 data.

This table provides an overview of the types of structures in which the nation's housing units have been located. Information about "units in structure" was first provided in the report on dwellings and families in the 1930 Census of Population, but not with the detail of later reports. The systematic enumeration of units in structure for both vacant and occupied units was initiated in the 1940 Census of Housing. Since then a "structure" has essentially been defined as having either open spaces on all four sides or vertical walls that divide it from all other structures from basement to roof. Changes to the categories of structures over the period have been primarily designed to differentiate more clearly among the classes of one- to four-unit structures that adjoin other structures. In 1940, for example, housing units that shared a structure with a business were identified separately, and a distinction was made between detached, attached, and semidetached one- and two-unit structures. Neither category was reported after 1950.

The 1940–1990 Censuses of Housing and the AHS contain data on units in structure by region, state, county, and metropolitan areas. These sources also present detailed information on structural

characteristics of the housing stock such as the number of total rooms, bedrooms and bathrooms, the quality of plumbing and kitchen facilities, and the types of sewage disposal, water supply, and heating fuel in use.

Series Dc670. Equals the sum of all categories shown in the table, series Dc671–678. It also equals the total housing units shown in series Dc653 for all years except 1970 and 1980. In these two years the Census Bureau did not collect information on units-in-structure (or, in fact, any other information) for seasonal and migratory housing. The aggregate shown in the tables for these years is referred to as year-round housing units.

Series Dc671. A one-unit detached structure has open spaces on all four sides, and it may contain a shed, a garage, or a business as well as the housing unit. Mobile homes are also considered one-unit detached units, but are shown separately in the table under series Dc677. A one-unit attached structure (series Dc672), on the other hand, is separated from all other structures by walls that extend from ground to roof. This category includes row houses, townhouses, or houses attached to nonresidential structures.

Series Dc674–675. The Census of Housing currently reports multiunit structures in several separate categories – those in 2- to 4-, 5- to 9-, 10- to 19-, 20- to 49-, and 50-or-more-unit structures. These have been combined in the table into only two categories.

Series Dc678. Included in this category are trailers, boats, and cabins with occupants who had no other usual place of residence. Such structures were not reported separately for 1950–1980.

TABLE Dc683-696 Housing units, by occupancy and ownership: 1965-1999[1]   [Current Population Survey/Housing Vacancy Survey]

Contributed by Kenneth A. Snowden

	Total	Vacant										Occupied		
			Year-round					Held off market						
Year	Total	Total	Total	For rent	For sale only	Rented or sold	Total	Occasional use	Residents have usual residence elsewhere	Other	Seasonal	Total	Owner-occupied	Renter-occupied
	Dc683	Dc684	Dc685	Dc686	Dc687	Dc688	Dc689	Dc690	Dc691	Dc692	Dc693	Dc694	Dc695	Dc696
	Thousand	Thousand	Thousand	Thousand	Thousand	Thousand	Thousand	Thousand	Thousand	Thousand	Thousand	Thousand	Thousand	Thousand
1965	64,213	6,712	4,853	1,884	548	330	2,092	504	379	1,209	1,860	57,501	36,230	21,271
1966	65,212	6,726	4,909	1,778	522	349	2,261	546	434	1,280	1,817	58,486	37,109	21,377
1967	66,014	6,538	4,762	1,566	499	348	2,349	571	460	1,318	1,776	59,476	37,842	21,634
1968	67,171	6,218	4,446	1,392	439	389	2,227	551	438	1,238	1,772	60,952	38,918	22,034
1969	68,479	6,218	4,437	1,296	408	402	2,332	619	454	1,258	1,782	62,261	40,049	22,211
1970	69,778	6,137	4,391	1,299	427	427	2,238	615	429	1,195	1,746	63,640	40,834	22,806
1971	71,320	6,238	4,559	1,353	422	478	2,307	652	416	1,239	1,680	65,081	41,816	23,266
1972	73,313	6,368	4,665	1,421	432	516	2,297	642	419	1,237	1,703	66,945	43,096	23,849
1973	75,407	6,558	4,851	1,521	467	524	2,340	588	433	1,320	1,706	68,849	44,424	24,425
1974	77,462	6,904	5,155	1,661	557	543	2,393	617	452	1,325	1,750	70,558	45,615	24,943
1975	78,821	6,896	5,202	1,647	591	536	2,429	649	470	1,309	1,694	71,925	46,463	25,462
1976	80,189	6,774	5,190	1,546	598	564	2,482	705	467	1,310	1,584	73,415	47,518	25,897
1977	81,645	6,861	5,224	1,472	574	651	2,528	707	438	1,383	1,637	74,784	48,461	26,324
1978	83,496	6,948	5,260	1,433	524	650	2,653	689	467	1,498	1,688	76,548	49,739	26,810
1979	85,735	7,589	5,893	1,579	607	705	3,003	794	591	1,618	1,696	78,146	50,972	27,174
1980	87,739	8,101	5,996	1,575	734	623	3,064	814	568	1,683	2,106	79,638	52,223	27,415
1981	88,988	7,967	6,034	1,500	746	585	3,203	884	605	1,715	1,934	81,020	53,007	28,013
1982	91,876	8,145	6,369	1,670	843	554	3,302	959	588	1,754	1,776	83,731	54,237	29,495
1983	93,044	8,479	6,693	1,810	862	633	3,389	926	642	1,821	1,787	84,565	54,671	29,894
1984	95,256	8,910	7,080	1,934	947	664	3,535	992	622	1,921	1,830	86,346	55,671	30,675
1985	97,333	9,446	7,400	2,221	1,006	664	3,510	977	659	1,875	2,046	87,887	56,152	31,736
1986	99,318	10,173	7,821	2,588	937	683	3,614	991	741	1,883	2,352	89,145	56,844	32,302
1987	101,811	11,294	8,265	2,752	978	688	3,848	1,066	787	1,996	3,029	90,517	57,915	32,602
1988	103,653	11,633	8,533	2,802	968	678	4,085	1,213	887	1,985	3,100	92,020	58,700	33,320
1989	105,729	12,240	9,349	2,732	1,082	705	4,830	1,565	1,014	2,251	2,891	93,489	59,755	33,734
1990	106,283	12,059	9,128	2,662	1,064	660	4,742	1,485	1,068	2,189	2,931	94,224	60,248	33,976
1991	107,276	12,023	9,137	2,780	1,070	602	4,686	1,494	1,084	2,107	2,886	95,253	61,010	34,242
1992	108,316	11,926	8,932	2,769	970	628	4,564	1,443	1,011	2,111	2,994	96,391	61,823	34,568
1993	109,611	11,894	8,937	2,809	894	625	4,609	1,508	994	2,108	2,957	97,717	62,533	35,184
1994	110,952	12,257	9,229	2,858	953	772	4,646	1,612	815	2,219	3,028	98,695	63,136	35,558
1995	112,655	12,669	9,570	2,946	1,022	810	4,793	1,667	801	2,325	3,099	99,985	64,739	35,246
1996	114,139	13,155	9,945	3,008	1,082	834	5,022	1,709	852	2,461	3,209	100,984	66,041	34,943
1997	115,621	13,419	10,114	2,978	1,133	867	5,136	1,818	885	2,433	3,305	102,202	67,143	35,059
1998	117,282	13,748	10,516	3,046	1,205	927	5,338	1,792	910	2,636	3,232	103,534	68,638	34,896
1999	119,044	14,116	10,848	3,119	1,184	956	5,589	1,948	965	2,676	3,268	104,928	70,097	34,831

[1] See text for information concerning the comparability of the data over time, the use of revised figures for certain years, and differences between these data and similar figures from the decennial Census of Housing.

Source

U.S. Bureau of the Census, Housing Vacancies and Homeownership: Annual (2000), I1-O00-H111-00-USA. Data were downloaded in January 2001 from the Census Bureau's Internet site.

Documentation

Annual estimates of the housing inventory and homeownership and vacancy rates (see Tables Dc781–825) are produced from data drawn from the Current Population Survey (CPS) and Housing Vacancy Survey (HVS) that are conducted by the U.S. Bureau of the Census. Since 1995 the annual reports of these series have been published as Internet documents, whereas for previous years these

(continued)

TABLE Dc683–696   Housing units, by occupancy and ownership: 1865–1999   *Continued*

[Current Population Survey/Housing Vacancy Survey]   *Continued*

Year		All units	Vacant				Occupied		
			Total	Year-round	Seasonal	Total	Owner-occupied	Renter-occupied	
1979	Unrevised	85,061	7,129	5,415	1,714	77,932	51,086	26,847
1979	Revised	85,735	7,589	5,893	1,696	78,146	50,972	27,174
1989	Unrevised	104,970	11,481	8,518	2,963	93,489	59,755	33,734
1989	Revised	105,729	12,240	9,349	2,891	93,489	59,755	33,734
1993	Unrevised	109,716	11,988	8,883	3,105	97,728	62,998	34,730
1993	Revised	109,611	11,894	8,937	2,957	97,717	62,533	35,184

data were reported in U.S. Bureau of the Census, Current Population Survey/Housing Vacancy Survey, Series H-111.

Not shown here are annual estimates of the housing inventory for regions and by age of householder that are available in the source. Biennial estimates of the housing inventory are available by state and for selected metropolitan areas in the American Housing Survey, while housing unit estimates for counties and smaller units are available only from the decennial censuses (see the text for Table Dc653–669 for information about both these sources).

Each month about 60,000 housing units, including both occupied and vacant, are contained in the CPS sample. Of these units, about 51,000 are occupied and are eligible for interview each month. In addition to the 51,000, about 9,000 are visited but found to be vacant or are otherwise not interviewed each month. About half of these 9,000 units are vacant and included in a supplemental survey known as the HVS.

Estimates of the inventory of occupied housing units are constructed from the data collected in the basic monthly CPS by weighting the data collected through the interviews and then inflating these results with independent estimates of the total civilian noninstitutional population of the United States by age, race, sex, and Hispanic categories. These independent estimates are based on statistics from the decennial censuses of population; statistics on births, deaths, immigration, and emigration; and statistics on the strength of the armed forces. The inventory of vacant houses is constructed from the 1990 HVS data in a similar fashion by weighting the sample results and then adjusting these using 1990 Census vacant counts. A second adjustment inflates these results based on the CPS coverage of occupied units by geographic areas. The annual estimates shown here are averages of the twelve monthly estimates made each year.

The CPS/HVS estimates are based on a sample, and they may differ from the figures that would have been obtained if a complete census had been taken using the same questionnaires, instructions, and enumerators. See the source for a discussion of the sampling and nonsampling errors associated with these data and the standard errors of the estimates.

Since its inception, the CPS/HVS has generally adopted the concepts and definitions of the Decennial Census of Housing (see below for some minor differences, and see Table Dc653–669 for data from the decennial census). A significant difference appeared in 1980, however, when the decennial censuses began to count vacant mobile homes as housing units, while the CPS/HVS did not. Coverage in the survey was extended to vacant seasonal mobile homes in 1986 and to year-round mobile homes in 1990, so that this difference with the Decennial Census of 1990 was removed. There have always been, of course, differences between the censuses and CPS/HVS in interviewing procedures, staff experience, and training, and in processing procedures and sample designs. Users of the data should be aware that the CPS/HVS and decennial censuses have produced some significantly different results over the years. It should also be noted that the housing inventory data in this table are an average for each year, whereas the census data for some of the same series shown in Table Dc653–669 are for April of the census years. Caution should be used, therefore, when making comparisons between the decennial census data and the CPS/HVS data shown in this table.

There are also some important issues concerning the continuity of CPS/HVS data over time. Mention has already been made of the inclusion of seasonal and year-round vacant mobile homes in 1987 and 1990. Analysis of seasonal vacancy data prior to 1987 has shown that this series was underestimated by approximately 28 percent before the change. In addition, the inclusion of year-round vacant mobile homes in 1990 increased the number of vacant units significantly for some regions; for earlier years the vacancy data may be misleading. Caution must also be taken in comparing data for 1980 with data from earlier years because several changes to the survey were implemented then to improve the reliability of the data, including a new supplemental sample and a refinement in estimation procedures. It is safe to assume, in fact, that prior to the implementation of these new procedures (that

is, 1955–1978), HVS produced underestimates of vacant units. A final problem in comparability over time is inherent in the CPS/HVS methodology because the weights used to inflate the sample data, and the composition of the sample itself, are changed every decade to reflect changes as measured in the most recent Census of Housing.

The source provides greater detail about each of these changes in coverage or procedures. It also provides revised and unrevised data for several individual years so that users of the data can gauge the magnitude of the discontinuities. Provided below is a comparison of the revised and unrevised data for the major categories in the table over the affected years; see the source to assess the impacts of revisions for components of these series.

The revised estimates are shown in this table for all three years; these are different from the original data published in the H-111 series. The source recommends particular caution in drawing conclusions about trends that extend from before 1980 to 1980 and beyond, and from before 1990 to 1990 and later.

Reference was made to minor differences between the definitions of a housing unit used in the CPS/HVS and the decennial censuses (these are discussed in the Series H-111 publication for years prior to 1985). A more recent difference appeared when the 1980 Decennial Census definition was changed so that a housing unit was no longer required to have complete kitchen facilities; beginning then, direct access to the facilities was deemed sufficient. The CPS/HVS did not adopt this change until 1990. A difference that continues between the census and survey, however, lies in the definition of group quarters. In the CPS/HVS, group quarters include living arrangements housing five or more unrelated persons, whereas in the census the requirement was raised to nine or more persons in 1980. The definitions that follow describe current CPS/HVS usage; see the text for Table Dc653–669 for those used in the Housing Census.

A housing unit is a house, an apartment, a group of rooms, or a single room occupied or intended for occupancy as separate living quarters. This means that the occupants live and eat only with other persons living in the unit and that all occupants of the unit have direct and common access from the outside. For vacant units, the criteria of separateness and direct access are applied to the intended occupants whenever possible. If this information cannot be obtained by way of the survey, the criteria are applied to the previous occupants of the unit. Boats are excluded as housing units if vacant, used for business, or used for extra sleeping space or vacations. Vacant seasonal or migratory mobile homes, on the other hand, are included in the count of vacant seasonal housing units.

Living quarters of the following types are excluded from the housing unit inventory: dormitories, bunkhouses, and barracks; quarters in predominantly transient hotels, motels, and the like, except those occupied by persons who consider the hotel their usual place of residence; and quarters in institutions, general hospitals, and military installations, except those occupied by staff members or resident employees who have separate living arrangements.

Series Dc684–693. A housing unit is vacant if no one lives in it at the time of the interview, unless its occupants are only temporarily absent. In addition, a vacant unit may be one that is entirely occupied by persons who have a usual residence elsewhere. New units not yet occupied are classified as vacant housing units if construction has reached a point at which all exterior windows and doors are installed and final usable floors are in place. Vacant units are excluded if they are exposed to the elements – that is, if the roof, walls, windows, or doors no longer protect the interior from the elements – or if there is positive evidence (such as a sign on the house or block) that the unit is to be demolished or is condemned. Also excluded are quarters being used entirely for nonresidential purposes, such as a store or an office, or quarters used for the storage of business supplies or inventory, machinery, or agricultural products.

Series Dc685–692. Year-round units are those intended for occupancy at any time of the year, even though they may not be in use year-round. In resort areas, a housing unit that is usually occupied on a year-round basis is considered a year-round unit. As indicated above, year-round units temporarily occupied by persons with usual residence elsewhere (URE) are included with year-round vacant units. Beginning in 1990, year-round vacant mobile homes were included as part of the year-round vacant count of housing units. Year-round vacant units are classified into four categories in the survey, and represent the sum of those categories. Vacant units for rent consist of vacant units offered for rent and those offered both for rent and for sale, whereas vacant units for sale only exclude units that are both for rent and sale. If a unit was located in a multiunit structure that was for sale as an entire structure and if the unit was not for rent, it was reported as "held off market." However, if the individual unit was intended to be occupied by the new owner, it was reported as "for sale." Vacant units rented or sold consist of year-round vacant units that have been rented or sold but the new renters or owners have not moved in as of the day of interview. Finally, vacant units held off the market include those units held for occasional use, temporarily occupied by persons with URE, or vacant for other reasons.

Series Dc690. A vacant unit is held off the market for occasional use if it is neither for rent nor for sale only, but is held for weekends or occasional use throughout the year. Time-shared units are classified in this category if the vacant unit is not for rent or for sale only, but is held for use for an individual during the time of interview.

Series Dc691. A housing unit that is occupied temporarily by persons who usually live elsewhere is interviewed as a vacant unit provided that a usual place of residence is held for the household, which is not offered for rent or for sale. Units occupied by persons with URE are further classified as seasonal vacant or year-round vacant units, and seasonal UREs are included with all seasonal vacant units.

Series Dc692. A unit can be held off the market and vacant for other reasons, such as for the use of a caretaker or janitor, or held for the settlement of an estate.

Series Dc693. Seasonal vacant units are those intended for occupancy only during certain seasons of the year and are found primarily in resort areas. Housing units held for occupancy by migratory labor employed in farm work during the crop season are tabulated as seasonal. Vacant seasonal mobile homes have been counted as a part of the seasonal housing inventory since 1986.

Series Dc694–696. A housing unit is occupied if a person or group of persons is living in it at the time of the interview, or if the occupants are only temporarily absent (for example, on vacation). The persons living in the unit must consider it their usual place of residence or have no usual place of residence elsewhere. The count of occupied housing units, therefore, is the same as the count of households. A unit is owner-occupied if the owner or co-owner lives in the unit, even if it is mortgaged or not fully paid for. A cooperative or condominium unit is "owner-occupied" only if the owner or co-owner lives in it. All other occupied units are classified as "renter-occupied," including units rented for cash rent and those occupied without payment of cash rent.

TABLE Dc697–760 Occupied housing units, by farm status, urban location, region, race, ethnicity, and ownership: 1890–1997[1]

Contributed by Kenneth A. Snowden

Occupied housing units

Year	Total	Farm status — Nonfarm	Farm status — Farm	Urban–rural — Urban	Urban–rural — Rural Total	Rural — Nonfarm	Rural — Farm	Region — Northeast	Region — North Central	Region — South	Region — West	Race — White	Race — Nonwhite Total	Race — Nonwhite Black	Race — Nonwhite Other	Race — Hispanic
	Dc697	Dc698	Dc699	Dc700	Dc701	Dc702	Dc703	Dc704	Dc705	Dc706	Dc707	Dc708	Dc709	Dc710	Dc711	Dc712
	Number	Number	Number	Number	Number	Number	Number	Number	Number	Number	Number	Number	Number	Number	Number	Number
1890[2]	12,690,152	7,922,973	4,767,179	—	—	—	—	3,712,242	4,598,605	3,758,887	620,418	11,255,169	1,434,983	1,410,769	24,214	—
1900	15,963,965	10,274,127	5,689,838	—	—	—	—	4,557,266	5,632,548	4,886,813	887,338	14,063,791	1,900,174	1,833,759	66,415	—
1910	20,255,555[4]	14,131,945	6,123,610	—	—	—	—	5,700,617	6,806,889	6,163,207	1,584,842	—	—	—	—	—
1920[3]	24,351,676	17,600,472	6,751,204	12,803,047	11,548,629	—	—	6,788,892	8,101,762	7,211,819	2,249,203	21,825,654	2,526,022	2,430,828	95,194	—
1930	29,904,663	23,235,982	6,668,681	17,372,524	12,532,139	5,927,502	6,604,637	8,355,879	9,680,704	8,653,481	3,214,599	26,982,994	2,921,669	2,803,756	117,913	—
1940	34,854,532	27,665,684	7,188,848	20,596,500	14,258,032	7,151,473	7,106,559	9,479,318	10,963,388	10,278,204	4,133,622	31,561,126	3,293,406	3,156,545	136,861	—
1950	42,826,281	—	—	28,492,186	14,334,095	8,613,073	5,721,022	11,228,076	12,971,966	12,632,607	5,993,632	39,043,595	3,782,686	3,633,480	149,206	—
1960	53,023,875	—	—	38,320,370	14,703,505	11,137,184	3,566,321	13,522,151	15,378,749	15,502,595	8,620,380	47,879,816	5,144,059	—	—	—
1970	63,449,747	—	—	47,562,681	15,887,066	—	—	15,482,778	17,537,256	19,258,163	11,171,550	56,529,374	6,920,373	6,180,260	740,113	—
1980	80,389,673	—	—	60,551,717	19,837,956	—	—	17,470,616	20,859,206	26,486,217	15,573,634	68,810,123	11,579,550	8,381,668	3,197,882	4,007,896
1990	91,947,410	—	—	70,045,167	21,902,243	—	—	18,872,713	22,316,975	31,822,254	18,935,468	76,880,105	15,067,305	9,976,161	5,091,144	6,001,718
1997	99,487,000	—	—	71,317,000	28,170,000	—	—	19,484,000	23,951,000	34,808,000	21,245,000	82,154,000	17,333,000	12,085,000	5,248,000	8,513,000

Occupied housing units reporting tenure – all units

Year	Total	Farm status — Nonfarm	Farm status — Farm	Urban–rural — Urban	Urban–rural — Rural Total	Rural — Nonfarm	Rural — Farm	Region — Northeast	Region — North Central	Region — South	Region — West	Race — White	Race — Nonwhite Total	Race — Nonwhite Black	Race — Nonwhite Other	Race — Hispanic
	Dc713	Dc714	Dc715	Dc716	Dc717	Dc718	Dc719	Dc720	Dc721	Dc722	Dc723	Dc724	Dc725	Dc726	Dc727	Dc728
	Number	Number	Number	Number	Number	Number	Number	Number	Number	Number	Number	Number	Number	Number	Number	Number
1890[2]	12,690,152	7,922,973	4,767,179	—	—	—	—	3,712,242	4,598,605	3,758,887	620,418	11,255,169	1,434,983	1,410,769	24,214	—
1900	15,428,987	9,779,979	5,649,008	—	—	—	—	4,429,374	5,489,238	4,667,166	843,209	13,659,106	1,769,881	1,708,726	61,155	—
1910	19,781,606[4]	13,672,044	6,109,562	—	—	—	—	5,592,425	6,665,723	5,997,444	1,526,014	—	—	—	—	—
1920[3]	23,810,558	17,229,394	6,581,164	12,587,063	11,223,495	—	—	6,687,566	7,936,278	6,996,714	2,190,000	21,379,163	2,431,395	2,342,348	89,047	—
1930	29,321,891	22,854,935	6,466,956	17,113,913	12,207,978	5,803,159	6,404,819	8,245,316	9,506,830	8,435,335	3,134,410	26,492,256	2,829,635	2,719,862	109,773	—
1940	34,854,532	27,665,684	7,188,848	20,596,500	14,258,032	7,151,473	7,106,559	9,479,318	10,963,388	10,278,204	4,133,622	31,561,126	3,293,406	3,156,545	136,861	—
1950	42,826,281	—	—	28,492,186	14,334,095	8,613,073	5,721,022	11,228,076	12,971,966	12,632,607	5,993,632	39,043,595	3,782,686	3,633,480	149,206	—
1960	53,023,875	—	—	38,320,370	14,703,505	11,137,184	3,566,321	13,522,151	15,378,749	15,502,595	8,620,380	47,879,816	5,144,059	—	—	—
1970	63,449,747	—	—	47,562,681	15,887,066	—	—	15,482,778	17,537,256	19,258,163	11,171,550	56,529,374	6,920,373	6,180,260	740,113	—
1980	80,389,673	—	—	60,551,717	19,837,956	—	—	17,470,616	20,859,206	26,486,217	15,573,634	68,810,123	11,579,550	8,381,668	3,197,882	4,007,896
1990	91,947,410	—	—	70,045,167	21,902,243	—	—	18,872,713	22,316,975	31,822,254	18,935,468	76,880,105	15,067,305	9,976,161	5,091,144	6,001,718
1997	99,487,000	—	—	71,317,000	28,170,000	—	—	19,484,000	23,951,000	34,808,000	21,245,000	82,154,000	17,333,000	12,085,000	5,248,000	8,513,000

Occupied housing units reporting tenure – owner-occupied units

Year	Total	Farm status		Urban–rural location				Region				Race and Hispanic origin				
	Total	Nonfarm	Farm	Urban	Rural			Northeast	North Central	South	West	White	Nonwhite			Hispanic
					Total	Nonfarm	Farm						Total	Black	Other	
	Dc729	Dc730	Dc731	Dc732	Dc733	Dc734	Dc735	Dc736	Dc737	Dc738	Dc739	Dc740	Dc741	Dc742	Dc743	Dc744
	Number	Number	Number	Number	Number	Number	Number	Number	Number	Number	Number	Number	Number	Number	Number	Number
1890 [2]	6,066,417	2,923,671	3,142,746	—	—	—	—	1,525,137	2,668,508	1,536,662	336,110	5,793,660	272,757	264,288	8,469	—
1900	7,205,212	3,566,809	3,638,403	—	—	—	—	1,691,307	3,072,890	1,981,296	459,719	6,788,069	417,143	373,450	43,693	—
1910 [4]	9,083,711	5,245,380	3,838,331	—	—	—	—	2,049,983	3,661,916	2,526,582	845,230	—	—	—	—	—
1920 [3]	10,866,960	7,041,283	3,825,677	4,707,715	6,159,245	—	—	2,532,447	4,270,823	2,957,723	1,105,967	10,286,267	580,693	542,654	38,039	—
1930	14,002,074	10,503,386	3,498,688	7,432,554	6,569,520	3,117,418	3,452,102	3,739,406	5,158,017	3,508,778	1,595,873	13,288,429	713,645	669,645	44,000	—
1940	15,195,763	11,358,218	3,837,545	7,714,960	7,480,803	3,698,076	3,782,727	3,624,622	5,383,127	4,183,022	2,004,992	14,418,092	777,671	719,771	57,900	—
1950	23,559,966	—	—	14,376,594	9,183,372	5,425,052	3,758,320	5,439,997	7,878,510	6,780,051	3,461,408	22,240,970	1,318,996	1,252,103	66,893	—
1960	32,796,720	—	—	22,334,781	10,461,939	7,829,055	2,632,884	7,588,017	10,307,662	9,612,875	5,288,206	30,823,194	1,973,526	—	—	—
1970	39,885,180	—	—	27,778,090	12,107,090	—	—	8,916,459	11,922,509	12,456,201	6,590,011	36,978,651	2,906,529	2,567,920	338,609	—
1980	51,794,545	—	—	35,946,411	15,848,134	—	—	10,303,760	14,356,776	17,742,997	9,391,012	46,670,775	5,123,770	3,724,251	1,399,519	1,738,920
1990	59,024,811	—	—	41,375,627	17,649,184	—	—	11,571,332	15,200,285	21,076,467	11,176,727	52,432,648	6,592,163	4,327,265	2,264,898	2,545,584
1997	65,487,000	—	—	42,282,000	23,205,000	—	—	12,241,000	16,902,000	23,650,000	12,694,000	57,781,000	7,705,000	5,457,000	2,248,000	3,646,000

Homeownership rate

Year	Overall	Farm status		Urban–rural location				Region				Race and Hispanic origin				
	Overall	Nonfarm	Farm	Urban	Rural			Northeast	North Central	South	West	White	Nonwhite			Hispanic
					Overall	Nonfarm	Farm						Overall	Black	Other race	
	Dc745	Dc746	Dc747	Dc748	Dc749	Dc750	Dc751	Dc752	Dc753	Dc754	Dc755	Dc756	Dc757	Dc758	Dc759	Dc760
	Percent	Percent	Percent	Percent	Percent	Percent	Percent	Percent	Percent	Percent	Percent	Percent	Percent	Percent	Percent	Percent
1890 [2]	47.8	36.9	65.9	—	—	—	—	41.1	58.0	40.9	54.2	51.5	19.0	18.7	35.0	—
1900	46.7	36.5	64.4	—	—	—	—	38.2	56.0	42.5	54.5	49.7	23.6	21.9	71.4	—
1910	45.9	38.4	62.8	—	—	—	—	36.7	54.9	42.1	55.4	—	—	—	—	—
1920 [3]	45.6	40.9	58.1	—	—	—	—	37.9	53.8	42.3	50.5	48.1	23.9	23.2	42.7	—
1930	47.8	46.0	54.1	43.4	53.8	53.7	53.9	45.4	54.3	41.6	50.9	50.2	25.2	24.6	40.1	—
1940	43.6	41.1	53.4	37.5	52.5	51.7	53.2	38.2	49.1	40.7	48.5	45.7	23.6	22.8	42.3	—
1950	55.0	—	—	50.5	64.1	63.0	65.7	48.4	60.7	53.7	57.8	57.0	34.9	34.5	44.8	—
1960	61.9	—	—	58.3	71.2	70.3	73.8	56.1	67.0	62.0	61.3	64.4	38.4	—	—	—
1970	62.9	—	—	58.4	76.2	—	—	57.6	68.0	64.7	59.0	65.4	42.0	41.6	45.8	—
1980	64.4	—	—	59.4	79.9	—	—	59.0	68.8	67.0	60.3	67.8	44.2	44.4	43.8	43.4
1990	64.2	—	—	59.1	80.6	—	—	61.3	68.1	66.2	59.0	68.2	43.8	43.4	44.5	42.4
1997	65.8	—	—	59.3	82.4	—	—	62.8	70.6	67.9	59.8	70.3	44.5	45.2	42.8	42.8

1 Terminology, methodology, and basic unit of enumeration changed over time; see text.

2 The Census Bureau distributed families that did not report tenure between the owner-occupied and rented categories in 1890.

3 The 1920 published report did not provide farm–nonfarm breakdown; such figures are drawn from the 1950 U.S. summary, Tables J and L.

4 Table CII in the 1910 report shows incorrect totals and includes data for Hawai'i and Alaska. Data for this year were also drawn from U.S. Housing and Finance Agency, Housing Statistics Yearbook, 1948, part 2, Chapter 2, Table 49.

Source

See the source for Table Dc653–669.

Documentation

The 1890–1930 Census of Population Reports on Families and Dwellings, the 1940–1990 Census of Housing, and the American Housing Survey (AHS) all contain data on occupancy by state, county, and metropolitan areas. The latter two sources also present detailed information such as persons per unit and per room, duration of occupancy, and occupancy by age groups.

This table breaks down the aggregate occupied and owner-occupied housing stock in the United States by several different classification schemes. Series Dc697, Dc713, Dc729, and Dc745 repeat the data on economy-wide occupancy, tenure, and rates of homeownership that are presented in Table Dc653–669. All of these terms are defined in the text for Table Dc653–669, which also discusses changes in census terminology and methodology over time. The aggregate picture is broken down

(continued)

TABLE Dc697–760   Occupied housing units, by farm status, urban location, region, race, ethnicity, and ownership: 1890–1997   *Continued*

in the rest of this table by using the distinctions that have been emphasized in the Censuses of Population and Housing since 1890 – between nonfarm and farm households, between urban and rural households, and among different regions and races, and since 1970 for persons of Hispanic origin. Over the past century the importance of these distinctions has changed as the U.S. economy has grown and matured, and the data reported in the published Census of Housing volumes have adapted to these trends. The data reveal marked differences in the level and trend of homeownership across different categories of households throughout the 1890–1990 period. Comparable data for 1997 drawn from the AHS are also shown in order to provide more recent information. The AHS is described in the text for Table Dc653–669.

The farm–nonfarm distinction dominated the published reports on housing and families before 1920, but between 1920 and 1940 data on occupancy and tenure began to be reported separately for the urban and rural areas of the country. The Census Bureau assigned urban–rural classification between 1920 and 1940 using the rule that urban households resided in incorporated cities and towns with populations greater than 2,500 persons. Some densely populated but unincorporated areas were also classified as urban by special rules to take account of peculiarities in local and state political boundaries.

In 1950 the Bureau of the Census introduced a new classification system in the population and housing censuses to better delineate urban and rural areas, especially those situated near large cities. The new class of "urbanized areas" continued to be dominated by incorporated places with populations greater than 2,500 but was broadened to include densely populated urban fringes around cities with populations greater than 50,000 and densely populated unincorporated "places" outside the urban fringe. All housing units located outside urbanized areas were classified as rural.

An estimated 7.5 million persons shifted from rural to urban classification between 1940 and 1950 because of the new urban–rural distinction. No such estimate was made for housing units, but the Census Bureau cautioned that the introduction of the urbanized area concept was likely to have been responsible for up to one third of the total increase in the urban residential housing stock over the decade. Since 1950 the urban–rural classification scheme has remained essentially the same, although more precise definitions of urbanized areas were introduced in 1960 and 1980. In 1970, moreover, some areas previously defined as urban were excluded from the category under the "extended city" concept, which was introduced to identify places that were essentially rural in character but had fallen within the expanding legal boundaries of many cities. The changes in the urban area definition after 1950 do not affect the comparability of urban–rural housing classification after 1950.

Any urban–rural classification cuts across the previously dominant farm–nonfarm categories, so in 1930 rural housing units began to be reported separately as rural farm and rural nonfarm housing units. Since that time the small number of farms that are located in urban areas have been classified as urban housing units. The number of "urban farms" in 1930 and 1940 is reflected in the small differences for those years between the number of total "farm" and "rural farm" housing units. In the 1950 Census of Housing the farm–nonfarm classification was abandoned altogether, although the 95,579 urban farm housing units in that year (about 1.5 percent of all farms) were noted separately in a few of the published tables. By 1960 the Census Bureau no longer identified or tabulated the number of urban farms, and from this date on no count of the total number (rural and urban combined) of farm and "nonfarm" housing units is available.

In 1950 the Census Bureau also began to introduce formal criteria to determine if a rural housing unit should be classified "rural farm" or "rural nonfarm." At first the test was relatively straightforward – a housing unit was excluded from the rural farm category if cash rent was paid for the housing unit and the land on which it was built. More restrictive criteria were implemented in 1960 when it was stipulated that a farm had to meet either a minimum acreage or a minimum farm output cutoff. In that year, moreover, all vacant housing units in rural areas began to be classified as nonfarm units. Finally, in 1970 the Census Bureau no longer attempted to distinguish between farm and nonfarm rural housing units on the basis of information gathered from all households. Instead, questions about

acreage and farm output value were included on the long form given to the "20 percent census sample," and the numbers of rural farm and nonfarm units have been estimated from these data. These estimates are not shown for the 1970–1990 period because all other data in this table are based on the full enumeration. Estimates of the rural farm–rural nonfarm breakdown can be found in the "Detailed Housing Characteristics" reports that are part of the 1970–1990 Censuses of Housing.

As the urban–rural classification system gradually supplanted the farm–nonfarm categorization, the Census of Housing data also began to be reported separately for areas inside and outside metropolitan areas. This disaggregation plays a prominent role in published census reports but is not shown in this table. The Standard Metropolitan Area system was not established until 1950, and then as a county-based system designed to increase the statistical uniformity of reports across federal agencies. In contrast, the urbanized area system reported here more accurately captures the social and economic differences that exist between urban and rural housing markets. As a general rule, the urbanized areas under the Census Bureau's definition are more territorially limited than the corresponding metropolitan areas because they exclude low population density places within metropolitan areas. Data disaggregated into housing units within and outside of metropolitan areas can be found in the 1930 and 1940 Censuses of Housing, and by Standard Metropolitan Areas beginning with 1950.

The regional classification system used in the Censuses of Population and Housing has changed only slightly for the period shown (see Table Ap-G in Appendix 2 regarding the composition of census regions and divisions). The data reported in this table have been organized by the standard four-region census classification system that has been in use since 1940 regardless of how the data were originally reported. State-level figures, and in most years county-level data, were also published throughout the period.

Race was generally assigned by the enumerator early on in the period shown in the table, but by 1940 it was being self-reported in categories that were commonly used at the time. The Census Bureau then determined the detail and specificity with which tabulations by race were published. As a result, several idiosyncrasies in the racial breakdowns that are reported occur over the decades. In 1910, units occupied by white and "colored" persons were reported separately only for the Southern states in which most blacks resided (national tabulations by race are unavailable for that date). In the 1930 published reports, Mexican-Americans were classified as "nonwhite," and the data shown for that year in the table had to be drawn from the 1940 revision of these figures. In 1960, separate tabulations were provided only for units occupied by white and "nonwhite" persons, although it was noted that blacks represented 95 percent of the latter category for the nation as a whole.

In this table, occupied housing units are reported for white and black families, and those of "all other races." In earlier years the last category primarily included persons of Native American, Chinese, and Japanese origin. Beginning in 1970, information was reported only for units occupied by white and black persons, and the "other races" category had to be constructed as a residual. The race classification system became much more detailed by 1980, when separate information was available for the "Asian and Pacific Islander" and the "American Indian, Eskimo, and Aleut" groups. These categories, along with the "other" category used by the Census Bureau, are included in the other categories reported here. The nonwhite category is reported for all years only because no more specific categories were available for 1960.

In 1960 the Census Bureau first tabulated units occupied by persons having Spanish surnames, but only for five Southwestern states. In 1970 a Hispanic category began to be reported for national data that cuts across racial classifications. In that year, however, only 1 percent of persons who reported being of Spanish origin also classified their race as "other." In 1980 the proportion increased to 40 percent, and the white and other race totals are therefore not comparable between these years.

Series Dc745–760. Homeownership rates for all groups have been calculated by expressing owner-occupied housing units as a percentage of occupied units reporting tenure.

TABLE Dc761–780   Home ownership rates, by region, sex, and race: 1900–1990

Contributed by William J. Collins and Robert A. Margo

	All household heads									
	United States		Northeast		Midwest		South		West	
	White	Black	White	Black	White	Black	White	Black	White	Black
	Dc761	Dc762	Dc763	Dc764	Dc765	Dc766	Dc767	Dc768	Dc769	Dc770
Year	Percent	Percent	Percent	Percent	Percent	Percent	Percent	Percent	Percent	Percent
1900	48.5	24.1	36.9	17.7	54.5	28.7	52.1	24.1	55.7	—
1910	47.2	25.3	34.8	15.9	53.7	32.1	49.7	25.3	57.1	—
1920	47.1	24.6	37.4	16.1	52.9	23.6	49.1	25.2	51.3	32.8
1940	42.1	20.5	35.7	10.3	45.6	19.9	42.8	21.8	46.3	30.8
1960	64.0	35.8	58.3	26.5	68.3	34.4	65.5	38.9	62.7	40.5
1970	66.2	39.9	62.2	27.8	70.9	41.8	68.3	44.4	61.2	39.6
1980	68.6	43.8	64.5	31.7	73.1	44.7	71.1	48.9	62.8	40.5
1990	66.5	40.9	65.4	31.7	71.1	40.1	68.5	45.7	59.1	33.9

	Male household heads									
	United States		Northeast		Midwest		South		West	
	White	Black	White	Black	White	Black	White	Black	White	Black
	Dc771	Dc772	Dc773	Dc774	Dc775	Dc776	Dc777	Dc778	Dc779	Dc780
Year	Percent	Percent	Percent	Percent	Percent	Percent	Percent	Percent	Percent	Percent
1900	48.4	23.8	36.8	19.1	54.2	30.3	51.5	23.5	56.3	—
1910	47.1	25.7	35.0	16.4	53.4	33.0	49.1	25.6	57.5	—
1920	47.2	24.6	37.7	16.7	52.8	22.8	48.7	25.2	52.0	34.3
1940	42.2	20.3	35.9	10.6	45.7	21.1	42.3	21.3	47.3	31.0
1960	66.4	39.1	61.4	30.5	70.5	38.7	67.1	41.2	65.7	44.6
1970	69.7	46.2	66.7	35.2	74.0	49.4	70.6	49.3	65.2	46.3
1980	73.4	53.9	71.0	42.7	77.7	56.2	74.7	58.0	67.8	48.3
1990	71.5	52.0	71.8	42.5	76.4	53.4	72.5	56.4	63.6	41.9

Source

Unpublished figures computed by William J. Collins and Robert A. Margo. See also William J. Collins and Robert A. Margo, "Race and Home Ownership: A Century-Long View," *Explorations in Economic History* 38 (1) (2001): 68–92.

Documentation

These series were tabulated from the Integrated Public Use Microdata Samples (IPUMS); see the Guide to the Millennial Edition for information on IPUMS. There is no sample for 1930, and the 1950 sample does not include housing information.

The figures give the number of homeowners per 100 household heads 20–64 years of age, expressed as a percentage.

Household heads who were enrolled in school were excluded. Rates for subgroups for which there were fewer than 100 observations in the IPUMS were not computed. Hispanics are included among whites in all years.

Figures were computed using IPUMS household weights. Figures for 1970 were computed from the Form 2 State Sample; for 1980, from the 1 Percent Metro B Sample; and for 1990, from the 1 Percent Unweighted Sample.

See Table Ap-G in Appendix 2 regarding the composition of census regions and divisions.

TABLE Dc781–809 Homeownership rates, by metropolitan location, region, age, marital and family status, race, and ethnicity: 1960–1999[1]

Contributed by Kenneth A. Snowden

	Overall	Metropolitan location				Region				Age of householder				
		Overall	Metropolitan		Nonmetropolitan	Northeast	Midwest	South	West	Under 35	35–44	45–54	55–64	Over 64
			Inside central cities	Outside central cities										
	Dc781	Dc782	Dc783	Dc784	Dc785	Dc786	Dc787	Dc788	Dc789	Dc790	Dc791	Dc792	Dc793	Dc794
Year	Percent	Percent	Percent	Percent	Percent	Percent	Percent	Percent	Percent	Percent	Percent	Percent	Percent	Percent
1960	62.1	59.0	—	—	66.8	55.5	66.4	63.4	62.2	—	—	—	—	—
1961	62.4	59.1	—	—	67.5	56.4	67.0	64.0	61.0	—	—	—	—	—
1962	63.0	60.2	—	—	67.7	56.9	67.9	64.4	61.2	—	—	—	—	—
1963	63.1	60.5	—	—	67.8	57.6	68.8	63.9	60.6	—	—	—	—	—
1964	63.1	60.1	—	—	68.7	57.7	68.7	64.4	59.7	—	—	—	—	—
1965	63.3	59.7	48.0	72.0	69.1	57.7	68.6	64.4	59.3	—	—	—	—	—
1966	63.4	60.0	48.3	72.0	69.9	57.7	68.5	65.3	60.5	—	—	—	—	—
1967	63.6	60.2	48.3	71.6	70.0	58.1	68.7	65.1	61.0	—	—	—	—	—
1968	63.9	60.5	48.6	71.8	70.3	59.1	68.9	65.0	60.6	—	—	—	—	—
1969	64.3	60.6	48.9	71.6	71.4	58.8	69.7	65.5	61.2	—	—	—	—	—
1970	64.2	60.3	48.9	70.6	71.6	58.1	69.5	66.0	60.0	—	—	—	—	—
1971	64.2	60.2	48.9	70.2	71.8	58.5	69.4	66.5	60.2	—	—	—	—	—
1972	64.4	60.7	49.8	70.6	72.2	58.7	69.3	66.4	61.0	—	—	—	—	—
1973	64.5	60.7	49.4	70.9	72.8	54.8 [2]	70.5	66.5	60.3	—	—	—	—	—
1974	64.6	61.0	49.7	70.9	72.6	58.8	70.4	66.3	60.6	—	—	—	—	—
1975	64.6	61.1	49.5	70.9	72.1	59.2	70.2	66.0	60.8	—	—	—	—	—
1976	64.7	61.3	49.5	71.0	72.2	59.8	69.7	66.4	60.9	—	—	—	—	—
1977	64.8	61.0	49.0	70.8	73.0	60.3	69.4	67.1	59.8	—	—	—	—	—
1978	65.0	61.2	49.4	70.7	73.0	60.6	69.3	67.9	59.2	—	—	—	—	—
1979	65.6	61.7	49.7	71.2	73.8	60.7	69.6	68.6	60.3	—	—	—	—	—
1980	65.6	61.6	49.6	70.8	74.1	60.8	69.8	68.7	60.0	—	—	—	—	—
1981	65.4	61.5	49.4	70.8	73.8	60.8	69.7	68.2	60.2	—	—	—	—	—
1982	64.8	61.0	49.1	70.0	73.0	61.1	69.4	66.7	59.4	41.2	70.0	77.4	80.0	74.4
1983	64.6	60.9	49.2	69.8	72.9	61.5	69.3	67.0	58.2	40.7	69.3	77.0	79.9	75.0
1984	64.5	60.8	49.0	69.7	72.3	61.2	68.4	67.0	58.5	40.5	68.9	76.5	80.0	75.1
1985	63.9	60.2	47.7	69.1	71.9	60.8	66.9	66.4	59.0	39.9	68.1	75.9	79.5	74.8
1986	63.8	61.2	48.5	70.8	72.3	61.4	66.9	66.1	58.3	39.6	67.3	76.0	79.9	75.0
1987	64.0	61.4	48.7	70.8	72.8	61.7	67.3	66.3	58.4	39.5	67.2	76.1	80.2	75.5
1988	63.8	61.3	48.3	70.6	72.6	61.3	67.5	65.8	58.5	39.3	66.9	75.6	79.5	75.6
1989	63.9	61.3	48.7	70.2	72.8	62.0	67.7	65.9	57.8	39.1	66.6	75.5	79.6	75.8
1990	63.9	61.3	48.7	70.1	73.2	62.6	67.5	65.7	58.0	38.5	66.3	75.2	79.3	76.3
1991	64.1	61.4	48.7	70.2	73.2	62.3	67.2	66.1	58.6	37.8	65.8	74.8	80.0	77.2
1992	64.1	61.6	49.3	70.1	72.8	62.5	67.2	65.8	59.3	37.6	65.1	75.1	80.2	77.1
1993	64.0	61.5	48.6	70.3	72.6	61.8	67.1	65.7	59.9	37.3	65.1	75.3	79.9	77.3
1994	64.0	61.7	48.5	70.3	72.0	61.5	67.7	65.6	59.4	37.3	64.5	75.2	79.3	77.4
1995	64.7	62.7	49.5	71.2	72.7	62.0	69.2	66.7	59.2	38.6	65.2	75.2	79.5	78.1
1996	65.4	63.4	49.7	72.2	73.5	62.2	70.6	67.5	59.2	39.1	65.5	75.6	80.0	78.9
1997	65.7	63.7	49.9	72.5	73.7	62.4	70.5	68.0	59.6	38.7	66.1	75.8	80.1	79.1
1998	66.3	64.2	50.0	73.2	74.7	62.6	71.1	68.6	60.5	39.3	66.9	75.7	80.9	79.3
1999	66.8	64.7	50.4	73.6	75.4	63.1	71.7	69.1	60.9	39.7	67.2	76.0	81.0	80.1

Notes appear at end of table

TABLE Dc781–809   Homeownership rates, by metropolitan location, region, age, marital and family status, race, and ethnicity: 1960–1999 *Continued*

	Marital and family status					Race of householder									
	Family					Annual averages of monthly figures						March data			
		No spouse present						American Indian, Aleut or Eskimo	Asian or Pacific Islander						
	Married couple	Male householder	Female householder	One person	Other multiperson	White	Black			Hispanic	Non-Hispanic	All races	White	Black	Hispanic
	Dc795 [3]	Dc796 [3]	Dc797 [3]	Dc798 [3]	Dc799 [3]	Dc800 [3]	Dc801 [3]	Dc802 [3]	Dc803 [3]	Dc804 [3]	Dc805 [3]	Dc806 [3]	Dc807 [3]	Dc808 [3]	Dc809 [3]
Year	Percent	Percent	Percent	Percent	Percent	Percent	Percent	Percent	Percent	Percent	Percent	Percent	Percent	Percent	Percent
1976	—	—	—	—	—	—	—	—	—	—	—	65.1	67.8	44.2	42.7
1977	—	—	—	—	—	—	—	—	—	—	—	64.9	67.6	44.1	42.3
1978	—	—	—	—	—	—	—	—	—	—	—	65.0	67.7	44.5	42.6
1979	—	—	—	—	—	—	—	—	—	—	—	67.6	70.2	48.2	46.0
1980	—	—	—	—	—	—	—	—	—	—	—	68.0	70.5	48.6	47.6
1981	—	—	—	—	—	—	—	—	—	—	—	67.8	70.6	47.8	46.6
1982	78.5	59.3	47.1	45.6	30.1	—	—	—	—	—	—	67.4	70.2	47.2	46.5
1983	78.3	59.2	47.0	46.2	30.6	—	—	—	—	—	—	64.9	67.6	45.3	41.2
1984	78.2	59.2	46.9	46.5	30.4	—	—	—	—	—	—	64.6	67.3	45.5	40.4
1985	78.2	57.8	45.8	45.8	31.1	—	—	—	—	—	—	64.3	67.3	44.1	41.1
1986	78.4	56.8	45.3	45.9	31.2	—	—	—	—	—	—	63.8	66.6	44.5	40.6
1987	78.7	56.5	45.8	46.3	31.6	—	—	—	—	—	—	64.0	66.8	45.4	40.6
1988	78.9	56.1	45.3	46.3	31.5	—	—	—	—	—	—	63.9	67.2	42.4	40.2
1989	78.3	55.7	44.1	48.2	31.2	—	—	—	—	—	—	64.0	67.4	41.8	41.6
1990	78.1	55.2	44.0	49.0	32.0	—	—	—	—	—	—	64.1	67.5	42.4	41.2
1991	78.5	54.3	43.9	49.4	32.5	—	—	—	—	—	—	64.0	67.3	42.4	39.0
1992	78.7	53.6	43.6	49.8	33.0	—	—	—	—	—	—	64.1	67.5	42.3	39.9
1993	78.7	53.7	43.9	49.8	33.5	—	—	—	—	—	—	64.6	68.1	42.2	40.1
1994	78.8	52.8	44.2	49.8	33.9	67.7	42.3	51.7	51.3	41.2	65.9	64.2	67.8	42.5	41.6
1995	79.6	55.3	45.1	50.5	33.8	68.7	42.7	55.8	50.8	42.1	66.7	64.7	68.6	41.9	42.4
1996	80.2	55.5	46.1	51.4	35.7	69.1	44.1	51.6	50.8	42.8	67.4	65.4	69.0	43.9	41.2
1997	80.8	54.0	46.1	51.8	37.3	69.3	44.8	51.7	52.8	43.3	67.8	65.7	69.2	45.5	43.1
1998	81.5	55.7	47.0	52.1	38.2	70.0	45.6	54.3	52.6	44.7	68.3	66.2	69.7	46.0	44.9
1999	81.8	56.1	48.2	52.7	38.9	70.5	46.3	56.1	53.1	45.5	68.9	66.7	70.3	45.5	45.2

[1] See text for information concerning the comparability of the data over time, the use of revised figures for certain years, and differences between these data and similar figures from the decennial Census of Housing.

[2] Rate is suspiciously low. The Housing and Household Economic Division of the U.S. Census Bureau has confirmed that 54.8 percent, even if mistaken, was the estimate originally reported.

[3] No data before 1976.

Sources

Series Dc781–805. 1960–1965: U.S. Bureau of the Census, Current Housing Reports/Housing Vacancies, Series H-111, number 43 (June 1966). 1965–1999: downloaded March 2001 from the Housing Statistics page on the Census Bureau's Internet site. The printed source for these series is U.S. Bureau of the Census, *Housing Vacancies and Homeownership: Annual* (1999), H111-99-USA.

Series Dc806–809. 1976–1999: U.S. Bureau of the Census, Current Population Reports, series P20-537, "America's Families and Living Arrangements: March 2000," downloaded September 2001 from the Census Bureau's Internet site.

Documentation

The data in this table are rates of homeownership that are derived from data collected in the Housing Vacancy Survey (HVS) and the Current Population Survey (CPS), which are conducted monthly by the U.S. Bureau of the Census. Refer to the text for Table Dc683–696 for a description of the CPS/HVS surveys and a discussion of the comparability of these data over time.

The homeownership rate is the number of owner-occupied housing units expressed as a percentage of all housing units. A housing unit is categorized as owner-occupied in the CPS/HVS if the owner or co-owner lives there, even if it is mortgaged or not fully paid for. A cooperative or condominium unit is also categorized as owner-occupied if, and only if, the owner or co-owner lives in it. All other occupied units are classified as "renter occupied," including units rented for cash rent and those occupied without payment of cash rent.

In the CPS/HVS, each household lives in an occupied housing unit – the two series are equal. The national homeownership rate in series Dc781, therefore, is equal to occupied housing units that are owner-occupied, series Dc695, expressed as a percentage of the total number of occupied units, series Dc694. The rate for all national subgroups shown in the table, correspondingly, is equal to the number of owner-occupied housing units with a given characteristic divided by the total number of occupied units with the same characteristic. All rates shown in this table have been calculated from CPS/HVS estimates of the housing inventory, and so they may differ from the figures that would have been obtained if a complete census had been taken using the same questionnaires, instructions, and enumerators. To underscore the point, note that the April 1990 Census produced a homeownership rate of 64.2 percent, whereas the CPS/HVS estimates were 63.9 percent for the first half of 1990. Users who require the standard errors associated with these estimates should consult the source.

Each decade the underlying CPS sample is reweighted to reflect more accurately the population patterns uncovered in the most recent decennial census. These alterations were made in 1994 and then used to revise the 1993 data so that the impact of the changes could be assessed. For the homeownership rates shown here, the impact of the reweighting was to reduce the national homeownership rate by 0.5 percent (or by 0.3–0.6 percent in each of the major regions of the country). For purposes of this table, the revised 1993 data, derived on the basis of 1990 Census results, are shown. Care should be taken in comparing homeownership rates in this and later years with those of earlier periods.

In the CPS/HVS a householder is defined as the person (or one of the persons) in whose name the housing unit is owned or rented or, if there is no such person, any adult member, excluding roomers, boarders, or paid employees. If the house is jointly owned by a married couple, either the husband or the wife may be listed first, thereby becoming the reference person, or householder, with whom the relationship of the other household members is recorded. One person in each household, therefore, is designated as the

(continued)

TABLE Dc781–809   Homeownership rates, by metropolitan location, region, age, marital and family status, race, and ethnicity: 1960–1999   *Continued*

"householder." The homeownership rates by age, race, and ethnicity refer to characteristics of this one individual within the household.

Series Dc782–785. Housing units are classified as lying inside or outside metropolitan areas according to standard definitions as issued by the Office of Management and Budget. The geographic boundaries of the nation's metropolitan areas are subject to change each decade, however, and were changed both in 1986 and 1994. At the same time, changes are made to the classification of areas as being within one of the nation's central cities or in a suburban metropolitan area. The source recommends special caution should be taken in comparing homeownership rates for these series across these two dates.

Series Dc786–789. The regional definitions conform to standard census usage. See Table Ap-G in Appendix 2 regarding the composition of census regions and divisions.

Series Dc795–799. These series examine the homeownership rate for different family types. A family in the CPS is a group of two or more persons (one of whom is the householder) related by birth, marriage, or adoption and residing together; all such persons (including related subfamily members) are considered members of one family. Beginning with the 1980 CPS, unrelated subfamilies (referred to in the past as secondary families) are no longer included in the count of families, nor are the members of unrelated subfamilies included in the count of family members. For purposes of this table, homeownership rates are shown for five major categories of families.

Series Dc795. A married-couple family is a husband and wife enumerated as members of the same household (the married couple may or may not have children living with them).

Series Dc796–797. The male householder, no wife present, category includes male householders living with at least one other relative in the household, but not with his wife. The male householder may be single or widowed; the wife may be absent because of separation or divorce; or the husband and wife may maintain separate residences for some other reason. The female householder, no husband present, category is defined analogously.

Series Dc798–799. A nonfamily householder in the CPS survey is a person maintaining a household while living either alone or only with nonrelatives.

Series Dc800–809. The CPS/HVS reports homeownership rates by race and ethnicity, but back only to 1994. Estimates of the numbers of occupied units and owner-occupied units separately for white, black, and Hispanic householders are available going back to 1976, however, as determined in the CPS Supplemental Survey that is conducted each March. These series were used to compute the homeownership rates that appear in series Dc806–809. The CPS/HVS and March homeownership rates should not be directly compared, however. The homeownership rates shown in series Dc800–805 are annual data constructed as averages of monthly figures; the rates in series Dc806–809, on the other hand, provide an estimate of the homeownership picture in only the spring of each year. Note also that the March homeownership rates for 1981 are revised figures based on population data from the 1980 Decennial Census.

Series Dc806–809. See the source for more detailed homeownership data by age, gender, and metropolitan areas.

TABLE Dc810–825 Rental and homeowner vacancy rates, by region and number of units in structure: 1956–1999[1]

Contributed by Kenneth A. Snowden

	Rental vacancy rate								Homeowner vacancy rate							
	Overall	Region				Number of units in structure			Overall	Region				Number of units in structure		
		Northeast	Midwest	South	West	One	Two to four	Five or more		Northeast	Midwest	South	West	One	Two to four	Five or more
	Dc810	Dc811	Dc812	Dc813	Dc814	Dc815	Dc816	Dc817	Dc818	Dc819	Dc820	Dc821	Dc822	Dc823	Dc824	Dc825
Year	Percent	Percent	Percent	Percent	Percent	Percent	Percent	Percent	Percent	Percent	Percent	Percent	Percent	Percent	Percent	Percent
1956	6.1	3.1	5.6	8.1	8.7	—	—	—	1.0	0.9	0.8	1.0	1.4	—	—	—
1957	5.6	3.4	5.4	6.7	7.4	—	—	—	1.0	0.7	0.9	0.9	1.3	—	—	—
1958	6.5	3.8	7.3	7.9	7.5	—	—	—	1.2	1.0	1.4	1.0	1.2	—	—	—
1959	7.0	3.9	7.1	9.4	8.5	—	—	—	1.2	1.0	1.1	1.2	1.4	—	—	—
1960	8.1	4.9	8.3	9.5	11.0	—	—	—	1.3	1.0	1.2	1.6	1.4	—	—	—
1961	8.7	4.9	9.3	10.4	10.7	—	—	—	1.4	1.1	1.2	1.7	1.3	—	—	—
1962	8.1	4.7	9.0	9.9	9.5	—	—	—	1.4	1.1	1.2	1.7	1.6	—	—	—
1963	8.3	5.1	8.7	9.2	10.2	—	—	—	1.5	1.0	1.4	1.9	1.9	—	—	—
1964	8.3	5.2	7.9	9.1	11.0	—	—	—	1.5	1.1	1.3	1.9	1.8	—	—	—
1965	8.3	5.6	7.2	9.0	11.9	—	—	—	1.5	1.0	1.2	2.0	1.9	—	—	—
1966	7.7	5.3	6.5	8.5	10.9	—	—	—	1.4	0.9	1.0	1.8	2.1	—	—	—
1967	6.8	4.8	5.7	8.0	8.9	—	—	—	1.3	0.7	1.0	1.7	2.0	—	—	—
1968	5.9	3.7	5.4	7.5	7.1	—	—	—	1.1	0.8	1.0	1.4	1.3	—	—	—
1969	5.5	3.0	5.7	7.2	6.1	—	—	—	1.0	0.8	0.9	1.2	1.2	—	—	—
1970	5.3	2.7	5.8	7.2	5.6	3.6	6.2	7.1	1.0	0.8	1.0	1.2	1.1	1.0	2.1	4.3
1971	5.4	3.0	5.7	7.3	5.7	3.6	6.4	7.9	1.0	0.7	0.9	1.2	1.2	0.9	2.4	8.5
1972	5.6	3.3	6.1	7.0	6.0	4.0	7.0	8.3	1.0	0.5	1.0	1.1	1.2	1.0	2.2	3.6
1973	5.8	3.9	5.9	7.1	6.3	4.3	7.0	8.1	1.0	0.6	1.0	1.2	1.4	1.0	3.3	9.3
1974	6.2	4.2	6.1	8.0	6.2	3.8	7.5	8.8	1.2	0.8	1.0	1.5	1.8	1.0	4.7	12.6
1975	6.0	4.1	5.7	7.7	6.2	3.6	7.3	8.3	1.2	1.0	1.0	1.5	1.5	1.0	5.4	14.4
1976	5.6	4.7	5.6	6.4	5.4	3.2	6.8	7.8	1.2	1.0	1.0	1.6	1.2	1.0	5.3	14.4
1977	5.2	5.1	5.1	5.7	5.0	3.1	6.4	7.1	1.2	0.9	0.9	1.7	0.9	0.9	5.4	16.3
1978	5.0	4.8	4.8	5.5	4.8	3.1	6.1	6.7	1.0	0.8	1.0	1.3	1.0	0.9	3.2	9.2
1979	5.4	4.5	5.7	6.1	5.3	3.2	6.6	7.6	1.2	1.0	1.2	1.1	1.3	1.0	3.7	6.6
1980	5.4	4.2	6.0	6.0	5.2	3.4	6.4	7.1	1.4	1.1	1.6	1.3	1.6	1.2	4.3	8.7
1981	5.0	3.7	5.9	5.4	5.1	3.3	6.0	6.4	1.4	1.1	1.4	1.3	1.7	1.1	5.4	10.8
1982	5.3	3.7	6.3	5.8	5.4	3.6	6.2	6.5	1.5	1.0	1.6	1.6	1.9	1.2	6.1	12.2
1983	5.7	4.0	6.1	6.9	5.2	3.7	6.7	7.1	1.5	1.0	1.5	1.8	1.8	1.3	5.2	8.8
1984	5.9	3.7	5.9	7.9	5.2	3.8	7.0	7.5	1.7	0.8	1.6	2.0	2.0	1.4	6.1	10.6
1985	6.5	3.5	5.9	9.1	6.2	3.8	7.9	8.8	1.7	1.0	1.6	2.1	2.1	1.4	6.6	10.1
1986	7.3	3.9	6.9	10.1	7.1	3.9	9.2	10.4	1.6	1.0	1.5	2.1	1.6	1.3	5.6	8.3
1987	7.7	4.1	6.8	10.9	7.3	4.0	9.7	11.2	1.7	1.2	1.4	2.0	1.8	1.4	5.8	8.6
1988	7.7	4.8	6.9	10.1	7.7	3.6	9.8	11.4	1.6	1.6	1.2	1.9	1.6	1.3	6.1	9.7
1989	7.4	4.7	6.8	9.7	7.1	4.2	9.2	10.1	1.8	1.5	1.4	2.2	1.6	1.4	7.1	9.6
1990	7.2	6.1	6.4	8.8	6.6	4.0	9.0	9.6	1.7	1.6	1.3	2.1	1.8	1.4	7.1	8.4
1991	7.4	6.9	6.7	8.9	6.5	3.9	9.4	10.4	1.7	1.5	1.3	2.2	1.7	1.4	6.8	7.9
1992	7.4	6.9	6.7	8.2	7.1	3.8	9.4	10.0	1.5	1.3	1.2	1.7	1.9	1.3	5.8	7.4
1993	7.3	7.0	6.6	7.9	7.4	3.7	9.4	10.2	1.4	1.3	1.1	1.7	1.4	1.2	5.3	6.8
1994	7.4	7.1	6.8	8.0	7.1	4.5	9.1	9.8	1.5	1.5	1.1	1.7	1.6	1.3	4.9	5.6
1995	7.6	7.2	7.2	8.3	7.5	5.4	9.0	9.5	1.5	1.5	1.3	1.7	1.7	1.4	4.8	5.1
1996	7.8	7.4	7.9	8.6	7.2	5.5	9.2	9.6	1.6	1.6	1.3	1.8	1.7	1.4	5.1	6.0
1997	7.7	6.7	8.0	9.1	6.6	5.8	9.0	9.1	1.6	1.6	1.2	1.9	1.8	1.5	4.4	4.6
1998	7.9	6.7	7.9	9.6	6.7	6.3	9.0	9.4	1.7	1.5	1.4	2.0	1.7	1.6	4.4	4.5
1999	8.1	6.3	8.6	10.3	6.2	7.3	8.7	8.9	1.7	1.4	1.2	2.0	1.7	1.5	3.6	3.8

Note appears on next page

(continued)

TABLE Dc810–825   Rental and homeowner vacancy rates, by region and number of units in structure: 1956–1999   Continued

¹ See text for information concerning the comparability of the data over time and the use of revised figures for certain years.

both revised and unrevised estimates for years directly preceding the introduction of substantial changes in basic procedures or the sample design used by the CPS/HVS:

		Rental vacancy rate					Homeowner vacancy rate				
		U.S.	Northeast	Midwest	South	West	U.S.	Northeast	Midwest	South	West
1979	Unrevised	5.0	4.0	5.1	5.8	4.9	1.1	0.9	1.1	1.1	1.3
1979	Revised	5.4	4.5	5.7	6.1	5.3	1.2	1.0	1.2	1.1	1.3
1989	Unrevised	7.1	4.7	6.5	9.1	6.9	1.6	1.5	1.3	2.0	1.4
1989	Revised	7.4	4.7	6.8	9.7	7.1	1.8	1.5	1.4	2.2	1.6
1993	Unrevised	7.4	7.1	6.6	8.0	7.5	1.4	1.3	1.1	1.6	1.4
1993	Revised	7.3	7.0	6.6	7.9	7.4	1.4	1.3	1.1	1.7	1.4

Sources

1956–1970: Current Housing Reports, Housing Vacancies, series H-111, number 43, Tables F and 1, and series H-111-73-5, Tables 1 and 4.

1970–1999: Current Population Survey / Housing Vacancy Survey, Series H-111, various issues.

Data after 1980 and for selected earlier years are also available and were downloaded from the Internet site of the U.S. Bureau of the Census.

Documentation

Rental and homeowner vacancy rates are available from the Housing Vacancy Survey (HVS) for the United States, regions, states, and the seventy-five largest metropolitan areas. The state and metropolitan area data are available annually, whereas national and regional data are available quarterly. Separate multifamily vacancy rates are available only nationally from the HVS. Overall vacancy rates (which include single- and multifamily units) are available by region, state, and for the sixty-one largest metropolitan areas. Separate multifamily vacancy rates are available from the American Housing Survey (AHS) by region, but only for every two years. The AHS also produces vacancy rates for the nation's forty-four largest metropolitan areas every four years on a rotating basis. The HVS collects data on residential units only. No data on commercial vacancy rates are collected at the U.S. Census Bureau.

Since 1956, the HVS has provided vacancy rates for rental and homeowner properties as well as characteristics of those units available for occupancy. These data are used extensively by public- and private-sector organizations to evaluate the need for new housing programs and initiatives. The rental vacancy rate is also a component of the index of leading economic indicators and is used by the federal government and economic forecasters to gauge the current economic climate. The HVS is a supplement to the Current Population Survey (CPS), as explained in the text for Table Dc683–696.

The vacancy rate for rental units is calculated as the proportion of year-round rental housing units that are for rent. In terms of the housing inventory estimates shown in Table Dc683–696, the vacancy rate is equal to the number of year-round vacant units for rent, series Dc686, expressed as a percentage of the following sum: the number of year-round vacant units for rent (series Dc686 itself), the number of occupied rental units (series Dc696), and the number of year-round vacant rental units rented but awaiting occupancy (not shown separately in Table Dc683–696).

The homeowner vacancy rate is the percentage of the homeowner housing inventory that is vacant for sale and is calculated in a similar manner as the rental vacancy rate. The total homeowner housing inventory is defined as the sum of housing units occupied by owner, housing units that are year-round vacant but sold and awaiting occupancy, and the year-round vacant units that are for sale. The percentage of the total homeowner inventory represented by the last component is the homeowner vacancy rate. The annual vacancy rates for the nation and its regions shown in this table are averages of twelve monthly vacancy rates. Users of these data should note that the vacancy rates shown in this table do not generally agree with those published in the Series H-111 report prior to 1972. Before that time, all previous annual data were recalculated on that basis.

Because they are calculated from CPS/HVS estimates of the housing inventory, these rates may differ from the figures that would have been obtained if a complete census had been taken using the same questionnaires, instructions, and enumerators. In fact, the rental vacancy rate from the April 1990 Census was 8.5 percent, whereas the CPS/HVS reported a rental vacancy rate of 7.2 percent for the first half of 1990. Similarly, the CPS/HVS had a homeowner vacancy rate of approximately 1.7 percent for the first half of 1990, whereas the decennial census for April of that year measured a homeowner vacancy rate of 2.1 percent. These differences illustrate that caution should be used when making comparisons between the 1990 Census and the CPS/HVS. They also underscore that the CPS/HVS vacancy rates are calculated using estimates of the housing inventory and are subject to sampling error. Users who require the standard errors associated with these estimates should consult the source.

Because the rental and homeowner vacancy rates are based on the CPS/HVS estimates of the housing inventory, they are subject to the same problems of comparability over time. The source provides

See the text for Table Dc683–696 and the source for a description of these revisions. In this table, the revised vacancy rates are shown for each of these years, and caution should be used in comparing rates before and after these dates. In particular, the source notes that it is safe to assume that HVS produced underestimates of vacant units prior to the implementation of new procedures in 1980, and that unrevised data prior to 1990 are not completely comparable to data for 1990 and after, owing to the inclusion of year-round vacant mobile homes beginning in that year. Thus, particular caution should be observed in drawing conclusions about trends in vacancy rates that extend from before 1980 to 1980 and beyond, or from before 1990 to 1990 and later.

The CPS/HVS quarterly reports provide separate vacancy rate estimates for units broken down by several different characteristics – rooms in the unit, the year the unit was built, monthly rent or home value, and, as shown in this table, the number of units in the structure. To derive the housing inventory estimates for occupied housing units according to each of these categories, the distributions of characteristics of occupied housing units are drawn from the AHS and are then applied to the independent CPS current housing inventory estimates to obtain the characteristics of occupied housing units used in this report. The supplemental HVS procedure obtains similar information for units found to be vacant. The use of data from the biennial AHS introduces yet another problem when comparing vacancy rates by units in structure (or any other characteristic covered by HVS) over time. This is because revisions are made in the sampling weights that are used to derive the CPS/HVS inventory estimates by housing characteristics each time the results of the most recent AHS are introduced into the estimation procedure. Refer to the text for Table Dc653–669 for a description of the AHS and information on the years in which significant revisions were made to the procedures used to produce the vacancy rates by units in structure.

In the CPS/HVS, a structure is defined as a separate building, which either has open space on all four sides or is separated from other structures by dividing walls that extend from ground to roof. In double houses, row houses, and houses attached to nonresidential structures, each building is a structure if the common wall between them goes from ground to roof. Sheds and private garages that adjoin houses are not counted as separate structures. In apartment developments, each building with open space on all sides is considered a separate structure. The count of housing units in a structure is the total number of units in the structure, both occupied and vacant units. In the tabulations, occupied mobile homes or trailers, tents, and boats are included in the "one housing unit in structure" category.

The vacancy rates by the number of units in the structure are calculated in a slightly different manner than the rates for the nation and regions. The total rental and homeowner housing inventories for this case do not include units rented or sold but awaiting occupancy. Instead, the total (rental or homeowner) housing inventory for each units-in-structure category is defined as the sum of the number of units occupied (by renters or owners) in that category and the number of year-round vacant units on the market (for rent or sale) in that category. The vacancy rates in these cases, therefore, represent the percentage of the rental and homeowner housing inventory that is currently for rent or sale.

See Table Ap-G in Appendix 2 regarding the composition of census regions and divisions.

TABLE Dc826-828   Single-family house price indexes and median asking price: 1890-1947

Contributed by Kenneth A. Snowden

	Price index		Median asking price in Washington, D.C.		Price index		Median asking price in Washington, D.C.		Price index		Median asking price in Washington, D.C.
	Unadjusted	Adjusted for depreciation			Unadjusted	Adjusted for depreciation			Unadjusted	Adjusted for depreciation	
	Dc826	Dc827	Dc828		Dc826	Dc827	Dc828		Dc826	Dc827	Dc828
Year	Index 1929 = 100	Index 1929 = 100	Dollars	Year	Index 1929 = 100	Index 1929 = 100	Dollars	Year	Index 1929 = 100	Index 1929 = 100	Dollars
1890	61.3	36.0	—	1910	74.2	57.3	—	1930	95.7	97.1	7,146
1891	55.3	32.9	—	1911	72.5	56.7	—	1931	87.9	90.4	6,796
1892	56.3	34.0	—	1912	75.3	59.7	—	1932	78.7	82.0	6,515
1893	58.7	35.9	—	1913	75.3	60.5	—	1933	75.7	80.0	5,759
1894	68.4	42.4	—	1914	78.1	63.7	—	1934	77.9	78.3	5,972
1895	62.1	39.0	—	1915	71.7	59.2	—	1935	—	—	6,296
1896	53.8	34.3	—	1916	78.5	65.8	—	1936	—	—	6,145
1897	55.5	35.9	—	1917	80.1	68.0	—	1937	—	—	6,622
1898	59.1	38.7	—	1918	85.2	73.3	4,821	1938	—	—	6,420
1899	56.5	37.5	—	1919	93.7	81.7	5,626	1939	—	—	6,416
1900	64.6	43.5	—	1920	102.7	90.8	6,296	1940	—	—	6,558
1901	54.2	37.0	—	1921	100.4	90.0	7,019	1941	—	—	6,954
1902	63.9	42.4	—	1922	101.8	92.5	7,197	1942	—	—	7,573
1903	64.9	45.5	—	1923	103.3	95.2	7,400	1943	—	—	8,011
1904	67.9	48.3	—	1924	103.5	96.7	7,720	1944	—	—	8,649
1905	59.5	42.9	—	1925	108.9	103.1	7,809	1945	—	—	10,131
1906	70.6	51.6	—	1926	104.5	100.4	7,748	1946	—	—	12,638
1907	77.9	37.7	—	1927	100.6	97.9	7,682	1947	—	—	12,309
1908	70.3	52.8	—	1928	102.1	100.7	7,333				
1909	68.7	52.3	—	1929	100.0	100.0	7,246				

Sources

Series Dc826-827. Leo Grebler, David M. Blank, and Louis Winnick, *Capital Formation in Residential Real Estate* (Princeton University Press, 1956), Tables C-1, C-3, pp. 347-51.

Series Dc828. Ernest M. Fisher, *Urban Real Estate Markets: Characteristics and Financing* (National Bureau of Economic Research, 1951), Table 6, p. 53.

Documentation

The development of price indexes for specific types of urban real estate is unusually difficult because of the great heterogeneity of the product and the local nature of real estate markets. Although the problem of heterogeneity is somewhat less serious in the case of single-family houses, before 1960 there were few attempts to compile national indexes of home prices. For a general discussion of the conceptual difficulties of using construction cost indexes for measuring price changes for homes and of distinguishing between prices for new and old homes, see Grebler, Blank, and Winnick (1956), Appendix C. In this discussion the authors also identify the few attempts that had been made to assemble price indexes for local urban markets, such as Herman Wyngarden, "An Index of Local Real Estate Prices," *Michigan Business Studies* 1 (2) (1927); William M. Hoad, "Real Estate Prices: A Study of Residential Real Estate Transfers in Lucas County, Ohio" (Ph.D. dissertation, University of Michigan, 1942); and data for Cleveland and Seattle given in Grebler, Blank, and Winnick (1956), Table C-2, p. 348. See Fisher (1951), pp. 51-6, for additional discussion of the problems associated with home price indexes.

Series Dc826-827. Grebler, Blank, and Winnick constructed their price indexes for owner-occupied houses as a check on the adequacy of their own residential construction cost index, which they assembled by extending the E. H. Boeckh residential construction cost index, series Dc210, back to the 1890-1915 period. To assemble the index, they secured detailed information about the value of homes for a sample of residential properties in twenty-two cities from U.S. Department of Commerce, *Financial Survey of Urban Housing, 1937*. The survey, in particular, ascertained the value of individual properties in 1934 and in the year that each property had been acquired by the then-present owner. Some of these homes, therefore, were acquired new whereas others were existing at the time of purchase. From these data the ratio of the total acquisition cost to self-reported market value in 1934 was calculated for single-family owner-occupied homes in twenty-two cities. Grebler, Blank, and Winnick's unadjusted price index represents the average across cities of the median ratio for each year of acquisition cost to 1934 value. The authors recognized that their index was subject to biases because it included the impact of both depreciation and structural additions and alterations as reflected in 1934 market values. To mitigate the first bias, an adjusted index was calculated that corrected for the net downward bias by allowing an annual rate of depreciation equal to 1.375 percent. See Grebler, Blank, and Winnick (1956), Appendix C, for complete details.

Series Dc828. Fisher's price index was assembled from the results of an experimental study by the National Housing Agency (a predecessor of the U.S. Department of Housing and Urban Development) of a sample of newspaper advertisements. Similar experimental indexes, but for shorter periods, were developed for 100 metropolitan areas. The principal limitations of the index, fully recognized by Fisher, are biases owing to the following: (1) changes in the types of homes in the sample from period to period; (2) the omission of a sizable number of houses that were advertised without a listing price or sold without newspaper advertisement; and (3) cyclical differences in the spread between asking prices and selling prices that were unaccounted for.

TABLE Dc829–857 Single-family home prices for new and previously occupied homes, by Federal Home Loan Bank District: 1963–1999
Contributed by Kenneth A. Snowden

	Average price			Median price											
				All houses											
					Federal Home Loan Bank District										
	Overall	New	Previously occupied	United States	Boston	New York	Pittsburgh	Atlanta	Cincinnati	Indianapolis	Chicago	Des Moines	Dallas	Topeka
Year	Dc829	Dc830	Dc831	Dc832	Dc833	Dc834	Dc835	Dc836	Dc837	Dc838	Dc839	Dc840	Dc841	Dc842
	Thousand dollars	Thousand dollars	Thousand dollars	Thousand dollars	Thousand dollars	Thousand dollars	Thousand dollars	Thousand dollars	Thousand dollars	Thousand dollars	Thousand dollars	Thousand dollars	Thousand dollars	Thousand dollars
1963	20.6	23.1	19.7	—	—	—	—	—	—	—	—	—	—	—
1964	21.8	24.3	20.9	—	—	—	—	—	—	—	—	—	—	—
1965	22.5	25.1	21.6	—	—	—	—	—	—	—	—	—	—	—
1966	23.3	26.6	22.2	—	—	—	—	—	—	—	—	—	—	—
1967	25.1	28.0	24.1	—	—	—	—	—	—	—	—	—	—	—
1968	26.9	30.7	25.6	—	—	—	—	—	—	—	—	—	—	—
1969	29.9	34.1	28.3	—	—	—	—	—	—	—	—	—	—	—
1970	31.5	35.5	30.0	—	—	—	—	—	—	—	—	—	—	—
1971	32.8	36.3	31.7	—	—	—	—	—	—	—	—	—	—	—
1972	34.3	37.3	33.4	—	—	—	—	—	—	—	—	—	—	—
1973	33.7	37.0	31.5	30.9	34.0	36.5	27.5	32.0	29.0	27.5	30.0	26.8	29.5	29.3
1974	37.6	40.1	35.5	34.5	36.5	39.5	29.9	34.5	32.0	29.5	33.0	29.5	33.2	32.0
1975	41.2	44.7	39.2	37.7	39.5	41.5	32.0	39.3	36.0	32.2	36.0	32.9	37.5	36.0
1976	44.3	49.1	42.0	40.0	41.5	43.0	35.0	40.0	36.0	34.5	40.0	36.4	38.9	38.5
1977	49.6	54.4	47.6	44.7	45.0	45.0	38.0	42.0	40.0	37.9	45.0	40.0	42.5	42.5
1978	57.1	62.8	54.5	50.7	49.9	50.0	42.0	46.9	45.0	44.6	52.0	46.9	47.5	48.5
1979	67.7	74.4	64.8	60.0	56.0	59.0	45.0	52.8	50.0	48.5	56.0	55.0	55.3	52.5
1980	73.4	83.2	68.3	63.0	60.0	65.0	50.0	60.0	51.7	48.0	60.0	55.0	62.5	55.0
1981	76.3	90.3	68.5	64.5	63.0	67.0	49.5	65.0	56.9	52.5	62.0	54.5	67.1	56.0
1982	78.4	94.1	70.7	66.0	65.0	73.0	48.0	65.0	57.9	47.0	60.0	60.0	68.4	60.8
1983	83.1	93.9	79.3	70.0	73.0	81.0	55.0	68.0	55.0	49.5	70.0	56.5	73.0	69.0
1984	86.6	96.8	82.2	73.0	80.0	82.6	58.5	68.0	56.0	52.5	67.0	58.0	73.0	69.0
1985	96.1	105.0	92.7	80.0	96.0	97.0	61.5	75.3	60.0	56.5	68.5	58.0	72.5	72.5
1986	110.6	119.8	108.5	95.0	126.0	119.4	68.5	87.6	65.5	63.0	73.0	70.0	88.0	78.9
1987	121.8	137.2	117.7	107.0	140.0	134.4	78.0	94.8	75.0	68.0	83.0	84.9	93.9	87.0
1988	131.6	150.5	126.6	116.0	148.0	148.0	80.0	100.0	82.5	76.0	86.0	83.0	90.0	90.0
1989	142.8	160.1	138.4	125.0	145.0	150.0	85.0	106.7	80.0	78.9	93.0	83.9	89.0	96.0
1990	142.6	154.1	140.3	126.0	140.0	145.5	92.0	110.9	81.0	81.0	95.0	82.0	96.1	94.0
1991	146.7	155.2	145.8	129.0	139.5	151.5	87.5	103.0	89.5	88.0	98.1	88.9	92.5	99.0
1992	146.4	158.1	144.1	125.0	148.0	149.0	115.0	124.0	98.0	90.0	117.0	97.0	104.9	98.5
1993	143.1	163.7	139.6	121.7	150.0	153.0	111.5	124.5	96.5	94.0	116.0	99.6	95.5	111.0
1994	142.0	170.7	136.4	120.3	149.9	160.0	105.0	117.0	97.5	98.8	127.0	98.9	87.0	120.1
1995	142.8	175.4	137.3	123.0	139.9	154.0	98.3	129.0	100.0	99.0	126.4	95.9	94.0	126.0
1996	155.1	182.6	150.2	131.9	145.0	164.0	105.9	132.0	110.0	96.0	134.9	106.0	115.0	126.0
1997	164.5	181.4	161.0	140.0	165.0	173.8	125.5	138.2	124.5	119.9	133.7	120.5	122.2	121.0
1998	173.4	195.0	169.5	145.0	175.0	180.0	129.0	141.5	130.0	125.0	140.0	126.0	122.3	116.0
1999	184.2	210.7	179.3	151.3	173.2	185.0	130.8	146.0	134.5	127.0	148.0	120.0	127.0	154.0

Median price

	All houses — Federal Home Loan Bank District		Previously occupied — Federal Home Loan Bank District													
	San Francisco	Seattle	United States	Boston	New York	Pittsburgh	Atlanta	Cincinnati	Indianapolis	Chicago	Des Moines	Dallas	Topeka	San Francisco	Seattle
	Dc843	Dc844	Dc845	Dc846	Dc847	Dc848	Dc849	Dc850	Dc851	Dc852	Dc853	Dc854	Dc855	Dc856	Dc857
Year	Thousand dollars	Thousand dollars	Thousand dollars	Thousand dollars	Thousand dollars	Thousand dollars	Thousand dollars	Thousand dollars	Thousand dollars	Thousand dollars	Thousand dollars	Thousand dollars	Thousand dollars	Thousand dollars	Thousand dollars
1963	—	—	—	—	—	—	—	—	—	—	—	—	—	—	—
1964	—	—	—	—	—	—	—	—	—	—	—	—	—	—	—
1965	—	—	—	—	—	—	—	—	—	—	—	—	—	—	—
1966	—	—	—	—	—	—	—	—	—	—	—	—	—	—	—
1967	—	—	—	—	—	—	—	—	—	—	—	—	—	—	—
1968	—	—	—	—	—	—	—	—	—	—	—	—	—	—	—
1969	—	—	—	—	—	—	—	—	—	—	—	—	—	—	—
1970	—	—	—	—	—	—	—	—	—	—	—	—	—	—	—
1971	—	—	—	—	—	—	—	—	—	—	—	—	—	—	—
1972	—	—	—	—	—	—	—	—	—	—	—	—	—	—	—
1973	32.3	30.0	28.5	32.5	35.8	24.7	28.3	26.5	24.9	28.0	24.0	25.0	25.0	32.0	27.0
1974	38.3	33.9	32.0	36.0	39.5	27.5	30.5	30.0	26.0	31.0	26.5	27.3	28.0	37.5	29.5
1975	44.5	36.5	35.0	38.5	40.5	30.0	36.0	33.0	29.9	34.0	28.0	32.3	33.0	45.0	33.0
1976	50.3	40.0	37.5	40.0	43.0	33.0	35.5	34.0	31.0	36.9	32.5	32.3	35.0	50.0	35.8
1977	59.0	45.0	42.0	43.5	44.5	36.0	39.0	38.0	34.9	42.5	37.0	37.6	38.5	59.0	41.0
1978	70.0	54.0	47.5	46.5	49.5	39.7	43.7	42.5	39.9	48.5	42.5	40.0	43.5	70.0	49.2
1979	80.9	65.0	57.0	53.0	58.0	41.0	48.0	46.4	42.8	52.5	51.0	49.6	46.5	80.0	58.3
1980	95.0	73.0	57.9	58.0	62.0	46.0	54.0	48.0	43.0	56.5	50.0	56.0	48.0	93.0	59.5
1981	97.0	70.0	57.0	59.0	63.0	46.0	55.9	51.0	45.0	60.0	50.0	60.0	48.5	94.0	70.0
1982	107.9	83.0	60.0	61.9	70.0	44.0	57.9	52.9	44.0	60.0	59.5	57.5	54.0	109.0	75.0
1983	115.0	86.6	67.0	70.0	80.0	51.5	63.5	52.5	48.5	66.5	55.0	69.0	64.0	115.0	81.0
1984	115.5	84.5	69.0	78.5	82.0	51.0	64.0	54.0	49.0	63.9	55.0	67.0	64.5	115.0	80.0
1985	127.5	83.0	76.0	95.0	97.0	57.5	70.0	57.0	53.9	66.9	57.9	69.5	67.0	128.0	80.0
1986	136.0	97.5	91.0	125.0	120.0	65.0	85.0	63.0	60.0	71.0	66.5	87.5	73.0	138.0	93.0
1987	144.0	101.0	100.0	138.0	132.5	69.5	89.9	68.5	65.0	79.5	80.0	89.5	82.5	145.0	95.0
1988	160.0	98.0	110.0	145.0	145.0	72.9	94.1	75.0	70.0	82.0	78.0	85.0	86.8	158.0	94.0
1989	175.8	102.0	120.0	145.0	149.0	73.5	97.5	74.0	72.0	86.3	84.0	84.7	87.5	175.9	95.0
1990	180.0	119.0	125.0	139.9	145.0	80.0	105.0	76.0	76.5	89.9	70.0	90.0	87.5	180.0	114.5
1991	190.0	130.0	126.0	137.8	150.0	84.5	98.0	85.6	85.6	92.0	83.0	85.0	92.5	190.0	128.0
1992	185.0	123.0	122.0	147.0	147.0	110.0	115.0	97.0	87.5	115.0	91.0	99.2	94.9	186.0	121.0
1993	170.0	124.0	118.0	150.0	152.0	109.9	117.5	95.0	90.0	112.0	96.0	88.0	105.0	171.0	122.5
1994	161.0	128.0	115.0	147.2	158.0	100.0	107.8	93.0	93.9	120.0	92.0	76.5	117.5	162.5	125.0
1995	150.0	135.0	118.0	137.0	152.0	92.0	120.0	94.2	95.0	120.0	93.5	89.5	121.5	148.9	134.0
1996	171.0	154.8	126.5	142.0	160.0	99.8	123.6	105.0	93.0	126.0	100.0	110.9	123.0	169.0	154.0
1997	179.6	160.0	136.8	165.0	171.0	122.9	135.0	122.5	118.0	129.0	119.0	119.5	117.5	173.0	160.0
1998	199.0	157.7	140.2	174.9	179.0	125.0	138.0	127.0	124.9	135.5	123.0	120.0	114.0	193.0	157.6
1999	217.0	166.0	146.5	170.0	183.0	126.3	142.3	129.9	124.0	145.0	117.0	124.5	146.5	210.0	166.0

(continued)

TABLE Dc829–857   Single-family home prices for new and previously occupied homes, by Federal Home Loan Bank District: 1963–1999   *Continued*

Source

Federal Housing Finance Board, Monthly Interest Rate Survey. The data for this table were downloaded from the Internet site of the Federal Housing Finance Board on June 26, 2000.

Documentation

The Federal Housing Finance Board (FHFB) releases the results of the Monthly Interest Rate Survey (MIRS) in monthly press releases and in periodic press releases summarizing historical data. The source provides additional information on interest rates, loan terms, and home prices by property type, loan type (fixed- or adjustable-rate), and lender type, as well as information on fifteen- and thirty-year fixed-rate loans (see Table Dc1210–1254). The MIRS Internet site also provides data on mortgage loans in major metropolitan areas and states.

The series in this table reflect the average and median purchase prices for homes bought with conventional mortgage loans (Veterans Administration, Federal Housing Administration, and refinancing loans are excluded). The data are compiled by the FHFB in its MIRS, in which information is gathered from a sample of major mortgage lenders including savings and loan associations, savings banks, commercial banks, and mortgage companies. Such lenders have accounted for more than 90 percent of all conventional home mortgage loan originations since 1972. FHFB has conducted the survey since October 1989; before then, the survey was conducted by the Federal Home Loan Bank Board. The survey covers all purchase loans closed (that

is, entered on the books) by participants during the first five working days of the month through October 1991, and the last five working days of each month after that date.

The Federal National Mortgage Association and the Federal Home Loan Mortgage Corporation are required to use information from MIRS to determine the maximum size of loan that they can purchase or guarantee.

All price series are weighted averages of home prices from conventional single-family nonfarm first mortgage loans. The weights for individual lenders are calculated according to single-family conventional mortgage holdings the institution has in relation to the holdings of all lenders in a stratum, the type of institution, and the geographic location of the institution. Geographic area averages pertain to the location of the property securing loans represented in the MIRS survey and may be subject to more fluctuation than the national averages.

Averages for the purchase of previously occupied homes are for properties that have had prior owners. Average prices for new homes are for properties where construction has been completed and the dwelling units (including detached and semidetached primary residences, condominium units, vacation, and second homes) have never been occupied. Average prices for new homes by home loan district are reported separately in MIRS, but are not shown here.

The purchase price reported by the lender represents the estimated current market value of the loan collateral.

TABLE Dc858–868   Existing single-family home sales and prices, by region: 1968–1999[1]

Contributed by Kenneth A. Snowden

	Home sales					Median sales price					
	Overall	Northeast	Midwest	South	West	Overall	Northeast	Midwest	South	West	Average sales price
	Dc858	Dc859	Dc860	Dc861	Dc862	Dc863	Dc864	Dc865	Dc866	Dc867	Dc868
Year	Thousand	Thousand	Thousand	Thousand	Thousand	Dollars	Dollars	Dollars	Dollars	Dollars	Dollars
1968	1,569	243	490	529	308	20,100	21,400	18,200	19,000	22,900	22,300
1969	1,594	240	508	538	308	21,800	23,700	19,000	20,300	23,900	23,700
1970	1,612	251	501	568	292	23,000	25,200	20,100	22,200	24,300	25,700
1971	2,018	311	583	735	389	24,800	27,100	22,100	24,300	26,500	28,000
1972	2,252	361	630	788	473	26,700	29,800	23,900	26,400	28,400	30,100
1973	2,334	367	674	847	446	28,900	32,800	25,300	29,000	31,000	32,900
1974	2,272	354	645	839	434	32,000	35,800	27,700	32,300	34,800	35,800
1975	2,476	370	701	862	543	35,300	39,300	30,100	34,800	39,600	39,000
1976	3,064	439	881	1,033	712	38,100	41,800	32,900	36,500	46,100	42,200
1977	3,650	515	1,101	1,231	803	42,900	44,000	36,700	39,800	57,300	47,900
1978	3,986	516	1,144	1,416	911	48,700	47,900	42,200	45,100	66,700	55,500
1979	3,827	526	1,061	1,353	887	55,700	53,600	47,800	51,300	77,400	64,200
1980	2,973	403	806	1,092	672	62,200	60,800	51,900	58,300	89,300	72,800
1981	2,419	353	632	917	516	66,400	63,700	54,300	64,400	96,200	78,300
1982	1,990	354	490	780	366	67,800	63,500	55,100	67,100	98,900	80,500
1983	2,697	477	692	1,004	524	70,300	72,200	56,600	69,200	94,900	83,100
1984	2,829	478	720	1,006	624	72,400	78,700	57,100	71,300	95,800	86,000
1985	3,134	561	806	1,063	704	75,500	88,900	58,900	75,200	95,400	90,800
1986	3,474	635	922	1,145	773	80,300	104,800	63,500	78,200	100,900	98,500
1987	3,436	618	892	1,163	763	85,600	133,300	66,000	80,400	113,200	106,300
1988	3,513	606	865	1,224	817	89,300	143,000	68,400	82,200	124,900	112,800
1989	3,325	490	832	1,185	818	93,100	145,200	71,300	84,500	139,900	118,100
1990	3,219	458	809	1,193	759	95,500	141,200	74,000	85,900	139,600	118,600
1991	3,186	463	812	1,173	737	100,300	141,900	77,800	88,900	147,200	128,400
1992	3,479	521	913	1,242	802	103,700	140,000	81,700	92,100	143,800	130,900
1993	3,786	550	967	1,386	882	106,800	139,500	85,200	95,000	142,600	133,500
1994	3,916	552	965	1,436	962	109,900	139,100	87,900	96,000	147,000	136,800
1995	3,888	547	945	1,433	964	113,100	136,900	93,600	97,800	148,300	139,100
1996	4,196	584	986	1,511	1,116	115,800	127,800	101,000	103,400	147,100	141,800
1997	4,382	607	1,005	1,595	1,174	121,800	131,800	107,000	109,600	155,200	150,500
1998	4,970	662	1,130	1,868	1,309	128,400	135,900	114,300	116,200	164,800	159,100
1999	5,205	656	1,148	2,015	1,386	133,300	139,000	119,600	120,300	173,900	168,300

TABLE Dc858–868   Existing single-family home sales and prices, by region: 1968–1999   *Continued*

[1] Data beginning in 1989 were rebenchmarked to homeowner information drawn from the 1990 Census and thus may not be comparable to data for earlier years.

Source

The 1998–1999 data shown here were downloaded from the Internet site of the National Association of Realtors on September 29, 2001. The data for all other years were taken from U.S. Department of Housing and Urban Development, *U.S. Housing Market Conditions* (4th quarter, 2000), Tables 7 and 9.

Documentation

The National Association of Realtors (NAR) has compiled information on existing home sales on a monthly basis for the United States and its regions, and on a quarterly basis for states, metropolitan areas, and some counties. Other proprietary data available from the NAR include sales of existing cooperatives and condominiums, and housing affordability indexes.

The Research Division of the NAR receives data each month on existing detached single-family home sales from nearly 700 Boards or multiple listing services (MLS) nationwide, which represent about 25 percent of all existing home sale transactions. The data sent by each Board/MLS include the total number of closed existing home sales and a breakdown of the total by price categories. Data from a nationally representative sample of 160 of these Boards/MLS are selected to construct monthly existing home sales. The

data on number of home sales from this sample are then inflated to provide monthly estimates for the nation and each region. The weights used in this adjustment are benchmarked every ten years to reflect shifts in regional demand. The annual existing sales totals shown here (series Dc858–862) represent the sum of the monthly seasonally unadjusted sales estimates. The existing sales estimates from 1989–1999 have been rebenchmarked to the 1990 Census. Caution should be used, therefore, in comparing sales volume across this break.

Median sales prices are also first computed for the nation and four census regions on a monthly basis. Sales prices are not seasonally adjusted nor are adjustments made for changes in the characteristics and size of homes that are sold. The distribution of home sales prices is generally not symmetric – it is positively skewed with a longer "tail" of high-priced homes than low-priced homes. In this case, the median sales price will be lower than the average (or mean) sales price, and it is generally thought to be a better overall measure of housing prices. In keeping with this practice, the median sales prices for the United States and its regions are shown in this table, but the average sales price for the United States is also shown for purposes of comparison.

Refer to the NAR's Internet site for additional details about these series.

See Table Ap-G in Appendix 2 regarding the composition of census regions and divisions.

TABLE Dc869–878   Repeat sales house price indexes, by region: 1975–2000

Contributed by Kenneth A. Snowden

Year	United States	New England	Middle Atlantic	South Atlantic	East South Central	West South Central	East North Central	West North Central	Mountain	Pacific
	Dc869	Dc870	Dc871	Dc872	Dc873	Dc874	Dc875	Dc876	Dc877	Dc878
	Index	Index	Index	Index	Index	Index	Index	Index	Index	Index
1975	62.5	66.2	72.2	69.7	71.4	57.4	64.2	65.0	54.2	43.2
1976	65.5	68.7	73.4	71.3	73.1	60.9	67.0	68.5	57.7	49.5
1977	70.7	73.5	73.7	74.0	78.8	67.8	73.1	72.3	65.1	59.6
1978	80.0	82.9	80.3	80.9	84.6	76.8	82.3	82.7	75.7	74.9
1979	91.7	97.2	91.5	90.7	96.3	90.0	94.4	93.8	90.8	85.5
1980	100.0	100.0	100.0	100.0	100.0	100.0	100.0	100.0	100.0	100.0
1981	105.7	108.4	106.5	107.9	103.9	105.6	102.5	101.6	105.1	109.2
1982	111.0	115.4	113.1	113.3	106.4	121.2	101.2	103.2	114.7	114.5
1983	114.1	122.3	113.0	117.7	111.1	125.9	102.1	105.8	123.0	116.4
1984	118.3	145.5	126.1	121.9	112.7	124.1	103.8	110.3	119.7	118.5
1985	124.8	170.8	142.9	127.5	118.3	124.3	107.4	114.1	122.1	123.5
1986	133.8	211.4	163.6	134.6	124.2	126.0	113.0	119.3	125.9	130.0
1987	145.1	255.6	194.5	142.9	131.7	123.4	121.2	124.5	128.9	141.2
1988	154.3	282.8	221.9	152.3	136.6	111.9	130.9	127.1	124.4	156.7
1989	163.1	287.0	232.4	161.8	139.1	110.4	139.5	129.6	123.9	185.0
1990	171.4	286.7	236.1	168.4	142.9	112.8	147.4	133.5	127.4	214.8
1991	172.4	267.1	230.5	169.5	145.5	114.6	152.8	135.6	131.4	219.5
1992	176.6	262.6	236.0	174.4	150.7	119.3	159.5	139.8	137.2	220.3
1993	178.5	258.2	236.2	176.3	155.1	122.3	165.0	143.9	144.5	215.1
1994	183.4	261.2	240.3	180.7	162.7	127.7	172.3	150.3	157.8	212.7
1995	184.9	254.8	232.6	180.8	169.9	128.9	180.9	158.2	171.0	206.2
1996	194.8	267.9	244.1	190.7	180.6	135.7	191.8	166.9	184.0	214.2
1997	199.4	271.9	243.3	194.6	187.5	137.7	201.7	173.8	191.2	216.1
1998	210.1	287.2	254.1	205.1	196.9	145.0	211.7	182.6	201.2	231.2
1999	220.8	308.3	264.4	213.7	206.1	151.0	222.5	192.2	210.2	247.3
2000	235.9	341.8	281.5	226.3	213.8	160.3	236.6	208.0	223.4	267.4

Source

U.S. Office of Federal Housing Enterprise Oversight (OFHEO), *House Price Index*, various issues. Data were downloaded from the Internet site of the OFHEO on January 16, 2001.

Documentation

These house price indexes are issued quarterly; the annual observations shown here are for the first quarter of each year. The index is based so that the first quarter of 1980 equals 100.

A repeat sales home price index measures average changes in the prices of a sample of homes that have been resold or refinanced during the period covered by the index. The advantage of this type of an index is that each price change used to construct the index is measured for the same house at two points in time so that housing quality and characteristics are held constant except for depreciation and additions or alterations. In contrast, a hedonic price index is constructed by estimating the prices of individual housing characteristics from market data and tracking the change in the price of a

(continued)

TABLE Dc869–878   Repeat sales house price indexes, by region: 1975–2000   *Continued*

fixed set of these characteristics over time. See the U.S. Bureau of Census's "fixed characteristics" price indexes for new homes in Table Dc585–607 for an index of this latter type.

An obvious disadvantage of the repeat sales index methodology is the difficulty associated with identifying a sufficiently large and representative sample to implement the methodology. The price indexes shown here are for detached single-family homes that were sold at least twice (or refinanced) with a conventional mortgage loan that was either purchased or held by the Federal National Mortgage Association (Fannie Mae) or the Federal Home Loan Mortgage Corporation (Freddie Mac). Both are government-sponsored enterprises (GSEs) that buy mortgages from commercial banks, thrift institutions, mortgage banks, and other primary lenders, and either hold these mortgages in their own portfolios or package them into mortgage-backed securities for resale to investors. Fannie Mae and Freddie Mac have a very large presence in the nation's secondary mortgage market, with combined assets of more than $2.4 trillion as of December 2000. The combined mortgage records of these GSEs, in fact, represent the nation's largest database of mortgage transactions, and the sample used to construct these indexes is very large – more than fourteen million repeat transactions between 1975 and 2000.

The large size of these samples permit the construction of price indexes for the nation and the census divisions shown here, as well as the state- and metropolitan-level indexes that are also available in the source. Users of these indexes should be aware, however, that important components of the housing market are not covered. Because these transactions involved only detached single-family homes, multifamily housing units and condominiums are not included. Because each transaction was financed by a conventional mortgage loan, the sample excludes transactions financed with loans that are guaranteed by the Veterans Administration or insured by the Federal Housing Administration. Finally, because Fannie Mae and Freddie Mac purchased or held the mortgage, which financed all of the sampled transactions, each had to conform to the underwriting guidelines and maximum size limit of these agencies. Excluded, therefore, are home sales or refinancings that were accomplished with nonconforming mortgages such as "jumbo" loans, which are above the maximum loan size Fannie Mae and Freddie Mac are allowed to accept.

These price indexes are produced by OFHEO, an independent agency within the U.S. Department of Housing and Urban Development. OFHEO serves as the federal regulator responsible for ensuring the financial safety and soundness of Fannie Mae and Freddie Mac. Although both GSEs are publicly owned corporations, each has a back-up credit line with the U.S. Treasury and therefore in 1992 Congress created OFHEO to administer quarterly risk-based capital stress tests on Fannie Mae and Freddie Mac. Performance of this test involves assessing changes in the loan-to-value ratio for mortgages held or guaranteed by the two GSEs, which requires, in turn, a home price index. Congress mandated that the OFHEO use the U.S. Commerce Department's annual Constant Quality Home Price Index (see series Dc597–598) or an "index of similar quality, authority and public availability that is regularly used by the Federal Government." OFHEO has concluded that an index of house prices based on properties secured by mortgages in Fannie Mae and Freddie Mac's own mortgage portfolios offered significant advantages over the one produced for the Commerce Department by the U.S. Bureau of the Census.

Before 1994, Fannie Mae and Freddie Mac both used data from their own portfolios to produce repeat sales indexes; in 1994, the two GSEs combined data to produce a single index. Currently, Fannie Mae and Freddie Mac provide information on their most recent mortgage transactions each quarter that is used to identify repeat transactions for the most recent quarter and for each quarter going back to 1975. The new repeat transactions that are identified are combined with the data since 1975 to establish price differentials on properties where more than one mortgage transaction has occurred. The data are then merged to create an updated historical database that is used to estimate the OFHEO's housing price index each quarter.

The methodology is a modified version of the Case–Shiller geometric weighted repeat sales procedure. Details about the construction of these series are available in Charles A. Calhoun, "OFHEO House Price Indexes: HPI Technical Description," Office of Federal Housing Enterprise Oversight, March 1996. This document is available at the OFHEO Internet site.

See Table Ap-G in Appendix 2 regarding the composition of census regions and divisions.

TABLE Dc879–888   Residential capital formation and wealth – nonfarm housekeeping structures and land: 1889–1953

Contributed by Kenneth A. Snowden

	Capital formation					Wealth				
								Structures		Land
	Gross	Net	Gross	Net	Residential construction cost index	Total (current dollars)	Constant dollars	Current dollars	As a percentage of total wealth	Value
	Dc879	Dc880	Dc881	Dc882	Dc883	Dc884	Dc885	Dc886	Dc887	Dc888
Year	Million dollars	Million dollars	Million 1929 dollars	Million 1929 dollars	1929 = 100	Million dollars	Million 1929 dollars	Million dollars	Percent	Million dollars
1889	891	712	2,284	1,826	39.0	14,333	22,050	8,600	40.0	5,733
1890	875	681	2,232	1,736	39.2	15,540	23,786	9,324	40.0	6,216
1891	694	493	1,831	1,301	37.9	15,742	25,087	9,508	39.6	6,234
1892	843	636	2,290	1,727	36.8	16,257	26,814	9,868	39.3	6,389
1893	662	444	1,804	1,210	36.7	16,833	28,024	10,285	38.9	6,548
1894	672	452	1,898	1,277	35.4	16,867	29,301	10,373	38.5	6,494
1895	756	529	2,167	1,515	34.9	17,403	30,816	10,755	38.2	6,648
1896	683	444	1,945	1,264	35.1	18,103	32,080	11,260	37.8	6,843
1897	719	474	2,090	1,379	34.4	18,387	33,459	11,510	37.4	6,877
1898	646	382	1,800	1,063	35.9	19,703	34,522	12,393	37.1	7,310
1899	679	386	1,763	1,003	38.5	21,607	35,525	13,677	36.7	7,930

Notes appear at end of table

TABLE Dc879–888   Residential capital formation and wealth – nonfarm housekeeping structures and land: 1889–1953   Continued

	Capital formation					Wealth				
								Structures		Land	
Year	Gross	Net	Gross	Net	Residential construction cost index	Total (current dollars)		Constant dollars	Current dollars	As a percentage of total wealth	Value
	Dc879	Dc880	Dc881	Dc882	Dc883	Dc884		Dc885	Dc886	Dc887	Dc888
	Million dollars	Million dollars	Million 1929 dollars	Million 1929 dollars	1929 = 100	Million dollars		Million 1929 dollars	Million dollars	Percent	Million dollars
1900	503	186	1,239	459	40.6	22,936		35,984	14,610	36.3	8,326
1901	683	364	1,703	908	40.1	23,116		36,892	14,794	36.0	8,322
1902	648	310	1,561	748	41.5	24,256		37,640	15,621	35.6	8,635
1903	691	335	1,607	778	43.0	25,494		38,418	16,520	35.2	8,974
1904	788	428	1,855	1,007	42.5	25,739		39,425	16,756	34.9	8,983
1905	1,264	872	2,840	1,960	44.5	28,118		41,385	18,416	34.5	9,702
1906	1,281	831	2,620	1,700	48.9	31,971		43,085	21,069	34.1	10,902
1907	1,148	661	2,246	1,293	51.1	34,255		44,378	22,677	33.8	11,578
1908	1,148	662	2,319	1,337	49.5	33,977		45,715	22,629	33.4	11,348
1909	1,390	869	2,705	1,691	51.4	36,369		47,406	24,367	33.0	12,002
1910	1,140	581	2,143	1,093	53.2	38,337		48,499	25,801	32.7	12,536
1911	1,109	545	2,113	1,040	52.5	38,417		49,539	26,008	32.3	12,409
1912	1,221	631	2,270	1,172	53.8	40,063		50,711	27,283	31.9	12,780
1913	1,214	631	2,339	1,216	51.9	39,401		51,927	26,950	31.6	12,451
1914	1,187	587	2,274	1,124	52.2	40,251		53,051	27,693	31.2	12,558
1915	1,300	671	2,430	1,255	53.5	41,986		54,306	29,054	30.8	12,932
1916	1,371	686	2,406	1,204	57.0	45,527		55,510	31,641	30.5	13,886
1917	879	69	1,320	103	66.6	52,987		55,613	37,038	30.1	15,949
1918	481	−479	608	−605	79.2	61,972		55,008	43,566	29.7	18,406
1919	1,398	285	1,518	309	92.1	72,163		55,317	50,947	29.4	21,216
1920	1,212	−231	1,021	−195	118.7	92,155		55,122	65,430 [2]	29.0	26,725 [2]
1921	1,980	815	2,076	854	95.4	74,791		55,976	53,401	28.6	21,390
1922	3,155	2,052	3,597	2,340	87.7	71,329		58,316	51,143	28.3	20,186
1923	4,170	2,879	4,242	2,929	98.3	83,501		61,245	60,204	27.9	23,297
1924	4,805	3,462	4,958	3,573	96.9	86,633		64,818	62,809	27.5	23,824
1925	5,160	3,749	5,364	3,897	96.2	90,802		68,715	66,104	27.2	24,698
1926	5,190	3,686	5,356	3,804	96.9	95,999		72,519	70,271	26.8	25,728
1927	4,830	3,270	5,052	3,420	95.6	98,639		75,939	72,598	26.4	26,041
1928	4,510	2,876	4,702	2,999	95.9	102,438		78,938	75,702	26.1	26,736
1929	3,380	1,625	3,380	1,625	100.0	108,429		80,563	80,563	25.7	27,866
1930	1,875	207	1,923	212	97.5	105,430		80,775	78,756	25.3	26,674
1931	1,495	−46	1,663	−51	89.9	96,761		80,724	72,571	25.0	24,190
1932	590	−706	775	−928	76.1	80,537		79,796	60,725	24.6	19,812
1933	435	−847	571	−1,111	76.2	79,100		78,685	59,958	24.2	19,142
1934	580	−797	699	−961	82.9	84,669		77,724	64,433	23.9	20,236
1935	960	−363	1,193	−451	80.5	81,314		77,273	62,205	23.5	19,109
1936	1,505	124	1,787	147	84.2	84,770		77,420	65,188	23.1	19,582
1937	1,795	255	1,916	272	93.7	94,297		77,692	72,797	22.8	21,500
1938	1,915	324	1,988	336	96.3	96,830 [2]		78,028	75,140	22.4	21,690
1939	2,590	958	2,643	978	98.0	99,264		79,006	77,426	22.0	21,838
1940	2,895	1,162	2,846	1,143	101.7	104,102		80,149	81,512	21.7	22,590
1941	3,415	1,519	3,116	1,386	109.6	113,548		81,535	89,362	21.3	24,186
1942	1,665	−353	1,438	−305	115.8	118,922		81,230	94,064	20.9	24,858
1943	870	−1,225	718	−1,011	121.2	122,450		80,219	97,225	20.6	25,225
1944	790	−1,464	598	−1,108	132.1	130,960		79,111	104,506	20.2	26,454
1945	1,060	−1,315	752	−933	140.9	137,348		78,178	110,153	19.8	27,195
1946	3,870	1,243 [2]	2,479	796	156.1	153,140		78,974	123,278	19.5	29,862
1947 [1]	6,185	2,955	3,269	1,562	189.2	188,396		80,556	152,412	19.1	35,984
1948 [1]	8,425	4,745	4,002	2,254	210.5	214,358		82,790	174,273	18.7	40,085
1949	8,082	4,415	3,956	2,161	204.3	212,430		84,951	173,555	18.3	38,875
1950	12,425	8,417	5,763	3,904	215.6	233,623		88,855	191,571	18.0	42,052
1951	10,783	6,310	4,648	2,720	232.0	257,833		91,575	212,454	17.6	45,379
1952	10,915	6,187	4,582	2,597	238.2	270,918		94,173	224,320	17.2	46,598
1953	11,638	6,691	4,801	2,760	242.4	282,751		96,933	234,966	16.9	47,785

Notes appear at end of table

(continued)

TABLE Dc879–888   Residential capital formation and wealth – nonfarm housekeeping structures and land: 1889–1953   *Continued*

[1] In calculating wealth in structures in constant 1929 dollars, the authors made an arithmetic error so that the 1947 value is $20 million too high and the increase between 1947 and 1948 is $20 million too small. These small offsetting errors are not corrected here because they are embedded in all of the wealth estimates (series Dc884–888) although only for these two years.

[2] Minor arithmetic errors that appear in the source have been corrected here.

Source

Leo Grebler, David M. Blank, and Louis Winnick, *Capital Formation in Residential Real Estate* (Princeton University Press, 1956), Tables B-6 (p. 338), B-8 (p. 340), B-10 (p. 342), and D-1 (pp. 360–1).

Documentation

The estimates in this table are for nonfarm housekeeping dwellings (that is, they do not cover transient hotels, clubs, motels, dormitories, and similar facilities). Figures for capital formation are for the year indicated; wealth estimates are for the end of the year.

Grebler, Blank, and Winnick combined evidence from U.S. Census Bureau, U.S. Bureau of Labor Statistics, and U.S. Department of Commerce sources to assemble their estimates of residential capital formation for the 1890–1953 period. Based on these estimates, Grebler, Blank, and Winnick concluded that the share of residential construction in gross national product had declined over this period, as had real per capita expenditure on residential housing. The second result was particularly controversial and led to a lively exchange concerning the methods used to construct these estimates, and their accuracy (see below). Grebler, Blank, and Winnick vigorously defended their estimates, and they remain the only comprehensive and continuous estimates of residential construction that extend back before 1925. See Table Dc889–902 for residential wealth estimates that cover more recent periods.

The source also provides separate annual estimates of expenditures on new residential construction, additions and alterations, and depreciation and demolitions. Chapters 3 and 4 of the source provide extensive discussion of the capital formation estimates, while Appendix D includes a detailed description of the wealth estimates. For a detailed, informative, and lively debate concerning the accuracy of these estimates, see Margaret G. Reid, "Capital Formation in Residential Real Estate," *Journal of Political Economy* 66 (April 1958): 131–54; Grebler, Blank, and Winnick, "Capital Formation in Residential Real Estate," *Journal of Political Economy* 67 (December 1959):

612–9; and short rejoinders by both Reid and Grebler, Blank, and Winnick that follow the second article.

Gross Capital Formation in Housekeeping Residential Real Estate

The gross capital formation series include expenditures on both new housing, and alterations and additions to existing housing. To derive the net capital formation series, estimates of depreciation and demolitions were subtracted from the gross capital formation series.

The conversion between constant- and current-dollar series was accomplished by a residential construction price index, series Dc883, which Grebler, Blank, and Winnick constructed by linking the Boeckh residential construction cost index, series Dc210, with their own weighted index of building wages and materials for the pre-1920 period.

Housekeeping Residential Wealth

Grebler, Blank, and Winnick constructed their estimates of housekeeping residential wealth from their residential capital formation series. The value of structures in 1929 dollars, series Dc885, was obtained by securing an estimate of year-end residential housing wealth for 1889 in 1929 dollars and then accumulating from that base their annual estimates of net capital formation in constant dollars, series Dc882. The initial estimate for year-end 1889 was based on the average value of owner-occupied nonfarm mortgaged homes reported in the 1890 Census report *Real Estate Mortgages* (see pp. 364–5 of the source). Because the census surveyed homeowners as of June 1, 1890, Grebler, Blank, and Winnick had to use extrapolation to derive year-end estimates.

The construction cost index (series Dc883) was used to convert the value of structures in 1929 dollars into current dollars (series Dc886). To construct estimates of current-dollar total residential wealth (series Dc884) from the current-dollar wealth-in-structures series, an estimate of the breakdown of residential wealth into its two basic components – land and structures – was required for each year. The series used for this purpose by Grebler, Blank, and Winnick (series Dc887) is a linear trend line fitted to a number of benchmarks, which is fully explained in Louis Winnick, "Wealth Estimates for Residential Real Estate, 1890–1950" (Ph.D. dissertation, Columbia University, 1953). Current-dollar wealth held in residential land, series Dc888, was then derived simply by subtracting wealth in structures from total wealth.

TABLE Dc889–902   Net stock of structures – private residential, current cost and chain-type quantity index, by type: 1925–1999

Contributed by Kenneth A. Snowden

	Current cost							Chain-type quantity indexes						
	All structures	Housing units				Improvements to structures	Other structures	All structures	All units	Housing units			Improvements to structures	Other structures
		In structures with								In structures with				
		All units	One to four units	Five or more units	Manufactured homes					One to four units	Five or more units	Manufactured homes		
	Dc889	Dc890	Dc891	Dc892	Dc893	Dc894	Dc895	Dc896	Dc897	Dc898	Dc899	Dc900	Dc901	Dc902
Year	Million dollars	Million dollars	Million dollars	Million dollars	Million dollars	Million dollars	Million dollars	1996 = 100	1996 = 100	1996 = 100	1996 = 100	1996 = 100	1996 = 100	1996 = 100
1925	100,037	92,419	85,856	6,562	0	6,663	955	17.50	19.59	21.57	11.55	0.00	6.90	43.16
1926	104,386	96,468	89,025	7,443	0	6,844	1,075	18.26	20.45	22.36	13.10	0.00	7.12	48.59
1927	107,849	99,655	91,314	8,341	0	7,034	1,160	18.96	21.22	23.05	14.75	0.00	7.36	52.70
1928	114,023	105,321	95,965	9,356	0	7,449	1,252	19.58	21.92	23.67	16.16	0.00	7.60	55.59
1929	117,911	108,814	98,810	10,004	0	7,772	1,325	19.98	22.34	24.04	17.05	0.00	7.85	58.01
1930	112,244	103,432	93,884	9,548	0	7,521	1,292	20.12	22.46	24.16	17.21	0.00	8.07	59.75
1931	96,959	89,328	81,079	8,249	0	6,521	1,110	20.19	22.53	24.23	17.28	0.00	8.13	59.60
1932	85,848	79,063	71,813	7,250	0	5,808	978	20.10	22.43	24.14	17.10	0.00	8.12	59.08
1933	89,671	82,530	74,985	7,545	0	6,125	1,016	19.99	22.28	23.99	16.92	0.00	8.19	58.46
1934	93,585	86,026	78,202	7,824	0	6,504	1,055	19.92	22.17	23.89	16.74	0.00	8.32	57.99
1935	95,238	87,355	79,467	7,888	0	6,817	1,066	19.94	22.15	23.88	16.61	0.00	8.57	57.66
1936	103,104	94,353	85,847	8,506	0	7,605	1,146	20.03	22.19	23.93	16.61	0.00	8.86	57.45
1937	110,721	101,068	91,958	9,110	0	8,428	1,225	20.14	22.28	24.02	16.66	0.00	9.15	57.47
1938	113,605	103,536	94,240	9,296	0	8,824	1,245	20.26	22.37	24.13	16.67	0.00	9.37	57.35
1939	117,912	107,366	97,743	9,623	0	9,268	1,277	20.53	22.65	24.44	16.85	0.00	9.64	57.50
1940	127,679	116,159	105,843	10,316	0	10,157	1,362	20.87	23.00	24.84	16.95	0.00	9.92	57.59
1941	140,237	127,433	116,253	11,180	0	11,332	1,473	21.24	23.39	25.29	17.01	0.00	10.23	57.61
1942	151,127	137,198	125,130	12,068	0	12,368	1,561	21.31	23.46	25.37	17.07	0.00	10.30	56.97
1943	163,417	148,348	135,095	13,253	0	13,414	1,655	21.26	23.41	25.29	17.21	0.00	10.26	55.85
1944	175,915	159,811	145,445	14,366	0	14,347	1,757	21.20	23.34	25.17	17.44	0.00	10.26	54.87
1945	189,402	171,976	156,619	15,358	0	15,553	1,873	21.13	23.24	25.07	17.36	0.00	10.39	54.04
1946	223,560	201,830	183,877	17,871	82	19,568	2,162	21.70	23.73	25.62	17.46	0.11	11.37	54.21
1947	264,427	237,177	216,107	20,829	241	24,795	2,456	22.50	24.45	26.40	17.83	0.32	12.61	53.98
1948	289,176	257,565	234,843	22,296	427	29,041	2,570	23.48	25.34	27.38	18.21	0.57	14.06	53.88
1949	305,674	270,913	247,076	23,316	521	32,134	2,627	24.35	26.15	28.26	18.68	0.67	15.28	54.00
1950	337,483	298,272	272,570	25,061	641	36,459	2,753	25.63	27.44	29.71	19.13	0.80	16.54	53.99
1951	367,749	323,922	296,742	26,427	753	40,937	2,890	26.62	28.41	30.83	19.23	0.93	17.71	54.03
1952	387,538	340,017	312,142	26,950	926	44,583	2,938	27.58	29.31	31.88	19.27	1.15	18.97	53.98
1953	403,669	352,729	324,438	27,216	1,075	47,959	2,981	28.56	30.24	32.94	19.37	1.38	20.26	54.46
1954	424,499	369,761	340,843	27,710	1,208	51,680	3,059	29.64	31.28	34.15	19.46	1.61	21.53	55.10
1955	454,490	394,948	364,914	28,553	1,482	56,356	3,185	30.93	32.57	35.63	19.54	2.03	22.90	55.94
1956	478,661	414,432	383,429	29,103	1,900	60,912	3,317	32.06	33.63	36.84	19.60	2.67	24.36	57.36
1957	493,204	424,677	392,899	29,497	2,281	65,235	3,292	33.07	34.54	37.84	19.83	3.33	25.86	59.06
1958	508,777	435,840	400,543	32,707	2,590	69,629	3,307	34.08	35.46	38.73	20.89	3.93	27.26	61.86
1959	530,858	452,637	414,745	35,019	2,873	74,743	3,478	35.45	36.77	40.02	22.37	4.60	28.89	64.85
1960	551,809	468,056	427,713	37,138	3,206	80,110	3,642	36.66	37.87	41.11	23.62	5.22	30.64	67.64
1961	572,067	483,067	439,882	39,892	3,293	85,113	3,887	37.86	38.95	42.10	25.25	5.81	32.39	71.88
1962	593,440	499,502	452,358	43,962	3,183	89,618	4,319	39.21	40.24	43.21	27.83	6.59	33.88	79.70
1963	608,409	508,895	456,942	48,516	3,437	94,938	4,575	40.77	41.77	44.46	31.27	7.63	35.43	86.04
1964	657,393	551,130	490,325	56,662	4,143	101,049	5,214	42.41	43.43	45.81	34.94	9.11	36.93	94.13

(continued)

TABLE Dc889–902 Net stock of structures – private residential, current cost and chain-type quantity index, by type: 1925–1999 *Continued*

	Current cost							Chain-type quantity indexes						
	All structures	Housing units				Improvements to structures	Other structures	All structures	Housing units				Improvements to structures	Other structures
		All units	In structures with		Manufactured homes				All units	In structures with		Manufactured homes		
			One to four units	Five or more units						One to four units	Five or more units			
	Dc889	Dc890	Dc891	Dc892	Dc893	Dc894	Dc895	Dc896	Dc897	Dc898	Dc899	Dc900	Dc901	Dc902
Year	Million dollars	Million dollars	Million dollars	Million dollars	Million dollars	Million dollars	Million dollars	1996 = 100	1996 = 100	1996 = 100	1996 = 100	1996 = 100	1996 = 100	1996 = 100
1965	698,950	586,250	518,567	62,947	4,735	106,843	5,857	43.96	44.98	47.13	37.82	10.92	38.33	102.86
1966	755,746	632,644	557,272	69,988	5,383	116,489	6,614	45.28	46.24	48.21	40.10	12.90	39.75	110.58
1967	805,824	672,714	590,161	76,197	6,356	125,915	7,195	46.50	47.42	49.24	41.96	15.13	41.17	115.95
1968	891,514	743,869	648,736	87,352	7,781	139,673	7,972	47.97	48.90	50.44	44.88	18.44	42.49	119.77
1969	954,338	790,758	683,119	97,201	10,438	155,215	8,364	49.47	50.45	51.57	48.62	22.65	43.74	122.09
1970	1,008,902	831,134	712,210	106,587	12,337	169,166	8,601	50.81	51.80	52.49	52.21	26.45	45.04	122.62
1971	1,133,357	937,281	795,726	126,920	14,635	186,761	9,315	52.69	53.81	53.97	56.96	31.82	46.42	122.08
1972	1,270,694	1,057,287	888,010	151,383	17,895	203,472	9,935	54.96	56.30	55.79	63.05	38.75	47.82	120.65
1973	1,458,373	1,218,191	1,011,615	183,982	22,593	229,351	10,832	57.20	58.80	57.60	69.20	45.88	48.97	119.45
1974	1,656,037	1,376,139	1,135,481	211,971	28,687	268,121	11,777	58.75	60.42	58.85	72.78	49.96	50.28	117.94
1975	1,791,838	1,486,896	1,228,143	227,829	30,924	292,522	12,420	59.95	61.53	60.00	73.51	51.88	51.89	117.27
1976	1,988,725	1,647,472	1,367,625	244,628	35,219	327,896	13,357	61.64	63.19	61.77	74.19	54.56	53.75	115.71
1977	2,322,070	1,933,732	1,606,894	286,368	40,469	373,461	14,877	63.86	65.49	64.20	75.43	58.10	55.70	113.56
1978	2,681,402	2,235,594	1,870,472	318,539	46,583	429,464	16,343	66.25	67.93	66.74	76.96	61.66	57.97	111.72
1979	3,115,959	2,600,353	2,185,906	360,211	54,236	497,460	18,147	68.46	70.14	68.95	78.99	65.09	60.28	109.61
1980	3,512,102	2,920,749	2,456,619	404,767	59,363	571,670	19,683	69.96	71.47	70.19	80.73	67.31	62.57	107.68
1981	3,775,982	3,122,266	2,612,932	445,429	63,906	633,297	20,419	71.22	72.59	71.21	82.35	69.55	64.53	106.30
1982	3,942,844	3,250,934	2,695,279	489,190	66,465	671,247	20,663	72.03	73.28	71.79	83.54	71.39	65.95	105.22
1983	4,102,122	3,375,060	2,787,104	517,813	70,143	706,306	20,756	73.64	74.90	73.32	85.56	74.61	67.51	104.48
1984	4,334,068	3,562,401	2,936,862	552,138	73,401	750,433	21,235	75.63	76.91	75.19	88.28	77.76	69.45	104.07
1985	4,564,634	3,750,265	3,078,954	595,226	76,085	792,755	21,614	77.61	78.87	77.00	91.02	80.48	71.58	103.47
1986	4,928,093	4,057,800	3,327,276	651,317	79,206	847,653	22,641	79.97	81.13	79.20	93.80	82.20	74.44	103.07
1987	5,240,876	4,314,316	3,553,034	678,554	82,729	902,957	23,603	82.31	83.39	81.54	95.73	83.74	77.16	103.52
1988	5,560,496	4,567,000	3,778,410	700,981	87,609	969,062	24,434	84.58	85.53	83.84	97.10	84.43	80.02	103.75
1989	5,863,816	4,801,409	4,006,406	702,712	92,291	1,037,058	25,349	86.69	87.47	85.90	98.41	85.24	82.94	104.07
1990	6,087,209	4,962,564	4,154,316	712,785	95,462	1,098,660	25,986	88.52	89.16	87.74	99.30	85.71	85.41	104.72
1991	6,209,567	5,047,097	4,221,407	728,770	96,920	1,136,901	25,569	89.86	90.48	89.26	99.61	85.60	86.88	103.39
1992	6,542,842	5,314,655	4,462,875	751,709	100,071	1,201,945	26,241	91.50	91.96	90.98	99.63	86.45	89.24	102.40
1993	6,935,300	5,653,036	4,789,188	754,846	109,002	1,254,782	27,483	93.50	93.79	93.11	99.41	88.29	92.05	102.09
1994	7,413,546	6,058,871	5,170,221	766,551	122,099	1,326,099	28,576	95.65	95.77	95.46	98.67	91.43	95.00	100.94
1995	7,723,255	6,301,480	5,383,917	785,209	132,353	1,392,844	28,930	97.67	97.75	97.59	99.23	95.46	97.25	100.33
1996	8,131,219	6,624,561	5,663,058	819,897	141,607	1,477,069	29,589	100.00	100.00	100.00	100.00	100.00	100.00	100.00
1997	8,580,822	6,995,180	5,959,363	885,605	150,211	1,555,124	30,518	102.31	102.25	102.38	100.94	104.68	102.65	100.33
1998	9,124,270	7,450,601	6,335,337	954,250	161,015	1,641,813	31,856	104.94	104.87	105.18	101.92	110.15	105.33	101.11
1999	9,765,940	7,984,113	6,817,362	995,323	171,428	1,747,986	33,841	107.78	107.67	108.19	103.09	114.50	108.42	102.74

Sources

See the source for Table Dc54–65. See also U.S. Bureau of Economic Analysis, *Fixed Reproducible Tangible Wealth in the United States, 1925–94* (August 1999), pp. M-22–M-23.

Documentation

This table presents year-end estimates for the six components of the net stock of private residential structures measured both in current cost and as a chain-type quantity index. The two totals presented here, series Dc889 and Dc896, repeat the estimates provided in series Dc55 and Dc67. These series were prepared by the U.S. Bureau of Economic Analysis (BEA) and the explanation of the methods used to construct them is provided in the text for Tables Dc54–77.

Underlying these stock estimates are the annual national income and product account (NIPA) investment flows for the years starting in 1929, as discussed below. The construction of net stock estimates beginning in 1925 requires annual investment flows for earlier periods. For the residential series shown here, the BEA draws these estimates from value-in-place estimates for 1915–1928 (see Tables Dc1–11 and Dc22–43), and those assembled for the 1889–1914 period by David M. Blank (see the text for Table Dc510–530).

For more details on all underlying residential investment series, see Bureau of Economic Analysis, *National Income and Product Accounts of the United States, 1929–1994*, volume I (April 1998), pp. M-32–33 and M-47–48.

Series Dc890 and Dc897. The current cost of the net stock of all private housing units is the sum of the stock of units in one- to four-unit structures, in five-or-more-unit structures, and in manufactured homes. The corresponding quantity index, series Dc897, is based on the sum of the same real investment flows.

Dc891–892 and Dc898–899. For permanent site housing, the NIPA accounts are based on the value-in-place estimates of residential construction that are produced by the U.S. Census Bureau and are shown here in Tables Dc1–53. See the text for Table Dc66–77 and the introduction to Current Construction Report C30/99-5, U.S. Census Bureau, *Value of Construction Put in Place* (May 1999), however, for a discussion of the adjustments the BEA makes to the value-in-place estimates before using them as investment flows.

Series Dc893 and Dc900. The NIPA investment series that are used to construct the net stock estimates for manufactured homes, on the other hand, are based on annual shipment figures provided by trade sources and a manufactured home retail price index prepared by the Census Bureau. See Table Dc637–652.

Series Dc894 and Dc901. The underlying investment series for residential improvements for owner-occupied dwellings is based on the consumer expenditures data drawn from quarterly surveys by the U.S. Bureau of Labor Statistics; for rental property the information on improvements is drawn from a Census Bureau survey.

Series Dc895 and Dc902. Consists primarily of group quarters, such as dormitories and fraternity and sorority houses.

RESIDENTIAL MORTGAGES

Kenneth A. Snowden

TABLE Dc903–928   Debt on nonfarm structures, by type of debt, property, and holder: 1896–1952

Contributed by Kenneth A. Snowden

			Mortgage debt, excluding real estate bonds										
			Residential structures								One- to four-family homes		
			All homes								Held by		
				Held by									
Year	Total	Real estate bonds	Total	Total	Noninstitutional lenders	Commercial banks	Mutual savings banks	Savings and loan associations	Life insurance companies	Other institutional lenders	Total	Noninstitutional lenders	Commercial banks
	Dc903	Dc904	Dc905	Dc906	Dc907	Dc908 [1]	Dc909	Dc910 [1]	Dc911	Dc912 [2]	Dc913	Dc914	Dc915 [1]
	Million dollars	Million dollars	Million dollars	Million dollars	Million dollars	Million dollars	Million dollars	Million dollars	Million dollars	Million dollars	Million dollars	Million dollars	Million dollars
1896	4,415	15	4,400	2,711	1,369	141	532	429	166	74	—	—	—
1897	4,459	20	4,439	2,746	1,411	140	550	403	169	73	—	—	—
1898	4,508	25	4,483	2,783	1,430	144	570	396	169	74	—	—	—
1899	4,577	30	4,547	2,835	1,466	148	595	376	172	78	—	—	—
1900	4,696	35	4,661	2,917	1,493	158	632	371	183	80	—	—	—
1901	4,833	40	4,793	3,011	1,535	173	658	367	194	84	—	—	—
1902	4,963	45	4,918	3,102	1,543	195	694	378	207	85	—	—	—
1903	5,095	50	5,045	3,194	1,539	221	727	394	223	90	—	—	—
1904	5,311	55	5,256	3,341	1,567	251	768	423	238	94	—	—	—
1905	5,577	60	5,517	3,520	1,600	293	822	448	254	103	—	—	—
1906	5,804	65	5,739	3,676	1,584	328	885	487	287	105	—	—	—
1907	5,973	70	5,903	3,795	1,565	337	925	538	316	114	—	—	—
1908	6,197	80	6,117	3,948	1,586	357	974	575	334	122	—	—	—
1909	6,524	90	6,434	4,168	1,598	408	1,042	628	361	131	—	—	—
1910	6,906	100	6,806	4,426	1,634	445	1,111	690	403	143	—	—	—
1911	7,230	115	7,115	4,644	1,643	461	1,184	768	439	149	—	—	—
1912	7,581	130	7,451	4,881	1,659	485	1,264	847	469	157	—	—	—
1913	8,253	150	8,103	5,329	1,907	493	1,331	930	499	169	—	—	—
1914	8,862	190	8,672	5,724	2,118	520	1,362	1,013	531	180	—	—	—
1915	9,305	230	9,075	6,012	2,222	566	1,416	1,098	522	188	—	—	—
1916	9,876	270	9,606	6,387	2,391	580	1,501	1,175	541	199	—	—	—
1917	10,932	320	10,612	7,082	2,836	621	1,554	1,293	563	215	—	—	—
1918	11,428	370	11,058	7,407	3,031	651	1,535	1,387	578	225	—	—	—
1919	12,089	472	11,617	7,809	3,129	733	1,613	1,552	549	233	—	—	—
1920	14,100	584	13,516	9,120	3,846	800	1,782	1,860	558	274	—	—	—
1921	15,384	640	14,744	10,017	4,041	860	1,945	2,179	698	294	—	—	—
1922	17,100	903	16,197	11,080	4,283	1,055	2,167	2,468	788	319	—	—	—
1923	20,072	1,306	18,766	12,924	4,940	1,323	2,437	2,917	946	361	—	—	—
1924	23,135	1,800	21,335	14,794	5,360	1,621	2,756	3,519	1,132	406	—	—	—
1925	27,589	2,905	24,684	17,231	6,469	1,858	3,037	3,994	1,408	465	12,984	4,892	1,384
1926	31,684	3,861	27,823	19,956	7,409	2,319	3,349	4,570	1,775	534	14,809	5,284	1,805
1927	35,710	4,668	31,042	22,491	8,379	2,508	3,700	5,214	2,088	602	16,433	5,690	1,934
1928	40,018	5,699	34,319	24,958	9,301	2,805	4,016	5,757	2,406	673	17,904	5,947	2,152
1929	42,949	6,098	36,851	27,001	10,350	2,896	4,135	6,182	2,704	734	18,912	6,107	2,213

Mortgage debt, excluding real estate bonds

			Residential structures										
			All homes								One- to four-family homes		
				Held by								Held by	
Year	Total	Real estate bonds	Total	Total	Noninstitutional lenders	Commercial banks [1]	Mutual savings banks	Savings and loan associations [1]	Life insurance companies	Other institutional lenders [2]	Total	Noninstitutional lenders	Commercial banks [1]
	Dc903	Dc904	Dc905	Dc906	Dc907	Dc908	Dc909	Dc910	Dc911	Dc912	Dc913	Dc914	Dc915
	Million dollars	Million dollars	Million dollars	Million dollars	Million dollars	Million dollars	Million dollars	Million dollars	Million dollars	Million dollars	Million dollars	Million dollars	Million dollars
1930	44,044	6,318	37,726	27,649	10,629	2,844	4,388	6,149	2,878	761	18,891	5,950	2,212
1931	43,011	6,500	36,511	26,673	9,940	2,769	4,568	5,704	2,948	744	18,104	5,566	2,128
1932	40,662	6,300	34,362	24,918	9,208	2,561	4,554	5,020	2,854	721	16,655	5,036	1,953
1933	36,418	5,952	30,466	23,083	8,356	2,528	4,293	4,473	2,626	807	15,352	4,447	1,901
1934	34,486	5,000	29,486	22,811	7,377	2,183	4,109	3,749	2,370	3,023	15,630	3,896	1,605
1935	32,615	4,200	28,415	22,211	6,984	2,225	3,984	3,301	2,200	3,517	15,437	3,788	1,657
1936	31,846	3,800	28,046	21,915	6,967	2,285	3,897	3,257	2,142	3,367	15,385	3,897	1,718
1937	31,395	3,400	27,995	21,924	7,089	2,415	3,851	3,414	2,163	2,992	15,518	4,082	1,845
1938	31,418	3,200	28,218	22,046	7,105	2,535	3,830	3,523	2,226	2,827	15,765	4,182	1,953
1939	31,903	3,000	28,903	22,740	7,156	2,719	3,875	3,748	2,557	2,685	16,337	4,295	2,128
1940	32,786	2,800	29,986	23,810	7,278	2,997	3,914	4,073	2,887	2,661	17,346	4,442	2,386
1941	33,850	2,600	31,250	24,875	7,462	3,308	3,884	4,481	3,235	2,505	18,358	4,654	2,683
1942	33,221	2,450	30,771	24,667	7,316	3,335	3,725	4,449	3,625	2,217	18,226	4,530	2,754
1943	32,156	2,250	29,906	24,056	7,181	3,256	3,558	4,422	3,835	1,804	17,835	4,559	2,706
1944	31,794	2,050	29,744	24,000	7,348	3,218	3,476	4,638	3,819	1,501	17,947	4,797	2,703
1945	32,642	1,850	30,792	24,643	7,874	3,395	3,387	5,162	3,632	1,193	18,543	5,249	2,875
1946	38,579	1,700	36,879	29,459	8,809	5,146	3,588	6,843	4,021	1,052	23,059	6,081	4,576
1947	45,453	1,600	43,853	35,061	9,679 [3]	6,933	3,937	8,475	5,005	1,032	28,161	6,718	6,303
1948	52,404	1,500	50,904	40,861	10,189	8,066	4,758	9,841	6,754	1,253	33,261	7,144	7,396
1949	58,477	1,400	57,077	45,896 [3]	10,461	8,676	5,569	11,117	8,232	1,841	37,496	7,408	7,956
1950	68,033	1,300	66,733	54,362	10,424 [3]	10,431	7,054	13,104	11,035	2,314	45,072	7,646	9,481
1951	76,755	1,200	75,555	62,026	10,604	11,270	8,595	14,801	13,865	2,891	51,872	7,952	10,275
1952	84,840	1,100	83,740	69,121	10,990	12,188	9,833	17,590	15,112	3,408	58,155	8,136	11,250

Notes appear at end of table

(continued)

TABLE Dc903-928   Debt on nonfarm structures, by type of debt, property, and holder: 1896–1952   *Continued*

Mortgage debt, excluding real estate bonds

	Residential structures									Multifamily structures			
	One- to four-family homes												
	Held by									Held by			
	Mutual savings banks	Savings and loan associations	Life insurance companies	Home Owners' Loan Corporation	Federal National Mortgage Association	Other institutional lenders	Total	Total (Federal Reserve)	Noninstitutional lenders	Commercial banks	Mutual savings banks	Life insurance companies	Other institutional lenders
	Dc916	Dc917 [1]	Dc918	Dc919	Dc920	Dc921 [2]	Dc922	Dc923	Dc924	Dc925	Dc926	Dc927	Dc928 [2]
Year	Million dollars	Million dollars	Million dollars	Million dollars	Million dollars	Million dollars	Million dollars	Billion dollars	Million dollars	Million dollars	Million dollars	Million dollars	Million dollars
1896	—	—	—	0	0	—	—	—	—	—	—	—	—
1897	—	—	—	0	0	—	—	—	—	—	—	—	—
1898	—	—	—	0	0	—	—	—	—	—	—	—	—
1899	—	—	—	0	0	—	—	—	—	—	—	—	—
1900	—	—	—	0	0	—	—	—	—	—	—	—	—
1901	—	—	—	0	0	—	—	—	—	—	—	—	—
1902	—	—	—	0	0	—	—	—	—	—	—	—	—
1903	—	—	—	0	0	—	—	—	—	—	—	—	—
1904	—	—	—	0	0	—	—	—	—	—	—	—	—
1905	—	—	—	0	0	—	—	—	—	—	—	—	—
1906	—	—	—	0	0	—	—	—	—	—	—	—	—
1907	—	—	—	0	0	—	—	—	—	—	—	—	—
1908	—	—	—	0	0	—	—	—	—	—	—	—	—
1909	—	—	—	0	0	—	—	—	—	—	—	—	—
1910	—	—	—	0	0	—	—	—	—	—	—	—	—
1911	—	—	—	0	0	—	—	—	—	—	—	—	—
1912	—	—	—	0	0	—	—	—	—	—	—	—	—
1913	—	—	—	0	0	—	—	—	—	—	—	—	—
1914	—	—	—	0	0	—	—	—	—	—	—	—	—
1915	—	—	—	0	0	—	—	—	—	—	—	—	—
1916	—	—	—	0	0	—	—	—	—	—	—	—	—
1917	—	—	—	0	0	—	—	—	—	—	—	—	—
1918	—	—	—	0	0	—	—	—	—	—	—	—	—
1919	—	—	—	0	0	—	—	—	—	—	—	—	—
1920	—	—	—	0	0	—	—	—	—	—	—	—	—
1921	—	—	—	0	0	—	—	—	—	—	—	—	—
1922	—	—	—	0	0	—	—	—	—	—	—	—	—
1923	—	—	—	0	0	—	—	—	—	—	—	—	—
1924	—	—	—	0	0	—	—	—	—	—	—	—	—
1925	1,547	3,994	837	0	0	330	4,247	4.2	1,577	474	1,490	571	135
1926	1,713	4,570	1,062	0	0	375	5,147	4.6	2,125	514	1,636	713	159
1927	1,922	5,214	1,254	0	0	419	6,058	5.0	2,689	574	1,778	834	183
1928	2,139	5,757	1,445	0	0	464	7,054	5.4	3,354	653	1,877	961	209
1929	2,286	6,182	1,626	0	0	498	8,089	6.0	4,243	683	1,849	1,078	236
1930	2,341	6,149	1,732	0	0	507	8,758	6.5	4,679	632	2,047	1,146	254
1931	2,436	5,704	1,775	0	0	495	8,569	6.2	4,374	641	2,132	1,173	249
1932	2,446	5,020	1,724	0	0	476	8,263	6.0	4,172	608	2,108	1,130	245
1933	2,354	4,473	1,599	132	0	446	7,731	5.7	3,909	627	1,939	1,027	229
1934	2,190	3,749	1,379	2,379	0	432	7,181	5.1	3,481	578	1,919	991	212

Mortgage debt, excluding real estate bonds

	One- to four-family homes									Multifamily structures			
	Residential structures												
	Held by									Held by			
Year	Mutual savings banks	Savings and loan associations [1]	Life insurance companies	Home Owners' Loan Corporation	Federal National Mortgage Association	Other institutional lenders [2]	Total	Total (Federal Reserve)	Noninstitutional lenders	Commercial banks	Mutual savings banks	Life insurance companies	Other institutional lenders [2]
	Dc916	Dc917	Dc918	Dc919	Dc920	Dc921	Dc922	Dc923	Dc924	Dc925	Dc926	Dc927	Dc928
	Million dollars	Million dollars	Million dollars	Million dollars	Million dollars	Million dollars	Million dollars	Billion dollars	Million dollars	Million dollars	Million dollars	Million dollars	Million dollars
1935	2,089	3,301	1,281	2,897	0	424	6,774	4.8	3,196	568	1,895	919	196
1936	2,082	3,257	1,245	2,763	0	423	6,530	4.6	3,070	567	1,815	897	181
1937	2,111	3,414	1,246	2,398	0	422	6,406	4.5	3,007	570	1,740	917	172
1938	2,119	3,523	1,320	2,169	80	419	6,281	4.4	2,923	582	1,711	906	159
1939	2,128	3,748	1,490	2,038	144	366	6,403	5.6	2,861	591	1,747	1,067	137
1940	2,162	4,073	1,758	1,956	178	391	6,464	5.7	2,836	611	1,752	1,129	136
1941	2,189	4,481	1,976	1,777	203	395	6,517	5.9	2,808	625	1,695	1,259	130
1942	2,128	4,449	2,255	1,567	206	337	6,441	5.8	2,786	581	1,597	1,370	107
1943	2,033	4,422	2,410	1,338	60	307	6,221	5.8	2,622	550	1,525	1,425	99
1944	1,937	4,638	2,458	1,091	50	273	6,053	5.6	2,551	515	1,539	1,361	87
1945	1,894	5,162	2,258	852	7	246	6,100	5.7	2,625	520	1,493	1,374	88
1946	2,033	6,843	2,570	636	6	314	6,400	6.1	2,728	570	1,555	1,451	96
1947	2,283	8,475	3,459	486	4	433	6,900	6.6	2,961	630	1,654	1,546	109
1948	2,835	9,841	4,925	369	198	553	7,600	7.5	3,045	670	1,923	1,829	133
1949	3,364	11,117	5,970	231	806	644	8,400	8.6	3,053	720	2,205	2,262	160
1950	4,312	13,104	8,392	10	1,328	799	9,290	10.1	2,778	950	2,742	2,643	177
1951	5,331	14,801	10,814	0	1,818	881	10,154	11.5	2,652	995	3,264	3,051	192
1952	6,180	17,590	11,800	0	2,210	989	10,966	12.3	2,854	938	3,653	3,312	209

[1] Includes both operating and closed commercial banks and savings and loan institutions.

[2] For 1896–1924, includes debt held by insurance companies other than life and mortgage companies; thereafter, also includes holdings of installment companies and, in the cases of series Dc921 and Dc928, Home Owners' Loan Corporation and the Federal National Mortgage Association.

[3] Estimates misprinted in the source have been corrected so that components sum to total.

Sources

Series Dc903–922 and Dc924–928. Leo Grebler, David M. Blank, and Louis Winnick, *Capital Formation in Residential Real Estate* (Princeton University Press, 1956), Chapter 9 and Tables L-2, L-3, N-2, N-4, and N-6.

Series Dc923. U.S. Bureau of the Census, *Historical Statistics of the United States* (1975), series N 276.

Documentation

These series measure several dimensions of the size and structure of the nonfarm residential mortgage market over a six-decade period: its relative importance in the total nonfarm mortgage market (which includes commercial as well as residential properties), the mix of mortgage debt outstanding on single-family and multifamily homes, the relative importance of institutional and noninstitutional mortgage lenders, and the importance of different groups of institutional lenders.

Grebler, Blank, and Winnick assembled these estimates by making extensive use of other sources, most notably: for the period up to 1925, Raymond W. Goldsmith, *A Study of Saving in the United States*, volume 1 (Princeton University Press, 1955), Tables R-34, R-35, and R-41; and for the period beginning in 1925, official Commerce Department estimates of nonfarm mortgage debt that appeared in U.S. Department of Commerce, *Survey of Current Business* 33 (September 1946): 12–18, and U.S. Department

of Commerce, *Survey of Current Business* 26 (September 1953): 13–19, as well as Federal Home Loan Bank Board estimates of institutional residential mortgage holdings beginning in 1925.

Users of these data should be aware that Grebler, Blank, and Winnick expressed reservations about the quality of some of the pre-1925 estimates shown in the table even after they had revised Goldsmith's estimates where appropriate and when possible (see Appendixes L and M of the source for details). As explained below, they were most concerned about the quality of the two most highly aggregated series for the earliest years shown in the table (series Dc905–906) and the volume of mortgage debt held by noninstitutional lenders (series Dc907). In contrast, the pre-1925 estimates of nonfarm residential mortgage debt held by major institutional lenders – commercial banks, mutual savings banks, savings and loan associations, and life insurance companies – are based on annual balance sheet data and tend to be of higher quality. Despite problems and caveats, therefore, the Grebler, Blank, and Winnick estimates remain the best and most comprehensive view of the size and structure of the American mortgage market before 1950.

For alternative estimates of mortgage debt for the 1945–1956 period, see Saul B. Klaman, *The Volume of Mortgage Debt in the Postwar Decade: Appraisal and Development of Statistics*, National Bureau of Economic Research, Technical Paper number 13 (1958), and Table Dc929–949.

For a discussion of the structure of the residential mortgage market before 1950, see J. E. Morton, *Urban Mortgage Lending: Comparative Markets and Experience* (Princeton University Press, 1956), Chapter 1.

These data are for total mortgage debt outstanding in each year. Estimates of the annual volume of new residential mortgage lending before 1952 can be found in Tables Dc983–995.

(continued)

TABLE Dc903–928   Debt on nonfarm structures, by type of debt, property, and holder: 1896–1952   *Continued*

Series Dc903. Total debt on nonfarm structures is the sum of real estate bonds outstanding, series Dc904, and nonfarm mortgage debt excluding real estate bonds, series Dc905.

Series Dc904. Includes bonds written on both commercial and the residential properties. The real estate bond series is from Goldsmith (1955), Table R41, except for minor revisions to the series that Grebler, Blank, and Winnick made for a few years between 1914 and 1934, and the extrapolation of Goldsmith's original series to cover the 1950–1952 segment. Real estate bonds played an important role in both the commercial and the residential real estate markets during the 1920s, and Goldsmith produced an estimate of outstanding residential real estate bonds (written primarily on apartment houses) by assuming that they comprised a fixed 40 percent of the total shown here after 1910. In this table, however, real estate bonds are not disaggregated into residential and commercial subcomponents, nor are they included in any of the residential mortgage debt series.

Series Dc905–906. In assessing their pre-1925 estimates of the total size of the nonfarm and nonfarm residential mortgage markets, Grebler, Blank, and Winnick (1956, Appendix L) caution that: "the [total nonfarm] residential mortgage debt series is especially weak for the pre-1925 period, based as it is on the two widely separated mortgage censuses of 1890 and 1920 and on the movement of total nonfarm mortgage debt, itself an inadequate series. . . . For the[se] earlier decades the series reflects approximate levels and underlying trends rather that accurate annual movements" (Grebler, Blank, and Winnick 1956, p. 442). After 1925 the two aggregate series are more reliable. Series Dc905, total nonfarm mortgage debt outstanding, was produced as an official Department of Commerce series, while series Dc906, total residential mortgage debt, is equal to the sum of separate estimates of the one- to four-family home and multifamily mortgage markets (series Dc913 and Dc922).

Series Dc905. The second component of total nonfarm real estate debt shown in the table is nonfarm mortgage debt excluding real estate bonds. This series includes mortgages on commercial as well as residential property, but excludes the mortgage indebtedness of railroads and other public utilities. For 1896–1912, the series is Grebler, Blank, and Winnick's revision of Goldsmith's original estimates (see Appendix L of the source and Goldsmith 1955, Table R-34). This earliest segment of the series was formed by fitting a trend to the levels of nonfarm mortgage indebtedness as measured in 1890 and 1922 and then interpolating between the 1896 and 1912 trend values using Goldsmith's annual series on the total amount of mortgage debt held by institutional lenders. The 1913–1928 segment of the series, on the other hand, is Goldsmith's original estimates, which were based on Department of Commerce estimates of total nonfarm mortgages that began in 1916 (see Goldsmith 1955, Table R-34, and the 1946 *Survey of Current Business* article cited above). Finally, for 1929–1952, series Dc905 is equal to official Commerce Department estimates.

Series Dc906. The residential component of nonfarm mortgage debt outstanding includes outstanding mortgage loans on one- to four-family and multifamily residential structures, as well as some mortgages written on smaller structures, which had mixed residential-commercial uses. Excluded from the residential mortgage series, on the other hand, are real estate bonds written on residential property and most mortgages made on hotels and transient residential buildings (Grebler, Blank, and Winnick 1956, p. 442). Before 1925 this series was estimated simply as a proportion of the total nonfarm mortgage debt shown in series Dc905. The proportion rose from 0.6161 in 1896 to 0.6934 in 1924, with the ratio in intervening years derived by interpolation between benchmark estimates for 1890, 1920, and 1925. For the first two of these years, the share of residential in total nonfarm mortgage debt was estimated on data drawn from the Censuses of Mortgage Indebtedness; beginning in 1925, the proportion was derived from separate estimates of mortgage debt on all nonfarm structures and on one- to four-family and multifamily residential structures. The interested reader is referred to Appendix L of Grebler, Blank, and Winnick (1956) for an extended discussion of the construction of series Dc906 before 1925, and its difference from Goldsmith's original estimates of this aggregate for the same period. Beginning in 1925,

series Dc906 is simply the sum of series Dc913 and Dc922 – mortgage debt on one- to four-family homes and on multifamily residential structures.

Series Dc907. Grebler, Blank, and Winnick measured noninstitutional residential mortgage holdings by compiling annual estimates of total nonfarm residential mortgage debt (series Dc906) and then subtracting from the latter all the measured institutional mortgage holdings. Estimated noninstitutional mortgage holdings (series Dc907) therefore were estimated as a residual series and as such are the weakest component of all the residential mortgage debt series shown in the table.

Series Dc908–912. For the 1896–1924 period, Grebler, Blank, and Winnick relied most heavily on Goldsmith's (1955, Tables M-3, M-4, and M-8) estimates of total nonfarm (residential and commercial) mortgage holdings in financial institutions. To derive estimates of institutional residential mortgage holdings over the period from these totals, they assumed that 42.1 percent of the mortgages held by commercial banks, 75.3 percent of those held by mutual savings banks, and 51.4 percent of mortgages held by life insurance companies were written on residential properties – or the same proportion that each intermediary held in 1925. For details on the derivation of these rates, see Tables N-2, N-8, N-9, and N-10 in the source. Savings and loan associations, on the other hand, were considered to hold only residential mortgages, and Grebler, Blank, and Winnick accepted Goldsmith's original estimates of these amounts before 1925 (Goldsmith, 1955, Table M-4). For both commercial banks and savings and loans, Grebler, Blank, and Winnick also derived estimates of residential mortgages held in institutions that had been closed, and added these to their estimates of loans held in operating institutions to form the totals shown in the table. See Table N-12 of the source for details.

Series Dc912. The "other financial institutions" category before 1925 includes only mortgage companies and other insurance companies for which Goldsmith derived annual estimates of residential mortgage holdings.

Series Dc913. This series was produced for the 1925–1952 period by the Federal Home Loan Bank Board (FHLBB).

Series Dc914 and Dc924. Beginning in 1925, the mortgage holdings of noninstitutional investors written on both one- to four-family homes and multifamily structures were calculated as the residual between the total mortgage debt outstanding in each market and the holdings of all institutional investors.

Series Dc915–920. Estimates of the total residential mortgage holding for each group of institutions for 1925–1952 are the sum of their holdings of mortgages on one- to four-family homes and multifamily structures. The one- to four-family mortgage series for operating commercial banks, mutual savings banks, operating savings and loan associations, and life insurance companies (series Dc915–918) were drawn from the FHLBB's publication *Estimated Home Mortgage Debt and Financing Activity, 1952*. For commercial banks and savings and loans, once again, the FHLBB's estimates were augmented by Grebler, Blank, and Winnick's own estimates of home mortgage loans held in closed institutions. The FHLBB publication was also the source for the single-family mortgage holdings of the Home Owners' Loan Corporation (HOLC) and the Federal National Mortgage Association (FNMA) (series Dc919–920). The HOLC holdings include both original HOLC loans and loans that the HOLC made when selling property it had acquired through foreclosure or similar proceedings. FNMA holdings cover all programs of that agency. (Under law, only mortgage loans insured by the Federal Housing Administration or guaranteed by the Veterans Administration were eligible for purchase by FNMA.)

Series Dc921 and Dc928. The amounts of both one- to four-family and multifamily mortgage debt held by other institutions between 1925 and 1952 combine estimates for non-life insurance companies, mortgage companies, and installment investment companies. In each case, Grebler, Blank, and Winnick used estimates originally made by Goldsmith (1955, Tables M-9 and M-10). Beginning in 1925, both series are included in the other institutions category for residential mortgage debt, series Dc912, along with the holdings of two government agencies – HOLC and FNMA (series Dc919–920).

TABLE Dc903–928   Debt on nonfarm structures, by type of debt, property, and holder: 1896–1952 *Continued*

Series Dc922–923. The multifamily mortgage debt figures shown in series Dc922 were drawn from Goldsmith (1955), Tables R-34 and R-35. Goldsmith derived his estimates by combining older Commerce Department estimates for 1929–1943 with estimates based on multifamily construction activity for earlier and later years. Although Grebler, Blank, and Winnick used Goldsmith's multifamily mortgage debt series for the 1925–1952 period (series Dc922), they questioned its quality (see the source, p. 442). The Federal Reserve produced its own, and presumably more accurate, estimates of mortgage debt on multifamily structures in later years (series Dc923). This series was published in *Historical Statistics of the United States* (1975), but without a clear source citation for the pre-1952 period. It is included here as an alternative measure of the size of the multifamily market even though it cannot be adequately documented. The uncertainty about which of these multifamily mortgage debt series is more accurate for the 1925–1952 period should

not be exaggerated, however: (1) reliable Commerce Department estimates for this period are available for combined multifamily residential and commercial mortgage debt – only the division between the two is in question; and (2) estimates of multifamily mortgage debt held by institutional lenders that are shown in the table are estimated separately from balance sheet data and so are of higher quality.

Series Dc925–927. Grebler, Blank, and Winnick derived estimates of institutional holdings of multifamily mortgages for the 1925–1952 period by combining and manipulating a variety of sources described in their Table N-6. Commercial bank holdings were derived from FHLBB and Federal Reserve Board estimates; mutual savings bank holdings as a share of Goldsmith's estimates the total mortgage holdings of these institutions; and life insurance company holdings by combining Goldsmith's and FHLBB estimates.

TABLE Dc929–949 Mortgage debt, by type of property, holder, and financing: 1939–1999

Contributed by Kenneth A. Snowden

			By type of property						By holder		
			Nonfarm						Major financial institutions		
					Residential					Savings institutions	
	Total	Farm	Total	Commercial	Total	One- to four-family homes	Multifamily	Total	Total	Savings and loan associations	Mutual savings banks
	Dc929	Dc930	Dc931	Dc932 [1]	Dc933	Dc934	Dc935	Dc936	Dc937 [2]	Dc938 [2]	Dc939 [2]
Year	Billion dollars	Billion dollars	Billion dollars	Billion dollars	Billion dollars	Billion dollars	Billion dollars	Billion dollars	Billion dollars	Billion dollars	Billion dollars
1939	35.5	6.6	28.9	7.0	21.9	16.3	5.6	18.6	8.6	3.8	4.8
1940	36.5	6.5	30.0	6.9	23.1	17.4	5.7	19.5	9.0	4.1	4.9
1941	37.6	6.4	31.2	7.0	24.3	18.4	5.9	20.7	9.4	4.6	4.8
1942	36.7	6.0	30.8	6.7	24.0	18.2	5.8	20.7	9.2	4.6	4.6
1943	35.3	5.4	29.9	6.3	23.6	17.8	5.8	20.2	9.0	4.6	4.4
1944	34.7	4.9	29.7	6.2	23.5	17.9	5.6	20.2	9.1	4.8	4.3
1945	35.5	4.8	30.8	6.4	24.3	18.6	5.7	21.0	9.6	5.4	4.2
1946	41.8	4.9	36.9	7.7	29.1	23.0	6.1	26.0	11.5	7.1	4.4
1947	48.9	5.1	43.9	9.1	34.8	28.2	6.6	31.8	13.8	8.9	4.9
1948	56.2	5.3	50.9	10.2	40.8	33.3	7.5	37.8	16.1	10.3	5.8
1949	62.3	5.6	56.7	10.8	45.9	37.3	8.6	42.9	18.3	11.6	6.7
1950	72.7	6.0	66.6	11.5	55.2	45.1	10.1	51.7	21.9	13.7	8.3
1951	82.1	6.6	75.6	12.5	63.1	51.6	11.5	59.5	25.5	15.6	9.9
1952	91.4	7.2	84.2	13.4	70.9	58.6	12.3	67.0	29.8	18.4	11.4
1953	101.2	7.7	93.5	14.6	79.0	66.1	12.9	75.1	34.8	22.0	12.9
1954	113.7	8.1	105.6	16.3	89.3	75.8	13.5	85.8	41.1	26.1	15.0
1955	130.1	9.0	121.1	18.4	102.7	88.4	14.3	99.5	48.9	31.4	17.5
1956	144.7	9.8	134.8	20.8	114.1	99.2	14.9	111.4	55.5	35.7	19.7
1957	156.7	10.4	146.3	23.2	123.1	107.8	15.3	120.0	61.2	40.0	21.2
1958	172.0	11.1	160.9	26.2	134.7	117.9	16.8	131.7	68.9	45.6	23.3
1959	190.9	12.1	178.8	29.2	149.6	130.9	18.7	145.6	78.1	53.1	25.0
1960	207.5	12.8	194.7	32.4	162.2	141.9	20.3	157.6	86.9	60.1	26.9
1961	228.1	13.9	214.2	36.5	177.7	154.7	23.0	172.7	98.0	68.8	29.1
1962	251.6	15.2	236.4	41.2	195.2	169.4	25.8	192.6	111.1	78.8	32.3
1963	278.7	16.8	261.9	46.3	215.6	186.6	29.0	217.4	127.2	90.9	36.2
1964	306.2	18.9	287.3	50.1	237.2	203.6	33.6	241.3	141.9	101.3	40.6
1965	333.7	21.2	312.5	54.5	258.0	220.8	37.2	265.0	154.9	110.3	44.6
1966	356.9	23.1	333.8	60.3	273.6	233.3	40.3	281.2	161.8	114.4	47.3
1967	381.6	25.1	356.5	64.8	291.6	247.7	43.9	299.2	172.3	121.8	50.5
1968	411.5	27.5	383.9	71.4	312.5	265.2	47.3	320.3	184.3	130.8	53.5
1969	442.3	29.4	412.9	77.1	335.8	283.6	52.2	339.8	196.4	140.2	56.1
1970	474.4	30.5	443.9	85.8	358.1	298.0	60.1	356.7	208.3	150.3	57.9
1971	525.1	32.4	492.7	96.1	396.7	326.6	70.1	395.2	236.2	174.3	62.0
1972	598.1	35.4	562.8	112.9	449.9	367.2	82.7	450.8	273.6	206.2	67.6
1973	673.4	39.8	633.6	132.0	501.5	408.4	93.1	506.3	305.0	231.7	73.2
1974	734.0	44.9	689.1	147.6	541.5	441.5	100.0	544.1	324.2	249.3	74.9
1975	793.5	49.9	743.7	160.3	583.4	482.8	100.6	582.9	355.8	278.6	77.2
1976	880.3	55.4	824.9	172.1	652.8	547.1	105.7	649.3	404.6	323.0	81.6
1977	1,012.0	63.8	948.2	190.7	757.5	643.5	114.0	747.0	469.4	381.2	88.2
1978	1,164.6	72.8	1,091.9	212.4	879.4	754.5	124.9	849.8	528.0	432.8	95.2
1979	1,330.0	86.8	1,243.3	237.5	1,005.7	870.9	134.8	939.9	574.6	475.7	98.9
1980	1,464.8	97.5	1,367.3	257.7	1,109.6	968.7	140.9	998.6	603.1	503.2	99.9
1981	1,590.1	107.2	1,482.9	296.5	1,186.4	1,047.6	138.8	1,042.8	618.5	518.5	100.0
1982	1,675.5	111.3	1,564.2	329.6	1,234.6	1,094.0	140.6	1,023.4	578.1	483.6	94.5
1983	1,869.0	113.7	1,755.2	384.6	1,370.7	1,216.9	153.8	1,109.9	626.6	494.8	131.9
1984	2,113.1	112.4	2,000.7	465.9	1,534.8	1,358.0	176.8	1,247.8	709.7	555.3	154.4
1985	2,376.8	105.9	2,271.0	533.6	1,737.4	1,532.4	205.0	1,363.5	760.5	583.2	177.3
1986	2,663.2	95.1	2,568.2	592.3	1,975.8	1,737.7	238.1	1,476.4	778.0	—	—
1987	3,001.4	87.7	2,913.7	684.3	2,229.4	1,968.8	260.6	1,667.6	860.5	—	—
1988	3,319.5	83.0	3,236.6	753.3	2,483.2	2,206.0	277.2	1,834.3	924.5	—	—
1989	3,590.4	80.5	3,509.9	779.2	2,730.7	2,443.0	287.7	1,934.2	910.3	—	—

Notes appear at end of table

TABLE Dc929–949   Mortgage debt, by type of property, holder, and financing: 1939–1999 *Continued*

				By type of property					By holder		
				Nonfarm					Major financial institutions		
						Residential				Savings institutions	
	Total	Farm	Total	Commercial	Total Total	One- to four-family homes	Multifamily	Total	Total	Savings and loan associations	Mutual savings banks
	Dc929	Dc930	Dc931	Dc932 [1]	Dc933	Dc934	Dc935	Dc936	Dc937 [2]	Dc938 [2]	Dc939 [2]
Year	Billion dollars	Billion dollars	Billion dollars	Billion dollars	Billion dollars	Billion dollars	Billion dollars	Billion dollars	Billion dollars	Billion dollars	Billion dollars
1990	3,807.9	78.9	3,729.0	796.8	2,932.2	2,646.6	285.6	1,918.8	801.6	—	—
1991	3,958.2	79.2	3,879.0	782.8	3,096.2	2,814.5	281.7	1,845.2	705.4	—	—
1992	4,073.9	79.7	3,994.1	740.1	3,254.0	2,984.7	269.3	1,770.4	627.9	—	—
1993	4,211.3	80.6	4,130.7	717.2	3,413.5	3,147.3	266.2	1,770.0	598.4	—	—
1994	4,383.1	83.0	4,300.1	704.6	3,595.5	3,330.2	265.3	1,824.7	596.2	—	—
1995	4,585.1	84.6	4,500.5	715.8	3,784.7	3,511.5	273.2	1,900.1	596.8	—	—
1996	4,868.3	87.1	4,781.2	773.6	4,007.5	3,718.7	288.8	1,981.9	628.3	—	—
1997	5,204.1	90.3	5,113.8	837.8	4,276.0	3,973.7	302.3	2,084.0	631.8	—	—
1998	5,737.2	96.5	5,640.7	945.8	4,694.8	4,362.7	332.1	2,194.8	644.0	—	—
1999	6,385.9	103.0	6,283.0	1,114.4	5,168.6	4,794.0	374.6	2,394.9	668.6	—	—

	By holder				By type of financing (nonfarm only)					
	Major financial institutions				Conventionally financed		Underwritten by federal agencies			
								On one- to four-family homes		
	Commercial banks	Life insurance companies	Federal and related agencies	Individual and other lenders	Total	One- to four-family homes	Total	Total	FHA	VA
	Dc940 [3]	Dc941	Dc942 [4]	Dc943	Dc944 [5]	Dc945 [5]	Dc946	Dc947	Dc948	Dc949
Year	Billion dollars	Billion dollars	Billion dollars	Billion dollars	Billion dollars	Billion dollars	Billion dollars	Billion dollars	Billion dollars	Billion dollars
1939	4.3	5.7	5.0	11.9	27.1	14.5	—	1.8	1.8	0.0
1940	4.6	6.0	4.9	12.0	27.7	15.1	—	2.3	2.3	0.0
1941	4.9	6.4	4.7	12.2	28.2	15.4	—	3.0	3.0	0.0
1942	4.7	6.7	4.3	11.7	27.1	14.5	—	3.7	3.7	0.0
1943	4.5	6.7	3.6	11.5	25.8	13.7	—	4.1	4.1	0.0
1944	4.4	6.7	3.0	11.5	25.5	13.7	—	4.2	4.2	0.0
1945	4.8	6.6	2.4	12.1	26.5	14.3	4.5	4.3	4.1	0.2
1946	7.2	7.2	2.0	13.8	30.6	16.9	6.3	6.1	3.7	2.4
1947	9.4	8.7	1.8	15.3	34.1	18.9	9.8	9.3	3.8	5.5
1948	10.9	10.8	1.8	16.6	37.3	20.8	13.6	12.5	5.3	7.2
1949	11.6	12.9	2.0	17.5	39.6	22.3	17.1	15.0	6.9	8.1
1950	13.7	16.1	2.6	18.4	44.6	26.2	22.1	18.8	8.5	10.3
1951	14.7	19.3	3.3	19.3	49.0	28.8	26.6	22.9	9.7	13.2
1952	16.0	21.3	3.9	20.4	55.0	33.2	29.3	25.4	10.8	14.6
1953	17.0	23.3	4.4	21.7	61.4	38.0	32.1	28.1	12.0	16.1
1954	18.7	26.0	4.7	23.2	69.4	43.7	36.2	32.1	12.8	19.3
1955	21.2	29.4	5.3	25.3	78.1	49.5	42.9	38.9	14.3	24.6
1956	22.9	33.0	6.2	27.1	87.0	55.3	47.8	43.9	15.5	28.4
1957	23.6	35.2	7.7	29.1	94.8	60.6	51.6	47.2	16.5	30.7
1958	25.8	37.1	8.0	32.3	105.8	67.8	55.2	50.1	19.7	30.4
1959	28.2	39.2	10.2	35.1	119.5	77.1	59.3	53.8	23.8	30.0
1960	28.9	41.8	11.5	38.4	132.3	85.5	62.3	56.4	26.7	29.7
1961	30.6	44.2	12.2	43.1	148.6	95.5	65.6	59.1	29.5	29.6
1962	34.7	46.9	12.6	46.3	167.1	107.3	69.4	62.2	32.3	29.9
1963	39.6	50.5	11.8	49.5	188.5	120.7	73.4	65.9	35.0	30.9
1964	44.3	55.2	12.2	52.7	210.1	134.3	77.2	69.2	38.3	30.9
1965	50.0	60.0	13.5	55.2	231.3	147.6	81.2	73.1	42.0	31.1
1966	54.8	64.6	17.5	58.2	249.7	157.2	84.1	76.1	44.8	31.3
1967	59.5	67.4	20.9	61.4	268.3	167.8	88.2	79.9	47.4	32.5
1968	66.1	70.0	25.1	66.1	290.5	180.8	93.4	84.4	50.6	33.8
1969	71.4	72.0	31.1	71.4	312.7	193.4	100.2	90.2	54.5	35.7

Notes appear at end of table

(continued)

TABLE Dc929–949   Mortgage debt, by type of property, holder, and financing: 1939–1999 *Continued*

	By holder				By type of financing (nonfarm only)					
	Major financial institutions				Conventionally financed		Underwritten by federal agencies			
								On one- to four-family homes		
	Commercial banks	Life insurance companies	Federal and related agencies	Individual and other lenders	Total	One- to four-family homes	Total	Total	FHA	VA
	Dc940 [3]	Dc941	Dc942 [4]	Dc943	Dc944 [5]	Dc945 [5]	Dc946	Dc947	Dc948	Dc949
Year	Billion dollars	Billion dollars	Billion dollars	Billion dollars	Billion dollars	Billion dollars	Billion dollars	Billion dollars	Billion dollars	Billion dollars
1970	74.1	74.4	38.3	79.4	334.7	200.7	109.2	97.3	59.9	37.3
1971	83.4	75.5	46.3	83.6	372.0	221.4	120.7	105.2	65.7	39.5
1972	100.2	76.9	54.5	92.8	431.7	254.2	131.1	113.0	68.2	44.7
1973	120.1	81.3	64.7	102.4	498.6	292.2	135.0	116.2	66.2	50.0
1974	133.6	86.2	82.2	107.7	548.8	320.2	140.2	121.3	65.1	56.2
1975	137.9	89.2	101.1	109.6	596.7	355.1	147.0	127.7	66.1	61.6
1976	153.1	91.6	116.7	114.4	670.8	413.6	154.1	133.5	66.5	67.0
1977	180.8	96.8	140.5	124.6	786.4	501.9	161.7	141.6	68.0	73.6
1978	215.7	106.2	170.6	144.3	915.5	601.1	176.4	153.4	71.4	82.0
1979	246.9	118.4	216.0	174.2	1,044.3	698.0	199.0	172.9	81.0	92.0
1980	264.5	131.1	256.8	209.4	1,142.2	773.6	225.1	195.2	93.6	101.6
1981	286.5	137.7	289.4	257.9	1,244.0	840.0	238.9	207.6	101.3	106.2
1982	303.4	142.0	355.4	296.7	1,315.3	876.1	248.9	217.9	108.0	109.9
1983	332.3	151.0	433.3	325.7	1,475.4	968.0	279.8	248.8	127.4	121.4
1984	381.4	156.7	490.6	374.7	1,705.8	1,092.1	294.8	265.9	136.7	129.1
1985	431.2	171.8	580.9	432.4	1,942.7	1,243.6	328.3	288.8	153.0	135.8
1986	504.7	193.7	733.7	453.1	2,197.7	1,409.1	370.5	328.6	185.5	143.1
1987	594.8	212.4	857.9	475.9	2,482.3	1,580.9	431.4	387.9	235.5	152.4
1988	676.9	232.9	937.8	547.5	2,776.9	1,791.9	459.7	414.2	258.8	155.4
1989	770.7	253.2	1,067.3	588.9	3,023.1	2,002.9	486.8	440.1	282.8	157.3
1990	849.3	267.9	1,258.9	630.2	3,211.1	2,175.7	517.9	470.9	310.9	160.0
1991	881.3	258.5	1,422.5	690.6	3,341.8	2,321.2	537.2	493.3	330.6	162.7
1992	900.5	242.0	1,558.1	745.3	3,460.8	2,494.9	533.3	489.8	326.0	163.8
1993	947.7	223.9	1,682.8	758.5	3,617.3	2,677.8	513.4	469.5	303.2	166.2
1994	1,012.7	215.8	1,787.6	770.8	3,740.8	2,816.0	559.3	514.2	336.8	177.3
1995	1,090.2	213.1	1,878.8	806.2	3,916.3	2,974.5	584.3	537.1	352.3	184.7
1996	1,145.4	208.2	2,006.5	879.9	4,160.8	3,147.5	620.3	571.2	379.2	192.0
1997	1,245.3	206.8	2,112.0	1,008.1	4,457.2	3,368.0	656.7	605.7	405.7	200.0
1998	1,337.2	213.6	2,312.0	1,230.3	4,966.6	3,738.9	674.1	623.8	417.9	205.9
1999	1,495.5	230.8	2,614.6	1,376.4	5,553.8	4,117.5	729.2	676.5	462.3	214.2

[1]   For earlier years, includes negligible amount of farm loans held by savings and loan associations.

[2]   Includes savings banks and savings and loan associations, which were reported separately until 1985. Data reported by institutions insured by the Federal Savings and Loan Insurance Corporation include loans in process for 1987 and exclude loans in process beginning 1988.

[3]   Includes loans held by nondeposit trust companies, but not by bank trust departments.

[4]   Composition changes over time; see text.

[5]   Derived for the source from Federal Reserve estimates; see text.

Source

1939–1985: Economic Report of the President (1987), Tables B-70, B-71. 1986–1999: Economic Report of the President (2001), Tables B-75, B-76, pp. 364–5.

Documentation

The estimates in this table are assembled by the Mortgage Debt Holding Group of the Federal Reserve Board and published each year in the President's annual economic report. Estimates of outstanding mortgage debt for recent years and quarters are published each month in the *Federal Reserve Bulletin*. The revised estimates for 1996–1999 shown in this table were first published in the April 2001 *Bulletin* (Table 1.54) and are subject to further revision. See Table Dc950–982 for estimates of outstanding residential

mortgage debt that are prepared by the Flow of Funds Group at the Federal Reserve Board. For a detailed explanation of the Federal Reserve's mortgage debt outstanding series for the earliest years in this table, see U.S. Board of Governors of the Federal Reserve System, *Flow of Funds in the United States, 1939–1953* (1955), pp. 345–56. This source also explains the relationship of the outstanding mortgage debt shown in this table to the flow of funds mortgage estimates for this early period.

The Mortgage Debt Holding Group of the Federal Reserve Board bases its estimates on data from a variety of governmental and institutional sources, which currently include the Federal Deposit Insurance Corporation, U.S. Departments of Agriculture and Commerce, Federal National Mortgage Association, Government National Mortgage Association, Federal Housing Administration, Public Housing Administration, Veterans Administration, Federal Home Loan Mortgage Corporation, Comptroller of the Currency, Federal Home Loan Bank Board, and the Institute of Life Insurance. For earlier years, the sources also include the Reconstruction Finance Corporation, the Home Owners' Loan Corporation, the Federal Farm Mortgage Corporation, and estimates of total mortgage debt outstanding compiled by the U.S. Department of Commerce.

This table presents three separate decompositions of total outstanding mortgage debt – by type of mortgaged property, by type of institutions or individuals holding the mortgage debt, and, for nonfarm debt only, by type of mortgage written on the property.

TABLE Dc929–949   Mortgage debt, by type of property, holder, and financing: 1939–1999   *Continued*

By Type of Mortgaged Property

The first breakdown shown in the table divides total outstanding mortgage debt into the amounts written on farm, commercial, and residential properties. The last two groups of mortgage debt added together comprise total nonfarm debt, while nonfarm residential mortgage debt comprises loans on one- to four-family homes and those written on multifamily structures. The latter are defined as structures containing residences for five or more families.

By Type of Institutions or Individuals Holding the Mortgage Debt

The second decomposition of total mortgage debt in this table divides it into the amounts held by major financial institutions, federal and related agencies, and individual and other noninstitutional lenders. Four types of institutions in the first category dominated the nation's mortgage market for most of the twentieth century – commercial banks, mutual savings banks, savings and loan associations, and life insurance companies. The holdings of these institutions taken together represented more than three quarters of total mortgage debt in the 1960s and 1970s, although their share had fallen to less than 40 percent by the end of the 1990s.

Series Dc937–941. The mortgage holdings of savings institutions are the sum of the holdings of savings and loan (S&L) associations and mutual savings banks. Savings institutions specialized in residential mortgage lending during the period shown in the table, and were the largest supplier of one- to four-family home mortgages until the mid-1980s. At that time the S&L industry experienced serious difficulties and the Federal Home Loan Bank Board, which had regulated the S&L industry since 1932, was soon replaced by the Office of Thrift Supervision in the Financial Institutions Reform, Recovery, and Enforcement Act of 1989. The same legislation transferred the insurance of S&L share accounts from the Federal Savings and Loan Insurance Corporation to the Federal Deposit Insurance Corporation, and created the Resolution Trust Corporation to dispose of the assets of insolvent S&Ls. The Federal Reserve has reported only the combined mortgage holdings of S&Ls and mutual savings banks since 1985. Before the 1980s, mutual savings banks were exclusively state-chartered institutions that were primarily located in the Northeast. For the later years shown in the table, the savings bank category includes both federal savings banks and Massachusetts Cooperative banks. The entire thrift industry is now regulated by the Office of Thrift Supervision, which publishes detailed information about the industry in its annual *Fact Book*.

Series Dc940. By the end of the twentieth century, commercial banks held the largest mortgage portfolio of the traditional intermediaries and lent on all types of property – farm, commercial, and single-family and multifamily residences. The mortgage holdings of commercial banks include loans held by nondeposit trust companies but exclude loans held by bank trust departments – the latter are included in the mortgage holdings of individual investors (series Dc943). Mortgage holdings of banks are derived from reports made to the Comptroller of the Currency or to state banking authorities.

Series Dc941. The mortgage holdings of life insurance companies have been reported in the annual *Life Insurance Fact Book* throughout the period shown in the table.

Series Dc942. The mortgage holdings of federal and federally related agencies include loans held by the Government National Mortgage Association (GNMA); the Federal Housing Administration (FHA); the Veterans Administration (VA); the Farmers Home Administration (FmHA); the Federal Deposit Insurance Corporation; and, prior to 1995, the Resolution Trust Corporation. For earlier years in the table, the category also includes the mortgage holdings of the Reconstruction Finance Corporation, the Home Owners' Loan Corporation, the Federal Farm Mortgage Corporation, and the Public Housing Administration. This series also includes U.S.-sponsored agencies such as the Federal National Mortgage Association (FNMA), the Federal Land Banks, the Federal Home Loan Mortgage Corporation (FHLMC), the Federal Home Loan Banks (beginning in 1997), and mortgage pass-through securities issued or guaranteed by GNMA, FHLMC, FNMA, or FmHA. See Tables Dc1105–1191 for additional detail about the institutional structure and mortgage holdings of these agencies.

Series Dc943. Includes mortgage loans held by bank trust departments, private mortgage pools, and U.S. agencies holding small or unmeasurable amounts of mortgage loans. The mortgage holdings of other types of insurance companies (such as property, health, or casualty) are also included in this series.

By Type of Mortgage Written on the Property (Nonfarm Only)

The third decomposition shown in the table breaks down outstanding mortgages on nonfarm properties (series Dc931) into those that were conventionally financed and those that were guaranteed or insured by federal agencies. The amount of both types of debt that was written on one- to four-family homes is also shown. Total federally underwritten debt on one- to four-family homes, in turn, is decomposed into FHA-insured and VA-guaranteed mortgages.

TABLE Dc950–982   Nonfarm residential mortgage debt, by holder and type of property: 1945–1999[1]

Contributed by Kenneth A. Snowden

			Home mortgages								
			All home mortgages								
			Total	Held by							
	Total (all nonfarm)	Total (nonfarm residential)	Total	Commercial banks	Savings institutions	Credit unions	Life insurance companies	State and local government	Federal government agencies	Government-sponsored enterprises	Federally related mortgage pools
	Dc950	Dc951	Dc952	Dc953	Dc954	Dc955	Dc956	Dc957	Dc958	Dc959	Dc960
Year	Million dollars	Million dollars	Million dollars	Million dollars	Million dollars	Million dollars	Million dollars	Million dollars	Million dollars	Million dollars	Million dollars
1945	35,700	23,500	18,600	2,900	7,000	0	2,300	0	900	0	0
1946	41,900	28,200	22,900	4,600	8,800	0	2,500	0	700	0	0
1947	49,000	33,800	28,000	6,300	10,600	0	3,500	100	600	0	0
1948	56,200	39,800	33,100	7,400	12,400	0	4,900	100	700	0	0
1949	62,700	45,200	37,400	8,000	14,200	100	6,100	200	1,200	0	0
1950	72,800	54,200	44,900	9,500	17,100	100	8,500	200	1,500	0	0
1951	82,200	62,000	51,400	10,300	19,800	100	10,600	300	2,100	0	0
1952	91,242	69,606	58,125	11,250	23,516	112	11,757	360	2,523	0	0
1953	101,096	77,792	65,671	12,025	28,126	136	13,195	420	2,770	0	0
1954	113,232	87,673	75,008	13,300	33,702	148	15,153	485	2,770	0	0
1955	129,368	100,971	87,481	15,075	40,926	174	17,661	523	2,929	86	0
1956	143,971	112,333	98,269	16,245	47,136	230	20,130	594	2,885	649	0
1957	156,185	121,529	106,918	16,385	52,546	265	21,441	789	3,051	1,636	0
1958	171,607	133,276	116,711	17,628	59,005	293	22,374	983	3,281	1,381	0
1959	190,655	148,326	129,626	19,200	67,108	345	23,583	1,222	4,206	2,050	0
1960	207,855	161,610	140,824	19,242	74,775	377	24,879	1,388	4,235	2,901	0
1961	228,209	176,889	153,267	20,038	83,272	407	25,776	1,564	4,448	2,870	0
1962	251,561	194,162	167,430	22,129	92,592	455	26,374	1,656	4,497	2,834	0
1963	278,174	214,048	184,024	24,910	104,272	502	27,331	1,681	4,124	2,050	0
1964	305,994	235,873	201,295	27,220	115,721	547	28,525	1,696	4,023	1,986	0
1965	333,524	256,676	218,463	30,401	125,840	580	29,589	1,705	3,900	2,510	50
1966	357,569	273,049	231,774	32,803	131,797	633	30,233	1,749	4,537	4,386	266
1967	381,110	289,844	245,029	35,275	138,760	668	29,763	1,741	5,253	5,513	652
1968	410,595	310,399	262,148	38,765	147,339	707	29,030	1,751	6,155	7,151	994
1969	441,468	333,422	280,246	41,356	156,709	731	27,649	1,809	6,361	10,919	1,369
1970	471,368	354,537	294,426	42,329	164,041	800	26,739	1,884	6,234	15,538	2,532
1971	520,087	391,010	320,948	48,020	180,071	847	24,645	1,978	5,615	17,615	6,717
1972	592,069	442,950	360,110	57,004	206,430	1,000	22,315	2,092	4,991	19,464	10,701
1973	668,962	495,983	402,851	67,998	231,222	1,441	20,426	2,642	4,211	22,939	13,636
1974	730,736	538,191	438,215	74,758	246,956	1,513	19,026	3,385	5,617	28,441	18,038
1975	788,418	578,305	477,696	77,018	268,800	1,993	17,590	4,154	9,668	30,934	25,339
1976	873,483	645,967	540,304	86,177	307,043	2,500	16,088	4,970	8,927	31,430	37,257
1977	1,002,198	747,574	633,582	105,079	358,842	2,800	14,740	5,173	11,386	31,918	52,988
1978	1,153,899	868,697	743,775	129,099	408,653	2,512	14,436	7,159	13,273	40,942	65,354
1979	1,320,566	996,291	861,457	148,882	450,903	3,102	16,144	11,835	15,592	50,128	88,429
1980	1,462,175	1,107,021	964,743	158,960	478,485	4,645	17,943	19,744	18,301	57,758	107,126
1981	1,584,148	1,180,408	1,038,384	167,684	494,944	3,686	17,201	25,566	20,690	63,990	125,011
1982	1,666,098	1,225,144	1,079,481	170,485	456,447	2,686	16,751	28,557	22,143	74,316	174,349
1983	1,856,122	1,357,778	1,197,082	179,150	483,384	4,381	15,319	33,712	22,891	83,685	239,539
1984	2,096,557	1,518,231	1,332,752	193,816	531,139	7,534	14,120	39,157	23,513	94,426	282,953
1985	2,378,097	1,738,481	1,533,452	211,188	561,668	11,086	12,381	45,042	24,403	106,577	361,508
1986	2,663,754	1,976,012	1,737,747	232,040	568,276	19,325	12,827	48,963	24,058	101,413	519,520
1987	2,965,986	2,198,114	1,940,409	268,905	573,181	29,872	13,226	50,127	20,751	98,911	653,892
1988	3,282,050	2,449,246	2,175,725	322,954	641,649	38,060	11,164	52,613	21,045	104,704	723,602
1989	3,552,628	2,690,361	2,404,467	373,429	630,975	44,846	12,231	57,312	21,319	110,033	843,800
1990	3,807,924	2,932,154	2,646,541	430,333	600,154	49,703	13,005	60,900	37,940	115,347	991,084
1991	3,959,200	3,096,247	2,814,527	452,443	538,358	52,798	10,642	62,901	37,087	126,402	1,130,351
1992	4,073,351	3,253,377	2,984,057	478,786	489,622	53,806	11,215	62,293	36,576	156,938	1,248,186
1993	4,210,314	3,412,767	3,146,535	532,217	470,000	55,966	8,855	56,328	32,979	196,718	1,334,285
1994	4,380,610	3,595,626	3,329,730	589,950	477,626	62,106	8,517	57,283	29,106	199,318	1,449,689
1995	4,581,936	3,783,942	3,510,460	646,545	482,353	66,461	8,890	60,498	24,070	205,222	1,543,402
1996	4,865,534	4,008,362	3,719,227	677,603	513,712	75,952	6,977	62,808	21,194	198,508	1,678,881
1997	5,197,904	4,273,925	3,971,531	745,510	520,672	86,038	7,187	65,763	19,136	194,301	1,788,052
1998	5,728,173	4,689,335	4,358,444	796,610	533,377	96,894	6,590	69,095	18,805	199,596	1,970,168
1999	6,375,459	5,163,667	4,790,696	878,731	548,526	110,979	5,934	72,589	18,388	189,324	2,234,793

Note appears at end of table

TABLE Dc950–982   Nonfarm residential mortgage debt, by holder and type of property: 1945–1999   *Continued*

				Home mortgages						
	All home mortgages				Home equity loans					
	Held by					Held by				
	Issuers of asset-backed securities	Mortgage companies	Finance companies	Individuals and others	Total	Commercial banks	Savings institutions	Credit unions	Issuers of asset-backed securities	Finance companies
	Dc961	Dc962	Dc963	Dc964	Dc965	Dc966	Dc967	Dc968	Dc969	Dc970
Year	Million dollars	Million dollars	Million dollars	Million dollars	Million dollars	Million dollars	Million dollars	Million dollars	Million dollars	Million dollars
1945	0	100	0	5,400	—	—	—	—	—	—
1946	0	100	0	6,200	—	—	—	—	—	—
1947	0	200	0	6,800	—	—	—	—	—	—
1948	0	200	0	7,300	—	—	—	—	—	—
1949	0	200	0	7,500	—	—	—	—	—	—
1950	0	400	0	7,700	—	—	—	—	—	—
1951	0	300	0	8,200	—	—	—	—	—	—
1952	0	501	0	8,106	—	—	—	—	—	—
1953	0	527	0	8,472	—	—	—	—	—	—
1954	0	722	0	8,728	—	—	—	—	—	—
1955	0	1,184	0	8,923	—	—	—	—	—	—
1956	0	1,102	0	9,298	—	—	—	—	—	—
1957	0	823	0	9,982	—	—	—	—	—	—
1958	0	1,222	0	10,544	—	—	—	—	—	—
1959	0	1,437	0	10,475	—	—	—	—	—	—
1960	0	1,404	0	11,623	—	—	—	—	—	—
1961	0	1,951	0	12,941	—	—	—	—	—	—
1962	0	2,334	0	14,559	—	—	—	—	—	—
1963	0	3,049	0	16,105	—	—	—	—	—	—
1964	0	3,366	0	18,211	—	—	—	—	—	—
1965	0	3,823	0	20,065	—	—	—	—	—	—
1966	0	3,330	0	22,040	—	—	—	—	—	—
1967	0	3,658	0	23,746	—	—	—	—	—	—
1968	0	4,201	0	26,055	—	—	—	—	—	—
1969	0	4,868	0	28,475	—	—	—	—	—	—
1970	0	5,343	628	28,358	—	—	—	—	—	—
1971	0	5,683	1,100	28,657	—	—	—	—	—	—
1972	0	6,236	1,571	28,306	—	—	—	—	—	—
1973	0	7,428	2,042	28,866	—	—	—	—	—	—
1974	0	6,240	2,514	31,727	—	—	—	—	—	—
1975	0	5,789	3,536	32,875	—	—	—	—	—	—
1976	0	6,222	5,230	34,460	—	—	—	—	—	—
1977	0	6,575	7,048	37,033	—	—	—	—	—	—
1978	0	9,226	8,941	44,180	—	—	—	—	—	—
1979	0	11,953	11,275	53,214	—	—	—	—	—	—
1980	0	11,010	13,803	76,968	—	—	—	—	—	—
1981	0	11,179	16,791	91,642	—	—	—	—	—	—
1982	0	13,428	18,688	101,631	—	—	—	—	—	—
1983	0	14,279	20,519	100,223	—	—	—	—	—	—
1984	11,000	15,659	23,787	95,648	—	—	—	—	—	—
1985	24,016	18,492	28,588	128,503	—	—	—	—	—	—
1986	16,617	29,507	34,201	131,000	—	—	—	—	—	—
1987	27,800	17,668	42,193	143,883	—	—	—	—	—	—
1988	34,865	22,622	47,304	155,143	—	—	—	—	—	—
1989	43,325	42,823	53,781	170,593	—	—	—	—	—	—
1990	55,408	41,874	64,978	185,815	235,858	115,148	60,153	20,147	2,073	38,337
1991	100,110	53,126	63,270	187,039	256,409	122,812	58,784	21,374	16,110	37,329
1992	151,369	52,708	65,806	176,752	255,570	122,680	53,606	20,525	19,933	38,826
1993	183,677	52,237	62,715	160,558	248,212	121,290	49,856	19,268	20,796	37,002
1994	205,969	28,273	66,892	155,001	264,366	129,716	49,423	20,861	24,900	39,466
1995	224,343	23,755	72,443	152,478	289,257	140,033	50,513	22,870	33,100	42,741
1996	256,172	31,981	52,116	143,323	335,285	153,836	52,257	25,476	51,600	52,116
1997	310,659	21,824	58,983	153,406	407,596	173,959	55,452	29,002	90,200	58,983
1998	405,153	24,918	75,733	161,505	462,467	176,855	55,938	29,741	124,200	75,733
1999	455,021	25,200	88,271	162,940	512,819	189,474	59,751	33,423	141,900	88,271

(continued)

TABLE Dc950–982   Nonfarm residential mortgage debt, by holder and type of property: 1945–1999   *Continued*

Multifamily mortgages

Held by

Year	Total	Commercial banks	Savings institutions	Life insurance companies	State and local government	Federal government agencies	Government-sponsored enterprises	Federally related mortgage pools	Issuers of asset-backed securities	Mortgage companies	Finance companies	Individuals and others
	Dc971	Dc972	Dc973	Dc974	Dc975	Dc976	Dc977	Dc978	Dc979	Dc980	Dc981	Dc982
	Million dollars	Million dollars	Million dollars	Million dollars	Million dollars	Million dollars	Million dollars	Million dollars	Million dollars	Million dollars	Million dollars	Million dollars
1945	4,900	500	1,600	1,400	0	—	0	0	0	0	0	1,400
1946	5,300	600	1,700	1,500	0	—	0	0	0	0	0	1,500
1947	5,800	600	1,800	1,600	0	—	0	0	0	0	0	1,700
1948	6,700	700	2,100	1,800	0	—	0	0	0	0	0	2,000
1949	7,800	700	2,400	2,300	0	—	0	0	0	0	0	2,300
1950	9,300	1,000	3,000	2,600	0	—	0	0	0	100	0	2,600
1951	10,600	1,000	3,600	3,000	0	100	0	0	0	0	0	2,900
1952	11,481	938	3,833	3,288	0	74	0	0	0	80	0	3,268
1953	12,121	900	4,071	3,363	0	184	0	0	0	79	0	3,524
1954	12,665	852	4,202	3,404	0	268	0	0	0	99	0	3,840
1955	13,490	813	4,344	3,552	0	383	0	0	0	150	0	4,248
1956	14,064	759	4,441	3,615	0	426	0	0	0	130	0	4,693
1957	14,611	762	4,493	3,551	0	469	0	0	0	92	0	5,244
1958	16,565	963	4,891	3,547	6	603	0	0	0	136	0	6,419
1959	18,700	1,120	5,272	3,666	12	904	0	0	0	160	0	7,566
1960	20,786	1,120	5,914	3,865	26	1,024	2	0	0	157	0	8,678
1961	23,622	1,187	6,966	4,250	91	1,107	2	0	0	224	0	9,795
1962	26,732	1,353	8,693	4,748	209	1,138	12	0	0	275	0	10,304
1963	30,024	1,566	10,800	5,343	394	1,055	12	1	0	365	0	10,488
1964	34,578	1,713	12,763	7,236	605	1,042	11	2	0	427	0	10,779
1965	38,213	1,986	14,405	8,811	785	1,040	10	4	0	494	0	10,678
1966	41,275	2,073	15,203	10,289	909	1,342	10	4	0	437	0	11,008
1967	44,815	2,367	16,428	11,717	1,041	1,557	9	9	0	491	0	11,196
1968	48,251	2,668	17,799	12,754	1,202	1,900	16	18	0	564	0	11,330
1969	53,176	3,217	19,326	14,235	1,588	2,581	31	35	0	675	0	11,488
1970	60,111	3,311	21,618	15,969	2,160	3,087	321	60	0	1,200	0	12,385
1971	70,062	3,984	27,185	16,747	2,876	3,486	1,140	114	0	2,359	0	12,171
1972	82,840	5,778	31,961	17,347	3,854	3,768	2,129	392	0	3,226	0	14,385
1973	93,132	6,932	35,122	18,451	4,771	4,066	3,963	616	0	3,652	0	15,559
1974	99,976	7,619	36,731	19,625	6,123	4,781	6,169	775	0	2,402	0	15,751
1975	100,609	5,915	39,339	19,629	6,871	5,993	6,410	1,175	0	1,625	0	13,652
1976	105,663	8,079	42,602	19,178	7,181	6,214	6,350	1,659	0	1,132	0	13,268
1977	113,992	9,213	47,550	18,823	7,469	6,511	6,403	2,584	0	1,404	0	14,035
1978	124,922	10,263	51,982	19,000	7,857	7,453	6,395	4,097	0	1,727	0	16,148
1979	134,834	11,153	54,136	19,215	9,233	8,570	6,583	5,318	0	1,991	0	18,635
1980	142,278	12,805	54,200	19,514	10,689	10,428	6,744	5,976	0	2,180	0	19,742
1981	142,024	14,829	53,659	19,283	11,938	11,386	5,482	3,228	0	2,086	0	20,133
1982	145,663	16,320	53,586	18,856	13,290	11,078	5,361	3,589	0	2,168	0	21,415
1983	160,696	18,223	60,526	19,107	15,686	10,731	5,284	4,820	0	1,776	0	24,543
1984	185,479	20,053	74,716	18,938	20,187	10,137	6,510	5,518	0	1,824	0	27,596
1985	205,029	23,150	89,183	19,894	23,367	10,160	8,457	6,998	0	2,029	0	21,791
1986	238,265	30,809	96,417	20,952	30,394	11,111	8,731	11,865	165	2,704	0	25,117
1987	257,705	32,207	103,494	22,524	37,389	11,480	8,425	16,378	529	1,755	0	23,524
1988	273,521	33,118	107,146	24,560	38,482	11,814	9,528	21,607	962	2,013	0	24,291
1989	285,894	37,844	104,362	26,907	39,697	12,266	12,029	25,690	939	1,825	0	24,335
1990	285,613	35,567	91,806	28,979	40,710	22,912	13,219	28,737	857	2,778	0	20,048
1991	281,720	35,086	79,881	29,342	41,676	31,856	14,198	26,102	3,150	2,690	0	17,739
1992	269,320	36,169	69,791	27,221	42,386	27,624	15,827	23,831	6,557	2,975	0	16,939
1993	266,232	37,004	67,366	27,545	42,773	24,550	17,517	22,458	8,373	3,081	0	15,565
1994	265,896	37,883	64,343	27,843	43,507	21,984	18,376	22,442	9,853	3,081	0	16,584
1995	273,482	42,521	61,987	28,714	44,148	17,321	19,011	26,893	12,021	4,196	0	16,670
1996	289,135	45,451	61,570	30,750	45,914	14,817	18,551	32,499	16,111	4,120	3,130	16,222
1997	302,394	49,670	59,543	30,402	46,488	13,897	17,302	37,794	21,154	5,166	2,930	18,048
1998	330,891	52,871	57,042	31,522	47,388	13,625	18,071	48,255	33,532	5,300	2,717	20,568
1999	372,971	66,013	59,370	32,818	48,334	13,628	22,891	57,478	41,729	5,334	5,105	20,271

[1] Quarterly flow of funds data begin in 1952. Mortgage holdings for prior years were reported annually at the end of the year and in billions of dollars. Some entries reported as zero may be less than $50 million. Components may not sum to totals for these years.

Source

Federal Reserve Board, "Flow of Funds Accounts of the United States, Historical Data," release date December 8, 2000, available from the Internet site of the Federal Reserve Board.

TABLE Dc950–982   Nonfarm residential mortgage debt, by holder and type of property: 1945–1999   *Continued*

Documentation

The data in this table represent amounts outstanding at end of the year, not seasonally adjusted. They are taken from the Federal Reserve's flow of funds accounts as they were published for the third quarter of 2000. The flow of funds accounts are constructed so that the sources of funds within the economy are equal to the uses of funds. Mortgage debt outstanding at the end of each year, therefore, represents both assets to lenders (the sources of funds shown in the table) and liabilities to the borrowers (primarily households and nonfarm noncorporate businesses). These data can be used to measure short-run macroeconomic developments, such as changes in total household mortgage debt in a given year or quarter, or to document longer-term trends such as changes in the institutional structure of the mortgage market itself.

The Federal Reserve compiles these accounts by collecting information on the quarterly flows of financial transactions from regulated financial institutions, government agencies, and private businesses. These quarterly flows are cumulated over time to form the level of financial assets outstanding at the end of each quarter – the annual data shown in this table, for example, are the mortgage debt levels at the end of each fourth quarter. These estimates are compiled separately from, and differ from, the Federal Reserve's series of mortgage debt outstanding shown in Table Dc929–949. The differences in the amounts shown are relatively small, however, because many of the same sources are used in compiling the two sets of estimates. Compared to the series shown in Table Dc929–949, the flow of funds accounts shown here provide greater detail about the mortgage holdings of financial institutions by type of residential property financed.

For detailed explanations for the earliest years in this table, see U.S. Board of Governors of the Federal Reserve System, *Flow of Funds in the United States, 1939–1953*, (1955), pp. 345–56. For a general introduction to the flow of funds accounts, see Albert M. Teplin, "The U.S. Flow of Funds Accounts and Their Uses," *Federal Reserve Bulletin* 87 (7)(2001):431–41. The complete description of the flow of funds accounts is provided in Board of Governors of the Federal Reserve System, *Guide to the Flow of Funds Accounts* (2000).

Series Dc950–952. Mortgage debt on all nonfarm properties (series Dc950) includes those on commercial properties (not shown) and residential properties (series Dc951).

Series Dc951–952 and Dc971. Series Dc951 equals the sum of home and multifamily mortgages, series Dc952 and Dc971. Multifamily residential mortgages include loans secured by residences with five or more dwelling units. Home mortgage loans, on the other hand, are secured by one- to four-family properties including condominium units. The total includes second mortgages, loans issued by sellers to finance home purchases, and construction and land development loans. Also included in the home mortgage series are loans taken out under home equity lines of credit and home equity loans secured by junior liens.

Series Dc952–964. Total home mortgage loans (series Dc952) are broken down into, and are equal to the sum of, the home mortgage holdings of twelve different groups of lenders. Six of these are privately owned, traditional financial intermediaries – commercial banks, savings institutions, credit unions, life insurance companies, mortgage companies, and finance companies. Note that the savings institutions category includes both savings and loan associations and savings banks for the entire period shown in the table. The remaining categories of mortgage holders may be less familiar; further details are provided below.

Series Dc957–960. State and local government agencies (including the District of Columbia) hold mortgages as shown in series Dc957. So does the federal government. Series Dc958 includes all federal agencies in the unified budget, but not government-sponsored, privately owned enterprises (GSEs) that have been specifically created to provide mortgage credit. The mortgage holdings of the GSEs are shown in series Dc959. Included in this series are the Federal Home Loan Banks, Federal National Mortgage Association (FNMA, Fannie Mae), Federal Home Loan Mortgage Corporation (FHLMC, Freddie Mac), and enterprises that were created to resolve the savings and loan crisis of the 1980s and 1990s (the Federal Savings and Loan Insurance Corporation Resolution Fund and the Resolution Trust Corporation). Fannie Mae and Freddie Mac hold mortgages in their portfolios but also form packages of mortgage loans and transfer them to off-balance-sheet entities known as mortgage pools. These pools raise funds, in turn, by issuing securities that are backed by the mortgages. Mortgages held in pools created by Fannie Mae and Freddie Mac are included in series Dc960; so too are the loans held in pools created by the Government National Mortgage Association. For more details on mortgage pools and the securities issued against them, see Table Dc1170–1191.

Series Dc961. Mortgage pools are also created by institutions that are neither sponsored nor owned by the federal government, such as commercial banks, thrift institutions, or finance companies. The legal entity created to pool mortgages in these cases is known as special-purpose vehicles. The mortgage loan holdings of these contractual entities are shown in series Dc961.

Series Dc964. The home mortgage holdings of individuals and others represent seven categories of mortgage holders that are reported separately in the flow of funds accounts. The two most important are households and nonfinancial corporate businesses, but the category also includes nonfarm noncorporate businesses, personal trusts and estates held in commercial banks, state and local government retirement funds, private pension funds, and real estate investment trusts.

Series Dc965–970. Total home equity loans are shown separately in the table, as well as their distribution across the five types of intermediaries that issue and hold them: commercial banks, savings institutions, credit unions, issuers of asset-backed securities, and finance companies. Users of these series should note that home equity loans are already included in total home mortgages (series Dc952) and within the mortgage amounts held for each of the affected lender groups (series Dc953–955, series Dc961, and series Dc963).

Series Dc971–982. Total multifamily mortgage holdings are divided into, and equal the sum of, eleven different groups of mortgage holdings shown in series Dc972–982. Each of these institutional groups is defined in the same way as for home mortgage loans.

TABLE Dc983–989   New mortgage loans on one- to four-family homes, by type of lender: 1925–1950

Contributed by Kenneth A. Snowden

		Lender					
	Total	Commercial banks	Mutual savings banks	Savings and loan associations	Life insurance companies	Home Owners' Loan Corporation	Individuals and others
	Dc983	Dc984	Dc985	Dc986	Dc987	Dc988	Dc989
Year	Million dollars	Million dollars	Million dollars	Million dollars	Million dollars	Million dollars	Million dollars
1925	4,240	650	450	1,620	400	0	1,120
1926	4,863	819	475	1,824	465	0	1,280
1927	4,857	585	517	1,895	500	0	1,360
1928	4,947	696	544	1,932	525	0	1,250
1929	4,442	538	468	1,791	525	0	1,120
1930	3,189	455	352	1,262	400	0	720
1931	2,232	368	353	892	169	0	450
1932	1,408	257	254	543	54	0	300
1933	1,093	233	104	414	10	132	200
1934	3,170	195	95	451	16	2,263	150
1935	2,259	474	118	564	77	583	443
1936	2,302	472	202	755	140	128	605
1937	2,588	513	196	897	232	27	723
1938	2,437	470	177	798	242	81	669
1939	2,912	604	157	986	274	151	740
1940	3,510	838	204	1,200	324	143	801
1941	3,931	847	243	1,379	371	63	1,028
1942	3,319	721	179	1,051	374	40	954
1943	3,362	654	160	1,184	272	54	1,038
1944	4,004	726	189	1,454	300	31	1,304
1945	4,867	923	267	1,913	209	4	1,551
1946	10,011	2,677	656	3,684	492	2	2,700
1947	11,207	2,986	658	3,811	906	2	2,844
1948	11,357	2,636	980	3,607	1,132	2	3,000
1949	11,069	2,236	990	3,636	1,093	2	3,112
1950	16,008	3,429	1,400	5,237	1,742	0	4,200

Source

Leo Grebler, David M. Blank, and Louis Winnick, *Capital Formation in Residential Real Estate* (Princeton University Press, 1956), Table N-13, pp. 489–90, and Table 47, p. 175.

Documentation

These series show the amount of new mortgage debt on one- to four-family homes that major lending groups issued each year between 1925 and 1950. Grebler, Blank, and Winnick cite as their source the Federal Home Loan Bank Board, *Estimated Home Mortgage Debt and Lending Activity, 1950*, which appears to have been an unpublished document (dated July 10, 1951) produced by the research staff of the Federal Home Loan Bank Board (FHLBB). It could not be located for the preparation of this table. An earlier version of the same group of series appeared for the years 1929–1940 in the *Ninth Annual Report* of the FHLBB (1941, p. 189). These earlier estimates of lending activity were virtually identical to those shown here for savings and loans, life insurance companies, and the Home Owners' Loan Corporation (HOLC).

Grebler, Blank, and Winnick report that the FHLBB discontinued compiling these estimates in 1950, even before these authors made use of them (p. 175). The FHLBB's estimates of new home mortgage loans made were based on the same balance sheet information that was used to compile the estimates of home mortgage debt outstanding that are shown in Table Dc903–928. New lending activity for a given year cannot be directly measured from balance sheet data measured at the beginning and end of that year, however, because changes in the amounts of mortgages held between the two dates are determined by both the volume of new lending and the volume of payoffs and cancellations of existing loans. As the regulator of savings and loans, the FHLBB had direct information about the actual lending activities of these institutions beginning in the mid-1930s. Grebler, Blank, and Winnick observe that the estimates for the other lenders were "probably less reliable" (p. 175). It should be noted, however, that the FHLBB also administered the HOLC and had supervisory authority over some life insurance companies. The weakest estimates in the table, therefore, are probably for the two banking groups (series Dc984–985) and the "individuals and others" category (series Dc989).

The description of these series as they appear in *Historical Statistics of the United States* (1975) appears to confirm this view: "These series represent only rough approximations except for the Home Owners' Loan Corporation and for savings and loan associations since the late thirties. The estimates were based on scattered reports of national and State supervisory authorities, special reports to the Home Loan Bank Board by life insurance companies, and, for 1939–1950, on mortgage recordings figures (see Table Dc990–995). Estimates for the earlier years, and for 'individuals and others' throughout, are highly tentative" (p. 637).

Series Dc989. The 1941 version of this table defined "individuals and others" as including fiduciaries; mortgage, title, and real estate companies; construction companies; philanthropic and educational institutions; fraternal organizations; and state and local governments. This is consistent with later definitions used by the FHLBB.

TABLE Dc990–995   Nonfarm mortgage recordings of $20,000 and less, by type of lender: 1939–1964

Contributed by Kenneth A. Snowden

Year	Total	Commercial banks	Mutual savings banks	Savings and loan associations	Life insurance companies	All others
	Dc990	Dc991	Dc992	Dc993	Dc994	Dc995
	Million dollars	Million dollars	Million dollars	Million dollars	Million dollars	Million dollars
1939	3,507	891	143	1,058	287	1,128
1940	4,031	1,006	170	1,284	334	1,238
1941	4,732	1,166	218	1,490	404	1,454
1942	3,943	886	166	1,171	362	1,359
1943	3,861	753	152	1,238	280	1,439
1944	4,606	878	165	1,560	257	1,746
1945	5,650	1,097	217	2,017	250	2,069
1946	10,589	2,712	548	3,483	503	3,343
1947	11,729	3,004	596	3,650	847	3,631
1948	11,882	2,664	745	3,629	1,016	3,829
1949	11,828	2,446	750	3,646	1,046	3,940
1950	16,179	3,365	1,064	5,060	1,618	5,073
1951	16,405	3,370	1,013	5,295	1,615	5,112
1952	18,018	3,600	1,137	6,452	1,420	5,409
1953	19,747	3,680	1,327	7,365	1,480	5,895
1954	22,974	4,239	1,501	8,312	1,768	7,154
1955	28,484	5,617	1,857	10,452	1,932	8,626
1956	27,088	5,458	1,824	9,532	1,799	8,475
1957	24,244	4,264	1,429	9,217	1,472	7,862
1958	27,388	5,204	1,640	10,516	1,460	8,568
1959	32,235	5,832	1,780	13,094	1,523	10,006
1960	29,341	4,520	1,557	12,158	1,318	9,788
1961	31,157	4,997	1,741	13,662	1,160	9,597
1962	34,187	5,851	1,958	15,144	1,212	10,022
1963	36,925	6,354	2,061	16,716	1,339	10,455
1964	36,921	6,656	2,182	15,769	1,408	10,916

Source

Federal Home Loan Bank Board, Housing and Home Finance Agency, *Savings and Home Financing Source Book,* annual issues.

Documentation

In compiling the series shown in Table Dc983–989 the Federal Home Loan Bank Board (FHLBB) measured the volume of new home mortgage lending each year from direct reports made by financial institutions. The series reported in this table represent a second approach the FHLBB used to estimate new mortgage lending – by measuring the flow of new residential mortgage loans as they were registered in county offices. In the late 1930s these reports were assembled with the help of the savings and loan associations, the U.S. Building and Loan League, the Mortgage Bankers Association, and the American Title Association. The national estimates were based on data drawn from sample counties, which grew in number over time; by 1964, approximately 500 areas containing about 54 percent of the nation's nonfarm single-family housing units were sampled. Activity in the remaining areas was usually estimated by reference to the closest reporting area. To relate the series as closely as possible to home-financing operations, it was limited to mortgages of $20,000 or less. As a result, the series include small mortgages secured by nonresidential real estate and exclude large mortgages secured by residences.

The *Savings and Home Financing Source Book, 1966* explained the series as follows:

Since almost every mortgage is recorded, the series provides an adequate means of determining trends in real estate financing activity, as well as the role being played by various types of lenders. Summaries are made on the basis of the originating mortgagees, and, for this reason, assignments of mortgages are not reflected in the series. To the extent that certain lenders (e.g., insurance companies) purchase mortgages originated and recorded by other lenders (e.g., mortgage companies), the recording statistics may overstate or understate the importance of a particular type of lender as the ultimate source of mortgage credit. It should also be pointed out that mortgage recording data are not directly comparable with estimates on home mortgage lending; the periods covered are not necessarily the same, because lending statistics are reported as of the date of loan commitment, while recording figures reflect the actual date of mortgage registration. Furthermore, alterations in the terms of an existing contract may necessitate a new registration. In the case of refinancing an institution's own mortgage, for example, the face amount of the instrument would appear in the recording totals, whereas only that portion which represented an increase of funds loaned would be included in the lending figures. (p. 46)

The source also reported that the mortgage recording series was to be discontinued after publication of the 1964 data.

The figures exclude Alaska and Hawai'i.

TABLE Dc996–1032   Originations, purchases, and sales of mortgages, by type of institutional lender: 1970–1997
[One- to four-family homes]

Contributed by Kenneth A. Snowden

	Total				Commercial banks				Mutual savings banks			
	Originations	Purchases	Sales	Net acquisition	Originations	Purchases	Sales	Net acquisition	Originations	Purchases	Sales	Net acquisition
	Dc996	Dc997	Dc998	Dc999	Dc1000	Dc1001	Dc1002	Dc1003	Dc1004	Dc1005	Dc1006	Dc1007
Year	Million dollars	Million dollars	Million dollars	Million dollars	Million dollars	Million dollars	Million dollars	Million dollars	Million dollars	Million dollars	Million dollars	Million dollars
1970	35,587	13,406	14,192	34,801	7,797	521	1,674	6,644	2,147	1,408	254	3,301
1971	57,788	18,292	18,534	57,546	12,598	1,130	1,971	11,757	3,540	1,874	175	5,239
1972	75,864	25,076	24,129	76,810	17,710	1,046	2,245	16,511	5,052	2,708	202	7,559
1973	79,126	22,573	24,862	76,837	18,782	925	2,010	17,698	5,912	1,958	161	7,709
1974	67,508	23,039	23,111	67,435	16,128	372	1,623	14,877	3,929	1,039	228	4,740
1975	77,913	31,881	29,652	80,142	14,450	236	2,932	11,755	4,333	1,103	235	5,202
1976	112,785	42,840	40,934	114,691	24,501	839	4,023	21,317	6,428	2,127	457	8,098
1977	161,973	55,712	55,361	162,324	36,675	1,756	5,839	32,592	8,660	2,947	221	11,387
1978	185,036	62,953	67,758	180,232	43,924	1,674	6,773	38,826	9,379	2,800	296	11,883
1979	187,091	69,771	76,536	180,326	41,415	2,112	6,526	37,002	8,963	2,633	521	11,075
1980	133,762	69,967	65,835	137,894	28,778	4,280	7,500	25,558	5,435	966	725	5,676
1981	98,212	55,999	53,194	101,018	21,689	3,120	4,497	20,313	4,022	245	446	3,822
1982	96,951	110,337	101,567	105,721	25,189	1,913	7,888	19,214	4,001	1,425	2,179	3,248
1983	201,863	173,902	152,123	223,642	44,830	3,484	14,842	33,471	10,775	2,412	2,617	10,570
1984	203,705	165,102	137,481	231,326	41,941	5,116	12,682	34,375	12,685	2,961	2,530	13,116
1985	289,783	238,875	270,847	257,812	57,031	6,276	21,730	41,577	7,477	1,190	8,325	342
1986	499,412	450,136	451,607	497,942	108,613	10,922	39,087	80,448	31,109	3,298	12,650	21,757
1987	507,231	444,748	452,267	499,711	124,551	21,246	50,258	95,539	34,232	3,329	12,568	24,992
1988	446,263	342,489	361,536	427,217	101,863	24,301	39,475	86,690	28,425	4,115	10,428	22,112
1989	452,907	417,363	416,951	453,319	123,193	26,565	46,166	103,592	23,196	1,432	12,451	12,177
1990	458,404	445,399	431,293	472,510	153,285	33,275	68,803	117,757	17,956	3,564	12,095	9,425
1991	562,074	503,837	516,580	549,331	153,323	26,553	67,242	112,634	18,516	4,243	10,751	12,008
1992	893,681	822,347	826,485	889,543	232,065	42,239	101,877	172,427	34,246	4,205	16,544	21,907
1993	1,019,861	1,035,652	985,921	1,069,592	268,985	59,134	136,015	192,104	39,411	6,448	22,205	23,654
1994	768,748	750,898	774,140	745,506	199,996	49,699	85,728	163,967	29,260	1,999	12,241	19,018
1995	639,436	655,839	648,779	646,496	155,359	81,612	72,862	164,109	23,258	6,867	8,933	21,192
1996	785,233	793,005	799,552	778,686	178,548	86,499	106,620	158,427	33,911	3,750	11,970	25,691
1997	859,124	1,022,452	1,023,084	858,492	206,591	78,239	85,385	199,445	21,828	2,863	6,047	18,644

	Savings and loan associations				Life insurance companies				Mortgage companies			
	Originations	Purchases	Sales	Net acquisition	Originations	Purchases	Sales	Net acquisition	Originations	Purchases	Sales	Net acquisition
	Dc1008 [1]	Dc1009 [1]	Dc1010 [1]	Dc1011 [1]	Dc1012	Dc1013	Dc1014	Dc1015	Dc1016	Dc1017	Dc1018	Dc1019
Year	Million dollars	Million dollars	Million dollars	Million dollars	Million dollars	Million dollars	Million dollars	Million dollars	Million dollars	Million dollars	Million dollars	Million dollars
1970	14,814	3,397	804	17,407	334	198	19	512	8,906	60	9,613	−647
1971	26,603	6,635	1,654	31,584	333	185	37	481	12,487	403	12,394	496
1972	36,739	9,502	2,886	43,356	401	207	5	603	13,326	1,431	14,315	442
1973	38,441	5,862	2,759	41,545	380	247	8	620	12,657	1,382	14,980	−941
1974	30,932	4,824	3,093	32,663	359	179	24	514	13,026	880	14,886	−980
1975	41,242	7,167	4,726	43,683	251	126	25	353	13,992	785	14,451	326
1976	61,900	11,106	7,714	65,292	365	114	3	477	15,744	2,221	17,332	633
1977	86,304	13,155	12,955	86,504	440	194	5	629	25,651	4,116	27,327	2,440
1978	89,952	10,283	14,999	85,236	848	814	20	1,642	34,448	3,826	35,037	3,237
1979	82,825	11,608	18,108	76,325	2,024	1,454	237	3,241	45,260	5,693	44,412	6,541
1980	61,095	12,440	15,523	58,012	1,711	1,329	134	2,906	29,419	3,422	31,500	1,341
1981	41,980	10,037	12,402	39,615	478	159	255	382	23,958	4,348	26,607	1,699
1982	34,783	20,156	50,776	4,163	544	234	238	540	27,995	4,947	29,635	3,307
1983	81,524	32,919	50,173	64,270	726	213	703	236	59,762	13,092	70,084	2,770
1984	96,187	44,660	54,169	86,678	826	214	841	199	47,589	10,885	55,232	3,242
1985	109,276	48,843	93,748	64,371	1,306	209	1,521	−6	110,004	31,252	138,423	2,833
1986	176,073	62,076	156,944	81,205	3,814	883	1,538	3,159	175,986	61,819	226,790	11,015
1987	174,549	56,726	116,059	115,216	3,209	1,336	1,071	3,474	167,053	86,812	265,704	−11,839
1988	160,446	49,492	97,858	112,080	3,331	2,266	3,668	1,929	148,004	60,197	203,247	4,954
1989	134,480	38,318	100,827	71,971	1,443	2,085	1,447	2,081	166,494	105,429	251,722	20,201

Notes appear at end of table

TABLE Dc996-1032   Originations, purchases, and sales of mortgages, by type of institutional lender: 1970-1997
[One- to four-family homes]   *Continued*

	Savings and loan associations				Life insurance companies				Mortgage companies			
	Originations	Purchases	Sales	Net acquisition	Originations	Purchases	Sales	Net acquisition	Originations	Purchases	Sales	Net acquisition
	Dc1008 [1]	Dc1009 [1]	Dc1010 [1]	Dc1011 [1]	Dc1012	Dc1013	Dc1014	Dc1015	Dc1016	Dc1017	Dc1018	Dc1019
Year	Million dollars	Million dollars	Million dollars	Million dollars	Million dollars	Million dollars	Million dollars	Million dollars	Million dollars	Million dollars	Million dollars	Million dollars
1990	121,034	37,512	108,614	49,932	606	774	442	938	161,153	51,265	213,367	−949
1991	121,900	50,036	120,359	51,577	564	418	491	491	263,917	38,125	290,790	11,252
1992	184,546	53,733	166,370	71,909	697	537	678	556	437,604	79,981	518,003	−418
1993	179,339	58,219	147,435	90,123	807	849	1,183	473	526,502	139,134	666,107	−471
1994	123,121	44,851	88,872	79,100	662	588	666	584	408,141	147,767	579,872	−23,964
1995	95,598	35,364	66,524	64,438	670	892	897	665	358,705	130,706	493,929	−4,518
1996	121,700	44,190	86,226	79,664	444	800	640	604	445,739	154,518	592,031	8,226
1997	130,897	48,564	96,750	82,711	391	712	579	524	494,530	265,462	744,670	15,322

	Federal credit agencies				Other institutions				Mortgage pools			Mortgage conduits	
	Originations	Purchases	Sales	Net acquisition	Originations	Purchases	Sales	Net acquisition	Purchases	Sales	Net acquisition	Purchases	Net acquisition
	Dc1020 [2]	Dc1021 [2]	Dc1022 [2]	Dc1023 [2]	Dc1024 [3]	Dc1025 [3]	Dc1026 [3]	Dc1027 [3]	Dc1028	Dc1029	Dc1030	Dc1031	Dc1032
Year	Million dollars	Million dollars	Million dollars	Million dollars	Million dollars	Million dollars	Million dollars	Million dollars	Million dollars	Million dollars	Million dollars	Million dollars	Million dollars
1970	1,366	5,371	1,631	5,106	222	610	77	756	1,841	119	1,722	0	0
1971	1,798	3,733	1,853	3,678	430	386	253	562	3,947	197	3,750	0	0
1972	2,044	4,996	3,799	3,240	592	430	522	500	4,756	157	4,599	0	0
1973	2,351	7,396	4,315	5,432	603	623	194	1,031	4,178	436	3,743	0	0
1974	2,467	8,801	2,534	8,734	668	638	29	1,276	6,305	692	5,612	0	0
1975	2,867	10,732	6,722	6,877	777	575	108	1,246	11,156	454	10,702	0	0
1976	2,652	9,573	10,831	1,394	1,195	492	39	1,649	16,367	534	15,832	0	0
1977	3,093	9,295	7,575	4,814	1,149	815	129	1,834	23,433	1,309	22,124	0	0
1978	4,843	18,779	9,088	14,534	1,642	1,576	118	3,098	23,202	1,427	21,775	0	0
1979	4,445	15,759	5,825	14,379	2,159	2,521	132	4,548	27,990	775	27,215	0	0
1980	4,378	14,381	7,226	11,533	2,946	6,432	24	9,354	26,717	3,203	23,514	0	0
1981	4,464	11,189	5,853	9,800	1,621	5,486	49	7,057	21,415	3,085	18,330	0	0
1982	3,504	18,411	7,973	13,942	935	3,132	29	4,038	57,070	2,849	54,221	3,049	3,049
1983	3,180	25,332	9,646	18,866	1,066	5,531	14	6,584	85,419	4,044	81,375	5,500	5,500
1984	3,223	23,842	7,853	19,212	1,255	5,687	41	6,900	64,080	4,133	59,947	7,658	7,658
1985	3,154	27,348	4,952	25,550	1,535	6,303	9	7,829	109,584	2,139	107,445	7,870	7,870
1986	2,676	35,403	13,307	24,772	1,142	6,029	283	6,888	253,527	1,008	252,519	16,179	16,179
1987	2,890	23,691	6,134	20,447	747	5,191	241	5,697	225,251	232	225,019	21,166	21,166
1988	2,858	29,135	6,326	25,667	1,336	6,803	276	7,863	142,769	258	142,511	23,411	23,411
1989	2,687	27,139	4,041	25,785	1,414	7,738	149	9,003	192,261	148	192,113	16,396	16,396
1990	3,022	63,890	27,955	38,957	1,348	5,232	17	6,563	229,740	0	229,740	20,147	20,147
1991	3,050	68,805	26,895	44,960	804	5,143	47	5,900	271,732	5	271,727	38,782	38,782
1992	3,362	95,766	22,951	76,177	1,161	4,541	56	5,646	463,158	6	463,152	78,187	78,187
1993	4,073	116,238	12,863	107,448	744	3,267	113	3,898	561,754	0	561,754	90,609	90,609
1994	5,502	85,259	6,681	84,080	2,066	5,532	67	7,531	353,348	13	353,335	61,855	61,855
1995	3,595	92,423	5,554	90,464	2,251	7,163	57	9,357	263,388	23	263,365	37,424	37,424
1996	2,928	99,516	2,025	100,419	1,963	7,062	40	8,985	357,914	0	357,914	38,756	38,756
1997	2,806	195,693	89,653	108,846	2,081	7,994	0	10,075	360,038	0	360,038	62,887	62,887

[1] Includes federally chartered savings banks beginning in 1984.

[2] Includes Resolution Trust Corporation beginning in 1990.

[3] Includes state and local government credit agencies and retirement funds, private pensions, and, for 1970-1982, real estate investment trusts.

Source

The data in this table were extracted from electronic copies of annual tables from the Survey of Mortgage Lending Activity, which was produced by the U.S. Department of Housing and Urban Development between 1970 and 1997.

Documentation

All revisions that were made to Survey of Mortgage Lending Activity (SMLA) data during this period are incorporated in these tables and so there are differences between the data shown here and those reported in published SMLA reports. For a description and details of the SMLA, see Office of

Financial Management, Financial Analysis Division, U.S. Department of Housing and Urban Development, *The Supply of Mortgage Credit, 1970–1979* (1980); and the following issues of "Survey of Mortgage Lending Activity" (published as news releases of the Office of Public Affairs, U.S. Department of Housing and Urban Development): 1985 Annual Report (HUD-number 86-67), Second Quarter 1987 (HUD-number 87-119), September 1987 (HUD-number 87-146), 1989 Annual report (HUD-number 90-43), January 1990 (HUD-number 90-49), September 1992 (HUD-number 93-18), December 1992 (HUD-number 93-35), March 1993 (HUD-number 93-61), June 1994 (HUD-number 94-167) and Second Quarter 1997 (HUD-number 97-289).

See Table Dc1033-1052 for SMLA home mortgage data by type of loan. See Tables Dc1053-1104 for SMLA multifamily mortgage data. Not shown in this volume are SMLA series on farm and commercial mortgages, loan commitments and home construction mortgages, and total mortgage

(continued)

TABLE Dc996–1032   Originations, purchases, and sales of mortgages, by type of institutional lender: 1970–1997 [One- to four-family homes]   *Continued*

holdings. All series, moreover, were reported monthly as well as annually in the SMLA. The Mortgage Bankers Association has produced less detailed estimates of mortgage originations since the SMLA was discontinued.

The monthly SMLA was undertaken by the Department of Housing and Urban Development (HUD) in 1970 to provide analysts and policymakers with a comprehensive statistical picture of the primary and secondary mortgage markets. The surveys were originally intended and produced as an internal HUD product, but were soon disseminated to the public on request and, finally, issued as regular press releases. Owing to budgetary, personnel, and priority considerations, the survey was discontinued in 1997. Nonetheless, it remains the most comprehensive statistical picture of the American mortgage market during a dramatic period of institutional and structural change.

Over its twenty-seven-year history, the SMLA captured the lending activities of between 1,500 and 1,700 institutions and agencies. Monthly reports made by these lenders were compiled by the Federal Home Loan Bank Board (and its successor Office of Thrift Supervision after 1990), the Mortgage Bankers Association of America, the American Council of Life Insurance, and the U.S. Census Bureau and HUD. In 1980 the SMLA was estimated to cover 95 percent of the nation's total mortgage lending activity; after 1980 the survey had to be restructured several times to more accurately reflect the changing composition of the market.

A home mortgage loan was defined in the SMLA as indebtedness incurred by a private borrower that was secured by a mortgage lien on a residential property designed to accommodate one to four families and located in the United States or its outlying parts. Included were purchase money mortgages (to purchase new or existing properties), and mortgage loans for refinancing, property improvement, and nonrealty purposes (including second mortgages and equity lines of credit). Excluded from the survey were loans issued by state or local governments or by industrial, railroad, or public utility corporations. Also excluded were loans to builders for which real estate was not the primary collateral, and any debts that were secured by mortgage loans.

This table shows the dollar value of home mortgage loans that were originated (made directly to the borrower) by the financial institutions that were covered by SMLA. Also shown is the dollar amount of mortgage loans that were purchased or sold (after origination) by these institutions. Purchases and sales of mortgage loans are generally transactions between different financial institutions and comprise what is called the secondary market for mortgage loans. By making use of the secondary market, a financial institution can choose to hold a different amount of mortgage debt, and a more diversified portfolio of mortgage loans, than if it holds every mortgage loan that it originates. The net acquisition of mortgage loans for each institutional group shown in the table is equal to the sum of its originations and purchases (called gross acquisitions) minus its sales.

Series Dc996–999 provide the total sum of originations, purchases, sales, and net acquisitions for all of the institutional groupings shown in the table, and therefore for all of the institutions that were covered by the SMLA. The first four of the groupings shown in the table dominated the U.S. residential mortgage market for most of the twentieth century: commercial banks, mutual savings banks, savings and loan associations (S&Ls), and life insurance companies. An important change in definition occurred in 1984 when the savings and loan category was broadened to include federal savings banks. These new types of thrift were first authorized by legislation in 1978 but by the early 1990s had grown to dominate the "savings and loan" SMLA category as more than 3,000 of the traditional mutual S&Ls disappeared through reorganization, failure, or merger. Beginning in 1990 any S&Ls that were liquidated through the auspices of the Resolution Trust Corporation (RTC) were shown in the SMLA as selling their mortgage loan portfolios to the RTC. See further discussion of these transactions below.

The SMLA estimated the mortgage lending activities of commercial and mutual savings banks by collecting survey data on originations, purchases, and sales for a sample of these institutions and then scaling these sample results up to an industry total using weights that were drawn from semi-annual Federal Deposit Insurance Corporation Call Reports. Modifications were made to these procedures in 1989, 1990, and 1992, and revisions were made to earlier data when it appeared that the activities of commercial banks were being underreported in the SMLA. Users of these data should also be aware that the SMLA excluded real estate loans held by foreign banking offices in the United States, and for this reason these figures differ from flow of funds estimates for banks that were prepared and published by the Federal Reserve Board.

Mortgage companies are intermediaries that specialize in originating mortgages and purchasing mortgage loans for the purpose of selling them to other financial institutions and long-term investors. Smaller mortgage companies became increasingly important in the mortgage market in the late 1980s, but were underrepresented in the SMLA. This gap in the survey's coverage led to both an underestimate of total originations and to a large divergence between the reported volume of mortgage purchases (which were well measured) and mortgage sales (which were not). After the problem was studied for two years, a major enhancement in the coverage of mortgage companies was introduced into the SMLA in January 1990, and data were revised going back to 1985.

Among the most important purchasers of loans from mortgage companies are federal credit agencies, mortgage pools, and mortgage conduits. Federal credit agencies within the SMLA included the Government National Mortgage Association (known as Ginnie Mae), government-sponsored enterprises (the Federal National Mortgage Association and the Federal Home Loan Mortgage Corporation, known as Fannie Mae and Freddie Mac), and, beginning in 1990, the RTC. The RTC was created to help liquidate failed S&Ls by absorbing these institutions and then disposing of their assets. These transactions were shown in the SMLA as a sale of mortgage loans from the failed S&L (series Dc1010) and a purchase by the RTC (series Dc1021). Following the acquisition of a thrift's mortgage loans, the RTC would normally securitize them so that yet another transaction was recorded in the SMLA – a sale by federal credit agencies (series Dc1022) and a purchase by a mortgage pool category (series Dc1029).

There was a dramatic increase, in fact, in the use of several different varieties of mortgage securitization structures during the 1980s and 1990s that are captured by the SMLA data. Securitization occurs when a financial institution "sells" a bundle of its mortgage loans to a specially created legal entity, which then issues securities using the mortgage loans as collateral. Much more important than those created by RTC during this period were mortgage pools that were created and guaranteed by Fannie Mae, Freddie Mac, and Ginnie Mae. Some securitization structures, in addition, were privately owned and were referred to as mortgage conduits in the SMLA. The purchase of mortgages by these conduits is shown here as series Dc1031. The total value of the mortgages purchased by the conduits is recorded in the SMLA rather than the face value of the securities that these mortgages were used to collateralize (which was generally less). See Table Dc1170–1191 for more detail on mortgage securitization activity.

Mortgage conduits were first introduced into the SMLA in 1983 as they began to increase in importance. To make room for the new category, real estate investment trusts (REITs) were no longer surveyed. In this table the transactions of the REITs between 1970 and 1982 are shown in the "other institutions" category (series Dc1024–1027). For all years this category also includes the credit agencies and retirement funds of state and local governments, and private pension funds. The activities of all three other groups were reported separately in the SMLA.

TABLE Dc1033–1052   Originations, purchases, and sales of mortgages, by type of property and loan: 1970–1997
[One- to four-family homes]

Contributed by Kenneth A. Snowden

	Originations									
	Total				New homes				Existing homes	
Year	Total	Insured by FHA	Guaranteed by VA	Conventional mortgages	Total	Insured by FHA	Guaranteed by VA	Conventional mortgages	Total	Insured by FHA
	Dc1033	Dc1034	Dc1035	Dc1036	Dc1037	Dc1038	Dc1039	Dc1040	Dc1041	Dc1042
	Million dollars	Million dollars	Million dollars	Million dollars	Million dollars	Million dollars	Million dollars	Million dollars	Million dollars	Million dollars
1970	35,587	8,769	3,846	22,972	12,601	2,724	1,389	8,488	22,986	6,044
1971	57,788	10,994	6,830	39,964	20,456	4,441	2,644	13,371	37,332	6,553
1972	75,864	8,456	7,749	59,659	25,832	3,415	3,037	19,380	50,031	5,041
1973	79,126	5,185	7,577	66,364	27,970	2,047	2,952	22,971	51,157	3,139
1974	67,508	4,532	7,889	55,088	24,131	1,389	2,512	20,230	43,377	3,143
1975	77,913	6,265	8,836	62,811	24,585	1,966	2,695	19,925	53,328	4,299
1976	112,785	6,998	10,426	95,361	32,158	1,933	2,867	27,358	80,627	5,065
1977	161,973	10,469	14,882	136,622	46,423	3,100	4,537	38,786	115,550	7,369
1978	185,036	14,581	16,026	154,429	58,015	5,313	5,844	46,858	127,021	9,268
1979	187,091	20,710	18,876	147,505	60,701	6,979	6,334	47,388	126,390	13,731
1980	133,762	14,955	12,102	106,704	49,138	6,501	5,153	37,483	84,624	8,454
1981	98,212	10,538	7,534	80,141	37,303	4,253	3,015	30,035	60,910	6,285
1982	96,951	11,482	7,687	77,782	30,588	4,112	2,736	23,740	66,363	7,370
1983	201,863	28,753	18,880	154,229	47,388	7,829	4,961	34,598	154,475	20,924
1984	203,705	16,600	12,024	175,081	53,731	5,392	3,947	44,392	149,974	11,208
1985	289,783	28,767	15,246	245,771	58,956	5,228	3,829	49,898	230,827	23,538
1986	499,412	64,770	23,149	411,493	72,488	8,295	3,856	60,336	426,924	56,474
1987	507,231	77,822	30,176	399,232	79,015	10,429	5,958	62,627	428,216	67,393
1988	446,263	46,655	15,875	383,733	85,198	7,139	3,928	74,131	361,065	39,516
1989	452,907	45,108	13,681	394,118	90,382	6,764	3,038	80,580	362,525	38,344
1990	458,404	59,803	21,901	376,700	110,678	7,459	5,637	97,582	347,726	52,344
1991	562,074	46,914	15,285	499,875	119,977	5,236	2,967	111,774	442,097	41,678
1992	893,681	50,275	24,543	818,863	132,386	4,945	3,217	124,224	761,295	45,330
1993	1,019,861	83,457	41,023	895,381	117,344	10,777	5,726	100,841	902,517	72,680
1994	768,748	94,913	48,190	625,645	114,551	10,377	6,085	98,089	654,197	84,536
1995	639,436	48,424	26,262	564,750	110,701	5,028	3,851	101,822	528,735	43,396
1996	785,233	72,727	35,211	677,295	178,165	14,306	7,839	156,020	607,068	58,421
1997	859,124	74,248	27,994	756,882	111,215	5,438	3,107	102,670	747,909	68,810

	Originations		Purchases				Sales			
	Existing homes									
Year	Guaranteed by VA	Conventional mortgages	Total	Insured by FHA	Guaranteed by VA	Conventional mortgages	Total	Insured by FHA	Guaranteed by VA	Conventional mortgages
	Dc1043	Dc1044	Dc1045	Dc1046	Dc1047	Dc1048	Dc1049	Dc1050	Dc1051	Dc1052
	Million dollars	Million dollars	Million dollars	Million dollars	Million dollars	Million dollars	Million dollars	Million dollars	Million dollars	Million dollars
1970	2,457	14,484	13,406	7,276	3,340	2,789	14,192	7,656	3,755	2,780
1971	4,186	26,594	18,292	9,704	4,852	3,736	18,534	9,956	4,949	3,630
1972	4,711	40,279	25,076	10,327	7,490	7,259	24,129	9,920	7,182	7,027
1973	4,625	43,393	22,573	7,428	6,464	8,681	24,862	8,827	7,010	9,025
1974	5,377	34,857	23,039	5,488	7,524	10,026	23,111	5,257	7,585	10,269
1975	6,142	42,886	31,881	8,917	8,980	13,984	29,652	6,611	9,094	13,947
1976	7,559	68,003	42,840	11,715	11,472	19,653	40,934	8,190	11,277	21,468
1977	10,345	97,836	55,712	11,976	14,997	28,739	55,361	10,470	14,112	30,779
1978	10,183	107,571	62,953	14,483	14,555	33,915	67,758	13,689	15,987	38,082
1979	12,543	100,117	69,771	18,767	16,921	34,082	76,536	19,458	18,001	39,077
1980	6,949	69,221	69,967	17,818	12,757	39,393	65,835	15,244	12,903	37,689
1981	4,519	50,106	55,999	13,318	8,174	34,507	53,194	12,194	8,902	32,098
1982	4,951	54,042	110,337	13,839	9,122	87,376	101,567	11,836	8,339	81,392
1983	13,919	119,632	173,902	40,025	26,232	107,645	152,123	33,485	21,506	97,132
1984	8,077	130,689	165,102	22,729	15,974	126,399	137,481	20,073	14,719	102,688

(continued)

TABLE Dc1033–1052   Originations, purchases, and sales of mortgages, by type of institutional lender: 1970–1997 [One- to four-family homes]   *Continued*

	Originations		Purchases				Sales			
	Existing homes									
	Guaranteed by VA	Conventional mortgages	Total	Insured by FHA	Guaranteed by VA	Conventional mortgages	Total	Insured by FHA	Guaranteed by VA	Conventional mortgages
	Dc1043	Dc1044	Dc1045	Dc1046	Dc1047	Dc1048	Dc1049	Dc1050	Dc1051	Dc1052
Year	Million dollars	Million dollars	Million dollars	Million dollars	Million dollars	Million dollars	Million dollars	Million dollars	Million dollars	Million dollars
1985	11,416	195,872	238,875	43,309	22,234	173,332	270,847	38,708	20,736	211,403
1986	19,293	351,157	450,136	107,389	42,474	300,274	451,607	93,310	34,882	323,415
1987	24,218	336,605	444,748	118,965	53,350	272,432	452,267	134,356	57,376	260,534
1988	11,947	309,602	342,489	75,458	27,583	239,448	361,536	77,652	28,174	255,709
1989	10,643	313,538	417,363	87,185	29,298	300,880	416,951	81,578	27,934	307,439
1990	16,264	279,118	445,399	72,031	24,137	349,231	431,293	74,959	28,392	327,942
1991	12,318	388,101	503,837	64,088	22,957	416,792	516,580	49,454	18,231	448,895
1992	21,326	694,639	822,347	66,289	33,211	722,847	826,485	62,459	30,072	733,954
1993	35,297	794,540	1,035,652	109,348	54,733	871,571	985,921	100,969	47,657	837,295
1994	42,105	527,556	750,898	115,056	61,629	574,213	774,140	134,047	68,761	571,332
1995	22,411	462,928	655,839	72,290	36,671	546,878	648,779	66,990	35,560	546,229
1996	27,372	521,275	793,005	104,619	45,858	642,528	799,552	105,928	47,942	645,682
1997	24,887	654,212	1,022,452	153,798	60,145	808,509	1,023,084	142,056	54,426	826,602

Source

See the source for Table Dc996–1032.

Documentation

See the text for Table Dc996–1032. The data shown in the table are for the major groups of lending institutions covered by the Survey of Mortgage Lending Activity.

TABLE Dc1053–1089   Originations, purchases, and sales of mortgages, by type of institutional lender: 1970–1997
[Multifamily residential property]

Contributed by Kenneth A. Snowden

	Total				Commercial banks				Mutual savings banks			
	Originations	Purchases	Sales	Net acquisition	Originations	Purchases	Sales	Net acquisition	Originations	Purchases	Sales	Net acquisition
	Dc1053	Dc1054	Dc1055	Dc1056	Dc1057	Dc1058	Dc1059	Dc1060	Dc1061	Dc1062	Dc1063	Dc1064
Year	Million dollars	Million dollars	Million dollars	Million dollars	Million dollars	Million dollars	Million dollars	Million dollars	Million dollars	Million dollars	Million dollars	Million dollars
1970	8,787	1,027	1,760	8,054	324	34	74	284	1,140	285	16	1,409
1971	12,455	1,275	2,220	11,510	726	6	34	698	1,870	266	59	2,077
1972	15,427	1,820	3,339	13,907	1,347	40	93	1,293	1,929	263	59	2,134
1973	14,022	2,144	2,866	13,299	1,122	24	75	1,071	2,088	275	64	2,299
1974	12,277	2,383	1,471	13,190	749	144	60	832	1,532	261	77	1,716
1975	10,642	3,154	2,196	11,601	767	30	27	770	1,459	343	32	1,770
1976	12,293	2,741	2,524	12,510	1,987	18	153	1,852	1,356	290	65	1,581
1977	15,826	4,162	3,821	16,167	1,890	16	104	1,802	1,492	324	33	1,783
1978	16,373	5,369	5,489	16,253	2,136	15	109	2,042	1,195	290	33	1,452
1979	15,209	5,201	5,018	15,392	2,032	46	85	1,994	906	129	26	1,009
1980	12,497	3,105	3,336	12,266	1,247	116	26	1,337	543	122	35	629
1981	11,971	3,095	4,480	10,586	1,491	209	36	1,664	593	28	25	596
1982	11,633	2,584	5,560	8,657	1,660	327	8	1,979	561	9	21	549
1983	21,441	6,702	4,994	23,149	3,517	197	127	3,587	1,968	104	241	1,832
1984	27,576	8,106	5,541	30,141	3,466	205	23	3,648	2,053	193	423	1,823
1985	31,931	12,035	10,629	33,337	4,498	432	54	4,875	870	89	1,371	−412
1986	49,868	13,458	12,176	51,150	7,176	115	48	7,243	2,892	49	225	2,716
1987	45,092	11,254	9,650	46,696	8,299	161	95	8,365	4,773	79	164	4,688
1988	38,158	10,905	9,421	39,643	6,920	81	80	6,921	3,065	164	332	2,896
1989	31,147	10,069	10,192	31,024	7,669	544	186	8,027	2,059	22	1,535	546
1990	32,563	20,874	12,369	41,068	10,966	402	962	10,406	1,529	115	45	1,599
1991	25,501	21,891	13,155	34,237	12,162	185	24	12,323	977	61	82	956
1992	25,731	14,864	11,556	29,039	11,742	598	1	12,339	1,055	0	4	1,051
1993	31,702	12,259	6,999	36,962	18,820	736	275	19,281	1,112	48	208	952
1994	32,685	14,245	5,381	41,549	20,924	670	122	21,472	2,141	0	293	1,848
1995	39,184	15,522	8,923	45,783	23,118	3,428	213	26,333	1,825	11	42	1,794
1996	47,138	16,680	17,237	46,581	22,619	1,662	697	23,584	1,898	43	0	1,941
1997	47,936	20,608	13,772	54,772	25,412	900	533	25,779	2,390	15	130	2,275

	Savings and loan associations				Life insurance companies				Mortgage companies			
	Originations	Purchases	Sales	Net acquisition	Originations	Purchases	Sales	Net acquisition	Originations	Purchases	Sales	Net acquisition
	Dc1065 [1]	Dc1066 [1]	Dc1067 [1]	Dc1068 [1]	Dc1069	Dc1070	Dc1071	Dc1072	Dc1073	Dc1074	Dc1075	Dc1076
Year	Million dollars	Million dollars	Million dollars	Million dollars	Million dollars	Million dollars	Million dollars	Million dollars	Million dollars	Million dollars	Million dollars	Million dollars
1970	1,927	229	92	2,064	2,238	281	3	2,516	1,433	0	1,438	−5
1971	3,711	467	187	3,992	1,708	149	8	1,849	1,960	12	1,583	389
1972	5,285	622	425	5,481	1,826	107	1	1,931	2,698	18	2,257	459
1973	4,171	539	414	4,297	2,293	124	1	2,416	928	11	1,871	−932
1974	3,262	433	228	3,467	2,046	128	5	2,170	595	9	639	−36
1975	3,562	393	102	3,853	1,139	76	0	1,215	778	24	807	−5
1976	5,113	820	388	5,545	756	34	0	789	609	4	593	19
1977	6,837	665	610	6,892	997	45	12	1,030	1,965	53	1,461	558
1978	6,225	366	381	6,210	1,845	59	24	1,881	1,848	162	1,771	239
1979	4,906	323	287	4,942	1,597	59	0	1,656	1,980	29	1,471	538
1980	3,100	253	331	3,022	1,427	56	4	1,479	1,633	10	1,322	321
1981	2,339	192	159	2,372	753	40	53	740	2,051	114	1,781	384
1982	3,171	608	1,761	2,018	438	21	3	456	960	5	682	283
1983	8,521	3,834	1,511	10,844	1,597	45	9	1,633	566	35	443	158
1984	13,160	4,236	2,463	14,933	1,466	20	27	1,459	443	212	545	110
1985	15,612	3,543	3,040	16,115	2,772	110	53	2,829	2,746	561	2,997	310
1986	19,877	2,359	3,218	19,018	3,723	79	35	3,767	7,172	275	6,519	928
1987	17,830	2,795	4,039	16,586	3,547	266	89	3,724	2,409	664	3,937	−864
1988	17,486	2,340	4,043	15,783	3,732	141	7	3,866	4,526	229	4,425	330
1989	11,410	1,040	3,800	8,650	2,786	214	76	2,924	4,443	13	4,573	−117

Notes appear at end of table

(continued)

TABLE Dc1053–1089   Originations, purchases, and sales of mortgages, by type of institutional lender: 1970–1997 [Multifamily residential property]   *Continued*

	Savings and loan associations				Life insurance companies				Mortgage companies			
	Originations	Purchases	Sales	Net acquisition	Originations	Purchases	Sales	Net acquisition	Originations	Purchases	Sales	Net acquisition
	Dc1065 [1]	Dc1066 [1]	Dc1067 [1]	Dc1068 [1]	Dc1069	Dc1070	Dc1071	Dc1072	Dc1073	Dc1074	Dc1075	Dc1076
Year	Million dollars	Million dollars	Million dollars	Million dollars	Million dollars	Million dollars	Million dollars	Million dollars	Million dollars	Million dollars	Million dollars	Million dollars
1990	9,225	1,101	2,084	8,242	2,172	432	58	2,546	5,536	276	4,859	953
1991	6,328	1,035	5,232	2,131	1,575	70	71	1,574	2,032	1,105	3,225	−88
1992	7,346	1,192	3,871	4,667	1,406	44	96	1,354	2,058	0	1,773	285
1993	6,181	1,176	2,171	5,186	1,486	61	74	1,473	2,000	0	1,890	110
1994	5,840	1,261	2,579	4,522	1,257	57	106	1,208	0	0	0	0
1995	3,875	1,015	1,595	3,295	1,611	91	117	1,585	6,108	101	4,967	1,242
1996	4,933	1,596	2,651	3,878	1,629	52	307	1,374	12,321	86	12,483	−76
1997	4,831	778	1,922	3,687	1,407	94	296	1,205	10,748	144	10,142	750

	Federal credit agencies				Other institutions				Mortgage pools			Mortgage conduits	
	Originations	Purchases	Sales	Net acquisition	Originations	Purchases	Sales	Net acquisition	Purchases	Sales	Net acquisition	Purchases	Net acquisition
	Dc1077 [2]	Dc1078 [2]	Dc1079 [2]	Dc1080 [2]	Dc1081 [3]	Dc1082 [3]	Dc1083 [3]	Dc1084 [3]	Dc1085	Dc1086	Dc1087	Dc1088	Dc1089
Year	Million dollars	Million dollars	Million dollars	Million dollars	Million dollars	Million dollars	Million dollars	Million dollars	Million dollars	Million dollars	Million dollars	Million dollars	Million dollars
1970	1,077	88	96	1,069	648	85	33	700	25	9	16	0	0
1971	1,372	242	56	1,558	1,106	80	284	902	52	8	44	0	0
1972	1,444	346	204	1,586	898	103	290	709	322	9	313	0	0
1973	2,218	701	306	2,613	1,201	201	120	1,282	268	15	254	0	0
1974	2,870	805	395	3,280	1,223	288	31	1,481	316	35	281	0	0
1975	1,725	1,261	892	2,094	1,213	435	305	1,342	594	32	562	0	0
1976	1,114	728	1,202	640	1,359	168	97	1,428	679	24	655	0	0
1977	1,029	1,410	1,363	1,076	1,614	224	159	1,678	1,428	81	1,347	0	0
1978	1,715	1,873	2,668	920	1,409	585	440	1,555	2,018	63	1,955	0	0
1979	2,632	1,511	3,022	1,121	1,155	674	127	1,702	2,430	0	2,430	0	0
1980	2,932	918	1,552	2,298	1,616	681	60	2,237	949	6	943	0	0
1981	3,215	580	2,415	1,380	1,529	1,095	7	2,617	836	4	832	0	0
1982	3,364	143	3,028	479	1,479	1,033	52	2,460	438	5	433	0	0
1983	2,837	227	2,655	409	2,435	1,007	1	3,441	1,252	7	1,245	0	0
1984	2,407	1,043	2,021	1,429	4,581	430	30	4,981	1,767	9	1,758	0	0
1985	2,000	4,359	892	5,467	3,433	347	72	3,708	2,594	2,150 [4]	444	0	0
1986	1,739	3,563	2,118	3,184	7,289	561	13	7,837	6,457	0	6,457	0	0
1987	1,120	1,445	1,100	1,465	7,114	420	226	7,308	5,424	0	5,424	0	0
1988	1,155	1,962	402	2,715	1,274	322	131	1,465	5,667	0	5,667	0	0
1989	1,194	3,728	0	4,922	1,586	272	22	1,836	4,236	0	4,236	0	0
1990	1,565	15,350	4,259	12,656	1,570	63	102	1,531	3,135	0	3,135	0	0
1991	918	14,604	4,521	11,001	1,509	193	0	1,702	4,638	0	4,638	0	0
1992	1,049	8,700	5,811	3,938	1,075	334	0	1,409	3,996	0	3,996	0	0
1993	933	4,888	2,381	3,440	1,170	620	0	1,790	2,486	0	2,486	2,244	2,244
1994	627	3,991	2,252	2,366	1,896	481	29	2,348	4,070	0	4,070	3,715	3,715
1995	733	3,454	1,989	2,198	1,914	449	0	2,363	5,902	0	5,902	1,071	1,071
1996	482	3,912	1,099	3,295	3,256	410	0	3,666	7,917	0	7,917	1,002	1,002
1997	492	3,559	749	3,302	2,656	373	0	3,029	7,274	0	7,274	7,471	7,471

[1] Includes federally chartered savings banks beginning in 1984.

[2] Includes Resolution Trust Corporation beginning in 1990.

[3] Includes state and local government credit agencies and retirement funds, private pensions, and, for 1970–1982, real estate investment trusts.

[4] According to the 1985 annual Survey of Mortgage Lending Activity report, the unusually high volume of multifamily mortgage loan sales by mortgage pools occurred during the second quarter of that year. No explanation was given in the report.

Source

See the source for Table Dc996–1032.

Documentation

See the text for Table Dc996–1032.

This table shows mortgage originations, purchases, and sales of loans on residential properties that were designed to be occupied by five or more families.

TABLE Dc1090–1104 Originations, purchases, and sales of mortgages, by type of property and loan: 1970–1997 [Multifamily residential property]

Contributed by Kenneth A. Snowden

	Originations									Purchases			Sales		
	Total			New structures			Existing structures								
Year	Total	Insured by FHA	Conventional mortgages	Total	Insured by FHA	Conventional mortgages	Total	Insured by FHA	Conventional mortgages	Total	Insured by FHA	Conventional mortgages	Total	Insured by FHA	Conventional mortgages
	Dc1090	Dc1091	Dc1092	Dc1093	Dc1094	Dc1095	Dc1096	Dc1097	Dc1098	Dc1099	Dc1100	Dc1101	Dc1102	Dc1103	Dc1104
	Million dollars	Million dollars	Million dollars	Million dollars	Million dollars	Million dollars	Million dollars	Million dollars	Million dollars	Million dollars	Million dollars	Million dollars	Million dollars	Million dollars	Million dollars
1970	8,787	1,921	6,866	6,981	1,798	5,184	1,806	123	1,682	1,027	164	862	1,760	719	1,041
1971	12,455	2,837	9,618	8,223	2,635	5,588	4,232	202	4,030	1,275	319	956	2,220	757	1,463
1972	15,427	3,247	12,179	9,214	2,844	6,370	6,212	403	5,809	1,820	502	1,318	3,339	1,167	2,173
1973	14,022	3,060	10,962	8,684	2,919	5,766	5,337	141	5,196	2,144	630	1,514	2,866	1,181	1,685
1974	12,277	3,350	8,928	8,417	3,113	5,305	3,860	237	3,623	2,383	548	1,835	1,471	539	931
1975	10,642	2,142	8,501	5,770	1,896	3,874	4,872	246	4,626	3,154	671	2,483	2,196	926	1,270
1976	12,293	1,972	10,321	4,473	1,250	3,223	7,820	722	7,098	2,741	845	1,896	2,524	1,247	1,277
1977	15,826	2,208	13,618	5,668	1,476	4,192	10,158	732	9,425	4,162	1,061	3,101	3,821	1,156	2,665
1978	16,373	3,225	13,147	6,776	2,018	4,758	9,596	1,207	8,389	5,369	1,083	4,286	5,489	2,245	3,244
1979	15,209	3,868	11,340	7,786	2,699	5,088	7,422	1,169	6,253	5,201	878	4,323	5,018	2,185	2,833
1980	12,497	3,888	8,609	8,633	3,629	5,003	3,864	258	3,606	3,105	969	2,136	3,336	2,084	1,252
1981	11,971	3,879	8,092	7,979	3,347	4,632	3,991	532	3,459	3,095	1,453	1,642	4,480	2,726	1,754
1982	11,633	4,081	7,552	6,250	3,270	2,979	5,383	811	4,572	2,584	1,105	1,479	5,560	3,560	2,000
1983	21,441	3,968	17,474	8,791	3,606	5,185	12,650	362	12,289	6,702	1,411	5,291	4,994	3,035	1,959
1984	27,576	4,651	22,925	11,144	4,285	6,858	16,432	365	16,066	8,106	1,188	6,918	5,541	2,301	3,240
1985	31,931	3,482	28,449	10,617	2,807	7,810	21,314	675	20,639	12,035	1,077	10,958	10,629	2,206	8,423
1986	49,868	8,740	41,127	15,250	5,377	9,873	34,618	3,363	31,254	13,458	2,043	11,415	12,176	3,850	8,326
1987	45,092	6,831	38,261	14,068	5,563	8,505	31,024	1,269	29,756	11,254	2,545	8,708	9,650	2,658	6,992
1988	38,158	2,960	35,198	8,962	744	8,218	29,196	2,216	26,980	10,905	2,334	8,571	9,421	2,798	6,623
1989	31,147	950	30,197	8,307	632	7,675	22,840	318	22,522	10,069	1,393	8,676	10,192	315	9,877
1990	32,563	2,004	30,559	6,517	974	5,543	26,046	1,030	25,016	20,874	1,111	19,763	12,369	1,332	11,037
1991	25,501	916	24,585	6,076	663	5,413	19,425	253	19,172	21,891	2,071	19,820	13,155	707	12,448
1992	25,731	576	25,155	4,866	380	4,486	20,865	196	20,669	14,864	998	13,866	11,556	116	11,440
1993	31,702	1,659	30,043	4,419	564	3,855	27,283	1,095	26,188	12,259	1,866	10,393	6,999	931	6,068
1994	32,685	963	31,722	4,535	690	3,845	28,150	273	27,877	14,245	1,887	12,358	5,381	41	5,340
1995	39,184	1,279	37,905	5,411	865	4,546	33,773	414	33,359	15,522	1,566	13,956	8,923	497	8,426
1996	47,138	3,440	43,698	8,386	1,762	6,624	38,752	1,678	37,074	16,680	1,988	14,692	17,237	1,979	15,258
1997	47,936	3,350	44,586	7,930	820	7,110	40,006	2,530	37,476	20,608	1,170	19,438	13,772	1,451	12,321

Source

See the source for Table Dc996–1032.

Documentation

See the text for Table Dc996–1032. This table shows conventional, Federal Housing Administration–insured, and total originations of mortgages on multifamily properties as reported in the Survey of Mortgage Lending Activity. Also shown is the amount of mortgage debt originated on new and existing multifamily properties each year, and the amounts that were bought and sold by the major participants in the market. Definitions used in this table are given in the text accompanying Table Dc996–1032.

TABLE Dc1105–1121   Home mortgage insurance and guarantee activity: 1935–1999

Contributed by Kenneth A. Snowden

	Home mortgages insured by the FHA						Loans guaranteed by the VA				Manufactured home loans		Private home mortgage insurance		Single-family units started under FHA or VA inspection		Privately insured home mortgage debt
	Total		New homes		Existing homes		Total		Home mortgages				Insurance certificates issued	New insurance written	FHA	VA	
Year	Dc1105	Dc1106	Dc1107	Dc1108	Dc1109	Dc1110	Dc1111	Dc1112	Dc1113	Dc1114	Dc1115	Dc1116	Dc1117	Dc1118	Dc1119	Dc1120	Dc1121
	Number	Face amount	Housing units	Face amount	Housing units	Face amount	Total Number	Face amount	Total Number	Face amount	Total Number	Face amount	Number	New insurance written	Number	Number	Million dollars
	Number	Thousand dollars	Number	Thousand dollars	Number	Thousand dollars	Number	Thousand dollars	Number	Thousand dollars	Number	Thousand dollars	Number	Million dollars	Number	Number	Million dollars
1935 [2]	23,397	93,882	5,091	22,331	20,362	71,551	0	0	0	0	0	0	0	0	13,226	0	0
1936	77,231	308,945	21,415	95,060	62,505	213,885	0	0	0	0	0	0	0	0	48,752	0	0
1937	102,076	424,373	38,479	168,867	72,371	255,506	0	0	0	0	0	0	0	0	56,980	0	0
1938	115,124	485,812	56,437	239,965	65,723	245,847	0	0	0	0	0	0	0	0	106,811	0	0
1939	164,530	694,764	113,969	486,366	57,263	208,398	0	0	0	0	0	0	0	0	144,657	0	0
1940	177,400	762,084	136,562	587,136	46,412	174,948	0	0	0	0	0	0	0	0	176,645	0	0
1941	210,310	910,770	169,242	727,758	46,535	183,012	0	0	0	0	0	0	0	0	217,091	0	0
1942	223,562	973,271	185,184	765,639	50,582	207,632	0	0	0	0	0	0	0	0	160,204	0	0
1943	166,402	763,097	140,767	553,145	48,966	209,952	0	0	0	0	0	0	0	0	126,119	0	0
1944	146,974	707,363	106,296	483,666	50,842	223,697	0	0	0	0	0	0	0	0	83,604	0	0
1945 [3]	96,776	474,344	54,829	257,243	48,589	217,101	43,000	192,000	43,000	192,000	0	0	0	0	38,897	8,800	0
1946	80,892	422,009	22,174	117,192	63,597	304,817	412,000	2,302,000	412,000	2,302,000	0	0	0	0	67,122	91,800	0
1947	141,387	894,716	71,384	476,927	78,730	417,789	542,000	3,283,000	542,000	3,283,000	0	0	0	0	178,269	160,300	—
1948	300,040	2,116,055	206,374	1,431,999	114,357	684,056	350,000	1,877,000	350,000	1,877,000	0	0	0	0	216,449	71,100	—
1949	305,718	2,211,508	185,385	1,317,362	134,406	894,146	277,000	1,424,000	277,000	1,424,000	0	0	0	0	252,626	90,800	—
1950	342,576	2,492,320	225,262	1,636,623	126,261	855,697	498,000	3,073,000	498,000	3,073,000	0	0	0	0	328,245	191,200	—
1951	252,541	1,929,105	161,572	1,216,207	99,558	712,898	447,000	4,252,000	447,000	4,252,000	0	0	0	0	186,924	148,600	—
1952	234,422	1,942,275	122,759	968,576	123,346	973,699	307,000	2,678,000	307,000	2,678,000	0	0	0	0	229,085	141,300	—
1953	261,541	2,288,627	151,777	1,258,559	120,522	1,030,068	322,000	2,464,000	322,000	2,464,000	0	0	0	0	216,509	156,500	—
1954	214,235	1,942,074	121,846	1,035,491	100,817	906,583	411,000	4,256,000	411,000	4,256,000	0	0	0	0	250,910	307,000	—
1955	310,882	3,084,767	131,116	1,269,179	187,350	1,815,588	650,000	7,154,000	650,000	7,154,000	0	0	0	0	268,655	392,900	0
1956	248,121	2,638,226	105,315	1,132,925	147,985	1,505,300	508,000	5,866,000	508,000	5,866,000	0	0	0	0	183,350	270,700	0
1957	198,428	2,251,200	74,601	880,279	127,852	1,370,921	307,000	3,758,000	307,000	3,758,000	0	0	—	—	150,126	128,300	—
1958	381,883	4,551,354	133,829	1,665,886	255,621	2,885,468	146,000	1,864,000	146,000	1,864,000	0	0	—	—	270,290	102,100	—
1959	495,172	6,069,418	200,222	2,562,611	305,271	3,506,807	213,000	2,788,000	213,000	2,788,000	0	0	—	—	307,035	109,300	—
1960	366,213	4,600,506	168,720	2,197,362	204,541	2,403,144	145,000	1,984,000	145,000	1,984,000	0	0	—	—	225,736	74,600	—
1961	368,561	4,765,216	132,248	1,782,899	244,000	2,982,317	134,000	1,836,000	134,000	1,836,000	0	0	—	—	198,756	83,300	—
1962	395,810	5,270,859	132,102	1,849,371	273,031	3,421,488	188,000	2,650,000	188,000	2,650,000	0	0	—	—	197,326	77,800	—
1963	412,779	5,569,103	114,362	1,664,196	309,018	3,904,907	211,000	3,042,000	211,000	3,042,000	0	0	—	—	166,151	71,000	—
1964	490,045	6,573,219	107,479	1,608,244	395,565	4,964,976	186,000	2,851,000	186,000	2,851,000	0	0	—	—	153,952	59,200	—
1965	537,851	7,464,588	109,553	1,704,975	444,500	5,759,613	163,000	2,652,000	163,000	2,652,000	0	0	—	—	159,906	49,400	—
1966	421,756	6,095,317	104,839	1,729,356	231,391	4,365,962	157,000	2,600,000	157,000	2,600,000	0	0	—	—	129,059	36,800	—
1967	395,814	5,884,638	78,980	1,368,609	332,834	4,516,030	201,000	3,405,000	201,000	3,405,000	0	0	—	—	141,946	52,500	—
1968	425,339	6,495,944	86,440	1,572,316	366,155	4,923,628	211,025	3,771,683	211,025	3,771,683	0	0	—	—	147,745	56,100	—
1969	450,079	7,120,628	82,535	1,550,706	408,737	5,569,922	213,940	4,073,410	213,940	4,073,410	0	0	—	—	153,593	51,200	—

	Home mortgages insured by the FHA						Loans guaranteed by the VA						Private home mortgage insurance		Single-family units started under FHA or VA inspection		Privately insured home mortgage debt
	Total		New homes[1]		Existing homes		Total		Home mortgages		Manufactured home loans		Insurance certificates issued	New insurance written	FHA	VA	
Year	Dc1105	Dc1106	Dc1107[1]	Dc1108[1]	Dc1109	Dc1110	Dc1111	Dc1112	Dc1113	Dc1114	Dc1115	Dc1116	Dc1117	Dc1118	Dc1119	Dc1120	Dc1121
	Number	Thousand dollars	Housing units	Thousand dollars	Housing units	Thousand dollars	Number	Thousand dollars	Number	Thousand dollars	Number	Thousand dollars	Number	Million dollars	Number	Number	Million dollars
1970	475,176	8,113,731	140,447	2,666,740	377,890	5,446,991	167,734	3,442,905	167,734	3,442,905	0	0	—	1,162	242,818	61,000	7,300
1971	565,417	10,374,542	198,223	3,899,650	409,943	6,474,892	284,358	6,082,943	282,278	6,065,519	2,080	17,424	—	3,430	278,705	94,000	9,600
1972	427,858	8,067,056	169,895	3,459,165	282,852	4,607,892	375,485	8,467,529	370,023	8,420,077	5,462	47,452	—	9,158	186,817	104,000	17,500
1973	240,004	4,473,303	80,251	1,674,828	171,385	2,798,475	321,522	7,520,962	315,509	7,466,941	6,013	54,021	—	12,627	76,166	86,000	27,400
1974	195,850	3,933,705	31,021	751,956	174,145	3,181,749	313,156	8,235,903	309,830	8,205,627	3,326	30,276	—	9,219	52,514	73,000	34,000
1975	255,061	6,166,115	39,087	1,148,704	227,907	5,017,411	301,443	8,902,089	299,768	8,883,968	1,675	8,121	—	10,024	69,821	77,000	39,900
1976	250,808	6,362,120	34,488	1,086,937	227,902	5,275,183	330,442	10,438,943	328,876	10,419,494	1,566	19,449	—	14,600	80,944	100,000	49,300
1977	321,118	8,840,836	50,581	1,663,669	283,015	7,177,167	392,557	13,902,404	389,098	13,856,152	3,459	46,252	617,398	21,595	81,547	131,000	63,030
1978	334,108	11,139,970	49,817	1,881,171	297,094	9,258,798	368,648	14,527,717	364,543	14,470,399	4,105	57,318	695,620	27,327	75,968	127,000	81,057
1979	457,054	18,166,744	77,046	3,408,780	395,356	14,757,964	364,656	16,661,683	356,105	16,505,497	8,551	156,186	578,038	25,324	77,536	122,000	95,211
1980	381,169	16,458,526	87,030	4,071,283	310,270	12,387,242	274,193	14,011,958	266,256	13,855,537	7,937	156,421	392,808	19,035	62,714	—	105,340
1981	224,829	10,278,136	66,236	3,176,628	172,240	7,101,508	151,811	8,098,996	142,180	7,905,929	9,631	193,067	334,565	18,719	43,108	—	114,318
1982	166,734	8,087,074	47,028	2,444,290	131,611	5,642,784	103,354	5,636,436	92,957	5,428,271	10,397	208,165	315,868	18,749	62,577	—	124,970
1983	503,425	26,571,818	75,249	4,209,263	460,694	22,362,555	300,568	18,278,267	285,696	17,965,656	14,872	312,611	652,214	46,197	95,329	—	148,222
1984	267,831	14,524,934	62,384	3,704,166	228,497	10,820,768	210,366	12,981,153	198,431	12,728,424	11,935	252,729	946,408	64,456	87,100	—	193,303
1985	409,547	23,963,947	60,644	3,998,739	383,645	19,965,208	201,313	13,222,172	193,178	13,047,557	8,135	174,615	729,597	50,956	131,398	—	227,107
1986	921,370	56,901,436	102,190	7,129,151	869,742	49,772,286	351,242	24,834,551	345,935	24,716,446	5,307	118,105	585,987	47,358	242,976	—	226,358
1987	1,319,987	81,880,506	145,543	10,364,768	1,244,960	71,515,739	455,627	33,213,672	451,136	33,110,209	4,491	103,463	511,058	45,175	160,894	—	227,107
1988	698,990	42,579,286	84,751	6,176,356	643,656	36,402,929	212,671	15,808,433	210,999	15,769,603	1,672	38,830	423,470	40,897	105,922	—	229,452
1989	726,359	45,893,236	84,973	6,434,522	667,469	39,458,714	183,209	14,057,141	182,559	14,041,800	650	15,341	365,497	39,093	106,870	—	238,339
1990	780,329	51,863,723	77,574	6,153,153	727,147	45,710,571	192,992	15,791,047	192,601	15,781,399	391	9,648	367,120	40,904	94,790	—	232,872
1991	685,905	46,990,047	63,164	5,196,399	642,400	41,793,648	186,561	15,951,904	186,205	15,943,046	356	8,858	494,259	53,967	78,345	—	255,917
1992	680,278	48,315,145	52,378	4,463,875	649,407	43,851,270	290,003	25,175,943	289,901	25,173,258	102	2,685	907,511	101,047	73,780	—	284,552
1993	1,065,832	79,131,259	54,936	4,855,528	1,042,139	74,275,731	457,693	41,585,275	457,693	41,583,238	86	2,037	1,198,307	136,767	72,016	—	337,708
1994	1,217,685	91,621,957	64,749	6,063,675	1,192,647	85,558,283	536,851	49,467,459	536,799	49,465,788	52	1,671	1,161,356	131,402	68,587	—	406,250
1995	568,399	45,310,805	42,843	4,045,810	552,880	41,264,995	243,772	23,931,719	243,741	23,931,254	31	465	960,756	109,625	57,694	—	460,817
1996	849,861	71,617,295	60,005	5,773,897	835,645	65,843,399	326,417	33,355,323	326,403	33,354,912	14	411	1,068,707	126,972	68,051	—	513,240
1997	839,712	74,243,458	55,799	5,455,876	831,746	68,787,582	254,691	26,865,493	254,688	26,865,435	3	58	974,298	120,896	56,081	—	546,133
1998	1,110,530	103,164,503	48,422	4,881,636	1,118,412	98,282,867	384,591	42,585,877	384,591	42,585,877	0	0	1,473,344	187,437	45,676	—	559,445
1999	1,246,433	122,291,308	49,600	5,355,483	1,255,570	116,935,825	441,548	49,575,466	441,548	49,575,466	0	0	1,455,403	188,871	52,995	—	598,515

[1] For 1938–1944, includes class 3 new small home loans, which were discontinued in 1944.

[2] The small amount of Federal Housing Administration activity in 1934 is included in 1935 totals.

[3] The small amount of Veterans Administration activity in 1944 is included in 1945 totals.

Sources

Series Dc1105–1110. 1935–1945: Federal Housing Administration (FHA): *Seventeenth Annual Report* (1950), Table 4, p. 27, with series Dc1107–1108 modified by FHA, *Eleventh Annual Report* (1944), Table 21. 1946–1999: FHA, unpublished mimeograph.

Series Dc1111–1116. 1945–1967: U.S. Bureau of the Census, *Historical Statistics of the United States* (1975), series N 185 and N 297; see also U.S. Department of Housing and Urban Development (HUD), *HUD Statistical Yearbooks*, various years. 1968–1999: Veteran's Administration, unpublished mimeograph.

Series Dc1117–1118 and Dc1121. Mortgage Insurance Companies of America (MICA), *Fact Book*, various years. The MICA *Fact Book* for the current year can be found at the MICA Internet site.

Series Dc1119. 1935–1954: FHA, *Twenty Sixth Annual Report* (1959), Table III-4, p. 18. 1955–1959: HUD, *Statistical Yearbook, 1966*, FHA Table 2, p. 85. 1960–1966: *1970 HUD Statistical Yearbook*, Table 160, p. 147. 1967–1999: FHA, unpublished mimeograph.

Series Dc1120. 1945–1969: U.S. Bureau of the Census, *Historical Statistics of the United States* (1975), series N 181; see also *HUD Statistical Yearbooks*, various years. 1970–1979: HUD, *1979 Statistical Yearbook*, Table 14, p. 283.

(continued)

TABLE Dc1105–1121 Home mortgage insurance and guarantee activity: 1935–1999 *Continued*

Documentation

Series Dc1105–1118 show the number and total face amounts of newly originated permanent home mortgages (on one- to four-family structures) that were guaranteed by the Veteran's Administration (VA) or insured by either the Federal Housing Administration (FHA) or a privately owned mortgage insurance company. The other series in this table provide additional information about each program – the number of homes started each year under the FHA and VA programs (series Dc1119–1120) and the total amount of privately insured home mortgage debt that was outstanding at the end of each year (series Dc1121; see series Dc948–949 for comparable data on outstanding FHA and VA mortgage debt). Not included in the series shown in this table are FHA loans that were insured under Title I provisions to finance the repair, improvement, or rehabilitation of an existing home. These loans are generally written for smaller amounts and shorter durations than the permanent home loans represented here.

The FHA was established by the National Housing Act of 1934 to increase the quantity and quality of the nation's housing stock by providing a system of mutual mortgage insurance. The FHA does not actually make mortgage loans; instead, the agency issues insurance policies that protect lenders from losses in the event that a borrower defaults on a loan. The reduced lending risk on an FHA loan results in lower interest rates charged to the borrower. Borrowers pay for the insurance provided by the FHA program by means of a premium charge in their monthly loan payment. To be eligible for FHA insurance, a home mortgage loan (1) must be issued by a qualified FHA lender, (2) must be written on property that meets FHA quality standards, (3) must meet FHA's minimum down payment requirement, and (4) must be on a home priced lower than the FHA ceiling, which varies over time and across markets.

The VA mortgage loan guarantee program was established in the Servicemen's Readjustment Act of 1944 (known as the "GI Bill of Rights"). VA-guaranteed loans are made by private lenders to eligible veterans for the purchase of a home. The VA does not guarantee the entire loan amount; instead, it protects the lender against losses up to a smaller amount that depends on the size of the loan and the price of the home being financed. Lenders usually require that the sum of the VA guaranty and the borrower's cash down payment equals at least 25 percent of the home's reasonable value or the sales price of the property, whichever is less. It is usually possible, therefore, for qualified veterans to obtain financing with no down payment. During the most recent years shown in the table, lenders have generally limited VA loan amounts so they could be easily sold in the secondary market – the maximum loan amount for any particular borrower, however, continues to depend on the maximum guaranty amount, the borrower's down payment and income, and the property's value. The VA guaranty program is financed by a funding fee that is charged at the time the loan is closed; there is no monthly premium under the program.

The modern private mortgage industry got its start in 1957 when the Mortgage Guaranty Insurance Corporation of Milwaukee was founded; by 2000, the industry comprised seven companies that issued policies to protect mortgage lenders from suffering losses if a borrower stopped making mortgage payments. Unlike FHA insurance, which covers 100 percent of the loan amount, private mortgage insurance generally covers the top 20–30 percent of the loan. Borrowers use private mortgage insurance, therefore, to qualify for a conventional mortgage when they cannot meet the traditional 20 percent down payment requirement. Private mortgage insurance companies are regulated by state agencies, which require them to hold contingency reserves and to meet minimum capital requirements as protection against insolvency. Premium payments for the insurance are typically folded into a borrower's monthly mortgage payment and vary according to the size of the down payment, the type of mortgage, and the amount of insurance coverage. The lender arranges for private mortgage insurance as part of the loan approval process.

Series Dc1105–1110 and Dc1119. The number of FHA cases each year represents the number of loans endorsed for insurance. A small number of these loans are used each year to finance more than one home, so the total number of cases (series Dc1105) is smaller than the total number of units covered by new FHA loans (series Dc1107 plus series Dc1109). The total dollar amount of FHA loans (series Dc1106), on the other hand, is equal to the sum of the face amounts of loans on newly built properties (series Dc1108) and loans made on existing homes (series Dc1110). The latter category includes mortgages used to purchase existing homes and those used to refinance existing mortgages. Since the inception of FHA, a great majority of loans on both new and existing homes have been written under its original authorizing statute (referred to as Section 203). Congress has broadened FHA's mission over time, however, to include new types of mortgage loans or to target particular underserved markets. Prominent among these special programs was Section 603, which authorized loan insurance to meet the housing needs of military personnel, civilian defense workers, and veterans during and just after World War II. Since the early 1960s, a large number of loans specifically designed to serve low- and moderate-income borrowers (Section 221) have also been issued.

Series Dc1111–1114 and Dc1120–1121. The source reported the data at a lower level of precision: series Dc1111, Dc1113, and Dc1120, in thousands through 1967 (through 1979 for series Dc1120); series Dc1112 and Dc1114, in million dollars through 1967; and series Dc1121, in billion dollars through 1976.

Series Dc1111–1116 and Dc1120. The total amount of loans written with VA guarantees (series Dc1112) represents the sum of the entire face value of each loan – not the sum of the smaller amounts guaranteed by the VA on each loan. Almost all VA loans have been written to finance the purchase of a newly built home, an existing home, or to refinance an existing mortgage. A small number of permanent VA loans have been written over the years to finance home improvements or, before 1970, to purchase mobile homes. The Veteran's Housing Act of 1970 explicitly authorized the VA to guarantee loans on manufactured homes, however, and since that date, the number and total amount of these loans have been reported separately (series Dc1115–1116). Series Dc1111–1112 represent the total number and amount of permanent VA loans used to finance either homes or manufactured homes. These total series, therefore, are equal to series Dc1113 plus series Dc1115, and series Dc1114 plus series Dc1116, respectively.

Series Dc1117–1118 and Dc1121. The number of mortgage loan originations insured by private mortgage companies is presented in series Dc1117 along with the total principal amounts of these new loans in series Dc1118. The actual dollar amount of losses that are insured each year under these policies is substantially smaller, of course, because private mortgage insurance typically covers only 20–30 percent of the entire loan amount. The same holds true for the outstanding face value of all privately insured mortgage loans at the end of each year, which is shown in series Dc1121 – this total is substantially larger than the total risk exposure of the private mortgage insurance industry. All three of these series refer only to private mortgage insurance on whole mortgage loans – these companies also write insurance on entire mortgage pools.

Series Dc1119–1120. The number of new, privately owned units started under both the FHA (series Dc1119) and VA (series Dc1120) programs represents homes under construction that have completed the first round of inspections required by these agencies so that newly built residential homes can be quickly approved for mortgage insurance or a loan guaranty. The importance of the FHA and VA loan programs to the homebuilding industry can be roughly assessed by comparing these series to Census Bureau estimates of the total number of private housing starts (see Table Dc510–530). Caution should be exercised when interpreting such comparisons, however, for a couple of reasons. Some homes that were started under FHA or VA inspection were later purchased with conventional mortgage loans; other previously unoccupied new homes, for which the builder did not apply for FHA insurance before or during construction, are classified as "existing homes" if they are later sold with an FHA-insured loan. The second problem was especially acute in earlier periods – in 1956 about one fifth of FHA-insured loans that financed the purchase of units classified as "existing construction" actually financed the purchase of a new, and previously unoccupied, home. By 1970, in contrast, fewer than 3 percent were so classified. For more detail concerning the appropriate use of FHA and VA start series, see U.S. Department of Commerce and U.S. Department of Labor, *Construction Review*, "FHA and VA Housing Statistics and the Housing Market" (June 1957). The VA no longer reports housing units started under its inspection program.

TABLE Dc1122–1128   Multifamily mortgage insurance by the Federal Housing Administration: 1935–1979

Contributed by Kenneth A. Snowden

							Units started under FHA inspection
			New units		**Existing units**		
	Units financed	Face amount	Units financed	Face amount	Units financed	Face amount	
	Dc1122	Dc1123	Dc1124	Dc1125	Dc1126	Dc1127	Dc1128 [1]
Year	Number	Thousand dollars	Number	Thousand dollars	Number	Thousand dollars	Number
1935	738	2,355	738	2,355	0	0	738
1936	624	2,101	624	2,101	0	0	624
1937	3,023	10,483	3,023	10,483	0	0	3,023
1938	11,930	47,638	11,930	47,638	0	0	11,930
1939	13,462	51,851	13,462	51,851	0	0	13,462
1940	3,559	12,949	3,446	12,489	113	460	3,446
1941	3,741	13,565	3,296	12,014	445	1,551	3,296
1942	5,842	21,215	5,458	19,533	384	1,682	5,458
1943	20,179	84,622	20,035	84,047	144	575	20,035
1944	12,430	56,096	9,655	46,105	2,775	9,991	9,655
1945	4,058	19,817	3,137	15,903	921	3,914	2,262
1946	2,232	13,175	1,579	10,889	653	2,286	1,911
1947	46,604	359,944	46,446	358,602	158	1,342	50,766
1948	79,184	608,711	77,808	605,800	1,376	2,911	77,610
1949	133,135 [2]	1,021,231 [2]	131,622 [2]	1,017,258 [2]	1,513	3,973	111,176
1950	154,597	1,156,682	153,477	1,154,680	1,120	2,002	158,436
1951	74,207	583,774	73,333	577,545	874	6,229	76,599
1952	39,839	321,911	39,839	321,911	0	0	50,816
1953	30,701	259,194	30,701	259,194	0	0	35,460
1954	28,257	234,022	28,257	234,022	0	0	25,397
1955	9,431	76,490	8,639	73,347	792	3,143	8,040
1956	11,177	130,247	10,933	129,585	244	662	5,791
1957	43,409	597,348	43,188	596,517	221	831	18,297
1958	64,958 [3]	908,671	64,851	908,208	107	463	25,147
1959	43,976	674,682	43,632	673,385	344	1,297	25,438
1960	49,101	723,501	47,974	717,994	1,127	5,507	35,213
1961	58,523	928,069	57,506	918,524	1,017	9,545	44,892
1962	64,134	1,087,132	60,393	1,047,800	3,741	39,332	62,198
1963	53,344	854,346	48,361	802,587	4,983	51,759	54,869
1964	54,248	898,808	50,913	862,881	3,335	35,927	50,654
1965	36,950	598,130	32,681	550,446	4,269	47,684	36,689
1966	32,814	577,095	29,928	537,503	2,886	39,592	29,322
1967	40,962	641,406	36,824	590,045	4,138	51,361	37,781
1968	76,195	1,129,301	68,397	1,023,350	7,798	105,951	72,118
1969	81,369	1,324,455	75,332	1,219,392	6,037	105,063	79,727
1970	200,660	3,256,795	177,288	2,963,773	23,372	293,022	187,514
1971	222,685	3,983,828	208,212	3,703,341	14,473	280,487	224,772
1972	188,224	3,447,750	169,964	3,091,751	18,260	355,999	172,322
1973	120,414	2,286,175	110,064	2,038,532	10,350	247,643	88,861
1974	54,820	1,213,460	46,935	1,019,815	7,885	193,645	37,763
1975	38,044	976,252	31,965	797,142	6,079	179,110	27,909
1976	78,292	2,314,957	62,056	1,674,095	16,236	640,862	63,424
1977	109,882	2,817,762	77,405	2,005,407	32,477	812,355	78,074
1978	121,712	3,270,380	78,725	2,213,275	42,987	1,057,105	83,960
1979	95,154	2,727,723	67,668	2,041,504	27,486	686,219	71,497

[1] Excludes mobile home spaces, nursing home and hospital beds, military housing classified as public housing, and lots for subdivisions. Beginning in 1968, excludes rehabilitation starts, which were included for earlier years.

[2] Data shown in the source for this year were corrected for a misclassification of Section 611 loans so that the series in this table agree with five-year totals that were published in later reports.

[3] Typographical error in the source was corrected so that components add up to the total.

Sources

Series Dc1128. 1935–1954: Federal Housing Administration (FHA), *Twenty Sixth Annual Report* (1959), Table III-4, p. 18; 1955–1959: U.S. Department of Housing and Urban Development (HUD), *Statistical Yearbook 1966*, FHA Table 2, p. 85; 1960–1969: *1970 HUD Statistical Yearbook*, Table 160, p. 147; 1970–1979: *1979 HUD Statistical Yearbook*, Table 2, p. 63.

All other series. 1935–1949: FHA, *Seventeenth Annual Report* (1950), Table 30, p. 70; 1950–1954: FHA, *Twenty Sixth Annual Report*, Table III-7, p. 23; 1955–1969: *1970 HUD Statistical Yearbook*, Table 164, p. 152; 1970–1979: *1979 HUD Statistical Yearbook*, Table 6, p. 74.

Documentation

This table presents information on the number of housing units financed and the total face amount of Federal Housing Administration (FHA)-insured mortgages on multifamily residential structures between 1935 and 1979. For information about FHA multifamily mortgage lending in later years, see Table Dc1129–1137 (but refer to the discussion there concerning the comparability of the data in the two tables).

The mutual insurance program offered by the FHA for multifamily units is similar in basic features to its single-family home program (see the text for Table Dc1105–1121 for a fuller discussion). There is, however, a marked

TABLE Dc1122–1128   Multifamily mortgage insurance by the Federal Housing Administration: 1935–1979
Continued

difference between the two programs: multifamily units are generally rented whereas a majority of FHA-financed homes are owner-occupied. Multifamily residential structures contain five or more housing units (or beds, if in congregate housing), and FHA loans on these structures can be used to build a new structure or to purchase, rehabilitate, or refinance an existing multifamily structure. A great majority of FHA multifamily loans during the period shown here were used to build new housing; relatively few loans were issued for the purchase or refinance of an existing structure.

Congress has enacted more than twenty amendments to the original 1934 FHA authorization to establish new multifamily mortgage programs that target specific needs. During the 1940s, for example, loans on rental structures for defense or war-related workers dominated FHA's multifamily insurance activity. In later years these special programs have targeted housing for the elderly and low-income populations, beds in nursing homes and hospitals, the construction of mobile home parks, and housing projects associated with urban renewal. See the source for a complete enumeration by specific program for each year.

The sources provide further breakdowns of annual insurance activity by particular program and property type.

Series Dc1122 represents the total number of units covered by FHA multifamily mortgage loans each year; this number is much larger than the number of loans (or individual projects) that were financed. Series Dc1123 represents the total face amount of the mortgages issued. These two aggregates are equal, respectively, to the sum of units and loan amounts on newly built multifamily structures and those used to purchase or refinance existing multifamily structures.

TABLE Dc1129–1137   Multifamily projects financed with Federal Housing Administration–insured mortgages: 1980–1999

Contributed by Kenneth A. Snowden

	New multifamily projects			Refinanced multifamily projects			Nursing home projects		
	Projects	Units	Mortgage amount	Projects	Units	Mortgage amount	Projects	Units	Mortgage amount
	Dc1129	Dc1130	Dc1131	Dc1132	Dc1133	Dc1134	Dc1135	Dc1136	Dc1137
Year	Number	Number	Million dollars	Number	Number	Million dollars	Number	Number	Million dollars
1980	79	14,671	560.8	32	6,459	89.1	25	3,187	78.1
1981	94	14,232	415.1	12	2,974	43.0	35	4,590	130.0
1982	98	14,303	460.4	28	7,431	95.2	50	7,096	200.0
1983	74	14,353	543.9	94	22,118	363.0	65	9,231	295.8
1984	96	14,158	566.2	88	21,655	428.2	45	5,697	175.2
1985	144	23,253	954.1	135	34,730	764.3	41	5,201	179.1
1986	154	22,006	1,117.5	245	32,554	1,550.1	22	3,123	111.2
1987	171	28,300	1,379.4	306	68,000	1,618.0	45	6,243	225.7
1988	140	21,180	922.2	234	49,443	1,402.3	47	5,537	197.1
1989	101	15,240	750.9	144	32,995	864.6	41	5,183	207.9
1990	61	9,910	411.4	69	13,848	295.3	53	6,166	263.2
1991	72	13,098	590.2	185	40,640	1,015.1	81	10,150	437.2
1992	54	7,823	358.5	119	24,960	547.1	66	8,229	367.4
1993	56	9,321	428.6	262	50,140	1,209.4	77	9,036	428.6
1994	84	12,988	658.5	321	61,416	1,587.0	94	13,688	701.7
1995	89	17,113	785.0	192	32,383	822.3	103	12,888	707.2
1996	128	23,554	1,178.8	268	51,760	1,391.1	152	20,069	927.5
1997	147	23,880	1,362.2	186	31,538	1,098.5	143	16,819	820.0
1998	149	25,237	1,420.7	158	19,271	576.3	89	7,965	541.0
1999	185	30,863	1,886.8	182	22,596	688.7	130	14,592	899.2

Source

Federal Housing Administration, Unassisted Multifamily Mortgage Insurance Activity: 1980–present, Table 17, *U.S. Housing Market Conditions* (May 2001), first quarter 2001.

Documentation

The series in this table represent the unassisted multifamily projects that were financed with Federal Housing Administration (FHA)-insured loans each year between 1980 and 1999. Multifamily refers to properties with five or more rental units, while the unassisted mortgage insurance programs of the FHA support housing projects that are not explicitly targeted to prospective tenants based on income, or to specific types of markets based on housing needs. These "basic" programs provide access only to FHA's mortgage insurance program; other U.S. Department of Housing and Urban Development (HUD) multifamily programs, which are excluded from this table, provide other housing assistance along with FHA insurance (such as federal rent subsidies, interest-free advances of capital for the project owner, or risk-sharing between the owner and HUD). The distinction between assisted and unassisted loan programs was not clearly made in FHA sources before 1980. Caution must be exercised, therefore, in using the series shown in this table in conjunction with the pre-1980 series that appear in Table Dc1122–1128.

FHA unassisted multifamily activity is broken down in the table into three categories – loans to finance the construction or substantial rehabilitation of multifamily structures, loans to refinance existing mortgages on multifamily structures, and loans used to finance a variety of housing used to serve the elderly or long-term health care needs. Reported for each category is the number of projects financed, the total number of housing units in those projects, and the combined face amount of the FHA-insured mortgages that were written on those projects during the year.

Series Dc1129 represents the number of FHA-insured loans made each year to finance projects that involved new construction or the substantial rehabilitation of an existing multifamily housing structure. Loans in this category are dominated by Section 221 loans – a category that helps private industry secure financing so that it can provide moderate-income households with affordable rental housing. Borrowers in these programs can be either "for-profit" or "nonprofit" organizations. Also included in this category are Section 220 FHA loans used to finance multifamily housing projects in urban renewal areas, code enforcement areas, and other areas where local governments have undertaken designated revitalization activities. Finally, loans from the original workhorse program of the FHA, Section 207, are included in this first category although few are now used for construction or rehabilitation of rental housing.

Section 207 mortgage insurance, in fact, is used much more frequently these days as a refinancing vehicle. Series Dc1132 represents the number of new FHA loans that are issued each year to refinance existing multifamily mortgages, which themselves can be either conventional or FHA-insured. Properties requiring substantial rehabilitation are not eligible for the FHA refinancing program, although noncritical repairs may be completed after a refinancing loan has been approved.

Series Dc1135 includes FHA-insured loans, which are issued under Section 231 to build or rehabilitate rental housing for the use of elderly persons and persons with disabilities. Few projects have been insured under Section 231 in recent years, so most loans in this category are Section 232 loans, which are used to finance the construction or rehabilitation of nursing homes and assisted-living facilities for people who need long-term care or medical attention.

TABLE Dc1138–1153   Secondary residential mortgage market activity of federal agencies: 1932–1970[1,2]

Contributed by Kenneth A. Snowden

Year	Federal Home Loan Bank (FHLB)				Federal National Mortgage Association (FNMA) and Government National Mortgage Association (GNMA)						FNMA's secondary market operations program					
	Advances	Repayments of advances	Year-end outstanding advances	Borrowing member institutions	Purchases	Sales	Repayments	Other liquidations	Year-end portfolio	Year-end purchase contracts outstanding	Purchases	Sales	Repayments	Other liquidations	Year-end portfolio	Year-end purchase contracts outstanding
	Dc1138	Dc1139	Dc1140	Dc1141	Dc1142	Dc1143	Dc1144	Dc1145	Dc1146	Dc1147	Dc1148	Dc1149	Dc1150	Dc1151	Dc1152	Dc1153
	Thousand dollars	Thousand dollars	Thousand dollars	Number	Million dollars	Million dollars	Million dollars	Million dollars	Million dollars	Million dollars	Million dollars	Million dollars	Million dollars	Million dollars	Million dollars	Million dollars
1932	838	—	838	—	0.0	0.0	0.0	0.0	0.0	0.0	0.0	0.0	0.0	0.0	0.0	0.0
1933	90,032	5,427	85,442	—	0.0	0.0	0.0	0.0	0.0	0.0	0.0	0.0	0.0	0.0	0.0	0.0
1934	38,676	37,515	86,603	1,769	0.0	0.0	0.0	0.0	0.0	0.0	0.0	0.0	0.0	0.0	0.0	0.0
1935	59,130	43,047	102,686	2,192	0.0	0.0	0.0	0.0	0.0	0.0	0.0	0.0	0.0	0.0	0.0	0.0
1936	93,257	50,716	145,227	2,483	0.0	0.0	0.0	0.0	0.0	0.0	0.0	0.0	0.0	0.0	0.0	0.0
1937	123,251	68,440	200,038	2,707	0.0	0.0	0.0	0.0	0.0	0.0	0.0	0.0	0.0	0.0	0.0	0.0
1938	81,958	83,154	198,842	2,607	82.2	0.0	1.9	0.0	80.3	17.5	0.0	0.0	0.0	0.0	0.0	0.0
1939	94,781	112,310	181,313	2,339	74.1	0.4	6.7	0.5	146.8	7.8	0.0	0.0	0.0	0.0	0.0	0.0
1940	134,212	114,033	201,492	2,262	48.0	(Z)	12.6	1.1	181.1	8.4	0.0	0.0	0.0	0.0	0.0	0.0
1941	157,600	139,646	219,446	2,057	42.3	(Z)	15.7	0.9	206.8	6.3	0.0	0.0	0.0	0.0	0.0	0.0
1942	99,462	189,695	129,213	1,388	23.2	0.0	18.8	0.3	210.9	0.4	0.0	0.0	0.0	0.0	0.0	0.0
1943	156,926	176,070	110,068	919	1.5	126.6	21.2	0.1	64.5	(Z)	0.0	0.0	0.0	0.0	0.0	0.0
1944	239,254	218,759	130,563	821	0.2	(Z)	12.3	(Z)	52.4	0.0	0.0	0.0	0.0	0.0	0.0	0.0
1945	277,748	213,439	194,872	916	0.1	38.6	6.5	0.0	7.4	(Z)	0.0	0.0	0.0	0.0	0.0	0.0
1946	329,232	230,649	293,455	1,420	0.0	(Z)	1.8	0.0	5.6	(Z)	0.0	0.0	0.0	0.0	0.0	0.0
1947	351,079	208,962	435,572	1,804	0.1	0.0	1.3	(Z)	4.4	0.7	0.0	0.0	0.0	0.0	0.0	0.0
1948	359,613	280,169	515,016	1,993	197.9	0.0	3.0	0.0	199.3	226.7	0.0	0.0	0.0	0.0	0.0	0.0
1949	255,663	337,250	433,429	1,800	672.2	19.8	21.1	2.2	828.4	824.1	0.0	0.0	0.0	0.0	0.0	0.0
1950	674,757	292,229	815,957	2,279	1,044.3	469.4	44.3	12.3	1,346.7	485.1	0.0	0.0	0.0	0.0	0.0	0.0
1951	422,977	432,997	805,937	2,221	677.3	111.1	55.5	7.9	1,849.5	239.1	0.0	0.0	0.0	0.0	0.0	0.0
1952	585,813	527,562	864,189	2,057	537.9	55.9	78.9	10.9	2,241.7	322.9	0.0	0.0	0.0	0.0	0.0	0.0
1953	727,517	640,150	951,555	2,147	542.5	221.1	93.7	7.7	2,461.7	637.9	0.0	0.0	0.0	0.0	0.0	0.0
1954	734,249	818,326	867,478	1,923	658.1	525.2	100.3	18.1	2,476.2	475.7	(Z)	(Z)	(Z)	(Z)	(Z)	0.2
1955	1,251,680	702,400	1,416,759	2,408	325.3	61.6	126.4	43.6	2,569.9	42.8	86.1	0.0	0.4	0.0	85.7	26.5
1956	744,936	933,539	1,228,156	2,241	28.6	0.2	118.2	48.0	2,432.1	8.1	574.6	5.0	6.2	0.4	648.7	283.4
1957	1,116,148	1,079,109	1,265,195	2,018	7.9	0.0	115.5	20.2	2,304.3	0.0	1,021.0	2.9	28.7	2.3	1,635.8	180.1
1958	1,363,699	1,330,574	1,298,320	2,040	0.0	3.3	141.3	21.0	2,138.7	0.0	259.5	465.6	39.1	9.9	1,380.7	79.9
1959	2,066,819	1,230,816	2,134,322	2,443	15.0	0.8	162.3	26.7	1,963.9	0.0	734.6	3.5	47.5	14.5	2,049.8	187.2
1960	1,943,164	2,096,711	1,980,775	2,371	143.5	311.3	122.4	14.2	1,659.5	0.0	980.4	42.0	64.1	21.1	2,903.0	164.9
1961	2,881,917	2,200,475	2,662,217	2,455	0.1	5.2	127.0	19.5	1,507.9	0.0	624.4	522.0	79.0	54.5	2,871.9	211.7
1962	4,110,764	3,293,958	3,479,958	2,722	0.7	15.4	135.0	18.4	1,339.8	0.0	547.5	390.7	104.0	78.1	2,846.6	28.0
1963	5,601,231	4,296,019	4,784,236	2,856	27.3	49.7	129.9	13.2	1,174.3	0.0	181.3	779.8	109.7	76.6	2,061.8	8.6
1964	5,563,456	5,023,164	5,324,528	2,795	124.9	43.8	122.0	19.7	1,113.7	0.0	197.5	78.1	120.1	64.2	1,996.9	38.6
1965	5,007,113	4,334,788	5,996,852	2,857	20.3	54.2	113.2	14.0	952.6	0.0	756.9	46.5	125.6	62.2	2,519.5	461.5
1966	3,803,545	2,865,719	6,934,678	2,580	418.6	0.0	92.0	10.4	1,268.8	0.0	2,080.6	0.1	133.0	70.7	4,396.3	214.3
1967	1,526,692	4,075,720	4,385,650	1,956	520.0	0.0	95.1	25.7	1,668.0	0.0	1,399.6	11.8	170.0	92.1	5,522.0	501.2
1968	2,734,468	1,861,107	5,259,010	2,193	451.2	0.0	109.2	40.2	1,969.8	0.0	1,944.3	0.1	217.8	81.1	7,167.2	1,287.5
1969	5,531,244	1,501,287	9,288,967	2,782	109.3	0.0	111.4	40.2	1,927.5	0.0	4,120.0	0.0	266.3	70.6	10,950.3	3,538.9
1970	3,255,378	1,929,814	10,614,532	2,391	31.6	0.0	105.8	32.7	1,820.6	0.7	5,078.8	20.3	339.2	177.8	15,491.8	5,145.1

(Z) Positive amount less than $50,000.

1 Includes Alaska and Hawai'i for all years.

2 Series Dc1142–1147 measure consolidated operations of Federal National Mortgage Association (FNMA) (1938 through November 1954); then management and liquidation of FNMA (November 1954 to 1967); and then secondary market operations program of Government National Mortgage Association (thereafter). Series Dc1148–1153 measure secondary market operations program of Government National Mortgage Association (thereafter); and then secondary market operations of privately owned FNMA (thereafter); see text.

Sources

Series Dc1138–1141. 1932–1954: *Federal Home Loan Bank Board Annual Report, 1964*, Table 6, p. 102. 1955–1970: Federal Home Loan Bank Board, *1980 Savings and Home Financing Book*, Table 2, p. 5.

Series Dc1142–1147. U.S. Department of Housing and Urban Development (HUD), *Statistical Yearbook 1970*, Table 95, p. 97

Series Dc1148–1153. 1954–1967, *1967 HUD Statistical Yearbook*, Federal National Mortgage Association Table 10, p. 216; 1968–1970, *HUD Statistical Yearbook*, various years.

Documentation

See Oliver Jones and Leo Grebler, *The Secondary Mortgage Market* (Real Estate Research Program, 1961), for a detailed examination of the pre-1970 secondary mortgage market in the United States. For more detail about the Federal Home Loan Bank (FHLB) system during this period, see the annual *Fact Book* that was published by the United States Savings and Loan League.

In the absence of a secondary market, the holder of a mortgage loan is forced to commit funds until the loan is repaid. The function of a secondary market, therefore, is to provide an opportunity for a mortgage investor to sell a mortgage loan, or to borrow against the loan, before it is repaid. The federal government established two facilities during the 1930s to serve as a secondary market for residential mortgage loans – the FHLB system in 1932 and the Federal National Mortgage Association (FNMA) in 1938. This table documents the secondary market activities of these two agencies until 1970. See Table Dc1154–1169 for the activities of these agencies after 1970.

The FHLB system is similar in structure to the Federal Reserve System; both comprise twelve district banks that regulate and serve member institutions within their regions. Almost all FHLB members were savings and loan associations (S&Ls) during the period shown in this table – over the same period, S&Ls were the nation's most important residential mortgage lenders. The most important benefit of FHLB membership is the privilege to borrow – these loans are called "advances." Advances from the FHLB can be short-term and unsecured; long-term advances, however, must be secured by mortgage loans in the borrowing member's portfolio. In this way, advances from the FHLB provide its members with a secondary loan market that they can use to balance current market demand for new mortgage loans with the available supply of loanable funds. The FHLB raises funds to finance its lending activities by selling its own stock (to member institutions) and by issuing debt in the bond market. To offset the cost of these funds, FHLB banks charge members interest on advances.

The table shows the number of FHLB members with advances outstanding at the end of each year (series Dc1141), as well as new advances made (series Dc1138) and repayments received on existing advances (series Dc1139). The change in the total amount of advances outstanding to members at the end of each year is shown in series Dc1140.

FNMA was chartered in 1938 to provide a different type of secondary market to a different group of mortgage originators and lenders. Unlike the FHLB system, FNMA was authorized to buy residential mortgage loans from qualified institutions – but only loans that were federally insured by the FHA or (after 1944) guaranteed by the VA. S&Ls had relatively little use for the services of FNMA because

they specialized in conventional loans and already had access to FHLB advances. So FNMA served other institutions in the residential mortgage market – commercial banks, mortgage companies, and life insurance companies. These types of lenders and originators were especially active in financing new homebuilding and made heavy use of FNMA's advance commitments. Through this device, FNMA agreed to purchase a mortgage loan in the future that was to be written on a home that had yet to be built. With the commitment for permanent financing in hand, homebuilders could more easily secure construction financing.

Although FNMA sold some of the mortgages it purchased, over time it accumulated a substantial portfolio of loans that it financed with marketable debt that it issued on its own account. FNMA was also called on by Congress and the President in its early years to purchase and hold mortgages that financed housing production in markets of great need and at times of high unemployment. As a result, FNMA came to perform three distinct functions: the management and liquidation of a very large mortgage portfolio, secondary market purchases and sales with qualified institutions, and the special assistance it provided for government housing initiatives. The Association was reorganized in 1954 to separate these three activities into distinct programs.

Series Dc1142–1147 measure all FNMA activity until 1954. From that date onward these series measure only one activity – FNMA's management and liquidation (M&L) program. This arrangement makes sense because the first task of the M&L program was to administer the entire mortgage portfolio that FNMA had accumulated up to that time. The newly separated Secondary Market Operations (SMO) program is shown in the table as series Dc1148–1153. Not shown in the table, or included in any of the series, is the activity of FNMA's Special Assistance (SA) program that was also created in 1954.

Between 1938 and 1954, total FNMA purchases for each year are shown in series Dc1142; all FNMA sales during this earliest period are measured in series Dc1143. Repayments and other liquidations (prepayments and foreclosure) on all mortgage loans held in FNMA's portfolio are shown in series Dc1144–1145 for each year up to 1954. The flow of purchases, sales, repayments, and liquidations together determined the amount of FNMA's total mortgage portfolio (series Dc1146). Finally, the outstanding advanced commitments FNMA had made to purchase mortgages at year-end are presented in series Dc1146. Beginning in November 1954, two sets of FNMA series are shown in the table (series Dc1142–1147 and series Dc1148–1153). Each set measures the same six variables that were defined above for FNMA's separate M&L and SMO programs.

The 1954 reorganization required institutions that used FNMA's secondary market operation program to purchase stock in the association. Before then, nearly all FNMA stock had been subscribed by the U.S. Treasury – a method of financing that had begun in 1938 in an attempt to substitute for, and then attract, private equity holders. The private ownership stake in FNMA began to grow, and by 1968, led to a second major reorganization of FNMA that was accomplished in the Housing Act of 1968. This legislation created a new government agency – the Government National Mortgage Association (Ginnie Mae) – to which the separate management and liquidation and special assistance programs of FNMA were transferred. Beginning in 1968, therefore, series Dc1142–1147 measure the activities of the same M&L program although it was housed within a new government agency between 1968 and 1970.

The secondary market operations program of the old FNMA was spun off entirely in 1968 as a government-sponsored, privately owned corporation. It is now known as Fannie Mae. As a result, between 1968 and 1970 series Dc1148–1153 measure the activities of a secondary mortgage market facility that had been operating within the old FNMA since 1954, but was under new ownership.

TABLE Dc1154–1169 Secondary residential mortgage market activity of federal-related agencies: 1970–1999

Contributed by Kenneth A. Snowden

	Federal Home Loan Bank (FHLB)					Fannie Mae							Freddie Mac			
	Advances	Year-end outstanding advances	Purchases			Retained portfolio				Purchases				Retained portfolio		
			Total	Single family	Multifamily	Total	Whole mortgage loans	Mortgage securities	Other mortgage-related securities	Total	Single family	Multifamily	Total	Whole mortgage loans	Mortgage securities	Other mortgage-related securities
Year	Dc1154	Dc1155	Dc1156	Dc1157	Dc1158	Dc1159	Dc1160	Dc1161	Dc1162	Dc1163	Dc1164	Dc1165	Dc1166	Dc1167	Dc1168	Dc1169
	Million dollars	Million dollars	Million dollars	Million dollars	Million dollars	Million dollars	Million dollars	Million dollars	Million dollars	Million dollars	Million dollars	Million dollars	Million dollars	Million dollars	Million dollars	Million dollars
1970	3,255	10,615	5,079	—	—	15,492	15,492	0	0	325	—	—	325	—	—	—
1971	2,714	7,936	4,040	2,742	1,298	18,515	18,515	0	0	778	—	—	935	—	—	—
1972	4,792	7,979	3,864	2,596	1,268	20,326	20,326	0	0	1,265	—	—	1,726	—	—	—
1973	10,013	15,147	6,252	4,170	2,082	24,459	24,459	0	0	1,334	—	—	2,521	—	—	—
1974	12,763	21,804	7,019	4,746	2,273	29,708	29,708	0	0	2,185	—	—	4,469	—	—	—
1975	5,468	17,845	4,320	3,646	674	31,916	31,916	0	0	1,716	—	—	4,878	—	—	—
1976	8,115	15,862	3,632	3,337	295	32,937	32,937	0	0	1,129	—	—	4,175	—	—	—
1977	13,757	20,173	4,784	4,650	134	34,377	34,377	0	0	4,124	—	—	3,204	—	—	—
1978	25,300	32,670	12,305	12,302	3	43,315	43,315	0	0	6,524	—	—	3,038	—	—	—
1979	29,184	41,838	10,807	10,798	9	51,097	51,096	1	0	5,716	—	—	4,003	—	—	—
1980	36,585	48,963	8,101	8,074	27	57,327	57,326	1	0	3,690	—	—	5,006	—	—	—
1981	53,941	65,194	6,829	6,827	2	61,412	61,411	1	0	3,744	—	—	5,178	—	—	—
1982	53,744	66,011	25,939	25,929	10	71,814	71,777	37	0	23,671	—	—	4,679	—	—	—
1983	44,724	58,977	26,479	26,339	140	78,256	77,983	273	0	22,952	—	—	7,485	—	—	—
1984	91,239	74,618	28,819	27,713	1,106	88,109	87,205	477	427	21,885	—	—	10,018	—	—	—
1985	133,651	88,852	43,743	42,543	1,200	98,649	97,421	435	793	44,012	42,110	1,902	13,547	—	—	—
1986	181,631	108,668	79,100	77,223	1,877	97,833	94,167	1,606	2,060	103,474	99,936	3,538	13,093	—	—	—
1987	194,451	133,054	75,675	73,942	1,733	96,746	89,618	4,226	2,902	76,840	74,824	2,016	12,354	—	—	—
1988	187,536	152,799	68,783	64,613	4,170	103,013	92,220	8,153	2,640	44,075	42,884	1,191	16,918	—	—	—
1989	218,876	141,807	84,835	80,510	4,325	110,721	95,729	11,720	3,272	78,589	76,765	1,824	21,448	—	—	—
1990	149,459	117,100	114,187	111,007	3,180	116,628	101,797	11,758	3,073	75,518	74,180	1,338	21,520	—	—	—
1991	175,673	79,065	136,755	133,551	3,204	128,983	109,251	16,700	3,032	99,965	99,729	236	26,667	—	—	—
1992	263,008	79,884	251,062	248,210	2,852	158,119	134,597	20,535	2,987	191,126	191,099	27	33,629	—	6,394	—
1993	579,374	103,131	293,961	289,826	4,135	190,861	163,149	24,219	3,493	229,242	229,051	191	55,938	—	15,877	—
1994	729,076	125,893	162,068	158,229	3,939	225,057	173,909	43,998	7,150	123,410	122,563	847	73,171	—	30,670	—
1995	689,673	132,264	130,969	126,003	4,966	253,511	171,481	69,729	12,301	91,536	89,971	1,565	107,706	44,035	56,006	7,665
1996	655,024	161,372	170,907	164,456	6,451	287,052	167,891	102,607	16,554	125,079	122,850	2,229	137,826	46,575	81,195	10,056
1997	832,005	202,265	166,455	159,921	6,534	316,678	160,102	130,444	26,132	117,401	115,160	2,241	164,543	48,576	103,400	12,567
1998	1,025,853	288,189	366,348	354,920	11,428	414,515	155,779	197,375	61,361	267,400	263,490	3,910	255,670	57,745	168,108	29,817
1999	2,577,096	395,747	326,148	316,136	10,012	523,941	149,105	281,714	93,122	239,793	232,612	7,181	322,914	55,147	211,198	56,569

Sources

Series Dc1154–1155. 1970–1987: Federal Home Loan Bank Board, *Savings and Home Financing Source Book*, Table E1–E2. 1988–1999: Federal Home Loan Bank, *Financial Report*, various years.

Series Dc1156–1169. Office of Federal Housing Enterprise Oversight, *2001 Report to Congress*, Appendix Tables 1, 5, 11, and 15, available at the Internet site of the Office of Federal Housing Enterprise Oversight.

Documentation

This table presents the secondary market activities of three federal-related agencies that came to dominate the secondary market for single-family residential mortgage loans during the last three decades of the twentieth century. Two of these agencies – the Federal Home Loan Bank (FHLB) system and the Federal National Mortgage Association (FNMA, generally known as Fannie Mae) – trace their origins back to the 1930s and are described in detail in the text for Table Dc1138–1153. The third agency shown here is the Federal Home Loan Mortgage Corporation, generally known as Freddie Mac, which was established by legislation as a federally sponsored, privately owned secondary market agency in 1970.

Four of the series in this table continue those shown in Table Dc1138–1153. For the FHLB system, in particular, the amount of advances made each year (series Dc1154) and the total amount of advances outstanding at year-end (series Dc1155) continue the same series from the earlier period. For

TABLE Dc1154–1169   Secondary residential mortgage market activity of federal-related agencies: 1970–1999
Continued

Fannie Mae, the continued series are total mortgage purchases each year (series Dc1156) and total year-end mortgage portfolio (series Dc1159). See the text in Table Dc1138-1153 for a description of these series.

There are some differences, however, between the FNMA series shown here and those shown in Table Dc1138-1153. To begin with, Fannie Mae was authorized in 1970 to purchase conventional mortgage loans for its portfolio in addition to the Federal Housing Administration (FHA)-insured and Veterans Administration (VA)-guaranteed loans to which it had been restricted before then. Second, total mortgage purchases by Fannie Mae for this period are divided in the table into those written on single-family and multifamily residential properties (series Dc1157–1158). (Single-family properties are those containing one to four dwelling units and multifamily properties are those containing five or more.) Finally, additional detail is also given in this table about the composition of Fannie Mae's retained mortgage portfolio at the end of the year (series Dc1159). Before 1970, Fannie Mae held mortgages that it purchased as whole loans in its portfolio, and whole mortgage loans (series Dc1160) continued to dominate its portfolio through the 1970s.

Beginning in the early 1980s, however, Fannie Mae began to purchase mortgage-backed securities (MBSs) in addition to whole loans, and by 1999 these new assets had supplanted whole loans as the most important asset on the company's balance sheet. In the table the MBSs held each year by Fannie Mae are shown in two series – those issued under Fannie Mae sponsorship (series Dc1161) and those issued through the programs of other federal-related or private agencies (series Dc1162). The company's total retained mortgage portfolio, therefore, is now equal to its holdings of whole mortgage loans plus its holdings of the two classes of mortgage-related securities.

Freddie Mac and Fannie Mae are similar institutions in several respects: both are privately owned but government-sponsored; both buy (and sell) residential mortgages from originators and institutional investors; both are authorized to purchase and hold conventional, FHA-insured, and VA-guaranteed mortgages loans; and both are active as both issuers and investors in the mortgage-related securities markets. The two agencies tend to serve different audiences, however: Fannie Mae caters disproportionately to mortgage companies, while Freddie Mac was originally restricted to serve only depository institutions (savings and loans, commercial banks, and mutual savings banks).

The series shown for Freddie Mac are identical in meaning to those described above for Fannie Mae. Both agencies are regulated by the Office of Housing Enterprise Oversight, which was the source of all the data shown in the table.

Series Dc1156. Includes cash purchases of loans from lenders and lender-originated securitizations; does not include purchases of mortgage-related securities issued by others or repurchases of previously issued Fannie Mae mortgage securities.

Series Dc1159 and Dc1166. Figures represent gross retained portfolio, net of amortized purchases, premiums, discounts, and deferred fees. Series Dc1159 equals total gross unpaid principal balance on whole loans and pooled mortgages.

Series Dc1163. Includes loans purchased from lenders; does not include purchases of mortgage-related securities issued by others or repurchases of previously issued Freddie Mac mortgage securities.

Series Dc1167. Includes purchase and sale premiums, discounts, and deferred fees and unrealized gain or loss on available-for-sale securities.

TABLE Dc1170–1191   Mortgage-related securities issued and outstanding, by type of security, guarantor, and property: 1970–1999

Contributed by Kenneth A. Snowden

	Mortgage-backed securities											
	Guaranteed by GNMA				Guaranteed by Freddie Mac				Guaranteed by Fannie Mae			
	Issued			Outstanding	Issued			Outstanding	Issued			Outstanding
	Total	Single family	Multifamily		Total	Single family	Multifamily		Total	Single family	Multifamily	
	Dc1170	Dc1171	Dc1172	Dc1173	Dc1174	Dc1175	Dc1176	Dc1177	Dc1178	Dc1179	Dc1180	Dc1181
Year	Million dollars	Million dollars	Million dollars	Million dollars	Million dollars	Million dollars	Million dollars	Million dollars	Million dollars	Million dollars	Million dollars	Million dollars
1970	452	—	—	347	0	0	0	0	0	0	0	0
1971	2,702	—	—	3,074	65	—	—	64	0	0	0	0
1972	2,662	—	—	5,504	494	—	—	444	0	0	0	0
1973	3,249	—	—	7,890	323	—	—	791	0	0	0	0
1974	4,784	—	—	11,769	46	—	—	780	0	0	0	0
1975	7,366	—	—	18,257	950	—	—	1,643	0	0	0	0
1976	—	—	—	30,572	1,360	—	—	2,765	0	0	0	0
1977	—	—	—	44,896	4,657	—	—	6,765	0	0	0	0
1978	15,358	—	—	54,347	6,412	—	—	12,017	0	0	0	0
1979	24,940	—	—	76,401	4,546	—	—	15,316	0	0	0	0
1980	20,600	—	—	93,874	2,526	—	—	16,962	0	0	0	0
1981	14,300	—	—	105,790	3,526	—	—	19,897	717	717	0	717
1982	16,000	—	—	118,940	24,169	—	—	42,952	13,970	13,970	0	14,450
1983	50,700	—	—	159,850	19,691	—	—	57,720	13,340	13,214	126	25,121
1984	28,097	27,223	874	179,981	18,684	—	—	70,026	13,546	13,087	459	35,738
1985	45,980	45,031	949	212,145	38,828	37,583	1,245	99,909	23,649	23,142	507	54,552
1986	101,433	99,492	1,941	262,697	100,198	96,798	3,400	169,186	60,566	60,017	549	95,568
1987	94,890	92,693	2,197	317,555	75,018	72,866	2,152	212,635	63,229	62,067	1,162	135,734
1988	55,181	52,918	2,263	340,527	39,777	39,490	287	226,406	54,878	51,120	3,758	170,097
1989	57,074	55,592	1,482	374,650	73,518	72,931	587	272,870	69,764	66,489	3,275	216,512
1990	64,395	63,095	1,300	403,613	73,815	71,998	1,817	316,359	96,695	96,006	689	288,075
1991	62,630	61,646	984	425,295	92,479	92,479	0	359,163	112,903	111,488	1,415	355,284
1992	81,917	81,016	901	419,516	179,207	179,202	5	407,514	194,037	193,187	850	424,444
1993	137,989	135,961	2,028	414,066	208,724	208,724	0	439,029	221,444	220,485	959	471,306
1994	111,185	109,241	1,944	450,934	117,110	116,901	209	460,656	130,622	128,385	2,237	486,345
1995	72,765	70,681	2,084	472,298	85,877	85,522	355	459,045	110,456	106,269	4,187	513,230
1996	100,915	98,552	2,363	506,200	119,702	118,932	770	473,065	149,869	144,201	5,668	548,173
1997	104,147	101,666	2,481	536,879	114,258	113,758	500	475,985	149,429	143,615	5,814	579,138
1998	150,205	147,080	3,125	537,446	250,564	249,627	937	478,351	326,148	315,120	11,028	637,143
1999	—	—	—	582,263	233,031	230,986	2,045	537,883	300,689	292,192	8,497	679,169

	Multiclass mortgage-backed securities						Mortgage-backed securities issued by privately organized mortgage pools			
	Guaranteed by GNMA		Guaranteed by Freddie Mac		Guaranteed by Fannie Mae		Issued			Outstanding
	Issued	Outstanding	Issued	Outstanding	Issued	Outstanding	Total	Single family	Multifamily	
	Dc1182	Dc1183	Dc1184	Dc1185	Dc1186	Dc1187	Dc1188	Dc1189	Dc1190	Dc1191
Year	Million dollars	Million dollars	Million dollars	Million dollars	Million dollars	Million dollars	Million dollars	Million dollars	Million dollars	Million dollars
1970	0	0	0	0	0	0	—	—	0	—
1971	0	0	0	0	0	0	—	—	0	—
1972	0	0	0	0	0	0	—	—	0	—
1973	0	0	0	0	0	0	—	—	0	—
1974	0	0	0	0	0	0	—	—	0	—
1975	0	0	0	0	0	0	—	—	0	—
1976	0	0	0	0	0	0	—	—	0	—
1977	0	0	0	0	0	0	—	—	0	—
1978	0	0	0	0	0	0	—	—	0	—
1979	0	0	0	0	0	0	—	—	0	—
1980	0	0	0	0	0	0	—	—	0	—
1981	0	0	0	0	0	0	—	—	0	—
1982	0	0	0	0	0	0	—	—	0	—
1983	0	0	1,685	1,669	0	0	—	—	0	—
1984	0	0	1,805	3,214	0	0	7,700	7,700	0	—

TABLE Dc1170–1191   Mortgage-related securities issued and outstanding, by type of security, guarantor, and property: 1970–1999   *Continued*

	Multiclass mortgage-backed securities						Mortgage-backed securities issued by privately organized mortgage pools			
	Guaranteed by GNMA		Guaranteed by Freddie Mac		Guaranteed by Fannie Mae		Issued			
	Issued	Outstanding	Issued	Outstanding	Issued	Outstanding	Total	Single family	Multifamily	Outstanding
	Dc1182	Dc1183	Dc1184	Dc1185	Dc1186	Dc1187	Dc1188	Dc1189	Dc1190	Dc1191
Year	Million dollars	Million dollars	Million dollars	Million dollars	Million dollars	Million dollars	Million dollars	Million dollars	Million dollars	Million dollars
1985	0	0	2,625	5,047	0	0	7,900	7,900	0	24,000
1986	0	0	2,233	5,333	2,400	0	16,200	16,200	0	16,800
1987	0	0	0	3,652	9,917	11,359	21,200	21,200	0	28,300
1988	0	0	12,985	15,621	17,005	26,660	23,400	23,400	0	35,800
1989	0	0	39,754	52,865	41,715	64,826	16,400	16,400	0	44,300
1990	0	0	40,479	88,124	68,291	127,278	20,100	20,100	0	56,300
1991	0	0	72,032	146,978	112,808	224,806	49,300	49,300	0	103,300
1992	0	0	131,284	218,747	170,205	312,369	89,500	89,500	0	157,900
1993	0	0	143,336	265,178	210,630	381,865	100,700	98,500	2,200	192,000
1994	3,100	—	73,131	264,152	73,365	378,733	66,900	63,200	3,700	215,700
1995	1,900	—	15,372	246,366	9,681	353,528	35,900	34,800	1,100	236,200
1996	9,500	—	34,145	237,939	30,780	339,798	39,500	38,500	1,000	272,100
1997	7,900	17,500	84,366	233,591	85,415	388,360	70,800	63,300	7,500	331,600
1998	13,600	29,000	135,162	260,504	84,147	361,613	151,500	134,500	17,000	438,900
1999	29,600	52,500	119,565	316,168	55,160	335,514	107,900	92,900	15,000	497,200

Sources

Series Dc1170–1172. 1970–1979: U.S. Department of Housing and Urban Development, *Statistical Yearbook*, various years. 1980–1983: Government National Mortgage Association estimates downloaded April 21, 2002, from the Internet site of the Bond Market Association. 1984–1998: Federal Home Loan Mortgage Corporation, *Secondary Mortgage Markets: Mortgage Market Trends 1997* (July 1997) and *Mortgage Market Trends 1999* (April 1999).

Series Dc1173. Federal Reserve Board, *Annual Statistical Digest*, various issues (1970–1979, 1980–1989, 1990–1995), and *Federal Reserve Bulletin*, various issues.

Series Dc1174–1181 and Dc1184–1187. Office of Federal Housing Enterprise Oversight, *2001 Report to Congress*, Appendix Tables 2, 4, 12, and 14, available from the Internet site of the Office of Federal Housing Enterprise Oversight.

Series Dc1182–1183. Downloaded April 21, 2002, from the Internet site of the Bond Market Association.

Series Dc1188–1191. Fannie Mae Economics, "2001 Statistical Summary of Housing and Mortgage Finance Activities," Tables 3, 15, and 17, available from the Internet site of Fannie Mae (the Federal National Mortgage Association).

Documentation

Beginning in 1970, Ginnie Mae (the Government National Mortgage Association, GNMA), Freddie Mac (the Federal Home Loan Mortgage Corporation), and eventually Fannie Mae (the Federal National Mortgage Association, FNMA) all began to sponsor programs through which groups of whole mortgage loans were assembled into pools. These pools were placed in trust, and new mortgage-backed securities were issued, representing claims on the future payments of interest and principal that borrowers were scheduled to make on the underlying whole mortgage loans. The introduction of these mortgage-backed securities transformed the secondary market for residential mortgages: instead of buying and selling whole mortgage loans, investors could now "purchase" the cash flow on a mortgage without actually owning the loan. It also placed the three federal-related agencies as key players in one of the most important financial innovations of the twentieth century.

Series Dc1170–1173. Ginnie Mae was the first of the agencies to securitize mortgages. In 1970 it began a program through which private portfolio lenders, such as commercial banks or savings and loans, could bundle a pool of Federal Housing Administration (FHA)-insured or Veterans Administration (VA)-guaranteed mortgages and issue and sell mortgage-backed bonds using the pool as collateral. Ginnie Mae used its status as a federal agency to guarantee both the principal and the interest payments that were to be "passed through" to the bondholders and, by doing so, stimulated the development of the mortgage-backed security (MBS) market. The volume of GNMA-guaranteed MBSs issued each year is shown in the table as series Dc1170. This total is equal to the sum of the securities issued that were backed with pools of single-family or multifamily mortgages. The total volume of GNMA-guaranteed mortgage securities outstanding at the end of each year is shown in series Dc1173.

Series Dc1174–1177. Freddie Mac began to pool mortgages and guarantee securities just one year after Ginnie Mae. These activities are shown in the table with four series identical in meaning to those described above for Ginnie Mae. There were important differences between the two cases, however. To begin with, Freddie Mac was oriented toward securitizing conventional mortgages, rather than those insured by the FHA or guaranteed by the VA. Second, because Freddie Mac was not a federal agency, the guarantee it made on its bonds was not backed by the full faith and credit of the national government. Because of its stature as a chartered enterprise of the federal government, however, Freddie Mac mortgage securities also gained rapid investor acceptance.

Series Dc1177 and Dc1181. Figures represent total MBSs outstanding, net of the company's holdings of its own securities.

Series Dc1178–1181 and Dc1186–1187. Fannie Mae lagged behind Ginnie Mae and Freddie Mac in issuing its own mortgage-backed and multiclass securities, but has become the largest issuer in both markets. The series for FNMA carry the same meanings as those described for the other agencies.

Series Dc1182–1187. In addition to the differences described above between Ginnie Mae and Freddie Mac, a third difference is that Freddie Mac continued to innovate by introducing "multiclass" mortgage securities in 1983. The earlier mortgage-backed bonds provided only proportional claims on the principal and interest payments that were generated by the underlying mortgage pool — each bond secured by a given pool earned the same cash flow over its life. A multiclass mortgage securitization structure, on the other hand, divides the principal and interest payments expected from the mortgage pool into cash flows with different time patterns and maturities by issuing a differentiated set of securities with these same characteristics. The volume of multiclass securities issued by Freddie Mac for each year is shown in the table as series Dc1184, while the amount of these securities that was outstanding at year-end is given in series Dc1185. The relatively late start and small size of the GNMA multiclass mortgage security program, on the other hand, is shown in series Dc1182–1183.

Series Dc1184–1186. The majority qualify as real estate mortgage investment conduits (REMICs), and are also known as structured securitizations.

TABLE Dc1170–1191   Mortgage-related securities issued and outstanding, by type of security, guarantor, and property: 1970–1999 *Continued*

Series Dc1184. For 1983-1986, data consist of collateralized mortgage obligations (CMOs) and mortgage cash flow obligations (MCFs).

Series Dc1185. For 1983-1999, data also includes original-issue CMOs and MCFs, and structured securitizations and Participation Certificates with mandatory purchase obligations.

Series Dc1188–1191. Also included in the table are the volumes of MBSs issued by privately organized mortgage pools. The source reported amounts in tenths of billions.

TABLE Dc1192–1209   Terms on nonfarm home mortgages, by type of mortgage and holder: 1920–1967

Contributed by Kenneth A. Snowden

	Lending terms on nonfarm home mortgages								
	Number of loans sampled			Average contract interest rate			Average contract length		
	Life insurance companies	Commercial banks	Savings and loan associations	Life insurance companies	Commercial banks	Savings and loan associations	Life insurance companies	Commercial banks	Savings and loan associations
	Dc1192	Dc1193	Dc1194	Dc1195	Dc1196	Dc1197	Dc1198	Dc1199	Dc1200
Year	Number	Number	Number	Percent	Percent	Percent	Years	Years	Years
1920	73	69	69	6.1	6.2	7.0	6.0	2.9	11.3
1921	119	58	58	6.2	6.2	7.3	7.9	1.8	10.6
1922	170	113	79	6.1	6.2	7.0	6.6	2.9	11.5
1923	209	147	84	5.9	6.2	7.0	5.9	2.9	11.2
1924	279	182	85	5.9	6.1	7.0	5.7	3.5	11.1
1925	358	200	129	5.9	6.1	6.9	6.0	3.1	10.9
1926	478	182	114	5.8	5.9	6.9	5.9	3.6	11.2
1927	414	188	129	5.9	6.1	6.8	6.7	2.5	11.4
1928	411	186	134	5.9	6.1	6.7	6.6	3.2	11.4
1929	396	134	129	6.0	6.1	6.8	6.8	3.7	11.2
1930	347	114	107	6.0	6.2	6.9	7.5	3.6	10.8
1931	299	114	50	6.0	5.8	6.6	7.8	3.0	10.8
1932	98	41	26	6.0	6.1	7.0	7.9	3.0	11.3
1933	15	32	24	5.9	6.3	6.5	6.3	2.1	11.1
1934	26	32	38	5.8	6.1	6.4	7.9	2.9	11.7
1935	64	87	63	5.5	5.6	6.2	13.0	9.8	11.9
1936	163	106	79	5.2	5.3	6.4	16.2	9.7	11.4
1937	192	136	111	5.1	5.3	6.0	16.7	9.6	12.8
1938	255	151	115	5.1	5.1	6.0	17.7	13.2	13.7
1939	285	198	146	4.9	5.0	6.0	18.3	14.8	12.9
1940	404	220	130	4.6	4.7	5.7	19.9	16.0	14.6
1941	584	194	168	4.6	4.7	5.6	20.6	14.4	13.9
1942	613	160	105	4.5	4.6	5.5	21.1	12.7	13.5
1943	459	152	135	4.5	4.7	5.6	21.7	12.4	13.4
1944	286	152	165	4.5	4.6	5.3	22.1	10.0	13.6
1945	235	164	195	4.4	4.5	5.1	20.0	9.3	14.3
1946	311	380	268	4.2	4.3	4.7	18.8	12.7	15.0
1947	72	81	184	4.0	4.4	4.7	19.5	14.8	15.2
1948	—	—	—	—	—	—	—	—	—
1949	—	—	—	—	—	—	—	—	—
1950	—	—	—	—	—	—	—	—	—
1951 [1]	—	—	—	—	—	—	—	—	—
1952 [1]	—	—	—	—	—	—	—	—	—
1953	—	—	—	—	—	—	—	—	—
1954	—	—	—	—	—	—	—	—	—
1955	—	—	—	—	—	—	—	—	—
1956	—	—	—	—	—	—	—	—	—
1957	—	—	—	—	—	—	—	—	—
1958	—	—	—	—	—	—	—	—	—
1959	—	—	—	—	—	—	—	—	—
1960	—	—	—	—	—	—	—	—	—
1961	—	—	—	—	—	—	—	—	—
1962	—	—	—	—	—	—	—	—	—
1963	—	—	—	—	—	—	—	—	—
1964	—	—	—	—	—	—	—	—	—
1965	—	—	—	—	—	—	—	—	—
1966	—	—	—	—	—	—	—	—	—
1967	—	—	—	—	—	—	—	—	—

Notes appear at end of table

TABLE Dc1192–1209   Terms on nonfarm home mortgages, by type of mortgage and holder: 1920–1967   *Continued*

	Lending terms on nonfarm home mortgages			Contract terms for mortgages on existing homes					
	Average loan-to-value ratio			Conventional mortgages by savings and loan associations		FHA-insured or VA-guaranteed mortgages			
						FHA-insured		VA-guaranteed	
	Life insurance companies	Commercial banks	Savings and loan associations	Median maturity	Median loan-to-purchase-price ratio	Average maturity	Average loan-to-value ratio	Average maturity	Average loan-to-value ratio
	Dc1201	Dc1202	Dc1203	Dc1204	Dc1205	Dc1206	Dc1207	Dc1208	Dc1209
Year	Percent	Percent	Percent	Years	Percent	Years	Percent	Years	Percent
1920	46	48	59	—	—	—	—	—	—
1921	44	49	56	—	—	—	—	—	—
1922	47	51	58	—	—	—	—	—	—
1923	48	50	57	—	—	—	—	—	—
1924	50	52	58	—	—	—	—	—	—
1925	49	50	60	—	—	—	—	—	—
1926	51	51	57	—	—	—	—	—	—
1927	51	54	56	—	—	—	—	—	—
1928	53	53	60	—	—	—	—	—	—
1929	52	53	61	—	—	—	—	—	—
1930	53	50	59	—	—	—	—	—	—
1931	52	50	59	—	—	—	—	—	—
1932	49	51	63	—	—	—	—	—	—
1933	46	57	56	—	—	—	—	—	—
1934	53	50	61	—	—	—	—	—	—
1935	53	60	60	—	—	—	—	—	—
1936	61	61	62	—	—	—	—	—	—
1937	64	60	62	—	—	—	—	—	—
1938	67	63	64	—	—	—	—	—	—
1939	69	69	64	—	—	—	—	—	—
1940	73	72	68	—	—	—	—	—	—
1941	76	68	68	—	—	—	—	—	—
1942	80	67	68	—	—	—	—	—	—
1943	81	66	70	—	—	—	—	—	—
1944	82	61	73	—	—	—	—	—	—
1945	76	61	73	—	—	—	—	—	—
1946	75	70	77	—	—	18.9	78.6	18.2	89.1
1947	69	69	74	—	—	19.1	77.3	16.7	89.2
1948	—	—	—	—	—	19.3	76.5	16.1	83.8
1949	—	—	—	—	—	19.8	76.6	17.4	84.6
1950	—	—	—	12.3	64.6	20.2	76.4	19.7	86.4
1951 [1]	—	—	—	13.6	63.6	21.1	73.6	18.2	80.7
1952 [1]	—	—	—	13.9	64.1	19.7	76.1	18.7	80.3
1953	—	—	—	13.9	63.9	19.9	77.5	19.3	82.0
1954	—	—	—	14.6	65.2	20.1	77.8	21.4	86.8
1955	—	—	—	15.1	67.9	22.7	82.2	22.4	88.4
1956	—	—	—	15.1	67.9	22.5	80.3	22.0	86.3
1957	—	—	—	15.2	67.3	22.5	82.5	21.3	85.8
1958	—	—	—	15.5	68.9	24.2	88.1	22.3	87.4
1959	—	—	—	16.1	71.1	25.1	89.7	23.6	89.0
1960	—	—	—	16.5	72.0	25.8	90.5	23.6	90.7
1961	—	—	—	16.9	73.1	26.7	91.4	25.4	92.5
1962	—	—	—	18.8	75.1	27.4	92.1	26.6	94.9
1963	—	—	—	20.2	75.6	27.9	92.5	27.3	95.8
1964	—	—	—	20.9	76.1	28.4	92.8	27.7	96.2
1965	—	—	—	22.2	75.3 [2]	28.6	92.7	27.8	96.2
1966	—	—	—	22.2	74.5 [2]	28.4	93.0	27.8	96.8
1967	—	—	—	23.1	75.2 [2]	28.5	93.0	28.0	97.6

[1] Selective government controls over maximum maturities and loan-to-value ratios were in effect for most of 1951 and 1952.

[2] Average loan-to-price for these years published by the Federal Home Loan Bank Board and are not strictly comparable with averages for earlier years.

Sources

Series Dc1192–1203. J. E. Morton, *Urban Mortgage Lending: Comparative Markets and Experience* (Princeton University Press, 1956), Appendix C.

Series Dc1204–1209. John P. Herzog and James S. Early, *Home Mortgage Delinquency and Foreclosure* (National Bureau of Economic Research, 1970), pp. 8–10.

Documentation

This table documents the rise of the long-term, low down payment, amortized home mortgage loan that became the staple of the American residential mortgage market in the twentieth century. There was broad recognition

(continued)

TABLE Dc1192–1209   Terms on nonfarm home mortgages, by type of mortgage and holder: 1920–1967   *Continued*

during the process that the home mortgage contract had been undergoing fundamental change since the 1920s, but by midcentury there was no systematic record of the process.

To remedy that situation, Morton (1956) designed and conducted a national survey of mortgage lending terms under the auspices of the Urban Real Estate Project of the National Bureau of Economic Research (NBER). Morton's study gathered information about contract terms on mortgages made on nonfarm, one- to four-family residential structures by the three most important groups of residential mortgage lenders – life insurance companies, commercial banks, and savings and loan associations. His survey requested information on 1 percent of the mortgage loans that each participating institution had issued or held over a three-decade period. Included in the survey were conventional, Federal Housing Administration (FHA)-insured (after 1938), and Veterans Administration (VA)-guaranteed (after 1944) mortgages. Responses were received from 24 of the 30 largest life insurance companies, from more than 300 commercial banks, and from nearly 200 savings and loan associations. See Appendix A of the Morton source for a complete description of the survey and an assessment of its potential biases.

This table summarizes four features of the mortgages that Morton captured in his survey. The first is the number of mortgage loans that survey participants reported having made for each year. These are shown in series Dc1192–1194. The number of loans for a given lending group and year

represents the sample size that was used to construct the average for the remaining mortgage characteristics – the average contract rate (not including additional fees and points), the average contact length (in years), and the average loan-to-value ratio.

The information on mortgage characteristics that Morton collected for the 1920–1947 period is supplemented in the table with information on average maturity and loan-to-value ratios for mortgages that were made during the post–World War II period. These series have been drawn from Herzog and Early's (1970) NBER-sponsored investigation of mortgage delinquency and foreclosure. They compiled these data from reports made by the Federal Housing Administration (for FHA-insured loans), from the Veterans Administration (for VA-guaranteed loans), and from the U.S. Savings and Loan League (for conventional mortgage loans made by savings and loan associations). Herzog and Early presented contract terms on mortgages written on both new and existing homes, but only the data for mortgages made on existing homes are shown here.

Series Dc1195–1203. Averages are weighted by the original amounts of the loans in the sample.

Series Dc1204–1205. The medians are estimated from the frequency distribution of the "most typical" maturities and loan-to-purchase-price ratios on mortgages reported each spring for a large sample of associations.

TABLE Dc1210–1254 Terms on conventional single-family residential mortgages, by type of property and mortgage: 1963–1999
Contributed by Kenneth A. Snowden

Monthly Interest Rate Survey (MIRS)

	All home mortgages									Mortgages on new homes					
	Contract interest rate	Rate charged for fees	Effective interest rate	Term to maturity	Loan amount	Home price	Loan-to-value ratio	Percentage with loan-to-value ratio greater than 80 percent	Percentage with adjustable rate	Contract interest rate	Rate charged for fees	Effective interest rate	Term to maturity	Loan amount	Home price
	Dc1210	Dc1211	Dc1212	Dc1213	Dc1214	Dc1215	Dc1216	Dc1217	Dc1218	Dc1219	Dc1220	Dc1221	Dc1222	Dc1223	Dc1224
Year	Percent	Percent	Percent	Years	Thousand dollars	Thousand dollars	Percent	Percent	Percent	Percent	Percent	Percent	Years	Thousand dollars	Thousand dollars
1963	5.90	0.62	6.00	21.3	14.8	20.6	71.7	—	—	5.80	0.58	5.89	24.1	16.9	23.1
1964	5.85	0.57	5.95	22.1	15.7	21.8	72.1	—	—	5.75	0.51	5.83	24.7	17.8	24.3
1965	5.83	0.53	5.92	22.6	16.4	22.5	73.0	—	—	5.74	0.49	5.81	25.0	18.5	25.1
1966	6.26	0.71	6.37	22.5	16.9	23.3	72.3	—	—	6.14	0.71	6.25	24.7	19.4	26.6
1967	6.38	0.77	6.50	23.1	18.3	25.1	72.9	—	—	6.33	0.81	6.46	25.2	20.6	28.0
1968	6.88	0.84	7.02	23.4	19.7	26.9	73.2	—	—	6.83	0.89	6.97	25.5	22.6	30.7
1969	7.67	0.89	7.82	23.5	21.5	29.9	71.9	—	—	7.66	0.91	7.81	25.5	24.9	34.1
1970	8.22	0.95	8.38	23.5	22.5	31.5	71.3	—	—	8.27	1.03	8.45	25.1	25.5	35.5
1971	7.56	0.80	7.69	24.7	24.2	32.8	74.0	—	—	7.59	0.87	7.74	26.2	27.0	36.3
1972	7.40	0.83	7.53	26.1	26.1	34.3	76.2	—	—	7.45	0.88	7.60	27.2	28.6	37.3
1973	7.80	1.01	7.97	24.0	24.6	33.7	74.8	37	—	7.78	1.12	7.96	26.2	27.9	37.0
1974	8.76	1.18	8.96	24.1	26.8	37.6	72.9	32	—	8.71	1.33	8.92	26.4	29.9	40.1
1975	8.92	1.28	9.13	24.9	29.7	41.2	73.7	33	—	8.75	1.53	9.00	27.0	33.4	44.7
1976	8.87	1.22	9.07	25.2	31.9	44.3	73.9	32	—	8.77	1.42	9.00	27.3	36.4	49.1
1977	8.82	1.22	9.02	26.3	36.3	49.6	75.0	32	—	8.80	1.32	9.02	27.9	40.5	54.4
1978	9.37	1.30	9.59	26.7	41.4	57.1	74.6	30	—	9.33	1.39	9.56	28.0	46.0	62.8
1979	10.59	1.50	10.85	27.4	48.2	67.7	73.5	26	—	10.49	1.66	10.78	28.5	53.3	74.4
1980	12.46	1.97	12.84	27.2	51.7	73.4	72.9	26	—	12.26	2.09	12.66	28.1	59.1	83.2
1981	14.39	2.39	14.91	26.4	53.7	76.3	73.1	32	—	14.13	2.66	14.70	27.7	65.2	90.3
1982	14.73	2.65	15.31	25.6	55.0	78.4	72.9	41	41	14.49	2.96	15.14	27.5	69.5	94.1
1983	12.26	2.39	12.73	26.0	59.9	83.1	74.5	40	40	12.11	2.39	12.57	26.7	70.6	93.9
1984	11.99	2.57	12.48	26.8	64.5	86.6	77.0	47	62	11.88	2.66	12.38	27.8	73.7	96.8
1985	11.17	2.51	11.64	25.9	70.2	96.1	75.8	40	51	11.09	2.52	11.55	27.0	78.2	105.0
1986	9.79	2.21	10.18	25.6	79.3	110.6	74.1	31	30	9.74	2.48	10.17	26.8	87.6	119.8
1987	8.95	2.08	9.30	26.8	89.1	121.8	75.2	31	43	8.94	2.26	9.31	27.8	100.6	137.2
1988	8.98	1.96	9.30	27.7	97.4	131.6	76.0	31	58	8.83	2.19	9.19	28.0	110.9	150.5
1989	9.81	1.87	10.13	27.7	104.5	142.8	74.8	27	38	9.77	2.08	10.13	28.1	117.4	160.1
1990	9.74	1.79	10.05	27.0	104.0	142.6	74.7	26	28	9.71	1.98	10.05	27.3	113.2	154.1
1991	9.07	1.58	9.34	26.5	106.3	146.7	74.4	27	23	9.03	1.72	9.32	26.8	114.2	155.2
1992	7.83	1.58	8.11	25.4	108.7	146.4	76.6	35	20	7.97	1.59	8.24	25.6	118.1	158.1
1993	6.93	1.20	7.13	25.5	107.0	143.1	77.2	37	20	7.00	1.29	7.20	26.1	123.2	163.7
1994	7.31	1.10	7.49	27.1	109.9	142.0	79.9	46	39	7.28	1.29	7.49	27.5	130.9	170.7
1995	7.69	0.97	7.85	27.4	110.4	142.8	79.9	45	32	7.67	1.20	7.87	27.7	134.3	175.4
1996	7.58	0.97	7.74	26.9	118.7	155.1	79.0	42	27	7.60	1.21	7.80	27.1	139.1	182.6
1997	7.52	0.98	7.68	27.5	126.6	164.5	79.4	42	22	7.55	1.01	7.71	28.2	141.2	181.4
1998	6.97	0.85	7.10	27.8	131.8	173.4	78.9	40	12	6.94	0.88	7.07	28.4	151.2	195.0
1999	7.14	0.74	7.25	28.2	139.3	184.2	78.5	38	21	6.93	0.76	7.04	28.8	161.8	210.7

(continued)

TABLE Dc1210–1254   Terms on conventional single-family residential mortgages, by type of property and mortgage: 1963–1999 *Continued*

Monthly Interest Rate Survey (MIRS)

	Mortgages on new homes			Mortgages on previously occupied homes									Fixed-rate home mortgages		
	Loan-to-value ratio	Percentage with loan-to-value ratio greater than 80 percent	Percentage with adjustable rate	Contract interest rate	Rate charged for fees	Effective interest rate	Term to maturity	Loan amount	Home price	Loan-to-value ratio	Percentage with loan-to-value ratio greater than 80 percent	Percentage with adjustable rate	Contract interest rate	Rate charged for fees	Effective interest rate
	Dc1225	Dc1226	Dc1227	Dc1228	Dc1229	Dc1230	Dc1231	Dc1232	Dc1233	Dc1234	Dc1235	Dc1236	Dc1237	Dc1238	Dc1239
Year	Percent	Percent	Percent	Percent	Percent	Percent	Years	Thousand dollars	Thousand dollars	Percent	Percent	Percent	Percent	Percent	Percent
1963	72.9	—	—	5.94	0.63	6.04	20.4	14.0	19.7	71.2	—	—	—	—	—
1964	73.3	—	—	5.89	0.59	5.99	21.3	15.0	20.9	71.7	—	—	—	—	—
1965	73.9	—	—	5.87	0.55	5.95	21.8	15.7	21.6	72.7	—	—	—	—	—
1966	73.0	—	—	6.30	0.72	6.41	21.7	16.0	22.2	72.0	—	—	—	—	—
1967	73.6	—	—	6.40	0.76	6.52	22.4	17.5	24.1	72.7	—	—	—	—	—
1968	73.9	—	—	6.90	0.83	7.03	22.7	18.7	25.6	73.0	—	—	—	—	—
1969	72.8	—	—	7.68	0.88	7.82	22.7	20.2	28.3	71.5	—	—	—	—	—
1970	71.7	—	—	8.20	0.92	8.36	22.8	21.3	30.0	71.1	—	—	—	—	—
1971	74.3	—	—	7.54	0.77	7.67	24.2	23.4	31.7	73.9	—	—	—	—	—
1972	76.8	—	—	7.38	0.81	7.51	25.7	25.4	33.4	76.0	—	—	—	—	—
1973	76.9	37	—	7.82	0.95	7.98	23.3	23.1	31.5	75.0	28	—	—	—	—
1974	75.9	32	—	8.78	1.10	8.97	23.3	25.0	35.5	72.4	20	—	—	—	—
1975	76.2	33	—	8.97	1.16	9.17	24.2	28.2	39.2	73.5	22	—	—	—	—
1976	75.7	32	—	8.90	1.14	9.10	24.6	30.2	42.0	73.8	23	—	—	—	—
1977	76.3	32	—	8.83	1.17	9.02	25.8	34.8	47.6	75.1	26	—	—	—	—
1978	75.2	30	—	9.40	1.26	9.61	26.4	39.6	54.5	75.0	28	—	—	—	—
1979	73.8	26	—	10.63	1.44	10.89	27.1	46.4	64.8	74.0	25	—	—	—	—
1980	73.2	26	—	12.53	1.91	12.90	26.9	48.4	68.3	73.5	26	—	—	—	—
1981	74.8	32	—	14.51	2.27	15.00	25.9	47.7	68.5	72.9	26	—	—	—	—
1982	76.6	41	41	14.78	2.55	15.33	24.9	48.7	70.7	71.9	27	39	—	—	—
1983	77.3	40	37	12.29	2.40	12.75	25.9	56.8	79.3	74.3	32	41	—	—	—
1984	78.6	47	59	12.00	2.54	12.49	26.5	60.9	82.2	76.8	39	64	—	—	—
1985	77.1	40	51	11.18	2.50	11.64	25.5	67.5	92.7	75.7	35	50	11.93	2.56	12.43
1986	75.3	31	27	9.80	2.13	10.18	25.4	77.4	108.5	73.9	27	31	10.09	2.31	10.50
1987	75.2	31	41	8.94	2.02	9.28	26.6	86.4	117.7	75.4	30	44	9.52	2.18	9.90
1988	75.6	31	19	9.01	1.88	9.32	27.7	94.3	126.6	76.4	32	24	10.04	2.07	10.41
1989	74.6	27	35	9.81	1.79	10.12	27.7	101.6	138.4	75.2	26	37	10.21	1.92	10.54
1990	74.9	27	31	9.75	1.74	10.05	27.0	102.5	140.3	74.9	26	27	10.06	1.87	10.39
1991	75.0	30	25	9.07	1.54	9.33	26.5	105.2	145.8	74.4	28	22	9.38	1.63	9.66
1992	76.6	39	17	7.81	1.58	8.08	25.4	106.9	144.1	76.5	35	21	8.21	1.61	8.50
1993	78.0	43	18	6.92	1.19	7.12	25.4	104.2	139.6	77.1	37	20	7.27	1.21	7.48
1994	78.7	45	41	7.31	1.07	7.49	27.1	105.9	136.4	80.1	46	39	7.98	1.14	8.17
1995	78.6	44	37	7.69	0.93	7.84	27.4	106.4	137.3	80.1	47	31	8.01	1.01	8.18
1996	78.1	42	26	7.57	0.93	7.73	26.8	115.1	150.2	79.1	42	27	7.81	1.03	7.98
1997	80.4	45	21	7.51	0.97	7.67	27.3	123.5	161.0	79.2	41	22	7.73	1.01	7.89
1998	80.1	43	17	6.97	0.84	7.10	27.7	128.4	169.5	78.7	40	12	7.05	0.86	7.19
1999	78.8	39	35	7.18	0.73	7.29	28.1	135.1	179.3	78.4	38	18	7.32	0.78	7.44

Monthly Interest Rate Survey (MIRS)

	Fixed-rate home mortgages						Adjustable-rate home mortgages				
	Term to maturity	Loan amount	Home price	Loan-to-value ratio	Contract interest rate	Rate charged for fees	Effective interest rate	Term to maturity	Loan amount	Home price	Loan-to-value ratio
Year	Dc1240	Dc1241	Dc1242	Dc1243	Dc1244	Dc1245	Dc1246	Dc1247	Dc1248	Dc1249	Dc1250
	Years	Thousand dollars	Thousand dollars	Percent	Percent	Percent	Percent	Years	Thousand dollars	Thousand dollars	Percent
1963	—	—	—	—	—	—	—	—	—	—	—
1964	—	—	—	—	—	—	—	—	—	—	—
1965	—	—	—	—	—	—	—	—	—	—	—
1966	—	—	—	—	—	—	—	—	—	—	—
1967	—	—	—	—	—	—	—	—	—	—	—
1968	—	—	—	—	—	—	—	—	—	—	—
1969	—	—	—	—	—	—	—	—	—	—	—
1970	—	—	—	—	—	—	—	—	—	—	—
1971	—	—	—	—	—	—	—	—	—	—	—
1972	—	—	—	—	—	—	—	—	—	—	—
1973	—	—	—	—	—	—	—	—	—	—	—
1974	—	—	—	—	—	—	—	—	—	—	—
1975	—	—	—	—	—	—	—	—	—	—	—
1976	—	—	—	—	—	—	—	—	—	—	—
1977	—	—	—	—	—	—	—	—	—	—	—
1978	—	—	—	—	—	—	—	—	—	—	—
1979	—	—	—	—	—	—	—	—	—	—	—
1980	—	—	—	—	—	—	—	—	—	—	—
1981	—	—	—	—	—	—	—	—	—	—	—
1982	—	—	—	—	—	—	—	—	—	—	—
1983	—	—	—	—	—	—	—	—	—	—	—
1984	—	—	—	—	—	—	—	—	—	—	—
1985	24.1	65.3	93.3	73.5	10.44	2.47	10.87	27.7	75.0	98.7	78.0
1986	24.9	75.5	107.7	73.2	9.10	1.97	9.42	27.3	88.0	117.7	76.1
1987	25.5	81.9	114.8	73.9	8.20	1.95	8.51	28.6	98.5	130.8	76.9
1988	26.0	82.8	117.3	73.7	8.21	1.88	8.51	28.9	107.9	141.7	77.7
1989	27.0	96.7	135.2	73.7	9.15	1.79	9.44	28.9	117.4	155.5	76.7
1990	26.1	97.4	136.1	73.9	8.90	1.56	9.15	29.3	122.3	160.4	77.1
1991	25.8	101.0	141.7	73.8	8.03	1.43	8.26	28.7	122.6	163.3	76.3
1992	24.4	104.4	141.4	76.5	6.37	1.44	6.59	29.1	125.3	165.9	76.7
1993	24.7	101.9	136.7	77.3	5.56	1.20	5.74	28.8	127.5	168.8	76.9
1994	25.8	96.1	125.3	79.7	6.27	1.05	6.42	29.2	131.3	167.7	80.1
1995	26.5	99.4	129.9	79.5	7.00	0.88	7.13	29.3	134.1	170.6	80.6
1996	26.1	107.2	141.6	78.6	6.94	0.81	7.06	29.0	150.5	192.1	79.9
1997	26.9	118.7	155.0	79.3	6.76	0.87	6.90	29.4	155.2	198.9	79.7
1998	27.5	124.9	164.3	79.0	6.35	0.75	6.46	29.6	180.7	237.4	78.2
1999	27.8	126.4	167.4	78.6	6.45	0.57	6.53	29.7	188.2	247.9	78.0

Primary Mortgage Market Survey (PMMS)

Year	Thirty-year fixed-rate mortgages		One-year adjustable-rate mortgages	
	Commitment rate	Points	Commitment rate	Points
	Dc1251	Dc1252	Dc1253	Dc1254
	Percent	Percent	Percent	Percent
1963	—	—	—	—
1964	—	—	—	—
1965	—	—	—	—
1966	—	—	—	—
1967	—	—	—	—
1968	—	—	—	—
1969	—	—	—	—
1970	—	—	—	—
1971	—	—	—	—
1972	7.38	0.9	—	—
1973	8.04	1.0	—	—
1974	9.19	1.2	—	—
1975	9.05	1.1	—	—
1976	8.87	1.2	—	—
1977	8.85	1.1	—	—
1978	9.64	1.3	—	—
1979	11.20	1.6	—	—
1980	13.74	1.8	—	—
1981	16.63	2.1	—	—
1982	16.04	2.2	—	—
1983	13.24	2.1	—	—
1984	13.88	2.5	11.51	2.5
1985	12.43	2.5	10.05	2.5
1986	10.19	2.2	8.43	2.3
1987	10.21	2.2	7.83	2.2
1988	10.34	2.1	7.90	2.3
1989	10.32	2.1	8.80	2.3
1990	10.13	2.1	8.36	2.1
1991	9.25	2.0	7.09	1.9
1992	8.39	1.7	5.62	1.7
1993	7.31	1.6	4.58	1.5
1994	8.38	1.8	5.36	1.5
1995	7.93	1.8	6.06	1.5
1996	7.81	1.7	5.67	1.4
1997	7.60	1.7	5.61	1.4
1998	6.94	1.1	5.58	1.1
1999	7.44	1.0	5.99	1.1

(continued)

Sources
Series Dc1210–1250. Federal Home Finance Board (FHFB), "Monthly Interest Rate Survey" (MIRS), available at the Internet site of the FHFB.

Series Dc1251–1254. Freddie Mac, "Primary Mortgage Market Summary" (PMMS), available at the Internet site of Freddie Mac (the Federal Home Loan Mortgage Corporation).

TABLE Dc1210–1254   Terms on conventional single-family residential mortgages, by type of property and mortgage: 1963–1999   Continued

Documentation

This table presents average contract terms for national samples of conventional, single-family home mortgage loans that have been compiled since 1963 in the Federal Home Finance Board's (FHFB) Monthly Interest Rate Survey (MIRS) and since 1971 by Freddie Mac in its Primary Mortgage Market Survey (PMMS). The MIRS is the nation's most comprehensive source of information on conventional mortgage rates and terms. PMMS results, on the other hand, are published extensively in the media and are routinely used by government agencies and private businesses. The thirty-year mortgage rate from PMMS, for example, is used by the Federal Reserve Board as its measure of the conventional mortgage rate in its list of selected interest rates (Statistical Release H.15).

The FHFB has been required by law to perform the MIRS since October 1989; before then the survey was conducted by the (now defunct) Federal Home Loan Bank Board. The information reported in MIRS is based on fully amortized mortgage loans that are used to purchase single-family, nonfarm homes. Excluded from the MIRS are loans used to refinance existing mortgages, nonamortized and balloon loans, and loans insured by the Federal Housing Administration (FHA) or guaranteed by the Veterans Administration (VA). FHFB notes in its documentation that the house prices reported in MIRS should not be interpreted as applying to all single-family homes because conventionally financed homes (which are covered) are generally priced higher than homes financed with FHA or VA mortgages (which are not).

The FHFB compiles MIRS data from a sample of major mortgage lenders that include savings and loan associations, savings banks, commercial banks, and mortgage companies; together these types of lenders have accounted for more than 90 percent of all conventional home mortgage loan originations since 1972. All of the MIRS series shown in the table (series Dc1210–1250) are weighted averages of the sample data; the weights reflect the relative volume of lending activity across the sampled lenders.

The table shows several average characteristics for each of the five broad loan types that are reported in the MIRS. Series Dc1210–1218 show average lending terms for all home mortgage loans in the survey. Series Dc1219–1236 provide the same information for loans that were written on newly built and previously occupied homes, respectively. Newly built homes are defined in MIRS as properties where construction has been completed and the dwelling units (including detached primary residences, condominium units, vacation, and second homes) have never been occupied; properties that had a

prior owner fall into the "previously occupied" category. The MIRS section of the table concludes with several series showing average lending terms on loans with fixed mortgage rates and, finally, adjustable rate mortgages. These last loan groups include loans on both newly built and previously occupied homes.

The total cost of borrowing associated with each of the five broad mortgage types is shown in the table as the effective interest rate series; these combine the separate contract interest rate and "charged for fees" series. The contract interest rate measured in MIRS is simply the initial interest rate paid by the borrower as specified in the loan contract for both fixed and adjustable rate mortgages. The "charged for fees" series captures additional costs that either the borrower or the seller of a home was required to pay to obtain the loan, including initial fees, charges, commissions, discounts, and "points." Excluded from the series are premiums paid for mortgage, credit, life, or property insurance; the costs associated with property transfer, title search, and title insurance; and the cost of private (that is, nongovernmental) mortgage insurance. "Charged for fees" is expressed in MIRS as a percentage of the loan amount; these charges are amortized over a ten-year period before being combined with the contract rate to form the effective interest rate series shown in the table.

Beyond the cost of borrowing, MIRS reports four other contractual terms for each type of loan – the average term to maturity (in years), mortgage loan amount, home purchase price, and loan-to-price ratio. The percentage of mortgages with adjustable rates and with loan-to-price ratios higher than 80 percent is also shown in the table for mortgages on all newly built and previously occupied homes.

While the MIRS survey is monthly, Freddie Mac has surveyed a national sample of lenders each week since 1971 to measure the interest rate and points that are currently being offered on thirty-year fixed-rate mortgage loans. The one-year adjustable rate mortgage and its points were added to PMMS in 1984, and the fifteen-year fixed-rate mortgage rate (not shown in this table) since 1991. Currently, 125 lenders are surveyed for PMMS each week and the mix of lender types – thrifts, commercial banks, and mortgage lending companies – is roughly proportional to the level of mortgage business that each type commands nationwide.

See the Internet site for the MIRS source for annual average and monthly contract terms by Federal Home Loan Bank District, state and metropolitan statistical area; historical monthly averages for all MIRS and PMMS series are available at their respective Internet sites.

TABLE Dc1255–1270 Mortgage foreclosures and delinquencies: 1926–1979

Contributed by Kenneth A. Snowden

	Nonfarm real estate				Nonfarm and farm foreclosures		FHA single-family home mortgages					VA single-family home mortgages				
	Foreclosures							In default		Foreclosures			In default		Foreclosures	
	Total	Index	Per 1,000 mortgaged structures	Mortgaged structures	Total	Per 1,000 mortgaged structures	In force	Total	Percentage	Total	Per 1,000 mortgages in force	In force	Total	Percentage	Total	Per 1,000 mortgages in force
	Dc1255	Dc1256	Dc1257	Dc1258	Dc1259	Dc1260	Dc1261	Dc1262	Dc1263	Dc1264	Dc1265	Dc1266	Dc1267	Dc1268	Dc1269	Dc1270
Year	Number	1939 = 100	Per 1,000	Thousand	Number	Per 1,000	Number	Number	Percent	Number	Per 1,000	Number	Number	Percent	Number	Per 1,000
1926	68,100	67.5	3.60	—	—	—	—	—	—	—	—	—	—	—	—	—
1927	91,000	90.1	4.80	—	—	—	—	—	—	—	—	—	—	—	—	—
1928	116,000	114.9	6.10	—	—	—	—	—	—	—	—	—	—	—	—	—
1929	134,900	133.6	7.10	—	—	—	—	—	—	—	—	—	—	—	—	—
1930	150,000	148.7	7.90	—	—	—	—	—	—	—	—	—	—	—	—	—
1931	193,800	192.0	10.20	—	—	—	—	—	—	—	—	—	—	—	—	—
1932	248,700	246.3	13.10	—	—	—	—	—	—	—	—	—	—	—	—	—
1933	252,400	250.0	13.30	—	—	—	—	—	—	—	—	—	—	—	—	—
1934	230,350	228.2	12.20	—	—	—	—	—	—	—	—	—	—	—	—	—
1935	228,713	226.5	12.10	—	—	—	—	—	—	—	—	—	—	—	—	—
1936	185,439	183.7	9.80	—	—	—	—	—	—	—	—	—	—	—	—	—
1937	151,366	149.9	8.00	—	—	—	—	—	—	—	—	—	—	—	—	—
1938	118,357	117.4	6.30	—	—	—	—	—	—	—	—	—	—	—	—	—
1939	100,410	100.0	5.30	—	—	—	437,472	8,617	1.97	—	—	—	—	—	—	—
1940	75,556	75.3	4.00	—	—	—	582,936	10,949	1.88	—	—	—	—	—	—	—
1941	58,559	58.5	3.40	—	—	—	755,480	9,405	1.24	—	—	—	—	—	—	—
1942	41,997	41.9	—	—	—	—	935,669	8,105	0.87	—	—	—	—	—	—	—
1943	25,281	25.5	—	—	—	—	1,022,877	7,301	0.71	—	—	—	—	—	—	—
1944	17,153	17.4	—	—	—	—	1,058,072	10,725	1.01	—	—	—	—	—	—	—
1945	12,706	14.3	—	—	—	—	1,037,030	10,500	1.01	—	—	—	—	—	—	—
1946	10,453	11.9	—	—	—	—	940,014	6,132	0.65	—	—	450,748	467	0.10	—	—
1947	10,559	10.5	—	—	—	—	911,905	4,443	0.49	—	—	971,807	8,460	0.87	—	—
1948	13,052	13.0	—	—	—	—	1,088,243	5,380	0.49	—	—	1,288,389	17,888	1.39	—	—
1949	17,635	17.6	—	—	—	—	1,302,203	12,461	0.96	—	—	1,526,689	31,826	2.08	—	—
1950	21,537	21.4	2.17	9,939	—	—	1,511,402	17,058	1.13	2,610	1.73	1,958,715	38,735	1.98	4,455	2.27
1951	18,141	—	1.67	10,888	—	—	1,654,276	18,007	1.09	1,523	0.92	2,323,892	39,639	1.71	2,603	1.12
1952	18,135	—	1.55	11,691	—	—	1,787,568	10,562	0.59	1,478	0.83	2,503,387	33,789	1.35	2,571	1.03
1953	21,473	—	1.70	12,633	—	—	1,925,485	10,778	0.56	1,132	0.59	2,723,006	28,541	1.05	2,458	0.90
1954	26,211	—	1.93	13,583	—	—	2,007,812	16,231	0.81	3,415	1.70	2,999,178	34,204	1.14	2,834	0.94
1955	28,529	—	1.94	14,715	—	—	2,140,936	14,988	0.70	4,021	1.88	3,441,453	33,346	0.97	3,719	1.08
1956	30,963	—	1.97	15,740	—	—	2,229,599	11,973	0.54	5,268	2.36	3,759,785	35,169	0.94	5,274	1.40
1957	34,204	—	2.08	16,477	—	—	2,310,367	10,333	0.45	3,405	1.47	3,906,536	38,189	0.98	6,706	1.72
1958	42,367	—	2.46	17,205	—	—	2,574,857	14,455	0.56	3,087	1.20	3,870,730	48,182	1.24	9,037	2.33
1959	44,075	—	2.44	18,043	—	—	2,873,788	16,969	0.59	5,223	1.82	3,859,235	44,775	1.16	10,643	2.76
1960	51,353	—	2.71	18,925	—	—	3,093,034	26,850	0.87	9,332	3.02	3,829,107	48,984	1.28	11,052	2.89
1961	73,074	—	3.70	19,754	—	—	3,297,421	40,713	1.23	20,718	6.28	3,766,481	55,217	1.47	16,060	4.26
1962	86,444	—	4.18	20,682	—	—	3,476,596	46,186	1.33	31,825	9.15	3,714,574	53,826	1.45	21,860	5.88
1963	98,195	—	4.52	21,703	—	—	3,643,981	51,551	1.41	37,863	10.39	3,658,980	56,702	1.55	23,155	6.33
1964	108,620	—	4.79	22,690	—	—	3,860,913	59,611	1.54	42,982	11.13	3,585,943	52,963	1.48	24,595	6.86

(continued)

	Nonfarm real estate				Nonfarm and farm foreclosures		FHA single-family home mortgages					VA single-family home mortgages				
	Foreclosures				Foreclosures		In force	In default		Foreclosures		In force	In default		Foreclosures	
	Total	Index	Per 1,000 mortgaged structures	Mortgaged structures	Total	Per 1,000 mortgaged structures		Total	Percentage	Total	Per 1,000 mortgages in force		Total	Percentage	Total	Per 1,000 mortgages in force
	Dc1255	Dc1256	Dc1257	Dc1258	Dc1259	Dc1260	Dc1261	Dc1262	Dc1263	Dc1264	Dc1265	Dc1266	Dc1267	Dc1268	Dc1269	Dc1270
Year	Number	1939 = 100	Per 1,000	Thousand	Number	Per 1,000	Number	Number	Percent	Number	Per 1,000	Number	Number	Percent	Number	Per 1,000
1965	116,664	—	4.93	23,647	—	—	4,090,458	64,018	1.57	46,624	11.40	3,508,558	53,590	1.53	23,195	6.61
1966	117,473	—	4.81	24,419	—	—	4,250,061	60,368	1.42	49,102	11.55	3,433,325	49,017	1.43	22,706	6.61
1967	110,541	—	4.38	25,237	134,203	5.05	4,401,885	63,184	1.44	42,198	9.59	3,452,000	—	—	18,670	5.41
1968	90,941	—	3.47	26,194	110,404	4.01	4,573,459	61,604	1.35	34,495	7.54	3,480,000	—	—	14,739	4.24
1969	—	—	—	—	95,856	3.37	4,792,523	70,832	1.48	27,541	5.75	3,537,000	—	—	11,152	3.15
1970	—	—	—	—	101,070	3.44	5,067,933	93,005	1.84	30,403	6.00	3,570,000	—	—	10,444	2.93
1971	—	—	—	—	116,704	4.62	5,339,974	120,818	2.26	41,062	7.69	3,666,000	—	—	10,493	2.86
1972	—	—	—	—	132,335	5.07	5,396,288	148,614	2.75	51,299	9.51	3,800,000	—	—	12,257	3.23
1973	—	—	—	—	135,803	5.12	5,194,953	134,086	2.58	60,515	11.65	3,695,000	—	—	15,741	4.26
1974	—	—	—	—	140,496	5.21	5,060,474	121,676	2.40	57,941	11.45	3,808,000	—	—	14,891	3.91
1975	—	—	—	—	142,803	5.19	4,983,297	110,826	2.22	46,739	9.38	3,891,000	—	—	15,566	4.00
1976	—	—	—	—	—	—	4,894,170	58,587	1.20	31,082	6.35	3,906,000	—	—	15,117	3.87
1977	—	—	—	—	—	—	4,798,302	54,651	1.14	27,897	5.81	3,955,000	—	—	14,639	3.70
1978	—	—	—	—	—	—	4,673,113	53,544	1.15	24,244	5.19	3,965,000	—	—	13,426	3.39
1979	—	—	—	—	—	—	4,757,789	51,637	1.09	18,941	3.98	4,028,000	—	—	11,673	2.90

Source

Series Dc1255–1258. 1926–1946: Housing and Home Finance Agency, *Housing Statistics Handbook* (1948), p. 150. 1947–1949: Housing and Home Finance Agency, *Housing in the Economy 1955*, p. 39. 1950–1968: U.S. Department of Housing and Urban Development (HUD), *Statistical Yearbook* (various years).

Series Dc1259–1260. 1967–1970: HUD, *Statistical Yearbook 1970*, p. 322. 1971–1975: Federal Home Loan Bank Board, *FHLBB Journal* (November 1976), p. 43.

Series Dc1261–1270. 1939–1944: Housing and Home Finance Agency, *Housing in the Economy 1955*, p. 40. 1945–1966: HUD, *Statistical Yearbook 1966*, p. 47–8. 1967–1979: HUD, *Statistical Yearbook 1979*, pp. 113, 294.

Documentation

The series in this table represent the earliest available measures of national trends in nonfarm mortgage delinquency and foreclosure. The broadest, and oldest, of these measures is the annual series of nonfarm foreclosures that was maintained by the Federal Home Loan Bank Board (FHLBB) from 1932 to 1975. Through 1968 the series was estimated based on reports from between 1,500 and 1,700 counties, cities, townships, or other governmental divisions; by 1968 these reporting areas contained between three fifths and two thirds of all nonfarm housing units. Foreclosures in remaining areas of the country were estimated based on the foreclosure experience in the closest reporting area.

Series Dc1255–1258. The basic series represents the estimated number of nonfarm properties, residential and nonresidential, that had been acquired during the year through completed foreclosure proceedings (series Dc1255); it does not include voluntary transfers to lenders in lieu of foreclosure, or defaults on real estate contracts. Before 1950, the FHLBB's foreclosure series was sometimes expressed as an index number; the index appears here as series Dc1256. Beginning in 1950, the FHLBB expressed

the series as a foreclosure rate (series Dc1257) by comparing it to annual estimates of the total number of nonfarm mortgaged structures (series Dc1258).

Series Dc1259–1260. The foreclosure series was redesigned in 1967 to include Alaska and Hawai'i and to measure farm as well as nonfarm foreclosures. The FHLBB noted that changes in the benchmark for the new series, as well as some technical problems, had led to significant understatements in the original series, which was discontinued (series Dc1255). The new series was published by FHLBB until 1975, when it was also discontinued.

Series Dc1261–1270. The Federal Housing Administration and Veterans Administration are liable for losses that lenders incur on mortgages that they have either insured or guaranteed. These agencies, therefore, systematically report the numbers of loans covered by FHA mortgage insurance and the VA loan guaranty programs, the number of these loans that have gone into default, and the number of affected properties that have been acquired by foreclosure. These data are shown for the single-family home mortgage programs for both of these agencies. FHA and VA loans represented up to one third of all single-family mortgage originations during the post–World War II decades and were issued in all areas of the nation. The users of these data should note, however, that both programs were designed to assist particular classes of borrowers and types of housing, which had different, and generally higher, rates of delinquency and foreclosure than conventionally financed, single-family mortgages.

Series Dc1262 and Dc1267. A loan reported in default was classified as remaining in default until delinquency was completely cured or until the claim was paid. Lenders were required to report a default to the FHA within ninety days of the missed due date; the VA required a report within ninety days of the missed due date or on initiation of foreclosure action if that occurred earlier.

Series Dc1264. Includes foreclosed properties held by mortgagees pending redemption period or final redemption.

Series Dc1269. Based on number of claims paid.

TABLE Dc1271–1288   Delinquency and foreclosure rates for single-family home mortgages: 1979–1999

Contributed by Kenneth A. Snowden

	Percentage of home mortgages delinquent								
	Total			30–59 days past due			60–89 days past due		
	Conventional	VA-guaranteed	FHA-insured	Conventional	VA-guaranteed	FHA-insured	Conventional	VA-guaranteed	FHA-insured
	Dc1271	Dc1272	Dc1273	Dc1274	Dc1275	Dc1276	Dc1277	Dc1278	Dc1279
Year	Percent	Percent	Percent	Percent	Percent	Percent	Percent	Percent	Percent
1979	2.79	4.83	6.22	2.11	3.42	4.57	0.43	0.85	0.99
1980	3.09	5.34	6.55	2.28	3.69	4.69	0.51	0.97	1.09
1981	3.27	5.67	6.80	2.38	3.95	4.82	0.55	0.97	1.13
1982	3.71	5.96	7.06	2.58	4.06	4.88	0.64	1.03	1.19
1983	3.88	6.09	7.06	2.65	4.12	4.86	0.66	1.02	1.16
1984	3.86	6.40	7.29	2.62	4.33	4.98	0.66	1.03	1.17
1985	4.05	6.63	7.44	2.78	4.37	5.02	0.66	1.12	1.22
1986	3.79	6.57	7.15	2.52	4.22	4.67	0.61	1.11	1.19
1987	3.15	6.22	6.57	2.06	4.01	4.31	0.49	1.04	1.06
1988	2.94	6.23	6.56	1.98	4.07	4.35	0.43	1.02	1.07
1989	3.06	6.43	6.69	2.15	4.30	4.52	0.44	1.06	1.10
1990	3.00	6.36	6.69	2.16	4.28	4.52	0.45	1.04	1.08
1991	3.25	6.77	7.30	2.29	4.52	4.88	0.51	1.14	1.18
1992	2.94	6.45	7.06	2.02	4.25	4.62	0.45	1.06	1.10
1993	2.65	6.29	7.14	1.81	4.13	4.66	0.40	1.01	1.08
1994	2.61	6.26	7.26	1.75	4.06	4.70	0.40	1.02	1.12
1995	2.78	6.45	7.58	1.94	4.23	4.94	0.42	1.06	1.17
1996	2.78	6.74	8.05	2.05	4.52	5.36	0.42	1.13	1.29
1997	2.82	6.93	8.13	2.08	4.59	5.53	0.43	1.19	1.37
1998	2.87	7.10	8.48	2.13	4.61	5.64	0.43	1.22	1.46
1999	2.52	6.80	8.58	1.90	4.41	5.62	0.36	1.15	1.46

	Percentage of home mortgages delinquent			Percentage of home mortgages upon which foreclosure started during year			Percentage of home mortgages in foreclosure at year end		
	90 or more days past due								
	Conventional	VA-guaranteed	FHA-insured	Conventional	FHA-insured	VA-guaranteed	Conventional	FHA-insured	VA-guaranteed
	Dc1280	Dc1281	Dc1282	Dc1283	Dc1284	Dc1285	Dc1286	Dc1287	Dc1288
Year	Percent	Percent	Percent	Percent	Percent	Percent	Percent	Percent	Percent
1979	0.25	0.56	0.65	0.07	0.18	0.20	0.10	0.38	0.44
1980	0.30	0.68	0.77	0.08	0.18	0.19	0.17	0.46	0.53
1981	0.34	0.75	0.85	0.10	0.18	0.21	0.24	0.55	0.57
1982	0.49	0.87	0.99	0.13	0.23	0.27	0.39	0.76	0.88
1983	0.58	0.94	1.05	0.16	0.24	0.26	0.46	0.76	0.84
1984	0.59	1.04	1.14	0.16	0.24	0.26	0.47	0.82	0.98
1985	0.61	1.14	1.20	0.17	0.26	0.28	0.61	0.88	1.01
1986	0.67	1.24	1.29	0.19	0.29	0.31	0.69	1.14	1.22
1987	0.61	1.17	1.19	0.18	0.32	0.34	0.67	1.28	1.44
1988	0.54	1.14	1.14	0.17	0.32	0.37	0.56	1.25	1.40
1989	0.48	1.07	1.08	0.21	0.42	0.46	0.59	1.30	1.42
1990	0.39	1.04	1.10	0.21	0.41	0.43	0.65	1.24	1.31
1991	0.46	1.11	1.25	0.27	0.42	0.43	0.79	1.32	1.36
1992	0.47	1.15	1.35	0.26	0.41	0.45	0.78	1.30	1.42
1993	0.45	1.16	1.40	0.24	0.42	0.48	0.72	1.34	1.43
1994	0.45	1.18	1.44	0.23	0.48	0.56	0.61	1.25	1.38
1995	0.43	1.17	1.47	0.23	0.50	0.53	0.66	1.27	1.33
1996	0.32	1.10	1.40	0.25	0.46	0.58	0.71	1.62	1.78
1997	0.32	1.15	1.24	0.26	0.51	0.62	0.76	1.75	2.05
1998	0.32	1.27	1.39	0.26	0.52	0.65	0.71	1.88	2.35
1999	0.27	1.24	1.50	0.22	0.44	0.59	0.63	1.71	2.01

Source

Mortgage Bankers Association of America, *National Delinquency Survey*, published quarterly. Data for this table were received electronically from the Mortgage Bankers Association on June 4, 2001.

Documentation

The National Delinquency Survey has been conducted since 1953 and currently covers more than 32 million loans on one- to four-unit residential properties or about one half of all "first-lien" residential mortgage loans outstanding in the United States. Data for earlier years are available on request. Loan status is currently reported by approximately 130 lenders, including mortgage bankers, commercial banks, thrifts, and life insurance companies.

Note that annual averages are from seasonally unadjusted data.

Series Dc1271–1282. A mortgage becomes delinquent when a scheduled installment payment is late by thirty days or more. The table first shows the overall percentage of each loan type that is delinquent and then decomposes

(continued)

TABLE Dc1271–1288   Delinquency and foreclosure rates for single-family home mortgages: 1979–1999   *Continued*

each total into loans that are 30–59 days past due, 60–89 days past due, and 90 or more days past due. None of these categories include loans that are in foreclosure. Components may not sum to totals due to rounding.

Series Dc1283–1285. Include loans that were placed in the process of foreclosure during the year. This category also includes deeds in lieu of foreclosure

and loans assigned to the Federal Housing Administrator, the Department of Veterans Affairs, or other insurers or investors.

Series Dc1286–1288. Indicate the percentage of loans of each type that remain in foreclosure at the end of each year.

CHAPTER Dd

Manufacturing

Editors: Jeremy Atack and Fred Bateman

MANUFACTURING

Jeremy Atack and Fred Bateman

Manufacturing is an economic activity that combines human effort (labor) with physical plant and equipment (capital) to transform raw materials into products that are neither available in nature nor resemble the various materials from which they were fabricated. At its most rudimentary level, this may require human skill and effort using only hand tools, and when this is so, it is referred to as craft or artisan production. At its most advanced and sophisticated level, manufacturing integrates a complex set of human skills (including managerial and entrepreneurial abilities) with automated techniques. Thus, although "manufacturing" literally refers to manual fabrication of goods, today's industrial production extends far beyond that original definition. We may generalize as follows.

Manufacturing differs from agriculture because its *process* is not essentially biological. It is distinguished from services in that the *product* is tangible. Certainly there are numerous exceptions to these general rules – the manufacture of cheese or butter, for example, or the manufacture of many industrial gases – but they suffice for the majority of cases.

Some manufactured products, classified as "consumer goods," are used by buyers in the form in which they leave the factory. Certain of these – those with life expectancies longer than three years – are called "durable goods." These include products such as automobiles, computers, and refrigerators. Others are considered consumer "nondurable" goods – products such as a loaf of bread or a pair of shoes. Still other products are manufactured not for immediate use by consumers but rather are created as inputs or components for other goods. These "intermediate" goods – steel, glass, or plastic parts, for example, may be used to produce an automobile. Finally, some manufactured output, referred to as "capital goods" or "producers' goods," provides machines and equipment for use in creating consumer goods or intermediate products. The pace and pattern of manufacturing development, the innovation and adoption of specific technologies, shifts in organizational structure, and the impact of manufactures on the growth and development of the American economy have all been subjects of extensive scholarly literature over the years. Key historical documents include works by Coxe (1814), Bishop (1861), Depew (1895), and Clark (1916–1928). Key works of modern synthesis are Porter (1973),

Chandler (1977), Cochran (1977), Bruchey (1990), and McGaw (1994).

Early Manufacturing

In his celebrated book *The Wealth of Nations*, the economist Adam Smith asserted that "the most opulent nations, indeed, excel all their neighbors in agriculture, as well as in manufacturing, but they are eminently more distinguished by their superiority in the latter than in the former." The United States' founders held divergent opinions on this issue. Alexander Hamilton, for example, tended to agree with Smith that a truly "developed" economy should have sectoral diversity that included manufacturing as well as agriculture. Indeed, he viewed manufacturing as the key to high levels of per capita income. Thomas Jefferson disagreed. He wrote, "Let the factories remain in Europe," distant from the rural, agricultural arcadia that he favored for the new nation. Jefferson's agrarian vision initially seemed compelling. Rich in land and other natural resources, and attractive to immigrants who had been farmers in their native lands or aspired to be, the early United States appeared destined to become and remain an agricultural nation, a consumer rather than producer of manufactures. Cultural and political attitudes fostering family farming as "a way of life" reinforced this economic tendency – what economists call "comparative advantage."

It was not that colonial America totally lacked industry. Shipbuilders on the New England shore thrived, converting lumber and other natural materials into ships sold abroad. Flour and lumber mills were present along the Eastern seaboard and supplied domestic and foreign markets. Craft shops making silverware, shoes, decorative objects, and other items could be found in cities such as Boston or New York. Itinerant craftspeople wandered the rural countryside selling pots, pans, and similar basic items. But the most ubiquitous industrial form was household manufacturing – individuals producing, literally manufacturing, their own clothing, furniture, soap, and other necessities of colonial life for use by and within the family. Farmers occupied themselves and their families in such manufacturing activities until well into the national period during their off-season, which, in the colder northern latitudes, could be lengthy. For quantitative evidence on the extent of this home manufacture, see Tables Ba4999–5081.

Between the American Revolution and the Civil War, however, industrial stirrings became increasingly more pronounced. An early impetus was provided by the interruption of trade that cut off Americans from access to English goods during the American Revolution and again during the Jeffersonian Embargo and the War of 1812. As a result, the new nation began to experiment with domestic manufacturing, often within households, but increasingly

Acknowledgments

Jeremy Atack and Fred Bateman thank their editors for helpful comments and suggestions.

for market sale by dedicated artisan shops, manufactories, mills, and factories. The textile mill of Almy and Brown established in 1790 in Pawtucket, Rhode Island, which pioneered the use of British textile machinery introduced by Samuel Slater, is one example. Indeed, after the Embargo of 1807 threatened to deprive the nation of much-needed manufactures, the House of Representatives passed a resolution requesting that Treasury Secretary Albert Gallatin report on how best to foster domestic industry. Gallatin protested that he did not have the resources to comply but noted that the Third Census would afford an ideal opportunity to collect the necessary information. Congress agreed and amended the act for the Third Census on May 1, 1810 – just three months before it was to be conducted – requiring that the enumerators render an accounting of the manufacturing establishments and their production in their districts according to whatever instructions the Secretary of the Treasury might give. Unfortunately, Gallatin gave them little direction about how this should be done, or even what questions should be asked. Enumerators, nevertheless, tried to discharge their duties to the best of their individual abilities, and the task of making sense of the resulting imperfect data fell to Tench Coxe (Coxe 1814). Despite the obvious inconsistencies in the underlying data, Coxe's efforts to present and interpret them have been praised by subsequent generations.

Perhaps a more far-reaching venture than Almy and Brown's was the establishment by Francis Cabot Lowell of the Boston Manufacturing Company – the first integrated spinning and weaving cotton mill – in Waltham, Massachusetts, in 1813. After the War of 1812, manufacturing at first faltered, but by the 1830s it had recovered, and by 1860 most settled areas had some manufacturing producers. The ups and downs of manufacturing initiatives during the period are nicely illustrated by data on new business incorporations in manufacturing, as shown in Table Ch330–379. The positive effects of the Embargo and War of 1812, the devastating effect of increased imports of cheap foreign manufactured goods following the peace, and the subsequent recovery and development of industry are all evident. Lebergott estimates that fully 14 percent of the labor force was engaged in manufacturing by the end of the antebellum period (Figure Dd-A).

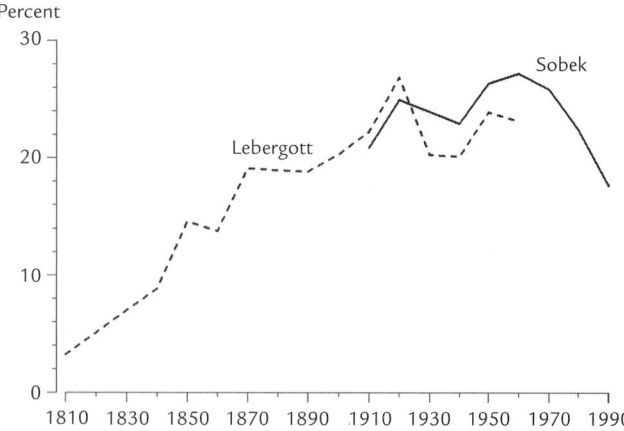

FIGURE Dd-A   Manufacturing as a percentage of total employment: 1810–1990

Sources

1810–1960: series Ba821 as a percentage of series Ba814. 1910–1990: the sum of series Ba657–658 as a percentage of series Ba652.

Although the older areas of the Northeast were home to some large (even by today's standards) cotton textile plants and ironworks, most manufacturing operations of the period were small businesses that served nearby local markets where they faced little competition. Few produced more than a limited range of products, and fewer still operated more than one plant, especially in separate locations. In the slaveowning South, however, even this rudimentary manufacturing was often absent (Bateman and Weiss 1981).

At the middle of the nineteenth century, most manufactured output originated in just five industries: flour and grist milling, lumber milling, textiles, iron and steel, and leather. All of these industries involved the processing of raw materials, which were relatively abundant in the American environment of the late eighteenth and early nineteenth centuries. It is also interesting that all of these industries were dramatically reduced over the subsequent century or were reclassified out of manufacturing. Measured in terms of tons per capita, flour and grist milling peaked about 1890 (series Aa7 and Dd368). The second largest industry at that time, lumber milling, is no longer classified as manufacturing, nor is blacksmithing, which in the antebellum period produced many of the nation's agricultural implements, wagons, and carriages as well as shoeing its horses. Details of the evolution of American manufacturing by industry group can be seen in Tables Dd366–436 and Dd561–625.

At the forefront of industrial innovation were factories – manufacturing establishments powered by inanimate sources – which were well established outside of the textile industry from New England west to Indiana by 1850. Some produced items such as clocks and guns, using interchangeable components to produce standardized products in what became known as the "American System" (Hounshell 1986). Despite the productivity gains from this method of manufacture, however, most manufactured goods produced in the antebellum period still originated in small local artisan shops or mills (Sokoloff 1984; Atack 1987).

The first comprehensive Census of Manufacturing was conducted in 1850. It revealed the aggregate value of industrial production was about one billion dollars, considerably below that of farming. At the time, there were almost 1.5 million individual farms, but only 123,000 industrial establishments employing slightly fewer than one million workers from a total national population of 23.2 million and a labor force of perhaps 8.25 million. Just three states – Massachusetts, New York, and Pennsylvania – accounted for 53 percent of all manufacturing capital and 54 percent of national manufactured output.

Power used to manufacture goods remained predominantly traditional until after the Civil War. Small shops and mills initially relied on human or animal power to convert raw materials from farms or mines into finished goods. Even larger, older, and more advanced enterprises in New England utilized the most ancient form of inanimate motive power, water, albeit using increasingly efficient and powerful water turbines in place of the traditional waterwheel. From the standpoint of locational choice, the availability of exploitable water power provides a major explanation for the earliest emergence of factories in that region, where natural waterfalls and waterways were abundant. Steam power was used only rarely until cheap coal could be shipped from Pennsylvania and Virginia (Hunter 1979; Atack, Bateman, and Weiss 1980).

Technology was equally simple and traditional. Hand tools continued to be used in shops as they had for centuries. Moreover, even where technology had become more complex – among Eastern textile producers, for example – it remained based on machines made of wood and employed belts made of leather, both abundant products closely related to the country's natural resource base.[1]

Manufacturing after the Civil War

During the Civil War, the industrial sector remained small outside of the Northeast. The war did not rely heavily on complex technology, so even the relatively unindustrialized Southern states could survive militarily for several years. Still, more basic issues such as clothing and feeding a large army created challenges. Overall, however, there is relatively little evidence that the war significantly stimulated or accelerated industrial change (Engerman 1966).

After the war, however, the nation embarked on its "Golden Age of Manufacturing." Virtually no segment of the American economy was left untouched. Steel produced in increasingly large Bessemer blast furnaces concentrated in just a few locations displaced iron made in small furnaces throughout the countryside. The confluence of the railroad, which began to create a national market, new technologies based on steel, and an expanded use of the corporate form led the nation into "the age of big business." A measure of the rising importance of steel production is displayed in Figure Dd-B, which graphs raw steel production per capita. Over the three decades beginning in 1870, this measure rose by more than a factor of 75. Other big business–related industries – tobacco, food processors and meat packers, chemical firms, and oil refiners – grew apace. Overall, manufacturing value added, in real terms, grew 660 percent between 1870 and 1900 (see Table Dd1–12).

The "modern business enterprise," as historian Alfred D. Chandler refers to it, lay at the center of this industrial transformation as manufacturing became large-scale, corporate, and national (Chandler 1977). Energy intensity also increased dramatically as manufacturers used higher pressures and temperatures in conjunction with mechanical conveyances to accelerate production. The first data quantifying the importance of the corporate form in manufacturing became available in 1899 and 1904. Even at these early dates, already 65 percent of manufacturing value added and 70.6 percent of manufacturing employees, respectively, were associated with manufacturing establishments owned by corporations, although they represented only a small fraction of the nation's manufacturing firms (see Table Dd903–904). The merger movement of the 1890s created many highly concentrated industries (Lamoreaux 1985). One measure of industrial concentration, or monopoly power, is the percentage of value added created by the four largest firms in an industry. For manufacturing in 1901, this figure stood at 32.4 percent, with individual industries ranging from a high of 100 percent in rubber to a low of only 0.5 percent in lumber and timber products (see Table Dd895–902).

Technological change also exerted more influence, as the prewar factory system blended into the corporate organization to serve a huge American market. Manufacturing output began to expand drastically, and the nation left behind its former agriculturally dominated economy and its small-scale, locally oriented industrial sector. The decade of the 1870s saw the United States abandon its old manufacturing forms to embark on becoming the world's industrial leader. This industrialization brought mass production to the mass

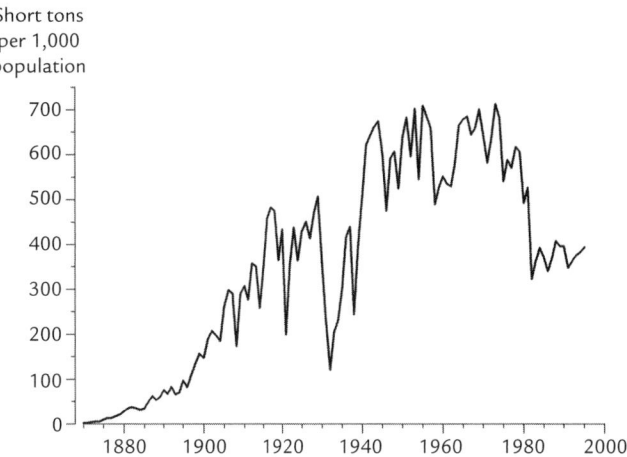

Short tons per 1,000 population

FIGURE Dd-B   Raw steel output per 1,000 population: 1870–1995

Sources
Series Aa7 and Dd399.

market. Even the "populist revolt" that occurred during the last third of the nineteenth century could not stop this transformation.[2] Industrialization nevertheless brought with it new problems such as pollution and exacerbated the social evils and extent of unemployment.

Manufacturing at the Turn of the Twentieth Century

The industrial transformation was swift: the modest manufacturing sector of 1850 had evolved into a complex multiplant, multiproduct producer of manufactured goods by 1900. Factories using new types of machinery and new power sources – steam and centrally generated electricity – were mass producing a wide variety of products in an industrial belt extending from southern New England to the Great Lakes (Hounshell 1986; Hunter and Bryant 1991). Chicago and nearby Gary, Indiana, where America's newly created largest industrial corporation, U.S. Steel, was headquartered, became the Western metropolis for this new industrial age (Meyer 1989). Even agriculture industrialized rapidly, adopting mechanical farm implements produced by Midwestern manufacturers and becoming increasingly reliant on the manufacture of chemical fertilizers (Atack and Bateman 1987). The resultant rise in agricultural labor productivity – output per labor hour – permitted more people to work in manufacturing without any diminution in the nation's food supply.

America had become the land of big business, an industrial economy comprising huge corporations mass producing standardized products for a national market. No product better symbolized this system's success than the automobile, a product that epitomized the nexus of mass production, consumer goods, and corporate organization. When Henry Ford adopted assembly-line techniques for producing a low-priced product, he brought together elements of the manufacturing sector that had individually evolved over the previous century. His product transformed American society profoundly. By 1929, the auto industry was the nation's largest

---

[1] For a detailed and highly readable account of manufacturing during the antebellum era, see Bruchey (1990), Chapter 5, pp. 137–64.

[2] For an influential and authoritative account of organizational change during this period, see Chandler (1977). See Lamoreaux (1985) on the merger movement of the 1890s.

industry (Davis 1988). Many scholars consider the automobile the single most influential manufactured product of the twentieth century (see Cochran 1957; Flink 1970).

The Great Depression of the 1930s caused a massive setback to the nation's industrial economy. Manufacturing production shrank dramatically, particularly for consumer durables such as the automobile and consequently for inputs used in its production such as steel. As industrial production declined, unemployment reached 25 percent of the national workforce. The Depression engulfed virtually every economic activity and was perceived as a massive failure of the nation's industrial system. Employment and output in manufacturing declined more than in other sectors of the economy. Particularly hard hit was the manufacture of consumer durables as households postponed their purchases of items such as automobiles, refrigerators, and other household appliances.

The nation's factories and its experienced labor force were still there, of course, and they were fully reemployed (and expanded) during World War II, a military conflict that relied heavily on industrial capacity. During the war, the manufacturing system attained new heights in output and productivity. Interchangeable parts, standard design, and the techniques of conveying products in assembly from work station to work station converted shipbuilding from a craft to a factory process with the production of more than 2,500 "Liberty" ships by shipyards that could turn out one ship in as little as 5 days (the *Robert E. Peary*) and where productivity grew at an average annual rate of 40 percent for three years (Thornton and Thompson 2001). Table Dd494–497 displays several indices of industrial production, all of which clearly show the dramatic decline during the Great Depression and its recovery and growth during World War II. Among the notable changes during this military conflict was the widespread employment of women workers in industries, such as shipbuilding, where none had been employed previously (Hartmann 1982, Chapter 5).

America emerged from World War II as the world's strongest economy and the leading producer of manufactured goods. In the early postwar era, products previously unknown or greatly improved burst onto the American market. From kitchen appliances to television receivers, new and attractive manufactured products appeared on the scene, most reliant on the spread of electricity to the home and a new spirit of optimism among increasingly wealthy consumers. After some twenty years of austerity and with large savings accounts created by overtime war-related work, pent-up demand increased the demand for manufactured products. Automobile production resumed its pre-Depression trend, as Americans replaced their aging cars, and as two-car household ownership became common. Manufacturers continued to serve the national consumer market virtually nonstop through the 1960s. The indexes of industrial production in Table Dd494–497 show the strength of this rapid and long-lasting expansion.

The 1970s marked a turning point for U.S. manufacturing. In particular, sharply higher oil prices rendered much of the nation's technology, which had evolved during decades of abundant and therefore low-priced energy, economically inefficient. Postwar industrial growth and the technology that lay behind it relied on a continuous flow of inexpensive energy, particularly that provided by petroleum. What economists term the "oil shock" broke that continuity, raised many industrial prices, and fundamentally altered the "rules of the game" for manufacturing. The remarkable rise in fuel oil prices in the 1970s is shown in series Cc25.

Prompted by the rise in gasoline prices, American consumers shifted their automobile purchases away from American-produced "gas guzzlers" toward the fuel-efficient cars produced by European and Japanese automakers. The effect on the economy was profound, as about 5 percent of the economy depended directly or indirectly on the auto industry.[3] At the same time, American manufacturers found themselves forced to deal with new environmental regulations. Traditional "smokestack" industries, epitomized by automobiles and steel, were particular targets. Manufacturing eventually began responding to the changed competitive environment and was reborn. "Downsizing" was among the first visible signs, as companies reduced their labor forces and substituted machines for people. No single new technology was more important in this transition than the computer. Automated factories, robotics, "just-in-time" inventory, and a host of other computer hardware and software innovations changed the way manufacturers operated and helped restore their competitiveness during the final two decades of the twentieth century. Both blue-collar and white-collar labor productivity grew as a consequence of new technologies and business reorganization. Better information systems, for example, reduced inventories and goods in process, and marketing was better able to identify and meet localized demand. By the turn of the century, American manufacturing had once again been transformed to meet new market realities.

Some observers viewed downsizing with alarm, suggesting that the United States was losing its industrial base. In terms of sheer numbers on the payroll, manufacturing employment peaked in the late 1970s. Since then, about 2.5 million jobs have disappeared in manufacturing, and numbers on the payroll have declined almost 15 percent (see series Dd661 or series Ba843). In terms of relative employment share, manufacturing peaked during World War II, when it employed about 40 percent of the nonagricultural workers, compared with less than 15 percent today. On the other hand, industrial production has generally risen (despite periodic downturns) and is now about 75 percent higher than it was at its employment peak in the late 1970s – evidence of rapid productivity growth in the manufacturing sector (see, for example, series Dd498). Nonetheless, despite this growth in manufacturing output and the sharp gains in productivity, other sectors have grown even more rapidly. As a result, the United States is relatively less industrial than it once was, and the manufacturing share of gross domestic product (GDP) has fallen from about 30 percent during the early 1950s to about 16 percent today.

The industrial product mix has also changed over the years, from the earliest days when small local manufacturers provided simple goods to predominantly rural buyers to the era of globally mass-produced consumer goods epitomized by the automobile to more recent production of consumer electronics and computers. In the 1950s, "Made in America" on a well-known brand meant just that: made in America. More recently, a purchaser might find that the "domestic content" – that portion of the product actually manufactured in the United States – might well be much less than 100 percent. An American brand of computer, with American-designed components manufactured into subassemblies in countries throughout South America, Africa, and Asia but assembled in the United States and controlled by an American-designed and

---

[3] See, for example, the Internet site of the Center for Automotive Research at the University of Michigan.

American-produced central processing unit, is an exemplar of the trend. Increasingly, manufactured goods have become multinational both in production and sales. Although many of the highest value-added activities remain on U.S. shores, less rewarding (or more polluting) activities are increasingly performed elsewhere.

Manufacturing Statistics and Sources

For the nineteenth century, the primary source of data on U.S. manufacturing comes from censuses (Fishbein 1973). In 1810, 1820, 1840, and every ten years thereafter, the Census of Manufactures was taken as a part of the decennial Census of Population required by the U.S. Constitution. The 1810–1840 Censuses had problems in geographic coverage, the range of industries embraced, and the level and economic sophistication of the questions asked, so the first truly comprehensive Census of Manufactures was not conducted until 1850. Thereafter, the economic component of the decennial census increased in precision and detail. The timing of the Census of Manufactures changed beginning in 1904, when they were collected at five-year intervals until interrupted by World War I. Thereafter, for a while they were taken even more frequently until war again interrupted their collection. The process was finally regularized in the 1960s, with manufacturing censuses taken every five years in years ending in "2" and "7." A variety of data is collected and tabulated, although the subjects covered vary by industry. Several key statistics are tabulated for all industries, including the number of establishments; number of employees; payroll; and various measures of output, value of shipments, and value added. However, no single statistic was collected at every census. For example, the definition of what constituted an establishment changed over time: what was meant by "manufacturing"; who should be included among the workforce (corporate officers and salaried staff as well as production line workers, for example); or how inventories should be treated. Indeed, early Census Bureau officials outspokenly criticized some statistics that they were required to report, most notably capital valuation.

Most records of the 1810 Manufacturing Census were lost when the British burned parts of Washington during the War of 1812. Other assorted manufacturing manuscript records have been lost over the years – some by accident (for example, in January 1921, a fire at the Commerce Department destroyed most of the returns of the 1890 Census), others by design, including most of the twentieth-century Censuses of Manufactures, which were destroyed by Congressional order.[4] Nevertheless, Americans have kept a voluminous quantitative record documenting the nation's industrialization. Among the more valuable, but certainly not the only, continuing data source is found in the published volumes of the federal Census of Manufactures. Some of the evidence in this chapter comes from this source. As time passed, however, other government documents such as patent filings, trade statistics, tax records, regulatory reports, and private sector sources that include corporate records, trade association data, and similar materials have become available to provide a fuller account of the emergence of manufacturing in the United States.

Although the complete enumerations provided by the census are invaluable, the insights that they provide are for discrete, widely separated intervals of time. These gaps are partly filled by a variety of programs, including the Annual Survey of Manufactures (ASM) and commodity surveys used to prepare Current Industrial Reports (CIRs). Although these data are more timely, they are not as detailed as those in the censuses. The ASM, which provides information for the years between the censuses, has been taken since 1949. Because it collects data from a sample of several tens of thousands of manufacturers (about 55,000 in 1991, for example), rather than all manufacturers as in the census, the ASM data are generally provided only for the nation and the states rather than at the level of Statistical Metropolitan Areas (SMAs). The CIR series provide monthly, quarterly, and annual data on production, shipments, and inventories of selected products or on special subjects. These data come from nearly 70 separate surveys of producers of particular product groups that cover about 4,400 of the 11,000 seven-digit Standard Industrial Classification (SIC) product categories. The CIRs deal mainly with the quantity and value of shipments of particular products and occasionally with information on production and inventories: unfilled orders, receipts, and consumption. They could also include comparative data on domestic production, exports, and imports of the products they cover. Some CIR data are displayed in Table Dd626–643.

Another source is the Enterprise Statistics program. This counts companies rather than plants. Summary statistics on companies and plants (establishments) are reported in Tables Ch440–509.

Readers seeking more detailed quantitative information bearing on American manufacturing should consult the abundant government documents available in many libraries, particularly those classified as "Government Depositories," and online at the Census Bureau's Internet site.

Trade associations for major industries publish statistical series, as do other private agencies. Indeed, some of these have taken over more of the government's role in collecting statistics – for example, the U.S. Bureau of Mines no longer disseminates data on petroleum products; rather, this has been taken over by the American Petroleum Institute. One consequence of this privatization is that statistical data are becoming more privileged and proprietary, and lack of knowledge poses problems in a free society. Annual reports issued by individual corporations can also provide statistical detail for their companies.

Those interested in details on early manufacturing are referred to a set of data samples by the authors that cover the years 1850, 1860, 1870, and 1880. In computer-ready format, they can be obtained through the Inter-University Consortium on Political and Social Research at the University of Michigan (Atack and Bateman 1992a, 1992b). There are many scholarly studies of individual industries at different points in time. A useful reference is McCloskey and Hersh (1990).

Lastly, note that shifts in the sources and in the fundamental nature of the data have also affected and influenced cyclical behavior, especially volatility and persistence. These concerns are dealt with at length by Romer (1985, 1991).

Definitions

The term "establishment" refers to a single facility or plant where the manufacturing business is conducted. The term "enterprise" refers to a business organization (sole proprietorship, partnership, cooperative, or corporation) under common control. Throughout most of the nineteenth century, "establishment," "plant," "firm,"

---

[4] For example, U.S. Congress 1912, 62d Congress 2d Session H Doc 460.

and "enterprise" were essentially synonymous; that is each enterprise operated just a single plant. This is no longer the case, and plants belonging to a single enterprise may be located in numerous locations anywhere around the world.

As noted, the definition of manufacturing defies any hard and fast categorization. In general, manufacturing industry is taken to encompass a specific range of products, although intended use or users play some role in the classification. Until recently, data have been organized according to what is known as the SIC coding system, which classifies establishments according to the principal type of products produced. This scheme dates back to the 1930s and has been revised several times, most recently in 1987. It has even been applied retrospectively to several nineteenth-century manufacturing statistics since firms were assigned to an industry by the principal product they produced (Niemi 1974). Beginning in 1997, however, the SIC classification scheme was superseded by the North American Industrial Classification System (NAICS).[5]

The statistics in this chapter are presented by SIC – the system under which many of them were originally collected and classified – although we have indicated the appropriate new NAICS code for each where possible. For manufacturing activities, this translation works tolerably well most of the time, but the mapping is not perfect, nor apparently will we ever have a complete measure of the distinctions between the two schemes in cold hard numbers. Although the Census Bureau has provided a subset of sector statistics assembled using both SIC and NAICS for the 1997 Census of Manufactures, this project is incomplete and is unlikely to be finished. This change will likely confound future efforts to extend most of these series.

References

Atack, Jeremy. 1987. "Economies of Scale and Efficiency Gains in the Rise of the Factory in America, 1820–1900." In Peter Kilby, editor. *Quantity and Quiddity: Essays in U.S. Economic History.* Wesleyan University Press.

Atack, Jeremy, and Fred Bateman. 1987. *To Their Own Soil: Agriculture in the Antebellum North.* Iowa State University Press.

Atack, Jeremy, and Fred Bateman. 1992a. *National Sample from the 1880 Census of Manufacturing.* Interuniversity Consortium for Political and Social Research, Project 9385, February 17.

Atack, Jeremy, and Fred Bateman. 1992b. *State Sample from the 1880 Census of Manufacturing.* Interuniversity Consortium for Political and Social Research, Project 9385, February 17.

Atack, Jeremy, Fred Bateman, and Thomas Weiss. 1980. "The Regional Diffusion and Adoption of the Steam Engine in American Manufacturing." *Journal of Economic History* 40 (2): 281–308.

Bateman, Fred, and Thomas Weiss. 1981. *A Deplorable Scarcity: The Failure of Industrialization in the Slave Economy.* University of North Carolina Press.

Bishop, J. Leander. 1861. *A History of American Manufactures from 1608 to 1860.* 3 volumes. E. Young.

Bruchey, Stuart. 1990. *Enterprise: The Dynamic Economy of a Free People.* Harvard University Press.

Chandler, Alfred Dupont, Jr. 1977. *The Visible Hand: The Managerial Revolution in American Business.* Belknap Press.

Clark, Victor S. 1916–1928. *History of Manufactures in the United States.* 2 volumes. Carnegie Institution of Washington.

Cochran, Thomas C. 1957. *The American Business System.* Harvard University Press.

Cochran, Thomas C. 1977. *200 Years of American Business.* Basic Books.

Coxe, Tench. 1814. *A Statement of the Arts and Manufactures of the United States of America, for the Year 1810.* A. Cornman.

Davis, Donald Finlay. 1988. *Conspicuous Production: Automobiles and Elites in Detroit, 1899–1933.* Temple University Press.

Depew, Chauncey M., editor. 1895. *1795–1895: One Hundred Years of American Commerce . . . A History of American Commerce.* 2 volumes. D. O. Haynes.

Engerman, Stanley L. 1966. "The Economic Impact of the Civil War." *Explorations in Economic History* 3: 176–99.

Fishbein, Meyer H. 1973. "The Censuses of Manufactures 1810–1890." Reference Information Paper number 50, General Services Administration, National Archives and Record Service.

Flink, James J. 1970. *America Adopts the Automobile, 1895–1910.* MIT Press.

Hartmann, Susan M. 1982. *The Home Front and Beyond: American Women in the 1940s.* Twayne Publishers.

Hounshell, David A. 1986. *From the American System to Mass Production, 1800–1932: The Development of Manufacturing Technology in the United States.* Johns Hopkins University Press.

Hunter, Louis C. 1979. *A History of Industrial Power in the United States, 1780–1930.* University Press of Virginia.

Hunter, Louis C., and Lynwood Bryant. 1991. *A History of Industrial Power in the United States, 1780–1930,* volume 3, *The Transmission of Power.* MIT Press.

Lamoreaux, Naomi R. 1985. *The Great Merger Movement in American Business, 1895–1904.* Cambridge University Press.

McCloskey, Donald N., and George K. Hersh Jr. 1990. *A Bibliography of Historical Economics to 1980.* Cambridge University Press.

McGaw, Judith A., editor. 1994. *Early American Technology: Making and Doing Things from the Colonial Era to 1850.* University of North Carolina Press.

Meyer, David R. 1989. "Midwestern Industrialization and the American Manufacturing Belt in the Nineteenth Century." *Journal of Economic History* 49 (4): 921–38.

Niemi, Albert W. 1974. *State and Regional Patterns in American Manufacturing, 1860–1900.* Greenwood Press.

Porter, Glenn. 1973. *The Rise of Big Business, 1860–1910.* Harlan Davidson.

Romer, Christina D. 1985. "The Instability of the Prewar Economy Reconsidered: A Critical Examination of Historical Macroeconomic Data." Ph.D. dissertation, Massachusetts Institute of Technology.

Romer, Christina D. 1991. "The Cyclical Behavior of Individual Production Series, 1889–1984." *Quarterly Journal of Economics* 106 (1): 1–31.

Sokoloff, Kenneth L. 1984. "Was the Transition from the Artisanal Shop to the Non-Mechanized Factory Associated with Gains in Efficiency? Evidence from the U.S. Manufactures Censuses of 1820 and 1850." *Explorations in Economic History* 21 (4): 351–82.

Thornton, Rebecca Achee, and Peter Thompson. 2001. "Learning from Experience and Learning from Others: An Exploration of Learning and Spillovers in Wartime Shipbuilding." *American Economic Review* 91 (5): 1350–68.

---

[5] See the Introduction to Part D for additional discussion of economic sectors, industrial classification, and the SIC and NAICS systems.

MANUFACTURING SUMMARY

Jeremy Atack and Fred Bateman

TABLE Dd1–12 Manufacturing summary – establishments, persons engaged, payroll, value added, capital expenditures, and inventories: 1849–1995[1],[2]

Contributed by Jeremy Atack and Fred Bateman

	Establishments		Persons engaged				Payroll			Value added	New capital expenditures	Inventories
	Total	With 20 or more employees	Proprietors and partners	Nonproduction employees	Production workers		Total	Salaries	Wages			
					Number	Man-hours						
	Dd1	Dd2	Dd3	Dd4	Dd5	Dd6	Dd7	Dd8	Dd9	Dd10 [3]	Dd11	Dd12
Year	Number	Number	Thousand	Thousand	Thousand	Million hours	Million dollars	Million dollars	Million dollars	Million dollars	Million dollars	Million dollars
1849	123,025	—	—	—	957	—	—	—	237	464	—	—
1859	140,433	—	—	—	1,311	—	—	—	379	854	—	—
1869	252,148	—	—	—	2,054	—	—	—	621	1,395	—	—
1879	253,852	—	—	—	2,733	—	—	—	948	1,973	—	—
1889	353,864	—	—	457	4,129	—	2,209	388	1,821	4,102	—	—
1899	509,490	—	—	380	5,098	—	2,596	389	2,207	5,475	—	—
1899	204,754	—	—	348	4,502	—	2,259	366	1,893	4,647	—	—
1904	213,444	—	225	493	5,182	—	2,991	550	2,441	6,019	—	—
1909	264,810	—	272	759	6,262	—	4,106	900	3,205	8,160	—	—
1914	268,436	—	259	911	6,602	—	5,016	1,234	3,782	9,386	—	—
1919	270,231	—	250	1,371	8,465	—	12,427	2,763	9,664	23,842	—	—
1921	192,059	—	172	1,081	6,476	—	9,870	2,419	7,451	17,253	—	—
1923	192,096	—	148	1,280	8,194	—	12,997	2,848	10,149	24,570	—	—
1925	183,877	—	133	1,271	7,871	—	12,958	2,978	9,980	25,668	—	—
1927	187,629	—	132	1,224	7,848	—	13,123	3,023	10,100	26,325	—	—
1929	206,663	—	133	1,290	8,370	—	14,284	3,399	10,885	30,591	—	—
1931	171,450	—	—	—	6,163	—	—	—	6,689	18,601	—	—
1933	139,325	—	72	770 [5]	5,788	—	6,238 [5]	1,298 [5]	4,940	14,008	—	—
1935	167,916	—	82	1,058	7,204	—	9,565	2,253	7,311	18,553	—	—
1937	166,794	—	99	1,217	8,569	—	12,830	2,717	10,113	25,174	—	9,863
1939 [4]	173,802	—	124	1,719	7,808	—	12,706	3,708	8,998	24,487	—	9,632
1947	240,807	—	189	2,376	11,918	24,317	39,696	9,452	30,244	74,291	5,998	26,129
1949	—	—	—	2,550	11,016	21,770	41,482	11,228	30,254	75,367	5,067	—
1950	260,000	—	—	2,688	11,779	23,717	46,643	12,043	34,600	89,750	5,041	—
1951	262,000	—	—	2,800	12,509	25,264	54,742	14,087	40,655	102,086	7,782	—
1952	267,000	—	—	3,026	12,706	25,618	59,598	15,834	43,764	109,162	7,883	—
1953	285,000	—	—	3,192	13,501	27,066	66,493	17,513	48,979	121,659	8,048	—
1954	286,814	90,470	198	3,273	12,372	24,334	62,963	18,372	44,591	117,032	8,201	40,341
1955	—	—	—	3,381	12,954	25,898	69,097	19,878	49,218	135,023	8,233	—
1956	—	—	—	3,563	13,131	26,089	74,015	21,974	52,041	144,909	11,233	—
1957	—	—	—	3,782	12,839	25,208	76,315	23,745	52,569	147,838	12,144	—
1958	299,017	95,278	186	3,742	11,681	22,679	73,875	24,270	49,605	141,541	9,544	49,947
1959	—	—	—	3,790	12,273	24,444	81,204	26,489	54,714	161,536	9,140	52,552
1960	—	—	—	3,940	12,210	24,174	83,673	28,117	55,556	163,999	10,098	53,560
1961	—	—	—	3,951	11,779	23,289	83,677	28,912	54,765	164,281	9,780	54,744
1962	—	—	—	4,028	12,127	24,270	89,819	30,685	59,134	179,071	10,436	58,067
1963	306,617	99,352	169	4,000	12,232	24,509	93,283	31,190	62,094	192,083	11,370	59,913
1964	—	—	—	4,082	12,403	25,246	98,685	32,846	65,839	206,194	13,294	63,211

Notes appear at end of table

(continued)

TABLE Dd1–12 Manufacturing summary – establishments, persons engaged, payroll, value added, capital expenditures, and inventories: 1849–1995
Continued

	Establishments		Persons engaged				Payroll			Value added	New capital expenditures	Inventories
	Total	With 20 or more employees	Proprietors and partners	Nonproduction employees	Production workers		Total	Salaries	Wages			
					Number	Man-hours						
	Dd1	Dd2	Dd3	Dd4	Dd5	Dd6	Dd7	Dd8	Dd9	Dd10 [3]	Dd11	Dd12
Year	Number	Number	Thousand	Thousand	Thousand	Million hours	Million dollars	Million dollars	Million dollars	Million dollars	Million dollars	Million dollars
1965	—	—	—	4,174	13,076	26,568	106,643	35,281	71,362	226,940	16,615	68,009
1966	—	—	—	4,374	13,827	28,103	117,157	38,901	78,256	250,880	20,236	77,721
1967	305,680	107,138	—	4,537	13,955	27,838	123,481	42,087	81,394	261,984	21,503	84,406
1968	—	—	—	4,640	14,041	28,157	132,568	45,088	87,480	285,059	20,613	90,505
1969	—	—	—	4,798	14,358	28,600	142,645	49,186	93,460	304,441	22,291	98,206
1970	—	—	—	4,462	13,528	26,669	141,886	50,277	91,609	300,228	22,164	101,285
1971	—	—	—	—	12,875	25,266	—	—	93,232	314,138	20,941	—
1972	320,710	114,195	—	—	13,527	26,697	—	—	105,495	353,974	24,073	—
1973	—	—	—	—	14,233	28,097	—	—	118,332	405,624	26,979	—
1974	—	—	—	—	13,971	27,239	—	—	124,983	452,468	35,696	—
1975	—	—	—	—	12,568	24,070	—	—	121,427	442,486	37,262	—
1976	—	—	—	—	13,051	25,354	—	—	137,564	511,471	78,632	—
1977	359,928	118,699	—	—	13,691	26,687	—	—	157,164	585,166	74,562	—
1978	—	—	—	—	14,229	27,677	—	—	176,417	657,412	61,931	—
1979	—	—	—	—	14,538	28,324	—	—	192,882	747,481	75,186	—
1980	—	—	—	—	13,900	26,746	—	—	198,164	773,831	83,058	—
1981	—	—	—	—	13,543	26,233	—	—	212,201	837,507	78,632	—
1982	358,061	123,163	—	—	12,401	23,538	—	—	204,787	824,118	74,562	—
1983	—	—	—	—	12,203	23,612	—	—	212,416	882,015	61,931	—
1984	—	—	—	—	12,573	24,637	—	—	231,784	983,228	75,186	—
1985	—	—	—	—	12,174	23,732	—	—	235,791	1,000,142	83,058	—
1986	—	—	—	—	11,765	23,178	—	—	236,599	1,035,437	76,355	—
1987	368,904	126,302	—	—	12,280	24,303	—	—	251,450	1,165,741	78,650	—
1988	—	—	—	—	12,439	24,815	—	—	265,147	1,269,313	81,593	—
1989	—	—	—	—	12,536	24,934	—	—	273,120	1,325,434	98,738	—
1990	—	—	—	—	12,233	24,463	—	—	275,208	1,346,970	105,018	—
1991	—	—	—	—	11,652	23,383	—	—	270,601	1,341,386	103,003	—
1992	381,696	124,822	—	—	11,641	23,563	—	—	281,538	1,424,700	103,188	—
1993	—	—	—	—	11,726	23,845	—	—	290,293	1,483,054	103,133	—
1994	—	—	—	—	11,947	24,560	—	—	304,663	1,605,980	112,784	—
1995	—	—	—	—	12,254	25,065	—	—	317,106	1,709,180	128,235	—

[1] The composition and coverage of the series change over time; see text.

[2] Figures through the first set of values for 1899 include factories and hand and neighborhood industries; thereafter, only factories.

[3] Computation of value added changes over time; see text.

[4] Figures revised by retabulation of returns to exclude data for establishments classified as manufacturing in 1939 but as nonmanufacturing beginning in 1947; see text for additional information and for exceptions.

[5] Excludes data for salaried officers of corporations and their salaries; therefore, not strictly comparable with other years.

Sources

Censuses of Manufactures and U.S. Bureau of the Census, *Annual Survey of Manufactures, 1970–71*, p. 10, and *1995*, pp. 1–7.

Documentation

The basic source of comprehensive data on manufactures has been the Census of Manufactures conducted by the U.S. Bureau of the Census. The first Census of Manufactures covered 1809. A census was taken at ten-year intervals thereafter to 1899 (with the exception of 1829), at five-year intervals for 1904–1919, and biennially for 1921–1939. The census was suspended during World War II but was resumed for 1947. Legislation enacted in 1948 provided for a Census of Manufactures every five years, with annual sample surveys authorized for interim years. The 1954 Census was the first to be taken as a result of this legislation. Subsequently, the census intervals were revised, and censuses were taken in 1958, 1963, and 1967. Annual surveys of manufacture were conducted every year beginning in 1949, except during census years. The data from the annual surveys represent estimates derived from a sample of manufacturing establishments canvassed. These estimates may differ from the results that would have been obtained from a complete canvass of all manufacturing establishments. The relative standard errors (measures of the potential differences) associated with these estimates are published in the annual survey volume.

There have been changes in scope from one Census of Manufactures to another. Through 1899, data cover factories as well as hand and neighborhood industries; thereafter, hand and neighborhood industries are excluded. Also, through 1899, data cover all establishments with products valued at $500 or more; for 1899–1919, establishments reporting value of shipments of $500 or more; for 1921–1939, establishments reporting a value of shipments of $5,000 or more; and beginning in 1947, establishments employing one or more persons at any time during the census year. These changes in the minimum size limit have not appreciably affected the historical comparability of the census figures except for data on number of establishments.

There have also been a number of changes in the definition of manufacturing industries. Among the more important were changes in the treatment of two industries – railroad repair shops and manufactured gas. These industries are included in the figures for 1899–1933 but excluded for 1935–1970. When the change results in the omission of an entire industry for which separate tabulations are available during each census, the adjustments are usually carried back through the previous censuses. Beginning with 1954, the figures cover the logging camps and contractors industry, which was not included within the scope of the 1947 Census; and establishments engaged in the processing and distribution of fluid milk, which were not included in the figures for earlier census years. Beginning with 1958, the figures cover establishments classified in the ready-mixed concrete industry, and establishments classified in the miscellaneous machinery industry that were engaged exclusively or almost exclusively in machine shop repair work. Data for such establishments are excluded for 1939–1957 but included for 1929 and earlier years.

Except as noted, the 1939 figures have been revised by retabulation of returns to exclude data for establishments classified as manufacturing in 1939 but as nonmanufacturing beginning in 1947. Value added by manufacture in 1939, prior to revision and on a basis comparable with prior years, was $24.7 billion. The exceptions occur in the series for proprietors and partners, nonproduction workers, and payroll. In series Dd3, the figure *includes* establishments classified as manufacturing in 1939 but as nonmanufacturing thereafter. And in series Dd4 and Dd7–9, figures were revised on the basis of estimates rather than by retabulation of 1939 reports. Such estimates were made as follows: for nonproduction employees, by multiplying the retabulated figures for number of production workers by the ratio of all employees to production workers computed from unrevised 1939 data; for salaries and wages, by multiplying the retabulated wage figure by the ratio for salaries and wages also derived from the unrevised 1939 data.

The reporting units in each census have been establishments rather than legal entities or companies. Conceptually, an establishment is a geographically isolated manufacturing unit maintaining independent bookkeeping records, regardless of its managerial or financial affiliations. An establishment may be a single plant, a group of closely located plants operated as a unit, or a group of closely located plants operated by a single company without separate records for each. The establishment is also the basic unit of industrial classification, being assigned to an industry on the basis of its reported product of chief total value. Establishments owned and operated by the federal government are excluded from coverage.

Series Dd3–5

The figures for 1939–1992 exclude personnel reported by manufacturing establishments as in distribution and in construction work (the 1939 and subsequent censuses required separate reporting for such employees). Therefore, the employee figures for earlier years probably are not strictly comparable with those for 1939–1970. It is not known how many of the wage earners and the salaried employees were engaged in distribution and construction, and how many were engaged in manufacturing.

Employees comprise all full-time and part-time employees on the payrolls of operating establishments who worked or received pay for any part of the pay period specified on the report form. Officers of corporations are included as employees; proprietors and partners of unincorporated firms are, however, excluded from the total. In recent censuses, employment at separate administrative offices and auxiliary units is excluded from this category.

Collection of data on proprietors and partners was discontinued after the 1963 Census.

The figures for nonproduction employees are derived by subtracting the figures for production workers from those for all employees shown in the source. For nonproduction employees, the figures through 1939 and earlier years refer to one payroll period, usually in October; for 1947, to an average of twelve monthly figures; for 1949–1954, to an average for the payroll period ending nearest the 12th of March, May, August, and November; and for 1955–1992, to the payroll period ending nearest the 12th of March.

For production workers, the figures through 1947 represent the average of twelve monthly figures; for 1949–1992, they are based on employment for the payroll period ending nearest the 12th of March, May, August, and November.

There has not been a consistent treatment of employees in central administrative offices. The latter are defined as offices that operate one or more manufacturing plants located in a city or cities other than that in which the administrative office is located. For the Censuses of 1909–1923, data on employees in such offices were collected on a separate "administrative schedule" and were tabulated and included with those for salaried employees (and, therefore, with all employees) of the manufacturing plants. Thereafter, these data were collected and tabulated for the Censuses of 1925, 1929, and 1937. Beginning with 1954, separate data on employment in administrative offices and auxiliary establishments were compiled in census years and are shown in Census of Manufactures publications. The figures for nonproduction employees for 1925 and 1929 include employees in central administrative offices. To make the 1937 figure for nonproduction employees more comparable with the figures for 1929 and earlier years (except 1927), 130,854 employees in central administrative offices should be added to the 1937 figure (*1937 Census of Manufactures*, p. 1652), and to make the 1954 figure more comparable with the figures for 1929 and earlier years (except 1927), 474,256 employees in administrative and auxiliary units should be added to the 1954 figure (*U.S. Census of Manufactures: 1954*, volume 2, part 1, p. 2).

Production workers are defined as workers (up through the working foreman level) engaged in fabricating, processing, assembling, inspection, receiving, storage, handling, packing, warehousing, shipping (but not delivering), maintenance, repair, janitorial, watchman services, product development, auxiliary production for plants' own use (for example, power plants), recordkeeping, and other services closely associated with these production operations at the establishment covered by the report. Supervisory employees above the working foreman level are excluded from this category. Decennial estimates of wage earners (production and related workers) excluding hand and neighborhood industries have been prepared for 1869–1899 by John W. Kendrick and Maude Pech for the National Bureau of Economic Research. The following is the estimated number of wage earners for each of these years (in thousands): 1869, 1,803; 1879, 2,454; 1889, 3,562; 1899, 4,496. This estimate for 1899 differs from the official Census Bureau estimate in series Dd5 by only one tenth of 1 percent. For details on the estimating procedure, see John W. Kendrick, *Productivity Trends in the United States* (National Bureau of Economic Research, 1961), Appendix D.

Series Dd5. The Bureau of Labor Statistics annual averages for employment in manufacturing indicates 1943 as the year of maximum employment, with 15,147,000 production workers.

Series Dd6. Covers all plant man-hours of production and related workers. It represents all man-hours worked or paid for except hours paid for vacations, holidays, or sick leave and includes actual overtime hours. Where employees elected to work during vacation periods, only the actual hours they worked were reported. The man-hour figures differ from those published by the Bureau of Labor Statistics, which cover all hours paid for, whether worked or not.

(continued)

TABLE Dd1–12   Manufacturing summary – establishments, persons engaged, payroll, value added, capital expenditures, and inventories: 1849–1995 Continued

Series Dd7–9. These figures include gross earnings paid in the calendar year to all employees on the payroll of operating manufacturing establishments. They include all forms of compensation, such as salaries, wages, commissions, dismissal pay, all bonuses, vacation and sick leave pay, and compensation in kind, prior to such deductions as employees' Social Security contributions, withholding taxes, group insurance, union dues, and savings bonds. Salaries of officers of these establishments are included for corporations; payments to proprietors and partners are excluded for unincorporated concerns. Also excluded are payments to members of armed forces and pensioners carried on the active payrolls of manufacturing establishments. Employers' Social Security contributions or other nonlabor costs such as pension plans, group insurance, and workmen's compensation are also excluded.

Series Dd10

The standard formula for calculating value added by manufacture beginning in 1954 differs from the one used for earlier years. Prior to 1954, the value added of an establishment was calculated by subtracting the cost of materials, supplies, containers, fuels, purchased electric energy, and contract work from the value of shipments for products manufactured plus miscellaneous receipts for services rendered. This is known as unadjusted value added. Thereafter, the measure of value added has been adjusted ("adjusted value added") for each establishment. Value added now includes the value added by merchandising (that is, the difference between the sales value and cost of merchandise sold without further manufacture, processing, or assembly), as well as an adjustment for the net change in finished goods and work-in-process inventories between the beginning and the end of the year. The resulting figure is referred to as the adjusted value added. This procedure avoids the duplication in the "value of shipments" figures that results from the use of products of some establishments as materials by others. The "value added by manufacture" concept should not be confused with "national income originating in manufacturing," as presented in national income estimates. The latter is obtained by subtracting from the value of shipments not only the cost of materials but also other costs, such as depreciation charges, state and local taxes (other than corporate income taxes), allowance for bad debts, and purchases of services from nonmanufacturing enterprises such as services of engineering and management consultants, advertising, telephone and telegraph expense, insurance, royalties, patent fees, and so forth. National income originating in manufacturing, therefore, is more of a "net" concept of value added than that used in the Census of Manufactures. Value added by manufacture in 1967, for example, exceeded national income originating in manufacturing, as estimated by the U.S. Office of Business Economics, by 34 percent.

For 1849–1933, the cost of contract work was not subtracted from the value of products in calculating value added by manufacture.

Robert E. Gallman prepared estimates of value added for the census years 1839–1879 by adjusting manufacturing totals to exclude nonmanufacturing industries and by correcting for industries omit-

ted from or poorly covered by the various censuses. See Robert E. Gallman, "Commodity Output in the United States, 1839–1899," *Studies in Income and Wealth* (National Bureau of Economic Research, 1960), volume 24, Table A13. His estimates are extrapolations based on data prepared by Richard A. Easterlin and published in "Estimates of Manufacturing Activity," in Everett S. Lee, Ann Ratner, Carol P. Brainerd, and Richard A. Easterlin, *Population Redistribution and Economic Growth, United States, 1870–1950*, volume 1 (American Philosophical Society, 1957), pp. 635–81.

The following are Gallman's estimates.

Value added by manufacture

Year	Million current dollars	Million 1879 dollars
1899	5,044	6,252
1889	3,727	4,156
1879	1,962	1,962
1769	1,631	1,078
1859	815	859
1849	447	488
1839	240	190

Series Dd11

Manufacturers were asked to report expenditures made during the year for permanent additions and major alterations to their plants, as well as for new machinery and equipment purchases that were chargeable to fixed-asset accounts of manufacturing establishments and were of a type for which depreciation accounts are ordinarily maintained. Excluded are costs of maintenance and repairs charged as current operating expense, new facilities and equipment leased from other companies, new facilities owned by the federal government but operated under contract by private companies, and plant and equipment furnished to manufacturers by communities and organizations. Beginning with 1951, the figures include expenditures for plants under construction and not yet in operation. In Table Dd13–231, however, such expenditures are included until 1958.

Series Dd12

Figures are as of end of year. Respondents were asked to report their inventories at approximate current costs if feasible, and otherwise at book values. See also the text for Table Dd626–643.

TABLE Dd13–231 Manufacturing summary, by industry division – establishments, employment and payroll, value added, capital expenditures, and aggregate power of equipment: 1899–1999[1,2]

Contributed by Jeremy Atack and Fred Bateman

	Food and kindred products											Tobacco manufactures			
	Establishments		Employment and payroll					Value added	Capital expenditures		Aggregate power of equipment	Establishments		Employment and payroll	
			All employees		Production workers									All employees	
	Total	With at least 20 employees	Number	Payroll	Number	Man-hours	Wages		New	Total		Total	With at least 20 employees	Number	Payroll
Year	Dd13	Dd14	Dd15	Dd16	Dd17	Dd18	Dd19	Dd20	Dd21	Dd22	Dd23	Dd24	Dd25	Dd26	Dd27
	Number	Number	Thousand	Million dollars	Thousand	Million	Million dollars	Million dollars	Million dollars	Million dollars	Thousand horsepower	Number	Number	Thousand	Million dollars
1899	—	—	—	—	—	—	—	—	—	—	—	14,959	—	140	57
1904	—	—	—	—	—	—	—	—	—	—	—	16,827	—	170	71
1909	—	—	—	—	—	—	—	—	—	—	—	15,822	—	180	86
1914	—	—	—	—	—	—	—	—	—	—	—	13,951	—	196	100
1919	—	—	—	—	—	—	—	—	—	—	—	10,291	—	173	153
1921	51,502	—	760	1,016	621	—	742	2,120	—	—	—	4,312	—	165	148
1923	51,173	—	818	1,084	676	—	792	2,506	—	—	3,723	3,672	—	162	151
1925	48,151	—	793	1,062	667	—	799	2,718	—	—	3,882	2,623	—	143	134
1927	48,947	—	796	1,104	668	—	817	2,840	—	—	4,135	2,156	—	141	129
1929	55,325	—	872	1,203	741	—	896	3,340	—	—	4,608	1,888	—	126	118
1931	48,729	—	—	—	647	—	740	2,745	—	—	—	1,228	—	—	—
1933	40,325	—	768	777	669	—	624	2,413	—	—	—	804	—	91	59
1935	48,982	—	932	1,068	800	—	804	2,804	—	—	—	890	—	96	71
1937	48,763	—	—	—	891	—	981	3,371	—	—	—	852	—	98	82
1939	43,667	—	—	—	802	—	888	3,485	—	—	5,642	765	—	96	87
1947	42,802	—	1,461	3,833	1,112	2,368	2,617	9,116	821	—	—	1,086	—	112	206
1949	—	—	1,463	4,199	1,077	2,222	2,707	9,426	723	—	—	—	—	101	208
1950	38,466	—	1,493	4,415	1,075	2,218	2,858	10,104	649	—	—	—	—	93	213
1951	38,237	—	1,474	4,819	1,079	2,218	3,143	10,579	687	—	—	—	—	94	230
1952	36,829	—	1,480	5,098	1,075	2,216	3,313	11,340	527	—	—	—	—	93	241
1953	—	—	1,455	5,267	1,059	2,160	3,436	11,938	545	—	—	—	—	95	253
1954	42,373	13,648	1,647	6,200	1,138	2,316	3,758	13,767	788	—	8,311	627	391	95	260
1955	—	—	1,674	6,544	1,154	2,344	3,940	14,790	798	—	—	—	—	96	271
1956	—	—	1,706	6,964	1,167	2,378	4,202	15,939	887	—	—	—	—	93	279
1957	—	—	1,688	7,141	1,133	2,304	4,244	16,347	923	—	—	—	—	88	284
1958	41,970	14,890	1,718	7,622	1,153	2,310	4,549	17,701	1,021	—	—	504	380	85	295
1959	—	—	1,718	7,910	1,155	2,345	4,702	18,646	1,078	—	—	—	—	83	304
1960	—	—	1,719	8,210	1,155	2,348	4,857	19,753	1,034	—	—	—	—	81	313
1961	—	—	1,702	8,363	1,138	2,317	4,934	20,124	1,044	—	—	—	—	78	317
1962	—	—	1,683	8,593	1,119	2,287	5,060	20,870	1,235	—	11,884	—	—	76	328
1963	37,521	14,113	1,643	8,637	1,098	2,228	5,159	21,826	1,249	—	—	394	231	77	331
1964	—	—	1,646	9,028	1,095	2,270	5,367	25,053	1,413	—	—	—	—	79	353

Notes appear at end of table

(continued)

TABLE Dd13–231 Manufacturing summary, by industry division – establishments, employment and payroll, value added, capital expenditures, and aggregate power of equipment: 1899–1999 *Continued*

	Food and kindred products											Tobacco manufactures			
	Establishments		Employment and payroll					Value added	Capital expenditures		Aggregate power of equipment	Establishments		Employment and payroll	
		With at least 20 employees	All employees		Production workers								With at least 20 employees	All employees	
	Total	Number	Number	Payroll	Number	Man-hours	Wages		New	Total		Total	Number	Number	Payroll
			Thousand	Million dollars	Thousand	Million	Million dollars	Million dollars	Million dollars	Million dollars	Thousand horsepower	Number		Thousand	Million dollars
Year	Dd13	Dd14	Dd15	Dd16	Dd17	Dd18	Dd19	Dd20	Dd21	Dd22	Dd23	Dd24	Dd25	Dd26	Dd27
1965	—	—	1,641	9,162	1,095	2,233	5,446	23,538	1,476	—	—	—	—	75	349
1966	—	—	1,643	9,542	1,098	2,240	5,676	24,896	1,692	—	—	—	—	72	356
1967	32,518	13,514	1,650	10,077	1,122	2,259	6,063	26,621	1,730	—	—	329	195	75	377
1968	—	—	1,632	10,497	1,114	2,234	6,390	28,202	1,740	—	—	—	—	74	396
1969	—	—	1,653	11,135	1,132	2,265	6,782	29,997	1,917	—	—	—	—	72	411
1970	—	—	1,619	11,698	1,105	2,216	7,095	32,289	2,144	—	—	—	—	71	448
1971	—	—	1,574	12,180	1,073	2,145	7,438	34,110	2,245	—	—	—	—	67	471
1972	28,183	12,325	1,569	12,922	1,085	2,167	8,007	35,617	2,355	—	—	272	154	66	502
1973	—	—	1,560	13,670	1,081	2,158	8,471	39,693	2,414	—	—	—	—	69	557
1974	—	—	1,553	14,788	1,075	2,126	9,196	44,948	3,006	—	—	—	—	67	604
1975	—	—	1,525	15,856	1,055	2,067	9,837	48,095	3,434	—	—	—	—	66	655
1976	—	—	1,536	17,289	1,067	2,103	10,806	52,760	3,817	—	—	—	—	65	704
1977	26,656	11,038	1,520	18,544	1,072	2,112	11,731	56,062	4,215	—	—	228	123	61	751
1978	—	—	1,547	20,308	1,097	2,158	12,864	62,911	4,807	—	—	—	—	59	813
1979	—	—	1,552	21,678	1,101	2,178	13,838	68,733	5,034	—	—	—	—	59	906
1980	—	—	1,538	23,222	1,090	2,153	14,797	75,302	5,852	—	—	—	—	58	1,045
1981	—	—	1,511	24,696	1,069	2,115	15,707	80,795	6,012	—	—	—	—	61	1,219
1982	22,130	10,681	1,488	26,088	1,047	2,033	16,440	88,419	6,727	—	—	163	107	58	1,324
1983	—	—	1,446	26,601	1,013	1,991	16,637	93,438	5,806	—	—	—	—	55	1,355
1984	—	—	1,437	27,350	1,010	1,977	17,061	98,037	6,433	—	—	—	—	52	1,354
1985	—	—	1,423	28,077	994	1,941	17,428	104,146	7,049	—	—	—	—	49	1,369
1986	—	—	1,409	28,567	990	1,932	17,789	112,191	6,966	—	—	—	—	46	1,360
1987	20,583	9,688	1,449	30,267	1,029	2,019	18,900	121,609	7,198	—	—	137	83	45	1,486
1988	—	—	1,474	31,671	1,053	2,075	19,806	129,700	7,651	—	—	—	—	45	1,498
1989	—	—	1,519	33,592	1,085	2,150	20,948	137,157	8,710	—	—	—	—	44	1,501
1990	—	—	1,497	34,221	1,084	2,185	21,564	143,774	9,332	—	—	—	—	41	1,506
1991	—	—	1,511	35,580	1,101	2,217	22,498	149,071	9,994	—	—	—	—	40	1,506
1992	20,798	9,329	1,503	36,772	1,100	2,243	23,352	157,260	9,899	—	—	114	80	38	1,524
1993	—	—	1,520	37,707	1,118	2,277	24,079	165,661	9,389	—	—	—	—	37	1,423
1994	—	—	1,511	38,471	1,112	2,299	24,691	171,986	10,093	—	—	—	—	34	1,441
1995	—	—	1,520	39,622	1,124	2,542	25,442	180,975	11,929	—	—	—	—	31	1,484
1996	—	—	1,517	40,380	1,113	2,301	25,702	178,783	11,717	—	—	—	—	31	1,522
1997	20,878	—	1,561	42,941	—	—	—	—	—	—	—	105	—	34	1,596
1997	26,361	—	1,467	38,366	1,112	2,234	25,186	163,675	—	10,799	—	105	—	34	1,596
1998	—	—	1,499	39,660	1,140	2,315	26,160	173,416	—	11,512	—	—	—	34	1,530
1999	—	—	1,488	41,211	1,139	2,345	27,128	177,659	—	13,208	—	—	—	28	1,445

Tobacco manufactures (Dd28–Dd34) and **Textile mill products** (Dd35–Dd42)

	Tobacco manufactures							Textile mill products							
	Employment and payroll — Production workers			Value added	Capital expenditures		Aggregate power of equipment	Establishments		Employment and payroll — All employees		Production workers			Value added
	Number	Man-hours	Wages		New	Total		Total	With at least 20 employees	Number	Payroll	Number	Man-hours	Wages	
Year	Thousand	Million	Million dollars	Million dollars	Million dollars	Million dollars	Thousand horsepower	Number	Number	Thousand	Million dollars	Thousand	Million	Million dollars	Million dollars
	Dd28	Dd29	Dd30	Dd31	Dd32	Dd33	Dd34	Dd35	Dd36	Dd37	Dd38	Dd39	Dd40	Dd41	Dd42
1899	133	—	48	—	—	—	22	5,930	—	716	250	698	—	224	441
1904	159	—	63	—	—	—	24	5,798	—	813	307	786	—	271	515
1909	167	—	69	—	—	—	28	6,490	—	—	—	932	—	362	752
1914	179	—	78	—	—	—	35	6,756	—	1,013	476	976	—	417	781
1919	157	—	124	—	—	—	43	7,869	—	1,139	1,108	1,076	—	932	2,300
1921	150	—	121	—	—	—	—	7,695	—	1,072	1,071	1,012	—	916	1,824
1923	146	—	121	—	—	—	44	8,249	—	1,263	1,345	1,190	—	1,152	2,413
1925	132	—	111	—	—	—	42	7,892	—	1,201	1,272	1,135	—	1,093	2,212
1927	129	—	105	—	—	—	52	7,633	—	1,208	1,314	1,143	—	1,128	2,273
1929	116	—	95	—	—	—	65	7,415	—	1,190	1,293	1,120	—	1,082	2,321
1931	100	—	69	370	—	—	—	6,490	—	—	—	904	—	762	1,525
1933	87	—	51	150	—	—	—	5,957	—	—	—	972	—	664	1,342
1935	91	—	59	284	—	—	—	6,433	—	1,130	986	1,070	—	847	1,461
1937	92	—	70	325	—	—	—	6,096	—	1,138	—	1,138	—	974	1,786
1939	88	—	69	350	—	—	100	6,388	—	1,082	—	1,082	—	907	1,818
1947	103	198	175	641	36	—	—	8,157	—	1,232	2,833	1,146	2,307	2,448	5,323
1949	93	174	174	779	22	—	—	—	—	1,170	2,973	1,066	2,071	2,510	4,741
1950	85	160	177	806	18	—	—	8,434	—	1,245	3,364	1,142	2,301	2,861	5,642
1951	86	162	192	856	18	—	—	7,758	—	1,195	3,438	1,097	2,155	2,925	5,421
1952	86	163	202	868	22	—	—	7,584	—	1,135	3,343	1,037	2,039	2,823	5,257
1953	87	166	213	987	29	—	—	—	—	1,158	3,455	1,060	2,086	2,910	5,412
1954	87	163	220	1,004	28	—	256	8,070	4,862	1,037	3,033	948	1,821	2,527	4,709
1955	88	166	230	1,083	27	—	—	—	—	1,059	3,241	966	1,921	2,708	5,312
1956	85	156	237	1,173	47	—	—	—	—	1,044	3,298	949	1,874	2,750	5,456
1957	81	151	240	1,246	42	—	—	—	—	989	3,183	893	1,736	2,632	5,197
1958	76	147	248	1,414	48	—	—	7,680	4,621	903	2,943	812	1,571	2,412	4,870
1959	75	145	255	1,480	53	—	—	—	—	930	3,252	835	1,689	2,681	5,692
1960	73	142	258	1,546	47	—	—	—	—	901	3,214	809	1,602	2,626	5,591
1961	69	135	258	1,590	49	—	—	—	—	876	3,183	782	1,552	2,575	5,609
1962	67	134	265	1,642	49	—	295	—	—	880	3,358	787	1,590	2,723	6,055
1963	69	132	272	1,681	54	—	—	7,104	4,368	863	3,385	775	1,568	2,768	6,123
1964	70	138	291	1,772	59	—	—	—	—	876	3,647	782	1,626	2,963	6,672

(continued)

TABLE Dd13–231 Manufacturing summary, by industry division – establishments, employment and payroll, value added, capital expenditures, and aggregate power of equipment: 1899–1999 Continued

Tobacco manufactures columns (Dd28–Dd34); Textile mill products columns (Dd35–Dd42).

	Tobacco manufactures							Textile mill products							
	Employment and payroll				Capital expenditures		Aggregate power of equipment	Establishments		Employment and payroll					
	Production workers			Value added						All employees		Production workers			Value added
	Number	Man-hours	Wages		New	Total		Total	With at least 20 employees	Number	Payroll	Number	Man-hours	Wages	
Year	Dd28	Dd29	Dd30	Dd31	Dd32	Dd33	Dd34	Dd35	Dd36	Dd37	Dd38	Dd39	Dd40	Dd41	Dd42
	Thousand	Million	Million dollars	Million dollars	Million dollars	Million dollars	Thousand horsepower	Number	Number	Thousand	Million dollars	Thousand	Million	Million dollars	Million dollars
1965	66	125	285	1,766	59	—	—	—	—	894	3,912	798	1,671	3,189	7,469
1966	64	122	289	1,872	58	—	—	—	—	927	4,244	828	1,728	3,446	8,028
1967	66	126	304	2,032	53	—	—	7,080	4,453	929	4,391	828	1,690	3,557	8,153
1968	65	121	323	2,141	50	—	—	—	—	959	4,850	854	1,758	3,945	9,184
1969	63	117	329	2,221	61	—	—	—	—	968	5,159	859	1,748	4,129	9,605
1970	63	119	362	2,489	56	—	—	—	—	925	5,082	813	1,629	4,036	9,334
1971	59	109	376	2,560	94	—	—	—	—	907	5,330	794	1,605	4,212	9,995
1972	57	107	401	2,637	133	—	—	7,201	4,503	953	6,052	636	1,726	4,807	11,718
1973	59	111	440	2,900	180	—	—	—	—	980	6,605	863	1,751	5,237	13,017
1974	58	107	477	3,179	185	—	—	—	—	933	6,684	813	1,589	5,195	13,199
1975	56	104	513	3,722	145	—	—	—	—	835	6,397	725	1,382	4,914	12,044
1976	55	103	544	4,128	130	—	—	—	—	876	7,368	765	1,519	5,769	14,495
1977	50	93	571	4,334	181	—	—	7,202	4,131	875	7,881	765	1,523	6,203	16,105
1978	49	92	612	4,607	254	—	—	—	—	862	8,368	753	1,496	6,592	17,131
1979	48	90	668	5,343	237	—	—	—	—	842	8,824	732	1,462	6,941	18,154
1980	47	88	768	6,148	354	—	—	—	—	816	9,228	706	1,392	7,212	18,983
1981	49	92	891	7,302	668	—	—	—	—	785	9,574	679	1,333	7,439	19,463
1982	45	84	957	8,965	697	—	—	6,630	3,663	717	9,046	616	1,159	6,936	18,550
1983	42	78	958	9,692	649	—	—	—	—	723	10,061	624	1,235	7,803	21,333
1984	39	73	933	10,787	670	—	—	—	—	710	10,192	611	1,198	7,852	22,110
1985	37	68	941	11,894	669	—	—	—	—	658	9,967	565	1,101	7,609	20,693
1986	34	63	912	12,725	659	—	—	—	—	644	10,306	555	1,111	7,898	22,232
1987	33	61	1,010	14,264	464	—	—	6,065	3,413	672	11,409	575	1,176	8,728	25,660
1988	33	60	1,006	17,130	410	—	—	—	—	668	11,557	570	1,154	8,821	26,237
1989	33	59	1,003	18,934	401	—	—	—	—	657	11,954	567	1,146	9,144	27,379
1990	30	57	1,006	22,487	278	—	—	—	—	630	11,596	544	1,105	8,828	26,406
1991	29	53	985	24,385	405	—	—	—	—	594	11,388	510	1,050	8,576	26,802
1992	27	51	996	27,207	389	—	—	5,886	3,201	616	12,398	529	1,084	9,343	30,060
1993	26	48	920	20,832	388	—	—	—	—	610	12,837	524	1,085	9,679	30,982
1994	24	46	955	22,131	387	—	—	—	—	624	13,594	534	1,101	10,221	32,972
1995	22	45	976	24,715	411	—	—	—	—	607	13,454	518	1,064	10,003	32,705
1996	23	46	1,009	25,860	649	—	—	—	—	576	13,215	489	1,016	9,775	32,555
1997	24	48	1,036	26,690	—	719	—	6,155	—	562	13,709	—	—	—	—
1997	—	—	—	—	—	—	—	4,706	—	392	10,058	332	696	7,439	23,697
1998	24	46	962	31,473	—	344	—	—	—	377	9,861	320	669	7,337	23,782
1999	20	38	894	38,059	—	310	—	—	—	357	9,466	301	635	6,989	22,954

Table continues across three industry groups: **Textile mill products** (Dd43–Dd45), **Apparel and other textile products** (Dd46–Dd56), and **Lumber and wood products** (Dd57–Dd58).

	Textile mill products			Apparel and other textile products											Lumber and wood products	
	Capital expenditures		Aggregate power of equipment	Establishments		Employment and payroll — All employees		Production workers			Value added	Capital expenditures		Aggregate power of equipment	Establishments	
	New	Total		Total	With at least 20 employees	Number	Payroll	Number	Man-hours	Wages		New	Total		Total	With at least 20 employees
Year	Dd43	Dd44	Dd45	Dd46	Dd47	Dd48	Dd49	Dd50	Dd51	Dd52	Dd53	Dd54	Dd55	Dd56	Dd57	Dd58
	Million dollars	Million dollars	Thousand horsepower	Number	Number	Thousand	Million dollars	Thousand	Million	Million dollars	Million dollars	Million dollars	Million dollars	Thousand horsepower	Number	Number
1899	—	—	—	12,619	—	364	150	338	—	123	309	—	—	—	32,456	—
1904	—	—	—	12,416	—	428	194	391	—	159	414	—	—	—	29,308	—
1909	—	—	—	16,747	—	618	356	537	—	247	614	—	—	—	44,822	—
1914	—	—	2,717	18,015	—	618	356	548	—	270	682	—	—	—	37,949	—
1919	—	—	3,248	22,501	—	640	769	554	—	578	1,618	—	—	—	35,872	—
1921	—	—	—	20,049	—	586	733	515	—	584	1,408	—	—	—	16,548	—
1923	—	—	3,783	20,333	—	635	816	545	—	627	1,748	—	—	40	16,471	—
1925	—	—	3,987	18,609	—	—	—	515	—	602	1,685	—	—	33	16,878	—
1927	—	—	4,173	22,077	—	648	859	571	—	673	1,878	—	—	34	14,949	—
1929	—	—	4,146	22,470	—	681	901	606	—	687	1,927	—	—	40	20,928	—
1931	—	—	—	19,750	—	—	—	531	—	503	1,370	—	—	—	11,141	—
1933	—	—	—	14,801	—	—	—	513	—	366	826	—	—	—	8,456	—
1935	—	—	—	18,952	—	—	—	631	—	545	1,123	—	—	—	11,280	—
1937	—	—	—	16,389	—	—	—	693	—	600	1,245	—	—	—	11,747	—
1939	—	—	3,670	20,375	—	—	—	753	—	656	1,386	—	—	24	13,208	—
1947	368	—	—	30,063	—	1,082	2,525	973	1,811	2,015	4,440	84	—	—	26,312	—
1949	419	—	—	—	—	1,161	2,717	1,009	1,813	2,094	4,245	54	—	—	—	—
1950	420	—	—	26,145	—	1,151	2,765	1,005	1,815	2,170	4,176	63	—	—	41,506	—
1951	406	—	—	28,931	—	1,123	2,955	1,002	1,819	2,295	4,699	69	—	—	—	—
1952	323	—	—	29,079	—	1,143	3,079	1,018	1,876	2,404	4,849	55	—	—	—	—
1953	256	—	—	—	—	1,227	3,358	1,106	1,995	2,652	5,415	60	—	—	—	—
1954	226	—	4,463	31,472	13,380	1,190	3,202	1,070	1,899	2,521	5,166	77	—	—	41,484	6,387
1955	262	—	—	—	—	1,248	3,408	1,117	2,000	2,684	5,650	86	—	—	—	—
1956	297	—	—	—	—	1,271	3,612	1,134	2,031	2,842	5,973	88	—	—	—	—
1957	289	—	—	—	—	1,264	3,664	1,123	1,989	2,867	6,067	107	—	—	—	—
1958	215	—	—	29,363	13,034	1,181	3,587	1,042	1,837	2,771	6,001	91	—	—	37,882	5,904
1959	300	—	—	—	—	1,237	3,827	1,090	1,990	3,001	6,495	88	—	—	—	—
1960	326	—	—	—	—	1,238	3,865	1,089	1,932	3,012	6,587	84	—	—	—	—
1961	322	—	—	—	—	1,214	3,877	1,066	1,891	3,000	6,707	80	—	—	—	—
1962	376	—	5,043	—	—	1,235	4,162	1,085	1,952	3,224	7,135	98	—	250	—	—
1963	382	—	—	28,457	13,011	1,280	4,423	1,133	2,053	3,482	7,861	129	—	—	36,150	5,765
1964	504	—	—	—	—	1,303	4,684	1,147	2,107	3,640	8,163	123	—	—	—	—

(continued)

TABLE Dd13–231 Manufacturing summary, by industry division – establishments, employment and payroll, value added, capital expenditures, and aggregate power of equipment: 1899–1999 Continued

	Textile mill products			Apparel and other textile products											Lumber and wood products	
	Capital expenditures		Aggregate power of equipment	Establishments		Employment and payroll					Value added	Capital expenditures		Aggregate power of equipment	Establishments	
	New	Total		Total	With at least 20 employees	All employees		Production workers				New	Total		Total	With at least 20 employees
						Number	Payroll	Number	Man-hours	Wages						
	Dd43	Dd44	Dd45	Dd46	Dd47	Dd48	Dd49	Dd50	Dd51	Dd52	Dd53	Dd54	Dd55	Dd56	Dd57	Dd58
Year	Million dollars	Million dollars	Thousand horsepower	Number	Number	Thousand	Million dollars	Thousand	Million	Million dollars	Million dollars	Million dollars	Million dollars	Thousand horsepower	Number	Number
1965	618	—	—	—	—	1,335	4,955	1,183	2,179	3,878	8,684	168	—	—	—	—
1966	887	—	—	—	—	1,360	5,207	1,202	2,213	4,038	9,181	206	—	—	—	—
1967	733	—	—	26,393	12,705	1,357	5,582	1,200	2,179	4,341	10,064	208	—	—	36,795	5,803
1968	691	—	—	—	—	1,356	6,012	1,194	2,177	4,681	10,881	267	—	—	—	—
1969	849	—	—	—	—	1,381	6,402	1,210	2,203	4,944	11,571	311	—	—	—	—
1970	811	—	—	—	—	1,341	6,267	1,171	2,119	4,807	11,598	300	—	—	—	—
1971	873	—	—	—	—	1,319	6,500	1,149	2,054	4,943	12,448	336	—	—	—	—
1972	1,128	—	—	24,438	12,226	1,368	7,212	1,198	2,161	5,461	13,488	364	—	—	33,949	6,868
1973	1,092	—	—	—	—	1,400	7,707	1,228	2,191	5,841	14,648	387	—	—	—	—
1974	1,170	—	—	—	—	1,317	7,642	1,147	2,041	5,753	14,926	391	—	—	—	—
1975	997	—	—	—	—	1,214	7,700	1,059	1,891	5,777	14,749	381	—	—	—	—
1976	1,087	—	—	—	—	1,271	8,563	1,109	2,004	6,460	16,860	423	—	—	—	—
1977	1,224	—	—	26,505	11,932	1,334	9,659	1,157	2,038	7,253	19,671	457	—	—	37,302	7,056
1978	1,356	—	—	—	—	1,322	10,191	1,152	2,021	7,671	21,287	514	—	—	—	—
1979	1,329	—	—	—	—	1,306	10,624	1,130	1,997	7,938	21,710	524	—	—	—	—
1980	1,488	—	—	—	—	1,307	11,354	1,130	2,001	8,503	23,426	608	—	—	—	—
1981	1,725	—	—	—	—	1,251	11,805	1,079	1,929	8,734	25,640	646	—	—	—	—
1982	1,579	—	—	24,391	10,907	1,189	12,129	1,010	1,804	8,832	26,061	654	—	—	33,984	6,313
1983	1,580	—	—	—	—	1,182	12,792	996	1,815	9,193	27,339	613	—	—	—	—
1984	2,002	—	—	—	—	1,148	12,877	977	1,735	9,280	28,859	742	—	—	—	—
1985	1,863	—	—	—	—	1,059	12,471	904	1,581	9,003	27,728	697	—	—	—	—
1986	1,598	—	—	—	—	1,017	12,471	863	1,535	8,949	28,451	684	—	—	—	—
1987	2,028	—	—	23,168	9,520	1,081	13,904	912	1,616	9,879	32,516	736	—	—	33,987	7,370
1988	2,261	—	—	—	—	1,071	14,416	899	1,585	10,137	32,782	692	—	—	—	—
1989	2,390	—	—	—	—	1,029	14,323	873	1,558	10,213	33,158	868	—	—	—	—
1990	2,372	—	—	—	—	1,010	14,524	857	1,543	10,322	34,018	857	—	—	—	—
1991	2,183	—	—	—	—	982	14,686	832	1,504	10,429	34,743	801	—	—	—	—
1992	2,225	—	—	23,093	8,584	985	15,325	824	1,514	10,776	36,423	945	—	—	35,807	6,886
1993	2,450	—	—	—	—	980	15,622	825	1,510	11,080	37,163	961	—	—	—	—
1994	2,961	—	—	—	—	954	15,620	799	1,484	11,047	38,777	1,091	—	—	—	—
1995	2,879	—	—	—	—	950	15,753	794	1,463	11,038	39,519	1,194	—	—	—	—
1996	2,666	—	—	—	—	865	14,920	727	1,356	10,397	38,366	964	—	—	—	—
1997	—	—	—	23,411	—	829	15,404	—	—	—	—	—	—	—	36,735	—
1997	—	2,692	—	17,065	—	711	12,582	592	1,060	8,799	33,780	—	941	—	17,411	—
1998	—	2,371	—	—	—	649	11,923	542	989	9,334	31,778	—	935	—	—	—
1999	—	2,231	—	—	—	576	11,022	470	868	7,333	30,594	—	986	—	—	—

Series Dd59–74 Lumber and wood products, and furniture and fixtures: 1899–1964

	Lumber and wood products									Furniture and fixtures						
	All employees		Production workers			Value added	Capital expenditures		Aggregate power of equipment	Establishments		All employees		Production workers		
	Number	Payroll	Number	Man-hours	Wages		New	Total		Total	With at least 20 employees	Number	Payroll	Number	Man-hours	Wages
	Dd59	Dd60	Dd61	Dd62	Dd63	Dd64	Dd65	Dd66	Dd67	Dd68	Dd69	Dd70	Dd71	Dd72	Dd73	Dd74
Year	Thousand	Million dollars	Thousand	Million	Million dollars	Million dollars	Million dollars	Million dollars	Thousand horsepower	Number	Number	Thousand	Million dollars	Thousand	Million	Million dollars
1899	—	—	563	—	209	437	—	—	—	2,614	—	—	—	98	—	40
1904	—	—	596	—	272	578	—	—	—	3,497	—	137	69	127	—	58
1909	—	—	758	—	347	708	—	—	—	4,337	—	—	—	142	—	73
1914	718	410	672	—	349	647	—	—	3,176	4,844	—	169	110	149	—	84
1919	715	774	663	—	668	1,299	—	—	3,410	4,821	—	183	214	160	—	162
1921	566	581	521	—	483	853	—	—	—	4,326	—	162	214	142	—	165
1923	746	820	693	—	701	1,399	—	—	3,336	4,532	—	217	293	192	—	232
1925	726	815	674	—	693	1,333	—	—	3,473	4,776	—	232	321	204	—	254
1927	649	748	602	—	632	1,179	—	—	3,332	4,666	—	237	338	210	—	266
1929	651	759	603	—	632	1,322	—	—	3,674	5,491	—	248	359	219	—	276
1931	—	—	327	—	277	524	—	—	—	4,554	—	137	111	147	—	147
1933	314	211	294	—	182	379	—	—	—	3,491	—	171	171	123	—	91
1935	415	340	384	—	283	542	—	—	—	4,319	—	—	—	151	—	133
1937	—	—	438	—	369	714	—	—	—	4,469	—	—	—	199	—	202
1939	—	—	423	—	355	731	—	—	2,998	5,178	—	—	—	189	—	187
1947	642	1,352	601	1,255	1,191	2,520	172	—	—	7,551	—	316	807	278	584	642
1949	649	1,422	601	1,083	1,210	2,284	147	—	—	—	—	310	862	270	549	653
1950	751	1,748	692	1,272	1,510	3,166	192	—	—	—	—	346	1,013	296	617	774
1951	771	2,015	714	1,308	1,738	3,523	240	—	—	8,369	—	336	1,077	290	590	818
1952	743	2,072	687	1,270	1,786	3,449	178	—	—	8,778	—	332	1,123	285	589	853
1953	720	2,087	658	1,236	1,803	3,501	183	—	—	—	—	361	1,259	310	629	973
1954	645	1,934	582	1,107	1,605	3,242	217	—	5,151	10,373	3,012	341	1,197	287	571	893
1955	693	2,187	628	1,202	1,820	3,744	302	—	—	—	—	366	1,329	309	627	996
1956	698	2,276	631	1,187	1,887	3,817	293	—	—	—	—	376	1,417	315	638	1,057
1957	646	2,111	579	1,072	1,723	3,285	204	—	—	—	—	375	1,432	311	618	1,049
1958	585	2,008	509	967	1,642	3,213	297	—	—	10,329	3,265	354	1,414	292	575	1,039
1959	617	2,230	552	1,071	1,850	3,806	301	—	—	—	—	368	1,522	309	628	1,131
1960	594	2,169	529	1,028	1,779	3,495	334	—	—	—	—	364	1,531	304	615	1,124
1961	556	2,084	494	961	1,714	3,413	242	—	—	—	—	351	1,503	293	590	1,097
1962	553	2,170	493	972	1,780	3,644	300	—	7,710	—	—	363	1,638	307	632	1,205
1963	563	2,339	497	979	1,943	4,021	395	—	—	10,478	3,133	377	1,727	315	640	1,290
1964	559	2,436	490	985	2,048	4,365	362	—	—	—	—	388	1,845	324	663	1,375

(continued)

TABLE Dd13–231 Manufacturing summary, by industry division – establishments, employment and payroll, value added, capital expenditures, and aggregate power of equipment: 1899–1999 Continued

Year	Lumber and wood products — All employees: Number Dd59 (Thousand)	All employees: Payroll Dd60 (Million dollars)	Production workers: Number Dd61 (Thousand)	Production workers: Man-hours Dd62 (Million)	Production workers: Wages Dd63 (Million dollars)	Value added Dd64 (Million dollars)	Capital expenditures: New Dd65 (Million dollars)	Capital expenditures: Total Dd66 (Million dollars)	Aggregate power of equipment Dd67 (Thousand horsepower)	Furniture and fixtures — Establishments: Total Dd68 (Number)	Establishments: With at least 20 employees Dd69 (Number)	All employees: Number Dd70 (Thousand)	All employees: Payroll Dd71 (Million dollars)	Production workers: Number Dd72 (Thousand)	Production workers: Man-hours Dd73 (Million)	Production workers: Wages Dd74 (Million dollars)
1965	572	2,586	507	1,009	2,124	4,474	482	—	—	—	—	407	2,013	342	699	1,487
1966	572	2,693	506	1,015	2,214	4,791	485	—	—	—	—	429	2,188	361	735	1,621
1967	554	2,799	496	977	2,291	4,973	426	—	—	10,008	3,449	425	2,258	358	716	1,654
1968	552	3,019	491	973	2,471	5,916	484	—	—	—	—	433	2,453	364	733	1,793
1969	566	3,246	502	986	2,630	6,331	590	—	—	—	—	456	2,693	381	761	1,968
1970	542	3,241	475	925	2,591	5,869	535	—	—	—	—	437	2,691	361	715	1,938
1971	530	3,462	465	909	2,782	6,761	716	—	—	—	—	436	2,821	360	711	2,034
1972	691	4,983	601	1,168	3,933	10,309	931	—	—	9,233	3,647	462	3,202	384	756	2,321
1973	722	5,471	628	1,214	4,311	12,357	953	—	—	—	—	479	3,532	404	791	2,561
1974	675	5,490	583	1,121	4,293	11,561	1,357	—	—	—	—	459	3,570	381	732	2,577
1975	588	5,231	506	946	4,050	10,356	1,264	—	—	—	—	396	3,310	325	605	2,339
1976	629	6,143	543	1,040	4,817	13,454	1,232	—	—	—	—	426	3,772	352	665	2,690
1977	692	7,425	595	1,147	5,795	16,223	1,563	—	—	10,234	3,587	464	4,446	384	736	3,190
1978	723	8,411	619	1,188	6,496	18,972	1,899	—	—	—	—	481	5,029	397	769	3,611
1979	743	9,042	632	1,221	6,989	20,107	2,068	—	—	—	—	483	5,362	398	770	3,814
1980	698	8,905	582	1,098	6,720	18,030	2,027	—	—	—	—	473	5,623	384	727	3,926
1981	649	8,991	544	1,035	6,753	17,321	1,781	—	—	—	—	460	5,983	374	716	4,189
1982	576	8,445	479	894	6,446	15,377	1,342	—	—	10,003	3,629	436	6,084	351	651	4,189
1983	629	9,715	531	1,019	7,508	19,531	1,205	—	—	—	—	444	6,615	359	682	4,564
1984	643	10,353	542	1,047	7,860	21,035	1,689	—	—	—	—	474	7,446	384	740	5,149
1985	613	10,407	514	996	7,836	21,066	1,664	—	—	—	—	472	7,755	380	727	5,346
1986	620	10,820	512	1,003	8,135	23,239	1,657	—	—	—	—	467	8,030	376	734	5,556
1987	698	12,707	582	1,151	9,524	28,664	1,825	—	—	11,636	4,072	511	9,082	410	805	6,253
1988	702	13,332	583	1,156	9,948	29,023	1,772	—	—	—	—	508	9,475	410	802	6,542
1989	684	13,362	568	1,127	9,973	29,673	2,024	—	—	—	—	510	9,807	409	798	6,671
1990	678	13,444	564	1,110	9,975	28,552	1,994	—	—	—	—	494	9,813	393	776	6,579
1991	624	12,668	518	1,021	9,414	26,935	1,732	—	—	—	—	459	9,438	362	708	6,216
1992	656	13,882	540	1,089	10,201	33,154	1,760	—	—	11,658	3,766	471	10,227	372	748	6,777
1993	685	14,955	569	1,161	11,043	37,582	1,950	—	—	—	—	482	10,703	384	764	7,177
1994	718	15,903	595	1,224	11,766	40,708	2,657	—	—	—	—	496	11,270	399	894	7,611
1995	741	16,622	614	1,248	12,241	40,937	2,974	—	—	—	—	514	11,907	415	833	8,051
1996	739	17,314	613	1,249	12,702	41,486	3,305	—	—	—	—	515	12,414	414	837	8,351
1997	757	18,669	—	—	—	—	—	—	—	12,095	—	524	13,344	—	—	—
1997	570	14,319	476	948	10,568	33,493	—	2,869	—	20,758	—	604	14,986	485	937	10,217
1998	578	15,113	484	977	11,123	34,469	—	2,799	—	—	—	625	16,048	506	993	10,935
1999	589	15,954	493	1,011	11,787	38,413	—	3,033	—	—	—	628	16,880	507	1,015	11,498

Furniture and fixtures (Dd75–Dd78) and **Paper and allied products** (Dd79–Dd89)

Year	Dd75 Value added (Million dollars)	Dd76 Capital exp. New (Million dollars)	Dd77 Capital exp. Total (Million dollars)	Dd78 Aggregate power of equipment (Thousand horsepower)	Dd79 Establishments Total (Number)	Dd80 Establishments with at least 20 employees (Number)	Dd81 All employees Number (Thousand)	Dd82 All employees Payroll (Million dollars)	Dd83 Production workers Number (Thousand)	Dd84 Production workers Man-hours (Million)	Dd85 Production workers Wages (Million dollars)	Dd86 Value added (Million dollars)	Dd87 Capital exp. New (Million dollars)	Dd88 Capital exp. Total (Million dollars)	Dd89 Aggregate power of equipment (Thousand horsepower)
1899	82	—	—	112	1,895	—	100	94	44	—	35	90	—	—	—
1904	116	—	—	163	2,031	—	129	62	120	—	51	122	—	—	—
1909	151	—	—	—	2,316	—	155	85	142	—	67	168	—	—	—
1914	174	—	—	240	2,344	—	182	114	164	—	87	201	—	—	1,697
1919	366	—	—	265	2,558	—	227	268	203	—	208	517	—	—	1,967
1921	347	—	—	—	2,511	—	202	256	181	—	198	392	—	—	—
1923	510	—	—	345	2,582	—	241	317	214	—	244	564	—	—	2,314
1925	562	—	—	403	2,614	—	242	327	216	—	256	612	—	—	2,575
1927	569	—	—	456	2,851	—	246	344	218	—	264	686	—	—	2,814
1929	615	—	—	504	2,973	—	258	373	229	—	282	782	—	—	3,167
1931	322	—	—	—	2,917	—	—	—	197	—	217	606	—	—	—
1933	193	—	—	—	2,697	—	221	220	196	—	173	518	—	—	—
1935	274	—	—	—	2,945	—	267	313	236	—	236	636	—	—	—
1937	424	—	—	—	3,084	—	—	—	267	—	310	863	—	—	—
1939	418	—	—	566	3,328	—	—	—	270	—	315	888	—	—	4,131
1947	1,346	77	—	—	4,100	—	454	1,295	392	857	1,018	2,913	407	—	—
1949	1,412	41	—	—	—	—	447	1,420	377	801	1,083	2,777	315	—	—
1950	1,667	58	—	—	4,849	—	478	1,607	401	874	1,240	3,438	299	—	—
1951	1,804	55	—	—	4,406	—	495	1,823	415	898	1,389	4,180	389	—	—
1952	1,904	55	—	—	4,334	—	482	1,878	402	868	1,425	3,883	371	—	—
1953	2,047	59	—	—	—	—	533	2,180	442	950	1,647	4,463	397	—	—
1954	1,998	62	—	949	5,004	3,277	528	2,205	436	920	1,657	4,630	533	—	8,256
1955	2,306	79	—	—	—	—	546	2,419	451	968	1,818	5,141	556	—	—
1956	2,510	92	—	—	—	—	563	2,616	461	982	1,952	5,610	750	—	—
1957	2,514	84	—	—	—	—	563	2,721	458	956	2,010	5,724	767	—	—
1958	2,396	83	—	—	5,259	3,214	551	2,759	445	927	2,022	5,669	634	—	—
1959	2,614	84	—	—	—	—	569	2,998	459	977	2,201	6,393	686	—	—
1960	2,619	76	—	—	—	—	575	3,089	461	964	2,235	6,509	659	—	—
1961	2,558	77	—	—	—	—	570	3,179	456	958	2,315	6,660	685	—	—
1962	2,841	96	—	1,265	—	—	576	3,336	460	971	2,424	6,997	742	—	12,477
1963	3,068	110	—	—	5,713	3,552	588	3,508	468	989	2,551	7,396	709	—	—
1964	3,227	108	—	—	—	—	593	3,686	471	1,007	2,678	7,806	902	—	—

(continued)

TABLE Dd13–231   Manufacturing summary, by industry division – establishments, employment and payroll, value added, capital expenditures, and aggregate power of equipment: 1899–1999 *Continued*

	Furniture and fixtures				Paper and allied products										
		Capital expenditures		Aggregate power of equipment	Establishments		Employment and payroll						Capital expenditures		Aggregate power of equipment
	Value added				Total	With at least 20 employees	All employees		Production workers			Value added			
		New	Total				Number	Payroll	Number	Man-hours	Wages		New	Total	
	Dd75	Dd76	Dd77	Dd78	Dd79	Dd80	Dd81	Dd82	Dd83	Dd84	Dd85	Dd86	Dd87	Dd88	Dd89
Year	Million dollars	Million dollars	Million dollars	Thousand horsepower	Number	Number	Thousand	Million dollars	Thousand	Million	Million dollars	Million dollars	Million dollars	Million dollars	Thousand horsepower
1965	3,612	151	—	—	—	—	610	3,896	485	1,029	2,829	8,464	1,186	—	—
1966	3,990	186	—	—	—	—	634	4,236	503	1,076	3,071	9,417	1,422	—	—
1967	4,170	198	—	—	5,890	3,812	639	4,436	508	1,071	3,206	9,756	1,585	—	—
1968	4,562	178	—	—	—	—	643	4,750	510	1,086	3,436	10,466	1,238	—	—
1969	5,031	190	—	—	—	—	670	5,200	531	1,128	3,757	11,426	1,421	—	—
1970	4,876	231	—	—	—	—	659	5,374	520	1,076	3,850	11,590	1,397	—	—
1971	5,227	196	—	—	—	—	632	5,537	495	1,025	3,951	11,682	1,197	—	—
1972	6,090	306	—	—	6,038	3,956	633	5,992	499	1,041	4,320	13,064	1,335	—	—
1973	6,736	344	—	—	—	—	645	6,482	509	1,056	4,695	15,166	1,530	—	—
1974	6,983	351	—	—	—	—	646	6,995	507	1,032	4,995	18,957	2,208	—	—
1975	6,290	252	—	—	—	—	589	6,990	454	901	4,873	17,943	2,718	—	—
1976	7,370	295	—	—	—	—	615	8,047	478	968	5,692	20,604	3,010	—	—
1977	8,917	388	—	—	6,545	3,999	629	8,943	486	986	6,323	22,171	3,295	—	—
1978	10,136	521	—	—	—	—	639	9,852	492	996	6,940	24,396	3,763	—	—
1979	10,999	526	—	—	—	—	658	10,810	509	1,030	7,636	27,136	4,447	—	—
1980	11,631	575	—	—	—	—	646	11,731	494	1,006	8,204	29,761	5,128	—	—
1981	12,642	573	—	—	—	—	636	12,644	487	994	8,820	32,367	4,656	—	—
1982	12,829	566	—	—	6,381	4,090	606	12,948	461	923	9,040	33,376	5,098	—	—
1983	14,282	601	—	—	—	—	606	13,827	461	937	9,737	35,612	4,987	—	—
1984	15,906	725	—	—	—	—	613	14,884	468	962	10,516	40,885	5,302	—	—
1985	16,479	763	—	—	—	—	604	15,346	462	943	10,780	40,422	6,273	—	—
1986	17,659	778	—	—	—	—	603	16,113	458	953	11,297	43,925	6,084	—	—
1987	20,310	895	—	—	6,292	4,144	611	16,860	466	972	11,776	50,489	5,752	—	—
1988	20,834	934	—	—	—	—	620	17,665	476	998	12,329	57,474	7,260	—	—
1989	21,360	1,039	—	—	—	—	633	18,500	486	1,018	12,897	61,222	9,579	—	—
1990	21,582	912	—	—	—	—	631	19,065	480	1,012	13,127	60,180	10,957	—	—
1991	20,586	723	—	—	—	—	625	19,542	477	1,005	13,463	58,756	9,206	—	—
1992	22,840	821	—	—	6,416	4,249	626	20,492	479	1,019	14,063	60,174	7,962	—	—
1993	23,994	974	—	—	—	—	626	20,901	479	1,024	14,429	59,257	7,370	—	—
1994	25,194	1,019	—	—	—	—	622	21,577	480	1,025	14,889	63,520	7,731	—	—
1995	26,238	1,232	—	—	—	—	630	22,237	486	1,041	15,353	79,836	8,219	—	—
1996	27,200	1,252	—	—	—	—	631	22,947	488	1,051	15,785	72,290	9,302	—	—
1997	34,839	—	1,745	—	6,496	—	574	22,312	440	936	15,188	70,300	—	8,595	—
1998	37,810	—	1,917	—	5,896	—	572	22,529	439	929	15,387	72,879	—	8,547	—
1999	40,296	—	2,172	—	—	—	560	22,789	432	924	15,641	74,602	—	7,051	—

	Printing and publishing											Chemicals and allied products			
	Establishments		Employment and payroll					Value added	Capital expenditures		Aggregate power of equipment	Establishments		Employment and payroll	
	Total	With at least 20 employees	All employees		Production workers							Total	With at least 20 employees	All employees	
			Number	Payroll	Number	Man-hours	Wages		New	Total				Number	Payroll
Year	Dd90	Dd91	Dd92	Dd93	Dd94	Dd95	Dd96	Dd97	Dd98	Dd99	Dd100	Dd101	Dd102	Dd103	Dd104
	Number	Number	Thousand	Million dollars	Thousand	Million	Million dollars	Million dollars	Million dollars	Million dollars	Thousand horsepower	Number	Number	Thousand	Million dollars
1899	24,363	—	244	144	202	—	104	300	—	—	—	7,669	—	170	80
1904	28,369	—	299	203	228	—	133	424	—	—	—	8,370	—	191	103
1909	32,137	—	374	281	270	—	174	519	—	—	—	10,380	—	235	144
1914	34,241	—	406	340	286	—	207	627	—	—	342	10,698	—	269	192
1919	33,262	—	448	594	304	—	352	1,091	—	—	379	10,688	—	388	497
1921	22,559	—	428	718	284	—	436	1,306	—	—	—	8,208	—	279	369
1923	22,897	—	481	838	310	—	494	1,527	—	—	430	8,253	—	340	459
1925	23,646	—	497	924	317	—	544	1,757	—	—	486	8,160	—	—	—
1927	25,375	—	524	1,027	331	—	589	1,936	—	—	570	8,594	—	348	492
1929	27,364	—	566	1,139	358	—	636	2,233	—	—	649	9,327	—	382	550
1931	24,664	—		—	315	—	535	1,768	—	—	—	8,324	—	—	—
1933	19,216	—	398	579	262	—	353	1,245	—	—	—	7,297	—	302	306
1935	22,505	—	473	792	303	—	444	1,547	—	—	—	8,225	—	—	—
1937	22,674	—	555	951	351	—	530	1,785	—	—	—	8,337	—	—	—
1939	24,878	—	552	978	324	—	493	1,765	—	—	771	8,839	—	—	—
1947	29,078	—	715	2,276	438	888	1,318	4,249	226	—	—	10,019	—	626	1,899
1949	—	—	756	2,744	462	994	1,569	4,659	254	—	—	—	—	612	2,092
1950	29,427	—	763	2,909	472	1,019	1,702	4,907	244	—	—	10,339	—	643	2,342
1951	29,704	—	765	3,068	474	991	1,791	5,289	244	—	—	10,909	—	703	2,784
1952	30,147	—	773	3,267	471	999	1,909	5,660	189	—	—	11,007	—	739	3,117
1953	—	—	760	3,387	474	924	2,014	5,916	195	—	—	—	—	768	3,400
1954	32,530	6,054	804	3,620	499	961	2,112	6,403	237	—	975	11,074	3,969	734	3,377
1955	—	—	823	3,837	507	985	2,225	6,938	254	—	—	—	—	741	3,566
1956	—	—	854	4,118	527	1,017	2,386	7,547	289	—	—	—	—	755	3,852
1957	—	—	867	4,295	533	1,019	2,466	7,913	327	—	—	—	—	757	4,036
1958	35,457	6,859	865	4,468	531	998	2,596	7,973	422	—	—	11,372	3,763	698	3,941
1959	—	—	885	4,812	553	1,054	2,799	8,788	403	—	—	—	—	718	4,233
1960	—	—	907	5,065	560	1,082	2,935	9,342	420	—	—	—	—	726	4,422
1961	—	—	913	5,201	559	1,075	2,983	9,551	414	—	—	—	—	713	4,524
1962	—	—	922	5,411	566	1,084	3,101	9,998	436	—	1,746	—	—	727	4,755
1963	38,090	7,215	913	5,515	560	1,083	3,191	10,476	464	—	—	11,996	3,985	737	4,970
1964	—	—	935	5,848	570	1,124	3,350	11,192	465	—	—	—	—	749	5,244

(continued)

TABLE Dd13–231   Manufacturing summary, by industry division – establishments, employment and payroll, value added, capital expenditures, and aggregate power of equipment: 1899–1999   Continued

	Printing and publishing											Chemicals and allied products			
	Establishments		Employment and payroll					Value added	Capital expenditures		Aggregate power of equipment	Establishments		Employment and payroll	
	Total	With at least 20 employees	All employees		Production workers				New	Total		Total	With at least 20 employees	All employees	
			Number	Payroll	Number	Man-hours	Wages							Number	Payroll
Year	Dd90	Dd91	Dd92	Dd93	Dd94	Dd95	Dd96	Dd97	Dd98	Dd99	Dd100	Dd101	Dd102	Dd103	Dd104
	Number	Number	Thousand	Million dollars	Thousand	Million	Million dollars	Million dollars	Million dollars	Million dollars	Thousand horsepower	Number	Number	Thousand	Million dollars
1965	—	—	982	6,269	597	1,156	3,575	12,099	543	—	—	—	—	780	5,594
1966	—	—	1,018	6,751	619	1,209	3,832	13,265	709	—	—	—	—	822	6,129
1967	37,989	8,035	1,031	7,152	632	1,196	4,011	14,355	788	—	—	11,799	4,348	841	6,443
1968	—	—	1,040	7,627	636	1,204	4,280	15,329	757	—	—	—	—	856	6,939
1969	—	—	1,091	8,338	667	1,262	4,702	16,793	853	—	—	—	—	883	7,603
1970	—	—	1,077	8,682	653	1,265	4,903	17,232	873	—	—	—	—	881	8,004
1971	—	—	1,049	8,976	626	1,192	5,010	18,086	942	—	—	—	—	849	8,260
1972	42,103	8,619	1,056	9,827	637	1,181	5,459	20,197	1,047	—	—	11,425	4,431	837	8,731
1973	—	—	1,084	10,523	649	1,203	5,830	21,871	1,090	—	—	—	—	852	9,440
1974	—	—	1,076	11,139	639	1,189	6,131	23,610	1,141	—	—	—	—	866	10,547
1975	—	—	1,070	11,655	626	1,138	6,220	24,641	1,175	—	—	—	—	842	11,227
1976	—	—	1,086	12,680	629	1,163	6,737	27,647	1,261	—	—	—	—	851	12,365
1977	49,767	9,132	1,092	14,025	626	1,153	7,322	31,980	1,598	—	—	12,173	4,602	880	13,839
1978	—	—	1,445	15,536	652	1,202	8,021	35,829	2,208	—	—	—	—	896	15,287
1979	—	—	1,223	16,953	698	1,294	8,761	40,004	2,449	—	—	—	—	895	16,516
1980	—	—	1,263	18,843	716	1,318	9,599	44,375	2,768	—	—	—	—	910	18,269
1981	—	—	1,270	20,609	720	1,343	10,454	49,352	3,076	—	—	—	—	892	19,723
1982	53,406	10,871	1,292	22,707	711	1,313	11,307	54,423	3,213	—	—	11,901	4,779	873	20,836
1983	—	—	1,301	24,212	723	1,339	12,053	60,062	3,237	—	—	—	—	851	21,411
1984	—	—	1,325	26,232	733	1,379	12,916	67,021	3,957	—	—	—	—	843	22,665
1985	—	—	1,360	28,169	742	1,384	13,554	73,054	4,715	—	—	—	—	826	23,345
1986	—	—	1,376	29,890	738	1,415	14,099	78,150	4,385	—	—	—	—	802	23,711
1987	61,791	12,616	1,494	33,440	797	1,538	15,659	90,162	4,908	—	—	12,040	4,897	814	25,017
1988	—	—	1,506	35,255	803	1,575	16,386	94,622	5,109	—	—	—	—	835	26,608
1989	—	—	1,518	37,131	815	1,580	16,928	98,960	5,962	—	—	—	—	867	29,105
1990	—	—	1,561	39,472	831	1,624	17,781	104,719	6,116	—	—	—	—	869	30,719
1991	—	—	1,518	39,629	804	1,576	17,702	105,825	5,447	—	—	—	—	867	31,851
1992	65,392	12,723	1,492	41,136	785	1,555	18,457	112,446	5,372	—	—	12,004	5,044	849	32,502
1993	—	—	1,495	42,059	784	1,547	18,485	116,767	4,874	—	—	—	—	839	33,094
1994	—	—	1,494	42,850	782	1,547	18,750	121,111	5,637	—	—	—	—	823	33,880
1995	—	—	1,534	44,747	809	1,593	19,507	125,936	5,617	—	—	—	—	839	35,424
1996	—	—	1,515	46,175	801	1,573	20,122	130,946	5,912	—	—	—	—	824	36,331
1997	62,355	—	1,534	50,092	—	—	—	—	—	—	—	12,371	—	820	37,240
1997	42,916	—	934	26,023	608	1,164	16,336	58,393	—	4,704	—	13,513	—	883	39,836
1998	—	—	843	26,847	617	1,210	16,906	60,248	—	4,493	—	—	—	895	41,581
1999	—	—	838	27,369	609	1,205	17,098	62,428	—	4,453	—	—	—	881	42,101

Chemicals and allied products — **Petroleum and coal products**

	Chemicals and allied products							Petroleum and coal products							
	Employment and payroll — Production workers			Value added	Capital expenditures		Aggregate power of equipment	Establishments		Employment and payroll — All employees		Production workers			Value added
	Number	Man-hours	Wages		New	Total		Total	With at least 20 employees	Number	Payroll	Number	Man-hours	Wages	
Year	Dd105	Dd106	Dd107	Dd108	Dd109	Dd110	Dd111	Dd112	Dd113	Dd114	Dd115	Dd116	Dd117	Dd118	Dd119
	Thousand	Million	Million dollars	Million dollars	Million dollars	Million dollars	Thousand horsepower	Number	Number	Thousand	Million dollars	Thousand	Million	Million dollars	Million dollars
1899	144	—	51	212	—	—	—	308	—	31	16	29	—	14	37
1904	158	—	56	286	—	—	—	376	—	39	23	36	—	19	57
1909	185	—	82	401	—	—	—	590	—	51	34	46	—	27	76
1914	208	—	106	457	—	—	1,459	591	—	60	49	51	—	36	112
1919	294	—	306	1,198	—	—	1,721	787	—	118	182	97	—	143	511
1921	212	—	218	834	—	—	—	692	—	103	176	87	—	136	430
1923	264	—	286	1,185	—	—	1,654	781	—	125	210	103	—	163	562
1925	261	—	297	1,320	—	—	1,748	750	—	113	193	97	—	154	635
1927	278	—	319	1,474	—	—	1,848	645	—	116	202	100	—	159	543
1929	307	—	352	1,737	—	—	2,312	922	—	—	—	112	—	180	829
1931	248	—	259	1,359	—	—	—	859	—	103	—	91	—	140	432
1933	254	—	217	1,121	—	—	—	835	—	124	141	90	—	113	395
1935	294	—	282	1,363	—	—	—	928	—	—	187	105	—	143	471
1937	303	—	366	1,732	—	—	—	934	—	—	—	116	—	189	638
1939	276	—	342	1,819	—	—	3,763	1,227	—	—	—	108	—	177	697
1947	464	975	1,236	5,317	805	—	—	1,411	—	208	726	165	354	543	1,991
1949	440	922	1,320	5,848	598	—	—	—	—	208	820	167	336	614	1,744
1950	457	955	1,471	7,237	603	—	—	1,142	—	208	850	162	330	624	2,139
1951	498	1,029	1,733	8,165	981	—	—	889	—	218	970	170	347	712	2,687
1952	513	1,063	1,904	8,539	1,019	—	—	1,024	—	220	1,036	170	338	751	2,619
1953	536	1,094	2,103	9,320	944	—	—	—	—	229	1,140	176	351	821	2,795
1954	499	1,011	1,994	9,547	927	—	13,521	1,262	659	183	953	136	269	659	2,241
1955	508	1,027	2,117	11,108	761	—	—	—	—	183	1,001	136	271	692	2,793
1956	515	1,040	2,266	11,894	1,082	—	—	—	—	184	1,083	136	271	744	3,318
1957	506	1,018	2,322	12,373	1,264	—	—	—	—	186	1,150	135	268	771	3,249
1958	453	908	2,242	12,308	1,244	—	—	1,708	821	179	1,117	131	255	758	2,518
1959	471	949	2,410	14,336	1,103	—	—	—	—	171	1,128	124	247	761	2,894
1960	470	944	2,473	14,415	1,285	—	—	—	—	171	1,145	124	250	773	3,308
1961	460	932	2,521	14,805	1,500	—	—	—	—	160	1,118	114	229	745	3,382
1962	470	953	2,647	16,009	1,382	—	20,553	—	—	154	1,097	110	222	724	3,439
1963	474	963	2,780	17,586	1,546	—	—	1,839	689	154	1,134	109	217	745	3,713
1964	480	986	2,928	19,166	1,862	—	—	—	—	148	1,127	105	214	743	3,780

(continued)

TABLE Dd13–231 Manufacturing summary, by industry division – establishments, employment and payroll, value added, capital expenditures, and aggregate power of equipment: 1899–1999 Continued

	Chemicals and allied products							Establishments		Petroleum and coal products					
	Employment and payroll — Production workers			Value added	Capital expenditures		Aggregate power of equipment	Total	With at least 20 employees	All employees		Employment and payroll — Production workers			Value added
	Number	Man-hours	Wages		New	Total				Number	Payroll	Number	Man-hours	Wages	
	Dd105	Dd106	Dd107	Dd108	Dd109	Dd110	Dd111	Dd112	Dd113	Dd114	Dd115	Dd116	Dd117	Dd118	Dd119
Year	Thousand	Million	Million dollars	Million dollars	Million dollars	Million dollars	Thousand horsepower	Number	Number	Thousand	Million dollars	Thousand	Million	Million dollars	Million dollars
1965	502	1,023	3,105	20,956	2,482	—	—	—	—	142	1,107	102	204	733	4,131
1966	529	1,077	3,400	22,656	2,899	—	—	—	—	140	1,128	99	198	742	4,754
1967	541	1,086	3,555	23,550	2,936	—	—	1,880	704	142	1,216	99	202	786	5,426
1968	551	1,116	3,845	25,810	2,789	—	—	—	—	141	1,284	98	201	825	5,567
1969	566	1,151	4,181	27,319	2,843	—	—	—	—	142	1,369	98	197	857	5,703
1970	556	1,121	4,327	27,930	3,111	—	—	—	—	144	1,487	100	205	942	5,478
1971	529	1,061	4,451	29,432	2,938	—	—	—	—	141	1,564	97	198	994	5,617
1972	525	1,053	4,734	32,414	2,948	—	—	2,016	720	140	1,638	98	201	1,064	5,793
1973	535	1,075	5,149	36,239	3,186	—	—	—	—	137	1,716	96	194	1,110	7,740
1974	542	1,085	5,697	44,488	4,957	—	—	—	—	146	1,920	101	208	1,241	9,951
1975	510	1,001	5,858	44,976	6,353	—	—	—	—	141	2,147	98	197	1,357	10,500
1976	520	1,032	6,518	51,408	7,122	—	—	—	—	145	2,437	100	206	1,578	13,169
1977	544	1,089	7,446	56,721	8,199	—	—	2,206	773	147	2,696	101	208	1,765	16,378
1978	548	1,099	8,156	61,506	7,919	—	—	—	—	148	3,001	103	217	1,983	16,301
1979	552	1,106	8,850	70,356	7,976	—	—	—	—	158	3,418	106	222	2,189	28,847
1980	545	1,080	9,483	74,384	8,770	—	—	—	—	149	3,615	100	200	2,134	24,816
1981	533	1,067	10,230	80,032	9,087	—	—	—	—	152	4,076	101	209	2,522	26,740
1982	509	1,004	10,544	77,315	9,087	—	—	2,322	848	152	4,339	100	205	2,613	22,069
1983	496	981	10,868	86,472	7,083	—	—	—	—	146	4,409	95	200	2,723	21,044
1984	491	979	11,444	94,728	7,643	—	—	—	—	137	4,380	90	192	2,649	16,163
1985	476	951	11,662	95,258	8,181	—	—	—	—	128	4,132	84	178	2,534	17,112
1986	458	928	11,756	100,013	7,907	—	—	—	—	125	4,215	82	168	2,598	17,496
1987	463	945	12,313	120,778	8,711	—	—	2,232	753	116	3,996	76	158	2,459	18,518
1988	477	983	12,985	139,090	11,006	—	—	—	—	115	4,150	76	158	2,527	25,333
1989	493	1,004	13,852	149,009	13,775	—	—	—	—	113	4,254	75	163	2,581	26,574
1990	489	1,006	14,462	156,665	15,645	—	—	—	—	112	4,497	73	162	2,705	27,375
1991	484	1,005	15,014	159,637	16,599	—	—	—	—	113	4,760	73	161	2,800	24,238
1992	479	1,008	15,396	164,346	16,381	—	—	2,124	688	114	4,967	74	165	2,922	23,408
1993	474	1,000	15,617	170,909	15,690	—	—	—	—	114	5,138	74	164	3,055	24,052
1994	472	992	16,116	181,601	15,411	—	—	—	—	111	5,224	72	166	3,140	29,079
1995	487	1,027	17,018	196,906	17,627	—	—	—	—	110	5,260	72	164	3,177	31,580
1996	477	1,014	17,469	194,412	20,041	—	—	—	—	106	5,238	69	161	3,159	31,656
1997	512	1,069	19,192	224,685	—	21,669	—	2,147	—	106	5,480	—	—	—	37,611
1998	516	1,070	19,878	230,219	—	21,739	—	2,155	—	108	5,546	72	162	3,421	31,649
1999	506	1,051	19,800	229,284	—	20,937	—	—	—	104	5,625	69	156	3,497	42,355

Group headings: **Petroleum and coal products** (Dd120–Dd122), **Rubber and plastic products** (Dd123–Dd133), **Leather and leather products** (Dd134–Dd135).

Dd120–Dd121 = Petroleum and coal products, Capital expenditures (New / Total). Dd122 = Aggregate power of equipment. Dd123–Dd124 = Rubber Establishments (Total / With at least 20 employees). Dd125–Dd126 = All employees (Number / Payroll). Dd127–Dd129 = Production workers (Number / Man-hours / Wages). Dd130 = Value added. Dd131–Dd132 = Capital expenditures (New / Total). Dd133 = Aggregate power of equipment. Dd134–Dd135 = Leather Establishments (Total / With at least 20 employees).

Year	Dd120	Dd121	Dd122	Dd123	Dd124	Dd125	Dd126	Dd127	Dd128	Dd129	Dd130	Dd131	Dd132	Dd133	Dd134	Dd135
	Million dollars	Million dollars	Thousand horsepower	Number	Number	Thousand	Million dollars	Thousand	Million	Million dollars	Million dollars	Million dollars	Million dollars	Thousand horsepower	Number	Number
1899	—	—	—	301	—	39	19	37	—	15	40	—	—	71	5,785	—
1904	—	—	—	365	—	48	25	44	—	20	68	—	—	86	5,476	—
1909	—	—	—	367	—	56	33	49	—	25	75	—	—	125	5,785	—
1914	—	—	465	342	—	89	60	74	—	44	138	—	—	199	6,798	—
1919	—	—	710	577	—	206	279	159	—	194	544	—	—	429	6,423	—
1921	—	—	—	596	—	115	171	103	—	124	327	—	—	—	4,827	—
1923	—	—	1,093	529	—	160	231	138	—	182	457	—	—	606	4,981	—
1925	—	—	1,242	530	—	—	—	142	—	191	539	—	—	660	4,352	—
1927	—	—	1,513	516	—	169	259	142	—	198	565	—	—	791	4,372	—
1929	—	—	1,755	525	—	172	263	149	—	207	539	—	—	821	4,285	—
1931	—	—	—	553	—	121	—	99	—	113	361	—	—	—	3,702	—
1933	—	—	—	408	—	132	125	106	—	99	261	—	—	—	3,265	—
1935	—	—	—	566	—	150	169	115	—	134	309	—	—	—	3,506	—
1937	—	—	—	578	—	150	216	130	—	171	369	—	—	—	3,249	—
1939	—	—	2,140	695	—	—	227	121	—	161	405	—	—	989	3,505	—
1947	400	—	—	872	—	258	781	214	424	613	1,300	110	—	—	5,308	—
1949	474	—	—	—	—	222	713	180	342	533	1,195	63	—	—	—	—
1950	332	—	—	838	—	239	837	196	392	644	1,620	80	—	—	4,903	—
1951	332	—	—	743	—	253	963	207	415	735	1,729	114	—	—	4,883	—
1952	612	—	—	730	—	255	1,042	206	409	786	1,744	127	—	—	5,012	—
1953	833	—	—	—	—	270	1,140	219	432	866	2,021	127	—	—	—	—
1954	674	—	6,506	1,406	753	247	1,059	196	377	776	1,954	128	—	2,211	4,445	2,267
1955	545	—	—	—	—	265	1,257	213	437	947	2,377	127	—	—	—	—
1956	701	—	—	—	—	265	1,260	211	415	931	2,418	152	—	—	—	—
1957	900	—	—	—	—	260	1,310	205	403	954	2,462	149	—	—	—	—
1958	682	—	—	4,562	1,827	348	1,723	271	531	1,211	3,277	197	—	—	4,549	2,227
1959	431	—	—	—	—	379	1,968	300	600	1,406	3,793	214	—	—	—	—
1960	485	—	—	—	—	378	1,998	296	590	1,400	3,773	299	—	—	—	—
1961	495	—	—	—	—	371	2,019	288	577	1,402	3,916	283	—	—	—	—
1962	479	—	9,916	—	—	398	2,250	314	637	1,585	4,316	354	—	3,549	—	—
1963	414	—	—	5,728	2,449	415	2,364	329	659	1,672	4,654	344	—	—	4,047	2,073
1964	413	—	—	—	—	430	2,457	341	696	1,799	4,991	399	—	—	—	—

(continued)

TABLE Dd13–231 Manufacturing summary, by industry division – establishments, employment and payroll, value added, capital expenditures, and aggregate power of equipment: 1899–1999 *Continued*

	Petroleum and coal products			Rubber and plastic products											Leather and leather products	
	Capital expenditures		Aggregate power of equipment	Establishments		Employment and payroll					Value added	Capital expenditures		Aggregate power of equipment	Establishments	
	New	Total		Total	With at least 20 employees	All employees		Production workers				New	Total		Total	With at least 20 employees
						Number	Payroll	Number	Man-hours	Wages						
	Dd120	Dd121	Dd122	Dd123	Dd124	Dd125	Dd126	Dd127	Dd128	Dd129	Dd130	Dd131	Dd132	Dd133	Dd134	Dd135
Year	Million dollars	Million dollars	Thousand horsepower	Number	Number	Thousand	Million dollars	Thousand	Million	Million dollars	Million dollars	Million dollars	Million dollars	Thousand horsepower	Number	Number
1965	604	—	—	—	—	465	2,814	369	747	1,985	5,681	516	—	—	—	—
1966	669	—	—	—	—	492	3,072	391	800	2,174	6,277	600	—	—	—	—
1967	999	—	—	6,456	3,122	517	3,287	410	816	2,313	6,800	677	—	—	3,685	1,967
1968	1,065	—	—	—	—	542	3,705	430	875	2,624	7,730	760	—	—	—	—
1969	1,072	—	—	—	—	567	4,026	451	916	2,846	8,431	857	—	—	—	—
1970	1,218	—	—	—	—	546	3,999	427	849	2,759	8,503	828	—	—	—	—
1971	1,304	—	—	—	—	544	4,286	422	844	2,968	9,521	724	—	—	—	—
1972	1,154	—	—	9,237	4,188	618	5,165	487	968	3,605	11,653	1,060	—	—	3,201	1,657
1973	1,107	—	—	—	—	672	5,812	532	1,042	4,080	13,440	1,305	—	—	—	—
1974	1,845	—	—	—	—	661	6,203	523	1,025	4,303	14,826	1,457	—	—	—	—
1975	2,418	—	—	—	—	585	5,923	451	873	3,985	13,599	1,140	—	—	—	—
1976	2,837	—	—	—	—	627	6,742	489	938	4,518	15,950	1,317	—	—	—	—
1977	2,261	—	—	11,943	5,294	721	8,536	564	1,111	5,842	19,740	1,645	—	—	3,075	1,486
1978	2,286	—	—	—	—	748	9,422	587	1,143	6,449	21,157	2,255	—	—	—	—
1979	3,273	—	—	—	—	754	10,146	593	1,150	6,939	23,112	2,208	—	—	—	—
1980	3,615	—	—	—	—	703	10,141	544	1,033	6,777	22,569	2,068	—	—	—	—
1981	5,158	—	—	—	—	691	11,047	542	1,050	7,393	26,006	2,217	—	—	—	—
1982	6,579	—	—	13,449	5,978	682	11,597	523	996	7,691	27,219	2,199	—	—	2,735	1,313
1983	4,583	—	—	—	—	684	12,305	527	1,036	8,229	29,805	1,767	—	—	—	—
1984	3,775	—	—	—	—	732	13,997	574	1,138	9,439	34,183	2,804	—	—	—	—
1985	3,438	—	—	—	—	743	13,723	578	1,138	9,794	35,708	3,430	—	—	—	—
1986	2,578	—	—	—	—	741	15,273	572	1,137	10,124	37,236	2,998	—	—	—	—
1987	2,341	—	—	14,587	7,300	831	17,575	643	1,283	11,694	44,418	3,410	—	—	2,198	915
1988	2,626	—	—	—	—	871	19,067	674	1,350	12,579	47,342	3,663	—	—	—	—
1989	3,394	—	—	—	—	903	20,414	697	1,392	13,373	49,309	4,776	—	—	—	—
1990	4,193	—	—	—	—	904	21,187	696	1,389	13,841	52,161	4,658	—	—	—	—
1991	5,942	—	—	—	—	886	21,566	677	1,350	13,937	53,325	4,633	—	—	—	—
1992	6,577	—	—	15,842	7,972	907	23,156	698	1,415	15,004	58,652	4,792	—	—	2,040	759
1993	6,302	—	—	—	—	936	24,467	726	1,476	16,024	63,204	5,001	—	—	—	—
1994	5,839	—	—	—	—	976	25,962	765	1,567	17,217	69,934	5,795	—	—	—	—
1995	6,213	—	—	—	—	1,018	27,301	801	1,635	18,088	73,023	6,651	—	—	—	—
1996	5,572	—	—	16,892	—	1,018	28,436	800	1,650	18,660	74,945	7,022	—	—	1,839	—
1997	—	4,755	—	16,876	—	1,037	30,255	806	1,608	19,829	81,349	—	7,837	—	1,870	—
1998	—	4,814	—	—	—	1,040	31,027	825	1,657	20,790	85,542	—	8,113	—	—	—
1999	—	4,569	—	—	—	1,069	32,638	848	1,720	21,823	91,346	—	8,680	—	—	—

Stone, clay, and glass products / Leather and leather products

Year	Leather and leather products — All employees Number (Dd136, Thousand)	Payroll (Dd137, Million dollars)	Production workers Number (Dd138, Thousand)	Man-hours (Dd139, Million)	Wages (Dd140, Million dollars)	Value added (Dd141, Million dollars)	Capital expenditures New (Dd142, Million dollars)	Capital expenditures Total (Dd143, Million dollars)	Aggregate power of equipment (Dd144, Thousand horsepower)	Stone, clay, and glass products — Establishments Total (Dd145, Number)	With at least 20 employees (Dd146, Number)	All employees Number (Dd147, Thousand)	Payroll (Dd148, Million dollars)	Production workers Number (Dd149, Thousand)	Man-hours (Dd150, Million)	Wages (Dd151, Million dollars)	Value added (Dd152, Million dollars)
1899	265	117	250	—	102	187	—	—	—	11,571	—	243	116	230	—	102	185
1904	284	141	266	—	121	246	—	—	—	10,744	—	305	171	286	—	149	271
1909	340	191	311	—	156	325	—	—	—	16,207	—	372	224	344	—	190	352
1914	341	214	308	—	170	353	—	—	311	14,793	—	405	249	335	—	206	379
1919	394	469	350	—	364	898	—	—	383	12,326	—	331	397	295	—	324	680
1921	314	385	280	—	315	610	—	—	—	8,227	—	282	377	251	—	305	605
1923	—	—	346	—	390	797	—	—	413	8,209	—	389	544	349	—	451	990
1925	350	—	314	—	355	751	—	—	413	8,491	—	392	565	351	—	466	1,043
1927	—	444	316	—	365	781	—	—	420	8,574	—	390	575	348	—	463	1,023
1929	351	444	319	—	360	774	—	—	436	8,788	—	372	548	331	—	436	1,054
1931	—	—	273	—	262	524	—	—	—	6,549	—	—	—	234	—	250	616
1933	302	254	282	—	223	452	—	—	—	4,757	—	—	—	175	—	144	404
1935	336	333	311	—	280	530	—	—	—	5,846	—	265	293	235	—	228	600
1937	—	—	329	—	308	584	—	—	—	6,114	—	331	420	297	—	346	860
1939	—	—	327	—	294	583	—	—	461	6,778	—	314	410	267	—	307	856
1947	383	874	349	677	725	1,533	31	—	—	11,643	—	461	1,207	405	838	992	2,299
1949	375	892	338	610	722	1,387	30	—	—	—	—	453	1,323	388	778	1,044	2,451
1950	385	949	342	629	773	1,499	26	—	—	9,707	—	491	1,530	418	863	1,220	3,138
1951	354	945	318	576	768	1,475	22	—	—	10,700	—	529	1,828	455	946	1,459	3,561
1952	361	1,016	324	605	834	1,597	19	—	—	10,435	—	510	1,842	436	895	1,457	3,531
1953	375	1,099	338	630	987	1,711	25	—	—	—	—	506	1,949	431	873	1,539	3,753
1954	357	1,027	321	587	834	1,641	28	—	—	11,162	—	492	1,938	412	827	1,496	3,866
1955	366	1,102	330	613	896	1,778	37	—	505	—	—	525	2,178	442	899	1,703	4,637
1956	367	1,149	329	607	939	1,882	37	—	—	—	—	536	2,345	450	911	1,815	5,036
1957	362	1,157	323	590	939	1,892	32	—	—	—	—	526	2,355	437	869	1,803	4,980
1958	349	1,146	310	566	912	1,898	32	—	—	15,047	4,484	553	2,586	446	884	1,935	5,333
1959	363	1,246	324	601	993	2,121	34	—	—	—	—	596	2,939	488	981	2,199	6,504
1960	358	1,227	317	582	972	2,044	35	—	—	—	—	581	2,950	474	960	2,187	6,370
1961	351	1,225	312	568	970	2,041	35	—	—	—	—	567	2,938	457	923	2,153	6,288
1962	346	1,256	308	569	1,000	2,102	36	—	587	—	—	573	3,103	463	939	2,280	6,589
1963	328	1,228	292	543	982	2,079	35	—	—	15,838	4,655	574	3,213	456	929	2,350	7,044
1964	327	1,286	292	553	1,022	2,265	38	—	—	—	—	581	3,369	459	949	2,447	7,493

(continued)

TABLE Dd13–231 Manufacturing summary, by industry division – establishments, employment and payroll, value added, capital expenditures, and aggregate power of equipment: 1899–1999 *Continued*

Leather and leather products

Year	All employees Number Dd136 (Thousand)	Payroll Dd137 (Million dollars)	Production workers Number Dd138 (Thousand)	Man-hours Dd139 (Million)	Wages Dd140 (Million dollars)	Value added Dd141 (Million dollars)	Capital expenditures New Dd142 (Million dollars)	Total Dd143 (Million dollars)	Aggregate power of equipment Dd144 (Thousand horsepower)
1965	336	1,348	299	563	1,065	2,322	47	—	—
1966	341	1,426	303	574	1,125	2,481	62	—	—
1967	329	1,459	239	549	1,147	2,627	62	—	—
1968	334	1,582	298	561	1,253	2,912	79	—	—
1969	327	1,593	291	538	1,252	2,898	64	—	—
1970	296	1,526	261	480	1,184	2,820	63	—	—
1971	274	1,501	240	442	1,155	2,761	69	—	—
1972	273	1,589	240	449	1,231	2,917	75	—	—
1973	268	1,595	235	434	1,230	2,962	81	—	—
1974	256	1,604	223	402	1,229	3,120	76	—	—
1975	240	1,651	209	378	1,250	3,187	78	—	—
1976	247	1,805	216	391	1,379	3,559	89	—	—
1977	243	1,860	212	382	1,408	3,719	96	—	—
1978	244	1,996	214	383	1,513	4,010	135	—	—
1979	239	2,085	207	363	1,542	4,249	130	—	—
1980	233	2,200	201	346	1,635	4,851	145	—	—
1981	228	2,364	197	347	1,766	5,230	200	—	—
1982	200	2,219	171	304	1,623	4,773	132	—	—
1983	189	2,225	162	290	1,613	4,853	122	—	—
1984	169	2,046	145	260	1,483	4,511	113	—	—
1985	147	1,863	125	225	1,342	4,108	103	—	—
1986	130	1,690	110	196	1,213	3,611	83	—	—
1987	129	1,831	109	206	1,301	4,378	101	—	—
1988	127	1,876	107	201	1,327	4,528	97	—	—
1989	119	1,852	100	189	1,303	4,540	117	—	—
1990	115	1,876	96	176	1,278	4,421	107	—	—
1991	103	1,737	85	153	1,188	4,072	89	—	—
1992	101	1,806	83	156	1,228	4,527	135	—	—
1993	99	1,818	82	156	1,260	4,642	131	—	—
1994	92	1,712	78	150	1,213	4,610	135	—	—
1995	86	1,632	72	136	1,125	4,126	126	—	—
1996	77	1,600	65	125	1,087	4,742	128	—	—
1997	85	1,832	69	134	1,186	5,408	—	167	—
1998	81	1,823	65	129	1,177	5,016	—	136	—
1999	74	1,760	60	118	1,146	4,551	—	155	—

Stone, clay, and glass products

Year	Establishments Total Dd145 (Number)	With at least 20 employees Dd146 (Number)	All employees Number Dd147 (Thousand)	Payroll Dd148 (Million dollars)	Production workers Number Dd149 (Thousand)	Man-hours Dd150 (Million)	Wages Dd151 (Million dollars)	Value added Dd152 (Million dollars)
1965	—	—	605	3,602	480	981	2,640	7,996
1966	—	—	616	3,838	488	999	2,812	8,495
1967	15,580	4,911	590	3,826	469	948	2,784	8,333
1968	—	—	590	4,065	469	951	2,971	9,212
1969	—	—	608	4,440	484	987	3,257	9,851
1970	—	—	591	4,531	470	951	3,321	9,786
1971	—	—	583	4,802	462	928	3,503	10,758
1972	16,015	5,301	623	5,547	493	998	4,037	12,587
1973	—	—	644	6,079	511	1,028	4,457	13,801
1974	—	—	637	6,414	508	1,013	4,720	14,566
1975	—	—	589	6,390	461	901	4,596	14,849
1976	—	—	599	7,086	474	939	5,145	16,773
1977	17,744	5,201	614	7,943	484	961	5,767	19,130
1978	—	—	639	9,077	509	1,019	6,622	22,535
1979	—	—	654	9,897	522	1,036	7,233	24,468
1980	—	—	613	10,062	480	946	7,190	24,051
1981	—	—	590	10,575	463	910	7,569	24,854
1982	16,545	4,753	532	10,097	408	796	7,164	22,986
1983	—	—	526	10,518	408	811	7,509	25,326
1984	—	—	533	11,224	416	831	8,039	27,707
1985	—	—	520	11,482	404	814	8,198	28,878
1986	—	—	514	11,745	399	814	8,352	30,677
1987	16,197	5,138	524	12,354	405	833	8,797	33,375
1988	—	—	522	12,745	401	817	9,031	34,243
1989	—	—	519	12,978	401	822	9,155	34,479
1990	—	—	508	13,201	392	808	9,274	34,164
1991	—	—	474	12,655	359	744	8,769	31,871
1992	16,254	4,851	469	13,113	357	743	9,035	34,641
1993	—	—	468	13,403	358	749	9,345	35,779
1994	—	—	485	14,144	374	788	9,864	39,504
1995	—	—	503	14,912	388	811	10,353	42,424
1996	—	—	520	15,857	402	836	10,934	46,055
1997	16,393	—	505	16,303	—	—	—	—
1997	—	—	501	16,172	389	798	11,319	49,425
1998	16,385	—	508	16,866	397	832	11,944	52,851
1999	—	—	526	17,948	411	871	12,620	56,538

Year	Stone, clay, and glass products — Capital expenditures New (Mil. $) Dd153	Total (Mil. $) Dd154	Aggregate power of equipment (Thous. hp) Dd155	Primary metal industries — Establishments Total Dd156	With at least 20 employees Dd157	All employees Number (Thous.) Dd158	All employees Payroll (Mil. $) Dd159	Production workers Number (Thous.) Dd160	Production workers Man-hours (Mil.) Dd161	Production workers Wages (Mil. $) Dd162	Value added (Mil. $) Dd163	Capital expenditures New (Mil. $) Dd164	Total (Mil. $) Dd165	Aggregate power of equipment (Thous. hp) Dd166	Fabricated metal products — Establishments Total Dd167	With at least 20 employees Dd168
1899	—	—	—	—	—	—	—	—	—	—	—	—	—	—	—	—
1904	—	—	—	—	—	—	—	—	—	—	—	—	—	—	—	—
1909	—	—	—	—	—	—	—	—	—	—	—	—	—	—	—	—
1914	—	—	1,494	—	—	—	—	—	—	—	—	—	—	—	—	—
1919	—	—	1,585	—	—	—	—	—	—	—	—	—	—	—	—	—
1921	—	—	—	—	—	—	—	—	—	—	—	—	—	—	—	—
1923	—	—	1,936	—	—	—	—	—	—	—	—	—	—	—	—	—
1925	—	—	2,348	—	—	—	—	—	—	—	—	—	—	—	—	—
1927	—	—	2,709	—	—	—	—	—	—	—	—	—	—	—	—	—
1929	—	—	2,854	—	—	—	—	—	—	—	—	—	—	—	—	—
1931	—	—	—	—	—	—	—	—	—	—	—	—	—	—	—	—
1933	—	—	—	—	—	—	—	—	—	—	—	—	—	—	—	—
1935	—	—	—	—	—	—	—	—	—	—	—	—	—	—	—	—
1937	—	—	—	3,245	—	—	—	792	—	1,205	2,520	—	—	—	8,688	—
1939	—	—	3,026	3,512	—	—	—	672	—	978	2,169	—	—	12,670	9,532	—
1947	285	—	—	5,465	—	1,158	3,602	1,012	2,054	2,983	5,733	592	—	—	16,877	—
1949	191	—	—	—	—	1,016	3,465	868	1,702	2,770	5,710	568	—	—	—	—
1950	222	—	—	5,322	—	1,129	4,158	978	2,009	3,400	7,951	548	—	—	17,975	—
1951	323	—	—	5,490	—	1,244	5,137	1,079	2,256	4,219	9,761	1,127	—	—	17,552	—
1952	251	—	—	5,500	—	1,240	5,215	1,066	2,071	4,204	9,051	1,603	—	—	17,953	—
1953	282	—	—	—	—	1,288	6,002	1,103	2,253	4,867	11,004	1,212	—	—	—	—
1954	301	—	4,811	—	—	1,152	5,260	967	1,866	4,105	9,772	910	—	25,546	22,516	7,348
1955	461	—	—	—	—	1,274	6,418	1,076	2,192	5,117	12,963	977	—	—	—	—
1956	725	—	—	—	—	1,319	6,893	1,110	2,195	5,444	13,848	1,651	—	—	—	—
1957	656	—	—	—	—	1,272	7,019	1,053	2,057	5,440	13,320	2,150	—	—	—	—
1958	489	—	—	6,447	3,412	1,092	6,281	883	1,670	4,696	11,542	1,544	—	—	24,783	8,323
1959	557	—	—	—	—	1,144	7,057	947	1,830	5,354	13,578	1,076	—	—	—	—
1960	541	—	—	—	—	1,175	7,215	957	1,837	5,424	13,283	1,615	—	—	—	—
1961	554	—	—	—	—	1,100	7,060	891	1,723	5,271	12,759	1,222	—	—	—	—
1962	549	—	8,716	6,513	3,583	1,128	7,482	917	1,796	5,658	13,678	1,159	—	33,304	27,075	9,210
1963	608	—	—	—	—	1,127	7,734	922	1,839	5,934	15,261	1,446	—	—	—	—
1964	627	—	—	—	—	1,181	8,488	973	1,994	6,578	16,692	1,886	—	—	—	—

(continued)

TABLE Dd13–231 Manufacturing summary, by industry division – establishments, employment and payroll, value added, capital expenditures, and aggregate power of equipment: 1899–1999 Continued

Column groups: **Stone, clay, and glass products** — Capital expenditures: New (Dd153), Total (Dd154), both Million dollars; Aggregate power of equipment (Dd155), Thousand horsepower. **Primary metal industries** — Establishments: Total (Dd156), With at least 20 employees (Dd157); Employment and payroll / All employees: Number (Dd158) Thousand, Payroll (Dd159) Million dollars; Production workers: Number (Dd160) Thousand, Man-hours (Dd161) Million, Wages (Dd162) Million dollars; Value added (Dd163) Million dollars; Capital expenditures: New (Dd164), Total (Dd165) Million dollars; Aggregate power of equipment (Dd166) Thousand horsepower. **Fabricated metal products** — Establishments: Total (Dd167) Number, With at least 20 employees (Dd168) Number.

Year	Dd153	Dd154	Dd155	Dd156	Dd157	Dd158	Dd159	Dd160	Dd161	Dd162	Dd163	Dd164	Dd165	Dd166	Dd167	Dd168
1965	773	—	—	—	—	1,250	9,238	1,026	2,105	7,176	18,924	2,257	—	—	—	—
1966	940	—	—	—	—	1,296	9,911	1,066	2,191	7,649	20,899	2,765	—	—	—	—
1967	821	—	—	6,837	4,082	1,281	9,851	1,042	2,089	7,457	19,978	3,134	—	—	27,418	10,741
1968	734	—	—	—	—	1,275	10,479	1,033	2,090	7,922	20,974	3,102	—	—	—	—
1969	908	—	—	—	—	1,311	11,447	1,064	2,172	8,688	22,729	2,816	—	—	—	—
1970	920	—	—	—	—	1,261	11,252	1,014	2,009	8,410	21,445	2,737	—	—	—	—
1971	928	—	—	—	—	1,169	11,205	931	1,832	8,301	21,120	2,198	—	—	—	—
1972	1,196	—	—	6,792	3,901	1,143	12,167	923	1,850	9,202	23,258	2,161	—	—	29,525	11,676
1973	1,391	—	—	—	—	1,222	14,148	996	2,028	10,873	28,614	2,334	—	—	—	—
1974	1,584	—	—	—	—	1,248	15,900	1,001	1,995	12,102	37,297	3,752	—	—	—	—
1975	1,581	—	—	—	—	1,089	14,994	856	1,638	11,030	30,367	4,165	—	—	—	—
1976	1,504	—	—	—	—	1,106	16,975	875	1,713	12,639	34,182	4,179	—	—	—	—
1977	1,881	—	—	7,375	3,980	1,114	18,745	885	1,744	14,065	37,568	4,497	—	—	33,712	12,739
1978	2,531	—	—	—	—	1,149	21,331	921	1,837	16,180	44,246	4,692	—	—	—	—
1979	2,606	—	—	—	—	1,190	23,996	953	1,888	18,185	50,882	5,129	—	—	—	—
1980	3,046	—	—	—	—	1,096	23,556	854	1,639	17,306	47,619	5,543	—	—	—	—
1981	2,581	—	—	—	—	1,063	25,322	826	1,600	18,564	49,551	6,339	—	—	—	—
1982	2,309	—	—	7,061	3,904	854	20,603	638	1,167	14,466	33,291	4,666	—	—	35,560	13,642
1983	1,746	—	—	—	—	771	19,260	585	1,122	13,642	35,997	4,362	—	—	—	—
1984	2,367	—	—	—	—	796	20,652	616	1,227	14,916	42,291	4,185	—	—	—	—
1985	2,774	—	—	—	—	747	19,962	574	1,138	14,315	38,239	4,680	—	—	—	—
1986	2,333	—	—	—	—	690	18,882	529	1,056	13,472	38,092	3,180	—	—	—	—
1987	2,416	—	—	6,661	3,688	702	19,800	542	1,115	14,176	46,136	3,851	—	—	36,098	13,891
1988	2,269	—	—	—	—	729	21,568	564	1,186	15,581	56,863	4,721	—	—	—	—
1989	2,924	—	—	—	—	743	22,658	576	1,229	16,134	56,751	5,594	—	—	—	—
1990	2,804	—	—	—	—	721	22,784	556	1,159	16,153	54,495	5,941	—	—	—	—
1991	2,481	—	—	—	—	690	22,049	526	1,083	15,469	48,110	6,082	—	—	—	—
1992	2,458	—	—	6,501	3,547	662	22,202	508	1,067	15,739	52,027	5,294	—	—	36,429	13,517
1993	2,415	—	—	—	—	653	22,708	504	1,074	16,232	55,444	4,744	—	—	—	—
1994	2,835	—	—	—	—	664	23,932	517	1,124	17,183	64,649	6,525	—	—	—	—
1995	3,365	—	—	—	—	688	25,075	541	1,556	17,967	69,594	6,718	—	—	—	—
1996	4,157	—	—	—	—	687	25,644	543	1,171	18,433	69,539	7,299	—	—	—	—
1997	—	4,799	—	6,275	—	692	26,830	480	1,025	17,355	68,749	—	6,516	—	37,985	—
1998	—	5,026	—	5,095	—	605	23,811	479	1,010	17,551	69,139	—	6,451	—	62,501	—
1999	—	5,355	—	—	—	602	24,146	466	985	17,236	66,733	—	6,096	—	—	—

Year	Fabricated metal products — All employees Number (Thousand) Dd169	All employees Payroll (Million dollars) Dd170	Production workers Number (Thousand) Dd171	Production workers Man-hours (Million) Dd172	Production workers Wages (Million dollars) Dd173	Value added (Million dollars) Dd174	Capital expenditures New (Million dollars) Dd175	Capital expenditures Total (Million dollars) Dd176	Aggregate power of equipment (Thousand horsepower) Dd177	Machinery, except electrical — Establishments Total (Number) Dd178	Establishments With at least 20 employees (Number) Dd179	All employees Number (Thousand) Dd180	All employees Payroll (Million dollars) Dd181	Production workers Number (Thousand) Dd182	Production workers Man-hours (Million) Dd183	Production workers Wages (Million dollars) Dd184
1899	—	—	—	—	—	—	—	—	—	—	—	—	—	—	—	—
1904	—	—	—	—	—	—	—	—	—	—	—	—	—	—	—	—
1909	—	—	—	—	—	—	—	—	—	—	—	—	—	—	—	—
1914	—	—	—	—	—	—	—	—	—	—	—	—	—	—	—	—
1919	—	—	—	—	—	—	—	—	—	—	—	—	—	—	—	—
1921	—	—	—	—	—	—	—	—	—	—	—	—	—	—	—	—
1923	—	—	—	—	—	—	—	—	—	—	—	—	—	—	—	—
1925	—	—	—	—	—	—	—	—	—	—	—	—	—	—	—	—
1927	—	—	—	—	—	—	—	—	—	—	—	—	—	—	—	—
1929	—	—	—	—	—	—	—	—	—	—	—	—	—	—	—	—
1931	—	—	—	—	—	—	—	—	—	—	—	—	—	—	—	—
1933	—	—	—	—	—	—	—	—	—	—	—	—	—	—	—	—
1935	—	—	—	—	—	—	—	—	—	—	—	—	—	—	—	—
1937	—	—	493	—	605	1,389	—	—	—	7,327	—	—	—	654	—	970
1939	—	—	451	—	547	1,401	—	—	1,740	8,860	—	—	—	536	—	770
1947	973	2,834	823	1,695	2,189	4,920	305	—	—	17,910	—	1,552	4,830	1,249	2,591	3,610
1949	872	2,884	710	1,429	2,088	4,834	231	—	—	18,734	—	1,295	4,559	1,005	2,013	3,175
1950	989	3,404	807	1,658	2,524	6,211	317	—	—	—	—	1,368	5,063	1,064	2,183	3,609
1951	1,035	3,988	853	1,765	2,970	7,139	354	—	—	—	—	1,604	6,729	1,260	2,693	4,914
1952	1,008	4,124	820	1,692	3,037	7,168	328	—	—	—	—	1,651	7,380	1,284	2,733	5,352
1953	1,118	4,765	916	1,885	3,555	8,144	446	—	—	—	—	1,691	7,876	1,307	2,744	5,686
1954	1,019	4,397	821	1,652	3,174	7,653	433	—	5,127	25,600	7,521	1,541	7,186	1,171	2,368	4,977
1955	1,094	4,863	885	1,787	3,533	8,775	459	—	—	—	—	1,647	7,812	1,222	2,513	5,438
1956	1,102	5,127	881	1,774	3,669	9,244	498	—	—	—	—	1,717	8,897	1,308	2,717	6,156
1957	1,114	5,383	880	1,751	3,803	9,544	528	—	—	—	—	1,707	9,050	1,266	2,573	6,061
1958	1,061	5,425	815	1,609	3,734	9,440	464	—	—	29,868	7,363	1,350	7,314	956	1,856	4,654
1959	1,089	5,805	843	1,714	4,004	10,488	505	—	—	—	—	1,414	8,203	1,022	2,062	5,310
1960	1,086	5,889	836	1,699	4,038	10,331	484	—	—	—	—	1,426	8,482	1,014	2,045	5,398
1961	1,050	5,810	803	1,629	3,953	10,291	416	—	—	—	—	1,382	8,405	984	1,961	5,248
1962	1,084	6,234	834	1,717	4,283	11,128	530	—	6,974	—	—	1,451	9,202	1,035	2,101	5,825
1963	1,082	6,388	844	1,721	4,484	11,791	570	—	—	33,703	8,426	1,459	9,571	1,045	2,151	6,209
1964	1,116	6,853	870	1,795	4,803	12,693	727	—	—	—	—	1,539	10,607	1,109	2,327	6,892

(continued)

TABLE Dd13–231   Manufacturing summary, by industry division – establishments, employment and payroll, value added, capital expenditures, and aggregate power of equipment: 1899–1999   *Continued*

The left-hand block of columns (Dd169–Dd177) refers to **Fabricated metal products**; the right-hand block (Dd178–Dd184) refers to **Machinery, except electrical**.

	Fabricated metal products									Machinery, except electrical						
	Employment and payroll					Value added	Capital expenditures		Aggregate power of equipment	Establishments		Employment and payroll				
	All employees		Production workers									All employees		Production workers		
	Number	Payroll	Number	Man-hours	Wages		New	Total		Total	With at least 20 employees	Number	Payroll	Number	Man-hours	Wages
Year	Dd169	Dd170	Dd171	Dd172	Dd173	Dd174	Dd175	Dd176	Dd177	Dd178	Dd179	Dd180	Dd181	Dd182	Dd183	Dd184
	Thousand	Million dollars	Thousand	Million	Million dollars	Million dollars	Million dollars	Million dollars	Thousand horsepower	Number	Number	Thousand	Million dollars	Thousand	Million	Million dollars
1965	1,173	7,414	915	1,901	5,182	14,171	806	—	—	—	—	1,653	11,742	1,196	2,515	7,660
1966	1,252	8,245	984	2,038	5,762	15,792	953	—	—	—	—	1,804	13,470	1,310	2,796	8,843
1967	1,342	9,320	1,057	2,161	6,542	18,043	1,118	—	—	37,892	10,627	1,865	14,226	1,349	2,785	9,236
1968	1,358	10,038	1,068	2,193	7,062	19,505	1,041	—	—	—	—	1,849	14,755	1,320	2,701	9,428
1969	1,399	10,773	1,097	2,228	7,551	20,740	1,287	—	—	—	—	1,944	16,442	1,377	2,830	10,402
1970	1,334	10,780	1,025	2,080	7,430	20,888	1,140	—	—	—	—	1,891	16,638	1,306	2,624	10,222
1971	1,279	11,022	981	1,971	7,578	21,966	1,043	—	—	—	—	1,744	16,235	1,187	2,335	9,740
1972	1,493	13,821	1,148	2,303	9,544	26,946	1,323	—	—	40,792	10,599	1,828	18,523	1,267	2,538	11,359
1973	1,567	15,374	1,213	2,440	10,742	30,573	1,735	—	—	—	—	1,994	21,598	1,400	2,843	13,494
1974	1,575	16,570	1,208	2,415	11,469	35,221	1,981	—	—	—	—	2,126	24,713	1,497	3,025	15,431
1975	1,417	16,334	1,070	2,085	11,030	34,203	2,074	—	—	—	—	1,967	24,555	1,341	2,645	14,778
1976	1,471	18,382	1,123	2,217	12,596	39,145	2,223	—	—	—	—	1,960	26,480	1,332	2,633	15,831
1977	1,556	21,036	1,192	2,374	14,429	45,512	2,606	—	—	48,197	12,446	2,083	30,558	1,414	2,803	18,298
1978	1,625	23,383	1,251	2,476	16,107	50,600	3,189	—	—	—	—	2,235	35,386	1,519	2,996	21,222
1979	1,671	25,610	1,286	2,539	17,553	56,893	3,345	—	—	—	—	2,410	40,682	1,641	3,267	24,306
1980	1,617	26,701	1,224	2,381	17,909	57,917	3,892	—	—	—	—	2,411	44,604	1,596	3,149	25,771
1981	1,568	28,531	1,183	2,337	19,134	61,558	4,573	—	—	—	—	2,380	48,643	1,561	3,086	27,762
1982	1,460	28,283	1,073	2,070	18,456	58,928	3,686	—	—	52,912	14,264	2,189	46,911	1,358	2,597	25,093
1983	1,418	28,824	1,050	2,073	18,979	61,327	2,773	—	—	—	—	1,990	45,107	1,234	2,380	23,588
1984	1,482	31,844	1,112	2,220	21,159	67,645	3,753	—	—	—	—	2,052	50,093	1,298	2,558	26,749
1985	1,473	33,150	1,104	2,200	21,977	69,162	4,346	—	—	—	—	1,991	50,905	1,237	2,437	26,534
1986	1,420	33,116	1,050	2,103	21,817	68,621	4,485	—	—	—	—	1,863	49,645	1,141	2,271	25,422
1987	1,460	35,027	1,079	2,186	22,791	75,011	4,820	—	—	52,087	13,845	1,844	50,548	1,143	2,314	26,089
1988	1,495	37,396	1,108	2,271	24,327	80,665	4,195	—	—	—	—	1,903	54,465	1,197	2,439	28,248
1989	1,487	37,874	1,101	2,243	24,702	82,048	4,636	—	—	—	—	1,929	56,780	1,224	2,500	29,891
1990	1,460	38,558	1,074	2,190	24,807	82,269	4,825	—	—	—	—	1,890	56,994	1,187	2,423	29,789
1991	1,387	37,851	1,013	2,069	24,129	79,758	4,178	—	—	—	—	1,790	55,742	1,104	2,246	28,452
1992	1,362	38,962	994	2,051	24,584	83,761	4,438	—	—	53,956	14,067	1,739	57,231	1,086	2,226	29,162
1993	1,371	40,065	1,016	2,106	25,638	88,319	5,774	—	—	—	—	1,750	58,557	1,111	2,296	30,554
1994	1,407	42,009	1,054	2,211	27,214	96,899	5,806	—	—	—	—	1,808	62,204	1,172	2,457	33,353
1995	1,465	44,577	1,100	2,300	28,796	102,672	7,106	—	—	—	—	1,926	67,478	1,259	2,630	36,288
1996	1,483	46,130	1,114	2,339	29,723	107,990	6,874	—	—	—	—	1,981	70,730	1,287	2,685	37,897
1997	1,549	50,904	—	—	—	—	—	—	—	56,383	—	1,978	74,550	—	—	—
1997	1,764	56,632	1,327	2,675	36,252	133,493	—	9,369	—	30,665	—	1,421	53,012	936	1,896	29,107
1998	1,811	59,344	1,370	2,808	38,061	139,741	—	9,939	—	—	—	1,433	54,039	944	1,910	29,732
1999	1,799	59,915	1,359	2,776	38,466	142,451	—	9,807	—	—	—	1,401	53,802	922	1,855	29,032

	Machinery, except electrical					Electrical equipment and supplies										
	Value added	Capital expenditures		Aggregate power of equipment		Establishments		Employment and payroll					Value added	Capital expenditures		Aggregate power of equipment
		New	Total			Total	With at least 20 employees	All employees		Production workers				New	Total	
								Number	Payroll	Number	Man-hours	Wages				
Year	Dd185	Dd186	Dd187	Dd188		Dd189	Dd190	Dd191	Dd192	Dd193	Dd194	Dd195	Dd196	Dd197	Dd198	Dd199
	Million dollars	Million dollars	Million dollars	Thousand horsepower		Number	Number	Thousand	Million dollars	Thousand	Million	Million dollars	Million dollars	Million dollars	Million dollars	Thousand horsepower
1899	—	—	—	—		592	—	49	26	43	—	21	44	—	—	41
1904	—	—	—	—		798	—	75	45	64	—	34	80	—	—	102
1909	—	—	—	—		1,027	—	111	73	93	—	52	121	—	—	158
1914	—	—	—	—		1,048	—	156	118	128	—	80	201	—	—	226
1919	—	—	—	—		1,570	—	305	379	241	—	272	672	—	—	438
1921	—	—	—	—		1,487	—	240	339	179	—	216	547	—	—	—
1923	—	—	—	—		1,782	—	332	474	255	—	330	806	—	—	480
1925	—	—	—	—		1,807	—	309	463	251	—	338	940	—	—	589
1927	—	—	—	—		1,837	—	322	509	256	—	356	1,049	—	—	661
1929	—	—	—	—		1,861	—	421	650	343	—	474	1,389	—	—	894
1931	—	—	—	—		1,596	—	—	—	217	—	240	763	—	—	—
1933	—	—	—	—		1,365	—	202	212	164	—	145	404	—	—	—
1935	—	—	—	—		1,589	—	275	348	224	—	241	686	—	—	—
1937	2,366	—	—	—		1,597	—	374	559	306	—	408	1,102	—	—	—
1939	2,031	—	—	2,613		1,979	—	—	—	248	—	323	941	—	—	1,019
1947	7,834	518	—	—		3,970	—	796	2,258	635	1,278	1,637	3,860	225	—	—
1949	7,689	351	—	—		—	—	663	2,145	506	1,026	1,460	3,902	187	—	—
1950	8,765	337	—	—		4,019	—	766	2,533	610	1,221	1,800	4,815	195	—	—
1951	11,219	631	—	—		4,294	—	877	3,193	692	1,396	2,278	5,753	296	—	—
1952	12,807	—	—	—		4,421	—	957	3,750	741	1,521	2,629	6,873	—	—	—
1953	13,381	755	—	—		—	—	1,096	4,425	851	1,703	3,078	7,876	406	—	—
1954	12,333	714	—	9,497		5,758	2,837	959	3,951	722	1,422	2,646	7,300	341	—	—
1955	13,753	653	—	—		—	—	1,001	4,314	759	1,521	2,896	8,002	335	—	—
1956	16,176	888	—	—		—	—	1,080	4,903	817	1,618	3,261	9,112	475	—	—
1957	15,978	1,038	—	—		—	—	1,084	5,133	795	1,565	3,292	9,620	524	—	—
1958	12,414	670	—	—		8,086	3,797	1,141	5,755	817	1,606	3,558	10,624	468	—	—
1959	14,582	607	—	—		—	—	1,274	6,752	927	1,855	4,196	12,826	554	—	—
1960	14,410	701	—	—		—	—	1,377	7,515	962	1,932	4,466	13,484	637	—	—
1961	14,240	658	—	—		—	—	1,432	8,207	970	1,951	4,681	14,433	639	—	—
1962	10,106	718	—	8,643		—	—	1,523	9,083	1,046	2,121	5,318	16,416	653	—	4,813
1963	17,311	783	—	—		9,948	4,722	1,512	9,284	1,049	2,091	5,406	17,011	702	—	—
1964	20,302	939	—	—		—	—	1,484	9,407	1,030	2,070	5,569	17,765	761	—	—

(continued)

TABLE Dd13–231 Manufacturing summary, by industry division – establishments, employment and payroll, value added, capital expenditures, and aggregate power of equipment: 1899–1999 Continued

Year	Machinery, except electrical — Value added	Machinery — Capital expenditures, New	Machinery — Capital expenditures, Total	Machinery — Aggregate power of equipment	Electrical — Establishments, Total	Electrical — Establishments, With at least 20 employees	Electrical — All employees, Number	Electrical — All employees, Payroll	Electrical — Production workers, Number	Electrical — Production workers, Man-hours	Electrical — Production workers, Wages	Electrical — Value added	Electrical — Capital expenditures, New	Electrical — Capital expenditures, Total	Electrical — Aggregate power of equipment
	Dd185	Dd186	Dd187	Dd188	Dd189	Dd190	Dd191	Dd192	Dd193	Dd194	Dd195	Dd196	Dd197	Dd198	Dd199
	Million dollars	Million dollars	Million dollars	Thousand horsepower	Number	Number	Thousand	Million dollars	Thousand	Million	Million dollars	Million dollars	Million dollars	Million dollars	Thousand horsepower
1965	22,762	1,228	—	—	—	—	1,605	10,450	1,139	2,313	6,232	20,162	1,046	—	—
1966	27,035	1,658	—	—	—	—	1,811	11,988	1,319	2,642	7,259	23,482	1,388	—	—
1967	27,836	1,868	—	—	10,706	5,572	1,875	12,968	1,324	2,611	7,607	24,487	1,537	—	—
1968	28,778	1,743	—	—	—	—	1,883	13,808	1,304	2,597	7,986	26,425	1,478	—	—
1969	32,009	1,866	—	—	—	—	1,918	14,830	1,324	2,619	8,446	28,211	1,641	—	—
1970	31,814	1,855	—	—	—	—	1,832	14,827	1,237	2,417	8,321	27,774	1,520	—	—
1971	30,681	1,696	—	—	—	—	1,659	14,437	1,119	2,183	8,040	27,874	1,399	—	—
1972	37,563	1,906	—	—	12,270	5,732	1,662	15,200	1,161	2,275	8,823	30,584	1,419	—	—
1973	44,559	2,344	—	—	—	—	1,797	17,151	1,278	2,505	10,190	34,984	1,996	—	—
1974	52,495	3,312	—	—	—	—	1,776	18,093	1,242	2,389	10,509	36,902	2,426	—	—
1975	51,044	3,355	—	—	—	—	1,524	17,401	1,020	1,950	9,632	34,845	1,877	—	—
1976	57,357	3,428	—	—	—	—	1,579	19,253	1,080	2,087	10,891	41,746	2,240	—	—
1977	67,223	4,402	—	—	14,973	6,338	1,723	22,544	1,191	2,309	12,952	50,366	2,867	—	—
1978	78,939	5,740	—	—	—	—	1,863	25,854	1,285	2,465	14,864	57,188	3,700	—	—
1979	92,528	6,817	—	—	—	—	1,953	29,144	1,337	2,588	16,593	66,476	4,566	—	—
1980	99,435	7,845	—	—	—	—	1,963	32,453	1,303	2,492	17,763	73,150	6,162	—	—
1981	111,394	8,822	—	—	—	—	1,959	35,989	1,278	2,453	19,192	79,720	6,645	—	—
1982	102,270	8,537	—	—	16,453	7,834	1,915	38,414	1,198	2,269	19,281	84,605	7,542	—	—
1983	94,753	6,425	—	—	—	—	1,896	41,209	1,188	2,282	20,370	92,520	7,261	—	—
1984	112,346	8,035	—	—	—	—	2,033	46,842	1,287	2,505	23,493	109,904	9,982	—	—
1985	110,436	8,323	—	—	—	—	2,007	48,504	1,233	2,374	23,659	110,499	10,466	—	—
1986	108,365	6,691	—	—	—	—	1,941	49,214	1,160	2,259	23,361	112,422	9,060	—	—
1987	118,178	6,954	—	—	15,922	7,544	1,565	38,738	1,000	1,959	19,719	95,815	6,875	—	—
1988	129,874	6,893	—	—	—	—	1,585	41,284	1,014	1,989	20,782	103,730	8,058	—	—
1989	135,497	8,148	—	—	—	—	1,578	42,833	1,012	1,987	21,078	107,164	9,029	—	—
1990	133,548	8,395	—	—	—	—	1,511	42,605	953	1,893	20,449	107,748	9,495	—	—
1991	126,078	7,468	—	—	—	—	1,445	42,328	901	1,815	20,089	107,688	8,465	—	—
1992	132,923	8,057	—	—	16,922	7,652	1,439	44,197	911	1,835	21,042	121,158	8,978	—	—
1993	141,053	7,909	—	—	—	—	1,438	45,306	915	1,847	21,499	128,620	9,988	—	—
1994	159,807	9,196	—	—	—	—	1,485	48,124	956	1,948	23,013	153,055	12,670	—	—
1995	172,945	9,998	—	—	—	—	1,534	51,121	995	2,005	24,278	173,920	17,247	—	—
1996	187,218	11,451	—	—	—	—	1,557	54,311	1,006	2,031	25,614	184,013	20,867	—	—
1997	137,935	—	8,836	—	17,104	—	1,582	58,256	—	—	—	—	—	—	—
1997	—	—	—	—	6,946	—	594	18,973	432	860	11,369	57,216	—	3,599	—
1998	141,269	—	9,528	—	—	—	593	19,529	432	862	11,681	59,124	—	4,012	—
1999	138,798	—	9,444	—	—	—	598	20,253	438	874	12,121	60,458	—	3,683	—

Transportation equipment / Instruments and related products

	Establishments		Employment and payroll					Value added	Capital expenditures		Aggregate power of equipment	Establishments		Employment and payroll	
	Total	With at least 20 employees	All employees		Production workers							Total	With at least 20 employees	All employees	
			Number	Payroll	Number	Man-hours	Wages		New	Total				Number	Payroll
	Dd200	Dd201	Dd202	Dd203	Dd204	Dd205	Dd206	Dd207	Dd208	Dd209	Dd210	Dd211	Dd212	Dd213	Dd214
Year	Number	Number	Thousand	Million dollars	Thousand	Million	Million dollars	Million dollars	Million dollars	Million dollars	Thousand horsepower	Number	Number	Thousand	Million dollars
1899	—	—	—	—	—	—	—	—	—	—	—	1,101	—	35	18
1904	—	—	—	—	—	—	—	—	—	—	—	1,027	—	46	26
1909	—	—	—	—	—	—	—	—	—	—	—	1,239	—	—	—
1914	—	—	—	—	—	—	—	—	—	—	—	1,572	—	71	50
1919	—	—	—	—	—	—	—	—	—	—	—	2,037	—	109	125
1921	—	—	—	—	—	—	—	—	—	—	—	1,592	—	83	109
1923	—	—	—	—	—	—	—	—	—	—	—	1,593	—	93	127
1925	—	—	—	—	—	—	—	—	—	—	—	1,286	—	88	124
1927	—	—	—	—	—	—	—	—	—	—	—	1,108	—	—	—
1929	—	—	—	—	—	—	—	—	—	—	—	1,109	—	98	149
1931	—	—	—	—	—	—	—	—	—	—	—	1,029	—	—	—
1933	—	—	—	—	—	—	—	—	—	—	—	830	—	—	—
1935	—	—	—	—	—	—	—	—	—	—	—	1,000	—	84	108
1937	1,958	—	—	—	662	—	1,029	1,987	—	—	—	1,026	—	—	—
1939	2,012	—	—	—	545	—	867	1,773	—	—	2,926	1,292	—	—	—
1947	3,703	—	1,175	3,695	981	1,961	2,921	5,842	353	—	—	2,605	—	245	706
1949	—	—	1,140	4,098	936	1,873	3,163	7,054	264	—	—	—	—	205	683
1950	2,780	—	1,218	4,680	1,006	2,060	3,657	8,547	343	—	—	2,697	—	226	813
1951	3,393	—	1,469	6,067	1,200	2,448	4,672	9,789	600	—	—	2,686	—	253	1,001
1952	—	—	1,650	7,423	1,317	2,750	5,585	12,042	—	—	—	—	—	279	1,179
1953	—	—	1,912	8,987	1,530	3,155	6,731	14,534	710	—	—	—	—	286	1,233
1954	5,349	2,318	1,706	8,300	1,328	2,711	6,006	13,428	925	—	901	3,141	984	273	1,200
1955	—	—	1,813	9,407	1,418	2,959	6,843	17,071	1,437	—	—	—	—	283	1,295
1956	—	—	1,793	9,707	1,358	2,793	6,743	16,633	1,142	—	—	—	—	297	1,458
1957	—	—	1,901	10,491	1,402	2,845	7,178	18,492	723	—	—	—	—	307	1,571
1958	6,634	2,674	1,562	9,186	1,139	2,275	6,037	15,315	630	—	—	3,518	1,189	286	1,510
1959	—	—	1,615	10,254	1,172	2,454	6,696	18,084	723	—	—	—	—	311	1,783
1960	—	—	1,593	10,360	1,161	2,393	6,842	18,369	731	—	—	—	—	326	1,908
1961	—	—	1,506	10,113	1,056	2,157	6,313	17,433	720	—	—	—	—	316	1,908
1962	—	—	1,601	11,334	1,129	2,367	7,169	20,872	856	—	10,699	—	—	308	1,871
1963	7,180	2,852	1,551	11,406	1,108	2,356	7,389	21,854	981	—	—	3,949	1,343	306	1,913
1964	—	—	1,563	11,887	1,120	2,370	7,772	22,734	1,177	—	—	—	—	308	2,014

(continued)

TABLE Dd13–231 Manufacturing summary, by industry division – establishments, employment and payroll, value added, capital expenditures, and aggregate power of equipment: 1899–1999 *Continued*

	Transportation equipment											Instruments and related products			
	Establishments		Employment and payroll					Value added	Capital expenditures		Aggregate power of equipment	Establishments		Employment and payroll	
	Total	With at least 20 employees	All employees		Production workers				New	Total		Total	With at least 20 employees	All employees	
			Number	Payroll	Number	Man-hours	Wages							Number	Payroll
Year	Dd200	Dd201	Dd202	Dd203	Dd204	Dd205	Dd206	Dd207	Dd208	Dd209	Dd210	Dd211	Dd212	Dd213	Dd214
	Number	Number	Thousand	Million dollars	Thousand	Million	Million dollars	Million dollars	Million dollars	Million dollars	Thousand horsepower	Number	Number	Thousand	Million dollars
1965	—	—	1,684	13,273	1,241	2,640	8,813	26,331	1,506	—	—	—	—	329	2,228
1966	—	—	1,830	14,852	1,355	2,844	9,858	28,277	1,880	—	—	—	1,614	362	2,509
1967	7,483	3,354	1,834	15,174	1,337	2,746	9,918	28,174	1,822	—	—	4,453	—	394	2,822
1968	—	—	1,888	16,811	1,377	2,893	11,135	32,866	1,599	—	—	—	—	400	3,002
1969	—	—	1,920	17,651	1,398	2,823	11,455	34,053	1,943	—	—	—	—	413	3,272
1970	—	—	1,689	16,073	1,201	2,393	10,230	29,990	1,612	—	—	—	—	405	3,358
1971	—	—	1,621	16,698	1,186	2,371	11,048	34,845	1,258	—	—	—	—	382	3,346
1972	8,802	3,618	1,719	19,880	1,246	2,527	12,849	39,799	2,660	—	—	5,983	2,066	454	4,297
1973	—	—	1,836	22,572	1,341	2,732	14,834	45,685	2,530	—	—	—	—	485	4,801
1974	—	—	1,738	22,609	1,250	2,470	14,554	44,973	3,176	—	—	—	—	524	5,560
1975	—	—	1,605	22,772	1,137	2,217	14,405	45,337	2,762	—	—	—	—	500	5,829
1976	—	—	1,668	26,442	1,206	2,419	17,296	55,657	3,131	—	—	—	—	518	6,598
1977	10,174	3,653	1,768	30,674	1,285	2,613	20,314	64,291	4,671	—	—	7,481	2,538	559	7,520
1978	—	—	1,866	34,962	1,365	2,751	23,261	72,956	5,843	—	—	—	—	600	8,570
1979	—	—	1,924	38,494	1,383	2,759	25,199	80,951	6,854	—	—	—	—	601	9,329
1980	—	—	1,772	38,878	1,213	2,373	24,109	76,592	7,958	—	—	—	—	616	10,672
1981	—	—	1,748	42,327	1,184	2,320	26,088	83,095	10,795	—	—	—	—	612	11,565
1982	9,443	3,800	1,596	40,812	1,060	2,052	24,379	84,932	7,214	—	—	8,045	3,015	624	12,883
1983	—	—	1,616	44,640	1,072	2,152	26,917	99,643	5,061	—	—	—	—	608	13,473
1984	—	—	1,709	50,311	1,160	2,425	30,768	113,599	8,027	—	—	—	—	612	14,321
1985	—	—	1,757	54,592	1,180	2,407	33,171	120,953	10,378	—	—	—	—	604	14,666
1986	—	—	1,770	56,708	1,169	2,381	33,626	125,706	11,295	—	—	—	—	585	14,818
1987	10,505	4,269	1,817	58,791	1,244	2,444	34,826	137,076	10,780	—	—	10,193	4,002	982	28,778
1988	—	—	1,822	61,459	1,199	2,457	36,456	143,514	7,241	—	—	—	—	998	30,343
1989	—	—	1,798	61,823	1,230	2,410	36,587	151,798	9,937	—	—	—	—	1,007	31,862
1990	—	—	1,791	63,283	1,161	2,318	36,279	146,959	10,860	—	—	—	—	983	32,793
1991	—	—	1,656	60,649	1,066	2,161	34,755	152,035	11,022	—	—	—	—	947	33,424
1992	11,287	4,305	1,650	62,734	1,080	2,166	36,553	158,326	11,038	—	—	11,354	4,285	907	33,067
1993	—	—	1,584	62,228	1,048	2,150	37,114	162,899	11,416	—	—	—	—	879	32,518
1994	—	—	1,544	63,690	1,061	2,219	39,313	173,284	11,751	—	—	—	—	828	31,882
1995	—	—	1,523	64,153	1,059	2,203	40,122	172,926	13,109	—	—	—	—	809	31,865
1996	—	—	1,467	63,532	1,032	2,153	39,762	176,598	13,498	—	—	—	—	821	33,783
1997	12,387	—	1,562	68,299	—	—	—	—	—	—	—	11,727	—	—	—
1997	12,980	—	1,842	79,617	1,341	2,735	51,450	227,511	—	19,251	—	—	—	—	—
1998	—	—	1,887	82,178	1,371	2,788	52,705	245,619	—	20,053	—	—	—	—	—
1999	—	—	1,876	86,806	1,371	2,856	57,106	268,511	—	18,992	—	—	—	—	—

Instruments and related products

Year	Number Dd215 (Thousand)	Man-hours Dd216 (Million)	Wages Dd217 (Million dollars)	Value added Dd218 (Million dollars)	Capital expenditures, new Dd219 (Million dollars)	Aggregate power of equipment Dd220 (Thousand horsepower)
1899	32	—	15	32	—	—
1904	42	—	21	46	—	—
1909	51	—	28	73	—	—
1914	60	—	36	98	—	—
1919	91	—	93	236	—	—
1921	67	—	78	189	—	—
1923	77	—	92	245	—	—
1925	73	—	91	263	—	—
1927	79	—	103	274	—	—
1929	82	—	108	301	—	—
1931	60	—	66	201	—	—
1933	50	—	46	142	—	—
1935	68	—	74	200	—	—
1937	84	—	113	298	—	—
1939	85	—	108	333	—	165
1947	194	390	502	1,141	56	—
1949	156	306	447	1,123	58	—
1950	169	342	532	1,389	64	—
1951	190	390	671	1,608	85	—
1952	205	420	779	1,995	—	—
1953	212	434	824	2,169	90	—
1954	196	391	760	2,131	94	667
1955	202	406	814	2,367	106	—
1956	211	426	897	2,690	145	—
1957	211	428	947	2,872	146	—
1958	197	390	898	2,781	115	—
1959	214	432	1,033	3,410	145	—
1960	217	437	1,067	3,641	162	—
1961	208	415	1,037	3,574	179	—
1962	206	416	1,051	3,690	178	860
1963	208	417	1,101	3,992	192	—
1964	209	421	1,149	4,314	192	—

Miscellaneous manufacturing industries

Year	Establishments Total Dd221 (Number)	Establishments With at least 20 employees Dd222 (Number)	All employees Number Dd223 (Thousand)	All employees Payroll Dd224 (Million dollars)	Production workers Number Dd225 (Thousand)	Production workers Man-hours Dd226 (Million)	Production workers Wages Dd227 (Million dollars)	Value added Dd228 (Million dollars)	Capital expenditures New Dd229 (Million dollars)	Capital expenditures Total Dd230 (Million dollars)	Aggregate power of equipment Dd231 (Thousand horsepower)
1899	—	—	—	—	—	—	—	—	—	—	—
1904	—	—	—	—	—	—	—	—	—	—	—
1909	—	—	—	—	—	—	—	—	—	—	—
1914	—	—	—	—	—	—	—	—	—	—	—
1919	—	—	—	—	—	—	—	—	—	—	—
1921	—	—	—	—	—	—	—	—	—	—	—
1923	—	—	—	—	—	—	—	—	—	—	—
1925	—	—	—	—	—	—	—	—	—	—	—
1927	—	—	—	—	—	—	—	—	—	—	—
1929	—	—	—	—	—	—	—	—	—	—	—
1931	—	—	—	—	—	—	—	—	—	—	—
1933	—	—	—	—	—	—	—	—	—	—	—
1935	—	—	—	—	—	—	—	—	—	—	—
1937	—	—	—	—	—	—	—	—	—	—	—
1939	—	—	—	—	—	—	—	—	—	—	—
1947	14,148	—	463	1,205	396	811	918	2,066	107	—	—
1949	—	—	447	1,263	370	728	917	2,109	77	—	—
1950	15,057	—	488	1,452	404	800	1,055	2,534	98	—	—
1951	—	—	519	1,711	432	862	1,233	2,842	—	—	—
1952	14,572	—	682	2,375	564	1,102	1,731	3,984	155	—	—
1953	—	—	844	3,232	686	1,368	2,366	5,272	205	—	—
1954	16,517	4,289	467	1,625	385	748	1,149	2,746	115	—	2,036
1955	—	—	489	1,734	404	783	1,225	3,042	117	—	—
1956	—	—	506	1,861	417	814	1,324	3,305	158	—	—
1957	—	—	495	1,886	403	776	1,313	3,327	122	—	—
1958	13,797	3,336	365	1,467	291	559	1,034	2,678	111	—	—
1959	—	—	376	1,556	305	591	1,084	2,888	124	—	—
1960	—	—	374	1,655	301	588	1,091	3,003	111	—	—
1961	—	—	375	1,608	303	585	1,097	3,082	113	—	—
1962	—	—	378	1,705	305	597	1,163	3,330	130	—	2,215
1963	14,723	3,618	391	1,812	315	613	1,254	3,562	131	—	—
1964	—	—	394	1,924	315	631	1,314	3,763	137	—	—

(continued)

TABLE Dd13–231   Manufacturing summary, by industry division – establishments, employment and payroll, value added, capital expenditures, and aggregate power of equipment: 1899–1999 *Continued*

Instruments and related products (Dd215–Dd220); Miscellaneous manufacturing industries (Dd221–Dd231)

Year	Instruments: Production workers Number Dd215 (Thousand)	Man-hours Dd216 (Million)	Wages Dd217 (Million dollars)	Value added Dd218 (Million dollars)	Capital expenditures, new Dd219 (Million dollars)	Aggregate power of equipment Dd220 (Thousand horsepower)	Misc.: Establishments Total Dd221 (Number)	With at least 20 employees Dd222 (Number)	All employees Number Dd223 (Thousand)	Payroll Dd224 (Million dollars)	Production workers Number Dd225 (Thousand)	Man-hours Dd226 (Million)	Wages Dd227 (Million dollars)	Value added Dd228 (Million dollars)	Capital expenditures New Dd229 (Million dollars)	Total Dd230 (Million dollars)	Aggregate power of equipment Dd231 (Thousand horsepower)
1965	226	452	1,275	5,002	232	—	—	—	416	2,042	340	661	1,393	4,092	166	—	—
1966	249	494	1,426	5,833	307	—	—	—	418	2,150	340	666	1,463	4,338	181	—	—
1967	266	530	1,569	6,418	392	—	14,072	3,845	423	2,291	344	662	1,553	4,599	214	—	—
1968	266	525	1,625	7,174	397	—	—	—	431	2,461	349	669	1,667	4,951	209	—	—
1969	271	535	1,757	7,676	388	—	—	—	449	2,665	363	690	1,796	5,296	240	—	—
1970	262	502	1,746	7,905	436	—	—	—	429	2,685	337	643	1,752	5,433	253	—	—
1971	245	465	1,733	8,386	393	—	—	—	411	2,740	319	604	1,773	5,707	263	—	—
1972	292	570	2,237	10,584	481	—	15,187	3,754	446	3,185	350	662	2,088	6,777	317	—	—
1973	316	614	2,490	12,224	636	—	—	—	447	3,351	352	660	2,188	7,166	341	—	—
1974	338	653	2,851	13,627	808	—	—	—	435	3,477	337	637	2,254	7,667	362	—	—
1975	309	588	2,818	14,158	794	—	—	—	393	3,487	303	565	2,168	7,580	302	—	—
1976	322	624	3,214	16,386	783	—	—	—	410	3,868	317	592	2,446	8,822	561	—	—
1977	347	678	3,743	18,762	939	—	17,257	3,793	440	4,408	338	626	2,742	10,282	473	—	—
1978	375	731	4,282	21,883	1,100	—	—	—	447	4,765	343	640	2,973	10,863	534	—	—
1979	371	723	4,562	24,598	1,419	—	—	—	443	5,014	339	642	3,148	11,935	595	—	—
1980	371	722	5,021	27,913	1,672	—	—	—	428	5,366	321	603	3,319	12,691	643	—	—
1981	368	717	5,537	31,494	2,024	—	—	—	413	5,630	308	581	3,447	13,953	613	—	—
1982	363	696	5,917	33,672	2,103	—	15,871	3,568	383	5,647	281	523	3,414	14,059	629	—	—
1983	348	671	6,100	35,258	1,804	—	—	—	375	5,675	280	518	3,416	13,703	461	—	—
1984	358	698	6,534	39,870	2,298	—	—	—	355	5,862	263	497	3,544	14,741	550	—	—
1985	348	676	6,693	40,278	2,581	—	—	—	328	5,726	235	453	3,415	14,032	667	—	—
1986	335	661	6,704	40,005	2,277	—	—	—	326	5,892	236	459	3,520	14,622	541	—	—
1987	503	1,004	11,531	70,975	3,872	—	16,573	3,674	374	6,872	271	520	4,025	17,409	711	—	—
1988	512	1,011	11,984	77,143	4,014	—	—	—	394	7,478	283	546	4,347	19,239	722	—	—
1989	512	1,023	12,259	80,416	4,596	—	—	—	389	7,678	279	536	4,428	20,007	840	—	—
1990	497	994	12,406	84,717	4,450	—	—	—	391	8,085	276	533	4,583	20,729	828	—	—
1991	473	945	12,198	86,627	4,700	—	—	—	369	8,123	258	514	4,517	20,844	852	—	—
1992	460	918	12,222	89,394	4,618	—	17,035	3,462	366	8,417	255	512	4,688	21,975	1,050	—	—
1993	444	883	12,046	92,514	4,469	—	—	—	379	8,858	267	531	5,017	23,380	938	—	—
1994	430	866	11,992	92,511	4,248	—	—	—	382	9,075	271	542	5,117	24,648	1,000	—	—
1995	418	836	11,870	92,534	4,367	—	—	—	397	9,685	280	555	5,413	25,672	1,253	—	—
1996	423	850	12,304	97,987	5,274	—	—	—	397	10,042	283	568	5,610	27,021	1,373	—	—
1997	—	—	—	—	—	—	18,043	—	394	10,563	—	—	—	—	—	—	—
1997	—	—	—	—	—	—	31,554	—	725	21,618	493	938	10,971	61,453	—	3,433	—
1998	—	—	—	—	—	—	—	—	749	22,913	511	983	11,645	64,875	—	3,852	—
1999	—	—	—	—	—	—	—	—	732	23,578	493	975	11,761	66,370	—	4,121	—

[1] The composition of many series changes over time, in some cases significantly affecting comparability; see text.

[2] The Census changed from the Standard Industrial Classification (SIC) system to the North American Industrial Classification System (NAICS) beginning in 1997. Data through the first set of 1997 values are based on the SIC classification; thereafter, the NAICS classification; see text. The Census provides one bridge between the two classification schemes, reporting 1997 NAICS matched to the 1987 SIC and the 1987 SIC matched to the 1997 NAICS.

Sources

Establishments. U.S. Bureau of the Census, Census of Manufactures. Data through 1929 are from *Fifteenth Census of the United States – Manufactures: 1929*, volume 2, *Report by Industries* (1933). Thereafter, data are from the census for the year shown, except when figures were revised by subsequent censuses, in which case the latest data are reported. At the time of compilation (2001), the complete 1997 Census of Manufactures data had not yet been released.

Employment, value added, and capital expenditures. U.S. Bureau of the Census. For those years in which establishment figures are reported, the data come from the same source indicated for the series on establishments. Otherwise, data taken from *Annual Survey of Manufactures* (various years), particularly the volumes entitled *Statistics for Industry Groups and Industries*. Recent volumes are available from the Internet site of the Census Bureau.

Horsepower rating of power equipment. U.S. Bureau of the Census. Through 1929: *Fifteenth Census of the United States – Manufactures: 1929*, volume 2, *Report by Industries* (1933), especially Table 8. 1939–1954: *U.S. Census of Manufactures: 1954, Industry Statistics*, Parts 1 and 2 (1957), especially Table 1 for each industry group. 1962: *1963 Census of Manufactures*, volume 1, *Summary and Subject Statistics* (1966), Chapter 6, especially pp. 6–10.

Documentation

See the Introduction to Part D for information on the North American Industry Classification System (NAICS) and the Standard Industrial Classification (SIC) system.

The adoption of the NAICS beginning with the 1997 Economic Census has had a major impact on the comparability of current and historic data. Approximately half of the industries in the manufacturing sector of NAICS do not have comparable industries in the SIC system that was used in the past. Some dimensions of the problem may be judged by a comparison of the data in this table, which report (some of) the data by two-digit SIC code in 1997 and by the single closest NAICS grouping for that year. The figures for some (tobacco, for example) are close. Others are not, and some did not separately exist under the SIC grouping.

Because these data are primarily historical rather than recent, the data are reported for consistent SIC industry groups along with the most comparable NAICS grouping.

General Note for Table Dd13-231

The first Census of Manufactures covered the year 1809. Between 1809 and 1963, a census was conducted at periodic intervals – every decade until 1899, every five years from 1904 through 1919, and every two years thereafter until World War II interrupted the sequence. The census resumed in 1947, and again in 1954, 1958, and 1963. Since then it has returned on a five-year cycle beginning in 1967. Census data are obtained for every manufacturing plant with one paid employee or more.

The Annual Survey of Manufactures (ASM), conducted for the first time in 1949, collects data for the years between censuses for the more general measure of manufacturing activity covered in detail by the censuses. The annual survey data are estimates derived from a scientifically selected sample of establishments. The 1996 annual survey is based on a sample of about 58,000 establishments of an approximate total of 230,000. These establishments represent all manufacturing establishments of multiunit companies, and all single-establishment manufacturing companies mailed schedules in the 1992 Census of Manufactures. For the current panel of the ASM sample, all establishments of companies with manufacturing shipments in 1992 in excess of $500 million were included in the survey with

certainty. For the remaining portion of the mail survey, the establishment was defined as the sampling unit. For this portion, all establishments with 250 employees or more and establishments with a very large value of shipments also were included. Therefore, of the 58,000 establishments included in the ASM panel, approximately 33,000 are selected with certainty. These establishments account for approximately 80 percent of total value of shipments in the 1992 census. Smaller establishments in the remaining portion of the mail survey were selected by sample.

The Censuses of Manufactures for 1947 through 1992 and the ASMs through 1996 cover operating manufacturing establishments as defined in the SIC Manual, issued by the U.S. Office of Management and Budget. One effort to aggregate nineteenth-century manufacturing census data in modern SIC groupings is found in Albert W. Niemi (*State and Regional Patterns in American Manufacturing, 1860–1900*, Greenwood Press, 1974), but given the manner in which these data are reported, they are not included here. The comparability of manufacturing data over time is affected by changes in the official definitions of industries as presented in the Manual. It is important to note, therefore, that the 1987 edition of the Manual was used for the 1987 and 1992 Censuses; and the 1972 edition of the Manual and the 1977 Supplement were used for the 1972 through 1982 Censuses. The Manual defines an industry as a number of establishments producing a single product or a closely related group of products. The division, however, was not always stable or clear and was complicated by the introduction and growth of new products – for example, the development of electronics and their substitution for many electrical components. In the main, an establishment is classified in a particular industry if its production of a product or product group exceeds in value added its production of any other product group. Although some establishments produce only the products of the industry in which they are classified, few within an industry specialize to that extent. The statistics on employment, payrolls, value added, inventories, and expenditures, therefore, reflect both the primary and secondary activities of the establishments in that industry. For this reason, care should be exercised in relating such statistics to the total shipments figures of products primary to the industry.

Under the NAICS, an establishment signifies a single physical plant site or factory. It is not necessarily identical to the business unit or company, which may consist of one or more establishments. A company operating establishments at more than one location is required to submit a separate report for each location. An establishment engaged in distinctly different lines of activity and maintaining separate payroll and inventory records is also required to submit separate reports.

Series on Establishments

These series include all those with a payroll at any time during the year. These are reported only for census years.

Series on Employees

This item includes all full-time and part-time employees on the payrolls of operating manufacturing establishments during any part of the pay period that included the 12th day of the months specified on the report form. Included are all persons on paid sick leave, paid holidays, and paid vacations during these pay periods. Officers of corporations are included as employees; proprietors and partners of unincorporated firms are excluded. The total for all employees is the average number of production workers plus the number of other employees in mid-March. The number of production workers is the average for the payroll periods including the 12th of March, May, August, and November.

Series on Payroll

This item includes the gross earnings of all employees on the payroll of operating manufacturing establishments paid in the calendar year. Respondents were told they could follow the definition of payrolls used for calculating the federal withholding tax. It includes all forms of compensation, such as salaries, wages, commissions, dismissal pay, bonuses, vacation and sick leave pay, and compensation in kind, prior to such deductions as employees' Social Security contributions, withholding taxes, group insurance, union dues, and savings bonds. The total includes salaries of officers of

(continued)

TABLE Dd13–231   Manufacturing summary, by industry division – establishments, employment and payroll, value added, capital expenditures, and aggregate power of equipment: 1899–1999   *Continued*

corporations; it excludes payments to proprietors or partners of unincorporated concerns. Also excluded are payments to members of the armed forces and pensioners carried on the active payroll of manufacturing establishments.

Series on Production Workers

This item includes workers (up through the line-supervisor level) engaged in fabricating, processing, assembling, inspecting, receiving, storing, handling, packing, warehousing, shipping (but not delivering), maintenance, repair, janitorial and guard services, product development, auxiliary production for plant's own use (power plant and the like), record-keeping, and other services closely associated with these production operations at the establishment covered by the report. Employees above the working-supervisor level are excluded from this item.

Series on Production-Worker Man-Hours

This item covers hours worked or paid for at the plant, including actual overtime hours (not straight-time equivalent hours). It excludes hours paid for vacations, holidays, or sick leave.

Series on Value Added by Manufacture

This measure of manufacturing activity is derived by subtracting the cost of materials, supplies, containers, fuel, purchased electricity, and contract work from the value of shipments (products manufactured plus receipts for services rendered). The result of this calculation is adjusted by the addition of value added by merchandising operations (the difference between the sales value and the cost of merchandise sold without further manufacture, processing, or assembly) plus the net change in finished goods and work-in-process inventories between the beginning- and end-of-year inventories. For those industries where value added is adjusted only for the change in value of shipments, value added is adjusted on the basis of production is collected instead of value of shipments, value added is adjusted only for the change in work-in-process inventories between the beginning and end of year. For those industries where value of work done is collected, the value added does not include an adjustment for the change in finished goods or work-in-process inventories. Value added avoids the duplication in value of shipments that results from the use of products of some establishments as materials by others. Value added is considered to be the best value measure available for comparing the relative economic importance of manufacturing among industries and geographic areas.

Series on New Capital Expenditures

For establishments in operation and any known plants under construction, manufacturers were asked to report their new expenditures for permanent additions and major alterations to manufacturing establishments, as well as for machinery and equipment used for replacement and additions to plant capacity if they were of the type for which depreciation accounts were ordinarily maintained. The totals for new expenditures include expenditures leased from nonmanufacturing concerns through capital leases. New facilities owned by the federal government but operated under private contract by private companies and plant and equipment furnished to the manufacturer by communities and nonprofit organizations are excluded.

Series on Total Capital Expenditures

From 1997 onward, includes "new capital expenditures" (see preceding explanation) plus the value of all used buildings and equipment purchased during the year at the purchase price. For any equipment or structure transferred for the use of the reporting establishment by the parent company or one of its subsidiaries, the value at which it was transferred to the establishment was to be reported. Furthermore, if the establishment changed ownership during the year, the cost of the fixed assets (building and equipment) was to be reported under used capital expenditures.

Series Dd13–23

SIC 20 (food and kindred products); NAICS 311 (food manufacturing).

This major group includes establishments manufacturing or processing foods and beverages for human consumption, and certain related products, such as manufactured ice, chewing gum, vegetable and animal fats and oils, and prepared feeds for animals and fowls.

The major difference with NAICS 311 "Food" is the reassignment of beverages to their own sub-category elsewhere (NAICS 3121).

Beginning in 1927, includes establishments engaged primarily in manufacture of vegetable cooking oils.

Beginning in 1933, excludes establishments primarily engaged in manufacture of ethyl alcohol.

Beginning in 1947, excludes driver-salesmen in bakery products industry. The number of driver-salesmen for 1939 was at least 120,000.

Beginning in 1954, includes milk bottling plants. Value added for this industry in 1954 was $1,476 million.

Series Dd24–34

SIC 21 (tobacco manufactures); NAICS 3122 (tobacco manufacturing).

Tobacco manufacturing includes two types of establishments: (1) those engaged in redrying and stemming tobacco, and (2) those that manufacture tobacco products, such as cigarettes and cigars.

Under the NAICS classification, tobacco manufacturing is now aggregated with beverages (including soft drinks and all alcoholic beverages) as NAICS 312 (subgroup 3122).

Series Dd35–45

SIC 22 (textile mill products); NAICS 313 (textile mills).

This major group includes establishments engaged in performing any of the following operations: (1) preparation of fiber and subsequent manufacturing of yarn, thread, braids, twine, and cordage; (2) manufacturing broad woven fabrics, narrow woven fabrics, knit fabrics, and carpets and rugs from yarn; (3) dyeing and finishing fiber, yarn, fabrics, and knit apparel; (4) coating, waterproofing, or otherwise treating fabrics; (5) the integrated manufacture of knit apparel and other finished articles from yarn; and (6) the manufacture of felt goods, lace goods, nonwoven fabrics, and miscellaneous textiles.

The SIC classification makes no distinction between the two types of organizations that operate in the textile industry: (1) the integrated mill, which purchases materials, produces textiles and related articles within the establishment, and sells the finished products; and (2) the contract or commission mill, which processes materials owned by others.

The NAICS classification 313 excludes establishments that knit or weave fabric from this subgroup if this activity extends to the production of a garment.

For 1937 and 1939, includes establishments that cut and stitch products from knit cloth made in separate mills of integrated companies.

Beginning in 1958, excludes establishments primarily producing hats, except cloth and millinery, and those primarily producing hard-surface floor covering, except asbestos, plastic, or rubber; therefore, data are not entirely comparable with those for earlier years. The 1957 employment was 12,428 for the hats except millinery industries and 8,736 for the hard-surface floor covering industry. Also, prior to 1958, excludes establishments primarily engaged in shrinking and sponging of cloth; such establishments had 1,723 employees in 1958.

Series Dd46–56

SIC 23 (apparel and other textile products); NAICS 315 (apparel).

This major group – known as the cutting-up and needle trades – includes establishments producing clothing and fabricating products by cutting and sewing purchased woven or knit textile fabrics and related materials, such as leather, rubberized fabrics, plastics, and furs. Also included are establishments that manufacture clothing by cutting and joining (for example, by adhesives) materials such as paper and nonwoven textiles. Included in the apparel industries are three types of establishments: (1) the regular or inside factories; (2) contract factories; and (3) apparel jobbers. The regular factories perform all of the usual manufacturing functions within their own plant; the contract factories manufacture apparel from materials owned by others; and apparel jobbers perform the entrepreneurial functions of a manufacturing company, such as buying raw materials, designing and preparing samples, arranging for the manufacture of clothing from their materials, and selling of the finished apparel.

Knitting mills are classified in SIC 2253 if primarily knitting outerwear, and in SIC 2254 if primarily knitting underwear and nightwear. Custom tailors and dressmakers not operating on a factory basis are classified in retail trade, SIC 5699. Establishments that purchase and resell finished garments but do not perform the functions of the apparel jobbers are classified in wholesale trade, industry group SIC 513.

The NAICS definition of this sector groups establishments with two distinct manufacturing processes: (1) cut and sew (that is, purchasing fabric and cutting and sewing to make a garment) and (2) the manufacture of garments in establishments that first knit fabric and then cut and sew the fabric into a garment. The apparel manufacturing subsector includes a diverse range of establishments manufacturing full lines of ready-to-wear apparel and custom apparel: apparel contractors, performing cutting or sewing operations on materials owned by others; jobbers, performing entrepreneurial functions involved in apparel manufacture; and tailors, manufacturing custom garments for individual clients, are all included. Knitting, when done alone, is classified in the textile mills subsector (NAICS 313), but when knitting is combined with the production of complete garments, the activity is classified in apparel manufacturing.

For 1937 and 1939, excludes establishments that cut and stitch products from knit cloth made in separate mills of integrated companies.

For the years prior to 1958, excludes establishments producing hats, except cloth and millinery. In 1954, these establishments had 12,958 employees and $61,866 thousand value added shrinking and sponging of cloth. In 1958, such establishments had 1,723 employees and $10,709 thousand value added by manufacture.

Series Dd56. In 1939, covers horsepower of prime movers only.

Series Dd57–67

SIC 24 (lumber and wood products); NAICS 321 (wood product manufacturing).

This major group includes establishments engaged in cutting timber and pulpwood; merchant sawmills, lath mills, shingle mills, cooperage stock mills, planing mills, and plywood mills and veneer mills engaged in producing lumber and wood basic materials; and establishments engaged in manufacturing finished articles made entirely or mainly of wood or related materials. Certain types of establishments producing wood products are classified elsewhere. For example, furniture and office and store fixtures are classified in major group SIC 25; musical instruments, toys and playground equipment, and caskets are classified in major group SIC 39. Woodworking in connection with construction, in the nature of reconditioning and repair, or performed to individual order, is classified in nonmanufacturing industries. Establishments engaged in integrated operations of logging combined with sawmills, pulp mills, or other converting activity, with the logging not separately reported, are classified according to the primary product shipped.

For 1899–1929, excludes establishments engaged primarily in manufacture of wood and vehicle stock. For 1931, on new basis comparable with 1929 is $523.8 million; 1931, on new basis, $524.4 million.

For 1899–1923, includes establishments engaged in manufacture of rules made of metal and other materials as well as wood; figures for later years include establishments making wooden rules only. For 1914, excludes establishments engaged in manufacture of laths and shingles; value added by manufacture on a basis comparable with prior years was $652 million.

Beginning in 1914, excludes establishments engaged primarily in manufacture of windows and door screens.

For 1937–1947, excludes logging contractors and independent logging camps not operating sawmills as well as establishments primarily engaged in manufacture of venetian blinds.

In 1949 and 1950, there was a significant undercoverage in the sample for this major group, especially in the logging camps and logging contractors industry.

For the years prior to 1958, excludes establishments engaged primarily in manufacture of hardpressed wood fiberboard and those primarily engaged in manufacturing fabricated hardboard products.

Series Dd68–78

SIC 25 (furniture and fixtures); NAICS 337 (furniture and related product manufacturing).

This major group includes establishments engaged in manufacturing household, office, public building, and restaurant furniture; and office and store fixtures. Establishments primarily engaged in the production of millwork are classified in industry SIC 2431; those manufacturing wood kitchen cabinets are classified in industry SIC 2434; those manufacturing cut stone and concrete furniture are classified in major group SIC 32; those manufacturing laboratory and hospital furniture, except hospital beds, are classified in major group SIC 38; those manufacturing beauty and barber shop furniture are classified in major group SIC 39; and those engaged in woodworking to individual order or in the nature of reconditioning and repair are classified in nonmanufacturing industries. This furniture was predominantly (but not exclusively) from wood. The growing use of other materials is recognized in the NAICS classification (NAICS 337), which describes the industry as the cutting, bending, molding, laminating, and assembly of such materials as wood, metal, glass, plastics, and rattan to make furniture. However, the production process for furniture is not solely bending metal, cutting and shaping wood, or extruding and molding plastics. Design and fashion trends play an important part in the production of furniture. The integrated design of the article for both aesthetic and functional qualities is also a major part of the process of manufacturing furniture. Design services may be performed by the furniture establishment's work force or may be purchased from industrial designers.

Furniture may be made of any material, but the most common ones used in North America are metal and wood. Furniture manufacturing establishments may specialize in making articles primarily from one material. Some of the equipment required to make a wooden table, for example, is different from that used to make a metal one. However, furniture is usually made from several materials. A wooden table might have metal brackets, and a wooden chair a fabric or plastic seat. Therefore, in NAICS, furniture initially is classified based on the type of furniture (application for which it is designed) rather than the material used. For example, an upholstered sofa is treated as household furniture, although it may also be used in hotels or offices.

When classifying furniture according to the component material from which it is made, furniture made from more than one material is classified based on the material used in the frame, or if there is no frame, the predominant component material. Upholstered household furniture (excluding kitchen and dining room chairs with upholstered seats) is classified without regard to the frame material. Kitchen or dining room chairs with upholstered seats are classified according to the frame material.

For 1899–1925, excludes establishments engaged primarily in manufacture of sewing machine cases, cabinets, and tables.

For 1899–1909, excludes establishments engaged primarily in manufacture of window and door screens. For 1914, value added by manufacture on a basis comparable with prior years was $169 million.

Beginning in 1937, includes establishments primarily engaged in manufacture of venetian blinds. For 1937, value added by manufacture on a basis comparable with prior years was $418 million. Beginning in 1939, includes establishments primarily engaged in manufacture of metal partitions. For 1939, value added by manufacture on a basis comparable with prior years was $411 million.

Series Dd79–89

SIC 26 (paper and allied products); NAICS 322 (paper manufacturing).

This major group includes establishments engaged primarily in the manufacture of pulps from wood and other cellulose fibers, and from rags; the manufacture of paper and paperboard; and the manufacture of paper and paperboard into converted products, such as paper coated off the paper machine, paper bags, paper boxes, and envelopes. Also included are establishments engaged primarily in manufacturing bags of plastic film and sheet. Certain types of converted paper products are

(continued)

TABLE Dd13–231   Manufacturing summary, by industry division – establishments, employment and payroll, value added, capital expenditures, and aggregate power of equipment: 1899–1999   Continued

classified elsewhere, such as abrasive paper, which is in industry SIC 3291; carbon paper, in industry SIC 3955; and photosensitized and blueprint paper, in industry SIC 3861.

Pulp mills and paperboard mills are essentially the same across the SIC and NAICS groupings. Significant differences occur in paper mills, stationery, paper bags, and converted paper products.

Beginning in 1931, includes establishments engaged primarily in the manufacture of papeteries. In 1931, value added by manufacture on a basis comparable with prior years was $600 million.

Beginning in 1937, includes establishments engaged primarily in the manufacture of fiber products, fiber conduits, and molded pulp products. In 1937, value added by manufacture on a basis comparable with prior years was $853 million.

Beginning in 1939, includes establishments engaged primarily in the manufacture of printed paper patterns and laminated enamel hard-pressed insulating wallboard of vegetable fiber. In 1939, value added by manufacture on a basis comparable with prior years was $870 million.

Beginning in 1947, includes establishments primarily engaged in the manufacture of tags.

Beginning in 1958, excludes hard-pressed wood fiberboard mills.

Series Dd90–100

SIC 27 (printing and publishing); NAICS 323 (printing and related activities).

This includes establishments engaged in printing by one or more common processes, such as letter-press; lithography (including offset); gravure, or screen; and those establishments that perform services for the printing trade, such as bookbinding and platemaking. This major group also includes establishments engaged in publishing newspapers, books, and periodicals, regardless of whether or not they do their own printing. News syndicates are classified in Services, industry SIC 7383. Establishments engaged primarily in textile printing and finishing fabrics are classified in major group SIC 22, and those engaged in printing and stamping on fabric articles are classified in industry SIC 2396. Establishments manufacturing products that contain incidental printing, such as advertising or instructions, are classified according to the nature of the products, for example, as cartons, bags, plastic film, or paper.

NAICS classifies the publishing of printed products in subsector 511, publishing industries. Although printing and publishing are often carried out by the same enterprise (a newspaper, for example), it is less and less the case that these distinct activities are carried out in the same establishment. When publishing and printing are done in the same establishment, the establishment is classified in sector 51, information, in the appropriate NAICS industry even if the receipts for printing exceed those for publishing. The result is a significant difference between SIC 27 and NAICS 323.

For 1909–1933, cost of contract work was subtracted from the value of products in calculating value added by manufacture only for the industries in which it was significant. For 1899 and 1904, cost of contract work was not subtracted from the value of products for any industries. In 1909, value added by manufacture on a basis comparable with prior years was $556 million.

For 1935, excludes establishments engaged solely in music publishing.

Prior to 1935, religious, social, charitable, educational, and other nonprofit organizations were not included. After 1935, only those whose employees are covered by the Social Security system are included.

Series Dd101–111

SIC 28 (chemicals and allied products); NAICS 325 (chemical manufacture).

This major group includes establishments producing basic chemicals, and establishments manufacturing products by predominantly chemical processes. Establishments classified in this major group

manufacture three general classes of products: (1) basic chemicals, such as acids, alkalies, salts, and organic chemicals; (2) chemical products to be used in further manufacture, such as synthetic fibers, plastic materials, dry colors, and pigments; and (3) finished chemical products to be used for ultimate consumption, such as drugs, cosmetics, and soaps; or to be used as materials or supplies in other industries, such as paints, fertilizers, and explosives. The mining of natural alkalies and other natural potassium, sodium, and boron compounds, of natural rock salt, and of other natural chemicals and fertilizers is classified in mining, SIC 147.

Establishments engaged primarily in manufacturing nonferrous metals and high-percentage ferroalloys are classified in major group 33; those manufacturing silicon carbide are classified in major group 32; those manufacturing baking powder, other leavening compounds, and starches are classified in major group 20; and those manufacturing artists' colors are classified in major group 39. Establishments primarily engaged in packaging, repackaging, and bottling of purchased chemical products, but not engaged in manufacturing chemicals and allied products, are classified in wholesale or retail trade industries.

Within various subgroups, there are significant differences in assignment between the SIC and the NAICS.

For 1899, includes establishments primarily engaged in manufacture of candles. In 1904, value added by manufacture on a basis comparable with 1899 was $287 million.

Beginning in 1925, excludes certain establishments engaged primarily in manufacture of rubber cement. In 1925, value added by manufacture on a basis comparable with prior years was $1,321 million.

Beginning in 1927, excludes establishments engaged primarily in manufacture of vegetable cooking oils.

Beginning in 1929, excludes establishments other than petroleum refineries engaged in manufacture of lubricating oils.

Beginning in 1933, includes establishments engaged primarily in manufacture of ethyl alcohol.

Beginning in 1937, excludes establishments engaged primarily in mining of rock salt or in smelting and refining of aluminum. In 1937, value added by manufacture on a basis comparable with prior years was $1,759 million.

Also beginning in 1937, excludes woods employees of the gum naval stores industry; in 1937, production workers numbered 30,880 with wages of $8.6 million.

Beginning in 1939, excludes establishments engaged primarily in manufacture of electrometallurgical products. In 1939, value added by manufacture on a basis comparable with prior years was $1,838 million.

Beginning in 1949, includes government-owned plants operated by private firms for the account of the federal government.

Note the substantial difference between the SIC and the NAICS basis figures with the removal of certain publishing from manufacturing to information services.

Series Dd112–122

SIC 29 (petroleum and coal products); NAICS 324 (petroleum and coal products).

This major group includes establishments engaged primarily in petroleum refining, manufacturing paving and roofing materials, and producing lubricating oils and greases from purchased materials. Establishments manufacturing and distributing gas to consumers are classified in public utilities industries, and those engaged primarily in producing coke and by-products are classified in major group SIC 33.

The SIC and NAICS classifications are very similar.

For 1899 and 1904, excludes fuel briquettes and roofing felts and coatings. In 1909, these industries represented 6 percent of the production workers and 9 percent of the value added by manufacture for this commodity group.

Beginning in 1929, excludes lubricants not elsewhere classified and paving mixtures and blocks. In 1929, these industries represented 4 percent of the production workers and 5 percent of the value added by the manufacture of this commodity group.

For 1935, excludes a few establishments engaged primarily in blending and compounding lubricating oils.

For the years prior to 1939, excludes by-product of coke ovens owned by city gas companies. In 1939, such ovens represented less than 2 percent of the total value of products for this commodity group.

For 1947, excludes by-products of coke plants operated in conjunction with public utilities manufacturing and distributing gas, and includes establishments engaged primarily in shipping lubricants and greases made from animal and vegetable oils.

Beginning in 1954, excludes beehive and by-product coke ovens.

Series Dd123–133

SIC 30 (rubber and plastics products not elsewhere classified); NAICS 326 (plastics and rubber products).

This major group includes establishments manufacturing products from plastics resins and from natural, synthetic, or reclaimed rubber, gutta percha, balata, or gutta siak. Numerous products made from these materials are included in other major groups, such as boats in major group SIC 37, and toys, buckles, and buttons in major group SIC 39. This group includes establishments primarily manufacturing tires, but establishments primarily recapping and retreading automobile tires are classified in services, industry SIC 7534. Establishments engaged primarily in manufacturing synthetic rubber and synthetic plastics resins are classified in industry group SIC 282.

The SIC and NAICS classifications are very similar.

For the years prior to 1939, for rubber and plastics products, excludes plastics products.

Beginning in 1925, includes establishments primarily engaged in manufacture of rubber cement and rubber toy balloons. In 1925, value added by manufacture on a basis comparable with prior years was $537 million.

Beginning in 1958, includes establishments engaged in molding plastics products for the trade and fabricating miscellaneous finished plastics products.

Series Dd134–144

SIC 31 (leather and leather products); NAICS 316 (leather and allied product manufacturing).

This major group includes establishments engaged in tanning, currying, and finishing hides and skins, leather converters, and establishments manufacturing finished leather and artificial leather products and some similar products made of other materials.

In 1997, detail was not given (under SIC) by the Census Bureau to prevent disclosure.

Series Dd145–155

SIC 32 (stone, clay, and glass products); NAICS 327 (nonmetallic mineral product manufacturing).

This major group includes establishments engaged in manufacturing flat glass and other glass products, cement, structural clay products, pottery, concrete and gypsum products, cut stone, abrasive and asbestos products, and other products from materials taken principally from the earth in the form of stone, clay, and sand. When separate reports are available for mines and quarries operated by manufacturing establishments classified in this major group, the mining and quarrying activities are classified in mining. When separate reports are not available, the mining and quarrying activities, other than those of industry SIC 3295, are classified herein with the manufacturing operations.

The SIC and NAICS classifications are very similar.

For 1939, 1947, and 1954, excludes establishments engaged primarily in producing ready-mixed concrete. In 1958, the value added in such establishments represented 12 percent of the total value added for this commodity group and, in 1937, less than 1 percent. The value added at quarries operated in conjunction with manufacturing establishments (including value added in producing mineral products consumed in the same establishment) was $194 million in 1954, $361 million in 1958, and $321 million in 1963.

Series Dd156–166

SIC 33 (primary metal industries); NAICS 331 (primary metals manufacturing).

Primary Metals establishments are engaged in smelting and refining ferrous and nonferrous metals from ore, pig, or scrap; in rolling, drawing, and alloying metals; in manufacturing castings and other basic metal products; and in manufacturing nails, spikes, and insulated wire and cable. This major group includes the production of coke. Establishments engaged primarily in manufacturing metal forgings or stampings are classified in industry group SIC 346.

Figures prior to 1937 are not reported because of serious noncomparability problems with respect to a number of the industries and activities included.

For 1937, includes establishments engaged primarily in producing certain nonferrous bearings and aluminum products (ship bunks, ornamental metal work, stampings, novelties, valves and fittings, machined castings, and tags) and excludes establishments engaged primarily in making electrometallurgical products, nonferrous die castings and forgings, cast aluminum cooking ware, and in the heat treatment of steel. In 1939, value added by manufacture on a basis comparable with 1937 was $2,131 million.

Beginning in 1954, includes beehive and by-product coke ovens.

Series Dd167–177

SIC 34 (fabricated metal products); NAICS 332 (fabricated metal product manufacturing).

This industry group includes establishments engaged in fabricating ferrous and nonferrous metal products, such as metal cans, tinware, handtools, cutlery, general hardware, nonelectric heating apparatus, fabricated structural metal products, metal forgings, metal stampings, ordnance (except vehicles and guided missiles), and a variety of metal and wire products not elsewhere classified. Certain important segments of the metal fabricating industries are classified in other major groups, such as machinery in major groups SIC 35 and 36; transportation equipment, including tanks, in major group SIC 37; professional scientific and controlling instruments, watches, and clocks in major group SIC 38; and jewelry and silverware in major group SIC 39. Establishments primarily engaged in producing ferrous and nonferrous metals and their alloys are classified in major group SIC 33.

The definition of this industry under the NAICS classification (332) is substantially different and, as a result, the SIC and NAICS groupings are not comparable. Industries in the fabricated metal product manufacturing subsector transform metal into intermediate or end products other than machinery, computers and electronics, and metal furniture or treating metals and metal formed products fabricated elsewhere. Important fabricated metal processes are forging, stamping, bending, forming, and machining, used to shape individual pieces of metal; and other processes, such as welding and assembling, used to join separate parts together. Establishments in this subsector may use one or a combination of these processes.

Figures prior to 1937 are not reported because of serious noncomparability problems with respect to a number of the industries and activities included. In particular, establishments stamping, pressing, and spinning aluminum ware were excluded earlier, while the manufacture of valves and fittings was included.

For 1937, excludes establishments engaged primarily in producing lawn sprinklers, spun ware, nonferrous metal novelties, tackle blocks, aluminum ornamental work, aluminum stampings, and machine knives (except metalworking) and includes establishments engaged primarily in making caulking guns, toilet seats, brooders, cast aluminum cooking ware, and hair clippers. In 1939, value added by manufacture on a basis comparable with 1937 was $1,340 million.

Series Dd178–188

SIC 35 (machinery, except electrical); NAICS 333 (machinery manufacture).

This major group includes establishments engaged in manufacturing industrial and commercial machinery and equipment and computers. Included are the manufacture of engines and turbines; farm and garden machinery; construction, mining, and oil field machinery; elevators and conveying equipment; hoists, cranes, monorails, and industrial trucks and tractors; metalworking machinery;

(continued)

TABLE Dd13–231   Manufacturing summary, by industry division – establishments, employment and payroll, value added, capital expenditures, and aggregate power of equipment: 1899–1999   Continued

special industry machinery; general industrial machinery; computer and peripheral equipment and office machinery; and refrigeration and service industry machinery. Machines powered by built-in or detachable motors ordinarily are included in this major group, with the exception of electrical household appliances. Power-driven handtools are included in this major group, whether electric or otherwise driven. Establishments engaged primarily in manufacturing electrical equipment are classified in major group 36, and those manufacturing handtools, except powered, are classified in major group 34.

Industries in some of the subgroups are defined in terms of end products, and the parts, attachments, and accessories for these items are included in the industry of the end product unless specifically classified elsewhere in the SIC. The volume of shipments of machinery parts and accessories in some industries constitutes a significant portion of total shipments. These parts producers are generally smaller establishments, but there are a large number of them. The machine shops subgroup includes plants producing a broad variety of miscellaneous parts made by job establishments.

Plants primarily rebuilding machinery or equipment are now classified according to the original industry this group. However, such rebuilding activities are now classified according to the original industry classification of the product being rebuilt. Plants primarily rebuilding automotive parts are included in the transportation equipment group. Plants primarily rebuilding machine tools, metalworking machinery, and office and store machines are included in the industry of the plants producing the original equipment.

Figures prior to 1937 are not reported because of serious noncomparability problems with respect to a number of the industries and activities included. In particular, the inclusion of aircraft engine manufacture and machine shop repairs.

For 1937, includes establishments engaged primarily in manufacture of thermostats and gauges, heat treating of steel, machine knives, and tackle blocks, and excludes establishments engaged primarily in manufacture of vacuum cleaners, turbo-generators and water-wheel generator sets, hair-clippers for animal use, brooders, nonferrous bearings, certain industrial furnaces and ovens, time-stamps and time-recording machines, dictating machines, certain valves and fittings (except plumbers'), and caulking guns. In 1939, value added by manufacture on a basis comparable with 1937 was $1,990 million.

Series Dd188. In 1954, includes electrical machinery.

Series Dd189–199

SIC 36 (electrical equipment and supplies) until 1997; thereafter, NAICS 335 (electrical equipment and appliance manufacturing).

This major group includes establishments engaged in manufacturing machinery, apparatus, and supplies for the generation, storage, transmission, transformation, and utilization of electrical energy. Included are the manufacturing of electricity distribution equipment; electrical industrial apparatus; household appliances; electrical lighting and wiring equipment; radio and television receiving equipment; communications equipment; electronic components and accessories; and other electrical equipment and supplies. The manufacture of household appliances is included in this group, but industrial machinery and equipment powered by built-in or detachable electric motors is classified in major group SIC 35. Establishments engaged primarily in manufacturing instruments are classified in major group SIC 38.

A number of products that are sometimes considered as belonging in electrical equipment are classified in other groups in the SIC. For example, machinery classified in other groups in the 1957 edition of the *SIC Manual* in use for 1963. For example, machinery or equipment powered by built-in or detachable electric motors, such as machine tools and other metalworking equipment, commercial laundry and dry cleaning equipment, industrial vacuum cleaners, and office and store machines are classified as machinery, except electrical. Establishments primarily

producing glass insulators, glass blanks for bulbs, and porcelain electrical supplies are classified in the stone, clay, glass, and concrete products group.

Industries included here are typically defined in terms of products and may include both electrical and electronic equipment. Electronic components are frequently produced and consumed at the same location by establishments classified in this group. Thus, there are (1) plants solely engaged in producing electronic components, (2) plants producing electronic components and assembling them into finished products, and (3) plants that assemble components produced elsewhere either in other plants of the same company or by other companies. Other types of components and equipment such as motors, generators, and motor-generator sets are not uncommonly produced for incorporation into other products made in the same plant.

The rapid development and expansion of the electronics industry led to the separation of electrical equipment (335) from electronic equipment (334) in the NAICS classification following a major revision and redefinition of this industry in 1987.

Beginning in 1909, excludes establishments engaged primarily in manufacture of signs and advertising novelties.

Beginning in 1927, excludes establishments engaged primarily in manufacture of certain types of mechanical refrigerators.

Beginning in 1935, excludes establishments engaged primarily in manufacture of certain types of beauty and barber shop equipment.

Beginning in 1939, excludes establishments engaged primarily in manufacture of vacuum cleaners, turbo-generators and water-wheel generator sets, dictating machines, and electric industrial furnaces and ovens. In 1939, value added by manufacture on a basis comparable with prior years was $1,000 million.

Beginning in 1947, includes establishments engaged primarily in manufacture of electric (dry) shavers.

Beginning in 1958, includes establishments engaged primarily in manufacture of household refrigerators and home farm freezers; household laundry equipment and sewing machines; water heaters, except electric; and other household appliances. Excludes those engaged primarily in manufacture of hearing aids; high frequency, induction, and dialectic heating apparatus; commercial food warming equipment; industrial electric heating units and devices; and insulated wire and cable made from purchased wire.

Major revision in the SIC definition of this industry in 1987 complicates comparisons before and after.

Series Dd199. In 1954, included under series Dd188.

Series Dd200–210

SIC 37 (transportation equipment); NAICS 336 (transportation equipment manufacturing).

This group covers establishments primarily manufacturing equipment for transportation of passengers and cargo by land, air, and water. Important products include motor vehicles, aircraft, ships, boats, railroad equipment, and miscellaneous transportation equipment such as motorcycles, bicycles, and so forth. It also includes, since 1967, guided missile components, not elsewhere classified; and receipts from research and development on aircraft parts, guided missile components, not elsewhere classified, and airplane and missile engines.

Certain products sometimes associated with or considered a part of transportation equipment are classified in other groups in the SIC. For example, wheeled tractors, tracklaying tractors, mining cars, and industrial trucks, tractors, trailers, and stackers are classified as machinery, except electrical; and ignition systems and storage batteries, as electrical equipment and supplies.

Railroad shops are not classified as manufacturing by the SIC and therefore such activities are not included in employment and other establishment totals for this group.

(continued)

Figures are not shown prior to 1937 because they are not sufficiently comparable with later years owing to their exclusion of establishments engaged primarily in manufacture of aircraft engines and of a number of large establishments classified prior to 1937 in other industry groups.

In the NAICS organization, establishments in this subsector utilize production processes similar to those of other machinery manufacturing establishments – bending, forming, welding, machining, and assembling metal or plastic parts into components and finished products. However, the assembly of components and subassemblies and their further assembly into finished vehicles tend to be a more common production process in this subsector than in the machinery manufacturing subsector.

NAICS classification of this industry has separate groups for the manufacture of equipment for each mode of transport – road, rail, air, and water. Parts for motor vehicles warrant a separate industry group because of their importance and because parts manufacture requires less assembly, and the establishments that manufacture only parts are not as vertically integrated as those that make complete vehicles.

For 1937, includes railroad repair shops. In 1939, value added by manufacture on a basis comparable with 1937 was $1,794 million.

Beginning in 1958, includes establishments engaged primarily in manufacture of truck and related engine and power take-off gears and excludes those engaged primarily in manufacture of parachutes.

Series Dd211–220

SIC 38 (instruments and related products).

This group covers establishments manufacturing primarily mechanical measuring, engineering, laboratory, and scientific research instruments; optical instruments and lenses; surgical, medical, and dental instruments, equipment, and supplies; ophthalmic goods; photographic equipment and supplies; and watches and clocks. Establishments primarily manufacturing instruments for indicating, measuring, and recording electrical quantities and characteristics are classified in electrical equipment and supplies.

During 1958 to 1963, reports received from some large establishments indicated a change from the manufacture primarily of such individual instruments as those used for indicating air speed, rate-of-climb, angle-of-yaw and similar flight characteristics, and gyroscopes that are sold separately to the manufacture primarily of complete instrumentation systems for navigation, guidance, checkout, and so forth. The major impact of this change has been on the classification of products and, consequently, with the SIC coding of these large establishments.

As a result, the annual data for 1958–1962 were revised. Because of the shift in recent years from instruments classified in this group to complete systems classified in the electrical equipment and supplies group, the year-to-year changes are of dubious validity for the industries considered separately. The two industries taken in combination, however, would yield significant measures of activity in the general area.

The composition of this industry was modified in 1987 when the SIC codes were revised. Its composition was altered so dramatically in the switch to NAICS that the NAICS figures are not even reported.

Beginning in 1914, includes establishments engaged primarily in manufacture of motion-picture machines. In 1914, value added by manufacture on a basis comparable with prior years was $96 million.

Beginning in 1925, excludes establishments engaged primarily in grinding lenses for spectacles and eyeglasses to individual prescription.

Beginning in 1927, excludes dental laboratories operating on a custom basis. In 1927, value added by manufacture on a basis comparable with prior years was $280 million. In 1929, value added on a basis comparable with prior years was $306 million. In 1929, excludes establishments engaged primarily in manufacture of gas machines. In 1935, includes establishments engaged primarily in manufacture of certain dental equipment and supplies (chairs, cabinets, and electrical devices).

Beginning in 1937, includes establishments engaged primarily in manufacture of certain mechanical measuring instruments. In 1937, value added by manufacture on a basis comparable with prior years was $295 million.

Beginning in 1939, includes establishments engaged primarily in manufacture of thermostats and gauges and excludes those engaged primarily in manufacture of time-recording stamps and machines. In 1939, value added on a basis comparable with prior years was $314 million.

For 1947 and 1954–1970, includes establishments engaged primarily in manufacture of automatic temperature controls.

Beginning in 1958, includes establishments engaged primarily in manufacture of laboratory precision balances, laboratory furniture, revolution counters, operating room and other hospital furniture, surgical corsets, and hearing aids and excludes those engaged primarily in manufacture of sanitary napkins and tampons.

In 1997, disclosure rules prevented the Census Bureau from revealing other statistics.

Series Dd221–231

SIC 39 (miscellaneous manufacturing industries); NAICS 339 (miscellaneous manufacturing).

This group covers establishments primarily manufacturing products not classified in any other group. Industries in this group fall into the following categories: jewelry, silverware, and plated ware; musical instruments; toys and sporting and athletic goods; pens, pencils, and other office and artists' materials; buttons, costume novelties, and miscellaneous notions; brooms and brushes; morticians' goods; and other miscellaneous manufacturing industries.

For 1953 and earlier years, data for ordnance and accessories are included with this group. For 1954 and subsequent years, data for the ordnance and accessories group are published separately in the source volumes.

Figures are not shown for years prior to 1947 because they are not sufficiently comparable with those for later years owing to their exclusion of establishments manufacturing primarily rubber dolls, carousels and other amusement park rides, electric vibrators, exercisers and reducers, blasting and detonating caps, safety fuses, and pressed and molded pulp goods; and inclusion of establishments primarily manufacturing cellophane bags, aluminum tags, and hair clippers for human use.

It is also clear from even a cursory comparison that the SIC grouping bears little relationship to the NAICS grouping, which is about twice as large.

For the years prior to 1955, includes ordnance and accessories.

Beginning in 1958, excludes establishments engaged primarily in manufacture of plastics products not elsewhere classified, cork products, soda-fountain and bar equipment, and jewelry, instrument, and musical instrument cases and includes those engaged primarily in manufacture of linoleum and other hard-surface floor covering not elsewhere classified.

Series Dd231. Includes ordnance in 1962.

TABLE Dd232–308   Manufacturing summary, by legal form of organization – establishments, employment and payroll, value added, and capital expenditures: 1939–1992[1]

Contributed by Jeremy Atack and Fred Bateman

Establishments

	All							Corporate						
	Establishments	Employment and payroll				Value added	New capital expenditures	Establishments	Employment and payroll				Value added	New capital expenditures
		All employees		Production workers					All employees		Production workers			
		Number	Payroll	Number	Wages				Number	Payroll	Number	Wages		
	Dd232	Dd233	Dd234	Dd235	Dd236	Dd237	Dd238	Dd239	Dd240	Dd241	Dd242	Dd243	Dd244	Dd245
Year	Number	Thousand	Million dollars	Thousand	Million dollars	Million dollars	Million dollars	Number	Thousand	Million dollars	Thousand	Million dollars	Million dollars	Million dollars
1939	184,230	—	—	7,887	—	24,683	—	95,187	—	—	7,051	—	22,790	—
1947	240,807	14,294	39,696	11,918	30,244	74,290	5,998	118,102	12,856	36,580	10,649	27,637	68,294	—
1954 [2]	286,814	15,645	62,963	12,372	44,591	117,032	8,201	148,461	14,273	59,051	11,206	41,480	109,669	7,752
1958	298,182	15,381	73,773	11,367	48,471	143,159	9,531	162,749	14,215	69,885	10,398	45,455	135,644	8,926
1963	306,617	16,235	93,289	12,232	62,394	192,103	11,371	176,190	15,245	89,356	11,426	59,064	184,100	10,791
1967 [3]	305,681	18,498	124,481 [4]	13,955	81,394	261,984	21,503	153,892	17,697	119,530	13,260	78,429	253,261	20,988
1972	320,710	19,029	174,206	13,528	105,502	353,994	24,078	233,213	18,547	171,162	13,120	103,264	347,086	23,625
1977	359,928	19,590	264,013	13,691	157,164	585,166	47,459	284,196	19,114	259,306	13,302	153,891	574,113	46,249
1982	358,061	19,094	379,627	12,401	204,787	824,118	74,562	283,196	18,524	372,338	11,960	199,778	807,553	72,952
1987	368,904	18,952	475,682	12,280	251,450	1,165,741	78,650	287,395	18,342	465,897	11,821	245,113	1,140,602	77,024
1992	381,696	18,205	559,087	11,641	281,538	1,424,670	103,188	311,516	17,746	549,995	11,308	276,086	1,400,995	101,574

Establishments

	Noncorporate							Individual proprietorships						
	Total													
	Establishments	Employment and payroll				Value added	New capital expenditures	Establishments	Employment and payroll				Value added	New capital expenditures
		All employees		Production workers					All employees		Production workers			
		Number	Payroll	Number	Wages				Number	Payroll	Number	Wages		
	Dd246	Dd247	Dd248	Dd249	Dd250	Dd251	Dd252	Dd253	Dd254	Dd255	Dd256	Dd257	Dd258	Dd259
Year	Number	Thousand	Million dollars	Thousand	Million dollars	Million dollars	Million dollars	Number	Thousand	Million dollars	Thousand	Million dollars	Million dollars	Million dollars
1939	89,043	—	—	836	—	1,893	—	53,834	—	—	443	—	957	—
1947	122,705	1,438	3,115	1,269	2,607	5,996	—	69,498	586	1,184	522	1,001	2,162	—
1954 [2]	138,353	1,372	3,912	1,166	3,111	7,863	449	83,224	593	1,527	507	1,237	2,735	176
1958	135,433	1,165	3,787	969	3,016	7,515	605	91,276	542	1,637	461	1,349	3,115	317
1963	130,427	990	3,932	806	3,030	8,002	580	99,174	536	2,033	440	1,595	3,916	315
1967 [3]	33,165	530	2,709	433	2,008	5,636	370	24,897	243	1,187	210	933	2,361	141
1972	87,497	482	3,043	408	2,237	6,908	453	42,507	213	1,303	183	963	2,885	186
1977	75,732	476	4,707	389	3,273	11,052	1,210	52,322	202	1,840	174	1,322	3,961	300
1982	74,865	570	7,288	441	5,010	16,564	1,609	45,630	221	2,306	180	1,747	4,950	294
1987	81,509	609	9,784	460	6,336	25,139	1,626	35,396	192	2,520	151	1,734	5,544	299
1992	70,180	459	9,092	333	5,452	23,705	1,615	49,191	198	3,116	154	2,103	7,317	401

Establishments / Noncorporate / Partnerships — and Companies / Multi-establishment

	Establishments	All employees	Payroll	Production workers	Wages	Value added	New capital expenditures	Establishments	All employees	Payroll	Production workers	Wages	Value added	New capital expenditures	Establishments	All employees	Payroll
		Number		Number					Number		Number					Number	
Year	Dd260	Dd261	Dd262	Dd263	Dd264	Dd265	Dd266	Dd267	Dd268	Dd269	Dd270	Dd271	Dd272	Dd273	Dd274	Dd275	Dd276
	Number	Thousand	Million dollars	Thousand	Million dollars	Million dollars	Million dollars	Number	Thousand	Million dollars	Thousand	Million dollars	Million dollars	Million dollars	Number	Thousand	Million dollars
1939	27,651	—	—	368	—	863	—	—	—	—	—	—	—	—	—	—	—
1947	50,771	757	1,687	673	1,432	3,347	—	—	—	—	—	—	—	—	—	—	—
1954 [2]	47,885	703	2,108	602	1,684	4,054	216	31,769	9,480	40,623	7,402	28,987	79,604	6,485	29,820	9,387	40,309
1958	41,958	543	1,836	452	1,458	3,663	223	41,871	10,064	51,785	7,174	33,469	105,306	7,525	39,048	9,964	51,407
1963	27,677	334	1,034	277	1,062	2,726	141	45,862	11,015	68,202	8,110	44,721	146,605	8,934	43,568	10,890	67,602
1967 [3]	6,731	193	971	157	730	1,895	114	51,706	13,310	93,687	9,790	60,875	206,437	18,596	50,168	13,206	93,053
1972	17,666	167	1,067	139	792	2,413	150	70,198	14,264	138,758	9,792	81,941	286,126	20,040	69,177	14,210	138,374
1977	18,315	123	1,213	100	829	2,681	206	81,241	14,957	214,227	10,097	124,854	485,018	40,975	80,102	14,850	213,006
1982	14,999	141	1,892	109	1,294	4,471	660	81,732	14,299	307,482	8,810	159,085	678,378	65,248	80,260	14,184	305,432
1987	13,181	146	2,510	109	1,603	6,693	676	80,909	13,846	377,336	8,558	191,808	953,608	66,511	79,794	13,747	375,085
1992	11,258	138	3,172	97	1,838	8,939	638	80,976	13,075	436,003	8,010	211,223	1,159,686	87,802	79,753	12,980	433,332

Companies — Multi-establishment (Corporate / Noncorporate) and Single-establishment (All)

	Production workers	Wages	Value added	New capital expenditures	Establishments	All employees	Payroll	Production workers	Wages	Value added	New capital expenditures	Establishments	All employees	Payroll	Production workers	Wages
	Number					Number		Number					Number		Number	
Year	Dd277	Dd278	Dd279	Dd280	Dd281	Dd282	Dd283	Dd284	Dd285	Dd286	Dd287	Dd288	Dd289	Dd290	Dd291	Dd292
	Thousand	Million dollars	Million dollars	Million dollars	Number	Thousand	Million dollars	Thousand	Million dollars	Million dollars	Million dollars	Number	Thousand	Million dollars	Thousand	Million dollars
1939	—	—	—	—	—	—	—	—	—	—	—	—	—	—	—	—
1947	—	—	—	—	—	—	—	—	—	—	—	—	—	—	—	—
1954 [2]	7,327	28,858	78,977	6,435	1,949	93	314	75	229	627	50	255,045	6,165	22,340	4,970	15,604
1958	7,197	33,103	104,475	7,465	2,823	100	378	77	266	831	60	256,311	5,317	21,887	4,193	15,102
1963	8,017	44,325	145,269	8,832	2,294	125	599	93	396	1,336	102	260,755	5,220	25,087	4,122	17,373
1967 [3]	9,718	60,499	204,986	18,463	1,538	104	634	71	376	1,451	133	135,352	4,917	28,482	3,904	19,563
1972	9,753	81,693	285,198	19,978	1,021	54	385	39	248	928	63	250,512	4,765	35,447	3,736	23,561
1977	10,018	124,040	481,685	40,377	1,139	107	1,221	79	814	3,333	598	278,687	4,633	49,786	3,594	32,310
1982	8,732	157,871	673,283	64,567	1,472	114	2,050	78	1,214	5,095	681	276,329	4,796	72,145	3,590	45,703
1987	8,487	190,413	946,227	66,126	1,115	99	2,251	71	1,395	7,380	385	287,995	5,105	98,345	3,723	59,641
1992	7,951	209,901	1,152,142	87,219	1,223	95	2,671	60	1,322	7,543	583	300,720	5,130	123,084	3,631	70,315

Notes appear at end of table

(continued)

TABLE Dd232–308 Manufacturing summary, by legal form of organization – establishments, employment and payroll, value added, and capital expenditures: 1939–1992 *Continued*

(This section: Companies — Single-establishment)

Year	All		Corporate							Noncorporate						
	Value added	New capital expenditures	Establishments	All employees Number	Payroll	Production workers Number	Wages	Value added	New capital expenditures	Establishments	All employees Number	Payroll	Production workers Number	Wages	Value added	New capital expenditures
	Dd293	Dd294	Dd295	Dd296	Dd297	Dd298	Dd299	Dd300	Dd301	Dd302	Dd303	Dd304	Dd305	Dd306	Dd307	Dd308
	Million dollars	Million dollars	Number	Thousand	Million dollars	Thousand	Million dollars	Million dollars	Million dollars	Number	Thousand	Million dollars	Thousand	Million dollars	Million dollars	Million dollars
1939	—	—	—	—	—	—	—	—	—	—	—	—	—	—	—	—
1947	—	—	—	—	—	—	—	—	—	—	—	—	—	—	—	—
1954 [2]	37,428	1,716	118,641	4,886	18,742	3,879	12,722	30,692	1,317	136,404	1,279	3,598	1,091	2,882	6,736	399
1958	37,853	2,006	123,701	4,252	18,478	3,301	12,352	31,169	1,461	132,610	1,065	3,409	892	2,750	6,684	545
1963	45,497	2,437	132,622	4,355	21,754	3,409	14,739	38,831	1,959	128,133	865	3,333	713	2,634	6,666	478
1967 [3]	52,460	2,762	103,723	4,491	26,408	3,542	17,931	48,275	2,525	31,629	425	2,075	361	1,632	4,185	237
1972	67,868	4,037	164,036	4,337	32,788	3,366	21,572	61,888	3,647	86,476	428	2,659	369	1,990	5,980	390
1977	100,147	6,484	204,094	4,264	46,300	3,285	29,851	92,428	5,872	74,593	369	3,486	310	2,459	7,719	612
1982	145,740	9,314	202,936	4,340	66,906	3,227	41,907	134,271	8,385	73,393	456	5,239	363	3,796	11,470	929
1987	212,133	12,139	207,601	4,595	90,813	3,334	54,700	194,375	10,898	80,394	510	7,533	389	4,941	17,758	1,241
1992	265,014	15,386	231,763	4,766	116,663	3,357	66,185	248,853	14,354	68,957	364	6,421	274	4,130	16,161	1,032

[1] See text regarding the lack of comparability of the value-added series over time.

[2] Figures exclude data for Alaska and Hawai'i, as well as industry Standard Industrial Classification (SIC) code 3273 (ready-mixed concrete) and establishments primarily engaged in machine shop repair from industry SIC 3599 (industrial machinery not elsewhere classified). See the Introduction to Part D for a discussion of SIC codes.

[3] For 118,622 establishments, information on the legal form of organization was not available; see text.

[4] Revised with 1992 Census of Manufactures.

Sources

Series Dd232–266. 1939: U.S. Bureau of the Census, *Sixteenth Census of the United States: 1940. Census of Manufactures, 1939*, volume 1, p. 230. 1947–1967: *1967 Census of Manufactures* (1971), volume 1, pp. 3–4. 1972–1992: *Census of Manufactures, 1992, General Summary* (1996), MC92-S-1, Table 3-7.

Series Dd267–308. *Census of Manufactures, 1992, General Summary* (1996), MC92-S-1, Table 3-7.

Documentation

Each establishment included in the manufacturing censuses was classified into one of the following legal forms of organization:

Corporate: an establishment (other than a cooperative) owned by an organization or company legally incorporated under state laws.

Noncorporate: individual proprietorships, partnerships, cooperatives, receiverships, public and quasi-public organizations, and, in addition, misassignments of small establishments that were not corrected because they were not statistically significant.

Individual proprietorship: an establishment owned by one person, who may or may not actively participate in the operation of the business.

Partnership: an establishment owned by two or more persons, each of whom has a financial interest in and responsibility for the business. A partner may or may not actively participate in the operation of the business.

In 1967, for 118,622 establishments information on the legal form of organization was not available in the administrative records used to compile the data, which probably explains much of the discontinuity between 1963 and 1972. This also accounts for the discrepancies between the totals in series Dd232–238 (which include these establishments) and the breakdowns in the rest of the table (which do not). The information for these establishments is as follows, with employment figures in thousands, and dollar figures in millions:

118,622	Establishments
271	Employees
1,313	Payroll
263	Production workers
957	Production worker wages
3,086	Value added
145	New capital expenditures

Information on particular series is provided later. See also the text for Table Dd13–231 for information on such series in the manufacturing censuses.

Series on All Employees

Includes production workers and all other employees. For 1958 and later censuses, figures were tabulated as of the pay period including the 12th of March. For 1954, they were tabulated as the average for the pay periods including the 12th of March, May, August, and November.

Series on Production Workers

The number of production workers is tabulated as the average for the pay periods including the 12th of March, May, August, and November. In 1939, figures represent the average for the year.

Series on Value Added

Beginning in 1982, all respondents were requested to report their inventories at cost or market prior to adjustment to LIFO (last in, first out) cost. This is a change from prior years in which respondents were permitted to value their inventories using any generally accepted accounting method. Consequently, data for value added by manufacture since 1982 are not comparable with earlier data.

OUTPUT

Jeremy Atack and Fred Bateman

TABLE Dd309–365 Manufacturing output and implicit price indexes, by type of commodity: 1869–1939[1]

Contributed by Jeremy Atack and Fred Bateman

					Value of output					
					Finished commodities					
					Perishable					Semidurables
	All finished commodities	Total	Food and kindred products		Cigars, cigarettes, and tobacco	Magazines, newspapers, miscellaneous paper supplies, etc.	Drug, toilet, and household preparations	Fuel and lighting products		Total	Dry goods and notions
			Manufactured	Nonmanufactured				Manufactured	Nonmanufactured		
	Dd309	Dd310	Dd311	Dd312	Dd313	Dd314	Dd315	Dd316	Dd317	Dd318	Dd319
Year	Million dollars	Million dollars	Million dollars	Million dollars	Million dollars	Million dollars	Million dollars	Million dollars	Million dollars	Million dollars	Million dollars
1869	2,813.3	1,594.2	673.1	699.1	74.7	30.6	37.7	29.4	49.7	665.4	224.5
1879	3,441.7	1,996.1	962.9	716.5	119.7	61.5	40.4	39.7	55.5	828.2	263.1
1889	5,080.4	2,905.7	1,434.3	956.6	202.5	93.9	81.6	59.5	77.2	1,132.9	281.7
1890	5,002.2	2,705.3	1,155.5	991.4	215.4	97.3	90.1	75.4	80.2	1,196.0	299.6
1891	5,284.3	2,964.9	1,308.5	1,079.2	226.6	101.2	97.9	62.7	88.9	1,196.9	289.3
1892	5,331.3	2,908.8	1,251.4	1,062.3	230.5	109.3	104.7	52.1	98.5	1,255.8	297.2
1893	5,500.4	3,314.4	1,555.3	1,182.7	218.5	98.3	104.9	54.0	100.7	1,124.2	259.4
1894	4,752.3	2,916.3	1,337.9	1,012.3	218.1	92.9	102.9	61.9	90.3	970.9	209.9
1895	5,227.2	3,119.1	1,443.7	1,079.0	202.4	94.1	111.3	95.8	92.9	1,114.7	265.7
1896	5,003.4	2,944.0	1,436.2	927.5	193.0	90.0	112.7	92.8	91.9	1,064.6	215.5
1897	5,376.1	3,222.6	1,633.7	1,032.1	197.3	92.6	115.6	62.4	89.0	1,154.0	232.3
1898	5,708.0	3,431.7	1,707.9	1,121.4	226.9	103.2	122.4	63.9	86.0	1,175.8	227.4
1899	6,586.2	3,820.9	1,955.5	1,160.9	267.4	113.0	134.6	87.7	101.8	1,374.4	255.8
1900	7,120.8	4,100.8	2,083.9	1,249.1	304.0	122.3	136.2	100.3	105.0	1,465.7	271.9
1901	7,782.2	4,620.5	2,365.0	1,420.9	327.9	134.9	155.2	84.7	132.0	1,528.5	271.1
1902	8,227.5	4,764.7	2,403.1	1,519.3	325.1	151.3	174.0	89.7	102.2	1,613.8	298.7
1903	8,702.1	5,012.7	2,516.7	1,518.9	346.0	154.2	183.1	111.5	182.3	1,734.7	302.1
1904	8,734.3	5,167.7	2,601.5	1,614.9	339.2	159.7	182.3	109.2	160.8	1,746.5	285.1
1905	9,451.0	5,403.6	2,856.7	1,540.0	357.2	172.5	215.8	94.4	167.0	1,925.3	318.3
1906	10,752.5	5,912.7	3,121.0	1,719.6	398.1	184.3	225.4	102.9	161.3	2,244.2	348.2
1907	11,524.3	6,452.7	3,389.7	1,886.9	405.2	196.7	249.3	128.5	196.5	2,310.1	375.5
1908	10,191.1	5,988.1	2,974.7	1,915.7	399.8	156.8	234.1	125.8	181.3	2,155.5	295.5
1909	11,825.3	6,922.1	3,617.7	2,112.5	430.5	210.6	250.3	124.7	175.8	2,447.0	368.0
1910	12,659.2 [2]	7,386.0	3,823.5	2,306.1	464.0	209.9	266.8	121.0	194.8	2,417.3	349.5
1911	12,749.4	7,491.3	3,980.1	2,235.7	460.4	211.3	278.8	119.1	205.9	2,571.4	326.3
1912	14,028.0	8,100.8	4,342.3	2,410.5	468.9	233.6	289.4	142.0	214.0	2,754.4	363.2
1913	14,632.8	8,230.2	4,441.9	2,315.9	506.8	243.9	294.9	191.3	235.3	2,900.2	348.6
1914	14,054.0	8,296.5	4,484.8	2,380.1	500.9	254.4	289.0	160.4	226.9	2,709.5	337.8
1915	13,986.1	8,079.8	4,342.1	2,310.3	478.6	255.6	331.0	141.7	220.5	2,635.7	317.0
1916	18,389.4	9,893.2	5,380.1	2,693.6	522.4	352.2	420.7	262.5	261.7	3,573.7	461.6
1917	24,545.5	13,174.1	6,925.7	3,907.2	629.5	407.5	511.5	425.7	366.9	4,790.6	620.3
1918	29,979.8	15,807.2	8,583.6	4,280.8	864.0	445.5	636.1	580.7	416.5	6,076.1	854.8
1919	33,265.3	17,215.5	9,312.4	4,709.0	1,000.0	458.7	660.1	630.7	444.5	6,770.2	890.9
1919	34,032.4	17,392.4	9,468.2	4,720.2	1,008.4	439.8	667.8	668.4	419.5	7,019.9	806.5
1920	37,285.2	19,236.2	10,301.4	4,696.3	1,195.5	675.9	765.6	1,044.8	556.8	7,872.8	903.6
1921	25,864.0	14,022.9	6,548.7	4,182.4	1,053.0	474.5	562.2	714.9	487.3	5,631.7	607.4
1922	27,393.8	14,059.4	6,837.6	3,843.0	1,002.1	499.9	624.6	888.4	363.9	6,313.9	681.5
1923	32,168.5	15,176.0	7,554.6	4,012.9	1,050.3	550.7	698.5	746.4	562.7	7,230.3	861.9
1924	30,957.7	15,573.6	7,981.3	3,948.0	1,073.2	563.0	718.6	781.3	508.2	6,401.4	700.7
1925	34,046.3	16,870.5	8,684.0	4,335.8	1,094.4	615.7	767.0	990.1	383.5	7,134.0	816.0
1926	35,856.6	17,784.6	9,039.8	4,467.4	1,127.2	632.8	783.3	1,220.7	513.4	7,295.6	803.5
1927	34,410.2	17,263.6	8,827.3	4,360.2	1,164.5	648.4	851.9	958.9	452.5	7,390.7	798.6
1928	35,892.9	17,911.1	9,111.7	4,466.9	1,168.7	661.6	932.3	1,153.3	416.4	7,383.2	769.1
1929	37,782.6	18,384.0	9,463.9	4,358.3	1,243.6	683.9	984.2	1,237.8	412.3	7,458.3	791.0
1930	31,260.7	16,590.5	8,497.5	3,996.8	1,141.8	644.8	891.0	1,052.2	366.3	6,069.4	574.4
1931	24,243.3	13,431.7	6,730.2	3,133.4	1,154.9	573.5	809.0	740.2	290.5	4,931.4	459.4 [3]
1932	17,727.8	10,754.9	5,183.0	2,408.1	1,006.6	492.6	624.4	830.6	209.5	3,526.1	317.5
1933	18,454.1	10,872.9	5,509.5	2,451.1	910.7	470.1	626.0	707.2	198.3	3,772.8	390.4
1934	23,166.7	12,987.2	—	—	—	—	—	—	—	4,501.6	—

Notes appear at end of table

(continued)

TABLE Dd309-365 Manufacturing output and implicit price indexes, by type of commodity: 1869-1939 *Continued*

	Value of output										
	Finished commodities										Semidurables
	Perishable										
	All finished commodities	Total	Food and kindred products		Cigars, cigarettes, and tobacco	Magazines, newspapers, miscellaneous paper supplies, etc.	Drug, toilet, and household preparations	Fuel and lighting products		Total	Dry goods and notions
			Manufactured	Nonmanufactured				Manufactured	Nonmanufactured		
	Dd309	Dd310	Dd311	Dd312	Dd313	Dd314	Dd315	Dd316	Dd317	Dd318	Dd319
Year	Million dollars	Million dollars	Million dollars	Million dollars	Million dollars	Million dollars	Million dollars	Million dollars	Million dollars	Million dollars	Million dollars
1935	26,744.7	14,571.7	7,884.9	3,183.6	1,096.4	527.2	727.7	952.2	199.7	4,937.6	576.0
1936	30,258.1	16,239.0	—	—	—	—	—	—	—	4,775.8	—
1937	33,667.8	17,295.3	9,402.3	3,683.0	1,274.1	601.9	818.4	1,335.0	180.6	5,591.3	712.9
1938	28,156.7	15,721.6	—	—	—	—	—	—	—	4,852.7	—
1939	31,277.7	16,073.5	—	—	—	—	—	—	—	5,490.6	—

	Value of output										
	Finished commodities										
	Semidurables					Consumer durables					
	Clothing and personal furnishings	Housefurnishings	Shoes and other footwear	Tires and tubes	Toys, games, and sporting goods	Total	Household furniture commodities	Printing and publishing books	Luggage commodities	China and household utensils	Monuments and tombstones
	Dd320	Dd321	Dd322	Dd323	Dd324	Dd325	Dd326	Dd327	Dd328	Dd329	Dd330
Year	Million dollars	Million dollars	Million dollars	Million dollars	Million dollars	Million dollars	Million dollars	Million dollars	Million dollars	Million dollars	Million dollars
1869	229.8	12.8	185.3	—	13.0	262.7	58.5	8.4	7.7	26.0	6.6
1879	358.2	16.2	173.7	—	17.0	304.3	65.2	19.1	7.1	31.2	7.5
1889	560.8	32.1	236.1	—	22.3	499.2	93.4	34.7	10.7	46.4	15.2
1890	588.8	34.5	249.8	—	23.3	538.7	95.3	33.9	13.4	49.3	17.3
1891	603.3	35.3	244.2	—	24.8	556.8	100.5	33.4	13.9	51.7	16.7
1892	632.8	37.0	263.8	—	25.0	579.3	115.0	34.9	15.6	52.9	16.6
1893	566.9	35.9	233.6	—	28.4	496.3	100.2	34.3	12.9	43.5	11.9
1894	478.1	32.4	228.0	—	22.4	429.3	82.4	28.4	11.1	39.3	14.9
1895	542.2	36.4	236.0	7.9	26.4	497.7	94.0	35.6	8.9	45.9	13.8
1896	549.5	35.5	228.9	9.8	25.4	475.2	90.2	34.6	9.2	51.0	13.4
1897	596.8	35.7	246.3	18.1	24.8	506.5	88.4	33.7	8.8	51.0	16.6
1898	608.2	35.9	261.9	19.0	23.4	528.9	89.4	40.8	8.8	52.0	17.5
1899	743.7	42.5	292.9	12.7	27.0	634.3	104.1	45.0	12.6	60.9	20.3
1900	817.4	49.8	289.8	7.8	29.0	658.7	106.9	44.3	12.0	69.5	18.4
1901	837.9	49.4	327.4	6.2	36.5	718.9	118.7	47.4	13.1	73.5	23.2
1902	892.8	53.2	325.9	5.5	37.8	786.3	129.4	49.2	14.9	78.5	27.9
1903	981.8	53.9	352.5	4.3	40.1	825.7	139.2	51.5	15.8	90.8	25.9
1904	992.6	52.9	368.9	5.7	41.3	826.9	142.4	53.6	18.9	91.7	25.7
1905	1,099.7	55.7	395.9	9.3	46.3	954.8	160.8	56.7	20.1	108.7	28.7
1906	1,314.7	69.5	448.9	12.5	50.4	1,129.5	190.3	55.9	23.9	122.6	34.5
1907	1,335.4	68.2	454.4	15.6	60.9	1,178.1	185.1	56.8	27.7	120.7	38.3
1908	1,287.0	60.1	452.1	17.5	43.3	1,011.0	152.6	53.8	23.6	93.6	40.9
1909	1,459.7	75.0	467.9	23.4	52.9	1,212.8	192.0	62.9	28.5	102.9	38.4
1910	1,408.3	83.0	486.0	36.0	54.4	1,331.6	202.4	60.3	32.8	114.1	42.6
1911	1,560.0	80.0	500.8	45.5	58.7	1,339.2	204.1	59.1	36.1	116.7	42.4
1912	1,656.7	85.5	531.4	58.3	59.3	1,538.4	220.5	66.3	33.9	122.4	40.3
1913	1,721.6	95.5	583.8	86.6	64.0	1,675.1	236.7	77.8	34.0	130.2	42.1
1914	1,598.1	90.0	523.8	92.7	67.1	1,570.4	222.5	68.1	26.5	125.9	41.0
1915	1,533.9	85.8	520.6	104.9	73.5	1,700.2	212.3	73.3	25.9	126.1	37.5
1916	2,025.3	112.2	705.5	156.1	113.0	2,396.1	271.7	76.7	39.6	160.9	37.9
1917	2,622.7	156.7	863.4	329.1	198.5	2,799.0	300.6	89.8	36.7	221.7	42.3
1918	3,361.1	199.9	1,043.2	491.3	125.8	2,646.9	329.0	99.2	52.2	197.6	50.0
1919	3,817.9	212.0	1,187.6	515.4	146.4	3,921.2	494.7	127.4	64.2	230.1	73.4
1919	3,932.9	324.0	1,254.2	546.6	155.8	4,075.6	509.0	128.2	70.4	201.7	73.4
1920	4,382.8	390.5	1,368.2	678.9	148.8	4,899.3	620.5	140.0	78.2	265.7	82.3
1921	3,345.3	277.9	953.5	323.5	124.1	3,270.3	466.6	122.0	51.0	166.8	46.9
1922	3,865.4	307.1	993.0	335.8	131.1	4,056.5	501.1	124.9	52.6	167.7	47.6
1923	4,347.4	377.3	1,128.2	348.3	167.1	5,366.7	578.9	130.7	69.2	239.0	65.6
1924	3,743.9	358.4	1,061.7	382.0	154.6	5,034.3	614.0	145.0	57.8	181.5	66.4

TABLE Dd309–365   Manufacturing output and implicit price indexes, by type of commodity: 1869–1939   *Continued*

Value of output

Finished commodities

	Semidurables					Consumer durables					
	Clothing and personal furnishings	Housefurnishings	Shoes and other footwear	Tires and tubes	Toys, games, and sporting goods	Total	Household furniture commodities	Printing and publishing books	Luggage commodities	China and household utensils	Monuments and tombstones
	Dd320	Dd321	Dd322	Dd323	Dd324	Dd325	Dd326	Dd327	Dd328	Dd329	Dd330
Year	Million dollars	Million dollars	Million dollars	Million dollars	Million dollars	Million dollars	Million dollars	Million dollars	Million dollars	Million dollars	Million dollars
1925	4,149.2	404.8	1,044.8	555.1	164.2	5,785.7	622.9	149.8	66.4	240.1	66.8
1926	4,186.6	438.1	1,073.9	616.3	177.2	6,109.0	638.2	155.4	66.4	271.6	63.8
1927	4,360.2	396.9	1,077.6	574.9	182.5	5,435.8	623.5	172.1	65.9	229.3	61.9
1928	4,385.6	401.5	1,074.9	551.0	200.9	5,936.1	629.3	179.7	67.9	275.7	61.0
1929	4,516.4	416.5	1,081.9	437.8	214.6	6,312.0	600.4	192.3	70.3	274.0	63.6
1930	3,767.8	347.8	860.3	336.9	182.2	4,272.6	441.4	174.3	44.5	196.4	54.9
1931	3,087.9	256.6	705.1	273.4	149.1	3,251.9	333.2	141.5	29.4	185.9	43.6
1932	2,183.4	187.5	546.3	194.5	96.9	2,047.4	205.4	102.9	18.4	138.9	25.7
1933	2,274.6	218.2	597.3	196.7	95.8	2,321.3	226.9	92.1	19.1	150.4	20.8
1934	—	—	—	—	—	3,307.2	—	—	—	—	—
1935	3,039.1	273.7	693.4	215.1	140.3	4,256.8	323.7	131.1	31.0	204.8	21.3
1936	—	—	—	—	—	5,158.0	—	—	—	—	—
1937	3,258.6	340.1	828.3	261.2	190.2	5,742.1	478.7	161.6	42.5	241.6	26.0
1938	—	—	—	—	—	3,747.3	—	—	—	—	—
1939	—	—	—	—	—	4,973.1	—	—	—	—	—

Value of output

Finished commodities

Consumer durables

	Heating and cooking apparatus, etc.	Electrical household appliances and supplies	Radios	Passenger vehicles (motor)	Motor vehicle accessories	Passenger vehicles (horse-drawn) and accessories	Motorcycles and bicycles	Pleasure craft	Jewelry, silverware, clocks, and watches	Ophthalmic products and artificial limbs	Housefurnishings	Musical instruments
	Dd331	Dd332	Dd333	Dd334	Dd335	Dd336	Dd337	Dd338	Dd339	Dd340	Dd341	Dd342
Year	Million dollars	Million dollars	Million dollars	Million dollars	Million dollars	Million dollars	Million dollars	Million dollars	Million dollars	Million dollars	Million dollars	Million dollars
1869	26.4	—	—	—	—	35.7	—	0.6	41.6	0.4	40.1	10.8
1879	23.0	—	—	—	—	35.1	—	0.9	43.3	0.8	56.7	14.3
1889	38.9	—	—	—	—	54.0	1.9	1.5	74.5	2.3	97.6	28.2
1890	37.9	—	—	—	—	60.4	—	1.5	90.2	2.6	103.9	32.9
1891	39.1	—	—	—	—	62.4	—	1.6	86.7	2.9	114.9	33.0
1892	38.9	—	—	—	—	63.3	—	1.5	90.3	3.2	112.6	34.6
1893	35.3	—	—	—	—	58.5	—	1.4	71.7	3.3	100.1	23.2
1894	31.0	—	—	—	—	50.9	—	1.0	58.3	3.3	88.9	19.9
1895	35.5	—	—	—	—	45.2	14.1	1.3	69.2	3.7	102.6	27.9
1896	45.6	—	—	—	—	39.3	14.9	1.2	58.5	3.8	90.6	22.8
1897	50.7	—	—	—	—	40.9	27.0	1.2	63.6	4.0	96.0	24.5
1898	46.3	—	—	—	—	43.5	27.8	1.4	74.0	4.3	95.4	27.8
1899	59.2	1.9	—	4.2	—	53.5	18.9	2.1	97.1	4.8	115.6	34.2
1900	61.9	2.4	—	6.0	—	50.1	10.5	2.7	100.0	4.7	126.8	42.4
1901	70.7	2.6	—	7.8	—	64.1	7.7	3.7	103.6	5.2	128.8	48.8
1902	78.6	3.2	—	9.3	—	58.8	6.4	3.5	117.0	5.7	146.8	57.2
1903	78.8	3.8	—	11.3	—	56.7	4.2	3.6	120.5	5.8	152.5	65.1
1904	73.6	3.3	—	21.4	2.5	57.8	2.5	3.1	120.9	5.6	146.2	57.7
1905	85.8	4.7	—	35.6	4.3	61.2	5.4	3.8	144.1	7.1	156.7	71.1
1906	103.4	8.0	—	62.7	7.8	62.4	4.9	4.3	174.0	7.9	185.8	81.2
1907	101.2	10.2	—	89.6	11.3	63.8	6.5	6.1	180.9	9.4	182.8	87.8
1908	84.2	7.7	—	132.2	17.3	48.8	4.9	3.4	128.6	9.3	147.1	63.0
1909	93.8	11.8	—	154.3	21.1	49.8	5.6	4.3	175.9	10.5	184.2	76.8
1910	97.3	16.3	—	203.8	26.9	53.3	7.3	4.4	186.1	10.7	195.7	77.6
1911	104.1	15.7	—	209.2	26.3	45.9	9.4	4.3	186.1	10.9	187.5	81.3
1912	131.5	19.7	—	311.3	39.3	41.6	12.0	3.9	190.9	10.6	199.1	95.2
1913	124.9	22.2	—	372.8	46.1	40.1	21.9	4.1	196.0	12.3	209.3	104.4
1914	110.5	18.8	—	399.6	49.9	35.6	16.2	3.6	154.6	15.5	190.7	91.6

(continued)

TABLE Dd309–365   Manufacturing output and implicit price indexes, by type of commodity: 1869–1939   *Continued*

Value of output

Finished commodities

Consumer durables

Year	Heating and cooking apparatus, etc.	Electrical household appliances and supplies	Radios	Passenger vehicles (motor)	Motor vehicle accessories	Passenger vehicles (horse-drawn) and accessories	Motorcycles and bicycles	Pleasure craft	Jewelry, silverware, clocks, and watches	Ophthalmic products and artificial limbs	Housefurnishings	Musical instruments
	Dd331	Dd332	Dd333	Dd334	Dd335	Dd336	Dd337	Dd338	Dd339	Dd340	Dd341	Dd342
	Million dollars	Million dollars	Million dollars	Million dollars	Million dollars	Million dollars	Million dollars	Million dollars	Million dollars	Million dollars	Million dollars	Million dollars
1915	119.4	23.7	—	537.8	61.0	30.5	13.3	3.4	144.1	20.2	181.4	90.2
1916	142.5	41.2	—	873.7	104.0	31.0	16.3	4.0	221.7	23.9	234.9	116.2
1917	194.2	58.8	—	996.7	120.5	38.8	16.7	3.3	219.2	36.5	288.6	134.7
1918	216.8	67.5	—	762.7	85.8	35.3	18.9	1.5	194.9	71.1	320.1	144.2
1919	263.5	84.5	—	1,286.9	168.0	26.4	19.0	5.1	409.7	45.0	375.2	248.3
1919	242.5	65.1	14.3	1,292.6	282.6	—	24.0	13.9	427.8	58.2	430.2	242.0
1920	345.6	82.8	17.0	1,628.3	313.4	—	20.8	14.7	383.2	67.8	574.8	264.2
1921	186.5	63.2	12.2	1,115.5	169.5	—	10.2	9.4	263.1	46.6	374.6	166.4
1922	239.2	58.6	26.9	1,546.1	243.4	—	8.9	6.2	327.0	48.6	470.0	187.7
1923	322.0	76.3	50.3	2,188.8	355.8	—	16.3	12.1	388.1	58.5	600.0	215.1
1924	322.2	83.4	139.3	1,922.5	337.2	—	13.0	14.0	363.9	48.6	547.1	178.5
1925	346.1	106.3	168.2	2,340.2	444.3	—	11.3	15.0	384.3	46.6	604.0	173.6
1926	364.3	137.5	206.7	2,504.3	440.2	—	11.9	22.4	398.9	46.6	591.6	189.3
1927	339.4	146.3	181.5	1,967.8	419.8	—	10.1	17.8	387.6	49.7	584.7	176.2
1928	314.2	152.7	298.7	2,294.9	411.7	—	12.0	17.4	396.3	48.7	627.5	148.6
1929	347.3	176.7	366.0	2,567.0	407.6	—	10.6	26.2	402.7	52.1	643.3	111.9
1930	254.2	160.0	230.6	1,538.0	326.1	—	9.2	24.6	263.8	48.3	402.7	103.4
1931	206.2	144.4	154.7	1,074.1	273.1	—	7.7	16.8	178.8	40.3	373.6	48.7
1932	123.0	82.2	94.2	603.2	211.9	—	4.6	9.3	108.5	32.0	252.0	35.0
1933	147.1	110.3	98.0	725.3	228.2	—	7.5	4.8	116.0	39.1	311.6	24.1
1934	—	—	—	—	—	—	—	—	—	—	—	—
1935	237.5	217.8	167.4	1,688.3	463.6	—	16.8	14.1	189.5	50.1	468.3	31.5
1936	—	—	—	—	—	—	—	—	—	—	—	—
1937	341.0	332.6	218.0	2,212.9	594.6	—	30.8	25.4	272.6	70.9	640.9	52.0
1938	—	—	—	—	—	—	—	—	—	—	—	—
1939	—	—	—	—	—	—	—	—	—	—	—	—

Value of output

Finished commodities

Producer durables

Year	Total	Carpenters' and mechanics' tools	Office and store furniture and fixtures	Farm equipment	Industrial machinery and equipment	Electrical equipment (industrial and commercial)	Office and store machinery and equipment	Miscellaneous equipment	Business vehicles (motor)	Tractors	Aircraft	Ships and boats
	Dd343	Dd344	Dd345	Dd346	Dd347	Dd348	Dd349	Dd350	Dd351	Dd352	Dd353	Dd354
	Million dollars	Million dollars	Million dollars	Million dollars	Million dollars	Million dollars	Million dollars	Million dollars	Million dollars	Million dollars	Million dollars	Million dollars
1869	291.0	10.5	13.6	50.0	110.4	—	3.1	31.4	—	—	—	11.5
1879	313.1	13.4	15.9	67.3	98.6	1.9	3.6	37.1	—	—	—	19.4
1889	542.6	20.8	25.6	83.9	184.5	13.1	8.2	63.3	—	—	—	24.7
1890	562.2	23.6	25.8	89.0	185.6	21.8	8.7	66.5	—	—	—	24.6
1891	565.7	24.7	26.8	75.3	185.5	23.7	9.0	69.5	—	—	—	26.9
1892	587.4	24.6	30.1	75.4	196.5	22.7	9.8	74.9	—	—	—	24.9
1893	565.5	22.5	26.1	71.2	184.9	16.6	9.5	71.7	—	—	—	23.9
1894	435.7	16.6	21.2	58.7	157.7	15.8	8.6	61.0	—	—	—	17.8
1895	495.7	19.1	23.7	59.3	193.1	20.0	10.7	64.8	—	—	—	22.7
1896	519.6	18.6	22.5	46.6	209.8	20.5	11.6	67.9	—	—	—	20.8
1897	492.9	16.8	21.8	58.4	182.3	24.4	9.7	64.2	—	—	—	20.7
1898	571.6	19.8	21.4	85.6	194.9	34.3	10.6	69.4	—	—	—	24.4
1899	756.6	24.5	24.2	99.4	267.5	56.1	14.3	83.9	—	—	—	36.1
1900	895.6	26.9	27.2	100.6	347.6	68.2	19.7	91.8	—	—	—	46.9
1901	914.3	29.2	30.2	110.4	330.3	68.5	18.9	89.5	—	—	—	64.7
1902	1,062.7	35.7	33.6	152.9	371.3	80.6	21.9	102.8	—	—	—	60.8
1903	1,129.0	37.7	37.8	120.2	405.9	91.9	23.9	110.4	—	—	—	61.3
1904	993.2	34.7	38.2	125.2	327.1	75.9	20.3	108.7	1.4	—	—	53.6

TABLE Dd309–365   Manufacturing output and implicit price indexes, by type of commodity: 1869–1939   *Continued*

Value of output

Finished commodities

Producer durables

Year	Total	Carpenters' and mechanics' tools	Office and store furniture and fixtures	Farm equipment	Industrial machinery and equipment	Electrical equipment (industrial and commercial)	Office and store machinery and equipment	Miscellaneous equipment	Business vehicles (motor)	Tractors	Aircraft	Ships and boats
	Dd343	Dd344	Dd345	Dd346	Dd347	Dd348	Dd349	Dd350	Dd351	Dd352	Dd353	Dd354
	Million dollars	Million dollars	Million dollars	Million dollars	Million dollars	Million dollars	Million dollars	Million dollars	Million dollars	Million dollars	Million dollars	Million dollars
1905	1,167.3	37.9	43.1	130.2	404.7	84.9	28.0	115.6	1.5	—	—	55.6
1906	1,466.1	43.4	50.7	160.5	504.6	119.9	38.8	135.2	1.8	—	—	54.8
1907	1,583.5	52.7	49.1	161.6	510.9	127.5	42.7	157.9	2.3	—	—	66.8
1908	1,036.5	35.7	40.4	137.7	331.2	83.2	27.9	157.4	3.5	—	—	34.4
1909	1,243.4	47.7	48.6	166.5	446.9	111.2	40.1	154.6	7.3	—	—	38.2
1910	1,524.2 [2]	49.1	50.1	170.6	512.4	144.4	48.4	151.6	12.5	—	—	40.8
1911	1,347.6	41.9	48.7	168.2	476.6	133.5	43.8	147.1	25.9	—	—	42.7
1912	1,634.5	48.5	54.3	187.3	517.1	162.1	50.2	152.8	49.9	8.1	0.3	44.4
1913	1,827.3	53.6	54.3	202.4	543.4	177.1	55.4	161.7	47.1	4.4	0.2	47.6
1914	1,477.6	49.6	50.8	187.8	460.2	147.0	50.9	171.0	36.2	16.7	0.2	43.5
1915	1,570.4	57.0	43.3	205.1	536.8	160.2	63.0	140.6	68.6	22.7	0.6	66.8
1916	2,526.3	97.5	51.6	237.1	906.0	253.9	98.8	205.6	111.6	25.8	1.4	103.7
1917	3,781.8	131.7	61.3	250.0	1,358.1	325.2	140.5	291.6	189.1	50.7	21.3	243.8
1918	5,449.7	210.6	65.7	301.8	1,575.8	339.9	157.8	360.7	417.0	136.6	174.7	805.3
1919	5,358.4	174.8	86.4	343.8	1,440.5	365.7	125.4	349.3	344.0	152.6	8.4	1,389.5
1919	5,544.5	120.6	100.3	394.6	1,434.3	460.8	156.4	347.6	344.3	171.6	10.0	1,381.3
1920	5,277.0	128.7	135.1	270.6	1,635.8	557.9	160.6	403.0	332.9	197.4	8.7	808.1
1921	2,939.1	62.1	115.5	248.1	922.8	406.6	114.0	208.6	170.4	49.6	6.1	272.7
1922	2,964.0	87.8	136.8	160.7	1,085.2	415.8	132.4	245.1	237.2	43.4	8.8	93.6
1923	4,395.5	115.4	201.3	315.5	1,510.9	598.1	182.0	302.1	321.8	63.5	11.5	73.1
1924	3,948.5	106.4	229.5	265.9	1,303.8	655.0	179.2	208.0	323.4	52.1	10.9	67.4
1925	4,256.0	109.8	236.1	306.5	1,486.4	666.2	196.4	300.4	389.6	70.3	10.5	55.7
1926	4,667.5	110.2	242.3	355.4	1,606.8	776.4	200.1	321.9	377.2	87.4	17.6	86.5
1927	4,320.2	104.2	249.0	340.4	1,476.0	741.2	201.2	318.4	302.3	91.3	19.4	70.8
1928	4,662.5	131.6	245.8	356.5	1,644.1	895.0	213.6	304.9	318.3	104.1	51.1	60.4
1929	5,628.4	124.6	288.7	386.5	2,017.2	1,000.1	217.8	369.7	510.8	121.8	56.0	78.2
1930	4,328.2	99.8	203.5	338.5	1,457.8	722.2	165.3	304.7	373.0	95.4	28.8	94.9
1931	2,628.3	53.9	151.7	163.4	938.2	499.5	116.5	199.9	247.0	19.6	30.0	82.0
1932	1,399.4	31.0	74.9	70.9	525.8	215.5	78.5	129.0	125.5	15.8	14.1	49.7
1933	1,487.1	49.1	70.3	78.8	577.1	200.9	78.8	168.1	159.0	12.6	16.5	30.4
1934	2,370.7	—	—	—	—	—	—	—	—	—	—	—
1935	2,978.6	66.3	111.1	345.3	1,126.0	361.2	140.6	198.8	359.3	133.3	19.1	48.2
1936	4,085.3	—	—	—	—	—	—	—	—	—	—	—
1937	5,039.1	95.3	176.8	668.5	1,883.7	673.8	204.9	269.9	496.6	223.7	48.4	128.6
1938	3,835.1	—	—	—	—	—	—	—	—	—	—	—
1939	4,740.5	—	—	—	—	—	—	—	—	—	—	—

	Value of output						Implicit price indexes				
	Finished commodities			Construction materials							
	Producer durables										
Year	Locomotive and railroad cars	Business vehicles (horse-drawn)	Professional and scientific equipment	Total	Manufactured	Nonmanufactured	Perishable	Semidurable	Consumer durable	Producer durable	Construction materials
	Dd355	Dd356	Dd357	Dd358	Dd359	Dd360	Dd361	Dd362	Dd363	Dd364	Dd365
	Million dollars	Million dollars	Million dollars	Million dollars	Million dollars	Million dollars	Index 1913 = 100	Index 1913 = 100	Index 1913 = 100	Index 1913 = 100	Index 1913 = 100
1869	40.8	18.1	1.6	377.4	324.8	52.6	141.2	158.5	119.4	163.8	107.4
1879	36.3	18.0	1.6	444.2	365.9	78.3	86.6	102.2	83.2	95.4	81.4
1889	87.3	28.4	2.9	838.9	712.2	126.7	88.3	95.6	81.9	88.2	85.0
1890	81.5	32.0	3.2	1,216.5	1,070.5	146.1	86.1	94.9	82.3	87.7	84.3
1891	87.6	33.5	3.2	1,076.0	940.0	136.0	84.8	92.6	82.1	81.1	80.2
1892	90.9	34.1	3.5	1,335.5	1,164.8	170.7	79.8	92.6	79.2	80.0	75.9
1893	104.1	32.1	3.0	1,074.8	933.1	141.3	84.7	90.5	74.8	78.4	75.4
1894	47.4	28.4	2.5	1,004.1	867.0	137.1	76.3	80.5	72.3	78.2	71.6

Notes appear at end of table

(continued)

TABLE Dd309–365   Manufacturing output and implicit price indexes, by type of commodity: 1869–1939   *Continued*

	Value of output						Implicit price indexes				
	Finished commodities				Construction materials						
	Producer durables											
	Locomotive and railroad cars	Business vehicles (horse-drawn)	Professional and scientific equipment	Total	Manufactured	Nonmanufactured	Perishable	Semidurable	Consumer durable	Producer durable	Construction materials
	Dd355	Dd356	Dd357	Dd358	Dd359	Dd360	Dd361	Dd362	Dd363	Dd364	Dd365
Year	Million dollars	Million dollars	Million dollars	Million dollars	Million dollars	Million dollars	Index 1913 = 100	Index 1913 = 100	Index 1913 = 100	Index 1913 = 100	Index 1913 = 100
1895	53.7	25.7	3.0	1,033.2	881.2	152.0	75.0	77.1	67.4	72.2	70.7
1896	75.2	23.0	3.2	880.3	751.4	128.9	70.9	75.5	63.8	66.1	71.8
1897	67.7	24.2	2.7	963.4	821.0	142.4	72.0	75.5	63.0	75.9	67.1
1898	82.1	25.9	3.2	937.8	795.8	141.9	74.9	77.3	67.5	82.5	69.9
1899	114.1	32.5	4.0	1,006.3	855.7	150.6	75.4	81.0	70.0	88.1	80.7
1900	130.0	31.4	5.3	1,222.7	1,046.8	175.8	80.2	86.7	77.0	90.0	85.8
1901	127.4	40.2	5.0	1,306.3	1,119.2	187.1	79.6	81.9	77.5	88.9	80.7
1902	157.8	37.9	7.5	1,493.6	1,270.6	223.0	84.1	83.5	79.9	89.7	82.5
1903	194.6	37.6	7.8	1,447.4	1,218.9	228.4	83.3	86.0	82.7	86.2	84.5
1904	162.7	38.9	6.4	1,394.3	1,167.3	227.0	85.5	86.0	83.5	88.8	81.7
1905	214.3	43.1	8.2	1,578.1	1,334.0	244.1	86.9	90.5	85.3	89.7	87.0
1906	299.4	46.2	10.7	1,911.1	1,622.8	288.3	84.9	98.2	89.1	90.6	96.6
1907	351.2	49.5	11.8	2,111.5	1,770.1	341.4	89.7	102.6	97.7	93.6	101.0
1908	137.1	40.2	8.0	1,820.1	1,513.9	306.3	92.3	96.0	96.6	89.3	93.3
1909	127.0	43.0	12.4	1,992.5	1,686.7	305.8	96.9	99.3	90.4	94.3	94.8
1910	203.3	48.3	12.6	2,049.7	1,728.0	321.7	100.0	100.9	93.5	95.3	97.6
1911	161.7	44.2	13.4	1,942.8	1,655.4	287.4	96.2	97.4	95.8	99.1	97.0
1912	303.4	41.9	14.2	2,154.1	1,854.9	299.2	102.8	98.6	66.2	97.6	97.9
1913	422.5	39.9	17.7	2,384.4	2,083.2	301.2	100.0	100.0	100.0	100.0	100.0
1914	203.2	36.9	23.7	2,043.8	1,758.7	285.2	101.4	96.5	94.4	100.3	93.1
1915	142.2	34.0	29.4	2,010.7	1,732.9	277.8	103.7	96.5	90.3	106.4	94.6
1916	363.4	37.4	32.5	2,627.8	2,309.5	318.2	120.6	117.6	90.4	120.5	119.0
1917	610.6	51.1	57.0	3,058.6	2,702.9	355.7	161.1	161.0	100.8	145.5	154.9
1918	734.0	50.6	119.2	3,217.5	2,824.6	392.8	182.8	206.2	121.9	175.7	174.5
1919	460.9	42.5	74.5	3,703.2	3,224.5	478.7	199.9	212.4	136.4	185.0	202.7
1919	560.7	—	62.0	3,508.1	—	—	196.5	219.0	134.5	184.1	202.7
1920	563.3	—	74.8	4,777.1	—	—	213.4	265.6	157.8	181.0	262.0
1921	313.6	—	48.8	2,956.7	—	—	146.5	173.8	139.8	164.5	172.2
1922	265.6	—	51.7	3,568.9	—	—	141.2	163.2	113.4	135.2	170.7
1923	635.5	—	64.7	4,647.3	—	—	147.7	177.6	108.2	138.7	190.4
1924	481.1	—	66.0	4,465.3	—	—	143.5	164.9	108.5	134.8	179.5
1925	353.1	—	74.9	4,950.4	—	—	154.3	160.0	103.3	135.0	178.5
1926	399.3	—	86.5	5,111.5	—	—	154.3	150.4	98.8	138.4	175.6
1927	318.5	—	87.7	4,845.2	—	—	146.9	137.4	104.0	138.5	166.6
1928	245.1	—	92.1	4,793.8	—	—	150.0	131.7	105.4	136.5	165.6
1929	347.6	—	109.6	5,007.5	—	—	147.4	130.7	106.4	131.1	167.8
1930	352.7	—	91.6	3,779.8	—	—	135.1	122.0	104.3	125.6	158.4
1931	78.0	—	48.6	2,552.1	—	—	114.1	109.2	99.8	117.2	140.2
1932	37.0	—	31.7	1,362.7	—	—	96.7	93.6	98.0	112.9	126.8
1933	13.6	—	32.0	1,536.1	—	—	95.0	105.0	96.8	104.6	136.0
1934	—	—	—	1,909.9	—	—	107.8 [4]	120.6 [4]	98.5 [4]	107.6 [4]	151.4
1935	33.0	—	36.4	2,375.0	—	—	122.4	119.2	93.6	99.6	149.8
1936	—	—	—	3,331.5	—	—	122.6 [4]	120.6 [4]	90.8 [4]	102.0 [4]	152.2
1937	119.1	—	49.8	3,945.8	—	—	126.4	132.6	91.9	112.1	167.3
1938	—	—	—	3,159.0	—	—	114.6 [4]	122.7 [4]	92.8 [4]	112.8 [4]	159.0
1939	—	—	—	3,701.6	—	—	110.6 [4]	123.1 [4]	92.1 [4]	110.4 [5]	159.0

[1] For 1869 through the first set of values for 1919, figures are Shaw's estimates; thereafter, figures are Kuznets's estimates adjusted by Shaw. See source, p. 104.

[2] Agrees with source; however, components do not add to total shown.

[3] Does not agree with source, which is in error.

[4] Derived by weighting the individual group indexes by the average current price estimates for 1933, 1935, and 1937. The composite indexes thus calculated were used to interpolate and extrapolate the implicit indexes for 1933, 1935, and 1937.

[5] Based on the movement of the National Bureau of Economic Research price index for processed capital equipment goods.

Source

William H. Shaw, *Value of Commodity Output since 1869* (National Bureau of Economic Research, 1947), pp. 30, 66, 290.

Documentation

Output figures represent the value of output of finished commodities and construction materials destined for domestic consumption at current producers' prices.

TABLE Dd366–436 Physical output of selected manufactured products: 1860–1997[1]
Contributed by Jeremy Atack and Fred Bateman

	Canned goods		Food and kindred products							Tobacco products			Textile mill products	
					Fats and oils		Beverages							
						Shortening		Distilled spirits						
	Corn	Tomatoes	Wheat flour	Refined sugar	Crude soybean oil	and salad and cooking oils	Beer	Total	Beverage	Manufactured tobacco and snuff	Cigars	Cigarettes	Finished knit cloth	Carpets and rugs
Year	Dd366	Dd367	Dd368	Dd369	Dd370	Dd371	Dd372	Dd373	Dd374	Dd375	Dd376	Dd377	Dd378	Dd379
	Thousand cases	Thousand cases	Thousand short tons	Thousand short tons	Million pounds	Million pounds	Thousand barrels	Thousand gallons	Thousand gallons	Million pounds	Million	Million	Thousand pounds	Thousand square yards
1860	—	—	3,900	394	—	—	—	—	—	—	—	—	—	—
1861	—	—	4,077	489	—	—	—	—	—	—	—	—	—	—
1862	—	—	4,155	295	—	—	—	—	—	—	—	—	—	—
1863	—	—	4,165	304	—	—	—	—	—	—	—	—	—	—
1864	—	—	4,155	283	—	—	—	—	—	—	—	—	—	—
1865	—	—	4,165	367	—	—	—	—	—	—	—	—	—	—
1866	—	—	4,194	443	—	—	—	—	—	—	—	—	—	—
1867	—	—	4,341	421	—	—	—	—	—	—	—	—	—	—
1868	—	—	4,400	575	—	—	—	—	—	—	—	—	—	—
1869	—	—	4,586	627	—	—	—	—	—	—	—	—	—	—
1870	—	—	4,694	598	—	—	6,600	72,600	—	102	1,183	16	—	—
1871	—	—	4,802	707	—	—	7,700	57,000	—	107	1,353	20	—	—
1872	—	—	4,822	727	—	—	8,700	69,400	—	112	1,578	24	—	—
1873	—	—	5,027	763	—	—	9,600	71,200	—	118	1,755	28	—	—
1874	—	—	5,253	819	—	—	9,600	69,600	—	124	1,835	35	—	—
1875	—	—	5,331	821	—	—	9,500	62,700	—	124	1,828	59	—	—
1876	—	—	5,498	792	—	—	9,900	58,600	—	124	1,776	113	—	—
1877	—	—	5,537	849	—	—	9,800	61,400	—	123	1,816	157	—	—
1878	—	—	5,860	889	—	—	10,200	57,300	—	125	1,923	210	—	—
1879	—	—	6,066	855	—	—	11,100	72,900	—	136	2,217	371	—	—
1880	—	—	6,301	994	—	—	13,300	91,400	—	146	2,510	533	—	—
1881	—	—	6,429	970	—	—	14,300	119,500	—	172	2,806	595	—	—
1882	—	—	6,644	1,184	—	—	17,000	107,300	—	159	3,118	599	—	—
1883	—	—	6,938	1,233	—	—	17,800	75,300	—	194	3,232	844	—	—
1884	—	—	7,105	1,366	—	—	19,000	76,500	—	172	3,373	920	—	—
1885	1,062	2,362	7,252	1,456	—	—	19,200	76,400	—	207	3,294	1,080	—	—
1886	1,675	3,921	7,419	1,475	—	—	20,700	81,800	—	210	3,462	1,607	—	—
1887	2,276	4,720	7,791	1,507	—	—	23,100	79,400	—	226	3,662	1,865	—	—
1888	3,437	5,580	7,791	1,524	—	—	24,700	71,700	—	209	3,668	2,212	—	—
1889	1,726	5,022	7,918	1,585	—	—	25,100	91,100	—	246	3,787	2,413	—	—
1890	1,523	5,280	8,163	1,617	—	—	27,600	111,100	—	253	4,229	2,505	—	—
1891	2,837	5,660	8,457	2,035	—	—	30,500	117,800	—	271	4,422	3,137	—	—
1892	3,417	5,502	9,026	1,948	—	—	31,900	118,400	—	274	4,675	3,282	—	—
1893	4,184	7,337	9,065	2,025	—	—	34,600	131,000	—	251	4,341	3,661	—	—
1894	3,278	10,971	9,183	2,141	—	—	33,400	92,200	—	269	4,164	3,621	—	—
1895	2,992	6,888	9,173	1,981	—	—	33,600	81,900	—	274	4,099	4,238	—	—
1896	2,539	5,845	9,457	1,979	—	—	35,900	90,000	—	261	4,048	4,967	—	—
1897	2,787	6,767	9,379	2,121	—	—	34,500	64,300	—	297	4,136	4,927	—	—
1898	4,315	9,651	9,829	2,054	—	—	37,500	83,700	—	275	4,459	4,843	—	—
1899	6,366	14,852	10,192	2,289	—	—	36,700	100,200	—	295	4,910	4,367	—	76,410

Notes appear at end of table   (continued)

TABLE Dd366–436   Physical output of selected manufactured products: 1860–1997   Continued

	Canned goods				Fats and oils		Beverages			Tobacco products			Textile mill products	
	Corn	Tomatoes	Wheat flour	Refined sugar	Crude soybean oil	Shortening and salad and cooking oils	Beer	Distilled spirits — Total	Distilled spirits — Beverage	Manufactured tobacco and snuff	Cigars	Cigarettes	Finished knit cloth	Carpets and rugs
	Dd366	Dd367	Dd368	Dd369	Dd370	Dd371	Dd372	Dd373	Dd374	Dd375	Dd376	Dd377	Dd378	Dd379
Year	Thousand cases	Thousand cases	Thousand short tons	Thousand short tons	Million pounds	Million pounds	Thousand barrels	Thousand gallons	Thousand gallons	Million pounds	Million	Million	Thousand pounds	Thousand square yards
1900	6,486	9,385	10,368	2,429	—	—	39,500	109,200	—	301	5,566	3,870	—	—
1901	5,028	7,227	10,623	2,578	—	—	40,600	128,600	—	314	6,139	3,503	—	—
1902	4,191	15,810	10,692	2,863	—	—	44,600	132,800	—	348	6,232	3,647	—	—
1903	4,861	17,335	10,956	2,734	—	—	46,700	148,200	—	351	6,806	3,959	—	—
1904	11,163	16,065	10,261	2,981	—	—	48,300	139,500	—	354	6,640	4,170	—	82,671
1905	13,019	9,517	10,329	2,850	—	—	49,500	153,300	—	368	6,748	4,477	—	—
1906	9,137	14,733	10,731	3,217	—	—	54,700	150,100	—	391	7,148	5,502	—	—
1907	6,654	22,051	10,927	3,226	—	—	58,600	174,700	—	388	7,302	6,345	—	—
1908	6,779	19,595	10,760	3,240	—	—	58,800	133,900	—	408	6,489	6,833	—	—
1909	5,787	18,750	10,535	3,493	—	—	56,300	139,900	—	431	6,668	7,880	—	81,219
1910	10,063	15,764	10,506	3,659	—	—	59,500	163,900	—	447	6,810	9,782	—	—
1911	14,301	16,642	10,858	3,675	—	—	63,300	183,400	—	424	7,049	11,700	—	—
1912	13,109	23,936	10,858	3,952	—	—	62,200	187,600	—	435	7,044	14,239	—	—
1913	7,283	24,250	11,133	4,137	—	—	65,300	193,600	—	444	7,572	16,530	—	—
1914	9,789	25,984	11,270	4,309	—	—	66,200	181,900	—	441	7,174	17,944	—	66,340
1915	10,124	14,457	11,682	—	—	—	59,800	140,700	—	442	6,599	18,945	—	—
1916	9,130	22,433	11,633	—	—	—	58,600	253,300	—	466	7,042	26,203	—	—
1917	10,803	25,735	11,348	—	—	—	60,800	286,100	—	483	7,560	36,323	—	—
1918	11,722	27,111	11,309	—	—	—	50,300	178,800	—	497	7,054	47,528	—	—
1919	13,550	18,452	12,005	4,739	—	—	27,700	100,800	—	424	7,072	53,865	—	52,182
1920	15,040	19,405	12,779	—	—	—	9,200	101,300	—	413	8,097	48,091	—	—
1921	8,843	6,857	9,526	4,793	—	—	9,200	87,900	—	387	6,726	52,770	—	52,906
1922	11,419	19,695	11,152	—	1	784	5,300	82,200	—	420	6,722	56,413	—	—
1923	14,106	25,045	11,241	5,179	1	751	6,300	124,600	—	413	6,950	67,239	—	83,242
1924	12,131	21,370	11,633	—	1	830	4,900	137,500	—	414	6,598	73,256	—	—
1925	24,320	33,747	11,515	6,486	3	1,153	5,100	167,500	—	414	6,463	82,712	—	72,100
1926	19,069	16,140	11,388	—	3	1,141	4,900	203,800	—	411	6,499	92,523	—	—
1927	10,347	22,425	11,956	6,023	3	1,179	4,400	185,500	—	396	6,519	100,260	—	67,193
1928	14,497	14,575	11,819	—	5	1,143	4,200	170,500	—	386	6,373	109,131	—	—
1929	17,487	24,146	12,113	6,188	11	1,220	3,900	203,300	—	381	6,519	122,822	—	73,411
1930	15,692	29,015	—	—	14	1,211	3,681	197,221	—	372	5,894	124,193	—	—
1931	19,415	16,341	11,270	5,586	39	1,172	3,137	170,394	—	371	5,348	117,402	—	44,181
1932	9,358	20,367	—	—	39	945	2,766	150,391	—	347	4,383	106,915	—	—
1933	10,193	20,461	9,526	5,566	27	953	9,798	123,405	—	342	4,300	115,087	41,484	41,876
1934	11,268	22,376	—	5,128	35	1,204	37,678	241,610	101,612	346	4,526	130,287	—	—
1935	21,471	26,985	10,427	5,446	105	1,547	45,229	349,772	183,668	343	4,685	140,147	49,587	59,152
1936	14,621	24,414	10,878	5,591	225	1,587	51,812	449,994	274,108	348	5,172	159,076	—	—
1937	23,541	26,235	10,721	5,842	194	1,595	58,748	482,138	299,207	341	5,303	170,171	76,377	64,799
1938	20,470	23,131	10,956	5,954	323	1,514	56,340	351,190	183,288	345	5,015	171,842	—	—
1939	14,567	24,465	11,182	5,875	458	1,404	53,871	346,344	166,763	343	5,198	180,828	79,756	63,676

	Food and kindred products									Tobacco products			Textile mill products	
	Canned goods				Fats and oils		Beverages							
						Shortening		Distilled spirits		Manufactured			Finished	Carpets
	Corn	Tomatoes	Wheat flour	Refined sugar	Crude soybean oil	and salad and cooking oils	Beer	Total	Beverage	tobacco and snuff	Cigars	Cigarettes	knit cloth	and rugs
	Dd366	Dd367	Dd368	Dd369	Dd370	Dd371	Dd372	Dd373	Dd374	Dd375	Dd376	Dd377	Dd378	Dd379
Year	Thousand cases	Thousand cases	Thousand short tons	Thousand short tons	Million pounds	Million pounds	Thousand barrels	Thousand gallons	Thousand gallons	Million pounds	Million	Million	Thousand pounds	Thousand square yards
1940	15,524	29,533	10,868	6,049	533	1,190	54,892	387,183	159,707	344	5,370	189,373	—	—
1941	26,109	31,759	11,045	6,719	586	1,409	55,214	474,054	192,416	342	5,610	218,083	—	—
1942	32,118	41,252	11,231	4,819	762	1,300	63,717	675,959	254,815	330	5,841	257,657	—	—
1943	28,755	29,269	12,034	5,318	1,234	1,438	71,018	772,267	246,262	327	5,363	296,305	112,560	—
1944	25,089	26,099	12,289	6,080	1,246	1,364	81,726	1,011,763	—	307	5,199	323,734	107,908	—
1945	28,237	16,758	13,828	5,602	1,392	1,441	86,604	1,174,391	87,515	331	5,275	332,345	129,958	—
1946	30,951	23,857	14,034	5,112	1,454	1,451	84,978	634,454	225,077	253	5,618	350,132	146,666	—
1947	26,089	27,709	15,357	6,877	1,543	1,375	87,857	563,956	219,656	242	5,488	369,763	153,778	91,160
1948	31,483	24,393	14,034	6,101	1,604	1,441	91,291	576,409	270,587	245	5,645	386,916	—	—
1949	29,795	21,537	11,789	6,618	1,859	1,487	89,736	617,558	291,722	239	5,453	385,046	147,853	—
1950	18,241	21,108	11,309	7,333	2,075	1,710	88,807	521,770	194,025	235	5,468	391,956	162,803	—
1951	25,576	31,770	11,525	6,638	2,473	1,403	88,976	846,388	342,768	227	5,664	418,803	148,747	—
1952	32,329	27,981	11,466	6,910	2,478	1,611	89,601	689,256	69,294	220	5,892	435,549	170,518	—
1953	30,982	22,334	11,162	6,950	2,515	1,675	90,434	619,456	135,240	209	5,973	423,070	164,193	—
1954	30,619	21,827	11,123	7,533	2,378	1,961	92,561	563,496	167,319	204	5,882	401,849	165,030	128,023
1955	24,075	24,727	11,329	7,380	2,827	1,975	89,791	593,982	194,888	199	5,834	412,309	181,884	77,822 [2]
1956	35,668	29,883	11,525	7,766	3,200	1,842	90,698	720,754	217,814	185	5,830	424,247	186,458	83,177 [2]
1957	31,533	21,686	11,976	7,575	3,475	1,809	89,882	650,366	207,946	179	5,952	442,328	193,518	99,651 [2]
1958	27,075	30,465	12,426	7,895	3,943	2,006	89,011	718,848	244,316	180	6,395	470,068	210,635	166,737
1959	33,810	24,126	12,554	8,041	4,344	4,061	90,974	754,539	271,797	176	7,298	489,865	243,042	132,523 [2]
1960	28,926	25,413	12,779	8,355	4,392	4,228	94,548	803,751	273,258	173	6,937	506,127	247,671	151,984 [2]
1961	37,857	27,908	13,034	8,420	4,442	4,580	93,496	801,799	248,439	173	6,648	518,031	276,048	178,625 [2]
1962	37,510	29,144	13,122	8,937	4,889	5,221	96,418	809,518	292,767	169	6,843	529,883	314,597	268,235
1963	36,205	27,094	13,014	8,873	5,053	4,945	97,961	800,830	266,648	168	6,657	543,688	345,607	305,470
1964	30,792	29,873	13,093	9,298	4,944	5,510	103,018	838,978	273,750	180	8,648	534,973	416,642	357,653
1965	32,075	29,532	12,534	9,213	5,236	5,566	108,015	865,240	275,616	167	8,883	562,368	450,128	411,220
1966	37,331	26,783	12,662	9,332	5,811	6,136	109,736	889,352	306,813	162	7,992	562,667	558,617	445,527
1967	40,400	32,084	12,270	9,419	6,150	6,148	116,564	873,010	301,949	158	7,303	572,790	603,951	467,909
1968	48,608	39,706	12,711	10,049	6,150	6,308	117,524	905,459	331,306	159	7,696	570,748	698,124	546,840
1969	40,497	26,270	12,711	9,908	6,805	6,624	122,657	985,641	336,456	161	7,499	573,002	744,003	597,885
1970	38,536	31,994	12,652	10,424	8,086	6,977	134,654	917,457	355,240	165	7,979	562,154	782,279	633,662
1971	—	—	12,491	10,529	8,082	7,015	134,092	715,251	231,161	154	7,868	585,057	937,401	755,159
1972	—	—	12,522	10,607	8,084	7,438	140,327	764,351	282,864	154	8,009	592,579	1,067,394	934,945
1973	—	—	12,733	10,491	7,540	9,157	143,014	859,152	281,520	152	11,422	615,563	1,992,672	1,025,389
1974	—	—	12,555	10,618	8,705	10,499	153,053	821,577	258,291	153	8,723	651,954	1,952,724	939,133
1975	—	—	12,949	9,429	7,862	10,448	157,870	717,550	277,524	152	8,324	626,760	1,911,841	834,037
1976	—	—	13,754	10,302	9,640	11,275	160,663	667,682	244,145	153	6,702	688,173	1,790,878	920,996
1977	—	—	13,789	10,277	8,837	11,067	169,745	656,128	224,926	155	5,848	672,640	1,715,438	1,024,572
1978	—	—	13,898	9,809	8,837	11,845	176,347	676,723	267,534	156	5,654	687,989	1,720,521	1,162,256
1979	—	—	14,203	9,608	11,323	12,283	182,741	720,342	246,786	159	5,149	706,976	1,865,573	1,206,030

Notes appear at end of table

(continued)

TABLE Dd366–436   Physical output of selected manufactured products: 1860–1997   Continued

Food and kindred products / Beverages / Tobacco products / Textile mill products

	Canned goods				Fats and oils		Beverages	Distilled spirits		Tobacco products			Textile mill products	
	Corn	Tomatoes	Wheat flour	Refined sugar	Crude soybean oil	Shortening and salad and cooking oils	Beer	Total	Beverage	Manufactured tobacco and snuff	Cigars	Cigarettes	Finished knit cloth	Carpets and rugs
	Dd366	Dd367	Dd368	Dd369	Dd370	Dd371	Dd372	Dd373	Dd374	Dd375	Dd376	Dd377	Dd378	Dd379
Year	Thousand cases	Thousand cases	Thousand short tons	Thousand short tons	Million pounds	Million pounds	Thousand barrels	Thousand gallons	Thousand gallons	Million pounds	Million	Million	Thousand pounds	Thousand square yards
1980	—	—	14,133	10,014	12,105	12,498	192,966	784,005	253,007	163	4,882	701,594	1,724,721	1,058,404
1981	—	—	14,198	10,118	11,270	12,564	194,542	752,556	336,321	163	5,020	743,721	1,420,485	990,619
1982	—	—	14,545	8,679	10,979	13,175	193,984	689,440	267,747	162	4,520	711,493	1,308,737	885,811
1983	—	—	15,579	8,098	12,040	13,304	195,664	839,305	779,640	161	4,315	668,089	1,510,425	1,090,071
1984	—	—	14,992	9,100	10,872	14,138	193,416	735,337	674,170	163	4,520	657,383	1,585,292	1,114,920
1985	—	—	15,691	8,164	11,470	11,382	193,795	795,583	754,555	158	4,190	664,752	1,496,557	1,159,155
1986	—	—	16,316	8,347	11,617	11,477	193,991	721,683	675,305	148	3,806	662,169	1,744,654	1,257,906
1987	—	—	17,078	8,872	12,798	11,079	196,169	795,558	730,724	144	3,454	677,964	1,840,788	1,263,302
1988	—	—	17,208	8,418	12,975	11,858	197,441	844,938	790,786	141	3,258	698,980	1,459,789	1,326,693
1989	—	—	17,138	8,811	11,737	11,938	198,011	1,009,298	923,851	141	3,098	680,395	1,998,044	1,365,498
1990	—	—	17,717	9,137	13,003	11,684	201,691	1,202,687	1,095,606	136	3,193	700,579	2,015,610	1,360,043
1991	—	—	18,116	9,296	13,686	11,831	203,707	1,291,584	1,188,482	142	3,034	707,759	1,948,198	1,255,876
1992	—	—	18,541	9,342	14,250	12,211	201,989	1,423,467	1,325,053	141	3,114	703,134	2,080,534	1,419,167
1993	—	—	19,371	9,009	13,789	12,994	202,277	1,417,556	1,296,575	137	3,064	687,326	2,184,283	1,491,453
1994	—	—	19,626	9,542	14,336	12,881	202,805	1,487,082	1,333,431	135	3,120	687,223	2,211,798	1,574,703
1995	—	—	19,434	9,741	15,636	12,700	200,302	1,548,858	—	135	3,470	756,931	2,130,635	1,570,025
1996	—	—	—	—	—	—	—	—	—	—	—	—	—	—
1997	—	—	—	—	—	—	—	—	—	—	—	—	—	—

Textile mill products / Apparel

	Yarns		Apparel	
	Rayon and acetate	Noncellulosic	Men's and boys' suits and coats	Women's, misses', and juniors' dresses
	Dd380	Dd381	Dd382	Dd383
Year	Million pounds	Million pounds	Thousand	Thousand
1860	—	—	—	—
1861	—	—	—	—
1862	—	—	—	—
1863	—	—	—	—
1864	—	—	—	—
1865	—	—	—	—
1866	—	—	—	—
1867	—	—	—	—
1868	—	—	—	—
1869	—	—	—	—

Chemicals and allied products / Refined petroleum products

| | Sodium hydroxide (caustic soda) | Sulfuric acid | Paints, varnishes, and lacquers | Anhydrous ammonia | Ammonia aqua | Superphosphates | Light products of distillation | Illuminating oils (kerosene) | Fuel oils | Lubricating oils | Paraffin wax |
| | Dd384 | Dd385 | Dd386 | Dd387 | Dd388 | Dd389 | Dd390 | Dd391 | Dd392 | Dd393 | Dd394 |
Year	Thousand short tons	Thousand short tons	Million gallons	Thousand short tons	Thousand short tons	Thousand short tons	Million barrels	Million barrels	Million barrels	Million barrels	Thousand barrels
1860	—	—	—	—	—	1	—	—	—	—	—
1861	—	—	—	—	—	—	—	—	—	—	—
1862	—	—	—	—	—	—	—	—	—	—	—
1863	—	—	—	—	—	—	—	—	—	—	—
1864	—	—	—	—	—	—	—	—	—	—	—
1865	—	—	—	—	—	—	—	—	—	—	—
1866	—	—	—	—	—	—	—	—	—	—	—
1867	—	—	—	—	—	—	—	—	—	—	—
1868	—	—	—	—	—	—	—	—	—	—	—
1869	—	—	—	—	—	—	—	—	—	—	—

	Textile mill products				Chemicals and allied products						Refined petroleum products				
	Yarns		Apparel												
Year	Rayon and acetate	Noncellulosic	Men's and boys' suits and coats	Women's, misses', and juniors' dresses	Sodium hydroxide (caustic soda)	Sulfuric acid	Paints, varnishes, and lacquers	Anhydrous ammonia	Ammonia aqua	Superphosphates	Light products of distillation	Illuminating oils (kerosene)	Fuel oils	Lubricating oils	Paraffin wax
	Dd380	Dd381	Dd382	Dd383	Dd384	Dd385	Dd386	Dd387	Dd388	Dd389	Dd390	Dd391	Dd392	Dd393	Dd394
	Million pounds	Million pounds	Thousand	Thousand	Thousand short tons	Thousand short tons	Million gallons	Thousand short tons	Thousand short tons	Thousand short tons	Million barrels	Million barrels	Million barrels	Million barrels	Thousand barrels
1870	—	—	—	—	—	—	—	—	—	—	—	—	—	—	—
1871	—	—	—	—	—	—	—	—	—	12	—	—	—	—	—
1872	—	—	—	—	—	—	—	—	—	—	—	—	—	—	—
1873	—	—	—	—	—	—	—	—	—	—	—	—	—	—	—
1874	—	—	—	—	—	—	—	—	—	—	—	—	—	—	—
1875	—	—	—	—	—	—	—	—	—	—	—	—	—	—	—
1876	—	—	—	—	—	—	—	—	—	—	—	—	—	—	—
1877	—	—	—	—	—	—	—	—	—	—	—	—	—	—	—
1878	—	—	—	—	—	—	—	—	—	—	—	—	—	—	—
1879	—	—	—	—	—	—	—	—	—	—	—	—	—	—	—
1880	—	—	—	—	—	—	—	—	—	35	—	—	—	—	—
1881	—	—	—	—	—	—	—	—	—	—	—	—	—	—	—
1882	—	—	—	—	—	—	—	—	—	—	—	—	—	—	—
1883	—	—	—	—	—	—	—	—	—	—	—	—	—	—	—
1884	—	—	—	—	—	—	—	—	—	—	—	—	—	—	—
1885	—	—	—	—	—	—	—	—	—	—	—	—	—	—	—
1886	—	—	—	—	—	—	—	—	—	—	—	—	—	—	—
1887	—	—	—	—	—	—	—	—	—	—	—	—	—	—	—
1888	—	—	—	—	—	—	—	—	—	—	—	—	—	—	—
1889	—	—	—	—	—	—	—	—	—	—	—	—	—	—	—
1890	—	—	—	—	—	—	—	—	—	84	—	—	—	—	—
1891	—	—	—	—	—	—	—	—	—	—	—	—	—	—	—
1892	—	—	—	—	—	—	—	—	—	—	—	—	—	—	—
1893	—	—	—	—	—	—	—	—	—	—	—	—	—	—	—
1894	—	—	—	—	—	—	—	—	—	—	—	—	—	—	—
1895	—	—	—	—	—	—	—	—	—	—	—	—	—	—	—
1896	—	—	—	—	—	—	—	—	—	—	—	—	—	—	—
1897	—	—	—	—	—	—	—	—	—	—	—	—	—	—	—
1898	—	—	—	—	—	—	—	—	—	—	—	—	—	—	—
1899	—	—	—	—	167 [9]	1,177	40	1 [9]	—	—	—	—	—	—	—
1900	—	—	—	—	—	—	—	—	—	—	—	—	—	—	—
1901	—	—	—	—	—	—	—	—	—	—	—	—	—	—	—
1902	—	—	—	—	—	—	—	—	—	—	—	—	—	—	—
1903	—	—	—	—	—	—	—	—	—	—	—	—	—	—	—
1904	—	—	—	—	87 [9]	1,421	46	3 [9]	—	—	—	—	—	—	—
1905	—	—	—	—	—	—	—	—	—	—	—	—	—	—	—
1906	—	—	—	—	—	—	—	—	—	—	—	—	—	—	—
1907	—	—	—	—	—	—	—	—	—	—	—	—	—	—	—
1908	—	—	—	—	—	—	—	—	—	—	—	—	—	—	—
1909	—	—	—	—	132 [9]	2,254	70	6 [9]	11 [9]	—	—	—	—	—	—
1910	—	—	—	—	—	—	—	—	—	—	—	—	—	—	—
1911	2.1	—	—	—	—	—	—	—	—	—	—	—	—	—	—
1912	2.9	—	—	—	—	—	—	—	—	—	—	—	—	—	—
1913	4.0	—	—	—	—	—	—	—	—	—	—	—	—	—	—
1914	5.1	—	—	—	—	—	—	—	—	—	—	—	—	—	—

Notes appear at end of table

(continued)

TABLE Dd366–436   Physical output of selected manufactured products: 1860–1997   Continued

	Textile mill products				Chemicals and allied products						Refined petroleum products				
	Yarns		Apparel												
	Rayon and acetate	Noncellulosic	Men's and boys' suits and coats	Women's, misses', and juniors' dresses	Sodium hydroxide (caustic soda)	Sulfuric acid	Paints, varnishes, and lacquers	Anhydrous ammonia	Ammonia aqua	Superphosphates	Light products of distillation	Illuminating oils (kerosene)	Fuel oils	Lubricating oils	Paraffin wax
	Million pounds	Million pounds	Thousand	Thousand	Thousand short tons	Thousand short tons	Million gallons	Thousand short tons	Thousand short tons	Thousand short tons	Million barrels	Million barrels	Million barrels	Million barrels	Thousand barrels
Year	Dd380	Dd381	Dd382	Dd383	Dd384	Dd385	Dd386	Dd387	Dd388	Dd389	Dd390	Dd391	Dd392	Dd393	Dd394
1915	6.6	—	—	—	292 [9]	3,096	77	8 [9]	18 [9]	—	—	—	—	—	—
1916	6.6	—	—	—	—	—	—	—	—	—	—	35	111	15	1,379
1917	6.8	—	—	—	—	—	—	—	—	—	—	41	155	18	1,719
1918	6.0	—	—	—	—	—	—	—	—	—	91	43	174	20	1,805
1919	9.3	—	—	—	313	4,222	109	14	23	—	101	56	182	20	1,668
1920	8.7	—	—	—	—	—	—	—	—	—	124	55	211	25	1,933
1921	19.8	—	—	—	239	3,323	94	15	39	863	132	46	230	21	1,553
1922	25.0	—	—	—	—	—	—	—	—	—	158	55	255	23	1,651
1923	32.8	—	—	—	437	4,984	152	12	34	—	196	56	287	26	1,665
1924	42.4	—	—	—	—	—	—	—	—	—	225	60	320	27	1,845
1925	58.4	—	—	—	497	5,325	176	16 [9]	51	—	269	60	365	31	2,135
1926	60.9	—	—	—	—	—	—	—	—	—	307	62	365	32	2,310
1927	100.1	—	31,846	109,080	573	5,577	201	23 [9]	25	—	340	56	393	32	2,089
1928	100.3	—	—	—	—	—	—	—	—	—	388	59	427	35	2,257
1929	131.8	—	30,342	162,837	762	6,456	239	87 [9]	15 [9]	—	445	56	449	34	2,261
1930	118.4	—	—	—	—	—	—	—	—	794	444	49	372	34	1,956
1931	157.8	—	21,624	167,192	659	4,627	171	64 [9]	9 [9]	478	442	42	337	27	1,705
1932	152.1	—	—	—	—	—	—	—	—	307	403	44	295	22	1,639
1933	211.9	—	19,300	145,238	687	—	—	75 [9]	6 [9]	463	411	49	316	24	1,677
1934	194.8	—	—	—	—	—	—	—	—	509	424	54	335	26	1,674
1935	252.8	—	24,287	172,247 [8]	759	4,890	219	69 [9]	12 [9]	532	470	56	360	28	1,608
1936	297.6	—	—	—	—	—	—	—	—	627	516	56	414	31	1,689
1937	267.2	—	23,743 [3]	178,300	969	6,029	280	108 [9]	13 [9]	805	571	65	459	35	1,863
1938	274.1	—	—	—	—	—	—	—	—	685	568	65	447	31	1,555
1939	359.9	—	27,354 [3]	194,383	1,045	4,795	265	311	16 [9]	758	611	69	468	35	1,659
1940	388.8	2.7	—	—	1,429	6,770	—	501	—	876	616	74	500	37	1,833
1941	452.5	7.5	—	—	1,574	7,754	—	543	—	955	704	73	532	40	2,393
1942	468.8	12.2	19,425	223,995	2,249	8,442	—	543	—	1,071	610	67	556	39	2,502
1943	494.2	17.7	20,729	204,878	2,328	9,242	—	544	—	1,273	609	72	629	39	2,697
1944	539.1	24.9	—	—	—	9,522	—	—	—	1,340	741	78	701	41	2,883
1945	602.4	29.4	35,086	213,073	2,322	9,203	—	549	—	1,447	793	81	719	42	2,921
1946	666.5	33.6	34,168	203,247	2,292	10,780	—	726	—	1,566	776	104	719	46	3,003
1947	729.3	43.7	32,005	227,279	2,909	11,456	520	1,114	24	1,857	842	110	760	52	3,624
1948	846.7	59.3	32,005	266,674	2,938	11,432	—	1,090	—	1,900	920	122	859	51	3,515
1949	782.8	75.6	29,737	248,195	2,650	13,029	—	1,294	—	1,891	961	102	766	45	3,208
1950	955.6	97.6	36,000	240,964	2,949	13,372	—	1,566	28	1,994	1,024	119	824	52	4,462
1951	865.5	134.4	30,471	258,263	3,106	13,310	—	1,777	35	2,045	1,140	136	945	61	4,814
1952	845.2	160.8	33,057	259,312	3,031	14,003	—	2,052	34	2,165	1,193	132	974	56	4,331
1953	865.6	186.4	34,659	248,169	3,263	14,376	421	2,288	34	2,147	1,266	123	978	53	4,978
1954	721.2	214.1	29,421	—	3,410	—	416 [10]	2,737	54	2,215	1,261	122	959	53	5,290

	Textile mill products				Chemicals and allied products						Refined petroleum products				
	Yarns		Apparel												
	Rayon and acetate	Noncellulosic	Men's and boys' suits and coats	Women's, misses', and juniors' dresses	Sodium hydroxide (caustic soda)	Sulfuric acid	Paints, varnishes, and lacquers	Anhydrous ammonia	Ammonia aqua	Superphosphates	Light products of distillation	Illuminating oils (kerosene)	Fuel oils	Lubricating oils	Paraffin wax
	Dd380	Dd381	Dd382	Dd383	Dd384	Dd385	Dd386	Dd387	Dd388	Dd389	Dd390	Dd391	Dd392	Dd393	Dd394
Year	Million pounds	Million pounds	Thousand	Thousand	Thousand short tons	Thousand short tons	Million gallons	Thousand short tons	Thousand short tons	Thousand short tons	Million barrels	Million barrels	Million barrels	Million barrels	Thousand barrels
1955	857.7	258.2	34,091	260,389	3,915	16,255	515 [10]	3,252	39	2,272	1,374	117	1,023	56	5,293
1956	727.0	273.1	35,640	257,336	4,227	16,495	503 [10]	3,378	37	2,439	1,429	123	1,092	59	5,367
1957	685.8	314.8	34,968	255,605	4,336	16,460	518 [10]	3,733	41	2,455	1,438	109	1,084	56	5,461
1958	643.5	311.3	33,053	243,273	3,993	15,950	595 [10]	3,879	51	2,381	1,440	110	995	51	5,252
1959	722.2	378.9	39,283	257,677	4,748	17,609	650	4,520	56	2,610	1,489	111	1,027	56	5,630
1960	624.9	400.8	40,622	253,606	4,972	17,883	663	4,818	45	2,672	1,522	136	999	59	5,896
1961	627.8	477.3	37,810	252,155	4,914	17,848	623	5,207	56	2,744	1,533	141	1,012	59	5,781
1962	668.9	570.7	41,937	251,734	5,486	19,701	643	5,810	64	2,823	1,583	156	1,015	61	5,353
1963	687.4	655.2	41,348	259,979	5,814	20,936	678	6,693	60	3,231	1,625	165	1,041	63	5,126
1964	768.6	797.4	40,815	271,718	6,399	22,924	725	7,634	63	3,482	1,687	168	1,009	64	5,352
1965	782.5	927.7	44,039 [4]	282,071	6,842	24,851	775	8,869	81	3,834	1,733	202	1,034	63	5,456
1966	780.8	1,081.9	44,641 [4]	273,080	7,596	28,385	837	10,605	73	4,450	1,822	228	1,050	65	5,772
1967	739.8	1,184.7	47,987 [5]	282,192	8,398	28,815	782	12,194	65	4,695	1,873	264	1,081	65	5,719
1968	794.5	1,555.7	50,320 [5]	277,971	8,868	28,544	843	12,120	42	4,149	1,968	295	1,116	66	5,887
1969	743.5	1,649.0	49,310 [5]	266,856	9,917	29,537	881	12,769	39	4,289	2,057	320	1,114	65	6,049
1970	699.6	1,803.8	43,642 [5]	251,540	10,064	29,577	827	13,570	33	4,596	2,136	314	1,155	66	6,294
1971	734.5	2,334.5	46,162	147,118	9,073	29,035	874	14,538	45	4,992	—	—	—	—	—
1972	643.6	2,914.3	49,856	137,594	9,895	31,184	927	15,169	38	5,482	—	—	—	—	—
1973	608.0	3,413.8	53,872	146,939	10,678	31,949	893	15,208	46	5,578	—	—	—	—	—
1974	482.6	3,234.4	49,542	134,173	11,184	34,177	—	15,733	55	5,367	—	—	—	—	—
1975	377.8	3,268.6	13,749	114,504	9,574	32,260	—	16,419	47	5,573	—	—	—	—	—
1976	339.6	3,211.2	16,224	116,308	9,238	34,878	—	16,716	57	5,824	—	—	—	—	—
1977	351.0	3,553.9	17,311	183,702	10,933	38,337	—	17,765	52	6,699	—	—	—	—	—
1978	363.3	3,694.1	23,050	176,695	10,746	41,314	—	17,119	60	7,176	—	—	—	—	—
1979	356.7	3,817.6	52,012	183,419	12,408	43,204	939	18,523	61	7,662	—	—	—	—	—
1980	325.0	3,551.6	46,443	175,701	11,301	44,272	890	18,984	—	8,088	—	—	—	—	—
1981	283.6	3,502.0	—	165,306	10,414	40,742	858	19,076	—	6,887	—	—	—	—	—
1982	206.1	2,917.7	40,926	171,748	9,141	33,233	803	15,801	—	5,687	—	—	—	—	—
1983	241.8	3,433.7	39,736	167,046	10,039	37,459	858	13,952	—	7,056	—	—	—	—	—
1984	228.3	3,398.6	37,858	158,968	11,224	41,802	938	16,702	—	8,014	—	—	—	—	—
1985	201.0	3,663.8	36,185	152,060	10,811	39,651	1,118	17,319	47	7,653	—	—	—	—	—
1986	209.1	3,747.3	35,762	133,412	11,055	35,993	1,163	14,474	57	6,108	—	—	—	—	—
1987	179.6	3,927.1	33,238	131,949	11,553	39,256	1,184	16,098	52	7,126	—	—	—	—	—
1988	200.2	4,045.9	34,707	142,163	10,526	42,580	1,229	16,821	60	7,968	—	—	—	—	—
1989	213.6	4,094.2	31,339	133,783	11,059	43,301	1,240	16,467	61	8,362	—	—	—	—	—
1990	196.9	4,143.3	11,304 [6]	172,320	12,030	44,044	1,282	16,795	—	8,982	—	—	—	—	—
1991	210.7	4,163.3	9,504 [6]	161,316	12,033	43,466	1,227	17,169	—	9,044	—	—	—	—	—
1992	215.0	4,505.1	64,908	157,896	12,244	44,524	1,236	17,924	—	9,696	—	—	—	—	—
1993	236.9	4,768.4	69,156	175,512	12,466	39,838	1,337	17,195	—	8,801	—	—	—	—	—
1994	223.2	5,318.7	76,013	198,503	12,921	44,842	1,431	17,869	—	10,042	—	—	—	—	—
1995	203.3	5,445.1	63,618 [7]	206,814	—	47,519	1,407	17,402	—	10,364	—	—	—	—	—
1996	208.2	5,665.8	64,157 [7]	187,904	—	—	1,430	17,762	—	—	—	—	—	—	—
1997	188.8	6,011.8	78,723	178,702	—	—	—	—	—	—	—	—	—	—	—

Notes appear at end of table

(continued)

TABLE Dd366–436   Physical output of selected manufactured products: 1860–1997   Continued

Year	Rubber products: pneumatic motor vehicle tires	Leather products: shoes (except athletic) Men's	Leather products: shoes (except athletic) Women's	Clay products: common and face bricks	Primary metals — Ferrous — Raw steel Total	Bessemer	Open hearth	Basic oxygen	Crucible	Electric arc	Hot rolled iron and steel	Structural iron and steel shapes	Rails	Nonferrous: copper and copper-based alloy products
	Dd395	Dd396	Dd397	Dd398	Dd399	Dd400	Dd401	Dd402	Dd403	Dd404	Dd405	Dd406	Dd407	Dd408
	Million	Million pairs	Million pairs	Billion	Thousand short tons	Thousand short tons	Thousand short tons	Thousand short tons	Thousand short tons	Thousand short tons	Thousand short tons	Thousand short tons	Thousand short tons	Thousand short tons
1860	—	—	—	—	13	—	—	—	13	—	—	—	205	—
1861	—	—	—	—	—	—	—	—	—	—	—	—	190	—
1862	—	—	—	—	—	—	—	—	—	—	—	—	214	—
1863	—	—	—	—	9	—	—	—	9	—	—	—	276	—
1864	—	—	—	—	10	—	—	—	10	—	872	—	335	—
1865	—	—	—	—	15	—	—	—	15	—	856	—	356	—
1866	—	—	—	—	19	—	—	—	19	—	1,026	—	431	—
1867	—	—	—	—	22	3	—	—	19	—	1,042	—	463	—
1868	—	—	—	—	30	9	—	—	22	—	1,105	—	506	—
1869	—	—	—	2.80	35	12	1	—	22	—	1,236	—	594	—
1870	—	—	—	—	77	42	2	—	34	—	1,325	—	620	—
1871	—	—	—	—	82	45	2	—	35	—	1,486	—	776	—
1872	—	—	—	—	160	120	3	—	37	—	1,942	—	1,000	—
1873	—	—	—	—	223	171	4	—	49	—	1,966	—	890	—
1874	—	—	—	—	242	192	7	—	43	—	1,840	—	729	—
1875	—	—	—	—	437	376	9	—	52	—	1,890	—	793	—
1876	—	—	—	—	597	526	21	—	50	—	1,922	—	880	—
1877	—	—	—	—	638	561	25	—	52	—	1,909	—	765	—
1878	—	—	—	—	820	732	36	—	51	—	2,115	—	883	—
1879	—	—	—	3.82	1,048	929	56	—	62	—	2,741	87	1,113	—
1880	—	—	—	—	1,397	1,203	113	—	81	—	3,301	—	1,462	—
1881	—	—	—	—	1,779	1,539	147	—	93	—	3,999	—	1,844	—
1882	—	—	—	—	1,945	1,696	161	—	88	—	3,955	—	1,689	—
1883	—	—	—	—	1,874	1,655	134	—	86	—	3,645	—	1,361	—
1884	—	—	—	—	1,737	1,541	132	—	65	—	3,077	—	1,145	—
1885	—	—	—	—	1,917	1,702	149	—	66	—	2,975	—	1,094	—
1886	—	—	—	—	2,870	2,541	245	—	83	—	4,853	—	1,793	—
1887	—	—	—	—	3,733	3,288	356	—	89	—	5,864	—	2,396	—
1888	—	—	—	—	3,238	2,813	345	—	80	—	5,171	—	1,572	—
1889	—	—	—	8.05	3,784	3,282	413	—	89	—	5,865	276	1,705	—
1890	—	—	—	—	4,779	4,131	566	—	82	—	6,746	—	2,112	—
1891	—	—	—	—	4,349	3,635	631	—	82	—	6,038	—	1,464	—
1892	—	—	—	—	5,492	4,663	732	—	96	—	6,906	508	1,738	—
1893	—	—	—	—	4,471	3,596	805	—	69	—	5,573	434	1,273	—
1894	—	—	—	—	4,899	3,995	845	—	58	—	5,199	404	1,144	—
1895	—	—	—	6.36	6,785	5,494	1,219	—	72	—	6,932	580	1,463	—
1896	—	—	—	5.97	5,849	4,388	1,396	—	65	—	6,178	555	1,257	—
1897	—	—	—	5.60	7,940	6,131	1,731	—	77	—	7,842	654	1,846	—
1898	—	—	—	6.16	9,888	7,401	2,388	—	99	—	9,535	786	2,219	—
1899	—	67.7	65.0	8.13	11,739	8,494	3,135	—	111	—	11,530	952	2,545	—

	Rubber products: pneumatic motor vehicle tires	Leather products: shoes (except athletic)		Clay products: common and face bricks	Primary metals									Nonferrous: copper and copper-based alloy products
					Ferrous									
					Raw steel									
		Men's	Women's		Total	Bessemer	Open hearth	Basic oxygen	Crucible	Electric arc	Hot rolled iron and steel	Structural iron and steel shapes	Rails	
	Dd395	Dd396	Dd397	Dd398	Dd399	Dd400	Dd401	Dd402	Dd403	Dd404	Dd405	Dd406	Dd407	Dd408
Year	Million	Million pairs	Million pairs	Billion	Thousand short tons	Thousand short tons	Thousand short tons	Thousand short tons	Thousand short tons	Thousand short tons	Thousand short tons	Thousand short tons	Thousand short tons	Thousand short tons
1900	—	—	—	7.49	11,227	7,481	3,638	—	109	—	10,626	913	2,672	—
1901	—	—	—	8.45	14,784	9,752	4,924	—	108	—	13,831	1,135	3,220	—
1902	—	—	—	8.93	16,402	10,222	6,054	—	126	—	15,617	1,456	3,302	—
1903	—	—	—	8.90	15,865	9,605	6,146	—	114	—	14,793	1,227	3,352	—
1904	—	83.4	69.5	9.10	15,205	8,787	6,325	—	93	—	13,455	1,063	2,559	—
1905	—	—	—	10.36	21,880	12,231	9,537	—	112	—	18,861	1,860	3,781	—
1906	—	—	—	10.64	25,443	13,712	11,594	—	137	—	21,939	2,373	4,455	—
1907	—	—	—	10.38	25,375	13,031	12,206	—	138	—	22,249	2,173	4,070	—
1908	—	—	—	8.40	15,383	6,828	8,492	—	63	—	13,248	1,213	2,152	—
1909	—	98.0	86.6	10.61	26,218	10,414	15,682	—	107	—	22,002	2,549	3,387	—
1910	—	—	—	9.92	28,330	10,478	17,672	—	122	58	24,216	2,539	4,072	—
1911	—	—	—	9.20	25,937	8,841	16,970	—	95	32	21,324	2,142	3,162	—
1912	—	—	—	9.37	34,079	11,492	22,457	—	114	17	27,616	3,188	3,727	—
1913	—	—	—	8.92	34,087	10,604	23,340	—	117	26	27,766	3,366	3,923	—
1914	12.0	98.0	80.9	7.96	25,606	6,895	18,603	—	88	20	20,575	2,275	2,179	—
1915	—	—	—	7.71	35,180	9,178	25,838	—	108	55	27,320	2,729	2,469	—
1916	—	—	—	8.40	46,793	12,234	34,278	—	135	146	36,266	3,394	3,197	—
1917	—	—	—	6.62	49,787	11,572	37,783	—	138	294	37,036	3,483	3,297	—
1918	—	—	—	3.91	49,010	10,335	38,065	—	128	482	34,894	3,192	2,846	—
1919	38.0 [11]	95.0	104.8	5.54	38,099	8,038	29,665	—	69	327	28,114	2,928	2,468	—
1920	—	—	—	5.64	46,183	9,841	35,846	—	79	417	36,230	3,704	2,917	—
1921	29.0 [11]	69.5	101.5	5.32	21,639	4,461	17,065	—	8	104	16,547	1,425	2,440	—
1922	—	90.0	105.4	7.32	38,945	6,578	32,106	—	31	230	29,626	3,045	2,432	—
1923	50.0 [11]	100.3	109.7	9.21	49,017	9,431	39,200	—	48	338	37,270	3,814	3,253	—
1924	—	84.7	104.1	9.19	41,446	6,551	34,597	—	24	274	31,457	3,678	2,725	—
1925	61.0 [11]	86.5	104.8	10.04	49,705	7,474	41,804	—	20	406	37,393	4,037	3,119	545 [16]
1926	—	86.6	110.4	9.96	52,902	7,721	44,764	—	16	401	39,755	4,381	3,604	558 [16]
1927	67.0 [11]	95.3	116.3	9.47	49,273	6,894	41,921	—	9	449	36,825	4,192	3,143	—
1928	—	91.0	123.8	8.83	56,623	7,385	48,689	—	7	542	42,182	4,588	2,965	—
1929	70.0 [12]	94.8	131.3	7.64	61,742	7,945	53,152	—	6	638	45,998	5,351	3,049	1,245
1930	—	77.1	112.6	5.11	44,591	5,623	38,587	—	2	379	33,055	3,934	2,098	—
1931	52.0 [11]	77.4	112.6	3.22	28,607	3,373	24,953	—	1	280	21,477	2,310	1,297	625
1932	—	74.5	113.9	1.40	15,123	1,712	13,243	—	(Z)	168	11,705	1,050	451	—
1933	45.0 [12]	88.8	130.7	1.29	25,725	2,717	22,653	—	(Z)	354	18,743	1,243	466	495
1934	—	91.4	133.0	1.40	29,182	2,422	26,355	—	1	405	21,246	1,596	1,131	—
1935	—	99.5	145.2	2.28	38,184	3,175	34,401	—	1	606	26,840	1,960	797	634
1936	53.0 [11]	103.8	161.9	3.82	53,500	3,873	48,760	—	1	865	37,858	3,245	1,366	—
1937	59.0 [11]	102.9	149.7	4.19	56,637	3,864	51,825	—	(Z)	947	41,178	3,670	1,619	1,060
1938	—	96.7	147.8	3.53	31,752	2,106	29,080	—	(Z)	566	23,569	2,083	698	—
1939	64.0 [11]	103.8	167.7	4.73	52,799	3,359	48,410	—	1	1,029	39,068	3,359	1,313	1,224

Notes appear at end of table

(continued)

TABLE Dd366–436 Physical output of selected manufactured products: 1860–1997 Continued

Year	Rubber products: pneumatic motor vehicle tires Dd395 (Million)	Leather products: shoes (except athletic) Men's Dd396 (Million pairs)	Women's Dd397 (Million pairs)	Clay products: common and face bricks Dd398 (Billion)	Primary metals — Ferrous — Raw steel: Total Dd399 (Thousand short tons)	Bessemer Dd400 (Thousand short tons)	Open hearth Dd401 (Thousand short tons)	Basic oxygen Dd402 (Thousand short tons)	Crucible Dd403 (Thousand short tons)	Electric arc Dd404 (Thousand short tons)	Hot rolled iron and steel Dd405 (Thousand short tons)	Structural iron and steel shapes Dd406 (Thousand short tons)	Rails Dd407 (Thousand short tons)	Nonferrous: copper and copper-based alloy products Dd408 (Thousand short tons)
1940	—	102.4	151.9	4.10	66,983	3,709	61,573	—	1	1,700	48,660	4,232	1,679	—
1941	—	135.8	184.9	—	82,839	5,578	74,390	—	2	2,869	62,324	5,724	1,928	—
1942	—	143.0	181.7	—	86,032	5,553	76,502	—	2	3,975	62,446	5,816	2,096	—
1943	—	129.3	154.7	1.92	88,837	5,625	78,622	—	(Z)	4,589	63,293	4,576	2,127	—
1944	—	108.5	118.1	1.88	89,642	5,040	80,364	—	(Z)	4,238	65,804	4,676	2,491	—
1945	—	107.7	120.2	2.29	79,702	4,305	71,940	—	(Z)	3,457	59,812	4,467	2,418	—
1946	—	106.0	181.4	4.87	66,603	3,328	60,712	—	—	2,563	50,937	4,388	1,966	—
1947	112.0	106.2	191.6	5.14	84,894	4,233	76,874	—	—	3,788	66,202	5,607	2,441	2,438
1948	—	104.4	176.5	5.84	88,640	4,243	79,340	—	—	5,057	69,192	5,456	2,208	—
1949	—	97.4	178.0	5.52	77,978	3,947	70,249	—	—	3,783	60,882	4,672	1,901	—
1950	—	102.5	195.2	6.33	96,836	4,535	86,263	—	—	6,039	75,191	5,442	1,850	—
1951	—	104.5	169.4	6.63	105,200	4,891	93,167	—	—	7,142	81,911	6,348	1,854	—
1952	—	100.7	183.9	5.89	93,168	3,524	82,846	—	—	6,798	71,349	5,355	1,472	2,465
1953	—	98.8	186.9	5.87	111,610	3,856	100,474	—	—	7,280	85,944	6,538	1,982	2,525
1954	102.0	91.1	202.0	6.72	88,312	2,548	80,327	—	—	5,436	68,465	5,706	1,171	2,114
1955	—	103.7	270.9	7.90	117,036	3,320	105,359	307	—	8,050	90,658	6,336	1,227	2,564
1956	—	106.9	273.4	8.09	115,216	3,228	102,841	506	—	8,641	89,284	7,167	1,301	2,435
1957	—	104.3	274.2	6.66	112,715	2,475	101,658	611	—	7,971	85,887	8,595	1,308	2,214
1958	112.0	101.4	270.7	6.32	85,255	1,396	75,879	1,323	—	6,656	65,105	5,220	587	2,021
1959	—	110.1	292.4	7.34	93,446	1,380	81,669	1,864	—	8,533	71,856	5,259	631	2,407
1960	—	100.6	279.8	6.94	99,282	1,189	86,368	3,346	—	8,379	76,446	6,125	711	2,149
1961	—	103.3	273.4	6.68	98,014	881	84,502	3,967	—	8,664	73,412	5,517	472	2,255
1962	—	112.7	288.2	6.89	98,328	805	82,957	5,553	—	9,013	74,998	5,278	544	2,478
1963	158.0	110.7	275.2	7.41	109,261	963	88,834	8,544	—	10,920	81,851	5,856	531	2,952
1964	—	117.7	278.0	7.87	127,076	858	98,097	15,442	—	12,678	93,635	6,809	701	2,950
1965	—	118.2	280.0	8.21	131,462	586	94,193	22,879	—	13,804	99,304	7,641	766	3,144
1966	186.0	126.9	284.2	8.26	134,101	278	85,025	33,928	—	14,870	99,205	7,687	878	3,447
1967	—	123.7	258.0	7.57	127,213	—[14]	70,690[14]	41,434	—	15,089	93,084	6,986	763	2,987
1968	—	125.6	283.7	7.91	131,462	—[14]	65,835[14]	48,812	—	16,814	99,115	7,098	847	2,912
1969	—	117.6	237.6	7.81	141,262	0	60,894	60,236	—	20,132	93,877[15]	5,766	830	3,274
1970	—	119.7	230.2	6.73	131,514	0	48,022	63,330	—	20,162	90,798[15]	5,566	900	2,821
1971	—	139.5	229.8	7.59	120,443	0	35,559	63,943	—	20,941	87,038	5,222	879	2,711
1972	265.1	150.0	219.5	8.28	133,241	0	34,936	74,584	—	23,721	91,805	5,237	921	2,985
1973	—	119.0	179.0	8.71	150,799	0	39,780	83,260	—	27,759	111,460	6,556	916	3,319
1974	—	—	—	7.56	145,720	0	35,499	81,552	—	28,669	109,472	6,548	924	2,813
1975	—	106.0	154.0	6.54	116,642	0	22,161	71,801	—	22,680	79,957	4,697	1,179	2,025
1976	—	111.0	157.0	7.34	128,000	0	23,470	79,918	—	24,612	89,447	3,857	1,303	2,517
1977	154.8	105.0	147.0	8.30	125,333	0	20,043	77,408	—	27,882	91,147	4,035	1,109	2,668
1978	—	103.0	145.0	8.70	137,031	0	21,310	83,484	—	32,237	97,935	4,667	946	2,712
1979	—	92.0	146.0	8.40	136,341	0	19,158	83,256	—	33,927	100,262	5,303	1,122	2,976

	Rubber products: pneumatic motor vehicle tires	Leather products: shoes (except athletic) Men's	Leather products: shoes (except athletic) Women's	Clay products: common and face bricks	Primary metals — Ferrous — Raw steel — Total	Raw steel Bessemer	Raw steel Open hearth	Raw steel Basic oxygen	Raw steel Crucible	Raw steel Electric arc	Hot rolled iron and steel	Structural iron and steel shapes	Rails	Nonferrous: copper and copper-based alloy products
	Dd395 [30]	Dd396	Dd397	Dd398	Dd399	Dd400	Dd401	Dd402	Dd403	Dd404	Dd405	Dd406	Dd407	Dd408 [30]
Year	Million	Million pairs	Million pairs	Billion	Thousand short tons	Thousand short tons	Thousand short tons	Thousand short tons	Thousand short tons	Thousand short tons	Thousand short tons	Thousand short tons	Thousand short tons	Thousand short tons
1980	—	91.0	141.0	6.51	111,835	0	13,054	67,615	—	31,166	83,853	4,861	1,085	2,467
1981	—	88.0	138.0	5.43	120,828	0	13,452	73,231	—	34,145	88,450	4,929	907	2,622
1982	190.5	72.0	132.0	4.81	74,577	0	6,110	45,309	—	23,158	61,567	3,313	498	2,014
1983	—	—	—	6.00	84,615	0	5,951	52,050	—	26,615	67,583	3,364	611	2,116
1984	—	72.0	115.0	7.11	92,528	0	8,336	52,822	—	31,369	73,739	3,868	933	2,717
1985	—	—	—	7.14	88,259	0	6,428	51,885	—	29,946	73,043	4,373	679	2,363
1986	—	58.0	83.0	7.51	81,606	0	3,330	47,885	—	30,390	70,263	4,233	444	2,318
1987	—[13]	57.0	79.0	7.64	89,151	0	2,666	52,496	—	33,989	76,654	4,839	351	2,624
1988	—	56.0	75.0	7.33	99,924	0	5,118	57,960	—	36,846	83,840	4,860	460	—
1989	—	51.0	69.0	8.03	97,943	0	4,442	58,348	—	35,154	84,100	4,987	458	—
1990	—	46.0	67.0	7.12	98,906	0	3,496	58,471	—	36,939	84,981	5,670	407	—
1991	—	41.0	56.0	5.94	87,896	0	1,408	52,714	—	33,774	78,846	5,245	382	—
1992	276.7	42.0	51.0	6.11	92,949	0	0	57,642	—	35,308	82,241	5,081	435	—
1993	—	45.0	51.0	6.62	97,877	0	0	59,353	—	38,524	89,022	4,973	544	—
1994	—	46.0	49.0	7.20	100,579	0	0	61,028	—	39,551	95,084	5,506	495	—
1995	—	39.0	41.0	7.01	104,930	0	0	62,523	—	42,407	97,494	5,710	528	—
1996	—	—	—	—	—	—	—	—	—	—	—	—	—	—
1997	—	—	—	—	—	—	—	—	—	—	—	—	—	—

	Fabricated metal products — Metal cans	Warm air furnaces	Nonelectric cooking stoves and ranges	Machinery, except electrical — Diesel engines	Gasoline engines	Metal cutting machines
	Dd409 [30]	Dd410 [30]	Dd411 [30]	Dd412 [30]	Dd413 [30]	Dd414 [30]
Year	Thousand base boxes	Thousand	Thousand	Thousand	Thousand	Thousand
1899	—	—	—	—	—	—
1900	—	—	—	—	—	—
1901	—	—	—	—	—	—
1902	—	—	—	—	—	—
1903	—	—	—	—	—	—
1904	—	—	—	—	—	—
1905	—	—	—	—	—	—
1906	—	—	—	—	—	—
1907	—	—	—	—	—	—
1908	—	—	—	—	—	—
1909	—	—	—	—	—	—

	Electrical machinery — Fractional horsepower motors	Integral horsepower motors and generators	Room air conditioners	Household appliances — Ranges	Refrigerators	Washing machines (mechanical)	Electric lamps — Large incandescent	Fluorescent (hot cathode)
	Dd415 [30]	Dd416 [30]	Dd417 [30]	Dd418 [30]	Dd419 [30]	Dd420 [30]	Dd421 [30]	Dd422 [30]
Year	Thousand	Thousand	Thousand	Thousand	Thousand	Thousand	Million	Million
1899	—	—	—	—	—	—	25	—
1900	—	—	—	—	—	—	—	—
1901	—	—	—	—	—	—	—	—
1902	—	—	—	—	—	—	—	—
1903	—	—	—	—	—	—	—	—
1904	—	—	—	—	—	—	—	—
1905	—	—	—	—	—	—	113	—
1906	—	—	—	—	—	—	—	—
1907	—	—	—	—	—	—	—	—
1908	—	—	—	—	—	—	—	—
1909	—	—	—	—	—	—	67	—

Notes appear at end of table

(continued)

TABLE Dd366–436   Physical output of selected manufactured products: 1860–1997   *Continued*

	Fabricated metal products			Machinery, except electrical			Electrical machinery						Electric lamps	
			Nonelectric cooking stoves and ranges							Household appliances				
	Metal cans	Warm air furnaces		Diesel engines	Gasoline engines	Metal cutting machines	Fractional horsepower motors	Integral horsepower motors and generators	Room air conditioners	Ranges	Refrigerators	Washing machines (mechanical)	Large incandescent	Fluorescent (hot cathode)
	Dd409 [30]	Dd410 [30]	Dd411 [30]	Dd412 [30]	Dd413 [30]	Dd414 [30]	Dd415 [30]	Dd416 [30]	Dd417 [30]	Dd418 [30]	Dd419 [30]	Dd420 [30]	Dd421 [30]	Dd422 [30]
Year	Thousand base boxes	Thousand	Thousand	Thousand	Thousand	Thousand	Thousand	Thousand	Thousand	Thousand	Thousand	Thousand	Million	Million
1910	—	—	—	—	—	—	—	—	—	—	—	—	—	—
1911	—	—	—	—	—	—	—	—	—	—	—	—	—	—
1912	—	—	—	—	—	—	—	—	—	—	—	—	—	—
1913	—	—	—	—	—	—	—	—	—	—	—	—	—	—
1914	—	—	—	—	—	—	64	283	—	—	—	—	89	—
1915	—	—	—	—	—	—	—	—	—	—	—	—	—	—
1916	—	—	—	—	—	—	—	—	—	—	—	—	—	—
1917	—	—	—	—	—	—	—	—	—	—	—	—	—	—
1918	—	—	—	—	—	—	—	—	—	—	—	—	—	—
1919	—	—	—	—	—	—	198	1,153	—	—	—	—	225	—
1920	—	—	—	—	—	—	—	—	—	—	—	—	—	—
1921	—	—	—	—	—	—	993	250	—	27	5	—	155	—
1922	—	—	—	—	—	—	—	—	—	—	—	—	—	—
1923	—	—	—	—	—	—	1,995	413	—	49 [20]	18	—	233	—
1924	—	—	—	—	—	—	—	—	—	—	—	—	—	—
1925	—	—	—	—	—	—	2,288	446	—	85	75	—	267	—
1926	—	—	—	—	—	—	—	—	—	—	—	—	—	—
1927	—	—	—	—	—	—	3,046	524	—	113	390	760	335	—
1928	—	—	—	—	—	—	—	—	—	—	—	—	—	—
1929	—	—	—	—	—	—	4,832	713	—	225	890	956	352	—
1930	—	—	—	—	—	—	—	—	—	—	—	—	—	—
1931	—	—	—	—	—	—	3,845	309	—	110	1,050	818	320	—
1932	—	—	—	—	—	—	—	—	—	—	—	—	—	—
1933	—	—	—	—	—	—	3,818	189	—	51	1,160	1,017	306	—
1934	—	—	—	—	—	—	—	—	—	—	—	—	—	—
1935	—	—	—	—	—	—	7,782	327	—	195	1,882	1,208	388	—
1936	—	—	—	—	—	—	—	—	—	—	—	—	—	—
1937	—	—	—	—	—	—	20,666	520	—	341	2,824	1,493	501	—
1938	—	—	—	—	—	—	—	—	—	—	—	—	—	—
1939	—	—	—	—	—	—	11,256	456	—	275	1,773	1,393	517	—
1940	—	—	—	—	—	—	—	—	—	—	—	—	—	—
1941	—	518 [17]	—	—	—	—	—	—	—	—	—	—	—	—
1942	—	256 [17]	—	—	—	—	—	—	—	—	—	—	—	—
1943	1,684	173 [17]	1,055 [18]	—	—	—	—	—	—	—	—	—	—	—
1944	2,072	281	1,424 [18]	—	—	—	—	—	—	—	—	—	—	—
1945	2,442	373	1,889 [18]	—	—	—	—	—	1	—	—	—	787	37
1946	2,760	699	2,811 [18]	—	—	—	—	—	30	—	—	—	774	52
1947	2,956	885	3,519	100	2,141	191	43,375	1,904	43	1,210	3,975	4,148	999	89
1948	3,245	777	3,532	—	—	—	—	—	74	—	—	—	1,030	94
1949	3,277	770	2,475	—	—	—	—	—	89	—	—	—	975	71

Group headers: **Fabricated metal products** (Dd409–Dd411) · **Machinery, except electrical** (Dd412–Dd414) · **Electrical machinery** (Dd415–Dd422), including **Household appliances** (Dd418–Dd420) and **Electric lamps** (Dd421–Dd422).

Year	Metal cans Dd409[30] (Thousand base boxes)	Warm air furnaces Dd410[30] (Thousand)	Nonelectric cooking stoves and ranges Dd411[30] (Thousand)	Diesel engines Dd412[30] (Thousand)	Gasoline engines Dd413[30] (Thousand)	Metal cutting machines Dd414[30] (Thousand)	Fractional horsepower motors Dd415[30] (Thousand)	Integral horsepower motors and generators Dd416[30] (Thousand)	Room air conditioners Dd417[30] (Thousand)	Ranges Dd418[30] (Thousand)	Refrigerators Dd419[30] (Thousand)	Washing machines (mechanical) Dd420[30] (Thousand)	Large incandescent Dd421[30] (Million)	Fluorescent (hot cathode) Dd422[30] (Million)
1950	3,893	1,100	3,388	99	2,458	—	—	—	194	—	—	—	1,200	98
1951	3,805	872	2,624	129	3,104	—	—	—	229 [19]	—	—	—	1,070	111
1952	3,842	928	2,424	121	2,945	—	—	—	372 [19]	—	—	—	864	65
1953	4,082	997	2,386	118	2,989	—	—	—	1,018 [19]	—	—	—	1,028	92
1954	4,143	1,152	2,203	105	3,670	121	57,643	1,744	1,353	1,209	3,387	3,697	960	93
1955	4,484	1,406	2,509	139	4,932	—	—	—	1,283	—	—	—	1,057	104
1956	4,786	1,355	2,274	141	5,883	—	—	—	1,828	—	—	—	1,132	126
1957	4,595	1,131	1,956	127	4,924	—	—	—	1,586	—	—	—	1,112	119
1958	4,761	1,235	1,825	132	5,756	110	58,877	1,639	1,675	789 [21]	3,038	3,974	1,052	113
1959	4,949	1,435	2,037	180	7,181	143	—	—	1,773	—	—	—	1,212	131
1960	4,862	1,253	1,822	139	6,022	134	76,027	1,409	1,523	—	—	—	1,142	140
1961	109,358	1,175	1,773	150	5,968	124	74,552	1,428	1,562	—	—	—	1,155	142
1962	114,506	1,238	1,878	155	7,126	139	81,373	1,724	1,628	—	—	—	1,238	164
1963	110,949	1,363	2,016	179	6,862	140	98,926	1,433	1,990	2,205	4,221	4,227	1,254	179
1964	116,213	1,535	2,068	238	6,734	154	106,587	1,923	2,592	—	—	—	1,264	198
1965	121,050	1,583	2,187	247	7,908	184	131,572	2,139	2,868	—	—	—	1,320	225
1966	129,389	1,528	2,132	254	8,900	243	136,820	2,595	3,269	—	—	—	1,394	256
1967	133,980	1,449	2,097	252	9,102	236	122,419	2,834	3,941	2,273	4,578	4,596	1,391	224
1968	145,862	1,741	2,326	252	9,822	226	142,696	2,726	3,887	—	—	—	1,467	258
1969	152,617	1,865	2,291	254	10,528	230	150,463	2,776	5,115	—	—	—	1,476	261
1970	159,299	1,783	2,114	226	9,558	188	135,134	2,836	5,438	—	—	—	1,582	267
1971	161,891	2,336	2,714	362	9,751	201	140,421	2,535	4,931	—	—	—	—	—
1972	170,672	2,668	2,919	439	11,007	252	157,598	3,020	3,923	3,693	6,069	6,125	1,738	289
1973	181,793	2,058	2,532	408	13,183	—	176,843	4,003	4,937	—	—	—	1,820	306
1974	187,758	1,453	1,966	565	13,822	227	166,031	5,325	4,495	—	—	—	1,460	277
1975	177,063	1,247	1,699	464	10,523	213	127,618	3,064	2,498	—	—	—	1,440	258
1976	180,141	1,496	2,040	488	10,804	220	190,423	3,778	2,805	—	—	—	1,656	293
1977	190,009	1,759	1,901	588	12,015	258	214,425	4,640	3,303	5,086	5,674	4,972	1,720	296
1978	—	1,885	2,039	594	12,076	263	235,916	5,089	3,903	—	—	—	1,622	314
1979	199,863	2,121	1,998	594	15,929	249	234,019	5,460	3,757	—	—	—	1,678	326
1980	192,729	1,532	1,720	903	14,431	235	197,547	4,116	3,179	—	—	—	1,656	335
1981	—	1,566	1,649	926	10,331	130	200,136	3,734	3,723	—	—	—	1,554	335
1982	—	1,265	1,486	653	9,685	101	177,824	3,545	2,883	5,070	4,609	4,013	1,499	323
1983	—	1,796	1,666	586	8,739	106	210,254	3,763	1,888	7,213	5,702	—	1,690	376
1984	—	1,995	1,893	775	11,757	94	235,088	4,151	3,039	8,959	6,317	—	1,735	414
1985	—	—	1,971	676	10,544	90	233,155	3,917	—	7,938	6,419	5,278	1,629	390
1986	—	—	2,243	574	10,951	93	230,265	7,698	—	7,801	6,940	5,425	1,626	420
1987	—	1,297	2,329	552	13,625	104	248,131	7,547	3,126	8,300	7,179	5,729	1,660	429
1988	—	2,099	2,174	635	14,289	104	311,377	6,467	3,708	7,944	7,968	6,200	1,680	467
1989	—	2,430	2,422	654	13,722	93	331,566	6,272	3,873	8,218	7,824	6,009	1,718	492
1990	—	2,137	2,448	639	16,326	78	292,579	7,026	3,454	7,500	7,016	6,072	1,681	477
1991	—	2,019	1,947	567	14,538	82	282,890	7,040	2,286	7,400	7,599	6,109	1,759	502
1992	—	2,417	1,991	648	18,217	88	263,875	6,483	2,519	7,452	9,676	6,001	1,799	555
1993	—	1,334	2,070	799	20,538	101	280,834	7,760	2,234	8,058	10,306	6,283	1,860	572
1994	—	1,523	2,158	885	23,316	118	307,959	9,624	3,265	7,246	11,287	6,600	1,815	599
1995	—	1,522	2,081	977	22,263	—	310,506	9,321	4,010	6,443	11,062	6,378	—	—
1996	—	—	—	—	—	—	—	—	—	—	—	—	—	—
1997	—	—	—	—	—	—	—	—	—	—	—	—	—	—

Notes appear at end of table

(continued)

TABLE Dd366–436 Physical output of selected manufactured products: 1860–1997 *Continued*

	Electrical machinery			Transportation equipment									Miscellaneous		
	Household electronics						Railroad cars			Horse-drawn vehicles					
	Radio receivers	Radio-phonograph combinations	Phonographs	Wheeled tractors	Truck trailers	Locomotives	Passenger	Freight	Bicycles	Carriages, buggies, and sulkies	Farm wagons, trucks, and business vehicles	Pianos	Organs	Typewriters
	Dd423	Dd424	Dd425	Dd426	Dd427	Dd428	Dd429	Dd430	Dd431	Dd432	Dd433	Dd434	Dd435	Dd436
Year	Thousand	Thousand	Thousand	Thousand	Thousand	Number	Number	Thousand	Million	Thousand	Thousand	Thousand	Thousand	Thousand
1860	—	—	—	—	—	—	—	—	—	—	—	—	—	—
1861	—	—	—	—	—	—	—	—	—	—	—	—	—	—
1862	—	—	—	—	—	—	—	—	—	—	—	—	—	—
1863	—	—	—	—	—	—	—	—	—	—	—	—	—	—
1864	—	—	—	—	—	—	—	—	—	—	—	—	—	—
1865	—	—	—	—	—	—	—	—	—	—	—	—	—	—
1866	—	—	—	—	—	—	—	—	—	—	—	—	—	—
1867	—	—	—	—	—	—	—	—	—	—	—	—	—	—
1868	—	—	—	—	—	—	—	—	—	—	—	—	—	—
1869	—	—	—	—	—	—	—	—	—	—	—	—	—	—
1870	—	—	—	—	—	—	—	—	—	—	—	—	—	—
1871	—	—	—	—	—	—	185	2	—	—	—	—	—	—
1872	—	—	—	—	—	—	387	9	—	—	—	—	—	—
1873	—	—	—	—	—	—	280	6	—	—	—	—	—	—
1874	—	—	—	—	—	—	256	5	—	—	—	—	—	—
1875	—	—	—	—	—	—	185	9	—	—	—	—	—	—
1876	—	—	—	—	—	—	836	8	—	—	—	—	—	—
1877	—	—	—	—	—	—	708	7	—	—	—	—	—	—
1878	—	—	—	—	—	—	211	9	—	—	—	—	—	—
1879	—	—	—	—	—	—	524	26	—	—	—	—	—	—
1880	—	—	—	—	—	1,405	685	46	—	—	—	—	—	—
1881	—	—	—	—	—	1,977	1,188	74	—	—	—	—	—	—
1882	—	—	—	—	—	2,282	1,711	68	—	—	—	—	—	—
1883	—	—	—	—	—	2,067	2,135	45	—	—	—	—	—	—
1884	—	—	—	—	—	1,149	1,063	25	—	—	—	—	—	—
1885	—	—	—	—	—	800	813	13	—	—	—	—	—	—
1886	—	—	—	—	—	1,436	953	42	—	—	—	—	—	—
1887	—	—	—	—	—	2,044	1,277	78	—	—	—	—	—	—
1888	—	—	—	—	—	2,180	1,452	72	—	—	—	—	—	—
1889	—	—	—	—	—	1,860	1,580	71	—	—	—	—	—	—
1890	—	—	—	—	—	2,300	1,654	104	—	—	—	—	—	—
1891	—	—	—	—	—	2,165	1,640	96	—	—	—	—	—	—
1892	—	—	—	—	—	2,012	2,195	98	—	—	—	—	—	—
1893	—	—	—	—	—	2,011	1,986	57	—	—	—	—	—	—
1894	—	—	—	—	—	695	516	17	—	—	—	—	—	—
1895	—	—	—	—	—	1,101	430	38	—	—	—	—	—	—
1896	—	—	—	—	—	1,175	474	51	—	—	—	—	—	—
1897	—	—	—	—	—	1,251	494	44	—	—	—	—	—	—
1898	—	—	—	—	—	1,875	699	100	—	—	—	—	—	—
1899	—	—	151	—	—	2,475	1,305	120	1.11	905	570	172	107	—

Year	Electrical machinery — Household electronics: Radio receivers Dd423 (Thousand)	Radio-phonograph combinations Dd424 (Thousand)	Phonographs Dd425 (Thousand)	Transportation equipment: Wheeled tractors Dd426 (Thousand)	Truck trailers Dd427 (Thousand)	Locomotives Dd428 (Number)	Railroad cars — Passenger Dd429 (Number)	Freight Dd430 (Thousand)	Bicycles Dd431 (Million)	Horse-drawn vehicles — Carriages, buggies, and sulkies Dd432 (Thousand)	Farm wagons, trucks, and business vehicles Dd433 (Thousand)	Miscellaneous — Pianos Dd434 (Thousand)	Organs Dd435 (Thousand)	Typewriters Dd436 (Thousand)
1900	—	—	—	—	—	3,153	1,636	116	—	—	—	—	—	145
1901	—	—	—	—	—	3,384	2,055	137	—	—	—	—	—	—
1902	—	—	—	—	—	4,070	1,948	163	—	—	—	—	—	—
1903	—	—	—	—	—	5,152	2,007	153	—	—	—	—	—	—
1904	—	—	—	—	—	3,441	2,144	61	0.23	937	644	261	113	—
1905	—	—	—	—	—	5,491	2,500	163	—	—	—	—	—	—
1906	—	—	—	—	—	6,952	3,084	233	—	—	—	—	—	—
1907	—	—	—	—	—	7,362	5,353	275	—	—	—	—	—	—
1908	—	—	—	—	—	2,342	1,637	68	—	—	—	—	—	—
1909	—	—	345	—	—	2,887	2,749	87	0.17	828	588	364	64	—
1910	—	—	—	—	—	4,755	4,288	171	—	—	—	—	—	—
1911	—	—	—	—	—	3,530	3,466	62	—	—	—	—	—	—
1912	—	—	—	—	—	4,915	2,818	126	—	—	—	—	—	—
1913	—	—	—	—	—	5,332	2,779	186	—	—	—	—	—	—
1914	—	—	514	—	—	2,235	3,366	98	0.30	538	534	323	41	—
1915	—	—	—	—	—	2,085	1,866	70	—	—	—	—	—	—
1916	—	—	—	—	—	4,075	1,802	129	—	—	—	—	—	—
1917	—	—	—	—	—	5,446	1,955	140	—	—	—	—	—	—
1918	—	—[22]	—	—	—	6,475	1,572	108	—	—	—	—	—	—
1919	—	—	2,230[22]	—	—	3,272	391	157	0.47	216	342	338	26	—
1920	—	—	—	—	—	3,672	903	76	—	—	—	—	—	—
1921	—	—[22]	596[22]	95	—	1,823	1,159	46	0.22	34	67	218	8	489
1922	190	—[22]	—	127	—	1,534	1,096	68	—	—	—	—	—	—
1923	—	—	997[22]	112	—	3,785	1,963	178	0.49	40	193	344	8	698
1924	—	—[22]	—	—	—	2,036	2,491	115	—	—	—	—	—	—
1925	2,350	—[22]	642[22]	158	—	1,285	2,383	109	0.30	22	196	303	4	742
1926	—	—	—	170	—	1,770	2,800	91	—	—	—	—	—	—
1927	1,980	59	988[22]	185	—	1,176	1,975	64	0.26	8	112	212	3	862
1928	—	—	—	152	—	747	1,462	48	—	—	—	—	—	—
1929	4,980	152	603[22]	196	—	1,161	2,202	85	0.31	4	106	121	3	962
1930	—	—	—	176	—	1,134	1,481	77	—	—	—	—	—	—
1931	3,743	74	—	62	—	222	290	14	0.26	1	27	51	1	529
1932	—	—	—	—	—	123	71	3	—	—	—	—	—	—
1933	3,648	30	—	—	—	63	7	2	0.32	1[26]	53	—	—	416
1934	—	—	—	—	—	110	195	25	—	—	—	—	—	—
1935	5,669	23	—	138	19	205	205	9	0.66	1	98	61	2	824
1936	—	—	—	194	—	202	191	47	—	—	—	—	—	—
1937	7,728	58	—	238	22	615	629	79	1.13	1	106	103	—	1,116
1938	—	—	—	172	—	346	434	17	—	—	—	—	—	—
1939	9,839	475	—	186	24	355	276	26	1.26	1	52	111	—	930

Notes appear at end of table

(continued)

TABLE Dd366–436   Physical output of selected manufactured products: 1860–1997   Continued

	Electrical machinery — Household electronics			Transportation equipment								Miscellaneous		
						Railroad cars				Horse-drawn vehicles				
Year	Radio receivers	Radio-phonograph combinations	Phonographs	Wheeled tractors	Truck trailers	Locomotives	Passenger	Freight	Bicycles	Carriages, buggies, and sulkies	Farm wagons, trucks, and business vehicles	Pianos	Organs	Typewriters
	Dd423	Dd424	Dd425	Dd426	Dd427	Dd428	Dd429	Dd430	Dd431	Dd432	Dd433	Dd434	Dd435	Dd436
	Thousand	Thousand	Thousand	Thousand	Thousand	Number	Number	Thousand	Million	Thousand	Thousand	Thousand	Thousand	Thousand
1940	—	—	—	249	27 [23]	560	257	64	—	—	—	—	—	—
1941	—	—	—	313	42 [23]	1,107	349	83	—	—	—	—	—	—
1942	—	—	—	172	80	1,018	418	71	—	—	—	—	—	—
1943	—	—	—	105	197	1,164	685	75	—	—	—	—	—	—
1944	—	—	—	249	209	1,438	1,003	82	—	—	—	—	—	—
1945	—	—	—	244	33 [23]	3,213	931	55	—	—	—	—	—	—
1946	—	—	—	258	73	—	1,337	60	—	—	—	—	—	—
1947	14,067	3,415	760	433	53	1,718	861	96	2.88	—	218	148	—	1,493 [28]
1948	—	—	—	530	47	—	891	115	—	—	—	—	—	1,173 [28]
1949	—	—	—	556	34	—	933	95	—	—	—	—	—	1,074 [28]
1950	—	—	—	499	66	—	964	44	—	—	—	—	—	1,408 [28]
1951	—	—	—	564	65	—	179	96	—	—	—	—	—	1,533
1952	6,556	566	830	415	55	—	117	79	—	—	—	—	—	1,383
1953	7,260	524	1,494	390	93	—	386	84	—	—	—	—	—	1,295
1954	6,448	377	2,659	246	52	1,409	315	36	1.75	—	108	152	—	1,111 [28]
1955	7,929	507	3,919	330	74	—	886	38	—	—	—	—	—	1,258
1956	8,974	602	3,949	215	64	—	396	67	—	—	—	—	—	1,501
1957	8,604	735	3,943	229	58	—	705	97	—	—	—	—	—	1,645
1958	8,012	787	3,750	241	49	1,140	116	32	2.05 [25]	—	107	159	89	1,224
1959	9,568	771	3,481	260	68	—	—	—	—	—	—	—	—	1,283
1960	9,763	654	3,242	152	58	—	—	—	—	—	—	—	—	1,191
1961	10,350	853	3,343	171	51	—	—	—	—	—	—	—	—	1,130
1962	10,112	1,243	3,668	188	68	—	—	—	—	—	—	—	—	1,306
1963	9,313	1,244	3,699	203	78	686	266	33	3.81 [25]	—	94	214	142 [27]	1,307
1964	9,404	1,454	3,242	213	87	—	—	—	—	—	—	—	—	1,438
1965	12,744	1,662	4,057	244	104	—	—	—	—	—	—	—	—	1,486
1966	13,536	1,702	4,323	271	113	—	—	—	—	—	—	—	—	1,889
1967	9,362	1,730	3,828	242	97	1,418 [24]	72	63	4.87 [25]	—	92	199	—	1,928
1968	7,455	1,982	3,705	213	114	—	—	—	—	—	—	—	—	1,842
1969	5,941	1,842	3,941	196	138	—	—	—	—	—	—	—	—	1,626
1970	4,359	1,660	3,051	172	106	—	—	—	—	—	—	—	—	1,371 [29]
1971	2,570	1,786	3,098	168	104	—	—	—	—	—	—	—	—	—
1972	2,050	2,466	3,996	197	141	—	—	43	8.47	—	—	206	—	1,297
1973	1,667	2,747	685	212	165	—	—	—	—	—	—	—	—	1,476
1974	762	2,909	601	210	210	—	—	—	—	—	—	—	—	1,270
1975	501	2,158	369	213	78	—	—	—	—	—	—	—	—	1,446
1976	897	2,581	676	194	105	—	—	—	—	—	—	—	—	1,406
1977	870	2,531	785	189	161	—	556	54	7.35	—	—	164	253	1,293
1978	438	1,553	855	137	195	—	—	—	—	—	—	—	—	1,925
1979	346	1,549	625	160	210	—	—	—	—	—	—	—	—	1,592
1980	206	1,050	—	118	137	—	—	—	—	—	—	—	—	1,479
1981	125	834	—	118	122	—	—	—	—	—	—	—	—	187
1982	845	1,069	—	65	104	—	—	—	5.59	—	—	181	128	230
1983	1,071	1,103	—	46	118	—	—	—	—	—	—	—	—	163
1984	—	—	—	50	214	—	—	—	—	—	—	—	—	—

	Electrical machinery					Transportation equipment						Miscellaneous		
	Household electronics					Railroad cars				Horse-drawn vehicles				
Year	Radio receivers	Radio-phonograph combinations	Phonographs	Wheeled tractors	Truck trailers	Locomotives	Passenger	Freight	Bicycles	Carriages, buggies, and sulkies	Farm wagons, trucks, and business vehicles	Pianos	Organs	Typewriters
	Dd423	Dd424	Dd425	Dd426	Dd427	Dd428	Dd429	Dd430	Dd431	Dd432	Dd433	Dd434	Dd435	Dd436
	Thousand	Thousand	Thousand	Thousand	Thousand	Number	Number	Thousand	Million	Thousand	Thousand	Thousand	Thousand	Thousand
1985	—	—	—	31	180	—	—	—	—	—	—	—	—	116
1986	—	—	—	24	167	—	—	—	—	—	—	—	—	—
1987	—	—	—	22	180	—	—	—	6.05	—	—	101	—	—
1988	—	—	—	—	186	—	—	—	—	—	—	—	—	—
1989	—	—	—	—	181	—	—	—	—	—	—	—	—	—
1990	—	—	—	—	149	—	—	—	—	—	—	—	—	—
1991	—	—	—	—	122	—	—	—	—	—	—	—	—	—
1992	—	—	—	—	165	—	—	—	4.07	—	—	59	—	—
1993	—	—	—	—	186	—	—	—	—	—	—	—	—	—
1994	—	—	—	—	234	—	—	—	—	—	—	—	—	—
1995	—	—	—	—	279	—	—	—	—	—	—	—	—	—
1996	—	—	—	—	—	—	—	—	—	—	—	—	—	—
1997	—	—	—	—	—	—	—	—	—	—	—	—	—	—

(Z) Less than 500 short tons.

1 Composition and coverage of many series changes over time; see text.
2 Tufted only.
3 Excludes separate coats.
4 Includes boys' uniform clothing.
5 Data for fifty-three weeks.
6 Suits only. In 1992, the Census Bureau reported production of 10,032 thousand suits and 53,184 thousand coats.
7 Coats only. In 1997, the Census Bureau reported production of 9,296 thousand suits and 69,427 thousand coats.
8 Includes children's and infants'.
9 Figures represent amount for sale.
10 Represents only reported quantities produced. Not adjusted to include estimated production for establishments not reporting.
11 Includes bicycle tires.
12 Excludes motorcycle tires.
13 Not reported because of disclosure rules.
14 Bessemer included in Open Hearth.
15 Represents shipments of steel products; comparable figure for 1968 is 91,856 thousand.
16 Excludes amount produced and consumed in same works.
17 Represents orders booked rather than shipments; comparable figure for 1944 is 226 thousand.
18 Production rather than shipments.
19 Listed as self-contained window sill type.
20 Includes disk stoves and hotplates.
21 Excludes other than free-standing ranges.
22 For phonographs, amount produced, 1921–1929. Radio-phonograph combinations included with phonographs, 1919–1925.
23 Civilian only.
24 Includes rebuilt locomotives.
25 Represents shipments. In 1963 and 1967, excludes children's two-wheel sidewalk cycles with semipneumatic tires.
26 Includes two-wheeled carts.
27 Represents electronic organs shipped.
28 Excludes specialized typewriters.
29 For October–December, excludes standard portable typewriters and specialized composing typewriters (that is, specialized composing typewriters, coded media typewriters, and input/output typewriters).
30 No data in series before 1899.

Series Dd366. 1885–1908: Arthur F. Burns, *Production Trends in the United States since 1870* (National Bureau of Economic Research, 1934), pp. 300–1, 341. 1909–1970: National Canners Association, *Canned Food Pack Statistics, 1971–72.*

Series Dd367. 1885–1898, 1900–1903, and 1905–1907: Arthur F. Burns, *Production Trends in the United States since 1870* (National Bureau of Economic Research, 1934), pp. 300–1, 341. 1899 and 1904: National Canners Association, *Canned Food Pack Statistics, 1969–70.* 1908–1970: National Canners Association, *Canned Food Pack Statistics, 1971–72.*

Series Dd368. 1860–1914: E. Frickey, *Production in the United States, 1860–1914* (Harvard University Press, 1947), pp. 8–9, 135–9. 1915–1929: Arthur F. Burns, *Production Trends in the United States since 1870* (National Bureau of Economic Research, 1934), pp. 299, 339. 1931–1933: Solomon Fabricant, *The Output of Manufacturing Industries, 1899–1937* (National Bureau of Economic Research, 1940), p. 395 (data from Census of Manufactures). 1935–1970: U.S. Department of Agriculture, Economic Research Service: *Food Consumption, Prices, and Expenditures,* Agricultural Economic Report number 138 and Supplement for 1970. 1971–1995: U.S. Department of Agriculture, Economic Research Service, *An Economic Research Service Report: Food Consumption, Prices, and Expenditures, 1970–1995.*

Series Dd369. 1860–1914: E. Frickey, *Production in the United States, 1860–1914* (Harvard University Press, 1947), pp. 8–9, 139–43. 1919–1933: Solomon Fabricant, *The Output of Manufacturing Industries, 1899–1937* (National Bureau of Economic Research, 1940), pp. 382, 387. 1934–1995: U.S. Department of Agriculture, *Agricultural Statistics* (1952, 1967, 1971, 1980, 1988, 1995–1996, 1997).

TABLE Dd366–436   Physical output of selected manufactured products: 1860–1997   *Continued*

Sources

Series Dd370–371. 1922–1940: U.S. Bureau of the Census, *Animal and Vegetable Fats and Oils* (annual issues). 1941–1995: U.S. Bureau of the Census, *Current Industrial Reports M20k – Fats and Oils: Production, Consumption, and Stocks,* Summary Report 1996 and earlier years (prior to 1958, issued as series M17-I, M17-2, and M28). This series now appears as M311N, where the numbering system derives from the North American Industrial Classification System (NAICS). See the Introduction to Part D for a discussion of NAICS.

Series Dd372. 1870–1929: Arthur F. Burns, *Production Trends in the United States since 1870* (National Bureau of Economic Research, 1934), pp. 292–3. 1930–1932: U.S. Internal Revenue Service (formerly Bureau of Internal Revenue), unpublished data. 1933: U.S. Internal Revenue Service, *Annual Report of the Commissioner of Internal Revenue, 1936.* 1934–1970: U.S. Bureau of Alcohol, Tobacco, and Firearms, *Alcohol, Tobacco and Firearms, Summary Statistics, 1973,* p. 41. 1971–1995: Bureau of Alcohol, Tobacco, and Firearms, *Alcohol, Tobacco and Firearms, Summary Statistics, 1981–1982* and *Statistical Release* (September each year beginning in 1977).

Series Dd373–374. 1870–1929: Arthur F. Burns, *Production Trends in the United States since 1870* (National Bureau of Economic Research, 1934), pp. 292–3. 1930–1933: U.S. Internal Revenue Service (formerly Bureau of Internal Revenue), *Annual Report of the Commissioner of Internal Revenue,* annual issues. 1934–1970: U.S. Bureau of Alcohol, Tobacco, and Firearms, *Alcohol, Tobacco and Firearms, Summary Statistics, 1973,* p. 20. 1971–1995: Bureau of Alcohol, Tobacco, and Firearms, *Alcohol, Tobacco and Firearms, Summary Statistics, 1981–1982* and *Statistical Release* (September each year).

Series Dd375–377. 1870–1879: Edwin Frickey, *Production in the United States, 1860–1914,* Harvard Economic Studies (Harvard University Press, 1947), pp. 14–15, 189–93. 1880–1929: Arthur F. Burns, *Production Trends in the United States since 1870* (National Bureau of Economic Research, 1934), pp. 296–9. 1930–1995: U.S. Department of Agriculture, *Agricultural Statistics* (1952, 1957, 1962, 1967, 1971, 1997).

Series Dd376–377. 1870–1879: Edwin Frickey, *Production in the United States, 1860–1914,* Harvard Economic Studies (Harvard University Press, 1947), pp. 14–15, 189–93. 1880–1929: Arthur F. Burns, *Production Trends in the United States since 1870* (National Bureau of Economic Research, 1934), pp. 296–9. 1930–1939 and 1941–1949: U.S. Internal Revenue Service (formerly Bureau of Internal Revenue), *Annual Report of the Commissioner of Internal Revenue* (various issues). 1940, 1950–1995: U.S. Department of the Treasury, *Alcohol and Tobacco Summary Statistics* (annual issues, usually September).

Series Dd378. 1933–1946: U.S. Bureau of the Census, *Current Industrial Reports: Underwear and Allied Products: Underwear, Knit Cloth, and Knit Fabric Gloves,* and *Underwear and Knit Cloth for Sale,* series M67C. 1947–1965: U.S. Bureau of the Census, *Knit Cloth for Sale.* 1966–1970: U.S. Bureau of the Census, *Shipments of Knit Cloth,* series M22X, series MQ22K (summary issues). 1971–1995: U.S. Bureau of the Census, *Current Industrial Reports: Shipments of Knit Cloth, Including Interplant Transfers* (summary issues).

Series Dd379. 1899–1947: U.S. Bureau of the Census, *Census of Manufactures* reports. 1954–1995: U.S. Bureau of the Census, *Current Industrial Reports, Carpets and Rugs,* series M22L and MQ22X (summary issues).

Series Dd380–381. 1911–1939: *Textile Organon-Base Book of Textile Statistics 33* (January 1962). 1940–1955: *Textile Organon 42* (January–February 1971). 1956–1970: *Textile Organon 42* (March 1971 and assorted issues thereafter). Beginning in 1989, the journal was renamed *Fiber Organon.* Most recent data (1982 onward) from *Fiber Organon 71* (March 2000), Tables 3 and 4.

Series Dd382–383. U.S. Bureau of the Census, *Current Industrial Reports: Annual Apparel Survey,* series MA23A or MQ23A (1997 and earlier years, summary issues).

Series Dd384 and Dd388. 1899–1939: U.S. Bureau of the Census, *Census of Manufactures* reports. 1940–1994: U.S. Bureau of the Census, *Current Industrial Reports: Inorganic Chemicals,* series M28A, and *Current Industrial Reports: Inorganic Fertilizer Chemicals,* series M28B (summary issues).

Series Dd385. 1899–1927: U.S. Bureau of the Census unpublished census data. 1929–1995: *Current Industrial Reports: Inorganic Chemicals,* series M28A (summary issues).

Series Dd386. 1899–1947: U.S. Bureau of the Census, *Census of Manufactures* (various census years). 1953–1996: U.S. Bureau of the Census, *Current Industrial Reports: Paint, Varnish, and Lacquer,* series MA28F (summary issues).

Series Dd389. 1860–1954: U.S. Department of Agriculture, *Statistics on Fertilizers and Liming Materials in the United States,* Statistical Bulletin number 191 (April 1957), p. 43. 1955–1957: U.S. Bureau of the Census, *Facts for Industry,* series M19D-06 and M19D-08. 1958–1995: U.S. Bureau of the Census, *Current Industrial Reports: Inorganic Fertilizer Materials and Related Acids,* series M28B (summary issues).

Series Dd395. U.S. Bureau of the Census, *Census of Manufactures* (various census years).

Series Dd396–397. 1899–1919: Solomon Fabricant, *The Output of Manufacturing Industries, 1899–1937* (National Bureau of Economic Research, 1940). 1921–1954: U.S. Bureau of the Census, *Statistical Abstract of the United States* (various issues). 1955–1995: U.S. Bureau of the Census, *Current Industrial Reports: Shoes and Slippers,* series M31A.

Series Dd398. 1869–1899 (decennially), 1904, 1909, 1914, 1919–1939 (biennially), 1947, 1954, 1958, 1963, and 1967: U.S. Bureau of the Census, *Census of Manufactures* (various years). 1895–1912: U.S. Geological Survey, *Mineral Resources of the United States* (various issues). 1913–1959: U.S. Bureau of the Census, *Facts for Industry: Clay Construction Products* (summary issues). 1960–1995: U.S. Bureau of the Census, *Current Industrial Reports,* series M320, *Clay Construction Products* (summary issues).

Series Dd399–405. American Iron and Steel Institute, *Annual Statistical Report* (various issues).

Series Dd406. 1879–1889: E. Frickey, *Production in the United States, 1860–1914* (Harvard University Press, 1947). 1892–1995: American Iron and Steel Institute, *Annual Statistical Report* (various issues).

Series Dd407. 1860–1872: E. Frickey, *Production in the United States, 1860–1914* (Harvard University Press, 1947). 1873–1995: American Iron and Steel Institute, *Annual Statistical Report* (various issues).

Series Dd408. 1925–1947: U.S. Bureau of the Census, *Census of Manufactures* (various census years). 1952–1987: *Current Industrial Reports,* series BDSAF-84, *Shipments of Copper-Base Mill and Foundry Products* (summary issues).

Series Dd409–414, Dd426, and Dd436. U.S. Bureau of the Census, *Current Industrial Reports* (summary issues), for the following series: series M34D, *Metal Cans;* series M34N, *Heating and Cooking Equipment (Except Electric);* series MA35L, *Internal Combustion Engines;* series M35S, *Tractors (Except Garden Tractors);* series M35W, *Metalworking Machinery;* and series M35C, *Typewriters.*

Series Dd415–416. 1914–1958: U.S. Bureau of the Census, *Census of Manufactures* (various census years). 1959–1995: U.S. Bureau of the Census, *Current Industrial Reports,* series M35H, *Motors and Generators* (summary issues).

Series Dd417. U.S. Bureau of the Census, *Current Industrial Reports,* series M35M, *Air-Conditioning and Refrigeration Equipment* (summary issues).

Series Dd418–420. 1921–1937: Solomon Fabricant, *The Output of Manufacturing Industries, 1899–1937* (National Bureau of Economic Research, 1940), p. 585. 1947–1977: U.S. Bureau of the Census, *Census of Manufactures* (various census years). 1982–1995: U.S. Bureau of the Census, *Current Industrial Reports,* series MA335F, *Major Household Appliances* (summary issues).

Series Dd421–425 and Dd427. Through 1939: U.S. Bureau of the Census, *Census of Manufactures* (various census years). Thereafter: U.S. Bureau of the Census, *Current Industrial Reports* (various issues), for the following series: series M36B and M36D, *Electric Lamps;* series MA36M, *Home-Type Radio Receivers and Television Sets, Automobile Radios, Phonographs, and Record Player Attachments;* and series M37L, *Truck Trailers.*

Series Dd428. 1880–1929: Arthur F. Burns, *Production Trends in the United States since 1870* (National Bureau of Economic Research, 1934), pp. 300–1. 1930–1945: American Railway Car Institute, *Railway Age, Annual Statistical and Outlook Number* (January 6, 1945), p. 91, and *Annual Statistical and Outlook Number* (January 5, 1946), p. 88. 1947–1967: U.S. Bureau of the Census, *Census of Manufactures* (various census years).

TABLE Dd366–436   Physical output of selected manufactured products: 1860–1997   *Continued*

Series Dd429–430. 1871-1914: Edwin Frickey, *Production in the United States, 1860–1914*, Harvard Economic Studies (Harvard University Press, 1947), pp. 14-15, 193-7. 1915-1919: American Railway Car Institute, *Railway Age, Annual Statistical and Outlook Number* (January 7, 1939), p. 83. 1920-1957: *Railway Age, Annual Statistical and Outlook Number* (most recently titled *Review and Outlook*) (various issues). 1958-1977: U.S. Bureau of the Census, *Census of Manufactures* (various census years).

Series Dd431–435. Through 1937: Solomon Fabricant, *The Output of Manufacturing Industries, 1899–1937* (National Bureau of Economic Research, 1940), pp. 585, 590, 597-8. Beginning 1939: U.S. Bureau of the Census, *Census of Manufactures* (various census years).

Documentation

Except as noted, figures represent commodities produced. Some of the exceptions are mentioned here; others are noted in this section or in the footnotes. Figures for the following represent commodities shipped: series Dd378-379, Dd408-411, Dd414-418, Dd420, Dd423-425, Dd427, and Dd436, except for the figures through 1939 for series Dd378, Dd408, Dd415-416, Dd418, Dd420, and Dd423-424, which represent amounts produced.

Series Dd366–367. A case consists of twenty-four number 2 cans. The successor trade association to the National Canners Association, the National Food Processors Association, no longer makes these production statistics available and they have not been updated beyond 1970.

Series Dd367. The figures for 1885-1907 were published in the unit case of twenty-four number 3 cans. They have been converted to a unit case of twenty-four number 2 cans by multiplying by 1.707. The conversion factor is taken from National Canners Association, *Canned Food Pack Statistics: 1940*, part 1, Vegetables (March 1941), p. 19. Except for some of the early historical data, which came from reports of the Bureau of the Census, the data have been compiled by the National Canners Association with the cooperation of state, regional, and commodity associations.

Series Dd368. Estimates are based on commercial production of wheat flour reported by the Bureau of the Census and the U.S. Department of Agriculture. They include flour milled from foreign wheat plus the estimated flour equivalent of farm wheat ground for flour or exchanged for flour for farm household use.

Series Dd369. Figures represent aggregate production of cane-sugar refineries and beet-sugar factories less imports of direct consumption sugar.

Series Dd371. Through 1958, figures cover shortening only; data for salad and cooking oils were not collected. Beginning in 1959, figures represent the sum of baking fats plus soybean and other cooking oils. Beginning in 1974, figures also include 100 percent vegetable oil.

Series Dd372–374 and Dd376. For 1971-1976, figures are for year ending June 30; thereafter, September 30.

Series Dd372. A barrel contains 31 wine gallons, each of 231 cubic inches. For the period 1920-1933, Prohibition restricted legal production to "near beer" with an alcohol content of less than 0.5 percent. Prohibition went into effect January 16, 1920 and ended effective April 7, 1933. The figure for 1933 includes 1,589 thousand barrels produced prior to April 7. Alcoholic content limited to 3.2 percent by weight from April 7 to December 5, 1933.

Series Dd373–374. Figures are in taxable gallons, which for spirits of 100 proof or more is equivalent to a proof gallon (which itself is the alcoholic equivalent of a U.S. gallon of 231 cubic inches at 60 degrees F, containing 50 percent ethyl alcohol), while for spirits of less than 100 proof is equivalent to a U.S. gallon of 231 cubic inches. The computation of taxable gallons excludes all fractional parts of a proof gallon less than one tenth. Pre-1977 figures are for years ending June 30 and include data for Hawai'i; beginning in 1928, they also include data for Puerto Rico. Beginning in 1977, figures cover periods from October of the previous year through September of the current year. For July, August, and September of 1976, production totaled 166,556 thousand taxable gallons and beverage availability totaled 154,030 thousand taxable gallons. Series Dd373 includes industrial alcohol for all years. Series Dd374 was derived by deducting figures for tax-free withdrawals (that is, industrial alcohol) from total distilled spirits production. Tax-free withdrawals

in 1995 were not reported on a comparable basis. Post-1995 data are not comparable with either series and are therefore not reported. According to the Bureau of Alcohol, Tobacco, and Firearms (ATF, a division of the U.S. Treasury), Statistics for July 1996 and beyond are not available. However, ATF has undertaken a project to automate the collection and compiling of these statistics.

Series Dd376–377. For 1940 and 1950-1970, includes large and small sizes.

Series Dd378. Beginning in 1974, series changed to total knit fabric.

Series Dd380–381. Figures represent yarns available.

Series Dd380. For 1941–1970, figures for rayon and acetate are as actually reported by the entire industry; earlier data are estimated totals based on reports obtained from 86 percent or more of the industry, with adjustments for complete coverage in accordance with information from the Census of Manufactures. Figures represent producers' domestic shipments plus imports of yarn and exclude staple, tow, waste, and other rayon and acetate products. Data for rayon relate to manmade fibers produced by the viscose, cuprammonium, and nitrocellulosic processes (the latter process discontinued after 1934). Rayon horsehair and straw are included in the filament yarn figures for 1952-1970 (for 1940-1951, production of these items averaged just under 1 million pounds per year). Acetate means manmade fibers composed of cellulose acetate and triacetate.

Series Dd381. Data include producers' domestic shipments plus imports of yarn and exclude staple and tow.

Series Dd382–383. Restrictions on the disclosure of information about individual companies has led to various inconsistencies in the reporting of recent data.

Series Dd382. Men's and boys' suits and separate coats represent (1) men's suits, excluding ski, slack, snow, and uniform; (2) men's tailored dress and sport coats and jackets, excluding uniform; (3) boys' tailored dress and sport coats; and (4) boys' suits, including students', cadets', and junior boys'.

Series Dd383. Beginning in 1972, covers dresses sold at a unit price. Women's, misses', and juniors' dresses include both dresses sold at a unit price and those sold at a dozen-price.

Series Dd384. For 1939-1949, figures exclude flakes and powders; for 1939-1942, also excludes solids.

Series Dd385. Figures are combined totals for sulfuric acid produced by the contact and chamber processes, including spent acid fortified in the contact plants with the simultaneous production of new acid. Production by government-owned plants during the World War II period, which was large, is not included because this production was available primarily for military use. However, for 1954-1970, appreciable amounts of sulfuric acid produced in government-owned privately operated plants are included. Figures for 1946-1950 include estimates based on annual totals of by-product operations of a few smelters reporting to the Bureau of Mines; the estimated data included vary from 4 percent in 1946 to 2 percent in 1950. For 1899-1939, figures are based on reports of the Census of Manufactures; they are shown in those reports on a 50 degree Baume basis but are here converted to 100 percent H_2SO_4. Beginning in January 1948, figures are not strictly comparable with earlier data because of the inclusion of additional plants; however, the addition of these plants increased the production of the specified chemical by less than 3.5 percent.

Series Dd387–388. Covers 100 percent NH_3. Series Dd388 ends in 1979.

Series Dd396–397. Includes nonrubber footwear and the production of shoes with vulcanized soles, excluding shoes for juveniles, athletic footwear, and slippers.

Series Dd398. The figures for 1869 and 1879 are for common brick only. For 1889, 1899, and 1904, the production of fancy or ornamental brick has been added to the production of face brick, the reason being that the best grade of face or front brick appears to have been classified as fancy or ornamental brick in these years. Beginning in 1943, common and face brick are classified as unglazed brick.

TABLE Dd366–436   Physical output of selected manufactured products: 1860–1997   *Continued*

Series Dd404. Beginning in 1946, includes crucible steel.

Series Dd405. Figures include rails, plates and sheets, merchant bar and skelp production, wire rods, and structural shapes.

Series Dd406–407. These are components of series Dd405, hot rolled iron and steel.

Series Dd406. Beginning in 1969, shipments of heavy steel structural shapes only; comparable figure for 1968 is 5,557 thousand short tons.

Series Dd408. Figures represent rolled, drawn, and extruded copper and copper-based alloy products shipped.

Series Dd407. Figures include both iron and steel rails, re-rolled rails, and girder and high T rails. For 1860–1867, figures include production of iron rails only.

Series Dd409. Through 1960, represents thousands of short tons of metal consumed in manufacture of cans. Comparable figure for 1961 is 5,039 thousand. Beginning in 1961, figures represent tinplate cans shipped. A base box is a unit of area equivalent to 31,360 square inches.

Series Dd410. Includes oil- and gas-fired furnaces sold as component parts of year-round air-conditioning units.

Series Dd412–413. Excludes engines for outboard, automotive, and aircraft purposes.

Series Dd418. For 1925–1937, covers 2.5 kilowatts and higher.

Series Dd419. Through 1937, figures represent sales.

Series Dd421. Figures through 1919 are not strictly comparable with later years because of changes in classification.

Series Dd422. Home-type radio receivers and radio–phonograph combinations for 1923–1939 include automobile sets.

Series Dd428. Beginning in 1947, figures represent shipments. For 1905–1945, Canadian output is included although the U.S. output is shown separately beginning with 1929 (see, for example, *Railway Age, Annual Statistical Number,* January 4, 1947). For 1880–1911, locomotives built in railroad repair shops are excluded. For 1942–1944, figures exclude locomotives built for U.S. Government and for the lend-lease program. This series was discontinued when the new traction power was supplied almost exclusively by diesel units. A locomotive may be composed of one or more diesel units.

Series Dd429–430. For 1871–1919, figures represent domestic production of passenger cars, exclusive of that in railroad repair shops. For 1920–1957, figures represent passenger train cars delivered; thereafter, shipments.

Series Dd431. For 1899–1921, figures relate to products made within the industry (as classified by the Bureau of the Census); for 1923–1967, figures relate to all products made regardless of the industry classification of the establishment.

Series Dd432. For 1899–1925, excludes sulkies.

Series Dd433. For 1899–1914, includes patrol wagons, ambulances, handcarts, and pushcarts. For 1919–1925, figures exclude mail carrier wagons and public conveyances and relate to products made within the industry (as classified by the Bureau of the Census).

Series Dd435. Represent reed organs for 1899–1935, electronic organs thereafter.

Series Dd436. Except as noted, standard electric and manual and portable models are included. Series discontinued.

TABLE Dd437–493 Value of output of finished commodities and construction materials destined for domestic consumption: 1869–1939[1]

Contributed by Jeremy Atack and Fred Bateman

			Finished commodities								Semidurable	
			Perishable									
			Food and kindred products		Cigars, cigarettes, and tobacco	Magazines, newspapers, misc. paper supplies, etc.	Drug, toilet, and household preparations	Fuel and lighting products			Dry goods and notions
	Total	Total	Manufactured	Nonmanufactured				Manufactured	Nonmanufactured	Total	
	Dd437	Dd438	Dd439	Dd440	Dd441	Dd442	Dd443	Dd444	Dd445	Dd446	Dd447
Year	Million dollars	Million dollars	Million dollars	Million dollars	Million dollars	Million dollars	Million dollars	Million dollars	Million dollars	Million dollars	Million dollars
1869	2,813.3	1,594.2	673.1	699.1	74.7	30.6	37.7	29.4	49.7	665.4	224.5
1879	3,441.7	1,996.1	962.9	716.5	119.7	61.5	40.4	39.7	55.5	828.2	263.1
1889	5,080.4	2,905.7	1,434.3	956.6	202.5	93.9	81.6	59.5	77.2	1,132.9	281.7
1890	5,002.2	2,705.3	1,155.5	991.4	215.4	97.3	90.1	75.4	80.2	1,196.0	299.6
1891	5,284.3	2,964.9	1,308.5	1,079.2	226.6	101.2	97.9	62.7	88.9	1,196.9	289.3
1892	5,331.3	2,908.8	1,251.4	1,062.3	230.5	109.3	104.7	52.1	98.5	1,255.8	297.2
1893	5,500.4	3,314.4	1,555.3	1,182.7	218.5	98.3	104.9	54.0	100.7	1,124.2	259.4
1894	4,752.3	2,916.3	1,337.9	1,012.3	218.1	92.9	102.9	61.9	90.3	970.9	209.9
1895	5,227.2	3,119.1	1,443.7	1,079.0	202.4	94.1	111.3	95.8	92.9	1,114.7	265.7
1896	5,003.2	2,944.0	1,436.2	927.5	193.0	90.0	112.7	92.8	91.9	1,064.6	215.5
1897	5,376.1	3,222.6	1,633.7	1,032.1	197.3	92.6	115.6	62.4	89.0	1,154.0	232.3
1898	5,708.0	3,431.7	1,707.9	1,121.4	226.9	103.2	122.4	63.9	86.0	1,175.8	227.4
1899	6,586.2	3,820.9	1,955.5	1,160.9	267.4	113.0	134.6	87.7	101.8	1,374.4	255.8
1900	7,120.8	4,100.8	2,083.9	1,249.1	304.0	122.3	136.2	100.3	105.0	1,465.7	271.9
1901	7,782.2	4,620.5	2,365.0	1,420.9	327.9	134.9	155.2	84.7	132.0	1,528.5	271.1
1902	8,227.5	4,764.7	2,403.1	1,519.3	325.1	151.3	174.0	89.7	102.2	1,613.8	298.7
1903	8,702.1	5,012.7	2,516.7	1,518.9	346.0	154.2	183.1	111.5	182.3	1,734.7	302.1
1904	8,734.3	5,167.7	2,601.5	1,614.9	339.2	159.7	182.3	109.2	160.8	1,746.5	285.1
1905	9,451.0	5,403.6	2,856.7	1,540.0	357.2	172.5	215.8	94.4	167.0	1,925.3	318.3
1906	10,752.5	5,912.7	3,121.0	1,719.6	398.1	184.3	225.4	102.9	161.3	2,244.2	348.2
1907	11,524.3	6,452.7	3,389.7	1,886.6	405.2	196.7	249.3	128.5	196.5	2,310.1	375.5
1908	10,191.1	5,988.1	2,974.7	1,915.7	399.8	156.8	234.1	125.8	181.3	2,155.5	295.5
1909	11,825.3	6,922.1	3,617.7	2,112.5	430.5	210.6	250.3	124.7	175.8	2,447.0	368.0
1910	12,659.2 [2]	7,386.0	3,823.5	2,306.1	464.0	209.9	266.8	121.0	194.8	2,417.3	349.5
1911	12,749.4	7,491.3	3,980.1	2,235.7	460.4	211.3	278.8	119.1	205.9	2,571.4	326.3
1912	14,028.0	8,100.8	4,342.3	2,410.5	468.9	233.6	289.4	142.0	214.0	2,754.4	363.2
1913	14,632.8	8,230.2	4,441.9	2,315.9	506.8	243.9	294.9	191.3	235.3	2,900.2	348.6
1914	14,054.0	8,296.5	4,484.8	2,380.1	500.9	254.4	289.0	160.4	226.9	2,709.5	337.8
1915	13,986.1	8,079.8	4,342.1	2,310.3	478.6	255.6	331.0	141.7	220.5	2,635.7	317.0
1916	18,389.4	9,893.2	5,380.1	2,693.6	522.4	352.2	420.7	262.5	261.7	3,573.7	461.6
1917	24,545.5	13,174.1	6,925.7	3,907.2	629.5	407.5	511.5	425.7	366.9	4,790.6	620.3
1918	29,979.8	15,807.2	8,583.6	4,280.8	864.0	445.5	636.1	580.7	416.5	6,076.1	854.8
1919 [1]	33,265.3	17,215.5	9,312.4	4,709.0	1,000.0	458.7	660.1	630.7	444.5	6,770.2	890.9
1919 [1]	34,032.4	17,392.4	9,468.2	4,720.2	1,008.4	439.8	667.8	668.4	419.5	7,019.9	806.5
1920	37,285.2	19,236.2	10,301.4	4,696.3	1,195.5	675.9	765.6	1,044.8	556.8	7,872.8	903.6
1921	25,864.0	14,022.9	6,548.7	4,182.4	1,053.0	474.5	562.2	714.9	487.3	5,631.7	607.4
1922	27,393.8	14,059.4	6,837.6	3,843.0	1,002.1	499.9	624.6	888.4	363.9	6,313.9	681.5
1923	32,168.5	15,176.0	7,554.6	4,012.9	1,050.3	550.7	698.5	746.4	562.7	7,230.3	861.9
1924	30,957.7	15,573.6	7,981.3	3,948.0	1,073.2	563.0	718.6	781.3	508.2	6,401.4	700.7
1925	34,046.3	16,870.5	8,684.0	4,335.8	1,094.4	615.7	767.0	990.1	383.5	7,134.0	816.0
1926	35,856.6	17,784.6	9,039.8	4,467.4	1,127.2	632.8	783.3	1,220.7	513.4	7,295.6	803.5
1927	34,410.2	17,263.6	8,827.3	4,360.2	1,164.5	648.4	851.9	958.9	452.5	7,390.7	798.6
1928	35,892.9	17,911.1	9,111.7	4,466.9	1,168.7	661.6	932.3	1,153.3	416.4	7,383.2	769.1
1929	37,782.6	18,384.0	9,463.9	4,358.3	1,243.6	683.9	984.2	1,237.8	412.3	7,458.3	791.0
1930	31,260.7	16,590.5	8,497.5	3,996.8	1,141.8	644.8	891.0	1,052.2	366.3	6,069.4	574.4
1931	24,243.3	13,431.7	6,730.2	3,133.4	1,154.9	573.5	809.0	740.2	290.5	4,931.4	459.4 [3]
1932	17,727.8	10,754.9	5,183.0	2,408.1	1,006.6	492.6	624.4	830.6	209.5	3,526.1	317.5
1933	18,454.1	10,872.9	5,509.5	2,451.1	910.7	470.1	626.0	707.2	198.3	3,772.8	390.4
1934	23,166.7	12,987.2	—	—	—	—	—	—	—	4,501.6	—
1935	26,744.7	14,571.7	7,884.9	3,183.6	1,096.4	527.2	727.7	952.2	199.7	4,937.6	576.0
1936	30,258.1	16,239.0	—	—	—	—	—	—	—	4,775.8	—
1937	33,667.8	17,295.3	9,402.3	3,683.0	1,274.1	601.9	818.4	1,335.0	180.6	5,591.3	712.9
1938	28,156.7	15,721.6	—	—	—	—	—	—	—	4,852.7	—
1939	31,277.7	16,073.5	—	—	—	—	—	—	—	5,490.6	—

Notes appear at end of table

(continued)

TABLE Dd437–493   Value of output of finished commodities and construction materials destined for domestic consumption: 1869–1939   *Continued*

	Finished commodities											
	Semidurable					Consumer durable						
	Clothing and personal furnishings	Housefurnishings	Tires and tubes	Shoes and other footwear	Toys, games, and sporting goods	Total	Housefurnishings	Household furniture	Printing and publishing books	China and household utensils	Monuments and tombstones	Luggage
	Dd448	Dd449	Dd450	Dd451	Dd452	Dd453	Dd454	Dd455	Dd456	Dd457	Dd458	Dd459
Year	Million dollars	Million dollars	Million dollars	Million dollars	Million dollars	Million dollars	Million dollars	Million dollars	Million dollars	Million dollars	Million dollars	Million dollars
1869	229.8	12.8	—	185.3	13.0	262.7	40.1	58.5	8.4	26.0	6.6	7.7
1879	358.2	16.2	—	173.7	17.0	304.3	56.7	65.2	19.1	31.2	7.5	7.1
1889	560.8	32.1	—	236.1	22.3	499.2	97.6	93.4	34.7	46.4	15.2	10.7
1890	588.8	34.5	—	249.8	23.3	538.7	103.9	95.3	33.9	49.3	17.3	13.4
1891	603.3	35.3	—	244.2	24.8	556.8	114.9	100.5	33.4	51.7	16.7	13.9
1892	632.8	37.0	—	263.8	25.0	579.3	112.6	115.0	34.9	52.9	16.6	15.6
1893	566.9	35.9	—	233.6	28.4	496.3	100.1	100.2	34.3	43.5	11.9	12.9
1894	478.1	32.4	—	228.0	22.4	429.3	88.9	82.4	28.4	39.3	14.9	11.1
1895	542.2	36.4	7.9	236.0	26.4	497.7	102.6	94.0	35.6	45.9	13.8	8.9
1896	549.5	35.5	9.8	228.9	25.4	475.2	90.6	90.2	34.6	51.0	13.4	9.2
1897	596.8	35.7	18.1	246.3	24.8	506.5	96.0	88.4	33.7	51.0	16.6	8.8
1898	608.2	35.9	19.0	261.9	23.4	528.9	95.4	89.4	40.8	52.0	17.5	8.8
1899	743.7	42.5	12.7	292.9	27.0	634.3	115.6	104.1	45.0	60.9	20.3	12.6
1900	817.4	49.8	7.8	289.8	29.0	658.7	126.8	106.9	44.3	69.5	18.4	12.0
1901	837.9	49.4	6.2	327.4	36.5	718.9	128.8	118.7	47.4	73.5	23.2	13.1
1902	892.8	53.2	5.5	325.9	37.8	786.3	146.8	129.4	49.2	78.5	27.9	14.9
1903	981.8	53.9	4.3	352.5	40.1	825.7	152.5	139.2	51.5	90.8	25.9	15.8
1904	992.6	52.9	5.7	368.9	41.3	826.9	146.2	142.4	53.6	91.7	25.7	18.9
1905	1,099.7	55.7	9.3	395.9	46.3	954.8	156.7	160.8	56.7	108.7	28.7	20.1
1906	1,314.7	69.5	12.5	448.9	50.4	1,129.5	185.8	190.3	55.9	122.6	34.5	23.9
1907	1,335.4	68.2	15.6	454.4	60.9	1,178.1	182.8	185.1	56.8	120.7	38.3	27.7
1908	1,287.0	60.1	17.5	452.1	43.3	1,011.0	147.1	152.6	53.8	93.6	40.9	23.6
1909	1,459.7	75.0	23.4	467.9	52.9	1,212.8	184.2	192.0	62.9	102.9	38.4	28.5
1910	1,408.3	83.0	36.0	486.0	54.4	1,331.6	195.7	202.4	60.3	114.1	42.6	32.8
1911	1,560.0	80.0	45.5	500.8	58.7	1,339.2	187.5	204.1	59.1	116.7	42.4	36.1
1912	1,656.7	85.5	58.3	531.4	59.3	1,538.4	199.1	220.5	66.3	122.4	40.3	33.9
1913	1,721.6	95.5	86.6	583.8	64.0	1,675.1	209.3	236.7	77.8	130.2	42.1	34.0
1914	1,598.1	90.0	92.7	523.8	67.1	1,570.4	190.7	222.5	68.1	125.9	41.0	26.5
1915	1,533.9	85.8	104.9	520.6	73.5	1,700.2	181.4	212.3	73.3	126.1	37.5	25.9
1916	2,025.3	112.2	156.1	705.5	113.0	2,396.1	234.9	271.7	76.7	160.9	37.9	39.6
1917	2,622.7	156.7	329.1	863.4	198.5	2,799.0	288.6	300.6	89.8	221.7	42.3	36.7
1918	3,361.1	199.9	491.3	1,043.2	125.8	2,646.9	320.1	329.0	99.2	197.6	50.0	52.2
1919 [1]	3,817.9	212.0	515.4	1,187.6	146.4	3,921.2	375.2	494.7	127.4	230.1	73.4	64.2
1919 [1]	3,932.9	324.0	546.6	1,254.2	155.8	4,075.6	430.2	509.0	128.2	201.7	73.4	70.4
1920	4,382.8	390.5	678.9	1,368.2	148.8	4,899.3	574.8	620.5	140.0	265.7	82.3	78.2
1921	3,345.3	277.9	323.5	953.5	124.1	3,270.3	374.6	466.6	122.0	166.8	46.9	51.0
1922	3,865.4	307.1	335.8	993.0	131.1	4,056.5	470.0	501.1	124.9	167.7	47.6	52.6
1923	4,347.4	377.3	348.3	1,128.2	167.1	5,366.7	600.0	578.9	130.7	239.0	65.6	69.2
1924	3,743.9	358.4	382.0	1,061.7	154.6	5,034.3	547.1	614.0	145.0	181.5	66.4	57.8
1925	4,149.2	404.8	555.1	1,044.8	164.2	5,785.7	604.0	622.9	149.8	240.1	66.8	66.4
1926	4,186.6	438.1	616.3	1,073.9	177.2	6,109.0	591.6	638.2	155.4	271.6	63.8	66.4
1927	4,360.2	396.9	574.9	1,077.6	182.5	5,435.8	584.7	625.5	172.1	229.3	61.9	65.9
1928	4,385.6	401.5	551.0	1,074.9	200.9	5,936.1	627.5	629.3	179.7	275.7	61.0	67.9
1929	4,516.4	416.5	437.8	1,081.9	214.6	6,312.0	643.3	600.4	192.3	274.0	63.6	70.3
1930	3,767.8	347.8	336.9	860.3	182.2	4,272.6	402.7	441.4	174.3	196.4	54.9	44.5
1931	3,087.9	256.6	273.4	705.1	149.1	3,251.9	373.6	333.2	141.5	185.9	43.6	29.4
1932	2,183.4	187.5	194.5	546.3	96.9	2,047.4	252.0	205.4	102.9	138.9	25.7	18.4
1933	2,274.6	218.2	196.7	597.3	95.8	2,321.3	311.6	226.9	92.1	150.4	20.8	19.1
1934	—	—	—	—	—	3,307.2	—	—	—	—	—	—
1935	3,039.1	273.7	215.1	693.4	140.3	4,256.8	468.3	323.7	131.1	204.8	21.3	31.0
1936	—	—	—	—	—	5,158.0	—	—	—	—	—	—
1937	3,258.6	340.1	261.2	828.3	190.2	5,742.1	640.9	478.7	161.6	241.6	26.0	42.5
1938	—	—	—	—	—	3,747.3	—	—	—	—	—	—
1939	—	—	—	—	—	4,973.1	—	—	—	—	—	—

Notes appear at end of table

TABLE Dd437–493   Value of output of finished commodities and construction materials destined for domestic consumption: 1869–1939   Continued

						Finished commodities					
						Consumer durable					
	Heating and cooking apparatus, etc.	Electrical household appliances and supplies	Radios	Passenger vehicles (motor)	Motor vehicle accessories	Pleasure craft	Motorcycles and bicycles	Passenger vehicles (horse-drawn) and accessories	Ophthalmic products and artificial limbs	Jewelry, silverware, clocks, and watches	Musical instruments
	Dd460	Dd461	Dd462	Dd463	Dd464	Dd465	Dd466	Dd467	Dd468	Dd469	Dd470
Year	Million dollars	Million dollars	Million dollars	Million dollars	Million dollars	Million dollars	Million dollars	Million dollars	Million dollars	Million dollars	Million dollars
1869	26.4	—	—	—	—	0.6	—	35.7	0.4	41.6	10.8
1879	23.0	—	—	—	—	0.9	—	35.1	0.8	43.3	14.3
1889	38.9	—	—	—	—	1.5	1.9	54.0	2.3	74.5	28.2
1890	37.9	—	—	—	—	1.5	—	60.4	2.6	90.2	32.9
1891	39.1	—	—	—	—	1.6	—	62.4	2.9	86.7	33.0
1892	38.9	—	—	—	—	1.5	—	63.3	3.2	90.3	34.6
1893	35.3	—	—	—	—	1.4	—	58.5	3.3	71.7	23.2
1894	31.0	—	—	—	—	1.0	—	50.9	3.3	58.3	19.9
1895	35.5	—	—	—	—	1.3	14.1	45.2	3.7	69.2	27.9
1896	45.6	—	—	—	—	1.2	14.9	39.3	3.8	58.5	22.8
1897	50.7	—	—	—	—	1.2	27.0	40.9	4.0	63.6	24.5
1898	46.3	—	—	—	—	1.4	27.8	43.5	4.3	74.0	27.8
1899	59.2	1.9	—	4.2	—	2.1	18.9	53.5	4.8	97.1	34.2
1900	61.9	2.4	—	6.0	—	2.7	10.5	50.1	4.7	100.0	42.4
1901	70.7	2.6	—	7.8	—	3.7	7.7	64.1	5.2	103.6	48.8
1902	78.6	3.2	—	9.3	—	3.5	6.4	58.8	5.7	117.0	57.2
1903	78.8	3.8	—	11.3	—	3.6	4.2	56.7	5.8	120.5	65.1
1904	73.6	3.3	—	21.4	2.5	3.1	2.5	57.8	5.6	120.9	57.7
1905	85.8	4.7	—	35.6	4.3	3.8	5.4	61.2	7.1	144.1	71.1
1906	103.4	8.0	—	62.7	7.8	4.3	4.9	62.4	7.9	174.0	81.2
1907	101.2	10.2	—	89.6	11.3	6.1	6.5	63.8	9.4	180.9	87.8
1908	84.2	7.7	—	132.2	17.3	3.4	4.9	48.8	9.3	128.6	63.0
1909	93.8	11.8	—	154.3	21.1	4.3	5.6	49.8	10.5	175.9	76.8
1910	97.3	16.3	—	203.8	26.9	4.4	7.3	53.3	10.7	186.1	77.6
1911	104.1	15.7	—	209.2	26.3	4.3	9.4	45.9	10.9	186.1	81.3
1912	131.5	19.7	—	311.3	39.3	3.9	12.0	41.6	10.6	190.9	95.2
1913	124.9	22.2	—	372.8	46.1	4.1	21.9	40.1	12.3	196.0	104.4
1914	110.5	18.8	—	399.6	49.9	3.6	16.2	35.6	15.5	154.6	91.6
1915	119.4	23.7	—	537.8	61.0	3.4	13.3	30.5	20.2	144.1	90.2
1916	142.5	41.2	—	873.7	104.0	4.0	16.3	31.0	23.9	221.7	116.2
1917	194.2	58.8	—	996.7	120.5	3.3	16.7	38.8	36.5	219.2	134.7
1918	216.8	67.5	—	762.7	85.8	1.5	18.9	35.3	71.1	194.9	144.2
1919 [1]	263.5	84.5	—	1,286.9	168.0	5.1	19.0	26.4	45.0	409.7	248.3
1919 [1]	242.5	65.1	14.3	1,292.6	282.6	13.9	24.0	—	58.2	427.8	242.0
1920	345.6	82.8	17.0	1,628.3	313.4	14.7	20.8	—	67.8	383.2	264.2
1921	186.5	63.2	12.2	1,115.5	169.5	9.4	10.2	—	46.6	263.1	166.4
1922	239.2	58.6	26.9	1,546.1	243.4	6.2	8.9	—	48.6	327.0	187.7
1923	322.0	76.3	50.3	2,188.8	355.8	12.1	16.3	—	58.5	388.1	215.1
1924	322.2	83.4	139.3	1,922.5	337.2	14.0	13.0	—	48.6	363.9	178.5
1925	346.1	106.3	168.2	2,340.2	444.3	15.0	11.3	—	46.6	384.3	173.6
1926	364.3	137.5	206.7	2,504.3	440.2	22.4	11.9	—	46.6	398.9	189.3
1927	339.4	146.3	181.5	1,967.8	419.8	17.8	10.1	—	49.7	387.6	176.2
1928	314.2	152.7	298.7	2,294.9	411.7	17.4	12.0	—	48.7	396.3	148.6
1929	347.3	176.7	366.0	2,567.0	407.6	26.2	10.6	—	52.1	402.7	111.9
1930	254.2	160.0	230.6	1,538.0	326.1	24.6	9.2	—	48.3	263.8	103.4
1931	206.2	144.4	154.7	1,074.1	273.1	16.8	7.7	—	40.3	178.8	48.7
1932	123.0	82.2	94.2	603.2	211.9	9.3	4.6	—	32.0	108.5	35.0
1933	147.1	110.3	98.0	725.3	228.2	4.8	7.5	—	39.1	116.0	24.1
1934	—	—	—	—	—	—	—	—	—	—	—
1935	237.5	217.8	167.4	1,688.3	463.6	14.1	16.8	—	50.1	189.5	31.5
1936	—	—	—	—	—	—	—	—	—	—	—
1937	341.0	332.6	218.0	2,212.9	594.6	25.4	30.8	—	70.9	272.6	52.0
1938	—	—	—	—	—	—	—	—	—	—	—
1939	—	—	—	—	—	—	—	—	—	—	—

Notes appear at end of table

(continued)

TABLE Dd437–493 Value of output of finished commodities and construction materials destined for domestic consumption: 1869–1939 Continued

					Finished commodities							
					Producer durable							
Year	Total	Office and store furniture fixtures	Carpenters' and mechanics' tools	Industrial machinery and equipment	Misc. subsidiary durable equipment	Farm equipment	Electrical equipment (industrial and commercial)	Office and store machinery and equipment	Tractors	Business vehicles (motor)	Aircraft	Ships and boats
	Dd471	Dd472	Dd473	Dd474	Dd475	Dd476	Dd477	Dd478	Dd479	Dd480	Dd481	Dd482
	Million dollars	Million dollars	Million dollars	Million dollars	Million dollars	Million dollars	Million dollars	Million dollars	Million dollars	Million dollars	Million dollars	Million dollars
1869	291.0	13.6	10.5	110.4	31.4	50.0	—	3.1	—	—	—	11.5
1879	313.1	15.9	13.4	98.6	37.1	67.3	1.9	3.6	—	—	—	19.4
1889	542.6	25.6	20.8	184.5	63.3	83.9	13.1	8.2	—	—	—	24.7
1890	562.2	25.8	23.6	185.6	66.5	89.0	21.8	8.7	—	—	—	24.6
1891	565.7	26.8	24.7	185.5	69.5	75.3	23.7	9.0	—	—	—	26.9
1892	587.4	30.1	24.6	196.5	74.9	75.4	22.7	9.8	—	—	—	24.9
1893	565.5	26.1	22.5	184.9	71.7	71.2	16.6	9.5	—	—	—	23.9
1894	435.7	21.2	16.6	157.7	61.0	58.7	15.8	8.6	—	—	—	17.8
1895	495.7	23.7	19.1	193.1	64.8	59.3	20.0	10.7	—	—	—	22.7
1896	519.6	22.5	18.6	209.8	67.9	46.6	20.5	11.6	—	—	—	20.8
1897	492.9	21.8	16.8	182.3	64.2	58.4	24.4	9.7	—	—	—	20.7
1898	571.6	21.4	19.8	194.9	69.4	85.6	34.3	10.6	—	—	—	24.4
1899	756.6	24.2	24.5	267.5	83.9	99.4	56.1	14.3	—	—	—	36.1
1900	895.6	27.2	26.9	347.6	91.8	100.6	68.2	19.7	—	—	—	46.9
1901	914.3	30.2	29.2	330.3	89.5	110.4	68.5	18.9	—	—	—	64.7
1902	1,062.7	33.6	35.7	371.3	102.8	152.9	80.6	21.9	—	—	—	60.8
1903	1,129.0	37.8	37.7	405.9	110.4	120.2	91.9	23.9	—	—	—	61.3
1904	993.2	38.2	34.7	327.1	108.7	125.2	75.9	20.3	—	1.4	—	53.6
1905	1,167.3	43.1	37.9	404.7	115.6	130.2	84.9	28.0	—	1.5	—	55.6
1906	1,466.1	50.7	43.4	504.6	135.2	160.5	119.9	38.8	—	1.8	—	54.8
1907	1,583.5	49.1	52.7	510.9	157.9	161.6	127.5	42.7	—	2.3	—	66.3
1908	1,036.5	40.4	35.7	331.2	157.4	137.7	83.2	27.9	—	3.5	—	34.4
1909	1,243.4	48.6	47.7	446.9	154.6	166.5	111.2	40.1	—	7.3	—	38.2
1910	1,524.2 [2]	50.1	49.1	512.4	151.6	170.6	144.4	48.4	—	12.5	—	40.8
1911	1,347.6	48.7	41.9	476.6	147.1	168.2	133.5	43.8	—	25.9	—	42.7
1912	1,634.5	54.3	48.5	517.1	152.8	187.3	162.1	50.2	8.1	49.9	0.3	44.4
1913	1,827.3	54.3	53.6	543.4	161.7	202.4	177.1	55.4	4.4	47.1	0.2	47.6
1914	1,477.6	50.8	49.6	460.2	171.0	187.8	147.0	50.9	16.7	36.2	0.2	43.5
1915	1,570.4	43.3	57.0	536.8	140.6	205.1	160.2	63.0	22.7	68.6	0.6	66.8
1916	2,526.3	51.6	97.5	906.0	205.6	237.1	253.9	98.8	25.8	111.6	1.4	103.7
1917	3,781.8	61.3	131.7	1,358.1	291.6	250.0	325.2	140.5	50.7	189.1	21.3	243.8
1918	5,449.7	65.7	210.6	1,575.8	360.7	301.8	339.9	157.8	136.6	417.0	174.7	805.3
1919 [1]	5,358.4	86.4	174.8	1,440.5	349.3	343.8	365.7	125.4	152.6	344.0	8.4	1,389.5
1919 [1]	5,544.5	100.3	120.6	1,434.3	347.6	394.6	460.8	156.4	171.6	344.3	10.0	1,381.3
1920	5,277.0	135.1	128.7	1,635.8	403.0	270.6	557.9	160.6	197.4	332.9	8.7	808.1
1921	2,939.1	115.5	62.1	922.8	208.6	248.1	406.6	114.0	49.6	170.4	6.1	272.7
1922	2,964.0	136.8	87.8	1,085.2	245.1	160.7	415.8	132.4	43.4	237.2	8.8	93.6
1923	4,395.5	201.3	115.4	1,510.9	302.1	315.5	598.1	182.0	63.5	321.8	11.5	73.1
1924	3,948.5	229.5	106.4	1,303.8	208.0	265.9	655.0	179.2	52.1	323.4	10.9	67.4
1925	4,256.0	236.1	109.8	1,486.4	300.4	306.5	666.2	196.4	70.3	389.6	10.5	55.7
1926	4,667.5	242.3	110.2	1,606.8	321.9	355.4	776.4	200.1	87.4	377.2	17.6	86.5
1927	4,320.2	249.0	104.2	1,476.0	318.4	340.4	741.2	201.2	91.3	302.3	19.4	70.8
1928	4,662.5	245.8	131.6	1,644.1	304.9	356.5	895.0	213.6	104.1	318.3	51.1	60.4
1929	5,628.4	288.7	124.6	2,017.2	369.7	386.5	1,000.1	217.8	121.8	510.8	56.0	78.2
1930	4,328.2	203.5	99.8	1,457.8	304.7	338.5	722.2	165.3	95.4	373.0	28.8	94.9
1931	2,628.3	151.7	53.9	938.2	199.9	163.4	499.5	116.5	19.6	247.0	30.0	82.0
1932	1,399.4	74.9	31.0	525.8	129.0	70.9	215.5	78.5	15.8	125.5	14.1	49.7
1933	1,487.1	70.3	49.1	577.1	168.1	78.8	200.9	78.8	12.6	159.0	16.5	30.4
1934	2,370.7	—	—	—	—	—	—	—	—	—	—	—
1935	2,978.6	111.1	66.3	1,126.0	198.8	345.3	361.2	140.6	133.3	359.3	19.1	48.2
1936	4,085.3	—	—	—	—	—	—	—	—	—	—	—
1937	5,039.1	176.8	95.3	1,883.7	269.9	668.5	673.8	204.9	223.7	496.6	48.4	128.6
1938	3,835.1	—	—	—	—	—	—	—	—	—	—	—
1939	4,740.5	—	—	—	—	—	—	—	—	—	—	—

Notes appear at end of table

TABLE Dd437–493   Value of output of finished commodities and construction materials destined for domestic consumption: 1869–1939   *Continued*

Year	Finished commodities — Producer durable: Locomotive and railroad cars Dd483 Million dollars	Business vehicles (horse-drawn) Dd484 Million dollars	Professional and scientific equipment Dd485 Million dollars	Construction materials: Total Dd486 Million dollars	Manufactured Dd487 Million dollars	Nonmanufactured Dd488 Million dollars	Implicit price indexes: Perishable Dd489 Index 1913 = 100	Semidurable Dd490 Index 1913 = 100	Consumer durable Dd491 Index 1913 = 100	Producer durable Dd492 Index 1913 = 100	Construction materials Dd493 Index 1913 = 100
1869	40.8	18.1	1.6	377.4	324.8	52.6	141.2	158.5	119.4	163.8	107.4
1879	36.3	18.0	1.6	444.2	365.9	78.3	86.6	102.2	83.2	95.4	81.4
1889	87.3	28.4	2.9	838.9	712.2	126.7	88.3	95.6	81.9	88.2	85.0
1890	81.5	32.0	3.2	1,216.5	1,070.5	146.1	86.1	94.9	82.3	87.7	84.3
1891	87.6	33.5	3.2	1,076.0	940.0	136.0	84.8	92.6	82.1	81.1	80.2
1892	90.9	34.1	3.5	1,335.5	1,164.8	170.7	79.8	92.6	79.2	80.0	75.9
1893	104.1	32.1	3.0	1,074.3	933.1	141.3	84.7	90.5	74.8	78.4	75.4
1894	47.4	28.4	2.5	1,004.1	867.0	137.1	76.3	80.5	72.3	78.2	71.6
1895	53.7	25.7	3.0	1,033.2	881.2	152.0	75.0	77.1	67.4	72.2	70.7
1896	75.2	23.0	3.2	880.3	751.4	128.9	70.9	75.5	63.8	66.1	71.8
1897	67.7	24.2	2.7	963.4	821.0	142.4	72.0	75.5	63.0	75.9	67.1
1898	82.1	25.9	3.2	937.8	795.8	141.9	74.9	77.3	67.5	82.5	69.9
1899	114.1	32.5	4.0	1,006.3	855.7	150.6	75.4	81.0	70.0	88.1	80.7
1900	130.0	31.4	5.3	1,222.7	1,046.8	175.8	80.2	86.7	77.0	90.0	85.8
1901	127.4	40.2	5.0	1,306.3	1,119.2	187.1	79.6	81.9	77.5	88.9	80.7
1902	157.8	37.9	7.5	1,493.6	1,270.6	223.0	84.1	83.5	79.9	89.7	82.5
1903	194.6	37.6	7.8	1,447.4	1,218.9	228.4	83.3	86.0	82.7	86.2	84.5
1904	162.7	38.9	6.4	1,394.3	1,167.3	227.0	85.5	86.0	83.5	88.8	81.7
1905	214.3	43.1	8.2	1,578.1	1,334.0	244.1	86.9	90.5	85.3	89.7	87.0
1906	299.4	46.2	10.7	1,911.1	1,622.8	288.3	84.9	98.2	89.1	90.6	96.6
1907	351.2	49.5	11.8	2,111.5	1,770.1	341.4	89.7	102.6	97.7	93.6	101.0
1908	137.1	40.2	8.0	1,820.1	1,513.9	306.3	92.3	96.0	96.6	89.3	93.3
1909	127.0	43.0	12.4	1,992.5	1,686.7	305.8	96.9	99.3	90.4	94.3	94.8
1910	203.3	48.3	12.6	2,049.7	1,728.0	321.7	100.0	100.9	93.5	95.3	97.6
1911	161.7	44.2	13.4	1,942.8	1,655.4	287.4	96.2	97.4	95.8	99.1	97.0
1912	303.4	41.9	14.2	2,154.1	1,854.9	299.2	102.8	98.6	66.2	97.6	97.9
1913	422.5	39.9	17.7	2,384.4	2,083.2	301.2	100.0	100.0	100.0	100.0	100.0
1914	203.2	36.9	23.7	2,043.8	1,758.7	285.2	101.4	96.5	94.4	100.3	93.1
1915	142.2	34.0	29.4	2,010.7	1,732.9	277.8	103.7	96.5	90.3	106.4	94.6
1916	363.4	37.4	32.5	2,627.8	2,309.5	318.2	120.6	117.6	90.4	120.5	119.0
1917	610.6	51.1	57.0	3,058.6	2,702.9	355.7	161.1	161.0	100.8	145.5	154.9
1918	734.0	50.6	119.2	3,217.5	2,824.6	392.8	182.8	206.2	121.9	175.7	174.5
1919 [1]	460.9	42.5	74.5	3,703.2	3,224.5	478.7	199.9	212.4	136.4	185.0	202.7
1919 [1]	560.7	—	62.0	3,508.1	—	—	196.5	219.0	134.5	184.1	202.7
1920	563.3	—	74.8	4,777.1	—	—	213.4	265.6	157.8	181.0	262.0
1921	313.6	—	48.8	2,956.7	—	—	146.5	173.8	139.8	164.5	172.2
1922	265.6	—	51.7	3,568.9	—	—	141.2	163.2	113.4	135.2	170.7
1923	635.5	—	64.7	4,647.3	—	—	147.7	177.6	108.2	138.7	190.4
1924	481.1	—	66.0	4,465.3	—	—	143.5	164.9	108.5	134.8	179.5
1925	353.1	—	74.9	4,950.4	—	—	154.3	160.0	103.3	135.0	178.5
1926	399.3	—	86.5	5,111.5	—	—	154.3	150.4	98.8	138.4	175.6
1927	318.5	—	87.7	4,845.2	—	—	146.9	137.4	104.0	138.5	166.6
1928	245.1	—	92.1	4,793.8	—	—	150.0	131.7	105.4	136.5	165.6
1929	347.6	—	109.6	5,007.5	—	—	147.4	130.7	106.4	131.1	167.8
1930	352.7	—	91.6	3,779.8	—	—	135.1	122.0	104.3	125.6	158.4
1931	78.0	—	48.6	2,552.1	—	—	114.1	109.2	99.8	117.2	140.2
1932	37.0	—	31.7	1,362.7	—	—	96.7	93.6	98.0	112.9	126.8
1933	13.6	—	32.0	1,536.1	—	—	95.0	105.0	96.8	104.6	136.0
1934	—	—	—	1,909.9	—	—	107.8 [4]	120.6 [4]	98.5 [4]	107.6 [4]	151.4
1935	33.0	—	36.4	2,375.0	—	—	122.4	119.2	93.6	99.6	149.8
1936	—	—	—	3,331.5	—	—	122.6 [4]	120.6 [4]	90.8 [4]	102.0 [4]	152.2
1937	119.1	—	49.8	3,945.8	—	—	126.4	132.6	91.9	112.1	167.3
1938	—	—	—	3,159.0	—	—	114.6 [4]	122.7 [4]	92.8 [4]	112.8 [4]	159.0
1939	—	—	—	3,701.6	—	—	110.6 [4]	123.1 [4]	92.1 [4]	110.4 [5]	159.0

[1] For 1869–1919, figures are Shaw's estimates; thereafter, Kuznets's estimates adjusted by Shaw. Both sets of values are shown for 1919. See Shaw, p. 104, for explanation.

[2] Agrees with source; however, figures for components do not add to total.

[3] Does not agree with source, which is in error.

[4] Indexes derived by weighting the individual group indexes by the average current price estimates for 1933, 1935, and 1937. The composite indexes thus calculated were used to interpolate and extrapolate the implicit indexes for 1933, 1935, and 1937.

[5] Based on the movement of the National Bureau of Economic Research price index for processed capital equipment goods.

(continued)

TABLE Dd437–493   Value of output of finished commodities and construction materials destined for domestic consumption: 1869–1939   *Continued*

Source
William H. Shaw, *Value of Commodity Output since 1869* (National Bureau of Economic Research, 1947), pp. 30, 66, 290.

Documentation
This table and its associated documentation have been reprinted, more or less without modification, from U.S. Bureau of the Census, *Historical Statistics of the United States* (1975), series P318–374.

These estimates are derived from Census of Manufactures data, supplemented by less complete data for nonmanufactured finished commodities and construction materials and for intercensal year interpolations. The estimates for the years prior to 1919 are based necessarily on less adequate information.

The estimates of finished commodities measure the value of commodities that have reached the form in which they are used by ultimate recipients – largely households in the case of consumers' goods, chiefly business and public enterprises in the case of producers' goods. The amount "destined for domestic consumption" is derived as the sum of domestic production, minus exports, plus imports. In most years and for most commodities,

the differences between domestic production of finished commodities and finished commodities destined for domestic consumption were modest. Changes in the latter, therefore, can be used as an approximate measure of changes in domestic manufacturing output. For figures on domestic output of finished commodities at producers' prices for 1919–1933, see Simon Kuznets, *Commodity Flow and Capital Formation*, volume 1 (National Bureau of Economic Research, 1938), pp. 136–8, 348.

The estimates presented here are at current producers' prices. They exclude transportation and distribution costs incurred after the production stage, and hence are not in terms of prices to final users. Nor do they measure domestic consumption, as they make no allowance for inventory changes.

Perishable commodities include those usually lasting less than six months; semidurable, those usually lasting from six months to three years; and durable, those usually lasting more than three years.

For a detailed discussion of sources and procedures, see the source: part 2 for estimates of the value of output; part 3 for exports and imports; and part 4 for price indexes.

TABLE Dd494–497   Indexes of manufacturing production: 1860–1966

Contributed by Jeremy Atack and Fred Bateman

	NBER						NBER			
	Kendrick	Fabricant	Census	Frickey			Kendrick	Fabricant	Census	Frickey
	Dd494	Dd495	Dd496	Dd497			Dd494	Dd495	Dd496	Dd497
Year	Index 1958 = 100	Index 1899 = 100	Index 1899 = 100	Index 1899 = 100		Year	Index 1958 = 100	Index 1899 = 100	Index 1899 = 100	Index 1899 = 100
1860	—	—	—	16		1895	—	—	—	81
1861	—	—	—	16		1896	—	—	—	74
1862	—	—	—	15		1897	—	—	—	80
1863	—	—	—	17		1898	—	—	—	91
1864	—	—	—	18		1899	—	100	100	100
1865	—	—	—	17		1900	—	102	—	100
1866	—	—	—	21		1901	—	115	—	111
1867	—	—	—	22		1902	—	129	—	127
1868	—	—	—	23		1903	—	132	—	126
1869	—	—	—	25		1904	—	124	122	121
1870	—	—	—	25		1905	—	148	—	140
1871	—	—	—	26		1906	—	159	—	152
1872	—	—	—	31		1907	—	161	—	156
1873	—	—	—	30		1908	—	133	—	127
1874	—	—	—	29		1909	—	158	159	166
1875	—	—	—	28		1910	—	168	—	172
1876	—	—	—	28		1911	—	161	—	162
1877	—	—	—	30		1912	—	185	—	194
1878	—	—	—	32		1913	—	198	—	203
1879	—	—	—	36		1914	—	186	170	192
1880	—	—	—	42		1915	—	218	—	—
1881	—	—	—	46		1916	—	259	—	—
1882	—	—	—	49		1917	—	257	—	—
1883	—	—	—	50		1918	—	254	—	—
1884	—	—	—	47		1919	—	222	214	—
1885	—	—	—	47		1920	—	242	—	—
1886	—	—	—	57		1921	—	194	169	—
1887	—	—	—	60		1922	—	249	—	—
1888	—	—	—	62		1923	—	280	263	—
1889	—	—	—	66		1924	—	266	—	—
1890	—	—	—	71		1925	—	298	275	—
1891	—	—	—	73		1926	—	316	—	—
1892	—	—	—	79		1927	—	317	274	—
1893	—	—	—	70		1928	—	332	—	—
1894	—	—	—	68		1929	56	364	311	—

TABLE Dd494–497   Indexes of manufacturing production: 1860–1966   *Continued*

	NBER						NBER			
	Kendrick	Fabricant	Census	Frickey			Kendrick	Fabricant	Census	Frickey
	Dd494	Dd495	Dd496	Dd497			Dd494	Dd495	Dd496	Dd497
Year	Index 1958 = 100	Index 1899 = 100	Index 1899 = 100	Index 1899 = 100		Year	Index 1958 = 100	Index 1899 = 100	Index 1899 = 100	Index 1899 = 100
1930	54	311	—	—		1950	87	—	—	—
1931	52	262	206	—		1951	86	—	—	—
1932	46	197	—	—		1952	86	—	—	—
1933	53	228	192	—		1953	90	—	—	—
1934	57	252	—	—		1954	91	—	—	—
1935	63	301	233	—		1955	98	—	—	—
1936	66	353	—	—		1956	99	—	—	—
1937	66	376	303	—		1957	100	—	—	—
1938	60	—	—	—		1958	100	—	—	—
1939	69	—	—	—		1959	107	—	—	—
1940	74	—	—	—		1960	109	—	—	—
1941	80	—	—	—		1961	113	—	—	—
1942	83	—	—	—		1962	117	—	—	—
1943	87	—	—	—		1963	121	—	—	—
1944	86	—	—	—		1964	125	—	—	—
1945	82	—	—	—		1965	129	—	—	—
1946	73	—	—	—		1966	131	—	—	—
1947	76	—	—	—						
1948	78	—	—	—						
1949	79	—	—	—						

Sources

Series Dd494. John W. Kendrick, *Postwar Productivity Trends in the United States, 1948–1969* (National Bureau of Economic Research, 1973), Table A 32.

Series Dd495–496. Base data from U.S. Bureau of the Census, unpublished data. Indexes from Solomon Fabricant, *The Output of Manufacturing Industries, 1899–1937* (National Bureau of Economic Research, 1940), Tables 1 and 2, pp. 44 and 48.

Series Dd497. Edwin Frickey, *Production in the United States, 1860–1914,* Harvard Economic Studies (Harvard University Press, 1947), p. 54.

Documentation

The indexes from the Federal Reserve Board (see Table Dd498–560) and Edwin Frickey (series Dd497) are measures of manufacturing production. Those by Fabricant and Day–Thomas (series Dd494–496) are measures of physical volume produced by all manufacturing industries. In some cases, these indexes were derived from physical output series. In other cases, they were based on gross product series deflated by price indexes. The breakdown and complete composition of each is not noted. These data were then benchmarked against the Census–Federal Reserve Board (FRB) production indexes for 1947, 1954, 1958, and 1963, interpolated and extrapolated to 1966 by the FRB indexes of manufacturing production.

Series Dd494. Kendrick's series uses (mostly) unpublished gross output indexes at the two-digit Standard Industrial Classification (SIC) level, assembled by the Office of Business Economics (subsequently renamed the Bureau of Economic Analysis) and described in a number of *Survey of Current Business* articles in the late 1960s, as the basis for his index of manufacturing output (see Kendrick 1973, pp. 177–80, 183–6). See the Introduction to Part D for a discussion of SIC codes. Making use of the figures for series Dd494–496 and other data, Kendrick has constructed another index of manufacturing (not reported here), with 1929 as the base, for benchmark years 1869, 1879, and 1889, and annually thereafter through 1953. See Appendix Table D-II for

figures and Appendix D for description of this index in Kendrick's *Productivity Trends in the United States* (National Bureau of Economic Research, 1961).

Series Dd495. Fabricant prepared a number of different indexes of manufacturing output based on physical production data, most of it derived from the census and based on indexes for individual industries with interpolation in noncensus years. The index reported here is that from Table 1, "All Manufacturing Industries Combined: Indexes of Physical Output" (p. 44), using an 1899 base, which was Fabricant's standard for comparison. The technical considerations underlying this index are set forth in Appendix A of *The Output of Manufacturing Industries,* and the individual underlying data are set out in Appendix B.

Series Dd496. This index was originally presented by Fabricant and is based on indexes derived by a number of researchers, several of them associated at various times with the Bureau of the Census. It is a composite of several different indexes all based on physical production data from the Censuses of Manufactures. The index for 1899–1914 was by W. M Persons and E. S. Coyle; for 1914–1925, by E. E. Day and Woodlief Thomas; for 1927–1931, by Aryness Joy; for 1933–1935, by V. S. Kolesnikoff; and for 1937, by C. L. Dedrick. See E. E. Day and Woodlief Thomas, *The Growth of Manufactures, 1899 to 1923,* Census Monograph number 7 (U.S. Bureau of the Census, 1928), pp. 23, 34; V. S. Kolesnikoff, "Index of Manufacturing Production Derived from Census Data, 1935," *Journal of the American Statistical Association* 32 (December 1937): 713–14; *Biennial Census of Manufactures: 1937,* part 1 (Bureau of the Census, 1939), pp. 12, 17.

Series Dd497. In deriving this index, Frickey employed the weighted arithmetic mean of quantity relatives. With respect to weighting, he took the value-added principle as his standard and conformed to this standard as nearly as possible with existing data. For details on constituent series, see Frickey (1947), Appendixes A and B.

TABLE Dd498–560   Indexes of industrial production, by market group: 1919–2001
Contributed by Jeremy Atack and Fred Bateman

Products — Final products — Consumer goods — Durable — Automotive — Autos and trucks — Other — Household appliances and electronics

Year	Final products Total Dd498	Consumer goods Total Dd499	Durable Total Dd500	Total Dd501	Total Dd502	Total Dd503	Autos and trucks Total Dd504	Auto Dd505	Light trucks Dd506	Auto parts and allied goods Dd507	Total Dd508	Household appliances and electronics Total Dd509	Appliances Dd510	Electronics Dd511	Carpeting and furniture Dd512	Miscellaneous Dd513
	Index 1992 = 100	Index 1992 = 100	Index 1992 = 100	Index 1992 = 100	Index 1992 = 100	Index 1992 = 100	Index 1992 = 100	Index 1992 = 100	Index 1992 = 100	Index 1992 = 100	Index 1992 = 100	Index 1992 = 100	Index 1992 = 100	Index 1992 = 100	Index 1992 = 100	Index 1992 = 100
1919	7.7	—	—	—	—	—	—	—	—	—	—	—	—	—	—	—
1920	8.1	—	—	—	—	—	—	—	—	—	—	—	—	—	—	—
1921	6.2	—	—	—	—	—	—	—	—	—	—	—	—	—	—	—
1922	7.9	—	—	—	—	—	—	—	—	—	—	—	—	—	—	—
1923	9.4	—	—	—	—	—	—	—	—	—	—	—	—	—	—	—
1924	8.9	—	—	—	—	—	—	—	—	—	—	—	—	—	—	—
1925	9.7	—	—	—	—	—	—	—	—	—	—	—	—	—	—	—
1926	10.3	—	—	—	—	—	—	—	—	—	—	—	—	—	—	—
1927	10.3	—	—	—	—	—	—	—	—	—	—	—	—	—	—	—
1928	10.7	—	—	—	—	—	—	—	—	—	—	—	—	—	—	—
1929	11.9	—	—	—	—	—	—	—	—	—	—	—	—	—	—	—
1930	9.9	—	—	—	—	—	—	—	—	—	—	—	—	—	—	—
1931	8.2	—	—	—	—	—	—	—	—	—	—	—	—	—	—	—
1932	6.4	—	—	—	—	—	—	—	—	—	—	—	—	—	—	—
1933	7.6	—	—	—	—	—	—	—	—	—	—	—	—	—	—	—
1934	8.2	—	—	—	—	—	—	—	—	—	—	—	—	—	—	—
1935	9.5	—	—	—	—	—	—	—	—	—	—	—	—	—	—	—
1936	11.2	—	—	—	—	—	—	—	—	—	—	—	—	—	—	—
1937	12.3	—	—	—	—	—	—	—	—	—	—	—	—	—	—	—
1938	9.7	—	—	—	—	—	—	—	—	—	—	—	—	—	—	—
1939	11.9	11.8	11.5	14.5	—	—	—	—	—	—	—	—	—	—	—	—
1940	13.8	13.2	12.9	15.3	—	—	—	—	—	—	—	—	—	—	—	—
1941	17.4	16.8	16.6	18.4	—	—	—	—	—	—	—	—	—	—	—	—
1942	20.0	19.2	19.5	17.0	—	—	—	—	—	—	—	—	—	—	—	—
1943	24.3	23.8	24.9	17.3	—	—	—	—	—	—	—	—	—	—	—	—
1944	26.1	25.9	27.3	18.1	—	—	—	—	—	—	—	—	—	—	—	—
1945	22.3	21.9	22.4	18.7	—	—	—	—	—	—	—	—	—	—	—	—
1946	19.3	19.1	18.9	22.4	—	—	—	—	—	—	—	—	—	—	—	—
1947	21.7	21.3	21.0	23.8	19.8	22.5	—	—	—	21.0	18.6	8.4	—	—	26.2	29.7
1948	22.6	22.2	21.8	24.5	20.7	23.5	—	—	—	20.6	19.4	9.0	—	—	28.1	29.7
1949	21.4	21.4	21.1	24.3	19.5	23.3	—	—	—	15.4	17.9	8.5	—	—	25.3	27.0
1950	24.7	24.4	23.8	27.8	26.3	29.4	—	—	—	18.2	24.9	14.9	—	—	31.9	30.2
1951	26.8	26.1	25.7	27.5	22.7	26.0	—	—	—	18.0	21.3	11.6	—	—	27.0	29.4
1952	27.9	27.5	27.6	28.1	22.0	23.5	—	—	—	17.8	21.3	11.4	—	—	28.7	29.3
1953	30.2	29.4	29.5	29.9	25.8	29.5	—	—	—	19.6	24.2	13.7	—	—	29.7	32.3
1954	28.5	28.1	27.8	29.6	23.9	27.3	—	—	—	19.1	22.2	12.3	—	—	31.7	28.5

	Products														
	Final products														
	Consumer goods														
						Durable									
						Automotive					Other				
						Autos and trucks					Household appliances and electronics				
	Total	Total	Total	Total	Total	Total	Total	Auto	Light trucks	Auto parts and allied goods	Total	Total	Appliances	Electronics	Carpeting and furniture	Miscellaneous
	Dd498	Dd499	Dd500	Dd501	Dd502	Dd503	Dd504	Dd505	Dd506	Dd507	Dd508	Dd509	Dd510	Dd511	Dd512	Dd513
Year	Index 1992 = 100	Index 1992 = 100	Index 1992 = 100	Index 1992 = 100	Index 1992 = 100	Index 1992 = 100	Index 1992 = 100	Index 1992 = 100	Index 1992 = 100	Index 1992 = 100	Index 1992 = 100	Index 1992 = 100	Index 1992 = 100	Index 1992 = 100	Index 1992 = 100	Index 1992 = 100
1955	32.1	30.8	30.1	33.1	29.5	36.7	—	—	—	22.4	26.3	14.2	—	—	36.9	34.4
1956	33.5	32.5	31.9	34.2	28.5	29.9	—	—	—	23.2	27.6	15.3	—	—	38.1	35.9
1957	34.0	33.2	32.8	35.1	28.5	31.6	—	—	—	24.4	27.0	14.2	—	—	38.5	35.7
1958	31.8	31.8	31.3	34.7	25.2	24.7	—	—	—	24.8	25.5	13.6	—	—	37.3	33.0
1959	35.6	35.0	34.4	38.2	30.0	31.5	—	—	—	27.9	29.3	16.3	—	—	42.5	37.0
1960	36.4	36.0	35.5	39.6	31.6	36.0	—	—	—	27.8	29.5	16.1	—	—	40.6	38.8
1961	36.7	36.3	35.8	40.4	31.2	33.0	—	—	—	29.0	30.4	16.8	—	—	39.7	40.5
1962	39.7	39.2	38.8	43.2	35.3	39.9	—	—	—	31.6	33.1	18.6	—	—	44.5	42.9
1963	42.2	41.5	41.1	45.6	38.3	43.6	—	—	—	33.5	35.7	20.5	—	—	47.8	46.0
1964	45.0	44.0	43.5	48.2	41.2	45.9	—	—	—	37.4	38.9	22.8	—	—	52.1	49.5
1965	49.5	47.9	47.7	51.9	48.2	56.3	—	—	—	40.9	44.1	26.8	—	—	56.2	56.1
1966	53.8	52.1	52.2	54.6	50.9	55.5	—	—	—	44.3	48.7	30.8	—	—	59.6	61.4
1967	55.0	54.3	54.4	56.0	49.1	49.2	51.9	—	10.0	44.3	49.3	30.3	53.9	—	59.7	63.3
1968	58.1	56.9	56.9	59.3	54.6	58.6	63.5	—	13.5	49.2	52.7	32.5	57.6	—	64.3	67.4
1969	60.7	59.0	58.8	61.5	57.1	59.1	62.5	—	15.1	52.7	56.3	34.7	62.1	—	66.6	73.0
1970	58.7	57.2	56.7	60.8	52.6	49.7	49.3	—	14.2	51.3	54.6	34.0	63.3	—	64.2	70.5
1971	59.5	58.0	57.2	64.3	59.6	63.3	67.7	—	20.0	55.1	57.7	35.8	65.5	—	69.1	74.3
1972	65.3	63.4	62.0	69.5	66.7	68.4	72.3	130.5	25.7	61.2	66.1	40.8	74.6	—	83.3	83.3
1973	70.6	68.0	66.7	72.6	71.8	75.2	82.8	141.9	33.3	62.8	70.0	45.7	84.4	—	88.5	84.1
1974	69.6	67.2	66.4	70.3	64.4	65.0	66.1	102.6	31.4	61.7	64.7	42.2	79.6	—	80.4	78.7
1975	63.5	62.8	62.6	67.7	58.7	61.8	60.7	93.7	28.0	61.6	56.9	34.4	64.2	—	70.2	73.7
1976	69.3	67.6	67.0	74.3	68.8	76.3	82.8	126.1	39.7	65.4	63.8	38.5	72.2	—	79.3	82.5
1977	74.9	73.2	72.4	79.5	77.9	87.2	95.4	136.3	49.9	73.6	71.8	44.4	80.2	—	89.7	91.2
1978	79.3	77.8	77.2	82.6	80.7	89.6	97.8	133.6	55.5	75.8	74.9	47.1	82.2	—	95.8	92.7
1979	82.0	80.2	79.7	81.5	76.7	81.4	87.5	123.8	46.6	70.4	73.6	47.3	84.2	—	96.4	88.3
1980	79.7	78.9	79.3	79.6	66.9	62.3	61.5	97.5	24.6	59.3	69.7	45.9	79.3	—	88.9	83.4
1981	81.0	80.4	81.2	80.1	67.2	61.6	61.2	93.9	27.0	58.3	70.7	46.2	79.7	—	87.8	86.3
1982	76.7	77.7	78.3	78.8	62.5	59.1	57.2	77.8	34.0	57.4	64.4	40.6	69.7	21.6	78.8	81.2
1983	79.5	80.2	80.0	83.2	73.8	74.3	79.9	110.5	45.7	64.7	73.1	54.0	82.0	33.9	87.8	82.6
1984	86.6	86.9	87.0	86.7	84.1	89.4	96.0	127.0	60.5	77.8	80.1	61.7	91.5	39.9	94.2	88.6
1985	88.0	89.2	89.3	87.6	84.7	95.4	103.9	134.8	68.0	81.6	77.3	58.1	85.4	38.1	92.9	85.9
1986	89.0	90.9	90.3	90.7	88.7	97.5	104.1	132.7	70.8	85.8	82.6	66.8	90.4	48.6	98.3	86.8
1987	93.2	95.1	93.3	93.7	93.9	100.7	104.0	123.9	80.1	94.1	89.1	73.0	95.7	55.2	103.5	94.2
1988	97.4	99.0	97.9	96.7	99.8	107.1	111.1	131.1	87.0	99.3	94.5	84.2	100.2	70.7	103.4	97.5
1989	99.1	100.6	99.9	97.7	101.3	108.9	114.0	131.5	92.5	99.2	95.9	86.3	101.7	73.3	103.5	99.0

(continued)

TABLE Dd498–560   Indexes of industrial production, by market group: 1919–2001   Continued

Year	Total Dd498	Total Dd499	Total Dd500	Total Dd501	Total Dd502	Total Dd503	Autos and trucks Total Dd504	Auto Dd505	Light trucks Dd506	Auto parts and allied goods Dd507	Total Dd508	Household appliances and electronics Total Dd509	Appliances Dd510	Electronics Dd511	Carpeting and furniture Dd512	Miscellaneous Dd513
	Index 1992=100	Index 1992=100	Index 1992=100	Index 1992=100	Index 1992=100	Index 1992=100	Index 1992=100	Index 1992=100	Index 1992=100	Index 1992=100	Index 1992=100	Index 1992=100	Index 1992=100	Index 1992=100	Index 1992=100	Index 1992=100
1990	98.9	100.1	99.5	97.3	98.0	100.9	103.3	115.2	88.4	96.1	96.0	87.7	98.2	78.9	100.8	99.4
1991	97.0	97.6	97.7	97.0	93.0	90.3	89.6	94.5	83.4	91.6	95.2	92.5	91.9	93.1	94.5	97.3
1992	100.0	100.0	100.0	100.0	100.0	100.0	100.0	100.0	100.0	100.0	100.0	100.0	100.0	100.0	100.0	100.0
1993	103.4	103.3	103.5	103.4	112.0	112.8	116.9	110.1	125.7	106.1	111.4	126.9	109.7	148.7	104.4	106.2
1994	109.1	107.6	108.0	107.8	124.2	126.2	136.5	128.6	146.6	110.1	122.8	159.6	123.7	211.7	108.4	111.0
1995	114.4	111.0	112.0	110.6	128.6	127.2	136.7	125.0	150.9	112.4	129.7	184.9	116.7	304.5	108.8	112.9
1996	119.6	115.0	116.4	112.6	131.8	129.6	138.4	118.6	161.1	115.9	133.4	197.7	118.8	341.2	110.4	114.0
1997	127.9	121.7	123.5	115.9	138.2	134.7	145.0	109.5	183.4	118.5	140.9	214.8	120.8	395.0	113.0	120.2
1998	134.5	126.8	128.9	118.3	146.4	140.1	150.1	106.5	196.6	124.5	151.7	253.0	128.9	506.8	122.1	121.7
1999	139.4	129.6	131.8	119.9	158.6	156.3	171.1	107.9	238.6	133.3	160.1	282.7	131.7	611.8	126.3	124.8
2000	145.7	133.5	135.8	121.9	161.2	157.0	169.8	104.4	239.5	137.2	164.6	304.9	138.0	679.6	128.8	125.0
2001	140.4	129.6	132.3	120.9	152.1	151.3	162.8	94.8	235.1	133.4	151.6	283.4	137.0	572.6	119.2	114.2

Year	Total Dd514 [1]	Total Dd515 [1]	Food and tobacco Dd516 [1]	Clothing Dd517 [1]	Chemical products Dd518 [1]	Paper products Dd519 [1]	Total Dd520 [1]	Fuels Dd521 [1]	Residential utilities Dd522 [1]	Total Dd523 [1]	Total Dd524 [1]	Total Dd525 [1]	Office and computing Dd526 [1]	Industrial Dd527 [1]	Total Dd528 [1]	Autos and trucks Dd529 [1]	Other Dd530 [1]
	Index 1992=100	Index 1992=100	Index 1992=100	Index 1992=100	Index 1992=100	Index 1992=100	Index 1992=100	Index 1992=100	Index 1992=100	Index 1992=100	Index 1992=100	Index 1992=100	Index 1992=100	Index 1992=100	Index 1992=100	Index 1992=100	Index 1992=100
1939	—	—	—	—	—	—	—	—	—	6.1	—	—	—	—	—	—	—
1940	—	—	—	—	—	—	—	—	—	8.6	—	—	—	—	—	—	—
1941	—	—	—	—	—	—	—	—	—	13.6	—	—	—	—	—	—	—
1942	—	—	—	—	—	—	—	—	—	24.4	—	—	—	—	—	—	—
1943	—	—	—	—	—	—	—	—	—	39.4	—	—	—	—	—	—	—
1944	—	—	—	—	—	—	—	—	—	44.9	—	—	—	—	—	—	—
1945	—	—	—	—	—	—	—	—	—	29.6	—	—	—	—	—	—	—
1946	—	—	—	—	—	—	—	—	—	12.8	—	—	—	—	—	—	—
1947	25.5	—	33.4	55.7	—	—	—	—	—	16.4	16.1	—	—	—	—	—	—
1948	26.2	—	32.9	58.2	—	—	—	—	—	17.2	16.8	—	—	—	—	—	—
1949	26.4	—	33.1	56.8	—	—	—	—	—	15.4	14.7	—	—	—	—	—	—

Products

Year	Total [1] Dd514	Consumer goods — Nondurable — Nonenergy — Total [1] Dd515	Food and tobacco [1] Dd516	Clothing [1] Dd517	Chemical products [1] Dd518	Paper products [1] Dd519	Total [1] Dd520	Energy — Fuels [1] Dd521	Residential utilities [1] Dd522	Total [1] Dd523	Final products — Total [1] Dd524	Equipment — Business — Information processing and related — Total [1] Dd525	Office and computing [1] Dd526	Industrial [1] Dd527	Transit — Total [1] Dd528	Autos and trucks [1] Dd529	Other [1] Dd530
	Index 1992=100	Index 1992=100	Index 1992=100	Index 1992=100	Index 1992=100	Index 1992=100	Index 1992=100	Index 1992=100	Index 1992=100	Index 1992=100	Index 1992=100	Index 1992=100	Index 1992=100	Index 1992=100	Index 1992=100	Index 1992=100	Index 1992=100
1950	28.6	—	34.3	62.7	—	—	—	—	—	16.7	15.7	—	—	—	—	—	—
1951	29.7	—	35.1	61.0	—	—	—	—	—	23.2	19.2	—	—	—	—	—	—
1952	30.9	—	35.9	64.1	—	—	—	—	—	27.8	21.7	—	—	—	—	—	—
1953	31.7	—	36.4	65.3	—	—	—	—	—	30.2	22.6	—	—	—	—	—	—
1954	32.1	—	36.9	63.4	11.6	33.3	25.3	46.6	18.0	26.4	19.8	—	—	—	22.1	—	—
1955	34.5	—	38.9	69.7	13.1	35.1	27.6	49.8	19.9	26.9	21.5	—	—	—	24.2	—	—
1956	36.7	—	41.1	71.3	15.0	36.9	30.4	53.4	22.2	29.6	24.9	—	—	—	29.3	—	—
1957	37.9	—	41.8	71.3	16.5	39.2	32.3	54.0	24.0	30.8	25.9	—	—	—	35.8	—	—
1958	39.0	—	43.0	70.2	17.9	40.2	33.8	52.6	25.9	27.5	21.8	—	—	—	27.0	—	—
1959	41.8	—	44.9	76.7	19.9	43.1	36.4	55.8	28.1	30.2	24.6	—	—	—	29.7	—	—
1960	43.1	—	46.3	76.5	21.1	44.8	38.6	56.9	30.2	31.1	25.2	—	—	—	30.8	—	—
1961	44.5	—	47.5	77.8	22.7	45.4	40.6	58.2	32.1	30.6	24.5	—	—	—	28.4	—	—
1962	46.6	—	49.0	81.1	24.7	46.6	43.5	60.8	34.7	34.1	26.6	—	—	—	30.8	—	—
1963	48.7	—	50.6	83.8	27.0	47.7	46.1	64.1	36.8	36.2	27.9	—	—	—	33.4	—	—
1964	51.1	—	52.9	87.1	28.6	50.2	49.1	65.3	40.0	38.2	31.3	—	—	—	37.1	—	—
1965	53.3	—	54.1	91.2	31.7	52.2	51.5	66.3	42.4	43.2	35.8	—	—	—	46.6	—	—
1966	55.9	—	55.9	93.1	34.6	55.9	54.9	69.3	45.6	50.4	41.5	—	—	—	58.2	—	—
1967	58.8	58.4	58.3	94.0	36.8	59.6	59.6	71.4	49.6	53.6	42.3	11.8	1.9	98.5	59.3	40.5	60.9
1968	61.1	60.4	59.8	97.3	40.2	59.0	63.8	75.2	53.8	55.1	44.1	13.3	2.1	97.7	66.2	48.4	62.3
1969	63.1	62.1	61.4	98.8	42.2	61.0	68.2	78.2	58.7	56.6	47.0	14.8	2.6	104.1	65.3	49.3	65.9
1970	64.2	62.8	62.3	95.9	45.9	58.9	72.1	81.8	62.7	52.5	45.3	15.3	2.7	100.9	57.3	39.4	63.0
1971	66.0	64.4	64.2	95.5	48.5	60.1	75.5	85.1	66.0	49.2	43.1	14.2	2.3	94.4	55.3	46.7	64.7
1972	70.3	68.6	67.8	103.9	53.0	60.6	79.8	89.3	69.9	53.8	49.1	16.6	2.8	104.7	60.4	50.1	79.7
1973	72.4	70.6	69.8	104.4	57.0	60.8	83.2	93.6	72.7	60.1	57.5	19.6	3.5	120.0	72.8	59.7	93.9
1974	72.4	70.7	70.2	99.3	59.7	62.1	82.3	90.4	72.8	62.0	60.0	21.8	4.1	126.0	70.3	54.2	92.9
1975	71.0	68.7	70.2	92.0	57.9	59.2	85.2	91.6	76.1	56.8	53.6	20.5	3.7	109.5	64.2	50.5	77.4
1976	76.2	74.3	74.3	103.8	63.2	63.4	86.8	97.2	76.0	58.8	55.5	22.3	4.5	108.8	61.8	61.5	86.9
1977	79.8	78.2	77.0	108.8	65.9	71.4	88.0	102.6	77.0	64.3	62.0	26.0	6.0	118.2	65.8	71.4	94.9
1978	82.9	81.6	80.0	111.4	70.1	76.1	89.8	102.6	79.7	71.0	69.3	31.8	8.9	125.3	76.7	74.9	97.4
1979	82.9	81.7	80.8	106.7	71.6	77.2	88.9	99.1	81.0	77.6	77.3	38.6	12.2	130.8	88.1	70.9	106.0
1980	83.8	83.4	82.4	107.5	75.0	77.9	85.8	91.1	82.7	79.1	76.7	43.3	16.4	126.5	81.3	53.6	95.7
1981	84.3	84.1	83.9	107.1	73.3	80.4	85.1	90.0	82.3	82.8	78.0	48.1	21.7	126.5	74.6	55.5	94.9
1982	84.2	84.1	84.7	105.8	71.0	82.1	85.2	89.1	83.3	77.7	70.6	51.2	25.2	103.7	62.0	49.3	84.1
1983	86.2	86.4	86.6	107.9	73.4	85.9	85.3	87.8	84.3	76.4	68.3	56.0	33.4	87.3	58.4	64.2	85.3
1984	87.5	87.5	88.2	106.4	73.5	90.1	87.7	91.6	86.0	87.6	79.2	67.9	48.6	98.1	67.0	80.9	95.2

Notes appear at end of table

(continued)

TABLE Dd498-560 Indexes of industrial production, by market group: 1919–2001 *Continued*

Products — Final products (years 1985–2001)

All series are Index 1992 = 100 [1].

Year	Consumer goods Total Dd514	Nonenergy Total Dd515	Food and tobacco Dd516	Clothing Dd517	Chemical products Dd518	Paper products Dd519	Energy Total Dd520	Fuels Dd521	Residential utilities Dd522	Equipment Total Dd523	Business Total Dd524	Info. processing Total Dd525	Office and computing Dd526	Industrial Dd527	Transit Total Dd528	Autos and trucks Dd529	Other Dd530
1985	88.5	88.5	90.6	100.8	74.5	92.1	88.5	91.2	87.3	91.8	82.5	74.9	58.8	97.4	73.0	91.6	90.5
1986	91.3	91.5	92.8	102.1	80.3	94.7	90.7	95.4	88.8	90.0	82.0	73.8	58.9	95.6	74.6	92.2	91.8
1987	93.6	93.8	95.3	104.2	83.0	96.4	92.7	95.6	91.3	92.9	85.1	78.9	67.3	95.4	75.4	92.5	98.4
1988	95.9	95.7	96.9	102.2	87.6	98.3	97.0	97.9	96.5	99.9	93.5	86.3	77.9	105.2	84.9	94.1	105.5
1989	96.7	96.4	97.4	100.1	89.7	100.2	98.3	98.2	98.2	103.7	98.8	90.7	88.4	109.6	94.4	96.0	109.5
1990	97.1	97.1	98.3	96.6	92.4	100.6	97.7	98.5	97.2	103.2	98.2	90.5	84.1	107.3	95.2	93.7	108.7
1991	98.1	97.8	98.5	97.6	95.1	99.6	100.4	99.0	100.9	98.8	95.7	91.1	79.9	100.9	96.4	91.6	98.2
1992	100.0	100.0	100.0	100.0	100.0	100.0	100.0	100.0	100.0	100.0	100.0	100.0	100.0	100.0	100.0	100.0	100.0
1993	101.3	100.7	99.2	102.3	102.1	102.5	105.2	102.5	106.3	103.7	105.6	106.9	112.1	106.4	100.1	110.6	108.6
1994	103.6	103.6	103.5	105.1	104.4	101.8	105.1	101.9	106.4	108.3	113.2	116.3	131.1	116.3	100.5	128.1	115.1
1995	106.0	106.0	105.8	104.4	108.6	103.7	107.7	104.3	109.0	114.5	122.0	130.6	172.8	126.7	97.4	130.1	121.8
1996	107.9	107.3	106.2	102.4	114.7	103.3	112.4	106.8	114.7	122.9	133.4	154.5	252.9	131.0	101.9	124.6	126.0
1997	110.5	110.3	107.2	101.3	121.8	110.4	111.5	109.3	112.0	136.9	152.3	187.1	367.1	136.8	123.1	139.7	136.5
1998	111.6	111.6	109.1	95.0	128.0	107.7	111.9	110.6	112.1	148.1	167.1	214.4	496.8	137.9	143.8	145.0	143.9
1999	110.8	110.4	108.0	91.9	129.7	103.9	113.8	111.4	114.6	153.5	176.6	247.5	678.9	135.1	149.3	167.2	137.4
2000	112.7	112.1	109.4	86.4	134.8	106.3	117.0	112.9	118.7	161.8	188.9	290.8	914.2	138.3	143.4	170.1	143.2
2001	113.4	112.8	108.7	78.4	145.4	105.7	117.2	114.0	118.7	152.7	176.3	279.8	948.1	125.3	128.6	147.2	139.2

Products — Final products (Equipment) / Intermediate products / Materials (years 1939–1949)

All series are Index 1992 = 100 [1].

Year	Defense and space Dd531	Oil and gas well drilling Dd532	Manufactured homes Dd533	Intermediate products Total Dd534	Construction supplies Dd535	Business supplies Dd536	Materials Total Dd537	Durable goods Total Dd538	Parts Consumer Dd539	Parts Equipment Dd540	Other Total Dd541	Basic metals Dd542	Nondurable Total Dd543	Textile Dd544	Paper Dd545
1939	—	—	—	13.4	—	—	12.0	—	—	—	—	—	—	—	—
1940	—	—	—	14.8	—	—	14.5	—	—	—	—	—	—	—	—
1941	—	—	—	17.8	—	—	18.2	—	—	—	—	—	—	—	—
1942	—	—	—	18.1	—	—	21.0	—	—	—	—	—	—	—	—
1943	—	—	—	19.2	—	—	24.8	—	—	—	—	—	—	—	—
1944	—	—	—	20.2	—	—	26.1	—	—	—	—	—	—	—	—
1945	—	—	—	19.8	—	—	22.9	—	—	—	—	—	—	—	—
1946	—	—	—	20.0	—	—	19.5	—	—	—	—	—	—	—	—
1947	8.2	—	—	22.5	31.2	17.2	22.0	18.3	32.7	6.1	—	54.5	—	—	—
1948	9.7	—	—	23.8	33.4	18.0	23.0	18.8	35.1	6.0	—	56.4	—	—	—
1949	10.1	—	—	22.6	30.6	17.8	21.0	16.9	37.3	5.3	—	47.3	—	—	—

	Products						Materials								
	Final products				Intermediate products				Durable goods				Nondurable goods		
		Equipment							Parts			Other			
Year	Defense and space	Oil and gas well drilling	Manufactured homes	Total	Construction supplies	Business supplies	Total	Total	Consumer	Equipment	Total	Basic metals	Total	Textile	Paper
	Dd531 [1]	Dd532 [1]	Dd533 [1]	Dd534 [1]	Dd535 [1]	Dd536 [1]	Dd537 [1]	Dd538 [1]	Dd539 [1]	Dd540 [1]	Dd541 [1]	Dd542 [1]	Dd543 [1]	Dd544 [1]	Dd545 [1]
	Index 1992 = 100	Index 1992 = 100	Index 1992 = 100	Index 1992 = 100	Index 1992 = 100	Index 1992 = 100	Index 1992 = 100	Index 1992 = 100	Index 1992 = 100	Index 1992 = 100	Index 1992 = 100	Index 1992 = 100	Index 1992 = 100	Index 1992 = 100	Index 1992 = 100
1950	11.9	—	—	26.3	36.8	19.8	25.1	21.2	50.2	6.5	—	59.1	—	—	—
1951	29.2	—	—	27.6	38.3	21.0	27.8	24.2	46.5	8.7	—	64.1	—	—	—
1952	41.1	—	—	27.4	38.1	20.9	28.1	24.7	43.7	10.1	—	59.3	—	—	—
1953	49.2	—	—	29.3	40.9	22.2	31.3	28.9	56.1	11.9	—	66.0	—	—	—
1954	43.3	86.5	—	29.2	40.2	22.5	28.8	24.9	47.0	10.1	35.0	55.6	23.0	—	—
1955	39.6	94.0	—	33.1	46.2	25.2	34.1	30.5	62.2	11.0	43.2	71.2	26.3	—	—
1956	38.7	97.0	—	34.6	47.6	26.7	35.0	30.6	55.4	12.2	44.0	71.5	27.5	—	—
1957	40.4	91.9	—	34.6	46.9	27.1	35.0	30.5	56.8	12.2	43.4	69.1	27.4	—	—
1958	40.6	81.8	—	33.8	45.3	26.8	31.5	25.7	44.7	10.2	37.9	57.1	27.2	—	—
1959	42.8	88.7	—	37.4	50.8	29.2	36.3	30.6	56.2	12.3	43.7	64.4	31.1	—	—
1960	44.0	83.1	—	37.6	49.6	30.2	36.8	31.0	57.7	12.2	44.4	66.1	31.6	—	—
1961	44.7	85.8	—	38.3	49.9	31.1	36.9	30.3	51.2	12.4	44.4	65.7	33.0	—	—
1962	51.8	91.0	—	40.7	53.0	33.1	40.1	33.6	59.5	14.1	47.8	69.8	35.7	—	—
1963	55.8	91.3	—	43.0	55.5	35.2	42.7	35.9	63.2	15.2	51.0	74.4	37.9	—	—
1964	54.1	97.0	—	45.8	58.9	37.7	46.2	39.2	65.5	16.7	56.7	84.0	41.2	—	—
1965	59.8	100.3	—	48.8	62.5	40.2	51.5	44.9	78.6	20.3	61.7	91.4	45.2	—	—
1966	70.3	99.3	—	51.8	65.2	43.3	56.1	49.4	80.7	24.0	67.6	98.0	48.8	—	—
1967	80.2	90.8	—	53.9	66.9	45.6	55.6	47.7	74.6	23.8	65.3	89.4	49.7	73.5	51.7
1968	80.4	94.7	—	57.0	70.3	48.4	59.2	50.5	84.1	24.3	68.7	93.1	54.6	81.2	54.1
1969	76.5	97.9	—	60.1	73.4	51.4	62.8	53.2	84.6	26.0	73.2	102.2	59.1	83.4	58.7
1970	64.8	85.2	—	59.2	70.8	51.7	60.5	48.3	71.0	23.8	68.3	97.2	59.4	80.3	58.2
1971	58.2	81.8	—	61.0	73.0	53.2	61.4	48.4	78.6	23.9	65.7	91.0	62.0	84.1	60.8
1972	56.6	93.9	146.6	68.1	82.9	58.5	67.7	54.8	87.4	27.4	74.4	101.3	68.3	88.6	64.9
1973	55.3	101.9	144.0	72.5	88.7	61.9	74.2	62.6	100.0	32.4	83.6	113.7	73.2	91.4	68.0
1974	54.5	126.4	101.7	69.9	83.1	61.4	72.6	60.8	89.5	33.0	82.0	110.5	73.6	84.9	67.4
1975	53.5	143.4	81.5	63.1	71.4	57.8	63.8	50.6	72.7	28.0	68.5	88.7	65.5	80.3	58.1
1976	54.3	144.1	107.1	69.5	79.8	62.9	71.3	58.4	92.2	31.4	76.6	98.4	74.2	91.0	66.4
1977	54.4	175.0	118.7	75.7	87.0	68.4	76.9	64.6	104.7	36.1	81.7	100.4	78.9	94.5	67.1
1978	55.9	196.4	126.0	79.9	92.1	72.0	81.0	70.2	107.9	41.4	88.1	108.9	81.6	93.2	69.3
1979	57.7	190.7	121.2	82.0	93.1	74.9	83.9	73.3	103.0	47.1	90.8	111.8	84.4	96.4	72.5
1980	63.2	236.8	99.6	77.7	84.9	73.2	80.3	67.7	82.3	49.6	81.4	94.3	80.7	93.7	72.6
1981	64.5	315.6	101.8	77.6	82.3	74.7	81.4	70.4	81.2	53.2	84.4	100.5	82.3	91.7	74.3
1982	72.6	296.0	89.3	75.8	75.7	75.8	75.1	62.6	71.0	51.5	70.1	73.3	74.6	82.0	72.2
1983	80.4	257.6	110.5	81.0	84.2	79.1	78.3	68.2	81.7	54.7	76.2	79.7	81.0	92.8	78.8
1984	89.5	296.1	104.7	86.9	90.4	84.9	85.9	79.5	94.0	67.0	85.2	89.6	84.5	92.5	83.1
1985	103.8	259.9	102.5	89.1	93.5	86.4	86.3	80.9	95.1	68.9	86.1	88.8	83.2	86.8	81.3
1986	113.0	143.3	102.7	92.7	98.4	89.3	86.3	82.3	92.3	73.3	85.9	83.7	85.7	91.8	85.8
1987	117.5	130.7	106.2	100.7	104.7	98.4	90.4	87.5	95.0	78.6	92.2	90.7	90.9	99.5	90.2
1988	117.1	150.0	103.0	102.5	106.3	100.3	95.1	93.6	100.4	85.3	97.9	99.6	94.8	98.6	93.7
1989	117.4	139.9	96.9	102.9	105.5	101.3	97.0	95.7	99.6	89.6	99.3	100.6	97.2	98.4	94.6

Notes appear at end of table

(continued)

TABLE Dd498–560 Indexes of industrial production, by market group: 1919–2001 *Continued*

Products / Materials

	Final products — Equipment				Intermediate products		Materials	Durable goods — Parts			Other		Nondurable goods		
Year	Defense and space Dd531 [1]	Oil and gas well drilling Dd532 [1]	Manufactured homes Dd533 [1]	Total Dd534 [1]	Construction supplies Dd535 [1]	Business supplies Dd536 [1]	Total Dd537 [1]	Total Dd538 [1]	Consumer Dd539 [1]	Equipment Dd540 [1]	Total Dd541 [1]	Basic metals Dd542 [1]	Total Dd543 [1]	Textile Dd544 [1]	Paper Dd545 [1]
	Index 1992 = 100	Index 1992 = 100	Index 1992 = 100	Index 1992 = 100	Index 1992 = 100	Index 1992 = 100	Index 1992 = 100	Index 1992 = 100	Index 1992 = 100	Index 1992 = 100	Index 1992 = 100	Index 1992 = 100	Index 1992 = 100	Index 1992 = 100	Index 1992 = 100
1990	115.9	151.1	94.0	101.9	102.9	101.4	97.2	95.3	93.2	92.3	98.8	100.9	98.1	94.4	96.3
1991	106.7	128.6	84.3	97.5	96.2	98.3	95.9	93.2	89.5	93.3	94.7	96.2	96.9	93.5	97.1
1992	100.0	100.0	100.0	100.0	100.0	100.0	100.0	100.0	100.0	100.0	100.0	100.0	100.0	100.0	100.0
1993	92.7	122.4	115.6	102.4	103.2	101.9	103.7	106.6	111.5	106.5	104.6	103.4	101.4	104.4	103.6
1994	86.1	126.2	127.3	106.1	110.5	103.5	111.6	118.9	127.5	121.3	113.2	110.4	105.7	111.1	108.2
1995	83.3	125.8	136.1	107.9	112.4	105.3	119.6	133.1	133.1	153.6	118.0	113.6	106.8	110.6	109.8
1996	80.1	137.5	144.6	110.7	117.7	106.6	127.0	147.4	138.0	189.8	121.9	116.4	106.0	107.8	108.7
1997	77.5	147.8	156.6	116.2	123.8	111.7	137.9	166.2	145.4	241.0	127.0	122.3	112.1	111.5	115.0
1998	80.8	131.6	169.2	120.2	131.3	113.7	146.9	184.3	151.1	301.1	129.6	124.6	112.9	111.2	114.8
1999	79.1	103.3	165.9	123.2	136.5	115.4	155.6	202.4	162.3	360.5	132.8	125.7	112.9	110.5	116.8
2000	74.4	132.0	120.3	126.4	141.5	117.5	166.4	225.4	167.2	459.6	134.7	127.7	113.0	106.3	115.6
2001	74.0	143.1	93.3	121.6	137.3	112.2	158.2	213.1	155.8	443.5	125.4	114.1	104.3	91.0	109.5

Materials

	Nondurable goods		Total	Energy	
Year	Chemical Dd546 [2]	Other Dd547 [2]	Dd548 [2]	Primary energy Dd549 [2]	Converted fuel Dd550 [2]
	Index 1992 = 100	Index 1992 = 100	Index 1992 = 100	Index 1992 = 100	Index 1992 = 100
1954	—	33.3	51.2	—	—
1955	—	35.7	57.7	—	—
1956	—	37.3	61.0	—	—
1957	—	37.2	61.7	—	—
1958	—	37.6	57.2	—	—
1959	—	40.1	60.5	—	—
1960	—	41.0	61.4	—	—
1961	—	42.7	61.8	—	—
1962	—	43.5	63.9	—	—
1963	—	45.0	67.8	—	—
1964	—	47.5	70.5	—	—
1965	—	50.3	73.7	—	—
1966	—	53.6	78.4	—	—
1967	38.8	56.8	81.1	90.6	72.6
1968	45.2	59.1	84.8	93.2	77.7
1969	50.2	63.4	89.1	96.4	83.0

Special aggregates

	Total, excluding					Consumer goods, excluding		Business equipment, excluding		Materials, excluding energy
Year	Autos and trucks Dd551 [2]	Motor vehicles and parts Dd552 [2]	Computer and office equipment Dd553 [2]	Computers and semiconductors Dd554 [2]	Computers, communications equipment, and semiconductors Dd555 [2]	Autos and trucks Dd556 [2]	Energy products Dd557 [2]	Autos and trucks Dd558 [2]	Computer and office equipment Dd559 [2]	Dd560 [2]
	Index 1992 = 100	Index 1992 = 100	Index 1992 = 100	Index 1992 = 100	Index 1992 = 100	Index 1992 = 100	Index 1992 = 100	Index 1992 = 100	Index 1992 = 100	Index 1992 = 100
1954	—	—	—	—	—	—	—	—	—	—
1955	—	—	—	—	—	—	—	—	—	—
1956	—	—	—	—	—	—	—	—	—	—
1957	—	—	—	—	—	—	—	—	—	—
1958	—	—	—	—	—	—	—	—	—	—
1959	—	—	—	—	—	—	—	—	—	—
1960	—	—	—	—	—	—	—	—	—	—
1961	—	—	—	—	—	—	—	—	—	—
1962	—	—	—	—	—	—	—	—	—	—
1963	—	—	—	—	—	—	—	—	—	—
1964	—	—	—	—	—	—	—	—	—	—
1965	—	—	—	—	—	—	—	—	—	—
1966	—	—	—	—	—	—	—	—	—	—
1967	55.4	55.2	58.8	61.9	63.3	56.4	55.4	42.6	60.9	47.8
1968	58.2	58.0	62.0	65.3	66.7	59.0	58.7	44.3	63.2	51.3
1969	61.0	60.8	64.8	68.1	69.6	61.5	60.7	47.1	66.4	54.5

Special aggregates

Year	Nondurable goods		Materials	Energy		Total, excluding					Consumer goods, excluding		Business equipment, excluding		Materials, excluding energy
	Chemical [2]	Other [2]	Total [2]	Primary energy [2]	Converted fuel [2]	Autos and trucks [2]	Motor vehicles and parts [2]	Computer and office equipment [2]	Computers and semiconductors [2]	Computers, communications equipment, and semiconductors [2]	Autos and trucks [2]	Energy products [2]	Autos and trucks [2]	Computer and office equipment [2]	[2]
	Dd546	Dd547	Dd548	Dd549	Dd550	Dd551	Dd552	Dd553	Dd554	Dd555	Dd556	Dd557	Dd558	Dd559	Dd560
	Index 1992 = 100	Index 1992 = 100	Index 1992 = 100	Index 1992 = 100	Index 1992 = 100	Index 1992 = 100	Index 1992 = 100	Index 1992 = 100	Index 1992 = 100	Index 1992 = 100	Index 1992 = 100	Index 1992 = 100	Index 1992 = 100	Index 1992 = 100	Index 1992 = 100
1970	51.4	64.5	93.6	101.0	87.5	59.3	59.3	62.6	65.7	67.2	61.9	59.5	45.8	63.4	51.3
1971	54.5	65.4	94.3	100.2	89.8	59.7	59.5	63.7	66.8	68.5	64.2	63.1	43.3	61.1	52.2
1972	63.4	69.2	98.0	101.9	95.5	65.5	65.3	69.7	72.9	74.7	69.4	68.3	49.4	68.9	58.5
1973	71.3	72.0	98.7	100.6	98.6	70.6	70.3	75.3	78.5	80.5	71.9	71.3	57.7	80.4	65.5
1974	74.1	72.6	96.0	98.1	95.7	70.0	69.8	73.9	77.1	78.9	70.8	69.0	60.8	82.8	64.3
1975	62.5	68.8	93.9	96.1	93.4	63.8	63.9	67.4	70.4	72.0	68.3	65.9	54.1	73.8	54.8
1976	72.5	74.5	96.2	95.5	99.2	69.2	69.0	73.4	76.5	78.4	73.7	72.9	55.5	75.0	62.7
1977	80.8	77.1	97.9	96.7	102.8	74.6	74.2	79.1	82.6	84.1	78.5	78.5	61.4	81.4	68.6
1978	85.0	79.8	98.9	98.5	102.3	79.1	78.6	83.3	86.8	88.2	81.6	81.7	69.0	88.6	73.4
1979	89.0	80.2	101.4	100.2	106.4	82.0	81.8	85.6	88.9	90.1	81.1	80.6	77.8	96.8	76.4
1980	81.5	79.6	102.2	102.1	104.8	80.2	80.4	82.8	85.7	86.5	80.5	78.8	78.4	93.0	71.4
1981	84.0	81.3	100.2	101.6	98.7	81.5	81.8	83.7	86.4	87.2	81.0	79.4	79.7	91.9	73.8
1982	71.1	78.9	96.7	100.1	90.0	77.1	77.6	78.9	81.0	81.6	79.9	78.0	72.2	80.7	66.0
1983	78.5	81.6	94.7	97.1	90.7	79.6	79.9	81.3	83.3	83.9	83.2	82.9	68.6	74.9	71.8
1984	83.1	84.6	99.5	102.2	94.5	86.5	86.6	88.0	89.7	90.2	86.1	86.6	79.0	84.1	80.9
1985	82.8	84.2	99.1	101.2	95.6	87.8	87.7	89.1	90.8	91.1	86.6	87.5	81.8	85.8	81.6
1986	83.4	87.0	95.2	99.7	87.3	88.8	88.8	90.0	91.6	91.8	89.9	90.7	81.2	85.2	83.3
1987	88.8	91.1	96.3	99.2	90.9	93.0	93.1	94.0	95.4	95.6	93.0	93.8	84.5	87.3	88.5
1988	95.2	93.1	98.5	100.5	94.9	97.2	97.3	97.9	99.2	99.4	95.8	96.7	93.5	95.3	94.0
1989	98.8	96.2	99.5	100.1	98.3	98.9	99.1	99.5	100.5	100.7	96.7	97.6	99.2	99.8	96.2
1990	100.3	97.3	100.6	101.7	98.5	98.9	99.1	99.3	100.1	100.2	97.0	97.3	98.6	99.6	96.1
1991	97.3	97.4	100.8	102.0	98.6	97.2	97.4	97.2	97.7	97.8	97.5	96.7	96.2	97.4	94.3
1992	100.0	100.0	100.0	100.0	100.0	100.0	100.0	100.0	100.0	100.0	100.0	100.0	100.0	100.0	100.0
1993	99.3	101.8	99.6	98.2	102.1	103.1	102.9	103.1	102.8	102.7	102.7	103.2	105.1	105.0	105.1
1994	103.7	104.4	101.3	100.0	103.8	108.5	108.0	108.5	107.3	107.0	106.3	108.2	111.7	111.6	114.9
1995	105.7	104.2	102.5	101.1	105.3	113.8	113.2	113.0	110.1	109.5	109.2	111.0	121.2	117.9	125.0
1996	105.1	104.4	103.7	101.9	107.1	119.3	118.8	117.5	112.7	111.7	111.2	112.6	134.4	125.0	134.2
1997	112.5	108.6	103.9	101.3	108.9	127.5	126.9	124.9	117.8	116.2	114.3	116.4	153.8	139.2	148.8
1998	112.1	113.1	103.9	100.7	110.2	134.1	133.5	130.5	120.9	119.1	116.6	119.1	169.6	149.2	161.0
1999	111.6	112.9	103.9	99.6	112.4	138.6	137.7	134.5	122.7	120.5	117.1	120.6	177.6	153.0	172.6
2000	113.4	112.8	104.6	98.9	116.2	145.1	144.2	139.8	124.9	122.0	119.3	122.5	191.2	159.6	187.2
2001	102.6	109.6	103.3	98.8	111.8	139.9	139.2	134.5	120.1	117.4	118.6	121.3	180.0	147.2	176.0

[1] Series has no data before 1939.

[2] Series has no data before 1954.

Source

Figures are arithmetic annual averages of seasonally adjusted indexes that appear in the Federal Reserve's monthly G-17 Statistical Release and are published subsequently in the Board of Governors of the Federal Reserve *Bulletin*. Data were downloaded February 13, 2002, from the Internet site of the Board of Governors of the Federal Reserve.

Documentation

The Federal Reserve Board's index of industrial production and related constituent indexes of manufacturing production are constructed from published and unpublished data from a wide variety of sources on a monthly basis. Individual indexes of industrial production are constructed from two main types of source data: (1) output measured in physical units, and (2) data on inputs to the production process, from which output is inferred. Data on physical products, such as tons of steel or barrels of oil, are obtained from private trade associations and from government agencies; data of this type

(continued)

TABLE Dd498–560   Indexes of industrial production, by market group: 1919–2001   Continued

are used to estimate monthly industrial production wherever possible and appropriate. Production indexes for a few industries are derived by dividing estimated nominal output (calculated using unit production or sales and unit values) by a corresponding Fisher price index; the most notable of these fall within the high-technology grouping and include computers and semiconductors. When suitable data on physical product are not available, estimates of output are based on either production-worker hours or electric power use by industry. The factors used to convert inputs into estimates of production are based on historical relationships between the inputs and the comprehensive annual data used to benchmark the industrial production indexes. These factors also may be influenced by technological or cyclical developments.

The annual data used in benchmarking the individual industrial production indexes are constructed from a variety of source data, such as the quinquennial *Censuses of Manufactures and Mineral Industries* and the *Annual Survey of Manufactures*, prepared by the Bureau of the Census; the *Minerals Yearbook*, prepared by the U.S. Geological Survey of the Department of the Interior; and publications of the Department of Energy.

The series are published monthly in the G-17 statistical release from the Federal Reserve and also appear in the *Federal Reserve Bulletin*. The sources of the current individual data series that go into each index are identified by the Federal Reserve in publications available at their Internet site. A more detailed description of the other methods used to compile the industrial production index, plus a history of its development, a glossary of terms, and a bibliography, are given in Federal Reserve Board of Governors, *Industrial Production – 1986 Edition*.

These series have been revised many times, adding new series and deleting old, so that the the base underlying the series has shifted. For example, in the revision described in the December 2000 G-17 Release, the Federal Reserve incorporated new production measures in four industries: communications equipment, computer and office equipment, drugs and medicines, and bearings. The new series measure production using detailed information on the major products of the industries. Some of the more recent revisions since 1990 are described in various issues of the *Federal Reserve Bulletin*.

At each revision, detailed adjustments are made to various series and carried back for some period. For example, the December 2000 revisions were carried back through 1986 while those for 1971 were carried back in detail to 1954 and in more limited fashion to 1939.

The index comparison base has been updated by the Federal Reserve to the single year, 1992, for all series, and conversion to the new base has been carried back to the beginning of each index.

As noted previously, the industrial production index itself measures the real output of the manufacturing, mining, and electric and gas utilities industries. The manufacturing indexes exclude mining and energy utilities and are reported at various levels of disaggregation.

For the period since 1997, the total industrial production index has been constructed from 276 individual series based on the 1987 Standard Industrial Classification (SIC) codes. See the Introduction to Part D for a discussion of SIC codes. These individual series are classified in two ways: market groups, shown in Table Dd498–560; and industry groups, shown in Table Dd561–607. Market groups consist of products and materials. Total products are the aggregate of final products, such as consumer goods and equipment, and intermediate products (which are inputs to nonindustrial sectors). Materials are inputs in the manufacture of products. Major industry groups include two-digit SIC industries and aggregates of these industries – for example, durable and nondurable manufacturing. Special aggregates that highlight the relative importance and contributions of several key industries, such as high-technology and motor vehicles, are also reported.

The Federal Reserve has yet to adopt the North American Industrial Classification System as its coding scheme for industries, making these indexes comparable over longer periods.

The industrial production index is a version of the Fisher-ideal index formula. The series that measure the output of an individual industry are combined using weights derived from their proportion in the total value-added output of all industries. The industrial production index, which extends back to 1919, has been built as an annually weighted chain-type index since 1977. Prior to that, weights were revised with the availability of census data. For example, 1963 weights were used for the 1963–1966 period, 1958 for the 1958–1962 period, and 1954 for the 1954–1957 period. The year 1947 was used as the weight base for the 1947–1952 period and 1939 weights applied to the 1939–1946 period. Between 1977 and 1992, the weights for months from January to June were drawn from the year containing the month being estimated and the preceding year; for months from July to December, the weights are drawn from the current and following year. Since mid-1992, the weights have been changed monthly, eliminating distortions in the contributions of several high-technology industries, particularly computers, computer peripherals, and semiconductors, where there have been rapid declines in the relative price – sectors where weights shift noticeably year to year. To assist users with calculations, the Federal Reserve's Internet site provides supplemental monthly statistics that represent the exact proportionate contribution of a monthly change in a component index to the monthly change in the total index. Historic weights, however, are harder to find at a centralized location.

Individual series are seasonally adjusted using Census X-12 ARIMA. For series based on production-worker hours, the current seasonal factors were estimated with data through October 2000; for other series, the factors were estimated with data through at least June 2000. Series are preadjusted for the effects of holidays or the business cycle when appropriate. For the data since 1977, all seasonally adjusted aggregate indexes are calculated by aggregating the seasonally adjusted indexes of the individual series.

For additional details on the construction of these indexes, see the *Federal Reserve Bulletin* 83 (February 1997): 67–92, which is available at the Federal Reserve Board's Internet site.

Series Dd509–511. Includes household appliances and home computing, video, and audio equipment.

TABLE Dd561–607   Indexes of industrial production, by industry group: 1919–2001

Contributed by Jeremy Atack and Fred Bateman

		Manufacturing			Durable goods				Primary metals					Industrial machinery and equipment	
	Total	Total	Primary processing	Advanced processing	Total	Lumber and products	Furniture and fixtures	Stone, clay, and glass products	Total	Iron and steel		Nonferrous metals	Fabricated metal products	Total	Computer and office equipment
										Total	Raw steel				
Year	Dd561	Dd562	Dd563	Dd564	Dd565	Dd566	Dd567	Dd568	Dd569	Dd570	Dd571	Dd572	Dd573	Dd574	Dd575
	Index 1992 = 100	Index 1992 = 100	Index 1992 = 100	Index 1992 = 100	Index 1992 = 100	Index 1992 = 100	Index 1992 = 100	Index 1992 = 100	Index 1992 = 100	Index 1992 = 100	Index 1992 = 100	Index 1992 = 100	Index 1992 = 100	Index 1992 = 100	Index 1992 = 100
1919	7.7	7.8	—	—	7.5	—	—	—	—	—	—	—	—	—	—
1920	8.1	8.0	—	—	8.3	—	—	—	—	—	—	—	—	—	—
1921	6.2	6.1	—	—	4.8	—	—	—	—	—	—	—	—	—	—
1922	7.9	8.0	—	—	7.2	—	—	—	—	—	—	—	—	—	—
1923	9.4	9.3	—	—	9.3	—	—	—	—	—	—	—	—	—	—
1924	8.9	8.7	—	—	8.5	—	—	—	—	—	—	—	—	—	—
1925	9.7	9.8	—	—	9.6	—	—	—	—	—	—	—	—	—	—
1926	10.3	10.3	—	—	10.2	—	—	—	—	—	—	—	—	—	—
1927	10.3	10.2	—	—	9.6	—	—	—	—	—	—	—	—	—	—
1928	10.7	10.8	—	—	10.5	—	—	—	—	—	—	—	—	—	—
1929	11.9	11.9	—	—	11.8	—	—	—	—	—	—	—	—	—	—
1930	9.9	9.7	—	—	8.8	—	—	—	—	—	—	—	—	—	—
1931	8.2	8.0	—	—	6.0	—	—	—	—	—	—	—	—	—	—
1932	6.4	6.2	—	—	3.7	—	—	—	—	—	—	—	—	—	—
1933	7.6	7.4	—	—	4.8	—	—	—	—	—	—	—	—	—	—
1934	8.2	8.0	—	—	5.8	—	—	—	—	—	—	—	—	—	—
1935	9.5	9.4	—	—	7.5	—	—	—	—	—	—	—	—	—	—
1936	11.2	11.3	—	—	9.7	—	—	—	—	—	—	—	—	—	—
1937	12.3	12.3	—	—	10.9	—	—	—	—	—	—	—	—	—	—
1938	9.7	9.4	—	—	7.0	—	—	—	—	—	—	—	—	—	—
1939	11.9	11.2	—	—	9.2	—	—	—	—	—	—	—	—	—	—
1940	13.8	13.2	—	—	12.3	—	—	—	—	—	—	—	—	—	—
1941	17.4	16.9	—	—	16.4	—	—	—	—	—	—	—	—	—	—
1942	20.0	19.7	—	—	20.9	—	—	—	—	—	—	—	—	—	—
1943	24.3	24.6	—	—	28.4	—	—	—	—	—	—	—	—	—	—
1944	26.1	26.6	—	—	31.3	—	—	—	—	—	—	—	—	—	—
1945	22.3	22.1	—	—	23.6	—	—	—	—	—	—	—	—	—	—
1946	19.3	18.4	—	—	16.5	—	—	—	—	—	—	—	—	—	—
1947	21.7	20.6	—	—	19.7	39.9	24.5	34.2	67.7	95.9	—	34.5	38.4	15.1	—
1948	22.6	21.3	—	—	20.5	41.6	25.4	36.4	70.5	100.4	—	35.3	39.1	15.2	—
1949	21.4	20.2	—	—	18.6	36.7	23.5	34.0	59.2	85.3	—	28.2	35.3	12.9	—
1950	24.7	23.5	—	—	22.7	44.5	28.7	41.1	74.8	105.8	—	38.1	43.1	14.5	—
1951	26.8	25.4	—	—	25.6	44.5	27.1	45.5	81.2	118.0	—	37.8	46.1	18.5	—
1952	27.9	26.4	—	—	27.1	43.9	27.8	43.5	73.9	102.7	—	38.9	45.0	20.1	—
1953	30.2	28.8	—	—	30.7	46.4	29.1	44.5	84.0	119.8	—	41.9	50.8	20.9	—
1954	28.5	26.8	—	—	27.0	46.1	31.2	44.1	68.0	93.1	87.8	37.8	45.7	17.8	0.3

(continued)

TABLE Dd561–607   Indexes of industrial production, by industry group: 1919–2001   Continued

Column groupings: Dd565–575 fall under *Manufacturing → Durable goods*. Dd569–572 = *Primary metals* (Dd570–571 = *Iron and steel*). Dd574–575 = *Industrial machinery and equipment*. All series: Index 1992 = 100.

Year	Total Dd561	Total Dd562	Primary processing Dd563	Advanced processing Dd564	Total Dd565	Lumber and products Dd566	Furniture and fixtures Dd567	Stone, clay, and glass products Dd568	Total Dd569	Iron and steel Total Dd570	Raw steel Dd571	Nonferrous metals Dd572	Fabricated metal products Dd573	Total Dd574	Computer and office equipment Dd575
1955	32.1	30.3	—	—	30.9	51.5	36.2	51.0	88.6	124.2	119.0	46.6	52.1	19.6	0.4
1956	33.5	31.5	—	—	31.8	50.9	37.6	54.0	87.1	120.2	115.5	47.6	52.9	22.4	0.4
1957	34.0	31.9	—	—	32.2	46.7	37.7	53.9	84.2	117.3	112.1	44.9	54.3	22.4	0.5
1958	31.8	29.7	—	—	28.1	47.5	35.5	51.2	67.3	89.2	86.1	40.0	48.6	18.8	0.5
1959	35.6	33.4	—	—	32.2	53.8	39.8	59.4	76.5	98.9	93.6	48.2	54.6	21.9	0.5
1960	36.4	34.1	—	—	32.8	50.7	39.4	57.4	77.1	102.3	98.2	45.9	54.7	22.0	0.6
1961	36.7	34.2	—	—	32.3	53.0	38.6	57.0	76.9	99.8	100.9	48.0	53.3	21.4	0.7
1962	39.7	37.2	—	—	35.8	55.9	42.5	60.6	81.4	102.1	99.5	54.6	58.0	24.0	0.7
1963	42.2	39.5	—	—	38.2	58.6	44.1	64.2	88.0	111.6	111.6	57.9	59.9	25.6	0.7
1964	45.0	42.3	—	—	40.9	62.8	47.4	67.2	99.6	127.5	129.3	64.0	63.5	29.2	0.9
1965	49.5	46.8	—	—	46.5	65.3	51.5	71.3	109.2	139.2	139.2	70.8	69.8	32.9	1.0
1966	53.8	51.1	—	—	51.7	67.8	55.4	73.4	116.2	143.9	146.0	80.2	74.8	38.2	1.5
1967	55.0	52.0	51.8	52.0	52.2	67.1	55.5	72.0	107.4	133.1	136.8	74.4	78.3	38.9	1.6
1968	58.1	54.9	55.9	54.1	54.8	69.1	57.5	76.2	111.0	136.8	140.0	77.6	82.4	39.3	1.8
1969	60.7	57.4	59.4	55.9	57.0	69.0	60.1	78.8	119.7	149.7	152.8	81.8	83.8	42.5	2.2
1970	58.7	54.8	56.9	53.3	52.7	68.6	56.2	74.8	111.2	139.0	139.2	75.9	77.7	41.1	2.3
1971	59.5	55.6	58.7	53.5	52.4	70.4	58.6	78.5	104.9	126.3	127.1	76.6	77.3	38.2	2.0
1972	65.3	61.5	66.1	58.3	58.5	80.6	70.7	86.9	118.3	141.5	143.9	87.0	84.8	44.3	2.4
1973	70.6	66.9	73.0	62.9	65.3	80.9	75.4	93.9	134.1	161.0	164.3	98.1	94.3	51.8	2.9
1974	69.6	65.9	70.6	62.7	64.0	73.4	70.1	92.4	129.7	155.7	163.1	94.8	90.5	55.2	3.5
1975	63.5	59.4	60.9	58.0	56.1	68.3	60.0	81.8	103.4	125.1	128.6	74.3	78.4	47.8	3.2
1976	69.3	65.4	69.6	62.5	61.8	77.8	67.0	91.5	115.7	137.9	140.9	85.7	86.9	50.2	3.9
1977	74.9	71.2	75.9	67.9	68.1	86.1	74.8	98.3	119.0	138.0	139.3	93.0	94.7	56.6	5.1
1978	79.3	75.8	79.9	72.8	73.6	87.5	80.4	106.0	128.0	147.5	154.9	101.1	98.2	63.3	7.5
1979	82.0	78.5	81.7	76.2	77.4	86.3	80.5	106.8	130.0	148.4	154.4	104.6	101.6	70.2	10.3
1980	79.7	75.5	74.7	75.8	73.4	80.4	79.1	96.5	108.0	119.0	126.9	92.4	94.4	70.5	13.9
1981	81.0	76.7	75.7	77.1	74.6	78.1	78.4	94.3	113.9	126.6	138.5	96.1	93.0	74.7	18.4
1982	76.7	72.1	68.6	74.3	68.2	70.3	74.6	84.2	80.5	80.5	82.6	80.7	84.9	65.8	21.3
1983	79.5	76.3	75.1	76.9	72.2	83.3	80.2	91.2	88.2	90.0	94.1	85.9	87.2	65.2	29.5
1984	86.6	83.8	82.8	84.4	82.7	89.9	88.6	98.6	98.7	98.9	102.6	98.6	95.2	78.9	42.0
1985	88.0	85.7	83.4	87.1	85.6	92.0	88.9	98.0	98.4	98.8	97.7	98.2	96.5	81.2	50.3
1986	89.0	88.1	85.0	89.9	87.4	99.6	93.3	101.7	91.2	86.8	89.4	97.6	95.6	81.8	53.7
1987	93.2	92.8	90.4	94.2	92.0	104.9	100.9	104.8	97.8	95.4	99.3	101.2	101.9	86.0	62.2
1988	97.4	97.1	94.6	98.6	98.1	105.1	101.1	107.5	106.2	107.6	111.3	104.6	106.1	97.1	74.6
1989	99.1	99.0	96.1	100.7	100.5	104.3	102.4	107.4	104.9	106.2	107.1	103.2	104.8	103.0	83.0
1990	98.9	98.5	96.1	99.9	99.0	101.6	100.9	105.0	104.0	106.4	108.4	100.9	101.2	100.1	81.4
1991	97.0	96.2	93.8	97.6	95.5	94.5	94.8	97.2	96.7	96.0	96.3	97.7	96.2	95.4	82.3
1992	100.0	100.0	100.0	100.0	100.0	100.0	100.0	100.0	100.0	100.0	100.0	100.0	100.0	100.0	100.0
1993	103.4	103.7	105.0	102.9	105.6	100.8	105.4	101.9	105.1	106.0	103.1	103.9	104.3	110.4	123.8
1994	109.1	110.0	114.3	107.6	114.8	105.9	109.5	107.9	113.8	114.4	107.6	113.0	112.1	126.0	155.7

Manufacturing — Durable goods

Year	Total Dd561	Total Dd562	Primary processing Dd563	Advanced processing Dd564	Total Dd565	Lumber and products Dd566	Furniture and fixtures Dd567	Stone, clay, and glass products Dd568	Total Dd569	Iron and steel Total Dd570	Raw steel Dd571	Nonferrous metals Dd572	Fabricated metal products Dd573	Industrial machinery and equipment Total Dd574	Computer and office equipment Dd575
	Index 1992 = 100	Index 1992 = 100	Index 1992 = 100	Index 1992 = 100	Index 1992 = 100	Index 1992 = 100	Index 1992 = 100	Index 1992 = 100	Index 1992 = 100	Index 1992 = 100	Index 1992 = 100	Index 1992 = 100	Index 1992 = 100	Index 1992 = 100	Index 1992 = 100
1995	114.4	115.8	122.3	112.0	124.4	107.9	113.6	110.8	116.2	116.6	112.2	115.7	116.3	144.7	216.9
1996	119.6	121.5	130.6	116.2	135.0	110.4	116.2	117.5	119.7	119.1	112.2	120.4	120.1	161.1	311.3
1997	127.9	131.1	143.9	123.8	149.6	113.1	126.2	121.0	125.5	123.9	114.2	127.3	126.5	178.3	438.3
1998	134.5	138.8	155.0	129.6	164.1	117.4	135.2	126.9	127.7	124.0	118.1	132.3	131.3	195.2	598.3
1999	139.4	144.7	165.6	133.0	176.3	122.0	141.9	130.8	129.4	123.9	113.8	136.1	132.4	207.9	804.6
2000	145.7	151.6	178.2	136.9	190.0	118.8	146.3	133.9	131.9	127.3	117.9	137.7	137.2	227.1	1,070.0
2001	140.4	145.0	168.1	132.2	179.7	113.2	139.0	130.6	117.2	113.3	103.0	122.2	130.3	213.5	1,088.1

Manufacturing

Year	Electrical machinery — Semiconductors and related components Total Dd576	Electrical machinery Total Dd577	Transportation equipment Total Dd578	Motor vehicles and parts Total Dd579	Autos and light trucks Dd580	Aerospace and miscellaneous Dd581	Instruments Dd582	Miscellaneous Dd583	Nondurable goods Total Dd584	Food Dd585	Tobacco products Dd586	Textile mill products Dd587	Apparel products Dd588	Paper products Dd589	Printing and publishing Dd590	Chemicals and products Dd591
	Index 1992 = 100	Index 1992 = 100	Index 1992 = 100	Index 1992 = 100	Index 1992 = 100	Index 1992 = 100	Index 1992 = 100	Index 1992 = 100	Index 1992 = 100	Index 1992 = 100	Index 1992 = 100	Index 1992 = 100	Index 1992 = 100	Index 1992 = 100	Index 1992 = 100	Index 1992 = 100
1919	—	—	—	—	—	—	—	—	8.0	—	—	—	—	—	—	—
1920	—	—	—	—	—	—	—	—	7.7	—	—	—	—	—	—	—
1921	—	—	—	—	—	—	—	—	7.3	—	—	—	—	—	—	—
1922	—	—	—	—	—	—	—	—	8.7	—	—	—	—	—	—	—
1923	—	—	—	—	—	—	—	—	9.4	—	—	—	—	—	—	—
1924	—	—	—	—	—	—	—	—	9.0	—	—	—	—	—	—	—
1925	—	—	—	—	—	—	—	—	9.9	—	—	—	—	—	—	—
1926	—	—	—	—	—	—	—	—	10.3	—	—	—	—	—	—	—
1927	—	—	—	—	—	—	—	—	10.8	—	—	—	—	—	—	—
1928	—	—	—	—	—	—	—	—	11.1	—	—	—	—	—	—	—
1929	—	—	—	—	—	—	—	—	12.0	—	—	—	—	—	—	—
1930	—	—	—	—	—	—	—	—	10.9	—	—	—	—	—	—	—
1931	—	—	—	—	—	—	—	—	10.3	—	—	—	—	—	—	—
1932	—	—	—	—	—	—	—	—	9.0	—	—	—	—	—	—	—
1933	—	—	—	—	—	—	—	—	10.3	—	—	—	—	—	—	—
1934	—	—	—	—	—	—	—	—	10.5	—	—	—	—	—	—	—

(continued)

TABLE Dd561–607   Indexes of industrial production, by industry group: 1919–2001   *Continued*

	Manufacturing															
	Durable goods									Nondurable goods						
	Electrical machinery			Transportation equipment												
		Semiconductors			Motor vehicles and parts											
	Total	and related components	Total	Total	Autos and light trucks	Aerospace and miscellaneous	Instruments	Miscellaneous	Total	Food	Tobacco products	Textile mill products	Apparel products	Paper products	Printing and publishing	Chemicals and products
	Dd576	Dd577	Dd578	Dd579	Dd580	Dd581	Dd582	Dd583	Dd584	Dd585	Dd586	Dd587	Dd588	Dd589	Dd590	Dd591
Year	Index 1992 = 100	Index 1992 = 100	Index 1992 = 100	Index 1992 = 100	Index 1992 = 100	Index 1992 = 100	Index 1992 = 100	Index 1992 = 100	Index 1992 = 100	Index 1992 = 100	Index 1992 = 100	Index 1992 = 100	Index 1992 = 100	Index 1992 = 100	Index 1992 = 100	Index 1992 = 100
1935	—	—	—	—	—	—	—	—	11.7	—	—	—	—	—	—	—
1936	—	—	—	—	—	—	—	—	13.1	—	—	—	—	—	—	—
1937	—	—	—	—	—	—	—	—	13.8	—	—	—	—	—	—	—
1938	—	—	—	—	—	—	—	—	12.3	—	—	—	—	—	—	—
1939	—	—	—	—	—	—	—	—	13.6	—	—	—	—	—	—	—
1940	—	—	—	—	—	—	—	—	14.3	—	—	—	—	—	—	—
1941	—	—	—	—	—	—	—	—	17.3	—	—	—	—	—	—	—
1942	—	—	—	—	—	—	—	—	18.0	—	—	—	—	—	—	—
1943	—	—	—	—	—	—	—	—	19.3	—	—	—	—	—	—	—
1944	—	—	—	—	—	—	—	—	20.0	—	—	—	—	—	—	—
1945	—	—	—	—	—	—	—	—	20.0	—	—	—	—	—	—	—
1946	—	—	—	—	—	—	—	—	20.6	—	—	—	—	—	—	—
1947	5.5	—	19.1	26.6	—	13.4	7.7	31.0	21.5	31.3	62.2	34.1	46.8	19.9	22.8	7.6
1948	5.7	—	20.8	28.9	—	14.9	7.9	33.1	22.2	31.0	63.8	36.4	48.8	20.4	23.9	8.2
1949	5.3	—	20.9	29.6	—	14.8	7.0	30.6	21.8	31.3	63.2	33.6	48.4	19.5	24.5	8.1
1950	7.4	—	25.0	38.0	—	15.1	8.2	34.4	24.3	32.4	64.1	38.3	52.1	23.5	25.7	10.1
1951	7.3	—	27.9	34.9	—	24.3	9.4	33.5	25.1	33.1	67.8	37.9	51.0	24.9	26.2	11.5
1952	8.4	—	32.5	29.9	—	38.7	11.2	34.3	25.5	33.8	70.1	37.6	53.8	23.7	26.1	12.0
1953	9.7	—	40.7	37.7	—	48.6	12.3	38.9	26.6	34.4	68.9	38.5	54.4	25.9	27.3	13.0
1954	8.6	0.3	35.3	32.3	—	42.8	12.4	35.8	26.7	35.1	66.8	36.0	53.8	25.7	28.4	13.1
1955	9.9	0.3	40.8	43.6	—	42.8	13.8	45.8	29.7	37.2	68.6	41.1	59.4	28.7	31.3	15.3
1956	10.7	0.4	39.4	35.0	—	48.8	15.2	48.1	31.2	39.2	70.0	42.2	60.7	30.5	33.2	16.5
1957	10.6	0.4	42.4	37.0	—	53.0	15.9	46.0	31.7	39.9	73.3	40.2	60.5	29.9	34.4	17.4
1958	9.7	0.4	33.2	27.0	—	44.0	14.9	41.8	31.9	40.9	78.9	39.7	58.9	30.2	33.6	18.0
1959	11.8	0.6	37.8	35.5	—	44.5	17.3	45.9	35.1	42.9	82.5	44.9	64.9	33.8	35.9	20.9
1960	12.8	0.7	39.1	40.0	—	42.3	18.1	47.7	36.0	44.1	84.2	44.0	66.1	34.5	37.3	21.7
1961	13.6	0.7	36.8	35.2	—	42.7	17.9	49.4	37.1	45.3	86.9	45.4	66.5	36.4	37.5	22.8
1962	15.6	0.9	42.6	42.8	—	46.9	18.7	52.6	39.3	46.8	88.0	48.4	69.2	38.6	38.9	25.3
1963	16.0	1.0	46.7	47.4	—	50.8	20.8	55.1	41.5	48.5	90.7	50.1	72.1	40.9	40.9	27.7
1964	17.0	1.2	48.0	48.7	—	52.1	22.5	58.0	44.2	50.7	91.9	54.2	74.6	43.3	43.4	30.3
1965	20.2	1.9	56.9	62.1	—	56.4	25.9	63.0	47.2	51.8	92.6	58.9	78.8	46.6	46.2	33.8
1966	24.3	2.7	60.9	60.6	—	67.6	28.4	65.7	50.2	53.8	92.6	62.6	80.9	50.3	49.7	36.9
1967	24.4	2.6	59.7	53.6	—	73.8	30.9	67.1	51.7	56.2	93.6	62.6	80.5	50.4	52.4	38.6
1968	25.7	2.8	64.8	64.2	—	72.4	34.0	70.3	55.1	57.7	93.8	69.8	82.4	53.1	53.3	43.3
1969	27.4	3.5	64.4	64.7	—	70.7	36.5	74.4	58.0	59.6	91.1	73.4	85.1	57.3	55.9	46.9
1970	26.2	3.5	54.1	52.0	—	62.3	36.2	72.1	58.0	60.6	94.3	71.8	81.8	56.7	54.4	48.8
1971	26.3	3.8	58.5	65.2	—	55.9	37.9	72.4	60.3	62.5	93.1	75.8	82.9	59.1	54.8	51.9
1972	30.1	4.8	62.4	71.1	—	57.7	42.5	84.6	65.7	65.8	96.6	83.1	87.9	64.3	58.5	58.4
1973	34.3	6.2	71.1	82.8	—	63.8	48.5	85.7	69.0	67.1	101.7	86.5	88.5	68.8	60.1	63.9
1974	33.9	6.4	64.6	71.4	—	62.0	51.4	81.9	68.5	68.0	99.4	78.7	84.5	68.2	59.1	66.2

	Manufacturing															
	Durable goods								Nondurable goods							
	Electrical machinery			Transportation equipment												
					Motor vehicles and parts											
Year	Total	Semiconductors and related components	Total	Total	Autos and light trucks	Aerospace and miscellaneous	Instruments	Miscellaneous	Total	Food	Tobacco products	Textile mill products	Apparel products	Paper products	Printing and publishing	Chemicals and products
	Dd576	Dd577	Dd578	Dd579	Dd580	Dd581	Dd582	Dd583	Dd584	Dd585	Dd586	Dd587	Dd588	Dd589	Dd590	Dd591
	Index 1992 = 100	Index 1992 = 100	Index 1992 = 100	Index 1992 = 100	Index 1992 = 100	Index 1992 = 100	Index 1992 = 100	Index 1992 = 100	Index 1992 = 100	Index 1992 = 100	Index 1992 = 100	Index 1992 = 100	Index 1992 = 100	Index 1992 = 100	Index 1992 = 100	Index 1992 = 100
1975	29.2	5.2	58.2	61.0	—	59.3	48.9	76.0	64.2	67.5	101.7	75.0	77.4	59.4	55.4	60.3
1976	32.8	6.9	66.3	80.0	—	56.6	53.7	82.5	70.7	71.4	106.8	83.3	91.1	67.4	60.5	67.5
1977	38.1	8.6	71.9	92.4	84.2	55.6	60.1	92.6	75.7	74.6	102.8	88.3	98.0	70.1	66.3	72.4
1978	42.2	10.6	77.5	96.8	87.5	62.2	66.2	92.7	78.9	77.2	107.4	88.6	100.4	73.4	70.1	76.4
1979	46.9	13.8	78.7	89.0	80.1	71.1	71.7	92.1	79.9	77.9	106.9	91.5	95.3	76.0	72.0	79.2
1980	48.6	16.6	70.3	65.8	58.1	74.3	73.6	86.9	78.3	79.7	108.5	89.0	95.4	75.2	72.4	75.9
1981	51.0	20.0	66.9	62.8	59.3	70.5	75.4	89.6	79.5	81.4	109.9	86.3	97.3	76.6	74.3	77.3
1982	51.7	24.3	63.0	56.9	54.4	68.3	76.3	85.5	77.7	82.4	106.2	80.1	96.3	74.3	77.5	71.0
1983	55.9	28.3	70.5	72.1	74.7	69.3	77.7	83.2	81.9	84.6	101.6	89.9	100.3	81.0	81.4	76.0
1984	66.7	38.9	80.5	87.3	90.7	75.1	86.0	87.6	85.3	86.4	101.7	90.4	102.2	85.0	87.0	79.3
1985	68.4	39.8	88.8	95.0	99.1	83.7	89.3	82.2	86.0	88.9	101.8	86.5	98.6	83.8	90.2	79.4
1986	71.0	42.9	94.1	94.2	99.2	94.2	88.8	83.5	89.1	91.2	100.3	90.5	101.8	88.3	93.4	82.4
1987	75.6	50.6	96.1	94.9	98.7	97.5	93.8	93.5	93.8	93.5	104.7	96.3	105.5	90.9	102.5	87.0
1988	82.5	57.3	101.1	100.2	103.1	102.1	97.2	99.8	96.0	94.9	106.5	95.0	103.6	93.8	103.4	92.2
1989	85.8	64.2	105.1	101.2	106.5	109.4	98.2	100.3	97.3	95.9	105.4	96.5	100.3	95.4	103.5	95.1
1990	87.7	71.7	102.3	95.3	99.3	109.8	98.4	100.0	97.9	97.0	105.4	93.2	97.2	96.0	103.1	97.3
1991	89.6	80.8	96.5	88.5	91.0	105.0	99.8	98.4	97.0	98.4	98.9	92.7	97.8	96.8	99.1	96.4
1992	100.0	100.0	100.0	100.0	100.0	100.0	100.0	100.0	100.0	100.0	100.0	100.0	100.0	100.0	100.0	100.0
1993	109.8	115.2	104.0	114.4	113.4	93.6	100.8	105.7	101.5	102.0	84.1	105.2	102.4	103.4	100.5	100.9
1994	131.3	153.7	108.8	133.6	130.2	84.9	99.8	110.0	104.8	103.6	104.4	110.6	106.5	107.0	100.5	103.7
1995	165.5	240.6	108.5	137.6	129.4	80.6	103.2	113.0	106.5	105.7	111.8	110.1	107.0	107.6	101.1	106.0
1996	206.3	359.3	110.2	137.6	130.5	83.8	107.8	116.5	107.4	105.4	113.5	108.6	105.1	106.8	101.1	108.8
1997	266.8	549.2	120.2	148.4	139.9	93.1	110.4	118.7	112.0	107.2	111.7	108.2	108.8	112.2	107.3	115.9
1998	334.5	829.4	130.6	154.7	143.6	107.6	114.0	120.7	113.4	110.6	107.6	106.2	105.5	113.8	106.3	118.3
1999	411.3	1,198.8	137.8	174.3	163.6	103.4	117.7	123.0	113.7	112.0	93.5	103.9	106.1	114.9	105.3	119.1
2000	536.6	1,855.9	137.1	177.6	164.6	99.1	118.6	124.9	114.8	113.8	93.0	98.9	101.9	113.9	106.9	122.0
2001	505.5	1,772.4	129.3	164.2	156.3	96.5	115.3	117.6	111.4	112.7	93.6	86.8	93.2	108.6	101.8	121.1

(continued)

TABLE Dd561–607 Indexes of industrial production, by industry group: 1919–2001 *Continued*

	Manufacturing — Nondurable goods			Mining					Utilities			Special aggregates			Manufacturing, excluding	
	Petroleum products	Rubber and plastic products	Leather and products	Total	Metal	Coal	Oil and gas	Stone and earth minerals	Total	Electric	Gas	Computers, communications equipment, and semiconductors	Motor vehicles and parts	Computer and office equipment	Computers and semiconductors	Computers, communications equipment, and semiconductors
	Dd592	Dd593	Dd594	Dd595	Dd596	Dd597	Dd598	Dd599	Dd600	Dd601	Dd602	Dd603	Dd604	Dd605	Dd606	Dd607
Year	Index 1992 = 100	Index 1992 = 100	Index 1992 = 100	Index 1992 = 100	Index 1992 = 100	Index 1992 = 100	Index 1992 = 100	Index 1992 = 100	Index 1992 = 100	Index 1992 = 100	Index 1992 = 100	Index 1992 = 100	Index 1992 = 100	Index 1992 = 100	Index 1992 = 100	Index 1992 = 100
1919	—	—	—	26.1	—	—	—	—	—	—	—	—	—	—	—	—
1920	—	—	—	30.3	—	—	—	—	—	—	—	—	—	—	—	—
1921	—	—	—	24.7	—	—	—	—	—	—	—	—	—	—	—	—
1922	—	—	—	26.0	—	—	—	—	—	—	—	—	—	—	—	—
1923	—	—	—	36.1	—	—	—	—	—	—	—	—	—	—	—	—
1924	—	—	—	33.1	—	—	—	—	—	—	—	—	—	—	—	—
1925	—	—	—	33.9	—	—	—	—	—	—	—	—	—	—	—	—
1926	—	—	—	36.7	—	—	—	—	—	—	—	—	—	—	—	—
1927	—	—	—	37.0	—	—	—	—	—	—	—	—	—	—	—	—
1928	—	—	—	36.4	—	—	—	—	—	—	—	—	—	—	—	—
1929	—	—	—	39.6	—	—	—	—	—	—	—	—	—	—	—	—
1930	—	—	—	34.5	—	—	—	—	—	—	—	—	—	—	—	—
1931	—	—	—	29.6	—	—	—	—	—	—	—	—	—	—	—	—
1932	—	—	—	24.7	—	—	—	—	—	—	—	—	—	—	—	—
1933	—	—	—	28.0	—	—	—	—	—	—	—	—	—	—	—	—
1934	—	—	—	29.5	—	—	—	—	—	—	—	—	—	—	—	—
1935	—	—	—	31.9	—	—	—	—	—	—	—	—	—	—	—	—
1936	—	—	—	36.7	—	—	—	—	—	—	—	—	—	—	—	—
1937	—	—	—	41.5	—	—	—	—	—	—	—	—	—	—	—	—
1938	—	—	—	35.9	—	—	—	—	—	—	—	—	—	—	—	—
1939	—	—	—	38.7	—	—	—	—	5.7	—	—	—	—	—	—	—
1940	—	—	—	43.0	—	—	—	—	6.2	—	—	—	—	—	—	—
1941	—	—	—	45.6	—	—	—	—	7.0	—	—	—	—	—	—	—
1942	—	—	—	47.1	—	—	—	—	7.9	—	—	—	—	—	—	—
1943	—	—	—	48.2	—	—	—	—	8.7	—	—	—	—	—	—	—
1944	—	—	—	51.7	—	—	—	—	9.3	—	—	—	—	—	—	—
1945	—	—	—	50.7	—	—	—	—	9.5	—	—	—	—	—	—	—
1946	—	—	—	49.7	—	—	—	—	9.9	—	—	—	—	—	—	—
1947	30.0	6.5	231.7	56.3	43.3	75.4	52.2	34.7	10.6	7.5	24.8	—	—	—	—	—
1948	32.5	6.7	220.7	59.2	44.7	72.3	57.5	37.8	11.9	8.4	27.5	—	—	—	—	—
1949	31.5	6.3	210.2	52.5	40.4	53.3	54.5	36.6	12.7	9.0	29.2	—	—	—	—	—
1950	34.7	8.2	227.2	58.6	46.2	61.3	59.7	41.7	14.4	10.1	34.2	—	—	—	—	—
1951	38.8	8.3	212.7	64.3	49.7	62.7	67.4	45.7	16.5	11.4	39.4	—	—	—	—	—
1952	39.7	8.5	226.9	63.8	46.6	55.1	69.7	47.7	17.9	12.5	42.4	—	—	—	—	—
1953	41.7	9.2	227.8	65.4	49.2	52.3	72.9	49.0	19.4	13.7	44.5	—	—	—	—	—
1954	43.4	9.4	223.0	64.1	44.9	44.4	73.5	49.3	20.8	14.6	49.0	—	—	—	—	—
1955	47.1	11.5	244.8	71.4	55.4	51.8	80.3	53.4	23.3	16.4	53.6	—	—	—	—	—
1956	50.0	11.5	247.2	75.2	58.8	56.0	83.8	57.0	25.6	18.0	58.9	—	—	—	—	—
1957	50.3	12.2	244.0	75.3	62.2	55.1	83.5	56.4	27.3	19.2	62.9	—	—	—	—	—
1958	50.3	12.0	240.2	69.0	55.1	46.0	78.4	55.7	28.6	20.1	66.2	—	—	—	—	—
1959	53.3	14.4	256.6	72.3	53.3	45.9	83.3	60.0	31.4	22.2	72.0	—	—	—	—	—

Year	Petroleum products Dd592	Rubber and plastic products Dd593	Leather and products Dd594	Mining Total Dd595	Metal Dd596	Coal Dd597	Oil and gas Dd598	Stone and earth minerals Dd599	Utilities Total Dd600	Electric Dd601	Gas Dd602	Computers, communications equipment, and semiconductors Dd603	Motor vehicles and parts Dd604	Computer and office equipment Dd605	Mfg. excl. Computers and semiconductors Dd606	Mfg. excl. Computers, communications equipment, and semiconductors Dd607
	Index 1992 = 100	Index 1992 = 100	Index 1992 = 100	Index 1992 = 100	Index 1992 = 100	Index 1992 = 100	Index 1992 = 100	Index 1992 = 100	Index 1992 = 100	Index 1992 = 100	Index 1992 = 100	Index 1992 = 100	Index 1992 = 100	Index 1992 = 100	Index 1992 = 100	Index 1992 = 100
1960	55.1	14.6	243.6	73.5	67.8	45.6	82.5	61.5	33.6	23.7	76.8	—	—	—	—	—
1961	57.3	15.2	242.2	74.1	63.5	44.0	84.5	62.9	35.5	25.2	79.4	—	—	—	—	—
1962	60.4	17.2	249.4	76.2	64.1	45.4	86.9	65.1	38.2	27.2	84.8	—	—	—	—	—
1963	63.2	18.5	245.4	79.3	63.3	49.6	90.2	68.5	40.8	29.3	88.6	—	—	—	—	—
1964	64.9	21.0	259.7	82.6	69.1	51.9	93.0	72.8	44.3	31.8	96.4	—	—	—	—	—
1965	66.2	24.0	264.2	85.6	70.2	54.1	95.9	78.2	47.1	34.2	98.1	—	—	—	—	—
1966	69.1	27.0	267.5	90.2	73.8	56.1	101.1	84.1	50.7	37.0	103.4	—	—	—	—	—
1967	71.7	27.6	264.0	91.9	60.2	57.8	105.9	84.4	53.2	40.0	110.0	5.8	52.0	56.2	60.3	61.6
1968	75.2	32.1	274.7	95.5	66.6	56.8	110.1	86.7	57.5	43.6	116.8	6.3	54.5	59.4	63.5	64.9
1969	77.3	35.0	250.5	99.2	74.6	58.3	113.3	91.7	62.6	47.7	124.9	7.0	57.1	61.8	66.0	67.5
1970	80.8	33.0	235.0	101.8	77.1	62.3	116.5	89.5	66.5	51.0	130.5	6.9	55.0	59.0	63.0	64.4
1971	83.5	35.9	225.7	99.3	68.6	57.3	115.2	89.9	69.6	53.9	134.4	6.5	55.2	60.1	64.0	65.7
1972	87.4	43.7	234.2	101.4	66.3	61.3	117.2	93.9	74.1	58.4	136.5	7.7	61.0	66.3	70.4	72.2
1973	92.2	49.0	217.9	102.3	70.0	60.7	116.6	102.5	77.0	62.3	134.4	9.1	66.2	72.0	76.4	78.3
1974	89.0	47.9	207.2	101.8	68.0	61.6	115.8	102.1	76.1	61.9	131.2	9.8	65.7	70.7	74.9	76.7
1975	88.0	41.6	206.6	99.5	63.5	66.2	113.1	91.9	76.8	64.0	125.2	8.9	59.4	63.7	67.6	69.0
1976	93.6	48.1	205.1	100.3	69.2	68.9	111.2	97.2	79.9	67.1	127.1	10.2	64.7	70.1	74.1	75.9
1977	101.5	56.0	200.6	103.4	61.1	70.6	116.8	99.4	82.0	70.7	120.7	12.4	70.3	76.1	80.2	81.9
1978	104.9	59.3	201.6	106.5	69.5	67.6	121.1	104.7	84.4	73.3	122.6	15.6	74.9	80.5	84.6	86.3
1979	103.9	58.7	184.4	108.3	72.2	78.6	119.5	107.1	86.8	75.2	126.6	19.8	78.1	82.9	86.8	88.2
1980	95.9	53.3	181.6	111.5	65.2	83.4	124.4	97.9	87.3	76.4	124.8	23.9	76.1	79.1	82.5	83.4
1981	91.2	57.5	176.0	115.6	73.5	82.9	129.7	94.1	85.0	78.0	109.3	27.8	77.5	79.8	82.9	83.8
1982	86.6	56.8	163.1	111.2	54.8	84.5	125.6	78.7	82.3	76.7	102.4	31.4	73.0	74.6	77.0	77.6
1983	86.9	64.0	158.3	106.6	52.8	79.0	120.2	84.0	83.7	79.2	100.4	36.7	76.5	78.3	80.6	81.2
1984	89.9	72.1	141.9	113.9	57.2	90.2	126.9	94.7	86.7	82.4	102.6	47.4	83.6	85.4	87.3	87.8
1985	89.5	73.8	126.1	111.0	56.6	89.1	123.0	97.9	88.8	84.6	104.3	52.5	85.2	86.9	88.9	89.1
1986	95.7	78.2	115.0	102.6	59.3	89.7	111.0	96.6	86.4	86.2	87.0	55.3	87.8	89.2	91.1	91.3
1987	97.0	86.0	112.4	102.1	61.9	92.5	108.9	100.9	89.4	89.4	89.0	61.2	92.7	93.7	95.4	95.7
1988	98.8	88.2	112.0	104.7	74.3	95.4	110.4	103.2	93.9	93.6	94.5	70.2	97.0	97.7	99.3	99.5
1989	99.3	91.2	111.9	103.2	85.6	98.9	106.1	101.8	97.1	96.8	98.1	76.6	98.9	99.4	100.7	100.9
1990	100.3	92.2	107.8	104.8	93.1	103.7	106.4	103.3	98.3	99.2	94.4	80.2	98.7	98.9	99.9	100.0
1991	99.1	90.7	98.4	102.6	93.3	100.1	104.7	96.7	100.4	101.2	97.3	83.7	96.7	96.5	97.0	97.2
1992	100.0	100.0	100.0	100.0	100.0	100.0	100.0	100.0	100.0	100.0	100.0	100.0	100.0	100.0	100.0	100.0
1993	102.9	106.9	100.9	100.0	98.7	94.0	101.1	102.3	104.0	103.9	104.3	115.8	103.1	103.3	102.9	102.8
1994	102.7	116.5	93.5	102.3	100.5	103.0	101.6	108.6	105.4	105.6	104.6	147.7	108.7	109.2	107.9	107.5
1995	104.5	119.7	86.8	102.0	101.8	102.6	100.4	112.9	109.1	109.6	107.2	208.6	114.6	114.3	110.9	110.2
1996	106.9	123.3	87.7	103.5	104.3	105.0	101.6	114.9	112.7	112.8	112.3	291.9	120.6	119.0	113.4	112.3
1997	111.0	130.9	86.4	105.3	108.8	108.2	102.5	120.1	112.7	113.2	110.5	418.4	130.1	127.6	119.2	117.5
1998	113.1	135.7	78.1	102.9	108.1	109.7	98.6	123.4	114.3	117.1	102.9	573.8	137.9	134.2	123.0	120.8
1999	113.4	142.5	74.5	98.2	99.8	107.8	92.5	127.5	117.3	120.0	106.2	771.2	142.9	138.9	125.0	122.5
2000	115.0	144.9	71.4	100.7	97.2	107.1	95.6	130.4	120.7	123.3	109.7	1,101.2	150.1	144.6	127.2	123.9
2001	114.1	137.2	63.3	101.5	89.7	111.8	96.3	132.0	120.0	123.2	107.7	1,053.0	144.0	138.2	121.4	118.3

Source

See the source for Table Dd498–560.

Documentation

See the text for Table Dd498–560.

TABLE Dd608–625   Indexes of manufacturing production, by industry group: 1899–1954

Contributed by Jeremy Atack and Fred Bateman

				Durable manufactures					
	All manufacturing industries	Lumber and furniture	Stone, clay, and glass products	Primary metals	Fabricated metal products	Machinery, except electrical	Electrical machinery	Transportation equipment	Instruments and miscellaneous
	Dd608	Dd609	Dd610	Dd611	Dd612	Dd613	Dd614	Dd615	Dd616
Year	Index 1947 = 100	Index 1947 = 100	Index 1947 = 100	Index 1947 = 100	Index 1947 = 100	Index 1947 = 100	Index 1947 = 100	Index 1947 = 100	Index 1947 = 100
1899	15	74	—	14	—	—	—	5	—
1904	19	69	—	18	—	—	—	5	—
1909	24	75	—	28	—	—	—	7	—
1914	29	75	—	29	—	—	—	13	—
1919	34	71	—	40	—	—	—	40	—
1921	30	76	—	26	—	—	—	25	—
1923	43	82	—	52	—	—	—	50	—
1925	46	93	81	53	—	—	—	50	—
1927	49	90	88	52	—	—	—	45	—
1929	56	91	89	65	—	—	—	66	—
1931	40	57	60	32	—	—	—	30	—
1933	35	42	42	27	—	—	—	22	—
1935	46	54	61	39	—	—	—	48	—
1937	58	69	88	58	51	—	—	60	—
1939	57	72	87	52	50	38	35	49	52
1947	100	100	100	100	100	100	100	100	100
1954	128	116	124	103	114	116	165	189	178

			Nondurable manufactures					
	Food	Tobacco	Textiles and apparel	Paper	Printing and publishing	Chemicals	Petroleum and coal products	Rubber products	Leather
	Dd617	Dd618	Dd619	Dd620	Dd621	Dd622	Dd623	Dd624	Dd625
Year	Index 1947 = 100	Index 1947 = 100	Index 1947 = 100	Index 1947 = 100	Index 1947 = 100	Index 1947 = 100	Index 1947 = 100	Index 1947 = 100	Index 1947 = 100
1899	19	16	26	10	12	6	5	—	50
1904	24	21	32	14	19	8	6	—	58
1909	28	24	41	19	25	11	9	—	65
1914	34	29	48	24	34	15	12	—	64
1919	32	38	45	27	39	18	21	30	142
1921	31	36	43	26	37	15	30	24	60
1923	38	41	56	36	52	22	34	41	75
1925	40	45	58	40	59	24	40	48	67
1927	42	50	63	46	65	29	45	52	76
1929	46	55	67	52	72	35	54	57	79
1931	41	51	58	45	60	30	45	39	142
1933	37	48	57	44	52	29	42	39	68
1935	52	56	67	53	62	35	49	45	79
1937	61	65	72	63	73	43	61	51	86
1939	65	66	80	68	69	46	65	55	87
1947	100	100	100	100	100	100	100	100	100
1954	109	108	109	131	126	164	131	114	90

Source

U.S. Bureau of the Census, unpublished data presented in U.S. Bureau of the Census, *Historical Statistics of the United States* (1975), series P40–57.

Documentation

This table and its associated documentation have been reprinted, more or less without modification, from U.S. Bureau of the Census, *Historical Statistics of the United States* (1975), series P40–57.

Series Dd616. Includes ordnance and accessories.

TABLE Dd626–643 Shipments, inventories, and orders, by durable and nondurable goods manufacturing industries: 1947–1995

Contributed by Jeremy Atack and Fred Bateman

	Shipments			Inventories			Inventory to sales ratio			By stage of manufacturing			Orders					
													New				Unfilled	
	Total	Durable goods	Nondurable goods	Total	Durable goods	Nondurable goods	Total	Durable goods	Nondurable goods	Materials and supplies	Work in progress	Finished goods	Total	Durable goods	Nondurable goods	Total	Durable goods	Nondurable goods
Year	Dd626	Dd627	Dd628	Dd629	Dd630	Dd631	Dd632	Dd633	Dd634	Dd635	Dd636	Dd637	Dd638	Dd639	Dd640	Dd641	Dd642	Dd643
	Billion dollars	Billion dollars	Billion dollars	Billion dollars	Billion dollars	Billion dollars	Ratio	Ratio	Ratio	Billion dollars	Billion dollars	Billion dollars	Billion dollars	Billion dollars	Billion dollars	Billion dollars	Billion dollars	Billion dollars
1947	186.0	80.2	106.0	26.1	13.1	13.0	1.69	1.96	1.47	—	—	—	183.1	77.0	106.4	34.3	28.4	6.0
1948	217.3	100.0	117.2	29.0	15.0	14.1	1.59	1.77	1.44	—	—	—	212.3	98.0	115.0	31.0	26.5	4.1
1949	193.1	86.0	107.1	26.5	13.1	13.4	1.65	1.83	1.50	10.3	6.8	9.4	187.4	80.0	108.0	24.0	20.0	4.4
1950	223.4	106.0	117.4	32.0	16.0	16.0	1.70	1.77	1.62	13.1	9.0	10.0	241.3	122.0	119.3	41.2	35.2	6.0
1951	260.4	126.0	135.0	39.2	21.1	18.0	1.80	2.01	1.60	16.0	11.0	12.4	287.0	154.1	133.0	67.0	63.1	4.0
1952	271.0	136.1	135.0	42.0	24.0	18.0	1.84	2.11	1.57	17.0	12.3	12.6	278.4	145.0	134.0	75.5	72.3	3.2
1953	298.0	160.0	138.0	44.2	26.0	18.2	1.79	1.95	1.59	17.8	13.1	13.4	282.4	145.3	137.1	60.3	58.0	2.5
1954	280.2	142.0	138.3	42.0	24.0	18.0	1.80	2.01	1.57	16.5	12.1	13.3	267.8	129.0	139.0	48.2	45.2	3.0
1955	318.0	169.0	149.0	45.2	26.4	19.0	1.71	1.88	1.51	18.2	13.2	14.0	329.1	179.4	150.0	60.0	56.4	4.0
1956	333.0	177.0	156.3	51.0	30.4	20.3	1.83	2.07	1.56	20.0	15.0	16.0	341.0	185.0	156.0	67.5	64.1	3.4
1957	345.0	183.0	162.0	52.0	32.0	20.3	1.81	2.07	1.50	20.0	16.0	17.0	330.2	169.0	161.3	53.3	50.5	2.8
1958	327.4	163.0	164.5	50.0	30.0	20.1	1.83	2.20	1.47	19.0	15.0	16.1	323.0	158.0	165.0	49.0	46.0	3.1
1959	363.0	187.0	176.1	52.5	31.5	21.0	1.74	2.02	1.43	20.0	16.0	17.0	368.1	191.4	177.0	54.1	50.4	4.0
1960	370.0	190.0	180.0	54.0	32.0	22.0	1.74	2.02	1.44	20.0	15.5	18.3	361.4	183.0	179.0	46.0	43.2	3.0
1961	371.0	187.0	184.2	55.0	32.2	23.0	1.77	2.08	1.47	20.1	16.0	19.0	373.0	188.4	184.4	48.0	45.0	3.0
1962	397.4	205.2	192.1	58.0	34.3	24.0	1.75	1.97	1.46	21.0	17.1	20.0	396.1	204.3	191.8	47.0	44.0	3.0
1963	420.4	219.0	201.4	60.0	36.0	24.3	1.71	1.95	1.45	21.3	18.1	20.4	424.0	222.3	202.0	50.2	47.3	3.0
1964	448.0	236.0	212.4	63.0	38.0	25.0	1.69	1.94	1.42	22.4	19.5	21.3	455.4	243.1	212.3	58.0	55.0	3.0
1965	492.0	267.0	225.5	68.0	42.0	26.0	1.66	1.89	1.39	24.1	22.0	22.3	502.0	276.0	226.0	67.2	64.0	3.1
1966	538.4	295.6	242.8	77.7	49.5	28.2	1.73	2.01	1.39	27.0	25.9	24.8	550.9	308.3	242.7	79.8	76.7	3.0
1967	557.8	303.2	254.6	84.4	54.6	29.7	1.71	2.00	1.35	28.5	29.1	26.8	564.7	310.0	254.8	104.5	100.6	4.0
1968	603.2	332.4	270.8	90.3	58.5	31.8	1.76	2.09	1.37	30.0	31.8	28.4	608.2	337.4	270.8	109.5	105.5	4.0
1969	642.4	353.7	288.8	97.8	64.2	33.5	1.81	2.18	1.36	31.8	35.1	30.9	647.6	358.6	289.0	114.6	110.5	4.2
1970	634.0	338.6	295.4	101.3	66.3	35.0	1.91	2.35	1.40	32.7	34.7	33.8	624.8	329.0	295.8	105.4	100.9	4.6
1971	671.1	359.7	311.4	102.3	65.8	36.5	1.76	2.11	1.34	33.8	34.0	34.6	671.9	360.1	311.8	106.2	101.3	5.0
1972	756.5	408.5	348.0	108.0	69.8	38.2	1.58	1.90	1.21	35.9	36.4	35.6	769.9	420.7	349.2	120.0	113.5	6.2
1973	875.4	476.4	399.0	124.4	80.7	43.6	1.63	2.01	1.20	44.6	41.9	37.9	914.2	514.2	400.0	158.4	151.3	7.2
1974	1,017.9	531.0	486.8	157.8	101.1	56.7	1.86	2.33	1.37	59.5	50.4	47.9	1,045.9	560.9	485.0	186.5	181.1	5.3
1975	1,039.4	524.1	515.3	158.2	101.1	57.1	1.74	2.24	1.24	57.5	51.1	49.6	1,021.0	503.4	517.5	168.0	160.5	7.6
1976	1,185.7	608.3	577.4	170.4	108.5	61.9	1.63	2.00	1.22	62.4	54.0	54.0	1,190.2	612.6	577.6	172.5	164.7	7.9
1977	1,330.1	696.1	634.0	180.1	114.9	65.2	1.53	1.87	1.16	64.7	56.6	58.8	1,349.4	714.7	634.7	191.8	183.3	8.5
1978	1,522.9	814.1	708.7	209.1	136.3	72.8	1.55	1.86	1.18	75.1	69.5	64.6	1,578.6	868.1	710.5	257.4	247.4	10.0
1979	1,727.2	912.7	814.5	239.1	158.5	80.6	1.61	2.10	1.10	85.6	81.6	71.9	1,768.8	953.4	815.4	299.0	288.0	10.9
1980	1,852.7	930.6	922.1	261.7	172.2	89.5	1.61	2.12	1.09	91.8	91.0	78.9	1,873.9	952.3	921.6	320.2	309.7	10.5
1981	2,017.5	1,006.5	1,011.1	279.5	183.6	95.8	1.74	2.33	1.17	96.2	95.2	88.1	2,013.0	1,002.6	1,010.4	315.7	305.9	9.8
1982	1,960.2	950.5	1,009.7	307.2	196.7	110.5	1.97	2.65	1.35	103.6	102.7	100.9	1,945.7	936.8	1,008.9	308.6	297.9	10.8
1983	2,070.6	1,025.8	1,044.8	307.7	196.0	111.7	1.67	2.09	1.23	105.7	102.8	99.2	2,105.4	1,057.7	1,047.7	343.5	329.8	13.7
1984	2,288.2	1,175.3	1,112.9	334.2	217.0	117.2	1.75	2.20	1.26	112.3	114.5	107.5	2,314.5	1,202.0	1,112.6	369.8	356.4	13.4

(continued)

TABLE Dd626–643   Shipments, inventories, and orders, by durable and nondurable goods manufacturing industries: 1947–1995   Continued

	Shipments			Inventories			Inventory to sales ratio			By stage of manufacturing			Orders					
													New			Unfilled		
	Total	Durable goods	Nondurable goods	Total	Durable goods	Nondurable goods	Total	Durable goods	Nondurable goods	Materials and supplies	Work in progress	Finished goods	Total	Durable goods	Nondurable goods	Total	Durable goods	Nondurable goods
	Dd626	Dd627	Dd628	Dd629	Dd630	Dd631	Dd632	Dd633	Dd634	Dd635	Dd636	Dd637	Dd638	Dd639	Dd640	Dd641	Dd642	Dd643
Year	Billion dollars	Billion dollars	Billion dollars	Billion dollars	Billion dollars	Billion dollars	Ratio	Ratio	Ratio	Billion dollars	Billion dollars	Billion dollars	Billion dollars	Billion dollars	Billion dollars	Billion dollars	Billion dollars	Billion dollars
1985	2,334.4	1,215.4	1,119.1	329.6	214.0	115.6	1.72	2.16	1.24	108.7	114.4	106.5	2,348.5	1,228.3	1,120.2	383.9	369.4	14.5
1986	2,335.9	1,238.9	1,097.0	317.6	207.9	109.7	1.63	2.01	1.19	104.3	111.9	101.4	2,342.4	1,243.8	1,098.7	390.4	374.3	16.2
1987	2,475.9	1,297.5	1,178.4	332.6	216.3	116.3	1.58	1.96	1.16	109.5	118.1	105.0	2,512.7	1,329.7	1,183.0	427.2	406.4	20.7
1988	2,695.4	1,421.5	1,273.9	363.3	237.5	125.8	1.56	1.93	1.14	119.7	129.6	114.0	2,739.2	1,464.9	1,274.3	471.0	449.9	21.1
1989	2,840.4	1,477.9	1,362.5	384.5	252.1	132.5	1.65	2.10	1.18	123.8	139.7	121.0	2,874.9	1,512.7	1,362.2	505.5	484.6	20.9
1990	2,912.2	1,485.3	1,426.9	397.9	257.4	140.5	1.70	2.23	1.18	127.0	142.5	128.3	2,934.1	1,507.0	1,427.1	527.3	506.3	21.0
1991	2,878.1	1,452.0	1,426.2	383.5	244.1	139.4	1.65	2.11	1.19	124.5	133.5	125.5	2,865.7	1,438.2	1,427.5	514.8	492.5	22.3
1992	3,004.7	1,541.9	1,462.9	374.9	232.3	142.6	1.47	1.77	1.15	124.0	124.0	126.9	2,978.5	1,515.7	1,462.9	488.7	466.3	22.3
1993	3,127.6	1,630.6	1,497.0	382.5	237.4	145.1	1.46	1.70	1.19	128.9	125.4	128.2	3,092.4	1,597.0	1,495.4	453.4	432.7	20.7
1994	3,343.8	1,787.0	1,556.8	397.4	248.4	149.0	1.39	1.64	1.11	136.6	128.8	132.0	3,354.7	1,794.1	1,560.7	464.3	439.7	24.6
1995	3,566.9	1,910.6	1,656.3	422.6	263.5	159.1	1.44	1.67	1.16	145.5	136.2	140.9	3,577.1	1,922.6	1,654.5	474.5	451.7	22.8

Source

U.S. Bureau of the Census, *Manufacturers' Shipments, Inventories, and Orders: 1947–1963 revised, 1961–1968, 1966–1972 revised, 1967–1978 revised, 1978–1984, and 1982–1995 revised*, series M3-1.

Documentation

Durable goods are defined as those with a life of three or more years. Nondurable goods have a life expectancy shorter than three years and include perishable products (those with a life expectancy of six months or less).

The manufacturers' shipments, inventories, and orders survey provides monthly figures that are comparable with the annual totals published each year in the Annual Survey of Manufactures. The sample panel is defined as a probability sample drawn as a subsample of the companies with 100 or more employees in the Annual Survey of Manufactures. The monthly reporting panel consists of approximately 5,000 reporting units and includes virtually all companies with 1,000 or more employees and a sample of the smaller ones.

Series Dd626–628. As used here, shipments represents manufacturers' receipts, billings, or the value of products shipped, less discounts, returns, and allowances during the calendar year. They exclude freight charges and excise taxes. Shipments for export as well as for domestic use are included, although shipments by foreign subsidiaries are excluded while shipments to a foreign subsidiary by a domestic firm are included. The shipments figures from the Annual Survey of Manufactures to which these series are benchmarked include interplant transfers as well as commercial sales.

Series Dd629–637. Inventory data are the book values of stocks on hand at the end of the period (December 31) and include materials and supplies, goods in process, and finished goods. Inventories associated with nonmanufacturing activities are excluded from the benchmark. In general, inventories are as valued by the manufacturer. Respondents are asked to report inventories of individual establishments at approximate current cost if feasible; otherwise, at book values. Because different methods of inventory valuation are used, the definition of the aggregate inventories for establishments in an industry is not precise. The figures on the change in inventories from one period to the next are of greater significance than the actual aggregates.

Series Dd632–634. Figures are the ratio of average inventories to average monthly sales. Beginning in 1967, figures are based on seasonally adjusted data.

Series Dd635–637. Inventories are reported by stage of fabrication: (a) finished goods; (b) work in process; and (c) materials, supplies, fuel, and other inventories. In using inventories by stage of fabrication at the all-manufacturing level, as well as for the durable and nondurable goods sectors, it should be noted that a finished product of one industry may be a raw material for another industry at the next stage of fabrication.

Series Dd638–640. New orders are net of cancellations received during the period. They include orders received during the period and also filled during the period as well as orders received for future delivery. They also include the net sales value of contract change documents that increase or decrease the sales value of the unfilled orders to which they relate. Orders include only those supported by binding legal documents such as signed contracts, letters of award, or letters of intent. In the case of letters of intent, the full amount of the sales value is included if the parties are in substantial agreement on the amount; otherwise, only the funds specifically authorized to be expended are included. New orders are derived from the shipments plus net change in unfilled orders for each industry category as of December 31.

Series Dd641–643. Unfilled orders at the end of a reporting period are orders that have not passed through the sales account and are equal to unfilled orders at the beginning of the period plus net new orders received during the period less net sales as of December 31. While both new orders and unfilled orders are used in reviewing individual company reports for consistency, only unfilled orders are estimated directly in the tabulated totals.

TABLE Dd644–660 Production capacity of selected manufacturing industries: 1887–1970

Contributed by Jeremy Atack and Fred Bateman

	Rayon and acetate yarn, staple, and tow	Paper and paperboard	Sulfuric acid	Phosphate fertilizers	Total combined nitrogen	Carbon black	Crude petroleum refining	Portland cement	Blast furnaces (pig iron)	Steel ingots and steel for castings	Coke Beehive	Coke By-product (slot type)	Copper refining	Aluminum ingots	Smelters and refiners of Missouri lead	Silver-lead refineries	Zinc refining
Year	Dd644	Dd645	Dd646	Dd647	Dd648	Dd649	Dd650	Dd651	Dd652	Dd653	Dd654	Dd655	Dd656 [1]	Dd657	Dd658	Dd659	Dd660 [1]
	Thousand short tons	Thousand short tons	Thousand short tons	Thousand short tons	Thousand short tons	Thousand short tons	42-gallon barrels	Thousand short tons	Thousand short tons	Thousand short tons	Thousand short tons	Thousand short tons	Thousand short tons	Thousand short tons	Thousand short tons	Thousand short tons	Thousand short tons
1887	—	—	—	—	—	—	—	—	—	5,852	—	—	—	—	—	—	—
1889	—	—	—	—	—	—	—	—	—	7,195	—	—	—	—	—	—	—
1891	—	—	—	—	—	—	—	—	—	—	—	—	—	(Z)	—	—	—
1892	—	—	—	—	—	—	—	—	—	8,332	—	—	—	(Z)	—	—	—
1894	—	—	—	—	—	—	—	—	—	10,780	—	—	—	(Z)	—	—	—
1895	—	—	—	—	—	—	—	—	—	—	—	—	—	—	—	—	—
1896	—	—	—	—	—	—	—	—	—	13,236	—	—	—	(Z)	—	—	—
1898	—	2,782	—	—	—	—	—	—	18,124	15,639	—	—	—	—	—	—	—
1900	—	—	—	336	—	—	—	—	—	—	—	—	—	—	—	—	—
1901	—	—	—	—	—	—	—	—	23,961	23,276	—	—	—	—	—	—	—
1904	—	3,858	—	—	—	—	—	—	27,262	26,919	—	—	—	—	—	—	—
1905	—	—	—	—	—	—	—	—	—	—	—	—	—	—	—	—	—
1907	—	—	—	—	—	—	—	—	—	—	—	—	568	—	—	—	—
1908	—	—	—	—	—	—	—	—	—	—	—	—	581	—	—	—	—
1909	—	5,293	—	943	—	—	—	—	34,074	36,545	57,100	(Z)	587	—	—	—	—
1910	—	—	—	—	—	—	—	17,578	—	—	58,200	(Z)	644	—	—	—	—
1911	1	—	—	—	—	—	—	18,362	—	—	59,100	8,600	724	17	—	—	—
1912	—	—	—	—	—	—	—	21,150	—	—	58,900	10,200	747	—	—	—	—
1913	—	—	—	—	—	—	—	20,680	48,448	—	57,900	12,800	824	—	—	—	—
1914	—	—	—	—	—	—	—	21,620	49,723	42,678	57,200	15,000	884	—	—	—	—
1915	—	6,440	—	—	—	—	—	21,620	49,734	44,454	56,300	16,600	889	45	—	—	—
1916	—	—	—	—	—	—	—	24,402	50,438	49,266	55,000	18,400	946	—	—	—	—
1917	—	—	—	—	—	—	—	25,132	51,368	53,914	55,000	21,600	1,244	—	—	—	—
1918	—	7,000	—	—	—	—	434	25,709	53,701	57,083	53,000	25,900	1,408	—	—	—	—
1919	—	7,500	—	—	—	—	473	25,869	55,182	59,174	51,000	33,700	1,408	63	—	—	—
1920	—	7,671	—	1,447	—	—	559	25,209	56,249	60,220	49,300	38,200	1,384	—	—	—	—
1921	—	8,540	—	—	—	—	689	27,523	57,950	61,928	—	42,821	1,348	—	342	—	1,439
1922	—	8,614	—	—	—	—	770	26,693	58,786	63,135	(Z)	43,854	1,348	—	348	—	1,439
1923	—	8,970	—	—	—	—	—	27,486	59,009	63,383	(Z)	43,763	1,348	—	372	—	1,409
1924	—	9,725	—	—	54	—	1,027	30,429	59,006	64,137	(Z)	45,058	1,318	—	372	—	1,485
1925	—	10,500	—	—	55	—	1,032	32,919	59,847	65,962	(Z)	46,809	1,335	—	427	—	1,478
1926	—	11,623	—	—	65	—	1,041	36,389	57,288	62,925	(Z)	48,184	1,375	—	437	—	1,625
1927	—	12,000	—	—	66	—	1,117	40,476	58,701	65,344	(Z)	52,666	1,490	82	437	—	1,692
1928	—	12,536	—	—	116	228	1,190	42,691	56,596	66,960	(Z)	57,852	1,520	83	437	711	1,697
1929	—	12,933	—	—	212	263	1,281	45,816	57,382	69,584	(Z)	60,357	1,520	100	407	711	1,575
1930	—	13,704	—	1,644	236	270	1,374	48,676	57,855	71,042	(Z)	60,167	1,528	113	407	771	1,491
1931	81	13,643	—	—	261	249	1,439	50,768	58,979	75,328	(Z)	61,468	1,630	125	417	775	1,447
1932	—	13,972	—	—	357	227	1,469	51,108	57,949	76,898	(Z)	63,491	1,612	132	417	781	1,424
1933	105	13,728	—	—	347	231	1,420	51,006	56,511	76,767	(Z)	62,645	1,612	134	417	823	1,458
1934	—	13,728	—	—	341	240	1,430	50,645	57,243	78,128	(Z)	63,050	1,624	132	417	895	1,489

Notes appear at end of table   (continued)

TABLE Dd644-660 Production capacity of selected manufacturing industries: 1887-1970 Continued

Year	Rayon and acetate yarn, staple, and tow Dd644 Thousand short tons	Paper and paperboard Dd645 Thousand short tons	Sulfuric acid Dd646 Thousand short tons	Phosphate fertilizers Dd647 Thousand short tons	Total combined nitrogen Dd648 Thousand short tons	Carbon black Dd649 Thousand short tons	Crude petroleum refining Dd650 42-gallon barrels	Portland cement Dd651 Thousand short tons	Blast furnaces (pig iron) Dd652 Thousand short tons	Steel ingots and steel for castings Dd653 Thousand short tons	Coke Beehive Dd654 Thousand short tons	Coke By-product (slot type) Dd655 Thousand short tons	Copper refining Dd656 Thousand short tons	Aluminum ingots Dd657 Thousand short tons	Lead refining Smelters and refiners of Missouri lead Dd658 Thousand short tons	Lead refining Silver-lead refineries Dd659 Thousand short tons	Zinc refining Dd660 Thousand short tons
1935	—	13,888	—	—	341	265	1,481	49,389	57,098	78,452	(Z)	62,757	1,624	130	333	799	1,489
1936	147	13,986	—	—	342	261	1,507	49,240	55,854	78,164	(Z)	62,403	1,613	130	333	785	1,379
1937	163	14,458	—	—	359	317	1,568	48,035	55,557	78,148	(Z)	62,076	1,642	133	317	809	1,368
1938	183	15,573	—	—	370	317	1,588	47,982	56,782	80,186	(Z)	62,727	1,642	144	317	863	1,413
1939	220	16,191	—	—	375	313	1,646	48,071	56,326	81,829	(Z)	61,272	1,642	131	317	851	1,346
1940	253	16,557	—	1,692	380	317	1,694	48,142	55,724	81,619	(Z)	62,955	1,572	188	317	851	1,313
1941	300	16,891	—	—	390	313	1,722	47,707	57,775	85,158	(Z)	62,220	1,549	245	313	845	787
1942	—	18,492	—	—	455	330	1,809	46,416	60,607	88,887	11,210	62,562	1,561	391	361	767	950
1943	—	18,755	—	—	797	395	1,789	46,669	64,188	90,589	10,409	64,555	1,563	771	(Z)	767	1,069
1944	370	18,830	—	—	1,191	472	1,864	45,319	67,921	93,854	11,230	71,378	1,595	1,164	279	767	1,097
1945	—	19,260	10,500	2,291	1,327	663	1,935	44,915	67,314	95,505	10,438	72,330	1,720	704	246	767	1,084
1946	446	20,282	—	—	1,384	668	1,940	45,108	67,341	91,891	8,095	71,399	1,720	785	238	737	1,100
1947	511	20,420	—	2,604	1,394	743	2,033	45,086	65,709	91,241	8,427	71,113	1,585	762	238	653	1,000
1948	586	22,025	—	2,834	1,389	736	2,209	46,362	67,439	94,233	8,844	72,549	1,557	676	238	653	1,000
1949	587	23,389	—	—	1,389	758	2,350	47,326	70,542	96,121	9,076	74,500	1,547	679	238	628	974
1950	641	25,048	13,000	2,896	1,565	744	2,444	48,000	71,560	99,983	8,672	73,710	1,557	633	238	628	986
1951	708	26,059	13,410	3,349	1,593	942	2,542	49,712	72,472	104,230	11,572	72,488	1,599	750	238	628	966
1952	745	26,789	14,220	3,432	1,955	1,030	2,684	52,156	73,782	108,588	13,859	74,228	1,599	846	238	628	995
1953	805	27,854	14,560	3,720	2,002	975	2,788	52,624	79,380	117,547	12,005	76,428	1,647	1,142	242	628	1,014
1954	826	29,089	15,970	4,329	2,474	966	2,923	54,050	82,001	124,330	10,073	78,258	1,896	1,311	258	628	1,094
1955	785	30,025	17,440	4,642	3,194	990	3,074	55,324	83,971	125,828	8,078	78,596	1,862	1,388	258	628	1,110
1956	750	33,169	18,600	4,590	3,631	1,016	3,159	58,562	85,485	128,363	6,285	79,676	2,064	1,589	258	628	1,161
1957	768	35,021	19,500	4,550	3,711	1,085	3,330	64,699	86,818	133,459	5,766	79,965	2,064	1,776	258	560	1,159
1958	709	37,351	15,950	2,423	3,879	1,028	3,434	70,385	91,000	140,743	5,503	80,299	2,109	2,230	248	560	1,173
1959	732	38,641	17,609	2,641	4,520	1,051	3,584	74,596	94,635	147,634	5,020	82,498	2,309	2,403	248	488	1,176
1960	734	40,232	17,883	2,672	4,818	1,174	3,624	77,906	96,521	148,571	4,369	81,448	2,332	2,464	248	488	1,191
1961	711	41,334	17,848	2,743	5,207	1,264	3,654	80,265	—	—	4,616	78,877	2,342	2,484	120	488	1,199
1962	727	42,800	19,701	2,823	5,810	1,287	3,682	81,878	—	—	—	—	2,335	2,489	120	488	1,203
1963	747	43,423	20,936	3,231	6,693	1,282	3,693	86,757	—	—	—	—	2,335	2,509	120	488	1,252
1964	818	44,671	22,924	3,482	7,634	1,327	3,801	88,451	—	—	—	—	2,365	2,553	120	488	1,267
1965	855	46,250	24,857	3,834	8,869	1,467	3,933	88,664	—	—	—	—	2,421	2,795	120	488	1,278
1966	860	48,073	28,385	4,450	10,605	1,464	3,830	89,194	—	—	—	—	2,431	2,968	120	402	1,264
1967	843	51,410	28,815	4,695	12,194	1,551	3,927	91,588	—	—	—	—	2,522	3,319	300	500	1,294
1968	858	53,978	28,544	4,149	12,120	1,668	4,221	93,521	—	—	—	—	2,643	3,668	390	422	1,310
1969	865	56,241	29,537	4,290	12,713	1,832	4,285	93,682	—	—	—	—	2,676	3,863	415	422	1,288
1970	857	58,372	29,676	4,496	13,135	1,877	4,407	93,349	—	—	—	—	2,676	4,121	435	350	1,253

(Z) Less than 500 tons.

[1] Components change over time; see text.

Sources

Series **Dd644.** 1911: *New York Times*, Special Chemistry Section, September 2, 1951. 1931–1970: Textile Economics Bureau, *Textile Organon* (prior to 1952, *Rayon Organon*), various issues.

Series **Dd645.** American Paper Institute, *The Statistics of Paper* (1957 and subsequent annual issues).

Series **Dd646.** 1945: *Chemical and Engineering News*, July 10, 1945. 1950–1970: U.S. Bureau of Domestic Commerce, *Chemical Industry Report* (various issues).

Series **Dd647.** 1900–1951: U.S. Agricultural Research Service, *Statistics on Fertilizers and Liming Materials in the United States*, Statistical Bulletin number 191, April 1957. 1952–1957: National Plant Food was used, based on 340 days a year for paper, 339 days for paperboard, and 326 days for construction paper and board and wet machine board. In 1970, practical maximum capacity was based on 346 days for all grades, 348 days for paper, 346 days for paperboard, and 334 days for construction paper and board and wet machine board. Includes Alaska and Hawai'i beginning in 1960.

Series Dd646. Capacity is based on 350 days a year.

Series Dd647. Available phosphoric oxide (P_2O_3). These data are the total of normal superphosphate, concentrated superphosphate, and miscellaneous phosphatic materials. Capacity of normal superphosphate is based on 300 two-shift days a year. Capacity of concentrated superphosphate and other phosphatic materials is based on 350 days a year, continuous operations.

Series Dd648. This series was titled "synthetic nitrogen" for 1924–1955. Capacity is based on 350 days a year, continuous operations.

Series Dd650. Capacity is defined as the maximum daily average throughout (converted to an annual basis) of the plant in complete operation, with allowance for necessary shutdown time for routine maintenance, repairs, and so forth. It approximates the maximum daily average crude runs to stills that can be maintained for an extended period. Capacity is based on November 1 for 1924. Includes Alaska for all years, Hawai'i beginning in 1960.

Series Dd651. A deduction from full-time operation is taken for estimated average number of days required for repair or other unavoidable shutdowns. Favorable labor, fuel, and transportation conditions are assumed. No capacity in Alaska; figures include Hawai'i beginning in 1960.

Series Dd652. Figures include a 6.1 percent deduction from full-time operation to allow for rebuilding, relining, and repairing the equipment. Capacity is based on April 1 for 1898; November 1 for 1901 and 1907; June 1, 1904; and the average of January 1 and July 1 for 1941–1944 and 1950.

Series Dd653. From open hearth, Bessemer, crucible, and electric furnaces. Figures include a 9.1 percent deduction from full-time operation to allow for rebuilding, relining, and repairing equipment, and for holiday shutdowns. Capacity is based on an average of January 1 and July 1 for 1941–1944.

Series Dd656. For 1907–1943, electrolytic capacity only; thereafter, includes electrolytic refining capacity plus Lake Superior and fire-refined.

Series Dd657. The general practice in this industry is to rate potline capacity on full-time operation. As an alternative source for data, see U.S. Bureau of Mines, *Minerals Yearbook* (various issues).

Series Dd660. Figures are not comparable throughout because of changes in components. For 1921–1925, figures represent distillation zinc; 1926–1940, distillation and electrolytic zinc; 1941–1970, slab zinc. As an alternative source for data, see U.S. Bureau of Mines, *Minerals Yearbook* (various issues).

Institute, *Plant Food Review*, volume 4, numbers 2 and 3 (1958). 1958–1970: U.S. Bureau of Domestic Commerce, unpublished data.

Series Dd648. 1924–1950: see source for series Dd647. 1951–1955: U.S. Business and Defense Services Administration, *Summary Information on Anhydrous Ammonia*, Bulletin number 142, February 1956. 1956–1970: U.S. Bureau of Domestic Commerce, unpublished data.

Series Dd649 and Dd651. U.S. Geological Survey, 1910–1923, *Mineral Resources of the United States* (annual volumes); U.S. Bureau of Mines, 1924–1931, *Mineral Resources of the United States* (annual volumes); 1932–1970, *Minerals Yearbook* (annual volumes).

Series Dd650. U.S. Bureau of Mines, 1918–1961, *Petroleum Refineries, Including Cracking Plants in the United States*, January 1, 1961 (also shown in *Minerals Yearbook*); 1962–1970, *Mineral Industry Survey, Petroleum Refineries in the United States and Puerto Rico* (January 1, annual issues).

Series Dd652–653. American Iron and Steel Institute, *Annual Directory* and *Annual Statistical Report* (various issues).

Series Dd654–655. 1909–1920: Edwin G. Nourse, *America's Capacity to Produce* (Brookings Institution Press, 1934), p. 557. 1921–1961: see sources cited for series Dd651.

Series Dd656. 1907–1930: Edwin G. Nourse, *America's Capacity to Produce* (Brookings Institution Press, 1934), p. 557. 1931–1970: American Bureau of Metal Statistics, *Year Book* (various issues).

Series Dd657. 1889–1895: J. D. Edwards and F. C. Frary, *The Aluminum Industry* (McGraw-Hill, 1930). 1910–1919: U.S. Business and Defense Services Administration, *Materials Survey, Aluminum* (1956). 1927–1938: U.S. Surplus Property Board, *Aluminum Plants and Facilities Report* (1945). 1939–1970: American Bureau of Metal Statistics, *Year Book* (various issues).

Series Dd658–660. American Bureau of Metal Statistics, *Year Book* (various issues).

Documentation

This table and its associated documentation have been reprinted, more or less without modification, from U.S. Bureau of the Census, *Historical Statistics of the United States* (1975), series P301–317.

Capacity is rarely calculated on the basis of full-time operation of an industry (that is, 365 days a year, 24 hours a day), but at varying criteria short of that. Capacity as of January 1 is generally used as the basis of computation. Exceptions to these general rules are noted in the text for each series, where applicable.

Except as noted for specific series, there was none or negligible capacity in Alaska and Hawai'i.

Series Dd644. Data for 1931–1938 are for yarn only; staple and tow data are not available for those years. Capacity is as of November for all years except 1933 (July) and 1944 (April). Allowance was made for periodic shutdowns of machines for repair, overhaul, or cleaning on a set time schedule.

Series Dd645. Historic capacity, used until 1955, is based on 310 days a year, 24 hours a day, for paper and building paper and 313 days for paperboard. From 1956 to 1969, practical maximum capacity

INPUTS – EMPLOYEES, CAPITAL, AND CONSUMPTION OF POWER AND SELECTED COMMODITIES

Jeremy Atack and Fred Bateman

TABLE Dd661–683   Employees of manufacturing firms, by industry division: 1919–1999
Contributed by Susan B. Carter

Year	Total Dd661 Thousand	Total Dd662 Thousand	Lumber and wood product Dd663 Thousand	Furniture and fixture Dd664 Thousand	Stone, clay, and glass Dd665 Thousand	Primary metal Dd666 Thousand	Fabricated metal products Dd667 Thousand	Industrial machinery and equipment Dd668 Thousand	Electronic and other electrical equipment Dd669 Thousand	Transportation equipment Dd670 Thousand	Instruments and related products Dd671 Thousand	Miscellaneous Dd672 Thousand
					Durable goods							
1919	10,659	—	—	—	—	—	—	—	—	—	—	—
1920	10,658	—	—	—	—	—	—	—	—	—	—	—
1921	8,257	—	—	—	—	—	—	—	—	—	—	—
1922	9,120	—	—	—	—	—	—	—	—	—	—	—
1923	10,300	—	—	—	—	—	—	—	—	—	—	—
1924	9,671	—	—	—	—	—	—	—	—	—	—	—
1925	9,939	—	—	—	—	—	—	—	—	—	—	—
1926	10,156	—	—	—	—	—	—	—	—	—	—	—
1927	10,001	—	—	—	—	—	—	—	—	—	—	—
1928	9,947	—	—	—	—	—	—	—	—	—	—	—
1929	10,702	—	—	—	—	—	—	—	—	—	—	—
1930	9,562	—	—	—	—	—	—	—	—	—	—	—
1931	8,170	—	—	—	—	—	—	—	—	—	—	—
1932	6,931	—	—	—	—	—	—	—	—	—	—	—
1933	7,397	—	—	—	—	—	—	—	—	—	—	—
1934	8,501	—	—	—	—	—	—	—	—	—	—	—
1935	9,069	—	—	—	—	—	—	—	—	—	—	—
1936	9,827	—	—	—	—	—	—	—	—	—	—	—
1937	10,794	—	—	—	—	—	—	—	—	—	—	—
1938	9,440	—	—	—	—	—	—	—	—	—	—	—
1939	10,278	4,754	—	—	350	—	—	—	369	638	—	—
1940	10,985	5,401	—	—	366	—	—	—	413	824	—	—
1941	13,192	7,006	—	—	431	—	—	—	550	1,281	—	—
1942	15,280	8,858	—	—	436	—	—	—	660	2,232	—	—
1943	17,602	11,112	—	—	422	—	—	—	849	3,622	—	—
1944	17,328	10,885	—	—	391	—	—	—	910	3,638	—	—
1945	15,524	9,108	—	—	386	—	—	—	820	2,517	—	—
1946	14,703	7,785	—	—	472	—	—	—	769	1,235	—	—
1947	15,545	8,358	882	320	508	1,225	1,049	1,386	855	1,261	451	421
1948	15,582	8,298	855	329	520	1,236	1,041	1,382	819	1,256	439	422
1949	14,441	7,462	775	301	486	1,087	935	1,192	713	1,196	393	385
1950	15,241	8,066	846	346	518	1,194	1,042	1,221	819	1,253	427	400
1951	16,393	9,059	879	340	556	1,307	1,158	1,470	927	1,516	501	406
1952	16,632	9,320	830	340	534	1,228	1,173	1,533	999	1,739	550	394
1953	17,549	10,080	813	352	550	1,325	1,287	1,573	1,128	2,022	610	421
1954	16,314	9,101	747	326	523	1,168	1,171	1,434	1,001	1,784	557	391

Year	Total	Total	Durable goods									
			Lumber and wood product	Furniture and fixture	Stone, clay, and glass	Primary metal	Fabricated metal products	Industrial machinery and equipment	Electronic and other electrical equipment	Transportation equipment	Instruments and related products	Miscellaneous
	Dd661	Dd662	Dd663	Dd664	Dd665	Dd666	Dd667	Dd668	Dd669	Dd670	Dd671	Dd672
	Thousand	Thousand	Thousand	Thousand	Thousand	Thousand	Thousand	Thousand	Thousand	Thousand	Thousand	Thousand
1955	16,882	9,511	781	347	557	1,267	1,222	1,465	1,039	1,874	563	396
1956	17,243	9,802	773	358	573	1,298	1,240	1,589	1,106	1,871	592	403
1957	17,176	9,825	697	357	564	1,298	1,267	1,603	1,123	1,928	600	387
1958	15,945	8,801	655	343	533	1,107	1,170	1,378	1,045	1,635	563	373
1959	16,675	9,342	703	367	572	1,133	1,219	1,469	1,166	1,715	611	388
1960	16,796	9,429	670	365	572	1,185	1,230	1,496	1,221	1,668	632	390
1961	16,326	9,041	624	350	551	1,100	1,181	1,435	1,222	1,574	625	378
1962	16,853	9,450	634	367	561	1,121	1,238	1,511	1,296	1,683	650	390
1963	16,995	9,586	641	371	569	1,127	1,264	1,548	1,282	1,749	648	387
1964	17,274	9,785	658	387	581	1,188	1,295	1,627	1,273	1,732	647	398
1965	18,062	10,374	665	410	595	1,253	1,372	1,754	1,368	1,853	684	420
1966	19,214	11,250	677	440	610	1,297	1,489	1,931	1,571	2,031	770	434
1967	19,447	11,408	662	434	595	1,261	1,556	1,991	1,615	2,058	801	428
1968	19,781	11,594	674	450	602	1,261	1,609	1,988	1,629	2,133	814	433
1969	20,167	11,862	691	461	622	1,305	1,665	2,055	1,664	2,120	838	441
1970	19,367	11,176	658	440	610	1,260	1,559	2,003	1,584	1,833	804	426
1971	18,623	10,604	681	444	611	1,171	1,479	1,834	1,477	1,743	753	412
1972	19,151	11,022	740	483	645	1,173	1,541	1,909	1,535	1,777	786	433
1973	20,154	11,863	774	507	680	1,259	1,645	2,111	1,667	1,915	851	454
1974	20,077	11,897	727	489	673	1,289	1,632	2,230	1,666	1,853	885	452
1975	18,323	10,662	627	417	598	1,139	1,453	2,076	1,442	1,700	804	407
1976	18,997	11,051	693	444	613	1,155	1,505	2,085	1,503	1,785	840	429
1977	19,682	11,570	736	464	636	1,182	1,577	2,195	1,591	1,857	895	438
1978	20,505	12,245	770	494	664	1,215	1,667	2,347	1,699	1,987	952	452
1979	21,040	12,730	782	498	674	1,254	1,713	2,508	1,793	2,059	1,006	445
1980	20,285	12,159	704	466	629	1,142	1,609	2,517	1,771	1,881	1,022	418
1981	20,170	12,082	680	464	606	1,122	1,586	2,521	1,774	1,879	1,041	408
1982	18,780	11,014	610	432	548	922	1,424	2,264	1,701	1,718	1,013	382
1983	18,432	10,707	671	448	541	832	1,368	2,053	1,704	1,730	990	370
1984	19,372	11,476	718	486	562	857	1,462	2,218	1,869	1,883	1,040	382
1985	19,248	11,458	711	493	557	808	1,464	2,195	1,859	1,960	1,045	367
1986	18,947	11,195	724	498	554	751	1,422	2,074	1,790	2,003	1,018	361
1987	18,999	11,154	754	515	554	746	1,399	2,028	1,750	2,028	1,011	370
1988	19,314	11,363	767	527	567	770	1,428	2,089	1,764	2,036	1,031	383
1989	19,391	11,394	756	524	568	772	1,445	2,125	1,744	2,052	1,026	381
1990	19,076	11,109	733	506	556	756	1,419	2,095	1,673	1,989	1,006	375
1991	18,406	10,569	675	475	522	723	1,355	2,000	1,591	1,890	974	366
1992	18,104	10,277	680	478	513	695	1,329	1,929	1,528	1,830	929	368
1993	18,075	10,221	709	487	517	683	1,339	1,931	1,526	1,756	896	378
1994	18,321	10,448	754	505	532	698	1,388	1,990	1,571	1,761	861	389
1995	18,524	10,683	769	510	540	712	1,437	2,067	1,625	1,790	843	390
1996	18,495	10,789	778	504	544	711	1,449	2,115	1,661	1,785	855	388
1997	18,675	11,010	796	512	552	711	1,479	2,168	1,689	1,845	866	392
1998	18,805	11,205	814	533	562	715	1,509	2,206	1,707	1,893	873	395
1999	18,543	11,103	828	548	563	700	1,517	2,141	1,670	1,884	856	395

(continued)

TABLE Dd661–683 Employees of manufacturing firms, by industry division: 1919–1999 *Continued*

Nondurable goods

Year	Total Dd673 [1] Thousand	Food and kindred products Dd674 [1] Thousand	Tobacco Dd675 [1] Thousand	Textile mill Dd676 [1] Thousand	Apparel and other textile Dd677 [1] Thousand	Paper and allied products Dd678 [1] Thousand	Printing and publishing Dd679 [1] Thousand	Chemicals and allied products Dd680 [1] Thousand	Petroleum and coal Dd681 [1] Thousand	Rubber and miscellaneous plastics products Dd682 [1] Thousand	Leather and leather products Dd683 [1] Thousand
1939	5,524	1,393	—	1,193	924	318	569	371	139	184	386
1940	5,584	1,414	—	1,176	929	331	570	399	146	198	374
1941	6,186	1,514	—	1,336	1,050	370	580	483	155	239	415
1942	6,422	1,617	—	1,342	1,088	374	565	571	160	246	413
1943	6,490	1,649	—	1,295	1,107	387	557	609	160	294	381
1944	6,443	1,685	—	1,197	1,079	386	558	650	174	309	359
1945	6,415	1,691	—	1,139	1,060	389	577	668	186	308	358
1946	6,918	1,767	—	1,264	1,146	444	669	633	208	345	408
1947	7,187	1,799	118	1,298	1,154	462	721	649	221	353	412
1948	7,285	1,801	114	1,332	1,190	469	739	655	228	344	412
1949	6,979	1,778	109	1,187	1,173	452	740	618	221	312	389
1950	7,175	1,790	103	1,256	1,202	482	748	640	218	342	395
1951	7,334	1,823	104	1,238	1,207	508	768	707	231	368	380
1952	7,313	1,828	106	1,163	1,216	500	780	730	235	371	384
1953	7,468	1,839	104	1,155	1,248	527	803	768	241	394	389
1954	7,213	1,818	103	1,042	1,184	528	814	753	238	360	373
1955	7,370	1,825	103	1,050	1,219	546	835	773	237	397	386
1956	7,442	1,842	100	1,032	1,223	564	862	797	236	404	383
1957	7,351	1,805	97	981	1,210	567	870	810	232	406	373
1958	7,144	1,773	95	919	1,172	560	873	794	224	376	359
1959	7,333	1,790	95	946	1,226	583	889	809	216	407	374
1960	7,367	1,790	94	924	1,233	597	911	828	212	413	363
1961	7,285	1,775	91	893	1,215	597	917	828	202	408	358
1962	7,403	1,763	91	902	1,264	610	926	849	195	442	361
1963	7,410	1,752	89	885	1,283	615	931	865	189	453	349
1964	7,489	1,750	90	892	1,303	621	952	879	184	471	348
1965	7,688	1,757	87	926	1,354	635	979	908	183	507	353
1966	7,963	1,777	84	964	1,402	663	1,017	961	184	547	364
1967	8,039	1,786	87	959	1,398	675	1,048	1,001	183	552	351
1968	8,187	1,782	85	994	1,406	687	1,065	1,030	187	598	355
1969	8,304	1,791	83	1,003	1,409	706	1,094	1,060	184	634	343
1970	8,190	1,786	83	975	1,364	701	1,104	1,049	191	617	320
1971	8,019	1,766	77	955	1,343	677	1,081	1,011	194	617	299
1972	8,129	1,745	75	986	1,383	679	1,094	1,009	195	667	296
1973	8,291	1,715	78	1,010	1,438	694	1,111	1,038	193	731	284
1974	8,181	1,707	77	965	1,363	696	1,111	1,061	197	733	271
1975	7,661	1,658	76	868	1,243	633	1,083	1,015	194	643	248
1976	7,946	1,689	77	919	1,318	666	1,099	1,043	199	675	263
1977	8,112	1,711	71	910	1,316	682	1,141	1,074	202	750	255
1978	8,259	1,724	71	899	1,332	689	1,192	1,096	208	793	257
1979	8,310	1,733	70	885	1,304	697	1,235	1,109	210	821	246
1980	8,127	1,708	69	848	1,264	685	1,252	1,107	198	764	233
1981	8,089	1,671	70	823	1,244	681	1,266	1,109	214	772	238
1982	7,766	1,636	69	749	1,161	655	1,272	1,075	201	729	219
1983	7,725	1,614	68	741	1,163	654	1,298	1,043	196	743	205
1984	7,896	1,611	64	746	1,185	674	1,375	1,049	189	813	189

Nondurable goods

Year	Total Dd673 [1]	Food and kindred products Dd674 [1]	Tobacco Dd675 [1]	Textile mill Dd676 [1]	Apparel and other textile Dd677 [1]	Paper and allied products Dd678 [1]	Printing and publishing Dd679 [1]	Chemicals and allied products Dd680 [1]	Petroleum and coal Dd681 [1]	Rubber and miscellaneous plastics products Dd682 [1]	Leather and leather products Dd683 [1]
	Thousand	Thousand	Thousand	Thousand	Thousand	Thousand	Thousand	Thousand	Thousand	Thousand	Thousand
1985	7,790	1,601	64	702	1,120	671	1,426	1,044	179	818	165
1986	7,752	1,607	59	703	1,100	667	1,456	1,021	169	823	149
1987	7,845	1,617	55	725	1,097	674	1,503	1,025	164	842	143
1988	7,951	1,626	54	728	1,085	689	1,543	1,057	160	866	143
1989	7,997	1,644	50	720	1,076	696	1,556	1,074	156	888	138
1990	7,968	1,661	49	691	1,036	697	1,569	1,086	157	888	133
1991	7,837	1,667	49	670	1,006	688	1,536	1,076	160	862	124
1992	7,827	1,663	48	674	1,007	690	1,507	1,084	158	878	120
1993	7,854	1,680	44	675	989	692	1,517	1,081	152	909	117
1994	7,873	1,678	43	676	974	692	1,537	1,057	149	953	113
1995	7,841	1,692	42	663	936	693	1,546	1,038	145	980	106
1996	7,706	1,692	41	627	868	684	1,540	1,034	142	983	96
1997	7,665	1,685	41	616	824	683	1,552	1,036	141	996	91
1998	7,600	1,683	41	598	766	677	1,565	1,043	139	1,005	84
1999	7,440	1,677	38	560	692	668	1,553	1,034	134	1,006	78

[1] Series has no data before 1939.

Source

U.S. Bureau of Labor Statistics Internet site, National Current Employment Statistics. See the source for Table Ba840–848.

Documentation

See the text for Table Ba840–848.

These series correspond to Standard Industrial Classification (SIC) codes as follows: series Dd663, SIC 24; series Dd664, SIC 25; series Dd665, SIC 32; series Dd666, SIC 32; series Dd667, SIC 34; series Dd668, SIC 35; series Dd669, SIC 36; series Dd670, SIC 37; series Dd671, SIC 38; series Dd672, SIC 39; series Dd673, SIC 20–23 and 26–31; series Dd674, SIC 20; series Dd675, SIC 21; series Dd676, SIC 22; series Dd677, SIC 23; series Dd678, SIC 26; series Dd679, SIC 27; series Dd680, SIC 28; series Dd681, SIC 29; series Dd682, SIC 30; series Dd683, SIC 31. See the Introduction to Part D for a discussion of SIC codes.

Series Dd661. Equals series Ba843, and is the sum of series Dd662 and Dd673.

Series Dd662. Equals the sum of series Dd663–672.

TABLE Dd684–699   Capital in manufacturing – purchases, depreciation, and net value of structures and equipment: 1863–1970

Contributed by Jeremy Atack and Fred Bateman

	Purchases of structures and equipment						Depreciation on structures and equipment						Real net value of assets			
	Current dollars			Constant dollars			Current dollars			Constant dollars			Structures and equipment			Government-owned but privately operated assets
	Total	Structures	Equipment	Total	Structures	Equipment	Total	Structures	Equipment	Total	Structures	Equipment	Total	Structures	Equipment	
	Dd684	Dd685	Dd686	Dd687	Dd688	Dd689	Dd690	Dd691	Dd692	Dd693	Dd694	Dd695	Dd696	Dd697	Dd698	Dd699
Year	Billion dollars	Billion dollars	Billion dollars	Billion 1958 dollars	Billion 1958 dollars	Billion 1958 dollars	Billion 1958 dollars	Billion dollars	Billion dollars	Billion 1958 dollars	Billion 1958 dollars	Billion 1958 dollars	Billion 1958 dollars	Billion 1958 dollars	Billion 1958 dollars	Billion 1958 dollars
1863	(Z)	0.0	(Z)	(Z)	0.0	(Z)	—	—	—	—	—	—	—	—	—	—
1864	(Z)	0.0	(Z)	(Z)	0.0	(Z)	—	—	—	—	—	—	—	—	—	—
1865	(Z)	(Z)	(Z)	0.1	0.1	(Z)	—	—	—	—	—	—	—	—	—	—
1866	(Z)	(Z)	(Z)	0.1	0.1	(Z)	—	—	—	—	—	—	—	—	—	—
1867	(Z)	(Z)	(Z)	0.2	0.2	(Z)	—	—	—	—	—	—	—	—	—	—
1868	(Z)	(Z)	(Z)	0.2	0.2	(Z)	—	—	—	—	—	—	—	—	—	—
1869	0.1	(Z)	(Z)	0.3	0.3	(Z)	—	—	—	—	—	—	—	—	—	—
1870	0.1	0.1	(Z)	0.4	0.4	0.1	—	—	—	—	—	—	—	—	—	—
1871	0.1	(Z)	(Z)	0.4	0.3	0.1	—	—	—	—	—	—	—	—	—	—
1872	0.1	(Z)	(Z)	0.4	0.3	0.1	—	—	—	—	—	—	—	—	—	—
1873	0.1	1.1	(Z)	0.4	0.4	0.1	—	—	—	—	—	—	—	—	—	—
1874	0.1	(Z)	(Z)	0.4	0.3	(Z)	—	—	—	—	—	—	—	—	—	—
1875	(Z)	(Z)	(Z)	0.2	0.2	(Z)	—	—	—	—	—	—	—	—	—	—
1876	0.1	(Z)	0.1	0.3	0.2	0.1	—	—	—	—	—	—	—	—	—	—
1877	0.1	(Z)	0.1	0.3	0.2	0.1	—	—	—	—	—	—	—	—	—	—
1878	0.1	(Z)	0.1	0.4	0.2	0.2	—	—	—	—	—	—	—	—	—	—
1879	0.1	(Z)	0.1	0.4	0.2	0.2	—	—	—	—	—	—	—	—	—	—
1880	0.1	(Z)	(Z)	0.4	0.2	0.2	—	—	—	—	—	—	—	—	—	—
1881	0.2	0.1	0.1	0.8	0.5	0.4	—	—	—	—	—	—	—	—	—	—
1882	0.2	0.1	0.1	0.9	0.5	0.4	—	—	—	—	—	—	—	—	—	—
1883	0.1	0.1	0.1	0.8	0.5	0.3	—	—	—	—	—	—	—	—	—	—
1884	0.1	0.1	0.1	0.9	0.6	0.3	—	—	—	—	—	—	—	—	—	—
1885	0.1	0.1	(Z)	0.7	0.5	0.2	—	—	—	—	—	—	—	—	—	—
1886	0.1	0.1	0.1	0.7	0.5	0.3	—	—	—	—	—	—	—	—	—	—
1887	0.2	0.1	0.1	1.0	0.5	0.4	—	—	—	—	—	—	—	—	—	—
1888	0.2	0.1	0.1	1.1	0.6	0.6	—	—	—	—	—	—	—	—	—	—
1889	0.2	0.1	0.1	1.6	1.0	0.6	—	—	—	—	—	—	—	—	—	—
1890	0.3	0.2	0.1	2.0	1.3	0.6	—	—	—	—	—	—	—	—	—	—
1891	0.3	0.2	0.1	2.2	1.4	0.7	—	—	—	—	—	—	—	—	—	—
1892	0.3	0.2	0.1	2.2	1.5	0.8	—	—	—	—	—	—	—	—	—	—
1893	0.3	0.2	0.1	2.2	1.5	0.7	—	—	—	—	—	—	—	—	—	—
1894	0.3	0.2	0.1	2.0	1.4	0.6	—	—	—	—	—	—	—	—	—	—
1895	0.3	0.2	0.1	2.5	1.6	0.8	—	—	—	—	—	—	—	—	—	—
1896	0.4	0.2	0.1	3.1	2.1	1.0	—	—	—	—	—	—	—	—	—	—
1897	0.3	0.2	0.1	2.7	2.1	0.7	—	—	—	—	—	—	—	—	—	—
1898	0.3	0.2	0.1	2.1	1.4	0.7	—	—	—	—	—	—	—	—	—	—
1899	0.3	0.2	0.2	2.2	1.3	0.8	—	—	—	—	—	—	—	—	—	—
1900	0.4	0.2	0.2	2.3	1.3	1.1	—	—	—	—	—	—	—	—	—	—
1901	0.4	0.2	0.2	2.6	1.5	1.1	—	—	—	—	—	—	—	—	—	—
1902	0.6	0.3	0.2	3.5	2.3	1.2	—	—	—	—	—	—	—	—	—	—
1903	0.6	0.3	0.3	3.7	2.2	1.5	—	—	—	—	—	—	—	—	—	—
1904	0.5	0.2	0.2	2.7	1.6	1.1	—	—	—	—	—	—	—	—	—	—

	Purchases of structures and equipment						Depreciation on structures and equipment						Real net value of assets			Government-owned
	Current dollars			Constant dollars			Current dollars			Constant dollars			Structures and equipment			but privately operated assets
	Total	Structures	Equipment	Total	Structures	Equipment	Total	Structures	Equipment	Total	Structures	Equipment	Total	Structures	Equipment	
	Dd684	Dd685	Dd686	Dd687	Dd688	Dd689	Dd690	Dd691	Dd692	Dd693	Dd694	Dd695	Dd696	Dd697	Dd698	Dd699
Year	Billion dollars	Billion dollars	Billion dollars	Billion 1958 dollars	Billion 1958 dollars	Billion 1958 dollars	Billion dollars	Billion dollars	Billion dollars	Billion 1958 dollars	Billion 1958 dollars	Billion 1958 dollars	Billion 1958 dollars	Billion 1958 dollars	Billion 1958 dollars	Billion 1958 dollars
1905	0.5	0.3	0.3	3.0	1.6	1.4	—	—	—	—	—	—	—	—	—	—
1906	0.7	0.3	0.3	3.6	1.9	1.7	—	—	—	—	—	—	—	—	—	—
1907	0.7	0.3	0.3	3.7	2.0	1.7	—	—	—	—	—	—	—	—	—	—
1908	0.5	0.3	0.2	3.2	2.0	1.1	—	—	—	—	—	—	—	—	—	—
1909	0.7	0.4	0.3	3.7	2.4	1.3	—	—	—	—	—	—	—	—	—	—
1910	0.7	0.4	0.3	4.1	2.5	1.5	—	—	—	—	—	—	—	—	—	—
1911	0.7	0.4	0.3	3.9	2.6	1.3	—	—	—	—	—	—	—	—	—	—
1912	0.9	0.5	0.3	4.6	3.1	1.5	—	—	—	—	—	—	—	—	—	—
1913	0.9	0.5	0.4	4.6	2.9	1.7	—	—	—	—	—	—	—	—	—	—
1914	0.6	0.3	0.3	3.4	2.1	1.3	—	—	—	—	—	—	—	—	—	—
1915	0.6	0.3	0.3	3.1	1.7	1.3	—	—	—	—	—	—	—	—	—	—
1916	1.0	0.4	0.6	4.0	2.0	2.0	—	—	—	—	—	—	—	—	—	—
1917	1.3	0.5	0.7	4.1	1.8	2.3	—	—	—	—	—	—	—	—	—	—
1918	1.4	0.5	0.9	3.6	1.6	2.1	—	—	—	—	—	—	—	—	—	—
1919	1.6	0.7	0.9	3.9	2.0	1.9	—	—	—	—	—	—	—	—	—	—
1920	2.4	1.4	1.1	5.4	3.1	2.3	—	—	—	—	—	—	—	—	—	—
1921	1.4	0.8	0.6	3.9	2.5	1.4	—	—	—	—	—	—	—	—	—	—
1922	1.4	0.7	0.7	4.2	2.4	1.8	—	—	—	—	—	—	—	—	—	—
1923	1.8	0.9	1.0	4.9	2.5	2.4	—	—	—	—	—	—	—	—	—	—
1924	1.6	0.7	0.9	4.2	2.1	2.1	—	—	—	—	—	—	—	—	—	—
1925	1.8	0.8	1.0	4.8	2.3	2.5	1.5	0.7	0.8	4.0	2.1	1.9	32.7	20.0	12.8	0.0
1926	2.2	1.1	1.1	6.0	3.3	2.7	1.6	0.7	0.8	4.2	2.2	2.0	34.4	21.1	13.3	0.0
1927	2.1	1.1	1.0	5.7	3.2	2.4	1.6	0.7	0.9	4.3	2.2	2.1	35.5	22.0	13.5	0.0
1928	2.3	1.2	1.1	6.3	3.7	2.6	1.7	0.8	0.9	4.4	2.3	2.1	37.2	23.3	13.9	0.0
1929	2.7	1.5	1.2	7.3	4.4	2.8	1.7	0.8	0.9	4.6	2.4	2.2	39.6	25.3	14.3	0.0
1930	1.7	0.8	0.9	4.8	2.7	2.1	1.6	0.8	0.9	4.7	2.4	2.2	39.6	25.5	14.1	0.0
1931	0.9	0.3	0.6	2.8	1.3	1.6	1.5	0.7	0.8	4.6	2.4	2.2	37.8	24.4	13.4	0.0
1932	0.4	0.1	0.3	1.4	0.5	0.9	1.3	0.6	0.8	4.5	2.4	2.1	34.9	22.7	12.2	0.0
1933	0.6	0.3	0.3	2.2	1.1	1.0	1.3	0.6	0.7	4.4	2.3	2.1	33.0	21.7	11.3	0.0
1934	0.8	0.3	0.5	2.3	1.1	1.2	1.4	0.6	0.8	4.3	2.3	2.0	31.4	20.7	10.7	0.0
1935	0.9	0.2	0.6	2.6	0.9	1.7	1.4	0.6	0.7	4.2	2.3	1.9	30.2	19.7	10.5	0.0
1936	1.3	0.4	0.9	3.7	1.4	2.3	1.4	0.6	0.8	4.2	2.2	2.0	30.1	19.2	10.9	0.0
1937	1.8	0.7	1.1	4.7	2.1	2.6	1.5	0.7	0.8	4.2	2.2	2.0	31.0	19.4	11.6	0.0
1938	1.1	0.4	0.8	2.9	1.1	1.8	1.6	0.7	0.9	4.2	2.2	2.0	30.1	18.7	11.4	0.0
1939	1.3	0.4	0.9	3.5	1.4	2.1	1.5	0.7	0.8	4.1	2.1	2.0	29.8	18.3	11.5	0.0

Note appears at end of table

(continued)

TABLE Dd684–699 Capital in manufacturing – purchases, depreciation, and net value of structures and equipment: 1863–1970 *Continued*

	Purchases of structures and equipment						Depreciation on structures and equipment						Real net value of assets			
	Current dollars			Constant dollars			Current dollars			Constant dollars			Structures and equipment			Government-owned but privately operated assets
	Total	Structures	Equipment	Total	Structures	Equipment	Total	Structures	Equipment	Total	Structures	Equipment	Total	Structures	Equipment	
	Dd684	Dd685	Dd686	Dd687	Dd688	Dd689	Dd690	Dd691	Dd692	Dd693	Dd694	Dd695	Dd696	Dd697	Dd698	Dd699
Year	Billion dollars	Billion dollars	Billion dollars	Billion 1958 dollars	Billion 1958 dollars	Billion 1958 dollars	Billion dollars	Billion dollars	Billion dollars	Billion 1958 dollars	Billion 1958 dollars	Billion 1958 dollars	Billion 1958 dollars	Billion 1958 dollars	Billion 1958 dollars	Billion 1958 dollars
1940	1.9	0.7	1.3	4.7	2.0	2.8	1.6	0.7	0.9	4.1	2.1	2.0	30.7	18.5	12.2	1.0
1941	2.6	1.1	1.6	6.0	2.9	3.1	1.7	0.8	1.0	4.2	2.1	2.0	32.7	19.5	13.2	5.0
1942	1.7	0.5	1.2	3.3	1.1	2.2	1.9	0.9	1.0	4.2	2.1	2.1	31.9	18.8	13.2	16.0
1943	1.4	0.2	1.2	2.5	0.4	2.1	1.9	0.9	1.0	4.1	2.1	2.1	30.5	17.4	13.1	22.2
1944	1.7	0.3	1.5	3.2	0.6	2.6	1.9	0.9	1.1	4.1	2.0	2.1	29.9	16.3	13.6	23.5
1945	2.9	0.8	2.1	5.5	1.7	3.7	2.0	0.9	1.1	4.1	1.9	2.2	31.7	16.6	15.1	22.8
1946	5.2	2.4	2.8	9.5	4.4	5.1	2.4	1.1	1.3	4.4	2.0	2.4	38.7	20.6	18.1	18.0
1947	6.7	2.4	4.3	10.6	3.6	6.9	3.0	1.4	1.6	4.8	2.1	2.8	45.9	23.2	22.6	14.3
1948	6.8	2.2	4.6	9.9	3.0	6.8	3.6	1.6	2.0	5.3	2.1	3.2	50.9	25.2	25.8	11.4
1949	5.6	1.7	3.9	7.8	2.4	5.4	3.9	1.6	2.4	5.7	2.2	3.5	52.8	25.9	26.9	9.7
1950	5.6	1.5	4.0	7.5	2.1	5.5	4.3	1.6	2.7	6.0	2.2	3.8	53.9	26.0	27.9	8.8
1951	8.0	2.6	5.4	9.9	3.1	6.8	5.0	1.8	3.2	6.3	2.2	4.1	56.8	26.8	30.0	8.7
1952	8.0	2.6	5.5	9.8	3.0	6.8	5.4	1.9	3.5	6.7	2.2	4.5	58.9	27.3	31.6	8.7
1953	8.4	2.6	5.8	10.0	3.0	7.1	5.8	1.9	3.9	7.0	2.2	4.8	61.0	27.8	33.2	9.3
1954	8.5	2.5	6.0	10.1	2.9	7.2	6.1	1.9	4.2	7.4	2.3	5.1	62.8	28.1	34.7	10.1
1955	8.6	2.4	6.2	10.0	2.8	7.1	6.5	2.0	4.6	7.7	2.3	5.4	64.5	28.7	35.8	10.3
1956	11.4	3.5	7.9	12.3	3.7	8.6	7.4	2.2	5.2	8.1	2.4	5.7	67.8	29.7	38.1	10.0
1957	12.3	3.9	8.4	12.5	3.9	8.6	8.3	2.4	5.9	8.5	2.4	6.1	70.8	30.9	39.9	9.4
1958	9.7	3.3	6.5	9.7	3.3	6.5	8.8	2.5	6.3	8.8	2.5	6.3	70.9	31.4	39.5	8.7
1959	9.0	2.5	6.6	8.8	2.4	6.4	9.1	2.6	6.6	8.9	2.5	6.4	70.1	31.2	39.0	8.0
1960	10.3	2.8	7.4	10.0	2.8	7.2	9.4	2.6	6.8	9.1	2.5	6.6	70.6	31.3	39.3	7.4
1961	9.9	2.7	7.2	9.6	2.7	7.0	9.6	2.7	7.0	9.3	2.6	6.7	70.7	31.5	39.3	7.1
1962	10.6	2.7	7.9	10.2	2.6	7.6	9.9	2.7	7.2	9.4	2.6	6.8	71.2	31.4	39.8	6.8
1963	11.5	3.0	8.5	11.0	2.8	8.2	10.2	2.8	7.3	9.6	2.6	7.0	72.2	31.6	40.7	6.5
1964	13.4	3.2	10.2	12.6	3.0	9.7	10.6	3.0	7.7	9.9	2.7	7.3	74.5	31.8	42.7	6.4
1965	16.7	4.2	12.6	15.4	3.7	11.7	11.3	3.1	8.2	10.3	2.7	7.6	79.0	32.7	46.2	6.3
1966	20.4	5.2	15.2	18.2	4.4	13.7	12.4	3.3	9.0	11.0	2.8	8.2	85.4	34.3	51.1	6.4
1967	21.7	5.7	16.0	18.7	4.7	14.0	13.6	3.6	10.1	11.7	2.9	8.8	91.3	36.0	55.3	6.4
1968	20.9	5.3	15.6	17.5	4.2	13.4	14.9	3.8	11.0	12.4	3.0	9.4	95.2	37.1	58.1	6.2
1969	22.5	5.8	16.7	18.1	4.2	14.0	16.4	4.3	12.1	13.1	3.1	10.0	99.2	38.2	61.0	5.8
1970	22.4	5.7	16.6	17.0	3.8	13.3	18.2	4.8	13.3	13.7	3.1	10.6	101.5	38.8	62.7	5.2

(Z) Less than $50 million.

Source

U.S. Bureau of Economic Analysis, *Fixed Nonresidential Business Capital in the United States, 1925–1970* (National Technical Information Service, January 1974), pp. T-25, 7–9, 50, 286–7, 397, 425–7, and 437–9; and unpublished data.

Documentation

This table and its associated documentation have been reprinted, more or less without modification, from U.S. Bureau of the Census, *Historical Statistics of the United States* (1975), series P107–122.

Series Dd684–689

Private purchases of structures and equipment for manufacturing establishments were derived from the estimates of gross private domestic investment in new industrial buildings and producers' durable equipment that are included in the gross national product estimates of the Department of Commerce.

The outlays on structures and equipment were adjusted to benchmarks based on expenditures for new plants and equipment in the Census of Manufactures for 1939, 1947, 1954, 1958, 1963, and 1966. The census controls were extended through 1970 by data from plant and equipment expenditure surveys conducted jointly by the Bureau of Economic Analysis (formerly Office of Business Economics) and the Securities and Exchange Commission.

The purchases of structures and equipment were converted to constant (1958) cost by the indexes used to deflate the corresponding individual series in the gross national product.

The Bureau of Economic Analysis discontinued these series, replacing them with new (and different) series, which are shown in Table Dd700–723.

For a more detailed discussion and for tabulations derived from these and related series, see the source.

TABLE Dd684–699   Capital in manufacturing – purchases, depreciation, and net value of structures and equipment: 1863–1970   *Continued*

Series Dd690–695

Information on the service lives of capital assets is deficient. Not enough is known either about the average service lives of the producers' durable equipment and structures that make up the stock of fixed capital or about how the service lives of individual items depart from average. Differences in the basic physical characteristics of capital assets, variations among the practices of their owners with respect to use and retirement, technological changes, and changes in demand all make for a large dispersion of service lives and help to explain the dearth of information about them. The useful life information was drawn largely from *Income Tax, Depreciation and Obsolescence, Estimated Useful Lives, and Depreciation Rates*, Bulletin F, Internal Revenue Service. The actual service lives used were 85 percent of Bulletin F for equipment, and 68 percent of Bulletin F for structures. See pp. T-4 and T-5 of source for reasons behind the use of shorter service lives.

Average service lives were estimated for each of the twenty types of equipment and ten types of structures that are detailed in the gross national product gross investment series with which the calculation starts. Average life for each type of nonfarm equipment was derived by assigning service lives as shown in Bulletin F to each of the equipment items of that type and deriving an average for the type for each year based on weights reflecting shipments of each item as shown in the censuses and Annual Surveys of Manufactures. Altogether, Bulletin F service lives for about 180 items of equipment were used in obtaining averages for the twenty types. Average lives for farm equipment were derived from several unpublished Department of Agriculture studies.

Depreciation at constant cost has been estimated by applying information on the length of useful lives to the constant dollar purchase of structures and equipment.

Underlying the average service life of a given type of asset is a distribution of discards. For example, trucks have an average service life of ten years, but some trucks are wrecked after a few months and others are used for fifteen or twenty years. To take into account that similar assets are discarded at different ages, a pattern labeled the Winfrey S-3 distribution was introduced. It is a minor modification of the original Winfrey S-3 curve. (See Robley Winfrey, *Statistical Analysis of Industrial Property Retirement*, Iowa Engineering Experiment Station Bulletin 125, December 11, 1935.) The new pattern is a bell-shaped distribution whose mean is the average service life of the asset in question, with discards starting at 45 percent of the average life and continuing until 155 percent of the average life has been attained. In the absence of sufficient information to support any alternative course, that service life distribution was applied uniformly to the gross investment series to derive the gross capital stocks and related estimates.

The Bureau of Economic Analysis discontinued these series, replacing them with new (and different) series, which are shown in Table Dd700–723.

Series Dd696–699

Estimates are for privately owned structures and equipment assets in manufacturing establishments (in contrast to the firm) and represent the undepreciated value remaining in past acquisitions, including the purchases of government surplus assets at original acquisition prices. The latter were derived from the estimates of gross private domestic investment in newly constructed nonresidential structures and producers' durable equipment that are included in the gross national product estimates of the Department of Commerce. The outlays on structures were adjusted to benchmarks, based mainly on expenditures for new plant construction by establishments included in the Census of Manufactures. Data on gross investment by manufacturing establishments from censuses and Annual Surveys of Manufactures were used as industry totals. The asset detail was developed on the basis of unpublished Internal Revenue Service studies on lives of depreciable assets and several specialized industry studies that provided detailed information on the composition of assets in manufacturing.

Purchases of equipment were converted to constant (1958) cost by the indexes used to deflate the corresponding component of the gross national product. Purchases of structures were deflated by "constant cost 2," which is a closer approximation to a price index than the alternative index, "constant cost 1." For the composition of these costs, see Table 4, pp. T-17 to T-19 of the source.

Depreciation was allocated over the useful life by the double declining balance method, under which twice the straight-line rate of depreciation is charged in the first year, and the same percentage rate is applied in successive years to the remaining value of the asset (see p. T-12 of the source).

Series Dd699. Includes structures and equipment – all agencies. For a discussion of the data and methodology of estimation of government-owned, privately operated assets for each of the four major owning agencies (Department of Defense, Atomic Energy Commission, Maritime Administration, and National Aeronautics and Space Administration), see pp. T-22 and T-23 of the source.

TABLE Dd700–723 Fixed assets and investment in manufacturing: 1901–2000

Contributed by Jeremy Atack and Fred Bateman

	Nonresidential fixed assets											
	Net stock									Depreciation		
	Current cost			Historical cost			Chain quantity index			Current cost		
	Total	Equipment and software	Structures	Total	Equipment and software	Structures	Total	Equipment and software	Structures	Total	Equipment and software	Structures
	Dd700 [1]	Dd701 [1]	Dd702 [1]	Dd703 [1]	Dd704 [1]	Dd705 [1]	Dd706 [1]	Dd707 [1]	Dd708 [1]	Dd709 [1]	Dd710 [1]	Dd711 [1]
Year	Million dollars	Million dollars	Million dollars	Million dollars	Million dollars	Million dollars	Index 1996 = 100	Index 1996 = 100	Index 1996 = 100	Million dollars	Million dollars	Million dollars
1925	17,465	7,320	10,145	13,351	6,660	6,691	14.28	8.08	25.89	1,112	797	314
1926	17,922	7,441	10,480	13,950	6,796	7,155	14.66	8.19	26.80	1,173	849	324
1927	18,316	7,564	10,752	14,558	6,910	7,648	15.04	8.26	27.84	1,173	841	331
1928	18,809	7,690	11,119	15,332	7,101	8,231	15.57	8.42	29.13	1,213	872	341
1929	18,896	7,766	11,130	16,443	7,493	8,950	16.40	8.82	30.82	1,249	895	354
1930	17,554	7,441	10,113	16,854	7,632	9,223	16.75	9.00	31.48	1,206	874	332
1931	15,761	6,891	8,870	16,623	7,463	9,160	16.56	8.85	31.26	1,106	814	291
1932	14,499	6,266	8,233	16,016	7,079	8,937	16.01	8.45	30.52	1,001	744	257
1933	15,323	6,434	8,889	15,659	6,830	8,829	15.74	8.24	30.19	925	668	256
1934	16,444	6,896	9,548	15,550	6,806	8,744	15.64	8.23	29.86	1,058	763	296
1935	16,802	7,069	9,733	15,574	6,955	8,619	15.64	8.42	29.38	1,075	778	297
1936	18,299	7,779	10,520	15,936	7,322	8,614	15.95	8.87	29.25	1,123	813	310
1937	20,031	8,816	11,216	16,797	7,961	8,836	16.58	9.53	29.64	1,296	948	348
1938	19,836	8,992	10,844	16,929	8,154	8,775	16.57	9.66	29.29	1,383	1,037	345
1939	20,287	9,398	10,889	17,212	8,466	8,747	16.72	9.94	29.06	1,368	1,039	329
1940	22,392	10,398	11,994	18,001	9,080	8,921	17.23	10.50	29.33	1,476	1,125	351
1941	25,978	11,785	14,192	19,513	9,945	9,568	18.17	11.23	30.58	1,695	1,294	401
1942	28,001	12,427	15,574	20,227	10,591	9,636	18.39	11.62	30.37	1,972	1,504	469
1943	28,092	12,577	15,515	20,447	10,966	9,481	18.32	11.85	29.70	1,940	1,446	494
1944	28,995	13,574	15,420	21,363	11,990	9,374	18.73	12.72	29.15	1,986	1,515	470
1945	32,966	15,478	17,488	23,025	13,343	9,682	19.58	13.87	29.35	2,086	1,594	492
1946	40,606	18,520	22,087	26,273	15,189	11,085	21.16	15.34	31.09	2,547	1,936	610
1947	49,028	22,666	26,362	30,470	18,022	12,448	22.87	17.34	32.36	3,070	2,309	761
1948	54,283	26,366	27,917	34,080	20,662	13,419	24.07	18.93	32.96	3,658	2,787	870
1949	55,749	28,311	27,439	36,021	22,036	13,985	24.49	19.49	33.12	3,981	3,123	858
1950	60,551	31,297	29,254	37,987	23,399	14,588	24.90	20.00	33.37	4,188	3,339	849
1951	67,802	34,961	32,841	42,219	25,998	16,221	26.02	21.06	34.59	4,825	3,839	986
1952	71,998	37,343	34,655	46,456	28,503	17,953	27.12	22.06	35.85	5,112	4,057	1,055
1953	74,876	39,664	35,212	50,325	30,836	19,490	28.08	22.94	36.93	5,403	4,310	1,093
1954	77,823	42,027	35,796	53,870	33,007	20,864	28.94	23.74	37.91	5,618	4,526	1,092
1955	84,688	46,083	38,605	57,467	35,116	22,351	29.82	24.48	39.00	5,938	4,803	1,135
1956	95,825	52,460	43,366	63,815	38,720	25,095	31.42	25.75	41.18	6,707	5,424	1,283
1957	103,201	57,498	45,702	70,400	42,693	27,708	32.91	27.00	43.08	7,460	6,057	1,404
1958	105,119	59,337	45,782	73,536	44,441	29,095	33.31	27.19	43.91	7,719	6,311	1,409
1959	107,680	61,573	46,108	76,184	46,066	30,118	33.56	27.30	44.42	7,996	6,576	1,420
1960	109,864	62,952	46,911	80,483	48,497	31,986	34.36	27.80	45.80	8,222	6,778	1,444
1961	112,634	63,726	48,908	84,290	50,502	33,788	35.05	28.18	47.12	8,333	6,849	1,485
1962	116,696	65,756	50,940	88,562	53,055	35,506	35.90	28.84	48.33	8,591	7,048	1,543
1963	121,087	68,047	53,040	93,289	55,894	37,395	36.91	29.66	49.67	8,880	7,270	1,610
1964	128,903	72,237	56,665	99,730	60,184	39,545	38.43	31.11	51.21	9,358	7,669	1,689
1965	139,368	78,352	61,016	109,128	66,379	42,748	40.82	33.43	53.59	10,073	8,262	1,811
1966	156,561	88,915	67,645	121,877	74,570	47,307	44.09	36.54	57.01	11,187	9,201	1,986
1967	171,865	98,256	73,609	133,420	81,822	51,598	46.85	39.07	60.07	12,490	10,316	2,174
1968	190,561	108,239	82,322	144,636	88,822	55,814	49.29	41.29	62.84	13,775	11,374	2,401
1969	210,835	118,226	92,609	156,942	96,285	60,657	51.81	43.53	65.78	15,118	12,418	2,701
1970	231,871	128,807	103,064	168,878	103,351	65,526	53.98	45.41	68.45	16,573	13,571	3,002
1971	252,779	136,811	115,968	179,164	109,176	69,988	55.54	46.67	70.52	17,975	14,609	3,366
1972	272,142	144,600	127,543	191,381	116,922	74,459	57.41	48.65	72.19	19,883	15,638	4,245
1973	300,846	158,079	142,767	205,462	125,681	79,780	59.55	50.87	74.18	20,983	16,711	4,272
1974	366,408	197,886	168,522	228,197	140,763	87,434	62.81	54.50	76.87	24,176	19,392	4,784
1975	407,393	230,631	176,762	250,216	156,326	93,890	65.04	57.00	78.62	29,508	24,127	5,382
1976	446,510	256,957	189,553	272,690	172,530	100,160	67.07	59.27	80.18	32,868	27,144	5,724
1977	500,333	291,169	209,164	299,091	192,423	106,669	69.34	61.98	81.60	36,732	30,510	6,222
1978	561,932	327,646	234,287	329,936	215,172	114,764	71.90	64.99	83.32	41,096	34,196	6,900
1979	644,802	376,168	268,634	365,353	241,388	123,965	74.44	68.01	84.96	47,024	38,852	8,172

Note appears at end of table

TABLE Dd700–723   Fixed assets and investment in manufacturing: 1901–2000   *Continued*

	Nonresidential fixed assets									Depreciation		
	Net stock									Current cost		
	Current cost			Historical cost			Chain quantity index			Current cost		
	Total	Equipment and software	Structures	Total	Equipment and software	Structures	Total	Equipment and software	Structures	Total	Equipment and software	Structures
	Dd700	Dd701	Dd702	Dd703	Dd704	Dd705	Dd706	Dd707	Dd708	Dd709	Dd710	Dd711
Year	Million dollars	Million dollars	Million dollars	Million dollars	Million dollars	Million dollars	Index 1996 = 100	Index 1996 = 100	Index 1996 = 100	Million dollars	Million dollars	Million dollars
1980	742,213	438,041	304,171	407,839	272,442	135,397	77.16	71.14	86.94	53,884	45,000	8,884
1981	817,620	484,397	333,223	456,238	308,576	147,661	79.95	74.46	88.80	61,584	51,680	9,904
1982	862,840	508,623	354,217	491,006	332,332	158,674	81.20	75.67	90.11	66,458	55,742	10,716
1983	879,072	512,951	366,121	514,155	347,702	166,453	81.47	75.84	90.52	68,306	57,090	11,215
1984	910,135	526,247	383,888	550,439	374,193	176,246	83.07	77.91	91.36	70,588	58,941	11,647
1985	960,227	559,903	400,324	592,405	404,813	187,592	85.14	80.56	92.49	74,882	62,742	12,140
1986	1,007,082	588,592	418,490	622,846	426,041	196,804	86.00	81.61	93.05	80,347	67,676	12,670
1987	1,050,012	615,563	434,448	651,122	446,164	204,958	86.53	82.31	93.31	85,047	71,861	13,187
1988	1,094,603	643,051	451,572	679,312	465,133	214,179	86.92	82.68	93.72	89,435	75,719	13,716
1989	1,151,234	678,985	472,249	723,523	497,079	226,444	88.49	84.63	94.69	93,942	79,638	14,303
1990	1,217,212	729,015	488,197	771,189	533,091	238,098	90.18	86.88	95.47	100,407	85,511	14,896
1991	1,247,572	755,482	492,090	814,023	565,933	248,090	91.44	88.63	95.91	106,206	90,979	15,227
1992	1,286,017	779,830	506,187	854,997	596,549	258,448	92.62	90.19	96.46	110,120	94,694	15,426
1993	1,326,548	800,706	525,842	890,542	622,585	267,957	93.43	91.32	96.77	113,891	97,853	16,038
1994	1,387,242	834,401	552,841	934,550	655,302	279,248	94.82	93.22	97.33	118,215	101,486	16,729
1995	1,457,326	884,474	572,852	994,212	700,124	294,088	97.17	96.37	98.41	125,002	107,428	17,575
1996	1,520,949	923,099	597,851	1,060,528	748,355	312,173	100.00	100.00	100.00	131,326	113,072	18,253
1997	1,584,240	954,401	629,839	1,126,190	795,225	330,964	102.82	103.61	101.62	137,632	118,709	18,923
1998	1,653,536	989,425	664,110	1,192,348	842,632	349,716	105.79	107.60	103.09	143,200	123,317	19,883
1999	1,713,357	1,016,341	697,016	1,245,710	878,572	367,138	107.93	110.45	104.23	149,642	128,652	20,990
2000	1,794,033	1,060,158	733,875	1,313,025	930,806	382,219	110.84	115.05	104.89	157,873	135,765	22,108

	Nonresidential fixed assets						Investment					
	Depreciation						Historical cost			Chain quantity index		
	Historical cost			Chain quantity index								
	Total	Equipment and software	Structures	Total	Equipment and software	Structures	Total	Equipment and software	Structures	Total	Equipment and software	Structures
	Dd712	Dd713	Dd714	Dd715	Dd716	Dd717	Dd718	Dd719	Dd720	Dd721	Dd722	Dd723
Year	Million dollars	Million dollars	Million dollars	Index 1996 = 100	Index 1996 = 100	Index 1996 = 100	Million dollars	Million dollars	Million dollars	Index 1996 = 100	Index 1996 = 100	Index 1996 = 100
1901	—	—	—	—	—	—	372	277	95	3.45	2.17	13.18
1902	—	—	—	—	—	—	471	305	166	4.40	2.43	22.77
1903	—	—	—	—	—	—	498	334	164	4.81	2.82	22.10
1904	—	—	—	—	—	—	370	264	106	3.40	2.08	14.25
1905	—	—	—	—	—	—	449	327	122	4.02	2.59	14.73
1906	—	—	—	—	—	—	569	403	166	5.11	3.25	19.42
1907	—	—	—	—	—	—	578	404	174	5.03	3.10	20.46
1908	—	—	—	—	—	—	429	257	172	3.91	2.11	20.47
1909	—	—	—	—	—	—	547	345	202	4.71	2.56	24.27
1910	—	—	—	—	—	—	600	390	210	5.12	2.90	24.56
1911	—	—	—	—	—	—	597	358	239	4.73	2.39	27.50
1912	—	—	—	—	—	—	697	396	301	5.66	2.80	33.85
1913	—	—	—	—	—	—	684	418	266	5.68	3.05	30.26
1914	—	—	—	—	—	—	525	349	176	4.17	2.37	19.97
1915	—	—	—	—	—	—	570	400	170	4.20	2.44	19.25
1916	—	—	—	—	—	—	852	632	220	5.51	3.47	20.52
1917	—	—	—	—	—	—	1,212	904	308	6.45	4.07	23.85
1918	—	—	—	—	—	—	1,298	954	344	5.71	3.50	23.09
1919	—	—	—	—	—	—	1,380	847	533	5.52	2.91	30.77
1920	—	—	—	—	—	—	1,826	685	1,141	7.15	2.20	67.69
1921	—	—	—	—	—	—	1,222	629	593	5.30	2.51	36.27
1922	—	—	—	—	—	—	1,146	642	504	5.28	2.92	30.07
1923	—	—	—	—	—	—	1,581	957	624	7.06	4.16	36.81
1924	—	—	—	—	—	—	1,168	691	477	5.32	3.16	27.47

(continued)

TABLE Dd700–723   Fixed assets and investment in manufacturing: 1901–2000 *Continued*

	Nonresidential fixed assets						Investment					
	Depreciation						Historical cost			Chain quantity index		
	Historical cost			Chain quantity index								
	Total	Equipment and software	Structures	Total	Equipment and software	Structures	Total	Equipment and software	Structures	Total	Equipment and software	Structures
	Dd712	Dd713	Dd714	Dd715	Dd716	Dd717	Dd718	Dd719	Dd720	Dd721	Dd722	Dd723
Year	Million dollars	Million dollars	Million dollars	Index 1996 = 100	Index 1996 = 100	Index 1996 = 100	Million dollars	Million dollars	Million dollars	Index 1996 = 100	Index 1996 = 100	Index 1996 = 100
1925	926	723	203	7.84	5.76	26.31	1,257	789	468	5.55	3.51	25.93
1926	969	755	214	8.27	6.14	26.96	1,445	764	681	6.38	3.43	37.28
1927	1,011	782	229	8.22	6.02	27.92	1,478	753	725	6.52	3.33	40.21
1928	1,049	803	245	8.51	6.21	29.07	1,673	841	832	7.43	3.72	46.82
1929	1,109	844	266	8.83	6.41	30.56	2,041	1,054	987	9.16	4.70	56.16
1930	1,153	872	281	9.13	6.62	31.73	1,401	844	557	6.82	4.03	35.01
1931	1,147	863	284	9.05	6.52	31.94	762	538	224	4.04	2.73	16.06
1932	1,110	830	280	8.84	6.35	31.44	378	318	60	2.16	1.72	4.78
1933	1,063	788	275	8.43	5.99	30.89	582	413	169	3.40	2.30	13.38
1934	1,050	778	272	8.51	6.10	30.56	810	620	190	4.26	3.18	12.87
1935	1,061	792	269	8.55	6.17	30.14	933	787	146	4.80	3.94	9.71
1936	1,090	823	267	8.82	6.47	29.82	1,275	1,011	264	6.55	5.10	16.68
1937	1,175	905	270	9.34	6.99	29.94	1,843	1,349	494	8.67	6.27	28.02
1938	1,239	966	273	9.79	7.44	29.95	1,210	996	214	5.60	4.53	12.19
1939	1,270	998	271	9.85	7.53	29.65	1,376	1,131	245	6.46	5.19	14.51
1940	1,323	1,049	274	10.23	7.91	29.65	1,917	1,467	450	8.63	6.49	25.09
1941	1,423	1,136	286	10.94	8.58	30.38	2,726	1,791	935	11.41	7.51	46.24
1942	1,527	1,230	297	11.43	9.04	30.87	2,129	1,762	367	8.14	6.85	15.86
1943	1,583	1,288	296	11.31	8.96	30.42	1,692	1,550	142	6.67	6.30	5.75
1944	1,630	1,339	292	11.47	9.18	29.80	2,395	2,209	186	9.45	8.95	7.80
1945	1,768	1,473	295	12.10	9.87	29.63	3,337	2,732	605	12.96	10.96	24.09
1946	2,038	1,717	322	13.28	11.04	30.61	5,272	3,546	1,726	18.49	13.19	57.30
1947	2,317	1,952	365	14.40	12.09	32.12	6,492	4,762	1,730	20.34	16.24	48.27
1948	2,701	2,299	402	15.74	13.48	33.05	6,219	4,845	1,374	17.89	15.26	34.51
1949	2,999	2,573	426	16.60	14.40	33.43	4,795	3,802	993	13.36	11.43	25.56
1950	3,207	2,764	444	17.09	14.91	33.62	4,998	3,950	1,048	13.64	11.49	27.56
1951	3,470	2,991	479	17.68	15.47	34.35	7,520	5,406	2,114	18.36	14.16	48.82
1952	3,786	3,254	532	18.34	16.05	35.60	7,833	5,569	2,264	18.74	14.37	50.50
1953	4,107	3,523	584	19.01	16.66	36.77	7,708	5,587	2,121	18.10	14.06	47.22
1954	4,405	3,775	630	19.65	17.25	37.80	7,664	5,661	2,003	17.94	14.04	45.92
1955	4,697	4,023	674	20.34	17.89	38.83	7,961	5,800	2,161	18.20	13.98	49.06
1956	5,064	4,325	739	21.14	18.58	40.42	11,062	7,579	3,483	23.20	16.72	72.82
1957	5,561	4,738	822	22.11	19.42	42.42	11,831	8,397	3,434	23.37	17.33	68.69
1958	5,912	5,027	885	22.60	19.80	43.79	8,706	6,435	2,271	17.08	13.02	46.71
1959	6,136	5,214	921	22.93	20.09	44.46	8,392	6,448	1,945	16.19	12.72	40.27
1960	6,413	5,447	966	23.25	20.34	45.38	10,309	7,475	2,834	19.65	14.49	59.03
1961	6,698	5,676	1,021	23.64	20.63	46.66	10,067	7,244	2,823	19.25	14.13	58.57
1962	7,012	5,938	1,075	24.15	21.05	47.86	10,818	8,025	2,793	20.56	15.59	57.19
1963	7,390	6,260	1,130	24.86	21.69	49.09	11,611	8,593	3,018	22.04	16.77	60.76
1964	7,871	6,680	1,192	25.86	22.62	50.50	13,837	10,495	3,342	26.00	20.33	66.05
1965	8,594	7,318	1,276	27.53	24.21	52.49	17,443	12,964	4,479	32.43	25.02	85.79
1966	9,603	8,204	1,399	29.94	26.49	55.48	21,727	15,770	5,957	39.82	30.25	110.03
1967	10,650	9,111	1,539	32.30	28.69	58.81	21,528	15,696	5,831	38.35	29.29	104.38
1968	11,627	9,954	1,674	34.31	30.54	61.80	22,183	16,294	5,889	38.10	29.46	100.28
1969	12,642	10,825	1,817	36.24	32.31	64.71	24,216	17,556	6,660	39.95	30.85	105.56
1970	13,642	11,672	1,970	37.95	33.87	67.58	24,826	17,987	6,839	39.16	30.42	101.89
1971	14,579	12,463	2,116	39.41	35.19	69.99	24,074	17,496	6,578	36.43	28.79	90.51
1972	16,004	13,456	2,549	42.24	36.99	81.15	27,431	20,411	7,020	40.29	33.27	88.55
1973	16,873	14,410	2,463	43.07	38.64	75.45	30,647	22,744	7,903	43.43	36.31	92.12
1974	18,544	15,933	2,611	45.48	41.27	76.06	40,438	30,177	10,261	52.72	44.66	107.61
1975	20,805	17,982	2,823	48.32	44.20	78.08	41,724	32,448	9,276	47.66	41.54	88.75
1976	23,121	20,082	3,039	50.67	46.55	80.31	44,578	35,273	9,305	48.23	42.53	86.11
1977	25,688	22,452	3,236	53.02	48.99	81.75	51,078	41,303	9,775	52.14	47.08	84.70
1978	28,511	25,066	3,445	55.34	51.45	82.78	58,823	47,287	11,536	56.26	50.81	91.32
1979	31,773	27,928	3,845	58.14	53.88	88.35	66,707	53,665	13,042	58.92	53.57	93.04

TABLE Dd700–723 Fixed assets and investment in manufacturing: 1901–2000 *Continued*

	Nonresidential fixed assets							Investment					
	Depreciation							Historical cost			Chain quantity index		
	Historical cost			Chain quantity index									
Year	Total	Equipment and software	Structures	Total	Equipment and software	Structures		Total	Equipment and software	Structures	Total	Equipment and software	Structures
	Dd712	Dd713	Dd714	Dd715	Dd716	Dd717		Dd718	Dd719	Dd720	Dd721	Dd722	Dd723
	Million dollars	Million dollars	Million dollars	Index 1996 = 100	Index 1996 = 100	Index 1996 = 100		Million dollars	Million dollars	Million dollars	Index 1996 = 100	Index 1996 = 100	Index 1996 = 100
1980	35,445	31,410	4,034	60.24	56.50	86.26		77,294	61,832	15,462	62.30	56.55	99.05
1981	40,356	35,957	4,399	63.44	59.85	88.15		88,057	71,397	16,660	65.81	60.71	97.77
1982	44,560	39,802	4,758	65.57	62.05	89.71		78,057	62,290	15,767	55.97	51.07	87.02
1983	47,206	42,137	5,069	66.38	62.77	91.09		69,144	56,300	12,844	49.04	45.86	68.81
1984	50,471	45,160	5,312	67.84	64.43	91.09		85,215	70,114	15,101	60.07	57.14	78.02
1985	55,289	49,658	5,631	71.01	67.91	92.00		96,086	79,113	16,973	67.14	64.22	85.01
1986	59,536	53,594	5,942	73.64	70.81	92.79		88,970	73,819	15,151	60.44	58.32	73.34
1987	62,836	56,631	6,205	75.28	72.63	93.15		90,056	75,700	14,356	59.25	57.97	67.03
1988	65,946	59,476	6,470	76.57	74.05	93.44		93,056	77,368	15,688	59.38	57.53	70.66
1989	69,743	62,941	6,802	78.34	75.98	94.11		112,658	93,596	19,062	70.11	68.00	82.94
1990	74,991	67,812	7,179	81.24	79.16	95.02		121,472	102,643	18,829	73.43	72.48	79.41
1991	80,353	72,819	7,533	84.09	82.32	95.74		122,299	104,776	17,523	72.45	72.43	72.84
1992	85,299	77,421	7,878	86.75	85.26	96.41		125,337	107,103	18,234	74.13	73.97	75.33
1993	89,658	81,447	8,211	89.06	87.83	96.99		123,803	106,091	17,712	72.87	73.26	70.84
1994	94,045	85,501	8,544	91.41	90.45	97.47		136,721	116,895	19,826	79.70	80.31	76.42
1995	100,073	91,100	8,973	95.08	94.54	98.45		158,523	134,724	23,799	91.19	91.75	88.18
1996	107,499	97,974	9,526	100.00	100.00	100.00		172,733	145,133	27,600	100.00	100.00	100.00
1997	114,917	105,024	9,893	105.06	105.82	100.44		179,027	150,954	28,073	104.50	105.66	98.55
1998	122,921	112,474	10,448	111.16	112.72	101.83		188,198	158,995	29,204	112.19	114.83	98.98
1999	129,904	118,892	11,012	116.72	119.06	103.17		181,386	152,926	28,461	109.22	112.60	92.69
2000	137,546	126,038	11,508	122.67	125.97	104.04		203,394	176,807	26,587	122.42	131.06	82.93

[1] Series has no data before 1925.

Source

U.S. Department of Commerce, Bureau of Economic Analysis (BEA), *Fixed Reproducible Tangible Wealth in the United States, 1925–94* (August 1999). Table A lists the various sources used for different ranges of years in assembling these data but without identifying the source(s) for individual numbers (see p. M-12). Data are available from the BEA Internet site.

Documentation
Series Dd700–717

The Bureau of Economic Analysis (BEA) replaced its series on fixed nonresidential business capital (which are embodied in Table Dd684–699) with a more comprehensive (and different) set of series on fixed reproducible tangible wealth. This includes series on the fixed private nonresidential capital stock in manufacturing and depreciation thereon. The Bureau also reports figures by Standard Industrial Classification industry group (1987 SIC) from 1947 on but cautions that these are less reliable than the more aggregated figures and therefore that the BEA has elected not to publish them in the *Survey of Current Business*. (They are available on the BEA Internet site.) One reason for the differential reliability of estimates is that the industry estimates are for establishments rather than companies where an establishment is an economic unit, generally at a single physical location, where business is conducted or where services or industrial operations are performed. A company, on the other hand, consists of one or more establishments owned by the same legal entity or group of affiliated entities. Establishments are classified into an SIC industry on the basis of their principal product or service, and companies are classified into an SIC industry on the basis of the principal SIC industry of all their establishments. Because large multi-establishment companies typically own establishments that are classified in different SIC industries, the industrial distributions of investment, capital stock, and capital consumption for establishments and companies can be significantly different. See the Introduction to Part D for a discussion of SIC codes.

The fixed asset estimates reported here derive from the national income and product accounts (NIPA) of the United States and incorporate the definitional and statistical improvements made in those accounts (including improvements in the calculation of depreciation). See "Improved Estimates of National Income and Product Accounts," *Survey of Current Business* 76 (January/February 1996): 1–31; and "The Measurement of Depreciation," *Survey of Current Business* 77 (July 1997): 7–23.

The net stock is the value of the stock of fixed assets after adjustment for depreciation, which captures the decline in value due to wear and tear, obsolescence, accidental damage, and aging. These depreciation allowances are predicated on the assumption that assets depreciate in the manner described by depreciation tables for specific types of assets over the service lives of those assets from their acquisition cost. These net stocks are for the most part calculated by the perpetual inventory method, which defines the net stock as the cumulative value of past gross investment less the cumulative value of past depreciation. Consequently, both the net stock and depreciation of any given type of asset are weighted summations of past investment in that asset.

Current-cost valuation expresses all assets in the capital stock in terms of the prices that prevailed in the period to which the stock estimates refer. For instance, the year-end 1994 capital stock estimate in current-cost valuation shows the assets that were in the stock at year-end 1994 expressed at the prices that would have been paid for them if they had been purchased at the market prices prevailing for those assets at year-end 1994.

In the historical cost valuations, assets are valued in terms of the prices prevailing *when they were purchased* and are prepared using current-dollar investment flows. They are generally similar to the book value estimates shown in company financial reports.

Real-cost estimates are quantity-type estimates that are often called "real" or "physical-volume" estimates. They are prepared for each type of asset using investment flows that have been deflated; that is, the effects of price change have been removed from the flows by dividing their nominal values by an appropriate price index. At the deflation level, identical assets are valued equally in the capital stock at a base-year price (here, the 1996 price) regardless of their actual prices in the years they were acquired. When valued in terms of real costs, depreciation charges on any individual asset over its lifetime will sum up to the asset's purchase price. Real-cost estimates of the net stock are the depreciated values of these deflated acquisition costs.

(continued)

TABLE Dd700–723   Fixed assets and investment in manufacturing: 1901–2000   *Continued*

Real-cost estimates of depreciation are the charges for a given period that are derived by writing off the deflated investment flows. These quantity indexes are aggregated using a Fisher chain-type index formula.

Series Dd718–723

Valuations are as described for series Dd700–717.

The BEA uses the term "investment" to denote any addition to fixed reproducible tangible wealth. Manufacturing industry estimates of capital expenditures for establishments with payroll are available from the Census of Manufactures for 1947, 1954, 1958, 1963, 1967, 1972, 1977, 1982, 1987, and 1992. Prior to 1978, investment estimates are not adjusted for establishments without payroll because no applicable data are available and because investment by these establishments is very small. For 1977–1994, adjustments are made for establishments without payroll. The census data for all manufacturing industries are adjusted to include investment by the CAOs (Central Administrative Offices), using investment data from Enterprise Statistics. Equipment and structures investment estimates for noncensus years in 1947–1994 are interpolated and extrapolated from census year estimates using capital expenditures data from the Annual Survey of Manufactures and NIPA series on investment. Prior to 1947, equipment investment estimates are extrapolated using the following series: for 1941–1946, the NIPA series for investment in industrial equipment; for 1921–1940, the estimates of Lowell J. Chawner, Simon Kuznets, and William H. Shaw

(see Lowell J. Chawner, "Capital Expenditures for Manufacturing Plant and Equipment – 1915 to 1940," *Survey of Current Business* 21 (March 1941): 9–15, "Capital Expenditures in Selected Manufacturing Industries," *Survey of Current Business* 21 (December 1941): 19–26, and "Capital Expenditures in Selected Manufacturing Industries, Part II," *Survey of Current Business* 22 (May 1942): 14–23; Simon Kuznets, *Capital in the American Economy: Its Formation and Financing* (Princeton University Press, 1961); and William H. Shaw, *Value of Commodity Output since 1869* (Princeton University Press, 1947)). Prior to 1947, structures estimates are extrapolated using the following series: for 1929–1946, the NIPA estimates of investment in industrial buildings; for 1915–1928, estimates of the value of new construction put in place for industrial buildings from the U.S. Department of Commerce's *Construction Statistics 1915–1964*; and for 1900–1914, balance sheet data from the Census of Manufactures for 1900, 1904, 1909, and 1914, and the F. W. Dodge series on the value of construction contract awards from U.S. Bureau of the Census, *Historical Statistics of the United States* (1975) for the noncensus years.

Motor vehicle industry equipment estimates prior to 1972 are adjusted to include investment in special tools and dies, which is excluded from the pre-1972 census data. Industrial machinery and equipment industry equipment estimates for census years prior to 1982 are adjusted to include the value of computers owned by the manufacturer and leased to other industries.

TABLE Dd724–831 Capital in manufacturing, by industry division: 1879–1957[1]

Contributed by Jeremy Atack and Fred Bateman

Current dollars

Year	Total			Food and kindred products									Textiles and textile products		
	Total	Fixed	Working	Total	Packinghouse	Canned	Mill	Bakery and confectionery	Sugar	Liquor and beverages	Other	Tobacco	Total	Cotton	Silk and rayon
	Dd724	Dd725	Dd726	Dd727	Dd728	Dd729	Dd730	Dd731	Dd732	Dd733	Dd734	Dd735	Dd736	Dd737	Dd738
	Million dollars	Million dollars	Million dollars	Million dollars	Million dollars	Million dollars	Million dollars	Million dollars	Million dollars	Million dollars	Million dollars	Million dollars	Million dollars	Million dollars	Million dollars
1879	2,718	—	—	498	49	9	177	28	28	135	32	40	602	246	19
1889	5,697	2,646	3,051	925	117	25	208	72	24	310	73	96	1,119	392	51
1899	8,663	4,223	4,440	1,647	189	59	219	123	204	534	195	124	1,494	528	81
1899	8,168	—	—	1,576	189	59	189	114	204	516	193	112	1,366	528	81
1904	11,588	5,596	5,992	2,230	238	90	265	173	221	660	259	324	1,783	702	110
1909	16,937	—	—	2,935	378	119	349	295	283	873	392	246	2,550	936	152
1914	20,784	—	—	3,668	537	172	380	426	316	1,016	517	304	2,881	1,039	210
1919	40,289	—	—	6,272	1,185	378	802	911	473	782	1,136	605	6,205	2,145	533
1929	59,072	27,410	31,662	8,881	1,385	853	471	1,568	1,053	692	1,709	1,150	7,687	1,603	869
1937	50,166	23,282	26,884	8,069	1,114	820	496	1,131	599	1,371	1,577	961	4,770	866	441
1948	113,617	45,891	67,726	16,071	1,975	1,681	1,060	1,757	780	3,158	3,302	2,330	10,397	3,693	—
1953	166,224	70,605	95,619	19,921	—	—	—	—	—	3,900	—	2,826	12,077	—	—
1957	214,613	97,210	117,403	22,495	—	—	—	—	—	4,282	—	3,044	12,417	—	—

Current dollars

Year	Textiles and textile products					Forest products				Printing, publishing, and allied industries	Chemicals and allied substances				Petroleum refining
	Woolen and worsted	Knit	Carpets, floor covering, tapestries, etc.	Other	Clothing	Total	Sawmill and planing mill	Other	Paper, pulp, and products		Total	Fertilizers	Chemicals proper	Allied chemical substances	
	Dd739	Dd740	Dd741	Dd742	Dd743	Dd744	Dd745	Dd746	Dd747	Dd748	Dd749	Dd750	Dd751	Dd752	Dd753
	Million dollars	Million dollars	Million dollars	Million dollars	Million dollars	Million dollars	Million dollars	Million dollars	Million dollars	Million dollars	Million dollars	Million dollars	Million dollars	Million dollars	Million dollars
1879	117	16	25	65	114	361	219	142	58	80	137	18	49	70	27
1889	203	51	43	87	292	825	518	307	115	234	288	41	96	151	77
1899	264	82	53	136	350	1,110	731	379	219	342	458	61	145	252	95
1899	264	82	53	101	257	872	520	352	218	342	457	61	144	252	95
1904	313	107	69	137	345	1,174	694	480	354	450	634	69	194	371	136
1909	429	164	97	204	568	1,767	1,122	645	523	611	911	122	273	516	182
1914	403	216	112	268	633	1,932	1,193	739	689	745	1,280	217	390	673	326
1919	868	516	179	517	1,447	2,726	1,730	996	1,195	1,189	2,594	312	941	1,341	1,170
1929	601	709	262	1,887	1,758	3,842	2,660	1,182	2,060	2,622	3,942	335	973	2,634	5,745
1937	415	433	199	1,380	1,036	2,405	1,562	843	1,942	2,320	3,537	198	1,125	2,214	5,814
1948	—	929	483	2,253	3,018	4,820	3,000	1,805	3,692	3,984	9,109	334	2,580	5,917	15,363
1953	—	—	—	—	3,924	6,347	—	—	5,499	5,202	14,450	—	—	—	19,960
1957	—	—	—	—	4,049	8,225	—	—	8,161	6,632	19,138	—	—	—	30,174

Note appears at end of table

(continued)

TABLE Dd724–831   Capital in manufacturing, by industry division: 1879–1957   Continued

Current dollars

	Rubber products			Leather products			Stone, clay, and glass products	Iron and steel and products				Nonferrous metals and products			Machinery, excluding transportation equipment	
	Total	Tires and tubes	Other	Total	Boots and shoes	Other		Total	Iron and steel	Metal building materials and supplies	Hardware, tools, etc.	Total	Precious metals	Other	Total	Electrical machinery and equipment
	Dd754	Dd755	Dd756	Dd757	Dd758	Dd759	Dd760	Dd761	Dd762	Dd763	Dd764	Dd765	Dd766	Dd767	Dd768	Dd769
Year	Million dollars	Million dollars	Million dollars	Million dollars	Million dollars	Million dollars	Million dollars	Million dollars	Million dollars	Million dollars	Million dollars	Million dollars	Million dollars	Million dollars	Million dollars	Million dollars
1879	9	—	—	157	43	114	83	318	258	10	49	86	29	57	242	2
1889	37	—	—	274	95	179	217	646	469	73	104	187	70	117	557	19
1899	78	—	—	369	102	267	351	860	657	87	117	381	97	284	924	86
1899	78	—	—	335	100	235	336	870	657	97	116	360	97	263	924	87
1904	99	—	—	452	123	329	554	1,544	1,185	202	156	455	126	329	1,309	183
1909	162	—	—	659	197	462	860	2,411	1,845	340	225	705	181	524	1,860	282
1914	268	130	138	743	255	488	990	2,836	2,147	417	273	827	196	631	2,331	390
1919	960	635	325	1,523	581	942	1,267	5,671	4,456	665	549	1,484	315	1,169	4,700	963
1929	1,088	918	170	1,167	625	542	2,351	6,226	4,155	756	1,315	2,194	352	1,842	5,833	1,514
1937	795	586	209	751	410	341	1,825	6,383	4,394	805	1,184	2,090	247	1,843	4,979	1,120
1948	1,791	1,383	361	1,303	710	592	2,934	13,609	9,521	2,309	1,177	2,655	515	2,663	14,674	4,874
1953	2,614	—	—	1,394	—	—	4,482	20,212	—	—	—	4,288	—	—	24,104	8,936
1957	3,369	—	—	1,542	—	—	6,681	26,572	—	—	—	6,516	—	—	29,735	10,014

Current dollars

	Machinery, excluding transportation equipment			Transportation equipment				
	Agricultural machinery	Office equipment, etc.	Factory, household, and miscellaneous machinery	Total	Motor vehicles	Airplanes	Locomotive and railroad equipment	Miscellaneous
	Dd770	Dd771	Dd772	Dd773	Dd774	Dd775	Dd776	Dd777
Year	Million dollars	Million dollars	Million dollars	Million dollars	Million dollars	Million dollars	Million dollars	Million dollars
1879	62	6	172	9	—	—	9	51
1889	145	8	385	73	2	—	71	123
1899	158	24	656	167	30	—	137	168
1899	158	24	655	173	36	—	137	166
1904	197	41	888	169	29	—	139	245
1909	256	72	1,250	390	184	—	206	411
1914	339	95	1,507	685	426	—	259	583
1919	367	167	3,203	2,326	1,816	18	491	1,007
1929	730	430	3,159	3,264	2,575	111	578	2,168
1937	749	413	2,697	3,294	2,504	180	610	1,192
1948	1,745	815	6,962	8,944	6,006	1,114	927	4,271
1953	—	—	—	17,885	9,982	—	—	7,789
1957	—	—	—	23,117	12,680	—	—	9,839

Constant dollars

	Total			Food and kindred products				
	Total	Fixed	Working	Total	Packinghouse	Canned	Mill	Bakery and confectionery
	Dd778	Dd779	Dd780	Dd781	Dd782	Dd783	Dd784	Dd785
Year	Million 1929 dollars	Million 1929 dollars	Million 1929 dollars	Million 1929 dollars	Million 1929 dollars	Million 1929 dollars	Million 1929 dollars	Million 1929 dollars
1879	4,821	—	—	879	88	16	319	50
1889	11,157	5,553	6,336	1,839	233	50	414	143
1899	18,626	9,651	8,975	3,760	432	135	500	281
1899	17,452	—	—	3,598	432	135	432	256
1904	23,295	12,316	10,979	4,656	497	188	553	361
1909	31,563	—	—	5,517	711	224	656	555
1914	36,737	—	—	6,515	954	306	675	757
1919	46,094	—	—	7,593	1,435	458	971	1,103
1929	63,022	30,853	32,169	9,591	1,496	921	509	1,693
1937	55,319	25,851	29,468	9,180	1,267	933	564	1,287
1948	78,067	36,639	41,428	10,488	1,288	1,097	691	1,146
1953	97,843	43,862	53,981	12,878	—	—	—	—
1957	110,455	51,061	59,394	13,361	—	—	—	—

Constant dollars

Year	Food and kindred products					Textiles and textile products								Forest products	
	Sugar	Liquor and beverages	Tobacco	Other	Total	Cotton	Silk and rayon	Woolen and worsted	Knit	Carpets, floor covering, tapestries, etc.	Other	Clothing	Total	Sawmill and planing mill	Other
	Dd786	Dd787	Dd788	Dd789	Dd790	Dd791	Dd792	Dd793	Dd794	Dd795	Dd796	Dd797	Dd798	Dd799	Dd800
	Million 1929 dollars	Million 1929 dollars	Million 1929 dollars	Million 1929 dollars	Million 1929 dollars	Million 1929 dollars	Million 1929 dollars	Million 1929 dollars	Million 1929 dollars	Million 1929 dollars	Million 1929 dollars	Million 1929 dollars	Million 1929 dollars	Million 1929 dollars	Million 1929 dollars
1879	50	243	72	58	998	408	32	194	27	41	108	189	847	514	333
1889	48	616	191	145	2,024	709	92	367	92	78	157	528	1,950	1,225	726
1899	466	1,219	283	445	3,145	1,112	171	556	173	112	286	737	2,868	1,889	979
1899	466	1,178	256	441	2,876	1,112	171	556	173	112	213	541	2,253	1,344	910
1904	461	1,378	676	541	3,482	1,371	215	611	209	135	268	674	2,662	1,574	1,088
1909	532	1,641	462	737	4,636	1,702	276	780	298	176	371	1,033	3,591	2,280	1,311
1914	561	1,805	540	918	5,163	1,862	376	722	387	201	480	1,134	3,475	2,146	1,329
1919	573	947	732	1,375	6,752	2,334	580	945	561	195	563	1,575	3,155	2,002	1,153
1929	1,137	747	1,242	1,846	8,195	1,709	926	641	756	279	2,012	1,874	4,083	2,827	1,256
1937	681	1,560	1,093	1,794	5,638	1,024	521	491	512	235	1,631	1,225	2,548	1,655	893
1948	509	2,061	1,520	2,154	6,892	2,447	—	—	616	320	1,493	2,001	2,934	1,826	1,099
1953	—	3,233	1,907	—	7,846	—	—	—	—	—	—	2,638	3,252	—	—
1957	—	3,092	1,948	—	7,758	—	—	—	—	—	—	2,657	3,634	—	—

Constant dollars

Year	Paper, pulp, and products	Printing, publishing, and allied industries	Chemicals and allied substances				Petroleum refining	Rubber products			Leather products			Stone, clay, and glass products	Iron and steel and products	
			Total	Fertilizers	Chemicals proper	Allied chemical substances		Total	Tires and tubes	Other	Total	Boots and shoes	Other		Total	Iron and steel
	Dd801	Dd802	Dd803	Dd804	Dd805	Dd806	Dd807	Dd808	Dd809	Dd810	Dd811	Dd812	Dd813	Dd814	Dd815	Dd816
	Million 1929 dollars	Million 1929 dollars	Million 1929 dollars	Million 1929 dollars	Million 1929 dollars	Million 1929 dollars	Million 1929 dollars	Million 1929 dollars	Million 1929 dollars	Million 1929 dollars	Million 1929 dollars	Million 1929 dollars	Million 1929 dollars	Million 1929 dollars	Million 1929 dollars	Million 1929 dollars
1879	90	144	206	27	74	105	37	10	—	—	328	90	238	156	472	388
1889	200	466	478	68	159	251	151	36	—	—	640	222	418	408	1,143	830
1899	455	801	871	116	276	479	195	74	—	—	891	246	645	741	1,581	1,208
1899	453	801	869	116	374	479	195	74	—	—	809	242	568	709	1,599	1,208
1904	670	939	1,134	123	347	664	254	93	—	—	1,066	290	776	1,138	2,886	2,215
1909	1,002	1,265	1,531	205	459	867	327	139	—	—	1,359	406	953	1,755	4,305	3,295
1914	1,246	1,444	2,078	352	633	1,093	552	265	129	136	1,351	464	887	1,937	5,166	3,911
1919	1,524	1,556	2,777	334	1,007	1,436	1,380	704	466	238	1,411	538	873	1,676	6,735	5,292
1929	2,239	2,737	4,221	359	1,042	2,820	6,092	1,131	954	177	1,213	650	563	2,592	6,666	4,449
1937	2,062	2,505	3,965	222	1,261	2,482	6,503	816	602	215	808	441	367	1,975	6,719	4,625
1948	2,476	2,571	6,487	237	1,830	4,196	11,188	1,422	1,098	287	817	445	371	2,128	9,649	6,598
1953	3,086	2,622	8,845	—	—	—	12,455	1,660	—	—	821	—	—	2,631	11,701	—
1957	4,039	2,832	10,564	—	—	—	16,134	1,842	—	—	940	—	—	3,375	13,090	—

(continued)

TABLE Dd724–831   Capital in manufacturing, by industry division: 1879–1957   Continued

Constant dollars

	Iron and steel and products		Nonferrous metals and products				Machinery, excluding transportation equipment				Transportation equipment				Miscellaneous
	Metal building materials and supplies	Hardware, tools, etc.	Total	Precious metals	Other	Total	Electrical machinery and equipment	Agricultural machinery	Office equipment, etc.	Factory, household, and miscellaneous machinery	Total	Motor vehicles	Airplanes	Locomotive and railroad equipment	
	Dd817	Dd818	Dd819	Dd820	Dd821	Dd822	Dd823	Dd824	Dd825	Dd826	Dd827	Dd828	Dd829	Dd830	Dd831
Year	Million 1929 dollars	Million 1929 dollars	Million 1929 dollars	Million 1929 dollars	Million 1929 dollars	Million 1929 dollars	Million 1929 dollars	Million 1929 dollars	Million 1929 dollars	Million 1929 dollars	Million 1929 dollars	Million 1929 dollars	Million 1929 dollars	Million 1929 dollars	Million 1929 dollars
1879	15	73	116	39	77	414	3	106	10	295	17	—	—	17	89
1889	129	184	276	103	173	1,160	40	302	17	802	156	4	—	152	230
1899	160	215	646	164	481	1,917	178	328	50	1,361	337	60	—	276	344
1899	178	213	610	164	446	1,917	180	328	50	1,359	349	73	—	276	340
1904	378	292	804	223	581	2,710	379	408	85	1,839	333	57	—	274	468
1909	607	402	1,203	309	894	3,654	554	503	141	2,456	567	267	—	299	712
1914	760	497	1,365	323	1,041	4,293	718	624	175	2,775	991	616	—	375	896
1919	790	652	1,808	384	1,424	5,595	1,146	437	199	3,813	2,480	1,936	19	523	948
1929	809	1,408	2,364	379	1,985	6,166	1,600	772	455	3,339	3,476	2,742	118	616	2,256
1937	847	1,246	2,338	276	2,062	5,286	1,189	795	438	2,863	3,672	2,792	201	680	1,304
1948	1,600	816	1,837	379	1,960	10,352	3,438	1,226	573	4,892	6,017	4,016	743	618	2,809
1953	—	—	2,508	—	—	13,773	5,517	—	—	—	9,387	5,425	—	—	4,378
1957	—	—	3,229	—	—	14,388	5,099	—	—	—	10,450	6,150	—	—	4,819

[1] Series coverage and composition change over time; see text.

Sources

1879–1937, Daniel Creamer, Sergei Dobrovolsky, and Israel Borenstein, *Capital in Manufacturing and Mining: Its Formation and Financing* (Princeton University Press, 1960), Appendix A, Tables 8 and 9.

1948–1957, Daniel Creamer, *Capital Expansion and Capacity in Postwar Manufacturing*, Studies in Business Economics, number 72 (National Industrial Conference Board, 1961), Appendix G, Tables G-1 and G-2.

Documentation

This table and its associated documentation have been reprinted, more or less without modification, from U.S. Bureau of the Census, *Historical Statistics of the United States* (1975), series P123–176.

Figures are expressed as book value. Data through the first set of values for 1899 include custom and neighborhood shops.

Beginning with the second set of values for 1899, figures cover factories having annual production of $500 or more; and beginning in 1929, $5,000 or more (both amounts in current dollars).

Beginning in 1949, some minor groups are not adjusted for investment in emergency facilities after "normal" depreciation or intangible assets; as a result, sum of detail does not equal totals. Firms engaged in shipbuilding are included beginning in 1953, but they are excluded in other years.

Series Dd751–752 and Dd805–806. Chemicals proper are items such as acids. Allied chemical substances are items such as drugs, oils, and so forth.

Series Dd765–767 and Dd819–821. Covers nonferrous metals, products, and processes.

TABLE Dd832-842   Consumption of selected commodities in manufacturing – coal, petroleum, and energy products: 1899-1981[1]

Contributed by Jeremy Atack and Fred Bateman

	Used for heat and power						Used as a raw material				
	Total energy	Coal	Coke	Fuel oil	Gas	Purchased electric energy	Coal	Coke	Crude petroleum	Fuel oil	Natural gas
	Dd832	Dd833	Dd834 [2]	Dd835	Dd836	Dd837	Dd838	Dd839	Dd840	Dd841	Dd842
Year	Billion kilowatt-hours	Thousand short tons	Thousand short tons	Million barrels	Billion cubic feet	Billion kilowatt-hours	Thousand short tons	Thousand short tons	Million barrels	Million barrels	Billion cubic feet
1899	—	—	—	—	—	—	—	—	52	—	—
1904	—	—	—	—	—	—	—	—	67	—	—
1909	1,630	165,593	38,530	19.7	309	—	—	—	121	—	—
1914	1,626	168,892	31,370	32.7	280	—	—	—	191	—	—
1919	2,097	202,576	41,785	69.6	566	—	—	—	365	—	—
1923	1,711 [3]	222,848	—	—	—	—	—	—	—	—	—
1927	1,533 [3]	199,705	—	—	—	—	—	—	—	—	—
1929	2,510	206,232	51,406	132.2	1,174	36	—	—	1,040	—	—
1937	2,588	169,523	42,194	136.3	2,489	46	—	—	—	—	—
1939	1,595	80,161	35,001	97.4	1,840	45	63,189	1,744	1,250	36.0	968
1947	3,195	110,869	66,171	215.6	4,866	103	108,053	2,551	1,884	—	485
1954	4,359	91,458	54,372	246.6	8,977	187	85,441	1,860	2,499	4.0	338
1958	4,184	81,784	49,806	226.9	8,628	253	77,817	1,265	2,850	6.0	365
1963	4,632	89,438	55,941	271.0	9,341	314	71,470	1,122	3,198	8.3	300
1967	5,348	75,100	61,105	262.3	11,638	427	92,940	1,390	3,621	11.1	607
1971	—	61,393	13,743	245.7	—	515	—	—	—	—	—
1974	—	47,807	15,215	284.9	—	617	—	—	—	—	—
1975	—	44,623	13,157	282.3	—	597	—	—	—	—	—
1976	—	47,903	18,536	321.3	—	640	—	—	—	—	—
1977	—	50,745	19,916	345.5	—	663	—	—	—	—	—
1978	—	51,484	21,063	343.9	—	676	—	—	—	—	—
1979	—	50,570	19,248	252.7	—	685	—	—	—	—	—
1980	—	50,479	15,594	187.5	—	659	—	—	—	—	—
1981	—	52,945	14,800	153.9	—	666	—	—	—	—	—

[1] Through 1937, use as raw material is included under use for heat and power, with the exception of crude petroleum. Thus, the total in series Dd832 includes energy equivalents for fuel used as raw material.

[2] Beginning in 1971, series differs from earlier data.

[3] Energy equivalent for coal only, including that used as raw material.

Sources

U.S. Bureau of the Census, *Thirteenth Census of the United States: 1910,* volume 10, p. 662; *Census of Manufactures: 1963,* volume 1, pp. 7-90 and 7-91; and *Census of Manufactures: 1967,* Special Report MC67(S)-4, *Fuels and Electric Energy Consumed,* pp. 8-9. U.S. Bureau of the Census, *Census of Manufactures, Fuels and Electric Energy Consumed* (1982), pp. 4-7, MC 82-S-4, part 1, pp. 4-7.

Documentation

Data for fuels consumed for heat and power were converted to kilowatt-hour equivalents, the international unit of energy, and then added to the quantity of purchased electric energy. The conversion factor used for each fuel is shown in the source reports. For fuels, quantities include both fuels purchased for use as fuel and fuels made and used in the same establishment.

TABLE Dd843–847   Consumption of selected commodities in manufacturing – coffee, cotton, wool, and silk: 1860–1995

Contributed by Jeremy Atack and Fred Bateman

	Coffee, imported	Raw cotton used in textiles	Mill consumption of cotton	Wool used in textiles	Unmanufactured silk imports for consumption		Coffee, imported	Raw cotton used in textiles	Mill consumption of cotton	Wool used in textiles	Unmanufactured silk imports for consumption
	Dd843 [1]	Dd844	Dd845	Dd846	Dd847		Dd843 [1]	Dd844	Dd845	Dd846	Dd847
Year	Million pounds	Thousand bales	Thousand bales	Million pounds	Million pounds	Year	Million pounds	Thousand bales	Thousand bales	Million pounds	Million pounds
1860	180	845	—	—	—	1915	1,137	6,009	6,398	—	30.8
1861	146	842	—	—	—	1916	1,132	7,279	6,789	—	32.0
1862	94	369	—	—	—	1917	1,218	7,658	6,566	—	36.0
1863	101	287	—	—	—	1918	1,014	7,685	5,766	399.3	32.3
1864	105	220	—	—	—	1919	1,256	6,224	6,420	329.1	44.3
1865	126	344	—	—	—	1920	1,248	6,762	4,893	314.2	29.3
1866	175	615	—	—	—	1921	1,304	5,409	5,910	343.4	44.9
1867	220	715	—	—	—	1922	1,220	6,549	6,666	406.5	50.1
1868	235	844	—	—	—	1923	1,388	7,312	5,681	422.4	49.1
1869	235	860	—	—	—	1924	1,395	6,217	6,193	342.2	50.5
1870	272	797	—	—	—	1925	1,269	6,852	6,456	349.9	63.1
1871	308	1,027	—	—	—	1926	1,482	7,260	7,190	342.7	65.6
1872	289	1,147	—	—	—	1927	1,419	7,996	6,834	354.1	72.7
1873	292	1,116	—	—	—	1928	1,447	7,614	7,091	333.2	74.4
1874	283	1,213	—	—	—	1929	1,475	7,970	6,106	368.1	85.9
1875	360	1,098	—	—	—	1930	1,585	6,911	5,263	263.2	80.6
1876	267	1,256	—	—	—	1931	1,730	5,977	4,866	311.0	87.6
1877	349	1,314	—	—	—	1932	1,484	5,503	6,137	230.1	77.6
1878	325	1,459	—	—	—	1933	1,574	6,898	5,700	317.1	73.0
1879	438	1,457	—	—	—	1934	1,514	6,467	5,361	229.6	60.4
1880	396	1,501	—	—	—	1935	1,745	6,080	6,351	417.5	72.4
1881	426	1,866	—	—	—	1936	1,732	7,085	7,950	406.1	67.5
1882	484	1,849	—	—	—	1937	1,689	8,769	5,748	380.8	64.2
1883	488	2,038	—	—	3.3	1938	1,981	6,463	6,858	284.5	57.1
1884	494	1,814	—	—	3.4	1939	2,001	7,709	7,784	396.5	55.3
1885	534	1,687	—	—	3.9	1940	2,044	8,845	9,722	407.9	47.6
1886	521	2,095	—	—	4.8	1941	2,250	11,081	11,170	648.0	25.6
1887	423	2,050	—	—	4.8	1942	1,712	12,658	11,100	603.6	0.2
1888	507	2,205	—	—	5.4	1943	2,194	12,401	9,943	636.2	—
1889	534	2,309	—	—	5.8	1944	2,604	11,308	9,568	622.8	—
1890	481	2,518	—	—	4.6	1945	2,705	11,049	9,163	645.1	1.0
1891	574	2,604	—	—	7.1	1946	2,664	10,218	10,025	737.5	13.5
1892	601	2,847	—	—	7.8	1947	2,458	11,009	9,354	698.3	3.2
1893	535	2,416	—	—	4.4	1948	2,752	10,510	7,795	693.1	7.4
1894	601	2,300	—	—	7.8	1949	2,913	9,201	8,851	500.4	4.0
1895	634	2,984	—	—	9.1	1950	2,429	10,467	10,654	634.8	10.5
1896	621	2,500	—	—	4.9	1951	2,678	12,050	9,120	484.1	7.2
1897	787	2,841	—	—	10.0	1952	2,665	10,426	9,424	466.4	12.6
1898	781	3,472	—	—	8.4	1953	2,767	10,783	8,576	494.0	7.8
1899	852	3,672	—	—	11.7	1954	2,234	9,900	8,841	380.8	8.5
1900	741	3,687	—	—	8.1	1955	2,569	10,315	9,141	413.8	11.0
1901	1,028	3,604	—	—	12.2	1956	2,776	10,930	8,728	440.7	12.7
1902	901	4,080	—	—	13.6	1957	2,713	10,166	7,973	368.8	8.3
1903	740	4,187	—	—	11.5	1958	2,667	9,101	8,671	331.1	5.3
1904	1,074	3,981	—	—	16.4	1959	3,066	9,913	9,025	435.3	8.0
1905	859	4,523	—	—	15.4	1960	2,917	10,471	8,252	411.0	6.9
1906	844	4,877	—	—	16.7	1961	2,954	9,560	9,071	412.1	6.7
1907	930	4,974	—	—	15.6	1962	3,238	10,292	8,391	429.1	6.5
1908	926	4,493	—	—	18.6	1963	3,185	9,747	8,554	411.7	6.4
1909	1,126	5,241	—	—	22.1	1964	3,054	9,967	9,171	356.7	6.7
1910	797	4,799	—	—	21.5	1965	2,844	10,557	9,497	387.0	5.8
1911	796	4,705	—	—	20.7	1966	2,918	10,950	9,449	307.2	4.6
1912	938	5,368	—	—	24.7	1967	2,819	10,650	9,071	315.5	2.8
1913	845	5,786	—	—	27.8	1968	3,357	10,072	8,215	329.7	4.0
1914	975	5,885	—	—	25.5	1969	2,676	9,367	7,965	312.8	3.3

Note appears at end of table

(continued)

TABLE Dd843–847 Consumption of selected commodities in manufacturing – coffee, cotton, wool, and silk: 1860–1995 *Continued*

Year	Coffee, imported Dd843 [1] Million pounds	Raw cotton used in textiles Dd844 Thousand bales	Mill consumption of cotton Dd845 Thousand bales	Wool used in textiles Dd846 Million pounds	Unmanufactured silk imports for consumption Dd847 Million pounds
1970	2,609	9,119	8,068	240.3	1.8
1971	2,905	—	8,010	191.0	1.7
1972	2,786	—	7,568	218.6	2.1
1973	2,933	—	7,150	151.3	2.8
1974	2,587	—	5,604	93.5	2.6
1975	2,727	—	6,965	110.0	1.0
1976	2,660	—	6,478	121.7	2.8
1977	1,990	—	6,217	108.0	1.6
1978	2,437	—	6,180	115.3	2.0
1979	2,607	—	6,209	117.0	1.5
1980	2,440	—	5,641	123.4	1.0
1981	2,225	—	5,043	138.6	1.9
1982	2,341	—	5,259	115.7	2.0
1983	2,211	—	5,628	140.6	1.6
1984	2,383	—	5,268	142.1	1.4

Year	Coffee, imported Dd843 [1] Million pounds	Raw cotton used in textiles Dd844 Thousand bales	Mill consumption of cotton Dd845 Thousand bales	Wool used in textiles Dd846 Million pounds	Unmanufactured silk imports for consumption Dd847 Million pounds
1985	2,513	—	6,198	116.6	1.5
1986	2,668	—	7,096	136.7	1.0
1987	2,675	—	7,294	142.8	1.4
1988	2,061	—	7,444	132.7	0.9
1989	2,604	—	8,383	127.1	1.1
1990	2,630	—	8,632	—	0.7
1991	2,533	—	9,373	—	1.0
1992	2,913	—	9,797	—	0.6
1993	2,421	—	10,408	—	0.8
1994	2,004	—	10,306	—	0.7
1995	2,135	—	—	—	0.5

[1] For 1956–1962 and beginning in 1971, figures are for imports for consumption of raw or green coffee.

Sources

Series Dd843. 1860–1914: Edwin Frickey, *Production in the United States, 1860–1914*, Harvard Economic Studies (Harvard University Press, 1947), pp. 8–9, 143–4. 1915–1929: Arthur F. Burns, *Production Trends in the United States since 1870* (National Bureau of Economic Research, 1934), pp. 292–3. 1930–1947: U.S. Bureau of the Census, *Foreign Commerce and Navigation of the United States* (1930–1947). 1945–1962: U.S. Bureau of the Census, *Quarterly Summary of Foreign Commerce of the United States* (1945–1962). 1963–1970: U.S. Bureau of the Census, *U.S. Imports of Merchandise for Consumption,* Reports FT 110, FT 125, and FT 135 (calendar year issues). 1971–1995: *An Economic Research Service Report, Foreign Agricultural Trade of the United States* (calendar year 1996 supplement).

Series Dd844. 1860–1909: U.S. Bureau of the Census, *Bulletin 160, Cotton Production and Distribution, 1926,* p. 49. 1910–1945: U.S. Bureau of the Census, *Bulletin 183, Cotton Production and Distribution, 1946,* pp. 26–31. 1946–1962: U.S. Bureau of the Census, *Cotton Production and Distribution,* annual reports. 1963–1970: U.S. Bureau of the Census, *Current Industrial Reports,* series M22P, *Cotton, Man-Made Fiber Staple, and Linters, Summary for Cotton Season* (various annual issues).

Series Dd845. 1915–1994: U.S. Department of Agriculture, *Agricultural Statistics* (various years, specifically 1936, 1943, 1949, 1956, 1962, 1967, 1972, 1977, 1984, 1989). Also for 1971–1994: for 1971–1974, U.S. Bureau of the Census, *Current Industrial Reports, Cotton, Manmade Fiber Staple, and Linters, Summary for Cotton Season* (1973–1974); and for 1975–1994, U.S. Bureau of the Census, *Current Industrial Reports, Consumption on the Cotton System, Summary for Cotton Season* (each year).

Series Dd846. 1922–1957: U.S. Bureau of the Census, *Facts for Industry, Wool Consumption and Stocks* (monthly issues) (title may vary). 1958–1995: U.S. Bureau of the Census, *Current Industrial Reports,* series M 220, *Consumption on the Woolen and Worsted Systems* (monthly issues).

Series Dd847. 1883–1929: Burns (1934), pp. 294–5. 1930–1931: U.S. Bureau of Foreign and Domestic Commerce, *Foreign Commerce and Navigation of the United States,* volume 1, for respective years. 1932: U.S. Bureau of the Census, *Statistical Abstract of the United States, 1940,* p. 732. 1933–1949: U.S. Bureau of the Census, *Statistical Abstract of the United States, 1950,* p. 638. 1950–1955: Textile Economics Bureau, *Textile Organon* 37 (3) (March 1966). 1955–1995: *Textile Organon* (continued as *Fiber Organon*) (various issues).

Documentation

Series Dd843. The data for 1860–1933 are described as net imports (general imports) minus foreign exports; for 1934–1970, they are described as imports for consumption minus foreign exports. However, on duty-free commodities such as coffee, general imports equal imports for consumption. Data cover U.S. customs area, which includes Alaska, Hawai'i, and Puerto Rico.

Series Dd844. Data are for years ending August 31 through 1910, July 31 thereafter. Figures are in running bales; except that for 1860–1870, they are in equivalent 500-pound bales. Data exclude linters for 1860–1908 and include them thereafter.

Series Dd845. Data are for years beginning August 1 of year given. Figures are in running bales.

Series Dd846. Figures relate to scoured wool plus greasy wool reduced to a scoured basis, assuming average yields varying with class, origin, grade, and whether shorn or pulled. For 1946–1970, they include raw wool consumed in woolen and worsted systems only. For a series on apparent consumption of all wool, 1870–1929, see Burns (1934), pp. 296–7.

Series Dd847. Figures are derived by subtracting foreign exports from general imports of all types of unmanufactured silk. Spun silk is not included. For a series on raw silk imports (excluding silk from cocoons and waste) for 1860–1914, see the source for series Dd847, pp. 8–9 and 153–5; and for 1870–1929, see Burns (1934), pp. 294–5.

TABLE Dd848–853   Power in manufacturing – horsepower of equipment: 1869–1962[1]

Contributed by Jeremy Atack and Fred Bateman

	Aggregate			Electric motors		
					Driven by energy	
Year	Number	Per 100 production workers	Prime movers	Total	Purchased	Generated at establishment
	Dd848	Dd849	Dd850	Dd851	Dd852	Dd853
	Thousand horsepower	Thousand horsepower	Thousand horsepower	Thousand horsepower	Thousand horsepower	Thousand horsepower
1869	—	114	2,346	—	—	—
1879	—	125	3,410	—	—	—
1889	—	140	5,939	15	—	—
1899	10,988	207	10,805	494	183	311
1899	9,811	218	9,633	475	178	297
1904	13,033	252	12,605	1,517	428	1,089
1909	18,062	288	16,393	4,582	1,669	2,913
1914	21,565	326	17,858	8,392	3,707	4,684
1919	28,397	333	19,432	15,612	8,965	6,647
1925	34,359	437	19,243	25,092	15,116	9,976
1927	37,126	473	18,902	29,153	18,224	10,929
1929	41,122	491	19,328	33,844	21,794	12,050
1939	49,893	652	21,077	44,827	28,816	16,011
1954	108,100	958	35,763	91,505	72,337	19,168
1962	151,498	1,249 [2]	45,770	126,783	105,728	21,054

[1] Through the first set of values for 1899, figures include hand trades and neighborhood industries.

[2] Figure comparable with 1954, based on 1954 industry coverage, is 1,365; see text. Figures for earlier censuses are comparable with 1962, except as noted in text.

Source

U.S. Bureau of the Census, *Census of Manufactures, 1963,* volume 1, pp. 6–9.

Documentation

This table and its associated documentation have been reprinted, more or less without modification, from U.S. Bureau of the Census, *Historical Statistics of the United States* (1975), series P68–73.

The first census of power equipment available in manufacturing establishments was taken by the Bureau of the Census in 1870, covering the year 1869. Because certain industries included in earlier censuses were not covered by the 1939 Census, the power equipment statistics for 1899–1929 were adjusted in 1939 to provide a comparable series for the seventy-year period. The comparability of the 1954 and 1962 statistics with those for 1939 is affected by (1) the exclusion from the 1954 and 1962 statistics inquiry of fractional horsepower motors included in the 1939 totals, and (2) the omission of data for selected industry groups in 1954 included in the 1939 and 1962 totals.

The aggregate horsepower figure, series Dd848, represents the unduplicated rating for total installed equipment and thus provides a measure of the mechanical power available in manufacturing establishments. The figure is derived by summing the horsepower rating of prime movers – the initial source of energy that engages the machine – and that for electric motors. To secure the latter figure, the total horsepower for electric motors was distributed, by establishment, into two categories: motors driven by purchased electricity and motors driven by energy generated at the establishment. For the relatively small number of establishments that both generate and purchase electricity, the total horsepower for electric motors was prorated on the basis of the ratio of the net quantity purchased to the net total for electricity consumed.

The horsepower ratings for prime movers include information for such types of power equipment as internal combustion engines, steam and hydraulic turbines, and reciprocating steam engines. The totals for prime movers are further separated between those driving electric generators and those used for other purposes. The statistics for prime movers not driving generators exclude data for automobiles, trucks, and other highway equipment.

Respondents were requested to report horsepower of standby equipment as well as equipment in operation at the end of the year, including all prime movers and motors in mobile (except automobiles, trucks, and other highway equipment) as well as in stationary equipment. Information for fractional horsepower motors, however, was not reported for either 1954 or 1962.

Horsepower data were not reported at later censuses.

Series Dd849. Data on aggregate horsepower per 100 (factory) production workers are comparable for all years, except for 1954 and for years prior to 1899. The figures for 1954 exclude data for all establishments in the printing trade services industry, and those in the apparel and other fabricated textile products industry except for miscellaneous apparel. The number of wage earners as published in the census reports prior to 1899 includes those in factory as well as in hand trades and neighborhood industries (such as carpentry, millinery, and painting) and custom grist milling, custom saw milling, and cotton ginning. Changes in the minimum size limit set for establishments included in the several censuses or the number of manufacturing establishments requested to report power equipment data are believed to have an insignificant effect on the totals.

TABLE Dd854–874   Power in manufacturing – consumption of offsite-produced energy, by industry group: 1974–1994[1]

Contributed by Jeremy Atack and Fred Bateman

Year	Total	Food and kindred products	Tobacco products	Textile mill products	Apparel and other textile products	Lumber and wood products	Furniture and fixtures	Paper and allied products	Printing and publishing	Chemicals and allied products	Petroleum and coal products
	Dd854	Dd855	Dd856	Dd857	Dd858	Dd859	Dd860	Dd861	Dd862	Dd863	Dd864
	Trillion BTU	Trillion BTU	Trillion BTU	Trillion BTU	Trillion BTU	Trillion BTU	Trillion BTU	Trillion BTU	Trillion BTU	Trillion BTU	Trillion BTU
1974	13,337	959	20	323	68	274	60	1,327	93	2,937	1,545
1975	12,037	916	19	307	56	229	46	1,210	87	2,780	1,357
1976	12,625	938	20	329	57	244	47	1,295	86	3,017	1,292
1977	12,929	952	21	339	66	228	53	1,308	92	2,979	1,303
1978	12,929	980	21	327	69	231	55	1,301	91	2,905	1,123
1979	12,867	949	21	315	61	223	51	1,300	90	2,889	1,245
1980	11,874	948	22	295	58	199	47	1,278	88	2,717	1,178
1981	11,563	913	23	292	61	185	46	1,262	91	2,630	1,137
1982	9,881	900	22	256	53	165	41	1,210	86	2,258	1,035
1983	9,990	889	21	274	49	179	43	1,299	83	2,285	982
1984	10,221	898	20	266	49	184	44	1,349	87	2,295	966
1985	9,698	876	20	247	31	167	41	1,340	76	2,170	917
1986	9,935	894	21	258	43	185	44	1,379	88	2,167	1,068
1987	10,461	921	24	278	48	201	51	1,402	103	2,436	972
1988	11,052	946	26	276	54	199	54	1,409	115	2,568	1,070
1989	11,184	946	26	280	50	205	55	1,446	114	2,631	1,106
1990	11,258	942	26	273	48	208	53	1,514	116	2,683	1,140
1991	10,837	922	26	272	44	197	46	1,540	108	2,674	1,138
1992	10,958	980	24	281	54	190	48	1,546	111	2,707	1,122
1993	11,453	1,027	24	303	59	205	51	1,570	114	2,823	1,123
1994	12,006	1,081	21	311	56	210	54	1,621	111	2,997	1,156

Year	Rubber and misc. plastics products	Leather and leather products	Stone, clay, and glass products	Primary metal industries	Fabricated metal products	Industrial machinery and equipment	Electronic and other electric equipment	Transportation equipment	Instruments and related products	Miscellaneous
	Dd865	Dd866	Dd867	Dd868	Dd869	Dd870	Dd871	Dd872	Dd873	Dd874
	Trillion BTU	Trillion BTU	Trillion BTU	Trillion BTU	Trillion BTU	Trillion BTU	Trillion BTU	Trillion BTU	Trillion BTU	Trillion BTU
1974	247	23	1,332	2,604	408	367	251	375	70	53
1975	227	23	1,159	2,235	367	330	227	348	70	45
1976	237	22	1,220	2,380	381	330	233	380	73	45
1977	272	23	1,252	2,539	395	340	249	390	78	49
1978	261	22	1,300	2,711	400	351	255	398	79	49
1979	249	20	1,266	2,689	386	353	250	385	80	46
1980	223	19	1,122	2,277	359	334	240	344	80	45
1981	223	18	1,077	2,241	352	325	235	329	79	43
1982	231	16	901	1,507	298	278	218	293	75	38
1983	238	16	916	1,528	288	257	229	307	72	36
1984	236	15	945	1,650	319	268	235	325	76	35
1985	211	13	878	1,537	297	241	209	322	74	30
1986	232	13	903	1,431	302	243	219	339	75	33
1987	250	14	921	1,560	323	261	207	348	103	39
1988	251	16	959	1,773	343	278	215	350	112	40
1989	260	15	978	1,720	345	284	217	356	110	41
1990	255	14	970	1,690	335	277	215	352	108	39
1991	235	12	877	1,563	305	236	196	318	97	31
1992	246	11	845	1,562	313	238	207	332	103	37
1993	270	11	887	1,679	340	244	222	353	106	44
1994	285	10	943	1,859	365	244	230	356	105	51

[1] Figures are based on the following: *Annual Survey of Manufactures* (1974–1976 and 1978–1981), *Census of Manufactures* (1977), and *Manufacturing Energy Consumption Survey* (1985, 1988, 1991, 1994); see text. Data for other years were derived as described in the text.

Source

U.S. Department of Energy, Energy Information Administration (EIA), *Manufacturing Energy Consumption Survey*, downloaded from the EIA Internet site.

Documentation

This table presents annual estimates of purchased energy used by the manufacturing sector. These estimates interpolate over gaps in the actual data collections by deriving estimates for the missing years 1982–1984 and 1986–1987. For the purposes of this table, "purchased" energy is energy brought from offsite for use at manufacturing establishments, whether the energy is purchased from an energy vendor or procured from some other source.

The actual data on purchased energy come from two sources, the U.S. Bureau of the Census's *Annual Survey of Manufactures* (ASM) and EIA's

(continued)

TABLE Dd854–874   Power in manufacturing – consumption of offsite-produced energy, by industry group: 1974–1994
Continued

Manufacturing Energy Consumption Survey (MECS). The ASM provides annual estimates for the years 1974–1981. However, in 1982 (and subsequent years) the scope of the ASM energy data was reduced to collect only electricity consumption and expenditures and total expenditures for other purchased energy. In 1985, EIA initiated the triennial MECS, collecting complete energy data. The series equivalent to the ASM is referred to in the MECS as "offsite-produced fuels." The completed annual series for 1974–1988 developed in this table links the ASM and MECS "offsite" series, estimating for the missing years. Estimates are provided for the manufacturing sector as a whole and at the two-digit Standard Industrial Classification (SIC) level for total energy consumption and for the consumption of individual fuels. (See the Introduction to Part D for a discussion of SIC codes.) There are no direct sources of data for the missing years (1982–1984, 1986–1987, 1989–1990, and 1992–1993). To derive consumption estimates, a comparison was made between the ASM, the MECS, and other economic series to see whether there were any good predictors for the missing data. Various estimation schemes were analyzed to fill in the gaps in data after 1981 by trying to match known data for the 1974–1981 period.

The most accurate methodology for deriving estimates for the missing years turned out to be a relatively simple process. The chosen procedure first estimates the total consumption of an industry for years for which no data are available. The method of estimation uses available consumption data from either the MECS or the ASM for endpoint years that bracket years with missing data. The relationship between the Federal Reserve Board production index (published in the *Statistical Abstract of the United States*) for the endpoint years and the intervening years is applied to the known consumption totals for the endpoint years to derive consumption totals for the missing years. Fuel-specific estimates are obtained by using a linear interpolation on the fuel shares for the endpoint years to determine shares for the intervening years, and applying these shares to the newly derived consumption totals for the intervening years.

INDUSTRY CONCENTRATION, LEGAL FORM, AND ECONOMIC PERFORMANCE

Jeremy Atack and Fred Bateman

TABLE Dd875–878 Manufacturing concentration – percentage of value added accounted for by the largest companies: 1947–1992

Contributed by Jeremy Atack and Fred Bateman

Year	Largest 50 Dd875 Percent	Largest 100 Dd876 Percent	Largest 150 Dd877 Percent	Largest 200 Dd878 Percent
1947	17	23	27	30
1954	23	30	34	37
1958	23	30	35	38
1962	24	32	36	40
1963	25	33	37	41
1966	25	33	38	42
1967	25	33	38	42
1970	24	33	38	43
1972	25	33	39	43
1976	24	33	39	44
1977	24	33	39	44
1982	24	33	39	43
1987	25	33	39	43
1992	24	32	38	42

Source

1947–1992: U.S. Bureau of the Census, *Census of Manufactures* (various issues). 1962 and 1966: U.S. Bureau of the Census, *Annual Survey of Manufactures*.

Documentation

Data for 1962 and 1966 are based on the *Annual Survey of Manufactures*; other years on the *Census of Manufactures*.

These data reflect the activity of the largest companies in the industrial sector as a whole. A company is defined as the total of its industrial establishments, including not only its manufacturing plants but also its auxiliary establishments such as warehouses and central administrative offices. Value added for all manufacturing establishments of a given company was aggregated irrespective of the industry classification of the individual establishments. The companies were then arrayed by magnitude of value added

in each specified year, and totals were computed for the 50, 100, 150, and 200 largest companies.

The rankings in 1947 and 1954 were based on unadjusted value added; those for later years on adjusted value added. See the text for series Dd10.

In Table Dd875–878, companies were classified in size groups in each particular year based on their size in that year. Thus, a size group does not necessarily include the same companies from year to year.

In Table Dd879–894, the largest companies in each year specified in the series titles were selected, and their proportion of value added in each of the years shown in the year stub was computed. Thus, these data measure the changes in concentration ratios for a fixed group of companies from one year to another. In case of mergers, the larger of the two at the time of merger was considered to be the predecessor company.

TABLE Dd879–894 Manufacturing concentration – percentage of value added accounted for by the largest companies: 1947–1970 [Consistent sets of companies]

Contributed by Jeremy Atack and Fred Bateman

	Largest companies as of 1947		Largest companies as of 1954		Largest companies as of 1958		Largest companies as of 1962		Largest companies as of 1963		Largest companies as of 1966		Largest companies as of 1967		Largest companies as of 1970	
	50	100	50	100	50	100	50	100	50	100	50	100	50	100	50	100
	Dd879	Dd880	Dd881	Dd882	Dd883	Dd884	Dd885	Dd886	Dd887	Dd888	Dd889	Dd890	Dd891	Dd892	Dd893	Dd894
Year	Percent	Percent	Percent	Percent	Percent	Percent	Percent	Percent	Percent	Percent	Percent	Percent	Percent	Percent	Percent	Percent
1947	17	23	16	21	16	22	15	21	15	22	14	21	15	20	12	18
1954	21	27	23	30	23	29	22	29	22	29	21	28	21	28	19	25
1958	20	27	23	30	23	30	23	30	23	30	22	29	22	29	20	26
1962	21	27	23	30	24	31	24	32	24	32	24	31	24	31	22	29
1963	21	28	24	31	24	32	25	32	25	33	24	32	24	32	23	29
1966	21	27	23	31	24	31	25	33	24	33	25	33	25	33	24	31
1967	20	27	23	31	23	31	24	33	24	32	24	32	25	33	23	31
1970	19	26	21	28	22	29	23	31	23	31	23	31	24	32	24	33

Source

U.S. Bureau of the Census: 1947–1967, 1967 Census of Manufactures, volume 1, p. 9-6; 1970, Annual Survey of Manufactures, Value of Shipment Concentration Ratios, M70 (AS)-9.

Documentation

This table has been reprinted, more or less without modification, from U.S. Bureau of the Census, Historical Statistics of the United States (1975), series P181-196. See the text for Table Dd875-878.

TABLE Dd895–902 Manufacturing concentration ratios, by industry group: 1901–1954

Contributed by Jeremy Atack and Fred Bateman

		Percentage of value added by "concentrated" 4-digit industry groups		Value added weights		Average concentration ratios			
						1947 employment weights		1954 employment weights	
		1901	1947	1947	1954	1947	1954	1947	1954
		Dd895 [1]	Dd896	Dd897	Dd898	Dd899	Dd900	Dd901	Dd902
Industry group	2-digit SIC code	Percent	Percent	Percent	Percent	Percent	Percent	Percent	Percent
Total, all industries, value-added weights	—	32.9	24.0	35.3	36.9	36.3	37.0	37.7	39.0
Total, all industries, employment weights	—	—	—	—	—	34.6	35.9	34.7	35.3
Food and kindred products	20	39.1	18.8	34.9	33.8	32.4	33.2	31.3	32.4
Tobacco manufactures	21	49.9	77.7	76.2	73.4	66.0	62.9	67.4	64.1
Textile mill products	22	20.3	9.0	24.3	26.5	27.6	28.8	26.5	27.8
Apparel and related products	23	—	2.2	12.6	13.0	14.0	14.7	13.6	14.8
Lumber and wood products	24	0.5	2.0	11.2	10.8	12.3	11.3	10.8	10.7
Furniture and fixtures	25	—	8.1	21.9	20.3	16.5	18.7	17.4	16.7
Pulp, paper, and products	26	71.0	1.6	21.2	24.8	24.2	24.3	24.5	24.4
Printing and publishing	27	1.0	0.0	19.7	17.7	18.8	17.2	18.6	16.9
Chemicals and products	28	24.3	33.7	51.0	48.6	25.8	29.7	29.7	32.5
Petroleum and coal products	29	46.8	13.6	39.5	36.6	39.5	37.0	39.4	36.7

		Percentage of value added by "concentrated" 4-digit industry groups		Average concentration ratios					
				Value added weights		1947 employment weights		1954 employment weights	
		1901 [1]	1947	1947	1954	1947	1954	1947	1954
		Dd895	Dd896	Dd897	Dd898	Dd899	Dd900	Dd901	Dd902
Industry group	2-digit SIC code	Percent	Percent	Percent	Percent	Percent	Percent	Percent	Percent
Rubber products	30	100.0	59.9	58.6	54.1	57.0	56.0	52.1	51.0
Leather and leather products	31	26.3	0.0	26.2	26.4	26.1	26.6	25.9	26.6
Stone, clay, and glass products	32	13.3	43.9	43.4	46.4	80.6	78.8	79.0	77.7
Primary metal products	33	45.7 [2]	21.0	43.8	49.5	40.6	45.3	41.4	46.7
Fabricated metal products	34	—	8.4	25.3	26.1	26.7	26.0	26.6	25.4
Machinery, except electrical	35	41.4 [3]	18.5	38.0	33.2	38.2	38.9	37.6	37.8
Electrical machinery	36	—	53.2	54.1	48.2	53.4	50.5	50.8	47.9
Transportation equipment	37	57.3	84.2	54.4	58.7	54.0	63.3	53.7	56.6
Instruments and related products	38	—	45.0	45.3	47.4	52.8	52.5	54.0	53.5
Miscellaneous manufactures	39	2.7	21.2	34.9	16.1	31.5	30.1	29.0	28.6

[1] Data are from various years in the 1895–1904 period, with the central date approximately 1901, but there weighting factors were as of 1899.

[2] Excludes steel works and rolling mills for which the concentration ratio is 78.8.

[3] Includes electrical machinery.

Sources

Series Dd895. G. Warren Nutter, *The Extent of Enterprise Monopoly in the United States* (University of Chicago Press, 1951), Tables 10 and 39.

Series Dd896. M. A. Adelman, "The Measurement of Industrial Concentration," *Review of Economics and Statistics 33* (November 1951), Table 14, which is based on U.S. House of Representatives, *Hearings before the Subcommittee on Study of Monopoly Power*, 81st Congress, 1st session, serial number 14, part 2-B, pp. 1436–56.

Series Dd897–898. Figures are tabulations prepared by the Bureau of the Census from data reported in the *Census of Manufactures*.

Series Dd899–902. Irving Rottenberg, "New Statistics on Companies and on Concentration in Manufacturing from the 1954 Census," *Proceedings of the American Statistical Association, Business and Economics Statistics Section* (1957), Table 5, p. 225.

Documentation

This table and its associated documentation have been reprinted, more or less without modification, from U.S. Bureau of the Census, *Historical Statistics of the United States* (1975), series P197–204.

The basic source of most of the data is the *Census of Manufactures*. The industry groups are based on the 1947 and 1954 Census classifications.

The concentration ratio is defined as the percentage of total industry sales (or value added) made by the four largest sellers.

This table uses two different measures of the degree of concentration, both based on the four-firm concentration ratio. Both cover all industries. The first takes the value added in all four-digit Standard Industrial Classification (SIC) industry groupings within a two-digit SIC group where the four-firm concentration exceeds 50 percent and expresses this as a percentage of value added in the two-digit industry group. The second consists of averages of the concentration ratios shown for the twenty industry groups. See the Introduction to Part D for a discussion of SIC codes.

Where the change in concentration from 1947 to 1954 as shown in series Dd897–898 differs substantially from the change shown in series Dd899–902, the difference is attributable to industry redefinition and to inclusion or exclusion of industries from the *Census of Manufactures*. A striking example is the miscellaneous manufactures group (SIC 39), from which the ordnance and accessories group (SIC 19) was omitted for national security reasons.

Series Dd895–896. Figures represent the value added by four-digit industry groups with concentration ratios of 50 or higher, expressed as a percentage of the total value added by all four-digit industry groups in the two-digit group. Series Dd895 covers 319 four-digit industry groups, and series Dd896 covers 452.

Series Dd897–902. Figures are average concentration ratios for each two-digit industry group. In computing these averages, the concentration ratio of each four-digit group is weighted in proportion to its employment or value added (as indicated) as a proportion of total employment or total value added by the entire two-digit group.

Series Dd897–898. Includes all four-digit industry groups for the given year – 452 in 1947, and 434 in 1954. Because of changes in four-digit industry definitions, concentration ratios are not fully comparable. Figures are based on weights for the year shown – for example, series Dd897 uses 1947 value-added weights.

Series Dd899–902. Figures are based on 375 comparable industries accounting for 85 percent of all value added by manufacture in 1947, and for 82 percent in 1954.

TABLE Dd903–904 Corporate control of manufacturing – percentage of workers and value added in establishments owned by corporations: 1899–1992

Contributed by Jeremy Atack and Fred Bateman

	Production workers	Value added			Production workers	Value added
	Dd903	Dd904 [1]			Dd903	Dd904 [1]
Year	Percent	Percent		Year	Percent	Percent
1899	—	65.0 [2]		1963	93.4	95.8
1904	70.6	71.9		1967	95.0	96.7
1909	75.6	77.2		1972	97.0	98.0
1914	80.8	83.2		1977	97.2	98.1
1919	86.6	87.7		1982	96.4	98.0
1929	89.9	91.5		1987	96.3	97.8
1939	89.4	92.3		1992	97.1	98.3
1947	89.4	91.9				
1954	90.6	93.7				
1958	91.7	94.7				

[1] Beginning in 1982, data are not comparable with earlier data; see text.

[2] Based on value of product.

Sources

1899: U.S. Bureau of the Census, *Census of Manufactures: 1905,* part 1, p. liv. 1904–1909: U.S. Bureau of the Census, *Thirteenth Census of the United States, 1910, Manufactures: 1909,* volume 8, p. 135. 1914–1919: U.S. Bureau of the Census, *Fourteenth Census of the United States, 1920, Manufactures: 1919,* volume 8, p. 108. 1929: U.S. Bureau of the Census, *Fifteenth Census of the United States, 1930, Manufactures: 1929,* volume 1, p. 95. 1939: U.S. Bureau of the Census, *Sixteenth Census of the United States, 1940, Manufactures: 1939,* volume 1, p. 229. 1947–1992: *U.S. Census of Manufactures* (various years).

Documentation

Percentages were computed from data reported in the various censuses cited in the sources.

Besides corporations, manufacturing establishments can be organized as individual proprietorships, partnerships, and other forms of ownership, mostly cooperative societies.

Beginning in 1982, all respondents were requested to report their inventories at cost or market prior to adjustment to LIFO (last in, first out) cost. This is a change from prior years in which respondents were permitted to value their inventories using any generally accepted accounting method. Consequently, data for value added by manufacture since 1982 are not comparable with earlier data.

Figures for 1899 include 66,143 establishments not covered by the Census of Manufactures. These establishments produced products valued at $290 million, compared with a total value of product of all manufactures of $11,701 million.

Series Dd903. The number of production workers is tabulated as the average for the pay periods that included the 12th of March, May, August, and November.

TABLE Dd905–918 Sales, profits, stockholder equity, cash dividends, and retained earnings of manufacturing corporations: 1947–1995[1,2]

Contributed by Jeremy Atack and Fred Bateman

	Total						Durable goods industries				Nondurable goods industries			
	Net sales	Net profits		Stockholders' equity	Cash dividends	Retained earnings	Net sales	Net profits		Stockholders' equity	Net sales	Net profits		Stockholders' equity
		Before income taxes	After income taxes					Before income taxes	After income taxes			Before income taxes	After income taxes	
Year	Dd905	Dd906[3]	Dd907	Dd908	Dd909	Dd910	Dd911	Dd912[3]	Dd913	Dd914	Dd915	Dd916[3]	Dd917	Dd918
	Billion dollars	Billion dollars	Billion dollars	Billion dollars	Billion dollars	Billion dollars	Billion dollars	Billion dollars	Billion dollars	Billion dollars	Billion dollars	Billion dollars	Billion dollars	Billion dollars
1947	150.7	16.6	10.1	65.1	3.7	6.4	66.6	7.6	4.5	31.1	84.1	9.0	5.6	34.0
1948	165.6	18.4	11.5	72.2	4.3	7.2	75.3	8.9	5.4	34.1	90.4	9.5	6.2	38.1
1949	154.9	14.4	9.0	77.6	4.5	4.5	70.3	7.5	4.5	37.0	84.6	7.0	4.6	40.6
1950	181.9	23.2	12.9	83.3	5.7	7.2	86.8	12.9	6.7	39.9	95.1	10.3	6.1	43.5
1951	245.0	27.4	11.9	98.3	5.5	6.3	116.8	15.4	6.1	47.2	128.1	12.1	5.7	51.1
1952	250.2	22.9	10.7	103.7	5.5	5.2	122.0	12.9	5.5	49.8	128.0	10.0	5.2	53.9
1953	265.9	24.4	11.3	108.2	5.6	5.7	137.9	14.0	5.8	52.4	128.0	10.4	5.5	55.7
1954	248.5	20.9	11.2	113.1	5.9	5.3	122.8	11.4	5.6	54.9	125.7	9.6	5.6	58.2
1955	278.4	28.6	15.1	120.1	6.8	8.3	142.1	16.5	8.1	58.8	136.3	12.1	7.0	61.3
1956	307.3	29.8	16.2	131.6	7.4	8.8	159.5	16.5	8.3	65.2	147.8	13.2	7.8	66.4
1957	320.0	28.2	15.4	141.1	7.6	7.9	166.0	15.8	7.9	70.5	154.1	12.4	7.5	70.6
1958	305.3	22.7	12.7	147.4	7.4	5.3	148.6	11.4	5.8	72.8	156.7	11.3	6.9	74.6
1959	338.0	29.7	16.3	157.1	7.9	8.4	169.4	15.8	8.1	77.9	168.5	13.9	8.3	79.2
1960	345.7	27.5	15.2	165.4	8.3	6.9	173.9	14.0	7.0	82.3	171.8	13.5	8.2	83.1
1961	356.4	27.5	15.3	172.6	8.6	6.8	175.2	13.6	6.9	84.9	181.2	13.9	8.5	87.7
1962	389.9	31.9	17.7	181.4	9.3	8.4	195.5	16.7	8.6	89.1	194.4	15.1	9.2	92.3
1963	412.7	34.9	19.5	189.7	9.9	9.6	209.0	18.5	9.5	93.3	203.6	16.4	10.0	96.3
1964	443.1	39.6	23.2	199.8	10.8	12.4	226.3	21.2	11.6	98.5	216.8	18.3	11.6	101.3
1965	492.2	46.5	27.5	211.7	12.0	15.5	257.0	26.2	14.5	105.4	235.2	20.3	13.0	106.3
1966	554.2	51.8	30.9	230.3	13.0	18.0	291.7	29.2	16.4	115.2	262.4	22.6	14.6	115.1
1967	575.4	47.8	29.0	247.6	13.3	15.7	300.6	25.7	14.6	125.0	274.8	22.0	14.4	122.6
1968	631.9	55.4	32.1	265.9	14.2	17.9	335.5	30.6	16.5	135.6	296.4	24.8	15.5	130.3
1969	694.6	58.1	33.2	289.9	15.1	18.2	366.5	31.5	16.9	147.6	328.1	26.6	16.4	142.8
1970	708.8	48.1	28.6	306.8	15.1	13.5	363.1	23.0	12.9	155.1	345.7	25.2	15.7	151.7
1971	751.1	52.9	31.0	320.8	—	—	381.8	26.5	14.5	160.4	369.3	26.5	16.5	160.5
1972	849.5	63.2	36.5	343.4	—	—	435.8	33.6	18.4	171.4	413.7	29.6	18.0	172.0
1973 [2]	1,017.2	81.4	48.1	374.1	—	—	527.3	43.6	24.8	188.7	489.9	37.8	23.3	185.4
1973 [2]	275.1	21.4	13.0	386.4	—	—	140.1	10.8	6.3	194.7	135.0	10.6	6.7	191.7
1973 [2]	236.6	20.6	13.2	368.0	—	—	122.7	10.1	6.2	185.8	113.9	10.5	7.0	182.1
1974	1,060.6	92.1	58.7	395.0	—	—	529.0	41.1	24.7	196.0	531.6	51.0	34.1	199.0
1975	1,065.2	79.9	49.1	423.4	—	—	521.1	35.3	21.4	208.1	544.1	44.6	27.7	215.3
1976	1,203.2	104.9	64.5	462.7	—	—	589.6	50.7	30.8	224.3	613.7	54.3	33.7	238.4
1977	1,328.1	115.1	70.4	496.7	—	—	657.3	57.9	34.8	239.9	670.8	57.2	35.5	256.8
1978	1,496.4	132.5	81.1	540.5	—	—	760.7	69.6	41.8	262.6	735.7	62.9	39.3	277.9
1979	1,741.8	154.2	98.7	600.5	—	—	865.7	72.4	45.2	292.5	876.1	81.8	53.5	308.0
1980	1,912.8	145.8	92.6	668.1	—	—	889.1	57.4	35.6	317.7	1,023.7	88.4	56.9	350.4
1981	2,144.7	158.6	101.3	743.4	—	—	979.5	67.2	41.6	350.4	1,165.2	91.3	59.6	393.0
1982	2,039.4	108.2	70.6	770.2	—	—	913.1	34.7	21.7	355.5	1,126.4	73.6	49.3	414.7
1983	2,114.3	133.1	85.8	812.8	—	—	973.5	48.7	30.0	372.4	1,140.8	84.4	55.8	440.4
1984	2,335.0	165.6	107.6	864.2	—	—	1,107.6	75.5	48.9	395.6	1,227.5	90.0	58.8	468.5

Notes appear at end of table   (continued)

TABLE Dd905–918   Sales, profits, stockholder equity, cash dividends, and retained earnings of manufacturing corporations: 1947–1995   Continued

	Total						Durable goods industries				Nondurable goods industries			
		Net profits		Stockholders' equity	Cash dividends	Retained earnings	Net sales	Net profits		Stockholders' equity	Net sales	Net profits		Stockholders' equity
	Net sales	Before income taxes	After income taxes					Before income taxes	After income taxes			Before income taxes	After income taxes	
	Dd905	Dd906 [3]	Dd907	Dd908	Dd909	Dd910	Dd911	Dd912 [3]	Dd913	Dd914	Dd915	Dd916 [3]	Dd917	Dd918
Year	Billion dollars	Billion dollars	Billion dollars	Billion dollars	Billion dollars	Billion dollars	Billion dollars	Billion dollars	Billion dollars	Billion dollars	Billion dollars	Billion dollars	Billion dollars	Billion dollars
1985	2,331.4	137.0	87.6	866.2	—	—	1,142.6	61.5	38.6	420.9	1,188.8	75.6	49.1	445.3
1986	2,220.9	129.3	83.1	874.7	—	—	1,125.5	52.1	32.6	436.3	1,095.4	77.2	50.5	438.4
1987	2,378.2	173.0	115.6	900.9	—	—	1,178.0	78.0	53.0	444.3	1,200.3	95.1	62.6	456.6
1988	2,596.2	216.1	154.6	957.6	—	—	1,284.7	91.7	67.1	468.7	1,311.5	124.4	87.5	488.9
1989	2,745.1	188.8	136.3	999.0	—	—	1,356.6	75.2	55.7	501.3	1,388.5	113.5	80.6	497.7
1990	2,810.7	159.6	111.6	1,043.8	—	—	1,357.2	57.6	40.9	515.0	1,453.5	102.0	70.6	528.9
1991	2,761.1	99.8	67.5	1,064.1	—	—	1,304.0	14.1	7.4	506.8	1,457.1	85.7	60.1	557.4
1992 [4]	2,890.2	32.5	23.2	1,034.7	—	—	1,389.8	−33.5	−23.7	473.9	1,500.4	66.0	47.0	560.8
1993	3,015.1	118.6	83.9	1,039.7	—	—	1,490.2	39.0	27.6	482.7	1,524.9	79.6	56.4	557.1
1994	3,255.8	245.3	176.6	1,110.1	—	—	1,657.6	121.6	87.6	533.3	1,598.2	123.7	89.1	576.8
1995	3,524.9	276.6	200.1	1,240.1	—	—	1,803.9	131.3	94.8	613.3	1,721.0	145.3	105.3	626.8

1 Beginning in 1969, total and nondurable series for sales, profits, and stockholder equity include newspapers.

2 See the text for discussion of changes in the series beginning in 1973. This table presents three sets of values for that year: annual data; then fourth-quarter data based on the old methods; and finally fourth-quarter data based on the new methods.

3 Through 1972, "income taxes" refers to federal income taxes only, as state and local income taxes had already been deducted; thereafter, no income taxes have been deducted.

4 Data for 1992 (most significantly 1992:1) reflect the early adoption of Financial Accounting Standards Board Statement 106 (Employer's Accounting for Post-Retirement Benefits Other Than Pensions) by a large number of companies during the fourth quarter of 1992. Data for 1993:1 also reflect adoption of Statement 106. Corporations must show the cumulative effect of a change in accounting principle in the first quarter of the year in which the change is adopted.

Sources

U.S. Council of Economic Advisers, *Economic Report of the President* (January 1972), Table B-74 and (February 1999), Table B-93.

Documentation

Data are from the U.S. Federal Trade Commission, U.S. Securities and Exchange Commission, and the U.S. Bureau of the Census, Economic Census and Surveys Division. The annual figures presented here appear originally in the Federal Trade Commission's *Quarterly Financial Report for Manufacturing Corporations* for the fourth quarter of the year and the continuation of these series by U.S. Bureau of the Census, Economic Census and Surveys Division, post-1974.

These data are based on uniform, confidential financial statements collected from a probability sample of all enterprises that are required to file Form 1120, U.S. Corporation Income Tax Return, and are classified as manufacturers. Included are domestic corporations organized within the United States, resident foreign corporations incorporated abroad but engaged in trade or business in the United States, associations and joint-stock companies that are taxed as corporations, and small business corporations electing to be taxed through their shareholders. Excluded are inactive corporations with no income or deductions, tax-exempt farmers' cooperatives, tax-exempt nonprofit organizations, and corporations not classified in their tax returns as manufacturers.

The first sample was drawn from Form 1120 for the taxable year 1943. A second sample was drawn for the taxable year 1949. The third sample was drawn for the taxable year 1954 and each taxable year thereafter. Each sample has been supplemented by a quarterly sample of applications for a Federal Social Security Employer's Identification Number filed with the Social Security Administration.

The first sample was used to provide estimates for each of the quarters in calendar years 1947 to 1951, inclusive; the second sample, from third quarter 1951 to second quarter 1956, inclusive; the third sample, from second quarter 1956 to 1970. To splice the estimates based on the first and second samples, an overlap was provided for the third and fourth quarters of 1951; to splice the estimates based on the second and third samples, an overlap was provided for the second quarter of 1956. Within the third sample, an overlap was provided for each quarter in calendar year 1958 to splice the estimates based upon the 1945 and 1957 editions of the *Standard Industrial Classification Manual* (*SIC Manual*). See the Introduction to Part D for a discussion of SIC codes.

The classification of a corporation has been determined, in general, on the basis of the consolidated operations of the reporting company (as opposed to the establishment). In the reports for 1947–1958, classification was based on the 1945 edition of the *SIC Manual*. Beginning in 1959, estimates were based on the classification of corporations within the framework of the 1957 edition. In 1963, the Enterprise Standard Industrial Classification (ESIC) was used in the classification of companies. The structure of the 1968 revision of the ESIC follows closely that of the 1967 edition of the *SIC Manual*.

When the original series began in 1947, corporations consolidated all their subsidiaries that were taxable under the U.S. Internal Revenue Code and the expectation was that this rule would eliminate most foreign operations. However, as the number of multinational corporations increased, new consolidation rules were put into effect that were designed to maximize coverage of quarterly financial reports while minimizing the effect of foreign operations. These changes are described in greater detail in U.S. Bureau of the Census, Economic Census and Surveys Division, *Quarterly Financial Report for Manufacturing, Mining, and Trade Corporations*. Specific information concerning significant changes and revisions is contained in various issues of the report: third quarter 1953, third quarter 1956, first quarter 1959, first quarter 1965, and fourth quarter 1974.

The following cautionary note is appended to these series: "Data are not necessarily comparable from one period to another due to changes in accounting principles, industry classifications, sampling procedures, etc." For explanatory notes and further discussion concerning compilation of these series, see U.S. Bureau of the Census, Economic Census and Surveys Division, *Quarterly Financial Report for Manufacturing, Mining, and Trade Corporations*.

Series Dd908, Dd914, and Dd918. Annual data are average equity for the year, using four end-of-quarter figures.

CHAPTER De

Distribution

Editor: Daniel M. G. Raff

DISTRIBUTION

Daniel M. G. Raff

Paul H. Nystrom, Professor of Marketing at the Columbia University Graduate School of Business, finished writing the third edition of his authoritative account of retailing shortly before the enumerators for the initial Census of Distribution took to the field in the springtime of 1930 (Nystrom 1930, volume 1, p. 4). There were roughly 6.4 million individual farms and 196,000 factory establishments in the American economy of the day, perhaps half producing goods for consumers. Americans themselves, he observed, numbered about 120 million. They were scattered over 3 million square miles. Nearly half of the population (49 percent) lived outside the 3,000 cities with populations of more than 2,500.[1] The scale of the problem of distribution is immediately apparent.

In that 1930 Census, distribution employed just shy of 5.8 million people, 19.7 percent of the nonagricultural work force. In 1900 the percentage had been 16.5, and by 2000 it was 21.1. By comparison, manufacturing in 1900 employed 36.0 percent, falling to 32.5 in 1930 and, as the economy continued to evolve and the world to change, manufacturing fell to 15.1 percent in 2000. The percentage share of distribution in gross domestic product (GDP) at the millennium was 16.0. Manufacturing stood at 14.1. Distribution has been a substantial part of the economy for a very long time. It is, in part for reasons that will be discussed, an increasingly important one.

The Contents of This Chapter

The body of this chapter gives time series, both aggregated and broken down, on retail and wholesale trade and on the related subject of advertising. The first Census of Retailing defined retailing as "the process of purveying goods to ultimate consumers for consumption or utilization, together with services incidental to the sale of goods " (U.S. Bureau of the Census 1933, volume 1, p. 13). The basic economic task carried out by retailers is thus the anticipation of the variety of wants and the convenient provision of candidate satisfactions. Wholesale trade was defined as a complementary category, thus including sales to retailers, intermediaries of various sorts, and to manufacturers who use the goods as intermediate or capital inputs.[2] The measurement has been carried forward without significant modification. The two together are important because they are what stands between manufacturing and consumption: they represent the distribution sector of the economy. Advertising is also covered in this chapter since it is reasonably viewed as an activity whose purpose is to encourage and facilitate distribution.

Some series in the chapter go back as far as the late 1860s.[3] Most begin in 1929, when the Census first began to cover distribution (as discussed later) or later as the coverage developed. Most of the data come from Bureau of the Census or Commerce Department sources or from trade journals. Some of the advertising data derive from the industrious research of Mr. Robert J. Coen of the advertising agency McCann–Erickson in New York.

The data are presented in four basic groupings. The first presents general statistics on the distribution sector. This includes series giving national income originating in wholesale trade, retail trade, and selected service industries, corresponding figures for employment, corresponding figures for wage and salary accruals, the number of establishments, sales, payroll, and employees all grouped by legal form of organization, and the book value of inventories industry category. The second gives finer detail for retail trade grouped by industries. It shows the number of establishments, sales, persons engaged, statistics on sales of multiunit firms and chain stores, and some limited information on trade margins, department store sales and stocks, and the number and sales of establishments in selected service industries. The third gives finer detail for wholesale trade by industries, showing establishments, sales, operating expenses, and employment by type of business, sales by industry, and more limited data on sales and stocks of merchant wholesalers and on trade margins of independent wholesalers. The fourth gives data on advertising expenditure (by medium) and finer data on newspaper advertising (by expenditure and by lineage) and magazine advertising.

The principal distinctions drawn in these tables are those between retail and wholesale and those between the industries. These distinctions carry over essentially intact (notes are given as appropriate) from the previous edition of *Historical Statistics of the*

Acknowledgments

Daniel Raff would like to thank the many industry executives who made time to speak with him on background. Colleagues George Day, Charles Fine, Louis Galambos, Robert Gordon, Janice Hammond, Leonard Lodish, David Reibstein, Walter Salmon, and Sidney Winter also contributed. Raff would like to thank Nicolas Fawzi, Faye Iosotaluno, Xian Li, Max Lin, and Preeta Roy for research assistance. This work was supported by the Wharton School's Huntsman Emerging Technologies Management Research Program, Jones Center for Management Policy, Strategy, and Organization, and Mack Center for Technological Innovation.

---

[1] Nystrom (1930), volume 1, pp. 3–4. After the category of "cities" came "towns," "villages," "hamlets," and only then "the country." That these distinctions seemed worth making at all speaks volumes.

[2] For the discussion in the report on the first Census of Distribution, see U.S. Bureau of the Census (1933), volume 1, pp. 3–4.

[3] The principal source of these nineteenth-century figures is the National Bureau of Economic Research study of Barger (1955).

United States. All data are given here on the Standard Industrial Classification (SIC) industry definitions. Subsequent editions will be more complex owing to the transition to North American Industrial Classification System (NAICS) definitions.[4]

History of the Institutions of Distribution

As with other sectors of the American economy such as agriculture and manufacturing, the distribution sector has changed dramatically in response to exogenous changes in transportation, information technology, population distribution and density, and the spatial configuration of our cities and communities. Some background knowledge about the evolving institutions of distribution in the economy is helpful for seeing what the statistical data do and do not reveal.[5]

Public or covered markets were present in some colonial cities, but market days and fairs do not appear to have been a durably significant factor in trade.[6] Lasting institutions of distribution began with general merchants in coastal cities of initial settlement. Trading posts with very modest offerings followed the fur trade and grew slightly in their breadth of merchandise as the westward migration began and farms and towns began to appear. Peddlers proceeding on foot or in wagons pursued trade in less populated regions. These brought the products of colonial craftsmen and New England industry (Nystrom mentions, for example, pins, needles, hooks and eyes, scissors, razors early on and eventually dry goods, hats, and hardware).[7]

As hinterland towns (or at least population centers) developed, so did general stores.[8] These sometimes ran as adjuncts to inns or farms, sometimes as freestanding enterprises. They were typically staffed by the owner or the owner's family and supplied the sort of goods a relatively rural and not terribly prosperous clientele would want: food, tools, and more materials out of which the industrious could make dresses and the like, rather than the dresses themselves. Stock was acquired on annual (or, as the mid-nineteenth century approached, sometimes semiannual) visits to trading centers such as Boston, New York, Philadelphia, and Baltimore.[9] Transactions were on a credit basis for much of the year. Pot-bellied stoves and a place to sit and chat were common features of these stores.

Perhaps information on the creditworthiness of the farmer-clients was gleaned from the gossip.

The coastal centers offered more. There, great merchants imported goods, sometimes by the boatload, from abroad and sold at both retail and wholesale (Bailyn 1955; Baxter 1945; Bruchey 1956; Porter 1931, 1937). In their capacity as wholesalers they did then what wholesalers do still: they sourced; they broke bulk; and they maintained for the benefit of the retailers with whom they did business broader and deeper inventories than the retailers – given their own locations and clienteles – could afford.[10] Thus, the variety of goods available to consumers was much wider than it otherwise would have been. These urban wholesalers owned the merchandise they sold. Smaller general stores also continued to trade in the urban areas, as did some more specialized shops where the population would support such a division of labor. A different category of wholesaler, the commission merchant, figured in these early years, principally though not entirely in the trade in agricultural commodities.[11] Commission merchants coordinated transactions for a fee but never took ownership of the goods and so stood no price risk. A particularly elaborate set of institutions developed in the South and the trading ports around the financing of the cotton trade. As a general matter, however, the commission merchant system died out by the 1870s.[12]

As the larger cities grew, particularly in the course of the nineteenth century, the most conspicuous change in this overall pattern was the tremendous growth in cities of specialized retailers selling an increasingly wide variety of goods in single-category establishments with assortments that would now be called narrow and deep. Hower, citing examination of city directories and advertisements during the period 1800–1855, lists books; boots and shoes; carpetings; china and glassware; cloaks and mantillas; combs and fancy goods; cutlery and hardware; fancy dry goods; feathers and mattresses; furniture; men's furnishings; groceries; hats, caps, and furs; hosiery and gloves; India rubber goods; laces and embroideries; millinery; saddles, trunks, and harness; silks and ribbons; tea and coffee; tobacco and snuff; upholstery; umbrellas and parasols; butter and cheese; and ready-to-wear clothing for men (Hower 1943, p. 83). There are suggestions from mid-century observers of finer divisions still (pp. 83–4). This was not the only development in the institutions of distribution. In the 1850s and 1860s, full-line wholesalers began to take over the trade of selling to retail stores. By the late 1860s they were central to it; and they did not fade away thereafter (Chandler 1977, pp. 209, 217–18).

A watershed event in this Smithian progress of the division of labor began with the emergence of department stores from the 1840s in New York and in succeeding decades elsewhere. The institution became established in cities of all sizes in the decades following the Civil War and represented the first tentative beginnings of mass distribution in retailing.[13] The outward form was a single

---

[4] See the Introduction to Part D for a discussion of industrial classification and a detailed discussion of the SIC and NAICS systems.

[5] The marketing and business historians give the same basic picture of institutional change so far as those literatures go. The locus classicus of books with a marketing perspective is Nystrom (1930), especially volume 1. A more recent source with a sweeping view (and more statistical data) is Bucklin (1972). The standard business history account is Chandler (1977). Its footnotes to the historical literature are especially thorough. See also Tedlow (1990). For reasons discussed later, the time is increasingly ripe for a new view.

[6] For an image of one market's structure, see Teitelman (2000).

[7] See Nystrom (1930), p. 77. Perhaps the most famous of these travelers was Mason Locke (Parson) Weems, who sold books for the Philadelphia publisher Matthew Carey and, in his idle hours, wrote a famous though less than entirely reliable biography of George Washington. See, vividly, his letters in Skeel (1929).

[8] The leading authority on these institutions is Lewis Atherton (1939, 1949). See also Martin (1939); Jones (1937); Hower (1943), pp. 77–82; and Massachusetts Bureau of Statistics of Labor (1900), pp. 58–64.

[9] Latterly also Cincinnati, Chicago, and St. Louis. This cycle changed with the coming of the railroad. See Atherton (1939), p. 82.

[10] For a more detailed portrait of the business of a somewhat less grand wholesaler of the day (Troth and Company, of Philadelphia), see Porter and Livesay (1971), pp. 29–34.

[11] For the general view, see Albion (1939), pp. 275–6.

[12] See Chandler (1977) on the cotton institutions (pp. 20–3) and on the transitions in the second half of the century (pp. 215–24).

[13] For histories of the leading establishments, see Elias (1992); Hower (1943); Twymann (1954); and Appel (1930). Some of the early department stores also did a wholesale trade for a time, but this was not a regular feature.

large establishment, typically located in the central business district and often at transportation terminus of some sort, containing many areas specialized in particular categories of goods, each one run by what was in effect a general manager with profit-and-loss responsibility for that category and responsibility for merchandising as well as selling. Department managers needed to be close to the selling: they ordered well ahead of demand and therefore needed to know their customers' tastes. The managers also had an indirect incentive to forecast well: the areas allocated to particular categories could be expanded and contracted as profitability suggested, since there were generally no masonry walls defining the spaces (as would have been the case in a congeries of free-standing stores). The numbers of departments and related services (restaurants, tearooms, and the like) were sometimes very large – Macy's reckoned sixty-five in 1902, while Marshall Field counted over one hundred fifty in 1904 – and the facilities overall were sometimes positively opulent. The central court in Wanamaker's central Philadelphia establishment was, for example, an arched and domed space five stories tall, outfitted with a massive pipe organ and a striking 2,500-pound sculpture of an American eagle. It was by common assent the most impressive interior space in any commercial building in the city. Altogether, the objective was to make the store into a destination for shoppers. Through consolidation of back-office operations and the general scale of orders and operations, unit costs, and by extension prices, could be kept relatively low. The volumes were, at least by the standards of the competing local specialty stores, enormous.[14]

The business of the leading department stores was indeed very large, but true mass distribution should be associated first with another late nineteenth-century institutional innovation, the mail order store.[15] The early history of Sears, Roebuck and Company is exemplary.[16] Richard Sears was an underemployed telegraph operator in Minnesota who became aware of a shipment of watches that proved to be unwanted by the consignee. The wholesaler offered Sears the watches at a wholesale price far below what the watches could bring at retail. Sears used the telegraph and his spare time very profitably to place the watches with railroad station agents who could sell the watches locally at a comfortable margin. This seemed altogether more promising than telegraphy, and he started his first company in 1886. Soon Sears was placing newspaper advertisements and making direct mail solicitations. He sold that company and worked briefly in banking, but found he preferred sales. He started Sears, Roebuck in 1893 and in that year mailed out his first catalogs. More than 300,000 went out in 1897 and the numbers were in the millions by 1904. The institution in effect rode

the back of the U.S. Post Office (for delivery of the catalogs) and expanding rail service to bring something like the selection of a department store to people who lived far from any urban center.[17] Sears was not himself a particularly effective manager, though he was a tremendously gifted salesman; but once the company hired someone with the requisite vision and skills for the top position and gained control of the massive coordination problems operations posed, the business really began to blossom.[18] The effect of all this upon the American sense of living standards was such that one historian has referred to the Sears catalog as "the Bible of the new rural consumption communities," and Franklin Roosevelt is said to have remarked that if he could put a single book into the hands of every (Soviet) Russian, it would be the Sears catalog (Boorstin 1973, p. 128; Tedlow 1990, p. 261). The company continued to grow for many years. In 1971 Sears was large enough to rank fourth in the Fortune 500 (*Fortune* 85 (May 1972): 190, 216). Its total revenues were roughly 1 percent of GDP (Katz 1987, p. vii).

Chains properly so-called are multiestablishment retail firms with centralized administration and merchandising. The earliest statistical data are given in Table De220–224 (from 1929, see Table De225–247). These enterprises first began to emerge in the late nineteenth century, not long after the completion of the nation's railroad and telegraph infrastructure, the immense expansion of productive capacity of the Second Industrial Revolution, and the enhanced interest in large-scale distribution that came along with these.[19] The growth of the chains attained its greatest salience in the 1920s and 1930s.[20] Chains by then were active both in categories with relatively narrow stock-keeping requirements, such as restaurants and cigar stores, and in categories with relatively broad ones, such as groceries and five-and-dime stores. The chains exploited a large target market (regional and even national) to place large orders and obtain their merchandise at unit costs that were very low relative to their local competitors. They sold no aura of exclusivity, nor did they offer particularly personal service. Procurement was centralized and local managers had relatively little autonomy. In particular, they had relatively little ability to adapt assortments to local demand patterns and preferences. The initial response of local small merchants appears to have been to seek political protection (see below). The initial response of department stores, which generally had more room to maneuver, was to retreat from categories in which the department stores could not sustain some such competitive advantage but remain active in those in which they

---

[14] For contemporary accounts from Massachusetts on the impact of department stores on retail trade in specific lines, see Massachusetts Bureau of Statistics of Labor (1900), pp. 39–56. Unfortunately, systematic national statistics about department stores begin only in 1919. See Table De291–292 for indexes. Barger (1955, p. 148) gives decadal estimates of total department store sales for 1869–1929. Department stores are broken out as a category within the "general merchandise" group coverage in the economic censuses starting in 1929.

[15] Barger (1955, p. 148) gives decadal estimates of total mail order sales for 1899–1929. Mail order stores are broken out as categories within the "general merchandise" group coverage in the economic censuses starting in 1929.

[16] See Emmet and Jeuck (1950) and Worthy (1984). On the other two large mail order companies, see Boorstin (1973), pp. 121–4, for Montgomery Ward; and see Smalley and Sturdivant (1973) for Spiegel.

[17] It is difficult to say precisely how many stock-keeping units the firm handled in this period, but a representative catalog contained twenty to thirty thousand items (some in a number of variants and sizes, some not).

[18] For more on coordination and complementarities in the history of the company, see Raff and Temin (1999). For a somewhat journalistic but still illuminating account of the company's later struggles, see Katz (1987).

[19] On the Second Industrial Revolution, see Chandler (1977), especially Parts III and IV. These developments had their roots in new production technologies suitable for very large-scale production; but administrative coordination of materials and product flows to fully exploit the new technology was a central part of the change. Second Industrial Revolution firms often integrated vertically beyond simple manufacturing, going forward toward distribution, backward into supply, or both, "reduc[ing] the number of transactions involved in the flow of goods, increas[ing] the speed and regularity of that flow, and so lower[ing] costs and improv[ing] ... productivity" overall (p. 209).

[20] On chain stores, see Beckman and Nolan (1938).

could.[21] The rural mail order business became less attractive in the 1920s and by the end of the decade both Sears and its great competitor Montgomery Ward had begun to open retail establishments, typically on the edge of cities and in suburban areas, whose economic basis resembled chain stores.

The institutional innovations of the fifty years following World War II derived to a substantial extent from the suburbanization of the population. As places of residence came on average to be less and less convenient to the central business districts of cities and towns, privately owned business districts in more peripheral locations emerged – first strip malls along highways, then enclosed local and regional malls generally near interstates.[22] The pace of overall growth was rapid. Retail space per capita was estimated by Bear Stearns to be 5.3 square feet per person in 1964 and 19 square feet in 1996. The largest malls were simply vast, enclosing 3–4 million square feet. Malls typically had several department stores or other types of general merchandise retailers as their anchor tenants, and had many smaller tenants as well. All the stores were, increasingly, operated as chains. Chained discount department stores also became common. These were typically sited in convenient suburban locations and offered merchandise that had failed to sell either at first price or on sale in traditional department stores or was simply of lower quality.[23]

In all of this, the chain phenomenon evolved in significant ways. The paradigm case is Wal-Mart. Superior management of merchandising and logistics, all supported by the intensive use of information technology and rapid scientific analysis of sales data, enabled Wal-Mart, originally a small-town general merchandise discount retailer in the southeastern United States, to operate many large stores with superior profitability and eventually to become the largest firm in the economy.[24] Inventory-keeping methods progressed slowly into the information age. But by the mid-1970s, it was possible to capture detailed information about sales in real time from checkout registers equipped with lasers and dedicated reading equipment to scan product bar codes while simultaneously adding up the customer's bill (Dunlop and Rivkin 1997, p. 5). Wal-Mart, exploiting this opportunity from 1981, shifted the traditional reliance from mass procurement well in advance of demand – in effect speculating on what consumers would want and pushing inventories onto the buying public – to high-frequency monitoring of sales, pulling goods in current high demand through the upstream channels, efficiently dispatching them to the stores that could use them, and in the course of all of this optimizing the use of (the inevitably limited) shelf space (Vance and Scott 1994, pp. 92–5; Abernathy, Dunlop, et al. 1999, pp. 49–50). Indeed, following out the logic of this has led Wal-Mart and other mass merchandisers to share sales data by stock-keeping unit – in apparel, for example, by size, style, and color – with manufacturers in order to ensure that the desired goods, manufactured in appropriate lot sizes, will always be on the shelf when needed (see, for example, Buzzell 1993). Overall investment levels required for this information-intensive mode were often very substantial, given the number of locations from which data needed to be gathered and transmitted, the massive amounts of data that needed to be processed, and all of the training required to implement this system. Wal-Mart's initial commitment was on the order of $700 million (Reid 1995).

In this transition, intrafirm distribution centers acting to some extent as internal wholesalers became a significant feature of the distribution system. Distribution centers function differently from traditional wholesalers' or chain store warehouses. Their main purpose is less to check inventory (against orders) and then hold it against future demand than to check it and then efficiently route it to a store that wants it immediately. Distribution centers therefore tend to be smaller than traditional warehouses but to have more extensive access and to have more sophisticated and efficient materials-handling systems. They certainly require much more sophisticated information-processing systems than older wholesale warehouses did, given the breadth of merchandising modern chain stores have adopted. A survey in the late 1990s showed ordinary-sized chain supermarket establishments carrying in the range of 25,000 to 40,000 stock-keeping units (distinct product variants), and especially large ones, 40,000 to 60,000. Mass merchandisers such as (conventionally sized) Wal-Marts and K-Marts stocked 100,000 to 150,000 units. Standard department store branches often kept 800,000, with flagship locations carrying between 1 and 2 million (Abernathy, Dunlop, et al. 1999, p. 41). Chains often had many hundreds of stores. The information-processing requirements were, relatively speaking, massive.

As information capture and analysis became cheap in the closing decades of the twentieth century, national chains emerged specializing in specific product categories and offering assortments in local stores that were tremendously broad both by earlier standards and even by the standards of comparable categories in the information-intensive general merchandise retailers. These became known as "category killers" because they were the death knell to department store trade in their categories. By comparison to the overall stock-keeping units figures given earlier, stores in such category-killer chains as Home Depot and Toys "R" Us carried roughly 80,000 (Abernathy, Dunlop, et al. 1999). Category-killer stores in the book trade at the time often carried 100,000 to 160,000 individual titles.

This was an affirmative response to a consuming public whose tastes were thought to have become increasingly differentiated

[21] See "Merchandise Type Promotion to Gain," *New York Times,* October 6, 1929, Section II, p. 21. For a more general perspective, see McNair (1958). There was also a movement toward the consolidation of department stores in the 1920s. See, for example, "Growth of Department Store Chains," *Dry Goods Economist* 78 (October 4, 1924): 11–12; "Department Store Consolidations," *Harvard Business Review* 4 (1925/1926): 459–70; and "Department Store Consolidation and Association," *Journal of Retailing* 2 (April 1926):14–15. In retrospect this movement seems to have had more to do with generational transitions and a buoyant stock market than the transformation of operations. For contemporary views of the nontransformation, see "Department Store Extension," *Harvard Business Review* 6 (1927/1928): 81–9; Falk (1929/1930); and Emmet (1930), p. 57.

[22] The pace of overall growth was rapid. Retail space per capita was estimated by Bear Stearns to be 5.3 square feet per person in 1964 and 19 in 1996. See Silverman (1997), pp. 1 and 10–11, for this and other data.

[23] These derive from low-price departments typically located in the basements of center city department stores. The most famous antecedent was that of Filene's in Boston. See Nystrom (1930), pp. 168–70, for some general background. Drew-Bear (1970) gives a number of firm histories.

[24] For some of the basic detail on Wal-Mart, see Bradley, Ghemawat, and Foley (1994). The company's total revenue reported in the 2003 *Fortune* 500 list was $246.5 million. The second-place firm, the automobile manufacturer General Motors (of which it was once famously said that what was good for the country was good for GM and what was good for GM was good for the country) came in at $186.8 million.

starting in the late 1960s.[25] Manufacturers' ability to keep such chain stores (and, indeed, their smaller competitors) continuously in stock did not improve apace. But the wholesale trade often invested in the required information infrastructure and did well out of it with both types of retailers. The chains ended up sourcing some of their merchandise direct to stores from manufacturers, some via wholesalers, and some via their own internal warehouses, with the proportions among these varying as costs and opportunities shifted. The smaller independent stores simply got improved wholesaler selection and service. All classes of retailers were able to keep lower levels of inventory per product in the stores.

The coming of the Internet in the 1990s promised to extend these developments. The Internet proper offered the prospect of faster, cheaper, and more reliable communications along the supply chain, in effect supercharging earlier efforts in product description standardization and electronic data interchange.[26] The World Wide Web offered the possibility of a final customer interface, thereby allowing the broad consuming public (or at least those who had Internet connections) access to a far wider range of goods than could profitably be kept in stock in any local retail store.[27] This was of course an attractive proposition only for goods that did not require direct examination prior to purchase and that could be shipped to customers reliably and reasonably promptly and inexpensively (via the private delivery services that had made major inroads into the Post Office's business). There were fewer of these categories than there appeared to be at the height of the boom in so-called technology stocks in the late 1990s, but it seems that some still exist. Many of these Internet firms remain heavily dependent on traditional (but technologically up-to-date) wholesalers for prompt order fulfillment. It is far too early as of this writing to tell whether Internet-based retailing will displace bricks-and-mortar retailing in any broad way: it may well expand the market somewhat and segment it to a smaller degree. Only time will tell. Internet competition is, however, clearly having an effect on the internal operations of many bricks-and-mortar firms, both in the services they offer and in their merchandising decisions.

Origins of Modern Statistical Data

Censuses of the manufacturing sector of the American economy have been conducted at regular intervals since 1810 (when it was a part of the third decennial census) (for a survey, see Bohme 1987). Mineral (extraction) industries and commercial fisheries – manufacturing industries more broadly construed – were added to the coverage later in the century. But the focus remained tightly on

directly productive activity. A broader and more problem-oriented interest in economic censuses emerged during and after World War I. After the war, questions of demobilization and postwar conversion seem to have been much on the minds of both the Census Bureau and the Congress. The idea of coordinating production and wants was increasingly in the air.

The first explicit mention in the Census *Annual Reports* of the idea of conducting a census of the distribution sector comes in 1926 at the end of a paragraph remarking that the central administrative offices of multiestablishment manufacturing sometimes administered distribution as well as production, thus making it difficult to measure manufacturing employment as cleanly as the Bureau would have preferred (U.S. Bureau of the Census 1926, p. 7). The next paragraph observes that many firms in the economy are concerned with distribution and that a census of them is therefore essential to a proper understanding of the manufacturing data as well as to any definite knowledge of the number and economic importance of such firms. It is unclear whether this latter was an afterthought. The Bureau commissioned a preliminary study, but it was paid for in part by the private sector. The results were published not by the Government Printing Office but by the U.S. Chamber of Commerce (U.S. Bureau of the Census 1927, p. 8; Chamber of Commerce 1928). It is possible that policy debates and grassroots concerns were a motivating factor.

Two debates might have been relevant. The first concerned retailing. Chain stores, as previously mentioned, had existed in America since the late nineteenth century; but only after World War I were they operating nationally and threatening both established mass retailers and small-town local ones. There was a major political backlash, leading to Federal Trade Commission (FTC) investigations and ultimately to retail price maintenance legislation.[28] The second debate concerned distribution more broadly. There had been public uneasiness about the efficiency of distribution in America at least since the Hoover Commission report of 1921 (Committee on Elimination of Waste in Industry of the Federated American Engineering Societies 1921). The 1920s were understood as a period of rapid productivity growth in manufacturing but slower growth in distribution (see Stewart and Dewhurst 1939, p. 3). The Census Bureau later commented that the American economy had by the turn of the twentieth century made a transition from not being able to produce enough to satisfy domestic wants to a state in which maximal supply was in excess of effective demand.[29] There was a widespread waste in distribution, that is, goods not being distributed in the most economical manner. The initial Census of Distribution was to be "the most comprehensive of all single efforts made in the field of distribution for the purpose of ascertaining the nature of the distribution mechanism, its component parts, and how it operates. It [was] hoped that the Census . . . [would] provide . . . a fairly complete picture of the complicated marketing system which has developed."

[25] The impression was widespread among retailing executives and commentators. For some suggestive evidence, see Pashigian (1988); and Pashigian and Bowen (1991). The neat summary statistic from the former article (pp. 941–2) is that sales of white shirts as a percentage of men's dress shirts fell from 72 percent in 1962 to 52 in 1967 and were only 21 percent by 1986. See also the discussion in Katz (1987), passim.

[26] On the development of the former, see Brown (1997). The Internet in its broadest sense represents an important vehicle for overall economic coordination. For a provisional view, see Litan and Rivlin (2001): Chapter 2 gives an overview of the effects on manufacturing in itself, Chapter 3 of the effects of coordinating consumer information with the supply chain.

[27] It also offered purchase opportunities at all hours of the day and night, a particular bonus for those whose jobs or other time demands made shopping during ordinary business hours difficult.

[28] On all of which see Lebhar (1963). Tedlow (1990), Chapter 4, gives a vivid overview. The series of FTC staff studies leading up to FTC (1935) are rich sources of information. For the doctrinal and legal history, see McCraw (1996). Bucklin (1972) is skeptical that in the end it mattered much: "The competitive press of new and large-scale retailers upon the fabric of the law caused it to give way and to fail to achieve the desired ends" (p. 150; for the detail, see pp. 150–6).

[29] See U.S. Bureau of the Census (1933), volume 2, p. 3, for this and the remainder of the paragraph.

In 1927, the Census Bureau conducted the preliminary study in eleven cities. These ranged in location from Atlanta to Seattle and in size from Chicago to Fargo and Springfield, Illinois. Data were gathered on establishment sales, employee numbers in various categories, salaries and wages, and inventory levels for retail and wholesale establishments. These were tabulated in summary form both in levels and in convenient ratios and were also broken down by lines of business (forty-six) and classes of commodities (seventy-three including "unclassified").[30] Data were also broken out to characterize the business of chain stores and independent stores, in particular giving distributions by establishment of annual sales for the independent stores in each line of business. Total sales, establishment numbers, and averages are given for the chains by line of business, but no indication is given of dispersion about the means. The chain means are generally larger than the independent store means, sometimes much larger. The pilot also made some use of population census data. Data on wholesale trade were also presented, though in less rich detail. Very detailed data for Chicago close out the study.

Building on the successful pilot, the 1930 Census of Distribution was completely full-blown in its geographical coverage. Enumerators – employed exclusively for the distribution census in places of 10,000 or more inhabitants, employed also for the population and agriculture census in smaller ones – visited all establishments (U.S. Bureau of the Census 1933, volume 1, p. 14). This involved visits to nearly 1.7 million worksites, a major undertaking even by Census Bureau standards. Efforts since then have only become more extensive and elaborate.

Trends in the Data

The basic statistics concerning the share of distribution in GDP and total employment were given in this essay's introduction. The broad pattern is distribution growing larger in its importance over the century just ended as manufacturing grows smaller. At century's end, distribution was larger on both measures. One implication of the large employment share is that productivity changes in distribution can be very important for national productivity growth even when the technology being deployed is less than state-of-the-art. One recent study suggests that 51 percent of the increase in productivity growth for 1995–1999 over 1987–1995 was attributable to wholesale and retail trade.[31] Some more detailed trends in aggregates, drawn from Tables De73–182 and De345–462, are as follows.[32]

Consistent with the narrative given earlier of post–World War II suburban development and mall-building, the ratio of population to total retail establishments has been in steady decline. The trend in total retail sales per establishment (deflated by the consumer price index) is downward too. Retail employment per establishment has grown fairly steadily since the early 1950s and deflated sales per employee has also trended upward, perhaps as more and more tasks are shifted to information systems and to customers themselves. The share of department stores in total retail sales has been relatively steadily in gentle decline since the first Census of Distribution. The pattern for general merchandise stores is more volatile – it is said that Sears, Roebuck furnished the homes in which the baby boomers were children and there has been more recent growth, particularly at lower price points – but the secular decline is pronounced.

The more positive phenomenon is the secular rise since World War II of the sales of multiunit firms as a fraction of total retail sales. Capital availability constrained their expansion during the 1930s relative to what might have been possible. Limited supplies during the war years probably had a similar effect. The postwar sharp upward trend in these firms' deflated total sales would certainly cheer any portfolio investor. The ratio of the number of retail establishments to wholesale establishments has been declining since the war.

Wholesale sales per wholesale establishment (deflated by the wholesale price index) are up secularly, and increasingly sharply. The same is true of deflated wholesale sales per wholesale employee. Employment per wholesale establishment is a relatively noisy series. It trends upward overall but not since the advent of information-technology-intensive distribution.

It would be in the spirit of the traditional perspective to measure the scale of new formats and to give evidence of the impact they are having across product categories. The outstanding open question of this sort as of this writing concerns the future of sales placed over the Internet. Internet firms have very different cost structures from traditional retail establishments as well as having very different cachement areas. If their active clientele became large, a number of the trends cited might be subject to change. Reliable measurement of Internet sales has begun but is not, as of this writing, advanced enough to be worth including in the tables.[33]

A different perspective suggests a more radical agenda. If the ultimate task of the distribution sector is not simply conveying produced output to those who want it but rather coordinating production and wants and, in particular, providing desired variety, then statistics on Internet trade are only the beginning of the new data that would be useful. The steady development of Amazon.com, the flagship of Internet retailing, from a purveyor of books to a company selling books, toys and games, electronics, apparel, and home and garden equipment suggests that some old groupings may be losing their bite. And it is undoubtedly true that a measurement agenda seeking to reflect changes in operations would now prioritize measuring variety on offer and the institutions supporting this. The old question of whether distribution costs too much has clearly become too simple. Establishment-level data on stock-keeping units, measurements of inventory levels that controlled for stock-keeping unit numbers (for example, variety), and data that helped track the changing boundaries between retail and wholesale activity would represent steps toward answering more illuminating questions.

---

[30] The cross-tabulations are sometimes quite revealing. Just shy of half of the items by value (49.5 percent) in the category "Clothing, men's and boy's" were purchased from men's ready-to-wear stores, for example, but nearly a quarter (24.4 percent) came from custom tailors and another 18.2 percent from department stores, so that these two – the closer substitutes as ready-to-wear chains pressed in on one of the department stores' core businesses – together amounted to 42.6 percent, not yet too far behind. Women's clothing stores and other sorts of establishments had the remainder of the trade. Chamber of Commerce (1928), p. 51 and elsewhere.

[31] See McKinsey Global Institute (2001). For a more historical perspective, see Field (1996).

[32] These tables also give more disaggregated data.

[33] Other series might also require adjustment as the Internet becomes a more stable and better understood phenomenon. During the bubble in technology stock prices, for example, a great deal of advertising for Internet firms was paid for through difficult-to-value exchanges of services rather than in cash.

Conclusion

The nation's productive capacities continue to increase, but the Second Industrial Revolution, whose impetus to vertical integration may have first planted in the mind of the Commissioner of the Census the idea of measuring the distribution sector, has come and gone (see Langlois 2003; Lamoreaux, Raff, and Temin 2003). Paul Nystrom was born in 1878 in Maiden Rock, Wisconsin, by the high bluffs above the Mississippi. The town was important to the farmers of the district because of the steamboats and, later, the railroad. Nystrom worked on a farm and in retail, taught school and became a principal, pursued advanced studies, taught at the Universities of Wisconsin and Minnesota, worked in business in the East, and was appointed to his job at Columbia at the age of forty-eight. He taught there for many years. He wrote prolifically, was the founding editor of the *Journal of Marketing*, and had a long and apparently productive retirement. He died in Spring Valley, New York, a once-rural town come within commuting distance of the great city, in August 1969. Americans were as a general matter far richer by then, and the world of goods of the American consumer was much larger than it had been. But there were no scanner units yet, no bar codes for the scanners' red glowing laser beams to shine onto, and no powerful cheap computers to decode the reflections, let alone to process and analyze the information about sales or to use the analyses to manage both assortments and the supply chain. There were facts, of course; but it was hard to see them. Nystrom's death notice in the *New York Times* suggested donations to the Lighthouse or to any other organization doing work for the blind (*New York Times*, August 19, 1969, p. 43). His death preceded slightly the revolution in information-capture and -processing practices that became feasible in the mid-seventies, began to gather momentum in the eighties, and seems to be in the process, as of this writing, of transforming the efficiency, and indeed the possibilities, of distribution. A next, and more penetrating, look at the wholesale and retail trade of the United States will explore those transformations more systematically than is possible today.

References

Abernathy, Frederick H., John T. Dunlop, Janice H. Hammond, and David Weil. 1999. *A Stitch in Time: Lean Retailing and the Transformation of Manufacturing – Lessons from the Apparel and Textile Industries.* Oxford University Press.

Albion, Robert Greenhalgh. 1939. *The Rise of New York Port, 1815–1860.* Charles Scribner's Sons.

Appel, Joseph. 1930. *The Business Biography of John Wanamaker, Founder and Builder, America's Merchant Pioneer.* Macmillan.

Atherton, Lewis. 1939. *The Pioneer Merchant in Mid-America.* University of Missouri Press.

Atherton, Lewis. 1949. *The Southern Country Store 1800–1860.* Louisiana State University Press.

Bailyn, Bernard. 1955. *The New England Merchants in the Seventeenth Century.* Harvard University Press.

Barger, Harold. 1955. *Distribution's Place in the American Economy since 1869.* Princeton University Press.

Baxter, William T. 1945. *The House of Hancock: Business in Boston, 1724–1775.* Harvard University Press.

Beckman, Theodore N., and Herman C. Nolan. 1938. *The Chain Store Problem: A Critical Analysis.* McGraw-Hill.

Bohme, Frederick G. 1987. "U.S. Economic Censuses, 1810 to the Present." *Government Information Quarterly* 4(3): 221–43.

Boorstin, Daniel J. 1973. *The Americans: The Democratic Experience.* Random House.

Bradley, Stephen P., Pankaj Ghemawat, and Sharon Foley. 1994. "Wal-Mart Stores, Inc." Case No. 9-794-024. Harvard Business School Publishing.

Brown, Stephen A. 1997. *Revolution at the Checkout Counter.* Harvard University Press.

Bruchey, Stuart W. 1956. *Robert Oliver, Merchant of Baltimore 1783–1819.* Johns Hopkins University Press.

Bucklin, Louis P. 1972. *Competition and Evolution in the Distributive Trades.* Prentice Hall.

Buzzell, Robert D. 1993. "Vanity Fair Mills: Market Response System" Case No. 9-593-111. Harvard Business School Publishing.

Chamber of Commerce of the United States, Domestic Distribution Department, Committee on the Collection of Business Figures. 1928. *Retail and Wholesale Trade of Eleven Cities, Atlanta, Ga., Baltimore, Md., Denver, Colo., Fargo, N.D., Kansas City, Mo., Providence, R.I., San Francisco, Calif., Seattle, Wash., Springfield, Ill., Syracuse, N.Y., Chicago, Ill., Based on a Census of Distribution Conducted by the United States Bureau of the Census.* Chamber of Commerce of the United States.

Chandler, Alfred D., Jr. 1977. *The Visible Hand: The Managerial Revolution in American Business.* Belknap Press.

Committee on Elimination of Waste in Industry of the Federated American Engineering Societies. 1921. *Waste in Industry.* McGraw-Hill.

Drew-Bear, Robert. 1970. *Mass Merchandising: Revolution and Evolution.* Fairchild.

Dunlop, John T., and Jan W. Rivkin. 1997. "Introduction." In Stephen A. Brown. *Revolution at the Checkout Counter.* Harvard University Press.

Elias, Stephen N. 1992. *Alexander T. Stewart: The Forgotten Merchant Prince.* Praeger.

Emmet, Boris. 1930. *Department Stores.* Stanford University Press.

Emmet, Boris, and John E. Jeuck. 1950. *Catalogues and Counters: A History of Sears, Roebuck and Company.* University of Chicago Press.

Falk, David R. 1929/1930. "Central Buying by Department Store Managers." *Harvard Business Review* 8: 265–73.

Federal Trade Commission. 1935. *Chain Stores: Final Report on the Chain-Store Investigation*, 74th Congress, 1st Session, S. Doc. 4. U.S. Government Printing Office.

Field, Alexander J. 1996. "The Relative Productivity of American Distribution 1869–1992." *Research in Economic History* 16: 1–37.

Hower, Ralph M. 1943. *History of Macy's of New York, 1858–1919.* Harvard University Press.

Jones, Fred Mitchell. 1937. "Middlemen in the Domestic Trade of the United States 1800–1850." *Illinois Studies in the Social Sciences* 21 (3), pp. 1–81.

Katz, Donald R. 1987. *The Big Store: Inside the Crisis and Revolution at Sears.* Viking.

Lamoreaux, Naomi R., Daniel M. G. Raff, and Peter Temin. 2003. "Beyond Markets and Hierarchies: Toward a New Synthesis of American Business History." *American Historical Review* 108 (April): 404–33.

Langlois, Richard N. 2003. "The Vanishing Hand: The Changing Dynamics of Industrial Capitalism." *Industrial and Corporate Change* 12 (April): 351–85.

Lebhar, Godfrey. 1963. *Chain Stores in America, 1859–1962.* Chain Store Publishing.

Litan, Robert E., and Alice M. Rivlin, eds. 2001. *The Economic Payoff from the Internet Revolution.* Brookings Institution.

Martin, Margaret E. 1939. "Merchants and Trade of the Connecticut River Valley 1750–1820." *Smith College Studies in History* 24 (1–4), pp. 1–284.

Massachusetts Bureau of Statistics of Labor. 1900. *Thirtieth Annual Report of the [Massachusetts] Bureau of Statistics of Labor.* Wright and Potter.

McCraw, Thomas K. 1996. "Competition and 'Fair Trade': History and Theory." *Research in Economic History* 16: 185–239.

McKinsey Global Institute. 2001. *US Productivity Growth 1995–2000: Understanding the Contribution of Information Technology Relative to Other Factors.* McKinsey & Company.

McNair, Malcolm P. 1958. "Significant Trends and Developments in the Post-War Period." In Albert B. Smith, editor. *Competitive Distribution in a Free High-Level Economy and Its Implications for the University.* University of Pittsburgh Press.

Nystrom, Paul H. 1930. *The Economics of Retailing.* Ronald Press.

Pashigian, B. Peter. 1988. "Demand Uncertainty and Sales: A Study of Fashion and Markdown Pricing." *American Economic Review* 78 (December): 936–53.

Pashigian, B. Peter, and Brian Bowen. 1991. "Why Are Products Sold on Sale? Explanations of Pricing Regularities." *Quarterly Journal of Economics* 106 (November): 1015–38.

Porter, Glenn, and Harold C. Livesay. 1971. *Merchants and Manufacturers: Studies in the Changing Structure of Nineteenth Century Marketing.* Johns Hopkins University Press.

Porter, Kenneth Wiggins. 1931. *John Jacob Astor, Business Man.* Harvard University Press.

Porter, Kenneth Wiggins. 1937. *The Jacksons and the Lees: Two Generations of Massachusetts Merchants, 1765–1844.* Harvard University Press.

Raff, Daniel M. G., and Peter Temin. 1999. "Sears Roebuck in the Twentieth Century: Competition, Complementarities, and the Problem of Wasting Assets." In Naomi R. Lamoreaux, Daniel M. G. Raff, and Peter Temin, editors. *Learning-by-Doing in Organizations, Markets, and Nations.* University of Chicago Press.

Reid, Michael. 1995. "Change at the Check-Out." *The Economist,* March 4, "Survey," p. 6.

Silverman, Dick. 1997. "Has Expansion Boom Finally Brought Retailing to Saturation Point?" *Women's Wear Daily,* October 30.

Skeel, Emily Ellsworth Ford, ed. 1929. *Mason Locke Weems, His Works and Ways.* N.p.

Smalley, Orange A., and Frederick D. Sturdivant. 1973. *The Credit Merchants: A History of Spiegel, Inc.* Southern Illinois University Press.

Stewart, Paul W., and J. Frederic Dewhurst. 1939. *Does Distribution Cost Too Much? A Review of the Costs Involved in Current Marketing Methods and a Program for Improvement.* Twentieth Century Fund.

Tedlow, Richard S. 1990. *New and Improved: The Story of Mass Marketing in America.* Basic Books.

Teitelman, S. Robert. 2000. *Birch's Views of Philadelphia: A Reduced Facsimile of the City of Philadelphia as It Appeared in the Year 1800 with Photographs of the Sites in 1960 and 2000 and Commentaries.* Free Library.

Twymann, Robert W. 1954. *History of Marshall Field & Co., 1852–1906.* University of Pennsylvania Press.

U.S. Bureau of the Census. 1926. *Annual Report of the Director of the Census to the Secretary of Commerce for the Fiscal Year Ended June 30th, 1926.* U.S. Government Printing Office.

U.S. Bureau of the Census. 1927. *Annual Report of the Director of the Census to the Secretary of Commerce for the Fiscal Year Ended June 30th, 1927.* U.S. Government Printing Office.

U.S. Bureau of the Census. 1933. *Fifteenth Census of the United States: Distribution.* U.S. Government Printing Office.

Vance, Sandra S., and Roy V. Scott. 1994. *Wal-Mart: A History of Sam Walton's Retail Phenomenon.* Twayne.

Worthy, James C. 1984. *Shaping an American Institution: Robert E. Wood and Sears, Roebuck.* University of Illinois Press.

GENERAL STATISTICS ON DISTRIBUTION

Daniel M. G. Raff

TABLE De1–13 National income originating and persons engaged in wholesale and retail trade: 1869–1929

Contributed by Susan B. Carter

	National income									Persons engaged			
		Employee compensation			Unincorporated business profits			Corporate profits	Interest	Wholesale		Retail	
	Total	Total	Wholesale	Retail	Total	Wholesale	Retail			Employees	Proprietors	Employees	Proprietors
	De1	De2	De3	De4	De5	De6	De7	De8	De9	De10	De11	De12	De13
Year	Million dollars	Million dollars	Million dollars	Million dollars	Million dollars	Million dollars	Million dollars	Million dollars	Million dollars	Thousand	Thousand	Thousand	Thousand
1869	730	270	160	100	460	120	340	(Z)	(Z)	208	52	196	429
1879	800	340	200	140	460	110	350	(Z)	(Z)	321	65	349	602
1889	1,420	720	380	340	700	150	550	(Z)	(Z)	529	83	698	862
1899	2,070	1,190	570	620	880	170	710	(Z)	(Z)	704	92	1,132	1,073
1909	3,570	1,940	840	1,110	1,030	180	850	600	(Z)	955	97	1,857	1,302
1919	8,980	5,410	2,180	3,230	2,310	370	1,930	1,230	40	1,142	103	2,480	1,485
1929	13,080	9,370	3,400	5,980	2,870	380	2,480	760	80	1,631	113	4,215	1,862

(Z) Amounts were assumed negligible and were reported as zero in the source.

Source

Harold Barger, "Income Originating in Trade, 1869–1929." In William N. Parker, ed. *Trends in the American Economy in the Nineteenth Century: Studies in Income and Wealth*, volume 24, Conference on Research in Income and Wealth, National Bureau of Economic Research (Princeton University Press, 1960), Tables 1 and 4, pp. 327, 331.

Documentation

Persons engaged are the number of persons with an occupation that might be associated with wholesale and retail trade.

National income is the factor incomes earned in the production of the gross national product (GNP). Factor incomes include the compensation of employees, proprietors' income, rental income of persons, corporate profits, and net interest.

Barger based his estimates of national income originating in trade on a variety of sources, including the decennial census estimates of persons engaged by occupation, scattered hours and earnings data, and estimates of business profits. Barger's estimates of national income originating in trade were developed using the same basic conceptual framework as those that underlie the National Income and Product Accounts (NIPA). They were meant to extend the series on national income by industry group back into the nineteenth century.

TABLE De14–25 Employees of wholesale and retail trade firms, by industry division: 1939–1999

Contributed by Susan B. Carter

	Wholesale trade			Retail trade								
	Total	Durable goods	Nondurable goods	Total	Building materials, hardware, etc.	General merchandise stores	Food stores	Automotive dealers and gasoline service stations	Apparel and accessory stores	Home furniture, furnishings, and equipment stores	Eating and drinking places	Establishments not elsewhere classified
	De14	De15	De16	De17	De18	De19	De20	De21	De22	De23	De24	De25
Year	Thousand	Thousand	Thousand	Thousand	Thousand	Thousand	Thousand	Thousand	Thousand	Thousand	Thousand	Thousand
1939	1,767	—	—	4,659	—	—	—	—	—	—	—	—
1940	1,841	—	—	4,909	—	—	—	—	—	—	—	—
1941	1,966	—	—	5,244	—	—	—	—	—	—	—	—
1942	1,912	—	—	5,206	—	—	—	—	—	—	—	—
1943	1,828	—	—	5,154	—	—	—	—	—	—	—	—
1944	1,851	—	—	5,208	—	—	—	—	—	—	—	—
1945	1,955	—	—	5,359	—	—	—	—	—	—	—	—
1946	2,298	—	—	6,077	—	—	—	—	—	—	—	—
1947	2,478	—	—	6,477	—	—	—	—	585	—	—	—
1948	2,612	—	—	6,659	—	—	—	—	600	—	—	—
1949	2,610	—	—	6,654	—	—	—	—	586	—	—	—
1950	2,643	—	—	6,743	—	—	—	—	573	—	—	—
1951	2,735	—	—	7,007	—	—	—	—	595	381	—	—
1952	2,821	—	—	7,184	—	—	—	—	608	384	—	—
1953	2,862	—	—	7,385	—	—	—	—	618	388	—	—
1954	2,875	—	—	7,360	—	—	—	—	609	383	—	—

(continued)

TABLE De14–25   Employees of wholesale and retail trade firms, by industry division: 1939–1999 *Continued*

	Wholesale trade			Retail trade								
	Total	Durable goods	Nondurable goods	Total	Building materials, hardware, etc.	General merchandise stores	Food stores	Automotive dealers and gasoline service stations	Apparel and accessory stores	Home furniture, furnishings, and equipment stores	Eating and drinking places	Establishments not elsewhere classified
	De14	De15	De16	De17	De18	De19	De20	De21	De22	De23	De24	De25
Year	Thousand	Thousand	Thousand	Thousand	Thousand	Thousand	Thousand	Thousand	Thousand	Thousand	Thousand	Thousand
1955	2,934	—	—	7,601	—	—	—	—	616	396	—	—
1956	3,027	—	—	7,831	—	—	—	—	630	406	—	—
1957	3,037	—	—	7,848	—	—	—	—	625	399	—	—
1958	2,989	—	—	7,761	—	—	1,265	1,208	611	388	1,529	—
1959	3,092	—	—	8,035	—	—	1,305	1,244	624	396	1,603	—
1960	3,153	—	—	8,238	—	—	1,356	1,267	639	400	1,654	—
1961	3,142	—	—	8,195	—	—	1,355	1,240	632	389	1,665	—
1962	3,207	—	—	8,359	—	—	1,364	1,273	637	389	1,721	—
1963	3,258	—	—	8,520	—	—	1,384	1,324	632	389	1,748	—
1964	3,347	—	—	8,812	—	—	1,419	1,367	636	395	1,848	—
1965	3,477	—	—	9,239	—	—	1,469	1,424	661	410	1,988	—
1966	3,608	—	—	9,637	—	—	1,536	1,462	681	420	2,118	—
1967	3,700	—	—	9,906	—	—	1,572	1,492	694	426	2,191	—
1968	3,791	—	—	10,308	—	—	1,620	1,549	725	440	2,309	—
1969	3,919	—	—	10,785	—	—	1,683	1,611	753	464	2,466	—
1970	4,006	—	—	11,034	—	—	1,731	1,617	761	472	2,575	—
1971	4,014	—	—	11,338	—	—	1,752	1,642	779	487	2,700	—
1972	4,127	2,336	1,791	11,822	508	2,149	1,805	1,723	784	513	2,860	1,480
1973	4,291	2,457	1,835	12,315	535	2,229	1,856	1,778	795	533	3,054	1,537
1974	4,447	2,578	1,869	12,539	542	2,210	1,948	1,666	811	538	3,231	1,594
1975	4,430	2,539	1,891	12,630	521	2,113	2,007	1,677	806	517	3,380	1,610
1976	4,562	2,615	1,946	13,193	546	2,155	2,039	1,744	842	540	3,656	1,672
1977	4,723	2,732	1,991	13,792	576	2,204	2,106	1,801	870	563	3,949	1,724
1978	4,985	2,917	2,068	14,556	608	2,308	2,199	1,861	909	595	4,277	1,800
1979	5,221	3,098	2,123	14,972	629	2,287	2,297	1,812	949	615	4,513	1,869
1980	5,292	3,139	2,153	15,018	617	2,245	2,384	1,689	957	606	4,626	1,895
1981	5,375	3,182	2,193	15,171	607	2,230	2,448	1,653	968	595	4,749	1,920
1982	5,295	3,107	2,188	15,158	588	2,184	2,477	1,632	942	583	4,829	1,922
1983	5,283	3,087	2,197	15,587	615	2,165	2,556	1,674	963	608	5,038	1,970
1984	5,568	3,291	2,277	16,512	659	2,267	2,636	1,798	1,008	677	5,381	2,087
1985	5,727	3,402	2,325	17,315	690	2,323	2,774	1,889	1,039	733	5,699	2,170
1986	5,761	3,395	2,365	17,880	704	2,365	2,896	1,941	1,075	767	5,902	2,231
1987	5,848	3,437	2,411	18,422	743	2,411	2,958	2,001	1,123	789	6,086	2,311
1988	6,030	3,564	2,466	19,023	779	2,472	3,074	2,071	1,165	802	6,258	2,402
1989	6,187	3,653	2,534	19,475	783	2,544	3,164	2,092	1,197	826	6,402	2,467
1990	6,173	3,614	2,559	19,601	771	2,540	3,215	2,063	1,183	820	6,509	2,499
1991	6,081	3,531	2,550	19,284	747	2,453	3,204	1,984	1,151	801	6,476	2,468
1992	5,997	3,446	2,552	19,356	758	2,451	3,180	1,966	1,131	800	6,609	2,461
1993	5,981	3,433	2,549	19,773	779	2,488	3,224	2,014	1,144	828	6,821	2,476
1994	6,162	3,559	2,604	20,507	833	2,583	3,291	2,116	1,144	889	7,078	2,573
1995	6,378	3,715	2,663	21,187	868	2,681	3,366	2,190	1,125	946	7,354	2,658
1996	6,482	3,805	2,677	21,597	894	2,702	3,436	2,267	1,098	975	7,517	2,709
1997	6,648	3,927	2,721	21,966	929	2,701	3,478	2,311	1,109	999	7,646	2,794
1998	6,800	4,043	2,757	22,295	948	2,730	3,484	2,332	1,141	1,025	7,768	2,868
1999	6,924	4,120	2,804	22,788	989	2,771	3,495	2,369	1,174	1,082	7,940	2,969

Source

U.S. Bureau of Labor Statistics Internet site, National Current Employment Statistics.

Documentation

See the text for Table Ba840–848.

Series correspond to Standard Industrial Classification (SIC) codes as follows: series De14, codes 50–51; series De15, code 50; series De16, code 51; series De17, codes 52–59; series De18, code 52; series De19, code 53; series De20, code 54; series De21, code 55; series De22, code 56; series De23, code 57; series De24, code 58; series De25, code 59.

Series De14 and De17. Their sum equals series Ba845. See the Introduction to Part D for a discussion of SIC codes.

Series De18. Includes garden supply and mobile home dealers.

TABLE De26–29 Wage and salary accruals per employee in wholesale and retail trade: 1929–1999[1]
Contributed by Daniel M.G. Raff

Year	Wholesale trade De26 Dollars	Retail trade De27 Dollars	Retail trade (including automobile services) De28 Dollars	Automobile repair, services, and parking De29 Dollars	Year	Wholesale trade De26 Dollars	Retail trade De27 Dollars	Retail trade (including automobile services) De28 Dollars	Automobile repair, services, and parking De29 Dollars
1929	2,072	—	1,409	—	1965	6,981	4,623	—	4,850
1930	2,039	—	1,384	—	1966	7,345	4,776	—	4,997
1931	1,934	—	1,324	—	1967	7,690	4,970	—	5,242
1932	1,672	—	1,173	—	1968	8,142	5,275	—	5,641
1933	1,477	—	1,066	—	1969	8,685	5,591	—	6,127
1934	1,550	—	1,102	—	1970	9,193	5,914	—	6,534
1935	1,640	—	1,139	—	1971	9,671	6,234	—	6,847
1936	1,652	—	1,159	—	1972	10,245	6,607	—	7,252
1937	1,693	—	1,218	—	1973	10,897	6,902	—	7,697
1938	1,686	—	1,217	—	1974	11,992	7,381	—	8,250
1939	1,698	—	1,224	—	1975	12,930	7,918	—	8,851
1940	1,754	—	1,236	—	1976	13,684	8,439	—	9,464
1941	1,943	—	1,299	—	1977	14,584	8,873	—	10,014
1942	2,177	—	1,395	—	1978	15,714	9,404	—	10,792
1943	2,416	—	1,555	—	1979	17,118	10,104	—	11,805
1944	2,600	—	1,709	—	1980	18,825	10,961	—	12,817
1945	2,751	—	1,879	—	1981	20,328	11,736	—	13,824
1946	3,021	—	2,141	—	1982	21,689	12,366	—	14,580
1947	3,322	—	2,368	—	1983	22,593	12,920	—	15,077
1948 [2]	3,661	—	2,530	—	1984	23,901	13,291	—	15,772
1948 [3]	3,597	2,509	—	2,520	1985	25,042	13,625	—	16,346
1949	3,621	2,596	—	2,553	1986	26,154	14,150	—	16,999
1950	3,806	2,711	—	2,658	1987 [2]	27,316	14,603	—	17,690
1951	4,028	2,785	—	2,864	1987 [3]	27,303	14,591	—	17,690
1952	4,134	2,891	—	3,000	1988	29,244	15,150	—	18,385
1953	4,320	3,035	—	3,181	1989	30,085	15,484	—	18,876
1954	4,442	3,136	—	3,254	1990	31,499	15,990	—	19,785
1955	4,616	3,267	—	3,318	1991	32,815	16,713	—	20,325
1956	4,883	3,374	—	3,445	1992	34,358	17,428	—	21,102
1957	5,119	3,514	—	3,621	1993	35,402	17,529	—	21,399
1958	5,294	3,626	—	3,712	1994	36,665	17,966	—	22,004
1959	5,558	3,785	—	3,877	1995	37,808	18,246	—	22,512
1960	5,756	3,911	—	4,000	1996	39,283	18,774	—	23,073
1961	5,932	4,001	—	4,162	1997	41,224	19,495	—	23,801
1962	6,172	4,156	—	4,396	1998	43,606	20,602	—	24,897
1963	6,419	4,297	—	4,534	1999	45,856	21,414	—	25,666
1964	6,703	4,454	—	4,715					

[1] Data are based on the following Standard Industrial Classification systems: 1869–1948 (1942 SIC), 1948–1987 (1972 SIC), and 1987–1999 (1987 SIC). Two sets of values are presented in some years to reflect such changes. See the Introduction to Part D for a discussion of SIC codes.

[2] Comparable with earlier years.

[3] Comparable with later years.

Source
U.S. Bureau of Economic Analysis Internet site, NIPA Tables 606a, 606b, and 606c, downloaded September 28, 2000.

Documentation
This table measures the average wage and salary income per full-time equivalent employee. Full-time equivalent employees equal the number of employees on full-time schedules plus the number of employees on part-time schedules converted to a full-time basis. Wages and salaries comprise all payments accruing to persons in an employee status as compensation for their work. They include commissions, tips, and bonuses, as well as cash payments commonly referred to as wages and salaries, together with the value of those payments in kind that clearly represent an addition to the recipient's income. Income in kind is valued, so far as possible, at its cost to the employer. Service industries in which it is a perceptible portion of wages and salaries include hotels and other lodging places, and educational services. Figures do not include dismissal pay, directors' fees, employer contributions to social insurance funds and private pension plans, or accident compensation payments.

TABLE De30–59 Retail and wholesale establishments – number, sales, payroll, and employees, by legal form of organization: 1935–1992[1]

Contributed by Daniel M.G. Raff

Units: Establishments and Paid employees in Number; Sales and Payroll in Thousand dollars.

Retail

Year	Total Establishments (De30)	Total Sales (De31)	Total Payroll Year (De32)	Total Payroll Workweek (De33)[2]	Total Paid employees (De34)[3]	Corporations Establishments (De35)	Corporations Sales (De36)	Corporations Payroll Year (De37)	Corporations Payroll Workweek (De38)[2]	Corporations Paid employees (De39)[3]	All other Establishments (De40)	All other Sales (De41)	All other Payroll Year (De42)	All other Payroll Workweek (De43)[2]	All other Paid employees (De44)[3]
1935	—	—	—	—	—	—	—	—	—	—	—	—	—	—	—
1939	1,770,355	42,041,790	4,529,499	—	4,600,217	210,570	19,810,302	2,824,195	—	2,453,828	1,559,785	22,231,488	1,705,304	—	2,146,389
1948	1,769,540	130,520,548	13,567,997	—	6,918,061	210,608	61,203,213	8,154,361	—	3,617,359	1,558,932	69,317,335	5,413,636	—	3,300,702
1954[4]	1,721,650	169,967,748	18,198,662	354,142	7,124,331	230,492	82,229,197	10,998,738	210,240	3,848,142	1,491,158	87,738,551	7,199,924	143,902	3,276,189
1958	1,788,325	199,646,463	21,589,339	412,650	7,911,081	277,805	106,098,594	13,658,964	257,516	4,438,378	1,510,520	93,547,869	7,930,375	155,134	3,472,703
1963	1,707,931	244,201,777	27,631,998	553,338	8,410,199	359,409	151,093,201	19,293,294	382,541	5,329,276	1,348,522	93,108,576	8,338,704	170,797	3,080,923
1967	1,763,324	310,214,393	36,174,723	8,811,937	9,380,616	451,386	209,152,555	27,067,819	6,461,839	6,376,852	1,311,938	101,061,838	9,106,904	2,350,098	3,003,764
1972	1,912,871	459,040,436	55,372,140	13,033,237	11,210,998	566,442	343,094,059	44,999,046	10,600,187	8,318,508	1,346,429	115,946,377	10,373,094	2,433,050	2,892,490
1977	1,855,068	723,134,221	85,853,987	20,263,279	13,040,082	695,441	576,853,514	72,772,842	17,059,909	10,194,651	1,159,627	146,280,707	13,081,145	3,203,370	2,845,431
1982	1,923,228	1,065,917,067	123,618,717	29,045,035	14,467,813	820,538	901,987,375	108,559,594	25,602,471	11,932,130	1,102,690	163,929,692	15,059,123	3,442,564	2,535,683
1987	1,503,593	1,493,308,759	177,547,927	41,599,090	17,779,942	964,915	1,327,199,364	157,872,607	37,034,571	15,032,154	538,678	166,109,395	19,675,320	4,564,519	2,747,788
1992	1,526,215	1,894,880,209	222,867,879	52,223,312	18,407,453	1,044,800	1,702,601,104	201,214,374	47,160,583	15,879,550	481,415	192,279,105	21,653,505	5,062,729	2,527,903

Wholesale

Year	Total Establishments (De45)	Total Sales (De46)	Total Payroll Year (De47)	Total Payroll Workweek (De48)[2]	Total Paid employees (De49)[3]	Corporations Establishments (De50)	Corporations Sales (De51)	Corporations Payroll Year (De52)	Corporations Payroll Workweek (De53)	Corporations Paid employees (De54)[3]	All other Establishments (De55)	All other Sales (De56)	All other Payroll Year (De57)	All other Payroll Workweek (De58)	All other Paid employees (De59)[3]
1935	176,756	42,802,913	2,022,262	—	1,260,553	88,471	32,986,801	1,736,298	—	1,000,819	88,285	9,816,112	285,964	—	259,734
1939	200,573	55,263,640	2,624,203	—	1,561,948	97,503[5]	41,012,835	2,186,268	—	1,180,693	103,070	14,250,805	437,935	—	381,255
1948	243,336	188,688,801	7,990,713	153,224	2,382,789	121,418	142,861,846	6,658,995	126,645	1,848,719	121,918	45,826,955	1,331,718	26,579	534,070
1954[4]	252,318	234,974,422	11,021,450	216,084	2,590,236	127,748	167,647,160	8,477,463		1,829,689	124,570	67,327,262	2,543,987		760,547
1958	285,996	284,970,807	13,198,744	269,113	2,797,341	162,184	225,124,487	10,997,160	221,953	2,179,579	123,812	59,846,320	2,201,584	47,160	617,762
1963	308,177	358,385,749	18,100,929	349,466	3,008,706	197,481	298,662,098	15,743,257	302,887	2,535,716	110,696	59,723,651	2,357,672	46,579	472,990
1967	311,464	459,475,967	23,921,680	5,796,114	3,518,969	200,392	393,997,036	21,097,900		2,949,786	111,072	65,478,931	2,823,780		569,183
1972	369,791	695,223,644	36,892,920	8,812,039	4,026,118	274,878	641,052,651	34,241,054		3,590,874	94,913	54,170,993	2,651,866		435,244
1977	382,837	1,258,400,268	58,289,573	13,829,556	4,397,089	306,892	1,177,558,378	54,973,566		4,012,923	75,945	80,841,890	3,316,007		384,166
1982	415,829	1,997,894,780	95,208,718	23,446,695	4,984,880	355,411	1,916,512,671	91,701,723		4,691,105	60,418	81,382,109	3,506,995		293,775
1987	469,539	2,524,726,802	133,359,426	32,030,202	5,609,024	403,166	2,442,374,373	129,176,488		5,312,984	66,373	82,352,429	4,182,938		296,040
1992	495,457	3,238,520,447	173,272,138	41,185,724	5,791,264	428,284	3,122,197,944	167,537,345		5,477,763	67,173	116,322,453	5,734,793		313,501

1 Data in series referring to workweek are for the week ending nearest November 15, except as noted.

2 Beginning in 1967, figures denote first quarter payroll, not payroll for the workweek ending nearest November 15.

3 Through 1939, figures are average annual number of full-time and part-time employees. Beginning 1967, figures are for paid employees for week including March 12.

4 Legal form of organization data were withheld for some selected services establishments to avoid disclosure.

5 Includes 17,530 petroleum bulk stations operated on a commission basis by operators with a proprietary interest in the business.

Sources

U.S. Bureau of the Census. 1935, *U.S. Census of Business: 1935, Wholesale Distribution*, volume 1, p. 119. 1939, *Sixteenth Census of the U.S.: 1940, Census of Business: 1939*, volume 1, p. 71; volume 2, p. 200; and volume 3, p. 104. 1948, U.S. Census of Business: 1948, volume 1, p. 6.05; volume 4, p. 5.02; and volume 6, p. 5.02. 1954, U.S. Census of Business: 1954, volume 1, p. 5-2; volume 3, p. 7-2; and volume 5, p. 5-2. 1958, U.S. Census of Business: 1958, volume 1, p. 5-2; volume 3, p. 5-2; and volume 5, p. 5-2. 1963, 1963 Census of Business, volume 1, p. 5-1; volume 4, p. 7-1; and volume 6, p. 5-1. 1967, 1967 Census of Business, BC67-RS5, p. 5-103; BC67-WS8, p. 8-126; and BC67-SS8, p. 8-57. 1972, 1972 Census of Retail Trade, volume 1, p. 1-118; 1972 Census of Wholesale Trade, volume 1; and 1972 Census of Selected Services Industries, volume 1, p. 1-129. 1977, 1977 Census of Retail Trade, RC77-S-1, p. 1-127; 1977 Census of Wholesale Trade, volume 1, p. 1-157; and 1977 Census of Service Industries, volume 1, p. 1-141. 1982, 1982 Census of Retail Trade, RC82-I-1, p. 1-146; 1982 Census of Wholesale Trade, WC82-I-1, p. 1-240; and 1982 Census of Service Industries, SC82-I-1, p. 1-213. 1987, 1987 Census of Retail Trade, RC87-S-1, p. 1-131; 1987 Census of Wholesale Trade, WC87-S-1, p. 1-231; and 1987 Census of Service Industries, SC87-S-1, p. 1-270. 1992, 1992 Census of Retail Trade, RC92-S-1, p. 1-140; 1992 Census of Wholesale Trade, WC92-S-1, p. 1-235; and 1992 Census of Service Industries, SC92-S-1, p. 1-258.

Documentation

Each establishment included in the censuses of business was classified into one of the following legal forms of organization. (1) Individual proprietorship – an establishment owned by one person, who may or may not actively participate in the operation of the business. (2) Partnership – an establishment owned by two or more persons, each of whom has a financial interest in and responsibility for the business. Any partner may or may not actively participate in the operation of the business. (3) Corporation – an establishment (other than a cooperative) owned by an organization or company legally incorporated under state laws. In the 1939 and 1948 Censuses of Business, cooperative associations incorporated either under regular corporation laws or under the special cooperative association laws of the states were classified as corporations. Beginning with the 1954 Census of Business, a separate legal form was established for cooperatives. (4) Cooperative – an establishment owned by an association of customers of the establishment whether or not they are incorporated. In general, the distinguishing features of a cooperative are patronage dividends based on the volume of expenditures by the member, and a limitation of one vote per member regardless of the amount of stock owned. The establishments are open to the public as a rule, but generally are patronized primarily by members of the association operating the business. In the 1939 and 1948 Censuses of Business, cooperatives were defined either as "corporations," if the cooperative was incorporated, or as "other legal forms." (5) Other legal forms – establishments whose legal form of organization is not one of those defined above. Included forms are liquor stores owned or operated by state, county, or municipal governments, and other miscellaneous ownership types such as estates, receiverships, some nonprofit organizations, and joint ventures. In the 1939 and 1948 Censuses of Business, cooperatives not incorporated were also included in this category.

TABLE De60-72 Book value of retail store and merchant wholesaler inventories, by type of business: 1938–1998[1,2]
Contributed by Daniel M. G. Raff

	Retail stores										Merchant wholesalers		
	Total	Durable goods				Nondurable goods					Total	Durable goods establishments	Nondurable goods establishments
		Total	Automotive dealers	Furniture, homefurnishings, and home equipment	Building materials	Total	Apparel and accessory stores	Food stores	General merchandise stores				
									Total	Department stores			
	De60	De61 [3]	De62	De63	De64 [4]	De65 [3]	De66	De67	De68	De69 [5]	De70 [6]	De71 [6]	De72 [6]
Year	Million dollars	Million dollars	Million dollars	Million dollars	Million dollars	Million dollars	Million dollars	Million dollars	Million dollars	Million dollars	Million dollars	Million dollars	Million dollars
1938	5,276	1,977	545	377	623	3,299	717	612	1,202	—	2,894	940	1,954
1939	5,534	2,088	575	395	640	3,446	748	656	1,269	—	3,052	1,008	2,044
1940	6,119	2,469	772	430	709	3,650	761	687	1,340	—	3,238	1,110	2,128
1941	7,776	3,175	951	599	881	4,601	948	961	1,590	—	4,044	1,388	2,656
1942	8,023	2,752	813	570	676	5,271	1,148	1,119	1,665	—	3,781	1,101	2,680
1943	7,561	2,209	562	446	593	5,352	1,207	1,080	1,679	—	3,684	1,073	2,611
1944	7,640	2,243	491	422	690	5,397	1,244	969	1,596	—	3,912	1,148	2,764
1945	7,948	2,431	517	480	683	5,517	1,116	1,034	1,686	—	4,555	1,497	3,058
1946 [7]	12,062	3,851	1,000	950	888	8,211	1,615	1,573	2,621	—	6,203	2,521	3,682
1946 [8]	11,852	3,949	977	938	1,056	7,903	1,567	1,596	2,603	—	6,583	2,595	3,988
1947	14,241	5,346	1,526	1,238	1,279	8,895	1,896	1,683	2,819	—	7,123	3,069	4,054
1948	16,007	6,572	1,992	1,483	1,532	9,435	2,126	1,780	2,855	—	7,957 [9]	3,999 [9]	3,958 [9]
1949	15,470	6,261	1,881	1,266	1,530	9,209	2,113	1,725	2,867	—	7,706	3,818	3,888
1950	19,460	8,290	2,455	1,881	2,098	11,170	2,488	2,171	3,508	—	9,284	4,691	4,593
1951	21,050	9,628	3,130	1,951	2,380	11,422	2,491	2,181	3,587	—	9,886	5,207	4,679
1952	21,031	9,491	3,033	1,905	2,400	11,540	2,489	2,196	3,736	—	10,210	5,312	4,898
1953	21,488	9,781	3,283	1,895	2,340	11,707	2,620	2,287	3,686	—	10,686	5,547	5,139
1954	20,926	9,270	3,013	1,785	2,281	11,656	2,601	2,469	3,401	—	10,637	5,477	5,160

Notes appear at end of table

(continued)

TABLE De60–72 Book value of retail store and merchant wholesaler inventories, by type of business: 1938–1998 _Continued_

		Retail stores									Merchant wholesalers		
		Durable goods				Nondurable goods			General merchandise stores				
Year	Total	Total	Automotive dealers	Furniture, homefurnishings, and home equipment	Building materials	Total	Apparel and accessory stores	Food stores	Total	Department stores	Total	Durable goods establishments	Nondurable goods establishments
	De60	De61 [3]	De62	De63	De64 [4]	De65 [3]	De66	De67	De68	De69 [5]	De70 [6]	De71 [6]	De72 [6]
	Million dollars	Million dollars	Million dollars	Million dollars	Million dollars	Million dollars	Million dollars	Million dollars	Million dollars	Million dollars	Million dollars	Million dollars	Million dollars
1955	22,769	10,532	4,012	1,878	2,355	12,237	2,682	2,560	3,706	—	11,678	6,261	5,417
1956	23,402	10,495	3,727	1,957	2,388	12,907	2,912	2,719	3,834	—	13,260	7,074	6,186
1957	24,451	11,283	4,520	1,922	2,394	13,168	3,024	2,852	3,843	—	12,730	7,115	5,615
1958	24,113	10,526	3,966	1,879	2,406	13,587	2,967	2,943	3,865	—	12,739	7,150	5,589
1959	25,305	11,029	4,105	1,983	2,435	14,276	3,194	2,984	4,198	—	13,879	7,861	6,018
1960	26,813	11,923	5,015	1,987	2,408	14,890	3,323	3,171	4,278	—	14,120	8,121	5,999
1961	26,221	11,062	4,487	1,802	2,381	15,159	3,044	3,132	4,917	—	14,488	8,315	6,173
1962	27,941	11,798	5,013	1,935	2,359	16,143	3,326	3,281	5,395	—	14,936	8,631	6,305
1963	29,386	12,572	5,623	2,080	2,403	16,814	3,288	3,435	5,709	—	16,048	9,119	6,929
1964	31,094	13,318	5,784	2,227	2,609	17,776	3,385	3,628	6,276	3,391	17,000	9,813	7,187
1965	34,405	15,253	7,316	2,392	2,529	19,152	3,751	3,856	6,827	3,748	18,317	10,588	7,729
1966	38,073	17,258	8,041	2,813	2,635	20,815	4,009	4,057	7,673	4,359	20,765	12,151	8,614
1967 [7]	38,952	17,277	7,395	2,903	2,663	21,675	4,084	4,239	8,022	4,689	21,885	12,698	9,187
1968 [7]	41,973	19,167	8,926	3,117	2,751	22,806	4,177	4,499	8,753	5,124	22,997	13,698	9,299
1969 [7]	45,376	20,647	9,866	3,315	2,719	24,729	4,518	4,849	9,567	5,541	24,910	14,919	9,991
1970 [7]	46,626	20,345	9,133	3,432	2,748	26,281	4,384	5,018	10,528	6,357	27,290	15,953	11,337
1971 [7]	52,571	23,864	11,776	3,608	3,358	28,707	4,642	5,514	12,095	7,199	29,695	17,704	11,991
1972 [7]	57,156	26,056	12,230	4,402	3,820	31,100	4,859	5,883	13,302	7,976	32,817	19,484	13,333
1973 [7]	65,229	29,593	14,813	4,684	4,296	35,636	5,382	6,865	15,439	8,988	38,302	21,892	16,410
1974 [7]	74,082	34,649	17,794	5,238	4,581	39,433	5,517	8,010	16,621	9,868	46,564	27,779	18,785
1967 [8]	35,299	14,151	6,839	2,732	2,742	21,148	3,748	4,280	7,266	5,161	24,955	15,360	9,595
1968 [8]	38,945	16,580	8,404	2,988	2,885	22,365	3,967	4,511	7,875	5,556	26,268	16,416	9,852
1969 [8]	42,517	18,206	9,381	3,216	2,900	24,311	4,421	4,908	8,538	5,923	28,762	18,043	10,719
1970 [8]	43,867	17,908	8,679	3,374	2,981	25,959	4,422	5,095	9,438	6,713	32,199	19,851	12,348
1971 [8]	50,063	21,687	11,363	3,585	3,683	28,376	4,820	5,601	10,728	7,499	35,210	22,160	13,050
1972 [8]	55,079	24,238	11,855	4,414	4,268	30,841	5,200	5,981	11,743	8,214	38,816	24,418	14,398
1973 [8]	63,237	28,418	14,356	4,800	4,844	34,819	5,791	6,946	13,137	9,016	45,556	27,605	17,951
1974 [8]	71,067	32,861	16,737	5,439	5,131	38,206	6,071	8,043	13,647	9,632	57,239	35,588	21,651
1975	71,744	33,356	16,347	5,717	5,474	38,388	6,029	8,069	13,521	9,848	56,972	36,972	20,000
1976	79,273	37,841	18,420	6,115	6,481	41,432	6,516	8,709	14,886	11,037	64,365	41,667	22,698
1977	89,444	43,071	21,879	6,610	7,502	46,373	7,646	9,362	17,307	13,145	72,801	47,425	25,376
1978	102,610	50,136	25,188	7,876	8,397	52,474	8,914	10,193	19,779	14,755	86,442	56,520	29,922
1979	110,906	54,108	26,933	8,681	8,981	56,798	9,514	11,343	20,865	15,518	99,348	64,014	35,334
1980 [7]	116,054	55,117	25,140	9,168	9,588	60,937	10,240	12,443	21,216	15,866	113,623	72,751	40,872
1981 [7]	126,656	60,327	27,636	9,749	10,051	66,329	11,555	13,492	23,324	17,769	118,438	77,940	40,498
1982 [7]	126,014	58,952	26,839	9,562	9,820	67,062	11,759	13,748	23,721	18,035	118,290	77,972	40,318
1983 [7]	139,123	66,845	31,322	11,000	11,464	72,278	13,103	14,404	26,198	20,307	120,476	77,331	43,145
1984 [7]	155,517	74,582	35,796	12,331	12,234	80,935	13,880	15,508	31,253	24,578	132,208	86,436	45,772

	Retail stores										Merchant wholesalers		
		Durable goods				Nondurable goods							
				Furniture, homefurnishings, and home equipment	Building materials	Total	Apparel and accessory stores	Food stores	General merchandise stores				Nondurable goods establishments
	Total	Total	Automotive dealers						Total	Department stores	Total	Durable goods establishments	
Year	De60	De61 [3]	De62	De63	De64 [4]	De65 [3]	De66	De67	De68	De69 [5]	De70 [6]	De71 [6]	De72 [6]
	Million dollars	Million dollars	Million dollars	Million dollars	Million dollars	Million dollars	Million dollars	Million dollars	Million dollars	Million dollars	Million dollars	Million dollars	Million dollars
1980 [8]	121,078	55,799	25,553	9,207	9,685	65,279	10,929	13,390	23,171	16,814	122,631	79,372	43,259
1981 [8]	132,719	61,050	28,026	9,795	10,180	71,669	12,234	14,649	25,951	19,279	129,654	85,856	43,798
1982 [8]	134,628	61,316	28,352	9,714	10,203	73,312	12,392	15,248	26,548	19,645	127,428	85,222	42,206
1983 [8]	147,833	68,856	32,919	11,217	11,716	78,977	13,466	16,282	28,651	21,196	130,075	85,180	44,895
1984 [8]	167,812	79,074	39,004	12,433	12,890	88,738	14,641	17,624	34,392	25,750	142,452	95,474	46,978
1985	181,881	88,315	45,798	13,762	13,683	93,566	15,689	19,283	34,683	25,525	147,409	97,371	50,038
1986	186,510	89,983	45,246	14,340	14,033	96,527	16,067	19,612	35,743	26,412	153,574	102,349	51,225
1987	207,836	105,481	56,161	15,050	14,868	102,355	17,280	19,898	38,285	28,450	163,903	108,112	55,791
1988	219,047	112,453	58,907	16,311	16,157	106,594	18,079	21,601	39,179	29,987	178,801	117,045	61,756
1989	237,234	121,347	64,072	17,280	17,122	115,887	19,422	23,543	43,107	33,678	187,009	122,237	64,772
1990	239,815	121,194	63,107	17,442	17,015	118,621	19,690	25,038	42,377	33,387	195,775	126,407	69,362
1991	243,389	119,189	60,881	17,649	16,718	124,200	20,263	25,580	45,764	36,110	200,376	127,342	73,034
1992	252,185	123,152	64,134	17,934	17,234	129,033	22,249	25,738	48,630	38,033	208,244	131,458	76,786
1993	269,303	135,088	69,730	20,232	18,895	134,215	22,453	26,043	52,305	41,091	216,974	137,042	79,932
1994	294,052	153,019	79,897	22,963	21,305	141,033	23,362	26,779	55,216	43,673	235,413	150,928	84,485
1995	310,276	165,108	87,354	24,377	22,742	145,168	22,811	27,551	58,189	46,402	253,565	163,474	90,091
1996	320,601	170,849	90,733	24,726	23,821	149,752	22,989	28,539	59,127	47,797	255,871	166,185	89,686
1997	330,308	176,483	94,244	24,263	25,080	153,825	24,600	28,853	59,239	48,863	273,885	177,746	96,139
1998	340,760	181,070	95,965	25,376	27,031	159,690	25,598	29,494	60,217	49,078	287,484	187,734	99,750

1 Two sets of values are presented for some years to reflect changes in the data series.

2 Data adjusted for seasonal variation.

3 Includes kinds of business not shown separately.

4 For 1967–1998, includes building materials; hardware; plants and garden supplies; and manufactured (mobile) homes.

5 Excluding leased departments.

6 Data prior to 1947 include estimates for nonmerchant wholesalers and are not comparable with data for later years.

7 Comparable with earlier years.

8 Comparable with later years.

9 Figures comparable with earlier years are as follows for series De70–72: $7,879, $3,683, and $4,186 million, respectively.

Sources

Series De60–69. 1938, unpublished data; 1939–1946, *1969 Business Statistics*, p. 63; 1947–1974, *1975 Business Statistics*, p. 64; 1967–1984, *Business Statistics: 1984*, pp. 40–41; 1980–1998, *Business Statistics of the United States: Fifth Edition, 1999*, p. 276.

Series De70–72. 1938–1945, *1953 Business Statistics*, p. 16; 1946, unpublished data; 1947–1974, *1975 Business Statistics*, p. 25; 1967–1984, *1984 Business Statistics*, p. 9; 1980–1998, *Business Statistics of the United States: Fifth Edition, 1999*, p. 277, except for series De71, 1990, which is from *Business Statistics of the United States: 1998 Edition*, p. 77, owing to a typographical error in the 1999 edition.

Documentation

Retail stores are defined as establishments primarily engaged in selling merchandise for personal or household consumption and rendering services incidental to the sales of goods. Merchant wholesalers are defined as establishments that take title to the goods they sell and are primarily engaged in selling merchandise to retailers; to commercial, professional, or institutional purchasers; or to other wholesalers.

Figures are as of the end of the year. Figures for 1980–1998 are not comparable to those for earlier years because of changes in valuation methods. Prior to 1980, inventories were defined as book values of stocks on hand at the end of the period and are valued according to the valuation method of the individual respondent retailers and wholesalers, resulting in a mixture of LIFO and non-LIFO values. Beginning in 1980, inventories are valued using methods other than LIFO in order to better reflect the current costs of goods held as inventory (see *Business Statistics of the United States: Fifth Edition, 1999*, the notes to pp. 276-7).

Series De60-69. These series were linked to the Census of Business for 1939 and 1948, the Internal Revenue Service's *Statistics of Income*, and Federal Reserve Board data on department store inventories. Data for 1946–1974, based on sample year-end estimates from the *1952–1974 Annual Retail Trade Reports* of the Bureau of the Census, reflect revisions to the 1957 Standard Industrial Classification (SIC) code and to the measurement of seasonal factors for each line of trade. Adjustments have been made to the data for 1961–1967 to make them directly comparable to retail sales estimates derived from a new sample introduced in 1968 and used through 1974 (see *Business Statistics: 1975*, the notes to p. 64). Classifications of businesses for the estimates for 1967–1984 are based on the 1972 or 1977 Standard Industrial Classification (SIC) Code and cause these years to be not comparable to earlier years. Data for 1967–1984 were recalculated with the new classifications, accounting for the overlap of years (see *Business Statistics: 1984*, the notes to p. 40). See the Introduction to Part D for a discussion of SIC codes.

Series De70-72. Includes wholesalers of farm products and raw materials. Figures for 1947–1958 are adjusted to the levels of the 1958 Census of Business. Figures for 1959–1975 are based on samples selected from the 1948 and 1954 Censuses of Business. Figures for 1959–1975 are based on a sample designed to conform to the 1963 Census of Business (see *Business Statistics: 1975*, the notes to p. 25). Figures for 1967–1984 are based on a sample designed to conform to the 1967, 1972, 1977, and 1984 Censuses of Wholesale Trade (see *Business Statistics: 1984*, notes to p. 9).

RETAIL TRADE

Daniel M. G. Raff

TABLE De73–109   Retail establishments, by type of business: 1929–1982[1]

Contributed by Daniel M.G. Raff

	All retail establishments	Food establishments						Eating establishments	Drinking establishments	General merchandise establishments		Variety stores
		Total	Grocery stores	Meat markets	Fruit stores, vegetable markets	Candy, nut, confectionery stores	Bakery product stores			Total	Department stores	
	De73 [2]	De74 [2]	De75	De76 [3]	De77	De78	De79	De80	De81	De82	De83	De84
Year	Number	Number	Number	Number	Number	Number	Number	Number	Number	Number	Number	Number
1929	1,476,365	481,891	307,425	43,788	22,904	63,265	12,013	134,293	—	54,636	4,221	12,110
1933	1,526,119	470,149	303,910	—	21,897	54,243	19,380	170,434	29,901	49,712	3,544	12,046
1935	1,587,718	532,010	354,971	32,555	32,632	55,197	14,150	153,468	98,005	44,651	4,201	11,741
1939	1,770,355	560,549	387,337	35,630	27,666	48,015	16,985	169,792	135,594	50,267	4,074	16,946
1948 [5]	1,769,540	504,439	377,939	24,242	15,763	32,876	20,152	194,123	152,433	52,544	2,580	20,210
1948 [6]	1,688,479	460,913	350,754	23,920	13,482	27,165	19,500	179,185	146,604	70,807	2,558	18,917
1954	1,721,650	384,616	287,572	22,896	13,136	20,507	19,034	195,128	123,887	76,198	2,761	20,917
1958	1,788,325	355,508	259,796	23,844	12,689	17,593	19,235	229,815	114,925	86,644	3,157	21,017
1963	1,707,931	319,433	244,838	16,457	8,874	14,979	18,631	223,876	110,605	62,063	4,251	22,378
1967	1,763,324	294,243	218,130	17,943	8,890	13,981	19,598	236,563	111,327	67,307	5,792	21,046
1972	1,912,871	267,352	194,346	16,586	8,371	12,872	19,203	253,136	106,388	56,245	7,742 [8]	21,852
1977	1,855,068	251,971	178,835	16,852	7,853	8,973	19,906	274,337	93,729	48,911	8,807 [8]	17,376
1982 [7]	1,923,228	—	—	—	—	—	—	—	—	—	—	—

	Apparel establishments			Furniture, homefurnishings, and appliance establishments			Automotive establishments			Tire, battery, and accessory dealers	Gasoline service stations
	Total	Shoe stores	Women's ready-to-wear stores	Total	Furniture stores	Household appliance, radio, and television establishments	Total	Passenger car dealers			
								Franchised	Nonfranchised		
	De85 [2]	De86	De87	De88 [2]	De89	De90	De91 [2]	De92	De93	De94	De95
Year	Number	Number	Number	Number	Number	Number	Number	Number	Number	Number	Number
1929	114,296	24,259	18,253	58,941	25,854	25,366	69,379	42,204	3,097	22,313	121,513
1933	86,548	18,836	17,759	42,976	17,418 [9]	17,922	48,545	30,646 [11]	— [11]	16,027	170,404
1935	95,968	18,967	21,975	45,215	17,043 [9]	18,396	50,459	30,294	4,751	14,343	197,568
1939	106,959	20,487	25,820	52,827	19,902 [9]	20,913	60,132	33,609	6,980	18,525	241,858
1948 [5]	115,246	19,551	30,677	85,585	29,031	36,931	86,162	43,999	16,874	20,628	188,253
1948 [6]	110,944	19,201	29,788	80,423	28,465	35,331	85,285	43,960	16,634	20,224	179,647
1954	119,743	23,847	—	91,797	—	40,542	85,953	41,407	20,140	18,845	181,747
1958	118,759	24,437	—	103,417	36,096	40,985	93,656	38,555	25,331	20,912	206,302
1963	116,223	24,568	29,696	93,649	37,216	30,685	98,514	33,349	27,984	25,899	211,473
1967	110,164	—	31,883	98,826	33,274	43,619 [10]	105,500	62,023 [11]	— [11]	29,189	216,059
1972	129,201	26,850	38,762	116,857	38,732	50,152 [10]	121,369	64,237	—	—	226,459
1977	140,126	27,891	44,894	138,579	40,801	55,988 [10]	139,006	67,899	—	—	176,465
1982 [7]	—	—	—	—	—	—	—	—	—	—	—

Notes appear at end of table

TABLE De73–109   Retail establishments, by type of business: 1929–1982   *Continued*

	Lumber, building, and hardware establishments				Other retail establishments									
	Total	Lumber and building materials dealers	Hardware stores	Farm equipment dealers	Total	Drug and proprietary stores	Liquor stores	Fuel and ice dealers	Hay, grain, and feed stores	Jewelry stores	Cigar stores and stands	Florists	Gift, novelty, and souvenir stores	Secondhand stores
	De96 [2]	De97	De98	De99	De100 [4]	De101	De102	De103	De104	De105	De106	De107	De108	De109
Year	Number	Number	Number	Number	Number	Number	Number	Number	Number	Number	Number	Number	Number	Number
1929	90,386	26,377	25,330	12,242	181,595	58,258	—	19,118 [12]	21,394	19,998	33,248	9,328	5,186	15,065
1933	76,098	21,015	22,844	9,958	149,134	58,407	3,767	23,875 [12]	—	14,313	20,175	7,728	—	20,869
1935	73,186	21,149	26,996	9,637	182,328	56,697	12,105	35,293	11,132	12,447	15,350	11,242	5,512	22,550
1939	79,313	25,067	29,147	10,499	215,492	57,903	19,136	41,172	16,772	14,559	18,504	16,055	7,429	23,962
1948 [5]	98,938	26,110	34,674	17,615	210,130	55,796	33,422	22,670	18,213	21,269	14,526	14,749	12,516	16,969
1948 [6]	97,342	25,978	34,009	17,509	198,233	55,282	32,949	21,473	17,970	20,550	12,791	13,565	10,266	13,387
1954	100,519	30,177	34,858	18,689	203,975	56,009	31,240	27,070	16,530	24,266	6,068	16,279	12,149	14,364
1958	108,248	34,867	34,670	19,008	217,628	56,232	37,068	28,559	16,782	23,751	5,336	19,176	13,987	16,737
1963	92,703	28,979	29,595	16,326	211,905	54,732	40,188	24,956	13,926	20,935	4,899	19,801	12,606	19,862
1967	86,373	—	27,162	16,739	167,399	53,722	39,719	22,258	—	23,689	5,560	22,451	—	—
1972	83,842	—	26,374	—	192,340	51,542	41,991	19,916	—	25,316	4,462	24,464	24,649	—
1977	90,357	28,932	26,451	—	215,319	49,570	44,354	20,246	—	34,104	3,629	29,375	34,041	—
1982 [7]	—	—	—	—	—	—	—	—	—	—	—	—	—	—

[1] Two sets of values are presented for some years to reflect changes in the data series.

[2] Total includes subclasses not shown separately.

[3] Beginning 1967, figures include fish (seafood) markets. Separate figures not available.

[4] Calculated as the sum of series De101–109.

[5] Comparable with earlier years.

[6] Comparable with later years.

[7] Excludes leased departments.

[8] Includes sales from catalog desks.

[9] Excludes interior decorators.

[10] Includes music stores.

[11] Nonfranchised dealers combined with franchised dealers.

[12] Excludes fuel oil dealers.

Sources

The sources for Tables De73–219 are from the U.S. Bureau of the Census, as follows. 1929: *Fifteenth Census of the United States, 1930*, Distribution, volume 1, Retail Distribution, part 1. 1933: *Census of American Business: 1933*, U.S. Summaries. 1935: *Census of Business: 1935*, Retail Distribution, part 1, volume 1, U.S. Summary. 1939: *Sixteenth Census of the United States, 1940*, Census of Business, volume 1, Retail Trade: 1939, part 1. 1948: *Census of Business: 1948*, volume 1, Retail Trade, General Statistics, part 1. 1954: *Census of Business: 1954*, volume 1, Retail Trade – Summary Statistics. 1958: *Census of Business: 1958*, volume 1, Retail Trade – Summary Statistics. 1963: *Census of Business: 1963*, volume I, Retail Trade – Summary Statistics, part 1. 1967: *Census of Business: 1967*, volume 1, Retail Trade – Subject Reports. 1972: *Census of Retail Trade – Area Statistics: 1972*, pp. 7–8. 1977: *Census of Retail Trade – Geographic Area Series: 1977*, pp. 10–11. 1982: *Census of Retail Trade – Geographic Area Series: 1982*, pp. 2–28. 1987: *Census of Retail Trade – Geographic Area Series: 1987*, pp. 2–29. 1992: *Census of Retail Trade – Geographic Area Series: 1992*, pp. 11–12. 1997: *Summary Statistics for the United States: 1997 – Geographic Area Series*, pp. 7–9; "1997 Economic Census: Comparative Statistics for the United States 1987, SIC Basis: Retail Trade," downloaded from the Census Bureau Internet site.

Documentation

General Note for Tables De73–219

Stores are classified according to their principal kind of business. Where a number of lines are carried, changes in relative importance may serve to shift a particular establishment from one category to another between censuses. Sales figures shown are for kinds of establishments, not kinds of products.

Certain of these series were adjusted or combined for some years prior to 1958 by Charles S. Goodman and Reavis Cox in order to provide historical series that are as comparable as possible. Figures for 1933, in particular, were adjusted for comparability. The reports of the Census of Business provide considerably more detail as to kinds of business.

Sales and excise taxes are included in sales figures for 1954 and later years and excluded for 1948 and 1939.

Figures for persons engaged represent the total number of reported number of active proprietors and employees for the week including March 12 for 1967, of active proprietors and employees for the payroll period ended nearest November 15 for 1939–1963, and of active proprietors plus the average annual number of full-time and part-time employees for 1939 and earlier years. Unpaid family workers are excluded from figures for persons engaged.

Establishments without paid employment and with less than $2,500 sales were excluded in 1954 and 1958. The 1948 figures exclude stores that operated the entire year but had sales of less than $500. The corresponding cutoff point for 1939 was $100. Nonemployer establishments that did not operate the entire year were included in 1963 and 1967 if their receipts during the period they operated were at a rate that would have reached an annual total of $2,500 or more had they operated the entire year.

There have been many changes in enumeration methods, in accuracy, and in classifications over the years. The principal ones are noted here; others are described in the various Census volumes. Users of the data are cautioned to consult original sources for more complete discussion of factors affecting the comparability of data. The 1954 and subsequent Censuses were conducted by mail canvasses of all firms included in the active records of the Internal Revenue Service as subject to the payment of Federal Insurance Contributions Act (FICA) taxes and which were in appropriate kind-of-business classifications. Such data cover only firms with paid employees. The nonemployer segment was derived from a 50 percent sample of 1954, 1958, and 1963 tax returns. This procedure was modified for the 1967 Census by the use of tax records instead of Census returns for small employers, and the use of tax records for all nonemployers rather than for a 50 percent sample. The 1948 and earlier censuses were conducted by field enumeration. The differences in enumeration affect particularly the coverage of establishments without easily recognized places of business (e.g., nonstore retailers) and those leaving business prior to the end of the year. The data for the 1954 and subsequent Censuses thus have better coverage in these areas. The 1933 and 1935 Censuses were not taken under mandatory reporting requirements and may be subject to some underenumeration.

Dairies, which processed milk and cream, were included as retailers in 1948 and earlier years if the major portion of their sales was by route delivery to the homes of consumers. They were excluded in 1954 and later years.

Nonstore retailers are treated as a separate kind of business for 1954 and later years. For earlier years, such retailers (to the extent enumerated) were classified in their appropriate kind of business. For 1954, each leased department is treated as a separate establishment; for all other years, data for such departments were consolidated with the establishments in which they were located.

(continued)

TABLE De73–109   Retail establishments, by type of business: 1929–1982 *Continued*

Two sets of data are shown for 1948. The data for 1948 (comparable with later years) represent retabulations of 1948 data to make them comparable with later years as to treatment of dairies, nonstore retailers, and cutoff points for tabulation. Similarly, two sets of data are shown for the number of persons engaged in retail establishments in 1939. The data for 1939 (comparable with later years) represent the sum of active proprietors and paid employees for the payroll period ended nearest November 15 and are comparable with data for 1948 and later years. The figures for 1939 (comparable with earlier years) represent the number of active proprietors and the average number of employees for the year, and are comparable with data for 1935 and earlier years.

The 1992 Census of Retail Trade, part of the 1992 Economic Census, covered retail trade as defined in the Standard Industrial Classification (SIC) Manual (1987). It included all establishments primarily engaged in selling merchandise for personal or household consumption and rendering services incidental to the sale of the goods. The Census excluded governmental organizations classified in the covered industries except for liquor stores operated by state and local governments. Data for direct sellers (SIC 5963) with no paid employees and post exchanges, ship stores, and similar establishments operated on military posts by agencies of the federal government

are not included. The basic tabulations in this report do not include data for establishments which are auxiliary (primary function is providing a service, such as warehouses) to retail establishments within the same organization. Data for auxiliaries are presented in a subsequent report issued as part of the 1992 Enterprise Statistics reports. See the Introduction to Part D for a discussion of SIC codes.

For the 1992 Census of Retail Trade, large- and medium-size firms, plus all firms known to operate more than one establishment, were sent questionnaires to be completed and returned to the Census Bureau by mail. For most very small firms, including those with no paid employees, data from existing administrative records of other federal agencies were used instead. These records provided basic information on location, kind of business, sales, payroll, number of employees, and legal form of organization. In addition, more detailed information for selected kinds of business was obtained on the various questionnaires.

1997 data are gathered as a combination of 1997 Economic Census Retail Trade Summary Statistics for the United States and 1997 Economic Census: Comparative Statistics for the United States 1987 SIC Basis: Retail Trade.

TABLE De110–146   Sales of retail establishments, by type of business: 1929–1997[1]

Contributed by Daniel M.G. Raff

		Food establishments						Eating establishments	Drinking establishments
	All retail establishments	Total	Grocery stores	Meat markets	Fruit stores, vegetable markets	Candy, nut, confectionery stores	Bakery product stores		
	De110 [2]	De111 [2]	De112	De113 [3]	De114	De115	De116	De117	De118
Year	Thousand dollars	Thousand dollars	Thousand dollars	Thousand dollars	Thousand dollars	Thousand dollars	Thousand dollars	Thousand dollars	Thousand dollars
1929	48,330,000	10,837,000	7,353,000	1,253,000	308,000	571,000	201,000	2,124,000	—
1933	25,037,000	6,776,000	5,004,000	—	170,000	271,000	188,000	1,324,000	105,000
1935	32,791,000	8,362,000	6,352,000	565,000	216,000	314,000	99,000	1,666,000	724,000
1939	42,042,000	10,165,000	7,722,000	700,000	222,000	295,000	168,000	2,135,000	1,385,000
1948 [7]	130,521,000	30,965,000	24,770,000	1,641,000	399,000	649,000	725,000	6,468,000	4,215,000
1948 [8]	128,849,000	29,207,000	24,730,000	1,641,000	394,000	586,000	722,000	6,440,000	4,204,000
1954	169,968,000	39,762,000	34,901,000	1,944,000	484,000	568,000	862,000	8,731,000	4,360,000
1958	199,646,000	49,022,000	43,696,000	2,327,000	505,000	528,000	905,000	11,038,000	4,164,000
1963	244,202,000	57,079,000	52,566,000	1,530,000	412,000	499,000	1,080,000	13,919,000	4,493,000
1967	310,214,000	70,251,000	65,074,000	1,831,000	448,000	541,000	1,340,000	18,879,000	4,964,000
1972	459,040,436	100,718,864	93,327,525	2,809,928	695,115	690,961	1,663,911	30,385,361	6,482,346
1977	723,134,221	157,940,457	147,750,535	3,779,993	1,088,102	642,578	2,300,101	55,580,643	7,695,030
1982 [9]	1,065,917,067	—	—	—	—	—	—	—	—
1987	1,493,308,759	301,846,804	285,481,116	5,616,255	1,802,222	1,182,238	4,870,760	139,281,605	9,494,892
1992	1,894,880,209	369,198,584	352,558,184	5,040,901	1,809,287	1,223,598	5,386,894	184,203,215	11,113,777
1997	2,460,886,012	401,764,499	368,250,471	4,347,021	2,106,828	1,515,510	890,310	—[10]	12,295,709

Notes appear at end of table

TABLE De110-146   Sales of retail establishments, by type of business: 1929-1997   *Continued*

	General merchandise establishments			Apparel establishments			Furniture, homefurnishings, and appliance establishments		
	Total	Department stores	Variety stores	Total	Shoe stores	Women's ready-to-wear stores	Total	Furniture stores	Household appliance, radio, and television establishments
	De119	De120 [4]	De121	De122 [2]	De123	De124	De125 [2]	De126	De127 [5]
Year	Thousand dollars	Thousand dollars	Thousand dollars	Thousand dollars	Thousand dollars	Thousand dollars	Thousand dollars	Thousand dollars	Thousand dollars
1929	6,444,000	4,350,000	904,000	4,240,000	806,000	1,087,000	2,754,000	1,578,000	950,000
1933	3,891,000	2,545,000	678,000	1,923,000	424,000	568,000	958,000	553,000 [12]	312,000
1935	4,620,000	3,311,000	780,000	2,656,000	511,000	795,000	1,289,000	694,000 [12]	438,000
1939	5,665,000	3,975,000	976,000	3,258,000	617,000	1,009,000	1,733,000	973,000 [12]	533,000
1948 [7]	15,975,000	10,645,000	2,506,000	9,803,000	1,467,000	3,305,000	6,914,000	3,427,000	2,543,000
1948 [8]	15,796,000	9,432,000	2,504,000	9,716,000	1,460,000	3,277,000	6,592,000	3,413,000	2,410,000
1954	17,872,000	10,558,000	3,066,000	11,078,000	1,895,000	—	8,619,000	—	3,237,000
1958	21,879,000	13,356,000	3,621,000	12,525,000	2,130,000	—	10,074,000	4,783,000	3,499,000
1963	30,003,000	20,537,000	4,538,000	14,040,000	2,390,000	4,428,000	10,926,000	5,317,000	3,385,000
1967	43,537,000	32,344,000	5,407,000	16,672,000	—	5,380,000	14,542,000	6,564,000	6,017,000
1972	65,090,832	51,083,522	7,343,967	24,741,375	4,074,583	8,451,228	22,533,328	10,442,856	8,468,927
1977	93,947,773	76,909,452	7,094,531	35,564,433	5,650,237	12,443,589	33,176,312	14,060,375	12,860,658
1982 [9]	—	—	—	—	—	—	—	—	—
1987	181,147,274	144,016,975	6,762,156	77,390,774	14,410,807	28,530,843 [11]	83,114,270	25,996,804	32,412,128
1992	245,329,695	186,422,670	9,056,820	101,714,474	17,883,367	31,326,346 [11]	101,361,468	30,416,124	43,042,174
1997	330,444,460	220,108,157	— [10]	136,397,645	20,543,252	27,257,683 [11]	140,252,144	40,968,335	77,477,189

	Automotive establishments					Lumber, building, and hardware establishments			
	Total	Passenger car dealers		Tire, battery, and accessory dealers	Gasoline service stations	Total	Lumber and building materials dealers	Hardware stores	Farm equipment dealers
		Franchised	Nonfranchised						
	De128 [2]	De129	De130	De131	De132	De133 [2]	De134	De135	De136
Year	Thousand dollars	Thousand dollars	Thousand dollars	Thousand dollars	Thousand dollars	Thousand dollars	Thousand dollars	Thousand dollars	Thousand dollars
1929	7,043,000	6,266,000	140,000	599,000	1,787,000	3,845,000	1,981,000	706,000	518,000
1933	2,367,000	2,127,000 [13]	— [13]	226,000	1,531,000	1,342,000	603,000	311,000	177,000
1935	4,236,000	3,725,000	122,000	373,000	1,967,000	1,864,000	866,000	467,000	291,000
1939	5,548,000	4,810,000	193,000	523,000	2,822,000	2,734,000	1,478,000	629,000	344,000
1948 [7]	20,104,000	15,952,000	2,441,000	1,359,000	6,483,000	11,151,000	5,127,000	2,493,000	2,386,000
1948 [8]	20,100,000	15,951,000	2,440,000	1,358,000	6,470,000	11,143,000	5,126,000	2,491,000	2,386,000
1954	29,915,000	25,108,000	2,423,000	1,814,000	10,743,000	13,123,000	6,502,000	2,694,000	2,804,000
1958	31,808,000	25,326,000	2,983,000	2,425,000	14,178,000	14,309,000	7,123,000	2,717,000	3,186,000
1963	45,376,000	37,375,000	3,087,000	3,336,000	17,760,000	14,606,000	7,023,000	2,560,000	3,626,000
1967	55,631,000	48,636,000 [14]	— [14]	4,236,000	22,709,000	17,200,000	—	2,813,000	4,832,000
1972	90,030,255	77,833,179 [14]	— [14]	—	33,655,378	23,844,148	—	3,957,373	—
1977	149,952,415	128,828,441 [14]	— [14]	—	56,468,144	38,859,865	24,725,764	6,086,879	—
1982 [9]	—	—	—	—	—	—	—	—	—
1987	333,419,982	—	—	23,169,210	101,997,440	60,525,420	55,283,957	10,534,934	—
1992	395,147,882	—	—	26,949,262 [15]	134,705,359	—	103,414,057	12,290,916	—
1997	553,652,292	—	—	62,824,978 [15]	170,660,068	—	68,300,659	13,605,263	—

Notes appear at end of table

(continued)

TABLE De110–146   Sales of retail establishments, by type of business: 1929–1997   *Continued*

					Other retail establishments					
	Total	Drug and proprietary stores	Liquor stores	Fuel and ice dealers	Hay, grain, and feed stores	Jewelry stores	Cigar stores and stands	Florists	Gift, novelty, and souvenir stores	Secondhand stores
	De137 [6]	De138	De139	De140	De141	De142	De143	De144	De145	De146
Year	Thousand dollars	Thousand dollars	Thousand dollars	Thousand dollars	Thousand dollars	Thousand dollars	Thousand dollars	Thousand dollars	Thousand dollars	Thousand dollars
1929	5,024,000	1,690,000	—	1,013,000 [16]	990,000	536,000	410,000	176,000	61,000	148,000
1933	2,240,000	1,066,000	16,000	623,000 [16]	—	175,000	189,000	66,000	—	105,000
1935	3,424,000	1,232,000	328,000	859,000	346,000	234,000	183,000	98,000	31,000	113,000
1939	4,692,000	1,562,000	586,000	1,013,000	624,000	361,000	207,000	148,000	53,000	138,000
1948 [7]	14,441,000	4,013,000	2,579,000	2,424,000	2,790,000	1,224,000	535,000	377,000	195,000	304,000
1948 [8]	14,262,000	4,011,000	2,578,000	2,425,000	2,796,000	1,209,000	385,000	375,000	185,000	298,000
1954	17,570,000	5,251,000	3,180,000	2,842,000	3,455,000	1,407,000	233,000	495,000	283,000	424,000
1958	20,877,000	6,779,000	4,202,000	3,473,000	3,117,000	1,495,000	233,000	638,000	389,000	551,000
1963	24,211,000	8,487,000	5,189,000	3,401,000	3,340,000	1,560,000	275,000	780,000	397,000	782,000
1967	24,852,000	10,930,000	6,663,000	3,598,000	—	2,207,000	352,000	1,102,000	—	—
1972	22,624,812	1,595,952	9,874,465	4,792,889	—	3,117,740	422,002	1,604,801	1,216,963	—
1977	57,196,103	23,196,366	12,967,473	10,171,097	—	5,428,732	460,133	2,400,028	2,572,274	—
1982 [9]	—	—	—	—	—	—	—	—	—	—
1987	114,903,891	53,824,463	18,596,981	14,198,230 [17]	—	11,994,271	518,146	4,810,359	7,459,217	3,502,224
1992	148,389,028	77,487,573	20,319,081	13,875,226 [17]	—	14,001,976	781,826 [18]	5,719,237	10,553,525	5,650,584
1997	194,664,088	98,630,857	22,684,120	22,622,249 [17]	—	18,511,350	3,068,352 [18]	6,555,088	14,497,296	8,094,776

[1] Two sets of values are presented for some years to reflect changes in the data series.

[2] Total includes subclasses not shown separately.

[3] Beginning with 1967, figures include fish (seafood) markets. Separate figures not available.

[4] Beginning with 1972, includes sales from catalog order desks. Beginning 1987, excludes leased departments.

[5] Beginning with 1967, includes music stores; beginning 1987, computer stores; and beginning 1997, software stores. Beginning with 1992, the radio and television component is called "radio, TV, and other electronics stores."

[6] Calculated as the sum of series De138–146.

[7] Comparable with earlier years.

[8] Comparable with later years.

[9] Source provides finer data only for establishments with payroll, not all establishments.

[10] Data withheld to avoid disclosure.

[11] Women's clothing stores.

[12] Excludes interior decorators.

[13] Nonfranchised dealers combined with franchised dealers.

[14] Nonfranchised dealers combined with franchised dealers.

[15] Includes automotive parts.

[16] Excludes fuel oil dealers.

[17] Fuel dealers only.

[18] Tobacco stores and stands.

Source

See the source for Table De73–109.

Documentation

For a general note, see the text for Table De73–109.

TABLE De147–182   Persons engaged by retail establishments, by type of business: 1929–1997[1]

Contributed by Daniel M.G. Raff

	Food establishments							
	Total	Grocery stores	Meat markets	Fruit stores, vegetable markets	Candy, nut, confectionery stores	Bakery product stores	Eating establishments	Drinking establishments
	De147 [2]	De148	De149 [3]	De150	De151	De152	De153	De154
Year	Thousand dollars	Thousand dollars	Thousand dollars	Thousand dollars	Thousand dollars	Thousand dollars	Thousand dollars	Thousand dollars
1929	1,174,665	719,765	113,407	46,277	127,311	41,907	615,385	—
1933	1,170,291	624,337	—	43,419	91,237	63,563	606,600	54,798
1935	1,235,069	844,483	77,236	56,463	91,164	28,939	652,334	252,167
1939 [8]	1,315,438	891,983	83,684	48,357	76,353	41,225	764,650	348,452
1939 [9]	1,331,722	905,015	85,485	48,564	77,170	43,217	777,884	358,398
1948	1,515,618	1,066,748	66,427	32,273	75,021	103,415	1,175,331	533,899
1954	1,439,397	1,132,789	71,836	27,691	46,892	104,929	1,280,398	438,559
1958	1,563,691	1,251,229	83,820	27,385	41,380	104,017	1,570,189	388,334
1963	1,579,759	1,315,615	50,274	19,347	34,233	110,882	1,705,797	381,954
1967	1,723,306	1,446,094	59,645	19,088	34,252	116,377	1,969,462	410,048
1972	2,158,419	1,587,276	59,059	17,887	32,926	130,583	2,449,570	383,688
1977	2,122,631	1,804,139	67,543	20,616	24,191	143,148	3,583,087	401,032
1982	2,347,603	2,031,453	61,755	16,789	23,154	158,709	4,340,832	324,998
1987	2,854,673	2,502,468	59,044	20,013	30,767	185,396	5,786,889	312,831
1992	2,969,317	2,682,153	45,139	16,258	25,504	157,136	6,243,862	304,046
1997	2,893,074	2,643,608	39,552	17,251	26,306	130,797	—	321,294

Notes appear at end of table

TABLE De147–182   Persons engaged by retail establishments, by type of business: 1929–1997   *Continued*

	General merchandise establishments			Apparel establishments			Furniture, homefurnishings, and appliance establishments		
	Total	Department stores	Variety stores	Total	Shoe stores	Women's ready-to-wear stores	Total	Furniture stores	Household appliance, radio, and television establishments
	De155	De156 [4]	De157	De158 [2]	De159	De160	De161 [2]	De162	De163 [5]
Year	Thousand dollars	Thousand dollars	Thousand dollars	Thousand dollars	Thousand dollars	Thousand dollars	Thousand dollars	Thousand dollars	Thousand dollars
1929	862,758	543,836	167,058	494,524	83,355	131,116	319,212	159,624	129,877
1933	570,157	365,936	163,002	341,202	63,193	99,702	197,663	93,419 [11]	79,446
1935	761,355	492,846	177,221	401,043	68,799	124,537	209,795	92,760 [11]	84,006
1939 [8]	903,369	566,612	221,658	471,066	76,151	154,297	256,126	121,512 [11]	88,342
1939 [9]	1,002,246	637,749	239,341	499,725	78,262	164,696	263,441	125,607 [11]	89,651
1948	1,391,319	843,740	345,812	685,156	87,203	255,426	456,186	190,551	165,307
1954	1,342,824	735,138	347,997	707,702	101,843	—	440,362	—	163,186
1958	1,406,092	807,898	340,422	749,614	111,153	—	489,654	217,214	169,810
1963	1,513,314	970,956	325,265	718,771	105,945	249,278	428,883	199,510	126,693
1967	1,696,237	1,175,402	297,346	741,706	—	261,224	487,372	205,610	191,150
1972	1,907,898	1,437,102	297,490	854,097	136,173	315,306	535,029	233,233	199,402
1977	2,034,378	1,644,098	221,328	902,362	130,163	345,432	595,284	241,153	220,711
1982	1,839,158	1,515,414	160,565	978,849	188,719	363,331	542,635	213,875	204,876
1987	2,003,181	1,651,465	120,684	1,121,011	205,237	418,972 [10]	702,583	246,772	279,995
1992	2,078,530	1,719,276	115,861	1,144,587	184,415	423,022 [10]	702,164	232,668	288,792
1997	2,507,540	1,795,577	—	1,280,153	185,803	305,685 [10]	482,845	251,300	423,832

	Automotive establishments					Lumber, building, and hardware establishments			
		Passenger car dealers		Tire, battery, and accessory dealers	Gasoline service stations		Lumber and building materials dealers	Hardware stores	Farm equipment dealers
	Total	Franchised	Nonfranchised			Total			
	De164 [2]	De165	De166	De167	De168	De169 [2]	De170	De171	De172
Year	Thousand dollars	Thousand dollars	Thousand dollars	Thousand dollars	Thousand dollars	Thousand dollars	Thousand dollars	Thousand dollars	Thousand dollars
1929	477,510	386,356	10,867	75,147	245,278	405,836	164,571	81,277	43,443
1933	285,817	237,185 [12]	— [12]	44,510	328,263	261,249	97,488	60,886	28,953
1935	356,374	282,638	14,603	56,135	383,623	253,829	101,677	72,130	31,879
1939 [8]	440,536	345,771	19,789	72,025	467,002	318,051	149,275	85,471	36,646
1939 [9]	451,404	353,757	20,552	74,224	478,075	323,396	152,959	86,707	35,831
1948	711,200	556,668	49,841	90,384	482,486	566,626	227,722	149,182	94,182
1954	788,246	623,740	56,552	91,292	558,449	540,326	232,329	143,323	99,825
1958	803,872	593,996	72,332	108,701	699,472	544,677	237,717	136,249	100,864
1963	871,525	630,817	72,857	131,141	732,542	473,759	205,927	114,058	92,437
1967	992,368	785,868 [13]	— [13]	158,799	800,331	476,186	—	108,028	103,869
1972	1,094,489	835,283 [13]	— [13]	—	895,281	444,511	—	110,769	—
1977	1,190,005	869,120 [13]	— [13]	—	789,447	518,327	264,514	128,944	—
1982	1,051,174	—	—	223,160	603,886	504,157	264,849	126,959	—
1987	1,373,238	—	—	259,770	701,690	668,448	379,984	137,860	—
1992	1,267,533	—	—	255,761 [14]	675,080	522,490	386,260	136,230	—
1997	1,138,995	—	—	477,200 [14]	741,040	624,926	523,636	137,831	—

Notes appear at end of table

(continued)

TABLE De147–182   Persons engaged by retail establishments, by type of business: 1929–1997   *Continued*

					Other retail establishments					
		Drug and proprietary stores	Liquor stores	Fuel and ice dealers	Hay, grain, and feed stores	Jewelry stores	Cigar stores and stands	Florists	Gift, novelty, and souvenir stores	Secondhand stores
	Total									
	De173 [6]	De174	De175	De176 [7]	De177	De178	De179	De180	De181	De182
Year	Thousand dollars	Thousand dollars	Thousand dollars	Thousand dollars	Thousand dollars	Thousand dollars	Thousand dollars	Thousand dollars	Thousand dollars	Thousand dollars
1929	623,879	233,210	—	109,191 [15]	66,072	62,853	67,377	37,889	13,771	33,516
1933	460,180	205,300	5,806	104,858 [15]	—	38,197	39,417	21,297	—	45,305
1935	531,429	207,493	25,234	123,199	28,376	36,805	28,828	28,296	9,655	43,543
1939 [8]	649,479	239,076	39,346	142,694	49,304	48,326	31,173	39,202	13,544	46,814
1939 [9]	664,448	241,969	40,735	149,094	50,321	50,686	31,197	38,635	13,665	48,146
1948	850,640	334,716	82,041	127,215	75,374	89,322	30,658	46,459	26,938	37,917
1954	860,375	354,261	85,244	121,292	75,725	90,908	14,255	50,111	27,538	41,041
1958	969,048	400,754	115,659	135,003	71,669	91,405	12,801	60,601	34,115	47,041
1963	965,734	405,798	129,256	120,891	65,550	79,275	12,551	63,865	31,860	56,688
1967	887,214	450,367	136,509	117,578	—	88,186	13,869	80,705	—	—
1972	989,697	472,472	147,614	110,774	—	101,256	11,935	88,296	57,350	—
1977	1,005,141	476,719	170,742	109,825	—	105,040	9,928	111,086	94,164	—
1982	950,928	496,217	167,286	95,092	—	—	8,980	103,804	—	79,549
1987	1,298,106	573,692	156,519	54,035	—	162,795	6,736	125,048	150,730	68,551
1992	1,335,548	587,943	132,989	81,506	—	147,888	5,530 [16]	122,114	164,311	93,267
1997	1,561,916	703,752	130,635	103,778	—	154,877	14,880 [16]	125,195	208,371	120,428

[1] Two sets of values are presented for some years to reflect changes in the data series.

[2] Total includes subclasses not shown separately.

[3] Beginning with 1967, figures include fish (seafood) markets. Separate figures not available.

[4] Beginning with 1972, includes sales from catalog order desks. Beginning 1992, excludes leased departments.

[5] Beginning with 1967, includes music stores; beginning 1987, computer stores; and beginning 1997, software stores. Beginning with 1992, the radio and television component is called "radio, TV, and other electronics stores."

[6] Calculated as the sum of series De174–182.

[7] Beginning with 1987, fuel dealers only.

[8] Comparable with earlier years.

[9] Comparable with later years.

[10] Women's clothing stores.

[11] Excludes interior decorators.

[12] Nonfranchised dealers combined with franchised dealers.

[13] Nonfranchised dealers combined with franchised dealers.

[14] Includes automotive parts.

[15] Excludes fuel oil dealers.

[16] Tobacco stores and stands.

Source
See the source for Table De73–109.

Documentation
For a general note, see the text for Table De73–109.

TABLE De183–219   Retail establishments, by type of business: 1939–1997   [Establishments with payroll]

Contributed by Daniel M. G. Raff

		Food establishments							
	All retail establishments	Total	Grocery stores	Meat markets	Fruit stores, vegetable markets	Candy, nut, confectionery stores	Bakery product stores	Eating establishments	Drinking establishments
	De183	De184 [1]	De185	De186	De187	De188	De189	De190	De191
Year	Number	Number	Number	Number	Number	Number	Number	Number	Number
1939	1,017,062	—	—	—	—	—	—	—	—
1948	1,118,692	232,532	168,131	—	—	—	—	141,163	104,316
1954	1,124,040	200,468	148,028	14,984	4,648	7,777	15,102	149,996	94,413
1958 [5]	1,185,036	190,074	138,176	16,810	4,323	6,147	14,483	172,701	82,223
1963	1,206,087	178,170	132,129	10,483	3,638	7,121	15,877	180,874	83,067
1967	1,191,546	171,700	128,675	9,243	3,222	6,284	15,711	189,418	81,764
1972	1,264,922	173,084	128,115	10,706	3,127	6,804	15,140	208,889	78,351
1977	—	171,592	126,635	11,066	3,091	4,685	15,949	237,728	—
1982	1,261,698	176,219	128,494	10,995	2,943	5,113	17,580	258,584	61,289
1987	1,626,017	190,706	137,584	11,364	3,271	6,124	21,790	332,611	58,692
1992	1,825,435	180,568	133,263	8,941	2,971	5,029	20,418	377,760	—
1997	1,118,447	148,528	96,542	7,081	3,179	4,473	18,502	423,082	52,825

Notes appear at end of table.

TABLE De183–219　Retail establishments, by type of business: 1939–1997　*Continued*

	General merchandise establishments			Apparel establishments			Furniture, homefurnishings, and appliance establishments		
	Total	Department stores	Variety stores	Total	Shoe stores	Women's ready-to-wear stores	Total	Furniture stores	Household appliance, radio, and television establishments
	De192	De193 [2]	De194	De195 [1]	De196	De197	De198 [1]	De199	De200 [3]
Year	Number	Number	Number	Number	Number	Number	Number	Number	Number
1939	—	—	—	—	—	—	—	—	—
1948	48,758	—	—	85,163	15,248	—	60,275	—	—
1954	50,554	2,761	17,639	97,829	19,723	26,893	65,773	25,475	27,774
1958 [5]	49,698	3,157	18,139	97,664	20,143	26,559	72,929	28,342	28,189
1963	51,417	4,251	20,176	96,015	21,450	26,066	69,393	26,982	24,793
1967	51,770	5,792	19,028	91,430	21,110	27,792	71,264	27,375	25,384
1972	44,409	7,742	18,393	105,717	23,390	33,375	82,473	30,043	34,792
1977	38,353	8,807	14,152	114,813	24,450	39,412	91,742	31,320	38,329
1982	34,145	9,981	10,989	134,137	36,277	44,163	93,734	29,609	48,208
1987	35,434	10,041	10,424	149,435	39,488	53,304 [6]	109,653	32,763	44,904
1992	34,606	11,001	12,561	145,490	37,206	50,174 [6]	110,073	32,478	44,578
1997	36,171	10,366	14,065	156,601	31,399	39,672 [6]	108,098 [7]	31,680	28,789

	Automotive establishments					Lumber, building, and hardware establishments			
		Passenger car dealers		Tire, battery, and accessory dealers	Gasoline service stations		Lumber and building materials dealers	Hardware stores	Farm equipment dealers
	Total	Franchised	Nonfranchised			Total			
	De201 [1]	De202	De203	De204	De205	De206 [1]	De207	De208	De209
Year	Number	Number	Number	Number	Number	Number	Number	Number	Number
1939	—	—	—	—	—	—	—	—	—
1948	72,655	—	—	—	112,372	79,899	—	—	15,944
1954	68,573	39,465	11,362	14,451	120,855	78,507	25,429	25,266	16,399
1958 [5]	71,464	36,869	13,199	15,992	149,004	80,644	27,539	24,522	16,028
1963	75,538	33,145	13,401	21,896	165,863	74,803	25,655	22,189	13,974
1967	76,887	32,898	11,502	22,521	165,190	69,015	24,296	19,339	13,342
1972	85,085	44,312	—	22,395	183,385	62,046	23,062	18,530	3,849
1977	94,800	44,080	—	30,761	146,523	65,788	24,698	19,351	6,921
1982	91,068	38,599	—	36,674	116,188	66,402	25,006	19,870	7,850
1987	102,704	43,268	—	41,590	114,748	73,805	27,497	20,059	10,692
1992	96,373	43,052	—	39,154 [8]	105,334	69,483	25,401	18,984	10,857
1997	49,237	—	—	17,288 [8]	98,846	41,412	25,664	15,748	—

	Other retail establishments									
	Total	Drug and proprietary stores	Liquor stores	Fuel and ice dealers	Hay, grain, and feed stores	Jewelry stores	Cigar stores and stands	Florists	Gift, novelty, and souvenir stores	Secondhand stores
	De210 [4]	De211	De212	De213	De214	De215	De216	De217	De218	De219
Year	Number	Number	Number	Number	Number	Number	Number	Number	Number	Number
1939	—	—	—	—	—	—	—	—	—	—
1948	101,348	47,628	21,282	17,855	—	14,583	—	—	—	—
1954	144,681	49,489	21,926	16,986	13,196	15,548	3,270	10,247	6,063	7,956
1958 [5]	157,312	50,792	28,040	18,557	13,512	15,223	2,680	11,662	7,179	9,667
1963	161,055	50,952	31,860	17,816	11,264	14,265	2,953	13,265	6,798	11,882
1967	158,067	49,079	31,039	16,596	11,625	14,626	2,852	14,587	7,501	10,162
1972	156,146	47,587	33,698	15,276	—	15,956	2,595	16,503	12,618	11,913
1977	170,606	47,169	35,144	14,655	—	19,670	2,293	20,092	17,101	14,482
1982	184,370	49,527	34,861	12,737	—	22,786	2,353	22,393	22,311	17,402
1987	203,915	52,181	35,194	12,743 [9]	—	28,050	1,948	26,683	32,245	14,871
1992	201,869	48,142	31,386	10,973 [9]	—	28,077	1,477 [10]	27,341	34,647	19,826
1997	205,036	43,615	29,613	12,532 [9]	—	28,336	3,884 [10]	26,200	37,285	23,571

Notes appear on next page

(continued)

TABLE De183–219 Retail establishments, by type of business: 1939–1997 *Continued*

[1] Total includes subclasses not shown separately.

[2] Beginning with 1982, excludes leased departments.

[3] Beginning with 1967, includes music stores; beginning 1987, computer stores; and beginning 1997, software stores. Beginning with 1992, the radio and television component is called "radio, TV, and other electronics stores."

[4] Calculated as the sum of series De211–219.

[5] Totals include Alaska and Hawai'i, which are not included in the series on individual kinds of business.

[6] Women's clothing stores.

[7] Sum of "furniture and home furnishings" and "household appliance stores" (SIC codes 57 and 572).

[8] Includes automotive parts.

[9] Fuel dealers only.

[10] Tobacco stores and stands.

Source
See the source for Table De73–109.

Documentation
For a general note, see the text for Table De73–109. For a discussion of Standard Industrial Classification (SIC) codes see the Introduction to Part D.

TABLE De220–224 Chain stores – number of chains, by type of business: 1872–1928

Contributed by Daniel M. G. Raff

| Year(s) | Total (26 lines of merchandise) | Grocery | Drug | Shoes | Ready-to-wear |
| | De220 | De221 | De222 | De223 | De224 |
	Number	Number	Number	Number	Number
1872	1	1	—	—	—
1873	2	1	—	—	—
1874	2	1	—	—	—
1875–1884	3	1	—	—	—
1885	4	2	—	—	—
1886	5	3	—	—	—
1887	6	3	1	—	—
1888	8	4	1	—	—
1889	9	5	1	—	—
1890	10	6	1	—	—
1891	12	7	1	—	—
1892	14	9	1	—	—
1893	17	10	1	—	—
1894	19	11	1	—	—
1895	21	11	1	1	1
1896	25	11	1	1	3
1897	35	14	2	1	4
1898	38	15	3	1	5
1899	42	17	3	2	5
1900	58	21	7	3	5
1901	66	23	9	4	7
1902	87	29	12	6	9
1903	107	36	13	7	10
1904	132	41	16	8	15

| Year(s) | Total (26 lines of merchandise) | Grocery | Drug | Shoes | Ready-to-wear |
| | De220 | De221 | De222 | De223 | De224 |
	Number	Number	Number	Number	Number
1905	154	44	19	9	21
1906	173	45	24	9	23
1907	193	49	25	10	28
1908	212	53	26	12	29
1909	231	59	30	12	31
1910	257	62	36	13	34
1911	292	69	39	17	39
1912	324	78	45	21	44
1913	376	85	52	27	52
1914	450	103	70	36	61
1915	505	112	81	38	73
1916	557	125	80	40	87
1917	607	135	86	44	96
1918	645	148	89	46	104
1919	733	168	101	63	110
1920	808	180	107	79	125
1921	905	198	117	95	137
1922	1,056	232	131	114	165
1923	1,164	249	145	128	184
1924	1,267	270	150	146	201
1925	1,440	301	162	167	231
1926	1,565	310	166	182	258
1927	1,689	335	175	206	281
1928	1,718	315	179	220	294

Source
U.S. Federal Trade Commission, *Chain Stores: Growth and Development of Chain Stores* (72d Congress, 1st session, Senate Document number 100), p. 80.

Documentation
Figures include chains of two or more stores reporting to the Federal Trade Commission or known to that agency. Grocery and meat chains have been combined with grocery chains. Ready-to-wear chains include men's ready-to-wear chains, women's ready-to-wear chains, and men's and women's ready-to-wear chains, but not chains specializing in furnishings, accessories, millinery, and the like, nor dry goods chains, whether carrying apparel or not. Data for each of the twenty-six lines of business shown in the total column are found in the source. The source publication also contains estimates of the number of chain outlets in different years, but such data embody substantial estimating difficulties.

TABLE De225–247   Sales of multiunit retail firms, by kind of business: 1929–1996[1]

Contributed by Daniel M. G. Raff

		Durable goods stores							Nondurable goods stores			
			Automotive		Furniture and appliances		Lumber, building, and hardware				Apparel	
	Total, all stores	Total	Motor vehicle and other automotive dealers	Tire, battery, and accessory dealers	Furniture and homefurnishings stores	Household appliance and radio stores	Total	Lumber and building materials dealers	Total	Total	Mens' and boys' wear stores	Women's apparel and accessory stores
	De225	De226 [2]	De227 [3,4]	De228	De229 [5]	De230 [5]	De231 [3]	De232 [3]	De233 [2]	De234 [2]	De235	De236
Year	Million dollars	Million dollars	Million dollars	Million dollars	Million dollars	Million dollars	Million dollars	Million dollars	Million dollars	Million dollars	Million dollars	Million dollars
1929	10,412	1,683	624	122	235	157	509	488	8,729	1,197	271	413
1933	6,618	528	115	76	86	60	180	162	6,090	589	112	214
1935	8,040	813	168	187	97	65	274	256	7,227	758	141	260
1936	8,960	986	190	208	127	81	351	330	7,974	913	174	326
1937	9,426	1,065	182	225	150	93	381	357	8,361	989	177	371
1938	8,872	931	115	221	126	77	362	339	7,941	913	156	349
1939	9,570	1,024	136	236	151	88	375	350	8,546	992	173	394
1940	10,500	1,157	165	241	175	104	427	385	9,343	1,062	182	428
1941	12,635	1,465	200	293	226	134	552	480	11,170	1,280	229	504
1942	14,376	1,291	79	236	211	101	588	486	13,085	1,594	237	668
1943	14,926	1,316	82	254	224	71	589	478	13,610	1,791	241	843
1944	16,234	1,416	91	270	240	81	636	500	14,818	1,957	264	923
1945	17,280	1,627	96	295	277	112	739	565	15,653	2,090	272	968
1946	22,514	2,510	191	467	436	281	998	715	20,004	2,434	355	1,013
1947	26,958	3,100	262	437	533	417	1,315	962	23,858	2,566	385	1,012
1948	29,737	3,407	287	454	562	465	1,505	1,107	26,330	2,729	366	1,117
1949	29,041	3,240	331	448	519	482	1,336	957	25,801	2,588	342	1,049
1950	31,232	3,863	408	551	592	622	1,561	1,147	27,369	2,588	338	1,042
1951	34,000	3,825	389	575	569	572	1,582	1,147	30,175	2,763	342	1,137
1952	30,120	2,605	—	611	317	383	1,224	785	27,515	2,068	214	834
1953	30,929	2,580	—	636	321	390	1,155	728	28,349	2,079	205	821
1954	31,690	2,582	—	609	346	378	1,178	750	29,108	2,041	187	794
1955	33,918	2,790	—	700	347	366	1,300	838	31,128	2,166	186	852
1956 [10]	36,291	2,836	—	732	—	784	1,316	818	33,455	2,249	175	863
1956 [11]	39,754	3,097	—	763	—	953	1,131	810	36,657	2,616	219	1,093
1957	41,900	3,031	—	815	—	924	1,053	723	38,868	2,696	232	1,141
1958	43,853	3,146	—	867	—	957	1,098	765	40,707	2,805	223	1,198
1959	46,673	3,365	—	973	—	965	1,192	825	43,308	3,046	231	1,302
1960 [12]	48,603	3,960	—	980	—	970	—	—	44,643	3,144	228	1,337
1960 [13]	50,681	3,985	—	990	—	999	—	—	46,696	3,515	348	1,414
1961	52,531	4,013	—	1,001	—	1,050	—	—	48,518	3,567	357	1,442
1962	55,576	4,271	—	1,087	—	1,070	—	—	51,305	3,683	351	1,490
1963	58,280	4,469	—	1,098	—	1,115	—	—	53,811	3,796	355	1,607
1964 [14]	63,191	5,032	—	1,196	—	1,246	—	—	58,159	4,145	387	1,757
1964 [15]	68,306	5,320	—	1,242	—	1,126	—	—	62,986	4,287	531	1,622
1965	73,356	5,506	—	1,312	—	1,193	—	—	67,850	4,445	557	1,656
1966	80,323	5,979	—	1,472	—	1,276	—	—	74,344	4,770	573	1,779
1967	85,203	6,184	—	1,529	—	1,362	—	—	79,019	5,069	612	1,855
1968 [16]	94,194	5,415	—	1,736	—	1,303	—	—	88,779	5,186	767	1,837
1969	103,070	5,892	—	1,816	—	1,354	—	—	97,178	5,921	905	2,090
1970 [17]	110,848	5,750	—	1,747	—	1,281	—	—	105,098	6,191	852	2,250
1970 [18]	117,245	8,617	—	1,827	—	1,508	—	—	108,628	5,475	819	1,875
1978	283,781	22,169	3,240	—	—	—	—	—	261,612	14,874	—	6,430
1979	309,398	24,344	3,438	—	—	—	—	—	285,054	16,031	—	6,894
1980	338,028	25,023	3,606	—	—	—	—	—	313,005	17,060	—	7,274
1981	372,443	27,216	3,846	—	—	—	—	—	345,227	18,798	—	7,960
1982	388,984	28,212	4,059	—	—	—	—	—	360,772	20,143	—	8,443
1983	415,631	32,795	4,416	—	—	—	—	—	382,836	22,237	—	9,547
1984	450,430	37,697	4,687	—	—	—	—	—	412,733	25,354	—	11,070
1985	472,244	40,049	4,895	—	—	—	—	—	432,195	28,120	—	12,392
1986	554,802	59,217	6,526	—	—	—	—	—	485,585	39,591	—	15,171
1987	583,102	68,181	7,220	—	—	—	—	—	514,921	43,148	—	16,091
1988	627,071	78,665	7,850	—	—	—	—	—	548,406	47,202	—	16,612
1989	679,919	86,540	8,560	—	—	—	—	—	593,379	53,337	—	18,416

Notes appear at end of table

(continued)

TABLE De225–247 Sales of multiunit retail firms, by kind of business: 1929–1996 *Continued*

		Durable goods stores							Nondurable goods stores			
		Automotive		Furniture and appliances		Lumber, building, and hardware			Apparel			
	Total, all stores	Total	Motor vehicle and other automotive dealers	Tire, battery, and accessory dealers	Furniture and homefurnishings stores	Household appliance and radio stores	Total	Lumber and building materials dealers	Total	Total	Mens' and boys' wear stores	Women's apparel and accessory stores
	De225	De226 [2]	De227 [3,4]	De228	De229 [5]	De230 [5]	De231 [3]	De232 [3]	De233 [2]	De234 [2]	De235	De236
Year	Million dollars	Million dollars	Million dollars	Million dollars	Million dollars	Million dollars	Million dollars	Million dollars	Million dollars	Million dollars	Million dollars	Million dollars
1990	733,429	96,481	9,600	—	—	—	—	—	636,948	57,955	—	19,523
1991	758,823	99,428	9,686	—	—	—	—	—	659,395	60,981	—	20,344
1992	804,807	109,573	10,323	—	—	—	—	—	695,288	65,548	—	21,969
1993	847,248	120,515	11,019	—	—	—	—	—	726,733	68,785	—	22,939
1994	901,056	138,353	11,986	—	—	—	—	—	762,703	72,190	—	22,336
1995	945,418	152,000	12,940	—	—	—	—	—	793,418	73,075	—	21,617
1996 [19]	990,747	163,594	14,000	—	—	—	—	—	827,153	75,413	—	20,576

		Nondurable goods stores									
	Apparel			Food				General merchandise stores			
	Family and other apparel stores	Shoe stores	Drug and proprietary stores	Eating and drinking places	Total	Grocery stores	Gasoline service stations	Total	Department stores, excluding mail order	Mail order (catalog sales)	Variety stores
	De237 [3,6]	De238	De239	De240 [7]	De241	De242	De243 [3]	De244 [2]	De245 [8,9]	De246 [3]	De247
Year	Million dollars	Million dollars	Million dollars	Million dollars	Million dollars	Million dollars	Million dollars	Million dollars	Million dollars	Million dollars	Million dollars
1929	144	369	312	299	3,475	2,833	605	2,275	1,013	447	815
1933	41	222	267	182	2,594	2,209	544	1,589	673	220	696
1935	78	279	317	248	2,916	2,468	423	2,124	898	386	801
1936	90	323	352	270	3,083	2,608	403	2,428	1,060	445	878
1937	90	351	378	290	3,170	2,643	375	2,590	1,155	467	917
1938	76	332	377	288	3,110	2,618	316	2,448	1,075	424	900
1939	80	345	400	304	3,340	2,833	288	2,693	1,226	464	952
1940	97	355	425	330	3,635	3,106	294	2,978	1,421	491	1,008
1941	135	412	479	374	4,328	3,729	331	3,666	1,828	621	1,147
1942	182	507	571	439	5,211	4,520	285	4,094	2,050	628	1,325
1943	232	475	654	518	5,111	4,318	234	4,222	2,125	581	1,406
1944	286	484	681	558	5,499	4,657	241	4,621	2,380	609	1,510
1945	329	521	704	593	5,614	4,705	271	4,925	2,630	608	1,559
1946	425	641	830	676	7,259	6,192	357	6,713	3,788	959	1,812
1947	483	686	864	714	9,418	8,284	416	7,916	4,636	1,171	1,937
1948	548	698	869	742	10,493	9,319	470	8,930	5,373	1,301	2,077
1949	517	680	847	721	10,636	9,468	505	8,560	5,159	1,156	2,077
1950	512	696	852	724	11,344	10,140	548	9,300	5,743	1,235	2,143
1951	539	745	905	779	12,921	11,569	609	9,950	6,149	1,284	2,326
1952	378	642	737	622	12,552	11,606	474	8,916	4,002	1,254	2,322
1953	402	651	759	671	13,392	12,404	498	8,962	4,058	1,233	2,350
1954	385	675	760	662	14,345	13,359	538	8,862	4,092	1,130	2,357
1955	404	724	785	707	15,250	14,223	561	9,726	4,575	1,233	2,508
1956 [10]	433	788	836	756	16,546	15,454	625	10,341	4,918	1,306	2,613
1956 [11]	534	770	943	821	16,636	15,895	732	12,805	7,630	—	2,619
1957	523	800	1,032	868	18,221	17,377	—	13,092	7,790	—	2,668
1958	532	852	1,118	871	19,461	18,590	—	13,414	7,939	—	2,779
1959	578	935	1,223	950	20,368	19,502	—	14,521	8,607	—	2,977
1960 [12]	—	992	1,309	999	21,472	20,602	—	14,991	8,839	—	3,053
1960 [13]	—	1,025	1,452	1,115	22,076	21,424	—	15,478	9,374	—	3,018
1961	—	1,030	1,526	1,141	22,774	22,119	—	16,249	9,875	—	3,147
1962	—	1,082	1,640	1,202	23,695	23,046	—	17,568	10,751	—	3,404
1963	—	1,054	1,728	1,253	24,357	23,692	—	19,018	11,817	—	3,542
1964 [14]	—	1,142	1,896	1,446	25,634	24,903	—	21,375	13,361	—	3,928
1964 [15]	—	1,155	2,029	1,677	27,081	26,198	—	23,645	15,807	—	3,770

Notes appear at end of table

TABLE De225-247   Sales of multiunit retail firms, by kind of business: 1929-1996   *Continued*

					Nondurable goods stores						
	Apparel				Food			General merchandise stores			
	Family and other apparel stores	Shoe stores	Drug and proprietary stores	Eating and drinking places	Total	Grocery stores	Gasoline service stations	Total	Department stores, excluding mail order	Mail order (catalog sales)	Variety stores
	De237 [3,6]	De238	De239	De240 [7]	De241	De242	De243 [3]	De244 [2]	De245 [8,9]	De246 [3]	De247
Year	Million dollars	Million dollars	Million dollars	Million dollars	Million dollars	Million dollars	Million dollars	Million dollars	Million dollars	Million dollars	Million dollars
1965	—	1,168	2,300	1,891	28,598	27,627	—	26,112	17,593	—	4,096
1966	—	1,269	2,663	2,222	30,940	29,906	—	28,988	19,653	—	4,593
1967	—	1,367	3,120	2,554	32,241	31,150	—	30,953	20,984	—	5,029
1968 [16]	—	1,335	3,373	2,122	34,707	34,295	—	38,395	26,184	—	4,821
1969	—	1,598	3,777	2,487	37,619	37,163	—	41,997	28,934	—	5,232
1970 [17]	—	1,712	4,307	2,683	40,965	40,557	—	45,302	31,105	—	5,627
1970 [18]	—	1,473	4,358	2,859	44,072	43,183	—	46,102	31,893	—	5,417
1978	3,810	3,116	12,331	14,745	94,216	93,155	—	93,962	80,367	—	5,829
1979	4,087	3,407	14,132	16,311	104,131	102,876	—	100,069	85,803	—	6,256
1980	4,333	3,694	16,137	18,237	115,059	113,630	—	105,982	90,949	—	6,625
1981	4,859	4,119	17,769	20,125	127,517	125,629	—	116,115	99,772	—	6,978
1982	5,414	4,337	19,095	22,138	135,387	133,475	—	119,163	102,857	—	7,091
1983	5,789	4,761	21,582	24,354	141,353	139,424	—	129,045	111,611	—	7,304
1984	6,766	5,099	24,387	26,999	148,957	146,983	—	142,334	123,652	—	7,627
1985	7,764	5,407	26,016	28,404	156,131	154,083	—	148,412	129,184	—	7,553
1986	12,294	8,640	29,397	36,381	168,645	166,390	—	162,775	132,178	—	5,980
1987	14,123	8,940	31,706	39,347	177,273	174,968	—	173,318	141,610	—	5,541
1988	16,145	9,811	33,797	41,375	188,492	185,983	—	183,842	148,601	—	5,550
1989	18,834	11,128	37,680	44,023	201,182	198,422	—	196,506	157,193	—	5,644
1990	21,018	11,835	42,605	45,714	217,230	214,098	—	205,101	162,786	—	5,529
1991	22,985	11,524	45,820	45,099	223,672	220,332	—	214,520	170,115	—	5,319
1992	25,166	12,218	48,109	47,345	223,414	223,338	—	233,533	183,689	—	6,483
1993	26,948	12,639	49,424	50,025	230,467	227,518	—	252,105	197,962	—	6,197
1994	29,511	12,987	51,607	50,904	238,583	235,533	—	271,684	216,283	—	5,504
1995	30,967	12,866	54,472	51,843	248,916	245,590	—	285,862	228,839	—	5,285
1996 [19]	34,140	13,003	58,312	51,722	259,002	255,392	—	298,565	239,585	—	5,849

[1] For 1929-1951, data give sales for firms with four or more stores; for 1952-1991, data give sales for firms with eleven or more stores.

[2] Includes data for kinds of business not shown separately.

[3] When series is not available separately, it continues to be included in total for group.

[4] Category is "Auto and home supply stores" beginning with 1978.

[5] For 1956-1970, furniture and homefurnishings stores (series De229) included with household appliance and radio stores (series De230).

[6] Category is "Family clothing stores" beginning with 1978.

[7] Category is "Eating places" beginning with 1978.

[8] Category is "Department stores" beginning with 1978.

[9] Beginning 1986, excludes leased departments within stores. The source has data that include leased departments.

[10] Old basis; based on the 1948 Census of Business.

[11] New basis; adjusted to reflect the classification, definition, and distribution of firms by size according to the 1954 Census of Business.

[12] Old basis; based on the 1954 Census of Business.

[13] New basis; adjusted to reflect the classification, definition, and distribution of firms by size according to the 1958 Census of Business.

[14] Old basis; based on the 1958 Census of Business.

[15] New basis; adjusted to reflect the classification, definition, and distribution of firms by size according to the 1963 Census of Business.

[16] Data for series De226-247 not comparable with previous years because of industry classification changes and the shift of "nonstore" operations into the General merchandise group.

[17] Old basis; based on the 1963 Census of Business.

[18] New basis; adjusted to reflect the classification, definition, and distribution of firms by size according to the 1967 Census of Business.

[19] Preliminary data.

Sources

U.S. Bureau of Economic Analysis (formerly Office of Business Economics), 1929-1938, unpublished data; 1939-1970, 1971 Business Statistics, p. 64, and unpublished data, except 1970 (new basis) and 1960 (old basis) from U.S. Bureau of the Census, Monthly Retail Trade Reports, January 1961 and December 1971 issues; 1978-1981, U.S. Bureau of the Census, Current Business Reports BR-13-87S, Monthly Retail Trade Survey Revised Retail Sales and Inventories, January 1978-1987; 1982-1996, U.S. Bureau of the Census, Current Business Reports BR/95-RV, Monthly Retail Trade Sales and Inventories, January 1982-1995, December 1996.

Documentation

For 1929-1951, these series were originally designated as "Retail Sales of Chain Stores and Mail-Order Houses" and represent sales of firms with four or more retail stores. Data from the Census of Business for 1929, 1933, 1935, 1939, and 1948 were used as benchmarks. The intercensal estimates were based on sample groups of organizations with four or more stores.

For 1951-1970, the series are based on a sample of firms that operated eleven or more retail units in the most recently available census. Adjustments reflecting changes in industry classification, and in the firms to be included in the sample, were made for 1956 based on 1954 Census results; for 1960 based on the 1958 Census; for 1964 based on the 1963 Census; and for 1970 based on the 1967 Census.

Since no adjustments were made for entries and exits from the "eleven or more" category between censuses, the data shown cannot be subtracted from total retail sales to obtain sales by organizations operating ten or fewer stores.

Series De235. Includes men's and boys' clothing and furnishing stores, and custom tailors.

Series De236. Includes women's ready-to-wear, other apparel, accessory, specialty shops; and furriers.

TABLE De248–267   Retail trade margins, by type of business: 1869–1947

Contributed by Daniel M.G. Raff

Year	All (weighted mean) De248 [1] Percent	Grocery Independent De249 Percent	Grocery Chain De250 Percent	Meat De251 Percent	Country general De252 Percent	Department De253 Percent	Mail order De254 Percent	Dry goods De255 Percent	Variety De256 Percent	Apparel De257 Percent
1869	23.2	18.0	—	—	—	—	—	—	—	21.1
1879	24.1	18.5	—	—	17.5	—	—	18.7	—	23.2
1889	25.1	19.0	—	29.0	17.8	22.2	24.4	19.2	—	25.4
1899	26.2	19.5	—	28.0	18.1	25.6	25.0	21.4	31.0	27.5
1909	27.6	19.5	17.0	26.8	18.7	29.3	25.6	27.0	33.3	29.6
1919	28.0	19.5	18.0	25.8	19.0	32.8	26.2	29.0	34.7	31.8
1929	28.6	19.5	18.5	24.7	18.4	33.4	26.8	28.0	34.7	34.1
1939	29.7	19.0	18.2	23.6	17.9	36.4	27.4	28.0	34.6	36.0
1947	29.7 [2]	18.0	17.5	20.3	17.9	35.6	28.0	28.0	36.0	37.7

Year	Shoes Independent De258 Percent	Shoes Chain De259 Percent	Furniture, independent De260 Percent	Automobile accessories De261 Percent	Filling stations De262 Percent	Coal and lumber De263 Percent	Hardware De264 Percent	Farm implements De265 Percent	Restaurants De266 Percent	Drugs De267 Percent
1869	21.4	—	—	—	—	18.0	—	23.0	—	—
1879	23.1	—	30.0	—	—	18.5	25.2	21.4	—	28.4
1889	24.7	—	30.6	—	—	19.0	23.7	19.6	—	30.2
1899	26.3	—	31.2	—	—	19.5	22.2	18.0	—	31.8
1909	28.0	33.5	31.2	26.5	22.0	20.5	23.6	18.0	52.0	33.6
1919	29.5	32.0	39.0	26.5	14.0	22.5	25.0	19.2	52.4	34.6
1929	31.2	30.5	41.2	29.1	16.5	24.0	26.4	20.6	54.3	34.6
1939	32.9	28.9	41.2	32.6	19.0	25.0	27.8	21.9	56.3	33.0
1947	34.5	27.6	40.0	32.6	19.5	25.8	29.0	23.0	58.0	33.0

[1] Includes classes not shown.

[2] 1948 data.

Source

Harold Barger, *Distribution's Place in the American Economy since 1869* (Princeton University Press, 1955), pp. 57, 60, and 81.

Documentation

The retail margin estimates are shown as a percent of retail value of sales, and include both net profit and expenses of doing business. With regard to the reliability of the data, the source volume notes that "because of the extremely heterogeneous nature of the source material, it is not possible to offer any measures of dispersion within categories for the data." The source concludes, however, that we may "have some confidence that at least the larger differences reported . . . have a real existence."

TABLE De268-290 Retail store sales, by type of business: 1929-1998[1,2]

Contributed by Daniel M. G. Raff

Year	Total, all stores	Durable goods stores								Nondurable goods stores	General merchandise stores		
		Building materials			Automotive		Furniture and appliances						
		Total	Building materials and supply stores	Hardware stores	Motor vehicle and miscellaneous automotive dealers	Auto and home supply stores	Total	Furniture and homefurnishings	Household appliances and electronics	Total	Total	Department stores	Variety stores
	De268	De269	De270	De271	De272	De273	De274[3]	De275	De276	De277	De278	De279[4]	De280
	Million dollars	Million dollars	Million dollars	Million dollars	Million dollars	Million dollars	Million dollars	Million dollars	Million dollars	Million dollars	Million dollars	Million dollars	Million dollars
1929	48,459	15,610	2,621	706	6,432	599	2,755	1,813	942	32,849	9,015	3,903	904
1933	24,517	5,384	854	311	2,142	226	959	646	313	19,133	4,982	—	756
1935	32,791	8,321	1,105	467	3,863	374	1,290	852	438	24,470	5,730	2,833	873
1936	38,339	10,751	1,463	576	5,102	457	1,615	1,082	533	27,588	6,366	—	967
1937	42,150	12,048	1,739	651	5,568	499	1,846	1,254	592	30,102	6,673	—	1,025
1938	38,053	9,475	1,530	563	3,909	457	1,490	1,014	476	28,578	6,145	—	1,015
1939	42,042	11,312	1,761	629	5,025	524	1,733	1,200	533	30,730	6,475	3,872	1,080
1940	46,375	13,576	2,023	712	6,429	560	2,011	1,386	625	32,799	6,859	4,128	1,153
1941	55,274	17,213	2,442	905	8,185	704	2,576	1,780	796	38,061	7,973	4,862	1,320
1942	57,212	12,320	2,332	973	3,404	623	2,370	1,776	594	44,892	9,204	5,389	1,536
1943	63,235	12,221	2,024	903	3,768	670	2,107	1,692	415	51,014	10,162	5,889	1,642
1944	70,208	13,942	2,102	1,030	4,420	739	2,310	1,848	462	56,266	11,076	6,488	1,774
1945	78,034	16,026	2,502	1,237	5,000	855	2,740	2,101	639	62,008	11,802	7,092	1,845
1946 [5]	104,802	28,231	3,935	1,836	10,912	1,420	5,132	3,366	1,766	76,571	14,755	8,431	2,197
1946 [6]	102,488	27,570	4,106	1,911	10,647	1,275	4,839	3,264	1,575	74,918	14,724	9,183	2,158
1947	122,406	37,542	5,204	2,171	16,198	1,423	6,760	4,167	2,593	84,864	16,088	9,108	2,363
1948	133,619	42,888	6,007	2,398	19,212	1,514	7,356	4,503	2,853	90,731	17,170	9,579	2,556
1949	133,783	44,983	5,648	2,248	22,211	1,417	7,240	4,284	2,956	88,800	16,339	9,083	2,555
1950	147,213	54,275	7,155	2,526	27,405	1,766	8,795	4,997	3,798	92,938	17,275	9,649	2,632
1951	156,548	54,479	7,470	2,738	26,282	1,874	8,604	5,095	3,509	102,069	18,202	10,095	2,859
1952	162,353	55,270	7,572	2,628	26,393	1,944	8,926	5,255	3,671	107,083	18,694	10,277	2,996
1953	169,094	60,371	7,715	2,706	31,498	1,822	9,125	5,136	3,989	108,723	19,006	10,370	3,095
1954	169,135	58,173	7,433	2,702	29,962	1,703	9,079	5,291	3,788	110,962	18,857	10,272	3,027
1955	183,851	66,978	8,242	2,788	36,267	1,959	10,055	6,116	3,939	116,873	20,100	10,882	3,295
1956	189,729	65,810	8,312	2,893	34,050	2,072	10,667	6,568	4,099	123,919	20,762	11,327	3,423
1957	200,002	68,352	7,950	2,737	36,298	2,292	10,584	6,601	3,983	131,650	21,157	—	3,523
1958	200,353	63,409	8,155	2,653	31,577	2,282	10,324	6,636	3,688	136,944	21,667	12,563	3,609
1959	215,413	71,608	9,086	2,737	36,901	2,560	11,042	—	—	143,805	23,420	—	—
1960	219,529	70,560	8,567	2,655	37,038	2,541	10,591	—	—	148,969	24,085	—	—
1961 [5]	218,811	66,968	8,316	2,495	34,523	2,492	10,370	—	—	151,843	—	—	—
1961 [6]	218,992	67,302	8,697	2,358	34,695	2,777	10,078	—	—	151,690	—	—	—
1962	235,563	74,894	9,017	2,401	40,472	3,010	10,497	—	—	166,669	—	—	—
1963	246,666	79,927	9,169	2,399	43,609	3,127	11,267	—	—	166,739	—	—	—
1964	261,870	84,593	9,089	2,505	46,029	3,268	12,724	—	—	177,277	—	22,224	—
1965	284,128	94,186	9,731	2,657	53,484	3,400	13,352	—	—	189,942	—	25,014	—
1966	303,956	98,301	9,769	2,804	54,144	3,945	14,558	—	—	205,655	—	27,868	—
1967 [5]	313,809	100,173	9,781	2,894	53,966	4,307	15,267	—	—	213,636	—	29,589	—
1968 [5]	341,876	111,210	11,107	3,180	61,021	4,695	16,749	10,256	5,409	230,666	49,039	33,065	6,110
1969 [5]	357,855	115,517	11,630	3,367	63,091	5,126	17,291	10,523	5,693	242,368	52,351	35,659	6,426

(continued)

Notes appear at end of table

TABLE De268–290   Retail store sales, by type of business: 1929–1998   *Continued*

		Durable goods stores								Nondurable goods stores			
			Building materials		Automotive		Furniture and appliances				General merchandise stores		
	Total, all stores	Total	Building materials and supply stores	Hardware stores	Motor vehicle and miscellaneous automotive dealers	Auto and home supply stores	Total	Furniture and homefurnishings	Household appliances and electronics	Total	Total	Department stores	Variety stores
	De268	De269	De270	De271	De272	De273	De274 [3]	De275	De276	De277	De278	De279 [4]	De280
Year	Million dollars	Million dollars	Million dollars	Million dollars	Million dollars	Million dollars	Million dollars	Million dollars	Million dollars	Million dollars	Million dollars	Million dollars	Million dollars
1970 [5]	375,527	114,288	11,995	3,351	59,388	5,578	17,778	10,483	6,073	261,239	55,812	37,295	6,959
1971 [5]	408,850	131,814	13,733	3,645	72,538	6,378	18,560	11,004	6,221	277,036	62,242	42,027	6,972
1972 [5]	448,379	149,659	15,973	4,091	81,521	7,091	21,315	12,550	7,029	298,720	68,936	46,560	7,498
1973 [5]	503,317	170,275	18,049	4,717	92,768	7,895	24,030	14,290	7,904	333,042	76,938	52,292	8,212
1974 [5]	537,782	167,313	18,328	5,163	84,773	8,316	25,544	15,364	8,006	370,649	82,535	55,871	8,714
1967 [6]	297,084	92,298	9,025	2,596	51,678	4,416	13,605	8,138	4,561	204,786	40,124	29,183	4,889
1968 [6]	329,336	106,023	10,370	2,841	59,426	4,888	15,257	9,309	5,005	223,313	44,019	32,341	5,302
1969 [6]	352,457	113,562	11,000	3,000	62,323	5,422	16,152	10,012	5,220	238,895	46,559	34,754	5,597
1970 [6]	374,989	114,586	11,343	2,979	59,243	5,998	17,043	10,442	5,571	260,403	49,163	36,187	6,082
1971 [6]	413,969	135,113	13,070	3,230	73,747	6,971	18,183	11,439	5,634	278,856	54,365	40,472	6,111
1972 [6]	458,267	155,937	15,112	3,620	84,477	7,858	21,199	13,480	6,274	302,330	59,656	44,451	6,598
1973 [6]	511,570	176,817	17,314	4,187	96,121	8,772	24,244	15,430	7,210	334,753	65,825	49,342	7,207
1974 [6]	541,686	172,497	17,874	4,604	88,310	9,241	25,982	18,544	7,427	369,189	69,540	52,059	7,594
1975	587,704	185,479	17,947	5,165	97,275	10,073	27,046	16,460	8,218	402,225	73,759	55,702	7,893
1976	655,859	219,908	22,484	5,591	119,063	11,116	30,300	18,383	9,129	435,951	79,500	61,500	7,101
1977	722,109	249,078	27,123	6,139	150,129	13,095	33,308	20,384	10,046	473,031	87,824	68,856	6,987
1978	804,019	280,899	31,910	6,652	168,065	14,165	36,832	22,538	10,780	523,120	97,215	76,137	7,176
1979	896,561	306,561	36,245	7,937	152,458	16,183	42,417	25,642	12,936	590,000	103,817	81,161	7,770
1980	956,921	298,618	34,997	8,349	146,190	17,959	44,238	26,332	14,010	658,303	108,955	85,464	7,791
1981	1,038,163	324,211	35,738	8,475	162,271	19,632	46,900	27,499	15,402	713,952	120,534	95,638	8,202
1982	1,068,747	335,587	35,144	8,727	172,359	20,081	46,761	27,093	15,774	733,160	124,624	99,841	8,211
1983	1,170,163	390,849	41,256	9,140	207,871	22,108	54,691	31,296	19,280	779,314	135,959	108,637	8,367
1984	1,286,914	454,481	47,127	10,354	250,193	23,127	61,432	35,587	21,474	832,433	150,283	120,487	8,700
1985	1,375,027	498,125	50,766	10,471	277,995	25,204	68,287	38,270	25,147	876,902	158,636	126,412	8,459
1986	1,449,636	540,688	56,510	10,734	301,083	25,055	75,714	43,030	27,037	908,948	169,397	134,486	7,447
1987	1,541,299	575,863	61,302	11,036	316,274	26,622	78,072	44,477	27,121	965,436	181,970	144,017	7,134
1988	1,656,202	629,154	66,796	11,894	343,217	29,353	85,390	47,617	30,608	1,027,048	192,521	151,523	7,458
1989	1,758,971	657,154	67,457	12,637	356,485	29,526	91,301	51,202	32,666	1,101,817	206,306	160,524	7,936
1990	1,844,611	668,835	70,341	12,524	356,764	30,841	91,545	50,524	33,035	1,175,776	215,514	165,808	8,306
1991	1,855,937	649,974	68,196	12,148	343,018	29,629	91,676	49,469	33,569	1,205,963	226,730	172,922	8,341
1992	1,951,589	703,604	75,358	12,729	377,118	29,817	96,947	52,348	35,802	1,247,985	246,420	186,423	9,516
1993	2,083,029	782,264	83,435	13,066	428,636	30,681	105,545	54,741	41,397	1,300,765	264,147	199,845	9,729
1994	2,250,033	887,443	95,209	13,852	492,662	32,717	119,171	59,013	49,745	1,362,590	282,332	217,499	9,464
1995	2,361,793	948,652	99,181	13,793	529,138	33,729	128,437	60,790	56,572	1,413,141	297,996	231,303	9,750
1996	2,506,141	1,020,861	106,859	13,989	573,557	35,224	135,149	63,887	59,792	1,485,280	313,342	244,783	10,481
1997	2,615,669	1,066,087	114,187	14,039	597,069	35,816	140,776	67,537	61,735	1,549,582	330,216	259,985	11,120
1998	2,746,011	1,138,286	124,365	14,630	631,689	36,969	152,044	71,377	68,532	1,607,725	351,436	276,697	11,480

		Food			Apparel and accessories						
	Total	Grocery stores	Gasoline service stations	Total	Men's and boys' clothing and furnishings	Women's clothing and accessories	Shoe stores	Eating and drinking places	Drug and proprietary stores	Liquor stores
	De281	De282	De283	De284	De285	De286	De287	De288	De289	De290
Year	Million dollars	Million dollars	Million dollars	Million dollars	Million dollars	Million dollars	Million dollars	Million dollars	Million dollars	Million dollars
1929	10,960	7,353	1,787 [7]	4,241	1,358	1,408	807	2,132	1,690	—
1933	6,772	5,004	1,532	1,930	542	754	425	1,434	1,066	17
1935	8,358	6,352	1,968	2,656	727	1,026	511	2,395	1,233	328
1936	9,008	6,850	2,318	3,102	855	1,205	586	2,748	1,409	475
1937	9,699	7,266	2,641	3,323	878	1,325	636	3,293	1,527	558
1938	9,505	7,187	2,696	2,998	765	1,211	591	3,188	1,474	539
1940	10,732	8,169	2,970	3,451	886	1,388	632	3,787	1,636	681
1939	10,156	7,722	2,822	3,259	840	1,323	617	3,529	1,563	586
1941	12,244	9,312	3,466	4,137	1,076	1,635	726	4,570	1,847	854
1942	14,788	11,368	3,089	5,089	1,268	2,042	914	5,699	2,213	1,212
1943	16,447	12,481	2,628	6,158	1,405	2,670	969	7,216	2,628	1,557
1944	17,918	13,665	2,812	6,704	1,524	2,964	1,001	8,305	2,924	1,926
1945	19,233	14,593	3,284	7,689	1,769	3,338	1,140	9,575	3,155	2,288
1946 [5]	23,315	18,980	4,922	9,054	2,331	3,706	1,417	11,152	3,759	2,823
1946 [6]	24,155	18,640	4,511	8,880	2,195	3,591	1,377	10,619	3,723	2,688
1947	27,577	22,907	5,979	9,467	2,451	3,753	1,487	11,183	3,904	2,782
1948	30,093	25,215	7,077	9,971	2,450	4,086	1,510	11,218	4,050	2,711
1949	30,101	25,248	7,590	9,493	2,317	3,817	1,498	10,994	4,074	2,598
1950	31,889	26,886	8,240	9,485	2,306	3,722	1,556	11,158	4,205	2,669
1951	35,951	30,346	9,151	10,209	2,461	4,049	1,684	12,207	4,547	2,975
1952	38,039	32,238	9,976	10,633	2,497	4,233	1,693	12,688	4,717	3,165
1953	39,130	33,623	10,536	10,256	2,249	4,089	1,736	13,003	4,790	3,325
1954	40,106	34,993	11,443	10,147	2,239	4,009	1,809	13,127	4,940	3,415
1955	42,010	36,919	12,411	10,791	2,294	4,207	2,009	13,662	5,232	3,546
1956	44,223	39,180	13,738	11,610	2,469	4,541	2,068	14,317	5,775	3,944
1957	47,786	42,444	15,070	12,277	2,487	4,914	2,091	14,787	6,325	4,212
1958	50,263	44,547	15,757	12,559	2,349	4,994	2,222	14,792	6,600	4,439
1959	51,739	46,132	16,793	13,239	2,544	5,271	2,330	15,618	7,150	4,743
1960	54,023	48,610	17,588	13,631	2,644	5,295	2,437	16,146	7,538	4,893
1961 [5]	55,739	—	17,959	13,601	—	—	—	16,488	7,752	4,927
1961 [6]	53,398	—	17,007	13,614	—	—	—	15,549	7,629	4,433
1962	55,643	—	17,644	14,164	—	—	—	16,434	7,917	4,892
1963	57,254	—	18,319	14,233	—	—	—	17,194	8,068	5,138
1964	60,224	—	19,196	15,295	—	—	—	18,462	8,476	5,410
1965	64,016	—	20,611	15,765	—	—	—	20,201	9,186	5,674
1966	68,137	—	21,792	17,291	—	—	—	22,098	9,988	6,081
1967 [5]	69,113	—	22,739	18,123	—	—	—	23,473	10,721	6,409
1968 [5]	74,111	68,975	24,801	19,159	4,515	7,389	3,232	25,673	11,581	6,963
1969 [5]	78,312	72,892	25,909	19,866	4,753	7,499	3,618	26,970	12,224	7,384

Nondurable goods stores

Notes appear at end of table

(continued)

TABLE De268–290   Retail store sales, by type of business: 1929–1998   Continued

	Food			Nondurable goods stores						
				Apparel and accessories						
Year	Total	Grocery stores	Gasoline service stations	Total	Men's and boys' clothing and furnishings	Women's clothing and accessories	Shoe stores	Eating and drinking places	Drug and proprietary stores	Liquor stores
	De281	De282	De283	De284	De285	De286	De287	De288	De289	De290
	Million dollars	Million dollars	Million dollars	Million dollars	Million dollars	Million dollars	Million dollars	Million dollars	Million dollars	Million dollars
1970 [5]	86,114	79,756	27,994	19,810	4,630	7,582	3,501	29,689	13,352	7,980
1971 [5]	89,239	82,793	29,163	20,804	4,727	8,193	3,532	31,131	13,736	8,773
1972 [5]	95,020	88,340	31,044	21,993	5,198	8,386	3,774	33,891	14,523	9,215
1973 [5]	105,731	98,392	34,432	24,062	5,609	9,119	4,229	37,925	15,474	9,602
1974 [5]	119,763	111,347	39,910	24,864	5,668	9,551	3,979	41,840	16,785	10,285
1967 [6]	70,456	65,036	22,362	17,900	3,519	6,812	3,606	22,518	11,359	6,652
1968 [6]	75,899	69,873	24,750	19,707	3,916	7,435	4,062	25,279	12,378	7,258
1969 [6]	81,258	74,836	26,301	21,384	4,382	7,842	4,577	27,173	13,200	7,739
1970 [6]	89,990	82,558	28,903	22,095	4,544	8,239	4,458	30,476	14,567	8,412
1971 [6]	94,002	86,419	30,620	24,178	4,903	9,222	4,524	32,321	15,143	9,294
1972 [6]	100,589	92,856	33,072	26,367	5,684	9,739	4,884	35,738	16,139	9,814
1973 [6]	111,817	103,555	36,942	29,109	6,193	10,732	5,600	40,290	17,190	10,288
1974 [6]	126,312	117,182	43,054	30,077	6,190	11,338	5,405	44,606	18,595	11,087
1975	138,665	129,087	47,603	32,398	6,619	12,438	5,751	51,067	19,995	11,896
1976	148,218	137,992	52,037	34,706	6,815	13,426	8,249	57,331	21,710	12,442
1977	158,444	148,116	56,638	37,165	7,042	12,537	7,058	63,370	23,381	13,031
1978	175,425	164,234	59,889	42,649	7,537	15,995	8,305	71,828	25,607	13,630
1979	197,985	185,318	73,521	46,070	7,763	17,030	9,693	82,110	28,455	15,194
1980	220,224	205,630	94,093	49,296	7,664	17,592	10,530	90,058	30,951	16,882
1981	236,188	220,580	103,072	53,998	7,910	19,060	11,821	98,118	33,999	17,702
1982	246,122	230,696	97,440	55,570	7,803	20,017	11,419	104,593	36,440	18,146
1983	256,018	240,402	102,927	60,192	7,958	21,847	11,949	113,281	40,591	19,121
1984	271,909	258,465	107,565	64,341	8,206	23,764	12,306	121,321	44,011	18,273
1985	285,062	269,546	113,341	70,195	8,458	26,149	13,054	127,949	46,994	19,532
1986	297,019	280,833	102,093	75,626	8,646	28,600	13,947	139,415	50,546	19,929
1987	309,461	290,979	104,769	79,322	9,017	29,208	14,594	153,461	54,142	19,826
1988	325,493	307,173	110,341	85,307	9,826	30,567	15,444	167,993	57,842	19,638
1989	347,045	328,072	122,882	92,341	10,507	32,231	17,290	177,829	63,343	20,099
1990	368,333	348,243	138,504	95,819	10,450	32,812	18,043	190,149	70,558	21,722
1991	374,523	354,331	137,295	97,441	10,435	32,865	17,504	194,424	75,540	22,454
1992	377,099	358,148	136,950	104,212	10,197	35,750	18,122	200,164	77,788	21,698
1993	382,930	363,625	141,603	107,588	9,986	36,426	18,509	212,690	79,784	21,561
1994	394,671	374,730	148,673	110,735	10,064	35,117	19,349	221,882	82,156	22,136
1995	403,205	382,378	156,939	111,970	9,353	33,831	19,755	229,526	86,093	22,053
1996	415,390	393,568	168,320	116,101	9,592	34,055	20,609	238,474	92,169	23,216
1997	425,170	402,540	171,527	120,575	10,123	34,222	20,802	253,551	99,301	24,147
1998	438,212	414,667	162,095	126,939	10,922	34,330	21,227	266,544	106,713	25,114

[1] Two sets of values are presented for some years to reflect changes in the data series. See text.

[2] Totals include subclasses not shown separately.

[3] Includes kinds of business not shown separately.

[4] Excludes leased departments.

[5] Comparable with earlier years.

[6] Comparable with later years.

[7] Excludes garages primarily selling gasoline and oil.

TABLE De268–290   Retail store sales, by type of business: 1929–1998   *Continued*

Sources

1929–1938, unpublished data; 1939–1946, *1969 Business Statistics*, pp. 58–59; 1947–1974, *1975 Business Statistics*, pp. 59–60; 1967–1995, *Business Statistics of the United States: 1996 Edition*, pp. 211–12; 1996–1998, *Business Statistics of the United States: Fifth Edition, 1999*, pp. 273–74.

Recent data are available at the Bureau of the Census Internet site.

Documentation

Retail stores are defined as establishments primarily engaged in selling merchandise for personal or household consumption and rendering services incidental to the sales of goods.

Sales figures include multiunit stores. The classification of durable goods stores and nondurable goods stores is based on the durability of the commodities accounting for a major portion of the sales of each kind-of-business group, tabulated under the appropriate classification defined in the Standard Industrial Classification (SIC) manual. See the Introduction to Part D for a discussion of SIC codes. Data from censuses of retail trade were used as benchmarks for annual 1929–1946 data. Estimates for intercensal years in this period were developed from sales tax collection data, special Internal Revenue Service compilations, business population trends, the Federal Reserve Board index of department store sales, and data from the Bureau of Public Roads and the American Petroleum Institute. Methods of compilation are described in *1969 Business Statistics*, p. 58.

Data for 1946–1961 were based on a new method of estimating retail sales and are not comparable with those shown for prior years. Estimates of retail sales were developed from a sample representing all sizes of stores, firms, or organizations, and all kinds of retail business. These data were not linked to a census of retail trade as were the old, a factor that accounts for most of the difference between the levels of retail sales indicated by the old and new series for 1946. In 1957 the data were revised back to January 1951 to exclude milk dealers engaged in processing on the premises. (This change conforms with the treatment of such establishments as manufacturing plants in the 1954 Census of Business.)

Data for 1961–1974 reflect a new sample design and classification changes resulting from the 1963 Census. In addition, data by kind-of-business group were revised by shifting all "nonstore" establishments into the general merchandise group. Nonstore establishments (mail order, house-to-house, and vending machine businesses) were previously shown in such kind-of-business groups as food, eating and drinking places, and furniture and appliance. The sampling procedure for the new series is described in *1971 Business Statistics*.

Data for 1967–1998 reflect classification of business based on the 1972 or 1977 Standard Industrial Classification (SIC) manual and cause these years to be not comparable to earlier years. Methods of benchmarking and adjusting are described in *Business Statistics: 1984*, notes to p. 3.

Series De270. Includes lumber yards; building materials dealers; and paint, plumbing, and electrical stores.

Series De274. Beginning with 1959, includes music stores, not shown separately.

Series De278. Includes nonstores, that is, establishments selling merchandise primarily through coin-operated vending machines, house-to-house canvass, and mail orders. Also includes sales made by mail order catalog desks located within department stores of mail order firms.

TABLE De291–292   Indexes of department store sales and stocks: 1919–1970

Contributed by Daniel M. G. Raff

Year	Sales De291 Index 1957–1959 = 100	Stocks De292 Index 1957–1959 = 100	Year	Sales De291 Index 1957–1959 = 100	Stocks De292 Index 1957–1959 = 100	Year	Sales De291 Index 1957–1959 = 100	Stocks De292 Index 1957–1959 = 100
1919	18	23	1940	25	24	1960	106	109
1920	22	30	1941	29	29	1961	109	110
1921	20	26	1942	33	40	1962	118	121
1922	20	26	1943	37	34	1963	127	135
1923	23	29	1944	41	36	1964	142	150
1924	23	30	1945	46	37	1965	160	166
1925	24	30	1946	60	48	1966	179	192
1926	24	30	1947	66	59	1967	190	213
1927	25	30	1948	70	67	1968	212	231
1928	25	30	1949	67	62	1969	230	250
1929	25	30	1950	72	69	1970	239	279
1930	24	28	1951	76	82			
1931	21	24	1952	77	76			
1932	16	20	1953	80	82			
1933	16	18	1954	80	80			
1934	18	20	1955	87	85			
1935	19	20	1956	94	95			
1936	20	21	1957	96	99			
1937	23	24	1958	98	97			
1938	21	22	1959	105	103			
1939	23	22						

Source

Board of Governors of the Federal Reserve System, unpublished data.

Documentation

The index for sales is based on the average per trading day. The stocks index is the annual average of monthly data of end-of-month stocks.

TABLE De293–344   Selected service establishments and receipts, by type of business: 1929–1992[1]

Contributed by Daniel M. G. Raff

	Establishments		Receipts							Active proprietors of unincorporated businesses
			All establishments	Establishments with payroll		Establishments without payroll		Annual payroll	Paid employees	
	Number	With payroll		Total	Average per establishment	Total	Average per establishment			
	De293	De294	De295	De296	De297	De298	De299	De300	De301 [2]	De302
Year	Number	Number	Million dollars	Million dollars	Dollars	Million dollars	Dollars	Million dollars	Thousand	Thousand
1929	—		—	—		—		—	—	—
1933	502,416	—	2,761	—	—	—	—	702	657 [7]	546
1935	631,309	—	3,001	—	—	—	—			
1939 [4]	646,028	—	3,420	—	—	—	—	1,070	1,102 [7]	652
1939 [5]	656,482	—	4,872	—	—	—	—	1,384	1,497	651
1948 [6]	665,475	—	13,296	12,164	32,879	1,132	3,830	4,164	2,100	667
1948 [5]	617,002	—	13,230	—	—	—	—	—	—	—
1954	785,589	375,149	23,508	21,263	56,680	2,245	5,469	6,534	2,362	782
1958	975,250	442,584	32,376	29,001	65,526	3,375	6,336	9,006	2,889	992
1963	1,061,673	504,356	44,586	41,023	81,338	3,563	6,393	12,192	3,262	1,017
1967	1,187,814	521,410	60,542	55,527	106,494	5,015	7,526	17,524	3,841	1,082
1972	1,590,248	683,614	112,970	103,237	151,017	9,733	10,735	33,424	5,305	—
1977	1,834,713	725,096	179,515	164,219	226,479	15,296	13,785	56,055	6,337	—
1982	—	1,261,698	—	426,982	338,419	—	—	158,625	11,106	—
1987	6,254,512	1,626,017	868,343	772,194	474,899	96,148	20,773	289,807	16,055	—
1992	8,593,491	1,825,435	1,345,146	1,202,613	658,809	142,533	21,060	452,697	19,290	—

	Personal services									
	Total		Barber, beauty shops		Funeral services, crematories		Shoe repair shops, shoeshine parlors, hat cleaning shops		Photographic studios	
	Number	Receipts	Number	Receipts	Number	Receipts	Number	Receipts	Number	Receipts
	De303 [3]	De304 [3]	De305	De306	De307	De308	De309	De310	De311	De312
Year	Number	Million dollars	Number	Million dollars	Number	Million dollars	Number	Million dollars	Number	Million dollars
1929	—	—	—	—	—	—	—	—	—	—
1933	320,863	1,223	159,905	321	12,655	172	57,452	97	8,330	32
1935	369,081	1,517	186,810	402	17,144	230	61,046	110	10,402	48
1939 [4]	388,918	1,820	205,268	481	18,196	262	59,371	119	10,957	64
1939 [5]	389,726	1,822	—	—	—	—	—	—	—	—
1948 [6]	351,985	4,440	169,081	845	18,675	572	44,151	219	14,712	212
1948 [5]	325,246	4,421	153,764	834	18,480	572	39,275	215	13,788	211
1954	348,843	5,773	169,684	1,206	18,387	744	29,385	202	17,293	334
1958	413,180	7,422	215,451	1,811	20,767	1,016	27,775	232	20,028	423
1963	447,080	9,163	257,236	2,525	20,529	1,299	21,486	208	19,544	495
1967	498,935	11,750	291,706	3,375	20,191	1,517 [9]	16,270	207	26,558	745
1972	503,378	14,050	280,896	3,910	20,854	2,218 [9]	12,924	210	29,973	768
1977	512,140	18,433	264,740	5,226	19,622	2,827	9,608	239	37,092	1,185
1982	167,749 [8]	22,980 [8]	79,160 [8]	5,304 [8]	15,051 [8]	3,737 [8]	2,800 [8]	186 [8]	7,079 [8]	1,409 [8]
1987	1,037,433	43,247	407,272	11,990	22,282	5,668	11,185 [10]	386 [10]	56,165	2,929
1992	1,320,920	59,598	471,643	15,951	25,164	7,588	2,702 [8,10]	276 [8,10]	64,316	4,280

Notes appear at end of table

TABLE De293–344   Selected service establishments and receipts, by type of business: 1929–1992   *Continued*

Personal services

	Laundry, cleaning, and garment services								Miscellaneous business services			
	Total		Dry cleaning plants		Coin-operated laundry and dry cleaning		Power laundries		Total		Advertising	
	Number	Receipts	Number	Receipts	Number	Receipts	Number	Receipts	Number	Receipts	Number	Receipts
	De313 [3]	De314 [3]	De315	De316	De317	De318	De319	De320	De321 [3]	De322 [3]	De323	De324
Year	Number	Million dollars	Number	Million dollars	Number	Million dollars	Number	Million dollars	Number	Million dollars	Number	Million dollars
1929	—	—	—	—	—	—	—	—	—	—	—	—
1933	79,907	587	3,864	98	—	—	5,122	296	36,442	469	1,479	190
1935	90,335	713	6,910	141	—	—	6,470	370	29,859	510	1,212 [11]	71 [11]
1939 [4]	90,048	874	12,616	193	—	—	6,773	454	26,188	487	1,628 [11]	97 [11]
1939 [5]	—	—	—	—	—	—	—	—	—	—	—	—
1948 [6]	101,127	2,533	25,534	844	8,523	65	6,783	913	32,007	1,630	5,986	652
1948 [5]	96,106	2,530	25,313	844	7,844	65	6,770	913	27,251	1,030	5,910	652
1954	106,520	3,180	29,200	1,138	—	—	9,612 [8]	914 [8]	88,661	6,317	8,239	3,498
1958	107,204	3,708	34,311	1,357	—	—	11,262 [8]	1,022 [8]	114,450	9,919	12,180	4,926
1963	109,740	4,357	33,580	1,511	26,153	373	10,050 [8]	1,040 [8]	147,668	15,193	12,896	6,384
1967	111,926	5,432	31,519 [8]	2,004 [8]	29,551	557	6,350 [8]	942 [8]	211,835	22,595	20,124	8,342
1972	97,340	5,800	28,422 [8]	1,759 [8]	31,642	879	3,094 [8]	670 [8]	326,077	37,802	28,440	10,605
1977	75,355	6,829	21,868 [8]	1,896 [8]	24,260	1,082	2,433 [8]	613 [8]	458,232	54,500	32,931	4,983
1982	43,912 [8]	9,324 [8]	20,202 [8]	2,873 [8]	10,943 [8]	1,168 [8]	2,145 [8]	699 [8]	215,125 [8]	106,866 [8]	12,950 [8]	8,325 [8]
1987	108,602	14,184	21,257 [8]	3,998 [8]	27,180	2,132	2,114 [8]	821 [8]	1,433,163	188,856	79,230	16,802
1992	124,436	18,805	23,213 [8]	5,067 [8]	29,067	2,931	1,853 [8]	867 [8]	2,056,212	309,439	91,586	22,673

Automobile repair, garage, and other services

	Total		Automobile repair shops		Automobile truck rentals (without drivers)		Automobile storage, parking		Automobile laundries	
	Number	Receipts	Number	Receipts	Number	Receipts	Number	Receipts	Number	Receipts
	De325 [3]	De326 [3]	De327	De328	De329	De330	De331	De332	De333	De334
Year	Number	Million dollars	Number	Million dollars	Number	Million dollars	Number	Million dollars	Number	Million dollars
1929	—	—	—	—	—	—	—	—	—	—
1933	100,149	585	93,760 [12]	550 [12]	381	5	5,275	27	733	2
1935	92,471	538	79,553	433	765	16	11,246	87	907	3
1939 [4]	78,881	441	66,178	316	648	20	11,095	102	960	3
1939 [5]	—	—	—	—	—	—	—	—	—	—
1948 [6]	95,444	1,561	84,875	1,272	1,011	84	8,533	190	792	10
1948 [5]	90,762	1,558	80,705	1,269	994	84	8,033	190	717	10
1954	94,342	2,223	79,709	1,589	2,872	278	8,572	292	1,657	44
1958	125,691	3,869	103,724	2,759	4,714	616	10,998	366	2,660	90
1963	139,611	5,444	114,459	3,588	4,323 [8]	1,187 [8]	11,269	416	2,338 [8]	139 [8]
1967	139,243	7,028	109,946	4,086	5,832 [8]	2,060 [8]	10,606	484	3,918 [8]	236 [8]
1972	168,959	12,081	127,203	7,045	10,474	3,559	10,505	725	6,267 [8]	429 [8]
1977	200,153	21,576	154,194	12,770	12,385	6,407	8,872	1,008	5,785 [8]	669 [8]
1982	115,481 [8]	30,695 [8]	88,445 [8]	17,904 [8]	9,024 [8]	9,642 [8]	8,256 [8]	1,576 [8]	5,868 [8]	861 [8]
1987	388,159	58,278	301,284	34,182	19,926	16,679	10,518	2,691	9,132 [8]	1,802 [8]
1992	454,317	78,512	334,480	46,200	22,230	20,906	11,830	3,744	11,589 [8]	2,644 [8]

Notes appear at end of table

(continued)

TABLE De293–344 Selected service establishments and receipts, by type of business: 1929–1992 *Continued*

Year	Miscellaneous repair services				Hotels, tourist courts, motels, trailer parks, and camps		Motion pictures		Amusement recreation services, except motion pictures	
	Total		Electrical repair shops							
	Number	Receipts	Number	Receipts	Number	Receipts	Number	Receipts	Number	Receipts
	De335 [3]	De336 [3]	De337	De338	De339	De340	De341	De342	De343	De344
	Number	Million dollars	Number	Million dollars	Number	Million dollars	Number	Million dollars	Number	Million dollars
1929	—	—	—	—	3,328 [15]	963 [15]	—	—	—	—
1933	53,010	91	6,892 [14]	17 [14]	29,462 [16]	516 [16]	10,265	415	19,472	105
1935	71,426 [13]	148 [13]	10,131	23	38,670	744	12,024	508	25,653	191
1939 [4]	72,130	195	15,644	48	41,508	900	15,115	673	29,802	325
1939 [5]	75,262	224	15,644	48	41,508	900	—	—	—	—
1948 [6]	80,023	947	19,440	215	55,569	2,368	18,631	1,614	31,716	735
1948 [5]	71,338	941	17,076	213	52,518	2,366	18,532	1,353	30,630	1,058
1954	113,429	1,796	32,195	502	66,962	3,027	20,843	2,352	52,509	2,021
1958	145,163	2,270	51,269	763	85,890	3,924	19,657	2,431	75,164	2,673
1963	146,116	3,022	61,186	1,116	84,706	5,049	16,381	2,583	79,451	3,990
1967	138,014	3,827	47,886	1,329	87,006	7,039	16,752	3,476	96,029	4,827
1972	148,925	5,855	53,357	2,142	79,685	10,638	21,254	4,753	124,729	8,692
1977	162,910	11,028	52,468	3,581	70,713	18,453	22,539	8,017	154,246	13,126
1982	54,421 [8]	14,133 [8]	16,703 [8]	4,108 [8]	41,231 [8]	33,125 [8]	17,249 [8]	13,693 [8]	49,966 [8]	19,422 [8]
1987	247,597	24,597	65,676	7,584	85,739	53,630	78,975	31,811	388,057	32,713
1992	269,751	35,237	71,611	11,875	92,882	71,038	103,948	51,543	587,787	52,013

[1] 1972–1982 data based on 1972 Standard Industrial Classification; 1987 and later data based on 1987 Standard Industrial Classification.

[2] Paid employees for week including March 12 for 1967 and later years. Workweek ended nearest November 15 for earlier years.

[3] Includes subclasses not shown separately.

[4] Comparable with earlier years. Data for series De305–334 comparable with both earlier and later years.

[5] Comparable with later years.

[6] Comparable with earlier years.

[7] Average annual number of full-time and part-time employees.

[8] Establishments with payroll only.

[9] Includes repayment of cash advances which are not part of the cost of the complete funeral service.

[10] Excludes hat cleaning shops.

[11] For advertising agencies only.

[12] Covers only general repair garages, paint shops, radiator shops, top and body repair shops, tire repair shops, and brake repair shops.

[13] Includes boat repair shops not included in other years.

[14] Excludes refrigerator repair and washing machine repair establishments.

[15] Limited to hotels with twenty-five or more guest rooms.

[16] Hotels only.

Sources

U.S. Bureau of the Census. 1929, unpublished data; 1933, *Census of American Business: 1933*, U.S. Summaries; 1935, *Census of Business: 1935, Service Establishments*, volume 1, *U.S. Summary and Census of Business: 1935*, Miscellaneous; 1939, *Census of Business: 1939*, volume 3, *Service Establishments*; 1948, *Census of Business: 1948*, volume 6, *Service Trade – General Statistics*; 1954, *Census of Business: 1954*, volume 5, *Selected Service Trades – Summary Statistics*; 1958, *Census of Business: 1958*, volume 5, *Selected Services – Summary Statistics*; 1963, *Census of Business: 1963*, volume 6, *Selected Services – Summary Statistics*; 1967, *Census of Business: 1967*, volume 5, *Selected Services – Area Statistics*, part 1; 1972, *Census of Service Industries: 1972*, volume 1, *Summary and Subject Statistics*; 1977, *Census of Service Industries*, volume 1, *Subject Statistics*; 1982, *Census of Service Industries: 1982, Industry Series*; 1987, *Census of Service Industries: 1987, Nonemployer Statistics Series*; 1992, *Census of Service Industries: 1992, Nonemployer Statistics Series*.

Documentation

Certain series have been combined for some years in order to provide as comparable historical series as possible. For some of the series, as noted in the following, data for some years were collected in other census programs. The series presented here cover that very limited segment of the services sector which bears greatest similarity to retail trade, specifically, personal, repair, and automotive services; hotels; and motels.

There have been numerous changes in enumeration methods, in accuracy, and in classifications over the years. The principal ones are noted here; others can be noted by reference to the various census volumes. The 1954 and later censuses were conducted by mail canvasses of firms included in the active records of the Internal Revenue Service as subject to the payment of Federal Insurance Contributions Act (FICA) taxes and that were in appropriate kind-of-business classifications. Such data cover only firms with paid employees. The nonemployer segment was derived from a 50 percent sample of 1954, 1958, and 1963 tax returns. In the 1967 Census, data for all nonemployers were compiled from tax records. The 1948 and earlier censuses were conducted by field enumeration. The differences in enumeration methods affect particularly the coverage of establishments without easily recognizable places of business and those leaving business prior to the end of the year. The 1954–1967 data are thus more complete in those areas. The 1933 and 1935 censuses were not taken under mandatory reporting requirements and may therefore be subject to some underenumeration. There are important gaps in enumerators' reports for 1933 so that substantial underenumeration, particularly of the smaller establishments, exists for 1933. Underenumerations have more effect on the number of establishments than on receipts.

In the 1963 and 1967 Censuses, nonemployer establishments that did not operate the entire year have been included if, during the period they operated, their receipts were at a rate which would have reached an annual total of $1,000 or more had they operated for the entire year. Establishments without paid employment and with less than $1,000 receipts were excluded in 1954 and 1958 tabulations. The data for 1948 (comparable with later years) show 1948 figures adjusted to this cutoff point. The data for 1948 (comparable with earlier years) exclude establishments that operated the entire year but had receipts less than $500. For 1939 and earlier years, establishments having receipts of $100 or more are included (except as noted). Where two estimates are shown for 1939, the figures for 1939 (comparable with later years) represent a revision to conform to 1948 kind-of-business definitions.

Receipts for 1954 and later years include sales and excise taxes; receipts for 1948 and 1939 exclude them.

Data for establishments without payroll are not available for 1982 because many businesses were misclassified by the IRS into miscellaneous categories rather than being classified into the specific kind of business. Numbers are reported for establishments with payroll only.

Establishments are classified according to their principal kinds of business. Changes in relative importance may thus serve to shift particular establishments among service categories or between service and retailing

TABLE De293–344   Selected service establishments and receipts, by type of business: 1929–1992   *Continued*

classifications from one census to another. Many service establishments derive some receipts from sales of merchandise; conversely, many establishments primarily engaged in the sale of goods, and hence included in retail trade, obtain some income from services. Receipts reported in each case *represent total receipts of establishments comprising the classification*, not receipts for the particular service indicated.

Series De303–304, total personal services. Data for 1933 and 1935 represent groupings that correspond most closely to the 1939 scope.

Series De311–312, photographic studios. Since the 1954–1967 data were obtained by mail canvass, they are believed to be substantially more complete than data for earlier years. For this industry, nonrecognizable establishments are likely to result in substantial underenumeration in a field canvass.

Series De313–318, laundry, cleaning, and garment services. Included in series De313 are power laundries, cleaning plants, press shops, linen supply, diaper service, industrial launderers, garment repair, and hand laundries. For 1933 and 1935, power laundries and dry cleaning plants with receipts of less than $5,000 were omitted. While series De315 does not include the count of outlets owned and operated by dry cleaning plants, series De316 does include the receipts of such outlets.

Series De319–320. Data prior to 1933 for establishments and receipts, respectively, are as follows (receipts in mil. dol.): 1914, 6,097 and 142.1; 1919 (comparable with 1914), 5,678 and 236.1; 1919 (comparable with later years), 4,881 and 233.8; 1925, 4,859 and 362.3; 1927, 6,013 and 454.0; 1929, 6,776 and 541.2; 1931, 6,400 and 466.0.

Series De327–328, automobile repair shops. Data for 1935 include specialized shops as enumerated in the census of service establishments, and general repair garages as enumerated in the *1935 Census of Business, Retail Distribution*, Table 1A. Data for 1933 cover only general repair garages, as enumerated in the *1933 Census of American Business, Retail Distribution*, Table 1A, and the following types of specialized shops as reported in *1933 Census of American Business, Service Industries:* Paint shops, radiator shops, top and body repair shops, tire repair shops, and brake repair shops.

Series De335–338, miscellaneous repair services. Separate data are available for some or all of the indicated years for several of the repair services in this group including shops engaged in armature rewinding, bicycle repair, blacksmithing, harness and leather goods repair, musical instrument repair, saw and tool repair, typewriter repair, upholstering and furniture repair, watch, clock, and jewelry repair, and so forth. Since the 1954–1967 data were obtained by mail canvass, they are believed to be substantially more complete than data for earlier years. In these industries, nonrecognizable establishments are likely to result in substantial underenumeration in a field canvass.

Series De339–340, hotels, tourist courts, motels, trailer parks, and camps. Data for 1954–1967 are for establishments with payrolls only.

WHOLESALE TRADE

Daniel M. G. Raff

TABLE De345–462   Wholesale establishments, sales, operating expenses, and employment, by type of business: 1929–1992[1]

Contributed by Daniel M. G. Raff

	All wholesale establishments						Merchant wholesalers				
					Persons engaged		Total				
	Establishments	Sales	Inventories, year end	Annual payroll	Paid employees	Active proprietors of unincorporated businesses	Establishments	Sales	Operating expenses as a percentage of sales	Inventories, year end	Annual payroll
	De345 [2]	De346 [2]	De347 [2,3]	De348 [2]	De349 [2]	De350 [2]	De351 [4]	De352 [4]	De353 [4]	De354 [4,3]	De355 [4]
Year	Number	Million dollars	Million dollars	Million dollars	Thousand	Thousand	Number	Million dollars	Percent	Million dollars	Million dollars
1929 [15]	163,830	65,378	5,195	2,922	1,550 [18]	87	79,840	29,556	11.7	3,383	1,713
1933 [15]	163,583	30,010	—	1,659	1,188 [18]	—	82,844	12,960	15.0	1,971	925
1935	176,756	42,803	3,107	2,022	1,261 [18]	97	88,931	17,662	7.6	2,068	1,162
1939 [15]	190,379	53,766	3,822	2,511	1,553 [18]	126	100,961	22,538	13.1	2,621	1,498
1948 [16]	243,366	188,689	10,167	7,991	2,383	163	146,518	79,767	11.6	7,207	5,064
1948 [17]	216,099	180,577	9,965	7,734	2,305	131	129,117	76,533	11.5	7,056	4,849
1954	250,322	233,976	13,046	10,868	2,555	150	163,157	100,103	13.0	9,492	6,865
1958	285,996	284,977	14,943	13,199	2,791	157	190,492	122,060	13.4	11,253	8,278
1963 [16]	308,177	358,386	20,150	18,101	3,089	138	208,997	157,392	13.5	14,992	11,545
1963 [17]	308,177	358,386	20,150	18,101	3,089	138	208,997	157,392	13.5	14,992	11,545
1967	311,464	459,476	28,117	23,922	3,519	122	212,993	206,055	13.5	21,463	15,368
1972	369,791	695,224	45,725	36,893	4,026	—	289,974	353,919	13.9	36,785	25,916
1977	382,837	1,258,400	82,288	58,290	4,397	—	307,264	676,058	12.7	67,036	42,067
1982	415,829	1,997,895	130,741	95,209	4,985	—	337,943	1,159,334	13.0	106,937	69,936
1987	469,539	2,524,727	165,092	133,359	5,596	—	390,982	1,478,169	14.5	141,083	100,416
1992	495,457	3,238,520	213,426	173,272	5,791	—	414,836	1,847,274	14.3	177,933	127,987

	Merchant wholesalers											
	Total			Groceries, confectionery, meat					Farm products (edible)			
	Persons engaged											
	Paid employees	Active proprietors of unincorporated businesses	Establishments	Sales	Operating expenses as a percentage of sales	Persons engaged	Paid employees	Establishments	Sales	Operating expenses as a percentage of sales	Persons engaged	Paid employees
	De356 [4]	De357 [4]	De358 [5]	De359 [5]	De360 [5]	De361 [5]	De362 [5]	De363 [6]	De364 [6]	De365 [6]	De366 [6]	De367 [6]
Year	Thousand	Thousand	Number	Million dollars	Percent	Number	Number	Number	Million dollars	Percent	Number	Number
1929 [15]	912	—	15,224	5,387	10.2	—	—	8,972	3,061	—	—	—
1933 [15]	636	—	18,088	3,121	12.8	—	—	10,386	1,590	14.8	—	—
1935	760	62	15,989	3,637	10.5	164,486	—	11,188	1,941	11.0	89,043	—
1939 [15]	949	72	15,681	3,941	11.3	165,550	—	10,945	2,111	13.0	104,508	—
1948 [16]	1,508	107	17,345	11,357	8.8	196,636	—	13,539	7,501	11.6	169,393	—
1948 [17]	1,441	85	15,707	11,213	8.8	195,072	—	10,966	5,859	9.0	106,809	—
1954	1,651	104	18,334	15,981	9.0	216,928	—	11,461	6,077	11.8	110,422	—
1958	1,843	120	18,582	18,712	8.6	213,231	—	11,440	6,489	12.0	100,599	—
1963 [16]	2,064	108	19,225	24,059	8.9	239,945	—	10,065	6,795	11.8	93,282	—
1963 [17]	2,064	104	19,814	25,333	8.7	243,445	—	10,065	6,795	11.8	92,905	—
1967	2,417	98	18,960	32,721	8.7	267,391	—	10,091	8,830	12.5	113,124	—
1972	3,023	—	18,831	50,238	9.0	—	289,368	11,079	13,844	14.1	—	147,824
1977	3,368	—	19,646	86,268	9.2	—	320,424	9,621	25,298	11.3	—	131,715
1982	3,918	—	20,249	135,916	9.9	—	363,149	8,836	38,771	11.7	—	140,172
1987	4,476	—	23,541	177,202	10.6	—	421,630	8,925	45,819	12.8	—	142,636
1992	4,588	—	24,485	223,605	10.6	—	436,965	8,739	55,612	12.7	—	141,682

Notes appear at end of table.

TABLE De345–462 Wholesale establishments, sales, operating expenses, and employment, by type of business: 1929–1992 *Continued*

	Merchant wholesalers									
	Beer, wine, and distilled alcoholic beverages					Tobacco and tobacco products				
	Establishments	Sales	Operating expenses as a percentage of sales	Persons engaged	Paid employees	Establishments	Sales	Operating expenses as a percentage of sales	Persons engaged	Paid employees
	De368	De369	De370	De371	De372	De373	De374	De375	De376	De377
Year	Number	Million dollars	Percent	Number	Number	Number	Million dollars	Percent	Number	Number
1929 [15]	—	—	—	—	—	1,721	858	7.4	—	—
1933 [15]	2,880	129	17.0	—	—	1,738	524	6.4	—	—
1935	5,496	699	13.1	37,266	—	2,253	783	5.5	16,862	—
1939 [15]	6,232	1,249	12.9	50,718	—	2,717	1,106	4.9	21,122	—
1948 [16]	7,195	4,070	10.9	69,059	—	3,019	2,530	5.2	28,886	—
1948 [17]	6,701	4,050	10.9	68,305	—	2,701	2,487	5.2	28,406	—
1954	7,309	5,687	12.0	78,340	—	2,858	3,209	5.9	30,848	—
1958	7,325	6,510	11.9	82,659	—	2,759	3,668	5.6	30,994	—
1963 [16]	7,164	8,195	12.0	87,769	—	2,753	4,682	5.6	33,570	—
1963 [17]	7,164	8,195	12.0	87,614	—	2,753	4,682	5.6	33,536	—
1967	6,862	10,444	11.9	95,435	—	2,515	5,315	5.9	35,370	—
1972	6,539	15,423	13.0	—	101,240	2,363	7,268	6.3	—	35,705
1977	6,323	22,446	14.3	—	112,123	2,124	9,587	6.8	—	34,637
1982	6,007	36,456	16.5	—	133,668	1,826	12,650	6.8	—	31,455
1987	5,470	41,588	17.8	—	137,878	1,758	19,572	7.3	—	38,362
1992	4,903	50,397	17.4	—	134,017	1,637	30,754	6.8	—	43,204

	Merchant wholesalers									
	Drugs, chemicals, and allied products					Dry goods, apparel				
	Establishments	Sales	Operating expenses as a percentage of sales	Persons engaged	Paid employees	Establishments	Sales	Operating expenses as a percentage of sales	Persons engaged	Paid employees
	De378 [7]	De379 [7]	De380 [7]	De381 [7]	De382 [7]	De383 [8]	De384 [8]	De385 [8]	De386 [8]	De387 [8]
Year	Number	Million dollars	Percent	Number	Number	Number	Million dollars	Percent	Number	Number
1929 [15]	2,376 [19]	948 [19]	15.9 [19]	—	—	7,543	2,849	13.4	—	—
1933 [15]	2,543	576	11.0	—	—	6,392	1,262	14.5	—	—
1935	2,989	723	15.6	35,926	—	7,567	1,634	12.8	69,624	—
1939 [15]	3,298	802	17.3	41,824	—	8,275	1,889	13.1	75,385	—
1948 [16]	4,671	2,282	15.8	58,679	—	11,733	5,728	11.8	88,745	—
1948 [17]	4,124	2,243	15.9	57,775	—	9,604	5,530	11.9	84,977	—
1954	5,837	3,370	15.9	71,366	—	9,389	5,690	13.3	83,811	—
1958	7,097	4,641	15.1	82,481	—	9,199	5,901	13.5	80,852	—
1963 [16]	7,792	5,996	15.9	91,590	—	9,227	7,027	13.5	80,161	—
1963 [17]	7,792	5,996	15.9	91,483	—	9,227	7,027	13.5	79,992	—
1967	7,701	7,808	15.5	107,182	—	8,846	8,861	14.2	95,887	—
1972	7,496	11,122	15.2	—	99,750	9,515	13,433	14.5	—	97,921
1977	8,912	20,030	15.4	—	114,547	9,713	17,906	16.0	—	96,387
1982	10,901	38,098	16.4	—	150,425	10,784	29,845	18.8	—	112,841
1987	13,374	60,437	14.1	—	160,663	13,393	46,572	19.9	—	146,059
1992	15,776	106,240	11.9	—	194,051	15,848	67,905	19.2	—	162,775

Notes appear at end of table

(continued)

TABLE De345–462   Wholesale establishments, sales, operating expenses, and employment, by type of business: 1929–1992 *Continued*

Merchant wholesalers

	Furniture, homefurnishings					Paper and allied products				
	Establishments	Sales	Operating expenses as a percentage of sales	Persons engaged	Paid employees	Establishments	Sales	Operating expenses as a percentage of sales	Persons engaged	Paid employees
	De388 [9]	De389 [9]	De390 [9]	De391 [9]	De392 [9]	De393	De394	De395	De396	De397
Year	Number	Million dollars	Percent	Number	Number	Number	Million dollars	Percent	Number	Number
1929 [15]	1,750	495	18.9	—	—	2,297	704	16.4	—	—
1933 [15]	1,788	175	22.5	—	—	2,221	333	20.7	—	—
1935	1,959	244	17.8	15,871	—	2,549	409	18.3	27,543	—
1939 [15]	2,214	374	17.2	20,265	—	2,898	575	17.2	33,605	—
1948 [16]	3,813	1,315	16.6	34,929	—	4,044	1,902	15.5	51,468	—
1948 [17]	3,189	1,249	17.3	34,402	—	3,630	1,880	15.5	50,553	—
1954	5,324	2,275	18.6	52,793	—	5,057	2,961	15.9	61,123	—
1958	5,359	2,510	19.2	54,162	—	5,182	3,564	15.3	67,424	—
1963 [16]	6,265	3,400	19.4	62,054	—	7,046	4,715	17.2	85,951	—
1963 [17]	6,265	3,400	19.4	61,956	—	7,046	4,715	17.2	85,851	—
1967	6,047	4,329	19.1	70,164	—	7,663	6,422	17.4	105,672	—
1972	7,130	6,788	19.9	—	78,203	8,231	8,216	18.8	—	99,237
1977	8,239	11,118	21.7	—	89,152	8,995	15,016	18.4	—	114,198
1982	9,436	17,663	23.2	—	105,688	11,061	25,937	19.6	—	146,068
1987	11,390	26,939	23.9	—	131,509	13,655	40,818	18.9	—	173,758
1992	13,133	33,200	23.8	—	137,274	15,995	54,802	18.4	—	200,622

Merchant wholesalers

	Farm products (raw materials)					Automobile vehicles, parts, and supplies				
	Establishments	Sales	Operating expenses as a percentage of sales	Persons engaged	Paid employees	Establishments	Sales	Operating expenses as a percentage of sales	Persons engaged	Paid employees
	De398	De399	De400	De401	De402	De403	De404	De405	De406	De407
Year	Number	Million dollars	Percent	Number	Number	Number	Million dollars	Percent	Number	Number
1929 [15]	3,240	3,666	4.5	—	—	3,451	1,383	15.0	—	—
1933 [15]	2,433	1,225	6.9	—	—	5,237	438	23.0	—	—
1935	2,199	1,563	6.7	23,712	—	5,672	780	16.8	53,820	—
1939 [15]	2,086	1,629	6.9	29,281	—	7,818	1,055	17.5	72,616	—
1948 [16]	2,594	6,904	3.6	26,592	—	14,693	4,092	17.8	146,459	—
1948 [17]	2,059	6,771	3.6	24,326	—	13,563	3,918	18.1	145,023	—
1954	3,853	9,232	4.0	41,317	—	15,540	3,978	22.6	144,532	—
1958	4,195	9,594	4.5	41,768	—	20,823	7,098	20.0	191,875	—
1963 [16]	3,565	13,690	3.3	36,968	—	26,500	10,304	19.5	237,749	—
1963 [17]	3,565	13,690	3.3	36,790	—	26,946	10,445	19.5	240,711	—
1967	4,044	16,176	3.4	39,217	—	28,513	14,093	18.5	274,698	—
1972	11,985	33,956	4.2	—	81,599	33,473	29,909	16.1	—	320,297
1977	12,182	85,755	3.4	—	97,490	35,711	55,090	14.2	—	350,580
1982	11,543	121,932	3.8	—	99,345	36,438	91,394	13.8	—	375,065
1987	10,755	91,386	5.0	—	86,141	42,926	156,214	11.8	—	422,783
1992	9,845	109,827	4.6	—	81,066	43,857	170,849	11.9	—	413,366

Notes appear at end of table

TABLE De345–462   Wholesale establishments, sales, operating expenses, and employment, by type of business: 1929–1992 *Continued*

Merchant wholesalers

	Electrical goods					Hardware, plumbing, and heating				
	Establishments	Sales	Operating expenses as a percentage of sales	Persons engaged	Paid employees	Establishments	Sales	Operating expenses as a percentage of sales	Persons engaged	Paid employees
	De408 [10]	De409 [10]	De410 [10]	De411 [10]	De412 [10]	De413 [10,11]	De414 [10,11]	De415 [10,11]	De416 [10,11]	De417 [10,11]
Year	Number	Million dollars	Percent	Number	Number	Number	Million dollars	Percent	Number	Number
1929 [15]	2,182	847	16.9	—	—	2,953	1,213	19.3	—	—
1933 [15]	2,125	276	22.3	—	—	2,614	485	22.5	—	—
1935	2,438	577	17.3	31,698	—	2,872	671	18.8	49,821	—
1939 [15]	3,072	788	16.6	40,147	—	3,568	972	18.4	64,358	—
1948 [16]	5,443	4,425	12.7	93,325	—	5,576	3,731	15.2	101,913	—
1948 [17]	5,041	4,309	12.8	91,772	—	5,189	3,680	15.2	100,721	—
1954	7,123	6,338	14.0	111,299	—	6,183	4,398	17.2	103,860	—
1958	9,488	7,928	14.4	128,346	—	7,526	5,307	17.8	112,029	—
1963 [16]	10,978	9,911	14.7	133,350	—	8,404	6,013	18.0	110,769	—
1963 [17]	10,978	9,911	14.7	133,170	—	8,404	6,013	18.0	110,661	—
1967	11,376	13,622	14.5	157,041	—	8,830	7,426	18.6	127,421	—
1972	14,278	18,848	15.5	—	168,573	14,336	13,328	19.1	—	159,613
1977	17,109	30,351	17.4	—	194,236	15,221	19,902	20.9	—	165,358
1982	20,562	55,837	18.5	—	259,326	17,392	29,255	23.4	—	189,569
1987	24,784	91,695	18.6	—	314,235	19,737	41,386	22.5	—	208,475
1992	29,105	115,387	17.6	—	320,770	20,972	53,063	21.6	—	210,911

Merchant wholesalers

	Lumber and other construction materials					Machinery, equipment, and supplies				
	Establishments	Sales	Operating expenses as a percentage of sales	Persons engaged	Paid employees	Establishments	Sales	Operating expenses as a percentage of sales	Persons engaged	Paid employees
	De418 [2]	De419 [2]	De420 [2]	De421 [2]	De422 [2]	De423 [10,11,12]	De424 [10,11,12]	De425 [10,11,12]	De426 [10,11,12]	De427 [10,11,12]
Year	Number	Million dollars	Percent	Number	Number	Number	Million dollars	Percent	Number	Number
1929 [15]	3,774	1,284	15.8	—	—	6,988	1,269	19.1	—	—
1933 [15]	2,636	279	22.7	—	—	6,226 [20]	506 [20]	25.4 [20]	—	—
1935	2,817	492	16.7	29,110	—	7,583 [20]	864 [20]	21.1 [20]	67,379 [20]	—
1939 [15]	3,303	804	15.2	38,918	—	11,270	1,440	20.0	96,311	—
1948 [16]	5,890	3,935	14.0	90,036	—	21,755	6,828	18.1	207,062	—
1948 [17]	5,576	3,890	14.1	89,427	—	19,573	6,723	18.2	203,642	—
1954	10,314	6,586	16.1	132,724	—	27,150	10,040	20.2	254,060	—
1958	9,463	6,272	13.4	102,748	—	32,593	13,259	20.5	299,285	—
1963 [16]	11,643	8,713	15.2	129,693	—	38,865	17,612	21.1	368,905	—
1963 [17]	11,643	8,713	15.2	129,483	—	38,419	17,471	21.1	363,964	—
1967	10,877	9,074	15.6	123,603	—	40,999	25,279	20.4	456,048	—
1972	12,601	16,914	14.7	—	145,131	59,323	42,497	20.8	—	560,629
1977	12,681	27,583	14.3	—	144,424	67,668	85,705	20.5	—	697,384
1982	14,137	33,118	17.6	—	156,940	79,973	140,896	23.4	—	871,989
1987	16,133	58,375	16.6	—	205,695	61,326	120,032	22.9	—	600,320
1992	16,355	63,765	15.9	—	180,832	62,138	149,216	22.2	—	593,869

Notes appear at end of table

(continued)

TABLE De345–462　Wholesale establishments, sales, operating expenses, and employment, by type of business: 1929–1992 *Continued*

Merchant wholesalers

	Metals and minerals					Scrap and waste materials				
	Establishments	Sales	Operating expenses as a percentage of sales	Persons engaged	Paid employees	Establishments	Sales	Operating expenses as a percentage of sales	Persons engaged	Paid employees
	De428	De429	De430	De431	De432	De433	De434	De435	De436	De437
Year	Number	Million dollars	Percent	Number	Number	Number	Million dollars	Percent	Number	Number
1929 [15]	856	673	8.1	—	—	3,919	475	12.3	—	—
1933 [15]	748	161	15.8	—	—	3,360	272	10.8	—	—
1935	810	282	13.2	11,343	—	4,793	400	14.5	34,830	—
1939 [15]	1,017	516	12.0	17,705	—	6,059	656	14.7	52,379	—
1948 [16]	1,803	2,057	12.1	34,395	—	7,717	2,699	11.9	67,227	—
1948 [17]	1,706	1,951	12.9	33,844	—	6,440	2,664	11.8	65,582	—
1954	3,235 [21]	3,363 [21]	14.5 [21]	53,641 [21]	—	8,189	2,406	17.8	75,499	—
1958	4,792	5,541	13.6	74,689	—	9,491	2,898	18.7	81,528	—
1963 [16]	5,547	7,935	12.4	83,261	—	8,174	3,484	17.8	78,391	—
1963 [17]	5,547	7,935	12.4	83,174	—	8,174	3,484	17.8	78,105	—
1967	5,395	11,863	11.9	103,459	—	7,814	4,423	17.3	84,536	—
1972	5,427	15,022	12.6	—	96,010	7,139	5,481	19.3	—	72,498
1977	6,584	32,847	10.9	—	106,747	7,219	9,819	19.9	—	82,414
1982	7,414	49,009	11.8	—	120,427	7,563	11,304	24.3	—	81,791
1987	8,682	64,498	11.0	—	122,710	8,278	17,047	21.6	—	83,504
1992	8,739	70,618	11.3	—	116,116	8,693	23,264	21.6	—	96,803

	Manufacturers' sales branches (with stocks)					Manufacturers' sales branches (without stocks)				
	Establishments	Sales	Operating expenses as a percentage of sales	Persons engaged	Paid employees	Establishments	Sales	Operating expenses as a percentage of sales	Persons engaged	Paid employees
	De438	De439	De440	De441	De442	De443	De444	De445	De446	De447
Year	Number	Million dollars	Percent	Number	Number	Number	Million dollars	Percent	Number	Number
1929 [15]	16,863 [22]	16,174 [22]	—	—	—	— [22]	— [22]	—	—	—
1933 [15]	12,444	5,145	14.9	—	—	4,429	2,413	7.4	—	—
1935	11,541	7,404	11.8	212,452 [23]	—	4,065	3,535	6.4	39,607 [23]	—
1939 [15]	12,844	9,610	12.5	267,774	—	5,082	4,643	6.9	47,699	—
1948 [16]	15,716	29,230	10.0	412,252	—	8,052	23,509	4.3	90,144	—
1948 [17]	15,687	28,609	10.0	410,199	—	8,019	22,191	4.0	89,992	—
1954	14,759 [21]	36,811 [21]	10.5 [21]	404,098 [21]	—	7,831 [24]	32,723 [24]	4.5 [24]	111,888 [24]	—
1958	15,088	41,798	10.8	419,415	—	10,093	45,960	4.8	140,954	—
1963 [16]	16,408	54,857	10.6	435,575	—	12,476	61,586	4.2	164,885	—
1963 [17]	16,408	54,857	10.6	435,573	—	12,476	61,586	4.2	164,855	—
1967	16,709	67,175	11.3	491,613	—	13,970	89,922	4.1	193,425	—
1972	32,611	124,459	11.0	—	574,886	14,586	131,221	4.1	—	219,805
1977	26,892	221,527	8.9	—	606,278	13,629	230,328	3.1	—	200,172
1982	22,121	312,644	9.1	—	569,849	16,113	314,342	4.5	—	261,142
1987	21,935	342,903	10.8	—	624,593	14,375	440,222	3.9	—	250,425
1992	22,329	462,674	11.5	—	666,547	13,624	577,055	4.1	—	270,561

Notes appear at end of table

TABLE De345–462   Wholesale establishments, sales, operating expenses, and employment, by type of business: 1929–1992 Continued

	Petroleum bulk stations, terminals						Agents and brokers	
	Establishments	Sales	Operating expenses as a percentage of sales	Persons engaged	Paid employees		Establishments	Sales
	De448 [13,14]	De449 [13,14]	De450 [13,14]	De451 [13,14]	De452 [13,14]		De453	De454
Year	Number	Million dollars	Percent	Number	Number		Number	Million dollars
1929 [15]	19,587	2,101	16.0	—	—		18,467	14,517
1933 [15]	26,176 [25]	1,885 [25]	19.8 [25]	—	—		13,818	6,502
1935	27,333	2,704	14.5	105,118 [23]	—		18,147	8,908
1939 [15]	30,825	3,808	11.0	123,017	—		21,083	11,780
1948 [16]	29,451	10,616	9.0	136,418	—		24,361	34,610
1948 [17]	28,351	10,483	9.0	134,897	—		18,138	32,840
1954	29,189	16,038	10.0	154,760	—		22,131	39,251
1958	30,424	20,131	11.9	147,351	—		26,567	46,423
1963 [16]	30,873	21,485	—	151,613	—		26,313	53,245
1963 [17]	30,873	21,485	—	151,541	—		25,313	53,245
1967	30,229	24,822	0.3	156,708	—		26,462	61,347
1972	26,035	33,358	—	—	152,132		32,620	85,626
1977	17,385	71,830	5.1	—	126,050		35,052	130,488
1982	12,920	163,769	3.8	—	131,057		39,652	211,575
1987	12,353	139,655	5.2	—	135,923		42,247	263,433
1992	12,098	167,696	5.0	—	130,047		44,668	351,518

	Agents and brokers				Assemblers (mainly farm products)				
	Operating expenses as a percentage of sales	Persons engaged	Paid employees		Establishments	Sales	Operating expenses as a percentage of sales	Persons engaged	Paid employees
	De455	De456	De457		De458	De459	De460	De461	De462
Year	Percent	Number	Number		Number	Million dollars	Percent	Number	Number
1929 [15]	3.2	—	—		34,143	4,452	—	—	—
1933 [15]	3.2	—	—		23,962	1,774	9.8	—	—
1935	2.9	88,064	—		26,515	2,463	6.7	115,381	—
1939 [15]	2.8	111,125	—		28,931	2,510	9.3	168,673	—
1948 [16]	2.6 [26]	123,470	—		19,268	10,958	6.1	169,182	—
1948 [17]	2.5 [26]	116,148	—		16,787	9,920	6.1	158,956	—
1954	3.1 [26]	148,595	—		13,255 [27]	9,051 [27]	8.1 [27]	130,337 [27]	—
1958	3.3 [26]	169,597	—		14,096	8,999	9.0	123,314	—
1963 [16]	3.6 [26]	184,678	—		14,110	9,820	9.0	117,986	—
1963 [17]	3.6 [26]	184,459	—		14,110	9,821	9.0	117,849	—
1967	4.0 [26]	195,838	—		11,101	10,156	8.6	88,564	—
1972	4.2	—	208,054		—	—	—	—	—
1977	4.6	—	222,431		10,348	37,817	6.9	—	103,764
1982	4.5	—	235,933		8,344	40,321	8.1	—	86,746
1987	4.8	—	258,127		7,686	40,536	9.0	—	80,612
1992	4.6	—	266,279		7,731	52,810	8.8	—	89,950

[1] 1972–1982 data based on 1972 Standard Industrial Classification; 1987 and later data based on 1987 Standard Industrial Classification.

[2] Excludes ready-mixed concrete distributors in 1954 and later years.

[3] Inventory valued at cost through 1972, by valuation method in 1977, and at cost or market beginning 1982.

[4] Includes subclasses not shown separately.

[5] Beginning 1977, includes food and beverage basic materials.

[6] Fresh fruit, vegetables, poultry, and dairy products. Milk bottling plants included through 1948 (unrevised).

[7] Beginning 1972, excludes paint and varnishes.

[8] Includes dressed furs.

[9] Beginning with 1954, includes musical instruments and sheet music wholesalers.

[10] Industrial controls classified under machinery, equipment, and supplies in 1987. Classified under electrical goods for all other years.

[11] Air conditioning and ventilation equipment classified under machinery, equipment, and supplies 1948–1967. Classified under hardware, plumbing, and heating in other years.

[12] Beginning with 1987, excludes commercial and professional machines, equipment, and supplies.

[13] Beginning with 1982, includes sale of crude oil from bulk storage facilities.

[14] Beginning with 1972, includes LP gas bulk stations and terminals.

[15] Data for series De345–350 revised for these years. Revised data not available for other series.

[16] Comparable with earlier years.

[17] Comparable with later years.

[18] Average annual number of full-time and part-time employees.

[19] Includes forty-two distilled spirits wholesalers with sales of $13 million and operating expenses of 24.7 percent.

[20] Excludes wholesalers of shoe finding and cut stock; in 1929, 555 such establishments had sales of $56 million. Persons engaged in optical goods segment partially estimated.

[21] For 1954, 142 sales branches (with stocks) and $172 million of sales from steel works and rolling mill companies are included in metal distributors rather than manufacturers' sales branches.

TABLE De345–462   Wholesale establishments, sales, operating expenses, and employment, by type of business: 1929–1992 *Continued*

[22] Figures include both manufacturers' sales branches with and without stocks.

[23] Partly estimated.

[24] Includes a moderate amount of underenumeration because in the mail canvass, activities of some branches and offices were reported as those of the manufacturing plant or an auxiliary establishment.

[25] Includes district and general sales offices.

[26] Commissions earned.

[27] Beginning with 1954, excludes fish and seafood assemblers included under grocery, confectionery, and meat series. In 1948 (adjusted) there were 544 such establishments with sales of $117 million and operating expenses of 23.5 percent.

Sources
U.S. Bureau of the Census. 1929, *Fifteenth Census of the United States*, 1930, Distribution, volume 2, *Wholesale Distribution*; 1933, *Census of American Business: 1933, U.S. Summaries*; 1935, *Census of Business: 1935, Wholesale Distribution*, part 1, volume 1, *U.S. Summary*; 1939, *Sixteenth Census of the United States, 1940, Census of Business*, volume 2, *Wholesale Trade: 1939*; 1948, *Census of Business: 1948*, volume 4, *Wholesale Trade – General Statistics and Commodity Line Sales Statistics*; 1954, *Census of Business: 1954*, volume 3, *Wholesale Trade – Summary Statistics*; 1958, *Census of Business: 1958*, volume 3, *Wholesale Trade – Summary Statistics*; 1963, *Census of Business: 1963*, volume 4, *Wholesale Trade – Summary Statistics*, part 1; 1967, *Census of Business: 1967*, volume 3, *Wholesale Trade – Subject Reports*; 1972, *Census of Wholesale Trade: 1972*, volume 1, *Summary and Subject Statistics*; 1977, *Census of Wholesale Trade: 1977*, volume 1, *Subject Statistics*; 1982, *Census of Wholesale Trade: 1982, Industry Series*; 1987, *Census of Wholesale Trade: 1987, Subject Series*; 1992, *Census of Wholesale Trade: 1992, Subject Series*.

Documentation
Data shown are for wholesale establishments, other than chain store warehouses. Merchant wholesalers include additional subclasses not separately shown. These estimates reflect adjustments made to the data prior to 1958 for certain years by Professors Charles S. Goodman and Reavis Cox. The estimates to 1967 were taken from *Historical Statistics of the United States* (1975), Series T274–371.

Establishment count is measured by the number of businesses at year end for 1982 and prior years. For 1987 and later years, establishment count includes businesses in operation anytime during the year.

Employment data represent the number of paid employees during the workweek nearest March 12 for 1967 and later years, the number of active proprietors and paid employees during the workweek nearest November 15 for 1948–1963, and the active proprietors plus the average annual number of full-time and part-time employees for 1939 and earlier years.

Data may not be compatible across time as there have been numerous changes in the definitions of kinds of business, scope of the census (especially size minimums for enumeration), enumeration methods, and completeness of data. The statistics shown have been adjusted where possible to maintain maximum comparability over time. Significant changes are noted in the following. For treatment of lesser differences, see source publications.

The 1954 and later censuses were conducted by mail canvass. Report forms were mailed to all firms included in the active records of the Internal Revenue Service as subject to the payment of Federal Insurance Contributions Act (FICA) taxes and that were classified in appropriate kinds of business or were unclassified at the time the forms were mailed. Data for such censuses, therefore, omit all wholesalers who had no employees subject to FICA taxes. The 1948 and earlier Censuses were conducted by field canvasses and were restricted to firms that operated from recognizable places of business, whether or not they had any employees subject to FICA taxes. The 1933 and 1935 Censuses were not taken under mandatory reporting requirements and may therefore be subject to some underenumeration.

Data for 1954 and later years are for establishments with paid employees. The original 1948 tabulations include all establishments with sales of $5,000 or more irrespective of employment. For 1939, the corresponding cutoff point was $500. No mention of cutoff point is made in sources of data for years prior to 1939.

The figures for 1948 (comparable with later years) have been revised to reflect 1954 coverage and to incorporate certain changes in classification.

The figures for 1963 (comparable with later years) have been revised to reflect the scope of the 1967 Census of Business. Significant changes are (1) kinds of business data for 1967 are in accordance with the 1967 edition of the U.S. Office of Management and Budget (formerly Bureau of the Budget) Standard Industrial Classification Manual, whereas the 1963 data are in conformity with the 1957 edition and its supplements; (2) the number of paid employees in 1967 was obtained from administrative records of the IRS while, in 1963, all census information was obtained directly from the companies; and (3) the number of active proprietors for 1967 is based on crediting sole proprietorships with one proprietor and partnerships with two proprietors for firms with first-quarter 1967 payroll; for 1963, on crediting proprietors similarly but for all sole proprietorships and partnerships operated at any time during 1963.

Figures for the years 1972, 1977, and 1982 are based on the 1972 Standard Industrial Classification (SIC). Figures for 1987 and later years are based on the 1987 SIC. Significant changes as a result of classification changes are noted in the footnotes where possible. See the Introduction to Part D for a discussion of SIC codes.

TABLE De463–465   Sales of wholesale establishments: 1939–1999[1]

Contributed by Daniel M. G. Raff

Year	Total De463 Billion dollars	Durable goods establishments De464 Billion dollars	Nondurable goods establishments De465 Billion dollars	Year	Total De463 Billion dollars	Durable goods establishments De464 Billion dollars	Nondurable goods establishments De465 Billion dollars	Year	Total De463 Billion dollars	Durable goods establishments De464 Billion dollars	Nondurable goods establishments De465 Billion dollars
1939	26.2	6.3	20.0	1960	148.0	53.3	94.7	1985	1,360.8	651.6	709.2
1940	28.9	7.5	21.4	1961	150.7	51.4	99.3	1986	1,379.3	681.9	697.4
1941	36.4	10.2	26.2	1962	156.7	54.2	102.5	1987	1,474.6	729.9	744.7
1942	41.1	9.6	31.5	1967	235.5	104.9	130.6	1988	1,611.5	799.9	811.6
1943	46.0	9.4	36.5	1968	251.4	115.9	135.4	1989	1,728.1	853.3	874.8
1944	49.8	10.1	39.7	1969	273.8	128.3	145.5	1990	1,792.9	880.7	912.3
1945	53.7	10.9	42.8	1970	290.1	133.9	156.3	1991	1,778.8	859.5	919.3
1946 [2]	71.9	17.6	54.3	1971	317.8	147.7	170.2	1992	1,843.5	905.7	937.7
1946 [3]	67.9	18.7	49.2	1972	358.5	169.0	189.6	1993	1,938.1	993.3	944.9
1947	82.9	26.0	57.0	1973	457.7	208.6	249.0	1994	2,075.9	1,099.0	976.9
1948	90.6	29.2	61.4	1974	575.3	255.8	319.5	1995	2,271.0	1,210.3	1,060.6
1949	86.6	27.2	59.3	1975	560.1	236.0	324.1	1996	2,391.0	1,258.0	1,133.0
1950	101.0	35.4	65.7	1976	606.1	262.7	343.4	1997	2,500.9	1,335.0	1,165.8
1951	112.4	39.6	72.8	1977	674.2	304.9	369.3	1998	2,554.1	1,381.8	1,172.3
1952	114.8	39.3	75.4	1978	798.0	372.4	425.7	1999	2,740.8	1,481.5	1,259.3
1953	117.7	41.4	76.3	1979	948.8	435.7	513.0				
1954	116.8	40.0	76.8	1980	1,113.8	485.0	628.7				
1955	127.4	48.2	79.2	1981	1,214.3	525.8	688.5				
1956	135.3	52.8	82.5	1982	1,142.7	480.3	662.3				
1957	135.2	50.5	84.8	1983	1,192.6	523.5	669.0				
1958	133.1	47.3	85.8	1984	1,344.4	621.3	723.1				
1959	147.5	55.4	92.1								

[1] Beginning with 1946, excludes wholesale establishments with no paid employment.

[2] Comparable with earlier data.

[3] Comparable with later data.

Sources

U.S. Bureau of Economic Analysis (formerly Office of Business Economics), 1939–1946, *Survey of Current Business*, October 1951, p. 24; 1946–1962, unpublished data (monthly averages published in *1963 Business Statistics*, p. 22); 1967–1999, unpublished data, U.S. Bureau of the Census.

Documentation

These estimates exclude sales of corporate manufacturers, sales branches and offices, and the marketing stations of petroleum refiners, which are included in the manufacturing series of the former Office of Business Economics. Sales of agents and brokers are included here on the basis of actual receipts of the agents and brokers rather than on the total value of goods sold. For 1939–1946, data are based on 1948 Census of Business definitions and classifications. The 1939 Census data have been recast to conform to the 1948 Census. Data for 1946–1962 are based on definitions and classifications in the 1954 Census of Business, with the 1948 Census data adjusted to the scope of the 1954 Census. 1967–1999 data are from a survey based on the Standard Industrial Classification (SIC) system by the U.S. Bureau of the Census. See the Introduction to Part D for a discussion of SIC codes.

Data for 1962–1966 are not available as the survey on the SIC basis began with 1967 data.

TABLE De466–474   Sales, stocks, and stock – sales ratios of merchant wholesalers: 1948–1998[1]

Contributed by Daniel M. G. Raff

	All establishments			Durable goods establishments			Nondurable goods establishments		
	Sales	Stocks, end of year	Stock–sales ratio	Sales	Stocks, end of year	Stock–sales ratio	Sales	Stocks, end of year	Stock–sales ratio
	De466	De467	De468	De469	De470	De471	De472	De473	De474
Year	Million dollars	Million dollars	Ratio	Million dollars	Million dollars	Ratio	Million dollars	Million dollars	Ratio
1948	81,699	7,797	1.15	31,010	3,831	1.48	50,598	3,966	0.94
1949	78,163	7,565	1.16	29,014	3,658	1.51	49,149	3,907	0.95
1950	92,336	9,133	1.19	37,695	4,494	1.43	54,641	4,639	1.02
1951	103,163	9,732	1.13	42,229	4,978	1.41	60,934	4,754	0.94
1952	105,379	10,059	1.15	41,905	5,073	1.45	63,474	4,986	0.94
1953	108,624	10,528	1.16	44,079	5,297	1.44	64,545	5,231	0.97
1954	107,290	10,521	1.18	42,639	5,258	1.48	65,281	5,263	0.97
1955	118,713	11,584	1.17	51,412	6,048	1.41	67,301	5,536	0.99
1956	126,153	13,229	1.26	56,308	6,876	1.47	69,845	6,353	1.09
1957	125,705	12,697	1.21	53,760	6,930	1.55	71,945	5,767	0.96
1958	123,083	12,715	1.24	50,437	6,964	1.66	72,646	5,751	0.95
1959	137,893	13,853	1.21	59,349	7,641	1.54	78,544	6,212	0.95
1960	139,866	14,085	1.21	58,581	7,898	1.62	81,285	6,187	0.91
1961	143,850	14,438	1.20	59,836	8,088	1.62	84,014	6,350	0.91
1962	152,082	14,817	1.17	64,541	8,391	1.56	87,541	6,426	0.88
1963	160,578	15,959	1.19	68,696	8,874	1.55	91,882	7,085	0.93
1964	174,351	16,927	1.17	75,733	9,602	1.52	98,618	7,325	0.89
1965	187,331	18,273	1.17	82,861	10,390	1.50	104,470	7,883	0.91
1966	203,847	20,771	1.22	91,128	11,959	1.57	112,719	8,812	0.94
1967	234,914	25,154	1.28	104,615	15,159	1.74	130,299	9,995	0.92
1968	252,145	26,437	1.26	116,297	16,211	1.67	135,848	10,226	0.90
1969	273,814	28,958	1.27	128,314	17,837	1.67	145,500	11,121	0.92
1970	289,999	32,509	1.35	133,778	19,622	1.76	156,221	12,887	0.99
1971	317,899	35,425	1.34	147,761	21,911	1.78	170,138	13,514	0.95
1972	358,388	39,181	1.31	168,879	24,129	1.71	189,509	15,052	0.95
1973	457,378	46,171	1.21	208,554	27,241	1.57	248,842	18,930	0.91
1974	575,786	57,870	1.21	255,863	35,164	1.65	319,923	22,706	0.85
1975	559,606	57,267	1.23	235,723	36,447	1.86	323,883	20,820	0.77
1976	608,381	64,633	1.27	263,605	41,026	1.87	344,776	23,607	0.82
1977	673,633	72,953	1.30	304,721	46,714	1.84	368,912	26,239	0.85
1978	796,961	86,600	1.30	372,176	55,729	1.80	424,785	30,871	0.87
1979	948,614	99,657	1.26	436,254	63,246	1.74	512,360	36,411	0.85
1980	1,117,187	124,015	1.33	486,509	78,849	1.94	630,678	45,166	0.86
1981	1,214,156	130,709	1.29	525,607	85,371	1.95	688,549	45,338	0.79
1982	1,142,535	128,514	1.35	480,318	84,806	2.12	662,217	43,708	0.79
1983	1,190,705	131,306	1.32	523,080	84,709	1.94	667,625	46,597	0.84
1984	1,346,392	143,458	1.28	622,361	94,895	1.83	724,031	48,563	0.80
1985	1,361,507	148,403	1.31	651,864	96,659	1.78	709,643	51,744	0.87
1986	1,379,514	154,081	1.34	681,691	101,369	1.78	697,828	52,712	0.91
1987	1,475,613	164,310	1.34	730,592	106,820	1.75	745,021	57,490	0.93
1988	1,614,249	179,828	1.34	801,751	115,613	1.73	812,498	64,215	0.95
1989	1,725,123	187,897	1.31	851,550	120,701	1.70	873,573	67,196	0.92
1990	1,794,072	196,881	1.32	880,767	124,839	1.70	913,305	72,042	0.95
1991	1,779,673	201,777	1.36	860,138	125,921	1.76	919,535	75,856	0.99
1992	1,849,798	209,675	1.36	908,917	130,044	1.72	940,881	79,631	1.02
1993	1,934,675	218,419	1.35	990,282	135,473	1.64	944,393	82,946	1.05
1994	2,066,847	236,710	1.37	1,091,483	149,016	1.64	975,364	87,694	1.08
1995	2,254,673	254,921	1.36	1,196,306	161,110	1.62	1,058,367	93,811	1.06
1996	2,384,019	256,490	1.29	1,246,078	163,621	1.58	1,137,941	92,869	0.98
1997	2,480,049	274,517	1.33	1,312,427	174,967	1.60	1,167,622	99,550	1.02
1998	2,535,008	287,997	1.36	1,359,989	184,769	1.63	1,175,019	103,228	1.05

[1] Beginning in 1980, valuation of inventory is not comparable with earlier data because of changes in valuation methods. See text.

Sources

U.S. Bureau of Economic Analysis (formerly Office of Business Economics). 1948–1963, *1979 Business Statistics*, p. 49; 1964–1966, *1984 Business Statistics*, p. 36; 1967–1969, *1996 Business Statistics* p. 214, *1988 Business Statistics*, p. 36; 1969–1998, *1988 Business Statistics*, p. 36, *1999 Business Statistics*, p. 277.

Documentation

The estimates are confined to merchant wholesalers since information on other types of wholesalers is not available except for years when the census of wholesale trade was taken. The data exclude manufacturers' sales branches and sales offices, petroleum bulk stations and terminals, agents and brokers, and assemblers of farm products.

Sales include sales of merchandise and receipts from repairs or other services to customers, after deduction of returns, allowances, and discounts;

TABLE De466–474   Sales, stocks, and stock – sales ratios of merchant wholesalers: 1948–1998   *Continued*

and sales of merchandise for others on a commission basis. Local and state sales taxes and federal excise taxes are included. Beginning in 1980, valuation of inventory is not comparable with earlier data because of changes in valuation methods. Value of stocks prior to 1980 are not value of stocks on hand at end of the period and are valued according to the valuation method used by each respondent. Thus, the aggregates are a mixture of LIFO (last in, first out) and non-LIFO values. Beginning with 1980, inventories are valued using methods other than LIFO in order to better reflect the current costs of goods held as inventory.

Data from *1999 Business Statistics* ran from 1970 to 1998 and have been used for those years. However, because of the change in valuation techniques, inventory values for years prior to 1980 are not found in *1999 Business Statistics*. Inventory values for 1970–1979 were taken from *1988 Business Statistics*, the most recent unrevised version that includes these values. Sales values

for 1967–1969 are from *1996 Business Statistics*, the volume that contains the most recent unrevised version of these values. Inventory values for these years were absent in the *1996 Business Statistics* so they have been taken from *1988 Business Statistics*, where they last appear. Values for 1964–1966 are from *1984 Business Statistics*, the volume that contains the most recent unrevised version of these values. 1948–1963 values are taken from *1979 Business Statistics*, the most recent unrevised version of these values.

The stock–sales ratio for a given year is derived by dividing seasonally unadjusted end-of-year inventories by yearly sales averaged per month. This is not equivalent to dividing the weighted average of seasonally adjusted end-of-month inventories (using the thirteen observations including the year-end figures for the given and previous year) by the monthly average sales for that year.

TABLE De475–481   Wholesale trade margins of independent wholesalers, by type of business: 1869–1947

Contributed by Daniel M. G. Raff

Year	Dry goods	Furniture	Automobile accessories	Gasoline and oil	Lumber	Hardware	Drug (general line)
	De475	De476	De477	De478	De479	De480	De481
	Percent	Percent	Percent	Percent	Percent	Percent	Percent
1869	14	14.0	—	—	10.0	19	10.0
1879	15	14.0	—	—	10.0	19	11.0
1889	16	14.0	—	—	10.0	19	12.2
1899	17	14.0	—	—	10.0	19	13.6
1909	18	15.0	25.0	18.0	11.5	20	15.2
1919	18	16.2	25.0	16.0	13.0	22	16.6
1929	18	18.0	25.5	17.8	14.2	23	16.0
1939	18	22.0	24.0	17.5	16.0	24	15.2
1947	18	22.0	23.0	16.5	17.0	24	15.6

Source

Harold Barger, *Distribution's Place in the American Economy since 1869* (Princeton University Press, 1955), pp. 57, 60, and 81.

Documentation

All figures are percent of wholesale value of sales. See the text for Table De248–267 for definition of "margin" and statement regarding reliability of the data.

Independent or regular wholesalers are types of wholesalers handling finished goods or construction materials for eventual distribution through some kind of retail outlet. This category excludes other kinds of wholesalers, such as brokers, commission merchants, manufacturers' sale branches, and chain store warehouses.

Daniel M. G. Raff

TABLE De482–515   Advertising expenditures, by medium: 1867–1998

Contributed by Daniel M. G. Raff

	All media			Newspapers			Magazines				Television						
												Broadcast					
Year	Total	National	Local	Total	National	Local	Total	Weeklies	Women's	Monthlies	Total	Total	Four TV networks	Three TV networks	Syndication	Spot (national)	Spot (local)
	De482	De483	De484	De485	De486	De487	De488	De489	De490	De491	De492 [1]	De493	De494	De495	De496 [2]	De497	De498
	Million dollars	Million dollars	Million dollars	Million dollars	Million dollars	Million dollars	Million dollars	Million dollars	Million dollars	Million dollars	Million dollars	Million dollars	Million dollars	Million dollars	Million dollars	Million dollars	Million dollars
1867	40	—	—	—	—	—	—	—	—	—	—	—	—	—	—	—	—
1876	150	—	—	—	—	—	—	—	—	—	—	—	—	—	—	—	—
1880	175	—	—	—	—	—	—	—	—	—	—	—	—	—	—	—	—
1890	300	—	—	—	—	—	—	—	—	—	—	—	—	—	—	—	—
1900	450	—	—	—	—	—	—	—	—	—	—	—	—	—	—	—	—
1904	750	—	—	—	—	—	—	—	—	—	—	—	—	—	—	—	—
1909	1,000	—	—	—	—	—	—	—	—	—	—	—	—	—	—	—	—
1914	1,100	—	—	—	—	—	—	—	—	—	—	—	—	—	—	—	—
1915	1,100	—	—	—	—	—	—	—	—	—	—	—	—	—	—	—	—
1916	1,240	—	—	—	—	—	—	—	—	—	—	—	—	—	—	—	—
1917	1,380	—	—	—	—	—	—	—	—	—	—	—	—	—	—	—	—
1918	1,240	—	—	—	—	—	—	—	—	—	—	—	—	—	—	—	—
1919	1,930	—	—	—	—	—	—	—	—	—	—	—	—	—	—	—	—
1920	2,480	—	—	—	—	—	—	—	—	—	—	—	—	—	—	—	—
1921	1,930	—	—	—	—	—	—	—	—	—	—	—	—	—	—	—	—
1922	2,200	—	—	—	—	—	—	—	—	—	—	—	—	—	—	—	—
1923	2,400	—	—	—	—	—	—	—	—	—	—	—	—	—	—	—	—
1924	2,480	—	—	—	—	—	—	—	—	—	—	—	—	—	—	—	—
1925	2,600	—	—	—	—	—	—	—	—	—	—	—	—	—	—	—	—
1926	2,700	—	—	—	—	—	—	—	—	—	—	—	—	—	—	—	—
1927	2,720	—	—	—	—	—	—	—	—	—	—	—	—	—	—	—	—
1928	2,760	—	—	—	—	—	—	—	—	—	—	—	—	—	—	—	—
1929	2,850	—	—	—	—	—	—	—	—	—	—	—	—	—	—	—	—
1930	2,450	—	—	—	—	—	—	—	—	—	—	—	—	—	—	—	—
1931	2,100	—	—	—	—	—	—	—	—	—	—	—	—	—	—	—	—
1932	1,620	—	—	—	—	—	—	—	—	—	—	—	—	—	—	—	—
1933	1,325	—	—	—	—	—	—	—	—	—	—	—	—	—	—	—	—
1934	1,650	—	—	—	—	—	—	—	—	—	—	—	—	—	—	—	—
1935	1,720	890	830	761	148	613	130	54	51	25	—	—	—	—	—	—	—
1936	1,930	1,030	900	842	166	676	154	67	57	30	—	—	—	—	—	—	—
1937	2,100	1,130	970	870	166	704	181	83	60	38	—	—	—	—	—	—	—
1938	1,930	1,060	870	782	148	634	158	75	52	31	—	—	—	—	—	—	—
1939	2,010	1,120	890	793	152	641	169	88	49	32	—	—	—	—	—	—	—
1940	2,110	1,190	920	815	161	654	186	103	49	34	—	—	—	—	—	—	—
1941	2,250	1,280	970	844	162	682	201	117	52	32	—	—	—	—	—	—	—
1942	2,160	1,220	940	797	141	656	179	107	52	20	—	—	—	—	—	—	—
1943	2,490	1,455	1,035	899	180	719	259	154	66	39	—	—	—	—	—	—	—
1944	2,700	1,655	1,045	886	191	695	305	172	82	51	—	—	—	—	—	—	—

Year	All media Total De482 (Million dollars)	National De483 (Million dollars)	Local De484 (Million dollars)	Newspapers Total De485 (Million dollars)	National De486 (Million dollars)	Local De487 (Million dollars)	Magazines Total De488 (Million dollars)	Weeklies De489 (Million dollars)	Women's De490 (Million dollars)	Monthlies De491 (Million dollars)	Television Total De492 [1] (Million dollars)	Broadcast Total De493 (Million dollars)	Four TV networks De494 (Million dollars)	Three TV networks De495 (Million dollars)	Syndication De496 [2] (Million dollars)	Spot (national) De497 (Million dollars)	Spot (local) De498 (Million dollars)
1945	2,840	1,740	1,100	919	203	716	344	188	97	59	—	—	—	—	—	—	—
1946	3,340	1,950	1,390	1,155	238	917	405	202	127	76	—	—	—	—	—	—	—
1947	4,260	2,500	1,760	1,471	323	1,148	464	246	133	85	—	—	—	—	—	—	—
1948	4,870	2,795	2,075	1,745	379	1,366	477	258	133	86	—	—	—	—	—	—	—
1949	5,210	2,990	2,220	1,911	463	1,448	458	245	129	84	58	58	—	30	—	9	19
1950	5,700	3,260	2,440	2,070	518	1,552	478	261	129	88	171	171	—	85	—	31	55
1951	6,420	3,710	2,710	2,251	529	1,722	535	297	143	95	332	332	—	181	—	70	81
1952	7,140	4,100	3,040	2,464	537	1,927	575	325	149	101	454	454	—	256	—	94	104
1953	7,740	4,515	3,225	2,632	606	2,026	627	351	158	118	606	606	—	320	—	145	141
1954	8,150	4,820	3,330	2,685	607	2,078	629	363	152	114	809	809	—	422	—	207	180
1955	9,150	5,380	3,770	3,077	712	2,365	691	397	161	133	1,035	1,035	—	550	—	260	225
1956	9,910	5,940	3,970	3,223	754	2,469	758	440	166	152	1,225	1,225	—	643	—	329	253
1957	10,270	6,250	4,020	3,260	760	2,500	777	451	165	161	1,286	1,286	—	690	—	352	244
1958	10,310	6,340	3,970	3,176	724	2,452	734	425	151	158	1,387	1,387	—	742	—	397	248
1959	11,270	6,855	4,415	3,526	773	2,753	832	479	168	185	1,529	1,529	—	776	—	486	267
1960	11,960	7,305	4,655	3,681	778	2,903	909	525	184	200	1,627	1,627	—	820	—	527	280
1961	11,860	7,315	4,545	3,601	744	2,857	895	508	187	200	1,691	1,691	—	887	—	548	256
1962	12,430	7,695	4,735	3,659	722	2,937	942	519	200	223	1,897	1,897	—	976	—	629	292
1963	13,100	8,120	4,980	3,780	702	3,078	1,002	540	218	244	2,032	2,032	—	1,025	—	698	309
1964	14,150	8,720	5,430	4,120	773	3,347	1,074	583	231	260	2,289	2,289	—	1,132	—	806	351
1965	15,250	9,340	5,910	4,426	784	3,642	1,161	610	269	282	2,515	2,515	—	1,237	—	892	386
1966	16,630	10,150	6,480	4,865	887	3,978	1,254	658	280	316	2,823	2,823	—	1,393	—	988	442
1967	16,870	10,210	6,660	4,910	846	4,064	1,245	651	282	312	2,909	2,909	—	1,455	—	988	466
1968	18,090	10,800	7,290	5,232	889	4,343	1,283	657	284	342	3,231	3,231	—	1,523	—	1,131	577
1969	19,420	11,400	8,020	5,714	943	4,771	1,344	662	308	374	3,585	3,585	—	1,678	—	1,253	654
1970	19,550	11,350	8,200	5,704	891	4,813	1,292	617	301	374	3,596	3,596	—	1,658	—	1,234	704
1971	20,700	11,755	8,945	6,167	972	5,195	1,370	626	340	404	3,534	3,534	—	1,593	—	1,145	796
1972	23,210	12,980	10,230	6,938	1,062	5,876	1,440	610	368	462	4,091	4,091	—	1,804	—	1,318	969
1973	24,980	13,700	11,280	7,481	1,049	6,432	1,448	583	362	503	4,460	4,460	—	1,968	—	1,377	1,115
1974	26,620	14,700	11,920	7,842	1,105	6,737	1,504	630	372	502	4,854	4,854	—	2,145	—	1,497	1,212
1975	27,900	15,200	12,700	8,234	1,109	7,125	1,465	612	368	485	5,263	5,263	—	2,306	—	1,623	1,334
1976	33,300	18,355	14,945	9,618	1,342	8,276	1,789	748	457	584	6,721	6,721	—	2,857	—	2,154	1,710
1977	37,440	20,595	16,845	10,751	1,472	9,279	2,162	903	565	694	7,612	7,612	—	3,460	—	2,204	1,948
1978	43,330	23,720	19,610	12,214	1,541	10,673	2,597	1,158	672	767	8,955	8,955	—	3,975	—	2,607	2,373
1979	48,780	26,695	22,085	13,863	1,770	12,093	2,932	1,327	730	875	10,154	10,154	—	4,599	—	2,873	2,682
1980	53,570	29,840	23,730	14,794	1,963	12,831	3,149	1,418	782	949	11,488	11,416	—	5,130	50	3,269	2,967
1981	60,460	33,930	26,530	16,528	2,259	14,269	3,533	1,598	853	1,082	12,889	12,729	—	5,540	75	3,746	3,368
1982	66,670	37,880	28,790	17,694	2,452	15,242	3,710	1,659	904	1,147	14,713	14,423	—	6,144	150	4,364	3,765
1983	76,000	42,660	33,340	20,582	2,734	17,848	4,233	1,917	1,056	1,260	16,879	16,427	—	6,955	300	4,827	4,345
1984	88,010	49,890	38,120	23,522	3,081	20,441	4,932	2,224	1,209	1,499	20,043	19,310	—	8,318	420	5,488	5,084
1985	94,900	53,510	41,390	25,170	3,352	21,818	5,155	2,297	1,294	1,564	21,287	20,298	—	8,060	520	6,004	5,714
1986	102,370	57,090	45,280	26,990	3,376	23,614	5,317	2,327	1,376	1,614	23,199	22,026	—	8,342	600	6,570	6,514
1987	110,270	60,920	49,350	29,412	3,494	25,918	5,607	2,445	1,417	1,745	24,262	22,941	—	8,500	762	6,846	6,833
1988	118,750	66,040	52,710	31,197	3,586	27,611	6,072	2,646	1,504	1,922	26,131	24,490	—	9,172	901	7,147	7,270
1989	124,770	69,495	55,275	32,368	3,704	28,664	6,716	2,813	1,710	2,193	27,459	25,364	—	9,110	1,288	7,354	7,612

Notes appear at end of table

(continued)

TABLE De482–515   Advertising expenditures, by medium: 1867–1998   Continued

	All media			Newspapers			Magazines				Television						
													Broadcast					
	Total	National	Local	Total	National	Local	Total	Weeklies	Women's	Monthlies	Total [1]	Total	Four TV networks	Three TV networks	Syndication [2]	Spot (national)	Spot (local)
	De482	De483	De484	De485	De486	De487	De488	De489	De490	De491	De492	De493	De494	De495	De496	De497	De498
Year	Million dollars	Million dollars	Million dollars	Million dollars	Million dollars	Million dollars	Million dollars	Million dollars	Million dollars	Million dollars	Million dollars	Million dollars	Million dollars	Million dollars	Million dollars	Million dollars	Million dollars
1990	129,590	73,380	56,210	32,281	3,867	28,414	6,803	—	—	—	29,073	26,616	9,863	9,383	1,109	7,788	7,856
1991	127,570	73,370	54,200	30,409	3,685	26,724	6,524	—	—	—	28,189	25,461	9,533	8,933	1,253	7,110	7,565
1992	132,650	76,710	55,940	30,737	3,602	27,135	7,000	—	—	—	30,450	27,249	10,249	9,549	1,370	7,551	8,079
1993	139,540	80,795	58,745	32,025	3,620	28,405	7,357	—	—	—	31,698	28,020	10,209	9,369	1,576	7,800	8,435
1994	151,680	88,250	63,430	34,356	3,906	30,450	7,916	—	—	—	35,435	31,133	10,942	9,959	1,734	8,993	9,464
1995	162,930	95,360	67,570	36,317	3,996	32,321	8,580	—	—	—	37,828	32,720	11,600	10,263	2,016	9,119	9,985
1996	175,230	103,040	72,190	38,402	4,400	34,002	9,010	—	—	—	42,484	36,046	13,081	11,423	2,218	9,803	10,944
1997	187,529	110,232	77,297	41,670	5,016	36,654	9,821	—	—	—	44,130	36,893	13,020	11,324	2,438	9,999	11,436
1998	201,594	118,966	82,628	44,292	5,402	38,890	10,518	—	—	—	47,474	39,173	13,736	12,105	2,609	10,659	12,169

	Television			Radio				Farm publications	Direct mail	Business papers	Outdoor			Internet	Miscellaneous		
	Cable																
	Total	Spot (local)	Networks	Total	Network	Spot (national)	Spot (local)				Total	National	Local		Total	National	Local
	De499	De500	De501	De502	De503	De504	De505	De506	De507	De508	De509	De510	De511	De512	De513	De514	De515
Year	Million dollars	Million dollars	Million dollars	Million dollars	Million dollars	Million dollars	Million dollars	Million dollars	Million dollars	Million dollars	Million dollars	Million dollars	Million dollars	Million dollars	Million dollars	Million dollars	Million dollars
1867	—	—	—	—	—	—	—	—	—	—	—	—	—	—	—	—	—
1876	—	—	—	—	—	—	—	—	—	—	—	—	—	—	—	—	—
1880	—	—	—	—	—	—	—	—	—	—	—	—	—	—	—	—	—
1890	—	—	—	—	—	—	—	—	—	—	—	—	—	—	—	—	—
1900	—	—	—	—	—	—	—	—	—	—	—	—	—	—	—	—	—
1904	—	—	—	—	—	—	—	—	—	—	—	—	—	—	—	—	—
1909	—	—	—	—	—	—	—	—	—	—	—	—	—	—	—	—	—
1914	—	—	—	—	—	—	—	—	—	—	—	—	—	—	—	—	—
1915	—	—	—	—	—	—	—	—	—	—	—	—	—	—	—	—	—
1916	—	—	—	—	—	—	—	—	—	—	—	—	—	—	—	—	—
1917	—	—	—	—	—	—	—	—	—	—	—	—	—	—	—	—	—
1918	—	—	—	—	—	—	—	—	—	—	—	—	—	—	—	—	—
1919	—	—	—	—	—	—	—	—	—	—	—	—	—	—	—	—	—
1920	—	—	—	—	—	—	—	—	—	—	—	—	—	—	—	—	—
1921	—	—	—	—	—	—	—	—	—	—	—	—	—	—	—	—	—
1922	—	—	—	—	—	—	—	—	—	—	—	—	—	—	—	—	—
1923	—	—	—	—	—	—	—	—	—	—	—	—	—	—	—	—	—
1924	—	—	—	—	—	—	—	—	—	—	—	—	—	—	—	—	—
1925	—	—	—	—	—	—	—	—	—	—	—	—	—	—	—	—	—
1926	—	—	—	—	—	—	—	—	—	—	—	—	—	—	—	—	—
1927	—	—	—	—	—	—	—	—	—	—	—	—	—	—	—	—	—
1928	—	—	—	—	—	—	—	—	—	—	—	—	—	—	—	—	—
1929	—	—	—	—	—	—	—	—	—	—	—	—	—	—	—	—	—

Year	Television Cable Total De499	Spot (local) De500	Networks De501	Radio Total De502	Network De503	Spot (national) De504	Spot (local) De505	Farm publications De506	Direct mail De507	Business papers De508	Outdoor Total De509	Outdoor National De510	Outdoor Local De511	Internet De512	Miscellaneous Total De513	Miscellaneous National De514	Miscellaneous Local De515
	Million dollars	Million dollars	Million dollars	Million dollars	Million dollars	Million dollars	Million dollars	Million dollars	Million dollars	Million dollars	Million dollars	Million dollars	Million dollars	Million dollars	Million dollars	Million dollars	Million dollars
1930	—	—	—	—	—	—	—	—	—	—	—	—	—	—	—	—	—
1931	—	—	—	—	—	—	—	—	—	—	—	—	—	—	—	—	—
1932	—	—	—	—	—	—	—	—	—	—	—	—	—	—	—	—	—
1933	—	—	—	—	—	—	—	—	—	—	—	—	—	—	—	—	—
1934	—	—	—	—	—	—	—	—	—	—	—	—	—	—	—	—	—
1935	—	—	—	113	63	15	35	10	282	51	31	23	8	—	342	168	174
1936	—	—	—	122	75	23	24	12	319	61	38	28	10	—	382	192	190
1937	—	—	—	165	89	28	48	19	333	70	44	33	11	—	418	211	207
1938	—	—	—	167	89	34	44	14	324	61	43	32	11	—	381	200	181
1939	—	—	—	184	99	35	50	17	333	69	44	33	11	—	401	213	188
1940	—	—	—	215	113	42	60	19	334	76	45	34	11	—	420	225	195
1941	—	—	—	247	125	52	70	19	353	89	53	37	16	—	444	242	202
1942	—	—	—	260	129	59	72	18	329	98	44	31	13	—	427	228	199
1943	—	—	—	314	157	71	86	25	322	142	42	29	13	—	487	270	217
1944	—	—	—	393	192	87	114	29	326	177	56	39	17	—	528	309	219
1945	—	—	—	424	198	92	134	32	290	204	72	50	22	—	555	327	228
1946	—	—	—	455	200	98	157	36	334	211	86	60	26	—	658	368	290
1947	—	—	—	506	201	106	199	49	579	233	121	79	42	—	837	466	371
1948	—	—	—	562	211	121	230	56	689	251	132	89	43	—	958	522	436
1949	—	—	—	571	203	123	245	55	756	248	131	88	43	—	1,022	557	465
1950	—	—	—	605	196	136	273	58	803	251	142	96	46	—	1,122	608	514
1951	—	—	—	606	180	138	288	64	924	292	149	101	48	—	1,267	696	571
1952	—	—	—	624	162	141	321	70	1,024	365	162	109	53	—	1,402	767	635
1953	—	—	—	611	141	146	324	71	1,099	395	176	119	57	—	1,523	846	677
1954	—	—	—	559	114	135	310	71	1,202	408	187	126	61	—	1,600	899	701
1955	—	—	—	545	84	134	327	72	1,299	446	192	130	62	—	1,793	1,002	791
1956	—	—	—	567	60	161	346	73	1,419	496	201	136	65	—	1,948	1,111	837
1957	—	—	—	618	63	187	368	71	1,471	568	199	134	65	—	2,012	1,169	843
1958	—	—	—	620	58	190	372	67	1,589	525	192	130	62	—	2,020	1,184	836
1959	—	—	—	656	44	206	406	71	1,688	569	193	130	63	—	2,206	1,280	926
1960	—	—	—	693	43	222	428	66	1,830	609	203	137	66	—	2,342	1,364	978
1961	—	—	—	683	43	220	420	62	1,850	578	180	122	58	—	2,320	1,366	954
1962	—	—	—	736	46	233	457	65	1,933	597	171	115	56	—	2,430	1,437	993
1963	—	—	—	789	56	243	490	66	2,078	615	171	115	56	—	2,567	1,520	1,047
1964	—	—	—	846	59	256	531	66	2,184	623	175	117	58	—	2,773	1,630	1,143
1965	—	—	—	917	60	275	582	71	2,324	671	180	120	60	—	2,985	1,745	1,240
1966	—	—	—	1,010	63	308	639	70	2,461	712	178	118	60	—	3,257	1,896	1,361
1967	—	—	—	1,048	64	314	670	68	2,488	707	191	126	65	—	3,304	1,909	1,395
1968	—	—	—	1,190	63	360	767	68	2,612	714	208	137	71	—	3,552	2,020	1,532
1969	—	—	—	1,264	59	368	837	64	2,670	752	213	138	75	—	3,814	2,131	1,683
1970	—	—	—	1,308	56	371	881	62	2,766	740	234	154	80	—	3,848	2,126	1,722
1971	—	—	—	1,445	63	395	987	57	3,067	720	261	172	89	—	4,079	2,201	1,878
1972	—	—	—	1,612	74	402	1,136	59	3,420	781	292	192	100	—	4,577	2,428	2,149
1973	—	—	—	1,723	68	400	1,255	65	3,698	865	308	200	108	—	4,932	2,562	2,370
1974	—	—	—	1,837	69	405	1,363	72	4,054	900	309	203	106	—	5,248	2,746	2,502

Notes appear at end of table   (continued)

TABLE De482-515   Advertising expenditures, by medium: 1867–1998   *Continued*

Year	Television Total De499 (Million dollars)	Cable Spot (local) De500 (Million dollars)	Cable Networks De501 (Million dollars)	Radio Total De502 (Million dollars)	Radio Network De503 (Million dollars)	Radio Spot (national) De504 (Million dollars)	Radio Spot (local) De505 (Million dollars)	Farm publications De506 (Million dollars)	Direct mail De507 (Million dollars)	Business papers De508 (Million dollars)	Outdoor Total De509 (Million dollars)	Outdoor National De510 (Million dollars)	Outdoor Local De511 (Million dollars)	Internet De512 (Million dollars)	Miscellaneous Total De513 (Million dollars)	Miscellaneous National De514 (Million dollars)	Miscellaneous Local De515 (Million dollars)
1975	—	—	—	1,980	83	436	1,461	74	4,124	919	335	220	115	—	5,506	2,841	2,665
1976	—	—	—	2,330	105	518	1,707	86	4,786	1,035	383	252	131	—	6,552	3,431	3,121
1977	—	—	—	2,634	137	546	1,951	90	5,164	1,221	418	290	128	—	7,388	3,849	3,539
1978	—	—	—	3,052	147	620	2,285	104	5,987	1,400	466	307	159	—	8,255	4,135	4,120
1979	—	—	—	3,310	161	665	2,484	120	6,653	1,575	540	355	185	—	9,633	4,992	4,641
1980	72	12	60	3,702	183	779	2,740	130	7,596	1,674	578	364	214	—	7,559	5,163	2,396
1981	160	26	134	4,230	230	879	3,121	146	8,944	1,841	650	419	231	—	8,399	5,804	2,595
1982	290	48	242	4,670	255	923	3,492	148	10,319	1,876	721	465	256	—	9,019	6,399	2,620
1983	452	76	376	5,210	296	1,038	3,876	163	11,795	1,990	794	512	282	—	9,954	6,952	3,002
1984	733	121	612	5,817	320	1,197	4,300	181	13,800	2,270	872	562	310	—	11,673	8,129	3,544
1985	989	196	793	6,490	365	1,335	4,790	186	15,500	2,375	945	610	335	—	11,992	8,560	3,432
1986	1,173	270	903	6,949	423	1,348	5,178	192	17,145	2,382	985	600	385	—	12,711	9,133	3,578
1987	1,321	306	1,015	7,206	413	1,330	5,463	196	19,111	2,458	1,025	615	410	—	13,693	9,743	3,950
1988	1,641	383	1,258	7,798	425	1,418	5,955	196	21,115	2,610	1,064	628	436	—	14,786	10,568	4,218
1989	2,095	497	1,598	8,323	476	1,547	6,300	212	21,945	2,763	1,111	653	458	—	15,543	11,118	4,425
1990	2,457	597	1,860	8,726	482	1,635	6,609	—	23,370	2,875	1,084	640	444	—	16,452	11,956	4,496
1991	2,728	704	2,024	8,476	490	1,575	6,411	—	24,460	2,982	1,077	637	440	—	16,271	11,935	4,336
1992	3,201	974	2,227	8,654	424	1,505	6,725	—	25,392	3,090	1,031	610	421	—	16,977	12,503	4,474
1993	3,678	1,092	2,586	9,457	458	1,657	7,342	—	27,266	3,260	1,090	605	485	—	17,870	13,171	4,699
1994	4,302	1,250	3,052	10,529	463	1,902	8,164	—	29,638	3,358	1,167	648	519	—	19,456	14,384	5,072
1995	5,108	1,573	3,535	11,338	480	1,959	8,899	—	32,866	3,559	1,263	701	562	—	20,943	15,539	5,404
1996	6,438	1,966	4,472	12,269	523	2,135	9,611	—	34,509	3,808	1,339	743	596	—	22,560	16,783	5,777
1997	7,237	2,170	5,067	13,491	560	2,455	10,476	—	36,890	4,109	1,455	795	660	600	23,940	17,751	6,189
1998	8,301	2,474	5,827	15,073	622	2,823	11,628	—	39,620	4,232	1,576	845	731	1,050	25,769	19,153	6,616

[1] Through 1989, includes series De495 in total; thereafter, includes series De494.

[2] Includes WB and UPN.

Source

Data prepared by Robert J. Coen of Universal McCann, from information furnished by the American Newspaper Publishers Association, A. C. Nielsen Company, Publishers' Information Bureau, Farm Publication Reports, Inc., the Direct Mail Advertising Association, A. R. Venezian, Outdoor Advertising, Inc., and the Federal Communications Commission.

Documentation

The data include the cost of preparation, and the cost of talent in the case of radio and television, as well as the charges for space and time.

TABLE De516–522   Newspaper advertising – linage for 52 cities: 1928–1970

Contributed by Daniel M. G. Raff

			Display				
	Total	Classified	Total	Automotive	Financial	General	Retail
	De516	De517	De518	De519	De520	De521	De522
Year	Thousand lines	Thousand lines	Thousand lines	Thousand lines	Thousand lines	Thousand lines	Thousand lines
1928	1,802,482	345,835	1,456,647	142,325	66,005	289,779	958,538
1929	1,897,213	345,441	1,551,772	150,473	74,177	338,875	988,248
1930	1,654,246	298,950	1,355,296	107,186	59,255	303,051	885,804
1931	1,464,868	265,270	1,199,598	80,613	40,984	261,817	816,183
1932	1,164,770	220,361	944,409	63,790	23,680	201,830	655,109
1933	1,065,515	197,262	868,253	62,642	20,179	188,045	597,386
1934	1,178,880	205,322	973,559	73,306	19,128	211,384	669,741
1935	1,246,942	228,972	1,017,969	72,929	21,309	216,976	706,755
1936	1,380,121	265,475	1,114,646	72,822	25,025	251,510	765,289
1937	1,409,666	283,416	1,126,250	67,802	22,480	247,155	788,813
1938	1,225,166	255,012	970,154	47,255	19,170	191,948	711,781
1939	1,243,550	252,725	990,825	52,678	20,308	191,859	725,980
1940	1,268,632	262,811	1,005,821	62,006	19,424	188,629	735,761
1941	1,313,233	272,568	1,040,666	56,445	20,478	194,053	769,690
1942	1,241,672	257,312	984,360	26,823	17,623	196,653	743,261
1943	1,396,418	335,042	1,061,377	32,358	17,758	247,424	763,837
1944	1,361,244	308,891	1,052,353	31,479	18,365	250,926	751,584
1945	1,391,629	320,156	1,071,474	34,656	22,090	246,052	768,676
1946	1,729,713	423,662	1,306,051	42,106	26,376	266,285	971,284
1947	2,008,536	473,600	1,534,936	68,672	24,417	314,605	1,127,242
1948	2,263,446	522,446	1,741,000	82,737	25,791	338,641	1,293,831
1949	2,301,968	484,024	1,817,944	105,485	25,345	354,781	1,332,333
1950	2,440,150	510,633	1,929,517	120,592	28,274	389,564	1,391,086
1951	2,478,463	582,014	1,896,449	109,996	30,164	366,661	1,389,629
1952	2,505,393	617,512	1,887,881	107,424	32,284	349,131	1,399,041
1953	2,610,670	648,841	1,961,829	140,145	33,424	368,049	1,420,212
1954	2,581,175	602,772	1,978,403	143,015	36,347	358,040	1,441,002
1955	2,843,395	704,461	2,138,934	191,034	40,593	376,201	1,531,107
1956	2,910,781	724,610	2,186,170	170,021	45,274	408,645	1,562,231
1957	2,829,132	685,470	2,143,662	181,400	47,515	377,714	1,537,033
1958	2,685,618	628,748	2,056,869	141,761	46,400	360,844	1,507,864
1959	2,865,238	727,574	2,137,664	155,080	54,704	363,580	1,564,299
1960	2,888,617	735,212	2,153,405	165,208	54,234	345,694	1,588,269
1961	2,776,958	697,740	2,079,217	147,598	59,175	323,043	1,549,401
1962	2,798,250	725,507	2,072,743	149,307	58,017	301,495	1,563,923
1963	2,856,483	749,734	2,106,749	150,555	58,841	285,778	1,611,576
1964	2,973,466	787,135	2,186,331	159,729	60,867	292,549	1,673,186
1965	3,164,577	865,631	2,298,946	170,366	63,350	288,528	1,776,702
1966	3,354,253	924,255	2,429,998	182,894	73,184	310,287	1,863,632
1967	3,297,750	878,114	2,419,636	158,506	66,943	297,106	1,897,081
1968	3,381,058	923,725	2,457,334	170,958	72,839	296,134	1,917,404
1969	3,575,126	1,017,084	2,558,042	173,263	81,677	300,080	2,003,022
1970	3,443,755	917,262	2,526,512	161,570	74,907	275,156	2,014,880

Sources

1928–1938, unpublished data; 1939–1946, *1969 Business Statistics*, p. 57; 1947–1970, *1971 Business Statistics*, p. 57.

Documentation

These series were discontinued; Table De523–526 replaces them.

Series De521. Covers advertising of specific products on general sale, as distinguished from the advertising of retail stores, and automotive or financial advertising.

TABLE De523–526   Newspaper advertising expenditures: 1950–2001

Contributed by Daniel M. G. Raff

Year	Total De523 Million dollars	Retail De524 Million dollars	National De525 Million dollars	Classified De526 Million dollars	Year	Total De523 Million dollars	Retail De524 Million dollars	National De525 Million dollars	Classified De526 Million dollars	Year	Total De523 Million dollars	Retail De524 Million dollars	National De525 Million dollars	Classified De526 Million dollars
1950	2,070	1,175	518	377	1970	5,704	3,292	891	1,521	1990	32,280	16,652	4,122	11,506
1951	2,251	1,259	529	463	1971	6,167	3,565	972	1,630	1991	30,349	15,839	3,924	10,587
1952	2,464	1,411	537	516	1972	6,939	3,964	1,062	1,913	1992	30,639	16,041	3,834	10,764
1953	2,632	1,455	606	571	1973	7,481	4,245	1,049	2,187	1993	31,869	16,859	3,853	11,157
1954	2,685	1,539	607	539	1974	7,842	4,563	1,105	2,174	1994	34,109	17,496	4,149	12,464
1955	3,077	1,755	712	610	1975	8,234	4,966	1,109	2,159	1995	36,092	18,099	4,251	13,742
1956	3,223	1,808	768	661	1976	9,618	5,668	1,342	2,608	1996	38,075	18,344	4,667	15,065
1957	3,268	1,835	738	665	1977	10,751	6,241	1,472	3,038	1997	41,330	19,242	5,315	16,773
1958	3,176	1,802	724	650	1978	12,213	7,023	1,541	3,649	1998	43,925	20,331	5,721	17,873
1959	3,526	2,014	774	738	1979	13,863	7,845	1,770	4,248	1999	46,289	20,907	6,732	18,650
1960	3,681	2,100	778	803	1980	14,794	8,609	1,963	4,222	2000	48,670	21,409	7,653	19,608
1961	3,601	2,053	744	804	1981	16,527	9,686	2,258	4,583	2001 [1]	44,317	20,690	7,005	16,622
1962	3,659	2,103	722	834	1982	17,694	10,390	2,452	4,852					
1963	3,780	2,211	702	867	1983	20,581	11,841	2,734	6,006					
1964	4,120	2,344	773	1,003	1984	23,522	12,784	3,081	7,657					
1965	4,426	2,429	783	1,214	1985	25,170	13,443	3,352	8,375					
1966	4,865	2,645	887	1,333	1986	26,990	14,311	3,376	9,303					
1967	4,910	2,760	846	1,304	1987	29,412	15,227	3,494	10,691					
1968	5,232	2,919	889	1,424	1988	31,197	15,790	3,821	11,586					
1969	5,714	3,166	943	1,605	1989	32,368	16,504	3,948	11,916					

[1] Preliminary estimate.

Source

Downloaded May 9, 2002, from the Internet site of the Newspaper Association of America (figures last updated March 2002).

Documentation

Prior to 1988, advertising linage data for approximately 700 daily and 500 Sunday newspapers were combined with data for newspaper advertising rates in order to obtain advertising expenditures. Adjustments were made for discounting practices. Beginning with 1988, newspaper advertising linage data have been generated by an industrywide survey by the Newspaper Advertising Bureau, Inc., and are not directly comparable to previous years. These series are updated by the Newspaper Association of America, which has taken over the function of the now defunct Newspaper Advertising Bureau.

The advertising of retail merchants is included under the classification "retail." The advertising of products is included under the classification "national." The retail advertiser is the merchant whose customers are the consumers. The national advertiser is the manufacturer, who distributes to these merchants.

TABLE De527–537   Magazine advertising expenditures, by product: 1948–1984

Contributed by Daniel M. G. Raff

Year	Total	Apparel and accessories	Automotive	Building materials	Drugs and toiletries	Foods, soft drinks, confectionery	Household equipment, supplies, furnishings	Industrial materials	Soaps, cleansers, etc.	Smoking materials	All other
	De527	De528	De529	De530	De531	De532	De533	De534	De535	De536	De537
	Million dollars	Million dollars	Million dollars	Million dollars	Million dollars	Million dollars	Million dollars	Million dollars	Million dollars	Million dollars	Million dollars
1948	458.7	47.6	38.2	19.1	50.3	57.4	27.1	59.2	21.6	9.4	12.0
1949	440.9	41.7	41.0	17.8	49.0	57.0	27.1	51.4	20.9	9.7	14.3
1950	458.5	39.0	42.0	20.1	50.1	60.1	26.6	59.1	24.5	8.2	13.0
1951	513.9	44.5	41.4	24.9	54.4	65.1	31.3	63.2	33.3	10.9	13.7
1952	553.8	44.6	46.9	28.2	58.0	70.0	30.1	62.5	40.6	9.9	14.6
1953	603.1	48.9	56.0	32.1	55.9	76.8	30.7	69.6	42.8	10.9	14.9
1954	597.1	48.6	54.3	30.2	55.8	81.1	30.8	64.5	42.7	8.7	16.4
1955	657.3	51.1	61.1	33.3	59.7	86.3	34.4	69.4	49.3	9.3	17.3
1956	691.7	54.0	58.1	35.8	62.7	86.9	31.7	72.0	59.2	11.5	16.4
1957	738.6	53.2	65.3	32.0	75.1	89.2	39.5	68.3	59.2	11.1	20.9
1958	693.1	49.1	64.8	29.4	71.2	86.3	40.7	55.0	45.1	10.5	24.4
1959	783.8	48.5	80.6	33.9	74.7	104.6	50.9	66.7	50.2	10.4	27.4
1960	853.2	56.7	93.6	35.8	80.0	117.3	50.9	67.5	55.4	9.1	26.2
1961	831.3	53.9	83.9	29.6	78.6	122.7	51.0	55.5	45.5	8.4	28.8
1962	875.3	54.9	94.8	27.8	85.6	126.9	54.1	59.6	44.7	9.3	33.1
1963	931.6	57.3	101.8	26.5	96.4	124.3	56.4	66.3	45.1	11.9	35.9
1964	996.6	62.0	110.6	27.1	108.8	134.8	58.1	71.6	48.5	15.9	38.2
1965	1,083.3	64.8	112.2	32.2	117.9	134.0	69.5	74.8	46.5	21.7	41.9
1966	1,170.5	68.0	124.6	34.2	134.0	125.2	79.2	80.2	55.4	17.6	39.6
1967	1,161.0	60.8	103.7	31.0	148.3	116.1	89.2	70.5	62.7	22.9	39.9
1968	1,163.6	62.9	112.5	28.2	142.0	104.7	93.0	73.3	56.8	22.1	39.4
1969	1,243.4	60.4	115.2	26.5	155.6	101.2	102.8	76.9	60.1	15.3	48.1
1970	1,185.7	50.9	95.3	20.8	156.6	99.4	98.0	71.1	43.8	16.4	64.7
1971	1,190.7	46.0	104.8	18.4	154.1	104.0	83.6	63.0	33.1	17.7	105.7
1972	1,210.6	44.2	102.1	21.0	145.0	113.6	81.0	72.9	29.4	20.5	94.6
1973	1,316.0	52.9	120.4	26.7	140.6	96.2	87.0	86.4	28.4	18.6	110.5
1974	1,372.3	50.8	104.7	24.7	143.2	91.1	103.4	79.6	35.4	17.6	136.7
1975	1,328.7	46.0	101.3	20.6	138.1	91.0	100.7	55.0	34.2	19.4	143.4
1976	1,626.7	57.8	142.3	28.3	167.4	120.7	111.0	83.4	47.0	25.0	161.8
1977	1,976.8	68.6	177.1	37.1	201.0	150.3	133.3	113.4	55.0	33.7	194.3
1978	2,364.8	85.8	220.8	46.3	221.9	186.7	192.8	148.8	58.4	37.4	203.0
1979	2,634.0	91.9	212.6	46.4	262.1	200.5	234.0	132.5	69.9	35.0	278.2
1980	2,872.6	112.2	231.1	52.5	280.8	211.9	239.2	139.6	71.0	30.0	290.3
1981	3,256.9	143.4	291.7	59.3	320.4	234.4	256.9	167.9	67.7	29.7	316.6
1982	3,428.9	155.7	333.5	52.2	330.6	263.8	257.6	147.4	50.9	26.6	358.6
1983	4,005.7	206.2	410.4	53.5	385.7	292.3	230.2	171.1	42.5	25.1	403.4
1984	4,668.0	240.0	473.5	68.7	463.6	334.9	242.1	191.6	48.0	34.6	422.6

Sources

1948–1960: U.S. Bureau of Economic Analysis, *1979 Business Statistics* (December 1989), p. 48. 1961–1984: U.S. Bureau of Economic Analysis, *Business Statistics, 1961–88* (December 1989), p. 35.

Documentation

Amounts represent advertising revenue of general magazines and national farm magazines; advertising in nationally distributed newspaper supplements and sections is not included in the data presented here (however, such data are provided in the original reports from Leading National Advertisers). Space cost is based on the one-time rate; special rates are used where applicable. Retail advertising and direct-mail advertising are not distributed according to individual classes but are included in "all other" advertising. Figures from year to year may not be strictly comparable, as minor publications are added or deleted.

CHAPTER Df

Transportation

Editor: Louis P. Cain

TRANSPORTATION

Louis P. Cain

Transportation refers to systems for carrying persons and goods from one place to another. It includes routes such as roadways, waterways, railways, airways, and pipelines. It also includes the means of conveyance such as carts, carriages, wagons, bicycles, automobiles, trucks, railroad engines and cars, ferries, barges, sailing ships, steamers, airplanes, and pipes.

Transportation systems have a direct impact on many aspects of a country's economy and society. This is because individuals, regions, and countries can increase their incomes by specializing in the production of those goods and services that they produce relatively efficiently, and then trading these with others. By reducing the costs of making those trades, transportation systems encourage this specialization and thereby promote the growth of income and wealth. Because of its large size and the diversity of its resources, the United States developed the potential to increase wealth through specialization and trade earlier than most countries. The legal structure of the United States also encouraged this specialization. The U.S. Constitution forbade states from establishing tariffs or other barriers to trade with other states and delegated to the federal government the power to regulate commerce among the states and with foreign nations. As a consequence of these clauses, trade barriers between the former colonies were removed, and the United States established a common, national set of tariff schedules with other countries. The Constitution thus created the framework for the various states to become a "common market" or free trade zone.

Technological advances also led to improvements in transportation. Notable inventions were the steam engine, internal combustion engine, and aircraft, as well as developments in the engineering of bridges and roadways. Much of the technology involved in transportation was invented and developed in the United States, and this makes American transportation history especially interesting.

Transportation is part of the infrastructure of the United States, that is, the underlying, basic structures such as transportation and communications systems, water and power lines, and public institutions such as post offices and schools that are considered vital to the functioning of an economy and society. Where people work and where they live, where goods are produced and where they are sold, are all determined in part by the transportation infrastructure.

One key to effective transportation systems is integration. It is far less costly to cross a river by bridge than to unload a wagon or train, board a boat, and then reload the goods before returning to an overland route. Integrated transportation systems are expensive, and, as a consequence, the transportation system of the United States was developed – by both private and governmental enterprises and in some cases by hybrid government–private enterprises. The subject of one of the earliest Constitutional debates was the Gallatin Report and concerned the role of the federal government in what were called "internal improvements." It was believed that the sheer size of the investment required for these improvements was too great for private entrepreneurs acting alone and that governments should ease this constraint. Two mechanisms were identified. Governments could make direct financial contributions to the development of transportation systems, or they could issue long-term bonds to help pay for construction.[1] In addition, governments became involved by issuing corporate charters to transportation companies. In the early years of this country, such charters implied a special relationship with the government. In granting corporate charters, political leaders could give transportation companies the right to contract loans, levy tolls, and even, in some cases, print money to support transportation enterprises. Government action is also necessary to secure right-of-way for railroads and highways, in many cases using the power of eminent domain to force the sale of private property. Consequently, state and local governments became vitally involved in the development of the U.S. transportation system almost from the beginning. The federal government, in spite of the suggestions of the Gallatin Report, did not become involved in a systematic and continuous way until the late nineteenth century.

Another consequence of the large size of integrated transportation systems was the challenges they presented to management. Business historian Alfred D. Chandler Jr. called the railroad companies, together with their associated telegraph companies, "the first modern business enterprises."

> They were the first to require a large number of full-time managers to coordinate, control, and evaluate the activities of a number of widely scattered operating units. For this reason, they provided the most relevant administrative models for enterprises in the production and distribution of goods and services when such enterprises began to build, on the basis of the new transportation and communication network, their own geographically extended, multiunit business empires. (Chandler 1977, p. 79)

The early history of transportation in the United States and its impact on the larger economy is a complex and fascinating story

Acknowledgments

Louis P. Cain thanks Thomas Geraghty and Peter Meyer for their help as research assistants for this chapter.

---

[1] Goodrich (1960), Chapter 1. The original scholarship on this point was done by Callender (1902).

that has been told in many important historical works, some of which are cited here. This essay examines the major modes of transportation sequentially, focusing on the available quantitative historical evidence that illustrates their growth and development (see Table Df-A).

Highways, Wagons, and Motor Vehicles

In colonial America, most "highways" were little more than earthen paths that turned to mud in rainy weather. This made overland transportation slow, costly, and undependable. Overland transportation

---

TABLE Df-A   Important events, legislation, and judicial decisions relating to transportation: 1787–1996

1787	A steamboat built by John Fitch is given a successful trial.
1794	The Lancaster Turnpike between Philadelphia and Lancaster is completed.
1804	Richard Trevithick of England invents the steam locomotive.
1806	Construction begins on the National Road (now U.S. Highway 40) that extends west from Cumberland (later, Baltimore), Maryland, and reaches Vandalia, Illinois, in 1837.
1807	Robert Fulton introduces the first commercially successful steamboat.
1808	Secretary of the Treasury Albert Gallatin delivers to Congress his report on internal improvements.
1811	First steamboat trip from Pittsburgh to New Orleans is completed.
1817	The Pittsburgh Pike is completed.
1818	Erie Canal construction begins with funding from New York State (a year earlier President James Madison had vetoed a bill providing federal funding).
1819	The *Savannah* becomes the first steam-powered vessel to cross the Atlantic Ocean, but it uses its engines during only 85 hours of a 27.5-day trip; the balance is under sail.
1821	Trade with Santa Fe begins.
1825	Construction begins on the Baltimore and Ohio Railroad.
1825	The Erie Canal between Buffalo and Albany is completed.
1825	The Schuylkill Navigation between Philadelphia and Port Carbon, Pennsylvania, a system of canals and slack water, is opened.
1825	The Stockton and Darlington Railway, built in England by George Stephenson, offers the first regularly scheduled steam-powered railway service.
1826	The Granite Railroad, actually a tramway, is completed in Quincy, Massachusetts.
1830	Peter Cooper builds the first steam locomotive in the United States.
1830	The Baltimore and Ohio Railroad begins passenger service.
1831	The South Carolina Canal and Railroad Company begins the first regularly scheduled steam-powered railway service in the United States.
1839	Charles Goodyear successfully vulcanizes rubber.
1843	A substantial flow of migration to Oregon begins.
1844	The first U.S. plank road is constructed in New York State.
1845	The *Rainbow*, the first clipper ship, is constructed in New York.
1847	The Mormon migration from Illinois to Utah begins.
1851	The Illinois Central Railroad is charted and given a federal land grant to subsidize construction.
1853	Elisha Otis introduces the elevator.
1859	The first oil well is drilled near Titusville, Pennsylvania.
1860	The *Pony Express* is in operation from St. Joseph, Missouri, to San Francisco.
1869	The first transcontinental railway line across the United States is completed at Promontory Point, Utah.
1872	George Pullman introduces his sleeper coach.
1876	Gustavus Swift successfully ships meat from Chicago to Boston in a refrigerated car.
1876	Refrigerated ships permit the export of beef from Argentina.
1877	*Munn v. Illinois* establishes the right of states to regulate private property in the public interest.
1883	The Brooklyn Bridge is opened.
1883	Railroads introduce standard time zones.
1886	Railroads adopt standard gauge.
1886	*Wabash v. Illinois* establishes that states cannot regulate private property in interstate commerce.
1887	The Interstate Commerce Act creates the Interstate Commerce Commission, the first federal regulatory body.
1888	The first U.S. electric trolley line is opened in Richmond, Virginia.
1893	Charles and Frank Duryea create the first American gasoline-powered automobile.
1897	Francis and Freelon Stanley introduce their steam-powered automobile.
1897	Rudolf Diesel of Germany successfully demonstrates the engine that bears his name.
1897	The first subway opens in Boston, Massachusetts.
1901	Hay–Paunce Treaty authorizes the United States to build a canal across the Central America isthmus.
1903	Wilbur and Orville Wright make the first successful airplane flight using a petrol engine.
1906	Cunard of Great Britain introduces the *Lusitania* and the *Mauretania*, the first giant passenger ships.
1908	Henry Ford introduces the first Model T.

TABLE Df-A Important events, legislation, and judicial decisions relating to transportation : 1787–1996 *Continued*

1911	First transcontinental flight takes place.
1913	Ford introduces the moving assembly line in Highland Park, Michigan.
1914	The first scheduled airline service begins across Tampa Bay between St. Petersburg and Tampa, but lasts only a few months.
1914	The Panama Canal is completed.
1916	The Federal Aid Roads Act creates a national road network.
1918	The U.S. government uses army pilots to initiate the first permanent airmail service.
1920	The first transcontinental airmail service begins.
1927	Charles Lindbergh makes the first nonstop transatlantic flight.
1932	The Boeing 247, the first modern airliner, is introduced.
1936	The DC-3, which will carry the majority of the U.S. air trade over the next decade, is introduced.
1937	Limited-access "superhighways" are introduced.
1954	The St. Laurence Seaway Act is passed.
1956	The United States creates the Interstate Highway System.
1957	Russia launches the *Sputnik* satellite.
1958	The National Aeronautics and Space Administration (NASA) is created.
1959	A Soviet probe hits the moon.
1959	The Boeing 707, the first jet airliner, is introduced.
1959	The *Savannah*, the first nuclear-powered merchant ship, is introduced.
1959	The St. Lawrence Seaway is opened.
1961	Alan Shepherd becomes the first American in space.
1965	Ralph Nader publishes *Unsafe at Any Speed*.
1966	The U.S. Department of Transportation is created as a cabinet-level department.
1966	The National Traffic and Motor Vehicle Safety Act is passed.
1969	The United States lands a man on the moon.
1970	The Boeing 747, the first jumbo jet airliner, is introduced.
1970	The Environmental Protection Agency is created.
1970	The first volume of *National Transportation Statistics* is published.
1970	The nationally owned Consolidated Rail Corporation (Conrail) is created.
1971	The National Rail Passenger Corporation (Amtrak) is created.
1976	The Concorde, the first supersonic airplane carrying passengers, is introduced by Air France and British Airways.
1977	The U.S. Department of Energy is created.
1978	The deregulation of airlines, railroads, and motor carriers begins.
1982	First commercial space launches.
1991	The Intermodal Surface Transportation Efficiency Act (ISTEA) creates the U.S. Bureau of Transportation Statistics (BTS).
1996	Congress abolishes the Interstate Commerce Commission and assigns its remaining functions to the Department of Transportation.

was subordinate to water, with roads built to facilitate connections with rivers, bays, and the ocean. This transportation system tended to facilitate communications between England and her American colonies while frustrating linkages among the colonies.

After the War of Independence, the new U.S. government sought to encourage interactions among the former colonies through the development of a national transportation system. In 1806, Congress approved a route and appointed a committee to plan the details of the National Road. But this federal initiative was an exception. The work of building the nation's highways was largely the result of private, state, and joint private–state initiatives.[2]

The first intercity highways were "turnpikes," toll roads that charged fees to travelers. Turnpikes offered more dependable road surfaces than the "common" or free highways. They were paved in

stone, gravel, and later with wooden plank. The hope of investors was that these improved roads would attract sufficient traffic to cover construction costs and return a profit. In the South, state governments took the lead. Oversight on these public turnpikes was the responsibility of public trustees and local road commissioners. In the North, private companies and some mixed private–public enterprises organized turnpike building projects. The most famous of these roads was the Lancaster Turnpike, constructed by the Philadelphia and Lancaster Turnpike Company, chartered in 1792. By 1800, there were seventy-two private turnpike companies in the Northern states; a decade later there were literally thousands. State–private ventures also flourished. In Pennsylvania, for example, public funds had been invested in fifty-six different construction companies by 1825.[3] Table Df25–26 demonstrates the growth in turnpike mileage and expenditures in New England, the Middle Atlantic states, and Maryland during their period of rapid development between 1810 and 1830. Development of turnpikes

---

[2] When it was first proposed in 1806, the National Road was to extend from Cumberland (now Baltimore), Maryland, to St. Louis, Missouri. The first section, called the Cumberland Road, extended to Wheeling, Virginia (now West Virginia), and was opened in 1818. At this point, the project was turned over to the states. When it was completed in 1833, the National Road extended to Vandalia, Illinois, and was the most ambitious road-building project of its time. See Jordan (1948).

---

[3] Most of the funds invested in turnpikes were private. Even in Pennsylvania, which had the most direct state government investment, the amount of public money was only 30 percent of the estimated total, a much smaller percentage than states would later invest in antebellum canal and railroad construction.

was slower in the South than in the North, partly because of the presence of rivers that penetrated the interior, providing alternative transportation routes, and also because of an absence of cities that concentrate travelers' routes. In the West, where there were few prepared roadbeds; routes such as the Oregon Trail and the Santa Fe Trail simply crossed the land following identifiable landmarks (see Table Df27–33). What turnpikes there were in the West were located adjacent to population centers, such as Chicago.

The typical turnpike company was a small enterprise that operated a relatively short length of road. Thus, several companies would serve a long-distance route, each charging a toll on its section. The profitability of these companies was often poor. Albert Fishlow estimated average profit rates of only 3 to 4 percent, well below the rate of return on alternative investments (Fishlow 1972). Part of the explanation for the low rate of return had to do with governmental regulation of the fee structures and activities of the turnpike companies. Turnpikes required substantial investments relative to other business opportunities at the time. To assemble the required capital, turnpike companies were organized as chartered corporations, and this made them subject to government regulation. Public officials regulated the tolls charged and restricted company activities to road operations. Regulations made tolls per ton-mile relatively low for the transportation of heavy loads over long distances and relatively high for the transportation of light loads over short distances. Because there were many more short journeys involving light loads and because travelers on such routes had the alternative of using "common" (free) roads, the toll structure worked against the turnpike companies. They did not attract the volume of traffic they might have, and their revenue consequently was lower than it might have been.

After about 1830, highways in the United States were eclipsed by canals and railroads as the dynamic component of the transportation infrastructure. But with the development and diffusion of the automobile, highways returned to prominence. Commercial production of automobiles began in the late 1890s and developed very quickly (Flink 1970). By 1900, when statistics on automobile ownership were first collected and compiled, the nation could claim 8,000 registered vehicles. During the next ten years the number rose to 458,000 (see Table Df339–342).

The growth and development of the automobile industry in this era had an enormous impact on American social and economic institutions. James J. Flink summarizes some of these consequences:

> With the introduction of the moving-belt assembly line and the $5-day in 1913–14, Henry Ford created a new class of semiskilled industrial worker and set a new standard of remuneration for manual labor. At General Motors under Alfred P. Sloan, the decentralized, multidivisional structure of the modern industrial corporation, modern management techniques, and consumer installment credit as we know it were pioneered in the 1920s. Applied to the manufacture of many other items, these innovations have called the tune and set the tempo of modern American life.... Since the 1920s the automobile industry has also been the lifeblood of the oil industry, one of the chief customers of the steel industry, and the biggest consumer of many other industrial products, including plate glass, rubber, and lacquers. Construction of streets and highways remains one of the largest items of governmental expenditure in the United States. The motorcar has also been responsible both for a continuing suburban real estate boom and for the rise of many new types

of small businesses, such as service stations and tourist accommodations.[4]

As early as the 1890s, the growing ranks of automobile owners joined with bicyclists to petition their elected officials for improved roads. Strong "good roads" planks were adopted into the state platforms of the two most popular political parties of the day (see Flink 1975, p. 8).

Systematic data on state and local highway finance were collected and published beginning in 1890 and are presented in Table Df305–317. These data can be used as a proxy for the pace and pattern of highway construction until data on surfaced mileage become available starting with 1904 (see Table Df184–186). Both tables indicate a rapid rate of growth in highway construction in the decades surrounding the turn of the twentieth century. By 1910, state spending on highways exceeded that of local governments, and all Eastern states had established highway departments. By this time, the streets and highways in most cities and towns were paved.

The continuing growth in automobile ownership began to generate demand for intercity connections and then a cross-country system of highways. The first proposal for a transcontinental highway to link New York and San Francisco was developed by a group of private citizens who solicited donations and enlisted the energies of towns along the way. Named the Lincoln Highway in an effort to bolster public support, organizers charted a route similar to that of present-day Interstate 80 and began construction (see Hokanson 1988).

The federal government also became involved in highway development (see Seely 1987). In 1893, it established the Office of Road Inquiry, an advisory center for road information, within the Department of Agriculture.[5] Congress appropriated funds for a federal program of rural highway construction in 1912 and passed the Federal–State Road Act, which provided federal subsidies to states for highway construction, in 1916. In 1921, it designated a portion of the federal highway subsidies for interstate and intercounty road construction. One of the requirements of the Federal-Aid Road Act of 1921 was that highways funded by the federal government be integrated into a nationwide system of roads. Many states along the path of the Lincoln Highway used these federal funds to complete the transcontinental link. Integration of the nation's highway system led to the abandonment of "named" highways such as the Lincoln Highway and the adoption of a national interstate highway numbering scheme. By 1925, the numbered-route system of intercity roads was in place. Route 1 was the north–south road along the Atlantic Coast advocated in the Gallatin Report; the National Road, an east–west route, became Route 40. The famous Route 66, linking Chicago and Los Angeles, was inaugurated in 1926. Route 101 was the north–south route on the West Coast.

In the 1930s with the onset of the Great Depression, the federal government initiated road-building projects as a method of alleviating unemployment. Herbert Hoover established the Reconstruction Finance Corporation, which was authorized to build public highways. Franklin Roosevelt allocated federal money for a large number of emergency public works, especially highways. It has

---

[4] Flink (1970), pp. 2–3. See also Cochran (1957), p. 44.
[5] The Office of Road Inquiry evolved into the Bureau of Public Roads twelve years later. Between 1939 and 1949, this Bureau was called the Public Roads Administration. Later it was renamed the Federal Highway Administration, and its functions were transferred to the Department of Transportation in 1967.

been estimated that between a third and a half of the labor force hired by federal relief projects during the Depression worked on building highways. The scale of governmental expenditures on this road-building was unprecedented (Hughes 1991). The Works Progress Administration itself constructed 572,000 miles of inter-city road, 67,000 miles of city streets, and 78,000 bridges (Seely 1993, p. 32). An important milestone was the construction of a section of Route 30 in Nebraska in 1935, which completed the first paved transcontinental highway.

The states were also active in highway construction. Several noted the advantage of limited-access highways in facilitating high-speed travel and reducing accidents. Thus, they fell back on eighteenth-century precedent and constructed toll roads. The first of these was the Pennsylvania Turnpike, construction of which be-gan in 1937. The roadway used the road bed and tunnels from the old New York Central railroad line built by Cornelius Vanderbilt in the nineteenth century. The turnpike entered service in 1940 and exhibited new concepts of superhighway design. It also demon-strated that revenue bonds could finance toll road construction in the twentieth century. Planners predicted that 1.3 million vehi-cles would use the turnpike each year, but early actual usage was 2.4 million vehicles; sometimes as many as 10,000 vehicles per day were recorded. The Pennsylvania Turnpike was an excellent ex-ample of public–private partnerships. Toll collections allowed the construction bonds to be retired early and reissued for capital im-provements to the road. Following the success of the Pennsylvania Turnpike, other states began plans to build their own toll roads after the war, including Ohio, Indiana, Illinois, New York, and New Jersey.

During the Second World War, both highway construction and automobile production were suspended in order to direct resources to the war effort; but with the return of peace, automobile sales soared, and the fraction of households owning one or more auto-mobiles rose from just over half in 1948 to almost three quarters just ten years later (see Table Df330–338). The prosperity of the postwar years, and particularly automobile-based suburbanization, further increased the demand for new roads. In 1952, Congress au-thorized funding of a national limited-access Interstate System. The 1956 Interstate Highway Act, with a preamble citing national defense concerns, authorized an additional 42,500-mile system of limited-access, high-speed roadways (Rose 1979). Although the actual roadway construction was undertaken by the states, the fed-eral government paid 90 percent of the total costs. Data on the financing of the highway system can be found in Tables Df225–329.

With the creation of the U.S. Department of Transportation (USDOT) in 1966, and with the passing of the Urban Mass Trans-portation Act two years later, the United States entered what Bruce Seely terms the "golden age of infrastructure development" (Seely 1993, p. 35). The Federal-Aid Highway Act of 1970 cre-ated the federal-aid urban system and increased the federal gov-ernment's share for non-interstate projects to 70 percent. In 1991, Congress passed the Inter-modal Surface Transportation Efficiency Act (ISTEA). The ISTEA restructured the federal-aid highway sys-tem and created the Bureau of Transportation Statistics.

As early as 1939, private automobiles accounted for almost 90 percent of domestic intercity passenger traffic, as shown in Figure Df-B. The exigencies of World War II diverted much of this traffic to the rails and buses, but automobiles resumed their importance immediately after the war's end. Since the mid-1960s,

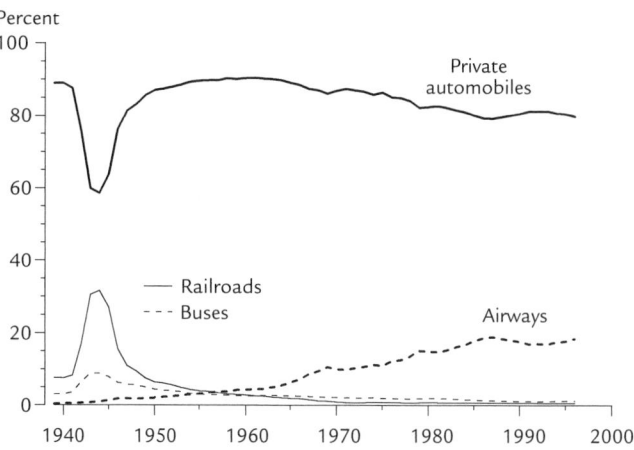

FIGURE Df-B   Domestic intercity passenger traffic – percentage of total, by type of transportation: 1939–1996

Sources

Series Df44–47.

Documentation

Percentages are based on the measurement of traffic in terms of passenger-miles.

private automobiles have lost ground relative to air transport as a means of intercity travel.

Highway safety was a public concern from the beginning of the automobile era. Data compilation on highway fatalities began in 1900 (see Table Df413–417). Although the number of traffic fatalities has increased enormously over time, the overall safety of automobile travel has improved. Measured in terms of millions of miles of annual vehicle travel, traffic fatalities fell from thirty-six to fewer than two over the course of the century. Despite the improve-ments in safety, the relative death rate attributable to automobile travel continued to increase into the 1940s as automobile travel became more extensive and medical advances reduced death rates from other causes. In the 1960s, there was a strong public reaction to highway fatalities. This prompted the legislation of a variety of vehicular safety features such as seatbelts and, later, airbags. Since 1970, motor vehicle death rates have been falling in the population as a whole, even among young drivers (see Figure Df-C).

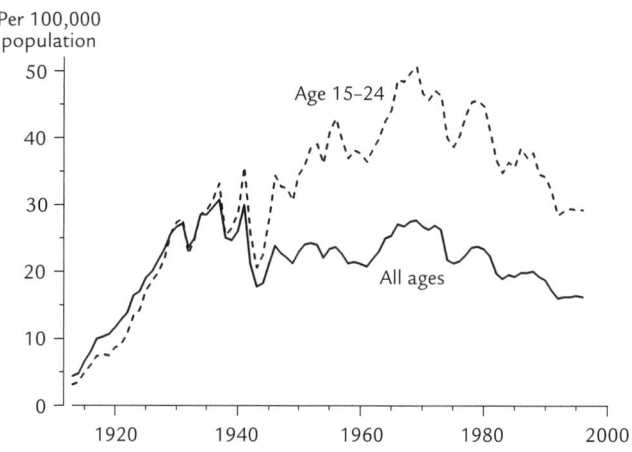

FIGURE Df-C   Motor vehicle death rates, by age: 1913–1996

Sources

Series Df465 and Df468.

Highway construction also facilitated the development of trucking as a means of transporting freight. As trucking developed, it was both complementary to and competitive with the railroad. The Railway Express Company emerged as the national firm that delivered what the railroad brought to town. With highway improvement (including bridges and tunnels) and technological developments in tires, brakes, and lights, the truck emerged in the 1920s as more than a replacement for the local horse and wagon. United Parcel Service, which began as a messenger service in Seattle in 1907, grew to become one of the important long-distance carriers of light freight by truck.

In the early 1930s, roughly two thirds of all trucking firms owned but a single vehicle (90 percent owned one or two), and these firms covered relatively short distances. A few consolidations emerged during the Depression, but both they and the railroads faced rate competition from the many small independent firms fighting for survival. This instability led the industry toward political solutions through trade associations and state laws. As William Childs notes, "Since it affected so much of the economy, motor trucking was bound to elicit collective attempts to control its development. The real issue was not whether the new technology should be controlled, but how and by whom" (Childs 1985, p. 48).

During the 1930s, the U.S. Supreme Court and the Interstate Commerce Commission (ICC) began to regulate the trucking industry. The Court clarified issues concerning truck regulation, while the ICC designed and promoted a structure in which trucking could be regulated. The attempt of the trucking industry to develop a National Recovery Act (NRA) code contributed to the creation of the American Trucking Association, which quickly became the agency through which the industry attempted to influence legislation to its advantage. The code was a failure as there was no efficient enforcement mechanism, and competitive rate-cutting continued in a still growing industry. Out of these pieces emerged the Motor Carrier Act of 1935, which contained the cartel features the NRA code lacked. Rates were to be regulated, as were safety, accounting procedures, mergers, and consolidations. Federal regulation, the ICC in particular, shaped the growth of the trucking industry in the twentieth century.

Although some consideration was given to coordinating the different transport modes, integration came about haphazardly and infrequently. Trucks began taking high-valued freight from the railroads in the mid-1920s, and, by 1940, they carried a large proportion of total freight. Just before World War II, trucking accounted for approximately 10 percent of domestic intercity freight traffic. This fell to just over 5 percent during the war, but it quickly recovered and began to grow steadily to where it was just under 30 percent in 1996 (see Table Df48–58 and Figure Df-D). Successful integration came to truck–rail transportation only in the final decades of the twentieth century. While "piggy back" service (truck trailers hauled on railroad flat cars) began expanding in the 1950s, the ground transportation component remained relatively inefficient until the 1980s. Federal policy contributed to the lack of efficient integration, but so did poor railroad management. Efficiency increased dramatically in the 1980s as a result of investment from the railroads. The trucking industry was prodded by competition to change the way they organized their work as, by this time, firms such as United Parcel and Federal Express were using airplanes to move light freight quickly across the country. Complete integration, however, is not feasible; it is limited by the

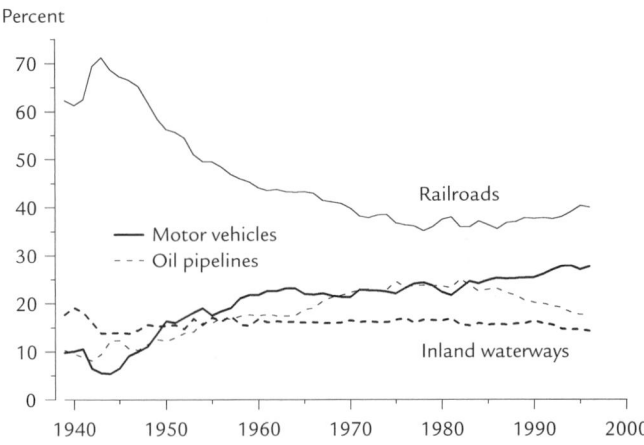

FIGURE Df-D   Domestic intercity freight traffic – percentage of total, by type of transportation: 1939–1996

Sources
Series Df54–57.

Documentation
Percentages are based on the measurement of traffic in terms of ton-miles.

technology. For example, with respect to household goods transportation, "piggy back" does not work well because the goods are more likely to become damaged on the rail haul than on the highway haul.

Water

Transportation over water was preferred in the years before the Civil War. Natural waterways such as rivers, lakes, and coastal routes were heavily used. Where natural waterways were absent, an elaborate system of canals was developed to link important commercial centers. As early as 1808, the Gallatin Report proposed that canals be cut through Cape Cod, between the Raritan and Delaware rivers, between Delaware Bay and Chesapeake Bay, and between the Chesapeake and Albemarle sounds. In addition, the Report suggested major east–west links: a northern link from the Hudson River to Lake Champlain, and from the Mohawk River to Lake Ontario and Lake Erie (Goodrich 1960, pp. 27–48).

The major era of American canal building commenced at the end of the War of 1812 and lasted until the Panic of 1837. The construction of canals, like the construction of Northern turnpikes, was undertaken by combinations of private and public enterprises. Of the total funds invested in canals before the Civil War, about three quarters came from state and local governments (Goodrich, Cranmer, et al. 1961, p. 215). Trends can be seen in Jerome Cranmer's data on investments in canals between 1815 and 1860, which are reported in Table Df684–689. Few entirely private canals were constructed. Economically, the most important canal was the 363-mile Erie Canal. The New York legislature hoped to receive federal aid for this project, but President Madison vetoed the funding bill in 1817. A month later, urged by Governor DeWitt Clinton, New York's legislature passed the necessary laws to build the canal with state resources and without federal help. Funding for this enterprise came from earmarked taxes, from borrowing on state credit, and from tolls that were collected when sections of the canal were opened. The initial public offering of Erie Canal bonds was in small denominations. These bonds were purchased mainly by

New Yorkers, with one New York City savings bank holding 30 percent of the outstanding debt in 1821.[6]

The Erie Canal opened in 1825 and was an immediate success; within ten years, cumulative toll collections exceeded construction costs. Those who shipped on the canal, within and through New York State, found their dollar costs fell in excess of 75 percent and their time costs fell by almost 67 percent. The Erie Canal had political implications as well. By providing a direct link between New York and the Northwest Territory, it strengthened the commercial advantage of the Northern relative to the Southern states. Prior to the construction of the Erie Canal, the Southern states had had the advantage of ease of access to the Ohio River and its tributaries. The completion of the Erie Canal helped shift the axis of Midwestern commerce from north–south to east–west. Further, with the help of the Erie Canal, New York City grew to become the largest port and largest city in the country. The ton-mile rates on the canal are reported in Table Df679–680; the tonnage moved on the Erie and other New York State canals appears in Table Df696–697.

The success of the Erie Canal prompted other states to initiate similar projects, but none of these were as financially remunerative for their investors. In Pennsylvania, for example, Philadelphia was already linked to the Susquehanna River by the Union Canal at the time of the Erie's completion. In 1826, the Pennsylvania legislature voted to build the Main Line Canal to connect the Susquehanna River with Pittsburgh, on the Allegheny and Monongahela rivers in the western part of the state. This proved to be a very complicated and expensive project because the canal had to cross the Appalachian Mountains. The Main Line Canal required 174 locks compared with 84 on the Erie and at its highest point was 2,200 feet above sea level compared with 650 feet for the Erie. The Main Line involved transfers of cargo from canal barges to surface transport (later to rail links) at several points. These breaks in transport put the Main Line at a competitive disadvantage with the Erie. When the 359-mile Main Line was completed in 1835, it was hailed as a technological and engineering wonder but earned only a 3 percent rate of return on investment and was finally sold to the Pennsylvania Railroad in 1857 (Rubin 1961). The Chesapeake and Ohio and the James River and Kanawha canals in Virginia were also financial disappointments for investors (Taylor 1951, pp. 42–5).

States of the Old Northwest[7] were also active in canal building even though their canals faced competition from railroads almost immediately on completion. Indiana built the longest waterway, the 450-mile Wabash and Erie Canal, from Evansville, Indiana, on the Ohio River to Toledo, Ohio, on Lake Erie. It was finished in the 1850s and almost immediately abandoned. Prior to Illinois's becoming a state, its northern border was extended by approximately 60 miles to ensure that a planned canal would be contained entirely within the state boundaries. A few years later, the state received a federal land grant to support construction of the Illinois and Michigan Canal, linking Lake Michigan at Chicago to the Illinois River at LaSalle. The canal opened in 1848, the same year as the first railroad train departed and the first telegraph message

arrived in the city. Despite this inauspicious beginning, the canal ultimately broke even financially, although its more important role in Chicago's history was that of an open sewer (see Cain 1978).

It has been suggested that the most important long-run consequence of canals in the United States was their encouragement of the development of manufacturing in the nation's hinterland. Although this manufacturing was largely involved in the processing of agricultural products, it made for a more even pattern of industrial development than would have been the case in the United States in the canals' absence.

The appearance of the railroad marked the end of the canal era. Railroads were much faster and more dependable (for example, ice halted canal transport in the winter months). These features attracted customers away from canals despite the railroads' higher freight rates.

The development of the steamboat was also important to economic growth before the Civil War. Robert Fulton's steam-powered *Clermont* traveled upstream on the Hudson River from New York City to Albany in 1807. By 1811, the steamboat was widely used. Before the advent of the steamboat, passengers and freight traveled downstream on these waterways using flatboats and keelboats. But without power, these vessels were unable to navigate upstream against the current. The steam-driven paddle wheeler was a major advance that improved speed and lowered cost in both directions. Upstream improvements were most dramatic and helped bring manufacturing products to the interior of the country. Improved downstream speed facilitated farmers' shipment of their crops to market (see Table Df641–650). Tables Df651–678 provide comparative data on travel times and freight rates in the two directions.

Steamboats proved particularly important in the West, where the Missouri, Ohio, and Mississippi rivers drain half the continental United States. Erik Haites, James Mak, and Gary Walton did the research that currently shapes our understanding of the river steamboat fleet and its tonnage on the Western rivers in the antebellum period. By the end of the 1850s, a fleet of some 800 steamboats with an average working life of 5.5 years serviced the interior rivers of the United States. Steamboats significantly reduced transit and turnaround times (see Tables Df632–638 and Df667–678). Douglass North's data on the general pattern of inland freight rates are presented in Table Df17–21. Freight rates for steamboats fell by 90 percent upstream in real terms between 1815 and 1860 and by nearly 40 percent downstream (see Table Df651–658). Vessels built in the 1850s were far more efficient than those built in earlier periods. Mak and Walton found that per-unit productivity increased by a factor of nearly nine from 1815 to 1860 (see Table Df639–640) (Mak and Walton 1972, p. 637). Map Df-E shows the extent of the canal system in 1860.

Transatlantic travel continued to be dominated by sailing ships through the mid-nineteenth century. In 1818, the Black Ball line began scheduled service between New York and London. Even before the Erie Canal was completed, this connection began the process of making New York City the dominant American transatlantic port. Over the remainder of the antebellum period the size and efficiency of sailing ships increased dramatically. The average sailing ship of the 1820s was approximately 300 tons. By the Civil War era, the average was more than three times as large. This was the era of the clipper ship that ruled ocean shipping from the early 1830s to the 1860s. Clippers were not the largest ships, but they were the fastest. For this reason, they were favored by passengers and shippers of high-value freight.

---

[6] With the success of the canal, other large investors and foreign buyers entered the canal bond market. By 1829, foreigners held half of the canal debt. See Olmstead (1972).

[7] The Old Northwest refers to a historical region in the north-central United States, control of which was a major issue in the War of 1812 with Britain. The area was later split into the present-day states of Ohio, Indiana, Illinois, Michigan, Wisconsin, and part of Minnesota.

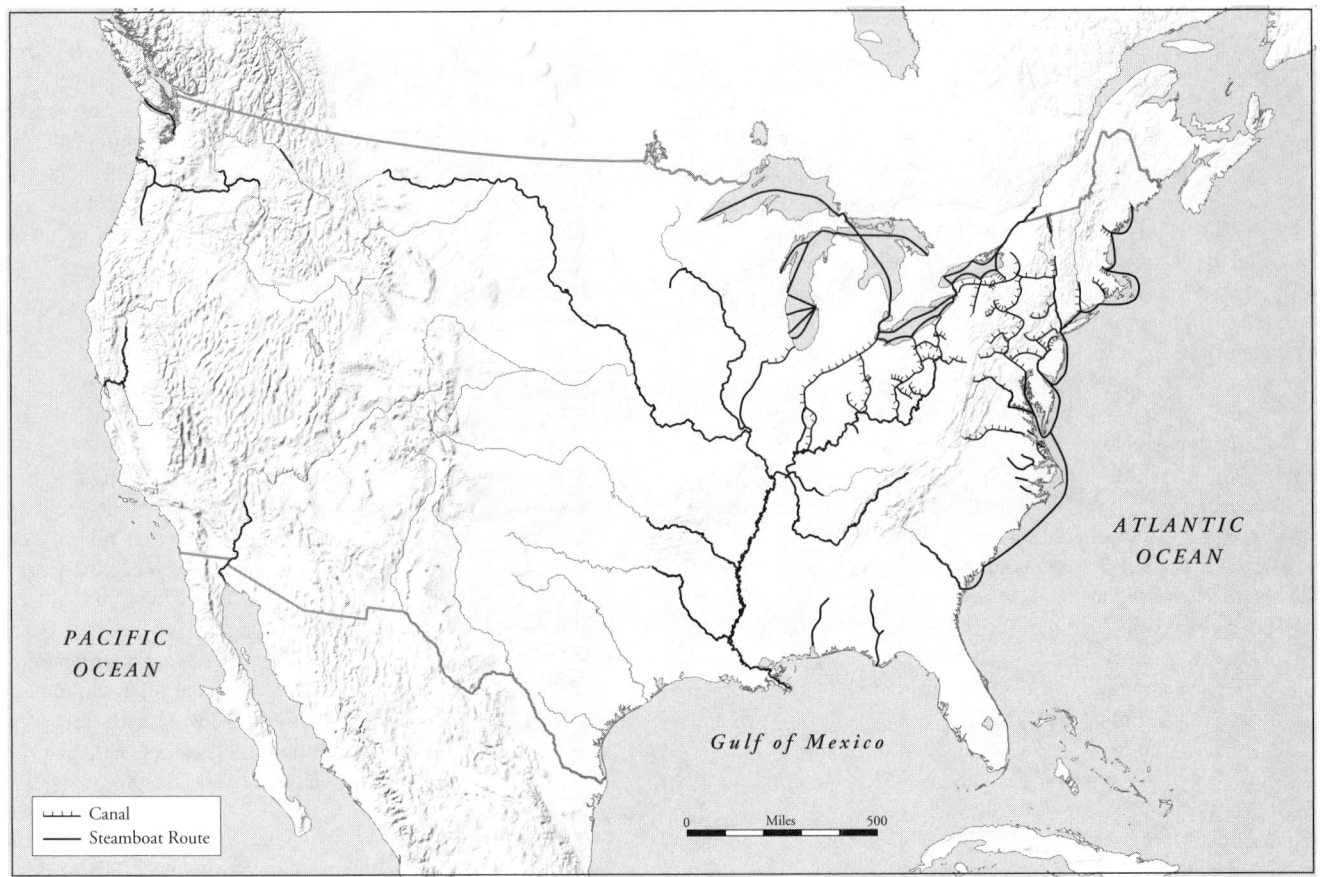

MAP Df-E   Canal and steamboat routes: 1860

Sources

National Geographic Society, *Historical Atlas of the United States* (National Geographic Society, 1993), p. 188. Underlying data are from H. A. Burr, *Mitchell's New National Map Exhibiting the U.S.* (Library of Congress, Geography and Map Division, 1858); *Distrunell's American and European Railway and Steamship Guide* (J. Distrunell, 1853); *The Great Lakes, or Inland Seas of America* (J. Distrunell, 1863); and Louis C. Hunter, *Steamboats on the Western Rivers: An Economic and Technological History* (Octagon Books, 1969). Also see Carter Goodrich, editor, *Canals and American Economic Development* (Columbia University Press, 1961), pp. 184–5.

Data on the number of ships constructed, tonnage, and the region in which construction took place are shown in Tables Df612–616, Df618–625, Df681–683, and Df698–702. These data reveal a rapid growth in the construction of wooden sailing vessels beginning in the 1840s and extending through the 1850s, with the maximum number produced in 1855. Productivity grew rapidly and the cost of transatlantic travel fell markedly throughout the first half of the nineteenth century. Douglass North's indices of this ocean-going shipping productivity and costs can be found in Table Df626–631, while George Rogers Taylor's estimates of cotton freight rates on the New York and New Orleans routes to Europe appear in Tables Df692–695.[8]

Even though steam-powered vessels became important on inland routes at a relatively early date, they did not come to dominate transatlantic travel until after the Civil War. In terms of construction, the number of ocean-going steam vessels did not surpass sail-powered ships until the 1880s. The locus of production was in New England throughout the nineteenth century, but it shifted to the Middle Atlantic and Gulf regions in the twentieth century (see

Tables Df618–625 and Df698–702). Tonnage on the Northern lakes and Western rivers became important after the Civil War and remained so until World War I (see Table Df703–707). Iron, coal, and grain were the important commodities that were shipped on inland waterways in this era (see Tables Df703–707 and Df716–721).

Steam eventually supplanted sail as a means of powering even ocean-going vessels. Two major innovations were crucial. The adoption of the screw propeller in place of the paddle wheel reduced fuel consumption and increased speed. The development of riveting techniques enabled engineers to produce iron-hull ships that proved to be stronger and longer lasting than wood (for data on the construction of American merchant vessels by type, see Table Df612–616). Both innovations were British, and, by the outbreak of the Civil War, British steamships were making considerable inroads against American sailing ships for transatlantic travel. In the 1820s, the American merchant marine carried more than 93 percent of America's imports and 87 percent of its exports in wooden sailing ships. By the decade of the 1850s, the American merchant marine share had fallen to 71 and 70 percent, respectively.

The Civil War accelerated the decline of the U.S. merchant marine, as shown in Figure Df-F. Virtually all antebellum U.S. international trade was conducted by shipping companies based in

---

[8] For a description of the American shipbuilding industry, see Goldenberg (1976) and McGowan (1980).

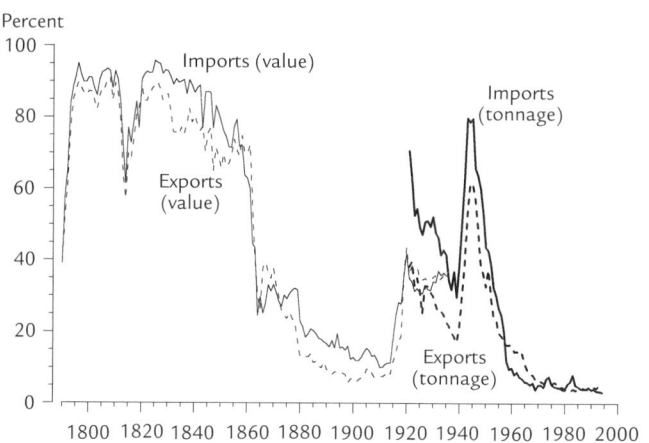

FIGURE Df-F   Waterborne imports and exports – percentage carried by U.S. vessels: 1790–1994

Sources

Computed from series Df606–607, Df609–610, Df736–737, and Df739–740.

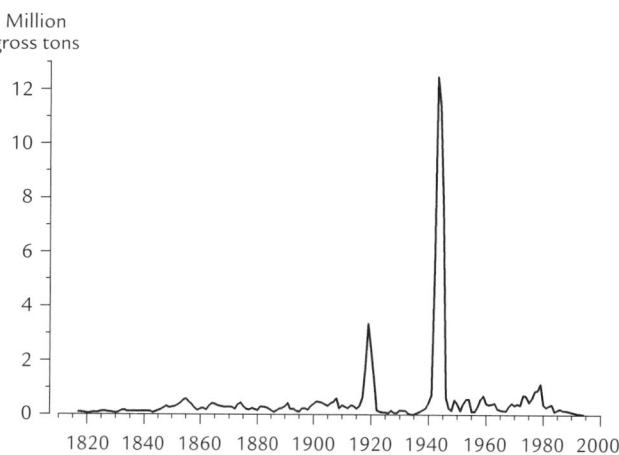

FIGURE Df-G   Merchant vessels built: 1817–1994

Sources

1817–1839: computed from series Df681 and Df683. 1840–1916: computed from series Df698 and Df702. Beginning 1917, series Df723.

New England; the Southern states had only a minimal commercial fleet. At the onset of the war, the Confederacy obtained from Great Britain a number of fast sailing ships that it used to successfully raid these Union merchant ships. A large number of Union ships were burned at sea, and an estimated 110,000 tons of Northern shipping was destroyed. Even more damaging to the American merchant marine was its loss of business to foreign fleets. The Southern raids pushed up insurance rates on Northern ships so high that shipping became unprofitable. Many ship owners were forced to sell their vessels to foreigners, while others transferred their allegiance and reregistered their ships under foreign flags. In total, over 800,000 tons of American shipping was reregistered in neutral countries; after the war, none of those ships were allowed to return to the U.S. registry (Gibson and Donovan 2000, pp. 67–9). Series Df590 shows the reduction in the size of the U.S. merchant marine during this period, while Table Df606–611 shows the reduction in the U.S. merchant marine's share of the value of U.S. waterborne exports and imports.

American merchant marine losses continued after the Civil War. By 1910, the American share of U.S. waterborne exports and imports had fallen to only 10 and 7.5 percent of the total, respectively. Scholars explain the American decline in terms of a shift in technology combined with a quirk in the American regulatory system. Wood was plentiful and inexpensive in the United States, whereas iron was relatively inexpensive in Britain. The shift from wooden to iron ships favored the British. The negative impact of the technological shift was reinforced by U.S. laws that restricted the American merchant marine fleet to American-made vessels.[9] The British also dominated the emerging transatlantic passenger business that catered to European emigrants. The Cunard Line was the most famous of these shipping companies (see Hyde 1975 and Taylor 1971). The same restrictions that crippled American international shipping protected American intercoastal and inland water trade. Despite strenuous competition from the railroad, the shipping industry exhibited modest growth during the second half of the nineteenth century (see series Df591).

The First and Second World Wars had a profound effect on the U.S. shipbuilding industry and merchant marine (see Figure Df-G). To protect transatlantic shipping from German submarine attacks and to transport troops and supplies to the theaters of war in Europe, the United States in 1917, shortly after its entry into the First World War, undertook an emergency shipbuilding program under the direction of the Emergency Fleet Corporation (EFC). The EFC, with a budget estimated at twice the value of the entire world merchant marine fleet, established new shipyards and began new construction. Because of the program's late start, the continuation of government-subsidized shipbuilding after the Armistice, and President Woodrow Wilson's restriction of government-built ships to the U.S. merchant marine, the volume of U.S. vessels involved in international trade increased dramatically. The quantitative impact of the wartime shipbuilding program can been seen in series Df579, which records a more than doubling of the tonnage of vessels in the U.S. merchant marine between 1916 and 1922.[10]

The enormous quantity of ships produced in the waning days of the First World War had a disastrous effect on the U.S. shipbuilding industry during the 1920s and 1930s. With so many ships afloat, there was little demand for new vessels. Between 1922 and 1928, not a single new ship for world commerce was built in the United States. Many famous and long-lived shipyards went out of business during these years. Political developments following the war favored a return to isolationism and an "America First" focus to federal policy. In response to these political developments and also to the fact that the large fleet of government-owned ships was expensive to maintain and operate, many ships were sold to private companies both in the United States and abroad (Gibson and Donovan, pp. 121–33).

The growing threat of hostilities in Europe in the mid-1930s changed U.S. mercantile policy dramatically. In 1936, Congress passed the Merchant Marine Act, a law that Gibson and Donovan call "a legislative landmark of unrivaled importance in the history

---

[9] For a lively discussion of these developments, see Chamberlain (1968), volume 1, pp. 39–40.

[10] For a detailed discussion of the role of sea power during World War I, the EFC shipbuilding program (including the characteristics of the ships it produced), and public policy toward shipbuilding and the merchant marine in the 1920s, see Gibson and Donovan (2000), pp. 103–21.

of U.S. maritime policy" (Gibson and Donovan, p. 141). The 1936 Merchant Marine Act formally recognized the importance of the maritime industry to the commercial prosperity and military security of the United States. It also acknowledged the need for federal subsidies to keep the industry viable in the face of international competition. Following passage of the legislation, shipbuilding subsidies were established. Government-initiated ship production commenced in 1939. As a carryover from World War I, the United States already had a large fleet. It also had experience with wartime shipbuilding. Nonetheless, the scale of World War II shipbuilding efforts reached unprecedented levels. Quantitative comparisons can be made using Tables Df681–683, Df698–702, and Df722–732. One measure of the human dimension of this effort is contained in the account by Gibson and Donovan of the work of Henry J. Kaiser, a successful industrialist who was drawn into the shipbuilding industry during the war.

> Henry J. Kaiser [was] a successful industrialist who had never built a ship before 1941. Unburdened by the limitations of vision and practices of traditional shipbuilding, Kaiser geared up for volume production. His ships were built of prefabricated modules that were then assembled in series construction. Welding, a skill that could be learned in a month, was used extensively for the first time instead of riveting. In the first year and a half, construction time for Liberty ships was reduced from 105 to 14 days; in a much publicized stunt one ship was built and launched in less than 5 days. By the end of the war Kaiser had built one-third of the Maritime Commission's vessels and had set the standard for all other yards.... A country that had constructed only 1 million tons of merchant shipping in 1941 built more than 17 million tons by 1943. By the war's end in 1945, a workforce of 4 million men and women had built 5,000 ships.... The speed with which this was done and the scale of the effort still defy comprehension. When operating at their peak rate of production, America's shipyards were capable of reproducing the entire world's prewar commercial tonnage in less than three years. (Gibson and Donovan, pp. 166–7)

This unprecedented shipbuilding effort had consequences far beyond the shipyards as well, affecting the geographic location of the population and the work experience of minority and especially women workers.

At the end of the war, America owned more than 60 percent of the tonnage of the world's ocean-going vessels. In an effort to help rebuild the war-torn countries of Europe and to stimulate the emerging economies of Latin America, the United States passed the 1946 Merchant Marine Sales Act that facilitated the sale of surplus ships. Following the conclusion of the war, countries of the Far East developed highly productive and competitive shipbuilding industries that soon dominated the international industry. Given this competition and American reluctance to subsidize water transport, the U.S. share of international waterborne commerce fell rapidly. By the end of the twentieth century, it was but a small fraction of the world total.

The shipbuilding frenzy of the Second World War also had a long-lasting effect on coastal and inland shipping. During the war years, the military demand for ships meant that domestic trade was shifted to rail and trucking. After the war, these alternative modes of transportation came to dominate. The shifting importance of water relative to other modes of domestic, intercity freight transportation is displayed in Table Df48–58.

Railroads

No innovation is more emblematic of the drama of nineteenth-century American economic history than the railroad. To earlier historians, the railroad was an empire-builder "opening the country," built at great risk "ahead of demand." By decreasing transportation costs, the railroad spurred economic growth. By stimulating the demand for iron and steel, the growth of the railroad helped to reduce unit costs in industries that were important inputs into a variety of industries across the economy. Modern cliometric scholarship on railroads, pioneered by Albert Fishlow and Robert Fogel, suggests that the claims of these early historians were exaggerated (Fogel 1964; Fishlow 1965). At the same time, it does not deny the broader proposition that the railroad had a transformative impact on the American economy in the nineteenth century.

The first railroad in the United States, the Baltimore and Ohio, began operations in 1830, five years after the Stockton and Darlington, the first English railroad. By the beginning of the Civil War, U.S. mileage exceeded that of railroads in the United Kingdom, France, and the German states combined. Fishlow estimated that total investment in railroads up to 1860 was more than five times the amount invested in canals (see Table Df865–873) (Fishlow 1972, p. 496). Government support encouraged this development. It was greatest in the South, where sparse population and competition with river transport reduced private profit possibilities. In New England and the Old Northwest, the governmental contribution was less necessary.

In the 1850s, the federal government, which had previously been reluctant to become involved in internal improvements, found a new and seemingly costless way to aid and encourage railroad development. Rather than provide cash subsidies or guarantee bonds as the states had done to promote canal and then railroad development, the federal government used its vast holdings of lands in the West and offered title and right of way to any company that agreed to build a railroad. When the land was offered, its value was virtually worthless, but if and when a railroad was completed and the land was connected to world markets, land values would rise dramatically. Thus, the land-grant system, like the modern system of stock options, encouraged entrepreneurs with the promise of capital gains.[11]

In 1851, the federal government made a land grant of 3.75 million acres to finance the building of the Illinois Central Railroad, a north–south route running parallel to the Mississippi River that, unlike the upper portion of that river, would not close in the winter (Gates 1934). Although this was not the first land grant for internal improvements, it was the largest of its time. It was also a sign of things to come; in the next seven years, forty-five railroad companies in ten states received federal land grants (see Table Df890).

Entrepreneurs responded enthusiastically to these incentives, which were sufficiently generous to energize an explosion of railroad construction. Between 1850 and the start of the Civil War in 1860, more than 20,000 miles of track were laid (see Table Df882–885). This period also witnessed rapid developments in the many industries associated with the railroads.

Discovery of gold in California in 1849 following America's triumph in its war with Mexico created both an economic and a

---

[11] The government profited from this system as well because it kept alternate land sections, which it then sold after railroad construction was completed and land values rose.

military interest in linking the newly acquired and newly rich state of California to the eastern part of the country. At the time, travel from the East Coast to California was a lengthy and dangerous process, whether pursued by wagon or by sail. The advantages and importance of a rail link between the two coasts were obvious.

The planning for a transcontinental railroad, particularly the determination of the site of its eastern terminus, aroused bitter political sectional debates in the years before the Civil War. The ultimate selection of Omaha, Nebraska, was sufficiently west that each eastern railroad could build its own connection to it. After the Civil War, four transcontinental railroads were granted 100 million acres, one tenth of the public domain, to facilitate construction. In total, the federal government granted 131 million acres, and states added an additional 49 million acres, to encourage railroad construction. The objective was to link the two coasts and create a nation that was transcontinental in settlement as well as in territorial claims. Success was achieved in 1869 when the Golden Spike at Promontory Point, Utah, completed the link. For data on public land grants to encourage the construction of railroads, wagon roads, canals, and river improvements, see Tables Cf83–87 and Df890.

After the Civil War, main-track mileage rose until World War I. Fishlow identifies three major construction booms: 1868–1873, 1879–1883, and 1886–1892 (see Table Df882–885 and Figure Df-H). By 1899, railroad tracks crisscrossed the nation. Every major American city had a rail head that was connected to the national system (see Map Df-I). Railroads were the life-blood of the American common market, and the links brought prosperity to the more remote outposts of a large, continental economy.

As railroad track mileage increased in the years after the Civil War, railroad companies grew in size and became complex, multi-state units with thousands of employees. They became America's first "big business" (Chandler 1965). As pioneers of large-scale enterprise, their management problems and methods defined U.S. industrial practice for years. Trading in railway bonds and stock became sufficiently active to lead to the development of organized stock and bond exchanges (see Table Df891–900). The evolution

of public policy toward all big business was heavily influenced by the nation's experience with the railroads. Railroads' size, rapid economic growth, and power not only excited imaginations and enthusiasm but also led to concerns about excessive concentration of power. In response to these concerns, the federal government established the first business regulatory agency in the country's history, the ICC. Established in 1887, the ICC was charged with the responsibility of regulating rates and overseeing railroad business practices. Railroad rate-setting practices were a main source of the public outcry that spurred the creation of the ICC, particularly what were felt to be high rates on routes with few railroad company competitors and the railroad company practice of giving rebates on transportation expenditures to favored shippers.[12]

There was another railroad construction boom in the first decade of the twentieth century and some construction in the 1920s, but, for the most part, the American rail network was gradually abandoned over the twentieth century. As Table Df927–955 indicates, there was very little new rail construction in the United States after 1920, and in most years the number of miles of rail abandoned was many times the level of new miles constructed. The railroads met with increasing competition for both the freight and passenger portions of their business from automobiles, trucks, and, later, airplanes.[13]

When statistics on the relative importance of various modes of transportation for passenger and freight shipment first became available in 1939, they indicated railways accounted for 62 percent of the volume of intercity freight traffic. Because railroads had accounted for virtually all of this traffic in 1900, this marked a dramatic drop in the railroad's share of this business. Even though this share rose during World War II, the conclusion of the war saw a return of the railroads' long-term losses to trucking and, more recently, to air. Intercity passenger travel was lost even more quickly (see Tables Df38–58, Df956–963, and Df965–979, as well as Figures Df-B and Df-D).

Air

The air transportation industry began in 1903 when Orville and Wilbur Wright made the first sustained flights in a heavier-than-air vehicle near Kitty Hawk, North Carolina. Commercial applications followed quickly. The Wright brothers concentrated their marketing efforts on the U.S. federal government, and their first order came from the Army Signal Corps, which purchased aircraft for military observation. The initial commercial market for aircraft was largely for sport and exhibition.

The first systematic data relevant to air transportation begin in 1913 and document the growth of total airplane production and sales through 1961 (see Table Df1165–1176). These data highlight the shifting importance of the industry's commercial and military customers. The military accounted for an important share of plane sales in most years through 1961, completely dominating sales during wartime. During war years, U.S. aircraft production occurred at record levels.

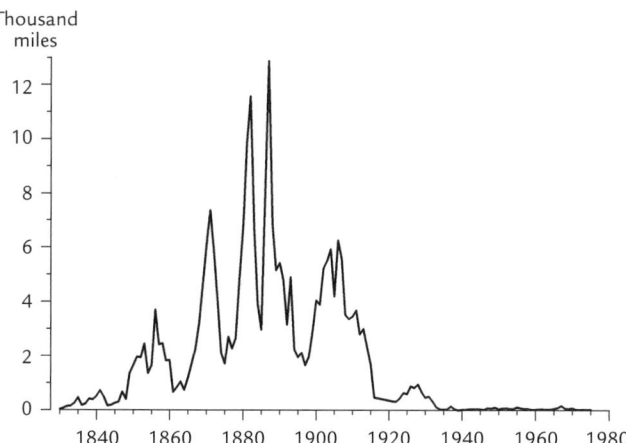

FIGURE Df-H   Railroad mileage built: 1830–1975

Sources

1830–1890, series Df884; 1891–1916, series Df885; and beginning 1921, series Df928.

Documentation

See the text for Table Df882–885 for discussion of the use of yearly changes in mileage operated and owned as proxies for mileage built.

---

[12] At the same time, the law and practice of railroad regulation grew out of earlier legal developments; see Hughes (1991).

[13] Some observers blame the decline of the railroads on the system of regulation that was put in place in the nineteenth century. For examples of different perspectives on this issue, see Caves (1980), Bryant (1988), and Martin (1992).

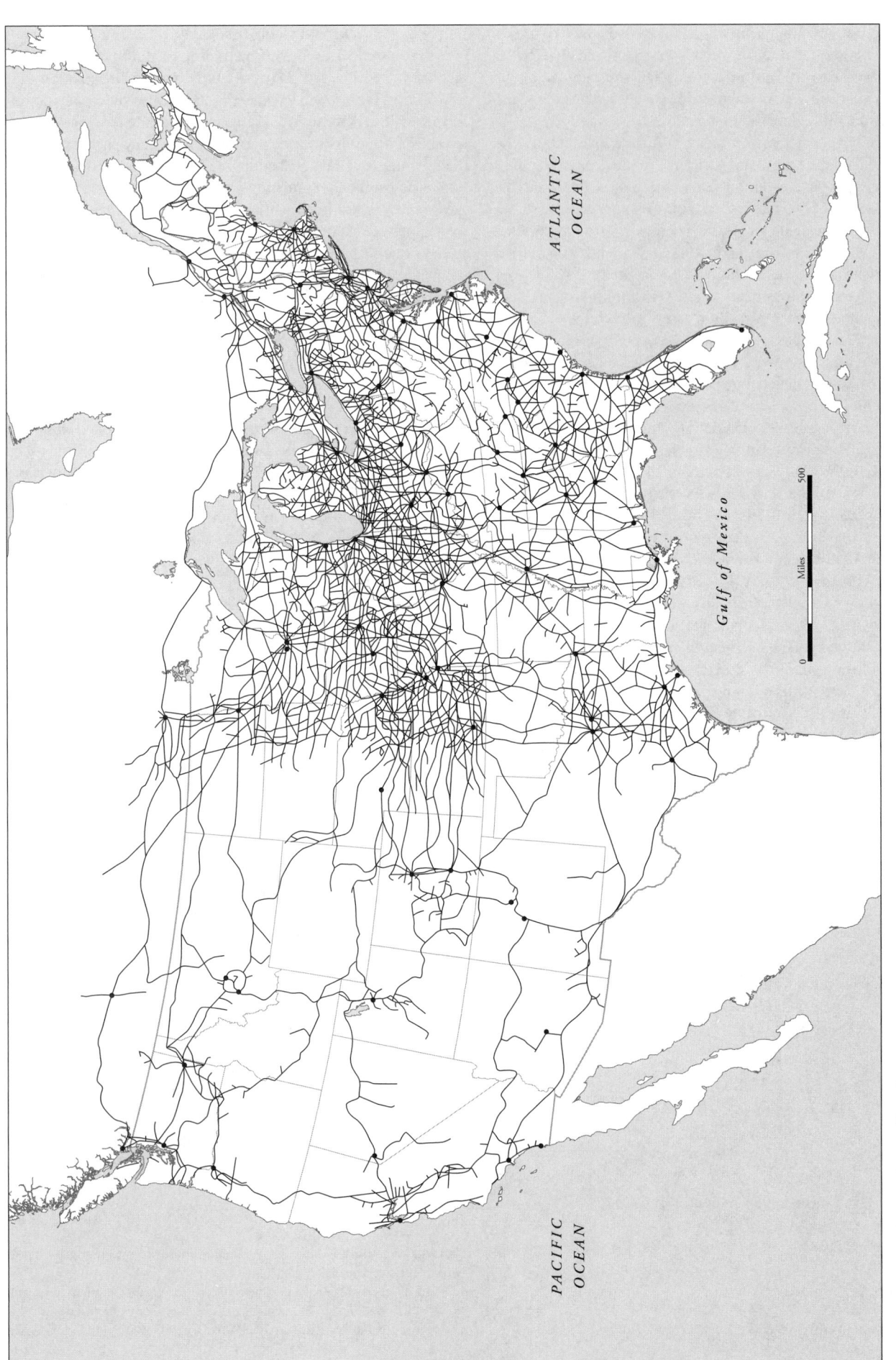

MAP Df-I   The North American railroad system: 1899

Source

James E. Vance Jr., *The North American Railroad: Its Origin, Evolution, and Geography* (Johns Hopkins University Press, 1995), endpaper in front of book. Underlying data are from *Travelers' Official Railway Guide*, January 1899.

PACIFIC OCEAN

ATLANTIC OCEAN

Gulf of Mexico

Miles

0   500

Technological change in the air transportation industry was rapid. The first transcontinental flight was accomplished in 1911, less than eight years after the first flight at Kitty Hawk. A mere three years later, the St. Petersburg–Tampa Airboat Line carried out the first commercial flight when it flew passengers the eighteen miles between those two cities. Beginning in 1920, pilots (including many trained during the First World War) participated in national air races (for example, the Pulitzer and Bendix Trophy Races) that proved a major inducement to progress in design, production, and performance, after the decline in government support for the industry following the conclusion of World War I. By 1928, when the first statistics on the number of scheduled aircraft in air transportation become available, the United States already had 268 aircraft in domestic operations and 57 in international operations (see Tables Df1112–1138).

With the outbreak of World War II, and the likelihood that air power would play an even more significant role than in the First World War, President Franklin D. Roosevelt asked Congress for an appropriation that greatly expanded U.S. airplane production. This appropriation also provided a spur to technological development, such as the helicopter and the jet engine.

The high level of aircraft production during World War II is clearly evident in the data on the number of aircraft produced. The Korean War stimulated an additional round of aircraft production. Unfortunately, the series on total and military aircraft production end in 1961, just before the escalation of the Vietnam conflict (see Table Df1165–1176).

The end of the Second World War also saw an important increase in the development and production of aircraft for civilian use. Series Df1167, which displays total civilian aircraft produced, show a sharp spike immediately after the war. Following the first successful test of a jet transport plane in 1951, civilian aircraft production began a sustained rise through the late 1970s, interrupted only during the Vietnam War era, when the demand for military aircraft competed with production for civilian use.

The rapid growth of airline travel in the post–World War II era is evident in Tables Df1112–1138 and Df1159–1164, which display statistics of U.S. domestic and international scheduled airline operations and international air passenger arrivals and departures. In the post–World War II era, airlines progressively displaced bus and rail as a mode of intercity passenger travel. While the airlines' share of freight transportation is still small, it too has been growing (see Tables Df38–58 and Figure Df-B).

The early and mid-1960s were among the most dramatic in aviation history.[14] The rate of technological change was at an all-time high, both in the airline industry and in the emerging "aerospace" industry, whose growth was spurred by the Cold War "race for space" that began in the late 1950s. See Table Cg236–240 for one measure of the aerospace industry's growth internationally, commercial space launches since 1982.

With the end of the Vietnam War in 1975 and the maturation of commercial aviation, aircraft production declined sharply and remained at a much-reduced level over the subsequent twenty-five years. Observers point to the decline of the NASA space program, an increase in international competition, and damage to the industry as a result of contracting and corruption scandals (Pattillo 1998, p. 317).

Alongside the history of air transportation's growth and technological change, there is a parallel history of government regulation and promotion of commercial air transportation, which began with passage of the Air Commerce Act of 1926. The Bureau of Air Commerce was created to help promote air safety by overseeing the licensing of pilots, checking the airworthiness of aircraft, and establishing and maintaining air traffic control. The positive impact of this regulation can be seen in Table Df1229–1245, which records data on airline safety since 1926.

The Aeronautics Branch of the Commerce Department initiated regular collection of national statistics in 1926. The growth in the number of airports, pilots, and the like can be seen in Table Df1139–1158. The Air Mail Act of 1925 opened an existing, federally operated airmail service to private competition and led to the development of aircraft to carry both passengers and mail. In 1926, the Postmaster General established a competition in which commercial airlines bid on routes for carrying airmail. Many of the famous pilots of the day, including Charles A. Lindbergh, began their aviation careers flying these airmail routes. The airmail contracts were crucial to the early development of passenger service because they guaranteed the airlines a known fee for flying a route, even in the absence of paying passengers and regardless of the volume of mail.

A new structure for airline regulation was initiated in 1934 following charges of collusion in the awarding of airmail contracts. President Franklin D. Roosevelt revoked all existing contracts and sponsored a new airmail act that divided responsibility for civil aviation among three agencies. The Post Office continued to award airmail contracts and set routes, the Interstate Commerce Commission fixed rates and payments, and a reorganized Bureau of Air Commerce (1934) assumed responsibility for establishing airways and creating licensing. The first comprehensive regulation was established in 1938 with the creation of the Civil Aeronautics Administration (CAA). Two years later a separate Civil Aeronautics Board (CAB) was created. In 1958, the Federal Aviation Agency assumed the function of the CAA and the safety functions of the CAB. It operated independently from the Commerce Department. In 1966, this agency was renamed the Federal Aviation Administration (FAA) and moved to the USDOT.

The FAA and the CAB carried out federal promotion and regulation of civil aviation. The FAA's principal activities address many aspects of airline safety, including the operation of air route traffic control centers, airport traffic control towers, and flight service stations. In addition, it became involved in the design, construction, maintenance, and inspection of navigation, traffic control, and communications equipment for the airways, as well as the promotion of air safety. The CAB was also involved in setting interstate routes and regulating fares for the commercial airlines. The responsibility for investigation of aviation accidents, originally held by the CAB, was transferred to the National Transportation Safety Board of the USDOT in 1966.

In 1978, federal regulation of the airline industry was dramatically curtailed when airline deregulation was implemented. The role of the CAB in setting interstate routes and regulating fares was reduced. On January 1, 1985, the CAB was eliminated. Its residual functions were assumed by the USDOT. The FAA continued to perform its functions within that department. Unfortunately, the USDOT does not publish many of the data series that had been reported by the CAB. Thus, one consequence of deregulation was a significant reduction in quantitative evidence on the commercial

---

[14] Pattillo (1998), p. 261. See also Morrison and Whinston (1995).

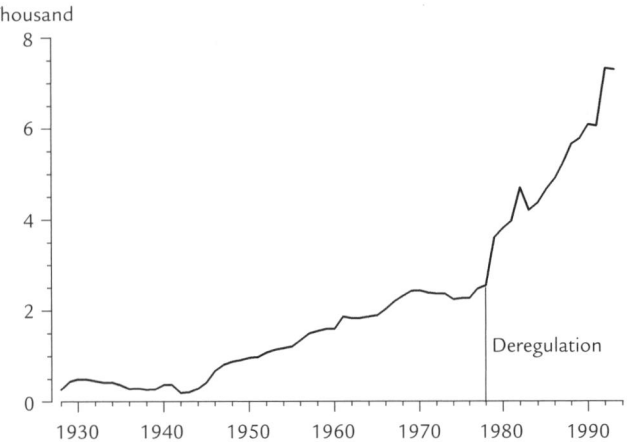

FIGURE Df-J **Scheduled domestic aircraft in operation: 1928–1993**

Source
Series Df1113.

airline industry. In particular, it has become more difficult to obtain information on airline routes and fares; as a result, the full impact of deregulation on the industry's activity and performance has been difficult to assess.[15]

Still, some effects of airline deregulation can be seen in the series on number of airline operators and aircraft in operation in domestic air transportation, shown in Table Df1112–1125 and Figure Df-J, and in the airline financial data presented in Tables Df1177–1228. Deregulation permitted the entry of many new airline companies, which brought a surge in the number of aircraft in operation. This heightened competition led to a much more turbulent financial situation for the industry, with many companies sustaining sizeable losses in the mid-1980s and early 1990s.

Pipelines

Pipelines are most commonly used for natural gas and petroleum products, but they are also used to transport slurry-coal, a thin mixture of fine particles of coal suspended in water. In some places, they are used to move water out of aquifers and to remove sludge from wastewater treatment plants.

Long-distance petroleum pipelines were first built in the United States in the 1870s, not long after Edwin Drake's first oil strike near Titusville, Pennsylvania, in 1859 (see the essay on mining, energy, fisheries, and forestry in Chapter Db). Independent crude-oil producers in the western Pennsylvania oil fields were trying to escape the control of the Standard Oil Trust over railroad rates on oil shipments. They organized themselves into the Tidewater Oil Company and built a pipeline as an alternative transportation mode to the railroad. At first, Standard Oil vigorously fought pipeline development. After the pipelines were built, however, Standard Oil was quick to see the advantages of this new form of transportation. Before pipelines were constructed, the high cost of shipping crude

oil meant that oil was refined in a large number of very small refineries that were located in out-of-the-way fields near the oil wells. Inexpensive pipeline transportation made it profitable to ship crude oil to a small number of very large refineries. This opportunity revolutionized petroleum manufacturing and the organization of the industry.[16]

Alfred D. Chandler Jr. emphasized the importance of pipelines in the development of the petroleum industry.

> Not only did it greatly reduce shipping costs, but it also provided magnificent storage areas and thus assured a much greater and steadier flow of crude oil into the refineries. The alliance quickly made an investment of more than $30 million in pipelines, at a time when the Standard Oil Company's total assets were valued at $3 million. As the new pipelines neared completion, the members of the Standard Oil alliance formed the Standard Oil Trust, which then rationalized the petroleum industry. (Chandler 1990, p. 94)

Oil and natural gas pipeline construction in the United States followed the geography of gas and oil discoveries and the location of refineries. Oil discoveries in Texas, Oklahoma, and Southern California in the 1920s instigated the development of a nationwide system of oil and natural gas pipelines. Table Df1246–1258 gives data on interstate pipelines and points to the substantial volume of pipeline construction in the 1920s. At its peak in the 1970s, pipelines accounted for almost a fourth of U.S. domestic intercity freight traffic (see series Df57 and Figure Df-D).[17] The discovery of oil at Prudhoe Bay on the Alaskan North Slope in 1968 prompted the construction of the Trans-Alaska Pipeline System during the mid-1970s. At the time, it was the largest privately financed construction project in world history. Because this project lay entirely within the state of Alaska, it is not included in the statistics shown in Table Df1246–1258, which refer to interstate pipeline projects only.[18]

Appendix: A Note on Data Sources

Because government involvement in the development of the nation's transportation infrastructure took place primarily at the state and local levels, and because of the heavy involvement of private enterprise, statistics on the early period of U.S. transportation history are to be found in the records of literally hundreds of separate local governmental jurisdictions and in those of private companies.

The federal 1880 Census made an effort to survey the extent and development of the nation's transportation system at the time, and the census continued quinquennial surveys of transportation systems through 1982. In 1957, the Census Bureau initiated a *Census of Transportation*.

Henry Varnum Poor, who operated a private credit assessment and reporting agency, began collecting and publishing statistics on selected transportation companies in 1851. His *History of the Railroads and Canals of the United States of America* (1860) is an important source of early data on these transportation modes.

---

[15] Both agencies published, and the FAA continues to publish, annual operational data on the use of airway facilities; data related to the location of air personnel, aircraft, and airports; the activity volume in the field of non–air carrier (general aviation) flying and aircraft production and registration.

[16] For a contemporary discussion of the implications of pipeline development, see Folger (1968), pp. 209–11.
[17] For a history of petroleum pipelines, see Johnson (1967). On natural gas pipelines, see Castaneda and Smith (1996).
[18] For a discussion of the Trans-Alaskan Pipeline, see Coates (1991).

Not until the formation of the ICC in 1887 did a truly coordinated and comprehensive national effort to collect and publish data on the transportation system begin. The ICC's data collection effort was undertaken to support its regulatory mission. Originally, the ICC had jurisdiction only over the railroads, but over time it came to regulate interstate activities of other transportation companies including those in trucking, passenger buses, freight forwarding, water carrying, oil and gas pipelines, transportation brokering, and express delivery. As these additional modes of transportation came under ICC jurisdiction, their statistics entered the ICC statistical base.

In 1966, the federal government created the USDOT with the mandate for "the development, collection, and dissemination of technological, statistical, economic, and other information relevant to domestic, and international, transportation." This department then conceived and developed a statistical compendium titled *National Transportation Statistics*. The first volume was published in 1970–1971, and it became an annual publication starting in 1978.

Deregulation of the airlines, railroads, and motor carriers between 1978 and 1980 significantly reduced or altogether eliminated data collection programs in the federal transportation regulatory agencies. The annual expenditures of the USDOT shrank dramatically between 1976 and 1986. In 1982, the Census Bureau terminated its quinquennial collection of data on commodity flows and passenger travel. No data on national multimodal commodity flows were collected between 1977 and 1993. The federal government conducted no comprehensive analyses of national transportation between 1979 and 1989. The few remaining data series published by the ICC ended when the ICC went out of existence in 1996 and its few remaining functions were transferred to the USDOT.

The Eno Transportation Foundation (ETF) is a nonprofit organization founded in 1921. Eno's *Transportation in America, Historical Compendium, 1939–1995*, and the annual edition of that volume are important continuations of historical series formerly produced and published by the federal government.

The Intermodal Surface Transportation Efficiency Act of 1991 (ISTEA) created the Bureau of Transportation Statistics (BTS). Many of the provisions in the act speak to recapturing past capabilities. How the BTS has responded to the mandates in ISTEA is addressed in its *Transportation Statistics Annual Report*. Further, the BTS has become responsible for the annual *National Transportation Statistics* volume. The BTS is mandated to develop an intermodal transportation data base on commodity and passenger flows, including public and private investment in intermodal transportation facilities and services. To that end, it has developed the Commodity Flow Survey and the American Travel Survey. It compiles locational and connection data on intermodal facilities and services for all modes as part of the National Transportation Atlas Database.

National Transportation Statistics contains a great deal more comparative data than existed in the past. Data since 1960 have been reported on measures such as average freight revenues (see Table Df104–108), the volume of intercity passenger and freight (see Tables Df38–58), length of haul (see Table Df126–133), passenger fares (see Tables Df109–113 and Df148–152), personal consumption expenditures on transportation (see Table Df153–157), and national freight bill as a component of aggregate income (see Table Df114–117).

The new *National Transportation Statistics* data are reported annually for the previous ten years. Earlier data are reported only in five-year increments – those ending in a 5 or 0. One unfortunate consequence of the new format is that, even though series continue to be revised, often as a result of changed definitions, the data are not being revised for the earlier years. Where this has happened in the data presented in the tables shown here, two numbers have been supplied. Researchers are referred to the original sources where this presents problems of comparability.

A second difficulty results from the fact that no attempt has been made to adjust the data in *National Transportation Statistics* for the effect of changes in methods of accounting and reporting; hence, the data for the various years are often only approximately comparable. This is in keeping with the way the data are reported in the source documents. Once again, concerned researchers should consult the original sources.

The best source for quantitative data on highways is the Federal Highway Administration's annual *Highway Statistics*, first published in 1945. This publication and its companion volume, published every ten years, the most recent being *Highway Statistics, Summary to 1995*, are the principal source of data on public roads, the ownership and operation of motor vehicles, and fuel consumption (see Tables Df370–412 and Df473–481). There have been several format changes over the years. For example, in 1985, the Federal Highway Administration stopped requesting that states supply data on county and rural governments separate from that of municipalities. In several cases, these format changes make it impossible to update historical tables in a consistent fashion to the present time.

Data on the motor vehicle and equipment industry and on retail, wholesale, and services aspects of this industry can be found in reports of the *Census of Manufactures*, the *Census of Business*, and the *Annual Survey of Manufactures*. Domestic sales, plus the imports and exports, of passenger cars and trucks are reported in Table Df347–352. Travel data on these vehicles can be found in Tables Df370–412. The Bureau of Public Roads published surveys of highway mileage, revenues, and expenditures that were conducted in 1904, 1909, and 1914.

Data on water traffic and the merchant marine can be found in a number of sources. For the earliest period, 1789–1823, the primary source is the *American State Papers: Class IV, Commerce and Navigation,* volumes 1 and 2. Between 1821 and 1946, there are the various annual issues of *Foreign Commerce and Navigation of the United States*. The *Annual Report of the Commissioner of Navigation* was issued between 1884 and 1923. Both the latter two reports were originally issued by the Register of the Treasury and later by the Treasury Department. They then moved to the Department of Commerce and Labor, which became simply the Department of Commerce.

The Bureau of Customs prepared annual issues of *Merchant Marine Statistics* between 1924 and 1965.[19] These were originally

---

[19] A number of copying and typesetting errors in the 1936 *Merchant Marine Statistics* report were corrected in the *Historical Statistics of the United States* (1975), Table II, p. 744. The corrections were limited to situations where the exact nature of the discrepancy could be determined beyond reasonable doubt. The text statements, and the correction of errors found in the published tables, are based on reference to the following primary sources: For 1789–1823, see *American State Papers: Class IV, Commerce and Navigation,* volumes 1 and 2 (published in 1834); for 1821–1892, see annual issues of *Commerce and*

prepared by the Department of Commerce as a successor to the statistical section of the *Annual Report of the Commissioner of Navigation*. These statistics were supplemented by records of the U.S. Coast Guard, and the various annual issues of the *Annual Report of the Office of the Chief of Engineers,* Corps of Engineers. Data for "documented merchant vessels" have not reported since the 1970s (see, for example, Table Df822–824). The *Statistical Abstract of the United States*, issued by the Bureau of the Census, also contains historical water-traffic and merchant-marine statistics.

Congressional documents are another source of historical series on the merchant marine, foreign commerce, and related areas. For 1789–1882, a particularly valuable collection of documents was bound together under the title *Decadence of American Shipping and Compulsory Pilotage*. The documents in this collection include: *Foreign Commerce* and *Decadence of American Shipping,* U.S. House of Representatives Ex. Document number 111, 41st Congress, 2d session; *Causes of the Reduction of American Tonnage and the Decline of Navigation Interest . . . ,* U.S. House of Representatives Report number 28, 41st Congress, 2d session; *Foreign Commerce and the Practical Workings of Maritime Reciprocity,* U.S. House of Representatives Ex. Document number 76, 41st Congress, 3d session; *Causes of the Decadence of Our Merchant Marine; Means for Its Restoration and the Extension of Our Foreign Commerce*, U.S. House of Representatives Report number 342, 46th Congress, 3d session; *American Shipping,* U.S. House of Representatives Report number 1827, 47th Congress, 2d session; *American Merchant Marine,* U.S. House of Representatives Report number 363, 48th Congress, 1st session; *Ship-Building and Ship-Owning Interests,* U.S. House of Representatives Report number 750, 48th Congress, 1st session; and reports of lesser interest, U.S. House of Representatives Miscellaneous Document number 37 and Report number 1848, both of the 48th Congress, 1st session.

The publications of the Maritime Commission and its predecessor agencies are another important source of data. *Ocean-Going Merchant Fleets of Principal Maritime Nations, Iron and Steel, Steam and Motor, Vessels of 2,000 Gross Tons and Over*, issued quarterly or semiannually, 1921–1941, provides data for each leading maritime nation on ocean-going merchant vessels of 2,000 gross tons and over, showing number and tonnage of such fleets classified by age, speed, size, boilers, engines, draft, and so forth, by major vessel type. *Employment of American Flag Steam and Motor Merchant Vessels of 1,000 Gross Tons and Over*, issued quarterly, 1923–1941, shows the number and tonnage of such vessels employed in U.S. foreign and domestic trade for seagoing merchant vessels of 1,000 gross tons and over, arranged by major vessel type, ownership (government and private), and area of operation (see Table Df758–821).

The Bureau of the Census (and its predecessor, the Census Office) published the results of five censuses of water transportation, for the years 1880, 1889, 1906, 1916, and 1926.[20] Although data

from these sources are not presented here, it is worth noting what is included in these volumes. The 1880 Census was limited to steam vessels; the report includes a detailed history of steam navigation in the United States with a separate discussion and single-year construction statistics by geographic region, from the beginning to 1880.[21] The report of the shipbuilding census, also taken the same year, includes a detailed technical history of shipbuilding in all aspects, with particular reference to sailing craft. Single-year figures are shown for New England shipbuilding, 1674–1714, classified by type of vessel and place where built.[22] The censuses of 1889 and 1906 included all classes of vessels; however, the 1889 Census included fishing vessels for the Pacific Division only, and the 1906 Census excluded fishing vessels. The Censuses of 1916 and 1926 provided data for all U.S. vessels and craft of five tons net register or more, documented and undocumented, whether propelled by machinery or sails, or unrigged, except that certain specified types of vessels were excluded.[23]

An early chronicler and critic of the railroads in the nineteenth century was Henry Varnum Poor, editor of the *American Railroad Journal* and later publisher of the *Manual of the Railroads of the United States*. As mentioned earlier, the vast majority of railroad (and canal) data available up to the time of the ICC is attributable to Poor. This includes information on the miles of road that was operated, equipment, passenger and freight service, and property investment, capital, income, and expenses. The ICC republished Poor's data in 1932 under the title *Railway Statistics Before 1890*. Elmus Wicker conducted a careful review of Poor's work and advises using these data with caution; anyone using Poor's data is advised to consult Wicker's essay.[24] The Tenth Census of 1880 also contained data on rail mileage through 1879. Similar data appeared in the Eleventh Census of 1890, but it was not strictly comparable. Beginning in 1893, *Railway Age* collected information similar to that reported in the Tenth Census (see Tables Df874–885, Df888–889, Df891–910, and Df919–926).

Beginning in 1890, the principal sources of the railroad series through the late 1970s are various issues of two annual publications of the ICC: *Statistics of Railways in the United States* for the years prior to 1954 and *Transport Statistics in the United States*, part 1, for 1954–1978 (see Tables Df927–1003 and Df1014–1033).

Beginning in 1911, the ICC classified operating companies on the basis of operating revenues. Those of Class I had annual revenues above $1,000,000; Class II, above $100,000; and Class III, below $100,000. Beginning in 1956, the minimum for Class I was raised to $3,000,000, and the other two classes were consolidated. Effective January 1965, the classification was changed to the following: Class I, $5,000,000 or more; and Class II, under $5,000,000. Companies with revenue falls that would move them into a new, lower, class were not reclassified until the revenue reduction appeared to be permanent. The relative importance of Class I railroads has increased since 1911 because of the growth of traffic and the absorption of small roads in larger systems. The

---

Navigation of the United States; for 1884–1923, see issues of *Annual Report of the Commissioner of Navigation;* for 1924–1945, see annual issues of *Merchant Marine Statistics*. Although the census reports of 1850 and 1860 contain some statistics relating to water transportation, these statistics apparently were collected by other agencies.

[20] For reports of these censuses, see *Tenth Census Reports*, volume 4, *Report on Agencies of Transportation* (1880); *Eleventh Census Reports, Report on Transportation Business*, Part 1, "Transportation by Water"; *Transportation by Water* (1906); *Water Transportation* (1916); and *Water Transportation* (1926).

[21] See T. C. Purdy, "Report on Steam Navigation in the United States," *Tenth Census Reports* (1880), volume 4.

[22] See Henry Hall, "Report on the Ship-Building Industry of the United States," *Tenth Census Reports* (1880), volume 8.

[23] See U.S. Bureau of the Census (1929), p. 5.

[24] Wicker (1960). George Rogers Taylor in a comment on Wicker in the same volume seconds Wicker's cautions. Both Fishlow and Fogel, whose work makes use of Poor's data, were aware of these cautions. It should also be noted that the original ICC publication contained typographical errors.

ratio of operating revenues of Class I line-haul companies to the total revenues of Classes I, II, and III was 96.48 percent in 1911, 97.45 in 1916, 98.07 in 1926, 98.76 in 1941, 99.06 in 1945, and 98.21 in 1969. Since the demise of the ICC, reported data are most consistent with what it reported as Class I railroads.

The vast majority of the freight statistics reported after deregulation are the work of the Association of American Railroads (AAR) and appear in one of that group's publications, particularly in its annual *Railroad Facts*. The AAR has been publishing data almost as long as the ICC. Its data are close, but not identical, to those of the ICC. The AAR does not collect as much data as the ICC did; consequently, some series simply cannot be continued to the present. Tables Df1034–1088 present the AAR data that parallel the old ICC data. In this volume, the tables on railroads that begin in 1960 were constructed to provide some overlap to the ICC data. It should be noted that the series reported in these tables often begin much earlier than 1960. Interested readers are referred to the source volumes.

The AAR no longer collects information on passenger service, as its members now handle freight exclusively. The federal government assumed responsibility for intercity-passenger service through Amtrak in 1970. Passenger service statistics come from Amtrak, and only recently did Amtrak begin publishing data on its operations. Over the past few years, Amtrak has included a ten-year "historical data appendix" as part of its *Annual Report*. Those data are reported in Tables Df1092–1111. Other data series relating to Amtrak are included in *National Transportation Statistics;* a few other series can be found in the *Statistical Abstract of the United States*. In most cases, the underlying source of these published numbers is private correspondence with Amtrak.

Through 1978, the railroads regulated by the ICC were still described legally as "steam railways," yet since 1957 most train and switching operations are performed by diesel locomotives, and some divisions of the railways included were electrified. The ICC also regulated a small (and diminishing) number of railways of the interurban electric type. These are not included in the ICC data reported here. Information on electric railways for the period 1890 through 1937 can be found in Table Df1004–1013.

An important source for information on public transportation is the American Public Transit Association's *Transit Fact Book*. There is some overlap between this source and Amtrak information on urban commuting. Multimode data on public transportation can be found in Tables Df158–183.

The FAA's annual *Statistical Handbook of Aviation* is the source for most of the air statistics presented in this volume.

References

Bright, Charles D. 1978. *The Jet Makers: The Aerospace Industry from 1945 to 1972*. Regents Press of Kansas.

Bryant, K. L. 1988. "Railroads in the Age of Regulation, 1900–1980." In *Encyclopedia of American Business History and Biography*. Facts On File.

Cain, Louis P. 1978. *Sanitation Strategy for a Lakefront Metropolis: The Case of Chicago*. Northern Illinois University Press.

Callender, Guy Stevens. 1902. "The Early Transportation and Banking Enterprises of the States in Relation to the Growth of Corporations." *Quarterly Journal of Economics* 17: 111–62.

Castaneda, Christopher J., and Clarance M. Smith. 1996. *Gas Pipelines and the Emergence of America's Regulatory State: A History of Panhandle Eastern Corporation, 1928–1993*. Cambridge University Press.

Caves, Douglas W. 1980. *Economic Performance in Regulated and Unregulated Environments: A Comparison of U.S. and Canadian Railroads*. Transportation Center, Northwestern University.

Chamberlain, Eugene T. 1968. "Our Merchant Marine." In Chauncey M. Depew, editor. *One Hundred Years of American Commerce, 1795–1895* [1895], volume 1. Greenwood Press.

Chandler, Alfred D., Jr. 1965. *The Railroads: The Nation's First Big Business*. Harcourt, Brace and World.

Chandler, Alfred D., Jr. 1977. *The Visible Hand: The Managerial Revolution in American Business*. Harvard University Press.

Chandler, Alfred D., Jr. 1990. *Scale and Scope: The Dynamics of Industrial Capitalism*. Harvard University Press.

Chapelle, Howard I. 1982 [1935]. *The History of American Sailing Ships*. Bonanza Books.

Chapelle, Howard I. 1967. *The Search for Speed under Sail, 1700–1855*. Norton.

Childs, William R. 1985. *Trucking and the Public Interest: The Emergence of Federal Regulation, 1914–1940*. University of Tennessee Press.

Coates, Peter A. 1991. *The Trans-Alaska Pipeline Controversy: Technology, Conservation, and the Frontier*. Associated University Press.

Cochran, Thomas C. 1957. *The American Business System*. Harvard University Press.

Davis, Lance E., Robert E. Gallman, and Karin Gleiter. 1997. *In Pursuit of Leviathan: Technology, Institutions, Productivity, and Profits in American Whaling, 1816–1906*. University of Chicago Press.

Fishlow, Albert. 1965. *American Railroads and the Transformation of the Ante-Bellum Economy*. Harvard University Press.

Fishlow, Albert. 1972. "Internal Transportation." In Lance Davis, Richard A. Easterlin, et al., editors. *American Economic Growth: An Economist's History of the United States*. Harper & Row.

Flink, James J. 1970. *America Adopts the Automobile, 1895–1910*. MIT Press.

Flink, James J. 1975. *The Car Culture*. MIT Press.

Fogel, Robert. 1964. *Railroads and American Economic Growth*. Johns Hopkins University Press.

Folger, Henry C., Jr. 1968. "Petroleum: Its Production and Products." In Chauncey M. Depew, editor. *One Hundred Years of American Commerce, 1795–1895* [1895], volume 1. Greenwood Press.

Gates, Paul W. 1934. *The Illinois Central Railroad and Its Colonization Work*. Harvard University Press.

Gibson, Andrew, and Arthur Donovan. 2000. *The Abandoned Ocean: A History of United States Maritime Policy*. University of South Carolina Press.

Goldenberg, Joseph A. 1976. *Shipbuilding in Colonial America*. University Press of Virginia for the Mariners Museum.

Goodrich, Carter. 1960. *Government Promotion of American Canals and Railroads 1800–1890*. Columbia University Press.

Goodrich, Carter, Jerome Cranmer, et al., editors. 1961. *Canals and American Economic Development*. Columbia University Press.

Haites, Erik, and James Mak. 1973. "The Decline of Steamboating on the Ante-Bellum Western Rivers: Some New Evidence and an Alternative Hypothesis." *Explorations in Economic History* 11 (1): 25–36.

Hokanson, Drake. 1988. *The Lincoln Highway: Main Street across America*. University of Iowa Press.

Hughes, Jonathan. 1991. *The Governmental Habit Redux*. Princeton University Press.

Hunter, Louis. 1949. *Steamboats on the Western Rivers*. Harvard University Press.

Hutchins, John G. B. 1941. *The American Maritime Industries and Public Policy, 1789–1914: An Economic History*. Harvard Economic Studies, volume 71. Harvard University Press.

Hyde, Francis Edwin. 1975. *Cunard and the North Atlantic, 1840–1973*: A History of Shipping and Financial Management. Macmillan.

Johnson, Arthur M. 1967. *Petroleum Pipelines and Public Policy, 1906–1959*. Harvard University Press.

Jordan, Philip D. 1948. *The National Road*. Peter Smith.

Lane, Frederick. 1951. *Ships for Victory: A History of Shipbuilding under the U.S. Maritime Commission to World War II*. Johns Hopkins University Press.

Mak, James, and Gary Walton. 1972. "Steamboats and the Great Productivity Surge in River Transportation." *Journal of Economic History* 32 (3): 619–40.

Martin, Albro. 1992. *Railroads Triumphant: The Growth, Rejection and Rebirth of a Vital American Force*. Oxford University Press.

McGowan, Alan. 1980. *The Century before Steam: The Development of the Sailing Ship, 1700–1820*. Volume 4 of *The Ship*, edited by Basil Greenhill. Her Majesty's Stationery Office.

Morris, James M. 1979. *Our Maritime Heritage: Maritime Developments and Their Impact on American Life*. University Press of America.

Morrison, Steven, and Clifford Whinston. 1995. *The Evolution of the Airline Industry*. Brookings Institution Press.

North, Douglass C. 1961. *The Economic Growth of the United States, 1790–1860*. Prentice Hall.

Olmstead, Alan L. 1972. "Investment Constraints and New York City Mutual Savings Bank Financing of Antebellum Development." *Journal of Economic History* 32: 811–40.

Pattillo, Donald M. 1998. *Pushing the Envelope: The American Aircraft Industry*. University of Michigan Press.

Poor, Henry Varnum. 1970 [1860]. *History of the Railroads and Canals of the United States of America*. Augustus M. Kelley.

Rose, Mark. 1979. *Interstate: Express Highway Politics, 1941–1956*. Regents Press of Kansas.

Rubin, Julius. 1961. "An Imitative Public Improvement: The Pennsylvania Mainline." In Carter Goodrich, Jerome Cranmer, et al., editors. *Canals and American Economic Development*. Columbia University Press.

Seely, Bruce. 1987. *Building the American Highway System: Engineers and Policy Makers*. Temple University Press.

Seely, Bruce. 1993. "A Republic Bound Together." *Wilson Quarterly* 17 (Winter): 19–40.

Taylor, George Rogers. 1951. *The Transportation Revolution 1815–1860*. Holt Rinehart.

Taylor, Philip A. M. 1971. *The Distant Magnet: European Emigration to the U.S.A.* Harper & Row.

U.S. Bureau of the Census. 1929. *Water Transportation, 1926*. U.S. Government Printing Office.

Wicker, E. R. 1960. "Railroad Investment before the Civil War." In *Trends in the American Economy in the Nineteenth Century: A Report of the National Bureau of Economic Research*. Studies in Income and Wealth, volume 24. Princeton University Press.

Wollenberg, Charles. 1990. *Marinship at War: Shipbuilding and Social Change in Wartime Sausalito*. Western Heritage Press.

ALL MODES

Louis P. Cain, Susan B. Carter, and Richard Sutch

TABLE Df1–7   Farmers' trips to market in rural Massachusetts – length of trip and hauling costs: 1750–1855

Contributed by Susan B. Carter

			Average per ton-mile cost				
			Total		Yoke of oxen	Vehicle	Driver
	Average length of trip	Median length of trip	Current dollars	Constant dollars	Yoke of oxen	Vehicle	Driver
	Df1	Df2	Df3	Df4	Df5	Df6	Df7
Period	Miles	Miles	Dollars per ton-mile	1795–1805 dollars per ton-mile	Dollars per ton-mile	Dollars per ton-mile	Dollars per ton-mile
1750–1775	23.7	17.8	0.095	0.151	0.031	0.015	0.049
1776–1790	18.7	17.3	0.151	0.177	0.049	0.029	0.073
1791–1805	27.0	17.7	0.143	0.146	0.044	0.032	0.067
1806–1820	24.5	18.9	0.182	0.156	0.083	0.027	0.072
1821–1835	18.7	12.7	0.181	0.171	0.074	0.033	0.074
1836–1855	17.2	13.6	0.220	0.180	0.085	0.027	0.108

Source

Winifred Barr Rothenberg, *From Market-Places to a Market Economy: The Transformation of Rural Massachusetts, 1750–1850* (University of Chicago Press, 1992), Tables 1, 4, and 8, pp. 85, 94, and 109–10.

Documentation

Rothenberg developed these estimates from data in the account books and daybooks of Massachusetts farmers. They are based on farmers' reports of what Rothenberg calls "marketing trips." These are trips that explicitly specify "hauling off the farm, 'with a load,' to a stated destination or a stated number of miles, by wagon, sled, or sleigh 'with team.'" Rothenberg did not include journeys by chaise, carriage, or on horseback because she hoped to avoid trips for "visiting, going to church or to meetings, arbitrating disputes, attending to paupers, appraising inventories, administering estates, surveying, [and] assessing." (Rothenberg 1992, p. 82).

The estimates reported in series Df1–2 are those in Rothenberg's Table 1, panel B, "truncated distribution," and exclude a small number of extraordinarily long trips. Rothenberg prefers these estimates because they were more representative of the typical experience of Massachusetts farmers at the time.

In calculating the costs of transportation, reported in series Df3–7, Rothenberg assumed that each full load weighed one ton. She also assumed that inputs hired by the day traveled ten miles; this is twice her assumed minimum farm-to-market distance of five miles. As she notes, to the extent this underestimates the distance, the cost is overestimated.

Most of the drivers in series Df7 were the farmers themselves. Rothenberg estimated the cost of farmers' own labor inputs as the daily wage for the most highly paid wage labor on the farm. In the earlier years, the most highly paid wage labor was for carting; in later years it was for haying.

The price index used to convert current to constant dollars in series Df4 was developed by Rothenberg. The base of that index is the average of prices observed from 1795 to 1805.

TABLE Df8–12   Travel times between New York City and other selected cities: 1800–1857

Contributed by Susan B. Carter and Richard Sutch

	Boston	Charleston, SC	New Orleans	Chicago	San Francisco
	Df8	Df9	Df10	Df11	Df12
Year	Days	Days	Days	Days	Days
1800	4.0	10	27	42	— [2]
1830	1.5	6	14	19	— [2]
1857	— [1]	2	5	2	28

[1] Less than one day.

[2] More than forty-two days.

Source

Charles O. Paullin. *Atlas of the Historical Geography of the United States* (Carnegie Institution, 1932), p. 133 and Plates 138A, 138B, and 138C.

Documentation

Paullin's estimates for 1800 and 1830 are based on a variety of sources. The estimates for 1857 come from G. F. Thomas, *Railway and Steam Navigation Guide* (D. Appleton, 1858), also known as Appleton's *Railway and Steam Navigation Guide.*

Paullin used the estimates to construct maps with isochronic lines connecting places equally distant in travel time from New York. He did not calculate travel times for cities more than six weeks away from New York City.

TABLE Df13-16   Federal aid for internal improvements – roads, canals, rivers, harbors, and railroads: 1803–1860

Contributed by Louis P. Cain

Year	Federal expenditures			Acreage granted to railroads	Year	Federal expenditures			Acreage granted to railroads
	Roads and canals	Rivers and harbors				Roads and canals	Rivers and harbors		
		Total United States	Mississippi and related rivers				Total United States	Mississippi and related rivers	
	Df13	Df14	Df15	Df16		Df13	Df14	Df15	Df16
	Thousand dollars	Thousand dollars	Thousand dollars	Thousand acres		Thousand dollars	Thousand dollars	Thousand dollars	Thousand acres
1803	2	—	—	—	1835	1,233	595	71	—
1804	3	—	—	—	1836	1,218	873	114	—
1806	2	—	—	—	1837	944	1,389	367	—
1807	12	—	—	—	1838	457	1,066	360	—
1808	11	—	—	—	1839	397	788	119	—
1809	3	—	—	—	1840	357	151	22	—
1810	56	—	—	—	1841	48	79	0	—
1811	31	—	—	—	1842	260	82	16	—
1812	68	—	—	—	1843	137	112	66	—
1813	78	—	—	—	1844	123	322	177	—
1814	73	—	—	—	1845	37	548	252	—
1815	114	—	—	—	1846	44	230	51	—
1816	109	—	—	—	1847	254	45	22	—
1817	361	—	—	—	1848	90	24	4	—
1818	349	—	—	—	1849	94	26	—	—
1819	510	—	—	—	1850	235	43	1	3,752
1820	147	—	—	—	1851	74	70	35	—
1821	84	—	—	—	1852	113	43	16	1,765
1822	41	—	—	—	1853	185	498	81	2,682
1823	38	—	—	—	1854	199	960	306	—
1824	110	26	3	—	1855	371	837	174	—
1825	363	40	11	—	1856	391	169	—	14,560
1826	563	87	16	—	1857	539	274	4	5,118
1827	352	136	36	—	1858	670	465	204	—
1828	401	188	53	—	1859	357	295	61	—
1829	782	530	57	—	1860	555	232	121	—
1830	639	576	59	—					
1831	363	653	157	—					
1832	695	540	86	—					
1833	1,053	710	87	—					
1834	867	606	56	—					

Sources

Stanley Lebergott, *The Americans: An Economic Record* (Norton, 1984). The underlying source for series Df13-15 is a tabulation of individual expenditure items listed in U.S. 47th Congress, 1st session, S.D. 196, *Statement of Appropriations and Expenditures 1789 to 1882* (1882). The underlying source for series Df16 is Thomas Donaldson, *The Public Domain*, volume 1 (1884), p. 273.

Documentation

Series Df13–14. Series are net expenditures. Series Df15 is expenditures by warrants.

TABLE Df17–21   Inland freight rates, by type of transportation: 1784–1900

Contributed by Louis P. Cain

		River			
	Wagon	Downstream	Upstream	Canal	Railroad
	Df17	Df18	Df19	Df20	Df21
Year	Cents per ton-mile	Cents per ton-mile	Cents per ton-mile	Cents per ton-mile	Cents per ton-mile
1784	38	—	—	—	—
1789	—	1.50	10.0	—	—
1794	30	—	—	—	—
1802	—	1.20	—	8.00	—
1804	—	—	8.0	—	—
1816	—	1.20	6.0	—	—
1817	—	—	—	5.50 [1]	—
1819	30	—	2.3	—	—
1822	15	0.70	1.5	—	—
1825	—	—	1.0	—	—
1828	—	0.55	—	—	—
1831	—	0.50	—	5.00	—
1833	—	—	—	—	6.20
1837	—	0.55	—	—	—
1840	—	0.50	—	1.80	—
1844	—	(Z)	—	1.10	—
1848	—	(Z)	—	0.80	5.50
1850	15	(Z)	—	—	—
1851	—	(Z)	—	—	4.00
1852	—	(Z)	—	0.70	3.10
1854	—	(Z)	—	—	3.10
1856	—	(Z)	—	1.05	3.40
1858	—	(Z)	—	0.80	3.10
1860	—	—	—	—	2.80
1861	—	0.60	—	—	—
1862	—	—	—	1.10	2.70
1864	—	1.00	—	1.40	3.00
1866	—	—	—	1.30	3.30
1868	—	—	—	1.20	3.25
1870	—	0.75	—	0.90	3.10
1872	—	0.60	—	1.00	2.40
1874	—	0.50	—	0.80	2.35
1876	—	(Z)	—	0.52	2.00
1878	—	(Z)	—	0.50	1.55
1880	—	(Z)	—	0.52	1.45
1882	—	—	—	—	1.15
1884	—	—	—	—	1.05
1888	—	—	—	—	1.00
1890	—	—	—	—	0.93
1892	—	—	—	—	0.90
1900	—	—	—	—	0.73

(Z) Less than 0.5 cents per ton-mile.

[1] Based on a single observation.

Source
Douglass C. North, "The Role of Transportation in the Economic Development of North America," in *Les Grandes Voies Maritimes dans le Monde XV–XIX Siécles* (École des Hautes Études en Sciences Sociales, 1965), pp. 244–5.

Documentation
The data are for those years when North believes "a representative or average rate could be obtained."

The chosen rates were used by the author only to indicate a pattern, but the graph of these numbers appears in a number of textbooks and other sources. They are not a systematic average of all rates, nor do they show any seasonal pattern or year-to-year changes. Downstream and upstream rates are presented separately until 1825, and then they are presented as a single number. That number is reported in series Df18.

TABLE Df22–24 Freight shipments from the Trans-Appalachian West through the Northern, Northeastern, and Southern Commercial Gateways: 1810–1860

Contributed by Susan B. Carter and Richard Sutch

Year	Northern Gateway Df22 Tons	Northeastern Gateway Df23 Tons	Southern Gateway (New Orleans) Df24 Tons	Year	Northern Gateway Df22 Tons	Northeastern Gateway Df23 Tons	Southern Gateway (New Orleans) Df24 Tons
1810	280	—	60,000 [2]	1840	181,200	27,900	537,400
1811	400	—	60,000 [2]	1841	241,800	26,900	542,500
1812	100	—	60,000 [2]	1842	244,700	32,900	566,500
1813	—	—	60,000 [2]	1843	264,100	46,600	782,600
1814	—	—	67,600	1844	324,800	39,600	652,000
1815	740	—	77,200	1845	316,000	41,300	868,000
1816	1,170	—	94,600	1846	518,900	52,100	971,700
1817	2,320	—	80,800	1847	831,300	82,800	937,600
1818	1,710	—	100,900	1848	655,600	60,200	1,025,900
1819	560	—	136,300	1849	776,000	57,000	1,009,900
1820	1,510	—	106,700	1850	848,800	82,800	886,000
1821	1,070	—	99,300	1851	1,058,900	97,000 [1]	1,058,200
1822	20	—	136,400	1852	1,258,700	111,800	1,160,500
1823	20	—	129,500	1853	1,364,400	59,900	1,328,800
1824	—	—	136,200	1854	1,318,100	144,200	1,286,300
1825	—	—	176,400	1855	1,396,800	179,200	1,247,200
1826	40	—	193,300	1856	1,660,600	234,300	1,500,200
1827	30	—	235,200	1857	1,448,100	221,200	1,431,800
1828	—	—	257,300	1858	1,882,600	312,400	1,572,700
1829	40	—	245,700	1859	1,559,200	264,900	1,803,400
1830	30	—	260,900	1860	2,599,800	299,700	2,187,600
1831	500	—	307,300				
1832	1,300	—	244,600				
1833	4,700	—	291,700				
1834	5,500	—	327,800				
1835	3,200	17,000	399,900				
1836	55,400	17,200	437,100				
1837	60,400	20,200	401,500				
1838	88,500	25,100	449,600				
1839	126,400	18,700	399,500				

[1] Interpolated.

[2] Estimated.

Source

Erik F. Haites, James Mak, and Gary M. Walton, *Western River Transportation: The Era of Early Internal Development, 1810–1860* (Johns Hopkins University Press, 1975), Appendix A, Tables A-1, A-2, and A-3.

Documentation

In the antebellum period (1776–1859) the "Trans-Appalachian West" referred to regions west of the Appalachian mountains that were experiencing American settlement. It included all or parts of the present-day states of Ohio, Indiana, Illinois, Michigan, Wisconsin, Iowa, Missouri, Kentucky, Tennessee, Arkansas, Mississippi, Louisiana, New York, Pennsylvania, Virginia, and West Virginia. Historians describe three "natural gateways" that linked this region with the Eastern Seaboard and the rest of the world. The Northern Gateway ran east from the Great Lakes, down the St. Lawrence, Hudson, and Mohawk rivers to New York City. The Northeastern Gateway linked Pittsburgh and Wheeling to Philadelphia and Baltimore. The Southern Gateway linked the Ohio, Missouri, and Mississippi river systems with New Orleans.

See the source for details on the conversion of raw data values into tons.

The series are based on different twelve-month date periods, as follows. Series Df22: year ending September 30 (1810–1842); a nine-month period

for 1843; and year ending June 30 thereafter. Series Df23: shipments made during navigation season of year shown. Series Df24: year ending September 30 (1810–1841) and August 31 thereafter.

Series Df22. Includes the following: exports to Canada or to the seaboard via the St. Lawrence Seaway; shipments on the Erie Canal (beginning 1836); shipments on the New York Central Railroad (beginning 1852); and shipments on the New York and Erie Railroad (beginning 1852). Exports for earlier years shown in the series may be understated owing to smuggling.

Series Df23. Includes freight shipments on the Pennsylvania canals (through 1852), as well as the Pennsylvania Railroad and the Baltimore and Ohio Railroad (beginning with 1853). The series excludes freight shipped via the National Road or the Pennsylvania Turnpike, both opened in 1817 (not likely to have exceeded 10,000 tons per year).

Series Df24. The data are the receipts of produce received at New Orleans by river. The series excludes articles rafted downstream but includes articles floated downstream by flatboats and barges. The data also include some receipts (1 to 6 percent of total) via Lake Pontchartrain.

TABLE Df25–26   Turnpike mileage and cost in New England, the Middle Atlantic, and Maryland: 1810–1830

Contributed by Louis P. Cain

Year	Cumulative mileage	Cumulative cost
	Df25	Df26
	Miles	Thousand dollars
1810	4,684	8,308
1820	9,930	22,534
1830 [1]	11,662	27,823

[1] Includes an estimate of 200 miles for the National Road (under construction at the time).

Source

Lance E. Davis, Richard A. Easterlin, et al. *American Economic Growth: An Economist's History of the United States.* (Harper & Row, 1972), p. 473.

Documentation

These estimates are based on literary accounts of individual New England turnpikes, various state reports, and other fragmentary references. The majority of the turnpike mileage was constructed in Maryland and the states to the north. Construction in the South was modest; few turnpikes were constructed in the West.

"Turnpikes" in this era meant toll roads. In the North, the work was largely privately financed, although there were several mixed private and public enterprises. In the South, the work was usually controlled by public trustees or local road commissioners. The tolls helped to cover the costs of grading, surfacing, and maintenance. Turnpikes were a marked improvement over the so-called common roads that accounted for the vast majority of roadways at the time.

TABLE Df27–33   Overland emigration to Oregon, California, and Utah – emigrants, travel time, and Indian–emigrant homicides: 1840–1860

Contributed by Susan B. Carter and Richard Sutch

Year	Emigrants to			Average travel time for journey from the Missouri River to		Homicides	
	Oregon	California	Utah	Placerville, California	Oregon City, Oregon	Emigrants by Indians	Indians by emigrants
	Df27	Df28	Df29	Df30	Df31	Df32	Df33
	Number	Number	Number	Days	Days	Number	Number
1840	13	0	0	—	—	0	0
1841	24	34	0	—	—	0	1
1842	125	0	0	—	—	0	0
1843	875	38	0	—	—	0	0
1844	1,475	53	0	157.7 [1]	169.1 [1]	0	0
1845	2,500	260	0	—	—	4	1
1846	1,200	1,500	0	—	—	4	20
1847	4,000	450	2,200	—	—	24	2
1848	1,300	400	2,400	—	—	2	2
1849	450	25,000	1,500	131.6	129.0	33	60
1850	6,000	44,000	2,500	107.9	125.0	48	76
1851	3,600	1,100	1,500	—	—	60	70
1852	10,000	50,000	10,000	—	—	45	70
1853	7,500	20,000	8,000	—	—	7	9
1854	6,000	12,000	3,167	—	—	35	40
1855	500	1,500	4,684	112.7 [2]	128.5 [2]	6	10
1856	1,000	8,000	2,400	—	—	20	15
1857	1,500	4,000	1,300	—	—	17 [3]	30
1858	1,500	6,000	150	—	—	—	—
1859	2,000	17,000	1,431	—	—	32 [3]	10
1860	1,500	9,000	1,630	—	—	25	10

[1] Average for 1841–1848.

[2] Average for 1850–1860.

[3] Excludes emigrants killed by so-called white Indians, or bandits: 8 in 1857 and 13 in 1859.

Source

John D. Unruh Jr., *The Plains Across: The Overland Emigrants and the Trans-Mississippi West, 1840–1860* (University of Illinois Press, 1979), Tables 1, 2, 4, and 10, pp. 119, 120, 185, and 403.

Documentation

"Oregon" here refers to the original Oregon Territory, including the present-day states of Oregon and Washington. Emigrants to Oregon, California, and Utah began their overland journey from cities on the western bank of the Missouri River, especially Independence, Westport (now Kansas City), and St. Joseph, Missouri.

The first group of overland emigrants to Utah were Mormons, led by Brigham Young, looking for an isolated place to set up a permanent settlement where they might be free from religious intolerance. Gold was discovered in California in 1849. Overland travel by covered wagon was

(continued)

TABLE Df27–33   Overland emigration to Oregon, California, and Utah – emigrants, travel time, and Indian–emigrant homicides: 1840–1860   *Continued*

abandoned shortly after the completion of the transcontinental railroad in 1869.

Series Df27–29. Unruh constructed his estimates of the number of travelers from contemporary statistics published in Oregon, California, Utah, Missouri, and Iowa newspapers. These newspapers reported the observations of the overland travelers themselves and the tabulations in the emigrant registers kept at Forts Kearny and Laramie during the peak gold rush years.

Series Df30–31. Unruh based his estimates of the average travel time on the overland trail on 258 Oregon Trail and California Trail diarists who indicated with reasonable precision the time at which they crossed the Missouri River and the time when they arrived at one of the common destination points on the West Coast. The sample of 258 includes the records of diarists whom Unruh found to have "sojourned for uncommonly long periods in Salt Lake City or at similar trail locations." Unruh had to exclude many gold rush diarists because "they eagerly plunged into mining activities shortly after crossing the Sierra summit" (p. 515). He attributes the reduction in travel times to phys-

ical improvements made to the trails and to the accumulation of knowledge regarding the routes.

Series Df30–31. Unruh constructed the estimates of the murders of emigrants and Indians on the overland trails from a large number of contemporary sources. Unruh terms the estimates "very tentative." He thought they understated the true number of murders, as he counted only those murders listed in what he terms "reasonably definite reports of death" (p. 457). Unruh believed that his estimates of murdered Indians were understated relative to his estimate of murdered whites because his sources were whites. They were often uncertain whether they had killed or wounded fleeing Indians and often did not provide a "definite report" of death (p. 458). Unruh excluded those killed in the famous Whitman massacre in Oregon Territory in 1847 because it took place after the emigrants concluded their trip. He also excluded the 120 emigrants killed in the Mountain Meadows massacre. He argued that "Indians, though very much involved, were not primarily responsible for the tragedy" (p. 457).

TABLE Df34–37   Indexes of passenger and freight traffic: 1889–1966

Contributed by Louis P. Cain

	All traffic		Passenger traffic	Freight traffic			All traffic		Passenger traffic	Freight traffic
	1939 = 100	1958 = 100					1939 = 100	1958 = 100		
	Df34	Df35	Df36	Df37			Df34	Df35	Df36	Df37
Year	Index 1939 = 100	Index 1958 = 100	Index 1939 = 100	Index 1939 = 100	Year		Index 1939 = 100	Index 1958 = 100	Index 1939 = 100	Index 1939 = 100
1889	19	—	26	17	1945		213	—	—	—
1920	103	—	127	96	1946		192	—	248	176
1921	81	—	115	72	1947		203	—	—	—
1922	88	—	116	81	1948		205	92.1	—	—
1923	102	—	122	96	1949		182	86.5	—	—
1924	98	—	121	91						
1925	102	—	120	97	1950		206	89.6	—	—
1926	108	—	121	104	1951		226	100.1	—	—
1927	106	—	119	102	1952		219	98.0	—	—
1928	106	—	117	103	1953		220	98.4	—	—
1929	110	—	118	108	1954		—	93.9	—	—
1930	97	—	108	95	1955		—	103.2	—	—
1931	82	—	94	79	1956		—	108.5	—	—
1932	66	—	79	62	1957		—	103.4	—	—
1933	70	—	76	68	1958		—	100.0	—	—
1934	76	—	84	74	1959		—	106.4	—	—
1935	79	—	87	77	1960		—	108.1	—	—
1936	93	—	99	92	1961		—	107.7	—	—
1937	101	—	103	101	1962		—	114.0	—	—
1938	89	—	97	87	1963		—	119.9	—	—
1939	100	—	100	100	1964		—	128.0	—	—
1940	110	—	108	114	1965		—	139.4	—	—
1941	137	—	—	—	1966		—	152.7	—	—
1942	183	—	—	—						
1943	216	—	—	—						
1944	222	—	—	—						

Sources
Series Df34 and Df36–37, 1889–1946, Harold Barger, *The Transportation Industries, 1889 to 1946* (National Bureau of Economic Research, 1951); series Df34–35, 1947–1966, estimates by John W. Kendrick, George Washington University.

Documentation
Barger's indexes begin in 1889, the year of what he called the first "satisfactory" Census of Water Transportation and the year in which the Interstate Commerce Commission began to collect railroad traffic statistics. His annual data do not begin until 1920. The industries he considers include railroads, street railways and buslines, trucking service, petroleum and gasoline pipelines, and water and air transportation. Rather than use unweighted

passenger miles and freight miles, Barger weighted passenger-miles (or passengers carried, where passenger-miles were not available) by revenue per passenger-mile (or per passenger) and ton-miles by revenue per ton-mile. For more information, see the source.

Series Df34–35. In combining passenger and freight traffic, passenger-miles were weighted by revenue per passenger-mile and ton-miles by revenue per ton-mile.

Series Df36. Includes airlines, intercity buslines, waterways, and steam railroads.

Series Df37. Includes motor trucking, pipelines, waterways, and steam railroads.

TABLE Df38–47   Domestic intercity passenger traffic – volume and percentage, by type of transportation: 1939–1996

Contributed by Louis P. Cain

	Volume						Percentage by type of transport			
	Total	Private automobile	Airways	Buses	Railroads	Inland waterways	Private automobile	Airways	Buses	Railroads
	Df38	Df39	Df40 [1]	Df41	Df42 [2]	Df43	Df44	Df45 [1]	Df46	Df47 [2]
Year	Billion passenger-miles	Billion passenger-miles	Billion passenger-miles	Billion passenger-miles	Billion passenger-miles	Billion passenger-miles	Percent	Percent	Percent	Percent
1939	309.5	275.4	0.9	9.5	23.7	—	88.98	0.29	3.07	7.66
1940	329.0	292.7	1.3	10.2	24.8	—	88.97	0.40	3.10	7.54
1941	369.9	324.0	1.8	13.5	30.6	—	87.59	0.49	3.65	8.27
1942	322.3	244.1	1.8	21.3	55.1	—	75.74	0.56	6.61	17.10
1943	293.8	176.0	2.0	25.9	89.9	—	59.90	0.68	8.82	30.60
1944	309.3	181.4	2.9	27.3	97.7	—	58.65	0.94	8.83	31.59
1945	345.5	220.3	4.3	27.4	93.5	—	63.76	1.24	7.93	27.06
1946	424.7	324.0	7.5	26.9	66.3	—	76.29	1.77	6.33	15.61
1947	427.1	347.8	7.7	24.8	46.8	—	81.43	1.80	5.81	10.96
1948	439.0	365.0	7.5	24.6	41.9	—	83.14	1.71	5.60	9.54
1949	478.0	409.4	8.6	24.0	36.0	—	85.65	1.80	5.02	7.53
1950	503.6	438.3	10.1	22.7	32.5	1.2	87.03	2.01	4.51	6.45
1951	569.9	498.1	12.9	23.6	35.3	1.3	87.40	2.26	4.14	6.19
1952	612.9	539.2	14.3	24.7	34.7	1.4	87.98	2.33	4.03	5.66
1953	649.9	575.8	17.4	24.4	32.3	1.5	88.60	2.68	3.75	4.97
1954	668.2	597.1	19.6	22.0	29.5	1.7	89.36	2.93	3.29	4.41
1955	710.8	637.4	22.8	21.9	28.7	1.7	89.67	3.21	3.08	4.04
1956	745.5	669.7	25.5	21.7	28.6	1.9	89.83	3.42	2.91	3.84
1957	746.4	670.5	28.1	21.5	26.3	1.9	89.83	3.76	2.88	3.52
1958	757.8	684.9	28.5	20.8	23.6	2.1	90.38	3.76	2.74	3.11
1959	762.8	687.4	32.6	20.4	22.4	2.0	90.12	4.27	2.67	2.94
1960	781.0	706.1	34.0	19.3	21.6	2.7	90.41	4.35	2.47	2.77
1961	789.0	713.6	34.6	20.3	20.5	2.3	90.44	4.39	2.57	2.60
1962	815.4	735.9	37.5	21.8	20.2	2.7	90.25	4.60	2.67	2.48
1963	849.8	765.9	42.8	22.5	18.6	2.8	90.13	5.04	2.65	2.19
1964	892.7	801.8	49.2	23.3	18.4	2.8	89.82	5.51	2.61	2.06
1965	917.2	817.7	58.1	23.8	17.6	3.1	89.15	6.33	2.59	1.92
1966	967.7	856.4	69.4	24.6	17.3	3.4	88.50	7.17	2.54	1.79
1967	1,017.2	889.8	87.2	24.9	15.3	3.4	87.48	8.57	2.45	1.50
1968	1,075.4	936.4	101.2	24.5	13.3	3.4	87.07	9.41	2.28	1.24
1969	1,134.1	977.0	119.9	24.9	12.3	3.8	86.15	10.57	2.20	1.08
1970	1,180.8	1,026.0	118.6	25.3	10.9	4.0	86.89	10.04	2.14	0.92
1971	1,225.3	1,071.0	119.9	25.5	8.9	4.1	87.41	9.79	2.08	0.73
1972	1,296.3	1,129.0	133.0	25.6	8.7	—	87.09	10.26	1.97	0.67
1973	1,341.6	1,162.8	143.1	26.4	9.3	—	86.67	10.67	1.97	0.69
1974	1,306.7	1,121.9	146.6	27.7	10.5	—	85.86	11.22	2.12	0.80
1975	1,354.5	1,170.7	148.3	25.4	10.1	—	86.43	10.95	1.88	0.75
1976	1,343.9	1,143.9	164.4	25.1	10.5	—	85.12	12.23	1.87	0.78
1977	1,412.9	1,199.5	177.0	26.0	10.4	—	84.90	12.53	1.84	0.74
1978	1,503.2	1,263.9	203.2	25.6	10.5	—	84.08	13.52	1.70	0.70
1979	1,511.8	1,244.3	228.2	27.7	11.6	—	82.31	15.09	1.83	0.77
1980	1,467.8	1,210.3	219.1	27.4	11.0	—	82.46	14.93	1.87	0.75
1981	1,468.7	1,215.0	216.0	27.1	10.6	—	82.73	14.71	1.85	0.72
1982	1,489.8	1,226.0	226.7	26.9	10.2	—	82.29	15.22	1.81	0.68
1983	1,524.4	1,243.6	244.9	25.6	10.3	—	81.58	16.07	1.68	0.68
1984	1,576.5	1,277.4	263.7	24.6	10.8	—	81.03	16.73	1.56	0.69
1985	1,635.5	1,310.3	290.1	23.8	11.3	—	80.12	17.74	1.46	0.69
1986	1,723.5	1,367.8	320.3	23.7	11.7	—	79.36	18.58	1.38	0.68
1987	1,806.8	1,430.3	341.3	23.0	12.2	—	79.16	18.89	1.27	0.68
1988	1,877.3	1,494.7	346.9	23.1	12.6	—	79.62	18.48	1.23	0.67
1989	1,936.2	1,550.8	348.3	24.0	13.1	—	80.10	17.99	1.24	0.68
1990	2,033.9	1,638.8	358.9	23.0	13.2	—	80.57	17.65	1.13	0.65
1991	2,068.5	1,681.5	350.3	23.1	13.6	—	81.29	16.93	1.12	0.66
1992	2,142.8	1,741.7	365.0	22.6	13.5	—	81.28	17.03	1.05	0.63
1993	2,196.0	1,786.0	372.3	24.7	13.0	—	81.33	16.95	1.12	0.59
1994	2,282.8	1,842.0	398.8	28.1	13.9	—	80.69	17.47	1.23	0.61
1995	2,336.8	1,881.1	414.4	27.7	13.6	—	80.50	17.73	1.19	0.58
1996	2,411.2	1,924.3	445.1	28.3	13.5	—	79.81	18.46	1.17	0.56

Notes appear on next page

(continued)

TABLE Df38–47   Domestic intercity passenger traffic – volume and percentage, by type of transportation: 1939–1996   *Continued*

[1] See text for discussion of computations used for data starting in 1975.

[2] Series composition and source changed in 1981. See text.

Sources

Except as noted, Eno Foundation for Transportation, Inc., *Transportation in America, Historical Compendium, 1939–1995* (Eno Transportation Foundation, 1997). Series Df43, 1950 to 1971, U.S. Interstate Commerce Commission (ICC), *Annual Report* and *Transport Economics*, various issues.

Documentation

A passenger-mile is one passenger carried one mile. Data pertain to public and private transport, both revenue and nonrevenue.

Series Df38, total traffic. Equals the sum of the volume figures for private automobiles, airways, buses, and railroads. Series that report percentages are based on that total.

Series Df39 and Df44. The Eno Foundation calculated automobile figures from 1973 onward by adding together interstate vehicle-mile auto and small-truck figures in the Federal Highway Administration (FHWA), *Highway Statistics*, and then multiplying the total by average occupancy, as determined by a separate FHWA study. The last year an auto passenger-mile figure was reported in *Transport Economics* was 1973.

Series Df40 and Df45. The air figures include both private pleasure and business flying and domestic commercial revenue service. Private flying figures

for 1975 onward are calculated by increasing the ICC's 1974 figure for air passenger-miles by the percentage changes in annual hours flown by general aviation aircraft, which include small air commuter and taxi operations, as published in Federal Aviation Administration, *Statistical Handbook of Aviation*. Domestic commercial figures are from the Department of Transportation's *Air Carrier Traffic Statistics*.

Series Df41 and Df46. The bus figures are derived from reports published by the American Bus Association, the ICC, and the FWHA. They exclude school buses.

Series Df42 and Df47. The railway figures prior to 1981 are taken from the Association of American Railroads (AAR), *Railroad Facts*, various issues and the ICC sources, and they include electric railroads. From 1981 onward, they represent intercity rail figures from Amtrak and Class I railroad data published by the AAR.

Series Df43. The inland waterway figures are derived from the ICC sources and include the Great Lakes. Throughout the period for which data are available, inland waterways were never more than 0.5 percent of the total. Because passenger information on inland waterways is no longer reported in a fashion that permits calculation of passenger-miles, only the volume information is reported here, and not for the same period as the other series.

TABLE Df48–58   Domestic intercity freight traffic – volume and percentage, by type of transportation: 1939–1996[1]

Contributed by Louis P. Cain

	Volume						Percentage by mode of transport				
	Total	Railroads	Motor vehicles	Inland waterways	Oil pipelines	Airways	Railroads	Motor vehicles	Inland waterways	Oil pipelines	Airways
	Df48	Df49	Df50	Df51 [2]	Df52	Df53	Df54	Df55	Df56 [2]	Df57	Df58
Year	Million ton-miles	Million ton-miles	Million ton-miles	Million ton-miles	Million ton-miles	Million ton-miles	Percent	Percent	Percent	Percent	Percent
1939	544	339	53	96	56	0.01	62.3	9.7	17.6	10.3	(Z)
1940	618	379	62	118	59	0.02	61.3	10.0	19.1	9.5	(Z)
1941	771	482	81	140	68	0.02	62.5	10.5	18.2	8.8	(Z)
1942	929	645	60	149	75	0.04	69.4	6.5	16.0	8.1	(Z)
1943	1,032	735	57	142	98	0.05	71.2	5.5	13.8	9.5	(Z)
1944	1,088	747	58	150	133	0.07	68.7	5.3	13.8	12.2	(Z)
1945	1,028	691	67	143	127	0.09	67.2	6.5	13.9	12.4	(Z)
1946	904	602	82	124	96	0.08	66.6	9.1	13.7	10.6	(Z)
1947	1,019	665	102	147	105	0.11	65.3	10.0	14.4	10.3	(Z)
1948	1,044	647	115	162 [3]	120	0.15	62.0	11.0	15.5 [3]	11.5	(Z)
1949	914	535	125	139	115	0.20	58.5	13.7	15.2	12.6	(Z)
1950	1,062	597	173	163	129	0.30	56.2	16.3	15.3	12.1	(Z)
1951	1,177	655	188	182 [3]	152	0.34	55.6	16.0	15.5 [3]	12.9	(Z)
1952	1,144	623	195	168	158	0.34	54.4	17.0	14.7	13.8	(Z)
1953	1,203	614	217	202 [3]	170	0.37	51.0	18.0	16.8 [3]	14.1	(Z)
1954	1,123	557	213	174	179	0.38	49.6	19.0	15.5	15.9	(Z)
1955	1,274	631	223	217	203	0.49	49.5	17.5	17.0	15.9	(Z)
1956	1,356	656	249	220	230	0.58	48.4	18.4	16.2	17.0	(Z)
1957	1,336	626	254	232	223	0.68	46.9	19.0	17.4	16.7	0.1
1958	1,216	559	256	189	211	0.70	46.0	21.1	15.5	17.4	0.1
1959	1,286	582	279	197	227	0.80	45.3	21.7	15.3	17.7	0.1
1960	1,314	579	285	220	229	0.89	44.1	21.7	16.7	17.4	0.1
1961	1,310	570	296	210	233	1.01	43.5	22.6	16.0	17.8	0.1
1962	1,371	600	309	223	238	1.30	43.8	22.5	16.3	17.4	0.1
1963	1,453	629	336	234	253	1.30	43.3	23.1	16.1	17.4	0.1
1964	1,543	666	356	250	269	1.50	43.2	23.1	16.2	17.4	0.1
1965	1,638	709	359	262	306	1.91	43.3	21.9	16.0	18.7	0.1
1966	1,748	751	381	281	333	2.25	43.0	21.8	16.1	19.0	0.1
1967	1,765	731	389	281	361	2.59	41.4	22.0	15.9	20.5	0.1
1968	1,838	757	396	291	391	2.90	41.2	21.5	15.8	21.3	0.2
1969	1,895	774	404	303	411	3.20	40.8	21.3	16.0	21.7	0.2

Notes appear at end of table

TABLE Df48–58   Domestic intercity freight traffic – volume and percentage, by type of transportation: 1939–1996
Continued

	Volume						Percentage by mode of transport				
	Total	Railroads	Motor vehicles	Inland waterways	Oil pipelines	Airways	Railroads	Motor vehicles	Inland waterways	Oil pipelines	Airways
	Df48	Df49	Df50	Df51 [2]	Df52	Df53	Df54	Df55	Df56 [2]	Df57	Df58
Year	Million ton-miles	Million ton-miles	Million ton-miles	Million ton-miles	Million ton-miles	Million ton-miles	Percent	Percent	Percent	Percent	Percent
1970	1,936	771	412	319	431	3.30	39.8	21.3	16.5	22.3	0.2
1971	1,954	746	445	315	444	3.50	38.2	22.8	16.1	22.7	0.2
1972	2,072	784	470	338	476	3.70	37.8	22.7	16.3	23.0	0.2
1973	2,232	858	505	358	507	3.95	38.4	22.6	16.0	22.7	0.2
1974	2,212	852	495	355	506	3.91	38.5	22.4	16.0	22.9	0.2
1975	2,066	759	454	342	507	3.73	36.7	22.0	16.6	24.5	0.2
1976	2,202	800	510	373	515	3.90	36.3	23.2	16.9	23.4	0.2
1977	2,307	834	555	368	546	4.18	36.1	24.1	16.0	23.7	0.2
1978	2,467	868	599	409	586	4.75	35.2	24.3	16.6	23.8	0.2
1979	2,573	927	608	425	608	4.64	36.0	23.6	16.5	23.6	0.2
1980	2,487	932	555	407	588	4.84	37.5	22.3	16.4	23.6	0.2
1981	2,430	924	527	410	564	5.09	38.0	21.7	16.9	23.2	0.2
1982	2,252	810	520	351	566	5.14	36.0	23.1	15.6	25.1	0.2
1983	2,337	841	575	359	556	5.87	36.0	24.6	15.4	23.8	0.3
1984	2,515	935	606	399	568	6.50	37.2	24.1	15.9	22.6	0.3
1985	2,458	895	610	382	564	6.71	36.4	24.8	15.5	22.9	0.3
1986	2,499	889	632	393	578	7.34	35.6	25.3	15.7	23.1	0.3
1987	2,642	972	663	411	587	8.67	36.8	25.1	15.6	22.2	0.3
1988	2,776	1,028	700	438	601	9.33	37.0	25.2	15.8	21.6	0.3
1989	2,828	1,070	716	448	584	10.21	37.8	25.3	15.8	20.6	0.4
1990	2,895	1,091	735	475	584	10.42	37.7	25.4	16.4	20.2	0.4
1991	2,906	1,100	758	459	579	9.96	37.9	26.1	15.8	19.9	0.3
1992	3,023	1,138	815	470	589	10.99	37.6	27.0	15.5	19.5	0.4
1993	3,105	1,183	861	456	593	11.54	38.1	27.7	14.7	19.1	0.4
1994	3,261	1,275	908	475	591	12.03	39.1	27.8	14.6	18.1	0.4
1995	3,407	1,375	921	497	601	12.72	40.4	27.0	14.6	17.6	0.4
1996	3,563	1,426	986	507	631	13.36	40.0	27.7	14.2	17.7	0.4

(Z) Less than 0.05 percent.

[1] See text for discussion of various series changes and computation or estimation methods.

[2] Includes Alaska for all years and Hawai'i beginning 1959.

[3] Part of this increase resulted from coverage of waterways previously existing but not covered.

Sources

1939–1959, U.S. Interstate Commerce Commission (ICC), *Inter-city Ton-Miles, 1939–1959*, Statement number 6103; 1960–1970, ICC, *Annual Report* and *Transport Economics*, various issues; 1971–1996, Rosalyn A. Wilson, *Transportation in America, Historical Compendium, 1939–1995* (Eno Transportation Foundation, 1997).

Documentation

Motor vehicles and airways, prior to 1959, and other types of transportation, prior to 1960, exclude Alaska and Hawai'i, except as noted. A ton-mile is a ton of freight (2,000 pounds) carried one mile. These definitions apply to all means of transport in this table. As far as possible, local switching, local delivery, lighterage, and rural-to-rural movements have been eliminated to confine operations to intercity only. Data include public and private traffic, both revenue and nonrevenue.

Information sufficient in quantity and accuracy is not available to cover all modes of transport on a comparable basis for years before 1939. Estimates of intercity ton-miles for a period sometime before 1939 through part of World War II are contained in the Bureau of Transport Economics and Statistics release, *Postwar Traffic Levels*, Statement number 4440, issued in 1944. These estimates, however, are not on bases comparable with those in the 1939–1959 series.

Series Df49 and Df54. Rail figures include electric railways, express, and mail. Through 1978, they include all classes of railroads and, prior to 1977, are taken from the ICC sources. The ICC furnished the number for 1978 directly to the Eno Foundation. Figures for 1979 onward include actual Class I railroad data taken from the Association of American Railroads' *Railroad Facts*, to which a percentage is then applied to represent the traffic of other classes of railroads.

Series Df50 and Df55. Motor vehicle figures through 1977 are from the ICC sources. ICC truck figures for 1978 were furnished by the American Trucking Association (ATA) to the Eno Foundation. From 1979 onward, Eno has estimated these based on ATA and ICC data. Non-ICC truck figures since 1978 are estimates based on both the actual changes in ICC truck ton-miles from ATA and changes in vehicle miles of combination and large single-unit trucks on the nation's nonurban highways as reported in the Federal Highway Association, *Highway Statistics*, Table VM-1. The vehicle-miles figure is multiplied by an estimated average load figure based on ICC truck data under the assumption that non-ICC trucks have the same characteristics as contract/specialized ICC trucks.

Series Df51 and Df56. Inland waterway figures, comprising the Great Lakes and rivers. For the years through 1990 the data are taken from U.S. Army Corps of Engineers, *Waterborne Commerce of the United States*, Part 5, National Summaries. The figures represent domestic traffic movements only; thus, these figures exclude a very small number of intraport movements. Eno has estimated figures since 1990 owing to the unavailability of current data. For 1948, 1951, and 1953, part of the increase resulted from the inclusion of waterways previously existing but not reporting.

Series Df52 and Df57. Oil pipeline figures through 1977 are taken from the ICC sources. Figures for 1978–1989 are taken from Association of Oil Pipe Lines, *Shifts in Petroleum Transportation*, various issues. After 1990, the figures are Eno Foundation estimates based on Department of Energy and Federal Energy Regulatory Commission reports.

Series Df53 and Df58. The air figures are for domestic revenue service exclusively and include both scheduled and nonscheduled carriers and are taken from the December issues of Department of Transportation, *Air Carrier Traffic Statistics*, "Traffic Data of Certified Route Air Carriers." Prior to 1980, figures were taken from the "All Services" section, plus separate freight ton-mile data for charter air carriers. Since 1980, figures are taken from the "All Services" section for freight, express, and mail revenue ton-miles. Beginning in 1978, data on traffic of Section 4128 air cargo carriers (mostly small freight shipments) have been added in special Department of Transportation reports.

TABLE Df59-71   Operating revenues, by type of transportation: 1936-1992[1]

Contributed by Louis P. Cain

	Electric railways	Railway express	Railroads	Waterlines	Oil pipelines	Domestic scheduled air carriers	Motor carriers of property	Motor carriers of passengers	Index				
									Railroads	Oil pipelines	Domestic scheduled air carriers	Motor carriers of property	Motor carriers of passengers
	Df59 [2]	Df60	Df61	Df62	Df63	Df64 [3]	Df65	Df66	Df67	Df68	Df69 [3]	Df70	Df71
Year	Million dollars	Million dollars	Million dollars	Million dollars	Million dollars	Million dollars	Million dollars	Million dollars	Index 1982-1984 = 100	Index 1982-1984 = 100	Index 1982-1984 = 100	Index 1982-1984 = 100	Index 1982-1984 = 100
1936	52	103	4,197	104	219	—	—	—	14.2	2.9	—	—	—
1937	51	110	4,321	108	249	—	—	—	14.6	3.3	—	—	—
1938	49	110	3,687	104	228	43	700	151	12.5	3.0	0.1	1.5	6.9
1939	50	112	4,140	111	212	56	796	168	14.0	2.8	0.2	1.7	7.6
1940	53	120	4,559	212	226	77	922	182	15.4	3.0	0.2	1.9	8.3
1941	59	135	5,541	258	252	97	1,095	237	18.7	3.4	0.3	2.3	10.8
1942	68	155	7,691	123	245	108	1,189	398	26.0	3.3	0.3	2.5	18.1
1943	99	208	9,288	196	277	123	1,347	544	31.4	3.7	0.4	2.8	24.7
1944	100	255	9,676	188	310	161	1,756	624	32.7	4.1	0.5	3.7	28.4
1945	87	284	9,136	173	304	215	1,840	652	30.9	4.1	0.7	3.9	29.7
1946	79	326	7,852	148	294	316	1,699	554	26.6	3.9	1.0	3.6	25.2
1947	80	313	8,973	225	325	365	2,214	534	30.4	4.3	1.1	4.7	24.3
1948	77	295	10,002	237	377	434	2,698	565	33.8	5.0	1.4	5.7	25.7
1949	70	251	8,885	275	376	486	2,911	554	30.1	5.0	1.5	6.1	25.2
1950	79	223	9,820	330	442	558	3,737	539	33.2	5.9	1.7	7.9	24.5
1951	81	223	10,773	336	524	702	4,169	578	36.5	7.0	2.2	8.8	26.3
1952	82	248	10,966	340	562	818	4,417	602	37.1	7.5	2.6	9.3	27.4
1953	78	242	11,063	391	591	937	4,926	614	37.4	7.9	2.9	10.4	27.9
1954	56	235	9,708	399	617	1,043	4,737	561	32.8	8.2	3.3	10.0	25.5
1955	60	241	10,495	452	678	1,215	5,535	560	35.5	9.1	3.8	11.6	25.5
1956	49	257	10,963	476	737	1,342	5,829	565	37.1	9.8	4.2	12.3	25.7
1957	45	248	10,920	450	730	1,515	6,166	599	36.9	9.8	4.7	13.0	27.3
1958	30	258	9,924	415	721	1,624	6,131	599	33.6	9.6	5.1	12.9	27.3
1959	25	247	10,207	430	765	1,955	7,145	631	34.5	10.2	6.1	15.0	28.7
1960	23	248	9,955	427	770	2,129	7,214	667	33.7	10.3	6.7	15.2	30.3
1961	22	257	9,540	389	787	2,245	7,463	690	32.3	10.5	7.0	15.7	31.4
1962	22	271	9,792	394	811	2,498	8,131	729	33.1	10.8	7.8	17.1	33.2
1963	14	275	9,921	395	840	2,723	8,548	759	33.6	11.2	8.5	18.0	34.5
1964	13	298	10,252	405	865	3,095	9,155	802	34.7	11.6	9.7	19.2	36.5
1965	13	316	10,738	426	904	3,609	10,068	885	36.3	12.1	11.3	21.2	40.3
1966	14	324	11,163	460	941	4,070	10,862	901	37.8	12.6	12.7	22.8	41.0
1967	12	323	10,875	426	995	4,887	11,308	945	36.8	13.3	15.3	23.8	43.0
1968	12	299	11,357	435	1,023	5,607	12,400	991	38.4	13.7	17.5	26.1	45.1
1969	13	270	11,951	450	1,103	6,857	13,958	1,007	40.4	14.7	21.5	29.3	45.8
1970	11	313	12,511	502	1,188	7,131	14,585	882	42.3	15.9	22.3	30.7	40.1
1971	11	263	13,332	525	1,249	8,085	16,700	1,091	45.1	16.7	25.3	35.1	49.6
1972	12	240	14,112	545	1,338	8,716	18,700	1,095	47.8	17.9	27.3	39.3	49.8
1973	12	264	15,634	618	1,446	9,782	20,800	1,172	52.9	19.3	30.6	43.7	53.3
1974	14	277	17,903	879	1,587	11,663	22,700	1,359	60.6	21.2	36.5	47.7	61.8
1975	14	133	17,357	946	1,874	12,315	22,000	1,217	58.7	25.0	38.5	46.3	55.4
1976	13	0	19,642	1,035	2,137	13,998	26,000	1,410	66.5	28.6	43.8	54.7	64.1
1977	14	0	21,214	924	2,792	15,936	31,000	1,410	71.8	37.3	49.9	65.2	64.1
1978	14	0	22,570	944	4,907	18,321	36,500	1,480	76.4	65.6	57.3	76.7	67.3
1979	—	0	25,735	854	5,585	22,217	41,200	1,655	87.1	74.6	69.5	86.6	75.3
1980	—	0	28,747	991	6,340	26,115	43,000	1,943	97.3	84.7	81.7	90.4	88.4
1981	—	0	31,465	1,029	6,678	28,750	47,100	2,068	106.5	89.2	90.0	99.0	94.1
1982	—	0	28,138	1,031	7,131	28,732	44,100	2,103	95.2	95.3	89.9	92.7	95.7
1983	—	0	28,536	1,133	7,472	31,207	46,500	2,211	96.6	99.8	97.7	97.8	100.6
1984	—	0	31,987	1,077	7,848	35,927	52,100	2,280	108.2	104.9	112.4	109.5	103.7
1985	—	0	30,792	1,069	7,484	38,587	54,200	2,234	104.2	100.0	120.8	113.9	101.6
1986	—	0	29,051	1,060	7,306	39,635	58,100	2,116	98.3	97.6	124.0	122.1	96.3
1987	—	0	29,645	1,092	7,109	44,196	61,000	2,011	100.3	95.0	138.3	128.2	91.5
1988	—	0	31,173	1,120	6,908	48,820	66,500	2,607	105.5	92.3	152.8	139.8	118.6
1989	—	0	31,267	1,080	6,579	51,637	70,500	2,166	105.8	87.9	161.6	148.2	98.5
1990	—	0	31,775	1,096	7,045	56,206	75,500	1,876	107.5	94.1	175.9	158.7	85.4
1991	—	0	31,253	1,092	6,805	54,682	76,700	2,006	105.7	90.9	171.1	161.2	91.3
1992	—	0	32,017	1,100	7,158	56,444	82,300	1,930	108.3	95.6	176.6	173.0	87.8

TABLE Df59–71   Operating revenues, by type of transportation: 1936–1992   *Continued*

[1] See text for discussion of various series changes and computation or estimation methods.

[2] The electric railway decrease is overstated through the years because of noncomparability of reporting.

[3] Includes Hawai'i for all years and Alaska beginning with 1955.

Sources

Rosalyn A. Wilson, *Transportation in America, Historical Compendium, 1939–1995* (Eno Transportation Foundation, 1997). See also U.S. Interstate Commerce Commission (ICC), *Annual Report* and *Transport Economics*.

Documentation

The reported figures are the sum of revenues from freight and passenger services for most carriers.

Series Df59. From ICC, *Transport Statistics in the United States*, Part 1.

Series Df60. The railway express figures are taken from Railway Express Agency reports. Through 1969, the payments to others for express privileges are excluded.

Series Df61 and Df67. The railroad freight figures beginning in 1980 are Class I railroad revenues plus a percentage representing the estimated share of total rail revenue for Class II and III railroads (4 percent in 1980, 7.5 percent in 1985, and then progressively higher to 8.7 percent in 1992). The figures for Class I carriers are taken from Association of American Railroads (AAR), *Railroad Facts* (various issues). Earlier years are taken from ICC, *Transport Statistics in the United States*, Part I. These figures include freight, mail, express, switching, and demurrage for all classes of carriers. The railroad passenger figures for 1985 onward are based on data in *Railroad Facts* and data Amtrak furnished directly to the Eno Foundation, and they include federal subsidies. The figures for 1975 and 1980 are taken from AAR, *Statistics of Railroads of Class I* (various issues), and include Class I passenger revenues, plus 1 percent for Class II railroads plus total operating revenue for Amtrak. The figures for earlier years are taken from the ICC, *Transport Statistics of the United States*. The figures include Pullman (prior to 1969), line-haul, switching, and terminal companies.

Series Df62. The waterlines freight data from 1980 onward are estimated based on ton-mile data in U.S. Army Corps of Engineers, *Waterborne Commerce of the United States*, and average revenue-per-ton data calculated using other data collected by the Eno Foundation. Water carrier passenger figures from 1980 onward are estimated assuming a 10 percent annual increase from the 1979 figure, the last figure published by the ICC. This includes only revenues from domestic traffic of carriers that were under the jurisdiction of the ICC. The Eno Foundation believes these numbers should be larger to reflect outlays for domestic cruises and ocean travel to and from Hawai'i and Alaska, but such data are not readily available. Prior to 1980, the figures appear in ICC, *Annual Report* and *Transport Statistics of the United States*.

Series Df63 and Df68. The oil pipeline figures from 1980 onward are based on Federal Energy Regulatory Commission (FERC) data compiled by the Oil Pipeline Research Institute. Data for 1975 are taken from an FERC table, "Transportation Revenue & Traffic of Large Pipe Line Companies." Prior to 1975, the data come from the ICC, *Annual Report* and *Transport Statistics of the United States*.

Series Df64 and Df69. The air freight and passenger figures are taken from the December issues of Department of Transportation (USDOT), *Air Carrier Financial Statistics*, plus data for Section 418 carriers from separate USDOT reports. This includes revenues for scheduled passenger cargo operations. Early data were taken from U.S. Federal Aviation Administration, *Statistical Handbook of Aviation*.

Series Df65 and Df70. Figures for motor carriers of property (trucks) for 1980 onward are taken from the American Trucking Association data, with an estimate of Class III carriers beginning in 1989. Prior to 1980, the data come from ICC, *Transport Statistics of the United States*.

Series Df66 and Df71. Figures for motor carriers of passengers (buses) from 1985 onward are estimated based on ICC data for Class I carriers. Data for 1980 were derived from the annual statistical reports of the American Bus Association. Earlier figures were taken from ICC, *Transport Statistics of the United States*.

TABLE Df72–80   Employees of transportation firms, by industry division: 1947–1999

Contributed by Richard Sutch

Year	Total Df72 Thousand	Railroad Df73 Thousand	Local and interurban passenger transit Df74 Thousand	Trucking and warehousing Df75 Thousand	Water Df76 Thousand	Air Df77 Thousand	Pipelines, except natural gas Df78 Thousand	Services firms Df79 Thousand	Other not separately classified Df80 Thousand
1947	—	1,557	—	—	—	—	—	—	—
1948	—	1,517	—	—	—	—	—	—	—
1949	—	1,367	—	—	—	—	—	—	—
1950	—	1,391	—	—	—	—	—	—	—
1951	—	1,449	—	—	—	—	—	—	—
1952	—	1,400	—	—	—	—	—	—	—
1953	—	1,377	—	—	—	—	—	—	—
1954	—	1,215	—	—	—	—	—	—	—
1955	—	1,205	—	—	—	—	—	—	—
1956	—	1,190	—	—	—	—	26	—	—
1957	—	1,121	—	—	—	—	27	—	—
1958	—	957	285	—	—	—	26	—	—
1959	—	925	281	—	—	—	24	—	—
1960	—	885	284	—	—	—	23	—	—
1961	—	817	277	—	—	—	22	—	—
1962	—	796	271	—	—	—	22	—	—
1963	—	772	269	—	—	—	21	—	—
1964	2,487	756	267	—	229	—	20	—	1,215
1965	2,530	735	269	—	228	—	20	—	1,278
1966	2,598	725	271	—	238	—	19	—	1,346
1967	2,655	698	279	—	241	—	19	—	1,418
1968	2,680	668	282	—	239	—	19	—	1,473
1969	2,722	649	281	—	229	—	18	—	1,545
1970	2,694	634	281	—	212	—	18	—	1,550
1971	2,639	606	279	—	194	—	17	—	1,543
1972	2,676	582	276	—	211	—	17	—	1,591
1973	2,746	579	278	—	199	—	17	—	1,674
1974	2,779	590	279	—	203	—	17	—	1,690
1975	2,634	548	270	—	194	—	18	—	1,604
1976	2,678	538	264	—	194	—	18	—	1,664
1977	2,781	545	262	—	195	—	19	—	1,762
1978	2,905	539	258	—	208	—	20	—	1,880
1979	3,019	556	263	—	214	—	20	—	1,966
1980	2,960	532	265	—	211	—	21	—	1,931
1981	2,920	495	265	—	218	—	22	—	1,921
1982	2,787	429	263	—	200	—	21	—	1,873
1983	2,742	376	257	—	189	—	20	—	1,901
1984	2,914	376	270	—	190	—	19	—	2,059
1985	2,997	359	277	—	185	—	19	—	2,158
1986	3,051	332	286	—	174	—	18	—	2,241
1987	3,156	309	294	—	172	—	19	—	2,362
1988	3,301	298	309	1,351	171	850	19	302	0
1989	3,404	293	326	1,379	172	897	19	319	0
1990	3,511	279	338	1,395	177	968	19	336	0
1991	3,495	262	354	1,378	184	962	19	336	0
1992	3,495	254	361	1,385	173	964	19	338	0
1993	3,598	248	379	1,444	168	988	18	352	0
1994	3,761	241	404	1,526	172	1,023	17	378	0
1995	3,904	238	419	1,587	175	1,068	15	401	0
1996	4,019	231	437	1,637	174	1,107	15	418	0
1997	4,123	227	452	1,677	179	1,134	14	441	0
1998	4,273	231	469	1,744	180	1,181	14	454	0
1999	4,409	230	485	1,805	187	1,227	13	463	0

Sources

U.S. Bureau of Labor Statistics (BLS), *Employment, Hours, and Earnings: United States, 1909–94*, Bulletin number 2445, 2 volumes (1994); BLS, *Employment, Hours, and Earnings: United States, 1990–95*, Bulletin number 2465 (1995); BLS, *National Employment, Hours, and Earnings*, Internet site. Also see *Employment and Earnings*, published monthly by the BLS.

Documentation

See the text for Table Ba840–848. See the Introduction to Part D for a discussion of Standard Industrial Classification (SIC) codes.

Series Df72. Includes SIC codes 40–42 and 44–47. SIC code 43 is the U.S. Postal Service; see Table Ea966–985.

Series Df73. SIC code 40. Includes line-haul and short-line railroads and support activities for rail transport such as switching and terminal establishments. For data on Class I line-haul railroads since 1924, see Table Df89.

Series Df74–77. Respectively, SIC codes 41, 42, 44, and 45. For disaggregations, see the relevant series in Tables Df81–88 and Df90–95.

Series Df78. SIC Code 46. Includes both crude and refined petroleum pipelines. Data on employees in natural gas pipelines are included in SIC code 131, "Crude Oil and Natural Gas."

TABLE Df72–80   Employees of transportation firms, by industry division: 1947–1999   *Continued*

Series Df79. SIC code 47. For an extended definition and detailed data, see Table Dh215–218.

Series Df80. For 1964 through 1987, this series is calculated as a residual and represents the sum of SIC codes 42, 45, and 47. BLS Bulletin number

2445 presents data for this time period and these three industries separately, but subsequent revisions of the industry definitions and new benchmarks make these data inconsistent with the data reproduced here.

TABLE Df81–88   Employees of passenger and freight land transportation firms, except railroads: 1947–1999

Contributed by Richard Sutch

	Local and interurban passenger transit					Trucking and warehousing		
		Local and suburban	Taxi service	Bus		Total	Trucking and courier services (except air)	Warehousing and storage firms
	Total			Intercity and rural	Private school			
	Df81	Df82	Df83	Df84	Df85	Df86	Df87	Df88
Year	Thousand	Thousand	Thousand	Thousand	Thousand	Thousand	Thousand	Thousand
1947	—	—	—	54	—	—	—	—
1948	—	—	—	55	—	—	—	—
1949	—	—	—	52	—	—	—	—
1950	—	—	—	47	—	—	—	—
1951	—	—	—	47	—	—	—	—
1952	—	—	—	48	—	—	—	—
1953	—	—	—	49	—	—	—	—
1954	—	—	—	44	—	—	—	—
1955	—	—	—	43	—	—	—	—
1956	—	—	—	43	—	—	—	—
1957	—	—	—	45	—	—	—	—
1958	285	—	121	43	—	—	—	86
1959	281	—	119	41	—	—	—	88
1960	284	—	121	41	—	—	—	85
1961	277	—	114	41	—	—	—	82
1962	271	—	113	41	—	—	—	82
1963	269	—	112	41	—	—	—	81
1964	267	—	110	42	—	—	—	82
1965	269	—	110	42	—	—	—	82
1966	271	—	109	42	—	—	—	84
1967	279	—	111	44	—	—	—	85
1968	282	—	111	43	—	—	—	85
1969	281	—	110	43	—	—	—	85
1970	281	—	106	43	—	—	—	84
1971	279	—	102	44	—	—	—	82
1972	276	75	96	42	53	—	—	81
1973	278	72	96	41	58	—	—	89
1974	279	71	94	42	61	—	—	89
1975	270	69	85	40	65	—	—	84
1976	264	68	77	40	68	—	—	81
1977	262	71	70	37	71	—	—	88
1978	258	72	64	36	73	—	—	91
1979	263	76	60	37	77	—	—	91
1980	265	79	53	38	80	—	—	91
1981	265	82	46	38	82	—	—	88
1982	263	82	42	39	82	—	—	84
1983	257	80	40	36	83	—	—	85
1984	270	87	39	37	87	—	—	91
1985	277	92	38	35	91	—	—	95
1986	286	99	36	33	97	—	—	99
1987	294	109	35	30	98	—	—	107
1988	309	118	35	29	102	1,351	1,236	111
1989	326	127	33	31	108	1,379	1,261	115
1990	338	141	32	26	111	1,395	1,274	117
1991	354	155	32	24	115	1,378	1,254	120
1992	361	162	30	23	118	1,385	1,257	124
1993	379	176	30	22	122	1,444	1,312	128
1994	404	194	31	24	126	1,526	1,384	138
1995	419	203	31	24	131	1,587	1,440	143
1996	437	218	31	24	132	1,637	1,482	150
1997	452	229	31	22	137	1,677	1,514	157
1998	468	236	31	24	141	1,744	1,569	169
1999	485	245	32	24	147	1,805	1,611	185

(continued)

TABLE Series Df81–88   Employees of passenger and freight land transportation firms, except railroads: 1947–1999
Continued

Sources
U.S. Bureau of Labor Statistics (BLS), *Employment, Hours, and Earnings: United States, 1909–94*, Bulletin number 2445, 2 volumes (1994); BLS, *Employment, Hours, and Earnings: United States, 1990–95*, Bulletin number 2465 (1995); BLS, *National Employment, Hours, and Earnings*, Internet site. Also see *Employment and Earnings*, published monthly by the BLS.

Documentation
See the text for Table Ba840–848. See the Introduction to Part D for a discussion of Standard Industrial Classification (SIC) codes.

Series Df81. The series is the sum of series Df82–85, plus a residual sector (not shown) that includes charter bus services (SIC code 414) and support activities for road transportation (SIC code 417).

Series Df82. SIC code 411. Includes commuter rail systems, bus and other motor vehicle transit systems, limousines, airport shuttles, ambulances, hearses, sightseeing buses, cable and cog railways, special needs transportation, and employee transportation. Only private firms are included.

Series Df83. SIC code 412. Self-employed taxicab drivers are not included.

Series Df84. SIC code 413.

Series Df85. SIC code 415.

Series Df86. The sum of series Df87–88, and SIC code 423 (not shown), support activities for motor freight transportation.

Series Df87. SIC code 421. There is data in BLS Bulletin number 2445 for this industry for 1964–1993. However, subsequent revisions of the industry's definition and new benchmarks make these data inconsistent with the series reproduced here.

Series Df88. SIC code 422. Includes general warehousing and storage, self-storage units, farm product storage, and refrigerated warehouses.

TABLE Df89   Employees of line-haul railroad transportation firms: 1924–1999

Contributed by Richard Sutch

Year	Employees Df89 Thousand	Year	Employees Df89 Thousand	Year	Employees Df89 Thousand
1924	1,754	1950	1,221	1975	498
1925	1,746	1951	1,276	1976	494
1926	1,782	1952	1,226	1977	502
1927	1,737	1953	1,207	1978	490
1928	1,656	1954	1,065	1979	503
1929	1,662	1955	1,057	1980	482
1930	1,488	1956	1,043	1981	457
1931	1,259	1957	985	1982	398
1932	1,032	1958	841	1983	348
1933	971	1959	815	1984	345
1934	1,009	1960	781	1985	323
1935	994	1961	718	1986	294
1936	1,066	1962	700	1987	271
1937	1,115	1963	679	1988	259
1938	940	1964	665	1989	252
1939	988	1965	640	1990	241
1940	1,027	1966	632	1991	231
1941	1,140	1967	610	1992	222
1942	1,271	1968	590	1993	218
1943	1,355	1969	578	1994	214
1944	1,414	1970	566	1995	212
1945	1,420	1971	546	1996	206
1946	1,359	1972	526	1997	202
1947	1,352	1973	524	1998	205
1948	1,327	1974	539	1999	204
1949	1,192				

Sources
U.S. Bureau of Labor Statistics (BLS), *Employment, Hours, and Earnings: United States, 1909–94*, Bulletin 2445, 2 volumes (1994); BLS, *Employment, Hours, and Earnings: United States, 1990–95*, Bulletin number 2465 (1995); BLS, *National Employment, Hours, and Earnings*, Internet site. Also see *Employment and Earnings*, published monthly by the BLS.

Documentation
See the text for Table Ba840–848.

Data cover Class I line-haul railroads.

TABLE Df90–95   Employees of passenger and freight water and air transportation firms: 1982–1998

Contributed by Richard Sutch

	Water transportation			Air transportation		
	Total	Inland-water freight	Services firms	Total	Scheduled and air courier	Airports, flying fields, and flight services
	Df90	Df91	Df92	Df93	Df94	Df95
Year	Thousand	Thousand	Thousand	Thousand	Thousand	Thousand
1982	200	—	—	—	—	51
1983	189	—	—	—	—	53
1984	190	—	—	—	—	57
1985	185	—	—	—	—	62
1986	174	—	—	—	—	67
1987	172	—	—	—	—	75
1988	171	14	111	850	744	86
1989	172	15	110	897	779	94
1990	177	15	112	968	841	99
1991	184	15	118	962	835	99
1992	173	14	109	964	836	99
1993	168	14	108	988	855	102
1994	172	13	112	1,023	883	104
1995	175	13	116	1,068	920	108
1996	174	14	115	1,107	952	113
1997	179	14	120	1,134	971	119
1998	180	15	120	1,183	1,008	128

Sources

U.S. Bureau of Labor Statistics (BLS), *Employment, Hours, and Earnings: United States, 1909–94*, Bulletin number 2445, 2 volumes (1994); BLS, *Employment, Hours, and Earnings: United States, 1990–95*, Bulletin number 2465 (1995); BLS, *National Employment, Hours, and Earnings*, Internet site. Also see *Employment and Earnings*, published monthly by the BLS.

Documentation

See the text for Table Ba840–848. See the Introduction to Part D for a discussion of Standard Industrial Classification (SIC) codes.

Series Df90. Equals the sum of series Df91–92 and a residual series (not shown) which includes deep-sea freight transportation (SIC code 441),

coastal and Great Lakes transportation of freight (SIC code 442), and water transportation of passengers (including ferries) (SIC code 448).

Series Df91. SIC code 444.

Series Df92. SIC code 449. Includes marine cargo handling, towing and tugboat services, marinas, and other water transportation services.

Series Df93. Equals the sum of series Df94–95 and a residual series (not shown) that includes charter and sightseeing flights and other nonscheduled air transportation.

Series Df94. SIC code 451. Includes scheduled passenger and freight air transportation and air courier services.

Series Df95. SIC code 458.

TABLE Df96–103   Workers, by mode of transportation to work: 1960–1990[1]

Contributed by Susan B. Carter

		Private car, truck, or van		Public transportation	Walk	Other means		Worked at home
	Total workers	Total	Carpool			Total	Bicycle	
	Df96	Df97	Df98	Df99	Df100	Df101	Df102	Df103
Year	Number	Number	Number	Number	Number	Number	Number	Number
1960	64,655,805	41,368,062	—	7,806,932 [3]	6,416,343	4,401,718 [5]	—	4,662,750
1970	76,852,389	59,722,550	9,025,000 [2]	6,810,458	5,689,819	1,944,418	—	2,685,144
1980	96,617,296	81,258,496	19,065,047	6,175,061	5,413,248	1,590,628	468,348	2,179,863
1990	115,070,274	99,592,932	15,377,634	6,032,092 [4]	4,488,886	1,550,339 [4]	466,856	3,406,025

[1] Workers at least 14 years old (1960–1970), and at least 16 years old thereafter.

[2] Value from different source; category was "Private automobile, passenger."

[3] Workers who used a taxicab are included under series Df101.

[4] Value for series Df99 differs from source: 37,497 workers who took ferryboats are included under series Df101.

[5] Includes 2,781,876 workers who did not report their means of transportation and some undisclosed number of workers who used a taxicab.

Source

U.S. Bureau of the Census Internet site, downloaded on September 11, 1999. The value for series Df98 for 1970 came from U.S. Bureau of the Census.

Statistical Abstract of the United States: 1976, 97th edition (1976), Table 1005, p. 601.

Documentation

Questions regarding the journey to work were asked in the decennial federal censuses beginning in 1960. See the Internet site for the U.S. Bureau of the Census, Population Division, Journey-to-Work Branch.

Series Df99. Includes bus or trolley bus, streetcar or trolley car, subway or elevated train, railroad, and taxicab.

Series Df101. Includes motorcycle, bicycle, ferryboat, and other means.

TABLE Df104–108   Freight revenue per ton-mile, by type of transportation: 1960–1998

Contributed by Louis P. Cain

Year	Air carrier, domestic, scheduled service Df104 Cents per ton-mile	Class I rail Df105 Cents per ton-mile	Truck Df106 Cents per ton-mile	Oil pipeline Df107 Cents per ton-mile	Barge Df108 Cents per ton-mile
1960	22.80	1.40	6.31	0.32	—
1961	22.08	1.37	6.30	0.32	—
1962	21.31	1.35	6.41	0.32	—
1963	21.72	1.31	6.38	0.32	—
1964	20.97	1.28	6.66	0.30	0.36
1965	20.46	1.27	6.46	0.28	0.35
1966	20.21	1.26	6.34	0.27	0.33
1967	19.90	1.27	6.65	0.26	0.29
1968	19.97	1.31	6.93	0.26	0.31
1969	21.03	1.35	7.08	0.27	0.29
1970	21.91	1.43	8.50	0.27	0.30
1971	22.58	1.59	9.30	0.29	0.34
1972	22.75	1.62	9.50	0.29	0.33
1973	23.31	1.62	9.80	0.29	0.38
1974	25.92	1.85	10.40	0.32	0.49
1975	28.22	2.04	11.60	0.37	0.52
1976	31.81	2.19	12.00	0.41	0.51
1977	34.22	2.29	12.70	0.62	0.56
1978	37.10	2.36	13.40	1.01 [2]	0.62
1979	41.02	2.61	15.20	1.12	0.67
1980	46.31	2.87	18.00	1.33	0.77
1981	50.15	3.18	20.00	1.45	0.85
1982	49.69	3.21	20.77	1.45	0.84
1983	49.30	3.12	21.23	1.62	0.82
1984	50.20	3.09	21.54	1.62	0.82
1985	48.77	3.04	22.90	1.57	0.80
1986	105.43 [1]	2.92	21.63	1.50	0.76
1987	109.79	2.73	22.48	1.45	0.73
1988	113.66	2.72	23.17	1.36	0.75
1989	96.84	2.67	23.91	1.33	0.77
1990	64.60	2.66	24.40	1.44	0.76
1991	64.80	2.59	24.80	1.40	0.78
1992	65.70	2.58	23.10	1.49	0.76
1993	71.40	2.52	25.00	1.42	0.76
1994	72.20	2.49	25.00	1.40	0.74
1995	76.50	2.40	25.10	1.51	0.73
1996	81.50	2.35	26.00	1.37	0.73
1997	79.70	2.40	26.10	1.37	0.73
1998	84.10	2.34	—	—	—

[1] Increase attributable to the inclusion of Federal Express and other freight carriers.

[2] Increase attributable to the entrance of the Alaska pipeline.

Sources

1960–1989, U.S. Bureau of Transportation Statistics, *National Transportation Statistics* (1993), Table 2; 1990–1998, U.S. Bureau of Transportation Statistics, *National Transportation Statistics* (1999), Table 2-17.

Documentation

Series Df106. Reports intercity service excluding carriers of household goods. Since 1970, this represents general freight common carriers, all of which are predominantly less-than-truckload carriers.

Series Df108. Reports barge lines operating on the Mississippi River and its tributaries.

TABLE Df109–113   Average passenger fares, by type of transportation: 1960–1997

Contributed by Louis P. Cain

Year	Air carrier, domestic, scheduled service	Class I bus, intercity	Local transit, all modes	Commuter rails	Intercity and Amtrak
	Df109	Df110	Df111 [1]	Df112	Df113 [2]
	Dollars	Dollars	Dollars	Dollars	Dollars
1960	34.12	2.46	0.14	0.64	4.22
1961	34.15	2.48	0.14	0.65	4.21
1962	34.18	2.50	0.15	0.66	4.20
1963	34.22	2.52	0.15	0.67	4.00
1964	34.13	2.55	0.15	0.68	3.86
1965	34.12	2.73	0.16	0.71	3.92
1966	33.41	2.71	0.16	0.72	3.83
1967	33.16	2.79	0.17	0.72	3.48
1968	33.70	2.91	0.19	0.75	3.16
1969	37.52	3.55	0.21	0.78	3.15
1970	40.65	3.81	0.22	0.84	3.19
1971	43.13	4.19	0.23	0.87	9.58
1972	43.87	4.25	0.24	0.93	9.31
1973	45.72	4.73	0.25	0.95	9.85
1974	51.43	5.13	0.27	1.00	12.20
1975	53.64	5.46	0.27	1.04	12.96
1976	57.47	5.76	0.27	1.15	12.88
1977	60.67	6.48	0.28	1.16	12.90
1978	61.07	6.89	0.29	1.20	13.16
1979	63.81	7.71	0.29	1.25	14.93
1980	84.55	10.57	0.30	1.41	17.72
1981	95.42	10.30	0.33	1.70	21.25
1982	92.08	10.90	0.38	1.89	22.38
1983	92.17	10.66	0.39	2.31	23.78
1984	97.10	11.09	0.50	2.92	24.80
1985	92.53	11.02	0.53	2.85	25.78
1986	84.99	12.35	0.58	3.07	26.35
1987	88.95	12.28	0.59	3.18	29.61
1988	96.67	17.15	0.60	3.35	32.70
1989	103.65	18.62	0.61	3.41	37.43
1990	107.86	20.18	0.67	2.90	38.51
1991	106.78	21.86	0.70	3.01	40.32
1992	103.60	21.15	0.72	3.09	40.19
1993	109.80	21.32	0.77	3.09	39.37
1994	103.21	19.77	0.85	3.19	38.16
1995	106.66	20.10	0.87	3.13	39.03
1996	110.37	22.85	0.93	3.25	42.54
1997	114.10	20.57	0.89	3.30	44.31

[1] Through 1983, excludes commuter railroad, automated guideway, urban ferryboat, demand response, and most rural and smaller systems.

[2] Amtrak operations are included beginning in 1971.

Sources

1960–1989, U.S. Bureau of Transportation Statistics, *National Transportation Statistics* (1993), Table 3; 1990–1997, U.S. Bureau of Transportation Statistics, *National Transportation Statistics* (1999), Table 2-15a.

Documentation

The 1993 edition of *National Transportation Statistics* reports annual data. The 1999 edition reports the data prior to 1990 at five-year intervals. There have been several revisions, but for series Df109–111 the data appear to be consistent over time. There have been revisions to series Df109 as follows: 1960, 33.01; 1965, 34.13; 1980, 84.60.

Series Df110. Reports regular route intercity service.

Series Df113. The switch between sources for this series takes place in 1987. The relevant number in the new series for 1985 is 26.15.

TABLE Df114–117   National freight and passenger transportation bills: 1960–1996

Contributed by Louis P. Cain

Year	Freight bill Df114 Billion dollars	Passenger bill Df115 Billion dollars	Transport bill Df116 Billion dollars	Transport bill as a percentage of GNP Df117 Percent
1960	47.8	60.5	106.6	20.7
1965	64.9	82.2	144.8	20.5
1970	84.0	114.3	195.2	19.2
1971	91.2	134.4	222.0	20.1
1972	97.2	149.2	242.3	20.0
1973	107.9	163.1	266.5	19.6
1974	116.0	171.3	282.6	19.2
1975	115.8	188.2	298.9	18.7
1976	133.4	223.8	351.1	19.7
1977	150.8	256.6	400.9	20.1
1978	172.9	287.7	453.4	20.2
1979	193.2	317.9	503.0	20.1
1980	213.7	338.1	542.9	19.8
1981	228.4	374.0	592.5	19.3
1982	222.1	379.2	591.4	18.6
1983	243.3	410.8	643.2	18.7
1984	268.0	459.5	715.6	18.8
1985	273.6	492.2	753.1	18.6
1986	281.0	492.5	760.9	17.2
1987	294.2	528.1	807.5	17.2
1988	313.0	571.9	869.0	17.2
1989	329.1	602.7	945.2	16.8
1990	350.8	630.4	963.8	16.7
1991	355.1	604.7	943.4	15.9
1992	375.1	641.1	999.0	16.0
1993	396.3	682.3	1,061.5	16.2
1994	419.9	715.2	1,117.7	16.1
1995	444.5	759.9	1,186.9	16.3
1996	467.2	796.8	1,245.6	16.3

Sources

Rosalyn A. Wilson, *Transportation in America, Historical Compendium, 1939–1995* (Eno Transportation Foundation, 1997), p. 8, and annual issues of same title.

Documentation

The Eno Foundation calculates the nation's total freight and passenger bills. The transport bill is the sum of these two minus duplications. The gross national product figure is taken from the U.S. Council of Economic Advisers, *Economic Report of the President* or *Economic Indicators*.

The 1996 data are identified in the source as preliminary.

TABLE Df118–125   Petroleum consumption, by type of transportation: 1965–1995

Contributed by Louis P. Cain

		Percentage of total						
		Highway						
Year	Total	Total	Auto and taxi	Truck	Bus	Rail	Air	Water
	Df118	Df119	Df120	Df121	Df122	Df123	Df124	Df125
	Million barrels	Percent	Percent	Percent	Percent	Percent	Percent	Percent
1965	2,005	84.4	59.6	23.7	1.0	4.4	6.6	4.6
1970	2,655	81.0	58.9	21.2	0.8	3.4	11.0	4.7
1972	2,980	83.9	58.4	24.5	0.7	3.2	8.9	4.0
1975	3,096	83.8	58.4	24.3	0.7	2.9	8.7	4.5
1976	3,288	83.8	56.8	26.0	0.7	2.9	8.3	5.0
1977	3,412	83.5	56.0	26.5	0.7	2.8	8.4	5.3
1978	3,587	83.2	55.4	26.7	0.7	2.7	7.7	6.4
1979	3,594	80.9	52.7	27.1	0.7	2.9	8.4	7.8
1980	3,407	80.4	51.3	28.1	0.8	3.0	8.6	8.0
1981	3,361	81.1	50.6	29.5	0.8	2.9	8.4	7.6
1982	3,274	82.4	52.8	28.7	0.8	2.5	8.5	6.5
1983	3,322	83.1	52.2	29.9	0.8	2.5	8.4	6.0
1984	3,423	82.5	49.3	32.2	0.7	2.4	9.1	6.0
1985	3,500	82.7	47.1	34.7	0.8	2.2	9.3	5.7
1986	3,616	82.6	46.9	34.8	0.8	2.1	9.8	5.6
1987	3,713	82.0	45.3	35.8	0.8	2.1	10.4	5.6
1988	3,791	82.0	45.2	35.9	0.8	2.1	10.4	5.5
1989	3,833	82.0	44.9	36.3	0.8	2.0	10.3	5.6
1990	3,860	80.8	44.4	35.6	0.7	2.1	11.1	6.0
1991	3,824	80.3	44.0	35.4	0.8	2.0	11.1	6.6
1992	3,898	79.7	45.1	34.7	0.8	1.9	9.8	6.4
1993	3,984	82.3	45.8	36.4	0.8	1.9	10.1	5.7
1994	3,968	83.0	40.5	42.4	0.7	2.0	7.8	5.2
1995	4,046	84.5	41.0	43.4	0.7	2.1	7.9	5.6

Sources

Rosalyn A. Wilson, *Transportation in America, Historical Compendium, 1939–1995* (Eno Transportation Foundation, 1997), p. 32. The rail freight figures are from the Association of American Railroads' *Railroad Facts* (various issues), with passenger information added from the American Public Transit Association's *Transit Fact Book* (various issues) and information from Amtrak. The air data are taken from the U.S. Department of Transportation's *National Transportation Statistics* and data from the Air Transport Association of America and the Aerospace Industries Association of America. The water data come from Federal Highway Administration, *Highway Statistics*, Table MF-24, and the American Petroleum Institute, *Basic Petroleum Data Book* (various issues).

The Eno Foundation assembles the highway materials from the Federal Highway Administration, *Highway Statistics*, Table VM-1; the National Safety Council's *Accident Facts* (various issues); and the American Public Transit Association's *Transit Fact Book* (various issues).

Documentation

Series Df119. Includes an amount, less than 0.5 percent, for motorcycles. Although series Df119 equals the sum of series Df120–122 for most years, there are discrepancies in this relationship beginning in 1992 that appear to go beyond mere rounding.

TABLE Df126-133   Average haul length for domestic interstate freight, by type of transportation: 1950-1996

Contributed by Louis P. Cain

	Air carriers	Oil pipelines		Railroads	Trucks	Water carriers		
		Crude	Products			Rivers and canals	Great Lakes	Coastwise
	Df126	Df127	Df128	Df129	Df130	Df131	Df132	Df133
Year	Miles	Miles	Miles	Miles	Miles	Miles	Miles	Miles
1950	720	—	—	454	235	—	—	—
1951	748	—	—	468	237	—	—	—
1952	797	—	—	467	240	—	—	—
1953	786	—	—	474	242	—	—	—
1954	779	—	—	480	233	—	—	—
1955	894	—	—	492	235	256	568	1,579
1956	953	—	—	522	230	274	540	1,491
1957	1,018	—	—	506	267	281	554	1,527
1958	943	—	—	487	270	280	469	1,515
1959	945	—	—	489	273	280	518	1,528
1960	953	—	—	489	272	282	522	1,496
1961	906	—	—	481	267	287	488	1,508
1962	867	—	—	474	263	284	486	1,474
1963	905	—	—	486	267	285	482	1,478
1964	940	—	—	481	256	285	484	1,516
1965	943	—	—	520	259	297	494	1,501
1966	961	—	—	529	263	301	496	1,472
1967	993	—	—	532	256	322	487	1,446
1968	993	—	—	539	258	324	498	1,421
1969	1,147	—	—	541	261	313	513	1,389
1970	1,014	—	—	546	263	330	506	1,509
1971	1,023	—	—	550	277	337	499	1,483
1972	992	583	492	543	280	350	504	1,449
1973	1,022	613	488	556	276	342	535	1,384
1974	1,050	653	483	572	280	359	540	1,383
1975	1,082	633	516	576	286	358	530	1,362
1976	1,075	661	446	551	290	376	535	1,367
1977	1,086	710	417	554	300	382	481	1,385
1978	1,115	803	423	586	339	392	535	1,770
1979	1,167	851	436	579	355	406	543	1,747
1980	1,052	871	414	587	363	425	536	1,915
1981	1,241	834	424	597	361	444	539	1,971
1982	1,224	804	422	600	358	438	494	2,034
1983	1,249	790	398	611	364	463	516	2,098
1984	1,204	798	399	614	361	448	508	1,931
1985	1,157	777	391	617	366	435	524	1,972
1986	1,165	797	395	613	377	443	495	1,886
1987	1,275	834	386	630	368	452	519	1,814
1988	1,333	846	384	633	366	458	530	1,727
1989	1,399	831	389	650	389	449	535	1,602
1990	1,389	805	389	646	391	469	554	1,602
1991	1,346	824	378	662	398	483	534	1,702
1992	1,391	827	376	634	410	480	523	1,761
1993	1,326	782	399	655	407	468	509	1,647
1994	1,191	756	400	670	392	482	504	1,653
1995	1,211	752	398	720	416	481	509	1,653
1996	1,260	761	394	722	426	481	509	1,653

Sources

Rosalyn A. Wilson, *Transportation in America, Historical Compendium, 1939–1995* (Eno Transportation Foundation, 1997), p. 71.

The data on air carriers prior to 1980 is taken from the Federal Aviation Agency, *Airport Activity Statistics of Certified Route Air Carriers* (various issues) and is defined to include both scheduled and nonscheduled carriers. For the years since 1980, the figures are taken from tables assembled by the Eno Foundation. Section 418 all-cargo carriers are also included. The oil pipeline data are derived from information assembled by the Eno Foundation in conjunction with estimates based on Federal Energy Regulatory Commission data. Railroad figures include material from Association of American Railroads,

Railroad Facts (various issues). The truck data are derived from American Trucking Association, *American Trucking Trends* (various issues) for total Class I motor carriers of freight. In 1990 and 1991, the Eno Foundation also used data from Transport Technical Services. Water carrier information before 1990 is taken from U.S. Army Corps of Engineers, *Waterborne Commerce of the United States*, Part 5, National Summaries. Since 1990, the data have been estimated by the Eno Foundation

Documentation

The 1996 data are identified in the source as preliminary.

TABLE Df134–147   Government expenditures for transportation services and facilities, by jurisdiction and type of transportation: 1947–1995

Contributed by Louis P. Cain

	Total	Federal							State and local					
		Total	Airways	Airports	Highways	Rivers and harbors	Railroads	Transit	Total	Airports	Highways	Rivers and harbors	Railroads	Transit
	Df134	Df135	Df136	Df137	Df138	Df139	Df140	Df141	Df142	Df143	Df144	Df145	Df146	Df147
Year	Million dollars	Million dollars	Percent	Percent	Percent	Percent	Percent	Percent	Million dollars	Percent	Percent	Percent	Percent	Percent
1947	3,208	512	12.9	4.1	65.8	17.2	0.0	0.0	2,696	2.6	93.8	3.6	0.0	0.0
1950	4,740	851	13.5	5.2	59.1	22.2	0.0	0.0	3,889	2.6	93.9	3.5	0.0	0.0
1955	7,450	1,025	10.5	1.4	76.5	11.6	0.0	0.0	6,425	1.8	95.8	2.4	0.0	0.0
1960	11,534	3,548	12.1	2.2	77.6	8.1	0.0	0.0	7,986	4.3	92.7	3.0	0.0	0.0
1965	15,349	5,326	12.2	1.8	77.7	7.3	0.0	1.0	10,023	4.1	93.0	2.8	0.0	0.1
1970	22,573	6,806	14.2	1.6	76.1	5.5	0.6	2.0	15,767	6.1	90.8	2.8	0.0	0.2
1971	25,184	7,988	17.5	2.7	70.7	4.8	0.7	3.6	17,196	6.2	90.5	2.9	0.0	0.4
1972	26,163	7,834	16.1	1.8	69.2	5.3	1.0	6.5	18,329	6.3	90.1	2.9	0.0	0.7
1973	27,934	8,291	17.7	3.3	62.1	5.3	1.2	10.4	19,643	7.2	88.6	3.1	(Z)	1.1
1974	30,115	9,645	15.9	3.0	64.5	5.3	1.3	9.9	20,470	6.4	89.3	3.1	0.1	1.2
1975	35,276	11,588	14.3	3.0	62.0	4.5	2.6	13.7	23,688	6.1	84.5	3.1	0.2	6.0
1976	37,803	13,510	13.3	2.4	58.8	4.4	3.6	17.6	24,293	6.2	83.6	2.9	0.3	7.1
1977	37,926	13,494	12.7	2.9	56.2	5.0	6.0	17.1	24,432	5.4	83.9	3.1	0.3	7.2
1978	42,366	15,079	12.4	4.1	53.6	5.7	6.1	18.1	27,287	5.9	83.3	2.8	0.4	7.5
1979	47,171	17,074	11.2	3.6	56.2	5.9	5.7	17.3	30,097	6.3	81.0	3.5	0.6	8.6
1980	55,272	20,928	10.2	3.1	57.5	5.5	5.1	18.5	34,344	7.3	79.1	3.4	0.6	9.6
1981	56,429	19,807	10.7	3.0	54.3	6.3	5.4	20.4	36,622	7.5	76.8	4.1	0.8	10.8
1982	57,979	18,572	8.7	2.2	57.8	6.5	5.7	19.1	39,407	7.2	77.5	3.6	1.0	10.7
1983	62,248	19,405	9.1	2.7	56.6	6.0	5.0	20.6	42,843	7.0	77.0	3.4	0.9	11.6
1984	70,415	23,523	11.4	3.3	54.3	5.1	9.3	16.6	46,892	7.6	74.8	2.8	1.3	13.4
1985	77,253	23,831	9.5	3.7	63.3	5.0	3.8	14.6	53,422	7.0	76.0	2.8	1.3	12.9
1986	84,114	24,496	13.2	3.8	61.9	4.4	8.2	8.5	59,618	7.1	76.7	2.9	2.2	11.1
1987	88,092	23,330	13.9	4.3	63.0	4.5	5.6	8.7	64,762	7.5	77.0	2.7	1.6	11.2
1988	91,596	24,308	14.4	3.6	64.1	4.7	4.9	8.5	67,288	8.0	76.5	2.7	1.6	11.3
1989	94,910	24,560	16.6	4.8	60.9	4.6	5.2	7.8	70,350	8.2	76.4	2.7	1.7	10.9
1990	100,864	25,930	20.3	4.9	58.4	5.0	4.6	6.8	74,934	8.7	76.3	2.6	1.7	10.8
1991	106,066	27,073	21.2	5.9	56.6	5.7	4.0	6.5	78,993	9.2	75.8	2.6	1.6	10.9
1992	113,416	28,633	22.6	6.1	54.9	5.2	4.1	7.0	84,783	9.4	76.7	2.4	1.5	10.1
1993	120,937	32,471	23.6	6.6	56.1	4.5	3.1	6.2	88,466	9.9	77.2	2.2	0.9	9.8
1994	110,085	28,963	25.0	5.8	52.9	4.7	2.1	9.4	81,122	11.6	73.8	2.3	0.3	12.0
1995	126,958	33,957	21.5	5.5	56.2	4.2	4.2	8.3	93,001	10.9	76.3	2.0	0.2	10.6

(Z) Less than 0.05 percent.

Sources

Rosalyn A. Wilson, *Transportation in America, Historical Compendium, 1939–1995* (Eno Transportation Foundation, 1997), p. 39. The underlying data are taken from *Budget of the United States,* with a few exceptions. Highway figures are from U.S. Federal Highway Administration, *Highway Statistics* (various issues). The state and local figures for airports and rivers and harbors come from U.S. Bureau of the Census, *Government Finances.* The information on railroads and transit come from American Public Transit Association, *Transit Fact Book* (various issues).

Documentation

There are no state and local government expenditures on airways.

Series Df140 and Df146. Federal railroad expenditures include Amtrak, the Northeast Corridor Project, and rail commutation capital grants. State and local railroad expenditures include rail commutation capital grants and operating subsidies. The transit figures exclude rail commutation, but include capital grants and operating subsidies.

TABLE Df148–152   Public transportation fares, by mode of transport: 1940–1978

Contributed by Louis P. Cain

Year	All modes Df148 Cents	Bus Df149 Cents	Subway and elevated Df150 Cents	Surface rail Df151 Cents	Trolley bus Df152 Cents
1940	6.7	6.9	5.4	7.3	5.9
1945	6.9	7.1	5.6	7.3	6.8
1950	10.0	9.6	9.9	11.6	9.6
1955	14.8	14.4	14.8	17.4	14.8
1956	15.4	15.2	15.1	18.7	15.3
1957	15.8	15.6	15.3	19.8	16.0
1958	16.5	16.3	15.9	20.1	16.9
1959	17.1	17.2	16.0	20.8	17.4
1960	17.8	18.0	16.1	22.1	18.1
1961	18.2	18.6	16.3	22.6	18.9
1962	18.7	19.1	16.4	23.4	20.4
1963	19.0	19.6	16.4	23.0	20.7
1964	19.4	20.1	16.6	22.7	21.0
1965	19.7	20.6	16.6	23.8	21.8
1966	20.8	21.2	18.8	24.6	22.1
1967	22.0	22.4	20.9	22.9	22.5
1968	22.7	23.2	21.0	23.5	22.9
1969	24.6	25.7	21.9	25.0	23.3
1970	27.6	29.4	23.4	27.0	23.8
1971	29.8	32.2	24.2	25.9	27.6
1972	31.4	33.1	27.8	26.9	31.6
1973	31.8	32.4	30.7	27.0	32.1
1974	32.2	31.8	33.9	27.9	28.9
1975	33.0	32.0	36.3	29.9	27.5
1976	35.7	32.8	45.6	29.9	27.8
1977	37.7	34.9	47.5	30.2	28.2
1978	38.1	35.8	46.1	33.4	28.1

Source

American Public Transit Association, *Transit Fact Book* (annual editions).

Documentation

There have been several changes over time in the way this information is reported. The *Transit Fact Book* does not report individual modes after 1978.

These data are the average fare per linked passenger trip. They include transfer charges; zone charges; and reduced-fare, free-fare, and free-transfer rides.

TABLE Df153–157   Personal consumption expenditures for transportation: 1960–1996[1]

Contributed by Louis P. Cain

	Total personal consumption	Transportation			
		Total	User-operated	Purchased local	Purchased intercity
	Df153	Df154	Df155	Df156	Df157
Year	Million dollars	Million dollars	Million dollars	Million dollars	Million dollars
1960	324,907	42,268	39,057	1,904	1,307
1961	334,997	40,883	37,640	1,865	1,378
1962	355,219	45,705	42,292	1,905	1,508
1963	374,581	49,395	45,963	1,910	1,522
1964	400,497	52,240	48,625	1,908	1,707
1965	430,378	58,290	54,461	1,925	1,904
1966	465,118	61,190	57,081	1,981	2,128
1967	490,262	63,196	58,680	2,091	2,425
1968	536,883	72,411	67,380	2,286	2,745
1969	581,781	78,577	72,920	2,443	3,214
1970	621,721	80,462	71,385	2,816	3,378
1971	700,326	90,050	83,311	3,084	3,655
1972	767,805	99,363	91,590	3,263	4,150
1973	848,146	107,380	99,427	3,280	4,673
1974	927,701	113,189	102,776	3,509	6,904
1975	1,024,898	123,282	112,180	3,833	7,269
1976	1,143,066	144,817	131,964	4,223	8,630
1977	1,271,531	165,385	150,916	4,527	9,942
1978	1,421,201	181,481	165,543	4,860	11,078
1979	1,583,706	204,193	185,940	5,286	12,967
1980	1,748,077	235,739	214,879	4,793	16,067
1981	1,926,235	258,995	236,417	5,011	17,517
1982	2,059,179	263,416	240,203	5,352	17,861
1983	2,257,546	292,832	268,136	5,966	18,730
1984	2,460,288	328,214	300,344	6,742	21,128
1985	2,667,396	363,265	333,536	7,361	22,368
1986	2,850,553	370,354	339,771	7,911	22,671
1987	3,052,223	384,773	351,432	8,018	25,323
1988	3,296,126	413,184	376,881	8,312	27,991
1989	3,523,070	437,269	399,633	8,142	29,494
1990	3,748,417	453,654	413,527	8,916	31,215
1990	3,839,300	463,300	426,900	7,800	28,510
1991	3,975,000	436,800	401,400	7,900	27,500
1992	4,219,700	471,500	435,700	8,000	27,900
1993	4,459,200	504,000	465,500	8,400	30,100
1994	4,717,000	542,200	502,600	8,900	30,700
1995	4,957,600	572,300	530,100	9,200	33,000
1996	5,207,600	602,200	557,700	10,100	34,400

[1] Revised data procedures effective 1990. Two data values are reported in that year. See text.

Sources

1960–1989, U.S. Bureau of Transportation Statistics, *National Transportation Statistics* (1993), Tables 52 and 53; 1990–1996, U.S. Bureau of Transportation Statistics, *National Transportation Statistics* (1998), Tables, 2-16 and 2-17.

Documentation

This table uses data excerpted from the U.S. Bureau of Economic Analysis. A revision took place between 1993 and 1998 that increased series Df154–155 and reduced series Df156–157. More recent editions provide revised data,

but only for every fifth year. For that reason, the nonrevised numbers are reported here through the first set of values for 1990; revised numbers are reported thereafter.

Series Df155. Includes expenditures on new and the net purchases of used automobiles, trucks, and recreation vehicles. Also includes expenditures for gasoline, oil and lubrication, tires and tubes, repairs, washing, parking, rental, tolls, and insurance.

Series Df156. Includes both transit systems and taxicabs.

Series Df157. Includes airline, bus, and rail other than commutation.

TABLE Df158-174   Public transit mileage, equipment, passengers, trips, employees, and passenger revenue: 1917–1994[1,2]

Contributed by Louis P. Cain

	Mileage			Equipment owned			Revenue and nonrevenue passengers									Railway passengers carried	
	Railway track	Trolley coach	Motor bus	Railway cars	Trolley coaches	Motor buses	Total	Railway	Trolley coach	Motor bus	Revenue passengers	Transit passenger trips	Passenger revenue	Employees	Employee payroll	Surface	Subway and elevated
	Df158	Df159	Df160	Df161	Df162	Df163	Df164	Df165	Df166	Df167	Df168[3]	Df169[3]	Df170[4]	Df171	Df172	Df173	Df174
Year	Miles	Miles	Miles	Number	Number	Number	Million	Million	Million	Million	Million	Million	Million dollars	Million	Million dollars	Million	Million
1917	—	—	—	—	—	—	—	14,507	—	—	—	—	—	—	—	—	—
1918	—	—	—	—	—	—	—	14,243	—	—	—	—	—	—	—	—	—
1919	—	—	—	—	—	—	—	14,916	—	—	—	—	—	—	—	—	—
1920	—	—	—	—	—	—	—	15,541	—	—	—	—	—	—	—	—	—
1921	—	—	—	—	—	—	—	14,574	—	—	—	—	—	—	—	—	—
1922	—	—	—	—	—	—	15,735	15,331	—	404	—	—	—	—	—	—	—
1923	—	—	—	—	—	—	16,311	15,650	—	661	—	—	—	—	—	—	—
1924	—	—	—	—	—	—	16,301	15,312	—	989	—	—	—	—	—	—	—
1925	—	—	—	—	—	—	16,651	15,167	—	1,484	—	—	—	—	—	—	—
1926	—	—	—	—	—	—	17,234	15,225	—	2,009	—	—	—	—	—	—	—
1927	—	—	—	—	—	—	17,201	14,901	—	2,300	—	—	—	—	—	—	—
1928	—	—	—	—	—	—	16,989	14,518	3	2,468	—	—	—	—	—	—	—
1929	—	—	—	—	—	—	16,985	14,358	5	2,622	—	—	—	—	—	—	—
1930	—	—	—	58,124	—	—	15,567	13,072	16	2,479	—	—	—	—	—	—	—
1931	—	—	—	54,118	—	—	13,924	11,583	28	2,313	—	—	—	—	—	—	—
1932	—	—	—	—	—	—	12,025	9,852	37	2,136	—	—	—	—	—	—	—
1933	28,500	—	—	—	310	17,200[5]	11,327	9,207	45	2,075	—	—	—	201	237	7,074	2,133
1934	—	423	54,700	—	441	18,700[5]	12,038	9,600	68	2,370	—	—	—	204	303	7,394	2,206
1935	26,700	548	58,100	50,466	578	23,800	12,226	9,512	96	2,618	9,782	—	642.3	204	311	7,276	2,236
1936	25,300	859	62,200	48,103	1,136	23,900	13,146	9,824	143	3,179	10,512	—	685.5	206	328	7,501	2,323
1937	23,770	1,166	67,000	45,312	1,655	27,500	13,246	9,468	289	3,489	10,436	—	689.7	209	348	7,161	2,307
1938	21,800	1,398	70,400	42,605	2,032	23,500	12,645	8,781	389	3,475	9,985	—	662.9	202	344	6,545	2,236
1939	20,600	1,543	74,300	40,372	2,184	32,600	12,837	8,539	445	3,853	10,252	—	681.5	202	352	6,171	2,368
1940	19,602	1,925	78,000	37,662	2,802	35,000	13,098	8,325	534	4,239	10,504	13,098	701.5	203	360	5,943	2,382
1941	18,342	2,041	82,100	37,670	3,029	39,300	14,085	8,502	652	4,931	11,302	—	758.8	205	386	6,074	2,421
1942	18,171	2,273	85,500	37,508	3,385	46,000	18,000	9,856	899	7,245	14,501	—	979.1	219	462	7,290	2,566
1943	18,181	2,248	87,000	37,505	3,501	47,100	22,000	11,806	1,175	9,019	17,918	—	1,235.6	209	554	9,150	2,656
1944	18,082	2,245	87,700	37,199	3,561	48,400	23,017	12,137	1,234	9,646	18,735	—	1,296.9	242	599	9,516	2,621
1945	17,702	2,313	90,400	36,377	3,711	49,670	23,254	12,124	1,244	9,886	18,982	23,254	1,313.7	242	632	9,426	2,698
1946	16,716	2,354	91,100	33,479	3,916	52,450	23,372	11,862	1,311	10,199	19,119	—	1,331.5	261	713	9,027	2,835
1947	14,976	2,699	95,300	30,158	4,707	56,917	22,540	10,852	1,356	10,332	18,287	—	1,324.2	266	790	8,096	2,756
1948	12,964	2,905	96,500	26,280	5,687	58,540	21,368	9,112	1,528	10,728	17,312	—	1,416.8	261	829	6,506	2,606
1949	11,931	3,337	96,400	24,728	6,366	57,085	19,008	7,185	1,661	10,162	15,251	—	1,419.7	253	841	4,839	2,346
1950	10,813	3,513	98,000	22,986	6,504	56,820	17,246	6,168	1,658	9,420	13,845	17,246	1,386.8	240	835	3,904	2,264
1951	9,457	3,678	99,700	20,604	7,071	57,660	16,125	5,290	1,633	9,202	12,281	—	1,411.6	232	872	3,101	2,189
1952	8,532	3,736	99,600	19,176	7,180	55,980	15,119	4,601	1,640	8,878	12,022	—	1,438.1	227	903	2,477	2,124
1953	7,352	3,663	100,000	17,234	6,941	54,700	13,902	4,076	1,566	8,260	11,036	—	1,448.6	220	913	2,036	2,040
1954	6,765	3,630	99,000	15,600	6,598	54,000	12,392	3,401	1,367	7,624	9,858	—	1,410.0	211	895	1,489	1,912
1955	6,197	3,428	99,800	14,532	6,157	52,400	11,529	3,077	1,202	7,250	9,189	11,529	1,358.9	198	864	1,207	1,870
1956	5,746	3,293	100,700	13,225	5,748	51,400	10,941	2,756	1,142	7,043	8,756	—	1,351.1	186	852	876	1,880
1957	5,019	3,007	102,400	12,759	5,412	50,800	10,389	2,522	993	6,874	8,338	—	1,319.8	177	840	679	1,843
1958	3,844	2,723	104,500	12,201	4,848	50,100	9,732	2,387	843	6,502	7,778	—	1,282.2	165	831	572	1,815
1959	3,445	2,491	106,300	11,983	4,297	49,500	9,557	2,349	749	6,459	7,650	—	1,308.0	159	832	521	1,828

Railway passengers carried

Year	Mileage — Railway track Df158 (Miles)	Mileage — Trolley coach Df159 (Miles)	Mileage — Motor bus Df160 (Miles)	Equipment owned — Railway cars Df161 (Number)	Equipment owned — Trolley coaches Df162 (Number)	Equipment owned — Motor buses Df163 (Number)	Revenue and nonrevenue passengers — Total Df164 (Million)	Revenue and nonrevenue passengers — Railway Df165 (Million)	Revenue and nonrevenue passengers — Trolley coach Df166 (Million)	Revenue and nonrevenue passengers — Motor bus Df167 (Million)	Revenue passengers Df168[3] (Million)	Transit passenger trips Df169[3] (Million)	Passenger revenue Df170[4] (Million dollars)	Employees Df171 (Million)	Employee payroll Df172 (Million dollars)	Surface Df173 (Million)	Subway and elevated Df174 (Million)
1960	3,143	2,196	108,700	11,866	3,826	49,600	9,395	2,313	657	6,425	7,521	9,395	1,334.9	156	857	463	1,350
1961	2,601	2,017	111,500	11,419	3,593	49,000	8,883	2,289	601	5,993	7,242	—	1,320.9	152	856	434	1,855
1962	2,557	1,849	114,300	11,084	3,161	48,800	8,695	2,283	547	5,865	7,122	—	1,330.2	149	878	284	1,704
1963	2,236	1,119	117,400	10,634	2,155	49,400	8,400	2,165	413	5,822	6,915	—	1,316.3	147	892	329	1,836
1964	2,173	986	118,300	10,614	1,865	49,200	8,328	2,166	349	5,813	6,854	—	1,326.0	145	917	289	1,877
1965	2,173	766	120,900	10,664	1,453	49,600	8,253	2,134	305	5,814	6,798	8,253	1,340.1	145	964	276	1,858
1966	2,153	676	122,100	10,680	1,326	50,130	8,083	2,035	284	5,764	6,671	8,083	1,385.4	144	995	282	1,753
1967	2,049	616	123,600	10,645	1,244	50,180	8,172	2,201	248	5,723	6,616	8,172	1,457.4	146	1,055	263	1,938
1968	2,045	616	121,000	10,745	1,185	50,000	8,019	2,181	228	5,610	6,491	8,019	1,470.2	144	1,110	253	1,928
1969	2,081	563	117,300	10,665	1,082	49,600	7,803	2,229	199	5,375	6,310	7,803	1,554.7	141	1,184	249	1,980
1970	2,081	563	112,700	10,600	1,050	49,700	7,332	2,116	182	5,034	5,932	7,332	1,639.1	138	1,274	235	1,881
1971	—	—	—	10,550	1,037	49,150	6,847	2,000	148	4,699	5,497	6,847	1,661.9	139	1,393	222	1,778
1972	—	—	—	10,599	1,030	49,075	6,567	1,942	130	4,495	5,253	6,567	1,650.7	138	1,455	211	1,731
1973	—	—	—	10,510	794	48,286	6,660	1,921	97	4,642	5,294	6,660	1,683.7	141	1,624	207	1,714
1974	—	—	—	10,471	718	48,700	6,935	1,876	83	4,976	5,606	6,935	1,805.2	153	1,967	150	1,726
1975	—	—	—	10,712	703	50,811	6,959	1,797	78	5,084	5,643	7,284	1,860.5	160	2,236	124	1,673
1976	—	—	—	10,720	685	52,382	7,066	1,744	75	5,247	5,673	7,393	2,025.6	163	2,404	112	1,632
1977	—	—	—	10,674	645	51,968	7,271	2,252	70	4,949	5,723	7,603	2,157.1	163	2,547	103	2,149
1978	—	—	—	10,554	593	52,866	7,601	2,389	70	5,142	5,963	7,935	2,271.0	165	2,741	104	2,285
1979	—	—	—	10,481	682	54,490	8,115	2,488	75	5,552	6,370	8,461	2,436.3	179	3,025	107	2,381
1980	—	—	—	10,654	823	59,411	8,220	2,241	142	5,837	6,358	8,567	2,556.8	187	3,281	133	2,108
1981	—	—	—	10,824	751	60,393	7,949	2,217	138	5,594	—	8,284	2,701.4	192	3,494	123	2,094
1982	—	—	—	10,831	763	62,114	7,726	2,251	151	5,324	—	8,052	3,077.0	194	3,731	136	2,115
1983	—	—	—	10,904	686	62,093	7,886	2,304	160	5,422	—	8,203	3,171.6	195	3,921	137	2,167
1984	—	—	—	9,816	664	67,294	8,439	2,366	165	5,908	—	8,829	4,447.7	263	5,488	135	2,231
1985	—	—	—	10,043	676	64,258	8,239	2,422	142	5,675	—	8,636	4,574.7	270	5,843	132	2,290
1986	—	—	—	11,083	680	66,218	8,355	2,463	139	5,753	—	8,777	5,113.1	278	6,119	130	2,333
1987	—	—	—	10,934	671	63,017	8,290	2,535	141	5,614	—	8,735	5,114.1	277	6,324	133	2,402
1988	—	—	—	11,370	710	62,572	8,188	2,462	136	5,590	—	8,666	5,224.6	276	6,675	154	2,308
1989	—	—	—	11,261	725	58,919	8,454	2,704	130	5,620	—	8,931	5,419.9	272	6,898	162	2,542
1990	—	—	—	11,332	832	58,714	8,324	2,521	126	5,677	—	8,799	5,890.8	273	7,226	175	2,346
1991	—	—	—	11,426	752	60,377	8,105	2,356	125	5,624	—	8,575	6,037.2	276	7,394	184	2,172
1992	—	—	—	11,303	907	63,080	8,038	2,395	126	5,517	—	8,501	6,152.5	279	7,670	188	2,207
1993	—	—	—	11,286	851	64,850	7,736	2,234	121	5,381	—	8,217	6,350.9	299	7,932	188	2,046
1994	—	—	—	11,192	877	67,492	7,929	2,409	118	5,402	—	8,435	6,840.5	312	8,649	203	2,206

[1] The range of transit operations covered in the source was expanded in 1984. See text.

[2] Mileage and equipment as of December 31.

[3] In 1977, the source title for series Df168 changed from "revenue passenger rides" to "linked transit passenger trips," and for series Df169 from "total passenger rides" to "unlinked transit passenger trips."

[4] Includes fare subsidies starting in 1991.

[5] Estimates probably understated.

Sources

American Public Transit Association, *Transit Fact Book* (annual editions); see also *The Transit Industry in the United States: Basic Data and Trends, 1943*; mimeographed release on number of passengers by the American Public Transit Association, January 3, 1938.

(continued)

TABLE Df158–174   Public transit mileage, equipment, passengers, trips, employees, and passenger revenue: 1917–1994   Continued

Documentation

Several of these series have undergone change. Before 1984, the *Transit Fact Book* figures were estimates based on reports for more than 85 percent of the industry, which included local motor buses, electric street railways (light rail), elevated and subway lines (heavy rail), interurban electric railways, and transit coach lines. That definition was expanded to include commuter rail lines, demand response, other forms of public transit (such as ferryboats), and most of the rural and smaller systems that comprised the other 15 percent. Consequently, none of these series can be considered continuous between 1983 and 1984. Specific examples are discussed in this section and in the table footnotes.

Unlike route miles, vehicle miles continue to be reported in a consistent manner (see Table Df175–183).

Series Df159. Miles of negative overhead wire.

Series Df160. Miles of route, round trip.

Series Df161–163. In 1984, the titles in the source changed from "passenger vehicles owned and leased" to "active passenger vehicles." This resulted in a significant reduction in series Df161, little change in series Df162, and a substantial increase in series Df163.

Series Df170. Prior to 1984, excludes commuter rail, automated guideway, urban ferryboat, demand response, fares retained by contractors, and most rural and smaller systems.

Series Df164–168. Revenue and nonrevenue passenger figures exceed revenue passenger figures chiefly because of free transfers. The inclusion of the rural and smaller systems, starting in 1984, had its largest effect on the motor bus figures.

Series Df165. Equals the sum of series Df173–174.

TABLE Df175–183   Public transit vehicle miles operated, by type of transportation: 1926–1994[1]

Contributed by Louis P. Cain

| | | | | | | Percentage of total | | | |
	Total	Surface railway	Subway and elevated railway	Trolley coach	Motor bus	Surface railway	Subway and elevated railway	Trolley coach	Motor bus
	Df175	Df176	Df177	Df178	Df179	Df180	Df181	Df182	Df183
Year	Million miles	Million miles	Million miles	Million miles	Million miles	Percent	Percent	Percent	Percent
1926	2,669.7	1,821.9	398.1	0.0	449.7	68.2	14.9	0.0	16.8
1927	2,753.0	1,753.6	410.2	0.0	589.2	63.7	14.9	0.0	21.4
1928	2,748.0	1,679.1	434.3	1.2	633.4	61.1	15.8	(Z)	23.0
1929	2,762.4	1,610.3	450.3	2.0	699.8	58.3	16.3	0.1	25.3
1930	2,707.0	1,540.4	454.8	6.0	705.8	56.9	16.8	0.2	26.1
1931	2,549.0	1,417.9	440.7	7.9	682.5	55.6	17.3	0.3	26.8
1932	2,363.0	1,266.7	423.5	9.5	663.3	53.6	17.9	0.4	28.1
1933	2,259.0	1,165.7	427.7	10.5	655.1	51.6	18.9	0.5	29.0
1934	2,312.0	1,147.7	438.6	14.6	711.1	49.6	19.0	0.6	30.8
1935	2,327.3	1,096.6	447.7	19.0	764.0	47.1	19.2	0.8	32.8
1936	2,433.0	1,080.9	461.6	26.3	864.2	44.4	19.0	1.1	35.5
1937	2,505.0	1,029.2	469.1	49.7	957.0	41.1	18.7	2.0	38.2
1938	2,434.0	922.3	457.4	67.9	986.4	37.9	18.8	2.8	40.5
1939	2,470.0	878.3	469.4	74.9	1,047.4	35.6	19.0	3.0	42.4
1940	2,596.0	844.7	470.8	86.0	1,194.5	32.5	18.1	3.3	46.0
1941	2,676.4	792.2	472.8	98.4	1,313.0	29.6	17.7	3.7	49.1
1942	3,047.7	850.4	469.6	115.7	1,612.0	27.9	15.4	3.8	52.9
1943	3,262.4	978.0	461.7	129.7	1,693.0	30.0	14.2	4.0	51.9
1944	3,284.5	977.9	461.0	132.3	1,713.3	29.8	14.0	4.0	52.2
1945	3,253.8	939.8	458.4	133.3	1,722.3	28.9	14.1	4.1	52.9
1946	3,304.3	894.5	458.9	143.7	1,807.2	27.1	13.9	4.3	54.7
1947	3,342.4	839.3	462.3	155.1	1,885.7	25.1	13.8	4.6	56.4
1948	3,311.1	699.3	458.1	178.0	1,975.7	21.1	13.8	5.4	59.7
1949	3,183.6	555.4	460.0	200.0	1,968.2	17.4	14.4	6.3	61.8
1950	3,007.6	463.1	443.4	205.7	1,895.4	15.4	14.7	6.8	63.0
1951	2,913.4	387.6	424.0	208.8	1,893.0	13.3	14.6	7.2	65.0
1952	2,814.5	321.2	400.4	215.2	1,877.7	11.4	14.2	7.6	66.7
1953	2,695.5	273.7	391.1	211.7	1,819.0	10.2	14.5	7.9	67.5
1954	2,548.8	215.1	376.3	196.7	1,760.7	8.4	14.8	7.7	69.1
1955	2,447.5	178.3	382.8	176.5	1,709.9	7.3	15.6	7.2	69.9
1956	2,366.6	132.9	387.1	165.7	1,680.9	5.6	16.4	7.0	71.0
1957	2,289.5	106.6	388.0	146.5	1,648.4	4.7	16.9	6.4	72.0
1958	2,201.0	89.9	386.5	131.0	1,593.6	4.1	17.6	6.0	72.4
1959	2,158.9	81.3	388.7	112.4	1,576.5	3.8	18.0	5.2	73.0

Notes appear at end of table

TABLE Df175–183   Public transit vehicle miles operated, by type of transportation: 1926–1994
Continued

	Total	Surface railway	Subway and elevated railway	Trolley coach	Motor bus	Percentage of total			
						Surface railway	Subway and elevated railway	Trolley coach	Motor bus
	Df175	Df176	Df177	Df178	Df179	Df180	Df181	Df182	Df183
Year	Million miles	Million miles	Million miles	Million miles	Million miles	Percent	Percent	Percent	Percent
1960	2,142.8	74.8	390.9	100.7	1,576.4	3.5	18.2	4.7	73.6
1961	2,077.1	69.4	385.1	92.9	1,529.7	3.3	18.5	4.5	73.6
1962	2,047.4	61.5	386.7	84.0	1,515.2	3.0	18.9	4.1	74.0
1963	2,021.7	48.9	387.3	62.4	1,523.1	2.4	19.2	3.1	75.3
1964	2,015.8	42.9	395.8	49.2	1,527.9	2.1	19.6	2.4	75.8
1965	2,008.2	41.6	395.3	43.0	1,528.3	2.1	19.7	2.1	76.1
1966	1,983.6	42.9	378.9	40.1	1,521.7	2.2	19.1	2.0	76.7
1967	1,996.8	37.8	396.5	36.5	1,526.0	1.9	19.9	1.8	76.4
1968	1,988.7	37.5	406.8	36.2	1,508.2	1.9	20.5	1.8	75.8
1969	1,966.7	36.0	416.6	35.8	1,478.3	1.8	21.2	1.8	75.2
1970	1,883.1	33.7	407.1	33.0	1,409.3	1.8	21.6	1.8	74.8
1971	1,846.4	32.7	407.4	30.8	1,375.5	1.8	22.1	1.7	74.5
1972	1,755.6	31.6	386.2	29.8	1,308.0	1.8	22.0	1.7	74.5
1973	1,834.6	31.2	407.3	25.7	1,370.4	1.7	22.2	1.4	74.7
1974	1,907.4	26.9	431.9	17.6	1,431.0	1.4	22.6	0.9	75.0
1975	1,988.2	23.8	423.1	15.3	1,526.0	1.2	21.3	0.8	76.8
1976	2,024.8	21.1	407.0	15.3	1,581.4	1.0	20.1	0.8	78.1
1977	2,019.8	20.4	361.3	14.8	1,623.3	1.0	17.9	0.7	80.4
1978	2,026.8	19.5	363.5	13.3	1,630.5	1.0	17.9	0.7	80.4
1979	2,044.9	19.1	380.5	11.7	1,633.6	0.9	18.6	0.6	79.9
1980	2,092.4	17.5	384.7	13.0	1,677.2	0.8	18.4	0.6	80.2
1981	2,133.1	16.5	420.1	11.9	1,684.6	0.8	19.7	0.6	79.0
1982	2,127.5	16.1	429.1	13.7	1,668.6	0.8	20.2	0.6	78.4
1983	2,116.3	16.0	407.5	15.0	1,677.8	0.8	19.3	0.7	79.3
1984	2,312.6	16.8	435.8	15.3	1,844.7	0.7	18.8	0.7	79.8
1985	2,345.7	16.5	450.8	15.5	1,862.9	0.7	19.2	0.7	79.4
1986	2,509.8	17.0	475.8	14.7	2,002.3	0.7	19.0	0.6	79.8
1987	2,603.0	18.4	490.2	15.0	2,079.4	0.7	18.8	0.6	79.9
1988	2,650.2	20.8	517.4	14.7	2,097.3	0.8	19.5	0.6	79.1
1989	2,677.2	21.3	532.1	14.5	2,109.3	0.8	19.9	0.5	78.8
1990	2,704.6	24.2	536.7	13.8	2,129.9	0.9	19.8	0.5	78.8
1991	2,735.0	27.6	527.2	13.6	2,166.6	1.0	19.3	0.5	79.2
1992	2,745.9	28.6	525.4	13.9	2,178.0	1.0	19.1	0.5	79.3
1993	2,772.4	27.7	522.1	13.0	2,209.6	1.0	18.8	0.5	79.7
1994	2,742.1	33.9	531.8	13.7	2,162.7	1.2	19.4	0.5	78.9

(Z) Less than 0.05 percent.

[1] The range of transit operations covered in the source was expanded in 1984. See text for Table Df158–174.

Source

American Public Transit Association, *Transit Fact Book* (annual editions).

Documentation

See the text for Table Df158–174 for a discussion of the source.

Series Df175 equals the total of the four modes reported; the percentages are based on that total.

ROADS AND VEHICLES

Louis P. Cain

TABLE Df184–186   Surfaced mileage of rural roads and municipal streets, by surface type: 1904–1979

Contributed by Louis P. Cain

		Under state control				Under state control	
	Total	High-type roads	Low-type roads		Total	High-type roads	Low-type roads
	Df184	Df185	Df186		Df184	Df185	Df186
Year	Thousand miles	Thousand miles	Thousand miles	Year	Thousand miles	Thousand miles	Thousand miles
1904	154	—	—	1945	1,721	168	312
1905	161	—	—	1946	1,730	170	317
1906	168	—	—	1947	1,780	170	332
1907	176	—	—	1948	1,815	172	338
1908	183	—	—	1949	1,865	174	350
1909	190	—	—	1950	1,939	227	316
1910	204	—	—	1951	1,998	236	323
1911	217	—	—	1952	2,070	245	328
1912	231	—	—	1953	2,160	252	332
1913	244	—	—	1954	2,228	262	333
1914	257	—	—	1955	2,273	270	340
1915	276	—	—	1956	2,323	281	335
1916	295	—	—	1957	2,371	290	338
1917	313	—	—	1958	2,448	301	338
1918	332	—	—	1959	2,503	314	338
1919	350	—	—	1960	2,557	322	338
1920	369	—	—	1961	2,588	331	338
1921	387	—	—	1962	2,647	341	337
1922	412	—	—	1963	2,693	350	336
1923	439	34	78	1964	2,730	359	334
1924	472	41	90	1965	2,776	367	333
1925	521	48	97	1966	2,800	376	334
1926	550	54	109	1967	2,827	386	331
1927	589	60	117	1968	2,870	392	330
1928	626	68	125	1969	2,914	403	324
1929	662	75	133	1970	2,946	411	322
1930	694	84	142	1971	2,983	419	319
1931	830	96	146	1972	3,021	426	316
1932	879	110	156	1973	3,042	431	312
1933	914	116	195	1974	3,067	432	308
1934	992	124	237	1975	3,101	433	311
1935	1,080	128	246	1976	3,135	439	307
1936	1,175	131	262	1977	3,164	432	309
1937	1,232	144	265	1978	3,203	441	302
1938	1,276	149	277	1979	3,167	449	286
1939	1,318	151	286				
1940	1,367	153	296				
1941	1,608	163	297				
1942	1,630	165	302				
1943	1,646	166	306				
1944	1,655	167	309				

Sources

1904–1940, U.S. Bureau of Public Roads, *Highway Statistics, Summary to 1955* (1957); 1941–1979, U.S. Federal Highway Administration, *Highway Statistics, Summary to 1985* (1987), Table M-203.

Documentation

Total surfaced mileage includes all surfaced mileage whether under state or local control; that under state control includes state highway extensions within cities.

High-type surfaced roads include bituminous penetration; sheet asphalt; bituminous concrete; Portland cement concrete; vitrified brick; and block pavements of asphalt, wood, and stone. For some years, they also include dual-type surfaces and a small amount of unclassified mileage.

Low-type surfaced roads include sand, clay, selected soil, untreated gravel, bituminous surface-treated, mixed bituminous and treated gravel, chert, shale, and waterbound macadam.

TABLE Df187–192   Mileage of rural roads and municipal streets, by jurisdiction: 1921–1979[1]

Contributed by Louis P. Cain

		Rural				
		State-administered				
	Total	Total	Primary	Secondary and county roads	County roads under local control	Municipal and other
	Df187	Df188	Df189	Df190	Df191 [2]	Df192
Year	Thousand miles	Thousand miles	Thousand miles	Thousand miles	Thousand miles	Thousand miles
1921	3,160	2,925	203	—	2,722	235
1922	3,196	2,960	227	—	2,733	236
1923	3,233	2,996	252	—	2,744	237
1924	3,243	3,004	261	—	2,743	239
1925	3,246	3,006	275	—	2,731	240
1926	3,242	3,000	288	—	2,712	242
1927	3,257	3,013	293	—	2,720	244
1928	3,262	3,016	306	—	2,710	246
1929	3,272	3,024	314	—	2,710	248
1930	3,259	3,009	324	—	2,685	250
1931	3,291	3,036	329	45	2,662	255
1932	3,296	3,040	358	84	2,598	256
1933	3,286	3,029	346	135	2,548	257
1934	3,309	3,034	325	170	2,539	275 [3]
1935	3,310	3,032	332	173	2,527	278 [3]
1936	3,267	2,920	340	177	2,403	347
1937	3,245	2,894	327	189	2,378	351
1938	3,257	2,898	327	194	2,377	359
1939	3,274	2,913	328	194	2,391	361
1940	3,287	2,920	329	195	2,396	367
1941	3,309	2,926	332	196	2,398	383
1942	3,309	2,925	334	199	2,392	384
1943	3,311	2,930	333	200	2,397	381
1944	3,311	2,932	335	200	2,397	379
1945	3,319	2,939	339	202	2,398	380
1946	3,316	2,934	342	205	2,387	382
1947	3,326	2,933	337	212	2,384	393
1948	3,323	2,929	350	206	2,373	394
1949	3,322	2,934	358	206	2,370	388
1950	3,313	2,922	363	210	2,349	391
1951	3,326	2,925	367	217	2,341	401
1952	3,343	2,925	371	219	2,335	418
1953	3,366	2,925	377	214	2,334	441
1954	3,395	2,941	379	218	2,344	454
1955	3,418	2,954	387	222	2,345	464
1956	3,430	2,945	389	226	2,330	485
1957	3,453	2,952	391	232	2,329	501
1958	3,479	2,959	395	234	2,330	520
1959	3,511	2,974	403	237	2,334	537
1960	3,546	2,989	403	241	2,345	557
1961	3,573	2,995	406	243	2,346	578
1962	3,600	3,005	407	247	2,351	595
1963	3,620	3,002	409	247	2,346	618
1964	3,644	3,003	411	248	2,344	641
1965	3,690	3,009	414	249	2,346	681
1966	3,698	3,002	418	251	2,333	696
1967	3,707	2,996	424	251	2,321	711
1968	3,685	2,951	425	252	2,274	734
1969	3,710	2,954	406	273	2,275	756
1970	3,731	2,956	408	273	2,275	775
1971	3,759	2,939	408	275	2,256	820
1972	3,787	2,937	408	277	2,252	850
1973	3,808	2,932	410	273	2,249	876
1974	3,816	2,925	410	267	2,248	891
1975	3,838	2,941	412	268	2,261	897
1976	3,857	2,943	411	268	2,264	914
1977	3,865	2,908	402	271	2,235	957
1978	3,885	2,929	402	272	2,255	956
1979	3,918	2,947	405	261	2,281	971

Notes appear on next page

(continued)

TABLE Df187–192   Mileage of rural roads and municipal streets, by jurisdiction: 1921–1979   *Continued*

[1] Mileage not on state or county systems was first included in 1936 (67,000 miles). Mileage on local city streets was first included in 1941 (274,000 miles).

[2] Includes municipal extensions of county, town, and township roads prior to 1962.

[3] Represents only mileage on municipal extensions of state systems that are state administered.

Source

U.S. Federal Highway Administration, *Highway Statistics, Summary to 1985* (1987), Table M-200.

Documentation

Municipal roads are defined as those roads located in incorporated communities or delimited places generally having more than 1,000 inhabitants. Rural roads lie outside such communities. Municipal extensions are continuations of state system roads through communities with more than 1,000 inhabitants.

In 1980, Table M-200 in *Highway Statistics* was superseded by Table HM-210. See Table Df193–196.

Series Df192. Includes mileage in national and state parks, forest, reservations, and the like that did not form part of the state or local road systems.

TABLE Df193–196   Mileage of public roads and streets, by jurisdiction: 1921–1995[1]

Contributed by Louis P. Cain

Year	Total Df193 Thousand miles	State Df194 Thousand miles	Local, county, town, and municipal Df195 Thousand miles	Other Df196 Thousand miles	Year	Total Df193 Thousand miles	State Df194 Thousand miles	Local, county, town, and municipal Df195 Thousand miles	Other Df196 Thousand miles
1921	3,160	203	2,957	0	1960	3,546	694	2,725	127
1922	3,196	227	2,969	0	1961	3,573	703	2,738	132
1923	3,233	252	2,981	0	1962	3,600	710	2,750	140
1924	3,243	261	2,982	0	1963	3,620	715	2,762	143
1925	3,246	275	2,971	0	1964	3,644	721	2,773	150
1926	3,242	288	2,954	0	1965	3,690	728	2,788	174
1927	3,257	293	2,964	0	1966	3,698	735	2,777	186
1928	3,262	306	2,956	0	1967	3,707	744	2,774	189
1929	3,272	314	2,958	0	1968	3,685	747	2,737	201
1930	3,259	324	2,935	0	1969	3,710	751	2,751	208
1931	3,291	374	2,917	0	1970	3,731	755	2,762	214
1932	3,296	442	2,854	0	1971	3,759	760	2,772	227
1933	3,286	481	2,805	0	1972	3,787	765	2,785	237
1934	3,309	511	2,798	0	1973	3,808	765	2,799	244
1935	3,310	523	2,787	0	1974	3,816	761	2,802	253
1936	3,267	536	2,664	67	1975	3,838	764	2,816	258
1937	3,245	538	2,641	66	1976	3,857	766	2,825	266
1938	3,257	545	2,642	70	1977	3,865	759	2,835	271
1939	3,274	549	2,658	67	1978	3,885	761	2,862	262
1940	3,287	551	2,666	70	1979	3,918	752	2,889	277
1941	3,309	558	2,672	79	1980	3,860	848	2,764	248
1942	3,309	564	2,666	79	1981	3,852	849	2,750	253
1943	3,311	565	2,671	75	1982	3,866	848	2,755	263
1944	3,311	567	2,671	73	1983	3,880	847	2,760	272
1945	3,319	574	2,672	73	1984	3,891	870	2,755	267
1946	3,316	580	2,661	75	1985	3,864	859	2,778	227
1947	3,326	582	2,667	77	1986	3,878	797	2,849	232
1948	3,323	591	2,654	78	1987	3,874	799	2,863	212
1949	3,322	599	2,645	78	1988	3,871	799	2,883	189
1950	3,313	609	2,623	81	1989	3,877	804	2,894	179
1951	3,326	621	2,623	82	1990	3,867	798	2,889	179
1952	3,343	628	2,630	85	1991	3,884	798	2,908	178
1953	3,366	630	2,637	99	1992	3,901	800	2,918	183
1954	3,395	638	2,655	102	1993	3,905	800	2,924	181
1955	3,418	651	2,664	103	1994	3,907	800	2,931	175
1956	3,430	658	2,666	106	1995	3,912	803	2,937	172
1957	3,453	668	2,673	112					
1958	3,479	676	2,688	115					
1959	3,511	688	2,702	121					

[1] See text concerning changes to data series in 1980.

Source

U.S. Federal Highway Administration, *Highway Statistics, Summary to 1995* (1997), Table HM-210.

Documentation

These series reflect a format that was adopted in 1980. Prior to 1980, some miles of nonpublic roadways are included. These series are aggregated from data supplied by the individual states; some years contain Federal Highway Administration estimates for missing data. See Table Df187–192 for more detailed data on rural and municipal streets prior to 1980.

The data include Alaska and Hawai'i beginning in 1953.

Series Df194. Includes state highway agency roadways prior to 1980, and includes state park, state toll, and other state agency roadways beginning in 1980.

TABLE Df187–192   Mileage of public roads and streets, by jurisdiction: 1921–1995   *Continued*

Series Df195. Includes mileage not identified by ownership.
Series Df196. Includes mileage in federal parks, forests, and reservations

that are not part of the state and local highway systems; prior to 1980, state park, forest, and reservation roads were included.

TABLE Df197–207   Mileage of public roads and streets, by urban–rural location and surface type: 1941–1995

Contributed by Louis P. Cain

		Rural					Urban				
	Total	Total	Unpaved	Low and intermediate type	High-type flexible	Rigid	Total	Unpaved	Low and intermediate type	High-type flexible	Rigid
	Df197	Df198	Df199	Df200	Df201	Df202	Df203	Df204	Df205	Df206	Df207
Year	Thousand miles	Thousand miles	Thousand miles	Thousand miles	Thousand miles	Thousand miles	Thousand miles	Thousand miles	Thousand miles	Thousand miles	Thousand miles
1941	3,310	3,006	2,554	265	83	104	304	157	48	99	0
1942	3,308	3,004	2,545	271	84	104	305	157	48	100	0
1943	3,311	3,005	2,531	282	88	104	306	157	49	100	0
1944	3,311	3,005	2,526	286	91	102	306	157	49	100	0
1945	3,319	3,012	2,525	296	92	100	307	157	50	100	0
1946	3,317	3,009	2,509	305	95	99	307	157	50	100	0
1947	3,326	3,010	2,484	328	98	99	317	157	54	106	0
1948	3,323	3,007	2,462	345	104	96	316	151	57	107	0
1949	3,322	3,003	2,436	364	107	95	319	145	62	113	0
1950	3,313	2,990	2,395	339	162	93	323	138	68	118	0
1951	3,327	2,987	2,371	354	174	89	339	141	73	125	0
1952	3,343	2,994	2,349	376	183	86	350	140	78	132	0
1953	3,366	3,013	2,328	403	199	83	354	119	103	132	0
1954	3,395	3,030	2,321	417	212	79	365	119	110	135	0
1955	3,418	3,045	2,304	439	225	77	373	119	114	140	0
1956	3,430	3,051	2,270	454	247	80	378	119	113	90	56
1957	3,453	3,064	2,249	476	260	78	389	118	116	109	46
1958	3,479	3,074	2,224	498	281	71	405	116	126	94	68
1959	3,511	3,094	2,206	522	297	70	416	115	131	115	55
1960	3,546	3,116	2,197	539	312	68	430	118	133	118	60
1961	3,573	3,127	2,181	544	336	66	446	119	139	143	46
1962	3,600	3,144	2,167	555	359	64	455	118	141	152	43
1963	3,620	3,146	2,136	567	381	62	475	118	149	157	52
1964	3,644	3,153	2,118	574	398	62	491	119	152	172	48
1965	3,690	3,183	2,122	587	413	62	506	113	171	168	54
1966	3,698	3,188	2,104	596	427	61	510	113	168	176	53
1967	3,705	3,184	2,076	615	432	61	521	110	194	164	54
1968	3,684	3,152	2,016	632	444	61	532	95	204	175	58
1969	3,710	3,162	2,000	656	445	61	549	92	221	178	57
1970	3,730	3,169	1,981	669	459	60	561	90	227	188	55
1971	3,759	3,166	1,970	668	470	59	593	94	239	202	57
1972	3,787	3,173	1,956	671	489	58	613	94	246	216	58
1973	3,807	3,176	1,951	668	499	57	631	95	253	225	58
1974	3,816	3,178	1,906	693	522	56	638	92	255	232	59
1975	3,838	3,199	1,894	715	533	56	640	89	252	240	59
1976	3,857	3,209	1,884	718	550	56	648	86	252	250	60
1977	3,867	3,180	1,818	776	530	55	687	89	279	258	62
1978	3,885	3,190	1,784	803	547	56	694	90	275	264	64
1979	3,917	3,224	1,845	732	587	60	694	87	265	277	65
1980	3,860	3,231	1,741	810	610	69	629	46	231	284	68
1981	3,852	3,221	1,732	803	616	69	632	46	231	286	68
1982	3,866	3,225	1,804	768	586	67	641	45	236	290	70
1983	3,880	3,216	1,818	742	592	65	663	47	244	301	72
1984	3,891	3,216	1,708	795	654	58	676	44	246	317	68
1985	3,864	3,173	1,705	763	650	55	691	45	252	327	68
1986	3,878	3,177	1,678	769	674	55	701	42	255	336	68
1987	3,874	3,164	1,651	753	704	55	710	42	257	343	69
1988	3,871	3,131	1,628	730	719	54	740	44	270	358	69
1989	3,877	3,123	1,569	756	743	54	754	44	275	366	70
1990	3,867	3,122	1,572	753	742	55	745	40	272	364	69
1991	3,884	3,134	1,569	754	756	55	750	36	276	369	70
1992	3,901	3,116	1,561	740	761	54	785	37	286	389	72
1993	3,905	3,099	1,589	718	740	53	806	39	292	401	74
1994	3,907	3,093	1,531	748	760	53	814	33	295	410	75
1995	3,912	3,093	1,501	764	774	53	820	33	298	414	75

(continued)

TABLE Df197–207   Mileage of public roads and streets, by urban–rural location and surface type: 1941–1995
Continued

Source
U.S. Federal Highway Administration, *Highway Statistics, Summary to 1995* (1997), Table HM-212 (1997).

Documentation
These series reflect a format that was adopted in 1980. Prior to 1980, some miles of nonpublic roadways are included. These series are aggregated from data supplied by the individual states; some years contain Federal Highway Administration estimates for missing data.

Paved mileage includes the following categories: Low Type, an earth, gravel, or stone roadway that has a bituminous surface course less than 1 inch thick – suitable for occasional heavy loads; Intermediate Type, a mixed bituminous or bituminous penetration road on a flexible base having a combined surface and base thickness of less than 7 inches; High-Type Flexible, a mixed bituminous or bituminous penetration roadway on a flexible base having a combined surface and base thickness of 7 inches or more (also includes brick, block, or combination roadways after 1979); High-Type Composite (included with High-Type Flexible), a mixed bituminous or bituminous penetration roadway of more than 1 inch of compacted material on a rigid base with a combined surface and base thickness of 7 inches or more; High-Type Rigid, a Portland cement concrete roadway with or without a bituminous wearing surface of less than 1 inch (includes brick, block, or combination roadways prior to 1980).

TABLE Df208–212   Mileage built by state highway departments, by road type: 1923–1975
Contributed by Louis P. Cain

	Total	Roads under state control					Total	Roads under state control			
		Total	Earth roads	High-type surface	Low-type surface			Total	Earth roads	High-type surface	Low-type surface
	Df208	Df209	Df210	Df211	Df212		Df208	Df209	Df210	Df211	Df212
Year	Miles	Miles	Miles	Miles	Miles	Year	Miles	Miles	Miles	Miles	Miles
1923	—	20,311	5,814	5,628	8,869	1950	55,487	44,265	1,784	13,379	29,102
1924	—	23,164	5,957	6,697	10,510	1951	51,471	41,864	1,603	15,122	25,139
1925	—	23,152	5,316	6,686	11,150	1952	57,847	46,354	1,238	17,811	27,305
1926	—	26,552	7,060	6,132	13,360	1953	52,886	41,744	1,264	17,807	22,673
1927	—	26,723	7,151	6,733	12,839	1954	55,488	42,053	866	19,730	21,457
1928	—	29,252	8,675	8,748	11,829	1955	53,559	41,120	694	17,672	22,754
1929	—	32,522	7,451	8,847	16,224	1956	57,454	44,016	486	20,726	22,804
1930	—	35,277	7,813	10,787	16,677	1957	53,235	39,675	374	19,476	19,825
1931	—	44,634	10,095	12,513	22,026	1958	54,753	39,824	313	23,644	15,867
1932	—	35,971	6,394	10,009	19,568	1959	50,232	36,282	185	21,892	14,205
1933	—	33,471	6,258	7,412	19,801	1960	49,443	36,944	328	22,013	14,603
1934	41,730	41,730	5,917	6,386	29,427	1961	44,279	33,449	372	20,554	12,523
1935	26,814	26,814	3,284	3,806	19,724	1962	52,585	41,052	433	26,305	14,314
1936	32,274	32,274	3,361	4,706	24,207	1963	49,947	36,980	210	23,623	13,147
1937	35,627	28,945	1,828	6,532	20,585	1964	45,298	36,203	275	22,664	13,264
1938	36,322	34,598	1,187	5,751	27,660	1965	47,573	36,442	278	24,194	11,970
1939	32,990	30,665	1,720	5,015	23,930	1966	80,142	38,968	249	27,152	11,567
1940	32,588	29,689	1,423	5,217	23,049	1967	80,798	36,763	209	24,915	11,639
1941	32,629	30,549	1,343	6,299	22,907	1968	78,939	37,279	403	23,617	13,259
1942	19,670	18,078	1,038	4,167	12,873	1969	76,810	30,034	212	20,394	9,428
1943	15,971	14,692	458	4,446	9,788	1970	74,287	33,834	68	24,637	9,129
1944	15,080	13,924	289	3,925	9,710	1971	65,469	30,792	180	22,131	8,481
1945	15,278	14,827	250	3,971	10,606	1972	64,288	25,431	62	19,027	6,342
1946	21,711	20,856	417	4,898	15,541	1973	64,542	26,774	57	20,724	5,993
1947	32,865	29,574	1,013	6,219	22,342	1974	69,492	28,416	36	19,837	8,543
1948	41,968	35,085	1,403	7,753	25,929	1975	58,429	24,890	51	18,868	5,971
1949	45,171	35,236	1,517	7,482	26,237						

Source
U.S. Federal Highway Administration, *Highway Statistics, Summary to 1975* (1977), Table SMB-201.

Documentation
The source table includes both primary state highways and secondary roads under state control. The secondary road category includes local roads under state control in several states; see the notes to the source table.

Mileage built is mileage on which construction work creates a newly located road or is regarded as significantly improving the condition of an existing road. It does not include work designed to maintain or restore the condition of an existing road without material betterment. Mileage resurfaced or rebuilt to higher standards is the bulk of mileage built.

Construction of earth roads consists of aligning, grading, and draining. See the text for Table Df184–186 for a description of road types.

Series Df208–209. The difference between these series is a category titled "other roads" in the source table. It includes mileage of local roads and streets on the federal-aid secondary system that were built by the state highway department or by a local authority and financed partially or entirely out of federal funds. This number increases substantially in 1966. In *Historical Statistics of the United States* (1975), the equivalent of series Df208 (series Q59) excluded mileage built with any federal funding; therefore, the figures here for 1966–1970 are larger.

TABLE Df213–217   Mileage and cost of federal-aid highway systems, by federal and state funds: 1917–1975

Contributed by Louis P. Cain

	Miles of highway		Cost					Miles of highway		Cost		
	Total designated as part of federal systems	Completed during the year	Total	Federal funds	State funds			Total designated as part of federal systems	Completed during the year	Total	Federal funds	State funds
	Df213 [1]	Df214	Df215 [2]	Df216 [2]	Df217 [2]			Df213 [1]	Df214	Df215 [2]	Df216 [2]	Df217 [2]
Year(s)	Miles	Miles	Million dollars	Million dollars	Million dollars		Year(s)	Miles	Miles	Million dollars	Million dollars	Million dollars
1917–1921	—	12,919	222	95	127		1950	643,939	19,876	753	390	364
1922	—	11,188	186	80	106		1951	664,464	17,060	772	390	382
1923	169,007	7,494	130	57	73		1952	675,121	22,147	978	505	472
1924	174,507	10,946	205	93	112		1953	704,150	21,136	1,078	559	519
1925	179,501	11,001	221	100	121		1954	725,963	20,548	1,146	591	555
1926	184,162	10,703	215	93	122		1955	749,166	22,571	1,287	666	621
1927	187,035	10,220	189	84	105		1956	777,514	23,609	1,444	757	687
1928	188,017	9,756	196	83	113		1957	810,466	22,424	1,714	969	746
1929	189,853	8,581	197	80	117		1958	830,569	28,137	2,744	1,669	1,075
1930	193,652	10,339	237	100	137		1959	854,294	32,633	3,709	2,518	1,191
1931	198,967	15,902	325	228	97		1960	866,841	20,969	3,264	2,273	992
1932	205,025	10,855	205	95	110		1961	879,539	21,313	3,265	2,339	925
1933	207,194	18,219	264	223	41		1962	886,678	21,051	3,423	2,437	986
1934	212,496	21,203	358	311	47		1963	891,927	19,561	3,790	2,767	1,023
1935	219,869	12,811	242	218	24		1964	901,120	19,487	4,560	3,385	1,175
1936	224,450	12,258	238	225	13		1965	908,722	17,433	4,569	3,430	1,139
1937	226,829	21,330	521	348	173		1966	910,720	16,281	5,362	4,151	1,211
1938	229,905	11,766	309	183	125		1967	911,248	14,150	5,178	4,039	1,139
1939	232,834	11,776	306	176	130		1968	911,519	11,871	4,132	3,167	965
1940	235,482	11,549	269	150	119		1969	914,552	10,569	4,826	3,706	1,120
1941	316,432	9,734	274	148	126		1970	919,010	10,745	4,625	3,515	1,110
1942	330,051	6,898	226	143	83		1971	929,251	11,494	4,788	3,623	1,165
1943	338,705	7,753	273	219	54		1972	934,345	9,806	4,714	3,602	1,112
1944	367,690	4,473	135	109	26		1973	940,402	8,677	5,195	3,960	1,235
1945	308,741	3,035	101	76	25		1974	955,712	7,342	4,118	3,102	1,015
1946	556,787	5,057	147	86	61		1975	974,286	7,221	4,249	3,221	1,028
1947	599,338	15,473	422	224	198							
1948	611,332	21,725	763	397	366							
1949	632,037	19,876	829	425	404							

[1] Includes estimates on federal-aid secondary systems beginning in 1942 and national system of interstate and defense highways beginning in 1951.

[2] Beginning with 1935, includes money spent on public works and defense highways. Beginning with 1940, includes secondary highways.

Sources

Series Df213, U.S. Federal Highway Administration, *Highway Statistics, Summary to 1975* (1977), Table FM-210.

Series Df214–217, U.S. Federal Highway Administration, *Highway Statistics, Summary to 1965* (1967), Table Fa-2, and annual issues thereafter.

Documentation

In 1912, the Congress authorized $500,000 for an experimental program of rural post-road construction. However, it was not until the Federal-Aid Road Act of 1916 that the cooperative federal–state highway program was established on a continuing basis. To accelerate the improvement of the main traveled roads, Congress in 1921 authorized designation of a system of principal interstate and intercounty roads, limited to 7 percent of the total rural mileage then existing. The use of federal aid was restricted to this system and to rural mileage only.

Urban highway improvement first came in for its share of the federal–state program when the Federal-Aid Highway Act of 1944 specifically authorized the use of funds for federal-aid highways in urban areas. In addition, the Act provided for the designation of a federal-aid secondary system and a National System of Interstate Highways. The Federal-Aid Highway Act of 1956 provided substantially increased sums for the federal-aid primary and secondary systems for a three-year period and established a long-range plan for financing accelerated completion of the 41,000-mile interstate system.

Federal funds were available for expenditure only on the designated federal-aid systems and, in general, had to be matched by an equal amount of state funds. However, under the Federal-Aid Highway Act of 1954 the federal share for the Interstate System was raised to 60 percent, and under the 1956 Act the proportion was increased to 90 percent. Federal aid could not be expended for maintenance. The cost of most federal-aid projects was paid initially out of state highway funds, or in some cases by counties or other local governments. The federal share was paid as reimbursement to the states as work progressed, with final payment made after completion.

Federal authorizations usually were made on a biennial basis and apportioned among the states for use within a three-year period. Figures for state funds shown here are based on legal matching ratios determined by applicable federal-aid acts. In states having public lands in excess of 5 percent of their total area, the federal share was proportionally increased.

Series Df213. Includes estimates on federal-aid primary system throughout. The estimates are as of the end of the calendar year.

Series Df214. Includes both new and rebuilt mileage.

Series Df215–217. Reports actual expenditures of funds on a calendar-year basis.

TABLE Df218-224   Highway construction contracts awarded, by jurisdiction: 1947-1979

Contributed by Louis P. Cain

Year	Highways			Federally aided projects		Independent state projects	
	Total	Federally owned	State-owned	Total value	Federal funds	Total value	Total facilities
	Df218 [1]	Df219	Df220	Df221	Df222	Df223	Df224
	Million dollars	Million dollars	Million dollars	Million dollars	Million dollars	Million dollars	Million dollars
1947	917	25	892	635	329	257	—
1948	1,436	28	1,145	740	386	405	46
1949	1,448	47	1,150	643	332	507	120
1950	1,528	36	1,492	798	415	694	228
1951	1,743	71	1,362	780	409	582	68
1952	2,088	90	1,654	912	476	743	146
1953	2,713	53	2,287	998	519	1,289	800
1954	2,746	62	2,300	1,218	630	1,082	459
1955	2,619	59	2,560	1,256	667	1,304	695
1956	3,303	92	2,718	1,737	963	981	337
1957	3,917	92	3,311	2,390	1,614	921	343
1958	4,585	96	3,996	3,489	2,504	507	44
1959	3,805	86	3,213	2,638	1,877	575	59
1960	4,030	129	3,901	3,097	2,218	804	165
1961	4,482	92	3,803	3,168	2,289	634	92
1962	4,336	95	4,241	3,253	2,506	988	326
1963	4,418	142	4,275	3,730	2,770	546	27
1964	4,868	123	4,745	4,055	3,084	690	82
1965	4,935	135	4,800	3,896	2,976	904	49
1966	5,459	127	5,332	4,173	3,131	1,159	99
1967	5,522	78	5,444	4,112	3,077	1,332	213
1968	5,305	84	5,220	3,711	2,766	1,510	63
1969	6,625	38	6,587	5,048	3,784	1,539	78
1970	6,520	52	6,468	4,877	3,619	1,591	49
1971	6,327	170	6,156	4,595	3,422	1,561	159
1972	6,505	206	6,299	4,876	3,598	1,423	99
1973	6,516	116	6,400	4,554	3,342	1,846	146
1974	7,313	158	7,154	5,256	4,222	1,898	13
1975	7,363	176	7,188	5,967	4,824	1,221	11
1976	6,205	168	6,037	5,030	4,004	1,007	35
1977	7,792	250	7,542	6,169	4,968	1,372	21
1978	9,141	256	8,885	6,843	5,488	2,042	13
1979	10,931	298	10,634	8,592	7,057	2,041	31

[1] Includes local from 1948 to 1961, except 1950, 1955, and 1960. Details do not sum to total in years that include local highways.

Source

U.S. Bureau of Domestic Commerce, *Construction Review* (various issues), Table D-2.

Documentation

This table covers federal- and state-owned highways only. It includes force-account construction authorized to start.

Highways include streets, roads, alleys, bridges, vehicular tunnels, viaducts, sidewalks, curbs, and gutters, except when installed by private builders as a part of land development; forest and park roads; new culverts and extension of old culverts; right-of-way drainage, erosion control, lighting, and guard rails; and earthwork protective structures in connection with road improvements.

The data for state- and locally owned highways were compiled by the Bureau of Domestic Commerce (formerly the Business and Defense Services Administration), Department of Commerce, from: (1) information published by a number of private construction news services; (2) information received from selected state and local government agencies; and (3) data compiled by the Bureau of Public Roads (now the Federal Highway Administration) and the Bureau of Labor Statistics (BLS).

Data on contracts awarded for federal-owned construction projects were compiled by the BLS from reports submitted by the various federal agencies having construction operations.

TABLE Df225–242   Federal government highway finance – revenues and disbursements, by fund: 1921–1995

Contributed by Louis P. Cain

	Revenues									
	Highway trust fund					Other funds				
	Total funds available	Motor-fuel and vehicle taxes	Investment income and other receipts	Intergovernmental payments	Funds drawn from reserves	Total funds available	Motor-fuel and vehicle taxes	Investment income and other receipts	Intergovernmental payments	Funds drawn from reserves
	Df225	Df226	Df227	Df228	Df229	Df230	Df231	Df232	Df233	Df234
Year	Million dollars	Million dollars	Million dollars	Million dollars	Million dollars	Million dollars	Million dollars	Million dollars	Million dollars	Million dollars
1921	—	—	—	—	—	6	92	0	−86	0
1922	—	—	—	—	—	5	80	0	−75	0
1923	—	—	—	—	—	10	85	0	−75	0
1924	—	—	—	—	—	11	109	0	−98	0
1925	—	—	—	—	—	11	103	0	−92	0
1926	—	—	—	—	—	14	91	0	−77	0
1927	—	—	—	—	—	10	90	0	−80	0
1928	—	—	—	—	—	16	97	0	−81	0
1929	—	—	—	—	—	13	89	0	−76	0
1930	—	—	—	—	—	14	112	0	−98	0
1931	—	—	—	—	—	27	272	0	−245	0
1932	—	—	—	—	—	18	154	0	−136	0
1933	—	—	—	—	—	80	283	0	−203	0
1934	—	—	—	—	—	384	739	4	−359	0
1935	—	—	—	—	—	256	474	4	−222	0
1936	—	—	—	—	—	687	1,040	0	−353	0
1937	—	—	—	—	—	483	753	0	−270	0
1938	—	—	—	—	—	853	1,057	0	−204	0
1939	—	—	—	—	—	707	926	0	−219	0
1940	—	—	—	—	—	548	751	0	−203	0
1941	—	—	—	—	—	382	553	0	−171	0
1942	—	—	—	—	—	233	393	1	−161	0
1943	—	—	—	—	—	40	196	2	−158	0
1944	—	—	—	—	—	23	115	2	−94	0
1945	—	—	—	—	—	23	90	0	−67	0
1946	—	—	—	—	—	28	180	0	−152	0
1947	—	—	—	—	—	46	338	0	−292	0
1948	—	—	—	—	—	47	417	0	−370	0
1949	—	—	—	—	—	65	504	0	−439	0
1950	—	—	—	—	—	62	490	0	−428	0
1951	—	—	—	—	—	58	486	0	−428	0
1952	—	—	—	—	—	69	562	0	−493	0
1953	—	—	—	—	—	82	649	0	−567	0
1954	—	—	—	—	—	84	690	0	−606	0
1955	—	—	—	—	—	89	783	0	−694	0
1956	—	—	—	—	—	97	396	0	−299	0
1957	17	1,467	3	−937	−516	124	178	0	−54	0
1958	20	2,009	18	−1,475	−532	139	194	0	−55	0
1959	30	2,066	14	−2,575	525	120	182	0	−62	0
1960	27	2,534	−3	−2,908	404	170	240	0	−70	0
1961	30	2,793	1	−2,584	−180	165	240	0	−75	0
1962	31	2,945	7	−2,749	−172	193	266	0	−73	0
1963	38	3,273	14	−2,973	−276	198	304	0	−106	0
1964	45	3,512	20	−3,593	106	190	316	0	−126	0
1965	55	3,651	11	−3,963	356	183	291	0	−108	0
1966	46	3,909	7	−3,911	41	304	470	0	−166	0
1967	55	4,433	14	−3,910	−482	306	514	0	−208	0
1968	62	4,386	34	−4,101	−257	302	522	0	−220	0
1969	65	4,632	53	−4,081	−539	283	574	0	−291	0
1970	83	5,349	115	−4,290	−1,091	342	696	0	−354	0
1971	94	5,536	184	−4,585	−1,041	395	746	0	−351	0
1972	170	5,315	206	−4,513	−838	351	697	0	−346	0
1973	175	5,657	247	−4,628	−1,101	331	1,030	0	−699	0
1974	218	6,252	415	−4,373	−2,076	308	1,232	0	−924	0

(continued)

TABLE Df225–242   Federal government highway finance – revenues and disbursements, by fund: 1921–1995
Continued

Revenues

	Highway trust fund					Other funds				
	Total funds available	Motor-fuel and vehicle taxes	Investment income and other receipts	Intergovernmental payments	Funds drawn from reserves	Total funds available	Motor-fuel and vehicle taxes	Investment income and other receipts	Intergovernmental payments	Funds drawn from reserves
	Df225	Df226	Df227	Df228	Df229	Df230	Df231	Df232	Df233	Df234
Year	Million dollars	Million dollars	Million dollars	Million dollars	Million dollars	Million dollars	Million dollars	Million dollars	Million dollars	Million dollars
1975	237	6,168	586	−4,586	−1,931	372	1,374	0	−1,002	0
1976 [1]	277	7,055	600	−7,967	589	422	1,465	0	−1,043	0
1977	240	6,690	593	−5,888	−1,155	480	1,715	0	−1,235	0
1978	269	6,876	662	−5,761	−1,508	522	1,993	0	−1,471	0
1979	277	7,144	857	−6,832	−892	648	2,544	0	−1,896	0
1980	315	6,588	1,027	−8,865	1,565	559	2,334	0	−1,775	0
1981	306	6,271	1,129	−8,834	1,740	879	2,789	0	−1,910	0
1982	238	6,710	1,079	−7,763	212	720	2,379	0	−1,659	0
1983	253	7,747	1,076	−8,555	−15	617	2,192	0	−1,575	0
1984	359	10,463	1,027	−9,981	−1,150	601	2,256	0	−1,655	0
1985	384	11,736	1,106	−12,308	−150	542	2,055	0	−1,513	0
1986	446	12,198	1,054	−13,681	875	471	1,891	0	−1,419	−1
1987	396	11,727	934	−12,340	75	499	1,624	0	−1,125	0
1988	364	12,764	809	−13,602	393	536	1,476	0	−940	0
1989	352	14,298	776	−13,190	−1,532	321	988	0	−667	0
1990	358	12,399	981	−13,944	922	306	1,196	0	−890	0
1991	363	14,398	810	−14,227	−618	293	1,145	0	−852	0
1992	421	15,571	908	−15,004	−1,054	295	1,386	0	−1,091	0
1993	788	15,892	817	−15,698	−223	312	1,154	0	−841	−1
1994	965	15,828	754	−17,623	2,006	341	1,272	0	−932	1
1995	1,033	18,285	548	−17,895	95	188	1,045	0	−858	1

Disbursements

	Highway trust fund				Other funds			
	Total	Capital outlay	Maintenance and traffic services	Administration and research	Total	Capital outlay	Maintenance and traffic services	Administration and research
	Df235	Df236	Df237	Df238	Df239	Df240	Df241	Df242
Year	Million dollars	Million dollars	Million dollars	Million dollars	Million dollars	Million dollars	Million dollars	Million dollars
1921	—	—	—	—	6	5	0	1
1922	—	—	—	—	5	4	0	1
1923	—	—	—	—	10	8	0	2
1924	—	—	—	—	11	9	0	2
1925	—	—	—	—	11	9	0	2
1926	—	—	—	—	14	12	0	2
1927	—	—	—	—	10	8	0	2
1928	—	—	—	—	16	14	0	2
1929	—	—	—	—	13	11	0	2
1930	—	—	—	—	14	12	0	2
1931	—	—	—	—	27	24	0	3
1932	—	—	—	—	18	15	0	3
1933	—	—	—	—	80	77	0	3
1934	—	—	—	—	384	376	2	6
1935	—	—	—	—	256	252	1	3
1936	—	—	—	—	687	680	2	5
1937	—	—	—	—	483	478	2	3
1938	—	—	—	—	853	849	2	2
1939	—	—	—	—	707	702	2	3

Notes appear at end of table

TABLE Df225–242   Federal government highway finance – revenues and disbursements, by fund: 1921–1995
Continued

	Disbursements							
	Highway trust fund				Other funds			
	Total	Capital outlay	Maintenance and traffic services	Administration and research	Total	Capital outlay	Maintenance and traffic services	Administration and research
	Df235	Df236	Df237	Df238	Df239	Df240	Df241	Df242
Year	Million dollars	Million dollars	Million dollars	Million dollars	Million dollars	Million dollars	Million dollars	Million dollars
1940	—	—	—	—	548	544	1	3
1941	—	—	—	—	382	378	1	3
1942	—	—	—	—	233	230	1	2
1943	—	—	—	—	40	38	1	1
1944	—	—	—	—	23	17	1	5
1945	—	—	—	—	23	17	1	5
1946	—	—	—	—	28	20	1	7
1947	—	—	—	—	46	34	4	8
1948	—	—	—	—	47	34	5	8
1949	—	—	—	—	65	50	5	10
1950	—	—	—	—	62	45	6	11
1951	—	—	—	—	58	41	6	11
1952	—	—	—	—	69	50	7	12
1953	—	—	—	—	82	63	7	12
1954	—	—	—	—	84	65	7	12
1955	—	—	—	—	89	70	7	12
1956	—	—	—	—	97	77	8	12
1957	17	1	0	16	124	99	24	1
1958	20	0	0	20	139	113	24	2
1959	30	1	0	29	120	94	25	1
1960	27	1	0	26	170 [2]	135	27	4
1961	30	1	0	29	165	133	28	4
1962	31	0	0	31	193	160	29	4
1963	38	1	0	37	198	183	12	3
1964	45	2	0	43	190	171	15	4
1965	55	7	0	48	183	162	18	3
1966	46	2	0	44	304	246	52	6
1967	55	3	0	52	306	241	51	14
1968	62	3	0	59	302	230	42	30
1969	65	1	0	64	283	210	44	29
1970	83	2	0	81	342	251	50	41
1971	94	5	0	89	395	281	56	58
1972	170	28	0	142	351	271	49	31
1973	175	22	0	153	331	247	57	27
1974	218	26	0	192	308	231	70	7
1975	237	30	0	207	372	277	89	6
1976 [1]	277	36	0	241	422	305	98	19
1977	240	27	0	213	480	369	93	18
1978	269	21	0	248	522	400	113	9
1979	277	23	0	254	648	506	127	15
1980	315	48	0	267	559	408	130	21
1981	306	45	0	261	879	706	127	46
1982	238	29	0	209	720	489	147	84
1983	253	53	0	200	617	415	133	69
1984	359	116	0	243	601	400	140	61
1985	384	135	0	249	542	334	140	68
1986	446	135	0	311	471	267	134	70
1987	396	134	0	262	499	271	151	77
1988	364	131	0	233	536	300	158	78
1989	352	125	0	227	321	109	102	110
1990	358	128	0	230	306	99	101	106
1991	363	126	0	237	293	110	73	110
1992	421	124	0	297	295	96	74	125
1993	788	168	0	620	312	170	68	74
1994	965	322	0	643	341	106	71	164
1995	1,033	392	2	639	188	40	69	79

Notes appear on next page

(continued)

TABLE Df225–242   Federal government highway finance – revenues and disbursements, by fund: 1921–1995
Continued

[1] Includes federal fiscal year transition quarter.

[2] Includes interest on debt ($4 million) that is not reported elsewhere.

Source
U.S. Federal Highway Administration, *Highway Statistics, Summary to 1995
1997)*, Table HF-210.

Documentation
Congress first authorized federal funds for highways in 1912 when $500,000
was allocated for an experimental rural post-road program. The Federal-Aid
Road Act of 1916 established the present program of federal–state cooperation on a continuing basis. In 1921, Congress authorized the creation of the
Federal-Aid Primary System, a system of principal and intercounty roads that
would be classified as "arterials" today. The system was limited to 7 percent
of the total rural mileage in each state. Federal aid was restricted to roads
in that system and only to rural mileage until 1933 when, as an emergency
measure, the program was extended to include extensions of such roads into
and through municipalities. Urban improvements received a specific share
of federal-aid funds in 1944.

That 1944 legislation also created the Federal-Aid Secondary System,
roads that would be classified as "major collectors" today, and a National
System of Interstate and Defense Highways, which was to be part of the
Federal-Aid Primary System. The Federal-Aid Highway Act of 1956 (and the
Highway Revenue Act of the same year) refined the purpose and extent of
the Interstate System and through various amendments provided funds for
its completion. Funds for the Interstate System were matched on the basis
of 90 percent federal for 10 percent state, with the federal share increased in
proportion to the federal land area to total area in each state. The Federal-
Aid Highway Act of 1970 created the Federal-Aid Urban System to serve
major centers of activity. Federal-Aid System funds were matched on a 75
percent federal to 25 percent state basis.

The federal-aid highway system is a federally assisted, state-administered
program. States develop the plans, let the contracts, and supervise the construction. Highways remain under the administrative control of the state or
local governments, which are responsible for their maintenance. The program is financed through motor-fuel and other highway-related excise taxes.
These monies are deposited in the Federal Highway Trust Fund (HTF), which

was created by the Highway Revenue Act of 1956. Beginning in April 1983,
one cent per gallon of motor-fuel taxes was deposited in the Mass Transit
Account within the HTF to cover the cost of transit system capital expenditures.

The Federal-Aid Highway Act of 1976 addressed the problem that many
highways were deteriorating. Up until that time, federal funds were generally
limited to new construction. That Act allocated funds for 3R-work (resurfac-
ing, restoration, and rehabilitation). The Surface Transportation Assistance
Act (STAA) of 1978 amended the Primary and Secondary programs to require 3R-work. The Urban program was brought in with the STAA of 1982.
The Federal-Aid Highway Act of 1981, which significantly increased funding,
defined 4R-work by adding reconstruction.

The Intermodal Surface Transportation Efficiency Act of 1991 (ISTEA)
replaced the federal-aid systems with the National Highway System (NHS),
which includes the Interstate System, most of the urban and rural principal
arterials, the Strategic Highway Network, and major connectors. 3R-work is
now funded under the Interstate Maintenance (IM) program with a federal
share of 90 percent. ISTEA also created the Surface Transportation Program
(STP), which provides flexible funding for roads and streets above the class
of "minor collector" and for bridges on any public road.

Other federal highway funds include the Mass Transit Account of the
HTF, Federal Highway Administration activities funded by general funds and
all other agencies, and funds that make appropriations for highways or that
receive highway-user revenues.

HTF data are based on the federal fiscal year.

Series Df225–229. It should be noted that the data reported in *Highway
Statistics – Summary to 1985* were on a calendar-year basis.

Series Df225–229 and Df235–238. The data in this table for 1956 reflect
general fund expenditures on a calendar-year basis, the majority of which
occurred prior to the creation of the HTF on July 1. Hence, those series begin
in 1957.

Series Df229 and Df234. A negative number indicates that funds were
placed in reserve.

TABLE Df243–256 State government highway finance – revenues, disbursements, and debt outstanding: 1890–1995[1]

Contributed by Louis P. Cain

	Revenues								Disbursements					
	Highway user revenue									For state-administered highways				
Year	Total	Total	Motor-fuel taxes	Motor vehicle and carrier taxes	Other	From federal funds	From issue of bonds, notes, etc.	Other	Total	Capital outlay for roads and bridges	Maintenance	Other	For county and local roads and streets	State highway debt outstanding
	Df243	Df244	Df245	Df246	Df247	Df248	Df249	Df250	Df251	Df252	Df253	Df254	Df255	Df256
	Million dollars	Million dollars	Million dollars	Million dollars	Million dollars	Million dollars	Million dollars	Million dollars	Million dollars	Million dollars	Million dollars	Million dollars	Million dollars	Million dollars
1890	—	—	—	—	—	—	—	—	—	—	—	—	—	(Z)
1891	—	—	—	—	—	—	—	—	—	—	—	—	—	(Z)
1892	—	—	—	—	—	—	—	—	—	—	—	—	—	(Z)
1893	—	—	—	—	—	—	—	—	—	—	—	—	—	0.5
1894	—	—	—	—	—	—	—	—	—	—	—	—	—	1.3
1895	—	—	—	—	—	—	—	—	—	—	—	—	—	2.6
1896	—	—	—	—	—	—	—	—	—	—	—	—	—	6.7
1897	—	—	—	—	—	—	—	—	—	—	—	—	—	8.2
1898	—	—	—	—	—	—	—	—	—	—	—	—	—	10.0
1899	—	—	—	—	—	—	—	—	—	—	—	—	—	12.2
1900	—	—	—	—	—	—	—	—	—	—	—	—	—	12.7
1901	—	—	—	—	—	—	—	—	—	—	—	—	—	13.1
1902	—	—	—	—	—	—	—	—	—	—	—	—	—	14.0
1903	—	—	—	—	—	—	—	—	—	—	—	—	—	14.5
1904	—	—	—	—	—	—	—	—	—	—	—	—	—	15.0
1905	—	—	—	—	—	—	—	—	—	—	—	—	—	15.4
1906	—	—	—	—	—	—	—	—	—	—	—	—	—	16.4
1907	—	—	—	—	—	—	—	—	—	—	—	—	—	18.4
1908	—	—	—	—	—	—	—	—	—	—	—	—	—	24.4
1909	—	—	—	—	—	—	—	—	—	—	—	—	—	31.6
1910	—	—	—	—	—	—	—	—	—	—	—	—	—	38.3
1911	—	—	—	—	—	—	—	—	—	—	—	—	—	52.4
1912	—	—	—	—	—	—	—	—	—	—	—	—	—	65.6
1913	—	—	—	—	—	—	—	—	—	—	—	—	—	94.2
1914	75.0	12.3	—	12.3	26.1	—	11.6	25.1	75.0	53.8	14.5	5.2	1.8	105.4
1915	90.0	18.2	—	18.2	20.1	—	25.3	27.0	88.0	55.9	19.2	5.8	7.5	130.2
1916	87.0	25.8	—	25.8	23.0	—	4.8	33.5	85.1	49.8	18.4	6.7	10.2	134.4
1917	116.0	37.5	—	37.5	6.3	—	21.6	50.8	113.2	61.6	27.6	10.2	14.1	154.0
1918	139.0	51.4	—	51.4	30.2	2.1	7.0	48.8	134.5	71.9	34.9	13.5	14.7	159.5
1919	221.0	65.7	1.0	64.6	27.7	11.7	34.3	81.7	216.1	124.9	53.0	19.2	19.0	191.4
1920	358.0	102.9	1.3	101.5	97.5	61.9	38.2	57.4	353.8	240.3	58.4	25.4	29.6	225.4
1921	425.9	123.5	4.1	119.4	69.7	77.7	114.8	40.1	437.1	300.6	64.8	41.9	29.8	372.9
1922	535.6	144.0	7.2	136.7	65.9	79.7	143.0	103.0	485.1	287.5	75.3	54.3	68.0	473.2
1923	507.1	202.5	24.3	178.2	62.5	73.3	88.2	80.6	487.6	280.0	75.3	74.4	57.8	565.5
1924	614.6	281.8	67.6	214.3	39.5	93.0	101.7	98.7	668.0	397.6	104.8	89.9	75.6	678.3
1925	764.3	386.8	138.8	248.0	56.2	93.3	141.4	86.5	740.6	403.8	119.3	116.0	101.5	789.3
1926	802.9	453.5	183.8	269.6	49.3	79.2	137.8	83.2	724.0	366.0	125.8	116.6	115.6	933.1
1927	855.4	535.9	252.9	283.0	52.0	80.2	91.0	96.4	823.8	418.8	139.1	129.4	136.5	1,085.9
1928	970.5	599.3	295.4	303.9	57.6	81.3	133.5	98.9	956.2	558.5	160.3	96.3	141.1	1,187.8
1929	1,177.1	746.6	420.3	326.3	75.8	78.0	191.2	85.5	1,057.0	575.5	173.6	136.9	171.0	1,439.0

Notes appear at end of table

(continued)

TABLE Df243–256 State government highway finance – revenues, disbursements, and debt outstanding: 1890–1995 Continued

	Revenues							Disbursements					State highway debt outstanding
	Total	Highway user revenue			From federal funds	From issue of bonds, notes, etc.	Other	Total	For state-administered highways			For county and local roads and streets	
		Total	Motor-fuel taxes	Motor vehicle and carrier taxes	Other						Capital outlay for roads and bridges	Maintenance	Other		
Year	Df243	Df244	Df245	Df246	Df247	Df248	Df249	Df250	Df251	Df252	Df253	Df254	Df255	Df256
	Million dollars	Million dollars	Million dollars	Million dollars	Million dollars	Million dollars	Million dollars	Million dollars	Million dollars	Million dollars	Million dollars	Million dollars	Million dollars	Million dollars
1930	1,256.9	810.7	478.3	332.4	55.2	94.1	222.3	74.6	1,290.5	728.9	193.9	167.2	200.5	1,572.5
1931	1,343.8	835.6	516.3	319.3	47.6	218.4	174.8	67.4	1,344.7	796.9	162.9	167.3	217.6	1,879.8
1932	1,072.4	741.6	464.3	277.4	48.4	138.9	104.7	38.8	1,135.7	571.1	178.2	190.1	196.3	2,038.5
1933	1,064.3	697.9	458.1	239.8	43.7	223.6	79.8	19.2	1,094.5	529.3	179.3	189.0	196.8	2,108.8
1934	1,237.5	732.6	472.2	260.4	27.6	354.8	103.1	19.5	1,169.4	580.4	181.5	191.2	216.4	2,114.8
1935	1,151.7	761.5	500.0	261.6	24.9	219.4	117.2	28.7	1,078.6	438.3	187.1	219.9	233.2	2,169.3
1936	1,383.6	850.7	557.4	293.3	25.3	349.7	134.2	23.6	1,367.5	631.8	222.0	256.4	257.3	2,210.4
1937	1,429.7	990.5	640.8	349.8	30.3	264.1	111.6	33.2	1,395.4	589.2	223.8	270.7	311.7	2,243.6
1938	1,376.8	974.3	640.9	333.4	33.5	197.7	146.0	25.4	1,418.1	558.4	232.6	332.2	294.9	2,250.2
1939	1,385.0	1,000.8	673.3	327.5	34.1	203.8	120.2	26.0	1,380.6	500.1	211.9	338.9	329.7	2,177.9
1940	1,537.2	1,077.8	715.1	362.7	38.2	196.1	202.3	22.8	1,432.7	563.1	218.8	322.5	328.4	2,159.0
1941	1,634.5	1,187.4	786.7	400.7	45.7	168.9	204.9	27.6	1,624.8	525.2	234.8	511.0	353.8	2,069.6
1942	1,322.0	1,071.2	706.3	364.8	44.5	154.9	33.0	18.3	1,242.0	401.7	216.7	269.0	354.6	1,962.1
1943	1,225.4	917.7	555.0	362.7	56.4	152.2	83.9	15.2	1,112.1	268.7	224.9	307.8	310.7	1,869.6
1944	1,178.0	953.8	591.7	362.2	44.4	91.9	72.2	15.7	1,058.9	210.3	259.0	294.6	295.1	1,794.5
1945	1,299.8	1,086.4	705.4	381.0	87.2	60.0	47.6	18.6	1,152.3	210.5	287.7	346.9	307.2	1,637.9
1946	1,954.8	1,449.7	979.3	470.4	176.5	147.2	150.0	31.3	1,635.2	502.3	327.3	407.7	397.9	1,571.6
1947	2,100.3	1,594.0	1,096.5	497.8	91.6	288.3	89.3	37.0	2,138.2	882.4	374.5	347.0	534.3	1,536.9
1948	2,676.9	1,807.7	1,250.8	556.9	144.2	364.9	312.8	47.4	2,600.4	1,138.7	465.6	347.7	648.4	1,735.4
1949	3,017.3	2,075.4	1,390.9	684.5	153.0	429.2	303.2	56.5	2,941.2	1,362.0	488.0	361.7	729.5	1,928.3
1950	3,287.4	2,270.1	1,536.9	733.1	116.1	425.6	410.1	65.6	3,235.8	1,533.9	501.5	453.2	747.2	2,141.1
1951	3,664.1	2,483.4	1,684.3	799.1	150.9	415.6	536.9	77.2	3,594.5	1,739.6	562.3	490.4	802.2	2,475.8
1952	4,326.0	2,771.3	1,881.6	889.7	182.1	485.3	798.6	88.7	3,922.0	1,941.9	602.6	479.0	898.7	3,116.1
1953	4,969.1	2,997.5	2,045.7	951.9	203.8	540.9	1,101.5	125.4	4,452.5	2,271.4	620.4	572.5	988.1	4,015.5
1954	6,502.6	3,238.4	2,185.2	1,053.2	220.3	587.9	2,338.0	118.1	5,307.4	2,962.6	647.8	660.9	1,036.2	6,164.0
1955	5,355.8	3,577.8	2,427.8	1,150.0	292.9	670.3	658.2	156.7	5,595.8	3,103.0	675.6	695.0	1,122.3	6,618.5
1956	6,293.6	3,903.3	2,652.8	1,250.5	389.1	775.7	1,064.6	160.9	6,402.0	3,662.0	756.5	757.4	1,226.2	7,495.9
1957	6,567.0	4,056.1	2,771.4	1,284.7	345.3	1,256.0	727.2	182.5	7,200.6	4,139.3	812.4	914.6	1,334.2	7,945.2
1958	7,939.3	4,192.3	2,862.8	1,329.5	387.7	2,246.8	916.1	196.4	7,962.9	4,713.6	867.1	970.7	1,411.4	8,605.0
1959	8,876.1	4,422.1	3,052.8	1,369.3	469.5	3,059.0	722.9	202.6	8,609.7	5,075.9	903.1	1,135.7	1,495.1	9,008.2
1960	8,679.4	4,724.6	3,258.9	1,465.7	519.1	2,521.5	707.3	207.0	8,358.4	4,669.3	985.6	1,167.3	1,536.2	9,383.0
1961	9,095.2	4,861.1	3,375.4	1,485.7	577.2	2,729.5	709.6	217.8	8,967.8	5,105.1	1,019.8	1,214.1	1,628.8	9,783.6
1962	9,996.1	5,147.9	3,590.6	1,557.3	605.2	2,933.1	1,077.9	231.9	9,743.4	5,608.4	1,093.3	1,378.3	1,663.4	10,472.1
1963	10,303.3	5,356.1	3,732.8	1,623.3	603.5	3,499.5	611.2	233.0	10,458.4	6,047.8	1,133.9	1,514.2	1,762.5	10,596.3
1964	11,426.5	5,688.6	3,977.0	1,711.6	670.0	4,000.7	783.7	283.5	11,075.7	6,362.4	1,210.3	1,592.5	1,910.6	10,930.7
1965	11,562.3	6,068.6	4,258.7	1,809.9	744.8	3,862.5	591.1	295.3	11,469.7	6,458.2	1,309.8	1,696.4	2,005.2	11,058.8
1966	13,217.5	6,577.5	4,494.2	2,083.3	755.2	4,229.7	1,295.3	359.7	12,548.3	7,056.4	1,402.3	1,904.1	2,185.6	11,813.9
1967	13,161.9	6,886.9	4,758.1	2,128.8	813.3	4,001.3	1,011.4	449.0	13,317.2	7,339.8	1,513.5	2,147.4	2,316.5	12,177.5
1968	14,563.7	7,426.5	5,122.8	2,303.7	921.6	4,431.0	1,374.7	409.8	14,252.6	7,866.4	1,593.7	2,319.7	2,472.9	12,903.3
1969	15,293.8	8,238.5	5,687.2	2,551.3	1,009.3	4,190.2	1,421.2	434.6	14,915.8	7,876.1	1,723.2	2,685.0	2,631.5	13,514.3
1970	16,501.5	8,843.1	6,091.0	2,752.2	1,175.1	4,737.2	1,301.6	444.5	16,532.6	8,866.0	1,928.8	2,821.7	2,916.0	14,020.1
1971	18,524.5	9,156.0	6,342.1	2,813.9	1,117.8	5,123.5	2,638.9	488.3	17,748.6	9,416.7	2,086.9	3,182.0	3,063.0	15,850.6
1972	18,887.5	10,236.1	7,104.3	3,131.8	1,210.3	4,848.7	2,080.0	512.6	18,174.5	9,383.9	2,236.2	3,333.1	3,221.4	17,119.7
1973	18,890.7	11,151.2	7,827.9	3,323.3	1,315.9	4,585.3	1,213.9	624.3	18,795.2	8,981.5	2,458.3	3,776.9	3,578.5	17,462.3
1974	19,407.1	11,217.0	7,731.0	3,486.0	1,473.7	5,068.4	881.4	766.6	19,694.8	9,390.8	2,656.4	3,938.9	3,708.7	17,631.2

Year	Revenues							Disbursements					
	Total	Highway user revenue			From federal funds	From issue of bonds, notes, etc.	Other	Total	For state-administered highways			For county and local roads and streets	State highway debt outstanding
		Total	Motor-fuel taxes	Motor vehicle and carrier taxes	Other					Capital outlay for roads and bridges	Maintenance	Other		
	Df243	Df244	Df245	Df246	Df247	Df248	Df249	Df250	Df251	Df252	Df253	Df254	Df255	Df256
	Million dollars	Million dollars	Million dollars	Million dollars	Million dollars	Million dollars	Million dollars	Million dollars	Million dollars	Million dollars	Million dollars	Million dollars	Million dollars	Million dollars
1975	21,066.3	11,324.7	7,802.3	3,522.4	1,624.3	5,964.7	1,410.1	742.5	21,122.6	10,168.5	2,946.2	4,183.8	3,824.0	18,136.5
1976	22,649.5	12,172.2	8,147.6	4,024.6	1,792.6	6,479.8	1,473.4	731.4	21,383.1	9,676.7	3,116.8	4,469.4	4,120.3	18,674.7
1977	23,052.7	12,714.7	8,582.0	4,132.7	2,012.8	6,140.0	1,417.7	767.4	21,444.6	8,882.9	3,465.8	4,814.3	4,281.6	19,129.1
1978	25,634.4	13,529.1	9,052.2	4,476.9	2,291.9	6,679.5	2,131.8	1,002.1	23,899.6	10,015.6	4,037.8	5,183.9	4,662.2	20,267.3
1979	26,344.1	13,710.8	9,080.7	4,630.1	2,363.6	8,106.9	965.5	1,197.3	26,852.7	11,798.1	4,352.6	5,637.0	5,065.0	20,162.9
1980	29,730.3	14,110.5	8,915.4	5,195.1	3,202.7	10,047.3	1,118.6	1,251.1	30,132.0	14,013.2	4,567.0	5,986.7	5,565.2	20,209.7
1981	29,729.2	14,868.4	9,189.4	5,679.0	3,140.0	8,689.9	1,493.5	1,537.4	30,210.6	12,430.8	4,886.2	7,234.4	5,659.2	18,994.6
1982	30,609.6	15,540.4	9,841.4	5,699.0	3,162.2	8,656.4	1,572.2	1,678.4	29,916.0	12,399.0	5,266.9	6,283.1	5,967.0	19,317.5
1983	32,995.4	17,166.6	10,606.0	6,560.6	3,898.7	9,243.4	1,114.3	1,572.4	32,392.3	13,713.1	5,487.1	6,724.9	6,467.2	19,128.9
1984	38,488.4	19,426.2	11,961.9	7,464.3	3,582.1	10,972.7	2,854.3	1,653.0	36,446.4	15,757.5	5,824.1	7,828.0	7,036.7	19,714.9
1985	45,739.4	21,309.9	12,913.7	8,396.2	4,107.9	13,085.4	5,374.3	1,861.9	42,938.5	18,882.2	6,385.5	10,182.3	7,488.6	21,276.8
1986	47,787.0	22,178.0	13,831.3	8,346.8	4,534.1	13,288.1	5,852.3	1,934.4	46,064.5	20,426.9	6,646.6	10,973.4	8,017.6	24,208.3
1987	48,780.9	24,335.0	15,417.3	8,917.7	4,684.1	13,140.2	4,335.7	2,285.9	48,401.7	21,221.5	7,179.7	11,514.2	8,486.5	24,793.6
1988	47,231.9	24,602.2	16,042.6	8,559.6	4,728.2	13,420.3	2,307.3	2,173.9	49,065.1	23,117.3	7,629.1	9,837.3	8,481.4	26,027.9
1989	51,996.7	26,260.2	16,992.6	9,267.6	5,572.6	13,620.1	3,700.8	2,843.0	51,284.6	23,035.5	7,798.0	11,438.9	9,012.2	26,862.7
1990	53,895.4	27,957.0	18,297.8	9,659.3	5,531.5	14,130.8	3,236.3	3,039.8	53,585.9	24,813.1	8,266.0	11,011.3	9,495.5	28,362.0
1991	58,753.9	29,530.3	19,303.2	10,227.1	5,596.6	14,376.5	6,119.2	3,131.3	57,997.7	25,716.0	8,209.1	14,475.6	9,596.9	30,257.7
1992	64,568.1	30,809.3	20,574.3	10,234.9	5,959.9	15,586.9	8,943.9	3,268.1	62,407.4	27,143.0	8,746.8	16,289.4	10,228.3	34,185.9
1993	68,602.2	32,743.1	22,016.4	10,726.7	6,445.3	16,242.6	9,769.8	3,401.5	67,944.6	28,275.1	9,485.3	19,223.4	10,960.8	35,408.0
1994	68,106.2	34,410.1	23,112.0	11,298.2	6,398.5	18,275.8	5,707.9	3,313.9	65,641.0	30,151.6	10,073.1	14,901.7	10,514.6	37,449.2
1995	68,529.3	35,825.8	24,074.8	11,751.0	6,912.8	18,050.4	4,670.7	3,069.7	67,614.6	30,550.2	10,358.8	14,429.7	12,275.9	39,227.9

(Z) Less than $50,000.

[1] Fiscal years and coverage vary. See text.

Sources

1890–1920, U.S. Bureau of Public Roads, *Highway Statistics, Summary to 1955* (1957); 1921–1995: U.S. Federal Highway Administration, *Highway Statistics, Summary to 1995* (1997), Tables SF-201, p. 202.

Documentation

Although the federal government conducted studies of highway finance as early as 1904, systematic annual surveys were not initiated until 1921. Between 1921 and 1933, state highway financial data were reported according to each state's fiscal year. From 1933 into the mid-1980s, the data were collected on a calendar-year basis, but, since the mid-1980s, many states have reverted to the earlier practice. A more detailed classification of receipts and disbursements was adopted in 1937, and, in 1945, the coverage was broadened to include the finances of special toll facility authorities. The data for 1921–1995 reflect the standards of classification and coverage in use in 1997. The data for years before 1950 have been adjusted to include receipts of certain toll authorities.

A state highway-user tax is defined as a special tax or fee levied on motor-vehicle users because of their use of the highways. The revenues reported exclude amounts that were not used for highways, such as collection expenses and mass transit. Highway-user taxes include motor-fuel taxes, motor-vehicle registration and associated fees, and special taxes applicable only to motor carriers; these taxes are separable and apart from property, excise, business, or other taxes paid by the general public.

In many states, specific portions of the revenue from each type of highway-user tax are allocated to particular highway purposes. A number of states, however, place all highway-user revenue in a highway fund, and a few have a general state fund into which go all types of revenue. For the latter group of states, each particular appropriation or expenditure for highway purposes is considered to have been made from motor-fuel taxes, motor-vehicle registration fees, and motor-carrier taxes in proportion to the relative amount of revenue received from each of these three sources.

The largest share of receipts from state highway-user taxes is expended on state highways, but a portion is also allocated for local roads and streets, and a small amount is used for nonhighway purposes.

Series Df247. Includes road, bridge, and ferry tolls, property taxes, and appropriations from general funds.

Series Df248. Includes funds of the Federal Highway Administration and other agencies paid as reimbursement to the states, but not direct federal expenditures for highways.

Series Df249. Includes issues for refunding purposes as well as toll revenue bonds.

Series Df250. Includes funds transferred from local governments and miscellaneous receipts.

Series Df251. Excludes amounts allocated for non-highway purposes, bonds redeemed by refunding, and the expense of collecting and administering highway-user revenue. In *Historical Statistics of the United States* (1975), these amounts were reported in series Q95, as well as the total disbursements series, series Q90.

Series Df254. Includes administration, engineering, and equipment; highway law enforcement and safety; interest on obligations for state highways; and retirement of obligations for state highways.

TABLE Df257–272   Local government highway finance – revenues and disbursements: 1921–1994

Contributed by Louis P. Cain

	Revenues									Disbursements						
	Total	Local revenues					Transfers from other governments			Total	Capital	Maintenance and operation	Administration and other [2]	Interest	Debt retirement [3]	Transfers to other governments
		Total	Local highway user imposts	Tolls	Borrowing	Property tax, general fund, miscellaneous	Total	Federal	State [1]							
Year	Df257	Df258	Df259	Df260	Df261	Df262	Df263	Df264	Df265	Df266	Df267	Df268	Df269	Df270	Df271	Df272
	Million dollars	Million dollars	Million dollars	Million dollars	Million dollars	Million dollars	Million dollars	Million dollars	Million dollars	Million dollars	Million dollars	Million dollars	Million dollars	Million dollars	Million dollars	Million dollars
1921	994.2	972.2	—	—	201.7	770.6	21.9	—	21.9	1,006.5	528.4	294.1	57.2	53.9	39.7	33.2
1922	1,106.8	1,020.8	—	—	150.0	870.8	86.0	—	86.0	1,108.8	543.0	300.0	59.0	64.0	48.0	94.8
1923	1,040.9	1,001.0	—	—	128.8	872.3	39.9	—	39.9	1,047.6	468.3	304.2	65.4	86.7	56.1	66.8
1924	1,263.4	1,219.5	—	—	248.5	971.0	43.8	—	43.8	1,180.4	540.8	325.0	50.3	99.5	76.8	88.0
1925	1,377.1	1,272.2	—	—	257.4	1,014.8	104.9	—	104.9	1,280.2	621.0	343.6	54.1	105.8	84.0	71.7
1926	1,504.6	1,391.9	—	—	268.6	1,123.3	112.7	—	112.7	1,395.6	637.7	380.2	70.1	128.7	106.1	72.8
1927	1,688.2	1,560.5	—	—	296.1	1,264.4	127.6	—	127.6	1,576.2	740.2	420.0	71.3	144.0	119.8	80.9
1928	1,676.8	1,533.1	—	—	265.2	1,267.9	143.6	—	143.6	1,577.1	723.3	439.8	67.3	153.8	123.3	69.6
1929	1,649.9	1,483.0	—	—	232.6	1,250.4	166.9	—	166.9	1,586.7	683.7	456.5	81.5	160.3	148.0	56.7
1930	1,728.2	1,521.7	—	—	206.7	1,315.0	206.6	—	206.6	1,797.7	769.6	481.2	70.1	173.6	264.6	38.6
1931	1,544.8	1,318.3	0.9	—	182.2	1,135.2	226.5	0.6	225.9	1,630.6	591.7	454.7	71.2	178.8	297.8	36.3
1932	1,194.9	971.0	1.0	—	108.5	861.5	223.8	0.4	223.5	1,300.3	376.5	400.8	54.4	174.1	275.2	19.4
1933	944.9	705.6	0.9	—	36.7	668.0	239.2	0.2	239.0	1,036.0	240.4	337.9	50.7	162.8	237.0	7.1
1934	897.1	648.4	0.9	—	60.3	587.3	248.6	3.9	244.7	878.4	197.9	335.3	50.7	155.9	134.1	4.6
1935	901.8	666.3	1.2	0.3	66.6	598.3	235.6	3.5	232.1	941.5	210.4	346.9	47.1	148.0	183.9	5.2
1936	953.6	692.0	1.4	0.3	75.5	614.9	261.6	2.1	259.5	993.8	234.9	376.4	49.8	132.5	181.4	18.8
1937	1,130.6	818.9	11.8	5.7	146.9	654.4	311.7	4.3	307.4	1,130.2	262.5	367.7	46.7	135.2	296.4	21.6
1938	1,078.0	761.6	17.2	7.4	160.2	576.8	316.4	10.0	306.4	1,061.8	283.2	382.5	50.4	130.0	203.2	12.5
1939	1,102.0	757.2	20.4	9.6	149.7	577.5	344.9	19.3	325.5	1,101.1	314.4	392.8	53.1	124.4	206.2	10.2
1940	1,133.0	776.5	10.7	12.0	154.5	599.3	356.6	9.7	346.9	1,121.8	308.4	381.9	41.9	118.7	262.7	8.1
1941	1,148.1	801.1	8.7	13.2	173.1	606.3	347.0	3.3	343.7	1,126.9	234.2	424.5	46.5	114.3	297.7	9.7
1942	995.0	677.4	7.6	15.5	123.8	530.4	317.6	1.4	316.2	922.8	175.6	413.9	40.7	97.3	190.7	4.6
1943	806.7	513.7	12.9	15.1	39.8	445.8	293.0	1.8	291.2	778.2	94.0	412.9	32.2	85.5	149.5	4.1
1944	822.5	535.7	14.7	15.6	46.9	458.5	286.9	1.9	284.9	873.6	110.6	464.0	31.9	79.6	183.9	3.6
1945	972.4	659.4	15.1	13.5	70.3	560.5	313.0	4.2	308.8	933.0	129.2	499.2	37.5	76.1	186.9	4.2
1946	1,184.2	781.9	16.4	16.5	116.2	632.7	402.3	3.1	399.2	1,135.8	246.6	592.7	48.9	71.9	160.2	15.5
1947	1,522.0	1,048.8	17.6	29.0	259.0	743.2	473.2	2.4	470.7	1,449.3	420.4	697.4	61.5	72.2	174.0	23.8
1948	1,704.0	1,151.2	21.2	34.2	233.9	861.9	552.8	4.7	548.1	1,669.9	507.8	802.2	76.7	72.1	176.5	34.5
1949	2,014.3	1,398.3	24.4	36.9	420.3	916.7	616.0	5.1	610.9	1,939.0	598.1	845.5	88.3	73.9	295.7	37.4
1950	1,973.3	1,318.4	24.9	43.4	291.4	958.7	654.9	6.4	648.5	1,917.7	594.7	903.3	94.2	71.2	215.2	39.1
1951	2,080.5	1,373.1	27.8	49.5	303.6	992.2	707.4	9.1	698.3	2,037.5	621.2	973.4	102.1	71.3	234.8	34.7
1952	2,543.3	1,763.7	37.8	54.1	563.9	1,107.8	779.6	18.0	761.6	2,421.8	733.4	1,027.2	120.7	71.2	425.6	43.7
1953	2,504.2	1,662.0	52.0	54.8	361.4	1,193.8	842.2	18.7	823.5	2,410.7	815.9	1,091.1	126.0	70.9	252.2	54.6
1954	2,669.8	1,763.3	53.3	56.9	402.4	1,250.8	906.5	18.7	887.8	2,591.5	900.1	1,132.5	131.4	78.7	300.4	48.4
1955	2,996.3	2,058.0	59.8	61.3	614.6	1,322.3	938.3	16.9	921.4	2,723.1	956.6	1,180.0	146.3	81.3	288.9	70.0
1956	3,046.6	2,033.4	59.8	64.2	492.8	1,416.6	1,013.2	21.3	991.9	2,975.1	1,037.5	1,305.8	169.8	78.2	329.0	54.8
1957	3,313.7	2,201.2	71.5	68.6	577.5	1,483.6	1,112.5	28.4	1,084.1	3,236.0	1,132.7	1,350.9	198.8	89.4	376.1	88.1
1958	3,357.8	2,204.7	65.5	72.3	513.8	1,553.1	1,153.1	26.4	1,126.7	3,450.1	1,204.6	1,460.5	235.7	95.1	357.1	97.2
1959	3,614.4	2,417.1	74.5	74.3	686.7	1,581.6	1,197.3	20.9	1,176.3	3,519.5	1,152.5	1,532.9	224.7	107.0	389.0	113.5

Revenues

Disbursements

Year	Total Df257	Local revenues					Transfers from other governments			Total Df266	Capital Df267	Maintenance and operation Df268	Administration and other Df269 [2]	Interest Df270	Debt retirement Df271 [3]	Transfers to other governments Df272
		Total Df258	Local highway user imposts Df259	Tolls Df260	Borrowing Df261	Property tax, general fund, miscellaneous Df262	Total Df263	Federal Df264	State Df265 [1]							
	Million dollars	Million dollars	Million dollars	Million dollars	Million dollars	Million dollars	Million dollars	Million dollars	Million dollars	Million dollars	Million dollars	Million dollars	Million dollars	Million dollars	Million dollars	Million dollars
1960	3,715.0	2,449.7	76.2	73.5	622.5	1,677.5	1,265.2	30.3	1,234.9	3,666.0	1,166.3	1,607.3	249.0	112.5	430.5	100.3
1961	3,881.3	2,569.3	75.7	69.7	635.7	1,788.3	1,312.0	30.9	1,281.1	3,798.1	1,224.7	1,659.8	261.4	123.0	424.0	105.1
1962	3,905.3	2,557.1	75.9	74.1	598.0	1,809.2	1,348.2	31.1	1,317.1	3,927.3	1,284.5	1,697.6	262.5	132.4	446.3	103.9
1963	4,129.3	2,695.9	70.7	76.8	633.6	1,914.7	1,433.4	34.8	1,398.6	4,061.1	1,312.2	1,747.7	298.6	138.6	466.8	97.1
1964	4,326.6	2,705.1	78.2	83.5	574.7	1,968.7	1,621.5	54.4	1,567.1	4,231.0	1,379.0	1,808.6	338.5	141.2	451.4	112.3
1965	4,577.5	2,862.7	83.2	95.9	609.4	2,074.1	1,714.8	53.6	1,661.2	4,477.9	1,403.0	1,933.9	366.5	149.4	511.2	114.0
1966	5,007.1	3,209.0	92.1	101.0	644.5	2,371.3	1,798.1	49.5	1,748.6	4,841.9	1,521.5	2,031.0	477.6	148.4	495.6	167.8
1967	5,350.1	3,436.6	94.4	102.3	770.8	2,469.1	1,913.5	47.7	1,865.9	5,320.0	1,656.5	2,174.9	545.8	163.8	573.1	205.9
1968	5,649.5	3,659.6	105.1	106.0	730.6	2,718.0	1,989.9	48.5	1,941.4	5,550.5	1,741.6	2,337.9	646.0	173.2	505.8	146.0
1969	6,111.2	3,908.9	133.2	110.1	683.4	2,982.1	2,202.3	63.1	2,139.2	6,035.4	1,863.1	2,527.8	742.3	192.8	575.1	134.3
1970	6,560.6	4,088.6	145.9	116.2	746.7	3,079.9	2,472.0	92.1	2,379.9	6,532.1	1,989.3	2,703.2	936.9	202.8	590.2	109.8
1971	7,157.4	4,635.9	161.3	120.4	923.8	3,430.6	2,521.5	101.3	2,420.2	7,036.2	2,086.8	2,917.5	1,043.0	224.3	639.2	125.3
1972	7,650.3	4,928.2	167.9	178.0	967.3	3,614.9	2,722.1	101.6	2,620.5	7,489.4	2,068.8	3,103.8	1,220.5	243.3	702.8	150.1
1973	8,634.3	5,225.7	183.4	184.1	921.1	3,937.0	3,408.7	420.9	2,987.8	8,211.3	2,367.7	3,382.3	1,366.0	266.7	663.8	164.8
1974	9,449.1	5,773.1	190.7	172.1	1,026.0	4,384.2	3,676.0	624.2	3,051.9	9,248.1	2,785.6	3,791.5	1,433.8	282.4	747.5	207.4
1975	10,404.7	6,678.0	185.6	199.3	1,075.7	5,217.4	3,726.7	707.5	3,019.1	10,264.0	3,060.6	4,210.8	1,720.4	307.2	762.1	203.0
1976	10,952.1	6,996.1	215.7	239.7	1,090.6	5,450.1	3,956.1	716.5	3,239.6	10,844.6	2,972.0	4,471.6	1,920.9	337.9	924.0	218.1
1977	11,901.9	7,573.1	222.6	245.8	1,307.4	5,797.4	4,328.8	963.8	3,365.0	11,617.3	2,972.2	5,003.1	2,078.1	354.8	988.4	220.6
1978	13,097.5	8,321.3	221.9	258.7	1,275.3	6,565.5	4,776.2	1,119.3	3,656.8	12,797.5	3,367.0	5,577.3	2,277.2	374.0	942.6	259.5
1979	13,872.4	9,099.4	182.5	127.5	1,225.4	7,564.0	4,773.0	1,100.4	3,672.5	13,753.4	3,828.4	5,914.8	2,454.6	388.4	942.1	225.1
1980	15,131.4	10,137.5	198.6	89.0	1,466.5	8,383.4	4,993.9	1,185.1	3,808.8	15,037.8	4,345.6	6,366.8	2,626.4	411.9	1,059.8	227.4
1981	16,410.4	10,931.9	166.4	191.2	1,958.5	8,615.8	5,478.5	1,394.4	4,084.1	16,176.0	4,736.2	6,736.9	2,694.1	595.0	1,139.6	274.1
1982	17,918.7	12,005.5	378.8	191.1	1,606.6	9,829.0	5,913.3	1,397.9	4,515.4	17,620.6	4,879.4	7,733.1	2,943.2	589.2	1,178.6	297.1
1983	19,288.9	12,746.0	388.5	219.3	1,826.6	10,311.6	6,543.0	1,319.9	5,223.0	18,800.2	4,904.0	8,428.8	3,109.9	697.3	1,332.2	327.9
1984	20,746.3	13,566.0	345.9	307.1	1,731.0	11,182.0	7,180.3	1,408.4	5,771.9	20,253.3	5,509.9	8,849.4	3,586.7	742.4	1,205.2	359.8
1985	23,636.5	16,551.0	469.0	264.8	3,427.9	12,389.3	7,085.5	1,350.2	5,735.3	22,620.6	5,762.4	9,868.1	3,779.6	852.3	1,959.0	399.2
1986	26,299.6	19,127.3	526.8	438.8	4,092.1	14,069.6	7,172.3	1,196.8	5,975.5	24,969.0	6,656.2	10,637.2	4,128.1	925.7	2,153.8	468.1
1987	26,446.7	18,770.0	305.8	632.9	2,924.7	14,906.6	7,676.8	1,066.8	6,610.0	26,319.5	7,333.4	10,728.9	4,528.3	1,069.2	2,064.7	595.0
1988	26,893.9	19,307.0	926.0	302.6	2,115.6	15,962.8	7,586.9	796.8	6,790.1	26,721.3	7,783.8	11,236.6	4,546.1	1,076.7	1,566.5	511.6
1989	28,244.9	20,100.1	375.5	673.9	2,826.7	16,223.9	8,144.8	655.0	7,489.8	28,549.3	8,388.3	10,978.6	5,177.0	1,165.4	2,085.0	755.0
1990	30,316.4	20,993.4	864.8	169.7	2,523.3	17,435.6	9,323.0	782.5	8,540.5	29,968.6	8,670.5	11,869.9	5,868.7	1,386.8	1,489.6	683.2
1991	32,214.6	21,876.5	931.9	358.5	3,260.5	17,325.8	10,338.1	877.5	9,460.5	31,814.5	9,301.2	12,892.4	5,432.4	1,319.6	1,793.7	1,075.3
1992	32,781.0	22,906.6	1,038.5	479.5	3,520.6	17,868.0	9,874.5	917.9	8,956.6	33,013.0	9,432.8	13,362.3	5,798.5	1,463.7	2,270.7	685.0
1993	35,070.7	23,830.3	1,175.5	454.2	4,070.6	18,130.0	11,240.4	814.7	10,425.7	33,840.9	9,056.3	13,300.3	5,879.5	1,578.4	2,718.4	1,308.0
1994	35,381.6	25,874.9	1,327.3	540.8	3,223.6	20,783.3	9,506.7	666.7	8,840.0	34,890.7	9,892.2	13,346.1	6,186.0	1,526.7	2,482.0	1,457.8

1 From 1931 to 1960, includes debt service for debts assumed by the state. Before 1985, includes proceeds from sale of short-term debt.

2 Highway law enforcement and safety expenditures were included as administrative expenditures by municipal governments before 1937 and by county governments before 1959.

3 Includes the retirement of short-term debt prior to 1990.

Source

U.S. Federal Highway Administration, *Highway Statistics, Summary to 1995* (1995), Tables LGF-201 and LGF-202.

Documentation

The Federal Highway Administration (FHWA), in cooperation with the states, began to collect information on local government highway finances in 1937. Each state elected either to canvass or to sample local agency records to obtain this information. The summaries were later pushed back to 1921 by the FHWA staff.

In 1983, the states were given the option of reporting this information biennially; FHWA staff would then estimate data for the missing year. About half the states elected to take this option. About the same time, the FHWA began requesting information on local governments, the sum of what they formerly reported separately as counties and townships (Table Df273–288) and municipalities (Table Df289–304).

TABLE Df273–288 County and township highway finance – revenues and disbursements: 1921–1984

Contributed by Louis P. Cain

	Revenues									Disbursements						
	Total	Local					Transfers from other governments			Total	Capital	Maintenance and operation	Administration and other	Interest	Debt retirement	Transfers to other governments
		Total	Local highway user imposts	Tolls	Borrowing	Property tax, general fund, miscellaneous	Total	Federal	State							
	Df273	Df274	Df275	Df276	Df277	Df278	Df279 [1]	Df280 [2]	Df281	Df282 [3]	Df283 [2]	Df284	Df285	Df286	Df287	Df288
Year	Million dollars	Million dollars	Million dollars	Million dollars	Million dollars	Million dollars	Million dollars	Million dollars	Million dollars	Million dollars	Million dollars	Million dollars	Million dollars	Million dollars	Million dollars	Million dollars
1921	657	635	0	0	202	433	22	0	22	670	337	186	40	34	40	33
1922	731	645	0	0	150	495	86	0	86	733	330	185	40	35	48	95
1923	638	598	0	0	129	469	40	0	40	645	242	184	46	50	56	67
1924	690	646	0	0	158	488	44	0	44	688	256	195	27	55	67	88
1925	683	581	0	0	144	437	102	0	102	689	265	197	29	52	74	72
1926	775	667	0	0	169	498	108	0	108	752	266	213	42	67	91	73
1927	841	716	0	0	181	535	125	0	125	829	289	238	41	75	105	81
1928	835	700	0	0	150	550	135	0	135	832	282	260	37	80	103	70
1929	790	636	0	0	111	525	154	0	154	808	257	260	50	78	106	57
1930	818	622	1	0	95	527	196	0	196	852	297	284	36	83	113	39
1931	812	602	1	0	109	492	210	1	209	847	248	262	38	91	165	41
1932	664	456	1	0	67	388	208	0	208	686	168	235	28	87	133	24
1933	567	320	1	0	24	295	247	25	222	576	130	191	27	81	124	12
1934	660	282	1	0	31	250	378	154	224	662	238	187	26	81	116	10
1935	624	314	1	0	50	263	310	95	215	629	194	202	23	80	120	9
1936	901	326	1	0	56	269	575	341	234	909	449	222	24	73	116	23
1937	869	389	0	1	108	280	480	223	257	876	353	234	19	72	168	26
1938	1,023	370	0	3	86	281	653	394	259	1,031	533	239	18	68	150	17
1939	987	354	0	3	69	282	633	362	271	989	495	240	19	63	152	14
1940	931	348	0	3	68	277	583	299	283	925	432	249	19	58	149	12
1941	847	364	1	4	94	265	483	191	292	836	311	254	22	55	175	13
1942	669	320	1	5	57	257	349	79	270	643	173	246	18	49	142	8
1943	516	266	1	5	18	242	250	2	248	470	52	237	18	45	107	7
1944	519	276	1	5	28	242	243	2	241	506	58	271	19	41	105	8
1945	575	310	1	5	39	265	265	4	261	556	74	308	20	38	103	9
1946	702	375	1	7	64	303	327	3	323	685	147	373	24	35	85	17
1947	856	485	1	8	127	349	371	2	369	826	208	432	27	33	96	27
1948	936	489	1	10	98	380	447	4	442	929	255	478	33	32	91	37
1949	1,010	538	2	11	120	405	472	5	466	990	279	498	39	31	96	39
1950	1,067	565	2	12	104	447	502	6	495	1,043	266	557	44	29	100	38
1951	1,128	582	2	12	98	470	546	9	536	1,106	285	596	47	29	101	35
1952	1,253	650	3	13	121	513	603	17	584	1,200	355	618	51	27	97	42
1953	1,329	691	3	13	126	549	638	18	619	1,297	401	649	55	28	102	51
1954	1,371	697	4	14	113	566	674	18	655	1,369	436	677	59	29	107	48
1955	1,531	835	4	15	229	587	696	17	678	1,429	450	701	64	29	109	62
1956	1,518	768	3	15	128	622	750	21	728	1,509	425	764	65	31	109	58
1957	1,619	810	4	16	141	649	809	28	779	1,603	518	784	76	32	112	72
1958	1,695	891	4	19	167	701	804	26	776	1,704	549	847	81	32	116	77
1959	1,762	926	9	20	184	713	836	21	812	1,745	521	874	92	32	126	99

	Revenues								Disbursements						
	Total	Local					Transfers from other governments			Total	Capital	Maintenance and operation	Administration and other	Interest	Debt retirement	Transfers to other governments
		Total	Local highway user imposts	Tolls	Borrowing	Property tax, general fund, miscellaneous	Total [1]	Federal [2]	State	Total [3]	[2]					
	Df273	Df274	Df275	Df276	Df277	Df278	Df279	Df280	Df281	Df282	Df283	Df284	Df285	Df286	Df287	Df288
Year	Million dollars	Million dollars	Million dollars	Million dollars	Million dollars	Million dollars	Million dollars	Million dollars	Million dollars	Million dollars	Million dollars	Million dollars	Million dollars	Million dollars	Million dollars	Million dollars
1960	1,753	878	9	19	115	735	875	28	845	1,737	500	923	95	33	108	78
1961	1,926	979	8	16	186	769	947	29	916	1,896	579	922	99	40	149	107
1962	1,990	1,035	9	16	220	790	955	30	922	1,934	605	939	99	41	144	106
1963	2,012	1,015	10	17	159	829	997	30	964	1,996	618	959	108	45	158	108
1964	2,135	1,053	11	18	203	821	1,082	33	1,044	2,068	649	1,008	123	45	148	95
1965	2,247	1,114	12	19	216	867	1,133	43	1,087	2,203	681	1,080	133	48	166	95
1966	2,410	1,216	18	20	201	977	1,194	45	1,146	2,345	714	1,138	146	46	162	139
1967	2,609	1,321	20	20	272	1,009	1,288	41	1,202	2,577	761	1,205	163	53	220	175
1968	2,693	1,372	18	21	272	1,061	1,321	44	1,255	2,639	806	1,272	201	55	167	138
1969	2,913	1,478	42	21	236	1,179	1,435	53	1,376	2,818	846	1,392	218	62	191	109
1970	3,075	1,511	50	24	222	1,216	1,565	72	1,485	3,028	915	1,463	269	65	193	124
1971	3,314	1,696	60	25	288	1,323	1,618	77	1,536	3,251	976	1,566	298	70	223	119
1972	3,434	1,709	65	27	292	1,325	1,725	85	1,638	3,370	1,009	1,637	296	78	208	142
1973	3,921	1,818	74	28	264	1,451	2,103	295	1,805	3,676	1,101	1,793	342	81	205	155
1974	4,271	2,021	65	22	235	1,700	2,250	386	1,857	4,226	1,313	2,021	385	85	234	187
1975	4,686	2,367	57	30	317	1,963	2,319	436	1,876	4,652	1,388	2,289	478	90	232	177
1976	4,943	2,501	81	33	298	2,089	2,442	429	2,009	4,789	1,332	2,414	533	100	251	160
1977	5,326	2,709	89	33	411	2,176	2,617	524	2,087	5,098	1,290	2,692	578	103	279	156
1978	5,726	2,871	87	36	355	2,392	2,856	550	2,299	5,631	1,528	2,931	623	105	269	176
1979	5,985	3,210	88	37	357	2,728	2,775	486	2,286	5,858	1,610	3,067	660	108	222	149
1980	6,559	3,646	119	37	331	3,158	2,913	531	2,373	6,473	1,817	3,229	720	119	260	169
1981	7,114	3,944	206	40	407	3,291	3,169	663	2,503	6,935	1,871	3,565	773	130	304	218
1982	7,650	4,269	235	47	511	3,476	3,351	620	2,714	7,438	1,952	3,961	760	162	314	225
1983	8,511	4,723	235	50	595	3,843	3,788	626	3,155	8,300	1,959	4,486	902	189	409	295
1984	9,037	4,967	229	54	646	4,039	4,070	773	3,291	8,627	2,196	4,585	1,017	201	297	306

[1] Includes a small amount of transfers from municipalities beginning in 1940.

[2] For the years 1933–1942, includes funds from the Works Progress Administration and other work-relief funds. The amounts, in millions of dollars, are 25, 150, 91, 339, 221, 389, 352, 295, 189, and 78, respectively.

[3] Between 1931 and 1959, includes a small amount of disbursements for non-highway purposes.

Source

U.S. Federal Highway Administration, *Highway Statistics, Summary to 1985* (1987), Tables LF-201 and LF-202.

Documentation

In the mid-1980s, the Federal Highway Administration (FHWA) stopped requesting separate information on counties and townships. The FHWA is now reporting only "local" government, the sum of counties, townships, and municipalities.

Series Df277. Includes both long-term and short-term notes. Short-term notes are defined as those for two years or less.

Series Df282. The majority of these funds were disbursements for local highways; however, some were for state-administered highways and local county streets.

Series Df286–287. Includes the debt service for both long-term and short-term notes.

TABLE Df289–304   Municipal highway finance – revenues and disbursements: 1921–1984

Contributed by Louis P. Cain

	Revenues									Disbursements						
	Total	Local					Transfers from other governments			Total	Capital	Maintenance and operation	Administration and other	Interest	Debt retirement	Transfers to other governments
		Total	Local highway user imposts	Tolls	Borrowing	Property tax, general fund, miscellaneous	Total	Federal	State							
	Df289	Df290	Df291	Df292	Df293	Df294	Df295 [1]	Df296	Df297	Df298 [2]	Df299	Df300	Df301	Df302	Df303	Df304
Year	Million dollars	Million dollars	Million dollars	Million dollars	Million dollars	Million dollars	Million dollars	Million dollars	Million dollars	Million dollars	Million dollars	Million dollars	Million dollars	Million dollars	Million dollars	Million dollars
1921	337	337	0	0	0	337	0	0	0	337	191	108	18	20	0	0
1922	376	376	0	0	0	376	0	0	0	376	213	115	19	29	0	0
1923	403	403	0	0	0	403	0	0	0	403	226	120	20	37	0	0
1924	573	573	0	0	91	482	0	0	0	492	285	130	22	45	10	0
1925	694	691	0	0	113	578	3	0	3	591	356	147	24	54	10	0
1926	729	724	0	0	100	624	5	0	5	644	372	167	28	62	15	0
1927	848	845	0	0	115	730	3	0	3	747	451	182	30	69	15	0
1928	841	833	0	0	115	718	8	0	8	745	441	180	30	74	20	0
1929	860	847	0	0	122	725	13	0	13	779	427	196	32	82	42	0
1930	910	899	0	0	112	787	11	0	11	946	473	197	33	91	152	0
1931	737	716	0	0	73	643	21	0	16	790	344	193	32	88	133	0
1932	536	516	0	0	42	474	20	0	15	630	208	166	27	87	142	0
1933	407	386	0	0	13	373	21	0	17	501	135	147	24	82	113	0
1934	392	366	0	0	29	337	26	0	21	376	110	148	25	75	18	0
1935	373	352	0	0	17	335	21	0	17	408	107	145	24	68	64	0
1936	396	367	0	0	19	348	29	0	25	430	125	154	26	60	65	0
1937	489	432	11	5	39	377	57	2	50	488	130	134	29	63	128	1
1938	448	393	17	5	74	297	55	5	47	433	140	144	31	62	53	1
1939	471	404	20	7	80	297	67	9	54	479	172	153	33	62	54	1
1940	504	429	10	9	86	324	75	6	63	509	171	133	24	60	114	2
1941	495	437	8	9	79	341	58	1	52	494	112	170	26	59	122	2
1942	407	358	7	11	66	274	49	0	46	372	81	168	21	48	49	2
1943	297	248	12	10	22	204	49	0	43	322	41	176	14	41	43	2
1944	310	261	14	11	19	217	49	0	43	381	53	193	13	39	79	2
1945	399	350	15	8	31	296	49	0	48	389	55	191	18	38	84	1
1946	485	407	16	10	53	328	78	0	76	463	100	220	24	37	75	4
1947	671	565	17	21	132	395	106	0	101	635	212	265	34	39	78	4
1948	776	662	20	24	136	482	114	0	106	756	253	324	43	40	86	7
1949	1,014	860	23	26	300	511	154	0	145	971	320	347	50	43	200	8
1950	918	753	23	31	187	512	165	0	154	901	329	346	51	42	115	13
1951	963	792	25	37	205	525	171	0	162	959	336	377	56	42	133	10
1952	1,302	1,113	35	41	443	594	189	1	178	1,256	379	409	70	44	329	14
1953	1,186	971	49	42	236	644	215	1	204	1,153	415	442	70	43	151	15
1954	1,314	1,068	49	43	290	686	246	1	232	1,269	464	456	71	50	194	16

	Revenues									Disbursements						
		Local					Transfers from other governments									
	Total	Total	Local highway user imposts	Tolls	Borrowing	Property tax, general fund, miscellaneous	Total [1]	Federal	State	Total [2]	Capital	Maintenance and operation	Administration and other	Interest	Debt retirement	Transfers to other governments
Year	Df289	Df290	Df291	Df292	Df293	Df294	Df295	Df296	Df297	Df298	Df299	Df300	Df301	Df302	Df303	Df304
	Million dollars	Million dollars	Million dollars	Million dollars	Million dollars	Million dollars	Million dollars	Million dollars	Million dollars	Million dollars	Million dollars	Million dollars	Million dollars	Million dollars	Million dollars	Million dollars
1955	1,485	1,224	56	46	385	737	261	0	243	1,347	507	479	82	52	180	25
1956	1,550	1,266	57	49	365	795	284	0	264	1,523	563	542	105	47	220	16
1957	1,725	1,390	68	52	436	834	335	1	305	1,682	615	567	123	57	264	38
1958	1,702	1,313	62	53	347	851	389	0	351	1,773	656	614	155	63	241	40
1959	1,892	1,491	66	54	503	868	401	0	364	1,815	631	659	133	75	263	54
1960	1,987	1,572	67	54	507	944	415	3	389	1,954	666	685	152	80	323	48
1961	2,003	1,592	67	53	450	1,022	411	2	365	1,949	645	738	163	83	275	45
1962	1,968	1,523	67	58	377	1,021	445	1	395	2,046	679	758	165	91	302	51
1963	2,170	1,680	61	60	475	1,084	490	5	435	2,117	694	789	189	94	309	42
1964	2,228	1,652	67	65	371	1,149	576	22	523	2,199	731	801	214	97	303	53
1965	2,362	1,748	71	77	394	1,206	614	11	574	2,305	722	854	234	101	345	49
1966	2,632	1,994	74	81	444	1,395	638	5	602	2,530	808	893	332	102	333	62
1967	2,826	2,116	74	82	499	1,461	710	6	664	2,786	894	970	381	111	354	76
1968	3,046	2,288	87	85	458	1,658	758	5	686	2,982	935	1,066	445	118	339	79
1969	3,269	2,430	91	89	447	1,803	839	10	764	3,273	1,017	1,136	525	131	384	80
1970	3,580	2,578	96	93	525	1,864	1,002	20	895	3,570	1,074	1,240	668	138	397	52
1971	3,933	2,940	102	95	635	2,108	992	24	884	3,852	1,111	1,352	745	154	417	73
1972	4,290	3,219	103	151	676	2,290	1,071	17	983	4,199	1,060	1,466	925	165	495	78
1973	4,805	3,408	109	156	657	2,486	1,397	126	1,182	4,614	1,267	1,590	1,024	186	458	88
1974	5,263	3,752	126	150	791	2,684	1,511	238	1,195	5,107	1,472	1,770	1,049	197	514	105
1975	5,802	4,311	129	170	759	3,254	1,491	272	1,143	5,695	1,673	1,922	1,242	218	531	110
1976	6,067	4,496	135	207	792	3,362	1,572	288	1,231	6,114	1,640	2,058	1,388	238	673	117
1977	6,631	4,864	134	213	896	3,621	1,767	440	1,278	6,575	1,682	2,311	1,500	252	709	121
1978	7,433	5,451	135	223	920	4,174	1,983	570	1,358	7,343	1,819	2,646	1,655	269	674	143
1979	8,134	6,071	139	226	869	4,836	2,063	614	1,387	8,141	2,219	2,848	1,794	280	720	142
1980	8,940	6,775	141	273	1,135	5,225	2,165	654	1,436	8,932	2,528	3,038	1,906	293	800	142
1981	9,745	7,343	166	301	1,552	5,325	2,401	732	1,581	9,690	2,865	3,171	1,921	465	835	149
1982	10,649	7,977	190	338	1,096	6,353	2,672	777	1,801	10,532	2,928	3,772	2,183	427	864	182
1983	11,138	8,255	227	337	1,232	6,459	2,873	694	2,069	10,860	2,948	3,942	2,208	508	923	151
1984	12,121	8,867	213	426	1,085	7,143	3,255	635	2,481	12,038	3,314	4,265	2,569	542	908	198

[1] Includes a small amount of transfers from county and township governments beginning in 1931.

[2] From 1937 to 1958, includes a small amount of disbursements for non-highway purposes.

Source

U.S. Federal Highway Administration, *Highway Statistics, Summary to 1985* (1987), Tables UF–201 and UF–202.

Documentation

In the mid-1980s, the Federal Highway Administration (FHWA) stopped requesting separate information on counties and townships. Since then, the FHWA has reported only "local" government, the sum of counties, townships, and municipalities.

Series Df293. Includes both long-term and short-term notes. Short-term notes are defined as those for two years or less.

Series Df298. The majority of these funds were disbursements for local highways; however, some were for state-administered highways and local county streets.

Series Df302–303. Includes the debt service for both long-term and short-term notes.

TABLE Df305–317   Highway debt of state and local governments – obligations issued, retired, and outstanding: 1890–1995[1]

Contributed by Louis P. Cain

	Obligations issued					Obligations retired					Obligations outstanding at the end of the year		
	State		Local			State		Local				Local	
				Long-term					Long-term					
						By current revenues or sinking fund	By refunding	By current revenues or sinking fund	By refunding	Short-term	State	Bonds	Notes
	Original	Refunding	Original	Refunding	Short-term								
	Df305	Df306	Df307	Df308	Df309	Df310	Df311	Df312	Df313	Df314	Df315	Df316	Df317
Year	Thousand dollars	Thousand dollars	Thousand dollars	Thousand dollars	Thousand dollars	Thousand dollars	Thousand dollars	Thousand dollars	Thousand dollars	Thousand dollars	Thousand dollars	Thousand dollars	Thousand dollars
1890	11	—	—	—	—	0	—	—	—	—	11	—	—
1891	29	—	—	—	—	0	—	—	—	—	40	—	—
1892	8	—	—	—	—	0	—	—	—	—	48	—	—
1893	490	—	—	—	—	3	—	—	—	—	535	—	—
1894	850	—	—	—	—	0	—	—	—	—	1,385	—	—
1895	1,250	—	—	—	—	0	—	—	—	—	2,635	—	—
1896	4,100	—	—	—	—	0	—	—	—	—	6,735	—	—
1897	1,500	—	—	—	—	0	—	—	—	—	8,235	—	—
1898	1,850	—	—	—	—	0	—	—	—	—	10,085	—	—
1899	2,150	—	—	—	—	0	—	—	—	—	12,235	—	—
1900	562	—	—	—	—	0	—	—	—	—	12,797	—	—
1901	350	—	—	—	—	38	—	—	—	—	13,109	—	—
1902	900	—	—	—	—	9	—	—	—	—	14,000	—	—
1903	605	—	—	—	—	38	—	—	—	—	14,567	—	—
1904	450	—	—	—	—	3	—	—	—	—	15,014	—	—
1905	450	—	—	—	—	33	—	—	—	—	15,431	—	—
1906	1,036	—	—	—	—	33	—	—	—	—	16,434	—	—
1907	2,338	—	—	—	—	45	—	—	—	—	18,727	—	—
1908	6,095	—	—	—	—	48	—	—	—	—	24,774	—	—
1909	7,449	—	—	—	—	48	—	—	—	—	32,175	—	—
1910	6,846	—	—	—	—	93	—	—	—	—	38,928	—	—
1911	14,414	—	—	—	—	103	—	—	—	—	53,239	—	—
1912	13,366	—	—	—	—	148	—	—	—	—	66,457	—	—
1913	29,059	—	—	—	—	243	—	—	—	—	95,273	—	—
1914	11,684	—	—	—	—	403	—	—	—	—	106,554	—	—
1915	25,319	—	—	—	—	569	—	—	—	—	131,304	—	—
1916	4,809	—	—	—	—	563	—	—	—	—	135,550	—	—
1917	21,698	—	—	—	—	1,358	—	—	—	—	155,890	—	—
1918	7,083	—	—	—	—	1,586	—	—	—	—	161,387	—	—
1919	34,322	—	—	—	—	1,683	—	—	—	—	194,026	—	—
1920	38,272	—	—	—	—	6,892	—	—	—	—	225,406	—	—
1921	150,627	—	—	—	—	3,088	—	—	—	—	372,945	—	—
1922	104,214	500	—	—	—	3,945	500	—	—	—	473,214	—	—
1923	105,622	610	—	—	—	13,386	610	—	—	—	565,450	—	—
1924	124,997	480	—	—	—	12,126	480	—	—	—	678,321	—	—
1925	123,079	9,577	—	—	—	12,053	9,577	—	—	—	789,347	—	—
1926	169,827	2,870	—	—	—	26,108	2,870	—	—	—	933,066	—	—
1927	194,139	4,766	—	—	—	41,338	4,766	—	—	—	1,085,867	—	—
1928	143,828	6,177	—	—	—	41,894	6,177	—	—	—	1,187,801	—	—
1929	289,218	10,268	—	—	—	38,025	10,268	—	—	—	1,438,994	—	—
1930	180,265	13,025	—	—	—	46,804	13,025	—	—	—	1,572,455	—	—
1931	351,206	5,493	—	—	—	43,864	5,493	—	—	—	1,879,797	—	—
1932	202,906	17,678	—	—	—	44,162	17,678	—	—	—	2,038,541	—	—
1933	122,818	6,536	—	—	—	52,520	6,536	—	—	—	2,108,839	—	—
1934	69,875	182,817	—	—	—	63,891	182,817	—	—	—	2,114,823	—	—
1935	145,289	73,064	—	—	—	90,813	73,064	—	—	—	2,169,299	—	—
1936	167,874	34,258	—	—	—	126,788	34,258	—	—	—	2,210,385	—	—
1937	136,965	19,373	73,723	61,454	10,592	103,702	19,373	224,065	58,793	12,971	2,243,648	2,260,284	21,602
1938	98,526	107,278	110,894	37,989	12,236	92,022	107,278	155,000	36,424	11,304	2,250,152	2,368,107	23,577
1939	98,106	15,232	102,378	33,328	13,355	170,375	15,232	158,579	31,760	12,792	2,177,883	2,336,067	25,073
1940	197,252	32,887	101,806	37,188	16,127	216,110	32,887	210,732	35,700	14,873	2,159,025	2,200,290	27,409
1941	35,735	169,674	92,044	69,885	11,210	125,121	169,674	212,219	69,105	16,345	2,069,639	2,060,274	22,976
1942	24,446	5,550	72,033	47,307	4,523	131,954	5,550	132,694	47,333	10,760	1,962,131	2,015,699	17,039
1943	75,420	11,465	22,396	15,694	2,215	167,992	11,465	127,145	15,269	6,719	1,869,559	1,940,976	13,441
1944	21,961	69,035	15,263	27,289	4,739	153,013	13,035	153,792	27,014	3,126	1,794,507	1,797,722	15,050

Note appears at end of table

TABLE Df305–317 Highway debt of state and local governments – obligations issued, retired, and outstanding: 1890–1995 *Continued*

	Obligations issued					Obligations retired					Obligations outstanding at the end of the year		
	State		Local			State		Local			Local		
			Long-term					Long-term					
	Original	Refunding	Original	Refunding	Short-term	By current revenues or sinking fund	By refunding	By current revenues or sinking fund	By refunding	Short-term	State	Bonds	Notes
	Df305	Df306	Df307	Df308	Df309	Df310	Df311	Df312	Df313	Df314	Df315	Df316	Df317
Year	Thousand dollars	Thousand dollars	Thousand dollars	Thousand dollars	Thousand dollars	Thousand dollars	Thousand dollars	Thousand dollars	Thousand dollars	Thousand dollars	Thousand dollars	Thousand dollars	Thousand dollars
1945	41,888	15,868	44,409	22,435	5,135	146,158	68,201	160,775	20,795	5,304	1,637,904	1,682,996	14,952
1946	104,623	57,066	95,100	10,528	11,284	174,650	53,366	146,338	9,948	3,791	1,571,577	1,638,731	22,333
1947	82,512	1,884	228,973	11,266	15,902	45,614	73,420	152,598	11,348	9,753	1,536,939	1,715,227	28,635
1948	275,572	47,764	204,636	7,247	20,706	124,149	764	155,839	6,966	13,793	1,735,362	1,761,076	36,444
1949	303,566	4,837	276,280	114,117	27,426	105,994	9,441	165,242	110,092	19,955	1,928,330	1,871,437	43,638
1950	400,123	6,220	252,000	8,530	29,447	142,632	50,983	178,292	8,319	28,117	2,141,058	1,939,125	64,453
1951	535,443	2,020	256,529	14,552	31,668	155,612	47,106	193,163	12,330	28,811	2,475,803	2,004,027	67,279
1952	796,836	12,025	309,149	211,312	37,290	156,632	11,913	186,248	208,209	30,443	3,116,119	2,119,045	74,316
1953	1,038,153	70,637	300,890	12,916	47,143	147,981	61,447	204,278	5,031	42,173	4,015,481	2,219,524	84,911
1954	2,316,881	49,234	341,920	13,973	44,694	171,362	46,234	242,172	7,290	49,132	6,164,000	2,342,451	82,110
1955	645,741	17,022	536,588	15,335	62,866	191,254	17,002	230,162	11,723	45,499	6,618,507	2,644,940	99,305
1956	1,067,017	0	405,669	13,019	74,036	185,619	4,002	232,614	3,485	92,100	7,495,903	2,833,992	81,241
1957	702,271	23,858	479,301	20,297	77,551	256,608	20,216	271,858	11,163	89,156	7,945,208	3,061,103	72,572
1958	913,536	622	432,716	8,759	71,392	251,975	2,378	291,197	1,960	63,913	8,605,013	3,208,548	86,866
1959	669,136	53,498	475,198	17,085	193,868	265,097	54,322	302,398	3,234	83,536	9,008,228	3,392,604	197,198
1960	680,237	33,352	470,265	71,360	80,160	299,760	39,069	300,844	1,792	128,149	9,382,988	3,754,491	143,630
1961	730,856	2,417	544,170	11,229	81,451	331,480	1,189	334,525	1,646	90,278	9,783,592	3,946,392	131,224
1962	1,023,723	72,102	504,470	20,092	72,491	340,648	66,667	339,071	6,598	100,683	10,472,102	4,087,191	101,754
1963	458,898	151,641	511,611	30,469	92,240	382,714	103,580	350,161	19,230	97,442	10,596,347	4,248,525	96,552
1964	635,882	153,530	454,271	13,993	106,090	381,779	73,306	371,308	4,546	75,691	10,930,674	4,335,311	126,412
1965	585,884	4,372	474,275	32,533	102,534	459,158	2,999	396,019	23,370	91,631	11,058,773	4,410,764	137,842
1966	1,170,559	147,696	514,194	12,042	115,006	519,401	43,706	396,473	2,233	97,545	11,813,921	4,538,341	155,303
1967	1,011,827	0	614,439	46,855	108,201	539,892	108,364	425,161	39,364	110,471	12,177,492	4,734,985	153,033
1968	1,383,057	4,899	614,292	8,019	107,700	656,912	5,231	414,488	3,884	91,513	12,903,305	4,938,977	162,621
1969	1,350,851	76,112	534,943	11,939	135,675	705,477	110,491	465,944	6,858	102,635	13,514,300	5,009,156	195,661
1970	1,304,860	640	580,429	6,069	157,219	781,813	17,906	469,988	470	118,402	14,020,081	5,132,980	228,396
1971	2,648,689	1,031	681,372	15,922	225,212	814,820	4,426	465,763	5,191	168,624	15,850,555	5,330,826	289,598
1972	1,684,889	418,374	786,226	14,630	168,638	834,098	0	487,611	3,615	204,243	17,119,720	5,640,436	252,993
1973	1,225,645	1,635	737,917	16,574	164,204	883,075	1,635	522,455	7,394	135,773	17,462,290	5,913,693	287,975
1974	1,015,989	40,000	737,652	18,220	269,614	887,039	0	551,278	14,948	182,426	17,631,240	6,097,678	375,162
1975	1,412,517	0	826,466	18,762	231,638	907,240	0	583,938	5,294	175,125	18,136,517	6,379,708	434,641
1976	1,461,600	14,850	761,451	91,392	238,819	938,255	0	647,111	20,705	262,028	18,674,712	6,561,000	411,433
1977	1,182,571	233,415	1,047,153	68,808	194,722	959,441	2,200	688,201	34,815	268,799	19,129,057	6,953,671	337,412
1978	941,529	1,209,155	941,046	113,237	222,230	983,706	28,710	638,981	70,004	227,771	20,267,325	7,193,556	318,886
1979	1,197,317	22,175	963,329	21,437	241,101	959,540	364,401	790,994	6,262	144,098	20,162,876	7,352,379	415,819
1980	1,154,040	6,440	927,743	293,791	250,662	1,026,827	86,845	658,010	214,779	173,605	20,209,684	7,405,928	489,005
1981	933,788	560,375	1,560,633	0	402,381	1,544,604	1,164,640	851,925	8,630	279,484	18,994,603	8,126,046	614,132
1982	1,555,255	30,640	1,355,914	0	254,228	1,137,035	125,915	887,448	0	292,456	19,317,548	8,821,686	587,401
1983	1,133,410	42,125	1,494,961	17,850	359,608	1,207,922	156,247	974,490	31,747	333,568	19,128,914	9,366,221	613,441
1984	1,714,746	1,215,599	1,435,961	0	297,568	1,505,399	838,981	899,770	0	305,649	19,714,879	9,908,587	547,382
1985	3,403,571	1,993,790	2,671,982	125,220	628,224	1,580,992	2,254,427	1,152,695	306,265	499,230	21,276,821	11,412,533	685,570
1986	4,836,977	1,926,442	2,991,137	938,384	165,162	1,897,614	1,934,341	914,733	930,880	310,094	24,208,285	14,183,935	540,895
1987	1,934,405	2,468,120	1,874,536	628,890	423,771	1,625,311	2,191,941	1,060,381	624,790	384,051	24,793,558	15,290,754	581,176
1988	2,628,927	317,555	1,876,823	15,537	236,234	1,407,016	305,171	1,338,885	28,567	199,310	26,027,853	15,786,637	627,084
1989	3,221,619	715,671	2,093,014	31,913	717,294	2,288,133	814,310	1,542,591	28,651	595,024	26,862,700	16,480,500	749,353
1990	3,102,611	44,543	2,409,980	150,777	514,886	1,603,330	44,543	1,321,887	150,682	512,414	28,361,981	18,223,840	751,826
1991	3,871,422	2,380,515	3,123,661	140,675	588,000	2,043,810	2,312,373	1,658,673	127,857	577,986	30,257,735	18,057,671	761,844
1992	6,395,019	3,064,960	3,326,801	201,141	686,262	2,675,563	2,856,207	1,990,827	285,806	603,744	34,185,944	19,352,962	850,228
1993	4,102,799	5,931,898	3,819,264	323,603	615,855	3,382,397	5,430,289	2,400,790	340,127	601,346	35,407,955	22,965,082	724,096
1994	4,192,510	1,546,787	4,977,617	115,989	608,997	2,246,135	1,451,896	2,364,516	115,989	553,385	37,449,221	25,612,877	779,704
1995	4,295,129	423,249	—	—	—	2,583,838	355,904	—	—	—	39,227,857		—

[1] State data are for calendar years; local data are for varying fiscal years.

Source

U.S. Federal Highway Administration, *Highway Statistics, Summary to 1995* (1997), Tables SB-202 and LGB-202.

Documentation

These data are regularly adjusted by the Federal Highway Administration (FHWA) to include only the portion for highway purposes. When bonds are issued for multiple purposes, their par value is assigned to highways and

(continued)

TABLE Df305–317   Highway debt of state and local governments – obligations issued, retired, and outstanding: 1890–1995   *Continued*

nonhighway purposes on the basis of the initial distribution of the net bond proceeds, and the nonhighway portion is excluded from this table. Such exclusions are part of an ongoing process. Consequently, the numbers in this table are not necessarily the same as those included in *Historical Statistics of the United States* (1975). Adjustments have taken place in the data reported in that volume. Table Df305–317 provides the most recent information concerning

obligations incurred for highway purposes. Table Df318–329 updates *Historical Statistics of the United States* (1975) until 1985, when the FHWA stopped requesting that states provide information on county and rural governments separately from that of municipal governments.

This table omits state notes and other obligations issued for terms of less than two years.

TABLE Df318–329   Long-term highway debt of state and local governments – obligations issued, retired, and outstanding, by jurisdiction: 1937–1984[1]

Contributed by Louis P. Cain

	Obligations issued				Obligations retired				Obligations outstanding at the end of the year			
	Total	State	County and local rural	Municipal	Total	State	County and local rural	Municipal	Total	State	County and local rural	Municipal
	Df318	Df319	Df320	Df321	Df322	Df323	Df324	Df325	Df326	Df327	Df328	Df329
Year	Million dollars	Million dollars	Million dollars	Million dollars	Million dollars	Million dollars	Million dollars	Million dollars	Million dollars	Million dollars	Million dollars	Million dollars
1937	211	137	47	27	328	104	106	118	4,504	2,244	1,274	986
1938	210	99	49	62	247	92	113	42	4,618	2,250	1,211	1,157
1939	201	98	35	68	329	170	117	42	4,514	2,178	1,129	1,207
1940	299	197	29	73	427	216	111	100	4,359	2,159	1,049	1,151
1941	128	36	31	61	337	125	109	103	4,130	2,070	972	1,088
1942	96	24	19	53	265	132	99	34	3,978	1,962	892	1,124
1943	97	75	6	16	296	168	92	36	3,811	1,870	806	1,135
1944	37	22	6	9	307	153	85	69	3,593	1,795	727	1,071
1945	86	42	22	22	307	146	87	74	3,321	1,638	664	1,019
1946	200	105	49	46	322	175	78	69	3,211	1,572	636	1,003
1947	312	83	107	122	198	46	78	74	3,252	1,537	664	1,051
1948	481	276	83	122	280	124	79	77	3,496	1,735	669	1,092
1949	580	304	98	178	271	106	81	84	3,799	1,928	687	1,184
1950	652	400	90	162	321	143	82	96	4,080	2,141	694	1,245
1951	793	535	79	179	349	156	82	111	4,480	2,476	691	1,313
1952	1,106	797	103	206	343	157	82	104	5,235	3,116	712	1,407
1953	1,339	1,038	106	195	352	148	85	119	6,234	4,015	732	1,487
1954	2,659	2,317	94	248	413	171	86	156	8,506	6,164	741	1,601
1955	1,182	646	205	331	421	191	89	141	9,264	6,619	858	1,787
1956	1,473	1,067	102	304	419	186	91	142	10,330	7,496	869	1,965
1957	1,181	702	114	365	529	257	92	180	11,006	7,945	900	2,161
1958	1,347	914	140	293	543	252	94	197	11,814	8,605	946	2,263
1959	1,144	669	145	330	567	265	92	210	12,400	9,008	1,006	2,386
1960	1,150	680	84	386	609	308	85	216	13,137	9,383	1,007	2,747
1961	1,275	731	152	392	665	331	117	217	13,730	9,784	1,252	2,694
1962	1,529	1,024	184	321	679	340	110	229	14,560	10,472	1,285	2,803
1963	971	459	114	398	733	383	114	236	14,844	10,596	1,281	2,967
1964	1,090	636	156	298	753	382	116	255	15,267	10,931	1,317	3,019
1965	1,060	586	166	308	855	459	123	273	15,470	11,059	1,363	3,048
1966	1,686	1,171	158	357	916	519	127	270	16,352	11,814	1,394	3,144
1967	1,627	1,012	192	423	965	540	136	289	16,912	12,177	1,450	3,285
1968	1,997	1,383	241	373	1,071	657	136	278	17,842	12,903	1,555	3,384
1969	1,886	1,351	175	360	1,170	705	146	319	18,523	13,514	1,579	3,430
1970	1,886	1,305	174	407	1,252	782	152	318	19,153	14,020	1,632	3,501
1971	3,331	2,649	196	486	1,281	815	145	321	21,182	15,851	1,678	3,653
1972	2,472	1,685	241	546	1,321	834	148	339	22,760	17,120	1,770	3,870
1973	1,964	1,226	210	528	1,405	883	158	364	23,375	17,462	1,810	4,103
1974	1,753	1,016	134	603	1,438	887	168	383	23,729	17,631	1,775	4,323
1975	2,240	1,413	222	605	1,491	907	166	418	24,516	18,137	1,822	4,557
1976	2,224	1,462	198	564	1,585	938	172	475	25,236	18,675	1,875	4,686
1977	2,229	1,183	339	707	1,647	959	178	510	26,082	19,129	2,036	4,917
1978	1,883	942	238	703	1,623	984	170	469	27,460	20,267	2,003	5,190
1979	2,160	1,197	279	684	1,751	960	177	614	27,516	20,163	2,106	5,247
1980	2,082	1,154	238	690	1,642	984	196	462	27,616	20,210	2,023	5,383
1981	2,495	934	298	1,263	1,812	960	193	659	27,122	18,995	2,164	5,963
1982	2,911	1,555	411	945	1,915	1,027	218	670	28,140	19,318	2,398	6,424
1983	2,628	1,133	475	1,020	2,519	1,545	301	673	28,495	19,129	2,606	6,760
1984	3,150	1,715	524	911	2,037	1,137	215	685	29,624	19,715	2,912	6,997

TABLE Df318–329   Long-term highway debt of state and local governments – obligations issued, retired, and outstanding, by jurisdiction: 1937–1984 *Continued*

[1] State data are for calendar years; local data are for varying fiscal years.

Source

U.S. Federal Highway Administration, *Highway Statistics, Summary to 1985* ('987), Tables SB-202, LB-202, and UB-202.

Documentation

See the text for Table Df305–317 for a discussion of the data source.

These series exclude the issue and redemption of refunding bonds. The totals exclude a small amount of duplicated and interunit obligations. Municipal obligations include all political subdivisions that are urban in character.

TABLE Df330–338   Automobile ownership and financing – percentage distributions by number of vehicles owned and payment method: 1947–1970[1]

Contributed by Louis P. Cain

	Percentage of families owning automobiles			Method of financing purchases of passenger cars						
				All cars		New cars		Used cars		
	One or more	One	Two or more	Full cash	Installment credit and other borrowing	Full cash	Installment credit and other borrowing	Full cash	Installment credit and other borrowing
	Df330	Df331	Df332	Df333	Df334	Df335	Df336	Df337	Df338
Year	Percent	Percent	Percent	Percent	Percent	Percent	Percent	Percent	Percent
1947	—	—	—	65	35	71	29	63	37
1948	54	—	—	59	39	66	33	55	42
1949	56	48 [2]	3 [2]	50	49	56	43	47	52
1950	59	52	7	47	52	54	46	41	57
1951	60	56	4	44	55	52	47	39	60
1952	60	56	4	35	63	41	57	33	65
1953	61	55	5	38	61	40	59	37	62
1954	66	58	8	37	61	38	61	36	61
1955	70	60	10	38	60	39	60	37	60
1956	72	61	9	36	61	34	63	38	60
1957	75	62	13	38	60	36	63	39	58
1958	70	60	10	43	56	36	63	45	54
1959	74	59	15	38	61	33	66	41	57
1960	77	62	15	38	62	33	67	41	59
1961	76	58	18	48	52	39	61	52	48
1962	74	57	17	44	56	38	62	48	50
1963	80	58	22	45	55	38	62	49	51
1964	78	55	22	47	53	40	60	51	49
1965	79	55	24	48	52	40	60	53	47
1966	79	54	25	48	52	37	63	52	48
1967	78	53	25	48	52	38	62	53	47
1968	79	53	26	42	58	31	69	50	50
1969	79	52	27	47	53	34	66	51	49
1970	82	54	28	47	53	34	66	52	48

[1] Excludes Alaska and Hawai'i.

[2] Based on spending units – persons living in the same dwelling and related by blood, marriage, or adoption who pooled their income for major items of expense.

Source

University of Michigan, Survey Research Center, *Survey of Consumer Finances* (Inter-University Consortium for Political and Social Research [distributor], various years).

Documentation

The data on financing purchases refer to purchases during the preceding year. They include cars received as gifts, whether purchased with cash or credit. They exclude buyers for whom the method of financing the purchase was not ascertainable. Full cash refers to the net price; therefore, it includes any trade-in allowance.

TABLE Df339–342   Motor vehicle registrations, by vehicle type: 1900–1995

Contributed by Louis P. Cain

	Total	Automobiles	Buses	Trucks		Total	Automobiles	Buses	Trucks
	Df339	Df340 [1]	Df341	Df342 [1]		Df339	Df340 [1]	Df341	Df342 [1]
Year	Thousand	Thousand	Thousand	Thousand	Year	Thousand	Thousand	Thousand	Thousand
1900	8.0	8.0	—	—	1950	49,161.7	40,339.1	223.7	8,599.0
1901	14.8	14.8	—	—	1951	51,912.8	42,688.3	230.5	8,994.0
1902	23.0	23.0	—	—	1952	53,262.4	43,823.1	240.5	9,198.8
1903	32.9	32.9	—	—	1953	56,217.4	46,429.3	244.3	9,543.9
1904	55.3	54.6	—	0.7	1954	58,505.4	48,468.4	248.3	9,788.6
1905	78.8	77.4	—	1.4	1955	62,688.8	52,144.7	255.2	10,288.8
1906	108.1	105.9	—	2.2	1956	65,148.3	54,210.9	258.8	10,678.6
1907	143.2	140.3	—	2.9	1957	67,124.9	55,917.9	264.1	10,942.9
1908	198.4	194.4	—	4.0	1958	68,296.6	56,890.6	270.2	11,135.9
1909	312.0	306.0	—	6.1	1959	71,354.4	59,454.0	265.1	11,635.3
1910	468.5	458.4	—	10.1	1960	73,857.8	61,671.4	272.1	11,914.2
1911	639.5	618.7	—	20.8	1961	75,961.4	63,420.6	279.7	12,261.2
1912	944.0	901.6	—	42.4	1962	79,150.3	66,085.3	285.2	12,779.8
1913	1,258.1	1,190.4	—	67.7	1963	82,696.7	69,038.4	297.9	13,360.4
1914	1,763.0	1,664.0	—	99.0	1964	86,313.3	71,994.8	305.4	14,013.1
1915	2,490.9	2,332.4	—	158.5	1965	90,357.7	75,257.6	314.3	14,785.8
1916	3,617.9	3,367.9	—	250.0	1966	93,949.9	78,124.7	322.2	15,503.0
1917	5,118.5	4,727.5	—	391.1	1967	96,905.9	80,399.0	337.9	16,169.0
1918	6,160.4	5,555.0	—	605.5	1968	100,898.1	83,604.5	351.8	16,941.8
1919	7,576.9	6,679.1	—	897.8	1969	105,096.4	86,857.8	364.2	17,874.4
1920	9,239.2	8,131.5	—	1,107.6	1970	108,418.2	89,243.6	377.6	18,797.1
1921	10,493.7	9,212.2	—	1,281.5	1971	112,986.3	92,718.4	397.1	19,870.9
1922	12,273.6	10,704.1	—	1,569.5	1972	118,796.7	97,082.1	406.9	21,307.7
1923	15,102.1	13,253.0	—	1,849.1	1973	125,653.9	101,985.4	424.9	23,243.6
1924	17,612.9	15,436.1	—	2,176.8	1974	129,933.6	104,856.3	447.0	24,630.2
1925	20,068.5	17,481.0	17.8	2,569.7	1975	132,948.7	106,705.9	462.2	25,780.6
1926	22,200.2	19,268.0	24.3	2,907.9	1976	138,542.9	110,188.6	478.3	27,875.9
1927	23,303.5	20,193.3	27.7	3,082.5	1977	142,092.6	112,287.5	490.8	29,314.3
1928	24,688.6	21,362.2	32.0	3,294.4	1978	148,414.6	116,573.4	505.4	31,335.9
1929	26,704.8	23,120.9	34.0	3,549.9	1979	151,869.3	118,428.7	526.8	32,913.8
1930	26,749.9	23,034.8	40.5	3,674.6	1980	155,796.2	121,600.8	528.8	33,666.6
1931	26,094.0	22,396.3	41.9	3,655.8	1981	158,286.4	123,098.4	543.9	34,644.1
1932	24,391.0	20,901.4	43.5	3,446.1	1982	159,643.2	123,701.7	559.2	35,382.4
1933	24,159.2	20,657.3	44.9	3,457.0	1983	163,749.3	126,443.8	582.9	36,722.6
1934	25,261.7	21,544.7	51.5	3,665.5	1984	166,248.8	128,157.7	583.7	37,507.5
1935	26,546.1	22,567.8	59.0	3,919.3	1985	171,688.9	127,885.2	593.5	43,210.2
1936	28,506.9	24,182.7	62.6	4,261.6	1986	175,700.3	130,003.6	593.9	45,102.9
1937	30,058.9	25,467.2	83.1	4,508.5	1987	178,909.8	131,482.1	602.1	46,825.6
1938	29,813.7	25,250.5	87.7	4,475.6	1988	184,392.7	133,835.5	615.7	49,941.5
1939	31,009.9	26,226.4	92.3	4,691.3	1989	187,356.1	134,559.2	625.0	52,171.9
1940	32,453.2	27,465.8	101.1	4,886.3	1990	188,797.9	133,700.5	627.0	54,470.4
1941	34,894.1	29,624.3	119.8	5,150.1	1991	188,136.5	128,299.6	631.3	59,205.6
1942	33,003.7	27,972.8	136.0	4,894.9	1992	190,362.2	126,581.1	644.7	63,136.3
1943	30,888.1	26,009.1	152.3	4,726.7	1993	194,063.5	127,327.2	654.4	66,081.9
1944	30,479.3	25,566.5	152.6	4,760.3	1994	198,045.4	127,883.5	670.4	69,491.5
1945	31,035.4	25,797.0	162.1	5,076.3	1995	201,530.0	128,386.8	685.5	72,457.7
1946	34,373.0	28,217.0	173.6	5,982.4					
1947	37,841.5	30,849.4	187.5	6,804.7					
1948	41,085.5	33,355.3	196.7	7,533.6					
1949	44,690.3	36,457.9	208.9	8,023.4					

[1] Beginning in 1985, personal passenger vans, passenger minivans, and utility-type vehicles are reclassified from automobiles to trucks.

Source

U.S. Federal Highway Administration, *Highway Statistics, Summary to 1995* (1997), Table MV-200.

Documentation

This table was compiled principally from information obtained from reports and unpublished data of state motor-vehicle registration departments, but it was necessary to draw on other sources and to make numerous estimates in order to present a complete series. Both privately and publicly owned vehicles are included.

Motor-vehicle data for the early years of the century are incomplete, largely because few states required registration of motor vehicles. By 1921, all states had adopted some form of motor-vehicle registration.

Accompanying the growth in motor-vehicle registrations has been a corresponding diversity in the registration practices among the states. In general, motor vehicles are classified as private passenger cars, passenger carriers for hire, trucks, trailers, motorcycles, and property carriers for hire. Several states, however, still register buses with either trucks or passenger cars. These differences have made it necessary for the data-compiling agency to supplement the data submitted by the states with information obtained from special studies and from other sources.

Trucks include pickups, panel trucks, and delivery vans. For the years in which no entries are given for buses and publicly owned vehicles, the available data on the relatively small number of such vehicles were not sufficiently detailed to differentiate by vehicle type.

TABLE Df343–346   Motor-vehicle factory sales, by vehicle type: 1900–1996[1]

Contributed by Louis P. Cain

	Passenger cars		Trucks and buses			Passenger cars		Trucks and buses	
	Number	Wholesale value	Number	Wholesale value		Number	Wholesale value	Number	Wholesale value
	Df343	Df344	Df345	Df346		Df343	Df344	Df345	Df346
Year	Thousand	Million dollars	Thousand	Million dollars	Year	Thousand	Million dollars	Thousand	Million dollars
1900	4.1	4	—	—	1950	6,665.8	8,468	1,337.1	1,707
1901	7.0	8	—	—	1951	5,338.4	7,241	1,426.8	2,323
1902	9.0	10	—	—	1952	4,320.7	6,455	1,218.1	2,319
1903	11.2	13	—	—	1953	6,116.9	9,002	1,206.2	2,089
1904	22.1	23	0.7	1	1954	5,558.8	8,218	1,042.1	1,660
1905	24.2	38	7.0	1	1955	7,920.1	12,452	1,249.1	2,020
1906	33.2	61	0.8	1	1956	5,816.1	9,754	1,104.4	2,077
1907	43.0	91	1.0	1	1957	6,113.3	11,198	1,107.1	2,082
1908	63.5	135	1.5	2	1958	4,257.8	8,010	877.2	1,730
1909	123.9	159	3.2	5	1959	5,591.2	10,543	1,137.3	2,338
1910	181.0	215	6.0	9	1960	6,674.7	12,164	1,194.4	2,350
1911	199.3	225	10.6	21	1961	5,542.7	10,285	1,133.8	2,155
1912	356.0	335	22.0	43	1962	6,933.2	13,071	1,240.1	2,581
1913	461.5	399	23.5	44	1963	7,637.7	14,427	1,462.7	3,090
1914	548.1	420	24.9	44	1964	7,751.8	14,836	1,540.4	3,223
1915	895.9	575	74.0	125	1965	9,305.5	18,380	1,751.6	3,733
1916	1,525.5	921	92.1	161	1966	8,598.3	17,554	1,731.0	3,953
1917	1,745.7	1,053	128.1	220	1967	7,436.7	15,653	1,539.4	3,592
1918	943.4	801	227.2	434	1968	8,822.1	19,352	1,896.0	4,670
1919	1,651.6	1,365	224.7	371	1969	8,223.7	18,751	1,923.1	4,936
1920	1,905.5	1,809	321.7	423	1970	6,546.8	14,630	1,692.4	4,820
1921	1,468.0	1,038	148.0	166	1971	8,584.6	21,410	2,053.1	5,964
1922	2,274.1	1,494	269.9	226	1972	8,823.9	23,133	2,446.8	7,654
1923	3,624.7	2,196	409.2	308	1973	9,657.6	16,240	2,979.7	9,544
1924	3,185.8	1,970	416.6	318	1974	7,331.3	21,653	2,727.3	10,163
1925	3,735.1	2,458	530.6	458	1975	6,712.9	23,400	2,272.2	9,900
1926	3,692.3	2,607	608.6	484	1976	8,500.3	—	2,979.5	—
1927	2,936.5	2,164	464.7	420	1977	9,200.8	—	3,441.5	—
1928	3,775.4	2,572	583.3	460	1978	9,165.2	—	3,706.2	—
1929	4,455.1	2,790	881.9	622	1979	8,419.2	—	3,036.7	—
1930	2,787.4	1,644	575.3	390	1980	6,440.0	—	1,667.3	—
1931	1,948.1	1,108	432.2	265	1981	6,255.3	—	1,700.9	—
1932	1,103.5	616	228.3	137	1982	5,049.2	—	1,906.5	—
1933	1,560.5	773	329.2	175	1983	6,739.2	—	2,433.9	—
1934	2,160.8	1,140	576.2	326	1984	7,621.2	—	3,175.8	—
1935	3,273.8	1,707	697.3	380	1985	8,002.3	—	3,464.3	—
1936	3,679.2	2,014	782.2	463	1986	7,516.2	—	3,500.9	—
1937	3,929.2	2,240	891.0	537	1987	7,085.1	—	3,821.4	—
1938	2,019.5	1,241	488.8	329	1988	7,104.6	—	4,120.6	—
1939	2,888.5	1,770	700.3	489	1989	6,807.4	—	5,062.0	—
1940	3,717.3	2,370	754.9	567	1990	6,049.7	—	3,725.2	—
1941	3,779.6	2,567	1,060.8	1,069	1991	5,407.1	—	3,387.5	—
1942	222.8	163	818.6	1,427	1992	5,685.3	—	4,062.0	—
1943	0.1	(Z)	699.6	1,451	1993	5,961.8	—	4,895.2	—
1944	0.6	(Z)	737.5	1,700	1994	6,548.6	—	5,640.3	—
1945	69.5	57	655.6	1,181	1995	6,309.8	—	5,713.5	—
1946	2,148.6	1,979	940.9	1,043	1996	6,140.5	—	5,775.7	—
1947	3,558.1	3,936	1,239.4	1,731					
1948	3,909.2	4,870	1,376.2	1,880					
1949	5,119.4	6,650	1,134.1	1,394					

(Z) Less than $500,000.

[1] Prior to July 1964, some firms counted military vehicles as factory sales; thereafter, all military vehicles were excluded.

Source

American Automobile Manufacturers Association, *Motor Vehicle Facts and Figures*, various issues. Known earlier as *Automobile Facts and Figures*.

Documentation

Production of passenger cars was discontinued in February 1942 to economize resources during World War II, but some vehicles remaining in factory stocks were sold under rationing orders in subsequent war years. The War Production Board authorized resumption of production as of July 1, 1945, but no new cars were actually produced until 1946.

Series Df344 and Df346. Based on vehicles with standard equipment. Figures exclude federal excise taxes.

Series Df346. Includes a substantial number of vehicles consisting of chassis only; the value of the bodies is excluded.

TABLE Df347–352   Domestic sales, imports, and exports of passenger cars and trucks: 1931–1996

Contributed by Louis P. Cain

	Passenger cars			Trucks		
	Domestic sales	Imports	Exports	Domestic sales	Imports	Exports
	Df347	Df348	Df349	Df350	Df351	Df352
Year	Thousand	Thousand	Thousand	Thousand	Thousand	Thousand
1931	1,903	—	—	328	—	—
1933	1,526	—	—	261	—	—
1935	2,867	—	—	552	—	—
1937	3,508	—	—	645	—	—
1939	2,724	—	—	521	—	—
1941	3,763	—	—	902	—	—
1951	5,143	21	—	1,111	—	—
1953	5,775	33	—	965	—	—
1955	7,408	58	—	1,012	3	—
1957	5,826	207	—	878	16	—
1959	5,486	614	—	928	37	—
1961	5,556	379	—	908	29	—
1962	6,753	339	—	1,068	32	—
1963	7,334	386	—	1,230	40	—
1964	7,617	484	—	1,351	42	—
1965	8,763	569	—	1,539	14	—
1966	8,377	651	—	1,619	17	—
1967	7,568	769	—	1,524	21	—
1968	8,625	1,031	—	1,807	24	—
1969	8,464	1,118	—	1,936	34	—
1970	7,119	1,280	—	1,746	65	—
1971	8,681	1,561	—	2,011	85	—
1972	9,327	1,614	—	2,486	143	—
1973	9,676	1,748	—	2,916	233	—
1974	7,454	1,399	—	2,512	176	—
1975	7,053	1,571	—	2,249	229	—
1976	8,611	1,499	—	2,944	237	—
1977	9,109	2,074	—	3,352	323	—
1978	9,312	2,002	234	3,773	336	—
1979	8,341	2,332	332	3,010	470	—
1980	6,581	2,398	352	2,001	487	—
1981	6,209	2,327	362	1,809	451	—
1982	5,759	2,224	282	2,146	414	—
1983	6,795	2,387	437	2,658	471	—
1984	7,951	2,439	493	3,475	618	—
1985	8,205	2,838	559	3,902	779	—
1986	8,215	3,245	673	3,921	941	205
1987	7,081	3,196	633	4,055	858	222
1988	7,256	3,004	781	4,508	641	230
1989	7,073	2,699	778	4,403	538	189
1990	6,897	2,403	794	4,215	631	151
1991	6,137	2,038	755	3,813	551	200
1992	6,277	1,937	851	4,481	422	152
1993	6,742	1,776	864	5,287	394	172
1994	7,255	1,735	1,019	5,995	426	267
1995	7,129	1,506	989	6,064	417	246
1996	7,254	1,273	974	6,478	452	308

Source

American Automobile Manufacturers Association, *Motor Vehicle Facts and Figures* (annual editions).

TABLE Df353–357   Automobile consumer installment credit and finance company interest rates: 1979–1996

Contributed by Louis P. Cain

Year	Credit held			Average finance company interest rate	
	Total	Commercial banks	Finance companies	New cars	Used cars
	Df353	Df354	Df355	Df356	Df357
	Billion dollars	Billion dollars	Billion dollars	Rate	Rate
1979	112.5	67.5	22.9	13.5	18.0
1980	112.0	61.5	29.4	14.8	19.1
1981	119.0	58.1	39.3	16.0	20.0
1982	125.9	59.6	44.1	15.9	20.8
1983	143.6	67.6	49.8	12.7	18.8
1984	173.6	83.9	51.9	14.6	17.9
1985	210.3	93.0	69.5	12.1	17.6
1986	247.5	101.5	92.5	9.4	16.0
1987	165.8	109.5	98.2	10.7	14.6
1988	184.3	123.4	97.2	12.6	15.1
1989	290.4	124.6	88.6	12.7	16.2
1990	288.3	126.6	79.8	12.6	16.0
1991	268.0	117.5	67.2	12.4	15.6
1992	257.6	110.7	59.4	9.8	13.7
1993	267.9	115.8	54.8	9.6	12.8
1994	299.6	132.6	59.6	9.8	13.4
1995	355.7	145.8	65.7	11.1	14.5
1996	367.6	151.9	74.2	9.9	13.5

Source

American Automobile Manufacturers Association, *Motor Vehicle Facts and Figures* (1997), p. 59, and other annual editions.

Documentation

Credit information is available in this source in earlier years, especially the dollars of credit held. These series begin in 1979 because that is the first year for which a consistent interest rate series is reported.

TABLE Df358–369   Automobile insurance premiums written and losses paid, by type of insurance: 1946–1970

Contributed by Louis P. Cain

	Total insurance			Automobile liability								Physical damage		
		Losses paid		Bodily injury			Property damage						Losses paid	
			As a percentage of premiums written		Losses paid			Losses paid						As a percentage of premiums written
	Premiums written	Total		Premiums written	Total	As a percentage of premiums written	Premiums written	Total	As a percentage of premiums written			Premiums written	Total	
	Df358	Df359	Df360	Df361	Df362	Df363	Df364	Df365	Df366			Df367	Df368	Df369
Year	Million dollars	Million dollars	Percent	Million dollars	Million dollars	Percent	Million dollars	Million dollars	Percent			Million dollars	Million dollars	Percent
1946	1,250	582	46.6	500	189	37.7	193	107	55.1			557	287	51.5
1947	1,657	673	40.6	636	235	36.9	289	138	37.9			732	300	41.0
1948	2,019	802	39.7	744	286	38.4	366	171	46.9			910	345	37.9
1949	2,332	901	38.7	879	343	39.0	453	205	45.3			999	353	41.0
1950 [1]	2,625	1,069	40.7	931	396	42.5	482	231	47.9			1,212	442	36.5
1951	2,995	1,406	47.0	1,126	493	43.8	575	313	54.5			1,294	600	46.3
1952	3,608	1,646	45.6	1,332	569	42.7	715	369	51.5			1,561	708	45.4
1953	4,165	1,810	43.5	1,562	661	42.3	833	374	44.9			1,770	775	43.8
1954	4,175	1,869	44.8	1,642	746	45.4	877	387	44.1			1,656	736	44.4
1955 [2]	4,644	2,122	45.7	1,735	820	47.3	896	415	46.3			2,013	887	43.6
1956	4,541	2,363	52.0	1,899	923	48.6	925	488	52.8			1,717	952	55.4
1957	5,037	2,714	53.9	2,180	1,141	52.3	989	541	54.7			1,868	1,032	55.2
1958	5,404	2,846	52.7	2,432	1,280	52.6	1,087	572	52.6			1,885	994	52.7
1959	6,060	3,445	56.8	2,596	1,615	62.2	1,185	655	55.3			2,279	1,175	51.6
1960 [3]	6,448	3,645	56.5	2,841	1,697	59.7	1,219	675	55.4			2,388	1,273	53.3
1961	6,668	3,723	55.8	2,977	1,744	58.6	1,285	705	54.9			2,406	1,274	53.0
1962	6,922	4,034	58.3	3,144	1,849	58.8	1,276	748	58.6			2,502	1,437	57.4
1963	7,341	4,459	60.7	3,333	2,017	60.5	1,328	826	62.2			2,680	1,616	60.3
1964	7,582	4,787	63.1	3,612	2,266	62.7	1,418	940	66.3			2,552	1,581	62.0
1965 [3]	8,358	5,221	62.5	3,948	2,459	62.3	1,567	1,025	65.4			2,843	1,737	61.1
1966	10,008	5,235	52.3	4,610	2,351	51.0	1,894	1,090	59.6			3,504	1,794	51.2
1967	10,800	5,814	53.8	4,991	2,580	51.7	2,091	1,224	58.5			3,718	2,011	54.1
1968	11,693	6,642	56.8	5,383	2,802	52.1	2,280	1,416	62.1			4,030	2,424	60.1
1969 [4]	12,906	7,715	59.8	5,892	3,093	52.5	2,544	1,693	66.5			4,470	2,929	65.5
1970 [5,6]	14,612	11,198	76.6	6,723	5,256	78.2	2,836	2,291	80.8			5,053	3,651	72.3

[1] Net basis.

[2] Direct writing basis.

[3] Direct premiums earned and direct losses incurred.

[4] Premiums written basis.

[5] Premiums earned basis.

[6] Losses paid include adjusting expenses.

Sources

The Spectator, Philadelphia, 1946–1954, *Insurance Yearbook* (annual); 1955–1965, *Insurance by States* (annual); 1966–1969, *Property Liability Insurance Review* (annual). 1970, National Underwriter Co., Cincinnati, *Argus F.C. & S. Chart* (annual).

Documentation

Property damage insurance covers real property against damage by automobiles. Physical damage insurance covers automobiles against theft and against damage from causes such as fires, collision, and acts of God.

TABLE Df370–382   Distance traveled, by motor vehicle type and highway category: 1921–1995

Contributed by Louis P. Cain

	All motor vehicles					Passenger vehicles				Trucks and combinations			
		Urban		Rural		Urban		Rural		Urban		Rural	
	Total	Total	Interstate	Total	Interstate	Total	Interstate	Total	Interstate	Total	Interstate	Total	Interstate
	Df370	Df371	Df372	Df373	Df374	Df375	Df376	Df377	Df378	Df379	Df380	Df381	Df382
Year	Million miles	Million miles	Million miles	Million miles	Million miles	Million miles	Million miles	Million miles	Million miles	Million miles	Million miles	Million miles	Million miles
1921	55,027	—	—	—	—	—	—	—	—	—	—	—	—
1922	67,697	—	—	—	—	—	—	—	—	—	—	—	—
1923	84,995	—	—	—	—	—	—	—	—	—	—	—	—
1924	104,838	—	—	—	—	—	—	—	—	—	—	—	—
1925	122,346					—	—	—	—	—	—	—	—
1926	140,735	—	—	—	—	—	—	—	—	—	—	—	—
1927	158,453	—	—	—	—	—	—	—	—	—	—	—	—
1928	172,856		—	—	—	—	—	—	—	—	—	—	—
1929	197,720	107,409	—	90,311	—	—	—	—	—	—	—	—	—
1930	206,320	111,202	—	95,118	—	—	—	—	—	—	—	—	—
1931	216,151	115,580	—	100,571	—	—	—	—	—	—	—	—	—
1932	200,517	106,366	—	94,151	—	—	—	—	—	—	—	—	—
1933	200,642	105,578	—	95,064	—	—	—	—	—	—	—	—	—
1934	215,563	112,513	—	103,050	—	—	—	—	—	—	—	—	—
1935	228,568	118,327	—	110,241	—	—	—	—	—	—	—	—	—
1936	252,128	129,450	—	122,678	—	110,419	—	100,710	—	19,031	—	21,968	—
1937	270,110	138,072	—	132,038	—	118,216	—	107,860	—	19,856	—	24,178	—
1938	271,177	136,264	—	134,913	—	117,537	—	109,084	—	18,727	—	25,829	—
1939	285,402	142,253	—	143,149	—	122,805	—	115,398	—	19,448	—	27,751	—
1940	302,188	149,993	—	152,195	—	130,269	—	122,029	—	19,724	—	30,166	—
1941	333,612	163,591	—	170,021	—	143,101	—	135,775	—	20,490	—	34,246	—
1942	268,224	138,235	—	129,989	—	119,653	—	101,867	—	18,582	—	28,122	—
1943	208,192	108,990	—	99,202	—	91,942	—	73,643	—	17,048	—	25,559	—
1944	212,713	110,750	—	101,963	—	93,679	—	76,695	—	17,071	—	25,268	—
1945	250,173	130,161	—	120,012	—	111,401	—	92,700	—	18,760	—	27,312	—
1946	340,880	170,049	—	170,831	—	148,497	—	136,729	—	21,552	—	34,102	—
1947	370,894	184,088	—	186,806	—	158,770	—	146,577	—	25,318	—	40,229	—
1948	397,957	199,082	—	198,875	—	170,331	—	153,223	—	28,751	—	45,652	—
1949	424,461	205,364	—	219,097	—	175,686	—	170,851	—	29,678	—	48,246	—
1950	458,246	218,248	—	239,998	—	184,476	—	185,066	—	33,772	—	54,932	—
1951	491,093	222,671	—	268,422	—	188,670	—	207,579	—	34,001	—	60,843	—
1952	513,581	224,118	—	289,463	—	189,987	—	224,534	—	34,131	—	64,929	—
1953	544,433	236,058	—	308,375	—	199,754	—	240,046	—	36,304	—	68,329	—
1954	561,963	247,551	—	314,412	—	210,671	—	246,733	—	36,880	—	67,679	—
1955	605,646	275,105	—	330,541	—	235,384	—	261,445	—	39,721	—	69,096	—
1956	631,161	287,200	—	343,961	—	246,961	—	271,955	—	40,239	—	72,006	—
1957	645,004	272,176	—	372,828	—	232,040	—	295,060	—	40,136	—	77,768	—
1958	664,653	285,661	—	378,992	—	244,321	—	300,424	—	41,340	—	78,568	—
1959	700,480	305,639	—	394,841	—	264,239	—	311,725	—	41,400	—	83,116	—
1960	718,762	318,299	—	400,463	—	275,403	—	315,955	—	42,896	—	84,508	—
1961	737,421	331,083	—	406,338	—	286,785	—	321,435	—	44,298	—	84,903	—
1962	766,734	347,255	—	419,479	—	300,885	—	330,971	—	46,370	—	88,508	—
1963	805,249	374,987	—	430,262	—	325,141	—	341,228	—	49,846	—	89,034	—
1964	846,298	402,917	—	443,381	—	348,552	—	351,899	—	54,365	—	91,482	—
1965	887,812	431,907	—	455,905	—	366,850	—	360,528	—	65,057	—	95,377	—
1966	925,899	449,760	50,414	476,139	48,900	394,906	43,020	387,102	38,293	54,854	7,394	89,037	10,607
1967	964,005	482,644	56,317	481,361	54,847	423,728	48,087	391,945	43,086	58,916	8,230	89,416	11,761
1968	1,015,869	509,851	63,973	506,018	62,300	446,374	54,413	408,839	48,770	63,477	9,560	97,179	13,530
1969	1,061,791	537,424	73,195	524,367	71,821	469,833	62,435	419,692	56,665	67,591	10,760	104,675	15,156
1970	1,109,724	570,252	81,532	539,472	79,516	497,586	69,646	426,637	62,681	72,666	11,886	112,835	16,835
1971	1,178,811	606,045	90,117	572,766	89,542	525,057	76,843	449,682	69,962	80,988	13,274	123,084	19,580
1972	1,259,786	670,004	100,556	589,782	99,024	573,298	84,950	457,746	76,341	96,706	15,606	132,036	22,683
1973	1,313,110	707,309	108,462	605,801	107,085	595,220	89,725	461,747	81,177	112,089	18,737	144,054	25,908
1974	1,280,544	695,194	109,304	585,350	104,621	578,357	89,250	440,023	77,685	116,837	20,054	145,327	26,936
1975	1,327,664	726,008	118,232	601,656	111,980	599,304	95,916	446,330	81,907	126,704	22,316	155,326	30,073
1976	1,402,380	777,479	136,791	624,901	122,505	637,201	109,851	453,275	87,628	140,278	26,940	171,626	34,877
1977	1,467,027	816,162	147,270	650,865	129,818	661,840	116,569	459,575	90,640	154,322	30,701	191,290	39,178
1978	1,544,704	862,218	158,861	682,486	138,214	689,436	124,497	470,115	94,612	172,782	34,364	212,371	43,602
1979	1,529,133	853,501	159,563	675,632	136,417	673,268	124,869	454,956	91,749	180,233	34,694	220,676	44,668

(continued)

TABLE Df370–382   Distance traveled, by motor vehicle type and highway category: 1921–1995   *Continued*

Year	All motor vehicles					Passenger vehicles				Trucks and combinations			
	Total	Urban		Rural		Urban		Rural		Urban		Rural	
		Total	Interstate	Total	Interstate	Total	Interstate	Total	Interstate	Total	Interstate	Total	Interstate
	Df370	Df371	Df372	Df373	Df374	Df375	Df376	Df377	Df378	Df379	Df380	Df381	Df382
	Million miles	Million miles	Million miles	Million miles	Million miles	Million miles	Million miles	Million miles	Million miles	Million miles	Million miles	Million miles	Million miles
1980	1,527,295	855,265	161,242	672,030	135,084	674,175	125,040	453,694	90,021	181,090	36,202	218,336	45,063
1981	1,555,308	867,000	166,479	688,308	139,304	683,835	128,528	466,428	92,305	183,165	37,951	221,880	46,999
1982	1,595,010	905,784	175,879	689,226	142,546	714,768	135,744	462,678	93,786	191,016	40,135	226,548	48,760
1983	1,652,788	952,271	192,470	700,517	145,250	743,379	146,760	465,634	94,409	208,892	45,710	234,883	50,841
1984	1,720,269	1,002,137	204,304	718,132	149,139	769,412	153,463	471,055	95,590	232,725	50,841	247,077	53,549
1985	1,774,826	1,044,098	216,188	730,728	154,357	781,655	157,857	478,706	97,043	262,443	58,331	252,022	57,314
1986	1,834,872	1,087,092	232,017	747,780	159,498	794,652	165,841	489,630	97,698	292,440	66,176	258,150	61,800
1987	1,921,204	1,140,754	244,836	780,450	170,493	816,499	170,055	514,318	103,423	324,255	74,781	266,132	67,070
1988	2,025,962	1,208,428	258,695	817,534	181,315	853,120	177,354	532,650	109,128	355,308	81,341	284,884	72,187
1989	2,096,487	1,249,262	270,735	847,225	191,085	870,628	183,351	546,635	114,233	378,634	87,384	300,590	76,852
1990	2,144,362	1,275,484	278,901	868,878	200,173	872,194	185,238	551,355	118,087	403,290	93,663	317,523	82,086
1991	2,172,050	1,288,497	285,325	883,553	205,011	838,762	180,148	534,351	115,072	449,735	105,177	349,202	89,939
1992	2,247,151	1,363,054	303,265	884,097	205,557	866,415	186,819	520,489	111,813	496,639	116,446	363,608	93,744
1993	2,296,378	1,409,672	317,399	886,706	208,308	880,591	193,577	510,149	110,925	529,081	123,822	376,557	97,383
1994	2,357,588	1,449,247	330,577	908,341	215,568	900,588	200,215	522,151	114,685	548,659	130,362	386,190	100,883
1995	2,422,823	1,489,534	341,528	933,289	223,382	922,805	206,077	531,786	116,701	566,729	135,451	401,503	106,681

Sources

1921–1935, U.S. Federal Works Agency, unpublished data, and U.S. Public Roads Administration, unpublished data; 1936–1995, U.S. Federal Highway Administration, *Highway Statistics, Summary to 1995* (1997), Table VM-201.

Documentation

Traffic volume information is obtained from automatic traffic recorders operating continuously at selected locations on the roads and streets of each state. The recorders are generally supplemented by periodic manual classification counts to determine the proportion of vehicles of each type, and by portable machine counts.

Highway travel estimates are compiled from data submitted by the fifty states and the District of Columbia. Travel data by vehicle type and stratification of trucks are calculated by the Federal Highway Administration. Entries have been revised to reflect updated estimation procedures, the 1992 Truck Inventory and Use Survey, and the new *Highway Statistics* format adopted in 1980.

Series Df375 and Df377. Include passenger cars, buses, and taxicabs.

TABLE Df383–412   Distance traveled, fuel consumption, and registered vehicles, by motor vehicle type: 1936–1995

Contributed by Louis P. Cain

	All motor vehicles							Passenger cars and motorcycles		
	Distance traveled	Registered vehicles	Average distance traveled per vehicle	Fuel consumption	Average fuel consumption per vehicle	Average mileage per gallon consumed		Distance traveled	Registered vehicles	Average distance traveled per vehicle
	Df383	Df384	Df385	Df386	Df387	Df388		Df389	Df390	Df391
Year	Million miles	Number	Miles	Million gallons	Gallons	Miles per gallon		Million miles	Number	Miles
1936	252,128	28,506,891	8,844	18,099	635	13.9		208,762	24,182,662	8,633
1937	270,110	30,058,892	8,986	19,455	647	13.9		223,584	25,467,229	8,779
1938	271,177	29,813,718	9,096	19,612	658	13.8		224,113	25,250,477	8,876
1939	285,402	31,009,927	9,204	20,714	668	13.8		235,649	26,226,371	8,985
1940	302,188	32,453,233	9,311	22,001	678	13.7		249,641	27,465,826	9,089
1941	333,612	34,894,134	9,561	24,192	693	13.8		276,056	29,624,269	9,319
1942	268,224	33,003,656	8,127	19,940	604	13.5		218,390	27,972,837	7,807
1943	208,192	30,888,134	6,740	16,004	518	13.0		162,220	26,009,073	6,237
1944	212,713	30,479,306	6,979	16,430	539	12.9		166,575	25,566,464	6,515
1945	250,173	31,035,420	8,061	19,149	617	13.1		200,267	25,796,985	7,763
1946	340,880	34,373,002	9,917	25,649	746	13.3		281,173	28,217,028	9,965
1947	370,894	37,841,498	9,801	28,216	746	13.1		301,096	30,849,353	9,760
1948	397,957	41,085,531	9,686	30,461	741	13.1		319,271	33,355,250	9,572
1949	424,461	44,690,296	9,498	32,438	726	13.1		342,285	36,457,943	9,388
1950	458,246	49,161,691	9,321	35,662	725	12.8		365,461	40,339,077	9,060
1951	491,093	51,912,755	9,460	38,139	735	12.9		392,131	42,688,309	9,186
1952	513,581	53,262,418	9,642	40,597	762	12.7		410,187	43,823,097	9,360
1953	544,433	56,217,443	9,684	42,746	760	12.7		435,351	46,429,270	9,377
1954	561,963	58,505,361	9,605	44,366	758	12.7		453,152	48,468,418	9,349
1955	605,646	62,688,792	9,661	47,732	761	12.7		492,635	52,144,739	9,447
1956	631,161	65,148,277	9,688	50,216	771	12.6		514,781	54,210,901	9,496
1957	645,004	67,124,904	9,609	51,866	773	12.4		522,747	55,917,897	9,348
1958	664,653	68,296,594	9,732	53,420	782	12.4		540,450	56,890,558	9,500
1959	700,480	71,354,420	9,817	56,334	789	12.4		571,626	59,453,984	9,615
1960	718,762	73,857,768	9,732	57,880	784	12.4		587,012	61,671,390	9,518
1961	737,421	75,961,437	9,708	59,306	781	12.4		603,827	63,420,580	9,521
1962	766,734	79,150,336	9,687	61,697	779	12.4		627,387	66,085,289	9,494
1963	805,249	82,696,732	9,737	64,516	780	12.5		661,884	69,038,443	9,587
1964	846,298	86,313,262	9,805	67,901	787	12.5		695,835	71,994,795	9,665
1965	887,812	90,357,667	9,826	71,104	787	12.5		722,696	75,257,588	9,603
1966	925,899	95,703,030	9,675	74,664	780	12.4		777,480	79,877,866	9,733
1967	964,005	98,858,898	9,751	77,731	786	12.4		811,046	82,351,989	9,849
1968	1,015,869	102,987,134	9,864	82,949	805	12.2		850,288	85,693,574	9,922
1969	1,061,791	107,412,077	9,885	88,135	821	12.0		884,705	89,173,502	9,921
1970	1,109,724	111,242,295	9,976	92,329	830	12.0		919,679	92,067,655	9,989
1971	1,178,811	116,330,037	10,133	97,559	839	12.1		969,937	96,062,090	10,097
1972	1,259,786	122,556,550	10,279	105,062	857	12.0		1,025,696	100,841,939	10,171
1973	1,313,110	130,024,945	10,099	110,473	850	11.9		1,051,175	106,356,453	9,884
1974	1,280,544	134,899,955	9,493	106,301	788	12.0		1,012,696	109,822,740	9,221
1975	1,327,664	137,912,779	9,627	108,984	790	12.2		1,039,579	111,670,004	9,309
1976	1,402,380	143,476,236	9,774	115,700	806	12.1		1,084,218	115,121,972	9,418
1977	1,467,027	147,025,824	9,978	119,625	814	12.3		1,115,592	117,220,778	9,517
1978	1,544,704	153,282,467	10,077	125,067	816	12.4		1,153,666	121,441,249	9,500
1979	1,529,133	157,291,431	9,722	122,115	776	12.5		1,122,277	123,850,862	9,062
1980	1,527,295	161,490,159	9,458	114,960	712	13.3		1,121,810	127,294,783	8,813
1981	1,555,308	164,117,547	9,477	114,453	697	13.6		1,144,022	128,929,543	8,873
1982	1,595,010	165,397,098	9,644	113,384	686	14.1		1,171,623	129,455,523	9,050
1983	1,652,788	169,334,393	9,760	116,081	686	14.2		1,203,814	132,028,894	9,118
1984	1,720,269	171,728,638	10,017	118,687	691	14.5		1,235,827	133,637,504	9,248
1985	1,774,826	177,133,282	10,020	121,301	685	14.6		1,255,884	133,329,597	9,419
1986	1,834,872	180,899,332	10,143	125,185	692	14.7		1,279,564	135,202,567	9,464
1987	1,921,204	183,795,545	10,453	127,528	694	15.1		1,325,488	136,367,895	9,720
1988	2,025,962	188,976,958	10,721	130,062	688	15.6		1,380,295	138,419,816	9,972
1989	2,096,487	191,776,526	10,932	131,852	688	15.9		1,411,592	138,979,613	10,157
1990	2,144,362	193,057,376	11,107	130,755	677	16.4		1,417,823	137,959,958	10,277
1991	2,172,050	192,313,834	11,294	128,563	669	16.9		1,367,363	132,476,966	10,322
1992	2,247,151	194,427,346	11,558	132,888	683	16.9		1,381,126	130,646,266	10,571
1993	2,296,378	198,041,338	11,595	137,262	693	16.7		1,384,615	131,305,045	10,545
1994	2,357,588	201,801,920	11,683	140,839	698	16.7		1,416,329	131,640,024	10,759
1995	2,422,823	205,297,050	11,802	143,268	698	16.9		1,448,207	132,153,804	10,958

(continued)

TABLE Df383–412   Distance traveled, fuel consumption, and registered vehicles, by motor vehicle type: 1936–1995
Continued

	Passenger cars and motorcycles				Buses					
	Fuel consumption	Average fuel consumption per vehicle	Average mileage per gallon consumed	Distance traveled	Registered vehicles	Average distance traveled per vehicle	Fuel consumption	Average fuel consumption per vehicle	Average mileage per gallon consumed
	Df392	Df393	Df394	Df395	Df396	Df397	Df398	Df399	Df400
Year	Million gallons	Gallons	Miles per gallon	Million miles	Number	Miles	Million gallons	Gallons	Miles per gallon
1936	13,648	564	15.3	2,367	62,618	37,801	378	6,037	6.3
1937	14,617	574	15.3	2,492	83,130	29,977	401	4,824	6.2
1938	14,663	581	15.3	2,508	87,664	28,609	406	4,631	6.2
1939	15,412	588	15.3	2,554	92,285	27,675	414	4,486	6.2
1940	16,323	594	15.3	2,657	101,145	26,269	436	4,311	6.1
1941	18,031	609	15.3	2,820	119,753	23,548	471	3,933	6.0
1942	14,428	516	15.1	3,130	135,957	23,022	542	3,987	5.8
1943	10,821	416	15.0	3,365	152,324	22,091	603	3,959	5.6
1944	11,108	434	15.0	3,799	152,592	24,896	697	4,568	5.5
1945	13,323	516	15.0	3,834	162,125	23,648	700	4,318	5.5
1946	18,759	665	15.0	4,053	173,585	23,349	743	4,280	5.5
1947	20,140	653	15.0	4,251	187,457	22,677	778	4,150	5.5
1948	21,369	641	14.9	4,283	196,726	21,771	780	3,965	5.5
1949	22,873	627	15.0	4,252	208,929	20,351	772	3,695	5.5
1950	24,305	603	15.0	4,081	223,652	18,247	732	3,273	5.6
1951	26,217	614	15.0	4,118	230,461	17,869	751	3,259	5.5
1952	27,982	639	14.7	4,334	240,485	18,022	766	3,185	5.7
1953	29,730	640	14.6	4,449	244,251	18,215	771	3,157	5.8
1954	31,070	641	14.6	4,252	248,346	17,121	755	3,040	5.6
1955	33,653	645	14.6	4,194	255,249	16,431	771	3,021	5.4
1956	35,436	654	14.5	4,135	258,764	15,980	802	3,099	5.2
1957	36,770	658	14.2	4,353	264,062	16,486	825	3,124	5.3
1958	38,097	670	14.2	4,295	270,163	15,897	809	2,994	5.3
1959	40,058	674	14.3	4,338	265,114	16,362	823	3,104	5.3
1960	41,171	668	14.3	4,346	272,129	15,970	827	3,039	5.3
1961	42,033	663	14.4	4,393	279,668	15,708	830	2,968	5.3
1962	43,771	662	14.3	4,469	285,219	15,668	837	2,935	5.3
1963	45,246	655	14.6	4,485	297,864	15,057	838	2,813	5.4
1964	47,561	661	14.6	4,616	305,355	15,116	870	2,849	5.3
1965	49,723	661	14.5	4,681	314,284	14,895	875	2,784	5.3
1966	54,987	688	14.1	4,528	322,170	14,055	835	2,593	5.4
1967	57,546	699	14.1	4,627	337,920	13,693	860	2,545	5.4
1968	61,176	714	13.9	4,925	351,758	14,001	907	2,578	5.4
1969	64,850	727	13.6	4,820	364,213	13,234	889	2,442	5.4
1970	67,879	737	13.5	4,544	377,562	12,035	820	2,172	5.5
1971	71,418	743	13.6	4,802	397,075	12,093	844	2,125	5.7
1972	76,024	754	13.5	5,348	406,866	13,144	924	2,270	5.8
1973	78,337	737	13.4	5,792	424,920	13,631	988	2,326	5.9
1974	74,337	677	13.6	5,684	447,048	12,715	965	2,159	5.9
1975	74,253	665	14.0	6,055	462,156	13,102	1,053	2,279	5.8
1976	78,417	681	13.8	6,258	478,339	13,083	1,046	2,188	6.0
1977	79,187	676	14.1	5,823	490,761	11,865	974	1,984	6.0
1978	80,795	665	14.3	5,885	505,354	11,645	989	1,957	5.9
1979	76,761	620	14.6	5,947	526,765	11,290	996	1,891	6.0
1980	70,186	551	16.0	6,059	528,789	11,458	1,018	1,926	6.0
1981	69,326	538	16.5	6,241	543,894	11,475	1,054	1,938	5.9
1982	69,314	535	16.9	5,823	559,200	10,413	982	1,756	5.9
1983	70,497	534	17.1	5,199	582,884	8,919	878	1,507	5.9
1984	70,839	530	17.4	4,640	583,671	7,950	816	1,398	5.7
1985	71,700	538	17.5	4,478	593,485	7,545	834	1,405	5.4
1986	73,362	543	17.4	4,717	593,853	7,944	889	1,496	5.3
1987	73,498	539	18.0	5,330	602,055	8,852	919	1,527	5.8
1988	73,546	531	18.8	5,475	615,669	8,893	938	1,523	5.8
1989	74,120	533	19.0	5,670	625,040	9,072	949	1,519	6.0
1990	69,759	506	20.3	5,726	626,987	9,133	895	1,428	6.4
1991	64,501	487	21.2	5,750	631,279	9,109	864	1,369	6.7
1992	65,627	502	21.0	5,778	644,732	8,962	878	1,362	6.6
1993	67,246	512	20.6	6,125	654,432	9,359	929	1,420	6.6
1994	68,079	517	20.8	6,409	670,423	9,560	964	1,438	6.6
1995	67,993	514	21.3	6,383	685,503	9,312	964	1,406	6.6

TABLE Df383–412   Distance traveled, fuel consumption, and registered vehicles, by motor vehicle type: 1936–1995
Continued

	Single-unit trucks						Combination trucks					
	Distance traveled	Registered vehicles	Average distance traveled per vehicle	Fuel consumption	Average fuel consumption per vehicle	Average mileage per gallon consumed	Distance traveled	Registered vehicles	Average distance traveled per vehicle	Fuel consumption	Average fuel consumption per vehicle	Average mileage per gallon consumed
	Df401	Df402	Df403	Df404	Df405	Df406	Df407	Df408	Df409	Df410	Df411	Df412
Year	Million miles	Number	Miles	Million gallons	Gallons	Miles per gallon	Million miles	Number	Miles	Million gallons	Gallons	Miles per gallon
1936	—	—	—	—	—	—	—	—	—	—	—	—
1937	—	—	—	—	—	—	—	—	—	—	—	—
1938	—	—	—	—	—	—	—	—	—	—	—	—
1939	—	—	—	—	—	—	—	—	—	—	—	—
1940	—	—	—	—	—	—	—	—	—	—	—	—
1941	—	—	—	—	—	—	—	—	—	—	—	—
1942	—	—	—	—	—	—	—	—	—	—	—	—
1943	—	—	—	—	—	—	—	—	—	—	—	—
1944	—	—	—	—	—	—	—	—	—	—	—	—
1945	—	—	—	—	—	—	—	—	—	—	—	—
1946	—	—	—	—	—	—	—	—	—	—	—	—
1947	—	—	—	—	—	—	—	—	—	—	—	—
1948	—	—	—	—	—	—	—	—	—	—	—	—
1949	—	—	—	—	—	—	—	—	—	—	—	—
1950	—	—	—	—	—	—	—	—	—	—	—	—
1951	—	—	—	—	—	—	—	—	—	—	—	—
1952	—	—	—	—	—	—	—	—	—	—	—	—
1953	—	—	—	—	—	—	—	—	—	—	—	—
1954	—	—	—	—	—	—	—	—	—	—	—	—
1955	—	—	—	—	—	—	—	—	—	—	—	—
1956	—	—	—	—	—	—	—	—	—	—	—	—
1957	—	—	—	—	—	—	—	—	—	—	—	—
1958	—	—	—	—	—	—	—	—	—	—	—	—
1959	—	—	—	—	—	—	—	—	—	—	—	—
1960	—	—	—	—	—	—	—	—	—	—	—	—
1961	—	—	—	—	—	—	—	—	—	—	—	—
1962	—	—	—	—	—	—	—	—	—	—	—	—
1963	108,779	12,654,403	8,596	12,348	976	8.8	30,101	706,022	42,634	6,084	8,617	4.9
1964	115,236	13,275,106	8,681	13,199	994	8.7	30,611	738,006	41,478	6,271	8,497	4.9
1965	128,769	13,999,285	9,198	13,848	989	9.3	31,665	786,510	40,260	6,658	8,465	4.8
1966	113,773	14,730,750	7,723	13,023	884	8.7	30,118	772,244	39,001	5,819	7,535	5.2
1967	116,859	15,387,066	7,595	13,221	859	8.8	31,473	781,923	40,250	6,104	7,806	5.2
1968	128,029	16,118,620	7,943	14,283	886	9.0	32,627	823,182	39,635	6,584	7,998	5.0
1969	138,386	16,998,807	8,141	15,326	902	9.0	33,880	875,555	38,695	7,069	8,074	4.8
1970	150,367	17,891,996	8,404	16,282	910	9.2	35,134	905,082	38,819	7,348	8,119	4.8
1971	166,855	18,951,803	8,804	17,702	934	9.4	37,217	919,069	40,494	7,595	8,264	4.9
1972	188,036	20,346,308	9,242	19,994	983	9.4	40,706	961,437	42,339	8,120	8,446	5.0
1973	210,494	22,214,663	9,475	22,122	996	9.5	45,649	1,028,909	44,366	9,026	8,772	5.1
1974	216,198	23,545,196	9,182	21,918	931	9.9	45,966	1,084,971	42,366	9,080	8,369	5.1
1975	235,306	24,649,872	9,546	24,501	994	9.6	46,724	1,130,747	41,321	9,177	8,116	5.1
1976	262,224	26,651,008	9,839	26,534	996	9.9	49,680	1,224,917	40,558	9,703	7,921	5.1
1977	289,930	28,074,672	10,327	28,650	1,021	10.1	55,682	1,239,613	44,919	10,814	8,724	5.1
1978	322,161	29,994,157	10,741	31,118	1,037	10.4	62,992	1,341,707	46,949	12,165	9,067	5.2
1979	333,917	31,527,430	10,591	31,494	999	10.6	66,992	1,386,374	48,322	12,864	9,279	5.2
1980	330,748	32,249,718	10,256	30,719	953	10.8	68,678	1,416,869	48,472	13,037	9,201	5.3
1981	335,911	33,382,908	10,062	30,564	916	11.0	69,134	1,261,202	54,816	13,509	10,711	5.1
1982	346,792	34,117,054	10,165	29,505	865	11.8	70,765	1,265,321	55,927	13,583	10,734	5.2
1983	370,189	35,418,574	10,452	30,910	873	12.0	73,586	1,304,041	56,429	13,796	10,579	5.3
1984	402,425	36,167,319	11,127	32,844	908	12.3	77,377	1,340,144	57,738	14,188	10,587	5.5
1985	436,402	41,806,934	10,438	34,763	832	12.6	78,063	1,403,266	55,629	14,005	9,980	5.6
1986	469,552	43,695,129	10,746	36,460	834	12.9	81,038	1,407,783	57,564	14,475	10,282	5.6
1987	504,892	45,295,771	11,147	38,121	842	13.2	85,495	1,529,824	55,886	14,990	9,799	5.7
1988	551,641	48,274,146	11,427	40,355	836	13.7	88,551	1,667,327	53,110	15,224	9,131	5.8
1989	587,346	50,464,691	11,639	41,050	813	14.3	91,879	1,707,182	53,819	15,733	9,216	5.8
1990	626,472	52,761,536	11,874	43,968	833	14.2	94,341	1,708,895	55,206	16,133	9,441	5.8
1991	702,292	57,514,258	12,211	46,389	807	15.1	96,645	1,691,331	57,141	16,809	9,938	5.7
1992	760,737	61,460,985	12,378	49,166	800	15.5	99,510	1,675,363	59,396	17,216	10,276	5.8
1993	802,522	64,401,556	12,461	51,339	797	15.6	103,116	1,680,305	61,367	17,748	10,562	5.8
1994	825,918	67,809,973	12,180	53,144	784	15.5	108,932	1,681,500	64,783	18,653	11,093	5.8
1995	852,778	70,761,992	12,051	54,609	772	15.6	115,455	1,695,751	68,085	19,702	11,619	5.9

(continued)

TABLE Df383–412   Distance traveled, fuel consumption, and registered vehicles, by motor vehicle type: 1936–1995
Continued

Source

U.S. Federal Highway Administration, *Highway Statistics, Summary to 1995* (1997), Table VM-201A.

Documentation

The fifty states and the District of Columbia report travel by highway category, number of motor vehicles registered, and total fuel consumed. The travel and fuel data by vehicle type, stratification of trucks, and related data are calculated by the Federal Highway Administration (FHWA). Estimation procedures include use of the 1992 Census of Transportation Truck Inventory and Use Survey (TIUS) and independent analysis of light truck travel.

Stratification of truck figures is made by the FHWA using the 1992 TIUS and historic FHWA records. The combinations represent approximately the number of tractor-trailers with semi-trailers and a majority of heavy single-unit trucks used regularly in combination with trailers.

Total fuel consumption figures are derived from state fuel tax records and reflect impacts of continuously improving tax compliance and changes in federal and state fuel tax laws. Distribution by vehicle type is derived from FHWA estimates of miles per gallon for both diesel- and gasoline-powered vehicles as calculated from the 1992 TIUS and other sources.

TABLE Df413–417   Motor vehicle traffic fatalities and fatality rates: 1900–1995[1]

Contributed by Louis P. Cain

		Motor vehicle traffic fatality rates			
	Total highway fatalities	Per 1,000 miles of road	Per 1,000,000 vehicle miles of travel	Per 100,000 registered motor vehicles	Per 1,000 licensed drivers
	Df413	Df414	Df415	Df416	Df417
Year	Number	Per 1,000	Per 1,000,000	Per 100,000	Per 1,000
1900	36	0.02	36.00	450.00	—
1901	54	0.02	31.76	364.86	—
1902	79	0.03	25.48	343.48	—
1903	117	0.05	25.43	355.41	—
1904	172	0.07	22.93	311.09	—
1905	252	0.11	25.98	319.80	—
1906	338	0.14	27.26	312.67	—
1907	581	0.24	40.35	405.73	—
1908	751	0.31	40.59	378.53	—
1909	1,174	0.49	45.33	376.28	—
1910	1,599	0.66	44.66	341.30	—
1911	2,043	0.83	40.54	319.47	—
1912	2,968	1.18	40.16	314.41	—
1913	4,079	1.57	39.80	324.23	—
1914	4,468	1.68	31.78	253.43	—
1915	6,779	2.47	34.71	272.15	—
1916	7,766	2.72	30.03	214.65	—
1917	9,630	3.29	31.39	188.14	—
1918	10,390	3.46	28.10	168.66	—
1919	10,896	3.57	24.70	143.81	—
1920	12,155	3.91	25.54	131.56	—
1921	13,253	4.19	24.08	126.30	—
1922	14,859	4.65	21.95	121.06	—
1923	17,870	5.53	21.02	118.33	—
1924	18,400	5.67	17.55	104.47	—
1925	20,771	6.40	16.98	103.50	—
1926	22,194	6.85	15.77	99.97	—
1927	24,470	7.51	15.44	105.01	—
1928	26,557	8.14	15.36	107.57	—
1929	29,592	9.04	14.97	110.81	—
1930	31,204	9.57	15.12	116.65	—
1931	31,963	9.71	14.79	122.49	—
1932	27,979	8.49	13.95	114.71	—
1933	29,746	9.05	14.83	123.12	—
1934	34,240	10.35	15.88	135.54	—
1935	34,494	10.42	15.09	129.94	—
1936	36,126	11.06	14.33	126.73	—
1937	37,819	11.65	14.00	125.82	—
1938	31,083	9.54	11.46	104.26	—
1939	30,895	9.44	10.83	99.63	—

Note appears at end of table

TABLE Df413–417   Motor vehicle traffic fatalities and fatality rates: 1900–1995   *Continued*

	Total highway fatalities	Per 1,000 miles of road	Motor vehicle traffic fatality rates		
			Per 1,000,000 vehicle miles of travel	Per 100,000 registered motor vehicles	Per 1,000 licensed drivers
	Df413	Df414	Df415	Df416	Df417
Year	Number	Per 1,000	Per 1,000,000	Per 100,000	Per 1,000
1940	32,914	10.01	10.89	101.42	—
1941	38,142	11.52	11.43	109.31	—
1942	27,007	8.16	10.07	81.83	—
1943	22,727	6.86	10.92	73.58	—
1944	23,165	7.00	10.89	76.00	—
1945	26,785	8.07	10.71	86.30	—
1946	31,874	9.61	9.35	92.73	—
1947	31,193	9.38	8.41	82.43	—
1948	30,775	9.26	7.73	74.90	—
1949	30,246	9.11	7.13	67.68	50.99
1950	33,186	10.02	7.24	67.50	53.36
1951	35,309	10.61	7.19	68.02	54.79
1952	36,088	10.79	7.03	67.76	54.00
1953	36,190	10.75	6.65	64.38	51.80
1954	33,890	9.98	6.03	57.93	47.14
1955	36,688	10.73	6.06	58.52	49.12
1956	37,965	11.07	6.05	58.27	48.89
1957	36,932	10.70	5.73	55.02	46.38
1958	35,331	10.16	5.32	51.73	43.33
1959	36,223	10.32	5.17	50.76	42.87
1960	36,399	10.27	5.06	49.28	41.72
1961	36,285	10.16	4.92	47.77	40.89
1962	38,980	10.83	5.08	49.25	43.03
1963	41,723	11.52	5.18	50.45	44.59
1964	45,645	12.53	5.39	52.88	47.81
1965	47,089	12.76	5.30	52.11	47.81
1966	50,894	13.76	5.50	54.17	50.39
1967	51,559	13.92	5.35	53.21	49.97
1968	53,763	14.59	5.29	53.28	51.00
1969	55,043	14.84	5.18	52.37	50.82
1970	53,816	14.43	4.85	49.64	48.25
1971	53,907	14.34	4.57	47.71	47.11
1972	55,600	14.68	4.41	46.80	46.95
1973	55,096	14.47	4.20	43.85	45.33
1974	46,049	12.07	3.60	35.44	36.71
1975	45,500	11.85	3.43	34.22	35.06
1976	45,523	11.80	3.25	32.86	33.96
1977	47,878	12.38	3.26	33.69	34.66
1978	50,331	12.96	3.26	33.91	35.74
1979	51,093	13.04	3.34	33.64	35.66
1980	51,091	13.24	3.35	32.79	35.16
1981	49,301	12.80	3.17	31.15	33.52
1982	43,945	11.37	2.76	27.53	29.25
1983	42,589	10.98	2.58	26.01	27.59
1984	44,257	11.37	2.57	26.62	28.48
1985	43,825	11.34	2.47	25.53	27.94
1986	46,087	11.88	2.51	26.16	28.90
1987	46,390	11.97	2.41	25.91	28.67
1988	47,087	12.16	2.32	25.54	28.91
1989	45,582	11.76	2.17	24.34	27.53
1990	44,599	11.53	2.08	23.64	26.70
1991	41,508	10.69	1.91	22.04	24.56
1992	39,230	10.06	1.75	20.61	22.66
1993	40,134	10.28	1.75	20.68	23.61
1994	40,718	10.42	1.73	20.88	23.21
1995	41,770	10.68	1.72	20.73	23.65

[1] Beginning in 1976, fatalities include only persons injured in a vehicular accident who died within thirty days.

Source

U.S. Federal Highway Administration, *Highway Statistics, Summary to 1995* (1997), Table FI-200.

TABLE Df418–433   Fatalities and injuries in motor vehicle accidents, by highway category: 1967–1995[1]

Contributed by Louis P. Cain

	Fatalities in motor-vehicle accidents								Nonfatal injuries in motor-vehicle accidents							
		Federal-aid highways								Federal-aid highways						
			National highway system								National highway system					
	Total	Total	Interstate	Other	Other	Non-federal-aid highways	Rural	Urban	Total	Total	Interstate	Other	Other	Non-federal-aid highways	Rural	Urban
	Df418	Df419	Df420	Df421	Df422	Df423	Df424	Df425	Df426	Df427	Df428	Df429	Df430	Df431	Df432	Df433
Year	Number	Number	Number	Number	Number	Number	Number	Number	Number	Number	Number	Number	Number	Number	Number	Number
1967	51,559	35,806	3,220	21,318	11,268	15,753	34,108	17,451	2,475,926	1,246,509	94,535	746,937	405,037	1,229,417	873,969	1,601,957
1968	53,763	37,911	3,759	21,615	12,537	15,852	35,592	18,171	2,617,406	1,306,054	114,344	758,616	433,094	1,311,352	952,449	1,664,957
1969	55,043	38,576	4,215	21,425	12,936	16,467	36,301	18,742	2,710,959	1,358,273	131,498	770,786	455,989	1,352,686	938,647	1,772,312
1970	53,816	38,079	4,326	20,704	13,049	15,737	35,753	18,063	2,735,610	1,388,044	139,607	772,662	475,775	1,347,566	950,432	1,785,178
1971	53,907	38,262	4,637	20,717	12,908	15,645	35,613	18,294	2,660,053	1,371,938	150,268	754,873	466,797	1,288,115	956,100	1,703,953
1972	55,600	40,774	4,835	20,715	15,224	14,826	35,745	19,855	2,788,046	1,618,348	163,531	777,135	677,682	1,169,698	968,625	1,819,421
1973	55,096	41,571	4,946	20,361	16,264	13,525	34,862	20,234	2,841,495	1,755,084	169,255	816,768	769,061	1,086,411	972,468	1,869,027
1974	46,049	33,747	3,321	15,788	14,638	12,302	28,455	17,594	2,653,057	1,674,401	128,352	742,385	803,664	978,656	872,344	1,780,713
1975	45,500	33,950	3,282	15,243	15,425	11,550	27,721	17,779	2,808,323	1,813,108	141,530	699,912	971,666	995,215	915,726	1,892,597
1976	45,523	33,407	3,541	15,440	14,426	12,116	27,754	17,769	2,903,109	1,962,598	153,328	729,430	1,079,840	940,511	1,016,958	1,886,151
1977	47,878	35,065	4,130	16,113	14,822	12,813	29,368	18,510	3,045,401	2,082,177	171,742	757,584	1,152,851	963,224	1,051,187	1,994,214
1978	50,331	37,446	4,644	16,762	16,040	12,885	30,958	19,373	3,168,788	2,198,343	192,802	763,807	1,241,734	970,445	1,089,046	2,079,742
1979	51,093	38,217	4,444	16,765	17,008	12,876	30,790	20,303	3,158,331	2,182,443	189,936	760,600	1,231,907	975,888	1,072,138	2,086,193
1980	51,091	38,034	4,447	16,845	16,742	13,057	29,545	21,546	3,057,409	2,008,079	181,150	717,217	1,109,712	1,049,330	984,312	2,073,097
1981	49,301	37,503	4,552	16,832	16,119	11,798	28,470	20,831	3,066,821	2,047,787	183,798	736,919	1,127,070	1,019,034	983,506	2,083,315
1982	43,945	33,514	4,099	14,679	14,736	10,431	25,031	18,914	2,993,495	2,018,885	183,872	716,889	1,118,124	974,610	974,449	2,019,046
1983	42,589	32,378	3,999	14,161	14,218	10,211	24,152	18,437	3,056,676	2,057,373	191,621	733,788	1,131,964	999,303	978,325	2,078,351
1984	44,377	34,031	4,320	14,369	15,342	10,346	25,036	19,341	3,211,788	2,170,044	203,814	764,009	1,202,221	1,041,744	1,028,543	2,183,245
1985	43,825	33,782	4,166	14,139	15,477	10,043	24,492	19,333	3,354,864	2,285,648	218,385	804,831	1,262,432	1,069,216	1,051,527	2,303,337
1986	46,087	34,882	4,302	14,750	15,830	11,205	26,189	19,898	3,431,292	2,297,821	221,337	826,223	1,250,261	1,133,471	1,102,044	2,329,248
1987	46,390	35,756	4,634	15,475	15,647	10,634	26,646	19,744	3,508,346	2,377,363	236,543	856,042	1,284,778	1,130,983	1,119,211	2,389,135
1988	47,087	35,957	5,125	15,022	15,810	11,130	27,635	19,452	3,605,786	2,442,061	255,713	853,250	1,333,098	1,163,725	1,154,173	2,451,613
1989	45,582	34,842	5,003	14,245	15,594	10,740	26,057	19,525	3,645,088	2,519,397	262,196	853,331	1,403,870	1,125,691	1,160,925	2,484,163
1990	44,599	34,064	4,959	13,769	15,336	10,535	25,786	18,813	3,599,043	2,521,324	261,285	840,709	1,419,330	1,077,719	1,064,821	2,534,222
1991	41,508	31,299	4,490	13,130	13,679	10,209	24,393	17,115	3,449,624	2,452,790	255,658	815,950	1,381,182	996,834	1,020,013	2,429,611
1992	39,230	29,485	4,205	10,098	15,182	9,745	20,931	18,299	3,242,134	2,316,265	221,778	931,409	1,163,078	925,869	788,345	2,453,789
1993	40,134	29,984	4,244	10,754	14,986	10,150	21,279	18,855	3,258,451	2,326,650	231,074	937,093	1,158,483	931,801	817,265	2,441,186
1994	40,718	30,916	4,312	4,434	22,170	9,802	21,653	19,065	3,303,136	2,371,960	242,310	347,465	1,782,185	931,176	820,521	2,482,615
1995	41,770	31,840	4,450	8,192	19,198	9,930	21,724	20,046	3,276,419	2,378,452	309,747	398,664	1,670,041	897,967	826,668	2,449,751

[1] Beginning in 1976, fatalities include only persons who died within thirty days of injury in a vehicular accident.

Source

U.S. Federal Highway Administration, *Highway Statistics, Summary to 1995* (1997), Tables FI-210, 211.

Documentation

Federal-Aid Systems include segments open to traffic.

Series Df420–421 and Df428–429. Based on the Federal-Aid Primary System until 1991, the interim National Highway System (NHS) for 1992 and 1993; the proposed NHS for 1994; and the approved NHS for 1995.

Series Df422 and Df430. Includes the Secondary and Urban Systems prior to 1992. Starting in 1992, includes all functional systems, except those classified as local and minor collector, or those that were part of the NHS.

TABLE Df434–447   Fatalities and injuries in motor vehicle accidents, by functional category of roadway: 1980–1995

Contributed by Louis P. Cain

	Fatalities in motor-vehicle accidents							Nonfatal injuries in motor-vehicle accidents						
	Total	Interstate	Other principal arterial	Minor arterial	Major collector	Minor collector	Local	Total	Interstate	Other principal arterial	Minor arterial	Major collector	Minor collector	Local
	Df434	Df435	Df436	Df437	Df438	Df439	Df440	Df441	Df442	Df443	Df444	Df445	Df446	Df447
Year	Number	Number	Number	Number	Number	Number	Number	Number	Number	Number	Number	Number	Number	Number
1980	51,091	4,447	8,337	11,923	12,710	4,280	9,394	3,057,409	181,150	228,732	782,262	705,441	302,600	857,224
1981	49,301	4,552	8,679	11,229	12,498	3,837	8,506	3,066,821	183,798	239,833	797,487	722,762	296,641	826,300
1982	43,945	4,099	6,028	11,570	11,669	3,194	7,385	2,993,495	183,872	222,935	819,239	686,737	264,442	816,270
1983	42,589	3,999	5,820	11,536	10,751	3,301	7,182	3,056,676	191,621	229,837	831,003	703,400	269,427	831,388
1984	44,377	4,320	5,897	12,083	11,368	3,378	7,331	3,211,788	203,814	236,681	873,702	749,284	284,650	863,657
1985	43,825	4,166	5,866	11,888	11,371	3,241	7,293	3,354,864	218,385	242,861	936,609	769,923	293,657	893,429
1986	46,087	4,302	6,384	11,997	11,774	3,467	8,163	3,431,292	221,337	273,453	937,989	763,213	302,813	932,487
1987	46,390	4,634	6,775	12,481	11,464	3,257	7,779	3,508,346	236,543	283,096	973,296	785,161	303,750	926,500
1988	47,087	5,125	6,490	12,211	11,726	3,412	8,123	3,605,786	255,713	295,312	947,684	841,218	305,231	960,628
1989	45,582	5,003	6,190	11,688	11,377	3,226	8,098	3,645,088	262,196	277,573	980,633	873,904	313,821	936,961
1990	44,599	4,959	5,910	11,742	10,955	3,307	7,726	3,599,043	261,285	281,586	998,043	845,690	312,346	900,093
1991	41,508	4,490	5,716	10,736	9,904	2,943	7,719	3,449,624	255,658	280,100	951,188	833,471	300,758	828,449
1992	39,230	4,205	4,566	9,575	8,845	3,876	8,163	3,242,134	221,778	232,910	832,515	764,538	328,782	861,611
1993	40,134	4,244	5,104	9,459	8,493	4,750	8,084	3,258,451	231,074	227,928	850,501	769,081	323,569	856,298
1994	40,718	4,312	6,358	8,497	9,131	4,083	8,337	3,303,136	242,310	236,115	822,391	825,058	303,195	874,067
1995	41,770	4,450	5,788	10,168	8,866	4,133	8,365	3,276,419	309,747	206,947	939,687	703,234	278,980	837,824

Source

U.S. Federal Highway Administration, *Highway Statistics, Summary to 1995* (1997), Tables FI-220, 221.

Documentation

Fatalities include only persons who died within thirty days of injury in a vehicular accident.

TABLE Df448–456   Motor vehicle accidents, death rates, and deaths, by type of accident: 1913–1996

Contributed by Louis P. Cain

		Traffic deaths					Traffic death rates		
				Collision accidents					
	Total accidents	Total	Noncollision accidents	With other motor vehicles	With pedestrians	With fixed objects	Per 100,000 population	Per 10,000 motor vehicles	Per 100 million vehicle miles
	Df448	Df449	Df450	Df451	Df452	Df453	Df454	Df455	Df456
Year	Thousand	Number	Number	Number	Number	Number	Per 100,000	Per 10,000	Per 100 million miles
1913	—	4,200	—	—	—	—	—	—	—
1914	—	4,700	—	—	—	—	—	—	—
1915	—	6,600	—	—	—	—	—	—	—
1916	—	8,200	—	—	—	—	—	—	—
1917	—	10,200	—	—	—	—	—	—	—
1918	—	10,700	—	—	—	—	—	—	—
1919	—	11,200	—	—	—	—	—	—	—
1920	—	12,500	—	—	—	—	—	—	—
1921	—	13,900	—	—	—	—	—	—	—
1922	—	15,300	—	—	—	—	—	—	—
1923	—	18,400	—	—	—	—	16.5	12.2	—
1924	—	19,400	—	—	—	—	17.1	11.0	—
1925	—	21,900	—	—	—	—	19.1	11.0	17.9
1926	—	23,400	—	—	—	—	20.1	10.6	18.0
1927	—	25,800	7,280	3,430	10,820	500	21.8	11.2	17.7
1928	—	28,000	7,360	4,310	11,420	540	23.4	11.4	17.4
1929	—	31,200	8,430	5,400	12,250	620	25.7	11.8	17.3
1930	—	32,900	8,730	5,880	12,900	720	26.7	12.4	17.4
1931	—	33,700	7,850	6,820	13,370	870	27.2	13.0	17.0
1932	—	29,500	7,000	6,070	11,490	800	23.6	12.2	16.1
1933	—	31,363	8,680	6,470	12,840	900	25.0	13.0	15.6
1934	—	36,101	9,820	8,110	14,480	1,040	28.6	14.3	16.8
1935	—	36,369	9,720	8,750	14,350	1,010	28.6	13.7	15.9
1936	—	38,089	9,410	9,500	15,250	1,060	29.7	13.4	15.1
1937	7,000	39,643	9,690	10,320	15,500	1,160	30.8	13.2	14.7
1938	5,800	32,582	7,350	8,900	12,850	940	25.1	10.9	12.0
1939	5,700	32,386	7,900	8,700	12,400	1,000	24.7	10.4	11.4

(continued)

TABLE Df448–456 Motor vehicle accidents, death rates, and deaths, by type of accident: 1913–1996 *Continued*

		Traffic deaths					Traffic death rates		
	Total accidents	Total	Noncollision accidents	With other motor vehicles	With pedestrians	With fixed objects	Per 100,000 population	Per 10,000 motor vehicles	Per 100 million vehicle miles
				Collision accidents					
	Df448	Df449	Df450	Df451	Df452	Df453	Df454	Df455	Df456
Year	Thousand	Number	Number	Number	Number	Number	Per 100,000	Per 10,000	Per 100 million miles
1940	6,100	34,501	7,800	10,100	12,700	1,100	26.1	10.6	11.4
1941	7,000	39,969	9,450	12,500	13,550	1,350	30.0	11.5	12.0
1942	5,200	28,309	6,740	7,300	10,650	850	21.1	8.6	10.6
1943	4,400	23,823	5,690	5,300	9,900	700	17.8	7.7	11.4
1944	4,800	24,282	5,600	5,700	9,900	700	18.3	8.0	11.4
1945	5,500	28,076	6,600	7,150	11,000	800	21.2	9.1	11.2
1946	6,150	33,411	8,900	9,400	11,600	950	23.9	9.7	9.8
1947	8,400	32,697	8,800	9,900	10,450	1,000	22.8	8.6	8.8
1948	8,200	32,259	8,950	10,200	9,950	1,000	22.1	7.9	8.1
1949	7,600	31,701	9,100	10,500	8,800	1,100	21.3	7.1	7.5
1950	8,300	34,763	10,600	11,650	9,000	1,300	23.0	7.1	7.6
1951	9,400	36,996	11,200	13,100	9,150	1,400	24.1	7.1	7.5
1952	9,500	37,794	11,900	13,500	8,900	1,450	24.3	7.1	7.4
1953	9,900	37,955	12,200	13,400	8,750	1,500	24.0	6.7	7.0
1954	9,550	35,586	11,500	12,800	8,000	1,500	22.1	6.1	6.3
1955	9,900	38,426	12,100	14,500	8,200	1,600	23.4	6.1	6.3
1956	10,300	39,628	13,000	15,200	7,900	1,600	23.7	6.1	6.3
1957	10,200	38,702	11,800	15,400	7,850	1,700	22.7	5.7	6.0
1958	10,000	36,981	11,600	14,200	7,650	1,650	21.3	5.4	5.6
1959	10,200	37,910	11,800	14,900	7,850	1,600	21.5	5.3	5.4
1960	10,400	38,137	11,900	14,800	7,850	1,700	21.2	5.1	5.3
1961	10,400	38,091	12,200	14,700	7,650	1,700	20.8	5.0	5.2
1962	11,000	40,804	12,900	16,400	7,900	1,750	22.0	5.1	5.3
1963	11,500	43,564	13,800	17,600	8,200	1,900	23.1	5.2	5.4
1964	12,300	47,700	14,600	19,600	9,000	2,100	25.0	5.5	5.6
1965	13,200	49,163	14,900	20,800	8,900	2,200	25.4	5.4	5.5
1966	13,600	53,041	16,300	22,200	9,400	2,500	27.1	5.5	5.7
1967	13,700	52,924	16,700	22,000	9,400	2,350	26.8	5.4	5.5
1968	14,600	54,862	17,400	22,400	9,900	2,700	27.5	5.3	5.4
1969	15,500	55,791	15,700	23,700	10,100	3,900	27.7	5.2	5.2
1970	16,000	54,633	15,400	23,200	9,900	3,800	26.8	4.9	4.9
1971	16,400	54,381	15,300	23,100	9,900	3,800	26.3	4.7	4.6
1972	17,000	56,278	15,800	23,900	10,300	3,900	26.9	4.6	4.4
1973	16,600	55,511	15,600	23,600	10,200	3,800	26.3	4.3	4.2
1974	15,600	46,402	12,800	19,700	8,500	3,100	21.8	3.4	3.6
1975	16,500	45,853	12,700	19,550	8,400	3,130	21.3	3.3	3.4
1976	16,800	47,038	13,000	20,100	8,600	3,200	21.6	3.3	3.3
1977	17,600	49,510	13,700	21,200	9,100	3,400	22.5	3.3	3.4
1978	18,300	52,411	14,500	22,400	9,600	3,600	23.6	3.4	3.4
1979	18,100	53,524	14,800	23,100	9,800	3,700	23.8	3.4	3.5
1980	17,900	53,172	14,700	23,000	9,700	3,700	23.4	3.3	3.5
1981	18,000	51,385	14,200	22,200	9,400	3,600	22.4	3.1	3.3
1982	18,100	45,779	12,600	19,800	8,400	3,200	19.7	2.8	2.9
1983	18,300	44,452	12,200	19,200	8,200	3,100	19.0	2.6	2.7
1984	18,800	46,263	12,700	20,000	8,500	3,200	19.6	2.7	2.7
1985	19,300	45,901	12,600	19,900	8,500	3,200	19.2	2.6	2.6
1986	17,700	47,865	13,100	20,800	8,900	3,300	19.9	2.6	2.6
1987	20,800	48,290	5,200	20,700	7,500	13,200	19.8	2.6	2.5
1988	20,600	49,078	5,300	20,900	7,700	13,400	20.1	2.6	2.4
1989	12,800	47,575	4,900	20,300	7,800	12,900	19.2	2.5	2.3
1990	11,500	46,814	4,900	19,900	7,300	13,100	18.8	2.4	2.2
1991	11,300	43,536	4,700	18,200	6,600	12,600	17.3	2.3	2.0
1992	10,000	40,982	4,100	17,600	6,300	11,700	16.1	2.1	1.8
1993	11,900	41,893	4,200	18,300	6,400	11,500	16.3	2.1	1.8
1994	11,200	42,524	4,300	19,300	5,900	11,800	16.3	2.1	1.8
1995	10,700	43,363	4,500	18,800	6,700	11,900	16.5	2.1	1.8
1996	11,200	43,300	4,600	19,300	6,100	12,000	16.3	2.1	1.8

Source

National Safety Council, Chicago, *Accident Facts* (1997), and earlier editions.

Documentation

Deaths generally include fatalities that occurred within one year of a traffic accident.

TABLE Df457–472 Motor vehicle deaths and death rates, by age: 1913–1996[1,2]

Contributed by Louis P. Cain

	Motor vehicle deaths								Motor vehicle death rates							
	All ages	Younger than 5	5–14	15–24	25–44	45–64	65–74	75 and older	All ages	Younger than 5	5–14	15–24	25–44	45–64	65–74	75 years and older
	Df457	Df458	Df459	Df460	Df461	Df462	Df463	Df464	Df465	Df466	Df467	Df468	Df469	Df470	Df471 [3]	Df472
Year	Number	Number	Number	Number	Number	Number	Number	Number	Per 100,000	Per 100,000	Per 100,000	Per 100,000	Per 100,000	Per 100,000	Per 100,000	Per 100,000
1913	4,200	300	1,100	600	1,100	800	300	—	4.4	2.3	5.5	3.1	3.8	5.3	8.5	—
1914	4,700	300	1,200	700	1,200	900	400	—	4.8	2.5	5.7	3.5	4.1	6.2	9.3	—
1915	6,600	400	1,500	1,000	1,700	1,400	600	—	6.6	3.5	7.3	5.0	5.6	8.8	13.5	—
1916	8,200	600	1,800	1,300	2,100	1,700	700	—	8.1	4.7	8.6	6.0	7.0	10.7	15.8	—
1917	10,200	700	2,400	1,400	2,700	2,100	900	—	10.0	5.6	10.6	7.4	8.6	12.6	18.6	—
1918	10,700	800	2,700	1,400	2,500	2,300	1,000	—	10.3	6.9	12.3	7.7	8.3	13.7	21.2	—
1919	11,200	900	3,000	1,400	2,500	2,100	1,300	—	10.7	7.5	13.9	7.5	8.1	12.4	24.1	—
1920	12,500	1,000	3,300	1,700	2,800	2,300	1,400	—	11.7	8.6	14.6	8.7	8.8	13.5	27.0	—
1921	13,900	1,100	3,400	1,800	3,300	2,700	1,600	—	12.9	9.0	14.5	9.2	10.2	15.4	31.0	—
1922	15,300	1,100	3,500	2,100	3,700	3,100	1,800	—	13.9	9.2	15.0	10.8	11.1	17.2	34.9	—
1923	18,400	1,200	3,700	2,800	4,600	3,900	2,200	—	16.5	9.7	15.6	13.4	13.6	21.0	40.5	—
1924	19,400	1,400	3,800	2,900	4,700	4,100	2,500	—	17.1	11.1	16.1	14.3	13.7	21.8	43.7	—
1925	21,900	1,400	3,900	3,600	5,400	4,800	2,800	—	19.1	11.0	15.6	17.2	15.8	25.0	48.9	—
1926	23,400	1,400	3,900	3,900	5,900	5,200	3,100	—	20.1	11.0	15.9	18.6	17.1	26.3	51.4	—
1927	25,800	1,600	4,000	4,300	6,600	5,800	3,500	—	21.8	12.8	16.0	20.0	18.8	28.9	56.9	—
1928	28,000	1,600	3,800	4,900	7,200	6,600	3,900	—	23.4	12.7	15.5	21.9	20.2	32.4	62.2	—
1929	31,200	1,600	3,900	5,700	8,000	7,500	4,500	—	25.7	13.4	15.6	25.6	22.3	35.6	68.6	—
1930	32,900	1,500	3,600	6,200	8,700	8,000	4,900	—	26.7	13.0	14.7	27.4	23.9	37.0	72.5	—
1931	33,700	1,500	3,600	6,300	9,100	8,200	5,000	—	27.2	13.3	14.5	27.9	24.8	37.4	70.6	—
1932	29,500	1,200	2,900	5,100	8,100	7,400	4,800	—	23.6	11.3	12.0	22.6	22.0	32.9	63.6	—
1933	31,363	1,274	3,121	5,649	8,730	7,947	4,642	—	25.0	12.0	12.7	24.8	23.4	34.7	63.1	—
1934	36,101	1,210	3,182	6,561	10,232	9,530	5,386	—	28.6	11.7	13.0	28.6	27.2	40.7	71.0	—
1935	36,369	1,253	2,951	6,755	10,474	9,562	5,374	—	28.6	12.3	12.2	29.2	27.6	39.9	68.9	—
1936	38,089	1,324	3,026	7,184	10,807	10,089	5,659	—	29.7	13.2	12.6	30.8	28.2	41.3	70.5	—
1937	39,643	1,303	2,991	7,800	10,877	10,475	6,197	—	30.8	13.0	12.7	33.2	28.2	42.0	75.1	—
1938	32,582	1,122	2,511	6,016	8,772	8,711	5,450	—	25.1	11.0	10.8	25.4	22.5	34.3	64.1	—
1939	32,386	1,192	2,339	6,318	8,917	8,292	5,328	—	24.7	11.2	10.4	26.5	22.6	32.2	60.2	—
1940	34,501	1,176	2,584	6,846	9,362	8,882	5,651	—	26.1	11.1	11.5	28.7	23.5	33.9	62.1	—
1941	39,969	1,378	2,838	8,414	11,069	9,829	6,441	—	30.0	12.7	12.6	35.7	27.5	37.0	68.6	—
1942	28,309	1,069	1,991	5,932	7,747	7,254	4,316	—	21.1	9.5	8.8	25.8	19.2	26.9	44.5	—
1943	23,823	1,132	1,959	4,522	6,454	5,996	3,760	—	17.8	9.4	8.6	20.6	16.1	21.9	37.6	—
1944	24,282	1,203	2,093	4,561	6,514	5,982	3,929	—	18.3	9.6	9.1	22.5	16.6	21.6	38.2	—
1945	28,076	1,290	2,386	5,358	7,578	6,794	4,670	—	21.2	10.0	10.3	27.8	19.7	24.2	44.1	—
1946	33,411	1,568	2,508	7,445	8,955	7,532	5,403	—	23.9	11.9	10.8	34.4	21.1	26.4	49.6	—
1947	32,697	1,502	2,275	7,251	8,775	7,468	5,426	—	22.8	10.5	9.7	32.8	20.3	25.7	48.2	—
1948	32,259	1,635	2,337	7,218	8,702	7,190	3,173	2,004	22.1	11.0	9.8	32.5	19.8	24.3	39.6	55.4
1949	31,701	1,667	2,158	6,772	8,892	7,073	3,116	2,023	21.3	10.7	9.0	30.7	19.9	23.4	37.8	53.9
1950	34,763	1,767	2,152	7,600	10,214	7,728	3,264	2,038	23.0	10.8	8.8	34.5	22.5	25.1	38.8	52.4
1951	36,996	1,875	2,300	7,713	11,253	8,276	3,444	2,135	24.1	10.9	9.2	36.0	24.7	26.5	39.5	53.0
1952	37,794	1,951	2,295	8,115	11,380	8,463	3,472	2,118	24.3	11.3	8.7	38.6	24.7	26.7	38.5	50.8
1953	37,956	2,019	2,368	8,169	11,302	8,318	3,508	2,271	24.0	11.5	8.5	39.1	24.5	25.8	37.7	52.6
1954	35,586	1,864	2,332	7,571	10,521	7,848	3,247	2,203	22.1	10.4	8.1	36.2	22.6	24.0	33.9	49.0

Notes appear at end of table   (continued)

Motor vehicle deaths (Df457–Df464) · **Motor vehicle death rates** (Df465–Df472)

Year	All ages Df457 Number	Younger than 5 Df458 Number	5–14 Df459 Number	15–24 Df460 Number	25–44 Df461 Number	45–64 Df462 Number	65–74 Df463 Number	75 and older Df464 Number	All ages Df465 Per 100,000	Younger than 5 Df466 Per 100,000	5–14 Df467 Per 100,000	15–24 Df468 Per 100,000	25–44 Df469 Per 100,000	45–64 Df470 Per 100,000	65–74 Df471 [3] Per 100,000	75 years and older Df472 Per 100,000
1955	38,426	1,875	2,406	8,656	11,448	8,372	3,455	2,214	23.4	10.2	8.0	40.9	24.5	25.2	35.1	47.1
1956	39,628	1,770	2,640	9,169	11,551	8,573	3,657	2,268	23.7	9.4	8.4	42.9	24.6	25.3	36.2	46.4
1957	38,702	1,785	2,604	8,667	11,230	8,545	3,560	2,311	22.7	9.2	8.0	39.7	23.9	24.8	34.4	45.5
1958	36,981	1,791	2,710	8,388	10,414	7,922	3,535	2,221	21.3	9.1	8.1	37.0	22.3	22.6	33.5	42.3
1959	37,910	1,842	2,719	8,969	10,358	8,263	3,487	2,272	21.5	9.1	7.9	38.2	22.2	23.2	32.3	41.8
1960	38,137	1,953	2,814	9,117	10,189	8,294	3,457	2,313	21.2	9.6	7.9	37.7	21.7	22.9	31.3	41.1
1961	38,091	1,891	2,802	9,088	10,212	8,267	3,467	2,364	20.8	9.2	7.6	36.5	21.8	22.5	30.7	40.5
1962	40,804	1,903	3,028	10,157	10,701	8,812	3,696	2,507	22.0	9.3	8.1	38.4	22.9	23.7	32.2	41.7
1963	43,564	1,991	3,063	11,123	11,356	9,506	3,786	2,739	23.1	9.8	8.0	40.0	24.3	25.2	32.6	44.3
1964	47,700	2,120	3,430	12,400	12,500	10,200	4,150	2,900	25.0	10.5	8.8	42.6	26.8	26.6	35.5	45.2
1965	49,163	2,059	3,526	13,395	12,595	10,509	4,077	3,002	25.4	10.4	8.9	44.2	27.0	27.0	34.6	45.4
1966	53,041	2,182	3,869	15,298	13,282	11,051	4,217	3,142	27.1	11.4	9.7	48.7	28.5	27.9	35.4	46.2
1967	52,924	2,067	3,845	15,646	12,987	10,902	4,285	3,192	26.8	11.2	9.5	48.4	27.8	27.1	35.6	45.4
1968	54,862	1,987	4,105	16,543	13,602	11,031	4,261	3,333	27.5	11.1	10.1	49.8	28.8	27.0	35.1	46.0
1969	55,791	2,077	4,045	17,443	13,868	11,012	4,210	3,136	27.7	12.0	9.9	50.7	29.1	26.6	34.3	42.0
1970	54,633	1,915	4,159	16,720	13,446	11,099	4,084	3,210	26.8	11.2	10.2	46.7	27.9	26.4	32.7	42.2
1971	54,381	1,885	4,256	17,103	13,307	10,471	4,108	3,251	26.3	10.9	10.5	45.7	27.4	24.7	32.4	41.3
1972	56,278	1,896	4,258	17,942	13,758	10,836	4,138	3,450	26.9	11.1	10.7	47.1	27.4	25.3	32.0	42.6
1973	55,511	1,998	4,124	18,032	14,013	10,216	3,892	3,236	26.3	11.9	10.5	46.3	27.2	23.6	29.4	39.1
1974	46,402	1,546	3,332	15,905	11,834	8,159	3,071	2,555	21.8	9.4	8.6	40.0	22.4	18.8	22.6	30.1
1975	45,853	1,576	3,286	15,672	11,969	7,663	3,047	2,640	21.3	9.8	8.6	38.7	22.1	17.5	21.9	30.1
1976	47,038	1,532	3,175	16,650	12,112	7,770	3,082	2,717	21.6	9.8	8.4	40.3	21.8	17.6	21.6	30.1
1977	49,510	1,472	3,142	18,092	13,031	8,000	3,060	2,713	22.5	9.5	8.5	43.3	22.7	18.1	20.9	29.3
1978	52,411	1,551	3,130	19,164	14,574	8,048	3,217	2,727	23.6	9.9	8.6	45.4	24.6	18.2	21.5	28.7
1979	53,524	1,461	2,952	19,369	15,658	8,162	3,171	2,751	23.8	9.1	8.3	45.6	25.6	18.4	20.7	28.1
1980	53,172	1,426	2,747	19,040	16,133	8,022	2,991	2,813	23.4	8.7	7.9	44.8	25.5	18.0	19.1	28.0
1981	51,385	1,256	2,575	17,363	16,447	7,818	3,090	2,836	22.4	7.4	7.5	41.1	25.2	17.6	19.4	27.5
1982	45,779	1,300	2,301	15,324	14,469	6,879	2,825	2,681	19.8	7.5	6.7	36.8	21.5	15.5	17.5	25.2
1983	44,452	1,233	2,341	14,289	14,323	6,690	2,827	2,849	19.0	7.0	6.6	34.8	20.6	15.0	17.2	26.0
1984	46,263	1,138	2,263	14,738	15,036	6,954	3,020	3,114	19.6	6.4	6.7	36.4	21.0	15.6	18.2	27.7
1985	45,901	1,195	2,319	14,277	15,034	6,885	3,014	3,177	19.3	6.7	6.9	35.7	20.5	15.4	17.9	27.5
1986	47,865	1,188	2,350	15,227	15,844	6,799	3,096	3,361	19.9	6.6	7.0	38.5	21.0	15.2	18.1	28.3
1987	48,290	1,190	2,397	14,447	16,405	7,021	3,277	3,553	19.9	6.6	7.1	37.1	21.3	15.7	18.8	29.1
1988	49,078	1,220	2,423	14,406	16,580	7,245	3,429	3,775	20.1	6.7	7.1	37.8	21.2	15.9	19.5	30.2
1989	47,575	1,221	2,266	12,941	16,571	7,287	3,465	3,824	19.3	6.6	6.5	34.6	20.8	15.9	19.4	29.8
1990	46,814	1,123	2,059	12,607	16,488	7,282	3,350	3,905	18.8	6.0	5.8	34.2	20.4	15.7	18.5	29.7
1991	43,536	1,076	2,011	11,664	15,082	6,616	3,193	3,894	17.3	5.6	5.6	32.1	18.3	14.2	17.5	28.9
1992	40,982	1,020	1,904	10,305	14,071	6,597	3,247	3,838	16.1	5.2	5.2	28.5	17.1	13.6	17.6	27.8
1993	41,893	1,081	1,963	10,500	14,283	6,711	3,116	4,239	16.3	5.5	5.3	29.1	17.3	13.5	16.7	30.0
1994	42,524	1,139	2,026	10,660	13,966	7,097	3,385	4,251	16.3	5.8	5.4	29.5	16.8	13.9	18.1	29.4
1995	43,363	900	2,100	10,600	14,900	7,300	3,300	4,300	16.5	4.6	5.5	29.3	17.9	14.0	17.6	29.1
1996	43,300	1,000	2,100	10,600	14,600	7,400	3,200	4,400	16.3	5.2	5.5	29.3	17.4	13.8	17.1	29.0

[1] Data from the National Center for Health Statistics (NCHS) data for registration states (1913–1932); National Safety Council estimates (1964, 1995, and 1996); and NCHS totals (other years).

[2] Through 1947, the last age category was 65 and older. Those numbers are reported here in the 65–74 age category.

[3] Includes "age unknown," which accounted for twenty-three deaths in 1967.

Source
National Safety Council, Chicago, *Accident Facts* (1997), and earlier editions.

Documentation
Death rates are per 100,000 population in each age group. The 1996 data are identified in the source as preliminary.

TABLE Df473–481   Motor fuel consumption, by highway and public–private uses and fuel type: 1919–1995[1,2]

Contributed by Louis P. Cain

		Highway				Nonhighway use of gasoline			Gasoline losses from evaporation, handling, etc.
	Total	Total	Private and commercial use		Public use of gasoline	Total	Private and commercial use	Public use	
			Gasoline	Special fuels					
	Df473	Df474	Df475	Df476	Df477	Df478	Df479	Df480	Df481
Year	Million gallons	Million gallons	Million gallons	Million gallons	Million gallons	Million gallons	Million gallons	Million gallons	Million gallons
1919	2,747	2,672	2,605	—	67	75	75	—	—
1920	3,448	3,346	3,264	—	82	102	102	—	—
1921	4,065	3,935	3,841	—	94	130	130	—	—
1922	5,014	4,841	4,728	—	113	173	173	—	—
1923	6,313	6,078	5,939	—	139	235	235	—	—
1924	7,809	7,497	7,328	—	169	312	312	—	—
1925	9,144	8,749	8,557	—	193	395	395	—	—
1926	10,552	10,064	9,849	—	215	488	488	—	—
1927	11,937	11,331	11,094	—	237	606	606	—	—
1928	13,090	12,361	12,106	—	255	729	729	—	—
1929	15,051	14,139	13,858	—	281	912	912	—	—
1930	15,778	14,754	14,454	—	300	1,024	1,024	—	—
1931	16,712	15,457	15,149	—	308	1,165	1,165	—	90
1932	15,517	14,339	14,013	—	327	1,088	1,088	—	89
1933	15,483	14,348	13,999	—	349	1,020	1,020	—	115
1934	16,726	15,415	15,034	—	381	1,108	1,087	21	203
1935	17,807	16,345	15,919	—	425	1,246	1,210	36	217
1936	19,738	18,099	17,641	—	458	1,401	1,360	41	238
1937	21,306	19,455	18,974	—	482	1,591	1,549	42	259
1938	21,578	19,612	19,110	—	501	1,641	1,592	49	326
1939	22,854	20,714	20,171	—	544	1,795	1,741	53	345
1940	24,335	22,001	21,418	—	584	1,967	1,906	61	366
1941	26,720	24,192	23,638	—	555	2,237	2,075	162	291
1942	22,692	19,940	19,473	—	467	2,499	2,358	141	254
1943	18,871	16,004	15,668	—	336	2,639	2,528	111	229
1944	19,524	16,430	16,090	—	340	2,862	2,748	115	232
1945	22,304	19,149	18,798	—	351	2,898	2,778	120	257
1946	29,201	25,649	25,269	—	380	3,228	3,113	115	325
1947	32,036	28,216	27,714	—	501	3,465	3,315	149	355
1948	34,707	30,461	29,909	—	552	3,869	3,707	162	378
1949	36,842	32,438	31,430	427	581	4,009	3,840	169	395
1950	40,288	35,662	34,506	537	619	4,178	3,999	179	449
1951	42,961	38,139	36,781	708	650	4,345	4,160	185	477
1952	45,538	40,597	39,074	837	686	4,453	4,258	195	489
1953	47,904	42,746	41,081	940	725	4,649	4,445	205	509
1954	49,637	44,366	42,532	1,047	787	4,753	4,531	223	517
1955	53,117	47,732	45,710	1,205	817	4,835	4,603	232	551
1956	55,712	50,216	47,956	1,410	849	4,935	4,691	244	561
1957	57,445	51,866	49,318	1,636	912	5,090	4,827	263	489
1958	59,088	53,420	50,588	1,857	975	5,171	4,892	279	497
1959	62,228	56,334	53,071	2,232	1,031	5,384	5,095	289	510
1960	63,716	57,880	54,330	2,451	1,099	5,332	5,031	302	504
1961	65,048	59,306	55,456	2,699	1,151	5,229	4,911	317	513
1962	66,637	61,697	57,572	2,948	1,177	4,405	4,075	330	535
1963	69,311	64,516	60,032	3,242	1,242	4,244	3,906	338	551
1964	72,666	67,901	62,985	3,633	1,284	4,196	3,839	357	569
1965	75,897	71,104	65,650	4,126	1,329	4,208	3,837	371	584
1966	79,593	74,664	68,588	4,691	1,385	4,315	3,928	386	614
1967	82,589	77,731	71,220	5,050	1,461	4,180	3,779	402	678
1968	87,878	82,949	75,734	5,691	1,525	4,207	3,788	419	721
1969	92,995	88,135	80,207	6,330	1,598	4,105	3,670	435	754
1970	97,117	92,329	83,999	6,731	1,599	4,003	3,593	410	785
1971	102,310	97,559	88,307	7,574	1,678	3,913	3,492	422	838
1972	109,766	105,062	94,791	8,519	1,752	3,824	3,381	443	880
1973	115,317	110,473	98,811	9,837	1,825	3,896	3,434	462	949
1974	110,818	106,301	94,719	9,796	1,785	3,623	3,163	459	894
1975	113,549	108,984	97,471	9,631	1,883	3,642	3,161	481	922
1976	120,448	115,700	103,059	10,722	1,919	3,778	3,280	497	970
1977	124,393	119,625	105,999	11,647	1,979	3,725	3,223	503	1,043
1978	129,669	125,067	110,262	12,828	1,977	3,577	3,059	518	1,025
1979	126,905	122,115	106,100	13,989	2,026	3,645	3,116	529	1,145

Notes appear at end of table

(continued)

TABLE Df473–481   Motor fuel consumption, by highway and public–private uses and fuel type: 1919–1995 *Continued*

		Highway				Nonhighway use of gasoline			Gasoline
	Total	Total	Private and commercial use		Public use of gasoline	Total	Private and commercial use	Public use	losses from evaporation, handling, etc.
			Gasoline	Special fuels					
	Df473	Df474	Df475	Df476	Df477	Df478	Df479	Df480	Df481
Year	Million gallons	Million gallons	Million gallons	Million gallons	Million gallons	Million gallons	Million gallons	Million gallons	Million gallons
1980	119,469	114,960	99,127	13,777	2,056	3,655	3,065	590	854
1981	118,713	114,453	97,516	14,856	2,081	3,515	2,883	632	746
1982	117,293	113,384	96,408	14,905	2,071	3,260	2,630	629	650
1983	119,938	116,081	97,627	15,975	2,480	3,204	2,445	759	653
1984	123,130	118,687	99,370	17,271	2,045	3,885	3,263	622	558
1985	125,942	121,301	101,218	17,756	2,328	4,044	3,343	701	596
1986	129,851	125,185	104,356	18,427	2,402	4,066	3,342	725	599
1987	132,282	127,528	105,989	19,088	2,452	4,109	3,371	738	645
1988	134,734	130,062	107,655	20,096	2,311	4,022	3,326	696	650
1989	136,532	131,852	108,327	21,275	2,250	3,981	3,308	673	699
1990	135,577	130,755	107,002	21,226	2,527	4,076	3,317	759	746
1991	133,440	128,563	106,103	20,650	1,810	4,309	3,764	545	569
1992	137,514	132,888	109,301	21,913	1,673	3,908	3,422	486	718
1993	140,848	137,262	111,636	23,594	2,032	2,911	2,817	94	675
1994	144,464	140,839	113,656	25,157	2,026	3,035	2,939	96	589
1995	147,084	143,268	114,988	26,207	2,073	3,192	3,097	95	623

[1] The District of Columbia is included beginning in 1929.

[2] Jet fuel is excluded beginning in 1962.

Source

U.S. Federal Highway Administration, *Highway Statistics, Summary to 1995* (1997), Table MF-221.

Documentation

Motor fuel includes all gasoline used for nonmilitary purposes, plus private and commercial use of diesel and other special fuels. The public use reported here is for federal-civilian, state, county, and municipal uses. Exports, including interstate shipments and dealer-to-dealer sales, are excluded.

Series Df473–474. Adjusted to correct for double-counting of series Df475 between 1919 and 1948 in the source table.

Series Df478–480. Nonhighway consumption includes all use off the highway, such as aeronautical, agricultural, marine, industrial, and so forth.

TABLE Df482–485   Motor vehicle fuel consumption: 1936–1995

Contributed by Louis P. Cain

Year	Passenger vehicles — Df482 [1] — Million gallons	Trucks and combinations — Df483 — Million gallons	Motor vehicle fuel usage per vehicle — Df484 — Gallons	Miles traveled per gallon used — Df485 — Miles per gallon
1936	14,026	4,003	635	14.0
1937	15,018	4,365	648	13.9
1938	15,069	4,465	658	13.9
1939	15,826	4,807	668	13.8
1940	16,759	5,156	678	13.8
1941	18,502	5,754	694	13.8
1942	14,974	4,889	604	13.5
1943	11,424	4,534	519	13.1
1944	11,805	4,576	540	13.0
1945	14,023	5,055	617	13.1
1946	19,502	6,068	747	13.3
1947	20,864	7,243	746	13.2
1948	22,149	8,189	741	13.1
1949	23,645	8,666	727	13.1
1950	25,037	10,566	728	12.9
1951	26,910	11,171	730	12.9
1952	28,735	11,849	766	12.7
1953	30,384	12,245	757	12.8
1954	31,670	12,541	757	12.7
1955	34,319	13,308	759	12.7
1956	36,128	13,978	768	12.5
1957	37,594	14,271	767	12.5
1958	38,904	14,514	776	12.4
1959	40,879	15,453	782	12.4
1960	41,996	15,882	777	12.4
1961	42,863	16,443	776	12.4
1962	44,608	17,089	774	12.4
1963	46,084	18,432	773	12.5
1964	48,431	19,470	778	12.5
1965	51,169	19,935	775	12.5
1966	54,208	20,415	778	12.5
1967	56,020	21,673	786	12.4
1968	59,456	23,482	804	12.3
1969	63,395	24,727	821	12.2

Year	Passenger vehicles — Df482 [1] — Million gallons	Trucks and combinations — Df483 — Million gallons	Motor vehicle fuel usage per vehicle — Df484 — Gallons	Miles traveled per gallon used — Df485 — Miles per gallon
1970	65,649	25,600	830	12.1
1971	—	—	—	—
1972	73,121	30,718	859	12.1
1973	77,619	31,615	851	11.8
1974	73,770	31,226	788	12.1
1975	76,010	31,632	790	12.2
1976	78,398	35,890	807	12.2
1977	80,225	37,964	804	12.3
1978	83,312	40,271	813	12.4
1979	79,793	40,859	765	12.5
1980	73,375	40,150	711	13.2
1981	71,720	41,287	697	13.5
1982	72,608	39,416	686	14.1
1983	73,150	41,662	685	14.3
1984	74,042	43,314	689	14.5
1985	69,268	51,037	685	14.6
1986	71,216	52,911	690	14.7
1987	70,573	55,850	694	15.1
1988	71,654	57,111	687	15.6
1989	72,749	57,912	688	15.9
1990	71,989	57,700	677	16.4
1991	70,692	56,821	668	16.9
1992	73,823	57,997	683	16.9
1993	73,553	62,472	693	16.7
1994	67,517	72,138	698	16.7
1995	68,317	73,789	698	16.9

[1] Includes travel by military vehicles beginning in 1942. Includes motorcycles before 1960.

Sources

1936–1965: U.S. Federal Highway Administration, *Highway Statistics, Summary to 1965* (annual editions); 1966–1969, *Analysis of Motor Fuel Consumption* (annual editions), Table G221, and unpublished data; 1970–1995, American Automobile Manufacturers Association, *Motor Vehicle Facts and Figures* (annual editions).

Documentation

These series were published in *Highway Statistics* into the late 1960s. They now appear in *Motor Vehicle Facts and Figures*, but the source is still the Federal Highway Administration (FHWA). Since 1970, they have been assembled from the annual editions of *Motor Vehicle Facts and Figures*. Because of a change in publication schedule, data for 1971 never appeared.

Fuel consumption data for states that did not report such figures have been estimated by the FHWA.

Motor fuel includes all gasoline used for any purpose (private and public), except military, plus any diesel or other fuels used solely for the propulsion of motor vehicles on public highways. Exports from the United States are excluded, and there is no duplication because of interstate shipment. Tractor fuels are not included. Nonhighway consumption includes all use off the highway, such as aviation-related, agricultural, marine, industrial, and so forth, and usually falls under the exemption or refund provisions of the motor-fuel tax law.

Series Df482. The data used to construct the series have changed over time, so interested individuals are strongly advised to consult the source.

Series Df485. Calculated by dividing miles traveled per vehicle by series Df484.

TABLE Df486–487   State and federal gasoline tax rates: 1930–1996

Contributed by Louis P. Cain

	State average	Federal		State average	Federal
	Df486	Df487		Df486	Df487
Year	Cents per gallon	Cents per gallon	Year	Cents per gallon	Cents per gallon
1930	3.35	—	1965	6.41	4.0
1931	3.48	—	1966	6.42	4.0
1932	3.60	1.0	1967	6.45	4.0
1933	3.65	1.5	1968	6.62	4.0
1934	3.66	1.0	1969	6.84	4.0
1935	3.80	1.0	1970	7.01	4.0
1936	3.85	1.0	1971	7.09	4.0
1937	3.91	1.0	1972	7.32	4.0
1938	3.96	1.0	1973	7.53	4.0
1939	3.96	1.0	1974	7.57	4.0
1940	3.96	1.5	1975	7.65	4.0
1941	3.99	1.5	1976	7.71	4.0
1942	3.99	1.5	1977	7.79	4.0
1943	4.05	1.5	1978	7.83	4.0
1944	4.06	1.5	1979	8.01	4.0
1945	4.10	1.5	1980	8.24	4.0
1946	4.16	1.5	1981	9.15	4.0
1947	4.25	1.5	1982	9.07	4.0
1948	4.35	1.5	1983	9.75	9.0
1949	4.52	1.5	1984	10.58	9.0
1950	4.65	1.5	1985	11.08	9.0
1951	4.74	2.0	1986	11.78	9.0
1952	4.83	2.0	1987	12.75	9.1
1953	5.10	2.0	1988	13.42	9.1
1954	5.19	2.0	1989	14.19	9.1
1955	5.35	2.0	1990	15.47	14.1
1956	5.54	3.0	1991	17.55	14.1
1957	5.58	3.0	1992	17.99	14.1
1958	5.65	3.0	1993	18.34	18.4
1959	5.86	4.0	1994	18.51	18.4
1960	5.94	4.0	1995	18.50	18.4
1961	6.09	4.0	1996	—	18.3
1962	6.18	4.0			
1963	6.22	4.0			
1964	6.31	4.0			

Source

U.S. Federal Highway Administration, *Highway Statistics, Summary to 1995* (1997), Tables FE-101a and MF-205.

Documentation

The tax rates given are those in effect at the end of the year. No data are shown before 1930, the first year in which all states had motor fuel taxes in effect for the whole year.

Series Df486. Data are weighted averages based on net gallons taxed.

Series Df487. The tax applies to all gallonage imported or produced, with some exceptions for farming, nonhighway uses, and use by local transit systems. Effective July 1, 1955, the entire tax became refundable for fuel used for farming; thereafter, the additional two cents (one cent levied July 1, 1956, and one cent levied October 1, 1959) became refundable for nonhighway uses and for use by local transit systems. The dates of the changes in the federal tax are as follows: June 21, 1932, 1 cent; June 17, 1933, 1.5 cents; January 1, 1934, 1 cent; July 1, 1940, 1.5 cents; November 1, 1951, 2 cents; July 1, 1956, 3 cents; October 1, 1959, 4 cents.

TABLE Df488–501   Carbon monoxide emissions, by vehicle and engine type: 1940–1997

Contributed by Louis P. Cain

		On-road vehicles						Nonroad engines and vehicles						
	Total emissions (all sources)	Emissions	Percentage of total	Percentage of on-road vehicle emissions from				Emissions	Percentage of total	Percentage of nonroad engine and vehicle emissions from				
				Light-duty gas vehicles and motorcycles	Light-duty gas trucks	Heavy-duty gas vehicles	Diesel vehicles			Gasoline	Diesel	Aircraft	Marine vessels	Railroads
	Df488	Df489	Df490	Df491	Df492	Df493	Df494	Df495	Df496	Df497	Df498	Df499	Df500	Df501
Year	Thousand short tons	Thousand short tons	Percent	Percent	Percent	Percent	Percent	Thousand short tons	Percent	Percent	Percent	Percent	Percent	Percent
1940	93,616	30,121	32.18	73.83	12.46	13.72	—	8,051	8.60	46.91	0.40	0.05	—	50.71
1950	102,609	45,196	44.05	69.68	13.52	16.68	0.12	11,610	11.31	63.14	0.46	8.04	—	26.49
1960	109,745	64,266	58.56	74.19	12.12	13.31	0.37	11,575	10.55	75.62	0.56	15.24	—	2.87
1970	128,716	88,034	68.39	72.73	18.82	7.62	0.82	10,702	8.31	88.54	5.99	4.73	0.13	0.61
1975	115,967	83,134	71.69	71.31	18.95	8.59	1.14	12,319	10.62	82.34	12.02	4.87	0.14	0.63
1980	116,701	78,049	66.88	68.62	20.68	9.21	1.49	13,757	11.79	79.97	13.66	5.40	0.27	0.70
1985	115,639	77,387	66.92	63.90	24.50	9.97	1.63	14,624	12.65	80.78	12.51	5.68	0.30	0.72
1987	108,353	71,250	65.76	63.64	24.24	10.31	1.81	14,439	13.33	85.08	7.66	6.14	0.35	0.78
1988	116,081	71,081	61.23	64.09	24.10	9.95	1.86	14,698	12.66	84.80	7.68	6.33	0.38	0.80
1989	103,480	66,050	63.83	63.94	24.13	9.85	2.07	14,820	14.32	84.60	7.75	6.44	0.40	0.82
1990	95,794	57,848	60.39	64.66	23.88	9.27	2.19	15,376	16.05	85.12	7.67	5.88	0.54	0.79
1991	97,790	62,074	63.48	64.87	24.19	8.79	2.15	15,368	15.72	85.01	7.85	5.78	0.57	0.78
1992	94,400	59,859	63.41	65.77	24.34	7.63	2.26	15,652	16.58	85.01	7.90	5.76	0.54	0.80
1993	94,526	60,202	63.69	65.05	25.24	7.43	2.27	15,828	16.74	85.00	8.01	5.72	0.51	0.76
1994	98,854	61,833	62.55	60.66	28.06	8.94	2.35	16,050	16.24	84.97	8.10	5.70	0.51	0.71
1995	89,151	54,106	60.69	62.29	27.41	7.62	2.69	16,271	18.25	84.84	8.17	5.79	0.50	0.70
1996	90,929	53,262	58.58	53.94	36.18	7.07	2.80	16,409	18.05	84.92	8.11	5.78	0.50	0.68
1997	87,451	50,257	57.47	—	—	—	—	16,755	19.16	85.00	7.76	6.04	0.51	0.69

Sources

U.S. Environmental Protection Agency, Office of Air Quality Planning and Standards, *National Air Pollution Emission Trends, 1900–1997*, Table 3-1, p. 3-10; *National Air Pollutant Emission Trends Update: 1970–1997*, Table A-1.

Documentation

Transportation accounted for slightly more than 40 percent of carbon monoxide emissions in 1940 and slightly less than 80 percent in 1997. Total emissions increased until 1970 and then decreased to where, in 1997, they were less in total than in 1940. Much of the decrease in emissions since 1970 is attributable to the air quality standards adopted as a result of the Amendments to the Clean Air Act in 1970, but part is the result of the disruptions in world oil markets in the early 1970s and the recession in the United States that followed shortly thereafter.

Series Df491–492. Light-duty gasoline vehicles do not include light-duty gasoline trucks.

TABLE Df502–515   Nitrogen oxides emissions, by vehicle and engine type: 1940–1997

Contributed by Louis P. Cain

		On-road vehicles						Nonroad engines and vehicles						
			Percentage of on-road vehicle emissions from						Percentage of nonroad engine and vehicle emissions from					
	Total emissions (all sources)	Emissions	Percentage of total	Light-duty gas vehicles and motorcycles	Light-duty gas trucks	Heavy-duty gas vehicles	Diesel vehicles	Emissions	Percentage of total	Gasoline	Diesel	Aircraft	Marine vessels	Railroads
	Df502	Df503	Df504	Df505	Df506	Df507	Df508	Df509	Df510	Df511	Df512	Df513	Df514	Df515
Year	Thousand short tons	Thousand short tons	Percent	Percent	Percent	Percent	Percent	Thousand short tons	Percent	Percent	Percent	Percent	Percent	Percent
1940	7,374	1,330	18.04	72.93	15.34	11.65	—	991	13.44	12.31	10.39	—	66.30	11.00
1950	10,093	2,143	21.23	66.03	15.82	13.81	4.34	1,538	15.24	16.19	12.16	0.13	64.50	7.02
1960	14,140	3,982	28.16	65.47	13.18	9.12	12.23	1,443	10.21	21.62	17.12	0.28	53.50	7.48
1970	21,179	7,390	34.89	56.27	17.29	3.76	22.68	2,182	10.30	3.44	68.74	3.30	22.69	1.83
1975	23,128	8,645	37.38	54.66	16.90	3.69	24.77	3,135	13.55	2.62	74.29	2.71	18.79	1.53
1980	24,866	8,621	34.67	51.28	16.33	3.48	28.92	4,011	16.13	2.39	74.02	2.64	18.22	2.74
1985	23,482	8,089	34.45	47.05	18.91	4.08	29.95	4,143	17.64	2.58	71.88	2.87	19.50	3.16
1987	22,767	7,651	33.61	45.64	18.77	4.34	31.24	3,908	17.17	2.84	68.24	3.28	21.85	3.81
1988	23,718	7,661	32.30	45.69	18.52	4.39	31.41	3,998	16.86	2.88	67.23	3.35	22.44	4.13
1989	23,414	7,682	32.81	45.48	18.04	4.46	32.00	4,049	17.29	2.86	66.61	3.41	22.80	4.32
1990	23,436	7,040	30.04	45.74	17.84	4.63	31.79	4,237	18.08	4.48	64.46	3.73	21.93	5.40
1991	23,520	7,373	31.35	46.98	18.16	4.42	30.44	4,265	18.13	4.38	64.57	3.63	21.78	5.65
1992	23,789	7,440	31.27	48.58	18.23	4.14	29.07	4,310	18.12	4.39	64.66	3.62	21.95	5.41
1993	24,046	7,510	31.23	49.00	18.91	4.19	27.88	4,339	18.04	4.36	65.15	3.60	21.78	5.12
1994	24,345	7,672	31.51	46.57	21.60	4.58	27.25	4,397	18.06	4.32	65.36	3.66	21.54	5.12
1995	23,768	7,323	30.81	47.03	20.76	4.53	27.69	4,507	18.96	4.53	64.81	3.66	21.97	5.04
1996	23,465	7,245	30.88	41.12	26.92	4.54	27.44	4,478	19.08	4.58	66.06	3.73	20.59	5.07
1997	23,582	7,035	29.83	40.87	27.02	4.63	27.46	4,560	19.34	4.63	65.50	3.90	20.81	5.15

Sources

U.S. Environmental Protection Agency, Office of Air Quality Planning and Standards, *National Air Pollution Emission Trends, 1900–1997*, Table 3-2, p. 3-11; *National Air Pollutant Emission Trends Update: 1970–1997*, Table A-2.

Documentation

Transportation accounted for slightly more than one third of nitrogen oxide emissions in 1940 and slightly less than one half in 1997. Nitrogen oxides are one of the primary contributors to ozone. Total emissions reached a maximum in 1980, but current levels are very close to those in 1980.

In 1900, on-road vehicles were an insignificant part of total emissions, but by 1920 they had increased to approximately 5 percent of the total. Between 1920 and 1940, they increased by a factor of three. They peaked in the late 1970s, and on-road vehicles currently account for just under one third of total emissions. By contrast, nonroad emissions have continued to increase to just under one fifth of the total.

Series Df505–506. Light-duty gas vehicles do not include light-duty gas trucks.

TABLE Df516–529   Volatile organic compounds emissions, by vehicle and engine type: 1940–1997

Contributed by Louis P. Cain

		On-road vehicles						Nonroad engines and vehicles						
			Percentage of on-road vehicle emissions from							Percentage of nonroad engine and vehicle emissions from				
Year	Total emissions (all sources)	Emissions	Percentage of total	Light-duty gas vehicles and motorcycles	Light-duty gas trucks	Heavy-duty gas vehicles	Diesel vehicles	Emissions	Percentage of total	Gasoline	Diesel	Aircraft	Marine vessels	Railroads
	Df516	Df517	Df518	Df519	Df520	Df521	Df522	Df523	Df524	Df525	Df526	Df527	Df528	Df529
	Thousand short tons	Thousand short tons	Percent	Percent	Percent	Percent	Percent	Thousand short tons	Percent	Percent	Percent	Percent	Percent	Percent
1940	17,161	4,817	28.07	75.71	13.95	10.34	—	778	4.53	26.74	1.54	—	—	—
1950	20,936	7,251	34.63	71.99	15.18	12.52	0.30	1,213	5.79	34.87	1.65	9.07	—	—
1960	24,459	10,506	42.95	76.70	13.64	8.81	0.85	1,215	4.97	43.29	1.89	18.11	—	—
1970	30,748	12,972	42.19	70.87	21.35	5.73	2.05	1,644	5.35	78.04	14.11	5.90	0.55	1.34
1975	25,894	10,545	40.72	68.73	21.71	6.23	3.33	1,892	7.31	72.52	19.34	6.13	0.58	1.43
1980	26,166	8,979	34.32	65.79	22.93	6.80	4.48	2,141	8.18	68.80	21.67	6.82	1.17	1.54
1985	24,225	9,376	38.70	62.54	25.86	7.64	3.95	2,239	9.24	69.67	20.01	7.37	1.34	1.65
1987	23,206	8,477	36.53	62.30	25.78	7.81	4.13	2,257	9.73	70.89	18.08	7.80	1.51	1.73
1988	24,027	8,290	34.50	62.59	25.68	7.55	4.16	2,293	9.54	70.61	17.92	8.07	1.66	1.79
1989	22,274	7,192	32.29	62.04	25.96	7.19	4.81	2,314	10.39	70.44	17.80	8.21	1.73	1.82
1990	20,935	6,313	30.16	62.52	25.69	6.84	4.94	2,452	11.71	71.53	17.01	7.34	2.00	2.12
1991	21,063	6,499	30.86	62.61	25.97	6.51	4.91	2,466	11.71	71.57	17.03	7.18	2.07	2.11
1992	20,642	6,072	29.42	63.11	26.15	5.50	5.24	2,498	12.10	71.74	16.97	7.17	2.00	2.16
1993	20,830	6,103	29.30	62.46	26.99	5.34	5.21	2,516	12.08	72.02	17.01	7.00	1.91	2.07
1994	21,465	6,401	29.82	58.55	29.82	6.47	5.17	2,538	11.82	72.18	17.06	6.93	1.93	1.93
1995	20,558	5,701	27.73	60.09	28.57	5.74	5.60	2,405	11.70	70.35	18.21	7.40	2.04	2.04
1996	19,293	5,490	28.46	52.37	37.52	5.34	4.79	2,397	12.42	70.30	18.27	7.38	2.00	2.00
1997	19,214	5,230	27.22	52.68	37.63	5.12	4.57	2,430	12.65	70.41	17.82	7.70	2.06	2.06

Sources

U.S. Environmental Protection Agency, Office of Air Quality Planning and Standards, *National Air Pollution Emission Trends, 1900–1997*, Table 3-3, p. 3-12; *National Air Pollutant Emission Trends Update: 1970–1997*, Table A-3.

Documentation

Transportation accounted for slightly less than one third of volatile organic compounds emissions in 1940 and slightly more than one half in 1997. Total emissions reached a maximum in 1980, but current levels are very close to those in 1980. Like nitrogen oxides, volatile organic compounds are one of the primary contributors to ozone.

In 1900, transportation accounted for about 4 percent of total emissions, and railroads were responsible for 99 percent of total transportation emissions. By 1920, railroad emissions constituted 20 percent of all emissions, but they have declined to less than 1 percent today. As is true of other pollutants, on-road emissions peaked in the late 1970s, but nonroad emissions continue to increase.

Series Df519–520. Light-duty gasoline vehicles do not include light-duty gasoline trucks.

TABLE Df530–539   Lead emissions, by vehicle and engine type: 1970–1997

Contributed by Louis P. Cain

		On-road vehicles					Nonroad engines and vehicles			
				Percentage of on-road vehicle emissions from					Percentage of nonroad engine and vehicle emissions from	
	Total emissions (all sources)	Emissions	Percentage of total	Light-duty gas vehicles and motorcycles	Light-duty gas trucks	Heavy-duty gas vehicles	Emissions	Percentage of total	Gasoline	Aircraft
	Df530	Df531	Df532	Df533	Df534	Df535	Df536	Df537	Df538	Df539
Year	Thousand short tons	Thousand short tons	Percent	Percent	Percent	Percent	Thousand short tons	Percent	Percent	Percent
1970	220,869	171,961	77.86	83.11	13.19	3.70	9,737	4.41	85.65	14.35
1975	159,659	130,206	81.55	82.08	14.93	2.99	6,130	3.84	81.76	18.24
1980	74,153	60,501	81.59	77.99	19.29	2.72	4,205	5.67	78.95	21.05
1985	22,890	18,052	78.86	75.54	22.50	1.96	921	4.02	24.86	75.14
1987	7,681	3,317	43.18	74.50	23.97	1.54	850	11.07	26.12	73.88
1988	7,053	2,566	36.38	74.79	23.58	1.64	885	12.55	23.84	76.16
1989	5,468	982	17.96	74.64	23.63	1.63	820	15.00	20.24	79.88
1990	4,975	421	8.46	74.58	23.75	1.66	776	15.60	20.36	79.77
1991	4,168	18	0.43	72.22	22.22	0.00	574	13.77	0.00	100.00
1992	3,808	18	0.47	77.78	22.22	0.00	565	14.84	0.00	100.00
1993	3,911	19	0.49	73.68	26.32	0.00	529	13.53	0.00	100.00
1994	4,043	19	0.47	73.68	26.32	0.00	525	12.99	0.00	100.00
1995	3,924	19	0.48	73.68	26.32	0.00	544	13.86	0.00	100.00
1996	3,910	20	0.51	60.00	35.00	0.00	505	12.92	0.00	100.00
1997	3,915	19	0.49	63.16	36.84	0.00	503	12.85	0.00	100.00

Sources

U.S. Environmental Protection Agency, Office of Air Quality Planning and Standards, *National Air Pollution Emission Trends, 1900–1997*, Table 3-6, p. 3-15; *National Air Pollutant Emission Trends Update: 1970–1997*, Table A-8.

Documentation

Historically, an overwhelming share of lead emissions were attributable to on-road vehicles. As late as 1985, this was approximately 85 percent of the total, but it has fallen dramatically as a result of regulatory actions eliminating lead from gasoline. Lead emissions by nonroad engines and vehicles are now greater in absolute and percentage amounts than those from on-road vehicles.

Series Df533–534. Light-duty gasoline vehicles do not include light-duty gasoline trucks.

TABLE Df540–551   Speed of motor vehicles on highways, by vehicle type and percentage exceeding selected thresholds: 1945–1970[1]

Contributed by Louis P. Cain

Year	Vehicles recorded	Average speed				Percentage of vehicles exceeding speed						
		All vehicles	Passenger cars	Trucks	Buses	40 miles per hour	45 miles per hour	50 miles per hour	55 miles per hour	60 miles per hour	65 miles per hour	70 miles per hour
	Df540	Df541	Df542	Df543	Df544	Df545	Df546	Df547	Df548	Df549	Df550	Df551
	Thousand	Miles per hour	Miles per hour	Miles per hour	Miles per hour	Percent	Percent	Percent	Percent	Percent	Percent	Percent
1945 [2]	96	44.0	45.0	39.8	45.5	64	42	24	11	5	—	—
1946	158	45.2	46.1	40.2	47.8	68	48	29	15	7	—	—
1947	132	46.9	48.1	42.5	48.4	75	56	34	18	8	—	—
1948	164	47.7	48.8	43.1	50.0	77	59	36	20	9	—	—
1949	223	47.6	48.7	43.5	50.3	78	60	38	21	9	—	—
1950	280	47.6	48.7	43.0	49.8	77	58	37	20	8	—	—
1951	273	48.9	50.1	44.4	51.2	82	63	42	24	11	—	—
1952	341	49.5	50.8	45.0	52.1	84	68	45	26	12	—	—
1953	241	49.7	51.1	44.9	51.5	85	69	47	27	13	—	—
1954	236	49.7	51.1	45.2	51.8	86	69	46	26	12	—	—
1955	395	50.5	52.0	45.6	52.3	87	72	50	29	14	—	—
1956	381	50.5	51.8	46.2	52.3	87	72	49	30	14	—	—
1957	344	51.4	52.6	47.0	52.6	89	75	52	33	15	—	—
1958	515	51.7	52.8	47.3	53.6	90	77	55	33	15	—	—
1959	396	52.0	53.3	47.3	53.5	90	77	56	36	16	—	—
1960	459	52.6	53.8	48.2	55.5	92	80	58	37	16	—	—
1961	574	52.6	53.7	48.2	55.3	92	80	60	38	18	—	—
1962	602	53.8	55.1	49.4	56.0	93	84	64	43	21	—	—
1963	539	55.8	57.1	51.3	58.1	95	88	72	52	29	—	—
1964	569	55.9	57.2	51.0	57.8	95	87	71	53	32	—	—
1965	552	56.4	57.8	51.8	57.4	95	88	73	56	34	—	—
1966	519	57.3	58.8	52.6	58.8	96	89	76	59	40	—	—
1967	478	58.0	59.5	53.1	59.4	96	91	79	64	44	24	12
1968	480	59.0	60.4	54.0	60.5	97	92	81	66	45	26	12
1969	388	60.0	61.3	54.9	59.4	98	93	82	67	46	27	13
1970	488	59.2	60.6	54.7	58.8	97	93	83	68	47	27	12

[1] Excludes Alaska and Hawai'i.

[2] August 15 to December 31.

Sources

U.S. Federal Highway Administration, Bureau of Public Roads, *Traffic Speed Trends* (various issues), and unpublished data.

Documentation

Data are based on the actual speed of each vehicle recorded on tangent sections of main rural highways during off-peak hours.

Comparatively few speed studies were conducted on main rural highways until immediately prior to World War II. At that time, the average speeds of trucks, passenger cars, and buses were forty-one, forty-five, and fifty-one miles per hour, respectively. The low average speeds during World War II resulted from wartime restrictions on travel speeds and from gasoline rationing.

Speeds of passenger cars did not return to their prewar level until 1947. Trucks reached their prewar level in 1946, and buses, in 1948. From 1948 through 1950, there was little change in vehicle speeds. Since then, speeds consistently increased until 1970, at which time the government chose not to continue this type of study.

TABLE Df552–564   Intercity motor carriers of passengers and property – finances, vehicles, and fares: 1939–1975[1]

Contributed by Louis P. Cain

	Carriers of passengers						Carriers of property					
	Carriers reporting	Operating revenue	Expenses	Net income after income taxes	Vehicles in service	Vehicle-miles	Average fare per passenger (intercity)	Carriers reporting	Operating revenues	Expenses	Net income after income taxes	Owned revenue vehicles	Intercity vehicle-miles
	Df552	Df553	Df554	Df555	Df556 [2]	Df557	Df558	Df559	Df560	Df561	Df562	Df563	Df564
Year	Number	Million dollars	Million dollars	Million dollars	Number	Million miles	Dollars	Number	Million dollars	Million dollars	Million dollars	Thousand	Million miles
1939	149	113	95	20	6,408	466	0.88	957	378	360	15	62	1,343
1940	135	115	98	15	6,678	482	0.84	991	431	412	13	69	1,761
1941	132	149	120	20	7,891	556	0.83	1,076	560	533	18	84	2,121
1942	136	251	164	24	9,677	702	0.80	1,083	588	556	17	84	2,040
1943	157	344	214	37	11,000	832	0.81	1,165	646	626	9	89	2,006
1944	194	375	245	36	12,019	905	0.80	1,337	711	696	8	98	2,132
1945	231	378	265	32	12,865	931	0.79	1,445	746	745	−2	100	2,165
1946	254	381	299	50	13,168	1,043	0.80	1,516	884	852	21	112	2,407
1947	253	367	313	33	14,149	1,056	0.80	1,603	1,233	1,174	37	128	3,059
1948	260	401	351	31	15,290	1,130	0.85	1,825	1,663	1,553	72	151	3,810
1949	262	380	346	20	14,863	1,066	0.91	2,012	1,895	1,794	64	169	4,338
1950	172	351	315	19	14,566	959	1.01	1,621	2,380	2,215	93	191	5,532
1951	166	393	345	25	13,431	1,011	1.12	1,737	2,728	2,603	58	213	5,848
1952	160	395	348	22	13,106	975	1.20	1,868	3,059	2,924	67	229	6,137
1953	161	395	354	18	12,940	972	1.24	2,027	3,493	3,360	60	251	6,802
1954	155	363	331	15	12,314	887	1.29	2,110	3,431	3,323	54	260	6,538
1955	146	362	331	16	13,127	859	1.37	2,244	4,030	3,870	82	289	7,559
1956	145	377	343	17	11,062	859	1.51	2,293	4,290	4,141	77	304	7,529
1957	144	407	371	20	11,301	867	1.70	837	3,836	3,702	62	238	6,399
1958	136	410	366	20	10,791	816	1.91	866	3,851	3,723	54	243	6,101
1959	143	439	380	29	10,763	810	2.00	890	4,590	4,392	92	265	7,085
1960	143	463	405	28	12,680	843	2.12	935	4,763	4,645	37	279	7,203
1961	144	485	423	31	11,036	865	2.20	972	4,908	4,718	84	285	7,023
1962	151	589	511	43	13,873	998	2.30	1,004	5,428	5,204	112	298	7,567
1963	148	610	529	48	13,608	1,009	2.38	1,004	5,756	5,520	122	309	7,882
1964	161	655	570	52	16,157	1,056	2.43	1,025	6,199	5,918	152	318	8,209
1965	156	607	514	52	13,287	947	2.73	1,114	7,131	6,760	209	355	9,154
1966	166	644	550	54	14,298	988	2.71	1,159	7,897	7,505	217	384	9,814
1967	177	670	591	52	15,406	997	2.79	1,198	8,091	7,796	144	394	9,815
1968	173	695	613	61	15,398	977	2.91	1,252	9,593	9,129	235	428	10,902
1969	70	677	594	56	12,992	869	3.55	1,311	10,770	10,337	200	466	11,699
1970	71	722	639	52	12,373	871	3.81	1,376	11,137	10,763	150	483	11,498
1971	71	758	664	64	12,038	856	4.19	1,355	13,011	12,238	410	493	12,661
1972	74	775	690	59	12,122	846	4.24	1,525	14,994	14,156	456	530	14,177
1973	75	815	738	55	12,794	851	4.73	1,442	16,600	15,787	431	554	14,901
1974	81	933	859	56	13,791	886	5.13	728	15,881	15,093	412	525	12,429
1975	77	942	880	56	9,691	835	5.52	748	15,476	14,761	299	531	11,479

[1] Class I for-hire motor carriers. See text for definition changes.

[2] Excludes intercity service before 1964, with the exception of 1950, 1955, and 1960.

Source

U.S. Interstate Commerce Commission, *Transport Statistics in the United States*, Part 7 (Part 2 beginning in 1974), annual issues.

Documentation

This table includes only Class I carriers subject to Interstate Commerce Commission (ICC) regulations. The definition of class I for-hire motor carriers changed over time. Prior to 1950, the ICC defined Class I carriers as those with gross annual operating revenue of $100,000 or more; for 1950–1958,

$200,000 for a three-year period; and, from 1969 onward, $1,000,000 for a three-year period.

Series Df552. Excludes carriers subject to ICC regulations engaged primarily in local or suburban services as well as carriers engaged in transporting both passengers and property.

Series Df556. Includes vehicles with regular intercity and local routes.

Series Df557. Includes all vehicles operated for revenues and those owned, leased, and operated under "purchased transportation" arrangements.

Series Df558. Equals intercity passenger revenue divided by the number of intercity passengers.

TABLE Df565–577   Trucking and courier services – expenses and operating revenue, by type of service: 1988–1997

Contributed by Louis P. Cain

	Operating revenue				Operating expenses					Trucking		Courier services	
	Total	Local trucking	Long-distance trucking	Nonmotor carrier	Total	Employee compensation	Purchased fuels	Purchased transportation	Other	Operating revenue	Operating expense	Operating revenue	Operating expense
	Df565	Df566	Df567	Df568	Df569	Df570	Df571	Df572	Df573	Df574	Df575	Df576	Df577
Year	Million dollars	Million dollars	Million dollars	Million dollars	Million dollars	Million dollars	Million dollars	Million dollars	Million dollars	Million dollars	Million dollars	Million dollars	Million dollars
1988	109,274	24,101	75,905	9,268	103,741	39,636	7,076	21,287	35,742	—	—	—	—
1989	116,937	26,560	82,085	8,292	110,669	42,505	8,419	21,478	38,267	—	—	—	—
1990	127,314	28,017	89,105	10,192	118,968	44,448	10,115	22,864	41,541	110,095	102,899	17,219	16,069
1991	126,772	27,281	90,451	9,040	118,855	45,405	10,203	22,507	40,740	109,007	102,553	17,765	16,302
1992	135,437	31,120	95,929	8,388	127,687	47,886	11,345	24,760	43,696	116,254	110,038	19,183	17,649
1993	142,547	36,649	98,351	7,547	133,857	50,841	11,589	26,130	45,297	122,452	115,203	20,095	18,654
1994	155,713	43,592	104,410	7,711	145,216	55,569	12,114	28,222	49,311	135,029	125,680	20,684	19,536
1995	161,806	48,731	105,150	7,925	151,628	59,144	12,051	28,757	51,676	140,659	131,573	21,147	20,055
1996	172,743	52,301	111,485	8,957	162,825	62,452	13,667	30,979	55,727	149,677	140,836	23,066	21,989
1997	183,153	59,354	114,530	9,269	170,998	66,233	13,777	34,323	56,665	159,679	147,880	23,474	23,118

Source

U.S. Bureau of the Census, *Current Business Reports*, BT/97, *Transportation Annual Survey: 1997* (formerly *Motor Freight Transportation and Warehousing Survey*) (January 1999), Table 2.

Documentation

The data are based on an annual sample survey of all employer firms with one or more establishments that are primarily engaged in providing commercial motor freight transport services or public warehousing services.

The data cover trucking and courier services, Standard Industrial Classification (SIC) 421. See the Introduction to Part D for a discussion of SIC codes.

The data exclude private motor carriers that operate as auxiliary establishments to nontransportation companies as well as independent owner-operators that have no paid employees. Courier services are defined to exclude air.

WATER

Louis P. Cain

TABLE Df578–593   Documented merchant vessels – number and tonnage, by type of vessel and trade: 1789–1970[1]

Contributed by Louis P. Cain

Year	Vessels	Total	Class						Sailing	Canal-boats and barges	Construction		Trade			
			Steam and motor				Motor									
				Steam												
	Number	Total	Total	Total	Coal-burning	Oil-burning	Total	Diesel and semidiesel engines			Metal	Wood	Foreign	Coastwise and internal	Whale fisheries	Cod and mackerel fisheries
	Df578	Df579	Df580	Df581	Df582	Df583	Df584	Df585	Df586	Df587	Df588	Df589	Df590	Df591	Df592	Df593
		Thousand gross tons	Thousand gross tons	Thousand gross tons	Thousand gross tons	Thousand gross tons	Thousand gross tons	Thousand gross tons	Thousand gross tons	Thousand gross tons	Thousand gross tons	Thousand gross tons	Thousand gross tons	Thousand gross tons	Thousand gross tons	Thousand gross tons
1789	—	202	—	—	—	—	—	—	202	—	—	—	124	69	—	9
1790	—	478	—	—	—	—	—	—	478	—	—	—	346	104	—	28
1791	—	502	—	—	—	—	—	—	502	—	—	—	363	106	—	33
1792	—	564	—	—	—	—	—	—	564	—	—	—	411	121	—	32
1793	—	521	—	—	—	—	—	—	521	—	—	—	368	122	—	31
1794	—	629	—	—	—	—	—	—	629	—	—	—	439	163	4	23
1795	—	748	—	—	—	—	—	—	748	—	—	—	529	184	3	31
1796	—	832	—	—	—	—	—	—	832	—	—	—	577	218	2	35
1797	—	877	—	—	—	—	—	—	877	—	—	—	598	237	1	41
1798	—	898	—	—	—	—	—	—	898	—	—	—	603	251	1	43
1799	—	939	—	—	—	—	—	—	939	—	—	—	657	247	6	30
1800	—	972	—	—	—	—	—	—	972	—	—	—	667	272	3	29
1801	—	948	—	—	—	—	—	—	948	—	—	—	631	275	3	39
1802	—	892	—	—	—	—	—	—	892	—	—	—	558	290	3	42
1803	—	949	—	—	—	—	—	—	949	—	—	—	586	299	12	52
1804	—	1,042	—	—	—	—	—	—	1,042	—	—	—	661	318	12	52
1805	—	1,140	—	—	—	—	—	—	1,140	—	—	—	744	333	6	57
1806	—	1,209	—	—	—	—	—	—	1,209	—	—	—	799	341	11	59
1807	—	1,269	(Z)	—	—	—	—	—	1,268	—	—	—	840	349	9	70
1808	—	1,243	(Z)	—	—	—	—	—	1,242	—	—	—	765	421	5	52
1809	—	1,350	1	—	—	—	—	—	1,350	—	—	—	907	405	4	34
1810	—	1,425	1	—	—	—	—	—	1,424	—	—	—	981	405	4	35
1811	—	1,233	1	—	—	—	—	—	1,231	—	—	—	764	420	5	43
1812	—	1,270	2	—	—	—	—	—	1,268	—	—	—	759	478	3	30
1813	—	1,167	3	—	—	—	—	—	1,164	—	—	—	673	471	3	20
1814	—	1,159	3	—	—	—	—	—	1,156	—	—	—	675	466	1	18
1815	—	1,368	3	—	—	—	—	—	1,365	—	—	—	854	476	1	37
1816	—	1,372	6	—	—	—	—	—	1,366	—	—	—	801	522	1	48
1817	—	1,400	9	—	—	—	—	—	1,391	—	—	—	805	525	5	65
1818	—	1,225	13	—	—	—	—	—	1,213	—	—	—	590	549	17	69
1819	—	1,261	17	—	—	—	—	—	1,243	—	—	—	581	571	32	76

Gross tonnage

	Vessels	Total	Class							Canal-boats and barges	Construction		Trade		Whale fisheries	Cod and mackerel fisheries
			Steam and motor						Sailing		Metal	Wood	Foreign	Coastwise and internal		
			Total	Steam			Motor									
				Total	Coal-burning	Oil-burning	Total	Diesel and semidiesel engines								
Year	Df578	Df579	Df580	Df581	Df582	Df583	Df584	Df585	Df586	Df587	Df588	Df589	Df590	Df591	Df592	Df593
	Number	Thousand gross tons	Thousand gross tons	Thousand gross tons	Thousand gross tons	Thousand gross tons	Thousand gross tons	Thousand gross tons	Thousand gross tons	Thousand gross tons	Thousand gross tons	Thousand gross tons	Thousand gross tons	Thousand gross tons	Thousand gross tons	Thousand gross tons
1820	—	1,280	22	—	—	—	—	—	1,258	—	—	—	584	588	36	72
1821	—	1,299	23	—	—	—	—	—	1,276	—	—	—	594	615	28	62
1822	—	1,325	23	—	—	—	—	—	1,304	—	—	—	583	624	49	69
1823	—	1,337	25	—	—	—	—	—	1,312	—	—	—	600	618	41	78
1824	—	1,389	22	—	—	—	—	—	1,368	—	—	—	637	642	33	77
1825	—	1,423	23	—	—	—	—	—	1,400	—	—	—	665	641	35	81
1826	—	1,534	34	—	—	—	—	—	1,500	—	—	—	696	722	42	74
1827	—	1,621	40	—	—	—	—	—	1,580	—	—	—	702	789	46	84
1828	—	1,741	39	—	—	—	—	—	1,702	—	—	—	758	843	55	86
1829	—	1,261	54	—	—	—	—	—	1,207	—	—	—	593	509	57	102
1830	—	1,192	64	—	—	—	—	—	1,127	—	—	—	538	517	40	98
1831	—	1,268	69	—	—	—	—	—	1,198	—	—	—	538	540	83	107
1832	—	1,439	91	—	—	—	—	—	1,349	—	—	—	614	650	73	102
1833	—	1,606	102	—	—	—	—	—	1,504	—	—	—	649	744	102	111
1834	—	1,759	123	—	—	—	—	—	1,636	—	—	—	749	784	108	117
1835	—	1,825	123	—	—	—	—	—	1,702	—	—	—	788	797	98	142
1836	—	1,882	146	—	—	—	—	—	1,737	—	—	—	753	873	146	110
1837	—	1,897	155	—	—	—	—	—	1,742	—	—	—	683	957	129	127
1838	—	1,996	193	—	—	—	—	—	1,802	—	—	—	703	1,041	125	127
1839	—	2,096	195	—	—	—	—	—	1,901	—	—	—	702	1,154	132	108
1840	—	2,181	202	—	—	—	—	—	1,978	—	—	—	763	1,177	137	104
1841	—	2,131	175	—	—	—	—	—	1,956	—	—	—	788	1,107	157	78
1842	—	2,092	230	—	—	—	—	—	1,863	—	—	—	824	1,046	152	71
1843	—	2,159	237	—	—	—	—	—	1,922	—	—	—	857	1,076	153	73
1844	—	2,280	272	—	—	—	—	—	2,008	—	—	—	900	1,110	169	101
1845	—	2,417	326	—	—	—	—	—	2,091	—	—	—	904	1,223	191	98
1846	—	2,562	348	—	—	—	—	—	2,214	—	—	—	943	1,316	187	116
1847	—	2,839	405	—	—	—	—	—	2,434	—	—	—	1,047	1,489	194	109
1848	—	3,154	428	—	—	—	—	—	2,726	—	—	—	1,169	1,659	193	133
1849	—	3,334	462	—	—	—	—	—	2,872	—	—	—	1,259	1,770	180	125
1850	—	3,535	526	—	—	—	—	—	3,010	—	—	—	1,440	1,798	146	152
1851	—	3,772	584	—	—	—	—	—	3,189	—	—	—	1,545	1,900	182	146
1852	—	4,138	643	—	—	—	—	—	3,495	—	—	—	1,706	2,056	194	183
1853	—	4,407	605	—	—	—	—	—	3,802	—	—	—	1,910	2,134	193	169
1854	—	4,803	677	—	—	—	—	—	4,126	—	—	—	2,152	2,322	182	147
1855	—	5,212	770	—	—	—	—	—	4,442	—	—	—	2,348	2,543	187	134
1856	—	4,872	673	—	—	—	—	—	4,199	—	—	—	2,302	2,248	189	132
1857	—	4,941	706	—	—	—	—	—	4,235	—	—	—	2,268	2,337	196	140
1858	—	5,050	729	—	—	—	—	—	4,320	—	—	—	2,301	2,401	199	149
1859	—	5,145	769	—	—	—	—	—	4,376	—	—	—	2,322	2,481	186	157

Notes appear at end of table　　　　　　　　　　　　　　　　　　　　　　　　　　　　(continued)

TABLE Df578–593   Documented merchant vessels – number and tonnage, by type of vessel and trade: 1789–1970   Continued

	Vessels	Gross tonnage									Construction		Trade			
		Total	Class — Steam and motor	Steam			Motor									
			Total	Total	Coal-burning	Oil-burning	Total	Diesel and semidiesel engines	Sailing	Canal-boats and barges	Metal	Wood	Foreign	Coastwise and internal	Whale fisheries	Cod and mackerel fisheries
Year	Number	Thousand gross tons	Thousand gross tons	Thousand gross tons	Thousand gross tons	Thousand gross tons	Thousand gross tons	Thousand gross tons	Thousand gross tons	Thousand gross tons	Thousand gross tons	Thousand gross tons	Thousand gross tons	Thousand gross tons	Thousand gross tons	Thousand gross tons
	Df578	Df579	Df580	Df581	Df582	Df583	Df584	Df585	Df586	Df587	Df588	Df589	Df590	Df591	Df592	Df593
1860	—	5,354	868	—	—	—	—	—	4,486	—	—	—	2,379	2,645	167	163
1861	—	5,540	877	—	—	—	—	—	4,663	—	—	—	2,497	2,705	146	193
1862	—	5,112	710	—	—	—	—	—	4,402	—	—	—	2,174	2,617	118	204
1863	—	5,155	576	—	—	—	—	—	4,580	—	—	—	1,927	2,961	99	168
1864	—	4,986	978	—	—	—	—	—	4,008	—	—	—	1,487	3,245	95	159
1865	—	5,097	1,067	—	—	—	—	—	4,030	—	—	—	1,518	3,382	84	113
1866	—	4,311	1,084	—	—	—	—	—	3,227	—	—	—	1,388	2,720	105	98
1867	—	4,304	1,192	—	—	—	—	—	3,113	—	—	—	1,516	2,660	52	76
1868	28,167	4,352	1,199	—	—	—	—	—	2,409	644	—	—	1,487	2,702	78	84
1869	27,487	4,145	1,104	—	—	—	—	—	2,400	641	—	—	1,496	2,516	70	63
1870	28,998	4,247	1,075	—	—	—	—	—	2,363	808	—	—	1,449	2,638	68	91
1871	29,651	4,283	1,088	—	—	—	—	—	2,286	909	—	—	1,364	2,765	61	93
1872	31,114	4,438	1,112	—	—	—	—	—	2,325	1,001	—	—	1,359	2,930	52	98
1873	32,672	4,696	1,156	—	—	—	—	—	2,383	1,156	—	—	1,379	3,163	45	110
1874	32,486	4,801	1,186	—	—	—	—	—	2,474	1,141	—	—	1,390	3,293	39	78
1875	32,285	4,854	1,169	—	—	—	—	—	2,585	1,100	—	—	1,516	3,220	38	80
1876	25,934	4,279	1,172	—	—	—	—	—	2,609	498	—	—	1,554	2,599	39	88
1877	25,386	4,243	1,171	—	—	—	—	—	2,580	491	—	—	1,571	2,540	41	91
1878	25,264	4,213	1,168	—	—	—	—	—	2,521	524	—	—	1,589	2,497	40	87
1879	25,211	4,170	1,176	—	—	—	—	—	2,423	571	—	—	1,452	2,598	40	80
1880	24,712	4,068	1,212	—	—	—	—	—	2,366	490	—	—	1,314	2,638	38	78
1881	24,065	4,058	1,265	—	—	—	—	—	2,350	442	—	—	1,297	2,646	39	76
1882	24,368	4,166	1,356	—	—	—	—	—	2,361	449	—	—	1,259	2,796	33	78
1883	24,217	4,235	1,413	—	—	—	—	—	2,387	436	—	—	1,270	2,838	32	95
1884	24,082	4,271	1,466	—	—	—	—	—	2,414	391	387	3,885	1,277	2,884	27	83
1885	23,963	4,266	1,495	—	—	—	—	—	2,374	397	430	3,836	1,263	2,895	25	83
1886	23,534	4,131	1,523	—	—	—	—	—	2,210	398	444	3,687	1,088	2,939	23	81
1887	23,063	4,106	1,543	—	—	—	—	—	2,170	393	475	3,631	989	3,011	26	80
1888	23,281	4,192	1,648	—	—	—	—	—	2,124	419	494	3,698	919	3,172	24	76
1889	23,623	4,307	1,766	—	—	—	—	—	2,099	443	554	3,753	1,000	3,211	22	74
1890	23,467	4,424	1,859	—	—	—	—	—	2,109	456	627	3,798	928	3,409	19	68
1891	23,899	4,685	2,016	—	—	—	—	—	2,172	497	742	3,943	989	3,610	17	69
1892	24,383	4,765	2,074	—	—	—	—	—	2,178	512	786	3,979	978	3,701	17	69
1893	24,512	4,825	2,183	—	—	—	—	—	2,118	524	896	3,930	883	3,855	17	71
1894	23,586	4,684	2,189	—	—	—	—	—	2,023	472	930	3,754	900	3,696	16	72
1895	23,240	4,636	2,213	—	—	—	—	—	1,965	458	970	3,666	822	3,729	16	69
1896	22,908	4,704	2,307	—	—	—	—	—	1,928	468	1,090	3,614	830	3,790	15	69
1897	22,633	4,769	2,359	—	—	—	—	—	1,904	506	1,207	3,562	793	3,897	13	67
1898	22,705	4,750	2,372	—	—	—	—	—	1,836	542	1,224	3,526	726	3,960	11	52
1899	22,728	4,864	2,476	—	—	—	—	—	1,825	563	1,376	3,489	837	3,965	11	51

		Gross tonnage														
		Class									**Construction**		**Trade**			
			Steam and motor													
				Steam			**Motor**									
	Vessels	**Total**	**Total**	**Total**	**Coal-burning**	**Oil-burning**	**Total**	**Diesel and semidiesel engines**	**Sailing**	**Canal-boats and barges**	**Metal**	**Wood**	**Foreign**	**Coastwise and internal**	**Whale fisheries**	**Cod and mackerel fisheries**
	Df578	**Df579**	**Df580**	**Df581**	**Df582**	**Df583**	**Df584**	**Df585**	**Df586**	**Df587**	**Df588**	**Df589**	**Df590**	**Df591**	**Df592**	**Df593**
Year	**Number**	Thousand gross tons	Thousand gross tons	Thousand gross tons	Thousand gross tons	Thousand gross tons	Thousand gross tons	Thousand gross tons	Thousand gross tons	Thousand gross tons	Thousand gross tons	Thousand gross tons	Thousand gross tons	Thousand gross tons	Thousand gross tons	Thousand gross tons
1900	23,333	5,165	2,658	—	—	—	—	—	1,885	622	1,593	3,572	817	4,287	10	52
1901	24,057	5,524	2,921	—	—	—	—	—	1,933	670	1,901	3,623	880	4,583	10	52
1902	24,273	5,798	3,177	—	—	—	—	—	1,942	679	2,180	3,618	873	4,859	9	57
1903	24,425	6,087	3,408	—	—	—	—	—	1,966	713	2,440	3,647	879	5,141	10	58
1904	24,558	6,292	3,595	—	—	—	—	—	1,945	751	2,669	3,623	889	5,335	10	58
1905	24,681	6,457	3,741	—	—	—	—	—	1,962	753	2,850	3,607	944	5,442	11	60
1906	25,006	6,675	3,975	—	—	—	—	—	1,899	801	3,115	3,560	928	5,674	11	61
1907	24,911	6,939	4,279	—	—	—	—	—	1,814	845	3,438	3,501	861	6,011	10	57
1908	25,425	7,365	4,711	—	—	—	—	—	1,761	893	3,860	3,505	930	6,372	10	54
1909	25,868	7,389	4,749	—	—	—	—	—	1,711	928	3,925	3,464	879	6,451	9	50
1910	25,740	7,508	4,900	—	—	—	—	—	1,655	952	4,117	3,391	783	6,669	9	47
1911	25,991	7,639	5,074	—	—	—	—	—	1,598	967	4,299	3,340	863	6,720	9	46
1912	26,528	7,714	5,180	—	—	—	—	—	1,539	995	4,433	3,282	923	6,737	9	45
1913	27,070	7,887	5,333	—	—	—	—	—	1,508	1,046	4,608	3,278	1,019	6,817	9	42
1914	26,943	7,929	5,428	—	—	—	—	—	1,433	1,069	4,733	3,196	1,066	6,818	10	34
1915	26,701	8,389	5,944	—	—	—	—	—	1,384	1,061	5,305	3,085	1,863	6,486	9	32
1916	26,444	8,470	6,070	—	—	—	—	—	1,311	1,089	5,476	2,994	2,185	6,245	7	33
1917	26,397	8,871	6,433	—	—	—	—	—	1,278	1,159	5,856	3,015	2,441	6,393	6	32
1918	26,711	9,925	7,471	—	—	—	—	—	1,210	1,244	6,814	3,110	3,599	6,282	4	38
1919	27,513	12,907	10,416	—	—	—	—	—	1,200	1,292	9,236	3,671	6,665	6,201	4	36
1920	28,183	16,324	13,823	13,466	7,551	5,915	357	24	1,272	1,228	12,448	3,876	9,925	6,358	4	38
1921	28,012	18,282	15,745	15,371	7,069	8,302	374	15	1,294	1,243	14,426	3,856	11,077	7,163	4	37
1922	27,358	18,463	15,982	15,607	6,908	8,699	376	16	1,288	1,193	14,805	3,658	10,720	7,703	4	36
1923	27,017	18,285	15,821	15,426	6,556	8,870	397	17	1,254	1,209	14,775	3,510	9,069	9,177	4	35
1924	26,575	17,741	15,315	14,870	5,921	8,947	445	128	1,185	1,240	14,627	3,114	8,794	8,911	3	32
1925	26,367	17,406	14,976	14,495	5,512	8,931	481	254	1,125	1,304	14,499	2,907	8,151	9,216	4	35
1926	26,343	17,311	14,848	14,318	5,370	8,895	530	293	1,092	1,371	14,473	2,838	7,719	9,552	3	38
1927	25,778	16,888	14,507	13,874	4,919	8,907	633	397	989	1,392	14,160	2,728	7,309	9,533	8	38
1928	25,385	16,680	14,344	13,614	4,557	9,002	730	494	915	1,421	14,064	2,619	6,934	9,706	7	36
1929	25,326	16,477	14,162	13,301	4,462	8,751	861	609	825	1,490	13,910	2,567	6,906	9,526	7	39
1930	25,214	16,068	13,757	12,775	4,209	8,429	982	715	757	1,554	13,514	2,554	6,296	9,723	7	42
1931	25,471	15,908	13,528	12,475	4,103	8,202	1,053	792	673	1,707	13,344	2,565	5,576	10,286	7	40
1932	25,156	15,839	13,568	12,499	3,991	8,308	1,069	810	625	1,646	13,421	2,417	5,071	10,728	2	38
1933	24,868	15,060	12,862	11,788	3,615	7,971	1,075	812	563	1,635	12,736	2,324	4,701	10,313	9	37
1934	24,904	14,862	12,687	11,599	3,539	7,860	1,087	824	500	1,675	12,601	2,261	4,598	10,220	9	35
1935	24,919	14,654	12,535	11,433	3,496	7,748	1,102	841	441	1,677	12,469	2,185	4,560	10,049	9	35
1936	25,392	14,497	12,267	11,161	3,371	7,617	1,105	867	379	1,851	12,263	2,234	4,159	10,300	9	28
1937	26,588	14,676	12,170	11,055	3,322	7,559	1,115	878	312	2,194	12,233	2,443	3,833	10,798	20	25
1938	27,155	14,651	12,007	10,835	3,325	7,510	1,172	1,005	261	2,384	12,130	2,521	3,551	11,064	21	16
1939	27,470	14,632	11,952	10,760	3,250	7,510	1,192	1,028	221	2,459	12,159	2,473	3,312	11,288	21	11

(continued)

TABLE Df578–593   Documented merchant vessels – number and tonnage, by type of vessel and trade: 1789–1970   Continued

Gross tonnage

	Vessels	Total	Class — Steam and motor						Sailing	Canal-boats and barges	Construction		Trade			
			Total	Steam			Motor				Metal	Wood	Foreign	Coastwise and internal	Whale fisheries	Cod and mackerel fisheries
				Total	Coal-burning	Oil-burning	Total	Diesel and semidiesel engines								
Year	Df578	Df579	Df580	Df581	Df582	Df583	Df584	Df585	Df586	Df587	Df588	Df589	Df590	Df591	Df592	Df593
	Number	Thousand gross tons	Thousand gross tons	Thousand gross tons	Thousand gross tons	Thousand gross tons	Thousand gross tons	Thousand gross tons	Thousand gross tons	Thousand gross tons	Thousand gross tons	Thousand gross tons	Thousand gross tons	Thousand gross tons	Thousand gross tons	Thousand gross tons
1940	27,212	14,018	11,353	10,102	3,159	6,943	1,251	1,090	200	2,466	—	—	3,638	10,352	20	8
1941	27,075	13,722	11,047	9,814	3,058	6,756	1,233	1,075	182	2,493	11,393	2,329	3,047	10,654	14	7
1942	27,325	13,860	11,072	9,704	2,965	6,739	1,369	1,213	166	2,621	11,641	2,218	4,109	9,744	2	6
1943	27,612	16,762	14,052	12,547	3,048	9,499	1,505	1,361	142	2,568	14,647	2,115	9,285	7,471	2	5
1944	28,690	25,795	23,217	21,674	3,014	18,660	1,543	1,392	129	2,449	23,837	1,959	18,685	7,105	1	4
1945	29,797	32,813	30,247	28,669	2,931	25,737	1,578	1,433	115	2,452	30,898	1,915	26,043	6,766	1	3
1946	31,386	38,501	35,928	33,779	2,884	30,895	2,149	2,002	98	2,475	36,571	1,929	29,705	8,791	1	3
1947	32,760	37,832	35,149	32,941	2,699	30,242	2,208	2,058	95	2,588	35,897	1,936	26,535	11,294	1	3
1948	33,843	33,167	30,469	28,401	2,606	25,796	2,067	1,902	87	2,611	31,211	1,956	22,021	11,143	1	3
1949	35,264	32,182	29,323	27,225	2,543	24,682	2,099	1,932	87	2,771	30,212	1,969	20,654	11,525	1	3
1950	36,083	31,215	28,327	26,273	2,507	23,765	2,055	1,885	82	2,806	29,263	1,952	19,154	12,048	11	2
1951	36,745	30,341	27,424	25,390	2,441	22,948	2,033	1,865	71	2,846	28,417	1,924	18,876	11,462	1	2
1952	37,389	30,416	27,459	25,356	2,405	22,951	2,103	1,923	66	2,891	28,559	1,857	19,280	11,134	1	2
1953	38,072	30,546	27,507	25,377	2,387	22,990	2,130	1,951	55	2,984	28,761	1,785	19,007	11,537	1	2
1954	39,008	30,764	27,631	25,489	2,321	23,168	2,142	1,960	46	3,087	28,982	1,782	18,974	11,787	1	2
1955	39,242	29,958	26,792	24,706	2,252	22,454	2,086	1,907	40	3,125	28,336	1,622	18,143	11,812	1	1
1956	39,499	29,610	26,251	24,210	2,204	22,005	2,041	1,886	34	3,326	28,073	1,537	17,765	11,843	1	1
1957	40,191	29,421	25,785	23,788	2,190	21,597	1,998	1,836	24	3,612	27,935	1,486	17,265	12,154	1	1
1958	41,276	28,586	24,599	22,596	2,171	20,426	2,002	1,844	23	3,965	27,118	1,469	16,206	12,376	1	1
1959	42,409	28,895	24,333	22,306	2,176	20,131	2,027	1,871	23	4,539	27,470	1,425	15,600	13,284	1	1
1960	43,088	28,581	23,553	21,526	2,125	19,401	2,027	1,876	23	5,005	27,184	1,397	14,737	13,833	1	1
1961	43,367	26,403	21,175	19,125	2,049	17,076	2,050	1,902	18	5,210	25,028	1,375	13,126	13,260	1	1
1962	43,566	25,456	20,076	17,990	1,903	16,088	2,085	1,942	18	5,362	24,107	1,349	12,393	12,775	1	1
1963	44,077	25,691	20,079	17,987	1,760	16,226	2,092	1,952	18	5,595	24,377	1,314	12,289	13,089	1	1
1964	44,669	26,160	20,018	17,896	1,664	16,232	2,122	1,988	17	6,125	24,900	1,260	12,580	13,276	1	1
1965	45,579	26,516	19,730	17,560	1,497	16,063	2,170	2,040	8	6,778	25,318	1,198	12,628	13,839	1	1
1966	47,223	26,522	—	—	—	—	—	—	—	—	—	—	—	—	—	—
1967	48,700	27,251	—	—	—	—	—	—	—	—	—	—	—	—	—	—
1968	49,545	27,932	19,396	16,871	—	—	2,525	—	6	8,530	—	—	—	—	—	—
1969	49,991	28,455	19,433	16,868	—	—	2,565	—	6	9,016	—	—	—	—	—	—
1970	49,993	28,613	19,074	16,447	—	—	2,627	—	6	9,583	—	—	—	—	—	—

(Z) Less than 500 gross tons.

1 Numerous exceptions, changes, and other special circumstances are discussed in the text.

Sources

Except as noted, U.S. Bureau of Marine Inspection and Navigation, *Merchant Marine Statistics, 1936* and *1965,* and U.S. Bureau of Customs, unpublished data. Series Df588–589, 1884, U.S. Department of the Treasury, *Annual Report of Commission of Navigation, 1884,* p. 161.

Documentation

The data are for ships of five tons or more. Figures are as of December 31 (1789–1834), September 30 (1835–1842), June 30 (1843–1940), and January 1 thereafter.

Gross tonnage refers to space measurement, 100 cubic feet equaling 1 ton; it is not a measure of weight. Gross tonnage is the capacity of the entire space within the frames and the ceiling of the hull, together with those closed-in spaces above deck available for cargo, stores, passengers, or crew, with certain minor exemptions. Before 1865, 95 cubic feet equaled 1 ton, and the admeasurement method differed in other respects. (Admeasurement is the calculation of gross and net tonnage of vessels.)

TABLE Df578–593   Documented merchant vessels – number and tonnage, by type of vessel and trade: 1789–1970   *Continued*

Net or registered tonnage is what remains after deducting from the gross tonnage the spaces occupied by the propelling machinery, fuel, crew quarters, master's cabin, and navigation spaces. It represents the space available for cargo and passengers. It is the usual basis for tonnage taxes and port charges. The net tonnage capacity of a ship recorded as "entered with cargo" may bear little relation to actual weight of cargo.

Documented vessels include all vessels granted registers, enrollments and licenses, or licenses, as "vessels of the United States," and as such have certain benefits and privileges. Vessels of five net tons or more owned by citizens of the United States and otherwise complying with the requirements for documentation may be documented to engage in the foreign or coasting trades or the fisheries.

Registers are ordinarily issued to vessels engaged in the foreign trade or the whale fisheries. Historically, this group has included the major portion of the whaling fleet.

Enrollments and licenses are issued to vessels of twenty net tons or more engaged in the coasting trade or fisheries.

Licenses may be issued to vessels of less than twenty net tons engaged in the coasting trade or fisheries.

Undocumented craft are those not registered, enrolled, or licensed. Barges, scows, lighters, and canal boats, without any propelling power of their own, operated exclusively in a harbor, on the canals or other internal waters of a state, or on the rivers or lakes of the United States, not in any case carrying passengers, and vessels of less than five net tons are exempt from the requirements of the laws governing documentation.

One way changes in maritime law can affect these statistics is illustrated by the Act of 18 April 1874 (18 Stat. 31), which exempted the greater amount of canal-boat and other unrigged tonnage from documentation (see U.S. Code, title 46, section 336). For 1874–1876, the "balance sheets of tonnage," published annually in the source volumes, record the removal of 879,000 tons of vessels for this reason alone.

At irregular intervals, steps were taken to remove from the tonnage accounts those vessels lost, abandoned, captured, sold to aliens, and so forth, which had not been officially reported for removal purposes. From the outset, the failure to remove such vessels annually resulted in a cumulative error that inflated the statistics of tonnage. When general clearances of this cumulative error were made, the effect was concentrated in a single year or a small group of years.

Recurrently, in the annual tonnage reports found in the source volumes, the problem is discussed, the announcement is made that the rolls have been finally cleared, and assurance is given that the problem has been solved for the future. However, as late as 1867, in spite of repeated clearances in earlier years, the *First Annual Report of the Director of the Bureau of Statistics* stated, "The tonnage returns were swelled with thousands of ghostly ships – ships that had gone to the bottom years ago" (see *Annual Report of the Secretary of Treasury*, 1867, p. 244). In 1869, the Register of the Treasury attributed the entire decline of tonnage reported for 1869 to this factor. (See *Treasury Report*, 1869, p. 300.)

There are additional factors that suggest early merchant-vessel statistics should be used with due caution. First, in some instances, there are systematic differences in identically described statistical series appearing in the source volumes; these reflect conflicting series of figures that possibly have originated from different primary sources of data. This reflects the corrections to the 1936 data described in U.S. Bureau of Marine Inspection and Navigation, *Merchant Marine Statistics, 1936* and *1965*. Second, transcription and typographical errors have crept into historical tables in the source volumes in the process of repeated recopying and retypesetting. Third, statistically significant footnotes that appeared in early reports frequently were dropped in later years. Finally, caution is suggested in referring back to the earlier volumes in the search for explanations of discrepancies or major changes because the earlier data may reflect the same or similar errors.

For 1789–1793, tonnage figures are the "duty tonnage," that is, the tonnage of vessels on which duties were collected during the year (see *American State Papers: Class IV, Commerce and Navigation*, volume 1 (1834), p. 895). The

"duty tonnage" appears to have been the tonnage on which duties were collected on registered vessels, including "the repeated voyages of the same vessel," plus tonnage of the enrolled and licensed vessels that paid tonnage duties once each year (see *American State Papers*, volume 1, pp. 494, 498, 528). Beginning in 1794, "district tonnage returns" were used, derived from reports of District Collectors of Customs, which gave the tonnage of vessels in each district based on registers, enrollments, and licenses outstanding, as of December 31.

For 1794–1801, the figures are district tonnage returns, with no attempt to correct for the cumulative error caused by failure to remove vessels lost, abandoned, sold to aliens, and so forth (see *American State Papers*, volume 1, pp. 494, 499). The figures for 1800–1801 ignore the first clearing of tonnage accounts that took place during these years (see *American State Papers*, volume 1, pp. 494–9, 527–31). The correction for the cumulative error for *registered vessels only* would reduce the 1800 total to 819,571 tons and the 1801 total to 903,235 tons. The sharp drop attributable to the clearing of tonnage accounts would thereby be shifted back to 1800 instead of appearing in 1802.

Figures for 1789 are for ships paying tonnage duties during the last five months of the year. Figures for 1790–1792 are for ships paying duties at some time during the year.

Series Df579. For 1802–1818, the figures consist of the "corrected registered" tonnage plus the uncorrected enrolled or licensed tonnage (see the 1813 tonnage report in *American State Papers*, volume 1, p. 1017). The figures for 1811 and 1818 reflect two additional attempts to clear out the cumulative error of registered vessels improperly retained on the registers (see *American State Papers*, volume 1, pp. 876, 958, and volume 2, p. 406).

Series Df581–585. For 1920–1937, tonnage for vessels with electric screws is included in the totals (series Df581 and Df584), but excluded from the components (series Df582–583 and Df585). Maximum such tonnage is 201,246 for series Df581 in 1933 and 91,470 for series Df584 in 1934.

Series Df584. Includes gasoline engines, not shown separately.

Series Df586. Includes canal-boats and barges prior to 1868.

Series Df588. Includes iron, steel, composite, concrete, bronze, and aluminum.

Series Df588–589. The source publication classifies tonnage of each material by type of propulsion (steam, motor, sail, canal-boat, and barge).

Series Df590–593. The source publication presents the number of vessels engaged in each type of trade as well as tonnage. The statutes do not recognize for documenting purposes any fisheries except cod, mackerel, and whale. Vessels engaged in catching any other fish, such as salmon or menhaden, are documented for the mackerel fishery.

Series Df592–593. Figures in early reports identified as "registered" or as "registered in foreign trade" commonly include the registered vessels engaged in the whale fishery. Accordingly, figures on whale fisheries that are found in early reports should be examined carefully to determine whether they represent the entire whaling fleet or only the "enrolled or licensed" portion. The term "fisheries" as used in early volumes refers to cod and later to cod and mackerel fisheries. It rarely includes the whale fishery.

Series Df590. Represents the total "registered" minus "registered whale fishery." The "registered" whaling tonnage, however, is included for 1794–1798.

Series Df591. Represents the portion of the enrolled or licensed group engaged in this trade. The rest of the group is in series Df593.

Series Df592. The "registered whale fishery" portion of the registered fleet plus the "whale fishery" portion of the enrolled or licensed fleet. For 1794–1798, however, the registered whaling tonnage is not included here, but in series Df590. The large increase in the series in the year 1950 is attributable to the documentation of one large vessel on the Atlantic Coast.

Series Df593. The cod and mackerel fishery portion of the enrolled or licensed fleet. The rest of the enrolled or licensed group is in series Df591. Beginning in 1937, the series reflects only the cod fishery (mackerel are excluded).

TABLE Df594–605   U.S. and foreign vessels entered and cleared – net tonnage, by type of port: 1789–1995[1,2,3]

Contributed by Louis P. Cain

	Vessels entered						Vessels cleared					
	All ports			Seaports			All ports			Seaports		
	Total	U.S. vessels	Foreign vessels	Total	U.S. vessels	Foreign vessels	Total	U.S. vessels	Foreign vessels	Total	U.S. vessels	Foreign vessels
	Df594	Df595	Df596	Df597	Df598	Df599	Df600	Df601	Df602	Df603	Df604	Df605
Year	Thousand net tons	Thousand net tons	Thousand net tons	Thousand net tons	Thousand net tons	Thousand net tons	Thousand net tons	Thousand net tons	Thousand net tons	Thousand net tons	Thousand net tons	Thousand net tons
1789	234	127	107	—	—	—	—	—	—	—	—	—
1790	606	355	251	—	—	—	—	—	—	—	—	—
1791	604	364	241	—	—	—	—	—	—	—	—	—
1792	659	415	244	—	—	—	—	—	—	—	—	—
1793	611	448	164	—	—	—	—	—	—	—	—	—
1794	609	526	83	—	—	—	—	—	—	—	—	—
1795	637	580	57	—	—	—	—	—	—	—	—	—
1796	722	675	47	—	—	—	—	—	—	—	—	—
1797	681	608	73	—	—	—	—	—	—	—	—	—
1798	610	522	88	—	—	—	—	—	—	—	—	—
1799	732	625	108	—	—	—	—	—	—	—	—	—
1800	804	683	121	—	—	—	—	—	—	—	—	—
1801	1,007	849	157	—	—	—	—	—	—	—	—	—
1802	944	799	146	—	—	—	—	—	—	—	—	—
1803	951	787	164	—	—	—	—	—	—	—	—	—
1804	944	822	122	—	—	—	—	—	—	—	—	—
1805	1,010	922	88	—	—	—	—	—	—	—	—	—
1806	1,135	1,044	91	—	—	—	—	—	—	—	—	—
1807	1,203	1,116	87	—	—	—	—	—	—	—	—	—
1808	586	539	47	—	—	—	—	—	—	—	—	—
1809	705	605	99	—	—	—	—	—	—	—	—	—
1810	989	909	80	—	—	—	—	—	—	—	—	—
1811	981	948	33	—	—	—	—	—	—	—	—	—
1812	715	668	47	—	—	—	—	—	—	—	—	—
1813	351	238	114	—	—	—	—	—	—	—	—	—
1814	108	60	48	—	—	—	—	—	—	—	—	—
1815	918	701	217	—	—	—	—	—	—	—	—	—
1816	1,136	877	259	—	—	—	—	—	—	—	—	—
1817	992	780	212	—	—	—	—	—	—	—	—	—
1818	917	755	161	—	—	—	—	—	—	—	—	—
1819	869	784	86	—	—	—	—	—	—	—	—	—
1820	880	801	79	—	—	—	—	—	—	—	—	—
1821	847	765	82	—	—	—	888	805	83	—	—	—
1822	889	788	101	—	—	—	911	814	97	—	—	—
1823	895	775	119	—	—	—	931	811	120	—	—	—
1824	952	850	102	—	—	—	1,022	919	103	—	—	—
1825	974	881	93	—	—	—	1,055	960	95	—	—	—
1826	1,048	942	106	—	—	—	1,052	953	99	—	—	—
1827	1,056	918	138	—	—	—	1,112	981	131	—	—	—
1828	1,019	868	150	—	—	—	1,048	897	151	—	—	—
1829	1,004	873	131	—	—	—	1,078	945	133	—	—	—
1830	1,099	967	132	—	—	—	1,105	972	133	—	—	—
1831	1,405	923	482	—	—	—	1,244	973	272	—	—	—
1832	1,343	950	393	—	—	—	1,362	975	388	—	—	—
1833	1,608	1,111	497	—	—	—	1,639	1,142	497	—	—	—
1834	1,643	1,075	568	—	—	—	1,712	1,134	578	—	—	—
1835	1,994	1,353	641	—	—	—	2,031	1,401	631	—	—	—
1836	1,936	1,255	680	—	—	—	1,990	1,316	674	—	—	—
1837	2,065	1,300	766	—	—	—	2,023	1,267	756	—	—	—
1838	1,895	1,303	592	—	—	—	2,013	1,409	604	—	—	—
1839	2,116	1,491	625	—	—	—	2,090	1,478	612	—	—	—
1840	2,289	1,577	712	1,788	—	—	2,353	1,647	706	1,861	—	—
1841	2,368	1,632	736	—	—	—	2,371	1,634	737	—	—	—
1842	2,243	1,510	733	—	—	—	2,277	1,536	740	—	—	—
1843	1,678	1,144	535	—	—	—	1,792	1,268	524	—	—	—
1844	2,894	1,977	917	1,897	—	—	2,918	2,011	907	—	—	—

Notes appear at end of table

TABLE Df594–605   U.S. and foreign vessels entered and cleared – net tonnage, by type of port: 1789–1995
Continued

	Vessels entered						Vessels cleared					
	All ports			Seaports			All ports			Seaports		
	Total	U.S. vessels	Foreign vessels	Total	U.S. vessels	Foreign vessels	Total	U.S. vessels	Foreign vessels	Total	U.S. vessels	Foreign vessels
	Df594	Df595	Df596	Df597	Df598	Df599	Df600	Df601	Df602	Df603	Df604	Df605
Year	Thousand net tons	Thousand net tons	Thousand net tons	Thousand net tons	Thousand net tons	Thousand net tons	Thousand net tons	Thousand net tons	Thousand net tons	Thousand net tons	Thousand net tons	Thousand net tons
1845	2,946	2,035	911	2,011	—	—	2,984	2,054	930	—	—	—
1846	3,111	2,151	960	2,022	—	—	3,189	2,221	968	—	—	—
1847	3,322	2,101	1,220	2,429	—	—	3,379	2,202	1,177	—	—	—
1848	3,799	2,393	1,405	2,503	—	—	3,865	2,461	1,404	—	—	—
1849	4,369	2,658	1,711	2,890	—	—	4,429	2,754	1,676	—	—	—
1850	3,749	2,573	1,176	3,013	—	—	4,361	2,633	1,728	3,167	—	—
1851	4,993	3,054	1,939	3,466	—	—	5,130	3,201	1,930	—	—	—
1852	5,293	3,236	2,057	3,926	—	—	5,278	3,231	2,048	—	—	—
1853	6,282	4,004	2,278	4,157	—	—	6,066	3,767	2,299	4,289	—	—
1854	5,884	3,752	2,132	4,343	—	—	6,019	3,911	2,108	4,524	—	—
1855	5,945	3,861	2,084	4,178	—	—	6,179	4,069	2,110	4,435	—	—
1856	6,872	4,385	2,487	4,464	3,194	1,270	7,000	4,538	2,462	4,695	—	—
1857	7,186	4,721	2,465	4,843	3,482	1,361	7,071	4,581	2,490	4,882	3,483	1,398
1858	6,905	4,396	2,209	4,338	3,051	1,287	7,803	4,490	3,313	4,436	3,128	1,309
1859	7,806	5,266	2,540	4,913	3,328	1,585	7,916	5,297	2,618	4,867	3,315	1,552
1860	8,275	5,921	2,354	5,000	3,302	1,698	8,790	6,166	2,624	5,257	3,501	1,756
1861	7,241	5,024	2,218	4,559	3,025	1,534	7,151	4,889	2,262	4,410	2,874	1,636
1862	7,363	5,118	2,245	4,191	2,629	1,562	7,339	4,962	2,377	4,205	2,568	1,637
1863	7,255	4,615	2,640	4,205	2,308	1,898	7,511	4,447	3,064	4,343	2,266	2,077
1864	6,538	3,066	3,471	4,167	1,655	2,512	6,832	3,091	3,741	4,279	1,662	2,617
1865	6,161	2,944	3,217	3,827	1,615	2,212	6,620	3,025	3,595	4,161	1,710	2,450
1866	7,782	3,372	4,410	5,008	1,891	3,117	7,822	3,383	4,438	5,161	2,030	3,131
1867	7,774	3,455	4,319	5,266	2,146	3,121	7,885	3,420	4,465	5,501	2,270	3,230
1868	8,046	3,551	4,495	5,572	2,466	3,106	8,279	3,718	4,561	5,811	2,625	3,186
1869	8,750	3,403	5,348	6,032	2,459	3,573	7,754	3,381	4,373	6,114	2,502	3,612
1870	9,156	3,486	5,670	6,270	2,452	3,818	9,169	3,507	5,662	6,362	2,530	3,832
1871	10,009	3,743	6,266	6,994	2,604	4,391	9,898	3,747	6,152	6,918	2,635	4,283
1872	10,806	3,712	7,095	7,770	2,585	5,185	10,734	3,682	7,051	7,739	2,598	5,141
1873	11,696	3,613	8,083	8,395	2,443	5,951	11,822	3,757	8,065	8,515	2,574	5,941
1874	13,092	3,894	9,198	10,010	2,915	7,095	13,189	3,982	9,207	10,058	2,961	7,097
1875	11,693	3,574	8,119	9,143	2,887	6,256	11,897	3,737	8,160	9,341	3,061	6,279
1876	12,511	3,611	8,899	9,716	2,928	6,788	12,655	3,732	8,923	9,839	3,037	6,802
1877	13,455	3,663	9,791	10,406	2,958	7,449	13,442	3,765	9,677	10,389	3,043	7,345
1878	14,464	3,642	10,821	11,531	3,009	8,521	14,808	3,872	10,935	11,844	3,196	8,647
1879	16,193	3,415	12,778	13,768	3,050	10,718	16,075	3,464	12,611	13,617	3,071	10,545
1880	18,011	3,437	14,574	15,251	3,140	12,111	18,043	3,397	14,646	15,296	3,078	12,218
1881	18,319	3,254	15,066	15,631	2,919	12,711	18,470	3,376	15,094	15,794	3,040	12,754
1882	17,601	3,341	14,260	14,656	2,968	11,688	17,757	3,318	14,439	14,846	2,936	11,911
1883	16,382	3,256	13,126	13,361	2,835	10,526	16,541	3,307	13,234	13,565	2,895	10,670
1884	15,069	3,202	11,867	12,085	2,821	9,264	15,205	3,237	11,968	12,206	2,845	9,361
1885	15,305	3,132	12,173	12,287	2,709	9,578	15,515	3,232	12,283	12,496	2,809	9,688
1886	15,136	3,232	11,904	12,230	2,762	9,468	15,328	3,303	12,024	12,413	2,806	9,607
1887	15,816	3,366	12,451	13,532	2,871	10,661	15,753	3,259	12,494	13,511	2,771	10,740
1888	15,393	3,367	12,026	12,956	2,914	10,042	15,669	3,415	12,254	13,252	2,944	10,308
1889	15,952	3,724	12,228	13,312	3,128	10,184	16,343	3,988	12,355	13,672	3,342	10,329
1890	18,107	4,083	14,024	15,366	3,405	11,961	18,149	4,067	14,082	15,429	3,390	12,039
1891	18,204	4,381	13,823	15,394	3,670	11,724	18,261	4,455	13,805	15,411	3,716	11,695
1892	21,013	4,470	16,543	18,180	3,747	14,434	21,161	4,536	16,625	18,258	3,751	14,507
1893	19,582	4,359	15,223	16,679	3,493	13,186	19,761	4,403	15,357	16,825	3,537	13,288
1894	19,990	4,655	15,335	17,025	3,649	13,376	20,272	4,740	15,532	17,306	3,747	13,560
1895	19,295	4,473	14,822	16,725	3,677	13,049	19,751	4,504	15,246	17,024	3,616	13,408
1896	20,989	5,196	15,793	17,453	3,673	13,779	21,415	5,330	16,085	17,819	3,741	14,078
1897	23,760	5,525	18,235	20,003	3,611	16,391	23,709	5,618	18,091	19,878	3,637	16,241
1898	25,579	5,240	20,339	21,700	3,362	18,338	25,748	5,111	20,637	21,892	3,231	18,661
1899	26,111	5,341	20,770	21,963	3,333	18,631	26,266	5,472	20,794	22,177	3,463	18,714

(continued)

TABLE Df594–605   U.S. and foreign vessels entered and cleared – net tonnage, by type of port: 1789–1995
Continued

	Vessels entered						Vessels cleared					
	All ports			Seaports			All ports			Seaports		
	Total	U.S. vessels	Foreign vessels	Total	U.S. vessels	Foreign vessels	Total	U.S. vessels	Foreign vessels	Total	U.S. vessels	Foreign vessels
	Df594	Df595	Df596	Df597	Df598	Df599	Df600	Df601	Df602	Df603	Df604	Df605
Year	Thousand net tons	Thousand net tons	Thousand net tons	Thousand net tons	Thousand net tons	Thousand net tons	Thousand net tons	Thousand net tons	Thousand net tons	Thousand net tons	Thousand net tons	Thousand net tons
1900	28,163	6,136	22,027	23,534	3,974	19,559	28,281	6,209	22,072	23,618	4,006	19,612
1901	29,768	6,381	24,791	24,791	3,980	20,811	29,820	6,417	23,403	24,889	4,020	20,870
1902	30,654	6,961	24,361	24,361	4,020	20,342	30,444	6,822	23,623	24,242	3,956	20,287
1903	31,094	6,907	24,698	24,698	3,881	20,817	31,316	6,975	24,341	24,823	3,931	20,892
1904	29,952	6,679	24,111	24,111	3,806	20,305	30,016	6,641	23,374	24,192	3,836	20,356
1905	30,983	7,081	24,793	24,793	4,120	20,673	31,158	7,203	23,955	25,020	4,259	20,760
1906	34,155	7,613	26,543	27,401	4,023	23,379	33,784	7,581	26,204	26,970	3,923	23,047
1907	36,622	8,116	28,507	29,248	3,924	25,324	35,990	8,093	27,898	28,499	3,797	24,702
1908	38,539	8,473	30,066	30,444	4,314	26,130	38,282	8,435	29,846	30,198	4,288	25,910
1909	39,058	8,771	30,287	30,243	4,403	25,840	38,196	8,492	29,705	29,604	4,215	25,389
1910	40,236	8,888	31,347	30,917	4,214	26,703	39,706	8,809	30,897	30,510	4,196	26,314
1911	42,675	9,693	32,982	32,457	4,302	28,155	42,437	9,753	32,684	32,299	4,427	27,871
1912	46,158	11,257	34,901	34,659	4,572	30,087	46,417	11,703	34,713	34,706	4,794	29,912
1913	50,639	13,073	37,567	37,973	5,241	32,732	51,152	13,946	37,206	37,566	5,289	32,277
1914	53,389	13,730	39,659	40,052	5,436	34,616	53,183	13,740	39,443	39,743	5,185	34,558
1915	46,710	13,275	33,435	35,032	6,830	28,202	46,885	13,418	33,467	35,458	7,110	28,347
1916	51,550	17,928	33,622	37,744	9,446	28,298	52,423	17,902	34,521	38,946	9,763	29,182
1917	50,472	18,725	31,747	36,521	10,898	25,623	52,077	19,146	32,931	38,094	11,339	26,755
1918	45,456	19,284	26,173	31,101	11,256	19,845	46,014	19,206	26,808	31,869	11,280	20,589
1919	46,702	21,933	24,769	36,381	16,224	20,157	51,257	24,992	26,265	40,751	19,133	21,617
1920	64,104	32,119	31,985	51,531	26,225	25,306	67,817	34,053	33,764	54,980	27,875	27,106
1921	62,285	31,185	31,100	49,958	24,402	25,556	62,665	30,181	32,484	50,423	23,432	26,991
1922	65,191	31,738	33,453	51,701	23,633	28,068	64,839	31,759	33,080	51,799	23,755	28,044
1923	66,319	27,725	38,594	52,775	20,984	31,791	66,624	27,932	38,692	53,215	21,305	31,910
1924	68,292	29,628	38,664	54,726	22,462	32,264	68,910	30,092	38,818	55,294	22,896	32,397
1925	69,378	27,947	41,431	55,636	21,148	34,487	70,229	27,808	42,421	57,160	21,394	35,766
1926	76,933	26,890	50,043	63,759	21,091	42,668	79,041	28,532	50,509	65,583	22,234	43,349
1927	74,310	29,289	45,021	58,921	22,001	36,920	75,440	29,793	45,647	59,759	22,078	37,681
1928	80,211	31,285	48,926	62,809	22,991	39,818	80,667	31,734	48,933	63,331	23,180	40,151
1929	82,602	32,241	50,361	66,853	25,208	41,645	82,343	31,927	50,416	67,030	25,045	41,985
1930	81,253	31,866	49,387	66,499	24,620	41,879	81,307	31,560	49,747	66,500	24,154	42,346
1931	72,782	26,907	45,875	60,427	21,499	38,929	73,501	26,854	46,647	61,204	21,417	39,787
1932	64,837	24,278	40,559	55,229	20,643	34,587	64,446	23,865	40,582	54,900	20,204	34,695
1933	60,936	22,488	38,448	51,564	19,051	32,513	61,287	22,434	38,853	52,083	19,093	32,990
1934	63,787	23,192	40,594	—	—	—	—	—	—	—	—	—
1935	64,612	22,372	42,240	54,289	18,893	35,395	64,887	22,126	42,761	54,722	18,651	36,071
1936	65,972	20,682	45,290	55,038	17,510	37,528	66,066	20,069	45,997	55,381	16,967	38,414
1937	71,560	19,527	52,033	59,980	16,747	43,233	72,880	19,938	52,942	61,177	17,134	44,043
1938	70,516	19,020	51,496	59,223	15,899	43,324	71,286	18,829	52,456	60,064	15,742	44,322
1939	68,992	17,769	51,223	57,973	14,553	43,421	70,306	18,156	52,150	59,218	14,903	44,316
1940	58,544	19,220	39,324	45,393	15,740	29,652	62,171	20,248	41,923	48,996	16,766	32,230
1941	59,061	20,940	38,121	42,616	16,767	25,849	62,596	21,869	40,726	46,142	17,701	28,441
1942	43,942	13,611	30,331	28,258	10,326	17,932	47,706	16,354	31,352	31,976	13,149	18,827
1943	61,084	29,292	31,792	44,739	24,508	20,231	66,716	33,682	33,034	50,232	28,826	21,406
1944	81,860	48,071	33,789	66,305	42,196	24,109	87,385	53,050	34,335	71,717	46,919	24,798
1945	94,021	61,375	32,646	81,182	56,499	24,682	94,559	61,460	33,099	81,452	56,332	25,120
1946	80,258	53,045	27,213	69,520	49,143	20,378	77,225	49,124	28,101	66,376	45,113	21,263
1947	93,796	53,627	40,170	80,889	49,044	31,844	97,160	54,088	43,072	84,508	49,558	34,949
1948	90,927	47,726	43,199	76,910	43,270	33,640	89,449	45,775	43,667	75,714	41,348	34,358
1949	85,700	41,251	44,451	74,701	37,626	37,076	84,286	39,681	44,604	73,063	36,136	36,927
1950	86,629	35,376	51,251	73,451	31,757	41,693	87,829	36,043	51,778	74,785	32,510	42,269
1951	108,086	44,571	63,515	93,674	40,482	53,192	110,236	46,763	63,472	96,257	43,024	53,233
1952	116,375	45,223	71,152	101,263	40,732	60,532	114,797	43,726	71,071	99,703	39,273	60,429
1953	112,559	39,319	43,240	97,344	34,969	62,375	112,935	39,188	73,747	97,627	34,775	62,852
1954	109,524	33,860	75,664	97,198	30,133	67,065	109,899	33,579	76,321	97,674	29,969	67,706

TABLE Df594–605   U.S. and foreign vessels entered and cleared – net tonnage, by type of port: 1789–1995
Continued

	Vessels entered						Vessels cleared					
	All ports			Seaports			All ports			Seaports		
	Total	U.S. vessels	Foreign vessels	Total	U.S. vessels	Foreign vessels	Total	U.S. vessels	Foreign vessels	Total	U.S. vessels	Foreign vessels
	Df594	Df595	Df596	Df597	Df598	Df599	Df600	Df601	Df602	Df603	Df604	Df605
Year	Thousand net tons	Thousand net tons	Thousand net tons	Thousand net tons	Thousand net tons	Thousand net tons	Thousand net tons	Thousand net tons	Thousand net tons	Thousand net tons	Thousand net tons	Thousand net tons
1955	128,405	34,321	94,084	113,807	30,407	83,400	129,368	34,407	94,961	114,806	30,615	84,192
1956	147,844	36,247	111,598	130,767	31,254	99,514	148,269	36,317	111,952	131,391	31,510	99,881
1957	162,925	35,898	127,027	146,144	31,189	114,956	162,578	35,118	127,460	145,954	30,569	115,385
1958	149,097	26,842	122,255	136,291	23,642	112,648	148,816	26,449	122,366	136,102	23,324	112,778
1959	154,213	26,417	127,796	137,845	21,897	115,947	155,505	26,623	128,883	139,262	22,042	117,221
1960	162,765	30,189	132,575	145,828	26,708	119,119	166,715	31,280	135,434	149,778	27,649	122,127
1961	166,548	31,144	135,404	148,955	28,266	120,688	168,878	31,941	136,936	151,295	29,062	122,233
1962	178,334	33,774	144,560	158,606	29,963	128,644	178,953	34,165	144,788	159,330	30,337	128,993
1963	186,700	33,300	153,400	165,124	29,677	135,447	187,539	34,106	153,433	166,103	30,440	135,663
1964	199,330	34,956	164,373	174,625	30,909	143,715	202,262	35,337	166,924	177,636	31,409	146,225
1965	209,000	34,041	174,960	183,724	30,919	152,806	208,736	34,016	174,721	183,540	31,048	152,492
1966	217,894	31,487	186,407	191,684	28,621	163,063	219,437	32,738	186,699	193,433	29,925	163,507
1967	220,681	30,830	189,848	195,871	26,990	168,878	220,231	30,827	189,404	195,845	27,089	168,756
1968	229,850	30,389	199,465	203,664	27,456	176,210	230,324	31,198	199,126	204,086	28,244	175,839
1969	238,085	26,662	211,423	213,008	25,264	187,741	237,986	27,235	210,758	212,746	25,738	187,013
1970	254,154	26,239	227,915	226,666	24,234	202,431	253,136	26,953	226,183	225,925	24,898	201,027
1971	255,779	23,549	232,230	229,024	22,003	207,021	258,082	24,242	233,841	231,201	22,752	208,449
1972	295,281	24,727	270,548	267,017	22,650	244,451	307,110	27,879	279,229	278,473	25,830	252,641
1973	344,772	32,924	311,845	314,169	30,770	283,397	348,043	34,719	313,325	317,047	32,521	284,525
1974	346,830	35,890	310,935	321,814	32,438	289,372	352,084	36,751	315,330	326,805	33,137	293,666
1975	355,179	32,037	323,148	326,427	29,590	296,839	363,176	33,885	329,290	333,778	31,144	302,630
1976	400,817	33,199	367,596	369,803	30,670	339,112	404,655	34,436	370,213	373,287	31,677	341,608
1977	440,080	34,115	405,952	407,175	30,765	376,397	429,809	34,404	395,398	396,514	30,895	365,613
1978	456,716	36,828	419,892	422,443	34,111	388,336	446,454	33,896	412,565	411,988	31,142	380,850
1979	498,584	44,874	453,701	462,248	42,043	420,198	496,298	47,520	448,767	459,386	44,443	414,933
1980	491,577	52,474	439,100	460,441	49,896	410,546	487,205	54,004	433,200	455,692	51,246	404,447
1981	469,761	56,097	413,655	438,796	53,703	385,086	476,639	56,309	420,333	445,248	53,643	391,611
1982	438,000	59,000	379,000	412,000	57,000	355,000	448,000	60,000	388,000	421,000	58,000	363,000
1983	442,000	62,000	380,000	416,000	60,000	355,000	449,000	62,000	387,000	423,000	60,000	363,000
1984	458,964	52,793	406,164	428,819	50,681	378,130	467,805	53,467	414,329	437,853	51,433	386,414
1985	451,784	53,422	398,347	425,464	51,241	374,218	461,199	55,174	406,021	435,081	52,963	382,119
1986	489,000	49,000	439,000	463,000	48,000	415,000	491,000	51,000	441,000	466,000	49,000	417,000
1987	518,000	48,000	470,000	492,000	47,000	445,000	521,000	49,000	472,000	495,000	48,000	447,000
1988	556,000	47,000	509,000	527,000	46,000	481,000	561,000	49,000	512,000	531,000	47,000	484,000
1989	587,000	44,000	543,000	558,000	42,000	516,000	590,000	45,000	545,000	561,000	44,000	517,000
1990	589,000	41,000	548,000	564,000	40,000	524,000	592,000	43,000	550,000	566,000	41,000	525,000
1991	516,000	39,000	476,000	494,000	38,000	455,000	521,000	40,000	480,000	498,000	39,000	459,000
1992	515,000	37,000	478,000	493,000	36,000	457,000	519,000	38,000	481,000	496,000	37,000	460,000
1993	515,000	35,000	480,000	493,000	33,000	460,000	519,000	36,000	483,000	497,000	35,000	462,000
1994	527,000	35,000	492,000	503,000	33,000	469,000	532,000	36,000	496,000	508,000	34,000	473,000
1995	539,000	32,000	507,000	514,000	30,000	484,000	540,000	33,000	508,000	517,000	31,000	485,000

[1] The data include Alaska, Hawai'i, Puerto Rico, and, beginning in 1935, the Virgin Islands.

[2] Excludes domestic trade. See text for other exclusions.

[3] Year-end date changes over time. See text.

Sources
Series Df594–596. 1789–1820, Fred J. Guetter and Albert E. McKinley, *Statistical Tables Relating to the Economic Growth of the United States* (McKinley, 1924), p. 39; 1821–1879, U.S. Bureau of Marine Inspection and Navigation, *Merchant Marine Statistics, 1936*, p. 93; 1880–1940, U.S. Bureau of the Census, *Statistical Abstract of the United States, 1880–1888* (1908), p. 286; 1889–1916, *Statistical Abstract* (1916), p. 338; 1917–1930, *Statistical Abstract* (1931), p. 474; 1931–1940, *Statistical Abstract* (1947), p. 558; 1941–1946, U.S. Bureau of the Census, *Foreign Commerce* and *Navigation of the United States* (various issues); 1947–1995, U.S. Bureau of the Census, *Vessel Entrances and Clearances*, Summary Report FT 975 (various issues), and unpublished data.

Series Df597. *Statistical Abstract of the United States, 1840* (1946), p. 546; 1844–1855, *Statistical Abstract* (1878), p. 134; 1856–1879, *Statistical Abstract* (1880), p. 138. 1880–1995, see sources for series Df594–596.

Series Df598. 1856–1879, see sources for series Df597; 1880–1995, see sources for series Df594–596.

Series Df599–602. See sources cited for specific periods for series Df594–596. The following page numbers apply, respectively, to the sources cited for 1821–1940: pp. 93, 287, 475, 558, and 592.

Series Df603. *Statistical Abstract of the United States, 1840* and *1850* (1946), p. 546; 1853–1879, *Statistical Abstract* (1881), p. 138. 1880–1995, see sources for series Df594–596.

Series Df604–605. 1857–1879, *Statistical Abstract* (1881), p. 136; 1880–1995, see sources for series Df594–596.

(continued)

TABLE Df594–605   U.S. and foreign vessels entered and cleared – net tonnage, by type of port: 1789–1995
Continued

Documentation

The data are for years ending September 20 (1789–1842), June 30 (1843–1918), and December 31 thereafter. The values for series Df594–605 during the transition period (July–December 1918) are as follows: 25,029, 11,006, 14,023, 16,113, 5,747, 10,366, 25,472, 11,223, 14,249, 16,112, 5,614, and 10,498, respectively. See the text for Table Df578–593 for a definition of gross tonnage and related discussion.

Net tonnage refers to the net or registered tonnage of the vessel, not the weight of cargo. The net tonnage is what remains after deducting from the gross tonnage the spaces occupied by the propelling machinery, fuel, crew quarters, master's cabin, and navigation spaces. It represents, substantially, space available for cargo and passengers. It is the usual basis for tonnage taxes and port charges. The net tonnage of a ship recorded as "entered with cargo" may bear little relation to the actual weight of cargo. Gross tonnage and net tonnage are both measures of cubic capacity, not of weight, 100 cubic feet equaling one ton. These terms should not be confused with the cargo ton of 2,000 pounds.

The tonnage figures shown in series Df595 and Df601 for U.S. vessels entered and cleared, respectively, in foreign trade are greater than the total tonnage of U.S. vessels documented for foreign trade because the "entered"

and "cleared" series include tonnage for each vessel each time it enters or clears during a year. The documented tonnage, series Df579, includes the tonnage of each vessel once for each year.

These figures include the tonnage of all types of watercraft engaged in foreign trade, whether entering or clearing with cargo or in ballast, which are required to make formal entrance and clearance under U.S. customs regulations. Vessels engaged in trade on the Great Lakes with Canada as well as in trade with Mexico are also included. Domestic trade is excluded. Vessels touching at a U.S. port in distress or for other temporary causes without discharging cargo and Army and Navy vessels carrying no commercial cargo are not required by customs regulations to enter or clear and thus are not included in the figures.

Vessels are reported as entered at the first port in the United States at which entry is made, regardless of whether any cargo is unladen at that port; arrivals at subsequent ports are not counted. Vessels are reported as cleared from the last port in the United States where loading of outward cargo is completed or where the vessel cleared in ballast; departures from prior ports are not counted. Seaports include all ports except northern border ports.

TABLE Df606–611   Value of waterborne imports and exports of merchandise, by flag of carrier: 1790–1994[1, 2]
Contributed by Louis P. Cain

	Imports			Exports				Imports			Exports		
	Total	U.S. vessels	Foreign vessels	Total	U.S. vessels	Foreign vessels		Total	U.S. vessels	Foreign vessels	Total	U.S. vessels	Foreign vessels
	Df606	Df607	Df608	Df609	Df610	Df611		Df606	Df607	Df608	Df609	Df610	Df611
Year	Million dollars	Million dollars	Million dollars	Million dollars	Million dollars	Million dollars	Year	Million dollars	Million dollars	Million dollars	Million dollars	Million dollars	Million dollars
1790	23	9	14	20	8	12	1850	178	140	38	152	100	52
1791	29	17	12	19	10	9	1851	216	164	53	218	152	66
1792	32	21	10	21	13	8	1852	208	155	53	210	139	70
1793	31	26	6	26	20	6	1853	268	192	76	231	155	76
1794	35	31	3	33	28	5	1854	301	215	86	276	191	84
1795	70	64	6	48	42	6	1855	261	202	59	275	203	72
1796	81	77	5	59	53	6	1856	315	250	65	327	232	95
1797	75	69	6	51	45	6	1857	361	259	102	363	251	112
1798	69	62	6	61	53	8	1858	283	204	79	325	243	81
1799	79	71	8	79	68	10	1859	339	216	123	357	250	107
1800	91	83	8	71	62	9	1860	362	228	134	400	279	121
1801	111	101	10	93	81	12	1861	336	202	134	249	180	69
1802	76	67	9	72	61	11	1862	206	92	113	230	125	105
1803	65	56	9	56	46	9	1863	253	110	143	332	132	200
1804	85	77	8	78	67	11	1864	330	81	248	340	103	237
1805	121	112	8	96	85	11	1865	249	74	174	356	93	263
1806	129	120	9	102	90	11	1866	446	112	333	565	214	352
1807	139	130	8	108	98	11	1867	418	117	301	461	181	281
1808	57	53	4	22	20	3	1868	372	123	249	477	175	302
1809	59	52	7	52	44	8	1869	437	137	301	439	153	286
1810	85	79	6	67	60	7	1870	462	153	309	530	200	330
1811	53	48	5	61	53	9	1871	526	163	363	583	190	393
1812	77	65	12	39	31	8	1872	623	177	445	562	168	394
1813	22	16	6	28	18	10	1873	647	175	472	666	172	495
1814	13	8	5	7	4	3	1874	581	176	405	708	174	534
1815	113	87	26	53	37	15	1875	541	158	383	658	156	502
1816	147	107	40	82	56	26	1876	465	143	321	660	168	492
1817	99	78	21	88	65	23	1877	481	152	330	695	165	530
1818	122	103	18	93	75	19	1878	454	146	307	736	167	570
1819	87	67	20	70	58	13	1879	454	144	310	729	128	601
1820	74	67	7	70	62	8	1880	653	149	503	830	109	721
1821	63	58	5	65	55	10	1881	625	134	492	894	117	777
1822	83	77	6	72	61	11	1882	702	130	572	738	97	641
1823	78	72	6	75	65	9	1883	700	136	564	799	104	694
1824	81	75	5	76	67	9	1884	648	135	513	714	99	615
1825	96	92	4	100	89	11	1885	556	113	444	718	82	636
1826	85	81	4	78	70	8	1886	611	119	492	660	78	582
1827	79	75	5	82	72	10	1887	665	121	543	695	73	622
1828	89	82	7	72	61	11	1888	692	124	568	674	67	606
1829	74	69	5	72	62	10	1889	707	121	586	714	83	631
1830	71	66	4	74	64	10	1890	749	125	624	825	78	747
1831	103	94	9	81	66	16	1891	804	127	677	853	79	774
1832	101	90	11	87	66	21	1892	788	139	649	997	81	916
1833	108	98	10	90	68	22	1893	822	127	695	804	71	733
1834	127	114	13	104	78	27	1894	625	122	504	843	74	769
1835	150	135	15	122	94	28	1895	699	108	591	758	62	695
1836	189	171	18	129	97	32	1896	744	117	627	821	70	751
1837	141	122	19	117	91	26	1897	729	109	620	986	80	906
1838	115	104	11	108	89	19	1898	586	94	492	1,158	68	1,090
1839	162	144	18	121	95	26	1899	664	82	582	1,143	79	1,065
1840	107	93	14	132	106	26	1900	806	104	701	1,284	91	1,193
1841	128	113	15	122	95	27	1901	776	93	683	1,376	84	1,292
1842	100	89	11	105	80	25	1902	847	102	745	1,258	84	1,174
1843	65	50	15	84	65	19	1903	960	124	836	1,281	91	1,190
1844	108	94	14	111	78	33	1904	923	132	791	1,308	97	1,211
1845	117	102	15	115	87	28	1905	1,039	161	878	1,355	130	1,225
1846	122	106	16	113	87	27	1906	1,140	168	971	1,550	154	1,396
1847	147	113	33	154	100	54	1907	1,340	177	1,164	1,662	142	1,521
1848	155	129	26	154	110	44	1908	1,123	152	971	1,670	121	1,550
1849	148	120	27	146	101	45	1909	1,241	151	1,090	1,481	108	1,373

Notes appear at end of table

(continued)

TABLE Df606–611   Value of waterborne imports and exports of merchandise, by flag of carrier: 1790–1994
Continued

Year	Imports Total Df606 (Million dollars)	Imports U.S. vessels Df607 (Million dollars)	Imports Foreign vessels Df608 (Million dollars)	Exports Total Df609 (Million dollars)	Exports U.S. vessels Df610 (Million dollars)	Exports Foreign vessels Df611 (Million dollars)
1910	1,467	147	1,319	1,516	114	1,403
1911	1,436	147	1,290	1,774	134	1,641
1912	1,551	171	1,380	1,880	152	1,729
1913	1,698	193	1,505	2,075	188	1,887
1914	1,738	199	1,539	2,048	170	1,878
1915	1,526	281	1,245	2,466	291	2,176
1916	2,157	532	1,625	4,820	665	4,155
1917	2,590	733	1,857	5,403	946	4,457
1918	2,577	717	1,860	5,226	986	4,240
1919	3,414	1,228	2,186	7,090	2,596	4,494
1920	4,731	1,988	2,743	7,252	3,165	4,087
1921	2,187	765	1,422	3,888	1,402	2,486
1922	2,704	921	1,783	3,281	1,261	2,020
1923	3,312	1,040	2,272	3,539	1,358	2,181
1924	3,145	1,012	2,133	4,010	1,532	2,478
1925	3,716	1,151	2,565	4,224	1,473	2,751
1926	3,891	1,195	2,696	4,050	1,401	2,649
1927	3,662	1,215	2,447	4,097	1,434	2,663
1928	3,550	1,133	2,418	4,277	1,472	2,804
1929	3,807	1,205	2,602	4,322	1,487	2,835
1930	2,635	898	1,737	3,168	1,117	2,051
1931	1,829	619	1,210	2,043	732	1,311
1932	1,164	431	734	1,385	476	909
1933	1,287	461	826	1,471	515	956
1934	1,446	528	917	1,837	658	1,179
1935	1,813	649	1,164	1,973	705	1,268
1936	—	—	—	—	—	—
1937	—	—	—	—	—	—
1938	—	—	—	—	—	—
1939	—	—	—	—	—	—
1940	—	—	—	—	—	—
1941	—	—	—	—	—	—
1942	—	—	—	—	—	—
1943	—	—	—	10,275	4,828	5,447
1944	—	—	—	11,382	5,582	5,800
1945	—	—	—	7,860	4,052	3,808
1946	3,691	2,239	1,452	7,705	4,692	3,013
1947	4,368	—	—	11,026	—	—
1948	5,197	—	—	8,877	—	—
1949	4,965	—	—	8,475	—	—
1950	6,754	—	—	7,097	—	—
1951	8,441	—	—	10,109	—	—
1952	8,118	—	—	9,031	—	—
1953	8,292	—	—	7,852	—	—
1954	7,334	—	—	8,286	—	—
1955	8,073	—	—	9,227	—	—
1956	8,899	—	—	11,045	—	—
1957	9,244	—	—	12,948	—	—
1958	9,700	—	—	10,664	—	—
1959	11,633	—	—	10,618	—	—
1960	11,140	—	—	13,164	—	—
1961	10,644	—	—	13,635	—	—
1962	11,805	—	—	13,705	—	—
1963	12,382	—	—	14,793	—	—
1964	13,441	—	—	17,089	—	—
1965	14,943	—	—	16,926	—	—
1966	17,319	—	—	18,520	—	—
1967	17,434	—	—	18,636	—	—
1968	21,139	—	—	19,359	—	—
1969	21,570	—	—	19,915	—	—
1970	24,728	—	—	24,394	—	—
1971	26,793	—	—	22,610	—	—
1972	33,617	—	—	25,520	—	—
1973	42,742	—	—	39,642	—	—
1974	67,148	—	—	55,506	—	—
1975	63,469	—	—	61,408	—	—
1976	81,171	—	—	64,712	—	—
1977	103,037	—	—	65,376	—	—
1978	135,480	—	—	77,338	—	—
1979	140,091	—	—	97,579	—	—
1980	164,924	—	—	118,835	—	—
1981	177,059	—	—	123,495	—	—
1982	155,493	—	—	115,885	—	—
1983	195,311	—	—	100,651	—	—
1984	191,113	—	—	101,803	—	—
1985	205,605	—	—	91,680	—	—
1986	217,776	—	—	87,946	—	—
1987	245,028	—	—	99,009	—	—
1988	254,766	—	—	126,192	—	—
1989	270,621	—	—	143,184	—	—
1990	283,412	—	—	150,739	—	—
1991	272,287	—	—	162,354	—	—
1992	293,099	—	—	170,313	—	—
1993	310,282	—	—	166,689	—	—
1994	338,809	—	—	177,333	—	—

[1] Data include reexports of merchandise; gold and silver coin bullion through 1879; imports and exports by land prior to 1871; and all waterborne foreign commerce of ports on the Great Lakes.

[2] Year-end date changes over time. See text.

Sources

1790–1820, Fred J. Guetter and Albert E. McKinley, *Statistical Tables Relating to the Economic Growth of the United States* (McKinley, 1924), p. 39; 1821–1858, U.S. Bureau of Marine Inspection and Navigation, *Merchant Marine Statistics, 1936*, p. 91; 1859–1935, U.S. Bureau of the Census, *Statistical Abstract of the United States, 1859–1866* (1895), pp. 399–400; 1867–1912, *Statistical Abstract* (1913), pp. 318–19; 1913–1923, *Statistical Abstract* (1924), p. 417; 1924–1935, *Statistical Abstract* (1946), p. 552; 1943–1946, U.S. Bureau of the Census, *Foreign Commerce and Navigation of the United States* (annual issues); 1947–1950, U.S. Bureau of the Census, *Waterborne Trade by United States Port*, FT 972 (annual issues); 1951–1970, U.S. Bureau of the Census, *Waterborne Foreign Trade Statistics*, FT 985 (annual issues) (title changed to *U.S. Waterborne Foreign Trade* in July 1965); 1970–1994, U.S. Bureau of the Census, *Waterborne Exports and General Imports* (annual issues).

Documentation

The primary source of figures for 1790–1820 is J. R. Soley, "The Maritime Industries of America," in *The United States of America*, edited by N. S. Shaler (D. Appleton & Company, 1894), volume 2, pp. 522–7, 534, 536, 538. The report gives the percentage of imports and exports in U.S. vessels. Guetter and McKinley (1924) have derived absolute figures by applying these percentages to total imports and exports of merchandise and specie. The primary source of figures for 1821–1935 is *Foreign Commerce and Navigation of the United States* (annual issues). Starting with 1943, import or export statistics by method of transportation, showing shipping weight as well as dollar value, have been compiled by the U.S. Bureau of the Census. The document in which the data are reported has experienced several name changes.

TABLE Df606–611   Value of waterborne imports and exports of merchandise, by flag of carrier: 1790–1994 Continued

The data were reported monthly to 1994, when the Census Bureau changed the format and started reporting it quarterly. The data reported here are from the annual summaries. Given the change in format, these series stop in 1994 to ensure consistency. Readers interested in more recent data are referred to the source documents.

The year-end dates are as follows: September 30 (1790–1842), June 30 (1843–1915), and December 31 thereafter. The data for the transition period (June–December 1915) for series Df606–611 are 817, 179, 638, 1,625, 200, and 1,425, respectively (in millions of dollars).

TABLE Df612–616   Merchant vessels built and documented – number and gross tonnage, by vessel type: 1797–1964[1, 2, 3]

Contributed by Louis P. Cain

	Number of vessels	Gross tons					Number of vessels	Gross tons			
		Total	Steam and motor vessels	Sailing vessels	Canal-boats and barges				Total	Steam and motor vessels	Sailing vessels	Canal-boats and barges
	Df612	Df613	Df614 [4]	Df615 [5]	Df616 [5]			Df612	Df613	Df614 [4]	Df615 [5]	Df616 [5]
Fiscal year	Number	Gross tons	Gross tons	Gross tons	Gross tons		Fiscal year	Number	Gross tons	Gross tons	Gross tons	Gross tons
1797	—	56,679	—	56,679	—		1845	1,038	146,018	40,926	105,092	—
1798	635	49,435	—	49,435	—		1846	1,420	188,203	51,778	136,425	—
1799	767	77,921	—	77,921	—		1847	1,598	243,732	53,979	189,753	—
1800	995	106,261	—	106,261	—		1848	1,851	318,075	66,652	251,423	—
1801	—	124,755	—	124,755	—		1849	1,547	256,577	61,241	195,336	—
1803	—	88,448	—	88,448	—		1850	1,360	272,218	56,911	215,307	—
1804	—	103,753	—	103,753	—		1851	1,357	298,203	78,197	220,006	—
1805	—	128,507	—	128,507	—		1852	1,444	351,493	98,624	252,869	—
1806	—	126,093	—	126,093	—		1853	1,710	425,572	109,402	316,170	—
1807	—	99,783	78	99,705	—		1854	1,774	535,616	91,037	444,579	—
1808 [6]	—	31,755	182	31,673	—		1855	2,024	583,450	78,127	505,323	—
1809	—	91,397	458	90,939	—		1856	1,703	469,393	74,865	394,528	—
1810	—	127,575	0	127,575	—		1857	1,443	378,804	74,459	304,345	—
1811	—	146,691	1,145	145,546	—		1858	1,241	244,712	65,374	179,338	—
1812	—	85,148	118	85,030	—		1859	875	156,602	35,305	121,297	—
1813	371	32,583	1,140	31,443	—		1860	1,071	214,798	69,370	145,428	—
1814	490	29,751	593	29,158	—		1861	1,146	233,194	60,986	172,208	—
1815	1,329	155,579	546	155,033	—		1862	864	175,076	55,449	119,627	—
1816	1,431	135,186	2,926	132,260	—		1863	1,816	311,045	94,233	216,812	—
1817	1,087	87,626	2,543	85,083	—		1864	2,388	415,740	147,499	268,241	—
1818	923	87,346	3,695	83,651	—		1865	1,789	394,523	146,438	248,090	—
1819	876	86,670	5,824	80,846	—		1866	1,898	336,146	125,183	210,963	—
1820	557	51,394	5,572	45,822	—		1867	1,518	305,594	72,010	233,584	—
1821	519	57,275	3,017	54,258	—		1868	1,802	285,304	63,940	142,742	78,622
1822	639	77,569	1,861	75,708	—		1869	1,726	275,230	65,066	149,029	61,135
1823	630	75,857	3,766	72,091	—		1870	1,618	276,953	70,621	146,340	59,992
1824	793	92,798	5,216	87,582	—		1871	1,755	273,227	87,842	97,179	88,206
1825	1,000	116,464	9,171	107,293	—		1872	1,643	209,052	62,210	76,291	70,551
1826	1,033	130,373	12,818	117,555	—		1873	2,261	359,246	88,011	144,629	126,606
1827	951	106,456	11,010	95,446	—		1874	2,147	432,725	101,930	216,316	114,479
1828	886	98,964	5,881	93,083	—		1875	1,301	297,639	62,460	206,884	28,295
1829	796	79,408	10,281	69,127	—		1876	1,112	203,586	69,251	118,672	15,663
1830	648	58,560	8,269	50,291	—		1877	1,029	176,592	47,514	106,331	22,747
1831	712	85,556	11,437	74,119	—		1878	1,258	235,504	81,860	106,066	47,578
1832	1,065	144,544	17,386	127,158	—		1879	1,132	193,031	86,361	66,867	39,803
1833	1,187	161,492	12,620	148,872	—		1880	902	157,410	78,854	59,057	19,499
1834	957	118,389	13,905	104,484	—		1881	1,108	280,459	118,070	81,209	81,180
1835 [7]	725	75,107	12,347	62,760	—		1882	1,371	282,270	121,843	118,798	41,629
1836	911	116,230	26,630	89,600	—		1883	1,268	265,430	107,229	137,046	21,155
1837	972	125,913	33,811	92,102	—		1884	1,190	225,514	91,328	120,621	13,565
1838	913	115,905	23,607	92,298	—		1885	920	159,056	84,333	65,362	9,361
1839	899	125,260	34,219	91,041	—		1886	715	95,453	44,468	41,238	9,747
1840	871	118,309	19,811	98,498	—		1887	844	150,450	100,074	34,633	15,743
1841	761	118,893	27,941	90,950	—		1888	1,014	218,087	142,007	48,590	27,490
1842	1,021	129,083	29,158	99,925	—		1889	1,077	231,134	159,318	50,570	21,246
1843 [7]	482	63,617	17,624	45,992	—							
1844	766	103,537	30,976	72,561	—							

Notes appear at end of table

(continued)

TABLE Df612–616 Merchant vessels built and documented – number and gross tonnage, by vessel type: 1797–1964 *Continued*

			Gross tons		
	Number of vessels	Total	Steam and motor vessels	Sailing vessels	Canal-boats and barges
	Df612	Df613	Df614 [4]	Df615 [5]	Df616 [5]
Fiscal year	Number	Gross tons	Gross tons	Gross tons	Gross tons
1890	1,051	294,123	159,046	102,873	32,204
1891	1,384	369,302	185,037	144,290	39,975
1892	1,395	199,633	92,531	83,217	23,885
1893	956	211,639	134,368	49,348	27,923
1894	838	131,195	83,720	37,827	9,648
1895	694	111,602	69,754	34,900	6,948
1896	723	227,097	138,029	65,236	23,832
1897	891	232,233	106,154	64,308	61,771
1898	952	180,458	105,838	34,416	40,204
1899	1,273	300,038	151,058	98,073	50,907
1900	1,447	393,790	202,528	116,460	74,802
1901	1,580	483,489	273,591	126,165	83,733
1902	1,491	468,831	308,178	97,698	62,955
1903	1,311	436,152	271,781	89,979	74,392
1904	1,184	378,542	255,744	64,908	57,890
1905	1,012	330,316	197,702	79,418	53,196
1906	1,221	418,745	315,707	35,209	67,829
1907	1,157	471,332	365,405	24,907	81,020
1908	1,457	614,216	481,624	31,981	100,611
1909	1,247	238,090	148,208	28,950	60,932
1910	1,361	342,068	257,993	19,358	64,717
1911	1,422	291,162	227,231	10,092	53,839
1912	1,505	232,669	153,493	21,221	57,955
1913	1,475	346,155	243,408	28,610	74,137
1914	1,151	316,250	224,225	13,749	78,276
1915	1,157	225,122	154,990	8,021	62,111
1916	937	325,413	250,125	14,765	60,523
1917	1,297	664,479	513,243	43,185	108,051
1918	1,528	1,300,868	1,090,996	83,629	126,243
1919	1,953	3,326,621	3,157,091	79,234	90,296
1920	2,067	3,880,639	3,660,023	132,184	88,432
1921	1,361	2,265,115	2,071,221	91,743	102,151
1922	845	661,232	597,137	25,459	38,636
1923	770	335,791	241,802	17,442	76,547
1924	1,049	223,968	145,493	914	77,561
1925	967	199,846	141,053	2,869	55,924
1926	924	224,673	140,586	263	83,824
1927	917	245,144	181,504	326	63,314
1928	969	257,180	172,901	230	84,049
1929	808	128,976	75,725	797	52,454

			Gross tons		
	Number of vessels	Total	Steam and motor vessels	Sailing vessels	Canal-boats and barges
	Df612	Df613	Df614 [4]	Df615 [5]	Df616 [5]
Fiscal year	Number	Gross tons	Gross tons	Gross tons	Gross tons
1930	1,020	254,296	172,969	210	81,117
1931	1,302	386,906	212,996	52	173,858
1932	722	212,892	164,620	18	48,254
1933	642	190,803	168,488	46	22,269
1934	724	66,649	26,916	33	39,700
1935	748	62,919	30,341	50	32,528
1936	1,207	224,084	59,020	79	164,985
1937	1,939	471,364	113,661	71	357,632
1938 [8]	753	237,374	—	—	—
1939	673	339,899	269,188	22	70,689
1940 [9]	319	193,229	172,433	17	20,779
1940 [9]	705	446,894	385,681	87	61,126
1941	703	647,097	586,443	0	60,654
1942	1,108	4,543,946	4,504,398	14	39,534
1943	1,901	10,431,734	10,339,670	23	92,041
1944	1,723	8,032,009	8,009,277	129	22,603
1945	1,744	6,313,977	6,258,608	0	55,369
1946	1,275	548,262	509,538	7	38,717
1947	1,259	267,331	186,109	16	81,206
1948	1,118	200,290	108,206	0	92,084
1949	978	195,190	85,288	39	109,863
1950	861	194,370	103,358	7	91,005
1951	992	308,825	165,064	0	143,761
1952	990	437,378	313,296	0	124,082
1953	1,190	633,966	477,421	28	156,517
1954	1,186	589,317	369,016	10	220,291
1955	1,116	400,076	117,011	24	283,041
1956	1,385	445,617	152,359	8	293,250
1957	1,582	585,048	248,801	0	336,247
1958	1,390	836,799	406,272	0	430,527
1959	1,180	791,640	385,874	0	405,766
1960	949	629,295	352,271	0	277,024
1961	877	620,287	388,927	0	231,360
1962	1,175	821,431	419,586	94	401,751
1963	1,365	942,809	460,442	6	482,361
1964	1,551	867,910	265,850	99	601,961

[1] Beginning with 1938, figures are not comparable with those for earlier years. See text.

[2] Data include Alaska, Hawai'i, Puerto Rico, Guam, and the Virgin Islands

[3] As of December 31 (1797–1834); September 30 (1835–1842); June 30 (1843–1939, as well as the first set of values shown for 1940); and January 1 thereafter.

[4] Statistics for motor vessels begin in 1893.

[5] Data for canal-boats and barges are included under sailing prior to 1868.

[6] The figures by class of vessel do not add to the total.

[7] The data are for a nine-month period.

[8] Understates number of vessels built as compared with earlier figures. Beginning in 1938, the figures represent vessels built during the previous twelve-month period that were still existent and documented as part of the merchant fleet at the end of the period. Hence, they exclude vessels that were lost, sold to the federal government, sold to aliens (especially the Allied Forces in Europe), or otherwise removed from merchant vessel documentation before the end of the period. A large number of

merchant vessels built at this time were sold either to the federal government or to the Allied Forces in Europe.

[9] First set of 1940 figures is comparable to earlier data; second set is comparable to later data.

Source
U.S. Bureau of Marine Inspection and Navigation, *Merchant Marine Statistics, 1936* and *1965* (annual report now published by the U.S. Coast Guard, *Boating Statistics*).

Documentation
The data are for documented vessels of five gross tons or more. See the text for Table Df578–593 for a definition of gross tonnage and related discussion.

The source publication also presents statistics separately for steam, motor, and sailing vessels; canal-boats; and barges.

TABLE Df617   Tonnage of documented vessels: 1800–1818

Contributed by Louis P. Cain

Year	Tonnage of documented vessels Df617 — Thousand gross tons	Year	Tonnage of documented vessels Df617 — Thousand gross tons
1800	768	1810	1,329
1801	850	1811	1,131
1802	865	1812	1,127
1803	917	1813	1,032
1804	983	1814	1,029
1805	1,085	1815	1,262
1806	1,166	1816	1,264
1807	1,208	1817	1,341
1808	1,173	1818	1,150
1809	1,266		

Source

U.S. Congress, *American State Papers* (1834), volumes 1 and 2.

Documentation

These figures were derived by a method authorized by Secretary of the Treasury Albert Gallatin. They were reported to Congress in the annual tonnage reports in *American State Papers* as being the "actual" or "more nearly correct" tonnage.

The data were obtained by taking the "corrected registered tonnage" and adding to it the "duty tonnage" for enrolled and licensed vessels. Because duties were paid only once each year on enrolled and licensed vessels, and owners were not likely to pay duties on nonexistent vessels, it was reasoned that the lower "duty tonnage" figure more accurately reflected the true total for the enrolled or licensed craft than did the district returns of tonnage based on outstanding marine documents. This correction for enrolled and licensed craft was dropped after 1818, probably because, beginning in 1819, the "duty tonnage" for this group exceeded the district tonnage.

In U.S. Congress (1834), volume 1, p. 499, the tonnage described as "actual tonnage" in the comparative table for 1794–1799 is, in fact, the district returns of tonnage without correction of any kind. Elsewhere in the tonnage report for 1800 (pp. 494-9), and in tonnage reports for later years, the term "actual tonnage" normally means the district returns based on outstanding marine documents (registers, enrollments, and licenses) corrected for cumulative error. Here the term "actual tonnage" is used in the latter sense.

See the text for Table Df578–593 for a related discussion.

TABLE Df618–625   Documented merchant vessels – gross tonnage, by region: 1811–1965[1]

Contributed by Louis P. Cain

	Seaboard					Western rivers	
	Total	New England	Mid-Atlantic and Gulf	New England, Mid-Atlantic, and Gulf	Pacific	Northern lakes	Official	Haites, Mak, and Walton
	Df618	Df619	Df620 [2]	Df621	Df622 [3]	Df623	Df624	Df625
Year	Thousand tons	Thousand tons	Thousand tons	Thousand tons	Thousand tons	Thousand tons	Thousand tons	Thousand tons
1811	—	—	—	—	—	—	—	0.4
1812	—	—	—	—	—	—	—	0.4
1813	—	—	—	—	—	—	—	0.4
1814	—	—	—	—	—	—	—	0.7
1815	—	—	—	—	—	—	—	1.5
1816	1,357	569	788	—	—	5	10	2.0
1817	1,320	562	758	—	—	7	13	3.0
1818	1,194	528	667	—	—	6	25	6.0
1819	1,228	551	678	—	—	7	25	13.0
1820	1,245	565	681	—	—	7	27	14.0
1821	1,265	580	684	—	—	7	27	14.0
1822	1,298	601	697	—	—	7	20	13.0
1823	1,312	600	711	—	—	7	18	12.0
1824	1,362	613	748	—	—	9	18	10.0
1825	1,397	641	756	—	—	7	19	13.0
1826	1,501	706	795	—	—	9	24	17.0
1827	1,590	714	876	—	—	9	22	20.0
1828	1,692	787	905	—	—	10	39	19.0
1829	—	—	—	—	—	—	—	22.0
1830	1,146	581	565	—	—	13	33	25.0
1831	1,215	576	639	—	—	9	44	29.0
1832	1,367	700	667	—	—	16	56	35.0
1833	1,530	811	718	—	—	17	60	37.0
1834	—	—	—	—	—	—	—	41.0
1835	1,735	896	840	—	—	17	73	50.0
1836	1,773	877	896	—	—	30	79	57.0
1837	1,771	889	882	—	—	35	91	64.0
1838	1,837	901	936	—	—	50	109	65.0
1839	—	—	—	—	—	—	—	78.0
1840	2,014	1,012	1,002	—	—	49	118	83.0
1841	1,936	984	951	—	—	58	137	85.0
1842	1,888	915	973	—	—	61	143	76.0
1843	1,940	923	1,017	—	—	66	152	80.0
1844	2,033	963	1,071	—	—	72	174	90.0
1845	2,143	1,010	1,133	—	—	86	188	96.0
1846	2,257	1,071	1,186	—	—	91	215	106.0
1847	2,464	1,125	1,339	—	—	134	241	122.0
1848	2,729	1,258	1,470	—	—	148	277	133.0
1849	2,874	1,289	1,584	—	1	174	286	130.0
1850	3,051	1,368	1,665	—	19	181	303	135.0
1851	3,259	1,414	1,785	—	59	196	318	143.0
1852	3,566	1,557	1,906	—	103	217	355	153.0
1853	3,872	1,679	2,088	—	105	254	282	169.0
1854	4,531	1,806	2,623	—	102	161	111	169.0
1855	4,877	2,004	2,779	—	93	206	129	173.0
1856	4,525	1,863	2,579	—	84	222	124	188.0
1857	4,562	1,777	2,701	—	85	238	140	200.0
1858	4,648	1,739	2,824	—	85	261	141	196.0
1859	4,675	1,833	2,754	—	88	329	142	193.0
1860	3,723	1,828	2,810	—	85	463	168	195.0
1861	4,888	1,839	2,959	—	90	479	173	165.0
1862	4,425	1,805	2,516	—	104	561	127	157.0
1863	4,382	1,646	2,618	—	118	631	142	160.0
1864	4,100	1,341	2,654	—	105	698	189	193.0
1865	4,180	1,269	2,756	—	154	671	246	229.0
1866	3,515	1,126	2,209	—	180	572	224	238.0
1867	3,340	1,008	2,171	—	161	613	352	232.0
1868	3,175	1,046	1,962	—	167	696	481	212.0
1869	3,090	1,066	1,839	—	185	661	393	—

Notes appear at end of table

TABLE Df618–625 Documented merchant vessels – gross tonnage, by region: 1811–1965 *Continued*

	Seaboard					Northern lakes	Western rivers	
	Total	New England	Mid-Atlantic and Gulf	New England, Mid-Atlantic, and Gulf	Pacific		Official	Haites, Mak, and Walton
	Df618	Df619	Df620 [2]	Df621	Df622 [3]	Df623	Df624	Df625
Year	Thousand tons	Thousand tons	Thousand tons	Thousand tons	Thousand tons	Thousand tons	Thousand tons	Thousand tons
1870	3,164	1,057	1,917	—	190	685	398	—
1871	3,164	1,050	1,947	—	167	712	407	—
1872	3,265	1,053	2,031	—	180	724	448	—
1873	3,489	1,055	2,243	—	191	788	418	—
1874	3,521	1,077	2,232	—	212	842	438	—
1875	3,597	1,143	2,225	—	229	838	419	—
1876	3,266	1,148	1,864	—	253	613	401	—
1877	3,196	1,146	1,799	—	252	610	436	—
1878	3,150	1,140	1,757	—	253	605	458	—
1879	3,070	1,095	1,705	—	270	597	502	—
1880	2,989	1,073	1,644	—	272	605	474	—
1881	3,000	1,045	1,669	—	286	663	394	—
1882	3,062	1,095	1,664	—	302	711	393	—
1883	3,151	1,121	1,702	—	328	724	361	—
1884	3,182	1,142	1,705	—	335	733	356	—
1885	3,170	1,090	1,720	—	361	750	346	—
1886	3,034	1,055	1,631	—	348	763	335	—
1887	2,995	998	1,640	—	356	784	327	—
1888	3,013	1,009	1,603	—	400	874	305	—
1889	3,036	957	1,643	—	436	972	299	—
1890	3,067	947	1,691	—	428	1,063	294	—
1891	3,222	944	1,836	—	441	1,155	308	—
1892	3,271	932	1,874	—	465	1,184	311	—
1893	3,265	907	1,901	—	457	1,261	299	—
1894	3,169	879	1,834	—	456	1,227	287	—
1895	3,113	846	1,834	—	434	1,241	281	—
1896	3,105	857	1,810	—	438	1,324	275	—
1897	3,087	818	1,830	—	439	1,410	272	—
1898	3,051	775	1,779	—	497	1,438	262	—
1899	3,155	742	1,873	—	540	1,446	263	—
1900	3,341	771	1,957	—	613	1,566	258	—
1901	3,568	750	2,104	—	714	1,706	249	—
1902	3,759	758	2,227	—	774	1,817	222	—
1903	3,970	772	2,386	—	812	1,903	215	—
1904	4,059	795	2,458	—	807	2,019	213	—
1905	4,220	813	2,586	—	822	2,062	174	—
1906	4,273	781	2,651	—	840	2,234	168	—
1907	4,328	784	2,656	—	887	2,440	172	—
1908	4,469	822	2,685	—	962	2,729	167	—
1909	4,444	828	2,681	—	934	2,782	163	—
1910	4,459	800	2,723	—	937	2,895	154	—
1911	4,544	775	2,795	—	974	2,944	168	—
1912	4,618	765	2,868	—	985	2,950	146	—
1913	4,800	766	2,986	—	1,049	2,940	146	—
1914	4,904	767	3,036	—	1,101	2,883	141	—
1915	5,433	658	3,652	—	1,123	2,818	139	—
1916	5,574	616	3,827	—	1,131	2,761	135	—
1917	5,959	604	4,146	—	1,210	2,779	133	—
1918	7,004	600	4,757	—	1,647	2,798	123	—
1919	9,762	616	6,329	—	2,816	3,024	122	—
1920	13,065	872	8,867	—	3,326	3,139	120	—
1921	15,320	920	10,932	—	3,468	2,840	122	—
1922	15,604	984	11,147	—	3,474	2,724	135	—
1923	15,388	1,113	10,780	—	3,496	2,758	138	—
1924	14,785	1,014	10,344	—	3,428	2,791	164	—
1925	14,390	953	10,155	—	3,282	2,853	162	—
1926	14,306	936	10,079	—	3,290	2,844	161	—
1927	13,914	918	9,747	—	3,249	2,805	168	—
1928	13,728	878	9,494	—	3,355	2,773	182	—
1929	13,527	815	9,447	—	3,264	2,771	179	—

Notes appear at end of table   (continued)

TABLE Df618–625   Documented merchant vessels – gross tonnage, by region: 1811–1965   *Continued*

	Seaboard						Western rivers	
	Total	New England	Mid-Atlantic and Gulf	New England, Mid-Atlantic, and Gulf	Pacific	Northern lakes	Official	Haites, Mak, and Walton
	Df618	Df619	Df620 [2]	Df621	Df622 [3]	Df623	Df624	Df625
Year	Thousand tons	Thousand tons	Thousand tons	Thousand tons	Thousand tons	Thousand tons	Thousand tons	Thousand tons
1930	13,131	798	9,106	—	3,227	2,758	178	—
1931	12,958	712	9,157	—	3,089	2,767	184	—
1932	13,793	708	9,970	—	3,115	1,857	189	—
1933	13,077	641	9,465	—	2,970	1,814	170	—
1934	12,883	620	9,312	—	2,951	1,802	177	—
1935	12,700	589	9,248	—	2,863	1,773	181	—
1936	12,512	517	9,254	—	2,741	1,767	218	—
1937	12,733	515	9,630	—	2,588	1,713	230	—
1938	12,666	454	9,730	—	2,483	1,739	246	—
1939	12,668	418	9,779	—	2,471	1,712	252	—
1940	12,064	453	9,563	—	2,047	1,669	285	—
1941	11,776	494	9,318	—	1,964	1,641	305	—
1942	11,856	544	9,372	—	1,939	1,624	379	—
1943	14,714	440	10,051	—	4,224	1,620	428	—
1944	23,569	972	13,596	—	9,001	1,793	434	—
1945	30,306	1,472	17,186	—	11,648	2,061	446	—
1946	35,829	1,644	19,927	—	14,258	2,183	489	—
1947	35,238	1,834	20,340	—	13,064	2,091	504	—
1948	30,484	1,719	18,397	—	10,368	2,079	604	—
1949	29,407	1,679	18,639	—	9,089	2,076	699	—
1950	28,866	1,505	18,915	—	8,446	1,628	721	—
1951	28,040	1,559	18,409	—	8,072	1,565	736	—
1952	28,136	1,335	19,604	—	7,196	1,556	725	—
1953	28,184	1,204	19,886	—	7,094	1,624	738	—
1954	28,299	1,239	19,908	—	7,152	1,616	849	—
1955	27,405	1,191	19,211	—	7,004	1,590	962	—
1956	26,952	1,091	18,732	—	7,129	1,558	1,100	—
1957	26,605	1,007	18,634	—	6,964	1,569	1,247	—
1958	25,520	898	17,955	—	6,667	1,638	1,429	—
1959	25,577	827	18,439	—	6,312	1,627	1,691	—
1960	24,708	814	18,112	—	5,782	1,728	2,145	—
1961	22,064	692	16,059	—	5,313	2,121	2,218	—
1962	21,010	555	15,922	—	4,533	2,056	2,389	—
1963	21,083	—	—	16,547	4,537	1,932	2,676	—
1964	21,482	—	—	17,077	4,405	1,858	2,820	—
1965	21,430	—	—	17,074	4,356	1,878	3,208	—

[1] As of December 31, 1816–1834; September 30, 1835–1842; June 30, 1843–1940; and January 1 thereafter.

[2] Includes Puerto Rico and the Virgin Islands.

[3] Includes Alaska, Hawai'i, and Guam.

Sources

Series Df618–624, U.S. Bureau of Marine Inspection and Navigation, *Merchant Marine Statistics, 1936* and *1965* (annual report now published by the U.S. Coast Guard, *Boating Statistics*). Series Df625, E. F. Haites, J. Mak, and G. M. Walton, *Western River Transportation during the Era of Early Internal Improvements, 1810–1860* (Johns Hopkins University Press, 1975), Appendix B.

Documentation

Figures are gross tonnage of documented vessels of five net tons or more. See the text for Table Df578–593 for a definition of gross tonnage and related discussion.

Series Df624–625. Series Df625 differs from series Df624 primarily in the treatment of the steamboats that ceased operation. Series Df625 excludes steamboats in the year during which they ceased to operate; series Df624 excludes such steamboats only at irregular intervals.

Series Df625. Calculated by the authors from W. M. Lytle, *Merchant Steam Vessels of the United States 1807–1868* (Steamship Historical Society of America, 1952), and *Supplements 2* (1954) and *3* (1958), edited by F. R. Holdcamper. The Lytle List is an alphabetical listing of steamboats based on the original records for documented merchant vessels constructed in the United States between 1807 and 1868. The entry for each steamboat includes its gross measured tonnage (by the pre-1865 calculation), year of construction, port of construction, and year of termination of service. Steamboats operating on the Western rivers during this era were of a special design. Other steamboats were not well suited to operate there. Western river steamboats did not generally leave the river system and were therefore isolated on the basis of their port of construction.

TABLE Df626–631   Indexes of ocean shipping costs and productivity: 1814–1860
Contributed by Louis P. Cain

Year	Wages	Shipbuilding capital costs	Warren-Pearson wholesale prices	Input prices	Freight rates	Total factor productivity
	Df626	Df627	Df628	Df629	Df630	Df631
	Index 1814 = 100	Index 1814 = 100	Index 1814 = 100	Index 1814 = 100	Index 1830 = 100	Index
1814	100.0	100.0	100.0	100.0	300.0	0.33
1815	100.0	103.0	93.4	96.7	363.3	0.27
1816	100.0	106.1	83.0	91.1	238.0	0.39 [1]
1817	84.6	109.2	83.0	89.0	109.2	0.82
1818	92.3	112.3	80.8	89.8	266.9	0.34
1819	92.3	115.4	68.7	83.2	122.2	0.68
1820	153.8	118.5	58.2	88.7	191.7	0.46
1821	84.6	121.6	56.0	75.6	148.3	0.51
1822	92.3	124.7	58.2	78.9	140.8	0.56
1823	92.3	127.8	56.6	78.7	147.1	0.54 [1]
1824	92.3	130.9	53.8	77.7	127.2	0.61
1825	100.0	133.9	56.6	81.5	134.1	0.63 [1]
1826	107.7	128.5	54.4	80.3	127.9	0.63
1827	107.7	123.1	53.8	78.8	125.0	0.63
1828	105.1	117.8	53.8	77.1	106.7	0.72
1829	102.5	112.4	52.7	74.8	100.1	0.75
1830	100.0	107.1	50.0	71.6	100.0	0.72
1831	107.7	110.8	51.2	74.5	124.5	0.60
1832	107.7	114.5	52.2	75.9	99.9	0.76
1833	100.0	118.2	52.2	75.3	87.8	0.86
1834	100.0	121.9	49.5	74.5	88.3	0.84
1835	107.7	125.6	54.9	79.9	87.0	0.92
1836	115.4	129.3	62.6	86.8	99.9	0.87
1837	107.7	133.0	63.2	86.6	110.8	0.78
1838	107.7	136.7	60.4	85.7	124.4	0.69
1839	107.7	140.4	61.5	87.2	109.1	0.80
1840	107.7	144.1	52.2	82.4	134.4	0.61
1841	107.7	147.8	50.5	82.2	83.2	0.98 [1]
1842	100.0	151.5	45.1	78.4	56.5	1.39
1843	100.0	155.2	41.2	76.8	66.7	1.15
1844	107.7	158.9	42.3	79.7	61.5	1.30
1845	107.7	151.8	45.6	80.2	66.7	1.20
1846	107.7	144.6	45.6	78.6	72.4	1.08 [1]
1847	115.4	137.5	49.5	80.8	85.1	0.95
1848	115.4	130.4	45.1	76.6	45.0	1.70
1849	115.4	123.2	45.1	75.0	43.5	1.72
1850	115.4	116.3	46.2	74.1	34.4	2.15
1851	115.4	117.7	45.6	74.1	35.6	2.08
1852	115.4	119.3	48.4	76.0	42.8	1.78
1853	115.4	120.9	53.3	79.4	51.1	1.55
1854	115.4	122.5	59.3	83.4	50.2	1.66
1855	115.4	124.1	60.4	84.3	47.4	1.78
1856	115.4	125.7	57.7	83.1	46.2	1.80
1857	115.4	127.3	61.0	85.5	35.6	2.40
1858	115.4	128.9	51.1	79.9	37.2	2.15
1859	115.4	130.5	52.2	80.8	40.4	2.00
1860	115.4	132.1	51.1	80.6	49.7	1.62

[1] Data given by the source is reported here. The value differs slightly from the result that would be obtained by dividing series Df629 by series Df630.

Sources
Douglass North, "Sources of Productivity Change in Ocean Shipping, 1600–1850," *Journal of Political Economy* 76 (5) (1968): 968–9. North took the wages series from Stanley Lebergott, *Manpower in Economic Growth* (McGraw-Hill, 1964).

Documentation
Series Df629. The sum of the "geometric ratio of 1814 and 1860 weights of each input," essentially 18 percent of series Df626, 22 percent of series Df627, and 60 percent of series Df628.

Series Df631. Total factor productivity is the input price index, series Df629, divided by the freight rate index, series Df630.

TABLE Df632–638   Steamboat trade from Louisville to New Orleans – average round trips, travel time, and days running: 1815–1860

Contributed by Louis P. Cain

	Round trips per year	Days per passage			Days per year		
		Round trip	Upstream	Downstream	Running time	Out of water	In port
	Df632	Df633	Df634	Df635	Df636	Df637	Df638
Period	Number	Days	Days	Days	Days	Days	Days
1815–1819	3	30.0	20.0	10.0	90	95	180
1820–1829	5	20.0	12.5	7.5	100	95	170
1830–1839	8	16.1	9.5	6.6	128	95	142
1840–1849	10	13.0	7.5	5.5	130	95	140
1850–1860	12	11.7	6.5	5.2	141	95	129

Source

Erik F. Haites, James Mak, and Gary M. Walton, *Western River Transportation: The Era of Early Internal Development, 1810–1860* (Johns Hopkins University Press, 1975), Table 16, p. 68.

Documentation

Data represent the average steamboat in the trade from Louisville to New Orleans.

Series Df633. Equals the sum of series Df634 and series Df635.

Series Df636. Equals the product of series Df632 and series Df633.

Series Df636–638. Series sum to 365 days.

TABLE Df639–640   Western river steamboating – total factor productivity and relative input–output prices: 1815–1860

Contributed by Louis P. Cain

Year	Index of total factor productivity	Index of input relative to output prices	Year	Index of total factor productivity	Index of input relative to output prices	Year	Index of total factor productivity	Index of input relative to output prices
	Df639 [1]	Df640		Df639 [1]	Df640		Df639 [1]	Df640
	Index 1840–1849 = 100	Index 1840–1849 = 100		Index 1840–1849 = 100	Index 1840–1849 = 100		Index 1840–1849 = 100	Index 1840–1849 = 100
1815	—	23	1830	—	59	1845	100	111
1816	—	24	1831	—	60	1846	—	102
1817	17	25	1832	—	63	1847	—	96
1818	—	24	1833	—	67	1848	—	106
1819	—	24	1834	—	68	1849	—	109
1820	—	43	1835	75	76	1850	—	129
1821	—	36	1836	—	84	1851	—	116
1822	—	41	1837	—	88	1852	—	127
1823	—	42	1838	—	86	1853	—	131
1824	—	43	1839	—	91	1854	—	102
1825	40	44	1840	—	97	1855	120	132
1826	—	43	1841	—	89	1856	—	103
1827	—	44	1842	—	93	1857	—	120
1828	—	45	1843	—	94	1858	—	132
1829	—	47	1844	—	110	1859	—	135
						1860	—	121

[1] Data are decadal averages for 1815–1819, 1820–1829, 1830–1839, 1840–1849, and, 1850–1860.

Source

Erik F. Haites, James Mak, and Gary M. Walton, *Western River Transportation: The Era of Early Internal Development, 1810–1860* (Johns Hopkins University Press, 1975), Appendix G, Tables G-1 and G-2, pp. 182–5.

Documentation

"Productivity" refers to the relationship between outputs and inputs in a production process. Thus, for steamboating, productivity refers to the number of passengers and freight transported relative to equipment, labor, and fuel used in the process. Productivity growth occurs when more output is produced from some given amount of inputs. Haites, Mak, and Walton developed two indexes of productivity growth in steamboating during the period of the "transportation revolution," 1815–1860. Their calculations refer to steamboating on the Mississippi River, on the route between St. Louis and New Orleans.

Series Df639. An index of "total factor productivity." It compares the *physical* output of steamboats (passengers and freight transported) with the *physical* inputs into steamboating. These include capital as measured by the average tonnage of a steamboat, labor as measured by the number of deckhands and other steamboat staff, and fuel as measured by wood consumption per ton of cargo transported.

Series Df640. An index of input relative to output *prices* in steamboating. The rising ratio means that the price of steamboat services fell relative to the price of the boats, labor, and fuel used to produce these services. For the output price to fall relative to the input prices, the steamboat industry had to have been making more productive use of its inputs. That is, a rising index of input relative to output prices means that productivity in steamboating was rising.

TABLE Df641–650   Steamboat cargo volume, passenger travel, and speed: 1815–1855

Contributed by Louis P. Cain

	Steamboats on trunk routes		Steamboats on tributary rivers		Speed		Volume of goods moved		Passenger travel	
	Number	Tonnage	Number	Tonnage	Upstream	Downstream	Upstream	Downstream	Upstream	Downstream
	Df641	Df642	Df643	Df644	Df645	Df646	Df647	Df648	Df649	Df650
Year	Number	Tons	Number	Tons	Miles per day	Miles per day	Million ton-miles	Million ton-miles	Million miles	Million miles
1815	7	1,516	—	—	68	135	1.2	3.5	1.8	3.2
1825	59	11,359	21	1,168	110	180	24.3	72.0	28.4	49.1
1835	107	28,961	217	21,162	145	210	150.7	458.0	159.9	282.8
1845	174	53,899	364	42,256	180	250	339.5	1,482.3	375.1	660.8
1855	357	129,411	339	43,284	205	260	315.3	3,442.1	931.5	1,646.2

Source

Erik F. Haites and James Mak, "Social Savings Due to Western River Steamboats," in *Research in Economic History*, volume 3 (JAI Press, 1978), Tables 10 and 11, pp. 291–3.

Documentation

These numbers are for steamboats on "Western" rivers, meaning those on the Mississippi, Ohio, Illinois, and Missouri rivers and their tributaries.

The authors assigned specific waterways to either "trunk route" or "tributary river." A "trunk route" is a major, downstream portion of either the Mississippi, the Ohio, or the Missouri river. A "tributary river" is a river or stream that contributes to one of these flows. See the source. All boats were assumed to operate on trunk routes in 1815. All boats less than 100 tons were assigned to tributary routes in 1825. For 1835, 1845, and 1855, the corresponding tonnage was 150, 200, and 200, respectively.

Series Df645–646. Calculated from data reported in Erik F. Haites, James Mak, and Gary M. Walton, *Western River Transportation: The Era of Early Internal Development, 1810–1860* (Johns Hopkins University Press, 1975), Table C-3. Average travel times on the 1,350-mile trip between Louisville and New Orleans.

TABLE Df651–658   Freight rates for steamboat, keelboat, and railroad: 1815–1855

Contributed by Louis P. Cain

	Upstream				Downstream			
	Steamboat				Steamboat			
	Trunk route	Tributary route	Keelboat	Railroad	Trunk route	Tributary route	Flatboat	Railroad
	Df651	Df652	Df653	Df654	Df655	Df656	Df657	Df658
Year	Cents per ton-mile	Cents per ton-mile	Cents per ton-mile	Cents per ton-mile	Cents per ton-mile	Cents per ton-mile	Cents per ton-mile	Cents per ton-mile
1815	8.05	—	7.41	—	1.61	—	1.22	—
1825	1.61	5.21	7.41	—	1.01	3.26	1.22	—
1835	0.81	2.61	7.41	7.03	0.81	2.61	1.22	1.22
1845	0.40	1.30	7.41	3.18	0.48	1.56	1.22	1.22
1855	0.40	1.30	7.41	2.08	0.52	1.69	1.22	1.22

Source

Erik F. Haites and James Mak, "Social Savings Due to Western River Steamboats," *Research in Economic History*, volume 3 (JAI Press, 1978), Table 12, p. 294.

Documentation

These numbers are for steamboats on "Western" rivers, meaning those on the Mississippi, Ohio, Illinois, and Missouri rivers and their tributaries, and for alternative transport in the same area.

Downstream freight was carried by flatboats. These were large, oblong, wooden boxes that floated with the river current and were difficult to navigate. Their advantage lay in their low cost and high carrying capacity. According to Erik F. Haites, James Mak, and Gary M. Walton, *Western Rivers Transportation: The Era of Early Internal Development, 1810–1860* (Johns Hopkins University Press, 1975), "The typical early flatboat . . . could carry 30 to 40 tons of freight and cost only about $50 to $60." Because of their cost advantage, "the flatboat was typically chosen over the costly alternative of land transportation. Little time and skill were required for its construction, and at the voyage's end it could be used as a temporary house or dismantled to construct a permanent home" (p. 14).

Before the advent of the steamboat, upstream freight was carried by keelboats. These were vessels built on a keel – a longitudinal beam in the hull of a vessel extending vertically into the water to provide lateral stability. Haites, Mak, and Walton (1975) cite Baldwin's description of the "ordinary keelboat" of the antebellum era as follows: "[It was] forty to eighty feet long and from seven to ten feet in beam, had a shallow keel, and was sharp at both ends. It drew about two feet of water when loaded. The middle part of the boat might be left open, but usually it was covered in whole or in part by a cabin or a cargo ox that had an inside clearance of about six feet. Here the goods were stored and here the passengers found shelter. . . . At the bow were the seats for the rowers, four to twelve in number, who sometimes received assistance from a square sail. The sail, however, was useless except on comparatively broad waters, so that many keelboats carried none" (p. 15).

The division between trunk and tributary routes is inferred. All boats were assumed to operate on trunk routes in 1815. All boats less than 100 tons were assigned to tributary routes in 1825. For 1835, 1845, and 1855, the corresponding tonnage was 150, 200, and 200, respectively.

Steamboat freight rates for the trip between Louisville and New Orleans are known for all years. The rates for trunk and tributary routes were calculated by assuming the same relationship existed between those routes and the Louisville–New Orleans route that existed in 1850. Namely, trunk rates were 8.1 percent higher and tributary rates were 251.4 percent higher.

TABLE Df659–666   Passenger fares for steamboat, keelboat, and railroad: 1815–1855

Contributed by Louis P. Cain

	Upstream				Downstream			
	Steamboat				Steamboat			
	Trunk route	Tributary route	Keelboat-overland	Railroad	Trunk route	Tributary route	Keelboat-flatboat	Railroad
	Df659	Df660	Df661	Df662	Df663	Df664	Df665	Df666
Year	Cents per mile	Cents per mile	Cents per mile	Cents per mile	Cents per mile	Cents per mile	Cents per mile	Cents per mile
1815	2.27	—	2.22	—	1.63	—	0.74	—
1825	0.91	2.27	2.22	—	0.54	1.36	0.74	—
1835	0.54	1.36	2.22	4.76	0.54	1.36	0.74	0.74
1845	0.36	0.91	2.22	2.56	0.36	0.91	0.74	0.74
1855	0.27	0.68	2.22	2.01	0.27	0.68	0.74	0.74

Source

Erik F. Haites and James Mak, "Social Savings Due to Western River Steamboats," *Research in Economic History*, volume 3 (JAI Press, 1978), Table 12, p. 295.

Documentation

These numbers are for steamboats on "Western" rivers, meaning those on the Mississippi, Ohio, Illinois, and Missouri rivers and their tributaries, and for alternative transport in the same area.

The division between trunk and tributary routes is inferred. All boats were assumed to operate on trunk routes in 1815. All boats less than 100 tons were assigned to tributary routes in 1825. For 1835, 1845, and 1855, the corresponding tonnage was 150, 200, and 200, respectively.

Steamboat deck passenger fares for the trip between Louisville and New Orleans are known for all years. The fares for trunk and tributary routes were calculated by assuming the same relationship existed between those routes and the Louisville–New Orleans route that existed in 1850. Namely, trunk fares were 22.5 percent higher than those on the Louisville–New Orleans route, while tributary fares were 2.5 times the trunk fares.

Haites and Mak estimate flatboat fares from Louisville to New Orleans to be $10. The return trip overland was estimated to be $30.

TABLE Df667–678   Average speeds and travel times for steamboat, keelboat, and railroad: 1815–1855

Contributed by Louis P. Cain

	Average speed						Travel time					
	Steamboat		Keelboat		Railroad		Freight			Passenger		
	Upstream	Downstream	Overland	Flatboat	Freight	Passenger	Steamboat	Keelboat-flatboat	Railroad	Steamboat	Keelboat-flatboat	Railroad
	Df667	Df668	Df669	Df670	Df671	Df672	Df673	Df674	Df675	Df676	Df677	Df678
Year	Miles per hour	Miles per hour	Miles per hour	Miles per hour	Miles per hour	Miles per hour	Million hours	Million hours	Million hours	Million hours	Million hours	Million hours
1815	2.8	5.60	0.45	1.75	—	—	0.84	3.98	—	0.89	4.80	—
1825	4.5	7.50	0.45	1.75	—	—	11.76	81.26	—	9.07	74.94	—
1835	6.0	8.75	0.45	1.75	14	7.0	60.24	510.49	65.43	40.70	425.56	20.20
1845	7.5	10.40	0.45	1.75	27	13.5	155.15	1,407.47	109.80	77.48	996.82	24.47
1855	8.5	10.80	0.45	1.75	34	17.0	326.61	2,487.41	202.48	175.77	2,478.40	48.42

Source

Erik F. Haites and James Mak, "Social Savings Due to Western River Steamboats," *Research in Economic History*, volume 3 (JAI Press, 1978), Table 13, p. 296.

Documentation

These numbers are for steamboats on "Western" rivers, meaning those on the Mississippi, Ohio, Illinois, and Missouri rivers and their tributaries, and for alternative transport in the same area.

Several of these observations are inferred. Where this has been done, Haites and Mak assumed numbers that were biased upward. The upstream trip from New Orleans to Louisville required three to four months of traveling by keelboat and foot. Haites and Mak assume it took 125 days, a rate of 0.45 miles per hour. The downstream trip from Louisville to New Orleans required about a month. Haites and Mak assume it took 32 days, a rate of 1.75 miles per hour. Passenger trains were assumed to travel 8 miles per hour in 1835, 15 miles per hour in 1845, and 20 miles per hour in 1855. These were then converted to equivalent speeds over river distances by dividing by 0.579. Freight train speeds were assumed to be half those of passenger trains.

TABLE Df679–680 Rates on New York and Ohio canals: 1817–1860[1]

Contributed by Louis P. Cain

Year	New York canal rates Df679 Cents per ton-mile	Ohio canal rates Df680 Cents per ton-mile
1817	19.12	—
1827	—	4.0
1840	1.68	4.8
1850	—	4.0
1853	1.10	—
1855	—	1.6
1857	0.80	—
1858	0.80	—
1859	0.67	—
1860	0.99	—

[1] Rate computation varies over time. See text.

Sources

Series Df679, George Rogers Taylor, *The Transportation Revolution, 1815–1860* (Holt, Rinehart and Winston, 1951), p. 137. Series Df680, Harry N. Scheiber, *Ohio Canal Era: A Case Study of Government and the Economy, 1820–1861* (Ohio University Press, 1987), Appendix 2.

Documentation

Series Df679. Represents the average rates (cents per ton-mile) on the Erie Canal system. The 1817 and 1840 rates are for the Buffalo to New York trip; the others are for the Buffalo to Albany trip. The 1840 rate is the rate in effect between 1830 and 1850. In that time period, the average rate for the New York to Buffalo trip was somewhat higher, 3.35 cents per ton-mile.

Series Df680. Represents the tolls for merchandise traveling up to 100 miles; tolls for additional miles were somewhat lower. These are tolls for northbound trips. The tolls for merchandise are the highest tolls quoted by Scheiber.

TABLE Df681–683 Merchant vessels built and documented – gross tonnage, by region: 1817–1850[1]

Contributed by Louis P. Cain

Year	The Coast Df681 [2] Gross tons	New England Df682 Gross tons	Western lakes and rivers Df683 Gross tons
1817	85,144	46,605	1,250
1818	82,232	48,823	189
1819	79,551	50,614	267
1820	47,696	29,353	88
1821	55,607	36,651	249
1822	75,242	44,206	105
1823	73,942	42,725	1,066
1824	89,166	52,445	1,773
1825	112,616	65,616	2,381
1826	121,908	72,668	4,530
1827	99,343	57,156	5,000
1828	95,349	54,282	3,027
1829	71,055	38,117	6,044
1830	52,686	24,169	5,398
1831	80,541	49,793	5,222
1832	130,064	100,585	14,475
1833	153,455	95,143	8,171
1834	105,683	61,779	12,647
1835	101,906	60,054	14,072
1836	98,130	58,330	15,497
1837	98,997	51,981	23,990
1838	100,074	53,054	13,061
1839	107,232	59,204	13,767
1840	109,706	65,189	8,603
1841	103,576	63,770	15,318
1842	108,302	56,234	20,782
1843	90,017	46,251	26,293
1844	71,732	36,268	31,805
1845	116,156	63,835	29,862
1846	149,332	82,347	38,872
1847	185,493	104,682	58,240
1848	262,581	146,111	55,495
1849	217,264	120,234	39,313
1850	247,847	142,367	24,372

[1] As of December 31, 1817–1834; September 30, 1835–1842; and June 30 thereafter.

[2] Includes New England.

Source

U.S. Department of the Treasury, *Annual Report of the Secretary of the Treasury* (1868), fold-in table on the history of shipbuilding (1817–1868).

Documentation

The data are for documented vessels of five gross tons or more. See the text for Table Df578–593 for a definition of gross tonnage and related discussion.

The source also presents figures separately for "the United States," "the Lakes," and "Western Rivers." For a discussion of these data see the *Annual Report.* The source table, with a more detailed discussion, appears as Plate 22 in House of Representatives, Ex. Document number 111, 41st Congress, 2d session, where the period covered is extended to 1869, and as Plate 10 (extended to 1870) in House of Representatives, Ex. Document number 76, 41st Congress, 3d session.

The figures in these three series do not sum to those in series Df613.

TABLE Df684–689   State and private investment in canals, by region: 1817–1860

Contributed by Louis P. Cain

Year	Total Df684 Million dollars	State Df685 Million dollars	Private Df686 Million dollars	Region Northeast Df687 Million dollars	Region South Df688 Million dollars	Region West Df689 Million dollars
1817	0.2	0.1	—	0.2	—	—
1818	0.7	0.6	0.1	0.6	—	—
1819	0.8	0.6	0.2	0.7	0.1	—
1820	1.1	0.8	0.2	0.8	0.3	—
1821	1.6	1.3	0.2	1.3	0.3	—
1822	2.7	2.3	0.3	2.2	0.4	—
1823	2.8	2.2	0.7	2.4	0.4	—
1824	2.5	1.8	0.7	1.9	0.6	—
1825	2.7	1.5	1.2	2.2	0.4	0.1
1826	4.0	1.5	2.5	3.0	0.3	0.8
1827	5.6	2.3	3.3	4.3	0.4	0.9
1828	7.8	4.0	3.7	6.0	0.7	1.0
1829	7.0	3.7	3.2	5.2	0.8	0.9
1830	7.5	5.1	2.4	6.1	0.5	1.0
1831	3.7	2.2	1.5	3.0	0.1	0.7
1832	4.6	2.9	1.7	4.2	0.1	0.4
1833	5.3	2.7	2.6	4.9	0.2	0.2
1834	4.4	2.8	1.6	3.9	0.1	0.4
1835	3.5	2.0	1.5	2.9	0.1	0.5
1836	4.4	1.8	2.6	2.9	0.3	1.2
1837	8.2	3.9	4.3	4.4	1.2	2.7
1838	12.3	7.2	5.1	6.0	1.9	4.4
1839	13.6	9.5	4.1	7.3	1.9	4.4
1840	14.3	11.3	3.0	8.4	1.2	4.7
1841	11.7	9.8	1.9	8.8	0.5	2.4
1842	3.1	2.6	0.6	1.8	0.3	1.1
1843	1.0	0.7	0.3	0.3	0.1	0.6
1844	1.0	0.7	0.3	0.2	0.0	0.8
1845	2.0	1.1	0.9	0.7	0.3	1.0
1846	1.8	0.8	1.0	0.5	0.7	0.7
1847	4.7	1.1	3.6	3.5	0.6	0.6
1848	4.5	1.5	3.0	3.9	0.3	0.3
1849	3.4	1.9	1.6	2.9	0.4	0.1
1850	4.9	2.3	2.5	4.2	0.7	0.0
1851	4.7	2.0	2.8	3.8	0.8	0.1
1852	3.4	1.9	1.5	2.8	0.5	0.1
1853	3.8	2.4	1.4	3.3	0.2	0.3
1854	4.7	3.8	0.9	4.0	0.3	0.5
1855	5.3	4.2	1.1	4.6	0.3	0.4
1856	4.2	3.2	1.0	3.6	0.4	0.2
1857	3.5	2.9	0.7	3.0	0.5	0.1
1858	2.8	1.6	1.1	2.3	0.4	0.1
1859	1.9	1.4	0.5	1.7	0.2	—
1860	1.2	1.0	0.1	1.1	0.1	—

Source

H. Jerome Cranmer, "Canal Investment, 1815–1860," in *Trends in the American Economy in the Nineteenth Century: A Report of the National Bureau of Economic Research*, Studies in Income and Wealth, volume 24 (Princeton University Press, 1960), pp. 555, 556.

Documentation

The development of data on annual canal investment was based on an averaging process applied to the experience of a sample of twenty-four canals for which annual expenditure figures were available. For a list of those canals and description of the estimating operations, see the source.

The Cranmer series begins in 1815, but the total for each of the first two years is less than $50,000; hence, the data reported here begin with 1817.

Adjusted estimates of annual expenditures were made for every canal or canal system undertaken between 1815 and 1860. Expenditures for river and harbor improvements were not included, nor were they included for slack water navigation except when the expenditures were part of a canal project. The estimates were then aggregated by region and by agency of enterprise within each region. The regional estimates were then aggregated to provide estimates of annual investment in canals for the entire United States, together with estimates for state and private enterprise.

The Northeast consists of the New England and Middle Atlantic states, including Maryland and the District of Columbia. The South encompasses the area south of the Potomac and Ohio rivers. The West is the region north of the Ohio River, with the addition of the Louisville and Portland Canal.

During this period, individual states, not the federal government, were responsible for the construction of canals.

TABLE Df690–691   Federal expenditures and appropriations for rivers and harbors: 1822–1994[1]

Contributed by Louis P. Cain

	Expenditures	Appropriations		Expenditures	Appropriations		Expenditures	Appropriations		Expenditures	Appropriations
	Df690 [2]	Df691		Df690 [2]	Df691		Df690 [2]	Df691		Df690 [2]	Df691
Year	Thousand dollars	Million dollars	Year	Thousand dollars	Million dollars	Year	Thousand dollars	Million dollars	Year	Thousand dollars	Million dollars
1822	1	—	1870	3,528	—	1915	46,834	—	1960	800,948	821
1824	26	—	1871	4,421	—	1916	32,450	—	1961	863,600	881
1825	40	—	1872	4,962	—	1917	30,487	—	1962	889,936	920
1826	87	—	1873	6,312	—	1918	29,594	—	1963	1,004,022	993
1827	136	—	1874	5,704	—	1919	33,078	—	1964	993,916	1,043
1828	188	—	1875	6,434	—	1920	47,188	—	1965	1,092,588	1,202
1829	524	—	1876	5,736	—	1921	57,166	—	1966	1,208,301	1,273
1830	574	—	1877	4,655	—	1922	43,393	—	1967	1,182,958	1,235
1831	652	—	1878	3,791	—	1923	47,478	—	1968	1,170,845	1,246
1832	538	—	1879	8,267	—	1924	62,025	—	1969	1,124,790	1,204
1833	704	—	1880	8,080	—	1925	69,882	—	1970	1,050,803	1,107
1834	598	—	1881	9,072	—	1926	63,464	—	1971	1,277,550	1,257
1835	569	—	1882	11,624	—	1927	60,620	—	1972	1,435,887	1,536
1836	869	—	1883	13,839	—	1928	70,197 [4]	—	1973	1,504,902	1,875
1837	1,362	—	1884	8,237	—	1929	57,299	—	1974	1,703,808	1,558
1838	1,054	—	1885	10,558	—	1930	73,970	—	1975	1,855,131	1,635
1839	780	—	1886	4,197	—	1931	80,903	—	1976 [3]	1,947,313	2,685
1840	145	—	1887	7,786	—	1932	84,260	—	1977	2,124,474	2,314
1841	79	—	1888	7,007	—	1933	76,788 [5]	—	1978	2,393,586	2,601
1842	82	—	1889	11,234	—	1934	104,873 [5]	—	1979	—	2,632
1843	111	—	1890	11,740	—	1935	162,375 [5]	—	1980	—	2,990
1844	313	—	1891	12,253	—	1936	106,239 [5]	—	1981	—	2,852
1845	529	—	1892	13,024	—	1937	178,825 [5]	—	1982	—	2,820
1846	219	—	1893	14,804	—	1938	135,921	—	1983	—	3,128
1847	44	—	1894	19,888	—	1939	115,987	—	1984	—	2,485
1848	24	—	1895	19,944	—	1940	107,082	—	1985	—	2,676
1849	26	—	1896	18,119	—	1941	86,530	—	1986	—	2,513
1850	42	—	1897	13,686	—	1942	88,664	—	1987	—	2,929
1851	70	—	1898	20,792	—	1943	84,368	—	1988	—	3,073
1852	40	—	1899	16,094	—	1944	64,366	—	1989	—	3,023
1853	489	—	1900	18,736	—	1945	57,146	—	1990	—	2,977
1854	937	—	1901	19,544	—	1946	79,542	—	1991	—	3,093
1855	791	—	1902	14,948	—	1947	89,170	—	1992	—	3,439
1856	161	—	1903	19,590	—	1948	115,728	—	1993	—	3,641
1857	268	—	1904	22,546	—	1949	160,431	—	1994	—	3,824
1858	427	—	1905	22,814	—	1950	190,456	—			
1859	290	—	1906	25,955	—	1951	204,699	—			
1860	228	—	1907	23,310	—	1952	214,957	—			
1861	172	—	1908	30,361	—	1953	272,130	—			
1862	37	—	1909	34,579	—	1954	475,418	—			
1863	65	—	1910	29,273	—	1955	455,612	—			
1864	102	—	1911	33,968	—	1956	489,118	—			
1865	305	—	1912	35,861	—	1957	545,032	—			
1866	295	—	1913	42,275	—	1958	624,558	595			
1867	1,217	—	1914	50,762	—	1959	721,767	764			
1868	3,457	—									
1869	3,545	—									

[1] Fiscal years.

[2] Includes expenditures for rivers, harbors, and flood control prior to 1928. In 1928, expenditures for flood control amounted to less than $13,500,000. Figures for 1929–1978 exclude expenditures for Mississippi River flood control, but not coastal flood control.

[3] Change in the fiscal year. Series Df690 excludes the transition quarter, whereas series Df691 includes it.

[4] Excludes $5,500,000 for purchase of Cape Cod Canal, expended by and accounted for by the U.S. Treasury Department.

[5] Includes amounts expended from emergency relief and U.S. Public Works Administration funds.

Sources

1822–1882, *Statement of Appropriations and Expenditures for Public Buildings, Rivers and Harbors, Forts, Arsenals, Armories, and Other Public Works from March 4, 1789, to June 30, 1882*, U.S. Senate Executive Document, volume 7, number 196, 47th Congress, 1st session (Treasury Department Document number 373), pp. 521–2; 1883–1919, Federal Works Agency, records (compiled from Treasury Department accounts); 1920–1994, U.S. Army Corps of Engineers, *Annual Report of the Chief of Engineers on Civil Works Activities*, volume 1 (annual issues).

Documentation

Series Df690 was not reported after 1978. Series Df691 reports the appropriations for the items included in series Df690. This series extends back further than 1960, but those numbers have not been included here because expenditures are a more accurate measure than appropriations.

In the source volumes, series Df690 excludes expropriations for "Flood Control – Mississippi River and Tributaries," but the amount reported for appropriations includes it. For consistency, series Df691 is the difference between total appropriations and appropriations for "Flood Control – Mississippi River and Tributaries."

TABLE Df692–693   Freight rates for cotton – New York to Europe: 1823–1855

Contributed by Louis P. Cain

Period	New York to Liverpool	New York to Le Havre
	Df692	Df693
	Pence per pound	Cents per pound
1823–1825	0.50	1.25 [1]
1826–1830	0.41	0.95
1831–1835	0.40	0.88
1836–1840	0.39	0.90
1841–1845	0.30	0.83
1846–1850	0.23	0.70
1851–1855	0.16	0.38

[1] 1824–1825.

Source

George Rogers Taylor, *The Transportation Revolution, 1815–1860* (Holt, Rinehart and Winston, 1951), p. 147.

Documentation

Figures are the average rates for shipping a pound of cotton over the given time period as measured on October 1.

TABLE Df694–695   Freight rates for cotton – New Orleans to Europe: 1822–1856

Contributed by Louis P. Cain

Year	New Orleans to Liverpool	New Orleans to Le Havre
	Df694	Df695
	Pence per pound	Cents per pound
1822	1.09	2.31
1826	0.86	1.91
1831	0.76	1.60
1836	0.65	1.44
1841	0.50	1.03
1846	0.53	1.10
1851	0.47	1.00
1856	0.47	1.00

Source

George Rogers Taylor, *The Transportation Revolution, 1815–1860* (Holt, Rinehart and Winston, 1951), p. 148.

Documentation

These data are the average monthly rates for shipping a pound of cotton over the given year as measured as close to the middle of the month as possible.

TABLE Df696–697   Cargo moved on New York State canals: 1837–1997

Contributed by Louis P. Cain

Year	All canals Df696 Short tons	Erie division, freight originating Df697 Short tons	Year	All canals Df696 Short tons	Erie division, freight originating Df697 Short tons	Year	All canals Df696 Short tons	Erie division, freight originating Df697 Short tons	Year	All canals Df696 Short tons	Erie division, freight originating Df697 Short tons
1837	1,171,296	667,151	1880	6,457,656	4,608,651	1920	1,421,434	891,221	1960	3,415,095	1,772,789
1838	1,333,011	744,848	1881	5,179,192	3,598,721	1921	1,270,407	993,639	1961	3,223,558	1,583,098
1839	1,435,713	845,007	1882	5,467,423	3,694,364	1922	1,873,434	1,485,109	1962	3,279,944	1,610,959
1840	1,416,046	829,960	1883	5,664,056	3,587,102	1923	2,006,284	1,626,062	1963	3,225,526	1,541,251
1841	1,521,661	906,442	1884	5,009,488	3,389,555	1924	2,032,317	1,691,766	1964	3,194,696	1,500,946
1842	1,236,931	712,310	1885	4,731,784	3,208,207	1925	2,344,013	1,945,466	1965	3,270,796	1,508,546
1843	1,513,439	819,216	1886	5,293,982	3,808,642	1926	2,369,367	1,935,278	1966	3,147,129	1,314,250
1844	1,816,586	945,944	1887	5,553,805	3,840,513	1927	2,581,892	2,047,774	1967	3,219,994	1,332,853
1845	1,977,565	1,038,700	1888	4,942,948	3,321,516	1928	3,089,998	2,535,684	1968	3,249,035	1,409,769
1846	2,268,662	1,264,408	1889	5,370,369	3,673,554	1929	2,876,160	2,422,204	1969	3,248,440	1,489,366
1847	2,869,810	1,661,575	1890	5,246,102	3,303,929	1930	3,605,457	3,044,271	1970	2,734,963	983,982
1848	2,796,230	1,599,965	1891	4,563,472	3,097,853	1931	3,722,012	3,277,936	1971	2,488,205	926,278
1849	2,894,732	1,622,444	1892	4,281,995	2,978,832	1932	3,643,433	3,186,094	1972	2,509,069	789,142
1850	3,076,617	1,635,089	1893	4,331,963	3,235,726	1933	4,074,002	3,574,951	1973	2,548,113	896,630
1851	3,582,733	1,955,265	1894	3,882,560	3,144,144	1934	4,142,728	3,645,125	1974	2,222,827	676,660
1852	3,863,441	2,129,334	1895	3,500,314	2,356,084	1935	4,489,172	3,898,506	1975	1,940,772	690,604
1853	4,247,853	2,196,308	1896	3,714,894	2,742,438	1936	5,014,206	4,220,397	1976	2,227,052	818,344
1854	4,165,862	2,224,008	1897	3,617,804	2,584,906	1937	5,010,464	4,173,700	1977	1,826,878	614,841
1855	4,022,617	2,202,463	1898	3,360,063	2,338,020	1938	4,709,488	3,349,250	1978	1,553,310	550,314
1856	4,116,082	2,107,678	1899	3,686,051	2,419,084	1939	4,689,037	3,643,782	1979	1,303,337	426,122
1857	3,344,061	1,566,624	1900	3,345,941	2,145,876	1940	4,768,160	3,587,086	1980	1,148,382	311,793
1858	3,665,192	1,767,004	1901	3,420,613	2,257,035	1941	4,505,059	3,512,829	1981	807,925	171,022
1859	8,781,684	1,753,954	1902	3,274,610	2,105,876	1942	8,539,101	2,760,596	1982	777,292	287,122
1860	4,650,214	2,253,533	1903	3,615,385	2,414,018	1943	2,824,160	2,166,393	1983	579,777	151,251
1861	4,507,635	2,500,782	1904	3,138,547	1,945,708	1944	2,506,840	1,729,448	1984	457,134	83,426
1862	5,598,785	3,204,277	1905	3,226,896	1,999,824	1945	2,968,682	1,665,447	1985	401,132	82,776
1863	5,557,692	2,955,302	1906	3,540,907	2,385,491	1946	2,820,541	1,685,516	1986	373,950	45,626
1864	4,852,941	2,535,792	1907	3,407,914	2,415,548	1947	3,790,050	2,514,643	1987	398,313	58,492
1865	4,729,654	2,523,490	1908	3,051,877	2,177,443	1948	4,513,817	3,121,411	1988	415,665	72,282
1866	5,775,220	2,896,027	1909	3,116,536	2,031,307	1949	3,949,739	2,685,635	1989	345,735	24,912
1867	5,688,325	2,920,578	1910	3,073,412	2,023,185	1950	4,615,613	3,620,346	1990	263,055	4,804
1868	6,442,225	3,346,986	1911	3,097,068	2,031,735	1951	5,211,472	3,673,104	1991	213,830	3,499
1869	5,859,080	2,845,072	1912	2,606,116	1,795,069	1952	4,487,858	3,112,480	1992	162,349	275
1870	6,173,769	3,083,132	1913	2,602,035	1,788,453	1953	4,497,231	3,211,932	1993	153,640	2,870
1871	6,467,888	3,580,922	1914	2,080,850	1,361,764	1954	3,859,335	2,395,291	1994	67,758	191
1872	6,673,870	3,562,560	1915	1,858,114	1,155,235	1955	4,616,399	2,779,491	1995	21,789	940
1873	6,364,782	3,602,535	1916	1,625,050	917,689	1956	4,858,044	3,053,219	1996	14,405	2,202
1874	5,804,588	3,097,122	1917	1,297,225	675,083	1957	4,468,539	2,675,853	1997	17,548	739
1875	4,859,958	2,787,226	1918	1,159,270	667,374	1958	4,000,580	2,056,733			
1876	4,172,129	2,418,422	1919	1,238,844	842,164	1959	3,719,919	1,976,739			
1877	4,955,963	3,254,367									
1878	5,171,320	3,608,634									
1879	5,362,372	3,820,027									

Sources

1837–1970, State of New York, Department of Public Works, *Annual Report of the Superintendent* (annual issues); 1971–1979, State of New York, Department of Transportation, data obtained through private correspondence with the New York State Canal Corporation; 1980–1997, New York State Thruway Authority, New York State Canal Corporation, *New York State Canal System Traffic Report* (annual issues).

Documentation

Series Df696. Includes data on all New York State canals. This includes the Champlain, Oswego, Cayuga and Seneca, and Black River canals as well as the Erie Canal.

Series Df697. Includes tonnage data for the Erie Canal exclusively. The Erie Canal opened in 1825, but the first year for which reliable tonnage data exists is 1837.

TABLE Df698–702   Merchant vessels built and documented – gross tonnage, by region: 1840–1936[1]

Contributed by Louis P. Cain

	Seaboard				Northern lakes and Western rivers
	Total	New England	Mid-Atlantic and Gulf	Pacific	
	Df698	Df699	Df700	Df701	Df702
Year	Gross tons	Gross tons	Gross tons	Gross tons	Gross tons
1840	110,683	65,189	45,494	—	7,626
1841	104,268	63,771	40,497	—	14,625
1842	109,100	64,237	44,863	—	19,983
1843 [2]	53,220	26,512	26,708	—	10,397
1844	71,832	36,268	35,564	—	31,705
1845	116,443	63,837	52,606	—	29,575
1846	149,571	82,347	67,224	—	38,632
1847	185,618	104,745	80,873	—	58,114
1848	264,268	146,113	118,155	—	53,807
1849	209,189	120,237	88,952	—	47,388
1850	248,865	142,369	106,374	122	23,353
1851	265,378	133,351	131,957	70	32,825
1852	301,274	179,804	121,470	—	50,218
1853	357,233	222,791	134,291	151	68,339
1854	454,933	289,599	164,311	1,023	80,683
1855	505,450	326,431	176,901	2,118	78,000
1856	369,679	252,974	116,343	362	99,714
1857	285,681	183,686	100,810	1,185	93,123
1858	177,799	103,864	71,811	2,124	64,487
1859	134,499	79,316	53,127	2,056	23,103
1860	169,836	134,289	33,524	2,023	44,962
1861	181,586	104,678	72,192	4,716	51,608
1862	112,486	45,597	64,365	2,524	62,589
1863	215,410	79,578	133,161	2,671	95,474
1864	328,710	112,615	211,242	4,853	87,030
1865	280,899	135,253	141,830	3,816	102,910
1866	232,788	121,335	105,329	6,124	103,358
1867	229,583	135,189	90,070	4,324	73,945
1868	173,722	98,915	67,956	6,851	111,582
1869	191,194	103,604	72,058	15,532	84,036
1870	182,836	110,584	59,532	12,720	94,117
1871	156,249	64,366	86,559	5,324	116,978
1872	128,097	46,269	79,552	2,276	80,955
1873	218,139	76,406	136,258	5,475	141,107
1874	277,093	136,251	129,983	10,859	155,632
1875	244,474	151,497	79,549	13,428	53,165
1876	163,826	95,288	51,716	16,822	39,760
1877	132,996	90,992	29,286	12,718	43,596
1878	155,138	90,386	53,419	11,333	80,366
1879	115,683	55,874	48,602	11,207	77,348
1880	101,720	46,374	46,403	8,943	55,690
1881	125,766	54,488	59,861	11,417	154,693
1882	188,084	93,965	78,342	15,777	94,186
1883	210,349	110,226	83,385	16,738	55,081
1884	178,419	84,046	83,753	10,620	47,095
1885	121,010	48,128	61,844	11,038	38,046
1886	64,458	30,624	27,920	5,914	30,995
1887	83,061	24,035	49,886	9,140	67,389
1888	105,125	33,813	49,356	21,956	112,962
1889	111,852	39,983	53,930	17,939	119,282
1890	169,091	78,577	78,179	12,335	125,032
1891	287,462	105,491	112,901	19,070	131,840
1892	138,863	60,624	57,469	20,770	60,770
1893	102,830	37,091	52,018	13,721	108,809
1894	80,099	28,665	46,042	5,392	51,096
1895	67,127	26,783	33,200	7,144	44,475
1896	102,544	39,582	52,143	10,819	124,553
1897	103,504	21,942	74,067	7,495	128,729
1898	112,879	23,944	39,146	49,789	67,579
1899	196,120	68,761	85,825	41,534	103,918

TABLE Df698–702   Merchant vessels built and documented – gross tonnage, by region: 1840–1936   Continued

	Seaboard				Northern lakes and Western rivers
	Total	New England	Mid-Atlantic and Gulf	Pacific	
	Df698	Df699	Df700	Df701	Df702
Year	Gross tons	Gross tons	Gross tons	Gross tons	Gross tons
1900	249,006	72,179	135,473	41,354	144,784
1901	291,516	82,971	153,977	54,568	191,973
1902	290,122	75,852	161,211	53,059	178,709
1903	288,196	66,973	177,887	43,336	147,956
1904	208,288	51,417	135,263	21,608	170,254
1905	230,716	119,377	91,224	20,115	99,600
1906	146,883	32,311	94,311	20,261	271,862
1907	219,753	44,428	140,134	35,191	251,579
1908	266,937	70,903	138,984	57,050	347,279
1909	131,748	27,237	81,752	22,759	106,342
1910	167,829	23,442	127,517	16,870	174,239
1911	190,612	23,653	139,725	27,234	100,550
1912	136,485	23,052	81,329	32,104	96,184
1913	247,318	27,131	175,523	44,664	98,837
1914	251,700	14,985	200,220	36,495	64,550
1915	203,156	18,551	152,906	31,699	21,966
1916	275,749	37,568	188,550	49,631	49,664
1917	518,958	52,526	298,958	167,474	145,521
1918	1,080,437	88,302	473,698	518,437	220,431
1919	2,815,733	177,758	1,274,472	1,868,503	510,888
1920	3,475,872	208,023	1,931,514	1,336,335	404,767
1921	2,147,555	150,745	1,383,185	613,625	117,560
1922	637,708	56,973	448,197	132,538	23,524
1923	262,769	13,057	199,026	50,686	73,022
1924	145,837	3,174	106,414	36,249	78,131
1925	123,933	5,615	76,784	41,534	75,913
1926	159,658	4,995	131,994	22,669	65,015
1927	176,207	6,574	124,068	45,565	68,937
1928	181,681	11,434	146,532	23,715	75,499
1929	104,769	12,766	71,750	20,253	24,207
1930	193,116	18,601	143,656	30,859	61,180
1931	355,771	26,639	287,884	41,248	31,135
1932	195,529	52,163	133,625	9,741	17,363
1933	181,593	25,851	151,823	3,919	9,210
1934	49,946	862	37,390	11,694	16,703
1935	49,054	1,910	38,452	8,692	13,865
1936	175,398	711	166,671	8,016	48,686

[1] As of September 30, through 1842; and June 30 thereafter.

[2] Figures are for a nine-month period.

Source

U.S. Bureau of Marine Inspection and Navigation, *Merchant Marine Statistics, 1936*, pp. 46–8 and Table 2.

Documentation

The data are for documented vessels of five gross tons or more. See the text for Table Df578–593 for a definition of gross tonnage and related discussion.

Figures for 1858, 1859, 1863, 1865, and 1867 do not sum to those in series Df613.

TABLE Df703–707   Freight traffic on the Sault Ste. Marie canals, by cargo type: 1855–1900

Contributed by Louis P. Cain

Year	Total	Iron ore	Coal	Grain	Stone
	Df703	Df704	Df705	Df706	Df707
	Thousand short tons	Thousand short tons	Thousand short tons	Thousand bushels	Thousand short tons
1855	15	1	1	—	—
1856	34	12	4	82	—
1857	52	26	5	41	—
1858	57	31	4	21	—
1859	122	66	9	72	—
1860	154	120	—	133	—
1861	88	45	12	77	—
1862	162	113	11	59	—
1863	237	182	8	78	—
1864	284	214	11	144	—
1865	182	147	—	—	—
1866	239	152	20	230	—
1867	325	223	23	249	—
1868	299	192	26	285	—
1869	368	239	28	324	—
1870	540	410	16	354	5
1871	586	327	47	1,686	6
1872	746	383	81	1,013	5
1873	888	504	97	2,430	2
1874	655	428	61	1,270	(Z)
1875	833	493	101	1,486	3
1876	1,074	610	125	2,396	2
1877	913	568	92	1,728	3
1878	937	556	92	2,138	3
1879	1,051	540	111	3,578	2
1880	1,322	677	171	4,659	2
1881	1,568	748	296	3,825	1
1882	2,030	987	430	4,202	5
1883	2,267	792	714	6,677	2
1884	2,875	1,136	706	12,503	6
1885	3,257	1,235	895	15,697	8
1886	4,528	2,088	1,010	19,707	9
1887	5,495	2,498	1,353	23,872	13
1888	6,411	2,571	2,105	20,619	34
1889	7,516	4,096	1,629	18,325	34
1890	9,041	4,775	2,177	18,262	48
1891	8,889	3,560	2,508	39,849	44
1892	11,214	4,901	2,904	42,661	40
1893	10,797	4,015	3,008	45,887	19
1894	13,196	6,549	2,797	36,414	21
1895	15,063	8,062	2,574	54,547	24
1896	16,239	7,909	3,023	90,705	18
1897	18,983	10,634	3,039	80,814	6
1898	21,235	11,707	3,776	88,418	5
1899	25,256	15,328	3,941	88,398	39
1900	25,643	16,444	4,487	56,664	49

(Z) Less than 500 short tons.

Source

U.S. Army Corps of Engineers, *Statistical Report of Lake Commerce Passing through Canals at Sault Ste. Marie* (1931).

Documentation

These series include traffic moving through the American and Canadian canals. Figures for later years may be obtained from various issues of Army Corps of Engineers, *Annual Report*, Part 2, *Commercial Statistics*. They are not shown here because they pertain only to traffic between Lake Superior and the other lakes. See Table Df716–721 for more comprehensive totals of Great Lakes traffic.

TABLE Df708–715　Merchant vessels launched and owned – number and tonnage, for the United States and all countries: 1895–1993[1,2]

Contributed by Louis P. Cain

Year	All countries				United States			
	Launched		Owned		Launched		Owned	
	Number	Gross tons	Number	Gross tons	Number	Gross tons	Number	Gross tons
	Df708	Df709	Df710	Df711	Df712	Df713	Df714	Df715
	Number	Thousand gross tons	Number	Thousand gross tons	Number	Thousand gross tons	Number	Thousand gross tons
1895	1,205	1,844	30,288	25,086	155	200	3,200	2,165
1900	1,611	2,354	27,840	28,957	242	347	3,135	2,750
1905	1,474	2,218	29,574	35,949	206	352	3,457	3,996
1910	1,426	2,588	29,943	41,884	140	222	3,380	5,018
1915	1,637	4,616	30,643	49,246	605	2,217	3,180	5,846
1920	942	2,582	31,484	57,281	99	315	5,381	15,997
1925	873	2,469	32,905	65,638	74	159	4,790	15,314
1930	484	1,020	32,713	69,608	25	83	4,105	13,947
1935	—[3]	—[4]	30,979	64,886	—[5]	—[6]	3,585	12,773
1939	—[3]	—[4]	31,186	69,440	—[5]	—[6]	3,270	11,874
1940	495	1,754	—	—	167	579	—	—
1941	489	2,487	—	—	184	1,035	—	—
1942	1,285	7,812	—	—	861	5,671	—	—
1943	2,067	13,881	—	—	1,620	11,577	—	—
1944	1,690	11,157	—	—	1,237	9,332	—	—
1945	1,311	7,189	—	—	880	5,968	—	—
1946	655	2,108	—	—	95	501	—	—
1947	741	2,093	—	—	61	163	—	—
1948	840	2,303	26,479	79,714	49	126	4,807	29,060
1949	899	3,126	27,194	81,954	66	633	4,605	27,707
1950	990	3,489	27,922	83,996	51	437	4,531	27,404
1951	1,002	3,639	28,374	86,678	58	164	4,484	27,226
1952	1,065	4,394	28,751	89,636	64	468	4,458	27,139
1953	1,134	5,095	29,174	92,826	68	528	4,431	27,144
1954	1,223	5,251	29,766	96,899	46	477	4,404	27,252
1955	1,437	5,315	29,967	100,069	26	73	4,225	26,343
1956	1,815	6,670	30,620	104,720	50	169	4,157	26,074
1957	1,950	8,501	31,421	109,778	54	359	4,116	25,843
1958	1,936	9,270	32,857	117,578	64	732	4,054	25,526
1959	1,808	8,746	33,924	124,494	47	597	3,964	25,227
1960	2,020	8,356	34,056	129,339	60	485	3,845	24,781
1961	1,990	7,940	35,465	135,477	56	343	3,728	24,184
1962	1,901	8,375	36,364	139,549	90	449	3,542	23,220
1963	2,001	8,539	37,310	145,438	78	294	3,506	23,082
1964	2,147	10,264	38,602	152,584	80	276	3,344	22,380
1965	2,280	12,216	39,628	159,979	130	270	3,224	21,478
1966	2,561	14,307	40,822	170,730	191	167	3,140	20,750
1967	2,778	15,780	42,234	181,709	231	242	3,115	20,286
1968	2,798	16,908	45,343	193,770	199	441	3,049	19,623
1969	2,819	19,315	48,246	211,294	174	400	2,972	19,507
1970	2,700	21,690	50,472	227,138	150	338	2,822	18,423
1971	2,645	24,860	55,041	247,203	242	482	3,327	16,266
1972	2,561	26,714	57,391	268,340	251	611	3,687	15,024
1973	2,864	31,520	59,606	289,927	280	890	4,063	14,912
1974	2,949	33,541	61,194	311,323	233	733	4,086	14,429
1975	2,730	34,203	63,794	342,162	127	476	4,346	14,587
1976	2,723	33,922	65,887	372,000	143	815	4,616	14,908
1977	2,796	27,531	67,945	393,678	129	1,012	4,740	15,300
1978	2,618	18,194	69,020	406,002	151	1,033	4,746	16,188
1979	2,466	14,289	71,129	413,021	182	1,352	5,088	17,542
1980	2,412	13,101	73,832	419,911	205	555	5,579	18,464
1981	2,269	16,932	73,864	420,835	223	360	5,869	18,908
1982	2,312	16,820	75,151	424,742	204	216	6,133	19,111
1983	2,276	15,911	76,106	422,590	159	381	6,437	19,358
1984	2,210	18,334	76,068	418,682	73	84	6,441	19,292

Notes appear at end of table

(continued)

TABLE Df708–715   Merchant vessels launched and owned – number and tonnage, for the United States and all countries: 1895–1993 *Continued*

	All countries				United States			
	Launched		Owned		Launched		Owned	
	Number	Gross tons	Number	Gross tons	Number	Gross tons	Number	Gross tons
	Df708	Df709	Df710	Df711	Df712	Df713	Df714	Df715
Year	Number	Thousand gross tons	Number	Thousand gross tons	Number	Thousand gross tons	Number	Thousand gross tons
1985	1,964	18,157	76,395	416,269	66	180	6,447	19,518
1986	1,634	16,845	75,266	404,910	36	223	6,496	19,901
1987	1,528	12,259	75,240	403,498	29	164	6,427	20,178
1988	1,575	10,909	75,680	403,406	60	11	6,442	20,832
1989	1,593	13,236	76,100	410,481	10	4	6,375	20,588
1990	1,672	15,885	78,336	423,627	16	15	6,348	21,328
1991	1,574	16,095	80,030	436,027	17	19	6,222	20,291
1992	1,506	18,633	79,845	444,305	27	54	5,737	18,228
1993	1,505	20,025	80,655	457,915	30	14	5,646	14,087

[1] The data are for vessels of 100 gross tons and over. They exclude sailing ships, non-propelled craft, and all ships built of wood.

[2] Figures for 1895–1935 represent annual averages for the five-year span beginning with the year shown.

[3] Total for 1935–1939, 1,040.

[4] Total for 1935–1939, 2,595.

[5] Total for 1935–1939, 117.

[6] Total for 1935–1939, 244.

Sources

The "Launched" data is taken from Lloyd's Register of Shipping, London, England, *Statistical Tables* (annual issues); the "Owned" data are from *Annual Summary of Merchant Ships Launched in the World* (various issues). Beginning in 1992, all data are taken from *World Fleet Statistics* (annual issues). These data are included in the *Statistical Abstract of the United States* (annual issues), and reported as coming from *World Fleet Statistics*.

Documentation

See the text for Table Df578–593 for a definition of gross tonnage and related discussion.

TABLE Df716–721   Bulk freight traffic on the Great Lakes, by cargo type: 1900–1997

Contributed by Louis P. Cain

	Dry bulk					Bulk trade in petroleum products
	Total	Iron ore	Coal	Grain	Stone	
	Df716	Df717	Df718	Df719	Df720	Df721 [1]
Year	Thousand short tons	Thousand short tons	Thousand short tons	Thousand short tons	Thousand short tons	Thousand short tons
1900	35,298	20,799	8,908	5,591	—	—
1901	37,064	22,576	9,820	4,668	—	—
1902	44,374	30,284	9,196	4,894	—	—
1903	45,571	26,488	13,351	5,732	—	—
1904	40,331	23,774	12,370	4,187	—	—
1905	58,008	37,494	14,401	6,113	—	—
1906	66,152	42,015	17,274	6,863	—	—
1907	74,743	46,245	21,487	7,011	—	—
1908	53,791	28,479	19,288	6,024	—	—
1909	71,954	46,686	18,617	6,651	—	—
1910	80,015	47,733	26,478	5,804	—	—
1911	68,646	35,987	25,700	6,959	—	—
1912	87,174	53,129	24,673	9,372	—	—
1913	100,018	54,959	33,362	11,697	—	—
1914	72,940	35,864	27,282	9,794	—	—
1915	93,050	51,877	26,220	11,099	3,854	—
1916	117,053	72,503	28,440	10,556	5,554	—
1917	115,102	69,998	31,193	7,162	6,749	—
1918	114,614	68,495	32,102	6,549	7,468	—
1919	91,762	52,839	26,424	6,092	6,407	—
1920	106,519	65,551	26,410	6,736	7,822	—
1921	68,034	24,977	26,661	12,470	3,926	—
1922	89,455	47,727	19,869	14,267	7,592	—
1923	121,029	66,122	33,137	11,850	9,920	—
1924	98,047	47,737	25,861	15,223	9,226	—
1925	113,292	60,571	28,049	13,320	11,352	—
1926	121,289	65,563	31,011	12,087	12,628	—
1927	120,760	57,240	34,794	14,693	14,033	—
1928	127,331	60,458	34,823	16,372	15,678	—
1929	138,574	73,028	39,255	10,021	16,270	—
1930	112,529	52,173	38,072	9,851	12,433	—
1931	74,149	26,284	31,176	9,480	7,209	—
1932	41,673	3,997	24,857	8,890	3,929	—
1933	71,373	24,218	31,777	8,713	6,665	—
1934	75,739	24,919	35,477	7,951	7,392	—
1935	82,887	31,766	35,289	6,750	9,082	—
1936	114,415	50,201	44,699	7,434	12,081	—
1937	134,688	70,111	44,319	5,829	14,429	—
1938	75,118	21,575	34,623	10,679	8,241	—
1939	114,230	50,482	40,368	11,172	12,208	—
1940	145,216	71,358	49,320	9,645	14,893	—
1941	172,287	89,732	53,535	11,387	17,633	9,387
1942	182,731	103,125	52,534	8,502	18,570	8,940
1943	175,653	94,534	51,969	11,810	17,340	9,450
1944	184,159	90,911	60,163	16,229	16,856	10,196
1945	175,083	84,801	55,246	18,718	16,318	9,364
1946	147,955	66,478	53,727	10,198	17,552	10,217
1947	177,606	87,246	58,060	11,409	20,891	10,145
1948	185,612	92,890	60,564	9,877	22,282	10,956
1949	151,697	77,902	40,930	12,543	20,322	12,607
1950	177,953	87,591	57,640	9,327	23,395	13,331
1951	189,750	99,783	50,946	13,150	25,871	16,297
1952	168,677	83,900	46,284	15,215	23,278	17,448
1953	199,697	107,346	51,035	14,317	26,999	16,810
1954	151,298	68,090	46,367	11,866	24,975	14,901
1955	193,759	99,871	53,378	10,788	29,722	15,532
1956	192,267	89,819	57,375	14,320	30,753	16,137
1957	196,206	97,752	56,780	11,235	30,439	16,628
1958	141,434	61,362	44,950	12,626	22,496	14,025
1959	144,622	57,625	47,228	13,609	26,160	14,410

Notes appear at end of table

(continued)

TABLE Df716–721   Bulk freight traffic on the Great Lakes, by cargo
type: 1900–1997   *Continued*

Year	Dry bulk					Bulk trade in petroleum products
	Total	Iron ore	Coal	Grain	Stone	
	Df716	Df717	Df718	Df719	Df720	Df721 [1]
	Thousand short tons	Thousand short tons	Thousand short tons	Thousand short tons	Thousand short tons	Thousand short tons
1960	169,857	81,842	46,701	14,135	27,179	14,295
1961	154,201	68,205	43,970	16,608	25,418	14,874
1962	157,490	70,656	46,184	15,919	24,731	13,893
1963	174,341	75,374	51,643	18,777	28,547	12,417
1964	192,041	87,489	52,143	21,637	30,771	10,790
1965	195,332	88,063	54,574	21,875	30,819	11,168
1966	210,128	95,506	55,585	25,014	34,022	12,980
1967	192,503	90,279	52,891	17,617	31,717	12,110
1968	191,947	93,667	48,862	16,325	33,093	12,834
1969	196,267	96,664	46,924	16,595	36,083	13,149
1970	209,531	97,550	49,684	23,820	38,477	13,873
1971	190,132	87,541	43,342	25,239	33,999	13,349
1972	190,171	90,897	43,235	26,692	37,346	13,768
1973	214,920	105,890	39,604	26,537	42,888	15,083
1974	195,762	98,087	34,989	19,589	43,096	12,692
1975	190,947	89,562	39,193	24,511	37,681	11,546
1976	196,197	97,013	37,493	23,488	38,204	13,241
1977	177,293	75,096	38,984	25,993	37,220	15,067
1978	209,159	99,548	37,767	32,090	39,754	13,322
1979	214,791	103,100	45,833	28,882	36,976	16,052
1980	182,550	81,723	41,306	31,510	28,011	12,699
1981	175,812	83,893	39,097	28,235	24,587	11,755
1982	123,253	43,134	36,760	28,283	15,076	14,285
1983	141,305	58,335	36,579	28,847	17,544	6,304
1984	156,513	64,137	43,134	28,153	21,089	6,208
1985	137,340	58,432	36,335	20,056	22,517	4,872
1986	130,478	51,017	36,267	20,156	23,038	4,495
1987	150,502	61,703	37,732	22,338	28,729	5,855
1988	159,035	68,306	40,521	19,102	31,106	6,228
1989	152,199	66,710	39,470	15,008	31,011	5,857
1990	152,792	68,877	37,994	15,841	30,080	7,342
1991	145,161	64,293	35,282	18,593	26,993	5,939
1992	144,940	67,112	35,397	15,186	27,245	4,907
1993	143,330	69,255	30,490	14,096	29,489	4,169
1994	156,064	70,117	35,002	18,107	32,838	4,628
1995	156,903	70,593	32,944	18,801	34,565	4,730
1996	156,466	71,248	34,822	15,297	35,099	4,753
1997	168,297	71,999	40,509	16,649	39,140	4,490 [2]

[1] Data beginning with 1983 are not strictly comparable with earlier data. See text.

[2] Includes an estimate for Canadian-flagged carriage, rather than the final total.

Source
Lake Carriers' Association, *Annual Report* (1997), pp. 39, 51, and each prior year.

Documentation
This table includes tonnage moving to or from Canadian or U.S. lake ports, in Canadian or U.S. bulk carriers. The survey was expanded to include more lake carriers in 1996; see the note on p. 40 of Lake Carriers' Association (1997). When reports from different years conflict, the one from a later year is shown here on the assumption that it is a correction.

Series Df716. Equals the sum of series Df717–720. Does not include potash or cement, which are increasingly important after 1978. Data for potash and cement are included in the original source; they have been excluded here for consistency with the data from the earlier years.

Series Df721. There is an error apparent in the sharp break in the reported figures between 1982 and 1983. This break reflects a change in the Canadian-flagged shipment data between Lake Carriers' Association (1991), p. 38, and Lake Carriers' Association (1992), p. 49. There is no comment in the source as to the cause of the disjuncture.

TABLE Df722–732   Merchant vessels built – number and tonnage, by vessel type: 1914–1994 [1,2]

Contributed by Louis P. Cain

	Merchant vessels		Passenger-cargo/transport			Cargo			Tanker		
	Number	Gross tons	Number	Gross tons	Deadweight tons	Number	Gross tons	Deadweight tons	Number	Gross tons	Deadweight tons
	Df722	Df723	Df724	Df725	Df726	Df727	Df728	Df729	Df730	Df731	Df732
Year	Number	Thousand gross tons	Number	Thousand gross tons	Thousand deadweight tons	Number	Thousand gross tons	Thousand deadweight tons	Number	Thousand gross tons	Thousand deadweight tons
1914	26	135	1	3	1	17	88	130	8	45	67
1915	24	128	3	20	13	17	88	131	4	20	30
1916	74	370	1	6	7	49	201	300	24	163	247
1917	125	642	1	10	10	92	414	627	32	218	314
1918	414	1,770	5	30	24	375	1,508	2,283	34	232	339
1919	723	3,370	2	10	11	679	3,086	4,680	42	273	395
1920	467	2,396	12	100	111	375	1,758	2,696	80	538	778
1921	183	1,359	22	256	243	57	317	485	104	786	1,158
1922	19	168	3	41	34	10	78	156	6	48	71
1923	18	117	7	34	26	9	68	110	2	16	23
1924	12	84	7	44	20	4	34	48	1	7	11
1925	12	84	3	19	11	9	65	92	—	—	—
1926	8	54	5	29	16	2	16	26	1	9	15
1927	19	155	7	51	27	9	73	104	3	30	50
1928	7	72	3	44	37	—	—	—	4	28	44
1929	8	65	2	24	20	5	33	49	1	9	15
1930	18	164	5	50	39	2	16	24	11	97	161
1931	14	151	9	109	85	—	—	—	5	42	70
1932	15	145	13	129	83	2	16	22	—	—	—
1933	4	50	4	50	32	—	—	—	—	—	—
1934	2	10	—	—	—	2	10	15	—	—	—
1935	2	19	—	—	—	—	—	—	2	19	30
1936	8	63	—	—	—	—	—	—	8	63	105
1937	15	122	—	—	—	—	—	—	15	122	192
1938	24	181	—	—	—	6	39	56	18	142	228
1939	28	241	3	30	20	14	92	128	11	119	193
1940	53	445	6	69	61	31	227	335	16	149	238
1941	95	749	6	58	57	61	423	598	28	268	434
1942	724	5,393	11	102	81	652	4,679	6,843	61	612	982
1943	1,661	12,486	20	220	180	1,410	10,103	14,921	231	2,163	3,420
1944	1,463	11,403	48	461	330	1,175	8,455	11,858	240	2,486	3,955
1945	1,041	7,615	46	509	311	807	5,336	7,206	188	1,770	2,787
1946	83	646	9	77	85	66	487	729	8	82	121
1947	39	247	8	74	68	28	154	224	3	19	36
1948	24	159	1	15	11	17	92	159	6	52	88
1949	33	541	—	—	—	—	—	—	33	541	863
1950	26	405	—	—	—	3	27	44	23	378	609
1951	10	148	2	47	24	4	29	43	4	71	116
1952	31	399	6	101	57	17	170	289	8	127	202
1953	45	570	1	4	4	22	212	324	22	354	555
1954	39	585	1	4	6	11	106	159	27	475	764
1955	9	119	—	—	—	7	84	95	2	35	55
1956	8	113	—	—	—	2	7	15	6	106	169
1957	19	297	—	—	—	3	8	6	16	289	457
1958	30	572	4	61	35	5	48	67	21	463	759
1959	30	714	1	5	1	3	40	73	26	668	1,095
1960	26	410	—	—	—	15	134	163	11	276	456
1961	25	369	—	—	—	18	190	224	7	179	298
1962	27	392	1	14	10	23	265	303	3	113	186
1963	35	418	6	51	31	23	250	289	6	117	200
1964	15	213	1	14	9	10	104	123	4	95	166
1965	13	173	—	—	—	11	121	154	2	52	92
1966	13	146	—	—	—	12	125	161	1	21	36
1967	12	143	—	—	—	12	143	150	—	—	—
1968	21	319	—	—	—	18	256	291	3	63	113
1969	22	418	—	—	—	14	217	247	8	201	381
1970	13	342	—	—	—	6	120	134	7	222	427
1971	14	394	—	—	—	6	151	170	8	243	473
1972	13	357	—	—	—	7	151	187	6	206	415
1973	24	734	—	—	—	18	419	450	6	315	653
1974	20	697	—	—	—	11	314	402	9	383	759

Notes appear at end of table

(continued)

TABLE Df722-732   Merchant vessels built – number and tonnage, by vessel type: 1914-1994   *Continued*

Year	Merchant vessels		Passenger-cargo/transport			Cargo			Tanker		
	Number	Gross tons	Number	Gross tons	Deadweight tons	Number	Gross tons	Deadweight tons	Number	Gross tons	Deadweight tons
	Df722	Df723	Df724	Df725	Df726	Df727	Df728	Df729	Df730	Df731	Df732
	Number	Thousand gross tons	Number	Thousand gross tons	Thousand deadweight tons	Number	Thousand gross tons	Thousand deadweight tons	Number	Thousand gross tons	Thousand deadweight tons
1975	15	452	—	—	—	3	65	71	12	387	742
1976	16	615	—	—	—	4	57	76	12	558	1,176
1977	17	884	—	—	—	2	25	37	15	859	1,585
1978	14	912	—	—	—	2	27	30	12	885	1,392
1979	15	1,149	—	—	—	4	53	47	11	1,096	1,901
1980	10	375	—	—	—	6	105	114	4	270	354
1981	12	275	—	—	—	2	53	73	10	222	358
1982	11	337	—	—	—	6	221	219	5	116	226
1983	13	376	—	—	—	6	228	219	7	148	277
1984	5	118	—	—	—	0	0	0	5	118	210
1985	8	172	—	—	—	4	113	97	4	59	92
1986	5	215	—	—	—	2	66	53	3	149	271
1987	4	153	—	—	—	3	58	63	1	95	209
1988	4	153	—	—	—	3	58	63	1	95	209
1992	3	44	—	—	—	1	32	29	2	12	16
1994	1	17	—	—	—	—	—	—	1	17	22

[1] Self-propelled steel vessels of 1,000 gross tons and over for domestic use (2,000 gross tons and more prior to 1961).

[2] Excludes Alaska and Hawai'i.

Sources

1914–1960, American Bureau of Shipping, New York, *The Bulletin* (annual issues); 1961–1995, U.S. Maritime Administration, *New Ship Construction* (annual issues).

Documentation

Data cover merchant vessels completed by U.S. shipyards. Passenger ships were not listed after 1964. See the text for Table Df578–593 for a definition of gross tonnage and related discussion.

TABLE Df733-735   Commercial traffic on the Panama Canal – transits, tolls, and cargo: 1915-1996[1]

Contributed by Louis P. Cain

	Transits	Tolls	Cargo		Transits	Tolls	Cargo
	Df733	Df734	Df735		Df733	Df734	Df735
Year	Number	Thousand dollars	Thousand long tons	Year	Number	Thousand dollars	Thousand long tons
1915 [2]	1,058	4,367	4,888	1960	10,795	50,939	59,258
1916 [3]	724	2,403	3,093	1961	10,866	54,128	63,670
1917	1,738	5,621	7,055	1962	11,149	57,290	67,525
1918	1,989	6,429	7,526	1963	11,017	56,368	62,247
1919	1,948	6,164	6,910	1964	11,808	61,098	70,550
1920	2,393	8,508	9,372	1965	11,834	65,443	76,573
1921	2,791	11,269	11,596	1966	11,925	69,095	81,704
1922	2,665	11,192	10,883	1967	12,412	76,769	86,193
1923	3,908	17,504	19,566	1968	13,199	83,907	96,550
1924	5,158	24,285	26,993	1969	13,146	87,423	101,373
1925	4,592	21,394	23,957	1970	13,658	94,620	114,257
1926	5,087	22,920	26,030	1971	14,020	97,380	118,627
1927	5,293	24,212	27,734	1972	13,766	98,765	109,234
1928	6,253	26,922	29,616	1973	13,841	111,032	126,104
1929	6,289	27,111	30,648	1974	14,033	119,423	147,907
1930	6,027	27,060	30,018	1975	13,609	141,898	140,101
1931	5,370	24,625	25,065	1976	12,157	134,204	117,212
1932	4,362	20,695	19,799	1977	11,896	163,827	122,979
1933	4,162	19,602	18,161	1978	12,677	194,773	142,518
1934	5,234	24,047	24,704	1979	12,935	208,377	154,111
1935	5,180	23,307	25,310	1980	13,507	291,839	167,215
1936	5,382	23,479	26,506	1981	13,884	301,763	171,222
1937	5,387	23,102	28,108	1982	14,009	323,958	185,452
1938	5,524	23,170	27,387	1983	11,707	285,984	145,591
1939	5,903	23,661	27,867	1984	11,230	286,678	140,471
1940	5,370	21,145	27,299	1985	11,515	298,498	138,643
1941	4,727	18,158	24,951	1986	11,925	321,074	139,945
1942	2,688	9,752	13,607	1987	12,230	328,373	148,690
1943	1,822	7,357	10,600	1988	12,234	337,866	156,483
1944	1,562	5,456	7,003	1989	11,989	327,851	151,636
1945	1,939	7,244	8,604	1990	11,941	353,726	157,073
1946	3,747	14,774	14,978	1991	12,572	372,280	162,696
1947	4,260	17,597	21,671	1992	12,454	365,716	159,273
1948	4,678	19,957	24,118	1993	12,086	398,232	157,704
1949	4,793	20,541	25,305	1994	12,337	416,803	170,538
1950	5,448	24,430	28,872	1995	13,459	460,044	190,303
1951	5,593	23,906	30,073	1996	13,536	483,115	198,068[1]
1952	6,524	26,923	33,611				
1953	7,410	31,918	36,095				
1954	7,784	33,248	39,095				
1955	7,997	33,849	40,646				
1956	8,209	36,154	45,119				
1957	8,579	38,444	49,702				
1958	9,187	41,796	48,125				
1959	9,718	45,529	51,153				

[1] Fiscal year ending June 30 (1915-1976); September 30 thereafter. Data for the transition quarter are not included, but appear in the source.

[2] Canal opened August 15, 1914.

[3] Canal closed about seven months by landslides.

Sources

1915-1924, Governor of the Panama Canal, *Annual Report* (1948), p. 10; 1925-1996, Panama Canal Company, *Annual Report* (various issues).

Documentation

These data do not include U.S. government or smaller commercial traffic, but both are available in the source.

Figures include oceangoing toll-paying vessels and foreign naval vessels of 300 net tons and more (Panama Canal measurement) for vessels rated on net tonnage, or 500 tons displacement and more for vessels rated on displacement tonnage.

TABLE Df736-741   Tonnage of waterborne imports and exports, by flag of carrier: 1921-1994[1]

Contributed by Louis P. Cain

	Imports			Exports		
	Total	U.S. vessels	Foreign vessels	Total	U.S. vessels	Foreign vessels
	Df736	Df737	Df738	Df739	Df740	Df741
Year	Thousand short tons	Thousand short tons	Thousand short tons	Thousand short tons	Thousand short tons	Thousand short tons
1921	37,167	26,269	10,898	54,477	20,784	33,692
1922	50,044	31,286	18,758	47,602	18,871	28,731
1923	48,491	25,518	22,973	54,970	18,131	36,838
1924	45,807	24,968	20,839	58,533	20,515	38,018
1925	48,311	23,760	24,551	55,626	17,603	38,024
1926	50,049	23,638	26,411	76,316	19,177	57,140
1927	47,245	24,033	23,212	63,768	20,939	42,829
1928	53,083	27,089	25,993	65,889	21,602	44,287
1929	57,103	28,260	28,844	64,372	20,071	44,301
1930	53,270	27,801	25,469	55,699	16,703	38,995
1931	40,168	19,168	21,000	44,855	12,396	32,459
1932	32,156	14,923	17,232	35,666	9,125	26,541
1933	29,755	12,340	17,415	36,272	9,357	26,914
1934	33,392	14,299	19,092	42,360	10,567	31,792
1935	38,042	15,820	22,221	42,723	9,789	32,935
1936	43,003	14,780	28,223	44,480	9,650	34,830
1937	47,110	14,967	32,143	61,105	12,189	48,916
1938	36,756	13,527	23,230	62,286	11,602	50,684
1939	42,054	12,459	29,595	61,697	10,557	51,140
1940	44,667	17,322	27,345	60,929	12,939	47,990
1941	—	—	—	—	—	—
1942	27,393	17,399	9,994	41,670	16,227	25,443
1943	30,988	24,740	6,248	47,765	25,302	22,463
1944	33,320	26,209	7,111	55,215	34,002	21,213
1945	39,426	31,415	8,011	61,603	37,729	23,874
1946	49,184	32,340	16,844	87,043	49,799	37,244
1947	59,203	37,682	21,521	124,317	61,062	63,254
1948	67,416	40,528	26,888	88,312	34,501	53,810
1949	77,371	41,364	36,007	71,865	26,136	45,729
1950	96,703	42,268	54,435	62,685	20,379	42,306
1951	100,603	42,836	57,767	115,690	43,232	72,458
1952	107,421	41,683	65,738	103,048	30,417	72,630
1953	119,003	38,468	80,535	80,549	19,448	61,101
1954	120,685	36,291	84,395	78,178	18,378	59,800
1955	141,123	37,409	103,715	112,796	22,144	90,652
1956	159,472	39,394	120,078	144,755	27,304	117,451
1957	172,030	34,558	137,472	165,796	29,092	136,704
1958	175,605	20,628	154,977	114,748	18,686	96,062
1959	200,481	19,219	181,262	108,281	17,724	90,557
1960	198,830	19,627	179,203	123,887	20,133	103,754
1961	187,887	15,155	172,732	127,519	18,411	109,108
1962	210,631	18,373	192,257	134,001	19,535	114,466
1963	212,542	15,682	196,860	156,122	20,885	135,237
1964	233,774	16,278	217,496	171,431	23,937	147,494
1965	255,596	15,573	240,023	171,811	19,048	152,762
1966	266,075	15,598	250,477	185,978	17,358	168,620
1967	256,806	13,526	243,280	187,427	15,365	172,062
1968	282,751	16,321	266,430	194,483	15,599	178,884
1969	288,620	10,985	277,635	199,286	13,060	186,226
1970	299,169	15,438	283,721	239,774	14,990	224,834
1971	313,165	16,376	296,789	204,148	12,777	191,371
1972	350,845	15,742	335,104	230,291	13,247	217,045
1973	441,624	30,540	411,085	274,257	16,409	257,848
1974	449,179	33,854	415,326	264,485	15,371	249,114
1975	427,865	23,009	404,856	269,182	14,471	254,711
1976	517,450	24,334	493,117	283,070	16,781	266,289
1977	612,798	27,524	585,275	274,413	15,061	259,352
1978	592,949	25,400	567,550	300,033	13,333	286,700
1979	597,495	27,917	569,579	357,793	13,773	344,020

Note appears at end of table

TABLE Df736–741   Tonnage of waterborne imports and exports,
by flag of carrier: 1921–1994   *Continued*

	Imports			Exports		
	Total	U.S. vessels	Foreign vessels	Total	U.S. vessels	Foreign vessels
	Df736	Df737	Df738	Df739	Df740	Df741
Year	Thousand short tons	Thousand short tons	Thousand short tons	Thousand short tons	Thousand short tons	Thousand short tons
1980	487,947	19,015	468,932	401,173	15,007	386,166
1981	464,420	25,551	438,869	406,796	15,712	391,084
1982	376,232	22,829	353,403	400,896	13,775	387,121
1983	366,427	29,451	336,976	361,405	14,128	347,277
1984	412,957	21,200	391,757	374,662	13,631	361,031
1985	394,237	18,494	375,744	349,933	14,480	335,453
1986	449,707	18,589	431,118	328,418	14,228	314,190
1987	471,693	18,499	453,194	357,285	14,894	342,391
1988	512,141	20,084	492,057	398,125	15,680	382,445
1989	543,997	24,455	519,542	419,522	16,795	402,727
1990	545,454	20,761	524,693	410,120	17,347	392,772
1991	494,781	19,443	475,338	429,459	19,770	409,689
1992	525,208	17,916	507,292	427,021	17,877	409,144
1993	585,150	19,729	565,420	387,745	20,518	367,226
1994	644,985	20,065	624,920	370,120	19,483	350,636

[1] Various exclusions as well as changing geographic coverage and weight and value thresholds are discussed in the text.

Sources

U.S. Bureau of the Census, 1921–1945, *Foreign Commerce and Navigation of the United States* (annual issues); 1946–1957, releases and unpublished data; 1958–1970, *Statistical Abstract of the United States* (various issues); 1970–1994, U.S. Bureau of the Census, *Waterborne Exports and General Imports* (annual issues).

Documentation

Prior to 1946, the data exclude cargoes (small in the aggregate) carried by ships of less than 100 tons gross capacity.

Beginning in 1942, U.S. Army and Navy cargo and the Great Lakes are excluded. Beginning in 1946, the Great Lakes are once again included, as are Alaska, Hawai'i, and Puerto Rico.

Beginning in July 1950, excludes commodities classified for security reasons as "special category."

Shipments less than $100 in value are excluded for all years. From July 1953 to December 1955 and July 1956 through December 1962, exports exclude shipments less than $500 in value regardless of shipping weight; for January–June 1956, exports exclude shipments less than $1,000. For 1963 and later years, exports exclude shipments to Canada individually valued less than $2,000 and to other countries less than $500. Beginning with 1954, imports exclude shipments less than 2,000 pounds shipping weight regardless of value, as well as shipments valued at less than $100 regardless of shipping weight. For January 1960 through June 1965, imports exclude formal entry shipments valued at less than $100 and informal entry shipments valued at less than $251. For July–December 1965 and later years, imports exclude all shipments less than $251.

The data were reported monthly to 1994, when the Census Bureau changed the format and started reporting it quarterly. The data reported here are from the annual summary. Given the change in format, these series stop in 1994 to ensure consistency. Readers interested in more recent data are referred to the source document.

Series Df736 and Df739. These series are the sum of the figures reported for dry cargo and tankers.

TABLE Df742–753   Waterborne cargo tonnage – foreign and domestic, by type of port and traffic: 1924–1996

Contributed by Louis P. Cain

		Foreign					Domestic					
			Through seaports		Great Lakes ports			Between ports		Local and intraport		
	Foreign and domestic	Total	Imports	Exports	Imports	Exports	Net total	Coastwise	Lakewise	Local and intraport	Internal	Intraterritory
	Df742	Df743	Df744	Df745	Df746	Df747	Df748 [1]	Df749	Df750	Df751	Df752 [2]	Df753 [2]
Year	Thousand short tons	Thousand short tons	Thousand short tons	Thousand short tons	Thousand short tons	Thousand short tons	Thousand short tons	Thousand short tons	Thousand short tons	Thousand short tons	Thousand short tons	Thousand short tons
1924	453,700	101,562	36,425	49,008	4,962	11,167	352,138	88,554	92,563	77,270	34,101	—
1925	483,400	108,548	42,793	49,251	7,317	9,187	374,852	105,090	110,626	59,981	49,787	—
1926	540,500	131,293	44,834	69,859	6,424	10,176	409,207	108,023	115,791	88,270	36,798	—
1927	532,500	120,523	43,388	56,550	8,098	12,487	411,977	121,036	112,805	78,020	40,559	—
1928	539,200	126,768	46,690	56,151	8,548	15,379	412,432	119,254	119,301	75,728	39,870	—
1929	583,800	127,510	51,591	55,761	6,385	13,773	456,290	124,999	135,838	89,528	41,995	—
1930	520,280	114,110	46,448	48,148	7,590	11,924	406,170	117,821	109,791	79,414	37,591	—
1931	445,648	89,525	37,375	38,841	4,016	9,293	356,123	113,949	71,788	67,530	37,327	—
1932	342,489	70,429	29,843	30,039	3,072	7,475	272,060	94,434	39,544	54,845	27,242	—
1933	394,104	69,466	27,670	31,197	3,034	7,565	324,638	110,675	68,911	55,207	26,030	—
1934	414,308	77,898	30,553	33,570	4,287	9,488	336,410	113,349	71,685	60,998	34,894	—
1935	453,331	81,639	33,942	33,922	4,716	9,059	371,692	115,561	83,628	76,583	35,720	—
1936	525,842	90,247	37,507	37,154	5,423	10,163	435,595	132,515	115,250	88,024	44,337	—
1937	583,100	114,413	43,764	52,910	4,102	13,637	468,687	149,740	135,075	91,059	55,295	—
1938	466,900	105,182	33,886	55,476	5,110	10,710	361,718	138,545	72,846	76,216	56,034	—
1939	569,400	112,667	37,854	57,711	4,941	12,161	456,733	150,983	113,309	87,710	62,014	—
1940	607,900	111,255	40,740	49,568	4,118	16,829	496,645	157,027	141,103	97,632	70,217	—
1941	653,600	120,652	54,616	40,605	4,628	20,802	532,948	155,927	163,161	98,728	85,368	—
1942	589,900	99,221	25,974	46,023	4,488	22,736	490,679	74,016	172,606	104,189	92,748	—
1943	580,581	127,284	33,077	63,086	7,120	24,001	453,297	60,009	159,458	106,278	93,689	—
1944	605,928	153,736	39,441	82,613	8,055	23,627	452,192	70,806	164,971	106,194	95,821	—
1945	618,906	172,094	44,526	100,333	6,511	20,724	446,812	90,705	157,900	97,822	87,073	—
1946	617,032	148,877	47,948	76,589	4,163	20,177	468,155	137,609	138,617	91,225	81,668	—
1947	766,817	188,256	57,366	101,996	4,796	24,098	578,561	153,098	163,180	112,668	149,615	—
1948	793,200	162,971	68,078	65,404	4,219	25,270	630,229	174,081	172,491	113,959	169,698	—
1949	740,721	165,358	77,153	65,740	4,839	17,626	575,363	161,431	145,592	102,637	165,703	—
1950	820,584	169,225	96,299	43,640	5,683	23,603	651,359	182,544	169,881	106,906	190,789	1,239
1951	924,128	232,056	101,813	97,603	6,935	25,705	692,073	186,759	178,463	112,029	213,405	1,417
1952	887,722	227,326	108,674	85,072	7,287	26,293	660,396	184,207	154,112	103,972	216,644	1,460
1953	923,548	217,396	120,595	63,780	7,387	26,635	706,151	188,758	188,621	102,562	224,957	1,253
1954	867,640	213,844	123,503	65,244	5,921	19,176	653,796	187,240	145,364	102,719	217,061	1,411
1955	1,016,136	271,103	144,276	95,404	8,681	22,742	745,033	195,718	184,809	112,863	249,693	1,951
1956	1,092,913	326,690	163,349	126,448	10,865	26,027	766,223	205,910	173,991	114,364	269,734	2,225
1957	1,131,401	358,540	176,236	146,890	10,116	25,298	772,862	196,419	182,150	110,824	281,066	2,403
1958	1,004,516	308,851	181,480	101,555	8,004	17,811	695,665	194,050	132,289	105,425	261,069	2,832
1959	1,052,402	325,670	198,608	91,629	14,878	20,555	726,732	205,509	131,220	106,747	282,269	987
1960	1,099,850	339,277	198,466	104,810	12,851	23,151	760,573	209,197	155,109	104,193	291,057	1,017
1961	1,062,155	329,330	188,179	105,959	11,986	23,205	732,825	206,899	136,841	93,929	294,052	1,104
1962	1,129,404	358,599	207,041	110,492	15,649	25,417	770,805	215,461	135,744	102,277	316,062	1,262
1963	1,173,767	385,659	209,370	129,782	18,006	28,502	788,108	213,853	141,741	98,981	331,902	1,630
1964	1,238,094	421,925	224,433	142,874	24,152	30,465	816,168	205,688	151,405	99,579	357,916	1,580
1965	1,272,896	443,727	244,874	142,121	24,961	31,771	829,169	201,508	153,695	102,865	369,615	1,486
1966	1,334,116	471,391	257,173	155,759	26,674	31,785	862,725	208,375	164,037	99,215	389,852	1,247
1967	1,336,606	465,972	248,245	162,443	27,720	27,564	870,634	214,647	153,597	102,320	398,593	1,478
1968	1,395,839	507,950	278,827	166,580	32,109	30,434	887,889	214,251	151,116	90,730	430,174	1,618
1969	1,448,712	521,312	295,648	168,944	24,645	32,075	927,399	216,708	160,844	87,536	460,945	1,366
1970	1,531,697	580,969	312,934	205,698	26,406	35,932	950,727	238,440	157,059	81,475	472,123	1,630
1971	1,510,327	565,986	333,777	172,759	25,969	33,481	944,341	242,916	140,955	81,253	479,218	2,257
1972	1,614,909	629,981	372,418	197,430	25,148	34,985	984,928	242,660	145,013	90,266	506,989	1,883
1973	1,757,269	767,394	461,828	238,807	28,260	38,498	989,875	236,795	156,621	93,223	503,237	4,283
1974	1,742,734	764,089	473,940	238,687	23,343	28,819	978,645	233,358	146,067	88,198	511,022	4,055
1975	1,692,182	748,707	455,117	236,708	21,455	35,426	943,475	231,932	129,331	78,279	503,932	2,852
1976	1,832,060	855,964	539,674	250,633	30,645	35,012	976,096	236,279	132,113	83,731	523,973	2,948
1977	1,904,569	935,257	625,309	240,784	32,828	36,336	969,312	248,083	109,080	83,444	528,705	3,654
1978	2,018,079	946,057	616,141	259,317	27,046	43,554	1,072,022	305,343	142,663	89,507	534,509	3,271
1979	2,069,757	993,445	607,899	311,786	25,097	48,663	1,076,312	304,666	143,564	93,114	534,969	4,001

Notes appear at end of table

TABLE Df742–753   Waterborne cargo tonnage – foreign and domestic, by type of port and traffic: 1924–1996
Continued

		Foreign					Domestic					
			Through seaports		Great Lakes ports			Between ports		Local and intraport		
	Foreign and domestic	Total	Imports	Exports	Imports	Exports	Net total	Coastwise	Lakewise		Internal	Intraterritory
	Df742	Df743	Df744	Df745	Df746	Df747	Df748 [1]	Df749	Df750	Df751	Df752 [2]	Df753 [2]
Year	Thousand short tons	Thousand short tons	Thousand short tons	Thousand short tons	Thousand short tons	Thousand short tons	Thousand short tons	Thousand short tons	Thousand short tons	Thousand short tons	Thousand short tons	Thousand short tons
1980	1,995,300	921,404	502,006	358,806	15,515	45,077	1,073,896	329,609	115,124	94,184	534,979	3,588
1981	1,938,425	887,102	457,467	366,424	19,724	43,486	1,051,327	321,990	115,418	93,250	520,669	3,130
1982	1,773,929	819,731	402,511	366,825	14,110	36,284	954,198	311,058	72,085	75,602	495,453	2,811
1983	1,704,501	751,140	371,773	330,956	16,074	32,337	953,361	309,637	83,447	73,145	487,132	3,160
1984	1,832,614	803,338	409,295	335,269	17,844	40,929	1,029,276	307,652	98,010	81,111	542,503	3,406
1985	1,785,033	774,323	395,577	327,426	17,110	34,210	1,010,710	309,802	91,987	74,263	534,658	3,401
1986	1,870,458	837,224	472,231	319,163	13,842	31,987	1,033,234	308,025	87,353	77,358	560,499	3,959
1987	1,962,760	890,980	493,828	351,226	13,876	32,049	1,071,780	323,518	96,484	81,951	569,827	4,698
1988	2,082,870	976,221	534,043	389,686	15,854	36,638	1,106,649	325,177	109,664	83,689	588,119	5,123
1989	2,135,237	1,037,910	571,733	411,338	17,771	37,068	1,097,327	302,027	109,086	80,208	606,006	5,205
1990	2,159,326	1,041,556	582,412	408,688	17,558	32,898	1,117,770	298,637	110,159	86,378	622,595	4,529
1991	2,087,550	1,013,557	541,067	430,655	14,288	27,548	1,073,993	294,543	103,427	75,635	600,386	4,559
1992	2,127,850	1,037,466	571,287	420,667	15,421	30,091	1,090,384	285,131	107,398	76,817	621,037	4,245
1993	2,123,256	1,060,041	630,700	385,698	18,083	25,560	1,063,215	271,717	109,854	74,390	607,253	4,965
1994	2,208,829	1,115,743	696,469	369,138	23,028	27,108	1,093,086	277,029	114,777	82,870	618,409	5,926
1995	2,233,525	1,147,358	653,760	441,732	18,897	32,968	1,086,167	266,612	116,127	83,104	620,324	6,868
1996	2,276,738	1,183,387	708,090	418,940	24,503	31,855	1,093,351	267,389	114,870	89,011 [3]	622,081 [3]	7,327

[1] Figures for 1924–1945 are approximations; there are some minor duplications in figures for foreign traffic. Domestic commerce for 1924–1946 includes "rivers, canals, and connecting channels," not shown separately.

[2] Beginning in 1959, excludes traffic in Alaska and Hawai'i; such traffic included in other domestic traffic categories.

[3] Excludes fish.

Sources
U.S. Army Corps of Engineers, 1924–1946, *Annual Report of the Chief of Engineers*, part 2; 1947–1996, *Waterborne Commerce of the United States*, part 5, *National Summaries*, Table 1–2 (annual issues).

Documentation
In 1954, part 2 of the Annual Report was superseded by a separate publication titled *Waterborne Commerce of the United States* (published in several regional parts). Part 5 of this report, *National Summaries*, presents separate figures for series Df746–747 for "Canadian" and "overseas."

Data are in short tons of 2,000 pounds. Cargo tonnage refers to the weight of cargo and should not be confused with gross tonnage or net or registered tonnage capacity, which are measures of cubic capacity, not of weight. See the text for Table Df578–593 for a definition of gross tonnage, and the text for Table Df594–605 for a description of net tonnage.

Domestic commerce includes all commercial movements between points in the United States, Puerto Rico, and the U.S. Virgin Islands. Traffic within the Canal Zone is treated as foreign commerce.

Foreign commerce includes all movements between the United States and foreign countries, and between Puerto Rico and the U.S. Virgin Islands (considered a single unit) and foreign countries. Trade between U.S. outlying areas (Guam, Wake, American Samoa, and so forth) and foreign countries is excluded.

Series Df748. Net totals are derived by deducting two types of duplications from unadjusted totals: (1) traffic between seaports and river points, and (2) "other duplications," comprising principally coastwise and lake traffic passing through canals and connecting channels other than the St. Mary's Falls Canal and the Detroit River.

Series Df749. "Coastwise" commerce refers to domestic traffic receiving a carriage over the ocean or the Gulf of Mexico, and to traffic between Great Lakes ports and seacoast ports, when having a carriage over the ocean.

Series Df750. "Lakewise" commerce refers to traffic between U.S. ports on the Great Lakes system.

Series Df751. "Local and intraport" commerce refers to movements of freight within the confines of a port, whether the port has only one or several arms or channels, except car-ferry and general ferry. The term is also applied to marine products, sand, and gravel taken directly from the Great Lakes. It includes figures for harbor traffic of New York, Philadelphia, and San Francisco; local traffic of other seaports, and local traffic of lake ports.

Series Df752. "Internal" commerce covers traffic between ports or landings where the entire movement takes place on inland waterways; movements involving carriage on both inland waterways and waters of the Great Lakes; inland movements that cross short stretches of open waters that link inland systems; marine products, sand, and gravel taken directly from beds of the oceans, the Gulf of Mexico, and important arms thereof; and movements between offshore installations and inland waterways.

Series Df753. "Intraterritory" commerce refers to traffic between ports in Puerto Rico and the U.S. Virgin Islands, which are considered as a single unit.

TABLE Df754–756   Employment and wage rates for able-bodied seamen on U.S. flag merchant vessels: 1929–1996[1]

Contributed by Louis P. Cain

	Employment	Monthly wage rate			Employment	Monthly wage rate	
		East Coast	West Coast			East Coast	West Coast
	Df754 [2]	Df755 [3]	Df756 [3]		Df754 [2]	Df755 [3]	Df756 [3]
Year	Thousand	Dollars	Dollars	Year	Thousand	Dollars	Dollars
1929	63.8 [4]	—	—	1965	39.1 [7]	393	539
1930	62.4 [4]	—	—	1966	51.9	393	558
1931	57.2 [4]	—	—	1967	54.6	423	578
1932	52.6 [4]	—	—	1968	54.2	444	600
1933	54.6 [4]	—	—	1969	47.5	444	600
1934	56.3 [4]	—	—	1970	37.6	470	652
1935	56.2	—	—	1971	30.4	499	704
1936	57.2	—	—	1972	27.7	528	756
1937	59.2	—	—	1973	25.2	555	806
1938	49.8	—	—	1974	24.8	583	856
1939	52.0	—	—	1975	20.5	612	900
1940	49.8	—	—	1976	21.2	688	1,001
1941	51.3	—	—	1977	20.9	737	1,072
1942	47.4	—	—	1978	19.9	804	1,172
1943	75.0 [5]	—	—	1979	19.7	865	1,287
1944	125.3 [5]	—	—	1980	19.6	967	1,414
1945	158.9 [5]	—	—	1981	18.3	1,120	1,535
1946	120.1 [5]	—	—	1982	16.7	1,204	1,686
1947	110.8 [6]	—	—	1983	15.3	1,320	1,862
1948	82.1	—	—	1984	13.7	1,419	2,029
1949	67.2	—	—	1985	13.1	1,419	2,069
1950	56.6	248 [8]	249 [8]	1986	11.5	1,419	2,132
1951	69.5	257	249	1987	10.4	1,419	2,132
1952	70.7	302	302	1988	10.7	1,419	2,175
1953	69.1	314	314	1989	9.9	1,448	2,218
1954	55.8	314	302 [10]	1990	11.1	1,505	2,218
1955	57.5	314	432 [11]	1991	11.7	1,581	2,329
1956	57.2	333	453 [10]	1992	9.2	1,655	2,438
1957	61.1	353	478 [10]	1993	9.3	1,721	2,438
1958	51.5	353	478 [10]	1994	9.1	1,790	2,536
1959	50.2	353	478	1995	7.9	1,918	2,637
1960	49.2	369 [9]	512 [10]	1996	7.5	2,014	2,769
1961	30.9 [7]	384	522 [10]				
1962	47.3	393	522				
1963	48.0	393	522				
1964	48.0	393	522				

[1] Except as indicated, employment data as of June 30. Wage rate data as of June 16 before 1969, January thereafter.

[2] Estimates of personnel employed on U.S. merchant ships, 1,000 gross tons and larger. Excludes vessels on inland waterways, Great Lakes, and those owned by, or operated for, the U.S. Army and Navy, and special types such as cable ships, tugs, and so forth.

[3] Seamen on both coasts receive extra pay for Saturdays and Sundays at sea. Beginning in 1955, the West Coast incorporated this extra pay into base wages but the East Coast did not.

[4] Average monthly employment.

[5] June 20.

[6] December 20.

[7] Decrease owing to seafaring strike.

[8] October 15.

[9] January.

[10] October.

[11] November.

Sources

1929–1965, U.S. Maritime Administration, *Seafaring Wage Rates*, and unpublished data; 1966–1996, U.S. Maritime Administration, *U.S. Merchant Marine Data Sheet* (monthly issues), and unpublished data cited in the *Statistical Abstract of the United States*.

Documentation

See the text for Table Df578–593 for related discussion.

The monthly wage rate represents basic wages, over and above subsistence (board and room), paid to seamen having qualifying experience and employed on U.S. flag merchant vessels.

TABLE Df757   Persons entering the United States by ship: 1933–1995

Contributed by Louis P. Cain

Fiscal year	Persons entering the United States by ship Df757 Thousand	Fiscal year	Persons entering the United States by ship Df757 Thousand	Fiscal year	Persons entering the United States by ship Df757 Thousand	Fiscal year	Persons entering the United States by ship Df757 Thousand
1933	795	1950	762	1965	782	1980	1,375
1934	754	1951	723	1966	767	1981	1,467
1935	812	1952	900	1967	719	1982	2,549
1936	898	1953	865	1968	715	1983	2,455
1937	1,011	1954	845	1969	728	1984	2,478
1938	1,072	1955	843	1970	723	1985	3,093
1939	1,019	1956	842	1971	745	1986	3,166
1940	733	1957	848	1972	806	1987	2,914
1941	443	1958	781	1973	873	1988	4,367
1942	305	1959	762	1974	939	1989	4,678
1943	389	1960	773	1975	841	1990	5,048
1944	676	1961	805	1976	960	1991	4,995
1945	1,286	1962	677	1977	900	1992	5,404
1946	1,660	1963	743	1978	1,226	1993	5,249
1947	548	1964 [1]	847	1979	1,269	1994	5,203
1948	641					1995	4,203
1949	676						

[1] Includes Puerto Rico.

Sources

U.S. Department of the Treasury, *Annual Report of the Secretary of the Treasury on the State of the Finances* (various issues). This report was not published after 1980. Beginning in 1981, the data appear in U.S. Customs Service, *Customs USA*, an annual publication that changed its name to *U.S. Customs Update* in 1990.

Documentation

The data include persons disembarking, as reported on U.S. Customs Service forms. They include persons entering by documented vessels, excluding ferryboats.

Data are for federal fiscal years. The 1976 transition quarter is not shown.

TABLE Df758-821 U.S. flag merchant vessels – number and tonnage, by type of vessel and traffic: 1934–1997[1,2,3]

Contributed by Louis P. Cain

	All vessel types															
	Total		Active												Inactive	
			Total		Foreign trade		Domestic trade									
							Total		Coastwise		Intercoastal and noncontiguous		Special service			
	Number	Tons	Number	Tons	Number	Tons	Number	Tons	Number	Tons	Number	Tons	Number	Tons	Number	Tons
Year	Df758	Df759	Df760	Df761	Df762	Df763	Df764	Df765	Df766	Df767	Df768	Df769	Df770	Df771	Df772	Df773
	Number	Thousand tons	Number	Thousand tons	Number	Thousand tons	Number	Thousand tons	Number	Thousand tons	Number	Thousand tons	Number	Thousand tons	Number	Thousand tons
1934	1,673	12,986	1,097	8,767	438	3,753	657	4,993	440	3,005	217	1,987	2	21	576	4,219
1935	1,637	12,809	1,145	9,194	434	3,748	709	5,425	488	3,479	221	1,946	2	21	492	3,615
1936	1,563	12,323	1,208	9,697	430	8,714	776	5,958	537	3,878	239	2,079	2	25	355	2,626
1937	1,517	12,335	1,231	10,251	426	3,643	805	6,608	563	4,467	242	2,141	—	—	286	2,085
1938	1,422	11,814	1,060	9,019	366	3,301	694	5,718	494	3,946	200	1,772	1	5	862	2,795
1939	1,398	11,699	1,092	9,808	319	2,804	772	6,499	543	4,359	229	2,141	—	—	306	2,391
1940	1,300	11,019	1,119	9,653	425	3,749	693	5,893	500	4,172	193	1,721	1	10	181	1,367
1941	1,168	10,096	1,137	9,919	471	4,052	663	5,836	488	4,261	175	1,575	3	31	31	177
1946[4]	4,852	50,263	2,762	29,127	1,890	20,592	442	4,807	297	3,483	145	1,324	430	3,728	2,090	21,136
1947[5]	3,696	38,882	2,114	23,651	1,603	17,238	511	6,413	381	5,104	130	1,309	—	—	1,582	15,231
1948	3,490	36,774	1,723	19,552	1,246	13,767	477	5,785	327	4,329	150	1,456	—	—	1,767	17,222
1949	3,379	36,228	1,386	16,044	1,004	11,416	382	4,628	262	3,437	120	1,191	—	—	1,993	20,184
1950	3,408	86,526	1,145	13,828	711	8,353	434	5,474	279	3,716	155	1,757	—	—	2,263	22,698
1951	3,386	36,336	1,654	19,284	988	11,425	426	5,333	287	3,924	139	1,408	240	2,523	1,732	17,053
1952	3,350	36,081	1,447	16,976	782	9,052	395	5,190	291	4,033	104	1,158	270	2,734	1,903	19,106
1953	3,349	36,255	1,415	16,738	629	7,390	437	5,725	303	4,275	134	1,450	349	3,623	1,934	19,517
1954	3,333	35,860	1,123	13,645	623	7,299	398	5,324	265	3,854	133	1,470	102	1,022	2,210	22,216
1955	3,235	35,017	1,163	14,232	601	6,992	425	5,880	271	3,999	154	1,881	137	1,360	2,072	20,786
1956	3,150	34,052	1,127	13,988	644	7,538	402	5,639	281	4,269	121	1,370	81	811	2,023	20,065
1957	3,032	32,900	1,199	14,874	721	8,406	399	5,595	262	4,082	137	1,513	79	873	1,833	18,027
1958	3,047	38,316	970	12,358	551	6,208	356	5,369	229	3,811	127	1,558	63	781	2,077	20,958
1959	3,047	33,565	963	12,636	533	5,935	375	5,912	229	4,054	146	1,858	55	789	2,084	20,930
1960	2,934	82,601	951	12,922	558	6,541	372	5,926	237	4,284	135	1,642	21	455	1,983	19,679
1961	2,810	31,525	644	8,837	415	5,066	182	3,107	115	2,325	67	783	47	664	2,166	22,690
1962	2,716	30,954	940	13,473	543	6,616	340	5,951	231	4,640	109	1,311	57	906	1,776	17,481
1963	2,691	30,753	946	13,812	587	7,344	299	5,479	207	4,344	108	1,829	60	989	1,745	16,940
1964	2,598	30,084	940	13,868	584	7,271	295	5,504	184	3,964	94	1,445	61	1,093	1,658	16,219
1965	2,425	28,755	779	11,821	512	6,877	217	3,953	118	2,667	99	1,286	50	993	1,646	16,934
1966	2,292	27,393	1,043	15,388	494	6,576	248	4,825	139	3,202	109	1,623	301	3,987	1,249	12,004
1967	2,209	26,560	1,107	16,273	460	6,037	233	4,654	142	3,333	91	1,323	414	5,582	1,102	10,286
1968	2,101	25,699	1,104	16,416	481	6,332	242	4,934	134	3,105	108	1,829	381	5,150	997	9,284
1969	2,013	25,079	1,013	15,180	447	6,021	199	4,062	105	2,619	94	1,445	367	5,097	1,000	9,898
1970	1,780	23,280	819	14,073	386	5,775	245	5,368	142	3,599	103	1,769	188	2,930	961	9,208
1971	1,478	20,474	690	12,971	321	5,273	236	5,418	130	3,541	106	1,879	133	2,280	788	—
1972	1,233	18,412	632	12,813	262	4,683	201	4,881	112	3,194	89	1,688	169	3,249	601	5,597
1973	1,051	17,297	595	12,847	312	6,618	196	4,725	113	3,026	83	1,699	87	1,504	456	4,450
1974	965	17,334	588	13,619	305	6,909	202	5,169	149	4,236	53	933	81	1,541	377	3,715

All vessel types

	Total		Active												Inactive	
			Total		Foreign trade		Domestic trade						Special service			
							Total		Coastwise		Intercoastal and noncontiguous					
	Number	Tons	Number	Tons	Number	Tons	Number	Tons	Number	Tons	Number	Tons	Number	Tons	Number	Tons
Year	Df758	Df759	Df760	Df761	Df762	Df763	Df764	Df765	Df766	Df767	Df768	Df769	Df770	Df771	Df772	Df773
	Number	Thousand tons	Number	Thousand tons	Number	Thousand tons	Number	Thousand tons	Number	Thousand tons	Number	Thousand tons	Number	Thousand tons	Number	Thousand tons
1975	891	17,608	532	13,105	267	6,204	205	5,687	153	4,653	52	1,034	60	1,214	359	4,503
1976	843	17,989	548	14,088	294	7,770	194	5,136	32	2,996	162	2,140	60	1,182	295	3,901
1977	841	19,468	564	15,542	281	6,817	214	7,442	125	3,931	89	3,511	69	1,283	277	3,926
1978	841	21,253	554	17,649	266	8,484	221	7,721	124	3,539	97	4,182	67	1,444	287	3,604
1979	871	22,997	552	18,948	276	10,109	208	7,629	114	3,473	94	4,156	68	1,210	319	4,049
1980	863	23,979	551	19,099	227	6,619	257	11,259	115	3,278	142	7,981	67	1,221	312	4,880
1981	863	24,477	539	18,561	216	5,141	235	10,951	87	2,884	148	8,067	88	2,469	324	5,916
1982	828	24,108	496	18,423	197	5,141	224	11,308	77	2,376	147	8,932	75	1,974	332	5,685
1983	819	24,737	420	17,553	184	5,700	204	10,335	80	2,617	124	7,718	72	1,518	359	7,184
1984	749	23,965	367	16,459	160	5,432	183	9,606	30	1,318	153	8,288	65	1,421	341	7,506
1985	748	24,439	403	16,695	161	5,448	171	9,568	28	1,136	143	8,432	71	1,679	345	7,744
1986	738	18,146	391	16,554	156	5,475	168	9,474	96	3,857	72	5,617	67	1,605	347	7,945
1987	724	31,467	367	15,823	135	4,702	170	9,581	92	3,726	78	5,855	62	1,540	357	9,291
1988	683	25,677	403	19,182	170	7,356	177	10,339	87	3,422	90	6,917	56	1,487	280	6,495
1989	661	24,457	383	17,720	164	7,251	158	8,967	89	3,632	69	5,335	61	1,502	278	6,739
1990	635	24,267	397	17,590	156	7,222	158	8,624	83	3,134	151	5,490	54	1,483	212	5,888
1991	636	24,266	449	19,038	149	7,068	160	8,804	77	2,752	83	6,052	68	1,934	187	5,228
1992	619	23,254	411	18,286	134	7,080	161	8,741	96	3,559	65	5,182	67	1,659	208	4,968
1993	603	22,461	365	16,765	158	7,367	143	7,695	77	2,983	66	4,982	50	1,274	238	5,696
1994	564	21,126	359	16,358	162	7,232	134	7,727	62	2,235	72	5,492	49	1,239	205	4,768
1995	543	19,968	343	15,279	154	6,605	129	7,318	66	2,476	63	4,842	48	1,228	200	4,689
1996	509	18,585	303	13,543	123	5,297	127	7,017	67	2,429	60	4,588	42	1,111	206	5,042
1997	495	17,511	291	13,076	114	4,926	130	7,058	70	2,554	60	4,504	38	992	204	4,435

Notes appear at end of table

(continued)

TABLE Df758–821   U.S. flag merchant vessels – number and tonnage, by type of vessel and traffic: 1934–1997   Continued

	Total		Cargo vessels												Inactive	
			Active													
			Total		Foreign trade		Domestic trade						Special service			
							Total		Coastwise		Intercoastal and noncontiguous					
	Number	Tons	Number	Tons	Number	Tons	Number	Tons	Number	Tons	Number	Tons	Number	Tons	Number	Tons
	Df774	Df775	Df776	Df777	Df778	Df779	Df780	Df781	Df782	Df783	Df784	Df785	Df786	Df787	Df788	Df789
Year	Number	Thousand tons	Number	Thousand tons	Number	Thousand tons	Number	Thousand tons	Number	Thousand tons	Number	Thousand tons	Number	Thousand tons	Number	Thousand tons
1934	1,079	7,946	596	4,382	258	2,168	336	2,194	200	1,025	136	1,169	2	21	483	3,564
1935	1,065	7,847	645	4,741	253	2,096	390	2,624	215	1,085	175	1,539	2	21	420	3,106
1936	1,007	7,405	694	5,072	250	2,087	442	2,961	243	1,227	199	1,734	2	25	313	2,333
1937	975	7,231	721	5,344	275	2,286	446	3,058	241	1,253	205	1,806	—	—	254	1,887
1938	882	6,557	592	4,436	213	1,808	379	2,629	205	1,073	174	1,556	—	—	290	2,121
1939	851	6,364	609	4,545	193	1,619	415	2,921	229	1,197	186	1,724	1	5	242	1,819
1940	790	6,020	642	4,892	291	2,443	350	2,438	188	988	162	1,450	1	10	148	1,129
1941	716	5,472	693	5,324	358	2,966	383	2,340	179	937	154	1,402	2	18	23	148
1946 4	3,829	36,675	2,220	21,408	1,607	16,200	226	1,910	101	730	125	1,180	387	3,298	1,609	15,267
1947 5	2,977	29,206	1,628	16,561	1,434	14,779	194	1,782	82	659	112	1,123	—	—	1,349	12,645
1948	2,887	28,674	1,221	12,424	1,023	10,592	198	1,832	68	569	130	1,263	—	—	1,666	16,250
1949	2,799	28,442	969	10,063	813	8,626	156	1,437	53	416	103	1,021	—	—	1,830	18,379
1950	2,846	28,927	682	7,075	505	5,367	177	1,708	66	559	111	1,149	—	—	2,164	21,851
1951	2,650	27,376	1,144	12,015	743	7,892	176	1,721	55	484	121	1,236	225	2,401	1,506	15,361
1952	2,629	27,210	967	10,047	582	6,177	135	1,302	58	517	77	786	250	2,567	1,662	17,164
1953	2,630	27,228	964	10,060	461	4,890	167	1,638	59	517	108	1,121	336	3,532	1,666	17,168
1954	2,636	26,435	730	6,876	489	5,226	154	1,581	44	396	110	1,185	87	69	1,906	19,559
1955	2,560	26,539	772	8,182	492	5,383	160	1,650	43	385	117	1,265	120	1,149	1,788	18,358
1956	2,511	26,007	738	7,864	524	5,688	149	1,569	42	411	107	1,158	65	607	1,773	18,140
1957	2,450	25,412	822	8,779	611	6,649	161	1,675	41	398	120	1,277	50	455	1,628	16,634
1958	2,425	25,125	657	7,051	487	5,348	133	1,366	37	345	96	1,021	37	337	1,768	18,076
1959	2,347	24,333	646	6,986	473	5,189	142	1,512	35	336	107	1,176	31	285	1,701	17,348
1960	2,204	22,813	633	6,907	479	5,265	148	1,589	35	373	113	1,215	6	53	1,571	15,906
1961	2,086	21,575	456	5,025	365	4,135	64	642	17	173	47	469	27	248	1,630	16,549
1962	2,018	21,024	628	7,083	482	5,554	115	1,233	32	362	83	872	31	296	1,390	13,941
1963	2,013	21,047	649	7,498	512	5,979	103	1,157	26	290	77	867	34	362	1,364	13,549
1964	1,959	20,612	642	7,493	509	5,971	100	1,137	19	220	81	918	33	385	1,317	13,121
1965	1,840	19,561	561	6,679	440	5,249	92	1,056	13	142	79	914	29	375	1,279	12,883
1966	1,739	18,565	760	8,913	420	5,093	83	1,050	11	160	72	890	257	2,770	979	9,652
1967	1,670	17,843	818	9,547	400	4,963	66	810	9	120	57	691	352	3,774	852	8,296
1968	1,581	16,993	811	9,569	421	5,180	65	797	9	123	56	674	325	3,592	770	7,425
1969	1,521	16,462	780	9,412	398	5,100	69	823	8	111	61	713	313	3,489	741	7,050
1970	1,302	14,298	557	7,173	344	4,605	68	837	10	116	58	721	145	1,731	745	7,125
1971	1,014	11,515	440	6,029	279	3,955	65	829	7	88	58	742	96	1,245	—	—
1972	792	9,366	393	5,631	224	3,452	57	751	6	87	51	665	112	1,428	399	3,736
1973	658	8,320	357	5,335	237	3,749	59	796	8	113	51	683	61	790	301	2,985
1974	594	7,981	345	5,553	241	4,082	53	800	20	341	33	459	51	671	249	2,428

	Total		Cargo vessels												Inactive	
			Active													
			Total		Foreign trade		Domestic trade						Special service			
							Total		Coastwise		Intercoastal and noncontiguous					
	Number	Tons	Number	Tons	Number	Tons	Number	Tons	Number	Tons	Number	Tons	Number	Tons	Number	Tons
Year	Df774	Df775	Df776	Df777	Df778	Df779	Df780	Df781	Df782	Df783	Df784	Df785	Df786	Df787	Df788	Df789
	Number	Thousand tons	Number	Thousand tons	Number	Thousand tons	Number	Thousand tons	Number	Thousand tons	Number	Thousand tons	Number	Thousand tons	Number	Thousand tons
1975	548	7,762	305	5,142	223	3,858	48	825	17	354	31	471	34	459	243	2,620
1976	521	7,519	316	5,357	230	4,140	50	731	10	147	40	584	36	486	205	2,162
1977	504	7,446	314	5,394	235	4,292	43	640	8	137	35	503	36	462	190	2,052
1978	552	7,807	293	5,044	204	3,829	46	685	6	111	40	574	43	530	259	2,763
1979	566	7,844	289	5,048	204	3,886	40	597	0	120	40	477	45	565	277	2,796
1980	553	7,872	285	5,099	195	3,826	46	713	12	200	34	513	44	560	268	2,773
1981	550	7,919	273	4,990	184	3,530	40	667	0	216	40	451	49	793	277	2,929
1982	524	7,597	250	4,597	171	3,426	42	651	0	91	42	560	37	520	274	3,000
1983	517	7,991	186	4,614	141	3,281	40	660	8	161	32	499	45	673	291	3,377
1984	477	7,876	160	4,508	122	3,108	41	813	5	148	29	665	38	587	276	3,368
1985	485	8,792	210	5,214	129	3,623	36	659	4	108	32	551	45	932	275	3,578
1986	484	9,106	201	5,103	123	3,468	37	775	8	226	29	549	41	860	283	4,003
1987	470	9,040	174	4,205	97	2,528	40	881	11	340	29	541	37	796	296	4,835
1988	432	8,887	201	5,479	128	3,861	42	875	7	220	35	655	31	743	231	3,408
1989	422	8,726	193	5,332	125	3,883	32	697	7	203	25	494	36	752	229	3,396
1990	402	8,618	237	6,227	117	3,709	37	774	7	156	30	618	30	749	165	2,386
1991	403	8,625	259	6,587	111	3,651	38	826	7	184	31	642	41	952	144	2,038
1992	393	8,261	229	6,021	97	3,348	40	894	14	384	26	510	44	990	164	2,240
1993	383	8,299	189	5,277	112	3,660	30	346	6	135	24	481	34	859	194	3,022
1994	354	8,078	189	5,332	115	3,791	28	580	3	60	25	520	33	818	165	2,746
1995	343	8,023	187	5,382	109	2,683	34	776	8	246	26	530	33	812	156	2,641
1996	328	7,557	166	4,838	89	3,200	35	731	8	178	27	553	32	806	162	2,719
1997	322	7,133	154	4,375	83	2,810	34	757	8	211	26	546	29	725	168	2,758

(continued)

Notes appear at end of table

TABLE Df758–821 U.S. flag merchant vessels – number and tonnage, by type of vessel and traffic: 1934–1997 Continued

Combination vessels

	Total		Active												Inactive	
			Total		Foreign trade		Domestic trade						Special service			
							Total		Coastwise		Intercoastal and noncontiguous					
	Number	Tons	Number	Tons	Number	Tons	Number	Tons	Number	Tons	Number	Tons	Number	Tons	Number	Tons
Year	Df790	Df791	Df792	Df793	Df794	Df795	Df796	Df797	Df798	Df799	Df800	Df801	Df802	Df803	Df804	Df805
	Number	Thousand tons	Number	Thousand tons	Number	Thousand tons	Number	Thousand tons	Number	Thousand tons	Number	Thousand tons	Number	Thousand tons	Number	Thousand tons
1934	233	1,389	184	1,123	111	823	73	300	50	143	23	157	—	—	49	266
1935	217	1,347	176	1,099	108	802	68	296	47	149	21	147	—	—	41	248
1936	201	1,281	171	1,083	104	770	67	313	46	170	21	143	—	—	30	198
1937	185	1,204	159	1,051	99	753	60	298	40	147	20	151	—	—	26	153
1938	167	1,108	125	764	76	562	49	202	38	145	11	57	—	—	42	344
1939	163	1,079	131	856	78	621	53	235	37	139	16	96	—	—	82	224
1940	140	873	112	696	66	514	46	182	36	129	10	53	—	—	28	176
1941	94	541	88	526	43	348	44	165	34	118	10	47	1	13	6	16
1946 [4]	117	800	56	412	15	127	10	38	0	0	10	38	31	247	61	388
1947 [5]	95	742	38	284	32	259	6	25	0	0	6	25	—	—	57	458
1948	77	601	48	385	41	357	7	28	0	0	7	28	—	—	29	216
1949	79	609	47	388	43	375	4	13	0	0	4	13	—	—	32	221
1950	83	639	51	417	45	389	6	28	0	0	6	28	—	—	32	222
1951	266	2,067	63	537	46	404	5	24	0	0	5	24	12	109	203	1,530
1952	260	2,044	62	552	44	393	1	4	0	0	1	4	17	155	198	1,491
1953	257	2,039	55	479	40	378	5	23	0	0	5	23	10	78	202	1,560
1954	252	1,695	54	466	39	361	5	23	0	0	5	23	10	82	198	1,230
1955	249	1,687	50	453	39	361	1	10	0	0	1	10	10	82	199	1,234
1956	247	1,683	48	443	38	359	1	10	0	0	1	10	9	74	199	1,240
1957	230	1,594	50	467	38	363	3	30	0	0	3	30	9	74	180	1,127
1958	238	1,638	44	413	36	344	3	30	0	0	3	30	5	39	194	1,225
1959	288	1,950	39	343	36	323	2	14	0	0	2	14	1	6	249	1,607
1960	305	2,038	36	320	34	305	2	14	0	0	2	14	0	0	269	1,717
1961	300	2,012	20	172	17	152	0	0	0	0	0	0	3	20	280	1,840
1962	289	1,925	34	294	29	260	2	14	0	0	2	14	3	20	255	1,630
1963	290	1,924	33	288	30	271	1	4	0	0	1	4	2	13	257	1,636
1964	271	1,787	35	307	32	290	1	4	0	0	1	4	2	13	236	1,480
1965	236	1,558	19	158	18	153	1	4	0	0	1	4	0	0	217	1,402
1966	225	1,476	29	250	26	233	1	4	0	0	1	4	2	13	196	1,225
1967	222	1,454	27	231	24	214	1	4	0	0	1	4	2	13	195	1,223
1968	205	1,343	26	227	22	200	1	4	0	0	1	4	3	23	179	1,116
1969	187	1,214	22	198	20	187	2	11	0	0	2	11	0	0	165	1,015
1970	177	1,147	13	117	10	94	2	13	0	0	2	13	1	10	164	1,031
1971	171	1,111	11	99	9	86	2	13	0	0	2	13	0	0	—	—
1972	158	999	7	61	5	46	1	6	0	0	1	6	1	9	151	937
1973	120	757	6	50	4	37	2	13	0	0	2	13	0	0	114	707
1974	96	614	5	41	4	34	1	7	0	0	1	7	0	0	91	573

Combination vessels

	Total		Active												Inactive	
			Total		Foreign trade		Domestic trade						Special service			
							Total		Coastwise		Intercoastal and noncontiguous					
	Number	Tons	Number	Tons	Number	Tons	Number	Tons	Number	Tons	Number	Tons	Number	Tons	Number	Tons
	Df790	Df791	Df792	Df793	Df794	Df795	Df796	Df797	Df798	Df799	Df800	Df801	Df802	Df803	Df804	Df805
Year	Number	Thousand tons	Number	Thousand tons	Number	Thousand tons	Number	Thousand tons	Number	Thousand tons	Number	Thousand tons	Number	Thousand tons	Number	Thousand tons
1975	64	413	6	50	5	43	1	7	0	0	1	7	0	0	58	363
1976	59	384	6	50	5	44	1	6	0	0	1	6	0	0	53	334
1977	62	404	11	88	5	44	1	6	0	0	3	6	5	38	51	316
1978	—	—	—	—	—	—	—	—	—	—	—	—	—	—	—	—
1979	—	—	—	—	—	—	—	—	—	—	—	—	—	—	—	—
1980	—	—	—	—	—	—	—	—	—	—	—	—	—	—	—	—
1981	—	—	—	—	—	—	—	—	—	—	—	—	—	—	—	—
1982	—	—	—	—	—	—	—	—	—	—	—	—	—	—	—	—
1983	—	—	—	—	—	—	—	—	—	—	—	—	—	—	—	—
1984	—	—	—	—	—	—	—	—	—	—	—	—	—	—	—	—
1985	—	—	—	—	—	—	—	—	—	—	—	—	—	—	—	—
1986	—	—	—	—	—	—	—	—	—	—	—	—	—	—	—	—
1987	—	—	—	—	—	—	—	—	—	—	—	—	—	—	—	—
1988	—	—	—	—	—	—	—	—	—	—	—	—	—	—	—	—
1989	—	—	—	—	—	—	—	—	—	—	—	—	—	—	—	—
1990	—	—	—	—	—	—	—	—	—	—	—	—	—	—	—	—
1991	—	—	—	—	—	—	—	—	—	—	—	—	—	—	—	—
1992	—	—	—	—	—	—	—	—	—	—	—	—	—	—	—	—
1993	—	—	—	—	—	—	—	—	—	—	—	—	—	—	—	—
1994	—	—	—	—	—	—	—	—	—	—	—	—	—	—	—	—
1995	—	—	—	—	—	—	—	—	—	—	—	—	—	—	—	—
1996	—	—	—	—	—	—	—	—	—	—	—	—	—	—	—	—
1997	—	—	—	—	—	—	—	—	—	—	—	—	—	—	—	—

Notes appear at end of table

(continued)

TABLE Df758–821   U.S. flag merchant vessels – number and tonnage, by type of vessel and traffic: 1934–1997   Continued

Tankers

Year	Total		Active: Total		Active: Foreign trade		Active: Domestic trade — Total		Active: Domestic trade — Coastwise		Active: Domestic trade — Intercoastal and noncontiguous		Active: Special service		Inactive	
	Df806	Df807	Df808	Df809	Df810	Df811	Df812	Df813	Df814	Df815	Df816	Df817	Df818	Df819	Df820	Df821
	Number	Thousand tons	Number	Thousand tons	Number	Thousand tons	Number	Thousand tons	Number	Thousand tons	Number	Thousand tons	Number	Thousand tons	Number	Thousand tons
1934	361	3,652	317	3,262	69	763	248	2,499	190	1,838	58	661	—	—	44	390
1935	355	3,615	324	3,354	73	850	251	2,504	226	2,245	25	260	—	—	31	261
1936	355	3,637	343	3,541	76	857	267	2,684	248	2,482	19	202	—	—	12	95
1937	357	3,900	351	3,856	52	604	299	3,252	282	3,067	17	184	—	—	6	44
1938	873	4,149	343	3,819	77	931	266	2,888	251	2,728	15	159	—	—	30	330
1939	384	4,256	352	3,908	48	565	304	3,343	277	3,022	27	320	—	—	32	348
1940	370	4,126	365	4,065	68	791	297	3,273	276	3,054	21	218	—	—	5	62
1941	358	4,083	356	4,070	70	739	286	3,331	275	3,205	11	125	—	—	2	13
1946 [4]	906	12,785	486	7,305	268	4,264	206	2,858	196	2,753	10	106	12	183	420	5,480
1947 [5]	624	8,934	448	6,806	137	2,200	311	4,606	299	4,445	12	161	—	—	176	2,128
1948	526	7,499	454	6,743	182	2,818	272	3,925	259	3,760	13	165	—	—	72	756
1949	501	7,177	370	5,593	148	2,415	222	3,178	209	3,021	13	157	—	—	181	1,584
1950	479	6,959	412	6,335	161	2,597	251	3,737	213	3,157	38	580	—	—	67	624
1951	470	6,893	447	6,731	199	3,129	245	3,587	232	3,440	13	146	3	13	23	162
1952	461	6,827	418	6,378	156	2,481	259	3,884	233	3,516	26	368	3	13	43	451
1953	462	6,988	396	6,199	128	2,122	265	4,064	244	3,758	21	306	3	13	66	790
1954	445	7,730	339	6,303	95	1,713	239	3,719	221	3,458	18	261	5	871	106	1,427
1955	426	6,790	341	5,597	70	1,248	264	4,220	228	3,614	36	606	7	129	85	1,193
1956	392	6,363	341	5,680	82	1,489	252	4,061	239	3,858	13	202	7	130	51	685
1957	352	5,894	327	5,628	72	1,398	235	3,891	221	3,684	14	207	20	844	25	266
1958	384	6,553	269	4,895	28	516	220	3,973	192	3,466	28	507	21	406	115	1,658
1959	412	7,283	278	5,306	24	422	231	4,386	194	3,718	37	668	23	498	134	1,977
1960	425	7,750	282	5,695	45	972	222	4,323	202	3,910	20	413	15	402	143	2,055
1961	424	7,941	168	3,641	33	781	118	2,465	98	2,152	20	313	17	395	256	4,301
1962	409	8,006	278	6,096	32	803	223	4,703	199	4,278	24	425	23	590	131	1,911
1963	388	7,784	264	6,027	45	1,095	195	4,318	181	4,059	14	259	24	614	124	1,756
1964	368	7,685	263	6,067	43	1,010	194	4,362	165	3,744	29	618	26	695	105	1,618
1965	349	7,636	199	4,985	54	1,475	124	2,892	105	2,525	19	368	21	618	150	2,651
1966	328	7,352	254	6,225	48	1,250	164	3,771	128	3,042	36	729	42	1,204	74	1,127
1967	317	7,263	262	6,495	36	860	166	3,840	133	3,213	33	628	60	1,795	55	767
1968	315	7,363	267	6,620	38	952	176	4,133	125	2,982	51	1,151	53	1,535	48	743
1969	305	7,403	211	5,570	29	734	128	3,228	97	2,508	31	721	54	1,608	94	1,833
1970	301	7,835	249	6,783	32	1,076	175	4,518	132	3,483	43	1,035	42	1,189	52	1,052
1971	293	7,848	239	6,843	33	1,232	169	4,576	123	3,453	46	1,124	37	1,035	—	—
1972	283	8,047	232	7,121	33	1,185	143	4,124	106	3,107	37	1,017	56	1,812	51	944
1973	273	8,220	232	7,462	71	2,832	135	3,916	105	2,913	30	1,003	26	714	41	728
1974	275	8,739	238	8,025	60	2,793	148	4,362	129	3,895	19	467	30	870	37	714

Tankers

Year	Total		Active												Inactive	
			Total		Foreign trade		Domestic trade						Special service			
							Total		Coastwise		Intercoastal and noncontiguous					
	Number	Tons	Number	Tons	Number	Tons	Number	Tons	Number	Tons	Number	Tons	Number	Tons	Number	Tons
	Df806	Df807	Df808	Df809	Df810	Df811	Df812	Df813	Df814	Df815	Df816	Df817	Df818	Df819	Df820	Df821
	Number	Thousand tons	Number	Thousand tons	Number	Thousand tons	Number	Thousand tons	Number	Thousand tons	Number	Thousand tons	Number	Thousand tons	Number	Thousand tons
1975	279	9,433	221	7,913	39	2,303	156	4,855	136	4,299	20	556	26	755	58	1,520
1976	263	10,086	226	8,681	59	3,586	143	4,399	22	2,849	121	1,550	24	696	37	1,405
1977	275	11,618	239	10,060	41	2,481	170	6,796	117	3,794	51	3,002	28	783	36	1,558
1978	289	13,446	261	12,605	62	4,655	175	7,036	118	3,428	57	3,608	24	914	28	841
1979	305	15,153	263	13,900	72	6,223	168	7,032	114	3,353	54	3,679	23	645	42	1,253
1980	310	16,107	266	14,000	32	2,793	211	10,546	103	3,078	108	7,468	23	661	44	2,107
1981	313	16,558	266	13,571	32	1,611	195	10,284	87	2,668	108	7,616	39	1,676	47	2,987
1982	304	16,511	246	13,826	26	1,715	182	10,657	77	2,285	105	8,372	38	1,454	58	2,685
1983	302	16,746	234	12,939	43	2,419	164	9,675	72	2,456	92	7,219	27	845	68	3,807
1984	272	16,089	207	11,951	38	2,324	142	8,793	25	1,170	117	7,623	27	834	65	4,138
1985	263	15,647	193	11,481	32	1,825	135	8,909	24	1,028	111	7,881	26	747	70	4,166
1986	254	9,040	190	11,451	33	2,007	131	8,699	88	3,631	43	5,068	26	745	64	3,942
1987	254	16,074	193	11,618	38	2,174	130	8,700	81	3,386	49	5,314	25	744	61	4,456
1988	251	16,790	202	13,703	42	3,495	135	9,464	80	3,202	55	6,262	25	744	49	3,087
1989	239	15,731	190	12,388	39	3,368	126	8,270	82	3,429	44	4,841	25	750	49	3,343
1990	233	15,649	160	11,363	39	3,513	121	7,850	76	2,978	121	4,872	24	734	47	3,502
1991	233	15,641	190	12,451	38	3,417	122	7,978	70	2,568	52	5,410	27	982	43	3,190
1992	226	14,993	182	12,265	37	3,732	121	7,847	82	3,175	39	4,672	23	669	44	2,728
1993	220	14,162	176	11,488	46	3,707	113	7,349	71	2,848	42	4,501	16	415	44	2,674
1994	210	13,048	170	11,026	47	3,441	106	7,147	59	2,175	47	4,972	16	421	40	2,022
1995	200	11,945	156	9,897	45	3,922	95	6,542	58	2,230	37	4,312	15	416	44	2,048
1996	181	11,028	137	8,705	34	2,097	92	6,286	59	2,251	33	4,035	10	305	44	2,323
1997	173	10,378	137	8,701	31	2,116	96	6,301	62	2,343	34	3,958	9	267	36	1,677

1 Beginning in 1978, the cargo and combination categories are combined in the cargo vessel series.

2 Prior to 1986, intercoastal traffic is categorized as coastwise; thereafter, such traffic is categorized as noncontiguous.

3 Except as indicated, data as of June 30 through 1979; as of September 30, 1980–1990 and 1992; as of January, 1991, 1993, and thereafter.

4 Data as of September 30.

5 Data as of December 31.

Sources

U.S. Maritime Administration, *Employment Report of United States Flag Merchant Fleet Oceangoing Vessels 1,000 Gross Tons and Over* (annual issues). See also *U.S. Merchant Marine Data Sheet* (monthly issues).

Documentation

All tonnage data are for dead-weight tonnage. The data cover oceangoing vessels of 1,000 gross tons and larger engaged in foreign and domestic trade, and inactive vessels. They exclude special types such as cable ships, tugs, and fishing trawlers; vessels operating in the Great Lakes and inland waterways; and those owned by the U.S. Army and Navy. They include as cargo vessels the new category of integrated tug/barges, but generally exclude tugs and barges. See the text for Table Df578–593 for a definition of gross tonnage and related discussion.

Series Df770–771, Df786–787, Df802–803, and Df818–819. As of 1955, the special service category meant U.S. Agency Operations, with subcategories merchant and military. Beginning in 1990, this category meant Military Sea Lift Command or M.S.C. Charter. Beginning with 1990, the special service category does not include government-owned vessels. More information is available in the annual *Statistical Abstract of the United States.*

TABLE Df822–824   Gross tonnage of documented merchant vessels, by type of service: 1934–1970[1, 2]

Contributed by Louis P. Cain

Year	Freight (dry cargo) Df822 Thousand gross tons	Tanker Df823 Thousand gross tons	All other Df824 Thousand gross tons
1934	8,887	2,674	3,301
1935	8,748	2,668	3,238
1936	8,702	2,686	3,109
1937	8,671	2,881	3,123
1938	8,702	2,989	2,960
1939	8,615	3,089	2,929
1940	8,267	3,028	2,723
1941	8,115	3,053	2,553
1942	8,226	3,261	2,373
1943	11,365	3,128	2,268
1944	18,878	4,802	2,115
1945	23,931	6,835	2,047
1946	28,087	8,836	2,077
1947	27,407	8,196	2,230
1948	24,047	6,856	2,264
1949	23,766	6,001	2,414
1950	23,209	5,554	2,452
1951	22,598	5,354	2,389
1952	22,556	5,451	2,409
1953	22,605	5,478	2,463
1954	22,818	5,520	2,427
1955	22,298	5,279	2,381
1956	22,280	4,945	2,386
1957	22,024	4,934	2,464
1958	21,420	4,632	2,534
1959	21,342	4,908	2,645
1960	20,637	5,261	2,683
1961	18,320	5,404	2,679
1962	17,236	5,535	2,685
1963	17,393	5,599	2,699
1964	17,731	5,645	2,784
1965	18,045	5,673	2,798
1966	—	—	—
1967	—	—	—
1968	18,823	5,976	3,134
1969	19,183	6,139	3,134
1970	18,896	6,412	3,305

[1] Includes Puerto Rico and Guam.

[2] Data as of June 30 (1934–1940) and January 1 thereafter.

Sources

U.S. Bureau of Marine Inspection and Navigation, *Merchant Marine Statistics, 1936* and *1965*, and U.S. Bureau of Customs, unpublished data.

Documentation

The data are for ships of five tons or more. See the text for Table Df578–593 for a definition of gross tonnage and related discussion.

Series Df824. Includes cable, cod, dredging, elevator, ferry, fireboat, fishing, ice breaker, lightering, oil exploitation, oystering, passenger, pile driving, pilot boat, police boat, patrol boat, refrigerator, towing, waterboat, whaling, welding, wrecking, and miscellaneous. The source presents details for each of these.

TABLE Df825–832   Vessel repairs and conversions in private shipyards – number and value, by vessel type: 1943–1982

Contributed by Louis P. Cain

Year	All vessels		Vessels less than 1,000 gross tons		Vessels more than 1,000 gross tons		Repair and conversion work in private yards	
	Number	Yards reporting	Number	Yards reporting	Number	Yards reporting	Commercial ships	Naval ships
	Df825	Df826	Df827	Df828	Df829	Df830	Df831	Df832
	Number	Number	Number	Number	Number	Number	Million dollars	Million dollars
1943	22,957	—	—	—	22,957	—	—	—
1944	22,014	—	—	—	22,014	—	—	—
1945	23,558	—	—	—	23,558	—	—	—
1946	38,091	126	19,462	107	18,629	87	—	—
1947	30,888	102	12,866	84	18,022	67	—	—
1948	30,937	105	14,651	97	16,286	70	—	—
1949	27,441	114	15,135	103	12,306	69	—	—
1950	33,287	118	17,993	111	15,294	80	—	—
1951	38,513	138	20,307	123	18,106	59	—	—
1952	42,774	131	20,878	113	21,896	82	—	—
1953	44,663	163	27,006	142	17,657	106	—	—
1954	39,870	154	24,458	136	15,412	99	—	—
1955	35,413	144	21,122	130	14,291	89	—	—
1956	45,555	165	29,401	144	16,154	93	359	143
1957	40,827	152	26,106	139	14,721	82	461	125
1958	42,809	154	28,331	134	14,478	88	327	124
1959	37,501	149	24,837	130	12,664	87	301	119
1960	37,774	159	24,991	132	12,783	93	274	122
1961	36,816	122	26,027	106	10,789	73	296	165
1962	42,686	151	29,912	137	12,774	95	279	171
1963	39,990	139	27,804	129	12,186	102	277	222
1964	37,500	146	26,777	132	10,723	93	330	205
1965	35,600	136	22,900	117	12,700	93	383	335
1966	33,100	135	19,600	110	13,500	75	447	413
1967	37,400	130	24,500	112	12,900	85	407	423
1968	37,200	128	24,300	114	12,900	81	458	363
1969	35,980	126	22,100	116	13,880	78	532	384
1970	39,200	122	26,800	110	12,400	75	431	359
1971	36,300	—	25,800	—	10,500	—	450	325
1972	36,000	—	27,600	—	8,400	—	484	387
1973	34,800	—	26,000	—	8,800	—	523	393
1974	—	—	—	—	8,500	—	713	533
1975	—	—	—	—	7,900	—	688	554
1976	—	—	—	—	8,000	—	715	644
1977	—	—	—	—	8,200	—	789	718
1978	—	—	—	—	8,200	—	809	912
1979	—	—	—	—	—	—	998	969
1980	—	—	—	—	—	—	1,335	1,134
1981	—	—	—	—	—	—	1,526 [1]	1,296 [1]
1982	—	—	—	—	—	—	1,498 [1]	1,321 [1]

[1] Estimate.

Source

Shipbuilders Council of America, Washington, D.C., *Annual Report* (various issues).

Documentation

See the text for Table Df578–593 for a definition of gross tonnage and related discussion.

Series Df825 and Df830. The series on the number of vessels add to the total; the series on yards reporting do not.

Series Df831–832. Data before 1956 are available, but the numbers vary. Interested readers may consult the source volumes. Military Sealift Command ships are considered to be commercial ships.

TABLE Df833–854 Shipbuilding in private shipyards – number and tonnage of commercial and naval vessels: 1949–1993[1]

Contributed by Louis P. Cain

	Number										
	Commercial vessels						Naval vessels				
	Under construction, Jan 1	Under construction, Dec 1	Contracted for during year	Canceled	Launched	Delivered	Under construction, Jan 1	Under construction, Dec 1	Contracted for during year	Launched	Delivered
	Df833	Df834	Df835	Df836	Df837	Df838	Df839	Df840	Df841	Df842	Df843
Year	Number	Number	Number	Number	Number	Number	Number	Number	Number	Number	Number
1949	71	40	5	—	39	34	21	11	—	—	7
1950	39	29	16	—	26	26	11	11	—	—	—
1951	29	96	77	—	10	10	11	32	22	7	1
1952	96	92	27	—	37	31	31	45	18	8	6
1953	92	48	4	—	41	45	45	31	2	16	16
1954	48	15	7	—	31	38	31	44	26	14	13
1955	15	25	18	—	3	8	44	43	13	13	14
1956	25	84	68	—	12	9	42	55	22	17	9
1957	84	93	35	—	26	23	55	46	14	15	23
1958	93	75	22	—	32	31	46	55	17	15	8
1959	75	60	19	—	28	32	55	52	13	15	16
1960	60	58	23	—	31	25	52	59	19	16	12
1961	57	66	34	—	20	25	59	67	24	13	16
1962	66	54	15	—	37	27	67	71	19	18	15
1963	54	45	25	—	18	34	71	83	29	23	17
1964	45	47	18	—	20	16	83	101	39	22	21
1965	47	45	16	—	17	18	101	106	23	15	18
1966	45	48	16	—	11	13	106	147	54	25	13
1967	48	64	29	—	15	13	147	134	8	15	21
1968	64	63	23	—	27	24	134	133	15	26	16
1969	63	49	8	—	13	22	133	108	6	28	31
1970	49	49	13	0	11	13	108	82	6	23	32
1971	49	59	24	—	—	14	82	64	15	—	33
1972	59	88	48	—	—	19	64	57	14	—	21
1973	88	97	43	—	—	34	57	56	7	—	8
1974	97	96	25	2	—	24	56	63	16	—	9
1975	96	79	14	12	—	19	63	76	16	—	3
1976	79	72	16	1	—	22	76	88	20	—	8
1977	72	60	13	0	—	25	88	91	15	—	12
1978	60	70	30	1	—	19	91	102	25	—	14
1979	70	69	21	1	—	21	102	99	13	—	16
1980	69	49	7	4	—	23	99	91	11	—	19
1981	49	35	9	1	—	22	91	93	28	—	26
1982	35	21	3	0	—	17	93	105	30	—	18
1983	21	10	4	0	—	15	105	111	27	—	21
1984	10	10	5	0	—	5	111	100	11	—	22
1985	10	7	0	0	—	3	100	85	11	—	26
1986	7	6	0	0	—	1	85	79	16	—	20
1987	6	0	0	2	—	4	79	83	20	—	16
1988	0	0	0	0	—	0	83	105	32	—	10
1989	0	0	0	0	—	0	105	98	16	—	23
1990	0	3	3	0	—	0	98	91	8	—	15
1991	3	3	0	0	—	0	91	90	13	—	14
1992	3	1	1	0	—	3	90	82	10	—	18
1993	1	1	0	0	—	0	82	73	12	—	19

Notes appear at end of table

TABLE Df833–854   Shipbuilding in private shipyards – number and tonnage of commercial and naval vessels: 1949–1993   *Continued*

	Tonnage										
	Commercial vessels						Naval vessels				
Year	Under construction, Jan 1	Under construction, Dec 1	Contracted for during year	Canceled	Launched	Delivered	Under construction, Jan 1	Under construction, Dec 1	Contracted for during year	Launched	Delivered
	Df844	Df845	Df846	Df847	Df848	Df849	Df850	Df851	Df852	Df853	Df854
	Thousand tons	Thousand tons	Thousand tons	Thousand tons	Thousand tons	Thousand tons	Thousand tons	Thousand tons	Thousand tons	Thousand tons	Thousand tons
1949	1,130	661	72	—	631	539	194	42	—	—	58
1950	636	401	181	—	422	415	42	42	—	—	—
1951	411	1,251	987	—	146	148	45	214	170	30	765
1952	1,222	1,303	478	—	428	397	158	254	107	33	14
1953	1,298	680	19	—	516	570	254	219	16	41	51
1954	672	210	122	—	473	564	212	303	138	132	48
1955	225	315	196	—	48	105	307	253	93	73	146
1956	312	1,902	1,715	—	156	126	247	284	87	110	49
1957	1,855	2,172	751	—	389	320	286	273	100	39	114
1958	2,156	1,543	176	—	719	573	281	335	78	56	24
1959	1,514	954	196	—	587	717	335	334	63	66	64
1960	979	844	270	—	471	404	334	410	115	170	39
1961	789	859 [2]	438 [2]	—	320	369	403 [2]	362	132	69	173
1962	859	648	174	—	429	385	362	385	99	79	76
1963	648	517	291	—	261	422	383 [2]	450	148	125	81
1964	517	550	244	—	239	223	450	537	195	133	108
1965	550	513	166	—	221	203	537	573	158	102	122
1966	513	596	244	—	134	161	573	745	246	129	74
1967	596	1,211 [3]	740	—	182	162	745	686	50	137	109
1968	1,211	1,495	613	—	454	329	686	701	153	138	138
1969	1,495	1,388	309	—	271	416	701	617	80	142	160
1970	1,388	1,609 [3]	580	0	322	370	621	588	132	117	166
1971	1,609	1,825	623	—	—	407	588	529	88	—	147
1972	1,819	2,983	1,565	—	—	491	529	520	86	—	95
1973	2,983	3,944	1,938	—	—	887	520	526	39	—	33
1974	4,005	5,053	1,766	33	—	684	526	659	171	—	38
1975	5,053	4,674	635	545	—	469	663	690	106	—	80
1976	4,674	4,238	339	21	—	755	690	712	91	—	70
1977	4,238	3,467	266	0	—	1,036	712	652	89	—	148
1978	3,467	2,635	397	199	—	1,027	652	677	119	—	95
1979	2,635	1,816	487	8	—	1,298	677	630	61	—	108
1980	1,816	937	116	207	—	788	630	628	101	—	102
1981	—	—	—	—	—	—	—	—	—	—	—
1982	—	—	—	—	—	—	—	—	—	—	—
1983	—	—	—	—	—	—	—	—	—	—	—
1984	—	—	—	—	—	—	—	—	—	—	—
1985	—	—	—	—	—	—	—	—	—	—	—
1986	—	—	—	—	—	—	—	—	—	—	—
1987	—	—	—	—	—	—	—	—	—	—	—
1988	—	—	—	—	—	—	—	—	—	—	—
1989	—	—	—	—	—	—	—	—	—	—	—
1990	—	—	—	—	—	—	—	—	—	—	—
1991	—	—	—	—	—	—	—	—	—	—	—
1992	—	—	—	—	—	—	—	—	—	—	—
1993	—	—	—	—	—	—	—	—	—	—	—

[1] Gross tons for commercial vessels; light displacement tons for naval vessels.

[2] Tonnages revised.

[3] Adjusted to account for major changes made during construction.

Source

Shipbuilders Council of America, Washington, D.C., *Annual Report* (various issues).

Documentation

The data are for steel self-propelled vessels of 1,000 tons or more. See the text for Table Df578–593 for a definition of gross tonnage and related discussion.

After 1980, the reported figures are those presented in the *Statistical Abstract of the United States* as coming from the basic source.

There are three years in which cancellation data are reported for naval vessels: two contracts were canceled during 1986, one during 1990, and two in August 1993.

TABLE Df855–864   Water transport vessels – number and tonnage, by vessel type: 1960–1997

Contributed by Louis P. Cain

		Inland water vessels								
		Non-self-propelled				Self-propelled			Oceangoing steam and motor ships	Recreational boats
	Total number	Total		Dry cargo barges and scows	Tankers	Total		Towboats and tugs		
		Number	Tonnage			Number	Tonnage			
	Df855	Df856	Df857	Df858	Df859	Df860	Df861	Df862	Df863	Df864
	Number	Number	Thousand net tons	Number	Number	Number	Thousand net tons	Number	Number	Number
Year										
1960	23,320	16,777	16,356	14,025	2,429	6,543	15,906	4,203	2,926	2,500,000
1961	—	16,505	16,356	13,856	2,515	—	—	4,178	—	—
1962	—	16,881	17,086	14,220	2,661	—	—	4,253	2,880	—
1963	—	17,154	18,006	14,415	2,739	—	—	4,205	2,785	—
1964	—	17,081	19,173	14,432	2,649	—	—	3,994	2,505	—
1965	22,872	16,789	19,554	14,241	2,548	6,083	—	4,054	2,376	6,400,000
1966	—	16,789	19,554	14,241	2,548	—	—	4,054	2,278	—
1967	—	18,611	21,186	15,830	2,781	—	—	4,395	2,162	4,458,893
1968	—	18,380	23,652	15,379	3,001	—	—	4,248	2,071	4,742,871
1969	—	19,171	24,028	15,890	3,281	—	—	4,248	1,937	4,864,074
1970	26,079	19,624	24,602	16,439	3,185	6,455	19,284	4,230	1,579	5,128,345
1971	27,201	20,947	27,197	17,527	3,420	6,254	18,083	4,059	1,372	5,510,092
1972	28,303	22,117	28,751	18,804	3,313	6,186	17,306	4,064	1,150	5,910,794
1973	29,333	23,147	30,271	19,772	3,375	6,186	17,306	4,035	1,016	6,339,678
1974	31,484	25,410	33,728	21,876	3,534	6,074	16,762	4,100	922	6,834,283
1975	32,931	26,787	35,645	23,164	3,623	6,144	16,762	4,240	857	7,303,286
1976	35,029	28,707	38,975	24,937	3,770	6,322	16,536	4,379	842	7,671,213
1977	35,270	28,707	38,975	24,937	3,770	6,563	18,726	4,379	840	7,975,587
1978	34,623	27,983	39,306	24,037	3,946	6,640	20,253	4,380	879	8,035,905
1979	36,192	29,420	42,428	25,420	4,000	6,772	21,106	4,492	865	8,278,723
1980	39,078	31,952	44,875	27,426	4,166	7,126	23,906	4,693	864	8,577,857
1981	42,019	34,388	49,933	29,479	4,909	7,631	26,278	4,890	853	8,905,097
1982	42,019	34,388	49,933	29,479	4,909	7,631	26,278	4,890	832	9,073,972
1983	—	—	—	—	—	—	—	—	788	9,165,094
1984	41,784	33,899	49,147	29,730	4,114	7,885	24,088	4,993	744	9,420,011
1985	41,119	33,597	49,476	29,287	4,252	7,522	21,196	4,954	737	9,589,483
1986	40,308	32,614	48,749	28,308	4,260	7,694	21,302	5,096	720	9,876,197
1987	39,865	32,035	49,104	27,741	4,247	7,830	19,747	5,171	709	9,963,696
1988	39,192	31,125	48,600	27,046	4,043	8,067	21,461	5,188	675	10,362,613
1989	39,209	31,081	48,835	27,073	3,978	8,128	19,905	5,242	655	10,777,370
1990	39,445	31,209	48,603	27,091	3,913	8,236	19,724	5,218	636	10,996,253
1991	—	—	—	—	—	—	—	—	619	11,068,440
1992	39,210	30,899	49,450	26,984	3,905	8,311	19,430	5,205	603	11,132,386
1993	39,108	30,785	49,546	26,913	3,862	8,323	17,654	5,224	565	11,282,736
1994	39,064	30,730	49,709	26,723	3,966	8,334	16,867	5,179	543	11,429,585
1995	39,641	31,360	51,140	27,342	3,985	8,281	15,783	5,127	509	11,734,710
1996	41,104	32,811	—	—	—	8,293	—	—	495	11,877,938
1997	—	—	—	—	—	—	—	—	—	12,312,982

Sources

Series Df855–863: U.S. Department of Transportation, *National Transportation Statistics* and *Inland Waterborne Commerce Statistics* (annual issues); series Df864: U.S Department of Transportation, United States Coast Guard, *Boating Statistics* (annual issues).

Documentation

These series have not been reported in a consistent manner over time. This is especially true of the period 1960–1982 for series Df856–859 and Df862. The annual issues from these years sometimes reported the identical number for two consecutive years because in some cases the figure was taken on December 31 one year and on January 1 the next. To try to resolve some of the confusion, the data from *National Transportation Statistics* were double-checked against the identical U.S. Army Corps of Engineers data as they appeared in an alternative source: The American Waterways Operators, Inc., *Inland Waterborne Commerce Statistics* (annual issues). The data reported here represent the best numbers available.

See the text for Table Df578–593 for a definition of gross tonnage and related discussion.

Series Df855. Equals the sum of series Df856 and Df860.

Series Df856. Include dry cargo barges and scows, tanker barges, and railroad car floats.

Series Df857. Reports the net tonnage of all these vessels. Net tonnage is a measure of volume for potential cargo and passengers; it is gross tonnage minus space used by equipment, workspace, and crew living space.

Series Df858–859. Report the dry cargo barges and scows and the tanker barges separately. The number of railroad floats is quite small, and in some years, particularly before 1980, the total number of non–self-propelled vessels is equal to the sum of the dry cargo barges and scows and the tankers.

Series Df860. Includes dry cargo and/or passenger vessels, railroad car ferries, tankers, towboats and tugs, and sailing vessels.

Series Df861. Reports net tonnage.

Series Df863. Ships of 1,000 gross tons and larger.

RAIL

Louis P. Cain

TABLE Df865–873   Railroad investment, by region: 1828–1860[1]

Contributed by Susan B. Carter and Richard Sutch

	United States			Gross investment by region					
	Gross investment		Net investment, 1860 dollars	New England	Middle Atlantic states	Ohio, Indiana, and Michigan	Illinois, Iowa, Wisconsin, Missouri, and California	The South	Louisiana and Texas
	Current dollars	1860 dollars							
	Df865	Df866	Df867	Df868	Df869	Df870	Df871	Df872	Df873
Year	Million dollars	Million 1860 dollars	Million 1860 dollars	Million dollars	Million dollars	Million dollars	Million dollars	Million dollars	Million dollars
1828	0.2	0.2	0.2	—	0.2	—	—	—	—
1829	1.0	1.0	1.0	—	1.0	—	—	—	—
1830	1.6	1.9	1.9	—	1.4	—	—	0.1	0.1
1831	3.4	4.0	4.0	0.1	2.6	—	—	0.5	0.1
1832	4.9	5.7	5.6	0.4	3.7	—	—	0.8	0.0
1833	5.6	6.0	5.7	1.1	3.6	—	—	0.9	0.0
1834	7.4	8.2	7.8	1.4	5.1	—	—	0.9	0.0
1835	8.8	9.9	9.4	1.7	5.4	0.2	—	1.5	0.1
1836	12.8	12.7	12.0	2.3	7.1	0.2	—	2.5	0.6
1837	15.6	15.3	14.3	2.5	7.2	0.9	0.1	4.3	0.6
1838	17.4	17.1	15.8	2.7	6.6	1.3	0.9	5.5	0.7
1839	17.7	17.0	15.4	4.2	5.3	0.9	1.3	5.6	0.4
1840	14.0	14.4	12.4	4.3	5.7	0.5	0.2	3.3	0.2
1841	14.1	12.6	10.3	3.7	4.8	0.6	0.2	2.0	0.2
1842	8.6	9.7	7.2	3.1	3.5	0.5	0.3	1.0	0.2
1843	6.5	6.6	3.9	2.2	1.7	1.7	0.0	0.9	0.0
1844	8.2	8.5	5.7	3.5	1.7	1.9	0.0	1.1	0.0
1845	10.0	10.3	7.3	5.4	1.1	1.9	0.0	1.6	0.0
1846	16.6	15.4	12.2	9.4	3.3	1.7	0.0	2.3	0.0
1847	27.3	26.0	22.5	15.2	7.4	2.8	0.2	1.6	0.0
1848	37.4	38.2	34.1	20.4	10.5	3.3	0.4	2.8	0.0
1849	36.7	39.4	34.6	17.0	12.1	2.4	0.4	4.7	0.0
1850	36.1	41.1	35.5	8.6	16.7	4.9	0.3	5.6	0.0
1851	50.9	57.8	51.4	8.6	17.4	15.7	2.6	6.5	0.0
1852	66.4	74.8	67.2	9.3	18.3	25.0	5.6	7.8	0.4
1853	93.4	94.7	86.6	6.3	21.3	25.3	23.6	16.5	0.4
1854	110.7	103.6	92.6	5.9	14.2	23.7	47.4	18.8	0.7
1855	74.2	75.9	62.8	3.1	7.6	18.3	33.4	10.7	1.1
1856	77.0	72.7	58.1	2.8	9.8	22.3	22.7	18.8	0.6
1857	84.2	77.7	61.7	2.4	12.3	21.7	24.6	22.5	0.8
1858	67.1	64.4	46.8	0.3	11.4	10.9	18.0	25.2	1.2
1859	60.8	60.4	41.5	0.2	8.1	5.3	12.3	30.1	4.7
1860	52.6	52.6	32.5	1.6	6.0	2.6	9.9	26.2	6.4

[1] Includes expenditures on failed projects through 1839; thereafter, excludes such expenditures.

Source

Albert Fishlow, *American Railroads and the Transformation of the Ante-Bellum Economy* (Harvard University Press, 1965), Tables 53 and 54, pp. 397, 399.

Documentation

"Gross investments" in railroads are defined as all current expenditures for railroads. These include expenditures for right-of-way, ties, rails, and rolling stock (engines, freight and passenger cars, and cabooses). Net expenditures deduct an estimate of the lost value of railroad capital owing to physical deterioration and obsolescence.

Series Df868. Includes Maine, New Hampshire, Vermont, Massachusetts, Rhode Island, and Connecticut.

Series Df869. Includes New York, New Jersey, Pennsylvania, Delaware, and Maryland.

Series Df872. "The South" is defined here as Virginia, West Virginia, Kentucky, Tennessee, Missouri, Alabama, Georgia, Florida, North Carolina, and South Carolina.

TABLE Df874–881   Railroad mileage and equipment: 1830–1890

Contributed by Louis P. Cain

	Mileage			Equipment				
					Revenue cars			
Year	Road operated	Road owned	All track	Locomotives	Total	Passenger	Freight	Baggage, mail, express
	Df874 [1]	Df875 [2]	Df876 [1]	Df877 [3]	Df878 [3]	Df879 [3]	Df880 [3]	Df881 [3]
	Miles	Miles	Miles	Thousand	Thousand	Thousand	Thousand	Thousand
1830	23	—	—	—	—	—	—	—
1831	95	—	—	—	—	—	—	—
1832	229	—	—	—	—	—	—	—
1833	380	—	—	—	—	—	—	—
1834	633	—	—	—	—	—	—	—
1835	1,098	—	—	—	—	—	—	—
1836	1,273	—	—	—	—	—	—	—
1837	1,497	—	—	—	—	—	—	—
1838	1,913	—	—	—	—	—	—	—
1839	2,302	—	—	—	—	—	—	—
1840	2,818	—	—	—	—	—	—	—
1841	3,535	—	—	—	—	—	—	—
1842	4,026	—	—	—	—	—	—	—
1843	4,185	—	—	—	—	—	—	—
1844	4,377	—	—	—	—	—	—	—
1845	4,633	—	—	—	—	—	—	—
1846	4,930	—	—	—	—	—	—	—
1847	5,598	—	—	—	—	—	—	—
1848	5,996	—	—	—	—	—	—	—
1849	7,365	—	—	—	—	—	—	—
1850	9,021	—	—	—	—	—	—	—
1851	10,982	—	—	—	—	—	—	—
1852	12,908	—	—	—	—	—	—	—
1853	15,360	—	—	—	—	—	—	—
1854	16,720	—	—	—	—	—	—	—
1855	18,374	—	—	—	—	—	—	—
1856	22,076	—	—	—	—	—	—	—
1857	24,503	—	—	—	—	—	—	—
1858	26,968	—	—	—	—	—	—	—
1859	28,789	—	—	—	—	—	—	—
1860	30,626	—	—	—	—	—	—	—
1861	31,286	—	—	—	—	—	—	—
1862	32,120	—	—	—	—	—	—	—
1863	33,170	—	—	—	—	—	—	—
1864	33,908	—	—	—	—	—	—	—
1865	35,085	—	—	—	—	—	—	—
1866	36,801	—	—	—	—	—	—	—
1867	39,050	—	—	—	—	—	—	—
1868	42,229	—	—	—	—	—	—	—
1869	46,844	—	—	—	—	—	—	—
1870	52,922	—	—	—	—	—	—	—
1871	60,301	51,455	—	—	—	—	—	—
1872	66,171	57,323	—	—	—	—	—	—
1873	70,268	70,651	—	—	—	—	—	—
1874	72,385	72,623	—	—	—	—	—	—
1875	74,096	74,096	—	—	—	—	—	—
1876	76,808	76,305	94,665	15.6	340	14.6 [4]	385	—
1877	79,082	79,208	97,308	15.9	408	12.1	392	3.9
1878	81,747	80,832	103,649	16.4	439	11.7	423	4.4
1879	86,556	84,893	104,756	17.1	497	12.0	480	4.5
1880	98,262	92,147	115,647	17.9	557	12.8	539	4.8
1881	108,108	103,530	130,455	19.9	667	13.9	648	5.0
1882	114,677	114,428	140,878	21.9	751	14.9	730	5.6
1883	121,422	120,519	149,101	23.4	801	16.2	779	5.8
1884	125,345	125,119	156,414	24.4	821	16.6	798	5.9
1885	128,320	127,689	160,506	25.7	828	16.5	806	6.0
1886	136,338	133,565	167,952	26.1	871	18.4	846	6.3
1887	149,214	147,953	184,935	27.3	977	19.3	951	6.6
1888	156,114	154,222	191,376	29.1	1,032	20.2	1,005	6.8
1889	161,276	159,934	202,088	30.6	1,081	21.5	1,051	7.1
1890	166,703	163,359	208,152	31.8	1,091	21.7	1,062	7.3

TABLE Df874–881   Railroad mileage and equipment: 1830–1890   *Continued*

[1] As of December 31.

[2] Prior to 1882, includes elevated railways.

[3] Prior to 1881, includes elevated railways.

[4] Includes baggage, mail, and express.

Source

U.S. Interstate Commerce Commission, *Railway Statistics before 1890*, Statement number 32151 (mimeographed) (1932).

Documentation

For discussion of the source, see the text for Table Df901–910.

TABLE Df882–885   Railroad mileage built: 1830–1925

Contributed by Richard Sutch

Year	1880 Census	Railroad Age	Change in miles operated	Change in miles owned	Year	1880 Census	Railroad Age	Change in miles operated	Change in miles owned
	Df882	Df883	Df884	Df885		Df882	Df883	Df884	Df885
	Miles	Miles	Miles	Miles		Miles	Miles	Miles	Miles
1830	40	—	23	—	1880	—	—	6,706	—
1831	99	—	72	—	1881	—	—	9,846	—
1832	191	—	134	—	1882	—	—	11,569	—
1833	116	—	151	—	1883	—	—	6,745	—
1834	214	—	253	—	1884	—	—	3,923	—
1835	138	—	465	—	1885	—	—	2,975	—
1836	280	—	175	—	1886	—	—	8,018	—
1837	348	—	224	—	1887	—	—	12,876	—
1838	453	—	416	—	1888	—	—	6,900	—
1839	386	—	389	—	1889	—	—	5,162	—
1840	491	—	516	—	1890	—	—	5,427	—
1841	606	—	717	—	1891	—	—	—	4,806
1842	505	—	491	—	1892	—	—	—	3,161
1843	288	—	159	—	1893	—	3,024	—	4,897
1844	180	—	192	—	1894	—	1,760	—	2,248
1845	277	—	256	—	1895	—	1,420	—	1,948
1846	333	—	297	—	1896	—	1,692	—	2,120
1847	263	—	668	—	1897	—	2,109	—	1,651
1848	1,056	—	398	—	1898	—	3,265	—	1,968
1849	1,048	—	1,369	—	1899	—	4,569	—	2,899
1850	1,261	—	1,656	—	1900	—	4,894	—	4,051
1851	1,274	—	1,961	—	1901	—	5,368	—	3,891
1852	2,288	—	1,926	—	1902	—	6,026	—	5,235
1853	2,170	—	2,452	—	1903	—	5,652	—	5,505
1854	3,442	—	1,360	—	1904	—	3,832	—	5,927
1855	2,453	—	1,654	—	1905	—	4,388	—	4,197
1856	1,471	—	3,702	—	1906	—	5,623	—	6,262
1857	2,077	—	2,427	—	1907	—	5,212	—	5,588
1858	1,966	—	2,465	—	1908	—	3,214	—	3,517
1859	1,707	—	1,821	—	1909	—	3,748	—	3,366
1860	1,500	—	1,837	—	1910	—	4,122	—	3,459
1861	1,016	—	660	—	1911	—	3,066	—	3,686
1862	720	—	834	—	1912	—	2,997	—	2,798
1863	574	—	1,050	—	1913	—	3,071	—	3,000
1864	947	—	738	—	1914	—	1,532	—	2,328
1865	819	—	1,177	—	1915	—	833	—	1,684
1866	1,404	—	1,716	—	1916	—	1,098	—	462
1867	2,541	—	2,249	—	1917	—	979	—	—
1868	2,468	—	3,179	—	1918	—	721	—	—
1869	4,103	—	4,615	—	1919	—	686	—	—
1870	5,658	—	6,078	—	1920	—	314	—	—
1871	6,660	—	7,379	—	1921	—	475	—	—
1872	7,439	—	5,870	—	1922	—	324	—	—
1873	5,217	—	4,097	—	1923	—	427	—	—
1874	2,584	—	2,117	—	1924	—	579	—	—
1875	1,606	—	1,711	—	1925	—	644	—	—
1876	2,575	—	2,712	—					
1877	2,280	—	2,274	—					
1878	2,428	—	2,665	—					
1879	5,006	—	4,809	—					

Notes appear on next page

(continued)

TABLE Df882–885   Railroad mileage built: 1830–1925   *Continued*

Sources

Series Df882. U.S. Bureau of the Census, Tenth Census Reports, volume 4, *Report on the Agencies of Transportation in the United States*, p. 289.

Series Df883. *Railway Age* 104 (1) (1938): 66.

Series Df884–885. Based on series Df874 and Df930.

Documentation

Series Df882. The U.S. Bureau of the Census's Tenth Census Report (pp. 289–93, 300–75) contains materials on the history of railroad construction, including figures on mileage built and existent, by groups of states, for individual companies, annually from 1830 to 1880. According to the Census Bureau, information was received from every railroad known to exist in 1880. The letter of instructions from the Superintendent of the Census to the railroads read: "In cases . . . in which the records have been lost, the officers of such companies and roads are requested to obtain . . . this information in the best form possible. The recollection of officers and employees long in the service of a road may be used . . . if more reliable data be not accessible." For a more detailed discussion of the problems of estimating miles of railroad built, see E. R. Wicker, "Railroad Investment before the Civil War," and the "Comments" by George R. Taylor and Charles J. Kennedy, in *Trends in the American Economy in the Nineteenth Century: A Report of the National Bureau of Economic Research,* Studies in Income and Wealth, volume 24 (Princeton University Press, 1960). The Census Bureau figures pertain only to miles in operation in the census year. The figures for any year are, therefore, understatements to the extent that mileage constructed in that year may have been abandoned by June 1, 1880, the date of the 1880 Census.

Series Df883. *Railway Age* obtained its figures at annual intervals from individual railroads and from state railroad commissions. One difficulty in interpreting these figures is that it is not clear precisely when a mile of road would be reported as built. Construction of some lines extended over several years. Each annual segment may have been reported when finished, or nothing may have been reported until the whole line was completed. The year of physical completion may have differed from the year in which traffic was first carried. In such cases, the mileage may have been assigned to either year.

Series Df884–885. No direct estimates of railroad mileage construction are available for the years 1880–1892, when railroad construction reached its peak. In an effort to track railroad mileage constructed during this important period, scholars have relied on two different measures. One is the year-to-year change in miles operated, series Df874. These data are shown in series Df884. Another is the year-to-year change in railroad miles owned, series Df930. These are shown in series Df885. The annual change in miles operated tend to overstate miles built to the extent to which they reflect railroads' acquisitions of track rights, as a result of which the same line may be counted in the operation of two or more railroads. The annual changes both in miles operated and in miles owned tend to understate the extent of mileage built to the extent to which they are deflated by abandonments during the year (regardless of when constructed). The value of these proxies may be judged by comparing them to the direct measures in series Df882–883.

TABLE Df886–887   Railroad receipts and freight traffic: 1848–1860

Contributed by Louis P. Cain

Year	Receipts Df886 Thousand dollars	Freight traffic Df887 Million ton-miles
1848	22,113	—
1849	26,026	—
1850	31,290	—
1851	37,615	—
1852	45,980	1,101
1853	56,463	1,158
1854	65,681	1,490
1855	77,580	1,719
1856	87,017	2,193
1857	98,950	2,200
1858	106,014	2,306
1859	—	2,521
1860	140,000	3,282

Source

Albert Fishlow, *American Railroads and the Transformation of the Ante-Bellum Economy* (Harvard University Press, 1965), Table 40, p. 316.

TABLE Df888–889   Road mileage operated by railroads: 1851–1890

Contributed by Louis P. Cain

Year	Roads reporting earnings, including elevated railways Df888 Miles	Roads reporting earnings and traffic statistics Df889 Miles
1851	8,836	—
1871	44,614	—
1872	57,323	—
1873	66,237	—
1874	69,273	—
1875	71,759	—
1876	73,508	—
1877	74,112	—
1878	78,960	—
1879	79,009	—
1880	82,146	—
1881	92,971	—
1882	104,971	95,752
1883	110,414	106,938
1884	115,704	113,172
1885	123,320	122,110
1886	125,185	125,146
1887	137,028	136,986
1888	145,387	145,341
1889	153,945	153,689
1890	158,037	157,976

Source

U.S. Interstate Commerce Commission, *Railway Statistics before 1890*, Statement number 32151 (mimeographed) (1932).

Documentation

For discussion of the source, see the text for Table Df901–910.

Earnings and traffic figures are understatements of actual levels.

TABLE Df890   Federal land grants used by railroads, by state: 1850–1871

Contributed by Louis P. Cain

State	Federal land grants used by railroads Df890 Acres
Alabama	2,747,479
Arizona	7,695,203
Arkansas	2,586,970
California	11,585,393
Colorado	3,757,673
Florida	2,218,705
Idaho	1,320,591
Illinois	2,595,133
Iowa	4,711,328
Kansas	8,234,013
Louisiana	1,375,000
Michigan	3,134,038
Minnesota	9,953,008
Mississippi	1,075,345
Missouri	2,328,674
Montana	14,736,919
Nebraska	7,272,623
Nevada	5,086,283
New Mexico	3,355,179
North Dakota	10,697,490
Oregon	3,655,390
Utah	2,230,085
Washington	9,582,878
Wisconsin	3,666,062
Wyoming	5,749,051

Source

U.S. Bureau of Land Management, *Annual Report of the Commissioner of the General Land Office* (1943), pp. 124–8.

Documentation

The federal government made approximately 200 million acres of land grants to the railroads between 1850 and 1871, but the railroads used only slightly more than 131 million of those acres. Typically, such grants were of alternating sections on both sides of the proposed route. None of this land was subject to the provisions of the Homestead Act. The idea was that the railroad would at least double the land value, so the government would at least break even.

TABLE Df891–900   Railroad property investment, capital, income, and expenses: 1850–1890
[Including elevated railways]

Contributed by Louis P. Cain

	Property investment and capital					Income and expense			Interest and dividends	
	Investment in railroad and equipment	Stock, mortgage bonds, equipment, obligations, etc.			Stock paying dividends	Total traffic earnings	Operating expenses	Net earnings	Dividends paid	Interest paid on funded debt
		Total	Capital stock	Bonded debt						
	Df891	Df892	Df893	Df894	Df895	Df896	Df897	Df898	Df899	Df900
Year	Million dollars	Million dollars	Million dollars	Million dollars	Million dollars	Million dollars	Million dollars	Million dollars	Million dollars	Million dollars
1850	—	318	—	—	—	—	—	346	85	226
1851	—	—	—	—	—	39	—	322	81	218
1855	—	763	424	299	—	84	—	301	80	207
1860	—	1,149	—	—	—	—	—	334	91	203
1861	—	—	—	—	—	130	—	300	81	189
1863	—	—	—	—	—	190	—	269	77	187
1867	—	1,172	756	416	—	334	—	270	94	178
1868	—	1,869	—	—	—	—	—	298	102	173
1869	—	2,041	—	—	—	—	—	280	102	150
1870	—	2,476	—	—	—	—	—	272	93	128
1871	—	2,664	1,481	—	—	403	—	255	77	107
1872	—	3,159	1,647	1,511 [2]	—	465	—	216	61	112
1873	—	3,784	1,947	1,836 [2]	—	526	302	187	53	103
1874	—	4,221	1,990	2,230 [2]	—	520	301	170	58	98
1875	—	4,658	2,198	2,459 [2]	—	503	310	186	68	93
1876	4,086	4,468 [1]	2,248	2,165	937	497	—	185	74	—
1877	4,180	—	4,806	2,313	2,255	—	472	330	189	67
1878	4,166	—	4,772	2,292	2,297	—	490	342	183	67
1879	4,416	—	4,872	2,395	2,319	—	525	—	165	64
1880	4,663	—	5,402	2,708	2,530	—	613	—	141	56
1881	5,577	—	6,278	3,177	2,878	—	701	—	—	—
1882	6,035	—	7,016	3,511	3,235	1,673	770	—	—	—
1883	6,684	—	7,477	3,708	3,500	1,713	823	—	—	—
1884	6,924	—	7,676	3,762	3,669	1,658	777	228	105	32
1885	7,037	—	7,842	3,817	3,765	1,304	772	—	—	—
1886	7,254	—	8,163	3,999	3,882	1,675	829	—	—	—
1887	7,799	—	8,673	4,191	4,186	1,805	940	—	—	—
1888	8,344	—	9,369	4,438	4,624	1,769	960	42	—	—
1889	8,598	—	9,680	4,495	4,828	1,790	1,002	—	—	—
1890	8,789	—	10,122	4,640	5,105	1,721	1,097	—	—	—

[1] Sum of capital stock, bonded debt, and $55 million Pacific R.R., U.S. subsidiary bonds.

[2] Includes other debt.

Source

U.S. Interstate Commerce Commission, *Railway Statistics before 1890*, Statement number 32151 (mimeographed) (1932).

Documentation

For discussion of the source, see the text for Table Df901–910.

TABLE Df901–910   Railroad passenger and freight service – revenue and volume: 1865–1890

Contributed by Louis P. Cain

	Passenger service				Freight service					Ton-miles carried, thirteen railroads
	Revenue	Passengers carried	Passenger miles	Revenue per passenger mile	Revenue	Revenue-tons carried	Ton-miles carried, all roads	Revenue per ton-mile	Revenue ton-miles per train-mile	
	Df901	Df902	Df903	Df904	Df905	Df906	Df907	Df908	Df909	Df910
Year	Million dollars	Million	Million passenger-miles	Cents per passenger-mile	Million dollars	Million tons	Million ton-miles	Cents per ton-mile	Ton-miles per train-mile	Billion ton-miles
1865	—	—	—	—	—	—	—	—	—	2.16
1866	—	—	—	—	—	—	—	—	—	2.62
1867	—	—	—	—	—	—	—	—	—	3.03
1868	—	—	—	—	—	—	—	—	—	3.44
1869	—	—	—	—	300	—	—	—	—	4.22
1870	—	—	—	—	—	—	—	—	—	4.92
1871	108	—	—	—	294	—	—	—	—	5.57
1872	132	—	—	—	340	—	—	—	—	6.42
1873	137	—	—	—	389	—	—	—	—	7.48
1874	140	—	—	—	379	—	—	—	—	7.73
1875	139	—	—	—	363	—	—	—	—	7.84
1876	136	—	—	—	361	—	—	—	—	8.74
1877	125	—	—	—	347	—	—	—	—	8.75
1878	124	—	—	—	365	—	—	—	—	10.68
1879	142	—	—	—	386	—	—	—	—	13.07
1880	147	—	—	—	467	—	—	—	—	14.48
1881	173	—	—	—	551	—	—	—	—	16.06
1882	188	289	7,688	2.447	485	360	39,302	1.236	128.81	16.23
1883	206	312	8,541	2.422	539	400	44,065	1.224	125.86	17.09
1884	206	334	8,779	2.356	502	399	44,725	1.124	133.58	16.81
1885	200	351	9,134	2.199	509	437	49,152	1.057	143.59	17.83
1886	211	382	9,660	2.194	550	482	52,802	1.042	150.99	—
1887	240	428	10,570	2.276	636	552	61,561	1.034	156.16	—
1888	251	451	11,191	2.246	639	590	65,423	0.977	159.36	—
1889	259	494	11,965	2.169	665	619	68,677	0.970	159.91	—
1890	272	520	12,522	2.174	734	691	79,193	0.927	163.99	—

Sources

Series Df901–909, U.S. Interstate Commerce Commission, *Railway Statistics before 1890*, Statement number 32151 (mimeographed) (1932). Series Df910, H. V. and H. W. Poor, *Manual of Railroads, New York City* (Standard and Poors, 1888), p. xxviii.

Documentation

Before 1890, the principal source of continuous information on railroads is the annual H. V. and H. W. Poor, *Manual of Railroads, New York City*. The figures in the *Manual* were revised in successive issues. The Interstate Commerce Commission consulted the issues from 1869 to 1900 and evidently took account of the revisions. Similar but not identical figures, with the degree of coverage similarly indicated in terms of mileage, appear in U.S. Bureau of the Census, *Report on Transportation Business in the United States at the Eleventh Census*, Part 1 (1890).

Following a careful review of the Poors' work, Elmus Wicker cautioned that these data should be used prudently; anyone using the Poors' data is advised to consult Wicker's "Railroad Investment before the Civil War," and the "Comments" by George R. Taylor and Charles J. Kennedy, in *Trends in the American Economy in the Nineteenth Century: A Report of the National Bureau of Economic Research*, Studies in Income and Wealth, volume 24 (Princeton University Press, 1960).

All figures are based on reports of individual railroads for fiscal years ending in the calendar year indicated. The period of time covered is, therefore, not the same for all carriers included.

Data for 1890 in these series do not agree with 1890 data in Table Df927–955 because of differences in the sources.

Earnings and traffic figures are understatements of the actual level.

Series Df906. 55.1 million revenue tons were carried in 1861 and 72.5 in 1870.

Series Df910. The roads represented are seven Eastern roads (Pennsylvania; Pittsburgh, Fort Wayne, and Chicago; New York Central; Lake Shore; Michigan Central; Boston and Albany; New York, Lake Erie, and Western) and six Western roads (Illinois Central; Chicago and Alton; Chicago and Rock Island; Chicago, Burlington, and Quincy; Chicago and Northwestern; Chicago, Milwaukee, and St. Paul).

TABLE Df911–918   Indexes of railroad output, inputs, and productivity: 1839–1910

Contributed by Susan B. Carter and Richard Sutch

Year	Output	Persons engaged	Capital			Fuel	Total input	Total factor productivity
			Total	Road	Equipment			
	Df911	Df912	Df913	Df914	Df915	Df916	Df917	Df918
	Index 1910 = 100	Index 1910 = 100	Index 1910 = 100	Index 1910 = 100	Index 1910 = 100	Index 1910 = 100	Index 1910 = 100	Index 1910 = 100
1839	0.08	0.3	0.8	0.9	0.2	0.07	0.5	16.0
1849	0.46	1.1	2.2	2.5	0.7	0.20	1.4	32.8
1859	2.21	5.0	10.1	11.4	3.6	1.50	6.6	33.5
1870	6.00	13.5	16.6	18.5	6.7	5.40	13.9	47.4
1880	13.80	24.5	31.5	34.2	17.3	11.70	25.9	53.4
1890	32.82	44.1	61.9	66.7	36.6	28.70	49.3	66.5
1900	54.84	59.9	72.3	77.4	45.2	45.90	63.2	86.7
1910	100.00	100.0	100.0	100.0	100.0	100.00	100.0	100.0

Sources

Series Df911 and Df918, 1839–1859.

Lance E. Davis, Richard Easterlin, et al., *American Economic Growth: An Economist's History of the United States* (Harper & Row, 1972), pp. 499, 508.

Series Df911 and Df918.

1870–1910, and series Df912–917, 1839–1910, Albert Fishlow, "Productivity and Technological Change in the Railroad Sector, 1840–1910," in *Output, Employment, and Productivity in the United States after 1800*, Studies in Income and Wealth, volume 30 (Columbia University Press, 1966), Table 10, p. 626.

Documentation

Fishlow recalculated the output index using 1910 weights for his "Internal Transportation" chapter in Davis, Easterlin, et al. (1972). Given the consistency with the input index, the recalculated index is reported here. Therefore,

the total factor productivity estimates are those presented in his revised tables.

Series Df917. This series summarizes the costs of various inputs into the production of railroad transportation services. These costs include the expenses of the employees, the railway roadbed, equipment, and fuel consumed in the production of railway services. The inputs were weighted by their relative shares in 1910 as reported in the Interstate Commerce Commission, *Statistics of Railways for the United States for 1910*. These input weights are 0.52 for employment, 0.38 for all capital, and 0.10 for fuel.

Series Df918. The ratio of the index of the value of total railroad output, series Df911, divided by Fishlow's index of the value of total railroad input, series Df917.

TABLE Df919–926   Railroad property investment, capital, income, and expenses: 1882–1890 [Excluding elevated railways]

Contributed by Louis P. Cain

Year	Stock, mortgage bonds, equipment, obligations, and the like			Income and expense			Interest and dividends	
	Total	Capital stock	Bonded debt	Total traffic earnings	Operating expenses	Net earnings	Dividends paid	Interest paid on funded debt
	Df919	Df920	Df921	Df922	Df923	Df924	Df925	Df926
	Million dollars	Million dollars	Million dollars	Million dollars	Million dollars	Million dollars	Million dollars	Million dollars
1882	6,960	3,478	3,214	—	—	—	—	—
1883	7,423	3,675	3,479	807	—	291	101	171 [1]
1884	7,617	3,726	3,647	763	—	266	93	167
1885	7,775	3,778	3,740	765	498	266	77	179
1886	8,089	3,956	3,853	822	524	297	80	182
1887	8,595	4,146	4,155	931	—	331	90	202
1888	9,281	4,392	4,585	950	—	297	78	205
1889	9,576	4,447	4,784	991	—	317	79	216
1890	10,020	4,590	5,055	1,086	—	342	83	224

[1] Includes other interest.

Source

U.S. Interstate Commerce Commission, *Railway Statistics before 1890*, Statement number 32151 (mimeographed) (1932).

Documentation

For discussion of the source, see the text for Table Df901–910.

TABLE Df927–955 Railroad mileage, equipment, and passenger traffic and revenue: 1890–1980[1,2,3]
Contributed by Louis P. Cain

				Mileage						New cars delivered for domestic use		Equipment			
					Track operated								Locomotives in service		
	Operating railroads	Constructed	Abandoned	Road owned	Total	First main track	Other main tracks	Yard tracks and sidings	Road operated, passenger service	Freight train	Passenger train	Total	Steam	Electric	Diesel
	Df927	Df928	Df929	Df930	Df931	Df932	Df933	Df934	Df935 [4]	Df936	Df937 [4]	Df938 [5]	Df939	Df940 [6]	Df941
Year	Number	Miles	Miles	Miles	Miles	Miles	Miles	Miles	Miles	Number	Number	Number	Number	Number	Number
1890	1,013	—	—	163,597	199,876	156,404	9,760	33,711	—	—	—	30,140	—	—	—
1891	991	—	—	168,403	207,446	161,275	10,428	35,742	—	—	—	32,139	—	—	—
1892	1,002	—	—	171,564	211,051	162,397	10,846	37,808	—	—	—	33,136	—	—	—
1893	1,034	—	—	176,461	221,864	169,780	11,633	40,451	—	—	—	34,788	—	—	—
1894	1,043	—	—	178,709	229,796	175,691	12,163	41,941	—	—	—	35,492	—	—	—
1895	1,104	—	—	180,657	233,276	177,746	12,348	43,181	—	—	—	35,699	—	—	—
1896	1,111	—	—	182,777	239,140	181,983	12,440	44,718	—	—	—	35,950	—	—	—
1897	1,158	—	—	184,428	242,013	183,284	12,795	45,934	—	—	—	35,986	—	—	—
1898	1,192	—	—	186,396	245,334	184,648	13,096	47,589	—	—	—	36,234	—	—	—
1899	1,206	—	—	189,295	250,143	187,535	13,384	49,224	—	—	—	36,703	—	—	—
1900	1,224	—	—	193,346	268,784	192,556	14,075	52,153	—	—	—	37,663	—	—	—
1901	1,213	—	—	197,237	265,352	195,562	14,876	54,915	—	—	—	39,584	—	—	—
1902	1,219	—	—	202,472	274,196	200,155	15,820	58,221	—	—	—	41,225	—	—	—
1903	1,281	—	—	207,977	283,822	205,314	16,948	61,560	—	—	—	43,871	—	—	—
1904	1,314	—	—	213,904	297,073	212,243	18,338	66,492	—	—	—	46,743	—	—	—
1905	1,380	—	—	218,101	306,797	216,974	19,881	69,942	—	—	—	48,357	—	—	—
1906	1,491	—	—	224,363	317,083	222,340	20,982	73,761	—	—	—	51,672	—	—	—
1907	1,564	—	—	229,951	327,975	227,455	22,771	77,749	—	—	—	55,388	—	—	—
1908	1,323	—	—	233,468	333,646	230,494	23,699	79,453	—	—	—	57,698	—	—	—
1909	1,316	—	—	236,834	342,351	235,402	24,573	82,377	—	—	—	58,219	—	—	—
1910	1,306	—	—	240,293	351,767	240,831	25,354	85,582	—	—	—	60,019	—	—	—
1911	1,312	—	—	243,979	362,824	246,238	27,613	88,974	—	—	—	62,463	—	—	—
1912	1,298	—	—	246,777	371,238	249,852	29,367	92,019	—	176,049 [10]	3,362 [10]	63,463	—	—	—
1913	1,296	—	—	249,777	379,508	253,470	30,827	95,211	—	97,626 [10]	2,509 [10]	65,597	—	—	—
1914	1,297	—	—	252,105	387,208	256,547	32,376	98,285	—	—	2,654 [10]	67,012	—	—	—
1915	1,260	—	—	253,789	391,142	257,569	33,662	99,910	—	58,226 [10]	3,589 [10]	66,502	66,229	278	—
1916 [9]	1,243	—	—	254,251	394,944	259,211	33,864	101,869	—	—	1,513 [10]	65,314	65,021	293	—
1916 [9]	1,216	—	—	254,037	397,014	259,705	34,325	102,984	—	111,516	1,344	65,595	65,253	342	—
1917	1,168	—	—	253,626	400,353	259,705	35,066	105,582	—	115,705	1,684	66,070	65,699	371	—
1918	1,131	—	—	253,529	402,343	258,507	36,228	107,608	—	67,063	750	67,936	67,563	373	—
1919	1,111	—	—	253,152	403,891	258,525	36,730	108,637	—	94,981	126	68,977	68,592	385	—
1920	1,085	—	—	252,845	406,580	259,941	36,894	109,744	—	60,955	831	68,942	68,554	388	—
1921	1,058	331	687	251,176	407,531	258,362	37,614	111,555	—	40,292	1,161	69,122	68,783	389	—
1922	1,041	318	1,188	250,413	409,359	257,425	37,888	114,046	—	66,289	977	68,518	68,121	397	—
1923	1,023	441	537	250,222	412,993	258,084	38,697	116,212	—	175,748	2,034	69,414	69,005	409	—
1924	995	635	617	250,156	415,028	258,238	39,916	116,874	—	113,711	2,517	69,486	69,114	372	—
1925	947	595	753	249,398	417,954	258,631	40,962	118,361	—	105,735	2,428	68,098	67,713	379	1
1926	929	881	892	249,138	421,341	258,815	41,686	120,840	—	88,862	2,814	66,847	66,381	435	11 [11]
1927	880	819	797	249,131	424,737	259,639	42,071	123,027	—	63,370	2,087	65,348	64,843	467	— [11]
1928	849	946	710	249,309	427,750	260,546	42,432	124,772	—	46,060	1,571	63,311	62,642	617	— [11]
1929	809	671	782	249,433	429,054	260,570	42,711	125,773	—	81,590	2,455	61,257	60,572	621	25

Notes appear at end of table

(continued)

TABLE Df927–955 Railroad mileage, equipment, and passenger traffic and revenue: 1890–1980 Continued

				Mileage						Equipment					
						Track operated				New cars delivered for domestic use		Locomotives in service			
Year	Operating railroads	Constructed	Abandoned	Road owned	Total	First main track	Other main tracks	Yard tracks and sidings	Road operated, passenger service	Freight train	Passenger train	Total	Steam	Electric	Diesel
	Df927	Df928	Df929	Df930	Df931	Df932	Df933	Df934	Df935 [4]	Df936	Df937 [4]	Df938 [5]	Df939	Df940 [6]	Df941
	Number	Miles	Miles	Miles	Miles	Miles	Miles	Miles	Miles	Number	Number	Number	Number	Number	Number
1930	775	460	954	249,052	429,883	260,440	42,742	126,701	—	74,920	1,534	60,189	59,406	663	77
1931	749	502	779	248,829	429,823	259,999	42,780	127,044	—	13,203	323	58,652	57,820	709	80
1932	709	321	1,370	247,595	428,402	258,869	42,556	126,977	—	3,252	77	56,732	55,831	764	80
1933	700	122	2,016	245,703	425,664	256,741	42,397	126,526	—	2,163	9	54,228	53,302	789	85
1934	678	33	1,784	243,857	422,401	254,882	42,109	125,410	—	25,176	275	51,423	50,465	805	104
1935	661	25	1,974	241,822	419,228	252,930	41,916	124,382	—	7,515	205	49,541	48,477	884	130
1936	641	38	1,577	240,104	416,381	251,542	41,731	123,108	178,491	46,612	191	48,009	46,923	858	175
1937	631	149	1,642	238,539	414,572	250,582	41,579	122,411	175,543	77,498	629	47,555	46,342	872	293
1938	611	35	1,621	236,842	411,324	248,474	41,589	121,261	173,616	16,470	434	46,544	45,210	882	403
1939	600	1	1,697	235,064	408,350	246,922	41,445	119,983	172,031	25,132	276	45,172	43,604	879	639
1940	574	19	1,284	233,670	405,975	245,740	41,373	118,862	170,429	62,341	257	44,333	42,410	900	967
1941	559	22	1,695	231,971	403,625	244,263	41,166	118,196	167,951	80,623	349	44,375	41,911	895	1,517
1942	543	38	2,886	229,174	399,627	241,737	41,137	116,753	163,658	62,873	418	44,671	41,755	892	1,978
1943	534	34	1,149	227,999	398,730	240,745	41,093	116,892	162,429	31,836	685	45,406	41,983	907	2,476
1944	524	46	705	227,335	398,437	240,215	41,178	117,044	162,290	43,003	1,003	46,305	41,921	902	3,432
1945	517	40	551	226,696	398,054	239,438	41,106	117,510	161,701	48,864	931	46,253	41,018	885	4,301
1946	513	20	381	226,438	398,037	239,069	41,015	117,953	161,407	41,955	1,337	45,511	39,592	867	5,008
1947	502	79	709	225,806	397,355	238,209	40,954	118,192	161,115	68,522	861	44,344	36,942	864	6,495
1948	485	71	529	225,149	397,203	237,756	40,845	118,602	160,140	112,640	891	44,474	34,581	867	8,981
1949	481	100	620	224,511	397,232	237,564	40,639	119,029	156,821	92,562	933	43,272	30,344	856	12,025
1950	471	33	755	223,779	396,380	236,857	40,456	119,067	146,468	43,991	964	42,951	26,680	827	15,396
1951	462	71	456	223,427	395,831	236,476	40,157	119,198	139,178	95,993	179	42,473	22,590	817	19,014
1952	454	76	965	222,508	394,631	235,545	39,977	119,109	132,903	77,833	117	39,697	16,737	790	22,118
1953	448	50	666	221,758	393,736	234,959	39,794	118,983	128,943	81,021	386	37,251	12,274	713	24,209
1954	443	49	694	221,098	392,580	234,342	39,520	118,718	124,572	35,696	349	35,033	9,041	669	25,256
1955	441	105	502	220,670	390,965	233,955	38,825	118,185	119,745	37,545	886	33,533	6,266	639	26,563
1956	422	74	613	220,221	389,668	233,509	37,908	118,251	115,951	67,080	396	32,593	3,918	616	28,001
1957	415	49	1,194	219,067	386,978	232,177	37,123	117,678	112,724	99,590	232	32,391	2,608	597	29,137
1958	412	50	941	218,399	385,264	231,494	36,448	117,322	107,131	42,760	143	31,616	1,488	562	29,515
1959	411	14	1,034	217,565	383,912	230,930	35,746	117,236	100,243	37,819	66	31,539	871	517	30,097
1960	407	21	693	217,552	381,745	230,169	34,800	116,776	93,816	57,047	251	31,178	374	498	30,240
1961	397	34	930	216,445	379,415	229,369	33,853	116,193	88,854	31,720	214	30,889	210	484	30,123
1962	395	41	1,353	215,090	376,290	227,851	32,719	115,720	86,302	36,554	304	30,701	136	441	30,057
1963	395	23	777	214,387	374,522	227,282	32,153	115,087	84,928	44,960	156	30,506	112	438	29,898
1964	380	24	882	212,059	372,300	226,753	31,535	114,012	81,795	69,330	399	30,296	93	402	29,745
1965	372	59	963	211,384	370,636	226,015	31,113	113,508	76,993	77,822	666	30,061	89	365	29,552
1966	375	89	786	210,573	370,104	225,528	30,906	113,670	73,173	90,104	113	30,124	76	347	29,644
1967	370	169	1,039	209,292	368,030	224,039	30,387	113,604	67,827	83,095	146	29,874	67	324	29,428
1968	360	63	747	208,111	366,238	222,924	30,002	113,312	59,259	56,232	65	29,448	—[11]	307	29,031
1969	361	49	1,166	207,005	364,915	222,164	29,564	113,187	56,484	69,028	240	29,090	—[11]	278	28,711

Mileage / Equipment

Year	Operating railroads Df927 (Number)	Constructed Df928 (Miles)	Abandoned Df929 (Miles)	Road owned Df930 (Miles)	Track operated — Total Df931 (Miles)	First main track Df932 (Miles)	Other main tracks Df933 (Miles)	Yard tracks and sidings Df934 (Miles)	Road operated, passenger service Df935[4] (Miles)	New cars delivered — Freight train Df936 (Number)	New cars delivered — Passenger train Df937[4] (Number)	Locomotives in service — Total Df938[5] (Number)	Steam Df939 (Number)	Electric Df940[6] (Number)	Diesel Df941 (Number)
1970	351	80	1,283	205,782	360,330	220,107	28,682	111,541	49,533	66,185	302	29,122	11	270	28,773
1971	341	21	1,073	204,696	359,194	219,945	28,532	110,717	—	—	—	29,185	—	255	28,831
1972	332	22	1,902	202,775	355,965	218,024	28,257	109,684	—	—	—	29,338	—	257	29,338
1973	331	28	1,650	201,067	353,687	216,405	28,072	109,210	—	—	—	29,926	—	243	29,419
1974	341	18	508	200,391	353,033	216,532	27,810	108,691	—	—	—	30,220	—	218	29,709
1975	340	16	845	199,126	347,958	215,105	27,500	105,353	—	72,392	—	30,195	—	216	29,688
1976	314	—	—	175,763	295,621	191,366	15,485	88,770	—	—	—	29,644	—	—	—
1977	320	—	—	190,390	331,585	209,332	21,238	101,015	—	—	—	29,703	—	—	—
1978	59	—	—	178,262	322,916	195,982	26,115	100,819	—	—	—	27,023	—	—	—
1979	63	—	—	162,503	311,744	187,976	25,915	97,853	—	—	—	27,885	—	—	—
1980	64	—	—	157,078	304,196	182,785	25,925	95,486	—	—	—	28,862	—	—	—

Equipment

Year	Locomotives in service — Other Df942 (Number)	Average tractive effort Df943[7] (Number)	Passenger-train cars in service — Railroad only Df944 (Number)	Class I railroads and Pullman Co. — Total Df945[8] (Number)	Air conditioned Df946[8] (Number)	Freight-train cars in service — Number Df947 (Number)	Average capacity Df948[7] (Tons)
1890	—	—	26,820	—	—	918,491	—
1891	—	—	27,949	—	—	947,300	—
1892	—	—	28,876	—	—	966,998	—
1893	—	—	31,384	—	—	1,013,307	—
1894	—	—	33,018	—	—	1,205,169	—
1895	—	—	33,112	—	—	1,196,169	—
1896	—	—	33,003	—	—	1,221,887	—
1897	—	—	33,626	—	—	1,221,730	—
1898	—	—	33,595	—	—	1,248,826	—
1899	—	—	33,850	—	—	1,295,510	—
1900	—	—	34,713	—	—	1,365,531	—
1901	—	—	35,969	—	—	1,464,328	—
1902	—	—	36,987	—	—	1,546,101	—
1903	—	21,781	38,140	—	—	1,653,782	29.4
1904	—	22,804	39,752	—	—	1,692,194	30.1

Passenger traffic and revenue

Year	Passengers Df949 (Thousand)	Passenger-miles — Total Df950 (Million passenger-miles)	Commutation Df951[4] (Million passenger-miles)	Coach Df952[4] (Million passenger-miles)	Parlor and sleeping car Df953[4] (Million passenger-miles)	Revenue — Total Df954 (Thousand dollars)	Per passenger-mile Df955 (Cents per passenger-mile)
1890	492,341	11,848	—	—	—	260,786	2.167
1891	531,184	12,844	—	—	—	281,179	2.142
1892	560,958	13,363	—	—	—	286,806	2.126
1893	593,561	14,229	—	—	—	301,492	2.108
1894	540,638	14,289	—	—	—	285,350	1.986
1895	507,421	12,188	—	—	—	252,246	2.040
1896	511,773	13,049	—	—	—	266,563	2.019
1897	489,445	12,257	—	—	—	251,136	2.022
1898	501,067	13,380	—	—	—	266,970	1.973
1899	523,177	14,591	—	—	—	291,113	1.978
1900	576,831	16,038	—	—	—	323,716	2.003
1901	607,278	17,354	—	—	—	351,356	2.013
1902	649,879	19,690	—	—	—	392,963	1.986
1903	694,892	20,916	—	—	—	421,705	2.006
1904	715,420	21,923	—	—	—	444,327	2.006

Notes appear at end of table

(continued)

TABLE Df927–955   Railroad mileage, equipment, and passenger traffic and revenue: 1890–1980   *Continued*

	Locomotives in service		Equipment					Passenger traffic and revenue						
			Passenger-train cars in service — Class I railroads and Pullman Co.			Freight-train cars in service			Passenger-miles				Revenue	
	Other	Average tractive effort [7]	Railroad only	Total [8]	Air conditioned [8]	Number	Average capacity [7]	Passengers	Total	Commutation	Coach	Parlor and sleeping car	Total	Per passenger-mile
Year	Df942 [4]	Df943	Df944	Df945	Df946	Df947	Df948	Df949	Df950 [4]	Df951 [4]	Df952 [4]	Df953 [4]	Df954	Df955
	Number	Number	Number	Number	Number	Number	Tons	Thousand	Million passenger-miles	Million passenger-miles	Million passenger-miles	Million passenger-miles	Thousand dollars	Cents per passenger-mile
1905	—	23,666	40,713	—	—	1,731,409	30.8	738,835	23,800	—	—	—	472,695	1.962
1906	—	24,741	42,262	—	—	1,837,914	32.2	797,946	25,167	—	—	—	510,033	2.003
1907	—	25,781	43,973	—	—	1,991,557	33.8	873,905	27,719	—	—	—	564,606	2.014
1908	—	26,356	45,292	—	—	2,100,784	34.9	890,010	29,083	—	—	—	566,833	1.937
1909	—	26,601	45,664	—	—	2,086,835	35.3	891,472	29,109	—	—	—	563,609	1.928
1910	—	27,282	47,179	—	—	2,148,478	35.9	971,683	32,338	—	—	—	628,992	1.938
1911	—	28,291	49,906	—	—	2,208,997	36.9	997,410	33,202	—	—	—	657,638	1.974
1912	—	29,049	51,583	—	—	2,229,163	37.4	1,004,081	33,132	—	—	—	660,373	1.987
1913	—	30,258	52,717	—	—	2,298,478	38.3	1,043,603	34,673	—	—	—	695,988 [12]	2.008 [12]
1914	—	31,006	54,492	—	—	2,349,734	39.1	1,063,249	35,357	—	—	—	703,484	1.990
1915	—	31,501	55,810	—	—	2,341,567	39.7	985,676	32,475	—	—	—	646,475	1.991
1916 [9]	—	32,380	54,774	—	—	2,343,378	40.5	1,015,338	34,309	—	—	—	689,627	2.010
1916 [9]	—	32,840	55,193	—	—	2,329,475	40.9	1,048,987	35,220	—	—	—	722,359	2.051
1917	—	33,932	55,939	—	—	2,379,472	41.5	1,109,943	40,100	—	—	—	840,910	2.097
1918	—	34,995	56,611	—	—	2,397,943	41.6	1,122,963	43,212	—	—	—	1,046,166	2.421
1919	—	35,789	56,290	—	—	2,426,889	41.9	1,211,022	46,838	—	—	—	1,193,431	2.548
1920	—	36,365	56,102	—	—	2,388,424	42.4	1,269,913	47,370	—	—	—	1,304,815	2.755
1921	—	36,935	56,950	—	—	2,378,510	42.5	1,061,131	37,706	—	—	—	1,166,252	3.093
1922	—	37,441	56,827	—	—	2,352,483	43.1	989,509	35,811	6,132	—	—	1,087,516	3.037
1923	—	39,177	57,159	—	—	2,379,131	43.8	1,008,538	38,294	6,401	—	—	1,158,925	3.026
1924	—	39,891	57,451	—	—	2,411,627	44.3	950,459	36,368	6,407	—	—	1,085,672	2.985
1925	5	40,666	56,814	—	—	2,414,083	44.8	901,963	36,167	6,592	—	—	1,064,806	2.944
1926	20	41,886	56,855	—	—	2,403,967	45.1	874,589	35,673	6,605	—	—	1,049,210	2.941
1927	38 [11]	42,798	55,729	—	—	2,378,800	45.5	840,030	33,798	6,650	—	—	980,528	2.901
1928	52 [11]	43,838	54,800	—	—	2,346,751	45.8	798,476	31,718	6,626	—	—	905,271	2.854
1929	39	44,801	53,838	—	—	2,323,683	46.3	786,432	31,165	6,898	—	—	875,929	2.811
1930	43	45,225	53,584	—	—	2,322,267	46.9	707,987	26,876	6,669	—	—	730,766	2.719
1931	43	45,764	52,096	—	—	2,245,904	47.0	599,227	21,933	6,018	—	—	551,726	2.515
1932	57	46,299	50,598	—	—	2,184,690	47.0	480,718	16,997	4,986	—	—	377,511	2.221
1933	52	46,916	47,677	—	—	2,072,632	47.5	434,848	16,368	4,308	—	—	329,816	2.015
1934	49	47,712	44,884	—	—	1,973,247	48.0	452,176	18,069	4,168	—	—	346,870	1.920
1935	50	48,367	42,426	—	—	1,867,381	48.3	448,059	18,509	4,118	—	—	358,423	1.936
1936	53	48,972	41,390	—	—	1,790,043	48.8	492,493	22,460	4,188	—	—	413,189	1.840
1937	48	49,412	40,949	—	—	1,776,428	49.2	499,688	24,695	4,116	12,417	8,126	443,532	1.796
1938	49	49,803	39,931	—	—	1,731,096	49.4	454,508	21,657	4,032	10,247	7,354	406,406	1.877
1939	50	50,395	38,977	—	—	1,680,519	49.7	454,032	22,713	4,012	11,118	7,527	417,716	1.839
1940	56	50,905	38,308	—	—	1,684,171	50.0	456,088	23,816	3,997	12,485	7,288	417,955	1.755
1941	52	51,217	38,334	—	—	1,732,673	50.3	488,668	29,406	4,088	16,106	9,166	515,851	1.754
1942	46	51,811	38,446	—	—	1,773,735	50.5	672,420	53,747	4,761	30,910	17,853	1,030,486	1.917
1943	40	52,451	38,331	45,764	13,165	1,784,472	50.7	887,674	87,925	5,261	57,909	24,675	1,655,814	1.883
1944	50	52,822	38,217	46,588	13,175	1,797,012	50.8	915,817	95,663	6,344	63,288	26,944	1,793,322	1.875

Equipment

Passenger traffic and revenue

Year	Locomotives in service — Other [7] Df942 (Number)	Locomotives in service — Average tractive effort [7] Df943 (Number)	Passenger-train cars in service (Class I railroads and Pullman Co.) — Railroad only Df944 (Number)	Passenger-train cars — Total [8] Df945 (Number)	Passenger-train cars — Air conditioned [8] Df946 (Number)	Freight-train cars in service Df947 (Number)	Freight-train cars — Average capacity [7] Df948 (Tons)	Passengers Df949 (Thousand)	Passenger-miles — Total Df950 (Million passenger-miles)	Passenger-miles — Commutation [4] Df951 (Million passenger-miles)	Passenger-miles — Coach [4] Df952 (Million passenger-miles)	Passenger-miles — Parlor and sleeping car [4] Df953 (Million passenger-miles)	Revenue — Total Df954 (Thousand dollars)	Revenue — Per passenger-mile Df955 (Cents per passenger-mile)
1945	49	53,217	38,633	46,863	12,685	1,787,073	51.1	897,384	91,826	5,418	59,415	26,912	1,719,316	1.872
1946	44	53,735	38,697	45,637	13,967	1,768,400	51.3	794,824	64,754	5,857	39,039	19,801	1,261,416	1.948
1947	43	54,506	39,057	44,841	14,628	1,759,758	51.5	706,551	45,972	6,011	27,660	12,261	965,005	2.099
1948	45	55,170	39,406	44,447	15,249	1,785,067	51.9	645,535	41,224	5,855	24,315	11,015	965,630	2.342
1949	47	56,333	38,006	43,578	16,008	1,778,811	52.4	556,741	35,133	5,478	20,273	9,349	862,139	2.454
1950	48	57,075	37,359	43,372	16,747	1,745,778	52.6	488,019	31,790	4,990	17,443	9,338	814,741	2.563
1951	52	58,476	36,326	42,406	16,502	1,777,878	52.9	485,468	34,640	4,866	19,524	10,226	901,019	2.601
1952	52	59,966	34,942	41,011	16,320	1,783,352	53.2	470,979	34,033	4,755	19,758	9,504	906,838	2.665
1953	55	61,339	34,106	39,532	16,231	1,801,874	53.5	458,252	31,679	4,757	18,955	7,950	842,663	2.660
1954	67	63,152	33,035	37,768	15,733	1,761,386	53.7	440,770	29,310	4,753	17,687	6,850	767,987	2.620
1955	65	65,005	32,118	35,455	14,784	1,723,747	53.7	433,308	28,548	4,776	17,314	6,441	743,688	2.605
1956	58	68,745	30,817	—	14,551	1,738,631	54.0	429,994	28,216	4,841	17,074	6,275	757,625	2.685
1957	49	61,515	29,564	32,231	14,323	1,777,557	54.5	412,625	25,914	4,901	15,803	5,185	786,408	2.842
1958	51	61,312	28,999	—	13,675	1,755,775	54.8	381,623	23,295	4,776	14,225	4,249	676,316	2.903
1959	54	61,408	27,419	29,160	12,993	1,708,116	55.0	353,647	22,075	4,549	13,704	3,798	652,316	2.955
1960	66	61,314	25,746	27,414	11,787	1,690,396	55.4	328,172	21,284	4,197	13,422	3,643	641,496	3.014
1961	72	61,969	24,433	26,899	11,259	1,635,342	55.7	318,359	20,308	4,132	12,893	3,262	625,874	3.082
1962	67	61,415	23,430	24,634	10,423	1,581,213	56.3	313,084	19,926	4,046	12,757	3,102	620,290	3.113
1963	58	61,533	22,616	23,568	9,950	1,542,456	56.8	310,999	18,519	4,101	11,785	2,611	589,621	3.183
1964	56	62,311	21,510	23,057	8,980	1,517,564	58.2	314,386	18,271	4,199	11,632	2,416	679,287	3.170
1965	55	63,096	20,022	21,327	8,079	1,515,169	59.8	305,822	17,454	4,128	11,069	2,191	555,986	3.185
1966	57	70,900	18,974	20,016	7,589	1,523,741	61.4	307,530	17,162	4,193	10,799	2,104	547,139	3.188
1967	55	65,267	17,822	18,610	7,159	1,510,963	63.4	304,028	15,264	4,281	9,329	1,592	488,549	3.201
1968	110 [11]	—	14,816	15,384	—	1,484,571	64.3	301,372	13,164	4,383	7,559	1,178	446,704	3.393
1969	101 [11]	—	12,630	14,619	—	1,464,194	65.8	301,673	12,214	4,546	6,601	1,021	441,503	3.615
1970	79 [11]	—	11,378	11,177	—	1,453,708	67.1	289,469	10,786	4,592	5,414	765	428,191	3.924
1971	99	—	8,869	7,548	—	1,440,873	68.4	275,534	8,863	—	—	—	384,116	4.334
1972	98	—	7,763	6,018	—	1,410,584	69.5	262,010	8,572	—	—	—	408,863	4.770
1973	63	—	7,363	5,412	—	1,386,990	70.5	255,444	9,308	—	—	—	444,412	4.774
1974	68	—	7,080	5,000	—	1,369,186	71.4	255,185	10,349	—	—	—	540,441	5.222
1975	65	—	6,658	4,558	—	1,344,979	73.0	270,209	9,948	—	—	—	539,033	5.412
1976	—	—	5,647	—	—	1,309,410	73.8	272,359	10,318	—	—	—	595,873	5.775
1977	—	—	5,674	—	—	1,275,542	75.5	276,187	10,306	—	—	—	611,702	5.936
1978	—	—	2,418	—	—	1,201,387	77.8	262,094	6,263	—	—	—	379,733	6.064
1979	—	—	2,389	—	—	1,148,705	79.7	273,665	6,500	—	—	—	409,764	6.304
1980	—	—	2,275	—	—	1,133,746	79.3	281,503	6,557	—	—	—	443,659	6.766

1 Includes intercorporate duplications.

2 Covers Class I, II, and III railroads, except that prior to 1908 includes returns for switching and terminal companies where applicable. Other exceptions are specifically noted.

3 Through the first set of values shown for 1916, data are for fiscal years ending June 30, except for series Df936–937, which correspond to calendar years. Thereafter, all data are for calendar years.

4 Class I railroads only.

5 For 1890–1927, number of locomotives; for 1928–1970, number of units, except for steam locomotives. See text.

6 For 1915–1922, identified as "other than steam," but most or all must have been electric.

7 For 1916–1956, represents steam locomotives and freight cars of Class I railroads excluding switching and terminal companies; for 1957–1967, includes all Class I locomotives excluding switching and terminal companies.

8 Beginning 1969, excludes Pullman Company.

9 First set of 1916 figures is comparable to earlier data; second set is comparable to later data.

10 Calendar-year data.

11 Steam or diesel locomotives included with "other."

12 Class I and II railroads only.

TABLE Df927-955   Railroad mileage, equipment, and passenger traffic and revenue: 1890-1980   *Continued*

Sources

For all series except series Df936-937, and for all years prior to 1954, U.S. Interstate Commerce Commission (ICC), *Statistics of Railways in the United States* (annual issues), and for 1954-1980, U.S. Interstate Commerce Commission, *Transport Statistics in the United States*, Part 1 (annual issues). For series Df936, 1913-1975, and series Df937, 1911-1956, American Railway Car Institute, New York, *Railroad Car Facts* (annual issues). For series Df937, 1957-1970, ICC, *Transport Statistics in the United States*, Part 1 (annual issues).

Documentation

Railway operating companies are those whose officers direct the actual transportation service and whose books contain operating as well as financial accounts. Lessor companies maintain a separate legal existence, but their properties are operated by the lessees. Proprietary companies are also nonoperating companies. Their outstanding capitalization is owned by other railway companies. The term "circular" refers to roads (operating or nonoperating) for which brief circulars showing date of incorporation, mileage, and a few other facts were filed with the ICC. They include intrastate roads and roads under construction.

Switching and terminal companies are those operating separately for joint account or for revenue. Services such as those of switching and terminal companies are mostly performed directly by the line-haul carriers as an ordinary part of their business. "Line haul" denotes train movements between terminals and stations on main and branch lines of the road, exclusive of switching.

Beginning in 1911, the ICC classified operating companies on the basis of operating revenues. Those of Class I had annual revenues of more than $1,000,000; Class II, more than $100,000; and Class III, less than $100,000. Beginning in 1956, the minimum for Class I was raised to $3,000,000, and the other two classes were consolidated. Effective January 1965, the classification was changed to the following: Class I, $5,000,000 or more; and Class II, less than $5,000,000. If the revenues of a company fall below the limit, the company is not reclassified until the decline appears to be permanent. The relative importance of Class I railroads has increased since 1911 because of the growth of traffic and the absorption of small roads into larger systems. The ratio of operating revenues of Class I line-haul companies to the total revenues of Classes I, II, and III was 96.48 percent in 1911, 97.45 in 1916, 98.07 in 1926, 98.76 in 1941, 99.06 in 1945, and 98.21 in 1969.

Series Df927. Includes circular and unofficial railroads.

Series Df928. Reports miles on which operations were begun during the year. The data exclude relocated road or road constructed to shorten distance without serving new territory.

Series Df929. Reports miles on which operation was permanently abandoned during the year, the cost of which was written out of the investment accounts or was scheduled to be written out at the end of the year.

Series Df930. Data are for first (main) track and includes lessors, proprietary, unofficial, and, through 1963, circular companies.

Series Df931. Includes only railroads reporting track by class and excludes circular and unofficial.

Series Df932. Reports first main track operated. This is equivalent to miles of road operated. The data exceed those for series Df930, road owned, in most years because of two or more roads operating on the same line under trackage agreements.

Series Df936-948. Include switching and terminal companies.

Series Df938. Starting in 1928, number of units, except for steam locomotives. A unit is the least number of wheel bases together with superstructure capable of independent propulsion, but not necessarily equipped with an independent control.

Series Df943. Reports a measure of the force in pounds exerted by locomotives as measured at the rim of the driving wheels.

Series Df944-946. Include coaches and parlor, sleeping, dining, club, lounge, observation, postal, baggage, express, and other cars, as well as cars serving a combination of purposes.

Series Df947-948. Exclude caboose cars.

Series Df954. Excludes revenue from services such as handling of excess baggage or mail; sleeping and parlor or chair car reservations; dining and buffet service on trains; station, train, and boat privileges; parcel rooms; storage of baggage; or other miscellaneous services and facilities connected with the transportation of passengers. Passenger revenue depends on the established tariffs (the published schedules of rates and fares) and includes extra fares on limited trains, additional railway fares for the exclusive use of space, mileage and scrip coupons honored, or revenue from the transportation of corpses.

Series Df955. Equals series Df954 divided by series Df950.

TABLE Df956–963   Railroad passenger and freight operations – per-car and per-train traffic volume, and speed: 1890–1980[1,2]

Contributed by Louis P. Cain

	Passenger			Freight				
	Revenue passengers				Revenue tons			
	Per car-mile	Per train-mile	Train-miles per train-hour	Per loaded car-mile	Per train-mile	Per mile of road	Train-miles per train-hour	Car-miles per car-day
	Df956	Df957	Df958	Df959	Df960	Df961	Df962	Df963
Year	Passengers per car	Passengers per train	Miles per hour	Tons per car	Tons per train	Ton-miles per mile	Miles per hour	Miles per day
1890	—	41.4	—	—	176.12	487,245	—	—
1891	—	41.7	—	—	181.67	502,705	—	—
1892	—	42.0	—	—	181.89	543,365	—	—
1893	—	42.4	—	—	183.97	551,232	—	—
1894	—	43.7	—	—	179.80	457,252	—	—
1895	—	38.3	—	—	189.69	479,490	—	—
1896	—	39.2	—	—	198.81	523,832	—	—
1897	—	36.6	—	—	204.62	519,079	—	—
1898	—	39.1	—	—	226.45	617,810	—	—
1899	—	41.2	—	—	243.52	659,565	—	—
1900	—	44.2	—	—	270.86	785,352	—	—
1901	—	45.1	—	16.55	281.26	760,414	—	—
1902	—	48.5	—	16.92	296.47	793,351	—	—
1903	—	49.2	—	17.60	310.54	855,442	—	—
1904	—	49.8	—	17.72	307.76	829,476	—	—
1905	—	51.7	—	18.14	322.26	861,396	—	—
1906	—	52.5	—	18.92	344.39	982,401	—	—
1907	—	54.5	—	19.68	357.35	1,052,119	—	—
1908	15.5	57.5	—	19.62	351.80	974,654	—	—
1909	15.4	57.5	—	19.26	362.57	953,986	—	—
1910	15.7	58.9	—	19.84	380.38	1,071,086	—	—
1911	15.6	57.9	—	19.74	383.10	1,053,566	—	—
1912	15.1	56.5	—	20.18	406.76	1,078,580	—	—
1913	15.4	58.5	—	21.12 [4]	445.43 [4]	1,190,397	—	—
1914	15.4	58.4	—	21.09	446.96	1,125,084	—	—
1915	15.0	56.0	—	21.14	476.13	1,075,962	—	—
1916 [3]	15.3	58.2	—	22.39	536.67	1,325,089	—	—
1916 [3]	15.5	59.2	—	22.83	552.26	1,409,957	—	—
1917	17.2	67.6	—	24.75	588.29	1,538,211	—	—
1918	19.9	79.4	—	26.96	620.68	1,582,796	—	—
1919	20.5	84.7	—	25.44	622.51	1,423,390	—	—
1920	19.8	82.4	—	26.71	639.03	1,697,133	10.3	—
1921	16.4	66.4	—	24.60	566.74	1,199,328	11.5	22.4
1922	15.9	64.6	—	24.31	599.12	1,330,460	11.1	23.5
1923	16.3	65.9	—	26.18	632.32	1,615,741	10.9	27.8
1924	15.3	62.1	—	24.47	634.43	1,518,556	11.5	26.8
1925	14.8	61.5	—	24.55	662.53	1,613,862	11.8	28.5
1926	14.2	60.4	—	24.96	688.56	1,732,295	11.9	30.4
1927	13.5	57.9	—	24.60	689.68	1,668,800	12.3	30.3
1928	12.9	55.1	—	24.31	705.86	1,677,089	12.9	31.2
1929	12.5	54.4	—	24.52	713.03	1,727,786	13.2	32.3
1930	11.3	48.9	—	24.28	699.27	1,481,199	13.8	28.7
1931	10.5	44.7	—	23.44	652.87	1,196,960	14.8	24.5
1932	9.8	39.9	—	22.56	585.49	908,296	15.5	19.8
1933	10.2	42.5	—	23.26	619.13	972,262	15.7	21.3
1934	10.9	46.7	—	23.19	623.62	1,058,609	15.9	24.2
1935	11.2	47.5	—	23.49	646.17	1,119,290	16.0	25.8
1936	13.6	55.4	34.0	24.32	687.49	1,353,406	15.8	30.7
1937	14.0	59.0	34.5	24.68	708.35	1,446,921	16.1	32.9
1938	13.1	54.5	34.7	23.80	676.57	1,171,637	16.6	28.5
1939	13.5	57.6	35.4	24.59	727.45	1,355,052	16.7	32.3
1940	14.0	60.3	35.8	25.40	764.30	1,525,579	16.7	35.6
1941	16.0	72.7	36.1	26.28	827.48	1,950,166	16.5	41.6
1942	23.7	124.9	35.7	29.76	947.87	2,638,067	15.8	47.4
1943	31.7	188.6	34.7	31.36	1,027.64	3,032,199	15.4	49.7
1944	32.2	199.8	34.8	30.62	1,045.67	3,084,195	15.7	50.6

Notes appear at end of table

(continued)

TABLE Df956–963   Railroad passenger and freight operations – per-car and per-train traffic volume, and speed: 1890–1980 Continued

	Passenger			Freight				
	Revenue passengers				Revenue tons			
	Per car-mile	Per train-mile	Train-miles per train-hour	Per loaded car-mile	Per train-mile	Per mile of road	Train-miles per train-hour	Car-miles per car-day
	Df956	Df957	Df958	Df959	Df960	Df961	Df962	Df963
Year	Passengers per car	Passengers per train	Miles per hour	Tons per car	Tons per train	Ton-miles per mile	Miles per hour	Miles per day
1945	30.4	189.7	34.7	30.18	1,034.49	2,852,615	15.7	47.7
1946	24.7	143.7	35.1	29.25	992.95	2,488,499	16.0	43.5
1947	21.1	110.2	36.1	30.61	1,052.43	2,752,915	16.0	46.9
1948	19.4	100.8	36.7	30.90	1,080.30	2,695,708	16.2	45.1
1949	18.0	92.0	37.0	29.48	1,044.83	2,229,430	16.9	40.3
1950	17.0	88.5	37.4	29.97	1,131.47	2,496,927	16.8	43.6
1951	18.1	97.2	37.7	31.38	1,211.06	2,748,700	17.0	45.0
1952	18.1	98.4	38.3	31.02	1,210.90	2,622,463	17.6	44.0
1953	17.7	94.8	39.1	30.66	1,219.03	2,592,188	18.2	44.3
1954	17.4	92.0	39.5	30.27	1,216.54	2,356,646	18.7	41.2
1955	17.8	95.2	39.8	30.94	1,296.86	2,679,482	18.6	45.7
1956	18.1	96.9	40.0	31.98	1,347.21	2,789,340	18.6	45.0
1957	18.1	93.9	40.2	32.42	1,369.56	2,676,573	18.8	43.7
1958	18.6	94.0	40.2	32.10	1,362.05	2,394,040	19.2	39.6
1959	18.9	97.6	40.3	32.32	1,374.99	2,506,800	19.5	41.2
1960	19.3	100.9	40.7	33.11	1,399.31	2,496,638	19.5	40.9
1961	19.8	101.5	40.9	33.80	1,441.87	2,460,997	19.9	40.6
1962	20.0	102.6	40.9	34.87	1,490.70	2,612,129	20.0	42.8
1963	19.6	97.3	40.9	36.27	1,537.72	2,750,078	20.1	44.6
1964	20.3	99.4	41.4	37.63	1,572.60	2,917,502	20.2	47.2
1965	19.5	100.9	41.3	39.02	1,638.44	3,120,778	20.1	49.0
1966	20.2	104.1	41.3	40.34	1,669.77	3,312,186	20.3	50.6
1967	20.7	101.5	41.7	41.24	1,693.38	3,237,648	20.3	49.1
1968	22.4	107.0	41.0	41.77	1,714.88	3,385,901	20.4	51.3
1969	24.7	113.6	41.0	42.75	1,754.54	3,456,667	20.1	52.6
1970	25.8	116.2	40.1	44.32	1,774.14	3,468,168	20.1	51.8
1971	—	—	—	44.88	1,708.41	3,014,641	—	—
1972	—	—	—	45.36	1,709.31	3,067,568	—	—
1973	—	—	—	47.27	1,803.92	3,563,903	—	—
1974	—	—	—	48.18	1,794.75	3,544,830	—	—
1975	—	—	—	49.89	1,861.54	3,160,745	—	—
1976	—	—	—	50.17	1,857.72	3,321,801	—	—
1977	—	—	—	50.71	1,922.57	3,542,813	—	—
1978	—	—	—	53.79	1,973.97	4,369,354	—	—
1979	—	—	—	57.36	2,063.86	4,669,420	—	—
1980	—	—	—	62.62	2,137.96	4,870,088	—	—

[1] Class I, II, and III railroads except as follows: series Df956, Class I beginning in 1911; series Df957, Class I beginning in 1933; and series Df958 and Df962-963, Class I for all years.

[2] Fiscal years ending June 30 through the first set of values shown for 1916; calendar years thereafter.

[3] First set of 1916 figures is comparable to earlier data; second set is comparable to later data.

[4] Class I and II railroads.

Sources

Series Df956–957. 1890–1965, U.S. Interstate Commerce Commission (ICC), *Revenue Traffic Statistics* (December issues); 1966–1970, ICC, *Transport Economics* (June 1970), and unpublished data.

Series Df958. 1936–1957, ICC, *Passenger Train Performance* (December issues); 1958–1968, ICC, *Annual Report* (1968 and 1969); 1969 and 1970, ICC, *Transport Economics* (June 1970), and unpublished data.

Series Df959–961. 1890–1953, ICC, *Statistics of Railways in the United States*, and 1954–1980, ICC, *Transport Statistics in the United States*, Part 1 (annual issues).

Series Df962. 1920–1955, ICC, *Freight Train Performance* (December issues); 1956–1965, ICC, *Annual Report* (1967 and 1969); 1966–1970, *Transport Economics* (June 1970), and unpublished data.

Series Df963. ICC, 1920–1953, *Statistics of Railways in the United States;* 1954–1955, ICC, *Transport Statistics in the United States*, Part 1; 1956–1962, ICC, *Annual Report* (various issues); 1963–1965, ICC, *Transport Statistics in the United States* (1967); 1966–1970, ICC, *Transport Economics* (June 1970), and unpublished data.

Documentation

The data in series Df956 for 1908–1919, and for series Df957 for 1890–1932, were computed by the National Bureau of Economic Research from figures for passenger-miles, car-miles, and train-miles presented in *Statistics of Railways in the United States*. Tons are 2,000 pounds.

See the text for Table Df927–955 for definitions of railroad company types.

Series Df958 and Df962. The train-hour figures on which the data in series Df958 and Df962 are based are reckoned from the time a train leaves its

TABLE Df956–963   Railroad passenger and freight operations – per-car and per-train traffic volume, and speed: 1890–1980   Continued

original terminal to the time it arrives at its final terminal. Time spent in stopping to take on and discharge traffic and other delays on the road are included.

Series Df959. The data were obtained by dividing the revenue ton-miles by the total loaded car-miles, the latter item including some cars loaded with

nonrevenue freight. The method is necessary to preserve comparability with figures for the earlier years; they differ slightly from the average "net tons per loaded car" shown in the regular monthly statements, *Freight and Passenger Service Operating Statistics*, based on revenue and nonrevenue ton-miles and car-miles.

TABLE Df964   Railroad mileage operated by receivers or trustees: 1894–1975[1]

Contributed by Louis P. Cain

| | Mileage operated by receivers or trustees | | Mileage operated by receivers or trustees | | Mileage operated by receivers or trustees | | Mileage operated by receivers or trustees |
| | Df964 | | Df964 | | Df964 | | Df964 |
Year	Miles	Year	Miles	Year	Miles	Year	Miles
1894	40,819	1915	30,223	1935	68,345	1955	11,685
1895	37,856	1916 [2]	37,353	1936	69,712	1956	1,594
1896	30,475	1916 [2]	34,804	1937	70,884	1957	1,022
1897	18,862	1917	17,376	1938	76,938	1958	1,040
1898	12,745	1918	19,208	1939	77,013	1959	1,097
1899	9,853	1919	16,590				
		1920	16,290	1940	75,270	1960	1,259
1900	4,178	1921	13,512	1941	69,859	1961	2,365
1901	2,497	1922	15,259	1942	66,904	1962	2,113
1902	1,475	1923	12,623	1943	64,758	1963	1,748
1903	1,185	1924	8,105	1944	50,497	1964	1,732
1904	1,323			1945	39,714	1965	1,690
1905	796	1925	18,687	1946	34,389	1966	1,612
1906	3,971	1926	17,632	1947	22,750	1967	2,476
1907	3,926	1927	16,752	1948	13,283	1968	650
1908	9,529	1928	5,256	1949	12,679	1969	649
1909	10,530	1929	5,703				
				1950	12,223	1970	23,190
1910	5,257	1930	9,486	1951	12,212	1971	24,137
1911	4,593	1931	12,970	1952	11,942	1972	26,963
1912	9,786	1932	22,545	1953	12,054	1973	26,773
1913	16,286	1933	41,698	1954	11,608	1974	26,701
1914	18,608	1934	42,168			1975	33,924

[1] Fiscal years through the first set of values shown for 1916; calendar years thereafter.

[2] First set of 1916 figures is comparable to earlier data; second set is comparable to later data.

Sources

For 1894–1953, U.S. Interstate Commerce Commission (ICC), *Statistics of*

Railways in the United States, and for 1954–1975, ICC, *Transport Statistics in the United States*, Part 1 (annual issues).

Documentation

Data are for Class I, II, and III railroads. See the text for Table Df927–955 for definitions of railroad company types.

TABLE Df965–979 Railroad freight traffic and revenue: 1890–1980[1,2]

Contributed by Louis P. Cain

	All tonnage	Revenue freight originated — In carloads						Less than carload	Revenue tons originated	Ton-miles	Haul per ton	Depreciation and retirements	Revenue — Total	Per ton	Per ton-mile
	Df965	Df966 Total	Df967 Products of agriculture	Df968 Animals and products	Df969 Products of mines	Df970 Products of forests	Df971 Manufactures and miscellaneous [3]	Df972	Df973	Df974	Df975	Df976	Df977	Df978	Df979
Year	Thousand tons	Thousand tons	Thousand tons	Thousand tons	Thousand tons	Thousand tons	Thousand tons	Thousand tons	Million tons	Million ton-miles	Miles per ton	Thousand dollars	Million dollars	Dollars per ton	Cents per ton-mile
1890	—	—	—	—	—	—	—	—	—	76,207	—	—	714	—	0.941
1891	—	—	—	—	—	—	—	—	—	81,074	—	—	737	—	0.895
1892	—	—	—	—	—	—	—	—	—	88,241	—	—	799	—	0.898
1893	—	—	—	—	—	—	—	—	—	93,588	—	—	829	—	0.878
1894	—	—	—	—	—	—	—	—	—	80,335	—	—	699	—	0.860
1895	—	—	—	—	—	—	—	—	—	85,228	—	—	730	—	0.839
1896	—	—	—	—	—	—	—	—	—	95,328	—	—	787	—	0.806
1897	—	—	—	—	—	—	—	—	—	95,139	—	—	773	—	0.798
1898	—	—	—	—	—	—	—	—	—	114,078	—	—	877	—	0.753
1899	—	—	—	—	—	—	—	—	502	123,667	246.58	—	914	1.82	0.724
1900	—	—	—	—	—	—	—	—	583	141,597	242.73	—	1,049	1.80	0.729
1901	—	—	—	—	—	—	—	—	584	147,077	251.98	—	1,119	1.92	0.750
1902	—	—	—	—	—	—	—	—	658	157,289	239.10	—	1,207	1.84	0.757
1903	—	—	—	—	—	—	—	—	715	173,221	242.35	—	1,338	1.87	0.763
1904	—	—	—	—	—	—	—	—	714	174,522	244.30	—	1,379	1.93	0.780
1905	—	—	—	—	—	—	—	—	785	186,463	237.56	—	1,451	1.85	0.766
1906	—	—	—	—	—	—	—	—	896	215,878	240.89	—	1,640	1.83	0.748
1907	—	—	—	—	—	—	—	—	977	236,601	242.05	—	1,824	1.87	0.759
1908	—	—	—	—	—	—	—	—	870	218,382	253.94	—	1,655	1.90	0.754
1909	—	—	—	—	—	—	—	—	881	218,803	251.10	—	1,678	1.90	0.763
1910	—	—	—	—	—	—	—	—	1,026	255,017	249.68	—	1,926	1.88	0.753
1911	901,573 [5]	866,398 [5]	81,780	22,833	483,861	79,345	163,380	35,175	1,003	253,784	254.10	—	1,926	1.92	0.757
1912	926,990 [5]	889,999 [5]	86,433	24,064	506,306	74,796	166,134	36,991	1,031	264,081	256.87	—	1,969	1.91	0.744
1913	1,067,978 [5]	1,026,817 [5]	102,658	25,669	592,164	93,762	196,947	41,161	1,183	301,730	255.15	—	2,199 [6]	1.86 [6]	0.729 [6]
1914	1,023,131 [5]	982,892 [5]	98,825	26,352	574,000	91,094	177,950	40,239	1,130	288,637	255.43	—	2,127	1.88	0.737
1915 [4]	925,697 [5]	878,761 [5]	109,483	26,001	507,250	76,674	157,085	46,936	1,024	277,135	270.69	—	2,038	1.99	0.735
1916 [4]	1,203,367 [5]	1,150,456 [5]	113,635	30,473	680,123	93,819	231,039	52,911	1,263	343,477	271.98	—	2,469	1.96	0.719
1917	1,264,016	1,210,247	104,629	31,858	732,653	100,838	240,269	53,769	1,317	366,173	277.98	—	2,631	2.00	0.719
1918	1,263,344	1,209,957	116,051	35,777	734,796	97,256	226,077	53,387	1,382	398,263	288.18	—	2,897	2.10	0.728
1919	1,096,449 [5]	1,045,148 [5]	115,033	35,494	589,951	94,076	210,256	51,301	1,377	408,778	296.89	—	3,522	2.56	0.862
1920	1,255,421 [5]	1,202,219 [5]	110,840	26,595	712,155	100,765	251,864	53,202	1,190	367,161	308.60	—	3,625	3.05	0.987
1921	940,183	898,191	114,069	24,263	511,271	76,419	172,169	41,992	1,363	413,699	303.52	—	4,421	3.24	1.069
1922	1,023,745	980,516	111,787	26,230	532,998	89,059	220,442	43,229	1,018	309,533	304.11	155,968	4,004	3.93	1.294
1923	1,279,030	1,234,692	109,318	28,254	713,735	115,618	267,767	44,338	1,112	342,188	307.77	169,808	4,086	3.67	1.194
1924	1,187,296	1,146,747	116,587	27,747	637,582	108,094	256,737	40,549	1,388	416,256	299.94	205,070	4,712	3.40	1.132
1925	1,247,242	1,206,655	109,313	26,324	678,336	107,391	285,291	40,587	1,287	391,945	304.44	208,064	4,437	3.45	1.132
1926	1,336,142	1,296,651	111,787	26,244	757,703	104,851	296,066	39,491	1,351	417,418	308.93	223,925	4,648	3.44	1.114
1927	1,281,611	1,243,171	113,342	26,003	713,402	99,351	291,073	38,440	1,440	447,444	310.81	231,497	4,906	3.41	1.096
1928	1,285,943	1,248,989	118,022	25,634	696,583	96,737	312,013	36,954	1,373	432,014	314.75	239,184	4,729	3.45	1.095
1929	1,339,091	1,303,048	115,343	24,907	737,879	94,855	330,064	36,043	1,371	436,087	318.00	241,719	4,772	3.48	1.094
1930	—	—	—	—	—	—	—	—	1,419	450,189	317.17	259,375	4,899	3.45	1.088

Revenue freight originated | Freight and revenue

				In carloads										Revenue	
Year	All tonnage	Total	Products of agriculture	Animals and products	Products of mines	Products of forests	Manufactures and miscellaneous [3]	Less than carload	Revenue tons originated	Ton-miles	Haul per ton	Depreciation and retirements	Total	Per ton	Per ton-mile
	Df965	Df966	Df967	Df968	Df969	Df970	Df971	Df972	Df973	Df974	Df975	Df976	Df977	Df978	Df979
	Thousand tons	Thousand tons	Thousand tons	Thousand tons	Thousand tons	Thousand tons	Thousand tons	Thousand tons	Million tons	Million ton-miles	Miles per ton	Thousand dollars	Million dollars	Dollars per ton	Cents per ton-mile
1930	1,153,197	1,123,530	110,728	23,129	642,537	69,371	277,765	29,667	1,220	385,815	316.21	243,253	4,145	3.40	1.074
1931	894,186	871,412	97,487	21,632	501,903	43,024	207,366	22,774	945	311,073	329.23	221,611	3,302	3.50	1.062
1932	646,223	630,989	80,917	18,055	362,226	26,109	143,682	15,234	679	235,309	346.63	209,111	2,485	3.66	1.056
1933	698,943	684,592	81,702	17,651	395,065	33,165	157,009	14,351	733	250,651	341.77	199,917	2,529	3.45	1.009
1934	765,296	750,951	79,305	20,363	436,380	35,650	179,253	14,345	802	270,292	336.91	192,387	2,672	3.33	0.989
1935	789,627	775,588	76,338	15,125	445,136	42,483	196,506	14,039	832	283,637	341.05	194,625	2,831	3.40	0.998
1936	958,830	942,538	86,648	16,209	541,488	53,156	245,037	16,292	1,012	341,182	337.29	193,502	3,357	3.32	0.984
1937	1,015,586	998,398	89,460	15,233	569,745	58,658	265,302	17,188	1,075	362,815	337.43	197,035	3,428	3.19	0.945
1938	771,862	757,470	95,390	14,760	408,835	43,973	194,512	14,392	820	291,866	356.05	201,825	2,901	3.54	0.994
1939	901,669	886,794	91,564	15,049	496,939	50,156	233,086	14,875	955	335,375	351.21	201,852	3,297	3.45	0.983
1940	1,009,421	994,728	88,821	15,456	570,220	58,221	262,010	14,693	1,069	375,369	351.13	205,860	3,584	3.35	0.955
1941	1,227,650	1,209,559	100,173	16,810	684,433	71,540	336,603	18,091	1,296	477,576	368.54	233,340	4,510	3.48	0.944
1942	1,421,187	1,408,612	117,318	20,620	804,577	84,570	376,527	17,575	1,498	640,992	427.76	338,181	6,026	4.02	0.940
1943	1,481,225	1,462,314	148,971	22,936	797,163	80,899	412,345	18,911	1,557	730,132	469.07	465,525	6,866	4.41	0.940
1944	1,491,491	1,471,366	145,685	25,413	785,265	83,731	431,272	20,125	1,565	740,586	473.28	540,461	7,087	4.53	0.957
1945	1,424,913	1,404,080	159,571	23,748	732,942	75,604	412,215	20,833	1,493	684,148	458.14	1,186,844	6,617	4.43	0.967
1946	1,366,617	1,342,230	149,941	21,587	717,806	84,817	368,079	24,387	1,432	594,943	415.48	365,902	5,866	4.10	0.986
1947	1,537,546	1,514,985	158,168	19,716	847,807	87,027	402,267	22,561	1,613	657,878	407.82	385,763	7,141	4.43	1.085
1948	1,506,878	1,488,612	145,176	16,865	845,640	86,104	394,827	18,266	1,580	641,104	405.64	409,310	8,090	5.12	1.262
1949	1,226,503	1,213,911	140,383	15,284	653,759	69,257	335,228	12,592	1,284	529,111	412.02	441,658	7,151	5.57	1.352
1950	1,354,196	1,343,308	129,175	14,321	746,808	78,860	374,144	10,888	1,421	591,550	416.32	466,589	7,934	5.58	1.341
1951	1,477,402	1,467,023	140,811	14,362	819,373	86,522	405,955	10,379	1,547	649,831	419.99	485,160	8,758	5.66	1.348
1952	1,382,604	1,373,294	138,415	14,601	752,699	83,480	384,097	9,310	1,447	617,942	426.93	513,059	8,915	6.16	1.443
1953	1,384,301	1,376,046	131,137	13,768	754,292	82,107	394,742	8,255	1,448	608,954	420.66	534,457	9,078	6.27	1.491
1954	1,223,969	1,217,005	131,733	13,128	650,074	75,650	346,420	6,964	1,279	552,197	431.65	547,267	7,915	6.19	1.433
1955	1,396,339	1,389,346	133,789	13,161	761,993	82,584	397,819	6,993	1,459	626,893	429.75	554,597	8,665	5.94	1.382
1956	1,447,422	1,440,937	138,093	13,198	796,480	87,799	405,367	6,485	1,521	651,188	428.08	569,605	9,089	5.97	1.396
1957	1,380,327	1,374,884	137,618	11,074	769,675	77,497	379,020	5,443	1,449	621,907	429.20	596,355	9,064	6.26	1.457
1958	1,190,353	1,185,951	146,746	9,895	628,911	73,287	327,112	4,402	1,247	554,534	444.55	618,062	8,193	6.57	1.477
1959	1,232,201	1,228,277	145,531	9,994	632,870	80,397	359,485	3,923	1,293	578,637	447.66	625,888	8,442	6.53	1.459
1960	1,240,789	1,237,575	150,350	9,463	649,228	79,211	349,323	3,213	1,301	575,360	442.14	634,778	8,152	6.26	1.417
1961	1,193,740	1,191,154	153,819	9,341	615,646	74,924	337,424	2,586	1,253	566,295	452.00	652,271	7,869	6.27	1.388
1962	1,233,597	1,231,415	155,301	9,452	634,747	78,105	353,809	2,183	1,294	595,774	460.57	660,586	8,115	6.27	1.362
1963	1,285,061	1,283,382	160,589	9,378	662,461	78,319	372,635	1,679	1,347	625,170	463.97	676,584	8,271	6.14	1.323
1964	1,354,612	1,353,117	—	—	—	—	—	1,496	1,420	662,089	466.17	685,785	8,575	6.04	1.295

Notes appear at end of table

(continued)

TABLE Df965–979   Railroad freight traffic and revenue: 1890–1980   Continued

	Revenue freight originated								Freight and revenue			Revenue		
	In carloads													
	All tonnage	Total	Products of agriculture	Animals and products	Products of mines	Products of forests	Manufactures and miscellaneous[3]	Less than carload	Revenue tons originated	Ton-miles	Haul per ton	Depreciation and retirements	Total	Per ton	Per ton-mile
	Df965	Df966	Df967	Df968	Df969	Df970	Df971	Df972	Df973	Df974	Df975	Df976	Df977	Df978	Df979
Year	Thousand tons	Thousand tons	Thousand tons	Thousand tons	Thousand tons	Thousand tons	Thousand tons	Thousand tons	Million tons	Million ton-miles	Miles per ton	Thousand dollars	Million dollars	Dollars per ton	Cents per ton-mile
1965	1,387,423	1,386,090	—	—	—	—	—	1,333	1,479	705,705	477.15	714,052	9,037	6.11	1.281
1966	1,448,901	1,447,852	—	—	—	—	—	1,049	1,544	746,699	483.70	744,800	9,487	6.15	1.271
1967	1,407,628	1,406,668	—	—	—	—	—	960	1,498	727,075	485.21	765,768	9,329	6.23	1.283
1968	1,481,308	1,430,441	—	—	—	—	—	867	1,515	750,468	495.37	775,356	9,942	6.56	1.325
1969	1,473,457	1,472,620	—	—	—	—	—	837	1,558	773,830	496.82	788,837	10,538	6.77	1.362
1970	1,484,919	1,484,110	—	—	—	—	—	809	1,572	771,012	490.41	812,684	11,124	7.08	1.443
1971	1,390,960	—	—	—	—	—	—	—	1,471	745,828	506.83	—	11,996	8.15	1.608
1972	1,447,864	—	—	—	—	—	—	—	1,531	782,597	511.08	—	12,790	8.35	1.634
1973	1,532,165	—	—	—	—	—	—	—	1,616	857,956	531.03	—	14,003	8.67	1.632
1974	1,530,686	—	—	—	—	—	—	—	1,619	852,262	526.53	—	15,993	9.88	1.876
1975	1,395,055	—	—	—	—	—	—	—	1,470	758,573	515.89	—	15,623	10.63	2.060
1976	1,370,167	—	—	—	—	—	—	—	1,481	799,727	540.00	—	17,707	11.96	2.214
1977	1,394,742	—	—	—	—	—	—	—	1,519	833,837	548.79	—	19,232	12.66	2.306
1978	1,390,603	—	—	—	—	—	—	—	1,430	867,832	606.65	—	20,610	14.41	2.375
1979	—	—	—	—	—	—	—	—	1,544	916,434	593.72	—	23,904	15.49	2.608
1980	—	—	—	—	—	—	—	—	1,537	932,748	606.88	—	26,757	17.41	2.869

[1] Except as noted, Class I railroads, series Df965–972, and Class I, II, and III railroads, series Df973–979.

[2] Fiscal years ending June 30 through the first set of values shown for 1916; calendar years thereafter.

[3] Includes forwarder traffic beginning in 1939.

[4] First set of 1916 figures is comparable to earlier data; second set is comparable to later data.

[5] Includes unassigned carload tonnage. See text.

[6] Class I and II railroads.

Sources

1890–1953, U.S. Interstate Commerce Commission (ICC), *Statistics of Railways in the United States*, and for 1954–1980, ICC, *Transport Statistics in the United States*, Part 1 (annual issues). In addition, for series Df965–966 and Df972, from 1964–1970, see ICC, *Freight Commodity Statistics of Class I Railroads in the United States* (annual issues).

Documentation

Revenue-tons and ton-miles exclude the movement of a railroad company's materials and supplies on its own lines. A carload is a shipment of 10,000 pounds or more of one commodity from one shipper to one consignee. Tons are 2,000 pounds. Ton-miles are computed by multiplying the weight of each shipment by the distance it moves.

Tons originated are tons identified as not having had previous line-haul transportation by other rail carriers; such shipments include import traffic and traffic from outlying possessions of the United States received from water carriers at the port of entry, and finished products from transit points.

See the text for Table Df927–955 for definitions of railroad company types.

Series Df965–966. Includes the following amounts of unassigned carload tonnage (thousands): 1911, 35,199; 1912, 32,266; 1913, 15,617; 1914, 14,671; 1915, 2,268; 1916, 1,367; and 1919, 338.

Series Df967. Includes raw farm products and simple manufactures such as flour, corn meal, cottonseed meal, cake, and linters. However, products such as vegetable oils, sugar and molasses, canned fruits and vegetables, and manufactured tobacco are included in series Df971, manufactures and miscellaneous.

Series Df969. Includes coke as well as coal and other raw minerals.

Series Df970. Includes lumber, shingles, lath; box, crate, and cooperage materials; veneer and built-up wood in addition to raw forest products.

Series Df975 and Df978. Defined in terms of the United States as a system, and so ton-miles or revenue of connecting roads are included in the numerator, whereas only tonnage originated is included in the denominator.

Series Df977. Includes revenue from the transportation of freight and from transit, stop, diversion, and reconsignment arrangements on the basis of tariffs. It excludes revenue from activities such as switching of freight-train cars; water transfers of freight, vehicles, and livestock; movement of freight trains at a rate per train-mile or for a lump sum; storage of freight; demurrage; operation of grain elevators or stockyards; or other miscellaneous services and facilities connected with the transportation of freight.

TABLE Df980–990   Railroad property investment, capital, and capital expenditures: 1890–1980[1,2]

Contributed by Louis P. Cain

	Property investment and capital								Capital expenditures for additions and betterments		
	Road and equipment		Railroad capital outstanding								
	Investment, book value	Depreciation reserve	Total	Common stock	Preferred stock	Funded debt unmatured	Net capitalization	Stock paying dividends	Total	Equipment	Roadway and structures
	Df980 [3]	Df981 [4]	Df982 [5]	Df983 [5]	Df984 [5]	Df985 [5]	Df986	Df987	Df988	Df989	Df990
Year	Million dollars	Million dollars	Million dollars	Million dollars	Million dollars	Million dollars	Million dollars	Million dollars	Million dollars	Million dollars	Million dollars
1890	8,133	—	8,984	3,803	606	4,575	7,577	1,598	—	—	—
1891	8,444	—	9,291	3,796	655	4,840	8,008	1,796	—	—	—
1892	8,690	—	9,686	3,979	654	5,053	8,295	1,825	—	—	—
1893	8,987	—	9,895	3,982	687	5,226	8,332	1,809	—	—	—
1894	9,073	—	10,191	4,104	730	5,357	8,647	1,767	—	—	—
1895	9,203	—	10,347	4,202	760	5,385	8,900	1,485	—	—	—
1896	9,500	—	10,567	4,257	970	5,340	9,066	1,559	—	—	—
1897	9,709	—	10,685	4,367	998	5,270	9,168	1,603	—	—	—
1898	9,760	—	10,819	4,269	1,119	5,431	9,297	1,818	—	—	—
1899	9,961	—	11,034	4,323	1,192	5,519	9,432	2,239	—	—	—
1900	10,263	—	11,491	4,522	1,323	5,646	9,548	2,668	—	—	—
1901	10,405	—	11,688	4,475	1,331	5,882	9,483	2,977	—	—	—
1902	10,658	—	12,134	4,722	1,302	6,110	9,926	3,337	—	—	—
1903	10,973	—	12,600	4,877	1,279	6,444	10,282	3,450	—	—	—
1904	11,511	—	13,213	5,051	1,289	6,873	10,712	3,643	—	—	—
1905	11,951	—	13,805	5,181	1,373	7,251	11,167	4,119	—	—	—
1906	12,420	—	14,570	5,403	1,401	7,766	11,672	4,526	—	—	—
1907	13,030	—	16,082	5,933	1,424	8,725	—	4,948	—	—	—
1908	13,213	—	16,768	5,911	1,463	9,394	12,834	4,843	—	—	—
1909	13,609	—	17,488	6,218	1,468	9,802	13,914	4,920	—	—	—
1910	14,557	—	18,417	6,710	1,403	10,304	14,376	5,412	—	—	—
1911	15,612	210	19,209	7,075	1,396	10,738	15,044	5,730	—	—	—
1912	16,004	259	19,753	7,249	1,374	11,130	15,126	5,581	—	—	—
1913	16,588	327	19,796	7,232	1,379	11,185	15,366	5,780	—	—	—
1914	17,153	435	20,247	7,304	1,376	11,567	15,759	5,667	—	—	—
1915	17,441	511	19,720	7,287	1,348	11,085	16,308	5,219	—	—	—
1916 [6]	17,689	571	21,092	7,603	1,456	12,033	16,336	5,279	—	—	—
1916 [6]	17,842	628	21,049	7,594	1,455	12,000	16,333	5,430	—	—	—
1917	18,574	796	21,249	7,454	1,848	11,947	16,402	5,610	—	—	—
1918	18,984	936	20,785	7,249	1,806	11,730	16,454	5,138	—	—	—
1919	19,300	1,009	20,950	7,193	1,898	11,859	16,550	5,298	—	—	—
1920	19,849	1,081	20,098	6,958	1,885	11,255	16,994	5,075	—	—	—
1921	20,329	1,237	22,292	7,275	1,801	13,216	17,083	5,059	557	319	237
1922	20,580	1,335	22,290	7,307	1,834	13,149	17,280	5,321	429	245	183
1923	21,372	1,408	22,839	7,398	1,852	13,589	17,810	5,646	1,059	681	377
1924	22,182	1,549	23,636	7,539	1,935	14,162	18,202	6,042	874	493	381
1925	23,217	1,681	21,734	7,492	1,921	12,321	18,191	6,278	748	338	410
1926	23,800	1,811	23,677	7,560	1,925	14,192	18,234	6,473	885	371	513
1927	24,453	1,946	23,614	7,683	1,980	13,951	18,137	6,701	771	288	482
1928	24,875	2,043	23,747	7,809	2,034	13,904	18,511	7,159	676	224	452
1929	25,465	2,169	23,983	7,853	2,065	14,065	18,680	7,506	853	321	532
1930	26,051	2,360	22,783	7,953	2,059	12,771	19,066	7,702	872	328	544
1931	26,094	2,520	24,344	8,031	2,049	14,264	18,941	7,325	361	73	288
1932	26,086	2,632	24,837	8,067	2,047	14,723	18,894	3,298	167	36	130
1933	25,901	2,707	24,723	8,057	2,042	14,624	18,831	3,119	103	15	88
1934	25,681	2,764	24,570	7,994	2,044	14,532	18,653	3,411	212	92	120
1935	25,500	2,771	22,080	7,907	2,018	12,155	18,342	3,412	188	79	108
1936	25,432	2,809	24,003	7,993	2,036	13,974	18,336	3,594	298	159	139
1937	25,636	2,950	24,123	8,064	2,050	14,009	18,319	3,890	509	322	186
1938	25,595	3,044	23,855	8,040	2,049	13,766	17,988	3,139	226	115	111
1939	25,538	3,102	23,609	8,025	2,050	13,534	17,698	3,190	262	133	128
1940	25,646	3,095	21,047	7,734	2,036	11,277	17,630	3,741	429	271	157
1941	25,668	3,240	20,708	7,546	1,953	11,209	17,568	3,861	543	367	175
1942	25,838	3,561	20,471	7,565	1,935	10,971	17,315	5,355	534	349	185
1943	26,145	3,939	19,914	7,517	1,912	10,485	16,755	5,466	454	255	198
1944	26,631	4,382	19,403	7,464	1,984	9,955	16,276	5,523	560	328	231

Notes appear at end of table

(continued)

TABLE Df980–990   Railroad property investment, capital, and capital expenditures: 1890–1980   *Continued*

	Property investment and capital								Capital expenditures for additions and betterments		
	Road and equipment		Railroad capital outstanding								
Year	Investment, book value	Depreciation reserve	Total	Common stock	Preferred stock	Funded debt unmatured	Net capitalization	Stock paying dividends	Total	Equipment	Roadway and structures
	Df980 [3]	Df981 [4]	Df982 [5]	Df983 [5]	Df984 [5]	Df985 [5]	Df986	Df987	Df988	Df989	Df990
	Million dollars	Million dollars	Million dollars	Million dollars	Million dollars	Million dollars	Million dollars	Million dollars	Million dollars	Million dollars	Million dollars
1945	26,967	5,549	18,681	7,442	1,981	9,258	15,667	5,383	562	314	248
1946	27,277	5,800	18,449	7,448	1,961	9,040	15,309	5,221	561	319	242
1947	27,686	6,037	18,050	7,250	1,975	8,825	15,301	5,184	864	565	298
1948	28,664	6,279	18,249	7,250	1,992	9,007	15,467	6,446	1,273	917	356
1949	29,519	6,438	18,343	7,234	1,988	9,121	15,609	5,924	1,312	981	330
1950	30,174	6,629	18,274	7,207	1,977	9,090	15,618	6,768	1,065	779	286
1951	31,077	6,837	18,220	7,235	1,977	9,008	15,489	6,700	1,413	1,050	363
1952	31,822	6,926	18,067	7,243	1,954	8,870	15,487	6,734	1,340	935	405
1953	32,416	7,009	17,658	7,023	1,868	8,767	15,365	7,252	1,259	857	401
1954	32,708	7,175	17,590	7,316	1,530	8,744	15,336	6,618	820	498	321
1955	33,034	7,313	17,422	7,341	1,310	8,771	15,171	7,300	909	568	341
1956	33,714	7,542	17,399	6,911	1,395	9,093	15,285	6,785	1,227	821	406
1957	34,614	7,800	16,775	6,291	1,369	9,115	14,682	6,465	1,394	1,007	386
1958	34,934	8,043	16,603	6,243	1,266	9,094	14,529	5,290	738	479	258
1959	35,157	8,295	16,365	6,233	1,246	8,886	14,287	5,750	818	567	250
1960	35,513	8,532	16,134	6,185	1,218	8,731	14,150	5,617	919	633	285
1961	35,541	8,792	15,179	5,526	1,212	8,441	13,184	4,361	646	427	219
1962	34,361	8,982	15,013	5,537	1,201	8,275	12,968	4,285	832	593	239
1963	34,519	9,143	15,011	5,592	1,189	8,230	12,840	4,462	1,043	784	258
1964	34,868	9,265	14,876	5,537	1,164	8,175	—	4,926	1,417	1,139	277
1965	35,489	9,341	14,857	5,580	1,116	8,161	—	4,845	1,630	1,303	327
1966	36,618	9,479	14,800	5,639	1,091	8,070	—	4,709	1,952	1,554	398
1967	37,250	9,664	14,690	5,828	889	7,973	—	4,727	1,522	1,148	374
1968	36,720	9,450	14,577	5,754	821	8,002	—	4,629	1,186	818	368
1969	37,383	9,688	14,701	5,758	814	8,129	—	4,347	1,509	1,088	420
1970	37,918	9,929	14,339	5,605	718	8,016	—	3,594	1,350	993	357
1971	38,022	10,078	13,588	5,656	728	7,204	—	3,598	1,267	916	351
1972	37,359	9,660	12,968	5,285	620	7,063	—	3,472	1,209	871	338
1973	37,897	9,868	13,092	5,301	593	7,198	—	3,359	1,321	954	367
1974	38,937	10,185	12,958	5,137	733	7,088	—	3,297	1,584	1,135	449
1975	40,197	10,650	13,473	5,150	690	7,633	—	3,402	993	732	261
1976	36,577	9,472	13,976	4,602	504	8,870	—	3,344	—	—	—
1977	38,343	9,994	14,781	4,342	629	9,810	—	3,745	—	—	—
1978	38,702	10,377	16,343	3,857	663	11,823	—	—	—	—	—
1979	40,133	10,488	17,089	3,710	962	12,417	—	—	—	—	—
1980	42,619	10,929	17,808	3,661	963	13,184	—	—	—	—	—

[1] Includes intercorporate duplications. Covers Class I, II, and III railroads and their lessors (see text for exceptions).

[2] Fiscal years through the first set of values shown for 1916; calendar years thereafter.

[3] See text for special circumstances and changes in the series over time.

[4] Includes depreciation on "miscellaneous physical property" prior to 1920 and amortization of defense projects accrued from 1941 through 1950.

[5] Prior to 1958, includes securities nominally issued and nominally outstanding as well as those outstanding.

[6] Two sets of values are given for 1916: The first set is comparable to data for earlier years; the second, to that for later years.

Sources

1890–1953, U.S. Interstate Commerce Commission (ICC), *Statistics of Railways in the United States*, and for 1954–1980, ICC, *Transport Statistics in the United States*, Part 1 (annual issues). For series Df988–990, Association of American Railroads, 1921–1950, *Railroad Transportation* (various issues), and for 1951–1975, *Yearbook of Railroad Facts* (annual issues).

Documentation

The data cover Class I, II, and III railroads and their lessors, with the following exceptions. The returns for switching and terminal companies are included prior to 1908 where applicable. Series Df988–990 cover Class I railroads. Series Df981 covers Class I railroads from 1911 to 1913. Series Df982–985 cover Class I and II railroads and their lessor subsidiaries for 1913 and 1914. See the text for Table Df927–955 for definitions of railroad company types.

Capital expenditure represents total money outlay without deductions for property retired.

Series Df980. Represents recorded value, in the accounts of carriers, of land, fixed improvements such as roadbed and track, rolling stock, and maintenance machinery owned by them. Includes property held under contract for purchase. The increase in investment over a period of years cannot be obtained accurately by subtraction of one year's investment from that of another owing to reorganization, sale or abandonment, reclassification, and so forth. The 1890–1892 data include $170 million estimated reserve for accrued depreciation to place the figures on a comparable basis with other years. The 1910 value represents 1893 investments less increases each year on account of change in classification in 1893. The 1921–1924 data include investment of lessor companies; the 1925–1970 data include investment of both lessor and proprietary companies.

TABLE Df980–990   Railroad property investment, capital, and capital expenditures: 1890–1980   *Continued*

Series Df981. Represents the accumulated accounting allowance for loss in service value not restored by current maintenance. The loss in value is incurred in connection with the consumption or prospective retirement of physical property in the course of service from causes against which carriers are not protected by insurance, which are known to be in current operation, and the effect of which can be forecast with a reasonable approach to accuracy.

Series Df985. Funded debt unmatured is debt maturing more than one year from date of issue.

Series Df986. Represents railway capital outstanding, series Df982, minus the stocks and debt of railroad companies held by other railroad companies.

Series Df988–990. Additions include the following: additional facilities such as equipment (rolling stock), tracks, buildings and other structures; additions to such facilities, such as extensions to tracks, buildings and other structures; additional ties laid in existing tracks; and additional devices applied to facilities such as airbrakes applied to cars not previously thus equipped. Betterments include improvements of existing facilities through the substitution of superior parts for inferior parts retired, such as the substitution of steel-tired wheels for cast wheels under equipment, the application of heavier rail in tracks, the strengthening of bridges by the substitution of heavier members, and the application of superior floors or roofs in buildings.

TABLE Df991–1001   Railroad income, expenses, interest, and dividends: 1890–1979[1,2,3]
Contributed by Louis P. Cain

	Income and expenses									Interest and dividends	
		Operating expenses									
Year	Operating revenue	Total	Maintenance of way and structures	Maintenance of equipment	Tax accruals	Operating income	Net operating income	Net income	Ratio of operating expenses to operating revenue	Dividends declared	Interest accrued on funded debt
	Df991	Df992	Df993	Df994	Df995	Df996	Df997	Df998	Df999	Df1000	Df1001
	Thousand dollars	Thousand dollars	Thousand dollars	Thousand dollars	Thousand dollars	Thousand dollars	Thousand dollars	Thousand dollars	Percent	Thousand dollars	Thousand dollars
1890	1,051,878	692,094	152,719	114,039	29,806	—	329,978	106,270	65.80	87,072	221,500
1891	1,096,761	731,888	153,672	117,048	32,052	—	332,822	114,965	66.73	91,118	219,521
1892	1,171,407	780,998	164,189	128,712	32,751	—	357,658	120,091	66.67	97,615	240,075
1893	1,220,752	827,921	169,258	136,876	35,071	—	357,760	114,015	67.82	100,930	250,177
1894	1,073,362	731,414	143,669	112,895	36,556	—	305,391	60,174	68.14	95,515	252,780
1895	1,075,371	725,720	143,976	113,789	38,146	—	311,505	60,133	67.48	85,288	252,513
1896	1,150,169	772,989	160,345	133,382	37,962	—	339,219	94,794	67.20	87,603	249,624
1897	1,122,090	752,525	159,434	122,762	41,119	—	328,446	85,802	67.06	87,111	247,880
1898	1,247,326	817,973	173,315	142,625	41,929	—	387,424	147,167	65.58	96,153	246,127
1899	1,313,610	856,969	180,411	150,919	44,397	—	412,244	177,225	65.24	111,010	251,158
1900	1,487,045	961,429	211,221	181,174	44,445	—	481,171	252,760	64.65	139,598	252,950
1901	1,588,526	1,030,397	231,057	190,300	46,708	—	511,421	273,450	64.86	156,736	262,095
1902	1,726,380	1,116,249	248,382	213,381	50,054	—	560,077	314,989	64.66	185,392	274,422
1903	1,900,847	1,257,539	266,422	240,430	53,522	—	590,056	338,324	66.16	196,728	283,953
1904	1,975,174	1,338,896	261,280	267,185	56,802	—	579,476	317,308	67.79	221,941	297,675
1905	2,082,482	1,390,602	275,046	288,441	58,712	—	633,168	364,811	66.78	237,964	310,632
1906	2,325,765	1,536,877	311,721	328,555	69,064	—	719,824	434,229	66.08	272,796	322,556
1907	2,589,106	1,748,516	343,545	368,062	73,743	—	766,846	488,014	67.53	308,089	344,243
1908	2,440,639	1,710,402	329,373	368,354	78,674	651,562	634,794	443,987	70.08	390,695	368,296
1909	2,473,205	1,650,034	308,450	363,913	85,140	738,032	710,474	441,063	66.72	321,072	382,675
1910	2,812,142	1,881,879	368,507	413,110	98,035	832,228	805,097	583,191	66.92	405,771	399,582
1911	2,852,855	1,976,332	366,025	428,367	102,657	773,866	744,669	547,281	69.28	460,195	410,327
1912	2,906,416	2,035,058	367,448	450,373	113,819	757,540	727,458	453,125	70.02	400,315	429,027
1913 [4]	3,193,118	2,235,923	421,232	511,561	122,005	835,190	805,266	546,761	70.02	369,078	434,753
1914	3,127,730	2,280,416	419,278 [6]	532,139 [6]	140,470	706,844	674,190	395,492	72.91	451,653	442,595
1915	2,956,193	2,088,683	381,532	509,819	137,775	729,069	694,276	354,787	70.65	328,478	464,186
1916 [5]	3,691,065	2,426,251	439,195	609,105	161,825	1,102,171	1,058,506	735,341	65.73	366,561	481,426
1916 [5]	3,472,642	2,277,202	421,501	570,326	150,015	1,044,603	1,002,935	671,398	65.58	342,109	474,535
1917	4,115,413	2,906,283	460,447	700,073	218,632	988,776	950,557	658,225	70.62	381,852	474,123
1918	4,985,290	4,071,522	673,084	1,120,611	229,533	684,004	646,223	442,336	81.67	339,186	468,286
1919	5,250,420	4,498,817	800,912	1,245,264	239,136	511,546	454,132	496,609	85.68	335,242	476,075
1920	6,310,151	5,954,394	1,069,436	1,613,950	289,272	75,402	12,101	481,951	94.36	331,103	500,354
1921	5,632,665	4,668,998	787,537	1,271,921	283,163	678,551	601,139	350,540	82.89	456,482	529,398
1922	5,674,483	4,509,991	755,030	1,269,971	308,145	854,779	769,411	434,459	79.48	338,806	538,594
1923	6,419,210	4,999,383	843,224	1,485,555	339,577	1,078,226	974,918	632,118	77.88	411,882	551,705
1924	6,045,252	4,608,807	821,793	1,279,680	347,437	1,086,578	984,463	623,399	76.24	385,130	588,301

Notes appear at end of table

(continued)

TABLE Df991–1001 Railroad income, expenses, interest, and dividends: 1890–1979 *Continued*

		Income and expenses								Interest and dividends	
		Operating expenses									
Year	Operating revenue	Total	Maintenance of way and structures	Maintenance of equipment	Tax accruals	Operating income	Net operating income	Net income	Ratio of operating expenses to operating revenue	Dividends declared	Interest accrued on funded debt
	Df991	Df992	Df993	Df994	Df995	Df996	Df997	Df998	Df999	Df1000	Df1001
	Thousand dollars	Thousand dollars	Thousand dollars	Thousand dollars	Thousand dollars	Thousand dollars	Thousand dollars	Thousand dollars	Percent	Thousand dollars	Thousand dollars
1925	6,246,884	4,633,497	844,186	1,278,227	365,790	1,245,622	1,136,728	771,053	74.17	409,645	583,875
1926	6,508,679	4,766,235	894,886	1,300,680	396,538	1,344,010	1,229,020	883,422	73.23	473,683 [7]	581,709
1927	6,245,716	4,662,521	895,063	1,234,655	383,112	1,198,547	1,077,842	741,924	74.65	567,281	583,452
1928	6,212,464	4,508,606	861,846	1,181,251	395,631	1,306,620	1,182,467	855,018	72.57	510,018	578,831
1929	6,373,004	4,579,162	877,067	1,216,045	402,698	1,389,955	1,262,636	977,230	71.85	560,902	580,770
1930	5,356,484	3,993,621	723,525	1,030,482	353,881	1,007,907	874,154	577,923	74.56	603,150	588,742
1931	4,246,385	3,273,906	544,300	825,923	308,492	663,084	528,204	169,287	77.10	401,463	592,866
1932	3,168,537	2,441,814	361,337	625,606	279,263	446,417	325,332	−121,630	77.06	150,774	591,340
1933	3,138,186	2,285,218	331,653	605,409	253,522	598,222	477,326	26,543	72.82	158,790	590,230
1934	3,316,861	2,479,997	375,410	644,989	243,646	592,034	465,896	23,282	74.77	211,767	569,760
1935	3,499,126	2,630,177	404,105	688,678	240,760	626,973	505,415	52,177	75.17	202,568	559,187
1936	4,108,658	2,973,366	466,284	790,240	324,858	810,434	675,600	221,591	72.37	231,733	548,452
1937	4,226,325	3,165,154	508,319	834,820	331,013	730,158	597,841	146,351	74.89	227,596	532,237
1938	3,616,072	2,762,681	431,021	683,529	346,236	507,155	376,865	−87,468	76.40	136,270	521,758
1939	4,050,047	2,959,438	477,697	773,080	361,617	728,992	595,961	141,134	73.07	179,412	512,283
1940	4,354,712	3,131,598	508,328	826,242	402,953	820,161	690,554	243,148	71.91	216,522	547,333
1941	5,413,972	3,709,921	615,533	1,000,375	555,970	1,148,081	1,009,592	557,672	68.52	239,438	543,954
1942	7,547,826	4,653,705	811,206	1,219,460	1,211,775	1,682,347	1,499,364	992,843	61.66	254,088	564,174
1943	9,138,419	5,714,804	1,125,873	1,449,356	1,862,940	1,560,675	1,370,568	946,150	62.54	263,919	515,617
1944	9,524,628	6,345,035	1,283,208	1,597,155	1,961,652	1,317,941	1,113,153	733,461	66.62	292,248	488,877
1945	8,986,954	7,115,391	1,431,221	2,157,678	835,434	1,036,130	858,864	502,250	79.17	295,294	449,917
1946	7,709,171	6,422,494	1,169,887	1,478,302	506,480	780,197	624,868	334,966	83.31	283,171	406,147
1947	8,784,214	6,869,806	1,234,978	1,568,124	949,273	965,136	790,534	537,405	78.21	280,397	374,150
1948	9,784,332	7,552,630	1,374,058	1,713,967	1,043,036	1,188,666	1,014,815	767,949	77.19	335,313	361,879
1949	8,680,791	6,968,296	1,309,857	1,617,800	845,089	867,406	693,957	496,103	80.27	306,995	365,393
1950	9,587,000	7,135,055	1,311,775	1,718,660	1,212,084	1,239,861	1,055,309	854,951	74.42	348,811	367,218
1951	10,511,612	8,122,521	1,505,488	1,956,438	1,223,644	1,165,447	956,699	757,934	77.27	373,574	367,244
1952	10,702,877	8,134,811	1,546,613	1,965,327	1,282,144	1,285,922	1,091,657	900,472	76.01	394,042	376,907
1953	10,787,891	8,218,223	1,612,390	1,993,602	1,205,366	1,364,302	1,122,512	939,887	76.18	445,145	378,218
1954	9,484,015	7,460,507	1,376,478	1,704,985	877,304	1,146,203	887,817	712,252	78.66	405,403	376,020
1955	10,229,600	7,724,496	1,412,877	1,798,579	1,100,920	1,404,185	1,144,347	958,849	75.51	476,207	373,502
1956	10,686,492	8,199,792	1,433,037	1,907,606	1,144,446	1,342,254	1,083,708	908,416	76.73	476,083	373,207
1957	10,625,452	8,321,577	1,458,888	1,928,912	1,090,818	1,213,057	934,645	765,227	78.32	466,415	382,175
1958	9,686,289	7,631,341	1,248,596	1,735,067	977,277	1,077,671	772,898	630,033	78.78	444,982 [8]	393,159
1959	9,954,828	7,796,835	1,262,683	1,813,550	1,070,093	1,087,900	760,140	607,924	78.32	431,860	390,467
1960	9,641,593	7,657,329	1,217,241	1,775,528	1,020,471	963,793	594,618	473,175	79.42	411,650	386,774
1961	9,309,696	7,361,751	1,141,223	1,698,617	1,011,814	936,131	547,045	410,140	79.08	385,017	383,313
1962	9,562,991	7,507,757	1,179,466	1,758,967	925,572	1,129,663	735,266	600,393	78.51	394,116	376,149
1963	9,684,636	7,542,306	1,207,801	1,747,395	906,456	1,235,874	815,952	681,325	77.88	412,815	377,556
1964	9,985,187	7,830,168	1,250,697	1,779,807	891,248	1,263,771	828,433	733,220	78.42	492,443	384,413
1965	10,425,052	8,002,685	1,273,099	1,802,103	949,215	1,473,152	980,066	865,899	76.76	532,649	402,889
1966	10,880,467	8,277,294	1,342,632	1,872,661	1,001,510	1,601,663	1,065,232	957,359	76.07	547,567	423,486
1967	10,581,560	8,359,369	1,326,630	1,895,376	941,272	1,280,919	689,548	367,689	79.00	582,088	455,059
1968	11,061,902	8,723,664	1,441,112	1,938,988	979,700	1,358,538	694,143	623,440	78.86	560,048	473,213
1969	11,658,525	9,209,137	1,540,481	2,025,511	1,065,134	1,384,254	667,157	517,066	78.99	534,849	501,856
1970	12,209,237	9,805,555	1,650,302	2,188,863	1,103,988	1,299,694	505,669	126,429	80.31	486,132	553,763
1971	13,821,880	11,016,038	1,969,915	2,486,656	1,198,079	1,607,764	705,029	295,295	79.70	531,908	578,391
1972	15,243,795	12,067,957	2,084,308	2,627,799	1,416,090	1,759,748	725,047	525,611	79.17	482,362	604,806
1973	17,458,315	13,758,455	2,408,781	2,941,712	1,872,298	1,614,287	538,744	558,418	78.81	643,538	680,153
1974	16,929,811	13,966,825	2,471,571	3,027,104	1,684,843	1,160,867	36,408	−11,750	82.50	457,666	715,630
1975	19,190,673	15,820,588	3,138,193	3,450,584	1,980,485	1,316,283	56,392	−145,483	82.44	477,286	714,035
1976	20,799,683	17,398,255	2,818,517	3,238,387	2,039,573	1,185,219	−136,086	−157,786	83.65	629,451	687,555
1977	22,138,387	21,424,214	4,137,362	5,519,728	2,096,989	714,173	451,318	283,831	96.77	520,633	773,566
1978	25,732,489	24,447,632	4,674,658	6,114,237	2,276,674	1,284,857	873,565	1,068,533	95.01	610,439	824,716
1979	28,708,496	26,761,302	5,025,472	6,506,184	2,107,056	1,947,194	1,364,081	1,261,606	93.22	644,545	967,483

TABLE Df991–1001   Railroad income, expenses, interest, and dividends: 1890–1979   *Continued*

[1] Includes intercorporate duplications. Covers Class I, II, and III railroads. See text for exceptions.

[2] The data appear to include discrepencies; see text for series Df996.

[3] Fiscal years through 1916; calendar years thereafter.

[4] Class I and II railroads only, except series Df1000.

[5] Two sets of values are given for 1916: The first set is comparable with data for earlier years; the second, with that for later years.

[6] Class I and II railroads.

[7] Includes unusual items, amounting to $76,300,000, not representing cash.

[8] Includes $10,000 dividend declared from "capital surplus."

Sources

1890–1953, U.S. Interstate Commerce Commission (ICC), *Statistics of Railways in the United States*, (annual issues) and for 1954–1980, ICC, *Transport Statistics in the United States*, Part 1 (annual issues).

Documentation

The data cover Class I, II, and III railroads, unless otherwise noted. Through 1907, where applicable, the returns for switching and terminal companies are included. See the text for Table Df927–955 for definitions of railroad company types.

Series Df991. Includes revenue from freight, passenger, and other transportation and incidental services.

Series Df992–994. Includes current depreciation.

Series Df995. Reports taxes imposed by any form of government, whether based on an assessed value of the property, on amounts of stocks and bonds, or on earnings, income, dividends declared, payroll, number of passengers, quantity of freight, length of road, rolling stock, or other basis. Tax accruals do not include special assessments for street and other improvements, or special benefit taxes such as water assessments.

Series Df996. Represents net revenue from railway operations: series Df991 minus series Df992 and Df995. These series do not sum properly in all years. The discrepancies are especially large in 1921, 1945, and 1974–1980. The sources offer no explanation for these discrepancies.

Series Df997. Equals operating income minus net payable balance of equipment and joint facility rents. The equipment rents deducted at this point are those for equipment leased for less than one year, or interchanged. They are usually on a per-day or per-mile basis.

Series Df998. Equals net operating income plus other income, minus miscellaneous deductions and fixed and contingent charges. Fixed charges are mainly rent for leased roads and equipment (that is, equipment leased for one year or more), and interest (except contingent interest). These data include lessors.

Series Df1000–1001. Interest and dividends after extraordinary and prior period items. Series Df1001 includes interest not paid during the year on debt in default of interest; it excludes interest on debt owed by the issuing company, or on debt incurred for new lines, extensions, additions, or betterments, accrued before such property is completed or comes into service.

TABLE Df1002–1003   Railroad employees and compensation: 1890–1980[1, 2, 3]

Contributed by Louis P. Cain

	Employees	Compensation		Employees	Compensation		Employees	Compensation
	Df1002	Df1003		Df1002	Df1003		Df1002	Df1003
Year	Thousand	Million dollars	Year	Thousand	Million dollars	Year	Thousand	Million dollars
1890	749	—	1920	2,076	3,754	1950	1,237	4,645
1891	784	—	1921	1,705	2,824	1951	1,292	5,328
1892	821	—	1922	1,670	2,693	1952	1,242	5,382
1893	874	—	1923	1,902	3,062	1953	1,221	5,381
1894	780	—	1924	1,795	2,883	1954	1,078	4,907
1895	785	446	1925	1,786	2,916	1955	1,071	5,045
1896	827	469	1926	1,822	3,002	1956	1,058	6,388
1897	823	466	1927	1,776	2,963	1957	999	5,422
1898	875	495	1928	1,692	2,874	1958	853	4,991
1899	929	523	1929	1,694	2,940	1959	828	5,049
1900	1,018	577	1930	1,517	2,589	1960	793	4,957
1901	1,071	611	1931	1,283	2,125	1961	727	4,684
1902	1,189	676	1932	1,052	1,535	1962	711	4,722
1903	1,313	757	1933	991	1,424	1963	691	4,690
1904	1,296	818	1934	1,027	1,541	1964	675	4,758
1905	1,382	840	1935	1,014	1,666	1965	655	4,887
1906	1,521	901	1936	1,086	1,874	1966	645	4,975
1907	1,672	1,072	1937	1,137	2,014	1967	624	5,026
1908	1,436	1,035	1938	958	1,771	1968	602	5,197
1909	1,503	988	1939	1,007	1,889	1969	590	5,451
1910	1,699	1,144	1940	1,046	1,991	1970	577	5,646
1911	1,670	1,208	1941	1,159	2,360	1971	555	5,990
1912	1,716	1,252	1942	1,291	2,966	1972	537	6,531
1913	1,815	1,374	1943	1,375	3,556	1973	533	7,294
1914	1,710	1,381	1944	1,434	3,898	1974	541	7,671
1915	1,548	1,278	1945	1,439	3,901	1975	502	7,674
1916 [4]	1,654	1,404	1946	1,378	4,214	1976	505	8,618
1916 [4]	1,701	1,507	1947	1,371	4,399	1977	510	9,357
1917	1,786	1,783	1948	1,345	4,821	1978	480	9,734
1918	1,892	2,665	1949	1,209	4,469	1979	492	11,105
1919	1,960	2,898				1980	469	11,537

[1] Includes intercorporate duplications.

[2] Classes I, II, and III railroads, with two exceptions: Through 1907, the returns for switching and terminal companies are included; and only Classes I and II railroads are included in 1913.

[3] Fiscal years through the first set of values shown for 1916; calendar years, thereafter. Time of year and frequency of measurement varies. See text.

[4] Two sets of values are given for 1916: The first set is comparable with data for earlier years; the second, with that for later years.

Sources

For 1890–1953, U.S. Interstate Commerce Commission (ICC), *Statistics of Railways in the United States* (annual issues), and for 1954–1980, ICC, *Transport Statistics in the United States*, Part 1 (annual issues).

Documentation

An employee is defined as a person in the service of a railroad, subject to its continuing authority to supervise and direct the manner of rendition of his or her service. Persons such as lawyers engaged to render only specifically defined service for specific cases and not under general or continuing retainer are not classed as employees.

For 1890–1914, the number of employees represents the number on the payroll June 30. Thereafter, the nature of the figures included for the smaller (Classes II and III) roads is not clear in the source. For Class I roads, they appear to be averages: four quarterly counts (1915–1920); two quarterly and six monthly counts (1921); and twelve monthly counts (beginning in 1922).

See the text for Table Df927–955 for definitions of railroad company types.

TABLE Df1004–1013   Electric railways – companies, employees, assets, and finances: 1890–1937

Contributed by Louis P. Cain

Fiscal year	Companies Df1004 [1] Number	Miles of line operated Df1005 Miles	Miles of track operated Df1006 [2] Miles	Value of road and equipment Df1007 Thousand dollars	Employees Df1008 [3] Number	Passenger cars Df1009 Number	Revenue passengers Df1010 Thousand dollars	Operating revenues Df1011 Thousand dollars	Operating expenses Df1012 Thousand dollars	Operating ratio Df1013 Percent
1890	789	5,783	8,123	389,357	70,764	32,505	2,023,010	90,617	62,011	68.4
1902	987	16,645	22,577	2,167,634	140,769	60,290	4,774,212	247,554	142,313	57.5
1907	1,236	25,547	34,382	3,637,669	221,429	70,016	7,441,115	418,188	251,309	60.1
1912	1,260	30,438	41,065	4,596,563	282,461	76,162	9,545,555	567,512	332,896	58.7
1917	1,307	32,548	44,835	5,186,442	294,826	79,914	11,304,660	709,825	452,595	63.8
1922	1,200	31,264	43,932	5,058,762	300,119	77,301	12,666,558	1,016,719 [7]	727,795 [7]	71.6
1927	963	27,948	40,722	—	264,575	70,309	12,174,592	927,774 [7]	694,460 [7]	74.9
1932	706	20,110	31,548	4,143,381	182,165 [5]	59,692	7,955,981 [6]	566,290	442,607	78.2
1937 [4]	478	14,214	23,770	4,399,768	152,476	44,864	7,485,290	513,129	406,119	79.1

[1] Beginning in 1917, the data includes certain companies in Pennsylvania that maintained separate organizations although controlled through stock ownership by other companies. For 1912 and earlier, these companies were treated as merged and not included in the number reported.

[2] Includes a few miles of track lying outside the United States.

[3] The specific dates to which the figures apply vary. See text.

[4] Excludes twenty-two companies operating on a part-year basis.

[5] Includes 334 trolley-bus operators.

[6] Includes 29,721,000 trolley-bus passengers.

[7] Includes auxiliary revenue or expenses. See text.

Source

U.S. Bureau of the Census, *Census of Electrical Industries, Report on Street Railways and Trolley-Bus and Motorbus Operations*, various years.

Documentation

The census of street railways, which was first taken in 1890, and which was taken at quinquennial intervals from 1902 through 1937, covers all street railways without regard to motive power, and all nonsteam interurban railways. The nonelectric railroads included are those operated principally by cable and gasoline engines. Operations of electrified divisions of steam-railway companies are not included. These series do not include data for motorbus and trolley-bus operations of electric street railways. For motorbus and trolley-bus statistics from census reports, see the source.

Series Df1008. The figure reported is as of June 30 for 1890, 1922, 1927, and 1932; for 1902, it is the average for the year; and for 1912, it is as of September 16. The figure for 1937 represents an average of numbers reported on June 30 and December 31.

Series Df1010. Includes pay-transfer.

Series Df1011–1012. Include auxiliary operating revenues of $91,242,000 for 1922 and $8,905,000 for 1927; and auxiliary expenses of $49,232,000 for 1922 and $7,822,000 for 1927. Data for operating revenues and operating expenses of auxiliary operations were excluded so far as possible for earlier years.

TABLE Df1014–1020   Railroad tax accruals: 1921–1975

Contributed by Louis P. Cain

		Federal government taxes					State and local taxes
	Total	Total	Old-age retirement	Unemployment insurance	Income and excess profits	Other federal	
	Df1014	Df1015	Df1016	Df1017	Df1018	Df1019	Df1020
Year	Million dollars	Million dollars	Million dollars	Million dollars	Million dollars	Million dollars	Million dollars
1921	275.9	37.3	—	—	—	—	238.6
1922	301.0	51.9	—	—	—	—	249.1
1923	331.9	77.1	—	—	—	—	254.8
1924	340.3	73.4	—	—	—	—	266.9
1925	358.5	86.5	—	—	—	—	272.0
1926	388.9	108.3	—	—	—	—	280.6
1927	376.1	84.6	—	—	—	—	291.5
1928	389.4	88.0	—	—	—	—	301.4
1929	396.7	89.4	—	—	—	—	307.2
1930	348.6	39.9	—	—	—	—	308.6
1931	303.5	10.2	—	—	—	—	293.3
1932	275.1	11.9	—	—	—	—	263.2
1933	249.6	19.3	—	—	12.7	6.6	230.3
1934	239.6	19.8	—	—	14.3	5.5	219.8
1935	236.9	24.7	—	—	18.9	5.8	212.2
1936	319.8	91.8	47.3	8.8	30.7	5.0	228.0
1937	325.7	66.7	25.1	4.5	32.0	5.1	259.0
1938	340.8	75.4	47.1	5.9	18.9	3.5	265.4
1939	355.7	118.7	50.3	28.7	32.8	6.9	237.0
1940	396.4	181.5	58.2	58.2	59.9	5.2	214.9
1941	547.2	323.3	69.1	69.0	173.8	11.4	223.9
1942	1,198.8	950.6	86.5	85.5	755.1	24.5	248.2
1943	1,849.2	1,578.5	110.0	101.6	1,335.1	31.8	270.7
1944	1,846.0	1,560.4	120.2	110.8	1,304.4	25.0	285.6
1945	823.5	548.0	119.8	110.8	305.7	11.9	275.5
1946	498.1	242.1	136.9	117.4	−15.7	3.4	256.0
1947	936.4	654.0	232.2	121.2	297.6	3.0	282.4
1948	1,028.5	721.2	243.9	21.1	448.4	7.9	307.3
1949	832.5	517.8	233.8	19.4	261.6	3.0	314.7
1950	1,194.6	866.5	242.1	20.2	601.2	3.0	328.1
1951	1,203.3	855.8	264.1	22.0	567.1	2.6	347.5
1952	1,261.8	906.4	269.8	21.6	612.6	2.4	355.4
1953	1,185.0	822.4	266.8	21.2	533.1	1.3	362.6
1954	861.3	499.6	250.6	20.0	226.4	2.6	361.7
1955	1,080.4	700.9	262.5	21.3	414.3	2.7	379.5
1956	1,121.3	728.5	269.3	64.9	392.0	2.3	392.8
1957	1,068.4	664.2	258.7	82.9	320.3	2.4	404.2
1958	957.2	559.0	225.5	90.3	240.9	2.2	398.2
1959	1,047.6	643.4	244.7	129.2	267.6	1.9	404.2
1960	998.8	598.6	253.2	141.0	202.9	1.6	400.2
1961	991.1	608.2	233.8	130.1	242.5	1.9	382.9
1962	905.0	540.0	246.0	135.8	156.8	1.5	365.0
1963	886.4	539.5	242.3	131.6	164.1	1.5	346.9
1964	870.6	524.0	256.3	128.3	137.9	1.6	346.6
1965	916.5	560.4	271.2	124.0	163.7	1.5	356.1
1966	968.4	626.4	318.1	121.0	186.3	1.0	342.0
1967	910.2	544.3	359.3	117.5	66.3	0.9	365.8
1968	946.6	579.6	398.9	113.8	66.1	0.8	366.7
1969	1,029.1	640.0	422.3	110.6	106.2	0.9	389.1
1970	1,068.5	665.3	468.3	107.6	88.4	1.0	403.2
1971	1,097.2	697.2	—	—	—	—	—
1972	1,157.3	752.4	—	—	—	—	—
1973	1,367.8	957.9	—	—	—	—	—
1974	1,819.9	1,376.5	—	—	—	—	—
1975	1,635.9	1,191.2	—	—	58.1	—	445.3

Sources

For 1890–1953, U.S. Interstate Commerce Commission (ICC), *Statistics of Railways in the United States* (annual issues), and for 1954–1975, ICC, *Transport Statistics in the United States*, Part 1 (annual issues).

Documentation

Data are for Class I railroads. See the text for Table Df927–955 for definitions of railroad company types.

Series Df1020. Consists primarily of property taxes levied by state or local governments.

TABLE Df1021–1023   Railroad highway grade crossings: 1925–1975

Contributed by Louis P. Cain

Year	Total Df1021 Number	Specially protected Df1022 Number	Eliminated during year by separation of grades Df1023 Number	Year	Total Df1021 Number	Specially protected Df1022 Number	Eliminated during year by separation of grades Df1023 Number	Year	Total Df1021 Number	Specially protected Df1022 Number	Eliminated during year by separation of grades Df1023 Number
1925	233,633	27,241	—	1945	226,153	33,321	7	1965	215,961	44,333	59
1926	235,158	27,927	195	1946	226,143	33,320	23	1966	214,417	44,432	173
1927	236,283	28,724	245	1947	226,501	33,789	24	1967	218,723	45,213	132
1928	240,089	29,215	270	1948	226,844	34,507	26	1968	211,993	45,502	207
1929	242,809	30,190	275	1949	226,791	35,243	53	1969	211,740	45,961	49
1930	240,673	30,287	403	1950	227,364	35,968	61	1970	210,954	46,674	95
1931	238,017	31,052	361	1951	227,415	36,682	50	1971	210,640	47,440	118
1932	237,035	30,809	189	1952	227,291	37,242	95	1972	209,780	48,335	28
1933	235,827	30,628	221	1953	227,110	37,990	53	1973	208,469	48,821	151
1934	234,820	30,226	231	1954	226,522	38,528	80	1974	209,468	49,436	106
1935	234,231	30,200	164	1955	226,318	39,060	84	1975	210,074	50,170	49
1936	232,902	30,466	521	1956	224,519	39,324	72				
1937	232,322	31,119	400	1957	223,381	39,884	113				
1938	231,400	31,448	235	1958	225,938	41,155	78				
1939	231,104	31,775	204	1959	225,394	41,720	130				
1940	230,285	32,421	209	1960	224,513	42,267	102				
1941	229,722	32,859	182	1961	223,735	42,256	100				
1942	227,496	33,075	149	1962	221,653	43,127	132				
1943	226,938	33,124	37	1963	220,165	43,484	72				
1944	226,357	33,211	14	1964	218,723	43,990	159				

Sources

For 1890–1953, U.S. Interstate Commerce Commission (ICC), *Statistics of Railways in the United States* (annual issues), and for 1954–1975, ICC, *Transport Statistics in the United States*, Part 1 (annual issues).

Documentation

Data are for Class I railroads and switching and terminal companies. See the text for Table Df927–955 for definitions of railroad company types.

Series Df1022. Includes crossings with operated gates, watchmen, or both, during at least part of the day, and those with audible signals, visible signals, or both. Excludes those with fixed signs only.

TABLE Df1024–1033   Railroad purchases, fuel received, and ties and rails laid: 1917–1975

Contributed by Louis P. Cain

	Fuel received				Cross-ties laid		Purchases			
	Bituminous coal	Fuel oil	Diesel oil	New rails laid	Total	Treated	Total, including miscellaneous	Fuel	Forest products	Iron and steel products
	Df1024 [1]	Df1025 [1]	Df1026 [1]	Df1027 [2]	Df1028 [2]	Df1029 [2]	Df1030	Df1031	Df1032	Df1033
Year	Thousand short tons	Million gallons	Million gallons	Thousand short tons	Thousand	Thousand	Million dollars	Million dollars	Million dollars	Million dollars
1917	—	—	—	2,293	79,070	—	—	—	—	—
1918	—	—	—	2,109	76,139	—	—	—	—	—
1919	—	—	—	2,615	80,903	—	—	—	—	—
1920	—	—	—	1,581	86,829	37,792	—	—	—	—
1921	127,630	—	—	1,640	86,522	36,072	—	—	—	—
1922	120,654	—	—	1,557	86,642	40,630	—	—	—	—
1923	157,900	3,017	—	1,937	84,435	41,656	1,739	618	233	465
1924	126,340	3,095	—	2,006	83,073	44,490	1,343	472	181	366
1925	131,452	3,114	—	2,184	82,717	50,090	1,392	459	170	419
1926	139,602	3,173	—	2,475	80,746	55,558	1,559	473	186	507
1927	130,606	2,921	—	2,477	86,243	62,963	1,896	439	176	407
1928	119,820	2,847	—	2,404	84,585	64,331	1,271	385	161	375
1929	124,152	3,208	—	2,281	81,964	64,724	1,330	364	158	407
1930	108,651	2,870	—	1,783	69,325	54,529	1,039	307	135	805
1931	91,136	2,380	—	1,154	54,449	41,851	695	245	76	189
1932	74,670	1,984	—	456	40,137	30,107	445	178	52	95
1933	75,487	1,943	—	457	38,007	26,818	466	181	42	104
1934	79,494	2,108	—	715	44,131	32,367	600	217	64	151
1935	81,286	2,282	—	658	45,260	33,939	593	233	57	135
1936	91,707	2,569	—	1,043	49,117	38,206	803	272	77	239
1937	91,718	2,875	—	1,163	49,738	39,674	966	294	105	311
1938	74,784	2,426	—	679	42,508	34,589	583	244	57	127
1939	81,813	2,573	44	992	46,410	39,654	769	257	70	236
1940	88,595	2,752	73	1,134	45,326	38,698	854	274	82	264
1941	104,100	3,368	114	1,355	50,077	43,872	1,161	350	104	380
1942	120,910	4,135	174	1,353	53,241	47,932	1,260	426	115	354
1943	129,738	4,802	219	1,448	49,344	44,822	1,394	527	150	340
1944	135,579	4,744	316	1,773	51,259	47,695	1,611	586	159	432
1945	123,007	4,706	441	1,823	46,624	43,657	1,572	555	137	418
1946	108,148	4,144	544	1,388	40,150	37,671	1,571	553	149	416
1947	109,884	4,052	785	1,639	40,206	37,920	1,909	692	172	504
1948	98,826	3,759	1,170	1,548	40,472	38,281	2,183	833	166	590
1949	64,671	2,638	1,486	1,448	32,926	31,198	1,641	564	142	454
1950	63,906	2,519	1,923	1,368	33,091	31,553	1,740	609	121	510
1951	54,226	2,335	2,323	1,282	32,457	30,804	2,176	621	188	704
1952	37,829	1,668	2,759	1,086	34,231	32,910	1,818	539	177	513
1953	28,005	1,153	3,067	1,302	33,462	32,144	1,920	510	176	613
1954	15,964	656	3,160	993	25,728	24,531	1,425	433	114	406
1955	15,188	613	3,453	963	27,173	26,490	1,637	454	119	510
1956	12,280	443	3,639	883	27,323	26,848	1,884	477	155	613
1957	8,160	279	3,633	782	25,123	24,497	1,816	460	128	609
1958	3,658	239	3,453	413	17,722	17,426	1,231	376	76	320
1959	2,717	237	3,620	481	18,267	18,077	1,430	392	93	419
1960	2,229	233	3,560	382	16,417	16,290	1,463	365	97	446
1961	1,870	224	3,507	293	13,427	13,357	1,262	366	70	334
1962	1,834	229	3,578	312	15,206	15,138	1,311	364	81	374
1963	1,566	221	3,636	370	15,120	15,027	1,401	376	85	396
1964	7	85	3,630	383	16,546	16,488	1,476	365	97	437
1965	4	77	3,742	446	16,982	16,731	1,498	374	104	447
1966	3	65	3,925	605	17,699	17,399	1,605	401	125	483
1967	2	47	3,889	474	17,458	17,319	1,591	415	126	462
1968	2	42	3,922	547	19,006	18,811	1,534	439	104	425
1969	1	33	3,924	575	20,088	19,895	1,654	446	123	454
1970	1	0	3,812	549	19,611	19,473	—	—	—	—
1971	1	—	3,819	649	22,777	22,542	—	—	—	—
1972	1	—	3,435	671	22,006	21,954	—	—	—	—
1973	1	—	3,346	683	19,897	19,826	—	—	—	—
1974	1	—	5,076	709	20,923	20,834	—	—	—	—
1975	1	—	10,834	537	20,546	20,430	—	—	—	—

TABLE Df1024–1033 Railroad purchases, fuel received, and ties and rails laid: 1917–1975 *Continued*

[1] Beginning in 1964, includes only fuel for the operation of locomotives and motorcars.

[2] Data for 1917–1926 include only rails laid in replacement.

Sources

Series Df1024–1029: For 1890–1953, U.S. Interstate Commerce Commission (ICC), *Statistics of Railways in the United States* (annual issues), and for 1954–1978, ICC, *Transport Statistics in the United States*, Part 1 (annual issues). Series Df1030–1033: For 1923–1964, Association of American Railroads, *Railroad Transportation* (various issues) and for 1965–1969, Association of American Railroads, *Yearbook of Railroad Facts* (annual issues).

Documentation

Data are for Class I line-haul railroads. See the text for Table Df927–955 for definitions of railroad company types.

Series Df1024–1026. Includes fuel for operation of trains and for station, shop, or other use.

Series Df1027–1029. Includes both rails laid in replacement and rails laid in additional tracks, new lines, and extensions.

Series Df1028–1029. Of the total ties laid in 1927, 78,340,000 were in replacement. Treated ties are those that have been subjected to some preservative process (for example, creosoting) before being placed in the track.

TABLE Df1034–1053 Railroad mileage, equipment, and passenger traffic and revenue: 1960–1996[1]

Contributed by Louis P. Cain

	Mileage				Equipment					
			Road operated		New cars delivered for domestic use		Locomotives in service			
	Operating railroads	Road owned	Total	Passenger service	Freight	Passenger	Total	Steam	Electric	Diesel
	Df1034	Df1035	Df1036	Df1037	Df1038	Df1039	Df1040	Df1041	Df1042	Df1043
Year	Number	Miles	Thousand miles	Miles	Number	Number	Number	Number	Number	Number
1960	—	217,552	382	93,816	57,047	251	29,080	261	492	28,278
1961	—	216,445	379	88,854	31,720	214	28,815	112	478	28,169
1962	—	215,090	376	86,302	36,554	304	28,639	51	434	28,104
1963	—	214,387	375	84,928	44,960	156	28,449	36	429	27,945
1964	—	212,059	372	81,795	69,330	399	28,300	34	393	27,837
1965	—	211,384	371	76,993	77,822	666	27,816	29	362	27,389
1966	—	210,573	370	73,173	90,104	113	27,886	25	344	27,481
1967	—	209,292	368	67,827	83,095	146	27,687	21	321	27,309
1968	—	208,111	366	59,259	56,232	65	27,376	21	305	27,017
1969	—	207,005	365	56,484	69,028	240	27,033	21	276	26,714
1970	71	206,625	336	—	66,185	302	27,086	13	268	26,796
1971	69	205,220	335	—	55,046	281	27,189	13	250	26,897
1972	68	203,299	331	—	47,322	334	27,073	13	252	27,064
1973	68	192,813	329	—	58,634	83	27,453	12	238	27,540
1974	67	192,991	327	—	66,798	85	27,627	12	215	27,857
1975	67	191,520	324	—	72,392	265	27,846	12	167	27,667
1976	52	182,395	313	—	52,323	349	27,215	12	217	27,383
1977	52	182,380	311	—	51,639	153	27,283	12	205	27,450
1978	52	177,710	310	—	67,440	43	26,960	12	204	27,184
1979	41	169,927	300	—	95,836	99	27,043	12	163	27,922
1980	40	164,822	292	24,000	85,920	152	28,094	12	79	28,003
1981	38	162,160	278	—	44,901	119	27,421	0	0	27,421
1982	33	159,123	275	—	17,236	102	26,795	0	0	26,795
1983	32	155,879	270	—	5,772	115	25,448	0	0	25,448
1984	29	151,998	264	—	12,396	128	24,117	0	0	24,117
1985	23	145,764	269	24,000	12,080	179	22,548	0	0	22,548
1986	22	140,061	262	—	11,508	140	20,790	0	0	20,790
1987	18	132,220	261	—	13,645	272	19,358	0	0	19,649
1988	17	127,555	251	—	22,524	74	19,364	0	0	19,501
1989	15	124,236	250	—	29,617	160	19,015	0	0	19,017
1990	14	119,758	244	24,000	32,063	83	18,835	0	0	18,835
1991	14	116,626	241	25,000	24,678	187	18,344	0	0	18,344
1992	13	113,056	234	25,000	25,761	110	18,004	0	0	18,004
1993	13	110,425	231	25,000	35,239	260	18,161	0	0	18,161
1994	13	109,332	222	25,000	48,819	—	18,505	0	0	18,496
1995	11	108,264	—	24,000	60,853	—	18,812	0	0	18,810
1996	10	105,779	—	25,000	57,877	—	19,269	0	0	19,267

Notes appear at end of table

(continued)

TABLE Df1034–1053 Railroad mileage, equipment, and passenger traffic and revenue: 1960–1996 *Continued*

	Equipment					Passenger traffic and revenue					
	Passenger-train cars in service		Freight-train cars in service				Passenger-miles			Revenue	
	Railroad only	Class I railroads and Pullman Co.	Number	Average capacity	Passengers	Total	Commutation	Coach, parlor, and sleeping car	Total	Per passenger-mile
	Df1044	Df1045 [2]	Df1046	Df1047 [3]	Df1048	Df1049	Df1050	Df1051	Df1052	Df1053
Year	Number	Number	Number	Number	Thousand	Million passenger-miles	Million passenger-miles	Million passenger-miles	Thousand dollars	Cents per passenger-mile
1960	25,746	27,414	1,658,292	55.4	327,172	21,261	4,197	17,065	641,496	3.03
1961	24,433	26,899	1,604,241	55.7	318,359	20,286	4,132	16,155	625,874	3.08
1962	23,430	24,634	1,550,067	56.3	313,084	19,905	4,046	15,859	620,290	3.10
1963	22,616	23,568	1,512,306	56.8	310,999	18,497	4,101	14,396	589,621	3.18
1964	21,510	23,057	1,488,385	58.2	314,386	18,247	4,199	14,048	679,287	3.16
1965	20,022	21,327	1,478,005	59.8	305,822	17,388	4,128	13,260	555,986	3.14
1966	18,974	20,016	1,488,115	61.4	307,530	17,096	4,193	12,903	547,139	3.13
1967	17,822	18,610	1,477,166	63.4	304,028	15,201	4,281	10,921	488,549	3.13
1968	14,816	15,384	1,453,883	64.3	301,372	13,120	4,383	8,737	446,704	3.33
1969	12,630	14,619	1,434,824	65.8	301,673	12,169	4,546	7,622	441,503	3.63
1970	11,378	11,177	1,423,921	67.1	289,469	10,771	4,592	6,179	423,191	4.02
1971	—	8,713	1,410,160	68.4	—	6,392	4,498	1,894	—	4.38
1972	—	7,589	1,381,038	69.6	—	7,267	4,229	3,038	—	4.42
1973	—	7,189	1,356,944	70.5	—	8,052	4,245	3,807	—	4.44
1974	—	6,848	1,339,223	71.6	—	8,792	4,533	4,259	—	5.29
1975	—	6,471	1,314,135	72.9	—	8,444	4,513	3,931	—	5.71
1976	—	5,478	1,268,735	73.8	—	8,738	4,470	4,268	—	5.62
1977	—	5,512	1,232,080	75.5	—	8,792	4,588	4,204	—	5.83
1978	—	4,493	1,166,517	76.9	—	10,367	6,213	4,154	—	6.08
1979	—	4,241	1,118,381	77.7	—	11,359	6,492	4,867	—	6.59
1980	—	4,347	1,168,114	78.5	—	11,019	6,516	4,503	—	8.18
1981	—	3,945	1,111,115	80.5	—	10,998	6,236	4,762	—	9.38
1982	—	3,736	1,039,016	81.6	—	10,199	6,027	4,172	—	10.19
1983	—	2,610	1,007,165	82.4	—	10,343	6,097	4,246	—	10.65
1984	—	2,580	948,171	83.4	—	10,759	6,207	4,552	—	10.91
1985	—	2,502	867,070	83.2	—	11,319	6,534	4,785	—	10.48
1986	—	2,307	798,631	84.1	—	11,734	6,723	5,011	—	10.60
1987	—	2,350	748,523	85.0	—	12,179	6,818	5,361	—	10.58
1988	—	2,332	724,840	86.4	—	12,650	6,964	5,686	—	11.46
1989	—	—	682,270	87.8	—	13,051	7,211	5,840	—	12.62
1990	—	—	658,902	87.5	—	13,123	7,082	6,041	—	12.85
1991	—	—	633,489	87.9	—	13,658	7,384	6,274	—	12.83
1992	—	—	605,189	88.0	—	13,400	7,344	6,100	—	—
1993	—	—	587,033	88.0	—	13,100	7,320	6,200	—	—
1994	—	—	590,930	88.1	—	13,900	6,939	5,900	—	—
1995	—	—	583,486	—	—	13,700	—	5,500	—	—
1996	—	—	570,865	—	—	13,500	—	5,100	—	—

[1] Includes intercorporate duplications.

[2] Beginning in 1969, excludes the Pullman Company.

[3] Through 1967, excludes switching and terminal companies.

Sources

Association of American Railroads, *Railroad Facts* (annual editions); U.S. Department of Transportation, *National Transportation Statistics* (annual editions).

Documentation

The data in this table are calculated from information reported by the Association of American Railroads for Class I railroads, except as noted. This information is slightly different from what was reported by the Interstate Commerce Commission (ICC).

See the text for Table Df927–955 for ICC definitions of railroad company types.

Series Df1035. Data are for first (main) track and includes lessors, proprietary, unofficial and, through 1963, circular companies.

Series Df1036. Includes only railroads reporting track by class and excludes circular and unofficial.

Series Df1038–1047. Include switching and terminal companies.

Series Df1040. Reports the number of units, except for steam locomotives. See text for series Df938.

Series Df1044–1045. Include coaches and parlor, sleeping, dining, club, lounge, observation, postal, baggage, express, and other cars, as well as cars serving a combination of purposes.

Series Df1046–1047. Exclude caboose cars.

Series Df1052. Excludes revenue from services such as handling of excess baggage or mail; sleeping and parlor or chair car reservations; dining and buffet service on trains; station, train, and boat privileges; parcel rooms; storage of baggage; or other miscellaneous services and facilities connected with the transportation of passengers. Passenger revenue depends on the established tariffs (the published schedules of rates and fares) and includes extra fares on limited trains, additional railway fares for the exclusive use of space, mileage and scrip coupons honored, or revenue from the transportation of corpses.

Series Df1053. Equals series Df1052 divided by series Df1049.

TABLE Df1054–1063   Railroad freight operations – per-car and per-train traffic volume, and speed: 1960–1997

Contributed by Louis P. Cain

Year	Revenue ton-miles Df1054 Million ton-miles	Road miles owned Df1055 Miles	Revenue ton-miles per mile of road Df1056 Tons per mile	Train miles Df1057 Thousand miles	Revenue ton-miles per train-mile Df1058 Tons per train	Net ton-miles Per train-mile Df1059 Tons per train	Net ton-miles Per loaded car-mile Df1060 Tons per car	Revenue ton-miles per loaded car-mile Df1061 Ton-miles per mile	Train-miles Per loaded car-mile Df1062 Trains per thousand cars	Train-miles Per train-hour Df1063 Miles per hour
1960	572,309	207,334	2,760,324	404,464	1,415	1,453	34.0	33.1	23.4	19.5
1961	563,361	216,445	2,602,791	386,410	1,458	1,495	34.7	33.8	23.2	19.9
1962	592,862	215,090	2,756,344	393,346	1,507	1,544	35.7	34.8	23.1	20.0
1963	621,737	214,387	2,900,069	399,897	1,555	1,590	37.1	36.3	23.3	20.1
1964	658,639	212,603	3,097,976	414,470	1,589	1,618	38.3	37.6	23.7	20.2
1965	697,878	199,798	3,492,918	420,964	1,658	1,685	39.6	39.0	23.5	20.1
1966	738,395	211,107	3,497,729	437,491	1,688	1,715	41.0	40.3	23.9	20.3
1967	719,498	198,603	3,622,795	420,365	1,712	1,740	42.0	41.3	24.1	20.3
1968	744,023	198,249	3,752,972	429,276	1,733	1,768	43.0	42.2	24.3	20.4
1969	767,841	197,414	3,889,496	433,371	1,772	1,804	43.5	42.7	24.1	20.1
1970	764,809	196,479	3,892,574	427,065	1,791	1,820	44.9	44.2	24.7	20.1
1971	738,395	195,840	3,770,399	429,530	1,719	1,751	45.6	44.8	26.0	20.4
1972	719,498	194,421	3,700,722	451,032	1,595	1,774	46.7	42.0	26.3	20.0
1973	744,023	192,813	3,858,780	468,992	1,586	1,844	48.7	41.9	26.4	19.8
1974	767,841	192,991	3,978,636	469,268	1,636	1,875	50.1	43.7	26.7	19.9
1975	754,252	191,520	3,938,241	402,557	1,874	1,938	51.7	50.0	26.7	20.0
1976	739,743	185,395	3,990,091	424,571	1,742	2,232	59.9	46.8	26.8	20.1
1977	776,746	182,380	4,258,943	427,686	1,816	2,029	53.2	47.6	26.2	19.8
1978	851,809	177,710	4,793,253	432,895	1,968	2,029	55.1	53.4	27.2	19.3
1979	850,961	169,927	5,007,803	437,848	1,944	2,096	57.9	53.7	27.6	17.2
1980	918,958	164,822	5,575,457	428,498	2,145	2,175	63.5	62.6	29.2	18.2
1981	910,169	162,160	5,612,784	407,520	2,233	2,263	67.1	66.2	29.7	19.0
1982	797,759	159,123	5,013,474	344,936	2,313	2,345	68.3	67.4	29.1	21.4
1983	828,275	155,879	5,313,577	345,916	2,394	2,432	61.2	60.3	25.2	20.3
1984	921,542	151,998	6,062,856	369,403	2,495	2,543	62.4	61.2	24.5	21.9
1985	876,984	145,764	6,016,465	347,292	2,525	2,574	62.7	61.5	24.4	21.9
1986	910,169	140,061	6,498,376	347,234	2,621	2,552	63.2	64.9	24.8	22.5
1987	797,759	132,220	6,033,573	360,692	2,212	2,644	64.0	53.5	24.2	22.3
1988	828,275	127,555	6,493,473	379,271	2,184	2,662	65.5	53.7	24.6	21.5
1989	921,542	124,236	7,417,673	382,661	2,408	2,683	67.0	60.1	25.0	23.0
1990	1,033,969	119,758	8,633,820	379,582	2,724	2,755	69.1	68.3	25.1	23.7
1991	1,038,875	116,626	8,907,748	374,974	2,771	2,796	71.6	70.9	25.6	23.7
1992	1,066,781	113,056	9,435,864	390,241	2,734	2,759	70.9	70.2	25.7	23.7
1993	1,109,309	110,425	10,045,814	405,446	2,736	2,759	71.6	71.0	26.0	23.1
1994	1,200,701	109,332	10,982,155	440,896	2,723	2,746	72.2	71.6	26.3	22.4
1995	1,305,688	108,264	12,060,223	458,271	2,849	2,870	73.6	73.1	25.6	21.8
1996	1,355,975	105,779	12,818,943	468,792	2,892	2,912	—	—	—	—
1997	1,348,926	102,188	13,200,434	474,954	2,840	2,861	—	—	—	—

Sources

Association of American Railroads, *Railroad Facts* (annual issues), and *Analysis of Class I Railroads* (annual issues).

Documentation

The data in this table are calculated from information reported by the Association of American Railroads for Class I railroads. This information is slightly different from what was reported by the Interstate Commerce Commission (ICC); hence, these series are not strictly comparable to series Df959–962.

See the text for Table Df927–955 for ICC definitions of railroad company types.

Tons are 2,000-pound tons.

The mileage figures in series Df1055 are road miles owned. Consequently, the ratio reported in series Df1056 has a different denominator than series Df961.

Series Df1063. The train-hour figures on which the data are based are reckoned from the time a train leaves its original terminal to the time it arrives at its final terminal. Time spent in stopping to take on and discharge traffic and other delays on the road are included.

TABLE Df1064–1069   Railroad freight traffic and revenue: 1960–1996

Contributed by Louis P. Cain

	Freight			Revenue		
	Revenue tons originated	Ton-miles	Haul per ton	Total	Per ton	Per ton-mile
	Df1064	Df1065	Df1066	Df1067	Df1068	Df1069
Year	Million tons	Million ton-miles	Miles per ton	Million dollars	Dollars per ton	Cents per ton-mile
1960	1,240.7	572,309	461.3	8,025	6.47	1.403
1961	1,193.7	563,361	—	7,739	—	1.374
1962	1,233.6	592,862	—	7,991	—	1.348
1963	1,284.8	621,737	—	8,146	—	1.310
1964	1,354.6	658,639	—	8,455	—	1.284
1965	1,387.4	697,878	503.0	8,836	6.37	1.266
1966	1,448.9	738,395	—	9,281	—	1.257
1967	1,407.6	719,498	—	9,130	—	1.269
1968	1,431.3	744,023	—	9,750	—	1.310
1969	1,473.5	767,841	—	10,346	—	1.347
1970	1,484.9	764,809	515.1	10,922	7.36	1.428
1971	1,391.0	739,743	—	11,786	—	1.593
1972	1,447.9	776,746	—	12,570	—	1.618
1973	1,532.2	851,809	—	13,771	—	1.617
1974	1,530.7	850,961	—	15,767	—	1.853
1975	1,395.1	754,252	540.7	15,390	11.03	2.041
1976	1,406.7	794,059	—	17,400	—	2.191
1977	1,394.7	826,292	—	18,892	—	2.286
1978	1,390.2	857,921	617.2	20,236	—	2.358
1979	1,502.3	904,956	611.0	23,447	—	2.599
1980	1,492.4	918,958	615.8	26,350	17.66	2.867
1981	1,453.0	910,169	626.4	28,925	19.91	3.178
1982	1,268.6	797,759	628.8	25,627	20.20	3.212
1983	1,292.6	828,275	640.8	25,836	19.99	3.119
1984	1,429.4	921,542	644.7	28,472	19.92	3.090
1985	1,319.8	876,984	664.5	26,688	20.22	3.043
1986	1,305.8	867,722	664.5	25,344	19.41	2.921
1987	1,372.3	943,747	687.7	25,797	18.80	2.733
1988	1,429.5	996,182	696.9	27,092	18.95	2.720
1989	1,402.6	1,013,841	722.8	27,059	19.29	2.669
1990	1,424.9	1,033,969	725.7	27,471	19.28	2.657
1991	1,382.7	1,038,875	751.3	26,949	19.49	2.594
1992	1,399.0	1,066,781	762.5	27,508	19.66	2.579
1993	1,396.8	1,109,309	794.2	27,991	20.04	2.523
1994	1,470.0	1,200,701	816.8	29,931	20.36	2.493
1995	1,549.6	1,305,688	842.6	31,356	20.23	2.401
1996	1,610.9	1,355,975	841.7	31,889	19.79	2.352

Source

Association of American Railroads, *Railroad Facts* (annual editions); Association of American Railroads, *National Transportation Statistics* (annual editions).

Documentation

The data in this table are calculated from information reported by the Association of American Railroads for Class I railroads. This information is slightly different from what was reported by the Interstate Commerce Commission (ICC).

See the text for Table Df927–955 for ICC definitions of railroad company types.

Revenue-tons and ton-miles exclude the movement of a railroad company's materials and supplies on its own lines. See text for Table Df965–979 for definitions of terms.

Series Df1066 and Df1068. The numerator is defined in terms of the United States as a system, and so ton-miles or revenue of connecting roads are included, whereas only tonnage originated is included in the denominator.

Series Df1067. Includes revenue from the transportation of freight and from transit, stop, diversion, and reconsignment arrangements upon the basis of tariffs. The series excludes revenue from activities such as switching of freight-train cars; water transfers of freight, vehicles, and livestock; movement of freight trains at a per-train-mile rate or for a lump sum; storage of freight; demurrage; operation of grain elevators or stockyards; or other miscellaneous services and facilities connected with the transportation of freight.

TABLE Df1070–1073   Railroad property investment and capital expenditures: 1960–1996[1]

Contributed by Louis P. Cain

Year	Road and equipment, net investment, book value	Capital expenditures for additions and betterments		
		Total	Equipment	Roadway and structures
	Df1070 [2]	Df1071	Df1072	Df1073
	Thousand dollars	Thousand dollars	Thousand dollars	Thousand dollars
1960	27,474,089	919,154	633,490	285,664
1961	27,180,557	646,425	427,130	219,295
1962	25,858,289	832,938	593,369	239,569
1963	25,772,832	1,043,788	784,874	258,914
1964	25,989,260	1,417,263	1,139,683	277,580
1965	26,318,532	1,630,687	1,303,603	327,084
1966	27,322,220	1,952,805	1,554,223	398,581
1967	27,732,601	1,522,478	1,148,381	374,097
1968	27,667,726	1,186,979	818,720	368,259
1969	27,891,688	1,509,394	1,088,712	420,681
1970	28,186,077	1,351,439	993,095	358,344
1971	28,096,047	1,177,627	863,517	314,110
1972	27,735,595	1,215,581	847,623	367,958
1973	27,979,177	1,342,138	892,690	449,448
1974	28,854,835	1,565,412	1,038,142	527,270
1975	29,739,673	1,789,725	1,303,308	486,417
1976	26,925,751	1,724,708	1,174,783	549,925
1977	28,222,310	2,290,439	1,539,549	750,890
1978	28,946,319	2,738,238	1,882,961	855,277
1979	30,438,804	3,324,174	2,284,855	1,039,319
1980	33,419,097	3,233,596	2,280,129	953,467
1981	34,997,185	2,749,757	1,501,707	1,248,050
1982	35,260,692	2,165,941	847,572	1,318,369
1983	43,483,411	2,760,909	455,279	2,305,630
1984	45,435,400	3,744,395	806,159	2,938,236
1985	46,236,917	4,422,903	964,888	3,458,015
1986	45,343,671	3,600,682	692,663	2,908,019
1987	45,689,605	2,970,805	656,853	2,313,952
1988	47,053,269	3,681,447	1,027,251	2,654,196
1989	47,370,438	3,708,662	1,170,728	2,537,934
1990	48,126,335	3,639,838	995,872	2,643,966
1991	48,565,225	3,437,363	1,067,958	2,369,405
1992	49,298,754	3,610,332	874,330	2,736,002
1993	51,324,734	4,177,069	1,381,699	2,795,370
1994	54,184,206	4,885,465	1,733,864	3,151,601
1995	62,746,424	5,994,368	2,342,904	3,651,464
1996	66,113,117	6,100,996	2,201,673	3,899,323

[1] Data prior to 1983 are not strictly comparable to later data. See text.

[2] Prior to 1970, includes investment of lessor and proprietary companies.

Source

Association of American Railroads, *Railroad Facts* (annual issues).

Documentation

The data are for Class I railroads; they include intercorporate duplications. See the text for Table Df927–955 for definitions of railroad company types. Also see the text for corresponding series in Table Df980–990.

Data starting in 1983 are not strictly comparable to the earlier data because of the industry's conversion to a standard depreciation accounting system which, on paper only, has the effect of decreasing annual costs. The Interstate Commerce Commission mandated that the railroads switch to this system. Prior to 1983, the system was a Retirement, Replacement, Betterment (RRB) system that used replacement cost rather than original cost to determine the asset consumption cost (see the preface to the 1984 edition of *Railroad Facts*).

TABLE Df1074–1082 Railroad income, expenses, interest, and dividends: 1960–1996[1,2]

Contributed by Louis P. Cain

		Income and expenses							Interest and dividends (dividends declared)
	Operating revenue	Operating expenses			Tax accruals	Net operating income	Net income	Ratio of operating expenses to operating revenue	
		Total	Maintenance of way and structures	Maintenance of equipment					
	Df1074	Df1075 [3]	Df1076 [3]	Df1077 [3]	Df1078	Df1079	Df1080	Df1081	Df1082
Year	Thousand dollars	Thousand dollars	Thousand dollars	Thousand dollars	Thousand dollars	Thousand dollars	Thousand dollars	Percent	Thousand dollars
1960	9,514,294	8,775,438	1,191,690	1,759,828	998,799	584,016	444,640	92.23	385,493
1961	9,189,138	—	1,117,680	1,683,363	991,083	537,771	382,444	—	357,561
1962	9,439,895	—	1,154,802	1,743,639	905,044	725,679	571,017	—	368,164
1963	9,559,522	—	1,182,507	1,731,735	886,387	805,658	651,637	—	378,549
1964	9,856,527	—	1,225,759	1,763,786	870,581	818,213	698,184	—	457,188
1965	10,207,850	8,947,607	1,235,801	1,774,878	916,494	961,516	814,629	87.65	470,800
1966	10,654,666	9,480,285	1,303,739	1,843,589	968,372	1,045,863	903,783	88.98	499,364
1967	10,366,041	9,679,650	1,287,834	1,867,788	910,178	676,434	553,789	93.38	502,570
1968	10,854,678	10,170,123	1,405,133	1,914,265	946,334	677,623	569,402	93.69	515,858
1969	11,450,325	10,747,308	1,502,958	2,002,316	1,029,067	654,670	514,238	93.86	487,440
1970	11,991,658	11,477,548	1,612,585	2,165,254	1,068,518	485,854	226,583	95.71	421,226
1971	12,689,016	11,947,362	1,813,141	2,350,875	1,190,046	595,171	246,729	94.16	386,551
1972	13,409,815	12,528,414	1,920,395	2,397,596	1,316,766	653,827	318,637	93.43	409,715
1973	14,770,082	13,844,765	2,035,613	2,531,380	1,547,109	649,828	359,343	93.74	416,100
1974	16,922,841	15,782,658	2,351,973	2,809,237	1,990,473	768,106	730,229	93.26	509,801
1975	16,401,860	15,935,542	2,408,980	2,856,203	1,706,411	350,682	144,362	97.16	434,246
1976	18,536,482	17,881,047	3,047,236	3,213,892	1,927,405	451,832	354,982	96.46	429,881
1977	20,090,482	19,533,970	3,460,153	3,613,494	2,063,572	343,093	325,582	97.23	497,208
1978	21,721,332	21,121,431	4,055,105	5,421,182	2,150,181	445,714	257,814	97.24	472,416
1979	25,219,115	24,089,500	4,581,742	6,018,672	2,418,414	860,684	883,718	95.52	562,684
1980	28,257,548	26,355,103	4,940,091	6,387,976	2,585,342	1,338,551	1,129,392	93.27	610,204
1981	30,898,610	28,586,890	5,535,815	6,866,503	3,280,178	1,360,611	2,041,265	92.52	662,400
1982	27,503,503	26,490,278	5,208,584	6,413,196	2,628,119	742,231	1,151,548	96.32	1,038,414
1983	26,729,392	24,106,254	4,107,246	6,070,391	3,013,608	1,837,854	1,777,916	90.19	1,084,508
1984	29,453,446	25,800,454	4,250,275	6,572,696	3,604,853	2,536,673	2,653,814	87.60	1,065,665
1985	27,586,441	25,225,295	4,332,663	6,394,579	3,168,603	1,746,386	1,788,151	91.44	1,443,688
1986	26,204,122	24,896,015	4,779,691	6,573,065	2,727,625	506,591	746,965	95.01	1,375,936
1987	26,622,482	23,878,116	4,338,334	6,093,534	3,552,724	1,756,460	1,965,475	89.69	1,252,127
1988	27,934,285	24,811,138	4,397,528	6,109,116	3,897,361	1,979,719	2,286,003	88.82	1,813,560
1989	27,955,959	25,037,666	4,431,101	6,178,666	3,742,233	1,894,315	2,009,094	89.56	—
1990	28,369,803	24,651,542	4,278,075	6,349,784	3,786,500	2,648,258	1,961,127	86.89	—
1991	27,845,206	28,061,187	5,215,582	6,300,006	2,649,438	−37,455	−90,849	100.78	—
1992	28,348,895	25,324,506	4,373,006	6,314,426	3,732,421	1,954,835	2,055,055	89.33	—
1993	28,824,852	24,516,966	4,353,206	6,459,363	4,343,294	2,517,138	2,258,037	85.05	—
1994	30,808,977	25,511,105	4,400,909	6,782,312	4,512,189	3,391,521	3,314,704	82.80	—
1995	32,279,491	27,896,748	5,446,567	7,018,921	4,075,222	2,857,691	2,438,999	86.42	—
1996	32,692,638	26,331,375	4,455,598	6,960,447	4,669,011	4,338,097	3,885,282	80.54	—

[1] Includes intercorporate duplications.

[2] Expense data after 1983 not comparable to earlier data because of the industry's conversion to a standard depreciation accounting system. See text.

[3] Revised after 1978 to include rent and taxes other than income taxes, as required by the Uniform System of Accounts that went into effect January 1, 1978.

Sources

Association of American Railroads, *Railroad Facts* (annual issues); *National Transportation Statistics* (annual issues).

Documentation

The data are for Class I railroads. See the text for Table Df927–955 for definitions of railroad company types.

Series Df1074. Includes revenue from freight, passenger, and other transportation and incidental services.

Series Df1075–1077. Include current depreciation.

Series Df1076–1081. The data after 1983 are not strictly comparable to earlier data because of the industry's conversion to a standard depreciation accounting system, which, on paper only, has the effect of decreasing annual costs. The Interstate Commerce Commission mandated that the railroads switch to this system. Prior to 1983, the system was a Retirement,

Replacement, Betterment (RRB) system that used replacement cost rather than original cost to determine the asset consumption cost. See the preface to the 1984 edition of *Railroad Facts*.

Series Df1078. Reports taxes imposed by any form of government, whether based on an assessed value of the property, amounts of stocks and bonds, earnings, income, dividends declared, payroll, number of passengers, quantity of freight, length of road, rolling stock, or other basis. Tax accruals do not include special assessments for street and other improvements, or special benefit taxes such as water assessments.

Series Df1079. Equals operating income minus net payable balance of equipment and joint facility rents. The equipment rents deducted at this point are those for equipment leased for less than one year, or interchanged. They are usually on a per-day or per-mile basis.

Series Df1080. Equals net operating income, series Df1079, plus other income minus miscellaneous deductions and fixed and contingent charges. Fixed charges are mainly rent for leased roads and equipment (that is, equipment leased for one year or more) and interest (except contingent interest). These data include lessors.

Series Df1082. Interest and dividends after extraordinary and prior period items.

TABLE Df1083–1088   Railroad purchases, and ties and rails laid: 1960–1996

Contributed by Louis P. Cain

	New rails laid	Cross-ties laid	Purchases	Diesel fuel		
			Total	Total cost	Gallons	Cost per gallon
	Df1083	Df1084	Df1085	Df1086	Df1087	Df1088
Year	Short tons	Thousand	Thousand dollars	Million dollars	Million gallons	Dollars per gallon
1960	382,277	16,417	1,463,245	313.5	3,471.8	0.0903
1961	292,750	13,426	1,262,220	313.5	3,382.0	0.0927
1962	312,128	15,206	1,311,293	317.2	3,462.7	0.0916
1963	370,418	15,120	1,401,424	322.9	3,544.7	0.0911
1964	383,311	16,546	1,475,599	320.9	3,630.3	0.0884
1965	445,863	16,982	1,498,059	340.6	3,742.4	0.0910
1966	605,338	17,699	1,604,862	360.7	3,925.4	0.0919
1967	470,659	17,458	1,590,737	373.7	3,888.8	0.0961
1968	546,859	19,006	1,534,100	389.9	3,922.5	0.0994
1969	574,918	20,088	1,653,748	399.1	3,924.1	0.1017
1970	548,505	19,611	—	408.6	3,807.7	0.1073
1971	648,625	22,777	—	415.9	3,822.9	0.1088
1972	675,796	22,251	—	438.5	3,997.0	0.1097
1973	698,506	19,983	—	561.3	4,160.7	0.1349
1974	708,362	21,175	—	1,110.2	4,175.4	0.2659
1975	537,537	20,548	—	1,120.9	3,736.5	0.3000
1976	802,441	27,002	—	1,261.4	3,895.5	0.3238
1977	952,144	27,270	—	1,449.8	3,985.1	0.3638
1978	838,001	27,219	—	1,508.2	3,980.4	0.3789
1979	1,064,829	26,667	—	2,350.5	4,080.8	0.5760
1980	881,783	25,984	—	3,269.2	3,956.0	0.8264
1981	800,340	26,529	—	3,782.5	3,774.2	1.0022
1982	502,718	20,726	—	3,032.9	3,178.1	0.9543
1983	538,597	20,086	—	2,607.7	3,137.3	0.8312
1984	659,285	23,581	—	2,797.6	3,388.2	0.8257
1985	699,774	20,736	—	2,463.2	3,144.2	0.7834
1986	456,066	18,104	—	1,496.1	3,039.1	0.4923
1987	377,282	14,768	—	1,662.8	3,102.2	0.5360
1988	357,371	14,046	—	1,564.1	3,182.3	0.4915
1989	348,186	13,458	—	1,795.5	3,190.8	0.5627
1990	338,867	14,309	—	2,169.7	3,134.4	0.6922
1991	299,385	12,844	—	1,967.4	2,926.0	0.6724
1992	456,674	13,690	—	1,912.1	3,022.1	0.6329
1993	441,381	13,233	—	1,962.1	3,112.0	0.6305
1994	434,349	12,896	—	2,009.1	3,355.8	0.5987
1995	443,084	12,784	—	2,102.2	3,503.1	0.6001
1996	491,488	14,269	—	2,436.2	3,600.6	0.6766

Source

Association of American Railroads, *Railroad Facts* (annual issues).

Documentation

The data are for Class I railroads. See the text for Table Df927–955 for definitions of railroad company types.

Series Df1083. Includes both rails laid in replacement and rails laid in additional tracks, new lines, and extensions. Treated ties are those that have been subjected to some preservative process (for example, creosoting) before being placed in the track.

TABLE Df1089–1091   Pullman Company operations – road mileage, passenger-miles, and employees: 1915–1968

Contributed by Louis P. Cain

	Average miles of road	Revenue passenger-miles	Employees		Average miles of road	Revenue passenger-miles	Employees
	Df1089	Df1090 [1]	Df1091		Df1089	Df1090 [1]	Df1091
Year	Miles	Million passenger-miles	Number	Year	Miles	Million passenger-miles	Number
1915	—	8,925	—	1945	95,765	27,276	41,601
1916	—	9,285	—	1946	100,653	20,672	36,982
1917	—	—	—	1947	105,950	13,516	29,046
1918	—	10,679	—	1948	104,940	12,172	23,724
1919	—	13,720	—	1949	104,287	10,544	22,286
1920	—	14,334	—	1950	102,722	10,558	22,820
1921	—	11,295	—	1951	99,592	9,893	23,862
1922	123,547	11,759	19,066	1952	96,390	9,336	22,588
1923	124,794	12,982	23,579	1953	94,518	8,200	21,529
1924	124,795	13,082	25,091	1954	91,920	7,271	19,866
1925	126,840	14,016	26,919	1955	89,124	6,882	18,061
1926	126,907	14,409	26,185	1956	87,472	6,630	16,793
1927	123,334	14,099	27,359	1957	85,068	5,388	14,890
1928	128,753	13,938	26,815	1958	79,555	4,300	10,234
1929	130,019	14,059	29,250	1959	71,448	3,462	8,020
1930	129,578	12,516	26,165	1960	67,467	3,358	7,320
1931	125,703	9,891	22,546	1961	63,035	3,046	6,688
1932	118,061	6,757	17,132	1962	61,278	2,905	6,392
1933	112,298	6,142	15,887	1963	59,798	2,516	5,902
1934	112,420	6,891	19,066	1964	52,994	2,218	5,544
1935	112,117	7,146	20,436	1965	51,057	2,014	5,347
1936	111,522	8,355	21,711	1966	45,807	1,969	4,905
1937	111,507	9,170	23,406	1967	42,713	1,434	4,179
1938	110,728	8,270	20,750	1968	33,464	1,002	2,945
1939	109,886	8,485	21,335				
1940	109,595	8,214	20,877				
1941	108,034	10,070	22,704				
1942	106,408	19,072	26,591				
1943	104,128	25,891	33,182				
1944	103,766	28,267	39,703				

[1] For the years 1939–1967, includes Pullman operations on Canadian and Mexican railroads and excludes chartered car operations.

Sources

U.S. Interstate Commerce Commission, *Statistics of Railways in the United States* and *Transport Statistics in the United States*, Part 2, and, beginning 1963, Part 1 (annual issues), and *The Pullman Company (Sleeping Car Companies)* (various annual issues); except series Df1090, 1915–1921, U.S. Office of Business Economics, *Survey of Current Business* (January 1939): 18.

Documentation

Series Df1090. Figures for this series exceed those in series Df953, parlor and sleeping car passenger-miles, mainly because travel of railroad employees (for which railroad companies receive no revenue) is not included in series Df953. If Pullman accommodations are paid for, the travel is included in series Df1090.

Series Df1091. The number of employees on the payroll at the end of the year. The Pullman Company ceased operation in 1969.

TABLE Df1092–1103   Amtrak finances – revenues, expenses, operating loss, and grants: 1987–1998

Contributed by Louis P. Cain

	Revenue			Expenses								
	Total	Passenger related	Commuter operating	Total	Employee compensation	Train operations	Facility and office related	Depreciation	Operating loss	Total federal grants	Noncash grants	Budget result
	Df1092	Df1093	Df1094	Df1095	Df1096	Df1097	Df1098	Df1099	Df1100	Df1101	Df1102	Df1103
Fiscal year	Million dollars	Million dollars	Million dollars	Million dollars	Million dollars	Million dollars	Million dollars	Million dollars	Million dollars	Million dollars	Million dollars	Million dollars
1987	974	666	49	1,672	863	344	112	163	−698	579	163	44
1988	1,107	775	79	1,757	967	317	121	154	−650	532	154	35
1989	1,269	879	83	1,935	1,034	354	131	166	−666	554	166	54
1990	1,308	942	90	2,012	1,076	381	144	182	−704	520	182	−2
1991	1,359	980	99	2,081	1,075	408	140	203	−722	488	203	−31
1992	1,325	950	116	2,037	1,076	382	148	206	−712	481	206	−25
1993	1,403	969	162	2,134	1,154	359	149	206	−731	498	206	−27
1994	1,413	913	184	2,246	1,205	358	153	245	−833	502	256	−76
1995	1,497	910	213	2,305	1,220	321	172	230	−808	542	254	−12
1996	1,555	965	234	2,318	1,211	321	181	238	−763	441	240	−82
1997	1,674	1,034	242	2,436	1,270	365	187	242	−762	444	248	−70
1998	2,285	1,001	260	2,638	1,418	356	190	294	−353 [1]	426	405	−99 [1]

[1] Operating loss excludes an item titled "federal payments and related interest" (–$577 million) that is included in the budget result.

Source

National Railroad Passenger Corporation, *Annual Report*, Statistical Appendix (various years).

Documentation

The data are for fiscal years that begin on October 1.

The subcategories for revenue and expenses are not exhaustive. The other categories of revenues are "reimbursable" and "other." The other categories of expenses are "postretirement benefits," "employee-related,"
"maintenance of way goods and services," "advertising services," "financial," "restructuring charges," and "other expenses."

Series Df1096. Employee compensation includes salaries, wages, and overtime, plus employee benefits.

Series Df1099 and Df1102. Noncash grants are equal to depreciation between 1987 and 1993.

Series Df1100. The operating loss is the difference between revenues and expenses.

Series Df1103. Equals the sum of series Df1100–1102.

TABLE Df1104–1111   Amtrak operations – ridership, ticket yield, trip length, and operating fleet: 1987–1998

Contributed by Louis P. Cain and Richard Sutch

	Passenger trips					Average length of trip	Operating fleet	
	Total ridership	Amtrak system	Contract commuter	Passenger miles	Ticket yield		Locomotive	Passenger car
	Df1104	Df1105	Df1106	Df1107	Df1108	Df1109	Df1110	Df1111
Fiscal year	Million	Million	Million	Million passenger-miles	Cents per mile	Miles	Number	Number
1987	30.6	20.4	10.2	5,221	11.8	255.4	289	1,705
1988	36.9	21.5	15.4	5,678	12.7	264.1	298	1,710
1989	38.8	21.4	17.4	5,859	14.0	274.2	312	1,742
1990	40.2	22.2	18.0	6,057	14.5	273.0	318	1,863
1991	40.1	22.0	18.1	6,273	14.5	284.1	316	1,786
1992	41.6	21.3	20.3	6,091	14.3	285.2	336	1,796
1993	55.0	22.1	32.9	6,199	14.3	280.9	360	1,853
1994	60.7	21.2	39.5	5,921	14.0	271.1	338	1,852
1995	62.9	20.7	42.2	5,545	14.9	267.6	313	1,722
1996	65.6	19.7	45.9	5,050	16.9	256.9	299	1,730
1997	68.7	20.2	48.5	5,166	17.7	255.8	332	1,728
1998	75.1	21.1	54.0	5,304	17.8	251.5	345	1,962

Source

National Railroad Passenger Corporation, *Annual Report*, Statistical Appendix (various years).

Documentation

The data are for fiscal years beginning October 1.

AIR

Louis P. Cain

TABLE Df1112–1125   Scheduled domestic air transportation – aircraft, passengers, cargo, mileage flown, and other characteristics: 1926–1996[1,2]

Contributed by Louis P. Cain and Richard Sutch

Year	Operators Df1112 [3]	Aircraft in service Df1113 [4]	Route mileage in operation Df1114 [5]	Average passenger-revenue per passenger-mile Df1115	Persons employed Df1116	Revenue miles flown Df1117	Revenue passengers carried — Duplicated Df1118 [6]	Enplanements Df1119 [7]	Revenue passenger-miles flown Df1120 [8]	Ton-miles flown — Express and freight Df1121 [9,10]	Mail Df1122 [10]	Fuel consumed Df1123	Average available seats Df1124	Average speed Df1125
	Number	Number	Number	Dollars per passenger-mile	Number	Thousand miles	Thousand	Thousand	Million passenger-miles	Thousand ton-miles	Thousand ton-miles	Million gallons	Number	Miles per hour
1926	13	—	—	0.1200	—	4,318	6	—	—	1	—	1	—	—
1927	18	—	—	0.1060	—	5,856	9	—	—	13	—	1	—	—
1928	34	268	—	0.1100	1,496 [13]	10,528	48	—	—	59	—	2	—	—
1929	38	442	—	0.1200	1,958	22,729	162	—	85	70	—	6	—	—
1930	43	497	30,293	0.0830	2,778	32,645	385	—	85	101	—	12	—	—
1931	39	490	30,857	0.0670	4,314	43,109	472	—	107	221	3,140 [14]	16	—	—
1932	32	456	28,956	0.0610	4,020	45,894	476	—	127	290	2,701 [14]	20	6.6	—
1933	25	418	28,283	0.0610	4,369	49,256	502	—	175	423	2,568 [14]	22	7.6	—
1934	24	423	28,609	0.0590	4,201	41,526	475	—	190	597	2,237 [15]	19	8.9	—
1935	26	363	29,190	0.0570	5,945	55,918	679	—	316	1,098	4,133	27	10.3	—
1936	24	280	29,797	0.0570	7,079	64,307	932	—	439	1,866	5,741	31	10.7	—
1937	22	291	32,006	0.0560	7,586	66,791	985	887	412	2,162	6,698	34	12.5	—
1938	16 [11]	260 [11]	34,879 [11]	0.0518	9,008 [11]	68,610	1,197	1,077	480	2,182	7,449	38	13.9	—
1939	18 [12]	276 [12]	36,654 [12]	0.0510	10,639 [12]	82,925	1,735	1,561	683	2,713	8,611	47	14.7	—
1940	19	369	42,757	0.0507	15,984	110,101	2,803	2,523	1,052	3,476	10,118	66	16.5	—
1941	19	370	45,163	0.0504	19,223	134,406	3,849	3,464	1,385	5,257	13,108	82	17.5	—
1942	19	186	41,596	0.0527	26,910	111,341	—	3,137	1,418	11,896	21,167	69	17.9	—
1943	18	204	42,537	0.0535	29,654	105,355	—	3,020	1,632	15,618	36,067	65	18.3	—
1944	18	288	47,384	0.0534	31,198	138,732	—	4,046	2,177	16,974	51,146	90	19.1	156
1945	19	421	48,516	0.0495	50,313	208,969	—	6,576	3,360	22,175	65,103	135	19.7	155
1946	23	674	53,981	0.0463	69,182	309,889	—	12,213	5,945	38,590	32,969	236	25.3	160
1947	27	810	62,215	0.0505	58,998	325,054	—	12,890	6,105	64,637	33,086	294	30.0	168
1948	39	878	68,702	0.0574	60,416	338,217	—	13,168	5,976	102,360	38,198	332	32.4	172
1949	51	913	72,667	0.0576	59,886	355,501	—	15,081	6,752	123,603	41,889	375	35.0	179
1950	52	960	77,440	0.0554	61,903	369,826	—	17,345	8,007	152,223	47,740	418	37.5	180
1951	49	981	78,913	0.0561	72,898	411,878	—	22,652	10,590	144,790	64,734	—	39.6	185
1952	46	1,078	77,894	0.0557	79,687	465,477	—	25,010	12,559	162,047	70,443	—	42.7	191
1953	44	1,139	78,384	0.0546	84,651	525,374	—	28,721	14,794	179,063	74,106	—	46.1	198
1954	43	1,175	78,294	0.0541	84,765	556,880	—	32,343	16,802	189,765	82,768	—	50.1	206
1955	42	1,212	78,992	0.0536	95,548	627,336	—	38,025	19,852	229,966	88,751	—	51.2	208
1956	40	1,347	84,189	0.0533	103,489	694,050	—	41,738	22,399	247,255	94,523	—	52.4	213
1957	40	1,494	88,325	0.0531	119,333	791,265	—	48,761	25,379	268,791	100,218	—	53.7	215
1958	39	1,546	89,569	0.0564	119,746	784,200	—	48,297	25,375	294,018	107,018	—	55.8	220
1959	39	1,596	95,063	0.0558	132,042	841,925	—	54,955	29,308	344,728	120,308	—	58.7	223

TABLE Df1112-1125 Scheduled domestic air transportation – aircraft, passengers, cargo, mileage flown, and other characteristics: 1926-1996 Continued

Year	Operators Df1112 [3] Number	Aircraft in service Df1113 [4] Number	Route mileage in operation Df1114 [5] Number	Average passenger-revenue per passenger-mile Df1115 Dollars per passenger-mile	Persons employed Df1116 Number	Revenue miles flown Df1117 Thousand miles	Revenue passengers carried — Duplicated Df1118 [6] Thousand	Revenue passengers carried — Enplanements Df1119 [7] Thousand	Revenue passenger-miles flown Df1120 [8] Million passenger-miles	Ton-miles flown — Express and freight Df1121 [9,10] Thousand ton-miles	Ton-miles flown — Mail Df1122 [10] Thousand ton-miles	Fuel consumed Df1123 Million gallons	Average available seats Df1124 Number	Average speed Df1125 Miles per hour
1960	42	1,594	101,414	0.0609	133,717	820,756	—	56,352	30,567	386,933	135,923	—	65.5	235
1961	41	1,867	102,309	0.0628	136,987	795,165	—	56,900	31,062	454,142	150,452	—	72.9	253
1962	40	1,831	112,944	0.0644	138,673	827,694	—	60,738	33,623	554,599	166,801	—	79.4	274
1963	40	1,832	114,089	0.0617	143,112	888,793	—	69,366	38,457	603,725	174,439	—	83.4	287
1964	40	1,863	115,147	0.0612	153,243	957,575	—	79,139	44,141	743,963	189,782	—	86.1	297
1965	40	1,896	114,110	0.0606	169,952	1,088,112	—	92,073	51,887	943,128	225,992	—	89.2	314
1966	40	2,027	111,488	0.0583	196,298	1,178,458	—	105,789	60,591	1,108,691	291,277	—	91.2	320
1967	39	2,194	119,768	0.0564	223,380	1,462,240	—	128,479	75,487	1,314,409	405,352	—	94.4	354
1968	38	2,317	125,581	0.0561	244,742	1,715,857	—	145,774	87,508	1,578,992	564,084	—	100.8	373
1969	33	2,423	150,431	0.0590	255,386	2,000,269	—	158,405	102,717	1,916,472	801,416	—	109.8	394
1970	33	2,437	171,615	0.0587	242,206	2,013,484	—	153,408	104,156	1,966,009	705,711	—	110.4	350
1971	34	2,389	180,373	0.0633	240,256	1,992,807	—	156,195	106,438	2,012,818	696,780	—	111.2	405
1972	33	2,361	173,485	0.0640	252,999	1,986,758	—	172,452	118,138	2,240,039	676,062	—	114.1	404
1973	31	2,361	175,917	0.0663	261,453	2,040,407	—	183,272	126,317	2,453,517	658,237	—	119.9	404
1974	31	2,244	168,667	0.0752	260,453	1,883,265	—	189,733	129,732	2,421,926	667,577	—	124.2	401
1975	32	2,267	172,076	0.0769	253,634	1,909,486	—	188,746	131,728	2,331,176	665,493	—	126.4	403
1976	35	2,271	175,105	0.0816	266,701	2,001,387	—	206,279	143,271	2,474,902	707,657	—	130.5	406
1977	—	2,473	—	0.0861	—	2,161,952	—	222,283	156,609	2,641,041	740,021	8,202	129.8	408
1978	34	2,545	—	0.0849	—	2,249,102	—	253,957	182,669	2,690,668	779,053	8,446	133.2	413
1979	—	3,609	—	0.0893	—	2,471,401	—	292,700	208,890	3,554,171	852,625	8,866	134.7	406
1980	72	3,808	—	0.1149	354,264	2,523,375	—	272,829	200,829	3,579,129	949,189	8,519	137.1	404
1981	—	3,970	—	0.1274	—	2,442,294	—	265,304	198,715	3,659,829	997,950	8,555	141.7	402
1982	—	4,702	—	0.1221	—	2,442,292	—	274,342	210,149	3,471,894	1,003,683	8,432	147.2	410
1983	—	4,204	—	0.1213	—	2,552,942	—	296,721	226,909	3,980,583	1,064,131	8,673	148.5	413
1984	—	4,371	—	0.1279	—	2,875,402	—	321,047	243,692	4,331,293	1,161,462	9,626	146.9	412
1985	—	4,678	—	0.1232	—	3,046,440	—	357,109	270,584	3,941,848	1,213,728	10,115	146.3	409
1986	—	4,909	—	0.1118	—	3,421,492	—	393,864	302,090	5,108,514	1,247,399	11,137	145.5	416
1987	—	5,250	—	0.1142	—	3,652,542	—	416,831	324,637	6,269,789	1,313,139	11,587	144.3	414
1988	—	5,660	—	0.1231	—	3,738,242	—	419,210	329,309	6,802,409	1,367,055	11,918	143.6	409
1989	—	5,778	—	0.1308	—	3,748,139	—	416,331	329,975	7,538,748	1,414,750	11,905	141.4	406
1990	62	6,083	—	0.1343	588,926	3,963,263	—	423,565	340,231	7,581,718	1,489,337	12,323	142.1	408
1991	—	6,054	—	0.1324	—	3,854,416	—	412,360	332,566	8,137,481	1,568,036	11,506	141.0	406
1992	—	7,320	—	0.1300	—	3,994,821	—	431,693	347,931	8,247,046	1,572,656	11,763	139.7	407
1993	—	7,297	—	0.1394	—	4,144,067	—	441,902	353,630	8,856,224	1,670,880	11,959	137.7	405
1994	82	—	—	0.1312	586,083	4,379,830	—	489,351	388,399	—	—	12,384	—	—
1995	86	—	—	0.1348	608,188	4,629,394	—	506,789	403,887	—	—	12,672	—	—
1996	96	—	—	0.1374	633,772	4,811,453	—	538,394	434,652	—	—	13,217	—	—

[1] Intra-Alaska carriers included beginning with 1941 for series Df1121-1122; 1948 for series Df1115 and Df1120; 1949 for series Df1117; and 1961 for series Df1116.

[2] As of December 31 or for years ending December 31.

[3] Beginning with 1979, includes international carriers.

[4] Beginning with 1961, includes international.

[5] Figures are for route mileage operated through 1961; thereafter, they represent the total route miles for passenger/cargo and all-cargo carriers, reported separately in the source.

[6] Prior to 1935, includes nonrevenue passengers.

[7] Prior to 1942, figures computed by the U.S. Civil Aeronautics Administration from reports of duplicated revenue passengers.

TABLE Df1112–1125   Scheduled domestic air transportation – aircraft, passengers, cargo, mileage flown, and other characteristics: 1926–1996   *Continued*

8 Prior to 1937, includes nonrevenue passenger-miles flown.

9 Prior to 1935, excludes Colonial Airlines, Inc., and Hawaiian Airlines, Ltd.

10 Beginning with 1979, includes both scheduled and nonscheduled service.

11 Excludes Colonial and Marine Airlines.

12 Excludes Marine Airlines.

13 Includes employees of Pan American Airways, in international service.

14 Excludes Colonial Airlines, Inc.

15 Excludes 224,236 ton-miles flown by the U.S. Army.

Sources

U.S. Federal Aviation Administration, *FAA Statistical Handbook of Aviation* (annual issues). More recent numbers are taken from Bureau of Transportation Statistics, *National Transportation Statistics, Air Carrier Profile* (various issues).

Documentation

U.S. domestic scheduled airline operations cover trunk airlines, local service airlines, helicopter carriers, and territorial airlines except those operations in Alaska. Scheduled intrastate airlines are omitted from these series. Statistics of international scheduled airline operations include not only operations to and from foreign countries but also overseas operations to American possessions. They also include the service of airlines between the United States and Alaska. Although several companies operate both domestic and international flights, statistics for these flights are presented separately, here and in Table Df1126–1138. Operations of scheduled carriers of cargo only are generally not included.

Before deregulation, the term "certificated route air carrier" refers to air carriers holding certificates of public convenience and necessity, issued by the Civil Aeronautics Board, authorizing the performance of scheduled air transportation over specified routes and a limited number of nonscheduled operations. Certificated route air carriers are often referred to as "scheduled airlines," although they also perform nonscheduled service. *Nonscheduled service* comprises revenue flights that are not operated in regular scheduled service, such as charter flights, and all nonrevenue flights incident to such flights. *Scheduled service* is transport service operated over an air carrier's certificated routes, based on published flight schedules, including extra sections and related nonrevenue flights.

Series Df1118–1119. Duplication exists where (1) the same passengers were carried on more than one route of an air carrier; and (2) where the same passengers were carried on more than one air carrier. In series Df1119, duplication has been eliminated where the same passengers were carried on more than one route of an air carrier, but still exists where the same passengers were carried by more than one carrier. This series is now reported as Revenue Passenger Emplanements.

Series Df1123. Aviation gasoline for 1926–1950. Jet fuel for 1977–1996. Data for fuel consumption during the years of transition from gasoline to jet fuel, 1951–1976, are available for the total of domestic and international air transportation for some years in the *FAA Statistical Handbook* for the relevant dates.

Series Df1124. Derived by dividing passenger seat-miles by revenue miles flown in passenger service.

TABLE Df1126–1138 Scheduled international air transportation – aircraft, passengers, cargo, mileage flown, and other characteristics: 1927–1996[1]

Contributed by Louis P. Cain and Richard Sutch

Year	Operators Df1126 [2]	Aircraft in service Df1127 [3]	Route mileage in operation Df1128	Average passenger-revenue per passenger-mile Df1129	Persons employed Df1130	Revenue miles flown Df1131	Revenue passengers carried Df1132 [5]	Revenue passenger-miles flown Df1133 [5]	Ton-miles flown: Express and freight Df1134 [6]	Ton-miles flown: Mail Df1135 [6]	Fuel consumed Df1136	Average available seats Df1137	Average speed Df1138
	Number	Number	Miles	Dollars per passenger-mile	Number	Thousand miles	Thousand	Million passenger-miles	Thousand ton-miles	Thousand ton-miles	Million gallons	Number	Miles per hour
1927	1	—	—	—	—	14	—	—	—	—	—	—	—
1928	1	57	—	—	—	146	1	—	—	—	—	—	—
1929	4	83	—	—	387	2,413	11	—	—	—	—	—	—
1930	3	103	19,256	—	697	4,301	33	19	—	—	1	—	—
1931	3	100	19,543	—	1,353	4,537	59	14	—	—	1	—	—
1932	3	108	19,574	—	1,590	5,278	72	21	—	—	2	—	—
1933	3	86	19,404	—	1,926	5,857	74	25	—	—	3	—	—
1934	2	99	22,192	—	2,276	7,539	97	37	—	—	4	—	—
1935	2	101	31,261	—	2,407	7,950	111	46	—	—	4	—	—
1936	2	94	31,990	—	2,916	6,904	88	42	—	—	6	—	—
1937	2	92	31,979	—	4,000	7,909	112	54	—	—	6	16.9	—
1938	2	73	34,968	0.0833	4,266	7,043	109	53	—	—	7	17.7	—
1939	2	84	43,455	0.0857	5,275	7,607	129	72	—	—	7	18.3	—
1940	3	68	52,322	0.0883	6,067	9,652	163	100	—	—	8	18.0	—
1941	3	83	—	0.0861	7,235	14,410	229	163	—	—	9	17.7	—
1942	4	68	—	0.0886	12,803	18,681	269	237	5,096	2,763	11	17.5	—
1943	4	70	27,211	0.0794	9,625	18,458	279	246	6,215	2,630	17	18.5	149
1944	4	70	29,708	0.0783	11,409	22,273	341	312	8,728	4,772	25	18.9	151
1945	5	97	38,885	0.0868	17,968	32,609	476	450	15,096	8,165	60	27.2	166
1946	5	147	66,419	0.0831	27,372	59,376	1,041	1,104	32,904	15,503	103	35.2	191
1947	5	154	95,503	0.0777	26,154	86,481	1,360	1,814	45,603	20,664	123	35.1	199
1948	5	175	105,853	0.0801	24,192	98,053	1,373	1,894	56,190	24,410	143	36.6	207
1949	5	177	109,011	0.0772	21,108	105,119	1,520	2,060	60,588	26,228	154	41.0	218
1950	6	160	106,401	0.0728	20,883	94,626	1,675	2,214	71,665	27,089	—	46.4	224
1951	6	140	108,763	0.0710	22,855	98,703	2,042	2,614	75,706	28,201	—	49.1	227
1952	7	149	110,465	0.0701	24,385	106,158	2,365	3,065	79,579	31,630	—	52.3	230
1953	8	161	111,826	0.0684	24,741	114,153	2,699	3,451	86,840	43,554	—	56.7	242
1954	9	161	112,488	0.0676	24,776	120,322	2,875	3,810	96,378	61,233	—	56.4	244
1955	9	147	117,282	0.0666	26,655	135,411	3,416	4,499	115,172	64,355	—	59.0	249
1956	11	196	113,694	0.0668	28,014	151,806	3,949	5,226	128,239	66,894	—	61.4	253
1957	10	170	133,884	0.0655	27,857	161,571	4,552	5,882	133,958	75,635	—	64.4	258
1958	12	185	140,105	0.0646	27,404	172,713	4,773	6,124	159,349	81,997	—	67.5	263
1959	13	173	139,820	0.0629	28,648	172,143	6,341	7,064	191,585	103,335	—	89.9	307
1960	13	174	148,303	0.0635	29,054	162,634	5,904	8,306	217,164	144,804	—	108.7	357
1961	11	—	138,668	0.0608	29,506	161,297	6,112	8,769	264,729	172,017	—	118.7	394
1962	10	—	153,219	0.0587	30,400	171,500	7,079	10,138	296,404	181,257	—	124.8	423
1963	10	—	153,294	0.0582	32,327	192,140	8,037	11,905	394,681	180,991	—	127.2	441
1964	10	—	154,096	0.0545	34,695	214,375	9,381	14,352	597,324	254,093	—	129.1	451
1965	10	—	152,293	0.0529	36,882	247,766	10,847	16,789	721,609	452,635	—	129.3	468
1966	10	—	156,745	0.0516	42,398	285,711	12,272	19,298	796,964	560,402	—	132.2	482
1967	10	—	158,823	0.0501	46,510	350,719	14,020	23,259	927,250	679,357	—	135.6	476
1968	9	—	163,534	0.0495	50,283	408,136	16,407	26,451	936,554	463,099	—	121.9	477
1969	3	—	193,554	0.0495	53,954	359,476	13,493	22,703	942,008	548,845	—	154.9	482

Notes appear at end of table

(continued)

TABLE Df1126–1138   Scheduled international air transportation – aircraft, passengers, cargo, mileage flown, and other characteristics: 1927–1996
Continued

Year	Operators [2] Df1126 Number	Aircraft in service [3] Df1127 Number	Route mileage in operation Df1128 Miles	Average passenger-revenue per passenger-mile Df1129 Dollars per passenger-mile	Persons employed Df1130 Number	Revenue miles flown Df1131 Thousand miles	Revenue passengers carried [5] Df1132 Thousand	Revenue passenger-miles flown [5] Df1133 Million passenger-miles	Ton-miles flown — Express and freight [6] Df1134 Thousand ton-miles	Ton-miles flown — Mail [6] Df1135 Thousand ton-miles	Fuel consumed [5] Df1136 Million gallons	Average available seats Df1137 Number	Average speed Df1138 Miles per hour
1970	3	—	205,666	0.0500	48,520	369,870	16,260	27,563	1,009,785	456,683	—	143.2	482
1971	14	—	204,604	0.0508	44,523	350,744	17,474	29,219	1,114,104	371,656	—	152.4	480
1972	14	—	206,111	0.0498	50,368	350,112	18,897	34,268	1,238,584	361,440	—	161.1	481
1973	14	—	217,158	0.0532	50,366	361,481	18,936	35,640	1,339,056	347,762	—	169.9	481
1974	14	—	204,467	0.0639	44,692	330,248	17,725	33,186	1,259,439	311,707	—	166.3	482
1975	14	—	198,750	0.0717	38,586	331,020	16,316	31,082	1,380,132	291,682	—	173.6	484
1976	14	—	196,299	0.0715	36,176	318,610	17,039	33,717	1,467,782	298,970	—	178.9	487
1977	—	—	—	0.0761	—	314,847	18,043	36,610	1,488,886	282,425	1,708	192.6	489
1978	14	—	—	0.0749	—	359,260	20,759	44,112	2,650,688	372,060	1,742	214.9	492
1979	—	—	—	0.0766	—	387,737	24,163	53,132	2,960,452	392,918	1,828	215.8	489
1980	—	—	—	0.0878	—	400,791	24,074	54,363	2,883,242	375,991	1,747	221.0	488
1981	—	—	—	0.0946	—	356,270	20,672	50,173	2,931,737	400,092	2,033	222.5	490
1982	—	—	—	0.0957	—	362,183	19,760	49,495	3,007,095	414,719	1,968	235.2	490
1983	—	—	—	0.1021	—	362,994	21,917	54,920	3,377,453	457,333	1,998	238.7	491
1984	—	—	—	0.0938	—	388,794	23,636	61,424	3,447,486	444,732	2,286	245.5	491
1985	—	—	—	0.0980	—	415,335	24,913	65,819	4,197,782	434,014	2,488	242.5	489
1986	—	—	—	0.1016	—	451,338	25,082	64,456	5,104,955	442,694	2,545	229.8	490
1987	—	—	—	0.0982	—	529,786	30,847	79,834	5,992,925	469,919	2,894	227.8	488
1988	—	—	—	0.1040	—	615,270	35,404	93,992	6,896,915	463,901	3,263	222.4	486
1989	—	—	—	0.1036	—	693,887	37,361	102,739	6,826,942	513,438	3,557	224.0	488
1990	—	—	—	0.1083	—	760,338	41,995	117,695	6,942,319	496,301	3,909	212.7	490
1991	—	—	—	0.1132	—	806,606	39,941	115,389	6,990,617	496,306	3,940	215.4	495
1992	—	—	—	0.1199	—	904,426	43,415	130,622	7,800,341	503,475	4,120	209.5	497
1993	—	—	—	0.1174	—	955,153	45,347	135,507	—	—	4,113	—	—
1994	—	—	—	—	—	979,765	42,702	133,300	—	—	4,279	—	—
1995	—	—	—	—	—	997,658	44,155	137,987	—	—	4,443	—	—
1996	—	—	—	—	—	1,043,313	46,302	145,331	—	—	4,618	—	—

[1] As of December 31 or for years ending December 31.

[2] Beginning with 1979, not distinguished from domestic operators. See series Df1112.

[3] Beginning with 1961, not distinguished from domestic. See series Df1113.

[4] Prior to 1938, includes nonrevenue passengers.

[5] Prior to 1938, includes nonrevenue passenger-miles flown.

[6] Beginning with 1979, includes both scheduled and nonscheduled service.

Sources

U.S. Federal Aviation Administration, *FAA Statistical Handbook of Aviation* (annual issues). More recent numbers are taken from Bureau of Transportation Statistics, *National Transportation Statistics, Air Carrier Profile* (various issues).

Documentation

See the text for Table Df1112–1125 for a description of air carriers and types of service and for corresponding data on domestic air transportation.

Series Df1132. Duplication has been eliminated where the same passengers were carried on more than one route of an air carrier, but still exists where the same passengers were carried by more than one carrier. This series is now reported as Revenue Passenger Enplanements.

Series Df1136. Aviation gasoline for 1927–1950. Jet fuel for 1977–1996. Data for fuel consumption during the years of transition from gasoline to jet fuel, 1951–1976, are available for the total of domestic and international air transportation for some years in the *FAA Statistical Handbook* for the relevant dates. Because the original data included fuel purchased abroad, the international total was divided in half to estimate domestic fuel use for international flights.

Series Df1137. Derived by dividing passenger seat-miles by revenue miles flown in passenger service.

TABLE Df1139–1158   Airports, aircraft, pilots, cargo, fuel consumed, and nonscheduled miles flown: 1926–1993[1, 2]

Contributed by Louis P. Cain

	Airports and landing fields		Federal aid to airports, cumulative since 1947				Certificated airplane pilots			
	Total	Lighted	Total funds	Federal funds	Sponsor funds	Total civil aircraft	Total	Airline transport	Commercial	Private
	Df1139 [3]	Df1140 [3]	Df1141	Df1142	Df1143	Df1144	Df1145 [4]	Df1146 [4]	Df1147 [4]	Df1148 [4]
Year	Number	Number	Million dollars	Million dollars	Million dollars	Number	Number	Number	Number	Number
1926	—	—	—	—	—	—	—	—	—	—
1927	1,036	—	—	—	—	2,740	1,572	—	—	—
1928	1,364	—	—	—	—	5,104	4,887	—	—	—
1929	1,550	—	—	—	—	9,922	10,430	—	6,165	4,265
1930	1,782	640	—	—	—	9,818	15,280	—	7,847	7,433
1931	2,093	680	—	—	—	10,780	17,739	—	8,513	9,226
1932	2,117	701	—	—	—	10,324	18,594	330	7,967	10,297
1933	2,188	626	—	—	—	9,284	13,960	554	7,635	5,771
1934	2,297	664	—	—	—	8,322	13,949	676	7,484	5,789
1935	2,368	698	—	—	—	9,072	14,805	736	7,362	6,707
1936	2,342	705	—	—	—	9,229	15,952	842	7,288	7,822
1937	2,299	720	—	—	—	10,836	17,681	1,064	6,411	10,206
1938	2,374	719	—	—	—	11,159	22,983	1,159	7,839	13,985
1939	2,280	735	—	—	—	13,772	33,706	1,197	11,677	20,832
1940	2,331	776	—	—	—	17,928	69,829	1,431	18,791	49,607
1941	2,484	662	—	—	—	26,013	129,947	1,587	34,578	93,782
1942	2,809	700	—	—	—	27,170	166,626	2,177	55,760	108,689
1943	2,769	859	—	—	—	27,180	173,206	2,315	63,940	106,951
1944	3,427	964	—	—	—	27,919	183,383	3,046	68,449	111,888
1945	4,026	1,007	—	—	—	37,789	296,895	5,815	162,873	128,207
1946	4,490	1,019	—	—	—	81,002	400,061	7,654	203,251	189,156
1947	5,759	1,447	142	68	74	94,821	433,241 [8]	7,059 [8]	181,912 [8]	244,270 [8]
1948	6,414	1,521	216	103	112	95,997	491,306 [9]	7,762 [9]	176,845 [9]	306,699 [9]
1949	6,484	1,480	277	133	144	92,622	525,174	9,025	187,769	328,380
1950	6,403	1,670	342	165	177	92,809	—	—	—	—
1951	6,237	—	368	182	186	88,545	580,574	10,813	197,900	371,861
1952	6,042	1,858	388	194	194	89,313	581,218	11,357	193,575	376,286
1953	6,760 [6]	1,050 [6]	388	193 [7]	195	91,102	585,974	12,757	195,363	377,854
1954	6,977	1,108	435	212	222	92,067	613,695	13,341	201,441	398,913
1955	6,839	1,247	460	224	236	85,320	643,201	13,700	211,142	418,359
1956	7,028	1,399	660	326	334	87,531	669,079	15,295	221,096	432,688
1957	6,412	1,713	782	385	397	93,189	702,519	16,900	237,149	448,470
1958	6,018	1,809	882	431	451	98,893	731,078	18,303	245,541	467,234
1959	6,426	1,943	1,047	509	538	105,309	758,368	19,364	255,377	483,627
1960	6,881	2,133	1,184	573	611	111,580	783,232	20,985	262,437	499,810
1961	7,715	2,299	1,198	578	620	117,904	804,707	22,042	268,707	513,958
1962	8,084	2,481	1,472	722	749	124,273	830,220	23,220	275,495	531,505
1963	8,814	2,672	1,624	799	825	129,975	378,700	20,269	96,341	152,209
1964	9,490	2,773	1,754	866	888	137,189	431,041	21,572	108,428	175,574
1965	9,566	2,878	1,887	935	952	142,078	479,770	22,440	116,665	196,393
1966	9,673	2,988	2,052	1,018	1,034	155,132	548,757	23,917	131,539	222,427
1967	10,126	3,149	2,193	1,090	1,103	166,598	617,931	25,817	150,135	253,312
1968	10,470	3,312	2,362	1,165	1,197	179,285	691,695	28,607	164,458	281,728
1969	11,050	3,430	2,447	1,198	1,249	190,749	720,028	31,442	176,585	299,491
1970	11,261	3,554	2,453	1,199	1,254	154,450	732,729	34,430	186,821	303,779
1971	12,070	3,759	—	—	—	131,148	741,009	35,949	192,409	312,656
1972	12,405	3,827	—	—	—	145,010	750,869	37,714	196,228	321,413
1973	12,700	3,880	—	—	—	153,311	714,607	38,139	182,444	298,921
1974	13,062	3,999	—	—	—	161,033	733,728	41,002	192,425	305,848
1975	13,251	4,171	—	—	—	168,049	728,187	42,592	189,342	305,863
1976	13,770	4,362	—	—	—	177,964	744,246	45,072	187,801	309,005
1977	14,117	4,483	—	—	—	184,294	783,932	50,149	188,763	327,424
1978	14,574	4,567	—	—	—	199,178	798,833	55,881	185,833	337,644
1979	14,746	4,631	—	—	—	210,339	814,667	63,562	182,097	343,276
1980	15,161	4,738	—	—	—	211,045	827,071	69,569	183,442	357,479
1981	15,476	4,796	—	—	—	213,226	764,182	70,311	168,580	328,562
1982	15,831	4,842	—	—	—	209,779	733,255	73,471	165,093	322,094
1983	16,029	4,878	—	—	—	213,293	718,004	75,938	159,495	318,643
1984	16,079	4,889	—	—	—	220,943	722,376	79,192	155,929	320,086

Notes appear at end of table

(continued)

TABLE Df1139–1158   Airports, aircraft, pilots, cargo, fuel consumed, and nonscheduled miles flown: 1926–1993
Continued

	Airports and landing fields		Federal aid to airports, cumulative since 1947			Total civil aircraft	Certificated airplane pilots			
	Total	Lighted	Total funds	Federal funds	Sponsor funds		Total	Airline transport	Commercial	Private
	Df1139 [3]	Df1140 [3]	Df1141	Df1142	Df1143	Df1144	Df1145 [4]	Df1146 [4]	Df1147 [4]	Df1148 [4]
Year	Number	Number	Million dollars	Million dollars	Million dollars	Number	Number	Number	Number	Number
1985	16,318	4,941	—	—	—	196,500	709,540	82,740	151,632	311,086
1986	16,582	4,954	—	—	—	205,300	709,118	87,186	147,798	305,736
1987	17,015	4,922	—	—	—	202,700	699,653	91,287	143,645	300,949
1988	17,327	4,890	—	—	—	196,200	694,016	96,968	143,030	299,786
1989	17,446	4,881	—	—	—	205,000	700,010	102,087	144,540	293,179
1990	17,490	4,822	—	—	—	198,000	702,659	107,732	149,666	299,111
1991	17,581	4,811	—	—	—	198,475	692,095	112,167	148,365	293,306
1992	17,846	4,831	—	—	—	184,434	682,959	115,855	146,385	288,078
1993	18,317	4,842	—	—	—	176,006	665,069	117,070	143,014	283,700

	Estimated miles flown in civil flying other than scheduled air carrier					Fuel consumed, general aviation	Domestic air cargo revenue ton-miles flown			
	Total	Business	Commercial	Instructional	Personal and other		Total	Scheduled carriers	Nonscheduled carriers	Supplemental carriers
	Df1149 [5]	Df1150 [5]	Df1151 [5]	Df1152 [5]	Df1153 [5]	Df1154 [5]	Df1155	Df1156	Df1157	Df1158
Year	Million miles	Million miles	Million miles	Million miles	Million miles	Million gallons	Million ton-miles	Million ton-miles	Million ton-miles	Million ton-miles
1926	19	—	—	—	—	2	—	—	—	—
1927	30	—	—	—	—	4	—	—	—	—
1928	60	—	—	—	—	8	—	—	—	—
1929	110	—	—	—	—	14	—	—	—	—
1930	108	—	—	—	—	14	—	—	—	—
1931	94	13	26	25	29	12	—	—	—	—
1932	78	12	22	18	26	11	—	—	—	—
1933	71	12	20	16	23	9	—	—	—	—
1934	76	12	21	17	26	10	—	—	—	—
1935	85	13	23	23	26	11	—	—	—	—
1936	93	12	25	30	27	11	—	—	—	—
1937	103	16	23	35	30	11	—	—	—	—
1938	129	19	25	46	39	10	—	—	—	—
1939	178	25	34	66	52	17	—	—	—	—
1940	264	26	32	126	80	23	—	—	—	—
1941	346	27	51	197	71	30	—	—	—	—
1942	294	30	47	188	29	26	—	—	—	—
1943	—	—	—	—	—	—	—	—	—	—
1944	—	—	—	—	—	—	—	—	—	—
1945	—	—	—	—	—	—	—	—	—	—
1946	875	122	108	479	166	101	—	—	—	—
1947	1,502	228	150	849	275	160	69	65	4	—
1948	1,470	299	143	755	273	183	109	102	7	—
1949	1,129	309	166	379	275	135	153	134	5	13
1950	1,062	340	181	287	255	134	239	211	16	13
1951	975	380	190	190	215	135	261	217	26	18
1952	972	420	218	144	190	141	259	244	5	10
1953	1,045	499	210	121	216	172	281	254	10	18
1954	1,119	553	226	124	216	180	277	248	6	24
1955	1,216	628	246	121	222	193	379	319	20	41
1956	1,315	672	247	158	238	201	457	351	47	59
1957	1,426	721	249	202	254	213	554	396	111	47
1958	1,660	847	299	232	282	209	567	387	119	61
1959	1,716	858	292	223	343	221	651	450	138	63
1960	1,769	881	299	194	395	246	724	476	185	112
1961	1,858	888	333	203	434	257	829	533	182	114
1962	1,965	935	367	256	407	264	1,102	637	351	115
1963	2,049	983	369	266	430	285	1,095	715	210	171
1964	2,181	1,047	393	284	458	307	1,288	894	209	185

Notes appear at end of table

TABLE Df1139-1158 Airports, aircraft, pilots, cargo, fuel consumed, and nonscheduled miles flown: 1926-1993
Continued

	Estimated miles flown in civil flying other than scheduled air carrier					Fuel consumed, general aviation	Domestic air cargo revenue ton-miles flown			
	Total	Business	Commercial	Instructional	Personal and other		Total	Scheduled carriers	Nonscheduled carriers	Supplemental carriers
	Df1149 [5]	Df1150 [5]	Df1151 [5]	Df1152 [5]	Df1153 [5]	Df1154 [5]	Df1155	Df1156	Df1157	Df1158
Year	Million miles	Million miles	Million miles	Million miles	Million miles	Million gallons	Million ton-miles	Million ton-miles	Million ton-miles	Million ton-miles
1965	2,562	1,204	461	359	538	378	1,661	1,112	330	220
1966	3,336	1,536	516	646	638	486	1,944	1,301	389	254
1967	3,440	1,431	569	713	727	541	2,168	1,498	406	264
1968	3,701	1,406	666	814	814	610	2,327	1,775	248	305
1969	3,926	1,426	723	910	867	690	2,769	2,126	365	278
1970	3,207	1,134	791	450	832	759	2,581	2,216	80	285
1971	3,143	1,129	507	651	857	—	2,747	2,278	164	306
1972	3,317	1,144	581	692	901	—	2,973	2,567	147	259
1973	3,728	1,344	688	779	918	—	3,267	2,922	54	292
1974	4,042	1,433	790	816	1,005	—	3,221	2,888	52	280
1975	4,238	1,487	818	829	1,104	—	3,020	2,718	40	263
1976	4,476	1,563	885	873	1,155	—	3,161	2,887	36	237
1977	—	—	—	—	—	—	—	—	—	—
1978	—	—	—	—	—	—	—	—	—	—
1979	—	—	—	—	—	—	—	—	—	—
1980	—	—	—	—	—	1,286	—	—	—	—
1981	—	—	—	—	—	—	—	—	—	—
1982	—	—	—	—	—	—	—	—	—	—
1983	—	—	—	—	—	—	—	—	—	—
1984	—	—	—	—	—	—	—	—	—	—
1985	—	—	—	—	—	—	—	—	—	—
1986	—	—	—	—	—	—	—	—	—	—
1987	—	—	—	—	—	—	—	—	—	—
1988	—	—	—	—	—	—	—	—	—	—
1989	—	—	—	—	—	—	—	—	—	—
1990	—	—	—	—	—	1,016	—	—	—	—
1991	—	—	—	—	—	—	—	—	—	—
1992	—	—	—	—	—	—	—	—	—	—
1993	—	—	—	—	—	—	—	—	—	—

[1] Includes Alaska, Hawai'i, and outlying areas for all years.

[2] As of December 31 or for years ending December 31, except as noted.

[3] Prior to 1954, all military fields included; beginning with 1954, only military fields having joint civil-military use included. Seaplane facilities excluded prior to 1953.

[4] Composition of series changes over time. See text.

[5] Figures for many years estimated, 1958-1968. See text.

[6] As of March 1, 1954.

[7] Data in source appears to be in error and cannot be corrected.

[8] As of April 1, 1948.

[9] As of May 1, 1949.

Sources

U.S. Federal Aviation Administration, *FAA Statistical Handbook of Aviation* (annual issues). Series Df1154, 1980-1990, Bureau of Transportation Statistics, *National Transportation Statistics, Air Carrier Profile* (various issues).

Documentation

Several of these series were affected by deregulation. Some are now reported in an altered form and included elsewhere in this chapter; some are not reported at all.

Series Df1139-1140. Figures for airports and landing fields include civil, military, and Federal Aviation Administration (FAA, formerly Civil Aeronautics Administration, CAA) fields, except as noted. Growth of airports after 1940 was stimulated by federal defense expenditures during World War II and by the federal-aid airport program thereafter.

Series Df1144. Includes gliders in the years 1946-1962. Beginning in 1950, both active and inactive aircraft are included. Beginning in 1971, only active civil aircraft are included.

Series Df1145-1148. Refer to persons certificated by the FAA in the various classifications. Some may not have been actively engaged in the classification for which they were certificated. The count of certificated pilots after 1941 is not directly comparable to those from the previous years because the aeronautics regulations were amended to permit pilot certificates currently effective on April 1, 1942, to continue in effect indefinitely. This amendment expired on July 1, 1947. The number of commercial pilots, series Df1147, rose sharply after 1944 because the CAA awarded many veterans commercial certificates on the basis of their military flying experience. The number of private pilots, series Df1147, increased sharply after 1939 because of the federally subsidized civilian pilot training program that was initiated in 1939. It gave preliminary training to hundreds of thousands of men who went into the military service. Beginning in 1963, the data are for active certified airplane pilots only. Also beginning in 1963, series Df1145 includes student, helicopter, glider, and other pilots, not shown separately.

Series Df1146. Airline transport rating became effective May 5, 1932.

Series Df1149. Includes corporation and individual business transportation, not for hire.

Series Df1149-1153. Include business flying (by corporate executives or employees or by individuals, including farmers, on personal business), commercial flying (contract, charter crop dusting, photographic, etc.), instructional pleasure flying, and other flying (testing, experimental, ferrying, Civil Air Patrol, etc.). The data for 1964-1968 were estimated from information received on Aircraft Use and Inspection Reports. Separate data on these five categories are given in the source.

Series Df1149-1154. No surveys were conducted in 1950, 1955, 1956, 1958-1961, and 1963. Data for 1958-1961 have been revised using a correction factor based on the 1962 survey of aircraft use in general aviation.

(continued)

TABLE Df1139-1158   Airports, aircraft, pilots, cargo, fuel consumed, and nonscheduled miles flown: 1926-1993
Continued

Data for 1963 are based on hours and use reported on aircraft inspection reports adjusted by the same correction factor. The 1962 general aviation survey excluded gliders, dirigibles, and balloons; these data have been adjusted to include them.

Series Df1150. Includes passenger and cargo transportation for hire, serial application (crop dusting, spraying, seeding, etc.), patrol, survey, and other miscellaneous work use.

Series Df1155–1158. Includes both express and freight ton-miles. Series Df1157 includes some military ton-miles and may include a small amount of international traffic. Series Df1158 includes both civil and military.

TABLE Df1159-1164   International air passenger arrivals and departures, by flag of carrier: 1975-1996

Contributed by Louis P. Cain

	Arrivals			Departures		
	Total	Flag of carrier		Total	Flag of carrier	
		United States	Foreign		United States	Foreign
	Df1159	Df1160	Df1161	Df1162	Df1163	Df1164
Year	Thousand	Thousand	Thousand	Thousand	Thousand	Thousand
1975	12,646	6,502	6,144	12,053	5,912	6,141
1977	14,701	7,487	7,214	13,804	6,889	6,915
1979	19,268	9,864	9,404	18,082	9,124	8,958
1981	20,881	10,265	10,615	19,911	9,581	10,330
1983	20,840	10,698	10,142	19,724	9,888	9,837
1985	24,156	11,798	12,357	22,487	10,696	11,791
1987	28,644	14,313	14,331	26,664	12,853	13,811
1989	33,217	17,174	16,044	31,153	15,687	15,466
1990	36,414	19,145	17,269	34,046	17,628	16,418
1991	35,464	18,910	16,554	33,286	17,530	15,756
1992	38,927	20,537	18,390	36,211	18,858	17,353
1993	41,558	21,940	19,618	38,254	20,232	18,022
1994	43,818	23,291	20,527	40,349	21,355	18,993
1995	46,910	24,582	22,328	43,026	22,231	20,795
1996	49,853	25,148	24,704	45,785	22,901	22,884

Source

U.S. Department of Transportation (USDOT), *National Transportation Statistics* (annual editions), as derived from USDOT/Research and Special Programs Administration/Volpe National Transportation Systems Center, *U.S. International Air Travel Statistics* (annual issues).

Documentation

The data count passengers on international commercial flights arriving or departing at U.S. airports. They exclude border crossers, crewmen, and military personnel. The data include travel between (1) U.S. airports in the fifty states, Puerto Rico, Guam, or the Virgin Islands and (2) any other outlying area. The data are compiled from flight reports of the U.S. Immigration and Naturalization Service.

The source tables also report passengers arriving from or departing to a number of countries including Australia, the Bahama Islands, Barbados, Belgium, Bermuda, Brazil, Canada, China/Taiwan, Colombia, Denmark, the Dominican Republic, France, Germany, Grand Cayman, Greece, Haiti, Hong Kong, Ireland, Israel, Italy, Jamaica, Japan, Mexico, the Netherlands, Netherlands Antilles, Panama Republic, the Philippines, South Korea, Spain, Switzerland, the United Kingdom, and Venezuela.

TABLE Df1165–1176   Aircraft production and exports, by type of aircraft: 1913–1993

Contributed by Louis P. Cain

			Aircraft produced								Exports		
			Civil								Aircraft exported		
					General aviation								
	Total	U.S. military	Total	Transports	Total	Single-engine	Multi-engine	Rotorcraft	Value of all products	Number	Value	Value of all exports
	Df1165	Df1166	Df1167	Df1168	Df1169	Df1170	Df1171	Df1172	Df1173 [1,2]	Df1174 [3,4]	Df1175 [3,4]	Df1176 [3,4,5]
Year	Number	Number	Number	Number	Number	Number	Number	Number	Thousand dollars	Number	Thousand dollars	Thousand dollars
1913	43	14	29	—	—	—	—	—	—	29	82	108
1914	49	15	34	—	—	—	—	—	790	34	189	226
1915	178	26	152	—	—	—	—	—	—	152	958	1,541
1916	411	142	269	—	—	—	—	—	—	269	2,158	7,002
1917	2,148	2,013	135	—	—	—	—	—	—	135	1,002	4,135
1918	14,020	13,991	29	—	—	—	—	—	—	20	206	9,084
1919	780	682	98	—	—	—	—	—	14,373	85	778	13,167
1920	328	256	72	—	—	—	—	—	—	65	598	1,153
1921	487	389	48	—	—	—	—	—	7,431	48	315	473
1922	263	226	37	—	—	—	—	—	—	37	157	495
1923	743	687	56	—	—	—	—	—	13,142	48	309	434
1924	377	317	60	—	—	—	—	—	—	59	413	798
1925	789	447	342	—	—	—	—	—	12,775	80	511	784
1926	1,186	532	654	—	—	—	—	—	17,695	50	303	1,027
1927	1,995	621	1,374	—	—	—	—	—	30,897	63	849	1,904
1928	4,346	1,219	3,127	—	—	—	—	—	64,662	162	1,760	3,665
1929	6,193	677	5,516	—	—	—	—	—	91,051	348	5,485	9,125
1930	3,437	747	2,690	—	—	—	—	—	60,846	321	4,820	8,818
1931	2,800	812	1,988	—	—	—	—	—	48,540	140	1,813	4,868
1932	1,396	593	803	—	—	—	—	—	34,861	280	4,359	7,947
1933	1,324	466	858	—	—	—	—	—	33,357	406	5,391	9,180
1934	1,615	437	1,178	—	—	—	—	—	43,892	490	8,195	17,663
1935	1,710	459	1,251	—	—	—	—	—	42,506	333	6,599	14,291
1936	3,010	1,141	1,869	—	—	—	—	—	78,149	527	11,601	23,143
1937	3,773	949	2,824	—	—	—	—	—	114,093	628	21,076	39,404
1938	3,623	1,800	1,823	—	—	—	—	—	198,293	875	37,977	68,228
1939	5,856	2,195	3,661	—	—	—	—	—	247,905	1,220	67,113	117,807
1940	12,813	6,028	6,785 [6]	—	—	—	—	—	370,000 [7]	3,522	196,261	311,871
1941	26,289	19,445	6,844 [6]	—	—	—	—	—	1,804,000	6,001	422,764	626,929
1942	47,675	47,675	—	—	—	—	—	—	5,817,000	10,448	879,995	1,357,345
1943	85,433	85,433	—	—	—	—	—	—	12,514,000	13,865	1,215,848	2,142,611
1944	95,272	95,272	—	—	—	—	—	—	16,047,000	16,544	1,589,801	2,825,927
1945	48,912	46,865	2,047	—	—	—	—	—	8,279,000 [8]	7,599	663,129	1,148,852
1946	36,418	1,417	35,001	433	34,568	—	—	—	—	2,302	65,258	115,320
1947	17,739	2,122	15,617	278	15,339	—	—	—	—	3,125	74,477	172,190
1948	9,838	2,536	7,302	263	7,039	—	—	—	—	2,259	66,354	153,629
1949	6,137	2,592	3,545	166	3,379	—	—	—	—	881	27,165	—
1950	6,293	2,773	3,520	129	3,391	—	—	—	—	756	44,287	—
1951	7,923	5,446	2,477	74	2,386	2,337	49	17	—	894	18,606	—
1952	12,811	9,302	3,509	194	3,247	3,137	110	68	—	1,180	26,620	—
1953	14,760	10,626	4,134	213	3,811	3,681	130	110	—	1,377	91,003	—
1954	12,129	8,740	3,389	191	3,072	2,717	355	126	—	1,053	102,736	—
1955	12,852	8,032	4,820	113	4,563	3,755	808	144	—	1,714	129,924	727,549
1956	13,307	6,102	7,205	205	6,765	5,715	1,050	235	—	1,711	171,097	1,064,838
1957	12,419	5,614	6,805	322	6,173	5,250	923	310	—	2,025	248,943	1,028,729
1958	11,117	4,235	6,882	218	6,478	5,609	869	186	—	1,689	204,051	971,541
1959	11,227	2,985	8,242	262	7,802	6,785	1,017	178	7,134,000	1,628	152,984	769,130
1960	10,324	2,143	8,181	238	7,726	6,438	1,288	217	6,429,000	2,336	537,133	1,329,494
1961	9,053	1,639	7,414	180	6,943	5,980	963	291	5,842,000	2,459	334,790	1,233,863
1962	—	—	7,249	146	6,797	5,765	1,032	306	5,900,000	2,131	323,340	1,435,477
1963	—	—	8,121	80	7,628	6,317	1,311	413	5,617,000	2,251	244,101	1,241,132
1964	—	—	10,067	158	9,459	7,812	1,647	450	6,431,000	2,577	287,345	1,212,442
1965	—	—	12,646	221	12,053	10,023	2,030	372	7,057,000	3,129	482,236	1,802,098
1966	—	—	16,397	322	15,723	13,226	2,497	352	8,725,000	3,611	553,908	1,393,422
1967	—	—	14,479	500	13,536	11,530	2,006	443	11,894,000	3,881	787,682	1,924,976
1968	—	—	14,969	702	13,749	11,479	2,270	518	13,850,000	3,682	1,403,930	2,817,654
1969	—	—	13,600	509	12,581	10,193	2,388	510	12,764,000	3,322	1,235,336	2,848,745

Notes appear at end of table

(continued)

TABLE Df1165–1176   Aircraft production and exports, by type of aircraft: 1913–1993 *Continued*

			Aircraft produced							Exports		
			Civil								Aircraft exported	
				General aviation								
Year	Total	U.S. military	Total	Transports	Total	Single-engine	Multi-engine	Rotorcraft	Value of all products	Number	Value	Value of all exports
	Df1165	Df1166	Df1167	Df1168	Df1169	Df1170	Df1171	Df1172	Df1173 [1,2]	Df1174 [3,4]	Df1175 [3,4]	Df1176 [3,4,5]
	Number	Number	Number	Number	Number	Number	Number	Number	Thousand dollars	Number	Thousand dollars	Thousand dollars
1970	—	—	8,190	313	7,381	6,029	1,352	496	13,466,000	2,383	1,316,041	2,769,345
1971	—	—	8,143	230	7,450	6,277	1,173	463	—	2,904	1,933,969	3,908,114
1972	—	—	10,523	230	9,765	7,898	1,867	528	—	3,042	1,599,439	3,494,344
1973	—	—	14,748	295	13,671	10,818	2,853	782	—	4,670	2,355,738	4,769,136
1974	—	—	15,117	263	14,026	11,470	2,556	828	—	5,714	3,368,780	6,556,129
1975	—	—	15,196	314	14,043	11,507	2,536	839	—	4,539	3,229,468	7,222,166
1976	—	—	16,446	238	15,648	13,029	2,619	560	—	4,531	3,217,360	7,059,787
1977	—	—	17,605	180	16,624	13,857	2,767	801	—	4,353	—	—
1978	—	—	17,397	225	16,456	14,043	2,413	716	—	4,399	3,616,077	9,746,630
1979	—	—	17,924	—	16,883	13,044	3,839	1,041	—	5,115	—	—
1980	—	—	13,130	—	11,777	8,175	3,602	1,353	—	4,434	—	—
1981	—	—	11,067	—	10,114	6,825	3,289	953	—	3,826	—	—
1982	—	—	4,669	—	4,055	2,546	1,509	614	—	1,557	—	—
1983	—	—	3,217	—	2,784	1,697	1,087	433	—	1,088	—	—
1984	—	—	3,028	—	2,635	1,578	1,057	393	—	1,045	—	—
1985	—	—	2,842	—	2,457	1,551	906	385	—	1,050	—	—
1986	—	—	2,888	—	1,858	—	—	493	—	1,277	—	—
1987	—	—	2,319	—	1,516	—	—	360	—	1,929	—	—
1988	—	—	2,681	—	1,734	—	—	517	—	2,784	—	—
1989	—	—	3,129	—	2,014	—	—	603	—	6,452	—	—
1990	—	—	2,785	—	1,759	—	—	582	—	4,814	—	—
1991	—	—	2,867	—	1,598	—	—	574	—	4,204	—	—
1992	—	—	2,517	—	1,539	—	—	308	—	2,374	—	—
1993	—	—	3,189	—	1,416	—	—	269	—	1,985	—	—

[1] Beginning with 1959, represents net sales of complete aircraft and parts plus aircraft engine and parts.

[2] 1940–1945 values are for military aircraft produced in the United States only. They are computed by the War Production Board in terms of August 1943 unit cost and are not meant to measure output at current prices or expenditures.

[3] 1913–1918, fiscal years; thereafter, calendar years. Data for the second half of 1918 are included with calendar year 1919.

[4] 1949–1954, civil aircraft only.

[5] Prior to 1922, engine values were not reported separately but were probably included with either other internal combustion engines or with parts of aircraft. Values for parachutes and their parts have been included only since 1932.

[6] Represents domestic civil aircraft only.

[7] Data for the second half of the year.

[8] Data for the first eight months of the year.

Source

U.S. Federal Aviation Administration, *FAA Statistical Handbook of Aviation* (annual issues).

Documentation

Series Df1173. Includes the value of the aircraft, engines, parts, parachutes, and the like. Values comparable with the prewar peacetime numbers are not available between 1946 and 1959.

Series Df1174–1176. Exclude gliders and barrage balloons.

Series Df1176. Includes the total value of aircraft, engines, parts, and the like.

TABLE Df1177–1189 Scheduled domestic airline revenues and expenses: 1938–1980[1]   [Pre-deregulation groupings]

Contributed by Louis P. Cain

	Operating revenue						Operating expenses				Aircraft			
	Total	Passenger	Mail (including subsidy)	Express and freight	Excess baggage	Other	Total	Total	Flying	Direct maintenance, flight equipment	Depreciation, flight equipment	Ground and indirect expense	Net operating income or loss
Year	Df1177	Df1178	Df1179	Df1180	Df1181	Df1182	Df1183 [2]	Df1184 [2]	Df1185 [2]	Df1186 [2,3]	Df1187 [2,3]	Df1188 [2,3]	Df1189
	Thousand dollars	Thousand dollars	Thousand dollars	Thousand dollars	Thousand dollars	Thousand dollars	Thousand dollars	Thousand dollars	Thousand dollars	Thousand dollars	Thousand dollars	Thousand dollars	Thousand dollars
1938	42,845	24,861	15,798	1,278	283	625	43,865 [5]	24,987	14,737	5,345	4,905	18,878	−1,020
1939	55,948	34,844	18,482	1,619	346	657	51,392 [6]	26,294	15,809	5,651	4,834	24,692	4,556
1940	76,864	53,308	20,090	2,078	551	837	70,897 [6]	35,179	22,093	7,496	5,590	35,028	5,967
1941	97,311	69,791	22,696	2,919	766	1,139	89,919	44,932	27,392	9,789	7,751	44,987	7,392
1942	108,249	74,819	23,470	6,978	1,260	1,722	84,366	36,392	21,866	8,664	5,862	47,974	23,882
1943	123,105	87,481	24,213	8,382	1,720	1,309	95,563	34,613	20,739	9,132	4,742	60,950	27,542
1944	160,928	116,441	33,317	8,306	2,031	833	124,522	45,150	28,238	11,893	5,019	79,372	36,406
1945	214,743	166,520	33,694	10,835	2,298	1,397	180,626	69,223	43,421	16,393	9,409	111,403	34,117
1946	316,233	275,594	20,982	13,620	2,993	3,044	322,219	129,250	70,410	33,273	25,567	192,969	−5,986
1947	364,840	308,576	29,445	19,378	3,572	3,869	386,199	169,165	88,840	42,903	37,422	217,034	−21,360
1948	434,295	343,290	59,309	24,372	3,953	3,371	431,634	199,991	109,636	49,035	41,320	231,643	2,661
1949	486,034	388,931	59,333	27,987	4,452	5,331	461,733	223,193	127,398	54,028	41,767	238,540	24,301
1950	557,803	444,506	63,788	35,122	5,077	9,310	494,645	241,060	141,816	57,841	41,403	253,585	63,158
1951	702,365 [4]	591,187	57,422	36,914	6,069	10,733	595,363 [4]	287,942	173,023	71,687	43,232	307,421	107,001
1952	817,680 [4]	695,456	58,887	42,828	7,348	13,152	723,409 [4]	361,464	208,665	92,696	60,103	361,939	94,271
1953	937,482 [4]	803,869	64,484	47,791	8,704	12,622	850,448 [4]	438,088	253,091	102,401	82,596	412,356	87,032
1954	1,042,793 [4]	905,840	65,726	49,901	10,631	10,680	941,582 [4]	487,376	279,971	110,299	97,106	454,200	101,211
1955	1,201,266 [4]	1,060,590	55,536	61,102	12,168	11,856	1,077,122	551,626	323,220	135,487	92,919	525,493	124,142
1956	1,359,480	1,193,370	66,558	64,004	15,175	20,373	1,258,423	637,082	371,623	168,490	96,969	621,341	101,057
1957	1,530,228	1,347,530	74,734	68,591	18,644	20,729	1,488,973	780,401	469,587	176,099	134,715	708,572	41,255
1958	1,636,231	1,432,207	81,814	77,622	19,490	25,098	1,538,700	786,406	474,654	186,690	125,062	752,294	97,531
1959	1,955,116	1,722,491	94,998	91,235	21,362	25,030	1,848,332	932,907	551,399	230,404	151,104	915,425	106,784
1960	2,129,311	1,860,369	113,123	102,766	21,365	31,688	2,091,423	1,043,016	600,840	257,788	184,388	1,048,407	37,888
1961	2,245,495	1,951,491	129,589	114,500	20,399	29,514	2,244,237	1,362,055	633,187	445,859	283,009	882,183	1,257
1962	2,497,900	2,167,476	139,451	135,947	19,661	35,366	2,407,935	1,448,288	659,136	496,408	292,744	959,646	89,965
1963	2,722,464	2,374,392	142,775	152,414	17,473	35,410	2,579,821	1,539,303	698,696	523,111	317,496	1,040,518	142,643
1964	3,094,628	2,701,111	149,122	181,396	16,674	46,325	2,777,925	1,614,993	755,846	580,092	279,055	1,162,932	316,703
1965	3,608,506	3,142,048	157,525	219,612	12,041	77,280	3,165,073	1,810,851	854,650	639,942	316,259	1,354,222	443,433
1966	4,070,323	3,534,335	161,796	251,344	5,954	116,894	3,589,659	2,007,928	974,179	680,413	353,336	1,581,731	480,664
1967	4,886,572	4,260,000	170,180	287,254	7,236	161,902	4,475,594	2,501,951	1,229,479	831,715	440,757	1,973,643	411,152
1968	5,607,054	4,911,881	185,654	343,392	8,943	157,184	5,297,594	2,948,964	1,505,477	911,297	532,190	2,348,630	309,460
1969	6,935,606	5,943,446	224,120	462,139	11,699	294,202	6,613,425	3,702,356	1,947,738	1,057,917	696,701	2,911,069	322,181
1970	7,180,121	6,246,416	206,679	498,322	12,134	216,570	7,180,938	4,005,322	2,119,362	1,135,808	750,152	3,175,616	−817
1971	7,701,402	6,736,350	224,283	485,182	13,562	242,027	7,443,222	4,108,607	2,235,004	1,124,526	749,077	3,334,614	258,181
1972	8,587,996	7,564,842	228,031	541,346	12,842	240,936	8,096,695	4,337,839	2,324,560	1,239,456	773,823	3,758,854	491,300
1973	9,604,652	8,379,396	257,745	615,099	14,289	338,124	9,116,173	4,837,337	2,605,723	1,397,007	834,607	4,278,836	488,479
1974	11,448,289	9,757,503	259,419	672,957	16,581	741,829	10,648,991	5,662,313	3,297,164	1,499,920	865,229	4,986,680	799,289
1975	11,910,894	10,123,503	185,336	696,135	18,869	897,469	11,781,406	6,347,332	3,869,405	1,595,358	882,569	5,434,073	129,488
1976	13,789,178	11,855,266	214,125	830,051	22,014	867,722	13,231,448	7,123,588	4,401,280	1,802,164	920,144	6,089,859	575,730
1977	15,690,236	13,489,111	277,518	960,857	20,913	941,837	15,036,431	8,175,282	5,229,115	1,986,460	959,707	6,861,149	653,805
1978	17,943,472	15,508,727	266,826	1,093,767	22,900	1,051,252	16,948,581	8,915,406	5,577,201	2,125,080	1,213,125	8,033,173	994,891
1979	21,336,853	18,719,830	328,542	1,161,845	27,681	1,098,939	21,213,615	11,640,030	7,867,090	2,421,163	1,351,777	9,573,453	123,238
1980	26,012,346	23,081,487	438,236	1,204,460	32,168	1,264,810	26,014,012	15,085,256	10,847,647	2,707,935	1,529,674	10,922,199	−1,666

Notes appear on next page

(continued)

TABLE Df1177–1189   Scheduled domestic airline revenues and expenses: 1938–1980   [Pre-deregulation groupings]   Continued

[1] Intra-Alaskan and intra-Hawaiian carriers included starting in 1956.

[2] Operating expenses before 1957 are not comparable to data for later years. See text.

[3] Data for 1961–1966 are not comparable to prior years. See text.

[4] The sum of the items does not agree with the total owing to the rounding procedure.

[5] Excludes Colonial Airlines, Inc.

[6] Includes total operating expenses for Colonial Airlines, Inc., for which distribution by type of expense was not available.

Sources

U.S. Federal Aviation Administration, *FAA Statistical Handbook of Aviation* (annual issues). More recent numbers are taken from U.S. Bureau of Transportation Statistics, *National Transportation Statistics, Air Carrier Profile* (annual issues).

Documentation

Tables Df1177–1228 are identical in form. The data in Tables Df1177–1202 reflect the pre-deregulation air carrier groupings; the numbers are for "passenger/cargo operators." The data in Tables Df1203–1228 reflect the post-deregulation grouping; the numbers are for "operators." The pre-deregulation groupings were discontinued after 1980. Tables Df1177–1189 and Df1203–1215 cover domestic air transportation, whereas Tables Df1190–1202 and Df1216–1228 present corresponding data on international air transportation. See Table Df1112–1125 for additional information on scheduled airlines.

Series Df1183–1188. Because of the revision in the *Uniform System of Accounts and Reports* put into effect on January 1, 1957, operating expense data before and after these data are not directly comparable. The time period covered and the number of air carriers involved precluded a full conversion to the new reporting system, and the Civil Aeronautics Board made only limited adjustments in the data for 1956.

Series Df1186–1188. For 1961–1966, items of aircraft operating expense are not comparable to prior years and include items of ground and indirect expenses as follows: (1) series Df1186 also includes direct maintenance ground equipment, and indirect maintenance; (2) series Df1187 also includes other depreciation and amortization expenses; (3) series Df1188 includes only those expenses chargeable to general services and administration.

TABLE Df1190–1202   Scheduled international airline revenues and expenses: 1938–1980   [Pre-deregulation groupings]

Contributed by Louis P. Cain

	Operating revenue						Operating expenses						Net operating income or loss
	Total	Passenger	Mail (including subsidy)	Express and freight	Excess baggage	Other	Total	Total	Aircraft			Ground and indirect expense	
									Flying	Direct maintenance, flight equipment	Depreciation, flight equipment		
Year	Df1190	Df1191	Df1192	Df1193	Df1194	Df1195	Df1196	Df1197 [1]	Df1198	Df1199 [1]	Df1200 [1]	Df1201 [1]	Df1202
	Thousand dollars	Thousand dollars	Thousand dollars	Thousand dollars	Thousand dollars	Thousand dollars	Thousand dollars	Thousand dollars	Thousand dollars	Thousand dollars	Thousand dollars	Thousand dollars	Thousand dollars
1938	15,153	4,435	8,599	562	219	1,338	14,303	—	—	—	—	—	850
1939	19,653	6,156	11,066	613	237	1,581	18,201	—	—	—	—	—	1,452
1940	26,922	8,812	13,439	893	306	3,472	25,666	—	—	—	—	—	1,256
1941	37,990	14,021	15,473	1,475	382	6,639	35,309	—	—	—	—	—	2,681
1942	40,870	20,971	9,039	4,319	936	5,605	35,223	—	—	—	—	—	5,647
1943	32,839	19,334	3,624	4,401	803	4,677	32,079	11,992	8,074	2,174	1,744	20,087	760
1944	38,882	24,287	2,889	5,405	1,066	5,235	39,227	13,353	8,471	3,030	1,852	25,874	–344
1945	69,111	38,859	12,246	7,315	1,571	9,120	61,765	22,918	15,297	5,199	2,422	38,847	7,346
1946	146,754	91,417	25,061	11,413	3,296	15,567	139,843	52,045	32,027	11,064	8,954	87,798	6,911
1947	209,009	140,652	32,300	17,526	4,388	14,143	209,294	93,766	53,189	21,997	18,580	115,528	–284
1948	249,234	151,338	57,331	20,809	4,135	15,621	235,287	110,993	67,163	24,241	19,589	124,294	13,947
1949	274,155	158,480	75,197	22,127	4,178	14,173	252,863	122,334	72,347	26,311	23,676	130,529	21,291
1950	260,131	160,672	55,689	21,664	3,244	18,862	248,323	122,776	70,980	26,158	25,638	125,547	11,808
1951	287,936	184,692	53,213	25,245	3,809	20,977	269,865	129,221	75,102	29,856	24,263	140,644	18,071
1952	315,141 [4]	212,581	51,532	26,910	4,822	19,290	304,423	146,965	87,442	33,043	26,480	157,456	10,718
1953	337,711 [4]	232,867	53,746	27,385	5,248	18,454	318,489	151,308	91,751	32,827	26,730	167,178	19,221
1954 [2]	359,491	254,653	49,191	29,784	6,997	18,866	333,337	157,728	99,044	30,856	27,828	175,610	26,155

	Operating revenue						Operating expenses						
	Total	Passenger	Mail (including subsidy)	Express and freight	Excess baggage	Other	Total	Aircraft				Ground and indirect expense [1]	Net operating income or loss
								Total	Flying	Direct maintenance, flight equipment [1]	Depreciation, flight equipment [1]		
Year	Df1190	Df1191	Df1192	Df1193	Df1194	Df1195	Df1196	Df1197	Df1198	Df1199	Df1200	Df1201	Df1202
	Thousand dollars	Thousand dollars	Thousand dollars	Thousand dollars	Thousand dollars	Thousand dollars	Thousand dollars	Thousand dollars	Thousand dollars	Thousand dollars	Thousand dollars	Thousand dollars	Thousand dollars
1955	385,157	295,442	27,221	32,013	7,385	23,093	366,562	171,427	108,954	34,867	27,606	195,135	18,597
1956 [3]	471,160	349,019	39,320	38,292	8,271	36,258	436,257	211,783	132,529	47,634	31,620	224,474	34,903
1957	508,827	385,183	32,895	42,879	9,228	38,642	480,495	241,820	150,763	44,828	46,229	238,675	28,332
1958	530,881	395,604	37,962	45,420	8,963	42,932	519,604	259,825	163,516	47,859	48,450	259,779	11,277
1959	592,226	444,618	40,469	51,877	8,845	46,417	573,653	281,988	170,391	57,522	54,075	291,665	18,573
1960	684,672	527,568	47,544	58,802	10,136	40,622	639,477	303,953	179,712	58,392	65,849	335,524	45,195
1961	722,390	533,159	59,527	63,265	9,570	56,869	698,685	400,537	186,561	109,493	104,483	298,148	23,706
1962	810,446	595,221	70,368	71,252	10,334	63,269	723,853	398,381	193,422	113,602	91,357	325,472	86,593
1963	920,303	692,801	73,989	80,378	11,665	61,470	799,462	430,073	216,834	117,729	95,510	369,389	120,841
1964	1,027,916	781,649	71,321	100,296	11,149	63,501	896,187	471,764	238,427	145,186	88,151	424,423	131,729
1965	1,199,403	887,335	82,158	131,119	13,481	85,310	1,001,362	508,710	262,597	146,043	100,070	492,651	198,041
1966	1,474,480	995,185	131,804	149,529	14,092	183,865	1,220,894	634,423	329,427	181,475	123,521	586,471	253,586
1967	1,769,682	1,165,862	145,051	163,558	13,419	281,792	1,496,540	792,026	424,135	211,874	156,017	704,514	273,142
1968	1,958,327	1,309,173	135,904	185,856	15,823	311,571	1,746,831	920,029	495,035	244,024	180,970	826,802	211,496
1969	1,689,387	1,176,349	99,041	185,502	14,232	214,263	1,638,275	832,503	456,431	219,053	157,019	805,772	51,112
1970	1,913,592	1,380,388	110,197	197,031	15,109	210,867	1,894,391	944,148	515,182	241,077	187,889	950,243	19,201
1971	2,080,262	1,483,973	90,188	220,553	15,672	269,874	2,050,095	1,032,259	573,008	269,031	190,220	1,017,834	30,167
1972	2,284,300	1,706,512	77,378	242,354	14,459	243,599	2,233,879	1,108,243	595,859	300,476	211,908	1,125,635	50,421
1973	2,526,878	1,894,914	71,366	268,055	15,231	277,314	2,458,971	1,210,890	680,521	316,597	213,772	1,248,081	67,907
1974	2,921,607	2,121,651	83,595	335,704	20,965	359,693	2,994,713	1,607,594	1,037,441	356,187	213,966	1,387,119	−73,104
1975	3,063,399	2,230,081	89,793	355,805	25,476	362,245	3,059,348	1,626,575	1,050,250	363,869	212,456	1,432,774	4,051
1976	3,316,136	2,410,987	77,620	382,053	27,259	418,217	3,182,236	1,650,456	1,089,387	368,190	192,879	1,531,780	133,900
1977	3,774,262	2,785,706	79,582	425,296	20,797	462,882	3,552,189	1,822,516	1,170,021	414,486	238,009	1,729,672	222,072
1978	4,331,776	3,305,236	82,457	444,087	20,020	480,221	4,007,653	1,971,852	1,210,641	457,787	303,424	2,035,801	324,124
1979	5,191,458	4,071,862	96,521	529,840	22,743	471,297	5,105,027	2,643,112	1,795,279	520,805	327,028	2,461,915	86,384
1980	6,364,238	4,777,026	138,821	590,894	24,749	810,899	6,521,824	3,641,521	2,668,042	598,375	375,104	2,880,303	−157,585

[1] Data for 1961–1967 are not comparable to prior years because they include items of ground and indirect expenses. See text.

[2] Excludes Midet Aviation Corporation owing to inadequacies in reporting.

[3] Operating expenses are not comparable to subsequent years. See text.

[4] The sum of the items does not agree with the total owing to rounding procedure.

Sources

U.S. Federal Aviation Administration, *FAA Statistical Handbook of Aviation* (annual issues). More recent numbers are taken from U.S. Bureau of Transportation Statistics, *National Transportation Statistics, Air Carrier Profile* (various issues).

Documentation

See the text for Table Df1177–1189 for a general discussion of Tables Df1177–1228 and for specific information relevant to series Df1196–1201.

TABLE Df1203–1215   Scheduled domestic airline revenues and expenses: 1972–1996   [Post-deregulation groupings]

Contributed by Louis P. Cain

	Operating revenue						Operating expenses						
								Aircraft					
Year	Total	Passenger	Mail (including subsidy)	Express and freight	Excess baggage	Other	Total	Total	Flying	Direct maintenance, flight equipment	Depreciation, flight equipment	Ground and indirect expense	Net operating income or loss
	Df1203	Df1204	Df1205	Df1206	Df1207	Df1208	Df1209	Df1210	Df1211	Df1212	Df1213	Df1214	Df1215
	Thousand dollars	Thousand dollars	Thousand dollars	Thousand dollars	Thousand dollars	Thousand dollars	Thousand dollars	Thousand dollars	Thousand dollars	Thousand dollars	Thousand dollars	Thousand dollars	Thousand dollars
1972	8,651,742	7,564,842	229,989	595,583	12,842	248,477	8,158,450	4,371,830	2,347,584	1,246,452	777,794	3,786,619	493,292
1973	9,694,007	8,379,396	262,626	693,610	14,289	344,086	9,200,212	4,884,897	2,638,061	1,407,618	839,218	4,315,314	493,795
1974	11,545,790	9,757,503	263,614	759,036	16,581	749,056	10,760,565	5,730,346	3,345,010	1,513,858	871,478	5,030,221	785,226
1975	12,020,059	10,123,503	252,750	781,638	18,869	843,298	11,902,956	6,421,027	3,919,059	1,610,751	891,217	5,481,929	117,103
1976	13,898,501	11,855,266	294,175	932,958	22,014	794,610	13,323,961	7,190,896	4,448,117	1,815,748	927,031	6,133,066	574,541
1977	15,822,428	13,489,111	355,117	1,085,888	20,913	871,129	15,165,899	8,256,059	5,287,884	2,001,329	966,846	6,909,839	656,529
1978	18,189,473	15,508,727	335,525	1,326,842	22,900	995,474	17,171,530	9,054,815	5,669,021	2,154,909	1,230,885	8,116,715	1,017,943
1979	21,652,405	18,719,830	415,737	1,455,828	27,681	1,033,313	21,522,972	11,828,881	7,998,440	2,457,497	1,372,944	9,693,961	129,433
1980	26,403,576	23,081,487	529,572	1,552,836	32,168	1,207,184	26,409,238	15,347,398	11,029,423	2,757,663	1,560,312	11,061,841	−5,662
1981	29,013,691	25,491,015	608,233	1,617,705	36,183	1,258,055	29,276,723	16,717,195	12,137,311	2,842,749	1,737,135	12,559,528	−263,032
1982	28,727,699	25,439,640	571,822	1,505,035	42,045	1,169,148	29,478,115	16,114,910	11,529,364	2,709,440	1,876,106	13,363,206	−750,416
1983	31,014,393	27,519,079	537,234	1,601,895	51,967	1,304,221	31,185,661	16,355,753	11,370,479	2,877,991	2,107,283	14,829,909	−171,268
1984	35,393,945	31,436,951	559,158	1,715,979	70,032	1,611,842	33,811,742	17,559,666	12,160,526	3,175,865	2,223,275	16,252,075	1,582,203
1985	37,628,540	33,343,005	740,384	1,580,914	78,113	1,886,123	36,610,744	18,606,531	12,684,018	3,604,447	2,318,066	18,004,213	1,017,796
1986	41,000,546	33,813,923	682,643	4,278,008	85,438	2,140,496	39,934,036	18,496,316	11,368,346	4,475,473	2,652,497	21,437,719	1,066,470
1987	45,657,800	37,492,065	706,178	4,951,924	66,756	2,440,877	43,925,149	20,314,080	12,508,716	4,950,558	2,854,806	23,611,068	1,732,650
1988	50,187,181	41,001,573	791,929	5,807,058	71,781	2,514,841	47,738,808	21,795,551	13,175,525	5,642,790	2,977,236	25,943,257	2,448,873
1989	54,314,210	43,670,025	770,333	5,408,336	69,761	4,395,754	52,459,535	24,011,087	14,749,292	6,184,193	3,077,602	28,448,448	1,854,675
1990	57,994,041	46,282,413	749,428	4,275,637	76,129	6,610,433	58,983,230	28,360,812	18,166,482	6,921,512	3,272,818	30,622,417	−989,189
1991	56,230,433	44,593,991	737,459	4,486,691	78,083	6,334,209	56,758,157	26,729,621	16,830,585	6,682,050	3,216,986	30,028,538	−527,724
1992	57,654,393	45,245,648	939,991	4,655,268	87,354	6,726,132	58,801,107	27,426,211	17,203,047	6,883,543	3,339,621	31,374,896	−1,146,714
1993	62,824,935	49,297,725	975,031	4,968,360	91,486	7,492,334	60,726,628	28,130,621	17,533,230	6,989,841	3,607,550	32,596,007	2,098,308
1994	65,948,993	—	—	—	—	—	63,757,937	—	—	—	—	—	2,191,056
1995	70,885,050	—	—	—	—	—	66,119,699	—	—	—	—	—	4,765,351
1996	76,720,068	—	—	—	—	—	71,388,319	—	—	—	—	—	5,331,749

Sources

U.S. Federal Aviation Administration, *FAA Statistical Handbook of Aviation* (annual issues). More recent numbers are taken from U.S. Bureau of Transportation Statistics, *National Transportation Statistics, Air Carrier Profile* (various issues).

Documentation

See the text for Table Df1177–1189 for a general discussion of Tables Df1177–1228.

TABLE Df1216–1228 Scheduled international airline revenues and expenses: 1972–1996 [Post-deregulation groupings]

Contributed by Louis P. Cain

	Operating revenue						Operating expenses						Net operating income or loss
	Total	Passenger	Mail (including subsidy)	Express and freight	Excess baggage	Other	Total	Aircraft				Ground and indirect expense	
								Total	Flying	Direct maintenance, flight equipment	Depreciation, flight equipment		
	Df1216	Df1217	Df1218	Df1219	Df1220	Df1221	Df1222	Df1223	Df1224	Df1225	Df1226	Df1227	Df1228
Year	Thousand dollars	Thousand dollars	Thousand dollars	Thousand dollars	Thousand dollars	Thousand dollars	Thousand dollars	Thousand dollars	Thousand dollars	Thousand dollars	Thousand dollars	Thousand dollars	Thousand dollars
1972	2,511,529	1,706,512	102,502	342,589	14,459	345,467	2,420,351	1,224,119	674,358	324,630	225,131	1,196,231	91,178
1973	2,724,771	1,894,914	101,350	381,024	15,231	332,250	2,633,299	1,314,894	751,582	338,089	225,223	1,318,405	67,907
1974	3,157,431	2,121,651	109,396	488,698	20,965	416,722	3,217,769	1,747,213	1,135,887	381,349	229,977	1,470,557	−60,338
1975	3,336,267	2,230,081	114,449	528,168	25,476	438,092	3,325,667	1,793,015	1,175,245	392,334	225,436	1,532,652	10,599
1976	3,604,687	2,410,987	103,981	564,257	27,259	498,204	3,457,412	1,819,356	1,215,273	398,914	205,169	1,638,057	147,275
1977	4,103,943	2,785,706	103,430	632,657	20,797	561,355	3,852,413	2,006,234	1,303,202	449,868	253,164	1,846,180	251,350
1978	4,702,663	3,305,236	107,903	660,040	20,020	610,168	4,355,044	2,172,961	1,351,126	498,483	323,352	2,182,082	347,620
1979	5,574,590	4,071,862	119,948	755,492	22,743	604,546	5,505,332	2,883,287	1,960,372	571,215	351,700	2,662,043	69,258
1980	6,543,033	4,777,026	163,204	875,682	24,749	702,372	6,765,623	3,776,709	2,775,331	615,982	385,396	2,988,914	−222,590
1981	6,390,140	4,749,683	151,422	857,002	34,282	299,075	6,595,039	3,701,729	2,753,907	561,836	385,986	2,893,309	−204,898
1982	6,434,904	4,959,347	176,930	989,620	25,358	283,448	6,451,807	3,504,088	2,596,134	511,795	396,159	2,947,719	−17,103
1983	7,163,275	5,604,902	152,455	999,405	23,012	383,502	6,692,776	3,426,525	2,490,076	547,741	388,708	3,266,252	470,499
1984	7,974,706	6,074,406	157,703	1,169,259	27,447	545,892	7,484,679	3,751,471	2,628,664	676,950	445,857	3,733,208	490,028
1985	8,302,279	6,451,324	160,543	1,130,050	27,832	531,528	7,983,705	3,988,017	2,738,439	768,018	481,560	3,995,687	318,574
1986	8,621,149	6,550,550	153,627	1,451,488	28,254	437,231	8,458,084	3,820,219	2,401,911	900,784	517,524	4,637,866	163,066
1987	10,924,837	8,374,295	180,052	1,782,832	32,688	554,971	10,226,388	4,464,809	2,836,095	1,095,635	533,079	5,761,579	698,450
1988	13,401,710	10,356,637	183,251	2,150,132	39,285	672,405	12,403,323	5,179,756	3,230,335	1,331,687	617,734	7,223,567	998,388
1989	14,910,912	11,181,198	188,284	2,416,980	46,759	1,077,692	14,953,533	6,388,537	3,918,537	1,723,953	746,047	8,564,996	−42,620
1990	17,990,355	13,467,960	223,840	2,601,668	43,244	1,653,644	18,914,480	8,391,811	5,453,830	2,051,246	886,735	10,522,670	−924,123
1991	18,928,061	14,102,721	222,833	3,134,202	49,584	1,418,721	20,185,077	8,680,434	5,636,310	2,152,099	892,025	11,504,643	−1,257,016
1992	20,485,850	15,663,944	247,628	2,980,441	46,702	1,547,135	21,783,598	9,023,321	5,842,677	2,147,512	1,033,132	12,760,276	−1,297,748
1993	20,969,851	15,909,921	237,201	3,173,381	49,410	1,599,937	21,631,934	8,943,459	5,903,332	1,965,431	1,074,696	12,688,476	−662,083
1994	22,364,429	—	—	—	—	—	21,842,021	—	—	—	—	—	522,408
1995	23,433,483	—	—	—	—	—	22,335,257	—	—	—	—	—	1,098,226
1996	24,967,512	—	—	—	—	—	24,075,018	—	—	—	—	—	892,494

Sources

U.S. Federal Aviation Administration, *FAA Statistical Handbook of Aviation* (annual issues). More recent numbers are taken from U.S. Bureau of Transportation Statistics, *National Transportation Statistics, Air Carrier Profile* (various issues).

Documentation

See the text for Table Df1177–1189 for a general discussion of tables Df1177–1228.

TABLE Df1229–1245 Air transportation accidents and fatalities – counts and rates, by type of carrier: 1927–1996[1]

Contributed by Louis P. Cain

	Domestic scheduled air carriers					International scheduled air carriers					Non-air-carrier flying operations						
	Total accidents	Fatal accidents	Total passenger fatalities	Plane-miles flown per fatal accident [2,3]	Passenger-fatalities per 100 million passenger-miles flown	Total accidents	Fatal accidents	Total passenger fatalities	Plane-miles flown per fatal accident [2,3]	Passenger-fatalities per 100 million passenger-miles flown	Total accidents	Total accidents Noncommuter	Fatal accidents Total	Fatal accidents Noncommuter	Fatalities Total	Fatalities Noncommuter	Miles flown per fatal accident
	Df1229	Df1230	Df1231	Df1232	Df1233	Df1234	Df1235	Df1236	Df1237	Df1238	Df1239	Df1240	Df1241	Df1242	Df1243	Df1244	Df1245
Year	Number	Number	Number	Thousand miles	Per 100 million passenger-miles	Number	Number	Number	Thousand miles	Per 100 million passenger-miles	Number	Number	Number	Number	Number	Number	Thousand miles
1927	25	4	1	1,464	—	—	—	—	—	—	253	—	95	—	146	—	—
1928	85	11	14	957	—	—	—	—	—	—	1,036	—	215	—	362	—	—
1929	124	21	14	1,082	—	—	—	—	—	—	1,586	—	287	—	467	—	—
1930	88	9	24	3,627	28.2000	3	0	0	—	—	2,029	—	300	—	504	—	360
1931	118	13	25	3,316	23.4000	8	1	1	4,537	7.100	2,197	—	251	—	398	—	375
1932	108	16	19	2,868	14.9000	7	1	6	5,278	28.900	1,936	—	207	—	318	—	377
1933	100	9	8	5,472	4.6000	1	0	0	—	—	1,589	—	177	—	299	—	402
1934	71	8	17	5,190	9.0000	2	2	4	3,769	10.900	1,491	—	184	—	323	—	410
1935	58	8	15	6,989	4.7000	4	0	0	—	—	1,503	—	161	—	253	—	526
1936	65	8	44	8,038	10.0000	5	2	2	3,452	4.800	1,674	—	155	—	261	—	602
1937	42	5	40	13,358	8.3000	8	1	11	7,909	13.900	1,900	—	184	—	280	—	560
1938	23	5	25	13,818	4.5000	9	3	7	2,347	13.000	1,861	—	176	—	274	—	734
1939	28	2	9	41,616	1.2000	6	1	10	7,042	12.800	2,222	—	203	—	315	—	876
1940	30	3	35	36,837	3.0000	6	0	0	—	—	3,471	—	232	—	359	—	1,137
1941	27	4	35	33,729	2.3000	5	1	2	14,410	1.200	4,252	—	217	—	312	—	1,595
1942	23	5	55	22,354	3.7000	2	0	0	—	—	3,324	—	143	—	220	—	2,053
1943	23	2	22	52,716	1.3000	2	1	10	18,457	3.900	3,871	—	167	—	257	—	—
1944	30	5	48	27,768	2.2000	7	1	17	22,272	5.300	3,343	—	169	—	257	—	—
1945	40	8	76	26,171	2.2000	5	2	17	16,304	3.700	4,652	—	322	—	508	—	1,267
1946	33	9	75	34,633	1.2000	14	2	40	30,355	3.500	7,618	—	690	—	1,009	—	1,703
1947	44	8	199	40,832	3.2000	9	3	20	29,392	1.100	9,253	—	882	—	1,352	—	1,728
1948	56	5	83	67,889	1.3000	12	2	44	50,144	1.000	7,850	—	850	—	1,384	—	2,008
1949	35	8	96	44,622	1.3000	9	0	0	—	—	5,459	—	562	—	896	—	2,127
1950	39	4	96	96,123	1.1000	6	2	48	47,956	2.100	4,505	—	499	—	871	—	2,211
1951	45	11	142	39,051	1.3000	10	1	31	102,534	1.100	3,824	—	441	—	750	—	2,424
1952	44	6	46	79,600	0.4000	11	3	94	36,275	3.000	3,657	—	401	—	691	—	2,701
1953	37	5	86	107,331	0.6000	6	2	2	59,250	0.100	3,232	—	387	—	635	—	2,848
1954	49 [4]	4	16	141,123	0.1000	5	0	0	—	—	3,381	—	393	—	684	—	3,166
1955	45 [5]	8	156	80,042	0.8000	5	1	2	144,921	0.040	3,343	—	384	—	619	—	3,693
1956	55	4	143	178,957	0.6000	3	0	0	—	—	3,474	—	356	—	669	—	3,256
1957	44	4	32	208,014	0.1000	7	1	36	179,624	0.600	4,200	—	438	—	800	—	4,323
1958	42	4	114	198,553	0.4000	12	2	10	89,387	0.200	4,584	—	384	—	717	—	3,813
1959	61	9	209	94,619	0.7000	6	1	59	178,667	0.800	4,576	—	450	—	823	—	4,122
1960	62	10 [6]	326	82,948	0.9000	5	2	10	84,246	0.100	4,793	—	429	—	787	—	4,361
1961	56	5	124	160,476	0.4000	2 [7]	0	0	—	—	4,625	—	426	—	761	—	4,568
1962	35	5	158	166,660	0.3000	8	0	0	—	—	4,840	—	430	—	857	—	4,250
1963	39	4	48	224,180	0.1000	10	1	73	198,337	0.600	4,690	—	482	—	893	—	4,327
1964	45	6	106	161,371	0.1000	8	3	94	73,635	0.600	5,070	—	504	—	1,056	—	—

	Domestic scheduled air carriers [1]					International scheduled air carriers					Non-air-carrier flying operations						
	Total accidents	Fatal accidents	Total passenger fatalities	Plane-miles flown per fatal accident [2,3]	Passenger-fatalities per 100 million passenger-miles flown	Total accidents	Fatal accidents	Total passenger fatalities	Plane-miles flown per fatal accident [2,3]	Passenger-fatalities per 100 million passenger-miles flown	Total accidents (Total)	Total accidents (Noncommuter)	Fatal accidents (Total)	Fatal accidents (Noncommuter)	Fatalities (Total)	Fatalities (Noncommuter)	Miles flown per fatal accident
	Df1229	Df1230	Df1231	Df1232	Df1233	Df1234	Df1235	Df1236	Df1237	Df1238	Df1239	Df1240	Df1241	Df1242	Df1243	Df1244	Df1245
Year	Number	Number	Number	Thousand miles	Per 100 million passenger-miles	Number	Number	Number	Thousand miles	Per 100 million passenger-miles	Number	Number	Number	Number	Number	Number	Thousand miles
1965	55	6	205	183,152	0.4000	8	1	21	254,587	0.100	5,196	—	538	—	1,029	—	4,762
1966	50	4	59	297,369	0.1000	3	0	0	—	—	5,712	—	573	—	1,151	—	5,822
1967	43	8	226	184,176	0.3000	8	0	0	—	—	6,115	—	603	—	1,228	—	5,705
1968	44	11	258	157,037	(Z)	10	2	47	209,282	0.200	4,968	—	692	—	1,399	—	5,348
1969	37	7	132	287,246	0.1000	11	0	0	—	—	4,767	—	647	—	1,495	—	6,068
1970	31	1	0	2,024,703	0.0000	8	1	2	390,630	(Z)	4,640	—	622	—	1,254	—	5,155
1971	33	6	194	332,135	0.1820	8	0	0	—	—	4,648	—	661	—	1,355	—	—
1972	37	6	185	331,126	0.1570	6	1	1	350,112	0.003	4,256	4,109	695	653	1,426	1,305	—
1973	27	4	138	510,102	0.0960	5	2	79	180,741	0.231	4,255	4,090	723	679	1,412	1,299	—
1974	31	3	168	627,755	0.1150	12	4	292	82,562	0.819	4,425	4,234	729	689	1,438	1,327	—
1975	21	2	122	954,743	0.0810	7	0	0	—	—	4,237	4,034	675	638	1,345	1,247	—
1976	17	1	1	2,001,387	0.0010	4	1	37	318,610	0.119	4,193	4,005	695	648	1,320	1,187	—
1977	15	2	75	1,080,976	0.0380	3	0	0	—	—	4,286	4,069	702	658	1,436	1,281	—
1978	18	4	16	562,276	0.0060	1	0	0	—	—	4,494	4,223	793	723	1,770	1,563	—
1979	14	4	279	617,850	0.1250	4	1	73	387,737	0.134	4,238	3,800	658	629	1,311	1,219	—
1980	8	1	13	2,523,375	0.0050	6	0	0	—	—	—	3,594	—	621	—	1,247	—
1981	25	4	4	610,574	0.0016	—	—	—	—	—	—	3,504	—	657	—	1,288	—
1982	15	3	233	814,097	0.0897	—	—	—	—	—	—	3,233	—	591	—	1,187	—
1983	22	4	15	638,236	0.0053	—	—	—	—	—	—	3,075	—	555	—	1,064	—
1984	13	1	4	2,875,402	0.0013	—	—	—	—	—	—	3,016	—	545	—	1,042	—
1985	17	4	197	761,610	0.0586	—	—	—	—	—	—	2,738	—	498	—	955	—
1986	21	2	5	1,710,746	0.0014	—	—	—	—	—	—	2,582	—	474	—	967	—
1987	32	4	231	913,136	0.0571	—	—	—	—	—	—	2,494	—	447	—	838	—
1988	28	3	285	1,246,081	0.0673	—	—	—	—	—	—	2,386	—	460	—	800	—
1989	24	8	131	468,517	0.0303	—	—	—	—	—	—	2,230	—	431	—	768	—
1990	22	6	39	660,544	0.0085	—	—	—	—	—	—	2,214	—	442	—	766	—
1991	25	4	62	963,604	0.0138	—	—	—	—	—	—	2,170	—	431	—	781	—
1992	16	4	33	998,705	0.0069	—	—	—	—	—	—	2,074	—	447	—	862	—
1993	23	1	1	4,144,067	0.0002	—	—	—	—	—	—	2,022	—	385	—	715	—
1994	19	4	239	1,094,958	0.0458	—	—	—	—	—	—	1,995	—	404	—	—	—
1995	34	2	166	2,314,697	0.0306	—	—	—	—	—	—	2,055	—	412	—	—	—
1996	32	3	342	1,603,818	0.0590	—	—	—	—	—	—	1,905	—	359	—	—	—

(Z) Fewer than 0.1 persons.

1 Data include military contract operations beginning in 1956 and scheduled cargo carriers beginning in 1949. Beginning in 1980, data for international carriers are included with domestic carriers.

2 Beginning with 1958, aircraft revenue-miles per fatal accident.

3 Data not strictly comparable over time; see text.

4 Includes one ground collision between two air-carrier aircraft, one in scheduled passenger service and one in other revenue operations.

5 Excludes sabotage disaster at Longmont, Colorado, in which five crew members and thirty-nine passengers were fatally injured.

6 Includes two midair collisions nonfatal to air-carrier occupants.

7 Midair collision, nonfatal to air-carrier occupants.

Sources

1927–1962, U.S. Federal Aviation Administration, *FAA Statistical Handbook of Aviation* (annual issues); 1963–1970, U.S. Civil Aeronautics Board, *Handbook of Airline Statistics* (annual issues). The data beginning in 1972 are taken from U.S. Bureau of Transportation Statistics, *National Transportation Statistics, Air Carrier Profile* (various issues).

TABLE Df1229–1245   Air transportation accidents and fatalities – counts and rates, by type of carrier: 1927–1996
Continued

Documentation

An aircraft accident is considered to be any occurrence, while the aircraft is operating as such, that results in fatal or serious injury to persons or appreciable damage to the aircraft. The aircraft is considered to be "operating as such" from the time the engine is started for the purposes of flight until the flight is completed; in the case of gliders, while they are under tow or gliding. Propeller accidents to persons are included. A collision between two or more aircraft is counted as one accident.

Domestic and international air carriers include scheduled revenue operators only.

Series Df1232. Data beginning with 1971 are not strictly comparable to earlier data. For the later period, figures were calculated as the ratio of revenue miles flown, series Df1117, to the number of fatal accidents involving domestic scheduled air carriers, series Df1230.

Series Df1233. Rates computed on the basis of total passengers carried and passenger-miles flown, revenue and nonrevenue. They apply to passenger-carrying service only and exclude passenger deaths occurring in dynamite/sabotage accidents.

Series Df1237. Data through 1970 are not strictly comparable to later data. Beginning in 1972, figures were calculated as the ratio of revenue miles flown, series Df1131, to the number of fatal accidents involving international scheduled air carriers, series Df1235.

Series Df1239, Df1241, and Df1243. Include commuter air carrier and on-demand air taxi service. These data were not reported after 1979. Beginning in 1972, alternative figures were reported that exclude commuter air carrier and on-demand air taxi service: series Df1240, Df1242, and Df1244.

Series Df1245. The rates for plane-miles flown per fatal accident are no longer reported. Series Df1245 is the ratio of the total estimated miles flown in civil flying (other than scheduled air carriers), series Df1149, to the number of fatal accidents in non–air-carrier flying operations, series Df1241.

PIPELINES

Louis P. Cain

TABLE Df1246–1258   Oil pipelines – companies, assets, finances, and oil delivered: 1921–1976

Contributed by Louis P. Cain

	Line operated	Oil originated		Oil delivered out of system			Companies reporting	Investment in carrier property	Current assets	Current liabilities	Retained income	Capitalization	Net income
		Crude	Refined	Total	To connecting carriers	Terminated							
	Df1246	Df1247	Df1248	Df1249	Df1250	Df1251	Df1252	Df1253	Df1254	Df1255	Df1256	Df1257	Df1258
Year	Miles	Million barrels	Million barrels	Million barrels	Million barrels	Million barrels	Number	Million dollars	Million dollars	Million dollars	Million dollars	Million dollars	Million dollars
1921	55,260	—	—	—	—	—	33	365	127	61	148	337	34
1922	57,349	—	—	—	—	—	36	382	130	36	152	472	59
1923	64,760	—	—	—	—	—	34	432	144	77	78	497	63
1924	68,185	—	—	—	—	—	36	496	159	54	107	496	72
1925	70,009	—	—	—	—	—	35	511	88	13	102	346	88
1926	72,846	—	—	—	—	—	33	539	93	22	130	342	80
1927	76,070	—	—	—	—	—	32	609	125	27	150	388	93
1928	81,676	—	—	—	—	—	33	659	130	30	186	388	117
1929	85,796	—	—	—	—	—	37	741	129	25	186	428	142
1930	88,728	—	—	—	—	—	40	773	133	36	167	458	124
1931	93,090	—	—	—	—	—	49	845	132	37	171	474	121
1932	92,782	—	—	—	—	—	46	764	77	21	89	368	112
1933	93,724	—	—	—	—	—	48	766	66	20	92	360	106
1934	93,070	—	—	—	—	—	51	758	72	11	101	348	84
1935	92,037	723	44	—	—	709	53	763	47	40	59	346	78
1936	93,926	755	52	—	—	788	52	774	42	43	38	309	92
1937	96,612	885	63	—	—	910	58	803	44	51	42	323	103
1938	95,938	793	65	—	—	868	59	808	35	45	40	295	93
1939	98,681	803	70	—	—	907	63	830	32	48	40	310	81
1940	100,156	886	72	1,407	451	956	66	842	47	52	51	295	80
1941	105,435	971	82	1,642	563	1,079	71	885	56	91	30	293	79
1942	106,485	981	92	1,764	692	1,072	69	919	81	75	62	301	57
1943	108,783	1,123	144	2,077	866	1,211	74	965	108	82	71	297	61
1944	111,615	1,277	147	2,389	1,043	1,347	75	1,001	104	91	93	283	66
1945	113,351	1,292	150	2,365	964	1,401	74	1,043	115	78	120	301	66
1946	116,544	1,319	154	2,260	766	1,494	70	1,106	104	83	129	298	56
1947	119,298	1,431	187	2,474	851	1,623	71	1,225	127	105	148	339	53
1948	124,092	1,586	227	2,697	880	1,817	73	1,381	168	110	180	439	57
1949	124,984	1,415	241	2,448	792	1,656	73	1,498	175	97	202	549	58
1950	128,589	1,525	297	2,740	937	1,803	76	1,656	192	126	219	660	81
1951	131,457	1,774	345	3,201	1,126	2,075	76	1,822	233	166	279	759	82
1952	132,715	1,810	385	3,359	1,198	2,161	75	2,064	323	182	328	1,024	97
1953	133,900	1,861	435	3,627	1,279	2,349	78	2,312	301	173	372	1,177	109
1954	138,962	1,829	502	3,705	1,355	2,349	81	2,501	316	155	403	1,266	124
1955	140,374	2,038	586	4,039	1,444	2,595	84	2,586	353	185	432	1,282	153
1956	142,686	2,195	663	4,458	1,613	2,845	83	2,716	368	217	467	1,304	178
1957	145,236	2,183	668	4,472	1,590	2,883	82	2,843	364	161	600	1,357	159
1958	144,354	2,018	757	4,317	1,509	2,807	82	2,949	347	154	633	1,383	162
1959	149,159	2,182	549	4,659	1,624	3,035	85	3,197	384	175	673	1,385	183
1960	151,968	2,239	909	4,783	1,639	3,144	87	3,300	393	187	701	1,439	169
1961	153,737	2,336	966	4,923	1,646	3,277	89	3,407	432	190	769	1,397	181
1962	155,053	2,379	1,078	5,109	1,624	3,485	92	3,518	432	184	798	1,383	204
1963	156,812	2,467	1,182	5,322	1,648	3,673	94	3,915	535	254	843	1,685	201
1964	159,583	2,567	1,381	5,565	1,684	3,881	90	4,040	530	293	812	1,620	210
1965	161,412	2,618	1,629	5,864	1,757	4,107	89	4,178	555	301	835	1,635	218
1966	163,155	2,826	1,774	6,238	1,770	4,468	87	4,433	572	333	858	1,790	236
1967	165,478	3,017	2,035	6,800	1,890	4,910	90	4,745	519	354	873	1,943	261 [1]
1968	169,307	3,203	2,203	7,269	2,048	5,221	97	5,139	562	431	950	2,130	262
1969	170,824	3,405	2,316	7,745	2,243	5,499	99	5,379	644	441	1,037	2,267	273

Note appears at end of table

(continued)

TABLE Df1246-1258 Oil pipelines – companies, assets, finances, and oil delivered: 1921-1976 *Continued*

Year	Line operated	Oil originated		Oil delivered out of system			Companies reporting	Investment in carrier property	Current assets	Current liabilities	Retained income	Capitalization	Net income
		Crude	Refined	Total	To connecting carriers	Terminated							
	Df1246	Df1247	Df1248	Df1249	Df1250	Df1251	Df1252	Df1253	Df1254	Df1255	Df1256	Df1257	Df1258
	Miles	Million barrels	Million barrels	Million barrels	Million barrels	Million barrels	Number	Million dollars	Million dollars	Million dollars	Million dollars	Million dollars	Million dollars
1970	175,735	3,568	2,449	8,147	2,320	5,827	101	5,786	628	480	1,124	2,518	312
1971	174,722	3,517	2,597	8,184	2,314	5,870	99	6,305	636	499	1,177	2,964	314
1972	173,532	3,615	2,896	8,889	2,552	6,336	99	6,759	672	549	1,263	3,184	332
1973	170,691	3,657	3,147	9,415	2,785	6,630	100	7,016	728	691	1,350	3,168	375
1974	173,341	3,575	3,073	9,333	2,748	6,585	103	8,065	1,038	887	1,406	4,093	352
1975	172,680	3,493	3,167	9,341	2,817	6,523	104	10,745	961	1,078	1,377	6,042	457
1976	174,072	3,434	3,230	9,757	2,976	6,781	111	13,704	1,055	1,571	1,486	8,143	599

[1] After extraordinary and prior period items.

Sources

U.S. Interstate Commerce Commission (ICC), 1921-1953, *Statistics of Railways in the United States* (various annual issues); 1954-1976, ICC, *Transport Statistics in the United States*, Part 6, Oil Pipe Lines, Table 1.

Documentation

Figures refer to pipelines operating in interstate commerce and regulated by the ICC. Because the Trans-Alaska Pipeline System, constructed during the mid-1970s, is entirely within the state of Alaska, it is not included in the statistics shown here.

For a discussion of statistics of oil pipelines, see ICC, *A Review of Statistics of Oil Pipe Lines, 1921–1941*, Statement number 4280 (mimeographed), 1942. The figure for mileage in 1938, which appears to have been revised, is from this Statement.

Figures for barrels of oil carried are as follows, in millions: 1925, 831; 1926, 836; 1927, 989; 1928, 1,053; 1929, 1,156; 1930, 1,172; 1931, 987. In these figures, a barrel handled by two or more pipelines in succession is counted each time it is handled. In the figures for barrels originated, series Df1247-1248, this duplication is avoided.

Series Df1247. Includes both gathering and trunk lines.

TABLE Df1259–1265   Oil and gas pipeline mileage, by type of line: 1960–1996

Contributed by Louis P. Cain

	Oil pipeline			Gas pipeline			
	Total	Crude lines	Product lines	Total	Distribution mains	Transmission pipelines	Field and gathering lines
	Df1259	Df1260	Df1261	Df1262	Df1263	Df1264 [1]	Df1265
Year	Thousand miles	Thousand miles	Thousand miles	Thousand miles	Thousand miles	Thousand miles	Thousand miles
1960	190.9	141.1	49.9	630.9	391.4	183.7	55.8
1961	195.8	144.2	51.5	659.0	410.4	191.9	56.7
1962	200.5	147.3	53.2	683.2	428.1	196.4	58.7
1963	204.0	148.0	55.9	709.9	448.3	200.9	60.7
1964	207.4	148.7	58.7	736.2	469.8	205.4	61.0
1965	210.9	149.4	61.4	767.5	494.5	211.3	61.7
1966	210.4	147.9	62.5	799.6	519.6	217.0	63.0
1967	209.9	146.4	63.5	828.3	539.2	225.4	63.7
1968	209.5	144.9	64.5	861.6	562.7	234.5	64.4
1969	214.1	145.6	68.5	891.6	578.6	248.1	64.9
1970	218.7	146.3	72.4	913.3	594.8	252.2	66.3
1971	219.9	146.0	73.9	931.4	610.4	254.8	66.2
1972	221.1	145.8	75.4	948.1	623.1	258.1	66.9
1973	223.5	145.5	78.0	962.9	633.8	263.1	65.9
1974	224.7	145.6	79.1	974.1	645.6	262.2	66.4
1975	225.9	145.7	80.2	979.3	648.2	262.6	68.5
1976	227.1	145.8	81.3	987.7	659.1	258.2	70.3
1977	220.1	145.1	75.0	998.9	666.9	260.5	71.5
1978	218.2	140.9	77.3	1,013.0	677.5	260.6	74.9
1979	216.0	130.1	85.9	1,029.8	688.5	263.5	77.8
1980	218.4	129.8	88.6	1,051.8	701.8	266.5	83.5
1981	215.0	125.6	89.5	1,069.8	714.1	269.5	86.2
1982	213.7	123.0	90.7	1,083.4	721.2	271.7	90.5
1983	211.9	118.5	93.4	1,095.1	729.7	273.5	91.9
1984	215.3	119.9	95.4	1,102.4	736.8	271.9	93.7
1985	213.6	117.8	95.8	1,118.9	753.4	271.2	94.3
1986	214.8	122.1	92.7	1,134.1	769.3	271.0	93.8
1987	215.9	122.0	94.0	1,151.2	783.8	273.8	93.6
1988	214.1	123.3	91.8	1,169.0	801.3	275.4	92.3
1989	211.5	117.6	90.9	1,185.0	818.4	276.3	90.6
1990	208.8	118.8	89.9	1,206.9	837.3	280.1	89.5
1991	203.8	115.9	88.0	1,225.3	857.4	281.6	86.3
1992	199.0	113.0	86.0	1,253.9	883.2	284.5	86.2
1993	199.0	113.0	86.0	1,251.1	908.3	269.6	73.1
1994	200.5	114.0	86.5	1,258.0	919.3	268.3	70.4
1995	200.5	—	—	1,262.2	935.0	264.9	62.2
1996	—	—	—	1,269.0	952.1	259.4	57.5

[1] After 1975 includes 5,000 to 6,200 miles of underground storage pipe.

Source

U.S. Interstate Commerce Commission, *National Transportation Statistics* (1998), Table 1-8.

Documentation

Series Df1259–1261. Include petroleum and other liquid product lines, including gathering lines.

Series Df1262–1265. Exclude service pipe. The data are not adjusted to a common diameter equivalent. Mileage as of the end of each year.

CHAPTER Dg
Communications

Editor: Alexander J. Field

COMMUNICATIONS

Alexander J. Field

The communications sector of an economy comprises a range of technologies, physical media, and institutions/rules that facilitate the storage of information through means other than a society's oral tradition and the transmission of that information over distances beyond the normal reach of human conversation. This chapter provides data on the historical evolution of a disparate range of industries and institutions contributing to the movement and storage of information in the United States over the past two centuries. These include the U.S. Postal Service, the newspaper industry, book publishing, the telegraph, wired and cellular telephone service, radio and television, and the Internet.

The communications sector, regrettably, has received relatively little attention from economic historians. None of the three volumes of the *Cambridge Economic History of the United States*, for example, dedicates a chapter to it (Engerman and Gallman 1996, 2000). Volume 1, on the colonial period, contains virtually nothing on the subject, not a single index entry even to the carriage of letters or the publication of newspapers or books. Volume 2 mentions, in passing, the post office, the telephone, and the telegraph, but there is no organized treatment of the origins or economic impacts of these systems. Volume 3 does reference communications in a number of its essays and provides some systematic discussion of late-twentieth-century telecommunications policy. But the technological and regulatory issues we continue to deal with in the first decade of the twenty-first century did not arrive full-blown with the breakup of the Bell System or the explosive growth of the Internet. There is a technological and historical context to these developments, and this essay, along with the statistical series whose interpretation it illumines, attempts to provide it.

Communications industries or sectors satisfy human needs directly by selling or providing goods or services to households. In addition, they provide services to other businesses as intermediate inputs in the production of final goods and services. In business-to-business transactions, communications services have been and remain especially important in implementing capital-saving strategies in customer industries. Such practices save resources by enabling a given stock of physical capital to be used more intensively. Innovative capital-saving strategies, along with labor-saving ones, have also loomed large in the history of communications industries

themselves. Where appropriate, the essay calls attention to these strategies.

Transactions in this sector can be roughly divided between those involving one transmitter and one receiver (point to point), and those that involve one transmitter and many receivers (broadcast). Different segments of the communications sector have facilitated different blends of these two main types of service, and the blends have sometimes changed over time. Further subdivisions and identification of intermediate categories are also possible.

In the one-transmitter/multiple-receiver case, for example, we may distinguish narrowcasting from broadcasting. In usages more inclusive than is common, I will characterize the maintenance of a Web site, as well as book, newspaper, and other print media publication, as broadcasting, alongside traditional examples from the radio and television industries, but treat junk mail delivery or email sent to an electronic mailing list as narrowcasting. The distinction, although not hard and fast, is that in the latter cases, audiences have been more selectively targeted by the sender than would result from the simple choice of a medium or channel.

In point-to-point communications, we may distinguish between those in which messages are exchanged in more or less real time (synchronous), and those in which sending and receiving are separated by an interval (asynchronous). Communication between two parties may be simplex (information flows in only one direction), half duplex (it flows in either direction, but only one way at a time), or full duplex (it flows at the same time in either direction). Generalizations about particular parts of the communications sector, although often robust over extended periods of time, are at risk in rapidly changing technological environments.

Changes in Communications to 2000

The intent of this chapter is to provide an overview and a statistical window into how the nation has moved and stored information for more than two centuries. The tables are organized into four groups: telegraph and telephone; radio and television; U.S. Postal Service and delivery services; and books, newspapers, and periodicals. This organization provides continuity, in the context of newly added series, with the organization of the preceding editions, although much has changed in the communications sector since 1970.

The first group of statistical tables, which now includes the Internet, covers the telegraph and telephone and the infrastructure necessary to deliver all of these services. The telegraph, an industry whose birth, growth, and senescence is chronicled in these pages, predominantly serviced demands for point-to-point communication, the major exceptions being the system for broadcasting stock prices to specialized printing telegraphs (stock tickers) and the technology used by wire services such as the Associated Press to provide raw material for newspapers.

Acknowledgments
Alexander Field thanks Peter Temin and Gavin Wright for comments on earlier versions of the essay.

Even more than the telegraph, the telephone network was specialized for two-way point-to-point communication, in spite of the fact that some of Alexander Graham Bell's early promotional stunts envisaged broadcast (for example, playing "The Star-Spangled Banner" in Boston so that an audience of 2,000 could hear it in Providence or having an opera singer in Providence entertain an audience in Boston) (Casson 1910, p. 51). Although telegraphic communication was traditionally asynchronous, the telephone satisfied the demand for synchronous communication. This distinction, however, has been weakening as a consequence of the diffusion of ancillary hardware and software, such as answering machines and voice mail. And certainly some telegraphic queries and responses, such as those encouraged by the TWX (teletypewriter exchange) system introduced by the American Telephone and Telegraph Company (AT&T) in 1932, were sufficiently close together in time that we may view the resulting communication as synchronous in the same way that emails or instant messages are rapidly exchanged over the Internet.

An emphasis on two-way communication as a distinguishing feature of telephony is also arguably vulnerable in the present technological environment, at least if both parties to the conversation are assumed to be individuals. Computerized systems can now provide customized one-way messages for automated reminders of dentist or doctor appointments or let one know that one's child did not show up for school. And customers can communicate directly with computers using voice menus, touch tone buttons, and increasingly more sophisticated voice recognition software. Thus, either the initiator or responder in a two-way exchange may now be a computer rather than another human. How widely these new modalities will ultimately penetrate into the traditional spheres of phone use remains to be seen. And whether the telephone itself, as a transmitting and receiving appliance, will ultimately remain distinct from the computer is an open question.

The Internet, understood best as an evolving set of rules or protocols for interconnecting computers and networks of computers, was barely a year old in 1970. In the last three decades of the twentieth century, these shared rules, in conjunction with rapid technological advance in the manufacture of computing equipment, facilitated a growing variety of cross-machine interchange involving remote access, file transfers, electronic mail, and transmission and receipt of text and graphical information using the hypertext markup language (HTML) format. Time-sharing technology predated the Internet, and many of these features were available prior to 1969 for users of a single mainframe. What is new with the Internet is the ability of users of different central-processing units easily to communicate and exchange data with one another.

Electronic mail (email), the most important use of the Net for its first two decades, satisfies, as did the telegraph to which it is most closely related, the demand for asynchronous point-to-point communication. The invention of the electronic mailing list shortly after the appearance of email, however, quickly enabled narrowcasting. With the opening of the Net to commercial use, more indiscriminate broadcast to email addresses, known as spamming, has engendered protests and resistance from users, as well as actions by Internet service providers (ISPs) to reduce its incidence.

From the standpoint of households, an ongoing social and policy issue will remain the appropriate segregation of commercial and personal communication within these new channels. In the past, lines of separation were clearly if somewhat arbitrarily drawn. Magazines and newspapers contained commercial messages, but

books did not. Radio and television were largely supported by advertising, but films were to a much lesser degree. The Postal Service might transmit "junk" commercial messages; the telephone, historically, did not.

In threatening traditional boundaries, changing technologies have led and will continue to lead to new debates and policy choices. Unsolicited narrowcasting over phone lines to fax machines, for example, is now legally restricted, as a result of complaints about the costs of materials required to print out advertisements. How will this play out with respect to voice communication? Recorded political messages narrowcast to thousands of phone lines are an increasingly common campaigning tool, and there is no technological obstacle to the use of this method for the transmission of commercial messages. Will such activity backfire by generating ill will for the sender? If it is acceptable for a human to cold-call and pitch a commercial product, why not a machine?

Conflicts between commercial and private communication space were originally less of an issue on the World Wide Web, as compared with email, fax, or phone, because individuals voluntarily choose access to commercial content, for the most part, whereas they disliked having it thrust before their ears or eyes. Nevertheless, the increasing sophistication and intrusiveness of pop-up and pop-under ads and their variants are softening this distinction. Sites on the Web, because of their interactivity, both broadcast and provide opportunities for point-to-point communication, typically over secure (encrypted) channels if money or confidential information is changing hands. Web sites, identified by their URL (uniform resource locator), are computer servers prepared on demand to transmit and receive material formatted in HTML according to the hypertext transfer protocol (HTTP). These protocols offer greater display flexibility and interactivity and quicker access to related data or sites than was possible in the 1980s with bulletin board systems, and they continue to become more sophisticated. In 1970, of course, there was no World Wide Web (its rules would not be set forth for another twenty-one years), let alone access to computer bulletin boards, and until 1992, the Internet was off bounds for openly commercial enterprise. The 1990s saw enormous growth in the commercial uses of the Web.

Conflicts between freedom of expression and perceived threats to public safety or morality remain active policy issues with respect to the Internet, as they have been with respect to radio and television broadcast and the publication of print or recorded media. Easier (and cheaper) access to some types of specialized information (that involving explosives manufacture or pornography, for example) has not met with universal acclaim, and there continues to be legal and public policy debate about such issues as the use of filtering technology in public access terminals (for example, those in libraries). Debates about the appropriate individual, political, or social control of information flows will undoubtedly persist.

At the end of the 1990s, as the stock market bubble reached its peak, many businesses, desirous of exploiting opportunities to make product data easily available, moved aggressively to take advantage of new ways of "grabbing eyeballs." At the same time, corporations struggled to protect proprietary information behind internal firewalls, and the growing popularity of wireless networks aggravated these problems. In 2000, households provide information about themselves at a much cheaper cost than was previously possible, and they enjoy much more convenient access to a wide range of information, goods, and transactions. But individuals have also had to come to terms with the consequences of inexpensive methods for keeping track of what one has been reading, watching, or buying, and with whom one has been communicating and about what. The transformation of the computer industry and telecommunications in the last three decades of the twentieth century raised, and continues to raise in heightened form, long-standing issues about personal privacy in a democratic society.

The second major group of tables of this chapter chronicles the radio and television industries and their associated infrastructure. Here, the main business model in the United States has entailed broadcasting to final consumers who support the services through advertising costs built into the prices of purchased goods and services, and, to a lesser degree, through direct fees for service, charitable contributions, or tax subsidies. Tables Dg131–161 provide data on advertising revenues for commercial radio and television, and Table Dg172–180 provides details on income sources for public broadcasting. Table Dg117–130 chronicles the growth in the total number of radio and TV broadcast stations, both commercial and noncommercial, along with trends in the number of radio and television sets produced. It also provides information on the growing importance of cable systems and videocassette recorders, each of which has offered customers access to greater diversity of content, and the option, for a price, of consuming entertainment without the interruptions of commercial messages. In 1970, the Public Broadcasting System and National Public Radio were in the process of being created, and home videocassette recorders (VCRs) were unavailable before 1975. At the end of the twentieth century, home VCR technology was a maturing technology, already being supplanted by digital video disks (DVDs) as well as digital video recorders (DVRs).

DVRs and accompanying services, such as those currently provided by TiVo, represent an evolving technology whose potential is only beginning to be appreciated by consumers and other commentators. These services download television listings for a two-week period over a modem, allowing the user to select and record programs far more easily than with a VCR. These programs can also be watched while they are still being recorded. TiVo makes it extremely easy to fast-forward through commercials. Thus, a program that usually runs from 9:00 to 10:00 P.M. with commercials can now effectively be watched starting at 9:20 P.M., or at any time thereafter, with virtually no commercial interruption.

Sophisticated computer users with high-speed Internet access can already swap all varieties of digitized compressed media – not just audio MP3 files but also video and feature-length movies, as well as episodes of popular television shows in MPEG and other formats. They can do so even after the demise of Napster, the free downloading service, through the use of peer-to-peer networks such as Kazaa. It remains to be seen whether legal challenges or the technological development and consumer acceptance of advanced copy-protection systems will extend the life of a commercial paradigm for marketing recorded media that has now endured for more than a century, since Edison's innovation of recorded music, remains to be seen.

In addition to the frequencies reserved for broadcast, portions of the radio spectrum have historically been set aside for "safety and special" radio services that facilitate point-to-point communication in applications where wired connections are impossible or impractical (Table Dg162–171). The technology of radio transmission, indeed, was originally developed as a means of extending the telegraph's and telephone's point-to-point capability over water.

Separate bands remain allocated for marine and aviation services and for police and taxicab dispatch, where mobile communication has been of great utility. Amateur radio operators (hams) can obtain licenses to broadcast on certain frequencies, and a small band of forty channels is reserved for short-distance communication by households over citizens band, for which, after 1983, licenses were no longer required (Table Dg162–171).

Unless encrypted, two-way radio communication is inherently less private than that which generally takes place over wires. Sometime this can be an advantage, as in marine communication, where ships can keep their radios tuned to a certain frequency for general postings or distress calls and switch to another if an individual conversation is desired. And in police work, it can be helpful for patrol cars to have an overall sense of the activity and problems in their region. On the other hand, exchanges are accessible to anyone with access to a scanner; one is communicating over the wireless equivalent of a party line.

In the last three decades of the twentieth century, the most important innovations in the area of radio transmission have been in the development of cellular and paging services using previously and newly allocated portions of the spectrum. AT&T first introduced mobile radiotelephones in 1946, but they were expensive and inconvenient. One had to rely on an operator to connect with land lines over the public switched network, and conversations were simplex, only one direction at a time, with a button on the microphone for switching between send and receive. An improved system was introduced in 1964 and further improved in 1969, but the number of users in any metropolitan area was limited because the system relied on one powerful central antenna that monopolized channels over large geographic areas. Thus, aside from the safety and special services, individuals had limited access to mobile communications.

The last two groups of tables in this chapter examine the Postal Service and the broadcast print media, including books, magazines and newspapers, as well as the libraries that store them. The Postal Service, which plays an important role in delivering these media to households, also transmits narrowcast "junk mail," as well as asynchronous point-to-point written communications among and between businesses, government entities, and households. These sectors rely on technologies less fundamentally revolutionized in the nineteenth and twentieth centuries than those covered in this section.

Nevertheless, each medium faces questions about its future in an age in which the costs of storing and sending data have fallen precipitously. The market for printed encyclopedias has been radically transformed, and greatly reduced, by the capability of providing this information cheaply on CD-ROMs, DVD disks, or over the Web. Back issues of a growing range of academic journals are now available through vehicles such as JSTOR, with the print market protected by a blackout window on electronic availability covering the most recent three to five years. On the other hand, the content of current issues of most major newspapers and many magazines and periodicals (but not, in general, back issues) can now be accessed free of charge via the Internet. Finally, an increasing number of books in the public domain are available electronically and can be freely downloaded onto handheld or personal computers as a result of initiatives such as those of Project Gutenberg. The ways in which libraries operate are being altered by the increased use of electronic reference tools, and the future of the Postal Service continues to be debated. It is too early to say how changes in the technologies and economics of communications will ultimately influence the markets for and pricing of print media.

Squeezing More out of Bandwidth

It is impossible to discuss telecommunications without encountering references to bandwidth. In analog communications, bandwidth refers to the difference between the highest and lowest frequency used by a given communications channel. Thus, because telephony transmits information within a subset of the audible spectrum (about 300 to 3,500 cycles per second, or hertz), the bandwidth of a voice channel is about 3,000 hertz. In digital communications, width is measured in bits per second. Higher bandwidth means speedier data transfer, but it does not actually mean that the individual units of data per se move more quickly. Electrons move over unshielded twisted pair (the standard telephone wiring used in homes, consisting of a pair of insulated copper wires twisted together to reduce crosstalk) at about two thirds the speed of light: 124,100 miles per second. This is approximately the same speed reached by photons over what is called a T3/DS3 fiber-optic cable, which provides the backbone of the Internet. By making the individual on/off signals of shorter duration, among other ways, these "pipes" can be made effectively wider, in the sense that they can handle a larger stream of bits (binary digits) per unit of time.

Whether in wired or wireless applications, communications channels are scarce, and much of the progress in this sector has involved attempts to use them more efficiently. Aside from tricks that speed up rates of "throughput," other economies have been achieved by reducing interference between channels (a major concern in wireless communications), by reducing the amount of time during which no data are effectively flowing through the pipe (through packet switching and channel reallocation), by increasing the information content of a given "bitstream" through data compression and through carrier-wave frequency division "multiplexing" (known as wavelength division multiplexing in fiber-optic applications), and by creating multiple channels in a medium that otherwise would accommodate only one. All of these strategies are discussed later in the essay.

Cellular telephone service represents a new implementation of established transmission technology made possible by advances in computing and multiplexing that facilitate automatic reallocation of channels as they become available, multiple simultaneous use of the same channel, and handoffs from one local cell to another. By lowering transmission power, and thereby allowing the same frequencies to be reused in nonadjacent cells, the coverage of a cellular system can be extended geographically without monopolizing channels over large areas.

The Advanced Mobile Phone (AMP) system is the analog system jointly developed by Motorola and AT&T and introduced in Chicago in 1983. In contrast to other two-way safety and special services, cell phone technology uses one channel for transmission, another for receiving. Advanced multiplexing and, in newer systems, digital compression technologies have vastly expanded the effective number of conversations that may be conducted simultaneously over a given allocation of spectrum. These techniques include frequency division multiple access (FDMA), standard in analog systems like the AMP, and time division multiple access (TDMA). In the former, each user gets a slice of spectrum in a particular region for the duration of a call or until handed off to a new cell, at which point the frequency may be reassigned to a new user. In TDMA, each channel itself is sliced into three very narrow

time slots, each of which is used to transmit a separate communication. Thus, one channel can serve to transmit three conversations simultaneously through the use of sequences of short interleaved bursts of data that are then demultiplexed and appropriately recombined at their receiving ends. GSM (global system for mobile communications) uses a variant of TDMA with encryption and is the standard in Europe. American GSM phones, however, operate at a different frequency than their European counterparts.

Code division multiple access (CDMA) is the most complex, using split spectrum technology borrowed from the military. A conversation is digitized and then split apart, with different parts assigned to different frequencies and then reassembled at the receiving end. This requires more expensive switching equipment but makes the most efficient use of spectrum. All of these multiplexing technologies have their origins in nineteenth-century solutions to challenges for squeezing more data through given wires in telegraphy and telephony. Although cellular service relies on radio transmission, data on the cellular phone industry are grouped along with those on wired telephones. Table Dg103–109 includes data on the growing number of employees, subscribers, cell sites, revenue, and capital investment.

Pagers represent another interesting and distinctive use of radio spectrum. Invented in 1949, they were a minor feature of the environment in 1970 but have greatly expanded in use in the intervening years. All pagers use a similar technology. A ground-based tower broadcasts a stream of data on a single frequency. Receivers monitor this frequency for messages containing a special address, or "cap code." Upon receipt of such a code, the earliest machines simply beeped, alerting the wearer to "phone home" to retrieve a message. In the 1970s, tone voice pagers appeared, beeping and playing a short voice message. But requiring considerable bandwidth, they have been less successful than devices, introduced in the late 1980s, that receive and display a short alphanumeric message on a liquid crystal display.

In 2000, many mobile individuals carry both a pager and a cellular telephone. Each has advantages, and to some degree they complement each other. The range of reception and battery life of a pager are superior to those of a cellular phone, but one cannot return a call on it. As in so many other aspects of the communications sector, much is in flux, and some convergence in equipment and services is now occurring with the development of short message systems for cellular telephones.

Finally, in 1970 there were no global positioning system (GPS) satellites, whose navigational beacons are available in 2000 without charge, courtesy of the U.S. Department of Defense. By triangulation involving very minute differences in the time at which radio signals from four or more different satellites are received, this specialized form of information transfer provides individuals with precise information on their longitude, latitude, and elevation above sea level, as well as the correct time, all without the intervention of any human operators. Military and other authorized users can pinpoint location within 22 meters on the ground and elevation to within about 28 meters. A slightly degraded service enables civilians using handheld receivers/computers to fix location within 100 meters horizontally and elevation within 156 meters.

Historical Perspective

The technological focus of the remainder of this essay is on systems of communication and on those sectors whose technologies have undergone the most radical transformation. Postal networks and the publication of books, newspapers, and other print media predate the nineteenth century, but virtually everything else – telegraphy, telephony, radio, television, and the Internet – were created after 1840 because they were dependent on advances in the generation, storage, and manipulation of electricity.

Better understanding of the past and present of the communications sector is also critical from an aggregate perspective. From the early 1970s through the mid-1990s, both labor and total factor productivity in the United States grew much more slowly than was true in the half century preceding. The limited total factor productivity (TFP) growth we have experienced has been highly concentrated in the telecommunications sector and the closely related manufacture of computers (Gordon 2000; Oliner and Sichel 2000). Productivity (including TFP) growth rates did move up in the late 1990s, but it is not clear in 2000 whether this acceleration will be sustained. The big question remains whether the investment of hundreds of billions of dollars in new computer and telecommunications equipment as intermediate inputs into the production of other goods and services has laid the groundwork for as-yet unrealized revolutions in practice that will boost labor productivity in consuming sectors above and beyond what one would otherwise expect from such capital deepening.

In 2000, the communications sector of the U.S. economy is in the throes of transformative change, the final impact of which remains difficult at this point definitively to discern. This is true both for industries that produce these services and for industries that use them. This essay offers the reader an explanation of what lies behind the historical series, an explanation that may facilitate attempts to peer ahead. It provides tools for thinking about the nature of convergences that will take place among communications modalities traditionally quite distinct, about what will change unrecognizably in the next decades, and about what will not. Some of the most recent developments mentioned here are not yet adequately chronicled in the accompanying historical series, but they almost certainly will be in future editons of this work.

Postal Service

We begin with the oldest public networks facilitating point-to-point communications. Prior to the development of sophisticated optical and electromagnetic telegraphs in the nineteenth century, detailed messages could move only on written media, and at speeds over land no faster than the fastest horse and over water no faster than the fastest sailing ship. Public-switched postal networks did exist in the classical world and were nowhere more highly developed than in the Roman Empire. But in the Middle Ages, such systems, along with Roman roads, fell into desuetude. Religious, state, and commercial organizations maintained private communication lines, but public systems appeared again only in the seventeenth century. Britain, for example, established a government postal service open to the public in 1635.

In postal matters, as in many other respects, colonial America took its lead from England. British and, more generally, European practice was based on the principle that the post office should be a revenue-generating institution. Like import tariffs, revenues were intended not only to cover expenses but also to help defray costs of other government activities. In 1691, the Crown granted Thomas Neale a franchise for a North American Post Office. In 1707, the Crown reacquired the franchise from Neale's successors, and from then until 1775, colonial mail service, like colonial defense, was provided by a branch of the British government, in this case, the General Post Office in London. Some colonial actions, such as that of the Massachusetts Bay legislature in 1639 designating a particular Boston tavern as a mail drop, affected postal service, but most of the shots were effectively called in the mother country.

The prerevolutionary economy, even more than was the case in England, was oriented externally. Water has always been the preferred means of moving goods in economies with poor internal transport because its low friction enables transit with less expense of energy than is associated with haulage of goods or people over land. Most seventeenth- and eighteenth-century written communication, like most merchandise trade in those centuries, moved over water between England, continental Europe, the Caribbean, and the colonies or, for intercolonial communication, on ships pursuing the coastal trade. The remainder traveled on a limited network of generally north–south post roads.

In 1775, as the American Revolution began, Benjamin Franklin took over operation of the system, but for the next seventeen years, it continued within largely colonial parameters. In 1789, the country had seventy-five post offices, almost all concentrated in coastal port cities, and linked by 1,875 miles of post roads. Service was virtually absent from the hinterland, and no explicit subsidies encouraged the circulation of printed matter.

With independence came increased demands for internal improvements, not only in the movement of goods and people but also in transfers of cash and written and printed materials. Article 1, Section 8 of the U.S. Constitution gave the federal government a monopoly on the movement of mail and gave Congress the right to establish post offices and post roads.

The Post Office Act of 1792 established a foundation for a system that dominated American internal communication for half a century. It led to the construction of a network that, within a few decades, annually carried hundreds of thousands of newspapers and periodicals, millions of dollars of cash payments, and a more limited number of first-class letters. In doing so, it played an important and often underappreciated role in nation building and commercial development within the young republic.

The Act formalized the preexisting exchange privilege allowing printers to swap ownership of newspapers freely, and it provided heavily subsidized carriage of newspapers from printers to subscribing households. These subsidies were a boon to the news industry but came at the expense of merchants, particularly in the Northeast, who had to pay higher rates for first-class service. In the early nineteenth century, the costs of producing a newspaper dropped owing both to breakthroughs in the making of paper from wood pulp (the Fourdrinier process, the basis of most modern papermaking, was invented in 1803) and to progress in putting ink on paper, in particular, the steam-powered rotary press (1814). These complemented cheap carriage and extension of the postal service into the hinterland to create, in the first half of the nineteenth century, a national market for newspapers and the information they transmitted (John 1995, p. 37). As Table Dg253–266 shows, by 1850 there were more than 250 daily newspapers publishing in America.

This national market preceded by several decades the establishment of similar markets in other commodities. Not until the 1850s does one begin to see national distribution of hard and soft goods, and not until the 1880s, with the availability of the railroad, the telegraph, and the refrigerator car, could perishables be marketed across the nation. News, like fish, gets stale quickly, but unlike fish it is the one perishable that does not require refrigeration. Because of this feature and the fact that it had a high value in comparison to the weight of its medium, it could easily be transported in a post rider's saddlebag.

The success of the antebellum American postal system was an administrative achievement, not one enabled fundamentally by new technology. Relying for actual carriage on contracts with stagecoach operators and post riders, and railroads when they became operational in the 1830s, it consisted of a sophisticated hub-and-spoke distribution system operated by an extensive three-level bureaucracy. Top-level management operated out of Washington. Second-level managers ran regional sorting stations. At the third level were thousands of local part-time postmasters. In 1831, the Postal Service employed more than three out of four civilian federal workers, and its corps of 8,764 postmasters was larger than that of the federal army of 6,332 (John 1995, p. 3). Not until the 1870s, with the Pennsylvania Railroad, would a private business enterprise exceed the Postal Service in employment.

Positions of postmaster in the United States were valued because of their steady salaries and the prestige associated with federal service. In 1835, for example, after serving in the state militia, Abraham Lincoln secured appointment as postmaster of New Salem, Illinois. In the antebellum United States, the local post office was the principal, if not the only, manifestation of the reach of the federal government into most Americans' lives.

In the first half of the nineteenth century, the United States became the first and, to that point, only country to abandon the view of the Postal Service as a cash cow for defraying other government expenses. As Congress eagerly designated new routes and offices, revenues that might otherwise have been surplus were effectively plowed back into the system, resulting in a rapid extension of service to all corners of the hinterland. In 1828, the United States had seventy-four post offices for every 100,000 inhabitants, versus seventeen in Great Britain and four in France. Canadian postal service was so poor that merchants routed interprovincial communication through the U.S. system (John 1995, p. 5).

As the data suggest, offices were built ahead of demand in a way sometimes criticized as wasteful. The fact that Congress, rather than the Postmaster General, determined new routes opened the process to political jockeying among communities vying for access to communications links with the outside world. But in conjunction with the subsidy for newspaper carriage, the resulting network enabled white males, regardless of their location, to participate actively in the political life of the nation. The character and extent of the service surely contributed to the high participation rates among eligible voters characteristic of the first century of U.S. history. Alexis de Tocqueville arrived in America expecting to find an information gradient as he journeyed away from the coast. In this he was disappointed, finding the rural backwoodsman in Michigan as well informed as his fellow citizen in coastal cities.

The history of the Postal Service makes its imprint in a number of ways in *Historical Statistics of the United States*. Series Dg181 provides the longest continuous series in this chapter, that for the number of post offices in the United States (see also Figure Dg-A). Beginning with the 75 reported for 1789, the number grew steadily, with a brief hiccup during the Civil War, until 1901, when it peaked at 76,945. Over the next century, the number of offices fell steadily (the series does not include branches and contract offices). The United States now has approximately the same number of post

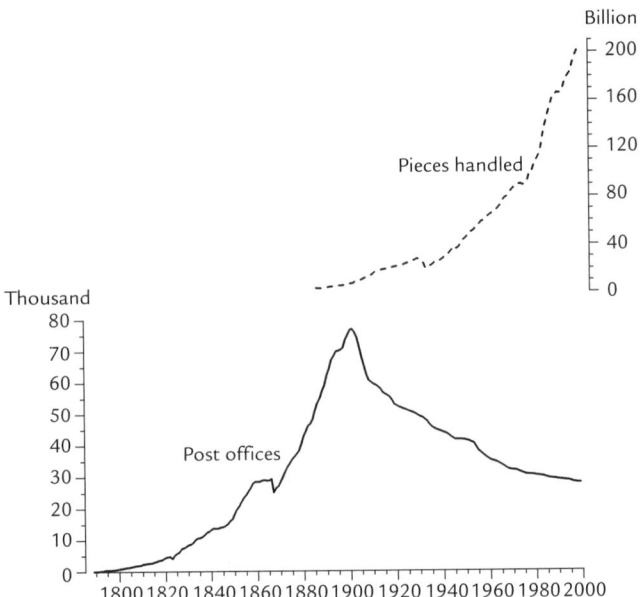

FIGURE Dg-A   Postal Service – post offices and pieces handled: 1789–1999

Sources
Series Dg181 and Dg189.

offices it had during the Civil War, although, of course, they service a much larger population and land area.

Series Dg182–184, showing revenues, expenses, and their difference, demonstrate that although the system has sometimes earned surpluses, it has also incurred deficits and has not, over time, been a source of revenue for the general government. The American polity has not insisted on surpluses and has been willing to tolerate deficits in its postal service, but not on a persisting basis. The Postal Reorganization Act of 1970, triggered by deficits, transformed the Post Office – between 1829 and 1971 a cabinet-level department of the federal government – into a governmentally owned corporation, the U.S. Postal Service (USPS). Taking the longer view, however, the divisive political issue in the United States has been less the degree of subsidization the Postal Service should provide to other government operations and more the question of the nature of cross subsidizations among different classes of mail.

In the first half of the nineteenth century, the politics of subsidizing newspaper delivery were complex. On balance, the printing industry clearly enjoyed the subsidy, but Western printers resisted calls to make carriage entirely free, fearing that if this were done, they would be swept out of business by cheaper imports from the East. Low rates for newspapers, defrayed by high first-class rates, engendered considerable griping among merchants, ministers, and others who felt the need to correspond. Although one could prepay postage in the first half of the century, most postal charges were paid by the recipient, thus giving the service an incentive to see that mail was delivered. But many complained bitterly about their correspondents who sent them letters that were not worth the reading, let alone the postage due.

Although the federal government enjoyed a legal monopoly on mail delivery, it did not move aggressively to prohibit private competitors, with the exception of the heavily trafficked and lucrative northeastern routes. When private mail service threatened the government enterprise there, it defended its monopoly in court. This was paired with a dramatic lowering of first-class rates reflected in the tariffs of 1845 and 1851 (Table Dg209) (John 1995, p. 48). Prior to 1845, mailing a first-class letter was an expensive proposition, costing the equivalent of half a day's wages for a laboring man (John 1995, p. 159).

Postage stamps, first introduced in 1847, represented a major reduction in the transaction costs associated with prepayment. Mandatory prepayment through the use of stamps took effect in 1855. Series Dg186, showing the number of individual stamps sold, has its first entry for 1848, grows very rapidly following the Postal Act of 1851 and its further reduction in first-class rates, and then more than doubles again between 1854 and 1856 as a consequence of the introduction of the prepayment requirement. The 1855 change is also evident in the disappearance of the prepaid category in the 1855 tariffs; see Table Dg209.

The nominal charge for mailing a half-ounce letter anywhere in the continental United States remained unchanged at 3 cents from 1851 to 1958. The 1845 and 1851 acts, which reduced the cost of postage as a deterrent to first-class letter writing, also enabled merchants as well as newspaper publishers to take advantage of low rates. The consequence was the advent of junk mail. Prior to these rate changes, it was relatively inexpensive to make political mass mailings, provided they were classed as newspapers, as illustrated by the abolitionist attempt in 1835 to mail thousands of antislavery papers to Southern slaveholders. But widespread commercial narrowcasting through the mails was not cost effective until the new midcentury rate schedules took effect.

Series Dg188 chronicles sales of the once-ubiquitous stamped postal cards, beginning in 1873. Postal cards appeared first in Austria in 1869 and were initially used in the United States for commercial advertisement. But in 1898, a new law allowed short personal messages to be included on half of the back of a card. Postcards introduced a new style of communication to America: shorter, because the message had to fit on half of one side of the card, and somewhat less intimate, since the message could be read by others.

Although billions of stamps continue to be sold, stamped envelopes, first issued in 1873, represent a product whose time has come and gone (series Dg187). Metered postage, pioneered by the Pitney-Bowes company, first became available in 1920, and in the late 1990s, the USPS approved systems using personal computers and printers that provide similar service. Nevertheless, the failure of stamped envelopes and metered postage to achieve widespread consumer acceptance suggests that the convenience of postage stamps, a nineteenth-century innovation, will likely assure a continued market for them into the future.

The structure of the U.S. postal system bears many similarities to a telecommunications network. The local post office can be thought of as analogous to a local exchange. The system is a switched network because, as is true in the phone system, routes do not directly connect all possible customers. Local depots segregate long distance mail and that remaining within the exchange. Long distance mail is sent, usually by truck, to a limited number of centralized switching (sorting) stations, where it may be sent on to another regional sorting station or to its final destination, usually through contract with commercial air carriers. For local delivery, long distance mail is blended with interexchange communication and distributed over the counter, through post office boxes, or, eventually, through local delivery service. Similarities between postal and telecommunications networks arise because they must address somewhat similar logistical issues and because, in their formative years, both telegraph and telephone systems drew heavily for experienced top management from the Post Office.

Whereas telephone communication occurs synchronously, mail interchange does not. Thus, although reducing delivery time is, for obvious reasons, not a pressing issue in telephony, it has for most of the past two centuries been a central and distinguishing priority of the U.S. postal system. A major innovation in the second half of the nineteenth century, beginning in 1862, was the use of railway cars as mobile sorting rooms. Prior to assuming the presidency of the Bell System for the first of his two terms, Theodore Vail directed this aspect of postal operation. With the growth of the road network in the twentieth century and the reduction in rail service, sorting stations on large trucks performed analogous functions between 1941 and 1969. In 1977, the last railroad post office, between New York and Washington, D.C., ceased operation. Continued reductions in the costs of air transport have returned sorting operations exclusively to stationary offices, as was true when the system began. The first cross-continent airmail moved in 1920; regular service began in 1924, and in 1929, data from this service begin to appear in our statistical tables (series Dg202–204). In 1977, airmail disappeared as a separate rate category for domestic service.

Table Dg190–208 provides a more detailed breakdown of revenues, expenses, and volume by class of mail. More recent data are from a mimeographed publication known from 1969 to 1983 as "Revenue and Cost Analysis" and from 1984 until the present as "Cost and Revenue Analysis." The data on employment can be compared with interest to that in other sectors of communications: In the 1990s, the number of direct employees in the Postal Service was in the same range as the number of employees in the telephone sector (see series Dg3 and Dg208).

The 1970 Postal Reorganization Act gave the system the right to raise its own capital for modernization, and the USPS received its last direct subsidy from Congress in 1982. The system continues to struggle to reduce the costs of routing heterogeneous physical media, principally through an aggressive automation program and incentives for large mailers to barcode and sort materials before drop-off. ZIP codes, introduced in 1963 (ZIP stands for Zone Improvement Plan), and "ZIP code plus four," introduced in 1983, combined with new automatic equipment, have been tools in the effort.

Sorting begins with manual segregation, in which packages, flats, and overseas envelopes are separated from envelopes that can be processed by machine. The latter are aligned (faced) by sensing machines that search for stamps and flip or rotate letters in preparation for automatic cancellation. For correspondence lacking bar codes, multiline optical character readers (MLOCRs) translate addresses into sprayed bar codes in order to facilitate subsequent sorting by automatic equipment. The post office is perceived as low tech, but character recognition software has now improved sufficiently that it can automatically barcode over 30 percent of handwritten letters. Where the machine cannot decipher a handwritten address, the MLOCR signals a remote location where, viewing the letter via video camera, an employee enters the correct addressing information, sent back electronically for bar coding.[1] Sorters read bar codes (evident, upon examination, on most mail received) to separate long distance from local traffic and to sort material into

---

[1] See the Internet site of the U.S. Postal Service for more information.

correct order for local delivery. At the end of the twentieth century, only 8 percent of letter mail received daily was processed manually, but it consumed half of all the labor costs associated with mail processing.

The postal system is distinguished within our communications sector by the degree to which the implementation of labor-saving technological change dominates the agenda. Automation remains key to cost control and an arena of both progress and challenge. Labor-saving technology aims ultimately to eliminate manual sorting, as telephone switches have eliminated manual switchers (telephone operators). How far the USPS will succeed in this effort without imposing greater uniformity on media and addresses remains uncertain.

Major increases in throughput speed, which, as we have seen, can effectively widen a given physical communication channel and thus save capital, have been much less a priority than in earlier decades, and in some respects, there has been retrogression. The situation with respect to capital costs in particular will worsen if the growth of electronic mail begins seriously to cut into printed correspondence. Series Dg189 suggests that throughout the 1990s, the growth of the Internet did not reduce our propensity to send written or printed communications any more than it has yet reduced the demand for paper in offices (see also Figure Dg-A). As this is written, however, there is evidence that the demand for first-class mail service may be declining, creating an incipient fiscal crisis for the Postal Service. Other uncertainties surround how the USPS express mail and package delivery service will fare in continued competition with private carriers, such as United Parcel Service and Federal Express.

Newspapers and Books

In contrast with the industries covered in the first two groups of tables of this chapter, those in the latter two groups employ paper as a medium for storing information, and none has depended fundamentally on advances in electrical engineering. This is true for newspapers and books as well as the Postal Service. These services and media were familiar to our Founding Fathers in a way none of those chronicled in the first two groups of tables would have been.

This is not to say that for two centuries, communication based on moving paper has been technologically stagnant. It is simply that the changes here have been less revolutionary. In the newspaper industry, reductions in the cost of making paper from wood pulp continued throughout the nineteenth century, with particular advance associated with improvements in mechanical grinding and the use of sulfites in the late 1860s. The Hoe press, an advanced steam-powered rotary press that printed on both sides of a web or roll of paper, was introduced in 1867 (Lacy 1996, p. 65). The late 1880s saw the introduction of the Mergenthaler linotype and Lanson monotype machines, which dramatically reduced the cost of typesetting. Together, these defined a technological paradigm for newspaper production that endured for a hundred years, until the introduction of computer-based typesetting in the 1980s.

As noted, the first daily newspaper in the United States began operation in 1783. By 1800, 24 papers published daily, with a combined circulation of about 50,000 (Lacy 1996, p. 65). These numbers can be compared with the first information from census data, for 1850, which shows 254 dailies with circulation of 750,000, with circulation increasing to 3.5 million in 1880 and over 15 million in 1900 (series Dg256; see also Figure Dg-B). Newsprint dropped in price from about 12 cents a pound in the 1880s to 3 cents a

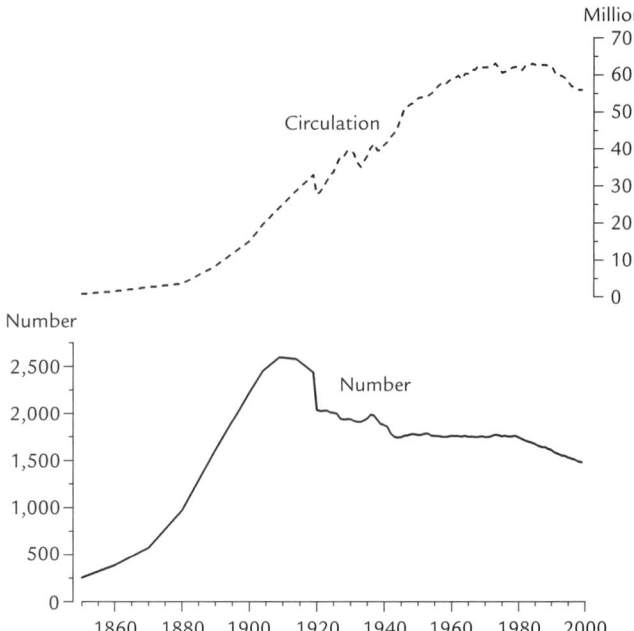

FIGURE Dg-B   Daily newspapers – number and circulation: 1850–1999

Sources
1850–1919: series Dg255–256. 1920–1999: series Dg267–268.

pound by 1900, and a daily paper at the date cost only 1 or 2 cents, barely covering the cost of paper. Its distribution was enabled by that burgeoning role of advertising.

Local newspaper production was further facilitated by postal legislation of 1879 that allowed free distribution within the county in which the newspapers were produced. The Act also provided, for the first time, a low national rate for shipping magazines, enabling periodicals to exploit the expanding rail network and develop a national audience. National magazines helped unify the country culturally and politically in a way analogous to the distribution of newspapers by subsidized carriage in the first half of the century (Lacy 1996, p. 72). The number of magazines in the United States, about 40 in 1800, grew to more than 5,500 by 1900. Series Dg280 picks up the story in 1935, showing at that date 6,546 periodicals.

Many of the technical changes affecting newspaper publishing have, along with improved binding technology, influenced the mechanics of book production. Table Dg225–252 provides data on the total number of books published and, after 1950, their topical distribution. Series Dg225, which includes both new books and new editions, confirms that reports of the demise of the printed book are as yet premature. Note that these totals do not include mass market paperbacks or imports, which are reported, respectively, in series Dg251–252. Thus, to calculate, for example, the share of new fiction books among the total new books published (excluding mass market paperbacks and new editions), one would divide series Dg233 by series Dg227, yielding about 8.5 percent for 1996.

It is remarkable that the publication of new books in the area of economics and sociology has grown so rapidly that it now comprises the largest single category here enumerated, more than 16.7 percent of the total in 1996, up from 11.8 percent in 1982, the first year for which comparable data are available (series Dg247). Perhaps a fifth of book industry sales derive from general fiction and nonfiction, what are called trade books. The remainder, and the vast bulk of the business, consists of textbooks and business, scientific, and technical publications.

Telegraph

So long as communication beyond the reach of face-to-face interchange was limited to the physical movement of written or printed media, its speed of transmission had binding constraints. With the possible exception of transport by carrier pigeons, it could not move faster than could people or goods. Most early efforts to break out of these barriers involved visual or optical telegraphy; for example, smoke signals mirrors to reflect the sun's light, or light beacons used at night. These primitive telegraphic technologies were the equivalent of narrow pipes: even under good conditions, you could not push much data through them. Developments in both hardware and software were necessary before visual telegraphy could make a major leap forward at the end of the eighteenth century.

Advances in optics in the seventeenth century had made it practical to produce relatively inexpensive telescopes, which significantly expanded the potential reach of semaphoric systems. The most successful of these systems was developed in France by Claude Chappe, with viable long distance service beginning in 1793. Chappe positioned stations at high points on mountains, tall buildings such as church belfries, or specially constructed towers. At each station, two men pointed telescopes in opposite directions. Operators composed signals on a Z-shaped semaphore, with each of the three segments independently rotatable throughout a 360-degree arc by means of hand controls located below. For signaling purposes, each arm could appear in one of eight orientations 45 degrees apart. The system used a basic transmission code of ninety-eight elements, meaning that each signal communicated about 6.5 ($\log_2 98$) binary digits, or bits of information. Carefully worked-out codebooks used these signals to maximum effect, making it possible in good weather, in conjunction with the hardware, to send a detailed message from Paris to Marseilles in about an hour and a half.

Napoleon used Chappe technology to extend his communications reach into French-controlled territory in the Low Countries, Germany, and Italy. But it was after peace in 1815 that the system reached its fullest development. At its peak, a network of 5,000 kilometers, with most of the lines radiating from Paris, made France the world leader in advanced communications technology (Field 1994). The Chappe system was not the only optical telegraph system, but it was far and away the most successful. During the Napoleonic wars, England employed the six-shutter Murray system to link London and Portsmouth, but the line was disbanded with peace. In the United States, semaphores operating over shorter distances were common in commercial cities like New York and San Francisco, where they announced the impending arrival of merchant ships. Their legacy is evident in place-names such as Telegraph Hill.

In the first part of the nineteenth century, Chappe technology was the acknowledged leader in long distance transmission, and its suitability for a coastal line linking New York to New Orleans was discussed in the United States as early as 1807. The project resurfaced periodically for several decades, with the most serious proposal for funding, endorsed by Andrew Jackson's Postmaster General Amos Kendall, put before Congress in 1836.

This proposal was vigorously opposed by Samuel F. B. Morse, a professor of painting and sculpture from New York. Morse had recently patented a new telegraphic technology exploiting electromagnetic principles, and he wanted Congress to support it instead. Although a practical and proven technology, Chappe telegraphs did have serious limitations. In addition to narrow bandwidth, they were always at the mercy of the weather (including fog and heat inversions) and never operated successfully at night. The advent of railroads offered some improvement in the speed at which information could reliably move independently of the weather or time of day, but far less than what people were prepared to pay for, especially in the markets for news and financial data.

Seventeenth-century scientific advance had also led to improved understanding of electricity and magnetism, providing foundations for a different solution to the problem of long distance communication, one that relied on fast movement of electrons along wires, as opposed to photons between eyeballs. Absent early nineteenth-century progress in producing and storing low-voltage high-amperage electricity, however, proposed implementations of electric telegraphy could not work over any but the shortest distances.

Prior to the beginning of the nineteenth century, scientists could store electrons by accumulating static electricity in a Leyden jar, a primitive capacitor. Such a power source appeared to be promising as a basis for long distance telegraphy. In 1753, Charles Morrison proposed running twenty-six wires from source to destination. In front of each he would hang a piece of paper suspended from a string, one corresponding to each letter of the alphabet. As he sent static electric charges down particular wires, they would cause displacement of the appropriate paper scrap (pith balls, in later proposals). Similar explorations used electric charges sent over wires to generate gas bubbles through chemical reactions in tubes of liquid. The main problem with all these proposals was reliance on static electricity: high voltage, low amperage, and subject to severe attenuation in signal strength, particularly in the presence of atmospheric disturbances.

Morse's ability to develop a commercially successful telegraph was predicated on Alessandro Volta's advances in battery technology (1800), which made available, as an alternative to static electricity, a source of lower-voltage, higher-amperage current whose signal strength was more reliable over distance. Morse also benefited from Hans Christian Ørsted's discovery in 1820 that electric current would deflect a magnetized needle. Charles Wheatstone's telegraph, developed in England and patented in 1837, exploited this discovery directly. Morse's device required the utilization of this knowledge to make an electromagnet. Building on Ørsted's work, Michael Faraday and Joseph Henry, of whom more later, provided Morse with this component.

Having contributed to the demise of the proposal for a U.S. long distance visual telegraph, Morse finally wrangled $30,000 from Congress in 1843 to build a demonstration line from Baltimore to Washington using his technology. Even though visual telegraphy was a well-understood technology, experimentation in electric telegraphy had about it a questionable penumbra owing to its attraction of a large number of charlatans and quacks. The bill providing for Morse's subvention passed in the House by the small margin of eighty-nine to eighty-three, with seventy abstentions, in a debate marked by sarcastic references to, and half serious proposals to fund, experiments in mesmerism (Standage 1998, p. 46).

The apparatus in this line used Joseph Henry's electromagnet, when activated by a transmitted electric signal, to move an armature holding a pencil, thus intermittently marking a paper-covered drum rotated by a clock mechanism. On May 24, 1844, Morse transmitted his first message, "What hath God wrought?" This question, which might better have been posed when the telephone was invented thirty-two years later, was rhetorical. The American public understood immediately what Morse had wrought, and to what uses it could be put, even if the initial financial success of the Washington-to-Baltimore line was disappointing (this was one consideration leading the U.S. government to spurn Morse's offer to sell the system to it).

Nevertheless, even before Morse's successful demonstration, telegraphs (irrespective of their mode or prospective mode of operation) were considered hot technologies in the United States. This is reflected not only in the early interest in importing Chappe systems but also in the forty-five newspapers that had by 1820 incorporated the word in their titles (John 1995, p. 87). Morse's achievement thus took place within a receptive political and commercial environment.

The next two decades were a period of rapid and at times chaotic growth of the telegraph industry under private ownership (Thompson 1947). The U.S. telegraph system grew rapidly and alongside of the railroad, with which it often shared rights-of-way and to which it provided logistical support. In this period, systems were set up based not only on the Morse patents but also on those of Alexander Bain, Royal E. House, and David E. Hughes. Some conservative investors stayed away because of fears that the government might change its mind again and step in to build or acquire its own system. Many of the fledgling firms faced difficulties raising cash, and thus acquired assets of other companies using stock, laying the foundation for later complaints about "watering." After a decade of growth involving fragmented systems using sometimes incompatible technology, consolidation began. The New York and Mississippi Valley Printing Telegraph Company brought together a number of smaller systems under its leadership, emerging in 1856 as the Western Union Telegraph Company, data from which appear prominently in our tables. Eventually, in a process culminating in 1866, shakeout occurred with consolidation under one firm.

In 1861, eight years prior to the driving of the golden stake at Promontory Point, the company linked San Francisco by telegraph to the East, receiving $400,000 from Congress and subventions from the California legislature to encourage the investment (Goldin 1947). And after a three-month abortive experiment with a poorly insulated cable in 1858, the United States and Europe were permanently linked by telegraph in 1866. Transmission speeds were initially low, limited to 2 words per minute (wpm), but rose to 20 wpm in 1870 with an improved receiving mechanism.

Congress watched the consolidation of the telegraph industry with growing unease. Whether or not Western Union was a *natural* monopoly, there is little question that it exercised monopoly power over national telegraphic traffic for at least two decades. This period extends roughly from 1866 to 1885, when the Postal Telegraph Company (subsequently part of the International Telephone and Telegraph Company, or ITT)[2] entered as a competitor, and the tele-

phone arguably began to serve as a competing technology within some heavily trafficked intercity routes, particularly the Boston–New York–Philadelphia corridor.

Between 1870 and 1896, at least twelve proposals emerged from congressional committees for government participation in the sector. The U.S. Postal Service run by the federal government, as well as European systems in which both post and telegraph systems were government owned, provided examples that fueled political pressure for nationalization, for government entry as a competitor, or for government subsidy of a competitor.

Complaints levied against Western Union echoed many of those raised against railroads at the time. High rates, of course, figured heavily. Average message rates in the United States fell from $1.09 in 1867 to $ .30 in 1898, although the economy-wide deflation over this period would have accounted for about half of this decline. Whatever one's views of the legitimacy of Western Union's rate structure, however, there is consensus that as a result of it, much more so than was true in Europe, the telegraph in the United States remained predominantly an instrument of commercial rather than individual household use.

Other complaints included poor service (errors of transmission, delayed messages, and violation of secrecy); the ability of stock speculators to obtain preferential access to the telegraph; free telegraph privileges granted to public officials to influence their votes; discrimination among regions and communities with respect to rates; long-term contracts with press agencies, such as the Associated Press, and with hotels and railroads that created barriers to entry for potential new entrants; and unfairness to workers (long hours, low wages, poor conditions) and to stockholders (stock watering). Perhaps the most damning complaint was the lack of technological progress, particularly in comparison with some of the European systems.

In addition to better insulation for undersea cables, advances in telegraphy in the second half of the nineteenth century included new input and output devices, as well as innovations that saved capital by increasing the rate of data flow. Morse's initial line was a single uninsulated wire, with the return part of the circuit through the ground, an implementation that remained standard throughout much of the remainder of the century. Underwater, however, cables had to be insulated; water (particularly salt water), unlike air, conducts electricity relatively easily. Gutta-percha, a nonstretch latex covering perfected in 1847, reliably insulated the first England-to-France telegraph cable in 1851. Gutta-percha and rubber remained the preferred insulation for undersea cables until 1947, when they were replaced by polyethylene sheathing.

In 1856, Morse replaced the marking device with a sounder, with telegraph operators decoding the sequences of sounds directly into letters, a system that unexpectedly speeded up the service. With the introduction of the sounder, U.S. telegraphic technology completed a framework that would remain in place throughout the remainder of the century, although there was some technological advance in peripheral equipment. Thomas Edison, who began his career in telegraphy, made his first major contributions with an improved stock ticker, a specialized printing telegraph used for broadcast that formed half of the telecommunications backbone of a national stock-trading technology that endured for the better part of a century, from the 1870s to the late 1960s (Field 1998). The other half of the system consisted of leased wires from brokerage houses across the country to New York for the transmission of orders and confirmations of execution.

---

[2] Postal Telegraph got its name because of repeated government proposals to strike a deal offering space in post offices for a private telegraph system competitive with Western Union. The deal was never consummated, but Postal Telegraph liked the name, even though the firm was as private an entity as Western Union.

Elsewhere I have described how the telegraph was used to implement capital-saving innovation. In customer industries, it permitted, for example, single-tracked railroad systems, higher rates of fixed capital utilization in manufacturing, and faster rates of inventory turn in wholesale and retail distribution (Field 1992). Capital-saving innovation was also critical in telegraphy.

For a quarter century, all telegraphic communication in the United States was simplex. The default position for a telegraph key was in closed position. Opening the key broke the circuit, alerting stations along a line to an imminent transmission. To interrupt an incoming message for an urgent outgoing transmission, a telegrapher opened his key. All sounders along a line then went dead, and the original transmitter would cease hearing his keystrokes echoed in his sounder. Ceasing transmission, he placed his key in closed position and awaited the incoming, presumably urgent, message. Only one message at a time could be transmitted.

Duplex technology, which enabled messages to be sent in both directions along one wire, originated in Germany and was improved upon in the United States by J. B. Stearns in 1871. In 1874, Thomas Edison patented a quadruplex system that enabled *two* messages to be sent in both directions at the same time.

In the area of multiplexing, considerable credit must also be given to the French engineer Jean-Maurice-Emile Baudot. Baudot brought us into the modern information age not only with a sophisticated time-division multiplexing technology in 1874 but also by developing the first true digital code. The Baudot multiplexing system consisted of a stationary face plate covered with five concentric copper rings, with the plate divided into six sectors, each of which was assigned to an individual user. At any moment of time, each sector of each ring either did or did not have an electric potential applied to it. A rotating armature with electric brushes swept the rings, producing bursts of on or off sequences, which were then demultiplexed at the receiving end by a synchronized device that sent signals to six separate receivers. Baudot's work on time-division multiplexing enabled 90 wpm transmission, and it laid foundations for the engineering triumphs of the late twentieth century that have permitted the rapid development of our ability to expand bandwidth by moving more information through channels in given periods of time. Baudot's work also facilitated the development of the teleprinter and teletypewriter in the twentieth century.

In visual as well as electromagnetic telegraphy, software was as important as hardware in expanding the utility of the systems. Morse code expanded in 1851 to include diacriticals (such as the *accent aigu* or *grave* in French) and became International Morse Code, which survives to this day. Although telegraphic transmission involves sequences of making and breaking a circuit, International Morse is not a true digital code because it involves five rather than two fundamental signals. The dot is the basic unit, with dashes defined as three times the duration of a dot. Dot-length pauses separate elements of a character code, triple-dot pauses separate characters, and seven-dot pauses separate words. Morse code requires skilled telegraph operators acting as coders and decoders. Because of the different lengths of dots and dashes and the different lengths of pauses, automated coding and decoding is cumbersome.

The five-bit Baudot code, patented in 1874, is the first true digital code because it relies almost entirely on sequences of two signals: on or off. With five bits, corresponding initially to the five concentric rings of his multiplexer, thirty-two (2^5) different symbols can easily be transmitted. To expand flexibility of his code, Baudot also pioneered by making two of them escape sequences,

signaling the shift to a different symbol set, such as numbers. Baudot's multiplexing equipment, subsequent advances such as Donald Murray's punch-tape stored-message transmission system (1903), and teletypewriters all used it or a modified version.

Morse's first devices printed code, and the cumbersome House machine, with which they initially competed, could print text directly. With the switch to sounder technology in 1856, however, the United States became conservative compared with Europe in its adoption of printing telegraphs (the exception being the specialized stock ticker). As early as 1855, for example, the American Hughes had invented a practical printing telegraph using a piano-style keyboard. These were used extensively in Europe, but not in the United States.

It was not until well into the twentieth century in the United States that teleprinter technology began to spread beyond its application in the area of finance. In 1915, the Associated Press began switching its sounders to teleprinters for receiving broadcasts "over the wire." The five-bit Baudot code, slightly modified, drove teletypewriters that could both send and receive keyboard or paper-tape input, which could be outputted along with print. Linked teletypewriters in corporate networks with administrative message switching provided the first crude electronic mail service. Paper tapes were used to store and forward messages on switched systems; these networks were known as torn tape systems. Beginning in the 1930s, the Telex and TWX (teletypewriter exchange) services made two-way point-to-point teletypewriter service available to individual businesses (Table Dg22–33).

Teletypewriter service was commercially successful for about fifty years, from the 1930s into the 1980s. TWX was introduced by AT&T in 1932; Telex began in Europe. Western Union brought Telex service to the United States in 1962 and bought TWX from AT&T in 1970 (the two systems could not talk directly to each other). After 1980, the technologies became virtually moribund, at least in the United States, replaced in their functions by fax (facsimile) and email, but their half-century heyday represented an important transitional step in the development of more sophisticated and flexible data transmission equipment, protocols, and peripherals. In 2000, everyone with a networked computer has the equivalent of a teletypewriter on the desktop, but its use has required an expanded basic symbol set, both to control output devices and, for example, to enable the use of both upper- and lowercase letters.

ASCII, the American Standard Code for Information Interchange, was first defined by the American National Standards Institute in 1968 (standard X3.4), and can be thought of as a direct descendant of Baudot with a larger number of basic symbols. Its original implementation was as a seven- rather than a five-bit code, thus enabling 128 (2^7) distinct symbols. With escape codes for shifting into different character sets, ASCII has subsequently been made even more flexible.

Critical to the ability of networks to handle increased quantities of digital data at faster speeds have been innovations in error-checking technology. An important example is the invention of the parity bit in 1948 by Richard Hamming of Bell Labs. In transmitting seven-bit ASCII code, for example, an eighth bit can be added such that the sum of all eight is either even or odd (one or the other convention must be selected). If even parity has been chosen, then a sequence of eight bits with an odd number of 1s indicates an error, and a request can automatically be made to retransmit the byte.

Data-compression algorithms, along with error-checking technology, have been critical in increasing the ability of given data "pipes" rapidly and reliably to move large quantities of information. Data compression, for example, makes it much easier to send large quantities of data, particularly graphics, over phone wires. A one-page fax transmission, for example, must provide data on more than 1.5 million pixels. Much of a printed page, however, consists of white space. By using run-time codes, one transmits the number of sequential white spaces, instead of using a code for each individual space. Transmission times are dramatically reduced, and the same physical infrastructure is capable of much larger flows of data. Both error-detection and data-compression software are capital-saving techniques: they enable more data to be reliably pushed through a given pipe in a given period of time.

The tables presented here encompass the rapid rise, maturation, and eclipse of telegraph technology, the first true electronic transmission medium. Railroad and telegraph service developed symbiotically in the nineteenth century. But the nature of the demands for both changed in the twentieth, and with competing technologies, in particular the telephone, the economic rationales for joint production faded. Series Dg20 identifies the string of losses suffered by Western Union beginning in 1932 and extending through 1952.

In 1949, the company ended its long-standing agreements with railroads, giving up all claims to ownership of poles, wire, or equipment. But whereas railroads survived competition from automobiles, trucks, and airplanes by specializing in the movement of bulk freight, Western Union was never quite able to reinvent itself or find a sustainable market niche. It limped along for another four decades, trying a number of new business plans, including specialization in the now moribund teletypewriter technology.

Peak message traffic is recorded for the last year of the Second World War, but series Dg8, Dg12, and Dg14 chart the subsequent slide in messages handled, number of telegraph offices, and employees thereafter. Figure Dg-C paints a similar picture. In 1988, the Western Union Telegraph company sold off its international

private-line business to a Swiss company, its Westar satellite to GM Hughes Electronics, and its business services group (for example, teletypewriters) to AT&T. Subsequently the Western Union corporation focused almost exclusively on money transfers, its original businesses eclipsed by rapidly changing technologies. But although the telegraph industry is effectively dead, its spirit lives on in the digitized information flows used for long-distance telephony and in the packet-switched Internet.

Telephone

The telegraph made it possible to transmit signals at close to the speed of light. In that sense it, rather than the telephone, marks the entry into the modern communications age. The main use of the telegraph was for long distance communication, a market in which, throughout the first decades of the twentieth century, the telephone effectively offered no competition. The telephone's initial success lay in satisfying a demand, then only latent, for convenient local communication. Because of the different nature of the service it provided, and because its use did not require the assistance of a skilled operator, telephone stations were installed in individual households and businesses, a rare event in telegraphy. (A telephone station is an installation capable of receiving and transmitting voice. Thus, a connected handset is a telephone station, and charges for calls without operator assistance are referred to as station-to-station rates.) As a consequence, the telephone gave rise to a range of advances in areas, such as switching and signaling, that eventually revolutionized and led to the convergence of technologies for transmitting data and voice.

Both Elisha Gray and Alexander Graham Bell were searching in the 1870s for capital-saving procedures that could move more than one message simultaneously over a single wire. Their experiments with harmonic telegraphs represented early attempts at frequency-division multiplexing. The idea underlying a harmonic telegraph was to use different tones to transmit different message streams at the same time, demultiplexing at the receiving end. The idea was a good one, although it could not then be practically implemented, and it was in multiplexing that astute investors saw the potential for big returns. Bell's financial backer and future father-in-law, George Hubbard, counseled him against working on a machine for voice transmission, "which would never be more than a scientific toy," and urged him to continue research on the harmonic telegraph, which, if successful, would "make him a millionaire" (Casson 1910, p. 25).

Bell's patent application described an improvement in telegraphy, but in fact the electronic foundations of telephony were different. The essence of Bell's innovation was the principle of transmitting voice over a *continuously completed* circuit, with fluctuations in sound waves generating corresponding fluctuations in direct current as a result of changing resistance in a medium that was produced as speech caused a diaphragm to vibrate.

Gray, a distinguished engineer whose telegraphic equipment firm Gray and Barton became Western Electric when brought under the control of Western Union, experimented with metal reeds tuned to specific frequencies that, when vibrated, induced fluctuating current in coils. The current, when transmitted to a similarly designed receiver, could make similarly tuned reeds vibrate. In 1874, he showed that a steel diaphragm placed in front of an electromagnetic coil (a forerunner of a loudspeaker) could reproduce any of the tones, but he was unable at the time to figure out a way to design a similarly flexible transmitter.

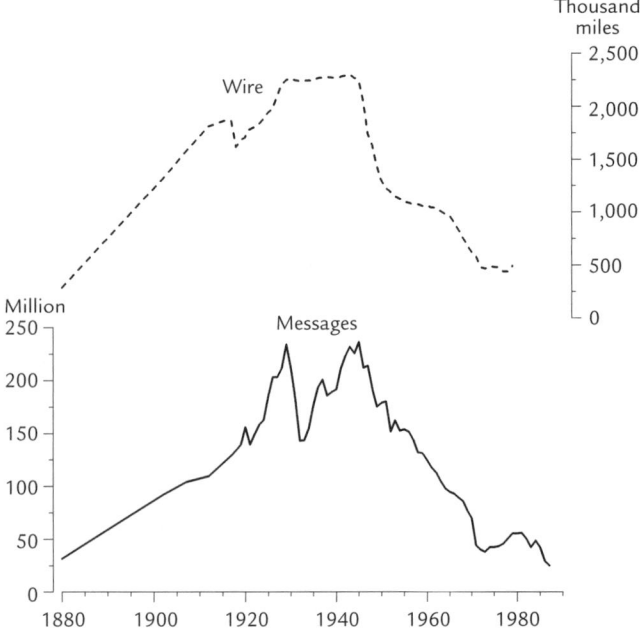

FIGURE Dg-C   Domestic telegraph industry – messages handled and miles of wire: 1880–1987

Sources
Series Dg8 and Dg10.

Bell also experimented with musical or multiple telegraphs. His breakthrough, which led to a device for transmitting speech, was in conceiving of the use of a membrane for transmission as well as reception, and it was on this basis that he filed a patent application for a telegraph and telephone system on February 14, 1876, just hours before Gray filed his intention (caveat) to patent similar devices.

Gray's caveat described a transmitter that attached a membrane to a metal rod inserted in a metal cup containing acid. Electric current from a battery flowed between the cup and rod, and variations in the distance separating them, as the diaphragm vibrated in the presence of speech, caused variations in resistance and, consequently, current flow. Bell used a similar mechanism three weeks later, when, spilling some acid on himself, he asked his assistant, Thomas Watson, to come to his assistance. March 10, 1876, marks the first successful telephonic voice transmission.

Bell took a selection of his apparatus to the centennial exposition in Philadelphia in the same year. Exhibited in a back corner amidst electric light bulbs, Gray's musical telegraph, and 60-wpm printing telegraphs from Western Union, Bell's creation, at first ignored, eventually became the hit of the exposition, admired by such pioneers as Joseph Henry and William Thomson – later Lord Kelvin – the chief engineer of the Atlantic cable. The public demonstrations in Philadelphia, which dispensed with both beaker and battery, showed a diaphragm attached to a magnet within an electric coil (magneto) that, in the presence of speech, induced current flows used to reproduce the sounds at the receiving end.

In spite of the favorable reception from scientific notables in Philadelphia, the telephone's reception by the public can charitably be described as tepid. Indeed, the press heaped ridicule on the scientific toy or, in some cases, branded it an outright hoax. Bell persevered with further tests, with simplex communication demonstrated over distance in Ontario in August 1876, and the first duplex (two-way) communication in October. May 1877 saw the first commercial application of the system, for a burglar alarm business in Boston. Bell's advertisements at this time stressed three advantages over telegraphy: (1) no skilled operator was required; (2) one could transmit 100–200 wpm versus 15–20 wpm using a Morse sounder; and (3) it required no battery. Bell's early telephones all used magnetos for transmission and did not require battery power until 1882.

With patents as its only capital, Bell, Hubbard, and Thomas Sanders organized the first Bell telephone company, giving themselves each 30 percent of the shares and Watson 10 percent. As Herbert Casson put it, "The four men had at this time an absolute monopoly of the telephone business, and everybody else was quite willing that they should have it." In the fall of 1876, Bell's financial backers, fearful about the commercial potential of their device and their ability to defend the patent, offered to sell their rights to Western Union for $100,000. The chief executive officer of Western Union turned them down: "What use," he said famously, "could this company make of an electrical toy?" (Casson 1910, p. 59). Western Union did not foresee the demand for communication over local networks, even though some telegraphic implementations in New York were evolving in that direction.

Western Union changed course rapidly when employees at one of its subsidiaries, the Gold and Stock Exchange Company, ripped out some of their printing telegraphs and replaced them with telephones. Western Union responded as might the software giant from Redmond, Washington, quickly organizing the American Speaking

Telephone Company, capitalized at $300,000, with three well-known and competent engineers, including Edison and Gray, as technical staff. Western Union ignored the Bell patent, assuming that it would triumph in court on the basis of Gray's caveat, and introduced, on its own, important technical advances, in particular, Edison's carbon transmitter.

Edison had exploited an unusual feature of carbon: its variability to conduct electricity depending on how much it is compressed. He situated granularized anthracite coal between two electrodes covered with a steel diaphragm. Vibrations in the diaphragm compressed the granules, moving the electrodes closer together, and changing the resistance to the electric current that passed between them. The component was easy to manufacture, inexpensive, and long lasting, and it remained the standard in telephone handpieces until supplanted in the 1980s by electret devices. The principle remains the same, although in these components, a metal-coated plastic diaphragm creates fluctuations in an electric field across an air gap between diaphragm and electrode, causing a varying electric current to move down the wires. Transistor amplifiers are needed to strengthen the signal variations with this technology.

Telephony requires not only the arrangement of a voice circuit between sending and receiving stations but also a means of signaling: ringing the called party or ringing the operator in a switched system. The solution was to use bursts of higher-voltage current to trigger ringers. Initially ringer current was generated by hand-cranked magnetos, but with the switch to central-office batteries, the current was supplied at the local exchange. Dial telephones used pulses of this higher-voltage current to trigger the movement of automatic electromechanical switching equipment.

The extent to which managers in the nineteenth century moved from and between the U.S. Postal Service, the telegraph industry, and the telephone industry is notable. In 1845, Morse hired Amos Kendall, Jackson's Postmaster General, to help him set up commercial telegraph service. Theodore Vail, whose cousin Alfred also worked closely with Morse, headed the government's railway postal service, and was responsible for introducing the system whereby mail was sorted in moving railway cars. In 1877, he began the first of two highly successful but nonconsecutive terms as president of Bell. Western Union's aggressive move into telephony actually rejuvenated the Bell company by legitimating a technology that many still were not taking seriously. The company was able, in exchange for stock rather than cash, to buy a transmitter as good as Edison's from an inventor named Francis Blake.

Meanwhile, Western Union was confidently attacking the Bell patent, declaring Gray the true inventor of the telephone. But after a year of litigation, Western Union's chief patent attorney concluded that Bell would win. In the peace treaty, Western Union agreed to admit that Bell was the inventor of telephony and that his patents were valid and to withdraw from the telephone business. Bell agreed to buy the fifty-five-city Western Union telephone system. In 1880, the American Bell Telephone Company was created, with capitalization of $6 million. By 1882, the firm booked over a million dollars of gross earnings, and on February 6 of the same year, it acquired Western Union's equipment subsidiary, Western Electric. In that year, Bell stock soared to over $1,000 per share.

In 1893 and 1894, the original Bell patents expired, and a multitude of independent local telephone companies entered the business. In 1897, these independents formed the National Telephone Association, the genesis of the United States Independent Telephone Association, known after the breakup of the Bell System as

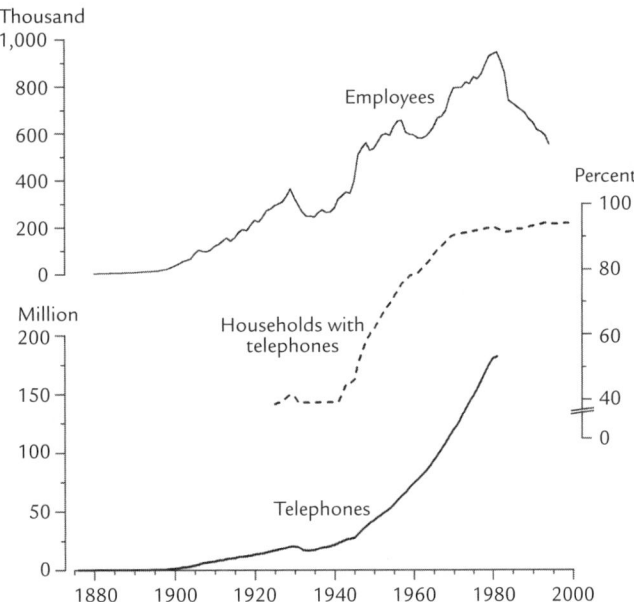

FIGURE Dg-D Telephone industry – telephones and employees: 1876–2000

Sources

Telephones: series Dg34 and Dg37. Employees: 1880–1974, series Dg41, which covers the Bell (AT&T) System; thereafter, series Dg40, which covers the entire U.S. telephone system.

the United States Telephone Association, and today as the United States Telecom Association. This organization is the main non-Bell source for the historical data recorded in the tables presented here. As series Dg34 and Figure Dg-D show, telephone use grew explosively. In New York City alone, the number of users jumped from 56,000 in 1900 to 810,000 in 1908. In 1879, the New York City telephone directory was one card with 252 names. By 1908, it had grown to an 800-page volume published quarterly.

Although there had been some exploration of switching technology within telegraphy, particularly in a network developed by a set of New York law offices (Fagen 1975, p. 729), switching had simply not been a major bottleneck or challenge in most applications. Most telegraph lines were single-wire ground return circuits, with many stations along them. Essentially, they were party lines. The bulk of telegraph use was long distance. Where routing required that a message switch from one line to another, it was simply decoded, recoded, and retransmitted on its next leg, a procedure replicated in the torn-tape teletypewriter networks of the twentieth century.

These retransmission lags were inconsequential given the asynchronous nature of telegraphic communication and the time required to move the message the "final mile." The telegraph system relied on messengers to deliver messages from the local office to the receiving household. Because the telephone did not require a skilled operator to encode and decode outgoing and incoming messages, and because it could service a demand for local communication much more conveniently than telegraphy, it made economic and technical sense to locate telephone stations in households, which had simply not been the case with telegraphs.

As the number of local users in a city grew, it immediately became apparent that economies could be garnered by connecting multiple stations to a central exchange, rather than trying to

connect each directly to all of the others. To illustrate the effect, consider that five subscribers require ten lines to connect each to the other $(4 + 3 + 2 + 1)$, only five "loops" if connected to a central switch. Ten subscribers require forty-five connections for station switching, ten if connected to a central switch, and the economies become greater as the number of users increases. The development of central switches was another important capital-saving innovation, as was the continued use of party lines (multiple stations on a single loop) in many sparsely settled regions of the country.

The telephone exchange originated in New Haven in 1878. The first central office exchange using a common battery system (eight or more storage cells) began operating in Lexington, Massachusetts, in 1893. Common battery systems gradually replaced the bulky and potentially dangerous power sources that home users had had to put up with from 1882 onward. The use of lead acid batteries, recharged by line voltage generators, and with backup internal combustion engine generators, remains, remarkably, standard practice to this day. The system produces reliable, clean (hum-free) direct current, and telephone service that often remains uninterrupted, even when a household's electrical power supply fails.

The construction of switchboards was a very serious technological challenge. As the numbers of subscribers in a local exchange began to rise above 500 or 1,000, the original boards became overwhelmed. Charles Scribner developed the multiple board, capable of serving up to 10,000 customers, which formed the upper limit to the number of lines that could effectively be switched manually in a local exchange.

When a customer picked up a handset, current flow began, and a small light lit on the switchboard. The operator inserted a plug into a jack (socket) below the light, obtained the desired destination from the customer, and used a key switch to send ringer current to the called customer. Upon answer, the operator plugged a second cord into that party's jack, connected these cords together, and was removed from the loop. With the use of these boards and experienced operators, local calls could be completed in a very short time. While the central exchange saved an enormous amount of wire, boards themselves were capital-using (they could cost more than a third of a million dollars) but labor-saving (they saved up to ten seconds a call) devices (Casson 1910, p. 147).

Initially, a three-letter alpha denoted the exchange and the last four numbers the line within it, reflecting the practical maximum of 10,000 local stations per exchange. Later, as the number of exchanges grew, the two–five system was adopted. The first three digits still identified the exchange, but the last of these could be any number, increasing the number of possible identifiers. Seven-digit phone numbers were introduced in 1958.

The hub-and-spoke system that was used to economize on physical capital in local exchanges also underlay the eventual construction of regional and long distance connections (Weiman 2002). And within firms and organizations, private branch exchanges (PBXs) replicated the structure at a lower level of the hierarchy. Calls within an organization were switched internally, those requiring an outside line routed to loops connected to a phone company's local exchange.

As noted, telephone switching was labor intensive, leading to potential economies from more automatic devices. The Strowger switch, patented in 1889, was an electromechanical device that arrayed 100 contacts in a ten-by-ten curved cylindrical matrix. An electrical brush stepped up or down within the cylinder or rotated to reach any of the 100 contacts. Callers drove movements of the brush directly by pulses of ringer current. In 1896, Almon B. Strowger devised a dial that would automatically generate the pulses. Although independent systems pioneered in introducing this innovation, the Bell System resisted it, claiming that it did not work well in urban settings, and often removed steppers in independent systems it bought. Not until 1919 did Bell begin installing automatic switching equipment itself.

The first crossbar switch, which permitted up to ten simultaneous connections, was installed in 1938. The Number 5 model, introduced in 1948, became standard in the Bell System and, in 1978, accounted for the largest number of automatically switched lines in the world. In 1965, Bell installed the first all-electronic switching system, the 1ESS. These early electronic switches still used metallic contacts – reed switches – that were opened or closed by application of a switched magnetic field. All-digital switches, essentially specialized computers, were introduced in 1974. Built on advances in semiconductor technology, the new switches did away with electromechanical switches in the same way that semiconductor technology would shortly render obsolete electromechanical desk calculators. Touch-tone dialing was introduced in 1963, in anticipation of moves to electronic switches, particularly in long distance communication.

Today, an unshielded twisted pair of copper wires drops down or up from one's phone to an entrance bridge. These wires run either directly to the phone switch (local exchange) in the area or to a digital concentrator, a refrigerator-size box that converts the analog signal into digital form (in a sense returning us to the old make-or-break methods of the original telegraph system) from which the digitized signal runs along with others through coaxial or fiber-optic cable to the main switch or local exchange.

When a caller picks up a handset, the telephone goes off hook, and direct current begins to flow to the receiver from the local exchange. The central office switch detects current flow and sends a dial tone back along the wires to the station. After the caller dials a number, the called number is located, and the central office switch sends a powerful surge of current at a specific frequency down the wire to it, triggering the ringer or alerter. When the called phone goes off hook, a connection is made between the two telephone stations, and in phone parlance, the call is completed. The basic protocols have been the same for a century. Indeed, if one takes a telephone from the 1920s and updates the plug, it will work flawlessly in the current environment.

Telegraph companies typically strung a single uninsulated steel wire on metal poles with glass insulators, with the return circuit through the ground. Such lines worked poorly for telephone transmission because interference degraded voice intelligibility much more easily than it could a telegraphic signal. The remedy was to run a twin-wire system, first demonstrated between Boston and Providence in 1883. Although this resulted in a major improvement in the quality of service, it was an expensive capital-using solution.

The second advance involved changes in the materials used to make wires. Steel wires gave rise to rapid signal attenuation. Copper was better, but brittle, and its weight, given the diameters of wire originally used, was incompatible with the typical 100-feet span between two poles. Hard-drawn copper, first introduced in 1884, solved this problem. Cross talk – interference among two or more simultaneous conversations – was addressed by twisting pairs of wires together, but areas of dense telephone demand, such as New York City, soon found their skies clouded with a web of wires, exposed to oxidation, ice, sleet, and other elements.

Putting telephone cables underground, however, required careful experimentation with insulators. At first, wires were wrapped in gutta-percha and soaked in oil (to eliminate moisture) in the manner of an undersea cable. Eventually, dry-core cables, with each wire wrapped in paper twine (so as to preserve some air as insulation) and then shrink-wrapped in lead, became the standard. By the turn of the century, more than 1,200 cables were often bunched in one sheath, accessible through manhole covers and at switching boxes where individual wires ran to customers (Casson 1910, p. 134). The cabling in a New York skyscraper at the turn of the century could weigh as much as fifty tons.

Copper wire was four times as good as steel for telephony, but it was also four times as expensive, and the immense technological payoffs to multiplexing in both telegraphy and telephony were driven by attempts to save on this capital – to increase its throughput or utilization rate. Another way to save capital was to use thinner wires.

The initial use of telephones, and their predominant use today, remains local calling, with residential demand figuring prominently. But from the very outset, Bell had conceived of a grand system in which the phone company linked local exchanges via long distance trunk lines, thus bringing major commercial centers into voice contact. When long distance telephony became possible, businesses rather than households drove demand for it. This was so because, unlike the telegraph, the telephone permitted quick, real-time message exchange involving nonstandardized information that was critical to the conduct of wholesale trade. For this type of negotiation, face-to-face communication was the preferred modality, but if that was not possible, the telephone was vastly preferred to the telegraph. Thus, the telephone substituted for railroad transportation as much as for telegraphic communication (Weiman 2002).

The development of long distance calling required technical advances beyond those necessary for local service. Better cabling, loading coils, and improved amplifiers were critical in the effort to deal with signal attenuation. Attenuation was doubly problematic because it differentially weakened signals of different frequencies, leading to distortion and degradation of intelligibility. The problem could be alleviated somewhat by increasing the cross section of the copper wire, but because of the physics of transmission, the cross section had to increase not proportionally but by the square of the distance multiple if one wished to extend range. Thus, to double the maximum range of intelligibility, one had to quadruple the cross section of the wire. The unsuitability of thick copper wires for aerial installations has already been noted. Because of the physics and economics of transmission, telephony was effectively limited to a maximum of thirty miles until the development of the loading coil and the solution to the mathematics of how it should be deployed. This range was adequate for the development of local exchange business but inadequate as a means of linking major commercial centers, such as New York and Chicago.

A loading coil is a metallic doughnut around which the copper wires going in both directions on a telephone line are wound. These coils were first tested in 1900, and by 1925, more than 1.25 million were in use. Introduced every several miles in a line, they reduced signal attenuation and distortion and increased the maximum range of telephony, in the absence of human repeaters, to about 1,000 miles. Equally important, they permitted the use of thinner wire, thus saving as much as $40 per mile of cable (Casson 1910, p. 139). Lighter wire also meant that aerial cables could be strung over longer distances using a smaller number of spans and, thus, fewer poles. The power of this capital-saving innovation is reflected in a conversation with an AT&T vice president that was reported by the inventor of the coil, Michael Pupin, in his autobiography. The executive told him that over twenty-two years, coils had saved AT&T more than $100 million in capital costs (Pupin 1923, p. 339). Pupin himself made a fortune from the sale of his patent rights to the company. A central part of his contribution was working out mathematically the optimal spacing of these devices (Wasserman 1985).

Although no longer used in long distance service, loading coils continue to be found in local exchange cabling. After almost a century of use, however, they are now being rapidly removed. Loading coils block high-frequency signals, improving the clarity of a phone message but rendering copper wires unsuitable for digital subscriber line (DSL) service. DSL is a technology for providing broadband access to the Internet over twisted pairs at frequencies above those used for voice; it thus multiplexes the final mile and permits continuous data access without tying up a phone line.

Loading coil technology and mechanical amplifiers (using the weakened signal to drive a loudspeaker placed near a carbon microphone) allowed telephony over substantial distances, as in the New York-to-Chicago service introduced in 1904. But mechanical coupling introduced distortion because not all frequencies were amplified proportionally. No more than three could practically be connected in series; therefore, such amplification could not enable a transcontinental line. For that, one needed Lee de Forest's vacuum tube. De Forest's patents, issued in 1907 and 1908, were for a "Device for Amplifying Feeble Electric Currents." The tube, which he called an audion, was also good at picking up modulated radio waves, and the inventor was principally interested in wireless applications (Fagen 1975, p. 260). It took five years for their potential in long distance wired telephony to be appreciated.

Using triodes as electronic amplifiers, AT&T opened the first transcontinental line, between New York and San Francisco, on January 25, 1915. Built with one-sixth-inch copper wire weighing 870 pounds per loop mile, it required 2,500 tons of wire on 130,000 poles, three vacuum tube repeaters, and loading coils at intervals of eight miles. Even so, upon inauguration, it allowed only one two-way conversation. The initial and subsequent costs of calls on this line, along with those for other long distance routes, are reported in Table Dg56–63.

In 1918, building on modulation technology developed for wireless broadcasting , Bell introduced carrier-wave frequency-division multiplexing over wires, which quadrupled the number of simultaneous phone conversations per line. The same technology could allow up to twenty-four simultaneously transmitted telegraphic signals on a single wired circuit. These improvements are again examples of the relentless search for capital-saving innovation in this sector.

More repeaters were added to the New York–to–San Francisco line in 1915 and 1918, and in 1920 all of the loading coils were removed. AT&T addressed the concomitant problem of signal loss instead by using twelve improved vacuum tube repeaters. In 1950, Western Union installed the first undersea vacuum tube repeaters, and in 1956, AT&T used them in the first transatlantic telephone cable. This use of tubes, which operated flawlessly for ten years, was an engineering triumph. But their days were numbered. Indeed, it was the Bell System's desire to find alternatives to the use of

tubes as repeaters (amplifiers) that drove the program of research in solid-state physics, culminating in 1947 in the invention of the transistor at Bell Labs (Mowery and Rosenberg 2000, p. 878). A transistor can perform the same functions as a vacuum tube, but it consumes less power, generates less heat, and is less prone to failure.

In telephony, advances in multiplexing have continued to be critical for getting more bandwidth out of existing pipes, be they copper, fiber-optic, coaxial, or microwave. So-called T1 service was developed in 1957 and widely introduced in 1962. T1, which is a transmission and not, per se, a cabling standard, digitally encodes twenty-four analog signals and multiplexes them into a 1.544 megabit per second (Mbps) signal that can be sent over copper wire. Digital transmission is based on pulse code modulation, a technology invented by Claude Shannon and others in 1948 at Bell Labs. Pulse code modulation encodes a voice or audio source by sampling it 8,000 times a second and representing each sample by eight bits of data. In other words, the height of the audio signal, which represents a complex combination of many sine waves with different phases, is measured at discrete time intervals as one of 256 (2^8) levels, or quantiles, and so encoded using eight binary digits.

Using time-division multiplexing, twenty-four different signals are then interleaved, along with a single synchronization bit, producing a 193-bit frame $[(24 \times 8) + 1]$. Sending 8,000 of these frames per second gives rise to the T1 bandwidth of 1.544 megabits per second ($8,000 \times 193$). Each individual channel is thus associated with a bitstream running at one twenty-fourth of this rate, or 64 kilobits per second (Kbps). Increasing bandwidth is thus enabled, not by sending individual bits faster, but by making each one of them shorter. T1 was designed to exploit the shortest bit duration and thus the maximum number of bits per second that could reliably be transmitted along the twenty-two-gauge copper wire common in most metropolitan systems. Pulse code modulation is the basic technique used to convert music into digital data on a CD-ROM, except that the sampling rate is higher (44,100 times per second for each channel), and a sixteen-bit rather than eight-bit value is created for each sample.

Bell had tried and failed in 1877 to make a telephone call over the Atlantic cable. Although a telephone cable was successfully introduced between San Francisco and Oakland in 1884, it would be more than seventy years before cabled telephone service reached across the Atlantic. Regular service by radio to Europe utilizing very powerful, long radio waves was introduced in 1927. Long waves, unlike the shorter microwaves, could bounce off the earth's ionosphere. Capacity was very limited, however, and the initial cost was $75 for a three-minute call (see Table Dg56–63).

The first transatlantic telephone cable in 1956 (actually, twin cables) used coaxial and tubed repeaters and was able to handle thirty calls. AT&T launched the Telstar satellite in 1963 with the intent to supplement the cable for transatlantic telephony. But because of the distances involved (these satellites travel in orbit at 22,300 miles above a fixed point on the earth), geosynchronous satellites introduce a total of about a half-second delay between send and receive. Signals must travel over 45,000 miles in each direction on a transatlantic call; electromagnetic radiation, such as radio waves, travels at about the speed of light in the ether: 186,000 miles per second. Experience has now shown that customers will not tolerate, without complaint, a delay of more than about a tenth of a second. Where satellite links are used today, the standard is to have conversation go in one direction by satellite and return by fiber-optic undersea cable. Geosynchronous satellites, which use very high frequency radio signals with high bandwidth channels, are ideally suited for one-way television and data transmission, such as sending a newspaper from one printing plant to another across the country. The commercially ill-fated Iridium system utilized a network of low-orbit satellites, which, because of their lower altitude, introduced less delay.

Over land, copper, fiber-optic, and coaxial cabling is supplemented with microwave links based on line-of-sight transmission from one station to another, situated at high points about thirty miles apart. They are the closest modern equivalents to the old Chappe telegraph stations. Although analog signals travel all or part of the way from a customer to the local exchange, today's long distance links consist exclusively of digitized data.

As a conclusion to this section on the telephone, a few words are in order about regulatory changes. Governmental concern about the monopoly power of AT&T was an issue periodically throughout the twentieth century. With the expiration of the original Bell patents in 1893 and 1894, and the explosion of independents, conflicts arose because of Bell's refusal to allow local systems to interconnect with the Bell long distance lines. And in 1909, as mentioned, Bell acquired control of Western Union, giving it a stranglehold on long distance and much local communication, but also providing convenience to consumers, for example, by making it possible for the first time to order a telegram over the telephone. Four years later, under government pressure, however, the company, in what is known as the Kingsbury Commitment, agreed to let go of Western Union, to connect its long distance lines to independent operators if certain conditions were met, and not to acquire an independent if the U.S. Department of Justice objected.

In 1974, Justice brought an antitrust suit against AT&T that was finally settled in 1982, with an historic divestiture agreement (the modified final consent decree) implemented in 1984. AT&T assets shrank at one fell swoop from $150 billion to $34 billion, as twenty-two regional telephone systems were grouped into seven Regional Holding Companies (RHCs), also known as Regional Bell Operating Companies (RBOCs), each with about 60,000 employees and $8 billion to $9 billion of assets (Vietor 2000, p. 1004). As a result of mergers, four remain today. AT&T kept long distance service, Bell Labs (later spun off as Lucent Technologies), and equipment manufacturing (Western Electric), with the RBOCs blocked from these sectors, but AT&T was to stay out of the provision of local service. Series Dg76–78 provide data on the revenues and net incomes of local exchange carriers.

The Telecommunications Act of 1996 relaxed many of the restraints of the modified final settlement, allowing new entrants (including AT&T) to provide local service and permitting RBOCs to offer long distance service. AT&T has since established significant ownership stakes in the cellular phone business (by purchasing McCaw Cellular Communications in 1994) and in cable television through its acquisition of TCI (Telecommunications, Inc.) and has continued to acquire cable systems, with the intent of providing local service through cable telephony. As this is written, the success of the strategy appears in doubt, as AT&T apparently intends to break itself into four smaller companies.

Radio and Television

By the 1890s, telecommunications engineers knew how to send data or voice signals over wire. What they did not know how to do well was send such information through the air. Semaphoric

systems could be used only for data, were vulnerable to the weather, and by necessity were land based. Semaphore enthusiasts did talk seriously about floating stations anchored eight to ten kilometers apart, but the logistical challenges of provisioning these stations, let alone maintaining clear lines of sight between them, were insurmountable. And although telegraphic data could be sent via the undersea cable, Bell had failed in his attempts to use it to transmit voice. None of these alternatives, moreover, was suitable for mobile communication, particularly that associated with communications between ships and between ships and shore. For practical purposes, telegraph and telephone transmissions were tethered to wire.

James Maxwell's theoretical work on electromagnetic waves paved the way for the first generation and measurement of radio waves by Heinrich Hertz. Between 1884 and 1888, Hertz demonstrated their existence, showed practically how to generate and detect them, and measured their velocity and wavelength. His generator used a battery-driven capacitor, which accumulated electricity until it was discharged across a spark gap connected to short lengths of wire, his broadcast antenna. His detector was even cruder: a circular piece of wire with a very small spark gap in one section. With this device, he generated and detected radio waves across short distances and, in principle, demonstrated the possibility of wireless telegraphy.

A number of scientists in France, England, and Russia contributed to the development of an improved detector based on an insulated tube filled with metal filings (Edouard Branly in France called it a coherer). In the presence of radio waves generated by sparks, the resistance of the filings changed, and it could be measured by a galvanometer or used to set off a bell. Guglielmo Marconi built on these investigations to create a commercially viable system. By 1896, using spark gap and coherer technology, he was able to transmit Morse code without wires over distances of up to two miles. He moved to England and set up the British Marconi Company, and on December 12, 1901, situated in Cornwall, he used a very long antenna raised by a kite to detect transmissions from a station in Newfoundland, more than 1,700 miles away. By 1907, Marconi had established a commercial service, focusing on ship-to-shore applications, which faced no competition from undersea cable. It was in this market that he had his greatest success in the first decade of the twentieth century, facilitated in part by the International Ship Act stipulating the presence of a wireless transmitter on every ocean-going vessel. These devices played a role in the *Titanic* tragedy, summoning assistance to the doomed vessel, although system incompatibility meant that some potential rescuers within thirty miles could not hear the distress signal.

The generation of radio waves by sparks, however, was wasteful of both energy and the spectrum. The average power of a transmission burst was less than the peak power, and the transmission was not closely concentrated in any one frequency, making tuning difficult and raising problems of signal interference as more users competed in a given geographical area. One could not simply treat the ether as one big wire; what was needed was a means of dividing the spectrum into different channels, or frequencies, so that users would not interfere with one another. In other words, one needed frequency-division multiplexing of the radio spectrum.

Figuring out how to do this also opened the way for radio telephony. Sound waves audible to humans vary in frequency from about 20 to 20,000 cycles per second (Hz). Telephones transmit sounds in the 300- to 3,500-Hz band (adequate for voice communication). A transducer, such as a microphone, converts these cycles to fluctuations of similar frequency in direct current, which can easily pass through a wire to the receiver. Sound waves per se cannot be broadcast very far.

Prior to Hertz's work on radio waves, Bell had actually demonstrated the transmission of speech over a beam of light and received a patent for a "photophone." But like the Chappe and all other optical systems at the time, any long distance transmission by light operated at the discretion of the weather. The big advantage of radio waves, much lower in frequency than light, is that their use is almost entirely unaffected by weather.

The trick that made wireless telephony (and the modern radio industry) possible is the use of a carrier wave of a specific frequency whose amplitude or frequency may be modulated in response to an audio signal, and then demodulated at the point of reception. To do this, one needed to generate a radio wave of steady frequency for use as a carrier. Early techniques for doing so were the rotary alternator, championed by Nicola Tesla and Reginald Fessenden, and the electric arc, favored by Valdemar Poulsen. But there was no practical way of modulating waves produced by these devices.

It was de Forest's invention of the triode in 1907 that formed the technical foundation for both broadcast and two-way radio communication as we know it, and also, as we have seen, advances in long distance wired telephony. Radio broadcast requires thousands of kilowatts of electric power, as opposed to the few milliwatts necessary for wired telephony. The vacuum tube could be used to generate carrier waves, to modulate them in response to an audio signal, to amplify the modulated signal so that it could be broadcast over an antenna, to detect the radio signals in a receiver, to extract the audio signal through the process of demodulation, and to amplify it so that it could drive a loudspeaker.

Edison had stumbled upon a diode by inserting an additional electrode into a light bulb, but he did not realize its potential use. In 1904, Ambrose Fleming, working for Marconi, invented the first vacuum tube. A diode (which he called a valve) is an evacuated bulb containing a metal cathode and anode. If an electrical potential is applied between them, current will flow across the gap between them. A diode can serve as a rectifier, turning alternating current (AC) into direct current (DC), and also as a radio wave detector (current flow fluctuates in the presence of such waves), which is what Fleming intended it for.

In 1907, de Forest patented the triode, a tube that inserts a grid between the cathode and the anode. A changing voltage applied to the grid, even at low power levels, will cause fluctuations in the current flow from the cathode to the anode, effectively allowing amplification of the power of a weak audio signal. De Forest's tube, which ushered in the age of modern electronics, made radio telephony possible and, as we have seen, enabled a vast improvement in long distance wired telephony. The triode could be used both as a detector and demodulator of radio waves and as a modulator, essential for wireless radio broadcast.

Building on de Forest's invention, Bell engineers in 1915 succeeded in using long radio waves to transmit speech from Arlington, Virginia, to Panama, Hawai'i, and Paris (Fagen 1975, pp. 368–9). It was essentially this line of research, delayed temporarily by the First World War, that underlay the inauguration in 1927 of radiotelephone service to Europe, the only vehicle for transoceanic voice communication until 1956. Except over oceans and in mobile services on land, wireless two-way point-to-point telephony could not compete with wired implementations, a

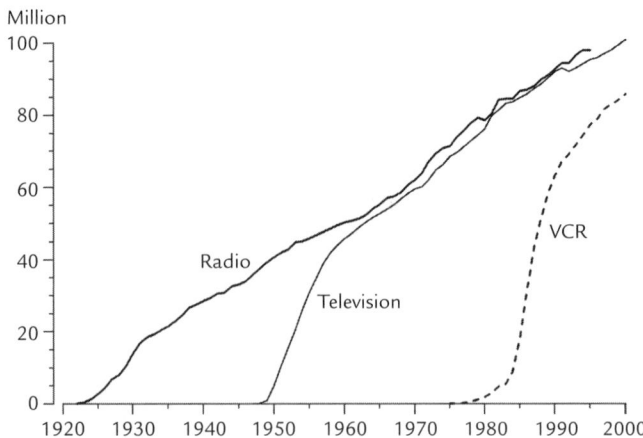

FIGURE Dg-E Households with radio sets, television sets, and videocassette recorders: 1922–2000

Sources

Series Dg128–130.

Documentation

Nearly 100 percent of households had radio sets as of the early 1950s, and so the plot for radios defines an approximate upper bound (for example, compare series Ae79 and Dg128).

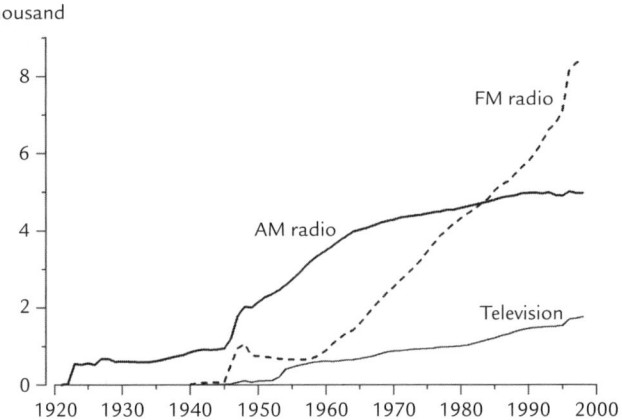

FIGURE Dg-F Operating radio and television broadcast stations: 1921–1998

Sources

AM radio: series Dg117. FM radio: series Dg118–119. Television: series Dg120–121.

Documentation

The graphs for FM radio and television include both commercial and non-commercial stations.

situation that remains only slightly altered today. Cellular telephone systems, obviously, have successfully demonstrated their potential to serve as an alternative to local wired service, but their appeal depends in part on their interconnection with the wired system, particularly for access to long distance calls.

Commercial broadcasting – the industry whose growth is charted in Table Dg117–130 and Figures Dg-E and Dg-F – began in 1921, but no one knew at its birth exactly how it would evolve. As noted, Bell had used telephonic broadcasts as a publicity stunt, and the modality resurfaced with the availability, thanks to de Forest, of powerful audio amplifiers. In 1919 in New York, AT&T used a system of a hundred loudspeakers over a three-block system in a war bond campaign, and on November 11, 1921, 150,000 people in

Arlington, Virginia, New York, and San Francisco, using open tele-phone lines, amplifiers, and loudspeakers, listened to the dedication of the Tomb of the Unknown Soldier (Fagen 1975, p. 425).

In the event, the radio and television broadcast industry de-veloped with wireless transmission used for local and regional distribution of content and land lines used to interconnect local transmitters in order to generate national radio networks. In the telecommunications industry, however, no generalization should ever be taken as final. Television broadcast now arrives in Ameri-can homes not only via traditional local broadcast stations but also over cable and via satellite. Radio and video are also increasingly available over the packet-switched Internet, a system that depends largely on land lines. So Bell's suggestion that broadcast might arrive over the telephone network is perhaps rising from the ashes, even if the modalities are far different from those he anticipated.

Unlike newspapers, magazines, or books, broadcasting via radio waves is regulated by the federal government. The traditional story is that in the absence of licensing for transmission on specified frequencies, wattages, and hours of operation, chaos developed because of interference from overlapping signals. Others argue that over the 1920–1926 period, priority-in-use rules derived from common law were adequate to address problems of interference (see Hazlett 1990). What is less in dispute is that the Radio Act of 1927, which created the Federal Radio Commission, had the consequence of permitting industry pioneers to obtain at low or no cost the equivalent of secure property rights to broadcast at certain frequencies, power levels, and times of day. An alternative to the actual regulatory structure adopted, one vigorously supported by Ronald Coase in a classic article in 1959, would have been for the government to auction off spectrum rights to the highest bidder. Coase's proposals were, in fact, implemented in the 1990s in auctions of cellular telephone frequencies, although the "give away in the public interest" principle appears to have informed the recent grant of frequencies for high definition television broadcast to the networks, valued by some estimates at roughly $70 billion.

The Federal Radio Commission became, in 1934, the Federal Communications Commission, one of whose functions remains the assignment of different users to different bands of frequencies. For example, AM (amplitude modulation) radio utilizes a band from 535 kilohertz (kHz) to 1.7 megahertz (MHz); VHF (very high frequency) television, 54–72, 76–88, and 174–216 MHz; and FM (frequency modulation) radio from 88 to 107 MHz. CB (citizens band) radio uses a band of forty channels in the 27-MHz range; garage door openers operate at 40 MHz; cordless phones have bands between 40 and 50 MHz and also 900 MHz; radio-controlled cars, 72 MHz; radio-controlled airplanes, 75 MHz; and so forth. The intent of regulatory allocation is to assign frequencies most appropriate for their use and to prevent signals from interfering with one another within specified time intervals or geographical areas.

The basic principles of the television broadcast industry rep-resent an extension of those developed for radio. A carrier wave is used to send a diplex modulated signal with input from both a video and an audio source. The video signal is carried through AM and the audio via FM. A difference between radio and television is that in radio, the transducer is a microphone, and in television it is a device that converts fluctuations of light into fluctuations of electric current.

The first completely electronic system for transmitting and receiving images over the air was demonstrated in 1927 by Philo T. Farnsworth. Vladimir Zworykin, working for the Radio Corporation of American (RCA), developed an image iconoscope in 1933, claiming priority for the invention of television on the basis of a 1923 application for a patent that was never awarded. David Sarnoff, head of RCA, was determined not to pay royalties to Farnsworth and filed a patent infringement suit against him. RCA's case was shaky, however, and after protracted litigation, Farnsworth prevailed, although his victory was Pyrrhic. World War II delayed the commercial exploitation of the medium, and by the late 1940s, many of his patents had expired. During the 1930s, RCA worked on refining what Farnsworth had invented, eventually developing the image orthicon tube, which was widely used in the early days of television (the name of the Emmy award for television programs is a corruption of "Immy," shorthand for these tubes). Video transducers today include those employing charge-coupled devices, integrated circuits capable of converting light to electricity.

Television requires a visual image to be scanned and broken down into pieces of information that can be transmitted electroni-cally and then reassembled. Just as pith ball telegraphy had antici-pated separate wires for each letter, so early schemes for television anticipated separate wires for each picture element. The break-through of sequentially scanned elements that rely on the persis-tence property of human vision to put them together in a moving picture allowed the possibility of transmission over a single circuit. Initial scanning technologies were mechanical, such as the Nipkow disk, a sheet of perforated metal in a spiral pattern that, when ro-tated, scanned a series of progressively smaller rings covering the picture. Light passing through these apertures struck a photoelec-tric substance, such as selenium, generating fluctuating current, which, when transmitted to a receiving site, could drive a light with varying intensity, such as a neon gas discharge tube, behind an identical and perfectly synchronized disk, thus regenerating the picture.

The problem was that mechanical scanning technologies could not scan at resolutions higher than about 200 lines. The image disector, invented by Farnsworth, used electromagnets to control a scanning electron beam that traced line-by-line patterns over a signal plate consisting of a mosaic of photoelectric substances acting as small capacitors. As the beam struck them successively, the stored charge was released, generating fluctuations in electric current that drove the video signal.

It was not until the 1939 World's Fair that television broadcast was introduced to a broad audience. Commercial television broad-casting began in the United States in 1941. During World War II, the production of all commercial television sets in the United States was banned, although, in contrast with Britain, a limited broadcast schedule did continue. Only after the war did television begin to take the American public by storm, as can be seen in Table Dg117–130. In 1947, Kodak and the National Broadcast-ing Company (NBC) introduced the kinescope, a motion picture camera adapted for filming a live television broadcast, thus per-mitting image storage and rebroadcast at a later date. Kinescopes remained the only available storage technology until the introduc-tion of videotape machines in 1956, and the films made with them are our only record of the early years of television broadcast.

The first coast-to-coast broadcast took place in 1951. That same year, the Columbia Broadcasting System (CBS) began color broad-casts using a mechanical scanning technology related to Nipkow disks, but at the end of the year, all color television broadcast was suspended owing to the outbreak of the Korean War. In 1953, the FCC approved a different RCA-pioneered all-electronic system, known today as NTSC (National Television System Committee). Broadcasts using this system began in November of 1953, and the first production model sets were released in 1954, meeting an initially cool reception from the public. The development of NTSC color television defined the basic technological paradigm for television that persisted through the end of the twentieth century.

Television broadcast has an effective range of about seventy-five miles. Network broadcast is enabled by the use of microwave relay stations about thirty miles apart or (today) by satellite broadcast. The delivery of signals to homes is increasingly over cable (AT&T invented coaxial cable in 1935) or by direct satellite transmission, as well as by local broadcast.

There were many technological improvements in the design of both broadcast and receiving equipment, including the replacement of tubes with transistors, and, in the mid-1970s, the introduction of home videocassette recorders. An analog version of high definition television (HDTV) was introduced in Japan in the early 1990s. Requiring an enormous bandwidth, the system has yet to be licensed in the United States, and at the beginning of the new century, only limited broadcasts of all-digital HDTV have begun in the United States.

Table Dg162–171 deals with the use of radio as a point-to-point communication medium. There is no corresponding table for television because, even more so than radio, TV has been almost exclusively a broadcast technology. Closed-circuit systems have been used for surveillance purposes from the inception of the technology, but these were simplex, not designed for two-way communication. AT&T introduced the duplex Picturephone service at the New York World's Fair in 1964, but it was never a commercial success because it would have tied up multiple telephone lines. High bandwidth requirements today are only slowly being overcome through compression techniques and drops in transmission costs. It is not clear that residential customers want video links, at least for local calling. For long distance, inexpensive cameras now permit crude point-to-point "television" over the Web. Video conferencing as an alternative to air travel is available to large corporations and universities, as well as to businesses that use off-site office services. The extent of the long-term demand for these services remains uncertain.

Internet

The Internet is, at its most fundamental level, a set of protocols for interconnecting networks of electronic devices, particularly computers. Its novelty lies not in the use of a binary code to represent information, nor in innovations in the data transmission pipes themselves, developed initially for telephony and telegraphy. Rather, it involves an entirely new set of procedures, or protocols, for moving data over this infrastructure, the most important element of which has been packet switching.[3]

The theory of packet switching was first adumbrated in a 1961 doctoral proposal by Leonard Kleinrock at the Massachusetts Institute of Technology. Bell engineers had long understood that multiplying the number of lines on a trunk circuit increased its effective capacity by more than the multiplicative factor because the law of large numbers means that less toll business would be lost owing

to peaks of congestion. Kleinrock's work envisaged an extension of the queuing theory developed for single-node systems to those involving multiple nodes, that is, situations where there was more than one possible route between source and destination. Packet switching involves sending a message not as a continual stream of data but as a bunch of packets, each with an address and sequencing label, and each of which might travel (depending upon congestion) by a different route to be assembled again at the endpoint.

Unlike a phone conversation, which ties up a completed circuit for its entire duration regardless of the long silences that may intersperse a difficult conversation, packet switching uses circuits only when there is data to transmit, and reduces congestion by reallocating packets on the fly to less congested routes. It is another of a long line of capital-saving innovations in the history of telecommunications. Most voice communication, and the modem links whereby the majority of home users at the end of the twentieth century connected to their ISPs, continue to be circuit switched. Some estimates suggest that if all voice communication were converted from circuit to packet switching, the effective capacity of the existing communications infrastructure could be doubled.

The principle of digitizing data is not new, going back at least to Baudot's innovations in the late nineteenth century. Claude Shannon's work on pulse code modulation in 1948 enabled the digitization of voice. Using analog-to-digital-to-analog conversion, long distance telephone conversations in the 1960s moved increasingly in digital form over T1 lines in the middle part of their journey. The development of mainframe computers in the 1950s and 1960s, and the desire to connect remote terminals to them via the telephone network, had posed the reverse problem: the need to convert digital to analog to digital. The solution was the development of modems, which enable digital data to move over part of its journey in analog form before being demodulated at the endpoint into digital form. But whether analog or digital, voice or data, telephone networks ultimately move information from one endpoint to another by establishing a continuous end-to-end circuit between the transmitter and the receiver. This is what packet switching dispensed with.

The Internet can be dated from 1969, with the interconnection of the first four hosts: the University of California at Los Angeles (Kleinrock was by then a professor there), the Stanford Research Institute (where the team included Douglas Englebart, who later invented the mouse), the University of California at Santa Barbara, and the University of Utah. The achievement lay in linking four physically separate computers produced by different manufacturers using different operating systems. Linkage was made possible by a piece of hardware called an interface message processor (IMP) attached to each machine and interconnected by leased phone lines. The IMP, whose modern descendant is the router, was a special kind of switch built under contract for the Pentagon by Bolt, Beranek and Newman, a Cambridge, Massachusetts, consulting firm. Designed for packet switching, and intended for enabling the first wide area network, IMPs also, in an unanticipated fashion, enabled the first local area networks (LANs) by permitting different computers on the same sites to communicate with each other. Series Dg110 charts the explosive growth in the number of Internet hosts.

With the time-sharing technology of the 1960s, terminals connected by leased wire or via modems over phone lines could access a mainframe from across town or across a country. But while connected, a terminal could talk only to a particular mainframe. An important impetus in developing the Internet was the facilitating of remote access to multiple mainframes, both to distribute computing

---

[3] See the Internet site of the Internet Society (ISOC).

load over time and to share data. This again reflected the search for innovations that could increase the utilization rates of scarce capital situated in geographically fixed locations.

Few anticipated that the main use of the network by researchers would be to send personal messages to each other via different mainframes. The protocols enabling computer networks to talk to each other ended up putting the equivalent of a souped-up printing telegraph on the desk of everyone who had access, and the value of this access has increased as more people have connected. In a manner totally unanticipated, electronic mail provided convenient, point-to-point asynchronous communication most analogous to that made possible by the telegraph in the mid-nineteenth century.

But the Internet did more than simply reinvent the telegraph. The convenience, ease of access, and low marginal cost made the system not just quantitatively but qualitatively different from anything that existed in the nineteenth century. Users of corporate teletypwriters sometimes had access to limited within-network electronic mail capability. And in time-sharing environments, different remote users of the same mainframe had been able to send messages to each other. But email among users of different machines, available on demand from desktops at zero marginal cost, was simply not possible before 1972. Most likely, the Defense Department would not have funded development of a network had it anticipated its main use; at the time, the telephone seemed perfectly adequate for desktop person-to-person communication.

At the heart of the Internet today are the rules embodied in the TCP-IP protocols. The Internet protocol (IP) defines the standard for addressing packets. The Transmission Control Protocol (TCP) governs the disassembly of messages into packets, attachment of address and sequence headers, selection of alternate routes through the network depending on congestion, reassembly (using the sequencing headers) at destination, and recovery from lost or degraded packets.

The original IP address system anticipated a maximum of 256 nodes. The assumption was that the Net would connect a limited number of large systems, rather than hundreds of thousands of smaller ones. The domain name system, whose growth and composition is charted in Table Dg110–116, was developed at the University of Wisconsin and first introduced in 1984. Twelve-digit IP addresses, which must be unique to each host, correspond to telephone numbers in telephony. Although easy to interpret by computers, they are difficult for humans to remember. Domain name servers solve the problem by translating domain names into twelve-digit IP addresses.

Because interoperability is a main goal of Internet protocols, and indeed a positive attribute of any communications network, the achievement of widely shared standards has been critical for the evolution of telecommunications. Although railroads can and did develop with different track widths, there are many advantages, particularly in the realm of saving capital, of standard gauges. Differences also exist in telecommunications. Standards-setting bodies have been and are important in its development. These include, for example, the International Telecommunications Union, responsible for standards that allow interoperability of national telephone and telegraph systems; the American National Standards Institute (ANSI), which has played a role in formalizing the ASCII code; and the Electronics Industry Association, which defined such conventions as the RS232C serial interface.

What is interesting in this regard is how much the rules of the Internet have *not* developed under the aegis of a standards-setting body. This is particularly the case with respect to the explosive growth of the World Wide Web in the 1990s. In 1992, Tim Berners-Lee at CERN (the European Organization for Nuclear Research) developed the protocols that define Web-based communication. These included addressing conventions (URLs), which also defined the type or scheme of Internet communication, as well as two sets of rules that defined the formatting and transmission of Web pages: HTML (hypertext markup language) and HTTP (hypertext transfer protocol). Berners-Lee's protocols ensure interoperability in the transmission and receipt of Web pages, which can ultimately include text, graphics, audio, and video imagery, all with hyperlinks – automatic connections to other pages, a system arguably anticipated by Vannevar Bush in an *Atlantic Monthly* article in 1945.

The Web protocols operate within the more encompassing TCP-IP conventions that permit other Net applications, such as email and file transfer, which can be integrated and made easily and conveniently accessible from Web pages. In January 1993, the first browser, Mosaic, was released, which led to Netscape and its main competitor, Microsoft's Internet Explorer. This software made possible easy access to HTML pages from distant servers. Because it is an open standard, various plug-ins are now available that permit HTML pages to provide audio and video display, for example.

The four original Internet hosts were connected by leased 45-Kbps telephone lines. Most business and organizations move data in and out using dedicated T1-size pipes to an Internet service provider. The Internet backbone – high bandwidth trunklines devoted to data traffic – was originally provided by the Defense Department through its Advanced Research Project Agency network, ARPANET, and for a time by the National Science Foundation (NSF) through its own network, NSFNET. The intent was to provide remote access to a fixed number of supercomputer facilities. In the event, NSF's motivation of achieving higher utilization rates for these centers was undercut by the rapid drop in the cost of computers: workstations became so powerful and inexpensive that the rationale for the NSFNET disappeared. In 1992, NSF got out of the business, and the backbone is now the responsibility of a number of commercial providers. Data over the backbone, which consists of the longest and fastest links in the packet-switched network, move over T3 links: full duplex fiber-optic pipes twenty-eight times larger than a T1 (about 45 Mbps, as opposed to 1.544 Mbps). T3 lines consist of two cables (one to receive and one to transmit), coaxial into and out of an organization and fiber-optic over most of their length. Data are formatted according to the DS3 standard, and the pipes are sometimes referred to using that designation.

Conclusion

This essay has shown that even prior to 1969, there were tendencies toward convergence, for example, among the technologies underlying telegraphy, telephony, and radio broadcast. The development of the Internet has accelerated these tendencies. It has put a printing telegraph on the desk of the millions who have access to it; now offers tolerably good and some would say superior substitutes for printed newspapers, journals, magazines, and books; provides decent alternatives to broadcast radio, if not television; and is closing the gap in telephony. The packet-switched technology of the Internet will, no doubt, continue to accentuate the blurring of traditional boundaries separating different communications sectors.

Yet we should be cautious in concluding that everything is, or will be, new. The Internet builds on modalities and technologies developed in the past. It is striking, in looking back over the sector's history to date, how revolutionary, technical change has led so frequently to relatively stable paradigms that endured for decades and even longer. To understand the lines along which the network will develop, and how it will influence modalities of moving and storing information that preceded it, we must be cognizant of its history and the infrastructure and media upon whose foundations it rests.

Much was written in the late 1990s, for example, about the contribution that interconnection would make to a world of distributed intelligence. But the theme is older, dating back at least to the mid-nineteenth century: "by means of electricity, the world of matter has become a great nerve, vibrating thousands of miles in a breathless point of time. . . . The round globe is a vast brain, instinct with intelligence." These words were penned by Nathaniel Hawthorne in *The House of the Seven Gables*. Here, Hawthorne has one of his characters describe the imagined impact of the electromagnetic telegraph (1851, Chapter 17). Major advances in communications technology, from Chappe's optical telegraph through the opening of the Atlantic cable through the development of television in the twentieth century, have frequently triggered powerful, sometimes utopian, or almost millenarian visions of their potential. With the benefit of hindsight, we can put some of these enthusiasms in perspective, and we will undoubtedly do the same looking back at the Internet hysteria of the late 1990s. At the same time, the collapse of stock valuations in this sector at the end of the twentieth century may lead to a reverse bias: underestimating the still only partially realized potential of these technologies to facilitate economic growth and improve human welfare.

References

Bush, Vannevar. 1945. "As We May Think." *Atlantic Monthly* (July): 101–8.

Casson, Herbert. 1910. *The History of the Telephone*. 1st edition. A. C. McClure.

Coase, R. H. 1959. "The Federal Communications Commission." *Journal of Law and Economics* 2 (October): 1–40.

Engerman, Stanley L., and Robert Gallman, editors. 1996, 2000. *The Cambridge Economic History of the United States*. 3 volumes. Cambridge University Press.

Fagen, M. D., editor. 1975. *A History of Engineering and Science in the Bell System*. Bell Telephone Laboratories.

Field, Alexander J. 1992. "The Magnetic Telegraph, Price and Quantity Data, and the New Management of Capital." *Journal of Economic History* 52 (June): 401–13.

Field, Alexander J. 1994. "French Optical Telegraphy, 1793–1855: Hardware, Software, Administration." *Technology and Culture* 35 (April): 315–47.

Field, Alexander J. 1998. "The Telegraphic Transmission of Financial Asset Prices and Orders to Trade: Implications for Economic Growth." In *Research in Economic History,* volume 18. JAI Press.

Geddes, Rick. 1998. "The Economic Effects of Postal Reorganization." *Journal of Regulatory Economics* 13: 139–56.

Goldin, H. H. 1947. "Governmental Policy and the Domestic Telegraph Industry." *Journal of Economic History* 7 (May): 53–68.

Gordon, Robert J. 2000. "Does the 'New Economy' Measure Up to the Great Inventions of the Past?" *Journal of Economic Perspectives* 14 (Fall): 49–74.

Hawthorne, Nathaniel. 1851 [1883]. *House of the Seven Gables*. Houghton Mifflin.

Hazlett, Thomas. 1990. "The Rationality of U.S. Regulation of the Broadcast Spectrum." *Journal of Law and Economics* 33 (April): 133–75.

John, Richard. 1995. *Spreading the News: The American Postal System from Franklin to Morse*. Harvard University Press.

Kleinrock, Leonard. 1961. "Information Flow in Large Communication Nets." Proposal for a doctoral dissertation, Massachusetts Institute of Technology. Available at Kleinrock's University of California at Los Angeles Internet site.

Lacy, Dan. 1996. *From Grunts to Gigabytes: Communications and Society*. University of Illinois Press.

Mowery, David, and Nathan Rosenberg. 2000. "Twentieth Century Technological Change." In Stanley L. Engerman and Robert Gallman, editors. *The Cambridge Economic History of the United States*, volume 3. Cambridge University Press.

Oliner, Steven D., and Daniel E. Sichel. 2000. "The Resurgence of Growth in the Late 1990s: Is Information Technology the Story?" *Journal of Economic Perspectives* 14 (Fall): 3–22.

Pupin, Michael. 1923. *From Immigrant to Inventor*. Scribner's.

Standage, Tom. 1998. *The Victorian Internet*. Walker.

Temin, Peter, and Louis Galambos. 1987. *The Fall of the Bell System*. Cambridge University Press.

Thompson, Robert Luther. 1947. *Wiring a Continent: The History of the Telegraph Industry in the United States*. Princeton University Press.

Vietor, Richard H. K. 1989. "AT&T and the Public Good: Regulation and Competition in Telecommunications, 1910–1987." In Stephen Bradley and Jerry Hausman, editors. *Future Competition in Telecommunications*. Harvard Business School Press.

Vietor, Richard H. K. 2000. "Government Regulation of Business." In Stanley L. Engerman and Robert Gallman, editors. *The Cambridge Economic History of the United States*, volume 3. Cambridge University Press.

Wasserman, Neil. 1985. *From Invention to Innovation*. Johns Hopkins University Press.

Weiman, David. 2002. "Building 'Universal Service' in the Early Bell System: The Co-Evolution of Regional Urban Systems and Long Distance Telephone Networks." In Timothy W. Guinnane, William Sundstrom, and Warren Whatley, editors. *History Matters: Essays on Economic Growth, Technology, and Demographic Change*. Stanford University Press.

EMPLOYEES

Alexander J. Field and Richard Sutch

TABLE Dg1–7   Employees of communications firms, by industry division: 1947–1999

Contributed by Alexander J. Field and Richard Sutch

Year	Total	Radiotelephone	Telephone	Radio and television broadcasting			Cable and other pay television
				Total	Radio	Television	
	Dg1	Dg2	Dg3	Dg4	Dg5	Dg6	Dg7
	Thousand	Thousand	Thousand	Thousand	Thousand	Thousand	Thousand
1947	—	14	572	—	—	—	—
1948	—	15	624	—	—	—	—
1949	—	15	622	—	—	—	—
1950	—	15	605	—	—	—	—
1951	—	15	629	—	—	—	—
1952	—	16	662	—	—	—	—
1953	—	17	686	—	—	—	—
1954	—	17	682	—	—	—	—
1955	—	17	690	—	—	—	—
1956	—	18	734	—	—	—	—
1957	—	18	750	—	—	—	—
1958	860	17	715	84	—	—	—
1959	837	17	690	86	—	—	—
1960	840	17	689	89	—	—	—
1961	829	16	677	90	—	—	—
1962	824	16	671	92	—	—	—
1963	824	16	669	95	—	—	—
1964	848	17	690	99	—	—	—
1965	881	17	718	103	—	—	—
1966	928	18	755	109	—	—	—
1967	970	19	788	115	—	—	—
1968	982	19	793	119	—	—	—
1969	1,049	21	850	126	—	—	—
1970	1,129	22	920	132	—	—	—
1971	1,143	22	929	138	—	—	—
1972	1,152	23	934	137	—	—	—
1973	1,180	23	958	139	—	—	—
1974	1,203	24	977	144	—	—	—
1975	1,176	23	944	149	—	—	—
1976	1,169	23	931	154	—	—	—
1977	1,185	23	935	162	—	—	—
1978	1,240	23	971	173	—	—	—
1979	1,309	25	1,023	181	—	—	—
1980	1,357	25	1,047	192	—	—	—
1981	1,391	25	1,052	200	—	—	—
1982	1,417	25	1,047	210	108	103	—
1983	1,324	23	934	217	110	106	—
1984	1,340	22	931	224	112	112	—
1985	1,319	22	899	228	113	115	—
1986	1,275	21	863	228	113	115	—
1987	1,282	21	881	224	115	109	—
1988	1,280	23	878	227	118	110	111
1989	1,272	30	856	230	119	112	117
1990	1,309	38	875	234	119	115	126
1991	1,299	46	864	230	117	114	128
1992	1,269	53	832	228	113	115	131
1993	1,269	63	816	230	113	116	136
1994	1,295	81	812	232	114	119	145
1995	1,318	103	797	236	113	123	156
1996	1,351	125	786	241	113	128	170
1997	1,419	151	820	243	114	129	174
1998	1,477	164	849	247	116	132	184
1999	1,552	177	892	248	116	132	201

(continued)

TABLE Dg1–7   Employees of communications firms, by industry division: 1947–1999   *Continued*

Source

U.S. Bureau of Labor Statistics Internet site, National Current Employment Statistics.

Documentation

See the text for Table Ba840–848. See the Introduction to Part D for a discussion of Standard Industrial Classification (SIC) codes.

Series Dg1. SIC code 48. This series, included in series Ba844, is the sum of series Dg2–4 and Dg7 and a residual category (not shown) comprising telegraph and semaphore communications (SIC 482) and taxi dispatch, ship-to-shore broadcasting, satellite communications, and other communications services (SIC 489).

Series Dg2. SIC code 4812. Includes paging and cellular carriers and resellers.

Series Dg3. SIC code 4813. Excludes radiotelephone.

Series Dg4. SIC code 483. This series is the sum of series Dg5–6.

Series Dg5. SIC code 4832. Includes both networks and stations.

Series Dg6. SIC code 4833. Includes both networks and stations.

Series Dg7. SIC code 484. Includes both networks and stations.

Alexander J. Field and David F. Weiman

TABLE Dg8–21   Domestic telegraph industry – messages, wire, offices, employees, and finances: 1866–1987[1,2]

Contributed by Alexander J. Field

Year	Messages handled		Miles of wire		Telegraph offices		Employees, system total	TWX teletypewriters	Book value capital stock		Operating revenues		Net income	
	Total	Western Union	Total	Western Union	Total	Western Union			Total	Western Union	Total	Western Union	Total	Western Union
	Dg8	Dg9	Dg10	Dg11	Dg12	Dg13	Dg14	Dg15	Dg16	Dg17	Dg18	Dg19	Dg20	Dg21
	Thousand	Thousand	Thousand miles	Thousand miles	Number	Number	Number	Number	Million dollars	Million dollars	Million dollars	Million dollars	Million dollars	Million dollars
1866	—	—	—	76	—	2,250	—	—	—	24,205	—	4,619	—	1,956
1867	—	5,879	—	85	—	2,565	—	—	—	47,426	—	5,964	—	2,082
1868	—	6,405	—	98	—	3,219	—	—	—	47,677	—	6,636	—	2,557
1869	—	7,935	—	105	—	3,607	—	—	—	48,402	—	6,672	—	2,226
1870	—	9,158	—	112	—	3,972	—	—	—	—	—	6,731	—	1,982
1871	—	10,646	—	121	—	4,606	—	—	—	—	—	7,384	—	2,224
1872	—	12,444	—	137	—	5,237	—	—	—	—	—	8,471	—	2,640
1873	—	14,457	—	154	—	5,740	—	—	—	53,331	—	8,612	—	1,995
1874	—	16,329	—	176	—	6,188	—	—	—	54,773	—	8,872	—	2,752
1875	—	17,154	—	179	—	6,565	—	—	—	54,673	—	4,330 [3]	—	1,304 [3]
1876	—	18,780	—	184	—	7,072	—	—	—	55,844	—	9,143	—	2,862
1877	—	21,159	—	194	—	7,500	—	—	—	56,318	—	9,039	—	2,694
1878	—	28,919	—	206	—	8,014	—	—	—	58,287	—	8,637	—	2,698
1879	—	25,070	—	212	—	8,534	—	—	—	62,699	—	9,118	—	3,836
1880	31,703	29,216	291	234	12,510	9,077	—	—	96,031	64,080	16,697	10,581	5,970	4,720
1881	—	32,500	—	327	—	10,737	—	—	—	87,123	—	11,552	—	5,713
1882	—	38,842	—	374	—	12,068	—	—	—	88,971	—	14,819	—	5,933
1883	—	41,181	—	433	—	12,917	—	—	—	90,961	—	16,596	—	6,132
1884	—	42,076	—	451	—	13,761	—	—	—	92,459	—	16,693	—	4,744
1885	—	42,097	—	462	—	14,184	—	—	—	92,616	—	15,298	—	4,274
1886	—	43,290	—	490	—	15,142	—	—	—	93,794	—	14,871	—	3,418
1887	—	47,395	—	525	—	15,658	—	—	—	96,481	—	15,683	—	3,557
1888	—	51,464	—	616	—	17,241	—	—	—	101,968	—	17,584	—	4,132
1889	—	54,108	—	648	—	18,470	—	—	—	108,430	—	19,075	—	5,651
1890	—	55,879	—	679	—	19,382	—	—	—	115,273	—	20,055	—	6,093
1891	—	59,148	—	716	—	20,098	—	—	—	116,255	—	21,135	—	5,719
1892	—	62,387	—	739	—	20,700	—	—	—	118,423	—	21,769	—	6,511
1893	—	66,592	—	769	—	21,078	—	—	—	120,364	—	22,983	—	6,602
1894	—	58,632	—	791	—	21,166	—	—	—	120,285	—	20,059	—	4,906
1895	—	58,307	—	803	—	21,360	—	—	—	121,278	—	20,421	—	5,244
1896	—	58,760	—	827	—	21,725	—	—	—	121,436	—	20,820	—	4,980
1897	—	58,152	—	841	—	21,769	—	—	—	123,484	—	20,630	—	4,849
1898	—	62,174	—	874	—	22,210	—	—	—	123,718	—	21,683	—	5,130
1899	—	61,398	—	905	—	22,285	—	—	—	123,818	—	22,048	—	4,980

Notes appear at end of table

(continued)

TABLE Dg8–21 Domestic telegraph industry – messages, wire, offices, employees, and finances: 1866–1987 *Continued*

Year	Messages handled — Total (Dg8) Thousand	Messages handled — Western Union (Dg9) Thousand	Miles of wire — Total (Dg10) Thousand miles	Miles of wire — Western Union (Dg11) Thousand miles	Telegraph offices — Total (Dg12) Number	Telegraph offices — Western Union (Dg13) Number	Employees, system total (Dg14) Number	TWX teletypewriters (Dg15) Number	Book value capital stock — Total (Dg16) Million dollars	Book value capital stock — Western Union (Dg17) Million dollars	Operating revenues — Total (Dg18) Million dollars	Operating revenues — Western Union (Dg19) Million dollars	Net income — Total (Dg20) Million dollars	Net income — Western Union (Dg21) Million dollars
1900	—	63,168	—	933	—	22,900	—	—	—	128,856	—	22,811	—	5,292
1901	—	65,657	—	973	—	23,238	—	—	—	129,715	—	23,865	—	6,703
1902	91,655	69,375	1,318	1,030	27,377	23,567	—	—	162,947	133,150	39,486	25,602	9,982	6,323
1903	—	69,791	—	1,089	—	23,120	—	—	—	138,409	—	26,525	—	8,450
1904	—	67,904	—	1,155	—	23,458	—	—	—	141,271	—	26,571	—	6,729
1905	—	67,477	—	1,185	—	23,814	—	—	—	145,993	—	26,347	—	5,959
1906	—	71,487	—	1,256	—	24,323	—	—	—	146,349	—	27,828	—	5,749
1907	103,794	74,805	1,578	1,321	29,110	24,760	—	—	220,294	153,585	49,685	29,939	9,704	4,903
1908	—	62,371	—	1,359	—	23,853	—	—	—	156,371	—	25,890	—	1,670
1909	—	68,053	—	1,383	—	24,321	—	—	—	159,246	—	27,600	—	5,614
1910	—	75,135	—	1,429	—	24,825	—	—	—	164,382	—	30,741	—	5,379
1911	—	—	—	1,487	—	24,926	—	—	—	166,762	—	33,598	—	5,371
1912	109,378	—	1,814	1,517	30,864	25,392	—	—	226,387	159,394	62,822	39,438	6,384	4,002
1913	—	—	—	1,543	—	25,060	—	—	—	158,855	—	45,784	—	3,235
1914	—	—	—	1,582	—	25,784	—	—	—	162,678	—	45,880	—	5,371
1915	—	—	—	1,584	—	25,142	—	—	—	167,338	—	51,100	—	10,168
1916	—	—	1,877	—	—	—	—	—	—	—	66,471	—	11,764	—
1917	129,273	—	1,863	—	—	—	60,122	—	184,351	—	81,623	—	12,336	—
1918	134,031	—	1,620	—	—	—	69,528	—	190,712	—	90,369	—	8,103	—
1919	139,435	—	1,686	—	—	—	65,181	—	203,010	—	105,409	—	9,595	—
1920	155,884	—	1,711	—	—	—	74,448	—	214,986	—	124,379	—	9,199	—
1921	139,544	—	1,787	—	—	—	64,395	—	224,876	—	111,707	—	7,932	—
1922	149,219	—	1,807	—	—	—	62,576	—	230,644	—	116,659	—	14,311	—
1923	158,468	—	1,836	—	—	—	69,045	—	238,923	—	124,172	—	13,094	—
1924	162,700	—	1,884	—	—	—	68,561	—	252,678	—	125,490	—	12,152	—
1925	185,187	—	1,944	—	—	—	73,262	—	266,571	—	141,680	—	15,153	—
1926	203,035	—	1,977	—	—	—	79,755	—	281,503	—	149,721	—	13,841	—
1927	203,365	—	2,095	—	—	—	76,183	—	292,817	—	147,845	—	14,105	—
1928	211,559	—	2,202	—	—	—	77,644	—	307,113	—	153,329	—	13,889	—
1929	234,050	—	2,251	—	—	—	87,435	—	357,343	—	163,358	—	12,796	—
1930	211,971	—	2,269	—	—	—	84,962	—	379,869	—	148,223	—	3,942	—
1931	183,373	—	2,250	—	—	—	72,916	1,479	382,737	—	126,697	—	537	—
1932	143,075	—	2,239	—	—	—	60,997	2,524	383,960	—	97,902	—	−5,099	—
1933	143,553	—	2,245	—	—	—	58,368	3,578	383,886	—	96,613	—	330	—
1934	155,215	—	2,247	—	—	—	62,839	5,776	383,165	—	102,557	—	−387	—
1935	176,250	—	2,245	—	—	—	62,257	7,894	383,216	—	106,262	—	3,213	—
1936	193,566	—	2,270	—	—	—	67,862	10,646	384,946	—	115,772	—	5,129	—
1937	200,711	—	2,275	—	—	—	64,084	12,499	387,749	—	117,228	—	−523	—
1938	185,639	—	2,279	—	—	—	57,190	14,266	387,897	—	106,813	—	−5,248	—
1939	189,055	—	2,277	—	—	—	57,513	14,855	388,837	—	109,899	—	−3,152	—
1940	191,645	—	2,269	—	—	—	59,670	16,130	375,021	—	114,587	—	372	—
1941	210,928	—	2,281	—	—	—	65,363	16,607	380,501	—	130,519	—	4,016	—
1942	223,148	—	2,294	—	—	—	64,674	16,013	384,352	—	145,789	—	3,836	—
1943	231,692	—	2,303	—	—	—	61,037	15,979	366,347	—	166,953	—	−746	—
1944	225,462	—	2,272	—	—	—	61,481	—	358,882	—	173,207	—	5,117	—

	Messages handled		Miles of wire		Telegraph offices		Employees, system total	TWX teletypewriters	Book value capital stock		Operating revenues		Net income	
	Total	Western Union	Total	Western Union	Total	Western Union			Total	Western Union	Total	Western Union	Total	Western Union
	Dg8	Dg9	Dg10	Dg11	Dg12	Dg13	Dg14	Dg15	Dg16	Dg17	Dg18	Dg19	Dg20	Dg21
Year	Thousand	Thousand	Thousand miles	Thousand miles	Number	Number	Number	Number	Million dollars	Million dollars	Million dollars	Million dollars	Million dollars	Million dollars
1945	236,169	—	2,247	—	—	—	63,446	13,031	357,784	—	182,048	—	-7,834	—
1946	212,072	—	2,044	—	—	—	57,644	14,838	361,618	—	175,536	—	-10,030	—
1947	213,780	—	1,743	—	—	—	53,572	20,208	314,275	—	199,654	—	906	—
1948	191,013	—	1,632	—	30,120	—	48,967	23,423	310,295	—	183,429	—	1,265	—
1949	175,323	—	1,438	—	29,401	—	41,660	25,526	306,316	—	171,393	—	-3,468	—
1950	178,904	—	1,298	—	28,631	—	40,482	28,393	294,451	—	177,994	—	7,353	—
1951	180,151	—	1,225	—	26,879	—	40,319	30,815	284,293	—	192,089	—	4,711	—
1952	151,712	—	1,194	—	25,639	—	39,853	33,338	286,372	—	184,336	—	-724	—
1953	162,188	—	1,151	—	24,745	—	38,957	35,272	289,448	—	208,578	—	13,242	—
1954	152,582	—	1,129	—	—	—	37,009	36,672	300,126	—	209,635	—	4,480	—
1955	153,910	—	1,100	—	—	—	37,785	38,946	310,968	—	228,816	—	10,331	—
1956	151,600	—	1,088	—	—	—	37,754	41,628	332,727	—	238,362	—	12,060	—
1957	143,947	—	1,078	—	—	—	36,467	44,923	350,860	—	245,549	—	12,911	—
1958	131,867	—	1,075	—	—	—	33,620	47,491	364,498	—	200,729	—	11,062	—
1959	130,993	—	1,058	—	—	—	33,151	51,631	380,216	—	260,849	—	14,755	—
1960	124,319	—	1,063	—	18,853	—	32,655	54,744	398,023	—	262,365	—	10,205	—
1961	117,263	—	1,044	—	17,051	—	31,425	57,920	434,933	—	265,727	—	11,833	—
1962	112,487	—	1,043	—	16,321	—	30,021	56,693	541,419	—	264,119	—	10,405	—
1963	104,220	—	1,010	—	15,096	—	28,015	57,598	596,587	—	286,822	—	24,931	—
1964	97,448	—	984	—	13,441	—	26,607	59,843	634,636	—	299,410	—	16,974	—
1965	94,302	—	964	—	12,706	—	26,179	56,675	688,757	—	305,615	—	17,833	—
1966	92,682	—	891	—	12,214	—	27,198	48,663	778,810	—	319,329	—	20,712	—
1967	89,078	—	829	—	—	—	26,524	47,200	871,425	—	334,983	—	22,062	—
1968	85,645	—	753	—	—	—	26,502	46,411	916,712	—	358,202	—	21,569	—
1969	77,059	—	683	—	—	—	25,164	42,605	968,401	—	391,338	—	22,724	—
1970	69,679	—	621	—	—	—	24,293	40,766	1,029,149	—	402,456	—	26,074	—
1971	44,103	—	583	—	8,141	—	20,566	—	1,235,248	—	396,841	—	23,752	—
1972	39,826	—	481	—	6,745	—	17,266	—	1,335,438	—	431,762	—	40,083	—
1973	37,572	—	467	—	5,745	—	15,121	—	1,414,861	—	454,726	—	13,319	—
1974	42,079	—	490	—	5,344	—	13,682	—	1,515,849	—	483,912	—	44,870	—
1975	41,968	—	483	—	5,052	—	13,167	—	1,581,052	—	504,760	—	48,583	—
1976	43,032	—	479	—	4,947	—	11,996	—	1,680,554	—	527,530	—	49,009	—
1977	45,306	—	439	—	5,212	—	11,988	—	1,766,735	—	554,908	—	59,535	—
1978	50,398	—	439	—	5,114	—	12,137	—	1,898,664	—	576,455	—	56,769	—
1979	55,148	—	489	—	4,937	—	11,733	—	2,009,765	—	636,061	—	51,039	—
1980	55,014	—	—	—	5,474	—	12,669	—	2,101,007	—	696,972	—	70,257	—
1981	55,560	—	—	—	5,968	—	13,026	—	2,209,121	—	779,172	—	107,518	—
1982	49,939	—	—	—	—	—	13,247	—	2,362,350	—	809,316	—	98,239	—
1983	42,000	—	—	—	—	—	—	—	—	—	—	—	—	—
1984	48,000	—	—	—	—	—	—	—	—	—	—	—	—	—
1985	42,000	—	—	—	—	—	—	—	—	—	—	—	—	—
1986	29,000	—	—	—	—	—	—	—	—	—	—	—	—	—
1987	25,000	—	—	—	—	—	—	—	—	—	—	—	—	—

(continued)

TABLE Dg8-21   Domestic telegraph industry – messages, wire, offices, employees, and finances: 1866-1987
Continued

[1] Beginning in 1944, Western Union is the sole domestic telegraph provider.

[2] In 1875, Western Union changed its fiscal year end from December 31 to June 30, and in 1913 changed back again to December 31.

[3] Data are for six months ending June 30.

Sources
Series Dg8, Dg10, Dg12, Dg14–16, Dg18, and Dg20. For 1866–1915: U.S. Bureau of the Census, *Compendium of the Tenth Census, 1880*, pp. 1310-25; U.S. Bureau of the Census, *Special Reports: Telephones and Telegraphs, 1902*, Tables 39, 41; U.S. Bureau of the Census, *Telegraph Systems: 1907*, Tables 1-8; U.S. Bureau of the Census, *Telephones and Telegraphs, 1912*, Tables 2, 3. For 1916-1928: U.S. Interstate Commerce Commission (ICC) and U.S. Federal Communications Commission (FCC), unpublished data (annual reports of Western Union Telegraph Company and Postal Telegraph-Cable Company to the ICC). For 1929-1955: FCC, *Statistics of the Communications Industry in the United States, 1955*, pp. 110-15. 1956-1987: FCC, *Statistics of Communications Common Carriers* (annual issues), and unpublished data (data are from the annual reports of Western Union Telegraph Company to the FCC).

Series Dg9, Dg11, Dg13, and Dg17. For 1866-1915, except 1913: Western Union Telegraph Company (annual reports). For 1913: Moody's Investors Service, *Moody's Public Utilities Reports, 1919*, New York.

Series Dg19 and Dg21. U.S. Bureau of Valuation, *Accounting Reports, The Western Union Telegraph Company* (December 31, 1915, and June 30, 1919).

Documentation
From the 1850s through the 1980s, the Western Union Telegraph Company was the dominant carrier in the domestic telegraph industry. This company, which was established in 1851 as the New York & Mississippi Valley Printing Telegraph Company, succeeded by 1866 in acquiring or merging dozens of competing telegraph firms and emerging as the sole telegraph company in the United States. (See Robert Luther Thompson, *Wiring a Continent: The History of the Telegraph Industry in the United States, 1832–1866* (Princeton University Press, 1947).) In subsequent decades, smaller telegraph companies were formed, serving a region or major cities, often with the intent of forcing Western Union to acquire them. Western Union developed close contractual ties with the railways. Telegraph pole lines were constructed along railroad rights-of-way. The lines were used jointly for general telegraph and railroad telegraph communication and signaling, and railroad stations and personnel were used for the pickup and delivery of telegraph messages.

Western Union's most serious telegraph rival, Postal Telegraph, was acquired by the Mackay interests in the 1880s as the domestic pickup and delivery agent for Mackay's Commercial Cable Company (later the International Telephone and Telegraph Company). Until the 1920s, Postal Telegraph competed with Western Union for the larger and more profitable routes. Beginning in the 1920s, Postal Telegraph attempted to provide a nationwide service in full competition with Western Union. Postal Telegraph expanded its own facilities and also made arrangements with the telephone companies, gasoline stations, and others for the pickup and delivery of telegrams.

The expansion of Postal Telegraph coincided roughly with the emergence of more effective competition from other sources. Predominantly, such competition came from the growth and development of toll telephone service, the expansion of domestic airmail, the introduction of the Bell System's teletypewriter exchange service (TWX), which was sold to Western Union in 1971, and the provision of domestic radiotelegraph service by the international radiotelegraph carriers RCA (Radio Corporation of America) Global Communications and the Mackay companies. (In 1942, as a war measure, domestic radiotelegraph service was discontinued and was not subsequently resumed.) Postal Telegraph's share of domestic telegraph revenues was less than 25 percent.

In 1943, Postal Telegraph merged with Western Union. (See U.S. Federal Communications Commission, *Reports*, volume 10, pp. 148-98, September 27, 1943, for FCC approval of the specific terms of the merger.) Thus, from 1943 onward, system statistics are identical to those for the Western Union Company.

In 1988, the Western Union Telegraph Company sold off its international private line business to a Swiss company, its Westar satellite to GM Hughes

Electronics, and its business services group (for example, teletypewriters) to American Telephone and Telegraph (AT&T). The Western Union corporation today focuses almost exclusively on money transfers.

The 1880 census data included many companies in addition to Western Union, and the later census data include Postal Telegraph, as well as reports from some fifteen to twenty small companies. Included in the Postal Telegraph data were the telephone operations of that company. The 1902 census data include several domestic ocean-cable systems, while the 1880, 1907, and 1912 Census figures exclude ocean-cable systems other than the Western Union Cable Division.

For 1916-1928, Western Union reported landline (domestic) and cable operations on a merged basis; therefore, supplementary material was obtained from Western Union relating to the landline operations. Necessarily, these involve estimates and allocations, the precise bases of which were not specified. For 1929-1955, figures were obtained from annual reports of the telegraph carriers to the ICC and the FCC, supplemented by correspondence and reference to the reports of the telegraph companies.

See *Historical Statistics of the United States* (1975) for sources on other available statistics. That edition also included census data for 1917, 1922, 1932, and 1937 (not shown here).

Series Dg8–9
Prior to 1935, the annual count of revenue messages handled was based on a count of messages during the month of January and was partly estimated. For 1935-1950, most of the Western Union message data were based on an actual count for two days in each month at some 400 of the largest offices, which together accounted for about 80 percent of total message revenues. The Postal Telegraph data continued to be based on counts and estimates for the month of January projected to annual totals. For 1950-1987, Western Union used a scientifically constructed random message sample, the results of which provide generally reliable monthly and annual message data by service classes and rate zones.

Data include telegraph traffic with Canada and Mexico. Such traffic forms only a small portion of the message data.

Series Dg10–11
Wire figures are not a satisfactory measure of the capacity of the domestic telegraph industry for various reasons, including the shift from less efficient open wire to more efficient cable; the introduction of multiplex terminal equipment, which has permitted a significant subdivision of each telegraph channel and the simultaneous transmission of messages on each such subdivision; the leasing from the Bell System telephone companies of voice-frequency channels and the subdivision of these channels into a substantially greater number of telegraph channels; operation by Western Union of its microwave radio system for the transmission of messages; and use of modernized routing and switching systems.

According to U.S. Bureau of the Census, *Compendium of the Seventh Census, 1854*, p. 189, there were 89 telegraph lines having 23,261 miles of wire in 1853. In 1854, the miles of wire were estimated at over 30,000.

Series Dg14.
Figures are number of employees reported at the end of June for 1929-1934, the end of December for 1935-1945, and the end of October for 1946-1970.

Series Dg15.
For 1931-1934, data are from responses to FCC, Telegraph Division Order number 12; for 1935-1938, from the FCC *Annual Report*. Bell TWX service was initiated November 21, 1931. The revenues from this service, as well as the private line telegraph revenues of telephone companies, are not included in total number operating revenues, which are limited to the revenues of domestic telegraph carriers. The TWX service of the telephone industry was purchased by Western Union in 1971.

Series Dg16
Effective January 1, 1914, the ICC prescribed a Uniform System of Accounts for telegraph and cable companies and required the carriers to keep their accounts in conformity with this system. All charges made to plant and equipment or other property accounts with respect to any property acquired on or after January 1, 1914, were to be the actual money costs of the property. The ICC did not attempt to prescribe the depreciation rates of the carriers.

TABLE Dg8–21   Domestic telegraph industry – messages, wire, offices, employees, and finances: 1866–1987
Continued

In 1940, the FCC adopted a revised uniform system of accounts for wire telegraph and ocean cable carriers, to go into effect January 1, 1942. The effective date was later postponed to January 1, 1943. The new system was designed to supplant the previous system in use since 1914. The FCC prescribed depreciation rates for the telegraph carrier, effective January 1, 1948. After the merger of Western Union and Postal Telegraph, the FCC required that the merged carrier reclassify its plant as of January 1, 1943.

Telegraph plant book costs for 1946–1970 were affected by two conflicting factors: accelerated retirement of old plant and addition of new plant as part of the general modernization program of the Western Union Telegraph Company begun in 1946. As part of its modernization program, the company leased substantial plant, in the form of voice channels, from the Bell System.

Census figures on book cost of plant include Western Union cables in all years. Note that before 1916, census data are used for system totals, but after 1916 they are not, although there are census year data available for 1922, 1927, 1932, and 1937. Census totals after 1916 exceed series presented here.

Series Dg18–21
Operating revenues are derived, in bulk, from various transmission and nontransmission telegraph services. However, a small proportion has been derived from incidental services, such as errand service, time service, and code registration. The operations of the former Postal Telegraph toll telephone system were included until February 1, 1952, when Western Union disposed of this service. Also included in operating revenues are revenues derived by the domestic telegraph carriers in handling the domestic haul of insular, mobile, and foreign cable and radiotelegraph communications. Such domestic haul is between the "gateway" cities and the interior of the nation.

To obtain data on total operating expenses, the domestic telegraph carriers (Western Union and Postal Telegraph) were required to subdivide their expense accounts between domestic and international operations in respect to compensation, overhead, materials and supplies, and other charges. Such allocations are subject to some arbitrariness.

No adjustments were made in the annual reported income statements. Thus, the net loss shown for 1945 resulted from a substantial retroactive wage award made by the War Labor Board. This was shown in the 1945 statement of the Western Union Telegraph Company as an extraordinary charge (less recoverable income taxes).

TABLE Dg22–33   Telegraph, teletypewriter exchange (TWX), and international cable and radiotelegraph rates between New York and selected cities: 1850–1980
Contributed by Alexander J. Field

	Telegraph				Teletypewriter exchange service (TWX)				International cable or radiotelegraph			
	Philadelphia	Chicago	Denver	San Francisco	Philadelphia	Chicago	Denver	San Francisco	London	Cairo	Tokyo	Buenos Aires
	Dg22 [1]	Dg23 [1]	Dg24 [1]	Dg25 [1]	Dg26 [2]	Dg27 [2]	Dg28 [2]	Dg29 [2]	Dg30 [3]	Dg31 [3]	Dg32 [3]	Dg33 [3]
Year	Dollars	Dollars	Dollars	Dollars	Dollars	Dollars	Dollars	Dollars	Dollars	Dollars	Dollars	Dollars
1850	0.25	1.55	—	—	—	—	—	—	—	—	—	—
1866	0.25	1.85	7.00	7.45	—	—	—	—	10.00	—	—	—
1868	—	—	—	—	—	—	—	—	1.58	—	—	—
1869	0.45	2.05	—	7.45	—	—	—	—	—	—	—	—
1870	0.25	1.00	—	5.00	—	—	—	—	—	—	—	—
1873	0.30	1.00	2.50	2.50	—	—	—	—	—	—	—	—
1875	—	0.25	—	—	—	—	—	—	—	—	—	—
1876	—	0.50	2.00	2.00	—	—	—	—	—	—	—	—
1877	—	0.60	—	—	—	—	—	—	—	—	—	—
1880	—	—	—	—	—	—	—	—	0.50	—	—	7.50
1882	—	—	—	—	—	—	—	—	0.50	—	—	4.60 [4]
1883	0.15	0.50	1.25	1.50	—	—	—	—	0.50	—	—	3.98
1884	—	0.50	—	1.00	—	—	—	—	0.40	—	—	3.98
1886	—	—	—	—	—	—	—	—	0.12	—	—	3.98
1888	0.25	0.50	0.75	1.00	—	—	—	—	0.25	—	—	3.98
1890	0.20	0.40	0.75	1.00	—	—	—	—	0.25	—	—	1.82
1892	—	—	—	—	—	—	—	—	0.25	—	2.21	1.70
1892	—	—	—	—	—	—	—	—	0.25	—	2.21	1.50
1901	—	—	—	—	—	—	—	—	0.25	—	1.76	1.00
1903	—	—	—	—	—	—	—	—	0.25	0.61	1.76	1.00
1903	—	—	—	—	—	—	—	—	0.25	—	1.53	1.00
1905	0.25	0.56	1.33	1.00	—	—	—	—	0.25	0.56	1.33	1.00
1908	0.25	0.50	0.75	1.00	—	—	—	—	0.25	—	1.33	1.00
1910	—	—	—	—	—	—	—	—	0.25	—	1.33	0.85
1912	—	—	—	—	—	—	—	—	0.25	—	1.33	0.65
1916	—	—	—	—	—	—	—	—	0.17	—	0.92	0.65
1917	—	—	—	—	—	—	—	—	0.25	—	1.33	0.50
1919	0.30	0.60	0.90	1.20	—	—	—	—	0.25	—	1.09	0.50
1921	0.30	0.60	0.90	1.20	—	—	—	—	0.18	—	0.85	0.50
1923	0.30	0.60	0.90	1.20	—	—	—	—	0.20	—	1.09	0.50
1924	0.30	0.60	0.90	1.20	—	—	—	—	0.20	—	0.85	0.50
1924	0.30	0.60	0.90	1.20	—	—	—	—	0.20	—	1.09	0.50
1925	0.30	0.60	0.90	1.20	—	—	—	—	0.20	0.42	0.85	0.42
1927	0.30	0.60	0.90	1.20	—	—	—	—	0.20	0.45	0.80	0.42
1928	0.30	0.60	0.90	1.20	—	—	—	—	0.20	0.39	0.80	0.42

Notes appear at end of table

(continued)

TABLE Dg22–33   Telegraph, teletypewriter exchange (TWX), and international cable and radiotelegraph rates between New York and selected cities: 1850–1980   *Continued*

	Telegraph				Teletypewriter exchange service (TWX)				International cable or radiotelegraph			
	Philadelphia	Chicago	Denver	San Francisco	Philadelphia	Chicago	Denver	San Francisco	London	Cairo	Tokyo	Buenos Aires
	Dg22 [1]	Dg23 [1]	Dg24 [1]	Dg25 [1]	Dg26 [2]	Dg27 [2]	Dg28 [2]	Dg29 [2]	Dg30 [3]	Dg31 [3]	Dg32 [3]	Dg33 [3]
Year	Dollars	Dollars	Dollars	Dollars	Dollars	Dollars	Dollars	Dollars	Dollars	Dollars	Dollars	Dollars
1931	0.30	0.60	0.90	1.20	0.35	1.10	1.80	2.40	0.20	0.39	0.80	0.42
1937	0.30	0.60	0.90	1.20	0.35	1.10	1.80	2.40	0.20	0.42	0.72	0.42
1940	0.30	0.60	0.90	1.20	0.35	1.10	1.80	2.40	0.20	0.42	0.72	0.26
1943	0.30	0.60	0.90	1.20	0.35	1.10	1.80	2.40	0.20	0.42	0.24	0.20
1945	0.30	0.60	0.90	1.20	0.35	1.10	1.80	2.40	0.20	0.30	0.20	0.20
1946	0.33	0.66	0.99	1.32	0.35	1.10	1.80	2.40	0.20	0.30	0.20	0.20
1946	0.36	0.72	1.08	1.44	0.35	1.05	1.55	1.75	0.25	0.30	0.30	0.22
1947	0.36	0.72	1.08	1.44	0.35	1.05	1.55	1.75	0.25	0.30	0.30	0.28
1948	0.36	0.72	1.08	1.44	0.35	1.05	1.55	1.75	0.25	0.40	0.40	0.35
1949	0.36	0.72	1.08	1.44	0.35	1.05	1.55	1.75	0.25	0.40	0.40	0.35
1950	0.40	0.75	1.25	1.45	0.35	1.05	1.55	1.75	0.19	0.30	0.30	0.27
1951	0.60	1.00	1.45	1.60	0.35	1.05	1.55	1.75	0.19	0.30	0.30	0.27
1952	0.65	1.10	1.55	1.70	0.35	1.05	1.55	1.75	0.19	0.30	0.30	0.27
1953	0.65	1.10	1.55	1.70	0.45	1.20	1.65	1.75	0.19	0.30	0.30	0.27
1954	0.85	1.25	1.70	1.70	0.45	1.20	1.65	1.75	0.19	0.30	0.30	0.27
1956	0.95	1.30	1.75	1.75	0.45	1.20	1.65	1.75	0.19	0.30	0.30	0.27
1958	1.05	1.40	1.85	1.85	0.45	1.20	1.65	1.75	0.21	0.34	0.34	0.31
1960	1.10	1.45	1.90	1.90	0.45	1.15	1.65	1.75	0.21	0.34	0.34	0.31
1963	1.20	1.60	2.10	2.10	0.45	1.15	1.65	1.75	0.21	0.34	0.34	0.31
1966	1.27	1.70	2.23	2.23	0.25	0.45	0.55	0.60	0.23	0.34	0.34	0.31
1968	2.25	2.25	2.25	2.25	0.25	0.45	0.55	0.60	0.23	0.34	0.34	0.31
1969	2.25	2.25	2.25	2.25	0.25	0.45	0.55	0.60	0.23	0.34	0.34	0.31
1971	3.75	3.75	3.75	3.75	0.25	0.45	0.55	0.60	0.23	0.34	0.34	0.31
1974	4.75	4.75	4.75	4.75	0.25	0.45	0.55	0.60	0.23	0.34	0.34	0.31
1978	4.95	4.95	4.95	4.95	0.40	0.48	0.52	0.52	0.23	0.34	0.34	0.31
1980	4.95	4.95	4.95	4.95	0.40	0.48	0.52	0.52	0.23	0.34	0.34	0.31

[1] Prior to September 1, 1951, charge for ten text words or less; subsequently, charge for fifteen text words or less.

[2] Prior to September 1966, telephone company rates for three minutes or less, two-way; thereafter, for each minute or fraction thereof. Starting in 1959, Western Union offered similar service known as "Telex" with a different rate structure.

[3] Per plain-language telegraph word, including address and signature.

[4] In addition to the figure shown, *Historical Statistics of the United States* (1975) also showed a rate of 3.98.

Sources

Series Dg22–29. For 1850–1970: U.S. Bureau of the Census, *Historical Statistics of the United States* (1975), series R71–74, based on unpublished data from the U.S. Federal Communications Commission (FCC). For 1971–1980: FCC, *Statistics of Communication, Common Carriers* (annual issues).

Series Dg30–33. For 1866–1970: *Historical Statistics of the United States* (1975), series R89–92, based on scattered sources as indicated below (1866–1928), and on unpublished data from the FCC (1929–1970). For 1971–1980: FCC, unpublished data and tariff releases; see U.S. Bureau of the Census, *Statistical Abstract of the United States* (1980), Table 989, p. 585.

Documentation

Series Dg22–29

Through 1970, the underlying sources for the data are as follows. The 1850 rates are cited in William Holmes, *History of Telegraph Rates, 1860 to 1913* (an unpublished study obtained by the FCC from the Western Union Telegraph Company), p. 2. The same source states, p. 8, that the New York–Chicago rate from 1866 to October 1, 1869, was $1.85, although James D. Reid, *The Telegraph in America* (Derby Brothers, 1879), p. 746, states that the Chicago rate was $2.05 between 1866 and 1869, and U.S. Senate, 60th Congress, 2d session, *Investigation of Western Union and Postal Telegraph Cable Companies*, Document number 725 (1909), p. 24, claims that in 1866 this rate was $2.20. Holmes, p. 8, is the source for the 1866 and 1869 New York–Philadelphia rates. Reid, p. 746, quotes the New York–San Francisco rates for 1866 and 1869. *Investigation of Western Union*, p. 24, is also the source for the New York–Denver rate as of 1866. The 1870 rates are mentioned in 51st Congress, 1st session, *Hearings before the House Committee on the Post-Office and Post-Roads*

on *Postal Telegraph Facilitie*s, p. 131. In addition, Holmes, p. 9, states that in 1870 the maximum rate from states north of Washington, D.C., to San Francisco was reduced from $7.45 in currency (or $6.75 if paid in gold) to $5.00 in currency (or $4.00 in gold). The 1873 rates are shown in *Investigation of Western Union*, p. 24. Holmes, p. 10, states that the $2.50 San Francisco rate became effective February 1, 1873, and a reason given was that $2.50 was the denomination of a coin in common use on the Pacific Coast. The same source, p. 12, describes the New York–Chicago rate in 1875 as having been 25 cents and in 1877 as being successively increased to 40 cents, 50 cents, and 60 cents. Holmes also states, p. 11, that the New York–Denver rate became $2.00 in March 1876 and that the San Francisco rate was reduced to $2.00 in August 1876. However, Reid mentions (p. 747) March 1877 as the date $2.00 was fixed as the maximum rate between New York City and points east of the Rocky Mountains. The 1883 rates are also from *Investigation of Western Union*, p. 24. Holmes, p. 17, states that the $1.00 San Francisco rate became effective in March 1884 as part of a general reduction that established $1.00 as the maximum rate for a ten-word full-rate telegram between any two points in the Western Union system. Holmes also reports, p. 17, that in June 1884, the rate between New York and Chicago charged by Western Union was 50 cents, by Postal Telegraph, 25 cents, and by the Baltimore and Ohio Telegraph Company, 40 cents. The 1888 rates are based on State of New York, *Report of the Joint Committee of the Senate and Assembly of the State of New York Appointed to Investigate Telephone and Telegraph Companies* (transmitted to the Legislature March 21, 1910), p. 687, and the annual report of Western Union to stockholders for 1888, p. 5. The 1890 rates are from *Hearings before the House Committee on the Post-Office and Post-Roads on Postal Telegraph Facilities*, p. 68. The rates in effect as of 1908 are from *Investigation of Western Union*, p. 24, although there is evidence from other sources that some of these rates were put into effect in 1907. The 1919 rates were the result of a 20 percent increase in domestic telegraph rates as set forth in the 1919 Western Union annual report to stockholders, p. 8. The 1931 TWX rates are from testimony on behalf of American Telephone and Telegraph (AT&T) by Carroll O. Bickelhaupt in the hearings pursuant to FCC, Telegraph Division Order number 12. Rates beginning with the 1946 increase are derived from official tariffs filed with the FCC.

TABLE Dg22–33   Telegraph, teletypewriter exchange (TWX), and international cable and radiotelegraph rates between New York and selected cities: 1850–1980   *Continued*

The census report, *Special Reports: Telephones and Telegraphs, 1902*, states (p. 14) that the first telegraph rate was applicable in 1845 between Baltimore and Washington and was 1 cent for each group of four characters. The rates shown here are mainly those of the Western Union Telegraph Company. During some of the early years, lower rates were sometimes published by competing companies. The frequent changes in the New York–Chicago rate illustrate particularly the effects of competition. The appearance of new companies offering lower rates on this basic route forced Western Union to meet the competition until such time as it succeeded in acquiring the competing company. Moreover, it is not certain that the published rates were adhered to uniformly, particularly in the early years of telegraph development and in periods of depression. Under the stress of competition, rebates were sometimes allowed.

The rate for the full-rate telegram is the keystone of the telegraph rate structure. Rates for most other public-message telegraph services (day letters, night letters, and so on) are a percentage of the rates for the full-time telegram. Between 1908 and 1946, there was no change in the level of the full-rate telegram, except for the increase effected in 1919. However, while maintaining the rate level on its full-rate telegrams, Western Union introduced various new classifications (including the fixed-text social message and serials), which in effect provided discounts to the message customer.

TWX was provided by the Bell System until this service was sold to Western Union in 1971. As contrasted with message telegraph service, which is a one-way (simplex) communication service, TWX provided two-way, instantaneous (duplex) communication service between TWX subscribers. The maximum number of words that could be transmitted in the three-minute rate period depended on the speed of the transmitting operator (provided by the subscriber) and the maximum rated speed of the TWX equipment. In addition to the charges for specific use (measured in time units and distance) of the facilities, TWX subscribers, beginning July 1, 1953, were billed a monthly service charge of $10. This was increased to $40 on September 1, 1966, and to $45 on February 1, 1970, for 60-speed service.

Series Dg30–33. The first overseas radiotelephone service was opened on January 7, 1927, between New York and London. Service to Buenos Aires began April 3, 1930, and that to Tokyo started December 8, 1934. The circuit to Cairo, opened August 8, 1932, operated via London until January 7, 1946, when a direct circuit to Cairo was placed in operation. As in the telegraph rate, the Tokyo radiotelephone rate included a landline haul charge until 1946 for the New York–San Francisco haul. Initially $9.00, the landline charge was reduced to $6.75 on July 1, 1937, and to $4.50 on August 1, 1940. All radiotelephone rates presented are for three-minute weekday person-to-person daytime calls. In addition, there were lower night and Sunday rates on some routes, and on three of the routes, station-to-station service was available at either a 25 percent or a 33⅓ percent discount from the person-to-person rates.

Series Dg30

The first successful transatlantic cable was laid in 1866. Reid (1979), p. 748, indicates that the first telegraph rate on the cable (presumably New York to London) was $100 for ten words. Three months later, the same source states, the rate was reduced to $50 and subsequently to $25. By 1868, the rate for ten words had declined to $15.75, and in 1885 it stood at 40 cents per word. A staff document of American Cable & Radio, Inc., prepared in connection with FCC Docket number 8777 (1948) indicates that the Western Union Telegraph Company had a 50-cents-per-word rate in 1884, and that on December 24 of that year, the Commercial Cable Company entered the field with a rate of 40 cents per word. The same source indicates that the cable companies other than Commercial Cable reduced their rates to 12 cents per word on May 6, 1886, and Commercial Cable in turn lowered its per-word rate from 40 cents to 25 cents. On September 16, 1887, Commercial Cable further reduced its rate to the 12-cent level. Then on September 1, 1888,

all the cable companies raised their rates between New York and London to 25 cents per word. Exhibit number 190, introduced by RCA (Radio Corporation of America) Communications, Inc., in the same hearing (Docket number 8777) shows the same rates, but with somewhat different effective dates; while William Holmes, *History of Telegraph Rates*, p. 23, cites rates that differ in part from those shown here.

In 1916, it became possible to send messages from New York to London through Canada via Marconi Wireless for 17 cents per full-rate word. According to the unpublished FCC "Report on the Radio Industry," p. 36, RCA, on March 1, 1920, began transmitting radiotelegraph messages to Great Britain. The rate initially was 17 cents per word, with an increase to 18 cents on January 1, 1921, and to 20 cents on April 15, 1923. At this point, the international cable companies reduced their rates to 20 cents to meet the radio competition. Since then, the rates for cable and radio have been identical.

The rate reductions effective May 1, 1945, provided for a uniform 20-cents-per-word basic rate from the U.S. "gateway" cities to a large part of the world (see FCC, *Eleventh Annual Report for Fiscal Year Ended June 30, 1945*, p. 45). Effective May 1, 1946, all international cable and radiotelephone rates were established on a country-to-country basis at 20 cents and 30 cents per word, respectively.

The reductions in rates, effective July 1, 1950, are the result of "unification" of the full rate and the code rate on all cable and radiotelegraph service. The rates were unified at 75 percent of the existing rate per full-rate word. This had the effect of lowering the charge for full-rate messages but increasing the charge for code messages, which at that time formed a substantial portion of international telegraph traffic.

Series Dg31. Telegraphic communication between New York and Cairo began, probably, in 1870 or shortly thereafter. A Commercial Cable Company tariff book dated January 1903 indicates a rate of 61 cents per word as of that time. A July 1905 tariff book of the Western Union Telegraph Company shows a New York–Cairo rate of 56 cents per word; 25 cents was the rate for the New York–London haul, and 31 cents was the rate for beyond London. No record of rates in effect between 1905 and 1925 has been found. Data since 1925 are from the FCC based on filed tariffs and correspondence with companies.

Series Dg32. No specific record has been found dating the beginning of telegraphic communication with Tokyo. In the hearings before the Senate Committee on Foreign Relations, 54th Congress, 1st session, Senate Document number 194 (1896), conflicting testimony was presented with respect to the early rates. The Commercial Cable Company tariff book of January 1903 stated that the rate at that time was $1.76 per word. Shortly thereafter, Commercial Pacific Cable Company opened its transpacific cable, and the rate fell to $1.53 per word. This rate included 12 cents per word for the domestic landline haul from New York to San Francisco, and $1.41 for the San Francisco–Tokyo leg. *Report on Communication Companies*, 73d Congress, 2d session, House Report number 1273, part 3, number 4, p. 3926, is the source of the New York–Tokyo rates between 1903 and 1929. The FCC is the source of rates since 1929. For data on radiotelegraph rates lower than cable rates prior to 1925, see FCC, "Report on the Radio Industry," p. 35, and testimony before the House Committee on the Merchant Marine and Fisheries, pursuant to House Report number 7357, 68th Congress, 1st session, p. 170.

Series Dg33. The 1880 rate is stated in the 1956 *Annual Report of the American Cable and Radio Corporation to Stockholders*, p. 16. Rates between 1882 and 1927 are derived from testimony before the Senate Committee on Interstate and Foreign Commerce, 71st Congress, 2d session, on S. (Senate) 6 (1929–1930) beginning p. 2201, and *A Half Century of Cable Service to the Three Americas* (1928), published by All America Cables, Inc. When radio service was opened in 1924, the rate was fixed at the same level as the existing cable rate. The FCC is the source for rates since 1929.

TABLE Dg34–45   Telephone industry – telephones, access lines, wire, employees, and plant: 1876–2000

Contributed by Alexander J. Field

	Telephones and access lines				Miles of wire		Employees		Telephone plant			
		Access lines		Percentage of households with telephones					Book value of capital stock		Depreciation reserves	
	Telephones	FCC data	USTA data		U.S. telephone system	Bell (AT&T) System	U.S. telephone system	Bell (AT&T) System	U.S. telephone system	Bell (AT&T) System	U.S. telephone system	Bell (AT&T) System
	Dg34	Dg35	Dg36	Dg37	Dg38	Dg39 [1]	Dg40	Dg41	Dg42	Dg43	Dg44	Dg45
Year	Number	Thousand	Thousand	Percent	Thousand	Thousand	Number	Number	Thousand dollars	Thousand dollars	Thousand dollars	Thousand dollars
1876	2,600	—	—	—	—	—	—	—	—	—	—	—
1877	9,300	—	—	—	—	—	—	—	—	—	—	—
1878	26,300	—	—	—	—	—	—	—	—	—	—	—
1879	30,900	—	—	—	—	—	—	—	—	—	—	—
1880	47,900	—	—	—	—	30	—	3,338	—	15,702	—	—
1881	71,400	—	—	—	—	52	—	—	—	—	—	—
1882	97,700	—	—	—	—	83	—	—	—	—	—	—
1883	123,600	—	—	—	—	115	—	—	—	—	—	—
1884	147,700	—	—	—	—	137	—	5,769	—	—	—	—
1885	155,800	—	—	—	—	156	—	5,766	—	38,619	—	—
1886	167,100	—	—	—	—	172	—	6,162	—	38,325	—	—
1887	180,700	—	—	—	—	203	—	6,683	—	40,799	—	—
1888	195,000	—	—	—	—	244	—	7,445	—	44,436	—	—
1889	211,500	—	—	—	—	280	—	7,550	—	51,572	—	—
1890	227,900	—	—	—	—	332	—	8,740	—	58,512	—	—
1891	239,300	—	—	—	—	382	—	9,713	—	62,190	—	—
1892	260,800	—	—	—	—	441	—	11,602	—	67,636	—	—
1893	266,400	—	—	—	—	508	—	11,862	—	73,186	—	—
1894	285,400	—	—	—	—	577	—	12,553	—	77,731	—	—
1895	339,500	—	—	—	—	675	—	14,699	—	87,859	—	—
1896	404,300	—	—	—	—	806	—	16,558	—	95,242	—	—
1897	515,200	—	—	—	—	951	—	19,603	—	104,488	—	—
1898	680,800	—	—	—	—	1,159	—	22,955	—	118,124	—	—
1899	1,004,700	—	—	—	—	1,519	—	29,818	—	145,511	—	—
1900	1,355,900	—	—	—	—	1,962	—	37,067	—	180,700	—	—
1901	1,801,100	—	—	—	—	2,445	—	45,990	—	211,780	—	—
1902	2,371,044	—	—	—	—	3,282	—	55,403	—	250,013	—	—
1903	2,808,900	—	—	—	—	4,359	—	61,476	—	284,568	—	—
1904	3,353,200	—	—	—	—	4,671	—	67,756	—	316,521	—	—
1905	4,126,900	—	—	—	—	5,780	—	89,661	—	368,065	—	—
1906	4,932,800	—	—	—	—	7,469	—	104,646	—	450,061	—	—
1907	6,118,578	—	—	—	—	8,611	—	100,789	—	502,988	—	12,246
1908	6,483,600	—	—	—	—	9,831	—	98,533	—	528,717	—	17,819
1909	6,995,700	—	—	—	—	10,480	—	104,956	—	557,417	—	38,980
1910	7,635,400	—	—	—	—	11,642	—	121,310	—	611,000	—	54,051
1911	8,348,700	—	—	—	—	12,933	—	129,724	—	666,661	—	73,832
1912	8,729,592	—	—	—	—	14,611	—	141,340	—	742,288	—	92,458
1913	9,542,500	—	—	—	—	16,111	—	156,928	—	797,159	—	105,720
1914	10,046,400	—	—	—	—	17,476	—	142,527	—	847,205	—	122,338

	Telephones and access lines				Miles of wire		Employees		Telephone plant			
		Access lines		Percentage of households with telephones					Book value of capital stock		Depreciation reserves	
	Telephones	FCC data	USTA data		U.S. telephone system	Bell (AT&T) System [1]	U.S. telephone system	Bell (AT&T) System	U.S. telephone system	Bell (AT&T) System	U.S. telephone system	Bell (AT&T) System
Year	Dg34	Dg35	Dg36	Dg37	Dg38	Dg39	Dg40	Dg41	Dg42	Dg43	Dg44	Dg45
	Number	Thousand	Thousand	Percent	Thousand	Thousand	Number	Number	Thousand dollars	Thousand dollars	Thousand dollars	Thousand dollars
1915	10,523,500	—	—	—	—	18,506	—	156,294	—	880,069	—	142,307
1916	11,241,400	—	—	—	—	19,850	—	179,032	1,204,710	946,293	—	168,044
1917	11,716,520	—	—	—	—	22,610	—	192,364	1,416,582	1,064,893	—	201,090
1918	12,077,600	—	—	—	—	23,349	—	187,458	—	1,142,498	—	235,395
1919	12,668,500	—	—	—	—	24,163	—	209,860	—	1,215,944	—	276,304
1920	13,411,400	—	—	35.0	—	25,377	—	231,316	1,713,621	1,363,826	—	309,556
1921	13,875,200	—	—	35.3	—	27,766	—	224,277	1,883,599	1,543,866	—	350,642
1922	14,347,395	—	—	35.6	—	30,617	—	243,045	2,151,324	1,729,220	—	395,297
1923	15,369,500	—	—	37.3	—	34,524	—	271,979	2,249,024	1,978,948	491,816	443,130
1924	16,208,900	—	—	37.8	—	39,894	—	278,838	2,538,530	2,266,923	529,169	485,661
1925	16,935,900	—	—	38.7	—	45,474	—	293,095	2,814,063	2,524,906	579,122	530,071
1926	17,746,200	—	—	39.2	—	50,861	—	300,557	3,110,473	2,783,023	626,839	576,216
1927	18,522,767	—	—	39.7	—	56,823	—	309,005	3,477,247	3,013,985	652,389	600,664
1928	19,341,300	—	—	40.8	—	62,193	—	333,794	3,652,642	3,275,687	706,905	650,621
1929	20,233,000	—	—	41.6	—	69,519	—	364,402	4,081,394	3,671,100	759,736	699,035
1930	20,201,600	—	—	40.9	—	76,248	—	324,343	4,461,878	4,043,422	799,764	740,006
1931	19,707,600	—	—	39.2	—	79,239	—	294,689	4,626,813	4,195,064	853,495	788,586
1932	17,424,406	—	—	33.5	—	80,491	—	266,288	4,711,383	4,188,749	888,162	820,195
1933	16,710,900	—	—	31.3	—	80,281	—	248,563	4,598,457	4,169,370	966,715	891,883
1934	16,968,800	—	—	31.4	—	80,118	—	248,996	4,552,604	4,177,950	1,039,477	968,214
1935	17,424,000	—	—	31.8	—	80,458	—	244,599	4,538,620	4,196,671	1,128,651	1,061,650
1936	18,433,000	—	—	33.1	—		—	262,888	4,726,942	4,380,881	1,227,116	1,156,227
1937	19,453,401	—	—	34.3	—	83,391	—	275,634	5,129,252	4,516,998	1,304,839	1,231,712
1938	19,953,000	—	—	34.6	—	85,295	—	264,275	4,979,386	4,621,914	1,362,872	1,286,582
1939	20,831,000	—	—	35.6	—	87,411	—	266,707	5,096,859	4,727,050	1,420,610	1,339,563
1940	21,928,000	—	—	36.9	—	91,273	—	282,224	5,271,215	4,887,900	1,482,792	1,397,339
1941	23,521,000	—	—	39.3	—	97,206	—	321,108	5,597,155	5,196,319	1,574,645	1,482,590
1942	24,919,000	—	—	42.2	—	99,709	—	334,957	5,862,911	5,450,471	1,700,896	1,601,916
1943	26,381,000	—	—	45.0	—	99,400	—	350,912	5,976,726	5,543,992	1,878,215	1,763,868
1944	26,859,000	—	—	45.1	—	100,271	—	345,703	6,109,841	5,670,879	2,061,389	1,934,419
1945	27,867,000	—	—	46.2	—	101,813	—	396,567	6,314,804	5,865,065	2,246,718	2,108,385
1946	31,611,000	—	—	51.4	—	107,343	—	508,391	6,972,578	6,474,011	2,438,911	2,286,952
1947	34,867,000	—	—	54.9	—	114,850	—	536,602	8,126,259	7,552,159	2,609,426	2,447,046
1948	38,205,000	—	—	58.2	—	126,424	—	559,408	9,516,334	8,848,572	2,772,106	2,597,371
1949	40,708,000	—	—	60.2	—	135,400	—	528,015	10,479,646	9,688,160	2,911,534	2,724,745
1950	43,003,800	—	—	61.8	147,000	144,264	565,000	534,751	11,253,267	10,375,100	3,108,085	2,904,820
1951	45,636,400	—	—	64.0	—	152,112	—	563,416	12,231,890	11,250,819	3,342,569	3,125,706
1952	48,056,000	—	—	66.0	—	162,120	—	591,783	13,426,069	12,301,975	3,592,182	3,352,297
1953	50,373,000	—	—	68.0	—	173,375	—	600,363	14,699,282	13,419,650	3,820,482	3,555,901
1954	52,813,000	—	—	69.6	—	185,809	—	591,364	15,969,666	14,525,346	4,059,538	3,766,530
1955	56,243,200	—	—	71.5	—	201,235	649,000	629,773	17,429,276	15,773,373	4,333,445	4,007,118
1956	60,190,400	—	—	73.8	—	220,154	—	653,074	19,482,433	17,555,690	4,593,582	4,228,966
1957	63,620,900	—	—	75.5	—	243,730	—	656,100	21,925,580	19,654,439	4,896,767	4,487,207
1958	66,629,600	—	—	76.4	—	260,464	—	606,340	23,834,321	21,225,314	5,221,052	4,760,297
1959	70,819,000	—	—	78.0	—	282,287	—	597,107	25,786,945	22,818,918	5,606,978	5,084,804

Note appears at end of table

(continued)

TABLE Dg34–45 Telephone industry – telephones, access lines, wire, employees, and plant: 1876–2000 Continued

	Telephones and access lines				Miles of wire		Employees		Telephone plant			
	Telephones	Access lines		Percentage of households with telephones					Book value of capital stock		Depreciation reserves	
		FCC data	USTA data		U.S. telephone system	Bell (AT&T) System [1]	U.S. telephone system	Bell (AT&T) System	U.S. telephone system	Bell (AT&T) System	U.S. telephone system	Bell (AT&T) System
	Dg34	Dg35	Dg36	Dg37	Dg38	Dg39	Dg40	Dg41	Dg42	Dg43	Dg44	Dg45
Year	Number	Thousand	Thousand	Percent	Thousand	Thousand	Number	Number	Thousand dollars	Thousand dollars	Thousand dollars	Thousand dollars
1960	74,341,100	—	—	78.3	316,000	307,876	627,000	594,860	28,117,695	24,721,830	6,002,739	5,402,334
1961	77,425,400	—	—	78.9	—	327,319	—	581,245	30,406,536	26,586,552	6,439,293	5,749,767
1962	80,971,700	—	—	80.2	—	346,697	—	578,403	32,991,205	28,656,559	6,919,166	6,126,180
1963	84,450,300	—	—	81.4	—	368,594	—	585,941	35,701,794	30,854,403	7,495,023	6,583,840
1964	88,787,400	—	—	82.8	—	394,360	—	604,577	38,837,289	33,384,997	8,197,248	7,158,004
1965	93,658,800	—	—	84.6	436,000	422,623	655,000	627,278	42,284,489	36,228,981	8,961,734	7,793,812
1966	98,785,600	—	—	86.3	—	453,521	—	666,982	46,194,358	39,316,832	9,884,503	8,551,263
1967	103,751,900	—	—	87.1	—	480,308	—	673,316	50,128,902	42,508,397	10,932,449	9,445,322
1968	109,255,600	—	—	88.5	—	512,250	—	696,749	54,805,529	46,091,402	12,217,232	10,511,655
1969	115,200,700	—	—	89.8	—	553,868	—	755,065	60,397,615	50,479,993	13,488,096	11,553,823
1970	120,221,000	—	—	90.5	628,000	601,912	839,000	793,196	67,346,779	56,171,376	14,812,977	12,609,552
1971	125,140,800	—	—	—	—	646,000	—	796,000	74,735,000	62,049,000	16,219,000	13,743,000
1972	131,602,500	—	—	—	—	695,000	—	797,000	82,721,000	68,446,000	16,963,000	14,182,000
1973	138,288,389	—	—	—	—	752,000	—	818,000	91,391,000	75,479,000	18,957,000	15,791,000
1974	143,971,452	—	—	—	—	800,000	—	812,000	100,359,000	82,683,000	20,181,000	16,582,000
1975	149,007,803	—	—	—	872,000	832,000	840,000	789,000	108,704,000	89,184,000	21,698,000	17,578,000
1976	155,173,288	—	—	—	—	871,000	832,000	778,000	119,041,000	95,798,000	23,418,000	18,673,000
1977	162,072,146	—	—	—	—	910,000	851,000	785,000	129,240,000	103,600,000	25,287,000	19,894,000
1978	169,026,948	—	—	—	1,022,000	962,000	894,000	823,000	142,379,000	113,000,000	27,263,000	21,200,000
1979	175,535,112	—	—	—	1,081,000	1,018,000	928,000	855,000	156,391,000	123,900,000	29,580,000	22,600,000
1980	180,424,023	—	—	92.9	1,131,000	1,068,000	938,000	868,000	171,486,000	135,500,000	31,820,000	24,000,000
1981	181,891,596	—	—	—	1,188,000	1,113,000	945,000	874,000	187,347,000	148,500,000	36,105,000	27,200,000
1982	—	—	—	91.4	1,223,000	1,152,000	909,000	840,000	208,263,000	159,700,000	41,000,000	30,800,000
1983	—	—	111,373	91.4	1,260,000	1,181,000	858,000	788,000	183,000,000	167,800,000	47,053,000	35,500,000
1984	—	100,000	114,474	91.9	1,290,000	—	742,000	574,000	195,000,000	144,058,000	42,900,000	—
1985	—	103,000	118,275	92.4	1,313,000	—	—	—	207,400,000	153,577,000	50,000,000	—
1986	—	106,000	122,203	92.3	1,338,000	—	—	—	222,000,000	159,700,000	58,700,000	—
1987	—	111,000	126,725	92.5	1,371,000	—	—	—	250,200,000	173,700,000	69,800,000	—
1988	—	122,000	129,709	93.0	1,483,000	—	688,000	—	260,100,000	193,200,000	84,700,000	—
1989	—	126,000	132,683	93.3	1,502,000	—	663,000	500,000	265,000,000	197,100,000	94,200,000	—
1990	—	130,000	136,337	93.4	1,528,000	—	648,000	487,000	270,000,000	197,000,000	98,000,000	—
1991	—	137,000	139,658	93.8	—	—	616,000	458,000	279,000,000	199,300,000	102,000,000	—
1992	—	140,000	143,325	94.2	—	—	608,000	456,000	289,000,000	—	108,000,000	—
1993	—	149,000	150,200	93.8	—	—	592,000	452,000	299,000,000	—	117,000,000	—
1994	—	157,000	—	93.9	—	—	553,000	—	—	—	127,000,000	—
1995	—	—	—	93.9	—	—	—	—	—	—	—	—
1996	—	—	—	93.8	—	—	—	—	—	—	—	—
1997	—	—	—	94.2	—	—	—	—	—	—	—	—
1998	—	—	—	94.1	—	—	—	—	—	—	—	—
1999	—	—	—	—	—	—	—	—	—	—	—	—
2000	—	—	—	94.1	—	—	—	—	—	—	—	—

TABLE Dg34–45   Telephone industry – telephones, access lines, wire, employees, and plant: 1876–2000   *Continued*

[1] Beginning 1957, excludes block and drop wire.

Sources

Series Dg34. For 1876–1934: taken from U.S. Federal Communications Commission (FCC) records consisting of *Special Investigation Docket No. 1*, "Report on Control of Telephone Communications," volume 3, Exhibit 2096-D, p. 11 (June 15, 1937, processed). For 1935–1956: supplied to the FCC by American Telephone and Telegraph (AT&T); substantially the same data are also available in the AT&T annual reports to stockholders. For 1957–1981: supplied by AT&T, compiled from annual reports and unpublished data. See FCC, *Statistics of Communications Common Carriers* (SOCC) (annual issues); United States Independent Telephone Association, *Statistics of the Independent Telephone for the Year 1981*, p. 2.

Series Dg35. FCC, *SOCC* (annual issues) and unpublished data.

Series Dg36. United States Telecom Association (formerly United States Telephone Association, formerly United States Independent Telephone Association), *Statistics of the Local Exchange Carriers* (annual issues).

Series Dg37. For 1920–1970: AT&T, unpublished data. For 1980: U.S. Bureau of the Census, *1980 Census of Population and Housing*. For 1983–2000: FCC, *SOCC* (2000), Table 5.2.

Series Dg38. FCC, *SOCC* (annual issues) and unpublished data.

Series Dg39. For 1880–1884: AT&T, unpublished financial reports. For 1885–1935: FCC, unpublished data consisting of *Special Investigation Docket No. 1*, "Report on American Telephone and Telegraph Company Corporate and Financial History," volume 1, Exhibit number 1360-A (January 16, 1937, processed), pp. 76, 115. For 1936–1956: AT&T annual reports, and FCC, unpublished data. For 1957–1983: AT&T, compiled from reports of Bell System, Southern New England and Cincinnati and Suburban companies, and unpublished data. See also FCC, *SOCC* (annual issues).

Series Dg40–41. For 1880: U.S. Bureau of the Census, *Compendium of the Tenth Census, 1880*, p. 1327. For 1884–1899 and 1907–1935: FCC, unpublished data consisting of *Special Investigation Docket No. 1*, Exhibit number 1360-A, pp. 76, 136, 147. For 1900–1906: AT&T, unpublished data. For 1936–1983: AT&T, annual reports to stockholders, unpublished data, and FCC, unpublished data. For 1984–1998: United States Telecom Association, *Statistics of the Local Exchange Carriers* (annual issues).

Series Dg42 and Dg44. For AT&T data, see source for series Dg43 and Dg45. For independent companies: 1916–1983, United States Independent Telephone Association, Washington, D.C., *Statistics of the Independent Telephone Industry*; 1984–1994, FCC, *SOCC* (annual issues).

Series Dg43 and Dg45. For 1880: *Compendium of the Tenth Census, 1880*, p. 1332. For 1885–1935, FCC, unpublished data consisting of *Special Investigation Docket No. 1*, "Report on American Telephone and Telegraph Company Corporate and Financial History," volume 1, Exhibit number 1360-A (January 16, 1937, processed), pp. 73, 102; volume 2, Exhibit number 1360-B, Schedule 2 (appendix); "Report on Associated Bell Telephone Companies Financial and Operating Data," Exhibit number 1364 (January 23, 1937), Schedule A-15. For 1936–1956: AT&T, annual reports, and FCC, unpublished data. For 1957–1970: AT&T, annual reports and unpublished data. For 1971–1983: AT&T, unpublished data compiled from reports of Bell System and Southern New England and Cincinnati Bell Companies. 1984–1994: data on successor companies contained in United States Telecom Association, *Statistics of the Local Exchange Carriers* (annual issues).

Documentation

The Bell System provided the great bulk of local exchange and interexchange or toll-telephone facilities and service in the United States until its dissolution in 1984. It included the parent company of the Bell operating telephone companies, consolidated with associated holding and operating companies in the United States, not including connected independent or sublicensee companies. When data are presented for the Bell System, the figures are "statements of the Bell Telephone business as a whole, eliminating all duplications and showing the figures and results as 'if operated by a single company.'" The parent company was known as the American Telephone and Telegraph Company after January 1, 1900; prior to that date it was the American Bell Telephone Company. The number of companies included within the Bell group varied from time to time. In 1914, approximately thirty-five companies were included, and in 1915–1916 the number increased to thirty-nine. Subsequent consolidations reduced the number to twenty-nine in 1920 and to twenty-five, including Cincinnati Bell, Inc., and Southern New England Telephone Company, in 1970. Beginning 1936, AT&T in its consolidated financial statements excluded these two large minority-interest companies. For comparability with previous years, however, the figures have been adjusted to include these two companies using reports filed by them with the FCC.

Included in the Bell organization in 1970 were the following:

1. AT&T, the parent company.
2. Twenty-one regional subsidiaries owned and controlled by AT&T, plus a subsidiary of one of these regional companies. These twenty-two Bell System principal telephone subsidiaries furnished exchange and intrastate toll service, as well as interstate toll-telephone service; they constituted, with the parent, the Bell System of 1970.
3. Two other major companies, Cincinnati Bell, Inc., and Southern New England Telephone Company, in which AT&T had substantial minority interests. These two companies, together with the twenty-two Bell System subsidiaries, were referred to as the Associated Companies.
4. Bell Telephone Laboratories, Inc., a scientific research and development organization, and Western Electric Company, Inc., the Bell manufacturing and supply organization.

In addition, a number of Bell Company affiliates had varying degrees of stock interest in other telephone companies. Data relating to the Bell companies exclude operations of Bell Telephone Laboratories and of Western Electric, except as their operations affected operating expenses and miscellaneous income of the Bell companies. Bell Telephone Laboratories operated on a nonprofit basis, and the profits of Western Electric on sales to the Bell companies are not eliminated in the consolidated statements.

The historical growth of the Western Electric Company is described in "Report of the Federal Communications Commission on the Investigation of the Telephone Industry in the United States," pp. 56–64. Additional data appear in the "Report on Preliminary Survey and Investigation of Western Electric Company, Inc.," prepared by a committee of National Association of Railroad and Utilities Commissioners and FCC representatives (July 15, 1948, processed), and in annual supplements since 1948. In 1970, AT&T's annual share of the net income of Western Electric was over $253 million.

Independent companies were referred to as non-Bell companies, although AT&T or Bell companies had financial interests in some of them. The independents participated with Bell in providing toll service and had contractual arrangements with AT&T and the Bell Associated Companies.

The Bell System continued to provide the bulk of U.S. local and long distance service until 1984. On August 24, 1982, Judge Harold Greene initiated the system's breakup by entering a decision known as the Modified Final Judgment (it modified a 1956 court decision limiting AT&T to the telephone business). Under the agreement, which became effective January 1, 1984, AT&T retained its long distance service along with its manufacturing capability and Bell Labs, but spun off seven Regional Bell Operating Companies. These companies were to provide local service within 160 local access and transport areas (LATAs); long distance carriers were to provide service between them. These legal barriers to entry were relaxed as a consequence of the Telecommunications Act of 1996.

As a result of the breakup, AT&T became a vastly different company. Overnight, according to the company Internet site, its assets dropped from $149.5 billion to $34 billion, and its employees from over a million to 373,000. On September 20, 1995, the company announced its further devolution into three separate publicly traded companies: Lucent Technologies, a systems and equipment company that retained Bell Labs (spun off on September 30, 1996); NCR (formerly National Cash Register), a computer company that AT&T had bought in 1991 (divested on January 1, 1997); and a communications services company that retained the name.

With its traditional stronghold in long distance wired communication weakening, the company moved aggressively into other areas. Through a

TABLE Dg34–45 Telephone industry – telephones, access lines, wire, employees, and plant: 1876–2000 *Continued*

variety of acquisitions including Telecommunications, Inc. (TCI) and Media One, AT&T became the nation's largest cable provider, and through purchase of McCaw Cellular, a major player in wireless communication as well. In October 2000, the company announced its intention to split again into four publicly traded companies: AT&T Broadband, AT&T Wireless, AT&T Business, and AT&T Consumer, reflecting its four principal areas of business, although as of this writing, the restructuring has not been consummated. For further information, see the AT&T Internet site.

The Regional Bell Operating Companies (RBOCs) were originally formed from the eighteen regional Bell subsidiaries remaining at the end of 1983. In 1984, there were seven: Ameritech, Bell Atlantic, Bell South, Nynex, Pacific Telesis, Southwestern Bell, and U.S. West. As a consequence of mergers, that number has fallen to four: SBC (which includes Ameritech, Pacific Telesis, and Southwestern Bell), Bell South, Qwest (which acquired U.S. West in 2000), and Verizon (which now includes Bell Atlantic and Nynex, as well as former independent GTE (General Telegraph and Electronics)).

The wrenching changes associated with the Bell breakup did away with the traditional distinction between the Bell System and "independents." Reflecting these changes, the trade association of non-Bell companies, the United States Independent Telephone Association, changed its name to the United States Telephone Association and admitted the original seven RBOCs to its membership. All vestiges of the Bell–independent distinction are now gone: the organization includes companies providing local exchange, long distance, wireless, and Internet and cable services and is known as the United States Telecom Association (see the organization's Internet site). At the same time, the Telecommunications Act of 1996, by removing the legal barriers to entry embodied in the Modified Final Judgment, is in the process of blurring the distinctions between long distance and local service providers.

Series Dg34. The number of telephones comprises the total number of instruments and extensions in the system. Telephones also include telegraph and teletypewriter stations provided by the Bell System (as opposed to Western Union or Postal Telegraph) through 1930 and private line telephones through 1934. Lines internal to a firm, organization, or household, on which outside calls to public (external) phones cannot be placed, constitute private-line telephones. *Historical Statistics of the United States* (1975) also includes a footnote indicating that beginning in 1920, data on the total number of telephones excludes private-line telephones, which conflicts with the general source note indicating that these telephones were included through 1934. It has not been possible to revise this discrepancy, but it is likely of relatively small import in determining trends in the overall series.

Series Dg34. *Historical Statistics of the United States* (1975) included census data for the years 1880, 1890, 1902, 1907, 1912, 1917, 1922, 1927, 1932, and 1937. In all but five of these census years, data are identical to those reported in series Dg34. See *Historical Statistics of the United States* (1975) for these alternate data points.

Series Dg35–36. Because of the proliferation of extensions, particularly in households, the tabulation of the number of telephones becomes increasingly less meaningful as a measure of telephone penetration in the 1980s. Data on the number of access lines now give a more accurate measure of the continuing expansion of the telephone network, used increasingly for data as well as voice transmission.

Series Dg37. Through 1970, telephone penetration was estimated by AT&T by dividing the total number of residential lines by the number of households. In the last part of the twentieth century, this methodology became increasingly unreliable owing to the proliferation of second lines and second homes. The statistic for 1980 is based on the percent of households reporting that they had a telephone. Subsequent data are based on the addition of a question to the Current Population Survey (CPS), a panel survey designed to track household behavior between the censuses. The presumption here is that this survey refers to the availability in the household of a wired line; in future years, it is possible that more households will rely on wireless (cellular) service exclusively.

Series Dg38. Includes Puerto Rico and the Virgin Islands; excludes intercompany duplications; includes company, service, and private. Miles of wire is an imperfect index of the growth in telephone capacity for a variety of reasons: the growth of microwave and satellite transmission links; the continued improvement in multiplexing technology permitting multiple transmissions to occur over single lines; and the shift from single-wire lines to complex cable systems, including multiple pairs of twisted copper wire, coaxial tubes, and fiber-optic lines.

Series Dg39 and Dg41. *Historical Statistics of the United States* (1975) included data for the eight census years listed in the text for series Dg34.

Series Dg40–41. Figures for 1885–1935 exclude Western Electric Company.

Series Dg42–45. Series Dg42 and Dg44 include the data for the AT&T system and, after 1984, its successors, reported in series Dg43 and Dg45, plus data for independent telephone companies. Data for independent companies include only reporting companies. The FCC's uniform system of accounts, which became effective January 1, 1937, required establishment of telephone plant accounts on the basis of original cost (cost at time of first dedication to the public use). This applied to all plants ordinarily having a service life of more than one year, as well as to franchises, patents, rights-of-way, leaseholds, and other interests in land. The depreciation policies of the Bell System underwent various changes, from a simple maintenance reserve set up for the purpose of equalizing maintenance charges over a period of years and providing for deferred maintenance expenses, to depreciation rates prescribed by the FCC. Prescription of depreciation rates for Bell companies began in 1949, and initial prescriptions were completed in 1953. For a discussion of Bell System depreciation policies, see "Report of the Federal Communications Commission on the Investigation of the Telephone Industry in the United States," pp. 325–49.

TABLE Dg46–55 Telephone industry – telephones and average daily conversations: 1876–1995

Contributed by David F. Weiman

	Telephones					Average daily conversations				
				Independent companies		Bell System		Independent companies		
	Residential	Business	Bell System companies	Not connected with the Bell System	Connected with the Bell System	Local	Toll	Local	Toll	Local exchange carriers
	Dg46	Dg47	Dg48	Dg49	Dg50	Dg51	Dg52	Dg53	Dg54	Dg55 [1]
Year	Thousand	Thousand	Thousand	Thousand	Thousand	Thousand	Thousand	Thousand	Thousand	Thousand
1876	—	—	3	—	—	—	—	—	—	—
1877	—	—	9	—	—	—	—	—	—	—
1878	—	—	26	—	—	—	—	—	—	—
1879	—	—	31	—	—	—	—	—	—	—
1880	—	—	48	—	—	237	2	—	—	—
1881	—	—	71	—	—	—	—	—	—	—
1882	—	—	98	—	—	—	—	—	—	—
1883	—	—	124	—	—	590	5	—	—	—
1884	—	—	148	—	—	698	8	—	—	—
1885	—	—	156	—	—	747	7	—	—	—
1886	—	—	167	—	—	856	7	—	—	—
1887	—	—	181	—	—	1,012	7	—	—	—
1888	—	—	195	—	—	1,052	7	—	—	—
1889	—	—	212	—	—	1,240	8	—	—	—
1890	—	—	228	—	—	1,438	10	—	—	—
1891	—	—	239	—	—	1,585	34	—	—	—
1892	—	—	261	—	—	1,868	41	—	—	—
1893	—	—	266	—	—	1,872	34	—	—	—
1894	—	—	270	—	15	2,088	38	—	—	—
1895	—	—	310	—	30	2,351	51	170	3	—
1896	—	—	354	—	50	2,630	63	—	—	—
1897	—	—	415	—	100	3,099	75	—	—	—
1898	—	—	496	—	185	3,823	95	—	—	—
1899	—	—	667	10	328	5,174	133	—	—	—
1900	—	—	836	20	500	4,773	149	2,916	44	—
1901	—	—	1,061	48	692	6,342	187	4,468	68	—
1902	—	—	1,317	84	970	7,850	240	6,146	94	—
1903	—	—	1,564	121	1,124	8,316	258	6,903	105	—
1904	—	—	1,838	167	1,348	9,388	301	7,884	120	—
1905	—	—	2,285	246	1,596	11,404	368	9,756	148	—
1906	—	—	2,774	297	1,862	13,875	461	11,430	175	—
1907	—	—	3,013	826	2,280	15,266	494	13,814	210	—
1908	—	—	3,176	1,188	2,119	15,576	463	15,717	239	—
1909	—	—	3,522	1,621	1,853	16,777	517	16,213	247	—
1910	—	—	3,933	1,950	1,753	18,256	602	17,043	260	—
1911	—	—	4,352	2,281	1,716	19,773	645	17,466	266	—
1912	—	—	4,804	2,496	1,430	21,532	738	18,064	275	—
1913	—	—	5,255	2,878	1,409	22,255	806	17,640	272	—
1914	—	—	5,585	3,074	1,388	22,775	799	17,198	262	—
1915	—	—	5,968	3,204	1,351	25,184	819	18,535	282	—
1916	—	—	6,545	3,348	1,348	28,530	890	19,856	302	—
1917	—	—	7,032	3,458	1,226	30,845	1,009	19,785	302	—
1918	—	—	7,202	3,864	1,012	30,001	1,067	18,753	285	—
1919	—	—	7,739	4,057	873	29,286	1,167	18,158	276	—
1920	9,021	4,252	8,736	3,810	727	31,836	1,327	18,371	280	—
1921	9,342	4,475	9,328	3,994	495	33,671	1,356	18,447	281	—
1922	9,642	4,652	9,950	3,912	432	36,831	1,523	18,329	317	—
1923	10,345	4,971	10,857	4,090	369	41,109	1,683	18,516	322	—
1924	10,773	5,242	11,857	3,908	250	43,981	1,835	18,260	324	—
1925	11,270	5,605	12,622	4,037	216	46,702	2,098	18,148	352	—
1926	11,689	5,991	13,402	4,106	172	49,980	2,375	18,453	372	—
1927	12,086	6,360	14,155	4,133	158	52,581	2,615	18,100	369	—
1928	12,645	6,611	14,955	4,157	144	56,196	2,839	17,895	370	—
1929	13,135	6,835	15,838	4,022	110	61,034	3,139	18,107	370	—
1930	13,153	6,950	15,983	4,017	103	62,365	2,933	17,860	362	—
1931	12,754	6,848	15,692	3,816	94	62,205	2,700	17,245	350	—
1932	11,054	6,287	14,011	3,246	84	58,813	2,251	15,637	299	—
1933	10,475	6,153	13,501	3,051	76	55,199	2,047	14,481	273	—
1934	10,683	6,186	13,805	2,992	72	56,648	2,142	14,332	278	—

Notes appear at end of table

(continued)

TABLE Dg46–55 Telephone industry – telephones and average daily conversations: 1876–1995 *Continued*

	Telephones					Average daily conversations				
				Independent companies		Bell System		Independent companies		
	Residential	Business	Bell System companies	Not connected with the Bell System	Connected with the Bell System	Local	Toll	Local	Toll	Local exchange carriers
	Dg46	Dg47	Dg48	Dg49	Dg50	Dg51	Dg52	Dg53	Dg54	Dg55 [1]
Year	Thousand	Thousand	Thousand	Thousand	Thousand	Thousand	Thousand	Thousand	Thousand	Thousand
1935	11,003	6,421	14,280	3,073	71	58,809	2,276	14,631	284	—
1936	11,654	6,779	15,192	3,170	71	64,960	2,589	14,124	281	—
1937	12,341	7,112	16,097	3,288	68	68,833	2,682	14,678	287	—
1938	12,727	7,226	16,536	3,349	68	70,070	2,596	14,739	283	—
1939	13,446	7,385	17,329	3,435	67	74,020	2,705	15,292	294	—
1940	14,271	7,657	18,311	3,550	67	79,515	2,852	16,110	306	—
1941	15,453	8,068	19,742	3,709	70	84,360	3,222	16,659	69	—
1942	16,619	8,300	21,000	3,853	66	86,314	3,544	17,141	68	—
1943	17,706	8,675	22,301	4,014	66	85,000	4,046	17,138	93	—
1944	17,791	9,068	22,653	4,190	16	84,618	4,377	17,227	107	—
1945	18,409	9,458	23,547	4,306	14	89,362	4,852	17,667	99	—
1946	21,239	10,372	26,900	4,697	14	103,827	5,544	18,645	82	—
1947	23,708	11,159	29,773	5,081	13	113,075	5,908	20,353	86	—
1948	26,314	11,891	32,698	5,495	12	123,481	6,065	22,520	90	—
1949	28,327	12,382	34,175	6,524	10	130,403	6,125	23,961	102	—
1950	30,077	12,927	36,795	6,200	9	138,881	6,118	25,539	85	—
1951	31,939	13,697	38,943	6,685	8	143,235	6,230	26,384	74	—
1952	33,667	14,389	41,014	7,038	4	147,400	6,358	27,292	73	—
1953	35,411	14,962	43,010	7,359	4	151,667	6,552	34,645	1,365	—
1954	37,272	15,534	45,039	7,764	3	157,423	6,799	35,946	1,380	—
1955	39,854	16,389	48,028	8,212	3	166,438	7,420	37,722	1,430	—
1956	42,832	17,358	51,344	8,843	3	175,848	8,015	41,863	1,518	—
1957	45,433	18,191	54,241	9,380	3	185,304	8,490	44,174	1,602	—
1958	47,831	18,814	56,759	9,886	(Z)	193,627	8,834	48,192	1,645	—
1959	—	—	60,110	10,710	(Z)	204,491	9,549	53,525	1,785	—
1960	53,537	20,805	62,989	11,353	(Z)	215,317	10,068	58,005	1,996	—
1961	55,737	21,685	65,507	11,915	—	222,320	10,539	62,177	2,074	—
1962	58,289	22,680	68,393	12,576	—	237,942	11,164	65,158	2,242	—
1963	60,876	23,577	71,152	13,301	—	246,282	11,784	68,400	2,400	—
1964	64,124	24,669	74,659	14,134	—	256,500	12,800	73,200	2,700	—
1965	67,729	25,927	78,632	15,024	—	273,400	14,000	77,400	3,000	—
1966	71,481	27,308	82,813	15,976	—	288,000	15,400	82,800	3,300	—
1967	74,963	28,789	86,776	16,976	—	298,600	16,700	87,100	3,600	—
1968	79,029	30,227	91,122	18,134	—	311,800	18,400	92,800	3,900	—
1969	83,210	32,012	95,943	19,279	—	337,900	20,700	97,500	4,100	—
1970	87,137	33,081	99,903	20,315	—	356,400	22,500	102,000	4,300	—
1971	91,000	34,000	104,000	21,000	—	375,000	24,000	112,000	5,000	—
1972	96,000	36,000	109,000	23,000	—	394,000	27,000	129,000	6,000	—
1973	101,000	37,000	114,000	24,000	—	414,000	30,000	125,000	7,000	—
1974	105,000	39,000	118,000	26,000	—	438,000	32,000	136,000	7,000	—
1975	110,000	39,000	122,000	27,000	—	448,000	33,000	144,000	8,000	—
1976	114,000	41,000	127,000	28,000	—	462,000	36,000	137,000	9,000	—
1977	120,000	52,000	132,000	30,000	—	479,000	40,000	150,000	10,000	—
1978	125,000	44,000	137,000	31,000	—	515,000	45,000	165,000	11,000	—
1979	130,000	46,000	143,000	32,000	—	526,000	50,000	156,000	14,000	—
1980	133,000	48,000	142,000	35,000	—	541,000	54,000	176,000	16,000	—
1981	135,000	47,000	147,000	35,000	—	545,000	56,000	182,000	17,000	—
1982	—	—	—	—	—	—	—	183,840	17,960	—
1983	—	—	—	—	—	—	—	188,070	21,130	—
1984	—	—	—	—	—	—	—	190,000	20,000	1,199,220
1985	—	—	—	—	—	—	—	203,138	20,314	1,263,537
1986	—	—	—	—	—	—	—	210,000	33,000	1,327,000
1987	—	—	—	—	—	—	—	251,000	50,000	1,662,000
1988	—	—	—	—	—	—	—	—	—	1,700,000
1989	—	—	—	—	—	—	—	—	—	9,569,000
1990	—	—	—	—	—	—	—	—	—	9,515,000
1991	—	—	—	—	—	—	—	—	—	9,773,000
1992	—	—	—	—	—	—	—	—	—	9,885,000
1993	—	—	—	—	—	—	—	—	—	10,665,000
1994	—	—	—	—	—	—	—	—	—	11,158,000
1995	—	—	—	—	—	—	—	—	—	11,641,000

TABLE Dg46–55   Telephone industry – telephones and average daily conversations: 1876–1995   *Continued*

(Z) Less than 500.

[1] Beginning in 1989, average business-day minutes of use.

Sources

For 1876–1934: U.S. Federal Communications Commission (FCC), unpublished data consisting of *Special Investigation Docket No. 1*, "Report on Control of Telephone Communications," volume 3, Exhibit number 2096-D, p. 11 (June 15, 1937, processed), and "Report on American Telephone and Telegraph Company Corporate and Financial History," volume 1, Exhibit number 1360-A, pp. 115, 150. For 1935–1981: American Telephone and Telegraph Company (AT&T), annual reports and unpublished data supplied to the FCC. For 1982–1989: United States Telephone Association (USTA), *Statistics of the Telephone Industry* (annual issues). For 1990–1995: USTA, *Statistics of Local Exchange Carriers* (annual issues). Recent data are reproduced in the U.S. Census Bureau, *Statistical Abstract of the United States* (various years).

Documentation

Historically, local exchange service meant telephone service within an exchange area. A local call was defined as a call originating in and completed within the same public-exchange area; a toll call was one that originated in one exchange destined to another exchange area, whether located nearby or across the continent. Prior to the breakup of the Bell System, in instances in which there was a high community of interest between exchanges, accompanied by considerable calling on a message toll basis, "extended-area service" was established under which adjacent and nearby exchanges were included in the subscriber's local service area. The growth of this type of service significantly affected the number of calls classified as local that otherwise would have been classified and charged as toll. Elimination of toll charges through the establishment of extended-area service tended to stimulate telephone usage within the service area as well.

Conversations are those completed calls originating from company and service telephones, excluding private-line telephones. Local calls include both completed and uncompleted calls. Bell System toll messages consisted of interstate and intrastate completed calls originated or terminated at Bell System Associated Company telephones, and toll messages originated or terminated at connecting (that is, independent) company telephones, provided their transmission utilized toll-line facilities of a Bell operating company. Toll messages handled wholly over facilities of connecting or nonconnecting independent companies are shown under independent companies. Toll-message figures include ship-to-shore messages and international messages. Because a toll ticket was made for each toll call, the count can be relatively exact. In very large exchanges, some counts of local calls were automatically accumulated in message registers, but in small exchanges the counts were estimates based upon samples.

Following the breakup of the Bell System, the relevant distinction becomes those calls made within local access and transport areas (inter-LATA calls), whose handling was, until the Telecommunications Act of 1996, restricted to Regional Bell Operating Companies, and calls made between LATA areas, the province until 1996 of long distance companies. See the text for Table Dg34–45.

Series Dg46–50. Telephones are measured in number of discrete physical units.

Series Dg49–50. These series show the extent to which independent companies were integrated into the Bell System through interconnection agreements, typically exclusive sublicense arrangements with a Bell operating company.

Series Dg51–55. Data are measures of the average number of business day conversations. Conversations are defined as originating calls for local calls, and as completed calls for toll or long distance calls. Beginning in 1989, average daily conversations are measured by the average business-day minutes of use.

TABLE Dg56–63   Telephone rates between New York and selected cities: 1902–1981

Contributed by Alexander J. Field

		Philadelphia	Chicago	Denver	San Francisco	London	Cairo	Tokyo	Buenos Aires
		Dg56	Dg57	Dg58	Dg59	Dg60	Dg61	Dg62	Dg63
Year	Month	Dollars	Dollars	Dollars	Dollars	Dollars	Dollars	Dollars	Dollars
1902	— [1]	0.55	5.45	—	—	—	—	—	—
1911	—	—	—	11.25	—	—	—	—	—
1915	Jan	—	—	11.25	20.70	—	—	—	—
1917	June	0.75 [3]	5.00 [3]	11.25	18.50	—	—	—	—
1917	Mar	—	—	11.25	19.80	—	—	—	—
1919	Jan	0.55	4.65	10.40	16.50	—	—	—	—
1926	Oct	0.60	3.40	7.25	11.30	—	—	—	—
1927	Dec	0.60	3.25	6.00	9.00	75.00	—	—	—
1928	—	0.60	3.25	6.00	9.00	45.00	—	—	—
1929	Feb	0.60	3.00	6.00	9.00	45.00	—	—	—
1930	Jan	0.50	3.00	6.00	9.00	30.00	—	—	36.00
1931	—	0.50	3.00	6.00	9.00	30.00	—	—	30.00
1932	—	0.50	3.00	6.00	9.00	30.00	36.00	—	30.00
1934	—	0.50	3.00	6.00	9.00	30.00	36.00	39.00	30.00
1936	Sept	0.50	2.50	5.25	7.50	21.00	30.00	33.00	21.00
1937	Jan	0.45	2.20	4.50	6.50	21.00	30.00	30.75	21.00
1939	—	0.45	2.20	4.50	6.50	21.00	30.00	30.75	15.00
1940	May	0.45	1.90	3.25	4.00	21.00	30.00	19.50	15.00
1941	July	0.45	1.75	3.25	4.00	21.00	30.00	19.50	15.00
1944	—	0.45	1.75	3.25	4.00	21.00	30.00	19.50	12.00
1945	July	0.45	1.75	2.35	2.50	12.00	30.00	19.50	12.00
1946	Feb	0.45	1.55	2.20	2.50	12.00	12.00	12.00	12.00
1952	Mar	0.50	1.50	2.20	2.50	12.00	12.00	12.00	12.00
1959	Sept	0.50	1.45	1.95	2.25	12.00	12.00	12.00	12.00
1960	Feb	0.50	1.45	1.80	2.25	12.00	12.00	12.00	12.00

Notes appear at end of table

(continued)

TABLE Dg56–63   Telephone rates between New York and selected cities: 1902–1981   *Continued*

| Year | Month | Philadelphia | Chicago | Denver | San Francisco | London | Cairo | Tokyo | Buenos Aires |
| | | Dg56 | Dg57 | Dg58 | Dg59 | Dg60 | Dg61 | Dg62 | Dg63 |
		Dollars	Dollars	Dollars	Dollars	Dollars	Dollars	Dollars	Dollars
1965	Dec	0.50	1.40	1.70	2.00	12.00	12.00	12.00	12.00
1967	Dec	0.50	1.40	1.60	1.75	12.00	12.00	12.00	12.00
1968	Aug	0.50	1.30	1.55	1.70	12.00	12.00	12.00	12.00
1970	Feb	0.50	1.05	1.25	1.35	9.60	12.00	12.00	12.00
1972	—	0.55	1.05	1.25	1.35	9.60	12.00	12.00	12.00
1973	—	0.60	1.15	1.35	1.45	9.60	12.00	12.00	12.00
1974	— [2]	0.60	1.15	1.35	1.45	3.60	9.00	9.00	8.00
1975	— [2]	0.90	1.20	1.30	1.36	3.60	9.00	9.00	8.00
1976	— [2]	0.99	1.18	1.24	1.30	3.60	9.00	9.00	8.00
1977	— [2]	1.01	1.18	1.24	1.30	3.60	9.00	9.00	8.00
1978	— [2]	1.01	1.18	1.24	1.30	4.50	9.00	7.80	8.00
1980	— [2]	1.05	1.25	1.31	1.37	4.80	9.45	7.80	7.05
1981	— [2]	1.22	1.45	1.52	1.58	3.00	9.45	4.95	4.50

[1] Toll rates were $0.006 per mile for all mileages.

[2] Rates in effect as of December 31.

[3] Rates in effect immediately prior to January 21, 1919, according to an item in the *New York Times* (January 23, 1919).

Sources

Series Dg56–59. For 1902: U.S. Bureau of the Census, *Special Reports: Telephones and Telegraphs, 1902*, p. 77. For 1911–1970: U.S. Federal Communications Commission (FCC), unpublished data. For 1972–1981: FCC, *Statistics of Communications, Common Carriers* (annual issues).

Series Dg60–63. See the sources for series Dg30–33.

Documentation
Series Dg56–59

Rates are for a station-to-station, daytime, three-minute telephone call.

Data for 1911–1917 are based on records of American Telephone and Telegraph (AT&T), newspapers, and other published reports. Data for 1919–1937 are based on rate and research information in FCC, "The Classified Toll Rate Structure and Basic Rate Practices for Message Toll Telephone Service," pp. 40–7 (January 15, 1938, processed). Data for 1940–1970 are based on unpublished data and tariffs of the FCC. Considerable historical toll-rate data also appear in the report of a committee of the National Association of Railroad and Utilities Commissioners (NARUC) and FCC representatives, "Message Toll Telephone Rates and Disparities" (annual issues in October).

The three major classes of toll-telephone messages were dial station-to-station, operator station-to-station, and person-to-person. In dial station-to-station service, the person originating the call from other than a coin telephone station dialed the telephone number desired, and the call was completed without the assistance of a telephone company operator.

In interstate toll service, operator station rates were over 10 percent higher than dial station rates, and person-to-person rates over twice the amount of the rates for dial station service. On station calls, the starting point was computed at the time communication was established between the calling and called stations; on person-to-person calls, the chargeable period began when the person called was reached. There was generally no rate differentiation between station and person service until January 21, 1919.

A paucity of historical data exists with respect to local exchange rates. Such data can only be laboriously constructed from the records of the Bell System companies and other telephone companies or from the tariffs filed with each state that has regulatory authority over the intrastate telephone rates. One source of data pertaining to exchange rates is the Census Bureau report *Telephones and Telegraphs and Municipal Electric Fire-Alarm and Police-Patrol Signaling Systems* (1912), pp. 49–156, which presents telephone rates of selected cities in thirty-eight states and the District of Columbia. Another source of exchange-rate data is provided by the responses of telephone companies to FCC's Telephone Division Order number 9, which called for rates in effect in selected-size exchanges between 1907 and 1933. These responses are on file at the FCC.

Series Dg60–63. Rates are for a three-minute telephone conversation – person-to-person for 1927–1970, and station-to-station for 1974–1981. Also see the text for series Dg30–33.

TABLE Dg64–75   Telephone industry finances – Bell and independent companies: 1880–1995

Contributed by David F. Weiman

	Bell companies						Independent companies					
	Operating revenues			Operating expenses	Federal income taxes	Net income	Operating revenues			Operating expenses	Federal income taxes	Net income
	Total	Local	Toll				Total	Local	Toll			
	Dg64	Dg65	Dg66	Dg67	Dg68	Dg69	Dg70	Dg71	Dg72	Dg73	Dg74	Dg75
Year	Thousand dollars	Thousand dollars	Thousand dollars	Thousand dollars	Thousand dollars	Thousand dollars	Thousand dollars	Thousand dollars	Thousand dollars	Thousand dollars	Thousand dollars	Thousand dollars
1880	3,098	—	—	2,374	—	—	—	—	—	—	—	—
1885	10,002	—	—	5,124	—	4,882	—	—	—	—	—	—
1886	—	—	—	—	—	5,160	—	—	—	—	—	—
1887	—	—	—	—	—	5,506	—	—	—	—	—	—
1888	—	—	—	—	—	5,747	—	—	—	—	—	—
1889	—	—	—	—	—	6,202	—	—	—	—	—	—
1890	16,153	—	—	9,068	—	6,866	—	—	—	—	—	—
1891	—	—	—	—	—	6,741	—	—	—	—	—	—
1892	—	—	—	—	—	8,114	—	—	—	—	—	—
1893	—	—	—	—	—	8,630	—	—	—	—	—	—
1894	—	—	—	—	—	7,708	—	—	—	—	—	—
1895	24,059	—	—	15,488	—	8,053	—	—	—	—	—	—
1896	—	—	—	—	—	8,833	—	—	—	—	—	—
1897	—	—	—	—	—	9,735	—	—	—	—	—	—
1898	—	—	—	—	—	10,577	—	—	—	—	—	—
1899	—	—	—	—	—	12,095	—	—	—	—	—	—
1900	46,086	32,414	12,098	30,632	—	13,364	—	—	—	—	—	—
1901	54,177	37,971	14,329	35,824	—	15,464	—	—	—	—	—	—
1902	64,176	44,845	16,906	44,338	—	16,129	—	—	—	—	—	—
1903	75,089	52,710	19,879	50,946	—	20,321	—	—	—	—	—	—
1904	85,296	59,841	22,638	58,152	—	22,487	—	—	—	—	—	—
1905	96,923	67,620	26,412	66,189	—	25,474	—	—	—	—	—	—
1906	11,108	77,243	30,192	77,967	—	25,582	—	—	—	—	—	—
1907	127,859	88,682	34,411	87,395	—	30,676	—	—	—	—	—	—
1908	137,363	93,964	35,800	93,377	—	33,894	—	—	—	—	—	—
1909	148,951	103,502	40,095	101,547	—	38,146	—	—	—	—	—	—
1910	164,245	114,896	45,004	114,618	—	39,438	—	—	—	—	—	—
1911	178,267	126,283	47,413	127,892	—	37,975	—	—	—	—	—	—
1912	197,798	139,630	53,037	142,285	—	42,681	—	—	—	—	—	—
1913	214,126	151,260	57,009	156,883	—	42,037	—	—	—	—	—	—
1914	224,500	160,311	58,466	166,102	603	40,307	—	—	—	—	—	—
1915	232,721	169,156	62,930	171,888	674	48,086	—	—	—	—	—	—
1916	263,095	188,888	72,972	197,772	1,103	52,921	48,591	—	—	34,521	—	9,268
1917	293,666	207,472	84,560	224,766	4,342	50,714	50,485	40,967	9,152	37,260	—	8,507
1918	326,524	—	—	—	5,893	46,383	—	—	—	—	—	—
1919	387,659	—	—	—	—	6,635	48,621	—	—	—	—	—
1920	448,233	301,283	141,883	376,171	4,246	47,785	80,561	—	—	67,548	—	7,559
1921	495,244	343,133	146,459	397,226	7,471	67,425	79,704	—	—	66,781	—	7,809
1922	543,747	374,719	163,098	426,302	10,162	86,623	85,130	—	—	67,945	—	11,036
1923	598,153	412,009	178,427	470,556	11,748	99,624	67,486	—	—	51,078	—	9,231
1924	653,459	454,326	190,318	511,905	13,091	107,246	69,236	—	—	52,163	—	9,936
1925	736,648	506,026	219,913	557,295	16,829	136,503	73,122	—	—	54,339	—	11,714
1926	817,928	557,490	248,087	611,675	22,712	155,061	78,240	—	—	57,376	1,661	12,476
1927	888,987	604,266	271,174	670,397	23,908	166,059	76,411	—	—	55,550	1,878	12,555
1928	969,237	644,209	309,334	728,544	25,591	191,088	83,866	—	—	59,446	1,740	14,966
1929	1,063,633	691,359	354,286	807,988	22,924	217,105	90,926	—	—	63,549	1,661	17,612
1930	1,094,883	728,709	348,541	852,703	21,931	201,646	90,884	—	—	63,860	1,454	16,628
1931	1,066,895	723,920	326,269	824,115	21,249	193,379	87,867	—	—	61,538	1,293	15,355
1932	943,540	670,737	263,148	747,713	19,073	139,336	77,067	—	—	55,725	1,147	9,616
1933	872,406	617,253	243,906	684,424	17,109	114,580	68,533	—	—	51,940	1,073	6,727
1934	884,532	607,676	258,691	685,951	19,586	125,352	63,934	—	—	48,466	1,283	6,229
1935	934,371	640,993	273,483	726,510	20,843	147,539	61,170	46,273	13,029	43,974	—	8,830
1936	1,020,698	685,110	311,489	766,287	28,807	201,624	65,500	49,041	14,803	47,481	—	10,259
1937	1,079,004	724,658	327,229	833,789	31,740	197,457	69,957	51,956	16,145	51,634	—	10,823
1938	1,080,591	734,687	317,290	849,079	35,015	167,896	71,508	53,678	15,923	53,366	—	10,573
1939	1,136,412	766,956	338,391	870,762	41,387	203,888	75,768	56,539	17,172	55,992	—	12,444

(continued)

TABLE Dg64–75 Telephone industry finances – Bell and independent companies: 1880–1995 *Continued*

	Bell companies						Independent companies					
	Operating revenues			Operating expenses	Federal income taxes	Net income	Operating revenues			Operating expenses	Federal income taxes	Net income
	Total	Local	Toll				Total	Local	Toll			
	Dg64	Dg65	Dg66	Dg67	Dg68	Dg69	Dg70	Dg71	Dg72	Dg73	Dg74	Dg75
Year	Thousand dollars	Thousand dollars	Thousand dollars	Thousand dollars	Thousand dollars	Thousand dollars	Thousand dollars	Thousand dollars	Thousand dollars	Thousand dollars	Thousand dollars	Thousand dollars
1940	1,205,435	811,400	360,792	913,023	64,419	223,941	80,846	59,993	18,676	61,478	—	11,768
1941	1,333,064	872,089	424,521	986,412	110,375	203,509	88,519	64,276	21,878	68,712	—	13,705
1942	1,507,336	923,765	544,234	1,089,074	195,906	174,232	97,071	68,786	25,801	66,459	11,875	12,725
1943	1,690,720	981,094	666,238	1,214,015	243,605	188,061	117,011	77,015	37,488	78,602	17,862	14,106
1944	1,814,113	1,017,244	746,694	1,308,926	283,062	180,163	126,081	80,752	42,519	86,482	18,704	14,329
1945	1,978,418	1,072,731	845,008	1,454,174	259,213	187,656	135,494	84,155	48,019	94,889	19,697	14,414
1946	2,146,894	1,198,802	874,497	1,789,686	104,121	219,966	154,757	93,857	56,754	117,195	12,522	18,781
1947	2,282,446	1,311,401	880,227	2,013,725	77,024	168,890	176,358	107,235	63,784	140,500	11,213	17,939
1948	2,693,027	1,551,742	1,030,474	2,324,762	105,154	235,264	203,578	124,219	72,898	161,499	12,843	21,621
1949	2,965,852	1,746,771	1,092,395	2,530,899	125,878	247,830	233,064	145,007	80,829	199,288	—	—
1950	3,341,308	1,995,659	1,207,509	2,652,421	248,328	367,377	270,347	170,536	91,512	211,493	18,762	28,765
1951	3,727,632	2,205,117	1,369,682	2,929,122	350,134	383,763	303,060	195,352	98,343	234,478	26,366	29,202
1952	4,135,537	2,460,438	1,500,063	3,240,896	403,031	427,459	347,307	226,436	109,943	265,597	31,140	36,368
1953	4,523,707	2,713,501	1,603,608	3,500,599	472,994	501,805	407,738	268,435	125,962	297,702	44,201	49,112
1954	4,901,162	2,914,754	1,755,241	3,746,294	524,995	577,303	449,464	295,965	137,820	327,318	48,841	55,136
1955	5,424,246	3,168,480	1,999,553	4,039,159	644,404	696,857	503,153	329,355	155,431	354,386	61,129	66,846
1956	5,964,876	3,457,640	2,220,488	4,437,810	714,260	792,632	570,929	370,587	178,728	402,318	67,472	76,686
1957	6,466,160	3,743,800	2,406,830	4,788,708	773,481	868,486	633,815	411,704	198,618	453,644	69,181	80,002
1958	6,936,364	4,049,465	2,543,114	4,910,866	939,687	1,001,709	703,792	459,906	217,470	502,806	76,461	86,409
1959	7,569,869	4,362,374	2,843,466	5,233,097	1,080,302	1,170,571	801,289	519,394	254,147	560,257	94,248	103,215
1960	8,108,793	4,665,115	3,058,181	5,584,190	1,172,131	1,274,101	905,744	585,004	289,400	630,187	107,092	116,998
1961	8,614,337	4,921,320	3,284,038	5,903,602	1,244,867	1,350,079	993,827	640,202	320,193	681,357	122,138	133,241
1962	9,192,520	5,219,431	3,543,591	6,271,299	1,360,144	1,456,158	1,119,531	710,073	372,005	754,569	137,506	157,003
1963	9,796,302	5,527,789	3,814,370	6,647,813	1,455,070	1,557,130	1,247,652	778,371	428,596	835,445	153,868	177,432
1964	10,549,386	5,778,936	4,291,054	7,233,111	1,476,741	1,743,574	1,386,143	849,035	491,720	934,421	161,036	201,013
1965	11,320,328	6,114,439	4,705,856	7,857,118	1,466,287	1,886,943	1,529,709	916,736	560,551	1,040,236	161,993	224,873
1966	12,419,140	6,517,473	5,378,439	8,577,644	1,633,247	2,076,305	1,734,341	1,000,283	668,752	1,183,853	174,322	257,241
1967	13,310,606	6,910,073	5,852,380	9,245,691	1,695,744	2,150,612	1,872,943	1,072,533	729,944	1,299,707	172,198	263,881
1968	14,428,866	7,366,128	6,472,036	10,025,833	1,990,741	2,152,630	2,152,316	1,178,891	891,800	1,477,393	214,630	293,484
1969	16,057,755	7,979,015	7,450,709	11,401,821	2,018,380	2,307,298	2,461,750	1,313,635	1,054,210	1,695,175	230,715	325,927
1970	17,368,544	8,685,479	8,042,160	12,867,499	1,608,526	2,303,227	2,791,304	1,453,662	1,232,084	1,952,904	224,326	356,094
1971	18,952,000	9,426,000	8,835,000	14,293,000	—	2,352,000	3,202,000	—	—	2,228,000	—	430,000
1972	21,388,000	10,630,000	9,983,000	16,032,000	—	2,658,000	3,661,000	—	—	2,540,000	—	495,000
1973	24,072,000	11,712,000	11,524,000	17,805,000	—	3,125,000	4,188,000	—	—	2,881,000	—	573,000
1974	26,761,000	13,131,000	12,729,000	19,814,000	—	3,306,000	4,714,000	—	—	3,254,000	—	641,000
1975	29,591,000	14,368,000	14,224,000	22,155,000	—	3,292,000	5,294,000	—	—	3,639,000	—	711,000
1976	33,518,000	15,977,000	16,399,000	24,802,000	—	3,999,000	6,072,000	—	—	4,159,000	—	837,000
1977	37,260,000	17,482,000	18,468,000	27,674,000	—	4,749,000	6,864,000	—	—	4,722,000	—	960,000
1978	41,953,000	19,224,000	21,207,000	30,969,000	—	5,605,000	7,807,000	—	—	5,405,000	—	1,073,000
1979	46,400,000	20,800,000	23,800,000	34,900,000	—	5,600,000	9,073,000	—	—	6,415,000	—	1,210,000
1980	51,900,000	23,000,000	26,700,000	39,300,000	—	6,100,000	10,177,000	—	—	7,279,000	—	1,268,000
1981	59,400,000	26,300,000	30,900,000	45,000,000	—	6,900,000	11,860,000	—	—	8,449,000	—	1,505,000
1982	65,700,000	29,600,000	33,900,000	51,400,000	—	6,600,000	13,445,000	—	—	10,699,000	—	1,751,000
1983	69,300,000	31,000,000	35,400,000	47,200,000	—	6,800,000	14,309,000	—	—	11,432,000	—	1,968,000
1984	—	—	—	—	—	—	15,403,000	—	—	12,305,000	—	2,199,000
1985	—	—	—	—	—	—	16,684,000	—	—	13,323,000	—	2,434,000
1986	—	—	—	—	—	—	17,555,000	—	—	12,548,000	—	2,617,000
1987	—	—	—	—	—	—	17,266,000	—	—	12,532,000	—	2,663,000
1989	—	—	—	—	—	—	21,700,000	—	—	15,300,000	—	3,300,000
1990	—	—	—	—	—	—	22,100,000	—	—	15,600,000	—	3,400,000
1991	—	—	—	—	—	—	23,100,000	—	—	16,200,000	—	3,500,000
1992	—	—	—	—	—	—	24,000,000	—	—	16,000,000	—	4,000,000
1993	—	—	—	—	—	—	24,200,000	—	—	17,300,000	—	2,000,000
1994	—	—	—	—	—	—	25,000,000	—	—	18,000,000	—	4,000,000
1995	—	—	—	—	—	—	26,000,000	—	—	20,000,000	—	3,000,000

TABLE Dg64–75   Telephone industry finances – Bell and independent companies: 1880–1995   *Continued*

Sources

Series Dg64–66 and Dg69. For 1880: U.S. Bureau of the Census, *Compendium of the Tenth Census, 1880*, p. 1329. For 1885–1914: U.S. Federal Communications Commission (FCC), unpublished data, consisting of *Special Investigation Docket No. 1*, Exhibit number 1360-A, pp. 39, 54, 73, 81, 89, 109 (for operating revenues and division between local and toll revenues, 1900–1914, Schedule B-2 of *Special Investigation Docket No. 1*, Exhibit number 1364 combined with long lines revenues from p. 395 of Exhibit 1360-B). For 1915–1956: American Telephone and Telegraph Company (AT&T), annual reports, and FCC, unpublished data. For 1957–1983: annual reports of AT&T, Southern Bell Telephone, and Cincinnati Bell Telephone and unpublished data.

Series Dg67. For 1880: U.S. Bureau of the Census, *Compendium of the Tenth Census, 1880*, p. 1329. For 1885–1907: FCC, unpublished data consisting of *Special Investigation Docket No. 1*, Exhibit number 1360-A, pp. 54, 73, 109 (figures for operating expenses derived by subtracting net earnings from revenues). For 1908–1935: AT&T, annual reports. For 1936–1956: AT&T, annual reports, and FCC, unpublished data. For 1957–1983: annual reports of AT&T, Southern Bell Telephone, and Cincinnati Bell Telephone and unpublished data.

Series Dg68. For 1914–1920: FCC, unpublished data (approximations derived from annual reports of individual Bell System companies to the U.S. Interstate Commerce Commission (ICC)). For 1921–1935: AT&T, unpublished data. For 1936–1956: AT&T, annual reports, and FCC, unpublished data. For 1957–1970: annual reports of AT&T, Southern Bell Telephone, and Cincinnati Bell Telephone and unpublished data.

Series Dg70–75. For 1916–1934: FCC, unpublished data. For 1935–1962: United States Independent Telephone Association (USITA), *Annual Statistical Volume of the United States Independent Telephone Association* (various years). For 1963–1982: USITA, *Statistics of the Independent Telephone Industry* (annual issues). For 1983–1989: United States Telephone Association (USTA), *Statistics of the Telephone Industry* (annual issues). For 1990–1995: USTA, *Statistics of Local Exchange Carriers* (annual issues).

Documentation
Series Dg64–69

Operating revenues included monthly service charges; amounts charged for connection, restoration, and termination of service, and for moves, instrument changes, and similar service requirements; initial nonrecurring charges for plant or equipment, except initial charges based on the cost of specially assembled private branch exchanges; and amounts of service charges for supplemental or auxiliary equipment such as extension stations and auxiliary receivers. Operating revenues included the telegraph services of the Bell System, including revenues derived from teletypewriter exchange service (TWX), and private-line service, international radiotelephone service, directory advertising and sales, and rent revenues.

Net income was calculated as net operating income and other income, including dividend income and interest income, including interest charged to construction, minus miscellaneous deductions from income and fixed charges (as interest deductions). All of the Bell System operations were included; however, prior to 1933 only the dividends from controlled companies not consolidated were included.

In calculations of operating expenses, for 1885–1907, the FCC's figures included all taxes (including federal income taxes) and interest expenses and miscellaneous income. For 1908–1913, figures also included federal income taxes. For 1914–1920, figures were adjusted to exclude estimated amounts of federal income taxes by use of annual reports of the individual Bell Telephone companies to the ICC. For 1921–1935, the federal income tax adjustment was obtained from AT&T unpublished data.

Figures include that portion of the expenses of Bell Telephone Laboratories absorbed by AT&T.

Following the breakup of the Bell System in January 1984, the series for the Bell System companies cease. The United States Telephone Association (USTA), which is now known as the United States Telecom Association and was formerly known as the United States Independent Telephone Association, continued to report data for "independent" telephone companies, companies that were independent of the Bell System prior to the divestiture of AT&T. The USTA also began reporting a new series on "All Telephone Companies" (see series Dg76–78), which include the Bell operating companies but not AT&T Corporation. The new series, therefore, only partially mends the discontinuity in the data resulting from the breakup because it does not include information on interexchange carriers like AT&T.

The Bell System did not operate in Alaska and Hawai'i.

Series Dg64–66. In *Historical Statistics of the United States* (1975), data on total, local, and toll operating revenues were also included for census years 1890, 1902, 1907, 1912, 1917, 1922, 1927, 1932, and 1937. The census data differ, often significantly, from those reported in series Dg64. The reader is referred to the 1975 edition for these alternate data points and to its source notes for the relevant references.

Series Dg64 and Dg66. Pre-1915 figures were adjusted by the FCC by subtracting uncollectible operating revenues so that they are comparable with figures for 1915–1970.

Series Dg70–75. The data include Alaska and Hawai'i.

TABLE Dg76-89 Telephone industry finances – local exchange and common carriers: 1950–1997

Contributed by David F. Weiman

	Local exchange carriers			Common carriers						Common carriers, excluding AT&T and Alascom				
	Operating revenues		Net income	Revenues			Operating expenses	Operating taxes	Net income	Revenues		Operating expenses	Operating taxes	Net income
	Total	Local		Total operating revenues	Local service	Toll service				Total operating revenues	Toll service			
Year	Dg76	Dg77	Dg78	Dg79	Dg80	Dg81	Dg82	Dg83	Dg84	Dg85	Dg86	Dg87	Dg88	Dg89
	Million dollars	Million dollars	Million dollars	Thousand dollars	Thousand dollars	Thousand dollars	Thousand dollars	Thousand dollars	Thousand dollars	Thousand dollars	Thousand dollars	Thousand dollars	Thousand dollars	Thousand dollars
1950	—	—	—	3,445,154	2,058,312	1,245,352	2,464,080	526,043	371,592	—	—	—	—	—
1951	—	—	—	3,817,537	2,258,926	1,403,479	2,698,098	659,279	377,423	—	—	—	—	—
1952	—	—	—	4,228,750	2,516,731	1,534,854	2,986,565	737,732	420,733	—	—	—	—	—
1953	—	—	—	4,628,118	2,777,054	1,641,990	3,222,873	835,053	496,507	—	—	—	—	—
1954	—	—	—	5,013,181	2,983,317	1,796,011	3,436,377	929,144	569,600	—	—	—	—	—
1955	—	—	—	5,561,530	3,252,550	2,048,868	3,703,953	1,093,585	694,119	—	—	—	—	—
1956	—	—	—	6,122,273	3,554,190	2,276,538	4,064,375	1,217,533	782,754	—	—	—	—	—
1957	—	—	—	6,869,237	4,013,345	2,525,273	4,516,814	1,378,194	891,703	—	—	—	—	—
1958	—	—	—	7,405,561	4,364,448	2,679,973	4,624,663	1,612,250	1,036,039	—	—	—	—	—
1959	—	—	—	8,116,573	4,726,045	3,008,483	4,917,171	1,844,233	1,203,109	—	—	—	—	—
1960	—	—	—	8,717,697	5,068,750	3,243,307	5,234,193	2,019,842	1,296,686	—	—	—	—	—
1961	—	—	—	9,291,843	5,366,202	3,495,054	5,530,943	2,166,262	1,390,952	—	—	—	—	—
1962	—	—	—	9,947,987	5,708,588	3,786,284	5,869,048	2,316,269	1,499,225	—	—	—	—	—
1963	—	—	—	10,639,453	6,066,207	4,095,280	6,231,098	2,482,843	1,607,762	—	—	—	—	—
1964	—	—	—	11,483,511	6,361,756	4,615,121	6,811,875	2,637,734	1,806,222	—	—	—	—	—
1965	—	—	—	12,383,400	6,758,792	5,091,582	7,445,761	2,711,975	1,956,652	—	—	—	—	—
1966	—	—	—	13,638,426	7,229,168	5,843,105	8,148,014	3,017,460	2,163,631	—	—	—	—	—
1967	—	—	—	14,654,905	7,685,209	6,375,078	8,802,634	3,192,647	2,266,882	—	—	—	—	—
1968	—	—	—	16,005,163	8,233,292	7,126,253	9,567,858	3,685,801	2,260,097	—	—	—	—	—
1969	—	—	—	17,883,442	8,957,415	8,231,896	10,918,121	3,929,506	2,403,117	—	—	—	—	—
1970	—	—	—	19,444,840	9,771,454	8,955,538	12,383,570	3,669,309	2,420,549	—	—	—	—	—
1971	—	—	—	21,399,387	10,659,981	9,961,937	13,840,268	3,836,820	2,534,459	—	—	—	—	—
1972	—	—	—	24,222,655	12,032,167	11,322,834	15,545,525	4,380,676	2,899,107	—	—	—	—	—
1973	—	—	—	27,367,688	13,306,226	13,126,213	17,306,988	5,016,653	3,454,407	—	—	—	—	—
1974	—	—	—	30,480,276	14,889,197	14,582,093	19,318,459	5,502,077	3,724,969	—	—	—	—	—
1975	—	—	—	33,409,910	16,214,529	16,098,270	21,463,220	5,850,154	3,859,667	—	—	—	—	—
1976	—	—	—	37,980,196	18,041,806	18,679,639	24,149,297	6,846,930	4,591,716	—	—	—	—	—
1977	—	—	—	42,403,722	19,794,050	21,159,394	27,121,749	7,599,718	5,420,093	—	—	—	—	—
1978	—	—	—	47,819,086	21,719,169	24,425,645	30,685,400	8,444,428	6,338,791	—	—	—	—	—
1979	—	—	—	53,035,149	23,476,086	27,598,607	35,067,495	8,346,971	6,487,697	—	—	—	—	—
1980	—	—	—	59,332,580	25,993,719	31,001,298	39,742,640	8,828,492	7,111,409	—	—	—	—	—
1981	—	—	—	68,133,171	29,636,252	36,094,193	45,626,311	10,200,835	8,043,987	—	—	—	—	—
1982	—	—	—	75,853,402	33,568,337	39,870,106	52,574,733	10,854,248	7,903,192	—	—	—	—	—
1983	—	—	—	80,243,637	35,270,701	41,769,192	54,422,054	12,430,767	8,322,636	—	—	—	—	—
1984	73,270	59,788	9,313	84,000,943	30,532,883	46,583,306	57,837,333	12,683,480	9,262,031	69,321,286	11,393,469	45,504,676	11,288,529	8,610,128
1985	77,864	63,679	10,063	89,446,126	32,292,761	48,330,601	61,137,208	13,800,826	10,341,116	73,218,346	11,289,509	48,014,363	11,955,753	9,325,641
1986	81,452	59,292	10,964	93,569,930	34,163,683	48,755,990	63,817,408	14,656,805	11,431,404	76,247,106	11,974,556	50,052,977	12,576,377	10,081,646
1987	82,246	61,431	11,192	94,647,428	34,558,925	48,130,830	66,148,058	12,904,964	12,026,172	76,971,071	12,649,928	51,706,124	11,245,688	10,510,914
1988	85,913	61,201	11,846	99,952,850	34,417,641	49,342,929	74,023,724	9,461,900	12,609,018	81,170,906	13,663,697	58,110,431	8,431,053	10,875,592
1989	87,900	63,900	11,500	102,389,550	35,277,597	48,675,494	76,812,870	9,435,654	12,370,414	82,693,554	13,848,578	60,494,285	8,206,106	10,363,755

	Local exchange carriers			Common carriers						Common carriers, excluding AT&T and Alascom				
	Operating revenues			Revenues						Revenues				
	Total	Local	Net income	Total operating revenues	Local service	Toll service	Operating expenses	Operating taxes	Net income	Total operating revenues	Toll service	Operating expenses	Operating taxes	Net income
	Dg76	Dg77	Dg78	Dg79	Dg80	Dg81	Dg82	Dg83	Dg84	Dg85	Dg86	Dg87	Dg88	Dg89
Year	Million dollars	Million dollars	Million dollars	Thousand dollars	Thousand dollars	Thousand dollars	Thousand dollars	Thousand dollars	Thousand dollars	Thousand dollars	Thousand dollars	Thousand dollars	Thousand dollars	Thousand dollars
1990	89,100	65,200	11,600	103,655,515	36,507,964	47,924,942	77,608,092	9,700,455	12,766,834	83,889,631	13,785,236	61,713,449	8,308,903	10,521,368
1991	91,000	67,100	11,100	105,989,423	38,183,594	47,988,755	80,434,159	9,808,006	11,895,133	85,505,175	13,266,972	63,444,681	8,453,100	9,938,910
1992	92,000	67,000	10,000	108,648,983	39,892,112	48,703,796	81,245,471	10,866,751	11,460,700	87,042,492	12,875,342	63,580,541	9,243,160	9,304,940
1993	95,500	70,000	7,000	112,643,343	41,683,031	49,084,947	84,659,931	10,978,739	7,820,648	90,206,192	13,034,450	66,495,913	9,323,827	5,399,692
1994	98,400	73,800	9,900	116,777,715	43,213,333	50,221,284	87,994,035	11,906,232	12,137,762	92,927,905	12,726,694	70,263,301	9,379,981	8,813,224
1995	101,100	76,500	11,300	—	—	—	—	—	—	95,646,207	10,797,831	72,177,953	9,798,872	11,061,353
1996	—	—	—	—	—	—	—	—	—	100,650,497	10,415,830	73,508,857	11,427,633	12,852,220
1997	—	—	—	—	—	—	—	—	—	103,134,290	9,245,891	75,484,924	11,274,458	11,542,555

Sources

Series Dg76–78. For 1984–1989: United States Telephone Association (USTA), *Statistics of the Telephone Industry* (annual issues). For 1990–1995: USTA, *Statistics of Local Exchange Carriers* (annual issues). The data are reproduced in U.S. Bureau of the Census, *Statistical Abstract of the United States* (various years).

Series Dg79–84. U.S. Federal Communications Commission (FCC), *1995 Statistics of Communications Common Carriers (SOCC)*, Tables 6.5, 6.6, and 6.7.

Series Dg85–89. FCC, *1997 SOCC*, Tables 6.5, 6.6, and 6.7.

Documentation

Series Dg76–78. Local exchange carriers provide services within metropolitan areas (known as local and toll services). Consequently, the data in these series do not include all providers of telephone services and, in particular, long distance or interexchange carriers such as AT&T Communications.

Series Dg79–84. The series on common carriers were compiled from previous editions of SOCC, formerly known as the *Statistics of the Communications Industry in the United States*. For the most part, the original data were gathered from the annual reports of Class A telephone carriers and, beginning in 1957, include the voluntary submissions of selected large telephone companies not subject to the FCC's reporting requirements. The 1950 data include information submitted by Class B carriers, which

are smaller companies that have less-detailed accounting requirements than do Class A carriers. Over the years, the number of carriers reporting to the FCC has varied because of mergers, carrier reclassification, and changes in the reporting criteria. In 1985, the annual operating revenue requirement for telephone carrier reporting was changed from $1 million to $100 million. As a result, twenty-one companies that had filed a report for 1984 were relieved of this requirement the following year. These carriers accounted for about $440 million in total operating revenues in 1984, with two thirds of them reporting less than $20 million. Also, because of the AT&T divestiture effective January 1, 1984, caution should be exercised in comparing the data for 1984 and later with the data reported for earlier years. On January 1, 1988, a revised uniform system of accounts (USOA) went into effect. As a result of these revisions, data submitted under the new rules may not be comparable on a one-to-one basis with data filed for previous years.

Series Dg85–89. In the 1995 edition of *SOCC*, the 1995 data did not include AT&T Communications or Alascom (which had been acquired by AT&T Corporation). Having decided that AT&T would no longer be considered a dominant carrier, the FCC eliminated the detailed reporting requirements for these carriers. In the 1996 edition, these tables were revised to exclude data for AT&T Communications and Alascom for 1984 and subsequent years – the period since AT&T's divestiture of the Bell operating companies. These revised data are reported here. The series on local revenues were unaffected by the FCC's decision, as neither of these carriers reported local service revenues.

TABLE Dg90–102 International telegraph and telephone industry – messages, calls, ocean cable, finances, and employment: 1907–1987
Contributed by Alexander J. Field

	Telegraph messages					Plant		International telegraph industry					
	Total	Cable	Overseas telephone calls	Ocean telegraph cable	Overseas countries served by direct radio telegraph circuits	Book value of capital stock	Depreciation reserves	Operating revenues	Operating expenses	Federal income taxes	Net income	Employees [1]	Wages and salaries [1]
	Dg90	Dg91	Dg92	Dg93	Dg94	Dg95	Dg96	Dg97	Dg98	Dg99	Dg100	Dg101 [1]	Dg102 [1]
Year	Thousand	Thousand	Thousand	Nautical miles	Number	Thousand dollars	Thousand dollars	Thousand dollars	Thousand dollars	Thousand dollars	Thousand dollars	Number	Thousand dollars
1907	6,024	5,869	—	46,000	—	57,438	—	7,672	2,205	—	4,029	1,207	915
1912	6,121	5,841	—	68,000	1	58,136	7,600	8,469	4,008	—	2,953	1,656	1,167
1916	—	378	—	68,000	4	63,256	21,349	10,878	4,706	—	3,318	—	—
1917	—	485	—	69,000	4	63,116	26,763	15,274	7,838	—	3,434	—	—
1918	—	418	—	69,000	4	64,058	31,481	17,299	10,425	—	2,965	—	—
1919	—	581	—	69,000	4	74,090	37,145	22,584	12,267	—	5,357	2,688	3,938
1920	4,387	4,037	—	75,000	8	83,799	42,059	40,507	24,287	—	11,463	3,062	4,882
1921	4,947	3,987	5	76,000	9	90,139	46,467	35,976	22,570	—	10,399	3,111	4,283
1922	5,437	3,992	10	73,000	10	92,073	49,142	34,191	22,539	—	11,058	2,603	3,902
1923	6,165	4,465	11	79,000	12	101,011	52,011	32,173	21,725	—	9,768	2,349	3,459
1924	7,088	5,198	12	83,000	14	107,357	54,834	33,636	21,360	—	10,962	2,340	3,463
1925	7,580	5,520	10	83,000	16	110,106	59,370	34,811	22,726	—	11,526	2,352	3,659
1926	15,493	13,298	9	88,000	20	116,179	60,904	32,672	22,293	—	11,159	2,309	3,469
1927	16,093	13,793	12	91,000	26	122,635	67,668	32,083	21,340	—	9,814	2,332	3,395
1928	17,562	14,812	23	93,000	30	126,770	69,124	34,264	21,643	—	11,368	2,299	3,392
1929	21,565	16,473	30	97,000	34	135,797	72,671	39,656	27,559	798	13,705	8,579	13,129
1930	20,409	15,258	33	98,000	42	147,236	64,994	35,360	27,010	366	9,775	8,999	13,604
1931	17,414	12,551	33	98,000	43	148,847	62,050	28,584	23,919	201	5,610	8,114	11,178
1932	14,940	10,443	28	98,000	46	145,913	73,066	23,442	21,707	169	2,368	7,553	10,009
1933	15,365	10,456	30	97,000	48	146,602	74,528	24,649	21,532	227	3,467	7,337	9,615
1934	14,464	9,287	27	97,000	49	147,662	75,473	25,449	23,177	259	1,395	7,851	10,754
1935	15,669	9,050	28	95,000	50	147,708	76,613	25,360	23,693	186	693	8,134	11,033
1936	17,641	9,819	48	95,000	52	147,723	78,082	27,173	24,042	306	2,004	8,182	11,538
1937	19,768	10,376	75	95,000	52	148,082	79,517	29,648	25,511	530	2,936	8,428	12,302
1938	18,306	9,612	75	95,000	53	147,747	81,263	26,895	25,577	219	−27	8,229	12,383
1939	18,725	9,300	76	95,000	55	146,236	81,860	30,612	26,518	524	2,074	8,176	12,663
1940	16,619	7,667	73	95,000	60	142,015	81,240	32,087	27,035	1,359	3,598	8,083	12,809
1941	16,511	7,434	117	95,000	61	141,292	82,723	36,022	28,425	3,201	3,814	8,206	13,723
1942	13,020	8,012	135	95,000	65	139,360	83,807	35,812	28,423	4,600	4,525	7,232	14,553
1943	15,991	10,159	154	95,000	68	138,436	83,909	40,254	29,450	6,424	6,508	7,591	16,513
1944	17,266	10,386	173	91,936	69	136,329	84,550	46,981	34,340	6,983	7,454	7,898	20,002
1945	21,047	10,531	360	90,700	72	137,623	86,197	49,879	37,905	7,190	7,907	9,579	25,153
1946	22,272	11,069	632	90,739	75	129,147	76,769	45,199	44,999	230	836	11,557	30,497
1947	23,960	11,835	664	90,748	76	132,534	79,426	45,579	49,358	263	−2,715	12,404	33,678
1948	22,136	11,022	798	90,362	81	135,626	82,087	46,348	47,435	519	−778	11,755	31,717
1949	20,891	10,390	853	87,784	83	134,332	82,897	46,595	45,959	525	619	11,150	31,269
1950	22,578	9,969	1,000	87,757	83	136,168	82,757	50,333	45,226	1,304	4,538	10,759	30,240
1951	24,043	10,059	1,263	78,181	85	127,310	73,929	56,949	49,087	3,504	4,526	11,081	33,120
1952	23,880	9,756	1,364	77,880	85	127,101	72,923	57,606	51,557	2,434	4,393	11,540	36,055
1953	23,725	10,085	1,440	77,835	85	131,168	75,348	59,727	53,217	4,308	3,390	11,686	37,507
1954	24,357	10,619	1,529	77,852	85	133,667	75,987	63,811	54,654	4,854	5,333	11,814	39,241

Year	Telegraph messages — Total (Dg90) Thousand	Telegraph messages — Cable (Dg91) Thousand	Overseas telephone calls (Dg92) Thousand	Ocean telegraph cable (Dg93) Nautical miles	Overseas countries served by direct radio telegraph circuits (Dg94) Number	Plant — Book value of capital stock (Dg95) Thousand dollars	Plant — Depreciation reserves (Dg96) Thousand dollars	Operating revenues (Dg97) Thousand dollars	Operating expenses (Dg98) Thousand dollars	Federal income taxes (Dg99) Thousand dollars	Net income (Dg100) Thousand dollars	Employees (Dg101) Number	Wages and salaries (Dg102) Thousand dollars
1955	25,642	10,671	1,742	75,764	85	135,178	76,432	68,050	58,366	6,328	5,020	11,844	40,548
1956	27,348	11,012	2,024	75,766	85	139,818	77,629	73,472	60,862	5,783	6,186	11,306	41,288
1957	27,838	10,647	2,421	75,713	84	149,439	80,069	76,845	66,258	5,386	5,921	11,502	41,994
1958	26,876	10,420	2,688	75,826	86	154,439	82,018	77,281	67,044	4,868	6,605	11,182	42,855
1959	28,133	10,807	3,039	75,129	83	157,557	83,679	84,377	71,726	5,815	8,328	11,239	44,531
1960	28,278	11,186	3,713	71,451	77	163,798	82,610	86,976	76,885	4,511	7,991	11,011	47,636
1961	28,345	11,323	4,365	71,450	74	172,050	85,210	90,049	78,379	4,926	8,467	10,734	48,876
1962	28,568	11,318	4,914	54,646	72	163,360	72,394	92,372	82,104	4,083	8,118	10,522	50,651
1963	29,390	11,260	5,290	42,281	71	153,465	66,939	97,822	85,102	3,611	−8,638 [2]	9,968	51,905
1964	30,102	9,365	6,382	38,253	70	191,412	71,452	107,560	91,109	5,439	9,158	9,041	53,131
1965	28,830	6,467	8,108	8,362	69	189,242	56,584	106,696	87,374	5,448	13,110	7,581	50,531
1966	29,925	6,663	9,932	8,362	68	213,359	62,623	121,516	96,133	6,550	14,779	7,437	52,217
1967	29,953	6,577	12,332	8,362	66	250,722	70,561	132,427	107,565	6,784	19,324	7,541	55,437
1968	30,705	6,560	15,166	8,362	64	282,412	79,225	153,547	123,997	8,527	21,212	7,727	59,873
1969	32,235	6,832	20,660	311	62	320,629	81,351	179,993	142,413	12,421	37,253	7,938	65,463
1970	32,241	6,548	25,813	311	60	351,674	93,355	193,808	155,707	11,887	42,346	7,599	71,709
1971	31,049	—	29,169	324	—	389,252	102,237	207,394	165,584	12,534	42,465	7,052	72,641
1972	29,098	—	36,444	324	—	422,243	120,186	227,588	180,398	11,868	45,990	6,547	77,346
1973	29,862	—	44,418	324	—	463,407	143,079	263,267	199,834	18,937	59,934	6,328	79,211
1974	29,257	—	53,671	324	—	546,252	151,622	298,854	224,515	24,940	76,574	6,346	90,229
1975	26,096	—	62,211	324	—	568,044	164,570	316,070	245,065	23,206	83,345	6,120	101,031
1976	24,130	—	75,792	324	—	622,431	187,740	343,842	264,912	23,909	74,509	5,732	106,981
1977	22,756	—	—	324	—	655,500	209,945	396,682	293,849	33,339	98,590	5,410	111,700
1978	21,870	—	133,894	325	—	695,628	230,389	455,058	336,459	35,729	118,182	5,309	120,389
1979	21,065	—	168,346	324	—	737,127	249,643	496,736	361,824	49,586	142,171	5,572	122,584
1980	20,456	—	199,631	—	—	802,232	—	534,817	—	—	—	5,680	—
1981	17,982	—	265,490	—	—	939,376	—	577,881	—	—	—	5,704	—
1982	14,908	—	310,832	—	—	1,051,947	—	613,404	—	—	—	5,837	—
1984	—	—	427,560	—	—	—	—	—	—	—	—	—	—
1985	—	—	411,735	—	—	—	—	—	—	—	—	—	—
1986	—	—	477,597	—	—	—	—	—	—	—	—	—	—
1987	—	—	579,554	—	—	—	—	—	—	—	—	—	—

[1] Prior to 1929, data represent incomplete reporting to the U.S. Federal Communications Commission (FCC) by all carriers.

[2] Net loss resulting from the sale, charged against income, of a cable system.

Sources

Series **Dg90–91, Dg93, and Dg95–102.** For 1907: U.S. Bureau of the Census, *Telegraph Systems: 1907*, pp. 10, 19. For 1912: U.S. Bureau of the Census, *Telephones and Telegraphs, 1912*, pp. 165, 167. For 1916–1928: U.S. Federal Communications Commission (FCC), unpublished data. For 1929–1956: U.S. Bureau of the Census, *Statistics of the Communications Industry in the United States* (1955, 1956), Table 19. For 1957–1982: FCC, *Statistics of Communications Common Carriers (SOCC)* (annual issues).

Series **Dg92.** For 1921–1970: 73d Congress, 2d session, "Report on Communication Companies," House Report number 1273, part 3, number 2, p. 1459 (1935); and American Telephone and Telegraph Company (AT&T), unpublished data. For 1971–1987: FCC, *SOCC* (annual issues).

Series **Dg94.** FCC, unpublished data (supplemented and confirmed in *Report of the Federal Trade Commission on the Radio Industry and Report on Communication Companies*, House Report number 1273, part 3, number 1, pp. 990, 998; part 3, number 4, pp. 3934, 3948, and 4188).

TABLE Dg90-102   International telegraph and telephone industry – messages, calls, ocean cable, finances, and employment: 1907–1987   *Continued*

Documentation

The first successful cable linking North America with Europe was laid in 1866. Radio was not a significant factor in overseas telegraphy until 1920 when the newly formed Radio Corporation of America (RCA) entered the field as successor to the Marconi Company of America. The record of hearings held in 1929 before the Committee on Interstate Commerce, U.S. Senate, 71st Congress, 1st session, on S. (Senate) 6, a "Bill to Provide for the Regulation of the Transmission of Intelligence by Wire or Wireless," contains a list of submarine cables of the world and the year in which each was laid (pp. 960–72). Few of these cables are now in use, having been replaced by circuits in telephone ocean cables beginning in the 1950s (the first telephone cable linking Europe and America was laid in 1956) and, since 1965, with the launching of Telstar, by circuits in microwave radio relayed by satellite. Information on the beginnings of international radiotelegraphy appears in the *Report of the Federal Trade Commission on the Radio Industry* (1924).

The first overseas radiotelephone service was opened in 1927 between New York and London by AT&T. The only overseas telephone service available during 1921–1926 was to and from Cuba by means of cable.

Census data for international telegraphy are available from the special quinquennial census reports of the telephone and telegraph industries. With respect to international telegraph, these reports suffer from two major shortcomings. First, the Census Bureau was unable to obtain from the Western Union Telegraph Company a division between its landline system and its cable operations with respect to plant and financial operations. Prior to the 1932 Census, Western Union provided separate data for its cable operations only in the categories of messages and cable mileage. In the Censuses of 1932 and 1937, Western Union also supplied operating revenue information for its cable system. The absence of Western Union's Cable Division from the census data on the ocean-cable companies largely accounts for the significant differences between the census data and the annual series with respect to telegraph plant book cost and depreciation reserves, operating revenues, operating expenses, and net income.

A second shortcoming of the census data is the lack of adequate coverage of the radiotelegraph industry. The financial information included in the 1922 and 1937 census compilations is seriously distorted because of the failure to exclude various activities of RCA not related to its telegraph communications business. In the 1932 Census, no information on radiotelegraphy appeared, whereas in the 1937 Census, the published statistics relate only to messages and operating revenue.

Because of these shortcomings, only the data for 1907 and 1912 in Table Dg90-102 are derived from these quinquennial censuses. For further detail, and data for other census years, please see the *Historical Statistics of the United States* (1975).

Series Dg90–91, Dg93, and Dg95–102. Annual data prior to 1929 were derived, in part, from annual reports of the carriers filed with the Inter-state Commerce Commission (ICC). In large part, these data were obtained through field examinations by the staff of the FCC and from data supplied by the carriers upon specific request. Figures include Hawai'i and Puerto Rico for all years. There is no international telegraph industry in Alaska; however, international telegrams originating or terminating there are included in series Dg90–91.

Series Dg90–91. Cable and radiotelegraph messages include communications sent from, received in, and transiting the United States and its outlying areas. In addition, radiotelegraph messages include ship-to-shore messages and domestic telegraph messages handled over radiotelegraph circuits prior to the closure of such circuits on June 30, 1942. The numbers of cable and radiotelegraph messages depend on whether they were reported by what were formerly known as cable or radio carriers. Since 1956, radio carriers have been using circuits in cables in addition to radio for transmission of messages; since 1965, cable carriers have been using radio circuits via satellite relay in addition to cables.

Series Dg92. Figures include calls to and from ships on the high seas and most international points. Additional data on radiotelephone service are contained in FCC, *Statistics of the Communications Industry in the United States* (various years). See also *Census of Electrical Industries: Telephones and Telegraphs, 1937*, Table 9.

Series Dg93. The miles of ocean cable as published have been adjusted in view of the fact that some of the cables were reported and tabulated in statute miles, rather than in nautical miles.

Series Dg94. This series became increasingly irrelevant in the 1960s as radiotelegraph service was supplanted by data service operating over telephone circuits through submarine cables or via satellite.

Series Dg95–96. Plant and depreciation figures are on the basis of the systems of accounts became effective in 1970. The radiotelegraph accounts became effective January 1, 1940, and the ocean-cable uniform system accounts became effective January 1, 1943 (replacing an earlier cable accounts system promulgated by the ICC, effective January 1, 1914).

Series Dg98–100. Federal income taxes prior to 1929 are included in operating expenses in amounts that are not ascertainable. The substantial decline in net income in 1912, compared with 1907, may have been accounted for in large measure by the introduction of depreciation charges that were absent from the 1907 accounts.

Series Dg101–102. Included in employees and compensation are the foreign employees of the carriers. The reporting dates for number of employees have varied: for 1929–1934, as of the end of June; for 1935–1945, as of the end of December; for 1946–1970, as of the end of October.

TABLE Dg103–109 Cellular telephone industry – systems, employees, subscribers, sites, revenue, and capital investment: 1984–2001

Contributed by Alexander J. Field

Year	Systems	Subscribers	Cell sites	Employees	Service revenue		Capital investment
					Total	Roamer	
	Dg103	Dg104	Dg105	Dg106	Dg107	Dg108	Dg109
	Number	Thousand	Number	Number	Million dollars	Million dollars	Million dollars
1984	32	92	346	1,404	178	—	—
1985	102	340	913	2,727	482	—	—
1986	166	682	1,531	4,334	823	—	1,437
1987	312	1,231	2,305	7,147	1,151	—	2,235
1988	517	2,069	3,209	11,400	1,959	89	3,274
1989	584	3,509	4,169	15,927	3,340	294	4,480
1990	751	5,283	5,616	21,382	4,548	456	6,282
1991	1,252	7,557	7,847	26,237	5,708	704	8,672
1992	1,506	11,033	10,307	34,348	7,822	974	11,262
1993	1,529	16,009	12,805	39,775	10,981	1,360	13,946
1994	1,581	24,134	17,920	53,902	14,229	1,830	18,939
1995	1,627	33,786	22,663	68,165	19,081	2,542	24,080
1996	1,740	44,043	30,045	84,161	23,635	2,781	32,574
1997	2,228	55,312	51,600	109,387	27,486	2,974	46,058
1998	3,073	69,209	65,887	134,754	33,133	3,501	60,543
1999	3,518	86,047	81,698	155,817	40,018	4,085	71,265
2000	2,440 [1]	109,478	104,288	184,449	52,466	3,883	89,624
2001	—	128,375	127,540	203,580	65,015	3,936	105,030

[1] Data not comparable to earlier years owing to consolidation of some systems.

Source

Cellular Telecommunications Industry Association, *Semi-Annual Wireless Survey* (various years).

Documentation

Data are as of December 31 of each year, with the exception of 1984, for which the survey was actually conducted in January of 1985. The data are based on a survey mailed to all cellular systems. For 1994, the response rate was 85 percent; for 2000, the response rate was 86.5 percent.

Series Dg108. Roamer revenue represents income earned through the servicing of subscribers of other systems.

TABLE Dg110-116   Internet hosts and Web sites, by type: 1969-2002   *Continued*

		Internet hosts						Web sites (www servers)
		Total	Education (.edu)	Commercial (.com)	Government (.gov)	Military (.mil)	Organization (.org)	
		Dg110	Dg111	Dg112	Dg113	Dg114	Dg115	Dg116
Year	Month	Number	Number	Number	Number	Number	Number	Number
1969	Dec	4	—	—	—	—	—	—
1970	Dec	13	—	—	—	—	—	—
1971	Apr	23	—	—	—	—	—	—
1974	June	62	—	—	—	—	—	—
1977	Mar	111	—	—	—	—	—	—
1981	Aug	213	—	—	—	—	—	—
1982	May	235	—	—	—	—	—	—
1983	Aug	562	—	—	—	—	—	—
1984	Oct	1,024	—	—	—	—	—	—
1985	Oct	1,961	—	—	—	—	—	—
1986	Nov	5,089	—	—	—	—	—	—
1987	Dec	28,174	—	—	—	—	—	—
1988	Oct	56,000	—	—	—	—	—	—
1989	Oct	159,000	—	—	—	—	—	—
1990	Oct	313,000	—	—	—	—	—	—
1991	July	535,000	205,648	143,868	35,569	25,536	14,747	—
1992	July	992,000	326,630	277,551	62,584	33,161	25,896	—
1993	July	1,776,000	539,668	460,848	109,550	88,163	39,359	130 [2]
1994	July	3,212,000	856,234	774,735	169,248	130,176	66,459	2,738 [2]
1995	July	6,642,000	1,411,013	1,743,390	273,855	224,778	201,905	23,500 [2]
1996	July	12,881,000	2,114,851	3,323,647	361,065	431,939	327,148	299,403
1997	July	19,540,000	2,942,714	4,501,039	418,576	542,295	434,654	1,203,096
1998	July	36,739,000	4,464,216	10,301,570	612,725	1,359,153	644,971	—
1999	July	56,218,000	5,141,774	18,773,097	683,363	1,561,756	821,933	—
2000	July	93,047,785	6,678,055	32,696,253	827,575	1,916,026	1,087,665	—
2001	July	125,888,197	7,183,493	37,502,747	786,984	1,881,091	1,281,090	—
2002	July	162,128,493	7,381,306	43,814,657	700,107	1,918,954	1,238,739	—

[1] New survey technique was used beginning 1998; results may not be comparable to earlier counts.

[2] June.

Series Dg110 (1981-2000) and series Dg111-115. Internet Domain Survey conducted by Network Wizards, from Internet software consortium's Web site.

Sources
Series Dg110 (1969-1977) and series Dg116. "Hobbes' Internet Time-line," by Robert H. Zakon (1993-1998), from Hobbes' Internet Timeline Internet site.

RADIO AND TELEVISION

Alexander J. Field

TABLE Dg117–130 Radio and television – stations, sets produced, and households with sets: 1921–2000

Contributed by Alexander J. Field

	Operating broadcast stations					Cable television		Radio sets		Television sets		Radio sets	Households with	
	Radio			Television										
	AM	FM												
		Commercial	Noncommercial	Commercial	Noncommercial	Systems	Subscribers	Produced in the United States	Total U.S. market	Produced in the United States	Total U.S. market		Television sets	Videocassette recorders
	Dg117 [1]	Dg118 [1]	Dg119 [1]	Dg120 [1]	Dg121 [1]	Dg122	Dg123	Dg124	Dg125	Dg126	Dg127	Dg128	Dg129 [2]	Dg130 [2]
Year	Number	Number	Number	Number	Number	Number	Thousand	Thousand	Thousand	Thousand	Thousand	Thousand	Thousand	Thousand
1921	1 [3]	—	—	—	—	—	—	—	—	—	—	—	—	—
1922	30	—	—	—	—	—	—	100	—	—	—	60	—	—
1923	556	—	—	—	—	—	—	500	—	—	—	400	—	—
1924	530	—	—	—	—	—	—	1,500	—	—	—	1,250	—	—
1925	571	—	—	—	—	—	—	2,000	—	—	—	2,750	—	—
1926	528	—	—	—	—	—	—	1,750	—	—	—	4,500	—	—
1927	681	—	—	—	—	—	—	2,350	—	—	—	6,750	—	—
1928	677	—	—	—	—	—	—	3,250	—	—	—	8,000	—	—
1929	606	—	—	—	—	—	—	4,428	—	—	—	10,250	—	—
1930	618	—	—	—	—	—	—	3,789	—	—	—	13,750	—	—
1931	612	—	—	—	—	—	—	3,594	—	—	—	16,700	—	—
1932	604	—	—	—	—	—	—	2,446	—	—	—	18,450	—	—
1933	598	—	—	—	—	—	—	4,157	—	—	—	19,250	—	—
1934	593	—	—	—	—	—	—	4,479	—	—	—	20,400	—	—
1935	623	—	—	—	—	—	—	6,030	—	—	—	21,456	—	—
1936	656	—	—	—	—	—	—	8,249	—	—	—	22,869	—	—
1937	704	—	—	—	—	—	—	8,083	—	—	—	24,500	—	—
1938	743	—	—	—	—	—	—	7,142	—	—	—	26,667	—	—
1939	778	—	—	—	—	—	—	10,763	—	—	—	27,500	—	—
1940	847	—	3	—	—	—	—	11,831	—	—	—	28,500	—	—
1941	897	49	7	2	—	—	—	13,642	—	—	—	29,300	—	—
1942	925	42	8	10	—	—	—	4,307	—	—	—	30,600	—	—
1943	912	48	7	8	—	—	—	—[4]	—	—	—	30,800	—	—
1944	924	52	8	9	—	—	—	—[4]	—	—	—	32,500	—	—
1945	955	53	12	9	—	—	—	—[4]	—	—	—	33,100	—	—
1946	1,215	511	24	30	—	—	—	15,955	—	6	—	33,998	8	—
1947	1,795	918	38	66	—	—	—	20,000	—	179	—	35,900	14	—
1948	2,034	1,020	46	108	—	—	—	16,500	—	975	—	37,623	172	—
1949	2,006	737	34	69	—	—	—	11,400	—	3,000	—	39,300	940	—
1950	2,144	691	62	104	—	—	—	13,468	—	7,464	—	40,700	5,030	—
1951	2,281	649	83	107	—	—	—	11,928	—	5,385	—	41,900	10,320	—
1952	2,355	629	92	108	—	70	14	10,431	—	6,096	—	42,800	15,300	—
1953	2,458	580	106	198	1	150	30	12,852	—	7,216	—	44,800	20,400	—
1954	2,583	553	117	402	6	300	65	10,028	10,243	7,347	—	45,100	26,000	—

Notes appear at end of table

(continued)

TABLE Dg117-130 Radio and television – stations, sets produced, and households with sets: 1921–2000 *Continued*

Year	AM Dg117[1] (Number)	FM Commercial Dg118[1] (Number)	FM Noncommercial Dg119[1] (Number)	TV Commercial Dg120[1] (Number)	TV Noncommercial Dg121[1] (Number)	Cable Systems Dg122 (Number)	Cable Subscribers Dg123 (Thousand)	Radio sets produced in the U.S. Dg124 (Thousand)	Radio sets total U.S. market Dg125 (Thousand)	TV sets produced in the U.S. Dg126 (Thousand)	TV sets total U.S. market Dg127 (Thousand)	Households with radio sets Dg128 (Thousand)	Households with TV sets Dg129[2] (Thousand)	Households with VCRs Dg130[2] (Thousand)
1955	2,732	540	124	458	11	400	150	14,133	14,190	7,757	—	45,900	30,700	—
1956	2,896	530	126	496	20	450	300	13,518	14,008	7,387	—	46,800	34,900	—
1957	3,079	530	135	519	26	500	350	14,505	15,448	6,399	—	47,600	38,900	—
1958	3,253	548	147	556	32	525	450	11,747	14,512	4,920	6,368	48,500	41,924	—
1959	3,377	622	154	566	43	560	550	15,622	21,273	6,349	5,829	49,450	43,950	—
1960	3,483	741	165	579	47	640	650	17,127	24,463	5,708	6,315	50,193	45,750	—
1961	3,602	889	186	553	54	700	725	17,374	29,222	6,178	7,134	50,695	47,200	—
1962	3,745	1,012	201	571	59	800	850	19,162	32,030	6,471	7,983	51,305	48,855	—
1963	3,860	1,120	221	581	70	1,000	950	18,282	31,548	7,130	9,764	52,300	50,300	—
1964	3,976	1,181	243	582	79	1,200	1,085	19,176	31,871	8,107	11,447	54,000	51,600	—
1965	4,025	1,343	262	589	92	1,325	1,275	24,119	41,726	8,382	12,714	55,200	52,700	—
1966	4,075	1,515	291	613	108	1,570	1,575	23,595	44,173	7,285	11,564	57,000	53,850	—
1967	4,135	1,708	318	626	127	1,770	2,100	21,698	41,211	5,104	13,211	57,500	55,130	—
1968	4,203	1,850	348	655	156	2,000	2,800	22,566	46,832	5,813	13,308	58,500	56,670	—
1969	4,254	2,018	375	680	177	2,260	3,600	20,549	51,353	5,309	12,220	60,600	58,250	—
1970	4,288	2,126	416	691	190	2,490	4,500	16,406	44,427	4,852	14,921	62,000	59,550	30
1971	4,343	2,250	461	695	199	2,639	5,300	—	47,610	—	17,084	63,900	60,100	80
1972	4,367	2,352	521	701	214	2,841	6,000	—	55,311	—	17,368	67,200	62,100	200
1973	4,392	2,447	599	705	228	2,996	7,300	—	50,198	—	17,368	69,400	64,800	600
1974	4,409	2,547	684	706	234	3,158	8,700	—	43,992	—	15,279	70,800	66,200	1,150
1975	4,448	2,698	757	706	243	3,506	9,800	—	34,515	7,984	10,637	71,400	68,500	1,850
1976	4,479	2,820	845	708	253	3,681	10,800	—	44,101	8,701	14,131	74,000	69,600	3,000
1977	4,502	2,972	913	725	259	3,832	11,900	—	52,926	9,374	15,431	75,800	71,200	4,850
1978	4,538	3,066	973	728	260	3,875	13,000	—	48,035	11,067	17,407	77,800	72,900	5,500
1979	4,551	3,151	1,037	738	264	4,150	14,100	—	40,029	10,249	16,617	79,300	74,500	9,000
1980	—	—	—	746	267	4,225	16,000	—	39,574	8,657	18,532	78,600	76,300	17,744
1981	—	—	—	765	269	4,375	18,300	—	44,359	9,551	18,479	80,500	79,900	31,000
1982	—	—	—	—	—	4,825	21,000	—	44,088	9,481	16,406	84,300	81,500	43,000
1983	4,754	3,658	1,165	893	287	5,600	25,000	—	51,577	6,459	19,683	84,600	83,300	51,000
1984	4,799	3,839	1,211	920	301	6,200	30,000	—	62,083	6,674	20,992	84,600	83,800	58,000
1985	4,856	3,936	1,254	982	303	6,600	32,000	—	37,071	8,391	20,749	86,700	84,900	63,181
1986	4,893	3,999	1,283	1,005	318	7,600	37,500	—	41,146	11,173	22,163	87,100	85,900	66,939
1987	4,915	4,116	1,356	1,049	333	7,900	41,000	—	40,936	11,445	22,900	88,100	87,400	69,075
1988	4,965	4,240	1,407	1,085	346	8,500	44,000	—	37,431	10,722	22,796	89,900	88,600	71,780
1989	4,978	4,357	1,435	1,112	353	9,050	47,500	—	36,647	—	23,362	91,100	90,400	74,420
1990	4,988	4,517	1,484	1,128	358	9,575	50,000	—	33,836	—	21,795	92,800	92,100	77,270
1991	4,963	4,742	1,570	1,144	361	10,704	51,000	—	32,627	—	20,258	94,400	93,100	78,830
1992	4,994	4,971	1,641	1,151	365	11,075	53,000	—	39,396	—	21,689	94,400	92,100	81,670
1993	4,919	5,076	1,715	1,157	363	11,100	55,000	—	38,084	—	23,554	96,600	93,100	82,910
1994	4,908	5,274	1,805	1,179	363	11,200	57,000	—	—	—	25,255	98,000	94,200	84,140
1995	5,013	6,017	2,136	1,323	383	11,126	58,000	—	—	—	—	98,000	95,400	85,810
1996	4,970	6,107	2,240	1,338	387	11,119	60,280	—	—	—	25,600	—	95,900	—
1997	4,979	6,168	2,277	1,379	391	10,950	64,050	—	—	—	—	—	97,000	—
1998	—	—	—	—	—	10,845	64,170	—	—	—	—	—	98,000	—
1999	—	—	—	—	—	10,700	65,500	—	—	—	—	—	99,400	—
2000	—	—	—	—	—	10,400	66,500	—	—	—	—	—	100,800	—

Similarly, statistics of licensed stations can be misleading. A station permittee who has completed construction in accordance with the specifications of the construction permit or a modification hereof usually receives a regular license, prior to the start of regular on-the-air program service. However, for a variety of reasons, the FCC has permitted stations to undertake regular broadcast service under a Special Temporary Authorization. Many stations have operated under such authority for a number of years. Here, again, this statement applies particularly to FM and TV stations.

Figures for these series are, for the most part, presented in terms of operating stations. Stations are recorded in FCC records as operating when they have received permission to conduct program tests. In some instances, considerable time may elapse before such stations are in regular, daily operation. Adjustments for this factor have been made by the FCC on the basis of trade sources, and such adjustments are incorporated here. In sum, the data on operating stations are not precise, but they are believed to be reasonably accurate.

Series include Alaska, Hawai'i, Puerto Rico, Guam, and the Virgin Islands. Prior to 1949, the FCC did not keep records on the number of stations on the air. Therefore, data for 1933–1948 are for authorized stations and may include a number that were not actually on the air. Data for 1949–1979 (in the case of the TV series, through 1982) reflect FCC data for stations on the air. Data for 1984–1999 report stations with operating authorizations, not including those under construction.

Series Dg117

Prior to 1948, data pertain to licensed stations that, in the amplitude modulation (AM) service, generally approximated operating stations.

Figures are not available annually on the number of noncommercial AM stations because there is no separate noncommercial service. Usually, such stations are supported by educational or public bodies. In the early growth of radio prior to 1927, educational institutions were prominent in radio (see S. E. Frost, *Education's Own Stations: The History of Broadcast Licenses Issued to Educational Institutions* (University of Chicago Press, 1937)). From 1945–1970, the number of noncommercial AM stations declined from about thirty-five to twenty-five. In addition, a small number of educational institutions have operated commercial stations.

The decline in the number of AM stations between 1927 and 1929 followed the transfer of the licensing function from the Secretary of Commerce to the FRC. The latter body tightened the licensing requirements, resulting in the withdrawal or deletion of a number of operating stations.

Series Dg118–119

FM was authorized as a regular service in 1940, effective January 1, 1941, and the first commercial station was licensed in 1941. Noncommercial FM is a separate service with a specific spectrum allocation. The stations are licensed to nonprofit educational organizations.

Series Dg120–121

Television was authorized on a regular commercial basis effective July 1, 1941, and two stations in New York began operating as of that date. Figures include very high frequency (VHF) stations, first authorized in 1941, and ultra high frequency stations (UHF), first authorized in 1952. Some stations (almost entirely UHF stations) began operation and subsequently ceased operation, but retained their FCC authorization. Such stations are not included in the years of nonoperation.

Series Dg124

Figures are based on reports of members of the Electronic Industries Association (formerly Radio–Electronics–Television Manufacturers Association), adjusted for estimated production of nonmembers. The figures also include sets produced for export. Radio set figures include home sets for all years; auto sets, 1930–1970; portable sets, 1939–1970; and clock sets, 1951–1970. As of 1970, automobile sets constituted over 40.3 percent of total radio-set production. As of 1970, year end, the Electronic Industries Association estimated that there were 336 million radio sets in working order in the United States, including 85 million in automobiles.

Series Dg125

Prior to 1971, data reflect factory sales by U.S. manufacturers plus those products imported directly by distributors or dealers for resale. Beginning in 1971, data reflect products produced or purchased by U.S. manufacturers plus those products imported directly by distributors or dealers for resale. Data for 1980 and subsequent years reflect imports reported by the Department of Commerce (home radio) and the sum of factory-installed auto radios plus sales of aftermarket auto radios.

(continued)

---

1 May include some stations not actually broadcasting in some years; see text.

2 Excludes Alaska and Hawai'i.

3 First station to receive regular license as of September 15; other stations in operation experimentally.

4 Authorization of new radio stations and production of radio receivers for commercial use halted from April 1942 until October 1945.

Sources

Series Dg117. For 1921: U.S. Federal Communications Commission (FCC), unpublished data. For 1922–1926: *Annual Report of the Secretary of Commerce* (various years). For 1927–1932: *Seventh Annual Report of the Federal Radio Commission for Fiscal Year 1933*, p. 18. For 1933–2000: FCC, *Annual Report* (various years).

Series Dg118–121. FCC, *Annual Report* (various years).

Series Dg122–123. For 1952–1970: John Blair & Company, *Statistical Trends in Broadcasting* (annual issues). For 1971–2000: *Television and Cable Factbook* (Television Digest, annual issues).

Series Dg124. For 1922–1934: Electronic Industries Association, Marketing Services Department, *Electronic Industry Fact Book* (1957), pp. 4, 5. For 1935–1970: *Electronic Market Data Book* (eBrain, 1971).

Series Dg125. *Television and Cable Factbook* (1995), p. I-18.

Series Dg126. For 1946–1970: *Electronic Market Data Book* (1971). For 1977–1990: *Electronic Market Data Book* (1985–1990).

Series Dg127. *Television and Cable Factbook* (1995), p. I-7.

Series Dg128. For 1922–1970: National Broadcasting Company (NBC), unpublished estimates. For 1971–1992: Radio Advertising Bureau, *Radio Facts* (annual issues). For 1993–1995: Radio Advertising Bureau, *Radio Marketing Guide and Fact Book for Advertisers* (annual issues); see also *Broadcasting and Cable Yearbook* (R. R. Bowker, 1997), p. B-217.

Series Dg129–130. For 1946–1949 and 1951–1970: NBC, unpublished estimates. For 1950: U.S. Bureau of the Census, *U.S. Census of Housing: 1950*, volume 1, part 1, Table 13. For 1971–2000: Television Bureau of Advertising (TBA), *Trends in Television* (various years). See also the TBA Internet site.

Documentation

Federal regulation of radio communication has been continuous since 1912 when the U.S. Department of Commerce was given authority to license radio equipment and radio operators, and then broadcast stations, which began operation in 1921. On February 23, 1927, Congress established the Federal Radio Commission (FRC) with broad authority for the regulation of radio. In 1934, the powers of the regulation of radio. In 1934, the powers of the Federal Radio Commission were transferred to the FCC.

Since 1937, the FCC has obtained annual financial reports from networks and broadcast stations. Statistical tabulations of the data so reported have been made available by the FCC in its annual reports, in its annual "Statistics of the Communications Industry in the United States," and in annual processed reports. Unlike the telephone and telegraph industries, radio broadcasting is not classified as a common carrier and is not subject to rate or earnings regulations. The FCC, therefore, does not prescribe a uniform system of accounts for the radio industry. However, the commission's Annual Report form number 324, and the accompanying instructions, ensures general uniformity in the reported data. The individual financial reports of networks and stations filed with the FCC are not available for public inspection. However, some individual network and station data have been published from time to time.

Series Dg117–121

Statistics of broadcast stations are commonly presented in terms of "authorized" and "licensed" stations. A broadcast station is authorized when it receives a construction permit from the FCC (or predecessor licensing agencies). Normally, a station is expected to complete construction and begin regular operation within eight months thereafter. However, not all authorized stations complete this process and become operating stations. This has occurred mainly in the broadcast services of frequency modulation (FM) and television (TV).

TABLE Dg117–130   Radio and television – stations, sets produced, and households with sets: 1921–2000   Continued

Series Dg126. Data calculated as factory production less imports.

Series Dg127. Prior to 1971, data reflect factory sales by U.S. manufacturers plus those products imported directly by distributors or dealers for resale. Beginning in 1971, data reflect products produced or purchased by U.S. manufacturers plus those products imported directly by distributors or dealers for resale.

Series Dg128

NBC credits data on radio ownership prior to 1950 to the National Association of Broadcasters (NAB), which is the national trade association of broadcasters, and to the Broadcast Measurement Bureau, a private survey group, which conducted a detailed nationwide survey of radio listening. A survey conducted by the Columbia Broadcasting System (CBS), the results of which were published as "Lost and Found," purported to show 2,450,000 households with radios not enumerated in the 1930 Census of Population. Accordingly, the NAB adjusted the 1930 Census figure to 14,499,000. Similarly, 964,026 occupied dwelling units did not report radio ownership in the 1940 Census of Population. The NAB estimated that 786,043 of these should be added to the 1940 Census figure of 28,048,219 occupied units with radio.

The figures include radio sets that may not have been in working order. Sets temporarily out of order or being repaired at the time of enumeration were included in the census data. The figures exclude radio sets in places of business, institutions, and hotels.

Data are as of December 31.

Series Dg129. An indication of the accuracy of the estimates is provided by several surveys of TV ownership in the nation's households conducted by the Census Bureau for the Advertising Research Foundation. These studies have yielded the following estimates:

	June 1955	March 1956	August 1956	January 1969
Sets in TV homes	33,269,000	37,277,000	39,568,000	79,660,000
TV homes	32,106,000	35,495,000	37,410,000	58,250,000
Second sets in TV homes	1,163,000	1,782,000	2,158,000	21,410,000
TV homes as a percentage of all homes	67.2	72.8	76.1	95

All figures exclude sets in places of business, institutions, and hotels, but include households with television sets that may not have been in current working order.

Series Dg130. Data are as of February.

TABLE Dg131–144   Radio – finances, employment, and advertising expenditures: 1935–1998
Contributed by Alexander J. Field

	Advertising expenditures				Networks reporting	Stations reporting	Broadcast revenues		Broadcast expenses		Broadcast income		Gross investment	Employees
	Total	Network	National spot	Local			Total	Network	Total	Network	Total	Network		
Year	Dg131	Dg132	Dg133	Dg134	Dg135	Dg136	Dg137	Dg138	Dg139	Dg140	Dg141	Dg142	Dg143	Dg144
	Million dollars	Million dollars	Million dollars	Million dollars	Number	Number	Million dollars	Million dollars	Million dollars	Million dollars	Million dollars	Million dollars	Million dollars	Thousand
1935	113	63	15	35	8	561	86	30	—	—	—	—	—	14.6
1936	122	76	23	24	—	—	—	—	—	—	—	—	—	—
1937	165	89	28	48	3	629	114	41	92	33	19	6	55	28.8
1938	167	89	34	44	3	660	111	45	93	36	19	8	61	22.5
1939	184	99	35	50	3	705	124	49	100	37	24	11	64	23.9
1940	216	113	42	60	8	765	147	53	114	39	33	13	71	25.7
1941	247	125	52	70	8	817	169	62	124	44	45	17	78	27.6
1942	260	129	59	73	10	856	179	63	134	47	45	17	81	29.6
1943	314	157	71	86	9	846	215	76	149	53	66	23	81	31.8
1944	394	192	87	114	9	879	275	95	185	68	90	26	83	34.3
1945	424	198	92	134	10	906	299	101	216	78	84	23	88	37.8
1946	454	200	98	157	8	1,033	323	102	246	73	76	19	108	40.0
1947	506	201	106	199	7	1,516	364	104	292	92	72	20	150	—
1948	562	211	121	230	7	1,927	407	109	343	91	64	18	202	48.3
1949	571	203	123	245	7	2,125	414	108	363	87	56	17	231	52.0
1950	605	196	136	273	7	2,229	443	111	372	92	71	19	244	—
1951	606	180	138	289	7	2,266	449	104	390	94	59	10	255	—
1952	624	162	142	321	7	2,380	469	101	408	89	61	11	267	—
1953	611	141	146	324	7	2,479	475	97	419	87	56	10	276	—
1954	559	114	135	309	7	2,598	449	89	406	80	43	8	279	—

Year	Advertising expenditures — Total Dg131 (Million dollars)	Network Dg132 (Million dollars)	National spot Dg133 (Million dollars)	Local Dg134 (Million dollars)	Networks reporting Dg135 (Number)	Stations reporting Dg136 (Number)	Broadcast revenues — Total Dg137 (Million dollars)	Network Dg138 (Million dollars)	Broadcast expenses — Total Dg139 (Million dollars)	Network Dg140 (Million dollars)	Broadcast income — Total Dg141 (Million dollars)	Network Dg142 (Million dollars)	Gross investment Dg143 (Million dollars)	Employees Dg144 (Thousand)
1955	545	84	134	326	7	2,742	452	78	406	72	46	6	287	45.3
1956	567	61	161	346	7	2,967	479	70	430	70	50	(Z)	298	47.6
1957	618	64	187	368	7	3,164	515	74	461	74	54	—	328	48.9
1958	619	58	190	372	7	3,290	521	69	483	73	38	−4	333	48.8
1959	656	44	206	406	4	3,528	556	60	512	65	44	−5	373	50.4
1960	692	43	222	428	4	3,688	598	63	552	66	46	−3	423	53.0
1961	683	43	221	420	4	3,859	584	62	552	61	32	(Z)	426	54.3
1962	736	46	233	457	4	3,977	627	64	580	62	47	2	466	56.1
1963	789	56	243	490	4	4,126	670	69	612	63	58	6	493	58.0
1964	846	59	256	531	4	4,202	719	71	645	67	73	4	521	60.2
1965	917	60	275	582	4	4,279	793	74	715	71	78	3	567	62.2
1966	1,010	64	308	638	4	4,400	872	79	775	76	97	4	623	64.8
1967	1,031	64	310	657	4	4,481	907	77	826	79	81	−2	671	67.2
1968	1,190	63	360	767	7	4,594	1,023	81	910	86	113	−5	723	70.6
1969	1,264	59	368	837	7	4,815	1,086	86	985	88	101	−2	780	70.0
1970	1,308	56	371	881	7	4,898	1,137	88	1,044	90	93	−1	823	71.0
1971	1,380	58	387	935	7	5,020	1,258	100	1,155	97	103	3	799	65.9
1972	1,612	74	402	1,136	7	5,136	1,407	112	1,273	103	134	9	842	67.5
1973	1,723	68	400	1,255	7	5,244	1,510	112	1,392	109	112	3	885	67.4
1974	1,837	69	405	1,363	7	5,436	1,603	116	1,519	116	84	0	933	68.8
1975	1,980	83	436	1,461	7	5,535	1,725	134	1,634	128	91	6	986	69.0
1976	2,330	105	518	1,707	7	5,638	2,019	166	1,841	157	179	9	1,058	70.2
1977	2,634	137	546	1,951	8	5,619	2,275	213	2,028	166	246	47	1,097	70.6
1978	3,052	147	620	2,285	8	5,748	2,635	236	2,324	193	311	44	1,510 [1]	91.7 [1]
1979	3,310	161	665	2,484	8	5,769	2,874	253	2,643	215	231	37	—	—
1980	3,702	183	779	2,740	8	5,878	3,206	293	3,047	285	159	27	—	—
1981	4,230	230	879	3,129	—	—	—	—	—	—	—	—	—	—
1982	4,670	255	923	3,492	—	—	—	—	—	—	—	—	—	—
1983	5,210	296	1,038	3,876	—	—	—	—	—	—	—	—	—	—
1984	5,817	320	1,197	4,300	—	—	—	—	—	—	—	—	—	—
1985	6,490	365	1,335	4,790	—	—	—	—	—	—	—	—	—	—
1986	6,949	423	1,348	5,178	—	—	—	—	—	—	—	—	—	—
1987	7,206	413	1,330	5,463	—	—	—	—	—	—	—	—	—	—
1988	7,798	425	1,418	5,955	—	—	—	—	—	—	—	—	—	—
1989	8,323	476	1,547	6,300	—	—	—	—	—	—	—	—	—	—
1990	8,726	482	1,635	6,609	—	—	6,954	—	6,317	—	637	—	—	—
1991	8,476	490	1,575	6,411	—	—	6,671	—	6,157	—	514	—	—	—
1992	8,654	424	1,505	6,725	—	—	6,795	—	6,137	—	658	—	—	—
1993	9,457	458	1,657	7,342	—	—	7,231	—	6,257	—	974	—	—	—
1994	10,529	463	1,902	8,164	—	—	7,980	—	6,769	—	1,211	—	—	—
1995	11,338	480	1,959	8,899	—	—	8,518	—	6,997	—	1,521	—	—	—
1996	12,269	523	2,135	9,611	—	—	9,305	—	7,499	—	1,806	—	—	—
1997	13,491	560	2,455	10,476	—	—	10,193	—	8,154	—	2,039	—	—	—
1998	15,073	622	2,823	11,628	—	—	11,206	—	8,747	—	2,459	—	—	—

Notes appear on next page

(continued)

TABLE Dg131-144 Radio – finances, employment, and advertising expenditures: 1935–1998 *Continued*

(Z) Less than $500,000.

1 Data not comparable with earlier years owing to substantial increase in coverage; see U.S. Bureau of the Census, *Annual Survey of Communication Services* (various issues) for details.

Sources

Series Dg131–134. For 1935–1956 and 1958–1968: *Printers' Ink Advertisers' Guide to Marketing* (various years). For 1957: *Printers' Ink* (February 6, 1959): 9. For 1969 and 1970: *Marketing Communications* (July 1971). For 1971–1995: McCann-Erickson, compiled for Crain Communications, in *Advertising Age* (various issues). See also the Television Bureau of Advertising Internet site.

Series Dg135–144. For 1935: U.S. Bureau of the Census, *Census of Business, 1935: Radio Broadcasting*, pp. 15, 25. For 1937–1947: U.S. Federal Communications Commission (FCC), *Annual Report* (various issues). For 1948–1980: *AM–FM Broadcast Financial Data* (various issues). For 1991–1998: U.S. Bureau of the Census, *Annual Survey of Communication Services* (various issues).

Documentation

Series Dg131–134 and Dg145–151

Historical time series on advertising expenditures were first developed by L. D. H. Weld of the McCann-Erickson Advertising Agency, New York City, in 1938. After Weld's death in 1946, McCann-Erickson continued to prepare the estimates under the supervision of Hans Zeisel and, since 1950, Robert J. Coen.

Total advertising expenditures in radio and television are total time sales of networks and stations, including commissions of advertising agencies and station representatives, as reported by the FCC, multiplied by estimated "adjustment" factors. For a description of the method used in developing the annual adjustment factors, see sources for series Dg135–144. Total advertising expenditures are larger than total broadcast revenues as reported by the FCC in two respects: the inclusion of commissions paid to advertising agencies and station representatives and the inclusion of sums paid by advertisers for talent, program, and production to organizations that do not operate networks or broadcast stations (included in the "adjustment" figures).

The networks included in radio were the four national networks: the American Broadcasting Company (ABC), the Columbia Broadcasting System (CBS), the National Broadcasting Company (NBC), and the Mutual Broadcasting System (MBS). The three large regional networks included for most years are the Don Lee Network, the Yankee Network, and the Texas State Network. The networks included in television were ABC, CBS, NBC (each of which operates a network in both radio and television), and, until September 1955, the DuMont Network. At that time, DuMont withdrew from the network field.

Series Dg132 and Dg146. Figures are total expenditures of network advertisers in radio or television for time (that is, access to the individual stations broadcasting the program); for the program, including talent and production; and for the production of the commercial announcements. Such sums include commissions to advertising agencies but exclude discounts and allowances received by the advertiser. The figures are before disbursements by the networks to their affiliated and owned stations, and exclude the nonnetwork time sales of the stations owned by the networks.

Series Dg133 and Dg147. This type of advertising is commonly confused with commercial, or spot, announcements. The term "spot" in this context refers to the purchase of time by national advertisers on individual stations "spotted" or selected in various communities. Predominantly, the advertiser expenditures are for commercial announcements adjacent to network or other programs carried by the individual stations. In addition, national spot advertisers sponsor programs or purchase "participations" in station-supplied programs. Thus, national spot-advertiser expenditures include total time sales (after discounts but including commissions to advertising agencies and station representatives) multiplied by an estimated "adjustment" factor for program and production.

Series Dg134 and Dg150. These expenditures include total time sales (after trade discounts but including commissions to advertising agencies) multiplied by an estimated "adjustment" factor for program and production. Local advertiser expenditures are made in connection with both the broadcast of commercial announcements and the supply of a program service. The main distinction between national spot and local advertising is as follows: National spot advertisers are connected with firms or companies that produce or distribute goods or services on a national or regional basis and that usually place their advertising message on a number of selected stations. Local advertisers are usually local retailers and other organizations whose goods or services are primarily for local distribution. As such, a local advertiser will place an advertising message only on the stations in that community or marketing area. However, in practice, the "national" and "local" categories are not completely differentiated.

Series Dg135–144 and Dg152–161

The basic sources are the annual report, *Statistics of the Communications Industry in the United States* (annual issues), and processed releases of the FCC.

The FCC began the regular annual collection of financial and operating data from networks and stations in 1937. The respondents each year usually include over 90 percent of commercial stations in operation, accounting for well over 95 percent of total industry revenues, expenses, and income. Statistics based on these reports, particularly prior to 1952, have included considerable detail. These statistics are reported in the annual report of the FCC, *Statistics of the Communications Industry in the United States* (annual issues), and in processed releases.

Network series cover network-owned-and-operated stations.

Series Dg135–136 and Dg152–153

Prior to 1949, the radio data are limited to commercial standard broadcasting (AM) stations and networks operating in the United States, Puerto Rico, and outlying areas. Since 1949, the radio data also include reports of joint AM-FM stations and reports of FM-only stations.

The television data include stations operating in the United States, Puerto Rico, and outlying areas.

Series Dg137–138 and Dg154–155. Figures include the amounts received by networks and stations from the sale of time (net of all trade and cash discounts and commissions to advertising agencies and station representatives) and from other broadcast activities as follows: gross amount received for services of talent under contract to and in the pay of networks or stations; net commissions, fees, and profits for services in obtaining, or for placing with others, talent not under contract to and in the pay of respondent; amounts received for furnishing manuscripts, transcriptions, productions, or other program materials or services; and amounts received for incidental broadcast activities, such as charges for studio facilities and special charges in connection with remote broadcasts, fees or other charges for conducting studio tours, and fees or profits received for the right to operate concessions.

Series Dg139–140 and Dg156–157. The expense categories reported include technical, program, selling, and general and administrative expenses. Among the expenses required to be included are the following: salaries and wages; talent expenses; film and transcription expenses; commissions to staff salesmen; insurance; depreciation and amortization of broadcast investments; rents paid for use of broadcast property; taxes (other than federal taxes on income); and losses on notes, accounts, and other amounts receivable.

Series Dg141–142 and Dg158–159. Figures represent net operating revenues (before federal income tax), excluding income derived by the networks and stations from sources and operations other than broadcasting.

Series Dg143 and Dg160. Figures represent investment in tangible broadcast property, before depreciation. The FCC report form requires that the costs be reported on an original-cost basis, and not on the basis of cost readjustments resulting from the sales or transfers of stations.

TABLE Dg131–144 Radio – finances, employment, and advertising expenditures: 1935–1998 *Continued*

Tangible broadcast property includes land and buildings, if owned, and transmitter and studio property; it excludes financial assets and goodwill. In the case of stations that have been sold, it represents that portion of the price assigned by the licensee to the property. Tangible broadcast property is, therefore, not a measure of total investment in broadcasting.

Series Dg144 and Dg161. Figures include all employees, staff and nonstaff, full and part time, not excluding general officers and other managerial officials, but excluding "uncompensated" employees.

Figures for 1935 are employees reported as of the fifteenth of each month, summed and divided by twelve; for 1938, week beginning December 11; for 1939–1943, middle week in October; for 1944–1946, as of December 31; for 1946–1948, middle week in October; for 1955–1970, as of December 31.

TABLE Dg145–161 Television – finances, employment, and advertising expenditures: 1945–1998

Contributed by Alexander J. Field

Year	Total Dg145	Broadcast network Dg146 [1]	National spot Dg147	Cable network Dg148	National syndication Dg149 [1]	Local spot Dg150	Cable nonnetwork Dg151	Networks reporting Dg152	Stations reporting Dg153	Total Dg154	Network Dg155	Total Dg156	Network Dg157	Total Dg158	Network Dg159	Gross broadcast investment Dg160	Employees Dg161
	Million dollars	Million dollars	Million dollars	Million dollars	Million dollars	Million dollars	Million dollars	Number	Number	Million dollars	Million dollars	Million dollars	Million dollars	Million dollars	Million dollars	Million dollars	Thousand
1945	—	—	—	—	—	—	—	—	6	(Z)	—	—	—	—	—	—	—
1946	—	—	—	—	—	—	—	—	10	1	—	—	—	—	—	—	—
1947	—	—	—	—	—	—	—	—	15	2	—	—	—	—	—	—	—
1948	58	29	—	—	—	—	—	—	47	9	5	24	11	−15	6	—	—
1949	58	29	9	—	—	19	—	4	98	34	19	60	31	−25	−12	56	—
1950	171	85	31	—	—	55	—	4	107	106	56	115	66	−9	−10	70	—
1951	332	181	70	—	—	82	—	4	108	236	128	194	117	42	11	93	—
1952	454	256	94	—	—	104	—	4	122	324	180	269	170	56	10	124	14.1
1953	606	320	146	—	—	141	—	4	334	433	232	361	214	71	18	233	18.2
1954	809	422	207	—	—	180	—	4	410	593	307	503	270	90	37	315	29.4
1955	1,035	550	260	—	—	225	—	4	437	745	374	595	306	150	68	365	32.3
1956	1,225	643	329	—	—	253	—	3	474	897	442	707	357	190	85	430	35.7
1957	1,286	690	352	—	—	244	—	3	501	943	468	783	397	160	71	478	37.8
1958	1,387	742	397	—	—	248	—	3	514	1,030	517	858	440	172	77	523	39.4
1959	1,529	776	486	—	—	267	—	3	519	1,164	576	942	488	222	88	563	40.3
1960	1,627	820	527	—	—	281	—	3	530	1,269	641	1,025	546	244	95	593	40.6
1961	1,691	887	548	—	—	256	—	3	540	1,318	675	1,081	588	237	87	631	40.1
1962	1,897	976	629	—	—	292	—	3	554	1,486	754	1,175	643	312	111	673	41.8
1963	2,032	1,025	698	—	—	309	—	3	565	1,597	820	1,254	684	343	136	—	43.6
1964	2,289	1,132	806	—	—	351	—	3	575	1,793	929	1,378	772	416	157	781	45.7
1965	2,515	1,237	892	—	—	386	—	3	588	1,965	1,024	1,517	862	448	162	860	47.8
1966	2,823	1,393	988	—	—	442	—	3	608	2,203	1,166	1,710	980	493	187	1,014	50.3
1967	2,909	1,455	988	—	—	466	—	3	637	2,275	1,217	1,861	1,057	415	160	1,185	51.7
1968	3,231	1,523	1,131	—	—	577	—	3	658	2,521	1,308	2,026	1,129	495	179	−1,307	55.2
1969	3,585	1,678	1,253	—	—	654	—	3	673	2,796	1,467	2,243	1,241	554	226	1,445	57.8
1970	3,596	1,658	1,234	—	—	704	—	3	686	2,808	1,457	2,354	1,290	454	167	1,497	58.4
1971	3,534	1,593	1,145	—	—	796	—	3	688	2,750	1,379	2,361	1,234	389	145	—	—
1972	4,091	1,804	1,318	—	—	969	—	3	690	3,179	1,598	2,627	1,385	552	213	—	—
1973	4,460	1,968	1,377	—	—	1,115	—	3	692	3,465	1,758	2,811	1,470	653	288	—	—
1974	4,854	2,145	1,497	—	—	1,212	—	3	694	3,781	1,921	3,043	1,590	738	331	—	—

Note appears at end of table

(continued)

TABLE Dg145–161   Television – finances, employment, and advertising expenditures: 1945–1998   Continued

	Advertising expenditures							Networks reporting	Stations reporting	Broadcast revenues		Broadcast expenses		Broadcast income		Gross broadcast investment	Employees
	Total	Broadcast network [1]	National spot	Cable network	National syndication [1]	Local spot	Cable nonnetwork			Total	Network	Total	Network	Total	Network		
	Dg145	Dg146	Dg147	Dg148	Dg149	Dg150	Dg151	Dg152	Dg153	Dg154	Dg155	Dg156	Dg157	Dg158	Dg159	Dg160	Dg161
Year	Million dollars	Million dollars	Million dollars	Million dollars	Million dollars	Million dollars	Million dollars	Number	Number	Million dollars	Million dollars	Million dollars	Million dollars	Million dollars	Million dollars	Million dollars	Thousand
1975	5,263	2,306	1,623	—	—	1,334	—	3	693	4,094	2,069	3,314	1,755	780	314	—	—
1976	6,821	2,857	2,154	—	—	1,710	—	3	701	5,198	2,604	3,948	2,150	1,250	455	—	—
1977	7,612	3,460	2,204	—	—	1,948	—	3	697	5,889	3,085	4,488	2,530	1,401	555	2,338	—
1978	8,955	3,975	2,607	—	—	2,373	—	3	714	6,950	3,549	5,297	2,989	1,653	560	2,691	64.1
1979	10,154	4,599	2,873	—	—	2,682	—	3	723	7,875	4,093	6,185	3,517	1,690	575	—	—
1980	11,488	5,130	3,269	60	50	2,967	12	3	725	8,808	4,566	7,154	4,031	1,654	534	—	—
1981	12,889	5,540	3,746	134	75	3,368	26	3	—	—	—	—	—	—	—	—	—
1982	14,713	6,144	4,364	242	150	3,765	48	3	—	—	—	—	—	—	—	—	—
1983	16,879	6,955	4,827	376	300	4,345	76	3	—	—	—	—	—	—	—	—	—
1984	20,043	8,318	5,488	612	420	5,084	121	3	—	—	—	—	—	—	—	—	—
1985	21,287	8,060	6,004	793	520	5,714	196	3	—	—	—	—	—	—	—	—	—
1986	23,199	8,342	6,570	903	600	6,514	270	3	—	—	—	—	—	—	—	—	—
1987	24,262	8,500	6,846	1,015	762	6,833	306	3	—	—	—	—	—	—	—	—	—
1988	26,131	9,172	7,147	1,258	901	7,270	383	3	—	—	—	—	—	—	—	—	—
1989	27,459	9,110	7,354	1,598	1,288	7,612	497	3	—	20,540	—	17,122	—	3,418	—	—	—
1990	29,073	9,863	7,788	1,860	1,109	7,856	597	4	—	21,063	—	17,828	—	3,235	—	—	—
1991	28,189	9,533	7,110	2,024	1,253	7,565	704	4	—	20,174	—	17,787	—	2,387	—	—	—
1992	30,450	10,249	7,551	2,227	1,370	8,079	974	4	—	21,064	—	17,998	—	3,066	—	—	—
1993	31,698	10,209	7,800	2,586	1,576	8,435	1,092	4	—	21,050	—	17,191	—	3,859	—	—	—
1994	35,435	10,942	8,993	3,052	1,734	9,464	1,250	4	—	23,084	—	18,269	—	4,815	—	—	—
1995	37,828	11,600	9,119	3,535	2,016	9,985	1,573	4	—	25,801	—	21,041	—	4,760	—	—	—
1996	42,484	13,081	9,803	4,472	2,218	10,944	1,966	4	—	28,237	—	23,222	—	5,015	—	—	—
1997	44,130	13,020	9,999	5,067	2,438	11,436	2,170	4	—	28,792	—	22,494	—	6,298	—	—	—
1998	47,474	13,736	10,659	5,827	2,609	12,169	2,474	4	—	31,256	—	24,870	—	6,386	—	—	—

(Z) Less than $500,000.

[1] Beginning 1990, Fox is included in TV networks, rather than syndication; thus, the data are not comparable with previous years.

Sources

Series Dg145–151. For 1945–1956 and 1958–1968: *Printers' Ink Advertisers' Guide to Marketing* (various issues). 1957: *Printers' Ink* (February 6, 1959): 9. For 1969 and 1970: *Marketing Communications* (July 1971). For 1971–1998: McCann-Erickson, compiled for Crain Communications, in *Advertising Age* (various issues). See also the Television Bureau of Advertising Internet site.

Series Dg152–161. For 1949–1980: *TV Broadcast Financial Data* (Federal Communications Commission, various issues) (publication discontinued after 1980). For 1989–1998: U.S. Bureau of the Census, *Annual Survey of Communication Services* (various years).

Documentation

See the text for Table Dg131–144.

TABLE Dg162–171 Radio – special and safety stations authorized, by class: 1913–1996

Contributed by Alexander J. Field

Year	Amateur and disaster services	Aviation services	Citizens' services	Industrial services	Land transportation services	Other private land mobile	Marine services	Public safety services	Experimental services	Radio operators
	Dg162	Dg163	Dg164	Dg165	Dg166	Dg167	Dg168	Dg169	Dg170	Dg171
	Number	Number	Number	Number	Number	Number	Number	Number	Number	Thousand
1913	1,312	—	—	—	—	—	701	—	—	—
1916	—	—	—	—	—	—	—	1	—	—
1920	5,719	—	—	—	—	—	—	1	—	—
1923	16,570	—	—	—	—	—	—	3	—	—
1924	15,540	—	—	—	—	—	2,741	3	—	—
1925	15,000	—	—	—	—	—	1,901	4	—	—
1926	14,902	—	—	—	—	—	1,954	—	—	—
1927	16,926	—	—	—	—	—	—	—	—	—
1928	16,928	—	—	—	—	—	—	—	—	—
1929	16,829	131	—	—	—	—	—	12	—	—
1930	18,994	281	—	—	—	—	2,173	20	—	—
1931	22,739	463	—	130	—	—	2,392	91	160	—
1932	30,374	579	—	134	—	—	2,225	123	168	—
1933	41,555	646	—	121	—	—	2,192	152	255	—
1934	46,390	671	—	129	—	—	2,195	220	681	—
1935	45,561	678	—	146	—	—	2,157	298	975	—
1936	46,850	852	—	195	—	—	2,219	403	1,576	—
1937	47,444	1,212	—	221	—	—	2,422	535	1,971	—
1938	49,911	1,460	—	232	—	—	3,516	662	2,842	—
1939	53,558	1,824	—	307	—	—	4,036	1,536	372	—
1940	56,295	2,099	—	340	—	—	4,945	2,334	295	—
1941	60,000	3,000	—	306	—	—	5,822	2,967	450	—
1942	60,000	4,713	—	356	—	—	—	3,455	497	—
1943	60,000	3,553	—	386	—	—	6,609	3,772	453	—
1944	60,000	3,445	—	468	—	—	6,817	4,144	572	—
1945	60,000	3,793	—	576	—	—	—	4,446	487	—
1946	70,000	6,205	—	702	156	—	8,676	4,760	1,374	—
1947	75,000	15,943	—	1,787	1,692	—	11,955	4,620	532	442
1948	78,434	20,858	—	2,855	3,122	—	15,024	4,903	652	506 [3]
1949	81,675	27,227	—	4,266	3,588	—	20,004	5,700	501	564 [3]
1950	87,967	23,794	335	6,099	3,495	—	24,921	7,607	466	624
1951	90,587	34,061	560	9,551	4,253	—	29,544	9,129	404	701
1952	113,163	32,603	1,401	13,680	5,027	—	35,500	11,143	369	790
1953	111,579	39,315	3,829	17,378	5,922	—	40,357	13,631	444	839
1954	124,324	40,154	7,054	21,598	6,891	—	46,299	15,697	586	963
1955	142,387	43,855	12,334	24,854	7,668	—	50,714	18,415	625	1,123
1956	154,337	48,745	18,602	30,597	8,990	—	56,915	20,718	716	1,259
1957	165,908	49,699	27,931	35,711	9,592	—	63,844	23,270	788	1,469
1958	187,362	62,684	38,611	39,978	10,190	—	72,514	26,512	834	1,682
1959	205,588	77,682	49,269	49,679	10,625	—	84,947	29,363	891	1,897
1960	228,206	91,180	126,034	64,804	11,452	—	97,411	32,906	728	2,154
1961	234,681	92,779	206,106	77,773	12,075	—	110,433	36,658	757	2,499
1962	251,659	106,923	305,138	93,073	13,278	—	127,633	38,676	757	2,789
1963	270,838	106,202	446,590	107,796	14,089	—	143,227	43,168	730	3,186
1964	280,818	107,557	682,307	124,347	14,815	—	161,593	47,389	698	2,870
1965	280,343	109,897	744,713	141,360	15,635	—	114,075	50,888	812	2,971
1966	285,600	105,133	865,414	152,315	16,914	—	137,469	54,839	928	3,088
1967	279,093	122,568	848,237	169,417	18,613	—	143,612	58,831	898	3,240
1968	282,525	140,799	867,552	185,046	20,016	—	164,000	63,160	966	3,405
1969	285,175	143,997	860,624	204,266	21,291	—	186,295	67,730	1,019	3,545
1970	283,461	150,955	886,951	222,500	22,262	—	206,251	72,215	1,049	3,688
1971	286,118	158,328	868,013	140,146	16,851	—	218,527	57,726	1,154	3,802
1972	284,235	161,223	851,610	171,387	18,318	—	238,415	66,209	1,159	3,914
1973	279,505	167,121	836,940	195,132	20,753	—	238,506	75,865	1,202	4,011
1974	273,780	172,466	931,640	231,158	21,695	—	243,276	86,411	1,206	4,110
1975	276,800	184,400	1,530,800	244,600	22,600	—	250,700	92,600	1,349	4,222
1976	292,800	188,500	5,613,600	277,100	23,000	—	262,600	105,900	1,110	4,386
1977	340,900	207,800	11,652,800	357,900	25,400	—	315,000	127,200	1,332	4,618
1978	369,500	216,000	14,249,000	426,200	28,000	—	345,300	138,700	1,432	4,779
1979	375,500	226,900	15,000,300	462,000	26,200	—	371,200	128,900	1,302	4,966

Notes appear at end of table   (continued)

TABLE Dg162–171   Radio – special and safety stations authorized, by class: 1913–1996   *Continued*

Year	Amateur and disaster services Dg162 Number	Aviation services Dg163 Number	Citizens' services Dg164 Number	Industrial services Dg165 Number	Land transportation services Dg166 Number	Other private land mobile Dg167 Number	Marine services Dg168 Number	Public safety services Dg169 Number	Experimental services Dg170 Number	Radio operators Dg171 Thousand
1980	389,900	231,600	14,560,200	504,900	28,000	—	398,300	137,100	1,513	5,154
1981	385,200	234,900	10,060,700	605,000	32,500	—	402,000	158,500	1,446	5,300
1982	410,600	238,000	5,759,000	649,000	34,400	—	434,700	166,200	1,195	5,400
1983	414,200	241,100	3,834,100 [1]	677,000	35,700	8,877	461,100	171,200	1,413	4,609
1984	413,200	245,300	—	767,900	35,800	95,988	497,500	184,200	1,575	—
1985	415,400	245,700	—	811,300	37,700	132,882	525,300	194,500	—	5,287
1986	423,700	244,300	—	864,400	39,800	171,979	561,200	207,100	1,397	5,803
1987	432,600	247,700	—	871,100	40,000	213,685	573,700	212,600	1,405	—
1988	439,100	248,500	—	875,600	40,100	252,514	605,400	221,400	1,594	—
1989	467,300	251,200	—	873,900	40,400	282,322	620,400	228,500	1,873	—
1990	495,700	250,900	—	864,800	40,100	305,887	622,900	234,500	1,527	—
1991	535,000	241,000	—	854,000	41,000	317,379	641,000	240,000	1,780	—
1992	583,000	210,000	—	840,000	41,000	339,447	634,000	245,000	1,820	—
1993	628,000	199,000	—	828,000	41,000	332,658	664,000	251,000	1,820	—
1994	652,000	192,000	—	795,000	40,000	309,812	686,000	252,000	1,626	—
1995	684,000	140,000	—	394,000	18,000	183,000	644,000	127,000	1,194 [2]	—
1996	664,000	140,000	—	392,000	16,000	183,000	644,000	127,000	—	—

[1] Reflects stations authorized as of April 30, 1983. Authorizations discontinued after that date.

[2] Includes 139 special temporary authorizations.

[3] Estimated.

Sources

For 1913–1926: U.S. Department of Commerce, *Annual Report of the Secretary of Commerce* (various years). For 1927–1934: Federal Radio Commission, *Annual Report* (various years). For 1935–1996: U.S. Federal Communications Commission (FCC), *Annual Report* (various years).

Documentation

Prior to 1948, the only data available to measure the use of radio in various nonbroadcast "safety and special" radio services were the number of authorized stations. The term "station," however, has not had a uniform significance among these services or within the same service over time. Primarily, the term reflects licensing procedures. A station is a single authorization issued by the FCC (or its predecessor licensing agencies) for the use of one or more transmitters on assigned frequencies. A station may include one of the following: one or more transmitters at a fixed (land or fixed stations) location; one or more mobile transmitters; a system including a transmitter at a fixed location and one or more mobile transmitters; or one of these in a combination with more than one frequency. Within most of the services, station authorizations have been changed from one to another form in an effort to simplify licensing procedures. As a result, year-to-year changes in the number of stations must be interpreted with caution, particularly if a decrease is shown.

Most of the nonbroadcast radio services are grouped together as the safety and special radio services, which constitute the greatest number of radio stations licensed by the FCC. Utilization of these services by individuals, industry, commerce, and state and local governments covers broad fields of operations in connection with the protection of life and property, industrial and agricultural production, transportation, disaster, and civil defense.

Series Dg167. Includes 200 megahertz (MHz) (authorized fiscal year 1992), 470–512 MHz (prior to 1984), 800 MHz (prior to 1983), 900 MHz (implemented October 1983), broadcast auxiliary, general mobile, and interactive video data.

Series Dg170. The Experimental Radio Service is the means by which the FCC encourages and promotes basic radio research and development of new radio techniques and systems.

TABLE Dg172–180   Public broadcasting – stations and income, by source: 1961–1997

Contributed by Alexander J. Field

	Public radio stations	Public or educational television stations		Public broadcasting system income						
					Source					
			Total	Federal government	State and local government	Subscribers and auction/marathon	Business and industry	Foundation	Other
	Dg172	Dg173	Dg174	Dg175	Dg176	Dg177	Dg178	Dg179	Dg180
Year	Number	Number	Million dollars	Million dollars	Million dollars	Million dollars	Million dollars	Million dollars	Million dollars
1961	—	56	—	—	—	—	—	—	—
1964	—	88	—	—	—	—	—	—	—
1966	—	115	—	—	—	—	—	—	—
1968	—	153	—	—	—	—	—	—	—
1970	—	190	—	—	—	—	—	—	—
1972	132	228	235	60	108	18	— [3]	25	24 [3]
1973	—	—	255	56	127	25	10	20	17
1974	159	247	290	67	139	32	16	18	19
1975	169	260	365	92	157	42	21	29	24
1976	176	266	433	130 [2]	176	54	29	23	21
1977	182	274	482	135	191	64	40	23	29
1978	199	280	552	161	218	75	49	17	32
1979	210	281	599	163	241	86	58	20	30
1980	217	290	705	193	264	102	72	24	50
1981	238	293	769	194	278	131	87	19	61
1982	255	299	845	198	301	163	101	22	62
1983	266	300	899	164	318	196	120	25	76
1984	275	304	974	167	335	215	145	28	85
1985	288	317	1,096	179	358	248	171	43	97
1986	295	322	1,134	186	379	269	171	38	92
1987	299	323	1,295	243	389	298	196	48	121
1988	308	324	1,368	248	416	321	213	51	120
1989	313	340	1,549	264	454	347	242	69	173
1990	318	341	1,581	267	474	364	262	71	143
1991	373	349	1,721	333	503	384	290	70	139
1992	391	349	1,790	374	485	404	300	80	148
1993	400	352	1,790	370	475	412	285	100	149
1994	403	351	1,795	330	510	420	301	97	137
1995	407	351	1,917	338	560	447	294	109	169
1996	408	352	1,956	339	518	—	—	—	—
1997	697 [1]	352	1,935	322	536	—	—	—	—

[1] Not comparable with previous years owing to different reporting standards.

[2] Includes transition quarter funding.

[3] Business and industry income included in other income.

Sources

Series Dg172 and Dg174–180. Corporation for Public Broadcasting (CPB), *Public Broadcasting Income* (annual issues) and unpublished data.

Series Dg173. For 1961–1971: National Instructional Television Center, *One Week of Educational Television* (National Instructional Television Center, 1971).

For 1972–1997: CPB, *Public Broadcasting Income* (annual issues) and unpublished data.

Documentation

Series Dg172. Covers CPB Qualified Public Radio Stations.

Series Dg175. Includes funding from the CPB as well as federal grants and contracts.

U.S. POSTAL SERVICE AND DELIVERY SERVICES

Alexander J. Field

TABLE Dg181–189   U.S. Postal Service – post offices, finances, pieces handled, and items issued: 1789–1999

Contributed by Alexander J. Field

Year	Post offices	Revenues	Expenditures	Surplus or deficit	Sales of postage stamps and other stamped paper	Issued			Pieces handled
						Ordinary postage stamps	Stamped envelopes and wrappers	Postal cards	
	Dg181	Dg182 [1]	Dg183 [1]	Dg184	Dg185	Dg186	Dg187	Dg188	Dg189
	Number	Thousand dollars	Thousand dollars	Thousand dollars	Thousand dollars	Thousand	Thousand	Thousand	Thousand
1789	75	8 [2]	8 [2]	—	—	—	—	—	—
1790	75	38	32	—	—	—	—	—	—
1791	89	46	37	—	—	—	—	—	—
1792	195	67	55	—	—	—	—	—	—
1793	209	105	72	—	—	—	—	—	—
1794	450	129	90	—	—	—	—	—	—
1795	453	161	118	—	—	—	—	—	—
1796	468	195	132	—	—	—	—	—	—
1797	554	214	150	—	—	—	—	—	—
1798	639	233	179	—	—	—	—	—	—
1799	677	265	188	—	—	—	—	—	—
1800	903	281	214	—	—	—	—	—	—
1801	1,025	320	255	—	—	—	—	—	—
1802	1,114	327	282	—	—	—	—	—	—
1803	1,258	352	322	—	—	—	—	—	—
1804	1,405	389	338	—	—	—	—	—	—
1805	1,558	421	377	—	—	—	—	—	—
1806	1,710	446	417	—	—	—	—	—	—
1807	1,848	479	454	—	—	—	—	—	—
1808	1,944	461	463	—	—	—	—	—	—
1809	2,012	507	498	—	—	—	—	—	—
1810	2,300	552	496	—	—	—	—	—	—
1811	2,403	587	499	—	—	—	—	—	—
1812	2,610	649	540	—	—	—	—	—	—
1813	2,708	703	631	—	—	—	—	—	—
1814	2,670	730	727	—	—	—	—	—	—
1815	3,000	1,043	748	—	—	—	—	—	—
1816	3,260	962	804	—	—	—	—	—	—
1817	3,459	1,003	917	—	—	—	—	—	—
1818	3,618	1,130	1,036	—	—	—	—	—	—
1819	4,000	1,205	1,118	—	—	—	—	—	—
1820	4,500	1,112	1,161	—	—	—	—	—	—
1821	4,650	1,059	1,165	—	—	—	—	—	—
1822	4,709	1,117	1,168	—	—	—	—	—	—
1823	4,043	1,130	1,157	—	—	—	—	—	—
1824	5,182	1,198	1,188	—	—	—	—	—	—
1825	5,677	1,307	1,229	—	—	—	—	—	—
1826	6,150	1,448	1,367	—	—	—	—	—	—
1827	7,300	1,525	1,470	—	—	—	—	—	—
1828	7,530	1,660	1,690	—	—	—	—	—	—
1829	8,004	1,707	1,782	—	—	—	—	—	—
1830	8,450	1,851	1,933	—	—	—	—	—	—
1831	8,686	1,998	1,936	—	—	—	—	—	—
1832	9,205	2,259	2,266	—	—	—	—	—	—
1833	10,127	2,617	2,930	—	—	—	—	—	—
1834	10,693	2,824	2,911	—	—	—	—	—	—
1835	10,770	2,994	2,757	—	—	—	—	—	—
1836	11,091	3,408	2,842	—	—	—	—	—	—
1837	11,767	4,102	3,288	—	—	—	—	—	—
1838	12,519	4,239	4,431	—	—	—	—	—	—
1839	12,780	4,485	4,637	—	—	—	—	—	—

Notes appear at end of table

TABLE Dg181–189   U.S. Postal Service – post offices, finances, pieces handled, and items issued: 1789–1999
Continued

					Sales of postage stamps and other stamped paper	Issued			
	Post offices	Revenues	Expenditures	Surplus or deficit		Ordinary postage stamps	Stamped envelopes and wrappers	Postal cards	Pieces handled
	Dg181	Dg182 [1]	Dg183 [1]	Dg184	Dg185	Dg186	Dg187	Dg188	Dg189
Year	Number	Thousand dollars	Thousand dollars	Thousand dollars	Thousand dollars	Thousand	Thousand	Thousand	Thousand
1840	13,468	4,544	4,718	—	—	—	—	—	—
1841	13,778	4,408	4,500	—	—	—	—	—	—
1842	13,733	4,547	4,628	—	—	—	—	—	—
1843	13,814	4,296	4,375	—	—	—	—	—	—
1844	14,103	4,237	4,299	—	—	—	—	—	—
1845	14,183	4,290	4,321	—	—	—	—	—	—
1846	14,601	3,487	4,076	—	—	—	—	—	—
1847	15,146	3,380	3,980	—	—	—	—	—	—
1848	16,159	4,555	4,327	—	—	860	—	—	—
1849	16,749	4,705	4,479	—	—	956	—	—	—
1850	18,417	5,500	5,213	—	—	1,541	—	—	—
1851	19,796	6,411	6,278	—	—	1,247	—	—	—
1852	20,901	5,185	7,108	—	—	54,136	—	—	—
1853	22,320	5,241	7,983	—	—	56,344	5,000	—	—
1854	23,548	6,256	8,577	—	—	56,330	21,384	—	—
1855	24,410	6,642	9,968	—	—	72,977	23,452	—	—
1856	25,565	6,921	10,405	—	—	126,045	33,764	—	—
1857	26,586	7,354	11,508	—	—	154,729	33,033	—	—
1858	27,977	7,487	12,722	—	—	176,761	30,971	—	—
1859	28,539	7,968	15,754	—	—	192,202	30,280	—	—
1860	28,498	8,518	14,875	—	—	216,371	29,280	—	—
1861	28,586	8,349	13,607	—	—	211,789	26,027	—	—
1862	28,875	8,300	11,125	—	—	251,307	27,234	—	—
1863	29,047	11,164	11,314	—	—	338,340	25,549	—	—
1864	28,878	12,438	12,645	—	—	334,055	28,219	—	—
1865	28,882	14,556	13,695	—	—	387,419	26,206	—	—
1866	29,389	14,387	15,352	—	—	347,734	39,095	—	—
1867	25,163	15,237	19,235	—	—	371,600	63,087	—	—
1868	26,481	16,292	22,731	—	—	383,471	73,365	—	—
1869	27,106	17,314	23,698	—	—	421,047	81,675	—	—
1870	28,492	18,880	23,999	—	—	468,118	86,290	—	—
1871	30,045	20,037	24,390	—	—	498,126	104,675	—	—
1872	31,863	21,915	26,658	—	—	541,445	113,926	—	—
1873	33,244	22,997	29,085	—	—	601,932	131,173	31,094	—
1874	34,294	26,471	32,126	—	—	632,733	136,419	91,079	—
1875	35,547	26,791	33,611	—	—	682,342	149,766	107,616	—
1876	36,383	28,644	33,263	—	—	698,799	165,520	150,815	—
1877	37,345	27,532	33,486	—	—	689,581	170,651	170,015	—
1878	38,253	29,278	34,165	—	—	742,462	183,500	200,630	—
1879	40,588	30,042	33,450	—	—	774,359	177,562	221,797	—
1880	42,989	33,315	36,543	—	—	875,682	207,137	272,550	—
1881	44,512	36,785	39,593	—	—	954,128	227,067	308,537	—
1882	46,231	41,876	40,482	—	—	1,114,560	256,565	351,498	—
1883	46,820	45,509	43,283	—	—	1,202,744	259,266	379,517	—
1884	48,434	43,326	47,225	—	—	1,459,768	322,232	362,877	—
1885	51,252	42,561	50,046	—	—	1,465,123	322,751	339,417	—
1886	53,614	43,948	51,005	—	—	1,620,784	354,008	355,648	3,747,000
1887	55,157	48,838	53,006	—	—	1,746,986	381,611	356,939	3,495,100
1888	57,376	52,695	56,458	—	—	1,867,173	433,636	381,798	3,576,100
1889	58,999	56,176	62,317	—	—	1,961,981	451,864	386,809	3,860,200
1890	62,401	60,882	66,260	—	—	2,219,737	513,833	429,515	4,005,408
1891	64,329	65,932	73,060	—	—	2,397,503	556,226	424,217	4,369,900
1892	67,119	70,930	76,981	—	—	2,543,270	593,685	511,434	4,776,575
1893	68,403	75,897	81,582	—	—	2,750,293	636,279	530,506	5,021,841
1894	69,805	75,080	84,994	—	—	2,602,278	571,475	468,500	4,919,090
1895	70,064	76,983	87,180	—	—	2,795,425	598,849	492,306	5,134,281
1896	70,360	82,499	90,933	—	—	3,025,481	616,040	524,820	5,693,719
1897	71,022	82,665	94,077	—	—	3,063,634	585,032	523,608	5,781,002
1898	73,570	89,013	98,054	—	—	3,418,458	606,447	556,381	6,214,447
1899	75,000	95,021	101,632	—	—	3,692,776	628,456	573,634	6,576,310

Notes appear at end of table   (continued)

TABLE Dg181-189   U.S. Postal Service - post offices, finances, pieces handled, and items issued: 1789-1999
Continued

				Sales of postage stamps and other stamped paper	Issued			
	Post offices	Revenues	Expenditures	Surplus or deficit		Ordinary postage stamps	Stamped envelopes and wrappers	Postal cards	Pieces handled
	Dg181	Dg182 [1]	Dg183 [1]	Dg184	Dg185	Dg186	Dg187	Dg188	Dg189
Year	Number	Thousand dollars	Thousand dollars	Thousand dollars	Thousand dollars	Thousand	Thousand	Thousand	Thousand
1900	76,688	102,354	107,740	—	—	3,998,545	707,555	587,815	7,129,990
1901	76,945	111,631	115,555	—	—	4,239,274	772,839	659,615	7,424,390
1902	75,924	121,848	124,786	—	—	4,621,286	853,128	547,204	8,085,447
1903	74,169	134,224	138,784	—	—	5,270,549	948,654	770,658	8,887,467
1904	71,131	143,582	152,362	—	—	5,330,887	1,020,255	702,907	9,502,460
1905	68,131	152,827	167,399	—	—	5,751,018	1,074,918	728,285	10,187,506
1906	65,600	167,933	178,450	—	—	6,284,450	1,230,288	798,918	11,361,091
1907	62,658	183,585	190,238	—	—	7,061,037	1,418,840	805,569	12,255,666
1908	60,704	191,479	208,352	—	—	7,651,400	1,266,003	809,427	13,364,069
1909	60,144	203,562	221,004	—	—	8,731,875	1,509,626	926,479	14,004,577
1910	59,580	224,129	229,977	—	—	9,067,165	1,506,862	726,441	14,850,102
1911	59,237	237,880	237,649	—	—	10,046,069	1,690,775	975,139	16,900,552
1912	58,729	246,744	248,525	—	—	9,929,174	1,684,624	909,411	17,588,659
1913	58,020	266,620	262,068	—	—	10,812,508	1,724,730	946,862	18,567,445
1914	56,810	287,935	283,544	—	—	11,112,254	1,864,714	962,072	—
1915	56,380	287,248	298,546	—	—	11,226,386	1,793,764	975,542	—
1916	55,935	312,058	306,204	—	—	11,671,842	1,853,791	1,047,895	—
1917	55,414	329,726	319,839	—	—	12,451,522	2,161,108	1,112,338	—
1918	54,347	388,976 [3]	324,834	—	—	13,065,785	1,819,307	707,111	—
1919	53,084	436,239 [3]	362,498	—	—	15,020,470	1,844,885	456,924	—
1920	52,641	437,150	454,323	—	—	13,212,790	2,350,073	986,156	—
1921	52,168	463,491	620,994	—	—	13,869,935	2,738,934	1,081,207	—
1922	51,950	484,854	545,644	—	—	14,261,949	2,364,373	1,111,124	—
1923	51,613	532,828	556,851	—	—	15,478,095	2,721,475	1,253,196	23,054,832
1924	51,266	572,949	587,377	—	—	15,954,475	2,964,464	1,293,185	—
1925	50,957	599,591	639,282	—	—	17,386,556	2,997,177	1,497,367	—
1926	50,601	659,820	679,704	−37,906	—	16,333,410	3,001,858	1,668,241	25,483,529
1927	50,266	683,122	714,577	−28,915	—	15,999,701	3,145,946	1,834,456	26,686,556
1928	49,944	693,634	725,700	−33,363	—	16,676,493	3,201,459	1,872,040	26,837,005
1929	49,482	606,918	782,344	−86,310	—	16,917,275	3,228,587	1,783,897	27,951,548
1930	49,063	705,484	803,667	−98,449	—	16,268,856	3,164,127	1,643,212	27,887,823
1931	48,733	656,463	802,485	−146,545	—	15,559,164	2,847,439	1,531,246	26,544,352
1932	48,159	588,172	793,684	−206,886	—	14,650,970	2,384,793	1,334,753	24,306,744
1933	47,641	587,631	699,887	−110,007	—	11,917,442	1,644,993	1,389,524	19,868,456
1934	46,506	586,733	630,733	−46,667	—	12,525,717	1,580,820	1,590,257	20,625,827
1935	45,686	630,795	696,503	−69,802	—	13,610,497	1,617,677	1,754,030	22,331,752
1936	45,230	665,343	753,616	−90,975	—	13,835,400	1,647,891	1,917,793	23,571,315
1937	44,877	726,201	772,743	−44,704	521,675	15,108,639	1,663,818	2,226,153	25,801,279
1938	44,586	728,634	772,308	−44,697	515,118	14,912,093	1,643,815	2,186,721	26,041,979
1939	44,327	745,955	784,550	−40,827	514,869	15,073,796	1,605,076	2,170,572	26,444,846
1940	44,024	766,949	807,629	−42,225	521,753	16,381,427	1,649,549	2,256,520	27,749,467
1941	43,739	812,828	836,859	−26,964	543,584	16,381,321	1,645,255	2,400,188	29,235,791
1942	43,358	859,817	873,950	−11,825	571,651	19,492,121	1,676,573	2,370,062	30,117,633
1943	42,654	966,227	952,529	1,335	658,054	19,123,977	1,797,400	2,316,990	32,818,262
1944	42,161	1,112,877	1,068,987	37,789	787,836	19,106,171	1,902,313	1,912,990	34,930,685
1945	41,792	1,314,240	1,145,002	162,642	953,770	20,239,986	2,064,773	2,282,280	37,912,067
1946	41,751	1,224,572	1,353,654	−148,083	843,417	19,180,427	1,815,916	2,477,854	36,318,158
1947	41,760	1,299,141	1,504,799	−263,368	801,437	19,542,257	1,996,450	2,951,300	37,427,706
1948	41,695	1,410,971	1,687,805	−308,972	820,904	20,432,059	2,117,573	3,656,591	40,280,374
1949	41,607	1,571,851	2,149,322	−551,130	856,266	21,047,376	2,219,744	3,468,719	43,555,108
1950	41,464	1,677,487	2,222,949	−545,462	862,313	20,647,165	2,052,156	3,872,301	45,063,737
1951	41,193	1,776,816	2,341,399	−564,583	883,357	21,521,807	2,004,569	4,183,748	46,908,410
1952	40,919	1,947,316	2,666,860	−719,544	948,430	22,067,083	2,274,660	2,984,124	49,905,875
1953	40,609	2,091,714	2,742,126	−650,412	985,172	22,960,962	2,338,622	2,330,921	50,948,156
1954	39,405	2,268,517	2,667,664	−399,147	998,965	22,219,068	2,265,309	2,360,534	52,213,170
1955	38,316	2,349,477	2,712,150	−362,673	999,985	23,105,454	2,189,521	2,515,392	55,233,564
1956	37,515	2,419,354	2,883,305	−463,951	1,010,523	23,722,489	2,571,416	2,911,276	56,441,216
1957	37,012	2,496,614	3,044,438	−547,824	1,015,237	24,257,860	1,966,336	2,046,515	59,077,633
1958	36,308	2,550,221	3,440,810	−890,577	1,016,930	22,879,828	2,040,211	2,375,065	60,129,911
1959	35,750	3,035,232	3,640,368	−605,117	1,245,231	27,980,885	2,228,813	2,969,055	61,247,220

TABLE Dg181–189   U.S. Postal Service – post offices, finances, pieces handled, and items issued: 1789–1999
Continued

					Sales of postage stamps and other stamped paper	Issued			
	Post offices	Revenues	Expenditures	Surplus or deficit		Ordinary postage stamps	Stamped envelopes and wrappers	Postal cards	Pieces handled
	Dg181	Dg182 [1]	Dg183 [1]	Dg184	Dg185	Dg186	Dg187	Dg188	Dg189
Year	Number	Thousand dollars	Thousand dollars	Thousand dollars	Thousand dollars	Thousand	Thousand	Thousand	Thousand
1960	35,238	3,276,588	3,873,953	−634,534	1,244,909	23,773,570	2,005,442	1,773,090	63,674,604
1961	34,955	3,423,059	4,249,414	−875,355	1,252,681	23,001,808	2,021,032	1,653,595	64,932,859
1962	34,797	3,557,041	4,331,617	−837,277	1,262,316	25,405,929	1,789,415	1,463,665	66,493,190
1963	34,498	3,879,128	4,698,528	−819,400	1,381,749	31,669,175	2,344,717	2,487,038	67,852,738
1964	34,040	4,276,123	4,927,825	−651,702	1,504,180	24,692,326	1,928,982	1,563,165	69,676,477
1965	33,624	4,483,390	5,275,840	−792,450	1,528,289	22,691,106	1,670,726	1,092,380	71,873,166
1966	33,121	4,784,186	5,726,523	−942,336	1,579,338	23,503,959	1,627,789	1,289,000	75,607,302
1967	32,626	5,101,982	6,249,027	−1,147,044	1,636,057	26,320,986	1,512,996	1,011,675	78,366,572
1968	32,260	6,423,515	6,543,920	−120,405	1,799,492	34,667,494	1,853,427	1,431,311	79,516,731
1969	32,064	7,025,898	7,168,489	−142,591	1,936,578	27,383,827	1,374,121	846,695	82,004,501
1970	32,002	7,701,695	7,867,269	−165,574	1,936,147	26,182,562	1,368,098	830,650	84,881,833
1971	31,947	8,751,000	8,955,000	−204,000	1,999,000	—	—	—	86,893,000
1972	31,686	9,347,000	9,522,000	−175,000	2,371,000	—	—	—	87,156,000
1973	31,385	9,913,000	9,926,000	−13,000	2,399,000	—	—	—	89,700,000
1974	31,000	10,857,000	11,295,000	−438,000	2,504,000	—	—	—	90,100,000
1975	30,754	11,590,000	12,578,000	−988,000	2,819,000	—	—	—	89,300,000
1976	30,521	12,747,000	13,923,000	−1,176,000	3,155,000	—	—	—	89,800,000
(TQ)	30,521	3,402,000	3,387,000	15,000	815,000	—	—	—	21,500,000
1977	30,521	14,622,000	15,310,000	−688,000	3,658,000	—	—	—	92,200,000
1978	30,518	15,841,000	16,220,000	−379,000	3,943,000	—	—	—	98,900,000
1979	30,449	17,999,000	17,529,000	470,000	4,382,000	—	—	—	99,800,000
1980	30,326	19,106,000	19,412,000	−306,000	4,287,000	—	—	—	106,300,000
1981	30,242	20,781,000	21,369,000	−588,000	4,625,000	—	—	—	110,100,000
1982	30,155	23,628,000	22,826,000	802,000	5,559,000	—	—	—	114,000,000
1983	29,990	24,699,000	24,083,000	616,000	5,709,000	—	—	—	119,400,000
1984	29,750	26,474,000	26,357,000	117,000	6,023,000	—	—	—	131,500,000
1985	29,557	28,956,000	29,207,000	−251,000	6,520,000	—	—	—	140,100,000
1986	29,334	31,021,000	30,716,000	305,000	6,969,000	—	—	—	147,400,000
1987	29,319	32,297,000	32,520,000	−223,000	7,246,000	—	—	—	153,900,000
1988	29,203	35,939,000	36,119,000	−180,000	7,784,000	—	—	—	161,000,000
1989	29,083	38,920,000	38,370,000	550,000	8,381,000	—	—	—	161,600,000
1990	28,959	40,074,000	40,490,000	−416,000	8,638,000	—	—	—	166,301,000
1991	28,912	44,202,000	43,291,000	911,000	9,148,000	—	—	—	165,851,000
1992	28,837	47,105,000	45,653,000	1,452,000	10,071,000	—	—	—	166,443,000
1993	28,728	47,986,000	46,322,000	1,664,000	10,357,000	—	—	—	171,220,000
1994	28,657	49,576,000	48,455,000	1,121,000	10,851,000	—	—	—	178,039,000
1995	28,392	54,509,000	50,730,000	3,779,000	11,846,000	—	—	—	180,734,000
1996	28,189	56,544,000	53,113,000	3,431,000	—	—	—	—	183,440,000
1997	28,060	58,331,000	54,873,000	3,458,000	—	—	—	—	190,888,000
1998	27,952	60,116,000	57,778,000	2,338,000	—	—	—	—	196,905,000
1999	27,893	62,755,000	60,631,000	2,124,000	—	—	—	—	201,576,000

(TQ) Transition quarter.

[1] Accounting basis changed from cash to accrual basis in 1954 and then to accrued cost basis in 1963.

[2] For three months only.

[3] Includes $44,500,000 (1918) and $71,392,000 (1919) in war-tax revenue accruing from increased postage.

Sources

For 1789–1969: U.S. Post Office Department, *Annual Report of the Postmaster General* (1970). For 1970–1983: *Revenue and Cost Analysis* (unpublished). For 1984–1999: *Cost and Revenue Analysis* (unpublished).

Documentation

Series Dg181. Excludes branches and stations.

Series Dg182–183. Comparability of figures from year to year is affected by various factors. For example, the Post Office discontinued payment of subsidies to airlines in 1954; the department also began receiving reimbursement for penalty and franked mail in 1954, costs that the Post Office had previously absorbed. Expenses include expenditures for plant and equipment of a capital nature and for inventories and supplies, but no provision for depreciation is made. Expenses also include certain public-service costs paid by the Post Office Department, but which the department considered to be unrelated to the determination of the proper operating costs of the Postal Service. These include unreimbursed services for other government agencies; specific rate subsidies for mailings of second- and third-class mail by certain nonprofit organizations, free-in-county second-class mail, classroom publications, and mail for the blind; excess rates paid to foreign air carriers; and custodial services for other government departments and agencies. Expenses of the Post Office Department do not include costs applicable to postal operations that are paid by other government departments and agencies for retirement pay accrual, workmen's compensation and unemployment compensation for postal employees, and certain custodial and maintenance expenses.

Series Dg184. The accounts of the department are maintained in such a way as to reflect the deficit in three ways – the cash deficit, the operating deficit, and the postal fund deficit. The cash deficit represents the excess

(continued)

TABLE Dg181–189   U.S. Postal Service – post offices, finances, pieces handled, and items issued: 1789–1999
Continued

of disbursements over receipts. The operating deficit, which is utilized in the series, represents the excess of expense over income. The postal fund deficit represents the excess of obligations incurred over postal revenues.

Series Dg186. Ordinary postage stamps were first issued under an act of March 3, 1847, and placed on sale in New York City on July 1, 1847.

Series Dg187. Stamped envelopes were first issued June 1853, under an act of August 31, 1852. Newspaper wrappers were first issued under an act of February 27, 1861; they were not made after October 9, 1934. Special-request envelopes were first issued in 1865.

Series Dg188. Postal cards were first issued May 1, 1873, under an act of June 8, 1872. The postcard, or private mailing card, was introduced in 1898.

The rate for this service has been practically identical with that of the postal cards. Business reply cards and letters as a postal service were initiated in 1928.

Series Dg189. Covers pieces of matter of all kinds. With the establishment of the cost ascertainment system in 1926, data on the volume of mail have been obtained from sample counts conducted quarterly for one week at representative post offices, ranging in number from 255 to over 500. These sample data were then projected to include all originating mail at all post offices in the United States. The methods of estimating the number of pieces of matter handled prior to 1926 could not be ascertained.

TABLE Dg190–208   U.S. Postal Service – employees, finances, and pieces handled, by class of mail: 1926–1999[1,2,3]
Contributed by Alexander J. Field

	First-class mail			Second-class mail			Third-class mail		
	Revenue	Expenses	Pieces	Revenue	Expenses	Pieces	Revenue	Expenses	Pieces
	Dg190 [4]	Dg191 [4]	Dg192 [4]	Dg193	Dg194	Dg195	Dg196	Dg197	Dg198
Year	Million dollars	Million dollars	Million	Million dollars	Million dollars	Million	Million dollars	Million dollars	Million
1926	321	247	15,266	34	118	4,658	69	71	3,962
1927	345	262	16,284	35	119	4,753	69	73	4,062
1928	356	268	16,706	35	120	4,678	66	72	3,838
1929	361	276	17,170	30	124	4,834	62	81	4,341
1930	359	279	16,901	31	120	4,968	61	83	4,325
1931	336	278	15,824	27	124	4,857	58	82	4,100
1932	310	277	14,598	23	125	4,552	51	80	3,641
1933	332	227	10,878	20	108	3,869	51	79	3,753
1934	325	206	11,557	21	99	3,956	50	67	3,612
1935	344	229	12,498	20	107	4,138	55	76	4,030
1936	355	247	12,731	22	113	4,353	63	86	4,674
1937	384	254	13,882	24	113	4,529	72	92	5,356
1938	389	259	14,226	24	114	4,877	71	95	5,272
1939	400	263	14,657	24	111	4,310	70	94	5,181
1940	413	267	15,224	25	110	4,577	75	101	5,556
1941	432	278	15,989	26	109	4,607	83	105	6,075
1942	459	293	16,972	27	113	4,571	74	98	5,435
1943	—	—	—	—	—	—	—	—	—
1944	540	370	20,510	29	138	4,635	63	88	4,409
1945	615	374	21,009	29	145	5,522	76	99	5,446
1946	598	454	20,059	33	181	5,832	83	135	6,055
1947	627	500	20,665	39	201	6,124	96	171	6,803
1948	668	518	21,948	41	210	6,344	112	201	8,183
1949	706	629	23,206	44	234	6,987	136	267	9,389
1950	741	665	24,500	45	242	6,265	154	292	10,343
1951	785	678	25,578	49	245	6,520	158	286	10,534
1952	843	787	26,502	51	288	6,956	171	361	11,630
1953	909	822	27,257	58	298	6,762	218	374	12,004
1954	908	845	27,085	62	293	6,483	252	399	13,866
1955	968	906	28,713	66	299	6,740	270	442	15,050
1956	1,014	978	30,078	66	318	6,915	266	472	14,676
1957	1,066	1,040	31,561	66	327	6,888	281	528	15,702
1958	1,092	1,229	32,218	66	351	7,148	288	611	15,849
1959	1,439	1,303	32,274	69	373	7,099	391	678	16,978
1960	1,510	1,395	33,235	81	412	7,535	441	711	17,910
1961	1,558	1,547	34,289	89	442	7,966	498	787	17,569
1962	1,615	1,605	35,333	94	455	8,090	510	787	17,837
1963	1,824	1,691	35,833	98	454	8,227	563	874	18,407
1964	2,109	1,814	36,943	108	481	8,559	612	899	18,599
1965	2,193	1,965	38,068	119	499	8,600	650	999	19,454
1966	2,334	2,176	40,422	126	524	8,634	682	1,041	20,305
1967	2,442	2,407	41,998	129	551	8,711	704	1,116	20,985
1968	2,722	2,660	43,183	134	569	8,907	743	1,144	20,665
1969	3,135	1,692	46,411	147	350	9,206	782	460	19,622

Notes appear at end of table

TABLE Dg190–208   U.S. Postal Service – employees, finances, and pieces handled, by class of mail: 1926–1999
Continued

	First-class mail			Second-class mail			Third-class mail		
	Revenue	Expenses	Pieces	Revenue	Expenses	Pieces	Revenue	Expenses	Pieces
	Dg190 [4]	Dg191 [4]	Dg192 [4]	Dg193	Dg194	Dg195	Dg196	Dg197	Dg198
Year	Million dollars	Million dollars	Million	Million dollars	Million dollars	Million	Million dollars	Million dollars	Million
1970	3,290	1,985	48,640	155	292	9,352	827	531	19,974
1971	3,506	2,105	50,000	157	343	9,604	844	584	20,532
1972	4,379	2,279	48,933	177	345	9,494	1,006	755	21,908
1973	4,578	2,414	51,000	186	362	9,034	1,162	760	22,689
1974	5,019	2,812	51,600	213	367	8,838	1,214	795	22,537
1975	5,798	3,457	51,400	236	456	9,085	1,348	1,050	21,867
1976	6,734	5,812	52,100	267	648	8,899	1,522	1,490	22,514
(TQ)	—	—	12,500	—	—	2,100	—	—	—
1977	7,831	6,561	53,668	363	759	8,673	1,748	1,913	24,050
1978	8,575	7,091	56,020	472	783	8,691	1,987	2,051	26,330
1979	9,733	5,307	57,976	644	717	8,400	2,216	2,153	27,513
1980	10,146	6,832	60,332	618	634	8,446	2,412	2,010	30,381
1981	11,457	7,338	61,476	885 [7]	766	9,956 [7]	2,643	2,240	33,607
1982	13,747	7,865	62,271	961	798	9,527	3,303	2,499	36,719
1983	14,255	8,446	64,320	958	805	9,220	3,677	2,795	40,735
1984	15,216	9,341	68,507	1,025	846	9,522	4,241	3,341	48,249
1985	16,740	10,292	72,517	1,093	986	10,380	4,887	3,722	52,170
1986	18,035	10,621	76,252	1,222	1,001	10,588	5,606	4,019	55,049
1987	18,786	11,385	78,933	1,280	1,113	10,324	6,148	4,641	59,734
1988	21,398	13,178	84,815	1,401	1,322	10,483	7,300	5,712	63,250
1989	23,234	14,198	85,926	1,519	1,414	10,523	7,924	5,948	62,779
1990	24,023	14,783	89,343	1,509	1,522	10,680	8,082	6,243	63,725
1991	26,649	15,758	90,356	1,668	1,591	10,399	8,956	6,496	62,430
1992	28,296	16,186	90,842	1,751	1,687	10,319	9,490	6,864	62,547
1993	28,828	16,467	92,229	1,740	1,614	10,306	9,817	6,824	65,773
1994	29,395	17,633	95,394	1,758	1,674	10,228	10,511	7,078	69,416
1995	31,955	18,442	96,349	1,972	1,765	10,194	11,792	7,496	71,112
1996	33,117	18,920	98,216	2,014	1,871	10,126	12,175	7,673	71,859
1997	33,398	17,710	99,660	2,068	1,989	10,411	12,876	8,199	77,254
1998	33,983	17,655	100,434	2,072	2,071	10,317	13,753	9,037	82,508
1999	34,933	19,264	101,936	2,115	2,290	10,274	14,436	10,239	85,662

	Fourth-class mail			Domestic airmail			Priority mail			Employees
	Revenue	Expenses	Pieces	Revenue	Expenses	Pieces	Revenue	Expenses	Pieces	
	Dg199	Dg200	Dg201	Dg202 [4,5,6]	Dg203 [4,5,6]	Dg204 [4,5,6]	Dg205	Dg206	Dg207	Dg208
Year	Million dollars	Million dollars	Million	Million dollars	Million dollars	Million	Million dollars	Million dollars	Million	Thousand
1926	145	148	770	—	—	—	—	—	—	329
1927	141	146	743	—	—	—	—	—	—	332
1928	144	151	752	—	—	—	—	—	—	337
1929	143	163	770	4	11	56	—	—	—	340
1930	152	167	837	5	15	69	—	—	—	340
1931	138	158	766	6	18	88	—	—	—	339
1932	114	146	617	6	24	89	—	—	—	333
1933	100	132	530	6	23	60	—	—	—	322
1934	102	121	531	6	15	57	—	—	—	314
1935	112	133	573	7	13	89	—	—	—	309
1936	122	140	618	10	17	134	—	—	—	324
1937	132	146	685	12	19	168	—	—	—	332
1938	129	146	670	15	22	210	—	—	—	345
1939	133	151	693	16	25	221	—	—	—	349
1940	134	156	712	19	28	259	—	—	—	353
1941	142	161	738	24	31	323	—	—	—	361
1942	151	169	779	33	37	463	—	—	—	360
1943	—	—	—	—	—	—	—	—	—	374
1944	202	217	961	79	49	1,092	—	—	—	390

Notes appear at end of table

(continued)

TABLE Dg190–208   U.S. Postal Service – employees, finances, and pieces handled, by class of mail: 1926–1999
Continued

	Fourth-class mail			Domestic airmail			Priority mail			Employees
	Revenue	Expenses	Pieces	Revenue	Expenses	Pieces	Revenue	Expenses	Pieces	
	Dg199	Dg200	Dg201	Dg202 [4,5,6]	Dg203 [4,5,6]	Dg204 [4,5,6]	Dg205	Dg206	Dg207	Dg208
Year	Million dollars	Million dollars	Million	Million dollars	Million dollars	Million	Million dollars	Million dollars	Million	Thousand
1945	233	232	1,028	81	50	876	—	—	—	436
1946	209	250	994	68	50	716	—	—	—	487
1947	235	298	1,067	54	68	772	—	—	—	471
1948	272	368	1,143	54	83	796	—	—	—	503
1949	356	485	1,209	65	104	856	—	—	—	518
1950	404	506	1,179	74	109	853	—	—	—	501
1951	431	537	1,235	95	116	1,094	—	—	—	498
1952	485	619	1,257	121	148	1,391	—	—	—	524
1953	491	623	1,245	121	157	1,430	—	—	—	507
1954	587	609	1,195	127	119	1,470	—	—	—	507
1955	595	593	1,136	130	109	1,467	—	—	—	512
1956	593	608	1,173	137	114	1,487	—	—	—	509
1957	586	641	1,184	140	119	1,483	—	—	—	521
1958	584	699	1,170	137	127	1,435	—	—	—	538
1959	576	709	1,038	153	131	1,368	—	—	—	550
1960	607	736	1,016	157	137	1,356	—	—	—	563
1961	626	774	978	171	151	1,453	—	—	—	582
1962	634	787	1,024	185	163	1,545	—	—	—	588
1963	645	806	1,076	200	172	1,545	—	—	—	587
1964	659	815	1,066	216	181	1,505	—	—	—	585
1965	702	846	1,045	243	198	1,629	—	—	—	596
1966	712	896	1,066	277	221	1,828	—	—	—	675
1967	742	933	1,070	329	271	2,111	—	—	—	717
1968	767	939	1,039	425	304	2,065	—	—	—	731
1969	831	542	1,031	485	165	1,836	—	—	—	739
1970	778	554	977	484	188	1,718	282	94	185	741
1971	819	546	968	198	213	1,493	303	103	197	729
1972	810	535	914	209	145	1,360	348	104	208	706
1973	759	527	893	213	189	1,291	352	151	209	701
1974	732	512	859	234	189	1,329	394	154	222	710
1975	718	765	801	218	220	1,082	411	165	207	702
1976	680	854	759	84	209	359	411	184	192	679
(TQ)	—	—	—	—	—	—	—	—	—	—
1977	769	1,029	762	6	110	—	468	235	202	655
1978	673	819	691	—	—	—	497	210	213	656
1979	747	687	614	—	—	—	561	275	229	663
1980	805	525	633	—	—	—	612	311	248	667
1981	786	565	590	—	—	—	758	344	269	670
1982	788	535	597	—	—	—	823	330	259	670
1983	753	614	568	—	—	—	849	354	271	679
1984	774	665	599	—	—	—	928	376	293	702
1985	763	716	576	—	—	—	960	438	308	744
1986	814	689	602	—	—	—	1,011	499	330	785
1987	823	777	615	—	—	—	1,086	507	354	791
1988	937	897	674	—	—	—	1,345	715	437	824
1989	908	840	626	—	—	—	1,416	813	471	817
1990	920	894	663	—	—	—	1,555	886	518	819
1991	1,001	993	695	—	—	—	1,765	1,013	530	808
1992	1,186	1,050	764	—	—	—	2,071	1,046	584	819
1993	1,183	1,230	744	—	—	—	2,300	1,166	664	818
1994	1,351	1,300	872	—	—	—	2,649	1,349	770	852
1995	1,525	1,261	936	—	—	—	3,075	1,359	869	875
1996	1,524	1,299	949	—	—	—	3,322	1,640	959	886
1997	1,628	1,478	988	—	—	—	3,857	2,201	1,068	893
1998	1,629	1,484	1,023	—	—	—	4,187	—	—	905
1999	1,828	1,728	1,043	—	—	—	4,533	—	—	906

TABLE Dg190–208   U.S. Postal Service – employees, finances, and pieces handled, by class of mail: 1926–1999
Continued

(TQ) Transition quarter.

[1] Box rent revenue classified as unassignable (through 1950), allocated to classes of mail (1951–1955), and classified as special service thereafter.

[2] In fiscal year 1969, the department changed from a fully distributed cost system to an attributable cost system. Attributable costs include volume variable costs and fixed costs exclusively associated with a class of mail. This change is first reflected in the data for fiscal year 1970.

[3] As of 1997, the category names for second, third, and fourth class became "Periodicals," "Standard Mail (A)," and "Standard Mail (B)," respectively.

[4] For 1926–1929, domestic airmail included with first-class mail. Includes express mail.

[5] Beginning 1947, includes airmail to and from armed forces overseas, previously included with foreign mail. Beginning 1954, excludes reimbursement for airmail transportation.

[6] As of October 11, 1975, surface mail service upgraded to level of airmail. Domestic airmail service was discontinued as of May 1, 1977. See text.

[7] Includes controlled circulation. See text.

Sources
Series Dg190–207. For 1926–1946: U.S. Post Office Department, "Budget Digest" (1949), Chapter 4, Tables 5–11. For 1947–1968: "Cost Ascertainment Report" (1956, 1958, and 1968). For 1969–1983: *Revenue and Cost Analysis* (various annual issues). For 1984–1999: *Cost and Revenue Analysis Report* (annual issues) and *Revenue, Pieces and Weight by Classes of Mail and Special Services* (quarterly issues).

Series Dg208. For 1926–1969: U.S. Post Office Department, *Annual Report of the Postmaster General* (1970). For 1970–1999: U.S. Postal Service, *Annual Report of the Postmaster General* (various years).

Documentation
Data through 1976 is for fiscal years ending June 30; thereafter, September 30. Geographical coverage includes Alaska, Hawai'i, Puerto Rico, and all outlying areas except the Canal Zone.

Postal revenues (except for about 10 percent, which can be directly allocated or computed) are derived from postage acquired in the form of stamps and stamped paper and from payments under permits, which may be used by the purchaser generally on any class of mail. The result is a large common pool of revenues from numerous sources. Similarly, the several classes of mail and the special services are, to a considerable extent, handled by the same employees using the same buildings, equipment, operating facilities, house services, and supplies.

Pursuant to the congressional Act of February 28, 1925 (39 U.S.C. 826), a regular, continuing cost ascertainment system was established in 1926 to collect and develop data on the revenue received (including volume and weight of mail) and costs incurred by the Post Office Department. Prior to 1970, the bulk of postal revenues and postal expenses could not be allocated directly to the various classes of mail handled or to special services performed. Beginning in 1970, costs represent attributable or incremental costs associated with particular categories of service. The latter system represents the culmination of many changes and improvements for *Revenue and Cost Analysis* (formerly *Cost Ascertainment Report*). The title of this report was changed to *Cost and Revenue Analysis* in 1984. Attributable costs include volume variable costs that can be assigned to specific subclasses of service and fixed specific costs that can be assigned to classes of service. For fiscal year 1986, 62 percent of total costs were attributable (U.S. Postal Service, *Cost and Revenue Analysis, Fiscal Year 1986*, p. 8, note 2.) For fiscal year 1996, 62.65 percent of total costs were attributable (U.S. Postal Service, *Cost and Revenue Analysis, Fiscal Year 1996*, p. 7, note 2).

The statistics of expenses as published annually are subject to later readjustments as a result of increases in the charges of railroad, air, or other transportation services, or increases in the salaries of department employees, if such increases are made retroactive to an earlier fiscal year.

Series Dg190–192. Figures cover letters, matter wholly or partially in writing or typewriting, and packages (including local delivery letters), single or double postal cards and postcards, bills and statements of account, and matter closed against postal inspection. Each piece may not weigh more than 70 pounds or measure more than 100 inches in length and girth combined.

Postage may be paid by adhesive stamps, stamped cards or envelopes, meter stamps, or permit imprint. For 1926–1929, domestic airmail could not be segregated and is included with first-class mail. Mail fees are included for 1950–1999. Box rent revenues, previously reported as unassignable, are allocated to classes of mail, 1951–1955, and classified with special services for 1956–1999. For 1951–1999, the expense of free mail from members of the armed forces is included in first-class mail expenditures. Beginning in 1979, the series include express mail revenues and expenses (service category established October 9, 1977).

Series Dg193–195
Newspapers and periodical publications, both domestic and foreign, that meet all of the requirements set forth in part 132, "Postal Service Manual," may be mailed at the second-class rates of postage. Revenues include postage payments (stamps or money order permit) and, since 1932, payment of fees for use of the second-class privilege; transient second-class matter (mailings of second-class publications by other than the publisher or news agents); publishers' second-class matter forwarded or returned, 1950–1999; mailing fees, 1951–1999; and box rent revenue allocation, 1951–1955.

Expenses include cost of publishers' second-class matter forwarded or returned, 1950–1999, and, for 1953–1999, also include the expense of sending notices to publishers regarding undelivered mail.

The category of controlled circulation was discontinued on March 22, 1982. Data for 1981 include controlled circulation (but see the text for series Dg196–201). Controlled circulation consisted of publications of at least twenty-four pages and containing at least 25 percent nonadvertising content issued quarterly or more frequently for mainly free distribution. It includes certain trade publications and "shopper" guides.

In 1997, the category "Second Class Mail" was replaced by "Periodicals."

Beginning in 1970, costs represent attributable or incremental costs associated with particular categories of service.

Series Dg196–198
Third-class mail embraces all matter less than 16 ounces in weight and not qualifying as first- or second-class or priority mail. A significant proportion of the matter mailed under third class is advertising material. Also included are keys, identification cards and tags, or similar identification devices that are without cover and bear, contain, or have securely attached the name and complete post office address of a person, organization, or concern, with instructions to return to such address and a statement guaranteeing the payment of the postage due on delivery. In 1928, a special "bulk rate" was made applicable to separately addressed identical pieces of third-class matter mailed at one time. The present law requires such matter to be mailed in quantities of at least 50 pounds or at least 200 pieces. Also, there is a single-piece third-class rate. Revenues include postage revenues and fees for permits; domestic mail fees, 1951–1999; and box rent revenue allocation, 1951–1955.

Prior to 1953, the revenues and expenses applicable to controlled-circulation publications (publications consisting primarily of advertising and distributed free or mainly free) were included with third-class and fourth-class services. For 1953–1980, controlled-circulation publications were reported separately; for 1981 they were included with second-class mail. See the text for series Dg193–195. The category was discontinued in 1982.

In 1997, the category "Third Class Mail" was replaced by "Standard Mail (A)."

Series Dg199–201
This class includes mailable matter 16 ounces or more in weight, not qualifying as first or second class. The major development in this class of mail was the establishment of the parcel post system effective January 1, 1913. Books, special fourth-class and library (now media) rate items, catalogs, and matter for the blind, included in fourth class, carry special rates. Mailers of fourth-class articles may use any method of paying postage. Revenues include domestic mail fees for 1951–1999; box rent revenue allocations, 1951–1955; and special handling fees, and before 1953, a portion of revenue from controlled-circulation publications (see the text for series Dg196–198).

In 1997, the category "Fourth Class Mail" was replaced by "Standard Mail (B)."

TABLE Dg190–208   U.S. Postal Service – employees, finances, and pieces handled, by class of mail: 1926–1999
Continued

Series Dg202–204. Beginning in September 1948, domestic airmail included a parcel post service and, after January 1949, airmail postal card and postcard service. Paid airmail to and from the armed forces overseas and the outlying areas of the United States, formerly in international airmail, was included with domestic airmail, 1947–1977. For 1951–1977, airmail expenses included the cost of free mail from members of the armed forces.

Airmail expenditures included subsequent payments, as of June 30, 1950, to airlines for retroactive rate increases where effective. The decline in airmail expenses between 1953 and 1954 resulted from the transfer of subsidy payments to airlines from the Post Office Department to the Civil Aeronautics Board, effective October 1, 1953. The *Cost Ascertainment Report* for 1953 and prior years shows division of service costs and subsidy payments.

Beginning in 1954, the department began experimenting with the transporting of all mail by air between a number of major cities. A separate category for domestic airmail ceased to exist in 1977.

Series Dg205–207. For 1970–1977, priority mail is mail otherwise qualified as first class or airmail but exceeding 12 ounces or 8 ounces, respectively. For 1978–1999, priority mail is mail otherwise qualified as first class but exceeding 13 ounces but less than 70 pounds.

Series Dg208. Included are regular or full-time employees and substitute, hourly rate, and part-time employees. Part-time employees are a substantial part of the Post Office labor force.

Prior to October 1933, the operating force for public buildings housing post offices and other government agencies was on the rolls of the U.S. Treasury Department. On that date, the personnel were transferred to the Post Office Department. This increased the regular labor force of the department by 8,000 employees.

TABLE Dg209   U.S. Postal Service – rates for single letters, by distance: 1792–1855

Contributed by Alexander J. Field

	Rate
	Dg209
Year and postal zone	Cents
1792	
Not more than 30 miles	6.0
31–60 miles	8.0
61–100 miles	10.0
101–150 miles	12.5
151–200 miles	15.0
201–250 miles	17.0
251–350 miles	20.0
351–450 miles	22.0
More than 450 miles	25.0
1794	
More than 500 miles	25.0
1799	
Not more than 40 miles	8.0
41–90 miles	10.0
91–150 miles	12.5
151–300 miles	17.0
301–500 miles	20.0
More than 500 miles	25.0 [1]

	Rate
	Dg209
Year and postal zone	Cents
1816	
Not more than 30 miles	6.0
31–80 miles	10.0
81–150 miles	12.5
151–400 miles	18.5 [2]
More than 400 miles	25.0
More than 500 miles	25.0 [1]
1845	
Not more than 300 miles	5.0
More than 300 miles	10.0
1851	
Not more than 3,000 miles, prepaid	3.0
Not more than 3,000 miles, not prepaid	5.0
More than 3,000 miles, prepaid	6.0
More than 3,000 miles, not prepaid	10.0
1855	
Not more than 3,000 miles	3.0
More than 3,000 miles, all prepaid	10.0

[1] In 1815, the rate for distances over 500 miles was increased 50 percent to 37.5 cents. The increase was repealed in 1816, and the rate dropped back to 25 cents for this category.

[2] Rate increased to 18.75 cents in 1825.

Source
U.S. Post Office Department, *United States Domestic Postage Rates, 1789–1956*, Table I.

Documentation
Rates shown are for a communication of one sheet. Proportionately higher rates were charged for letters of two, three, and four or more sheets (packet).

As of 1794, the top rate of 25 cents applied to points more than 500 (rather than 450) miles apart. Also, starting in 1794 and continuing through 1863, extra fees were charged for city delivery service. The proceeds went to the letter carrier.

Ship and steamboat letters carried special rates, 1792–1863.

Various acts between 1847 and 1850 established special rates for the western and southwestern United States.

Also see text for series Dg210.

TABLE Dg210–220 U.S. Postal Service – rates, by zone and type of mail: 1861–2001
Contributed by Alexander J. Field

Year or date of rate change	Letters, first class	Postcards	Airmail Letters	Airmail Postcards	Express mail	Zone 1	Zone 2	Zone 3	All, excluding Canada and Mexico	Postcards	Aerogrammes
	Dg210	Dg211	Dg212	Dg213	Dg214	Dg215 [1]	Dg216	Dg217	Dg218	Dg219	Dg220
	Cents	Cents	Cents	Cents	Dollars	Cents	Cents	Cents	Cents	Cents	Cents
1861	3	—	—	—	—	—	—	—	—	—	—
1863	3	—	—	—	—	—	—	—	—	—	—
1873	3	1	—	—	—	—	—	—	—	—	—
1883	2	1	—	—	—	—	—	—	—	—	—
1885	2	1	—	—	—	—	—	—	—	—	—
1917	3	2	—	—	—	—	—	—	—	—	—
1919	2	1	—	—	—	—	—	—	—	—	—
1926	2	1	—	—	—	—	—	—	—	—	—
Feb 1, 1927	2	1	10 [2]	—	—	—	—	—	—	—	—
Aug 1, 1928	2	1	5	—	—	—	—	—	—	—	—
1932	3	1	8	—	—	—	—	—	—	—	—
July 1, 1934	3	1	6	—	—	—	—	—	—	—	—
1940	3	1	6	—	—	—	—	—	—	—	—
Mar 26, 1944	3	1	8	—	—	—	—	—	—	—	—
Sept 1, 1948	3	1	5	—	—	—	—	—	—	—	—
Jan 1, 1949	3	1	6	4	—	—	—	—	—	—	—
Jan 1, 1952	3	2	6	4	—	—	—	—	—	—	—
Aug 1, 1958	4	3	7	5	—	—	—	—	—	—	—
July 11, 1961	4	3	7	5	—	13	15	25	—	11	11
Jan 7, 1963	5	4	8	6	—	15	20	25	—	13	13
May 1, 1967	5	4	8	6	—	15	20	25	—	13	13
Jan 7, 1968	6	5	10	8	—	15	20	25	—	13	13
May 16, 1971	8	6	11	9	—	15	20	25	—	13	13
July 1, 1971	8	6	11	9	—	17	21	21	—	13	13
Mar 2, 1974	10	8	13	11	—	21	26	26	—	18	18
Sept 14, 1975	10	7	13	11	—	21	26	26	—	18	18
Dec 31, 1975	13	9	17	14	—	21	26	26	—	18	22
Jan 3, 1976	13	9	17	14	—	25	31	31	—	21	22
May 29, 1978	15	10	—	—	—	25	31	31	—	21	22
Jan 1, 1981	15	10	—	—	—	35	40	40	—	28	30
Mar 22, 1981	18	12	—	—	—	35	40	40	—	28	30
Nov 1, 1981	20	13	—	—	9.35	35	40	40	—	28	30
Jan 1, 1985	20	13	—	—	9.35	35	40	40	—	28	30
Feb 17, 1988	22	14	—	—	10.75	39	44	44	—	33	36
Feb 3, 1988	22	14	—	—	10.75	45	45	45	—	36	36
Apr 3, 1991	25	15	—	—	12.00	45	45	45	—	36	39
Feb 3, 1995	29	19	—	—	13.95	—	—	—	50	40	45
Jan 1, 1995	32	20	—	—	15.00	—	—	—	50	40	50
July 9, 1995	32	20	—	—	15.00	—	—	—	60	50	50
Jan 10, 1999	33	20	—	—	15.75	—	—	—	60	50	50
Jan 17, 2001	34	20	—	—	16.00	—	—	—	80 [3]	70	70
July 1, 2001	34	21	—	—	16.25	—	—	—	80	70	70

[1] See text for special circumstances affecting South America.

[2] Rate per half ounce.

[3] Maximum weight increased to one ounce.

Sources
For 1861–1956: U.S. Post Office Department, *United States Domestic Postage Rates, 1789–1956*, Table I. For 1958–1970: Public Law 85-126 (Postal Policy Act of 1958), Public Law 87-793 (Postal Service and Employee Salary Act of 1962), and Public Law 90-206 (Postal Service and Employee Salary Act of 1967). For 1971–2001: *United States Domestic Postage Rates: Recent History* (1974) and unpublished data.

Documentation
Series Dg210–213
The postage rates in effect in 1789 were those fixed by the Continental Congress in the Ordinance of 1782. These rates were continued until 1792.

It was not until 1863 that mail was divided into "classes." In the early days of the Postal Service, the recipient rather than the sender ordinarily paid the postage. In 1847, postage stamps were introduced, and in 1885, compulsory prepayment for all domestic letter mail was established.

The rates shown are for regular service. During the earlier years of the westward expansion, special local rates were often improvised. Thus, the first letter rate on the "pony express," which operated between Missouri and California from 1860 to 1861, was $5 for a half ounce, reduced in May 1861 to $2 for a half ounce and in July 1861 to $1 for a half ounce because of a government subsidy.

A considerable part of the domestic mail service between 1792 and 1863 was carried by ship and was subject to shipletter rates. These rates are detailed in *United States Domestic Postage Rates, 1789–1956*, Table II, p. 24. In 1863, a ship and steamboat rate, double the regular rate, was made applicable to domestic mail conveyed by ships not regularly employed in carrying

TABLE Dg210–220   U.S. Postal Service – rates, by zone and type of mail: 1861–2001   *Continued*

mail. This classification is omitted after 1879 because of its diminishing importance, but the double rate is still in effect although little or no matter is mailed under these rates.

In 1863, first-class mail was defined to include letters and matter wholly or partly in writing, except book manuscripts and corrected proof sheets. In 1872, first-class mail was described as including letters and all correspondence, wholly or partly in writing, except book manuscripts and corrected proof sheets passing between authors and publishers. In 1879, it was redefined to include letters, postal cards, and all matter wholly or partly in writing, except such writing as is authorized to be placed on mail of other classes. See Jane Kennedy, "Development of Postal Rates: 1845–1955," *Land Economics* (May 1957): 93–112, for additional materials on postal rates, particularly rates for second-, third-, and fourth-class mail.

Series Dg210. The rate for 1861 applied between points east of the Rockies and any state or territory on the Pacific. The 1855 rates shown in Table Dg209 applied for other routes. Since the 1855 rate for less than 3,000 miles was 3 cents per half ounce, the 1861 change effectively established the uniform national domestic rate for letters recognized in the establishment of the first-class mail category in 1863. In 1863, a uniform rate regardless of distance and a free city delivery service were introduced, and letters of up to one half ounce (instead of the former "single letter") became eligible for the basic rate. In 1885, this weight limit was increased to 1 ounce. As a result of a policy change in 1940, the 3-cent letter rate was not applied to first-class matter for local delivery or for delivery within a county with a population of more than 1 million if the county was entirely within a corporate city. In 1975, the Postal Service began charging reduced rates for additional ounces beyond the first ounce; rates shown in this series are for the first ounce.

Series Dg211. Government postal cards were first authorized in 1872, first issued in 1873.

Series Dg212–213

Rates are for the first ounce, except as noted. For information on the complexities of airmail rates prior to 1927, consult *Historical Statistics of the United States* (1975), series R191.

Until 1948, domestic airmail rates applied not only to letters but also to other mailable matter, including sealed parcels up to specified maxima (prescribed according to weight or according to length and girth). Effective September 1, 1948, Air Parcel Post Service was established. Matter carried by air weighing 8 ounces or less was classified as "airmail," and that weighing more than 8 ounces, "air parcel post." In 1968, air parcel post and first-class mail weighing more than 13 ounces were combined and classified "priority mail."

As of October 11, 1975, surface mail service was upgraded to the level of airmail. Domestic airmail service was discontinued as of May 1, 1977.

Series Dg214. Rates are for domestic express mail – for 1981–1988, up to 2 pounds, all zones, and beginning after April 3, 1988, more than 8 ounces and up to 2 pounds. Prior to November 1, 1981, rates varied by both weight and distance.

Series Dg215–218. As of March 2, 1974, the Postal Service began charging reduced rates for additional ounces beyond the first half ounce. Rates shown are for the first half ounce. Zone 1 included the Caribbean and Central and South America. For 1961–1967, the airmail letter rate to South America was the same as that to Europe. Beginning January 3, 1976, the airmail letter rate to all South American countries except Colombia and Venezuela was the same as that to Europe. Zone 2 included Europe and Mediterranean Africa. Zone 3 included the rest of the world, except for Canada and Mexico. In 1991, the international airmail zone system was eliminated; rates for an airmail letter were collapsed into a single schedule, except for airmail to Canada and Mexico, which continues to have lower rates (not shown).

TABLE Dg221–224   United Parcel Service employees, vehicles, volume, and customers: 1907–1996

Contributed by Louis P. Cain

	Employees	Vehicles	Volume	Customers		Employees	Vehicles	Volume	Customers
	Dg221	Dg222	Dg223	Dg224		Dg221	Dg222	Dg223	Dg224
Year	Number	Number	Million	Number	Year	Number	Number	Million	Number
1907	— [1]	0	—	—	1975	79,700 [2]	40,400	930	351,000
1913	30 [2]	—	—	—	1976	86,200	45,400	950	388,000
1924	200 [2]	—	—	—	1977	99,200	47,900	1,178	426,000
1927	435	350	—	—	1978	103,100	51,700	1,309	469,000
1932	650	—	—	—	1979	114,000	58,200	1,437	508,000
1934	1,600 [2]	—	—	—	1980	111,000	59,300	1,495	538,000
1947	7,000 [2]	4,050	—	—	1981	114,300	60,900	1,588	573,000
1949	—	4,055	—	—	1982	117,800	62,400	1,625	604,000
1950	7,500	—	—	—	1983	124,200	63,400	1,781	645,000
1951	7,500	—	—	—	1984	141,100	72,400	1,956	669,000
1952	7,700	4,696	—	—	1985	152,400	80,200	2,061	740,000
1954	—	5,000	—	—	1986	168,200	85,500	2,261	804,000
1955	—	5,612	—	—	1987	191,600	94,700	2,492	872,000
1957	—	6,400	—	23,000	1988	219,400	103,700	2,685	933,000
1958	10,000	6,636	—	28,000	1989	237,700	116,000	2,778	1,007,000
1959	11,083	7,207	183	—	1990	246,800	122,000	2,860	1,054,000
1960	13,000	8,511	—	46,000	1991	256,000	129,000	2,886	1,119,000
1961	13,040	9,123	207	52,000	1992	265,000	131,000	2,941	1,209,000
1962	15,000	9,875	—	60,000	1993	286,000	—	2,945	1,289,000
1963	17,300	11,035	250	73,000	1994	320,000	135,000	3,028	1,350,000
1964	21,000	13,000	296	86,000	1995	337,000	147,000	3,090	1,450,000
1965	24,000	15,000	342	100,000	1996	338,000	157,000	3,150	1,460,000
1966	29,000	17,000	374	113,000					
1967	30,400	18,000	409	125,000					
1968	33,731	20,000	421	139,000					
1969	41,168	22,400	514	—					
1970	45,371	24,500	553	—					
1971	53,195	27,600	608	200,000					
1972	58,642	30,100	712	250,000					
1973	67,398	33,900	798	280,000					
1974	67,900 [2]	37,600	837	308,000					

[1] Fewer than 10.

[2] Approximate.

Source

Data supplied by United Parcel Service. With the exception of the 1952 value for series Dg221, these data can be found in the *Annual Report*, beginning in 1947.

Documentation

United Parcel Service (UPS) was founded in Seattle, Washington, in 1907 as a messenger service. It acquired its first Model T Ford in 1913 and provided a local delivery service for stores. Six years later, it expanded to Oakland, California. Air service began on the West Coast in the late 1920s but ended as a result of the Great Depression. In 1930, three New York stores contracted with UPS for package delivery. By 1975, UPS was delivering to every address in the United States and had begun service in Ontario, Canada. Air service resumed in the early 1950s, but it was not until 1981 that UPS acquired its first airplane. By 1996, UPS owned 197 aircraft and had 302 chartered aircraft. Its success attracted several competitors, and so these data provide an underestimate of the growth of this important component of transportation services.

Series Dg221. Data are essentially estimates because there is considerable turnover, and employment varies by season.

Series Dg222. Includes ground vehicles only, not planes.

Series Dg223. Values are number of packages.

Series Dg224. Figures are places receiving regular pickup service.

BOOKS, NEWSPAPERS, AND PERIODICALS

Alexander J. Field

TABLE Dg225–252 Books published, by subject: 1880–1999[1,2]

Contributed by Alexander J. Field

	Total	New editions	New books and editions	New books										
			Total	Agriculture	Art	Biography	Business	Education	Fiction	General works	History	Home economics	Juvenile	Language
	Dg225	Dg226	Dg227	Dg228	Dg229	Dg230	Dg231	Dg232	Dg233	Dg234	Dg235	Dg236	Dg237	Dg238
Year	Number	Number	Number	Number	Number	Number	Number	Number	Number	Number	Number	Number	Number	Number
1880	2,076	—	—	—	—	—	—	—	—	—	—	—	—	—
1881	2,991	—	—	—	—	—	—	—	—	—	—	—	—	—
1882	3,472	—	—	—	—	—	—	—	—	—	—	—	—	—
1883	3,481	—	—	—	—	—	—	—	—	—	—	—	—	—
1884	4,088	—	—	—	—	—	—	—	—	—	—	—	—	—
1885	4,030	—	—	—	—	—	—	—	—	—	—	—	—	—
1886	4,676	—	—	—	—	—	—	—	—	—	—	—	—	—
1887	4,437	—	—	—	—	—	—	—	—	—	—	—	—	—
1888	4,631	—	—	—	—	—	—	—	—	—	—	—	—	—
1889	4,014	—	—	—	—	—	—	—	—	—	—	—	—	—
1890	4,559	446	4,113	—	—	—	—	—	—	—	—	—	—	—
1891	4,665	—	—	—	—	—	—	—	—	—	—	—	—	—
1892	4,862	788	4,074	—	—	—	—	—	—	—	—	—	—	—
1893	5,134	853	4,281	—	—	—	—	—	—	—	—	—	—	—
1894	4,484	647	3,837	—	—	—	—	—	—	—	—	—	—	—
1895	5,469	368	5,101	—	—	—	—	—	—	—	—	—	—	—
1896	5,703	514	5,189	—	—	—	—	—	—	—	—	—	—	—
1897	4,928	757	4,171	—	—	—	—	—	—	—	—	—	—	—
1898	4,886	554	4,332	—	—	—	—	—	—	—	—	—	—	—
1899	5,321	572	4,749	—	—	—	—	—	—	—	—	—	—	—
1900	6,356	1,866	4,490	—	—	—	—	—	—	—	—	—	—	—
1901	8,141	2,645	5,496	—	—	—	—	—	—	—	—	—	—	—
1902	7,833	2,348	5,485	—	—	—	—	—	—	—	—	—	—	—
1903	7,865	2,072	5,793	—	—	—	—	—	—	—	—	—	—	—
1904	8,291	1,320	6,971	—	—	—	—	—	—	—	—	—	—	—
1905	8,112	598	7,514	—	—	—	—	—	—	—	—	—	—	—
1906	7,139	415	6,724	—	—	—	—	—	—	—	—	—	—	—
1907	9,620	695	8,925	—	—	—	—	—	—	—	—	—	—	—
1908	9,254	509	8,745	—	—	—	—	—	—	—	—	—	—	—
1909	10,901	708	10,193	—	—	—	—	—	—	—	—	—	—	—
1910	13,470	1,799	11,671	—	—	—	—	—	—	—	—	—	—	—
1911 [5]	11,123	783	10,440	—	—	—	—	—	—	—	—	—	—	—
1912	10,903	768	10,135	—	—	—	—	—	—	—	—	—	—	—
1913	12,230	1,623	10,607	—	—	—	—	—	—	—	—	—	—	—
1914	12,010	1,835	10,175	—	—	—	—	—	—	—	—	—	—	—

New books and editions

Year	Total Dg225 Number	New editions Dg226 Number	New books and editions — Total Dg227 Number	Agriculture Dg228 Number	Art Dg229 Number	Biography Dg230 Number	Business Dg231 Number	Education Dg232 Number	Fiction Dg233 Number	General works Dg234 Number	History Dg235 Number	Home economics Dg236 Number	Juvenile Dg237 Number	Language Dg238 Number
1915	9,734	1,385	8,349	—	—	—	—	—	—	—	—	—	—	—
1916	10,445	1,285	9,160	—	—	—	—	—	—	—	—	—	—	—
1917	10,060	1,211	8,849	—	—	—	—	—	—	—	—	—	—	—
1918	9,237	1,152	8,085	—	—	—	—	—	—	—	—	—	—	—
1919	8,594	969	7,625	—	—	—	—	—	—	—	—	—	—	—
1920	8,422	1,086	5,101	—	—	—	—	—	—	—	—	—	—	—
1921	8,329	1,008	5,438	—	—	—	—	—	—	—	—	—	—	—
1922	8,638	865	5,998	—	—	—	—	—	—	—	—	—	—	—
1923	8,863	921	6,257	—	—	—	—	—	—	—	—	—	—	—
1924	9,012	1,158	6,380	—	—	—	—	—	—	—	—	—	—	—
1925	9,574	1,493	6,680	—	—	—	—	—	—	—	—	—	—	—
1926	9,925	1,527	6,832	—	—	—	—	—	—	—	—	—	—	—
1927	10,153	1,449	7,450	—	—	—	—	—	—	—	—	—	—	—
1928	10,354	1,562	7,614	—	—	—	—	—	—	—	—	—	—	—
1929	10,187	1,845	8,342	—	—	—	—	—	—	—	—	—	—	—
1930	10,027	1,893	8,134	—	—	—	—	—	—	—	—	—	—	—
1931	10,307	1,801	8,506	—	—	—	—	—	—	—	—	—	—	—
1932	9,035	1,479	7,556	—	—	—	—	—	—	—	—	—	—	—
1933	8,092	1,279	6,813	—	—	—	—	—	—	—	—	—	—	—
1934	8,198	1,410	6,788	—	—	—	—	—	—	—	—	—	—	—
1935	8,766	1,852	6,914	—	—	—	—	—	—	—	—	—	—	—
1936	10,436	1,852	8,584	—	—	—	—	—	—	—	—	—	—	—
1937	10,912	1,639	9,273	—	—	—	—	—	—	—	—	—	—	—
1938	11,067	1,603	9,464	—	—	—	—	—	—	—	—	—	—	—
1939	10,640	1,625	9,015	—	—	—	—	—	—	—	—	—	—	—
1940	11,328	1,813	9,515	—	—	—	—	—	—	—	—	—	—	—
1941	11,112	1,775	9,337	—	—	—	—	—	—	—	—	—	—	—
1942	9,525	1,739	7,786	—	—	—	—	—	—	—	—	—	—	—
1943	8,325	1,561	6,764	—	—	—	—	—	—	—	—	—	—	—
1944	6,970	1,163	5,807	—	—	—	—	—	—	—	—	—	—	—
1945	6,548	1,162	5,386	—	—	—	—	—	—	—	—	—	—	—
1946	7,735	1,565	6,170	—	—	—	—	—	—	—	—	—	—	—
1947	9,182	1,939	7,243	—	—	—	—	—	—	—	—	—	—	—
1948	9,897	2,090	7,807	—	—	—	—	—	—	—	—	—	—	—
1949	10,892	2,432	8,460	—	—	—	—	—	—	—	—	—	—	—
1950	11,022	2,388	8,634	111	317	538	190	209	1,211	262	456	150	907	—
1951	11,255	2,490	8,765	105	272	586	180	229	1,329	329	435	186	982	—
1952	11,840	2,441	9,399	114	267	650	180	238	1,354	336	454	237	1,094	—
1953	12,050	2,326	9,724	126	265	710	225	201	1,495	360	495	197	1,264	—
1954	11,901	2,211	9,690	111	285	687	196	223	1,512	339	529	192	1,193	—
1955	12,589	2,363	10,226	125	305	735	228	231	1,459	315	572	205	1,372	—
1956	12,538	2,531	10,007	106	283	676	222	229	1,500	305	521	159	1,384	—
1957	13,142	2,581	10,561	120	304	699	266	254	1,433	360	773	115	1,420	—
1958	13,462	2,450	11,012	122	409	608	283	276	1,592	213	750	142	1,424	—
1959	14,876	2,859	12,017	101	354	671	327	368	1,675	326	750	141	1,540	—

Notes appear at end of table

(continued)

TABLE Dg225–252 Books published, by subject: 1880–1999 Continued

			New books and editions						New books					
	Total	New editions	Total	Agriculture	Art	Biography	Business	Education	Fiction	General works	History	Home economics	Juvenile	Language
	Dg225	Dg226	Dg227	Dg228	Dg229	Dg230	Dg231	Dg232	Dg233	Dg234	Dg235	Dg236	Dg237	Dg238
Year	Number	Number	Number	Number	Number	Number	Number	Number	Number	Number	Number	Number	Number	Number
1960	15,012	2,943	12,069	121	422	746	240	308	1,642	233	695	155	1,628	—
1961	18,060	3,822	14,238	194	539	622	286	461	1,645	231	796	143	1,513	248
1962	21,904	5,456	16,448	215	590	667	308	559	1,787	279	812	156	2,328	226
1963	25,784	6,727	19,057	219	664	680	396	777	1,859	346	847	205	2,605	334
1964	28,451	7,909	20,542	209	776	697	411	934	1,703	361	834	188	2,533	414
1965	28,595	8,361	20,234	214	763	455	437	789	1,615	384	909	241	2,473	385
1966	30,050	8,231	21,819	212	779	819	478	886	1,699	410	959	219	2,375	459
1967	28,762	6,885	21,877	218	844	783	509	781	1,981	426	1,015	203	2,390	382
1968	30,387	7,066	23,321	191	930	786	644	917	1,822	521	1,048	245	2,318	387
1969	29,579	7,792	21,787	216	856	718	566	721	1,816	508	1,191	267	1,321	355
1970	36,071	11,783	24,288	200	852	735	658	842	1,998	568	1,010	235	2,472	339
1971	37,692	12,166	25,526	241	932	853	550	1,020	2,066	715	949	381	1,991	400
1972	38,053	11,185	26,868	286	1,097	1,086	529	1,041	2,109	802	906	479	2,126	354
1973	39,951	11,811	28,140	292	1,105	1,369	615	999	2,591	833	869	536	1,834	325
1974	40,846	10,271	30,575	299	1,220	1,380	732	963	2,382	872	801	666	2,336	315
1975	39,372	9,368	30,004	350	1,254	1,348	657	877	2,407	857	1,190	583	2,098	338
1976	41,698	9,346	32,352	464	1,368	1,545	779	918	2,336	1,042	1,634	660	2,272	403
1977	42,780	9,488	33,292	455	1,481	1,563	839	997	2,317	1,151	1,427	695	2,626	407
1978	41,216	9,414	31,802	408	1,229	1,454	925	871	2,455	1,047	1,361	717	2,617	303
1979	45,182	9,070	36,112	432	1,718	1,557	1,057	952	2,313	1,248	1,546	767	2,704	435
1980	42,377	8,347	34,030	382	1,437	1,399	935	876	1,918	1,428	1,569	767	2,585	433
1981	44,618	7,359	37,259	393	1,450	1,407	931	1,006	1,906	1,428	1,813	848	2,761	629
1982	42,950	6,712	36,238	338	1,453	1,447	979	887	2,042	2,055	1,696	886	2,677	447
1983	49,545	7,309	42,236	451	1,650	1,818	1,289	925	2,258	2,410	1,776	1,109	2,838	522
1984	47,255	6,691	40,564	405	1,619	1,791	1,301	885	2,400	2,671	1,827	1,088	2,747	522
1985	46,263	6,510	39,753	450	1,392	1,604	1,142	885	2,290	2,549	1,913	999	3,183	519
1986	48,917	6,992	41,925	477	1,504	1,805	1,197	866	2,687	2,144	2,015	900	3,849	528
1987	52,111	7,473	44,638	548	1,460	1,903	1,088	906	3,264	2,232	2,310	930	4,000	544
1988	52,462	7,569	44,893	561	1,384	1,898	1,195	940	3,329	2,086	2,478	838	4,410	503
1989	49,724	6,802	42,922	464	1,358	1,855	1,163	871	3,131	1,937	2,093	740	4,867	454
1990	42,775	5,726	37,049	428	1,113	1,674	880	867	2,725	1,456	1,840	595	4,496	487
1991	44,771	6,730	38,041	418	1,131	1,814	1,036	973	2,888	1,562	1,892	610	4,335	446
1992	45,450	6,538	38,912	465	1,227	1,671	1,025	1,015	2,922	1,776	1,924	637	4,379	481
1993	46,193	6,347	39,846	434	1,345	1,778	1,088	1,040	3,014	1,565	1,962	684	4,796	529
1994	49,205	6,751	42,454	429	1,417	1,936	1,254	1,130	3,276	1,855	2,133	817	4,860	567
1995	57,353	7,385	49,968	539	1,958	2,287	1,467	1,281	3,676	2,331	2,601	1,185	5,032	583
1996	63,689	8,388	55,301	575	1,858	2,636	1,380	1,324	4,704	2,552	3,068	1,231	4,881	703
1997	61,700	8,525	53,175	729	1,710	2,669	1,300	1,210	4,753	2,561	3,191	1,349	3,253	793
1997 [3]	119,262	—	—	1,303	4,565	2,993	4,015	3,278	9,312	1,561	9,704	2,481	8,631	3,199
1998	120,244	—	—	1,201	4,934	3,206	3,844	3,391	11,016	1,504	7,346	2,518	9,195	2,862
1999	119,357	—	—	1,037	4,795	4,051	3,789	3,408	12,372	1,456	7,486	2,564	9,438	2,565

New books and editions — New books

Year	Law Dg239 [6]	Literature Dg240 [6]	Medicine Dg241 [6]	Music Dg242 [6]	Philosophy and psychology Dg243 [6]	Poetry and drama Dg244 [6]	Religion Dg245 [6]	Science Dg246 [6]	Sociology and economics Dg247 [6]	Sports and recreation Dg248 [6]	Technology Dg249 [4,6]	Travel Dg250 [6]	Mass market paperbacks Dg251 [6]	Imports (hardbound and trade paperbacks), including new editions Dg252 [6]
	Number	Number	Number	Number	Number	Number	Number	Number	Number	Number	Number	Number	Number	Number
1950	228	510	312	88	380	453	626	499	447	153	366	221	—	—
1951	223	445	336	80	393	400	636	521	430	151	287	230	—	—
1952	236	518	350	71	427	424	715	513	478	168	311	264	—	—
1953	196	485	328	58	425	412	725	522	467	194	294	280	—	—
1954	226	493	345	69	386	389	774	522	463	201	325	230	—	—
1955	240	529	407	85	362	423	747	623	443	175	355	290	—	—
1956	221	570	334	88	425	337	810	531	448	160	404	294	—	—
1957	252	477	359	73	480	378	883	697	416	195	316	291	—	—
1958	245	495	393	89	467	373	941	781	494	201	443	271	—	—
1959	245	630	445	93	505	395	984	814	566	204	585	298	—	—
1960	303	560	388	82	496	404	983	833	651	233	574	372	—	—
1961	203	617	595	114	433	517	1,098	1,193	1,289	381	665	455	—	—
1962	219	771	688	137	436	505	1,174	1,309	1,603	367	780	532	—	—
1963	269	861	752	139	505	578	1,459	1,648	1,932	427	960	595	—	—
1964	256	1,038	876	156	528	681	1,441	1,923	2,445	452	939	747	—	—
1965	291	1,166	871	183	582	775	1,428	1,850	2,372	474	942	635	—	—
1966	316	1,185	1,007	207	629	728	1,477	2,079	2,632	441	1,091	732	—	—
1967	392	1,172	935	165	633	739	1,502	1,835	2,761	391	1,051	769	—	—
1968	432	1,301	1,022	210	669	791	1,511	2,011	3,107	501	1,072	885	—	—
1969	363	1,348	928	227	678	944	1,278	1,999	3,216	585	884	802	—	—
1970	355	1,349	1,144	217	843	973	1,315	1,955	3,867	583	930	848	—	—
1971	415	1,383	1,252	214	947	932	1,140	2,225	4,268	645	1,057	950	—	—
1972	418	1,398	1,404	215	829	883	1,233	2,143	4,688	686	1,184	972	—	—
1973	494	1,249	1,602	175	858	1,117	1,374	2,268	4,644	814	1,112	1,065	—	—
1974	743	1,304	1,799	172	1,003	1,155	1,458	2,574	5,068	839	1,298	1,196	—	—
1975	703	1,203	1,790	201	988	1,127	1,414	2,461	5,219	981	1,385	573	—	—
1976	668	1,130	2,027	213	1,052	1,254	1,638	2,378	5,627	1,009	1,518	412	—	—
1977	725	1,200	2,233	207	1,089	1,043	1,736	2,474	5,602	907	1,784	334	—	—
1978	786	1,254	2,177	231	1,048	972	1,750	2,155	5,259	948	1,511	324	—	—
1979	873	1,298	2,609	219	1,082	1,084	1,861	2,563	6,422	931	1,922	519	—	—
1980	816	1,317	2,667	236	1,097	962	1,635	2,551	5,876	808	1,923	413	—	—
1981	1,128	1,477	3,128	296	1,141	1,047	1,905	2,781	6,627	921	1,866	372	4,125	—
1982	1,065	1,454	2,691	265	1,151	925	1,762	2,604	6,319	832	1,911	352	3,985	4,278
1983	1,356	1,675	3,308	335	1,227	1,111	2,108	3,079	7,142	1,005	2,396	448	4,035	5,918
1984	1,059	1,715	2,989	307	1,216	1,085	2,172	2,704	6,600	966	2,083	412	3,803	6,337
1985	1,036	1,669	2,925	277	1,220	1,075	2,211	2,808	6,285	876	2,079	366	3,807	7,349
1986	1,018	1,788	2,845	270	1,323	1,180	2,464	2,782	6,815	843	2,213	412	3,720	7,749
1987	1,149	2,024	3,281	283	1,424	1,141	2,474	3,046	6,987	901	2,259	484	3,916	8,229
1988	965	1,954	3,187	273	1,582	1,127	2,401	3,091	7,158	837	2,209	487	3,021	8,626
1989	802	1,988	2,765	306	1,652	1,053	2,306	2,698	6,907	801	2,196	515	3,722	7,315

Notes appear at end of table

(continued)

TABLE Dg225–252 Books published, by subject: 1880–1999 *Continued*

Year	Law [6] Dg239	Literature [6] Dg240	Medicine [6] Dg241	Music [6] Dg242	Philosophy and psychology [6] Dg243	Poetry and drama [6] Dg244	Religion [6] Dg245	Science [6] Dg246	Sociology and economics [6] Dg247	Sports and recreation [6] Dg248	Technology [4],[6] Dg249	Travel [6] Dg250	Mass market paperbacks [6] Dg251	Imports (hardbound and trade paperbacks), including new editions [6] Dg252
	Number	Number	Number	Number	Number	Number	Number	Number	Number	Number	Number	Number	Number	Number
1990	649	1,802	2,438	223	1,350	826	2,005	2,276	6,146	721	1,687	365	3,698	6,414
1991	821	1,815	2,389	243	1,431	832	2,006	2,158	6,214	794	1,903	330	3,375	5,687
1992	729	1,918	2,499	289	1,444	841	2,167	2,182	6,427	850	1,692	352	3,826	6,506
1993	807	1,919	2,367	312	1,466	948	2,247	2,187	6,443	872	1,714	329	3,564	7,055
1994	784	2,031	2,359	277	1,485	1,004	2,396	2,500	6,976	892	1,668	408	2,658	8,172
1995	845	2,212	2,813	370	1,673	1,328	2,914	2,786	8,241	1,314	2,027	505	4,686	8,359
1996	952	2,689	3,280	381	1,903	1,443	3,298	3,105	9,247	1,470	2,116	505	4,486	9,271
1997	981	2,308	3,197	360	1,845	1,482	3,285	3,310	8,645	1,388	2,279	577	6,475	—
1997 [3]	2,452	3,467	7,117	1,643	5,622	2,770	5,748	9,304	14,611	3,664	9,496	2,326	—	—
1998	3,007	3,784	6,718	1,398	5,965	3,018	6,347	8,486	14,645	3,718	9,103	3,038	—	—
1999	3,078	3,646	6,153	1,593	5,861	2,455	6,044	7,862	14,579	3,252	8,896	2,977	—	—

Columns Dg240–Dg252 fall under the spanning heading "New books and editions"; subject columns Dg240–Dg249 fall under the nested heading "New books."

1 For 1880–1919, includes pamphlets; for 1920–1928, pamphlets included in total only; thereafter, pamphlets excluded.

2 The definition of a book was changed in 1959, and counting methods were changed in 1967. Data before and after each of these two changes, therefore, are not strictly comparable. See text.

3 Beginning in 1997, the R. R. Bowker Company introduced a new and more comprehensive system for tabulating books published in the United States. See text.

4 Prior to 1961, includes military.

5 Agrees with source; however, figures for components do not add to total shown.

6 Series has no data before 1950.

Sources

Series Dg225 and Dg227. For 1890: *Bookman Literary Yearbook* (Dodd, Mead, 1898).

All other data. Through 1970: reprinted from *Publishers Weekly* (R. R. Bowker, various issues). For 1971–1999: *The Bowker Annual Library and Book Trade Almanac* (R. R. Bowker).

Documentation

Figures represent the number of titles published, not the number of books that were printed.

These data exclude government publications, books sold only by subscription, dissertations, periodicals and quarterlies, and pamphlets under forty-nine pages. Unless otherwise noted, data exclude new editions.

Beginning in 1959, the United Nations Educational, Scientific, and Cultural Organization definition of a "book" (a volume of more than forty-nine pages) was adopted. Previously, all hardbound books and all paperbacks that were specialized (workbooks, laboratory manuals, and so on) and were more than sixty-five pages, or had mass market distribution, were counted. Beginning in 1967, books were counted by title rather than by volume.

Prior to 1997, the method of tabulation restricted books to those cataloged by the Library of Congress, particularly those passing through the Cataloging in Publication program. As a consequence, inexpensive editions, annuals, and much of the output of small presses and self-publishers were missed. Beginning in 1997, Bowker began compiling these data using its Books in Print database. See *The Bowker Annual Library and Book Trade Almanac 2000*, pp. 508–9. Data for 1997 are reported using both the old tabulation system and the new; data for subsequent years reflect the new procedures.

Series Dg251. Prior to 1981, mass market paperback books were not accurately counted. Beginning in 1981, they were counted as a separate category, and they are not included in totals.

Series Dg252. Beginning in 1982, imports of hardbacks and trade paperbacks were tabulated separately, and they are not included in totals.

TABLE Dg253–266 Newspapers and periodicals – number and circulation, by type: 1850–1967[1,2]

Contributed by Alexander J. Field

	Newspapers		Daily		Sunday		Weekly		Other		Periodicals		Weekly	
	Number	Circulation	Number	Circulation	Number	Circulation	Number	Circulation	Number	Circulation	Number	Circulation	Number	Circulation
Year	Dg253[3]	Dg254[3]	Dg255	Dg256	Dg257	Dg258	Dg259	Dg260	Dg261	Dg262	Dg263	Dg264	Dg265	Dg266
	Number	Thousand	Number	Thousand	Number	Thousand	Number	Thousand	Number	Thousand	Number	Thousand	Number	Thousand
1850	—	—	254	758	—	—	—	—	—	—	—	—	—	—
1860	—	—	387	1,478	—	—	—	—	—	—	—	—	—	—
1870	—	—	574	2,602	—	—	—	—	—	—	—	—	—	—
1880	—	—	971	3,566	—	—	—	—	—	—	—	—	—	—
1890	—	—	1,610	8,387	—	—	—	—	—	—	—	—	—	—
1900	—	—	2,226	15,102	—	—	—	—	—	—	—	—	—	—
1904	16,459	50,464	2,452	19,633	494	12,022	13,513	18,809	—	—	—	—	1,493	17,418
1909	17,023	58,505	2,600	24,212	520	13,347	13,903	20,946	—	—	—	—	1,194	19,877
1914	16,944	67,108	2,580	28,777	571	16,480	13,793	21,851	—	—	—	—	1,379	28,486
1919	15,697	73,139	2,441	33,029	604	19,369	12,145	20,741	507	—	4,796	—	1,230	31,162
1921	9,419	75,411	2,334	33,742	538	20,853	6,059	20,816	488	—	3,747	—	995	23,090
1923	9,248	76,408	2,271	35,471	602	24,512	5,903	16,425	472	—	3,829	—	984	31,436
1925	9,569	80,705	2,116	37,407	597	25,630	6,435	15,990	421	1,678	4,496	179,281	1,133	34,826
1927	9,693	87,617	2,091	41,368	511	27,696	6,661	16,879	430	1,674	4,659	191,000	1,099	39,107
1929	10,176	91,778	2,086	42,015	578	29,012	7,075	18,884	437	1,867	5,157	202,022	1,158	34,495
1931	9,299	86,457	2,044	41,294	555	27,453	6,313	16,173	387	1,537	4,887	183,527	1,066	30,782
1933	6,884	76,298	1,903	37,630	489	25,454	4,218	12,048	274	1,166	3,459	174,759	878	39,365
1935	8,266	87,096	2,037	40,871	523	29,196	5,337	15,185	369	1,844	4,019	178,621	966	42,648
1937	8,826	95,296	2,065	43,345	528	32,713	5,839	17,287	394	1,951	4,202	224,275	954	56,115
1939	9,173	96,477	2,040	42,966	542	33,007	6,212	18,295	379	2,209	4,985	239,693	1,109	55,825
1947	10,282	119,568	1,854	53,287	416	42,736	7,705	21,408	307	2,137	4,610	384,628	892	69,393
1954	9,022	136,353	1,820	56,410	510	46,350	6,249	30,336	443	3,257	3,427	449,285	487	82,066
1958	8,645	136,803	1,778	58,713	552	48,262	6,315	26,177	—	3,651	4,455	408,364	478	105,147
1963	7,703	136,600	1,766	63,831	560	51,669	5,377	17,500 [4]	—	3,600 [5]	—	427,915	—	—
1967	—	—	—	66,527	—	52,129	—	—	—	—	—	—	—	—

[1] Criteria for including establishments changed over time; see text.

[2] Through 1900, newspaper data include a small number of periodicals.

[3] Does not include the number and circulation of other newspapers because data are not available prior to 1919 and 1925, respectively.

[4] Estimates based on the yearly subscription rate of reporting newspapers, as many small newspapers did not report circulation.

[5] Includes a small number of periodicals.

Sources

For 1850–1900: *Twelfth Census Reports, Manufactures*, volume 9, part 3. For 1904–1909: *Thirteenth Census Reports, Manufactures*, volume 10. For 1914–1927: Census of Manufactures for each census year. For 1929–1947: *Census of Manufactures, 1947: Product Supplement*, pp. 67 and 68. For 1954: *U.S. Census of Manufactures: 1954*, volume 2, part 1, p. 27A-16. For 1958: *U.S. Census of Manufactures: 1958*, volume 2, part 1, p. 27A-28. For 1963: *U.S. Census of Manufactures: 1963*, volume 2, part 1, p. 27A-35. For 1967: *U.S. Census of Manufactures: 1967*, volume 2, part 1, p. 27A-23.

Documentation

Data for 1921–1939 are for establishments reporting annual receipts of $5,000 or more. For prior years the corresponding limit was $500. Circulation figures are the totals of average circulation per issue. Data for 1947 and 1954 are for establishments having one or more regularly paid employees for whom a Social Security account was maintained at the Bureau of Old-Age and Survivors Insurance.

For data prior to 1850, which are not comparable to the subsequent data, see S. N. D. North, *Tenth Census Reports: History and Present Conditions of the Newspaper and Periodical Press of the United States* (U.S. Government Printing Office, 1884) p. 47; and W. S. Rossiter, *A Century of Population Growth in the United States* (U.S. Government Printing Office, 1909), p. 32.

TABLE Dg267–274   Newspapers – number and circulation, by type: 1920–1999[1]
Contributed by Alexander J. Field

			Daily				Sunday	
			Morning		Evening			
	Number	Circulation	Number	Circulation	Number	Circulation	Number	Circulation
	Dg267	Dg268	Dg269	Dg270	Dg271	Dg272	Dg273	Dg274
Year	Number	Thousand	Number	Thousand	Number	Thousand	Number	Thousand
1920	2,042	27,791	437	—	1,605	—	522	17,084
1921	2,028	28,424	427	—	1,601	—	545	19,041
1922	2,033	29,780	426	—	1,607	—	546	19,713
1923	2,036	31,454	426	—	1,610	—	547	21,463
1924	2,014	32,999	429	—	1,585	—	539	22,220
1925	2,008	33,739	427	—	1,581	—	548	23,355
1926	2,001	36,002	425	—	1,576	—	545	24,435
1927	1,949	37,967	411	—	1,538	—	526	25,469
1928	1,939	37,973	397	—	1,542	—	522	25,772
1929	1,944	39,426	381	—	1,563	—	528	26,880
1930	1,942	39,589	388	—	1,554	—	521	26,413
1931	1,923	38,761	384	—	1,539	—	513	25,702
1932	1,913	36,408	380	—	1,533	—	518	24,860
1933	1,911	35,175	378	—	1,533	—	506	24,041
1934	1,929	36,709	385	—	1,544	—	505	26,545
1935	1,950	38,156	390	—	1,560	—	518	28,147
1936	1,989	40,292	405	—	1,584	—	520	29,962
1937	1,983	41,419	406	—	1,577	—	539	30,957
1938	1,936	39,572	398	—	1,538	—	523	30,481
1939	1,888	39,671	383	—	1,505	—	524	31,519
1940	1,878	41,132	380	16,114	1,498	25,018	525	32,371
1941	1,857	42,080	377	16,519	1,480	25,561	510	33,436
1942	1,787	43,375	345	17,111	1,442	26,264	474	35,294
1943	1,754	44,393	333	17,078	1,421	27,315	467	37,292
1944	1,744	45,955	338	18,059	1,406	27,896	481	37,946
1945	1,749	48,384	330	19,240	1,419	29,144	485	39,680
1946	1,763	50,928	334	20,546	1,429	30,382	497	43,665
1947	1,769	51,673	328	20,762	1,441	30,911	511	45,151
1948	1,781	52,285	328	21,082	1,453	31,203	530	46,308
1949	1,780	52,846	329	21,005	1,451	31,841	546	46,399
1950	1,772	53,829	322	21,266	1,450	32,563	549	46,582
1951	1,773	54,018	319	21,223	1,454	32,795	543	46,279
1952	1,786	53,951	327	21,160	1,459	32,791	545	46,210
1953	1,785	54,472	327	21,412	1,458	33,060	544	45,949
1954	1,765	55,072	317	21,705	1,448	33,367	544	46,176
1955	1,760	56,147	316	22,183	1,454	33,964	541	46,448
1956	1,761	57,102	314	22,492	1,454	34,610	546	47,162
1957	1,755	57,805	309	23,171	1,453	34,635	544	47,044
1958	1,751	57,418	307	23,161	1,456	34,258	556	46,955
1959	1,755	58,300	306	23,547	1,455	34,753	564	47,848
1960	1,763	58,882	312	24,029	1,459	34,853	563	47,699
1961	1,761	59,261	312	24,094	1,458	35,167	558	48,216
1962	1,760	59,849	318	24,563	1,451	35,286	558	48,888
1963	1,754	58,905	311	23,459	1,453	35,446	550	46,830
1964	1,763	60,412	323	24,365	1,452	36,048	561	48,383
1965	1,751	60,358	320	24,107	1,444	36,251	562	48,600
1966	1,754	61,397	324	24,806	1,444	36,592	578	49,282
1967	1,749	61,561	327	25,282	1,438	36,279	573	49,224
1968	1,752	62,535	328	25,838	1,443	36,697	578	49,693
1969	1,758	62,060	333	25,812	1,443	36,248	585	49,675
1970	1,748	62,108	334	25,934	1,429	36,174	586	49,217
1971	1,749	62,231	339	26,116	1,425	36,115	590	49,665
1972	1,761	62,510	337	26,078	1,441	36,432	603	49,339
1973	1,774	63,147	343	26,524	1,451	36,623	634	51,717
1974	1,768	61,877	340	26,145	1,449	35,732	641	51,679
1975	1,756	60,655	339	25,490	1,436	35,165	639	51,096
1976	1,762	60,977	346	25,858	1,435	35,119	650	51,565
1977	1,753	61,500	352	26,700	1,435	34,800	668	52,400
1978	1,756	62,000	355	27,700	1,419	34,300	696	54,000
1979	1,763	62,200	382	28,600	1,405	33,600	720	54,400

TABLE Dg267–274 Newspapers – number and circulation, by type: 1920–1999 *Continued*

			Daily						Sunday	
	Number	Circulation	Morning		Evening			Number	Circulation
			Number	Circulation	Number	Circulation			
	Dg267	Dg268	Dg269	Dg270	Dg271	Dg272		Dg273	Dg274
Year	Number	Thousand	Number	Thousand	Number	Thousand		Number	Thousand
1980	1,745	62,200	387	29,400	1,388	32,800		736	54,700
1981	1,730	61,400	408	30,600	1,352	30,900		755	55,200
1982	1,711	62,500	434	33,200	1,310	29,300		768	56,300
1983	1,701	62,600	446	33,800	1,284	28,800		772	56,700
1984	1,688	63,100	458	35,400	1,257	27,700		783	57,500
1985	1,676	62,800	482	36,400	1,220	26,400		798	58,800
1986	1,657	62,500	499	37,400	1,188	25,100		802	58,900
1987	1,645	62,800	511	39,100	1,166	23,700		820	60,100
1988	1,642	62,700	529	40,400	1,141	22,200		840	61,500
1989	1,626	62,600	530	40,700	1,125	21,800		847	62,000
1990	1,611	62,300	559	41,300	1,084	21,000		863	62,600
1991	1,586	60,700	571	41,500	1,042	19,200		875	62,100
1992	1,570	60,100	596	42,400	996	17,800		891	62,200
1993	1,556	59,812	623	43,100	954	16,700		884	62,566
1994	1,548	59,300	635	43,400	935	15,900		886	62,300
1995	1,533	58,200	656	44,300	891	13,900		888	61,500
1996	1,520	57,000	686	44,800	846	12,200		890	60,800
1997	1,509	56,700	705	45,400	816	11,300		903	60,500
1998	1,489	56,100	721	45,600	781	10,500		898	60,100
1999	1,483	56,000	736	46,000	760	10,000		905	59,900

[1] Starting in 1954, the daily number is adjusted to account for "all-day" papers listed in both morning and evening figures: they are counted only once in the total, but their circulation is divided between the morning and evening totals.

Source

Editor and Publisher Company, *Editor and Publisher International Year Book* (various issues).

Documentation

The term "daily" refers to papers that are published either morning or evening.

About 90 percent of the circulation figures are credited by the Audit Bureau of Circulations. The remaining 10 percent are based on publishers' statements to the U.S. Post Office Department. The compilation is checked annually with a questionnaire to every daily newspaper in the country. The source also presents data for individual states.

Values given are as of October 1 of each year.

TABLE Dg275–286 Newspapers and periodicals – number, by type: 1935–1999

Contributed by Alexander J. Field

	Newspapers					Periodicals						
	Total	Semiweekly	Weekly	Daily	Other	Total	Weekly	Semiweekly	Monthly	Bimonthly	Quarterly	Other
	Dg275	Dg276	Dg277	Dg278	Dg279	Dg280	Dg281	Dg282 [1]	Dg283	Dg284	Dg285	Dg286
Year	Number	Number	Number	Number	Number	Number	Number	Number	Number	Number	Number	Number
1935	14,091	369	11,438	2,197	87	6,546	1,484	203	3,608	196	493	562
1936	13,928	368	11,288	2,189	83	6,670	1,546	216	3,622	197	497	592
1937	14,336	401	11,592	2,272	71	6,320	1,251	253	3,512	203	530	571
1938	14,112	383	11,421	2,242	66	6,412	1,220	202	3,663	219	530	578
1939	14,213	380	11,516	2,216	101	6,846	1,408	213	3,821	250	563	591
1940	13,314	368	10,860	2,086 [3]	— [3]	6,432	1,399	427 [1]	3,466	241	538	361
1941	14,284	397	11,617	2,153	117	7,141	1,449	222	3,966	277	595	632
1942	14,100	408	11,474	2,131	87	7,374	1,609	248	3,983	288	601	645
1943	13,456	356	10,967	2,043	90	7,040	1,489	215	3,826	274	586	650
1944	12,889	308	10,504	2,006	71	6,672	1,456	226	3,500	285	588	617
1945	12,791	283	10,430	2,004	74	6,569	1,359	246	3,503	309	578	574
1946	12,804	286	10,424	2,020	74	6,693	1,331	253	3,595	345	595	574
1947	12,877	284	10,523	2,003	67	7,083	1,394	272	3,805	401	609	602
1948	12,900	301	10,511	2,001	87	7,346	1,498	262	3,970	412	576	628
1949	12,814	326	10,386	2,014	88	7,570	1,537	244	4,073	458	635	623
1950	12,115	337	9,794	1,894	90	6,960	1,443	416 [1]	3,694	436	604	367
1951	13,009	362	10,514	2,018	115	7,635	1,491	239	4,132	517	633	623
1952	12,833	341	10,381	1,998	113	7,711	1,485	246	4,118	558	665	639
1953	12,645	346	10,173	2,009	117	7,792	1,494	242	4,115	598	673	670
1954	12,398	328	9,960	1,999	111	8,092	1,584	260	4,218	604	695	731

Notes appear at end of table   (continued)

TABLE Dg275–286   Newspapers and periodicals – number, by type: 1935–1999 *Continued*

Year	Newspapers					Periodicals						
	Total	Semiweekly	Weekly	Daily	Other	Total	Weekly	Semiweekly	Monthly	Bimonthly	Quarterly	Other
	Dg275	Dg276	Dg277	Dg278	Dg279	Dg280	Dg281	Dg282 [1]	Dg283	Dg284	Dg285	Dg286
	Number	Number	Number	Number	Number	Number	Number	Number	Number	Number	Number	Number
1955	11,415	324	9,126	1,860	105	7,648	1,602	503 [1]	3,782	608	674	479
1956	12,256	338	9,813	1,963	142	8,718	1,748	283	4,450	614	831	792
1957	12,299	354	9,854	1,946	145	8,722	1,681	288	4,457	639	842	815
1958	12,207	332	9,768	1,969	138	8,927	1,705	292	4,490	676	914	850
1959	12,294	359	9,812	1,977	146	9,004	1,592	302	4,577	712	950	871
1960	11,315	324	8,979	1,854	158	8,422	1,580	527 [1]	4,113	743	895	564
1961	12,285	361	9,783	1,968	173	9,275	1,656	301	4,634	801	998	885
1962	12,293	376	9,774	1,970	173	9,483	1,740	305	4,705	826	1,030	877
1963	12,295	391	9,739	1,974	191	9,643	1,792	313	4,744	858	1,025	911
1964	12,332	390	9,761	1,963	218	9,798	1,724	334	4,847	910	1,065	918
1965	11,383	357	8,989	1,843	194	8,990	1,716	550 [1]	4,195	876	1,030	623
1966	12,365	382	9,785	1,972	226	10,002	1,884	335	4,796	912	1,119	956
1967	11,307	366	8,915	2,026 [3]	— [3]	9,238	1,808	573 [1]	4,296	859	1,051	651
1968	11,293	387	8,858	1,833	215	9,400	1,796	606	4,331	899	1,078	690
1969	11,336	413	8,855	1,833	235	9,434	1,787	587	4,353	899	1,084	724
1970	11,383	423	8,903	1,838	219	9,573	1,856	589	4,314	957	1,108	749
1971	11,350	412	8,888	1,818	232	9,657	1,873	544	4,277	1,005	1,124	834
1972	11,299	398	8,682	1,809	410	9,062	1,606	493	4,093	852	1,106	912
1973	11,324	459	8,804	1,792	269	9,630	2,022	506	4,107	925	1,148	922
1974	11,296	523	8,711	1,806	256	9,755	2,027	529	4,123	942	1,164	970
1975	11,400	506	8,824	1,819	251	9,657	1,918	537	4,087	1,009	1,093	1,013
1976	11,298	511	8,735	1,813	239	9,872	1,915	557	4,144	1,058	1,161	1,037
1977	11,089 [2]	550	8,506	1,811	225	9,732	1,882	548	4,019	1,045	1,149	1,089
1978	10,538	569	7,980	1,783	206	9,582	1,827	541	3,846	1,031	1,172	1,165
1979	9,827	543	7,357	1,744	183	9,719	1,764	594	3,850	1,043	1,261	1,207
1980	9,620	537	7,159	1,744	180	10,236	1,716	645	3,985	1,114	1,444	1,332
1981	9,676	508	7,238	1,747	183	10,873	1,921	667	4,199	1,193	1,484	1,409
1982	9,183	498	6,806	1,712	167	10,688	1,672	689	4,078	1,237	1,554	1,458
1983	9,205	508	6,855	1,735	107	10,952	1,626	724	4,108	1,307	1,627	1,560
1984	9,151	525	6,798	1,711	117	10,809	1,376	658	4,096	1,348	1,711	1,620
1985	9,134	517	6,811	1,701	105	11,090	1,367	801	4,088	1,361	1,759	1,714
1986	9,144	495	6,857	1,671	121	11,328	1,383	789	4,066	1,387	1,985	1,718
1987	9,031	510	6,750	1,646	125	11,593	1,400	858	4,031	1,402	1,984	1,918
1988	10,088	555	7,438	1,745	350	11,229	880	619	4,192	1,558	2,245	1,735
1989	10,457	567	7,622	1,773	495	11,556	828	622	4,445	1,880	2,513	1,268
1990	11,471	579	8,420	1,788	684	11,092	553	435	4,239	2,087	2,758	1,020
1991	11,689	574	8,546	1,781	788	11,239	511	412	4,340	2,116	2,861	999
1992	11,339	562	8,293	1,755	729	11,143	466	371	4,326	2,143	3,024	813
1993	12,597	639	9,177	1,850	931	11,863	485	199	4,545	2,359	3,199	1,076
1994	12,513	661	9,067	1,831	954	12,136	487	209	4,494	2,475	3,370	1,101
1995	12,246	705	9,011	1,710	820	11,179	513	216	4,067	2,568	3,621	194
1996	10,466	612	7,655	1,537	662	9,843	442	307	3,554	2,216	3,280	44
1997	10,042	558	7,191	1,582	711	8,530	350	139	3,067	1,943	2,893	138
1998	10,504	557	7,267	1,461	1,219	12,448	382	262	3,378	2,184	3,386	2,856
1999	10,521	560	7,471	1,647	843	9,893	388	260	3,447	2,220	3,429	149

[1] Includes fortnightly beginning 1970, and in indicated years.

[2] Owing to processing errors, detail does not add exactly to total.

[3] "Other" included under daily.

Sources

For 1935–1970: N. W. Ayer and Son, *Ayer Directory of Newspapers, Magazines and Trade Publications* (annual issues). For 1971–1999: Gale Research Company, *Gale Directory of Publications and Broadcast Media* (various years).

Documentation

Data refer to year of compilation, generally the year preceding the year shown.

TABLE Dg287–292   Newspapers – newsprint consumption and pages per issue: 1940–1978

Contributed by Alexander J. Field

Year	Newsprint consumption				Newspaper pages per issue	
	Total	Newspaper			Daily	Sunday
		Total	Advertising	Not advertising		
	Dg287	Dg288	Dg289	Dg290	Dg291	Dg292
	Thousand short tons	Thousand short tons	Thousand short tons	Thousand short tons	Number	Number
1940	3,739	3,507	1,403	2,104	27	86
1941	3,922	3,694	1,481	2,213	27	88
1942	3,721	3,587	1,442	2,145	26	82
1943	3,559	3,409	1,568	1,841	26	78
1944	3,218	3,048	1,530	1,518	23	68
1945	3,451	3,237	1,667	1,570	22	70
1946	4,192	3,995	2,177	1,818	27	84
1947	4,658	4,420	2,550	1,870	29	94
1948	5,136	4,781	2,811	1,970	32	102
1949	5,532	5,142	2,977	2,165	34	107
1950	5,863	5,521	3,279	2,242	36	112
1951	5,872	5,557	3,295	2,262	36	113
1952	5,915	5,569	3,286	2,283	36	117
1953	6,109	5,713	3,394	2,319	37	121
1954	6,103	5,732	3,376	2,356	36	122
1955	6,484	6,173	3,827	2,346	40	132
1956	6,807	6,320	3,925	2,395	41	135
1957	6,768	6,300	3,843	2,457	40	138
1958	6,515	6,059	3,635	2,424	39	135
1959	7,073	6,578	4,026	2,552	42	141
1960	7,312	6,800	4,148	2,652	43	142
1961	7,358	6,843	4,126	2,717	43	139
1962	7,412	6,893	4,205	2,688	45	145
1963	7,577	7,047	4,313	2,734	46	148
1964	8,092	7,482	4,616	2,866	47	154
1965	8,442	7,851	4,750	3,101	50	167
1966	9,099	8,462	5,221	3,241	53	180
1967	9,159	8,518	5,213	3,305	53	178
1968	9,162	8,521	5,274	3,247	55	186
1969	9,820	9,133	5,662	3,471	56	191
1970	9,764	9,081	5,585	3,496	48	153
1971	10,318	9,569	6,017	3,579	51	162
1972	10,594	9,852	6,345	3,507	56	176
1973	10,686	9,938	6,509	3,429	59	182
1974	10,134	9,425	6,183	3,242	60	188
1975	—	—	—	—	57	180
1976	—	—	—	—	55	177
1977	—	—	—	—	64	177
1978	—	—	—	—	60	196

Sources

For 1940–1970: U.S. Domestic and International Business Administration, unpublished data. For 1971–1978: U.S. Bureau of Domestic Commerce, unpublished data.

Documentation

Series Dg287–290. Represents apparent consumption – production plus imports minus exports, adjusted for year-end changes in newspaper publishers' inventories and domestic mill stocks.

Series Dg288–292. Based on information of Media Records, Inc.

Series Dg291–292. Through 1968, based on average in 39 cities; thereafter, based on average in 110 cities.

CHAPTER Dh

Services and Utilities

Editor: Thomas Weiss

Associate Editor: Susan B. Carter

INTRODUCTION

Susan B. Carter and Richard Sutch

Services are functions such as repairing, restoring, and facilitating that maintain or improve the quality of a product but are not physical products themselves. Services also include activities such as education, health and personal care, entertainment, and protective services that are designed to enhance the standard of living and quality of life. In the context of the National Income and Product Accounts as reported here, "services" refers to the activities of private businesses and public agencies that are engaged in these maintenance and enhancement activities. Utilities are services or commodities provided by the government or by government-regulated entities. The major utilities are communications, electricity, natural gas, running water, sanitary services, and refuse collection.

The North American Industry Classification System (NAICS) classifies seventeen major economic sectors under the broad heading of Service Sector. It classifies Utilities under the broad heading of Secondary Sector. For a full listing of the NAICS system, see the Introduction to Part D.

Because of their size and complexity, statistics for a number of services and utilities are presented as separate chapters of *Historical Statistics of the United States*. The most notable of these are health care (Chapter Bd), social assistance (Chapter Bf), educational services (Chapter Bc), finance and insurance (Chapter Cj), public administration (Chapter Ea), communications (Chapter Dg), and electric and natural gas utilities (Chapter Db). See the Introduction to Part D for a concordance between the official list of the service and utilities sectors and the chapters of *Historical Statistics of the United States*.

This chapter presents a global discussion of the service sector by Thomas Weiss, followed by a similar discussion of the utilities sector by Susan Carter. The data displayed in the accompanying tables refer to the global definitions of these sectors (and thus span

and serve to summarize material scattered across many chapters) and provide details on the industries and activities not elsewhere presented.

SERVICES

Thomas Weiss

The service sector is composed of a heterogeneous assortment of industries. Narrowly defined – as, for example, in the national accounts – services include the following: hotels and other lodging places; personal services, which include a wide range of industries servicing individuals and the home, such as barbering, tax return preparation services, and funeral services; business services, such as advertising, direct mail, and secretarial services; automotive repair services and parking; miscellaneous repair services, including electrical repair, computer repair, and the like; motion pictures; amusement and recreation services; health services; legal services; educational services; social services; membership organizations; other miscellaneous services; and the value of services provided by those employed in private households.[1] In addition, there are other industries whose products are entirely or largely services: transportation and public utilities; wholesale trade; retail trade; finance, insurance, and real estate (FIRE); and government services. These individual industries are so important to the economy that they are identified and listed separately in the national accounts. Nonetheless, a comprehensive definition of the service sector would include these as well as the more narrowly defined service industries.

Over time, almost all of these industries have become an increasingly important component of the American economy, especially those services identified in the national income accounts. The rapid growth in the service component of the U.S. economy can be seen in Figure Dh-A. This growth has sparked alarm among social critics. Some call the shift out of manufacturing and into services "deindustrialization" and see it as a cause of slower growth of productivity and in the standard of living overall. One popular view is that the United States is becoming a nation of "hamburger flippers" who do not contribute much to the growth or vitality of the nation's economy.

Acknowledgments

Thomas Weiss thanks Alka Gandhi and Astrid Marschatz for their assistance in preparing the tables in this chapter, as well as all those people at the various arts and sports associations who provided some of the data presented here. Richard Sutch, Susan Carter, and Monty Hindman provided valuable comments on the essay. The work was supported in part by funding from the Department of Economics of the University of Kansas.

Susan B. Carter thanks Richard Sutch, Thomas Weiss, and Gavin Wright for their valuable comments on an early draft. This work was made possible in part by funding from the National Science Foundation.

[1] In the Census of Service Industries, the government provides further detail, identifying other categories such as museums, art galleries, and zoological and botanical gardens; and engineering and management services.

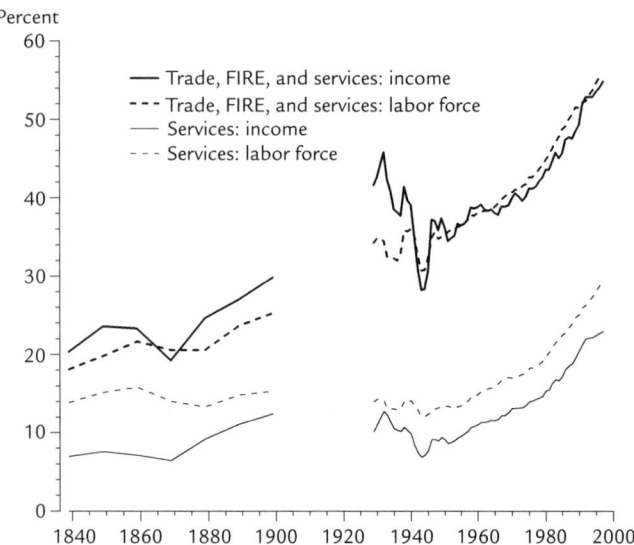

Percent

Legend:
— Trade, FIRE, and services: income
- - - Trade, FIRE, and services: labor force
— Services: income
- - - Services: labor force

FIGURE Dh-A   Percentage of the labor force and national income in services and related industries: 1839–1997

Sources

Series Ba1–2, Ba40–41, Ba471, Ba481, Ca4, Ca10, Dh1–3, Dh7–9, and Dh25–32.

Documentation

This figure presents a long-term view of services and related industries as a share of the larger economy – specifically, wholesale and retail trade; finance, insurance, and real estate (FIRE); and selected service industries. In order to construct this figure, various series of roughly comparable coverage and scope have been spliced together as described here.

   Value added in trade, FIRE, and service industries, 1839–1899: series Dh1–3 (or series Dh3 in the case of just services). National income originating in trade, FIRE, and service industries, 1929–1997: series Dh25–28 (or series Dh28 in the case of just services).

   Gross domestic product for the entire economy, 1839–1928: series Ca10, with straight-line interpolation based on the change for 1840–1841 to create a value for 1839. National income for the entire economy, 1929–1997, series Ca4.

   Gainful workers in trade, FIRE, and service industries, 1839–1899: series Dh7–9 (or series Dh9 in the case of just services). Persons engaged in trade, FIRE, and service industries, 1929–1996: series Dh29–32 (or series Dh32 in the case of just services).

   Labor force for the entire economy: 1839–1899, the sum of series Ba1–2 and Ba40–41, with straight-line interpolation; 1900–1937, series Ba471; 1938–1996, series Ba481.

   The data in this chapter tell a different story. The shift to services has been a more complex phenomenon, involving "high-tech" industries along with fast food chains, and it has been going on for a long time. Some of the shift toward services reflects increased investment in skills, health, and other proficiencies that may be expected to improve economy-wide productivity in the long run. Other components of the shift toward services involve the maturation of activities such as accounting services, out of individual firms and into stand-alone firms that supply services to many firms in different industries. To the extent that such specialization and division of labor enhance productivity and reduce business costs, the growth of the service sector means productivity growth – not decline – for the economy as a whole.

   The rise of the service sector with economic development is a seemingly universal pattern among industrializing nations, as service output and employment grow disproportionately fast as per capita income rises. With per capita income in the United States

having risen at more than 1.0 percent per year since the 1820s or so, the composition of the nation's output and the industrial distribution of its labor force have been steadily shifting toward services for well over 150 years. The same is true elsewhere. While other advanced countries display slightly different patterns in the pace and timing of the shift toward services, and while the patterns are not the same for the labor force as for output, there are few exceptions to the general rule.

The Service Sector Defined

Whether one is interested in the more recent history or the longer-term story, the timing, pace, and pattern of the shift toward services depend on the definition of services and on how one measures the sector and its component parts. Services can be defined in different ways, and their output measured accordingly. For some questions it may be appropriate to use a narrower definition that excludes specific industries (for example, finance) even though they provide a service, while in other instances a broader definition that includes all of the intermediate-type services, such as transportation and trade, would be more useful. Or, industries could be categorized according to the final use of their services or by the industry in which they were produced. In the former case, for example, tax returns prepared for households would be considered a professional service; in the latter instance, bookkeeping services supplied to a manufacturer would be classified in the accounting industry.

   In the national product statistics shown in Chapter Ca, the focus is on the end user of the goods and services. In that framework, service output is measured as the value of services, such as medical care or recreation, flowing to consumers. It also includes the value of shelter services, including an imputed value for those who occupy their own homes, and expenditures on household operations for items such as electricity and gas. The figures include the value of transportation services purchased by consumers but exclude transportation services and other intermediate services that were used to distribute durable and nondurable goods to the consumers.[2] This focus on final goods and services has its use, but it downplays the importance of intermediate services in our economy and the extent to which workers are employed in the production of those services.

   Another way to view the service sector, then, is to look at output and employment by industry of origin. In this scheme of things, transportation, wholesale and retail trade, finance, and business services are identified as separate industries. The output of each industry is measured as the value added by that industry and excluded from the value of any other industry, so that the sum of these value-added figures adds up to an unduplicated total of the nation's output.

   In this industry-of-origin scheme, the service sector could be defined broadly to include everything from the highly labor-intensive personal and repair services to the most capital-intensive transportation services and the most technologically sophisticated finance firms. When defined so broadly, the sector appears very heterogeneous, and it becomes difficult to draw generalizations about the sector's performance. For this reason, it can be useful to focus on a more homogeneous subset of the much larger service sector.

_____

[2] Even in this scheme of things, there can be disagreement about the definition of the service sector. More detailed discussion about the various ways of defining the sector can be found in Fuchs (1968) or Ofer (1967).

It is just such a category that is labeled as "services" when the national income accounts are presented on an industry-of-origin basis. Although this reduces the heterogeneity, it does not eliminate it. Within services one finds a diverse collection of industries and products, such as barbershops and shoe repair shops, as well as movie production, engineering services, and kidney dialysis centers.

Another view of services sees them as growing in importance only after a nation has passed through earlier stages of development. In its least advanced stage, an economy would be concentrated predominantly in primary industries – agriculture, fishing, forestry – those industries and products without which the populace could not survive. As the economy developed and incomes rose, some resources would shift toward a second group of industries, primarily manufacturing. In this scheme of things, services are seen as becoming important in the third stage of development, and so have been referred to as the tertiary sector.[3] This pattern, however, does not apply equally to all service items or activities, especially not to those services, such as trade and transportation, that make up part of the more broadly defined sector. Those intermediate services would be necessary even at low income levels to simply distribute the primary and secondary goods, and their behavior over time has differed from those final services, such as recreational services, that become more widely used only at higher incomes.

It is also important to bear in mind the distinction between the type of product, such as accounting services, and the industry, such as manufacturing or business services, in which it is produced. Intermediate services consist primarily of business-type services that are used by firms in many industries in order to produce and deliver their products to the ultimate user. Some intermediate services, such as transportation and retail trade, have been important throughout much of American history. There are, however, a number of other business services, such as finance, accounting, and more recently computer software services and consulting, that have grown in importance as economic growth took place. The exact extent to which such intermediate services may have grown in importance is difficult to trace because of the way in which data are collected and reported, and because of the extent to which some services are embodied in the final good. If we were to measure service output at any point in time based on the type of firm in which the output was produced, some business services would be excluded because they would have taken place within a firm in some different industry, such as manufacturing or construction.[4] Over time, however, some of these services became so specialized that they were shifted out of the manufacturing or construction firm into separate service firms and industries. As a result, we would observe a rise of services, measured on an industrial basis, even though there may be no additional services taking place in the economy.

These movements from the services being provided within a firm to their provision by outside service firms is a well-known phenomenon today – called outsourcing – but it has also taken place over the long term. Moreover, as is true today, the shifts can and did go in both directions.[5] The available statistics describing the growth of some of the business-type services, therefore, represent the net shifting of services within and without firms and do not sort those changes into new growth versus substitution. Obviously, when measured in this way, the statistics capture only a portion of the total volume of services being produced.

In the remainder of this discussion, the term "service sector" is used to represent a broader definition that includes some of the intermediate service industries; the term "service industries" pertains to the narrowly defined "services" embodied in the national income accounts. The data presented in the accompanying tables focus on the industry-of-origin classification rather than the final use. The chapter focuses primarily on the service industries but begins by first describing the service sector, broadly defined, to include the intermediate industries of wholesale and retail trade and finance. Additional data about the trade and finance components, as well as other industries, such as transportation and government, that could also be classified as services, are presented in separate chapters.

The Long-Term Shift toward Services

At the close of the twentieth century, services comprised a sizable chunk of the U.S. economy whether we look at the value of final services purchased by consumers (see Chapter Cd) or the governmentally defined "services" reported on an industrial basis (that is, the service industries) in Table Dh17–28. Final services amounted to $3.4 trillion or 38 percent of gross domestic product (GDP) in 1999.[6] The service industries comprised 20 percent of GDP when measured in current prices. The former percentage is larger than the latter primarily because it includes some transportation, housing, and other services, such as electricity, related to the operation of households. In the industry-of-origin approach, these services are classified as separate industries or placed in some other intermediate service industry; housing services, for example, are placed in the finance, insurance, and real estate industry. If in the industry-of-origin scheme we were to define services broadly to include wholesale and retail trade, transportation, and finance, then the sector dominates the economy, accounting for 64 percent of GDP in current prices. If government services were also included, then the service sector's share of GDP would be higher by another 12 percentage points. When measured by the number of workers engaged, the picture is similar but not exactly the same. The labor force share is the same as the output share for the entire service sector, but not for the subset of service industries. For that subset, the share of persons engaged at 30 percent is noticeably larger than the output share of 20 percent.

The rise to prominence occurred over a very long time. Since 1840, the earliest year for which we have reliable and comprehensive statistics that describe the composition of the economy, the service industries have been increasing in importance (Table Dh1–16). The increases in the service share of the economy were

[3] Fisher (1935) and Clark (1957) were among the first to identify the service industries as the tertiary or residual part of the economy. The historical pattern has been well documented empirically by Kuznets (1966, 1971) and Maddison (1995).

[4] The obvious examples of this sort of service are business services such as accounting, legal services, or consulting, but there are also complementarities between some consumer goods and services, such as maintenance contracts on durable consumer goods or instructional services for items of technology. See Stanback, Bearse, et al. (1981, Chapter 2) for a discussion of these complementarities.

[5] Our knowledge of these countermovements over time, however, is not well documented, and this would seem to be an area in which further research would enhance our statistical picture of the rise of services.

[6] If housing were excluded, the share would have been 29 percent. If we further excluded transportation, the figure would be 26 percent.

gradual at some times, and the pace and timing of the increases varied across the different service industries, but the upshot has been an inexorable increase in importance. And, the increases have occurred more prominently in the labor force than in output. The upward movement was such that Victor Fuchs could assert that the United States had become "the world's first service economy – that is, the first nation in which more than half the employed population is [involved in the production of services]" (Fuchs 1968, p. 1). He dated this as having occurred in the period following World War II, but if he had defined the sector to include transportation, the milestone would have been reached a decade or so earlier.

The relatively rapid rise in service output can be explained in part by changes in the country's level of economic development, or its statistical counterpart – increases in per capita output or income – just as appears to be true elsewhere. Over time, increases in per capita income are seen as one of the basic forces underlying the rise in the service sector. Of course, the level of economic development or per capita income is a proxy for a wide variety of factors – such as urbanization, changing educational levels, and technological progress – that are associated with it.[7] The upshot of all of those factors is that increased incomes in the United States led to increased demand for service industry output and tended to have a more noticeable effect on final services than on intermediate ones. The United States became the first service economy because its income rose to greater heights sooner than it did in all other nations, not because the United States had unusually strong preferences for services (Weiss 1984). Indeed, as Baumol and others argue, the United States has been shifting toward services more slowly than other nations (Baumol, Blackman, and Wolff 1992, Chapter 6).

The impact on the size of the service labor force was indirect; the increased demand for service products created a derived demand for workers in the service industries. All else equal, the service labor force would have risen as output rose in response to the increased demand. Not all things were equal; differential changes in productivity have contributed to the rising importance of the service labor force. Productivity changes are discussed in Chapter Cg, but suffice it to say here that slower productivity growth in services has been a major determinant of labor force growth in the twentieth century (Fuchs 1968, Chapter 2; Baumol, Blackman, and Wolff 1992, Chapter 6). In the nineteenth century, slower productivity growth also played a part, but it was not nearly as important a force as in the twentieth century (Weiss 1984).

The Nineteenth Century

The service sector was surprisingly large in the nineteenth century and increased in importance during the century. In 1840, the service sector produced approximately 23 percent of the nation's

output and engaged about 18 percent of the labor force.[8] By the end of the century, those shares were 31 percent and 25 percent, respectively. Clearly, the importance of services emerged at lower levels of income and development than would have been predicted by those who see an economy as progressing from a primary stage in which agriculture dominates, to a secondary stage where manufacturing becomes important, and then to a third and later stage in which services become prominent.

That services were relatively important and increased in importance so early in the U.S. growth process reflects the heterogeneous nature of both manufacturing and services. Some components of the service sector experienced rapid growth early on in the nation's growth process, while some manufacturing industries – such as flour milling and saw milling – grew slowly, with the consequence that the overall rate of growth of services was about the same as that of manufacturing. This growth should not be surprising because intermediate services are necessary to produce and market all the agricultural and manufactured goods and so can be expected to experience increases in demand that parallel those for all other products. The group of intermediate services was the larger throughout the nineteenth century, and especially so earlier in the century. Trade and finance accounted for roughly two thirds of the sector's output before the Civil War and still well over half at the end of the century (Table Dh1–16). Thus, service output was weighted heavily toward industries that served other sectors and that grew at approximately the same rate over the long term, although it varied from decade to decade.

The other portion of the sector – services such as education and personal services that flowed primarily to consumers – also experienced growth during the nineteenth century, especially in the post–Civil War period. This portion of the service sector increased more rapidly than manufacturing, and much more rapidly than the entire goods-producing sector, suggesting that rising per capita income must have favored this group of services even at the levels of income that prevailed in the nineteenth century.[9]

The composition of the labor force and the changes that took place in that composition over the nineteenth century were quite a bit different from those on the output side. Whereas intermediate services produced the bulk of the sector's output, their share of the workforce was much smaller. In 1840, trade and finance engaged slightly less than one fourth the service sector labor force. This reflects the fact that a large number of gainful workers in the United States, including a large number of slaves in the antebellum South, worked in personal services. In 1840 personal service (which included the repair trades) engaged nearly two thirds of all the workers in the service sector (see Table Dh1–16). Output per worker in these personal service industries was, and still is, relatively small *on average*, so the labor force share was noticeably higher than the output share. The importance of this industry's

---

[7] The relationship between the level of development and the service share may not be as strong as that for the other industrial sectors; nevertheless, it is positive, and its impact shows up more clearly in the workforce shares than in output. The cross-sectional evidence for the economically advanced nations suggests that there would or should have been a smaller rise in the service sector workforce than that which occurred historically in those countries that have experienced long-term economic growth (Kuznets 1971, pp. 276–80). On the other hand, if the historical evidence is expanded to include countries with lower incomes per capita – those countries that industrialized more recently and for a shorter length of time – predictions based on the cross-sectional evidence would overstate the rise in the service workforce (Kuznets 1971, pp. 281ff.). See also Baumol, Blackman, and Wolff (1992, Chapter 6).

[8] Figures are taken from Weiss (1969), Tables 2, 6, A-1, and A-12. The output shares are based on value added with shelter services being excluded from both the service sector total and the U.S. total. The output and number of workers in transportation and government have been excluded from the service sector total for this calculation. If they were included, the sector's shares of output would have been 32 percent in 1840 and 42 percent in 1900, and the labor force shares would have been 20 percent in 1840 and 33 percent in 1900.

[9] It is likely that price trends worked against the growth of services because the prices of final service output probably rose relative to the prices of other services and commodities.

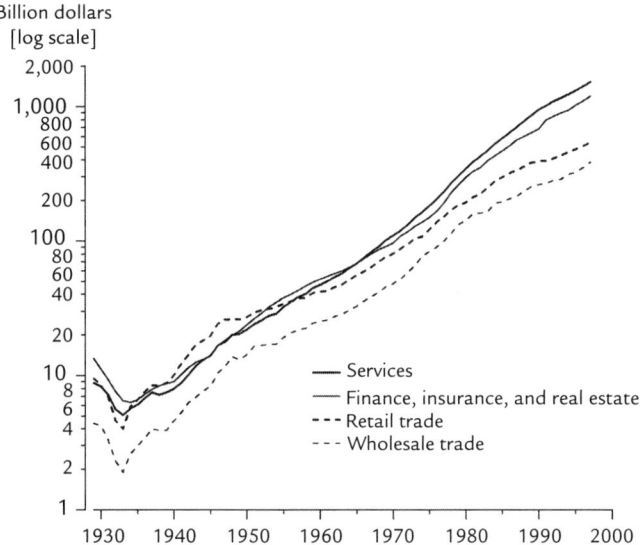

FIGURE Dh-B National income in service, finance, and trade industries: 1929–1997

Sources
Series Dh25–28.

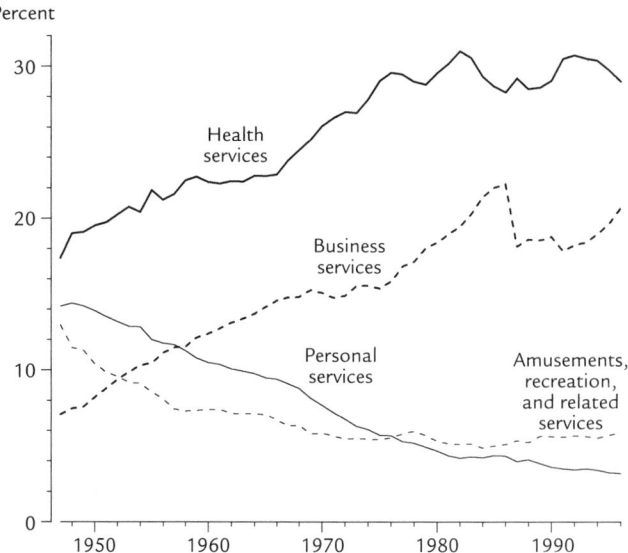

FIGURE Dh-C Gross product in selected service industries as a percentage of total service industry gross product: 1947–1996

Sources
Series Dh39–40 and Dh42–43, each expressed as a percentage of series Dh37.

Documentation
This figure provides a percentage breakdown for the services total displayed in Figure Dh-B. Although Figure Dh-B refers to national income and Figure Dh-C refers to gross product, the distributive shares are approximately the same.

The lesser categories from Table Dh37–47 are not shown (series Dh38, Dh41, and Dh44–47). Over the period shown, these categories accounted for 40–50 percent of the total in series Dh37.

workforce dwindled substantially over time, especially after the Civil War, and closed the century around 45 percent.[10] Meanwhile trade and finance had risen to 39 percent of the sector.

The Twentieth Century

The same upward trends in output and the labor force that characterized the nineteenth century continued through the twentieth, but the compositional changes were different in the two centuries (Tables Dh1–69). The twentieth century is the era of the "service industries" – that subset of the service sector made up of consumer services and business services other than trade and finance. It is also the era in which some people have become concerned about the continued rise of services – or, viewed differently, the deindustrialization of America.

The growth of the service sector can be seen in Figures Dh-B and Dh-C. All of the major components in Figure Dh-B increased from 1929 to the present, but the two trade components increased only modestly, while finance and all of the other service industries grew more rapidly. Since World War II the differential growth is even more striking. The service industries' output of around $18 billion in 1947 was not quite equal to that in retail trade ($26 billion), but by the close of the twentieth century, the service industries were producing nearly two and one half times as much as retail trade. The labor force shows similar movement: Between 1929 and 1997, the number of persons engaged in the service industries rose more rapidly than any of the other major components of the service sector, and fully twice as fast as that in retail trade.

The rise of the service industries in the twentieth century can be traced in large part to the explosion of business and health care services (Figure Dh-C). While gross product for the entire set of service industries increased between 1947 and 1997, business

service output rose three times as much, and health services increased by nearly twice as much. Over the longer term from 1929 to 1997, when the number of persons engaged in the entire service industry subsector rose by 460 percent, the number in business services increased by nearly eight times as much; its share of the service industry workforce rose from 3 percent to 21 percent.

At the opposite extreme were the personal services and all other services. The former dropped from 16 percent in 1929 to only 5 percent of the subsector in 1997, while the latter fell from being the dominant component at 56 percent in 1929 to only 28 percent in 1997. The category called "all other services" was comprised primarily of persons engaged in private households in 1929 (87 percent of that category), but by 1997 such workers comprised only 16 percent of this category, having declined from 2.3 million workers in 1929 to only 796 thousand in 1997.

Perhaps one of the more striking developments revealed by the statistics on persons engaged is the change in the relative importance of self-employment. It was thought by many that the rise of services would have provided greater opportunity for individuals to go into business for themselves. The chief reason for this expectation was that the capital requirements were lower in services than in manufacturing or agriculture. In addition, the personalized nature of some of the service outputs (such as beauty shops), and the absence of economies of scale in those and others were compatible with self-employment (Fuchs 1968, Chapter 8). Many people did behave as predicted and became self-employed in services; in 1997 there were 4.2 million self-employed persons engaged in the service industries, three times as many as the 1.4 million or so engaged in 1929. Likewise in finance, insurance, and real estate the number

---

[10] These calculations exclude transportation workers. Had they been included, the personal service share would have been 51 percent in 1840 and 28 percent in 1900.

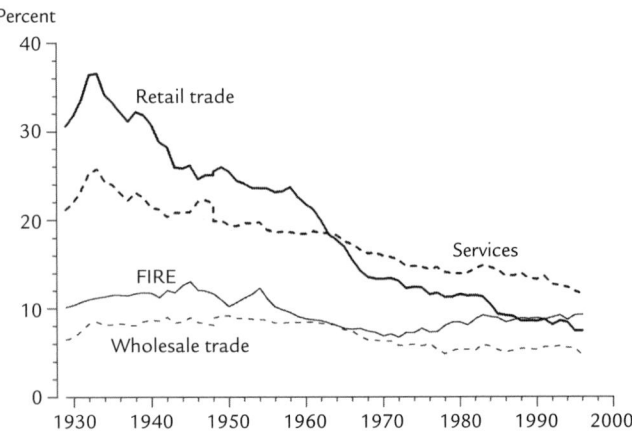

FIGURE Dh-D   The self-employed as a percentage of persons engaged in trade, finance, and service industries: 1929–1996

Source
Table Dh29–36.

Documentation
FIRE stands for finance, insurance, and real estate.

of self-employed persons increased, quadrupling between 1929 and 1997. But in retail trade there are now fewer self-employed persons than there were in 1929, and in wholesale trade the number is only slightly larger. More surprising, perhaps, is that self-employment is relatively less important today even in the service industries. As can be seen in Figure Dh-D, the self-employed share of the workforce has declined in each of the major components of the service sector.

The Implications of the Rise in Services

Does the rise in the importance of services mean de-industrialization and in general bode poorly for the U.S. economy? Since 1970 or so there has been concern that the shift to services could have undesirable consequences for the U.S. economy (see, for example, Urquhart 1984, pp. 15–22; Kutscher and Personick 1986, pp. 3–13; Inman 1985). The issues were first aired by Victor Fuchs in the late 1960s (Fuchs 1968, especially Chapter 8). At that time, the service industries employed about 13 percent of the labor force, while the broader service sector employed 55 percent. Today the fractions are even higher, approximately 30 percent and 62 percent, respectively. Fuchs found that the major explanation for the rise of the service workforce between 1929 and 1965 was the relatively slower growth of productivity in services versus goods-producing industries, and it was natural to be worried about a continuation of those trends. Baumol labeled this sort of phenomenon the "cost-disease of the service sector" (Baumol 1967; Baumol, Blackman, and Wolff 1992). The concern was further heightened by the productivity slowdown that appeared to be afflicting the U.S. economy beginning in the early 1970s. Those seeking an explanation for that phenomenon brought up a number of possibilities, the rise of services being one. With productivity growing slower in the service industries, the structural shift toward that sector meant retardation in the rate of growth of productivity for the nation as a whole, a slowing of the nation's economic growth, and increased difficulty in producing for export.

Some of that concern appears to have been exaggerated and misdirected. The argument reflects to a large extent the mistaken view that manufacturing and manufactured exports in particular are the keys to economic success, a view that can be traced back to mercantilist ideas about the economy.[11] The concern about the rise of services has also overlooked the fact, as shown previously, that the U.S. economy has been shifting to services for over a century. There is of course a difference between the structural shift in the nineteenth century and that which has taken place more recently. In the nineteenth century, the shift came at the expense of agriculture; both services and manufacturing increased in relative importance while agriculture dwindled. With agriculture having declined to a negligible share of the labor force today, any shift toward services must come in part from manufacturing. Even today, however, the shift is predominantly a relative one, with the industrial workforce increasing, although more slowly than that in services.[12] Perhaps the United States could have grown even faster before 1970 if there had been less of a shift to services, but the point is that the economy's performance before 1970 was considered a success. The country experienced what seemed to be an acceptable rate of economic growth accompanied by shifts in the composition of output that met consumers' changing desires.

The fears were exaggerated in part because the slowdown in productivity that prompted the concern had been misjudged. It appeared to be a very striking retardation when contrasted with the economy's performance after World War II. In retrospect, however, that immediate postwar performance was the anomaly, being noticeably above the longer term trend in the U.S. economy. Baumol, Blackman, and Wolff present a more balanced or cautious view (Baumol, Blackman, and Wolff 1992, Chapter 4). In particular, they stress the value of taking the long-term view: what appeared to have been a slowdown in productivity could be viewed more realistically as a return to normalcy. Thus, the shift to services, or the other possible sources of the slowdown, was not as worrisome as it had been made out to be.

The phenomenon of slow productivity advance in services, however, has not and likely will not go away. Certain service industries will continue to lag behind in productivity growth. The provision of child care services is an example. It seems generally agreed that there is a limit to the number of children who can be provided with adequate day care by an individual provider. Additional children can be accommodated only by hiring additional day care workers, virtually ruling out an increase in output per worker.[13] The service sector is broad and heterogeneous, however, and includes some services that have experienced rapid productivity growth, such as railroads in the nineteenth century and broadcasting in the twentieth, as well as those with substantial potential for continued productivity advance, such as electronic banking and Internet-related services. Nevertheless, the sector may be comprised of a disproportionately large number of industries in which productivity advance

---

[11] To the extent the concern is with the balance of payments, it is worth bearing in mind that the United States runs a surplus in the balance of trade in services, and it has been increasing (see Chapter Ee).

[12] During cyclical downturns, such as that of the mid-1970s or early 1980s, the level of employment in manufacturing dipped but subsequently recovered to about its previous level. For goods-producing industries as a whole, the level of employment has been more stable. See Kutscher and Personick (1986), Table 1. Ironically, during the 1970s when the productivity slowdown became an issue, manufacturing employment rose steadily (except for that cyclical downturn) and reached a peak in 1981 (U.S. Bureau of Economic Analysis, Internet site).

[13] For a discussion of the difficulties of increasing productivity in the arts, see Baumol and Bowen (1966).

seems limited, so continued shifts toward services will continue to hold aggregate productivity growth in check.[14]

Consumer Behavior

Whatever the consequences for productivity growth, the shift toward services is being driven in part by consumers expressing their preferences for services as incomes rise. The share of GDP made up of consumer expenditures on services has risen from 21 percent in 1947 to 38 percent today, and there is no reason to think the trend will not continue. In the past, some have expressed concern that these are frivolous expenditures – "a luxury that can not be afforded" – especially when made by lower income households (see Costa 1997, p. 22). When one realizes that a substantial chunk of the 38 percent includes expenditures on nonrecreational items, such as education and medical care, the concern abates somewhat. Still, there is the group of recreational services whose increase may be decried by some because they object to passive recreation such as spectator sports or movie going. Perhaps they are echoing ideas of Marx about the unproductiveness of services, or the physiocrats on the importance of agriculture, or those with a more puritanical viewpoint who hold that expenditures on such services are frivolous, immoral, or even wasteful. Agreement on what those frivolous services might be could be hard to come by, but one way of gauging them is to look at the expenditures on recreational services, such as purchases of movie tickets or pari-mutuel receipts (Table Dh309–318). The rise in those expenditures has certainly occurred, but surprisingly the expenditure on recreational goods, such as toys, audio equipment, and potted plants, has continued apace. As can be seen in Figure Dh-E, consumer expenditures on recreational services relative to expenditures on recreational goods have been increasing since 1970 or so, but it is still the minority portion of this set of expenditures. Perhaps more startling is that recreational services today are no more important relative to recreational goods than they were in the 1920s and 1930s.

Moreover, the distinction between recreational goods and services can be misleading, and the dollar figures may not accurately reflect all the services consumers are getting in today's economy. For example, the dollars spent on the purchase of a boat add to the goods total, but the purpose of such expenditure is to engage in a service activity over a long period of time. The national income accounts make just such a distinction with housing, incorporating a separate estimate of the value of shelter services derived from owner-occupied housing into the total value of consumer purchases of services. No similar calculation has been made for other durable goods whose purpose is to provide service. As can be seen in Table Dh339–353, the number of recreational boats owned has doubled since 1970. Although this has been a relatively slow growing part of recreational participation, its value as a service is neglected entirely.

The dollars spent on recreational services do not measure fully the value of all such services being consumed in the United States.

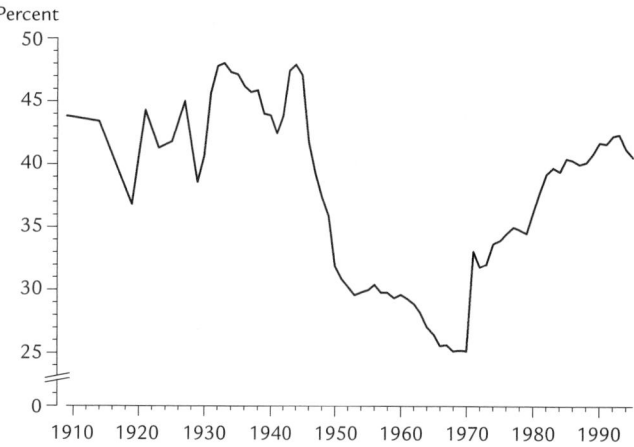

FIGURE Dh-E   Personal consumption expenditures for recreational services as a percentage of total recreational expenditures on goods and services: 1909–1995

Sources
Series Dh309 expressed as a percentage of the sum of series Dh298 and Dh309.

For one thing, there has been an increase in the provision of public spaces, such as museums, national and state parks, artificial lakes, municipal golf courses, and tennis courts, where recreational services can be enjoyed for free or for a low, subsidized user fee. There are also services provided by the private sector or by nongovernmental agencies that are subsidized. Ticket prices for, say, symphony concerts or dance performances come readily to mind as being subsidized by grants from the National Endowment for the Arts or by various state and local governments. But ticket prices for professional sports, as high as they may seem to some, are also subsidized by the many tax exemptions and financing schemes used to lure teams to a city. Whatever the merits of the subsidies for arts and sports, the consequences are the undervaluation of the services being consumed and, as intended, the increased consumption of these services. To the extent this has occurred, the subsidies would appear to have had far greater impact on sports than the arts (see Tables Dh327–391).

Although recreational services amount to only a small fraction of the nation's GDP, their history can serve to illuminate the status of services in the U.S. economy. Concern about the rise of services must be tempered by the facts; this ascendance is not a major problem for the American economy. To be sure, the service industries have increased in importance, but that rise has not been sudden or sharp; it has been going on for a long time, and it will almost certainly continue. There are legitimate concerns, especially about the slower growth of productivity in some of the service industries, but this may not be so different from what can be found within the goods-producing sector. More importantly, the inexorable growth of services has been primarily the result of individual decision making as the nation experienced its long history of economic development, characterized by not only sustained increases in incomes but by increased leisure as well. Services that may have been luxury items in the nineteenth century are today being enjoyed by much of society. The increased accessibility and consumption of services has improved the standards of living of all, including those in the lower income groups (Costa 1997, 1999).

---

[14] Fuchs (1968), Chapters 3–5, and Baumol, Blackman, and Wolff (1992), Chapter 6. Some of the slow productivity growth reflects the fact that it is difficult to measure output in some service industries, such as government, health care, and banking, and in consequence the growth of output and productivity may be understated in these industries and the service sector as a whole. See Fuchs (1968), Chapter 6; Reder (1969); and Gorman (1969).

References

Baumol, William J. 1967. "The Macroeconomics of Unbalanced Growth." *American Economic Review* 57: 415–26.

Baumol, William J., and William G. Bowen. 1966. *Performing Arts – The Economic Dilemma.* Twentieth Century Fund.

Baumol, William J., Sue Anne Batey Blackman, and Edward N. Wolff. 1992. *Productivity and American Leadership.* MIT Press.

Clark, Colin. 1957. *The Conditions of Economic Progress,* 3rd edition. Macmillan.

Costa, Dora. 1997. "Less of a Luxury: The Rise of Recreation since 1888." National Bureau of Economic Research, Working Paper number 6054.

Costa, Dora. 1999. "American Living Standards: Evidence from Recreational Expenditures." National Bureau of Economic Research, Working Paper number 7148.

Fisher, A. G. B. 1935. *The Clash of Progress and Security.* Macmillan.

Fuchs, Victor R. 1968. *The Service Economy.* Columbia University Press.

Fuchs, Victor R., editor. 1969. *Production and Productivity in the Service Industries.* National Bureau of Economic Research.

Gorman, John A. 1969. "Alternative Measures of the Real Output and Productivity of Commercial Banks." In Victor R. Fuchs, editor. *Production and Productivity in the Service Industries.* National Bureau of Economic Research.

Inman, Robert, editor. 1985. *Managing the Service Economy: Problems and Prospects.* Cambridge University Press.

Kutscher, Ronald, and Valerie Personick. 1986. "Deindustrialization and the Shift to Services." *Monthly Labor Review* 109 (June): 3–13.

Kuznets, Simon. 1966. "Trends in Industrial Structure." In Simon Kuznets, editor. *Modern Economic Growth.* Yale University Press.

Kuznets, Simon. 1971. *The Economic Growth of Nations.* Harvard University Press.

Maddison, Angus. 1995. *Monitoring the World Economy, 1820–1992.* Development Centre of the Organization for Economic Cooperation and Development.

Ofer, Gur. 1967. *The Service Industries in a Developing Economy.* Praeger.

Reder, Melvin W. 1969. "Some Problems in the Measurement of Productivity in the Medical Care Industry." In Victor Fuchs, editor. *Production and Productivity in the Service Industry.* National Bureau of Economic Research.

Stanback, Thomas M., Jr., Peter J. Bearse, et al. 1981. *Services: The New Economy.* Allanheld, Osmun.

Urquhart, Michael. 1984. "The Employment Shift to Services: Where Did It Come From?" *Monthly Labor Review* 107 (April): 15–22.

Weiss, Thomas. 1969. "The Service Industries in the Nineteenth Century." In Victor R. Fuchs, editor. *Production and Productivity in the Service Industries.* National Bureau of Economic Research.

Weiss, Thomas. 1984. "The Nineteenth Century Origins of the American Service Industry Workforce." *Essays in Economic and Business History* 3: 48–67.

UTILITIES

Susan B. Carter

Utilities take their name from the usefulness of the services they provide. These include tap water, sanitation, electricity, gas, telephone, and transportation. Today, utilities are virtually synonymous with public utilities. As the latter name suggests, utilities are often owned by government, and when they are in private hands, they are most often regulated by government.

In the United States, the appearance of utilities was spurred by the development of urban places. In rural areas, individuals typically supply their own water, sanitation, energy, and transportation. In cities, such individual procurement is ineffective and counterproductive. One person's water supply is another's latrine;

one person's yard is another's garbage dump. Foraging chickens, pigs, and goats mean animal waste and dead animal carcasses on streets and in vacant lots.

Individuals are poorly situated to address such problems on their own. One reason has to do with the "public good" aspect of such situations. Clean water at my local watering hole benefits not only me, but also my neighbors. The incentive for me to clean up is less than the value of such cleanup to the community as a whole. In an environment where individuals are responsible for their own cleanup, such services are underprovided and individuals are better off if water is supplied by an agency that responds to the needs of the community as a whole.

Another reason why utilities are difficult to procure individually has to do with the nature of the technology. Water provision, waste disposal, and electricity, gas, telephone, and transportation services involve extensive networks of pipes and wires, and of distribution, collection, and disposal routes. Utilities are extremely expensive if they are not networked in this fashion.

Networking reduces the average cost to consumers, but it also means economic power for the provider since more than one network would be redundant. In economic terms, this characteristic makes utilities "natural monopolies" because a single company can offer services at lower cost than two competitors. Market pressures push for the elimination of all but one provider. Once a single firm is the sole provider in a market, however, that firm has an incentive to charge customers high rates. Since the service is necessary and there is no competition, consumers have little choice except to pay.

Because of their tendency toward natural monopoly, utilities are often owned by governments; when held privately, they are heavily regulated. An important objective of government ownership and regulation is to set prices close to costs, including as a part of costs a "fair" or normal return on the capital invested. Governments also oblige utilities to provide services to all citizens, even those for whom service might come at high cost. An example of a high-cost utility provision is the rural electrification program begun in 1935 that built more than one third of a mile of electrical line for each customer serviced, considerably more line per customer than in densely packed urban areas (see series Dh277–278). By the 1950s, more than 95 percent of rural residents had access to electricity (series Db239). Privately owned utilities do not appear to have taken the mandate to provide services to all citizens as seriously as those that are owned by the government. For example, Troesken (2001) shows that public water companies provided black communities with better service than did private water companies.

The ownership and regulation of utilities are often matters of intense public debate. Conditions that seem to justify regulation during one phase of history may change because of new technologies and new industries offering substitutes. The development of government ownership and regulation of utilities is the subject of a large body of literature.[1]

An important characteristic of utilities is their "networked" character. Utilities themselves are networks, that is, complex, large-scale systems that cross and interconnect in ways that require coordination and management. In addition, utilities form part of

---

[1] See, for example, Demsetz (1968), North (1990), Troesken (1996, 1997), and Williamson (1985). For an analysis of the recent *deregulation* of utilities, see Hirsh (1999).

even larger networked systems that include housing, industry, technology, civic organization, and labor. The interconnectedness of utilities with other institutions, combined with their physical durability, gives *history* a role in the impact of utilities on any particular region's economic and social development. The contrasting suburban developments surrounding Boston versus Los Angeles are one example. Boston's high-density suburbs reflect the impact of the trolleys that dominated intraurban transit at the time of their growth in the late nineteenth century; Los Angeles's post–World War I growth with its suburban sprawl reflects the impact of the automobile.

Another example, developed by Norris Hundley Jr., concerns the consequences of water rights laws in affecting the differential growth of Los Angeles and San Francisco. It is surprising today that these two cities' size and structure are so different. In many ways, their growth and development followed similar routes. Initially, both cities relied on local water resources. As they grew, their semi-arid environments meant that they had to develop more distant water-supply sources. San Francisco ultimately found water by damming the Toulumne River in the Hetch Hetchy Valley, 170 miles to the east of the city, and Los Angeles did so by diverting the Owens River, 235 miles to the north and on the eastern side of the Sierras. At the same time, certain differences in the legal environments in which the two cities operated produced important differences in their size and organization. By the time San Francisco city officials appreciated the need for distant water resources, a private company, Spring Valley Water Works, had already gained control over the local water supply. Much of the drama of that city's growth during the late nineteenth and early twentieth centuries involved the process of establishing public control over this private company. By contrast, Los Angeles, which developed later, possessed control of its local water resources from the beginning. Growth of the city took place in a legal environment that permitted the sale of local water to city residents only. The superiority of the Los Angeles River flow in Southern California combined with the legal restriction on the sale to city residents prompted a large number of neighboring communities to apply for absorption into the rapidly sprawling metropolis. Today, when much of Los Angeles's water comes from distant sources not covered by the initial agreement, the city still governs a large geographic area.[2]

The essay in Chapter Db discusses the development of electricity and its impact on the layout of manufacturing plants, machine design, and the organization of work. Similar stories could be told about the impact of municipal water provision.[3] Information on utilities may be found in several chapters of *Historical Statistics of the United States*. Electricity and gas are discussed in Chapter Db; railroads, public transportation, and roads, in Chapter Df; and the telephone and telegraph, in Chapter Dg. The purpose of this essay is to bring together these disparate elements, to discuss data on utilities as a whole, and to comment on those utilities not treated elsewhere.

---

[2] For a comparative history of San Francisco and Los Angeles water procurement, see Hundley (1992), Chapter 4, pp. 121–202.

[3] For overviews, see Baker (1899), Armstrong (1976), Tarr (1996), Jacobson (2000), and Melosi (2000). For region- and city-specific histories, see Cain (1978) on Chicago; Hundley (1992) on California; Taylor (1926) on San Francisco; Ostrom (1953), Kahrl (1982, 1993), and Mulholland (2000) on Los Angeles; and Weidner (1974) on New York.

Waterworks

Waterworks emerged as the first utility, their growth and development following that of urban places. It is easy to understand why this was the case. The rural practice of procuring water directly from local wells and streams worked poorly in cities. In sparsely populated rural environments, natural groundwater collectors would carry over water from wet years into dry so as to permit a continuous flow. In densely populated urban regions, growing populations quickly drained groundwater reserves from wet years, creating crises during dry seasons. In an effort to combat the problem, cities developed public waterworks that dammed rivers, tapped distant resources, and recycled nominally undrinkable water for public water supplies. As early as 1652, the basic structure of Boston's public waterworks was already in place. By 1800, sixteen American cities, or half of all urban places, boasted waterworks plants (Table Dh240–241).

As the urban population expanded in the eighteenth and early nineteenth centuries, many of these city water systems became contaminated with human, animal, and industrial waste. Water contamination and accumulations of refuse bred disease. Periodic urban epidemics killed rich and poor and young and old alike. In the late eighteenth and nineteenth centuries, massive cholera and yellow fever epidemics hit major U.S. cities. In 1793, more than 5,000 died in a yellow fever epidemic in Philadelphia. In 1832, cholera took the lives of more than 3,000 people in New York and more than 4,000 in New Orleans. In 1853 and again in 1867, yellow fever killed more than 7,000 and 3,000 persons, respectively, in New Orleans (Rosenberg 1962). As medical theories of disease contagion gained acceptance over the nineteenth century, people came to appreciate the environment as a source of disease, and city governments began to take on responsibility for water purity. The resulting surge in city waterworks is shown in Table Dh236–239.

Early waterworks were most often financed and controlled by private investors. In 1800 among the sixteen waterworks nationwide, all but one was privately owned (Baker 1899, pp. 13–14). Over the course of the nineteenth century, the number of waterworks increased, and, at the same time, their ownership shifted from private to public hands (series Dh239). This transfer of waterworks from private to public ownership was evident in all communities, but it was especially pronounced in the larger cities. Larger cities developed mechanisms for raising money, especially the right to tax their citizens and to issue bonds. Private utility ownership resulted in high prices and management improprieties (Baker 1899, pp. 31–50). As a consequence, over the course of the nineteenth century, older cities with privately held waterworks purchased them on behalf of the public. New cities were increasingly likely to begin their operation with public services. Case studies of the transfer of waterworks from private to public ownership make for lively reading (see, for example, Hundley 1992).

Data on public expenditures on waterworks are available beginning in 1900 and are displayed in Figure Dh-F. They indicate substantial growth of real per capita governmental expenditures over the twentieth century. One reason for the growth is that an increasing share of the population was served by these public utilities. Another is that individuals and firms – both industrial and agricultural – used more water once it was conveniently supplied by tap. For data on per capita water usage over time, see Table Cf156–167. Third, the shift of population out of the moist East and to the arid West meant higher costs for water delivery.

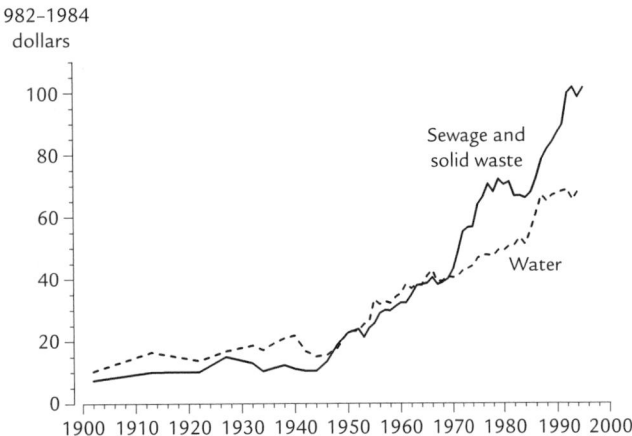

FIGURE Dh-F   Per capita government expenditures on water and sanitation: 1902–1995

Sources

Series Ea100 and Ea114, converted to per capita terms using series Aa7, and then to constant dollar terms using series Cc1.

Dams, Reservoirs, and Aqueducts

In 1790, American cities relied almost exclusively on local sources for their water supply. Rapid city growth during the first part of the nineteenth century forced cities to look beyond their boundaries to expand their total supply and to ensure additional supplies during dry years. Cities began building dams, creating reservoirs, building aqueducts, and laying pipes to collect and store distant water and to make it available to their denizens. Many of the early projects appear to have been initiated after a public emergency such as an epidemic or a fire. Statistical information on the timing and cost of these water-storage and delivery projects are available in the municipal records of individual cities. As far as I am aware, no one has aggregated this information on dams and aqueducts into an overview for the nation as a whole.

Prominent early projects include Boston's aqueduct from nearby Jamaica Pond, completed in 1796; Philadelphia's 1801 use of steam engines to shift the city's water supply from the contaminated Delaware River to the sanitary Schuylkill River; New York's forty-mile-long Croton Aqueduct, completed in 1842; and Boston's twenty-mile-long Cochituate Aqueduct, completed in 1848 (Blake 1956). Chicago gained worldwide attention in 1871 when it first attempted to reverse the flow of the Chicago River as a way of keeping contaminants out of Lake Michigan. The project finally succeeded in 1900 (Cain 1978).

Settlement of the arid West led to even more ambitious water projects. The small quantity and the strong seasonality of rain in the West required large storage reservoirs capable of capturing winter rains and spring floods for release in the late summer and early fall. More than 600 such projects were launched after the establishment in 1902 of the U.S. Bureau of Reclamation, whose mandate was to "reclaim" Western lands through irrigated agriculture and the provision of family homesteads. Operating in seventeen Western states, the Bureau of Reclamation quickly became a world leader in dam engineering and construction. Its two most famous projects are the Hoover Dam on the Colorado River, completed in 1936, and the Grand Coulee Dam on the Columbia River, completed in 1942. A hundred years after its founding, the Bureau of Reclamation is the nation's largest water wholesaler and its second-largest producer of hydroelectric energy.[4]

Some cities received their drinking water from the Bureau of Reclamation's water system, but others, most notably San Francisco and Los Angeles, built their own. The merits of these projects remain controversial to this day.[5]

The Tennessee Valley Authority (TVA) and the Bonneville Power Administration are two major water projects that were constructed and run independently of the Bureau of Reclamation. These extensive public projects were built primarily to generate hydroelectric power and for flood control rather than for water supply. Both were part of the New Deal legislation of the 1930s. The TVA was launched in 1933 over the entire Tennessee River basin. It came to encompass thirty-one separate dams (see Table Dh268–273). The Bonneville system on the Columbia River between Washington and Oregon was built between 1933 and 1943. Both systems are major sources of hydroelectric power generation.

Sewers

Today sewers and water mains are coordinated systems, but in the nineteenth century most cities – including those with highly developed water systems – relied on privy vaults and cesspools for sewage disposal. The differential in expenditures for the two systems is shown in Table Dh287–292. Sewers were late to develop because at least initially privy vaults and cesspools were acceptable methods of liquid waste disposal, and they were considerably less expensive to build and operate than sewers.

Sewers began to replace privy vaults and cesspools as running water became more common and its use grew. The convenience and low price of running water led to a great increase in per capita usage. The consequent increase in the volume of waste water overwhelmed and undermined the efficacy of cesspools and privy vaults. According to Martin Melosi, "the great volume of water used in homes, businesses, and industrial plants flooded cesspools and privy vaults, inundated yards and lots, and posed not just a nuisance but a major health hazard" (Melosi 2000, p. 91).

Joel Tarr also notes the impact of the increasing popularity of water closets over the later part of the nineteenth century (Tarr 1996, p. 183). Water closets further increased the consumption of water, thus contributing to the discharge of contaminated fluids.

Once the decision to build sewers and integrate them with the water mains was made, cities had to grapple with enormous technical, management, finance, and political issues before the systems were successful. Joanne Abel Goldman's detailed study of the building of New York City's sewers illustrates the nature of these problems (Goldman 1997). Tables Dc364–389 and Dc476–493 provide information on water and sewer line construction. Governmental expenditures on sewage are shown in Table Ea61–124.

4 U.S. Bureau of Reclamation Internet site; Pfaff (2000); and Robinson (1979); also see Table Dh268–273.
5 See, for example, Hundley (1992), Taylor (1926), Ostrom (1953), Kahrl (1982, 1993), and Mulholland (2000). For a listing of California's major dams and reservoirs, see the Division of Safety of Dams Statistical File, available from the Internet site of the California Department of Water Resources.

Solid Waste

Solid waste disposal is a relatively recent problem. In earlier times, people did not own many objects, and those they did own were pressed into service in a variety of ways. Thus a broken bottle, excavated from a colonial-era Virginia plantation, was found to have been transformed into a "bowl" and a "funnel" (Strasser 1999, p. 21). Objects discarded by one family were often collected by others. "Swill children" went from house to house in nineteenth-century cities collecting kitchen refuse to sell for fertilizer and hog feed. Well into the twentieth century itinerant rag-pickers and paper-collectors went from house to house offering money or housewares in exchange for discards. Susan Strasser provides a detailed account of the transformation of an early culture that valued the "stewardship of objects" into our modern world in which the plethora of discards has made trash disposal a serious social problem (Strasser 1999).

The first solid waste disposal problem to attract the attention of policymakers was a consequence of an increase in the use of urban horses over the nineteenth century. Manure was one problem.

> Sanitary experts in the early part of the twentieth century agreed that the normal city horse produced between fifteen and thirty pounds of manure a day, with the average being about twenty-two pounds. In a city like Milwaukee in 1907, for instance, with a human population of 350,000 and a horse population of 12,500, this meant 133 tons of manure a day, or an average of nearly three-quarters of a pound of manure per person per day. Or, as the health officials in Rochester calculated in 1900, the 15,000 horses in that city produced enough manure in a year to make a pile covering an acre of ground 175 feet high and breeding sixteen billion flies. (Tarr 1996, pp. 323–4)

The carcasses of dead horses were another.

> A description of Broadway appearing in the *Atlantic Monthly* in 1866 spoke of the street as being clogged with "dead horses and vehicular entanglements." In 1880 New York City removed 15,000 dead horses from its streets; and as late as 1912, Chicago carted away nearly 10,000 horse carcasses. (A contemporary book on the collection of municipal refuse advised that, since the average weight of dead horses was 1,300 pounds, "trucks of the removal of dead horses should be hung low, to avoid an excessive lift.") (Tarr 1996, p. 327)

Ironically, social critics of the time looked to the development of the "horseless carriage," or the automobile, as a solution to cities' sanitary problems.

By this time, scientists had already made the connection between cleanliness and health, publicly managed water and sewer systems were the norm, and Progressive social reform movements had identified cleanliness with civic pride and good government. Thus, recognition of the trash problem rather quickly led to the appearance of public solid waste disposal systems (see Melosi 2000, Chapters 13, 20).

The rise of per capita real income and the development of a "consumer society" over the twentieth century intensified the garbage problem. Rags, paper, and other such items that commanded a market in the nineteenth century were transformed into garbage during the twentieth. An increasing fraction of purchases, especially food products, were dispensed in packaging formats that were disposable. Strasser offers a detailed and highly readable account of the

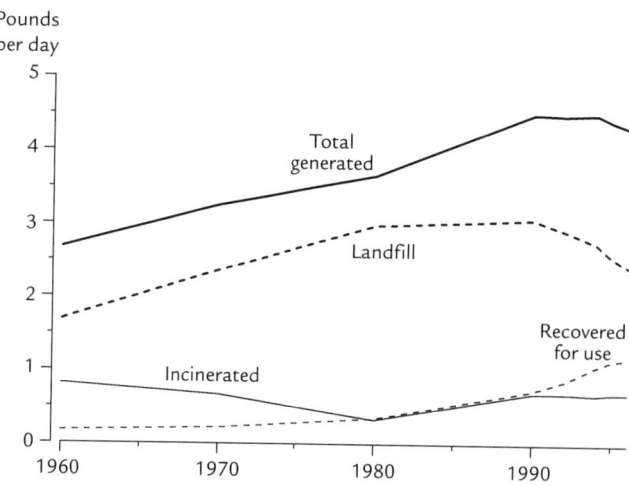

FIGURE Dh-G Solid waste generation and disposal per capita: 1960–1996

Sources

Series Dh293–294 and Dh296–297.

process as a whole and of individual products that were emblematic of the transformation (Strasser 1999). Statistics on per capita solid waste generation indicate that the average American was generating 2.68 pounds of solid waste per day in 1960, and that this statistic rose by two thirds over the next thirty years.

Alarmed by these developments, counterculture groups began to practice waste restriction and recycling in the 1960s. Over time these efforts gained supporters and led to an overall reduction in solid waste production per capita and to a rapidly rising share of solid waste that is composted and recycled. Beginning in 1960, the U.S. Environmental Protection Agency reported statistics on solid waste disposal by type. These statistics are provided in Tables Cf211–216 and Dh293–297 and are shown in Figure Dh-G.

References

Armstrong, Ellis L., editor. 1976. *History of Public Works in the United States, 1776–1976*. American Public Works Association.

Baker, M. N. 1899. "Water-Works." In Edward W. Bemis, editor. *Municipal Monopolies*. Thomas Y. Crowell.

Blake, Nelson Manfred. 1956. *Water for the Cities: A History of the Urban Water Supply Problem in the United States*. Syracuse University Press.

Cain, Louis P. 1978. *Sanitation Strategy for a Lakefront Metropolis: The Case of Chicago*. Northern Illinois University Press.

Demsetz, Harold. 1968. "Why Regulate Utilities?" *Journal of Law and Economics* 11: 55–65.

Goldman, Joanne Abel. 1997. *Building New York's Sewers: Developing Mechanisms of Urban Management*. Purdue University Press.

Hirsh, Richard F. 1999. *Power Loss: The Origins of Deregulation and Restructuring in the American Electric Utility System*. MIT Press.

Hundley, Norris. 1992. *The Great Thirst: Californians and Water, 1770s–1990s*. University of California Press.

Jacobson, Charles David. 2000. *Ties That Bind: Economic and Political Dilemmas of Urban Utility Networks, 1800–1990*. University of Pittsburgh Press.

Kahrl, William L. 1982. *Water and Power: The Conflict over Los Angeles' Water Supply in the Owens Valley*. University of California Press.

Kahrl, William L. 1993. "Acquisitions and Aqueducts: How California's Water System Evolved." *Pacific Discovery* 46 (1): 21–5.

Melosi, Martin V. 2000. *The Sanitary City: Urban Infrastructure in America from Colonial Times to the Present*. Johns Hopkins University Press.

Mulholland, Catherine. 2000. *William Mulholland and the Rise of Los Angeles.* University of California Press.

North, Douglass. 1990. *Institutions, Institutional Change, and Economic Performance.* Cambridge University Press.

Ostrom, Vincent. 1953. *Water and Politics: A Study of Water Policies and Administration in the Development of Los Angeles.* Haynes Foundation.

Pfaff, Christine. 2000. *The Bureau of Reclamation and the Civilian Conservation Corps, 1933–1942.* U.S. Bureau of Reclamation.

Robinson, Michael C. 1979. *Water for the West: The Bureau of Reclamation, 1902–1977.* Public Works Historical Society.

Rosenberg, Charles E. 1962. *The Cholera Years.* University of Chicago Press.

Strasser, Susan. 1999. *Waste and Want: A Social History of Trash.* Metropolitan Books.

Tarr, Joel A. 1996. *The Search for the Ultimate Sink: Urban Pollution in Historical Perspective.* University of Akron Press.

Taylor, Ray W. 1926. *Hetch Hetchy: The Story of San Francisco's Struggle to Provide a Water Supply for Her Future Needs.* R. J. Orozco.

Troesken, Werner. 1996. *Why Regulate Utilities? The New Institutional Economics and the Chicago Gas Industry, 1849–1924.* University of Michigan Press.

Troesken, Werner. 1997. "The Sources of Public Ownership: Historical Evidence from the Gas Industry." *Journal of Law, Economics, and Organization* 13 (1): 1–27.

Troesken, Werner. 2001. "Race, Disease, and the Provision of Water in American Cities, 1889–1921." *Journal of Economic History* 61 (3): 750–76.

Waterman, Earle Lytton. 1938. *Elements of Water Supply Engineering.* Wiley.

Weidner, Charles H. 1974. *Water for a City: A History of New York City's Problem from the Beginning to the Delaware River System.* Rutgers University Press.

Williamson, Oliver. 1985. *The Economic Institutions of Capitalism.* Free Press.

OUTPUT AND EMPLOYMENT

Thomas Weiss

TABLE Dh1–16 Value added, gainful workers, and income originating in trade, finance, and selected service industries: 1839–1929

Contributed by Thomas Weiss

	Value added						Gainful workers engaged						National income originating in		Persons engaged	
	Wholesale and retail trade	Finance, insurance, and real estate	Selected service industries	Personal services	Education	Other services not elsewhere classified	Wholesale and retail trade	Finance, insurance, and real estate	Selected service industries	Personal services	Education	Other services not elsewhere classified	Wholesale trade	Retail trade	Wholesale trade	Retail trade
	Dh1	Dh2	Dh3	Dh4	Dh5	Dh6	Dh7	Dh8	Dh9	Dh10	Dh11	Dh12	Dh13	Dh14	Dh15	Dh16
Year	Million dollars	Million dollars	Million dollars	Million dollars	Million dollars	Million dollars	Thousand	Thousand	Thousand	Thousand	Thousand	Thousand	Million dollars	Million dollars	Thousand	Thousand
1839	197	32	119	65 [1]	8	46	232	5	781	671 [1]	45	65	—	—	—	—
1849	346	29	178	90 [1]	15	73	360	7	1,206	1,010 [1]	83	113	—	—	—	—
1859	661	51	313	168 [1]	31	114	614	23	1,739	1,457 [1]	119	163	—	—	—	—
1869	970	129	552	259	86	208	781	43	1,774	1,423	170	181	210	500	169	716
1879	1,294	201	890	374	98	418	1,161	63	2,256	1,753	228	275	220	560	250	1,087
1889	1,944	372	1,610	715	172	723	1,855	163	3,404	2,587	347	470	360	1,020	397	1,775
1899	2,653	558	2,302	919	266	1,117	2,527	302	4,367	3,263	446	658	810	1,340	783	2,218
1909	—	—	—	—	—	—	—	—	—	—	—	—	1,300	2,320	1,034	3,177
1919	—	—	—	—	—	—	—	—	—	—	—	—	3,130	5,920	1,233	3,977
1929	—	—	—	—	—	—	—	—	—	—	—	—	4,120	8,960	1,744	6,077

[1] Revised slightly by Weiss to reflect new evidence about the number of slave domestics.

Sources

Robert Gallman and Thomas Weiss, "The Service Industries in the Nineteenth Century," in Victor R. Fuchs, editor, *Production and Productivity in the Service Industries*, Studies in Income and Wealth, volume 34 (National Bureau of Economic Research, 1969), Tables A-12 and A-17. Thomas Weiss, *The Service Sector in the United States, 1839 through 1899* (Arno Press, 1975), Chapters 3, 5. Harold Barger, "Income Originating in Trade, 1869–1929," in *Trends in the American Economy in the Nineteenth Century: A Report of the National Bureau of Economic Research, New York*, Studies in Income and Wealth, volume 24 (Princeton University Press, 1960), Tables 1, 4.

Documentation

Value added is the difference between an industry's output and the value of intermediate inputs consumed in the production of that output. It is comparable in scope and definition to the concept of gross product reported in the national income and product accounts today, and thus to the figures reported in Tables Dh17–28 and Dh37–47. The nineteenth-century estimates of value added were prepared as though they represented national product rather than domestic product, but because of the paucity of data sources and the ambiguities in the scope of the data available for the period, the distinction between national product and domestic product is not as clear-cut as in the measures prepared today.

National income represents the income earned by those involved in the production of the services. Whereas the value-added figures represent the market value of the services produced, the national income figures are valued at factor costs. The value-added figures are gross of capital consumption, while the national income figures are a net measure. For additional information about these concepts,

see the text for Table Ca1–8.

The national income figures shown here are those reported in *Historical Statistics of the United States* (1975), series T1, T2, T15, and T16, which included an allocation of corporate profits and interest that Barger had not presented in his original work (Table 4).

The gainful worker measure is based on the census counts of workers. Anyone who reported an occupation to the census taker was counted as a gainful worker even though he or she may have been unemployed and not looking for work at the time of the census. The gainful worker measure might also exclude new labor market entrants who are looking for work but have not yet found their first job. The concept thus differs from the modern definition of the labor force and differs from the count of persons engaged. The latter figures measure the labor input in terms of full-time equivalent employment, which measures person-years of full-time employment and its equivalent work performed by part-time workers. The figures include the self-employed, but not unpaid family workers who have been excluded owing to unresolved difficulties in their definition and measurement. The figures include males and females aged 10 and over, and for the years 1839 to 1859 include slave workers as well as free.

The value-added and national income figures for the nineteenth century were estimated; no official or unofficial statistics of this sort were collected then. The details of the estimations are explained in the sources cited. Those sources used the available nineteenth-century statistics to estimate the series according to the modern national income and product accounts definitions. It should be noted also that the nineteenth-century data, including the gainful worker data, were not reported on an industrial basis. The industrial distribution of output was based in part on the distribution of workers, which was constructed from the census counts of workers. Because those census figures were reported by occupation, the industrial distribution was derived by allocating workers with various occupations to the industries in which they most likely were engaged, as explained in the sources.

(continued)

TABLE Dh1–16   Value added, gainful workers, and income originating in trade, finance, and selected service industries: 1839–1929 *Continued*

When the series in this table were originally estimated, the classification of output and workers was based on a much earlier scheme of industrial classification; no attempt was made to reorganize the data according to the most recent scheme. Thus, retail trade includes automobile repair, services, and garages. Moreover, the paucity of data precluded some distinctions. As a consequence, the value-added figures for trade include some small amounts of output (that of auctioneers and undertakers) that would be placed in business services according to more recent classification schemes. The personal service industry encompasses much more than it does in today's accounts, including hotels and boardinghouses, miscellaneous repair services, and ser-

vants, who are classified in the private household sector in the twentieth century. The category of other services not elsewhere classified includes primarily professional services, defined broadly to include medical and legal services, and includes as well actors and musicians, who would be classified in amusements, or services not elsewhere classified, in the more recent scheme of classification.

Series Dh4 and Dh10. Includes personal services, hotels and boardinghouses, miscellaneous repair services, and domestic service.

Series Dh6 and Dh12. Includes professional, medical, and legal services, some amusement services, and services not elsewhere classified.

TABLE Dh17–28   Gross product and national income in trade, finance, and service industries: 1929–1997[1]

Contributed by Thomas Weiss

	Gross product				Real gross product				National income			
	Wholesale trade	Retail trade	Finance, insurance, and real estate	Services	Wholesale trade	Retail trade	Finance, insurance, and real estate	Services	Wholesale trade	Retail trade	Finance, insurance, and real estate	Services
	Dh17	Dh18	Dh19	Dh20	Dh21	Dh22	Dh23	Dh24	Dh25	Dh26 [2]	Dh27	Dh28
Year	Billion dollars	Billion dollars	Billion dollars	Billion dollars	Billion chained 1992 dollars	Billion chained 1992 dollars	Billion chained 1992 dollars	Billion chained 1992 dollars	Billion dollars	Billion dollars	Billion dollars	Billion dollars
1929	—	—	—	—	—	—	—	—	4.4	9.5	13.4	8.8
1930	—	—	—	—	—	—	—	—	4.2	8.5	11.2	8.3
1931	—	—	—	—	—	—	—	—	3.3	6.9	9.3	7.2
1932	—	—	—	—	—	—	—	—	2.3	4.6	7.6	5.6
1933	—	—	—	—	—	—	—	—	1.9	4.0	6.5	5.1
1934	—	—	—	—	—	—	—	—	2.6	5.9	6.3	5.7
1935	—	—	—	—	—	—	—	—	3.0	6.6	6.6	6.1
1936	—	—	—	—	—	—	—	—	3.4	7.6	7.3	6.8
1937	—	—	—	—	—	—	—	—	4.0	8.5	7.9	7.5
1938	—	—	—	—	—	—	—	—	3.9	8.4	8.4	7.2
1939	—	—	—	—	—	—	—	—	3.9	8.8	8.7	7.5
1940	—	—	—	—	—	—	—	—	4.6	10.1	9.0	8.0
1941	—	—	—	—	—	—	—	—	5.3	12.2	10.2	8.8
1942	—	—	—	—	—	—	—	—	6.3	14.3	11.5	10.2
1943	—	—	—	—	—	—	—	—	6.9	17.1	12.5	11.8
1944	—	—	—	—	—	—	—	—	7.7	18.2	13.2	13.1
1945	—	—	—	—	—	—	—	—	8.3	19.8	14.0	14.1
1946	—	—	—	—	—	—	—	—	10.5	24.2	16.6	16.6
1947	16.6	27.6	24.0	20.1	—	—	—	—	11.7	26.0	17.7	18.1
1948	18.3	30.1	27.0	21.9	—	—	—	—	13.8	26.3	19.9	20.0
1949	17.6	30.3	29.3	22.6	—	—	—	—	13.1	26.1	21.4	20.4
1950	19.8	31.7	32.2	24.2	—	—	—	—	14.3	27.1	23.9	22.0
1951	22.5	34.3	35.6	26.4	—	—	—	—	16.5	29.3	26.3	24.0
1952	22.7	36.3	39.3	28.2	—	—	—	—	16.8	30.7	29.0	25.7
1953	23.3	37.2	43.5	30.2	—	—	—	—	17.0	31.3	32.2	27.7
1954	23.5	38.1	47.3	31.6	—	—	—	—	17.1	32.3	35.0	28.8
1955	26.6	40.5	51.2	35.2	—	—	—	—	19.2	34.3	37.6	32.3
1956	29.0	42.4	54.8	38.7	—	—	—	—	20.8	35.5	39.9	35.3
1957	30.5	44.6	58.9	41.8	—	—	—	—	21.9	37.1	42.6	38.1
1958	31.1	45.3	63.7	44.1	—	—	—	—	22.4	37.7	45.9	40.2
1959	36.0	49.1	68.6	48.4	—	—	—	—	24.5	40.9	49.1	44.4
1960	37.6	50.4	73.2	51.6	—	—	—	—	25.2	41.6	52.0	47.0
1961	38.7	51.7	77.7	55.0	—	—	—	—	25.9	42.4	54.7	50.1
1962	41.3	55.4	82.2	59.3	—	—	—	—	27.5	45.2	57.3	54.0
1963	43.0	57.9	86.8	63.4	—	—	—	—	28.6	47.2	59.9	57.6
1964	46.3	63.5	92.7	69.1	—	—	—	—	30.7	51.7	63.5	62.9
1965	49.9	68.0	99.7	74.7	—	—	—	—	32.8	55.5	68.3	68.0
1966	54.3	72.7	107.8	82.7	—	—	—	—	35.8	59.3	74.1	75.6
1967	57.7	78.2	117.0	90.8	—	—	—	—	38.0	63.8	80.1	83.3
1968	63.3	86.6	126.6	99.4	—	—	—	—	41.5	70.2	86.1	91.1
1969	68.4	94.2	136.1	110.8	—	—	—	—	45.3	75.9	91.0	101.2

Notes appear at end of table

TABLE Dh17–28   Gross product and national income in trade, finance, and service industries: 1929–1997   *Continued*

	Gross product				Real gross product				National income			
	Wholesale trade	Retail trade	Finance, insurance, and real estate	Services	Wholesale trade	Retail trade	Finance, insurance, and real estate	Services	Wholesale trade	Retail trade	Finance, insurance, and real estate	Services
	Dh17	Dh18	Dh19	Dh20	Dh21	Dh22	Dh23	Dh24	Dh25	Dh26 [2]	Dh27	Dh28
Year	Billion dollars	Billion dollars	Billion dollars	Billion dollars	Billion chained 1992 dollars	Billion chained 1992 dollars	Billion chained 1992 dollars	Billion chained 1992 dollars	Billion dollars	Billion dollars	Billion dollars	Billion dollars
1970	72.1	100.2	146.0	120.5	—	—	—	—	47.9	80.4	96.9	109.9
1971	77.9	109.2	162.8	130.4	—	—	—	—	51.6	87.4	108.7	119.0
1972	87.0	118.8	176.2	144.9	—	—	—	—	58.3	94.3	117.1	132.2
1973	97.6	130.9	192.9	163.1	—	—	—	—	65.6	104.2	128.0	148.7
1974	111.0	136.7	208.7	179.3	—	—	—	—	76.9	107.9	137.9	163.6
1975	121.0	152.8	226.6	199.1	—	—	—	—	83.3	121.8	149.4	181.9
1976	129.0	172.2	250.0	223.9	—	—	—	—	90.2	137.8	166.5	205.0
1977	142.2	190.2	283.4	255.5	201.0	364.5	742.7	712.5	100.2	151.9	191.8	234.0
1978	160.9	215.6	328.0	294.6	215.5	389.9	786.0	759.5	114.2	170.9	228.8	269.3
1979	182.3	234.2	370.6	333.2	228.2	389.1	830.7	787.3	132.4	184.3	261.8	304.7
1980	195.2	245.9	418.3	377.3	226.0	374.5	862.8	810.8	143.1	192.6	296.6	344.6
1981	216.3	270.4	470.9	426.2	241.1	386.2	878.1	830.0	159.2	211.5	329.7	387.0
1982	219.5	288.1	504.0	471.8	246.5	387.9	875.8	838.1	161.4	223.5	351.2	425.4
1983	229.1	321.9	565.3	521.5	251.5	422.6	900.0	862.8	164.9	249.5	395.2	469.9
1984	264.3	362.2	625.6	590.4	286.8	465.0	945.0	920.8	190.5	278.5	427.8	527.0
1985	280.7	395.0	690.6	651.1	298.1	496.8	968.1	963.9	196.2	298.1	466.6	581.2
1986	293.5	415.2	760.4	712.2	333.0	526.6	969.0	996.8	206.2	319.2	508.3	638.4
1987	300.1	436.5	829.3	785.1	322.0	510.1	1,015.2	1,041.9	214.8	336.2	561.6	704.0
1987	300.8	435.8	829.7	784.6	322.8	509.2	1,015.7	1,041.4	214.8	336.2	561.6	704.0
1988	336.3	459.3	891.4	877.8	343.8	537.6	1,069.4	1,099.1	235.6	357.0	600.7	781.7
1989	356.3	490.2	959.3	965.5	363.3	553.4	1,101.8	1,149.5	252.7	381.2	639.5	859.0
1990	367.2	503.5	1,024.1	1,059.4	360.5	546.4	1,109.0	1,181.7	261.7	392.3	684.2	949.4
1991	388.1	517.4	1,081.6	1,107.6	381.2	534.1	1,105.7	1,174.2	270.0	392.7	795.5	1,011.1
1992	406.4	544.3	1,147.9	1,200.8	406.4	544.3	1,147.9	1,200.8	281.7	410.7	848.9	1,098.5
1993	423.3	573.2	1,218.1	1,267.0	416.5	566.2	1,174.3	1,223.5	287.2	430.7	898.6	1,159.6
1994	468.0	615.3	1,267.6	1,350.4	448.6	601.2	1,196.9	1,256.5	312.1	457.0	938.8	1,230.7
1995	484.4	637.6	1,361.3	1,440.3	457.5	622.5	1,231.1	1,298.8	325.4	480.1	1,024.4	1,318.1
1996	516.8	667.9	1,448.5	1,539.5	493.3	648.5	1,258.5	1,342.9	349.1	503.7	1,095.3	1,410.1
1997	—	—	—	—	—	—	—	—	383.3	538.4	1,192.0	1,515.0

[1] The table contains two sets of data for 1987 to reflect changes in the industrial classification system. See text.

[2] Through 1948, automobile repair, services, and garages are included with retail trade.

Sources

Sherlene K. S. Lum and Robert E. Yuskavage, "Gross Product by Industry, 1947–96," *Survey of Current Business* (November 1997), Tables 11, 12. *National Income and Product Accounts of the United States*, volume 1 (1929–1958), Tables 6.1A, 6.1B; and volume 2 (1959–1988), Tables 6.1B, 6.1C. *Survey of Current Business* (August 1993, January/February 1996, January 1997, February 1998), Tables 6.1C.

Updates for these series are published in the *Survey of Current Business* and are also available at the Internet site of the U.S. Bureau of Economic Analysis. The data will also be available through STAT-USA's Economic Bulletin Board.

Documentation

For a discussion of the concepts employed, see the text for Table Dh1–16.

The series are based on different and changing Standard Industrial Classification (SIC) systems. The gross product series, both nominal and real, for years through 1986 are based on the 1972 SIC; thereafter they are based on the 1987 SIC. The national income data for 1929–1945 are based on the 1942 SIC; those for 1946–1986 are based on the 1972 SIC; and thereafter they are based on the 1987 SIC. In 1987, two figures are shown for each series, the first comparable in scope to the earlier years, the second comparable to the later years. See the Introduction to Part D for a discussion of SIC codes.

Series Dh25–28. Figures do not include a capital consumption adjustment.

TABLE Dh29-36   Persons engaged in trade, finance, and service industries: 1929–1996[1]

Contributed by Thomas Weiss

					Self-employed			
	Wholesale trade	Retail trade	Finance, insurance, and real estate	Services	Wholesale trade	Retail trade	Finance, insurance, and real estate	Services
	Dh29	Dh30 [2]	Dh31	Dh32	Dh33	Dh34	Dh35	Dh36
Year	Thousand	Thousand	Thousand	Thousand	Thousand	Thousand	Thousand	Thousand
1929	1,744	6,077	1,575	6,484	113	1,862	160	1,372
1930	1,685	5,839	1,551	6,318	114	1,859	161	1,390
1931	1,533	5,507	1,488	5,934	115	1,851	160	1,387
1932	1,395	5,058	1,423	5,443	116	1,841	157	1,375
1933	1,393	5,038	1,373	5,275	118	1,841	154	1,356
1934	1,530	5,431	1,401	5,658	124	1,855	159	1,378
1935	1,572	5,608	1,425	5,850	129	1,865	164	1,402
1936	1,690	5,949	1,475	6,167	140	1,915	170	1,419
1937	1,857	6,305	1,520	6,429	151	1,965	174	1,429
1938	1,857	6,218	1,520	6,241	150	2,002	178	1,441
1939	1,942	6,440	1,560	6,396	166	2,051	184	1,439
1940	2,015	6,768	1,611	6,707	175	2,082	189	1,433
1941	2,136	7,126	1,647	6,784	184	2,051	185	1,437
1942	2,041	6,916	1,636	6,926	184	1,950	197	1,408
1943	1,912	6,648	1,575	6,598	160	1,722	186	1,372
1944	1,936	6,598	1,561	6,522	165	1,702	197	1,357
1945	2,052	6,862	1,602	6,549	184	1,792	209	1,368
1946	2,419	7,973	1,813	7,068	204	1,962	219	1,558
1947	2,620	8,376	1,864	7,444	217	2,096	223	1,653
1948	2,642	8,639	1,890	7,650	214	2,162	220	1,668
1948	2,839	7,851	1,885	7,707	253	1,999	220	1,530
1949	2,783	7,839	1,868	7,688	255	2,034	205	1,531
1950	2,818	7,971	1,941	7,911	259	2,029	199	1,539
1951	2,980	8,302	2,045	8,033	265	2,027	219	1,550
1952	3,056	8,409	2,141	8,006	272	2,025	239	1,572
1953	3,103	8,483	2,247	8,097	273	2,001	261	1,584
1954	3,092	8,379	2,349	8,019	271	1,974	289	1,582
1955	3,164	8,593	2,433	8,382	273	2,023	270	1,581
1956	3,307	8,820	2,525	8,720	276	2,039	257	1,623
1957	3,318	8,867	2,594	9,006	277	2,056	255	1,683
1958	3,295	8,775	2,628	9,158	278	2,077	251	1,706
1959	3,351	8,911	2,668	9,430	282	2,011	242	1,736
1960	3,421	9,075	2,754	9,817	289	1,975	243	1,812
1961	3,419	8,934	2,784	10,005	289	1,894	243	1,872
1962	3,448	8,985	2,836	10,310	287	1,787	244	1,912
1963	3,480	9,019	2,909	10,597	287	1,655	243	1,958
1964	3,555	9,294	2,969	10,920	287	1,651	240	1,997
1965	3,648	9,565	3,075	11,306	276	1,624	238	1,989
1966	3,782	9,833	3,166	11,874	281	1,532	242	2,052
1967	3,849	9,973	3,332	12,443	264	1,432	258	2,074
1968	3,920	10,259	3,493	12,821	252	1,392	260	2,080
1969	4,041	10,596	3,653	13,313	259	1,416	266	2,177
1970	4,123	10,766	3,749	13,380	259	1,437	258	2,133
1971	4,154	11,004	3,836	13,577	263	1,480	272	2,149
1972	4,252	11,236	3,959	14,200	247	1,472	267	2,197
1973	4,492	11,717	4,202	14,879	262	1,436	306	2,199
1974	4,617	11,948	4,334	15,313	275	1,483	314	2,268
1975	4,521	11,979	4,405	15,650	261	1,478	341	2,299
1976	4,690	12,407	4,507	16,252	282	1,432	329	2,346
1977	4,832	13,008	4,708	17,035	258	1,527	347	2,494
1978	5,074	13,758	5,059	18,045	248	1,545	408	2,549
1979	5,345	14,124	5,333	18,911	280	1,597	451	2,639
1980	5,406	14,053	5,497	19,581	294	1,628	463	2,732
1981	5,534	14,153	5,619	20,331	297	1,612	456	2,854
1982	5,423	14,068	5,650	20,891	284	1,610	496	3,025
1983	5,424	14,455	5,834	21,701	320	1,634	539	3,223
1984	5,714	15,402	6,073	23,048	326	1,614	550	3,378

Notes appear at end of table

TABLE Dh29–36   Persons engaged in trade, finance, and service industries: 1929–1996   *Continued*

	Wholesale trade	Retail trade	Finance, insurance, and real estate	Services	Self-employed Wholesale trade	Retail trade	Finance, insurance, and real estate	Services
	Dh29	Dh30 [2]	Dh31	Dh32	Dh33	Dh34	Dh35	Dh36
Year	Thousand	Thousand	Thousand	Thousand	Thousand	Thousand	Thousand	Thousand
1985	5,816	16,025	6,304	24,085	308	1,499	563	3,461
1986	5,846	16,434	6,593	24,939	297	1,512	557	3,416
1987	6,002	17,039	6,892	26,317	315	1,549	598	3,609
1987	6,023	17,018	6,900	26,309	315	1,549	598	3,609
1988	6,179	17,479	7,005	27,538	337	1,498	624	3,850
1989	6,415	18,021	7,045	29,018	349	1,548	621	3,899
1990	6,291	18,036	7,114	29,739	334	1,539	634	3,955
1991	6,201	17,668	7,067	30,505	350	1,544	618	4,163
1992	6,207	17,695	6,999	31,128	349	1,439	630	3,963
1993	6,141	18,260	7,162	32,377	354	1,569	661	4,065
1994	6,324	18,897	7,251	33,627	353	1,590	631	4,166
1995	6,559	19,476	7,216	35,048	359	1,447	666	4,184
1996	6,589	19,866	7,315	36,442	311	1,483	680	4,220

[1] The table contains two sets of data for both 1948 and 1987 to reflect changes in the industrial classification system. See text.

[2] Through 1948, automobile repair, services, and garages are included with retail trade.

Sources

Series Dh29 through Dh32. 1929–1948, from *National Income and Product Accounts of the United States,* volume 1 (1929–1958), Table 6.8B; 1948–1996, from Sherlene K. S. Lum and Robert E. Yuskavage, "Gross Product by Industry, 1947–96," *Survey of Current Business* (November 1997): 20–34.

Series Dh33 through Dh36. *National Income and Product Accounts of the United States, 1929–94,* volume 2, Tables 6.7A, 6.7B, and 6.7C, pp. 37–38, and *Survey of Current Business* (January/February 1996, August 1997), Tables 6.7C.

Updates for these series are published in the *Survey of Current Business* and are also available at Internet site of the U.S. Bureau of Economic Analysis. The data will also be available through STAT-USA's Economic Bulletin Board.

Documentation

Persons engaged equals the number of full-time equivalent employees plus the number of self-employed persons. Unpaid family workers are not included owing to unresolved difficulties in their definition and measurement.

Full-time equivalent employees equals the number of employees on full-time schedules plus the number of employees on part-time schedules converted to a full-time basis. The conversion is based on the number of hours employed. The number of full-time equivalent employees in each industry is the product of the total number of employees and the ratio of average weekly hours per employee for all employees to average weekly hours per employee on full-time schedules. Although the number of full-time equivalent employees in each industry is not shown in this table, it equals the difference between the number of persons engaged and the number of self-employed in that industry. Self-employed persons consist of active proprietors or partners who devote a majority of the working hours to their unincorporated business.

The industry series are based on different and changing Standard Industrial Classification (SIC) systems. The data for 1929–1948 are based on the 1942 SIC, those for 1948–1987 are based on the 1972 SIC, and those for 1987–1999 are based on the 1987 SIC. In 1948 and 1987, two figures are shown for each series, the first comparable in scope to the earlier years, the second comparable to the later years. See the Introduction to Part D for a discussion of SIC codes.

TABLE Dh37–47   Gross product in selected service industries: 1947–1996[1]

Contributed by Thomas Weiss

	All selected service industries	Hotels and other lodging places	Personal services	Business services	Automotive repair services and parking	Amusements, recreation, and related services	Health services	Legal services	Educational services	Social services and membership organizations	Other services
	Dh37	Dh38	Dh39	Dh40	Dh41	Dh42	Dh43	Dh44	Dh45	Dh46	Dh47
Year	Million dollars	Million dollars	Million dollars	Million dollars	Million dollars	Million dollars	Million dollars	Million dollars	Million dollars	Million dollars	Million dollars
1947	20,081	1,540	2,852	1,421	941	2,603	3,490	1,047	790	1,370	4,027
1948	21,921	1,657	3,155	1,637	930	2,515	4,162	1,214	912	1,519	4,220
1949	22,577	1,696	3,210	1,708	904	2,553	4,309	1,302	964	1,737	4,194
1950	24,173	1,732	3,359	1,980	992	2,520	4,713	1,425	1,024	1,872	4,556
1951	26,373	1,841	3,563	2,316	1,122	2,606	5,198	1,556	1,079	2,065	5,027
1952	28,167	1,939	3,714	2,636	1,190	2,696	5,698	1,636	1,120	2,211	5,327
1953	30,238	1,985	3,894	2,983	1,320	2,780	6,270	1,746	1,186	2,446	5,628
1954	31,612	2,083	4,057	3,254	1,402	2,887	6,447	1,926	1,282	2,644	5,630
1955	35,200	2,176	4,223	3,680	1,601	3,013	7,688	2,099	1,391	2,856	6,473
1956	38,720	2,321	4,554	4,306	1,982	3,138	8,213	2,174	1,584	3,081	7,367
1957	41,826	2,515	4,883	4,800	2,102	3,110	9,025	2,346	1,742	3,351	7,952
1958	44,112	2,496	4,976	5,086	2,242	3,221	9,909	2,468	1,878	3,645	8,191
1959	48,401	2,703	5,226	5,865	2,489	3,562	10,994	2,878	2,041	4,106	8,537

Note appears at end of table

(continued)

TABLE Dh37–47   Gross product in selected service industries: 1947–1996   *Continued*

Year	All selected service industries	Hotels and other lodging places	Personal services	Business services	Automotive repair services and parking	Amusements, recreation, and related services	Health services	Legal services	Educational services	Social services and membership organizations	Other services
	Dh37	Dh38	Dh39	Dh40	Dh41	Dh42	Dh43	Dh44	Dh45	Dh46	Dh47
	Million dollars	Million dollars	Million dollars	Million dollars	Million dollars	Million dollars	Million dollars	Million dollars	Million dollars	Million dollars	Million dollars
1960	51,556	2,777	5,416	6,381	2,772	3,822	11,539	2,966	2,245	4,559	9,079
1961	55,008	2,866	5,706	7,000	2,895	4,076	12,252	3,358	2,502	4,950	9,403
1962	59,310	3,089	5,982	7,767	3,208	4,239	13,302	3,571	2,813	5,400	9,939
1963	63,434	3,370	6,297	8,477	3,499	4,518	14,204	3,876	3,079	5,691	10,423
1964	69,121	3,531	6,751	9,458	3,899	4,927	15,754	4,215	3,410	6,016	11,160
1965	74,735	3,949	7,087	10,560	4,080	5,282	17,007	4,599	3,838	6,442	11,891
1966	82,650	4,358	7,766	12,029	4,425	5,542	18,905	5,110	4,328	7,138	13,049
1967	90,800	4,844	8,261	13,399	4,797	5,735	21,602	5,450	4,768	7,826	14,118
1968	99,431	5,298	8,741	14,712	5,302	6,330	24,332	5,747	5,385	8,451	15,133
1969	110,766	5,813	9,040	16,882	5,995	6,427	27,886	6,317	6,311	9,581	16,514
1970	120,479	6,331	9,274	18,149	6,349	7,025	31,413	7,268	7,147	10,048	17,475
1971	130,356	6,706	9,390	19,212	7,293	7,347	34,673	8,112	8,028	10,961	18,634
1972	144,925	7,526	9,793	21,555	8,221	7,894	39,130	9,124	9,174	11,808	20,700
1973	163,080	8,331	10,246	25,302	9,451	8,976	43,911	10,364	10,002	13,057	23,440
1974	179,283	8,871	10,891	27,858	10,278	9,724	49,928	11,466	10,554	14,231	25,482
1975	199,140	9,738	11,363	30,557	11,222	10,755	57,859	12,485	11,421	15,915	27,825
1976	223,916	11,153	12,706	35,412	12,933	12,403	66,226	13,696	11,736	17,079	30,572
1977	255,464	12,856	13,496	42,980	13,301	14,827	75,307	16,841	12,153	18,738	34,965
1978	294,562	15,909	15,232	50,498	15,950	17,568	85,392	18,779	13,197	21,339	40,698
1979	333,245	18,194	16,405	60,070	18,227	18,905	95,984	21,237	14,494	23,480	46,249
1980	377,313	19,980	17,606	69,419	19,143	20,021	111,509	24,798	16,390	26,171	52,276
1981	426,220	22,582	18,546	80,741	20,607	21,884	128,640	27,758	18,013	28,320	59,129
1982	471,787	24,351	19,720	91,764	22,064	24,091	146,332	32,735	19,776	29,932	61,022
1983	521,530	25,402	22,273	105,780	24,955	26,681	159,446	36,424	21,930	33,059	65,580
1984	590,393	28,307	24,916	126,438	29,332	28,728	173,282	43,033	24,529	36,398	75,430
1985	651,125	31,440	28,437	143,263	34,570	32,522	186,771	47,652	26,440	38,818	81,212
1986	712,225	33,575	30,816	158,653	36,791	36,282	201,568	55,396	27,983	43,022	88,139
1987	785,059	36,534	32,591	175,079	39,765	39,816	229,371	61,366	31,178	46,808	92,551
1987	784,630	36,534	31,176	142,385	39,765	41,897	229,371	61,137	31,178	46,807	124,380
1988	877,846	39,871	36,034	163,345	44,063	45,830	250,414	69,365	34,068	52,716	142,140
1989	965,537	43,708	37,029	178,995	45,191	54,436	276,302	74,170	36,965	58,627	160,114
1990	1,059,393	46,080	38,162	198,996	48,918	59,418	307,909	80,698	39,752	64,582	174,878
1991	1,107,558	48,375	38,720	197,728	49,608	61,720	337,708	83,653	43,912	70,505	175,629
1992	1,200,834	50,978	40,951	218,911	51,111	67,863	369,052	90,147	46,250	75,799	189,772
1993	1,266,965	53,819	44,281	233,472	54,274	71,205	386,594	91,576	48,893	82,015	200,836
1994	1,350,363	57,401	45,820	256,020	59,302	74,417	410,248	93,823	52,290	88,238	212,804
1995	1,440,342	60,622	46,583	283,284	61,139	82,160	428,873	96,456	55,054	93,703	232,468
1996	1,539,525	63,746	49,073	318,526	65,041	90,685	446,961	100,004	58,199	98,157	249,133

[1] The table contains two sets of data for 1987 to reflect changes in the industrial classification system. See text.

Sources

Sherlene K. S. Lum and Robert E. Yuskavage, "Gross Product by Industry, 1947–96," *Survey of Current Business* (November 1997): 20–34.

Updates for these series are published in the *Survey of Current Business* and are also available at the Internet site of the U.S. Bureau of Economic Analysis. The data will also be available through STAT-USA's Economic Bulletin Board.

Documentation

For a discussion of the concepts employed, see the text for Table Dh1–16.

The series are based on different and changing Standard Industrial Classification (SIC) systems. The data for 1948–1987 are shown on the basis of the 1972 SIC; those for 1987–1999 are shown on the basis of the 1987 SIC. See the Introduction to Part D for a discussion of SIC codes.

Series Dh42. Includes motion pictures.

Series Dh45. Includes commercial and trade schools, and employment agencies.

Series Dh47. Includes other services not elsewhere classified, miscellaneous repair services, miscellaneous professional services, and private households.

TABLE Dh48–58   Persons engaged in selected service industries: 1929–1996[1]

Contributed by Thomas Weiss

Year	Services	Hotels and other lodging places	Personal services	Business services	Automotive repair services and parking	Amusements, recreation, and related services	Health services	Legal services	Educational services	Social services and membership organizations	Other services not elsewhere classified
	Dh48	Dh49	Dh50	Dh51	Dh52 [2]	Dh53	Dh54	Dh55	Dh56	Dh57	Dh58
	Thousand	Thousand	Thousand	Thousand	Thousand	Thousand	Thousand	Thousand	Thousand	Thousand	Thousand
1929	6,484	518	1,008	209	—	448	750	194	311	351	2,695
1930	6,318	504	996	207	—	430	749	202	313	358	2,559
1931	5,934	465	941	192	—	395	725	212	312	354	2,338
1932	5,443	417	886	198	—	328	691	214	304	341	2,064
1933	5,275	403	860	204	—	304	679	217	300	335	1,973
1934	5,658	453	910	231	—	334	695	216	302	339	2,178
1935	5,850	469	950	233	—	352	711	223	311	338	2,263
1936	6,167	494	994	265	—	383	750	225	317	342	2,397
1937	6,429	520	1,034	269	—	414	785	230	326	332	2,519
1938	6,241	522	1,008	276	—	390	807	236	333	331	2,338
1939	6,396	526	996	290	—	402	813	242	338	328	2,461
1940	6,707	538	1,050	296	—	421	841	244	340	390	2,587
1941	6,784	557	1,095	314	—	447	861	245	355	427	2,483
1942	6,926	561	1,115	310	—	455	878	228	380	448	2,551
1943	6,598	573	1,090	305	—	445	894	211	398	455	2,227
1944	6,522	584	1,053	320	—	453	895	200	385	479	2,153
1945	6,549	584	1,073	343	—	454	892	195	372	493	2,143
1946	7,068	632	1,210	418	—	511	983	210	394	572	2,138
1947	7,444	636	1,243	455	—	521	1,071	212	423	599	2,284
1948	7,650	636	1,240	480	—	522	1,141	210	492	647	2,282
1948	7,707	634	1,243	382	340	522	1,132	217	462	678	2,097
1949	7,688	605	1,216	383	325	516	1,160	227	469	717	2,070
1950	7,911	606	1,209	395	312	507	1,222	237	473	737	2,213
1951	8,033	630	1,210	422	305	495	1,272	242	470	766	2,221
1952	8,006	645	1,200	451	307	481	1,305	244	469	782	2,122
1953	8,097	665	1,187	481	305	473	1,354	249	477	816	2,090
1954	8,019	653	1,173	496	301	464	1,402	252	485	840	1,953
1955	8,382	634	1,168	542	311	465	1,455	253	505	886	2,163
1956	8,720	642	1,185	604	324	465	1,520	257	519	927	2,277
1957	9,006	656	1,221	653	336	462	1,600	262	557	966	2,293
1958	9,158	649	1,198	679	351	453	1,675	271	583	1,004	2,295
1959	9,430	666	1,185	755	361	459	1,730	292	595	1,107	2,280
1960	9,817	692	1,222	819	391	472	1,777	304	623	1,217	2,300
1961	10,005	701	1,229	870	398	474	1,803	308	654	1,285	2,283
1962	10,310	722	1,241	942	404	478	1,856	321	692	1,360	2,294
1963	10,597	758	1,268	995	423	489	1,929	322	724	1,391	2,298
1964	10,920	797	1,289	1,071	440	497	2,012	336	743	1,430	2,305
1965	11,306	835	1,318	1,162	450	503	2,123	343	794	1,477	2,301
1966	11,874	875	1,373	1,284	465	517	2,286	362	839	1,573	2,300
1967	12,443	911	1,394	1,402	487	552	2,450	373	889	1,670	2,315
1968	12,821	944	1,390	1,491	492	565	2,612	373	927	1,731	2,296
1969	13,313	996	1,394	1,624	504	586	2,796	390	964	1,779	2,280
1970	13,380	1,003	1,341	1,666	508	583	2,905	401	1,001	1,756	2,216
1971	13,577	992	1,275	1,684	546	603	3,098	410	1,050	1,763	2,156
1972	14,200	1,018	1,246	1,798	574	656	3,404	419	1,073	1,832	2,180
1973	14,879	1,067	1,235	1,984	607	706	3,658	451	1,092	1,838	2,241
1974	15,313	1,112	1,200	2,095	617	729	3,877	479	1,130	1,868	2,206
1975	15,650	1,117	1,182	2,054	638	737	4,114	501	1,151	2,025	2,131
1976	16,252	1,119	1,219	2,186	681	777	4,288	536	1,154	2,079	2,213
1977	17,035	1,181	1,251	2,363	724	821	4,496	583	1,151	2,119	2,346
1978	18,045	1,212	1,294	2,627	788	866	4,751	621	1,177	2,239	2,470
1979	18,911	1,239	1,331	2,886	842	906	4,974	666	1,206	2,306	2,555
1980	19,581	1,267	1,341	3,083	847	935	5,233	699	1,216	2,366	2,594
1981	20,331	1,318	1,353	3,262	876	968	5,493	745	1,252	2,379	2,685
1982	20,891	1,354	1,355	3,354	926	976	5,711	800	1,314	2,402	2,699
1983	21,701	1,395	1,399	3,706	935	997	5,859	847	1,357	2,498	2,708
1984	23,048	1,470	1,468	4,279	1,032	1,036	6,014	903	1,411	2,573	2,862

Notes appear at end of table

(continued)

TABLE Dh48–58   Persons engaged in selected service industries: 1929–1996   *Continued*

Year	Services	Hotels and other lodging places	Personal services	Business services	Automotive repair services and parking	Amusements, recreation, and related services	Health services	Legal services	Educational services	Social services and membership organizations	Other services not elsewhere classified
	Dh48	Dh49	Dh50	Dh51	Dh52 [2]	Dh53	Dh54	Dh55	Dh56	Dh57	Dh58
	Thousand	Thousand	Thousand	Thousand	Thousand	Thousand	Thousand	Thousand	Thousand	Thousand	Thousand
1985	24,085	1,578	1,525	4,652	1,122	1,041	6,189	942	1,439	2,635	2,962
1986	24,939	1,616	1,544	5,005	1,146	1,067	6,400	972	1,450	2,754	2,985
1987	26,317	1,677	1,613	5,470	1,187	1,098	6,694	1,067	1,532	2,939	3,040
1987	26,309	1,677	1,568	4,646	1,187	1,244	6,694	1,059	1,532	2,939	3,763
1988	27,538	1,778	1,627	5,040	1,235	1,284	6,824	1,117	1,558	3,139	3,936
1989	29,018	1,837	1,605	5,356	1,254	1,411	7,190	1,153	1,603	3,301	4,308
1990	29,739	1,828	1,565	5,551	1,263	1,428	7,507	1,110	1,616	3,546	4,325
1991	30,505	1,826	1,661	5,544	1,245	1,475	7,829	1,148	1,657	3,857	4,263
1992	31,128	1,483	1,707	5,552	1,267	1,550	8,205	1,148	1,758	3,905	4,553
1993	32,377	1,508	1,737	6,012	1,325	1,637	8,451	1,163	1,815	4,066	4,663
1994	33,627	1,549	1,725	6,538	1,338	1,762	8,677	1,184	1,860	4,351	4,643
1995	35,048	1,587	1,776	7,109	1,362	1,870	8,903	1,173	1,915	4,504	4,849
1996	36,442	1,625	1,805	7,664	1,480	2,003	9,168	1,147	1,986	4,623	4,941

[1] The table contains two sets of data for both 1948 and 1987 to reflect changes in the industrial classification system. See text.

[2] Through 1948, automobile repair, services, and garages are included with retail trade.

Sources

The figures for 1929–1948 are from *National Income and Product Accounts of the United States,* volume 1 (1929–1958), Table 6.8B; those for 1948–1996 are from Sherlene K. S. Lum and Robert E. Yuskavage, "Gross Product by Industry, 1947–96," *Survey of Current Business* (November 1997): 20–34.

Updates for these series are published in the *Survey of Current Business* and are also available at the Internet site of the U.S. Bureau of Economic Analysis. The data will also be available through STAT-USA's Economic Bulletin Board.

Documentation

See the text for Table Dh29–36 for the definition and coverage of persons engaged.

In 1948 and 1987, two figures are shown for each series, the first comparable in scope to the earlier years and the second comparable to the later years.

Series Dh53. Includes motion pictures.

Series Dh56. Includes commercial and trade schools, and employment agencies.

Series Dh58. Includes other services not elsewhere classified, miscellaneous repair services, miscellaneous professional services, and private households.

TABLE Dh59–69   National income originating in selected service industries: 1929–1979[1]

Contributed by Thomas Weiss

Year	Services	Hotels and other lodging places	Personal services	Business services	Automotive repair services and parking	Amusements, recreation, and related services	Health services	Legal services	Educational services	Social services and membership organizations	Other services not elsewhere classified
	Dh59	Dh60	Dh61	Dh62	Dh63 [2]	Dh64	Dh65	Dh66	Dh67	Dh68	Dh69
	Million dollars	Million dollars	Million dollars	Million dollars	Million dollars	Million dollars	Million dollars	Million dollars	Million dollars	Million dollars	Million dollars
1929	8,751	623	1,287	568	—	819	1,532	689	393	601	2,239
1930	8,277	577	1,218	568	—	774	1,472	683	401	609	1,975
1931	7,142	465	1,040	450	—	629	1,302	701	393	586	1,576
1932	5,565	335	814	363	—	371	1,033	591	364	528	1,166
1933	5,046	291	707	338	—	364	945	561	332	486	1,022
1934	5,688	361	790	432	—	480	1,033	600	333	492	1,167
1935	6,090	383	865	483	—	540	1,112	624	344	488	1,251
1936	6,755	418	962	578	—	644	1,250	647	359	506	1,391
1937	7,426	473	1,113	610	—	742	1,320	680	386	509	1,593
1938	7,140	460	1,028	601	—	692	1,328	666	398	518	1,449
1939	7,471	485	1,053	642	—	722	1,378	692	404	521	1,574
1940	7,945	532	1,154	668	—	758	1,460	719	415	564	1,675
1941	8,789	585	1,292	781	—	881	1,571	763	457	605	1,854
1942	10,193	675	1,552	829	—	1,040	1,802	793	537	681	2,284
1943	11,726	878	1,899	916	—	1,266	1,985	814	630	784	2,554
1944	13,090	990	2,015	1,056	—	1,389	2,336	874	637	882	2,911
1945	14,065	1,087	2,121	1,182	—	1,542	2,454	930	616	950	3,183
1946	16,621	1,322	2,563	1,482	—	1,945	3,021	957	724	1,164	3,443
1947	18,043	1,292	2,643	1,639	—	1,843	3,539	1,036	896	1,278	3,877
1948	19,483	1,344	2,842	1,856	—	1,734	4,016	1,176	970	1,462	4,083
1948	19,976	1,344	2,842	1,488	909	1,734	3,939	1,177	899	1,512	4,132
1949	20,410	1,359	2,914	1,541	842	1,690	4,057	1,258	950	1,723	4,076

Notes appear at end of table

TABLE Dh59–69   National income originating in selected service industries: 1929–1979   *Continued*

Year	Services	Hotels and other lodging places	Personal services	Business services	Automotive repair services and parking	Amusements, recreation, and related services	Health services	Legal services	Educational services	Social services and membership organizations	Other services not elsewhere classified
	Dh59	Dh60	Dh61	Dh62	Dh63 [2]	Dh64	Dh65	Dh66	Dh67	Dh68	Dh69
	Million dollars	Million dollars	Million dollars	Million dollars	Million dollars	Million dollars	Million dollars	Million dollars	Million dollars	Million dollars	Million dollars
1950	21,702	1,380	3,028	1,760	865	1,656	4,426	1,345	1,003	1,860	4,379
1951	23,473	1,450	3,175	2,029	933	1,699	4,847	1,456	1,050	2,051	4,783
1952	24,983	1,539	3,292	2,296	959	1,751	5,294	1,516	1,085	2,195	5,056
1953	26,743	1,569	3,433	2,586	1,013	1,837	5,823	1,607	1,147	2,429	5,299
1954	27,687	1,594	3,518	2,782	1,035	1,999	5,895	1,759	1,233	2,625	5,247
1955	31,053	1,681	3,679	3,135	1,173	2,109	7,121	1,927	1,337	2,835	6,056
1956	33,816	1,770	3,936	3,630	1,337	2,156	7,563	1,981	1,521	3,055	6,867
1957	36,375	1,857	4,216	4,008	1,324	2,146	8,310	2,133	1,668	3,322	7,391
1958	38,328	1,835	4,253	4,284	1,448	2,212	9,105	2,234	1,801	3,612	7,544
1959	42,089	1,992	4,474	4,965	1,606	2,406	10,164	2,612	1,968	4,085	7,817
1960	44,677	2,031	4,607	5,387	1,748	2,555	10,666	2,692	2,165	4,537	8,289
1961	47,487	2,036	4,786	5,892	1,810	2,712	11,330	3,060	2,414	4,926	8,521
1962	50,935	2,176	4,991	6,503	1,980	2,728	12,285	3,235	2,716	5,373	8,948
1963	54,328	2,343	5,237	7,064	2,126	2,882	13,137	3,536	2,978	5,661	9,364
1964	59,254	2,496	5,643	7,956	2,310	3,160	14,587	3,842	3,304	5,982	9,974
1965	64,254	2,839	5,950	8,906	2,395	3,408	15,771	4,207	3,724	6,406	10,648
1966	71,507	3,272	6,524	10,149	2,582	3,771	17,560	4,678	4,208	7,096	11,667
1967	78,713	3,573	6,914	11,316	2,827	3,929	20,137	5,004	4,632	7,779	12,602
1968	86,107	3,898	7,299	12,272	3,103	4,354	22,767	5,306	5,230	8,386	13,492
1969	95,942	4,235	7,530	13,950	3,458	4,383	26,093	5,840	6,148	9,509	14,796
1970	104,094	4,498	7,621	14,960	3,651	4,824	29,411	6,725	6,951	9,969	15,484
1971	112,388	4,829	7,593	15,753	4,138	4,983	32,482	7,575	7,784	10,855	16,396
1972	124,036	5,301	7,677	17,386	4,558	5,302	36,570	8,484	9,018	11,743	17,997
1973	138,771	5,904	7,987	20,333	5,222	6,067	40,938	9,628	9,667	12,851	20,174
1974	151,705	6,221	8,337	22,036	5,523	6,391	46,449	10,657	10,253	13,954	21,884
1975	168,678	7,032	8,634	24,049	6,152	7,108	54,052	11,530	10,974	15,563	23,584
1976	188,685	8,049	9,399	27,770	7,022	8,405	60,818	12,710	11,444	16,791	26,277
1977	212,431	9,002	10,362	32,272	8,049	9,643	68,590	14,447	11,790	18,336	29,940
1978	240,332	10,743	11,579	38,227	9,531	10,828	75,445	16,052	12,786	20,500	34,641
1979	275,334	12,342	12,727	45,882	10,985	12,044	86,898	18,083	14,091	22,749	39,533

[1] The table contains two sets of data for 1948 to reflect changes in the industrial classification system. See text.

[2] Through 1948, automobile repair, services, and garages are included with retail trade.

Sources

National Income and Product Accounts of the United States, 1929–76, Table 6.3A and 6.3B; and *Survey of Current Business,* Special Supplement (July 1981), Table 6.3B.

Documentation

The U.S. Bureau of Economic Analysis no longer publishes national income originating in the detailed industries shown here, and the figures for 1948–1979 were not revised in the last revision of the national income and product accounts. The series have been included because they do provide aggregate series at the detailed industrial level that go back further in time than the gross product series.

National income represents the income earned by those involved in the production of the services. Whereas the gross product figures represent the market value of the services produced, the national income figures are valued at factor costs. These national income figures are those without a capital consumption adjustment by industry. For additional information about these concepts, see the text for Table Ca1–8.

Data for 1929–1948 are based on the 1942 Standard Industrial Classification (SIC) system; data for 1948–1979 are based on the 1957 SIC system. In 1948, two figures are shown for each series: the first comparable in scope to the earlier years and the second comparable to the later years. See the Introduction to Part D for a discussion of SIC codes.

Series Dh64. Includes motion pictures.

Series Dh67. Includes commercial and trade schools, and employment agencies.

Series Dh69. Includes other services not elsewhere classified, miscellaneous repair services, miscellaneous professional services, and private households.

ESTABLISHMENTS, RECEIPTS, AND EMPLOYEES

Thomas Weiss

TABLE Dh70-83 Establishments in selected service industries: 1933–1992[1] [Establishments with or without payroll and subject to federal income tax]

Contributed by Thomas Weiss

Year	Total Dh70	Hotels, rooming houses, camps, and other lodging places Dh71	Personal services Dh72	Business services Dh73	Automotive repair services and parking Dh74	Miscellaneous repair services Dh75	Amusements, recreation, and related services Dh76	Health services Dh77	Legal services Dh78	Engineering, accounting, research, management, and related services Dh79	All other services — Total Dh80	Selected educational services Dh81[2]	Social services Dh82	Services not elsewhere classified Dh83
	Number	Number	Number	Number	Number	Number	Number	Number	Number	Number	Number	Number	Number	Number
1933	502,416	35,308	311,416	39,412[8]	13,695	68,985	29,737	—	—	—	3,863	—	—	3,863[10]
1935	645,213[6]	38,670	369,464	29,556[8]	92,471	71,426	37,677	—	—	—	5,949	—	—	5,949[11]
1939[3]	656,482	41,508[7]	389,726	26,188	78,881	75,262	44,917	—	—	—	—	—	—	—
1948	665,475	55,569[7]	351,985	32,007	95,544	80,023	50,347	—	—	—	—	—	—	—
1948	619,926	52,518[7]	325,246	30,900	90,762	71,338	49,162	—	—	—	—	—	—	—
1954	785,589	66,962	348,843	88,661	94,342	113,429	73,352	—	—	—	—	—	—	—
1958	975,250	85,580	411,507	99,155	125,240	144,759	94,241	—	—	14,768	—	—	—	—
1963	1,061,673	84,706	447,080	120,323	139,611	146,776	95,832	—	—	27,345	—	—	—	—
1967	1,187,814	87,006	498,935	172,721	139,243	138,014	112,781	—	—	39,114	—	—	—	—
1972[4]	1,590,248	79,685	503,378	244,175	168,959	148,925	145,983	8,543[9]	144,452	146,148	—	—	—	—
1977[5]	2,778,900	79,747	512,140	314,432	200,153	162,910	176,785	444,062	167,896	345,512	375,263	85,082	267,397	22,784[12]
1987	6,254,512	85,739	1,037,433	1,433,163	388,159	247,597	467,032	800,571	273,196	876,632	644,990	155,896	319,472	169,622
1992	8,593,491	92,882	1,320,920	2,056,212	454,317	269,751	691,735	1,005,520	326,860	1,317,066	1,058,228	240,708	617,412	200,108

1 The table contains two sets of data for 1948 to reflect changes in the establishments that were included. The first is more compatible with earlier years, and the second, with later years. See text.

2 Includes Puerto Rico.

3 Includes tax-exempt firms with payrolls.

4 Includes taxable nongovernmental establishments and organizations that were reported separately.

5 Excludes custom industries reported in the original census, but includes data reported separately in the census for hotels and tourist camps, and establishments providing amusement services.

6 Includes only hotels and tourist courts.

7 Includes dental laboratories, which in 1972 and later are included in series Dh77. Also includes warehousing.

8 Covers only dental laboratories.

9 In 1977, includes elementary and secondary schools except those operated by religious organizations; excludes elementary and secondary schools thereafter.

10 Includes only "other miscellaneous service" reported in the original census. Most establishments originally classified in miscellaneous services have been included with other industries.

11 Includes landscape gardening, livery stables, and other miscellaneous services.

12 Includes arrangement of transportation.

Sources

Census of American Business: 1933, United States Summaries, Part 1; *Census of Business: 1935, Service Establishments*, volume 1, *U.S. Summary* and *Census of Business: 1935, Tourist Camps*, Table 1, and *Statistical Abstract of the United States* (1940), Table 887; *Census of Business: 1939*, volume 3, *Service Establishments*, pp. 2–3, 503, 623; *Census of Business: 1948*, volume 6, *Service Trade – General Statistics*, Tables 1a, 1b; *Census of Business: 1954*, volume 5, *Selected Service Trades – Summary Statistics*, Table 1a; *Census of Business*, volume 5, *Selected Services Summary Statistics*, Table 2; *Census of Business: 1963*, volume 6, *Selected Business – Area Statistics*, Table 2; *Census of Business: 1967*, volume 5, *Selected Services – Area Statistics*, Part 1, Table 2; *Census of Selected Services, 1972, Summary and Subject Statistics*, volume 1, Table 1; *Census of Service Industries 1977*, volume 2, *Geographic Area Series*, Part 1, U.S. Summary, Table 1, and part 4, Other Service Industries, pp. x, xi; *1982 Census of Service Industries, Geographic Area Series*, number 52, Table 1a; *1987 Census of Service Industries, Geographic Area Series*, number 52, Table 1a, and *1987 Census of Service Industries, Miscellaneous Subjects*, Table 68; *1992 Census of Service Industries, Geographic Area Series*, number 52, Table 1a, and *1992 Census of Service Industries, Nonemployer Statistics Series – Summary*, Table 1.

Documentation

These series have been compiled from the censuses of business that have been taken every five years since 1967 and at various dates before that. The series are identified here by the titles of two-digit industries listed in the *Standard Industrial Classification Manual: 1987*, except for series on "all other services." That category is the residual of all establishments not found in one of the industries specified, and so is not the same as services not elsewhere classified (Standard Industrial Classification (SIC) code 89) used in the census reports. See the Introduction to Part D for a discussion of SIC codes. An establishment is a single physical location at which business is conducted. It is not necessarily identical with a business, company, or firm, which may consist of one or more establishments. There have been numerous changes in enumeration methods, in accuracy, and in classification over time. The principal ones are not noted here; others can be found in the various census volumes.

The 1954 and later censuses combine information for firms with and without employees. Information for large firms with employees and for a sample of "small employers" was obtained by mail canvasses of firms that were included in the active records of the Internal Revenue Service as subject to the payment of Federal Insurance Contributions Act (FICA) taxes and that were in appropriate kind-of-business classifications. Data for the nonemployer segment was derived from tax returns; a 50 percent sample of returns was used in 1954, 1958, and 1963, while in the 1967 and later censuses data for all nonemployers were compiled from tax records. The 1948 and earlier censuses were conducted by field enumeration. The differences in enumeration methods particularly affect the coverage of establishments without easily recognizable places of business and those leaving business prior to the end of the year. The post-1954 data are thus more complete in those areas. The 1933 and 1935 censuses were not taken under mandatory reporting requirements and may therefore be subject to some underenumeration. There are important gaps in enumerators' reports for 1933 so that substantial underenumeration, particularly of the smaller establishments, exists for that year. Underenumerations have more effect on the number of establishments than on receipts.

In the 1963 and later censuses, nonemployer establishments that did not operate the entire year have been included if, during the period they operated, their receipts were at a rate that would have reached an annual total of $1,000 or more had they operated the entire year. Establishments without paid employment and with less than $1,000 in receipts were excluded in the 1954 and 1958 tabulations. The 1948 data shown as being comparable with later years were adjusted to the 1954 cutoff point. The 1948 data shown as comparable with earlier years exclude establishments that operated the entire year but had receipts less than $500. For 1939 and earlier, establishments having receipts of $100 or more are included. Receipts for 1954 and later years include sales and excise taxes; receipts for 1948 and 1939 exclude them, except as indicated.

Establishments are classified according to their principal kinds of business. Changes in the relative importance of that principal business may thus serve to shift particular establishments among service categories or between service and retailing classifications from one census to another. Many service establishments derive some receipts from sales of merchandise; conversely, many establishments primarily engaged in the sale of goods, and hence included in retail trade, obtain some income from services.

Over the years, the industrial classification system was changed, so there is not strict comparability in each industry's coverage from year to year. The various census volumes identify the major

changes from one year to the next. In preparing these series, the original census data were reorganized somewhat in order to improve the comparability of the historical series. The most noticeable reorganization involved "Engineering, accounting, research, management, and related services" (SIC code 87), which was reported as a separate industry for the first time in 1987. Given its numerical importance in recent years, it seemed appropriate to reclassify some of the three- and four-digit industries that were placed in business services more generally defined in earlier years. The series "all other services" is composed of four industries identified by the following titles from the 1987 SIC manual: selected educational services, social services, selected membership organizations, and services not elsewhere classified.

The table does not contain data for 1982. Data for nonemployers and the combined data for all establishments are not available because many businesses were miscoded into miscellaneous categories rather than specific kinds of business.

Series Dh80–83. "All other services" is composed of four industries identified by the following titles from the 1987 SIC manual: selected educational services, social services, selected membership organizations, and services not elsewhere classified. The last of these includes establishments that should be classified in services but could not be placed into a particular industry. In each year the kind of business of some of these establishments is identified (e.g., landscape gardening in 1933) but not all. These other establishments are listed as being in other miscellaneous services. The scope and coverage of this industry changed over time. The few components identified in the earliest years are noted in the tables. Since 1977, services not elsewhere classified has included noncommercial educational, scientific, and research organizations and related consulting services, as well as other services not elsewhere classified. Since 1992, the census also identified authors, composers, and other arts-related services.

In 1997, in order to facilitate comparisons between U.S. and international data, the Economic Censuses replaced the SIC classification system with the North American Industry Classification System (NAICS) (pronounced "nakes"). See the Introduction to Part D. No NAICS sector corresponds exactly to any SIC sector. The lack of correspondence is particularly great in the service sectors. For this reason, it is generally not possible to update the data shown in series Dh70–197 beyond 1992. For certain series, however, the *1997 Economic Census* reported data according to both the SIC and NAICS classification systems. This reporting enables one to extend the end date for certain series through to 1997. Where updates to 1997 were possible, they are displayed in tables for series Dh84–197.

TABLE Dh84–97 Establishments in selected service industries: 1954–1997 [Establishments with payroll and subject to federal income tax]

Contributed by Thomas Weiss

	Total	Hotels, rooming houses, camps, and other lodging places	Personal services	Business services	Automotive repair services and parking	Miscellaneous repair services	Amusements, recreation, and related services	Health services	Legal services	Engineering, accounting, research, management, and related services	All other services			
											Total	Selected educational services [1]	Social services	Services not elsewhere classified
	Dh84	Dh85	Dh86	Dh87	Dh88	Dh89	Dh90	Dh91	Dh92	Dh93	Dh94	Dh95	Dh96	Dh97
Year	Number	Number	Number	Number	Number	Number	Number	Number	Number	Number	Number	Number	Number	Number
1954	375,149	38,558	163,007	40,061	48,176	33,125	52,222	—	—	6,692	—	—	—	—
1958	442,584	48,304	181,597	48,411	65,160	37,283	55,137	—	—	12,039	—	—	—	—
1963	504,356	53,071	200,468	61,466	76,480	41,610	59,222	—	—	16,942	—	—	—	—
1967	521,410	53,650	204,634	68,046	77,111	42,422	58,605	5,131 [4]	77,282	50,643	—	—	—	—
1972 [2]	683,614	46,509	196,989	108,914	90,536	46,677	66,064	278,686	94,882	102,171	48,808	9,143	23,104	16,561 [6]
1977 [3]	1,088,757	44,726	170,162	126,321	106,248	54,992	61,761	346,565 [5]	115,407	143,202	41,263	7,222	27,638	6,403
1982	1,261,698	41,231	167,749	169,164	115,481	54,421	67,215	406,753	138,222	204,963	75,713	10,596	43,071	22,046
1987	1,626,017	46,793	185,443	251,900	151,218	65,532	99,480	441,705	151,737	232,885	88,445	14,735	59,123	14,587
1992	1,825,435	48,619	197,101	306,551	171,970	71,576	114,846	466,421	165,757	292,162	109,280	21,283	69,713	18,284
1997	2,077,666	55,912	204,455	397,264	191,907	66,607	127,901							

1 Includes tax-exempt firms.

2 Includes taxable nongovernmental establishments and organizations that were reported separately.

3 Covers only dental laboratories.

4 Excludes hospitals.

5 In 1977, includes elementary and secondary schools except those operated by religious organizations; excludes elementary and secondary schools thereafter.

6 Includes arrangement of transportation.

Sources

For sources for the years 1954 through 1992, see sources for those years as reported in Table Dh70–83. Data for 1997 come from the *1997 Economic Census, Core Business Statistics Series: Comparative Statistics,* available on the Census Bureau Internet site.

Documentation

See text for Table Dh70–83. The difference between the data reported in Table Dh70–83 and those reported here is that Table Dh70–83 data include establishments operated by self-employed proprietors, perhaps with the assistance of unpaid family labor, while those reported here include only those establishments employing hired labor.

TABLE Dh98–108 Establishments in selected service industries: 1977–1997 [Tax-exempt establishments with payroll]

Contributed by Thomas Weiss

	Total	Hotels, rooming houses, camps, and other lodging places	Amusements, recreation, and related services	Health services	Legal services	Engineering, accounting, research, management, and related services	All other services				
							Total	Selected educational services [1]	Social services	Selected membership organizations	Services not elsewhere classified
	Dh98	Dh99	Dh100	Dh101	Dh102	Dh103	Dh104	Dh105	Dh106	Dh107	Dh108
Year	Number	Number	Number	Number	Number	Number	Number	Number	Number	Number	Number
1977	165,614	3,922	9,390	12,307	1,101	446	138,448	9,160	40,983	82,666 [3]	5,639
1982	147,061	4,148	10,526	10,010 [2]	1,302	959	120,116	4,263	52,571	61,336	1,946
1987	175,829	3,533	12,045	19,106	1,439	3,979	135,727	4,728	63,002	67,997	0
1992	208,911	3,198	14,435	23,651	1,725	5,507	160,395	6,283	81,726	72,386	0
1997	224,980	— [4]	20,476	33,146	2,532	— [4]	— [4]	5,801	92,156	65,075	0

TABLE Dh109–122 Receipts in selected service industries: 1933–1992[1] [Establishments with or without payroll and subject to federal income tax]

Contributed by Thomas Weiss

Year	Total	Hotels, rooming houses, camps, and other lodging places	Personal services	Miscellaneous business services	Automotive repair services and parking	Miscellaneous repair services	Amusements, recreation, and related services	Health services	Legal services	Engineering, accounting, research, management, and related services	All other services			
											Total	Selected educational services [2]	Social services	Services not elsewhere classified
	Dh109	Dh110	Dh111	Dh112	Dh113	Dh114	Dh115	Dh116	Dh117	Dh118	Dh119	Dh120	Dh121	Dh122
	Million dollars	Million dollars	Million dollars	Million dollars	Million dollars	Million dollars	Million dollars	Million dollars	Million dollars	Million dollars	Million dollars	Million dollars	Million dollars	Million dollars
1933	2,761	524	811	671 [8]	65	149	520	—	—	—	21	—	—	21 [11]
1935	4,302 [6]	744	1,507	608 [8]	538	148	699	—	—	—	58	—	—	58 [12]
1939 [3]	4,872	900 [7]	1,822	487	441	224	998 [9]	—	—	—	—	—	—	—
1948	13,619	2,368 [7]	4,440	1,630	1,561	947	2,673 [9]	—	—	—	—	—	—	—
1948	13,326	2,366 [7]	4,421	1,629	1,558	941	2,411	—	—	—	—	—	—	—
1954	23,508	3,027	5,773	6,317	2,223	1,796	4,372	—	—	—	—	—	—	—
1958	32,376	3,888	7,394	8,710	3,853	2,262	5,082	—	—	1,187	—	—	—	—
1963	44,586	5,049	9,163	12,789	5,444	3,022	6,715	—	—	2,404	—	—	—	—
1967	60,542	7,039	11,750	19,509	7,028	3,827	8,303	—	—	3,087	—	—	—	—
1972 [4]	112,970	10,638	14,050	33,545	12,081	5,855	13,445	573 [10]	10,938	11,845	—	—	—	—
1977 [5]	255,726	18,755	18,433	46,158	21,576	11,028	21,143	59,130	18,696	31,070	9,737	2,278	5,211	2,248 [13]
1987	868,343	53,630	43,247	188,856	58,278	24,597	64,524	196,211	72,115	141,228	25,656	6,102	9,561	9,993
1992	1,345,146	71,038	59,598	309,439	78,512	35,237	103,556	321,650	108,443	215,624	42,050	9,158	18,201	14,691

[1] The table contains two sets of data for 1948 to reflect changes in the establishments that were included. The first is more compatible with earlier years, and the second, with later years. See text for Table Dh70–83.

[2] Includes Puerto Rico.

[3] Includes tax-exempt.

[4] Includes taxable nongovernmental establishments and organizations that were reported separately.

[5] Excludes custom industries reported in the original census, but includes data reported separately in the census for hotels and tourist camps, and establishments providing amusement services.

[6] Includes only hotels and tourist courts.

[7] Includes dental laboratories, which in 1972 and later are included in series Dh116. Also includes warehousing.

[8] Includes federal, state, and local amusement, sales, and excise taxes collected directly from the customer and paid directly to the taxing agency.

[9] Covers only dental laboratories.

[10] In 1977, includes elementary and secondary schools except those operated by religious organizations; excludes elementary and secondary schools thereafter.

[11] Includes only "other miscellaneous service" reported in the original census. Most establishments originally classified in miscellaneous services have been included with other industries.

[12] Includes landscape gardening, livery stables, and other miscellaneous services.

[13] Includes arrangement of transportation.

Sources

See Table Dh70–83 for sources.

Documentation

See the text for Table Dh70–83.

Establishments have been classified according to their *principal* kinds of business. Many service establishments derive some receipts from sales of merchandise; conversely, many establishments

(continued)

---

[1] In 1977, includes elementary and secondary schools except those operated by religious organizations; excludes elementary and secondary schools thereafter.

[2] Excludes hospitals.

[3] Includes labor unions and political organizations.

[4] Available data not comparable to data for earlier years.

Sources

For sources for the years 1977 through 1992, see sources for those years as reported in Table Dh70–83. Data for 1997 come from the *1997 Economic Census, Core Business Statistics Series: Comparative Statistics*, available on the Census Bureau Internet site.

Documentation

In the 1972 and later censuses, establishments whose income was tax-exempt under section 501 of the Internal Revenue Service code were included in the published data. In 1972, taxable and tax-exempt establishments were not distinguished and so could not be included here. In 1977 and later censuses, data for tax-exempt firms were reported separately from those subject to tax. It is not known how many tax-exempt firms may be included in the census counts obtained by field survey in the earlier years, but it is likely few, if any. In earlier years, the industries in which most tax-exempt firms were found (such as education or health services) were not included in the scope of the census.

See also the text for Table Dh70–83.

TABLE Dh109–122 Receipts in selected service industries: 1933–1992 [Establishments with or without payroll and subject to federal income tax]
Continued

primarily engaged in the sale of goods, and hence included in retail trade, obtain some income from services. Receipts reported in each case represent total receipts of establishments comprising the classification, not receipts for the particular service indicated.

Receipts include receipts from customers or clients for services rendered, from the use of facilities, and from merchandise sold during the year, whether or not payment was received in that year. Beginning with the 1987 Census, health practitioners and legal, architectural, engineering, and surveying services, which report on a cash basis, are an exception, reporting payments received in the year regardless of when services were rendered. Receipts are net after deductions for refunds and allowances for merchandise returned by customers. Receipts exclude income from other sources such as contributions, gifts, grants, dividends, interest, investments, or sale and rental of real estate. Excise taxes on gasoline, liquor, tobacco, and the like that are paid by the manufacturer or wholesaler and passed on in the cost of goods purchased by the service establishments are included. Local and state sales taxes, or federal excise taxes collected by the service establishment directly from the customer and paid directly to the taxing agency, were included in 1954 through 1972; they have been excluded since 1977 and in the censuses before 1954, except as indicated.

The table does not contain data for 1982. Data for nonemployers and the combined data for all establishments are not available because many businesses were miscoded into miscellaneous categories rather than specific kinds of business.

TABLE Dh123–136 Receipts in selected service industries: 1954–1997 [Establishments with payroll and subject to federal income tax]
Contributed by Thomas Weiss

Year	Total	Hotels, rooming houses, camps, and other lodging places	Personal services	Business services	Automotive repair services and parking	Miscellaneous repair services	Amusements, recreation, and related services	Health services	Legal services	Engineering, accounting, research, management, and related services	All other services			
											Total	Selected educational services	Social services	Services not elsewhere classified
	Dh123	Dh124	Dh125	Dh126	Dh127	Dh128	Dh129	Dh130	Dh131	Dh132	Dh133	Dh134 [1]	Dh135	Dh136
	Million dollars	Million dollars	Million dollars	Million dollars	Million dollars	Million dollars	Million dollars	Million dollars	Million dollars	Million dollars	Million dollars	Million dollars	Million dollars	Million dollars
1954	21,263	2,846	4,935	6,014	1,895	1,357	4,218	—	—	—	—	—	—	—
1958	29,001	3,609	6,200	8,369	3,309	1,581	4,808	—	—	1,125	—	—	—	—
1963	41,023	4,816	7,877	12,415	4,858	2,305	6,455	—	—	2,296	—	—	—	—
1967	55,527	6,738	10,003	17,299	6,368	3,089	7,901	519 [4]	—	4,128	—	—	—	—
1972 [2]	103,237	10,197	11,692	30,306	10,929	4,836	12,660		9,724	12,892	—	—	—	—
1977 [3]	232,342	18,127	15,297	40,634	19,659	9,558	19,756	55,508	17,147	30,690	5,965	1,806	2,038	2,121 [6]
1982	426,982	33,215	22,980	85,492	30,695	14,133	33,115	95,610 [5]	34,325	70,285	7,132	2,400	3,636	1,096
1987	772,194	51,865	31,491	166,322	51,423	20,838	57,638	182,289	66,998	127,344	15,988	4,882	7,330	3,775
1992	1,202,613	69,204	43,280	274,892	70,033	30,732	92,915	299,067	101,114	192,819	28,558	7,242	13,349	7,966
1997	1,843,792	97,892	53,132	528,516	99,575	37,303	150,176	398,505	122,617	302,005	107,203	12,440	18,894	75,869

1 Includes tax-exempt firms for which expenses are reported rather than receipts.

2 Includes taxable nongovernmental establishments and organizations that were reported separately.

3 Covers only dental laboratories.

4 Excludes hospitals.

5 In 1977, includes elementary and secondary schools except those operated by religious organizations; excludes elementary and secondary schools thereafter.

6 Includes arrangement of transportation.

Sources

For sources for the years 1954 through 1992, see sources for those years as reported in Table Dh70–83. Data for 1997 come from the *1997 Economic Census, Core Business Statistics Series: Comparative Statistics*, available on the Census Bureau Internet site.

Documentation

See the text for Tables Dh70–83 and Dh98–122.

TABLE Dh137–147   Revenue in selected service industries: 1977–1992   [Tax-exempt establishments with payroll]

Contributed by Thomas Weiss

		Hotels, rooming houses, camps, and other lodging places	Amusements, recreation, and related services	Health services	Legal services	Engineering, accounting, research, management, and related services			All other services			
	Total						Total	Selected educational services [1]	Social services	Selected membership organizations	Services not elsewhere classified
	Dh137	Dh138	Dh139	Dh140	Dh141	Dh142	Dh143	Dh144	Dh145	Dh146	Dh147
Year	Million dollars	Million dollars	Million dollars	Million dollars	Million dollars	Million dollars	Million dollars	Million dollars	Million dollars	Million dollars	Million dollars
1977 [2]	85,372	303	2,743	43,961	259	1,214	36,892	14,026	8,295	12,068 [4]	2,503
1982	61,488	543	6,665	10,882 [3]	442	2,604	40,352	1,198	19,959	16,290	2,905
1987	267,490	604	8,455	191,795	665	9,206	56,765	1,753	31,552	23,459	—
1992	446,256	807	12,191	324,414	1,161	14,782	92,901	2,973	53,672	36,256	—

[1] In 1977, includes elementary and secondary schools except those operated by religious organizations; excludes elementary and secondary schools thereafter.

[2] Expenses were reported, not revenue.

[3] Excludes hospitals.

[4] Includes labor unions and political organizations.

Revenue for tax-exempt firms includes revenue from customers or clients for services rendered and from merchandise sold during the year, whether or not payment was received in that year. Revenues also include income from other sources such as contributions, gifts, grants, dividends, interest, rents, royalties, dues from members and affiliates, and receipts from fund-raising activities. Receipts from taxable business activities of firms exempt from federal income tax are also included. Revenue does not include sales, admissions, or other taxes collected by the organization from the customer and paid directly to the taxing agency.

Sources

See sources for the years 1977 through 1992 as reported in Table Dh70–83.

Documentation

See the text for Tables Dh70–83 and Dh98–108.

TABLE Dh148–161   Payroll in selected service industries: 1933–1997   [Establishments subject to federal income tax]

Contributed by Thomas Weiss

		Hotels, rooming houses, camps, and other lodging places	Personal services	Business services	Automotive repair services and parking	Miscellaneous repair services	Amusements, recreation, and related services	Health services	Legal services	Engineering, accounting, research, management, and related services	All other services			
	Total										Total	Selected educational services [1]	Social services	Services not elsewhere classified
	Dh148	Dh149	Dh150	Dh151	Dh152	Dh153	Dh154	Dh155	Dh156	Dh157	Dh158	Dh159	Dh160	Dh161
Year	Million dollars	Million dollars	Million dollars	Million dollars	Million dollars	Million dollars	Million dollars	Million dollars	Million dollars	Million dollars	Million dollars	Million dollars	Million dollars	Million dollars
1933	702	147	183	198 [8]	18	30	117	—	—	—	7	—	—	7
1935	859 [6]	194	228	213 [8]	44	25	132	—	—	—	22	—	—	22
1939 [2]	1,384	247 [7]	572	199	98	43	225	—	—	—	—	—	—	—
1948 [3]	4,164	683 [7]	1,583	701	355	232	610	—	—	—	—	—	—	—
1954	6,534	896	1,960	1,483	488	455	1,252	—	—	—	—	—	—	—
1958	9,006	1,145	2,447	2,077	854	501	1,481	—	—	502	—	—	—	—
1963	12,192	1,439	2,933	3,035	1,135	744	1,837	—	—	1,068	—	—	—	—
1967	17,524	1,990	3,923	4,739	1,468	1,046	2,398	—	—	1,960	—	—	—	—
1972 [4]	33,424	2,971	4,325	9,827	2,553	1,586	3,848	218 [9]	2,318	5,997	—	—	—	—
1977 [5]	83,821	5,190	5,478	16,862	4,456	2,992	5,272	22,745	5,217	13,199	2,411	706	866	839 [11]
1982	158,625	9,289	7,956	33,665	7,057	4,559	8,805	42,632 [10]	12,554	29,401	2,706	822	1,477	407
1987	289,807	14,452	10,853	66,456	11,690	6,416	15,474	78,820	26,078	53,508	6,061	1,657	2,971	1,433
1992	452,697	19,633	14,379	109,299	15,550	9,695	25,357	129,093	39,328	79,344	11,019	2,457	5,466	3,095
1997	688,873	26,558	17,796	211,485	22,643	11,366	38,506	173,455	47,410	121,659	17,995	4,198	8,026	5,771

Notes appear on next page

(continued)

TABLE Dh148–161   Payroll in selected service industries: 1933–1997   [Establishments subject to federal income tax]   Continued

1 In 1977, includes elementary and secondary schools except those operated by religious organizations; excludes elementary and secondary schools thereafter.
2 Includes Puerto Rico.
3 Comparable with earlier years. For a discussion of changes in the establishments that were included, see the text for Table Dh70-83.
4 Includes tax-exempt firms.
5 Includes taxable nongovernmental establishments and organizations that were reported separately.
6 Excludes custom industries reported in the original census, but includes data reported separately in the census for hotels and tourist camps, and establishments providing amusement services.
7 Includes only hotels and tourist courts.
8 Includes dental laboratories and warehousing.
9 Covers only dental laboratories.
10 Excludes hospitals.
11 Includes arrangement of transportation.

Sources

For data through 1992, see sources reported in Table Dh70-83. Data for 1997 come from the *1997 Economic Census, Core Business Statistics Series: Comparative Statistics*, available on the Census Bureau Internet site.

Documentation

Annual payroll includes all forms of compensation such as salaries, wages, commissions, bonuses, vacation allowances, sick-leave pay, and the value of payments in kind (for example, meals and lodging) paid during the year to all employees. Beginning with the 1967 Census, tips and gratuities received by employees and reported to employers are included. Amounts paid to officers and executives of corporations are included, but profit or other compensation of proprietors or partners in unincorporated business is excluded. The payroll figure is before deductions for Social Security, income tax, insurance, union dues, and so forth.

See also the text for Table Dh70-83.

TABLE Dh162–172   Payroll in selected service industries: 1977–1997   [Tax-exempt establishments]
Contributed by Thomas Weiss

	Total	Hotels, rooming houses, camps, and other lodging places	Amusements, recreation, and related services	Health services	Legal services	Engineering, accounting, research, management, and related services	Total	Selected educational services [1]	All other services		
									Social services	Selected membership organizations	Services not elsewhere classified
Year	Dh162	Dh163	Dh164	Dh165	Dh166	Dh167	Dh168	Dh169	Dh170	Dh171	Dh172
	Million dollars	Million dollars	Million dollars	Million dollars	Million dollars	Million dollars	Million dollars	Million dollars	Million dollars	Million dollars	Million dollars
1977	41,691	79	1,207	22,849	153	595	16,808	7,224	4,124	4,407 [3]	1,052
1982	23,142	155	2,105	5,197 [2]	252	1,251	14,182	487	7,521	5,196	977
1987	117,976	156	3,068	91,588	373	3,460	19,332	615	11,617	7,100	—
1992	186,672	204	4,618	145,500	629	5,220	30,501	981	19,331	10,188	—
1997	224,131	— [4]	6,749	172,584	797	— [4]	— [4]	— [5]	25,999	— [4]	— [4]

1 In 1977, includes elementary and secondary schools except those operated by religious organizations; excludes elementary and secondary schools thereafter.
2 Excludes hospitals.
3 Includes labor unions and political organizations.
4 Available data not comparable with data for earlier years.
5 Data withheld to avoid disclosure of sources.

Sources

For sources for the years 1977 through 1992, see sources for those years as reported in Table Dh70-83. Data for 1997 come from the *1997 Economic Census, Core Business Statistics Series: Comparative Statistics*, available on the Census Bureau Internet site.

Documentation

See the text for Tables Dh70-83 and Dh148-161.

The 1997 figures for series Dh163, Dh167, Dh168, Dh171, and Dh172 as reported in the *1997 Economic Census, Core Business Statistics Series: Comparative Statistics* are not comparable with earlier data.

The 1997 figures for series Dh169 were withheld to avoid disclosure of reporting sources.

TABLE Dh173–186   Employees in selected service industries: 1933–1997[1]   [Establishments subject to federal income tax]

Contributed by Thomas Weiss

Year	Total	Hotels, rooming houses, camps, and other lodging places	Personal services	Business services	Automotive repair services and parking	Miscellaneous repair services	Amusements, recreation, and related services	Health services	Legal services	Engineering, accounting, research, management, and related services	All other services			
											Total	Selected educational services[2]	Social services	Services not elsewhere classified
	Dh173	Dh174	Dh175	Dh176	Dh177	Dh178	Dh179	Dh180	Dh181	Dh182	Dh183	Dh184	Dh185	Dh186
	Number	Number	Number	Number	Number	Number	Number	Number	Number	Number	Number	Number	Number	Number
1933	859,986 [7]	238,297	254,336	184,585 [10]	20,343	36,580	118,159	—	—	—	7,686	—	—	7,686
1935	988,474 [8]	296,977	299,191	174,526 [10]	45,075	28,840	126,383	—	—	—	17,482	—	—	17,482
1939 [3]	1,497,112	337,154 [9]	653,072	143,491	96,424	43,284	223,687	—	—	—	—	—	—	—
1948 [4]	2,099,692	415,265 [9]	851,024	242,982	153,576	94,914	341,931	—	—	—	—	—	—	—
1954	2,361,821	420,352	820,281	404,755	157,437	125,685	433,311	—	—	—	—	—	—	—
1958	2,889,183	502,265	919,476	523,665	255,891	133,596	461,429	—	—	92,861	—	—	—	—
1963	3,261,541	526,050	954,179	711,223	288,025	161,533	456,889	—	—	163,642	—	—	—	—
1967	3,841,174	616,841	1,029,763	976,460	316,209	179,111	486,840	—	—	235,950	—	—	—	—
1972 [5]	5,305,181	726,577	976,709	1,550,995	392,498	206,842	653,047	29,827 [11]	267,656	530,857	—	—	—	—
1977 [6]	8,924,920	918,685	910,445	2,014,843	483,191	279,147	660,321	2,023,623	392,048	886,598	356,019	94,819	177,449	83,751 [13]
1982	11,106,144	1,102,097	970,472	2,699,068	553,245	299,662	803,776	2,433,061 [12]	569,359	1,364,251	311,153	68,477	222,048	20,628
1987	16,054,738	1,410,792	1,104,961	4,414,436	785,290	345,836	1,094,396	3,592,482	807,599	1,969,187	529,759	109,432	357,343	62,984
1992	19,290,352	1,489,058	1,217,634	5,542,417	863,856	428,103	1,381,853	4,452,539	923,617	2,271,478	719,797	133,260	505,401	81,136
1997	25,278,399	1,685,659	1,302,628	8,652,013	1,094,161	418,722	1,809,602	5,519,988	956,074	2,931,608	907,944	188,606	662,201	57,137

[1] Data represent the sum of the average number of full- and part-time employees (1933–1935); the number of employees as of the workweek ending nearest November 15 (1939–1963); and thereafter employment for the pay period including March 12.

[2] In 1977, includes elementary and secondary schools except those operated by religious organizations; excludes elementary and secondary schools thereafter.

[3] Includes Puerto Rico.

[4] Comparable with earlier years. For a discussion of changes in the establishments that were included, see the text for Table Dh70–83.

[5] Includes tax-exempt firms.

[6] Includes taxable nongovernmental establishments and organizations that were reported separately.

[7] Data in the original source have been revised.

[8] Excludes custom industries reported in the original census, but includes data reported separately in the census for hotels and tourist camps, and establishments providing amusement services.

[9] Includes only hotels and tourist courts.

[10] Includes dental laboratories and warehousing.

[11] Covers only dental laboratories.

[12] Excludes hospitals.

[13] Includes arrangement of transportation.

Sources

See Table Dh70–83 for sources for 1933 through 1992. Data for 1997 come from the *1997 Economic Census, Core Business Statistics Series: Comparative Statistics*, available on the Census Bureau Internet site.

Documentation

See the text for Table Dh70–83.

TABLE Dh187–197 Employees in selected service industries: 1977–1997 [Tax-exempt establishments]

Contributed by Thomas Weiss

	Total	Hotels, rooming houses, camps, and other lodging places	Amusements, recreation, and related services	Health services	Legal services	Engineering, accounting, research, management, and related services	All other services				
							Total	Selected educational services [1]	Social services	Selected membership organizations	Services not elsewhere classified
	Dh187	Dh188	Dh189	Dh190	Dh191	Dh192	Dh193	Dh194	Dh195	Dh196	Dh197
Year	Number	Number	Number	Number	Number	Number	Number	Number	Number	Number	Number
1977	4,950,531	16,381	154,179	2,431,015	12,440	35,634	2,300,882	932,343	676,473	600,062 [3]	92,004
1982	2,280,054	22,820	213,621	476,224 [2]	14,462	53,550	1,499,377	52,704	903,878	492,923	49,872
1987	6,736,670	16,957	236,105	4,648,435	16,191	121,300	1,697,682	49,278	1,109,536	538,868	—
1992	8,108,944	17,634	285,453	5,564,611	21,341	147,406	2,072,499	63,036	1,406,936	602,527	—
1997	8,563,199	— [4]	386,312	5,814,763	23,316	— [4]	— [4]	— [4]	1,586,186	— [4]	— [4]

[1] In 1977, includes elementary and secondary schools except those operated by religious organizations; excludes elementary and secondary schools thereafter.

[2] Excludes hospitals.

[3] Includes labor unions and political organizations.

[4] Available data not comparable with data from earlier years.

Documentation

See the text for Table Dh70–83.

The data represent employment for the pay period including March 12.

Sources

See Table Dh70–83 for sources for 1933 through 1992. Data for 1997 come from the *1997 Economic Census, Core Business Statistics Series: Comparative Statistics*, available on the Census Bureau Internet site.

TABLE Dh198–214 Employees of service firms, by industry division: 1958–1999

Contributed by Susan B. Carter

| | Total | Hotels, rooming houses, camps, and other lodging places | Personal services | Business services | Automotive repair services and parking | Miscellaneous repair services | Motion pictures | Amusement and recreation services | Health services | Legal services | Educational services | Social services | Museums, art galleries, and botanical and zoological gardens | Membership organizations | Engineering, accounting, research, management, and related services | Agricultural services | Services not elsewhere classified |
| | Dh198 | Dh199 | Dh200 | Dh201 | Dh202 | Dh203 | Dh204 | Dh205 | Dh206 | Dh207 | Dh208 | Dh209 | Dh210 | Dh211 | Dh212 | Dh213 | Dh214 |
Year	Thousand	Thousand	Thousand	Thousand	Thousand	Thousand	Thousand	Thousand	Thousand	Thousand	Thousand	Thousand	Thousand	Thousand	Thousand	Thousand	Thousand
1958	6,765	—	796	555	—	—	—	—	1,365	—	572	—	—	—	—	—	—
1959	7,087	—	809	608	—	—	—	—	1,454	—	598	—	—	—	—	—	—
1960	7,378	—	812	656	—	—	—	—	1,548	—	616	—	—	—	—	—	—
1961	7,619	—	816	693	—	—	—	—	1,640	—	637	—	—	—	—	—	—
1962	7,982	—	831	754	—	—	—	—	1,739	—	679	—	—	—	—	—	—
1963	8,277	—	845	814	—	—	—	—	1,837	—	708	—	—	—	—	—	—
1964	8,660	—	866	881	—	149	—	—	1,963	—	743	—	—	—	—	—	—
1965	9,036	—	895	955	—	155	—	—	2,080	—	772	—	—	—	—	—	—
1966	9,498	—	924	1,052	—	161	—	—	2,204	—	804	—	—	—	—	—	—
1967	10,045	—	933	1,145	—	168	—	—	2,434	—	842	—	—	—	—	—	—
1968	10,567	—	937	1,210	—	174	—	—	2,639	—	891	—	—	—	—	—	—
1969	11,169	—	931	1,329	—	184	—	—	2,862	—	930	—	—	—	—	—	—

Year	Total Dh198	Hotels, rooming houses, camps, and other lodging places Dh199	Personal services Dh200	Business services Dh201	Automotive repair services and parking Dh202	Miscellaneous repair services Dh203	Motion pictures Dh204	Amusement and recreation services Dh205	Health services Dh206	Legal services Dh207	Educational services Dh208	Social services Dh209	Museums, art galleries, and botanical and zoological gardens Dh210	Membership organizations Dh211	Engineering, accounting, research, management, and related services Dh212	Agricultural services Dh213	Services not elsewhere classified Dh214
	Thousand	Thousand	Thousand	Thousand	Thousand	Thousand	Thousand	Thousand	Thousand	Thousand	Thousand	Thousand	Thousand	Thousand	Thousand	Thousand	Thousand
1970	11,548	—	898	1,397	—	189	—	—	3,053	—	940	—	—	—	—	—	—
1971	11,797	—	848	1,402	—	193	—	—	3,239	—	948	—	—	—	—	—	—
1972	12,276	813	828	1,491	399	199	—	—	3,412	271	958	553	—	1,403	—	—	—
1973	12,857	854	823	1,610	422	205	—	—	3,641	296	975	552	—	1,410	—	—	—
1974	13,441	878	807	1,686	430	217	—	—	3,887	326	990	625	—	1,438	—	—	—
1975	13,892	898	782	1,697	439	218	—	—	4,134	341	1,001	690	—	1,452	—	—	—
1976	14,551	929	790	1,806	466	227	—	—	4,350	364	1,013	763	—	1,487	—	184	—
1977	15,302	956	806	1,958	498	241	—	—	4,584	394	1,031	855	—	1,495	—	197	—
1978	16,252	988	827	2,181	549	261	—	—	4,792	427	1,062	991	—	1,502	—	217	—
1979	17,112	1,060	821	2,410	575	282	—	—	4,993	460	1,090	1,081	—	1,516	—	234	—
1980	17,890	1,076	818	2,564	571	289	—	—	5,278	498	1,138	1,134	—	1,539	—	246	—
1981	18,615	1,119	828	2,700	574	293	—	—	5,562	532	1,179	1,149	—	1,527	—	258	—
1982	19,021	1,133	844	2,722	589	287	—	—	5,811	565	1,199	1,149	—	1,526	—	267	—
1983	19,664	1,172	869	2,948	619	287	—	—	5,986	602	1,225	1,188	—	1,510	—	287	—
1984	20,746	1,263	918	3,353	682	310	—	—	6,118	645	1,270	1,222	—	1,504	—	328	—
1985	21,927	1,331	957	3,679	730	319	—	—	6,293	692	1,359	1,325	—	1,517	—	361	—
1986	22,957	1,378	991	3,957	762	322	—	—	6,528	747	1,421	1,406	—	1,536	—	389	—
1987	24,110	1,464	1,027	4,278	794	321	—	—	6,794	801	1,449	1,454	—	1,614	—	411	—
1988	25,504	1,540	1,056	4,638	834	350	341	977	7,105	845	1,567	1,552	58	1,740	2,230	447	32
1989	26,907	1,596	1,086	4,941	884	374	375	1,033	7,463	880	1,647	1,644	62	1,836	2,389	465	36
1990	27,934	1,631	1,104	5,139	914	374	408	1,076	7,814	908	1,661	1,734	66	1,946	2,478	490	39
1991	28,336	1,589	1,112	5,086	882	341	411	1,122	8,183	912	1,710	1,845	69	1,982	2,433	487	40
1992	29,052	1,576	1,116	5,315	881	347	401	1,188	8,490	914	1,678	1,959	73	1,973	2,471	490	41
1993	30,197	1,596	1,137	5,735	925	349	412	1,258	8,756	924	1,711	2,070	76	2,035	2,521	519	41
1994	31,579	1,631	1,140	6,281	968	338	441	1,334	8,992	924	1,850	2,200	79	2,082	2,579	564	41
1995	33,117	1,668	1,163	6,812	1,020	359	488	1,417	9,230	921	1,965	2,336	80	2,146	2,731	582	45
1996	34,454	1,715	1,180	7,293	1,080	372	525	1,476	9,478	928	2,030	2,413	85	2,201	2,844	627	47
1997	36,040	1,746	1,186	7,988	1,120	374	550	1,552	9,703	944	2,104	2,518	90	2,277	2,988	678	49
1998	37,533	1,789	1,201	8,618	1,145	376	576	1,594	9,853	971	2,178	2,646	94	2,372	3,139	708	51
1999	39,027	1,848	1,233	9,267	1,184	377	610	1,660	9,989	997	2,276	2,800	98	2,425	3,254	766	52

Source

U.S. Bureau of Labor Statistics Internet site, National Current Employment Statistics.

Documentation

See the text for Table Ba840–848.

Series correspond to Standard Industrial Classification (SIC) codes as follows: series Dh199, code 70; series Dh200, code 72; series Dh201, code 73; series Dh202, code 75; series Dh203, code 76; series Dh204, code 78; series Dh205, code 79; series Dh206, code 80; series Dh207, code 81; series Dh208, code 82; series Dh209, code 83; series Dh210, code 84; series Dh211, code 86; series Dh212, code 87; series Dh213, code 07; series Dh214, code 89. See the Introduction to Part D for a discussion of SIC codes.

Series Dh198. Equals series Ba847 and is the sum of series Dh199–214 plus the total in unclassifiable firms, SIC 99 (not shown).

TABLE Dh215–218   Employees of transportation service firms: 1988–1999

Contributed by Richard Sutch

Year	Total	Passenger transportation arrangement firms		Freight transportation arrangement firms
		Total	Travel agencies	
	Dh215	Dh216	Dh217	Dh218
	Thousand	Thousand	Thousand	Thousand
1988	302	171	134	107
1989	319	180	142	114
1990	336	188	150	120
1991	336	182	146	125
1992	338	184	147	124
1993	352	187	150	130
1994	378	198	159	142
1995	401	205	163	155
1996	418	212	168	162
1997	441	217	171	175
1998	454	219	173	181
1999	463	221	174	187

Source

U.S. Bureau of Labor Statistics Internet site, National Current Employment Statistics.

Documentation

See the text for Table Ba840–848.

Series Dh215. Standard Industrial Classification (SIC) code 49. See the Introduction to Part D for a discussion of SIC codes. The series equals series Df79 and is the sum of series Dh216 and Dh218, and a residual se-

ries (not shown) consisting of the rental of railroad cars (SIC code 474) and packing and crating and other transportation services (SIC 478).

Series Dh216. Includes travel agencies, tour operators, and the arrangement of carpools and vanpools.

Series Dh217. Does not include self-employed travel agents.

Series Dh218. SIC code 473.

UTILITIES

Susan B. Carter

TABLE Dh219–223   Indexes of output and productivity in electric and gas utilities: 1899–1942

Contributed by Susan B. Carter

Year	Electric light and power Dh219 Index 1929 = 100	Manufactured gas Dh220 Index 1929 = 100	Natural gas Dh221 Index 1929 = 100	Combined electric and gas (weighted indexes) Output Dh222 Index 1929 = 100	Output per worker Dh223 Index 1929 = 100
1899	—	15.6	17.0	—	—
1900	—	—	18.1	—	—
1901	—	23.7	20.2	—	—
1902	3.6	21.6	21.5	7.6	38.0
1903	—	24.7	22.8	—	—
1904	—	26.6	23.7	—	—
1905	—	27.0	26.8	—	—
1906	—	30.2	29.7	—	—
1907	7.5	33.3	32.5	13.4	47.0
1908	—	35.9	33.2	—	—
1909	—	38.0	38.1	—	—
1910	—	39.6	41.2	—	—
1911	—	42.2	41.9	—	—
1912	13.0	47.3	46.1	21.0	51.8
1913	13.6	50.0	46.2	21.9	—
1914	15.2	52.8	48.4	23.9	—
1915	16.6	53.1	51.6	25.3	—
1916	21.1	58.8	59.5	30.4	—
1917	24.5	65.8	63.7	34.6	69.9
1918	31.4	66.0	60.5	39.6	—
1919	36.0	71.2	60.8	44.1	82.4
1920	39.3	71.6	65.4	47.1	—
1921	36.3	69.2	52.3	43.3	—
1922	41.2	73.2	59.4	48.3	—
1923	50.0	79.5	64.7	56.4	—
1924	54.9	82.0	68.2	60.8	—
1925	63.5	83.6	69.2	67.4	84.9
1926	73.5	92.2	76.4	77.0	—
1927	81.7	97.3	80.2	84.2	—
1928	89.5	98.2	87.3	90.7	—
1929	100.0	100.0	100.0	100.0	100.0
1930	103.5	100.6	102.3	102.9	102.5
1931	101.9	98.0	99.9	101.0	107.5
1932	92.7	90.6	94.9	92.6	111.4
1933	92.8	85.4	92.1	91.5	113.3
1934	99.2	85.9	100.0	97.1	115.0
1935	108.2	85.9	107.9	104.5	121.3
1936	123.4	81.0	124.8	116.4	126.3
1937	136.3	81.9	132.1	126.3	130.7
1938	136.8	81.9	126.0	125.9	134.4
1939	151.6	83.6	135.8	137.5	147.0
1940	167.7	88.5	150.0	151.4	157.2
1941	190.5	90.9	159.9	168.4	172.6
1942	212.0	96.8	178.4	186.6	209.0

Source

Jacob Martin Gould, *Output and Productivity in the Electric and Gas Utilities, 1899–1942* (National Bureau of Economic Research, 1946), Table 40, p. 131; Table 42, p. 136.

Documentation

Gould's estimates of output and productivity in the electric light and power and in the manufactured and natural gas utilities were constructed as part of a larger project, organized by the National Bureau of Economic Research in the 1930s and 1940s, to investigate the historical growth of the American economy. Using concepts developed by Simon Kuznets that formed the basis for official data collection efforts beginning in the 1930s, Gould and his colleagues made estimates of what output and productivity would have been in the period prior to the collection of official statistics if the modern definitions had been in use during that earlier time. Gould based his estimates on a variety of sources, including census and industry data. Gould's estimates are conceptually similar to, though not identical to, the official output and productivity estimates that begin in 1947 and are shown in Tables Cg336–340 and Dh226–229.

TABLE Dh224–225 Gross domestic product originating in the electric, gas, and sanitary service industries: 1947–2000[1]

Contributed by Susan B. Carter

Year	Current dollars Dh224 Million dollars	Constant dollars Dh225 Million chained 1996 dollars	Year	Current dollars Dh224 Million dollars	Constant dollars Dh225 Million chained 1996 dollars	Year	Current dollars Dh224 Million dollars	Constant dollars Dh225 Million chained 1996 dollars
1947	3,840	—	1970	24,444	—	1990	165,435	189,988
1948	4,351	—	1971	27,606	—	1991	176,492	195,903
1949	4,953	—	1972	30,433	—	1992	181,160	193,198
1950	5,467	—	1973	32,743	—	1993	188,711	193,315
1951	6,283	—	1974	34,320	—	1994	197,443	196,693
1952	6,873	—	1975	42,703	—	1995	206,874	207,208
1953	7,534	—	1976	47,763	—	1996	208,253	208,253
1954	8,374	—	1977	53,172	—	1997	205,891	202,022
1955	9,018	—	1978	58,766	—	1998	204,844	193,743
1956	9,809	—	1979	60,787	—	1999	215,558	212,912
1957	10,516	—	1980	70,492	—	2000	230,030	217,913
1958	11,269	—	1981	83,230	—			
1959	12,452	—	1982	96,981	—			
1960	13,617	—	1983	105,754	—			
1961	14,341	—	1984	119,520	—			
1962	15,198	—	1985	126,926	—			
1963	15,919	—	1986	130,784	—			
1964	16,880	—	1987	141,774	—			
1965	17,614	—	1987	141,853	165,834			
1966	18,737	—	1988	146,985	171,252			
1967	19,766	—	1989	158,985	182,525			
1968	21,500	—						
1969	23,131	—						

[1] Figures through the first set of values for 1987 are on a 1972 Standard Industrial Classification (SIC) basis; beginning with the second set of values for 1987, figures are on a 1987 SIC basis. See the Introduction to Part D for a discussion of SIC codes.

Source

U.S. Bureau of Economic Analysis (BEA), Industry Economics Division. Downloaded from the BEA Internet site, July 8, 2002.

Documentation

Gross domestic product (GDP) by industry is the contribution of each private industry and government to GDP. An industry's GDP, often referred to as its value added, is equal to its gross output (sales or receipts and other operating income, commodity taxes, and inventory change) minus its intermediate inputs (consumption of goods and services purchased from other industries or imported). These estimates provide the industrial distribution of GDP as shown in the national income and product accounts (NIPA). They incorporate the NIPA annual revision released in August 2001, as well as newly available source data.

TABLE Dh226–229   Index of industrial production – all utilities: 1939–2001

Contributed by Susan B. Carter

	All industries	Utilities				All industries	Utilities		
		All	Electrical	Gas			All	Electrical	Gas
	Dh226	Dh227	Dh228	Dh229		Dh226	Dh227	Dh228	Dh229
Year	Index 1992 = 100	Index 1992 = 100	Index 1992 = 100	Index 1992 = 100	Year	Index 1992 = 100	Index 1992 = 100	Index 1992 = 100	Index 1992 = 100
1939	11.9	5.7	—	—	1970	58.7	66.5	51.0	130.5
1940	13.8	6.2	—	—	1971	59.5	69.6	53.9	134.4
1941	17.4	7.0	—	—	1972	65.3	74.1	58.4	136.5
1942	20.0	7.9	—	—	1973	70.6	77.0	62.3	134.4
1943	24.2	8.7	—	—	1974	69.6	76.1	61.9	131.2
1944	26.1	9.3	—	—	1975	63.4	76.8	64.0	125.2
1945	22.4	9.5	—	—	1976	69.3	79.9	67.1	127.1
1946	19.3	9.9	—	—	1977	74.9	82.0	70.7	120.7
1947	21.7	10.6	7.5	24.8	1978	79.3	84.4	73.3	122.6
1948	22.6	11.9	8.4	27.5	1979	82.0	86.8	75.2	126.6
1949	21.4	12.7	9.0	29.2	1980	79.7	87.3	76.4	124.8
1950	24.7	14.4	10.1	34.2	1981	81.0	85.0	78.0	109.3
1951	26.8	16.5	11.4	39.4	1982	76.7	82.3	76.7	102.4
1952	27.8	17.9	12.5	42.4	1983	79.5	83.7	79.2	100.4
1953	30.2	19.4	13.7	44.5	1984	86.6	86.7	82.4	102.6
1954	28.6	20.8	14.6	49.0	1985	88.0	88.8	84.6	104.3
1955	32.2	23.3	16.4	53.6	1986	89.0	86.4	86.2	87.0
1956	33.6	25.6	18.0	58.9	1987	93.2	89.4	89.4	89.0
1957	34.1	27.3	19.2	62.9	1988	97.4	93.9	93.6	94.5
1958	31.9	28.6	20.1	66.2	1989	99.1	97.1	96.8	98.1
1959	35.7	31.4	22.2	72.0	1990	98.9	98.3	99.2	94.4
1960	36.5	33.6	23.7	76.8	1991	97.0	100.4	101.2	97.3
1961	36.7	35.5	25.2	79.4	1992	100.0	100.0	100.0	100.0
1962	39.8	38.2	27.2	84.8	1993	103.4	104.0	103.9	104.3
1963	42.1	40.8	29.3	88.6	1994	109.1	105.4	105.6	104.6
1964	45.0	44.3	31.8	96.4	1995	114.4	109.1	109.6	107.2
1965	49.5	47.1	34.2	98.1	1996	119.6	112.7	112.8	112.3
1966	53.8	50.7	37.0	103.4	1997	127.9	112.7	113.2	110.5
1967	55.0	53.2	40.0	110.0	1998	134.5	114.3	117.1	102.9
1968	58.1	57.5	43.6	116.8	1999	139.4	117.3	120.0	106.2
1969	60.7	62.6	47.7	124.9	2000	145.7	120.7	123.3	109.9
					2001	140.1	119.9	123.1	107.5

Source
Board of Governors, Federal Reserve Board (FRB). Downloaded from the FRB Internet site, June 11, 2002.

Documentation
The industrial production (IP) index measures the real output of the manufacturing, mining, and electric and gas utilities industries; the reference period for the index is 1992. For the period since 1997, the total IP index has been constructed from 276 individual series based on the 1987 Standard Industrial Classification (SIC) codes. (See the Introduction to Part D for a discussion of SIC codes.) These individual series are classified in two ways: (1) market groups and (2) industry groups. Market groups consist of products and materials. Total products are the aggregate of final products, such as consumer goods and equipment, and intermediate products (which are inputs to nonindustrial sectors). Materials are inputs in the manufacture of products. Major industry groups include two-digit SIC industries and aggregates of these industries – for example, durable and nondurable manufacturing, mining, and utilities. This table presents the industrial production index for all utilities (SIC code 49) and for electrical utilities (SIC code 491 and part of SIC 493) and gas utilities (SIC code 492 and part of SIC 493) separately. For a fuller description of the computation of the industrial production index, see the *Federal Reserve Bulletin*, February 1997 and March 2001 issues.

TABLE Dh230–235   Employees of utility firms, by industry division: 1947–1999

Contributed by Susan B. Carter

	Total	Electric	Gas	Water and steam	Combination	Sanitary services
	Dh230	Dh231	Dh232	Dh233	Dh234	Dh235
Year	Thousand	Thousand	Thousand	Thousand	Thousand	Thousand
1947	—	213	—	—	—	—
1948	—	227	—	—	—	—
1949	—	236	—	—	—	—
1950	—	239	118	—	169	—
1951	—	240	124	—	169	—
1952	—	244	128	—	171	—
1953	—	248	133	—	171	—
1954	—	249	139	—	169	—
1955	—	249	141	—	173	—
1956	—	250	145	—	176	—
1957	—	258	149	—	175	—
1958	—	254	152	—	175	—
1959	—	254	154	—	174	—
1960	—	253	155	—	175	—
1961	—	249	156	—	175	—
1962	—	247	155	—	173	—
1963	—	246	153	—	174	—
1964	617	249	153	—	174	—
1965	625	253	154	—	177	—
1966	631	257	153	—	178	—
1967	644	261	156	—	180	—
1968	656	269	158	—	180	—
1969	672	277	160	—	184	—
1970	692	290	161	—	186	—
1971	698	300	159	—	183	—
1972	713	312	161	20	183	37
1973	731	321	163	21	188	38
1974	744	330	163	21	190	39
1975	733	323	162	22	187	40
1976	735	327	159	22	185	41
1977	747	336	159	22	188	42
1978	778	354	164	23	193	45
1979	807	374	167	23	195	49
1980	829	391	168	23	197	50
1981	854	406	174	24	199	52
1982	877	422	177	24	202	53
1983	886	433	174	24	201	55
1984	902	441	173	25	202	60
1985	916	448	175	26	203	65
1986	921	449	167	26	207	72
1987	925	449	165	27	202	82
1988	931	452	164	28	194	93
1989	938	448	163	29	192	105
1990	957	454	165	30	193	115
1991	961	448	166	31	194	123
1992	954	440	163	30	193	128
1993	944	428	161	31	189	136
1994	928	417	159	31	178	144
1995	911	404	154	32	167	154
1996	884	383	147	32	163	158
1997	866	369	141	33	161	162
1998	861	364	137	34	159	167
1999	865	360	133	37	156	179

Source

U.S. Bureau of Labor Statistics Internet site, National Current Employment Statistics.

Documentation

See the text for Table Ba840–848.

Series Dh230. Standard Industrial Classification (SIC) code 49. See the Introduction to Part D for a discussion of SIC codes. The series is the sum of series Dh231–235. Note that government-owned utilities are not included.

Series Dh231. SIC code 491.

Series Dh232. SIC code 492.

Series Dh233. This series was calculated as a residual by subtracting series Dh231–232 and Dh234–235 from series Dh230. This sector includes water supply (SIC code 494), steam and air conditioning supply (SIC code 496), and irrigation systems (SIC code 497).

Series Dh234. SIC code 493.

Series Dh235. SIC code 495.

TABLE Dh236–239   City waterworks, by type of ownership: 1800–1924

Contributed by Susan B. Carter

	Waterworks		Cities with waterworks	
	Number	Percentage publicly owned	Number	Percentage
	Dh236	Dh237	Dh238	Dh239
Year	Number	Percent	Number	Percent
1800	17	5.9	33	51
1810	27	18.5	46	59
1820	31	16.1	61	51
1830	45	20.0	90	50
1840	65	35.4	131	50
1850	84	39.3	236	36
1860	137	41.7	392	35
1870	244	47.5	663	37
1880	599	48.9	939	64
1890	1,879	42.9	—	—
1896	3,197 [1]	52.9	—	—
1924	9,850	70.0	—	—

[1] Includes seventeen undocumented systems.

Source

Martin V. Melosi, *The Sanitary City: Urban Infrastructure in America from Colonial Times to the Present* (Johns Hopkins University Press, 2000), Table 1.1, p. 29; Table 1.3, p. 36; Table 4.1, p. 74; Table 4.3, p. 74; Table 7.1, p. 120.

Documentation

The data cover cities with population of at least 2,500.

TABLE Dh240–241   Waterworks at the close of 1800 – year built and year changed to public ownership: 1652–1891

Contributed by Susan B. Carter

	Year built	Year changed to public ownership
	Dh240	Dh241
Location	—	Number
Boston, Mass.	1652	1848
Bethlehem, Pa.	1761	1871
Providence, R.I.	1772	1871
Geneva, N.Y.	1787	1896
Plymouth, Mass.	1796	1855
Salem, Mass.	1796	1873
Hartford, Conn.	1797	1854
Portsmouth, N.H.	1798	1891
Worcester, Mass.	1798	1852
Albany, N.Y.	1798 or 1799	1851
Peabody, Mass.	1799	1873
New York, N.Y.	1799	1843
Morristown, N.J.	1799	— [1]
Lynchburg, Va.	1799	1828
Winchester, Va.	Before 1800	— [2]
Newark, N.J.	1800	1860

[1] Still private.

[2] Always public.

Source

M. N. Baker, "Water-Works," in Edward W. Bemis, editor, *Municipal Monopolies* (Thomas Y. Crowell, 1899), Table 1, p. 15.

Documentation

Baker compiled these statistics from various issues of *The Manual of American Water-Works,* published by the Engineering Publishing Company, New York, and edited by Mr. Baker.

TABLE Dh242–251   Los Angeles water supply and consumption, by source and use: 1920–1950

Contributed by Susan B. Carter

	Supply							Consumption		
	Local			Owens Wells and Mono Basin			Municipal Water District	Total	Commercial and industrial	Irrigation
	Total	Los Angeles River basin	Wells on coastal plain	Total	Mono Basin	Owens Wells				
	Dh242	Dh243	Dh244	Dh245	Dh246	Dh247	Dh248	Dh249	Dh250	Dh251
Year	Cubic feet per second	Cubic feet per second	Cubic feet per second	Cubic feet per second	Cubic feet per second	Cubic feet per second	Cubic feet per second	Cubic feet per second	Cubic feet per second	Cubic feet per second
1920	68	55.8	12.2	283.3	—	19.2	—	232	126	106
1921	78	63.7	14.3	262.5	—	19.0	—	243	139	104
1922	86	73.7	12.3	346.2	—	14.4	—	252	152	100
1923	93	74.3	18.7	269.3	—	16.1	—	287	169	118
1924	98	78.6	19.5	198.8	—	26.4	—	267	189	78
1925	122	97.1	24.9	269.9	—	46.2	—	280	203	77
1926	107	87.3	19.7	250.6	—	43.2	—	303	214	89
1927	93	73.2	19.8	367.3	—	13.3	—	295	217	78
1928	101	84.8	16.2	296.9	—	52.3	—	337	231	106
1929	116	94.8	21.2	268.3	—	73.2	—	378	255	123
1930	97	73.7	23.3	347.0	—	171.3	—	356 [1]	249	108
1931	102	83.1	19.0	342.4	—	197.3	—	348	243	105
1932	65	52.9	12.1	346.7	—	4.0	—	320	234	85
1933	66	54.0	12.0	341.0	—	8.5	—	314	227	87
1934	102	90.8	11.2	326.0	—	56.1	—	308	220	88
1935	80	70.0	10.0	357.0	—	9.1	—	310	223	87
1936	80	78.5	1.5	306.0	3.6	7.1	—	359	249	110
1937	72	69.9	2.2	376.0	—	12.1	—	356	260	96
1938	67	66.1	1.0	398.0	8.6	23.3	—	347	265	82
1939	64	63.9	0.1	360.0	9.5	25.6	—	350	269	81
1940	71	71.2	0.0	341.0	26.8	13.8	—	347	272	75
1941	61	60.5	0.5	353.0	70.8	10.5	0.5	334 [1]	272	63
1942	64	63.3	0.7	442.0	33.0	15.7	0.7	388	293	95
1943	79	77.3	1.7	409.0	36.8	14.3	0.1	424	326	98
1944	85	82.6	2.4	398.0	92.8	14.7	0.5	440	352	88
1945	118	111.4	6.6	401.0	25.6	15.5	2.3	482	381	101
1946	112	105.1	6.9	458.0	19.0	16.3	9.8	495	398	97
1947	123	114.5	8.5	457.0	61.2	15.4	13.0	527	423	104
1948	119	112.4	6.6	440.0	138.5	12.1	24.2	542	434	108
1949	118	110.6	7.4	438.0	132.0	9.7	16.3	541	442	99
1950	119	105.3	13.7	441.0	148.0	9.0	8.1	532 [1]	444	87

[1] Error in addition in the original.

Source

Vincent Ostrom, *Water and Politics: A Study of Water Policies and Administration in the Development of Los Angeles* (Haynes Foundation, 1953), Table 1, p. 23.

Documentation

All figures are annual mean flow in cubic feet per second. One cubic foot per second flow is a measure of the rate of flow required for one cubic foot of water (7.48 gallons) to pass a given point each second.

Series Dh242. Includes wells on the coastal plain.

Series Dh243. Includes all water above the Narrows.

Series Dh245. Refers to the supply as measured at Cartago station near intake of Haiwee reservoir.

Series Dh246. Measured at the east portal of Mono tunnels.

Series Dh247. The Owens Valley well water production including normal artesian flow.

Series Dh248. Refers to the Colorado River water supplied by the water district to meet special demands.

TABLE Dh252–267 Developed and undeveloped water power, by geographic division: 1920–1970
Contributed by Susan B. Carter

	Developed water power								Undeveloped water power							
	United States	New England	Middle Atlantic	North Central	South Atlantic	South Central	Mountain	Pacific	United States	New England	Middle Atlantic	North Central	South Atlantic	South Central	Mountain	Pacific
	Dh252	Dh253	Dh254	Dh255	Dh256	Dh257	Dh258	Dh259	Dh260	Dh261	Dh262	Dh263	Dh264	Dh265	Dh266	Dh267
Year	Thousand kilowatts	Thousand kilowatts	Thousand kilowatts	Thousand kilowatts	Thousand kilowatts	Thousand kilowatts	Thousand kilowatts	Thousand kilowatts	Thousand kilowatts	Thousand kilowatts	Thousand kilowatts	Thousand kilowatts	Thousand kilowatts	Thousand kilowatts	Thousand kilowatts	Thousand kilowatts
1920	3,704	291	662	629	589	174	487	872	—	—	—	—	—	—	—	—
1921	3,902	314	741	632	536	187	494	998	—	—	—	—	—	—	—	—
1922	4,128	337	757	664	534	195	509	1,132	—	—	—	—	—	—	—	—
1923	4,507	350	766	705	659	248	520	1,259	—	—	—	—	—	—	—	—
1924	5,024	381	905	741	760	280	544	1,413	—	—	—	—	—	—	—	—
1925	5,922	415	1,027	813	878	482	570	1,738	—	—	—	—	—	—	—	—
1926	6,405	474	1,115	835	945	618	592	1,826	—	—	—	—	—	—	—	—
1927	6,802	496	1,151	842	963	700	673	1,977	—	—	—	—	—	—	—	—
1928	7,702	557	1,205	862	1,346	840	679	2,213	—	—	—	—	—	—	—	—
1929	7,831	554	1,218	879	1,351	841	680	2,308	—	—	—	—	—	—	—	—
1930	8,585	753	1,290	881	1,603	882	784	2,391	—	—	—	—	—	—	—	—
1931	9,091	762	1,338	1,056	1,635	945	788	2,566	—	—	—	—	—	—	—	—
1932	9,258	768	1,457	1,058	1,634	954	788	2,599	—	—	—	—	—	—	—	—
1933	9,334	768	1,489	1,065	1,680	916	791	2,624	—	—	—	—	—	—	—	—
1934	9,345	767	1,489	1,071	1,680	924	782	2,631	—	—	—	—	—	—	—	—
1935	9,399	804	1,517	1,071	1,678	924	792	2,613	—	—	—	—	—	—	—	—
1936	10,037	832	1,533	1,111	1,709	1,079	1,152	2,622	—	—	—	—	—	—	—	—
1937	10,176	832	1,550	1,147	1,710	1,114	1,160	2,662	—	—	—	—	—	—	—	—
1938	10,657	824	1,561	1,204	1,728	1,223	1,381	2,736	—	—	—	—	—	—	—	—
1939	11,004	833	1,563	1,204	1,803	1,279	1,581	2,741	—	—	—	—	—	—	—	—
1940	11,224	858	1,588	1,219	1,882	1,397	1,612	2,668	—	—	—	—	—	—	—	—
1941	11,817	855	1,589	1,280	1,912	1,588	1,692	2,902	—	—	—	—	—	—	—	—
1942	12,842	891	1,596	1,294	2,084	1,936	1,784	3,256	—	—	—	—	—	—	—	—
1943	13,884	893	1,587	1,314	2,085	2,151	1,924	3,929	—	—	—	—	—	—	—	—
1944	14,586	894	1,593	1,303	2,086	2,393	2,003	4,314	—	—	—	—	—	—	—	—
1945	14,912	895	1,591	1,300	2,222	2,592	2,002	4,309	—	—	—	—	—	—	—	—
1946	15,828	1,167	1,669	1,434	2,663	2,618	2,008	4,269	—	—	—	—	—	—	—	—
1947	15,956	1,165	1,662	1,435	2,662	2,618	2,026	4,387	77,130	3,348	5,175	7,309	7,462	7,446	17,755	28,635
1948	16,635	1,192	1,668	1,437	2,662	2,731	2,056	4,888	—	—	—	—	—	—	—	—
1949	17,622	1,202	1,687	1,469	2,687	2,993	2,202	5,423	88,070	3,249	6,503	8,192	8,184	8,374	23,426	30,142
1950	18,675	1,239	1,678	1,530	2,767	3,195	2,286	5,980	87,604	3,250	6,572	8,119	8,151	8,304	23,440	29,768
1951	19,871	1,254	1,677	1,559	2,785	3,547	2,627	6,421	86,174	3,239	6,598	8,117	8,255	8,168	22,089	29,708
1952	21,416	1,262	1,707	1,564	2,834	4,054	3,181	6,814	87,992	3,233	6,415	9,480	8,677	7,784	21,895	30,508
1953	23,055	1,282	1,704	1,620	3,212	4,374	3,438	7,425	85,562	3,122	6,449	9,412	8,281	7,464	21,618	29,216
1954	24,238	1,335	1,750	1,783	3,423	4,418	3,629	7,901	82,804	2,990	6,395	9,211	8,058	7,035	20,105	29,010
1955	25,742	1,385	1,789	1,905	3,536	4,524	3,706	8,898	86,895	2,586	8,023	9,335	7,943	7,213	20,668	31,127
1956	26,386	1,388	1,479	2,243	3,611	4,524	3,701	9,440	90,102	2,728	8,012	9,000	7,586	7,721	21,333	33,722
1957	27,761	1,528	1,600	2,277	3,732	4,674	3,785	10,165	90,242	2,728	8,382	8,967	7,645	7,480	21,245	33,795
1958	30,089	1,521	2,113	2,276	3,732	4,697	4,157	11,592	93,783	2,708	7,869	9,323	8,393	7,854	23,141	34,495
1959	31,794	1,513	2,475	2,369	3,788	4,697	4,511	12,439	114,287	2,858	7,465	9,591	8,388	8,499	23,243	54,243

(continued)

TABLE Dh252–267   Developed and undeveloped water power, by geographic division: 1920–1970   Continued

	Developed water power								Undeveloped water power							
	United States	New England	Middle Atlantic	North Central	South Atlantic	South Central	Mountain	Pacific	United States	New England	Middle Atlantic	North Central	South Atlantic	South Central	Mountain	Pacific
	Dh252	Dh253	Dh254	Dh255	Dh256	Dh257	Dh258	Dh259	Dh260	Dh261	Dh262	Dh263	Dh264	Dh265	Dh266	Dh267
Year	Thousand kilowatts	Thousand kilowatts	Thousand kilowatts	Thousand kilowatts	Thousand kilowatts	Thousand kilowatts	Thousand kilowatts	Thousand kilowatts	Thousand kilowatts	Thousand kilowatts	Thousand kilowatts	Thousand kilowatts	Thousand kilowatts	Thousand kilowatts	Thousand kilowatts	Thousand kilowatts
1960	33,180	1,520	2,472	2,522	3,773	4,695	4,621	13,578	114,200	2,900	7,600	9,400	8,400	8,500	23,600	53,800
1961	36,193	1,518	3,852	2,618	3,795	4,897	4,821	14,694	112,700	2,800	5,700	9,000	8,900	8,100	24,100	54,100
1962	37,835	1,508	4,239	2,942	4,099	5,164	4,773	15,110	116,100	3,100	5,200	6,800	11,000	8,200	26,900	54,900
1963	40,230	1,497	4,218	3,197	4,600	5,419	4,845	16,454	115,734	3,128	5,179	5,866	9,903	8,023	26,652	56,983
1964	41,827	1,491	4,237	3,302	4,635	5,851	5,218	17,093	117,793	3,125	4,950	5,691	10,017	7,549	27,253	59,208
1965	42,948	1,488	4,237	3,460	4,700	6,088	5,551	17,424	124,087	3,240	4,986	5,497	9,977	7,343	26,530	66,514
1966	44,288	1,487	4,246	3,625	5,184	6,298	6,022	17,426	130,640	3,312	4,332	5,312	9,812	7,031	26,822	74,019
1967	45,826	1,491	4,247	3,703	5,349	6,530	6,083	18,425	130,444	3,304	4,514	5,619	9,468	7,008	26,891	73,640
1968	48,741	1,487	4,243	3,665	5,255	6,874	6,095	21,122	129,709	3,302	4,545	5,892	9,716	7,063	26,923	72,268
1969	50,248	1,495	4,231	3,718	5,271	6,951	6,097	22,481	128,900	3,300	4,545	5,892	9,708	7,054	26,923	71,478
1970	51,952	1,473	4,264	3,664	5,265	7,170	6,202	23,914	127,990	3,330	4,455	5,966	9,556	7,089	26,655	70,939

Source

U.S. Federal Power Commission, *Electric Power Statistics*, annual summaries and related monthly reports.

Documentation

The data for developed water power are based on monthly reports submitted to the Federal Power Commission (FPC) by the electric utilities. FPC practice is to record generating unit capacity as that given by the manufacturer on the nameplate that is placed on each generator. Included are plants of the privately owned electric utilities, municipal utilities, federal projects, public utility power districts, and state power projects. For 1946–1970, the data also include hydroelectric plants of industrial establishments based on their monthly reports to the FPC.

The data for undeveloped water power resources are based on river basin studies of the years shown. The discovery of new sites, changing criteria, and reevaluation of needs, as well as the development of sites and a host of other reasons, may cause the listed amounts of undeveloped water resources to increase or decrease from year to year. Therefore, the yearly changes in the figures for undeveloped water power resources cannot be directly related to the amounts of developed water power resources.

See Table Ap-G in Appendix 2 regarding the composition of census regions and divisions.

Series Dh252–259. Nameplate capacity of existing installations. Includes capacity at electric utility and industrial plants, but excludes pumped storage capacity. Prior to 1946, includes capacity at electric utility plants only.

TABLE Dh268–273   Dams and hydroelectric power plants owned by the federal government and the Tennessee Valley Authority – number and capacity: 1904–1999

Contributed by Susan B. Carter and Dustin Chambers

	Federal government hydroelectric power plants, by year put into service				Tennessee Valley Authority dams, by year completed	
	Operated by the U.S. Bureau of Reclamation		Operated by other entities			
	Number	Capacity	Number	Capacity	Number	Capacity
	Dh268	Dh269	Dh270	Dh271	Dh272	Dh273
Year	Number	Megawatts	Number	Megawatts	Number	Megawatts
1904	—	—	1	10.3	—	—
1909	1	27.7	—	—	—	—
1911	—	—	2	2.8	1	22.0
1912	1	1.5	1	1.4	1	12.0
1913	—	—	1	1.1	1	18.0
1914	—	—	1	3.0	—	—
1916	—	—	—	—	1	37.0
1924	—	—	—	—	1	629.0
1925	2	11.8	—	—	—	—
1926	—	—	1	57.9	—	—
1927	1	6.4	1	129.6	—	—
1930	—	—	1	10.4	1	13.0
1933	—	—	1	3.0	—	—
1936	1	2,078.8	—	—	2	495.3
1937	—	—	1	0.3	—	—
1938	—	—	—	—	1	228.0
1939	1	51.8	—	—	1	116.0
1940	1	27.9	—	—	2	245.0
1941	1	6,809.0	2	29.4	1	75.0
1942	1	120.0	—	—	3	212.0
1943	1	26.0	—	—	3	198.1
1944	1	629.0	—	—	3	1,000,241.0
1948	1	5.0	—	—	1	68.0
1949	1	117.0	—	—	—	—
1950	3	121.0	—	—	1	46.0
1951	2	248.1	—	—	—	—
1952	2	443.0	—	—	1	83.0
1953	1	50.0	1	10.0	1	32.0
1954	2	132.7	—	—	—	—
1955	3	253.6	—	—	—	—
1956	1	12.0	—	—	—	—
1957	1	176.6	—	—	—	—
1958	3	55.9	2	5.9	—	—
1959	1	4.5	—	—	—	—
1960	2	84.1	—	—	—	—
1961	—	—	1	33.0	—	—
1962	2	13.5	—	—	—	—
1963	2	306.4	—	—	1	75.0
1964	4	1,616.4	—	—	—	—
1966	1	250.0	1	7.2	—	—
1967	2	111.6	—	—	1	96.0
1968	2	212.0	—	—	—	—
1970	1	173.3	—	—	1	37.0
1973	—	—	1	36.0	—	—
1978	1	28.0	—	—	1	16,000.0
1979	1	300.0	—	—	1	140.0
1981	1	200.0	—	—	—	—
1982	—	—	1	4.0	—	—
1983	—	—	1	3.9	—	—
1984	—	—	1	6.0	—	—

(continued)

TABLE Dh268–273   Dams and hydroelectric power plants owned by the federal government and the Tennessee Valley Authority – number and capacity: 1904–1999 *Continued*

Year	Federal government hydroelectric power plants, by year put into service				Tennessee Valley Authority dams, by year completed	
	Operated by the U.S. Bureau of Reclamation		Operated by other entities			
	Number	Capacity	Number	Capacity	Number	Capacity
	Dh268	Dh269	Dh270	Dh271	Dh272	Dh273
	Number	Megawatts	Number	Megawatts	Number	Megawatts
1987	—	—	1	4.6	—	—
1988	1	3.7	—	—	—	—
1989	—	—	1	0.1	—	—
1992	3	22.3	—	—	—	—
1993	1	11.5	1	36.0	—	—
1994	1	4.5	—	—	—	—
1995	—	—	1	0.3	—	—
1999	—	—	1	1.9	—	—

Source

Computed from detailed listings by power plant and dam from the U.S. Bureau of Reclamation Internet site. Downloaded August 15, 2002.

Documentation

Series Dh268–271

The U.S. Bureau of Reclamation was established with the Reclamation Act of 1902, which authorized the Secretary of the Interior to undertake certain water resource development activities in the Western United States. Under the 1902 Act, Congress authorized construction of federally financed water projects to reclaim arid lands west of the 100th meridian by providing water for irrigation. In turn, the Secretary of the Interior established the Reclamation Service within the U.S. Geological Survey to carry out these activities. The Reclamation Service was renamed the Bureau of Reclamation in 1923.

The Bureau of Reclamation has statutory responsibilities for comprehensive planning, development, and management of multipurpose water projects in the seventeen Western states. Historically, the primary purposes of reclamation projects have been irrigation; flood control; and water for domestic, industrial, and municipal use. Hydroelectric power generally has been a secondary purpose. Although not a primary objective, power is considered for inclusion in multipurpose federal reclamation projects when it is in the national interest, economically justified, feasible by engineering and environmental standards, and capable of repaying its share of the federal investment in accordance with the reclamation law.

Electric power generated at reclamation dam sites was initially used to process materials as well as to construct the engineering works. The plants powered sawmills, concrete plants, cableways, hoists, giant shovels, and draglines; they also powered lights that facilitated round-the-clock operations at some dam sites. Following completion of the construction, the energy powered pumps that provided drainage or conveyed water to lands unreachable by gravity canal systems. Under provisions of the Town Sites and Power Development Act of 1906, surplus power was sold to municipal and farm consumers and helped meet local industrial demands for electricity. The hydroelectric features were included in project construction costs repaid by the water and power users under provisions of the 1902 Reclamation Act.

Series Dh270–271. These facilities are those whose ownership is with the federal government, but whose operations, maintenance, and marketing are performed by other entities.

Series Dh272–273

The Tennessee Valley Authority (TVA) is an independent U.S. government corporate agency, created in 1933 by an act of Congress. The mandate of the agency is to stimulate the economic development of the region. From its beginnings, the TVA was viewed as an ambitious experiment in governmental initiative. President Franklin Delano Roosevelt, who proposed the project during the depths of the Great Depression of the 1930s, envisioned the TVA as a totally different kind of governmental agency. He asked Congress to create "a corporation clothed with the power of government but possessed of the flexibility and initiative of a private enterprise."

The TVA took over administration of federal dams built prior to its establishment and oversaw the construction and administration of its own new projects.

The series here cover both previously built dams that were incorporated under the TVA umbrella and the new dams that were built under TVA auspices.

TABLE Dh274–286 Rural Electrification Administration and Rural Utilities Service – electric program, summary of operations: 1935–2000
Contributed by Dustin Chambers

	Net loans approved		Systems in operation			Borrowers' operations during year				Average monthly consumption per consumer		Total utility plant	Employees
	Borrowers	Amount	Systems	Miles energized	Consumers served	Energy Generated	Purchased	Sold	Revenue	All consumers	Residential consumers		
	Dh274 [1]	Dh275 [1]	Dh276 [2]	Dh277 [2]	Dh278 [2]	Dh279 [3]	Dh280 [3]	Dh281 [3]	Dh282 [3]	Dh283	Dh284	Dh285	Dh286
Year	Number	Million dollars	Number	Thousand	Thousand	Million kilowatt-hours	Million kilowatt-hours	Million kilowatt-hours	Million dollars	Kilowatt-hours	Kilowatt-hours	Million dollars	Number
1935	—	7	2	—	—	—	—	—	—	—	—	—	—
1936	—	44	29	3	8	—	—	—	—	—	—	—	—
1937	—	82	126	17	44	—	—	—	—	—	—	—	—
1938	—	181	350	67	176	—	—	—	—	—	—	—	—
1939	688	268	548	181	436	—	—	—	—	—	—	—	—
1940	791	351	685	268	674	34	402	311	17	—	—	—	—
1941	869	434	773	348	902	83	854	724	35	—	—	—	—
1942	868	460	803	378	1,012	131	1,305	1,151	47	—	—	—	—
1943	873	474	811	390	1,088	199	1,721	1,572	54	—	—	—	—
1944	904	518	826	410	1,217	213	1,974	1,795	63	—	—	—	—
1945	961	667	848	450	1,409	258	2,159	1,951	71	—	—	—	—
1946	1,009	958	869	507	1,684	320	2,497	2,244	87	—	—	—	—
1947	1,029	1,191	911	603	2,046	443	3,379	3,056	111	—	—	—	—
1948	1,044	1,575	952	759	2,518	718	4,514	4,252	145	153	121	—	—
1949	1,066	1,999	995	943	3,040	903	5,879	5,564	188	166	134	—	—
1950	1,076	2,312	1,007	1,089	3,413	1,077	7,270	6,884	229	180	147	—	—
1951	1,076	2,484	1,016	1,179	3,666	1,413	8,828	8,567	270	206	166	—	—
1952	1,081	2,669	1,020	1,245	3,858	1,640	10,351	10,128	306	230	182	2,143	—
1953	1,078	2,778	1,022	1,297	4,025	2,103	11,786	11,804	343	254	201	2,351	—
1954	1,075	2,946	1,024	1,333	4,174	2,721	13,450	13,829	383	285	223	2,542	—
1955	1,077	3,125	1,026	1,362	4,251	3,255	14,996	15,739	420	312	242	2,706	—
1956	1,077	3,343	1,026	1,383	4,362	3,612	17,266	18,197	460	345	263	2,879	—
1957	1,079	3,634	1,030	1,405	4,466	3,291	19,266	19,677	490	364	283	3,059	—
1958	1,081	3,847	1,030	1,424	4,596	3,482	21,500	21,902	525	393	311	3,244	—
1959	1,085	4,011	1,032	1,446	4,722	4,464	24,033	25,071	575	432	334	3,486	—
1960	1,087	4,256	1,038	1,465	4,826	4,922	26,057	27,269	615	466	357	3,697	—
1961	1,091	4,509	1,038	1,483	4,956	5,118	27,754	28,967	651	487	375	3,897	28,084
1962	1,096	4,786	1,042	1,504	5,095	6,043	30,134	31,880	697	526	401	4,104	29,046
1963	1,101	5,073	1,046	1,527	5,238	7,002	33,005	35,357	746	565	425	4,406	29,816
1964	1,105	5,477	1,051	1,547	5,386	8,039	36,907	39,837	802	616	456	4,696	30,799
1965	1,103	5,793	1,052	1,567	5,541	8,834	39,104	42,668	847	654	479	4,979	31,702
1966	1,101	6,145	1,051	1,587	5,653	11,547	42,825	48,439	912	708	515	5,353	32,597
1967	1,101	6,403	1,052	1,606	5,806	13,710	45,400	52,880	977	751	543	5,776	33,457
1968	1,101	6,822	1,052	1,627	5,986	14,509	50,917	58,304	1,060	812	593	6,167	34,563
1969	1,098	7,151	1,049	1,650	6,197	18,073	56,031	66,421	1,168	876	643	6,593	35,771
1970	1,096	7,496	1,050	1,676	6,442	23,814	60,478	76,009	1,309	948	687	7,175	37,013
1971	1,094	7,835	1,048	1,700	6,748	27,760	65,494	84,283	1,482	998	711	7,708	38,197
1972	1,092	8,356	1,047	1,733	7,076	32,290	70,610	92,534	1,681	1,063	754	8,313	39,779
1973	1,091	8,945	1,046	1,767	7,457	32,045	79,235	100,688	1,913	1,120	793	9,043	41,422
1974	1,094	9,674	1,047	1,798	7,768	32,795	84,520	105,691	2,316	1,149	803	10,109	42,908

Notes appear at end of table.

(continued)

TABLE Dh274–286   Rural Electrification Administration and Rural Utilities Service – electric program, summary of operations: 1935–2000 *Continued*

	Net loans approved		Systems in operation			Borrowers' operations during year				Average monthly consumption per consumer			
	Borrowers [1]	Amount [1]	Systems [2]	Miles energized [2]	Consumers served [2]	Energy Generated [3]	Energy Purchased [3]	Sold [3]	Revenue [3]	All consumers	Residential consumers	Total utility plant	Employees
	Dh274	Dh275	Dh276	Dh277	Dh278	Dh279	Dh280	Dh281	Dh282	Dh283	Dh284	Dh285	Dh286
Year	Number	Million dollars	Number	Thousand	Thousand	Million kilowatt-hours	Million kilowatt-hours	Million kilowatt-hours	Million dollars	Kilowatt-hours	Kilowatt-hours	Million dollars	Number
1975	1,095	10,440	1,050	1,828	8,018	33,463	91,875	112,670	2,972	1,191	840	11,845	43,629
1976	1,093	11,181	1,048	1,857	8,312	38,660	100,140	124,004	3,556	1,254	866	14,031	44,655
1977	1,097	12,068	1,051	1,890	8,631	46,015	102,627	131,548	4,212	1,313	910	17,266	46,463
1978	1,101	12,993	1,052	1,918	8,963	52,472	107,477 [4]	141,908	5,017	1,339	937	20,352	48,837
1979	1,098	13,951	1,050	1,950	9,275	60,181	109,061 [4]	150,055	5,770	1,335	919	23,620	50,806
1980	1,099	14,857	1,050	1,979	9,524	69,537	111,232	160,243	6,908	1,361	935	28,444	52,729
1981	1,103	15,635	1,051	2,010	9,844	77,231	111,516	167,688	8,295	1,334	901	34,634	54,486
1982	1,105	16,589	1,055	2,036	10,096	81,568	111,574	172,732	9,692	1,326	905	40,046	55,258
1983	1,106	17,373	1,060	2,058	10,555	93,059	117,966	187,194	11,175	1,317	896	45,067	55,471
1984	1,105	18,098	1,060	2,082	10,836	106,753	125,172	209,064	12,218	1,364	914	48,278	56,327
1985	1,105	18,618	1,059	2,100	11,110	120,373	118,619	215,175	13,076	—	906	51,467	57,109
1986	1,103	19,413	1,057	2,123	11,357	120,832	115,457	215,599	13,502	1,351	920	54,499	57,684
1987	1,103	19,948	1,058	2,142	11,628	137,302	107,963	223,965	13,901	1,358	925	55,454	56,337
1988	1,102	20,566	1,057	2,150	11,798	147,852	111,687	236,468	14,482	1,419	951	54,039	56,651
1989	1,101	21,124	1,056	2,179	12,139	154,165	109,323	239,666	15,092	1,427	952	57,288	57,962
1990	1,098	21,605	1,053	2,198	12,383	156,281	117,819	252,151	15,813	—	961	—	58,674
1991	1,098	22,103	1,053	2,211	12,612	151,132	124,246	252,569	15,631	1,483	984	58,998	58,074
1992	1,097	22,743	1,052	2,230	12,906	154,129	128,722	260,492	16,490	1,458	958	60,670	58,591
1993	1,094	23,518	1,049	2,248	13,170	157,375	144,160	277,205	17,169	1,530	1,021	62,654	58,168
1994	1,095	24,022	—	—	—	—	—	—	—	1,540	1,001	61,273	—
1995	1,093	24,653	—	—	—	—	—	—	—	1,570	1,035	64,655	—
1996	1,089	25,174	—	—	—	—	—	—	—	1,632	1,071	61,395	—
1997	1,079	25,684	—	—	—	—	—	—	—	1,612	1,037	60,771	—
1998	1,072	26,316	—	—	—	—	—	—	—	1,670	1,073	61,721	—
1999	1,066	26,548	—	—	—	—	—	—	—	1,668	1,067	62,684	—
2000	1,063	26,874	—	—	—	—	—	—	—	1,716	1,093	66,353	—

[1] Excludes loans rescinded. Cumulative as of December 31. Prior to 1948, includes amounts not yet under loan contract.

[2] Figures are as of December 31. Includes data at time of repayment of loan for borrowers whose loans have been repaid in full.

[3] Excludes energy sales and revenues of power sold from one Rural Electrification Administration borrower to another, except for 1940–1942, for which such sales and revenues are included.

[4] Excludes energy sales to non-Rural Electrification Administration financed electric utilities for resale.

Sources

U.S. Rural Electrification Administration, *Annual Statistical Report – Rural Electrification Borrowers* (various issues).

Documentation

The Rural Electrification Administration (REA) was established in May 1935 to initiate, formulate, administer, and supervise a program of approved projects with respect to the generation, transmission, and distribution of electric energy in rural areas. Later, the REA was authorized to make loans for a maximum of thirty-five years with interest at 2 percent per annum for the construction or improvement of rural electric systems.

The following definitions are used by REA:

Borrowers: Organizations, mainly cooperatives, to which loans for extending central station electric service in rural areas are made.

Systems: Rural electric distribution, generation, and transmission systems in operation by REA borrowers.

Miles energized: Pole miles of electric distribution and transmission lines in service.

Consumers served: The number of individual customers receiving service by borrowers as of the end of the calendar year.

Energy generated: The kilowatt-hours of energy produced during the calendar year by electricity-generating plants owned by the borrowers of REA loan funds.

Energy purchased: The kilowatt-hours of energy purchased during the calendar year by REA borrowers from all suppliers.

Revenue: Gross revenue received by REA borrowers mainly from the sale of electric energy.

In 1994, the REA was abolished, and its responsibilities were assumed by the Rural Utilities Service (RUS). Although the RUS continues to publish the *Annual Statistical Report – Rural Electrification Borrowers*, several data series have been discontinued.

Series Dh276–282 and Dh286. These series were discontinued in 1994 when the RUS assumed the functions of the REA.

Series Dh284. Includes rural-nonfarm and farm consumers.

TABLE Dh287–292   Average operating and capital costs for sanitation works in selected cities: 1899–1929

Contributed by Louis P. Cain and Thomas Weiss

	Operating costs			Capital acquisition costs		
	Waterworks	Sewer works	Refuse collection and disposal systems	Waterworks	Sewer works	Refuse collection and disposal systems
	Dh287	Dh288	Dh289	Dh290	Dh291	Dh292
Year	Dollars	Dollars	Dollars	Dollars	Dollars	Dollars
1899	466,077	69,634	—	380,371	262,854	—
1900	551,587	106,682	196,503	544,314	402,184	—
1901	593,261	96,705	204,840	411,867	329,323	—
1902	509,819	101,093	143,049	566,090	265,193	—
1903	619,665	101,215	169,724	—	—	—
1904	685,995	138,063	181,242	908,571	585,749	—
1905	650,707	137,120	246,035	747,688	613,676	—
1906	678,287	151,446	182,094	1,019,998	597,895	—
1907	693,363	177,208	226,687	1,519,213	695,522	—
1908	774,145	191,478	237,992	1,472,971	710,554	—
1909	762,352	182,022	247,382	1,840,302	725,353	—
1910	753,505	166,920	245,668	1,979,694	684,011	32,315
1911	797,814	178,706	924,878	2,305,635	694,828	39,699
1912	857,305	195,271	991,405	2,006,491	821,570	40,444
1915	878,513	204,244	1,068,999	1,498,704	1,345,028	61,075
1916	912,182	202,080	1,085,985	1,137,455	1,041,289	40,551
1917	917,344	185,239	1,113,471	1,000,356	913,393	72,853
1918	1,013,156	205,574	1,250,617	900,114	885,454	67,440
1919	1,140,588	226,974	1,426,393	661,741	794,147	94,003
1921	1,681,311	—	—	—	—	—
1923	1,776,091	405,667	953,744	2,216,546	1,716,961	244,459
1924	1,857,920	505,582	983,783	3,114,627	2,036,529	322,375
1925	1,762,345	549,222	1,038,012	2,968,902	2,703,576	200,767
1926	1,849,867	575,685	1,105,042	2,788,278	3,076,917	164,317
1927	2,005,847	710,690	1,093,817	2,718,838	3,670,982	225,342
1928	2,111,000	728,908	1,158,561	2,211,250	4,020,338	179,823
1929	2,005,163	774,010	1,164,722	2,244,465	2,573,771	126,837

Sources

U.S. Bureau of the Census, *Bulletin*, numbers 20, 50, 105, 118, and 126; U.S. Bureau of the Census, *Financial Statistics of Cities Having a Population of over 30,000* (U.S. Government Printing Office, 1909–1934; 1909–1911 issued as *Special Reports*; no issues were published for 1913–1914 and 1920).

Documentation

Annual operating costs include all payments for general expenses. Those data, as well as the data for capital acquisition costs, were published in various census bulletins up to 1903 and in *Financial Statistics of Cities* (U.S. Bureau of the Census) beginning in 1905.

The averages pertain to operations in the twenty-four cities with a 1929 population of 300,000 or more: Baltimore, Milwaukee, Boston, Minneapolis, Buffalo, New Orleans, Chicago, New York, Cincinnati, Newark, Cleveland, Philadelphia, Detroit, Pittsburgh, Indianapolis, Rochester, Jersey City, San Francisco, Kansas City (Missouri), Seattle, Los Angeles, St. Louis, Louisville, and Washington.

Not every city reported a number for every series in every year, so the coverage varies slightly from year to year. There are few direct figures available for 1904. The census volume, *Financial Statistics of Cities,* was not published in 1913, 1914, or 1920. For 1921 and 1922, the information reported for sewerage and refuse was not consistent with that for other years.

Series Dh287 and Dh290. In 1899, there were three cities with private waterworks (Indianapolis, New Orleans, and San Francisco); in 1929, only that of Indianapolis was private.

TABLE Dh293–297   Solid waste generation and disposal per capita: 1960–1996

Contributed by Louis P. Cain and Thomas Weiss

	Total generated	Recovered for use	Discarded after recovery		
			Total	Disposed of by combustion	Discarded to landfill
	Dh293	Dh294	Dh295	Dh296	Dh297
Year	Pounds per day	Pounds per day	Pounds per day	Pounds per day	Pounds per day
1960	2.68	0.17	2.51	0.82	1.69
1970	3.25	0.22	3.04	0.67	2.36
1980	3.66	0.35	3.31	0.33	2.98
1990	4.51	0.74	3.77	0.70	3.07
1992	4.49	0.87	3.62	0.70	2.92
1994	4.51	1.07	3.44	0.68	2.75
1995	4.41	1.15	3.26	0.70	2.56
1996	4.33	1.18	3.15	0.70	2.44

Sources

U.S. Environmental Protection Agency, "Characterization of Municipal Solid Waste in the United States, 1997 Update," Report number EPA 530-R-98-007.

The annual update of this report is available at the Environmental Protection Agency's Internet site.

Documentation

Series Dh294. Recovered for purposes of recycling and composting.

Series Dh297. Includes other unspecified methods of disposal.

Thomas Weiss

TABLE Dh298-308   Personal consumption expenditures for recreational goods: 1909-1963

Contributed by Thomas Weiss

		Books, maps, magazines, newspapers, and sheet music			Nondurable toys, sports supplies, wheel goods, sports and photographic equipment, boats, and pleasure aircraft			Video and audio products, computing equipment, musical instruments, and radio and television repair			
	Recreational goods	Total	Books and maps	Magazines, newspapers, and sheet music	Total	Nondurable toys and sports supplies	Wheel goods, sports and photographic equipment, boats, and pleasure aircraft	Total	Video and audio products, computing equipment, and musical instruments	Radio and television repairs	Flowers, seeds, and potted plants
	Dh298	Dh299 [1]	Dh300	Dh301	Dh302	Dh303	Dh304	Dh305	Dh306	Dh307	Dh308
Year	Million dollars	Million dollars	Million dollars	Million dollars	Million dollars	Million dollars	Million dollars	Million dollars	Million dollars	Million dollars	Million dollars
1909	483	104	—	—	143	—	—	166	—	—	70
1914	566	131	—	—	186	—	—	193	—	—	56
1919	1,383	204	—	—	377	—	—	667	—	—	135
1921	1,144	239	—	—	338	—	—	439	—	—	128
1923	1,538	270	—	—	455	—	—	637	—	—	176
1925	1,650	318	—	—	411	—	—	739	—	—	182
1927	1,715	349	—	—	470	—	—	713	—	—	183
1929	2,661	847	309	538	555	336	219	1,038	1,012	26	221
1930	2,367	776	264	512	453	281	172	948	921	27	190
1931	1,793	732	253	479	425	266	159	502	478	24	134
1932	1,274	581	153	428	317	207	110	287	268	19	89
1933	1,144	571	152	419	274	181	93	209	195	14	90
1934	1,286	606	165	441	318	200	118	246	229	17	116
1935	1,390	639	183	456	352	216	136	269	248	21	130
1936	1,624	698	208	490	413	242	171	354	333	21	159
1937	1,834	761	243	518	479	269	210	408	385	23	186
1938	1,753	735	221	514	478	268	210	364	339	25	176
1939	1,932	780	226	554	513	285	228	448	420	28	191
1940	2,110	823	234	589	560	306	254	526	494	32	201
1941	2,439	891	255	636	676	362	314	643	607	36	229
1942	2,625	994	291	703	710	404	306	680	634	46	241
1943	2,605	1,204	366	838	664	393	271	463	403	60	274
1944	2,822	1,330	450	880	782	459	323	383	311	72	327
1945	3,248	1,485	520	965	953	553	400	432	344	88	378
1946	4,968	1,688	589	1,099	1,633	840	793	1,231	1,116	115	416
1947	5,616	1,774	531	1,243	1,862	907	955	1,538	1,398	140	442
1948	6,063	1,958	584	1,374	2,041	1,076	965	1,624	1,450	174	440
1949	6,415	2,081	627	1,454	2,006	1,170	836	1,877	1,675	202	451
1950	7,593	2,169	674	1,495	2,263	1,394	869	2,704	2,421	283	457
1951	7,992	2,349	776	1,573	2,559	1,662	897	2,589	2,236	353	495
1952	8,442	2,477	788	1,689	2,697	1,708	989	2,742	2,349	393	526
1953	8,957	2,606	830	1,776	2,784	1,694	1,090	3,022	2,588	434	545
1954	9,177	2,631	806	1,825	2,798	1,624	1,174	3,208	2,726	482	540
1955	9,856	2,736	867	1,869	3,189	1,803	1,386	3,385	2,869	516	546
1956	10,420	2,831	951	1,880	3,524	1,951	1,573	3,511	2,938	573	554
1957	10,763	2,956	983	1,973	3,767	2,047	1,720	3,453	2,825	628	587
1958	11,104	3,083	1,022	2,061	3,960	2,115	1,845	3,517	2,836	681	544
1959	12,277	3,269	1,159	2,110	4,344	2,306	2,038	4,065	3,330	735	599
1960	12,874	3,497	1,304	2,193	4,523	2,417	2,106	4,213	3,412	801	641
1961	13,784	3,744	1,396	2,348	4,831	2,702	2,129	4,507	3,668	839	702
1962	14,555	3,938	1,523	2,415	5,061	2,792	2,269	4,817	3,935	882	739
1963	15,952	4,141	1,620	2,521	5,524	2,986	2,538	5,445	4,539	906	842

[1] The values through 1927 represent 42 percent of the estimated expenditures for books, maps, magazines, newspapers, and sheet music; the remaining 58 percent was classified as educational outlays.

Sources

1909-1927: Twentieth Century Fund, unpublished data (prepared for *Survey of Time, Work, and Leisure*). 1929-1963: U.S. Bureau of Economic Analysis (formerly Office of Business Economics), *The National Income and Product Accounts of the United States, 1929-1965*.

Documentation

The Twentieth Century Fund figures are presented here because they have been widely cited in the scholarly literature. Recently, Stanley Lebergott constructed annual estimates of the consumption of recreational as well as other

(continued)

TABLE Dh298–308   Personal consumption expenditures for recreational goods: 1909–1963   *Continued*

goods and services for the period 1900 through 1929. See Stanley Lebergott, *Consumer Expenditures: New Measures and Old Motives* (Princeton University Press, 1996), Table A1. Lebergott's estimates are presented in Table Cd1–77.

The Bureau of Economic Analysis (BEA) produces annual (and monthly) estimates of consumer expenditures on all items, including recreational goods. These are shown in Table Cd153–263 for the period 1929 through 1999, denominated in billions of dollars. Here we provide additional detail for the period 1929 through 1963 by denominating the figures in millions of dollars.

The data represent the market value of purchases of recreational services by individuals and nonprofit institutions. They exclude expenditures for other

items, such as clothing or food and drink, that were made for the purposes of recreation.

Table Dh298–308 presents data on consumption expenditures for recreational goods, and Table Dh309–318 presents data on consumption expenditures for recreational services, with the exceptions noted next.

Series Dh305 and Dh307. Because expenditures for radio and television repairs cannot be separated from expenditures on video and audio products in the years 1909–1927, expenditures for these repair services are included in Table Dh298–308 rather than in Table Dh309–318.

TABLE Dh309–318   Personal consumption expenditures for recreational services: 1909–1963

Contributed by Thomas Weiss

		Admissions				Commercial participant amusements and pari-mutuel net receipts			
									Other
	Recreational services	Spectator amusements	Motion picture theaters	Legitimate theaters and opera and entertainment by nonprofit institutions	Spectator sports	Dues and fees paid to clubs and fraternal organizations	Total	Commercial participant amusements	Pari-mutuel net receipts	recreational goods and services
	Dh309	Dh310	Dh311	Dh312	Dh313	Dh314	Dh315	Dh316	Dh317	Dh318
Year	Million dollars	Million dollars	Million dollars	Million dollars	Million dollars	Million dollars	Million dollars	Million dollars	Million dollars	Million dollars
1909	377	167	—	—	—	121	22	—	—	67
1914	434	191	—	—	—	140	25	—	—	78
1919	806	336	—	—	—	242	55	—	—	173
1921	911	412	301	81	30	242	128	—	—	129
1923	1,082	528	336	146	46	242	148	—	—	164
1925	1,185	588	367	174	47	275	145	—	—	177
1927	1,405	769	526	195	48	288	159	—	—	189
1929	1,670	913	720	127	66	302	215	207	8	240
1930	1,623	892	732	95	65	294	210	203	7	227
1931	1,509	854	719	78	57	277	181	175	6	197
1932	1,168	631	527	57	47	242	136	132	4	159
1933	1,058	573	482	41	50	208	127	121	6	150
1934	1,155	625	518	42	65	199	154	135	19	177
1935	1,240	672	556	44	72	197	167	141	26	204
1936	1,396	759	626	50	83	198	194	165	29	245
1937	1,547	818	676	53	89	203	232	194	38	294
1938	1,488	816	663	58	95	200	208	164	44	264
1939	1,520	821	659	64	98	199	224	183	41	276
1940	1,651	904	735	71	98	203	252	197	55	292
1941	1,800	995	809	79	107	203	275	210	65	327
1942	2,052	1,204	1,022	92	90	205	282	213	69	361
1943	2,356	1,455	1,275	118	62	217	294	215	79	390
1944	2,600	1,563	1,341	142	80	236	372	241	131	429
1945	2,891	1,714	1,450	148	116	281	437	284	153	459
1946	3,571	2,066	1,692	174	200	359	620	379	241	526
1947	3,633	2,003	1,594	187	222	397	659	404	255	574
1948	3,629	1,918	1,506	180	232	435	682	425	257	594
1949	3,595	1,872	1,451	182	239	454	675	428	247	594
1950	3,554	1,781	1,376	183	222	462	687	448	239	624
1951	3,572	1,716	1,310	186	220	477	727	472	255	652
1952	3,660	1,655	1,246	189	220	498	816	489	327	691
1953	3,763	1,605	1,187	197	221	517	886	514	372	755
1954	3,900	1,672	1,228	220	224	539	896	528	368	793
1955	4,222	1,801	1,326	245	230	569	965	584	381	887
1956	4,559	1,899	1,394	268	237	611	1,068	654	414	981
1957	4,570	1,655	1,126	287	242	653	1,176	738	438	1,086
1958	4,713	1,538	992	297	249	692	1,302	848	454	1,181
1959	5,104	1,571	958	344	269	721	1,484	991	493	1,328
1960	5,421	1,606	951	365	290	733	1,678	1,161	517	1,404
1961	5,722	1,625	921	398	306	763	1,835	1,299	536	1,499
1962	5,919	1,646	903	417	326	773	1,930	1,366	564	1,570
1963	6,261	1,692	904	446	342	808	2,069	1,443	626	1,692

TABLE Dh309–318 Personal consumption expenditures for recreational services: 1909–1963 *Continued*

Sources

1909–1927: Twentieth Century Fund, unpublished data (prepared for *Survey of Time, Work, and Leisure*). 1929–1963: U.S. Bureau of Economic Analysis (formerly Office of Business Economics), *The National Income and Product Accounts of the United States, 1929–1965.*

Documentation

See the text for Table Dh298–308.

Series Dh312. Excludes athletics.

Series Dh318. Includes expenditures for both goods and services. For 1909 to 1927, this figure is the residual amount included in the total expenditures for recreation but not reported separately in *Historical Statistics of the United States* (1975).

TABLE Dh319–326 Americans traveling overseas and foreign visitors to the United States: 1820–2000[1]

Contributed by Thomas Weiss

	Ocean-bound tourists		Arrivals and departures of U.S. citizens		U.S. travelers		Foreign visitors and travelers to the United States	
	U.S. tourists abroad	Foreign tourists in the United States	Arrivals	Departures	Overseas	All destinations	Visitors	Travelers
	Dh319 [2]	Dh320 [2]	Dh321	Dh322	Dh323	Dh324	Dh325	Dh326
Year	Thousand	Thousand	Thousand	Thousand	Thousand	Thousand	Thousand	Thousand
1820	2.0	0.2	1.9	—	—	—	—	—
1821	2.6	0.2	2.5	—	—	—	—	—
1822	1.7	0.1	1.6	—	—	—	—	—
1823	2.0	0.1	1.9	—	—	—	—	—
1824	1.8	0.2	1.7	—	—	—	—	—
1825	2.7	0.2	2.7	—	—	—	—	—
1826	3.2	0.2	3.1	—	—	—	—	—
1827	3.0	0.4	2.9	—	—	—	—	—
1828	2.9	0.5	2.8	—	—	—	—	—
1829	2.1	0.5	2.0	—	—	—	—	—
1830	1.6	0.5	1.5	—	—	—	—	—
1831	1.3	0.5	1.2	—	—	—	—	—
1832	1.2	1.2	1.2 [3]	—	—	—	—	—
1833	1.3	1.2	1.3	—	—	—	—	—
1834	2.7	1.3	2.6	—	—	—	—	—
1835	3.4	0.9	3.3	—	—	—	—	—
1836	4.9	1.5	4.7	—	—	—	—	—
1837	5.8	1.6	5.6	—	—	—	—	—
1838	6.4	0.8	6.2	—	—	—	—	—
1839	6.8	1.4	6.6	—	—	—	—	—
1840	8.4	0.8	8.1	—	—	—	—	—
1841	7.7	0.8	7.5	—	—	—	—	—
1842	6.6	1.0	6.4	—	—	—	—	—
1843	4.2	0.5	4.0 [4]	—	—	—	—	—
1844	6.3	0.8	6.1	—	—	—	—	—
1845	5.7	1.1	5.5	—	—	—	—	—
1846	4.4	1.5	4.2	—	—	—	—	—
1847	4.6	2.4	4.5	—	—	—	—	—
1848	3.0	2.3	3.0	—	—	—	—	—
1849	2.7	3.0	2.7	—	—	—	—	—
1850	11.3	3.7	10.9 [3]	—	—	—	—	—
1851	30.2	3.8	29.4	—	—	—	—	—
1852	26.5	3.7	25.7	—	—	—	—	—
1853	33.3	3.7	32.3	—	—	—	—	—
1854	33.6	4.3	32.6	—	—	—	—	—
1855	30.5	2.0	29.6	—	—	—	—	—
1856	24.8	2.1	24.1	—	—	—	—	—
1857	21.3	2.0	20.7	—	—	—	—	—
1858	22.4	1.7	21.8	—	—	—	—	—
1859	35.3	1.2	34.2	—	—	—	—	—
1860	26.8	1.6	26.1	—	—	—	—	—
1861	24.1	0.6	20.8	—	—	—	—	—
1862	22.3	0.6	22.5	—	—	—	—	—
1863	23.7	0.6	23.5	—	—	—	—	—
1864	26.6	0.2	28.1	—	—	—	—	—

Notes appear at end of table

(continued)

TABLE Dh319–326   Americans traveling overseas and foreign visitors to the United States: 1820–2000   *Continued*

	Ocean-bound tourists		Arrivals and departures of U.S. citizens		U.S. travelers		Foreign visitors and travelers to the United States	
	U.S. tourists abroad	Foreign tourists in the United States	Arrivals	Departures	Overseas	All destinations	Visitors	Travelers
	Dh319 [2]	Dh320 [2]	Dh321	Dh322	Dh323	Dh324	Dh325	Dh326
Year	Thousand	Thousand	Thousand	Thousand	Thousand	Thousand	Thousand	Thousand
1865	34.7	0.1	39.3	—	—	—	—	—
1866	38.9	1.1	18.2 [5]	—	—	—	—	—
1867	40.3	1.0	39.1	—	—	—	—	—
1868	41.3	1.5	40.1	—	—	—	—	—
1869	27.6	2.6	26.8	—	—	—	—	—
1870	34.9	3.9	33.9	—	—	—	—	—
1871	45.0	6.6	43.7	—	—	—	—	—
1872	50.5	4.5	49.1	—	—	—	—	—
1873	49.2	3.0	47.7	—	—	—	—	—
1874	49.2	4.0	47.7	—	—	—	—	—
1875	51.6	4.1	50.9	—	—	—	—	—
1876	49.4	5.8	48.0	—	—	—	—	—
1877	42.7	5.6	41.5	—	—	—	—	—
1878	42.9	5.7	41.7	—	—	—	—	—
1879	56.9	6.3	55.3	—	—	—	—	—
1880	51.8	7.0	50.3	—	—	—	—	—
1881	50.0	8.4	48.5	—	—	—	—	—
1882	54.5	9.1	52.9	—	—	—	—	—
1883	69.3	18.0	67.3	—	—	—	—	—
1884	91.6	22.2	88.9	—	—	—	—	—
1885	100.2	24.5	97.3	—	—	—	—	—
1886	89.0	17.5	86.4 [6]	—	—	—	—	—
1887	95.1	17.8	92.3 [6]	—	—	—	—	—
1888	98.4	17.2	95.5 [6]	—	—	—	—	—
1889	83.7	17.3	81.2 [6]	—	—	—	—	—
1890	90.7	18.1	88.0	—	—	—	—	—
1891	91.9	13.8	—	—	—	—	—	—
1892	95.1	16.0	—	—	—	—	—	—
1893	93.4	37.9	—	—	—	—	—	—
1894	68.7	30.7	—	—	—	—	—	—
1895	103.7	15.6	—	—	—	—	—	—
1896	101.3	16.9	—	—	—	—	—	—
1897	98.8	16.9	—	—	—	—	—	—
1898	96.4	16.8	—	—	—	—	—	—
1899	98.1	18.3	—	—	—	—	—	—
1900	124.1	20.3	—	—	—	—	—	—
1908	—	—	200.4	159.9	—	—	—	—
1909	—	—	217.2	215.8	—	—	—	—
1910	—	—	220.3	271.3	—	—	—	—
1911	—	—	236.7	258.5	—	—	—	—
1912	—	—	240.4	274.1	—	—	—	—
1913	—	—	230.6	256.4	—	—	—	—
1914	—	—	240.9	299.5	—	—	—	—
1915	—	—	192.7	142.3	—	—	—	—
1916	—	—	88.8	87.5	—	—	—	—
1917	—	—	82.7	81.2	—	—	—	—
1918	—	—	44.8	232.4	—	—	—	—
1919	—	—	73.5	194.3	152	—	47	—
1920	—	—	135.5	167.6	302	—	81	—
1921	—	—	203.7	247.5	294	—	75	—
1922	—	—	228.1	293.3	320	—	53	—
1923	—	—	287.3	260.8	291	—	65	—
1924	—	—	285.5	267.1	351	—	79	—
1925	—	—	304.3	314.3	408	—	65	—
1926	—	—	359.3	360.3	433	—	70	—
1927	—	—	367.9	358.3	471	—	73	—
1928	—	—	422.4	414.3	518	—	78	—
1929	—	—	441.8	414.4	517	—	78	—

Notes appear at end of table

TABLE Dh319–326 Americans traveling overseas and foreign visitors to the United States: 1820–2000 *Continued*

	Ocean-bound tourists		Arrivals and departures of U.S. citizens		U.S. travelers		Foreign visitors and travelers to the United States	
	U.S. tourists abroad	Foreign tourists in the United States	Arrivals	Departures	Overseas	All destinations	Visitors	Travelers
	Dh319 [2]	Dh320 [2]	Dh321	Dh322	Dh323	Dh324	Dh325	Dh326
Year	Thousand	Thousand	Thousand	Thousand	Thousand	Thousand	Thousand	Thousand
1930	—	—	467.3	445.5	538	—	83	—
1931	—	—	420.2	429.2	438	—	66	—
1932	—	—	326.7	350.8	393	—	49	—
1933	—	—	295.8	322.6	300	—	60	—
1934	—	—	264.1	255.1	302	—	75	—
1935	—	—	275.2	265.1	314	—	69	—
1936	—	—	308.0	306.1	381	—	81	—
1937	—	—	373.1	386.1	435	—	96	—
1938	—	—	392.8	393.2	370	—	98	—
1939	—	—	343.1	327.8	282	—	100	—
1940	—	—	250.9	218.5	156	—	81	—
1941	—	—	169.1	163.3	170	—	46	—
1942	—	—	112.1	108.5	71	—	42	—
1943	—	—	99.2	59.1	57	—	50	—
1944	—	—	101.1	60.6	75	—	70	—
1945	—	—	168.7	100.5	117	—	102	—
1946	—	—	263.3	226.3	329	—	117	—
1947	—	—	428.0	446.3	435	—	229	—
1948	—	—	533.5	474.0	495	—	282	—
1949	—	—	607.0	548.4	573	—	258	—
1950	—	—	651.9	651.6	676	—	242	—
1951	—	—	749.7	663.8	684	—	255	—
1952	—	—	797.1	812.6	772	—	296	—
1953	—	—	921.4	923.6	827	—	287	—
1954	—	—	1,009.5	971.0	912	—	307	—
1955	—	—	1,167.6	1,096.1	1,075	—	328	332
1956	—	—	1,281.1	1,272.5	1,239	—	345	360
1957	—	—	1,365.1	1,402.1	1,369	—	419	450
1958	—	—	1,469.3	1,483.9	1,398	—	447	472
1959	—	—	1,804.4	1,739.0	1,516	—	520	544
1960	—	—	1,920.6	1,935.0	1,634	—	572	602
1961	—	—	2,043.4	1,969.1	1,575	—	602	624
1962	—	—	2,199.3	2,159.9	1,767	—	671	713
1963	—	—	2,433.5	2,421.3	1,990	—	780	847
1964	—	—	2,786.9	2,709.2	2,220	—	937	1,098
1965	—	—	3,100.0	3,084.9	2,623	—	1,130	1,204
1966	—	—	3,613.9	3,542.8	2,975	—	1,274	1,360
1967	—	—	4,073.5	4,033.3	3,425	—	1,431	1,729
1968	—	—	4,645.0	4,587.4	3,885	—	1,825	1,798
1969	—	—	5,457.3	5,221.6	4,623	—	1,894	2,010
1970	—	—	6,208.2	6,107.3	5,260	—	2,193	2,288
1971	—	—	—	—	5,667	—	—	2,490
1972	—	—	—	—	6,790	—	—	2,861
1973	—	—	—	—	6,933	—	—	3,554
1974	—	—	—	—	6,467	—	—	3,700
1975	—	—	—	—	6,354	—	—	3,674
1976	—	—	—	—	6,897	—	—	4,456
1977	—	—	—	—	7,390	—	—	4,509
1978	—	—	—	—	7,790	—	—	5,764
1979	—	—	—	—	7,835	—	—	7,230
1980	—	—	—	—	8,163	—	—	8,200
1981	—	—	—	—	8,040	—	—	9,069
1982	—	—	—	—	8,510	—	—	8,761
1983	—	—	—	—	9,628	—	—	7,873
1984	—	—	—	—	11,755	—	—	7,528
1985	—	—	—	—	12,696	34,715	—	7,537
1986	—	—	—	—	12,038	37,158	—	8,860
1987	—	—	—	—	13,616	39,410	—	10,535
1988	—	—	—	—	14,443	40,669	—	12,512
1989	—	—	—	—	14,791	41,138	—	13,999

Notes appear at end of table

(continued)

TABLE Dh319–326   Americans traveling overseas and foreign visitors to the United States: 1820–2000 *Continued*

	Ocean-bound tourists		Arrivals and departures of U.S. citizens		U.S. travelers		Foreign visitors and travelers to the United States	
	U.S. tourists abroad	Foreign tourists in the United States	Arrivals	Departures	Overseas	All destinations	Visitors	Travelers
	Dh319 [2]	Dh320 [2]	Dh321	Dh322	Dh323	Dh324	Dh325	Dh326
Year	Thousand	Thousand	Thousand	Thousand	Thousand	Thousand	Thousand	Thousand
1990	—	—	—	—	15,990	44,623	—	15,060
1991	—	—	—	—	14,521	41,566	—	16,156
1992	—	—	—	—	15,965	43,898	—	17,791
1993	—	—	—	—	17,102	44,411	—	18,661
1994	—	—	—	—	18,149	46,450	—	18,458
1995	—	—	—	—	19,059	50,763	—	20,639
1996	—	—	—	—	19,786	52,311	—	22,659
1997	—	—	—	—	21,634	52,944	—	24,196
1998	—	—	—	—	23,069	56,300	—	23,698
1999	—	—	—	—	24,579	57,502	—	24,466
2000	—	—	—	—	26,853	60,816	—	25,973

[1] The data for series Dh323–326 are for the calendar year. Other series are for fiscal years ending as follows: September 30 for 1820–1831 and 1843–1849; December 31 for 1832–1842 and 1850–1865; and June 30 for 1866–1970.

[2] The figures are not strictly tourists, as they include commercial travelers.

[3] Fifteen months ending December 31 of the year indicated.

[4] Nine months ending September 30.

[5] Six months.

[6] Includes some number of Chinese returning through the port of San Francisco.

Sources

Series Dh319–320. For 1820–1860, Douglass North, "The United States Balance of Payments, 1790–1860," in *Trends in the American Economy in the Nineteenth Century*, National Bureau of Economic Research Studies in Income and Wealth, volume 24 (Princeton University Press, 1960), pp. 611–19. For 1861–1900, Matthew Simon, "The United States Balance of Payments, 1861–1900," in *Trends in the American Economy in the Nineteenth Century*, National Bureau of Economic Research Studies in Income and Wealth, volume 24 (Princeton University Press, 1960), pp. 661–75, especially Tables 16, 17.

Series Dh321–322. For 1820–1890, *Statistical Abstract of the United States* (1890), pp. 214–17, Tables 153, 154. For 1908–1930, U.S. Bureau of Immigration, *Annual Report of the Commissioner General of Immigration*. For 1931–1949, U.S. Immigration and Naturalization Service, *Report of Passenger Travel between the United States and Foreign Countries* (annual issues). For 1950–1970, *Annual Report of the Immigration and Naturalization Service* (annual issues).

Series Dh323. For 1919–1970, *Historical Statistics of the United States* (1975), series H921; thereafter, *Statistical Abstract of the United States* (annual issues).

Series Dh324 and Dh326. *Statistical Abstract of the United States* (annual issues).

Series Dh325. *Historical Statistics of the United States* (1975), series H941.

Documentation

These series are intended to measure the number of Americans traveling internationally and the number of foreign visitors admitted to the United States for a temporary period of time for purposes of business or pleasure. These travelers are also known as nonimmigrants. In order to achieve this coverage, the series on American travelers attempted to exclude U.S. citizens residing abroad, cruise travelers, and crewmen, as well as military personnel and other government employees and their dependents stationed abroad. The series on foreign visitors excluded immigrants, transmigrants, migratory labor from Canada and Mexico, government personnel, and foreign businessmen employed in the United States. Before 1985, the series cover only overseas travelers, and thus exclude travel over international land borders to and from Canada and Mexico, and travel between the coterminous United States and Alaska, Hawai'i, Puerto Rico, and the Virgin Islands.

Series Dh319–320. The series on ocean-bound tourists for 1820–1900 were compiled by Douglass North and Matthew Simon in order to allow estimation of the value of tourist expenditures included in the balance of payments. This required estimates of the number of tourists abroad during the year, which was not necessarily the number of tourists who departed that year. They estimated the stock of U.S. tourists abroad by inflating the number of U.S. citizens returning in each year to account for those who may have remained abroad. To estimate ocean-bound foreign tourists in the United States, they adjusted the total number of passengers arriving to account for those who were immigrants to the United States, transmigrants (primarily to Canada and the West Indies), and Canadian and Mexican tourists and farm laborers. The figures are intended to measure overseas travelers but, before 1885, may include some number of visitors arriving from Canada, the West Indies, and Mexico. For 1820–1860, the figures were obtained by dividing North's estimate of tourist expenditures by the per capita figures he reported of $750 for American tourists and $1,000 for foreign tourists.

Series Dh321–322. Arrivals from the British North American possessions and Mexico were not included after July 1, 1885. Prior to that date they were included if they arrived by ship. Statistics on passenger travel were obtained from passenger manifests or lists required by law to be prepared by carriers for vessels and aircraft traveling between the United States and foreign countries. Arrival manifests were first required under the Act of 1819, and similar manifests of departing passengers were first required under the Act of 1907. Prior to 1908, statistical information on passenger travel is incomplete. From 1820 through 1855, reports showed the number of U.S. citizens and the total number of alien passengers arrived. During the years 1856–1890, data reflected the arrivals of U.S. citizens returning, immigrants, and nonimmigrant aliens. Data relating to the inward and outward movement of passengers became complete in 1908, when, as the result of the Act of 1907, departure records were first compiled.

Series Dh322. Excludes travel over international land borders, crewmen, military personnel, and travelers between the United States and its outlying areas.

Series Dh323. Excludes the following: travel to Canada and Mexico; travel between the coterminous United States and Alaska, Hawai'i, Puerto Rico, and the Virgin Islands; cruise travelers; military personnel and other government employees and their dependents stationed abroad; and U.S. citizens residing abroad.

Series Dh325. The data on foreign visitors for 1919–1932 include all classes of nonimmigrants except aliens returning to the United States to resume residence after a temporary stay abroad of less than one year. The data on foreign visitors for 1933–1970 include only nonimmigrant aliens admitted as temporary visitors for business or pleasure, foreigners in transit through the United States, and students.

TABLE Dh327–338   Attendance at selected professional sports: 1933–1999

Contributed by Thomas Weiss

	Major League Baseball			National Basketball Association		National Football League		National Hockey League				
	Regular season											
	American League	National League	World Series	Regular season	Postseason	Regular season	Postseason	Regular season	Postseason	U.S. open tennis championship	Horse racing	National Finals Rodeo
	Dh327	Dh328	Dh329	Dh330	Dh331	Dh332 [1]	Dh333	Dh334	Dh335	Dh336 [2]	Dh337	Dh338
Year	Thousand	Thousand	Thousand	Thousand	Thousand	Thousand	Thousand	Thousand	Thousand	Thousand	Thousand	Thousand
1933	2,926	3,163	163	—	—	—	—	—	—	—	—	—
1934	2,764	3,200	282	—	—	493	35	—	—	—	—	—
1935	3,688	3,657	287	—	—	638	15	—	—	—	—	—
1936	4,179	3,904	303	—	—	816	30	—	—	—	—	—
1937	4,736	4,204	238	—	—	963	16	—	—	—	—	—
1938	4,446	4,561	201	—	—	937	48	—	—	—	—	—
1939	4,271	4,707	184	—	—	1,071	32	—	—	—	—	—
1940	5,434	4,390	282	—	—	1,063	36	—	—	—	—	—
1941	4,912	4,778	236	—	—	1,109	56	—	—	—	—	—
1942	4,200	4,353	277	—	—	888	36	—	—	—	—	—
1943	3,697	3,769	277	—	—	969	71	—	—	—	—	—
1944	4,798	3,975	207	—	—	1,020	46	—	—	—	—	—
1945	5,580	5,261	333	—	—	1,270	32	—	—	—	—	—
1946	9,621	8,902	250	—	—	1,732	58	—	—	—	—	—
1947	9,486	10,388	390	—	—	1,837	66	—	—	—	—	—
1948	11,150	9,771	358	—	—	1,525	36	—	—	—	—	—
1949	10,731	9,485	237	—	—	1,392	28	—	—	—	—	—
1950	9,142	8,321	196	—	—	1,978	137	—	—	—	29,291	—
1951	8,883	7,244	342	—	—	1,913	58	—	—	—	31,865	—
1952	8,294	6,339	341	—	—	2,052	98	—	—	—	35,065	—
1953	6,964	7,420	307	1,127	—	2,165	55	—	—	—	38,249	—
1954	7,922	8,014	252	982	—	2,191	44	—	—	—	38,637	—
1955	8,943	7,674	362	900	—	2,522	86	—	—	—	38,503	—
1956	7,894	8,995	346	1,102	—	2,551	57	—	—	—	39,871	—
1957	8,196	8,820	395	1,199	—	2,836	120	—	—	—	41,365	—
1958	7,296	10,165	394	1,167	—	3,006	124	—	—	—	43,373	—
1959	9,149	9,995	421	1,249	—	3,140	58	—	—	—	45,451	—
1960	9,227	10,685	350	1,297	—	4,054	100	—	—	—	46,879	—
1961	10,163	8,732	223	1,456	—	4,989	69	2,317	242	—	49,560	—
1962	10,015	11,360	377	1,434	—	5,151	103	2,435	277	—	50,582	—
1963	9,094	11,382	247	1,658	—	5,372	109	2,591	221	—	55,754	—
1964	9,235	12,045	322	1,796	—	6,011	120	2,733	309	—	60,595	—
1965	8,861	13,581	364	1,805	—	6,416	131	2,823	304	—	62,887	47
1966	10,167	15,051	221	2,022	—	7,497	116	2,941	249	—	63,577	50
1967	11,337	12,971	304	2,553	—	8,235	220	3,085	248	—	63,373	55
1968	11,317	11,758	380	2,936	—	8,517	330	4,938	495	97	65,460	59
1969	12,135	15,095	272	3,722	506	8,940	329	5,551	432	101	68,099	66
1970	12,085	16,662	253	4,341	556	9,533	459	5,992	462	123	69,704	75
1971	11,869	17,325	351	5,330	489	10,076	484	7,258	708	121	73,619	72
1972	11,439	15,530	363	5,618	525	10,446	483	7,609	583	130	70,807	79
1973	13,434	16,675	358	5,852	608	10,731	525	8,576	625	137	74,683	84
1974	13,047	16,978	260	5,910	593	10,236	439	8,641	600	153	74,948	89
1975	13,189	16,600	308	6,892	685	10,213	476	9,522	784	217	78,662	89
1976	14,658	16,661	223	7,512	698	11,071	493	9,104	726	251	79,307	89
1977	19,640	19,070	338	9,899	807	11,019	535	8,564	646	218	75,987	89
1978	20,530	20,107	337	9,874	798	12,772	624	8,527	687	275	75,324	98
1979	22,372	21,178	368	9,761	904	13,182	630	7,758	695	305	72,783	117
1980	21,890	21,124	325	9,938	740	13,392	624	10,534	977	331	74,690	117
1981	14,066	12,478	338	9,449	765	13,607	638	10,726	966	351	75,463	117
1982	23,080	21,507	349	9,965	727	7,367 [6]	1,033	10,711	1,059	360	76,858	117
1983	23,991	21,549	304	9,638	606	13,277	676	11,021	1,088	377	75,693	117
1984	23,961	20,781	272	10,015	1,096	13,398	665	11,359	1,107	392	74,076	117
1985	24,532	22,292	327	10,506	985	13,345	711	11,634	1,108	409	73,346	142
1986	25,173	22,333	322	11,215	979	13,589	734	11,621	1,153	414	70,580	147
1987	27,277	24,734	387	12,065	1,091	11,406 [7]	657	11,856	1,384	406	70,105	152
1988	28,500	24,499	260	12,654	1,397	13,540	658	12,118	1,337	404	68,949	165
1989	29,849	25,324	223	15,465	1,077	13,626	686	12,418	1,327	417	59,893	169

Notes appear at end of table

(continued)

TABLE Dh327–338   Attendance at selected professional sports: 1933–1999   *Continued*

Year	Major League Baseball			National Basketball Association		National Football League		National Hockey League		U.S. open tennis championship	Horse racing	National Finals Rodeo
	Regular season											
	American League	National League	World Series	Regular season	Postseason	Regular season	Postseason	Regular season	Postseason			
	Dh327	Dh328	Dh329	Dh330	Dh331	Dh332 [1]	Dh333	Dh334	Dh335	Dh336 [2]	Dh337	Dh338
	Thousand	Thousand	Thousand	Thousand	Thousand	Thousand	Thousand	Thousand	Thousand	Thousand	Thousand	Thousand
1990	30,332	24,492	209	17,369	1,203	13,960	848	12,580	1,356	422	63,803	171
1991	32,118	24,696	373	16,876	1,109	13,841	813	12,344	1,442	483	52,874	171
1992	31,760	24,113	311	17,367	1,228	13,829	816	12,770	1,328	521	49,275	171
1993	33,333	36,924	344	17,778	1,339	13,967	815	14,158	1,346	531	45,688	170
1994	24,202	25,808	0 [4]	17,984	1,349	14,030	780	16,106	1,440	530	42,065	171
1995	25,359	25,110	286	18,516	1,347	15,044	791	9,234	1,329 [8]	506	38,934	169
1996	29,718	30,379	325	20,513	1,284	14,612	769	17,042	1,540	506	43,367	171
1997	31,283	31,885	404	20,305	1,352	14,967	802	17,641	1,495	560	41,846	169
1998	31,915	38,424 [3]	243	20,373	1,409	15,365	823	17,265	1,507	535	—	175
1999	31,817	38,323	216	12,135 [5]	1,315	16,207	—	18,002	1,509	584	—	—

[1] For 1960–1969, the figures include attendance at both National Football League and American Football League games in order to make them consistent with the data beginning in 1970 when the two leagues had merged.

[2] Night sessions were first held in 1975. Sessions were first held at the U.S Tennis Association National Tennis Center in 1978. Starting in 1995, figures refer to paid attendance only.

[3] Milwaukee was shifted to the National League.

[4] No World Series because of a labor dispute.

[5] The season was shortened, and there was no All-Star game because of a labor dispute.

[6] Season shortened because of a strike of the players.

[7] Season shortened because of a strike. Value includes games played by replacement players.

[8] Labor dispute forced the cancellation of 468 games.

Sources

Baseball data are from National League of Professional Baseball Clubs, *National League Green Book* (Sporting News, annual); American League of Professional Baseball Clubs, *American League Red Book* (Sporting News, annual); and Sporting News, *Official Major League Fact Book* (Sporting News, 1999). Basketball data are from NBA Properties, Inc., *Official NBA Guide* (annual). Football data were provided by the NFL Broadcasting Department. National Hockey League, *National Hockey League Official Guide and Record Book* (annual). Tennis data were obtained from *U.S. Open Media Guide* (H. O. Zimman, 1998) and from the U.S. Tennis Association Communications Office. Horse racing data provided by Association of Racing Commissioners International. Professional Rodeo Cowboys Association, *Media Guide* (annual).

These data are updated annually in the publications cited, and most are updated in the annual edition of *Statistical Abstract of the United States*.

Documentation

There are inconsistencies and ambiguities in the measurement of attendance. In some cases, attendance reflects tickets sold; in others, it is a count of tickets collected. The difference can be large depending on whether the event was televised. Furthermore, the count of tickets sometimes includes complimentary tickets, while at other times it covers only paid attendance, which may include no-shows. The exact coverage is not always clear in the original source. Attendance at horse racing covers most states, but not all. Large fluctuations in attendance from year to year reflect either expansion of the league and a concomitant increase in the number of games in each of these years, or a shortened season caused by a labor dispute.

Series Dh330 and Dh335. For seasons ending in year shown.

Series Dh333. Includes playoff games and the Pro Bowl game.

TABLE Dh339–353 Participation in selected recreational activities – bowling, golfing, and boating: 1896–1999
Contributed by Thomas Weiss

	Members				Number shipped		Boats					Estimated retail expenditure on boating	Recreational boats owned	Golfers who played	
	Bowling associations	American Bowling Congress	Women's International Bowling Congress	Young American Bowling Alliance	Outboard motors	Sterndrive and inboard engines	Total	Motorized	Sailboats	Canoes	Miscellaneous			15 or more rounds	1 or more rounds
	Dh339	Dh340	Dh341	Dh342	Dh343	Dh344	Dh345	Dh346	Dh347	Dh348	Dh349	Dh350	Dh351	Dh352	Dh353
Year	Thousand	Thousand	Thousand	Thousand	Thousand	Thousand	Thousand	Thousand	Thousand	Thousand	Thousand	Million dollars	Thousand	Thousand	Thousand
1896	0.3	0.3	—	—	—	—	—	—	—	—	—	—	—	—	—
1897	0.4	0.4	—	—	—	—	—	—	—	—	—	—	—	—	—
1898	0.5	0.5	—	—	—	—	—	—	—	—	—	—	—	—	—
1899	0.6	0.6	—	—	—	—	—	—	—	—	—	—	—	—	—
1900	0.8	0.8	—	—	—	—	—	—	—	—	—	—	—	—	—
1901	1.0	1.0	—	—	—	—	—	—	—	—	—	—	—	—	—
1902	1.1	1.1	—	—	—	—	—	—	—	—	—	—	—	—	—
1903	2.0	2.0	—	—	—	—	—	—	—	—	—	—	—	—	—
1904	1.9	1.9	—	—	—	—	—	—	—	—	—	—	—	—	—
1905	3.2	3.2	—	—	—	—	—	—	—	—	—	—	—	—	—
1906	4.9	4.9	—	—	—	—	—	—	—	—	—	—	—	—	—
1907	6.1	6.1	—	—	—	—	—	—	—	—	—	—	—	—	—
1908	6.6	6.6	—	—	—	—	—	—	—	—	—	—	—	—	—
1909	6.6	6.6	—	—	—	—	—	—	—	—	—	—	—	—	—
1910	6.8	6.8	—	—	—	—	—	—	—	—	—	—	—	—	—
1911	7.3	7.3	—	—	—	—	—	—	—	—	—	—	—	—	—
1912	6.4	6.4	—	—	—	—	—	—	—	—	—	—	—	—	—
1913	7.7	7.7	—	—	—	—	—	—	—	—	—	—	—	—	—
1914	8.9	8.9	—	—	—	—	—	—	—	—	—	—	—	—	—
1915	10.5	10.5	—	—	—	—	—	—	—	—	—	—	—	—	—
1916	16.4	16.4	—	—	—	—	—	—	—	—	—	—	—	—	—
1917	16.8	16.7	(Z)	—	—	—	—	—	—	—	—	—	—	—	—
1918	16.2	15.8	0.4	—	—	—	—	—	—	—	—	—	—	—	—
1919	14.3	13.6	0.6	—	12	—	—	—	—	—	—	—	—	—	—
1920	26.9	25.9	1.0	—	17	—	—	—	—	—	—	—	—	—	—
1921	25.6	24.4	1.2	—	12	—	—	—	—	—	—	—	—	—	—
1922	31.9	30.0	1.9	—	16	—	—	—	—	—	—	—	—	—	—
1923	60.2	58.0	2.2	—	21	—	—	—	—	—	—	—	—	—	—
1924	53.9	51.0	2.9	—	21	—	—	—	—	—	—	—	—	—	—
1925	67.8	64.0	3.8	—	27	—	—	—	—	—	—	—	—	—	—
1926	80.6	76.0	4.6	—	33	—	—	—	—	—	—	—	—	—	—
1927	99.4	94.0	5.4	—	42	—	—	—	—	—	—	—	—	—	—
1928	116.1	110.0	6.1	—	54	—	—	—	—	—	—	—	—	—	—
1929	146.8	139.0	7.8	—	59	—	—	—	—	—	—	—	—	—	—
1930	219.0	210.0	9.0	—	44	—	—	—	—	—	—	—	—	—	—
1931	224.4	215.0	9.4	—	14	—	—	—	—	—	—	—	—	—	—
1932	196.7	187.0	9.7	—	12	—	—	—	—	—	—	—	—	—	—
1933	148.4	140.0	8.4	—	15	—	—	—	—	—	—	—	—	—	—
1934	168.5	158.0	10.5	—	23	—	—	—	—	—	—	—	—	—	—

Notes appear at end of table

(continued)

TABLE Dh339–353   Participation in selected recreational activities – bowling, golfing, and boating: 1896–1999 *Continued*

	Members				Number shipped									Golfers who played	
	Bowling associations	American Bowling Congress	Women's International Bowling Congress	Young American Bowling Alliance	Outboard motors	Sterndrive and inboard engines	Boats Total	Motorized	Sailboats	Canoes	Miscellaneous	Estimated retail expenditure on boating	Recreational boats owned	15 or more rounds	1 or more rounds
	Dh339	Dh340	Dh341	Dh342	Dh343	Dh344	Dh345	Dh346	Dh347	Dh348	Dh349	Dh350	Dh351	Dh352	Dh353
Year	Thousand	Thousand	Thousand	Thousand	Thousand	Thousand	Thousand	Thousand	Thousand	Thousand	Thousand	Million dollars	Thousand	Thousand	Thousand
1935	216.4	203.0	13.4	—	41	—	—	—	—	—	—	—	—	—	—
1936	266.9	251.0	15.9	—	50	—	—	—	—	—	—	—	—	—	—
1937	329.3	307.0	22.3	—	100	—	—	—	—	—	—	—	—	—	—
1938	482.2	446.0	36.2	—	100	—	—	—	—	—	—	—	—	—	—
1939	534.9	483.0	51.9	—	120	—	—	—	—	—	—	—	—	—	—
1940	683.8	602.0	81.8	—	130	—	—	—	—	—	—	—	—	—	—
1941	873.7	746.0	127.7	—	170	—	—	—	—	—	—	—	—	—	—
1942	1,058.7	875.0	183.7	—	—	—	—	—	—	—	—	—	—	—	—
1943	894.6	694.0	200.6	—	—	—	—	—	—	—	—	—	—	—	—
1944	909.6	697.0	212.6	—	—	—	—	—	—	—	—	—	—	—	—
1945	1,047.5	795.0	252.5	—	—	—	—	—	—	—	—	—	—	—	—
1946	1,060.5	810.0	250.5	8.9	398	—	—	—	—	—	—	—	—	—	—
1947	1,415.0	1,105.0	301.1	13.2	584	—	—	—	—	—	—	—	—	2,517	—
1948	1,635.0	1,259.0	362.8	20.1	499	—	—	—	—	—	—	—	—	2,742	—
1949	1,821.0	1,368.0	432.9	—	329	—	—	—	—	—	—	—	—	3,112	—
1950	1,936.9	1,417.0	495.9	24.0	367	—	—	—	—	—	—	—	—	3,215	—
1951	1,999.0	1,430.0	542.7	26.3	284 [1]	—	—	—	—	—	—	—	—	3,237	—
1952	2,096.0	1,482.0	582.7	31.3	337	—	—	—	—	—	—	—	—	3,265	—
1953	2,238.0	1,569.0	630.4	38.6	463	—	—	—	—	—	—	—	—	3,336	—
1954	2,363.0	1,651.0	665.4	46.6	479 [2]	—	—	—	—	—	—	—	—	3,400	—
1955	2,514.2	1,741.0	706.2	67.0	515	—	—	—	—	—	—	—	—	3,500	—
1956	2,787.0	1,929.0	764.5	93.5	647	—	—	—	—	—	—	—	—	3,680	—
1957	3,222.0	2,225.0	865.6	131.4	550	—	—	—	—	—	—	—	—	3,812	—
1958	3,686.0	2,500.0	1,005.2	180.8	504	—	—	—	—	—	—	—	—	3,970	—
1959	4,449.0	3,000.0	1,231.5	217.5	540	—	—	—	—	—	—	—	—	4,125	—
1960	5,373.4	3,500.0	1,543.4	330.0	468	—	—	—	—	—	—	—	—	4,400	—
1961	6,316.1	4,000.0	1,906.1	410.0	343	—	—	—	—	—	—	—	—	5,000	—
1962	6,930.3	4,275.0	2,212.3	443.0	360	—	—	—	—	—	—	—	—	5,500	—
1963	7,404.8	4,500.0	2,453.8	451.0	362	—	—	—	—	—	—	—	—	6,250	—
1964	7,497.4	4,575.0	2,607.4	315.0	390	—	—	—	—	—	—	—	—	7,000	—
1965	7,616.4	4,550.0	2,736.4	330.0	393	—	—	—	—	—	—	—	—	7,750	—
1966	7,545.7	4,375.0	2,821.7	349.0	440	—	—	—	—	—	—	—	—	8,525	—
1967	7,573.4	4,298.7	2,896.7	378.0	444	—	—	—	—	—	—	—	—	9,100	—
1968	7,588.0	4,204.3	2,941.7	442.0	500	—	—	—	—	—	—	—	—	9,300	—
1969	7,480.5	4,023.2	2,968.3	489.0	510	—	—	—	—	—	—	—	8,814	9,500	—
1970	7,510.2	3,987.2	2,988.1	535.0	430	86.0	436.5	345.5	51.0	40.0	—	3,440	—	9,700	11,245
1971	7,653.4	3,984.4	3,059.0	610.0	495	88.0	447.5	344.5	59.0	44.0	—	3,610	—	10,000	—
1972	7,911.3	4,047.6	3,184.7	679.0	535	109.0	631.0	461.0	114.0	56.0	—	3,900	—	10,400	—
1973	8,195.6	4,131.6	3,344.0	720.0	585	113.0	726.0	538.0	120.0	68.0	—	4,245	—	11,000	—
1974	8,499.7	4,217.6	3,531.1	751.0	545	105.0	729.0	506.0	143.0	80.0	—	4,607	—	11,660	—

	Members				Number shipped — Boats							Number shipped		Golfers who played	
Year	Bowling associations (Dh339)	American Bowling Congress (Dh340)	Women's International Bowling Congress (Dh341)	Young American Bowling Alliance (Dh342)	Outboard motors (Dh343)	Sterndrive and inboard engines (Dh344)	Total (Dh345)	Motorized (Dh346)	Sailboats (Dh347)	Canoes (Dh348)	Miscellaneous (Dh349)	Estimated retail expenditure on boating (Dh350)	Recreational boats owned (Dh351)	15 or more rounds (Dh352)	1 or more rounds (Dh353)
	Thousand	Thousand	Thousand	Thousand	Thousand	Thousand	Thousand	Thousand	Thousand	Thousand	Thousand	Million dollars	Thousand	Thousand	Thousand
1975	8,749.9	4,298.2	3,692.7	759.0	435	103.0	592.1	408.2	107.9	76.0	—	4,800	—	12,036	13,036
1976	9,201.0	4,504.0	3,870.9	826.0	468	117.0	597.9	432.0	88.9	77.0	—	5,333	—	12,328	—
1977	9,453.1	4,583.5	4,043.6	826.0	462	123.0	571.6	431.5	58.1	82.0	—	5,920	—	12,451	—
1978	9,790.3	4,727.1	4,209.2	854.0	450	128.0	584.3	433.1	63.2	80.0	8.0	6,690	—	12,665	—
1979	9,833.6	4,777.4	4,232.1	824.0	375	135.0	614.7	423.6	71.9	90.0	29.2	7,500	—	12,870	14,612
1980	9,775.2	4,799.2	4,187.1	789.0	315	87.8	569.7	354.2	73.1	105.0	37.4	7,370	—	13,000	15,112
1981	9,794.8	4,755.8	4,112.0	927.0	318	81.5	594.5	340.4	77.1	126.0	51.0	8,250	11,832	13,650	15,566
1982	9,549.9	4,685.0	4,064.9	800.0	293	85.7	499.5	299.3	53.4	101.0	45.8	8,100	—	14,100	16,003
1983	9,269.7	4,556.9	3,947.2	765.5	337	104.1	570.7	363.4	43.7	107.0	56.6	9,375	—	14,300	16,514
1984	8,422.0	3,791.1	3,886.7	744.2	411	148.0	657.7	440.3	40.8	103.0	73.7	12,340	—	14,500	17,009
1985	8,063.8	3,656.9	3,713.8	693.2	392	155.0	636.8	436.7	37.8	78.8	83.5	13,284	13,778	—	17,520
1986	7,843.7	3,624.6	3,555.7	663.4	410	161.9	660.0	452.0	37.2	80.2	90.6	14,479	—	—	19,897
1987	7,421.8	3,424.2	3,351.4	646.2	444	210.8	724.7	505.7	33.5	85.3	100.2	16,500	14,515	—	21,316
1988	7,163.4	3,313.5	3,184.2	665.7	460	211.9	749.0	523.9	38.1	89.8	97.2	17,927	15,093	—	22,951
1989	6,867.0	3,165.5	3,026.5	675.1	430	190.7	637.5	445.4	27.2	80.1	84.8	17,143	15,658	—	24,191
1990	6,590.0	3,036.9	2,859.6	693.5	352	134.1	504.1	339.0	21.2	75.3	68.6	13,731	15,987	—	27,761
1991	6,255.1	2,922.8	2,711.9	620.4	289	92.4	448.0	277.8	8.7	72.3	89.2	10,564	16,262	—	24,796
1992	5,874.1	2,713.0	2,523.4	637.8	272	94.6	466.8	277.0	10.6	78.0	101.2	10,317	16,262	—	24,775
1993	5,600.6	2,576.8	2,403.2	620.6	283	94.7	498.8	290.2	11.9	89.7	107.0	11,254	16,212	—	24,563
1994	5,201.5	2,454.7	2,191.1	555.7	308	114.0	576.2	321.4	13.0	99.8	142.0	14,071	16,239	—	24,338
1995	4,924.5	2,370.2	2,035.8	518.5	317	120.0	663.8	337.0	14.3	97.8	214.7	17,226	15,375	—	25,012
1996	4,662.6	2,261.5	1,916.8	484.4	308	120.0	634.8	320.9	15.9	92.9	205.1	17,753	15,830	—	24,737
1997	4,405.0	2,135.1	1,797.8	472.1	302	116.1	610.1	304.4	14.4	103.6	187.7	19,344	16,230	—	26,474
1998	4,155.9	2,026.7	1,678.5	450.7	314	116.9	571.1	305.4	19.4	107.8	138.5	19,148	16,654	—	26,427
1999	3,933.6	1,936.6	1,565.9	431.0	331	120.5	605.5	345.1	27.8	121.0	111.6	22,987	16,834	—	—

(Z) Fewer than 50.

1 Production disrupted as a result of material allocations under the Controlled Material Plan.

2 Production disrupted because of labor arbitration.

Sources

American Bowling Congress, *Bowler's Encyclopedia*, fourth edition (American Bowling Congress, 2000). National Marine Manufacturing Association, *Boating* (National Marine Manufacturing Association, annual). National Golf Foundation, *Trends in the Golf Industry, 1986–1996* (National Golf Foundation), and annual information sheets.

These data are updated annually in the publications cited, and most are updated in the annual edition of *Statistical Abstract of the United States*. Data can also be found at the Internet sites of the National Marine Manufacturing Association and the National Golf Foundation.

Documentation

Series Dh339. Ending year of each bowling season.

Series Dh342. The Young American Bowling Alliance was formed in 1982 with the merger of the American Junior Bowling Congress, the Youth Bowling Association, and the Collegiate Division of the American Bowling Congress/Women's International Bowling Congress. Statistics for earlier years pertain to only the American Junior Bowling Congress.

Series Dh346. Includes outboard, inboard, and sterndrive boats.

Series Dh347. Includes nonpowered and auxiliary-powered sailboats.

Series Dh349. Includes personal watercraft, inflatable boats, sailboards, and jet boats.

Series Dh351. Based on the actual state and Coast Guard registrations and estimates of nonregistered boats.

Series Dh352–353. Based on a survey of households. Series Dh352 includes those who played fifteen or more rounds. Series Dh353 includes those age 12 and older who played at least one round of golf during the year.

TABLE Dh354–365   Attendance at NCAA basketball and football games: 1939–1999

Contributed by Thomas Weiss

	Men's basketball					Women's basketball				Men's football		
		Division I					Division I					
	Total	Total	Regular season	Championship tournament	Divisions II and III	Total	Total	Championship tournament	Divisions II and III	Total	Division I	Divisions I-AA, II, and III
	Dh354	Dh355	Dh356	Dh357	Dh358	Dh359	Dh360 [1]	Dh361	Dh362	Dh363 [2]	Dh364	Dh365
Year	Thousand	Thousand	Thousand	Thousand	Thousand	Thousand	Thousand	Thousand	Thousand	Thousand	Thousand	Thousand
1939	—	—	—	15	—	—	—	—	—	—	—	—
1940	—	—	—	37	—	—	—	—	—	—	—	—
1941	—	—	—	48	—	—	—	—	—	—	—	—
1942	—	—	—	24	—	—	—	—	—	—	—	—
1943	—	—	—	57	—	—	—	—	—	—	—	—
1944	—	—	—	59	—	—	—	—	—	—	—	—
1945	—	—	—	68	—	—	—	—	—	—	—	—
1946	—	—	—	73	—	—	—	—	—	—	—	—
1947	—	—	—	73	—	—	—	—	—	19,134	—	—
1948	—	—	—	73	—	—	—	—	—	19,652	—	—
1949	—	—	—	66	—	—	—	—	—	18,962	—	—
1950	—	—	—	75	—	—	—	—	—	17,481	—	—
1951	—	—	—	111	—	—	—	—	—	17,288	—	—
1952	—	—	—	116	—	—	—	—	—	16,682	—	—
1953	—	—	—	127	—	—	—	—	—	17,049	—	—
1954	—	—	—	115	—	—	—	—	—	17,267	—	—
1955	—	—	—	117	—	—	—	—	—	18,032	—	—
1956	—	—	—	133	—	—	—	—	—	18,291	—	—
1957	—	—	—	109	—	—	—	—	—	19,281	—	—
1958	—	—	—	177	—	—	—	—	—	19,615	—	—
1959	—	—	—	162	—	—	—	—	—	20,403	—	—
1960	—	—	—	155	—	—	—	—	—	20,678	—	—
1961	—	—	—	170	—	—	—	—	—	21,227	—	—
1962	—	—	—	177	—	—	—	—	—	22,237	—	—
1963	—	—	—	153	—	—	—	—	—	23,354	—	—
1964	—	—	—	141	—	—	—	—	—	24,683	—	—
1965	—	—	—	141	—	—	—	—	—	25,276	—	—
1966	—	—	—	141	—	—	—	—	—	26,431	—	—
1967	—	—	—	160	—	—	—	—	—	27,026	—	—
1968	—	—	—	161	—	—	—	—	—	27,626	—	—
1969	—	—	—	166	—	—	—	—	—	29,466	—	—
1970	—	—	—	147	—	—	—	—	—	30,455	—	—
1971	—	—	—	207	—	—	—	—	—	30,829	—	—
1972	—	—	—	147	—	—	—	—	—	31,283	—	—
1973	—	—	—	163	—	—	—	—	—	31,235	—	—
1974	—	—	—	154	—	—	—	—	—	31,688	—	—
1975	—	—	—	184	—	—	—	—	—	32,012	23,918	8,094
1976	—	15,060	14,857	203	—	—	—	—	—	32,905	24,613	8,292
1977	23,324	16,469	16,228	242	6,855	—	—	—	—	32,370	25,018	7,352
1978	23,591	17,669	17,442	227	5,922	—	—	—	—	32,875	25,863	7,012
1979	24,483	18,649	18,387	262	5,833	—	—	—	—	33,708	26,499	7,209
1980	24,862	19,053	18,731	321	5,809	—	—	—	—	34,230	26,589	7,642
1981	25,159	19,356	19,008	347	5,804	—	—	—	—	35,176	24,772	10,404
1982	25,416	19,790	19,362	427	5,626	1,927	1,148	67	779	34,817	25,382	9,436
1983	26,123	20,488	20,124	364	5,634	2,429	1,480	74	949	35,211	25,784	9,427
1984	26,272	20,715	20,318	397	5,556	2,251	1,378	85	873	34,952	25,434	9,517
1985	26,584	21,394	20,972	423	5,190	2,309	1,496	99	848	35,031	25,692	9,339
1986	26,369	21,245	20,745	500	5,124	2,349	1,501	97	773	35,008	25,472	9,536
1987	26,798	21,757	21,102	655	5,041	2,440	1,667	122	792	34,324	25,079	9,244
1988	27,453	22,463	21,904	559	4,989	2,649	1,857	134	762	35,116	25,308	9,808
1989	28,270	23,059	22,446	613	5,211	2,867	2,105	168	856	35,330	25,513	9,817
1990	28,741	23,582	23,045	537	5,159	3,184	2,328	192	1,005	35,528	25,646	9,882
1991	29,250	23,777	23,112	666	5,472	3,407	2,402	154	945	35,225	25,402	9,823
1992	29,378	23,894	23,314	580	5,484	3,828	2,883	198	1,020	34,871	25,305	9,565
1993	28,527	23,232	22,524	708	5,296	4,193	3,173	231	955	36,460	25,590	10,870
1994	28,390	23,275	22,697	578	5,115	4,557	3,603	279	992	35,638	25,836	9,801
1995	28,548	23,560	23,021	539	4,988	4,962	3,970	249	1,071	36,083	26,621	9,462
1996	28,225	23,543	22,899	643	4,683	5,234	4,163	274	1,871	36,858	27,566	9,292
1997	27,738	23,191	22,556	635	4,547	6,734	4,863	226	2,005	37,491	27,674	9,817
1998	28,032	23,283	22,600	683	4,749	7,387	5,382	285	2,169	—	—	—
1999	28,733	23,815	23,095	721	4,918	8,010	5,841	301	—	—	—	—

TABLE Dh354–365   Attendance at NCAA basketball and football games: 1939–1999   *Continued*

[1] Beginning in 1997, figures include attendance at double-headers with men in which separate attendance was taken by half time of the women's game.

[2] Through 1977, includes attendance at non-NCAA (National Collegiate Athletic Association) games.

Sources

Official NCAA Basketball and *Official NCAA Football* (National Collegiate Athletic Association, various years).

These data are updated annually in the publications cited and can also be found at the NCAA Internet site.

Documentation

Data based on regular season ending in the year shown.

Series Dh358 and Dh362. Includes attendance at all regular season games, at home and at neutral sites, plus attendance at tournament games.

ARTS AND HUMANITIES

Thomas Weiss

TABLE Dh366–371   Attendance for selected arts: 1958–1999

Contributed by Thomas Weiss

Year	Broadway shows	Nonprofit professional theaters	Opera		Symphony orchestra performances	Museums of art
			Total professional	Main season performances		
	Dh366	Dh367	Dh368	Dh369	Dh370	Dh371
	Million	Million	Million	Million	Million	Million
1958	7.2	—	—	—	—	—
1959	7.7	—	—	—	—	—
1960	7.9	—	—	—	—	—
1961	7.7	—	—	—	—	—
1962	6.8	—	—	—	—	—
1963	7.4	—	—	—	—	—
1964	6.8	—	—	—	—	—
1965	8.2	—	—	—	11.6	—
1966	9.6	—	—	—	—	—
1967	9.3	—	—	—	—	—
1968	9.5	—	—	—	—	—
1969	8.6	—	—	—	—	—
1970	7.1	—	—	—	12.7	—
1971	7.4	—	—	—	—	—
1972	6.5	—	—	—	—	—
1973	5.4	—	—	—	—	—
1974	5.7	—	—	—	—	—
1975	6.6	5.4	—	—	18.3	—
1976	7.3	—	—	—	20.0	—
1977	8.8	—	—	—	21.0	—
1978	9.6	—	—	—	21.4	—
1979	9.6	—	—	—	22.4	—
1980	9.6	14.2	—	—	22.6	—
1981	11.0	—	5.5	—	22.8	—
1982	10.1	13.1	5.6	—	22.0	—
1983	8.4	13.7	6.1	2.5	22.0	—
1984	7.9	15.5	6.1	2.5	23.2	—
1985	7.3	14.2	5.9	2.9	24.0	43.5
1986	6.5	14.8	6.7	3.3	25.4	43.2
1987	7.1	14.6	6.2	3.4	24.5	41.5
1988	8.1	13.9	6.6	3.8	27.4	46.6
1989	8.1	18.7	6.8	4.0	25.8	47.7
1990	8.0	15.2	7.5	4.0	24.7	45.6
1991	7.3	16.9	7.6	4.3	26.7	47.2
1992	7.4	16.0	7.1	4.3	26.3	45.7
1993	7.9	16.5	6.1	3.9	24.0	47.1
1994	8.1	20.7	6.5	4.1	24.4	46.0
1995	9.0	18.6	7.1	4.3	30.9	45.1
1996	9.5	17.1	7.1	4.3	31.1	48.7
1997	10.6	17.2	7.5	4.1	31.9	42.8
1998	11.5	—	7.1	4.0	—	42.0
1999	11.7	—	—	—	—	—

Sources

For Broadway shows, the League of American Theatres and Producers, Inc., New York; for opera, OPERA America, Washington, DC; for museums, the Association of Art Museum Directors, *Statistics Survey* (annual). The statistics for nonprofit theaters and orchestras were taken from annual editions of the *Statistical Abstract of the United States*. Those statistics had been reported originally by Theatre Communications Group, New York, and the American Symphony Orchestra League, Washington, DC.

Documentation

The statistics for Broadway theaters pertain to the season running from June 1 through May 31. The opera season runs September through August 31.

The statistics for nonprofit theaters and orchestras pertain to the season ending before August 31 of the year shown. The museum figures are for the calendar year.

Series Dh368. Includes educational performances and outreach activities. Professional opera companies are those with budgets in excess of $100,000 and include Canadian companies.

Series Dh370. Excludes college groups and youth orchestras.

Series Dh371. Coverage varies depending on response rate of museums. Figures include some Canadian museums.

TABLE Dh372–380   Revenues and expenses of selected arts: 1955–1999

Contributed by Thomas Weiss

Year	Gross box office receipts, Broadway shows	Gross income, nonprofit professional theaters	Expenses, professional opera companies	Symphony orchestras					
				Earned income	Contributed income	Gross revenues	Governmental and private support	Gross expenses	Operating expenses
	Dh372	Dh373	Dh374	Dh375	Dh376	Dh377	Dh378	Dh379	Dh380 [1]
	Million dollars	Million dollars	Million dollars	Million dollars	Million dollars	Million dollars	Million dollars	Million dollars	Million dollars
1955	31	—	—	—	—	—	—	—	—
1956	35	—	—	—	—	—	—	13.8	—
1957	37	—	—	—	—	—	—	—	—
1958	38	—	—	—	—	—	—	—	—
1959	40	—	—	—	—	—	—	—	—
1960	46	—	—	—	—	—	—	—	—
1961	44	—	—	—	—	—	—	—	—
1962	44	—	—	—	—	—	—	—	—
1963	44	—	—	—	—	—	—	—	—
1964	40	—	—	—	—	—	—	—	—
1965	50	—	—	—	—	—	—	—	—
1966	54	—	—	—	—	—	—	27.7	—
1967	55	—	—	—	—	—	—	—	—
1968	59	—	—	—	—	—	—	—	—
1969	58	—	—	—	—	—	—	—	—
1970	53	—	—	43.1	30.2	—	—	—	—
1971	55	—	—	—	—	—	—	76.4	—
1972	52	—	—	—	—	—	—	—	—
1973	45	—	—	—	—	—	—	—	—
1974	46	—	—	—	—	—	—	—	—
1975	57	34.5	—	70.9	53.6	—	—	129.5	—
1976	71	—	—	78.3	—	—	—	141.5	—
1977	93	—	76.4	89.0	—	—	—	160.9	—
1978	114	—	85.1	102.5	75.6	—	—	183.1	—
1979	134	—	100.5	122.6	94.2	—	—	221.0	—
1980	146	113.6	112.9	141.2	105.1	—	—	252.1	—
1981	197	—	130.3	163.3	125.6	—	—	289.3	—
1982	223	142.5	148.8	187.6	137.9	—	—	315.3	—
1983	209	186.0	174.7	201.8	147.1	—	—	352.2	—
1984	227	226.6	195.5	220.2	158.8	—	—	389.8	—
1985	209	234.7	220.4	250.7	184.7	252.4	188.1	441.8	426.1
1986	190	263.8	235.7	282.4	196.1	281.2	188.1	491.2	469.7
1987	208	271.2	252.6	305.9	217.7	306.9	219.4	525.4	503.5
1988	253	276.4	290.3	332.9	228.9	325.3	229.2	571.3	541.2
1989	262	349.0	323.4	363.3	256.2	353.2	249.0	600.0	583.5
1990	282	307.6	341.7	405.4	274.5	377.5	257.7	665.4	621.7
1991	267	333.9	393.8	412.1	290.4	394.5	281.2	688.8	662.2
1992	293	359.1	407.8	—	—	414.0	279.6	—	683.0
1993	328	342.5	427.1	—	—	430.5	293.0	—	689.9
1994	356	455.1	440.5	—	—	442.5	293.1	—	710.0
1995	406	444.4	472.4	—	—	536.2	351.0	—	858.8
1996	436	450.7	506.8	—	—	558.9	382.9	—	892.4
1997	499	565.0	575.8	—	—	575.5	401.1	—	937.1
1998	558	—	599.0	—	—	—	—	—	—
1999	588	—	—	—	—	—	—	—	—

[1] U.S. companies only, beginning 1993; prior to that, Canadian companies were included. Also, coverage increased in 1995 from 254 companies to 1,200.

Sources

For Broadway shows, the League of American Theatres and Producers, Inc., New York; for opera, OPERA America, Washington, DC; for museums, the Association of Art Museum Directors, *Statistics Survey* (annual). The statistics for nonprofit theaters and orchestras were taken from annual editions of the *Statistical Abstract of the United States*. Those statistics had been reported originally by Theatre Communications Group, New York, and the American Symphony Orchestra League, Washington, DC.

Documentation

Data are for the season ending on or prior to August 31 of the year shown.

Series Dh375–380. Excludes college groups and youth orchestras.

Series Dh375–377. Gross revenue of symphony orchestras since 1985 includes concert income, endowment income, and other earned income, and it appears similar in concept and coverage to the earned income figures reported for 1970–1991. The gross revenue figures exclude tax-supported grants and private sector support.

Series Dh379–380. Operating expenses of symphony orchestras for 1985–1999 include costs of artistic personnel, concert production, advertising and promotion, general and administrative costs, and other expenses. The gross expense figures for 1970–1991 appear to be similar to the figures for the later period, but precise coverage was not specified.

TABLE Dh381–387 National Endowment for the Arts and National Endowment for the Humanities – appropriations, grants, awards, and gifts: 1966–1999

Contributed by Thomas Weiss

	Appropriations for			Grants and awards obligated by		Gifts to	
	National Endowment for the Arts	National Endowment for the Humanities	Administrative funds	National Endowment for the Arts	National Endowment for the Humanities	National Endowment for the Arts	National Endowment for the Humanities
	Dh381	Dh382	Dh383 [1]	Dh384 [2]	Dh385	Dh386	Dh387 [3]
Fiscal year	Thousand dollars	Thousand dollars	Thousand dollars	Thousand dollars	Thousand dollars	Thousand dollars	Thousand dollars
1966	2,898	5,864	727	2,485	39	34	0
1967	8,476	5,510	1,020	7,632	4,105	1,983	106
1968	7,774	4,600	1,200	10,670	3,842	674	325
1969	8,457	6,400	1,400	6,371	5,454	2,357	1,262
1970	9,055	8,855	1,610	12,978 [5]	10,516	2,000	2,000
1971	16,420	14,890	2,660	17,640 [5]	14,184 [6]	2,500	2,500
1972	31,480	29,730	3,460	33,103 [5]	31,939 [6]	3,500	3,500
1973	40,857	40,657	5,314	42,031	40,452 [6]	3,632	4,395
1974	64,025	54,250	6,500	67,616	60,244 [6]	7,281	6,114
1975	80,142	79,142	10,783	81,665	73,176	7,710	6,050
1976	87,455	84,955	10,910	92,647	86,568	7,520	5,970
(TQ)	35,301	22,614	2,727	35,708	26,279	510	1,598
1977	99,872	99,372	11,742	112,644	116,802	16,601	18,503
1978	123,850	121,000	—	141,922	148,980	25,865	33,422
1979	149,585	145,231	—	178,491	185,063	37,508	43,900
1980	154,610	150,100	—	166,363	185,514	42,996	42,900
1981	158,795	151,299	—	135,757	144,366	34,870	38,600
1982	143,456	130,560	—	129,188	115,818	—	—
1983	143,875	130,247	—	126,951	123,315	—	—
1984	162,223	140,118	—	147,444	127,571	—	—
1985	163,660	139,478	—	149,400	125,672	—	—
1986	158,822	134,582 [4]	—	146,627	121,125 [4]	—	—
1987	165,281	138,890 [4]	—	151,369	128,407 [4]	—	—
1988	167,731	140,435	—	156,256	125,230	—	—
1989	169,090	153,000	—	148,276	137,076	—	—
1990	171,255	156,910	—	157,618	141,048	—	—
1991	174,081	170,002	—	157,962	149,832	—	—
1992	175,955	175,955	—	154,563	159,103	—	—
1993	174,459	177,413	—	148,414	160,275	—	—
1994	170,228	177,491	—	145,193	158,953	—	—
1995	162,311	172,003	—	147,908	151,777	—	—
1996	99,470	109,981	—	72,238	93,359	—	—
1997	99,494	110,000	—	94,366	94,770	—	—
1998	98,000	110,700	—	—	92,655	—	—
1999	97,966	110,700	—	—	—	—	—

(TQ) indicates transition quarter.

[1] Shown for illustrative purposes. One half of these amounts has been included in the appropriation figures for each agency. See text.

[2] Figures include Challenge Grant funds in the year in which they were obligated rather than spent.

[3] The agencies stopped reporting gifts in fiscal year 1981 because they no longer had to be deposited with the endowments. See text.

[4] Includes funds for the National Capital Arts and Cultural Affairs.

[5] Excludes funds transferred to the National Endowment for the Humanities.

[6] Excludes funds transferred to the National Endowment for the Arts.

Sources

National Endowment for the Arts, *Annual Report to the President,* and National Endowment for the Humanities, *Annual Report to the President,* and data supplied by each of the agencies.

Recent data may be obtained from agencies' annual reports and Internet sites.

Documentation

These agencies began in 1966 with the establishment of the National Foundation on the Arts and Humanities. Federal appropriations are the major source of funds, but not the only one. From the beginning, each endowment was allowed to accept private gifts and donations, which were matched by funds from a special Treasury fund. The appropriation figures exclude the value of any gifts but include the amounts allocated to match those gifts. In some years, gifts received were less than funds available for appropriation; in those years, the appropriation figures overstate the amount of funds available for obligations. In some years, gifts exceeded the level of Treasury funds authorized for matching purposes.

The appropriation figures reflect congressional actions, such as a rescission in fiscal year 1999 that reduced the amount from the levels originally approved.

From fiscal year 1966 through 1977, administrative funds were appropriated to the Foundation, not to each agency. The appropriation figures shown for each endowment include one half of the administrative funds, the total of which is shown separately.

Through 1981, all gifts were sent to the endowments as a condition of their being matched and were represented as receipts in the annual reports. Beginning in fiscal year 1982, gifts were no longer deposited with the endowments and so are no longer reported as receipts. Matching Treasury funds have been released upon receipt of certification that a grantee had received a gift that met the federal matching requirements.

In many years, the endowments made multiyear commitments or made commitments to be funded in the next fiscal year. This has been especially true of Challenge Grant funds. The funds obligated for each fiscal year include amounts obligated by a prior year's commitment but exclude grants that will be funded in future years.

The figures shown here were compiled from the annual reports of each endowment and in some cases the amounts may differ from the final allocations due to variation in the obligations of multiyear monies or receipts of gifts or transfers from other agencies. The differences appear to be larger before 1977.

TABLE Dh388–391   Motion picture attendance, box office receipts, and admission prices: 1922–1998

Contributed by Thomas Weiss

	Attendance		Box office receipts	Average admission price			Attendance		Box office receipts	Average admission price
	Average weekly	Annual					Average weekly	Annual		
	Dh388	Dh389	Dh390	Dh391			Dh388	Dh389	Dh390	Dh391
Year	Million	Million	Million	Dollars		Year	Million	Million	Million	Dollars
1922	40	—	—	—		1965	44	—	1,067	—
1923	43	—	—	—		1966	—	—	1,119	—
1924	46	—	—	—		1967	—	—	1,128	1.22
1925	46	—	—	—		1968	—	—	1,294	—
1926	50	—	—	—		1969	—	—	1,400	—
1927	57	—	—	—		1970	—	920.6	1,429	1.55
1928	65	—	—	—		1971	—	820.3	1,350	1.65
1929	80	—	720	—		1972	—	934.1	1,583	1.70 [1]
1930	90	—	732	—		1973	—	864.6	1,524	1.76 [1]
1931	75	—	719	—		1974	—	1,010.7	1,725 [1]	1.89 [1]
1932	60	—	527	—		1975	—	1,032.8	2,115	2.03
1933	60	—	482	—		1976	—	957.1	2,036	2.13
1934	70	—	518	—		1977	—	1,063.2	2,372	2.23
1935	80	—	556	—		1978	—	1,128.2	2,643	2.34
1936	88	—	626	—		1979	—	1,120.9	2,821	2.47
1937	88	—	676	—		1980	—	1,021.5	2,749	2.69
1938	85	—	663	—		1981	—	1,067.0	2,966	2.78
1939	85	—	659	—		1982	—	1,175.4	3,453	2.94
1940	80	—	735	—		1983	—	1,196.9	3,766	3.15
1941	85	—	809	—		1984	—	1,199.1	4,031	3.36
1942	85	—	1,022	—		1985	—	1,056.0	3,749	3.55
1943	85	—	1,275	—		1986	—	1,017.2	3,778	3.71
1944	85	—	1,341	—		1987	—	1,088.5	4,253	3.91
1945	85	—	1,450	—		1988	—	1,084.8	4,458	4.11
1946	90	—	1,692	—		1989	—	1,263.0	5,033	4.44
1947	90	—	1,594	—		1990	—	1,188.6	5,022	4.22
1948	90	—	1,506	0.36		1991	—	1,140.6	4,803	4.21
1949	70	—	1,451	—		1992	—	1,173.2	4,871	4.15
1950	60	—	1,376	—		1993	—	1,244.0	5,154	4.14
1951	54	—	1,310	—		1994	—	1,291.7	5,396	4.18
1952	51	—	1,246	—		1995	—	1,262.6	5,494	4.35
1953	46	—	1,187	—		1996	—	1,338.6	5,912	4.42
1954	49	—	1,228	0.49		1997	—	1,387.7	6,366	4.59
1955	46	—	1,326	—		1998	—	1,480.7	6,949	4.69
1956	47	—	1,394	—						
1957	45	—	1,126	—						
1958	40	—	992	0.68						
1959	42	—	954	—						
1960	40	—	956	—						
1961	42	—	955	—						
1962	43	—	945	—						
1963	42	—	942	0.86						
1964	44	—	951	—						

[1] As reported in *Statistical Abstract of the United States* (1975).

Source

Motion Picture Association of America, Inc. Recent data can be found at the Motion Picture Association of America's Internet site.

INDEX

Note: The number before the colon is the volume; the number after the colon is the page. A number range indicates inclusive pages in the same volume. Numbers in italics refer to pages in essays; numbers not in italics refer to pages in statistical tables.

Numbers in italics refer to pages in essays; numbers not in italics refer to pages in statistical tables.

Numbers in italics refer to pages in essays; numbers not in italics refer to pages in statistical tables.

Numbers in italics refer to pages in essays; numbers not in italics refer to pages in statistical tables.

Numbers in italics refer to pages in essays; numbers not in italics refer to pages in statistical tables.

Numbers in italics refer to pages in essays; numbers not in italics refer to pages in statistical tables.

Numbers in italics refer to pages in essays; numbers not in italics refer to pages in statistical tables.

Numbers in italics refer to pages in essays; numbers not in italics refer to pages in statistical tables.

Numbers in italics refer to pages in essays; numbers not in italics refer to pages in statistical tables.

Numbers in italics refer to pages in essays; numbers not in italics refer to pages in statistical tables.

Numbers in italics refer to pages in essays; numbers not in italics refer to pages in statistical tables.

Numbers in italics refer to pages in essays; numbers not in italics refer to pages in statistical tables.

Numbers in italics refer to pages in essays; numbers not in italics refer to pages in statistical tables.

Numbers in italics refer to pages in essays; numbers not in italics refer to pages in statistical tables.

Numbers in italics refer to pages in essays; numbers not in italics refer to pages in statistical tables.

Numbers in italics refer to pages in essays; numbers not in italics refer to pages in statistical tables.

Numbers in italics refer to pages in essays; numbers not in italics refer to pages in statistical tables.

Numbers in italics refer to pages in essays; numbers not in italics refer to pages in statistical tables.

Numbers in italics refer to pages in essays; numbers not in italics refer to pages in statistical tables.